ILLINOIS

COURT RULES

AND

PROCEDURE

VOLUME I – STATE

2016

Mat # 41778218

ISBN 978-0-314-68055-6

PREFACE

Designed for use in the office or courtroom, this pamphlet contains the Illinois State Court Rules.

WHAT'S NEW

Illinois Court Rules and Procedure, Volume I – State, 2016, includes rules and associated material governing practice before the Illinois state courts. It is current with amendments received through April 1, 2016.

CONTACT US

For additional information or research assistance, call the reference attorneys at 1-800-REFATTY (1-800-733-2889). Contact our U.S. legal editorial department directly with your questions and suggestions by e-mail at editors.us-legal@tr.com.

Thank you for subscribing to this product. Should you have any questions regarding this product please contact Customer Service at 1-800-328-4880 or by fax at 1-800-340-9378. If you would like to inquire about related publications, or to place an order, please contact us at 1-800-344-5009 or visit us online.

THE PUBLISHER

May 2016

TABLE OF CONTENTS

TABLE OF CONTENTS

CHAPTER 735

CIVIL PROCEDURE

ACT 5. CODE OF CIVIL PROCEDURE

Enactment

Provisions now comprising this chapter were enacted by P.A. 82–280, effective July 1, 1982. It combines into one Act the provisions of the Civil Practice Act and many other acts relating to civil procedure.

Section 19c–101 of P.A. 82–280, provides:

"(a) This Act takes effect July 1, 1982, and shall apply to all cases and proceedings commenced on or after that date.

"(b) For cases and proceedings commenced prior to and still pending on July 1, 1982, this Act shall apply only to those proceedings which take place on or after that date."

ARTICLE I. GENERAL PROVISIONS

5/1–101. Short titles

§ 1–101. Short titles. (a) This Act shall be known and may be cited as the "Code of Civil Procedure".

(b) Article II shall be known as the "Civil Practice Law" and may be referred to by that designation.

(c) Article III shall be known as the "Administrative Review Law" and may be referred to by that designation.

P.A. 82–280, § 1–101, eff. July 1, 1982.

Formerly Ill.Rev.Stat.1991, ch. 110, ¶ 1–101.

Title of Act:

    An Act to codify civil procedure. P.A. 82–280, approved Aug. 19, 1981, eff. July 1, 1982.

5/1–102. Continuation of prior statutes

§ 1–102. Continuation of prior statutes. The provisions of this Act insofar as they are the same or substantially the same as those of any prior statute, shall be construed as a continuation of such prior statute and not as a new enactment.

If in any other statute reference is made to an Act of the General Assembly, or an Article or a Section of such an Act, which is continued in this Act, such reference shall refer to the Act, Article, or Section thereof so continued in this Act.

P.A. 82–280, § 1–102, eff. July 1, 1982.

Formerly Ill.Rev.Stat.1991, ch. 110, ¶ 1–102.

5/1–103. Effect of headings

§ 1–103. Effect of headings. Article, Part and Section headings contained herein shall not be deemed to govern, limit, modify or in any manner affect the scope, meaning or intent of the provisions of any Article, Part or Section of this Act.

P.A. 82–280, § 1–103, eff. July 1, 1982.

Formerly Ill.Rev.Stat.1991, ch. 110, ¶ 1–103.

5/1–104. Power of courts to make rules

§ 1–104. Power of courts to make rules. (a) The Supreme Court of this State has power to make rules of pleading, practice and procedure for the circuit, Appellate and Supreme Courts supplementary to, but not inconsistent with the provisions of this Act, and to amend the same, for the purpose of making this Act effective for the convenient administration of justice, and otherwise simplifying judicial procedure, and power to make rules governing pleading, practice and procedure in small claims actions, including service of process in connection therewith. Unless otherwise indicated by the text, references in this Act to rules are to rules of the Supreme Court.

(b) Subject to the rules of the Supreme Court, the circuit and Appellate Courts may make rules regulating their dockets, calendars, and business.

P.A. 82–280, § 1–104, eff. July 1, 1982.

Formerly Ill.Rev.Stat.1991, ch. 110, ¶ 1–104.

5/1–105. Enforcement of Act and rules

§ 1–105. Enforcement of Act and rules. The Supreme Court may provide by rule for the orderly and expeditious administration and enforcement of this Act and of the rules, including the striking of pleadings, the dismissal of claims, the entry of defaults, the assessment of costs, the assessment against an offending party of the reasonable expenses, including attorney's fees, which any violation causes another party to incur, or other action that may be appropriate.

P.A. 82–280, § 1–105, eff. July 1, 1982.

Formerly Ill.Rev.Stat.1991, ch. 110, ¶ 1–105.

5/1–106. Act to be liberally construed

§ 1–106. Act to be liberally construed. This Act shall be liberally construed, to the end that controversies may be speedily and finally determined according to the substantive rights of the parties. The rule that statutes in derogation of the common law must be strictly construed does not apply to this Act or to the rules made in relation thereto.

P.A. 82–280, § 1–106, eff. July 1, 1982.

Formerly Ill.Rev.Stat.1991, ch. 110, ¶ 1–106.

5/1–107. Appeals

§ 1–107. Appeals. Appeals may be taken as provided for civil cases.

P.A. 82–280, § 1–107, eff. July 1, 1982.

Formerly Ill.Rev.Stat.1991, ch. 110, ¶ 1–107.

5/1–108. Civil Practice Law applies

§ 1–108. Civil Practice Law applies. (a) The provisions of Article II of this Act apply to all proceedings covered by Articles III through XIX of this Act except as otherwise provided in each of the Articles III through XIX, respectively.

(b) In proceedings in which the procedure is regulated by statutes other than those contained in this Act, such other statutes control to the extent to which they regulate procedure but Article II of this Act applies to matters of procedure not regulated by such other statutes.

(c) As to all matters not regulated by statute or rule of court, the practice at common law prevails.

P.A. 82–280, § 1–108, eff. July 1, 1982.

Formerly Ill.Rev.Stat.1991, ch. 110, ¶ 1–108.

5/1–109. Verification by certification

§ 1–109. Verification by certification. Unless otherwise expressly provided by rule of the Supreme Court, whenever in this Code any complaint, petition, answer, reply, bill of particulars, answer to interrogatories, affidavit, return or proof of service, or other document or pleading filed in any court of this State is required or permitted to be verified, or made, sworn to or verified under oath, such requirement or permission is hereby defined to include a certification of such pleading, affidavit or other document under penalty of perjury as provided in this Section.

Whenever any such pleading, affidavit or other document is so certified, the several matters stated shall be stated positively or upon information and belief only, according to the fact. The person or persons having knowledge of the matters stated in a pleading, affidavit or other document certified in accordance with this Section shall subscribe to a certification in substantially the following form: Under penalties as provided by law pursuant to Section 1–109 of the Code of Civil Procedure, the undersigned certifies that the statements set forth in this instrument are true and correct, except as to matters therein stated to be on information and belief and as to such matters the undersigned certifies as aforesaid that he verily believes the same to be true.

Any pleading, affidavit or other document certified in accordance with this Section may be used in the same manner and with the same force and effect as though subscribed and sworn to under oath.

Any person who makes a false statement, material to the issue or point in question, which he does not believe to be true, in any pleading, affidavit or other document certified by such person in accordance with this Section shall be guilty of a Class 3 felony.

P.A. 82–280, § 1–109, added by P.A. 83–916, § 1, eff. Jan. 1, 1984.

Formerly Ill.Rev.Stat.1991, ch. 110, ¶ 1–109.

ARTICLE II. CIVIL PRACTICE

PART 1. VENUE

5/2–101. Generally

§ 2–101. Generally. Except as otherwise provided in this Act, every action must be commenced (1) in the county of residence of any defendant who is joined in good faith and with probable cause for the purpose of obtaining a judgment against him or her and not solely for the purpose of fixing venue in that county, or (2) in the county in which the transaction or some part thereof occurred out of which the cause of action arose.

If a check, draft, money order, or other instrument for the payment of child support payable to or delivered to the State Disbursement Unit established under Section 10–26 of the Illinois Public Aid Code [1] is returned by the bank or depository for any reason, venue for the enforcement of any criminal proceedings or civil cause of action for recovery and attorney fees shall be in the county where the principal office of the State Disbursement Unit is located.

If all defendants are nonresidents of the State, an action may be commenced in any county.

If the corporate limits of a city, village or town extend into more than one county, then the venue of an action or proceeding instituted by that municipality to enforce any fine, imprisonment, penalty or forfeiture for violation of any ordinance of that municipality, regardless of the county in which the violation was committed or occurred, may be in the appropriate court (i) in the county wherein the office of the clerk of the municipality is located or (ii) in any county in which at least 35% of the territory within the municipality's corporate limits is located.

P.A. 82–280, § 2–101, eff. July 1, 1982. Amended by P.A. 83–707, § 1, eff. Sept. 23, 1983; P.A. 89–28, § 5, eff. Jan. 1, 1996; P.A. 91–212, § 22, eff. July 20, 1999.

Formerly Ill.Rev.Stat.1991, ch. 110, ¶ 2–101.
[1] 305 ILCS 5/10–26.

5/2–102. Residence of corporations, voluntary unincorporated associations and partnerships defined

§ 2–102. Residence of corporations, voluntary unincorporated associations and partnerships defined. For purpose of venue, the following definitions apply:

(a) Any private corporation or railroad or bridge company, organized under the laws of this State, and any foreign corporation authorized to transact business in this State is a resident of any county in which it has its registered office or other office or is doing business. A foreign corporation not authorized to transact business in this State is a nonresident of this State.

(b) A partnership sued in its firm name is a resident of any county in which any partner resides or in which the partnership has an office or is doing business. A partnership sued in its firm name, of which all partners are nonresidents of this State and which does not have an office or do business in this State, is a nonresident of this State.

(c) A voluntary unincorporated association sued in its own name is a resident of any county in which the association has an office or, if on due inquiry no office can be found, in which any officer of the association resides. A voluntary unincorporated association sued in its own name, of which all its members are nonresidents of this State and which does not have an office or do business in this State, is a nonresident of this State.

P.A. 82–280, § 2–102, eff. July 1, 1982. Amended by P.A. 83–901, § 1, eff. Jan. 1, 1984.

Formerly Ill.Rev.Stat.1991, ch. 110, ¶ 2–102.

5/2–103. Public corporations—Local actions— Libel—Insurance companies

§ 2–103. Public corporations—Local actions—Libel—Insurance companies.

(a) Actions must be brought against a public, municipal, governmental or quasi-municipal corporation in the county in which its principal office is located or in the county in which the transaction or some part thereof occurred out of which the cause of action arose. Except as otherwise provided in Section 7–102 of this Code, if the cause of action is related to an airport owned by a unit of local government or the property or aircraft operations thereof, however, including an action challenging the constitutionality of this amendatory Act of the 93rd General Assembly, the action must be brought in the county in which the unit of local government's principal office is located. Actions to recover damage to real estate which may be overflowed or otherwise damaged by reason of any act of the corporation may be brought in the county where the real estate or some part of it is situated, or in the county where the corporation is located, at the option of the party claiming to be injured. Except as otherwise provided in Section 7–102 of this Code, any cause of action that is related to an airport owned by a unit of local government, and that is pending on or after the effective date of this amendatory Act of the 93rd General Assembly in a county other than the county in which the unit of local government's principal office is located, shall be transferred, upon motion of any party under Section 2–106 of this Code, to the county in which the unit of local government's principal office is located.

(b) Any action to quiet title to real estate, or to partition or recover possession thereof or to foreclose a mortgage or other lien thereon, must be brought in the county in which the real estate or some part of it is situated.

(c) Any action which is made local by any statute must be brought in the county designated in the statute.

(d) Every action against any owner, publisher, editor, author or printer of a newspaper or magazine of general circulation for libel contained in that newspaper or magazine may be commenced only in the county in which the defendant resides or has his, her or its principal office or in which the article was composed or printed, except when the defendant resides or the article was printed without this State, in either of which cases the action may be commenced in any county in which the libel was circulated or published.

(e) Actions against any insurance company incorporated under the law of this State or doing business in this State may also be brought in any county in which the plaintiff or one of the plaintiffs may reside.

P.A. 82–280, § 2–103, eff. July 1, 1982. Amended by P.A. 85–887, § 1, eff. Nov. 6, 1987; P.A. 93–450, § 95, eff. Aug. 6, 2003.

Formerly Ill.Rev.Stat.1991, ch. 110, ¶ 2–103.

Applicability

Section 99 of P.A. 93–450 provides:

"Effective date. This Act takes effect upon its becoming law, and Section 95 of this Act applies to cases pending on or after the effective date."

P.A. 93–450 became law effective August 6, 2003.

5/2–104. Wrong venue—Waiver—Motion to transfer

§ 2–104. Wrong venue—Waiver—Motion to transfer. (a) No order or judgment is void because rendered in the wrong venue, except in case of judgment by confession as provided in subsection (c) of Section 2–1301 of this Act. No action shall abate or be dismissed because commenced in the wrong venue if there is a proper venue to which the cause may be transferred.

(b) All objections of improper venue are waived by a defendant unless a motion to transfer to a proper venue is made by the defendant on or before the date upon which he or she is required to appear or within any further time that may be granted him or her to answer or move with respect to the complaint, except that if a defendant upon whose residence venue depends is dismissed upon motion of plaintiff, a remaining defendant may promptly move for transfer as though the dismissed defendant had not been a party.

(c) Motions for transfer to a proper venue may be supported and opposed by affidavit. In determining issues of fact raised by affidavits, any competent evidence adduced by the parties shall also be considered. The determination of any issue of fact in connection with a motion to transfer does not constitute a determination of the merits of the case or any aspect thereof.

P.A. 82–280, § 2–104, eff. July 1, 1982. Amended by P.A. 83–707, § 1, eff. Sept. 23, 1983.

Formerly Ill.Rev.Stat.1991, ch. 110, ¶ 2–104.

5/2–105. Defendants in different counties—Review

§ 2–105. Defendants in different counties—Review. In any action involving defendants residing in different counties in which venue is based on residence and an appropriate and timely motion to transfer is made by a defendant not residing in the county, the overruling of the motion is not ground for reversal if he or she proceeds to trial on the merits, unless he or she renews the motion at the close of all the evidence and it appears from the record or the evidence that the defendant residing within the county was joined without probable cause and not in good faith for the purpose of obtaining a judgment against him or her but solely for the purpose of fixing venue in that county.

P.A. 82–280, § 2–105, eff. July 1, 1982.

Formerly Ill.Rev.Stat.1991, ch. 110, ¶ 2–105.

5/2–106. Transfer

§ 2–106. Transfer. (a) Transfer for wrong venue. If a motion to transfer is allowed on the ground that the action was commenced in a wrong venue, the cause shall be transferred to the court in a proper venue, subject to any equitable terms and conditions that may be prescribed.

(b) Method of transfer. The clerk of the court from which a transfer is granted shall immediately certify and transmit to the clerk of the court to which the transfer is ordered the originals of all papers filed in the case together with copies of all orders entered therein. In the event of a severance, certified copies of papers filed and orders entered shall be transmitted. The clerk of the court to which the transfer is ordered shall file the papers and transcript transmitted to him or her and docket the case, and the action shall proceed and be determined as if it had originated in that court.

P.A. 82–280, § 2–106, eff. July 1, 1982.

Formerly Ill.Rev.Stat.1991, ch. 110, ¶ 2–106.

5/2–107. Costs and expenses of transfer

§ 2–107. Costs and expenses of transfer. The costs attending a transfer shall be taxed by the clerk of the court from which the transfer is granted, and, together with the filing fee in the transferee court, shall be paid by plaintiff. If the court granting the transfer finds that venue was fixed by plaintiff in bad faith and without probable cause, then it may order the reasonable expenses of defendant in attending and obtaining a transfer to a proper venue, including a reasonable attorney's fee, to be paid by plaintiff. If the costs and expenses are not paid within a reasonable time, the transferring court shall on motion dismiss the action.

P.A. 82–280, § 2–107, eff. July 1, 1982.

Formerly Ill.Rev.Stat.1991, ch. 110, ¶ 2–107.

5/2–108. Place of trial

§ 2–108. Place of trial. All actions shall be tried in the county in which they are commenced, except as otherwise provided by law.

P.A. 82–280, § 2–108, eff. July 1, 1982.

Formerly Ill.Rev.Stat.1991, ch. 110, ¶ 2–108.

5/2–109. Malicious prosecution—medical malpractice

§ 2–109. Malicious prosecution—medical malpractice. In all cases alleging malicious prosecution aris-

ing out of proceedings which sought damages for injuries or death by reason of medical, hospital, or other healing art malpractice, the plaintiff need not plead or prove special injury to sustain his or her cause of action. In all such cases alleging malicious prosecution, no exemplary or punitive damages shall be allowed.

P.A. 82–280, § 2–114, added by P.A. 84–7, § 1, eff. Aug. 15, 1985. Renumbered § 2–109 and amended by P.A. 84–1308, Art. II, § 107, eff. Aug. 25, 1986. Amended by P.A. 91–357, § 250, eff. July 29, 1999.

Formerly Ill.Rev.Stat.1991, ch. 110, ¶ 2–109.

5/2–114. § 2–114. Renumbered § 2–109 by P.A. 84–1308, Art. II, § 107, eff. Aug. 25, 1986

PART 2. PROCESS

5/2–201. Commencement of actions—Forms of process

§ 2–201. Commencement of actions—Forms of process. (a) Every action, unless otherwise expressly provided by statute, shall be commenced by the filing of a complaint. The clerk shall issue summons upon request of the plaintiff. The form and substance of the summons, and of all other process, and the issuance of alias process, and the service of copies of pleadings shall be according to rules.

(b) One or more duplicate original summonses may be issued, marked "First Duplicate," "Second Duplicate," etc., as the case may be, whenever it will facilitate the service of summons in any one or more counties, including the county of venue.

P.A. 82–280, § 2–201, eff. July 1, 1982.

Formerly Ill.Rev.Stat.1991, ch. 110, ¶ 2–201.

5/2–202. Persons authorized to serve process; Place of service; Failure to make return

§ 2–202. Persons authorized to serve process; Place of service; Failure to make return.

(a) Process shall be served by a sheriff, or if the sheriff is disqualified, by a coroner of some county of the State. In matters where the county or State is an interested party, process may be served by a special investigator appointed by the State's Attorney of the county, as defined in Section 3–9005 of the Counties Code. A sheriff of a county with a population of less than 2,000,000 may employ civilian personnel to serve process. In counties with a population of less than 2,000,000, process may be served, without special appointment, by a person who is licensed or registered as a private detective under the Private Detective, Private Alarm, Private Security, Fingerprint Vendor, and Locksmith Act of 2004[1] or by a registered employee of a private detective agency certified under that Act as defined in Section (a–5). A private detective or licensed employee must supply the sheriff of any county in which he serves process with a copy of his license or certificate; however, the failure of a person to supply the copy shall not in any way impair the validity of process served by the person. The court may, in its discretion upon motion, order service to be made by a private person over 18 years of age and not a party to the action. It is not necessary that service be made by a sheriff or coroner of the county in which service is made. If served or sought to be served by a sheriff or coroner, he or she shall endorse his or her return thereon, and if by a private person the return shall be by affidavit.

(a–5) Upon motion and in its discretion, the court may appoint as a special process server a private detective agency certified under the Private Detective, Private Alarm, Private Security, Fingerprint Vendor, and Locksmith Act of 2004. Under the appointment, any employee of the private detective agency who is registered under that Act may serve the process. The motion and the order of appointment must contain the number of the certificate issued to the private detective agency by the Department of Professional Regulation under the Private Detective, Private Alarm, Private Security, Fingerprint Vendor, and Locksmith Act of 2004. A private detective or private detective agency shall send, one time only, a copy of his, her, or its individual private detective license or private detective agency certificate to the county sheriff in each county in which the detective or detective agency or his, her, or its employees serve process, regardless of size of the population of the county. As long as the license or certificate is valid and meets the requirements of the Department of Financial and Professional Regulation, a new copy of the current license or certificate need not be sent to the sheriff. A private detective agency shall maintain a list of its registered employees. Registered employees shall consist of:

(1) an employee who works for the agency holding a valid Permanent Employee Registration Card;

(2) a person who has applied for a Permanent Employee Registration Card, has had his or her fingerprints processed and cleared by the Department of State Police and the FBI, and as to whom the Department of Financial and Professional Regulation website shows that the person's application for a Permanent Employee Registration Card is pending;

(3) a person employed by a private detective agency who is exempt from a Permanent Employee Registration Card requirement because the person is a current peace officer; and

(4) a private detective who works for a private detective agency as an employee.

A detective agency shall maintain this list and forward it to any sheriff's department that requests this list within 5 business days after the receipt of the request.

(b) Summons may be served upon the defendants wherever they may be found in the State, by any person authorized to serve process. An officer may serve summons in his or her official capacity outside his or her county, but fees for mileage outside the county of the officer cannot be taxed as costs. The person serving the process in a foreign county may make return by mail.

(c) If any sheriff, coroner, or other person to whom any process is delivered, neglects or refuses to make return of the same, the plaintiff may petition the court to enter a rule requiring the sheriff, coroner, or other person, to make return of the process on a day to be fixed by the court, or to show cause on that day why that person should not be attached for contempt of the court. The plaintiff shall then cause a written notice of the rule to be served on the sheriff, coroner, or other person. If good and sufficient cause be not shown to excuse the officer or other person, the court shall adjudge him or her guilty of a contempt, and shall impose punishment as in other cases of contempt.

(d) If process is served by a sheriff, coroner, or special investigator appointed by the State's Attorney, the court may tax the fee of the sheriff, coroner, or State's Attorney's special investigator as costs in the proceeding. If process is served by a private person or entity, the court may establish a fee therefor and tax such fee as costs in the proceedings.

(e) In addition to the powers stated in Section 8.1a of the Housing Authorities Act,[2] in counties with a population of 3,000,000 or more inhabitants, members of a housing authority police force may serve process for forcible entry and detainer actions commenced by that housing authority and may execute orders of possession for that housing authority.

(f) In counties with a population of 3,000,000 or more, process may be served, with special appointment by the court, by a private process server or a law enforcement agency other than the county sheriff in proceedings instituted under the Forcible Entry and Detainer Article of this Code as a result of a lessor or lessor's assignee declaring a lease void pursuant to Section 11 of the Controlled Substance and Cannabis Nuisance Act.[3]

P.A. 82–280, § 2–202, eff. July 1, 1982. Amended by P.A. 84–942, § 1, eff. Sept. 25, 1985; P.A. 85–907, Art. II, § 1, eff. Nov. 23, 1987; P.A. 86–660, § 1, eff. Jan. 1, 1990; P.A. 89–594, § 370, eff. Aug. 1, 1996; P.A. 90–557, § 5, eff. June 1, 1998; P.A. 91–95, § 5, eff. July 9, 1999; P.A. 93–438, Art. 90, § 90–35, eff. Aug. 5, 2003; P.A. 95–613, § 50, eff. Sept. 11, 2007; P.A. 96–1451, § 5, eff. Aug. 20, 2010; P.A. 97–427, § 5, eff. Jan. 1, 2012; P.A. 99–169, § 10, eff. July 28, 2015.

Formerly Ill.Rev.Stat.1991, ch. 110, ¶ 2–202.

[1] 225 ILCS 447/5–5, et seq.
[2] 310 ILCS 10/8.1a.
[3] 740 ILCS 40/11.

5/2–203.   Service on individuals

§ 2–203.   Service on individuals.

(a) Except as otherwise expressly provided, service of summons upon an individual defendant shall be made (1) by leaving a copy of the summons with the defendant personally, (2) by leaving a copy at the defendant's usual place of abode, with some person of the family or a person residing there, of the age of 13 years or upwards, and informing that person of the contents of the summons, provided the officer or other person making service shall also send a copy of the summons in a sealed envelope with postage fully prepaid, addressed to the defendant at his or her usual place of abode, or (3) as provided in Section 1–2–9.2 of the Illinois Municipal Code[1] with respect to violation of an ordinance governing parking or standing of vehicles in cities with a population over 500,000. The certificate of the officer or affidavit of the person that he or she has sent the copy in pursuance of this Section is evidence that he or she has done so. No employee of a facility licensed under the Nursing Home Care Act, the Specialized Mental Health Rehabilitation Act of 2013, the ID/DD Community Care Act, or the MC/DD Act shall obstruct an officer or other person making service in compliance with this Section. An employee of a gated residential community shall grant entry into the community, including its common areas and common elements, to a process server authorized under Section 2–202 of this Code who is attempting to serve process on a defendant or witness who resides within or is known to be within the community. As used in this Section, "gated residential community" includes a condominium association, housing cooperative, or private community.

(b) The officer, in his or her certificate or in a record filed and maintained in the Sheriff's office, or other person making service, in his or her affidavit or in a record filed and maintained in his or her employer's office, shall (1) identify as to sex, race, and approximate age the defendant or other person with whom the summons was left and (2) state the place where (whenever possible in terms of an exact street address) and the date and time of the day when the summons was left with the defendant or other person.

(c) Any person who knowingly sets forth in the certificate or affidavit any false statement, shall be liable in civil contempt. When the court holds a person in civil contempt under this Section, it shall award such damages as it determines to be just and, when the contempt is prosecuted by a private attorney, may award reasonable attorney's fees.

P.A. 82–280, § 2–203, eff. July 1, 1982. Amended by P.A. 82–783, Art. 4, § 27, eff. July 13, 1982; P.A. 86–947, § 3, eff. Nov. 13, 1989; P.A. 88–340, § 5, eff. Jan. 1, 1994; P.A. 95–858, § 5, eff. Aug. 18, 2008; P.A. 96–339, § 90–190, eff. July 1, 2010; P.A. 97–38, § 90–210, eff. June 28, 2011; P.A. 97–227, § 150, eff. Jan. 1, 2012; P.A. 97–813, § 670, eff. July 13, 2012; P.A. 98–104, § 6–285, eff. July 22, 2013; P.A. 98–966, § 5, eff. Jan. 1, 2015; P.A. 99–180, § 235, eff. July 29, 2015.

Formerly Ill.Rev.Stat.1991, ch. 110, ¶ 2–203.

[1] 65 ILCS 5/1–2–9.2.

5/2–203.1.   Service by special order of court

§ 2–203.1.   Service by special order of court. If service upon an individual defendant is impractical under items (1) and (2) of subsection (a) of Section 2–203, the plaintiff may move, without notice, that the court enter an order directing a comparable method of service. The motion shall be accompanied with an affidavit stating the nature and extent of the investigation made to determine the whereabouts of the defendant and the reasons why service is impractical under items (1) and (2) of subsection (a) of Section 2–203, including a specific statement showing that a diligent inquiry as to the location of the individual defendant was made and reasonable efforts to make service have been unsuccessful. The court may order service to be made in any manner consistent with due process.

P.A. 82–280, § 2–203.1, added by P.A. 87–1165, § 1, eff. Jan. 1, 1993.

Formerly Ill.Rev.Stat., ch. 110, ¶ 2–203.1.

5/2–203.2.   Service on an inmate

§ 2–203.2.   Service on an inmate. For the security of a correctional institution or facility or jail, a process server may be refused entry into that correctional institution or facility or jail. Each correctional institution or facility or jail shall designate a representative to accept service from a licensed or registered private detective or agency for purposes of effectuating service upon an inmate in the custody of the institution, facility, or jail. With respect to an inmate incarcerated in an Illinois Department of Corrections facility, the process server shall contact the chief administrative officer in advance to arrange and designate the time and date, during regularly scheduled business hours, that the facility representative will meet with and accept service from the process server. Service upon a warden's or sheriff's representative shall constitute substitute service and a mailing to the inmate of the process shall be completed by the server in accordance with Section 2–202. A warden's or sheriff's representative accepting substitute service shall forward the process to the inmate, but if for any reason the process is not forwarded to the inmate, the sheriff, sheriff's representative, warden, or warden's representative shall not be responsible for any civil fine or penalty, or have other liability. If for any reason an inmate is not in the correctional institution or facility or jail at the time of the service of process, a warden's or sheriff's representative may refuse to accept service for the inmate. If it is determined after the process has been left with the designated representative, that the inmate is not present at that institution or facility or jail, the designated representative shall promptly return it to the licensed or registered private detective or agency, indicating that the substitute service could not be effectuated. The process server shall promptly notify the court of the unsuccessful service.

P.A. 82–280, § 2–203.2, added by P.A. 96–1451, § 5, eff. Aug. 20, 2010.

5/2–204. Service on private corporations

§ 2–204. Service on private corporations. A private corporation may be served (1) by leaving a copy of the process with its registered agent or any officer or agent of the corporation found anywhere in the State; or (2) in any other manner now or hereafter permitted by law. A private corporation may also be notified by publication and mail in like manner and with like effect as individuals.

P.A. 82–280, § 2–204, eff. July 1, 1982. Amended by P.A. 83–707, § 1, eff. Sept. 23, 1983.

Formerly Ill.Rev.Stat.1991, ch. 110, ¶ 2–204.

5/2–205. Service on partnership and partners

§ 2–205. Service on partnership and partners. (a) A partnership sued in its firm name may be served by leaving a copy of the process with any partner personally or with any agent of the partnership found anywhere in the State. A partnership sued in its firm name may also be notified by publication and mail in like manner and with like effect as individuals.

(b) When a personal judgment is sought against a known partner for a partnership liability the partner may be served (1) in any manner provided for service on individuals or (2) by leaving a copy of the summons for him or her with any other partner and mailing a copy of the summons in a sealed envelope with postage prepaid, addressed to the partner against whom

the judgment is sought at his or her usual place of abode as shown by an affidavit filed in the cause. The certificate of the officer or the affidavit of the other person making service that he or she has mailed the copy in pursuance of this section is evidence that he or she has done so. Service on a nonresident partner against whom a personal judgment is sought may be made by leaving a copy with any other partner, and mailing, as provided herein, only if the cause of action sued on is a partnership liability arising out of the transaction of business within the State.

(c) When a personal judgment is sought against an unknown owner in an action authorized under Section 6 of "An Act in relation to the use of an assumed name in the conduct or transaction of business in this State", approved July 17, 1941, as amended,[1] service may be made by leaving a copy of the summons with any agent of the business and publishing notice in the manner provided by Section 2–206 of this Act.

P.A. 82–280, § 2–205, eff. July 1, 1982. Amended by P.A. 82–783, Art. IV, § 27, eff. July 13, 1982; P.A. 83–707, § 1, eff. Sept. 23, 1983.

Formerly Ill.Rev.Stat.1991, ch. 110, ¶ 2–205.
[1] 805 ILCS 405/6.

5/2–205.1. Service on voluntary unincorporated associations

§ 2–205.1. Service on voluntary unincorporated associations. A voluntary unincorporated association sued in its own name may be served by leaving a copy of the process with any officer of the association personally or by leaving a copy of the process at the office of the association with an agent of the association. A voluntary unincorporated association sued in its own name may also be notified by publication and mail in like manner and with like effect as individuals.

P.A. 82–280, § 2–205.1, added by P.A. 83–901, § 1, eff. Jan. 1, 1984.

Formerly Ill.Rev.Stat.1991, ch. 110, ¶ 2–205.1.

5/2–206. Service by publication; affidavit; mailing; certificate

§ 2–206. Service by publication; affidavit; mailing; certificate.

(a) Whenever, in any action affecting property or status within the jurisdiction of the court, including an action to obtain the specific performance, reformation, or rescission of a contract for the conveyance of land, plaintiff or his or her attorney shall file, at the office of the clerk of the court in which the action is pending, an affidavit showing that the defendant resides or has gone out of this State, or on due inquiry cannot be found, or is concealed within this State, so that process cannot be served upon him or her, and stating the place of residence of the defendant, if known, or that upon diligent inquiry his or her place of residence cannot be ascertained, the clerk shall cause publication to be made in some newspaper published in the county in which the action is pending. If there is no newspaper published in that county, then the publication shall be in a newspaper published in an adjoining county in this State, having a circulation in the county in which action is pending. The publication shall contain notice of the pendency of the action, the title of the court, the title of the case, showing the names of the first named plaintiff and the first named defendant, the number of the case, the names of the parties to be served by publication, and the date on or after which default may be entered against such party. The clerk shall also, within 10 days of the first publication of the notice, send a copy thereof by mail, addressed to each defendant whose place of residence is stated in such affidavit. The certificate of the clerk that he or she has sent the copy in pursuance of this Section is evidence that he or she has done so.

(b) In any action brought by a unit of local government to cause the demolition, repair, or enclosure of a dangerous and unsafe or uncompleted or abandoned building, notice by publication under this Section may be commenced during the time during which attempts are made to locate the defendant for personal service. In that case, the unit of local government shall file with the clerk an affidavit stating that the action meets the requirements of this subsection and that all required attempts are being made to locate the defendant. Upon the filing of the affidavit, the clerk shall cause publication to be made under this Section. Upon completing the attempts to locate the defendant required by this Section, the municipality shall file with the clerk an affidavit meeting the requirements of subsection (a). Service under this subsection shall not be deemed to have been made until the affidavit is filed and service by publication in the manner prescribed in subsection (a) is completed.

P.A. 82–280, § 2–206, eff. July 1, 1982. Amended by P.A. 87–1276, § 3, eff. March 12, 1993.

Formerly Ill.Rev.Stat.1991, ch. 110, ¶ 2–206.

5/2–207. Period of Publication—Default

§ 2–207. Period of Publication—Default. The notice required in the preceding section may be given at any time after the commencement of the action, and shall be published at least once in each week for 3 successive weeks. No default or proceeding shall be taken against any defendant not served with summons, or a copy of the complaint, and not appearing, unless the first publication be at least 30 days prior to the time when the default or other proceeding is sought to be taken.

P.A. 82–280, § 2–207, eff. July 1, 1982.

Formerly Ill.Rev.Stat.1991, ch. 110, ¶ 2–207.

5/2–208. Personal service outside State

§ 2–208. Personal service outside State. (a) Personal service of summons may be made upon any party outside the State. If upon a citizen or resident of this State or upon a person who has submitted to the jurisdiction of the courts of this State, it shall have the force and effect of personal service of summons within this State; otherwise it shall have the force and effect of service by publication.

(b) The service of summons shall be made in like manner as service within this State, by any person over 18 years of age not a party to the action. No order of court is required. An affidavit of the server shall be filed stating the time, manner and place of service. The court may consider the affidavit, or any other competent proofs, in determining whether service has been properly made.

(c) No default shall be entered until the expiration of at least 30 days after service. A default judgment entered on such service may be set aside only on a showing which would be timely and sufficient to set aside a default judgment entered on personal service within this State.

P.A. 82–280, § 2–208, eff. July 1, 1982.

Formerly Ill.Rev.Stat.1991, ch. 110, ¶ 2–208.

5/2–209. Act submitting to jurisdiction—Process

§ 2–209. Act submitting to jurisdiction—Process.

(a) Any person, whether or not a citizen or resident of this State, who in person or through an agent does any of the acts hereinafter enumerated, thereby submits such person, and, if an individual, his or her personal representative, to the jurisdiction of the courts of this State as to any cause of action arising from the doing of any of such acts:

(1) The transaction of any business within this State;

(2) The commission of a tortious act within this State;

(3) The ownership, use, or possession of any real estate situated in this State;

(4) Contracting to insure any person, property or risk located within this State at the time of contracting;

(5) With respect to actions of dissolution of marriage, declaration of invalidity of marriage and legal separation, the maintenance in this State of a matrimonial domicile at the time this cause of action arose or the commission in this State of any act giving rise to the cause of action;

(6) With respect to actions brought under the Illinois Parentage Act of 1984,[1] as now or hereafter amended, or under the Illinois Parentage Act of 2015 [2] on and after the effective date of that Act, the performance of an act of sexual intercourse within this State during the possible period of conception;

(7) The making or performance of any contract or promise substantially connected with this State;

9

(8) The performance of sexual intercourse within this State which is claimed to have resulted in the conception of a child who resides in this State;

(9) The failure to support a child, spouse or former spouse who has continued to reside in this State since the person either formerly resided with them in this State or directed them to reside in this State;

(10) The acquisition of ownership, possession or control of any asset or thing of value present within this State when ownership, possession or control was acquired;

(11) The breach of any fiduciary duty within this State;

(12) The performance of duties as a director or officer of a corporation organized under the laws of this State or having its principal place of business within this State;

(13) The ownership of an interest in any trust administered within this State; or

(14) The exercise of powers granted under the authority of this State as a fiduciary.

(b) A court may exercise jurisdiction in any action arising within or without this State against any person who:

(1) Is a natural person present within this State when served;

(2) Is a natural person domiciled or resident within this State when the cause of action arose, the action was commenced, or process was served;

(3) Is a corporation organized under the laws of this State; or

(4) Is a natural person or corporation doing business within this State.

(b–5) Foreign defamation judgment. The courts of this State shall have personal jurisdiction over any person who obtains a judgment in a defamation proceeding outside the United States against any person who is a resident of Illinois or, if not a natural person, has its principal place of business in Illinois, for the purposes of rendering declaratory relief with respect to that resident's liability for the judgment, or for the purpose of determining whether said judgment should be deemed non-recognizable pursuant to this Code, to the fullest extent permitted by the United States Constitution, provided:

(1) the publication at issue was published in Illinois, and

(2) that resident (i) has assets in Illinois which might be used to satisfy the foreign defamation judgment, or (ii) may have to take actions in Illinois to comply with the foreign defamation judgment.

The provisions of this subsection (b–5) shall apply to persons who obtained judgments in defamation proceedings outside the United States prior to, on, or after the effective date of this amendatory Act of the 95th General Assembly.

(c) A court may also exercise jurisdiction on any other basis now or hereafter permitted by the Illinois Constitution and the Constitution of the United States.

(d) Service of process upon any person who is subject to the jurisdiction of the courts of this State, as provided in this Section, may be made by personally serving the summons upon the defendant outside this State, as provided in this Act, with the same force and effect as though summons had been personally served within this State.

(e) Service of process upon any person who resides or whose business address is outside the United States and who is subject to the jurisdiction of the courts of this State, as provided in this Section, in any action based upon product liability may be made by serving a copy of the summons with a copy of the complaint attached upon the Secretary of State. The summons shall be accompanied by a $5 fee payable to the Secretary of State. The plaintiff shall forthwith mail a copy of the summons, upon which the date of service upon the Secretary is clearly shown, together with a copy of the complaint to the defendant at his or her last known place of residence or business address. Plaintiff shall file with the circuit clerk an affidavit of the plaintiff or his or her attorney stating the last known place of residence or the last known business address of the defendant and a certificate of mailing a copy of the summons and complaint to the defendant at such address as required by this subsection (e). The certificate of mailing shall be prima facie evidence that the plaintiff or his or her attorney mailed a copy of the summons and complaint to the defendant as required. Service of the summons shall be deemed to have been made upon the defendant on the date it is served upon the Secretary and shall have the same force and effect as though summons had been personally served upon the defendant within this State.

(f) Only causes of action arising from acts enumerated herein may be asserted against a defendant in an action in which jurisdiction over him or her is based upon subsection (a).

(g) Nothing herein contained limits or affects the right to serve any process in any other manner now or hereafter provided by law.

P.A. 82–280, § 2–209, eff. July 1,1982. Amended by P.A. 82–783, Art. III, § 43, eff. July 13, 1982; P.A. 85–907, Art. II, § 1, eff. Nov. 23, 1987; P.A. 85–1156, Art. I, § 7, eff. Jan. 1, 1989; P.A. 86–840, § 1, eff. Sept. 7, 1989; P.A. 95–865, § 5, eff. Aug. 19, 2008; P.A. 99–85, § 964, eff. Jan. 1, 2016.

Formerly Ill.Rev.Stat.1991, ch. 110, ¶ 2–209.

1 750 ILCS 45/1 et seq.

2 750 ILCS 46/101 et seq.

5/2–209.1. Actions by and against voluntary associations

§ 2–209.1. Actions by and against voluntary associations. A voluntary unincorporated association may sue and be sued in its own name, and may complain and defend in all actions. For the purposes of this Code, "voluntary unincorporated association" means any organization of 2 or more individuals formed for a common purpose, excluding a partnership or corporation.

P.A. 82–280, § 2–209.1, added by P.A. 83–901, § 1, eff. Jan. 1, 1984. Amended by P.A. 84–1043, § 1, eff. Nov. 26, 1985.

Formerly Ill.Rev.Stat.1991, ch. 110, ¶ 2–209.1.

5/2–210. Aircraft and Watercraft

§ 2–210. Aircraft and Watercraft. (a) For the purposes of this Section:

"aircraft" means any contrivance now known, or hereafter invented, used or designed for flight in the air;

"watercraft" means any boat, vessel, craft or floating thing designed for navigation in the water; and

"waters of this State" means the Illinois portion of all boundary lakes and rivers, and all lakes, rivers, streams, ponds and canals within the State of Illinois.

(b) The use and operation by any person of an aircraft on the land of or in the air over this State or the use and operation by any person of a watercraft in the waters of this State, shall be deemed an appointment by such person of the Secretary of State, to be his or her true and lawful attorney upon whom may be served all legal process in any action or proceeding against him or her, growing out of such use or resulting in damage or loss to person or property, and such use or operation shall be signification of his or her agreement that any such process against him or her which is so served, shall be of the same legal force and validity as though served upon him or her personally if such person is a nonresident of this State or at the time a cause of action arises is a resident of this State but subsequently becomes a nonresident of this State. Service of such process shall be made by serving a copy upon the Secretary of State, or by filing such copy in his or her office, together with a fee of $2.00, and such service shall be sufficient service upon such person; if notice of such service and a copy of the process are, within 10 days thereafter, sent by registered mail by the plaintiff to the defendant, at the last known address of the defendant, and the plaintiff's affidavit of compliance herewith is appended to the summons. The court in which the action is pending may order such continuances as may be necessary to afford the defendant reasonable opportunity to defend the action. The fee of $2.00 paid by the plaintiff to the Secretary of State at the time of the service shall be taxed in his or her costs, if he or she prevails in the action. The Secretary of State shall keep a record of all such processes, which shall show the day and hours of such services.

(c) When a final judgment is entered against any non-resident defendant who has not received notice of service and a copy of the process by registered mail, required to be sent to him or her as above provided, and such person, his or her heirs, legatees, executor, administrator or other legal representatives, as the case may require, shall within one year after the written notice is given to him or her of such judgment, or within 5 years after such judgment, if no such notice has been given, as above stated, appear and petition the court to be heard regarding such judgment, and shall pay such costs as the court may deem reasonable in that behalf, the person so petitioning may appear and answer the plaintiff's allegations, and thereupon such proceeding shall be had as if the defendant had appeared in due time and no judgment had been entered. If it appears upon the hearing that the judgment ought not to have been entered against the defendant, the judgment may be set aside, altered or amended as shall appear just; otherwise, it shall be ordered that the judgment stands confirmed against such defendant. The judgment shall after 5 years from the entry thereof, if not set aside in the manner stated above, be deemed and adjudged confirmed against such defendant, and all persons claiming under him or her by virtue of any act done subsequent to the commencement of such action, and at the end of the 5 years, the court may enter such further orders as shall be required for the enforcement of the judgment.

P.A. 82–280, § 2–210, eff. July 1, 1982. Amended by P.A. 83–707, § 1, eff. Sept. 23, 1983; P.A. 84–549, § 22, eff. Sept. 18, 1985.

Formerly Ill.Rev.Stat.1991, ch. 110, ¶ 2–210.

5/2–211. Service on public, municipal, governmental and quasi-municipal corporations

§ 2–211. Service on public, municipal, governmental and quasi-municipal corporations. In actions against public, municipal, governmental or quasi-municipal corporations, summons may be served by leaving a copy with the chairperson of the county board or county clerk in the case of a county, with the mayor or city clerk in the case of a city, with the president of the board of trustees or village clerk in the case of a village, with the supervisor or town clerk in the case of a town, and with the president or clerk or other officer corresponding thereto in the case of any other public, municipal, governmental or quasi-municipal corporation or body.

P.A. 82–280, § 2–211, eff. July 1, 1982.

Formerly Ill.Rev.Stat.1991, ch. 110, ¶ 2–211.

5/2–212. Service on trustee of corporation or receiver

§ 2–212. Service on trustee of corporation or receiver. Any trustee of a corporation or its property or any receiver may be served with summons (1) in any manner provided for service on individuals or corporations, as is appropriate, or (2) by leaving a copy thereof with any agent in the employ of the trustee or receiver anywhere in the State. The trustee or receiver may also be notified by publication and mail in like manner and with like effect as individuals. P.A. 82–280, § 2–212, eff. July 1, 1982.

Formerly Ill.Rev.Stat.1991, ch. 110, ¶ 2–212.

5/2–213. Waiver of service

§ 2–213. Waiver of service. (a) Notice and request for waiver. A plaintiff may notify a defendant of the commencement of an action and request that the defendant waive service of a summons. The notice and request shall be in writing in a form prescribed by Supreme Court rule. The notice and request shall:

(1) be addressed to an individual who is the defendant or who could be served as representative of an entity that is the defendant;

(2) be dispatched through first class U.S. mail or other equally reliable means;

(3) contain a copy of the complaint and identify the court in which it has been filed;

(4) inform the defendant of the consequences of compliance and of a failure to comply with the request;

(5) allow the defendant a reasonable time to return the waiver, which shall be at least (i) 30 days from the date on which the request is sent or (ii) 60 days if the defendant is addressed outside the United States; and

(6) provide the defendant with an extra copy of the notice and request and prepaid means of compliance in writing.

(b) Limits on waiver. A defendant who waives service of a summons in the manner provided in subsection (a) does not thereby waive any objection to the venue or to the jurisdiction of the court over the person of the defendant.

(c) Time to appear or answer. A defendant who returns a timely waiver of service is not required to appear or serve an answer to the complaint until (i) 60 days from the date on which the request for waiver of service was sent or (ii) 90 days if the defendant was addressed outside of the United States.

(d) Effect of filing. When a waiver of service is filed by the plaintiff with the court, the action shall proceed as if a summons and complaint had been served at the time of filing of the waiver, and no proof of service shall be required.

(e) Right to refuse to waive service; effect of refusal. A defendant may refuse to waive service of a summons. If a defendant does not return the waiver provided for in subsection (a), the plaintiff must serve summons on that defendant as otherwise provided by this Code and Supreme Court rules.

P.A. 82–280, § 2–213, added by P.A. 87–352, § 1, eff. Jan. 1, 1992.

Formerly Ill.Rev.Stat.1991, ch. 110, ¶ 2–213.

PART 3. APPEARANCE

Section

5/2–301. Objections to jurisdiction over the person

§ 2–301. Objections to jurisdiction over the person.

(a) Prior to the filing of any other pleading or motion other than a motion for an extension of time to answer or otherwise appear, a party may object to the court's jurisdiction over the party's person, either on the ground that the party is not amenable to process of a court of this State or on the ground of insufficiency of process or insufficiency of service of process, by filing a motion to dismiss the entire proceeding or any cause of action involved in the proceeding or by filing a motion to quash service of process. Such a motion may be made singly or included with others in a combined motion, but the parts of a combined motion must be identified in the manner described in Section 2–619.1. Unless the facts that constitute the basis for the objection are apparent from papers already on file in the case, the motion must be supported by an affidavit setting forth those facts.

(a–5) If the objecting party files a responsive pleading or a motion (other than a motion for an extension of time to answer or otherwise appear) prior to the filing of a motion in compliance with subsection (a), that party waives all objections to the court's jurisdiction over the party's person.

(b) In disposing of a motion objecting to the court's jurisdiction over the person of the objecting party, the court shall consider all matters apparent from the papers on file in the case, affidavits submitted by any party, and any evidence adduced upon contested issues of fact. The court shall enter an appropriate order sustaining or overruling the objection. No determination of any issue of fact in connection with the objection is a determination of the merits of the case or any aspect thereof. A decision adverse to the objector does not preclude the objector from making any motion or defense which he or she might otherwise have made.

(c) Error in ruling against the objecting party on the objection is waived by the party's taking part in further proceedings unless the objection is on the ground that the party is not amenable to process issued by a court of this State.

P.A. 82–280, § 2–301, eff. July 1, 1982. Amended by P.A. 91–145, § 10, eff. Jan. 1, 2000.

Formerly Ill.Rev.Stat.1991, ch. 110, ¶ 2–301.

PART 4. PARTIES

5/2–401. Designation of parties—Misnomer

§ 2–401. Designation of parties—Misnomer. (a) The party commencing an action shall be called the plaintiff. The adverse party shall be called the defendant.

(b) Misnomer of a party is not a ground for dismissal but the name of any party may be corrected at any time, before or after judgment, on motion, upon any terms and proof that the court requires.

(c) A party shall set forth in the body of his or her pleading the names of all parties for and against whom relief is sought thereby.

(d) Unless a contrary meaning is indicated, wherever used in this Act and in rules adopted pursuant hereto the term "plaintiff" includes counterclaimants and third-party plaintiffs, and the term "defendant" includes third-party defendants and parties against whom relief is sought by counterclaim.

(e) Upon application and for good cause shown the parties may appear under fictitious names.

P.A. 82–280, § 2–401, eff. July 1, 1982. Amended by P.A. 85–907, Art. II, § 1, eff. Nov. 23, 1987.

Formerly Ill.Rev.Stat.1991, ch. 110, ¶ 2–401.

5/2–402. Respondents in discovery

§ 2–402. Respondents in discovery. The plaintiff in any civil action may designate as respondents in discovery in his or her pleading those individuals or other entities, other than the named defendants, be-lieved by the plaintiff to have information essential to the determination of who should properly be named as additional defendants in the action.

Persons or entities so named as respondents in discovery shall be required to respond to discovery by the plaintiff in the same manner as are defendants and may, on motion of the plaintiff, be added as defendants if the evidence discloses the existence of probable cause for such action.

A person or entity named a respondent in discovery may upon his or her own motion be made a defendant in the action, in which case the provisions of this Section are no longer applicable to that person.

A copy of the complaint shall be served on each person or entity named as a respondent in discovery.

Each respondent in discovery shall be paid expenses and fees as provided for witnesses.

A person or entity named as a respondent in discovery in any civil action may be made a defendant in the same action at any time within 6 months after being named as a respondent in discovery, even though the time during which an action may otherwise be initiated against him or her may have expired during such 6 month period. An extension from the original 6–month period for good cause may be granted only once for up to 90 days for (i) withdrawal of plaintiff's counsel or (ii) good cause. Notwithstanding the limitations in this Section, the court may grant additional reasonable extensions from this 6–month period for a failure or refusal on the part of the respondent to comply with timely filed discovery.

The plaintiff shall serve upon the respondent or respondents a copy of the complaint together with a summons in a form substantially as follows:

"STATE OF ILLINOIS

COUNTY OF . . . .

IN THE CIRCUIT COURT OF . . . .
COUNTY, ILLINOIS

COUNTY DEPARTMENT, LAW DIVISION

(or, in the Circuit Court of the . . . . Judicial Circuit)

. . . .

Plaintiff(s),

v.   No.

. . . .

. . . . ,

Defendant(s),

and   PLEASE SERVE:

. . . .

. . . . ,

Respondent(s) in Discovery.

SUMMONS FOR DISCOVERY

TO RESPONDENT IN DISCOVERY:

YOU ARE HEREBY NOTIFIED that on . . . ., 20 . . . . . , a complaint, a copy of which is attached, was filed in the above Court naming you as a Respondent in Discovery. Pursuant to the Illinois Code of Civil Procedure Section 2–402 and Supreme Court Rules 201 et. seq., and/or Court Order entered on . . . ., the above named Plaintiff(s) are authorized to proceed with the discovery of the named Respondent(s) in Discovery.

YOU ARE SUMMONED AND COMMANDED to appear for deposition, before a notary public (answer the attached written interrogatories), (respond to the attached request to produce), (or other appropriate discovery tool).

We are scheduled to take the oral discovery deposition of the above named Respondent, ..., on . . . ., 20 . . . . . , at the hour of . . . . . a.m./p.m., at the office . . . ., Illinois, in accordance with the rules and provisions of this Court. Witness and mileage fees in the amount of . . . . are attached (or)

(serve the following interrogatories, request to produce, or other appropriate discovery tool upon Respondent, ... to be answered under oath by Respondent, ..., and delivered to the office of . . . ., Illinois, within 28 days from date of service).

TO THE OFFICER/SPECIAL PROCESS SERVER:

This summons must be returned by the officer or other person to whom it was given for service, with endorsement or affidavit of service and fees and an endorsement or affidavit of payment to the Respondent of witness and mileage fees, if any, immediately after service. If service cannot be made, this summons shall be returned so endorsed.

WITNESS, ...

. . . .

Clerk of Court

Date of Service: . . . ., 20 . . . . .

(To be inserted by officer on copy left

with Respondent or other person)

Attorney No.

Name:

Attorney for:

Address:

City/State/Zip:

Telephone:".

This amendatory Act of the 94th General Assembly applies to causes of action pending on or after its effective date.

P.A. 82–280, § 2–402, eff. July 1, 1982. Amended by P.A. 86–483, § 1, eff. Sept. 1, 1989; P.A. 89–7, § 15, eff. March 9, 1995; P.A. 94–582, § 5, eff. Jan. 1, 2006.

Formerly Ill.Rev.Stat.1991, ch. 110, ¶ 2–402.

Validity

Public Act 89–7, which amended this section, has been held unconstitutional in its entirety by the Illinois Supreme Court in the case of Best v. Taylor Machine Works, 1997, 689 N.E.2d 1057, 228 Ill.Dec. 636, 179 Ill.2d 367. P.A. 94–582 did not include amendments by P.A. 89–7.

P.A. 89–7, in the first paragraph, added a sentence relating to naming fictitious defendants in a complaint; in the sixth paragraph, added a sentence requiring a plaintiff to show a failure or refusal on the part of the respondent to comply with timely filed discovery in order to receive an extension; and added a seventh paragraph.

5/2–403. Who may be plaintiff—Assignments—Subrogation

§ 2–403. Who may be plaintiff—Assignments—Subrogation. (a) The assignee and owner of a nonnegotiable chose in action may sue thereon in his or her own name. Such person shall in his or her pleading on oath allege that he or she is the actual bona fide owner thereof, and set forth how and when he or she acquired title. The action is subject to any defense or set-off existing before notice of the assignment.

(b) In all cases in which the chose in action consists of wages due or to become due to the assignor thereof from the defendant in the action, at least 5 days' written notice of the pendency of the action shall be served upon the assignor, before the trial of the same. Upon application of the assignor of the chose in action the court shall allow him or her to intervene and be made a party to the action. The assignor, or the defendant to the action on behalf of the assignor, shall be allowed to set up or affirmatively maintain any just setoff, discount or defense which the assignor may have to the assignment of the chose in action, or to the indebtedness, the payment of which is secured by the assignment of the chose in action. The court, by jury or otherwise, shall ascertain the amount of the indebtedness remaining due and unpaid from the assignor to the assignee of the chose in action. The judgment, if any, against the defendant shall not exceed the amount so found to be due and unpaid from the assignor to the assignee of the chose in action. Judgment for the balance, if any, remaining due from the defendant, upon the assigned chose in action, shall be rendered in favor of the assignor and against the defendant in the action or proceeding. The court may enter any order as to costs in the proceeding that may be equitable.

(c) Any action hereafter brought by virtue of the subrogation provision of any contract or by virtue of subrogation by operation of law shall be brought either in the name or for the use of the subrogee; and the subrogee shall in his or her pleading on oath, or by his or her affidavit if pleading is not required, allege that he or she is the actual bona fide subrogee and set forth how and when he or she became subrogee.

(d) A judgment in an action brought and conducted by a subrogee by virtue of the subrogation provision of any contract or by virtue of any subrogation by operation of law, whether in the name of the subrogor or otherwise, is not a bar or a determination on the merits of the case or any aspect thereof in an action by the subrogor to recover upon any other cause of action arising out of the same transaction or series of transactions.

P.A. 82–280, § 2–403, eff. July 1, 1982. Amended by P.A. 83–707, § 1, eff. Sept. 23, 1983.

Formerly Ill.Rev.Stat.1991, ch. 110, ¶ 2–403.

5/2–404. Joinder of plaintiffs

§ 2–404. Joinder of plaintiffs. All persons may join in one action as plaintiffs, in whom any right to relief in respect of or arising out of the same transaction or series of transactions is alleged to exist, whether jointly, severally or in the alternative, whenever if those persons had brought separate actions any common question of law or fact would arise. If upon the application of any party it shall appear that joinder may embarrass or delay the trial of the action, the court may order separate trials or enter any other order that may be expedient. Judgment may be entered for any one or more of the plaintiffs who may be found to be entitled to relief, for the relief to which he or she or they may be entitled.

If any one who is a necessary plaintiff, counterclaimant or third-party plaintiff declines to join, he or she may be made a defendant, cross defendant or third-party defendant, as the case may be, the reason therefor being stated in the complaint, counterclaim or third-party complaint.

P.A. 82–280, § 2–404, eff. July 1, 1982. Amended by P.A. 83–707, § 1, eff. Sept. 23, 1983.

Formerly Ill.Rev.Stat.1991, ch. 110, ¶ 2–404.

5/2–405. Joinder of defendants

§ 2–405. Joinder of defendants. (a) Any person may be made a defendant who, either jointly, severally or in the alternative, is alleged to have or claim an interest in the controversy, or in any part thereof, or in the transaction or series of transactions out of which the controversy arose, or whom it is necessary to make a party for the complete determination or settlement of any question involved therein, or against whom a liability is asserted either jointly, severally or

in the alternative arising out of the same transaction or series of transactions, regardless of the number of causes of action joined.

(b) It is not necessary that each defendant be interested as to all the relief prayed for, or as to every cause of action included in any proceeding against him or her; but the court may make any order that may be just to prevent any defendant from being embarrassed or put to expense by being required to attend any proceedings in which such defendant may have no interest.

(c) If the plaintiff is in doubt as to the person from whom he or she is entitled to redress, he or she may join two or more defendants, and state his or her claim against them in the alternative in the same count or plead separate counts in the alternative against different defendants, to the intent that the question which, if any, of the defendants is liable, and to what extent, may be determined as between the parties.

P.A. 82–280, § 2–405, eff. July 1, 1982.

Formerly Ill.Rev.Stat.1991, ch. 110, ¶ 2–405.

5/2–406. Bringing in new parties—Third-party proceedings

§ 2–406. Bringing in new parties—Third-party proceedings. (a) If a complete determination of a controversy cannot be had without the presence of other parties, the court may direct them to be brought in. If a person, not a party, has an interest or title which the judgment may affect, the court, on application, shall direct such person to be made a party.

(b) Within the time for filing his or her answer or thereafter by leave of court, a defendant may by third-party complaint bring in as a defendant a person not a party to the action who is or may be liable to him or her for all or part of the plaintiff's claim against him or her. Subsequent pleadings shall be filed as in the case of a complaint and with like designation and effect. The third-party defendant may assert any defenses which he or she has to the third-party complaint or which the third-party plaintiff has to the plaintiff's claim and shall have the same right to file a counterclaim or third-party complaint as any other defendant. If the plaintiff desires to assert against the third-party defendant any claim which the plaintiff might have asserted against the third-party defendant had he or she been joined originally as a defendant, the plaintiff shall do so by an appropriate pleading. When a counterclaim is filed against a party, the party may in like manner proceed against third parties. Nothing herein applies to liability insurers.

(c) An action is commenced against a new party by the filing of an appropriate pleading or the entry of an order naming him or her a party. Service of process shall be had upon a new party in like manner as is provided for service on a defendant.

P.A. 82–280, § 2–406, eff. July 1, 1982.

Formerly Ill.Rev.Stat.1991, ch. 110, ¶ 2–406.

5/2–407. Nonjoinder and misjoinder of parties— Change of parties

§ 2–407. Nonjoinder and misjoinder of parties— Change of parties. No action shall be dismissed for misjoinder of parties, or dismissed for nonjoinder of necessary parties without first affording reasonable opportunity to add them as parties. New parties may be added and parties misjoined may be dropped by order of the court, at any stage of the cause, before or after judgment, as the ends of justice may require and on terms which the court may fix.

P.A. 82–280, § 2–407, eff. July 1, 1982.

Formerly Ill.Rev.Stat.1991, ch. 110, ¶ 2–407.

5/2–408. Intervention

§ 2–408. Intervention. (a) Upon timely application anyone shall be permitted as of right to intervene in an action: (1) when a statute confers an unconditional right to intervene; or (2) when the representation of the applicant's interest by existing parties is or may be inadequate and the applicant will or may be bound by an order or judgment in the action; or (3) when the applicant is so situated as to be adversely affected by a distribution or other disposition of property in the custody or subject to the control or disposition of the court or a court officer.

(b) Upon timely application anyone may in the discretion of the court be permitted to intervene in an action: (1) when a statute confers a conditional right to intervene; or (2) when an applicant's claim or defense and the main action have a question of law or fact in common.

(c) In all cases involving the validity of a constitutional provision, statute or regulation of this State and affecting the public interest, the State upon timely application may in the discretion of the court be permitted to intervene.

(d) In all cases involving the validity of an ordinance or regulation of a municipality or governmental subdivision of this State and affecting the public interest, the municipality or governmental subdivision upon timely application may in the discretion of the court be permitted to intervene.

(e) A person desiring to intervene shall present a petition setting forth the grounds for intervention, accompanied by the initial pleading or motion which he or she proposes to file. In cases in which the allowance of intervention is discretionary, the court shall consider whether the intervention will unduly delay or prejudice the adjudication of the rights of the original parties.

(f) An intervenor shall have all the rights of an original party, except that the court may in its order allowing intervention, whether discretionary or a matter of right, provide that the applicant shall be bound by orders or judgments, theretofore entered or by evidence theretofore received, that the applicant shall not raise issues which might more properly have been raised at an earlier stage of the proceeding, that the applicant shall not raise new issues or add new parties, or that in other respects the applicant shall not interfere with the control of the litigation, as justice and the avoidance of undue delay may require.

P.A. 82–280, § 2–408, eff. July 1, 1982. Amended by P.A. 82–783, art. IV, § 27, eff. July 13, 1982.

Formerly Ill.Rev.Stat.1991, ch. 110, ¶ 2–408.

5/2–409. Interpleader

§ 2–409. Interpleader. Persons having claims against the plaintiff arising out of the same or related subject matter may be joined as defendants and required to interplead when their claims may expose plaintiff to double or multiple liability. It is not a ground for objection to interpleader that the claims of the several claimants or the titles upon which their claims depend do not have a common origin or are not identical, or are adverse to or independent of one another, or that the plaintiff avers that he or she is not liable in whole or in part to any of or all the claimants. A defendant under similar circumstances may obtain like relief by counterclaim. The provisions hereof are not a limitation upon the joinder of parties or causes of action.

P.A. 82–280, § 2–409, eff. July 1, 1982.

Formerly Ill.Rev.Stat.1991, ch. 110, ¶ 2–409.

5/2–410. Actions against joint debtors or partners

§ 2–410. Actions against joint debtors or partners. All parties to a joint obligation, including a partnership obligation, may be sued jointly, or separate actions may be brought against one or more of them. A judgment against fewer than all the parties to a joint or partnership obligation does not bar an action against those not included in the judgment or not sued. Nothing herein permits more than one satisfaction.

P.A. 82–280, § 2–410, eff. July 1, 1982.

Formerly Ill.Rev.Stat.1991, ch. 110, ¶ 2–410.

5/2–411. Actions by or against partnerships

§ 2–411. Actions by or against partnerships. (a) A partnership may sue or be sued in the names of the partners as individuals doing business as the partnership, or in the firm name, or both.

(b) An unsatisfied judgment against a partnership in its firm name does not bar an action to enforce the individual liability of any partner.

P.A. 82–280, § 2–411, eff. July 1, 1982. Amended by P.A. 86–483, § 1, eff. Sept. 1, 1989.

Formerly Ill.Rev.Stat.1991, ch. 110, ¶ 2–411.

5/2–412. Saving clause as to change of parties

§ 2–412. Saving clause as to change of parties. No change in parties, made by order of court or otherwise, impairs any previous attachment of the estate or body of any person remaining a defendant in the action, or bonds or recognizances of any person remaining a party, either as against such person or his or her sureties, or receipts to an officer for property attached; and, when parties are changed, the court may order new bonds if new bonds are necessary.

P.A. 82–280, § 2–412, eff. July 1, 1982.

Formerly Ill.Rev.Stat.1991, ch. 110, ¶ 2–412.

5/2–413. Unknown parties

§ 2–413. Unknown parties. If in any action there are persons interested therein whose names are unknown, it shall be lawful to make them parties to the action by the name and description of unknown owners, or unknown heirs or legatees of any deceased person, who may have been interested in the subject matter of the action previous to his or her death; but an affidavit shall be filed by the party desiring to make those persons parties stating that their names are unknown. Process may then issue and publication may be had against those persons by the name and description so given, and judgments entered in respect to them shall be of the same effect as though they had been designated by their proper names. If there has been a person who may have been interested in the action, and upon diligent inquiry it cannot be ascertained whether the person is living or dead, it shall be lawful to make those persons who would be his or her heirs and legatees parties defendant as unknown owners, the same as if he or she were known to be dead, but in all those cases an affidavit shall be filed by the party desiring to make any unknown persons who would be the heirs or legatees of the person not known to be living or dead parties, stating that upon due and diligent inquiry it cannot be ascertained whether or not the person is living or dead and further stating that the names of the persons who would be his or her heirs or legatees are unknown. Process may then issue and publication may be had against all parties by the name and description of unknown owners, and judgments entered in respect to the unknown parties shall be of the same effect as though they had been designated by their proper names. Only one affidavit is necessary under the

provisions of this section for the purpose of making persons described herein parties to the action.

P.A. 82–280, § 2–413, eff. July 1, 1982. Amended by P.A. 83–707, § 1, eff. Sept. 23, 1983.

Formerly Ill.Rev.Stat.1991, ch. 110, ¶ 2–413.

5/2–414. Joint or consolidated affidavits—validation of judgments

§ 2–414. Joint or consolidated affidavits—validation of judgments. (a) If in any action or proceeding the affidavits required by Section 2–206 and Section 2–413 of this Act are joined and submitted as a single affidavit, or as two affidavits on one sheet, the fact of joinder or of consolidation of the two affidavits into one shall not deprive the court of the jurisdiction it would have had if the affidavits had been filed as two distinct affidavits; however, the facts with reference to the nonresident defendants required by Section 2–206 of this Act, and the facts relative to the unknown parties required by Section 2–413 of this Act, are otherwise correctly set forth and properly related in the one affidavit.

(b) Any judgment heretofore entered by the court based upon joint affidavits or a consolidated affidavit which is regular in other respects is validated as though the affidavits were separate and distinct.

P.A. 82–280, § 2–414, eff. July 1, 1982.

Formerly Ill.Rev.Stat.1991, ch. 110, ¶ 2–414.

5/2–415. Appointment of and actions against receivers

§ 2–415. Appointment of and actions against receivers. (a) Before any receiver shall be appointed the party making the application shall give bond to the adverse party in such penalty as the court may order and with security to be approved by the court conditioned to pay all damages including reasonable attorney's fees sustained by reason of the appointment and acts of such receiver, in case the appointment of such receiver is revoked or set aside. Bond need not be required, when for good cause shown, and upon notice and full hearing, the court is of the opinion that a receiver ought to be appointed without such bond.

(b) On an application for the appointment of a receiver, the court may, in lieu of appointing a receiver, permit the party in possession to retain such possession upon giving bond with such penalty and with such security and upon such condition as the court may order and approve; and the court may remove a receiver and restore the property to the possession of the party from whom it was taken upon the giving of a like bond.

(c) Every receiver of any property appointed by any court of this State may be sued in respect of any act or transaction of the receiver in carrying on the business connected with the property, without the previous leave of the court in which the receiver was appointed; but the action shall be subject to the jurisdiction of the court in which the receiver was appointed, so far as the same is necessary to the ends of justice.

P.A. 82–280, § 2–415, eff. July 1, 1982. Amended by P.A. 83–707, § 1, eff. Sept. 23, 1983.

Formerly Ill.Rev.Stat.1991, ch. 110, ¶ 2–415.

5/2–416. Representation of corporations in small claims

§ 2–416. Representation of corporations in small claims. A corporation may prosecute as plaintiff or defend as defendant any small claims proceeding in any court of this State through any officer, director, manager, department manager or supervisor of the corporation, as though such corporation were appearing in its proper person.

No corporation may appear as assignee or subrogee in a small claims proceeding.

For the purposes of this Section, the term "officer" means the president, vice-president, registered agent or other person vested with the responsibility of managing the affairs of the corporation, and "small claims proceeding" means a civil action based on either tort or contract for money not in excess of $2,500, exclusive of interests and costs, or for collection of taxes not in excess of that amount.

P.A. 82–280, § 2–416, added by P.A. 83–909, § 4, eff. Jan. 1, 1984. Amended by P.A. 84–1043, § 1, eff. Nov. 26, 1985.

Formerly Ill.Rev.Stat.1991, ch. 110, ¶ 2–416.

5/2–417. Actions under Illinois Educational Labor Relations Act

§ 2–417. Actions under Illinois Educational Labor Relations Act. Whenever the Illinois Educational Labor Relations Board commences an action under subsection (b) of Section 16 of the Illinois Educational Labor Relations Act [1] seeking to enforce a final order of the Board or alleging a violation of a final order, such action shall be commenced by petition filed in the name of the people of the State of Illinois as Petitioner and any persons charged with alleged violation of such final order shall be designated Respondents. Persons charged with alleged violation of such final order may not raise as defenses in such action any matters that such persons could have raised by initiating judicial review of such final order in accordance with subsection (a) of Section 16 of the Illinois Educational Labor Relations Act and Section 3–104 of the Administrative Review Law.[2]

P.A. 82–280, § 2–417, added by P.A. 84–123, § 2, eff. July 30, 1985.

Formerly Ill.Rev.Stat.1991, ch. 110, ¶ 2–417.
[1] 115 ILCS 5/16.
[2] 735 ILCS 5/3–104.

PART 5. APPOINTMENT OF GUARDIANS

5/2–501. Guardian for persons not in being

§ 2–501. Guardian for persons not in being. In any action, whether a trust is involved or not, any person or persons not in being are or may become entitled to, or may upon coming into being claim to be entitled to, any future interest, legal or equitable, whether arising by way of remainder, reversion, possibility of reverter, executory devise, upon the happening of a condition subsequent, or otherwise, in any property, real or personal, involved in such action, the court may, whenever it may deem it necessary for the proper and complete determination of such cause, appoint some competent and disinterested person as guardian ad litem of such person or persons not in being; and any judgment or order entered in such action shall be as binding and effectual for all purposes as though such person or persons were in being and were parties to such action. By such appointment, the person so appointed guardian ad litem, shall not be rendered liable to pay costs of the action; and shall be allowed a reasonable fee for the services as such guardian, to be fixed by the court.

P.A. 82–280, § 2–501, eff. July 1, 1982.

Formerly Ill.Rev.Stat.1991, ch. 110, ¶ 2–501.

5/2–502. Guardians for minors

§ 2–502. Guardians for minors. Guardianships for minors shall be governed by Section 11–13 of the "Probate Act of 1975", as amended.[1]

P.A. 82–280, § 2–502, eff. July 1, 1982.

Formerly Ill.Rev.Stat.1991, ch. 110, ¶ 2–502.
[1] 755 ILCS 5/11–13.

PART 6. PLEADING

5/2–601. Substance of pleadings

§ 2–601. Substance of pleadings. In all actions, pleadings shall be as specified in Article II of this Act and the rules. This section does not affect in any way the substantial allegations of fact necessary to state any cause of action.

P.A. 82–280, § 2–601, eff. July 1, 1982.

Formerly Ill.Rev.Stat.1991, ch. 110, ¶ 2–601.

5/2–602. Designation and order of pleadings

§ 2–602. Designation and order of pleadings. The first pleading by the plaintiff shall be designated a complaint. The first pleading by the defendant shall be designated an answer. If new matter by way of defense is pleaded in the answer, a reply shall be filed by the plaintiff, but the filing of a reply is not an admission of the legal sufficiency of the new matter. Further pleadings may be permitted as required by the court.

P.A. 82–280, § 2–602, eff. July 1, 1982.

Formerly Ill.Rev.Stat.1991, ch. 110, ¶ 2–602.

5/2–603. Form of pleadings

§ 2–603. Form of pleadings. (a) All pleadings shall contain a plain and concise statement of the pleader's cause of action, counterclaim, defense, or reply.

(b) Each separate cause of action upon which a separate recovery might be had shall be stated in a separate count or counterclaim, as the case may be and each count, counterclaim, defense or reply, shall be separately pleaded, designated and numbered, and each shall be divided into paragraphs numbered consecutively, each paragraph containing, as nearly as may be, a separate allegation.

(c) Pleadings shall be liberally construed with a view to doing substantial justice between the parties.

P.A. 82–280, § 2–603, eff. July 1, 1982.

Formerly Ill.Rev.Stat.1991, ch. 110, ¶ 2–603.

5/2–604. Prayer for relief

§ 2–604. Prayer for relief. Every count in every complaint and counterclaim shall contain specific prayers for the relief to which the pleader deems himself or herself entitled except that in actions for injury to the person, no ad damnum may be pleaded except to the minimum extent necessary to comply with the circuit rules of assignment where the claim is filed. Relief may be requested in the alternative. Prayers for relief which the allegations of the pleadings do not sustain may be objected to on motion or in the answering pleading. In actions for injury to the person, any complaint filed which contains an ad damnum, except to the minimum extent necessary to comply with the circuit rules of assignment where the claim is filed, shall, on motion of a defendant or on the court's own motion, be dismissed without prejudice. Except in case of default, the prayer for relief does not limit the relief obtainable, but where other relief is sought the court shall, by proper orders, and upon terms that may be just, protect the adverse party against prejudice by reason of surprise. In case of default, if relief is sought, whether by amendment, counterclaim, or otherwise, beyond that prayed in the pleading to which the party is in default, notice shall be given the defaulted party as provided by rule.

Nothing in this Section shall be construed as prohibiting the defendant from requesting of the plaintiff by interrogatory the amount of damages which will be sought.

P.A. 82–280, § 2–604, eff. July 1, 1982. Amended by P.A. 83–707, § 1, eff. Sept. 23, 1983; P.A. 93–387, § 5, eff. July 25, 2003.

Formerly Ill.Rev.Stat.1991, ch. 110, ¶ 2–604.

5/2–604.1. Pleading of punitive damages

§ 2–604.1. Pleading of punitive damages. In all actions on account of bodily injury or physical damage to property, based on negligence, or product liability based on any theory or doctrine, where punitive damages are permitted no complaint shall be filed containing a prayer for relief seeking punitive damages. However, a plaintiff may, pursuant to a pretrial motion and after a hearing before the court, amend the complaint to include a prayer for relief seeking punitive damages. The court shall allow the motion to amend the complaint if the plaintiff establishes at such hearing a reasonable likelihood of proving facts at trial sufficient to support an award of punitive damages. Any motion to amend the complaint to include a prayer for relief seeking punitive damages shall be made not later than 30 days after the close of discovery. A prayer for relief added pursuant to this Section shall not be barred by lapse of time under any statute prescribing or limiting the time within which an action may be brought or right asserted if the time prescribed or limited had not expired when the original pleading was filed.

P.A. 82–280, § 2–604.1, added by P.A. 84–1431, Art. 3, § 1, eff. Nov. 25, 1986. Amended by P.A. 89–7, § 15, eff. March 9, 1995.

Formerly Ill.Rev.Stat.1991, ch. 110, ¶ 2–604.1.

Validity

Public Act 89–7, which amended this section, has been held unconstitutional in its entirety by the Illinois Supreme Court in the case of Best v. Taylor Machine Works, 1997, 689 N.E.2d 1057, 228 Ill.Dec. 636, 179 Ill.2d 367.

P.A. 89–7, in the first sentence, substituted "any theory or doctrine" for "strict tort liability".

Prior to amendment by P.A. 89–7, this section read:

"Pleading of punitive damages. In all actions on account of bodily injury or physical damage to property, based on negligence, or product liability based on strict tort liability, where punitive damages are permitted no complaint shall be filed containing a prayer for relief seeking punitive damages. However, a plaintiff may, pursuant to a pretrial motion and after a hearing before the court, amend the complaint to include a prayer for relief seeking punitive damages. The court shall allow the motion to amend the complaint if the plaintiff establishes at such hearing a reasonable likelihood of proving facts at trial sufficient to support an award of punitive damages. Any motion to amend the complaint to include a prayer for relief seeking punitive damages shall be made not later than 30 days after the close of discovery. A prayer for relief added pursuant to this Section shall not be barred by lapse of time under any statute prescribing or limiting the time within which an action may be brought or right asserted if the time prescribed or limited had not expired when the original pleading was filed."

Section 995 of P.A. 89–7, approved March 9, 1995, provides:

"Effective date. This Act takes effect upon becoming law, and applies to causes of action as specified in each Section or part of this Act."

5/2–605.　Verification of pleadings

§ 2–605. Verification of pleadings. (a) Any pleading, although not required to be sworn to, may be verified by the oath of the party filing it or of any other person or persons having knowledge of the facts pleaded. Corporations may verify by the oath of any officer or agent having knowledge of the facts. If any pleading is so verified, every subsequent pleading must also be verified, unless verification is excused by the court. In pleadings which are so verified, the several matters stated shall be stated positively or upon information and belief only, according to the fact. Verified allegations do not constitute evidence except by way of admission.

(b) The allegation of the execution or assignment of any written instrument is admitted unless denied in a pleading verified by oath, except in cases in which verification is excused by the court. If the party making the denial is not the person alleged to have executed or assigned the instrument, the denial may be made on the information and belief of that party. P.A. 82–280, § 2–605, eff. July 1, 1982.

Formerly Ill.Rev.Stat.1991, ch. 110, ¶ 2–605.

5/2–606.　Exhibits

§ 2–606. Exhibits. If a claim or defense is founded upon a written instrument, a copy thereof, or of so much of the same as is relevant, must be attached to the pleading as an exhibit or recited therein, unless the pleader attaches to his or her pleading an affidavit stating facts showing that the instrument is not accessible to him or her. In pleading any written instrument a copy thereof may be attached to the pleading as an exhibit. In either case the exhibit constitutes a part of the pleading for all purposes. P.A. 82–280, § 2–606, eff. July 1, 1982.

Formerly Ill.Rev.Stat.1991, ch. 110, ¶ 2–606.

5/2–607.　Bills of particulars

§ 2–607. Bills of particulars. (a) Within the time a party is to respond to a pleading, that party may, if allegations are so wanting in details that the responding party should be entitled to a bill of particulars, file and serve a notice demanding it. The notice shall point out specifically the defects complained of or the details desired. The pleader shall have 28 days to file and serve the bill of particulars, and the party who requested the bill shall have 28 days to plead after being served with the bill.

(b) If the pleader does not file and serve a bill of particulars within 28 days of the demand, or if the bill of particulars delivered is insufficient, the court may, on motion and in its discretion, strike the pleading, allow further time to furnish the bill of particulars or require a more particular bill to be filed and served.

(c) If a bill of particulars, in an action based on a contract, contains the statement of items of indebtedness and is verified by oath, the items thereof are admitted except in so far as the opposite party files an affidavit specifically denying them, and as to each item denied states the facts upon which the denial is based, unless the affidavit is excused by the court.

(d) If the party on whom a demand for a bill of particulars has been made believes that the party demanding it is not entitled to the particulars asked for, he or she may move the court that the demand be denied or modified.

P.A. 82–280, § 2–607, eff. July 1, 1982. Amended by P.A. 83–707, § 1, eff. Sept. 23, 1983; P.A. 86–646, § 1, eff. Sept. 1, 1989.

Formerly Ill.Rev.Stat.1991, ch. 110, ¶ 2–607.

5/2–608.　Counterclaims

§ 2–608. Counterclaims. (a) Any claim by one or more defendants against one or more plaintiffs, or against one or more codefendants, whether in the nature of setoff, recoupment, cross claim or otherwise, and whether in tort or contract, for liquidated or unliquidated damages, or for other relief, may be pleaded as a cross claim in any action, and when so pleaded shall be called a counterclaim.

(b) The counterclaim shall be a part of the answer, and shall be designated as a counterclaim. Service of process on parties already before the court is not necessary.

(c) Every counterclaim shall be pleaded in the same manner and with the same particularity as a complaint, and shall be complete in itself, but allegations set forth in other parts of the answer may be incorporated by specific reference instead of being repeated.

(d) An answer to a counterclaim and pleadings subsequent thereto shall be filed as in the case of a complaint and with like designation and effect.

P.A. 82–280, § 2–608, eff. July 1, 1982.

Formerly Ill.Rev.Stat.1991, ch. 110, ¶ 2–608.

5/2–609. Supplemental pleadings

§ 2–609. Supplemental pleadings. Supplemental pleadings, setting up matters which arise after the original pleadings are filed, may be filed within a reasonable time by either party by leave of court and upon terms.

P.A. 82–280, § 2–609, eff. July 1, 1982.

Formerly Ill.Rev.Stat.1991, ch. 110, ¶ 2–609.

5/2–610. Pleadings to be specific

§ 2–610. Pleadings to be specific. (a) Every answer and subsequent pleading shall contain an explicit admission or denial of each allegation of the pleading to which it relates.

(b) Every allegation, except allegations of damages, not explicitly denied is admitted, unless the party states in his or her pleading that he or she has no knowledge thereof sufficient to form a belief, and attaches an affidavit of the truth of the statement of want of knowledge, or unless the party has had no opportunity to deny.

(c) Denials must not be evasive, but must fairly answer the substance of the allegation denied.

(d) If a party wishes to raise an issue as to the amount of damages only, he or she may do so by stating in his or her pleading that he or she desires to contest only the amount of the damages.

P.A. 82–280, § 2–610, eff. July 1, 1982. Amended by P.A. 83–354, § 1, eff. Sept. 14, 1983.

Formerly Ill.Rev.Stat.1991, ch. 110, ¶ 2–610.

5/2–611, 5/2–611.1. §§ 2–611, 2–611.1. Repealed by P.A. 86–1156, § 7, eff. Aug. 10, 1990

5/2–612. Insufficient pleadings

§ 2–612. Insufficient pleadings. (a) If any pleading is insufficient in substance or form the court may order a fuller or more particular statement. If the pleadings do not sufficiently define the issues the court may order other pleadings prepared.

(b) No pleading is bad in substance which contains such information as reasonably informs the opposite party of the nature of the claim or defense which he or she is called upon to meet.

(c) All defects in pleadings, either in form or substance, not objected to in the trial court are waived.

P.A. 82–280, § 2–612, eff. July 1, 1982.

Formerly Ill.Rev.Stat.1991, ch. 110, ¶ 2–612.

5/2–613. Separate counts and defenses

§ 2–613. Separate counts and defenses. (a) Parties may plead as many causes of action, counterclaims, defenses, and matters in reply as they may have, and each shall be separately designated and numbered.

(b) When a party is in doubt as to which of two or more statements of fact is true, he or she may, regardless of consistency, state them in the alternative or hypothetically in the same or different counts or defenses. A bad alternative does not affect a good one.

(c) Defenses to jurisdiction of the subject matter or in abatement or in bar may be pleaded together, without waiving any defense so pleaded, but the court may order defenses to jurisdiction of the subject matter or in abatement to be tried first. An answer containing only defenses to jurisdiction of the subject matter or in abatement does not constitute an admission of the facts alleged in the complaint, counterclaim or third-party complaint.

(d) The facts constituting any affirmative defense, such as payment, release, satisfaction, discharge, license, fraud, duress, estoppel, laches, statute of frauds, illegality, that the negligence of a complaining party contributed in whole or in part to the injury of which he complains, that an instrument or transaction is either void or voidable in point of law, or cannot be recovered upon by reason of any statute or by reason of nondelivery, want or failure of consideration in whole or in part, and any defense which by other affirmative matter seeks to avoid the legal effect of or defeat the cause of action set forth in the complaint, counterclaim, or third-party complaint, in whole or in part, and any ground or defense, whether affirmative or not, which, if not expressly stated in the pleading, would be likely to take the opposite party by surprise, must be plainly set forth in the answer or reply.

P.A. 82–280, § 2–613, eff. July 1, 1982. Amended by P.A. 84–624, § 1, eff. Sept. 20, 1985.

Formerly Ill.Rev.Stat.1991, ch. 110, ¶ 2–613.

5/2–614. Joinder of causes of action and use of counterclaims

§ 2–614. Joinder of causes of action and use of counterclaims. (a) Any plaintiff or plaintiffs may join any causes of action, against any defendant or defendants; and the defendant may set up in his or her answer any and all cross claims whatever, whether in the nature of recoupment, setoff or otherwise, which shall be designated counterclaims.

(b) The court may, in its discretion, order separate trial of any causes of action, counterclaim or third-party claim if it cannot be conveniently disposed of with the other issues in the case. Legal and equitable issues may be tried together if no jury is employed. P.A. 82–280, § 2–614, eff. July 1, 1982.

Formerly Ill.Rev.Stat.1991, ch. 110, ¶ 2–614.

5/2–615. Motions with respect to pleadings

§ 2–615. Motions with respect to pleadings. (a) All objections to pleadings shall be raised by motion. The motion shall point out specifically the defects complained of, and shall ask for appropriate relief, such as: that a pleading or portion thereof be stricken because substantially insufficient in law, or that the action be dismissed, or that a pleading be made more definite and certain in a specified particular, or that designated immaterial matter be stricken out, or that necessary parties be added, or that designated misjoined parties be dismissed, and so forth.

(b) If a pleading or a division thereof is objected to by a motion to dismiss or for judgment or to strike out the pleading, because it is substantially insufficient in law, the motion must specify wherein the pleading or division thereof is insufficient.

(c) Upon motions based upon defects in pleadings, substantial defects in prior pleadings may be considered.

(d) After rulings on motions, the court may enter appropriate orders either to permit or require pleading over or amending or to terminate the litigation in whole or in part.

(e) Any party may seasonably move for judgment on the pleadings. P.A. 82–280, § 2–615, eff. July 1, 1982.

Formerly Ill.Rev.Stat.1991, ch. 110, ¶ 2–615.

5/2–616. Amendments

§ 2–616. Amendments. (a) At any time before final judgment amendments may be allowed on just and reasonable terms, introducing any party who ought to have been joined as plaintiff or defendant, dismissing any party, changing the cause of action or defense or adding new causes of action or defenses, and in any matter, either of form or substance, in any process, pleading, bill of particulars or proceedings, which may enable the plaintiff to sustain the claim for which it was intended to be brought or the defendant to make a defense or assert a cross claim.

(b) The cause of action, cross claim or defense set up in any amended pleading shall not be barred by lapse of time under any statute or contract prescribing or limiting the time within which an action may be brought or right asserted, if the time prescribed or

limited had not expired when the original pleading was filed, and if it shall appear from the original and amended pleadings that the cause of action asserted, or the defense or cross claim interposed in the amended pleading grew out of the same transaction or occurrence set up in the original pleading, even though the original pleading was defective in that it failed to allege the performance of some act or the existence of some fact or some other matter which is a necessary condition precedent to the right of recovery or defense asserted, if the condition precedent has in fact been performed, and for the purpose of preserving the cause of action, cross claim or defense set up in the amended pleading, and for that purpose only, an amendment to any pleading shall be held to relate back to the date of the filing of the original pleading so amended.

(c) A pleading may be amended at any time, before or after judgment, to conform the pleadings to the proofs, upon terms as to costs and continuance that may be just.

(d) A cause of action against a person not originally named a defendant is not barred by lapse of time under any statute or contract prescribing or limiting the time within which an action may be brought or right asserted, if all the following terms and conditions are met: (1) the time prescribed or limited had not expired when the original action was commenced; (2) the person, within the time that the action might have been brought or the right asserted against him or her plus the time for service permitted under Supreme Court Rule 103(b), received such notice of the commencement of the action that the person will not be prejudiced in maintaining a defense on the merits and knew or should have known that, but for a mistake concerning the identity of the proper party, the action would have been brought against him or her; and (3) it appears from the original and amended pleadings that the cause of action asserted in the amended pleading grew out of the same transaction or occurrence set up in the original pleading, even though the original pleading was defective in that it failed to allege the performance of some act or the existence of some fact or some other matter which is a necessary condition precedent to the right of recovery when the condition precedent has in fact been performed, and even though the person was not named originally as a defendant. For the purpose of preserving the cause of action under those conditions, an amendment adding the person as a defendant relates back to the date of the filing of the original pleading so amended.

(e) A cause of action against a beneficiary of a land trust not originally named a defendant is not barred by lapse of time under any statute or contract prescribing or limiting the time within which an action may be brought or right asserted, if all the following terms and conditions are met: (1) the cause of action arises from the ownership, use or possession of real estate, record title whereto is held by a land trustee;

(2) the time prescribed or limited had not expired when the original action was commenced; (3) the land trustee of record is named as a defendant; and (4) the plaintiff proceeds with reasonable diligence subsequent to the commencement of the action to serve process upon the land trustee, to determine the identity of the beneficiary, and to amend the complaint to name the beneficiary as a defendant.

(f) The changes made by this amendatory Act of the 92nd General Assembly apply to all complaints filed on or after the effective date of this amendatory Act, and to complaints filed before the effective date of this amendatory Act if the limitation period has not ended before the effective date.

P.A. 82–280, § 2–616, eff. July 1, 1982. Amended by P.A. 85–907, Art. II, § 1, eff. Nov. 23, 1987; P.A. 92–116, § 5, eff. Jan. 1, 2002.

Formerly Ill.Rev.Stat.1991, ch. 110, ¶ 2–616.

5/2–617. Seeking wrong remedy not fatal

§ 2–617. Seeking wrong remedy not fatal. Where relief is sought and the court determines, on motion directed to the pleadings, or on motion for summary judgment or upon trial, that the plaintiff has pleaded or established facts which entitled the plaintiff to relief but that the plaintiff has sought the wrong remedy, the court shall permit the pleadings to be amended, on just and reasonable terms, and the court shall grant the relief to which the plaintiff is entitled on the amended pleadings or upon the evidence. In considering whether a proposed amendment is just and reasonable, the court shall consider the right of the defendant to assert additional defenses, to demand a trial by jury, to plead a counterclaim or third party complaint, and to order the plaintiff to take additional steps which were not required under the pleadings as previously filed.

P.A. 82–280, § 2–617, eff. July 1, 1982.

Formerly Ill.Rev.Stat.1991, ch. 110, ¶ 2–617.

5/2–618. Lost pleadings

§ 2–618. Lost pleadings. If any pleading or paper filed in a cause has been lost or mislaid, the court may permit the filing of a copy authenticated by such affidavits as the court may require.

P.A. 82–280, § 2–618, eff. July 1, 1982.

Formerly Ill.Rev.Stat.1991, ch. 110, ¶ 2–618.

5/2–619. Involuntary dismissal based upon certain defects or defenses

§ 2–619. Involuntary dismissal based upon certain defects or defenses. (a) Defendant may, within the time for pleading, file a motion for dismissal of the action or for other appropriate relief upon any of the following grounds. If the grounds do not appear on

the face of the pleading attacked the motion shall be supported by affidavit:

(1) That the court does not have jurisdiction of the subject matter of the action, provided the defect cannot be removed by a transfer of the case to a court having jurisdiction.

(2) That the plaintiff does not have legal capacity to sue or that the defendant does not have legal capacity to be sued.

(3) That there is another action pending between the same parties for the same cause.

(4) That the cause of action is barred by a prior judgment.

(5) That the action was not commenced within the time limited by law.

(6) That the claim set forth in the plaintiff's pleading has been released, satisfied of record, or discharged in bankruptcy.

(7) That the claim asserted is unenforceable under the provisions of the Statute of Frauds.

(8) That the claim asserted against defendant is unenforceable because of his or her minority or other disability.

(9) That the claim asserted against defendant is barred by other affirmative matter avoiding the legal effect of or defeating the claim.

(b) A similar motion may be made by any other party against whom a claim is asserted.

(c) If, upon the hearing of the motion, the opposite party presents affidavits or other proof denying the facts alleged or establishing facts obviating the grounds of defect, the court may hear and determine the same and may grant or deny the motion. If a material and genuine disputed question of fact is raised the court may decide the motion upon the affidavits and evidence offered by the parties, or may deny the motion without prejudice to the right to raise the subject matter of the motion by answer and shall so deny it if the action is one in which a party is entitled to a trial by jury and a jury demand has been filed by the opposite party in apt time.

(d) The raising of any of the foregoing matters by motion under this Section does not preclude the raising of them subsequently by answer unless the court has disposed of the motion on its merits; and a failure to raise any of them by motion does not preclude raising them by answer.

(e) Pleading over after denial by the court of a motion under this Section is not a waiver of any error in the decision denying the motion.

(f) The form and contents of and procedure relating to affidavits under this Section shall be as provided by rule.

P.A. 82–280, § 2–619, eff. July 1, 1982. Amended by P.A. 83–707, § 1, eff. Sept. 23, 1983.

Formerly Ill.Rev.Stat.1991, ch. 110, ¶ 2–619.

5/2–619.1. Combined motions

§ 2–619.1. Combined motions. Motions with respect to pleadings under Section 2–615, motions for involuntary dismissal or other relief under Section 2–619, and motions for summary judgment under Section 2–1005 may be filed together as a single motion in any combination. A combined motion, however, shall be in parts. Each part shall be limited to and shall specify that it is made under one of Sections 2–615, 2–619, or 2–1005. Each part shall also clearly show the points or grounds relied upon under the Section upon which it is based.

P.A. 82–280, § 2–619.1, added by P.A. 86–1156, § 6, eff. Aug. 10, 1990.

Formerly Ill.Rev.Stat.1991, ch. 110, ¶ 2–619.1.

5/2–620. Practice on motions

§ 2–620. Practice on motions. The form and contents of motions, notices regarding the same, hearings on motions, and all other matters of procedure relative thereto, shall be according to rules.

P.A. 82–280, § 2–620, eff. July 1, 1982.

Formerly Ill.Rev.Stat.1991, ch. 110, ¶ 2–620.

5/2–621. Product liability actions

§ 2–621. Product liability actions. (a) In any product liability action based on any theory or doctrine commenced or maintained against a defendant or defendants other than the manufacturer, that party shall upon answering or otherwise pleading file an affidavit certifying the correct identity of the manufacturer of the product allegedly causing injury, death or damage. The commencement of a product liability action based on any theory or doctrine against such defendant or defendants shall toll the applicable statute of limitation and statute of repose relative to the defendant or defendants for purposes of asserting a strict liability in tort cause of action.

(b) Once the plaintiff has filed a complaint against the manufacturer or manufacturers, and the manufacturer or manufacturers have or are required to have answered or otherwise pleaded, the court shall order the dismissal of a product liability action based on any theory or doctrine against the certifying defendant or defendants, provided the certifying defendant or defendants are not within the categories set forth in subsection (c) of this Section. Due diligence shall be exercised by the certifying defendant or defendants in providing the plaintiff with the correct identity of the manufacturer or manufacturers, and due diligence shall be exercised by the plaintiff in filing an action and obtaining jurisdiction over the manufacturer or manufacturers.

The plaintiff may at any time subsequent to the dismissal move to vacate the order of dismissal and reinstate the certifying defendant or defendants, provided plaintiff can show one or more of the following:

(1) That the applicable period of statute of limitation or statute of repose bars the assertion of a cause of action against the manufacturer or manufacturers of the product allegedly causing the injury, death or damage; or

(2) That the identity of the manufacturer given to the plaintiff by the certifying defendant or defendants was incorrect. Once the correct identity of the manufacturer has been given by the certifying defendant or defendants the court shall again dismiss the certifying defendant or defendants; or

(3) That the manufacturer no longer exists, cannot be subject to the jurisdiction of the courts of this State, or, despite due diligence, the manufacturer is not amenable to service of process; or

(4) That the manufacturer is unable to satisfy any judgment as determined by the court; or

(5) That the court determines that the manufacturer would be unable to satisfy a reasonable settlement or other agreement with plaintiff.

(c) A court shall not enter a dismissal order relative to any certifying defendant or defendants other than the manufacturer even though full compliance with subsection (a) of this Section has been made where the plaintiff can show one or more of the following:

(1) That the defendant has exercised some significant control over the design or manufacture of the product, or has provided instructions or warnings to the manufacturer relative to the alleged defect in the product which caused the injury, death or damage; or

(2) That the defendant had actual knowledge of the defect in the product which caused the injury, death or damage; or

(3) That the defendant created the defect in the product which caused the injury, death or damage.

(d) Nothing contained in this Section shall be construed to grant a cause of action on any legal theory or doctrine, or to affect the right of any person to seek and obtain indemnity or contribution.

(e) This Section applies to all causes of action accruing on or after September 24, 1979.

P.A. 82–280, § 2–621, added by P.A. 83–350, § 1, eff. Sept. 14, 1983. Amended by P.A. 84–1043, § 1, eff. Nov. 26, 1985; P.A. 89–7, § 15, eff. March 9, 1995.

Formerly Ill.Rev.Stat.1991, ch. 110, ¶ 2–621.

Validity

Public Act 89–7, which amended this section, has been held unconstitutional in its entirety by the Illinois Supreme Court in the case of Best v. Taylor Machine Works, 1997, 689 N.E.2d 1057, 228 Ill.Dec. 636, 179 Ill.2d 367.

Historical and Statutory Notes

P.A. 84–1043 in subd. (b)(3), substituted "amenable" for "amendable".

P.A. 89–7, in subsec. (a), in the first and second sentences, substituted "on any theory or doctrine" for "in whole or in part on the doctrine of strict liability in tort"; in subsec. (b), in the first paragraph, substituted "product liability action based on any theory or doctrine" for "strict liability in tort claim", and in subpar. (1) of the second paragraph, deleted "strict liability in tort" preceding "cause of action"; and in subsec. (d), substituted "on any legal theory or doctrine" for "in strict liability in tort or any other legal theory".

Prior to amendment by P.A. 89–7, this section read:

"Product liability actions. (a) In any product liability action based in whole or in part on the doctrine of strict liability in tort commenced or maintained against a defendant or defendants other than the manufacturer, that party shall upon answering or otherwise pleading file an affidavit certifying the correct identity of the manufacturer of the product allegedly causing injury, death or damage. The commencement of a product liability action based in whole or in part on the doctrine of strict liability in tort claim against such defendant or defendants shall toll the applicable statute of limitation and statute of repose relative to the defendant or defendants for purposes of asserting a strict liability in tort cause of action.

"(b) Once the plaintiff has filed a complaint against the manufacturer or manufacturers, and the manufacturer or manufacturers have or are required to have answered or otherwise pleaded, the court shall order the dismissal of a strict liability in tort claim against the certifying defendant or defendants, provided the certifying defendant or defendants are not within the categories set forth in subsection (c) of this Section. Due diligence shall be exercised by the certifying defendant or defendants in providing the plaintiff with the correct identity of the manufacturer or manufacturers, and due diligence shall be exercised by the plaintiff in filing an action and obtaining jurisdiction over the manufacturer or manufacturers.

"The plaintiff may at any time subsequent to the dismissal move to vacate the order of dismissal and reinstate the certifying defendant or defendants, provided plaintiff can show one or more of the following:

"(1) That the applicable period of statute of limitation or statute of repose bars the assertion of a strict liability in tort cause of action against the manufacturer or manufacturers of the product allegedly causing the injury, death or damage; or

"(2) That the identity of the manufacturer given to the plaintiff by the certifying defendant or defendants was incorrect. Once the correct identity of the manufacturer has been given by the certifying defendant or defendants the court shall again dismiss the certifying defendant or defendants; or

"(3) That the manufacturer no longer exists, cannot be subject to the jurisdiction of the courts of this State, or, despite due diligence, the manufacturer is not amenable to service of process; or

"(4) That the manufacturer is unable to satisfy any judgment as determined by the court; or

"(5) That the court determines that the manufacturer would be unable to satisfy a reasonable settlement or other agreement with plaintiff.

"(c) A court shall not enter a dismissal order relative to any certifying defendant or defendants other than the manufacturer even though full compliance with subsection (a) of this Section has been made where the plaintiff can show one or more of the following:

"(1) That the defendant has exercised some significant control over the design or manufacture of the product, or has provided instructions or warnings to the manufacturer relative to the alleged defect in the product which caused the injury, death or damage; or

"(2) That the defendant had actual knowledge of the defect in the product which caused the injury, death or damage; or

"(3) That the defendant created the defect in the product which caused the injury, death or damage.

"(d) Nothing contained in this Section shall be construed to grant a cause of action in strict liability in tort or any other legal theory, or to affect the right of any person to seek and obtain indemnity or contribution.

"(e) This Section applies to all causes of action accruing on or after September 24, 1979."

Section 995 of P.A. 89–7, approved March 9, 1995, provides:

"Effective date. This Act takes effect upon becoming law, and applies to causes of action as specified in each Section or part of this Act."

Prior Laws:

P.A. 81–1056, §§ 1 to 5.

Ill.Rev.Stat. 1981, ch. 110, ¶¶ 801 to 805.

5/2–622. Healing art malpractice

§ 2–622. Healing art malpractice.

(a) In any action, whether in tort, contract or otherwise, in which the plaintiff seeks damages for injuries or death by reason of medical, hospital, or other healing art malpractice, the plaintiff's attorney or the plaintiff, if the plaintiff is proceeding pro se, shall file an affidavit, attached to the original and all copies of the complaint, declaring one of the following:

1. That the affiant has consulted and reviewed the facts of the case with a health professional who the affiant reasonably believes: (i) is knowledgeable in the relevant issues involved in the particular action; (ii) practices or has practiced within the last 6 years or teaches or has taught within the last 6 years in the same area of health care or medicine that is at issue in the particular action; and (iii) is qualified by experience or demonstrated competence in the subject of the case; that the reviewing health professional has determined in a written report, after a review of the medical record and other relevant material involved in the particular action that there is a reasonable and meritorious cause for the filing of such action; and that the affiant has concluded on the basis of the reviewing health professional's review and consultation that there is a reasonable and meritorious cause for filing of such action. If the affidavit is filed as to a defendant who is a physician licensed to treat human ailments without the use of drugs or medicines and without operative surgery, a dentist, a podiatric physician, a psychologist, or a naprapath, the written report must be from a health professional licensed in the same profession, with the same class of license, as the defendant. For affidavits filed as to all other defendants, the written report must be from a physician licensed to practice medicine in all its branches. In either event, the affidavit must identify the profession of the reviewing health professional. A copy of the written report, clearly identifying the plaintiff and the reasons for the reviewing health professional's determination that a reasonable and meritorious cause for the filing of the action exists, must be attached to the affidavit, but information which would identify the reviewing health professional may be deleted from the copy so attached.

2. That the affiant was unable to obtain a consultation required by paragraph 1 because a statute of limitations would impair the action and the consultation required could not be obtained before the expiration of the statute of limitations. If an affidavit is executed pursuant to this paragraph, the certificate and written report required by paragraph 1 shall be filed within 90 days after the filing of the complaint. The defendant shall be excused from answering or otherwise pleading until 30 days after being served with a certificate required by paragraph 1.

3. That a request has been made by the plaintiff or his attorney for examination and copying of records pursuant to Part 20 of Article VIII of this Code [1] and the party required to comply under those Sections has failed to produce such records within 60 days of the receipt of the request. If an affidavit is executed pursuant to this paragraph, the certificate and written report required by paragraph 1 shall be filed within 90 days following receipt of the requested records. All defendants except those whose failure to comply with Part 20 of Article VIII of this Code is the basis for an affidavit under this paragraph shall be excused from answering or otherwise pleading until 30 days after being served with the certificate required by paragraph 1.

(b) Where a certificate and written report are required pursuant to this Section a separate certificate and written report shall be filed as to each defendant who has been named in the complaint and shall be filed as to each defendant named at a later time.

(c) Where the plaintiff intends to rely on the doctrine of "res ipsa loquitur", as defined by Section 2–1113 of this Code, the certificate and written report must state that, in the opinion of the reviewing health professional, negligence has occurred in the course of medical treatment. The affiant shall certify upon filing of the complaint that he is relying on the doctrine of "res ipsa loquitur".

(d) When the attorney intends to rely on the doctrine of failure to inform of the consequences of the procedure, the attorney shall certify upon the filing of the complaint that the reviewing health professional has, after reviewing the medical record and other relevant materials involved in the particular action, concluded that a reasonable health professional would have informed the patient of the consequences of the procedure.

(e) Allegations and denials in the affidavit, made without reasonable cause and found to be untrue, shall subject the party pleading them or his attorney, or both, to the payment of reasonable expenses, actually incurred by the other party by reason of the untrue pleading, together with reasonable attorneys' fees to be summarily taxed by the court upon motion made within 30 days of the judgment or dismissal. In no event shall the award for attorneys' fees and expenses exceed those actually paid by the moving party, including the insurer, if any. In proceedings under this paragraph (e), the moving party shall have the right to depose and examine any and all reviewing health professionals who prepared reports used in conjunction with an affidavit required by this Section.

(f) A reviewing health professional who in good faith prepares a report used in conjunction with an affidavit required by this Section shall have civil immunity from liability which otherwise might result from the preparation of such report.

(g) The failure to file a certificate required by this Section shall be grounds for dismissal under Section 2–619.

(h) (Blank).

(i) (Blank).

P.A. 82–280, § 2–622, added by P.A. 84–7, § 1, eff. Aug. 15, 1985. Amended by P.A. 86–646, § 1, eff. Sept. 1, 1989; P.A. 89–7, § 15, eff. March 9, 1995; P.A. 90–579, § 5, eff. May 1, 1998; P.A. 94–677, § 330, eff. Aug. 25, 2005. Re-enacted and amended by P.A. 97–1145, § 5, eff. Jan. 18, 2013. Amended by P.A. 98–214, § 110, eff. Aug. 9, 2013.

Formerly Ill.Rev.Stat.1991, ch. 110, ¶ 2–622.

[1] 735 ILCS 5/8–2001 et seq.

Validity

P.A. 94–677, effective August 25, 2005, a comprehensive revision of the law relating to health care and medical malpractice actions, is unconstitutional in its entirety because (i) provisions limiting the recovery of damages for non-economic losses in medical malpractice actions violate the separation of powers principle of the Illinois Constitution (ILCON Art. II, Sec. 1) and (ii) other provisions are inseverable. Lebron v. Gottlieb Memorial Hospital, 237 Ill.2d 217 (2010). P.A. 97–1145 re-enacted this section so as to remove any question as to its validity.

Public Act 89–7, which amended this section, has been held unconstitutional in its entirety by the Illinois Supreme Court in the case of Best v. Taylor Machine Works, 1997, 689 N.E.2d 1057, 228 Ill.Dec. 636, 179 Ill.2d 367. P.A. 94–677 did not include the changes made by P.A. 89–7. P.A. 97–1145 re-enacted this section so as to remove any question as to its validity.

P.A. 94–677 did not include the changes made by P.A. 89–7, which was held unconstitutional.

5/2–623. Certificate of merit; product liability

§ 2–623. Certificate of merit; product liability.

(a) In a product liability action, as defined in Section 2–2101, in which the plaintiff seeks damages for harm, the plaintiff's attorney or the plaintiff, if the plaintiff is proceeding pro se, shall file an affidavit, attached to the original and all copies of the complaint, declaring one of the following:

(1) That the affiant has consulted and reviewed the facts of the case with a qualified expert, as defined in subsection (c), who has completed a written report, after examination of the product or a review of literature pertaining to the product, in accordance with the following requirements:

(A) In an action based on strict liability in tort or implied warranty, the report must:

(i) identify specific defects in the product that have a potential for harm beyond that which would be objectively contemplated by the ordinary user of the product; and

(ii) contain a determination that the product was unreasonably dangerous and in a defective condition when it left the control of the manufacturer.

(B) In any other product liability action, the report must identify the specific act or omission or other fault, as defined in Section 2–1116, on the part of the defendant.

(C) In any product liability action, the report must contain a determination that the defective condition of the product or other fault was a proximate cause of the plaintiff's harm.

(2) That the plaintiff has not previously voluntarily dismissed an action based upon the same or substantially the same acts, omissions, or occurrences and that the affiant was unable to obtain a consultation required by paragraph (1) because either a statute of limitations would impair the action and the consultation required could not be obtained before the expiration of the statute of limitations or despite a good faith effort to comply with this Section, the plaintiff was prevented by another person from inspecting or conducting nondestructive testing of the product. If an affidavit is executed pursuant to this paragraph, the affidavit required by paragraph (1) shall be filed within 90 days after the filing of the complaint. The defendant shall be excused from answering or otherwise pleading until 30 days after being served with an affidavit required by paragraph (1). No plaintiff shall be afforded the 90–day extension of time provided by this paragraph (2) if he or she has voluntarily dismissed an action for the same harm against the same defendant.

(b) When the defective condition referred to in the written report required under paragraph (1) of subsection (a) is based on a design defect, the affiant shall further state that the qualified expert, as defined in subsection (c), has identified in the written report required under subsection (a) either: (i) a feasible alternative design that existed at the time the product left the manufacturer's control; or (ii) an applicable government or industry standard to which the product did not conform.

(c) A qualified expert, for the purposes of subsections (a) and (b), is someone who possesses scientific, technical, or other specialized knowledge regarding the product at issue or similar products and who is qualified to prepare the report required by subsections (a) and (b).

(d) A copy of the written report required by subsections (a) and (b) shall be attached to the original and all copies of the complaint. The report shall include the name and address of the expert.

(e) The failure to file an affidavit required by subsections (a) and (b) shall be grounds for dismissal under Section 2–619.

(f) Any related allegations concerning healing art malpractice must include an affidavit under Section 2–622.

(g) This amendatory Act of 1995 applies only to causes of action filed on or after its effective date.
P.A. 82–280, § 2–623, added by P.A. 89–7, § 15, eff. March 9, 1995.

Validity

Public Act 89–7, which added this section, has been held unconstitutional in its entirety by the Illinois Supreme Court in the case of Best v. Taylor Machine Works, 1997, 689 N.E.2d 1057, 228 Ill.Dec. 636, 179 Ill.2d 367.

5/2–624. § 2–624. **Repealed by P.A. 97–1145, § 15, eff. Jan. 18, 2013**

PART 7.   ACTION FOR DECLARATORY JUDGMENT

5/2–701. Declaratory judgments

§ 2–701. Declaratory judgments. (a) No action or proceeding is open to objection on the ground that a merely declaratory judgment or order is sought thereby. The court may, in cases of actual controversy, make binding declarations of rights, having the force of final judgments, whether or not any consequential relief is or could be claimed, including the determination, at the instance of anyone interested in the controversy, of the construction of any statute, municipal ordinance, or other governmental regulation, or of any deed, will, contract or other written instrument, and a declaration of the rights of the parties interested. The foregoing enumeration does not exclude other cases of actual controversy. The court shall refuse to enter a declaratory judgment or order, if it appears that the judgment or order, would not terminate the controversy or some part thereof, giving rise to the proceeding. In no event shall the court entertain any action or proceeding for a declaratory judgment or order involving any political question where the defendant is a State officer whose election is provided for by the Constitution; however, nothing herein shall prevent the court from entertaining any such action or proceeding for a declaratory judgment or order if such question also involves a constitutional convention or the construction of a statute involving a constitutional convention.

(b) Declarations of rights, as herein provided for, may be obtained by means of a pleading seeking that relief alone, or as incident to or part of a complaint, counterclaim or other pleading seeking other relief as well, and if a declaration of rights is the only relief asked, the case may be set for early hearing as in the case of a motion.

(c) If further relief based upon a declaration of right becomes necessary or proper after the declaration has been made, application may be made by petition to any court having jurisdiction for an order directed to any party or parties whose rights have been determined by the declaration to show cause why the further relief should not be granted forthwith, upon reasonable notice prescribed by the court in its order.

(d) If a proceeding under this Section involves the determination of issues of fact triable by a jury, they shall be tried and determined in the same manner as issues of fact are tried and determined in other civil actions in the court in which the proceeding is pending.

(e) Unless the parties agree by stipulation as to the allowance thereof, costs in proceedings authorized by this Section shall be allowed in accordance with rules. In the absence of rules the practice in other civil actions shall be followed if applicable, and if not applicable, the costs may be taxed as to the court seems just.

P.A. 82–280, § 2–701, eff. July 1, 1982.

Formerly Ill.Rev.Stat.1991, ch. 110, ¶ 2–701.

5/2–702. Petition for a certificate of innocence that the petitioner was innocent of all offenses for which he or she was incarcerated

§ 2–702. Petition for a certificate of innocence that the petitioner was innocent of all offenses for which he or she was incarcerated.

(a) The General Assembly finds and declares that innocent persons who have been wrongly convicted of crimes in Illinois and subsequently imprisoned have been frustrated in seeking legal redress due to a variety of substantive and technical obstacles in the law and that such persons should have an available avenue to obtain a finding of innocence so that they may obtain relief through a petition in the Court of Claims. The General Assembly further finds misleading the current legal nomenclature which compels an innocent person to seek a pardon for being wrongfully

incarcerated. It is the intent of the General Assembly that the court, in exercising its discretion as permitted by law regarding the weight and admissibility of evidence submitted pursuant to this Section, shall, in the interest of justice, give due consideration to difficulties of proof caused by the passage of time, the death or unavailability of witnesses, the destruction of evidence or other factors not caused by such persons or those acting on their behalf.

(b) Any person convicted and subsequently imprisoned for one or more felonies by the State of Illinois which he or she did not commit may, under the conditions hereinafter provided, file a petition for certificate of innocence in the circuit court of the county in which the person was convicted. The petition shall request a certificate of innocence finding that the petitioner was innocent of all offenses for which he or she was incarcerated.

(c) In order to present the claim for certificate of innocence of an unjust conviction and imprisonment, the petitioner must attach to his or her petition documentation demonstrating that:

(1) he or she has been convicted of one or more felonies by the State of Illinois and subsequently sentenced to a term of imprisonment, and has served all or any part of the sentence; and

(2) his or her judgment of conviction was reversed or vacated, and the indictment or information dismissed or, if a new trial was ordered, either he or she was found not guilty at the new trial or he or she was not retried and the indictment or information dismissed; or the statute, or application thereof, on which the indictment or information was based violated the Constitution of the United States or the State of Illinois; and

(3) his or her claim is not time barred by the provisions of subsection (i) of this Section.

(d) The petition shall state facts in sufficient detail to permit the court to find that the petitioner is likely to succeed at trial in proving that the petitioner is innocent of the offenses charged in the indictment or information or his or her acts or omissions charged in the indictment or information did not constitute a felony or misdemeanor against the State of Illinois, and the petitioner did not by his or her own conduct voluntarily cause or bring about his or her conviction. The petition shall be verified by the petitioner.

(e) A copy of the petition shall be served on the Attorney General and the State's Attorney of the county where the conviction was had. The Attorney General and the State's Attorney of the county where the conviction was had shall have the right to intervene as parties.

(f) In any hearing seeking a certificate of innocence, the court may take judicial notice of prior sworn testimony or evidence admitted in the criminal proceedings related to the convictions which resulted in the alleged wrongful incarceration, if the petitioner was either represented by counsel at such prior proceedings or the right to counsel was knowingly waived.

(g) In order to obtain a certificate of innocence the petitioner must prove by a preponderance of evidence that:

(1) the petitioner was convicted of one or more felonies by the State of Illinois and subsequently sentenced to a term of imprisonment, and has served all or any part of the sentence;

(2)(A) the judgment of conviction was reversed or vacated, and the indictment or information dismissed or, if a new trial was ordered, either the petitioner was found not guilty at the new trial or the petitioner was not retried and the indictment or information dismissed; or (B) the statute, or application thereof, on which the indictment or information was based violated the Constitution of the United States or the State of Illinois;

(3) the petitioner is innocent of the offenses charged in the indictment or information or his or her acts or omissions charged in the indictment or information did not constitute a felony or misdemeanor against the State; and

(4) the petitioner did not by his or her own conduct voluntarily cause or bring about his or her conviction.

(h) If the court finds that the petitioner is entitled to a judgment, it shall enter a certificate of innocence finding that the petitioner was innocent of all offenses for which he or she was incarcerated. Upon entry of the certificate of innocence or pardon from the Governor stating that such pardon was issued on the ground of innocence of the crime for which he or she was imprisoned, (1) the clerk of the court shall transmit a copy of the certificate of innocence to the clerk of the Court of Claims, together with the claimant's current address; and (2) the court shall enter an order expunging the record of arrest from the official records of the arresting authority and order that the records of the clerk of the circuit court and Department of State Police be sealed until further order of the court upon good cause shown or as otherwise provided herein, and the name of the defendant obliterated from the official index requested to be kept by the circuit court clerk under Section 16 of the Clerks of Courts Act in connection with the arrest and conviction for the offense but the order shall not affect any index issued by the circuit court clerk before the entry of the order. The court shall enter the expungement order regardless of whether the petitioner has prior criminal convictions.

All records sealed by the Department of State Police may be disseminated by the Department only as required by law or to the arresting authority, the State's Attorney, the court upon a later arrest for the same or similar offense, or for the purpose of sentencing for any subsequent felony. Upon conviction for any subsequent offense, the Department of Corrections shall have access to all sealed records of the Department pertaining to that individual.

Upon entry of the order of expungement, the clerk of the circuit court shall promptly mail a copy of the order to the person whose records were expunged and sealed.

(i) Any person seeking a certificate of innocence under this Section based on the dismissal of an indictment or information or acquittal that occurred before the effective date of this amendatory Act of the 95th General Assembly shall file his or her petition within 2 years after the effective date of this amendatory Act of the 95th General Assembly. Any person seeking a certificate of innocence under this Section based on the dismissal of an indictment or information or acquittal that occurred on or after the effective date of this amendatory Act of the 95th General Assembly shall file his or her petition within 2 years after the dismissal.

(j) The decision to grant or deny a certificate of innocence shall be binding only with respect to claims filed in the Court of Claims and shall not have a res judicata effect on any other proceedings.
P.A. 82–280, § 2–702, added by P.A. 95–970, § 15, eff. Sept. 22, 2008. Amended by P.A. 96–1550, § 15, eff. July 1, 2011; P.A. 98–133, § 15, eff. Jan. 1, 2014.

PART 8. CLASS ACTION

5/2–801. Prerequisites for the maintenance of a class action

§ 2–801. Prerequisites for the maintenance of a class action. An action may be maintained as a class action in any court of this State and a party may sue or be sued as a representative party of the class only if the court finds:

(1) The class is so numerous that joinder of all members is impracticable.

(2) There are questions of fact or law common to the class, which common questions predominate over any questions affecting only individual members.

(3) The representative parties will fairly and adequately protect the interest of the class.

(4) The class action is an appropriate method for the fair and efficient adjudication of the controversy.
P.A. 82–280, § 2–801, eff. July 1, 1982.

Formerly Ill.Rev.Stat.1991, ch. 110, ¶ 2–801.

5/2–802. Order and findings relative to the class

§ 2–802. Order and findings relative to the class. (a) Determination of Class. As soon as practicable after the commencement of an action brought as a class action, the court shall determine by order whether it may be so maintained and describe those whom the court finds to be members of the class. This order may be conditional and may be amended before a decision on the merits.

(b) Class Action on Limited Issues and Sub-classes. When appropriate, an action may be brought or maintained as a class action with respect to particular issues, or divided into sub-classes and each sub-class treated as a class. The provisions of this rule shall then be construed and applied accordingly.

P.A. 82–280, § 2–802, eff. July 1, 1982.

Formerly Ill.Rev.Stat.1991, ch. 110, ¶ 2–802.

5/2–803. Notice in class cases

§ 2–803. Notice in class cases. Upon a determination that an action may be maintained as a class action, or at any time during the conduct of the action, the court in its discretion may order such notice that it deems necessary to protect the interests of the class and the parties.

An order entered under subsection (a) or Section 2–802 of this Act, determining that an action may be maintained as a class action, may be conditioned upon the giving of such notice as the court deems appropriate.

P.A. 82–280, § 2–803, eff. July 1, 1982. Amended by P.A. 83–707, § 1, eff. Sept. 23, 1983.

Formerly Ill.Rev.Stat.1991, ch. 110, ¶ 2–803.

5/2–804. Intervention by and exclusion of class members

§ 2–804. Intervention by and exclusion of class members. (a) Intervention. Any class member seeking to intervene or otherwise appear in the action may do so with leave of court and such leave shall be liberally granted except when the court finds that such intervention will disrupt the conduct of the action or otherwise prejudice the rights of the parties or the class.

(b) Exclusion. Any class member seeking to be excluded from a class action may request such exclusion and any judgment entered in the action shall not apply to persons who properly request to be excluded.

P.A. 82–280, § 2–804, eff. July 1, 1982.

Formerly Ill.Rev.Stat.1991, ch. 110, ¶ 2–804.

5/2–805. Judgments in class cases

§ 2–805. Judgments in class cases. Any judgment entered in a class action brought under Section 2–801 of this Act shall be binding on all class members, as the class is defined by the court, except those who have been properly excluded from the class under subsection (b) of Section 2–804 of this Act.

P.A. 82–280, § 2–805, eff. July 1, 1982.

Formerly Ill.Rev.Stat.1991, ch. 110, ¶ 2–805.

5/2–806. Dismissal or compromise of class cases

§ 2–806. Dismissal or compromise of class cases. Any action brought as a class action under Section 2–801 of this Act shall not be compromised or dismissed except with the approval of the court and, unless excused for good cause shown, upon notice as the court may direct.

P.A. 82–280, § 2–806, eff. July 1, 1982.

Formerly Ill.Rev.Stat.1991, ch. 110, ¶ 2–806.

5/2–807. Residual funds in a common fund created in a class action

§ 2–807. Residual funds in a common fund created in a class action.

(a) Definitions. As used in this Section:

"Eligible organization" means a not-for-profit organization that:

    (i) has been in existence for no less than 3 years;

    (ii) has been tax exempt for no less than 3 years from the payment of federal taxes under Section 501(c)(3) of the Internal Revenue Code;

    (iii) is in compliance with registration and filing requirements applicable pursuant to the Charitable Trust Act and the Solicitation for Charity Act; and

    (iv) has a principal purpose of promoting or providing services that would be eligible for funding under the Illinois Equal Justice Act.

"Residual funds" means all unclaimed funds, including uncashed checks or other unclaimed payments, that remain in a common fund created in a class action after court-approved payments are made for the following:

    (i) class member claims;

    (ii) attorney's fees and costs; and

    (iii) any reversions to a defendant agreed upon by the parties.

(b) Settlement. An order approving a proposed settlement of a class action that results in the creation of a common fund for the benefit of the class shall, consistent with the other Sections of this Part, establish a process for the administration of the settlement and shall provide for the distribution of any residual funds to one or more eligible organizations, except that up to 50% of the residual funds may be distributed to one or more other nonprofit charitable organizations or other organizations that serve the public good if the court finds there is good cause to approve such a distribution as part of a settlement.

(c) Judgment. A judgment in favor of the plaintiff in a class action that results in the creation of a common fund for the benefit of the class shall provide for the distribution of any residual funds to one or more eligible organizations.

(d) State and its political subdivisions. This Section does not apply to any class action lawsuit against the State of Illinois or any of its political subdivisions.

(e) Application. This Section applies to all actions commenced on or after the effective date of this amendatory Act of the 95th General Assembly and to all actions pending on the effective date of this amendatory Act of the 95th General Assembly for which no court order has been entered preliminarily approving a proposed settlement for a class of plaintiffs.

P.A. 82–280, § 2–807, added by P.A. 95–479, § 5, eff. July 1, 2008.

PART 9. ACTION ON PENAL BOND

5/2–901. Actions on penal bonds

§ 2–901. Actions on penal bonds. In an action on a penal bond the plaintiff may allege as many breaches as the plaintiff may think fit. Damages shall be assessed for the breaches which are proved. The judgment for the penalty stands as security for all other breaches which may occur thereafter. The court may at any time thereafter, upon motion of plaintiff and 10 days' notice, assess damages for each subsequent breach. An order shall be entered after each assessment of damages for the enforcement of the judgment for the amount of the additional damages assessed, until the full amount of the judgment is paid.

P.A. 82–280, § 2–901, eff. July 1, 1982.

Formerly Ill.Rev.Stat.1991, ch. 110, ¶ 2–901.

PART 10. PRE–TRIAL STEPS

5/2–1001. Substitution of judge

§ 2–1001. Substitution of judge.

(a) A substitution of judge in any civil action may be had in the following situations:

(1) Involvement of judge. When the judge is a party or interested in the action, or his or her testimony is material to either of the parties to the action, or he or she is related to or has been counsel for any party in regard to the matter in controversy. In any such situation a substitution of judge may be awarded by the court with or without the application of either party.

(2) Substitution as of right. When a party timely exercises his or her right to a substitution without cause as provided in this paragraph (2).

(i) Each party shall be entitled to one substitution of judge without cause as a matter of right.

(ii) An application for substitution of judge as of right shall be made by motion and shall be granted if it is presented before trial or hearing begins and before the judge to whom it is presented has ruled on any substantial issue in the case, or if it is presented by consent of the parties.

(iii) If any party has not entered an appearance in the case and has not been found in default, rulings in the case by the judge on any substantial issue before the party's appearance shall not be grounds for denying an otherwise timely application for substitution of judge as of right by the party.

(3) Substitution for cause. When cause exists.

(i) Each party shall be entitled to a substitution or substitutions of judge for cause.

(ii) Every application for substitution of judge for cause shall be made by petition, setting forth the specific cause for substitution and praying a substitution of judge. The petition shall be verified by the affidavit of the applicant.

(iii) Upon the filing of a petition for substitution of judge for cause, a hearing to determine whether the cause exists shall be conducted as soon as possible by a judge other than the judge named in the petition. The judge named in the petition need not testify but may submit an affidavit if the judge wishes. If the petition is allowed, the case shall be assigned to a judge not named in the petition. If the petition is denied, the case shall be assigned back to the judge named in the petition.

(4) Substitution in contempt proceedings. When any defendant in a proceeding for contempt arising from an attack upon the character or conduct of a judge occurring otherwise than in open court, and the proceeding is pending before the judge whose character or conduct was impugned, fears that he or she will not receive a fair and impartial trial before that judge. In any such situation the application

shall be by petition, verified by the applicant, and shall be filed before the trial of the contempt proceeding.

(b) An application for substitution of judge may be made to the court in which the case is pending, reasonable notice of the application having been given to the adverse party or his or her attorney.

(c) When a substitution of judge is granted, the case may be assigned to some other judge in the same county, or in some other convenient county, to which there is no valid objection. If the case is assigned to a judge in some other county, the provisions of subsections (f) through (m) of Section 2–1001.5 shall apply.
P.A. 82–280, § 2–1001, eff. July 1, 1982. Resectioned §§ 2–1001, 2–1001.5 and amended by P.A. 87–949, § 1, eff. Jan. 1, 1993. Amended by P.A. 88–35, § 1, eff. July 6, 1993; P.A. 94–531, § 5, eff. Jan. 1, 2006.

Formerly Ill.Rev.Stat.1991, ch. 110, ¶ 2–1001.

5/2–1001.5. Change of venue

§ 2–1001.5. Change of venue.

(a) A change of venue in any civil action may be had when the court determines that any party may not receive a fair trial in the court in which the action is pending because the inhabitants of the county are prejudiced against the party, or his or her attorney, or the adverse party has an undue influence over the minds of the inhabitants.

(b) Every application for a change of venue by a party or his or her attorney shall be by petition, verified by the affidavit of the applicant. The petition shall set forth the facts upon which the petitioner bases his or her belief of prejudice of the inhabitants of the county or the undue influence of the adverse party over their minds, and must be supported by the affidavits of at least 2 other reputable persons residing in the county. The adverse party may controvert the petition by counter affidavits, and the court may grant or deny the petition as shall appear to be according to the right of the case.

(c) A petition for change of venue shall not be granted unless it is presented before trial or hearing begins and before the judge to whom it is presented has ruled on any substantial issue in the case, but if any ground for change of venue occurs thereafter, a petition for change of venue may be presented based upon that ground.

(d) The application may be made to the court in which the case is pending, reasonable notice thereof having been given to the adverse party or his or her attorney.

(e) When a change of venue is granted, it shall be to some other convenient county to which there is no valid objection.

(f) The order for a change of venue may be made subject to such equitable terms and conditions as

safety to the rights of the parties may seem to require, and the court in its discretion may prescribe.

(g) The expenses attending a change of venue shall be taxed by the clerk of the court from which the case is certified according to the rates established by law for like services, and shall be paid by the petitioner and not allowed as part of the costs in the action.

(h) The order shall be void unless the party obtaining a change of venue shall, within 15 days, or such shorter time as the court may prescribe, pay to the clerk the expenses attending the change.

(i) Where the venue is changed without the application of either party, the costs of such change shall abide the event of the action.

(j) In all cases of change of venue, the clerk of the court from which the change is granted shall immediately prepare a full transcript of the record and proceedings in the case, and of the petition, affidavits and order for the change of venue, and transmit the same, together with all the papers filed in the case, to the proper court, but when the venue is changed, on behalf of a part of the defendants in a condemnation proceeding, it shall not be necessary to transmit the original papers in the case, and it shall be sufficient to transmit certified copies of so much thereof as pertains to the case so changed. Such transcript and papers or copies may be transmitted by mail, or in such other ways as the court may direct.

(k) The clerk of the court to which the change of venue is granted shall file the transcript and papers transmitted and docket the cause, and such cause shall be proceeded in and determined before and after judgment, as if it had originated in such court.

(l) All questions concerning the regularity of the proceedings in a change of venue, and the right of the court to which the change is made to try the cause and enforce the judgment, shall be considered as waived after trial and verdict.

(m) Upon the entry of judgment of any civil cause in which the venue has been changed, it shall be lawful for the party in whose favor judgment is entered, to file in the office of the clerk of the court where the action was instituted a transcript of such judgment, and the clerk shall file the same of record, and enforcement may be had thereon, and the same shall, from the time of filing such transcript, have the same operation and effect as if originally recovered in such court.
Formerly § 2–1001. Resectioned in part § 2–1001.5 and amended by P.A. 87–949, § 1, eff. Jan. 1, 1993.

Formerly Ill.Rev.Stat., ch. 110, ¶ 2–1001.5.

5/2–1002.   § 2–1002. Repealed by P.A. 87–949, § 2, eff. Jan. 1, 1993

5/2–1003.   Discovery and depositions

§ 2–1003. Discovery and depositions.

(a) Discovery, such as admissions of fact and of genuineness of documents, physical and mental examinations of parties and other persons, the taking of any depositions, and interrogatories, shall be in accordance with rules.

(b) (Blank).

(c) (Blank).

(d) Whenever the defendant in any litigation in this State has the right to demand a physical or mental examination of the plaintiff pursuant to statute or Supreme Court Rule, relative to the occurrence and extent of injuries or damages for which claim is made, or in connection with the plaintiff's capacity to exercise any right plaintiff has, or would have but for a finding based upon such examination, the plaintiff has the right to have his or her attorney, or such other person as the plaintiff may wish, present at such physical or mental examination.

(e) No person or organization shall be required to furnish claims, loss or risk management information held or provided by an insurer, which information is described in Section 143.10a of the "Illinois Insurance Code".[1]

P.A. 82–280, § 2–1003, eff. July 1, 1982. Amended by P.A. 84–1431, Art. 8, § 3, eff. Nov. 25, 1986; P.A. 89–7, § 15, eff. March 9, 1995; P.A. 99–110, § 5, eff. Jan. 1, 2016.

Formerly Ill.Rev.Stat.1991, ch. 110, ¶ 2–1003.

[1] 215 ILCS 5/143.10a.

Validity

Public Act 89–7, which amended this section, has been held unconstitutional in its entirety by the Illinois Supreme Court in the case of Best v. Taylor Machine Works, 1997, 689 N.E.2d 1057, 228 Ill.Dec. 636, 179 Ill.2d 367.

This section as amended by P.A. 89–7 also has been held unconstitutional by the Illinois Supreme Court in the case of Kunkel v. Walton, 1997, 689 N.E.2d 1047, 228 Ill.Dec. 626, 179 Ill.2d 519.

P.A. 89–7 inserted subsec. (a); redesignated former subsec. (a) as (a–1); and added subsec. (f). Prior to amendment by P.A. 89–7, the section read:

"Discovery and depositions. (a) Discovery, admissions of fact and of genuineness of documents and answers to interrogatories shall be in accordance with rules.

"(b) The taking of depositions, whether for use in evidence or for purposes of discovery in proceedings in this State or elsewhere, and fees and charges in connection therewith, shall be in accordance with rules.

"(c) A party shall not be required to furnish the names or addresses of his or her witnesses, except that upon motion of any party disclosure of the identity of expert witnesses shall be made to all parties and the court in sufficient time in advance of trial so as to insure a fair and equitable preparation of the case by all parties.

"(d) Whenever the defendant in any litigation in this State has the right to demand a physical or mental examination of the plaintiff pursuant to statute or Supreme Court Rule, relative to the occurrence and extent of injuries or damages for which claim is made, or in connection with the plaintiff's capacity to exercise any right plaintiff has, or would have but for a finding based upon such examination, the plaintiff has the right to have his or her attorney, or such other person as the plaintiff may wish, present at such physical or mental examination.

"(e) No person or organization shall be required to furnish claims, loss or risk management information held or provided by an insurer, which information is described in Section 143.10a of the 'Illinois Insurance Code'."

Section 995 of P.A. 89–7, approved March 9, 1995, provides:

"Effective date. This Act takes effect upon becoming law, and applies to causes of action as specified in each Section or part of this Act."

5/2–1004. Pretrial procedure

§ 2–1004. Pretrial procedure. The holding of pretrial conferences shall be in accordance with rules. P.A. 82–280, § 2–1004, eff. July 1, 1982.

Formerly Ill.Rev.Stat.1991, ch. 110, ¶ 2–1004.

5/2–1005. Summary judgments

§ 2–1005. Summary judgments. (a) For plaintiff. Any time after the opposite party has appeared or after the time within which he or she is required to appear has expired, a plaintiff may move with or without supporting affidavits for a summary judgment in his or her favor for all or any part of the relief sought.

(b) For defendant. A defendant may, at any time, move with or without supporting affidavits for a summary judgment in his or her favor as to all or any part of the relief sought against him or her.

(c) Procedure. The opposite party may prior to or at the time of the hearing on the motion file counteraffidavits. The judgment sought shall be rendered without delay if the pleadings, depositions, and admissions on file, together with the affidavits, if any, show that there is no genuine issue as to any material fact and that the moving party is entitled to a judgment as a matter of law. A summary judgment, interlocutory in character, may be rendered on the issue of liability alone although there is a genuine issue as to the amount of damages.

(d) Summary determination of major issues. If the court determines that there is no genuine issue of material fact as to one or more of the major issues in the case, but that substantial controversy exists with respect to other major issues, or if a party moves for a summary determination of one or more, but less than all, of the major issues in the case, and the court finds that there is no genuine issue of material fact as to that issue or those issues, the court shall thereupon draw an order specifying the major issue or issues that appear without substantial controversy, and directing such further proceedings upon the remaining undetermined issues as are just. Upon the trial of the case, the facts so specified shall be deemed established, and the trial shall be conducted accordingly.

(e) Form of affidavits. The form and contents of and procedure relating to affidavits under this Section shall be as provided by rule.

(f) Affidavits made in bad faith. If it appears to the satisfaction of the court at any time that any affidavit presented pursuant to this Section is presented in bad faith or solely for the purpose of delay, the court shall without delay order the party employing it to pay to the other party the amount of the reasonable expenses which the filing of the affidavit caused him or her to incur, including reasonable attorney's fees, and any offending party or attorney may be adjudged guilty of contempt.

(g) Amendment of pleading. Before or after the entry of a summary judgment, the court shall permit pleadings to be amended upon just and reasonable terms.

P.A. 82–280, § 2–1005, eff. July 1, 1982. Amended by P.A. 84–316, § 1, eff. Sept. 14, 1985.

Formerly Ill.Rev.Stat.1991, ch. 110, ¶ 2–1005.

5/2–1006. Consolidation and severance of cases

§ 2–1006. Consolidation and severance of cases. An action may be severed, and actions pending in the same court may be consolidated, as an aid to convenience, whenever it can be done without prejudice to a substantial right.

P.A. 82–280, § 2–1006, eff. July 1, 1982.

Formerly Ill.Rev.Stat.1991, ch. 110, ¶ 2–1006.

5/2–1007. Extension of time and continuances

§ 2–1007. Extension of time and continuances. On good cause shown, in the discretion of the court and on just terms, additional time may be granted for the doing of any act or the taking of any step or proceeding prior to judgment.

The circumstances, terms and conditions under which continuances may be granted, the time and manner in which application therefor shall be made, and the effect thereof, shall be according to rules. However, in actions involving building code violations or violations of municipal ordinances caused by the failure of a building or structure to conform to the minimum standards of health and safety, the court shall grant a continuance only upon a written motion by the party seeking the continuance specifying the reason why such continuance should be granted.

It is sufficient cause for the continuance of any action that any party applying therefor or his or her attorney is a member of either house of the General Assembly during the time the General Assembly is in session, or if any party's attorney is a bona fide member of a religious faith that dictates that the individual refrain from normal business activity or attend religious services as a part of the observance of a religious holiday and requests a continuance to observe such religious holiday when the date of a scheduled court proceeding conflicts with the date of such holiday, or if any party applying therefor or his or her attorney is a delegate to a State Constitutional Convention during the time the Constitutional Convention is in session, if the presence of such party is necessary for the full and fair trial of the action and, in the case of his or her attorney, if such attorney was retained by such party prior to the time the cause was set for trial.

P.A. 82–280, § 2–1007, eff. July 1, 1982. Amended by P.A. 83–703, § 1, eff. July 1, 1984; P.A. 84–931, § 1, eff. Sept. 23, 1985.

Formerly Ill.Rev.Stat.1991, ch. 110, ¶ 2–1007.

5/2–1007.1. Preference in setting for trial

§ 2–1007.1. Preference in setting for trial. (a) A party who is an individual and has reached the age of 70 years shall, upon motion by that party, be entitled to preference in setting for trial unless the court finds that the party does not have a substantial interest in the case as a whole.

(b) The court may, in its discretion, grant a motion for preference in setting for trial where a party shows good cause that the interests of justice will be served by granting a preference in setting for trial.

P.A. 82–280, § 2–1007.1, added by P.A. 86–854, § 1, eff. Jan. 1, 1990.

Formerly Ill.Rev.Stat.1991, ch. 110, ¶ 2–1007.1.

5/2–1008. Abatement; change of interest or liability; substitution of parties

§ 2–1008. Abatement; change of interest or liability; substitution of parties.

(a) Change of interest or liability. If by reason of marriage, bankruptcy, assignment, or any other event occurring after the commencement of a cause or proceeding, either before or after judgment, causing a change or transmission of interest or liability, or by reason of any person interested coming into existence after commencement of the action, it becomes necessary or desirable that any person not already a party be before the court, or that any person already a party be made party in another capacity, the action does not abate, but on motion an order may be entered that the proper parties be substituted or added, and that the cause or proceeding be carried on with the remaining parties and new parties, with or without a change in the title of the cause.

(b) Death. If a party to an action dies and the action is one which survives, the proper party or parties may be substituted by order of court upon motion as follows:

(1) If no petition for letters of office for the decedent's estate has been filed, the court may appoint a special representative for the deceased for the purpose of prosecuting the action. The appointment shall be on verified motion of any party who appears entitled to participate in the deceased's estate, reciting the names and last known addresses of all known heirs and the legatees and executor

named in any will that has been filed. The court's determination that a person appears entitled to participate in the deceased's estate shall be solely for purposes of this Section and not determinative of rights in final disposition. Within 90 days after appointment, the special representative shall notify the heirs and legatees of the following information by mail: that an appointment has been made, the court in which the case was filed, the caption of the case, and a description of the nature of the case. The special representative shall publish notice to unknown heirs and legatees as provided in the Probate Act of 1975.[1] If a will is filed within 90 days after the appointment of the special representative, the same notice shall be given to any additional executors and legatees named in the will. At any time that an estate is opened with a representative other than the special representative, the court may upon motion substitute the representative for the special representative. In this case, the court shall allow disbursements and fees of the special representative and his or her attorney as a claim against any proceeds received. The proceeds of any judgment or settlement shall be distributed under the provisions of the Probate Act of 1975. This paragraph (1) does not apply to actions pending under the Wrongful Death Act.[2]

(2) If a person against whom an action has been brought dies, and the cause of action survives and is not otherwise barred, his or her personal representative shall be substituted as a party. If no petition has been filed for letters of office for the deceased's estate, the court, upon the motion of a person bringing an action and after the notice to the party's heirs or legatees as the court directs and without opening an estate, may appoint a special representative for the deceased party for the purposes of defending the action. If a party elects to have a special representative appointed under this paragraph (2), the recovery shall be limited to the proceeds of any liability insurance protecting the estate and shall not bar the estate from enforcing any claims that might have been available to it as counterclaims.

If a motion to substitute is not filed within 90 days after the death is suggested of record, the action may be dismissed as to the deceased party.

In the event of the death of a party in an action in which the right sought to be enforced survives only as to the remaining parties to the action, the action does not abate. The death shall be suggested of record and the action shall proceed in favor of or against the remaining parties.

No action brought for the use of another abates by reason of the death of the plaintiff whose name is used but may be maintained by the party for whose use it was brought in his or her own name upon suggesting the death of record and the entry of an order of substitution.

(c) Legal disability. If a party is declared to be a person under legal disability, that fact shall be suggested of record and the prosecution or defense shall be maintained by his or her representative, guardian ad litem or next friend, as may be appropriate.

(d) Trustees; public officers. If any trustee or any public officer ceases to hold the trust or office and that fact is suggested of record, the action shall proceed in favor of or against his or her successor.

(e) Service of process. Parties against whom relief is sought, substituted under subsection (a) hereof, shall be brought in by service of process. Service of process on parties substituted under subsections (b), (c), and (d) hereof is not required, but notice shall be given as the court may direct.

P.A. 82–280, § 2–1008, eff. July 1, 1982. Amended by P.A. 83–707, § 1, eff. Sept. 23, 1983; P.A. 90–111, § 5, eff. July 14, 1997.

Formerly Ill.Rev.Stat.1991, ch. 110, ¶ 2–1008.

[1] 755 ILCS 5/1–1 et seq.
[2] 740 ILCS 180/0.01 et seq.

5/2–1009. Voluntary dismissal

§ 2–1009. Voluntary dismissal. (a) The plaintiff may, at any time before trial or hearing begins, upon notice to each party who has appeared or each such party's attorney, and upon payment of costs, dismiss his or her action or any part thereof as to any defendant, without prejudice, by order filed in the cause.

(b) The court may hear and decide a motion that has been filed prior to a motion filed under subsection (a) of this Section when that prior filed motion, if favorably ruled on by the court, could result in a final disposition of the cause.

(c) After trial or hearing begins, the plaintiff may dismiss, only on terms fixed by the court (1) upon filing a stipulation to that effect signed by the defendant, or (2) on motion specifying the ground for dismissal, which shall be supported by affidavit or other proof.

(d) A dismissal under subsection (a) of this Section does not dismiss a pending counterclaim or third party complaint.

(e) Counterclaimants and third-party plaintiffs may dismiss upon the same terms and conditions as plaintiffs.

P.A. 82–280, § 2–1009, eff. July 1, 1982. Amended by P.A. 88–157, § 5, eff. Jan. 1, 1994.

Formerly Ill.Rev.Stat.1991, ch. 110, ¶ 2–1009.

5/2–1010. Healing art malpractice; affidavit in lieu of answer or other pleading

§ 2–1010. (a) In any action, whether in tort, contract or otherwise, in which the plaintiff seeks damages for injuries or death by reason of medical, hospital, or other healing art malpractice, a party may, in lieu of answering or otherwise pleading, file an affidavit certifying that he or she was not directly or indirectly involved in the occurrence or occurrences alleged in the action. In the event such an affidavit is filed, the court shall order the dismissal of the claim against the certifying party, except as provided for in subparagraph (b).

(b) Any party may oppose the dismissal or move to vacate the order of dismissal and reinstate the certifying party, provided he or she can show that the certifying party was directly or indirectly involved in the occurrence or occurrences alleged in the action. The party opposing the dismissal may, after the filing of an affidavit under this Section, have discovery with respect to the involvement or noninvolvement of the party filing the affidavit, provided that such discovery is completed within 60 days of the filing of such affidavit.

(c) This Section does not apply to or affect any actions pending at the time of its effective date, but applies to cases filed on or after its effective date.
P.A. 82–280, § 2–1010, added by P.A. 84–7, § 1, eff. Aug. 15, 1985.

Formerly Ill.Rev.Stat.1991, ch. 110, ¶ 2–1010.

5/2–1011. Deposits with Court

§ 2–1011. Deposits with Court. (a) In any action in which any part of the relief sought is a judgment for a sum of money or a determination by the court as to the disposition of a sum of money and a party to the action deposits all or part of that sum with the clerk of the court, the clerk shall deposit that money in an interest bearing account as provided in this Section. When a judgment is entered as to the disposition of the principal deposited, the court shall also direct disposition of the interest accrued to the parties as it deems appropriate.

(b) Unless otherwise ordered by the court as to a specified deposit or deposits, all funds so deposited with the court may be intermingled. The accounts established by the clerk of the circuit court under this Section shall be in banks or savings and loan associations doing business in this State. The accounts must be insured by an agency of the United States to the full extent of the amounts held in the accounts. The clerk shall keep complete and accurate records of the amounts deposited with the court in each action and of the accounts containing those deposits. The records and accounts shall be subject to audit, as provided by law. The clerk shall, upon request of any party in an action in which a sum of money has been deposited with the court under this Section, furnish to that party a statement showing the condition of the deposit or of the account containing the deposit.

(c) Payment out of money deposited with the court shall be made only upon order of the court after a finding that:

(1) the order is consistent with the account records as to the amount involved; and

(2) the order correctly identifies affected parties and specifies to whom payments are to be made and the amount each is to receive.

(d) No moneys on deposit under this Section shall be paid out except by a check of the clerk.

(e) Orders to pay out may be made under terms and conditions as the court may, in its discretion, deem appropriate, subject to the provisions of this Section. The orders may be stayed pending appeal upon application under Supreme Court Rule 305.
P.A. 82–280, § 2–1011, added by P.A. 86–1329, § 3, eff. Jan. 1, 1991.

Formerly Ill.Rev.Stat.1991, ch. 110, ¶ 2–1011.

5/2–1012 to 5/2–1020. §§ 2–1012 to 2–1020.
Repealed by P.A. 86–1028, Art. III, § 3–34, eff. Feb. 5, 1990

PART 10A. MANDATORY ARBITRATION SYSTEM

Section

Date Effective

Part 10A was added by P.A. 84–844, § 1, eff. Jan. 1, 1986.

5/2–1001A. Authorization

§ 2–1001A. Authorization. The Supreme Court of Illinois, by rule, may provide for mandatory arbitration of such civil actions as the Court deems appropriate in order to expedite in a less costly manner any litigation wherein a party asserts a claim not exceeding $50,000 or any lesser amount as authorized by the Supreme Court for a particular Circuit, or a judge of the circuit court, at a pretrial conference, determines that no greater amount than that authorized for the Circuit appears to be genuinely in controversy.
P.A. 82–280, § 2–1001A, added by P.A. 84–844, § 1, eff. Jan. 1, 1986. Amended by P.A. 88–108, § 5, eff. July 20, 1993.

Formerly Ill.Rev.Stat.1991, ch.110, ¶ 2–1001A.

5/2–1002A. Implementation by Supreme Court Rules

§ 2–1002A. Implementation by Supreme Court Rules. The Supreme Court shall by rule adopt procedures adapted to each judicial circuit to implement mandatory arbitration under this Act.

P.A. 82–280, § 2–1002A, added by P.A. 84–844, § 1, eff. Jan. 1, 1986.

Formerly Ill.Rev.Stat.1991, ch.110, ¶ 2–1002A.

5/2–1003A. Qualification, Appointment, and Compensation of Arbitrators

§ 2–1003A. Qualification, Appointment, and Compensation of Arbitrators. The qualification and the method of appointment of arbitrators shall be prescribed by rule. Arbitrators shall be entitled to reasonable compensation for their services. Arbitration hearings shall be conducted by arbitrators sitting in panels of three or of such lesser number as may be stipulated by the parties.

P.A. 82–280, § 2–1003A, added by P.A. 84–844, § 1, eff. Jan. 1, 1986.

Formerly Ill.Rev.Stat.1991, ch.110, ¶ 2–1003A.

5/2–1004A. Decision and Award

§ 2–1004A. Decision and Award. Following an arbitration hearing as prescribed by rule, the arbitrators' decision shall be filed with the circuit court, together with proof of service on the parties. Within the time prescribed by rule, any party to the proceeding may file with the clerk of the court a written notice of the rejection of the award. In case of such rejection, the parties may, upon payment of appropriate costs and fees imposed by Supreme Court Rule as a consequence of the rejection, proceed to trial before a judge or jury. Costs and fees received by the clerk of the circuit court pursuant to this Section shall be remitted within one month after receipt to the State Treasurer for deposit into the Mandatory Arbitration Fund.

P.A. 82–280, § 2–1004A, added by P.A. 84–844, § 1, eff. Jan. 1, 1986. Amended by P.A. 85–408, § 2, eff. Sept. 15, 1987; P.A. 85–1007, § 1, eff. Jan. 21, 1988.

Formerly Ill.Rev.Stat.1991, ch.110, ¶ 2–1004A.

5/2–1005A. Judgment of the Court

§ 2–1005A. Judgment of the Court. If no rejection of the award is filed, a judge of the circuit court may enter the award as the judgment of the court.

P.A. 82–280, § 2–1005A, added by P.A. 84–844, § 1, eff. Jan. 1, 1986.

Formerly Ill.Rev.Stat.1991, ch.110, ¶ 2–1005A.

5/2–1006A. Uniform Arbitration Act

§ 2–1006A. Uniform Arbitration Act. The provisions of the Uniform Arbitration Act shall not be applicable to the proceedings under this Part 10A of Article II.

P.A. 82–280, § 2–1006A, added by P.A. 84–844, § 1, eff. Jan. 1, 1986. Amended by P.A. 84–1308, Art. II, § 107, eff. Aug. 25, 1986.

Formerly Ill.Rev.Stat.1991, ch.110, ¶ 2–1006A.

5/2–1007A. Expenses

§ 2–1007A. The expenses of conducting mandatory arbitration programs in the circuit court, including arbitrator fees, and the expenses related to conducting such other alternative dispute resolution programs as may be authorized by circuit court rule for operation in counties that have implemented mandatory arbitration, shall be determined by the Supreme Court and paid from the State Treasury on the warrant of the Comptroller out of appropriations made for that purpose by the General Assembly.

P.A. 82–280, § 2–1007A, added by P.A. 85–408, § 2, eff. Sept. 15, 1987. Amended by P.A. 89–532, § 10, eff. July 19, 1996.

Formerly Ill.Rev.Stat.1991, ch. 110, ¶ 2–1007A.

5/2–1008A. § 2–1008A. Repealed by P.A. 97–1099, § 10, eff. Aug. 24, 2012

5/2–1009A. Filing Fees

§ 2–1009A. Filing Fees. In each county authorized by the Supreme Court to utilize mandatory arbitration, the clerk of the circuit court shall charge and collect, in addition to any other fees, an arbitration fee of $8, except in counties with 3,000,000 or more inhabitants the fee shall be $10, at the time of filing the first pleading, paper or other appearance filed by each party in all civil cases, but no additional fee shall be required if more than one party is represented in a single pleading, paper or other appearance. Arbitration fees received by the clerk of the circuit court pursuant to this Section shall be remitted within one month after receipt to the State Treasurer for deposit into the Mandatory Arbitration Fund, a special fund in the State treasury for the purpose of funding mandatory arbitration programs and such other alternative dispute resolution programs as may be authorized by circuit court rule for operation in counties that have implemented mandatory arbitration, with a separate account being maintained for each county. Notwithstanding any other provision of this Section to the contrary, the Mandatory Arbitration Fund may be used for any other purpose authorized by the Supreme Court.

P.A. 82–280, § 2–1009A, added by P.A. 85–1007, § 1, eff. Jan. 21, 1988. Amended by P.A. 85–1281, § 1, eff. Aug. 30, 1988; P.A. 88–108, § 5, eff. July 20, 1993; P.A. 89–532, § 10, eff. July 19, 1996; P.A. 93–25, Art. 50, § 50–35, eff. June 20, 2003; P.A. 93–839, Art. 10, § 10–178, eff. July 30, 2004; P.A. 94–91, Art. 70, § 70–15, eff. July 1, 2005; P.A. 94–839, Art. 5, § 5–100, eff. June 6, 2006; P.A. 95–707, Art. 5, § 5–55, eff. Jan. 11, 2008.

Formerly Ill.Rev.Stat.1991, ch. 110, ¶ 2–1009A.

PART 11. TRIAL

5/2–1101. Subpoenas

§ 2–1101. Subpoenas. The clerk of any court in which an action is pending shall, from time to time, issue subpoenas for those witnesses and to those counties in the State as may be required by either party. Every clerk who shall refuse so to do shall be guilty of a petty offense and fined any sum not to exceed $100. An attorney admitted to practice in the State of Illinois, as an officer of the court, may also issue subpoenas on behalf of the court for witnesses and to counties in a pending action. An order of court is not required to obtain the issuance by the clerk or by an attorney of a subpoena duces tecum. For good cause shown, the court on motion may quash or modify any subpoena or, in the case of a subpoena duces tecum, condition the denial of the motion upon payment in advance by the person in whose behalf the subpoena is issued of the reasonable expense of producing any item therein specified.

In the event that a party has subpoenaed an expert witness including, but not limited to physicians or medical providers, and the expert witness appears in court, and a conflict arises between the party subpoenaing the expert witness and the expert witness over the fees charged by the expert witness, the trial court shall be advised of the conflict. The trial court shall conduct a hearing subsequent to the testimony of the expert witness and shall determine the reasonable fee to be paid to the expert witness.

P.A. 82–280, § 2–1101, eff. July 1, 1982. Amended by P.A. 87–418, eff. Jan. 1, 1992; P.A. 95–1033, § 5, eff. June 1, 2009.

Formerly Ill.Rev.Stat.1991, ch. 110, ¶ 2–1101.

5/2–1102. Examination of adverse party or agent

§ 2–1102. Examination of adverse party or agent. Upon the trial of any case any party thereto or any person for whose immediate benefit the action is prosecuted or defended, or the officers, directors, managing agents or foreman of any party to the action, may be called and examined as if under cross-examination at the instance of any adverse party. The party calling for the examination is not concluded thereby but may rebut the testimony thus given by countertestimony and may impeach the witness by proof of prior inconsistent statements.

P.A. 82–280, § 2–1102, eff. July 1, 1982.

Formerly Ill.Rev.Stat.1991, ch. 110, ¶ 2–1102.

5/2–1103. Affidavits

§ 2–1103. Affidavits. (a) All affidavits presented to the court shall be filed with the clerk.

(b) If evidence is necessary concerning any fact which according to law and the practice of the court may now be supplied by affidavit, the court may, in its discretion, require the evidence to be presented, wholly or in part, by oral examination of the witnesses in open court upon notice to all parties not in default, or their attorneys. If the evidence is presented by oral examination, an adverse party shall have the right to cross-examination. This Section does not apply to applications for change of venue on grounds of prejudice.

P.A. 82–280, § 2–1103, eff. July 1, 1982.

Formerly Ill.Rev.Stat.1991, ch. 110, ¶ 2–1103.

5/2–1104. Party need not submit to lie detector

§ 2–1104. Party need not submit to lie detector. In the course of any civil trial or pre-trial proceeding the court shall not require that the plaintiff or defendant submit to a polygraphic detection deception test, commonly known as a lie detector test or require, suggest or request that the plaintiff or defendant submit to questioning under the effect of thiopental sodium or to any other test or questioning by means of any chemical substance.

P.A. 82–280, § 2–1104, eff. July 1, 1982.

Formerly Ill.Rev.Stat.1991, ch. 110, ¶ 2–1104.

5/2–1105. Jury demand

§ 2–1105. Jury demand.

(a) A plaintiff desirous of a trial by jury must file a demand therefor with the clerk at the time the action is commenced. A defendant desirous of a trial by jury must file a demand therefor not later than the filing of his or her answer. Otherwise, the party waives a jury. If an action is filed seeking equitable relief and the court thereafter determines that one or more of the parties is or are entitled to a trial by jury, the plaintiff, within 3 days from the entry of such order by the court, or the defendant, within 6 days from the entry of such order by the court, may file his or her demand for trial by jury with the clerk of the court. If the plaintiff files a jury demand and thereafter waives a jury, any defendant and, in the case of multiple defendants, if the defendant who filed a jury demand thereafter waives a jury, any other defendant shall be granted a jury trial upon demand therefor made promptly after being advised of the waiver and upon payment of the proper fees, if any, to the clerk.

(b) All jury cases shall be tried by a jury of 6. If alternate jurors are requested, an additional fee established by the county shall be charged for each alternate juror requested. For all cases filed prior to the effective date of this amendatory Act of the 98th General Assembly, if a party has paid for a jury of 12, that party may demand a jury of 12 upon proof of payment.

P.A. 82–280, § 2–1105, eff. July 1, 1982. Amended by P.A. 83–378, § 1, eff. Sept. 14, 1983; P.A. 83–707, § 1, eff. Sept. 23, 1983; P.A. 83–1362, Art. II, § 109, eff. Sept. 11, 1984; P.A. 94–206, § 5, eff. Jan. 1, 2006; P.A. 98–1132, § 10, eff. June 1, 2015.

Formerly Ill.Rev.Stat.1991, ch. 110, ¶ 2–1105.

Small Claims

Procedure in small claims cases, i.e., civil actions for money not in excess of $5,000, exclusive of interest and costs, is governed by Supreme Court Rules 281 to 289.

5/2–1105.1. Challenge for cause

§ 2–1105.1. Challenge for cause. Each party may challenge jurors for cause. If a prospective juror has a physical impairment, the court shall consider such prospective juror's ability to perceive and appreciate the evidence when considering a challenge for cause.

P.A. 82–280, § 2–1105.1, added by P.A. 83–461, § 3, eff. Jan. 1, 1984.

Formerly Ill.Rev.Stat.1991, ch. 110, ¶ 2–1105.1.

5/2–1106. Peremptory challenges—Alternate jurors

§ 2–1106. Peremptory challenges—Alternate jurors. (a) Each side shall be entitled to 5 peremptory challenges. If there is more than one party on any side, the court may allow each side additional peremptory challenges, not to exceed 3, on account of each additional party on the side having the greatest number of parties. Each side shall be allowed an equal number of peremptory challenges. If the parties on a side are unable to agree upon the allocation of peremptory challenges among themselves, the allocation shall be determined by the court.

(b) The court may direct that 1 or 2 jurors in addition to the regular panel be impanelled to serve as alternate jurors. Alternate jurors, in the sequence in which they are ordered into the jury box, shall replace jurors who, prior to the time the jury retires to consider its verdict, become unable to perform their duties. Alternate jurors shall be drawn in the same manner, have the same qualifications, be subject to the same examination and challenges, take the same oath, and have the same functions, powers, facilities, and privileges as the principal jurors. An alternate juror who does not replace a principal juror shall be discharged at the time the jury retires to consider its verdict. If alternate jurors are called each side shall be allowed one additional peremptory challenge, regardless of the number of alternate jurors called. The additional peremptory challenge may be used only against an alternate juror, but any unexercised peremptory challenges may be used against an alternate juror.

P.A. 82–280, § 2–1106, eff. July 1, 1982. Amended by P.A. 83–707, § 1, eff. Sept. 23, 1983.

Formerly Ill.Rev.Stat.1991, ch. 110, ¶ 2–1106.

5/2–1107. Instructing the jury—Taking instructions and papers to the jury room

§ 2–1107. Instructing the jury—Taking instructions and papers to the jury room. (a) The court shall give instructions to the jury only in writing, unless the parties agree otherwise, and only as to the law of the case. An original and one copy of each instruction asked by any party shall be tendered to the court. The copies shall be numbered and shall indicate who tendered them. Copies of instructions given on the court's own motion or modified by the court shall be so identified. When instructions are asked which the court refuses to give, the court shall on the margin of the original and copy write the word "refused" and shall write the word "given" on the margin of the original and copy of those given. The court shall in no case, after instructions are given, clarify, modify or in any manner explain them to the jury, otherwise than in writing, unless the parties agree otherwise.

(b) The original written instructions given by the court to the jury shall be taken by the jury to the jury room, and shall be returned by the jury with its verdict into court. The originals and copies of all instructions, whether given, modified or refused, shall be filed as a part of the proceedings in the cause.

(c) At the close of the evidence or at any earlier time during the trial that the court reasonably directs, any party may tender instructions and shall at the same time deliver copies thereof to counsel for other parties. If the number or length of the instructions tendered is unreasonable, the court after examining the instructions may require counsel to reduce the number or length thereof. The court shall hold a conference with counsel to settle the instructions and shall inform counsel of the court's proposed action thereon prior to the arguments to the jury. If as a result of the arguments to the jury the court determines that additional instructions are desirable, the court may after a further conference with counsel approve additional instructions. The court shall instruct the jury after the arguments are completed. Conferences on instructions must be out of the presence of the jury.

(d) Papers read or received in evidence, other than depositions, may be taken by the jury to the jury room for use during the jury's deliberation.

P.A. 82–280, § 2–1107, eff. July 1, 1982. Amended by P.A. 83–707, § 1, eff. Sept. 23, 1983.

Formerly Ill.Rev.Stat.1991, ch. 110, ¶ 2–1107.

5/2–1107.1.   Jury instruction in tort actions

§ 2–1107.1. Jury instruction in tort actions. In all actions on account of bodily injury or death or physical damage to property based on negligence, or product liability based on any theory or doctrine, the court shall instruct the jury in writing, to the extent that it is true, that any award of compensatory damages or punitive damages will not be taxable under federal or State income tax law. The court shall not inform or instruct the jury that the defendant shall be found not liable if the jury finds that the contributory fault of the plaintiff is more than 50% of the proximate cause of the injury or damage for which recovery is sought, but it shall be the duty of the court to deny recovery if the jury finds that the plaintiff's contributory fault is more than 50% of the proximate cause of the injury or damage. The court shall not inform or instruct the jury concerning any limitations in the amount of non-economic damages or punitive damages that are recoverable, but it shall be the duty of the trial court upon entering judgment to reduce any award in excess of such limitation to no more than the proper limitation.

This amendatory Act of 1995 applies to causes of action filed on or after its effective date.

P.A. 82–280, § 2–1107.1, added by P.A. 84–1431, Art. 4, § 1, eff. Nov. 25, 1986. Amended by P.A. 89–7, § 15, eff. March 9, 1995.

Formerly Ill.Rev.Stat.1991, ch. 110, ¶ 2–1107.1.

Validity
Public Act 89–7, which amended this section, has been held unconstitutional in its

entirely by the Illinois Supreme Court in the case of Best v. Taylor Machine Works, 1997, 689 N.E.2d 1057, 228 Ill.Dec. 636, 179 Ill.2d 367.

P.A. 89–7 rewrote this section, which prior thereto read:

"Jury instruction in tort actions. In all actions on account of bodily injury or death or physical damage to property based on negligence, or product liability based on strict tort liability, the court shall instruct the jury in writing that the defendant shall be found not liable if the jury finds that the contributory fault of the plaintiff is more than 50% of the proximate cause of the injury or damage for which recovery is sought."

5/2–1108.   Verdict—Special interrogatories

§ 2–1108. Verdict—Special interrogatories. Unless the nature of the case requires otherwise, the jury shall render a general verdict. The jury may be required by the court, and must be required on request of any party, to find specially upon any material question or questions of fact submitted to the jury in writing. Special interrogatories shall be tendered, objected to, ruled upon and submitted to the jury as in the case of instructions. Submitting or refusing to submit a question of fact to the jury may be reviewed on appeal, as a ruling on a question of law. When the special finding of fact is inconsistent with the general verdict, the former controls the latter and the court may enter judgment accordingly.

P.A. 82–280, § 2–1108, eff. July 1, 1982. Amended by P.A. 83–707, § 1, eff. Sept. 23, 1983.

Formerly Ill.Rev.Stat.1991, ch. 110, ¶ 2–1108.

5/2–1109.   Itemized verdicts

§ 2–1109. Itemized verdicts. In every case where damages for bodily injury or death are assessed by the jury the verdict shall be itemized so as to reflect the monetary distribution, if any, among economic loss and non-economic loss as defined in Section 2–1115.2 and, in healing art malpractice cases, further itemized so as to reflect the distribution of economic loss by category, such itemization of economic loss by category to include: (a) amounts intended to compensate for reasonable expenses which have been incurred, or which will be incurred, for necessary medical, surgical, x-ray, dental, or other health or rehabilitative services, drugs, and therapy; (b) amounts intended to compensate for lost wages or loss of earning capacity; and (c) all other economic losses claimed by the plaintiff or granted by the jury. Each category of economic loss shall be further itemized into amounts intended to compensate for losses which have been incurred prior to the verdict and amounts intended to compensate for future losses.

This amendatory Act of 1995 applies to causes of action filed on or after its effective date.

P.A. 82–280, § 2–1109, eff. July 1, 1982. Amended by P.A. 84–7, § 1, eff. Aug. 15, 1985; P.A. 89–7, § 15, eff. March 9, 1995.

Formerly Ill.Rev.Stat.1991, ch. 110, ¶ 2–1109.

Validity

Public Act 89–7, which amended this section, has been held unconstitutional in its entirety by the Illinois Supreme Court in the case of Best v. Taylor Machine Works, 1997, 689 N.E.2d 1057, 228 Ill.Dec. 636, 179 Ill.2d 367.

P.A. 89–7, in the paragraph requiring itemized verdicts, in the sentence relating to itemization of economic loss by category, substituted "bodily injury or death" for "injury to the person" and "as defined in Section 2–1115.2 and, in healing art malpractice cases" for ", if any, and, in medical malpractice cases" and inserted ", if any,", and in the sentence relating to further itemization, substituted "future losses" for "losses which will be incurred in the future"; and added the paragraph relating to the applicability of this amendatory Act.

Prior to amendment by P.A. 89–7, this section read:

"Itemized verdicts. In every case where damages for injury to the person are assessed by the jury the verdict shall be itemized so as to reflect the monetary distribution among economic loss and non-economic loss, if any, and, in medical malpractice cases, further itemized so as to reflect the distribution of economic loss by category, such itemization of economic loss by category to include: (a) amounts intended to compensate for reasonable expenses which have been incurred, or which will be incurred, for necessary medical, surgical, x-ray, dental, or other health or rehabilitative services, drugs, and therapy; (b) amounts intended to compensate for lost wages or loss of earning capacity; and (c) all other economic losses claimed by the plaintiff or granted by the jury. Each category of economic loss shall be further itemized into amounts intended to compensate for losses which have been incurred prior to the verdict and amounts intended to compensate for losses which will be incurred in the future."

5/2–1110. Motion in non-jury case to find for defendant at close of plaintiff's evidence

§ 2–1110. Motion in non-jury case to find for defendant at close of plaintiff's evidence. In all cases tried without a jury, defendant may, at the close of plaintiff's case, move for a finding or judgment in his or her favor. In ruling on the motion the court shall weigh the evidence, considering the credibility of the witnesses and the weight and quality of the evidence. If the ruling on the motion is favorable to the defendant, a judgment dismissing the action shall be entered. If the ruling on the motion is adverse to the defendant, the defendant may proceed to adduce evidence in support of his or her defense, in which event the motion is waived.

P.A. 82–280, § 2–1110, eff. July 1, 1982.

Formerly Ill.Rev.Stat.1991, ch. 110, ¶ 2–1110.

5/2–1111. Juries in cases seeking equitable relief

§ 2–1111. Juries in cases seeking equitable relief. The court may in its discretion direct an issue or issues to be tried by a jury, whenever it is judged necessary in any action seeking equitable relief.

P.A. 82–280, § 2–1111, eff. July 1, 1982.

Formerly Ill.Rev.Stat.1991, ch. 110, ¶ 2–1111.

5/2–1112. Oral testimony in actions seeking equitable relief

§ 2–1112. Oral testimony in actions seeking equitable relief. On the trial of every action seeking equitable relief, oral testimony shall be taken when desired by either party.

P.A. 82–280, § 2–1112, eff. July 1, 1982.

Formerly Ill.Rev.Stat.1991, ch. 110, ¶ 2–1112.

5/2–1113. Medical malpractice—res ipsa loquitur

§ 2–1113. Medical malpractice—res ipsa loquitur. In all cases of alleged medical or dental malpractice, where the plaintiff relies upon the doctrine of res ipsa loquitur, the court shall determine whether that doctrine applies. In making that determination, the court shall rely upon either the common knowledge of laymen, if it determines that to be adequate, or upon expert medical testimony, that the medical result complained of would not have ordinarily occurred in the absence of negligence on the part of the defendant. Proof of an unusual, unexpected or untoward medical result which ordinarily does not occur in the absence of negligence will suffice in the application of the doctrine.

P.A. 82–280, § 2–1113, added by P.A. 82–783, Art. III, § 43, eff. July 13, 1982.

Formerly Ill.Rev.Stat.1991, ch. 110, ¶ 2–1113.

5/2–1114. Contingent fees for attorneys in medical malpractice actions

§ 2–1114. Contingent fees for attorneys in medical malpractice actions.

(a) In all medical malpractice actions the total contingent fee for plaintiff's attorney or attorneys shall not exceed 33 1/3% of all sums recovered.

(b) For purposes of determining any lump sum contingent fee, any future damages recoverable by the plaintiff in periodic installments shall be reduced to a lump sum value.

(c) (Blank).

(d) As used in this Section, "contingent fee basis" includes any fee arrangement under which the compensation is to be determined in whole or in part on the result obtained.

P.A. 82–280, § 2–1114, added by P.A. 84–7, § 1, eff. Aug. 15, 1985. Amended by P.A. 97–1145, § 10, eff. Jan. 18, 2013.

Formerly Ill.Rev.Stat.1991, ch. 110, ¶ 2–1114.

5/2–1115. Punitive damages not recoverable in healing art and legal malpractice cases

§ 2–1115. Punitive damages not recoverable in healing art and legal malpractice cases. In all cases, whether in tort, contract or otherwise, in which the plaintiff seeks damages by reason of legal, medical, hospital, or other healing art malpractice, no punitive, exemplary, vindictive or aggravated damages shall be allowed.

P.A. 82–280, § 2–1115, added by P.A. 84–7, § 1, eff. Aug. 15, 1985.

Formerly Ill.Rev.Stat.1991, ch. 110, ¶ 2–1115.

5/2–1115.05. Limitations on recovery of punitive damages in cases other than healing art or legal malpractice cases

§ 2–1115.05. Limitations on recovery of punitive damages in cases other than healing art or legal malpractice cases.

(a) In all cases on account of bodily injury, or physical damage to property based on negligence, or product liability based on any theory or doctrine, other than those cases described in Section 2–1115, punitive damages may be awarded only if actual damages are awarded. The amount of punitive damages that may be awarded for a claim in any civil action subject to this Section shall not exceed 3 times the amount awarded to the claimant for the economic damages on which such claim is based.

(b) To recover punitive damages in cases described in subsection (a), a plaintiff must show by clear and convincing evidence that the defendant's conduct was with evil motive or with a reckless and outrageous indifference to a highly unreasonable risk of harm and with a conscious indifference to the rights and safety of others. "Clear and convincing evidence" means that measure or degree of proof that will produce in the mind of the trier of fact a high degree of certainty as to the truth of the allegations sought to be established. This evidence requires a greater degree of persuasion than is necessary to meet the preponderance of the evidence standard.

(c) In any action including a claim for punitive damages, a defendant may request that the issues relating to punitive damages be tried separately from the other issues in the action. If such a request is made, the trier of fact shall first hear evidence relevant to, and render a verdict upon, the defendant's liability for compensatory damages and the amount thereof. If the trier of fact makes an award of actual damages, the same trier of fact shall immediately hear any additional evidence relevant to, and render a verdict upon, the defendant's liability for punitive damages and the amount thereof. If no award of actual damages is made, the claim for punitive damages shall be dismissed. If the defendant requests a separate proceeding concerning liability for punitive damages pursuant to this Section, and the proceeding is held, evidence relevant only to the claim of punitive damages shall be inadmissible in any proceeding to determine whether compensatory damages are to be awarded.

(d) The limitations of subsection (a) shall not apply in a case in which a plaintiff seeks damages against an individual on account of death, bodily injury, or physical damage to property based on any theory or doctrine due to an incident or occurrence for which the individual has been charged and convicted of a criminal act for which a period of incarceration is or may be a part of the sentence.

(e) Nothing in this Section shall be construed to create a right to recover punitive damages.

(f) This amendatory Act of 1995 applies to causes of action accruing on or after its effective date.

P.A. 82–280, § 2–1115.05, added by P.A. 89–7, § 15, eff. March 9, 1995.

Validity

Public Act 89–7, which added this section, has been held unconstitutional in its entirety by the Illinois Supreme Court in the case of Best v. Taylor Machine Works, 1997, 689 N.E.2d 1057, 228 Ill.Dec. 636, 179 Ill.2d 367.

5/2–1115.1. Limitations on recovery of non-economic damages

§ 2–1115.1. Limitations on recovery of non-economic damages.

(a) In all common law, statutory or other actions that seek damages on account of death, bodily injury, or physical damage to property based on negligence, or product liability based on any theory or doctrine, recovery of non-economic damages shall be limited to $500,000 per plaintiff. There shall be no recovery for hedonic damages.

(b) Beginning in 1997, every January 20, the liability limit established in subsection (a) shall automatically be increased or decreased, as applicable, by a percentage equal to the percentage change in the consumer price index-u during the preceding 12-month calendar year. "Consumer price index-u" means the index published by the Bureau of Labor Statistics of the United States Department of Labor that measures the average change in prices of goods and services purchased by all urban consumers, United States city average, all items, 1982–84 = 100. The new amount resulting from each annual adjustment shall be determined by the Comptroller and made available to the chief judge of each judicial circuit.

(c) The liability limits at the time at which damages subject to such limits are awarded by final judgment or settlement shall be utilized by the courts.

(d) Nothing in this Section shall be construed to create a right to recover non-economic damages.

(e) This amendatory Act of 1995 applies to causes of action accruing on or after its effective date.

P.A. 82–280, § 2–1115.1, added by P.A. 89–7, § 15, eff. March 9, 1995. Amended by P.A. 95–331, § 1085, eff. Aug. 21, 2007.

Public Act 89–7, which added this section, has been held unconstitutional in its entirety by the Illinois Supreme Court in the case of Best v. Taylor Machine Works, 1997, 689 N.E.2d 1057, 228 Ill.Dec. 636, 179 Ill.2d 367.

P.A. 95–331 amended this section, which was added by P.A. 89–7. P.A. 89–7 has been held unconstitutional. See italic Validity notes, ante.

5/2–1115.2. Economic and non-economic loss

§ 2–1115.2. Economic and non-economic loss. In all actions on account of bodily injury, death, physical damage to property based on negligence, or a product liability action as defined in Section 2–2101, the following terms have the following meanings:

(a) "Economic loss" or "economic damages" means all damages which are tangible, such as damages for past and future medical expenses, loss of income or earnings and other property loss.

(b) "Non-economic loss" or "non-economic damages" means damages which are intangible, including but not limited to damages for pain and suffering, disability, disfigurement, loss of consortium, and loss of society.

(c) "Compensatory damages" or "actual damages" are the sum of economic and non-economic damages.

This amendatory Act of 1995 applies to causes of action filed on or after its effective date.

P.A. 82–280, § 2–1115.2, added by P.A. 89–7, § 15, eff. March 9, 1995.

Validity

Public Act 89–7, which added this section, has been held unconstitutional in its entirety by the Illinois Supreme Court in the case of Best v. Taylor Machine Works, 1997, 689 N.E.2d 1057, 228 Ill.Dec. 636, 179 Ill.2d 367.

5/2–1116. Limitation on recovery in tort actions; fault

§ 2–1116. Limitation on recovery in tort actions; fault.

(a) The purpose of this Section is to allocate the responsibility of bearing or paying damages in actions brought on account of death, bodily injury, or physical damage to property according to the proportionate fault of the persons who proximately caused the damage.

(b) As used in this Section:

"Fault" means any act or omission that (i) is negligent, willful and wanton, or reckless, is a breach of an express or implied warranty, gives rise to strict liability in tort, or gives rise to liability under the provisions of any State statute, rule, or local ordinance and (ii) is a proximate cause of death, bodily injury to person, or physical damage to property for which recovery is sought.

"Contributory fault" means any fault on the part of the plaintiff (including but not limited to negligence, assumption of the risk, or willful and wanton misconduct) which is a proximate cause of the death, bodily injury to person, or physical damage to property for which recovery is sought.

"Tortfeasor" means any person, excluding the injured person, whose fault is a proximate cause of the death, bodily injury to person, or physical damage to property for which recovery is sought, regardless of whether that person is the plaintiff's employer, regardless of whether that person is joined as a party to the action, and regardless of whether that person may have settled with the plaintiff.

(c) In all actions on account of death, bodily injury or physical damage to property in which recovery is predicated upon fault, the contributory fault chargeable to the plaintiff shall be compared with the fault of all tortfeasors whose fault was a proximate cause of the death, injury, loss, or damage for which recovery is sought. The plaintiff shall be barred from recovering damages if the trier of fact finds that the contributory fault on the part of the plaintiff is more than 50% of the proximate cause of the injury or damage for which recovery is sought. The plaintiff shall not be barred from recovering damages if the trier of fact finds that the contributory fault on the part of the plaintiff is not more than 50% of the proximate cause of the injury or damage for which recovery is sought, but any economic or non-economic damages allowed shall be diminished in the proportion to the amount of fault attributable to the plaintiff.

(d) Nothing in this Section shall be construed to create a cause of action.

(e) This amendatory Act of 1995 applies to causes of action accruing on or after its effective date.

P.A. 82–280, § 2–1116, added by P.A. 84–1431, Art. 4, § 1, eff. Nov. 25, 1986. Amended by P.A. 89–7, § 15, eff. March 9, 1995.

Formerly Ill.Rev.Stat.1991, ch. 110, ¶ 2–1116.

Validity

Public Act 89–7, which amended this section, has been held unconstitutional in its entirety by the Illinois Supreme Court in the case of Best v. Taylor Machine Works, 1997, 689 N.E.2d 1057, 228 Ill.Dec. 636, 179 Ill.2d 367.

P.A. 89–7 rewrote this section, which prior thereto read:

"Limitation on recovery in tort actions. In all actions on account of bodily injury or death or physical damage to property, based on negligence, or product liability based on strict tort liability, the plaintiff shall be barred from recovering damages if the trier of fact finds that the contributory fault on the part of the plaintiff is more than 50% of the proximate cause of the injury or damage for which recovery is sought. The plaintiff shall not be barred from recovering damages if the trier of fact finds that the contributory fault on the part of the plaintiff is not more than 50% of the proximate cause of the injury or damage for which recovery is sought, but any damages allowed shall be diminished in the proportion to the amount of fault attributable to the plaintiff."

5/2–1117. Joint liability

§ 2–1117. Joint liability.

Except as provided in Section 2–1118, in actions on account of bodily injury or death or physical damage to property, based on negligence, or product liability based on strict tort liability, all defendants found liable are jointly and severally liable for plaintiff's past and future medical and medically related expenses. Any defendant whose fault, as determined by the trier of fact, is less than 25% of the total fault attributable to the plaintiff, the defendants sued by the plaintiff, and any third party defendant except the plaintiff's employer, shall be severally liable for all other damages. Any defendant whose fault, as determined by the trier of fact, is 25% or greater of the total fault attributable to the plaintiff, the defendants sued by the plaintiff, and any third party defendants except the plaintiff's employer, shall be jointly and severally liable for all other damages.

P.A. 82–280, § 2–1117, added by P.A. 84–1431, Art. 5, § 1, eff. Nov. 25, 1986. Amended by P.A. 89–7, § 15, eff. March 9, 1995; P.A. 93–10, § 5, eff. June 4, 2003; P.A. 93–12, § 5, eff. June 4, 2003.

Formerly Ill.Rev.Stat.1991, ch. 110, ¶ 2–1117.

Validity

Public Act 89–7, which amended this section, was held unconstitutional in its entirety by the Illinois Supreme Court in the case of Best v. Taylor Machine Works, 1997, 689 N.E.2d 1057, 228 Ill.Dec. 636, 179 Ill.2d 367. Later amendments by P.A. 93–10 and P.A. 93–12 did not include the amendment by P.A. 89–7.

P.A. 89–7 rewrote this section, which prior thereto read:

"Joint Liability. Except as provided in Section 2–1118, in actions on account of bodily injury or death or physical damage to property, based on negligence, or product liability based on strict tort liability, all defendants found liable are jointly and severally liable for plaintiff's past and future medical and medically related expenses. Any defendant whose fault, as determined by the trier of fact, is less than 25% of the total fault attributable to the plaintiff, the defendants sued by the plaintiff, and any third party defendant who could have been sued by the plaintiff, shall be severally liable for all other damages. Any defendant whose fault, as determined by the trier of fact, is 25% or greater of the total fault attributable to the plaintiff, the defendants sued by the plaintiff, and any third party defendants who could have been sued by the plaintiff, shall be jointly and severally liable for all other damages."

As amended by P.A. 89–7, the section would have read:

"§ 2–1117. Several liability.

"(a) In any action brought on account of death, bodily injury to person, or physical damage to property in which recovery is predicated upon fault as defined in Section 2–1116, a defendant is severally liable only and is liable only for that proportion of recoverable economic and non-economic damages, if any, that the amount of that defendant's fault, if any, bears to the aggregate amount of fault of all other tortfeasors, as defined in Section 2–1116, whose fault was a proximate cause of the death, bodily injury, economic loss, or physical damage to property for which recovery is sought.

"(b) Notwithstanding the provisions of subsection (a), in any healing art malpractice action based on negligence or wrongful death, any defendants found liable shall be jointly and severally liable if the limitations on non-economic damages in Section 2–1115.1 of this Act are for any reason deemed or found to be invalid.

"This amendatory Act of 1995 applies to causes of action filed on or after its effective date."

Section 995 of P.A. 89–7, approved March 9, 1995, provides:

"Effective date. This Act takes effect upon becoming law, and applies to causes of action as specified in each Section or part of this Act."

P.A. 93–10 did not include the amendment by P.A. 89–7, which was held unconstitutional.

P.A. 93–12 did not include the amendment by P.A. 89–7, which was held unconstitutional.

P.A. 93–12 incorporated the amendment by H.B. 2784 of the 2003 Regular Session of the 93rd General Assembly, which became P.A. 93–10.

5/2–1118. Exceptions

§ 2–1118. Exceptions. Notwithstanding the provisions of Section 2–1117, in any action in which the trier of fact determines that the injury or damage for which recovery is sought was caused by an act involving the discharge into the environment of any pollutant, including any waste, hazardous substance, irritant or contaminant, including, but not limited to smoke, vapor, soot, fumes, acids, alkalis, asbestos, toxic or corrosive chemicals, radioactive waste or mine tailings, and including any such material intended to be recycled, reconditioned or reclaimed, any defendants found liable shall be jointly and severally liable for such damage. However, Section 2–1117 shall apply to a defendant who is a response action contractor. As used in this Section, "response action contractor" means an individual, partnership, corporation, association, joint venture or other commercial entity or an employee, agent, sub-contractor, or consultant thereof which enters into a contract, for the performance of remedial or response action, or for the identification, handling, storage, treatment or disposal of a pollutant, which is entered into between any person or entity and a response action contractor when such response action contractor is not liable for the creation or maintenance of the condition to be ameliorated under the contract.

Notwithstanding the provisions of Section 2–1117, in any medical malpractice action, as defined in Section 2–1704, based upon negligence, any defendants found liable shall be jointly and severally liable.

P.A. 82–280, § 2–1118, added by P.A. 84–1431, Art. 5, § 1, eff. Nov. 25, 1986.

Formerly Ill.Rev.Stat.1991, ch. 110, ¶ 2–1118.

Validity

Public Act 89–7, which repealed this section effective March 9, 1995, has been held unconstitutional in its entirety by the Illinois Supreme Court in the case of Best v. Taylor Machine Works, 1997, 689 N.E.2d 1057, 228 Ill.Dec. 636, 179 Ill.2d 367.

5/2–1119. Tampering with anhydrous ammonia equipment, containers, or storage facilities

§ 2–1119. Tampering with anhydrous ammonia equipment, containers, or storage facilities.

(a) A person tampering with anhydrous ammonia equipment, containers, or storage facilities does not have a cause of action against the owner of the equipment, containers, or storage facilities, any person responsible for the installation or operation of the equipment, containers, or storage facilities, the person lawfully selling anhydrous ammonia, the person who lawfully purchases anhydrous ammonia for agricultural purposes, or the person who operates or uses anhydrous ammonia equipment, containers, or storage facilities when lawfully applying anhydrous ammonia for agricultural purposes.

(b) No person may commence a derivative action against the owner of anhydrous ammonia equipment, containers, or storage facilities, any person responsible for the installation or operation of the equipment, containers, or storage facilities, the person lawfully selling anhydrous ammonia, the person who lawfully purchases anhydrous ammonia for agricultural purposes, or the person who operates or uses anhydrous ammonia equipment, containers, or storage facilities when lawfully applying anhydrous ammonia for agricultural purposes when the injured person has tampered with anhydrous ammonia equipment, containers, or storage facilities.

(c) Tampering with anhydrous ammonia equipment, containers, or storage facilities occurs when any person who is not authorized by the owner of the anhydrous ammonia or anhydrous ammonia equipment, containers, or storage facilities transfers or attempts to transfer anhydrous ammonia to another container or causes damage to anhydrous ammonia equipment, containers, or storage facilities.

(d) For purposes of this Section:

"Anhydrous ammonia" means the compound defined in paragraph (d) of Section 3 of the Illinois Fertilizer Act of 1961. [1]

"Anhydrous ammonia equipment", "anhydrous ammonia storage containers", and "anhydrous ammonia storage facilities" are defined in the rules adopted under the Illinois Fertilizer Act of 1961. [2]

(e) The immunity to civil liability provided in this Section does not apply to any act or omission caused by the willful and wanton negligence of any person. P.A. 82–280, § 2–1119, added by P.A. 91–263, § 15, eff. Jan. 1, 2000.

[1] 505 ILCS 80/3.
[2] 505 ILCS 80/1 et seq.

PART 12. POST–TRIAL

5/2–1201. Return of verdict—Separate counts—Defective or unproved counts

§ 2–1201. Return of verdict—Separate counts—Defective or unproved counts. (a) It is sufficient for the jury to pronounce its verdict by its foreman in open court, without reducing it to writing, if it is a general verdict. The clerk shall enter it in form, under the direction of the court.

(b) Promptly upon the return of a verdict, the court shall enter judgment thereon.

(c) If there are several counts in a complaint, counterclaim or third-party complaint based on different claims upon which separate recoveries might be had, the court shall, on the motion of any party, direct the jury to find a separate verdict upon each claim.

(d) If several grounds of recovery are pleaded in support of the same claim, whether in the same or different counts, an entire verdict rendered for that claim shall not be set aside or reversed for the reason that any ground is defective, if one or more of the grounds is sufficient to sustain the verdict; nor shall the verdict be set aside or reversed for the reason that the evidence in support of any ground is insufficient to sustain a recovery thereon, unless before the case was submitted to the jury a motion was made to withdraw that ground from the jury on account of insufficient evidence and it appears that the denial of the motion was prejudicial.
P.A. 82–280, § 2–1201, eff. July 1, 1982. Amended by P.A. 83–707, § 1, eff. Sept. 23, 1983.

Formerly Ill.Rev.Stat.1991, ch. 110, ¶ 2–1201.

5/2–1202. Reserved ruling on motion for directed verdict—Post-trial motions in jury cases

§ 2–1202. Reserved ruling on motion for directed verdict—Post-trial motions in jury cases. (a) If at the close of the evidence, and before the case is submitted to the jury, any party moves for a directed verdict the court may (1) grant the motion or (2) deny the motion or reserve its ruling thereon and submit the case to the jury. If the court denies the motion or reserves its ruling thereon, the motion is waived unless the request is renewed in the post-trial motion.

(b) Relief desired after trial in jury cases, heretofore sought by reserved motions for directed verdict or motions for judgment notwithstanding the verdict, in arrest of judgment or for new trial, must be sought in a single post-trial motion. Relief after trial may include the entry of judgment if under the evidence in the case it would have been the duty of the court to direct a verdict without submitting the case to the jury, even though no motion for directed verdict was made or if made was denied or ruling thereon reserved. The post-trial motion must contain the points relied upon, particularly specifying the grounds in support thereof, and must state the relief desired, as for example, the entry of a judgment, the granting of a new trial or other appropriate relief. Relief sought in post-trial motions may be in the alternative or may be conditioned upon the denial of other relief asked in preference thereto, as for example, a new trial may be requested in the event a request for judgment is denied.

(c) Post-trial motions must be filed within 30 days after the entry of judgment or the discharge of the jury, if no verdict is reached, or within any further time the court may allow within the 30 days or any extensions thereof. A party against whom judgment is entered pursuant to post-trial motion shall have like time after the entry of the judgment within which to file a post-trial motion.

(d) A post-trial motion filed in apt time stays enforcement of the judgment.

(e) Any party who fails to seek a new trial in his or her post-trial motion, either conditionally or unconditionally, as herein provided, waives the right to apply for a new trial, except in cases in which the jury has failed to reach a verdict.

(f) The court must rule upon all relief sought in all post-trial motions. Although the ruling on a portion of the relief sought renders unnecessary a ruling on other relief sought for purposes of further proceedings in the trial court, the court must nevertheless rule conditionally on the other relief sought by determining whether it should be granted if the unconditional rulings are thereafter reversed, set aside or vacated. The conditional rulings become effective in the event the unconditional rulings are reversed, set aside or vacated.

P.A. 82–280, § 2–1202, eff. July 1, 1982.

Formerly Ill.Rev.Stat.1991, ch. 110, ¶ 2–1202.

5/2–1203. Motions after judgment in non-jury cases

§ 2–1203. Motions after judgment in non-jury cases.

(a) In all cases tried without a jury, any party may, within 30 days after the entry of the judgment or within any further time the court may allow within the 30 days or any extensions thereof, file a motion for a rehearing, or a retrial, or modification of the judgment or to vacate the judgment or for other relief.

(b) Except as provided in subsection (a) of Section 413 of the Illinois Marriage and Dissolution of Mar-

riage Act, a motion filed in apt time stays enforcement of the judgment except that a judgment granting injunctive or declaratory relief shall be stayed only by a court order that follows a separate application that sets forth just cause for staying the enforcement.
P.A. 82–280, § 2–1203, eff. July 1, 1982. Amended by P.A. 95–902, § 5, eff. Jan. 1, 2009; P.A. 96–1072, § 5, eff. Jan. 1, 2011.

Formerly Ill.Rev.Stat.1991, ch. 110, ¶ 2–1203.

5/2–1204. Arrest of judgment

§ 2–1204. Arrest of judgment. If judgment is arrested pursuant to post-trial motion for any defect in the record, the plaintiff need not commence his or her action anew. If appropriate, the court shall order new pleadings.
P.A. 82–280, § 2–1204, eff. July 1, 1982.

Formerly Ill.Rev.Stat.1991, ch. 110, ¶ 2–1204.

5/2–1205. Reduction in amount of recovery

§ 2–1205. Reduction in amount of recovery. An amount equal to the sum of (i) 50% of the benefits provided for lost wages or private or governmental disability income programs, which have been paid, or which have become payable to the injured person by any other person, corporation, insurance company or fund in relation to a particular injury, and (ii) 100% of the benefits provided for medical charges, hospital charges, or nursing or caretaking charges, which have been paid, or which have become payable to the injured person by any other person, corporation, insurance company or fund in relation to a particular injury, shall be deducted from any judgment in an action to recover for that injury based on an allegation of negligence or other wrongful act, not including intentional torts, on the part of a licensed hospital or physician; provided, however, that:

(1) Application is made within 30 days to reduce the judgment;

(2) Such reduction shall not apply to the extent that there is a right of recoupment through subrogation, trust agreement, lien, or otherwise;

(3) The reduction shall not reduce the judgment by more than 50% of the total amount of the judgment entered on the verdict;

(4) The damages awarded shall be increased by the amount of any insurance premiums or the direct costs paid by the plaintiff for such benefits in the 2 years prior to plaintiff's injury or death or to be paid by the plaintiff in the future for such benefits; and

(5) There shall be no reduction for charges paid for medical expenses which were directly attributable to the adjudged negligent acts or omissions of the defendants found liable.

P.A. 82–280, § 2–1205, eff. July 1, 1982. Amended by P.A. 84–7, § 1, eff. Aug. 15, 1985.

Formerly Ill.Rev.Stat.1991, ch. 110, ¶ 2–1205.

5/2–1205.1. Reduction in amount of recovery

§ 2–1205.1. Reduction in amount of recovery. In all cases on account of bodily injury or death or physical damage to property, based on negligence, or product liability based on any theory or doctrine, to which Section 2–1205 does not apply, the amount in excess of $25,000 of the benefits provided for medical charges, hospital charges, or nursing or caretaking charges, which have been paid, or which have become payable by the date of judgment to the injured person by any other insurance company or fund in relation to a particular injury, shall be deducted from any judgment. Provided, however, that:

(1) Application is made within 30 days to reduce the judgment;

(2) Such reduction shall not apply to the extent that there is a right of recoupment through subrogation, trust agreement, contract, lien, operation of law or otherwise;

(3) The reduction shall not reduce the judgment by more than 50% of the total amount of the judgment entered on the verdict; and

(4) The damages awarded shall be increased by the amount of any insurance premiums or the direct costs paid by the plaintiff for such benefits in the 2 years prior to plaintiff's injury or death or to be paid by the plaintiff in the future for such benefits.

P.A. 82–280, § 2–1205.1, added by P.A. 84–1431, Art. 6, § 1, eff. Nov. 25, 1986. Amended by P.A. 89–7, § 15, eff. March 9, 1995.

Formerly Ill.Rev.Stat.1991, ch. 110, ¶ 2–1205.1.

Validity

Public Act 89–7, which amended this section, has been held unconstitutional in its entirety by the Illinois Supreme Court in the case of Best v. Taylor Machine Works, 1997, 689 N.E.2d 1057, 228 Ill.Dec. 636, 179 Ill.2d 367.

P.A. 89–7, in the introductory paragraph, substituted "any theory or doctrine" for "strict tort liability".

Prior to amendment by P.A. 89–7, this section read:

"Reduction in amount of recovery. In all cases on account of bodily injury or death or physical damage to property, based on negligence, or product liability based on strict tort liability, to which Section 2–1205 does not apply, the amount in excess of $25,000 of the benefits provided for medical charges, hospital charges, or nursing or caretaking charges, which have been paid, or which have become payable by the date of judgment to the injured person by any other insurance company or fund in relation to a particular injury, shall be deducted from any judgment. Provided, however, that:

"(1) Application is made within 30 days to reduce the judgment;

"(2) Such reduction shall not apply to the extent that there is a right of recoupment through subrogation, trust agreement, contract, lien, operation of law or otherwise;

"(3) The reduction shall not reduce the judgment by more than 50% of the total amount of the judgment entered on the verdict; and

"(4) The damages awarded shall be increased by the amount of any insurance premiums or the direct costs paid by the plaintiff for such

benefits in the 2 years prior to plaintiff's injury or death or to be paid by the plaintiff in the future for such benefits."

5/2–1206. Assessment of damages

§ 2–1206. Assessment of damages. (a) Upon default, when the damages are to be assessed, the court may hear the evidence and assess the damages without a jury for that purpose. If interlocutory judgment is entered in an action brought upon a penal bond, or upon any instrument in writing, for the payment of money only, and the damages rest in computation, the court may refer the matter to the clerk, to assess and report the damages, and may enter judgment therefor. However, either party may have the damages assessed by a jury.

(b) Unless a jury has been waived, the trial court shall empanel a jury to assess damages: (1) if the ruling on a post-trial motion is in favor of a party entitled to recover damages and there is no verdict assessing his or her damages; or (2) the reviewing court remands solely for the purpose of assessing damages.

P.A. 82–280, § 2–1206, eff. July 1, 1982.

Formerly Ill.Rev.Stat.1991, ch. 110, ¶ 2–1206.

5/2–1207. Punitive damages

§ 2–1207. Punitive damages. The trial court may, in its discretion, with respect to punitive damages, determine whether a jury award for punitive damages is excessive, and if so, enter a remittitur and a conditional new trial.

The trial court may also in its discretion, apportion the punitive damage award among the plaintiff, the plaintiff's attorney and the State of Illinois Department of Human Services. The amount of the award paid from the punitive damages to the plaintiff's attorney shall be reasonable and without regard to any contingent fee contract, except that such amount shall not exceed the amount authorized by the contingent fee contract. In apportioning punitive damages as provided in this Section, the court shall consider, among other factors it deems relevant, whether any special duty was owed by the defendant to the plaintiff.

P.A. 82–280, § 2–1207, added by P.A. 84–1431, Art. 3, § 1, eff. Nov. 25, 1986. Amended by P.A. 89–507, Art. 90, § 90E–28, eff. July 1, 1997.

Formerly Ill.Rev.Stat.1991, ch. 110, ¶ 2–1207.

PART 13. JUDGMENT

5/2–1301. Judgments—Default—Confession

§ 2–1301. Judgments—Default—Confession. (a) The court shall determine the rights of the parties and grant to any party any affirmative relief to which the party may be entitled on the pleadings and proofs. Judgments shall be in the form required by the nature of the case and by the recovery or relief awarded. More than one judgment may be rendered in the same cause. If relief is granted against a party who upon satisfying the same in whole or in part will be entitled by operation of law to be reimbursed by another party to the action, the court may determine the rights of the parties as between themselves, and may thereafter upon motion and notice in the cause, and upon a showing that satisfaction has been made render a final judgment against the other party accordingly.

(b) A determination in favor of the plaintiff on an issue as to the truth or validity of any defense in abatement shall be that the defendant answer or otherwise plead.

(c) Except as otherwise limited by this subsection (c), any person for a debt bona fide due may confess judgment by himself or herself or attorney duly authorized, without process. The application to confess judgment shall be made in the county in which the note or obligation was executed or in the county in which one or more of the defendants reside or in any county in which is located any property, real or personal, owned by any one or more of the defendants. A judgment entered by any court in any county other than those herein specified has no force or validity, anything in the power to confess to the contrary notwithstanding.

No power to confess judgment shall be required or given after September 24, 1979 in any instrument used in a consumer transaction; any power to confess given in violation hereof is null and void and any judgment entered by a court based on such power shall be unenforceable. "Consumer transaction" as used in this Section means a sale, lease, assignment, loan, or other disposition of an item of goods, a consumer service, or an intangible to an individual for purposes that are primarily personal, family, or household.

(d) Judgment by default may be entered for want of an appearance, or for failure to plead, but the court may in either case, require proof of the allegations of the pleadings upon which relief is sought.

(e) The court may in its discretion, before final order or judgment, set aside any default, and may on motion filed within 30 days after entry thereof set aside any final order or judgment upon any terms and conditions that shall be reasonable.

(f) The fact that any order or judgment is joint does not deprive the court of power to set it aside as to fewer than all the parties, and if so set aside it remains in full force and effect as to the other parties.

(g) If any final judgment is entered against any defendant who has been served by publication with notice of the commencement of the action and who has not been served with a copy of the complaint, or received the notice required to be sent him or her by mail, or otherwise brought into court, and such defendant or his or her heirs, legatees, or personal representatives, as the case may require, shall, within 90 days after notice in writing given him or her of the judgment, or within 1 year after the judgment, if no notice has been given, appear in open court and petition to be heard touching the matter of the judgment, the court shall upon notice being given to the parties to such action who appeared therein and the purchaser at a sale made pursuant to the judgment, or their attorneys, set the petition for hearing and may allow the parties and the purchaser to answer the petition. If upon the hearing it appears that the judgment ought not to have been made against the defendant, it may be set aside, altered or amended as appears just; otherwise the petition shall be dismissed at petitioner's costs. If, however, a sale has been had under and pursuant to the final judgment, the court, in altering or amending the judgment may, upon terms just and equitable to the defendant, permit the sale to stand. If upon the hearing of the petition it appears that the defendant was entitled under the law to redeem from the sale, the court shall permit redemption to be made at any time within 90 days thereafter, upon terms that are equitable and just.
P.A. 82–280, § 2–1301, eff. July 1, 1982. Amended by P.A. 83–707, § 1, eff. Sept. 23, 1983.

Formerly Ill.Rev.Stat.1991, ch. 110, ¶ 2–1301.

5/2–1302. Notice of entry of default order

§ 2–1302. Notice of entry of default order. (a) Upon the entry of an order of default, the attorney for the moving party shall immediately give notice thereof to each party who has appeared, against whom the order was entered, or such party's attorney of record. However, the failure of the attorney to give the notice does not impair the force, validity or effect of the order.

(b) The notice shall contain the title, number, court, date of entry, name of the judge, and state that the order was one of default. The notice may be given by postal card or in any manner provided by rules.

(c) In the case of an action for foreclosure of a mortgage or a deed in trust, in addition to the information required by subsection (b) of this Section, the notice shall state that the defendant or defendants may redeem the property within the time and in the manner provided by law.

(d) No notice of the entry of an order of dismissal for want of prosecution shall be necessary provided plaintiff has been notified in advance that the court is considering the entry of such an order, unless required by local rule.

P.A. 82–280, § 2–1302, eff. July 1, 1982. Amended by P.A. 82–783, Art. III, § 43, eff. July 13, 1982; P.A. 84–614, § 1, eff. Jan. 1, 1986.

Formerly Ill.Rev.Stat.1991, ch. 110, ¶ 2–1302.

5/2–1303. Interest on judgment

§ 2–1303. Interest on judgment. Judgments recovered in any court shall draw interest at the rate of 9% per annum from the date of the judgment until satisfied or 6% per annum when the judgment debtor is a unit of local government, as defined in Section 1 of Article VII of the Constitution, a school district, a community college district, or any other governmental entity. When judgment is entered upon any award, report or verdict, interest shall be computed at the above rate, from the time when made or rendered to the time of entering judgment upon the same, and included in the judgment. Interest shall be computed and charged only on the unsatisfied portion of the judgment as it exists from time to time. The judgment debtor may by tender of payment of judgment, costs and interest accrued to the date of tender, stop the further accrual of interest on such judgment notwithstanding the prosecution of an appeal, or other steps to reverse, vacate or modify the judgment.

P.A. 82–280, § 2–1303, eff. July 1, 1982. Amended by P.A. 83–707, § 1, eff. Sept. 23, 1983; P.A. 85–907, Art. I, § 1, eff. Nov. 23, 1987.

Formerly Ill.Rev.Stat.1991, ch. 110, ¶ 2–1303.

5/2–1304. Orders for liens and conveyances

§ 2–1304. Orders for liens and conveyances. (a) Whenever, by any order, any party to an action is required to perform any act other than the payment of money, or to refrain from performing any act, the court may, in such order, provide that the same shall be a lien upon the real or personal estate, or both, of such party until such order is fully complied with; and such lien shall have the same force and effect, and be subject to the same limitations and restrictions, as judgments for the payment of money, including the time and manner when the same shall take effect and the time and manner when the lien upon a revival thereof shall take effect.

(b) Whenever an order is entered, directing the execution of any deed or other writing, it shall be lawful for any judge of the court to execute or for the court to direct the sheriff to execute such deed or other writing, in case the parties under no disability fail to execute such deed or other writing, in a time to be named in the order, or on behalf of minors or persons under legal disability who have guardians; and the execution thereof shall be valid in law to pass, release or extinguish the right, title and interest of the party on whose behalf it is executed, as if executed by the party in proper person, and he or she were under no disability; and whenever any property is sold in open court, it shall be lawful for any judge to execute a deed, certificate or sale or bill of sale or for the court to direct the sheriff to execute a deed, certificate of sale or bill of sale to the purchaser thereat and the execution thereof shall be valid in law to pass, release or extinguish all right, title and interest of the parties to the action with the same force and effect as though such sale had been held by the sheriff pursuant to the court's order; and such deed or other writing, if it relates to land, shall promptly after its execution by a judge or the sheriff, be recorded in the recorder's office of the county wherein the land is situated.

P.A. 82–280, § 2–1304, eff. July 1, 1982. Amended by P.A. 83–351, § 1, eff. Sept. 14, 1983.

Formerly Ill.Rev.Stat.1991, ch. 110, ¶ 2–1304.

5/2–1305. Motion to stay

§ 2–1305. Motion to stay. A party intending to move to set aside any judgment, bond or other proceeding may apply to the court or to the judge in chamber for a certificate (which the judge may, in his or her discretion, grant) that there is probable cause for staying further proceedings until the order of the court on the motion. Service of a copy of the certificate at the time of or after the service of the notice of the motion stays all further proceedings accordingly. In no case shall the judge grant the certificate if the error complained of may, by the direction of the judge to the clerk issuing the process, be corrected, but the judge shall order and the clerk shall make the correction in the process, nor unless the applicant has given notice of the motion to the opposite party, or his or her attorney of record, if they or either of them can be found in the county where the judgment was entered.

P.A. 82–280, § 2–1305, eff. July 1, 1982.

Formerly Ill.Rev.Stat.1991, ch. 110, ¶ 2–1305.

5/2–1306. Supersedeas bonds

§ 2–1306. Supersedeas bonds.

(a) In civil litigation under any legal theory involving a signatory, a successor to a signatory, or a parent or an affiliate of a signatory to the Master Settlement Agreement described in Section 6z–43 of the State Finance Act, execution of the judgment shall be stayed during the entire course of appellate review upon the posting of a supersedeas bond or other form of security in accordance with applicable laws or court rules, except that the total amount of the supersedeas bond or other form of security that is required of all appellants collectively shall not exceed $250,000,000, regardless of the amount of the judgment, provided that this limitation shall apply only if appellants file at least 30% of the total amount in the form of cash, a letter of credit, a certificate of deposit, or other cash equivalent with the court. The cash or cash equivalent shall be deposited by the clerk of the court in the account of the court, and any interest earned shall be utilized as provided by law.

(b) Notwithstanding subsection (a) of this Section, if an appellee proves by a preponderance of the evidence that an appellant is dissipating assets outside the ordinary course of business to avoid payment of a judgment, a court may require the appellant to post a supersedeas bond in an amount up to the total amount of the judgment.

(c) This Section applies to pending actions as well as actions commenced on or after its effective date, and to judgments entered or reinstated on or after its effective date.

P.A. 82–280, § 2–1306, added by P.A. 97–1145, § 10, eff. Jan. 18, 2013.

PART 14. POST–JUDGMENT

5/2–1401. Relief from judgments

§ 2–1401. Relief from judgments.

(a) Relief from final orders and judgments, after 30 days from the entry thereof, may be had upon petition as provided in this Section. Writs of error coram nobis and coram vobis, bills of review and bills in the nature of bills of review are abolished. All relief heretofore obtainable and the grounds for such relief heretofore available, whether by any of the foregoing remedies or otherwise, shall be available in every case, by proceedings hereunder, regardless of the nature of the order or judgment from which relief is sought or of the proceedings in which it was entered. Except as provided in the Illinois Parentage Act of 2015,[1] there shall be no distinction between actions and other proceedings, statutory or otherwise, as to availability of relief, grounds for relief or the relief obtainable.

(b) The petition must be filed in the same proceeding in which the order or judgment was entered but is not a continuation thereof. The petition must be supported by affidavit or other appropriate showing as to matters not of record. All parties to the petition shall be notified as provided by rule.

(b–5) A movant may present a meritorious claim under this Section if the allegations in the petition establish each of the following by a preponderance of the evidence:

(1) the movant was convicted of a forcible felony;

(2) the movant's participation in the offense was related to him or her previously having been a victim of domestic violence as perpetrated by an intimate partner;

(3) no evidence of domestic violence against the movant was presented at the movant's sentencing hearing;

(4) the movant was unaware of the mitigating nature of the evidence of the domestic violence at the time of sentencing and could not have learned of its significance sooner through diligence; and

(5) the new evidence of domestic violence against the movant is material and noncumulative to other evidence offered at the sentencing hearing, and is of such a conclusive character that it would likely change the sentence imposed by the original trial court.

Nothing in this subsection (b–5) shall prevent a movant from applying for any other relief under this Section or any other law otherwise available to him or her.

As used in this subsection (b–5):

"Domestic violence" means abuse as defined in Section 103 of the Illinois Domestic Violence Act of 1986.

"Forcible felony" has the meaning ascribed to the term in Section 2–8 of the Criminal Code of 2012.

"Intimate partner" means a spouse or former spouse, persons who have or allegedly have had a child in common, or persons who have or have had a dating or engagement relationship.

(c) Except as provided in Section 20b of the Adoption Act[2] and Section 2–32 of the Juvenile Court Act of 1987[3] or in a petition based upon Section 116–3 of the Code of Criminal Procedure of 1963,[4] the petition must be filed not later than 2 years after the entry of the order or judgment. Time during which the person seeking relief is under legal disability or duress or the ground for relief is fraudulently concealed shall be excluded in computing the period of 2 years.

(d) The filing of a petition under this Section does not affect the order or judgment, or suspend its operation.

(e) Unless lack of jurisdiction affirmatively appears from the record proper, the vacation or modification of an order or judgment pursuant to the provisions of this Section does not affect the right, title or interest in or to any real or personal property of any person, not a party to the original action, acquired for value after the entry of the order or judgment but before the filing of the petition, nor affect any right of any person not a party to the original action under any certificate of sale issued before the filing of the petition, pursuant to a sale based on the order or judgment.

(f) Nothing contained in this Section affects any existing right to relief from a void order or judgment, or to employ any existing method to procure that relief.

P.A. 82–280, § 2–1401, eff. July 1, 1982. Amended by P.A. 88–550, Art. 9, § 970, eff. July 3, 1994; P.A. 90–18, § 90, eff. July 1, 1997; P.A. 90–27, § 40, eff. Jan. 1, 1998; P.A. 90–141, § 10, eff. Jan. 1, 1998; P.A. 90–655, § 166, eff. July 30, 1998; P.A. 95–331, § 1085, eff. Aug. 21, 2007; P.A. 99–85, § 964, eff. Jan. 1, 2016; P.A. 99–384, § 10, eff. Jan. 1, 2016.

Formerly Ill.Rev.Stat.1991, ch. 110, ¶ 2–1401.

[1] 750 ILCS 46/101 et seq.
[2] 750 ILCS 50/20b.
[3] 705 ILCS 405/3–32.
[4] 725 ILCS 5/116–3.

P.A. 99–85, § 964, in subsec. (a), substituted "in the Illinois Parentage Act of 2015" for "in Section 6 of the Illinois Parentage Act of 1984".

P.A. 99–384, § 10, inserted subsec. (b–5).

See 5 ILCS 70/6 as to effect of (1) more than one amendment of a section at the same session of the General Assembly or (2) two or more acts relating to the same subject matter enacted by the same General Assembly.

5/2–1401.1. Relief from default judgment; military personnel in military service

§ 2–1401.1. Relief from default judgment; military personnel in military service.

(a) In this Section:

"Military service" means any full-time training or duty, no matter how described under federal or State law, for which a service member is ordered to report by the President, Governor of a state, commonwealth, or territory of the United States, or other appropriate military authority.

"Service member" means a resident of Illinois who is a member of any component of the U.S. Armed Forces or the National Guard of any state, the District of Columbia, or commonwealth, or a territory of the United States.

(b) Relief from and vacation of final orders and judgments after 30 days from the entry thereof entered by default against a service member that has entered military service may be had upon petition as provided in this Section. All relief heretofore obtainable and the grounds for such relief heretofore available shall be available in every case, by proceedings commenced pursuant to this Section, regardless of the nature of the order or judgment from which relief is sought or of the proceedings in which it was entered. Except as provided in Section 6 of the Illinois Parentage Act of 1984, there shall be no distinction between actions and other proceedings, statutory or otherwise, as to availability of relief, grounds for relief or the relief obtainable.

(c) The petition must be filed in the same proceeding in which the order or judgment was entered but is not a continuation thereof. The petition must be supported by affidavit or other appropriate showing as to matters not of record and show that the service member did not appear in the proceeding, the person's military service materially affected the service member's ability to defend the case, the person has a meritorious or legal defense to the action, and the petition must be filed within 90 days after the service member's date of release from military service. All parties to the petition shall be notified as provided by rule.

(d) Except as provided in Section 20b of the Adoption Act and Section 2–32 of the Juvenile Court Act of 1987 or in a petition based upon Section 116–3 of the Code of Criminal Procedure of 1963, the petition must be filed not later than 90 days after the service member's release from military service. Time during which the person seeking relief is under legal disability or duress or the ground for relief is fraudulently concealed shall be excluded in computing the period for filing.

(e) The filing of a petition under this Section does not affect the order or judgment, or suspend its operation.

(f) Unless lack of jurisdiction affirmatively appears from the record proper, the vacation or modification of an order or judgment pursuant to the provisions of this Section does not affect the right, title or interest in or to any real or personal property of any person, not a party to the original action, acquired for value after the entry of the order or judgment but before the filing of the petition, nor affect any right of any person not a party to the original action under any certificate of sale issued before the filing of the petition, pursuant to a sale based on the order or judgment.

(g) Nothing contained in this Section affects any existing right to relief from a void order or judgment, or to employ any existing method to procure that relief.

P.A. 82–280, § 2–1401.1, added by P.A. 97–913, § 940, eff. Jan. 1, 2013.

5/2–1402. Supplementary proceedings

§ 2–1402. Supplementary proceedings.

(a) A judgment creditor, or his or her successor in interest when that interest is made to appear of record, is entitled to prosecute supplementary proceedings for the purposes of examining the judgment debtor or any other person to discover assets or income of the debtor not exempt from the enforcement of the judgment, a deduction order or garnishment, and of compelling the application of non-exempt assets or income discovered toward the payment of the amount due under the judgment. A supplementary proceeding shall be commenced by the service of a citation issued by the clerk. The procedure for conducting supplementary proceedings shall be prescribed by rules. It is not a prerequisite to the commencement of a supplementary proceeding that a certified copy of the judgment has been returned wholly or partly unsatisfied. All citations issued by the clerk shall have the following language, or language substantially similar thereto, stated prominently on the front, in capital letters: "IF YOU FAIL TO APPEAR IN COURT AS DIRECTED IN THIS NOTICE, YOU MAY BE ARRESTED AND BROUGHT BEFORE THE COURT TO ANSWER TO A CHARGE OF CONTEMPT OF COURT, WHICH MAY BE PUNISHABLE BY IMPRISONMENT IN THE COUNTY JAIL." The court shall not grant a continuance of the supplementary proceeding except upon good cause shown.

(b) Any citation served upon a judgment debtor or any other person shall include a certification by the attorney for the judgment creditor or the judgment creditor setting forth the amount of the judgment, the date of the judgment, or its revival date, the balance due thereon, the name of the court, and the number of the case, and a copy of the citation notice required by this subsection. Whenever a citation is served upon a person or party other than the judgment debtor, the officer or person serving the citation shall send to the judgment debtor, within three business days of the service upon the cited party, a copy of the citation and the citation notice, which may be sent by regular first-class mail to the judgment debtor's last known address. In no event shall a citation hearing be held sooner than five business days after the mailing of the citation and citation notice to the judgment debtor, except by agreement of the parties. The citation notice need not be mailed to a corporation, partnership, or association. The citation notice shall be in substantially the following form:

"CITATION NOTICE

(Name and address of Court)

Name of Case: (Name of Judgment Creditor),

    Judgment Creditor v.

(Name of Judgment Debtor),

    Judgment Debtor.

Address of Judgment Debtor: (Insert last known address)

Name and address of Attorney for Judgment

    Creditor or of Judgment Creditor (If no

    attorney is listed): (Insert name and address)

Amount of Judgment: $ (Insert amount)

Name of Person Receiving Citation: (Insert name)

Court Date and Time: (Insert return date and time

    specified in citation)

NOTICE: The court has issued a citation against the person named above. The citation directs that person to appear in court to be examined for the purpose of allowing the judgment creditor to discover income and assets belonging to the judgment debtor or in which the judgment debtor has an interest. The citation was issued on the basis of a judgment against the judgment debtor in favor of the judgment creditor in the amount stated above. On or after the court date stated above, the court may compel the application of any discovered income or assets toward payment on the judgment.

The amount of income or assets that may be applied toward the judgment is limited by federal and Illinois law. The JUDGMENT DEBTOR HAS THE RIGHT TO ASSERT STATUTORY EXEMPTIONS AGAINST CERTAIN INCOME OR ASSETS OF THE JUDGMENT DEBTOR WHICH MAY NOT BE USED TO SATISFY THE JUDGMENT IN THE AMOUNT STATED ABOVE:

(1) Under Illinois or federal law, the exemptions of personal property owned by the debtor include the debtor's equity interest, not to exceed $4,000 in value, in any personal property as chosen by the debtor; Social Security and SSI benefits; public assistance benefits; unemployment compensation benefits; worker's compensation benefits; veteran's benefits; circuit breaker property tax relief benefits; the debtor's equity interest, not to exceed $2,400 in value, in any one motor vehicle, and the debtor's equity interest, not to exceed $1,500 in value, in any implements, professional books, or tools of the trade of the debtor.

(2) Under Illinois law, every person is entitled to an estate in homestead, when it is owned and occupied as a residence, to the extent in value of $15,000, which homestead is exempt from judgment.

(3) Under Illinois law, the amount of wages that may be applied toward a judgment is limited to the lesser of (i) 15% of gross weekly wages or (ii) the amount by which disposable earnings for a week exceed the total of 45 times the federal minimum hourly wage or, under a wage deduction summons served on or after January 1, 2006, the Illinois minimum hourly wage, whichever is greater.

(4) Under federal law, the amount of wages that may be applied toward a judgment is limited to the lesser of (i) 25% of disposable earnings for a week or (ii) the amount by which disposable earnings for a week exceed 30 times the federal minimum hourly wage.

(5) Pension and retirement benefits and refunds may be claimed as exempt under Illinois law.

The judgment debtor may have other possible exemptions under the law.

THE JUDGMENT DEBTOR HAS THE RIGHT AT THE CITATION HEARING TO DECLARE EXEMPT CERTAIN INCOME OR ASSETS OR BOTH. The judgment debtor also has the right to seek a declaration at an earlier date, by notifying the clerk in writing at (insert address of clerk). When so notified, the Clerk of the Court will obtain a prompt hearing date from the court and will provide the necessary forms that must be prepared by the judgment debtor or the attorney for the judgment debtor and sent to the judgment creditor and the judgment creditor's attorney regarding the time and location of the hearing. This notice may be sent by regular first class mail."

(b–1) Any citation served upon a judgment debtor who is a natural person shall be served by personal service or abode service as provided in Supreme Court Rule 105 and shall include a copy of the Income and Asset Form set forth in subsection (b–5).

(b–5) The Income and Asset Form required to be served by the judgment creditor in subsection (b–1) shall be in substantially the following form:

INCOME AND ASSET FORM

To Judgment Debtor: Please complete this form and bring it with you to the hearing referenced in the enclosed citation notice. You should also bring to the hearing any documents you have to support the information you provide in this form, such as pay stubs and account statements. The information you provide will help the court determine whether you have any property or income that can be used to satisfy the judgment entered against you in this matter. The information you provide must be accurate to the best of your knowledge.

If you fail to appear at this hearing, you could be held in contempt of court and possibly arrested.

In answer to the citation and supplemental proceedings served upon the judgment debtor, he or she answers as follows:

Name: ....
Home Phone Number: ......
Home Address: ....
Date of Birth: ....
Marital Status: ....
I have .... dependents.
Do you have a job? YES NO
Company's name I work for:
....
Company's address: ....

Job:
    I earn $.......... per..........
    If self employed, list here your business name and
address:
    ....
    Income from self employment is $.......... per year.
    I have the following benefits with my employer:
    ....
I do not have a job, but I support myself through:
    Government Assistance $.......... per month
    Unemployment $.......... per month
    Social Security $.......... per month
    SSI $.......... per month
    Pension $.......... per month

Other $......... per month
Real Estate:
Do you own any real estate? YES NO
I own real estate at ...., with names of other owners
....
Additional real estate I own: ....
I have a beneficial interest in a land trust. The name and address of the trustee is: ....
The beneficial
interest is listed in my name and ....
There is a mortgage on my real estate. State the mortgage company's name and address for each parcel of real
estate owned:
....
An assignment of beneficial interest in the land trust was signed to secure a loan from....................
I have the following accounts:
    Checking account at ....;
      account balance $......
    Savings account at ....;
      account balance $......
    Money market or certificate of deposit at........
    Safe deposit box at...........................
    Other accounts (please identify): ....
I own:
    A vehicle (state year, make, model, and VIN):
    ....
    Jewelry (please specify): ....
Other property described as: ....
    Stocks/Bonds ....
    Personal computer .....
    DVD player ....
    Television ....
    Stove ....
    Microwave ....
    Work tools ....
    Business equipment ....
    Farm equipment ....
    Other property (please specify):
    ....
Signature: ....

(b–10) Any action properly initiated under this Section may proceed notwithstanding an absent or incomplete Income and Asset Form, and a judgment debtor may be examined for the purpose of allowing the judgment creditor to discover income and assets belonging to the judgment debtor or in which the judgment debtor has an interest.

(c) When assets or income of the judgment debtor not exempt from the satisfaction of a judgment, a deduction order or garnishment are discovered, the court may, by appropriate order or judgment:

(1) Compel the judgment debtor to deliver up, to be applied in satisfaction of the judgment, in whole or in part, money, choses in action, property or effects in his or her possession or control, so discovered, capable of delivery and to which his or her title or right of possession is not substantially disputed.

(2) Compel the judgment debtor to pay to the judgment creditor or apply on the judgment, in installments, a portion of his or her income, however or whenever earned or acquired, as the court may deem proper, having due regard for the reasonable requirements of the judgment debtor and his or her family, if dependent upon him or her, as well as any payments required to be made by prior order of court or under wage assignments outstanding; provided that the judgment debtor shall not be compelled to pay income which would be considered exempt as wages under the Wage Deduction Statute. The court may modify an order for installment payments, from time to time, upon application of either party upon notice to the other.

(3) Compel any person cited, other than the judgment debtor, to deliver up any assets so discovered, to be applied in satisfaction of the judgment, in whole or in part, when those assets are held under such circumstances that in an action by the judgment debtor he or she could recover them in specie or obtain a judgment for the proceeds or value thereof as for conversion or embezzlement. A judgment creditor may recover a corporate judgment debtor's property on behalf of the judgment debtor for use of the judgment creditor by filing an appropriate petition within the citation proceedings.

(4) Enter any order upon or judgment against the person cited that could be entered in any garnishment proceeding.

(5) Compel any person cited to execute an assignment of any chose in action or a conveyance of title to real or personal property or resign memberships in exchanges, clubs, or other entities in the same manner and to the same extent as a court could do in any proceeding by a judgment creditor to enforce payment of a judgment or in aid of the enforcement of a judgment.

(6) Authorize the judgment creditor to maintain an action against any person or corporation that, it appears upon proof satisfactory to the court, is indebted to the judgment debtor, for the recovery of the debt, forbid the transfer or other disposition of the debt until an action can be commenced and prosecuted to judgment, direct that the papers or proof in the possession or control of the debtor and necessary in the prosecution of the action be delivered to the creditor or impounded in court, and provide for the disposition of any moneys in excess of the sum required to pay the judgment creditor's judgment and costs allowed by the court.

(c–5) If a citation is directed to a judgment debtor who is a natural person, no payment order shall be entered under subsection (c) unless the Income and Asset Form was served upon the judgment debtor as required by subsection (b–1), the judgment debtor has had an opportunity to assert exemptions, and the payments are from non-exempt sources.

(d) No order or judgment shall be entered under subsection (c) in favor of the judgment creditor unless there appears of record a certification of mailing showing that a copy of the citation and a copy of the citation notice was mailed to the judgment debtor as required by subsection (b).

(d–5) If upon examination the court determines that the judgment debtor does not possess any non-exempt income or assets, then the citation shall be dismissed.

(e) All property ordered to be delivered up shall, except as otherwise provided in this Section, be delivered to the sheriff to be collected by the sheriff or sold at public sale and the proceeds thereof applied towards the payment of costs and the satisfaction of the judgment. If the judgment debtor's property is of such a nature that it is not readily delivered up to the sheriff for public sale or if another method of sale is more appropriate to liquidate the property or enhance its value at sale, the court may order the sale of such property by the debtor, third party respondent, or by a selling agent other than the sheriff upon such terms as are just and equitable. The proceeds of sale, after deducting reasonable and necessary expenses, are to be turned over to the creditor and applied to the balance due on the judgment.

(f)(1) The citation may prohibit the party to whom it is directed from making or allowing any transfer or other disposition of, or interfering with, any property not exempt from the enforcement of a judgment therefrom, a deduction order or garnishment, belonging to the judgment debtor or to which he or she may be entitled or which may thereafter be acquired by or become due to him or her, and from paying over or otherwise disposing of any moneys not so exempt which are due or to become due to the judgment debtor, until the further order of the court or the termination of the proceeding, whichever occurs first. The third party may not be obliged to withhold the payment of any moneys beyond double the amount of the balance due sought to be enforced by the judgment creditor. The court may punish any party who violates the restraining provision of a citation as and for a contempt, or if the party is a third party may enter judgment against him or her in the amount of the unpaid portion of the judgment and costs allowable under this Section, or in the amount of the value of the property transferred, whichever is lesser.

(2) The court may enjoin any person, whether or not a party to the supplementary proceeding, from making or allowing any transfer or other disposition of, or interference with, the property of the judgment debtor not exempt from the enforcement of a judgment, a deduction order or garnishment, or the property or debt not so exempt concerning which any person is required to attend and be examined until further direction in the premises. The injunction order shall remain in effect until vacated by the

court or until the proceeding is terminated, whichever first occurs.

(g) If it appears that any property, chose in action, credit or effect discovered, or any interest therein, is claimed by any person, the court shall, as in garnishment proceedings, permit or require the claimant to appear and maintain his or her right. The rights of the person cited and the rights of any adverse claimant shall be asserted and determined pursuant to the law relating to garnishment proceedings.

(h) Costs in proceedings authorized by this Section shall be allowed, assessed and paid in accordance with rules, provided that if the court determines, in its discretion, that costs incurred by the judgment creditor were improperly incurred, those costs shall be paid by the judgment creditor.

(i) This Section is in addition to and does not affect enforcement of judgments or proceedings supplementary thereto, by any other methods now or hereafter provided by law.

(j) This Section does not grant the power to any court to order installment or other payments from, or compel the sale, delivery, surrender, assignment or conveyance of any property exempt by statute from the enforcement of a judgment thereon, a deduction order, garnishment, attachment, sequestration, process or other levy or seizure.

(k) (Blank).

(k–3) The court may enter any order upon or judgment against the respondent cited that could be entered in any garnishment proceeding under Part 7 of Article XII of this Code. This subsection (k–3) shall be construed as being declarative of existing law and not as a new enactment.

(k–5) If the court determines that any property held by a third party respondent is wages pursuant to Section 12–801, the court shall proceed as if a wage deduction proceeding had been filed and proceed to enter such necessary and proper orders as would have been entered in a wage deduction proceeding including but not limited to the granting of the statutory exemptions allowed by Section 12–803 and all other remedies allowed plaintiff and defendant pursuant to Part 8 of Article 12 of this Act.

(k–10) If a creditor discovers personal property of the judgment debtor that is subject to the lien of a citation to discover assets, the creditor may have the court impress a lien against a specific item of personal property, including a beneficial interest in a land trust. The lien survives the termination of the citation proceedings and remains as a lien against the personal property in the same manner that a judgment lien recorded against real property pursuant to Section 12–101 remains a lien on real property. If the judgment is revived before dormancy, the lien shall remain. A lien against personal property may, but need not, be recorded in the office of the recorder or filed as an informational filing pursuant to the Uniform Commercial Code.

(*l*) At any citation hearing at which the judgment debtor appears and seeks a declaration that certain of his or her income or assets are exempt, the court shall proceed to determine whether the property which the judgment debtor declares to be exempt is exempt from judgment. At any time before the return date specified on the citation, the judgment debtor may request, in writing, a hearing to declare exempt certain income and assets by notifying the clerk of the court before that time, using forms as may be provided by the clerk of the court. The clerk of the court will obtain a prompt hearing date from the court and will provide the necessary forms that must be prepared by the judgment debtor or the attorney for the judgment debtor and sent to the judgment creditor, or the judgment creditor's attorney, regarding the time and location of the hearing. This notice may be sent by regular first class mail. At the hearing, the court shall immediately, unless for good cause shown that the hearing is to be continued, shall proceed to determine whether the property which the judgment debtor declares to be exempt is exempt from judgment. The restraining provisions of subsection (f) shall not apply to any property determined by the court to be exempt.

(m) The judgment or balance due on the judgment becomes a lien when a citation is served in accordance with subsection (a) of this Section. The lien binds nonexempt personal property, including money, choses in action, and effects of the judgment debtor as follows:

(1) When the citation is directed against the judgment debtor, upon all personal property belonging to the judgment debtor in the possession or control of the judgment debtor or which may thereafter be acquired or come due to the judgment debtor to the time of the disposition of the citation.

(2) When the citation is directed against a third party, upon all personal property belonging to the judgment debtor in the possession or control of the third party or which thereafter may be acquired or come due the judgment debtor and comes into the possession or control of the third party to the time of the disposition of the citation.

The lien established under this Section does not affect the rights of citation respondents in property prior to the service of the citation upon them and does not affect the rights of bona fide purchasers or lenders without notice of the citation. The lien is effective for the period specified by Supreme Court Rule.

This subsection (m), as added by Public Act 88–48, is a declaration of existing law.

(n) If any provision of this Act or its application to any person or circumstance is held invalid, the invalidity of that provision or application does not affect the provisions or applications of the Act that can be given effect without the invalid provision or application.

(*o*) The changes to this Section made by this amendatory Act of the 97th General Assembly apply only to supplementary proceedings commenced under this Section on or after the effective date of this amendatory Act of the 97th General Assembly. The requirements or limitations set forth in subsections (b–1), (b–5), (b–10), (c–5), and (d–5) do not apply to the enforcement of any order or judgment resulting from an adjudication of a municipal ordinance violation that is subject to Supreme Court Rules 570 through 579, or from an administrative adjudication of such an ordinance violation.

P.A. 82–280, § 2–1402, eff. July 1, 1982. Amended by P.A. 84–1043, § 1, eff. Nov. 26, 1985; P.A. 88–48, § 5, eff. July 6, 1993; P.A. 88–299, § 5, eff. Jan. 1, 1994; P.A. 88–667, § 20, eff. Sept. 16, 1994; P.A. 88–670, Art. 2, § 2–67, eff. Dec. 2, 1994; P.A. 89–364, § 45, eff. Jan. 1, 1996; P.A. 94–293, § 5, eff. Jan. 1, 2006; P.A. 94–306, § 5, eff. Jan. 1, 2006; P.A. 95–331, § 1085, eff. Aug. 21, 2007; P.A. 95–661, § 5, eff. Jan. 1, 2008; P.A. 97–350, § 5, eff. Jan. 1, 2012; P.A. 97–848, § 5, eff. July 25, 2012; P.A. 98–557, § 5, eff. Jan. 1, 2014.

Formerly Ill.Rev.Stat.1991, ch. 110, ¶ 2–1402.

5/2–1403. Judgment debtor as beneficiary of trust

§ 2–1403. Judgment debtor as beneficiary of trust. No court, except as otherwise provided in this Section, shall order the satisfaction of a judgment out of any property held in trust for the judgment debtor if such trust has, in good faith, been created by, or the fund so held in trust has proceeded from, a person other than the judgment debtor.

The income or principal of a trust shall be subject to withholding for the purpose of securing collection of unpaid child support obligations owed by the beneficiary as provided in Section 4.1 of the "Non-Support of Spouse and Children Act",[1] Section 22 of the Non-Support Punishment Act,[2] and similar Sections of other Acts which provide for support of a child as follows:

(1) income may be withheld if the beneficiary is entitled to a specified dollar amount or percentage of the income of the trust, or is the sole income beneficiary; and

(2) principal may be withheld if the beneficiary has a right to withdraw principal, but not in excess of the amount subject to withdrawal under the instrument, or if the beneficiary is the only beneficiary to whom discretionary payments of principal may be made by the trustee.

P.A. 82–280, § 2–1403, added by P.A. 83–314, § 1, eff. Sept. 14, 1983. Amended by P.A. 85–218, § 1, eff. Aug. 23, 1987; P.A. 85–907, Art. II, § 1, eff. Nov. 23, 1987; P.A. 85–1209, Art. II, § 2–53, eff. Aug. 30, 1988; P.A. 91–613, § 960, eff. Oct. 1, 1999.

Formerly Ill.Rev.Stat.1991, ch. 110, ¶ 2–1403.

[1] 750 ILCS 15/4.1 (repealed; see, now, generally 750 ILCS 16/1, et seq.).

[2] 750 ILCS 16/22.

5/2–1404. Preservation of trust estates

§ 2–1404. Preservation of trust estates. In all cases where a trustee has been or shall be appointed by order of a circuit court, such court has authority to authorize the payment of interest on any mortgage which is a lien upon the trust estate, to authorize the payment of taxes and assessments levied upon or assessed against the trust estate, to authorize the payment of the insurance premiums on any policy of insurance on the buildings and personal property of the trust estate, and to authorize the making of repairs and the payment therefor, when it appears for the best interests of the estate; and where a trustee has paid any such interest, taxes, assessments, insurance premiums, or for repairs, and it appears that such payments were for the best interests of the estate and the protection and preservation thereof, the court, on application or by report, has authority to approve such payments.

P.A. 82–280, § 2–1404, added by P.A. 84–621, § 2, eff. Sept. 20, 1985.

Formerly Ill.Rev.Stat.1991, ch. 110, ¶ 2–1404.

PART 15. ABOLITION OF WRITS

Section
5/2–1501. Writs abolished.

5/2–1501. Writs abolished

§ 2–1501. Writs abolished. The function which was prior to January 1, 1979, performed by a writ of execution to enforce a judgment or order for the payment of money, or by the writs of mandamus, injunction, prohibition, sequestration, habeas corpus, replevin, ne exeat or attachment, or by the writ of possession in an action of ejectment, or by the writ of restitution in an action of forcible entry and detainer, or by the writ of assistance for the possession of real estate, or by a temporary restraining order, shall hereafter be performed by a copy of the order or judgment to be enforced, certified by the clerk of the court which entered the judgment or order.

The clerk's certification shall bear a legend substantially as follows:

I hereby certify the above to be correct.

Dated . . . .

(Seal of Clerk of Circuit Court)

. . . .

Clerk of the Circuit Court of . . . . Illinois.

This order is the command of the Circuit Court and violation thereof is subject to the penalty of the law.
P.A. 82–280, § 2–1501, eff. July 1, 1982. Amended by P.A. 83–707, § 1, eff. Sept. 23, 1983.

Formerly Ill.Rev.Stat.1991, ch. 110, ¶ 2–1501.

PART 16. REVIVAL OF JUDGMENT

Section
5/2–1601. Scire facias abolished.
5/2–1602. Revival of judgment.

5/2–1601. Scire facias abolished

§ 2–1601. Scire facias abolished. Any relief which heretofore might have been obtained by scire facias may be had by employing a petition filed in the case in which the original judgment was entered in accordance with Section 2–1602.

P.A. 82–280, § 2–1601, eff. July 1, 1982. Amended by P.A. 92–817, § 5, eff. Aug. 21, 2002.

Formerly Ill.Rev.Stat.1991, ch. 110, ¶ 2–1601.

5/2–1602. Revival of judgment

§ 2–1602. Revival of judgment.

(a) A judgment may be revived by filing a petition to revive the judgment in the seventh year after its entry, or in the seventh year after its last revival, or in the twentieth year after its entry, or at any other time within 20 years after its entry if the judgment becomes dormant. The provisions of this amendatory Act of the 96th General Assembly are declarative of existing law.

(b) A petition to revive a judgment shall be filed in the original case in which the judgment was entered. The petition shall include a statement as to the original date and amount of the judgment, court costs expended, accrued interest, and credits to the judgment, if any.

(c) Service of notice of the petition to revive a judgment shall be made in accordance with Supreme Court Rule 106.

(d) An order reviving a judgment shall be for the original amount of the judgment. The plaintiff may recover interest and court costs from the date of the original judgment. Credits to the judgment shall be reflected by the plaintiff in supplemental proceedings or execution.

(e) If a judgment debtor has filed for protection under the United States Bankruptcy Code [1] and failed to successfully adjudicate and remove a lien filed by a judgment creditor, then the judgment may be revived only as to the property to which a lien attached before the filing of the bankruptcy action.

(f) A judgment may be revived as to fewer than all judgment debtors, and such order for revival of judgment shall be final, appealable, and enforceable.

(g) This Section does not apply to a child support judgment or to a judgment recovered in an action for damages for an injury described in Section 13–214.1, which need not be revived as provided in this Section and which may be enforced at any time as provided in Section 12–108.

(h) If a judgment becomes dormant during the pendency of an enforcement proceeding against wages under Part 14 of this Article or under Article XII, the enforcement may continue to conclusion without revival of the underlying judgment so long as the enforcement is done under court supervision and includes a wage deduction order or turn over order and is against an employer, garnishee, or other third party respondent.

P.A. 82–280, § 2–1602, added by P.A. 92–817, § 5, eff. Aug. 21, 2002. Amended by P.A. 96–305, § 5, eff. Aug. 11, 2009; P.A. 97–350, § 5, eff. Jan. 1, 2012; P.A. 98–557, § 5, eff. Jan. 1, 2014.

[1] 11 U.S.C.A. § 101 et seq.

PART 17. HEALING ART MALPRACTICE

Section
5/2–1701. Application.
5/2–1702. Economic/Non–Economic Loss.
5/2–1703. Past/Future Damages.
5/2–1704. Medical Malpractice Action.
5/2–1704.5. Repealed.
5/2–1705. Election for Periodic Payment.
5/2–1706. Special findings required.
5/2–1706.5. Repealed.
5/2–1707. Calculation of future damages.
5/2–1708. Basis for determining judgment to be entered.
5/2–1709. Payment of periodic installment obligations.
5/2–1710. Form of security.
5/2–1711. Posting and maintaining security.
5/2–1712. Equivalent lump sum value.
5/2–1713. Effect of death.
5/2–1714. Liability insurance policy limits.
5/2–1715. Assignment of periodic installments.
5/2–1716. Exemption of benefits.
5/2–1717. Settlement agreements and consent judgments.
5/2–1718. Satisfaction of judgments.
5/2–1719. Duties of Director of Insurance.

Date Effective

Part 17, Healing Art Malpractice, comprised of §§ 2–1701 to 2–1719, was added to the Code of Civil Procedure by P.A. 84–7, § 1, eff. Aug. 15, 1985.

Renumbering

Another Part 17, Lis Pendens, §§ 2–1701 to 2–1703, was added by P.A. 84–622, § 1, and was renumbered as Part 19, §§ 2–1901 to 2–1903, by P.A. 84–1308, Art. II, § 107.

5/2–1701. Application

§ 2–1701. Application. Subject to the provisions of Section 2–1705, in all medical malpractice actions the provisions of this Act shall be applicable.

P.A. 82–280, § 2–1701, added by P.A. 84–7, § 1, eff. Aug. 15, 1985.

Formerly Ill.Rev.Stat.1991, ch. 110, ¶ 2–1701.

5/2–1702. Economic/Non–Economic Loss

§ 2–1702. Economic/Non–Economic Loss. As used in this Part, "economic loss" and "non-economic loss" are defined as in Section 2–1115.2.

P.A. 82–280, § 2–1702, added by P.A. 84–7, § 1, eff. Aug. 15, 1985. Amended by P.A. 89–7, § 15, eff. March 9, 1995.

Formerly Ill.Rev.Stat.1991, ch. 110, ¶ 2–1702.

Validity

Public Act 89–7, which amended this section, has been held unconstitutional in its entirety by the Illinois Supreme Court in the case of Best v. Taylor Machine Works, 1997, 689 N.E.2d 1057, 228 Ill.Dec. 636, 179 Ill.2d 367.

P.A. 89–7 rewrote this section, which prior thereto read:

"Economic/Non-Economic Loss. As used in this Part:

"(a) "Economic loss" means all pecuniary harm for which damages are recoverable.

"(b) "Non-economic loss" means loss of consortium and all nonpecuniary harm for which damages are recoverable, including, without limitation, damages for pain and suffering, inconvenience, disfigurement, and physical impairment."

5/2–1703. Past/Future Damages

§ 2–1703. Past/Future Damages. As used in this Part:

(a) "Past damages" means damages that have accrued when the damages findings are made.

(b) "Future damages" includes all damages which the trier of fact finds will accrue after the damages findings are made, including, without limitation, damages for future medical or health treatment, care or custody, loss of future earnings, loss of bodily function, future pain and suffering, and future physical impairment and inconvenience.

P.A. 82–280, § 2–1703, added by P.A. 84–7, § 1, eff. Aug. 15, 1985.

Formerly Ill.Rev.Stat.1991, ch. 110, ¶ 2–1703.

5/2–1704. Medical Malpractice Action

§ 2–1704. Medical Malpractice Action. As used in this Part, "medical malpractice action" means any action, whether in tort, contract or otherwise, in which the plaintiff seeks damages for injuries or death by reason of medical, hospital, or other healing art malpractice. The term "healing art" shall not include care and treatment by spiritual means through prayer in accord with the tenets and practices of a recognized church or religious denomination.

P.A. 82–280, § 2–1704, added by P.A. 84–7, § 1, eff. Aug. 15, 1985.

Formerly Ill.Rev.Stat.1991, ch. 110, ¶ 2–1704.

5/2–1704.5. § 2–1704.5. Repealed by P.A. 97–1145, § 15, eff. Jan. 18, 2013

5/2–1705. Election for Periodic Payment

§ 2–1705. Election for Periodic Payment. (a) In order to invoke the provisions of Section 2–1706 through 2–1718, a party to a medical malpractice action must make an effective election in accordance with this Section.

(b) The election must be made by motion not less than 60 days before commencement of a trial involving issues of future damages unless leave of court is obtained. Any objection to the election must be made not more than 30 days after the election.

(c) An election is effective if:

(1) all parties have consented; or

(2) no timely objection is filed by any party; or

(3) a timely objection is filed, but:

(i) the electing party is a plaintiff and shows there is a good faith claim that future damages will exceed $250,000, or

(ii) the electing party is responding to a claim for future damages in excess of $250,000 and shows both that security in the amount of the claim for past and future damages or $500,000, whichever is less, can be provided and that future damages are likely to accrue over more than one year.

(d) If an effective election is made prior to the commencement of trial, all actions, including third-party claims, counterclaims, and actions consolidated for trial, must be tried under Sections 2–1706 through 2–1718, unless the court finds that the purposes of these Sections would not be served by doing so or in the interest of justice a separate trial or proceeding should be held on some or all of the claims that are not subject of the election.

(e) An effective election can be withdrawn only by consent of all parties to the claim to which the election relates.

P.A. 82–280, § 2–1705, added by P.A. 84–7, § 1, eff. Aug. 15, 1985.

Formerly Ill.Rev.Stat.1991, ch. 110, ¶ 2–1705.

5/2–1706. Special findings required

§ 2–1706. Special findings required. (a) If liability is found in a trial under Sections 2–1706 through 2–1718, the trier of fact, in addition to other appropriate findings, shall make separate findings for each plaintiff specifying the amount of:

(1) any past damages; and

(2) any future damages for each of the following types:

(i) medical and other costs of health care;

(ii) other economic loss; and

(iii) non-economic loss.

(b) If the trier of fact finds that certain future damages will accrue for a definite number of years, the amount of periodic payments for those damages must be calculated based on that definite number of years. Payment for such damages shall be made periodically for that number of years.

(c) If the trier of fact finds that certain future damages will accrue for the remainder of the plaintiff's life, the trier of fact shall make a specific finding specifying the remaining life expectancy of the plaintiff and the amount of periodic payments for those damages must be calculated based on the remaining life expectancy of the plaintiff. Payment for such damages shall be made periodically and shall continue until the plaintiff's remaining life expectancy is reached or the plaintiff dies, whichever is later.

P.A. 82–280, § 2–1706, added by P.A. 84–7, § 1, eff. Aug. 15, 1985.

Formerly Ill.Rev.Stat.1991, ch. 110, ¶ 2–1706.

5/2–1706.5. § 2–1706.5. Repealed by P.A. 97–1145, § 15, eff. Jan. 18, 2013

5/2–1707. Calculation of future damages

§ 2–1707. Calculation of future damages. (a) In all trials under Sections 2–1706 through 2–1718, future damages must be calculated by the trier of fact without discounting future damages to present value.

(b) In all jury trials in which special damages findings are required under Sections 2–1706 through 2–1718, the jury must be informed that with respect to future damages:

(1) the law takes into account the fact that those payments may be made in the future rather than in one lump sum now; and

(2) the jury will make their findings on the assumption that appropriate adjustments for the present value of those payments will be made later and that the jury should not discount those payments to present value.

P.A. 82–280, § 2–1707, added by P.A. 84–7, § 1, eff. Aug. 15, 1985.

Formerly Ill.Rev.Stat.1991, ch. 110, ¶ 2–1707.

5/2–1708. Basis for determining judgment to be entered

§ 2–1708. Basis for determining judgment to be entered. In order to determine what judgment is to be entered on a verdict requiring findings of special damages under Sections 2–1706 through 2–1718, the court shall proceed as follows:

(1) The court shall apply to the findings of past and future damages any applicable rules of law, including set-offs, comparative fault, additurs, and remittiturs, in calculating the respective amounts of past and future damages each plaintiff is entitled to recover and each party is obligated to pay.

(2) The court shall calculate the equivalent lump sum value of future damages in accordance with Section 2–1712.

(3) Any contingent attorneys' fees shall be calculated based on the sum of the past damages recoverable and equivalent lump sum value of future damages recoverable. Any judgment for periodic installments must specify payment of attorneys' fees and litigation expenses in lump sum, separate from the periodic installments payable to the plaintiff, pursuant to an agreement entered into between the plaintiff and his or her attorney.

(4) Upon election of a subrogee, including an employer or insurer who provides workers' compensation, filed within 10 days after verdict, any part of future damages allocable to reimbursement of payments previously made by the subrogee is payable in equivalent lump sum to the subrogee.

(5) The court shall determine the amount of future damages to be awarded in equivalent lump sum. This amount shall be that part of the equivalent lump sum value of future damages which does not exceed $250,000. In the event that the equivalent lump sum value of the total amount of future damages recoverable is $500,000 or more, the court may, upon a showing by the plaintiff that he will incur greater expenses for future damages immediately after judgment in order to secure appropriate necessities including, but not limited to, equipment, supplies, medication, residence or other items, allow additional amounts of future damages to be awarded in equivalent lump sum value so that the total amount awarded in equivalent lump sum is sufficient to secure the aforementioned items, but in no event shall any increase under this sentence cause more than 50% of the equivalent lump sum value of total future damages recoverable to be awarded in lump sum. The amount of future damages awarded in equivalent lump sum shall be added to the total amount of past damages recoverable and this total shall be known as the present award. The periodic award shall consist of the total amount of future damages without reduction to an equivalent lump sum value, reduced in the proportion that the equivalent lump sum value of the amount of future damages included in the lump sum present award bears to the equivalent lump sum value of the total amount of future damages.

(6) Any attorneys' fees and litigation expenses shall be allocated proportionately between the amount of the present award and the amount of the periodic award.

(7) The court shall enter judgment in lump sum for the present award including that portion of attorneys' fees and litigation expenses allocable to the present award, for amounts payable under subsection (4), and

for that portion of attorneys' fees and litigation expenses allocable to the periodic award.

(8) The court shall enter judgment in accordance with Section 2–1709 for the payment in installments of the periodic award, less that part of future damages allocable to reimbursement of payments previously made by a subrogee under subsection (4), and less that portion of attorney's fees and litigation expenses allocable to the periodic award.

(9) In an action for wrongful death, the calculation of all amounts, values, and awards under this Section must be based on the total recovery for all beneficiaries of the action.

(10) Upon petition of a party before entry of judgment and upon a finding of incapacity to post the required security, the court, at the election of the plaintiff or beneficiaries in an action for wrongful death, shall:

(i) enter a judgment in accordance with subsections (7) and (8); or

(ii) determine the equivalent lump sum value under Section 2–1712 in the amount otherwise to be paid in periodic installments under subsection (8) and enter judgment for that equivalent lump sum value and for those amounts payable under subsection (7).

P.A. 82–280, § 2–1708, added by P.A. 84–7, § 1, eff. Aug. 15, 1985.

Formerly Ill.Rev.Stat.1991, ch. 110, ¶ 2–1708.

5/2–1709. Payment of periodic installment obligations

§ 2–1709. Payment of periodic installment obligations. (a) Except in those cases specified in this Part concerning the death of the person receiving periodic payments, the amount of periodic payments may not be adjusted or otherwise modified following final judgment.

(b) Unless the court directs otherwise or the parties otherwise agree, payments must be scheduled at one-month intervals. Payments for damages accruing during the scheduled intervals are due at the beginning of the intervals.

(c) If the trier of fact has found that different elements of future damages will accrue over different periods of time the court shall direct that amounts to be periodically paid in the future be proportionately divided into the same periods of time.

P.A. 82–280, § 2–1709, added by P.A. 84–7, § 1, eff. Aug. 15, 1985.

Formerly Ill.Rev.Stat.1991, ch. 110, ¶ 2–1709.

5/2–1710. Form of security

§ 2–1710. Form of security. (a) Security authorized or required for payment of a judgment for periodic installments entered in accordance with this Sec-

tion must be in one or more of the following forms and approved as to quality by the court:

(1) bond executed by a qualified insurer;

(2) annuity contract executed by a qualified insurer;

(3) evidence of applicable and collectible liability insurance with one or more qualified insurers;

(4) an agreement by one or more qualified insurers to guarantee payment of the judgment; or

(5) any other satisfactory form of security.

(b) Security complying with this Section serves also as a required supersedeas bond.

P.A. 82–280, § 2–1710, added by P.A. 84–7, § 1, eff. Aug. 15, 1985.

Formerly Ill.Rev.Stat.1991, ch. 110, ¶ 2–1710.

5/2–1711. Posting and maintaining security

§ 2–1711. Posting and maintaining security. (a) If the court enters a judgment for period installments, each party liable for all or a portion of the judgment, unless found to be incapable of doing so under subsection (10) of Section 2–1708, shall separately or jointly with one or more others post security in an amount equal to the equivalent lump sum value of the unpaid judgment, including past damages, in a form prescribed in Section 2–1710, within 30 days after the date the judgment is subject to enforcement. A liability insurer having a contractual obligation and any other person adjudged to have an obligation to pay all or part of a judgment for periodic installments on behalf of a judgment debtor is obligated to post security to the extent of its contractual or adjudged obligation if the judgment debtor has not done so.

(b) A judgment creditor or successor in interest and any party having rights under subsection (d) may move that the court find that security has not been posted and maintained with regard to a judgment obligation owing to the moving party. Upon so finding, the court shall order that security complying with this Section be posted within 30 days. If the security is not posted within that time, the court shall calculate the equivalent lump sum value of the obligation and enter a judgment for that amount in favor of the moving party.

(c) If a judgment debtor who is the only person liable for all or a portion of a judgment requiring security under this Section fails to post and maintain security, the right to lump sum payment described in subsection (b) applies only against that judgment debtor and the portion of the judgment so owed.

(d) If more than one party is liable for all or a portion of a judgment requiring security and the required security is posted by one or more but fewer than all of the parties liable, the security requirements are satisfied and those posting security may proceed under subsection (b) to enforce rights for security or

lump sum payment to satisfy or protect rights of reimbursement from a party not posting security.
P.A. 82–280, § 2–1711, added by P.A. 84–7, § 1, eff. Aug. 15, 1985.

Formerly Ill.Rev.Stat.1991, ch. 110, ¶ 2–1711.

5/2–1712. Equivalent lump sum value

§ 2–1712. Equivalent lump sum value. When required to do so under Part 17 of Article II of the "Code of Civil Procedure", the court shall determine the equivalent lump sum value in accordance with this Section.

Non-economic loss shall not, under any Section of this Part, be subject to discounting. The only portion of damages subject to discounting in this Part is future economic loss.

The court shall determine the equivalent lump sum value of any future economic loss by applying the discount factor, compounded annually, to those elements of damages for future economic loss, and then adding, without discounting, those elements of damages for future non-economic loss. The discount factor shall be 6%.
P.A. 82–280, § 2–1712, added by P.A. 84–7, § 1, eff. Aug. 15, 1985.

Formerly Ill.Rev.Stat.1991, ch. 110, ¶ 2–1712.

5/2–1713. Effect of death

§ 2–1713. Effect of death. (a) For all future damages which the trier of fact has determined will accrue for the remainder of the plaintiff's life, payment for those damages shall continue until the later of the plaintiff's death or the time when the remaining life expectancy is reached. For all future damages which the trier of fact has determined will accrue for a definite number of years, payment for those damages shall continue for that number of years irrespective of the plaintiff's death.

(b) If, in an action for wrongful death, a judgment for periodic installments provides payments to more than one person entitled to receive benefits for losses that do not terminate under subsection (a) and one or more but fewer than all of them die, the surviving beneficiaries succeed to the shares of the deceased beneficiaries. The surviving beneficiaries are entitled to shares proportionate to their shares in the periodic installments not yet paid, but they are not entitled to receive payments beyond the respective periods specified for them in the judgment.

(c) If, in an action other than one for wrongful death, a judgment for period installments is entered and a person entitled to receive benefits for losses that do not terminate under subsection (a) under the judgment dies and is survived by one or more qualifying survivors, any periodic installments not yet due at the death must be shared equitably by those survivors.

(d) "Qualifying survivor" means a person who, had the death been caused under circumstances giving rise to a cause of action for wrongful death, would have qualified as a beneficiary at the time of death according to the law that would have applied in an action for wrongful death by the jurisdiction under which the issue of liability was resolved in entering the judgment for periodic installments.
P.A. 82–280, § 2–1713, added by P.A. 84–7, § 1, eff. Aug. 15, 1985.

Formerly Ill.Rev.Stat.1991, ch. 110, ¶ 2–1713.

5/2–1714. Liability insurance policy limits

§ 2–1714. Liability insurance policy limits. (a) In determining whether or to what extent a judgment for periodic installments exceeds limits under a liability insurance policy, the present equivalent lump sum value of future periodic payments must be added to the amount of the judgment awarded in lump sum. The sum so calculated must be compared to applicable limits under the policy.

(b) If the sum calculated under subsection (a) does not exceed applicable policy limits when the judgment is entered, amounts due by reason of future periodic payments are entirely within those limits.

(c) If the sum calculated under subsection (a) exceeds applicable policy limits when the judgment is entered, the future periodic payments must be allocated proportionately to amounts within and amounts in excess of those limits.
P.A. 82–280, § 2–1714, added by P.A. 84–7, § 1, eff. Aug. 15, 1985.

Formerly Ill.Rev.Stat.1991, ch. 110, ¶ 2–1714.

5/2–1715. Assignment of periodic installments

§ 2–1715. Assignment of periodic installments. An assignment of or an agreement to assign any right to periodic installments for future damages contained in a judgment is enforceable only as to amounts:

(1) to secure payment of alimony, maintenance, or child support;

(2) for the costs of products, services, or accommodations provided or to be provided by the assignee for medical or other health care; or

(3) for attorney's fees and other expenses of litigation incurred in securing the judgment.
P.A. 82–280, § 2–1715, added by P.A. 84–7, § 1, eff. Aug. 15, 1985.

Formerly Ill.Rev.Stat.1991, ch. 110, ¶ 2–1715.

5/2–1716. Exemption of benefits

§ 2–1716. Exemption of benefits. Periodic installments for future damages for loss of earnings are exempt from garnishment, attachment, execution, and any other process or claim to the extent that wages or

61

earnings are exempt under any applicable law. Except to the extent that they may be assigned under Section 2–1715, periodic installments for all future damages are exempt from garnishment, attachment, execution, and any other process or claim.

P.A. 82–280, § 2–1716, added by P.A. 84–7, § 1, eff. Aug. 15, 1985.

Formerly Ill.Rev.Stat.1991, ch. 110, ¶ 2–1716.

5/2–1717. Settlement agreements and consent judgments

§ 2–1717. Settlement agreements and consent judgments. (a) Parties to a medical malpractice action may file with the clerk of the court in which the action is pending or, if none is pending, with the clerk of a court of competent jurisdiction over the claim, a settlement agreement for future damages payable in periodic installments. The settlement agreement may provide that one or more of Sections 2–1705 through 2–1718 apply to it.

(b) Upon petition of the parties, a court of competent jurisdiction may enter a consent judgment adopting one or more of Sections 2–1705 through 2–1718.

P.A. 82–280, § 2–1717, added by P.A. 84–7, § 1, eff. Aug. 15, 1985.

Formerly Ill.Rev.Stat.1991, ch. 110, ¶ 2–1717.

5/2–1718. Satisfaction of judgments

§ 2–1718. Satisfaction of judgments. If security is posted in accordance with Section 2–1711 and approved under a final judgment, the judgment is satisfied and the judgment debtor on whose behalf the security is posted is discharged.

P.A. 82–280, § 2–1718, added by P.A. 84–7, § 1, eff. Aug. 15, 1985.

Formerly Ill.Rev.Stat.1991, ch. 110, ¶ 2–1718.

5/2–1719. Duties of Director of Insurance

§ 2–1719. Duties of Director of Insurance. The Director of Insurance shall establish rules and procedures:

(1) for determining which insurers, self-insurers, plans, arrangements, reciprocals or other entities under his or her regulation are financially qualified to provide the security required under Section 2–1711 and to be designated as qualified insurers;

(2) to require insurers to post security under Section 2–1711 if found by the court to be obligated and capable of posting security; and

(3) for publishing prior to January 1 of each year the rate of discount per annum set out in subsection (c) of Section 2–1709.

P.A. 82–280, § 2–1719, added by P.A. 84–7, § 1, eff. Aug. 15, 1985.

Formerly Ill.Rev.Stat.1991, ch. 110, ¶ 2–1719.

PART 18. MITTIMUS

Section
5/2–1801. Mittimus.

Date Effective

Part 18 was added by P.A. 84–622,
§ 1, eff. Sept. 20, 1985.

5/2–1801. Mittimus

§ 2–1801. Mittimus. (a) In all cases, including criminal, quasi-criminal and civil, when a person is imprisoned, incarcerated, confined or committed to the custody of a sheriff, warden, Department of Corrections or other executive officer by virtue of a judgment or order which is signed by a judge, a copy of such judgment or order shall, in each case, constitute the mittimus, and no separate mittimus need be issued.

(b) Where no written judgment or order was signed by a judge, the practice heretofore prevailing in such cases in the courts of this State shall be followed.

P.A. 82–280, § 2–1801, added by P.A. 84–622, § 1, eff. Sept. 20, 1985.

Formerly Ill.Rev.Stat.1991, ch. 110, ¶ 2–1801.

PART 19. LIS PENDENS

Section
5/2–1901. Lis pendens—Operative date of notice.
5/2–1902. Lis pendens—Bankruptcy.
5/2–1903. Lis Pendens—Limitation as to Public Officers.

Date Effective

Part 19, Lis Pendens, was added to the
Code of Civil Procedure as Part 17, consist-
ing of §§ 2–1701 to 2–1703, by P.A. 84–622,
§ 1, eff. Sept. 20, 1985 and renumbered as
Part 19, consisting of §§ 2–1901 to 2–1903,
by P.A. 84–1308, Art. II, § 107, eff. Aug. 25,
1986.

5/2–1901. Lis pendens—Operative date of notice

§ 2–1901. Lis Pendens—Operative date of notice. Except as otherwise provided in Section 15–1503, every condemnation proceeding, proceeding to sell real estate of decedent to pay debts, or other action seeking equitable relief, affecting or involving real property shall, from the time of the filing in the office of the recorder in the county where the real estate is located, of a notice signed by any party to the action or his attorney of record or attorney in fact, on his or her behalf, setting forth the title of the action, the parties to it, the court where it was brought and a description of the real estate, be constructive notice to every person subsequently acquiring an interest in or a lien on the property affected thereby, and every such person and every person acquiring an interest or lien as above stated, not in possession of the property and whose interest or lien is not shown of record at the time of filing such notice, shall, for the purposes of this Section, be deemed a subsequent purchaser and shall be bound by the proceedings to the same extent and in the same manner as if he or she were a party thereto. If in any such action plaintiff or petitioner neglects or fails for the period of 6 months after the filing of the complaint or petition to cause notice to be given the defendant or defendants, either by service of summons or publication as required by law, then such notice shall cease to be such constructive notice until service of summons or publication as required by law is had.

This Section authorizes a notice of any of these actions concerning real property pending in any United States district court to be recorded and indexed in the same manner and in the same place as herein provided with respect to notices of such actions pending in courts of this State.

However, no such action or proceeding shall be constructive notice, either before or after service of summons or publication, as to property subject to the provisions of "An Act concerning land titles", approved May 1, 1897, as amended,[1] until the provisions of Section 84 of that Act [2] are complied with.

At any time during the pendency of an action or proceeding initiated after July 1, 1959, which is constructive notice, the court, upon motion, may for good cause shown, provided a finding of specific performance is not necessary for final judgment in the action or proceeding, and upon such terms and conditions, including the posting of suitable bond, if any, as it may deem equitable, authorize the making of a deed, mortgage, lease or other conveyance of any or all of the real estate affected or involved, in which event the party to whom the deed, mortgage, lease or other conveyance of the real estate is made and those claiming under him or her shall not be bound by such action or proceeding.

P.A. 82–280, § 2–1701, added by P.A. 84–622, § 1, eff. Sept. 20, 1985. Renumbered § 2–1901 and amended by P.A. 84–1308, Art. II, § 107, eff. Aug. 25, 1986. Amended by P.A. 85–907, Art. I, § 1, eff. Nov. 23, 1987.

Formerly Ill.Rev.Stat.1991, ch. 110, ¶ 2–1901.
1 765 ILCS 35/0.01 et seq.
2 765 ILCS 35/84.

5/2–1902. Lis pendens—Bankruptcy

§ 2–1902. Lis Pendens—Bankruptcy. A certified copy of a petition, with schedules omitted, commencing a proceeding under the Bankruptcy Act of the United States [1] or of the order of adjudication in such proceeding, or of the order approving the bond of the trustee appointed in the proceedings, may be filed, indexed and recorded in the office of the recorder where conveyances of real estate are recorded in the same manner as deeds. It shall be the duty of the recorder to file, index under the name of the bankrupt, and record such certified copies filed for record in the same manner as deeds, for which services the recorder shall be entitled to the same fees as are provided by law for filing, indexing and recording deeds.

P.A. 82–280, § 2–1702, added by P.A. 84–622, § 1, eff. Sept. 20, 1985. Renumbered § 2–1902 and amended by P.A. 84–1308, Art. II, § 107, eff. Aug. 25, 1986.

Formerly Ill.Rev.Stat.1991, ch. 110, ¶ 2–1902.
1 11 U.S.C.A. § 101 et seq.

5/2–1903. Lis Pendens—Limitation as to Public Officers

§ 2–1903. Lis Pendens—Limitation as to Public Officers. In the absence of a permanent or preliminary injunction or temporary restraining order of a court, the bringing or pendency of any action alone, heretofore, or hereafter brought, to defeat or enjoin the disbursement by public officers of public funds to the persons, uses, or purposes for which they are appropriated or set apart, including the payment of the salaries and wages of all officers and employees of the State, or of any county, city, village, town or other municipality of the State, shall in no way change the liability of any public officer in the disbursement of public funds on account of any notice of matters contained in the pleadings in any action, but such liability shall remain the same, insofar as the bringing or pendency of any such action alone is concerned, as if no such action had been brought.

P.A. 82–280, § 2–1703, added by P.A. 84–622, § 1, eff. Sept. 20, 1985. Renumbered § 2–1903 and amended by P.A. 84–1308, Art. II, § 107, eff. Aug. 25, 1986.

Formerly Ill.Rev.Stat.1991, ch. 110, ¶ 2–1903.

PART 20. CRIME VICTIMS

Section
5/2–2001. Crime victims.

Date Effective

Part 20 was added by P.A. 88–378, § 10, eff. Aug. 17, 1993.

5/2–2001. Crime victims

§ 2–2001. Crime victims. A victim of crime as defined in Section 2.3 of the Criminal Victims' Asset Discovery Act [1] shall have a cause of action against a defendant who has been convicted of a crime, or found not guilty by reason of insanity or guilty but mentally ill of a crime, to recover damages suffered by the victim of the crime.

The Civil Practice Law shall apply in the proceedings, and the case shall be tried as in other civil cases.

If the victim is deceased, the next of kin may maintain the action.

P.A. 82–280, § 2-2001, added by P.A. 88–378, § 10, eff. Aug. 17, 1993.

1 725 ILCS 145/2.3.

PART 21. PRODUCT LIABILITY

Date Effective

Part 21 was added by P.A. 89–7, § 15, eff. March 9, 1995.

Validity

Public Act 89–7, which added this part, has been held unconstitutional in its entirety by the Illinois Supreme Court in the case of Best v. Taylor Machine Works, 1997, 689 N.E.2d 1057, 228 Ill.Dec. 636, 179 Ill.2d 367.

5/2–2101. Definitions

§ 2–2101. Definitions. For purposes of this Part, the terms listed have the following meanings:

"Clear and convincing evidence" means that measure or degree of proof that will produce in the mind of the trier of fact a high degree of certainty as to the truth of the allegations sought to be established. This evidence requires a greater degree of persuasion than is necessary to meet the preponderance of the evidence standard.

"Harm" means (i) damage to property other than the product itself; (ii) personal physical injury, illness, or death; (iii) mental anguish or emotional harm to the extent recognized by applicable law; (iv) any loss of consortium or services; or (v) other loss deriving from any type of harm described in item (i), (ii), (iii), or (iv).

"Manufacturer" means (i) any person who is engaged in a business to design or formulate and to produce, create, make, or construct any product or component part of a product; (ii) a product seller with respect to all component parts of a product or a component part of a product that is created or affected when, before placing the product in the stream of commerce, the product seller designs or formulates and produces, creates, makes, or constructs an aspect

of a product or a component part of a product made by another; or (iii) any product seller not described in (ii) that holds itself out as a manufacturer to the user of the product.

"Product liability action" means a civil action brought on any theory against a manufacturer or product seller for harm caused by a product.

"Product seller" means a person who, in the course of a business conducted for that purpose, sells, distributes, leases, installs, prepares, blends, packages, labels, markets, repairs, maintains, or otherwise is involved in placing a product in the stream of commerce.

P.A. 82–280, § 2-2101, added by P.A. 89–7, § 15, eff. March 9, 1995.

Validity

Public Act 89–7, which added this section, has been held unconstitutional in its entirety by the Illinois Supreme Court in the case of Best v. Taylor Machine Works, 1997, 689 N.E.2d 1057, 228 Ill.Dec. 636, 179 Ill.2d 367.

For applicability of P.A. 89–7, see note following 735 ILCS 5/2–402.

5/2–2102. Effect on other laws

§ 2–2102. Effect on other laws. Except as may be provided by other laws, any civil action that conforms to the definition of a product liability action as defined in Section 2–2101 of this Part shall be governed by the provisions of this Part.

P.A. 82–820, § 2-2102, added by P.A. 89–7, § 15, eff. March 9, 1995.

Validity

Public Act 89–7, which added this section, has been held unconstitutional in its entirety by the Illinois Supreme Court in the case of Best v. Taylor Machine Works, 1997, 689 N.E.2d 1057, 228 Ill.Dec. 636, 179 Ill.2d 367.

For applicability of P.A. 89–7, see note following 735 ILCS 5/2–402

5/2–2103. Federal and State standards; presumption

§ 2–2103. Federal and State standards; presumption. In a product liability action, a product or product component shall be presumed to be reasonably safe if the aspect of the product or product component that allegedly caused the harm was specified or required, or if the aspect is specifically exempted for particular applications or users, by a federal or State statute or regulation promulgated by an agency of the federal or State government responsible for the safety or use of the product before the product was distributed into the stream of commerce.

P.A. 82–280, § 2-2103, added by P.A. 89–7, § 15, eff. March 9, 1995.

Validity

For applicability of P.A. 89–7, see note following 735 ILCS 5/2–402

5/2–2104. No practical and feasible alternative design; presumption

§ 2–2104. No practical and feasible alternative design; presumption. If the design of a product or product component is in issue in a product liability action, the design shall be presumed to be reasonably safe unless, at the time the product left the control of the manufacturer, a practical and technically feasible alternative design was available that would have prevented the harm without significantly impairing the usefulness, desirability, or marketability of the product. An alternative design is practical and feasible if the technical, medical, or scientific knowledge relating to safety of the alternative design was, at the time the product left the control of the manufacturer, available and developed for commercial use and acceptable in the marketplace.

P.A. 82–280, § 2–2104, added by P.A. 89–7, § 15, eff. March 9, 1995.

Validity

For applicability of P.A. 89–7, see note following 735 ILCS 5/2–402

5/2–2105. Changes in design or warning; inadmissibility

§ 2–2105. Changes in design or warning; inadmissibility. When measures are taken which, if taken previously, would have made an event less likely to occur, evidence of the subsequent measures is not admissible to prove a defect in a product, negligence, or culpable conduct in connection with the event. In a product liability action brought under any theory or doctrine, if the feasibility of a design change or change in warnings is not controverted, then a subsequent design change or change in warnings shall not be admissible into evidence. This rule does not require the exclusion of evidence of subsequent measures when offered for another purpose such as proving ownership, control, or impeachment.

P.A. 82–280, § 2–2105, added by P.A. 89–7, § 15, eff. March 9, 1995.

Validity

For applicability of P.A. 89–7, see note following 735 ILCS 5/2–402

5/2–2106. Provision of written warnings to users of product; nonliability

§ 2–2106. Provision of written warnings to users of product; nonliability.

(a) The warning, instructing, or labeling of a product or specific product component shall be deemed to be adequate if pamphlets, booklets, labels, or other written warnings were provided that gave adequate notice to reasonably anticipated users or knowledgeable intermediaries of the material risks of injury, death, or property damage connected with the reasonably anticipated use of the product and instructions as to the reasonably anticipated uses, applications, or limitations of the product anticipated by the defendant.

(b) In the defense of a product liability action, warnings, instructions or labeling shall be deemed to be adequate if the warnings, instructions or labels furnished with the product were in conformity with the generally recognized standards in the industry at the time the product was distributed into the stream of commerce.

(c) Notwithstanding subsections (a) and (b), a defendant shall not be liable for failure to warn of material risks that were obvious to a reasonably prudent product user and material risks that were a matter of common knowledge to persons in the same position as or similar positions to that of the plaintiff in a product liability action.

(d) In any product liability action brought against a manufacturer or product seller for harm allegedly caused by a failure to provide adequate warnings or instructions, a defendant manufacturer or product seller shall not be liable if, at the time the product left the control of the manufacturer, the knowledge of the danger that caused the harm was not reasonably available or obtainable in light of existing scientific, technical, or medical information.

P.A. 82–280, § 2–2106, added by P.A. 89–7, § 15, eff. March 9, 1995.

Validity

For applicability of P.A. 89–7, see note following 735 ILCS 5/2–402

5/2–2106.5. Inherent characteristics of products; nonliability

§ 2–2106.5. Inherent characteristics of products; nonliability. In a product liability action, a manufacturer or product seller shall not be liable for harm allegedly caused by a product if the alleged harm was caused by an inherent characteristic of the product which is a generic aspect of the product that cannot be eliminated without substantially compromising the product's usefulness or desirability and which is recognized by the ordinary person with the ordinary knowledge common to the community.

P.A. 82–280, § 2–2106.5, added by P.A. 89–7, § 15, eff. March 9, 1995.

Validity

Public Act 89–7, which added this section, has been held unconstitutional in its entirety by the Illinois Supreme Court in the case of Best v. Taylor Machine Works, 1997, 689 N.E.2d 1057, 228 Ill.Dec. 636, 179 Ill.2d 367.

For applicability of P.A. 89–7, see note following 735 ILCS 5/2–402

5/2–2107. Punitive damages

§ 2–2107. Punitive damages. In a product liability action, punitive damages shall not be awarded against a manufacturer or product seller if the conduct of the defendant manufacturer, seller, or reseller that allegedly caused the harm was approved by or was in compliance with standards set forth in an applicable federal or State statute or in a regulation or other administrative action promulgated by an agency of the federal or State government responsible for the safety or use of the product, which statute or regulation was in effect at the time of the manufacturer's or product seller's alleged misconduct, unless the plaintiff proves by clear and convincing evidence that the manufacturer or product seller intentionally withheld from or misrepresented to Congress, the State legislature, or the relevant federal or State agency material information relative to the safety or use of the product that would or could have resulted in a changed decision relative to the law, standard, or other administrative action.

P.A. 82–280, § 2–2107, added by P.A. 89–7, § 15, eff. March 9, 1995.

Validity

Public Act 89–7, which added this section, has been held unconstitutional in its entirety by the Illinois Supreme Court in the case of Best v. Taylor Machine Works, 1997, 689 N.E.2d 1057, 228 Ill.Dec. 636, 179 Ill.2d 367.

For applicability of P.A. 89–7, see note following 735 ILCS 5/2–402

5/2–2108. No cause of action created

§ 2–2108. No cause of action created. Nothing in this Part shall be construed to create a cause of action.

P.A. 82–280, § 2–2108, added by P.A. 89–7, § 15, eff. March 9, 1995.

Validity

Public Act 89–7, which added this section, has been held unconstitutional in its entirety by the Illinois Supreme Court in the case of Best v. Taylor Machine Works, 1997, 689 N.E.2d 1057, 228 Ill.Dec. 636, 179 Ill.2d 367.

For applicability of P.A. 89–7, see note following 735 ILCS 5/2–402

5/2–2109. Applicability

§ 2–2109. This amendatory Act of 1995 adding Part 21 to the Code of Civil Procedure applies to causes of action accruing on or after its effective date.

P.A. 82–280, § 2–2109, added by P.A. 89–7, § 15, eff. March 9, 1995.

Validity

Public Act 89–7, which added this section, has been held unconstitutional in its entirety by the Illinois Supreme Court in the case of Best v. Taylor Machine Works, 1997, 689 N.E.2d 1057, 228 Ill.Dec. 636, 179 Ill.2d 367.

For applicability of P.A. 89–7, see note following 735 ILCS 5/2–402

PART 22. INSURANCE PLACEMENT LIABILITY

Section
5/2–2201. Ordinary care; civil liability.

Date Effective

Part 22 was added by P.A. 89–638, § 5, eff. Jan. 1, 1997.

5/2–2201. Ordinary care; civil liability

§ 2–2201. Ordinary care; civil liability.

(a) An insurance producer, registered firm, and limited insurance representative shall exercise ordinary care and skill in renewing, procuring, binding, or placing the coverage requested by the insured or proposed insured.

(b) No cause of action brought by any person or entity against any insurance producer, registered firm, or limited insurance representative concerning the sale, placement, procurement, renewal, binding, cancellation of, or failure to procure any policy of insurance shall subject the insurance producer, registered firm, or limited insurance representative to civil liability under standards governing the conduct of a fiduciary or a fiduciary relationship except when the conduct upon which the cause of action is based involves the wrongful retention or misappropriation by the insurance producer, registered firm, or limited insurance representative of any money that was received as premiums, as a premium deposit, or as payment of a claim.

(c) The provisions of this Section are not meant to impair or invalidate any of the terms or conditions of a contractual agreement between an insurance producer, registered firm, or limited insurance representative and a company that has authority to transact the kinds of insurance defined in Class 1 or clause (a), (b), (c), (d), (e), (f), (h), (i), or (k) of Class 2 of Section 4 of the Illinois Insurance Code.[1]

(d) While limiting the scope of liability of an insurance producer, registered firm, or limited insurance representative under standards governing the conduct of a fiduciary or a fiduciary relationship, the provisions of this Section do not limit or release an insurance producer, registered firm, or limited insurance representative from liability for negligence concerning the sale, placement, procurement, renewal, binding, cancellation of, or failure to procure any policy of insurance.

P.A. 82–280, § 2–2201, added by P.A. 89–638, § 5, eff. Jan. 1, 1997.

[1] 215 ILCS 5/4.

PART 23. SETTLEMENT

Section
5/2–2301. Settlement of claims; payment.

5/2–2301. Settlement of claims; payment

§ 2–2301. Settlement of claims; payment.

(a) In a personal injury, property damage, wrongful death, or tort action involving a claim for money damages, a release must be tendered to the plaintiff by the settling defendant within 14 days of written confirmation of the settlement. Written confirmation includes all communication by written means.

(b) In a personal injury, property damage, wrongful death, or tort action involving a claim for money damages in which the law requires court approval of a settlement, the plaintiff shall tender to the defendant a copy of the court order approving the settlement.

(c) In a personal injury, property damage, wrongful death, or tort action involving a claim for money damages in which there is a known third-party right of recovery or subrogation interest (including attorney's liens, healthcare provider liens, or rights of recovery claimed by Medicare, the Centers for Medicare and Medicaid Services, the Illinois Department of Healthcare and Family Services, or private health insurance companies), the plaintiff may protect the third-party's right of recovery or subrogation interest, where applicable, by tendering to the defendant:

(1) A signed release of the attorney's lien.

(2) Either:

(i) a signed release of a healthcare provider lien; or

(ii) a letter from the plaintiff's attorney agreeing to hold the full amount of the claimed lien in the plaintiff's attorney's client fund account pending final resolution of the lien amount; or

(iii) an offer that the defendant hold the full amount of the claimed right to recovery pending final resolution of the amount of the right of recovery; or

(iv) documentation of any other method of resolution of the liens as agreed by the parties.

(3) Either:

(i) documentation of the agreement between the plaintiff and Medicare, the Centers for Medicare and Medicaid Services, the Illinois Department of Healthcare and Family Services, or the private health insurance company as to the amount of the settlement that will be accepted in satisfaction of right of recovery; or

(ii) a letter from the plaintiff's attorney agreeing to hold the full amount of the claimed right to recovery in the plaintiff's attorney's client fund account pending final resolution of the amount of the right to recovery; or

(iii) an offer that the defendant hold the full amount of the claimed right to recovery pending final resolution of the amount of the right of recovery; or

(iv) documentation of any other method of resolution of the liens as agreed by the parties.

(d) A settling defendant shall pay all sums due to the plaintiff within 30 days of tender by the plaintiff of the executed release and all applicable documents in compliance with subsections (a), (b), and (c) of this Section.

(e) If, after a hearing, the court having jurisdiction over the parties finds that timely payment has not been made by a defendant pursuant to subsection (d) of this Section, judgment shall be entered against that defendant for the amount set forth in the executed release, plus costs incurred in obtaining the judgment and interest at the rate specified under Section 2–1303 of this Code, calculated from the date of the tender by the plaintiff under subsection (d) of this Section.

(f) As used in this Section, "tender" means personal delivery or delivery by a means providing a return receipt.

(g) This Section applies to all personal injury, property damage, wrongful death, and tort actions involving a claim for money damages, except as otherwise agreed by the parties. This Section does not apply to:

(1) the State of Illinois;

(2) any State agency, board, or Commission, as defined in Section 1–7 of the Illinois State Auditing Act; [1]

(3) any State officer or employee sued in his or her official capacity;

(4) any person or entity that is being represented by the Attorney General and provided indemnification by the State pursuant to the State Employee Indemnification Act;

(5) any municipality or unit of local government as defined under Article VII of the Illinois Constitution; and

(6) class action lawsuits.

P.A. 82–280, § 2–2301, added by P.A. 98–548, § 5, eff. Jan. 1, 2014.

¹ 30 ILCS 5/1–7.

ARTICLE III. ADMINISTRATIVE REVIEW

5/3–101. Definitions

§ 3–101. Definitions. For the purpose of this Act:

"Administrative agency" means a person, body of persons, group, officer, board, bureau, commission or department (other than a court or judge) of the State, or of any political subdivision of the State or municipal corporation in the State, having power under law to make administrative decisions.

"Administrative decision" or "decision" means any decision, order or determination of any administrative agency rendered in a particular case, which affects the legal rights, duties or privileges of parties and which terminates the proceedings before the administrative agency. In all cases in which a statute or a rule of the administrative agency requires or permits an application for a rehearing or other method of administrative review to be filed within a specified time (as distinguished from a statute which permits the application for rehearing or administrative review to be filed at any time before judgment by the administrative agency against the applicant or within a specified time after the entry of such judgment), and an application for such rehearing or review is made, no administrative decision of such agency shall be final as to the party applying therefor until such rehearing or review is had or denied. However, if the particular statute permits an application for rehearing or other method of administrative review to be filed with the administrative agency for an indefinite period of time after the administrative decision has been rendered (such as permitting such application to be filed at any time before judgment by the administrative agency against the applicant or within a specified time after the entry

of such judgment), then the authorization for the filing of such application for rehearing or review shall not postpone the time when the administrative decision as to which such application shall be filed would otherwise become final, but the filing of the application for rehearing or review with the administrative agency in this type of case shall constitute the commencement of a new proceeding before such agency, and the decision rendered in order to dispose of such rehearing or other review proceeding shall constitute a new and independent administrative decision. If such new and independent decision consists merely of the denial of the application for rehearing or other method of administrative review, the record upon judicial review of such decision shall be limited to the application for rehearing or other review and the order or decision denying such application and shall not include the record of proceedings had before the rendering of the administrative decision as to which the application for rehearing or other administrative review shall have been filed unless the suit for judicial review is commenced within the time in which it would be authorized by this Act to have been commenced if no application for rehearing or other method of administrative review had been filed. On the other hand, if the rehearing or other administrative review is granted by the administrative agency, then the record on judicial review of the resulting administrative decision rendered pursuant to the rehearing or other administrative review may consist not only of the record of proceedings had before the administrative agency in such rehearing or other administrative review proceeding, but also of the record of proceedings had before such administrative agency prior to its rendering of the administrative decision as to which the rehearing or other administrative review shall have been granted. The term "administrative decision" or "decision" does not mean or include rules, regulations, standards, or statements of policy of general application issued by an administrative agency to implement, interpret, or make specific the legislation enforced or administered by it unless such a rule, regulation, standard or statement of policy is involved in a proceeding before the agency and its applicability or validity is in issue in such proceeding, nor does it mean or include regulations concerning the internal management of the agency not affecting private rights or interests.

P.A. 82–280, § 3–101, eff. July 1, 1982. Amended by P.A. 83–707, § 1, eff. Sept. 23, 1983; P.A. 88–1, § 6, eff. Jan. 1, 1994; P.A. 92–651, § 84, eff. July 11, 2002.

Formerly Ill.Rev.Stat.1991, ch. 110, ¶ 3–101.

5/3–102. Scope of Article

§ 3–102. Scope of Article. Article III of this Act shall apply to and govern every action to review judicially a final decision of any administrative agency where the Act creating or conferring power on such agency, by express reference, adopts the provisions of

Article III of this Act or its predecessor, the Administrative Review Act.[1] This Article shall be known as the "Administrative Review Law". In all such cases, any other statutory, equitable or common law mode of review of decisions of administrative agencies heretofore available shall not hereafter be employed.

Unless review is sought of an administrative decision within the time and in the manner herein provided, the parties to the proceeding before the administrative agency shall be barred from obtaining judicial review of such administrative decision. In an action to review any final decision of any administrative agency brought under Article III, if a judgment is reversed or entered against the plaintiff, or the action is voluntarily dismissed by the plaintiff, or the action is dismissed for want of prosecution, or the action is dismissed by a United States District Court for lack of jurisdiction, neither the plaintiff nor his or her heirs, executors, or administrators may commence a new action within one year or within the remaining period of limitation, whichever is greater. All proceedings in the court for revision of such final decision shall terminate upon the date of the entry of any Order under either Section 2–1009 or Section 13–217. Such Order shall cause the final administrative decision of any administrative agency to become immediately enforceable. If under the terms of the Act governing the procedure before an administrative agency an administrative decision has become final because of the failure to file any document in the nature of objections, protests, petition for hearing or application for administrative review within the time allowed by such Act, such decision shall not be subject to judicial review hereunder excepting only for the purpose of questioning the jurisdiction of the administrative agency over the person or subject matter.

P.A. 82–280, § 3–102, eff. July 1, 1982. Amended by P.A. 84–221, Art. I, § 2, eff. Sept. 1, 1985; P.A. 88–1, § 6, eff. Jan. 1, 1994.

Formerly Ill.Rev.Stat.1991, ch. 110, ¶ 3–102.

[1] Former Ill.Rev.Stat.1991, ch. 110, ¶ 264 et seq. (repealed; see, now, 735 ILCS 5/3–101 et seq.).

5/3–103. Commencement of action

§ 3–103. Commencement of action. Every action to review a final administrative decision shall be commenced by the filing of a complaint and the issuance of summons within 35 days from the date that a copy of the decision sought to be reviewed was served upon the party affected by the decision, except that in municipalities with a population of 500,000 or less a complaint filed within the time limit established by this Section may be subsequently amended to add a police chief or a fire chief in cases brought under the Illinois Municipal Code's provisions providing for the discipline of fire fighters and police officers.

The method of service of the decision shall be as provided in the Act governing the procedure before the administrative agency, but if no method is provided, a decision shall be deemed to have been served either when a copy of the decision is personally delivered or when a copy of the decision is deposited in the United States mail, in a sealed envelope or package, with postage prepaid, addressed to the party affected by the decision at his or her last known residence or place of business.

The form of the summons and the issuance of alias summons shall be according to rules of the Supreme Court.

This amendatory Act of 1993 applies to all cases involving discipline of fire fighters and police officers pending on its effective date and to all cases filed on or after its effective date.

The changes to this Section made by this amendatory Act of the 95th General Assembly apply to all actions filed on or after the effective date of this amendatory Act of the 95th General Assembly.

P.A. 82–280, § 3–103, eff. July 1, 1982. Amended by P.A. 88–1, § 6, eff. Jan. 1, 1994; P.A. 88–110, § 5, eff. July 20, 1993; P.A. 88–670, Art. 2, § 2–67, eff. Dec. 2, 1994; P.A. 89–685, § 25, eff. June 1, 1997; P.A. 95–831, § 5, eff. Aug. 14, 2008.

Formerly Ill.Rev.Stat.1991, ch. 110, ¶ 3–103.

Validity

The Appellate Court of Illinois, First District, has held that a population classification concerning a plaintiff's right to amend an administrative review complaint by adding a defendant constitutes special legislation in violation of Section 13 of Article IV of the Illinois Constitution in the case of Lacny v. Police Bd. of the City of Chicago, App. 1 Dist.1997, 225 Ill.Dec. 602, 291 Ill. App.3d 397, 683 N.E.2d 1265.

5/3–104. Jurisdiction and venue

§ 3–104. Jurisdiction and venue. Jurisdiction to review final administrative decisions is vested in the Circuit Courts, except as to a final order of the Illinois Educational Labor Relations Board in which case jurisdiction to review a final order is vested in the Appellate Court of a judicial district in which the Board maintains an office. If the venue of the action to review a final administrative decision is expressly prescribed in the particular statute under authority of which the decision was made, such venue shall control, but if the venue is not so prescribed, an action to review a final administrative decision may be commenced in the Circuit Court of any county in which (1) any part of the hearing or proceeding culminating in the decision of the administrative agency was held, or (2) any part of the subject matter involved is situated, or (3) any part of the transaction which gave rise to the proceedings before the agency occurred. The court first acquiring jurisdiction of any action to review a final administrative decision shall have and retain jurisdiction of the action until final disposition of the action.

P.A. 82–280, § 3–104, eff. July 1, 1982. Amended by P.A. 84–123, § 2, eff. July 30, 1985; P.A. 85–924, § 4, eff. July 1, 1988; P.A. 88–1, § 6, eff. Jan. 1, 1994.

Formerly Ill.Rev.Stat.1991, ch. 110, ¶ 3–104.

5/3–105. Service of summons

§ 3–105. Service of summons. Summons issued in any action to review the final administrative decision of any administrative agency shall be served by registered or certified mail on the administrative agency and on each of the other defendants except in the case of a review of a final administrative decision of the regional board of school trustees, regional superintendent of schools, or State Superintendent of Education, as the case may be, when a committee of 10 has been designated as provided in Section 7–6 of the School Code, and in such case only the administrative agency involved and each of the committee of 10 shall be served. The method of service shall be as provided in the Act governing the procedure before the administrative agency, but if no method is provided, summons shall be deemed to have been served either when a copy of the summons is personally delivered or when a copy of the decision is deposited in the United States mail, in a sealed envelope or package, with postage prepaid, addressed to the party affected by the decision at his or her last known residence or place of business. The form of the summons and the issuance of alias summons shall be according to rules of the Supreme Court. No action for administrative review shall be dismissed for lack of jurisdiction based upon the failure to serve summons on an employee, agent, or member of an administrative agency, board, committee, or government entity, acting in his or her official capacity, where the administrative agency, board, committee, or government entity has been served as provided in this Section. Service on the director or agency head, in his or her official capacity, shall be deemed service on the administrative agency, board, committee, or government entity. No action for administrative review shall be dismissed for lack of jurisdiction based upon the failure to serve summons on an administrative agency, board, committee, or government entity, acting, where the director or agency head, in his or her official capacity, has been served as provided in this Section. Service on the administrative agency shall be made by the clerk of the court by sending a copy of the summons addressed to the agency at its main office in the State. The clerk of the court shall also mail a copy of the summons to each of the other defendants, addressed to the last known place of residence or principal place of business of each such defendant. The plaintiff shall, by affidavit filed with the complaint, designate the last known address of each defendant upon whom service shall be made. The certificate of the clerk of the court that he

or she has served such summons in pursuance of this Section shall be evidence that he or she has done so.

The changes to this Section made by this amendatory Act of the 95th General Assembly apply to all actions filed on or after the effective date of this amendatory Act of the 95th General Assembly.

P.A. 82–280, § 3–105, eff. July 1, 1982. Amended by P.A. 82–783, Art. III, § 43, eff. July 3, 1982; P.A. 87–210, § 1, eff. Sept. 3, 1991; P.A. 88–1, § 6, eff. Jan. 1, 1994; P.A. 89–685, § 25, eff. June 1, 1997; P.A. 95–831, § 5, eff. Aug. 14, 2008.

Formerly Ill.Rev.Stat.1991, ch. 110, ¶ 3–105.

5/3–106. Appearance of defendants

§ 3–106. Appearance of defendants. In any action to review any final decision of any administrative agency, the agency shall appear by filing an answer consisting of a record of the proceedings had before it, or a written motion in the cause or a written appearance. All other defendants desiring to appear shall appear by filing a written appearance. Every appearance shall be filed within the time fixed by rule of the Supreme Court, and shall state with particularity an address where service of notices or papers may be made upon the defendant so appearing, or his or her attorney.

P.A. 82–280, § 3–106, eff. July 1, 1982. Amended by P.A. 88–1, § 6, eff. Jan. 1, 1994.

Formerly Ill.Rev.Stat.1991, ch. 110, ¶ 3–106.

5/3–107. Defendants

§ 3–107. Defendants.

(a) Except as provided in subsection (b) or (c), in any action to review any final decision of an administrative agency, the administrative agency and all persons, other than the plaintiff, who were parties of record to the proceedings before the administrative agency shall be made defendants. The method of service of the decision shall be as provided in the Act governing the procedure before the administrative agency, but if no method is provided, a decision shall be deemed to have been served either when a copy of the decision is personally delivered or when a copy of the decision is deposited in the United States mail, in a sealed envelope or package, with postage prepaid, addressed to the party affected by the decision at his or her last known residence or place of business. The form of the summons and the issuance of alias summons shall be according to rules of the Supreme Court.

No action for administrative review shall be dismissed for lack of jurisdiction based upon the failure to name an employee, agent, or member, who acted in his or her official capacity, of an administrative agency, board, committee, or government entity, where the administrative agency, board, committee, or government entity, has been named as a defendant as provided in this Section. Naming the director or agency head, in his or her official capacity, shall be deemed to include as defendant the administrative agency, board, committee, or government entity that the named defendants direct or head. No action for administrative review shall be dismissed for lack of jurisdiction based upon the failure to name an administrative agency, board, committee, or government entity, where the director or agency head, in his or her official capacity, has been named as a defendant as provided in this Section.

If, during the course of a review action, the court determines that an agency or a party of record to the administrative proceedings was not made a defendant as required by the preceding paragraph, then the court shall grant the plaintiff 35 days from the date of the determination in which to name and serve the unnamed agency or party as a defendant. The court shall permit the newly served defendant to participate in the proceedings to the extent the interests of justice may require.

(b) With respect to actions to review decisions of a zoning board of appeals in a municipality with a population of 500,000 or more inhabitants under Division 13 of Article 11 of the Illinois Municipal Code,[1] "parties of record" means only the zoning board of appeals and applicants before the zoning board of appeals. The plaintiff shall send a notice of filing of the action by certified mail to each other person who appeared before and submitted oral testimony or written statements to the zoning board of appeals with respect to the decision appealed from. The notice shall be mailed within 2 days of the filing of the action. The notice shall state the caption of the action, the court in which the action is filed, and the names of the plaintiff in the action and the applicant to the zoning board of appeals. The notice shall inform the person of his or her right to intervene. Each person who appeared before and submitted oral testimony or written statements to the zoning board of appeals with respect to the decision appealed from shall have a right to intervene as a defendant in the action upon application made to the court within 30 days of the mailing of the notice.

(c) With respect to actions to review decisions of a hearing officer or a county zoning board of appeals under Division 5–12 of Article 5 of the Counties Code, "parties of record" means only the hearing officer or the zoning board of appeals and applicants before the hearing officer or the zoning board of appeals. The plaintiff shall send a notice of filing of the action by certified mail to each other person who appeared before and submitted oral testimony or written statements to the hearing officer or the zoning board of appeals with respect to the decision appealed from. The notice shall be mailed within 2 days of the filing of the action. The notice shall state the caption of the action, the court in which the action is filed, and the name of the plaintiff in the action and the applicant to the hearing officer or the zoning board of appeals.

The notice shall inform the person of his or her right to intervene. Each person who appeared before and submitted oral testimony or written statements to the hearing officer or the zoning board of appeals with respect to the decision appealed from shall have a right to intervene as a defendant in the action upon application made to the court within 30 days of the mailing of the notice. This subsection (c) applies to zoning proceedings commenced on or after the effective date of this amendatory Act of the 95th General Assembly.

(d) The changes to this Section made by this amendatory Act of the 95th General Assembly apply to all actions filed on or after the effective date of this amendatory Act of the 95th General Assembly.

P.A. 82–280, § 3–107, eff. July 1, 1982. Amended by P.A. 87–497, § 1, eff. Jan. 1, 1992; P.A. 88–1, § 6, eff. Jan. 1, 1994; P.A. 88–655, § 5, eff. Sept. 16, 1994; P.A. 89–438, § 3, eff. Dec. 15, 1995; P.A. 89–685, § 25, eff. June 1, 1997; P.A. 95–321, § 5, eff. Aug. 21, 2007; P.A. 95–831, § 5, eff. Aug. 14, 2008.

Formerly Ill.Rev.Stat.1991, ch. 110, ¶ 3–107.

[1] 65 ILCS 5/11–13–1 et seq.

P.A. 95–831 incorporated the amendment by P.A. 95–321.

5/3–108. Pleadings and record on review

§ 3–108. Pleadings and record on review. (a) Complaint. The complaint shall contain a statement of the decision or part of the decision sought to be reviewed. It shall specify whether the transcript of evidence, if any, or what portion thereof, shall be filed by the agency as part of the record. Upon motion of any defendant, or upon its own motion, the court may require of the plaintiff a specification of the errors relied upon for reversal.

(b) Answer. Except as herein otherwise provided, the administrative agency shall file an answer which shall consist of the original or a certified copy of the entire record of proceedings under review, including such evidence as may have been heard by it and the findings and decisions made by it. By order of court or by stipulation of all parties to the review, the record may be shortened by the elimination of any portion thereof. If the complaint specifies that none or only a part of the transcript of evidence shall be filed as part of the answer and if the administrative agency or any other defendant objects thereto, the court shall hear the parties upon this question and make a finding as to whether all, or if less than all, what parts of the transcript shall be included in the answer. No pleadings other than as herein enumerated shall be filed by any party unless required by the court.

(c) Record after remandment. If the cause is remanded to the administrative agency and a review shall thereafter be sought of the administrative decision, the original and supplemental record, or so much thereof as shall be determined by court order or the stipulation of all the parties, shall constitute the record on review.

P.A. 82–280, § 3–108, eff. July 1, 1982. Amended by P.A. 83–707, § 1, eff. Sept. 23, 1983; P.A. 88–1, § 6, eff. Jan. 1, 1994.

Formerly Ill.Rev.Stat.1991, ch. 110, ¶ 3–108.

5/3–109. Costs of preparing and certifying record of proceedings before agency

§ 3–109. Costs of preparing and certifying record of proceedings before agency. If the statute under authority of which the administrative decision was entered provides or requires that the plaintiff in the review proceeding shall pay to the agency the costs of preparing and certifying the record of proceedings before the agency, the failure to make that payment shall relieve the agency of the necessity of filing the answer required in Section 3–108 of this Act and shall be authority for the entry of an order by the court, on motion therefor by the agency or any other defendant, dismissing the complaint and (in the case of an administrative decision which requires the payment of money) entering a judgment against the plaintiff and in favor of the administrative agency for the amount shown by the administrative decision that is involved to be due, and for costs.

P.A. 82–280, § 3–109, eff. July 1, 1982. Amended by P.A. 88–1, § 6, eff. Jan. 1, 1994.

Formerly Ill.Rev.Stat.1991, ch. 110, ¶ 3–109.

5/3–110. Scope of review

§ 3–110. Scope of review. Every action to review any final administrative decision shall be heard and determined by the court with all convenient speed. The hearing and determination shall extend to all questions of law and fact presented by the entire record before the court. No new or additional evidence in support of or in opposition to any finding, order, determination or decision of the administrative agency shall be heard by the court. The findings and conclusions of the administrative agency on questions of fact shall be held to be prima facie true and correct.

P.A. 82–280, § 3–110, eff. July 1, 1982. Amended by P.A. 88–1, § 6, eff. Jan. 1, 1994.

Formerly Ill.Rev.Stat.1991, ch. 110, ¶ 3–110.

5/3–111. Powers of circuit court

§ 3–111. Powers of circuit court.

(a) The Circuit Court has power:

(1) with or without requiring bond (except if otherwise provided in the particular statute under authority of which the administrative decision was entered), and before or after answer filed, upon notice to the agency and good cause shown, to stay the decision of the administrative agency in whole or in part pending the final disposition of the case.

For the purpose of this subsection, "good cause" requires the applicant to show (i) that an immediate stay is required in order to preserve the status quo without endangering the public, (ii) that it is not contrary to public policy, and (iii) that there exists a reasonable likelihood of success on the merits;

(2) to make any order that it deems proper for the amendment, completion or filing of the record of proceedings of the administrative agency;

(3) to allow substitution of parties by reason of marriage, death, bankruptcy, assignment or other cause;

(4) to dismiss parties, to correct misnomers, to realign parties, or to join agencies or parties;

(5) to affirm or reverse the decision in whole or in part;

(6) where a hearing has been held by the agency, to reverse and remand the decision in whole or in part, and, in that case, to state the questions requiring further hearing or proceedings and to give such other instructions as may be proper;

(7) where a hearing has been held by the agency, to remand for the purpose of taking additional evidence when from the state of the record of the administrative agency or otherwise it shall appear that such action is just. However, no remandment shall be made on the ground of newly discovered evidence unless it appears to the satisfaction of the court that such evidence has in fact been discovered subsequent to the termination of the proceedings before the administrative agency and that it could not by the exercise of reasonable diligence have been obtained at such proceedings; and that such evidence is material to the issues and is not cumulative;

(8) in case of affirmance or partial affirmance of an administrative decision which requires the payment of money, to enter judgment for the amount justified by the record and for costs, which judgment may be enforced as other judgments for the recovery of money;

(9) when the particular statute under authority of which the administrative decision was entered requires the plaintiff to file a satisfactory bond and provides for the dismissal of the action for the plaintiff's failure to comply with this requirement unless the court is authorized by the particular statute to enter, and does enter, an order imposing a lien upon the plaintiff's property, to take such proofs and to enter such orders as may be appropriate to carry out the provisions of the particular statute. However, the court shall not approve the bond, nor enter an order for the lien, in any amount which is less than that prescribed by the particular statute under authority of which the administrative decision was entered if the statute provides what the minimum amount of the bond or lien shall be or provides how said minimum amount shall be deter-

mined. No such bond shall be approved by the court without notice to, and an opportunity to be heard thereon by, the administrative agency affected. The lien, created by the entry of a court order in lieu of a bond, shall not apply to property exempted from the lien by the particular statute under authority of which the administrative decision was entered. The lien shall not be effective against real property whose title is registered under the provisions of the Registered Titles (Torrens) Act [1] until the provisions of Section 85 [2] of that Act are complied with.

(b) Technical errors in the proceedings before the administrative agency or its failure to observe the technical rules of evidence shall not constitute grounds for the reversal of the administrative decision unless it appears to the court that such error or failure materially affected the rights of any party and resulted in substantial injustice to him or her.

(c) On motion of either party, the circuit court shall make findings of fact or state the propositions of law upon which its judgment is based.

(d) The changes to this Section made by this amendatory Act of the 95th General Assembly apply to all actions filed on or after the effective date of this amendatory Act of the 95th General Assembly.

P.A. 82-280, § 3-111, eff. July 1, 1982. Amended by P.A. 88-1, § 6, eff. Jan. 1, 1994; P.A. 88-184, § 10, eff. Aug. 4, 1993; P.A. 88-670, Art. 2, § 2-67, eff. Dec. 2, 1994; P.A. 95-831, § 5, eff. Aug. 14, 2008.

Formerly Ill.Rev.Stat.1991, ch. 110, ¶ 3-111.

[1] 765 ILCS 35/0.01 et seq.

[2] 765 ILCS 35/85 (repealed).

5/3–112.   Appeals

§ 3–112. Appeals. A final decision, order, or judgment of the Circuit Court, entered in an action to review a decision of an administrative agency, is reviewable by appeal as in other civil cases.

P.A. 82-280, § 3-112, eff. July 1, 1982. Amended by P.A. 88-1, § 6, eff. Jan. 1, 1994.

Formerly Ill.Rev.Stat.1991, ch. 110, ¶ 3-112.

5/3–113.   Direct review of administrative orders by the appellate court

§ 3–113. Direct review of administrative orders by the appellate court.

(a) Unless another time is provided specifically by the law authorizing the review, an action for direct review of a final administrative decision of an administrative agency by the appellate court shall be commenced by the filing of a petition for review in the appellate court within 35 days from the date that a copy of the decision sought to be reviewed was served upon the party affected by the decision. The method of service of the decision shall be as provided in the Act governing the procedure before the administrative agency, but if no method is provided, a decision shall be deemed to have been served either when a copy of the decision is personally delivered or when a copy of the decision is deposited in the United States mail, in a sealed envelope or package, with postage prepaid, addressed to the party affected by the decision at his or her last known residence or place of business.

(b) The petition for review shall be filed in the appellate court and shall specify the parties seeking review and shall designate the respondent and the order or part thereof to be reviewed. The administrative agency and all persons, other than the petitioner, who were parties of record to the proceedings before the administrative agency shall be made respondents. The method of service of the decision shall be as provided in the Act governing the procedure before the administrative agency, but if no method is provided, a decision shall be deemed to have been served either when a copy of the decision is personally delivered or when a copy of the decision is deposited in the United States mail, in a sealed envelope or package, with postage prepaid, addressed to the party affected by the decision at his or her last known residence or place of business. The form of the summons and the issuance of alias summons shall be according to rules of the Supreme Court.

If, during the course of a review action, the court determines that an agency or a party of record to the administrative proceedings was not made a defendant as required by the preceding paragraph, then the court shall grant the plaintiff 35 days from the date of the determination in which to name and serve the unnamed agency or party as a defendant. The court shall permit the newly served defendant to participate in the proceedings to the extent the interests of justice may require.

(c) The changes to this Section made by this amendatory Act of the 95th General Assembly apply to all actions filed on or after the effective date of this amendatory Act of the 95th General Assembly.

P.A. 82-280, § 3-113, added by P.A. 88-1, § 6, eff. Jan. 1, 1994. Amended by P.A. 89-438, § 3, eff. Dec. 15, 1995; P.A. 95-831, § 5, eff. Aug. 14, 2008.

Formerly Ill.Rev.Stat.1991, ch. 110, ¶ 3-113.

ARTICLE IV.   ATTACHMENT

PART 1.   IN GENERAL

5/4–101. Cause

§ 4–101. Cause. In any court having competent jurisdiction, a creditor having a money claim, whether liquidated or unliquidated, and whether sounding in contract or tort, or based upon a statutory cause of action created by law in favor of the People of the State of Illinois, or any agency of the State, may have an attachment against the property of his or her debtor, or that of any one or more of several debtors, either at the time of commencement of the action or thereafter, when the claim exceeds $20, in any one of the following cases:

1. Where the debtor is not a resident of this State.

2. When the debtor conceals himself or herself or stands in defiance of an officer, so that process cannot be served upon him or her.

3. Where the debtor has departed from this State with the intention of having his or her effects removed from this State.

4. Where the debtor is about to depart from this State with the intention of having his or her effects removed from this State.

5. Where the debtor is about to remove his or her property from this State to the injury of such creditor.

6. Where the debtor has within 2 years preceding the filing of the affidavit required, fraudulently conveyed or assigned his or her effects, or a part thereof, so as to hinder or delay his or her creditors.

7. Where the debtor has, within 2 years prior to the filing of such affidavit, fraudulently concealed or disposed of his or her property so as to hinder or delay his or her creditors.

8. Where the debtor is about fraudulently to conceal, assign, or otherwise dispose of his or her property or effects, so as to hinder or delay his or her creditors.

9. Where the debt sued for was fraudulently contracted on the part of the debtor. The statements of the debtor, his or her agent or attorney, which constitute the fraud, shall have been reduced to writing, and his or her signature attached thereto, by himself or herself, agent or attorney.

10. When the debtor is a person convicted of first degree murder, a Class X felony, or aggravated kidnapping, or found not guilty by reason of insanity or guilty but mentally ill of first degree murder, a Class X felony, or aggravated kidnapping, against the creditor and that crime makes the creditor a "victim" under the Criminal Victims' Asset Discovery Act.[1]

11. When the debtor is referred by the Department of Corrections to the Attorney General under Section 3–7–6 of the Unified Code of Corrections[2] to recover the expenses incurred as a result of that debtor's cost of incarceration.

P.A. 82–280, § 4–101, eff. July 1, 1982. Amended by P.A. 87–1157, § 2, eff. Sept. 18, 1992; P.A. 88–378, § 10, eff. Aug. 17, 1993; P.A. 89–428, Art. 6, § 615, eff. Dec. 13, 1995; P.A. 90–85, § 10, eff. July 10, 1997; P.A. 93–508, § 5, eff. Jan. 1, 2004.

Formerly Ill.Rev.Stat.1991, ch. 110, ¶ 4–101.

[1] 725 ILCS 145/1 et seq.
[2] 730 ILCS 5/3–7–6.

5/4–102. Construed for detection of fraud

§ 4–102. Construed for detection of fraud. This Act shall be construed in all courts in the most liberal manner for the detection of fraud.

P.A. 82–280, § 4–102, eff. July 1, 1982.

Formerly Ill.Rev.Stat.1991, ch. 110, ¶ 4–102.

5/4–103. Venue

§ 4–103. Venue. The venue provisions applicable to other civil cases shall apply to attachment proceedings; and in addition thereto, attachment proceedings may be brought in the county where property or credits of the debtor are found.

P.A. 82–280, § 4–103, eff. July 1, 1982. Amended by P.A. 83–707, § 1, eff. Sept. 23, 1983.

Formerly Ill.Rev.Stat.1991, ch. 110, ¶ 4–103.

5/4–104. Affidavit

§ 4–104. Affidavit. A plaintiff seeking the entry of an order for attachment shall file with the court an affidavit based upon the personal knowledge of the affiant and showing:

1. the amount of the claim, so far as practicable, after allowing all just credits and set-offs;

2. facts establishing any one or more of the causes set forth in Section 4–101 of this Act;

3. the place of residence of the defendant, if known, and if not known, that upon diligent inquiry the affiant has been unable to ascertain the place of residence; and

4. facts establishing the cause of action against the defendant.

The plaintiff shall file an additional statement in writing, either embodied in such affidavit or separately, to the effect that the action invoked by such affidavit does or does not sound in tort and a designation of the return day for the summons to be issued in the action; and the court, if it is satisfied that the affidavit has established a prima facie case, shall enter an order for attachment.

In all actions sounding in tort, before an order for attachment is entered, the plaintiff, his or her agent or attorney, shall apply to the circuit court of the county in which the action is to be brought or is pending and be examined, under oath, by the court concerning the cause of action; and, thereupon, the court shall indorse upon the affidavit the amount of damages for which the order for attachment shall be entered, and no greater amount shall be claimed.

P.A. 82–280, § 4–104, eff. July 1, 1982. Amended by P.A. 83–707, § 1, eff. Sept. 23, 1983.

Formerly Ill.Rev.Stat.1991, ch. 110, ¶ 4–104.

5/4–105. Form of affidavit

§ 4–105. Form of affidavit. Affidavits for attachment in courts may be substantially in the following form:

STATE OF ILLINOIS,)
) ss.
. . . . County)

A B, being duly sworn, says: That (here state if affiant is agent or attorney of the creditor; if the action is by an individual or corporation, the name of the individual or corporation, and if the action is by a firm, the name of the partners) has a just claim against (name of debtor), on account of (here state facts giving rise to the cause of action and amount of the claim), and the affiant believes (the name of the creditor) is entitled to recover of (name of debtor), after allowing all just credits and set-offs . . . . dollars and . . . . cents, which is now due, and that he, she or it has good reason to believe and does believe that (name of debtor) (here state facts which give rise to some one or more of the causes which authorize an attachment). (name of debtor) resides at (here state the residence of the debtor if known, or if not, that the affiant has made diligent inquiry and cannot ascertain his or her or its place of residence.)

Affiant has personal knowledge that the foregoing statements are true.

. . . .

Subscribed and sworn to before me on this . . . . day of . . . . , ... ,

. . . .

My commission expires . . . . , ... ,

(If action sounds in tort here include the endorsement of the court as to amount of damages for which order shall be entered)

P.A. 82–280, § 4–105, eff. July 1, 1982. Amended by P.A. 83–707, § 1, eff. Sept. 23, 1983.

Formerly Ill.Rev.Stat.1991, ch. 110, ¶ 4–105.

5/4–106. Designation of names

§ 4–106. Designation of names. It shall be sufficient, in all cases of attachment, to designate defendants by their reputed names, by surnames, and joint defendants by their separate or partnership names, or by such names, styles or titles as they are usually known; and heirs, executors and administrators of deceased defendants shall be subject to the provisions of Part 1 of Article IV of this Act, in all cases in which it may be applicable to them.

P.A. 82–280, § 4–106, eff. July 1, 1982. Amended by P.A. 83–707, § 1, eff. Sept. 23, 1983.

Formerly Ill.Rev.Stat.1991, ch. 110, ¶ 4–106.

5/4–107. Bond

§ 4–107. Bond. Before the entry of an order for attachment, as hereinabove stated, the court shall take bond and sufficient security, payable to the People of the State of Illinois, for the use of the person or persons interested in the property attached, in double the sum sworn to be due, conditioned for satisfying all costs which may be awarded to such defendant, or to any others interested in the proceedings, and all damages and costs which shall be recovered against the plaintiff, for wrongfully obtaining the attachment order, which bond, with affidavit of the party complaining, or his, her or its agent or attorney, shall be filed in the court entering the order for attachment. Every order for attachment entered without a bond and affidavit taken, is hereby declared illegal and void, and shall be dismissed. Nothing herein contained shall be construed to require the State of Illinois, or any Department of Government thereof, or any State officer, to file a bond as plaintiff in any proceeding instituted under Part 1 of Article IV of this Act.

P.A. 82–280, § 4–107, eff. July 1, 1982. Amended by P.A. 83–707, § 1, eff. Sept. 23, 1983.

Formerly Ill.Rev.Stat.1991, ch. 110, ¶ 4–107.

5/4–108. Fixing of bond

§ 4–108. Fixing of bond. The court, upon ex parte motion, without notice, supported by affidavit of the plaintiff, his or her agent or attorney, substantially describing the property to be attached, and the value thereof, may, if satisfied of the bona fides of the application and sufficiency of the bond under the circumstances of the case, including proposed garnishments, fix the amount of the bond in double the value of the property to be attached, instead of double the sum sworn to be due, and in such event the order shall direct the officer to attach such specifically described property, but the value of such property to be attached shall not be in excess of an amount sufficient to satisfy the debt claimed and costs. The court may require that such affidavit be supplemented by additional showing, by appraisal or otherwise, as to the value of such property, and may, upon motion of any party to the action claiming an interest in such property, either before or after actual attachment, require additional security, or order release of the attachment to the extent not covered by adequate double security.

P.A. 82–280, § 4–108, eff. July 1, 1982.

Formerly Ill.Rev.Stat.1991, ch. 110, ¶ 4–108.

5/4–109. Condition of bond

§ 4–109. Condition of bond. The condition of the bond shall be applicable to additional certified copies of the order for attachment as well as to the first certified copy of the order for attachment and shall be substantially in the following form:

The condition of this obligation is such, that whereas the plaintiff has on (insert date) applied for an order for attachment in the above entitled action of . . . against the estate of the above named . . . . Now, if the . . . shall prosecute the action with effect, or in the case of failure therein shall satisfy all costs which may be awarded to . . . or to any person or persons interested in the property attached, and all damages and costs which shall be recovered against the plaintiff for wrongfully obtaining the order for attachment, then the above obligation to be void; otherwise to remain in full force and effect.

Additional bonds shall not be required for obtaining additional certified copies, except as provided in Section 4–115 of this Act.

P.A. 82–280, § 4–109, eff. July 1, 1982. Amended by P.A. 83–707, § 1, eff. Sept. 23, 1983; P.A. 91–357, § 250, eff. July 29, 1999.

Formerly Ill.Rev.Stat.1991, ch. 110, ¶ 4–109.

5/4–110. Order for attachment

§ 4–110. Order for attachment. The order for attachment required in the preceding section shall be directed to the sheriff (and, for purpose only of service of summons, to any person authorized to serve summons), or in case the sheriff is interested, or otherwise disqualified or prevented from acting, to the coroner of the county in which the action is commenced, and shall be made returnable on a return day designated by the plaintiff, which day shall be not less than 10 days or more than 60 days after its date. Such order shall order the officer to attach so much of the estate, real or personal, of the defendant, to be found in the county, as shall be of value sufficient to satisfy the debt and costs, according to the affidavit, but in case any specific property of the defendant, found in the county, shall be described in the order, then the officer shall attach the described property only, and no other property. Such estate or property shall be so attached in the possession of the officer to secure, or so to provide, that the same may be liable to further proceedings thereupon, according to law. The order shall also direct that the officer summon the defendant to appear and answer the complaint of the plaintiff in court at a specified time or, at defendant's option, to appear at any time prior thereto and move the court to set a hearing on the order for the attachment or affidavit; and that the officer also summon any specified garnishees, to be and appear in court at a specified time to answer to what may be held by them for the defendant.

P.A. 82–280, § 4–110, eff. July 1, 1982. Amended by P.A. 83–707, § 1, eff. Sept. 23, 1983.

Formerly Ill.Rev.Stat.1991, ch. 110, ¶ 4–110.

5/4–111. Attachment against joint debtors

§ 4–111. Attachment against joint debtors. In all cases where two or more persons are jointly indebted, either as partners or otherwise, and an affidavit is filed as provided in Part 1 of Article IV of this Act, so as to bring one or more of such joint debtors within its provisions, and amenable to an action for attachment, then the order for attachment shall be entered against the property and the effects of such as are so brought within the provisions of Part 1 of Article IV of this Act; and the officer shall be also directed to summon, all defendants to the action, whether the action for attachment is against them or not, to answer the action, as in other cases of joint defendants.

P.A. 82–280, § 4–111, eff. July 1, 1982. Amended by P.A. 83–707, § 1, eff. Sept. 23, 1983.

Formerly Ill.Rev.Stat.1991, ch. 110, ¶ 4–111.

5/4–112. Serving of order

§ 4–112. Serving of order. Such officer shall without delay serve the order for attachment upon the property described in the order, or in the absence of such description, upon the lands, tenements, goods, chattels, rights, credits, moneys and effects of the debtor, or upon any lands and tenements in and to which such debtor has or may claim any equitable interest or title, of sufficient value to satisfy the claim sworn to, with costs of the action.

Except as provided in Section 4–116 of this Act, the order for attachment may be levied only in the county in which the order is entered, and by a proper officer of that county.

P.A. 82–280, § 4–112, eff. July 1, 1982. Amended by P.A. 83–707, § 1, eff. Sept. 23, 1983.

Formerly Ill.Rev.Stat.1991, ch. 110, ¶ 4–112.

5/4–113. Certificate of levy

§ 4–113. Certificate of levy. When an order for attachment is levied upon any real estate, in any case, it shall be the duty of the officer making the levy to file a certificate of such fact with the recorder of the county where such land is situated; and from and after the filing of the same, such levy shall take effect, as to creditors and bona fide purchasers, without notice, and not before.

P.A. 82–280, § 4–113, eff. July 1, 1982. Amended by P.A. 83–707, § 1, eff. Sept. 23, 1983.

Formerly Ill.Rev.Stat.1991, ch. 110, ¶ 4–113.

5/4–114. Serving defendant

§ 4–114. Serving defendant. The officer shall also serve a certified copy of the order upon the defendant therein, if he or she can be found, in like manner as provided for service of summons in other civil cases. Such service upon the defendant shall be made as soon as possible after the entry of the order for attachment upon the property described in the order, but in no event later than 5 days thereafter. Failure to make such service upon the defendant within the time provided shall in the absence of good cause shown for such delay, be ground for vacating of the attachment order upon motion of the defendant made at any time. The return of the order shall state the particular manner in which the order was served. If the certified copy of the order is served upon the defendant less than 10 days before the return day thereof, the defendant shall not be compelled to appear or plead until 15 days after the return day

designated in the order. The certified copy of the order for attachment may be served as a summons upon defendants wherever they may be found in the State, by any person authorized to serve process in like manner as summons in other civil cases.

P.A. 82–280, § 4–114, eff. July 1, 1982. Amended by P.A. 83–707, § 1, eff. Sept. 23, 1983.

Formerly Ill.Rev.Stat.1991, ch. 110, ¶ 4–114.

5/4–115. Additional certified copies

§ 4–115. Additional certified copies. (a) When it appears by the return of the officer that the defendant or property of the defendant is not found, or that a garnishee designated by the order for attachment has not been served, additional certified copies of the order for attachment may be issued by the clerk of court on the application of the plaintiff.

(b) Additional certified copies of the order for attachment may also issue on the application of the plaintiff where the property attached, or the property found to be in the possession of the garnishee or garnishees, is not of a value sufficient to satisfy the claim sworn to, with costs of the action. The provisions of this subsection shall not be applicable to cases in which the court order describes specific property to be attached.

(c) When the order for attachment is directed against specific property of the defendant and only a portion of the property described is attached, or the property found to be in the possession of the garnishee or garnishees, is not of a value sufficient to satisfy the claim sworn to, with costs of action, a certified copy of the order for attachment against the remainder of the property described, may be issued by the clerk of court upon the application of the plaintiff. A certified copy of the order for attachment may also issue where additional specific property is desired to be attached, but before such certified copy shall issue the plaintiff shall furnish an additional bond in accordance with Section 4–108 of this Act, in double the value of the additional specific property. Where an order for attachment covering specific property has been entered, a certified copy of the order for attachment may be issued by the clerk of court on the application of the plaintiff directing the sheriff to attach sufficient property of the defendant, which, together with the specific property already attached, if any, will equal the amount of the plaintiff's claim, and before such certified copy shall issue the plaintiff shall furnish in accordance with Section 4–107 of this Act an additional bond in amount double the value of the additional property to be attached.

(d) When an additional certified copy is issued, the defendant shall be served, if he or she can be found, and return shall be made, and the same proceedings shall be had, as though such additional certified copy was the original certified copy.

P.A. 82–280, § 4–115, eff. July 1, 1982. Amended by P.A. 83–707, § 1, eff. Sept. 23, 1983.

Formerly Ill.Rev.Stat.1991, ch. 110, ¶ 4–115.

5/4–116. Pursuit of property

§ 4–116. Pursuit of property. If the defendant, or any person for him or her, shall be in the act of removing any personal property, the officer may pursue and take the same in any county in this State, and return the same to the county from which such order for attachment issued.

P.A. 82–280, § 4–116, eff. July 1, 1982. Amended by P.A. 83–707, § 1, eff. Sept. 23, 1983.

Formerly Ill.Rev.Stat.1991, ch. 110, ¶ 4–116.

5/4–117. Serving on Sunday

§ 4–117. Serving on Sunday. If it shall appear, by the affidavit, that a debtor is actually absconding, or concealed, or stands in defiance of an officer duly authorized to arrest him or her on civil process, or has departed this State with the intention of having his or her effects and personal estate removed out of the State, or intends to depart with such intention, it shall be lawful for the clerk to issue, and sheriff or other officer to serve a certified copy of the order for attachment against such debtor, on a Sunday as on any other day.

P.A. 82–280, § 4–117, eff. July 1, 1982. Amended by P.A. 83–707, § 1, eff. Sept. 23, 1983.

Formerly Ill.Rev.Stat.1991, ch. 110, ¶ 4–117.

5/4–118. Certified copies of order to other county

§ 4–118. Certified copies of order to other county. The creditor may, at the same time, or at any time before judgment, cause a certified copy of an order for attachment to be issued to any other county in the State where the debtor may have property liable to be attached, which shall be levied as other certified copies of orders for attachment.

P.A. 82–280, § 4–118, eff. July 1, 1982. Amended by P.A. 83–707, § 1, eff. Sept. 23, 1983.

Formerly Ill.Rev.Stat.1991, ch. 110, ¶ 4–118.

5/4–119. Forthcoming bond

§ 4–119. Forthcoming bond. The officer serving the order for attachment shall take and retain the custody and possession of the property attached, to answer and abide by the judgment of the court, unless the person in whose possession the same is found shall enter into bond and security to the officer, to be approved by the officer, in double the value of the property so attached with condition that the estate and property shall be forthcoming to answer the judgment of the court in the action. The sheriff, or other officer shall return such bond to the court in which the action was brought, on the day to which such order for attachment is returnable.

P.A. 82–280, § 4–119, eff. July 1, 1982. Amended by P.A. 83–707, § 1, eff. Sept. 23, 1983.

Formerly Ill.Rev.Stat.1991, ch. 110, ¶ 4–119.

5/4–120. Bond or recognizance to pay judgment

§ 4–120. Bond or recognizance to pay judgment. Any defendant in attachment, desiring the return of property attached, may, at his or her option, instead of or in substitution for the bond required in the preceding section, give like bond and security, in a sum sufficient to cover the amount due sworn to in behalf of the plaintiff, with all interest, damages and costs of the action, conditioned that the defendant will pay the plaintiff the amount of the judgment and costs which may be entered against him or her in that action, on a final trial, within 90 days after such judgment shall be entered or a recognizance, in substance hereinabove stated, may be taken by the court, and filed of record, in which case the court shall approve of the security and the recognizance made to the plaintiff, and upon a forfeiture of such recognizance judgment may be entered and enforced as in other cases of recognizance. In either case, the attachment shall be dissolved, and the property taken restored, and all previous proceedings, either against the sheriff or against the garnishees, set aside, and the cause shall proceed as if the defendant had been seasonably served with a summons.

P.A. 82–280, § 4–120, eff. July 1, 1982. Amended by P.A. 83–707, § 1, eff. Sept. 23, 1983.

Formerly Ill.Rev.Stat.1991, ch. 110, ¶ 4–120.

5/4–121. Neglect of officer to take bond

§ 4–121. Neglect of officer to take bond. If the sheriff fails to return a bond taken by virtue of the provisions of Part 1 of Article IV of this Act, or has neglected to take one when he or she ought to have done so, in any attachment entered under any of the provisions of Part 1 of Article IV of this Act, the plaintiff in the attachment may cause a rule to be entered at any time during the first 10 days after the day on which the order is returnable requiring the sheriff to return the bond; or in case no bond has been taken, to show cause why such bond was not taken. If the sheriff does not return the bond within one day thereafter, or show legal and sufficient cause why the bond has not been taken, judgment shall be entered against the sheriff for the amount of the plaintiff's claim, with costs of the action. Enforcement may thereupon be had after judgment is entered against the defendant in the attachment action.

P.A. 82–280, § 4–121, eff. July 1, 1982. Amended by P.A. 83–707, § 1, eff. Sept. 23, 1983.

Formerly Ill.Rev.Stat.1991, ch. 110, ¶ 4–121.

5/4–122. Neglect to return sufficient bond

§ 4–122. Neglect to return sufficient bond. The plaintiff may, within 30 days after the return of such bond, except to the sufficiency thereof, reasonable notice of such exception having been given to the sheriff or other officer who took the same, and if, upon hearing, the court shall adjudge such security insufficient, such sheriff shall be subject to the same judgment and recovery and have the same liberty of defense as if the sheriff had been made defendant in the attachment, unless good and sufficient security shall be given within such time as may be directed by the court, and enforcement may be had thereupon as in other cases of judgment for the payment of money. Whenever the judgment of the plaintiff, or any part thereof shall be paid or satisfied by any such sheriff, he or she shall have the same remedy against the defendant for the amount so paid by him or her as is now provided by law for bail against their principal where a judgment is paid or satisfied by them.

P.A. 82–280, § 4–122, eff. July 1, 1982.

Formerly Ill.Rev.Stat.1991, ch. 110, ¶ 4–122.

5/4–123. Action on bond

§ 4–123. Action on bond. If the plaintiff does not object to the bond taken by the sheriff, or the objections are not sustained, and such bond is forfeited, the plaintiff in the attachment may bring an action thereon in his or her own name, the same as if such bond had been assigned to him or her, and judgment shall be entered for the plaintiff against the obligors in the bond for the value of the property, or if the property is greater than the amount due upon the judgment, then for the amount due and costs of the action.

P.A. 82–280, § 4–123, eff. July 1, 1982.

Formerly Ill.Rev.Stat.1991, ch. 110, ¶ 4–123.

5/4–124. Live stock

§ 4–124. Live stock. When any sheriff or other officer enforces an order for attachment by taking possession of horses, cattle or live stock, and the same are not immediately replevied or restored to the debtor, such officer shall provide sufficient sustenance for the support of such live stock until the live stock is sold or discharged from such attachment. The sheriff or other officer shall receive therefor a reasonable compensation, to be ascertained and determined by the court in which the attachment order was entered, and charged in the fee bill of such officer, and shall be collectible as part of the costs.

P.A. 82–280, § 4–124, eff. July 1, 1982. Amended by P.A. 83–707, § 1, eff. Sept. 23, 1983.

Formerly Ill.Rev.Stat.1991, ch. 110, ¶ 4–124.

5/4–125. Perishable property

§ 4–125. Perishable property. When any goods and chattels are levied on by virtue for any order of attachment, and the sheriff or other officer having custody of such goods and chattels is of the opinion that they are of a perishable nature and in danger of immediate waste or decay, such sheriff or other officer shall demand that the plaintiff in such attachment obtain from the court which entered the order for attachment an order permitting such property to be sold not later than 24 hours after the levy has been made, upon due notice of sale to the defendant and to the public as the court in its order shall require. The money derived from such sale shall be applied to satisfy the judgment entered in the attachment action, and deposited with the clerk of the court to which the certified copy of the order for attachment is returnable.

If the plaintiff in the attachment fails or refuses to obtain such an order for sale of perishable property, the sheriff or other officer making the levy shall be absolved of all responsibility to any person for loss occasioned by the failure to sell or care for such perishable property. The demand of the sheriff or other officer shall be in writing and shall be delivered to the plaintiff or his or her attorney or agent, and to the defendant if found. If defendant is not found, a copy of the demand shall be posted on the premises where the perishable items are located. Plaintiff's motion for an order of sale of perishable property shall be treated as an emergency motion.

P.A. 82–280, § 4–125, eff. July 1, 1982. Amended by P.A. 83–707, § 1, eff. Sept. 23, 1983.

Formerly Ill.Rev.Stat.1991, ch. 110, ¶ 4–125.

5/4–126. Summoning garnishees

§ 4–126. Summoning garnishees. The sheriff or any other person authorized to serve summons shall, in like manner as summons are served in ordinary civil cases, summon, wherever they may be found in the State, the persons mentioned in such order for attachment as garnishees and all other persons whom the creditor shall designate as having any property, effects, choses in action or credits in their possession or power, belonging to the defendant, or who are in anyway indebted to such defendant, the same as if their names had been inserted in such order for attachment. The persons so summoned shall be considered as garnishees. The return shall state the names of all persons so summoned, and the date of such service on each.

Persons summoned as garnishees shall thereafter hold any property, effects, choses in action or credits in their possession or power belonging to the defendant which are not exempt, subject to the court's order in such proceeding, and shall not pay to the defendant any indebtedness owed to him or her subject to such order, and such property, effects, choses in action, credits and debts shall be considered to have been attached and the plaintiff's claim to have become a lien thereon pending such action.

P.A. 82–280, § 4–126, eff. July 1, 1982. Amended by P.A. 83–707, § 1, eff. Sept. 23, 1983; P.A. 89–364, § 45, eff. Jan. 1, 1996.

Formerly Ill.Rev.Stat.1991, ch. 110, ¶ 4–126.

5/4–127. Notice by publication and mail

§ 4–127. Notice by publication and mail. When it shall appear by the affidavit filed or by the return of the officer, that a defendant in any attachment action is not a resident of this State, or the defendant has departed from this State, or on due inquiry cannot be found, or is concealed within this State, so that the order for attachment cannot be served upon him or her, and that property of the defendant has been attached, or that persons having such property or effects, choses in action or credits belonging to defendant, or owing debts to him or her, have been summoned as garnishees, it shall be the duty of the clerk of the court in which the action is pending to give notice, by publication at least once in each week for 3 weeks successively, in some newspaper published in this State, most convenient to the place where the court is held, of such attachment or garnishment, and at whose action, against whose estate, for what sum, and before what court the same is pending, and that unless the defendant shall appear, give bail, and plead within the time limited for his or her appearance in such case, judgment will be entered, and the estate so attached or garnisheed, sold or otherwise disposed of as provided by law. Such clerk shall, within 10 days after the first publication of such notice, send a copy thereof by mail, addressed to such defendant, if the place of residence is stated in such affidavit; and the certificate of the clerk that he or she has sent such notice in pursuance of this section, shall be evidence of that fact.

P.A. 82–280, § 4–127, eff. July 1, 1982. Amended by P.A. 83–707, § 1, eff. Sept. 23, 1983.

Formerly Ill.Rev.Stat.1991, ch. 110, ¶ 4–127.

5/4–128. Default

§ 4–128. Default. No default or proceeding shall be taken against any defendant not served with summons within the State and not appearing, unless the first publication or personal service outside of the State be at least 30 days prior to the day at which such default or proceeding is proposed to be taken.

P.A. 82–280, § 4–128, eff. July 1, 1982.

Formerly Ill.Rev.Stat.1991, ch. 110, ¶ 4–128.

5/4–129. Continuance for want of publication

§ 4–129. Continuance for want of publication. If for want of due publication or service the cause is continued, the same proceedings shall be had at a subsequent return day to be fixed by the court, as might have been had at the return day at which the certified copy of the order for attachment was returnable.

P.A. 82–280, § 4–129, eff. July 1, 1982. Amended by P.A. 83–707, § 1, eff. Sept. 23, 1983.

Formerly Ill.Rev.Stat.1991, ch. 110, ¶ 4–129.

5/4–130. Filing complaint

§ 4–130. Filing complaint. The complaint shall be filed 10 days before the return day of the certified copy of the order for attachment, and if so filed the defendant, subject to the provisions of Section 4–114 of this Act, shall file his or her answer or otherwise plead on or before that day. If the complaint is not so filed the defendant shall not be compelled to appear or answer until 15 days after the return day designated in the order for attachment and if the complaint is not filed within 5 days after the return day designated in the order for attachment the defendant may, in the discretion of the court have the action dismissed.

P.A. 82–280, § 4–130, eff. July 1, 1982. Amended by P.A. 83–707, § 1, eff. Sept. 23, 1983.

Formerly Ill.Rev.Stat.1991, ch. 110, ¶ 4–130.

5/4–131. Pleadings

§ 4–131. Pleadings. The defendant may answer, denying the facts stated in the affidavit upon which the order for attachment was entered which answer shall be verified by affidavit; and if, upon the trial thereon, the issue is found for the plaintiff, the defendant may answer the complaint or file a motion directed thereto as in other civil cases, but if found for the defendant, the order for attachment shall be set aside, and the costs of the attachment shall be adjudged against the plaintiff, but the action shall proceed to final judgment as in other civil cases.

P.A. 82–280, § 4–131, eff. July 1, 1982. Amended by P.A. 83–707, § 1, eff. Sept. 23, 1983.

Formerly Ill.Rev.Stat.1991, ch. 110, ¶ 4–131.

5/4–132. Amendments

§ 4–132. Amendments. Subject to the requirements of Section 4–137 of this Act, no order for attachment shall be vacated, nor the property taken thereon restored, nor any garnishee discharged, nor any bond by him or her given canceled, nor any rule entered against the sheriff discharged, on account of any insufficiency of the original affidavit, order for attachment or attachment bond, if the plaintiff, or some credible person for him, her or it shall cause a legal and sufficient affidavit or attachment bond to be filed, or the order to be amended, in such time and manner as the court shall direct; and in that event the cause shall proceed as if such proceedings had originally been sufficient.

P.A. 82–280, § 4–132, eff. July 1, 1982. Amended by P.A. 83–707, § 1, eff. Sept. 23, 1983.

Formerly Ill.Rev.Stat.1991, ch. 110, ¶ 4–132.

5/4–133. Seeking wrong remedy not fatal

§ 4–133. Seeking wrong remedy not fatal. Where relief is sought under Part 1 of Article IV of this Act and the court determines, on motion directed to the pleadings, or on motion for summary judgment or upon trial, that the plaintiff has pleaded or established facts which entitle the plaintiff to relief but that the plaintiff has sought the wrong remedy, the court shall permit the pleadings to be amended, on just and reasonable terms, and the court shall grant the relief to which plaintiff is entitled on the amended pleadings or upon the evidence. In considering whether a proposed amendment is just and reasonable, the court shall consider the right of the defendant to assert additional defenses, to demand a trial by jury, to plead a counterclaim or third party complaint, and to order the plaintiff to take additional steps which were not required under the pleadings as previously filed.

P.A. 82–280, § 4–133, eff. July 1, 1982.

Formerly Ill.Rev.Stat.1991, ch. 110, ¶ 4–133.

5/4–134. Intervention

§ 4–134. Intervention. In all cases of attachment, any person, other than the defendant, claiming the property attached, or garnisheed may intervene, verifying his or her petition by affidavit, without giving bond, but such property shall not thereby be replevied; and the court shall immediately (unless good cause be shown by either party for a continuance) direct a jury to be impaneled to inquire into the right of the property. In all cases where the jury finds for the claimant, and that such claimant is also entitled to the possession of all or any part of such property, the court shall enter judgment for such claimant accordingly and order the property attached or garnisheed to which such claimant is entitled to be delivered to such claimant, and the payment of his or her costs in such action. In cases where the jury finds for a claimant but further finds that such claimant is not then entitled to the possession of any such property, such claimant shall be entitled to his or her costs; and where the jury find for the plaintiff in the attachment, such plaintiff shall recover his or her costs against such claimant. If such claimant is a non-resident of the State he or she shall file security for costs as in cases of non-resident plaintiffs.

P.A. 82–280, § 4–134, eff. July 1, 1982.

Formerly Ill.Rev.Stat.1991, ch. 110, ¶ 4–134.

5/4–135. Counterclaim

§ 4–135. Counterclaim. Any defendant against whom an order for attachment is entered under Part 1 of Article IV of this Act, may avail himself or herself of any counterclaim as provided in Section 2–608 of this Act.

P.A. 82–280, § 4–135, eff. July 1, 1982. Amended by P.A. 83–707, § 1, eff. Sept. 23, 1983.

Formerly Ill.Rev.Stat.1991, ch. 110, ¶ 4–135.

5/4–136. Substitution of parties

§ 4–136. Substitution of parties. The provisions in regard to joinder, nonjoinder or misjoinder of parties applicable to other civil cases, shall be applicable to attachment proceedings; and when any action has been commenced in the name of the wrong party as plaintiff, the court, if satisfied that it has been so commenced through mistake, and that it is necessary for the determination of the real matter in dispute so to do, may allow any other party or parties to be substituted.

No change of parties made, or any other amendment made by order of court, shall impair any previous attachment of the estate of any defendant remaining in the action, nor impair any recognizance or bond given by any party remaining either as against the defendant, defendants, his, hers, its, or their sureties. No sureties shall be released by reason of any amendment made by order of court.

P.A. 82–280, § 4–136, eff. July 1, 1982. Amended by P.A. 83–707, § 1, eff. Sept. 23, 1983.

Formerly Ill.Rev.Stat.1991, ch. 110, ¶ 4–136.

5/4–137. Prompt hearing

§ 4–137. Prompt hearing. At any time after the entry of an order for attachment, upon motion of the defendant, the court shall set a hearing on the order or affidavit. The hearing shall be held as soon as possible after the motion by the defendant, but shall not be more than 5 days after service of notice on the plaintiff.

At the hearing, either party may introduce affidavits or oral testimony. The order for attachment shall be vacated unless the plaintiff shows by a preponderance of evidence that a cause for the entry of the order exists, and unless the plaintiff demonstrates to the court the probability that he, she or it will ultimately prevail in the action.

P.A. 82–280, § 4–137, eff. July 1, 1982. Amended by P.A. 83–707, § 1, eff. Sept. 23, 1983.

Formerly Ill.Rev.Stat.1991, ch. 110, ¶ 4–137.

5/4–138. Proceedings in aid

§ 4–138. Proceedings in aid. Upon the return of certified copies of orders for attachment issued in aid of actions pending, unless it shall appear that the defendant or defendants have been served with process in the original action, notice of the pendency of the action, and of the issue and levy of the order for attachment, shall be given as is required in cases of original attachment; and such notification shall be sufficient to entitle the plaintiff to judgment, and the right to proceed thereon against the property and estate attached, and against garnishees, in the same manner and with like effect as if the action had been commenced as an original action for attachment.

P.A. 82–280, § 4–138, eff. July 1, 1982. Amended by P.A. 83–707, § 1, eff. Sept. 23, 1983.

Formerly Ill.Rev.Stat.1991, ch. 110, ¶ 4–138.

5/4–139. Effect of judgment

§ 4–139. Effect of judgment. When the defendant has been served with the order for attachment, or appears in the action, the judgment shall have the same force and effect as in other civil cases; and enforcement may be had thereon, not only against the property attached, but the other property of the defendant.

P.A. 82–280, § 4–139, eff. July 1, 1982. Amended by P.A. 83–707, § 1, eff. Sept. 23, 1983.

Formerly Ill.Rev.Stat.1991, ch. 110, ¶ 4–139.

5/4–140. Judgment by default

§ 4–140. Judgment by default. When the defendant is notified as hereinabove stated, but not served with an order for attachment within the State, and does not appear and answer the action, judgment by default may be entered, which may be proceeded upon to final judgment as in other cases of default, but in no case shall judgment be entered against the defendant for a greater sum than appears, by the affidavit of the plaintiff, to have been due at the time of obtaining the order for attachment, with interest, damages and costs; and such judgment shall bind, and enforcement had against the property, credits and effects attached, and such judgment shall not be enforced from any other property of the defendant; nor shall such judgment be any evidence of debt against the defendant in any subsequent cases.

P.A. 82–280, § 4–140, eff. July 1, 1982. Amended by P.A. 83–707, § 1, eff. Sept. 23, 1983.

Formerly Ill.Rev.Stat.1991, ch. 110, ¶ 4–140.

5/4–141. Property levied upon

§ 4–141. Property levied upon. The property attached may be levied upon by judgment entered in the attachment action, whether in the possession of the officer or secured by bond as provided in Part 1 of Article IV of this Act, and shall be sold as other property levied upon for the enforcement of a judgment for the payment of money.

P.A. 82–280, § 4–141, eff. July 1, 1982. Amended by P.A. 82–783, Art. IV, § 27, eff. July 13, 1982.

Formerly Ill.Rev.Stat.1991, ch. 110, ¶ 4–141.

5/4–142. Division of proceeds

§ 4–142. Division of proceeds. All judgments for the payment of money in actions for attachment against the same defendant, returnable on the same day, and all judgments in other civil cases or orders for attachment against such defendant, recovered within 30 days from the day when the judgment in the first attachment upon which judgment is recovered is entered, shall share pro rata, according to the amount of the several judgments, in the proceeds of the property attached, either in the possession of a garnishee or otherwise. If the property is attached while the defendant is removing the same or after the same has been removed from the county, and the same is overtaken and returned, or while the same is secreted by the defendant, or placed out of his or her possession for the purpose of defrauding his or her creditors, the court may allow the creditor or creditors through whose diligence the same has been secured a priority over other attachment or judgment creditors.

P.A. 82–280, § 4–142, eff. July 1, 1982. Amended by P.A. 83–707, § 1, eff. Sept. 23, 1983.

Formerly Ill.Rev.Stat.1991, ch. 110, ¶ 4–142.

5/4–143. Officer to divide proceeds

§ 4–143. Officer to divide proceeds. Upon issuing a certified copy of a judgment for the enforcement thereof against any property attached, the proceeds of which shall be required to be divided, the clerk shall, at the same time, prepare and deliver to the sheriff or other officer to whom the certified copy of the judgment is delivered, a statement of all judgments, with the costs thereon, which shall be entitled to share in such proceeds, and when any judgment creditor shall have been allowed a priority over the other judgment creditors, the same shall be stated. Upon the receipt of such proceeds by the sheriff or other officer, he or she shall divide and pay over the same to the several judgment creditors entitled to share in the same in the proportion they shall be entitled thereto.

P.A. 82–280, § 4–143, eff. July 1, 1982.

Formerly Ill.Rev.Stat.1991, ch. 110, ¶ 4–143.

5/4–144. Payment into court

§ 4–144. Payment into court. The court may, at any time before the proceeds of any attached property have been paid over to the judgment creditors, order the whole or any part thereof to be deposited with the clerk of the court, and the court may enter any and all orders concerning the same as it deems just.

P.A. 82–280, § 4–144, eff. July 1, 1982.

Formerly Ill.Rev.Stat.1991, ch. 110, ¶ 4–144.

5/4–145. Sale of live stock

§ 4–145. Sale of live stock. When any live stock is levied upon in any attachment proceeding, the plaintiff may apply to the court in which the action is pending for an order of sale thereof, and if it shall appear that the stock is fit for market, or that if not sold will depreciate in value, then the court shall order a sale of the property on such terms as shall seem proper, and the proceeds shall be deposited with the clerk of the court in which the action is pending until determined by the court, and then be paid to the successful party in the action.

P.A. 82–280, § 4–145, eff. July 1, 1982.

Formerly Ill.Rev.Stat.1991, ch. 110, ¶ 4–145.

PART 2. WATERCRAFT

5/4–201. Liens in general

§ 4–201. Liens in general. Every sail vessel, steamboat, steam dredge, tug boat, scow, canal boat, barge, lighter, and other water craft of above five tons burthen, used or intended to be used in navigating the waters or canals of this State, or used in trade and commerce between ports and places within this State, or having their home port in this State, shall be subject to a lien thereon, which lien shall extend to the tackle, apparel and furniture of such craft, as follows:

1. For all debts contracted by the owner or part owner, master, clerk, steward, agent or ship's husband of such craft, on account of supplies and provisions furnished for the use of such water craft, on account of work done or services rendered on board of such craft by any seaman, master or other employee thereof, or on account of work done or materials furnished by mechanics, tradesmen or others, in or about the building, repairing, fitting, furnishing or equipping such craft.

2. For all sums due for wharfage, anchorage or dock hire, including the use of dry docks.

3. For sums due for towage, labor at pumping out or raising, when sunk or disabled, and to shipshusband or agent of such water craft, for disbursement due by the owner on account of such water craft.

4. For all damages arising for the nonperformance of any contract of affreightment, or of any contract touching the transportation of property entered into by the master, owner, agent or consignee of such water craft, where any such contract is made in this state.

5. For all damages arising from injuries done to persons or property by such water craft, whether the same are aboard said vessel or not, where the same shall have occurred through the negligence or misconduct of the owner, agent, master or employee thereon; but the craft shall not be liable for any injury or damage received by one of the crew from another member of the crew.

P.A. 82–280, § 4–201, eff. July 1, 1982. Amended by P.A. 95–331, § 1085, eff. Aug. 21, 2007.

Formerly Ill.Rev.Stat.1991, ch. 110, ¶ 4–201.

5/4–202. Lien on goods for freight

§ 4–202. Lien on goods for freight. There shall also be a lien upon the goods, wares and merchandise shipped, taken in and put aboard any such water craft for sums due for freight, advanced charges and demurrage, which shall be collected against the goods, wares and merchandise in the same manner as hereinafter provided in Part 2 of Article IV of this Act, in cases of sums due against such water craft.

P.A. 82–280, § 4–202, eff. July 1, 1982. Amended by P.A. 83–707, § 1, eff. Sept. 23, 1983.

Formerly Ill.Rev.Stat.1991, ch. 110, ¶ 4–202.

5/4–203. Limitation

§ 4–203. Limitation. Any such lien may be enforced in the manner herein provided at any time within 5 years. However, no creditor shall be allowed to enforce such lien as against, or to the prejudice of any other creditor or subsequent incumbrancer, or bona fide purchaser, unless proceedings are instituted to enforce such lien within 9 months after the indebtedness accrues or becomes due.

P.A. 82–280, § 4–203, eff. July 1, 1982.

Formerly Ill.Rev.Stat.1991, ch. 110, ¶ 4–203.

5/4–204. Complaint

§ 4–204. Complaint. The person claiming to have a lien under the provisions of Part 2 of Article IV of this Act may file in the circuit court, in the county where any such water craft may be found, a complaint, setting forth the nature of his or her claim, the amount due after allowing all payments and just offsets, the name of the water craft, and the name and residence of each owner known to the plaintiff; and when any owner or his or her place of residence is not known to the plaintiff, he or she shall so state, and that he or she has made inquiry and is unable to ascertain the same, which complaint shall be verified by the affidavit of the plaintiff or his or her agent or attorney. If the claim is upon an account or instrument in writing, a copy of the same shall be attached to the complaint.

P.A. 82–280, § 4–204, eff. July 1, 1982.

Formerly Ill.Rev.Stat.1991, ch. 110, ¶ 4–204.

5/4–205. Bond

§ 4–205. Bond. The plaintiff, or his or her agent or attorney, shall also file with such complaint a bond, payable to the owner of the craft to be attached, or, if unknown, to the unknown owners thereof, in at least double the amount of the claim, with security to be approved by the court, conditioned that the plaintiff shall prosecute his or her action with effect, or, in case of failure therein, will pay all costs and damages which the owner or other person interested in such water craft may sustain, in consequence of the wrongful suing out of such attachment, which bond may be sued by any owner or person interested, in the same manner as if it had been given to such person by his or her proper name. Only such persons shall be required to join in such suit as have a joint interest. Others may allege breaches and have assessment of damages, as in other actions on penal bonds.

P.A. 82–280, § 4–205, eff. July 1, 1982. Amended by P.A. 84–631, § 1, eff. Jan. 1, 1986.

Formerly Ill.Rev.Stat.1991, ch. 110, ¶ 4–205.

5/4–206. Designation of defendants

§ 4–206. Designation of defendants. Upon the filing of such complaint and bond, the court shall enter an order for attachment against the owners of such water craft, directed to the sheriff of the county, or other officer if the sheriff is disqualified or unavailable to attach such water craft. Such owners may be designated by their reputed names, by surnames, and joint defendants by their separate or partnership names, or by such names, styles or titles as they are usually known. If the name of any owner is unknown, he or she may be designated as unknown owner.

P.A. 82–280, § 4–206, eff. July 1, 1982. Amended by P.A. 84–631, § 1, eff. Jan. 1, 1986.

Formerly Ill.Rev.Stat.1991, ch. 110, ¶ 4–206.

5/4–207. Order

§ 4–207. Order. The order shall command the sheriff or other officer to attach the vessel, its tackle, apparel and furniture, to satisfy such claim and costs, and all such claims as shall be exhibited against such vessel according to law, and having attached the same, to summon the owners of such vessel, to be and appear before the court on a specified date to answer what may be claimed against them and the vessel.

P.A. 82–280, § 4–207, eff. July 1, 1982.

Formerly Ill.Rev.Stat.1991, ch. 110, ¶ 4–207.

5/4–208. Serving of order

§ 4–208. Serving of order. The sheriff or other officer to whom such order for attachment is directed shall forthwith serve a certified copy of the order upon such defendant as summons is served in other civil cases, and attaching the vessel, her tackle, apparel and furniture, and shall keep the same until disposed of as hereinafter provided. The sheriff or other officer shall also, on or before the return day in such order, or at any time after the service thereof, make a return to the court, stating therein particularly his or her doings in the premises, and shall make, subscribe and annex thereto a just and true inventory of all the property so attached.

P.A. 82–280, § 4–208, eff. July 1, 1982. Amended by P.A. 83–707, § 1, eff. Sept. 23, 1983.

Formerly Ill.Rev.Stat.1991, ch. 110, ¶ 4–208.

5/4–209. Only one attachment

§ 4–209. Only one attachment. Whenever such order for attachment is entered and served, no other order for attachment shall be entered against the same water craft, unless the first attachment is discharged, or the vessel is bonded.

P.A. 82–280, § 4–209, eff. July 1, 1982. Amended by P.A. 83–707, § 1, eff. Sept. 23, 1983.

Formerly Ill.Rev.Stat.1991, ch. 110, ¶ 4–209.

5/4–210. Notice by publication and mail

§ 4–210. Notice by publication and mail. Upon return being made to such order, unless the vessel has been bonded, as hereinafter provided, the clerk shall immediately cause notice to be given in the same manner as required in other cases of attachment. The notice shall contain, in addition to that required in other cases of attachment, a notice to all persons to intervene for their interests on a day certain, or that the claim will be heard ex parte.

P.A. 82–280, § 4–210, eff. July 1, 1982. Amended by P.A. 83–707, § 1, eff. Sept. 23, 1983.

Formerly Ill.Rev.Stat.1991, ch. 110, ¶ 4–210.

5/4–211. Seeking wrong remedy not fatal

§ 4–211. Seeking wrong remedy not fatal. Where relief is sought under Part 2 of Article IV of this Act and the court determines, on motion directed to the pleadings, or on motion for summary judgment or upon trial, that the plaintiff has pleaded or established facts which entitle the plaintiff to relief but that the plaintiff has sought the wrong remedy, the court shall permit the pleadings to be amended, on just and reasonable terms, and the court shall grant the relief to which the plaintiff is entitled on the amended pleadings or upon the evidence. In considering whether a proposed amendment is just and reasonable, the court shall consider the right of the defendant to assert additional defenses, to demand a trial by jury, to plead a counterclaim or third party complaint, and to order the plaintiff to take additional steps which were not required under the pleadings as previously filed.

P.A. 82–280, § 4–211, eff. July 1, 1982.

Formerly Ill.Rev.Stat.1991, ch. 110, ¶ 4–211.

5/4–212. Intervention

§ 4–212. Intervention. Any person having a lien upon or any interest in the water craft attached, may intervene to protect such interest, by filing a petition, entitled an intervening petition; and any person interested may be made a defendant at his or her request, or that of any party to the action, and may defend any petition by filing an answer as hereinafter provided, and giving security, satisfactory to the court, to pay any costs arising from such defense; and upon the filing of any intervening petition, a summons, as hereinbefore provided, shall issue; and if the same shall be returned not served, notice by publication may be given as hereinabove stated and several intervening petitioners may be united with each other, or the original, in one notice.

P.A. 82–280, § 4–212, eff. July 1, 1982.

Formerly Ill.Rev.Stat.1991, ch. 110, ¶ 4–212.

5/4–213. Bond by intervenor

§ 4–213. Bond by intervenor. Any person intervening to enforce any lien or claims adverse to the owners of the craft attached shall, at the time of filing the petition, file with the clerk a bond as in the case of original attachment.

P.A. 82–280, § 4–213, eff. July 1, 1982.

Formerly Ill.Rev.Stat.1991, ch. 110, ¶ 4–213.

5/4–214. Intervening petition

§ 4–214. Intervening petition. Intervening petitions may be filed at any time before the vessel is bonded, as provided in Section 4–216 of this Act, or, if the same is not so bonded, before order for distribution of the proceeds of the sale of the craft, and the same proceeding shall thereupon be had as in the case of claims filed before sale.

P.A. 82–280, § 4–214, eff. July 1, 1982.

Formerly Ill.Rev.Stat.1991, ch. 110, ¶ 4–214.

5/4–215. Liens not filed cease

§ 4–215. Liens not filed cease. All liens upon any water craft which are not filed hereunder before sale under judgment, as hereinafter provided, shall cease.

P.A. 82–280, § 4–215, eff. July 1, 1982.

Formerly Ill.Rev.Stat.1991, ch. 110, ¶ 4–215.

5/4–216. Bonding vessel

§ 4–216. Bonding vessel. The owner, his or her agent or attorney, or any other person interested in such water craft, desiring the return of the property attached, having first given notice to the plaintiff, his or her agent or attorney, of his or her intention to bond the same, may, at any time before judgment, file with the court in which the action is pending, a bond to the parties, having previously filed a complaint or intervening petition against such craft, in a penalty at least double the aggregate of all sums alleged to be due the several plaintiffs or intervening petitioners, with security to be approved by the court, conditioned that the obligors will pay all moneys adjudged to be due such claimants, with costs of the action.

P.A. 82–280, § 4–216, eff. July 1, 1982.

Formerly Ill.Rev.Stat.1991, ch. 110, ¶ 4–216.

5/4–217. Appraisement—Restitution—Sale

§ 4–217. Appraisement—Restitution—Sale. If the owner, his or her agent or attorney, or other party in interest, so elect, in place of bonding, as heretofore provided, such person may apply to the court upon like notice, for an order of appraisement of such water-craft so seized, by three competent persons to be appointed by the court and named in the order, and upon such party depositing with the clerk the amount of such appraisement in money, or executing or filing with the clerk a bond for such amount, executed as provided in the preceding section, the court shall enter an order of restitution, as provided in the next section, and if the claimant of such water-craft shall decline any such application, or neglect within 20 days to accept such appraisement and make the deposit, or give bond as hereinabove stated, or the property seized shall be liable to decay, depreciation or injury from delay, the court, in its discretion, may order the same or part thereof to be sold, and the proceeds thereof to be brought into court to abide the results of the action.

P.A. 82–280, § 4–217, eff. July 1, 1982. Amended by P.A. 84–631, § 1, eff. Jan. 1, 1986.

Formerly Ill.Rev.Stat.1991, ch. 110, ¶ 4–217.

5/4–218. Order of restitution

§ 4–218. Order of restitution. Upon receiving a bond or deposit, as provided in either of the foregoing sections, the court shall enter an order of restitution, directing the officer who attached the water-craft to deliver the same to the person from whose possession it was taken, and the water-craft shall be discharged from all the liens secured by such bond or deposit, unless the court, upon motion, orders it again into custody on account of the insufficiency or insolvency of the surety.

P.A. 82–280, § 4–218, eff. July 1, 1982. Amended by P.A. 84–631, § 1, eff. Jan. 1, 1986.

Formerly Ill.Rev.Stat.1991, ch. 110, ¶ 4–218.

5/4–219. Additional security

§ 4–219. Additional security. If any plaintiff or intervening petitioner, at any time, deems his or her security insufficient, or has become imperiled, he or she may, by motion supported by affidavit filed, and upon notice served with copy of such affidavit and motion, move the court to direct the giving of additional security, which motion shall be promptly heard and determined, and such order made therein as justice shall require; and the court may enforce all orders so made by attachment for contempt against persons, or by orders against such water-craft, or otherwise.

P.A. 82–280, § 4–219, eff. July 1, 1982. Amended by P.A. 83–707, § 1, eff. Sept. 23, 1983.

Formerly Ill.Rev.Stat.1991, ch. 110, ¶ 4–219.

5/4–220. Answer—Default

§ 4–220. Answer—Default. Within 3 days after the return day of summons—if personally served 10 days before the day on which it is returnable, or within 13 days after such return day, if personally served less than 10 days prior thereto, or if not personally served, then within the time prescribed in the published notice—the owner or any person interested adversely to the claims mentioned in the notice, unless on cause shown, further time shall be allowed by the court, shall plead to the complaint as in other civil cases. If an answer is filed, the answer shall respond completely and distinctly to each allegation of the complaint, and shall be supported by affidavit. If no such answer or motion, together with an affidavit is filed within the time above specified, the plaintiff is entitled to an order of default, and the claim may be proved and judgment entered as in other civil cases.

P.A. 82–280, § 4–220, eff. July 1, 1982.

Formerly Ill.Rev.Stat.1991, ch. 110, ¶ 4–220.

5/4–221. Judgment when vessel discharged

§ 4–221. Judgment when vessel discharged. If, after trial, judgment is entered in favor of the plaintiff, and the water craft has been discharged from custody as herein provided, the judgment shall be entered against the principal and sureties in the bond. In no case shall the judgment exceed the penalty of the bond, and the subsequent proceedings shall be the same as now provided by law in actions in personam. If the release has been upon deposit, the judgment shall be paid out of the deposit.

P.A. 82–280, § 4–221, eff. July 1, 1982. Amended by P.A. 83–707, § 1, eff. Sept. 23, 1983.

Formerly Ill.Rev.Stat.1991, ch. 110, ¶ 4–221.

5/4–222. Judgment when vessel in custody

§ 4–222. Judgment when vessel in custody. In case the water craft has not been discharged from custody, the judgment shall be that the same, with the appurtenances, be sold at public sale by the sheriff, after notice of the time and place of the sale, published as herein required in cases of seizure, at least 10 days before such sale. In case of petition filed prior to distribution, the judgment shall be for payment out of the proceeds of sale, and in case of claims filed against surplus proceeds, the judgment, if in favor of the petitioner, shall, in substance, affirm the claim to be sustained, and direct payment thereof from the surplus proceeds.

P.A. 82–280, § 4–222, eff. July 1, 1982. Amended by P.A. 83–707, § 1, eff. Sept. 23, 1983.

Formerly Ill.Rev.Stat.1991, ch. 110, ¶ 4–222.

5/4–223. Order of sale

§ 4–223. Order of sale. The court shall thereupon enter an order of sale, commanding the sheriff to sell such water craft as directed in the judgment, and to return the certified copy of the order of sale within 24 hours after the sale, with his or her doings in the premises, and with proof by affidavit of the requisite notice, with a copy of such notice.

P.A. 82–280, § 4–223, eff. July 1, 1982.

Formerly Ill.Rev.Stat.1991, ch. 110, ¶ 4–223.

5/4–224. Proceedings on sale

§ 4–224. Proceedings on sale. It shall be the duty of the sheriff, upon receiving the amount of the bid at any sale, either before or after judgment, from the purchaser, or in case the purchaser is the plaintiff or an intervenor, upon receiving so much of the bid as the court directs by order, reference being had to the relative amount of the buyer's claim, to deliver such water craft and appurtenances to the purchaser, with

a bill of sale thereof, and to return and to deliver to the clerk of court the amount received on such sale.
P.A. 82–280, § 4–224, eff. July 1, 1982.

Formerly Ill.Rev.Stat.1991, ch. 110, ¶ 4–224.

5/4–225. Bill of sale

§ 4–225. Bill of sale. A copy of the last enrollment, if any, of such water craft shall be recited in the bill of sale if such copy can be obtained, and a copy of the judgment, with the order of sale, or if such craft is sold pursuant to an order before judgment, a copy of such order shall also be recited in such bill of sale, certified by the clerk, under the seal of the court; and such bill of sale shall be full and complete evidence of the regularity of the judgment or order and sale, in all courts and places, and shall supersede the necessity of any other proof thereof to validate the bill of sale; and all bills of sale containing such recital, and supported by such proof, are effectual to pass the title of such water craft.
P.A. 82–280, § 4–225, eff. July 1, 1982.

Formerly Ill.Rev.Stat.1991, ch. 110, ¶ 4–225.

5/4–226. Distribution

§ 4–226. Distribution. The sum delivered by the sheriff to the clerk of court as above set out, shall be distributed by the court upon motion of any party in interest of record, and due notice to the other parties, and after the following manner:

First—The costs accruing upon all complaints filed before distribution, and on which judgment is or may be thereafter entered in favor of plaintiff.

Second—Seamen's (which term shall include the master) wages due upon the last two voyages, or if shipped by the month the last two months.

Third—All other claims filed prior to order of distribution on which judgment may be entered in favor of plaintiff, together with whatever balance may be due seamen.
P.A. 82–280, § 4–226, eff. July 1, 1982. Amended by P.A. 83–707, § 1, eff. Sept. 23, 1983.

Formerly Ill.Rev.Stat.1991, ch. 110, ¶ 4–226.

5/4–227. Remnants

§ 4–227. Remnants. Any portion of the sum so paid by the sheriff to the clerk, or of a deposit remaining after such distribution as hereinabove provided, shall be denominated remnants and surplus proceeds, and where any claim or complaint is filed against the same as provided in Part 2 of Article IV of this Act, distribution shall be directed by the court after judgment upon motion and notice, as provided in Section 4–226 of this Act, and after the following order:

First—All costs upon claims passing into judgment which were filed after distribution.

Second—All other liens enforceable under Part 2 of Article IV of this Act against the water craft prior to distribution.

Third—All claims upon mortgages of such water craft or other incumbrances by the owner, in proportion to the interest they cover and priority.

Fourth—Upon petition of the creditor, all judgments against the owner, and which ought equitably to be paid out of the proceeds in preference to the owner.

Fifth—The owner.
P.A. 82–280, § 4–227, eff. July 1, 1982. Amended by P.A. 91–357, § 250, eff. July 29, 1999.

Formerly Ill.Rev.Stat.1991, ch. 110, ¶ 4–227.

5/4–228. Power of court in distribution

§ 4–228. Power of court in distribution. In case the sum for which the water craft is sold is sufficient to pay all the claims filed before distribution, with costs thereon, and an appeal is taken as provided by law, the court may order distribution of such portion of the sum brought on sale upon judgments unappealed from as may seem just and proper.
P.A. 82–280, § 4–228, eff. July 1, 1982.

Formerly Ill.Rev.Stat.1991, ch. 110, ¶ 4–228.

ARTICLE V. COSTS

5/5–101. Security for costs

§ 5–101. Security for costs. In all actions in any court on official bonds for the use of any person, actions on the bonds of executors, administrators or guardians, qui tam actions, actions on a penal statute, and in all civil actions, where the plaintiff, or person for whose use an action is to be commenced, is not a resident of this State, the plaintiff, or person for whose use the action is to be commenced, shall, before he or she institutes such action, file, or cause to be filed, with the clerk of the court in which the action is to be commenced, security for costs, substantially in the following form:

A B v. C D—(Title of court.)

I, (E.F.) enter myself security for all costs which may accrue in the above entitled action.

Dated this . . . . day of . . . . , ...

(Signed) E.F.

P.A. 82–280, § 5–101, eff. July 1, 1982. Amended by P.A. 83–707, § 1, eff. Sept. 23, 1983.

Formerly Ill.Rev.Stat.1991, ch. 110, ¶ 5–101.

5/5–102. Approval—Effect of bond

§ 5–102. Approval—Effect of bond. Such instrument shall be signed by some responsible person, being a resident of this State, and be approved by the clerk, and shall bind such person to pay all costs which may accrue in such action, either to the opposing party or to any of the officers of the court in which the action is commenced, or to which it is removed by change of place of trial or appeal.

P.A. 82–280, § 5–102, eff. July 1, 1982. Amended by P.A. 83–707, § 1, eff. Sept. 23, 1983.

Formerly Ill.Rev.Stat.1991, ch. 110, ¶ 5–102.

5/5–103. Dismissal for want of security

§ 5–103. Dismissal for want of security. If any such action is commenced without filing such written instrument, the court, on motion, shall dismiss the same, and the attorney of the plaintiff shall pay all costs accruing thereon, unless the security for costs is filed within such time as is allowed by the court, and when so filed it shall relate back to the commencement of the action; the right to require security for costs shall not be waived by any proceeding in the action.

P.A. 82–280, § 5–103, eff. July 1, 1982. Amended by P.A. 83–707, § 1, eff. Sept. 23, 1983.

Formerly Ill.Rev.Stat.1991, ch. 110, ¶ 5–103.

5/5–104. Events after filing action

§ 5–104. Events after filing action. If at any time after the commencement of any action by a resident of this state, he or she becomes non-resident; or if in any case the court is satisfied that any plaintiff is unable to pay the costs of the action, or that he or she is so unsettled as to endanger the officers of the court with respect to their legal claims, it shall be the duty of the court, on motion of the defendant or any officer of the court, to order the plaintiff, on or before a day in such order stated, to give security for the payment of costs in such action. If such plaintiff neglects or refuses, on or before the day in such order stated, to file a written instrument of some responsible person, being a resident of this state, whereby he or she shall bind himself or herself to pay all costs which have accrued, or may accrue in such action, the court shall, on motion, dismiss the action. The defendant or officer making such motion shall file therewith his or her affidavit, or the affidavit of some credible person, stating that he or she has reason to believe, and does believe, that in case such action is prosecuted to a conclusion, a judgment will be entered against such plaintiff for such costs.

P.A. 82–280, § 5–104, eff. July 1, 1982. Amended by P.A. 83–707, § 1, eff. Sept. 23, 1983.

Formerly Ill.Rev.Stat.1991, ch. 110, ¶ 5–104.

5/5–105. Leave to sue or defend as an indigent person

§ 5–105. Leave to sue or defend as an indigent person.

(a) As used in this Section:

(1) "Fees, costs, and charges" means payments imposed on a party in connection with the prosecution or defense of a civil action, including, but not limited to: filing fees; appearance fees; fees for service of process and other papers served either within or outside this State, including service by publication pursuant to Section 2–206 of this Code and publication of necessary legal notices; motion fees; jury demand fees; charges for participation in, or attendance at, any mandatory process or procedure including, but not limited to, conciliation, mediation, arbitration, counseling, evaluation, "Children First", "Focus on Children" or similar programs; fees for supplementary proceedings; charges for translation services; guardian ad litem fees; charges for certified copies of court documents; and all other processes and procedures deemed by the court to be necessary to commence, prosecute, defend, or enforce relief in a civil action.

(2) "Indigent person" means any person who meets one or more of the following criteria:

(i) He or she is receiving assistance under one or more of the following public benefits programs: Supplemental Security Income (SSI), Aid to the Aged, Blind and Disabled (AABD), Temporary Assistance for Needy Families (TANF), Food Stamps, General Assistance, Transitional Assistance, or State Children and Family Assistance.

(ii) His or her available income is 125% or less of the current poverty level as established by the United States Department of Health and Human Services, unless the applicant's assets that are not exempt under Part 9 or 10 of Article XII of this Code are of a nature and value that the court determines that the applicant is able to pay the fees, costs, and charges.

(iii) He or she is, in the discretion of the court, unable to proceed in an action without payment of fees, costs, and charges and whose payment of those fees, costs, and charges would result in substantial hardship to the person or his or her family.

(iv) He or she is an indigent person pursuant to Section 5–105.5 of this Code.

(b) On the application of any person, before, or after the commencement of an action, a court, on finding that the applicant is an indigent person, shall grant the applicant leave to sue or defend the action without payment of the fees, costs, and charges of the action.

(c) An application for leave to sue or defend an action as an indigent person shall be in writing and supported by the affidavit of the applicant or, if the applicant is a minor or an incompetent adult, by the affidavit of another person having knowledge of the facts. The contents of the affidavit shall be established by Supreme Court Rule. The court shall provide, through the office of the clerk of the court, simplified forms consistent with the requirements of this Section and applicable Supreme Court Rules to any person seeking to sue or defend an action who indicates an inability to pay the fees, costs, and charges of the action. The application and supporting affidavit may be incorporated into one simplified form. The clerk of the court shall post in a conspicuous place in the courthouse a notice no smaller than 8.5 x 11 inches, using no smaller than 30–point typeface printed in English and in Spanish, advising the public that they may ask the court for permission to sue or defend a civil action without payment of fees, costs, and charges. The notice shall be substantially as follows:

"If you are unable to pay the fees, costs, and charges of an action you may ask the court to allow you to proceed without paying them. Ask the clerk of the court for forms."

(d) The court shall rule on applications under this Section in a timely manner based on information contained in the application unless the court, in its discretion, requires the applicant to personally appear to explain or clarify information contained in the application. If the court finds that the applicant is an indigent person, the court shall enter an order permitting the applicant to sue or defend without payment of fees, costs, or charges. If the application is denied, the court shall enter an order to that effect stating the specific reasons for the denial. The clerk of the court shall promptly mail or deliver a copy of the order to the applicant.

(e) The clerk of the court shall not refuse to accept and file any complaint, appearance, or other paper presented by the applicant if accompanied by an application to sue or defend in forma pauperis, and those papers shall be considered filed on the date the application is presented. If the application is denied, the order shall state a date certain by which the necessary fees, costs, and charges must be paid. The court, for good cause shown, may allow an applicant whose application is denied to defer payment of fees, costs, and charges, make installment payments, or make payment upon reasonable terms and conditions stated in the order. The court may dismiss the claims or defenses of any party failing to pay the fees, costs, or charges within the time and in the manner ordered by the court. A determination concerning an application to sue or defend in forma pauperis shall not be construed as a ruling on the merits.

(f) The court may order an indigent person to pay all or a portion of the fees, costs, or charges waived pursuant to this Section out of moneys recovered by the indigent person pursuant to a judgment or settlement resulting from the civil action. However, nothing in this Section shall be construed to limit the authority of a court to order another party to the action to pay the fees, costs, or charges of the action.

(g) A court, in its discretion, may appoint counsel to represent an indigent person, and that counsel shall perform his or her duties without fees, charges, or reward.

(h) Nothing in this Section shall be construed to affect the right of a party to sue or defend an action in forma pauperis without the payment of fees, costs, or charges, or the right of a party to court-appointed counsel, as authorized by any other provision of law or by the rules of the Illinois Supreme Court.

(i) The provisions of this Section are severable under Section 1.31 of the Statute on Statutes. [1]

P.A. 82–280, § 5–105, eff. July 1, 1982. Amended by P.A. 83–707, § 1, eff. Sept. 23, 1983; P.A. 91–621, § 5, eff. Aug. 19, 1999; P.A. 97–689, § 104, eff. June 14, 2012; P.A. 97–813, § 670, eff. July 13, 2012.

Formerly Ill.Rev.Stat.1991, ch. 110, ¶ 5–105.

[1] 5 ILCS 70/1.31

P.A. 97–689, § 104, in clause (a)(2)(i), deleted "State" preceding "Transitional Assistance"; and in subsec. (f), in the second sentence, substituted "nothing in this" for "nothing is this".

P.A. 97–813, the First 2012 General Revisory Act, amended various Acts to delete obsolete text, to correct patent and technical errors, to revise cross references, to resolve multiple actions in the 96th and 97th General Assemblies and to make certain technical corrections in P.A. 96–1480 through P.A. 97–625.

See 5 ILCS 70/6 as to effect of (1) more than one amendment of a section at the same session of the General Assembly or (2) two or more acts relating to the same subject matter enacted by the same General Assembly.

5/5–105.5. Representation by civil legal services provider

§ 5–105.5. Representation by civil legal services provider.

(a) As used in this Section:

"Civil legal services" means legal services in non-criminal matters provided without charge to indigent persons who have been found eligible under financial eligibility guidelines established by the civil legal services provider.

"Civil legal services provider" means a not-for-profit corporation that (i) employs one or more attorneys who are licensed to practice law in the State of Illinois and who directly provide free civil legal services or (ii) is established for the purpose of providing free civil legal services by an organized panel of pro bono attorneys.

"Court-sponsored pro bono program" means a pro bono program established by or in partnership with a court in this State for the purpose of providing free civil legal services by an organized panel of pro bono attorneys.

"Eligible client" means an indigent person who has been found eligible for civil legal services by a civil legal services provider or court-sponsored pro bono program.

"Indigent person" means a person whose income is 125% or less of the current official federal poverty income guidelines or who is otherwise eligible to receive civil legal services under the eligibility guidelines of the civil legal services provider or court-sponsored pro bono program.

(b) When a party is represented in a civil action by a civil legal services provider or attorney in a court-sponsored pro bono program, all fees and costs relating to filing, appearing, transcripts on appeal, and service of process shall be waived without the necessity of a motion for that purpose, and the case shall be given an index number or other appropriate filing number, provided that (i) a determination has been made by the civil legal services provider or attorney in a court-sponsored pro bono program that the party is an indigent person and (ii) an attorney's certification that that determination has been made is filed with the clerk of the court along with the complaint, the appearance, or any other paper that would otherwise require payment of a fee.

(c) The changes made to this Section by this amendatory Act of the 98th General Assembly apply to all actions commenced on or after July 1, 2013. The changes made to this Section by this amendatory Act of the 98th General Assembly also apply to all actions pending on or after the effective date of this amendatory Act of the 98th General Assembly, but only with respect to fees and costs that become due in those actions after July 1, 2013.

P.A. 82–280, § 5–105.5, added by P.A. 88–41, § 5, eff. Jan. 1, 1994. Amended by P.A. 98–351, § 45, eff. Aug. 15, 2013.

5/5–106. Lien of officer

§ 5–106. Lien of officer. Where any person has been permitted by any court to commence and prosecute or to defend an action as a poor person without the payment of costs and expenses, the clerk of the court and the sheriff shall each have a lien upon every claim, including every claim for unliquidated damages, asserted in such action by the party who has thus been permitted to sue or defend as a poor person, and upon the proceeds thereof, for the amount of all fees and charges, becoming due such officer under the provisions of Section 5–105 of this Act, and remaining unpaid. Of the existence of such lien the order of court permitting the party to proceed as a poor person shall be sufficient notice to all other parties in the cause, as well as to any insurer or other third party in anyway liable for payment of any such claim or portion thereof, who shall have been called upon to defend against the same or otherwise notified of the commencement of such action and the assertion of such claim.

On petition filed in the court in which the action has been commenced, the court shall, on not less than 5 days' notice to all parties concerned, adjudicate the rights of the petitioning officer or officers and enforce the lien or liens by all appropriate means.

P.A. 82–280, § 5–106, eff. July 1, 1982. Amended by P.A. 83–707, § 1, eff. Sept. 23, 1983.

Formerly Ill.Rev.Stat.1991, ch. 110, ¶ 5–106.

5/5–107. Affidavit

§ 5–107. Affidavit. If, prior to the commencement of an action in a court, a person desiring to commence such action in such court, files with the clerk thereof an affidavit, stating that the affiant is a poor person and unable to pay costs, and that his or her cause of action is meritorious, the clerk shall issue, and the sheriff shall serve, all necessary process without requiring costs; if judgment is entered against such plaintiff, it shall be for costs, unless the court shall otherwise order.

P.A. 82–280, § 5–107, eff. July 1, 1982.

Formerly Ill.Rev.Stat.1991, ch. 110, ¶ 5–107.

5/5–108. Plaintiff to recover costs

§ 5–108. Plaintiff to recover costs. If any person sues in any court of this state in any action for damages personal to the plaintiff, and recovers in such action, then judgment shall be entered in favor of the plaintiff to recover costs against the defendant, to be taxed, and the same shall be recovered and enforced as other judgments for the payment of money, except in the cases hereinafter provided.

P.A. 82–280, § 5–108, eff. July 1, 1982. Amended by P.A. 83–707, § 1, eff. Sept. 23, 1983.

Formerly Ill.Rev.Stat.1991, ch. 110, ¶ 5–108.

5/5–109. Defendant to recover costs

§ 5–109. Defendant to recover costs. If any person sues in any court of this state, in any action, wherein the plaintiff may have costs in case judgment is entered in favor of the plaintiff and the action is voluntarily dismissed by the plaintiff or is dismissed for want of prosecution or judgment is entered against the plaintiff, then judgment shall be entered in favor of defendant to recover defendant's costs against the plaintiff (except against executors or administrators prosecuting in the right of their testator or intestate), to be taxed, and the costs shall be recovered of the plaintiff, by like process as the plaintiff may have had against the defendant, in case judgment had been entered for such plaintiff.

P.A. 82–280, § 5–109, eff. July 1, 1982.

Formerly Ill.Rev.Stat.1991, ch. 110, ¶ 5–109.

5/5–110. Judgment on motion

§ 5–110. Judgment on motion. If in any action, judgment upon any motion directed to the complaint, answer or reply, by either party to the action, is entered against the plaintiff, the defendant shall recover costs against the plaintiff. If such judgment is entered in favor of the plaintiff, the plaintiff shall recover costs against the defendant; and the person so recovering costs may collect same in the same manner as judgments for the payment of money are enforced.

P.A. 82–280, § 5–110, eff. July 1, 1982.

Formerly Ill.Rev.Stat.1991, ch. 110, ¶ 5–110.

5/5–111. Pleading several matters

§ 5–111. Pleading several matters. Where any defendant in any action, or plaintiff in replevin, pleads several matters, and any of such matters, upon a motion directed to the complaint, answer or reply, is adjudged insufficient, or if judgment is entered, in any issues of the cause, for the plaintiff, costs shall be awarded at the discretion of the court.

P.A. 82–280, § 5–111, eff. July 1, 1982.

Formerly Ill.Rev.Stat.1991, ch. 110, ¶ 5–111.

5/5–112. Several counts

§ 5–112. Several counts. Where there are several counts in any complaint, and any one of them is adjudged insufficient, or a judgment on any issue

joined thereon is entered for the defendant, costs shall be awarded in the discretion of the court.

P.A. 82–280, § 5–112, eff. July 1, 1982.

Formerly Ill.Rev.Stat.1991, ch. 110, ¶ 5–112.

5/5–113. Several defendants

§ 5–113. Several defendants. Where several persons are made defendant to any action, if judgment is entered in favor of any one or more of the defendants, each defendant shall recover costs in the action.

P.A. 82–280, § 5–113, eff. July 1, 1982.

Formerly Ill.Rev.Stat.1991, ch. 110, ¶ 5–113.

5/5–114. Scire facias and prohibition

§ 5–114. Scire facias and prohibition. In all actions of scire facias, or prohibition, the plaintiff recovering judgment after an answer was filed, or a motion directed to the complaint, shall recover his or her costs of the action. If the action is voluntarily dismissed by the plaintiff or is dismissed for want of prosecution or judgment is entered against the plaintiff, the defendant shall recover his or her costs.

P.A. 82–280, § 5–114, eff. July 1, 1982.

Formerly Ill.Rev.Stat.1991, ch. 110, ¶ 5–114.

5/5–115. Number of witnesses

§ 5–115. Number of witnesses. The court may limit the number of witnesses whose fees are to be taxed against any party to such number, not less than 2, as shall appear to the court to be necessary.

P.A. 82–280, § 5–115, eff. July 1, 1982.

Formerly Ill.Rev.Stat.1991, ch. 110, ¶ 5–115.

5/5–116. Dismissals

§ 5–116. Dismissals. In all cases, where any action is voluntarily dismissed by the plaintiff or is dismissed for want of prosecution by reason that the plaintiff neglects to prosecute the same, the defendant shall recover judgment for his or her costs, to be taxed and to be collected in the same manner as judgments for the payment of money are enforced.

P.A. 82–280, § 5–116, eff. July 1, 1982. Amended by P.A. 83–707, § 1, eff. Sept. 23, 1983.

Formerly Ill.Rev.Stat.1991, ch. 110, ¶ 5–116.

5/5–117. Action by State

§ 5–117. Action by State. In all actions commenced or to be commenced for and on behalf of the people of this state, or the governor thereof, or for or on behalf of any county of this state, or in the name of any person for the use of the people of this state, or any county, then and in every such case, if the plaintiff recovers in such action, the plaintiff shall recover costs as any other person in like cases; but if the action is voluntarily dismissed by the plaintiff or is dismissed for want of prosecution or judgment is entered against the plaintiff, the defendant shall not recover any costs whatever. Nothing in this section contained shall extend to any popular action, nor to any action to be prosecuted by any person in behalf of himself or herself and the people or a county, upon any penal statute.

P.A. 82–280, § 5–117, eff. July 1, 1982. Amended by P.A. 83–707, § 1, eff. Sept. 23, 1983.

Formerly Ill.Rev.Stat.1991, ch. 110, ¶ 5–117.

5/5–118. Costs on dismissal

§ 5–118. Costs on dismissal. Upon the action being dismissed, or the defendant dismissing the same for want of prosecution, the defendant shall recover against the plaintiff full costs; and in all other civil cases, not otherwise directed by law, it shall be in the discretion of the court to award costs or not; and the payment of costs, when awarded, may be collected in the same manner as judgments for the payment of money are enforced.

P.A. 82–280, § 5–118, eff. July 1, 1982.

Formerly Ill.Rev.Stat.1991, ch. 110, ¶ 5–118.

5/5–119. Action for use of another

§ 5–119. Action for use of another. When judgment for costs is entered against a plaintiff suing for the use of another, such judgment shall also be against the person for whose use the action is brought, in like manner as if he or she had been a joint plaintiff, and the same may be collected in the same manner as judgments for the payment of money are enforced.

P.A. 82–280, § 5–119, eff. July 1, 1982.

Formerly Ill.Rev.Stat.1991, ch. 110, ¶ 5–119.

5/5–120. Affirmance or reversal on appeal

§ 5–120. Affirmance or reversal on appeal. If any person takes an appeal to review the judgment of any other court, and the judgment is affirmed or the appeal is dismissed, the appellee shall recover costs, which may be collected in the same manner as judgments for the payment of money are enforced; and if the judgment is reversed, the appellant shall recover costs, which may be collected in the same manner as judgments for the payment of money are enforced.

P.A. 82–280, § 5–120, eff. July 1, 1982.

Formerly Ill.Rev.Stat.1991, ch. 110, ¶ 5–120.

5/5–120.5. Administrative review, code compliance

§ 5–120.5. Administrative review, code compliance.

(a) In an administrative review action under Article III of this Code, if the court reverses the decision of a municipal code hearing officer in an action set forth under subsection (c) of this Section, then the court may award the plaintiff all reasonable costs, including court costs and attorney's fees, associated with the action if the court finds that: (i) the decision of the hearing officer was arbitrary and capricious; or (ii) the defendant failed to file a record under Section 3–108 of this Code that is sufficient to allow the court to determine whether the decision of the hearing officer was arbitrary and capricious.

(b) The court may award the municipality reasonable costs, including court costs and attorney's fees, if the court finds that the plaintiff's action under Article III of this Code for administrative review of a decision by the municipal code hearing officer is not reasonably well grounded in fact, is not warranted by existing law, or is not accompanied by a reasonable argument for the extension, modification, or reversal of existing law.

(c) This Section applies only to the decision of a code hearing officer that imposes a fine or penalty against the owner of a single-family or multi-family residential dwelling for a violation related to the condition or use of that residential property. This Section does not apply to any administrative decision of a municipality with a population of more than 500,000.

(d) The provisions of this Section are mutually dependent and inseverable; if any provision is held invalid, then the entire Section is invalid.

P.A. 82–280, § 5–120.5, added by P.A. 98–1105, § 5, eff. Jan. 1, 2015.

5/5–121. Clerks to tax costs

§ 5–121. Clerks to tax costs. The clerk of any court in this state is hereby authorized and required to tax and subscribe all bills of costs arising in any action or proceeding instituted in which such person is clerk, agreeably to the rates which shall, at that time, be allowed or specified by law and shall in no case allow any item or charge unless the clerk shall be satisfied that the service for which it was made was actually performed in the action or proceeding.

P.A. 82–280, § 5–121, eff. July 1, 1982. Amended by P.A. 83–707, § 1, eff. Sept. 23, 1983.

Formerly Ill.Rev.Stat.1991, ch. 110, ¶ 5–121.

5/5–122. Postage as costs

§ 5–122. Postage as costs. When service or return of process is made by mail, the postage and postal fees may be recovered as costs.

P.A. 82–280, § 5–122, eff. July 1, 1982.

Formerly Ill.Rev.Stat.1991, ch. 110, ¶ 5–122.

5/5–123. Retaxing costs

§ 5–123. Retaxing costs. Any person who is dissatisfied by the taxation of any bill of costs by the clerk may apply to the court in which the action or proceeding was had to retax the same, according to law. If the court finds any charge allowed for services not performed, or for which the person charged is not liable, or any item charged higher than is allowed by law, then the court shall correct such taxation; and if the dissatisfied party has paid such unlawful charge, the clerk shall pay to the dissatisfied party, out of fees in the possession of the clerk, the amount which such party has paid by reason of the unlawful charge.

P.A. 82–280, § 5–123, eff. July 1, 1982. Amended by P.A. 84–552, § 1, eff. Sept. 18, 1985.

Formerly Ill.Rev.Stat.1991, ch. 110, ¶ 5–123.

5/5–124. Stay of enforcement of fee bill

§ 5–124. Stay of enforcement of fee bill. When collection of any fee bill is attempted, the dissatisfied party may stay the enforcement of the fee bill by giving to the officer attempting collection, bond with sufficient sureties, to be approved by such officer, in the amount of such fee bill, conditioned for the payment of such fee bill if the same is not quashed; and upon receiving such bond, such officer shall forthwith return the fee bill and bond to the court. If it appears to the court that any item or charge contained in such fee bill is not authorized by law, or is for services not actually rendered, or any item is charged in an amount which is higher than is allowed by law, the court shall quash such fee bill and bond, and correct the taxation of the costs for which such fee bill was issued, and upon such correction being made, such costs may be collected in the same manner as judgments for the payment of money are enforced.

P.A. 82–280, § 5–124, eff. July 1, 1982. Amended by P.A. 84–553, § 1, eff. Sept. 18, 1985.

Formerly Ill.Rev.Stat.1991, ch. 110, ¶ 5–124.

5/5–125. Enforcement of fee bill

§ 5–125. Enforcement of fee bill. In all cases where either party is adjudged to pay costs before final judgment, by reason of setting aside a voluntary dismissal, a dismissal for want of prosecution or a default, or the granting of a continuance or new trial, or otherwise, and in all cases where there is security for costs, or attorney liable for costs, or an action brought to the use of another, and the plaintiff is adjudged to pay the costs, either before or upon final judgment, it shall be lawful for the clerk to prepare and tax a bill of costs so adjudged to be paid, against the party adjudged to pay the same, and against his or her security for costs, or other person liable for the payment thereof, or either of them, and certify the same under the seal of the court, which being delivered to the sheriff of the proper county, the sheriff shall demand payment from the person therein charged; if payment is not made accordingly, within 30 days after such demand, the sheriff shall levy the same on the goods and chattels, lands and tenements of the person so chargeable, and proceed therein in the same manner as judgments for the payment of money are enforced.

P.A. 82–280, § 5–125, eff. July 1, 1982.

Formerly Ill.Rev.Stat.1991, ch. 110, ¶ 5–125.

5/5–126. Costs after tender

§ 5–126. Costs after tender. Whoever is guilty of a trespass or injury or whoever owes another unliquidated damages or demands arising out of a contract may at any time, before or after suit is brought, tender what he or she shall conceive sufficient amends for the injury done or to pay the unliquidated damages or demands; and if suit has been commenced, also the costs of suit up to the time of making the tender. If it appears that the sum tendered was sufficient amends for the injury done or to pay the damages, and if suit has been commenced was also sufficient to pay the costs of suit up to the time of making the tender, the plaintiff shall not be allowed to recover any costs incurred after the tender, but shall be liable to the defendant for the defendant's costs incurred after that time.

P.A. 82–280, § 5–126, added by P.A. 87–409, Art. 5, § 5–5, eff. Sept. 10, 1991.

Formerly Ill.Rev.Stat.1991, ch. 110, ¶ 5–126.

5/5–126.5. Expenses

§ 5–126.5. Expenses. The plaintiff shall be allowed to recover as costs those expenses required by law or a law enforcement or court officer for the purposes of enforcing a judgment including levy bonds, replevin bonds, certification of court orders, recording certified orders or memoranda of judgment, and expenses for those assisting a sheriff or other court officer in enforcing court orders including, but not limited to, orders for possession, replevin orders, and personal property levies.

P.A. 82–280, § 5–126.5, added by P.A. 95–661, § 5, eff. Jan. 1, 2008.

ARTICLE VI. EJECTMENT

5/6–101. Bringing action

§ 6–101. Bringing action. An action of ejectment may be brought in the cases and manner heretofore accustomed, subject to the provisions contained in Article VI of this Act.

P.A. 82–280, § 6–101, eff. July 1, 1982.

Formerly Ill.Rev.Stat.1991, ch. 110, ¶ 6–101.

5/6–102. Interest in land

§ 6–102. Interest in land. It may also be brought to recover lands, tenements or hereditaments, and by any person claiming an estate therein, in fee for life or for years, whether as heir, legatee or purchaser.

P.A. 82–280, § 6–102, eff. July 1, 1982.

Formerly Ill.Rev.Stat.1991, ch. 110, ¶ 6–102.

5/6–103. Lessee of United States or of this State

§ 6–103. Lessee of United States or of this State. In all cases in which any person has heretofore entered upon and occupied or shall hereafter enter upon and occupy, any lands, tenements or hereditaments within this state, by virtue of any lease or permit from the United States or this state, such person, his, her or their legatees, executors, administrators, heirs or assigns, may have and maintain an action of ejectment against any person who has or may enter upon such lands, tenements or hereditaments without the consent of such lessee, his, her or their legatees, executors, administrators, heirs or assigns, and proof of the right of possession shall be sufficient to authorize a recovery.

P.A. 82–280, § 6–103, eff. July 1, 1982. Amended by P.A. 83–707, § 1, eff. Sept. 23, 1983.

Formerly Ill.Rev.Stat.1991, ch. 110, ¶ 6–103.

5/6–104. Interest of plaintiff

§ 6–104. Interest of plaintiff. No person shall recover in ejectment unless he or she has, at the time of commencing the action, a valid subsisting interest in the premises claimed, and a right to recover the same, or to recover the possession thereof, or of some share, interest or portion thereof, to be proved and established at the trial.

P.A. 82–280, § 6–104, eff. July 1, 1982.

Formerly Ill.Rev.Stat.1991, ch. 110, ¶ 6–104.

5/6–105. Joinder of plaintiffs

§ 6–105. Joinder of plaintiffs. Any two or more persons claiming the same premises as joint tenants or tenants in common, may join in an action for the recovery thereof, or any one may sue alone for his or her share.

P.A. 82–280, § 6–105, eff. July 1, 1982.

Formerly Ill.Rev.Stat.1991, ch. 110, ¶ 6–105.

5/6–106. Joinder of defendants

§ 6–106. Joinder of defendants. If the premises for which the action is brought are actually occupied by any person, such actual occupant shall be named defendant in the action; and all other persons claiming title or interest to or in the same may also be joined as defendants.

P.A. 82–280, § 6–106, eff. July 1, 1982.

Formerly Ill.Rev.Stat.1991, ch. 110, ¶ 6–106.

5/6–107. Vacant land

§ 6–107. Vacant land. If the premises are not occupied, the action shall be brought against some person exercising ownership on the premises claimed, or claiming title thereto, or some interest therein, at the commencement of the action.

P.A. 82–280, § 6–107, eff. July 1, 1982.

Formerly Ill.Rev.Stat.1991, ch. 110, ¶ 6–107.

5/6–108. Pleading as in other civil cases

§ 6–108. Pleading as in other civil cases. The time of filing complaints in actions of ejectment shall be the same as in other civil cases; and the rules of pleading and practice in other civil cases shall apply to actions of ejectment, so far as they are applicable, and except as is otherwise provided by Article VI of this Act.

P.A. 82–280, § 6–108, eff. July 1, 1982.

Formerly Ill.Rev.Stat.1991, ch. 110, ¶ 6–108.

5/6–109. Allegations in complaint

§ 6–109. Allegations in complaint. It shall be sufficient for the plaintiff to allege in the complaint that (on some day therein to be specified, and which shall be after his or her title accrued), he or she was possessed of the premises involved (describing them as hereinafter provided), and, being so possessed thereof, that the defendant afterwards (on some day to be stated) entered into such premises, and that he or she unlawfully withholds from the plaintiff the possession thereof, to his or her damage any nominal sum the plaintiff deems proper to state.

P.A. 82–280, § 6–109, eff. July 1, 1982.

Formerly Ill.Rev.Stat.1991, ch. 110, ¶ 6–109.

5/6–110. Description of premises

§ 6–110. Description of premises. The premises so claimed shall be described in such complaint with convenient certainty, so that, from such description possession of the premises claimed may be delivered. If the plaintiff claims any undivided share of interest in any premises, he or she shall state the same particularly in the complaint; but the plaintiff, in any case, may recover such part, share or interest in the premises as he or she shall appear on the trial to be entitled to.

P.A. 82–280, § 6–110, eff. July 1, 1982.

Formerly Ill.Rev.Stat.1991, ch. 110, ¶ 6–110.

5/6–111. Interest claimed

§ 6–111. Interest claimed. The plaintiff shall state whether he or she claims in fee, or whether he or she claims for his or her own life, or the life of another, or for a term of years, specifying such life or the duration of such term.

P.A. 82–280, § 6–111, eff. July 1, 1982.

Formerly Ill.Rev.Stat.1991, ch. 110, ¶ 6–111.

5/6–112. Limited to matters which are germane

§ 6–112. Limited to matters which are germane. The complaint may contain several counts, and several parties may be named as plaintiffs, jointly in one count and separately in others. Except as provided in this Article, no matters not germane to the distinctive purpose of the action shall be introduced by joinder, counterclaim or otherwise.

P.A. 82–280, § 6–112, eff. July 1, 1982.

Formerly Ill.Rev.Stat.1991, ch. 110, ¶ 6–112.

5/6–113. Summons as in other civil cases

§ 6–113. Summons as in other civil cases. Summons shall be issued, tested, served and returned as summons in other civil cases.

P.A. 82–280, § 6–113, eff. July 1, 1982.

Formerly Ill.Rev.Stat.1991, ch. 110, ¶ 6–113.

5/6–114. Notice to landlord

§ 6–114. Notice to landlord. Every tenant who is sued in ejectment by any person other than his or her landlord, shall forthwith give notice thereof to his or her landlord, or to his or her agent or attorney, under the penalty of forfeiting 2 years' rent of the premises involved, or the value thereof, to be recovered by such landlord by civil action.

P.A. 82–280, § 6–114, eff. July 1, 1982.

Formerly Ill.Rev.Stat.1991, ch. 110, ¶ 6–114.

5/6–115. Landlord as defendant

§ 6–115. Landlord as defendant. The landlord, whose tenant is sued in ejectment, may, upon his or her own motion or that of the plaintiff, be made defendant in such action, upon such terms as may be ordered by the court.

P.A. 82–280, § 6–115, eff. July 1, 1982.

Formerly Ill.Rev.Stat.1991, ch. 110, ¶ 6–115.

5/6–116. Pleading by defendant

§ 6–116. Pleading by defendant. The defendant may file any appropriate motion as in ordinary civil cases, and may answer as hereinafter provided by way of general denial, or specific denial or affirmative defense, and such motion or answer shall constitute an appearance in the case.

P.A. 82–280, § 6–116, eff. July 1, 1982.

Formerly Ill.Rev.Stat.1991, ch. 110, ¶ 6–116.

5/6–117. General denial

§ 6–117. General denial. Under a general denial which alleges generally that the defendant is not guilty of unlawfully withholding the premises claimed by the plaintiff, the defendant may offer in evidence any matter that may tend to defeat the plaintiff's action, except that it shall not put in issue the possession of the premises by the defendant or that he or she claims title or interest in the premises.

P.A. 82–280, § 6–117, eff. July 1, 1982.

Formerly Ill.Rev.Stat.1991, ch. 110, ¶ 6–117.

5/6–118. Plaintiff's proof

§ 6–118. Plaintiff's proof. It is not necessary for the plaintiff to prove that the defendant was in possession of the premises, or claims title or interest therein at the time of bringing the action, or that the plaintiff demanded the possession of the premises, unless the defendant in his or her answer verified by affidavit specifically denies that he or she was in such possession, or claims title or interest therein, or that demand of possession was made.

P.A. 82–280, § 6–118, eff. July 1, 1982.

Formerly Ill.Rev.Stat.1991, ch. 110, ¶ 6–118.

5/6–119. Plaintiff's proof—Continued

§ 6–119. Plaintiff's proof—Continued. It is not necessary for the plaintiff to prove an actual entry under title, nor the actual receipt of any of the profits of the premises demanded; but it shall be sufficient for the plaintiff to prove a right to the possession of such premises at the time of the commencement of the action, as heir, legatee, purchaser or otherwise.

P.A. 82–280, § 6–119, eff. July 1, 1982.

Formerly Ill.Rev.Stat.1991, ch. 110, ¶ 6–119.

5/6–120. Evidence

§ 6–120. Evidence. It is not necessary on the trial for the defendant to admit, nor for the plaintiff to prove lease, entry and ouster, or either of them, except in actions by one or more tenants in common, or joint tenants against their co-tenants; but this section shall not be construed to impair, nor in any way to affect, any of the rules of evidence now in force in regard to the maintenance and defense of the action.

P.A. 82–280, § 6–120, eff. July 1, 1982.

Formerly Ill.Rev.Stat.1991, ch. 110, ¶ 6–120.

5/6–121. Claim of title through common source

§ 6–121. Claim of title through common source. If the plaintiff, or his or her agent or attorney, states under oath that he or she claims title through a common source with the defendant, it is sufficient for the plaintiff to show title from such common source, unless the defendant, or his or her agent or attorney, denies, on oath, that he or she claims title through such source, or swears that he or she claims title through some other source.

P.A. 82–280, § 6–121, eff. July 1, 1982.

Formerly Ill.Rev.Stat.1991, ch. 110, ¶ 6–121.

5/6–122. Action against co-tenants

§ 6–122. Action against co-tenants. If the action is brought by one or more tenants in common, or joint tenants against their co-tenants, the plaintiff, in addition to all other evidence which he or she may be bound to introduce, shall be required to prove on the trial of the cause, that the defendant actually ousted

the plaintiff, or did some other act amounting to a total denial of his or her right as such co-tenant.

P.A. 82–280, § 6–122, eff. July 1, 1982.

Formerly Ill.Rev.Stat.1991, ch. 110, ¶ 6–122.

5/6–123. Proof of interest

§ 6–123. Proof of interest. It is not an objection to a recovery in an action of ejectment that any one of several plaintiffs do not prove any interest in the premises claimed, but those entitled shall have judgment, according to their rights, for the whole or such part or portion as he, she or they might have recovered if he, she or they had sued in his, her or their name or names only.

P.A. 82–280, § 6–123, eff. July 1, 1982.

Formerly Ill.Rev.Stat.1991, ch. 110, ¶ 6–123.

5/6–124. Action against several

§ 6–124. Action against several. If the action is against several, and the plaintiff is entitled to recover, he or she shall recover against all who are in joint possession or claim the title, whether they have pleaded separately or jointly.

P.A. 82–280, § 6–124, eff. July 1, 1982.

Formerly Ill.Rev.Stat.1991, ch. 110, ¶ 6–124.

5/6–125. Proof of occupancy

§ 6–125. Proof of occupancy. When the action is against several defendants, if it is proved on the trial that any of them occupy distinct parcels in severalty or jointly, the plaintiff shall elect, at the trial, against which he or she will proceed; and such election shall be made before the evidence in the action is closed, and the action shall be dismissed as to the defendants not so proceeded against.

P.A. 82–280, § 6–125, eff. July 1, 1982.

Formerly Ill.Rev.Stat.1991, ch. 110, ¶ 6–125.

5/6–126. Specificity of verdict

§ 6–126. Specificity of verdict. In the following cases, if tried by a jury, the verdict shall be rendered as follows:

1. If it is proved on the trial that all the plaintiffs have a right to recover the possession of the premises, the verdict shall be for the plaintiffs generally.

2. If it is proved that one or more of the plaintiffs has a right to the possession of the premises, and that one or more does not have such right, the verdict shall specify for which plaintiff the jury finds, and as to which plaintiff the jury finds for the defendant.

3. If the verdict is for any plaintiff, and there are several defendants, the verdict shall be rendered against such of them as were in possession of the

premises or as claimed title thereto at the commencement of the action.

4. If the verdict is for all the premises claimed, as specified in the complaint, it shall, in that respect, be for such premises generally.

5. If the verdict is for a part of the premises described in such complaint, the verdict shall particularly specify such part, as the same was proved, with the same certainty hereinbefore required in the description of the premises claimed.

6. If the verdict is for an undivided share or interest in the premises claimed, it shall specify such share or interest; and if for an undivided share in a part of the premises claimed, it shall specify such share, and shall describe such part of the premises as hereinbefore required.

The verdict shall also specify the estate which has been established on the trial, by the plaintiff in whose favor it is rendered, whether such estate is in fee or for his or her own life or for the life of another, stating such lives, or whether it is for a term of years, and specifying the duration of such term.

P.A. 82–280, § 6–126, eff. July 1, 1982.

Formerly Ill.Rev.Stat.1991, ch. 110, ¶ 6–126.

5/6–127. Expiration of plaintiff's right or termination of plaintiff's title before trial

§ 6–127. Expiration of plaintiff's right or termination of plaintiff's title before trial. If the right of a plaintiff in ejectment expires or the plaintiff's title terminates after the commencement of the action, but before trial, the verdict, if tried by a jury, shall be returned according to the fact, and judgment shall be entered that the plaintiff recover his or her damages by reason of the withholding of the premises, by the defendant, to be assessed, and that as to the premises claimed, the action shall be dismissed; and such damages may be thereupon assessed by the court or jury trying the case.

P.A. 82–280, § 6–127, eff. July 1, 1982.

Formerly Ill.Rev.Stat.1991, ch. 110, ¶ 6–127.

5/6–128. Suggestion of death

§ 6–128. Suggestion of death. If there are several plaintiffs in an action of ejectment, and any of them die before final judgment, the death of such party may be suggested of record, and the executor, administrator, heir or legatee of the deceased party shall be allowed to proceed with the action jointly with the survivor, in the same manner as if he or she had originally joined with him or her in commencing the action.

P.A. 82–280, § 6–128, eff. July 1, 1982. Amended by P.A. 83–707, § 1, eff. Sept. 23, 1983.

Formerly Ill.Rev.Stat.1991, ch. 110, ¶ 6–128.

5/6–129. Judgment

§ 6–129. Judgment. In cases where no other provision is made, the judgment in the action, if the plaintiff prevails, shall be that the plaintiff recover the possession of the premises, according to the verdict of the jury, if there was such a verdict, or the finding of the court, if the case is tried without a jury, or according to the description thereof in the complaint, with costs to be taxed, if the judgment is by default.

P.A. 82–280, § 6–129, eff. July 1, 1982.

Formerly Ill.Rev.Stat.1991, ch. 110, ¶ 6–129.

5/6–130. Recovery of rents and profits

§ 6–130. Recovery of rents and profits. The plaintiff recovering judgment in ejectment in any of the cases in which such action may be maintained, shall also be entitled to recover damages against the defendant for the rents and profits of the premises recovered.

P.A. 82–280, § 6–130, eff. July 1, 1982.

Formerly Ill.Rev.Stat.1991, ch. 110, ¶ 6–130.

5/6–131. Conclusiveness of judgment

§ 6–131. Conclusiveness of judgment. Every judgment in the action of ejectment shall be conclusive as to the title established in such action upon the party against whom the same is rendered, and against all persons claiming from, through or under such party, by title accruing after the commencement of such action, subject to the exceptions hereinafter named.

P.A. 82–280, § 6–131, eff. July 1, 1982.

Formerly Ill.Rev.Stat.1991, ch. 110, ¶ 6–131.

5/6–132. New trial as in other civil cases

§ 6–132. New trial as in other civil cases. The court may grant a new trial before or after final judgment, as in other civil cases.

P.A. 82–280, § 6–132, eff. July 1, 1982.

Formerly Ill.Rev.Stat.1991, ch. 110, ¶ 6–132.

5/6–133. Petition for damages

§ 6–133. Petition for damages. Instead of a separate action for the recovery of mesne profits, the plaintiff seeking to recover such damages shall, within one year after the entering of the judgment, file a petition in the ejectment action.

P.A. 82–280, § 6–133, eff. July 1, 1982.

Formerly Ill.Rev.Stat.1991, ch. 110, ¶ 6–133.

5/6–134. Petition stands as complaint

§ 6–134. Petition stands as complaint. Such petition shall be substantially in the same form as is now in use in other civil cases for complaints and the same rules of pleading shall be observed as in other civil cases.

P.A. 82–280, § 6–134, eff. July 1, 1982.

Formerly Ill.Rev.Stat.1991, ch. 110, ¶ 6–134.

5/6–135. Service of copy of petition

§ 6–135. Service of copy of petition. Upon the filing of such petition, the defendant shall be served with a copy thereof.

P.A. 82–280, § 6–135, eff. July 1, 1982.

Formerly Ill.Rev.Stat.1991, ch. 110, ¶ 6–135.

5/6–136. Pleadings

§ 6–136. Pleadings. The pleadings following the filing of the petition and the proceedings thereon shall be the same as in ordinary civil actions, but no matters shall be pleaded or presented which were or might have been denied in such action of ejectment. The defendant may plead a recovery by such defendant, or any other person, of the same premises, or of part thereof, subsequent to the verdict of the jury if tried by a jury, or to the finding of the court if tried without a jury, in such action of ejectment, in bar or in mitigation of the damages claimed by the plaintiff.

P.A. 82–280, § 6–136, eff. July 1, 1982.

Formerly Ill.Rev.Stat.1991, ch. 110, ¶ 6–136.

5/6–137. Issue of fact on petition

§ 6–137. Issue of fact on petition. If any issue of fact is presented on such petition, it shall be tried as in other civil cases; and if such issue is found for the plaintiff, or if demand for trial by jury has been made in accordance with law, a jury may assess damages in the amount of the mesne profits received by the defendant since he or she entered into possession of the premises, subject to the restrictions contained in Article VI of this Act.

P.A. 82–280, § 6–137, eff. July 1, 1982. Amended by P.A. 84–1043, § 1, eff. Nov. 26, 1985.

Formerly Ill.Rev.Stat.1991, ch. 110, ¶ 6–137.

5/6–138. Extent of recovery

§ 6–138. Extent of recovery. On the trial of such issue, the plaintiff is required to establish and the defendant may deny, the time when such defendant entered into the possession of the premises, the time during which he or she enjoyed the mesne profits thereof, and the value of such profits; and the record of the recovery in the action of ejectment shall not be evidence of such time. On such trial, the defendant shall have the same right to set off any improvements made on the premises, to the amount of the plaintiff's claim, as is now or shall hereafter be judicially allowed; and in estimating the plaintiff's damages, the value of the use by the defendant of any improvements made by him or her shall not be allowed to the plaintiff.

P.A. 82–280, § 6–138, eff. July 1, 1982. Amended by P.A. 83–707, § 1, eff. Sept. 23, 1983.

Formerly Ill.Rev.Stat.1991, ch. 110, ¶ 6–138.

5/6–139. Death of plaintiff

§ 6–139. Death of plaintiff. If the plaintiff in ejectment dies after issue joined or judgment entered therein, the decedent's personal representatives may offer a suggestion of such death, of the granting of letters of office to them, and may claim their right to the mesne profits of the premises recovered, in the same manner, and with the like effect, as the decedent; and the same proceedings shall in all respects be had thereon.

P.A. 82–280, § 6–139, eff. July 1, 1982. Amended by P.A. 83–707, § 1, eff. Sept. 23, 1983.

Formerly Ill.Rev.Stat.1991, ch. 110, ¶ 6–139.

5/6–140. When mesne profits not recoverable

§ 6–140. When mesne profits not recoverable. Every person who is hereafter evicted from any land for which he or she can show a plain, clear and connected title deduced from the record of some public office, without actual notice of an adverse title in like manner derived from record, shall be exempt and free from all and every species of action, process or prosecution for or on account of any rents, profits, or damages, which have been done, accrued or incurred at any time prior to receipt of actual notice of the adverse claim by which the eviction may be effected, provided such person obtained peaceable possession of the land.

P.A. 82–280, § 6–140, eff. July 1, 1982.

Formerly Ill.Rev.Stat.1991, ch. 110, ¶ 6–140.

5/6–141. Notice of adverse claim

§ 6–141. Notice of adverse claim. Notice of any adverse claim or title to the land within the meaning of this Article is to be given by bringing an action for the same, by the one or the other of the parties, and may hereafter be given by bringing an action, as above provided, or by delivering an attested copy of the entry, survey or patent, from which he or she derives his or her title or claim, or leaving any such copy with the party or the spouse of such party. Notice given by the delivery of an attested copy, as above set out, is void, unless an action is filed within one year thereafter. In no case shall the proprietor of the better title be obliged to pay to the occupying claimant, for improvements made after notice, more than what is equal to the rents and profits above set forth.

P.A. 82–280, § 6–141, eff. July 1, 1982.

Formerly Ill.Rev.Stat.1991, ch. 110, ¶ 6–141.

5/6–142. Notice to occupying claimant

§ 6–142. Notice to occupying claimant. Notice to any occupying claimant shall bind all those claiming from, by or through such occupying claimant, to the extent of such claim.

P.A. 82–280, § 6–142, eff. July 1, 1982.

Formerly Ill.Rev.Stat.1991, ch. 110, ¶ 6–142.

5/6–143 to 5/6–148. §§ 6–143 to 6–148. Repealed by P.A. 84–623, § 1, eff. Sept. 20, 1985

5/6–149. Stay of waste—Security

§ 6–149. Stay of waste—Security. Nothing herein contained shall be construed so as to prevent any court from entering an order to stay waste, and ordering a party to give bond and security in such manner as the court may deem appropriate.

P.A. 82–280, § 6–149, eff. July 1, 1982.

Formerly Ill.Rev.Stat.1991, ch. 110, ¶ 6–149.

5/6–150. Abolition of common law fictions

§ 6–150. Abolition of common law fictions. The following common law fictions are abolished:

(1) The use of fictitious names of plaintiffs or defendants and of the names of any other than the real claimants and the real defendants, and the statements of any lease or demise to the plaintiff, and of an ejectment by a casual or nominal ejector.

(2) The consent rule.

P.A. 82–280, § 6–150, eff. July 1, 1982.

Formerly Ill.Rev.Stat.1991, ch. 110, ¶ 6–150.

ARTICLE VII. EMINENT DOMAIN

5/7–101 to 5/7–103.45. §§ 101 to 103.45. Repealed by P.A. 94–1055, Art. 95, § 95–1–5, effective January 1, 2007

5/7–103.46 to 5/7–103.95. §§ 103.46 to 103.95. Repealed by P.A. 94–1055, Art. 95, § 95–1–5, effective January 1, 2007

5/7–103.96 to 5/7–104. §§ 103.96 to 104. Repealed by P.A. 94–1055, Art. 95, § 95–1–5, effective January 1, 2007

5/7–105 to 5/7–129. §§ 105 to 129. Repealed by P.A. 94–1055, Art. 95, § 95–1–5, effective January 1, 2007

ARTICLE VIII. EVIDENCE

PART 1. INTERESTED PERSON AS WITNESS

5/8–101. Interested witness

§ 8–101. Interested witness. No person shall be disqualified as a witness in any action or proceeding, except as hereinafter stated, by reason of his or her interest in the event thereof, as a party or otherwise, or by reason of his or her conviction of any crime; but such interest or conviction may be shown for the purpose of affecting the credibility of such witness; and the fact of such conviction may be proven like any fact not of record, either by the witness himself or herself (who shall be compelled to testify thereto) or by any other witness cognizant of such conviction, as impeaching testimony, or by any other competent evidence.

P.A. 82–280, § 8–101, eff. July 1, 1982.

Formerly Ill.Rev.Stat.1991, ch. 110, ¶ 8–101.

PART 2. DEAD–MAN'S ACT

5/8–201. Dead-Man's Act

§ 8–201. Dead–Man's Act. In the trial of any action in which any party sues or defends as the representative of a deceased person or person under a legal disability, no adverse party or person directly interested in the action shall be allowed to testify on his or her own behalf to any conversation with the deceased or person under legal disability or to any event which took place in the presence of the deceased or person under legal disability, except in the following instances:

(a) If any person testifies on behalf of the representative to any conversation with the deceased or person under legal disability or to any event which took place in the presence of the deceased or person under legal disability, any adverse party or interested person, if otherwise competent, may testify concerning the same conversation or event.

(b) If the deposition of the deceased or person under legal disability is admitted in evidence on behalf of the representative, any adverse party or interested person, if otherwise competent, may testify concerning the same matters admitted in evidence.

(c) Any testimony competent under Section 8–401 of this Act, is not barred by this Section.

(d) No person shall be barred from testifying as to any fact relating to the heirship of a decedent.

As used in this Section:

(a) "Person under legal disability" means any person who is adjudged by the court in the pending civil action to be unable to testify by reason of mental illness, an intellectual disability, or deterioration of mentality.

(b) "Representative" means an executor, administrator, heir or legatee of a deceased person and any guardian or trustee of any such heir or legatee, or a guardian or guardian ad litem for a person under legal disability.

(c) "Person directly interested in the action" or "interested person" does not include a person who is interested solely as executor, trustee or in any other fiduciary capacity, whether or not he or she receives or expects to receive compensation for acting in that capacity.

(d) This Section applies to proceedings filed on or after October 1, 1973.

P.A. 82–280, § 8–201, eff. July 1, 1982. Amended by P.A. 97–227, § 150, eff. Jan. 1, 2012.

Formerly Ill.Rev.Stat.1991, ch. 110, ¶ 8–201.

PART 3. SURVIVING PARTNER OR JOINT–CONTRACTOR

Section
5/8–301. Surviving partner or joint-contractor.

5/8–301. Surviving partner or joint-contractor

§ 8–301. Surviving partner or joint-contractor. In any action or proceeding by or against any surviving partner or partners, or joint contractor or joint contractors, no adverse party or person adversely interested in the event thereof, shall, by virtue of Section 8–101 of this Act, be rendered a competent witness to testify to any admission or conversation by any deceased partner or joint contractor, unless some one or more of the surviving partners or joint contractors were also present at the time of such admission or conversation; and in every action or proceeding a party to the same who has contracted with an agent of the adverse party—the agent having since died—shall not be a competent witness as to any admission or conversation between himself or herself and such agent, unless such admission or conversation with the deceased agent was had or made in the presence of a surviving agent or agents of such adverse party, and then only except where the conditions are such that under the provisions of Sections 8–201 and 8–401 of this Act he or she would have been permitted to testify if the deceased person had been a principal and not an agent.

P.A. 82–280, § 8–301, eff. July 1, 1982.

Formerly Ill.Rev.Stat.1991, ch. 110, ¶ 8–301.

PART 4. ACCOUNT BOOKS AND RECORDS

Section
5/8–401. Account books and records.
5/8–402. Production of books and writings.

5/8–401. Account books and records

§ 8–401. Account books and records. Where in any action or proceeding, the claim or defense is founded on a book account or any other record or document, any party or interested person may testify to his or her account book, or any other record or document and the items therein contained; that the same is a book, record, or document of original entries, and that the entries therein were made by himself or herself, and are true and just; or that the same were made by a deceased person, or by a disinterested person, a non-resident person of the state at the time of the trial, and where made by such deceased or non-resident person in the usual course of trade, and of his or her duty or employment to the party so testifying; and thereupon the account book and entries or any other record or document shall be admitted as evidence in the cause. Where such book of original entries or any other record or document has been photographed, microphotographed, microfilmed, optical imaged, or otherwise reproduced either in the usual course of business, or pursuant to any statute of this State authorizing the reproduction of public records, papers or documents, and the reproduction, in either case, complies with the minimum standards of quality for permanent records approved by the State Records Commission, then such reproduction shall be deemed to be an original record, book or document for all purposes, including introduction in evidence in all courts or administrative agencies.

P.A. 82–280, § 8–401, eff. July 1, 1982. Amended by P.A. 87–205, Art. 2, § 2–3, eff. July 1, 1992; P.A. 88–609, § 5, eff. Sept. 1, 1994.

Formerly Ill.Rev.Stat.1991, ch. 110, ¶ 8–401.

5/8–402. Production of books and writings

§ 8–402. Production of books and writings. The circuit courts shall have power, in any action pending before them, upon motion, and good and sufficient cause shown, and reasonable notice thereof given, to require the parties, or either of them, to produce books or writings in their possession or power which contain evidence pertinent to the issue.

P.A. 82–280, § 8–402, eff. July 1, 1982. Amended by P.A. 92–651, § 84, eff. July 11, 2002.

Formerly Ill.Rev.Stat.1991, ch. 110, ¶ 8–402.

PART 5. EFFECT OF RELEASE OR ASSIGNMENT

Section
5/8–501.   Release or assignment.

5/8–501. Release or assignment

§ 8–501. Release or assignment. In any action or proceeding, any person who would, if a party thereto, be incompetent to testify therein under the provisions of Section 8–201 or Section 8–401 of this Act, shall not become competent by reason of any assignment or release of his or her claim, made for the purpose of allowing such person to testify.

P.A. 82–280, § 8–501, eff. July 1, 1982. Amended by P.A. 87–760, § 1, eff. Jan. 1, 1992.

Formerly Ill.Rev.Stat.1991, ch. 110, ¶ 8–501.

PART 6. CERTAIN LAWS UNAFFECTED

Section
5/8–601.   Laws not affected.

5/8–601. Laws not affected

§ 8–601. Laws not affected. Nothing in this Article shall in any manner affect the laws now existing relating to the settlement of the estates of deceased persons, minors, persons under legal disability who have guardians, or to the acknowledgment or proof of deeds and other conveyances relating to real estate, in order to entitle the same to be recorded, or to the attestation of the execution of last wills or of any other instrument required by law to be attested.

P.A. 82–280, § 8–601, eff. July 1, 1982.

Formerly Ill.Rev.Stat.1991, ch. 110, ¶ 8–601.

PART 7. BROADCAST OR TELEVISED TESTIMONY

Section
5/8–701.   Broadcast or televised testimony.

5/8–701. Broadcast or televised testimony

§ 8–701. Broadcast or televised testimony. No witness shall be compelled to testify in any proceeding conducted by a commission, administrative agency or other tribunal in this State if any portion of his or her testimony is to be broadcast or televised or if motion pictures are to be taken of him or her while he or she is testifying. This Section shall not apply to judicial proceedings.

P.A. 82–280, § 8–701, eff. July 1, 1982. Amended by P.A. 97–1099, § 5, eff. Aug. 24, 2012.

Formerly Ill.Rev.Stat.1991, ch. 110, ¶ 8–701.

PART 8. PRIVILEGED COMMUNICATIONS

Section
5/8–801.   Husband and wife.
5/8–802.   Physician and patient.
5/8–802.1.   Confidentiality of Statements Made to Rape Crisis Personnel.
5/8–802.2.   Confidentiality of statements made to personnel counseling victims of violent crime.
5/8–802.3.   Informant's privilege.
5/8–803.   Clergy.
5/8–803.5.   Union agent and union member.
5/8–804.   Confidential advisor.

5/8–801. Husband and wife

§ 8–801. Husband and wife. In all actions, husband and wife may testify for or against each other, provided that neither may testify as to any communication or admission made by either of them to the other or as to any conversation between them during marriage, except in actions between such husband and wife, and in actions where the custody, support, health or welfare of their children or children in either spouse's care, custody or control is directly in issue, and as to matters in which either has acted as agent for the other.

P.A. 82–280, § 8–801, eff. July 1, 1982. Amended by P.A. 83–408, § 2, eff. Jan. 1, 1984.

Formerly Ill.Rev.Stat.1991, ch. 110, ¶ 8–801.

5/8–802. Physician and patient

§ 8–802. Physician and patient. No physician or surgeon shall be permitted to disclose any information he or she may have acquired in attending any patient in a professional character, necessary to enable him or her professionally to serve the patient, except only (1) in trials for homicide when the disclosure relates directly to the fact or immediate circumstances of the homicide, (2) in actions, civil or criminal, against the physician for malpractice, (3) with the expressed consent of the patient, or in case of his or her death or disability, of his or her personal representative or other person authorized to sue for personal injury or of the beneficiary of an insurance policy on his or her life, health, or physical condition, or as authorized by Section 8–2001.5, (4) in all actions brought by or against the patient, his or her personal representative, a beneficiary under a policy of insurance, or the executor or administrator of his or her estate wherein the patient's physical or mental condition is an issue, (5) upon an issue as to the validity of a document as a will of the patient, (6) in any criminal action where the charge is either first degree murder by abortion, attempted abortion or abortion, (7) in actions, civil or criminal, arising from the filing of a report in compliance with the Abused and Neglected Child Reporting Act,[1] (8) to any department, agency, institution or facility which has custody of the patient pursuant to State statute or any court order of commitment, (9) in prosecutions where written results of blood alcohol tests are admissible pursuant to Section 11–501.4 of the Illinois Vehicle Code,[2] (10) in prosecutions where written results of blood alcohol tests are admissible under Section 5–11a of the Boat Registration and Safety Act,[3] (11) in criminal actions arising from the filing of a report of suspected terrorist offense in compliance with Section 29D–10(p)(7) of the Criminal Code of 2012,[4] (12) upon the issuance of a subpoena pursuant to Section 38 of the Medical Practice Act of 1987; the issuance of a subpoena pursuant to Section 25.1 of the Illinois Dental Practice Act; the issuance of a subpoena pursuant to Section 22 of the Nursing Home Administrators Licensing and Disciplinary Act; or the issuance of a subpoena pursuant to Section 25.5 of the Workers' Compensation Act, (13) upon the issuance of a grand jury subpoena pursuant to Article 112 of the Code of Criminal Procedure of 1963, or (14) to or through a health information exchange, as that term is defined in Section 2 of the Mental Health and Developmental Disabilities Confidentiality Act, in accordance with State or federal law.

Upon disclosure under item (13) of this Section, in any criminal action where the charge is domestic battery, aggravated domestic battery, or an offense under Article 11 of the Criminal Code of 2012 or where the patient is under the age of 18 years or upon the request of the patient, the State's Attorney shall petition the court for a protective order pursuant to Supreme Court Rule 415.

In the event of a conflict between the application of this Section and the Mental Health and Developmental Disabilities Confidentiality Act[5] to a specific situation, the provisions of the Mental Health and Developmental Disabilities Confidentiality Act shall control. P.A. 82–280, § 8–802, eff. July 1, 1982. Amended by P.A. 82–783, Art. III, § 43, eff. July 13, 1982; P.A. 84–1450, § 8, eff. July 1, 1987; P.A. 85–992, § 2, eff. Jan. 5, 1988; P.A. 87–803, § 2, eff. July 1, 1992; P.A. 92–854, § 40, eff. Dec. 5, 2002; P.A. 95–478, § 5, eff. Aug. 27, 2007; P.A. 97–18, § 10, eff. June 28, 2011; P.A. 97–623, § 5, eff. Nov. 23, 2011; P.A. 97–813, § 670, eff. July 13, 2012; P.A. 97–1150, § 705, eff. Jan. 25, 2013; P.A. 98–954, § 5, eff. Jan. 1, 2015; P.A. 98–1046, § 30, eff. Jan. 1, 2015; P.A. 99–78, § 535, eff. July 20, 2015.

Formerly Ill.Rev.Stat.1991, ch. 110, ¶ 8–802.
[1] 325 ILCS 5/1 et seq.
[2] 625 ILCS 5/11–501.4.
[3] 625 ILCS 45/5–11a (renumbered as 625 ILCS 45/5–16a).
[4] 720 ILCS 5/29D–10.
[5] 740 ILCS 110/1 et seq.

Validity

Public Act 89–7, which amended this section, has been held unconstitutional in its entirety by the Illinois Supreme Court in the case of Best v. Taylor Machine Works, 1997, 689 N.E.2d 1057, 228 Ill.Dec. 636, 179 Ill.2d 367. Later amendments did not included the amendment by P.A. 89–7.

P.A. 89–7 rewrote this section, which prior thereto read:

"Physician and patient. No physician or surgeon shall be permitted to disclose any information he or she may have acquired in attending any patient in a professional character, necessary to enable him or her professionally to serve the patient, except only (1) in trials for homicide when the disclosure relates directly to the fact or immediate circumstances of the homicide, (2) in actions, civil or criminal, against the physician for malpractice, (3) with the expressed consent of the patient, or in case of his or her death or disability, of his or her personal representative or other person authorized to sue for personal injury or of the beneficiary of an insurance policy on his or her life, health, or physical condition, (4) in all actions brought by or against the patient, his or her personal representative, a beneficiary under a policy of insurance, or the executor or administrator of his or her estate wherein the patient's physical or mental condition is an issue, (5) upon an issue as to the validity of a document as a will of the patient, (6) in any criminal action where the charge is either first degree murder by abortion, attempted abortion or abortion, (7) in actions, civil or criminal, arising from the filing of a report in compliance with the Abused and Neglected Child Reporting Act, (8) to any department, agency, institution or facility which has custody of the patient pursuant to State statute or any court order of commitment, (9) in prosecutions where written results of blood alcohol tests are admissible pursuant to Section 11–501.4 of the Illinois Vehicle Code or (10) in prosecutions where written results of blood alcohol tests are admissible under Section 5–11a of the Boat Registration and Safety Act.

"In the event of a conflict between the application of this Section and the Mental Health and Developmental Disabilities Confidentiality Act to a specific situation, the provisions of the Mental Health and Developmental Disabilities Confidentiality Act shall control."

Section 995 of P.A. 89–7, approved March 9, 1995, provides:

"Effective date. This Act takes effect upon becoming law, and applies to causes of action as specified in each Section or part of this Act."

Public Act 89–7, which amended this section, has been held unconstitutional in its entirety by the Illinois Supreme Court in the case of Best v. Taylor Machine Works, 1997, 689 N.E.2d 1057, 228 Ill.Dec. 636, 179 Ill.2d 367. P.A. 92–854 did not recognize the changes made by P.A. 89–7. See note, post, for changes made by P.A. 92–854.

5/8–802.1.   Confidentiality of Statements Made to Rape Crisis Personnel

§ 8–802.1. Confidentiality of Statements Made to Rape Crisis Personnel.

(a) Purpose. This Section is intended to protect victims of rape from public disclosure of statements they make in confidence to counselors of organizations established to help them. On or after July 1, 1984, "rape" means an act of forced sexual penetration or sexual conduct, as defined in Section 11–0.1 of the Criminal Code of 2012,[1] including acts prohibited under Sections 11–1.20 through 11–1.60 or 12–13 through 12–16 of the Criminal Code of 1961 or the Criminal Code of 2012.[2] Because of the fear and stigma that often results from those crimes, many victims hesitate to seek help even where it is available at no cost to them. As a result they not only fail to receive needed medical care and emergency counseling, but may lack the psychological support necessary to report the crime and aid police in preventing future crimes.

(b) Definitions. As used in this Act:

(1) "Rape crisis organization" means any organization or association the major purpose of which is providing information, counseling, and psychological support to victims of any or all of the crimes of aggravated criminal sexual assault, predatory criminal sexual assault of a child, criminal sexual assault, sexual relations between siblings, criminal sexual abuse and aggravated criminal sexual abuse.

(2) "Rape crisis counselor" means a person who is a psychologist, social worker, employee, or volunteer in any organization or association defined as a rape crisis organization under this Section, who has undergone 40 hours of training and is under the control of a direct services supervisor of a rape crisis organization.

(3) "Victim" means a person who is the subject of, or who seeks information, counseling, or advocacy services as a result of an aggravated criminal sexual assault, predatory criminal sexual assault of a child, criminal sexual assault, sexual relations within families, criminal sexual abuse, aggravated criminal sexual abuse, sexual exploitation of a child, indecent solicitation of a child, public indecency, exploitation of a child, promoting juvenile prostitution as described in subdivision (a)(4) of Section 11–14.4, or an attempt to commit any of these offenses.

(4) "Confidential communication" means any communication between a victim and a rape crisis counselor in the course of providing information, counseling, and advocacy. The term includes all records kept by the counselor or by the organization in the course of providing services to an alleged victim concerning the alleged victim and the services provided.

(c) Waiver of privilege.

(1) The confidential nature of the communication is not waived by: the presence of a third person who further expresses the interests of the victim at the time of the communication; group counseling; or disclosure to a third person with the consent of the victim when reasonably necessary to accomplish the purpose for which the counselor is consulted.

(2) The confidential nature of counseling records is not waived when: the victim inspects the records; or in the case of a minor child less than 12 years of age, a parent or guardian whose interests are not adverse to the minor inspects the records; or in the case of a minor victim 12 years or older, a parent or guardian whose interests are not adverse to the minor inspects the records with the victim's consent, or in the case of an adult who has a guardian of his or her person, the guardian inspects the records with the victim's consent.

(3) When a victim is deceased, the executor or administrator of the victim's estate may waive the privilege established by this Section, unless the executor or administrator has an interest adverse to the victim.

(4) A minor victim 12 years of age or older may knowingly waive the privilege established in this Section. When a minor is, in the opinion of the Court, incapable of knowingly waiving the privilege, the parent or guardian of the minor may waive the privilege on behalf of the minor, unless the parent or guardian has been charged with a violent crime against the victim or otherwise has any interest adverse to that of the minor with respect to the waiver of the privilege.

(5) An adult victim who has a guardian of his or her person may knowingly waive the privilege established in this Section. When the victim is, in the opinion of the court, incapable of knowingly waiving the privilege, the guardian of the adult victim may waive the privilege on behalf of the victim, unless the guardian has been charged with a violent crime against the victim or otherwise has any interest adverse to the victim with respect to the privilege.

(d) Confidentiality. Except as provided in this Act, no rape crisis counselor shall disclose any confidential communication or be examined as a witness in any civil or criminal proceeding as to any confidential communication without the written consent of the victim or a representative of the victim as provided in subparagraph (c).

(e) A rape crisis counselor may disclose a confidential communication without the consent of the victim if failure to disclose is likely to result in a clear, imminent risk of serious physical injury or death of the victim or another person. Any rape crisis counselor or rape crisis organization participating in good faith in the disclosing of records and communications under this Act shall have immunity from any liability, civil, criminal, or otherwise that might result from the action. In any proceeding, civil or criminal, arising out of a disclosure under this Section, the good faith of any rape crisis counselor or rape crisis organization who disclosed the confidential communication shall be presumed.

(f) Any rape crisis counselor who knowingly discloses any confidential communication in violation of this Act commits a Class C misdemeanor.

P.A. 82–280, § 8–802.1, added by P.A. 82–783, Art. III, § 43, eff. July 13, 1983. Amended by P.A. 83–678, § 1, eff. Jan. 1, 1984; P.A. 83–1067, § 20, eff. July 1, 1984; P.A. 83–1362, Art. II, § 109, eff. Sept. 11, 1984; P.A. 87–954, § 1, eff. Jan. 1, 1993; P.A. 88–33, § 5, eff. Jan. 1, 1994; P.A. 89–428, Art. 2, § 290, eff. Dec. 13, 1995; P.A. 89–462, Art. 2, § 290, eff. May 29, 1996; P.A. 96–1010, § 5, eff. Jan. 1, 2011; P.A. 96–1551, Art. 2, § 1085, eff. July 1, 2011; P.A. 97–1150, § 705, eff. Jan. 25, 2013.

Formerly Ill.Rev.Stat.1991, ch. 110, ¶ 8–802.1.

1 720 ILCS 5/11–0.1.

2 720 ILCS 5/11–1.20 to 5/11–1.60 or 5/12–13 to 5/12–16.

5/8–802.2. Confidentiality of statements made to personnel counseling victims of violent crime

§ 8–802.2. Confidentiality of statements made to personnel counseling victims of violent crimes. (a) Purpose. This Section is intended to protect victims of violent crimes from public disclosure of statements they make in confidence to counselors of organizations established to help them. Because of the fear and trauma that often result from violent crimes, many victims hesitate to seek help even where it is available and may therefore lack the psychological support necessary to report the crime and aid police in preventing future crimes.

(b) Definitions. As used in this Act, "violent crimes" include, but are not limited to, any felony in which force or threat of force was used against the victim or any misdemeanor which results in death or great bodily harm to the victim.

(c) Confidentiality. Where any victim of a violent crime makes a statement relating to the crime or its circumstances during the course of therapy or consultation to any counselor, employee or volunteer of a victim aid organization, the statement or contents thereof shall not be disclosed by the organization or any of its personnel unless the maker of the statement consents in writing or unless otherwise directed pursuant to this Section.

If in any judicial proceeding, a party alleges that such statements are necessary to the determination of any issue before the court and written consent to disclosure has not been given, the party may ask the court to consider the relevance and admissibility of the statements. In such a case, the court shall hold a hearing in camera on the relevance of the statements. If the court finds them relevant and admissible to the issue, the court shall order the statements to be disclosed.

P.A. 82–280, § 8–802.2, added by P.A. 86–538, § 2, eff. Jan. 1, 1990.

Formerly Ill.Rev.Stat.1991, ch. 110, ¶ 8–802.2.

5/8–802.3. Informant's privilege

§ 8–802.3. Informant's privilege.

(a) Except as provided in subsection (b), if an individual (i) submits information concerning a criminal act to a law enforcement agency or to a community organization that acts as an intermediary in reporting to law enforcement and (ii) requests anonymity, then the identity of that individual is privileged and confidential and is not subject to discovery or admissible in evidence in a proceeding.

(b) There is no privilege under subsection (a) if a court, after a hearing in camera, finds that the party seeking discovery or the proponent of the evidence has shown that:

(1) the identity of an individual who submits information concerning a criminal act is sought or offered in a court proceeding involving a felony or misdemeanor;

(2) the evidence is not otherwise available; and

(3) nondisclosure infringes upon a constitutional right of an accused, or there is a need for the evidence that substantially outweighs the interest in protecting confidentiality.

(c) The court may impose such sanctions as are necessary to enforce its order.

P.A. 82–280, § 8–802.3, added by P.A. 94–174, § 5, eff. Jan. 1, 2006.

5/8–803. Clergy

§ 8–803. Clergy. A clergyman or practitioner of any religious denomination accredited by the religious body to which he or she belongs, shall not be compelled to disclose in any court, or to any administrative board or agency, or to any public officer, a confession or admission made to him or her in his or her professional character or as a spiritual advisor in the course of the discipline enjoined by the rules or practices of such religious body or of the religion which he or she professes, nor be compelled to divulge any information which has been obtained by him or her in such professional character or as such spiritual advisor.

P.A. 82–280, § 8–803, eff. July 1, 1982.

Formerly Ill.Rev.Stat.1991, ch. 110, ¶ 8–803.

5/8–803.5. Union agent and union member

§ 8–803.5. Union agent and union member.

(a) Except when required in subsection (b) of this Section, a union agent, during the agency or representative relationship or after termination of the agency or representative relationship with the bargaining unit member, shall not be compelled to disclose, in any court or to any administrative board or agency arbitration or proceeding, whether civil or criminal, any information he or she may have acquired in attending to his or her professional duties or while acting in his or her representative capacity.

(b) A union agent may use or reveal information obtained during the course of fulfilling his or her professional representative duties:

(1) to the extent it appears necessary to prevent the commission of a crime that is likely to result in a clear, imminent risk of serious physical injury or death of another person;

(2) in actions, civil or criminal, against the union agent in his or her personal or official representa-

tive capacity, or against the local union or subordinate body thereof or international union or affiliated or subordinate body thereof or any agent thereof in their personal or official representative capacities;

(3) when required by court order; or

(4) when, after full disclosure has been provided, the written or oral consent of the bargaining unit member has been obtained or, if the bargaining unit member is deceased or has been adjudged incompetent by a court of competent jurisdiction, the written or oral consent of the bargaining unit member's estate.

(c) In the event of a conflict between the application of this Section and any federal or State labor law to a specific situation, the provisions of the federal or State labor law shall control.

P.A. 82–280, § 8–803.5, added by P.A. 94–22, § 5, eff. Jan. 1, 2006.

5/8–804. Confidential advisor

§ 8–804. Confidential advisor.

(a) This Section is intended to protect students at higher education institutions in this State who are survivors of sexual violence from public disclosure of communications they make in confidence to confidential advisors. Because of the fear, stigma, and trauma that often result from incidents of sexual violence, many survivors hesitate to report or seek help, even when it is available at no cost to them. As a result, they not only fail to receive needed medical care and emergency counseling, but may lack the psychological support necessary to report the incident of sexual violence to the higher education institution or law enforcement.

(b) In this Section:

"Confidential advisor" means a person who is employed or contracted by a higher education institution to provide emergency and ongoing support to survivors of sexual violence with the training, duties, and responsibilities described in Section 20 of the Preventing Sexual Violence in Higher Education Act.

"Higher education institution" means a public university, a public community college, or an independent, not-for-profit or for-profit higher education institution located in this State.

"Sexual violence" means physical sexual acts attempted or perpetrated against a person's will or when a person is incapable of giving consent, including without limitation rape, sexual assault, sexual battery, sexual abuse, and sexual coercion.

"Survivor" means a student who has experienced sexual violence while enrolled at a higher education institution.

(c) All communications between a confidential advisor and a survivor pertaining to an incident of sexual violence shall remain confidential, unless the survivor consents to the disclosure of the communication in writing, the disclosure falls within one of the exceptions outlined in subsection (d) of this Section, or failure to disclose the communication would violate State or federal law. Communications include all records kept by the confidential advisor in the course of providing the survivor with services related to the incident of sexual violence.

(d) The confidential advisor may disclose confidential communications between the confidential advisor and the survivor if failure to disclose would result in a clear, imminent risk of serious physical injury to or death of the survivor or another person.

The confidential advisor shall have no obligation to report crimes to the higher education institution or law enforcement, except to report to the Title IX coordinator, as defined by Title IX of the federal Education Amendments of 1972, on a monthly basis the number and type of incidents of sexual violence reported exclusively to the confidential advisor in accordance with the higher education institution's reporting requirements under subsection (b) of Section 9.21 of the Board of Higher Education Act and under federal law.

If, in any judicial proceeding, a party alleges that the communications are necessary to the determination of any issue before the court and written consent to disclosure has not been given, the party may ask the court to consider ordering the disclosure of the communications. In such a case, communications may be disclosed if the court finds, after in camera examination of the communication, that the communication is relevant, probative, and not unduly prejudicial or inflammatory or is otherwise clearly admissible; that other evidence is demonstrably unsatisfactory as evidence of the facts sought to be established by the communication or communications; and that disclosure is more important to the interests of substantial justice than protection from injury to the confidential advisor-survivor relationship, to the survivor, or to any other individual whom disclosure is likely to harm.

(e) This privilege shall not preclude an individual from asserting a greater privilege under federal or State law that applies.

P.A. 82–280, § 8–804, added by P.A. 99–426, § 85, eff. Aug. 21, 2015.

PART 9. REPORTER'S PRIVILEGE

5/8–901. Source of information

§ 8–901. Source of information. No court may compel any person to disclose the source of any information obtained by a reporter except as provided in Part 9 of Article VIII of this Act.

P.A. 82–280, § 8–901, eff. July 1, 1982. Amended by P.A. 82–783, Art. IV, § 27, eff. July 13, 1982; P.A. 83–707, § 1, eff. Sept. 23, 1983; P.A. 84–398, § 1, eff. Sept. 16, 1985.

Formerly Ill.Rev.Stat.1991, ch. 110, ¶ 8–901.

5/8–902. Definitions

§ 8–902. Definitions. As used in this Act:

(a) "reporter" means any person regularly engaged in the business of collecting, writing or editing news for publication through a news medium on a full-time or part-time basis; and includes any person who was a reporter at the time the information sought was procured or obtained.

(b) "news medium" means any newspaper or other periodical issued at regular intervals whether in print or electronic format and having a general circulation; a news service whether in print or electronic format; a radio station; a television station; a television network; a community antenna television service; and any person or corporation engaged in the making of news reels or other motion picture news for public showing.

(c) "source" means the person or means from or through which the news or information was obtained.

P.A. 82–280, § 8–902, eff. July 1, 1982. Amended by P.A. 84–398, § 1, eff. Sept. 16, 1985; P.A. 92–335, § 35, eff. Aug. 10, 2001.

Formerly Ill.Rev.Stat.1991, ch. 110, ¶ 8–902.

5/8–903. Application to court

§ 8–903. Application to court. (a) In any case, except a libel or slander case, where a person claims the privilege conferred by Part 9 of Article VIII of this Act, the person or party, body or officer seeking the information so privileged may apply in writing to the circuit court serving the county where the hearing, action or proceeding in which the information is sought for an order divesting the person named therein of such privilege and ordering him or her to disclose his or her source of the information.

(b) In libel or slander cases where a person claims the privilege conferred by Part 9 of Article VIII of this Act, the plaintiff may apply in writing to the court for an order divesting the person named therein of such privilege and ordering him or her to disclose his or her source of information.

P.A. 82–280, § 8–903, eff. July 1, 1982. Amended by P.A. 83–707, § 1, eff. Sept. 23, 1983; P.A. 84–398, § 1, eff. Sept. 16, 1985.

Formerly Ill.Rev.Stat.1991, ch. 110, ¶ 8–903.

5/8–904. Contents of application

§ 8–904. Contents of application. The application provided in Section 8–903 of this Act shall allege: the name of the reporter and of the news medium with which he or she was connected at the time the information sought was obtained; the specific information sought and its relevancy to the proceedings; and, either, a specific public interest which would be adversely affected if the factual information sought were not disclosed, or, in libel or slander cases, the necessity of disclosure of the information sought to the proof of plaintiff's case. Additionally, in libel or slander cases, the plaintiff must include in the application provided in Section 8–903 a prima facie showing of falsity of the alleged defamation and actual harm or injury due to the alleged defamation.

P.A. 82–280, § 8–904, eff. July 1, 1982. Amended by P.A. 84–398, § 1, eff. Sept. 16, 1985.

Formerly Ill.Rev.Stat.1991, ch. 110, ¶ 8–904.

5/8–905. Civil proceeding

§ 8–905. Civil proceeding. All proceedings in connection with obtaining an adjudication upon the application not otherwise provided in Part 9 of Article VIII of this Act shall be as in other civil cases.

P.A. 82–280, § 8–905, eff. July 1, 1982.

Formerly Ill.Rev.Stat.1991, ch. 110, ¶ 8–905.

5/8–906. Consideration by Court

§ 8–906. Consideration by Court. In granting or denying divestiture of the privilege provided in Part 9 of Article VIII of this Act the court shall have due regard to the nature of the proceedings, the merits of the claim or defense, the adequacy of the remedy otherwise available, if any, the relevancy of the source, and the possibility of establishing by other means that which it is alleged the source requested will tend to prove.

P.A. 82–280, § 8–906, eff. July 1, 1982. Amended by P.A. 83–707, § 1, eff. Sept. 23, 1983.

Formerly Ill.Rev.Stat.1991, ch. 110, ¶ 8–906.

5/8–907. Court's findings

§ 8–907. Court's findings. An order granting divestiture of the privilege provided in Part 9 of Article VIII of this Act shall be granted only if the court, after hearing the parties, finds:

(1) that the information sought does not concern matters, or details in any proceeding, required to be kept secret under the laws of this State or of the Federal government; and

(2) that all other available sources of information have been exhausted and, either, disclosure of the information sought is essential to the protection of the public interest involved or, in libel or slander cases,

the plaintiff's need for disclosure of the information sought outweighs the public interest in protecting the confidentiality of sources of information used by a reporter as part of the news gathering process under the particular facts and circumstances of each particular case.

If the court enters an order divesting the person of the privilege granted in Part 9 of Article VIII of this Act it shall also order the person to disclose the information it has determined should be disclosed, subject to any protective conditions as the court may deem necessary or appropriate.

P.A. 82–280, § 8–907, eff. July 1, 1982. Amended by P.A. 83–707, § 1, eff. Sept. 23, 1983; P.A. 84–398, § 1, eff. Sept. 16, 1985.

Formerly Ill.Rev.Stat.1991, ch. 110, ¶ 8–907.

5/8–908. Privilege continues during pendency of appeal

§ 8–908. Privilege continues during pendency of appeal. In case of an appeal the privilege conferred by Part 9 of Article VIII of this Act remains in full force and effect during the pendency of such appeal. P.A. 82–280, § 8–908, eff. July 1, 1982. Amended by P.A. 83–707, § 1, eff. Sept. 23, 1983.

Formerly Ill.Rev.Stat.1991, ch. 110, ¶ 8–908.

5/8–909. Contempt

§ 8–909. Contempt. A person refusing to testify or otherwise comply with the order to disclose the source of the information as specified in such order, after such order becomes final, may be adjudged in contempt of court and punished accordingly. P.A. 82–280, § 8–909, eff. July 1, 1982.

Formerly Ill.Rev.Stat.1991, ch. 110, ¶ 8–909.

PART 9.1. VOTER'S PRIVILEGE

Section
5/8–910. Voter's privilege.

Date Effective

Part 9.1 was added by P.A. 84–344, § 1, eff. Jan. 1, 1986.

5/8–910. Voter's privilege

§ 8–910. No person shall be compelled to disclose, in any proceeding conducted by a court, commission, administrative agency or other tribunal in the State, the name of any candidate for whose nomination, election or retention in office the person voted, or whether the person voted for or against any question of public policy, as defined in Section 1–3 of The Election Code,[1] at any election held within this State. P.A. 82–280, § 8–910, added by P.A. 84–344, § 1, eff. Jan. 1, 1986.

Formerly Ill.Rev.Stat.1991, ch. 110, ¶ 8–910.
[1] 10 ILCS 5/1–3.

PART 9.2. INTERPRETER'S PRIVILEGE

Section
5/8–911. Language interpreter's privilege.
5/8–912. Interpreter for the deaf and hard of hearing's privilege.

Date Effective

Part 9.2 was added by P.A. 87–409, Art. 5, § 5–5, eff. Sept. 10, 1991.

5/8–911. Language interpreter's privilege

§ 8–911. Language interpreter's privilege.

(a) A "language interpreter" is a person who aids a communication when at least one party to the communication has a language difficulty.

(b) If a communication is otherwise privileged, that underlying privilege is not waived because of the presence of the language interpreter.

(c) The language interpreter shall not disclose the communication without the express consent of the person who has the right to claim the underlying privilege.

P.A. 82–280, § 8–911, added by P.A. 87–409, Art. 5, § 5–5, eff. Sept. 10, 1991. Amended by P.A. 95–617, § 915, eff. Sept. 12, 2007.

Formerly Ill.Rev.Stat.1991, ch. 110, ¶ 8–911.

5/8–912. Interpreter for the deaf and hard of hearing's privilege

§ 8–912. Interpreter for the deaf and hard of hearing's privilege.

(a) An "interpreter for the deaf and hard of hearing" is a person who aids communication when at least one party to the communication has a hearing loss.

(b) An interpreter for the deaf and hard of hearing who interprets a conversation between a hearing person and a deaf person is deemed a conduit for the conversation and may not disclose or be compelled to disclose by subpoena the contents of the conversation that he or she facilitated without the written consent of all persons involved who received his or her professional services.

(c) All communications that are recognized by law as privileged shall remain privileged even in cases where an interpreter for the deaf and hard of hearing is utilized to facilitate such communications.

(d) Communications may be voluntarily disclosed under the following circumstances:

(1) the formal reporting, conferring, or consulting with administrative superiors, colleagues, or consultants who share similar professional responsibility, in which instance all recipients of such information

are similarly bound to regard the communication as privileged;

(2) a person waives the privilege by bringing any public charges against an interpreter for the deaf and hard of hearing, including a person licensed under the Interpreter for the Deaf Licensure Act of 2007; and

(3) a communication reveals the intended commission of a crime or harmful act and such disclosure is judged necessary by the interpreter for the deaf and hard of hearing to protect any person from a clear, imminent risk of serious mental or physical harm or injury or to forestall a serious threat to public safety.

(e) (Blank).

P.A. 82–280, § 8–912, added by P.A. 95–617, § 915, eff. Sept. 12, 2007. Amended by P.A. 96–552, § 5, eff. Jan. 1, 2010.

PART 10. JUDICIAL NOTICE

5/8–1001. Courts of original jurisdiction

§ 8–1001. Courts of original jurisdiction. Every court of original jurisdiction, in addition to the matters of which courts of original jurisdiction have heretofore been required to take judicial notice, shall take judicial notice of the following:

All general ordinances of every municipal corporation within the State.

All ordinances of every county within the State.

All laws of a public nature enacted by any state or territory of the United States.

All rules of practice in force in the court from which a case has been transferred by change of place of trial or otherwise.

P.A. 82–280, § 8–1001, eff. July 1, 1982.

Formerly Ill.Rev.Stat.1991, ch. 110, ¶ 8–1001.

5/8–1002. Courts of appellate jurisdiction

§ 8–1002. Courts of appellate jurisdiction. Upon the review by any court of appellate jurisdiction of a judgment or order of a circuit court the court of appellate jurisdiction shall take judicial notice of all matters of which the circuit court was required to take judicial notice, including all rules of practice adopted by the circuit court. In case of the review by the Supreme Court of a judgment or order of the appel-

late court, the Supreme Court shall take judicial notice of all matters of which the circuit court was required to take judicial notice as well as of the rules of practice adopted by the circuit court, the judgment or order of which has been reviewed by the appellate court.

P.A. 82–280, § 8–1002, eff. July 1, 1982.

Formerly Ill.Rev.Stat.1991, ch. 110, ¶ 8–1002.

5/8–1003. Common law and statutes

§ 8–1003. Common law and statutes. Every court of this state shall take judicial notice of the common law and statutes of every state, territory and other jurisdiction of the United States.

P.A. 82–280, § 8–1003, eff. July 1, 1982.

Formerly Ill.Rev.Stat.1991, ch. 110, ¶ 8–1003.

5/8–1004. Information of the court

§ 8–1004. Information of the court. The court may inform itself of such laws in such manner as it may deem proper, and the court may call upon counsel to aid it in obtaining such information.

P.A. 82–280, § 8–1004, eff. July 1, 1982.

Formerly Ill.Rev.Stat.1991, ch. 110, ¶ 8–1004.

5/8–1005. Ruling reviewable

§ 8–1005. Ruling reviewable. The determination of such laws shall be made by the court and not by the jury, and shall be reviewable.

P.A. 82–280, § 8–1005, eff. July 1, 1982.

Formerly Ill.Rev.Stat.1991, ch. 110, ¶ 8–1005.

5/8–1006. Evidence as to laws of other jurisdictions

§ 8–1006. Evidence as to laws of other jurisdictions. Any party may also present to the trial court any admissible evidence of such laws, but, to enable a party to offer evidence of the law in another jurisdiction or to ask that judicial notice be taken thereof, reasonable notice shall be given to the adverse parties either in the pleadings or otherwise.

P.A. 82–280, § 8–1006, eff. July 1, 1982.

Formerly Ill.Rev.Stat.1991, ch. 110, ¶ 8–1006.

5/8–1007. Foreign country

§ 8–1007. Foreign country. The law of a jurisdiction other than those referred to in Section 8–1003 of this Act shall be an issue for the court, but shall not be subject to the foregoing provisions concerning judicial notice.

P.A. 82–280, § 8–1007, eff. July 1, 1982.

Formerly Ill.Rev.Stat.1991, ch. 110, ¶ 8–1007.

5/8–1008. Interpretation

§ 8–1008. Interpretation. Sections 8–1003 through 8–1007 of this Act shall be so interpreted and construed as to effectuate its general purpose to make uniform the law of those states which enact it.

P.A. 82–280, § 8–1008, eff. July 1, 1982.

Formerly Ill.Rev.Stat.1991, ch. 110, ¶ 8–1008.

5/8–1009. Short title of uniform Act

§ 8–1009. Short title of uniform Act. Sections 8–1003 through 8–1008 of this Act may be cited as the Uniform Judicial Notice of Foreign Law Act.

P.A. 82–280, § 8–1009, eff. July 1, 1982.

Formerly Ill.Rev.Stat.1991, ch. 110, ¶ 8–1009.

PART 11. STATUTES AND REPORTS

5/8–1101. Publications covered by uniform Act

§ 8–1101. Publications covered by uniform Act. Printed books or pamphlets purporting on their face to be the session or other statutes of any of the United States, or the territories thereof, or of any foreign jurisdiction, and to have been printed and published by the authority of any such state, territory or foreign jurisdiction or proved to be commonly recognized in its courts, shall be received in the courts of this State as prima facie evidence of such statutes.

P.A. 82–280, § 8–1101, eff. July 1, 1982.

Formerly Ill.Rev.Stat.1991, ch. 110, ¶ 8–1101.

5/8–1102. Uniformity of interpretation

§ 8–1102. Uniformity of interpretation. Section 8–1101 of this Act shall be so interpreted and construed as to effectuate its general purposes to make uniform the law of those states which enact it.

P.A. 82–280, § 8–1102, eff. July 1, 1982.

Formerly Ill.Rev.Stat.1991, ch. 110, ¶ 8–1102.

5/8–1103. Short title of uniform Act

§ 8–1103. Short title of uniform Act. Sections 8–1101 and 8–1102 of this Act may be cited as the Uniform Proof of Statutes Act.

P.A. 82–280, § 8–1103, eff. July 1, 1982.

Formerly Ill.Rev.Stat.1991, ch. 110, ¶ 8–1103.

5/8–1104. Printed statutes

§ 8–1104. Printed statutes. (a) The printed statute books of the United States, and of this State, and of the several states, of the territories and late territories of the United States, purporting to be printed under the authority of the United States, any state or territory, shall be evidence in all courts and places in this State, of the Acts therein contained.

(b) The acts and laws of the territory of Illinois and all of the laws and joint resolutions passed prior to January 1, 1917, at all regular and special sessions of the General Assemblies, printed and published by the State of Illinois, shall be admissible in evidence in all courts and proceedings in this State, and shall be considered as duly authenticated copies of the originals.

P.A. 82–280, § 8–1104, eff. July 1, 1982.

Formerly Ill.Rev.Stat.1991, ch. 110, ¶ 8–1104.

5/8–1105. Foreign statutes

§ 8–1105. Foreign statutes. The laws of the other states and territories, when certified by the Secretary of State of that state or territory, shall be admissible as evidence in any court of this State.

P.A. 82–280, § 8–1105, eff. July 1, 1982. Amended by P.A. 83–520, § 1, eff. Sept. 17, 1983.

Formerly Ill.Rev.Stat.1991, ch. 110, ¶ 8–1105.

5/8–1106. Reports of courts

§ 8–1106. Reports of courts. The books of reports of decisions of the supreme court, and other courts of the United States, of this state, and of the several states and the territories thereof, purporting to be published by authority, may be read as evidence of the decisions of such courts.

P.A. 82–280, § 8–1106, eff. July 1, 1982.

Formerly Ill.Rev.Stat.1991, ch. 110, ¶ 8–1106.

PART 12. RECORDS AND PATENTS

5/8–1201. Printed copies

§ 8–1201. Printed copies. Printed copies of schedules, classifications and tariffs of rates, fares and charges, and supplements to any such schedules, classifications and tariffs filed with the Interstate Commerce Commission, which show respectively an Interstate Commerce Commission number, which may be stated in abbreviated form, as I.C.C. No. _____, and an effective date, shall be presumed to be correct copies of the original schedules, classifications, tariffs and supplements on file with the Interstate Commerce Commission, and shall be received as good and sufficient evidence, without certification, in any court of this State to prove such schedules, classifications, tariffs and supplements.

P.A. 82–280, § 8–1201, eff. July 1, 1982.

Formerly Ill.Rev.Stat.1991, ch. 110, ¶ 8–1201.

5/8–1202. Court records

§ 8–1202. Court records. The papers, entries and records of courts may be proved by a copy thereof certified under the signature of the clerk having the custody thereof, and the seal of the court, or by the judge of the court if there is no clerk.

P.A. 82–280, § 8–1202, eff. July 1, 1982. Amended by P.A. 83–707, § 1, eff. Sept. 23, 1983.

Formerly Ill.Rev.Stat.1991, ch. 110, ¶ 8–1202.

5/8–1203. Municipal records

§ 8–1203. Municipal records. The papers, entries, records and ordinances, or parts thereof, of any city, village, town or county, may be proved by a copy thereof, certified under the signature of the clerk or the keeper thereof, and the corporate seal, if there is any; if not, under his or her signature and private seal.

P.A. 82–280, § 8–1203, eff. July 1, 1982. Amended by P.A. 83–707, § 1, eff. Sept. 23, 1983.

Formerly Ill.Rev.Stat.1991, ch. 110, ¶ 8–1203.

5/8–1204. Corporate records

§ 8–1204. Corporate records. The papers, entries and records of any corporation or incorporated association may be proved by a copy thereof, certified under the signature of the secretary, clerk, cashier or other keeper of the same. If the corporation or incorporated association has a seal, the same shall be affixed to such certificate.

P.A. 82–280, § 8–1204, eff. July 1, 1982.

Formerly Ill.Rev.Stat.1991, ch. 110, ¶ 8–1204.

5/8–1205. Form of certificate

§ 8–1205. Form of certificate. The certificate of any such clerk of a court, city, village, town, county, or secretary, clerk, cashier or other keeper of any such papers, entries, records or ordinances, shall contain a statement that such person is the keeper of the same, and if there is no seal, shall so state.

P.A. 82–280, § 8–1205, eff. July 1, 1982.

Formerly Ill.Rev.Stat.1991, ch. 110, ¶ 8–1205.

5/8–1206. Sworn copies

§ 8–1206. Sworn copies. Any such papers, entries, records and ordinances may be proved by copies examined and sworn to by credible witnesses.

P.A. 82–280, § 8–1206, eff. July 1, 1982.

Formerly Ill.Rev.Stat.1991, ch. 110, ¶ 8–1206.

5/8–1207. Penalty

§ 8–1207. Penalty. If any officer, clerk, secretary, cashier, or other person authorized to certify copies of any papers, entries, records or ordinances, knowingly makes a false certificate, he or she is punishable in the same manner as if he or she were guilty of perjury.

P.A. 82–280, § 8–1207, eff. July 1, 1982.

Formerly Ill.Rev.Stat.1991, ch. 110, ¶ 8–1207.

5/8–1208. Official certificate—Land office

§ 8–1208. Official certificate—Land office. The official certificate of any register or receiver of any land office of the United States, to any fact or matter on record in his or her office, shall be received in evidence in any court in this State, and shall be competent to prove the fact so certified. The certificate of any such register, of the entry or purchase of any tract of land within his or her district, shall be deemed and taken to be evidence of title in the party who made such entry or purchase, or his or her legatees, heirs or assigns, and shall enable such party, his or her legatees, heirs or assigns, to recover or protect the possession of the land described in such certificate, in any action of ejectment or forcible entry and detainer, unless a better legal and paramount title be exhibited for the same. The signature of such register or receiver may be proved by a certificate of the Secretary of State, under his or her seal, that such signature is genuine.

P.A. 82–280, § 8–1208, eff. July 1, 1982. Amended by P.A. 83–707, § 1, eff. Sept. 23, 1983.

Formerly Ill.Rev.Stat.1991, ch. 110, ¶ 8–1208.

5/8–1209. Patents for land

§ 8–1209. Patents for land. A patent for land shall be deemed and considered a better legal and paramount title in the patentee, his or her legatees, heirs or assigns, than the official certificate of any register of a land office of the United States, of the entry or purchase of the same land.

P.A. 82–280, § 8–1209, eff. July 1, 1982. Amended by P.A. 83–707, § 1, eff. Sept. 23, 1983.

Formerly Ill.Rev.Stat.1991, ch. 110, ¶ 8–1209.

5/8–1210. State patents

§ 8–1210. State patents. In all cases where any lands or lots have been or may be sold by this State or any of the officers thereof, under the authority of any law of this State, whereof the patent is issued by the Governor, under the seal of this State, and in case the patent has been or shall purport to be recorded in the recorder's office of the county where the lands or lots are situated, and the patent is lost, or out of the power of the party desiring to use it to produce in evidence, a copy of the record of such patent, certified by the recorder of the county, may be read in evidence in place of the original patent, which copy certified as above stated, shall be prima facie evidence of the issuing of such patent, and of the contents thereof. The provisions of this section shall apply to deeds executed by the trustees of the Illinois and Michigan canal, and to patents for land issued or granted by the United States.

P.A. 82–280, § 8–1210, eff. July 1, 1982. Amended by P.A. 83–707, § 1, eff. Sept. 23, 1983.

Formerly Ill.Rev.Stat.1991, ch. 110, ¶ 8–1210.

5/8–1211. State land sales

§ 8–1211. State land sales. Copies of the books and entries of the sale of all lands or lots heretofore or that hereafter may be sold by this State or any of the officers thereof under any law of this State, certified to be true and correct copies of such books and entries by the proper person or officer in whose custody said books and entries may properly be, shall be prima facie evidence of the facts stated in such books and entries. The certificate of such officer of the purchase of or issuing of a patent for any tract of land sold by this State or any agent of the same, shall be deemed as evidence of title in the party certified to have made such purchase or obtained such patent, his or her legatees, heirs or assigns, unless a better and paramount title is exhibited for the same. The patent for land shall be deemed a better and paramount title in the patentee, his or her legatees, heirs and assigns, than such certificate, and when any swamp and overflowed lands and lots heretofore have been or hereafter may be sold under any law of this State by any proper person or officer of the county in which such lands are located, copies of the books and entries of the sales of such swamp and overflowed lands and lots certified to be true and correct copies of such books and entries by the proper person or officer in whose custody such books and entries may properly be, shall be prima facie evidence of the facts stated in such books and entries. The certificate of such officer of the sale or entry of any tract or tracts of such swamp and overflowed land or lots and of the execution of a deed for the same, giving the date of such sale or entry, the date of the execution of the deed, the name of the purchaser and description of the land, under the seal of his or her office, may, if the original deed is lost, or it is out of the power of the party wishing to use the same to produce it in evidence, and the original deed has never been recorded, be read in evidence in place of said original deed, and shall be prima facie evidence of the execution and delivery of a proper deed for such land and shall be deemed as evidence of title in the person certified to have made such entry or purchase, his or her legatees, heirs and assigns, until a better and paramount title is exhibited for the same. Whenever it appears that the original deed made upon any entry or sale of such swamp and overflowed lands is lost, or not in the power of the party wishing to use the same to produce in evidence, and the same has never been recorded as above stated and that the books and original entries of sale of such swamp and overflowed lands or lots have also been lost or destroyed, and the clerk of the circuit court or other proper officer has made return of such sales and entries to the State Comptroller according to law, a certified copy of such return by the Comptroller, under his or her seal of office, may be used in evidence with the like force and effect as hereinbefore provided.

P.A. 82–280, § 8–1211, eff. July 1, 1982. Amended by P.A. 83–707, § 1, eff. Sept. 23, 1983; P.A. 86–657, § 3, eff. Jan. 1, 1990.

Formerly Ill.Rev.Stat.1991, ch. 110, ¶ 8–1211.

PART 13. SURVEYS

Section
5/8–1301. Surveys.

5/8–1301. Surveys

§ 8–1301. Surveys. All testimony that has been or may hereafter be taken by commissions of surveyors for the establishing of original corners of land, shall be filed with their report in court, and may hereafter be read as evidence in all actions in reference to such corners.

P.A. 82–280, § 8–1301, eff. July 1, 1982.

Formerly Ill.Rev.Stat.1991, ch. 110, ¶ 8–1301.

PART 14. INTERPRETERS

Section
5/8–1401. Language interpreter.
5/8–1402. Accommodation for hearing disability.
5/8–1403. Interpreters for civil cases.

5/8–1401. Language interpreter

§ 8–1401. Language interpreter. Interpreters may be sworn truly to interpret, when necessary.

P.A. 82–280, § 8–1401, eff. July 1, 1982.

Formerly Ill.Rev.Stat.1991, ch. 110, ¶ 8–1401.

5/8–1402. Accommodation for hearing disability

§ 8–1402. Accommodation for hearing disability. Whenever any deaf person is a party to any legal proceeding of any nature, or a juror or witness therein, the court in all instances shall appoint a qualified interpreter of the deaf sign-language to interpret the proceedings to and the testimony of such deaf person. In the case of a deaf juror, the interpreter shall be available throughout the actual trial and may accompany and communicate with such juror throughout any period during which the jury is sequestered or engaged in its deliberations. Accommodations shall be made in accordance with the federal Americans with Disabilities Act of 1990 [1] so that a qualified individual with a hearing disability may participate as a party, witness, juror, or spectator in any legal proceeding. The court shall determine and allow a reasonable fee for all services provided under this Section which shall be paid out of general county funds.

P.A. 82–280, § 8–1402, eff. July 1, 1982. Amended by P.A. 83–461, § 3, eff. Jan. 1, 1984; P.A. 91–381, § 5, eff. Jan. 1, 2000.

Formerly Ill.Rev.Stat.1991, ch. 110, ¶ 8–1402.

[1] 42 U.S.C.A. § 12101 et seq.

5/8–1403. Interpreters for civil cases

§ 8–1403. Interpreters for civil cases.

(a) Whenever any person is a party or witness in a civil action in this State, the court shall, upon its own motion or that of a party, determine whether the person is capable of understanding the English language and is capable of expressing himself or herself in the English language so as to be understood directly by counsel, court, or jury. If the court finds the person incapable of so understanding or so expressing himself or herself, the court shall appoint an interpreter for the person whom he or she can understand and who can understand him or her. All appointments for court interpreters in civil matters shall be pursuant to the Illinois Supreme Court Language Access Policy and the judicial circuit's Language Access Plan that is appropriate for the demands and resources specific to the Illinois courts within that particular circuit.

(b) The court shall enter an order of its appointment of the interpreter who shall be sworn to truly interpret or translate all questions propounded or answers given as directed by the court.

(c) As used in this Section, "interpreter" includes a sign language interpreter.

P.A. 82–280, § 8–1403, added by P.A. 99–133, § 5, eff. Jan. 1, 2016.

PART 15. PROOF OF HANDWRITING

Section
5/8–1501. Comparison.

Section
5/8–1502. Notice.
5/8–1503. Opportunity to examine.

5/8–1501. Comparison

§ 8–1501. Comparison. In all courts of this State it shall be lawful to prove handwriting by comparison made by the witness or jury with writings properly in the files of records of the case, admitted in evidence or treated as genuine or admitted to be genuine, by the party against whom the evidence is offered, or proved to be genuine to the satisfaction of the court.

P.A. 82–280, § 8–1501, eff. July 1, 1982.

Formerly Ill.Rev.Stat.1991, ch. 110, ¶ 8–1501.

5/8–1502. Notice

§ 8–1502. Notice. Before a standard of writing is admitted in evidence by the court for comparison, such notice thereof as under all circumstances of the case is reasonable shall first be given to the opposite party or his or her attorney.

P.A. 82–280, § 8–1502, eff. July 1, 1982.

Formerly Ill.Rev.Stat.1991, ch. 110, ¶ 8–1502.

5/8–1503. Opportunity to examine

§ 8–1503. Opportunity to examine. A reasonable opportunity to examine such proposed standards shall on motion duly made be accorded the opposite party, his or her attorney and witnesses, prior to the introduction in evidence of such standards and the court may, in its discretion, impound the same with the clerk of the court for that purpose.

P.A. 82–280, § 8–1503, eff. July 1, 1982.

Formerly Ill.Rev.Stat.1991, ch. 110, ¶ 8–1503.

PART 16. PROOF OF DEEDS AND WRITINGS

Section
5/8–1601. Execution of deed.

5/8–1601. Execution of deed

§ 8–1601. Execution of deed. Whenever any deed, mortgage, conveyance, release, power of attorney or other writing of, or relating to the sale, conveyance or other disposition of real estate, or any interest therein, or any other instrument in writing not required by law to be attested by a subscribing witness, may be offered in evidence in any action pending in any court of this state, and the same appears to have been so attested, and it becomes necessary to prove the execution of such deed or other writing otherwise than as now provided by law, it shall not be necessary to prove the execution of the same by a subscribing witness to the exclusion of other evidence, but the execution of such instrument may be proved by secondary evidence without producing or accounting for the absence of the subscribing witness or witnesses.

P.A. 82–280, § 8–1601, eff. July 1, 1982.

Formerly Ill.Rev.Stat.1991, ch. 110, ¶ 8–1601.

PART 17. TITLE TO LAND OF ILLINOIS CENTRAL RAILROAD

Section
5/8–1701. Commissioner's tract list, map, etc.—Evidence.
5/8–1702. Appointment of trustees.

5/8–1701. Commissioner's tract list, map, etc.— Evidence

§ 8–1701. Commissioner's tract list, map, etc.— Evidence. Whenever it becomes necessary, in any judicial proceeding, to prove the title of the Illinois Central Railroad Company, or of the trustees of the railroad company, or of any person claiming title through or under the company or trustees, to any of the lands granted by the State to the railroad company under the provisions of the Act incorporating such company, the record in the proper county (or a transcript of such record, duly certified by the custodian thereof), of the list purporting to contain the tracts of land selected by the railroad company in such county, and purporting to be certified by the commissioner of the general land office as being a true abstract from the original list of selections by the company, shall be sufficient prima facie evidence of title in the railroad company or the trustees thereof, as the case may be, to the lands embraced in such list; and the record in the proper county (or a duly certified copy thereof by the custodian of such record) of the map or profile of the railroad or branches, shall be sufficient prima facie evidence of the line of location of the railroad or its branches in such county.

P.A. 82–280, § 8–1701, eff. July 1, 1982.

Formerly Ill.Rev.Stat.1991, ch. 110, ¶ 8–1701.

5/8–1702. Appointment of trustees

§ 8–1702. Appointment of trustees. A copy of the commission issued by the governor or by the president of the railroad company to any successor of any of the original trustees (or any of their successors) named in the Act of incorporation, certified by the Secretary of State under the great seal of the State, or by the commissioner of the land department of the railroad company or its president, under the common seal of the company, as the case may be, shall be sufficient prima facie evidence of the regular appointment and due authority of the person named as trustee in such commission.

P.A. 82–280, § 8–1702, eff. July 1, 1982.

Formerly Ill.Rev.Stat.1991, ch. 110, ¶ 8–1702.

PART 18. CLAIMS REGARDING WORK ON REALTY

Section
5/8–1801. Presumptive proof.

5/8–1801. Presumptive proof

§ 8–1801. Presumptive proof. Any work or service on real property or any product incorporated therein to become part of such real property which does not cause injury or property damage within 6 years after such performance, manufacture, assembly, engineering or design, shall be presumptive proof that such work, service or product was performed, manufactured, assembled, engineered or designed with reasonable care by every person doing any of such acts. However, all written guarantees are excluded from this Section.

P.A. 82–280, § 8–1801, eff. July 1, 1982.

Formerly Ill.Rev.Stat.1991, ch. 110, ¶ 8–1801.

PART 19. ADMISSION OF LIABILITY

Section
5/8–1901. Admission of liability—Effect.

5/8–1901. Admission of liability—Effect

§ 8–1901. Admission of liability - Effect. The providing of, or payment for, medical, surgical, hospital, or rehabilitation services, facilities, or equipment by or on behalf of any person, or the offer to provide, or pay for, any one or more of the foregoing, shall not be construed as an admission of any liability by such person or persons. Testimony, writings, records, reports or information with respect to the foregoing shall not be admissible in evidence as an admission of any liability in any action of any kind in any court or before any commission, administrative agency, or other tribunal in this State, except at the instance of the person or persons so making any such provision, payment or offer.

P.A. 82–280, § 8–1901, eff. July 1, 1982. Amended by P.A. 94–677, § 330, eff. Aug. 25, 2005. Re-enacted by P.A. 97–1145, § 5, eff. Jan. 18, 2013.

Formerly Ill.Rev.Stat.1991, ch. 110, ¶ 8–1901.

Validity

P.A. 94–677, effective August 25, 2005, a comprehensive revision of the law relating to health care and medical malpractice actions, is unconstitutional in its entirety because (i) provisions limiting the recovery of damages for non-economic losses in medical malpractice actions violate the separation of powers principle of the Illinois Constitution (IL-CON Art. II, Sec. 1) and (ii) other provisions are inseverable. Lebron v. Gottlieb Memori-

al Hospital, 237 Ill.2d 217 (2010). P.A. 97–1145 re-enacted this section so as to remove any question as to its validity.

PART 20. INSPECTION OF RECORDS

Date Amended

P.A. 92–228, § 5, eff. September 1, 2001, changed the heading of Part 20 from "Inspection of Hospital Records" to "Inspection of Records"

5/8–2001. Examination of health care records

§ 8–2001. Examination of health care records.

(a) In this Section:

"Health care facility" or "facility" means a public or private hospital, ambulatory surgical treatment center, nursing home, independent practice association, or physician hospital organization, or any other entity where health care services are provided to any person. The term does not include a health care practitioner.

"Health care practitioner" means any health care practitioner, including a physician, dentist, podiatric physician, advanced practice nurse, physician assistant, clinical psychologist, or clinical social worker. The term includes a medical office, health care clinic, health department, group practice, and any other organizational structure for a licensed professional to provide health care services. The term does not include a health care facility.

(b) Every private and public health care facility shall, upon the request of any patient who has been treated in such health care facility, or any person, entity, or organization presenting a valid authorization for the release of records signed by the patient or the patient's legally authorized representative, or as authorized by Section 8–2001.5, permit the patient, his or her health care practitioner, authorized attorney, or any person, entity, or organization presenting a valid authorization for the release of records signed by the patient or the patient's legally authorized representative to examine the health care facility patient care records, including but not limited to the history, bedside notes, charts, pictures and plates, kept in connection with the treatment of such patient, and permit copies of such records to be made by him or her or his or her health care practitioner or authorized attorney.

(c) Every health care practitioner shall, upon the request of any patient who has been treated by the health care practitioner, or any person, entity, or organization presenting a valid authorization for the release of records signed by the patient or the patient's legally authorized representative, permit the patient and the patient's health care practitioner or authorized attorney, or any person, entity, or organization presenting a valid authorization for the release of records signed by the patient or the patient's legally authorized representative, to examine and copy the patient's records, including but not limited to those relating to the diagnosis, treatment, prognosis, history, charts, pictures and plates, kept in connection with the treatment of such patient.

(d) A request for copies of the records shall be in writing and shall be delivered to the administrator or manager of such health care facility or to the health care practitioner. The person (including patients, health care practitioners and attorneys) requesting copies of records shall reimburse the facility or the health care practitioner at the time of such copying for all reasonable expenses, including the costs of independent copy service companies, incurred in connection with such copying not to exceed a $20 handling charge for processing the request and the actual postage or shipping charge, if any, plus: (1) for paper copies 75 cents per page for the first through 25th pages, 50 cents per page for the 26th through 50th pages, and 25 cents per page for all pages in excess of 50 (except that the charge shall not exceed $1.25 per page for any copies made from microfiche or microfilm; records retrieved from scanning, digital imaging, electronic information or other digital format do not qualify as microfiche or microfilm retrieval for purposes of calculating charges); and (2) for electronic records, retrieved from a scanning, digital imaging, electronic information or other digital format in an electronic document, a charge of 50% of the per page charge for paper copies under subdivision (d)(1). This per page charge includes the cost of each CD Rom, DVD, or other storage media. Records already maintained in an electronic or digital format shall be provided in an electronic format when so requested. If the records system does not allow for the creation or transmission of an electronic or digital record, then the facility or practitioner shall inform the requester in writing of the reason the records can not be provided electronically. The written explanation may be included with the production of paper copies, if the requester chooses to order paper copies. These rates shall be automatically adjusted as set forth in Section 8–2006. The facility or health care practitioner may, however, charge for the reasonable cost of all duplication of record material or information that cannot routinely be copied or duplicated on a standard commercial photocopy machine such as x-ray films or pictures.

(d–5) The handling fee shall not be collected from the patient or the patient's personal representative who obtains copies of records under Section 8–2001.5.

(e) The requirements of this Section shall be satisfied within 30 days of the receipt of a written request by a patient or by his or her legally authorized representative, health care practitioner, authorized attorney, or any person, entity, or organization presenting a valid authorization for the release of records signed by the patient or the patient's legally authorized representative. If the facility or health care practitioner needs more time to comply with the request, then within 30 days after receiving the request, the facility or health care practitioner must provide the requesting party with a written statement of the reasons for the delay and the date by which the requested information will be provided. In any event, the facility or health care practitioner must provide the requested information no later than 60 days after receiving the request.

(f) A health care facility or health care practitioner must provide the public with at least 30 days prior notice of the closure of the facility or the health care practitioner's practice. The notice must include an explanation of how copies of the facility's records may be accessed by patients. The notice may be given by publication in a newspaper of general circulation in the area in which the health care facility or health care practitioner is located.

(g) Failure to comply with the time limit requirement of this Section shall subject the denying party to expenses and reasonable attorneys' fees incurred in connection with any court ordered enforcement of the provisions of this Section.

P.A. 82–280, § 8–2001, eff. July 1, 1982. Amended by P.A. 84–7, § 1, eff. Aug. 15, 1985; P.A. 89–7, § 15, eff. March 9, 1995; P.A. 92–228, § 5, eff. Sept. 1, 2001; P.A. 93–87, § 5, eff. July 2, 2003; P.A. 94–155, § 5, eff. Jan. 1, 2006; P.A. 95–478, § 5, eff. Jan. 1, 2008; P.A. 95–480, § 5, eff. Jan. 1, 2008; P.A. 97–623, § 5, eff. Nov. 23, 2011; P.A. 97–867, § 5, eff. July 30, 2012; P.A. 98–214, § 110, eff. Aug. 9, 2013; P.A. 98–756, § 725, eff. July 16, 2014.

Formerly Ill.Rev.Stat.1991, ch. 110, ¶ 8–2001.

Validity

Public Act 89–7, which amended this section, has been held unconstitutional in its entirety by the Illinois Supreme Court in the case of Best v. Taylor Machine Works, 1997, 689 N.E.2d 1057, 228 Ill.Dec. 636, 179 Ill.2d 367. Later amendments did not included the amendment by P.A. 89–7.

P.A. 89–7, in the paragraph permitting the examination of records, inserted "or the holder of a Consent pursuant to Section 2–1003" in three places and made a nonsubstantive change; and added the paragraph relating to the applicability of this amendatory Act.

Prior to the amendment by P.A. 89–7, this section read:

"Examination of records. Every private and public hospital shall, upon the request of any patient who has been treated in such hospital and after his or her discharge therefrom, permit the patient, his or her physician or authorized attorney to examine the hospital records, including but not limited to the history, bedside notes, charts, pictures and plates, kept in connection with the treatment of such patient, and permit copies of such records to be made by him or her or his or her physician or authorized attorney. A request for examination of the records shall be in writing and shall be delivered to the administrator of such hospital.

"The requirements of this Section shall be satisfied within 60 days of the receipt of a request by a patient, for his or her physician, authorized attorney, or own person.

"Failure to comply with the time limit requirement of this Section shall subject the denying party to expenses and reasonable attorneys' fees incurred in connection with any court ordered enforcement of the provisions of this Section."

As amended by P.A. 89–7, § 15 this section read:

"§ 8–2001. Examination of records. Every private and public hospital shall, upon the request of any patient who has been treated in such hospital and after his or her discharge therefrom, permit the patient or his or her physician or authorized attorney or the holder of a Consent pursuant to Section 2–1003 to examine the hospital records, including but not limited to the history, bedside notes, charts, pictures and plates, kept in connection with the treatment of such patient, and permit copies of such records to be made by him or her or his or her physician or authorized attorney or the holder of a Consent pursuant to Section 2–1003. A request for examination of the records shall be in writing and shall be delivered to the administrator of such hospital.

"The requirements of this Section shall be satisfied within 60 days of the receipt of a request by a patient, for his or her physician, authorized attorney, or own person or the holder of a Consent pursuant to Section 2– 1003.

"Failure to comply with the time limit requirement of this Section shall subject the denying party to expenses and reasonable attorneys' fees incurred in connection with any court ordered enforcement of the provisions of this Section.

"This amendatory Act of 1995 applies to causes of action filed on or after its effective date."

Section 995 of P.A. 89–7, approved March 9, 1995, provides:

"Effective date. This Act takes effect upon becoming law, and applies to causes of action as specified in each Section or part of this Act."

P.A. 95–478, § 5, rewrote this section, which prior thereto read:

"§ 8–2001. Examination of records.

"In this Section, 'health care facility' or 'facility' means a public or private hospital, ambulatory surgical treatment center, nursing home, independent practice association, or physician hospital organization, or any other entity where health care services are provided to any person. The term does not include an organizational structure whose records are subject to Section 8–2003.

"Every private and public health care facility shall, upon the request of any patient who has been treated in such health care facility, or any person, entity, or organization presenting a valid authorization for the release of records signed by the patient or the patient's legally authorized representative, permit the patient, his or her physician, authorized attorney, or any person, entity, or organization presenting a valid authorization for the release of records signed by the patient or the patient's legally authorized representative to examine the health care facility patient care records, including but not limited to the history, bedside notes, charts, pictures and plates, kept in connection with the treatment of such patient, and permit copies of such records to be made by him or her or his or her physician or authorized attorney. A request for copies of the records shall be in writing and shall be delivered to the administrator or manager of such health care facility. The health care facility shall be reimbursed by the person requesting copies of records at the time of such copying for all reasonable expenses, including the costs of independent copy service companies, incurred by the health care facility in connection with such copying not to exceed a $20 handling charge for processing the request for copies, and 75 cents per page for the first through 25th pages, 50 cents per page for the 26th through 50th pages, and 25 cents per page for all pages in excess of 50 (except that the charge shall not exceed $1.25 per page for any copies made from microfiche or microfilm), and actual shipping costs. These rates shall be automatically adjusted as set forth in Section 8-2006. The health care facility may, however, charge for the reasonable cost of all duplication of record material or information that cannot routinely be copied or duplicated on a standard commercial photocopy machine such as x-ray films or pictures.

"The requirements of this Section shall be satisfied within 30 days of the receipt of a written request by a patient or by his or her legally authorized representative, physician, authorized attorney, or any person, entity, or organization presenting a valid authorization for the release of records signed by the patient or the patient's legally authorized representative. If the health care facility needs more time to comply with the request, then within 30 days after receiving the request, the facility must provide the requesting party with a written statement of the reasons for the delay and the date by which the requested information will be provided. In any event, the facility must provide the requested information no later than 60 days after receiving the request.

"A health care facility must provide the public with at least 30 days prior notice of the closure of the facility. The notice must include an explanation of how copies of the facility's records may be accessed by patients. The notice may be given by publication in a newspaper of general circulation in the area in which the health care facility is located.

"Failure to comply with the time limit requirement of this Section shall subject the denying party to expenses and reasonable attorneys' fees incurred in connection with any court ordered enforcement of the provisions of this Section."

P.A. 95–480, § 5, in subsec. (d), substituted "50% of the per page charge for paper copies under subdivision (d)(1). This per page charge includes the cost of" for "75 cents for" and inserted the sixth sentence to read: "The written explanation may be included with the production of paper copies, if the requester chooses to order paper copies."

5/8–2001.5. Authorization for release of a deceased patient's records

§ 8–2001.5. Authorization for release of a deceased patient's records.

(a) In addition to disclosure allowed under Section 8–802, a deceased person's health care records must be released upon written request of the executor or administrator of the deceased person's estate or to an agent appointed by the deceased under a power of attorney for health care. When no executor, administrator, or agent exists, and the person did not specifically object to disclosure of his or her records in writing, then a deceased person's health care records must be released upon the written request of a person, who is considered to be a personal representative of the patient for the purpose of the release of a deceased patient's health care records, in one of these categories:

(1) the deceased person's surviving spouse; or

(2) if there is no surviving spouse, any one or more of the following: (i) an adult son or daughter of the deceased, (ii) a parent of the deceased, or (iii) an adult brother or sister of the deceased.

(b) Health care facilities and practitioners are authorized to provide a copy of a deceased patient's records based upon a person's payment of the statutory fee and signed "Authorized Relative Certification", attesting to the fact that the person is authorized to receive such records under this Section.

(c) Any person who, in good faith, relies on a copy of an Authorized Relative Certification shall have the same immunities from criminal and civil liability as those who rely on a power of attorney for health care as provided by Illinois law.

(d) Upon request for records of a deceased patient, the named authorized relative shall provide the facility or practitioner with a certified copy of the death certificate and a certification in substantially the following form:

AUTHORIZED RELATIVE CERTIFICATION

I, (insert name of authorized relative), certify that I am an authorized relative of the deceased (insert name of deceased). (A certified copy of the death certificate must be attached.)

I certify that to the best of my knowledge and belief that no executor or administrator has been appointed for the deceased's estate, that no agent was authorized to act for the deceased under a power of attorney for health care, and the deceased has not specifically objected to disclosure in writing.

I certify that I am the surviving spouse of the deceased; or

I certify that there is no surviving spouse and my relationship to the deceased is (circle one):

(1) An adult son or daughter of the deceased.

(2) Either parent of the deceased.

(3) An adult brother or sister of the deceased.

I certify that I am seeking the records as a personal representative who is acting in a representative capacity and who is authorized to seek these records under Section 8–2001.5 of the Code of Civil Procedure.

This certification is made under penalty of perjury.*

Dated: (insert date)

. . . .
(Print Authorized Relative's Name)

. . . .
(Authorized Relative's Signature)

. . . .
(Authorized Relative's Address)

* (Note: Perjury is defined in Section 32–2 of the Criminal Code of 2012, and is a Class 3 felony.)

P.A. 82–280, § 8–2001.5, added by P.A. 97–623, § 5, eff. Nov. 23, 2011. Amended by P.A. 97–867, § 5, eff. July 30, 2012; P.A. 97–1150, § 705, eff. Jan. 25, 2013.

P.A. 97–1150 incorporated the amendments by P.A. 97–623 and 97–867.

5/8–2002. Application

§ 8–2002. Application.

(a) Part 20 of Article VIII of this Act does not apply to the records of patients, inmates, or persons being examined, observed or treated in any institution, division, program or service now existing, or hereafter acquired or created under the jurisdiction of the Department of Human Services as successor to the Department of Mental Health and Developmental

Disabilities and the Department of Alcoholism and Substance Abuse, or over which, in that capacity, the Department of Human Services exercises executive or administrative supervision.

(b) In the event of a conflict between the application of Part 20 of Article VIII of this Act and the Mental Health and Developmental Disabilities Confidentiality Act [1] or subsection (bb) of Section 30–5 of the Alcoholism and Other Drug Abuse and Dependency Act [2] to a specific situation, the provisions of the Mental Health and Developmental Disabilities Confidentiality Act or subsection (bb) of Section 30–5 of the Alcoholism and Other Drug Abuse and Dependency Act shall control. The provisions of federal law concerning the confidentiality of alcohol and drug abuse patient records, as contained in Title 21 of the United States Code, Section 1175; Title 42 of the United States Code, Section 4582; 42 CFR Part 2; and any other regulations promulgated pursuant thereto, all as now or hereafter amended, shall supersede all other laws and regulations concerning such confidentiality, except where any such otherwise applicable laws or regulations are more stringent, in which case the most stringent shall apply.

P.A. 82–280, § 8–2002, eff. July 1, 1982. Amended by P.A. 83–707, § 1, eff. Sept. 23, 1983; P.A. 83–969, Art. VI, § 62, eff. July 1, 1984; P.A. 83–1362, Art. II, § 109, eff. Sept. 11, 1984; P.A. 85–965, Art. XII, § 6, eff. July 1, 1988; P.A. 88–670, Art. 3, § 3–87, eff. Dec. 2, 1994; P.A. 89–507, Art. 90, § 90D–90, eff. July 1, 1997.

Formerly Ill.Rev.Stat.1991, ch. 110, ¶ 8–2002.

[1] 740 ILCS 110/1 et seq.

[2] 20 ILCS 301/30–5.

5/8–2003. § 8–2003. Repealed by P.A. 95–478, § 90, eff. Jan. 1, 2008

5/8–2004. § 8–2004. Repealed by P.A. 93–87, § 6, eff. July 2, 2003

5/8–2005. Attorney's records

§ 8–2005. Attorney's records. This Section applies only if a client and his or her authorized attorney have complied with all applicable legal requirements regarding examination and copying of client files, including but not limited to satisfaction of expenses and attorney retaining liens.

Upon the request of a client, an attorney shall permit the client's authorized attorney to examine and copy the records kept by the attorney in connection with the representation of the client, with the exception of attorney work product. The request for examination and copying of the records shall be in writing and shall be delivered to the attorney. Within a reasonable time after the attorney receives the written request, the attorney shall comply with the written request at his or her office or any other place designated by him or her. At the time of copying, the person requesting the records shall reimburse the attorney for all reasonable expenses, including the costs of independent copy service companies, incurred by the attorney in connection with the copying not to exceed a $20 handling charge for processing the request, and the actual postage or shipping charges, if any, plus (1) for paper copies 75 cents per page for the first through 25th pages, 50 cents per page for the 26th through 50th pages, and 25 cents per page for all pages in excess of 50 (except that the charge shall not exceed $1.25 per page for any copies made from microfiche or microfilm; records retrieved from scanning, digital imaging, electronic information or other digital format do not qualify as microfiche or microfilm retrieval for purposes of calculating charges); and (2) for electronic records, retrieved from a scanning, digital imaging, electronic information or other digital format in an electronic document, a charge of 50% of the per page charge for paper copies under subdivision (d)(1). This per page charge includes the cost of each CD Rom, DVD, or other storage media. Records already maintained in an electronic or digital format shall be provided in an electronic format when so requested. If the records system does not allow for the creation or transmission of an electronic or digital record, then the attorney shall inform the requester in writing of the reason the records cannot be provided electronically. The written explanation may be included with the production of paper copies, if the requester chooses to order paper copies. These rates shall be automatically adjusted as set forth in Section 8–2006. The attorney may, however, charge for the reasonable cost of all duplication of record material or information that cannot routinely be copied or duplicated on a standard commercial photocopy machine such as pictures.

An attorney shall satisfy the requirements of this Section within 60 days after he or she receives a request from a client or his or her authorized attorney. An attorney who fails to comply with the time limit requirement of this Section shall be required to pay expenses and reasonable attorney's fees incurred in connection with any court-ordered enforcement of the requirements of this Section.

P.A. 82–280, § 8–2005, added by P.A. 92–228, § 5, eff. Sept. 1, 2001. Amended by P.A. 95–478, § 5, eff. Jan. 1, 2008; P.A. 95–480, § 5, eff. Jan. 1, 2008; P.A. 98–756, § 725, eff. July 16, 2014.

5/8–2006. Copying fees; adjustment for inflation

§ 8–2006. Copying fees; adjustment for inflation. Beginning in 2003, every January 20, the copying fee limits established in Sections 8–2001 and 8–2005 shall automatically be increased or decreased, as applicable, by a percentage equal to the percentage change in the consumer price index-u during the preceding 12-month calendar year. "Consumer price index-u" means the index published by the Bureau of Labor Statistics of the United States Department of Labor that measures the average change in prices of goods and services purchased by all urban consumers, United States city average, all items, 1982-84 = 100. The new amount resulting from each annual adjustment shall be determined by the Comptroller and made available to the public via the Comptroller's official website by January 31 of every year.

P.A. 95–478, § 5, eff. Jan. 1, 2008.

PART 21. MEDICAL STUDIES

Section
5/8–2101. Information obtained.
5/8–2102. Admissibility as evidence.
5/8–2103. Furnishing information.
5/8–2104. Interviews.
5/8–2105. Improper disclosure.

5/8–2101. Information obtained

§ 8–2101. Information obtained. All information, interviews, reports, statements, memoranda, recommendations, letters of reference or other third party confidential assessments of a health care practitioner's professional competence, or other data of the Illinois Department of Public Health, local health departments, the Department of Human Services (as successor to the Department of Mental Health and Developmental Disabilities), the Mental Health and Developmental Disabilities Medical Review Board, Illinois State Medical Society, allied medical societies, health maintenance organizations, medical organizations under contract with health maintenance organizations or with insurance or other health care delivery entities or facilities, tissue banks, organ procurement agencies, physician-owned insurance companies and their agents, committees of ambulatory surgical treatment centers or post-surgical recovery centers or their medical staffs, or committees of licensed or accredited hospitals or their medical staffs, including Patient Care Audit Committees, Medical Care Evaluation Committees, Utilization Review Committees, Credential Committees and Executive Committees, or their designees (but not the medical records pertaining to the patient), used in the course of internal quality control or of medical study for the purpose of reducing morbidity or mortality, or for improving patient care or increasing organ and tissue donation, shall be privileged, strictly confidential and shall be used only for medical research, increasing organ and tissue donation, the evaluation and improvement of quality care, or granting, limiting or revoking staff privileges or agreements for services, except that in any health maintenance organization proceeding to decide upon a physician's services or any hospital or ambulatory surgical treatment center proceeding to decide upon a physician's staff privileges, or in any judicial review of either, the claim of confidentiality shall not be invoked to deny such physician access to or use of data upon which such a decision was based.

P.A. 82–280, § 8–2101, eff. July 1, 1982. Amended by P.A. 82–783, Art. III, § 43, eff. July 13, 1982; P.A. 83–1001, § 1, eff. July 1, 1984; P.A. 84–544, § 1, eff. Jan. 1, 1986; P.A. 84–902, § 4, eff. Jan. 1, 1986; P.A. 84–1308, Art. II, § 107, eff. Aug. 25, 1986; P.A. 85–284, § 1, eff. Jan. 1, 1988; P.A. 89–393, § 15, eff. Aug. 20, 1995; P.A. 89–507, Art. 90, § 90D–90, eff. July 1, 1997; P.A. 92–644, § 5, eff. Jan. 1, 2003.

Formerly Ill.Rev.Stat.1991, ch. 110, ¶ 8–2101.

5/8–2102. Admissibility as evidence

§ 8–2102. Admissibility as evidence. Such information, records, reports, statements, notes, memoranda, or other data, shall not be admissible as evidence, nor discoverable in any action of any kind in any court or before any tribunal, board, agency or person. The disclosure of any such information or data, whether proper, or improper, shall not waive or have any effect upon its confidentiality, nondiscoverability, or nonadmissibility.

P.A. 82–280, § 8–2102, eff. July 1, 1982. Amended by P.A. 82–783, Art. III, § 43, eff. July 13, 1982; P.A. 85–907, Art. II, § 1, eff. Nov. 23, 1987.

Formerly Ill.Rev.Stat.1991, ch. 110, ¶ 8–2102.

5/8–2103. Furnishing information

§ 8–2103. Furnishing information. The furnishing of such information in the course of a research project to the Illinois Department of Public Health, Illinois State Medical Society, allied medical societies or to in-hospital staff committees or their authorized representatives, shall not subject any person, hospital, sanitarium, nursing or rest home or any such agency to any action for damages or other relief.

P.A. 82–280, § 8–2103, eff. July 1, 1982.

Formerly Ill.Rev.Stat.1991, ch. 110, ¶ 8–2103.

5/8–2104. Interviews

§ 8–2104. Interviews. No patient, patient's relatives, or patient's friends named in any medical study, shall be interviewed for the purpose of such study unless consent of the attending physician and surgeon is first obtained.

P.A. 82–280, § 8–2104, eff. July 1, 1982.

Formerly Ill.Rev.Stat.1991, ch. 110, ¶ 8–2104.

5/8–2105. Improper disclosure

§ 8–2105. Improper disclosure. The disclosure of any information, records, reports, statements, notes, memoranda or other data obtained in any such medical study except that necessary for the purpose of the specific study is unlawful, and any person convicted of violating any of the provisions of Part 21 of Article VIII of this Act is guilty of a Class A misdemeanor.

P.A. 82–280, § 8–2105, eff. July 1, 1982. Amended by P.A. 83–707, § 1, eff. Sept. 23, 1983.

Formerly Ill.Rev.Stat.1991, ch. 110, ¶ 8–2105.

PART 22. CORONER'S RECORDS

Section
5/8–2201. Admissibility of coroner's records.

5/8–2201. Admissibility of coroner's records

§ 8–2201. Admissibility of coroner's records. In actions or proceedings for the recovery of damages arising from or growing out of injuries caused by the negligence of any person, firm or corporation resulting in the death of any person or for the collection of a policy of insurance, neither the coroner's verdict returned upon the inquisition, nor a copy thereof, shall be admissible as evidence to prove or establish any of the facts in controversy in such action or proceeding.

P.A. 82–280, § 8–2201, eff. July 1, 1982.

Formerly Ill.Rev.Stat.1991, ch. 110, ¶ 8–2201.

PART 23. PERPETUATING TESTIMONY

Section
5/8–2301. Perpetuation of testimony.

5/8–2301. Perpetuation of testimony

§ 8–2301. Perpetuation of testimony. Any person may take the deposition of a witness to perpetuate the remembrance of any fact, matter or thing, relating to the boundaries or improvements of land, the name or former name of water course, the name or former name of any portion or district of the county, the ancient customs, laws or usages of the inhabitants of any part of this country, as far as they may pertain to the future settlement of land claims or the marriage or pedigree of any person, any other matter or thing necessary to the security of any estate, or to any private right by filing a petition supported by affidavit in the circuit court of the proper county. The petition shall set forth, briefly and substantially, the petitioner's interest, claim or title in or to the subject concerning which the petitioner desires to perpetuate evidence, the fact intended to be established, the names of all other persons interested or supposed to be interested therein, whether there are any persons interested therein whose names are unknown to the petitioner (who shall be designated as unknown owners), and the name of the witness proposed to be examined. Except as in this Section otherwise provided, the procedure for the giving of notice to interested persons, including unknown owners, and the manner of taking the deposition shall be that provided by the rules of the Supreme Court now or hereafter in effect for the taking of depositions for the perpetuation of testimony. A deposition taken under this Section may be used as evidence in any case in the same manner and subject to the same conditions and objections as if it had originally been taken in that case. The deposition is admissible against parties notified as unknown owners to the same extent as it is against other notified parties.

P.A. 82–280, § 8–2301, eff. July 1, 1982.

Formerly Ill.Rev.Stat.1991, ch. 110, ¶ 8–2301.

PART 24. APPLICATION TO CRIMINAL CASES

Section
5/8–2401. Application to criminal cases.

5/8–2401. Application to criminal cases

§ 8–2401. Application to criminal cases. The provisions of Article VIII of this Act shall apply to criminal cases, unless expressly provided otherwise or unless such construction would be inconsistent with the manifest intention of the context.

P.A. 82–280, § 8–2401, eff. July 1, 1982. Amended by P.A. 83–707, § 1, eff. Sept. 23, 1983.

Formerly Ill.Rev.Stat.1991, ch. 110, ¶ 8–2401.

PART 25. EXPERT WITNESS STANDARDS

Section
5/8–2501. Expert Witness Standards.

Date Effective

Part 25 was added by P.A. 84–7, § 1, eff. Aug. 15, 1985.

5/8–2501. Expert Witness Standards

§ 8–2501. Expert Witness Standards. In any case in which the standard of care given by a medical profession is at issue, the court shall apply the following standards to determine if a witness qualifies as an expert witness and can testify on the issue of the appropriate standard of care.

(a) Relationship of the medical specialties of the witness to the medical problem or problems and the type of treatment administered in the case;

(b) Whether the witness has devoted a substantial portion of his or her time to the practice of medicine, teaching or University based research in relation to the medical care and type of treatment at issue which gave rise to the medical problem of which the plaintiff complains;

(c) whether the witness is licensed in the same profession as the defendant; and

(d) whether, in the case against a nonspecialist, the witness can demonstrate a sufficient familiarity with the standard of care practiced in this State.

P.A. 82–280, § 8–2501, added by P.A. 84–7, § 1, eff. Aug. 15, 1985. Amended by P.A. 89–7, § 15, eff. March 9, 1995; P.A. 94–677, § 330, eff. Aug. 25, 2005. Re-enacted by P.A. 97–1145, § 5, eff. Jan. 18, 2013.

Formerly Ill.Rev.Stat.1991, ch. 110, ¶ 8–2501.

Validity

P.A. 94–677, effective August 25, 2005, a comprehensive revision of the law relating to health care and medical malpractice actions, is unconstitutional in its entirety because (i) provisions limiting the recovery of damages for non-economic losses in medical malpractice actions violate the separation of powers principle of the Illinois Constitution (IL-CON Art. II, Sec. 1) and (ii) other provisions are inseverable. Lebron v. Gottlieb Memorial Hospital, 237 Ill.2d 217 (2010). P.A. 97–1145 re-enacted this section so as to remove any question as to its validity.

Public Act 89–7, which amended this section, has been held unconstitutional in its entirety by the Illinois Supreme Court in the case of Best v. Taylor Machine Works, 1997, 689 N.E.2d 1057, 228 Ill.Dec. 636, 179 Ill.2d 367. P.A. 94–677, effective August 25, 2005, specifically re-enacted this section. P.A. 97–1145 re-enacted this section so as to remove any question as to its validity.

For applicability of P.A. 89–7, see note following 735 ILCS 5/2–402 Section 995 of P.A. 89–7, approved March 9, 1995, provides:

"Effective date. This Act takes effect upon becoming law, and applies to causes of action as specified in each Section or part of this Act."

P.A. 94–677 did not include the changes made by P.A. 89–7, which was held unconstitutional.

PART 26. MINORS

Section
5/8–2601. Admissibility of evidence; out-of-court statements; child abuse.

Date Effective

Part 26 was added by P.A. 85–1440, Art. III, § 3–26, eff. Feb. 1, 1989.

5/8–2601. Admissibility of evidence; out-of-court statements; child abuse

§ 8–2601. (a) An out-of-court statement made by a child under the age of 13 describing any act of child abuse or any conduct involving an unlawful sexual act performed in the presence of, with, by, or on the declarant child, or testimony by such of an out-of-court statement made by such child that he or she complained of such acts to another, is admissible in any civil proceeding, if: (1) the court conducts a hearing outside the presence of the jury and finds that the time, content, and circumstances of the statement provide sufficient safeguards of reliability; and (2) the child either: (i) testifies at the proceeding; or (ii) is unavailable as a witness and there is corroborative evidence of the act which is the subject of the statement.

(b) If a statement is admitted pursuant to this Section, the court shall instruct the jury that it is for the jury to determine the weight and credibility to be given to the statement and that, in making its determination, it shall consider the age and maturity of the child, the nature of the statement, the circumstances

under which the statement was made, and any other relevant factors.

(c) The proponent of the statement shall give the adverse party reasonable notice of an intention to offer the statement and the particulars of the statement.

P.A. 82–280, § 8–2601, added by P.A. 85–1440, Art. III, § 3–26, eff. Feb. 1, 1989.

Formerly Ill.Rev.Stat.1991, ch. 110, ¶ 8–2601.

PART 27. ELDER ADULTS

Section
5/8–2701. Admissibility of evidence; out of court statements; elder abuse.

Date Effective

Part 27 was added by P.A. 90–628, § 20, eff. January 1, 1999.

5/8–2701. Admissibility of evidence; out of court statements; elder abuse

§ 8–2701. Admissibility of evidence; out of court statements; elder abuse.

(a) An out of court statement made by an eligible adult, as defined in the Adult Protective Services Act,[1] who has been diagnosed by a physician to suffer from (i) any form of dementia, developmental disability, or other form of mental incapacity or (ii) any physical infirmity which prevents the eligible adult's appearance in court, describing any act of elder abuse, neglect, or financial exploitation, or testimony by an eligible adult of an out of court statement made by the eligible adult that he or she complained of such acts to another, is admissible in any civil proceeding, if:

(1) the court conducts a hearing outside the presence of the jury and finds that the time, content, and circumstances of the statement provide sufficient safeguards of reliability; and

(2) the eligible adult either:

(A) testifies at the proceeding; or

(B) is unavailable as a witness and there is corroborative evidence of the act which is the subject of the statement.

(b) If a statement is admitted pursuant to this Section, the court shall instruct the jury that it is for the jury to determine the weight and credibility to be given to the statement and that, in making its determination, it shall consider the condition of the eligible adult, the nature of the statement, the circumstances under which the statement was made, and any other relevant factors.

(c) The proponent of the statement shall give the adverse party reasonable notice of an intention to offer the statement and the particulars of the statement.

P.A. 82–280, § 8–2701, added by P.A. 90–628, § 20, eff. Jan. 1, 1999. Amended by P.A. 98–49, § 110, eff. July 1, 2013.

[1] 320 ILCS 20/1 et seq.

PART 28. PRIOR SEXUAL ACTIVITY OR REPUTATION AS EVIDENCE

Section
5/8–2801. Admissibility of evidence; prior sexual activity or reputation.

5/8–2801. Admissibility of evidence; prior sexual activity or reputation

§ 8–2801. Admissibility of evidence; prior sexual activity or reputation.

(a) Evidence generally inadmissible. The following evidence is not admissible in any civil proceeding except as provided in subsections (b) and (c):

(1) evidence offered to prove that any victim engaged in other sexual behavior; or

(2) evidence offered to prove any victim's sexual predisposition.

(b) Exceptions.

(1) In a civil case, the following evidence is admissible, if otherwise admissible under this Act:

(A) evidence of specific instances of sexual behavior by the victim offered to prove that a person other than the accused was the source of semen, injury, or other physical evidence; and

(B) evidence of specific instances of sexual behavior by the victim with respect to the person accused of the sexual misconduct offered by the accused to prove consent by the victim.

(c) Procedure to determine admissibility.

(1) A party intending to offer evidence under subsection (b) must:

(A) file a written motion at least 14 days before trial specifically describing the evidence and stating the purpose for which it is offered unless the court, for good cause requires a different time for filing or permits filing during trial; and

(B) serve the motion on all parties and notify the victim or, when appropriate, the victim's guardian or representative.

(2) Before admitting evidence under this Section the court must conduct a hearing in camera and afford the victim and parties a right to attend and be heard. The motion, related papers, and the record of the hearing must be sealed and remain under seal unless the court orders otherwise.

P.A. 82–280, § 8–2801, added by P.A. 96–307, § 5, eff. Jan. 1, 2010.

ARTICLE IX. FORCIBLE ENTRY AND DETAINER

Part
1. In General.
2. Recovery of Rent; Termination of Certain Tenancies.
3. Distress for Rent.

PART 1. IN GENERAL

5/9–101. Forcible entry prohibited

§ 9–101. Forcible entry prohibited. No person shall make an entry into lands or tenements except in cases where entry is allowed by law, and in such cases he or she shall not enter with force, but in a peaceable manner.

P.A. 82–280, § 9–101, eff. July 1, 1982.

Formerly Ill.Rev.Stat.1991, ch. 110, ¶ 9–101.

5/9–102. When action may be maintained

§ 9–102. When action may be maintained.

(a) The person entitled to the possession of lands or tenements may be restored thereto under any of the following circumstances:

(1) When a forcible entry is made thereon.

(2) When a peaceable entry is made and the possession unlawfully withheld.

(3) When entry is made into vacant or unoccupied lands or tenements without right or title.

(4) When any lessee of the lands or tenements, or any person holding under such lessee, holds possession without right after the termination of the lease or tenancy by its own limitation, condition or terms, or by notice to quit or otherwise.

(5) When a vendee having obtained possession under a written or verbal agreement to purchase lands or tenements, and having failed to comply with the agreement, withholds possession thereof, after demand in writing by the person entitled to such possession; provided, however, that any such agreement for residential real estate as defined in the Illinois Mortgage Foreclosure Law [1] entered into on or after July 1, 1987 where the purchase price is to be paid in installments over a period in excess of 5 years and the amount unpaid under the terms of the contract at the time of the filing of a foreclosure complaint under Article XV, including principal and due and unpaid interest, is less than 80% of the original purchase price shall be foreclosed under the Illinois Mortgage Foreclosure Law.

This amendatory Act of 1993 is declarative of existing law.

(6) When lands or tenements have been conveyed by any grantor in possession, or sold under the order or judgment of any court in this State, or by virtue of any sale in any mortgage or deed of trust contained and the grantor in possession or party to such order or judgment or to such mortgage or deed of trust, after the expiration of the time of redemption, when redemption is allowed by law, refuses or neglects to surrender possession thereof, after demand in writing by the person entitled thereto, or his or her agent.

(7) When any property is subject to the provisions of the Condominium Property Act, [2] the owner of a unit fails or refuses to pay when due his or her proportionate share of the common expenses of such property, or of any other expenses lawfully agreed upon or any unpaid fine, the Board of Managers or its agents have served the demand set forth in Section 9–104.1 of this Article in the manner provided for in that Section and the unit owner has failed to pay the amount claimed within the time prescribed in the demand; or if the lessor-owner of a unit fails to comply with the leasing requirements prescribed by subsection (n) of Section 18 of the Condominium Property Act [3] or by the declaration, by-laws, and rules and regulations of the condominium, or if a lessee of an owner is in breach of any covenants, rules, regulations, or by-laws of the condominium, and the Board of Managers or its agents have served the demand set forth in Section 9–104.2 of this Article in the manner provided in that Section.

(8) When any property is subject to the provisions of a declaration establishing a common interest community and requiring the unit owner to pay regular or special assessments for the maintenance or repair of common areas owned in common by all of the owners of the common interest community or by the community association and maintained for the use of the unit owners or of any other expenses of the association lawfully agreed upon, and the unit owner fails or refuses to pay when due his or her proportionate share of such assessments or expenses and the board or its agents have served the demand set forth in Section 9–104.1 of this Article in the manner provided for in that Section and the unit owner has failed to pay the amount claimed within the time prescribed in the demand.

(b) The provisions of paragraph (8) of subsection (a) of Section 9–102 and Section 9–104.3 of this Act shall not apply to any common interest community unless (1) the association is a not-for-profit corporation or a limited liability company, (2) unit owners are authorized to attend meetings of the board of directors or board of managers of the association in the same manner as provided for condominiums under the Condominium Property Act, and (3) the board of managers or board of directors of the common interest community association has, subsequent to the effective date of this amendatory Act of 1984 voted to have the provisions of this Article apply to such association and has delivered or mailed notice of such action to the unit owners or unless the declaration of the association is recorded after the effective date of this amendatory Act of 1985.

(c) For purposes of this Article:

(1) "Common interest community" means real estate other than a condominium or cooperative with respect to which any person by virtue of his or her ownership of a partial interest or unit therein is obligated to pay for maintenance, improvement, insurance premiums, or real estate taxes of other real estate described in a declaration which is administered by an association.

(2) "Declaration" means any duly recorded instruments, however designated, that have created a common interest community and any duly recorded amendments to those instruments.

(3) "Unit" means a physical portion of the common interest community designated by separate ownership or occupancy by boundaries which are described in a declaration.

(4) "Unit owners' association" or "association" means the association of all owners of units in the common interest community acting pursuant to the declaration.

(d) If the board of a common interest community elects to have the provisions of this Article apply to such association or the declaration of the association is recorded after the effective date of this amendatory Act of 1985, the provisions of subsections (c) through (h) of Section 18.5 of the Condominium Property Act applicable to a Master Association and condominium unit subject to such association under subsections (c) through (h) of Section 18.5 shall be applicable to the community associations and to its unit owners.

P.A. 82–280, § 9–102, eff. July 1, 1982. Amended by P.A. 83–645, § 2, eff. Jan. 1, 1984; P.A. 83–1271, § 3, eff. Aug. 30, 1984; P.A. 84–722, § 2, eff. Sept. 21, 1985; P.A. 84–1464, § 3, eff. Jan. 13, 1987; P.A. 85–907, Art. I, § 1, eff. Nov. 23, 1987; P.A. 87–895, Art. 3, § 3–64, eff. Aug. 14, 1992; P.A. 88–47, § 5, eff. Jan. 1, 1994; P.A. 89–41, § 10, eff. June 23, 1995; P.A. 89–626, Art. 3, § 3–39, eff. Aug. 9, 1996; P.A. 99–41, § 5, eff. July 14, 2015.

Formerly Ill.Rev.Stat.1991, ch. 110, ¶ 9–102.

[1] 735 ILCS 5/15–1101 et seq.
[2] 765 ILCS 605/1 et seq.
[3] 765 ILCS 605/18.

5/9–103. Mobile home site

§ 9–103. Mobile home site. The rental of land upon which a mobile home is placed or the rental of a mobile home and the land on which it is placed, for more than 30 days, shall be construed as a lease of real property. However, nothing in this Section shall be construed to affect the classification of mobile homes as real or personal property for purposes of taxation.

P.A. 82–280, § 9–103, eff. July 1, 1982.

Formerly Ill.Rev.Stat.1991, ch. 110, ¶ 9–103.

5/9–104. Demand—Notice—Return

§ 9–104. Demand—Notice—Return. The demand required by Section 9–102 of this Act may be made by delivering a copy thereof to the tenant, or by leaving such a copy with some person of the age of 13 years or upwards, residing on, or being in charge of, the premises; or in case no one is in the actual possession of the premises, then by posting the same on the premises; or if those in possession are unknown occupants who are not parties to any written lease, rental agreement, or right to possession agreement for the premises, then by delivering a copy of the notice, directed to "unknown occupants", to the occupant or by leaving a copy of the notice with some person of the age of 13 years or upwards occupying the premises, or by posting a copy of the notice on the premises directed to "unknown occupants". When such demand is made by an officer authorized to serve process, his or her return is prima facie evidence of the facts therein

stated, and if such demand is made by any person not an officer, the return may be sworn to by the person serving the same, and is then prima facie evidence of the facts therein stated. The demand for possession may be in the following form: To . . .

I hereby demand immediate possession of the following described premises: (describing the same.)

The demand shall be signed by the person claiming such possession, his or her agent, or attorney.

P.A. 82–280, § 9–104, eff. July 1, 1982. Amended by P.A. 83–355, § 1, eff. Sept. 14, 1983; P.A. 83–645, § 2, eff. Jan. 1, 1984; P.A. 83–1362, Art. II, § 109, eff. Sept. 11, 1984; P.A. 92–823, § 5, eff. Aug. 21, 2002.

Formerly Ill.Rev.Stat.1991, ch. 110, ¶ 9–104.

5/9–104.1. Demand; Notice; Return; Condominium and Contract Purchasers

§ 9–104.1. Demand; Notice; Return; Condominium and Contract Purchasers.

(a) In case there is a contract for the purchase of such lands or tenements or in case of condominium property, the demand shall give the purchaser under such contract, or to the condominium unit owner, as the case may be, at least 30 days to satisfy the terms of the demand before an action is filed. In case of a condominium unit, the demand shall set forth the amount claimed which must be paid within the time prescribed in the demand and the time period or periods when the amounts were originally due, unless the demand is for compliance with Section 18(n) of the Condominium Property Act,[1] in which case the demand shall set forth the nature of the lease and memorandum of lease or the leasing requirement not satisfied. The amount claimed shall include regular or special assessments, late charges or interest for delinquent assessments, and attorneys' fees claimed for services incurred prior to the demand. Attorneys' fees claimed by condominium associations in the demand shall be subject to review by the courts in any forcible entry and detainer proceeding under subsection (b) of Section 9–111 of this Act. The demand shall be signed by the person claiming such possession, his or her agent, or attorney.

(b) In the case of a condominium unit, the demand is not invalidated by partial payment of amounts due if the payments do not, at the end of the notice period, total the amounts demanded in the notice for common expenses, unpaid fines, interest, late charges, reasonable attorney fees incurred prior to the initiation of any court action and costs of collection. The person claiming possession, or his or her agent or attorney, may, however, agree in writing to withdraw the demand in exchange for receiving partial payment. To prevent invalidation, the notice must prominently state:

"Only FULL PAYMENT of all amounts demanded in this notice will invalidate the demand, unless the person claiming possession, or his or her agent or attorney, agrees in writing to withdraw the demand in exchange for receiving partial payment."

(c) The demand set forth in subsection (a) of this Section shall be served either personally upon such purchaser or condominium unit owner or by sending the demand thereof by registered or certified mail with return receipt requested to the last known address of such purchaser or condominium unit owner or in case no one is in the actual possession of the premises, then by posting the same on the premises. When such demand is made by an officer authorized to serve process, his or her return is prima facie evidence of the facts therein stated and if such demand is made by any person not an officer, the return may be sworn to by the person serving the same, and is then prima facie evidence of the facts therein stated. To be effective service under this Section, a demand sent by certified or registered mail to the last known address need not be received by the purchaser or condominium unit owner. No other demand shall be required as a prerequisite to filing an action under paragraph (7) of subsection (a) of Section 9–102 of this Act. Service of the demand by registered or certified mail shall be deemed effective upon deposit in the United States mail with proper postage prepaid and addressed as provided in this subsection.

P.A. 82–280, § 9–104.1, added by P.A. 83–645, § 2, eff. Jan. 1, 1984. Amended by P.A. 83–1362, Art. IV, § 20, eff. Sept. 11, 1984; P.A. 84–722, § 2, eff. Sept. 21, 1985; P.A. 84–1043, § 1, eff. Nov. 26, 1985; P.A. 84–1308, Art. II, § 107, eff. Aug. 25, 1986; P.A. 86–1156, § 6, eff. Aug. 10, 1990; P.A. 87–746, § 2, eff. Sept. 26, 1991; P.A. 90–496, § 2, eff. Aug. 18, 1997.

Formerly Ill.Rev.Stat.1991, ch. 110, ¶ 9–104.1.
1 765 ILCS 605/18.

5/9–104.2. Demand—Notice—Termination of Lease and Possession of a Condominium

§ 9–104.2. Demand—Notice—Termination of Lease and Possession of a Condominium.

(a) Unless the Board of Managers is seeking to terminate the right of possession of a tenant or other occupant of a unit under an existing lease or other arrangement with the owner of a unit, no demand nor summons need be served upon the tenant or other occupant in connection with an action brought under paragraph (7) of subsection (a) of Section 9–102 of this Article.

(a–5) The Board of Managers may seek to terminate the right of possession of a tenant or other occupant of a unit under an existing lease or other arrangement between the tenant or other occupant and the defaulting owner of a unit, either within the same action against the unit owner under paragraph (7) of subsection (a) of Section 9–102 of this Article or independently thereafter under other paragraphs of that subsection. If a tenant or other occupant of a unit is joined within the same action against the defaulting unit owner under paragraph (7), only the

unit owner and not the tenant or other occupant need to be served with 30 days prior written notice as provided in this Article. The tenant or other occupant may be joined as additional defendants at the time the suit is filed or at any time thereafter prior to execution of judgment for possession by filing, with or without prior leave of the court, an amended complaint and summons for trial. If the complaint alleges that the unit is occupied or may be occupied by persons other than or in addition to the unit owner of record, that the identities of the persons are concealed and unknown, they may be named and joined as defendant "Unknown Occupants". Summons may be served on the defendant "Unknown Occupants" by the sheriff or court appointed process server by leaving a copy at the unit with any person residing at the unit of the age of 13 years or greater, and if the summons is returned without service stating that service cannot be obtained, constructive service may be obtained pursuant to Section 9–107 of this Code with notice mailed to "Unknown Occupants" at the address of the unit. If prior to execution of judgment for possession the identity of a defendant or defendants served in this manner is discovered, his or her name or names and the record may be corrected upon hearing pursuant to notice of motion served upon the identified defendant or defendants at the unit in the manner provided by court rule for service of notice of motion. If however an action under paragraph (7) was brought against the defaulting unit owner only, and after obtaining judgment for possession and expiration of the stay on enforcement the Board of Managers elects not to accept a tenant or occupant in possession as its own and to commence a separate action, written notice of the judgment against the unit owner and demand to quit the premises shall be served on the tenant or other occupant in the manner provided under Section 9–211 at least 10 days prior to bringing suit to recover possession from the tenant or other occupant.

(b) If a judgment for possession is granted to the Board of Managers under Section 9–111, any interest of the unit owner to receive rents under any lease arrangement shall be deemed assigned to the Board of Managers until such time as the judgment is vacated.

(c) If a judgment for possession is entered, the Board of Managers may obtain from the clerk of the court an informational certificate notifying any tenants not parties to the proceeding of the assignment of the unit owner's interest in the lease arrangement to the Board of Managers as a result of the entry of the judgment for possession and stating that any rent hereinafter due the unit owner or his agent under the lease arrangement should be paid to the Board of Managers until further order of court. If the tenant pays his rent to the association pursuant to the entry of such a judgement for possession, the unit owner may not sue said tenant for any such amounts the tenant pays the association. Upon service of the certificate on the tenant in the manner provided by

Section 9–211 of this Code, the tenant shall be obligated to pay the rent under the lease arrangement to the Board of Managers as it becomes due. If the tenant thereafter fails and refuses to pay the rent, the Board of Managers may bring an action for possession after making a demand for rent in accordance with Section 9–209 of this Code.

(c–5) In an action against the unit owner and lessee to evict a lessee for failure of the lessor/owner of the condominium unit to comply with the leasing requirements prescribed by subsection (n) of Section 18 of the Condominium Property Act [1] or by the declaration, bylaws, and rules and regulations of the condominium, or against a lessee for any other breach by the lessee of any covenants, rules, regulations, or bylaws of the condominium, the demand shall give the lessee at least 10 days to quit and vacate the unit. The notice shall be substantially in the following form:

"TO A.B. You are hereby notified that in consequence of (here insert lessor-owner name) failure to comply with the leasing requirements prescribed by Section 18(n) of the Condominium Property Act or by the declaration, bylaws, and rules and regulations of the condominium, or your default of any covenants, rules, regulations or bylaws of the condominium, in (here insert the character of the default) of the premises now occupied by you, being (here described the premises) the Board of Managers of (here describe the condominium) Association elects to terminate your lease, and you are hereby notified to quit and vacate same within 10 days of this date.".

The demand shall be signed by the Board of Managers, its agent, or attorney and shall be served either personally upon the lessee with a copy to the unit owner or by sending the demand thereof by registered or certified mail with return receipt requested to the unit occupied by the lessee and to the last known address of the unit owner, and no other demand of termination of such tenancy shall be required. To be effective service under this Section, a demand sent by certified mail, return receipt requested, to the unit occupied by the lessee and to the last known address of the unit owner need not be received by the lessee or condominium unit owner.

(d) Nothing in this Section 9–104.2 is intended to confer upon a Board of Managers any greater authority with respect to possession of a unit after a judgment than was previously established by this Act.

P.A. 82–280, § 9–104.2, added by P.A. 83–1271, § 3, eff. Aug. 30, 1984. Amended by P.A. 89–41, § 10, eff. June 23, 1995; P.A. 90–496, § 2, eff. Aug. 18, 1997; P.A. 91–196, § 5, eff. July 20, 1999.

Formerly Ill.Rev.Stat.1991, ch. 110, ¶ 9–104.2
[1] 765 ILCS 605/18.

5/9–104.3. Applicability of Article

§ 9–104.3. Applicability of Article. All common interest community associations electing pursuant to paragraph (8) of subsection (a) of Section 9–102 to have this Article made applicable to such association shall follow the same procedures and have the same rights and responsibilities as condominium associations under this Article.

P.A. 82–280, § 9–104.3, added by P.A. 83–1271, § 3, eff. Aug. 30, 1984. Amended by P.A. 84–722, § 2, eff. Sept. 21, 1985; P.A. 84–1043, § 1, eff. Nov. 26, 1985; P.A. 84–1308, Art. II, § 107, eff. Aug. 25, 1986.

Formerly Ill.Rev.Stat.1991, ch. 110, ¶ 9–104.3.

5/9–105. Growing crops

§ 9–105. Growing crops. In case of forfeiture under contract of purchase, the purchaser shall be entitled to cultivate and gather the crops, if any, planted by him or her and grown or growing on the premises at the time of the filing of the action, and shall have the right to enter for the purpose of removing such crops, first paying or tendering to the party entitled to the possession a reasonable compensation for such use of the land before removing such crops.

P.A. 82–280, § 9–105, eff. July 1, 1982.

Formerly Ill.Rev.Stat.1991, ch. 110, ¶ 9–105.

5/9–106. Pleadings and evidence

§ 9–106. Pleadings and evidence. On complaint by the party or parties entitled to the possession of such premises being filed in the circuit court for the county where such premises are situated, stating that such party is entitled to the possession of such premises (describing the same with reasonable certainty), and that the defendant (naming the defendant) unlawfully withholds the possession thereof from him, her or them, the clerk of the court shall issue a summons.

The defendant may under a general denial of the allegations of the complaint offer in evidence any matter in defense of the action. Except as otherwise provided in Section 9–120, no matters not germane to the distinctive purpose of the proceeding shall be introduced by joinder, counterclaim or otherwise. However, a claim for rent may be joined in the complaint, and judgment may be entered for the amount of rent found due.

P.A. 82–280, § 9–106, eff. July 1, 1982. Amended by P.A. 90–360, § 5, eff. Jan. 1, 1998.

Formerly Ill.Rev.Stat.1991, ch. 110, ¶ 9–106.

5/9–106.1. Action for condominium assessments not barred or waived by acceptance of assessments for time periods not covered by demand

§ 9–106.1. Action for condominium assessments not barred or waived by acceptance of assessments for time periods not covered by demand. An action brought under paragraph (7) of subsection (a) of Section 9–102 of this Act is neither barred nor waived by the action of a Board of Managers in accepting payments from a unit owner for his or her proportionate share of the common expenses or of any other expenses lawfully agreed upon for any time period other than that covered by the demand.

P.A. 82–280, § 9–106.1, added by P.A. 83–645, § 2, eff. Jan. 1, 1984. Amended by P.A. 84–722, § 2, eff. Sept. 21, 1985; P.A. 84–1043, § 1, eff. Nov. 26, 1985; P.A. 84–1308, Art. II, § 107, eff. Aug. 25, 1986.

Formerly Ill.Rev.Stat.1991, ch. 110, ¶ 9–106.1.

5/9–106.2. Affirmative defense for violence; barring persons from property

§ 9–106.2. Affirmative defense for violence; barring persons from property.

(a) It shall be an affirmative defense to an action maintained under this Article IX if the court makes one of the following findings that the demand for possession is:

(1) based solely on the tenant's, lessee's, or household member's status as a victim of domestic violence or sexual violence as those terms are defined in Section 10 of the Safe Homes Act, stalking as that term is defined in the Criminal Code of 2012, or dating violence;

(2) based solely upon an incident of actual or threatened domestic violence, dating violence, stalking, or sexual violence against a tenant, lessee, or household member;

(3) based solely upon criminal activity directly relating to domestic violence, dating violence, stalking, or sexual violence engaged in by a member of a tenant's or lessee's household or any guest or other person under the tenant's, lessee's, or household member's control, and against the tenant, lessee, or household member; or

(4) based upon a demand for possession pursuant to subsection (f) where the tenant, lessee, or household member who was the victim of domestic violence, sexual violence, stalking, or dating violence did not knowingly consent to the barred person entering the premises or a valid court order permitted the barred person's entry onto the premises.

(b) When asserting the affirmative defense, at least one form of the following types of evidence shall be provided to support the affirmative defense: medical, court, or police records documenting the violence or a statement from an employee of a victim service organization or from a medical professional from whom the tenant, lessee, or household member has sought services.

(c) Nothing in subsection (a) shall prevent the landlord from seeking possession solely against a tenant,

household member, or lessee of the premises who perpetrated the violence referred to in subsection (a).

(d) Nothing in subsection (a) shall prevent the landlord from seeking possession against the entire household, including the tenant, lessee, or household member who is a victim of domestic violence, dating violence, stalking, or sexual violence if the tenant, lessee, or household member's continued tenancy would pose an actual and imminent threat to other tenants, lessees, household members, the landlord or their agents at the property.

(e) Nothing in subsection (a) shall prevent the landlord from seeking possession against the tenant, lessee, or household member who is a victim of domestic violence, dating violence, stalking, or sexual violence if that tenant, lessee, or household member has committed the criminal activity on which the demand for possession is based.

(f) A landlord shall have the power to bar the presence of a person from the premises owned by the landlord who is not a tenant or lessee or who is not a member of the tenant's or lessee's household. A landlord bars a person from the premises by providing written notice to the tenant or lessee that the person is no longer allowed on the premises. That notice shall state that if the tenant invites the barred person onto any portion of the premises, then the landlord may treat this as a breach of the lease, whether or not this provision is contained in the lease. Subject to paragraph (4) of subsection (a), the landlord may evict the tenant.

(g) Further, a landlord may give notice to a person that the person is barred from the premises owned by the landlord. A person has received notice from the landlord within the meaning of this subsection if he has been notified personally, either orally or in writing including a valid court order as defined by subsection (7) of Section 112A–3 of the Code of Criminal Procedure of 1963 granting remedy (2) of subsection (b) of Section 112A–14 of that Code, or if a printed or written notice forbidding such entry has been conspicuously posted or exhibited at the main entrance to such land or the forbidden part thereof. Any person entering the landlord's premises after such notice has been given shall be guilty of criminal trespass to real property as set forth in Section 21–3 of the Criminal Code of 2012. After notice has been given, an invitation to the person to enter the premises shall be void if made by a tenant, lessee, or member of the tenant's or lessee's household and shall not constitute a valid invitation to come upon the premises or a defense to a criminal trespass to real property.

P.A. 82–280, § 9–106.2, added by P.A. 96–1188, § 5, eff. July 22, 2010. Amended by P.A. 97–1150, § 705, eff. Jan. 25, 2013.

5/9–107. Constructive service

§ 9–107. Constructive service. If the plaintiff, his or her agent, or attorney files a forcible detainer action, with or without joinder of a claim for rent in the complaint, and is unable to obtain personal service on the defendant or unknown occupant and a summons duly issued in such action is returned without service stating that service can not be obtained, then the plaintiff, his or her agent or attorney may file an affidavit stating that the defendant or unknown occupant is not a resident of this State, or has departed from this State, or on due inquiry cannot be found, or is concealed within this State so that process cannot be served upon him or her, and also stating the place of residence of the defendant or unknown occupant, if known, or if not known, that upon diligent inquiry the affiant has not been able to ascertain the defendant's or unknown occupant's place of residence, then in all such forcible detainer cases whether or not a claim for rent is joined with the complaint for possession, the defendant or unknown occupant may be notified by posting and mailing of notices; or by publication and mailing, as provided for in Section 2–206 of this Act. However, in cases where the defendant or unknown occupant is notified by posting and mailing of notices or by publication and mailing, and the defendant or unknown occupant does not appear generally, the court may rule only on the portion of the complaint which seeks judgment for possession, and the court shall not enter judgment as to any rent claim joined in the complaint or enter personal judgment for any amount owed by a unit owner for his or her proportionate share of the common expenses, however, an in rem judgment may be entered against the unit for the amount of common expenses due, any other expenses lawfully agreed upon or the amount of any unpaid fine, together with reasonable attorney fees, if any, and costs. The claim for rent may remain pending until such time as the defendant or unknown occupant appears generally or is served with summons, but the order for possession shall be final, enforceable and appealable if the court makes an express written finding that there is no just reason for delaying enforcement or appeal, as provided by Supreme Court rule of this State.

Such notice shall be in the name of the clerk of the court, be directed to the defendant or unknown occupant, shall state the nature of the cause against the defendant or unknown occupant and at whose instance issued and the time and place for trial, and shall also state that unless the defendant or unknown occupant appears at the time and place fixed for trial, judgment will be entered by default, and shall specify the character of the judgment that will be entered in such cause. The sheriff shall post 3 copies of the notice in 3 public places in the neighborhood of the court where the cause is to be tried, at least 10 days prior to the day set for the appearance, and, if the place of residence of the defendant or unknown occupant is stated in any affidavit on file, shall at the same time mail one copy of the notice addressed to such defendant or unknown occupant at such place of residence shown in such affidavit. On or before the day set for the

appearance, the sheriff shall file the notice with an endorsement thereon stating the time when and places where the sheriff posted and to whom and at what address he or she mailed copies as required by this Section. For want of sufficient notice any cause may be continued from time to time until the court has jurisdiction of the defendant or unknown occupant.

P.A. 82–280, § 9–107, eff. July 1, 1982. Amended by P.A. 83–645, § 2, eff. Jan. 1, 1984; P.A. 83–707, § 1, eff. Sept. 23, 1983; P.A. 83–1271, § 3, eff. Aug. 30, 1984; P.A. 83–1362, Art. II, § 109, eff. Sept. 11, 1984; P.A. 83–1528, Art. II, § 28, eff. Jan. 17, 1985; P.A. 92–823, § 5, eff. Aug. 21, 2002.

Formerly Ill.Rev.Stat.1991, ch. 110, ¶ 9–107.

5/9–107.5. Notice to unknown occupants

§ 9–107.5. Notice to unknown occupants.

(a) Service of process upon an unknown occupant may be had by delivering a copy of the summons and complaint naming "unknown occupants" to the tenant or any unknown occupant or person of the age of 13 or upwards occupying the premises.

(b) If unknown occupants are not named in the initial summons and complaint and a judgment for possession in favor of the plaintiff is entered, but the order does not include unknown occupants and the sheriff determines when executing the judgment for possession that persons not included in the order are in possession of the premises, then the sheriff shall leave with a person of the age of 13 years or upwards occupying the premises, a copy of the order, or if no one is present in the premises to accept the order or refuses to accept the order, then by posting a copy of the order on the premises. In addition to leaving a copy of the order or posting of the order, the sheriff shall also leave or post a notice addressed to "unknown occupants" that states unless any unknown occupants file a written petition with the clerk that sets forth the unknown occupant's legal claim for possession within 7 days of the date the notice is posted or left with any unknown occupant, the unknown occupants shall be evicted from the premises. If any unknown occupants file such a petition, a hearing on the merits of the unknown occupant's petition shall be held by the court within 7 days of the filing of the petition with the clerk. The unknown occupants shall have the burden of proof in establishing a legal right to continued possession.

(c) The plaintiff may obtain a judgment for possession only and not for rent as to any unknown occupants.

(d) Nothing in this Section may be construed so as to vest any rights to persons who are criminal trespassers, nor may this Section be construed in any way that interferes with the ability of law enforcement officials removing persons or property from the premises when there is a criminal trespass.

P.A. 82–280, § 9–107.5, added by P.A. 92–823, § 5, eff. Aug. 21, 2002.

5/9–107.10. Military personnel in military service; action for possession

§ 9–107.10. Military personnel in military service; action for possession.

(a) In this Section:

"Military service" means any full-time training or duty, no matter how described under federal or State law, for which a service member is ordered to report by the President, Governor of a state, commonwealth, or territory of the United States, or other appropriate military authority.

"Service member" means a resident of Illinois who is a member of any component of the U.S. Armed Forces or the National Guard of any state, the District of Columbia, a commonwealth, or a territory of the United States.

(b) In an action for possession of residential premises of a tenant, including a tenant who is a resident of a mobile home park, who is a service member that has entered military service, or of any member of the tenant's family who resides with the tenant, if the tenant entered into the rental agreement on or after the effective date of this amendatory Act of the 94th General Assembly, the court may, on its own motion, and shall, upon motion made by or on behalf of the tenant, do either of the following if the tenant's ability to pay the agreed rent is materially affected by the tenant's military service:

(1) Stay the proceedings for a period of 90 days, unless, in the opinion of the court, justice and equity require a longer or shorter period of time.

(2) Adjust the obligation under the rental agreement to preserve the interest of all parties to it.

(c) In order to be eligible for the benefits granted to service members under this Section, a service member or a member of the service member's family who resides with the service member must provide the landlord or mobile home park operator with a copy of the orders calling the service member to military service in excess of 29 consecutive days and of any orders further extending the period of service.

(d) If a stay is granted under this Section, the court may grant the landlord or mobile home park operator such relief as equity may require.

(e) A violation of this Section constitutes a civil rights violation under the Illinois Human Rights Act. All proceeds from the collection of any civil penalty imposed pursuant to the Illinois Human Rights Act

under this subsection shall be deposited into the Illinois Military Family Relief Fund.

P.A. 82–280, § 9–107.10, added by P.A. 94–635, § 915, eff. Aug. 22, 2005. Amended by P.A. 95–392, § 30, eff. Aug. 23, 2007; P.A. 97–913, § 940, eff. Jan. 1, 2013.

5/9–108. Jury trial

§ 9–108. Jury trial. In any case relating to premises used for residence purposes, either party may demand trial by jury, notwithstanding any waiver of jury trial contained in any lease or contract.

P.A. 82–280, § 9–108, eff. July 1, 1982.

Formerly Ill.Rev.Stat.1991, ch. 110, ¶ 9–108.

5/9–109. Trial ex parte

§ 9–109. Trial ex parte. If the defendant does not appear, having been duly summoned as herein provided the trial may proceed ex parte, and may be tried by the court, without a jury.

P.A. 82–280, § 9–109, eff. July 1, 1982.

Formerly Ill.Rev.Stat.1991, ch. 110, ¶ 9–109.

5/9–109.5. Standard of Proof

§ 9–109.5. Standard of Proof. After a trial, if the court finds, by a preponderance of the evidence, that the allegations in the complaint have been proven, the court shall enter judgment for possession of the premises in favor of the plaintiff.

P.A. 82–280, § 9–109.5, added by P.A. 90–557, § 5, eff. June 1, 1998.

5/9–109.7. Stay of enforcement; drug related action

§ 9–109.7. Stay of enforcement; drug related action. A judgment for possession of the premises entered in an action brought by a lessor or lessor's assignee, if the action was brought as a result of a lessor or lessor's assignee declaring a lease void pursuant to Section 11 of the Controlled Substance and Cannabis Nuisance Act,[1] may not be stayed for any period in excess of 7 days by the court. Thereafter the plaintiff shall be entitled to re-enter the premises immediately. The sheriff or other lawfully deputized officers shall execute an order entered pursuant to this Section within 7 days of its entry, or within 7 days of the expiration of a stay of judgment, if one is entered.

P.A. 82–280, § 9–109.7, added by P.A. 90–557, § 5, eff. June 1, 1998.

[1] 740 ILCS 40/11.

5/9–110. Judgment for whole premises—Stay of enforcement

§ 9–110. Judgment for whole premises—Stay of enforcement. If it appears on the trial that the plaintiff is entitled to the possession of the whole of the premises claimed, judgment for the possession thereof and for costs shall be entered in favor of the plaintiff. However, if the action is brought under Article IX of this Code and is based upon a breach of a contract entered into on or after July 1, 1962 for the purchase of such premises, the court, by order, may stay the enforcement of the judgment for a period not to exceed 60 days from the date of the judgment, or if the court finds that the amount unpaid on the contract is less than 75% of the original purchase price, then the court shall stay the enforcement of the judgment for a period of 180 days from the date of the judgment. The court may order a stay of less than 180 days (but in no event less than 60 days) if it is shown that the plaintiff, prior to the filing of the action under Article IX of this Act, granted the defendant previous extensions of time to pay the amounts due under the contract, or for other good cause shown. If during such period of stay the defendant pays the entire amount then due and payable under the terms of the contract other than such portion of the principal balance due under the contract as would not be due had no default occurred and costs and, if the contract provides therefor, reasonable attorney's fees as fixed by the court, and cures all other defaults then existing, the contract shall remain in force the same as if no default had occurred. The relief granted to a defendant by this Section shall not be exhausted by a single use thereof but shall not be again available with respect to the same contract for a period of 5 years from the date of such judgment. Whenever defendant cures the default under the contract pursuant to this Section, the defendant may within the period of stay file a motion to vacate the judgment in the court in which the judgment was entered, and, if the court, upon the hearing of such motion, is satisfied that such default has been cured, such judgment shall be vacated. Unless defendant files such motion to vacate in the court or the judgment is otherwise stayed, enforcement of the judgment may proceed immediately upon the expiration of such period of stay and all rights of the defendant in and to the premises and in and to the real estate described in the contract are terminated.

Nothing herein contained shall be construed as affecting the right of a seller of such premises to any lawful remedy or relief other than that provided by Part 1 of Article IX of this Act.

P.A. 82–280, § 9–110, eff. July 1, 1982. Amended by P.A. 85–907, Art. I, § 1, eff. Nov. 23, 1987.

Formerly Ill.Rev.Stat.1991, ch. 110, ¶ 9–110.

5/9–111. Condominium property

§ 9–111. Condominium property.

(a) As to property subject to the provisions of the "Condominium Property Act", approved June 20, 1963, as amended,[1] when the action is based upon the failure of an owner of a unit therein to pay when due

his or her proportionate share of the common expenses of the property, or of any other expenses lawfully agreed upon or the amount of any unpaid fine, and if the court finds that the expenses or fines are due to the plaintiff, the plaintiff shall be entitled to the possession of the whole of the premises claimed, and judgment in favor of the plaintiff shall be entered for the possession thereof and for the amount found due by the court including interest and late charges, if any, together with reasonable attorney's fees, if any, and for the plaintiff's costs. The awarding of reasonable attorney's fees shall be pursuant to the standards set forth in subsection (b) of this Section 9–111. The court shall, by order, stay the enforcement of the judgment for possession for a period of not less than 60 days from the date of the judgment and may stay the enforcement of the judgment for a period not to exceed 180 days from such date. Any judgment for money or any rent assignment under subsection (b) of Section 9–104.2 is not subject to this stay. The judgment for possession is not subject to an exemption of homestead under Part 9 of Article XII of this Code. If at any time, either during or after the period of stay, the defendant pays such expenses found due by the court, and costs, and reasonable attorney's fees as fixed by the court, and the defendant is not in arrears on his or her share of the common expenses for the period subsequent to that covered by the judgment, the defendant may file a motion to vacate the judgment in the court in which the judgment was entered, and, if the court, upon the hearing of such motion, is satisfied that the default in payment of the proportionate share of expenses has been cured, and if the court finds that the premises are not presently let by the board of managers as provided in Section 9–111.1 of this Act, the judgment shall be vacated. If the premises are being let by the board of managers as provided in Section 9–111.1 of this Act, when any judgment is sought to be vacated, the court shall vacate the judgment effective concurrent with the expiration of the lease term. Unless defendant files such motion to vacate in the court or the judgment is otherwise stayed, enforcement of the judgment may proceed immediately upon the expiration of the period of stay and all rights of the defendant to possession of his or her unit shall cease and determine until the date that the judgment may thereafter be vacated in accordance with the foregoing provisions, and notwithstanding payment of the amount of any money judgment if the unit owner or occupant is in arrears for the period after the date of entry of the judgment as provided in this Section. Nothing herein contained shall be construed as affecting the right of the board of managers, or its agents, to any lawful remedy or relief other than that provided by Part 1 of Article IX of this Act.

This amendatory Act of the 92nd General Assembly is intended as a clarification of existing law and not as a new enactment.

(b) For purposes of determining reasonable attorney's fees under subsection (a), the court shall consider:

(i) the time expended by the attorney;

(ii) the reasonableness of the hourly rate for the work performed;

(iii) the reasonableness of the amount of time expended for the work performed; and

(iv) the amount in controversy and the nature of the action.

P.A. 82–280, § 9–111, eff. July 1, 1982. Amended by P.A. 83–645, § 2, eff. Jan. 1, 1984; P.A. 83–1271, § 3, eff. Aug. 30, 1984; P.A. 84–722, § 2, eff. Sept. 21, 1985; P.A. 85–1386, § 2, eff. Jan. 1, 1989; P.A. 88–417, § 5, eff. Jan. 1, 1994; P.A. 91–196, § 5, eff. July 20, 1999; P.A. 92–540, § 5, eff. June 12, 2002.

Formerly Ill.Rev.Stat.1991, ch. 110, ¶ 9–111.
[1] 765 ILCS 605/1 et seq.

5/9–111.1. Lease to bona fide tenant

§ 9–111.1. Lease to bona fide tenant. Upon the entry of a judgment in favor of a board of managers for possession of property under the Condominium Property Act,[1] as provided in Section 9–111 of this Act, and upon delivery of possession of the premises by the sheriff or other authorized official to the board of managers pursuant to execution upon the judgment, the board of managers shall have the right and authority, incidental to the right of possession of a unit under the judgment, but not the obligation, to lease the unit to a bona fide tenant (whether the tenant is in occupancy or not) pursuant to a written lease for a term which may commence at any time within 8 months after the month in which the date of expiration of the stay of judgment occurs. The term may not exceed 13 months from the date of commencement of the lease. The court may, upon motion of the board of managers and with notice to the dispossessed unit owner, permit or extend a lease for one or more additional terms not to exceed 13 months per term. The board of managers shall first apply all rental income to assessments and other charges sued upon in the action for possession plus statutory interest on a monetary judgment, if any, attorneys' fees, and court costs incurred; and then to other expenses lawfully agreed upon (including late charges), any fines and reasonable expenses necessary to make the unit rentable, and lastly to assessments accrued thereafter until assessments are current. Any surplus shall be remitted to the unit owner. The court shall retain jurisdiction to determine the reasonableness of the expense of making the unit rentable.

P.A. 82–280, § 9–111.1, added by P.A. 88–417, § 5, eff. Jan. 1, 1994. Amended by P.A. 91–357, § 250, eff. July 29, 1999; P.A. 98–996, § 5, eff. Jan. 1, 2015.
[1] 765 ILCS 605/1 et seq.

5/9–112. Judgment for part of premises

§ 9–112. Judgment for part of premises. If it shall appear that the plaintiff is entitled to the possession of only a part of the premises claimed, the judgment shall be entered for that part only and for costs, and for the residue defendant shall be dismissed.

P.A. 82–280, § 9–112, eff. July 1, 1982.

Formerly Ill.Rev.Stat.1991, ch. 110, ¶ 9–112.

5/9–113. Joinder of several tenants

§ 9–113. Joinder of several tenants. Whenever there is one lease for the whole of certain premises, and the actual possession thereof, at the time of the filing of the action, is divided in severalty among persons with, or other than the lessee, in one or more portions or parcels, separately or severally held or occupied, all or so many of such persons, with the lessee, as the plaintiff may elect, may be joined as defendants in one action, and the recovery against them, with costs, shall be several, according as their actual holdings are judicially determined.

P.A. 82–280, § 9–113, eff. July 1, 1982.

Formerly Ill.Rev.Stat.1991, ch. 110, ¶ 9–113.

5/9–114. Judgment against plaintiff

§ 9–114. Judgment against plaintiff. If the plaintiff voluntarily dismisses the action, or fails to prove the plaintiff's right to the possession, judgment for costs shall be entered in favor of the defendant.

P.A. 82–280, § 9–114, eff. July 1, 1982.

Formerly Ill.Rev.Stat.1991, ch. 110, ¶ 9–114.

5/9–115. Dismissal as to part

§ 9–115. Dismissal as to part. The plaintiff may at any time dismiss his or her action as to any one or more of the defendants, and the jury or court may find any one or more of the defendants liable, and the others not liable, and the court shall thereupon enter judgment according to such finding.

P.A. 82–280, § 9–115, eff. July 1, 1982.

Formerly Ill.Rev.Stat.1991, ch. 110, ¶ 9–115.

5/9–116. Pending appeal

§ 9–116. Pending appeal. If the plaintiff appeals, then, during and notwithstanding the pendency of such appeal, the plaintiff is entitled to enforce, or accept from the defendant or from any person claiming under him or her, performance of all obligations imposed upon such defendant by the terms of any lease, contract, covenant or agreement under which the defendant claims the right to possession, or by law, as if such appeal has not been taken, without thereby affecting the appeal or the judgment appealed from, and without thereby creating or reinstating any tenancy or other relationship of the parties. However, if the result of the prosecution of such appeal and entry of final judgment is that the defendant was obligated to the plaintiff during the pendency thereof in a different form, manner or amount than that in which any payment or payments made under the provision of this Section was or were enforced or accepted, or in a different form, manner or amount than that adjudged in any judgment entered by any court in any other proceedings instituted by virtue of the provisions of this Section during the pendency of the appeal, such payment or payments shall be deemed to have been made to apply in the form, manner and amount resulting or arising from the prosecution of such appeal, on account of the defendant's obligation.

P.A. 82–280, § 9–116, eff. July 1, 1982.

Formerly Ill.Rev.Stat.1991, ch. 110, ¶ 9–116.

5/9–117. Expiration of Judgment

§ 9–117. Expiration of Judgment. No judgment for possession obtained in an action brought under this Article may be enforced more than 120 days after judgment is entered, unless upon motion by the plaintiff the court grants an extension of the period of enforcement of the judgment. Plaintiff's notice of motion shall contain the following notice directed to the defendant:

"Your landlord, (insert name), obtained an eviction judgment against you on (insert date), but the sheriff did not evict you within the 120 days that the landlord has to evict after a judgment in court. On the date stated in this notice, your landlord will be asking the court to allow the sheriff to evict you based on that judgment. You must attend the court hearing if you want the court to stop the landlord from having you evicted. To prevent the eviction, you must be able to prove that (1) the landlord and you made an agreement after the judgment (for instance, to pay up back rent or to comply with the lease) and you have lived up to the agreement; or (2) the reason the landlord brought the original eviction case has been resolved or forgiven, and the eviction the landlord now wants the court to grant is based on a new or different reason; or (3) that you have another legal or equitable reason why the court should not grant the landlord's request for your eviction."

The court shall grant the motion for the extension of the judgment of possession unless the defendant establishes that the tenancy has been reinstated, that the breach upon which the judgment was issued has been cured or waived, that the plaintiff and defendant entered into a post-judgment agreement whose terms the defendant has performed, or that other legal or equitable grounds exist that bar enforcement of the judgment. This Section does not apply to any action

based upon a breach of a contract entered into on or after July 1, 1962, for the purchase of premises in which the court has entered a stay under Section 9–110; nor shall this Section apply to any action to which the provisions of Section 9–111 apply; nor shall this Section affect the rights of Boards of Managers under Section 9–104.2.

P.A. 82–280, § 9–117, added by P.A. 86–1280, § 1, eff. Jan. 1, 1991. Amended by P.A. 96–60, § 5, eff. July 23, 2009.

Formerly Ill.Rev.Stat.1991, ch. 110, ¶ 9–117.

5/9–118. Emergency housing eviction proceedings

§ 9–118. Emergency housing eviction proceedings.

(a) As used in this Section:

"Cannabis" has the meaning ascribed to that term in the Cannabis Control Act.[1]

"Narcotics" and "controlled substance" have the meanings ascribed to those terms in the Illinois Controlled Substances Act.[2]

(b) This Section applies only if all of the following conditions are met:

(1) The complaint seeks possession of premises that are owned or managed by a housing authority established under the Housing Authorities Act [3] or privately owned and managed.

(2) The verified complaint alleges that there is direct evidence of any of the following:

(A) unlawful possessing, serving, storing, manufacturing, cultivating, delivering, using, selling, giving away, or trafficking in cannabis, methamphetamine, narcotics, or controlled substances within or upon the premises by or with the knowledge and consent of, or in concert with the person or persons named in the complaint; or

(B) the possession, use, sale, or delivery of a firearm which is otherwise prohibited by State law within or upon the premises by or with the knowledge and consent of, or in concert with, the person or persons named in the complaint; or

(C) murder, attempted murder, kidnapping, attempted kidnapping, arson, attempted arson, aggravated battery, criminal sexual assault, attempted criminal sexual assault, aggravated criminal sexual assault, predatory criminal sexual assault of a child, or criminal sexual abuse within or upon the premises by or with the knowledge and consent of, or in concert with, the person or persons named in the complaint.

(3) Notice by verified complaint setting forth the relevant facts, and a demand for possession of the type specified in Section 9–104 is served on the tenant or occupant of the premises at least 14 days before a hearing on the complaint is held, and proof of service of the complaint is submitted by the plaintiff to the court.

(b–5) In all actions brought under this Section 9–118, no predicate notice of termination or demand for possession shall be required to initiate an eviction action.

(c) When a complaint has been filed under this Section, a hearing on the complaint shall be scheduled on any day after the expiration of 14 days following the filing of the complaint. The summons shall advise the defendant that a hearing on the complaint shall be held at the specified date and time, and that the defendant should be prepared to present any evidence on his or her behalf at that time.

If a plaintiff which is a public housing authority accepts rent from the defendant after an action is initiated under this Section, the acceptance of rent shall not be a cause for dismissal of the complaint.

(d) If the defendant does not appear at the hearing, judgment for possession of the premises in favor of the plaintiff shall be entered by default. If the defendant appears, a trial shall be held immediately as is prescribed in other proceedings for possession. The matter shall not be continued beyond 7 days from the date set for the first hearing on the complaint except by agreement of both the plaintiff and the defendant. After a trial, if the court finds, by a preponderance of the evidence, that the allegations in the complaint have been proven, the court shall enter judgment for possession of the premises in favor of the plaintiff and the court shall order that the plaintiff shall be entitled to re-enter the premises immediately.

(d–5) If cannabis, methamphetamine, narcotics, or controlled substances are found or used anywhere in the premises, there is a rebuttable presumption either (1) that the cannabis, methamphetamine, narcotics, or controlled substances were used or possessed by a tenant or occupant or (2) that a tenant or occupant permitted the premises to be used for that use or possession, and knew or should have reasonably known that the substance was used or possessed.

(e) A judgment for possession entered under this Section may not be stayed for any period in excess of 7 days by the court. Thereafter the plaintiff shall be entitled to re-enter the premises immediately. The sheriff or other lawfully deputized officers shall give priority to service and execution of orders entered under this Section over other possession orders.

(f) This Section shall not be construed to prohibit the use or possession of cannabis, methamphetamine, narcotics, or a controlled substance that has been legally obtained in accordance with a valid prescription for the personal use of a lawful occupant of a dwelling unit.

P.A. 82–280, § 9–118, added by P.A. 87–933, § 1, eff. Jan. 1, 1993. Amended by P.A. 88–587, § 5, eff. Jan. 1, 1995; P.A. 90–557, § 5, eff. June 1, 1998; P.A. 90–768, § 5, eff. Aug. 14, 1998; P.A. 91–504, § 5, eff. Aug. 13, 1999; P.A. 94–556, § 1115, eff. Sept. 11, 2005.

Formerly Ill.Rev.Stat., ch. 110, ¶ 9–118.

1 720 ILCS 550/1 et seq.
2 720 ILCS 570/100 et seq.
3 310 ILCS 10/1 et seq.

5/9–119. Emergency subsidized housing eviction proceedings

§ 9–119. Emergency subsidized housing eviction proceedings.

(a) As used in this Section:

"FmHA" means the Farmers Home Administration or a local housing authority administering an FmHA program.

"HUD" means the United States Department of Housing and Urban Development, or the Federal Housing Administration or a local housing authority administering a HUD program.

"Section 8 contract" means a contract with HUD or FmHA which provides rent subsidies entered into pursuant to Section 8 of the United States Housing Act of 1937 [1] or the Section 8 Existing Housing Program (24 C.F.R. Part 882).

"Subsidized housing" means:

(1) any housing or unit of housing subject to a Section 8 contract;

(2) any housing or unit of housing owned, operated, or managed by a housing authority established under the Housing Authorities Act; or

(3) any housing or unit of housing financed by a loan or mortgage held by the Illinois Housing Development Authority, a local housing authority, or the federal Department of Housing and Urban Development ("HUD") that is:

(i) insured or held by HUD under Section 221(d)(3) of the National Housing Act [2] and assisted under Section 101 of the Housing and Urban Development Act of 1965 [3] or Section 8 of the United States Housing Act of 1937;

(ii) insured or held by HUD and bears interest at a rate determined under the proviso of Section 221(d)(3) of the National Housing Act;

(iii) insured, assisted, or held by HUD under Section 202 or 236 of the National Housing Act; [4]

(iv) insured or held by HUD under Section 514 or 515 of the Housing Act of 1949; [5]

(v) insured or held by HUD under the United States Housing Act of 1937; [6] or

(vi) held by HUD and formerly insured under a program listed in subdivision (i), (ii), (iii), (iv), or (v).

(b) This Section applies only if all of the following conditions are met:

(1) The verified complaint seeks possession of premises that are subsidized housing as defined under this Section.

(2) The verified complaint alleges that there is direct evidence of refusal by the tenant to allow the

landlord or agent of the landlord or other person authorized by State or federal law or regulations or local ordinance to inspect the premises, provided that all of the following conditions have been met:

(A) on 2 separate occasions within a 30 day period the tenant, or another person on the premises with the consent of the tenant, refuses to allow the landlord or agent of the landlord or other person authorized by State or federal law or regulations or local ordinance to inspect the premises;

(B) the landlord then sends written notice to the tenant stating that (i) the tenant, or a person on the premises with the consent of the tenant, failed twice within a 30 day period to allow the landlord or agent of the landlord or other person authorized by State or federal law or regulations or local ordinance to inspect the premises and (ii) the tenant must allow the landlord or agent of the landlord or other person authorized by State or federal law or regulations or local ordinance to inspect the premises within the next 30 days or face emergency eviction proceedings under this Section;

(C) the tenant subsequently fails to allow the landlord or agent of the landlord or other person authorized by State or federal law or regulations or local ordinance to inspect the premises within 30 days of receiving the notice from the landlord; and

(D) the tenant's written lease states that the occurrence of the events described in items (A), (B), and (C) may result in eviction.

(3) Notice, by verified complaint setting forth the relevant facts, and a demand for possession of the type specified in Section 9–104 is served on the tenant or occupant of the premises at least 14 days before a hearing on the complaint is held, and proof of service of the complaint is submitted by the plaintiff to the court.

(c) When a complaint has been filed under this Section, a hearing on the complaint shall be scheduled on any day after the expiration of 14 days following the filing of the complaint. The summons shall advise the defendant that a hearing on the complaint shall be held at the specified date and time, and that the defendant should be prepared to present any evidence on his or her behalf at that time.

(d) If the defendant does not appear at the hearing, judgment for possession of the premises in favor of the plaintiff shall be entered by default. If the defendant appears, a trial shall be held immediately as is prescribed in other proceedings for possession. The matter shall not be continued beyond 7 days from the date set for the first hearing on the complaint except by agreement of both the plaintiff and the defendant. After a trial, if the court finds, by a preponderance of the evidence, that the allegations in the complaint have been proven, the court shall enter judgment for

possession of the premises in favor of the plaintiff and the court shall order that the plaintiff shall be entitled to re-enter the premises immediately.

(e) A judgment for possession entered under this Section may not be stayed for any period in excess of 7 days by the court. Thereafter the plaintiff shall be entitled to re-enter the premises immediately. The sheriff or other lawfully deputized officers shall give priority to service and execution of orders entered under this Section over other possession orders.

P.A. 82–280, § 9–119, added by P.A. 89–660, § 5, eff. Jan. 1, 1997.

[1] 42 U.S.C.A. § 1437f.
[2] 12 U.S.C.A. § 1715l.
[3] 12 U.S.C.A. § 1701s.
[4] 12 U.S.C.A. § 1701q or 1715z–1.
[5] 42 U.S.C.A. § 1484 or 1485.
[6] 42 U.S.C.A. § 1437 et seq.

5/9–120. Leased premises used in furtherance of a criminal offense; lease void at option of lessor or assignee

§ 9–120. Leased premises used in furtherance of a criminal offense; lease void at option of lessor or assignee.

(a) If any lessee or occupant, on one or more occasions, uses or permits the use of leased premises for the commission of any act that would constitute a felony or a Class A misdemeanor under the laws of this State, the lease or rental agreement shall, at the option of the lessor or the lessor's assignee become void, and the owner or lessor shall be entitled to recover possession of the leased premises as against a tenant holding over after the expiration of his or her term. A written lease shall notify the lessee that if any lessee or occupant, on one or more occasions, uses or permits the use of the leased premises for the commission of a felony or Class A misdemeanor under the laws of this State, the lessor shall have the right to void the lease and recover the leased premises. Failure to include this language in a written lease or the use of an oral lease shall not waive or impair the rights of the lessor or lessor's assignee under this Section or the lease. This Section shall not be construed so as to diminish the rights of a lessor, if any, to terminate a lease for other reasons permitted under law or pursuant to the lease agreement.

(b) The owner or lessor may bring a forcible entry and detainer action, or, if the State's Attorney of the county in which the real property is located or the corporation counsel of the municipality in which the real property is located agrees, assign to that State's Attorney or corporation counsel the right to bring a forcible entry and detainer action on behalf of the owner or lessor, against the lessee and all occupants of the leased premises. The assignment must be in writing on a form prepared by the State's Attorney of the county in which the real property is located or the corporation counsel of the municipality in which the real property is located, as applicable. If the owner or lessor assigns the right to bring a forcible entry and detainer action, the assignment shall be limited to those rights and duties up to and including delivery of the order of eviction to the sheriff for execution. The owner or lessor shall remain liable for the cost of the eviction whether or not the right to bring the forcible entry and detainer action has been assigned.

(c) A person does not forfeit any part of his or her security deposit due solely to an eviction under the provisions of this Section, except that a security deposit may be used to pay fees charged by the sheriff for carrying out an eviction.

(d) If a lessor or the lessor's assignee voids a lease or contract under the provisions of this Section and the tenant or occupant has not vacated the premises within 5 days after receipt of a written notice to vacate the premises, the lessor or lessor's assignee may seek relief under this Article IX. Notwithstanding Sections 9–112, 9–113, and 9–114 of this Code, judgment for costs against a plaintiff seeking possession of the premises under this Section shall not be awarded to the defendant unless the action was brought by the plaintiff in bad faith. An action to possess premises under this Section shall not be deemed to be in bad faith when the plaintiff based his or her cause of action on information provided to him or her by a law enforcement agency, the State's Attorney, or the municipality.

(e) After a trial, if the court finds, by a preponderance of the evidence, that the allegations in the complaint have been proven, the court shall enter judgment for possession of the premises in favor of the plaintiff and the court shall order that the plaintiff shall be entitled to re-enter the premises immediately.

(f) A judgment for possession of the premises entered in an action brought by a lessor or lessor's assignee, if the action was brought as a result of a lessor or lessor's assignee declaring a lease void pursuant to this Section, may not be stayed for any period in excess of 7 days by the court unless all parties agree to a longer period. Thereafter the plaintiff shall be entitled to re-enter the premises immediately. The sheriff or other lawfully deputized officers shall execute an order entered pursuant to this Section within 7 days of its entry, or within 7 days of the expiration of a stay of judgment, if one is entered.

(g) Nothing in this Section shall limit the rights of an owner or lessor to bring a forcible entry and detainer action on the basis of other applicable law. P.A. 82–280, § 9–120, added by P.A. 90–360, § 5, eff. Jan. 1, 1998. Amended by P.A. 97–236, § 5, eff. Aug. 2, 2011.

5/9–121. Sealing of court file

§ 9–121. Sealing of court file.

(a) Definition. As used in this Section, "court file" means the court file created when a forcible entry and detainer action is filed with the court.

(b) Discretionary sealing of court file. The court may order that a court file in a forcible entry and detainer action be placed under seal if the court finds that the plaintiff's action is sufficiently without a basis in fact or law, which may include a lack of jurisdiction, that placing the court file under seal is clearly in the interests of justice, and that those interests are not outweighed by the public's interest in knowing about the record.

(c) Mandatory sealing of court file. The court file relating to a forcible entry and detainer action brought against a tenant under Section 9–207.5 of this Code or as set forth in subdivision (h)(6) of Section 15–1701 of this Code shall be placed under seal. P.A. 82–280, § 9–121, added by P.A. 96–1131, § 5, eff. July 20, 2010. Amended by P.A. 98–514, § 5, eff. Nov. 19, 2013.

PART 2. RECOVERY OF RENT; TERMINATION OF CERTAIN TENANCIES

5/9–201. Recovery of rent

§ 9–201. Recovery of rent. The owner of lands, his or her executors or administrators, may sue for and recover rent therefor, or a fair and reasonable satisfaction for the use and occupation thereof, by a civil action in any of the following instances:

1. When rent is due and in arrears on a lease for life or lives.

2. When lands are held and occupied by any person without any special agreement for rent.

3. When possession is obtained under an agreement, written or verbal, for the purchase of the premises, and before a deed is given the right to possession is terminated by forfeiture or non-compliance with the agreement, and possession is wrongfully refused or neglected to be given upon demand, made in writing, by the party entitled thereto. All payments made by the vendee, or his or her representatives or assigns, may be set off against such rent.

4. When land has been sold upon a judgment of court, when the party to such judgment or person holding under him or her, wrongfully refuses or neglects to surrender possession of the same, after demand, in writing, by the person entitled to the possession.

5. When the lands have been sold upon a mortgage or trust deed, and the mortgagor or grantor, or person holding under him or her, wrongfully refuses or neglects to surrender possession of the same, after demand, in writing, by the person entitled to the possession.

P.A. 82–280, § 9–201, eff. July 1, 1982. Amended by P.A. 83–707, § 1, eff. Sept. 23, 1983.

Formerly Ill.Rev.Stat.1991, ch. 110, ¶ 9–201.

5/9–202. Wilfully holding over

§ 9–202. Wilfully holding over. If any tenant or any person who is in or comes into possession of any lands, tenements or hereditaments, by, from or under, or by collusion with the tenant, wilfully holds over any lands, tenements or hereditaments, after the expiration of his or her term or terms, and after demand made in writing, for the possession thereof, by his or her landlord, or the person to whom the remainder or reversion of such lands, tenements or hereditaments belongs, the person so holding over, shall, for the time the landlord or rightful owner is so kept out of possession, pay to the person so kept out of possession, or his or her legal representatives, at the rate of double the yearly value of the lands, tenements or hereditaments so detained to be recovered by a civil action.

P.A. 82–280, § 9–202, eff. July 1, 1982. Amended by P.A. 83–707, § 1, eff. Sept. 23, 1983.

Formerly Ill.Rev.Stat.1991, ch. 110, ¶ 9–202.

5/9–203. Holding over after notice

§ 9–203. Holding over after notice. If any tenant gives notice of his or her intention to quit the premises which are held by him or her, at a time mentioned in such notice, at which time the tenant would have a right to quit by the lease, and does not accordingly deliver up possession thereof, such tenant shall pay to the landlord or lessor double the rent or sum which would otherwise be due, to be collected in the same manner as the rent otherwise due should have been collected.

P.A. 82–280, § 9–203, eff. July 1, 1982. Amended by P.A. 82–783, Art. IV, § 27, eff. July 13, 1982.

Formerly Ill.Rev.Stat.1991, ch. 110, ¶ 9–203.

5/9–204. Rent in arrears—Re-entry

§ 9–204. Rent in arrears—Re-entry. In all cases between landlord and tenant, where one-half year's rent is in arrears and unpaid, and the landlord or lessor to whom such rent is due has the right by law to re-enter for non-payment thereof, such landlord or lessor may, without any formal demand or re-entry, commence an action of ejectment for the recovery of the demised premises. In case judgment is entered in favor of the plaintiff in the action of ejectment before the rent in arrearage and costs of the action are paid, then the lease of the lands shall cease and be determined, unless the lessee shall by appeal reverse the judgment, or by petition filed within 6 months after the entry of such judgment, obtain relief from the same. However, any tenant may, at any time before final judgment on the ejectment, pay or tender to the landlord or lessor of the premises the amount of rent in arrears and costs of the action, whereupon the action of ejectment shall be dismissed.

P.A. 82–280, § 9–204, eff. July 1, 1982.

Formerly Ill.Rev.Stat.1991, ch. 110, ¶ 9–204.

5/9–205. Notice to terminate tenancy from year to year

§ 9–205. Notice to terminate tenancy from year to year. Except as provided in Section 9–206 and Section 9–207.5 of this Act, in all cases of tenancy from year to year, 60 days' notice, in writing, shall be sufficient to terminate the tenancy at the end of the year. The notice may be given at any time within 4 months preceding the last 60 days of the year.

P.A. 82–280, § 9–205, eff. July 1, 1982. Amended by P.A. 98–514, § 5, eff. Nov. 19, 2013.

Formerly Ill.Rev.Stat.1991, ch. 110, ¶ 9–205.

5/9–206. Notice to terminate tenancy of farm land

§ 9–206. Notice to terminate tenancy of farm land. Subject to the provisions of Section 16 of the Landlord and Tenant Act, in order to terminate tenancies from year to year of farm lands, occupied on a crop share, livestock share, cash rent or other rental basis, the notice to quit shall be given in writing not less than 4 months prior to the end of the year of letting. Such notice may not be waived in a verbal lease. The notice to quit may be substantially in the following form:

To A.B.: You are hereby notified that I have elected to terminate your lease of the farm premises now occupied by you, being (here describe the premises) and you are hereby further notified to quit and deliver up possession of the same to me at the end of the lease year, the last day of such year being (here insert the last day of the lease year).

P.A. 82–280, § 9–206, eff. July 1, 1982. Amended by P.A. 97–913, § 940, eff. Jan. 1, 2013.

Formerly Ill.Rev.Stat.1991, ch. 110, ¶ 9–206.

5/9–206.1. Life tenancy termination; farmland leases

§ 9–206.1. Life tenancy termination; farmland leases.

(a) Tenancies from year to year of farmland occupied on a crop share, livestock share, cash rent, or other rental basis in which the lessor is the life tenant or the representative of the life tenant shall continue until the end of the current lease year in which the life tenant's interest terminates unless otherwise provided in writing by the lessor and the lessee.

(b) Whenever the life tenancy of the lessor terminates not more than 6 months before the end of the tenancy of the lessee but before the beginning of the next crop year, the lessee of the farmlands is entitled to reasonable costs incurred in field preparation for the next crop year, payable by the succeeding life tenant or remainderman.

As used in this Section "farmland" means any property used primarily for the growing and harvesting of crops; the feeding, breeding and management of livestock; dairying, or any other agricultural or horticultural use or combination thereof, including, but not limited to, hay, grain, fruit, truck or vegetable crops, floriculture, mushroom growing, plant or tree nurseries, orchards, forestry, sod farming and greenhouses; the keeping, raising and feeding of livestock or poultry, including poultry, swine, sheep, beef cattle, ponies or horses; dairy farming; fur farming; beekeeping; or fish or wildlife farming.

P.A. 82–280, § 9–206.1, added by P.A. 89–549, § 5, eff. Jan. 1, 1997.

5/9–207. Notice to terminate tenancy for less than a year

§ 9–207. Notice to terminate tenancy for less than a year.

(a) Except as provided in Section 9–207.5 of this Code, in all cases of tenancy from week to week, where the tenant holds over without special agreement, the landlord may terminate the tenancy by 7 days' notice, in writing, and may maintain an action for forcible entry and detainer or ejectment.

(b) Except as provided in Section 9–207.5 of this Code, in all cases of tenancy for any term less than one year, other than tenancy from week to week, where the tenant holds over without special agreement, the landlord may terminate the tenancy by 30

days' notice, in writing, and may maintain an action for forcible entry and detainer or ejectment.

P.A. 82–280, § 9–207, eff. July 1, 1982. Amended by P.A. 98–514, § 5, eff. Nov. 19, 2013.

Formerly Ill.Rev.Stat.1991, ch. 110, ¶ 9–207.

5/9–207.5. Termination of bona fide leases in residential real estate in foreclosure

§ 9–207.5. Termination of bona fide leases in residential real estate in foreclosure.

(a) A mortgagee, receiver, holder of the certificate of sale, holder of the deed issued pursuant to that certificate, or, if no certificate or deed was issued, the purchaser at a judicial sale under Section 15–1507 of this Code, who assumes control of the residential real estate in foreclosure, as defined in Section 15–1225 of this Code, may terminate a bona fide lease, as defined in Section 15–1224 of this Code, only: (i) at the end of the term of the bona fide lease, by no less than 90 days' written notice or (ii) in the case of a bona fide lease that is for a month-to-month or week-to-week term, by no less than 90 days' written notice.

(b) Notwithstanding the provisions of subsection (a) of this Section, an individual who assumes control of residential real estate in foreclosure pursuant to a judicial sale and who will occupy a dwelling unit of the residential real estate in foreclosure as his or her primary residence may terminate the bona fide lease for the dwelling unit subject to the 90–day notice requirement of subsection (a) of this Section.

(c) Nothing in this Section or Section 15–1224 of this Code shall abrogate the rights of a mortgagee, receiver, holder of the certificate of sale, holder of the deed issued pursuant to that certificate, or, if no certificate or deed was issued, the purchaser at a judicial sale, who assumes control of the residential real estate in foreclosure to terminate a bona fide lease of a dwelling unit in residential real estate in foreclosure under Section 9–118, 9–119, 9–120, 9–201, 9–202, 9–203, 9–204, 9–209, or 9–210 of this Code.

P.A. 82–280, § 9–207.5, added by P.A. 98–514, § 5, eff. Nov. 19, 2013.

5/9–208. Further demand

§ 9–208. Further demand. Where a tenancy is terminated by notice, under either of the 2 preceding sections, no further demand is necessary before bringing an action under the statute in relation to forcible detainer or ejectment.

P.A. 82–280, § 9–208, eff. July 1, 1982. Amended by P.A. 83–707, § 1, eff. Sept. 23, 1983.

Formerly Ill.Rev.Stat.1991, ch. 110, ¶ 9–208.

5/9–209. Demand for rent—Action for possession

§ 9–209. Demand for rent—Action for possession. A landlord or his or her agent may, any time after rent is due, demand payment thereof and notify the tenant, in writing, that unless payment is made within a time mentioned in such notice, not less than 5 days after service thereof, the lease will be terminated. If the tenant does not within the time mentioned in such notice, pay the rent due, the landlord may consider the lease ended, and sue for the possession under the statute in relation to forcible entry and detainer, or maintain ejectment without further notice or demand. A claim for rent may be joined in the complaint, including a request for the pro rata amount of rent due for any period that a judgment is stayed, and a judgment obtained for the amount of rent found due, in any action or proceeding brought, in an action of forcible entry and detainer for the possession of the leased premises, under this Section.

Notice made pursuant to this Section shall, as hereinafter stated, not be invalidated by payments of past due rent demanded in the notice, when the payments do not, at the end of the notice period, total the amount demanded in the notice. The landlord may, however, agree in writing to continue the lease in exchange for receiving partial payment. To prevent invalidation, the notice must prominently state:

"Only FULL PAYMENT of the rent demanded in this notice will waive the landlord's right to terminate the lease under this notice, unless the landlord agrees in writing to continue the lease in exchange for receiving partial payment."

Collection by the landlord of past rent due after the filing of a suit for possession or ejectment pursuant to failure of the tenant to pay the rent demanded in the notice shall not invalidate the suit.

P.A. 82–280, § 9–209, eff. July 1, 1982. Amended by P.A. 83–1398, § 5, eff. Sept. 12, 1984; P.A. 97–247, § 5, eff. Jan. 1, 2012.

Formerly Ill.Rev.Stat.1991, ch. 110, ¶ 9–209.

5/9–210. Notice to quit

§ 9–210. Notice to quit. When default is made in any of the terms of a lease, it is not necessary to give more than 10 days' notice to quit, or of the termination of such tenancy, and the same may be terminated on giving such notice to quit at any time after such default in any of the terms of such lease. Such notice may be substantially in the following form:

"To A.B.: You are hereby notified that in consequence of your default in (here insert the character of the default) of the premises now occupied by you, being, etc., (here describe the premises) I have elected to terminate your lease, and you are hereby notified to quit and deliver up possession of the same to me within 10 days of this date (dated, etc.)."

The notice is to be signed by the lessor or his or her agent, and no other notice or demand of possession or termination of such tenancy is necessary.

P.A. 82–280, § 9–210, eff. July 1, 1982.

Formerly Ill.Rev.Stat.1991, ch. 110, ¶ 9–210.

5/9–211. Service of demand or notice

§ 9–211. Service of demand or notice. Any demand may be made or notice served by delivering a written or printed, or partly written and printed, copy thereof to the tenant, or by leaving the same with some person of the age of 13 years or upwards, residing on or in possession of the premises; or by sending a copy of the notice to the tenant by certified or registered mail, with a returned receipt from the addressee; and in case no one is in the actual possession of the premises, then by posting the same on the premises.

P.A. 82–280, § 9–211, eff. July 1, 1982. Amended by P.A. 83–355, § 1, eff. Sept. 14, 1983.

Formerly Ill.Rev.Stat.1991, ch. 110, ¶ 9–211.

5/9–212. Evidence of service

§ 9–212. Evidence of service. When such demand is made or notice served by an officer authorized to serve process, the officer's return is prima facie evidence of the facts therein stated, and if such demand is made or notice served by any person not an officer, the return may be sworn to by the person serving the same, and is then prima facie evidence of the facts therein stated.

P.A. 82–280, § 9–212, eff. July 1, 1982.

Formerly Ill.Rev.Stat.1991, ch. 110, ¶ 9–212.

5/9–213. Expiration of term

§ 9–213. Expiration of term. When the tenancy is for a certain period, and the term expires by the terms of the lease, the tenant is then bound to surrender possession, and no notice to quit or demand of possession is necessary.

P.A. 82–280, § 9–213, eff. July 1, 1982.

Formerly Ill.Rev.Stat.1991, ch. 110, ¶ 9–213.

5/9–213.1. Duty of landlord to mitigate damages

§ 9–213.1. Duty of landlord to mitigate damages. After January 1, 1984, a landlord or his or her agent shall take reasonable measures to mitigate the damages recoverable against a defaulting lessee.

P.A. 82–280, § 9–213.1, added by P.A. 83–521, § 1, eff. Jan. 1, 1984. Amended by P.A. 84–1043, § 1, eff. Nov. 26, 1985.

Formerly Ill.Rev.Stat.1991, ch. 110, ¶ 9–213.1.

5/9–214. Lease defined

§ 9–214. Lease defined. The term "lease," as used in Part 2 of Article IX of this Act, includes every letting, whether by verbal or written agreement.
P.A. 82–280, § 9–214, eff. July 1, 1982.

Formerly Ill.Rev.Stat.1991, ch. 110, ¶ 9–214.

5/9–215. Remedies available to grantee

§ 9–215. Remedies available to grantee. The grantees of any leased lands, tenements, rents or other hereditaments, or of the reversion thereof, the assignees of the lessor of any lease, and the heirs, legatees and personal representatives of the lessor, grantee or assignee, shall have the same remedies by action or otherwise, for the non-performance of any agreement in the lease, or for the recovery of any rent, or for the doing of any waste or other cause of forfeiture, as their grantor or lessor might have had if such reversion had remained in such lessor or grantor.
P.A. 82–280, § 9–215, eff. July 1, 1982. Amended by P.A. 83–707, § 1, eff. Sept. 23, 1983.

Formerly Ill.Rev.Stat.1991, ch. 110, ¶ 9–215.

5/9–216. Remedies available to lessee

§ 9–216. Remedies available to lessee. The lessees of any lands, their assigns or personal representatives, shall have the same remedy, by action or otherwise, against the lessor, his or her grantees, assignees or his, her or their representatives, for the breach of any agreement in such lease, as such lessee might have had against his or her immediate lessor. This section shall have no application to the covenants against incumbrances, or relating to the title or possession of the premises demised.
P.A. 82–280, § 9–216, eff. July 1, 1982.

Formerly Ill.Rev.Stat.1991, ch. 110, ¶ 9–216.

5/9–217. Rent recoverable by representative, from subtenant

§ 9–217. Rent recoverable by representative, from subtenant. When a tenant for life demises[1] any lands and dies on or after the day when any rent becomes due and payable, his or her executor or administrator may recover from the subtenant the whole rent due, but if such tenant for life dies, before the day when any rent is to become due, his or her executor or administrator may recover the portion of rent which accrued before his or her death, and the remainderman shall recover for the residue.
P.A. 82–280, § 9–217, eff. July 1, 1982.

Formerly Ill.Rev.Stat.1991, ch. 110, ¶ 9–217.
 [1] So in enrolled bill.

5/9–218. Rent payments at business office

§ 9–218. Rent payments at business office.

(a) If the lessor, or agent of the lessor, of residential real property, containing 100 or more residential units in either a single building or a complex of buildings, maintains a business office on the premises of the building or complex that has regularly scheduled office hours, then the lessor, or agent of the lessor, must accept rent payments from a lessee of any of those residential units at that business office during the regularly scheduled office hours and the lessor may not impose any penalty, fee, or charge for making rent payments in this manner that are otherwise considered timely under the lease, but the landlord may refuse to accept payment by cash when rent payments are made in this manner.

(b) This Section applies to each lease and other rental agreement in effect on the effective date of this amendatory Act of the 94th General Assembly unless there is specific language in that lease or other rental agreement that conflicts with the provisions of this Section. If any provision of a lease or other rental agreement entered into, extended, or renewed on or after the effective date of this amendatory Act of the 94th General Assembly conflicts with the provisions of this Section, then that provision of the lease or other rental agreement is void and unenforceable.
P.A. 82–280, § 9–218, added by P.A. 94–2, § 5, eff. May 31, 2005.

PART 3. DISTRESS FOR RENT

5/9–301. Property subject to distraint

§ 9–301. Property subject to distraint. In all cases of distress for rent, the landlord, by himself or herself, his or her agent or attorney, may seize for rent any personal property of his or her tenant that may be found in the county where such tenant resides, and in no case shall the property of any other person, although the same may be found on the premises, be liable to seizure for rent due from such tenant.

P.A. 82–280, § 9–301, eff. July 1, 1982.

Formerly Ill.Rev.Stat.1991, ch. 110, ¶ 9–301.

5/9–302. Filing of distress warrant with inventory

§ 9–302. Filing of distress warrant with inventory. The person making such distress shall immediately file with the clerk of the circuit court a copy of the distress warrant, together with an inventory of the property levied upon.

P.A. 82–280, § 9–302, eff. July 1, 1982.

Formerly Ill.Rev.Stat.1991, ch. 110, ¶ 9–302.

5/9–303. Summons and return

§ 9–303. Summons and return. Upon the filing of such copy of distress warrant and inventory, the clerk shall issue a summons against the party against whom the distress warrant has been issued, returnable as summons in other civil cases.

P.A. 82–280, § 9–303, eff. July 1, 1982.

Formerly Ill.Rev.Stat.1991, ch. 110, ¶ 9–303.

5/9–304. Notice to non-residents

§ 9–304. Notice to non-residents. When it appears, by affidavit filed in the court where such proceeding is pending, that the defendant is a nonresident or has departed from this state, or on due inquiry cannot be found, or is concealed within this state, and the affiant states the place of residence of the defendant, if known, and if not known, that upon diligent inquiry he or she has not been able to ascertain the same, notice may be given as in attachment cases.

P.A. 82–280, § 9–304, eff. July 1, 1982.

Formerly Ill.Rev.Stat.1991, ch. 110, ¶ 9–304.

5/9–305. Proceedings—Pleading

§ 9–305. Proceedings—Pleading. The action shall thereafter proceed in the same manner as in case of attachment before the court. It shall not be necessary for the plaintiff in any case to file a complaint, but the distress warrant shall stand as a complaint and shall be amendable, as complaints in other civil cases, but no such amendment shall in any way affect any liabilities that have accrued in the execution of such warrant.

P.A. 82–280, § 9–305, eff. July 1, 1982.

Formerly Ill.Rev.Stat.1991, ch. 110, ¶ 9–305.

5/9–306. Counterclaim—Defenses

§ 9–306. Counterclaim—Defenses. The defendant may file a counterclaim as in other civil actions or other defense which would have been proper if the action had been for the rent, and with like effect.

P.A. 82–280, § 9–306, eff. July 1, 1982.

Formerly Ill.Rev.Stat.1991, ch. 110, ¶ 9–306.

5/9–307. Judgment for plaintiff

§ 9–307. Judgment for plaintiff. If the plaintiff recovers, judgment shall be entered in favor of plaintiff, for the amount which the court finds to be due the plaintiff.

P.A. 82–280, § 9–307, eff. July 1, 1982.

Formerly Ill.Rev.Stat.1991, ch. 110, ¶ 9–307.

5/9–308. Effect of judgment against defendant

§ 9–308. Effect of judgment against defendant. After the defendant is served with process or appears in the action, the judgment shall have the same force and effect as if served by summons, and the judgment may be enforced, not only against the property distrained, but also against the other property of the defendant. But the property distrained, if the same has not been replevied or released from seizure, shall be first sold.

P.A. 82–280, § 9–308, eff. July 1, 1982.

Formerly Ill.Rev.Stat.1991, ch. 110, ¶ 9–308.

5/9–309. Judgment by default

§ 9–309. Judgment by default. When publication of notice, as provided by law, but the defendant is not served with process and does not appear, judgment by default may be entered, and the plaintiff may recover the amount due him or her for rent at the time of issuing the distress warrant, and enforcement may be had against the property distrained, but no enforcement may be had against any other property of the defendant.

P.A. 82–280, § 9–309, eff. July 1, 1982.

Formerly Ill.Rev.Stat.1991, ch. 110, ¶ 9–309.

5/9–310. Judgment in favor of defendant—Counterclaim

§ 9–310. Judgment in favor of defendant—Counterclaim. If the judgment is in favor of the defendant, the defendant shall recover costs and judgment shall be entered for the return to the defendant of the property distrained, unless the same has been replevied or released from such distress. If a counterclaim is interposed, and it is determined by the court that a balance is due from the plaintiff to the defendant, judgment shall be entered in favor of the defendant.

P.A. 82–280, § 9–310, eff. July 1, 1982.

Formerly Ill.Rev.Stat.1991, ch. 110, ¶ 9–310.

5/9–311. Bond for release of property

§ 9–311. Bond for release of property. When any distress warrant is levied, the person whose property is distrained, may release the same by entering into bond in double the amount of the rent claimed, payable to the landlord, with sufficient sureties, to be approved by the person making the levy, if the bond is tendered before the filing of a copy of the warrant, as provided in Part 3 of Article IX of this Act, or if after, by the clerk of the court in which the action if pending, conditioned to pay whatever judgment the landlord may recover in the action, with costs of the action. If the bond is taken before the filing of a copy of the distress warrant, such bond shall be filed therewith, and if taken after the filing of a copy of the distress warrant, it shall be filed in the office of the clerk of the court where the action is pending.

P.A. 82–280, § 9–311, eff. July 1, 1982. Amended by P.A. 83–707, § 1, eff. Sept. 23, 1983.

Formerly Ill.Rev.Stat.1991, ch. 110, ¶ 9–311.

5/9–312. Perishable property

§ 9–312. Perishable property. If any property distrained is of a perishable nature and in danger of immediate waste or decay, and is not replevied or bonded, the landlord or his or her agent or attorney may, upon giving notice to the defendant or his or her attorney, or if neither can be found, without any notice, apply to the court in which the action is pending describing the property, and showing that it is so in danger, and if the court is satisfied that the property is of a perishable nature and in danger of immediate waste or decay, and if the defendant or his or her attorney is not served with notice, or does not appear, that neither the defendant nor the attorney can be found, the court may enter an order to the person having possession of the property, directing the sale thereof upon such time and notice, terms and conditions as the court shall deem for the best interests of the parties concerned. The money resulting from such sale shall be deposited with the clerk of the court in which the action is pending, there to abide the event of the action.

P.A. 82–280, § 9–312, eff. July 1, 1982.

Formerly Ill.Rev.Stat.1991, ch. 110, ¶ 9–312.

5/9–313. Limitation

§ 9–313. Limitation. The right of the landlord to distrain the personal goods of the tenant, shall continue for the period of 6 months after the expiration of the term for which the premises were demised or the tenancy is terminated.

P.A. 82–280, § 9–313, eff. July 1, 1982.

Formerly Ill.Rev.Stat.1991, ch. 110, ¶ 9–313.

5/9–314. Distress for products and labor

§ 9–314. Distress for products and labor. When the rent is payable wholly or in part in specific articles of property or products of the premises, or labor, the landlord may distrain for the value of such articles, products or labor.

P.A. 82–280, § 9–314, eff. July 1, 1982.

Formerly Ill.Rev.Stat.1991, ch. 110, ¶ 9–314.

5/9–315. Exemption

§ 9–315. Exemption. The same articles of personal property which are, by law, exempt from the enforcement of a judgment thereon, except the crops grown or growing upon the demised premises, shall also be exempt from distress for rent.

P.A. 82–280, § 9–315, eff. July 1, 1982. Amended by P.A. 83–707, § 1, eff. Sept. 23, 1983.

Formerly Ill.Rev.Stat.1991, ch. 110, ¶ 9–315.

5/9–316. Lien upon crops

§ 9–316. Lien upon crops. Every landlord shall have a lien upon the crops grown or growing upon the demised premises for the rent thereof, whether the same is payable wholly or in part in money or specific articles of property or products of the premises, or labor, and also for the faithful performance of the terms of the lease. Such lien shall continue for the period of 6 months after the expiration of the term for which the premises are demised, and may be enforced by distraint as provided in Part 3 of Article IX of this Act.

A good faith purchaser shall, however, take such crops free of any landlord's lien unless, within 6 months prior to the purchase, the landlord provides written notice of his lien to the purchaser by registered or certified mail. Such notice shall contain the names and addresses of the landlord and tenant, and clearly identify the leased property.

A landlord may require that, prior to his tenant's selling any crops grown on the demised premises, the tenant disclose the name of the person to whom the tenant intends to sell those crops. Where such a requirement has been imposed, the tenant shall not sell the crops to any person other than a person who has been disclosed to the landlord as a potential buyer of the crops.

A lien arising under this Section shall have priority over any agricultural lien as defined in, and over any security interest arising under, provisions of Article 9 of the Uniform Commercial Code.[1]

P.A. 82–280, § 9–316, eff. July 1, 1982. Amended by P.A. 83–70, § 1, eff. Aug. 16, 1983; P.A. 91–893, § 33, eff. July 1, 2001; P.A. 92–819, § 5, eff. Aug. 21, 2002.

Formerly Ill.Rev.Stat.1991, ch. 110, ¶ 9–316.
[1] 810 ILCS 5/9–101.

5/9–316.1. Tenant's duty to disclose to landlord identity of vendee of crops

§ 9–316.1. Tenant's duty to disclose to landlord identity of vendee of crops. (a) Where, pursuant to Section 9–316, a landlord has required that, before the tenant sells crops grown on the demised premises, the tenant disclose to the landlord the persons to whom the tenant intends to sell such crops, it is unlawful for the tenant to sell the crops to a person other than a person so disclosed to the landlord.

(b) An individual who knowingly violates this Section is guilty of a Class A misdemeanor.

(c) A corporation convicted of a violation of this Section is guilty of a business offense and shall be fined not less than $2000 nor more than $10,000.

(d) In the event the tenant is a corporation or a partnership, any officer, director, manager or managerial agent of the tenant who violates this Section or causes the tenant to violate this Section is guilty of a Class A misdemeanor.

(e) It is an affirmative defense to a prosecution for the violation of this Section that the tenant has paid to the landlord the proceeds from the sale of the crops within 10 days after such sale.

P.A. 82–280, § 9–316.1, added by P.A. 83–70, § 1, eff. Aug. 16, 1983. Amended by P.A. 84–1043, § 1, eff. Nov. 26, 1985.

Formerly Ill.Rev.Stat.1991, ch. 110, ¶ 9–316.1.

5/9–317. Landlord's right against sublessee

§ 9–317. Landlord's right against sublessee. In all cases when the leased premises are sublet, or the lease is assigned, the landlord shall have the same right to enforce his or her lien against the sublessee or assignee, that the landlord has against the tenant to whom the premises were leased.

P.A. 82–280, § 9–317, eff. July 1, 1982.

Formerly Ill.Rev.Stat.1991, ch. 110, ¶ 9–317.

5/9–318. Abandonment of premises

§ 9–318. Abandonment of premises. When a tenant abandons or removes from the premises or any part thereof, the landlord or his or her agent or attorney may seize upon any grain or other crops grown or growing upon the premises or part thereof so abandoned, whether the rent is due or not. If such grain or other crops or any part thereof is not fully grown or matured, the landlord or his or her agent or attorney shall cause the same to be properly cultivated and harvested or gathered, and may sell and dispose of the same, and apply the proceeds, so far as may be necessary, to compensate for his or her labor and expenses, and to pay the rent. The tenant may, at any time before the sale of the property so seized, redeem the same by tendering the rent due and the reasonable compensation and expenses of the cultiva-tion and harvesting or gathering the same, or the tenant may replevy the property seized.

P.A. 82–280, § 9–318, eff. July 1, 1982.

Formerly Ill.Rev.Stat.1991, ch. 110, ¶ 9–318.

5/9–319. Removal of fixture

§ 9–319. Removal of fixture. Subject to the right of the landlord to distrain for rent, a tenant has the right to remove from the leased premises all removable fixtures erected thereon by him or her during the term of the lease, or of any renewal thereof, or of any successive leasing of the premises while the tenant remains in possession in the character of a tenant.

P.A. 82–280, § 9–319, eff. July 1, 1982.

Formerly Ill.Rev.Stat.1991, ch. 110, ¶ 9–319.

5/9–320. Notice by nonresident owner

§ 9–320. Notice by nonresident owner. (a) An owner of residential real property containing more than 4 living units, who does not reside or maintain an office therein and does not employ a manager or agent who resides or maintains an office therein, shall:

(1) post or cause to be posted on such residential real property adjacent to the mailboxes or within the interior of such residential real property in a location visible to all the residents, a notice of not less than 20 square inches in size bearing:

(i) the name, address and telephone number of the person responsible for managing the building; and

(ii) the name, address and telephone number of the company or companies insuring such residential real property against loss or damage by fire or explosion or if the residential real property is not insured, that shall be stated in the notice; and

(2) within 24 hours from the time such owner is notified that any company or companies insuring such residential real property against loss or damage by fire or explosion has cancelled such insurance, post or cause to be posted in the manner provided in subparagraph (1) notice of such cancellation.

(b) In lieu of the requirement for posting the notices prescribed in subsection (a) of this Section and the owner's managing agent may include such notice in a written rental or lease agreement or may give such notice by first class mail addressed to the lessee or renter.

(c) Failure to give any notice required by this Section is a petty offense and shall subject the owner to pay a fine of not more than $100 per day of violation.

P.A. 82–280, § 9–320, eff. July 1, 1982. Amended by P.A. 83–707, § 1, eff. Sept. 23, 1983.

Formerly Ill.Rev.Stat.1991, ch. 110, ¶ 9–320.

5/9–321.   Distress before rent due

§ 9–321. Distress before rent due. If any tenant shall, without the consent of his or her landlord, sell and remove, or permit to be removed, or be about to sell and remove, or permit to be removed, from the demised premises, such part or portion of the crops raised thereon, as shall endanger the lien of the landlord upon such crops for the rent agreed to be paid, it is lawful for the landlord to institute proceedings by distress before the rent is due, as is now provided by law, in case of the removal of the tenant from the demised premises; and thereafter the proceedings shall be conducted in the same manner as is now provided by law in ordinary cases of distress, where the rent is due and unpaid.

P.A. 82–280, § 9–321, eff. July 1, 1982.

Formerly Ill.Rev.Stat.1991, ch. 110, ¶ 9–321.

ARTICLE X.   HABEAS CORPUS

5/10–101.   Action commenced by plaintiff

§ 10–101. Action commenced by plaintiff. In all proceedings commenced under Article X of this Act, the name of the person seeking the relief afforded by this Article shall be set out as plaintiff without the use of the phrase "People ex rel." or "People on the relation of".

P.A. 82–280, § 10–101, eff. July 1, 1982.

Formerly Ill.Rev.Stat.1991, ch. 110, ¶ 10–101.

5/10–102.   Who may file

§ 10–102. Who may file. Every person imprisoned or otherwise restrained of his or her liberty, except as herein otherwise provided, may apply for habeas corpus in the manner provided in Article X of this Act, to obtain relief from such imprisonment or restraint, if it proved to be unlawful.

P.A. 82–280, § 10–102, eff. July 1, 1982.

Formerly Ill.Rev.Stat.1991, ch. 110, ¶ 10–102.

5/10–103.   Application

§ 10–103. Application. Application for the relief shall be made to the Supreme Court or to the circuit court of the county in which the person in whose behalf the application is made, is imprisoned or restrained, or to the circuit court of the county from which such person was sentenced or committed. Application shall be made by complaint signed by the person for whose relief it is intended, or by some person in his or her behalf, and verified by affidavit. Application for relief under this Article may not be commenced on behalf of a person who has been sentenced to death without the written consent of that person, unless the person, because of a mental or physical condition, is incapable of asserting his or her own claim.

P.A. 82–280, § 10–103, eff. July 1, 1982. Amended by P.A. 89–684, § 15, eff. June 1, 1997.

Formerly Ill.Rev.Stat.1991, ch. 110, ¶ 10–103.

5/10–104.   Substance of complaint

§ 10–104. Substance of complaint. The complaint shall state in substance:

1. That the person in whose behalf the relief is applied for is imprisoned or restrained of his or her liberty, and the place where—naming all the parties if they are known, or describing them if they are not known.

2. The cause or pretense of the restraint, according to the best knowledge and belief of the applicant, and that such person is not committed or detained by virtue of any process, or judgment, specified in Section 10–123 of this Act.

3. If the commitment or restraint is by virtue of any warrant or process, a copy thereof shall be annexed, or it shall be stated that by reason of such prisoner being removed or concealed before application, a demand of such copy could not be made, or that

such demand was made, and the legal fees therefor tendered to the officer or person having such prisoner in his or her custody, and that such copy was refused. P.A. 82–280, § 10–104, eff. July 1, 1982.

Formerly Ill.Rev.Stat.1991, ch. 110, ¶ 10–104.

5/10–105. Copy of process

§ 10–105. Copy of process. Any sheriff or other officer or person having custody of any prisoner committed on any civil or criminal process of any court who shall neglect to give such prisoner a copy of the process or order of commitment by which he or she is imprisoned within 6 hours after demand made by the prisoner, or anyone on behalf of the prisoner, shall forfeit to the prisoner or party affected not exceeding $500. This Section shall not apply to the Illinois Department of Corrections. P.A. 82–280, § 10–105, eff. July 1, 1982. Amended by P.A. 85–907, Art. II, § 1, eff. Nov. 23, 1987.

Formerly Ill.Rev.Stat.1991, ch. 110, ¶ 10–105.

5/10–106. Grant of relief—Penalty

§ 10–106. Grant of relief—Penalty. Unless it shall appear from the complaint itself, or from the documents thereto annexed, that the party can neither be discharged, admitted to bail nor otherwise relieved, the court shall forthwith award relief by habeas corpus. Any judge empowered to grant relief by habeas corpus who shall corruptly refuse to grant the relief when legally applied for in a case where it may lawfully be granted, or who shall for the purpose of oppression unreasonably delay the granting of such relief shall, for every such offense, forfeit to the prisoner or party affected a sum not exceeding $1,000. P.A. 82–280, § 10–106, eff. July 1, 1982. Amended by P.A. 83–707, § 1, eff. Sept. 23, 1983.

Formerly Ill.Rev.Stat.1991, ch. 110, ¶ 10–106.

5/10–107. Form of orders

§ 10–107. Form of orders. If the relief is allowed by an order of a court it shall be certified by the clerk under the seal of the court; if by a judge, it shall be under the judge's signature, and shall be directed to the person in whose custody or under whose restraint the prisoner is, and may be substantially in the following form: The People of the State of Illinois, to the Sheriff of .... county (or, "to A B," as the case may be):

You are hereby commanded to have the body of C D, imprisoned and detained by you, together with the time and cause of such imprisonment and detention by whatsoever name C D is called or charged, before .... court of .... County (or before E F, judge of, etc.), at, etc., immediately after being served with a certified copy of this order, to be dealt with according to law; and you are to deliver a certified copy of this order with a return thereon of your performance in carrying out this order. P.A. 82–280, § 10–107, eff. July 1, 1982. Amended by P.A. 82–783, Art. IV, § 27, eff. July 13, 1982; P.A. 83–707, § 1, eff. Sept. 23, 1983.

Formerly Ill.Rev.Stat.1991, ch. 110, ¶ 10–107.

5/10–108. Indorsement

§ 10–108. Indorsement. With the intent that no officer or person to whom such order is directed may pretend ignorance thereof, every such order shall be indorsed with these words: "By the habeas corpus law." P.A. 82–280, § 10–108, eff. July 1, 1982.

Formerly Ill.Rev.Stat.1991, ch. 110, ¶ 10–108.

5/10–109. Subpoena—Service

§ 10–109. Subpoena—Service. When the party has been committed upon a criminal charge, unless the court deems it unnecessary, a subpoena shall also be issued to summon the witnesses whose names have been endorsed upon the warrant of commitment, to appear before such court at the time and place when and where such order of habeas corpus is returnable, and it shall be the duty of the sheriff, or other officer to whom the subpoena is issued, to serve the same, if it is possible, in time to enable such witnesses to attend. P.A. 82–280, § 10–109, eff. July 1, 1982.

Formerly Ill.Rev.Stat.1991, ch. 110, ¶ 10–109.

5/10–110. Service of order

§ 10–110. Service of order. The habeas corpus order may be served by the sheriff, coroner or any person appointed for that purpose by the court which entered the order; if served by a person not an officer, he or she shall have the same power, and be liable to the same penalty for non-performance of his or her duty, as though he or she were sheriff. P.A. 82–280, § 10–110, eff. July 1, 1982. Amended by P.A. 83–707, § 1, eff. Sept. 23, 1983.

Formerly Ill.Rev.Stat.1991, ch. 110, ¶ 10–110.

5/10–111. Manner of service

§ 10–111. Manner of service. Service shall be made by leaving a copy of the order with the person to whom it is directed, or with any of his or her under officers who may be at the place where the prisoner is detained; or if he or she can not be found, or has not the person imprisoned or restrained in custody, the service may be made upon any person who has the person in custody with the same effect as though he or she had been made a defendant therein. P.A. 82–280, § 10–111, eff. July 1, 1982.

Formerly Ill.Rev.Stat.1991, ch. 110, ¶ 10–111.

5/10–112. Expense involved

§ 10–112. Expense involved. When the person confined or restrained is in the custody of a civil officer, the court entering the order shall certify thereon the sum to be paid for the expense of bringing the person from the place of imprisonment, not exceeding 10 cents per mile, and the officer shall not be bound to obey it unless the sum so certified is paid or tendered to him or her, and security is given to pay the charges of carrying the party back if he or she should be remanded. If the court is satisfied that the party so confined or restrained is a poor person and unable to pay such expense, then the court shall so state in the order, and in such case no tender or payment of expenses need be made or security given but the officer shall be bound to obey such order.
P.A. 82–280, § 10–112, eff. July 1, 1982.

Formerly Ill.Rev.Stat.1991, ch. 110, ¶ 10–112.

5/10–113. Form of return

§ 10–113. Form of return. The officer or person upon whom such order is served shall state in his or her return, plainly and unequivocally:

1. Whether he or she has or has not the party in his or her custody or control, or under his or her restraint, and if he or she has not, whether he or she has had the party in his or her custody or control, or under his or her restraint, at any and what time prior or subsequent to the date of the order.

2. If he or she has the party in his or her custody or control, or under his or her restraint, the authority and true cause of such imprisonment or restraint, setting forth the same in detail.

3. If the party is detained by virtue of any order, warrant or other written authority, a copy thereof shall be attached to the return, and the original shall be produced and exhibited on the return of the order to the court before whom the same is returnable.

4. If the person upon whom the order is served has had the party in his or her custody or control or under his or her restraint, at any time prior or subsequent to the date of the order but has transferred such custody or restraint to another, the return shall state particularly to whom, at what time, for what cause and by what authority such transfer took place. The return shall be signed by the person making the same, and except where such person is a sworn public officer and makes the return in his or her official capacity, it shall be verified by oath.
P.A. 82–280, § 10–113, eff. July 1, 1982.

Formerly Ill.Rev.Stat.1991, ch. 110, ¶ 10–113.

5/10–114. Bringing of body

§ 10–114. Bringing of body. The officer or person making the return, shall, at the same time, bring the body of the party, if in his or her custody or power or under his or her restraint, according to the command of the order unless prevented by the sickness or infirmity of the party.
P.A. 82–280, § 10–114, eff. July 1, 1982.

Formerly Ill.Rev.Stat.1991, ch. 110, ¶ 10–114.

5/10–115. Sickness or infirmity

§ 10–115. Sickness or infirmity. When, from the sickness or infirmity of the party, he or she cannot without danger, be brought to the place designated for the return of the order, that fact shall be stated in the return, and if it is proved to the satisfaction of the judge, he or she may proceed to the jail or other place where the party is confined, and there make an examination, or the judge may adjourn the same to such other time, or make such other order in the case as law and justice require.
P.A. 82–280, § 10–115, eff. July 1, 1982.

Formerly Ill.Rev.Stat.1991, ch. 110, ¶ 10–115.

5/10–116. Neglect to obey order

§ 10–116. Neglect to obey order. If the officer or person upon whom such order is served refuses or neglects to obey the same, by producing the party named in the order and making a full and explicit return thereto within the time required by Article X of this Act, and no sufficient excuse is shown for such refusal or neglect, the court before whom the order is returnable, upon proof of the service thereof, shall enforce obedience by attachment as for contempt, and the officer or person so refusing or neglecting shall forfeit to the party a sum not exceeding $500, and be incapable of holding office.
P.A. 82–280, § 10–116, eff. July 1, 1982.

Formerly Ill.Rev.Stat.1991, ch. 110, ¶ 10–116.

5/10–117. Order in case of neglect

§ 10–117. Order in case of neglect. The court may also, at the same time or afterwards, enter an order to the sheriff or other person to whom such attachment is directed, commanding him or her to bring forthwith before the court the party for whose benefit the habeas corpus order was entered, who shall thereafter remain in the custody of such sheriff, or other person, until the party is discharged, bailed or remanded, as the court directs.
P.A. 82–280, § 10–117, eff. July 1, 1982.

Formerly Ill.Rev.Stat.1991, ch. 110, ¶ 10–117.

5/10–118. Proceedings in case of emergency

§ 10–118. Proceedings in case of emergency. Whenever it appears by the complaint, or by affidavit, that any one is illegally held in custody or restraint, and that there is good reason to believe that such person will be taken out of the jurisdiction of the court in which the application for a habeas corpus is made, or will suffer some irreparable injury before compliance with the order can be enforced, the court may enter an order directed to the sheriff or other proper officer, commanding him or her to take the prisoner thus held in custody or restraint, and forthwith bring him or her before the court to be dealt with according to law. The court may also, if it is deemed necessary, order the apprehension of the person charged with causing the illegal restraint. The officer shall execute the order by bringing the person therein named before the court, and the like return and proceedings shall be had as in other orders of habeas corpus. P.A. 82–280, § 10–118, eff. July 1, 1982. Amended by P.A. 83–707, § 1, eff. Sept. 23, 1983.

Formerly Ill.Rev.Stat.1991, ch. 110, ¶ 10–118.

5/10–119. Examination

§ 10–119. Examination. Upon the return of an order of habeas corpus, the court shall, without delay, proceed to examine the cause of the imprisonment or restraint, but the examination may be adjourned from time to time as circumstances require. P.A. 82–280, § 10–119, eff. July 1, 1982.

Formerly Ill.Rev.Stat.1991, ch. 110, ¶ 10–119.

5/10–120. Denial of allegations in return

§ 10–120. Denial of allegations in return. The party imprisoned or restrained may file a reply to the return and deny any of the material facts set forth in the return, and may allege any other facts that may be material in the case, which denial or allegation shall be on oath; and the court shall proceed promptly to examine the cause of the imprisonment or restraint, hear the evidence produced by any person interested or authorized to appear, both in support of such imprisonment or restraint and against it, and thereupon shall determine the matter according to law. P.A. 82–280, § 10–120, eff. July 1, 1982.

Formerly Ill.Rev.Stat.1991, ch. 110, ¶ 10–120.

5/10–121. Seeking wrong remedy not fatal

§ 10–121. Seeking wrong remedy not fatal. Where relief is sought under Article X of this Act and the court determines, on motion directed to the pleadings, or on motion for summary judgment or upon trial, that the plaintiff has pleaded or established facts which entitle the plaintiff to relief but that the plaintiff has sought the wrong remedy, the court shall permit the pleadings to be amended, on just and reasonable terms, and the court shall grant the relief to which the plaintiff is entitled on the amended pleadings or upon the evidence. In considering whether a proposed amendment is just and reasonable, the court shall consider the right of the defendant to assert additional defenses, to demand a trial by jury, to plead a coun-

terclaim or third party complaint, and to order the plaintiff to take additional steps which were not required under the pleadings as previously filed. P.A. 82–280, § 10–121, eff. July 1, 1982.

Formerly Ill.Rev.Stat.1991, ch. 110, ¶ 10–121.

5/10–122. Amendments

§ 10–122. Amendments. The return, as well as any denial or allegation, may be amended at any time by leave of the court. P.A. 82–280, § 10–122, eff. July 1, 1982.

Formerly Ill.Rev.Stat.1991, ch. 110, ¶ 10–122.

5/10–123. When prisoner not entitled to discharge

§ 10–123. When prisoner not entitled to discharge. No person shall be discharged under the provisions of this Act, if he or she is in custody:

1. By virtue of process of any court of the United States, in a case where such court has exclusive jurisdiction; or,

2. By virtue of a final judgment of any circuit court, or of any proceeding for the enforcement of such judgment, unless the time during which such party may be legally detained has expired; or,

3. For any treason, felony or other crime committed in any other state or territory of the United States, for which such person ought, by the Constitution and laws of the United States, to be delivered to the executive power of such state or territory. P.A. 82–280, § 10–123, eff. July 1, 1982.

Formerly Ill.Rev.Stat.1991, ch. 110, ¶ 10–123.

5/10–124. Causes for discharge when in custody on process of court

§ 10–124. Causes for discharge when in custody on process of court. If it appears that the prisoner is in custody by virtue of process from any court legally constituted, he or she may be discharged only for one or more of the following causes:

1. Where the court has exceeded the limit of its jurisdiction, either as to the matter, place, sum or person.

2. Where, though the original imprisonment was lawful, nevertheless, by some act, omission or event which has subsequently taken place, the party has become entitled to be discharged.

3. Where the process is defective in some substantial form required by law.

4. Where the process, though in proper form, has been issued in a case or under circumstances where the law does not allow process to issue or orders to be entered for imprisonment or arrest.

5. Where, although in proper form, the process has been issued in a case or under circumstances unauthorized to issue or execute the same, or where the person having the custody of the prisoner under such process is not the person empowered by law to detain him or her.

6. Where the process appears to have been obtained by false pretense or bribery.

7. Where there is no general law, nor any judgment or order of a court to authorize the process if in a civil action, nor any conviction if in a criminal proceeding. No court, on the return of a habeas corpus, shall, in any other matter, inquire into the legality or justice of a judgment of a court legally constituted.

P.A. 82–280, § 10–124, eff. July 1, 1982.

Formerly Ill.Rev.Stat.1991, ch. 110, ¶ 10–124.

5/10–125. New commitment

§ 10–125. New commitment. In all cases where the imprisonment is for a criminal, or supposed criminal matter, if it appears to the court that there is sufficient legal cause for the commitment of the prisoner, although such commitment may have been informally made, or without due authority, or the process may have been executed by a person not duly authorized, the court shall make a new commitment in proper form, and direct it to the proper officer, or admit the party to bail if the case is bailable. The court shall also, when necessary, take the recognizance of all material witnesses against the prisoner, as in other cases. The recognizances shall be in the form provided by law, and returned as other recognizances. If any judge shall neglect or refuse to bind any such prisoner or witness by recognizance, or to return a recognizance when taken as hereinabove stated, he or she shall be guilty of a Class A misdemeanor in office, and be proceeded against accordingly.

P.A. 82–280, § 10–125, eff. July 1, 1982.

Formerly Ill.Rev.Stat.1991, ch. 110, ¶ 10–125.

5/10–126. Remand

§ 10–126. Remand. When any prisoner brought up on a habeas corpus is remanded to prison, it shall be the duty of the court remanding the prisoner to deliver to the sheriff, or other person to whose custody the prisoner is remanded, an order in writing, stating the cause of remanding the prisoner. If such prisoner obtains a second order of habeas corpus, it shall be the duty of such sheriff, or other person to whom the same is directed, to return therewith the order above stated; and if it appears that the prisoner was remanded for an offense adjudged not bailable, it shall be taken and received as conclusive, and the prisoner shall be remanded without further proceedings.

P.A. 82–280, § 10–126, eff. July 1, 1982.

Formerly Ill.Rev.Stat.1991, ch. 110, ¶ 10–126.

5/10–127. Grant of habeas corpus

§ 10–127. Grant of habeas corpus. It is not lawful for any court, on a second order of habeas corpus obtained by such prisoner, to discharge the prisoner, if he or she is clearly and specifically charged in the warrant of commitment with a criminal offense; but the court shall, on the return of such second order, have power only to admit such prisoner to bail where the offense is bailable by law, or remand him or her to prison where the offense is not bailable, or being bailable, where such prisoner fails to give the bail required.

P.A. 82–280, § 10–127, eff. July 1, 1982.

Formerly Ill.Rev.Stat.1991, ch. 110, ¶ 10–127.

5/10–128. Person discharged again imprisoned

§ 10–128. Person discharged again imprisoned. No person who has been discharged by order of the court on a habeas corpus, shall be again imprisoned, restrained or kept in custody for the same cause, unless he or she is afterwards indicted for the same offense, nor unless by the legal order or process of the court wherein he or she is bound by recognizance to appear. The following shall not be deemed to be the same cause:

1. If, after a discharge for a defect of proof, or any material defect in the commitment, in a criminal case, the prisoner is again arrested on sufficient proof, and committed by legal process for the same offense.

2. If, in a civil action, the party has been discharged for any illegality in the judgment or process, and is afterwards imprisoned by legal process for the same cause of action.

3. Generally, whenever the discharge is ordered on account of the non-observance of any of the forms required by law, the party may be a second time imprisoned if the cause is legal and the forms required by law observed.

P.A. 82–280, § 10–128, eff. July 1, 1982.

Formerly Ill.Rev.Stat.1991, ch. 110, ¶ 10–128.

5/10–129. Penalty for rearrest of person discharged

§ 10–129. Penalty for rearrest of person discharged. Any person who, knowing that another has been discharged by order of a competent court on a habeas corpus, shall, contrary to the provisions of Article X of this Act, arrest or detain him or her again for the same cause which was shown on the return to such order, shall forfeit $500 for the first offense, and $1,000 for every subsequent offense.

P.A. 82–280, § 10–129, eff. July 1, 1982.

Formerly Ill.Rev.Stat.1991, ch. 110, ¶ 10–129.

5/10–130. Prisoner not to be removed from county

§ 10–130. Prisoner not to be removed from county. To prevent any person from avoiding or delaying his or her trial, it shall not be lawful to remove any prisoner on habeas corpus under Article X of this Act out of the county in which he or she is confined, within 15 days next preceding the first day of the calendar month in which such person ought to be tried unless it is done to convey him or her into the county where the offense with which he or she stands charged is properly cognizable.

P.A. 82–280, § 10–130, eff. July 1, 1982.

Formerly Ill.Rev.Stat.1991, ch. 110, ¶ 10–130.

5/10–131. Custody not to be changed

§ 10–131. Custody not to be changed. Any person being committed to any prison, or in the custody of any sheriff or other officer or person for any criminal or supposed criminal matter, shall not be removed therefrom into any other prison or custody, unless it is done by habeas corpus order or some other legal process or when it is expressly allowed by law. If any person removes, or causes to be removed any prisoner so committed, except as above provided, he or she shall forfeit to the party affected a sum not exceeding $300.

P.A. 82–280, § 10–131, eff. July 1, 1982. Amended by P.A. 83–707, § 1, eff. Sept. 23, 1983.

Formerly Ill.Rev.Stat.1991, ch. 110, ¶ 10–131.

5/10–132. Avoidance of order—Punishment

§ 10–132. Avoidance of order—Punishment. Any one having a person in his or her custody, or under his or her restraint, power or control, for whose relief an order of habeas corpus is entered, who, with intent to avoid the effect of such order, transfers such person to the custody or places him or her under the control of another, or conceals him or her, or changes the place of his or her confinement, with intent to avoid the operation of such order, or with intent to remove him or her out of the State, shall, for every such offense, be guilty of a Class 4 felony. In any prosecution for the penalty incurred under this Section, it shall not be necessary to show that the order of habeas corpus had been entered at the time of the removal, transfer or concealment therein mentioned, if it is proven that the acts therein forbidden were done with the intent to avoid the operation of such order.

P.A. 82–280, § 10–132, eff. July 1, 1982. Amended by P.A. 83–707, § 1, eff. Sept. 23, 1983.

Formerly Ill.Rev.Stat.1991, ch. 110, ¶ 10–132.

5/10–133. Penalties—How recovered

§ 10–133. Penalties—How recovered. All the pecuniary forfeitures incurred under this Act shall inure to the use of the party for whose benefit the order of habeas corpus was entered, and shall be sued for and recovered with costs, by the Attorney General or State's Attorney, in the name of the State, by complaint; and the amount, when recovered, shall, without any deduction, be paid to the party entitled thereto.

P.A. 82–280, § 10–133, eff. July 1, 1982.

Formerly Ill.Rev.Stat.1991, ch. 110, ¶ 10–133.

5/10–134. No bar to civil damages

§ 10–134. No bar to civil damages. The recovery of the penalties shall be no bar to a civil action for damages.

P.A. 82–280, § 10–134, eff. July 1, 1982.

Formerly Ill.Rev.Stat.1991, ch. 110, ¶ 10–134.

5/10–135. Habeas corpus to testify

§ 10–135. Habeas corpus to testify. The several courts having authority to grant relief by habeas corpus, may enter orders, when necessary, to bring before them any prisoner to testify, or to be surrendered in discharge of bail, or for trial upon any criminal charge lawfully pending in the same court or to testify in a criminal proceeding in another state as provided for by Section 2 of the "Uniform Act to secure the attendance of witnesses from within or without a state in criminal proceedings", approved July 23, 1959, as heretofore or hereafter amended;[1] and the order may be directed to any county in the State, and there be served and returned by any officer to whom it is directed.

P.A. 82–280, § 10–135, eff. July 1, 1982.

Formerly Ill.Rev.Stat.1991, ch. 110, ¶ 10–135.
[1] 725 ILCS 220/2.

5/10–136. Prisoner remanded or punished

§ 10–136. Prisoner remanded or punished. After a prisoner has given his or her testimony, or been surrendered, or his or her bail discharged, or he or she has been tried for the crime with which he or she is charged, he or she shall be returned to the jail or other place of confinement from which he or she was taken for that purpose. If such prisoner is convicted of a crime punishable with death or imprisonment in the penitentiary, he or she may be punished accordingly; but in any case where the prisoner has been taken from the penitentiary, and his or her punishment is by imprisonment, the time of such imprisonment shall not commence to run until the expiration of the time of service under any former sentence.

P.A. 82–280, § 10–136, eff. July 1, 1982.

Formerly Ill.Rev.Stat.1991, ch. 110, ¶ 10–136.

5/10-137. Contempt—Discharge

§ 10-137. Contempt—Discharge. Any person imprisoned for any contempt of court for the non-performance of any order or judgment for the payment of money, is entitled to relief by habeas corpus, and if it appears, on full examination of such person and such witnesses, and other evidence as may be adduced, that he or she is unable to comply with such order or judgment, or to endure the confinement, and that all persons interested in the order or judgment have had reasonable notice of the time and place of trial, the court may discharge him or her from imprisonment, but no such discharge shall operate to release the lien of such order or judgment, but the same may be enforced against the property of such person as other orders and judgments are enforced in civil cases.

P.A. 82–280, § 10–137, eff. July 1, 1982.

Formerly Ill.Rev.Stat.1991, ch. 110, ¶ 10–137.

ARTICLE XI. INJUNCTION

Part
1. In General.
2. Domestic Violence.
3. Disbursement of Public Moneys.

PART 1. IN GENERAL

5/11-101. Temporary restraining order

§ 11–101. Temporary restraining order. No temporary restraining order shall be granted without notice to the adverse party unless it clearly appears from specific facts shown by affidavit or by the verified complaint that immediate and irreparable injury, loss, or damage will result to the applicant before notice can be served and a hearing had thereon. Every temporary restraining order granted without notice shall be indorsed with the date and hour of signing; shall be filed forthwith in the clerk's office; shall define the injury and state why it is irreparable and why the order was granted without notice; and shall expire by its terms within such time after the signing of the order, not to exceed 10 days, as the court fixes, unless within the time so fixed the order,

for good cause shown, is extended for a like period or unless the party against whom the order is directed consents that it may be extended for a longer period. The reasons for the granting of the extension shall be stated in the written order of the court. In case a temporary restraining order is granted without notice, the motion for a preliminary injunction shall be set for hearing at the earliest possible time and takes precedence over all matters except older matters of the same character; and when the motion comes on for hearing the party who obtained the temporary restraining order shall proceed with the application for a preliminary injunction and, if he or she does not do so, the court shall dissolve the temporary restraining order.

On 2 days' notice to the party who obtained the temporary restraining order without notice or on such shorter notice to that party as the court may prescribe, the adverse party may appear and move its dissolution or modification and in that event the court shall proceed to hear and determine such motion as expeditiously as the ends of justice require.

Every order granting an injunction and every restraining order shall set forth the reasons for its entry; shall be specific in terms; shall describe in reasonable detail, and not by reference to the complaint or other document, the act or acts sought to be restrained; and is binding only upon the parties to the action, their officers, agents, employees, and attorneys, and upon those persons in active concert or participation with them who receive actual notice of the order by personal service or otherwise.

P.A. 82–280, § 11–101, eff. July 1, 1982. Amended by P.A. 84–554, § 1, eff. Sept. 18, 1985.

Formerly Ill.Rev.Stat.1991, ch. 110, ¶ 11–101.

5/11-102. Preliminary injunction

§ 11–102. Preliminary injunction. No court or judge shall grant a preliminary injunction without previous notice of the time and place of the application having been given the adverse party.

P.A. 82–280, § 11–102, eff. July 1, 1982. Amended by P.A. 84–282, § 1, eff. Jan. 1, 1986.

Formerly Ill.Rev.Stat.1991, ch. 110, ¶ 11–102.

5/11-103. Bond

§ 11–103. Bond. The court in its discretion, may before entering a restraining order or a preliminary injunction, require the applicant to give bond in such sum, upon such condition and with such security as may be deemed proper by the court, for the payment of such costs and damages as may be incurred or suffered by any party who is found to have been wrongfully enjoined or restrained.

No such bond shall be required of any governmental office or agency.

A surety upon a bond or undertaking under Article XI of this Act submits to the jurisdiction of the court and irrevocably appoints the clerk of the court as the surety's agent upon whom any papers affecting the surety's liability on the bond or undertaking may be served. Such liability may be enforced on motion without the necessity of an independent action. The motion and such notice of motion as the court prescribes may be served on the clerk of the court who shall forthwith mail copies to the persons giving the security if their addresses are known.

P.A. 82–280, § 11–103, eff. July 1, 1982. Amended by P.A. 83–707, § 1, eff. Sept. 23, 1983.

Formerly Ill.Rev.Stat.1991, ch. 110, ¶ 11–103.

5/11–104. Bond before court or clerk

§ 11–104. Bond before court or clerk. The bond may be entered into before the court granting or ordering the injunction, or before the clerk of the court, if the court has approved the security.

P.A. 82–280, § 11–104, eff. July 1, 1982.

Formerly Ill.Rev.Stat.1991, ch. 110, ¶ 11–104.

5/11–105. Filing of bond

§ 11–105. Filing of bond. All bonds required by Article XI of this Act shall be filed with the clerk of the court who is to certify the injunctive order or judgment.

P.A. 82–280, § 11–105, eff. July 1, 1982. Amended by P.A. 83–707, § 1, eff. Sept. 23, 1983.

Formerly Ill.Rev.Stat.1991, ch. 110, ¶ 11–105.

5/11–106. Injunctive relief on Saturday, Sunday or legal holiday

§ 11–106. Injunctive relief on Saturday, Sunday or legal holiday. When an application is made on a Saturday, Sunday, legal holiday or on a day when courts are not in session for injunctive relief and there is filed with the complaint an affidavit of the plaintiff, or his, her or their agent or attorney, stating that the benefits of injunctive relief will be lost or endangered, or irremediable damage occasioned unless such injunctive relief is immediately granted, and stating the bases for such alleged consequence, and if it appears to the court from such affidavit that the benefits of injunctive relief will be lost or endangered, or irremediable damage occasioned unless such injunctive relief is immediately granted, and if the plaintiff otherwise is entitled to such relief under the law, the court may grant injunctive relief on a Saturday, Sunday, legal holiday, or on a day when courts are not in session; and it shall be lawful for the clerk to certify, and for the sheriff or coroner to serve such order for injunctive relief on a Saturday, Sunday, legal holiday or on a day when courts are not in session as on any other day, and all affidavits and bonds made and

proceedings had in such case shall have the same force and effect as if made or had on any other day.

P.A. 82–280, § 11–106, eff. July 1, 1982. Amended by P.A. 98–756, § 725, eff. July 16, 2014.

Formerly Ill.Rev.Stat.1991, ch. 110, ¶ 11–106.

5/11–107. Seeking wrong remedy not fatal

§ 11–107. Seeking wrong remedy not fatal. Where relief is sought under Article XI of this Act and the court determines, on motion directed to the pleadings, or on motion for summary judgment or upon trial, that the plaintiff has pleaded or established facts which entitle the plaintiff to relief but that the plaintiff has sought the wrong remedy, the court shall permit the pleadings to be amended, on just and reasonable terms, and the court shall grant the relief to which plaintiff is entitled on the amended pleadings or upon the evidence. In considering whether a proposed amendment is just and reasonable, the court shall consider the right of the defendant to assert additional defenses, to demand a trial by jury, to plead a counterclaim or third party complaint, and to order the plaintiff to take additional steps which were not required under the pleadings as previously filed.

P.A. 82–280, § 11–107, eff. July 1, 1982.

Formerly Ill.Rev.Stat.1991, ch. 110, ¶ 11–107.

5/11–107.1. Injunctive relief for the father of an unborn child in an abortion related decision by the mother

§ 11–107.1. Injunctive relief for the father of an unborn child in an abortion related decision by the mother. In any case when a married woman wishes to have an abortion performed upon her, and her spouse, who is the father of the unborn child, is opposed to the performance of that abortion, a court may hear testimony from both parties and balance the rights and interests of those parties.

When the interests of the husband in preventing the abortion outweigh those of the wife in having an abortion performed after the unborn child is viable, the court may issue an injunction against the performance of the abortion but only where the court makes a finding that the mother's life or physical health are not in danger.

P.A. 82–280, § 11–107.1, added by P.A. 84–1000, § 1, eff. Oct. 30, 1985.

Formerly Ill.Rev.Stat.1991, ch. 110, ¶ 11–107.1.

5/11–108. Motion to dissolve

§ 11–108. Motion to dissolve. A motion to dissolve an injunction may be made at any time before or after answer is filed. Upon a motion to dissolve an injunction after answer is filed the court shall decide the motion upon the weight of the evidence.

P.A. 82–280, § 11–108, eff. July 1, 1982.

Formerly Ill.Rev.Stat.1991, ch. 110, ¶ 11–108.

5/11–109. Affidavits in support of motion to dissolve

§ 11–109. Affidavits in support of motion to dissolve. The plaintiff may support the complaint and the defendant may support the answer by affidavits filed with the same, which may be read in evidence on the hearing of the motion to dissolve the injunction.

P.A. 82–280, § 11–109, eff. July 1, 1982.

Formerly Ill.Rev.Stat.1991, ch. 110, ¶ 11–109.

5/11–110. Assessing damages

§ 11–110. Assessing damages. In all cases where a temporary restraining order or a preliminary injunction is dissolved by the circuit court or by the reviewing court, the circuit court, after the dissolution of the temporary restraining order or preliminary injunction, and before finally disposing of the action shall, upon the party claiming damages by reason of such temporary restraining order or preliminary injunction, filing a petition under oath setting forth the nature and amount of damages suffered, determine and enter judgment in favor of the party who was injured by such temporary restraining order or preliminary injunction for the damages which the party suffered as a result thereof, which judgment may be enforced as other judgments for the payment of money. However, a failure so to assess damages as hereinabove set out shall not operate as a bar to an action upon the injunction bond.

P.A. 82–280, § 11–110, eff. July 1, 1982.

Formerly Ill.Rev.Stat.1991, ch. 110, ¶ 11–110.

PART 2. DOMESTIC VIOLENCE

Section
5/11–201. Repealed.

5/11–201. § 11–201. Repealed by P.A. 82–783, Art. III, § 44, eff. July 13, 1982

PART 3. DISBURSEMENT OF PUBLIC MONEYS

Section
5/11–301. Who may file action.
5/11–302. Action by Attorney General.
5/11–303. Action by private citizen.
5/11–304. Summons—Pleadings.

5/11–301. Who may file action

§ 11–301. Who may file action. An action to restrain and enjoin the disbursement of public funds by any officer or officers of the State government may be maintained either by the Attorney General or by any citizen and taxpayer of the State.

P.A. 82–280, § 11–301, eff. July 1, 1982.

Formerly Ill.Rev.Stat.1991, ch. 110, ¶ 11–301.

5/11–302. Action by Attorney General

§ 11–302. Action by Attorney General. Such action may be maintained by the Attorney General, by filing in the office of the clerk of the circuit court of the proper county a complaint in the name of the People of the State of Illinois. When such complaint is filed, it shall be presented to the court and an order shall be entered thereon showing the day of presentation and the day, which shall not be less than 5 days and not more than 10 days thereafter, when the court will hear the same.

P.A. 82–280, § 11–302, eff. July 1, 1982. Amended by P.A. 83–707, § 1, eff. Sept. 23, 1983.

Formerly Ill.Rev.Stat.1991, ch. 110, ¶ 11–302.

5/11–303. Action by private citizen

§ 11–303. Action by private citizen. Such action, when prosecuted by a citizen and taxpayer of the State, shall be commenced by petition for leave to file an action to restrain and enjoin the defendant or defendants from disbursing the public funds of the State. Such petition shall have attached thereto a copy of the complaint, leave to file which is petitioned for. Upon the filing of such petition, it shall be presented to the court, and the court shall enter an order stating the date of the presentation of the petition and fixing a day, which shall not be less than 5 nor more than 10 days thereafter, when such petition for leave to file the action will be heard. The court shall also order the petitioner to give notice in writing to each defendant named therein and to the Attorney General, specifying in such notice the fact of the presentation of such petition and the date and time when the same will be heard. Such notice shall be served upon the defendants and upon the Attorney General, as the case may be, at least 5 days before the hearing of such petition.

Upon such hearing, if the court is satisfied that there is reasonable ground for the filing of such action, the court may grant the petition and order the complaint to be filed and process to issue. The court may, in its discretion, grant leave to file the complaint as to certain items, parts or portions of any appropriation Act sought to be enjoined and mentioned in such complaint, and may deny leave as to the rest.

P.A. 82–280, § 11–303, eff. July 1, 1982.

Formerly Ill.Rev.Stat.1991, ch. 110, ¶ 11–303.

5/11–304. Summons—Pleadings

§ 11–304. Summons—Pleadings. Upon the filing of the complaint, summons shall be issued commanding the defendant or defendants to appear on the day named therein, which shall not be less than 5 days nor more than 10 days thereafter, as shall be directed by the court. Such summons shall be served at least 5 days before the return day thereof in the same manner as summons is served in other civil cases.

Every defendant who is summoned shall appear by filing a pleading or motion in the cause on the return day of the summons as in other civil cases, and such action shall be given preference in hearing over all other cases.

P.A. 82–280, § 11–304, eff. July 1, 1982.

Formerly Ill.Rev.Stat.1991, ch. 110, ¶ 11–304.

ARTICLE XII. JUDGMENTS—ENFORCEMENT

PART 1. IN GENERAL

5/12–101. Lien of judgment

§ 12–101. Lien of judgment. With respect to the creation of liens on real estate by judgments, all real estate in the State of Illinois is divided into 2 classes.

The first class consists of all real property, the title to which is registered under "An Act concerning land titles", approved May 1, 1897, as amended. [1]

The second class consists of all real property not registered under "An Act concerning land titles".

As to real estate in class one, a judgment is a lien on the real estate of the person against whom it is entered for the same period as in class two, when Section 85 of "An Act concerning land titles", [2] has been complied with.

As to real estate included within class two, a judgment is a lien on the real estate of the person against whom it is entered in any county in this State, including the county in which it is entered, only from the time a transcript, certified copy or memorandum of the judgment is filed in the office of the recorder in the county in which the real estate is located. The lien may be foreclosed by an action brought in the name of the judgment creditor or its assignee of record under Article XV in the same manner as a mortgage of real property, except that the redemption period shall be 6 months from the date of sale and the real estate homestead exemption under Section 12–901 shall apply. A judgment resulting from the entry of an order requiring child support payments shall be a lien upon the real estate of the person obligated to make the child support payments, but shall not be enforceable in any county of this State until a transcript, certified copy, or memorandum of the lien is filed in the office of the recorder in the county in which the real estate is located. Any lien hereunder arising out of an order for support shall be a lien only as to and from the time that an installment or payment is due under the terms of the order. Further, the order for support shall not be a lien on real estate to the extent of payments made as evidenced by the records of the Clerk of the Circuit Court or State agency receiving payments pursuant to the order. In the event payments made pursuant to that order are not paid to the Clerk of the Circuit Court or a State agency, then each lien imposed by this Section may be released in the following manner:

(a) A Notice of Filing and an affidavit stating that all installments of child support required to be paid pursuant to the order under which the lien or liens were imposed have been paid shall be filed with the office of recorder in each county in which each such lien appears of record, together with proof of service of such notice and affidavit upon the recipient of such payments.

(b) Service of such affidavit shall be by any means authorized under Sections 2–203 and 2–208 of the Code of Civil Procedure [3] or under Supreme Court Rules 11 or 105(b).

(c) The Notice of Filing shall set forth the name and address of the judgment debtor and the judgment creditor, the court file number of the order giving rise to the judgment and, in capital letters, the following statement:

YOU ARE HEREBY NOTIFIED THAT ON (insert date) THE ATTACHED AFFIDAVIT WAS FILED IN THE OFFICE OF THE RECORDER OF … COUNTY, ILLINOIS, WHOSE ADDRESS IS ...., ILLINOIS. IF, WITHIN 28 DAYS OF THE DATE OF THIS NOTICE, YOU FAIL TO FILE AN AFFIDAVIT OBJECTING TO THE RELEASE OF THE STATED JUDGMENT LIEN OR LIENS, IN THE ABOVE OFFICE, SUCH JUDGMENT LIEN WILL BE DEEMED TO BE RELEASED AND NO LONGER SUBJECT TO FORECLOSURE. THIS RELEASE OF LIEN WILL NOT ACT AS A SATISFACTION OF SUCH JUDGMENT.

(d) If no affidavit objecting to the release of the lien or liens is filed within 28 days of the Notice described in paragraph (c) of this Section such lien or liens shall be deemed to be released and no longer subject to foreclosure.

A judgment is not a lien on real estate for longer than 7 years from the time it is entered or revived, unless the judgment is revived within 7 years after its entry or last revival and a new memorandum of judgment is recorded prior to the judgment and its recorded memorandum of judgment becoming dormant.

When a judgment is revived it is a lien on the real estate of the person against whom it was entered in any county in this State from the time a transcript, certified copy or memorandum of the order of revival is filed in the office of the recorder in the county in which the real estate is located.

A foreign judgment registered or filed pursuant to Sections 12–630 through 12–672 of this Act is a lien upon the real estate of the person against whom it was entered only from the time (1) a copy of the affidavit required by Section 12–653 with a copy of the foreign judgment attached showing the filing in a court of this State or (2) a transcript, certified copy or memorandum of a final judgment of the court of this State entered on an action to enforce a foreign judgment is filed in the office of the recorder in the county in which the real estate is located. However, no such judgment shall be a lien on any real estate registered under "An Act concerning land titles", as amended, until Section 85 of that Act has been complied with.

The release of any transcript, certified copy or memorandum of judgment or order of revival which has been recorded shall be filed by the person receiving the release in the office of the recorder in which such judgment or order has been recorded.

Such release shall contain in legible letters a statement as follows:

FOR THE PROTECTION OF THE OWNER, THIS RELEASE SHALL BE FILED WITH THE RECORDER OR THE REGISTRAR OF TITLES IN WHOSE OFFICE THE LIEN WAS FILED.

The term "memorandum" as used in this Section means a memorandum or copy of the judgment signed by a judge or a copy attested by the clerk of the court entering it and showing the court in which entered, date, amount, number of the case in which it was entered, name of the party in whose favor and name and last known address of the party against whom entered. If the address of the party against whom the judgment was entered is not known, the memorandum or copy of judgment shall so state.

The term "memorandum" as used in this Section also means a memorandum or copy of a child support order signed by a judge or a copy attested by the clerk of the court entering it or a copy attested by the administrative body entering it.

This Section shall not be construed as showing an intention of the legislature to create a new classification of real estate, but shall be construed as showing an intention of the legislature to continue a classification already existing.

P.A. 82–280, § 12–101, eff. July 1, 1982. Amended by P.A. 82–783, Art. III, § 43, eff. July 13, 1982; P.A. 83–358, § 76, eff. Sept. 14, 1983; P.A. 84–333, § 1, eff. Jan. 1, 1986; P.A. 85–2, § 6, eff. May 1, 1987; P.A. 85–1156, Art. I, § 7, eff. Jan. 1, 1989; P.A. 86–1329, § 1, eff. Jan. 1, 1991; P.A. 90–18, § 90, eff. July 1, 1997; P.A. 91–357, § 250, eff. July 29, 1999; P.A. 92–817, § 5, eff. Aug. 21, 2002; P.A. 97–350, § 5, eff. Jan. 1, 2012; P.A. 98–557, § 5, eff. Jan. 1, 2014.

Formerly Ill.Rev.Stat.1991, ch. 110, ¶ 12–101.

1 765 ILCS 35/0.01 et seq.

2 765 ILCS 35/85 (repealed).

3 735 ILCS 5/2–203 and 5/2–208.

5/12–102. Judgment against partnership

§ 12–102. Judgment against partnership. A judgment entered against a partnership in its firm name is enforceable only against property of the partnership and does not constitute a lien upon real estate other than that held in the firm name.

P.A. 82–280, § 12–102, eff. July 1, 1982.

Formerly Ill.Rev.Stat.1991, ch. 110, ¶ 12–102.

5/12–103. Representative capacity

§ 12–103. Representative capacity. A judgment entered against a person not as a result of a contract made by him or her or a tort committed by him or her but solely because he or she is the holder of title to property as receiver, trustee of a specifically identified trust, representative as defined in Section 1–2.11 of the Probate Act of 1975,[1] or in any other fiduciary capacity, shall be enforced only against property held in the particular representative capacity, but no judgment shall be enforced against nor shall the judgment constitute a lien upon, other property owned by such person, whether individually or in some other designated identifiable representative capacity.

P.A. 82–280, § 12–103, eff. July 1, 1982.

Formerly Ill.Rev.Stat.1991, ch. 110, ¶ 12–103.

1 See 755 ILCS 5/1–2.15.

5/12–104. Time of restraint deducted

§ 12–104. Time of restraint deducted. When the party in whose favor a judgment is entered is restrained, by injunction, or by stay on appeal, or by the order of a court, or is delayed, on account of the death of the defendant from enforcement of the judgment, the time he or she is so restrained or delayed shall not

be considered as any part of the time mentioned in Sections 12–101 or 12–108 of this Act.

P.A. 82–280, § 12–104, eff. July 1, 1982.

Formerly Ill.Rev.Stat.1991, ch. 110, ¶ 12–104.

5/12–105. Definition of "real estate"

§ 12–105. Definition of "real estate". The term "real estate," when used in Part 1 of Article XII of this Act includes lands, tenements, hereditaments, and all legal and equitable rights and interests therein and thereto, including estates for the life of the debtor or of another person, and estates for years, and leasehold estates, when the unexpired term exceeds 5 years.

P.A. 82–280, § 12–105, eff. July 1, 1982.

Formerly Ill.Rev.Stat.1991, ch. 110, ¶ 12–105.

5/12–106. Enforcement in other counties

§ 12–106. Enforcement in other counties. The person in whose favor any judgment is entered, may have the judgment enforced by the proper officer of any county, in this State, against the lands and tenements, goods and chattels of the person against whom the judgment is entered, or against his or her body, when the same is authorized by law. Upon the filing in the office of the clerk of any circuit court in any county in this State of a transcript of a judgment entered in any other county of this State, enforcement may be had thereon in that county, in like manner as in the county where originally entered.

P.A. 82–280, § 12–106, eff. July 1, 1982. Amended by P.A. 83–707, § 1, eff. Sept. 23, 1983.

Formerly Ill.Rev.Stat.1991, ch. 110, ¶ 12–106.

5/12–107. Incarceration of judgment debtor

§ 12–107. Incarceration of judgment debtor. No order shall be entered for the incarceration of a judgment debtor as a means of satisfying a money judgment except when the judgment is entered for a tort committed by such judgment debtor, and it appears from a special finding of the jury, or from a special finding by the court, if the case is tried by the court without a jury, that malice is the gist of the action, and except when the judgment debtor refuses to deliver up his or her estate for the benefit of his or her creditors.

P.A. 82–280, § 12–107, eff. July 1, 1982.

Formerly Ill.Rev.Stat.1991, ch. 110, ¶ 12–107.

5/12–107.5. Body attachment order

§ 12–107.5. Body attachment order.

(a) No order of body attachment or other civil order for the incarceration or detention of a natural person respondent to answer for a charge of indirect civil contempt shall issue unless the respondent has first had an opportunity, after personal service or abode service of notice as provided in Supreme Court Rule 105, to appear in court to show cause why the respondent should not be held in contempt.

(b) The notice shall be an order to show cause.

(c) Any order issued pursuant to subsection (a) shall expire one year after the date of issue.

(d) The first order issued pursuant to subsection (a) and directed to a respondent may be in the nature of a recognizance bond in the sum of no more than $1,000.

(e) Upon discharge of any bond secured by the posting of funds, the funds shall be returned to the respondent or other party posting the bond, less applicable fees, unless the court after inquiry determines that: (1) the judgment debtor willfully has refused to comply with a payment order entered in accordance with Section 2–1402 or an otherwise validly entered order; (2) the bond money belongs to the debtor as opposed to a third party; and (3) that any part of the funds constitute non-exempt funds of the judgment debtor, in which case the court may cause the non-exempt portion of the funds to be paid over to the judgment creditor.

(f) The requirements or limitations of this Section do not apply to the enforcement of any order or judgment for child support, any order or judgment resulting from an adjudication of a municipal ordinance violation that is subject to Supreme Court Rules 570 through 579, or from an administrative adjudication of such an ordinance violation.

P.A. 82–280, § 12–107.5, added by P.A. 97–848, § 5, eff. July 25, 2012. Amended by P.A. 98–417, § 5, eff. Jan. 1, 2014.

5/12–108. Limitation on enforcement

§ 12–108. Limitation on enforcement. (a) Except as herein provided, no judgment shall be enforced after the expiration of 7 years from the time the same is rendered, except upon the revival of the same by a proceeding provided by Section 2–1601 of this Act; but real estate, levied upon within the 7 years, may be sold to enforce the judgment at any time within one year after the expiration of the 7 years. A judgment recovered in an action for damages for an injury described in Section 13–214.1 may be enforced at any time. Child support judgments, including those arising by operation of law, may be enforced at any time.

(b) No judgment shall be enforced against a police officer employed by a municipality if the corporate authority of the municipality files with the clerk of the court in which the judgment was entered a statement certifying: (1) such police officer was employed by the municipality and was within the scope and course of his employment at the time of the occurrence giving rise to the action in which the judgment is entered and (2) the municipality indemnifies the police officer in the amount of the judgment and interest thereon. In such event, the judgment creditor may enforce the judgment against the municipality in the same manner and to the same extent as if the municipality were the judgment debtor.

P.A. 82–280, § 12–108, eff. July 1, 1982. Amended by P.A. 83–143, § 1, eff. Jan. 1, 1984; P.A. 83–293, § 1, eff. Sept. 14, 1983; P.A. 83–1362, Art. II, § 109, eff. Sept. 11, 1984; P.A. 85–293, Art. III, § 25, eff. Sept. 8, 1987; P.A. 90–18, § 90, eff. July 1, 1997.

Formerly Ill.Rev.Stat.1991, ch. 110, ¶ 12–108.

5/12–109. Interest on judgments

§ 12–109. Interest on judgments.

(a) Every judgment except those arising by operation of law from child support orders shall bear interest thereon as provided in Section 2–1303.

(b) Every judgment arising by operation of law from a child support order shall bear interest as provided in this subsection. The interest on judgments arising by operation of law from child support orders shall be calculated by applying one-twelfth of the current statutory interest rate as provided in Section 2–1303 to the unpaid child support balance as of the end of each calendar month. The unpaid child support balance at the end of the month is the total amount of child support ordered, excluding the child support that was due for that month to the extent that it was not paid in that month and including judgments for retroactive child support, less all payments received and applied as set forth in this subsection. The accrued interest shall not be included in the unpaid child support balance when calculating interest at the end of the month. The unpaid child support balance as of the end of each month shall be determined by calculating the current monthly child support obligation and applying all payments received for that month, except federal income tax refund intercepts, first to the current monthly child support obligation and then applying any payments in excess of the current monthly child support obligation to the unpaid child support balance owed from previous months. The current monthly child support obligation shall be determined from the document that established the support obligation. Federal income tax refund intercepts and any payments in excess of the current monthly child support obligation shall be applied to the unpaid child support balance. Any payments in excess of the current monthly child support obligation and the unpaid child support balance shall be applied to the accrued interest on the unpaid child support balance. Interest on child support obligations may be collected by any means available under State law for the collection of child support judgments.

P.A. 82–280, § 12–109, eff. July 1, 1982. Amended by P.A. 83–1398, § 5, eff. Sept. 12, 1984; P.A. 85–2, § 6, eff. May 1, 1987; P.A. 94–90, § 10, eff. Jan. 1, 2006; P.A. 98–563, § 10, eff. Aug. 27, 2013.

Formerly Ill.Rev.Stat.1991, ch. 110, ¶ 12–109.

5/12–110. Certified copy returnable

§ 12–110. Certified copy returnable. Certified copies of judgments which are delivered to an appropriate officer for enforcement shall be returnable within 90 days after the issuance of the certified copy by the clerk of court.

P.A. 82–280, § 12–110, eff. July 1, 1982.

Formerly Ill.Rev.Stat.1991, ch. 110, ¶ 12–110.

5/12–111. When binding on personalty

§ 12–111. When binding on personalty. No judgment shall bind the goods and chattels of the person against whom it is entered, until a certified copy thereof is delivered to the sheriff or other proper officer to be served; and for the better manifestation of the time, the sheriff or other officer shall, on receipt of such certified copy, indorse upon the back thereof the day of the month and year and hour when he or she received the same.

P.A. 82–280, § 12–111, eff. July 1, 1982.

Formerly Ill.Rev.Stat.1991, ch. 110, ¶ 12–111.

5/12–112. What liable to enforcement

§ 12–112. What liable to enforcement. All the lands, tenements, real estate, goods and chattels (except such as is by law declared to be exempt) of every person against whom any judgment has been or shall be hereafter entered in any court, for any debt, damages, costs, or other sum of money, shall be liable to be sold upon such judgment. Any real property, any beneficial interest in a land trust, or any interest in real property held in a revocable inter vivos trust or revocable inter vivos trusts created for estate planning purposes, held in tenancy by the entirety shall not be liable to be sold upon judgment entered on or after October 1, 1990 against only one of the tenants, except if the property was transferred into tenancy by the entirety with the sole intent to avoid the payment of debts existing at the time of the transfer beyond the transferor's ability to pay those debts as they become due. However, any income from such property shall be subject to garnishment as provided in Part 7 of this Article XII, [1]whether judgment has been entered against one or both of the tenants.

If the court authorizes the piercing of the ownership veil pursuant to Section 505 of the Illinois Marriage and Dissolution of Marriage Act [2] or Section 805 of the Illinois Parentage Act of 2015, [3] any assets determined to be those of the non-custodial parent, although not held in name of the non-custodial parent, shall be subject to attachment or other provisional remedy in accordance with the procedure prescribed by this Code. The court may not authorize attachment of property or any other provisional remedy under this paragraph unless it has obtained jurisdiction over the entity holding title to the property by proper service on that entity. With respect to assets which are real property, no order entered as described in this paragraph shall affect the rights of bona fide purchasers, mortgagees, judgment creditors, or other lien holders who acquire their interests in the property prior to the time a notice of lis pendens pursuant to this Code or a copy of the order is placed of record in the office of the recorder of deeds for the county in which the real property is located.

This amendatory Act of 1995 (P.A. 89–438) is declarative of existing law.

This amendatory Act of 1997 (P.A. 90–514) is intended as a clarification of existing law and not as a new enactment.

P.A. 82–280, § 12–112, eff. July 1, 1982. Amended by P.A. 86–966, Art. 2, § 5, eff. Oct. 1, 1990; P.A. 86–1028, Art. III, § 3–33, eff. Feb. 5, 1990; P.A. 87–421, § 3, eff. Jan. 1, 1992; P.A. 89–88, § 3, eff. June 30, 1995; P.A. 89–438, § 5, eff. Dec. 15, 1995; P.A. 90–476, § 5, eff. Jan. 1, 1998; P.A. 90–514, § 10, eff. Aug. 22, 1997; P.A. 90–655, § 166, eff. July 30, 1998; P.A. 96–1145, § 5, eff. Jan. 1, 2011; P.A. 99–85, § 964, eff. Jan. 1, 2016.

Formerly Ill.Rev.Stat.1991, ch. 110, ¶ 12–112.

[1] 735 ILCS 5/12–701 et seq.
[2] 750 ILCS 5/505 et seq.
[3] 750 ILCS 46/805 et seq.

5/12–112.5. Charging orders

§ 12–112.5. Charging orders. If a statute or case requires or permits a judgment creditor to use the remedy of a charging order, said remedy may be brought and obtained by serving any of the various enforcement procedures set forth within this Article XII or by serving a citation pursuant to Section 2–1402. If the court does not otherwise have jurisdiction of the parties, the law relating to the type of enforcement served shall be used to determine issues ancillary to the entry of a charging order such as jurisdiction, liens, and priority of liens.

P.A. 82–280, § 12–112.5, added by P.A. 97–350, § 5, eff. Jan. 1, 2012.

5/12–113. Election of property

§ 12–113. Election of property. Except as to any sale had by virtue of a judgment of foreclosure entered in accordance with Article XV, the judgment creditor may elect on what property not exempt from enforcement of a judgment he or she will have the same levied, provided personal property shall be last taken, except that a judgment in favor of any city, village or incorporated town may, at the option of the city, village or incorporated town, be levied against either personal or real property with no restriction as to priority.

P.A. 82–280, § 12–113, eff. July 1, 1982. Amended by P.A. 84–1462, § 2, eff. July 1, 1987.

Formerly Ill.Rev.Stat.1991, ch. 110, ¶ 12–113.

5/12–114. Sale in separate items

§ 12–114. Sale in separate items. Except as to any sale had by virtue of a judgment of foreclosure entered in accordance with Article XV, when real or personal property is taken in the enforcement of a judgment, if the property is susceptible of division it shall be sold in separate tracts, lots or articles, and only so much shall be sold as is necessary to satisfy the judgment and costs.

P.A. 82–280, § 12–114, eff. July 1, 1982. Amended by P.A. 84–1462, § 2, eff. July 1, 1987.

Formerly Ill.Rev.Stat.1991, ch. 110, ¶ 12–114.

5/12–115. Notice of sale of real estate

§ 12–115. Notice of sale of real estate. Except as to any sale had by virtue of a judgment of foreclosure entered in accordance with Article XV, no real estate shall be sold by virtue of any judgment, except at public sale, between the hours of 9 in the morning and the setting of the sun of the same day, nor unless the time (specifying the particular hour of day at which the sale shall commence) and the place of holding such sale shall have been previously advertised 3 successive weeks, once in each week, in a newspaper published in the county where the sale is made (if there is any newspaper published in such county), and by placing written or printed notices thereof in at least 3 of the most public places in the county where the real estate is situated, specifying the name of the judgment creditor and judgment debtor in the judgment in all of which notices the real estate to be sold shall be described with reasonable certainty, and if there is more than one newspaper published in such county, the judgment creditor or his or her attorney may designate the newspaper in which such notice shall be published.

P.A. 82–280, § 12–115, eff. July 1, 1982. Amended by P.A. 84–1462, § 2, eff. July 1, 1987.

Formerly Ill.Rev.Stat.1991, ch. 110, ¶ 12–115.

5/12–116. Penalty for neglect of officer

§ 12–116. Penalty for neglect of officer. If any sheriff or other officer sells any real estate by virtue of any judgment, otherwise than in the manner provided by law, or without such previous notice, the officer so offending shall, for every such offense, forfeit and pay the sum of $50, to be recovered with costs of the action by the person whose property is sold.

However, no such offense, nor any irregularity on the part of the sheriff, or other officer having the certified copy of the judgment for enforcement, shall affect the validity of any sale made under it, unless the purchaser had notice thereof.

P.A. 82–280, § 12–116, eff. July 1, 1982.

Formerly Ill.Rev.Stat.1991, ch. 110, ¶ 12–116.

5/12–117, 5/12–118. §§ 12–117, 12–118. Repealed by P.A. 84–1462, § 7, eff. July 1, 1987

5/12–119. Certificate

§ 12–119. Certificate. When any real estate is sold by virtue of a judgment, or enforcement of mechanic's lien, or vendor's lien, or for the payment of money, the sheriff or other officer, except as otherwise provided in Part 1 of Article XII of this Act, instead of executing a deed for the premises sold, shall give to the purchaser a certificate describing the premises purchased by him or her, showing the amount paid therefor, or if purchased by the judgment creditor, the amount of his or her bid, and the time when the purchaser will be entitled to a deed unless the premises are redeemed, as provided in Part 1 of Article XII of this Act.

P.A. 82–280, § 12–119, eff. July 1, 1982. Amended by P.A. 83–707, § 1, eff. Sept. 23, 1983; P.A. 85–907, Art. I, § 1, eff. Nov. 23, 1987.

Formerly Ill.Rev.Stat.1991, ch. 110, ¶ 12–119.

5/12–120. Deposit of money—Receipt of other document

§ 12–120. Deposit of money—Receipt of other document. With respect to any sale made in open court, wherever provisions are made in Part 1 of Article XII of this Act for any payment of money to or deposit of any receipt or other document with the officer who made the sale or who sold the real estate, such payment shall be made to or deposit made with the sheriff of the county in which the sale is held.

P.A. 82–280, § 12–120, eff. July 1, 1982. Amended by P.A. 83–707, § 1, eff. Sept. 23, 1983.

Formerly Ill.Rev.Stat.1991, ch. 110, ¶ 12–120.

5/12–121. Certificate recorded

§ 12–121. Certificate recorded. The purchaser shall, within 10 days from such sale, file in the office of the recorder of the county in which the property is situated, such certificate, which shall be recorded by such recorder; and such certificate or duplicate, or record, and certified copy of the record thereof, shall be evidence of the facts therein stated.

P.A. 82–280, § 12–121, eff. July 1, 1982. Amended by P.A. 84–314, § 1, eff. Jan. 1, 1986.

Formerly Ill.Rev.Stat.1991, ch. 110, ¶ 12–121.

5/12–122. Redemption

§ 12–122. Redemption. Any defendant, his or her heirs, executors, administrators, assigns, or any person interested in the premises, through or under the defendant, may, except as to any sale had by virtue of a judgment of foreclosure in accordance with Article XV of this Act, within 6 months from the sale, redeem the real estate so sold by paying to the purchaser thereof, his or her heirs, executors, administrators or assigns or to the sheriff or other officer who sold the same, or his or her successor in office, for the benefit of such purchaser, his or her heirs, executors, administrators, or assigns, the sum of money for which the premises were sold or bid off, with interest thereon at the rate of 10% per annum from the time of such sale, whereupon such sale and certificate shall be null and void. If there has been a prior redemption by a judgment creditor, his or her heirs, executors, administrators or assigns, then redemption by a defendant, his or her heirs, executors, administrators or assigns, or any person interested in the premises through or under the defendant, shall be in accordance with Section 12-137 of this Act.

P.A. 82-280, § 12-122, eff. July 1, 1982. Amended by P.A. 82-783, Art. III, § 43, eff. July 13, 1982; P.A. 83-707, § 1, eff. Sept. 23, 1983; P.A. 83-1271, § 3, eff. Aug. 30, 1984; P.A. 84-1462, § 2, eff. July 1, 1987.

Formerly Ill.Rev.Stat.1991, ch. 110, ¶ 12-122.

5/12-123 to 5/12-130. §§ 12-123 to 12-130. Repealed by P.A. 84-1462, § 7, eff. July 1, 1987

5/12-131. Certificate of redemption

§ 12-131. Certificate of redemption. Except as to any sale had by virtue of a judgment of foreclosure entered in accordance with Article XV, in all cases of redemption of land from sale had under any judgment or order, it shall be the duty of the purchaser, sheriff, or other officer or person from whom such redemption takes place, to prepare an instrument in writing, under his or her signature and seal, evidencing the redemption, which shall be recorded in the recorder's office of the proper county, in like manner as other writings affecting the title to real estate are filed and recorded, which recording shall be paid for by the party redeeming.

P.A. 82-280, § 12-131, eff. July 1, 1982. Amended by P.A. 83-707, § 1, eff. Sept. 23, 1983; P.A. 84-1462, § 2, eff. July 1, 1987.

Formerly Ill.Rev.Stat.1991, ch. 110, ¶ 12-131.

5/12-132. Redemption by creditors

§ 12-132. Redemption by creditors. If a redemption is not made, pursuant to Section 12-122 of this Act where applicable, prior to the making of redemption under this Section, any judgment creditor, his or her heirs, executors, administrators or assigns may, after the expiration of 3 months and within 6 months after the sale, redeem the premises in the following manner: such creditor, so entitled to redeem, his or her heirs, executors, administrators or assigns may obtain a certified copy of the judgment, and place the same with the sheriff or other proper officer for enforcement, and the sheriff or other proper officer shall endorse upon the back thereof a levy of the premises desired to be redeemed; and the person so entitled and desiring to make such redemption shall pay to such officer the amount for which the premises to be redeemed were sold, with interest thereon at the rate of 10% per annum from the date of the sale, for the use of the purchaser of such premises, his or her heirs, executors, administrators or assigns, whereupon such officer shall prepare and file in the office of the recorder of the county in which the premises are situated a certificate of such redemption, and shall advertise and offer the premises for sale under the judgment as in other cases of sale under a judgment.

P.A. 82-280, § 12-132, eff. July 1, 1982. Amended by P.A. 82-783, Art. III, § 43, eff. July 13, 1982; P.A. 83-353, § 1, eff. Sept. 14, 1983; P.A. 83-707, § 1, eff. Sept. 23, 1983; P.A. 83-1362, Art. II, § 109, eff. Sept. 11, 1984; P.A. 83-1528, Art. II, § 28, eff. Jan. 17, 1985; P.A. 84-1462, § 2, eff. July 1, 1987.

Formerly Ill.Rev.Stat.1991, ch. 110, ¶ 12-132.

5/12-133. Redemption money bid

§ 12-133. Redemption money bid. The creditor, his or her heirs, executors, administrators or assigns, having so redeemed, shall be considered as having bid at such sale the amount of the redemption money so paid by him or her, with interest thereon at the rate of 6% per annum from the date of such redemption to the day of sale, with the cost of such redemption and sale, and if no greater amount is bid at such sale, the premises shall be struck off to the person making such redemption. If at the time of issuance thereof, any person is entitled to redeem under Section 12-137 of this Act the officer shall forthwith execute a certificate of purchase to him or her in like form and manner as upon the first sale, for a deed of the premises so sold. If no person is so entitled to redeem under Section 12-137 of this Act, such officer shall execute a deed of the premises and no other redemption shall be allowed.

P.A. 82-280, § 12-133, eff. July 1, 1982. Amended by P.A. 83-707, § 1, eff. Sept. 23, 1983.

Formerly Ill.Rev.Stat.1991, ch. 110, ¶ 12-133.

5/12-134. Bid at more than redemption money

§ 12-134. Bid at more than redemption money. If at any sale held pursuant to Section 12-132 of this Act, a greater amount is bid and the premises sold for more than the amount of such redemption money, interest and costs, the excess shall be applied on the judgment under which the redemption was made; and a certificate of the purchase shall be delivered to the new purchaser in like form and manner as upon the first sale, for a deed of the premises so sold, in 60 days from the date of such sale, unless the same are redeemed before the expiration of that time, by some other judgment creditor, his or her heirs, executors, administrators or assigns, or by any defendant, his or her heirs, executors, administrators, assigns, or any person interested in the premises through or under the defendant, as provided in Section 12–137 of this Act.

P.A. 82–280, § 12–134, eff. July 1, 1982. Amended by P.A. 83–707, § 1, eff. Sept. 23, 1983.

Formerly Ill.Rev.Stat.1991, ch. 110, ¶ 12–134.

5/12–135. Further redemptions

§ 12–135. Further redemptions. Successive redemptions may be made of the premises at any time within 60 days of the last sale at which they were sold for more than the amount of the redemption money, interest and costs, and the premises again sold in the same manner and upon the same terms and conditions, and certificate shall be made in like form and manner as upon the sale on the first redemption, and the person redeeming shall be considered to have bid the amount of his or her redemption money, interest and costs; and if at any such sale the premises are not sold for a greater sum, the sheriff or other officer shall forthwith execute a deed to the purchaser, and no other redemption shall be allowed.

P.A. 82–280, § 12–135, eff. July 1, 1982.

Formerly Ill.Rev.Stat.1991, ch. 110, ¶ 12–135.

5/12–136. Preference in redemptions

§ 12–136. Preference in redemptions. When there are several judgment creditors, the creditor having the senior judgment shall have the preference to redeem during the first 2 days after the commencement of the period in which judgment creditors may redeem, and the other creditors shall respectively have preference to redeem during a like time, in the order of seniority of their several judgments; but where 2 or more judgments bear equal date, the creditor first paying the redemption money shall have preference.

P.A. 82–280, § 12–136, eff. July 1, 1982. Amended by P.A. 83–707, § 1, eff. Sept. 23, 1983.

Formerly Ill.Rev.Stat.1991, ch. 110, ¶ 12–136.

5/12–137. Subsequent redemptions

§ 12–137. Subsequent redemptions. Any redemption made under Sections 12–132 through 12–136 of this Act, by any judgment creditor, his or her heirs, executors, administrators or assigns after the expiration of 3 months and within 6 months after the original sale, is subject to subsequent redemption within 6 months after the date of the original sale by any defendant, his or her heirs, executors, administrators, assigns, or any person interested in the premises through or under the defendant, in the manner provided in this Section. In the event there is a redemption by any defendant, his or her heirs, executors, administrators, assigns, or any person interested in

the premises through or under the defendant, in accordance with Section 12–122 or this Section 12–137, the right to further redemption by any judgment creditor, his or her heirs, executors, administrators or assigns, is terminated, notwithstanding any other provisions of this Act. Any such defendant, his or her heirs, executors, administrators, assigns, or any person interested in the premises through or under the defendant, having a right to redeem, may redeem by paying to the sheriff or other proper officer the amount at which the premises were last redeemed by the judgment creditor, his or her heirs, executors, administrators or assigns, with interest thereon at the rate of 10% per annum, from the date of the last redemption; however, if the premises were sold pursuant to such last redemption for an amount greater than the redemption money, interest and costs, then the amount payable shall be the amount for which the premises were sold, together with interest on that amount at the rate of 10% per annum from the time of such sale, and costs of sale.

P.A. 82–280, § 12–137, eff. July 1, 1982. Amended by P.A. 82–783, Art. III, § 43, eff. July 13, 1982; P.A. 83–353, § 1, eff. Sept. 14, 1983; P.A. 83–707, § 1, eff. Sept. 23, 1983; P.A. 84–1462, § 2, eff. July 1, 1987.

Formerly Ill.Rev.Stat.1991, ch. 110, ¶ 12–137.

5/12–138. Redemptions of parts as sold

§ 12–138. Redemptions of parts as sold. Any person entitled to redeem may redeem the whole or any part of the premises sold, in like district parcels or quantities in which the same were sold.

P.A. 82–280, § 12–138, eff. July 1, 1982.

Formerly Ill.Rev.Stat.1991, ch. 110, ¶ 12–138.

5/12–139. Redemption by joint owner

§ 12–139. Redemption by joint owner. Except as to any sale had by virtue of a judgment of foreclosure in accordance with Article XV of this Code, any joint owner, his or her heirs, executors, administrators or assigns, or a judgment creditor of such joint owner, may redeem the interest of such joint owner in the premises sold under judgment, in the manner and upon the conditions hereinbefore provided, upon the payment of his or her proportion of the amount which would be necessary to redeem the whole.

P.A. 82–280, § 12–139, eff. July 1, 1982. Amended by P.A. 83–707, § 1, eff. Sept. 23, 1983; P.A. 85–907, Art. I, § 1, eff. Nov. 23, 1987.

Formerly Ill.Rev.Stat.1991, ch. 110, ¶ 12–139.

5/12–140. Redemption on claims allowed in probate

§ 12–140. Redemption on claims allowed in probate. For the purpose of redemption from the sale of real estate of a deceased debtor, any person whose claim has been allowed in probate against the estate of such deceased debtor, shall be considered a judgment creditor, and for the purpose of enabling such creditor to redeem from such sale, a certified copy of the order allowing the claim issued by the clerk of the court wherein letters of office were granted, may be delivered to the sheriff of the proper county, upon redemption having been made, to levy upon and sell the premises so sought to be redeemed, and like proceedings shall be had as upon other judgments.

P.A. 82–280, § 12–140, eff. July 1, 1982. Amended by P.A. 83–707, § 1, eff. Sept. 23, 1983.

Formerly Ill.Rev.Stat.1991, ch. 110, ¶ 12–140.

5/12–141. Taxes and assessments during period of redemption

§ 12–141. Taxes and assessments during period of redemption. Except as to any sale had by virtue of a judgment of foreclosure in accordance with Article XV of this Act, whenever any real estate is sold under any judgment of any court, the holder of the certificate of that sale, may pay all taxes and assessments which are or may become a lien on that real estate during the time of redemption running on the sale. Whenever redemption is made from that sale the party or parties entitled to redeem shall pay to the holder of the certificate of sale, or grantee under such deed, or to the sheriff or other officer who sold the real estate, or his successor in office, in addition to the amount due on the certificate, or deed, the amount paid by the holder thereof or grantee therein for the taxes and assessments, together with interest thereon at the rate of 10% per annum, if before the redemption is made a receipt for those taxes or assessments is filed with the sheriff or other officer who made the sale or exhibited by the holder of the certificate if redemption is made directly to the holder of the certificate, or the grantee in such deed.

P.A. 82–280, § 12–141, eff. July 1, 1982. Amended by P.A. 82–783, Art. III, § 43, eff. July 13, 1982; P.A. 83–707, § 1, eff. Sept. 23, 1983; P.A. 84–1462, § 2, eff. July 1, 1987.

Formerly Ill.Rev.Stat.1991, ch. 110, ¶ 12–141.

5/12–142. Realty sold to satisfy junior lien

§ 12–142. Realty sold to satisfy junior lien. Except as to any sale had by virtue of a judgment of foreclosure in accordance with Article XV of this Act, whenever any real estate has been or is sold at judicial or judgment sale to enforce a lien thereon and the real estate is subject to a mortgage lien which is prior and superior to the lien so foreclosed through that sale, the holder of the certificate of sale, may from time to time during the period of redemption pay any interest, principal or other obligation which is due and payable in accordance with the terms of the superior mortgage. If redemption is made from the sale, the party or parties entitled to redeem shall pay to the holder of the certificate of sale, or grantee under such deed, or to the sheriff or other officer who

sold the real estate or his or her successor in office, in addition to the amount due on the certificate, or deed, the amount paid by the holder thereof or grantee therein for interest, principal or other obligation, together with interest thereon at the rate of 10% per annum, if before the redemption is made a receipt evidencing the payments of interest, principal and other obligations is filed with the sheriff or other officer who made the sale or his or her successor in office or exhibited by the holder of the certificate or grantee in such deed to the party redeeming if the redemption payment is made directly to the holder of the certificate, or the grantee in such deed.

P.A. 82–280, § 12–142, eff. July 1, 1982. Amended by P.A. 82–783, Art. III, § 43, eff. July 13, 1982; P.A. 83–707, § 1, eff. Sept. 23, 1983; P.A. 84–1462, § 2, eff. July 1, 1987.

Formerly Ill.Rev.Stat.1991, ch. 110, ¶ 12–142.

5/12–143. Commissions

§ 12–143. Commissions. No commission upon the amount of the redemption money paid in any case shall be allowed to the officer receiving the same, but the usual commission shall be allowed to the officer selling the premises, on the excess made over and above the amount of the redemption money and interest.

P.A. 82–280, § 12–143, eff. July 1, 1982.

Formerly Ill.Rev.Stat.1991, ch. 110, ¶ 12–143.

5/12–144. Certificate assignable

§ 12–144. Certificate assignable. Every certificate which is given by any officer to any purchaser, under the provisions of Part 1 of Article XII of this Act is assignable by endorsement thereon, under the signature of such purchaser or his or her heirs, executors, administrators or assigns, and every person to whom the same is so assigned is entitled to the same benefits therefrom in every respect, that the person therein named would be if the same was not assigned.

P.A. 82–280, § 12–144, eff. July 1, 1982. Amended by P.A. 83–707, § 1, eff. Sept. 23, 1983.

Formerly Ill.Rev.Stat.1991, ch. 110, ¶ 12–144.

5/12–144.5. Report of sale and confirmation of sale

§ 12–144.5. Report of sale and confirmation of sale.

(a) When the premises mentioned in the certificate are not redeemed in pursuance of law, the legal holder of the certificate shall promptly make a report to the court that issued the underlying judgment. The report shall include a copy of the certificate of sale; an affidavit, under oath, containing a good faith appraisal of the fair market value of the property; and a listing of all liens and mortgages including the value thereof.

(b) Upon motion and notice in accordance with court rules applicable to motions generally, including notice to the judgment debtor, the court issuing the underlying judgment shall conduct a hearing to confirm the sale. Unless the court finds that (i) notice as required by law was not given, (ii) the terms of the sale were unconscionable, (iii) the sale was conducted fraudulently, or (iv) justice was otherwise not done, the court shall then enter an order confirming the sale. In making these findings, the court shall take into account the purchase price at the sale in relation to the fair market value of the property less the value of any mortgages and liens.

P.A. 82–280, § 12–144.5, added by P.A. 91–924, § 10, eff. Jan. 1, 2001.

5/12–145. Time of execution of deed

§ 12–145. Time of execution of deed. When the premises mentioned in such certificate are not redeemed in pursuance of law, and the court issuing the underlying judgment has entered an order confirming the sale in accordance with Section 12–144.5, the legal holder of the certificate is entitled to a deed therefor at any time within 5 years from the expiration of the time of redemption. The deed shall be executed by the sheriff or other officer who made the sale, or by his or her successor in office, or by some person specially appointed by the court for the purpose. If the deed is not taken within the time limited by Part 1 of Article XII of this Act, the certificate of purchase is void unless the purchaser under the certificate of sale has gone into possession of the premises under and in reliance on the certificate of sale within the 5 year period. If, however, the deed is wrongfully withheld by the officer whose duty it is to execute it, or if the execution of the deed is restrained by injunction or order of a court, the time during which the deed is so withheld or the execution thereof restrained shall not be considered as any part of the 5 years within which the holder is required to take a deed.

P.A. 82–280, § 12–145, eff. July 1, 1982. Amended by P.A. 83–707, § 1, eff. Sept. 23, 1983; P.A. 91–924, § 10, eff. Jan. 1, 2001.

Formerly Ill.Rev.Stat.1991, ch. 110, ¶ 12–145.

5/12–146. Foreclosures subject to prior law

§ 12–146. Foreclosures subject to prior law. Any sales of real estate made pursuant to a judgment foreclosing a mortgage or trust deed executed on or after July 1, 1917 and before July 1, 1921 shall be governed by the law in effect at the time such mortgage or trust deed was executed.

P.A. 82–280, § 12–146, eff. July 1, 1982.

Formerly Ill.Rev.Stat.1991, ch. 110, ¶ 12–146.

5/12–147. Form of deed

§ 12–147. Form of deed. The deed may be substantially, in the following form:

Whereas, A.B. ... in the ... court of ... county recovered a judgment against C.D. for the sum of ... and costs on (insert date) and a certified copy of the judgment, issued on (insert date), by virtue of which ... levied upon the premises hereinafter described, and the time and place of the sale thereof having been duly advertised according to law, the same were struck off and sold to ..., he or she being the highest and best bidder therefor. (If the certificate has been transferred, recite the fact.)

Now, therefore, I, ..., of the county of ..., in consideration of the premises, hereby convey to ..., his or her heirs and assigns, the following described lot or parcel of land (here describe the premises) to have and to hold the same with all the appurtenances thereto belonging forever.

.................(Date) ....(Signature)

P.A. 82–280, § 12–147, eff. July 1, 1982. Amended by P.A. 83–707, § 1, eff. Sept. 23, 1983; P.A. 91–357, § 250, eff. July 29, 1999.

Formerly Ill.Rev.Stat.1991, ch. 110, ¶ 12–147.

5/12–148. Effect of deed

§ 12–148. Effect of deed. Such deed shall convey to the grantee therein named all the title, estate and interest of the judgment debtor, of every nature and kind, in and to the premises thereby conveyed, but such deed shall not be construed to contain any covenant on the part of the officer executing the same.

P.A. 82–280, § 12–148, eff. July 1, 1982.

Formerly Ill.Rev.Stat.1991, ch. 110, ¶ 12–148.

5/12–149. Title acquired at sale

§ 12–149. Title acquired at sale. The right, title and interest of any purchaser acquired at a sale made under or pursuant to any judgment in a proceeding in which the court had jurisdiction of the subject matter and of the parties, and who was not a party to such proceeding, and the right, title and interest of any bona fide assignee or pledgee for value of the certificate of sale under such certificate issued pursuant to a sale based on such judgment rendered in such proceeding who was not a party to such proceeding (whether the purchaser at such sale was a party or not), shall not be affected by any reversal, modification or order setting aside such judgment made in any proceeding to review such judgment, unless at the time of such sale, assignment or pledge, an appeal was pending which operated as a stay of enforcement of the judgment or a petition under Section 2–1401 of this Act had been filed.

P.A. 82–280, § 12–149, eff. July 1, 1982.

Formerly Ill.Rev.Stat.1991, ch. 110, ¶ 12–149.

5/12–150. Deed as evidence

§ 12–150. Deed as evidence. Any deed which has been heretofore, or which may hereafter be so executed, or which has been executed pursuant to Article XV of this Act, or a certified copy of the record thereof, shall be prima facie evidence that the provisions of the law in relation to the sale of the property for which it is or may be given were complied with; and in case of the loss or destruction of the record of the judgment, or levy thereon, such deed or certified copy of the record thereof shall be prima facie evidence of the entry and existence of the judgment and levy thereunder as therein recited.

P.A. 82–280, § 12–150, eff. July 1, 1982. Amended by P.A. 84–1462, § 2, eff. July 1, 1987.

Formerly Ill.Rev.Stat.1991, ch. 110, ¶ 12–150.

5/12–151. § 12–151. Repealed by P.A. 84–1462, § 7, eff. July 1, 1987

5/12–152. Certificate of levy

§ 12–152. Certificate of levy. When a certified copy of a judgment is issued from a circuit court of any county in this State, and levied upon any real estate, the officer making such levy shall execute a certificate thereof and file the same in the office of the recorder of the county in which such real estate is located or in the office of the registrar of titles of such county if the real estate levied upon is registered under "An Act concerning land titles", approved May 1, 1897, as amended.[1] Unless a transcript, certified copy or memorandum has been filed in the office of the recorder or in the office of the registrar of titles of such county, as the case may be, as provided by Section 12–101 of this Act, no judgment or order shall become a lien upon either nonregistered or registered real property until such certificate of levy has been filed as provided in this Section and, if the real property levied upon is registered, a memorial thereof is entered upon the register of the last certificate of title to be affected.

P.A. 82–280, § 12–152, eff. July 1, 1982. Amended by P.A. 83–358, § 76, eff. Sept. 14, 1983.

Formerly Ill.Rev.Stat.1991, ch. 110, ¶ 12–152.

[1] 765 ILCS 35/0.01 et seq.

5/12–153. Form of certificate

§ 12–153. Form of certificate. The certificate may be substantially in the following form:

STATE OF ILLINOIS,   )
)   ss.
.... County.   )

I (here state the name of the officer and the title of his or her office) do hereby certify that by virtue of a judgment from the ... court of ... county, in favor of ..., against ..., dated (insert date), I did, on (insert date), levy upon the following premises. (Here describe the premises.)

(Signature.)

P.A. 82–280, § 12–153, eff. July 1, 1982. Amended by P.A. 91–357, § 250, eff. July 29, 1999.

Formerly Ill.Rev.Stat.1991, ch. 110, ¶ 12–153.

5/12–154. Recordation of certificate

§ 12–154. Recordation of certificate. Such certificate shall be recorded by the recorder, in a book to be kept for that purpose. The fee for recording such certificate shall be collected as other costs.

P.A. 82–280, § 12–154, eff. July 1, 1982.

Formerly Ill.Rev.Stat.1991, ch. 110, ¶ 12–154.

5/12–155. Death of judgment creditor

§ 12–155. Death of judgment creditor. The collection of a judgment shall not be delayed or hindered, or the lien created by law abate, by reason of the death of any person in whose favor such judgment stands; but the executor or administrator may cause his or her letters of office to be filed in such court, after which the judgment may be enforced and proceeding had in the name of the executor or administrator as such, in the same manner as if the judgment had been recovered in his or her name.

P.A. 82–280, § 12–155, eff. July 1, 1982. Amended by P.A. 83–707, § 1, eff. Sept. 23, 1983.

Formerly Ill.Rev.Stat.1991, ch. 110, ¶ 12–155.

5/12–156. Representative may purchase realty

§ 12–156. Representative may purchase realty. When it is necessary in order to secure the collection of a judgment belonging to any estate the executor or administrator shall bid for and become the purchaser of real estate at the sale thereof by the sheriff, or other officer. The premises so purchased shall be assets in his or her possession, and may be again sold by him or her, with the approval of the circuit court, and the moneys arising from such sale shall be accounted for and paid over as other moneys in his or her possession.

P.A. 82–280, § 12–156, eff. July 1, 1982.

Formerly Ill.Rev.Stat.1991, ch. 110, ¶ 12–156.

5/12–157. Death of judgment debtor

§ 12–157. Death of judgment debtor. If a person dies, after a court enters on judgment for the payment of money against him or her, the judgment may be enforced against the real estate of such deceased person, or a sale may be made under such judgment, without reviving the judgment against his or her heirs, legatees or legal representatives. No sale shall be made until after the expiration of 12 months from the death of such deceased person, nor shall any sale be had on such judgment until the person in whose favor the judgment is sought to be enforced shall give to the executor or administrator, or if there is neither, the heirs of the deceased, at least 3 months' notice of the existence of such judgment, before proceeding to sell, which notice shall be in writing if the parties required to be notified reside or may be found within the State, and their place of residence known, otherwise publication notice shall be given in the same manner as is provided for other civil cases.

P.A. 82–280, § 12–157, eff. July 1, 1982.　Amended by P.A. 83–707, § 1, eff. Sept. 23, 1983.

Formerly Ill.Rev.Stat.1991, ch. 110, ¶ 12–157.

5/12–158.　Goods and chattels

§ 12–158.　Goods and chattels.　All goods and chattels, real and personal, may be taken and sold to satisfy a judgment, except as otherwise provided by law.

When any officer levies a judgment on livestock, or other personal property, which is not immediately replevied or restored to the debtor, such officer shall provide sufficient sustenance for the support of such livestock and shall provide for the proper care and storage of such personal property until it is replevied, sold or discharged from such judgment.　The officer shall receive a reasonable compensation therefor, to be determined by the court which entered the judgment, to be advanced to him or her, from time to time, by the judgment creditor, and the amount of such compensation shall be collected as a part of the costs in the case.

If any goods or chattels levied upon are, in the opinion of the officer making the levy, of a perishable nature and in danger of immediate waste or decay, the officer shall request the judgment creditor to obtain from the court which entered the judgment an order permitting that property to be sold not later than 24 hours after the levy was made, upon due notice of sale to the judgment debtor and to the public, as the court in its order may require.　The money from such a sale shall be retained by the sheriff or other officer until the balance of the property levied upon is sold, at which time it shall be paid to the judgment creditor with the proceeds of the sale of the balance of the property.　If the judgment creditor fails or refuses to obtain such an order for sale of perishable property, the sheriff or other officer making the levy shall be absolved of all responsibility to any person for loss occasioned by the failure to sell or care for such perishable property.　The request of the sheriff or other officer shall be in writing and shall be delivered to the judgment creditor or his or her attorney or agent and to the judgment debtor if found.　If the judgment debtor is not found a copy of the request shall be posted on the premises where the perishable

items are located.　The judgment creditor's motion for an order of sale of perishable property shall be treated as an emergency motion.

P.A. 82–280, § 12–158, eff. July 1, 1982.

Formerly Ill.Rev.Stat.1991, ch. 110, ¶ 12–158.

5/12–159.　Gold and silver

§ 12–159.　Gold and silver.　Current gold or silver coin, or other legal tender, may be levied upon for the enforcement of a judgment and may be paid over to the creditor as money collected.

P.A. 82–280, § 12–159, eff. July 1, 1982.

Formerly Ill.Rev.Stat.1991, ch. 110, ¶ 12–159.

5/12–160.　Bills

§ 12–160.　Bills.　Bank bills, and all other bills or evidence of debt, issued by a moneyed corporation and circulated as money, may be levied upon for the enforcement of a judgment and paid to the creditor, at their par value, as money collected, if he or she is willing to receive them; otherwise they shall be sold like other chattels.

P.A. 82–280, § 12–160, eff. July 1, 1982.

Formerly Ill.Rev.Stat.1991, ch. 110, ¶ 12–160.

5/12–161.　Security

§ 12–161.　Security.　If there is reasonable doubt as to the ownership of the goods, or as to their liability to be levied upon to satisfy the judgment, the officer may require sufficient security to indemnify him or her for levying upon them.

P.A. 82–280, § 12–161, eff. July 1, 1982.

Formerly Ill.Rev.Stat.1991, ch. 110, ¶ 12–161.

5/12–162.　Delivery bond

§ 12–162.　Delivery bond.　When personal property is levied upon, or about to be levied upon, if the judgment debtor gives bond with sufficient security, to be approved by the officer, payable to the creditor, in double the amount of the judgment, conditioned to deliver the property levied upon undamaged at the time and place where the same is to be sold, which shall be named in the condition, the sheriff may allow the property to remain with the judgment debtor.

P.A. 82–280, § 12–162, eff. July 1, 1982.

Formerly Ill.Rev.Stat.1991, ch. 110, ¶ 12–162.

5/12–163.　When property not delivered

§ 12–163.　When property not delivered.　If the property is not delivered according to the condition of the bond, the officer having the certified copy of the judgment may proceed to enforce the same in the same manner as if no levy had been made.

P.A. 82–280, § 12–163, eff. July 1, 1982.

Formerly Ill.Rev.Stat.1991, ch. 110, ¶ 12–163.

5/12–164. Proceedings on delivery bond

§ 12–164. Proceedings on delivery bond. If the officer does not obtain satisfaction of the judgment, he or she shall return the bond with the certified copy of the judgment, and the creditor shall be allowed to recover thereon the amount of the judgment, with interest and costs, or if the value of the property so levied upon is shown by the judgment debtor to be less than such judgment and costs, the value thereof, with 10% damages for the delay.

P.A. 82–280, § 12–164, eff. July 1, 1982. Amended by P.A. 91–357, § 250, eff. July 29, 1999.

Formerly Ill.Rev.Stat.1991, ch. 110, ¶ 12–164.

5/12–165. Second delivery bond

§ 12–165. Second delivery bond. No second delivery bond shall be taken in behalf of a judgment debtor so failing to comply with the first, nor shall a delivery bond be taken of his or her surety without the consent of the judgment creditor.

P.A. 82–280, § 12–165, eff. July 1, 1982.

Formerly Ill.Rev.Stat.1991, ch. 110, ¶ 12–165.

5/12–166. Notice of sale of personalty

§ 12–166. Notice of sale of personalty. Before any goods or chattels are sold to satisfy a judgment, at least 10 days' previous notice of such sale shall be given by posting notices thereof in 3 of the most public places in the county where such sale is to be held, specifying the time when and place where the same are to be sold.

P.A. 82–280, § 12–166, eff. July 1, 1982.

Formerly Ill.Rev.Stat.1991, ch. 110, ¶ 12–166.

5/12–167. Postponing sale

§ 12–167. Postponing sale. The officer may postpone such sale from time to time, not exceeding 10 days at one time, whenever, for want of bidders or other good cause, he or she deems it for the interest of the parties concerned. Notice of such postponement may be given at the time and place fixed for the sale, or by posting notices as hereinbefore provided, but if the postponement exceeds one day, the officer shall post notices thereof.

P.A. 82–280, § 12–167, eff. July 1, 1982.

Formerly Ill.Rev.Stat.1991, ch. 110, ¶ 12–167.

5/12–168. Return—Liability

§ 12–168. Return—Liability. The officer making such sale shall, in his or her return of the certified copy of the judgment particularly describe the goods sold, and the sum for which each article was sold; and if he or she is guilty of fraud in the sale or return, he or she shall be liable, in a civil action to the party damaged, for 5 times the amount of the actual damage sustained by reason of such fraud.

P.A. 82–280, § 12–168, eff. July 1, 1982.

Formerly Ill.Rev.Stat.1991, ch. 110, ¶ 12–168.

5/12–169. Marshalling proceeds

§ 12–169. Marshalling proceeds. If the goods or chattels sold to satisfy the judgment have been attached by another creditor or seized on another judgment either by the same or any other officer, or if before the payment of the residue, after the satisfaction of the judgment to the debtor, another attachment or judgment against the judgment debtor is delivered to the officer who made the sale, the proceeds of the sale shall be applied to the discharge of the several judgments in the order in which the respective attachments or judgments become a lien or are entitled by law to share, and the residue, if any, shall be returned to the debtor or his or her assigns.

P.A. 82–280, § 12–169, eff. July 1, 1982.

Formerly Ill.Rev.Stat.1991, ch. 110, ¶ 12–169.

5/12–170. Levy upon corporate stock

§ 12–170. Levy upon corporate stock. The share or interest of a stockholder in any corporation may be levied upon in the enforcement of a judgment, and sold as hereinafter provided; but in all cases, where such share or interest has been sold or pledged in good faith for a valuable consideration, and the certificate thereof has been delivered upon such sale or pledge, such shares or interest shall not be liable to be levied upon in the enforcement of a judgment against the vendor, or pledgor, except for the excess of the value thereof over and above the sum for which the same may have been pledged and the certificate thereof delivered.

P.A. 82–280, § 12–170, eff. July 1, 1982.

Formerly Ill.Rev.Stat.1991, ch. 110, ¶ 12–170.

5/12–171. Mode of levy on corporate stock

§ 12–171. Mode of levy on corporate stock. If the property has not been attached in the same action, the officer shall leave a copy of the judgment with the clerk, treasurer or cashier of the company, if there is such officer, otherwise with any officer or person having the custody of the books and papers of the corporation; and the property shall be considered as seized in the enforcement of the judgment when the copy is so left, and shall be sold in like manner as goods and chattels.

P.A. 82–280, § 12–171, eff. July 1, 1982.

Formerly Ill.Rev.Stat.1991, ch. 110, ¶ 12–171.

5/12–172. Mode of sale of corporate stock

§ 12–172. Mode of sale of corporate stock. If the share is already attached in the same action, the officer shall proceed in seizing and selling it to satisfy the judgment, in the same manner as in selling goods and chattels.

P.A. 82–280, § 12–172, eff. July 1, 1982.

Formerly Ill.Rev.Stat.1991, ch. 110, ¶ 12–172.

5/12–173. Certificate of corporate officer

§ 12–173. Certificate of corporate officer. The officer of the company who keeps a record or account of the shares or interest of the stockholders therein, shall, upon the exhibiting to him or her of the certified copy of the judgment, be bound to give a certificate of the number of shares or amount of the interest held by the judgment debtor. If he or she refuses to do so, or willfully gives a false certificate thereof, he or she shall be liable for double the amount of all damages occasioned by such refusal or false certificate, to be recovered in a civil action, unless the judgment is satisfied by the judgment debtor.

P.A. 82–280, § 12–173, eff. July 1, 1982.

Formerly Ill.Rev.Stat.1991, ch. 110, ¶ 12–173.

5/12–174. Rights of purchaser

§ 12–174. Rights of purchaser. A certified copy of the judgment and of the return thereon shall, within 15 days after the sale, be left with the officer of the company whose duty it is to record transfers of shares; and the purchaser shall thereupon be entitled to a certificate or certificates of the shares bought by him or her upon paying the fees therefor and for recording the transfer.

P.A. 82–280, § 12–174, eff. July 1, 1982.

Formerly Ill.Rev.Stat.1991, ch. 110, ¶ 12–174.

5/12–175. Right to dividends

§ 12–175. Right to dividends. If the shares or interest of the judgment debtor had been attached in the action in which the judgment was entered, the purchaser shall be entitled to all the dividends which have accrued after the attachment.

P.A. 82–280, § 12–175, eff. July 1, 1982.

Formerly Ill.Rev.Stat.1991, ch. 110, ¶ 12–175.

5/12–176. Judgments between parties

§ 12–176. Judgments between parties. Judgments between the same parties may be set off, one against another, if required by either party, as prescribed in the following Section.

P.A. 82–280, § 12–176, eff. July 1, 1982.

Formerly Ill.Rev.Stat.1991, ch. 110, ¶ 12–176.

5/12–177. Multiple judgments

§ 12–177. Multiple judgments. When one of the judgments is delivered to an officer to be enforced, the debtor therein may deliver his or her judgment to the same officer, and the officer shall apply it, as far as it will extend, to the satisfaction of the first judgment, and the balance due on the larger judgment may be collected and paid in the same manner as if there had been no set-off.

P.A. 82–280, § 12–177, eff. July 1, 1982.

Formerly Ill.Rev.Stat.1991, ch. 110, ¶ 12–177.

5/12–178. Cases excepted

§ 12–178. Cases excepted. Such set-off shall not be allowed in the following cases:

1. When the creditor in one of the judgments is not in the same capacity and trust as the debtor in the other.

2. When the sum due on the first judgment was lawfully and in good faith assigned to another person, before the creditor in the second judgment became entitled to the sum due thereon.

3. When there are several creditors in one judgment, and the sum due on the other is due from a part of them only.

4. When there are several debtors in one judgment, and the sum due on the other is due to a part of them only.

5. It shall not be allowed as to so much of the first judgment as is due to the attorney in that action for his or her fees and disbursements therein.

P.A. 82–280, § 12–178, eff. July 1, 1982.

Formerly Ill.Rev.Stat.1991, ch. 110, ¶ 12–178.

5/12–179 to 5/12–182. §§ 12–179 to 12–182. Repealed by P.A. 83–352, § 2, eff. Sept. 14, 1983

5/12–183. Release of judgment

§ 12–183. Release of judgment.

(a) Every judgment creditor, his or her assignee of record or other legal representative having received full satisfaction or payment of all such sums of money as are really due to him or her from the judgment debtor on any judgment rendered in a court shall, at the request of the judgment debtor or his or her legal representative, execute and deliver to the judgment debtor or his or her legal representative an instrument in writing releasing such judgment.

(b) If the judgment creditor, his or her assigns of record or other legal representative to whom tender has been made of all sums of money due him or her from the judgment debtor including interest, on any judgment entered by a court, wilfully fails or refuses, at the request of the judgment debtor or his or her legal representative to execute and deliver to the judgment debtor or his or her legal representative an instrument in writing releasing such judgment, the judgment debtor may petition the court in which such judgment is of record, making tender therewith to the court of all sums due in principal and interest on such judgment, for the use of the judgment creditor, his or her executors, administrators or assigns, whereupon the court shall enter an order satisfying the judgment and releasing all liens based on such judgment.

(c) For the recording of assignment of any judgment the clerk of the court in which such judgment is of record is allowed a fee of $2.

(d) A satisfaction of a judgment may be delivered to the judgment debtor, his or her attorney or to the clerk of the court in which such judgment is of record.

(e) The clerk shall not be allowed any fee for recording the satisfaction of judgment. The clerk of the court shall make appropriate notation on the judgment docket of the book and page where any release or assignment of any judgment is recorded.

(f) No judgment shall be released of record except by an instrument in writing recorded in the court in which such judgment is of record. However, nothing contained in this Section affects in any manner the validity of any release of judgment made, prior to January 1, 1952, in judgment and execution dockets by the judgment creditor, his or her attorney, assignee or other legal representative.

(g) The writ of audita querela is abolished and all relief heretofore obtainable and grounds for such relief heretofore available, whether by the writ of audita querela or otherwise, shall be available in every case by petition hereunder, regardless of the nature of the order or judgment from which relief is sought or of the proceeding in which it was entered. There shall be no distinction between actions and other proceedings, statutory or otherwise, as to availability of relief, grounds for relief or relief obtainable. The petition shall be filed in the same proceeding in which the order or judgment was entered and shall be supported by affidavit or other appropriate showing as to matters not of record. All parties to the petition shall be notified as provided by rule.

(h) Upon the filing of a release or satisfaction in full satisfaction of judgment, signed by the party in whose favor the judgment was entered or his or her attorney, the court shall vacate the judgment, and dismiss the action.

(i) Any judgment arising out of an order for support shall not be a judgment to the extent of payments made as evidenced by the records of the Clerk of the Circuit Court or State agency receiving payments pursuant to the order. In the event payments made pursuant to that order are not paid to the Clerk of the Circuit Court or a State agency, then any judgment arising out of each order for support may be released in the following manner:

(1) A Notice of Filing and an affidavit stating that all installments of child support required to be paid pursuant to the order under which the judgment or judgments were entered have been paid shall be filed with the office of the court or agency entering said order for support, together with proof of service of such notice and affidavit upon the recipient of such payments.

(2) Service of such affidavit shall be by any means authorized under Sections 2–203 and 2–208 of the Code of Civil Procedure [1] or under Supreme Court Rules 11 or 105(b).

(3) The Notice of Filing shall set forth the name and address of the judgment debtor and the judgment creditor, the court file number of the order giving rise to the judgment and, in capital letters, the following statement:

YOU ARE HEREBY NOTIFIED THAT ON (insert date) THE ATTACHED AFFIDAVIT WAS FILED IN THE OFFICE OF THE CLERK OF THE CIRCUIT COURT OF ... COUNTY, ILLINOIS, WHOSE ADDRESS IS ...., ILLINOIS. IF, WITHIN 28 DAYS OF THE DATE OF THIS NOTICE, YOU FAIL TO FILE AN AFFIDAVIT OBJECTING TO THE SATISFACTION OF THE STATED JUDGMENT OR JUDGMENTS IN THE ABOVE OFFICE, THE SAID JUDGMENTS WILL BE DEEMED TO BE SATISFIED AND NOT ENFORCEABLE. THE SATISFACTION WILL NOT PREVENT YOU FROM ENFORCING THE ORDER FOR SUPPORT THROUGH THE COURT.

(4) If no affidavit objecting to the satisfaction of the judgment or judgments is filed within 28 days of the Notice described in paragraph (3) of this subsection (i), such judgment or judgments shall be deemed to be satisfied and not enforceable.

P.A. 82–280, § 12–183, eff. July 1, 1982. Amended by P.A. 82–783, Art. IV, § 27, eff. July 13, 1982; P.A. 82–1057, Art. III, § 10, eff. Feb. 11, 1983; P.A. 85–2, § 6, eff. May 1, 1987; P.A. 85–1156, Art. I, § 7, eff. Jan. 1, 1989; P.A. 91–357, § 250, eff. July 29, 1999.

Formerly Ill.Rev.Stat.1991, ch. 110, ¶ 12–183.
[1] 735 ILCS 5/2–203 and 5/2–208.

PART 2. TRIAL OF RIGHT OF PROPERTY

5/12–201. Procedure

§ 12–201. Procedure. (a) Whenever a judgment or order of attachment, entered by any court, shall be levied by any sheriff or coroner upon any personal property, and such property is claimed by any person other than the judgment debtor or defendant in such attachment, or is claimed by the judgment debtor or defendant in attachment as exempt from levy or attachment by virtue of the exemption laws of the State, by giving to the sheriff or coroner notice, in writing, of his or her claim, and intention to prosecute the same, it shall be the duty of such sheriff or coroner to notify the circuit court of such claim.

(b) The court shall thereupon cause the proceeding to be entered of record, and the claimant shall be made plaintiff in the proceeding, and the judgment creditor or plaintiff in attachment shall be made defendant in such proceeding.

(c) The clerk of the circuit court shall thereupon issue a notice, directed to the judgment creditor or plaintiff in attachment, notifying him or her of such claim, and of the time and place of trial, which time shall be not more than 10 days nor less than 5 days from the date of such notice.

(d) Such notice shall be served in the same manner as provided for the service of summons in other civil cases, at least 5 days before the day of trial; and if such notice is served less than 5 days before the day of trial, the trial shall, on demand of either party, be continued for a period not exceeding 10 days.

(e) In case return is made on such notice that the judgment creditor or plaintiff in attachment cannot be found, the proceeding shall be continued for a period not exceeding 90 days, and the judgment creditor or plaintiff in attachment shall be notified of such proceeding by publication as in other civil cases.

(f) If the judgment creditor or plaintiff in attachment, or his or her attorney, shall at least 5 days before the day of trial, file with the clerk of the circuit court his or her appearance in such proceeding, then it shall not be necessary to notify such person as above provided.

P.A. 82–280, § 12–201, eff. July 1, 1982.

Formerly Ill.Rev.Stat.1991, ch. 110, ¶ 12–201.

5/12–202. Trial

§ 12–202. Trial. The trial shall proceed without written pleadings in the same manner as in other civil cases, and may be by a jury if either party demands one.

P.A. 82–280, § 12–202, eff. July 1, 1982. Amended by P.A. 83–707, § 1, eff. Sept. 23, 1983.

Formerly Ill.Rev.Stat.1991, ch. 110, ¶ 12–202.

5/12–203. Subpoenas

§ 12–203. Subpoenas. The clerk of the court shall issue subpoenas for witnesses at the request of any party or the party's attorney.

P.A. 82–280, § 12–203, eff. July 1, 1982.

Formerly Ill.Rev.Stat.1991, ch. 110, ¶ 12–203.

5/12–204. Trial and judgment

§ 12–204. Trial and judgment. The court or the jury shall determine the rights of the parties and the court shall enter judgment accordingly, and the court shall direct the sheriff or coroner as to the disposition of the property in the possession of the sheriff or coroner. In case the property appears to belong to the claimant, when the claimant is any person other than the judgment debtor or the defendant in the attachment, or in case the property is found to be exempt from enforcement of a judgment thereon or attachment, when the claimant is the judgment debtor or the defendant in the attachment, judgment shall be entered against the judgment creditor or plaintiff in the attachment for the costs, and the property levied on shall be released, and in case it further appears that such claimant is entitled to the immediate possession of such property, the court shall order that such property be delivered to such claimant. If it appears that the property does not belong to the claimant, or is not exempt from the enforcement of a judgment thereon or attachment, as the case may be, judgment shall be entered against the claimant for costs, and an order shall be entered that the sheriff or coroner proceed to sell the property levied on. The judgment in such cases shall be a complete indemnity to the sheriff or coroner in selling or restoring any such property, as the case may be.

P.A. 82–280, § 12–204, eff. July 1, 1982.

Formerly Ill.Rev.Stat.1991, ch. 110, ¶ 12–204.

5/12–205. Costs

§ 12–205. Costs. If the judgment is entered in favor of the claimant as to part of the property, and in favor of another party as to part, then the court shall in its discretion apportion the costs; and the sheriff, coroner and clerk of the court shall be entitled to the same fees as are allowed by law for similar services.

P.A. 82–280, § 12–205, eff. July 1, 1982.

Formerly Ill.Rev.Stat.1991, ch. 110, ¶ 12–205.

PART 3. CONCEALING PROPERTY

Section
5/12–301. Contempt for concealing property.

5/12–301. Contempt for concealing property

§ 12–301. Contempt for concealing property. Any person who hides or conceals any property so that it cannot be taken by virtue of an order or judgment or, on the officer's request therefor, refuses to deliver property to the officer having an order or judgment for the taking of the property is guilty of contempt of court and subject to punishment therefor.

P.A. 82–280, § 12–301, eff. July 1, 1982. Amended by P.A. 83–352, § 1, eff. Sept. 14, 1983.

Formerly Ill.Rev.Stat.1991, ch. 110, ¶ 12–301.

PART 4. REDEMPTION BY STATE

5/12–401. Right of State as judgment creditor

§ 12–401. Right of State as judgment creditor. Except as to any sale had by virtue of a judgment of foreclosure in accordance with Article XV of this Act, whenever any real estate has been or is sold at a judicial or judgment sale and such real estate is then subject to a lien or claim for lien in favor of the People of the State of Illinois, which is junior and inferior to the lien so enforced or foreclosed by or through that sale, the right of the State to redeem by virtue of its lien from that sale or from the lien so foreclosed or enforced ceases and terminates at the end of 12 months from the date upon which it is filed for record in the Office of the Recorder for the County in which the lands so sold are situated, if such lands are unregistered, or in the Office of the Registrar of Titles for such County, if such lands are registered, a certified copy of the original or duplicate recorded or registered certificate of such sale, such certified copy being endorsed by the State's Attorney of such County, or his or her assistant, showing service of a copy of such certificate upon him or her, and upon such service such officer shall make such endorsement. Service may be made by United States registered or certified mail.

P.A. 82–280, § 12–401, eff. July 1, 1982. Amended by P.A. 83–358, § 76, eff. Sept. 14, 1983; P.A. 83–485, § 2, eff. Sept. 17, 1983; P.A. 83–1362, Art. II, § 109, eff. Sept. 11, 1984; P.A. 84–1462, § 2, eff. July 1, 1987.

Formerly Ill.Rev.Stat.1991, ch. 110, ¶ 12–401.

5/12–402. § 12–402. Repealed by P.A. 84–1462, § 7, eff. July 1, 1987

5/12–403. Application

§ 12–403. Application. The provisions of Part 4 of Article XII of this Act shall not apply to any lien in favor of the State of Illinois or notice of such lien arising under any other Act containing provisions relating to the right of the State of Illinois to redeem real estate sold at judicial or judgment sale.

P.A. 82–280, § 12–403, eff. July 1, 1982. Amended by P.A. 83–707, § 1, eff. Sept. 23, 1983.

Formerly Ill.Rev.Stat.1991, ch. 110, ¶ 12–403.

5/12–404. Does not include where State is nominal party

§ 12–404. Does not include where State is nominal party. The term "lien or claim for lien in favor of the People of the State of Illinois," as used in Part 4 of Article XII of this Act, means and includes a lien or claim for lien in which the State of Illinois is a real party in interest, and not a lien or claim for lien in the name of the People of the State of Illinois as nominal plaintiff for the sole use or benefit of others.

P.A. 82–280, § 12–404, eff. July 1, 1982. Amended by P.A. 83–707, § 1, eff. Sept. 23, 1983.

Formerly Ill.Rev.Stat.1991, ch. 110, ¶ 12–404.

PART 5. FEDERAL JUDGMENTS

5/12–501. Registration of Federal judgments

§ 12–501. Registration of Federal judgments. Judgments of courts of the United States held, within this State, and all process, returns, certificates of the levy of a process, and records of such courts may be registered, recorded, docketed, indexed or otherwise dealt with in, the public offices of this State, so as to make them conform to the rules and requirements relating to judgments of courts of this State. A certified copy of a federal judgment order entered in this State may be filed in any circuit court and shall be afforded recognition as if it were a judgment entered in any other circuit court of this State.

P.A. 82–280, § 12–501, eff. July 1, 1982. Amended by P.A. 83–707, § 1, eff. Sept. 23, 1983; P.A. 95–661, § 5, eff. Jan. 1, 2008.

Formerly Ill.Rev.Stat.1991, ch. 110, ¶ 12–501.

5/12–501A. § 12–501A. Repealed by P.A. 84–1389, § 7, eff. Jan. 1, 1987

5/12–502. Lien of Federal judgments

§ 12–502. Lien of Federal judgments. Upon filing in the office of the recorder in any county of this State of a transcript, certified copy or memorandum of a judgment entered in this State by a court of the United States, such judgment shall be a lien upon the real estate of the person against whom the same is entered, in the county where filed, in like manner as judgments of courts of this State. The term "memorandum" as used in this Section means a memorandum or copy of the judgment signed by a judge of the court entering it and showing the court in which entered, date, amount, case number of the case in which entered, name of the party in whose favor and name of the party against whom entered. However, no such judgment shall be a lien on any real estate, registered under the provisions of "An Act concerning land titles", approved May 1, 1897, as amended,[1] until the provisions of Section 85 of that Act[2] have been complied with.

P.A. 82–280, § 12–502, eff. July 1, 1982. Amended by P.A. 83–358, § 76, eff. Sept. 14, 1983.

Formerly Ill.Rev.Stat.1991, ch. 110, ¶ 12–502.

[1] 765 ILCS 35/1 et seq. (repealed).
[2] 765 ILCS 35/85 (repealed).

PART 6. FOREIGN JUDGMENTS AND FOREIGN–MONEY CLAIMS

5/12–601 to 5/12–617. §§ 12–601 to 12–617. Repealed by P.A. 87–358, § 2, eff. Sept. 9, 1991

UNIFORM FOREIGN MONEY–JUDGMENTS RECOGNITION ACT

5/12–618 to 5/12–626. §§ 12–618 to 12–626. Repealed by P.A. 97–140, § 10, eff. Jan. 1, 2012

5/12–627 to 5/12–629. §§ 12–627 to 12–629. Renumbered as §§12–651 to 12–653 and amended by P.A. 87–895, Art. 2, § 2–50, eff. Aug. 14, 1992

UNIFORM FOREIGN–MONEY CLAIMS ACT

5/12–630. Short title; Uniform Foreign–Money Claims Act

§ 12–630. Short title; Uniform Foreign–Money Claims Act. Sections 12–630 through 12–645 may be cited as the Uniform Foreign–Money Claims Act. In those Sections, "this Act" means the Uniform Foreign–Money Claims Act.

P.A. 82–280, § 12–630, added by P.A. 86–1291, Art. 2, § 2002, eff. Jan. 1, 1991.

Formerly Ill.Rev.Stat., ch. 110, ¶ 12–650.

5/12–631. Definitions

§ 12–631. Definitions. In this Act:

(1) "Action" means a judicial proceeding or arbitration in which a payment in money may be awarded or enforced with respect to a foreign-money claim.

(2) "Bank-offered spot rate" means the spot rate of exchange at which a bank will sell foreign money at a spot rate.

(3) "Conversion date" means the banking day next preceding the date on which money, in accordance with this Act, is:

(i) paid to a claimant in an action or distribution proceeding;

(ii) paid to the official designated by law to enforce a judgment or award on behalf of a claimant; or

(iii) used to recoup, set-off, or counterclaim in different moneys in an action or distribution proceeding.

(4) "Distribution proceeding" means a judicial or nonjudicial proceeding for the distribution of a fund in which one or more foreign-money claims is asserted and includes an accounting, an assignment for the benefit of creditors, a foreclosure, the liquidation or rehabilitation of a corporation or other entity, and the distribution of an estate, trust, or other fund.

(5) "Foreign money" means money other than money of the United States of America.

(6) "Foreign-money claim" means a claim upon an obligation to pay, or a claim for recovery of a loss, expressed in or measured by a foreign money.

(7) "Money" means a medium of exchange for the payment of obligations or a store of value authorized or adopted by a government or by inter-governmental agreement.

(8) "Money of the claim" means the money determined as proper pursuant to Section 12–634.

(9) "Person" means an individual, a corporation, government or governmental subdivision or agency, business trust, estate, trust, joint venture, partnership, association, 2 or more persons having a joint or common interest, or any other legal or commercial entity.

(10) "Rate of exchange" means the rate at which money of one country may be converted into money of another country in a free financial market convenient to or reasonably usable by a person obligated to pay or to state a rate of conversion. If separate rates of exchange apply to different kinds of transactions, the term means the rate applicable to the particular transaction giving rise to the foreign-money claim.

(11) "Spot rate" means the rate of exchange at which foreign money is sold by a bank or other dealer in foreign exchange for immediate or next day availability or for settlement by immediate payment in cash or equivalent, by charge to an account, or by an agreed delayed settlement not exceeding 2 days.

(12) "State" means a State of the United States, the District of Columbia, the Commonwealth of Puerto Rico, or a territory or insular possession subject to the jurisdiction of the United States.

P.A. 82–280, § 12–631, added by P.A. 86–1291, Art. 2, § 2002, eff. Jan. 1, 1991.

Formerly Ill.Rev.Stat.1991, ch. 110, ¶ 12–631.

5/12–632. Scope

§ 12–632. Scope. (a) This Act applies only to a foreign-money claim in an action or distribution proceeding.

(b) This Act applies to foreign-money issues even if other law under the conflict of laws rules of this State applies to other issues in the action or distribution proceeding.

P.A. 82–280, § 12–632, added by P.A. 86–1291, Art. 2, § 2002, eff. Jan. 1, 1991.

Formerly Ill.Rev.Stat.1991, ch. 110, ¶ 12–632.

5/12–633. Variation by agreement

§ 12–633. Variation by agreement.

(a) The effect of this Act may be varied by agreement of the parties made before or after commencement of an action or distribution proceeding or the entry of judgment.

(b) Parties to a transaction may agree upon the money to be used in a transaction giving rise to a foreign-money claim and may agree to use different moneys for different aspects of the transaction. Stating the price in a foreign money for one aspect of a transaction does not alone require the use of that money for other aspects of the transaction.

P.A. 82–280, § 12–633, added by P.A. 86–1291, Art. 2, § 2002, eff. Jan. 1, 1991.

Formerly Ill.Rev.Stat.1991, ch. 110, ¶ 12–633.

5/12–634. Determining money of the claim

§ 12–634. Determining money of the claim.

(a) The money in which the parties to a transaction have agreed that payment is to be made is the proper money of the claim for payment.

(b) If the parties to a transaction have not otherwise agreed, the proper money of the claim, as in each case may be appropriate, is the money:

(1) regularly used between the parties as a matter of usage or course of dealing;

(2) used at the time of a transaction in international trade, by trade usage or common practice, for valuing or settling transactions in the particular commodity or service involved; or

(3) in which the loss was ultimately felt or will be incurred by the party claimant.

P.A. 82–280, § 12–634, added by P.A. 86–1291, Art. 2, § 2002, eff. Jan. 1, 1991.

Formerly Ill.Rev.Stat.1991, ch. 110, ¶ 12–634.

5/12–635. Determining amount of the money of certain contract claims

§ 12–635. Determining amount of the money of certain contract claims.

(a) If an amount contracted to be paid in a foreign money is measured by a specified amount of a different money, the amount to be paid is determined on the conversion date.

(b) If an amount contracted to be paid in a foreign money is to be measured by a different money at the rate of exchange prevailing on a date before default, that rate of exchange applies only to payments made within a reasonable time after default, not exceeding 30 days. Thereafter, conversion is made at the bank-offered spot rate on the conversion date.

(c) A monetary claim is neither usurious nor unconscionable because the agreement on which it is based provides that the amount of the debtor's obligation to be paid in the debtor's money, when received by the creditor, must equal a specified amount of the foreign money of the country of the creditor. If, because of unexcused delay in payment of a judgment or award, the amount received by the creditor does not equal the amount of the foreign money specified in the agreement, the court or arbitrator shall amend the judgment or award accordingly.

P.A. 82–280, § 12–635, added by P.A. 86–1291, Art. 2, § 2002, eff. Jan. 1, 1991.

Formerly Ill.Rev.Stat.1991, ch. 110, ¶ 12–635.

5/12–636.　Asserting and defending foreign-money claim

§ 12–636. Asserting and defending foreign-money claim.

(a) A person may assert a claim in a specified foreign money. If a foreign-money claim is not asserted, the claimant makes the claim in United States dollars.

(b) An opposing party may allege and prove that a claim, in whole or in part, is in a different money than that asserted by the claimant.

(c) A person may assert a defense, set-off, recoupment, or counterclaim in any money without regard to the money of other claims.

(d) The determination of the proper money of the claim is a question of law.

P.A. 82–280, § 12–636, added by P.A. 86–1291, Art. 2, § 2002, eff. Jan. 1, 1991.

Formerly Ill.Rev.Stat.1991, ch. 110, ¶ 12–636.

5/12–637.　Judgments and awards on foreign-money claims; times of money conversion; form of judgment

§ 12–637. Judgments and awards on foreign-money claims; times of money conversion; form of judgment.

(a) Except as provided in subsection (c), a judgment or award on a foreign-money claim must be stated in an amount of the money of the claim.

(b) A judgment or award on a foreign-money claim is payable in that foreign money or, at the option of the debtor, in the amount of United States dollars which will purchase that foreign money on the conversion date at a bank-offered spot rate.

(c) Assessed costs must be entered in United States dollars.

(d) Each payment in United States dollars must be accepted and credited on a judgment or award on a foreign-money claim in the amount of the foreign money that could be purchased by the dollars at a bank-offered spot rate of exchange at or near the close of business on the conversion date for that payment.

(e) A judgment or award made in an action or distribution proceeding on both (i) a defense, set-off, recoupment, or counterclaim and (ii) the adverse party's claim, must be netted by converting the money of the smaller into the money of the larger, and by subtracting the smaller from the larger, and specify the rates of exchange used.

(f) A judgment substantially in the following form complies with subsection (a):

IT IS ADJUDGED AND ORDERED, that Defendant (insert name) pay to Plaintiff (insert name) the sum of (insert amount in the foreign money) plus interest on that sum at the rate of (insert rate—see Section 12–639) percent a year or, at the option of the judgment debtor, the number of United States dollars which will purchase the (insert name of foreign money) with interest due, at a bank-offered spot rate at or near the close of business on the banking day next before the day of payment, together with assessed costs of (insert amount) United States dollars.

(g) If a contract claim is of the type covered by Section 12–635(a) or (b), the judgment or award must be entered for the amount of money stated to measure the obligation to be paid in the money specified for payment or, at the option of the debtor, the number of United States dollars which will purchase the computed amount of the money of payment on the conversion date at a bank-offered spot rate.

(h) A judgment must be filed and indexed in foreign money in the same manner, and has the same effect as a lien, as other judgments. It may be discharged by payment.

P.A. 82–280, § 12–637, added by P.A. 86–1291, Art. 2, § 2002, eff. Jan. 1, 1991.

Formerly Ill.Rev.Stat.1991, ch. 110, ¶ 12–637.

5/12–638.　Conversions of foreign money in distribution proceeding

§ 12–638. Conversions of foreign money in distribution proceeding. The rate of exchange prevailing at or near the close of business on the day the distribution proceeding is initiated governs all exchanges of foreign money in a distribution proceeding. A foreign-money claimant in a distribution proceeding shall assert its claim in the named foreign money and show the amount of the United States dollars resulting from a conversion as of the date the proceeding was initiated.

P.A. 82–280, § 12–638, added by P.A. 86–1291, Art. 2, § 2002, eff. Jan. 1, 1991.

Formerly Ill.Rev.Stat.1991, ch. 110, ¶ 12–638.

5/12–639. Pre-judgment and judgment interest

§ 12–639. Pre-judgment and judgment interest.

(a) With respect to a foreign-money claim, recovery of pre-judgment or pre-award interest and the rate of interest to be applied in the action or distribution proceeding, except as provided in subsection (b), are matters of the substantive law governing the right to recovery under the conflict-of-laws rules of this State.

(b) The court or arbitrator shall increase or decrease the amount of pre-judgment or pre-award interest otherwise payable in a judgment or award in foreign-money to the extent required by the law of this State governing a failure to make or accept an offer of settlement or offer of judgment, or conduct by a party or its attorney causing undue delay or expense.

(c) A judgment or award on a foreign-money claim bears interest at the rate applicable to judgments of this State.

P.A. 82–280, § 12–639, added by P.A. 86–1291, Art. 2, § 2002, eff. Jan. 1, 1991.

Formerly Ill.Rev.Stat.1991, ch. 110, ¶ 12–639.

5/12–640. Enforcement of foreign judgments

§ 12–640. Enforcement of foreign judgments.

(a) If an action is brought to enforce a judgment of another jurisdiction expressed in a foreign money and the judgment is recognized in this State as enforceable, the enforcing judgment must be entered as provided in Section 12–637, whether or not the foreign judgment confers an option to pay in an equivalent amount of United States dollars.

(b) A foreign judgment may be filed in accordance with any rule or statute of this State providing a procedure for its recognition and enforcement.

(c) A satisfaction or partial payment made upon the foreign judgment, on proof thereof, must be credited against the amount of foreign money specified in the judgment, notwithstanding the entry of judgment in this State.

(d) A judgment entered on a foreign-money claim only in United States dollars in another state must be enforced in this State in United States dollars only.

P.A. 82–280, § 12–640, added by P.A. 86–1291, Art. 2, § 2002, eff. Jan. 1, 1991.

Formerly Ill.Rev.Stat.1991, ch. 110, ¶ 12–640.

5/12–641. Determining United States dollar value of foreign-money claims for limited purposes

§ 12–641. Determining United States dollar value of foreign-money claims for limited purposes.

(a) Computations under this Section are for the limited purposes of the Section and do not affect computation of the United States dollar equivalent of the money of the judgment for the purpose of payment.

(b) For the limited purpose of facilitating the enforcement of provisional remedies in an action, the value in United States dollars of assets to be seized or restrained pursuant to a writ of attachment, garnishment, execution, or other legal process, the amount of United States dollars at issue for assessing costs, or the amount of United States dollars involved for a surety bond or other court-required undertaking, must be ascertained as provided in subsections (c) and (d).

(c) A party seeking process, costs, bond, or other undertaking under subsection (b) shall compute in United States dollars the amount of the foreign money claimed from a bank-offered spot rate prevailing at or near the close of business on the banking day next preceding the filing of a request or application for the issuance of process or for the determination of costs, or an application for a bond or other court-required undertaking.

(d) A party seeking the process, costs, bond, or other undertaking under subsection (b) shall file with each request or application an affidavit or certificate executed in good faith by its counsel or a bank officer, stating the market quotation used and how it was obtained, and setting forth the calculation. Affected court officials incur no liability, after a filing of the affidavit or certificate, for acting as if the judgment were in the amount of United States dollars stated in the affidavit or certificate.

P.A. 82–280, § 12–641, added by P.A. 86–1291, Art. 2, § 2002, eff. Jan. 1, 1991.

Formerly Ill.Rev.Stat.1991, ch. 110, ¶ 12–641.

5/12–642. Effect of currency revalorization

§ 12–642. Effect of currency revalorization.

(a) If, after an obligation is expressed or a loss is incurred in a foreign money, the country issuing or adopting that money substitutes a new money in place of that money, the obligation or the loss is treated as if expressed or incurred in the new money at the rate of conversion the issuing country establishes for the payment of like obligations or losses denominated in the former money.

(b) If substitution under subsection (a) occurs after a judgment or award is entered on a foreign-money claim, the court or arbitrator shall amend the judgment or award by a like conversion of the former money.

P.A. 82–280, § 12–642, added by P.A. 86–1291, Art. 2, § 2002, eff. Jan. 1, 1991.

Formerly Ill.Rev.Stat.1991, ch. 110, ¶ 12–642.

5/12–643. Supplementary general principles of law

§ 12–643. Supplementary general principles of law. Unless displaced by particular provisions of this Act, the principles of law and equity, including the law merchant, and the law relative to capacity to contract, principal and agent, estoppel, fraud, misrepresentation, duress, coercion, mistake, bankruptcy, or other validating or invalidating causes supplement its provisions.

P.A. 82–280, § 12–643, added by P.A. 86–1291, Art. 2, § 2002, eff. Jan. 1, 1991.

Formerly Ill.Rev.Stat.1991, ch. 110, ¶ 12–643.

5/12–644. Uniformity of application and construction

§ 12–644. Uniformity of application and construction. This Act shall be applied and construed to effectuate its general purpose to make uniform the law with respect to the subject of this Act among states enacting it.

P.A. 82–280, § 12–644, added by P.A. 86–1291, Art. 2, § 2002, eff. Jan. 1, 1991.

Formerly Ill.Rev.Stat.1991, ch. 110, ¶ 12–644.

5/12–645. Transitional provision

§ 12–645. Transitional provision. This Act applies to actions and distribution proceedings commenced after its effective date.

P.A. 82–280, § 12–645, added by P.A. 86–1291, Art. 2, § 2002, eff. Jan. 1, 1991.

Formerly Ill.Rev.Stat.1991, ch. 110, ¶ 12–645.

UNIFORM ENFORCEMENT OF FOREIGN JUDGMENTS ACT

5/12–650. Short Title

§ 12–650. Short Title. Sections 12–650 through 12–657 of this Act may be cited as the Uniform Enforcement of Foreign Judgments Act.

P.A. 82–280, § 12–634, added by P.A. 87–358, § 1, eff. Sept. 9, 1991. Renumbered as § 12–650 and amended by P.A. 87–895, Art. 2, § 2–50, eff. Aug. 14, 1992.

Formerly Ill.Rev.Stat., ch. 110, ¶ 12–650.

5/12–651. Definition

§ 12–651. Definition. As used in Sections 12–650 through 12–657, "foreign judgment" means any judgment, decree, or order of a court of the United States or of any other court which is entitled to full faith and credit in this State.

P.A. 82–280, § 12–627, added by P.A. 87–358, § 1, eff. Sept. 9, 1991. Renumbered as § 12–651 and amended by P.A. 87–895, Art. 2, § 2–50, eff. Aug. 14, 1992.

Formerly Ill.Rev.Stat., ch. 110, ¶ 12–651.

5/12–652. Filing and Status of Foreign Judgments

§ 12–652. Filing and Status of Foreign Judgments.

(a) A copy of any foreign judgment authenticated in accordance with the acts of Congress or the statutes of this State may be filed in the office of the circuit clerk for any county of this State. The clerk shall treat the foreign judgment in the same manner as a judgment of the circuit court for any county of this State. A judgment so filed has the same effect and is subject to the same procedures, defenses and proceedings for reopening, vacating, or staying as a judgment of a circuit court for any county of this State and may be enforced or satisfied in like manner. A judgment filed or registered under this Act shall be construed to be an original Illinois judgment from the date it is filed with the clerk of the circuit court and for purposes of enforcement and revival, shall be treated in exactly the same manner as an Illinois judgment entered on that same date.

(b) A foreign judgment or lien arising by operation of law, and resulting from an order requiring child support payments shall be entitled to full faith and credit in this State, shall be enforceable in the same manner as any judgment or lien of this State resulting from an order requiring child support payments, and shall not be required to be filed with the office of the circuit clerk in any county of this State, except as provided for in Sections 10–25 and 10–25.5 of the Illinois Public Aid Code.[1]

(c) A foreign order of protection issued by the court of another state, tribe, or United States territory is entitled to full faith and credit in this State, is enforceable in the same manner as any order of protection issued by a circuit court for any county of this State, and may be filed with the circuit clerk in any county of this State as provided in Section 222.5 of the Illinois Domestic Violence Act of 1986[2] or Section 22.5 of the Code of Criminal Procedure of 1963.[3] A foreign order of protection shall not be required to be filed with the circuit clerk to be entitled to full faith and credit in this State.

P.A. 82–280, § 12–628, added by P.A. 87–358, § 1, eff. Sept. 9, 1991. Renumbered as § 12–652 and amended by P.A. 87–895, Art. 2, § 2–50, eff. Aug. 14, 1992. Amended by P.A. 90–18, § 90, eff. July 1, 1997; P.A. 91–903, § 15, eff. Jan. 1, 2001; P.A. 97–350, § 5, eff. Jan. 1, 2012.

Formerly Ill.Rev.Stat., ch. 110, ¶ 12–652.
[1] 305 ILCS 5/10–25 and 305 ILCS 5/10–25.5.

2 750 ILCS 60/222.5.
3 725 ILCS 5/112A–22.5.

5/12–653. Notice of Filing

§ 12–653. Notice of Filing.

(a) At the time of the filing of the foreign judgment, the judgment creditor or his lawyer shall make and file with the circuit clerk an affidavit setting forth the name and last known post office address of the judgment debtor, and the judgment creditor.

(b) Promptly upon the filing of a foreign judgment (other than a foreign order of protection) and the affidavit, the clerk shall mail notice of the filing of the foreign judgment to the judgment debtor at the address given and shall make a note of the mailing in the docket. The notice shall include the name and post office address of the judgment creditor and the judgment creditor's lawyer, if any, in this State. In addition, the judgment creditor may mail a notice of the filing of the judgment to the judgment debtor and may file proof of mailing with the clerk. Lack of mailing notice of filing by the clerk shall not affect the enforcement proceedings if proof of mailing by the judgment creditor has been filed.

(c) The clerk shall not mail notice of the filing of a foreign order of protection to the respondent named in the order.

P.A. 82–280, § 12–629, added by P.A. 87–358, § 1, eff. Sept. 9, 1991. Renumbered as § 12–653 and amended by P.A. 87–895, Art. 2, § 2–50, eff. Aug. 14, 1992. Amended by P.A. 89–686, Art. 10, § 10–5, eff. Dec. 31, 1996; P.A. 91–903, § 15, eff. Jan. 1, 2001.

Formerly Ill.Rev.Stat., ch. 110, ¶ 12–653.

5/12–654. Stay

§ 12–654. Stay. (a) If the judgment debtor shows the circuit court that an appeal from the foreign judgment is pending or will be taken, or that a stay of execution has been granted, the court shall stay enforcement of the foreign judgment until the appeal is concluded, the time for appeal expires, or the stay of execution expires or is vacated, upon proof that the judgment debtor has furnished the security for the satisfaction of the judgment required by the state in which it was rendered.

(b) If the judgment debtor shows the circuit court any ground upon which enforcement of a judgment of any circuit court for any county of this State would be stayed, the court shall stay enforcement of the foreign judgment for an appropriate period, upon requiring the same security for satisfaction of the judgment which is required in this State.

P.A. 82–280, § 12–630, added by P.A. 87–358, § 1, eff. Sept. 9, 1991. Renumbered as § 12–654 and amended by P.A. 87–895, Art. 2, § 2–50, eff. Aug. 14, 1992.

Formerly Ill.Rev.Stat., ch. 110, ¶ 12–654.

5/12–655. Fees

§ 12–655. Fees.

(a) Any person filing a foreign judgment shall pay a fee to the circuit clerk equivalent to the fee which would be required were the person filing a complaint seeking the amount awarded in the foreign judgment. Fees for docketing, transcription or other enforcement proceedings shall be as provided for judgments of the circuit court.

(b) The clerk shall not charge a fee to any person to register a foreign order of protection.

P.A. 82–280, § 12–631, added by P.A. 87–358, § 1, eff. Sept. 9, 1991. Renumbered as § 12–655 and amended by P.A. 87–895, Art. 2, § 2–50, eff. Aug. 14, 1992. Amended by P.A. 91–903, § 15, eff. Jan. 1, 2001.

Formerly Ill.Rev.Stat., ch. 110, ¶ 12–655.

5/12–656. Optional Procedure

§ 12–656. Optional Procedure. The right of a judgment creditor to bring an action to enforce his judgment instead of proceeding under this Act remains unimpaired.

P.A. 82–280, § 12–632, added by P.A. 87–358, § 1, eff. Sept. 9, 1991. Renumbered as § 12–656 and amended by P.A. 87–895, Art. 2, § 2–50, eff. Aug. 14, 1992.

Formerly Ill.Rev.Stat., ch. 110, ¶ 12–656.

5/12–657. Uniformity of Interpretation

§ 12–657. Uniformity of Interpretation. This Act shall be so interpreted and construed as to effectuate its general purpose to make uniform the law of those states which enact it.

P.A. 82–280, § 12–633, added by P.A. 87–358, § 1, eff. Sept. 9, 1991. Renumbered as § 12–657 and amended by P.A. 87–895, Art. 2, § 2–50, eff. Aug. 14, 1992.

Formerly Ill.Rev.Stat., ch. 110, ¶ 12–657.

UNIFORM FOREIGN–COUNTRY MONEY
JUDGMENTS RECOGNITION ACT

5/12–661. Short title

§ 12–661. Short title. Sections 12–661 through 12–672 may be cited as the Uniform Foreign–Country Money Judgments Recognition Act. In those Sections, "this Act" means the Uniform Foreign–Country Money Judgments Recognition Act.

P.A. 82–280, § 12–661, added by P.A. 97–140, § 5, eff. Jan. 1, 2012.

5/12–662. Definitions

§ 12–662. Definitions. In this Act:

"Foreign country" means a government other than:

(A) the United States;

(B) a state, district, commonwealth, territory, or insular possession of the United States; or

(C) any other government with regard to which the decision in this State as to whether to recognize a judgment of that government's courts is initially subject to determination under the Full Faith and Credit Clause of the United States Constitution.

"Foreign-country judgment" means a judgment of a court of a foreign country.

P.A. 82–280, § 12–662, added by P.A. 97–140, § 5, eff. Jan. 1, 2012.

5/12–663. Applicability

§ 12–663. Applicability.

(a) Except as otherwise provided in subsection (b), this Act applies to a foreign-country judgment to the extent that the judgment:

(1) grants or denies recovery of a sum of money; and

(2) under the law of the foreign country where rendered, is final, conclusive, and enforceable.

(b) This Act does not apply to a foreign-country judgment, even if the judgment grants or denies recovery of a sum of money, to the extent that the judgment is:

(1) a judgment for taxes;

(2) a fine or other penalty; or

(3) a judgment for divorce, support, or maintenance, or other judgment rendered in connection with domestic relations.

(c) A party seeking recognition of a foreign-country judgment has the burden of establishing that this Act applies to the foreign-country judgment.

P.A. 82–280, § 12–663, added by P.A. 97–140, § 5, eff. Jan. 1, 2012.

5/12–664. Standards for recognition of foreign-country judgment

§ 12–664. Standards for recognition of foreign-country judgment.

(a) Except as otherwise provided in subsections (b) and (c), a court of this State shall recognize a foreign-country judgment to which this Act applies.

(b) A court of this State may not recognize a foreign-country judgment if:

(1) the judgment was rendered under a judicial system that does not provide impartial tribunals or procedures compatible with the requirements of due process of law;

(2) the foreign court did not have personal jurisdiction over the defendant; or

(3) the foreign court did not have jurisdiction over the subject matter.

(c) A court of this State need not recognize a foreign-country judgment if:

(1) the defendant in the proceeding in the foreign court did not receive notice of the proceeding in sufficient time to enable the defendant to defend;

(2) the judgment was obtained by fraud that deprived the losing party of an adequate opportunity to present its case;

(3) the judgment or the cause of action on which the judgment is based is repugnant to the public policy of this State or of the United States;

(4) the judgment conflicts with another final and conclusive judgment;

(5) the proceeding in the foreign court was contrary to an agreement between the parties under which the dispute in question was to be determined otherwise than by proceedings in that foreign court;

(6) in the case of jurisdiction based only on personal service, the foreign court was a seriously inconvenient forum for the trial of the action;

(7) the judgment was rendered in circumstances that raise substantial doubt about the integrity of the rendering court with respect to the judgment; or

(8) the specific proceeding in the foreign court leading to the judgment was not compatible with the requirements of due process of law.

(d) A party resisting recognition of a foreign-country judgment has the burden of establishing that a ground for nonrecognition stated in subsection (b) or (c) exists.

P.A. 82–280, § 12–664, added by P.A. 97–140, § 5, eff. Jan. 1, 2012.

5/12–665. Personal jurisdiction

§ 12–665. Personal jurisdiction.

(a) A foreign-country judgment may not be refused recognition for lack of personal jurisdiction if:

(1) the defendant was served with process personally in the foreign country;

(2) the defendant voluntarily appeared in the proceeding, other than for the purpose of protecting property seized or threatened with seizure in the proceeding or of contesting the jurisdiction of the court over the defendant;

(3) the defendant, before the commencement of the proceeding, had agreed to submit to the jurisdiction of the foreign court with respect to the subject matter involved;

(4) the defendant was domiciled in the foreign country when the proceeding was instituted or was a corporation or other form of business organization that had its principal place of business in, or was organized under the laws of, the foreign country;

(5) the defendant had a business office in the foreign country and the proceeding in the foreign court involved a cause of action arising out of busi-

ness done by the defendant through that office in the foreign country; or

(6) the defendant operated a motor vehicle or airplane in the foreign country and the proceeding involved a cause of action arising out of that operation.

(b) The list of bases for personal jurisdiction in subsection (a) is not exclusive. The courts of this State may recognize bases of personal jurisdiction other than those listed in subsection (a) as sufficient to support a foreign-country judgment.

P.A. 82–280, § 12–665, added by P.A. 97–140, § 5, eff. Jan. 1, 2012.

5/12–666. Procedure for recognition of foreign-country judgment

§ 12–666. Procedure for recognition of foreign-country judgment.

(a) If recognition of a foreign-country judgment is sought as an original matter, the issue of recognition shall be raised by filing an action seeking recognition of the foreign-country judgment.

(b) If recognition of a foreign-country judgment is sought in a pending action, the issue of recognition may be raised by counterclaim, cross-claim, or affirmative defense.

P.A. 82–280, § 12–666, added by P.A. 97–140, § 5, eff. Jan. 1, 2012.

5/12–667. Effect of recognition of foreign-country judgment

§ 12–667. Effect of recognition of foreign-country judgment. If the court in a proceeding under Section 12–666 finds that the foreign-country judgment is entitled to recognition under this Act then, to the extent that the foreign-country judgment grants or denies recovery of a sum of money, the foreign-country judgment is:

(1) conclusive between the parties to the same extent as the judgment of a sister state entitled to full faith and credit in this State would be conclusive; and

(2) enforceable in the same manner and to the same extent as a judgment rendered in this State.

P.A. 82–280, § 12–667, added by P.A. 97–140, § 5, eff. Jan. 1, 2012.

5/12–668. Stay of proceedings pending appeal of foreign-country judgment

§ 12–668. Stay of proceedings pending appeal of foreign-country judgment. If a party establishes that an appeal from a foreign-country judgment is pending or will be taken, the court may stay any proceedings with regard to the foreign-country judgment until the appeal is concluded, the time for appeal expires, or the

appellant has had sufficient time to prosecute the appeal and has failed to do so.

P.A. 82–280, § 12–668, added by P.A. 97–140, § 5, eff. Jan. 1, 2012.

5/12–669. Statute of limitations

§ 12–669. Statute of limitations. An action to recognize a foreign-country judgment must be commenced within the earlier of the time during which the foreign-country judgment is effective in the foreign country or 15 years from the date that the foreign-country judgment became effective in the foreign country.

P.A. 82–280, § 12–669, added by P.A. 97–140, § 5, eff. Jan. 1, 2012.

5/12–670. Uniformity of interpretation

§ 12–670. Uniformity of interpretation. In applying and construing this uniform Act, consideration must be given to the need to promote uniformity of the law with respect to its subject matter among states that enact it.

P.A. 82–280, § 12–670, added by P.A. 97–140, § 5, eff. Jan. 1, 2012.

5/12–671. Saving clause

§ 12–671. Saving clause. This Act does not prevent the recognition under principles of comity or otherwise of a foreign-country judgment not within the scope of this Act.

P.A. 82–280, § 12–671, added by P.A. 97–140, § 5, eff. Jan. 1, 2012.

5/12–672. Act application

§ 12–672. Act application. This Act applies to all actions commenced on or after the effective date of this amendatory Act of the 97th General Assembly in which the issue of recognition of a foreign-country judgment is raised.

P.A. 82–280, § 12–672, added by P.A. 97–140, § 5, eff. Jan. 1, 2012.

PART 7. GARNISHMENT

Section
5/12–715. Refusal or neglect of garnishee to deliver proper-
           ty.
5/12–716. Costs and fees.
5/12–717. Death of garnishee and procedure thereafter.
5/12–718. Powers of court.
5/12–719. Transfer of interest by heir or legatee.

5/12–701.   Affidavit for garnishment; Contents

§ 12–701. Affidavit for garnishment; Contents.
Upon the filing by a judgment creditor, its attorney or
other designee of (1) an affidavit that the affiant
believes any person is indebted to the judgment debt-
or, other than for wages, or has in his or her possession, custody or control any other property belonging
to the judgment debtor, or in which the judgment
debtor has an interest, which person shall be identified as the garnishee, and includes the last address of
the judgment debtor known to the affiant as well as
the name of the judgment debtor, (2) the garnishment
notice required by Section 12–705, and (3) written
interrogatories to be answered by the garnishee with
respect to the indebtedness or other property, the
clerk of the court in which the judgment was entered
shall issue summons against the person named in the
affidavit commanding him or her to appear in the
court as garnishee and answer the interrogatories in
writing under oath. The interrogatories shall require
that the garnishee certify that a copy of the completed
interrogatories, as specified in subsection (b) of Section 12–707, has been mailed to the judgment debtor
and shall be in a form consistent with local court rules.
P.A. 82–280, § 12–701, eff. July 1, 1982. Amended by P.A.
87–1252, § 2, eff. Jan. 7, 1993.

Formerly Ill.Rev.Stat.1991, ch. 110, ¶ 12–701.

5/12–702.   § 12–702. Repealed by P.A. 89–364, § 50, eff. Jan. 1, 1996

5/12–703.   Garnishment of administrators and executors

§ 12–703. Garnishment of administrators and executors. Administrators and executors may be summoned as garnishees regarding indebtedness or other
property belonging to any heir or distributee of any
estate, but judgment shall not be rendered against an
administrator or an executor until an order of distribution is entered by the court which appointed him or
her.
P.A. 82–280, § 12–703, eff. July 1, 1982.

Formerly Ill.Rev.Stat.1991, ch. 110, ¶ 12–703.

5/12–704.   Exemptions from garnishment

§ 12–704. Exemptions from garnishment. Benefits and refunds payable by pension or retirement
funds or systems and any assets of employees held by
such funds or systems, and any monies an employee is
required to pay to such funds or systems are exempt
and are not subject to garnishment under Part 7 of
Article XII of this Act.
P.A. 82–280, § 12–704, eff. July 1, 1982. Amended by P.A.
83–707, § 1, eff. Sept. 23, 1983.

Formerly Ill.Rev.Stat.1991, ch. 110, ¶ 12–704.

5/12–705.   Summons

§ 12–705. Summons.

(a) Summons shall be returnable not less than 21
nor more than 30 days after the date of issuance.
Summons with 4 copies of the interrogatories shall be
served and returned as in other civil cases. If the
garnishee is served with summons less than 10 days
prior to the return date, the court shall continue the
case to a new return date 14 days after the return
date stated on the summons. The summons shall be
in a form consistent with local court rules. The
summons shall be accompanied by a copy of the
underlying judgment or a certification by the clerk of
the court that entered the judgment, or by the attorney for the judgment creditor, setting forth the
amount of the judgment, the name of the court and
the number of the case and one copy of a garnishment
notice in substantially the following form:

“GARNISHMENT NOTICE

(Name and address of Court)

Name of Case: (Name of Judgment Creditor),

     Judgment Creditor v.

     (Name of Judgment Debtor),

     Judgment Debtor.

Address of Judgment Debtor: (Insert last known
address)

Name and address of Attorney for Judgment

Creditor or of Judgment Creditor (If no

attorney is listed): (Insert name and address)

Amount of Judgment: $(Insert amount)

Name of Garnishee: (Insert name)

Return Date: (Insert return date specified in summons)

NOTICE: The court has issued a garnishment summons against the garnishee named above for money or
property (other than wages) belonging to the judgment debtor or in which the judgment debtor has an
interest. The garnishment summons was issued on
the basis of a judgment against the judgment debtor
in favor of the judgment creditor in the amount stated
above.

The amount of money or property (other than
wages) that may be garnished is limited by federal
and Illinois law. The judgment debtor has the right
to assert statutory exemptions against certain money
or property of the judgment debtor which may not be

used to satisfy the judgment in the amount stated above.

Under Illinois or federal law, the exemptions of personal property owned by the debtor include the debtor's equity interest, not to exceed $4,000 in value, in any personal property as chosen by the debtor; Social Security and SSI benefits; public assistance benefits; unemployment compensation benefits; workers' compensation benefits; veterans' benefits; circuit breaker property tax relief benefits; the debtor's equity interest, not to exceed $2,400 in value, in any one motor vehicle, and the debtor's equity interest, not to exceed $1,500 in value, in any implements, professional books or tools of the trade of the debtor.

The judgment debtor may have other possible exemptions from garnishment under the law.

The judgment debtor has the right to request a hearing before the court to dispute the garnishment or to declare exempt from garnishment certain money or property or both. To obtain a hearing in counties with a population of 1,000,000 or more, the judgment debtor must notify the Clerk of the Court in person and in writing at (insert address of Clerk) before the return date specified above or appear in court on the date and time on that return date. To obtain a hearing in counties with a population of less than 1,000,000, the judgment debtor must notify the Clerk of the Court in writing at (insert address of Clerk) on or before the return date specified above. The Clerk of the Court will provide a hearing date and the necessary forms that must be prepared by the judgment debtor or the attorney for the judgment debtor and sent to the judgment creditor and the garnishee regarding the time and location of the hearing. This notice may be sent by regular first class mail."

(b) An officer or other person authorized by law to serve process shall serve the summons, interrogatories and the garnishment notice required by subsection (a) of this Section upon the garnishee and shall, (1) within 2 business days of the service upon the garnishee, mail a copy of the garnishment notice and the summons to the judgment debtor by first class mail at the judgment debtor's address indicated in the garnishment notice and (2) within 4 business days of the service upon the garnishee file with the clerk of the court a certificate of mailing in substantially the following form:

"CERTIFICATE OF MAILING

I hereby certify that, within 2 business days of service upon the garnishee of the garnishment summons, interrogatories and garnishment notice, I served upon the judgment debtor in this cause a copy of the garnishment summons and garnishment notice by first class mail to the judgment debtor's address as indicated in the garnishment notice.

Date:................ ....

Signature"

In the case of service of the summons for garnishment upon the garnishee by certified or registered mail, as provided in subsection (c) of this Section, no sooner than 2 business days nor later than 4 business days after the date of mailing, the clerk shall mail a copy of the garnishment notice and the summons to the judgment debtor by first class mail at the judgment debtor's address indicated in the garnishment notice, shall prepare the Certificate of Mailing described by this subsection, and shall include the Certificate of Mailing in a permanent record.

(c) In a county with a population of less than 1,000,000, unless otherwise provided by circuit court rule, at the request of the judgment creditor or his or her attorney and instead of personal service, service of a summons for garnishment may be made as follows:

(1) For each garnishee to be served, the judgment creditor or his or her attorney shall pay to the clerk of the court a fee of $2, plus the cost of mailing, and furnish to the clerk an original and 2 copies of a summons, an original and one copy of the interrogatories, an affidavit setting forth the garnishee's mailing address, an original and 2 copies of the garnishment notice required by subsection (a) of this Section, and a copy of the judgment or certification described in subsection (a) of this Section. The original judgment shall be retained by the clerk.

(2) The clerk shall mail to the garnishee, at the address appearing in the affidavit, the copy of the judgment or certification described in subsection (a) of this Section, the summons, the interrogatories, and the garnishment notice required by subsection (a) of this Section, by certified or registered mail, return receipt requested, showing to whom delivered and the date and address of delivery. This Mailing shall be mailed on a "restricted delivery" basis when service is directed to a natural person. The envelope and return receipt shall bear the return address of the clerk, and the return receipt shall be stamped with the docket number of the case. The receipt for certified or registered mail shall state the name and address of the addressee, the date of the mailing, shall identify the documents mailed, and shall be attached to the original summons.

(3) The return receipt must be attached to the original summons and, if it shows delivery at least 10 days before the day for the return date, shall constitute proof of service of any documents identified on the return receipt as having been mailed.

(4) The clerk shall note the fact of service in a permanent record.

(d) The garnishment summons may be served and returned in the manner provided by Supreme Court

Rule for service, otherwise than by publication, of a notice for additional relief upon a party in default.
P.A. 82–280, § 12–705, eff. July 1, 1982. Amended by P.A. 87–1252, § 2, eff. Jan. 7, 1993; P.A. 88–492, § 5, eff. Jan. 1, 1994; P.A. 94–293, § 5, eff. Jan. 1, 2006; P.A. 98–557, § 5, eff. Jan. 1, 2014; P.A. 99–78, § 535, eff. July 20, 2015.

Formerly Ill.Rev.Stat.1991, ch. 110, ¶ 12–705.

5/12–706. Conditional judgment

§ 12–706. Conditional judgment. (a) When any person summoned as garnishee fails to appear and answer as required by Part 7 of Article XII of this Act, the court may enter a conditional judgment against the garnishee for the amount due upon the judgment against the judgment debtor. A summons to confirm the conditional judgment may issue against the garnishee, returnable in the same manner as provided in Section 12–705 of this Act, commanding the garnishee to show cause why the judgment should not be made final. If the garnishee, after being served with summons to confirm the conditional judgment or after being notified as provided in subsection (b) hereof, fails to appear and answer, the court shall confirm such judgment to the amount of the judgment against the judgment debtor and award costs. If the garnishee appears and answers, the same proceedings may be had as in other cases.

(b) If any garnishee becomes a non-resident, goes out of this State, or is concealed within this State so that the summons to confirm the conditional judgment cannot be served upon him or her, upon the filing by the plaintiff or his or her agent of an affidavit as in cases of non-resident defendants in attachments, the garnishee may be notified in the same manner as a non-resident defendant in attachment; and upon notice being given to him or her as above stated, he or she may be proceeded against in the same manner as if he or she had been personally served with summons to confirm the conditional judgment.
P.A. 82–280, § 12–706, eff. July 1, 1982. Amended by P.A. 83–707, § 1, eff. Sept. 23, 1983.

Formerly Ill.Rev.Stat. 1991, ch. 110, ¶ 12–706.

5/12–707. Duties of garnishee

§ 12–707. Duties of garnishee.

(a) To the extent of the amount due upon the judgment and costs, the garnishee shall hold, subject to the order of the court any non-exempt indebtedness or other non-exempt property in his or her possession, custody or control belonging to the judgment debtor or in which the judgment debtor has any interest. The judgment or balance due thereon becomes a lien on the indebtedness and other property held by the garnishee at the time of the service of garnishment summons and remains a lien thereon pending the garnishment proceeding.

(b) The garnishee shall file, on or before the return date, or within the further time that the court for cause may allow, a written answer under oath to the interrogatories, setting forth as of the date of service of the garnishment summons any indebtedness due or to become due to the judgment debtor and any other property in his, her or its possession, custody or control belonging to the judgment debtor or in which the judgment debtor has an interest. The garnishee shall mail, by first class mail, a copy of the answer to the judgment creditor or its attorney and to the judgment debtor at the address specified in the affidavit filed under Section 12–701 of this Act, or at any other address or location of the judgment debtor known to the garnishee, and shall certify in the answer that it was so mailed to the judgment debtor.
P.A. 82–280, § 12–707, eff. July 1, 1982. Amended by P.A. 83–707, § 1, eff. Sept. 23, 1983; P.A. 87–1252, § 2, eff. Jan. 7, 1993.

Formerly Ill.Rev.Stat.1991, ch. 110, ¶ 12–707.

5/12–708. Deductions and set-offs of garnishee

§ 12–708. Deductions and set-offs of garnishee. The garnishee is entitled to assert against the indebtedness due to the judgment debtor offsetting claims against either or both the judgment creditor and the judgment debtor, whether due at the time of service of the garnishment summons or thereafter to become due and whether liquidated or unliquidated, except claims for unliquidated damages for actions sounding in tort. To the extent that other property belonging to the judgment debtor or in which the judgment debtor has an interest is pledged to or held by the garnishee in good faith as security or that the garnishee has other just claim against the other property, the garnishee is entitled to retain the other property. The garnishee is liable for the balance of the indebtedness due to the judgment debtor after the offsetting claims are adjusted and for the balance of other property after deducting property to which the garnishee has just claim. The verdict or finding and judgment shall show the amount of offsetting claims or deductions allowed against each party.
P.A. 82–280, § 12–708, eff. July 1, 1982. Amended by P.A. 83–707, § 1, eff. Sept. 23, 1983.

Formerly Ill.Rev.Stat.1991, ch. 110, ¶ 12–708.

5/12–709. Negotiable paper

§ 12–709. Negotiable paper. No person shall be liable as a garnishee by reason of having drawn, accepted, made or endorsed a negotiable instrument in the possession of the judgment debtor at the time of either (1) service of the garnishment summons or (2) entry of judgment when the negotiable instrument is not due.
P.A. 82–280, § 12–709, eff. July 1, 1982.

Formerly Ill.Rev.Stat.1991, ch. 110, ¶ 12–709.

5/12–710. Adverse claims; Trial

§ 12–710. Adverse claims; Trial.

(a) In the event any indebtedness or other property due from or in the possession of a garnishee is claimed by any other person, the court shall permit the claimant to appear and maintain his or her claim. A claimant not voluntarily appearing shall be served with notice as the court shall direct. If a claimant fails to appear after being served with notice in the manner directed, he or she shall be concluded by the judgment entered in the garnishment proceeding.

(b) If the adverse claimant appears and, within the time the court allows, files his or her claim and serves a copy thereof upon the judgment creditor, the judgment debtor, and the garnishee, he or she is then a party to the garnishment proceeding; and his or her claim shall be tried and determined with the other issues in the garnishment action. Upon certification by the Department of Healthcare and Family Services (formerly Illinois Department of Public Aid) that a person who is receiving support payments under this Section is a public aid recipient, any support payments subsequently received by the clerk of the court shall be transmitted to the Department until the Department gives notice to cease such transmittal. If the adverse claimant is entitled to all or part of the indebtedness or other property, the court shall enter judgment in accordance with the interests of the parties.

(c) Claims for the support of a spouse or dependent children shall be superior to all other claims for garnishment of property.

P.A. 82–280, § 12–710, eff. July 1, 1982. Amended by P.A. 87–1252, § 2, eff. Jan. 7, 1993; P.A. 95–331, § 1085, eff. Aug. 21, 2007.

Formerly Ill.Rev.Stat.1991, ch. 110, ¶ 12–710.

5/12–711. Contest of answer and trial

§ 12–711. Contest of answer and trial.

(a) The judgment creditor or the judgment debtor may contest the truth or sufficiency of the garnishee's answer and the court shall immediately, unless for good cause the hearing is postponed, proceed to try the issues. The answer of the garnishee shall be considered denied without further pleading.

(b) At any time on or before the return date, the judgment debtor may request a hearing to dispute the garnishment or to seek exemptions for certain moneys or property by notifying the clerk of the court before that time, using forms as may be provided by the clerk of the court. To obtain a hearing in counties with a population of 1,000,000 or more, the judgment debtor must notify the clerk of the court in person and in writing at the clerk's office before the return date specified in the summons, or appear in court on the date and time specified in the summons. To obtain a hearing in counties with a population of less than 1,000,000, the judgment debtor must notify the clerk of the court in writing at the clerk's office on or before the return date specified in the summons. The clerk of the court will provide a prompt hearing date and the necessary forms that must be prepared by the judgment debtor or the attorney for the judgment debtor and sent to the judgment creditor and the garnishee, or their attorneys, regarding the time and location of the hearing. This notice may be sent by regular first class mail. At the hearing the court shall immediately, unless for good cause the hearing is continued, proceed to try the issues.

(c) The trial shall be conducted as in other civil cases.

(d) If the finding or verdict is against a garnishee, appropriate judgment or other orders shall be entered against the garnishee and in favor of the judgment debtor to whom the garnishee is indebted, or for whom the garnishee holds property, for the use of the judgment creditor, in the same manner as if the facts are admitted.

(e) No garnishment order shall be entered in favor of the judgment creditor unless the certificate of mailing required by subsection (b) of Section 12–705 is filed and the garnishee's answer to the interrogatories certifies that a copy of the answer was mailed to the judgment debtor in accordance with Section 12–707 of this Act.

P.A. 82–280, § 12–711, eff. July 1, 1982. Amended by P.A. 87–1252, § 2, eff. Jan. 7, 1993.

Formerly Ill.Rev.Stat.1991, ch. 110, ¶ 12–711.

5/12–712. Effect of judgment—Discharge no bar

§ 12–712. Effect of judgment—Discharge no bar. Judgment against a garnishee shall be enforceable as in other civil cases and shall discharge the garnishee of all claims by the judgment debtor for the indebtedness or other property paid, delivered or accounted for by the garnishee by virtue of the judgment in garnishment. The discharge of a garnishee is no bar to an action by the judgment debtor for the same claim.

P.A. 82–280, § 12–712, eff. July 1, 1982.

Formerly Ill.Rev.Stat.1991, ch. 110, ¶ 12–712.

5/12–713. No judgment until debt due

§ 12–713. No judgment until debt due. If the debt from the garnishee to the judgment debtor is not due, judgment shall not be entered against the garnishee until the debt is due, either by the terms of the agreement giving rise thereto or by acceleration as therein provided.

P.A. 82–280, § 12–713, eff. July 1, 1982.

Formerly Ill.Rev.Stat.1991, ch. 110, ¶ 12–713.

5/12–714. Property surrendered in enforcement of a judgment and disposition thereof

§ 12–714. Property surrendered in enforcement of a judgment and disposition thereof. (a) A garnishee having property other than money belonging to the judgment debtor, which the garnishee is obligated to deliver to the judgment debtor, shall deliver to the officer holding a certified copy of the judgment for the enforcement thereof against the judgment debtor so much thereof as is necessary to satisfy the amount due upon the judgment and costs.

(b) If mortgaged or pledged property is in the possession of a garnishee, or property is held for the payment of a debt to the garnishee, the judgment creditor may, under order of court, pay or tender the amount due to the garnishee; and the garnishee shall thereupon deliver the property to the officer holding the certified copy of the judgment for the enforcement thereof against the judgment debtor.

(c) Nothing contained in Part 7 of Article XII of this Act shall be construed to prevent the garnishee from selling property in his or her possession for the payment of claims for which it is mortgaged, pledged or otherwise held at any time before the amount due to the garnishee is paid or tendered, if the sale would be authorized as between the garnishee and the judgment debtor.

(d) If property is held for purposes other than to secure the payment of money, and if the promise, condition or other act to be performed can be performed by the judgment creditor without damage to other parties, the court may permit performance by the judgment creditor. Upon performance, or a tender of performance, by the judgment creditor the garnishee shall deliver the property to the officer holding the certified copy of the judgment for the enforcement thereof against the judgment debtor.

(e) Property received by an officer as described in this Section shall be sold in the same manner as if levied upon for the satisfaction of a judgment for the payment of money and from the proceeds of sale the officer shall repay the judgment creditor the amount paid the garnishee for the redemption, with interest, or shall indemnify the judgment creditor for acts done or performed pursuant to order of court in the redemption.

P.A. 82–280, § 12–714, eff. July 1, 1982. Amended by P.A. 83–707, § 1, eff. Sept. 23, 1983.

Formerly Ill.Rev.Stat.1991, ch. 110, ¶ 12–714.

5/12–715. Refusal or neglect of garnishee to deliver property

§ 12–715. Refusal or neglect of garnishee to deliver property. If a garnishee refuses or neglects to deliver property in his or her possession when ordered by the court or upon request by the officer holding a certified copy of the judgment for enforcement thereof against the judgment debtor, the garnishee may be attached and punished for contempt; or the court may enter judgment against the garnishee for the value of the property or the amount due upon the judgment and costs, whichever is the lesser, and have same enforced against the garnishee.

P.A. 82–280, § 12–715, eff. July 1, 1982.

Formerly Ill.Rev.Stat.1991, ch. 110, ¶ 12–715.

5/12–716. Costs and fees

§ 12–716. Costs and fees. (a) The costs of obtaining a garnishment order shall be charged to the judgment debtor, unless the court determines, in its discretion, that costs incurred by the judgment creditor were improperly incurred, in which case those costs shall be paid by the judgment creditor.

(b) No fee shall be paid by a garnishee for filing his, her or its appearance, answer or satisfaction of judgment against him, her or it.

(c) No fee shall be paid to a garnishee at the time of service of the garnishment summons or at any time thereafter, unless he or she is subpoenaed to appear as a witness, in which case he or she is entitled to witness fees as in other civil cases.

P.A. 82–280, § 12–716, eff. July 1, 1982. Amended by P.A. 87–1252, § 2, eff. Jan. 7, 1993.

Formerly Ill.Rev.Stat.1991, ch. 110, ¶ 12–716.

5/12–717. Death of garnishee and procedure thereafter

§ 12–717. Death of garnishee and procedure thereafter. Upon the death of a garnishee, the procedure shall be the same as in the case of the death of a defendant in other civil cases.

P.A. 82–280, § 12–717, eff. July 1, 1982.

Formerly Ill.Rev.Stat.1991, ch. 110, ¶ 12–717.

5/12–718. Powers of court

§ 12–718. Powers of court. If the garnishee has in his or her possession, custody or control any property belonging to the defendant or which he or she is obligated to deliver to the defendant, with or without condition, the court may enter all proper orders for the delivery thereof to the proper officer, the sale or disposition of the same, and the discharging of any lien thereon, and may authorize the garnishee to collect any indebtedness or to sell any other property and account for the proceeds. The court, when necessary to further the purposes and provisions of Part 7 of Article XII of this Act, may compel the judgment debtor to do or to refrain from doing any specific act or deed; or the court may appoint a receiver to collect any indebtedness or to take possession, sell or otherwise dispose of any other property, and enter all orders in regard thereto which are necessary and equitable between the parties.

P.A. 82–280, § 12–718, eff. July 1, 1982. Amended by P.A. 83–707, § 1, eff. Sept. 23, 1983.

Formerly Ill.Rev.Stat.1991, ch. 110, ¶ 12–718.

5/12–719. Transfer of interest by heir or legatee

§ 12–719. Transfer of interest by heir or legatee. No assignment, transfer or other disposition by an heir or distributee of his or her interest in the possession of an administrator or executor shall defeat the garnishment, unless (1) prior to the service of garnishment summons upon the administrator or executor, the transfer or other disposition is reduced to writing and (2) the writing is filed in the office of the clerk of the court appointing the executor or administrator.

P.A. 82–280, § 12–719, eff. July 1, 1982.

Formerly Ill.Rev.Stat.1991, ch. 110, ¶ 12–719.

PART 8. WAGE DEDUCTIONS

5/12–801. Definitions

§ 12–801. Definitions. As used in Part 8 of Article XII of this Act:

"Deduction order" means an order entered pursuant to Section 12–811 of this Act.

"Employer" means the person named as employer in the affidavit filed under Section 12–805.

"Federal agency employer" means an agency of the federal government as defined in 5 USC 5520a(a)(1), as amended from time to time.

"Judgment creditor" means the recipient of any judgment, except a judgment by confession which has not been confirmed as provided in Part 8 of Article XII of this Act.

"Judgment debtor" means a person against whom a judgment has been obtained.

"Wages" means any hourly pay, salaries, commissions, bonuses, or other compensation owed by an employer to a judgment debtor.

P.A. 82–280, § 12–801, eff. July 1, 1982. Amended by P.A. 83–707, § 1, eff. Sept. 23, 1983; P.A. 86–1268, § 1, eff. Nov. 5, 1990; P.A. 89–28, § 5, eff. June 23, 1995.

Formerly Ill.Rev.Stat.1991, ch. 110, ¶ 12–801.

5/12–802. Force and effect of order

§ 12–802. Force and effect of order. A deduction order entered under Part 8 of Article XII of this Act shall have the force and effect and be enforceable as a judgment.

P.A. 82–280, § 12–802, eff. July 1, 1982.

Formerly Ill.Rev.Stat.1991, ch. 110, ¶ 12–802.

5/12–803. Wages subject to collection

§ 12–803. Wages subject to collection. The wages, salary, commissions and bonuses subject to collection under a deduction order, for any work week shall be the lesser of (1) 15% of such gross amount paid for that week or (2) the amount by which disposable earnings for a week exceed 45 times the Federal Minimum Hourly Wage prescribed by Section 206(a)(1) of Title 29 of the United States Code, as amended, or, under a wage deduction summons served on or after January 1, 2006, the minimum hourly wage prescribed by Section 4 of the Minimum Wage Law, whichever is greater, in effect at the time the amounts are payable. This provision (and no other) applies irrespective of the place where the compensation was earned or payable and the State where the employee resides. No amounts required by law to be withheld may be taken from the amount collected by the creditor. The term "disposable earnings" means that part of the earnings of any individual remaining after the deduction from those earnings of any amounts required by law to be withheld.

P.A. 82–280, § 12–803, eff. July 1, 1982. Amended by P.A. 85–187, § 1, eff. Aug. 21, 1987; P.A. 87–569, § 1, eff. Jan. 1, 1992; P.A. 94–306, § 5, eff. Jan. 1, 2008; P.A. 95–661, § 5, eff. Jan. 1, 2008.

Formerly Ill.Rev.Stat.1991, ch. 110, ¶ 12–803.

5/12–804. Exemptions from deduction orders

§ 12–804. Exemptions from deduction orders. Benefits and refunds payable by pension or retirement funds or systems and any assets of employees held by such funds or systems, and any monies an employee is required to contribute to such funds or systems are exempt and are not subject to a deduction order under Part 8 of Article XII of this Act. A plan governed by the Employee Retirement Income Security Act of 1974 [1] shall be considered a retirement fund for purposes of this Part 8.

P.A. 82–280, § 12–804, eff. July 1, 1982. Amended by P.A. 87–1252, § 2, eff. Jan. 7, 1993.

Formerly Ill.Rev.Stat.1991, ch. 110, ¶ 12–804.

[1] 29 U.S.C.A. § 1001 et seq.

5/12–805. Summons; Issuance

§ 12–805. Summons; Issuance.

(a) Upon the filing by a judgment creditor, its attorney or other designee of (1) an affidavit that the affiant believes any person is indebted to the judgment debtor for wages due or to become due, as provided in Part 8 of Article XII of this Act, and includes the last address of the judgment debtor known to the affiant as well as the name of the judgment debtor, and a certification by the judgment creditor or his attorney that, before filing the affidavit, the wage deduction notice has been mailed to the judgment debtor by first class mail at the judgment debtor's last known address, and (2) written interrogatories to be answered by the employer with respect to the indebtedness, the clerk of the court in which the judgment was entered shall issue summons against the person named in the affidavit as employer commanding the employer to appear in the court and answer the interrogatories in writing under oath. The interrogatories shall elicit all the information necessary to determine the proper amount of non-exempt wages. The interrogatories shall require that the employer certify that a copy of the completed interrogatories as specified in subsection (c) of Section 12–808 has been mailed or hand delivered to the judgment debtor and shall be in a form consistent with local court rules. The summons shall further command federal agency employers, upon effective service of summons pursuant to 5 USC 5520a, to commence to pay over deducted wages in accordance with Section 12–808. The summons shall be in a form consistent with local court rules. The summons shall be accompanied by a copy of the underlying judgment or a certification by the clerk of the court that entered the judgment, or by the attorney for the judgment creditor, setting forth the date and amount of the judgment, allowable costs expended, interest accumulated, credits paid by or on behalf of the judgment debtor and the balance due the judgment creditor, and one copy of a wage deduction notice in substantially the following form:

"WAGE DEDUCTION NOTICE

(Name and address of Court)
Name of Case: (Name of Judgment Creditor),
   Judgment Creditor v.
   (Name of Judgment Debtor),
   Judgment Debtor.

Address of Judgment Debtor: (Insert last known address)
Name and Address of Attorney for Judgment Creditor or of Judgment Creditor (if no attorney is listed): (Insert name and address)
Amount of Judgment: $. . . . .
Employer: (Name of Employer)
Return Date: (Insert return date specified in summons)

NOTICE: The court shall be asked to issue a wage deduction summons against the employer named above for wages due or about to become due to you. The wage deduction summons may be issued on the basis of a judgment against you in favor of the judgment creditor in the amount stated above.

The amount of wages that may be deducted is limited by federal and Illinois law.

(1) Under Illinois law, the amount of wages that may be deducted is limited to the lesser of (i) 15% of gross weekly wages or (ii) the amount by which disposable earnings for a week exceed the total of 45 times the federal minimum hourly wage or, under a wage deduction summons served on or after January 1, 2006, the minimum hourly wage prescribed by Section 4 of the Minimum Wage Law, whichever is greater.

(2) Under federal law, the amount of wages that may be deducted is limited to the lesser of (i) 25% of disposable earnings for a week or (ii) the amount by which disposable earnings for a week exceed 30 times the federal minimum hourly wage.

(3) Pension and retirement benefits and refunds may be claimed as exempt from wage deduction under Illinois law.

You have the right to request a hearing before the court to dispute the wage deduction because the wages are exempt. To obtain a hearing in counties with a population of 1,000,000 or more, you must notify the Clerk of the Court in person and in writing at (insert address of Clerk) before the Return Date specified above or appear in court on the date and time on that Return Date. To obtain a hearing in counties with a population of less than 1,000,000, you must notify the Clerk of the Court in writing at (insert address of clerk) on or before the Return Date specified above. The Clerk of the Court will provide a hearing date and the necessary forms that must be prepared by you or your attorney and sent to the judgment creditor and the employer, or their attorney, regarding the time and location of the hearing. This notice may be sent by regular first class mail."

(b) In a county with a population of less than 1,000,000, unless otherwise provided by circuit court rule, at the request of the judgment creditor or his or her attorney and instead of personal service, service of a summons for a wage deduction may be made as follows:

(1) For each employer to be served, the judgment creditor or his or her attorney shall pay to the clerk of the court a fee of $2, plus the cost of mailing, and furnish to the clerk an original and one copy of a summons, an original and one copy of the interrogatories and an affidavit setting forth the employer's mailing address, an original and one copy of the wage deduction notice required by subsection (a) of this Section, and a copy of the judgment or certification described in subsection (a) of this Section. The original judgment shall be retained by the clerk.

(2) The clerk shall mail to the employer, at the address appearing in the affidavit, the copy of the judgment or certification described in subsection (a) of this Section, the summons, the interrogatories, and the wage deduction notice required by subsection (a) of this Section, by certified or registered mail, return receipt requested, showing to whom delivered and the date and address of delivery. This Mailing shall be mailed on a "restricted delivery" basis when service is directed to a natural person. The envelope and return receipt shall bear the return address of the clerk, and the return receipt shall be stamped with the docket number of the case. The receipt for certified or registered mail shall state the name and address of the addressee, the date of the mailing, shall identify the documents mailed, and shall be attached to the original summons.

(3) The return receipt must be attached to the original summons and, if it shows delivery at least 3 days before the return date, shall constitute proof of service of any documents identified on the return receipt as having been mailed.

(4) The clerk shall note the fact of service in a permanent record.

(c) Instead of personal service, a summons for a wage deduction may be served and returned in the manner provided by Supreme Court rule for service, otherwise than by publication, of a notice for additional relief upon a party in default.

P.A. 82–280, § 12–805, eff. July 1, 1982. Amended by P.A. 83–707, § 1, eff. Sept. 23, 1983; P.A. 86–1268, § 1, eff. Nov. 5, 1990; P.A. 87–569, § 1, eff. Jan. 1, 1992; P.A. 87–696, § 1, eff. Sept. 23, 1991; P.A. 87–895, Art. 2, § 2–50, eff. Aug. 14, 1992; P.A. 88–492, § 5, eff. Jan. 1, 1994; P.A. 89–28, § 5, eff. June 23, 1995; P.A. 90–677, § 5, eff. Jan. 1, 1999; P.A. 94–306, § 5, eff. Jan. 1, 2006.

Formerly Ill.Rev.Stat.1991, ch. 110, ¶ 12–805.

5/12–806. Service and return of summons

§ 12–806. Service and return of summons. Summons shall be returnable not less than 21 nor more than 40 days after the date of issuance. Summons with 4 copies of the interrogatories and one copy of the judgment or certification and one copy of the wage deduction notice specified in Section 12–805 of this Act shall be served on the employer and returned as in other civil cases.

If the employer is served with summons less than 3 days prior to the return date, the court shall continue the case to a new return date not less than 21 days after the service of the summons.

P.A. 82–280, § 12–806, eff. July 1, 1982. Amended by P.A. 86–1268, § 1, eff. Nov. 5, 1990; P.A. 87–569, § 1, eff. Jan. 1, 1992; P.A. 90–677, § 5, eff. Jan. 1, 1999.

Formerly Ill.Rev.Stat.1991, ch. 110, ¶ 12–806.

5/12–807. Failure of employer to appear

§ 12–807. Failure of employer to appear. (a) If an employer fails to appear and answer as required by Part 8 of Article XII of this Act, the court may enter a conditional judgment against the employer for the amount due upon the judgment against the judgment debtor. A summons to confirm the conditional judgment may issue against the employer returnable not less than 21 nor more than 30 days after the date of issuance, commanding the employer to show cause why the judgment should not be made final. If the employer, after being served with summons to confirm the conditional judgment or after being notified as provided in subsection (b) hereof, fails to appear and answer, the court shall confirm such judgment to the amount of the judgment against the judgment debtor and award costs. If the employer appears and answers, the same proceedings may be had as in other cases.

(b) If an employer becomes a non-resident, goes out of this State, or is concealed within this State so that the summons to confirm the conditional judgment cannot be served upon him or her, upon the filing by the plaintiff or his or her agent of an affidavit as in cases of non-resident defendants in attachments, the employer may be notified in the same manner as a non-resident defendant in attachment; and upon notice being given to him or her as above stated, he or she may be proceeded against in the same manner as if he or she had been personally served with summons to confirm the conditional judgment.

P.A. 82–280, § 12–807, eff. July 1, 1982. Amended by P.A. 83–707, § 1, eff. Sept. 23, 1983; P.A. 86–603, S 1, eff. Jan. 1, 1990.

Formerly Ill.Rev.Stat.1991, ch. 110, ¶ 12–807.

5/12–808. Duty of employer

§ 12–808. Duty of employer.

(a) An employer served as herein provided shall pay the employee the amount of his or her exempt wages.

(b) To the extent of the amount due upon the judgment and costs, the employer shall hold, subject to order of court, any non-exempt wages due or which subsequently come due. The judgment or balance due thereon is a lien on wages due at the time of the service of summons, and such lien shall continue as to subsequent earnings until the total amount due upon the judgment and costs is paid, except that such lien on subsequent earnings shall terminate sooner if the employment relationship is terminated or if the underlying judgment is vacated or modified.

(b–5) If the employer is a federal agency employer and the creditor is represented by an attorney, then the employer, upon service of summons and to the extent of the amount due upon the judgment and costs, shall commence to pay over to the attorney for the judgment creditor any non-exempt wages due or that subsequently come due. The attorney for the judgment creditor shall thereafter hold the deducted wages subject to further order of the court and shall make answer to the court regarding amounts received from the federal agency employer. The federal agency employer's periodic payments shall be considered a sufficient answer to the interrogatories.

(c) Except as provided in subsection (b–5), the employer shall file, on or before the return date or within the further time that the court for cause may allow, a written answer under oath to the interrogatories, setting forth the amount due as wages to the judgment debtor for the payroll periods ending immediately prior to the service of the summons and a summary of the computation used to determine the amount of non-exempt wages. Except as provided in subsection (b–5), the employer shall mail by first class mail or hand deliver a copy of the answer to the judgment debtor at the address specified in the affidavit filed under Section 12–805 of this Act, or at any other address or location of the judgment debtor known to the employer.

A lien obtained hereunder shall have priority over any subsequent lien obtained hereunder, except that liens for the support of a spouse or dependent children shall have priority over all other liens obtained hereunder. Subsequent summonses shall be effective in the order in which they are served.

(d) The Illinois Supreme Court may by rule allow an employer to file answers to interrogatories by facsimile transmission.

(e) Pursuant to answer under oath to the interrogatories by the employer, an order shall be entered compelling the employer to deduct from wages of the judgment debtor subject to collection under a deduction order an amount which is the lesser of (i) 15% of the gross amount of the wages or (ii) the amount by which disposable earnings for a week exceed 45 times the Federal Minimum Hourly Wage prescribed by Section 206(a)(1) of Title 29 of the United States Code, as amended,[1] in effect at the time the amounts are payable, for each pay period in which statutory exemptions under Section 12–804 and child support garnishments, if any, leave funds to be remitted or, under a wage deduction summons served on or after January 1, 2006, the minimum hourly wage prescribed by Section 4 of the Minimum Wage Law, whichever is greater. The order shall further provide that deducted wages shall be remitted to the creditor or creditor's attorney on a monthly basis.

(f) If after the entry of a deduction order, the employer ceases to remit funds to the plaintiff pursuant to the order without a lawful excuse (which would terminate the employer's obligation under the deduction order such as the debtor having filed a bankruptcy, the debtor having left employment or the employer having received service of a support order against the judgment debtor having priority over the wage deduction proceedings), the court shall, upon plaintiff's motion, enter a conditional judgment against the employer for the balance due on the judgment. The plaintiff may then issue a Summons After Conditional Judgment. After service of the Summons After Conditional Judgment, the employer may show cause why the conditional judgment, or some portion thereof should not be made a final judgment. If the employer shall fail to respond or show cause why the conditional judgment or some portion thereof should not be made final, the court shall confirm the conditional judgment and make it final as to the employer plus additional court costs.

P.A. 82–280, § 12–808, eff. July 1, 1982. Amended by P.A. 86–1268, § 1, eff. Nov. 5, 1990; P.A. 87–569, § 1, eff. Jan. 1, 1992; P.A. 87–1252, § 2, eff. Jan. 7, 1993; P.A. 89–28, § 5, eff. June 23, 1995; P.A. 90–677, § 5, eff. Jan. 1, 1999; P.A. 94–306, § 5, eff. Jan. 1, 2006; P.A. 95–661, § 5, eff. Jan. 1, 2008.

Formerly Ill.Rev.Stat.1991, ch. 110, ¶ 12–808.
  1 29 U.S.C.A. § 206.

5/12–808.5.   Certification of judgment balance

§ 12–808.5.   Certification of judgment balance. Whenever a wage deduction order has not been fully satisfied by the end of the first full calendar quarter following the date of service of the wage deduction summons:

(1) The judgment creditor or his attorney shall prepare a certification that states the amount of the judgment remaining unsatisfied as of the last calendar day of each full calendar quarter for which the wage deduction order continues in effect.

(2) The certification shall be mailed or delivered to the employer by the judgment creditor or his or her attorney within 15 days after the end of each calendar quarter for which the wage deduction order continues in effect. The employer shall hand deliver or mail by first class mail a copy of the certification to the judgment debtor at the judgment debtor's last known address.

(3) In the event that the plaintiff fails to provide the certification required by this Section, the employer must continue to withhold funds from the defendant's wages but may hold the funds without remitting to the plaintiff until such time as it receives a certification required by this Section. A

certification of judgment balance need not be filed with the court.

(4) Any party to the wage deduction proceeding may, upon motion with notice to all other parties, ask the court to review the balance due claimed by the judgment creditor.

P.A. 82–280, § 12–808.5, added by P.A. 90–677, § 5, eff. Jan. 1, 1999; P.A. 95–661, § 5, eff. Jan. 1, 2008.

5/12–809. Offsetting claims

§ 12–809. Offsetting claims. The employer is entitled to assert against indebtedness due to the judgment debtor offsetting claims against either or both the judgment creditor and the judgment debtor, whether (1) due at the time of service of the summons or thereafter to become due and (2) liquidated or unliquidated, except demands for unliquidated claims for actions sounding in tort. The employer is liable for the balance of indebtedness due the judgment debtor after the offsetting claims are adjusted. The verdict or finding and judgment shall show the amount of offsetting claims or deductions allowed against each party.

P.A. 82–280, § 12–809, eff. July 1, 1982.

Formerly Ill.Rev.Stat.1991, ch. 110, ¶ 12–809.

5/12–810. Adverse claims

§ 12–810. Adverse claims. (a) In the event any indebtedness or other property due from or in the possession of any employer is claimed by any other person, the court shall permit the claimant to appear and maintain his or her claim. A claimant not voluntarily appearing shall be served with notice in person or by certified or registered mail. If a claimant fails to appear after being served with notice in the manner directed, he or she shall be concluded by the judgment entered in the proceeding against any claim on the wages involved in that proceeding.

(b) If the adverse claimant appears and, within the time the court allows, files his or her claim and serves a copy thereof upon the judgment creditor and the employer, he or she is then a party to the proceeding, and his or her claim shall be tried and determined with the other issues in the action. If the adverse claimant is entitled to all or part of the indebtedness or other property, the court shall enter judgment in accordance with the interest of the parties.

P.A. 82–280, § 12–810, eff. July 1, 1982.

Formerly Ill.Rev.Stat.1991, ch. 110, ¶ 12–810.

5/12–811. Trial and judgment

§ 12–811. Trial and judgment.

(a) The judgment creditor or the judgment debtor may contest the truth or sufficiency of the employer's answer and, in accordance with local court rules, the court shall immediately, unless for good cause the hearing is postponed, proceed to try the issues. The answer of the employer may be contested without further pleading.

(b) At any time on or before the return date, the judgment debtor may request a hearing to dispute the wage deduction because the wages are exempt by notifying the clerk of court before that time, using forms as may be provided by the clerk of the court. To obtain a hearing in counties with a population of 1,000,000 or more, the judgment debtor must notify the clerk of court in person and in writing at the clerk's office before the return date specified in the summons or appear in court on the date and time specified in the summons. To obtain a hearing in counties with a population of less than 1,000,000, the judgment debtor must notify the clerk of the court in writing at the clerk's office on or before the return date specified in the summons. The Clerk of Court will provide a hearing date and the necessary forms that must be prepared by the judgment debtor or the attorney for the judgment debtor and sent to the judgment creditor and the employer, or their attorney, regarding the time and location of the hearing. This notice may be sent by regular first class mail. At the hearing the court shall immediately, unless for good cause the hearing is continued, proceed to try the issues.

(c) The trial shall be conducted as in other civil cases.

(d) If the finding is against an employer, a deduction order shall be entered against the employer and in favor of the judgment debtor to whom the employer is indebted, in the same manner as if the facts are admitted.

(e) No deduction order shall be entered in favor of the judgment creditor unless the affidavit filed by the judgment creditor certifies that a copy of the wage deduction notice has been mailed to the judgment debtor, under Section 12–805, and the employer's answer provides a summary of the computation used to determine the amount of non-exempt wages. If the employer is a federal agency employer, a deduction order shall be entered in favor of the judgment creditor if (i) the affidavit filed by the judgment creditor certifies that a copy of the wage deduction notice has been mailed to the judgment debtor under Section 12–805 and (ii) the federal agency employer identifies, on or with its periodic payments made under subsection (b–5) of Section 12–808, the computation method used to determine the amount of non-exempt wages. A federal agency employer shall not be required to provide a summary of the computation used to determine the amount of non-exempt wages.

P.A. 82–280, § 12–811, eff. July 1, 1982. Amended by P.A. 86–1268, § 1, eff. Nov. 5, 1990; P.A. 89–28, § 5, eff. June 23, 1995.

Formerly Ill.Rev.Stat.1991, ch. 110, ¶ 12–811.

5/12–812.   Effect of order

§ 12–812.   Effect of order.   A deduction order against an employer shall be enforceable as in other civil cases and shall discharge the employer of all claims by the judgment debtor for the indebtedness paid, delivered or accounted for by the employer by virtue of the order.   The discharge of an employer is no bar to an action by the judgment debtor for the same claim.

Entry of the deduction order shall discharge the federal agency employer of all claims by the judgment debtor for the indebtedness paid and delivered by the employer and accounted for by the attorney for the judgment creditor under this Section.
P.A. 82–280, § 12–812, eff. July 1, 1982. Amended by P.A. 89–28, § 5, eff. June 23, 1995.

Formerly Ill.Rev.Stat.1991, ch. 110, ¶ 12–812.

5/12–813.   Judgment by confession

§ 12–813.   Judgment by confession.   A judgment by confession without service of process on the defendant shall not be the basis for seeking a deduction order, unless such judgment is confirmed after service of process by a trial de novo, as if such confession of judgment had not been obtained, except that if it appears by the return of the officer on the first summons that the employee is not found, alias summonses subsequently issued may be served upon the employee by leaving a copy thereof with the employee's employer, or leaving a copy thereof at the usual place of business of the employer with his or her superintendent, manager, cashier, general agent or clerk, pursuant to an affidavit filed by the creditor with the clerk of the court stating the identity of the employee's employer, and that the employee is actively employed at the time such alias is sought, and except that if a notice of defense has been filed to a wage assignment as provided in Section 4.1 of "An Act to promote the welfare of wage earners by regulating the assignment of wages, and prescribing a penalty for the violation thereof", approved July 1, 1935, as amended,[1] the debtor may be served by registered or certified mail within 6 months after the filing of such defense on a wage assignment in the action to confirm the judgment by confession and such mailing by the creditor to the address shown on the notice of defense shall constitute service of the summons.
P.A. 82–280, § 12–813, eff. July 1, 1982. Amended by P.A. 83–707, § 1, eff. Sept. 23, 1983.

Formerly Ill.Rev.Stat.1991, ch. 110, ¶ 12–813.
[1] 740 ILCS 170/4.1.

5/12–814.   Costs and fees

§ 12–814.   Costs and fees.

(a) The costs of obtaining a deduction order shall be charged to the judgment debtor, unless the court determines, in its discretion, that costs incurred by the judgment creditor were improperly incurred, in which case those costs shall be paid by the judgment creditor.

(b) No fee shall be paid by an employer for filing his or her appearance, answer or satisfaction of judgment against him or her.

(c) A fee consisting of 2% of the amount required to be deducted by any deduction order shall be allowed and paid to the employer, and the amount so paid shall be charged to the judgment debtor.

(d) No other fee shall be paid to an employer at the time of service of the summons or at any other time thereafter unless he or she is subpoenaed to appear as a witness, in which case he or she is entitled to witness fees as in other civil cases.
P.A. 82–280, § 12–814, eff. July 1, 1982. Amended by P.A. 87–569, § 1, eff. Jan. 1, 1992; P.A. 95–661, § 5, eff. Jan. 1, 2008.

Formerly Ill.Rev.Stat.1991, ch. 110, ¶ 12–814.

5/12–815.   Death of employer

§ 12–815.   Death of employer.   Upon the death of an employer the procedure shall be the same as in the case of the death of a defendant in other civil cases.
P.A. 82–280, § 12–815, eff. July 1, 1982.

Formerly Ill.Rev.Stat.1991, ch. 110, ¶ 12–815.

5/12–816.   Assignment, transfer or other disposition

§ 12–816.   Assignment, transfer or other disposition.   No assignment, transfer or other disposition by an heir or distributee of his or her interest in the possession of an administrator or executor shall defeat the deduction order, unless (1) prior to the service of summons upon the administrator or executor, the transfer or other disposition is reduced to writing and (2) the writing is filed in the office of the clerk of the court appointing the executor or administrator.
P.A. 82–280, § 12–816, eff. July 1, 1982.

Formerly Ill.Rev.Stat.1991, ch. 110, ¶ 12–816.

5/12–817.   Wrongful issuance of summons

§ 12–817.   Wrongful issuance of summons.   If any person wrongfully causes summons to issue for a deduction order, he or she shall be liable to the employee and the employer for all damages occasioned by such action including reasonable attorney's fees, which damages or attorney's fees may be proved in the same action in which the summons was wrongfully issued.
P.A. 82–280, § 12–817, eff. July 1, 1982.

Formerly Ill.Rev.Stat.1991, ch. 110, ¶ 12–817.

5/12–818. Discharge or suspension of employee prohibited

§ 12–818. Discharge or suspension of employee prohibited. No employer may discharge or suspend any employee by reason of the fact that his or her earnings have been subjected to a deduction order for any one indebtedness. Any person violating this Section shall be guilty of a Class A misdemeanor.

P.A. 82–280, § 12–818, eff. July 1, 1982.

Formerly Ill.Rev.Stat.1991, ch. 110, ¶ 12–818.

5/12–819. Limitations on part 8 of Article XII

§ 12–819. Limitations on part 8 of Article XII. The provisions of this Part 8 of Article XII of this Act do not apply to orders for withholding of income entered by the court under provisions of The Illinois Public Aid Code,[1] the Illinois Marriage and Dissolution of Marriage Act,[2] the Non–Support of Spouse and Children Act,[3] the Non–Support Punishment Act,[4] the Revised Uniform Reciprocal Enforcement of Support Act,[5] the Illinois Parentage Act of 1984,[6] and the Illinois Parentage Act of 2015[7] for support of a child or maintenance of a spouse.

P.A. 82–280, § 12–819, added by P.A. 83–658, § 7, eff. Jan. 1, 1984. Amended by P.A. 84–1043, § 1, eff. Nov. 26, 1985; P.A. 91–613, § 960, eff. Oct. 1, 1999; P.A. 99–85, § 964, eff. Jan. 1, 2016.

Formerly Ill.Rev.Stat.1991, ch. 110, ¶ 12–819.

[1] 305 ILCS 5/1–1 et seq.

[2] 750 ILCS 5/101 et seq.

[3] 750 ILCS 15/1 et seq. (repealed; see, now, generally, 750 ILCS 16/1).

[4] 750 ILCS 16/1 et seq.

[5] 750 ILCS 20/1 et seq. (repealed; see, now, 750 ILCS 22/101 et. seq.).

[6] 750 ILCS 45/1 et seq.

[7] 750 ILCS 46/101 et seq.

PART 9. EXEMPTION OF HOMESTEAD

5/12–901. Amount

§ 12–901. Amount. Every individual is entitled to an estate of homestead to the extent in value of $15,000 of his or her interest in a farm or lot of land and buildings thereon, a condominium, or personal property, owned or rightly possessed by lease or otherwise and occupied by him or her as a residence, or in a cooperative that owns property that the individual uses as a residence. That homestead and all right in and title to that homestead is exempt from attachment, judgment, levy, or judgment sale for the payment of his or her debts or other purposes and from the laws of conveyance, descent, and legacy, except as provided in this Code or in Section 20–6 of the Probate Act of 1975.[1] This Section is not applicable between joint tenants or tenants in common but it is applicable as to any creditors of those persons. If 2 or more individuals own property that is exempt as a homestead, the value of the exemption of each individual may not exceed his or her proportionate share of $30,000 based upon percentage of ownership.

P.A. 82–280, § 12–901, eff. July 1, 1982. Amended by P.A. 82–783, Art. III, § 43, eff. July 13, 1982; P.A. 83–707, § 1, eff. Sept. 23, 1983; P.A. 88–672, § 25, eff. Dec. 14, 1994; P.A. 94–293, § 5, eff. Jan. 1, 2006.

Formerly Ill.Rev.Stat.1991, ch. 110, ¶ 12–901.

[1] 755 ILCS 5/20–6.

5/12–902. Exemption after death or desertion

§ 12–902. Exemption after death or desertion. Such exemption shall continue after the death of such individual, for the benefit of the spouse surviving, so long as he or she continues to occupy such homestead, and of the children until the youngest child becomes 18 years of age; and in case the spouse deserts his or her family, the exemption shall continue in favor of the one occupying the premises as a residence.

P.A. 82–280, § 12–902, eff. July 1, 1982. Amended by P.A. 82–783, Art. III, § 43, eff. July 13, 1982.

Formerly Ill.Rev.Stat.1991, ch. 110, ¶ 12–902.

5/12–903. Extent of exemption

§ 12–903. Extent of exemption. No property shall, by virtue of Part 9 of Article XII of this Act, be exempt from sale for nonpayment of taxes or assessments, or for a debt or liability incurred for the purchase or improvement thereof, or for enforcement of a lien thereon pursuant to paragraph (g)(1) of Section 9 of the "Condominium Property Act", approved June 20, 1963, as amended,[1] or be exempt from enforcement of a judgment for possession pursuant to paragraph (a)(7) or (a)(8) of Section 9–102 of this Code.

This amendatory Act of the 92nd General Assembly is intended as a clarification of existing law and not as a new enactment.

P.A. 82–280, § 12–903, eff. July 1, 1982. Amended by P.A. 83–707, § 1, eff. Sept. 23, 1983; P.A. 92–540, § 5, eff. June 12, 2002.

Formerly Ill.Rev.Stat.1991, ch. 110, ¶ 12–903.

[1] 765 ILCS 605/9.

5/12–903.5.   Drug asset forfeitures

§ 12–903.5. Drug asset forfeitures.

(a) The homestead exemption under this Part 9 of Article XII [1] does not apply to property subject to forfeiture under Section 505 of the Illinois Controlled Substances Act, Section 12 of the Cannabis Control Act, Section 85 of the Methamphetamine Control and Community Protection Act, or Section 5 of the Narcotics Profit Forfeiture Act.[2]

(b) This Section applies to actions pending on or commenced on or after the effective date of this Section.

P.A. 82–280, § 12–903.5, added by P.A. 89–404, § 45, eff. Aug. 20, 1995. Amended by P.A. 90–593, § 45, eff. June 19, 1998; P.A. 94–556, § 1115, eff. Sept. 11, 2005.

[1] 735 ILCS 5/12–901 et seq.
[2] 720 ILCS 570/505, 720 ILCS 550/12, or 725 ILCS 175/5.

Validity

Public Act 89–404, which added this section, has been held unconstitutional in its entirety for violating the single-subject rule of the state Constitution by the Supreme Court of Illinois in the case of People v. Reedy, 1999, 186 Ill.2d 1, 237 Ill.Dec. 74, 708 N.E.2d 1114, rehearing denied. P.A. 90–593 reenacted this section.

5/12–904.   Release, waiver or conveyance

§ 12–904. Release, waiver or conveyance. No release, waiver or conveyance of the estate so exempted shall be valid, unless the same is in writing, signed by the individual and his or her spouse, if he or she have one, or possession is abandoned or given pursuant to the conveyance; or if the exception is continued to a child or children without the order of a court directing a release thereof; but if a conveyance is made by an individual as grantor to his or her spouse, such conveyance shall be effectual to pass the title expressed therein to be conveyed thereby, whether or not the grantor in such conveyance is joined therein by his or her spouse. In any case where such release, waiver or conveyance is taken by way of mortgage or security, the same shall only be operative as to such specific release, waiver or conveyance; and when the same includes different pieces of land, or the homestead is of greater value than $15,000, the other lands shall first be sold before resorting to the homestead, and in case of the sale of such homestead, if any balance remains after the payment of the debt and costs, such balance shall, to the extent of $15,000 be exempt, and be applied upon such homestead exemption in the manner provided by law.

P.A. 82–280, § 12–904, eff. July 1, 1982. Amended by P.A. 82–783, Art. III, § 43, eff. July 13, 1982; P.A. 94–293, § 5, eff. Jan. 1, 2006.

Formerly Ill.Rev.Stat.1991, ch. 110, ¶ 12–904.

5/12–905.   Dissolution of marriage

§ 12–905. Dissolution of marriage. In case of a dissolution of marriage, the court granting the dissolution of marriage may dispose of the homestead estate according to the equities of the case.

P.A. 82–280, § 12–905, eff. July 1, 1982.

Formerly Ill.Rev.Stat.1991, ch. 110, ¶ 12–905.

5/12–906.   Proceeds of sale

§ 12–906. Proceeds of sale. When a homestead is conveyed by the owner thereof, such conveyance shall not subject the premises to any lien or incumbrance to which it would not be subject in the possession of such owner; and the proceeds thereof, to the extent of the amount of $15,000, shall be exempt from judgment or other process, for one year after the receipt thereof, by the person entitled to the exemption, and if reinvested in a homestead the same shall be entitled to the same exemption as the original homestead.

P.A. 82–280, § 12–906, eff. July 1, 1982. Amended by P.A. 82–783, Art. III, § 43, eff. July 13, 1982; P.A. 94–293, § 5, eff. Jan. 1, 2006.

Formerly Ill.Rev.Stat.1991, ch. 110, ¶ 12–906.

5/12–907.   Insurance proceeds

§ 12–907. Insurance proceeds. Whenever a building, exempted as a homestead, is insured in favor of the person entitled to the exemption, and a loss occurs, entitling such person to the insurance, such insurance money shall be exempt to the same extent as the building would have been had it not been destroyed.

P.A. 82–280, § 12–907, eff. July 1, 1982.

Formerly Ill.Rev.Stat.1991, ch. 110, ¶ 12–907.

5/12–908.   Enforcement of lien

§ 12–908. Enforcement of lien. In the enforcement of a lien in the circuit court upon premises, including the homestead, if such right is not waived or released, as provided in Part 9 of Article XII of this Act, the court may set off the homestead and order the sale of the balance of the premises, or, if the value of the premises exceeds the exemption, and the premises cannot be divided, the court may order the sale of the whole and the payment of the amount of the exemption to the person entitled thereto.

P.A. 82–280, § 12–908, eff. July 1, 1982. Amended by P.A. 83–707, § 1, eff. Sept. 23, 1983.

Formerly Ill.Rev.Stat.1991, ch. 110, ¶ 12–908.

5/12–909.   Bid for less than exempted amount

§ 12–909. Bid for less than exempted amount. No sale shall be made of the premises on such judgment unless a greater sum than $15,000 is bid therefor. If a greater sum is not so bid, the judgment may be set aside or modified, or the enforcement of the judgment released, as for lack of property.

P.A. 82–280, § 12–909, eff. July 1, 1982. Amended by P.A. 82–783, Art. III, § 43, eff. July 13, 1982; P.A. 94–293, § 5, eff. Jan. 1, 2006.

Formerly Ill.Rev.Stat.1991, ch. 110, ¶ 12–909.

5/12–910. Proceedings to enforce judgment

§ 12–910. Proceedings to enforce judgment. If in the opinion of the judgment creditors, or the officer holding a certified copy of a judgment for enforcement against such individuals, the premises claimed by him or her as exempt are worth more than $15,000, such officer shall summon 3 individuals, as commissioners, who shall, upon oath, to be administered to them by the officer, appraise the premises, and if, in their opinion, the property may be divided without damage to the interest of the parties, they shall set off so much of the premises, including the dwelling house, as in their opinion is worth $15,000, and the residue of the premises may be advertised and sold by such officer. Each commissioner shall receive for his or her services the sum of $5 per day for each day necessarily engaged in such service. The officer summoning such commissioners shall receive such fees as may be allowed for serving summons, but shall be entitled to charge mileage for only the actual distance traveled from the premises to be appraised, to the residence of the commissioners summoned. The officer shall not be required to summon commissioners until the judgment creditor, or some one for him or her, shall advance to the officer one day's fees for the commissioners, and unless the creditor shall advance such fees the officer shall not be required to enforce the judgment. The costs of such appraisement shall not be taxed against the judgment debtor unless such appraisement shows that the judgment debtor has property subject to such judgment.

P.A. 82–280, § 12–910, eff. July 1, 1982. Amended by P.A. 82–783, Art. III, § 43, eff. July 13, 1982; P.A. 83–707, § 1, eff. Sept. 23, 1983; P.A. 94–293, § 5, eff. Jan. 1, 2006.

Formerly Ill.Rev.Stat.1991, ch. 110, ¶ 12–910.

5/12–911. Notice to judgment debtor

§ 12–911. Notice to judgment debtor. In case the value of the premises is, in the opinion of the commissioners, more than $15,000, and cannot be divided as is provided for in Section 12–910 of this Act, they shall make and sign an appraisal of the value thereof, and deliver the same to the officer, who shall deliver a copy thereof to the judgment debtor, or to some one of the family of the age of 13 years or upwards, with a notice thereto attached that unless the judgment debtor pays to such officer the surplus over and above

$15,000 on the amount due on the judgment within 60 days thereafter, such premises will be sold.

P.A. 82–280, § 12–911, eff. July 1, 1982. Amended by P.A. 82–783, Art. III, § 43, eff. July 13, 1982; P.A. 83–356, § 1, eff. Sept. 14, 1983; P.A. 94–293, § 5, eff. Jan. 1, 2006.

Formerly Ill.Rev.Stat.1991, ch. 110, ¶ 12–911.

5/12–912. Sale of premises—Distribution of proceeds

§ 12–912. Sale of premises—Distribution of proceeds. In case of such surplus, or the amount due on the judgment is not paid within the 60 days, the officer may advertise and sell the premises, and out of the proceeds of such sale pay to such judgment debtor the sum of $15,000, and apply the balance on the judgment.

P.A. 82–280, § 12–912, eff. July 1, 1982. Amended by P.A. 82–783, Art. III, § 43, eff. July 13, 1982; P.A. 94–293, § 5, eff. Jan. 1, 2006.

Formerly Ill.Rev.Stat.1991, ch. 110, ¶ 12–912.

PART 10. EXEMPTION OF PERSONAL PROPERTY

5/12–1001. Personal property exempt

§ 12–1001. Personal property exempt. The following personal property, owned by the debtor, is exempt from judgment, attachment, or distress for rent:

(a) The necessary wearing apparel, bible, school books, and family pictures of the debtor and the debtor's dependents;

(b) The debtor's equity interest, not to exceed $4,000 in value, in any other property;

(c) The debtor's interest, not to exceed $2,400 in value, in any one motor vehicle;

(d) The debtor's equity interest, not to exceed $1,500 in value, in any implements, professional books, or tools of the trade of the debtor;

(e) Professionally prescribed health aids for the debtor or a dependent of the debtor;

(f) All proceeds payable because of the death of the insured and the aggregate net cash value of any or all life insurance and endowment policies and annuity contracts payable to a wife or husband of the insured, or to a child, parent, or other person dependent upon the insured, or to a revocable or irrevocable trust which names the wife or husband of the insured or which names a child, parent, or other person dependent upon the insured as the primary beneficiary of the trust, whether the power to change the beneficiary is reserved to the insured or not and whether the insured or the insured's estate is a contingent beneficiary or not;

(g) The debtor's right to receive:

(1) a social security benefit, unemployment compensation, or public assistance benefit;

(2) a veteran's benefit;

(3) a disability, illness, or unemployment benefit; and

(4) alimony, support, or separate maintenance, to the extent reasonably necessary for the support of the debtor and any dependent of the debtor.

(h) The debtor's right to receive, or property that is traceable to:

(1) an award under a crime victim's reparation law;

(2) a payment on account of the wrongful death of an individual of whom the debtor was a dependent, to the extent reasonably necessary for the support of the debtor;

(3) a payment under a life insurance contract that insured the life of an individual of whom the debtor was a dependent, to the extent reasonably necessary for the support of the debtor or a dependent of the debtor;

(4) a payment, not to exceed $15,000 in value, on account of personal bodily injury of the debtor or an individual of whom the debtor was a dependent; and

(5) any restitution payments made to persons pursuant to the federal Civil Liberties Act of 1988[1] and the Aleutian and Pribilof Island Restitution Act, P.L. 100–383.[2]

For purposes of this subsection (h), a debtor's right to receive an award or payment shall be exempt for a maximum of 2 years after the debtor's right to receive the award or payment accrues; property traceable to an award or payment shall be exempt for a maximum of 5 years after the award or payment accrues; and an award or payment and property traceable to an award or payment shall be exempt only to the extent of the amount of the award or payment, without interest or appreciation from the date of the award or payment.

(i) The debtor's right to receive an award under Part 20 of Article II of this Code[3] relating to crime victims' awards.

(j) Moneys held in an account invested in the Illinois College Savings Pool of which the debtor is a participant or donor, except the following nonexempt contributions:

(1) any contribution to such account by the debtor as participant or donor that is made with the actual intent to hinder, delay, or defraud any creditor of the debtor;

(2) any contributions to such account by the debtor as participant during the 365 day period prior to the date of filing of the debtor's petition for bankruptcy that, in the aggregate during such period, exceed the amount of the annual gift tax exclusion under Section 2503(b) of the Internal Revenue Code of 1986, as amended, in effect at the time of contribution; or

(3) any contributions to such account by the debtor as participant during the period commencing 730 days prior to and ending 366 days prior to the date of filing of the debtor's petition for bankruptcy that, in the aggregate during such period, exceed the amount of the annual gift tax exclusion under Section 2503(b) of the Internal Revenue Code of 1986, as amended, in effect at the time of contribution.

For purposes of this subsection (j), "account" includes all accounts for a particular designated beneficiary, of which the debtor is a participant or donor.

Money due the debtor from the sale of any personal property that was exempt from judgment, attachment, or distress for rent at the time of the sale is exempt from attachment and garnishment to the same extent that the property would be exempt had the same not been sold by the debtor.

If a debtor owns property exempt under this Section and he or she purchased that property with the intent of converting nonexempt property into exempt property or in fraud of his or her creditors, that property shall not be exempt from judgment, attachment, or distress for rent. Property acquired within 6 months of the filing of the petition for bankruptcy shall be presumed to have been acquired in contemplation of bankruptcy.

The personal property exemptions set forth in this Section shall apply only to individuals and only to personal property that is used for personal rather than business purposes. The personal property exemptions set forth in this Section shall not apply to or be allowed against any money, salary, or wages due or to become due to the debtor that are required to be withheld in a wage deduction proceeding under Part 8 of this Article XII.[4]

P.A. 82–280, § 12–1001, eff. July 1, 1982. Amended by P.A. 82–783, Art. III, § 43, eff. July 13, 1982; P.A. 83–707, § 1, eff. Sept. 23, 1983; P.A. 83–968, § 1, eff. Dec. 2, 1983; P.A. 83–1362, Art. II, § 109, eff. Sept. 11, 1984; P.A. 86–393, § 1, eff. Aug. 30, 1989; P.A. 87–565, § 2, eff. Sept. 17, 1991; P.A. 87–569, § 1, eff. Jan. 1, 1992; P.A. 87–895, Art. 2, § 2–50, eff. Aug. 14, 1992; P.A. 88–378, § 10, eff. Aug. 17, 1993; P.A. 89–686, Art. 10, § 10–5, eff. Dec. 31, 1996; P.A. 94–293, § 5, eff. Jan. 1, 2006; P.A. 95–306, § 10, eff. Jan. 1, 2008; P.A. 97–1030, § 5, eff. Aug. 17, 2012.

Formerly Ill.Rev.Stat.1991, ch. 110, ¶ 12–1001.

1 50 App. U.S.C.A. § 1989b et seq.
2 50 App. U.S.C.A. § 1989c et seq.
3 735 ILCS 5/2–2001 et seq.
4 735 ILCS 5/12–801 et seq.

5/12–1002. Schedule of property

§ 12–1002. Schedule of property. It shall not be necessary for the debtor against whom a judgment or attachment was entered or distress warrant was issued to make a schedule of his or her personal property to enable him or her to secure the exemption and to retain the property enumerated in paragraph (b) of Section 12–1001 of this Act, but whenever any debtor against whom a judgment or attachment was entered or distress warrant was issued, desires to avail himself or herself of the benefit of this Act to make a selection of certain household furniture (in case such property is worth more than the amount he or she is entitled to retain) or to select other personal property instead of household furniture or to select part household furniture and part other personal property he or she shall, within 10 days after a copy of the judgment, attachment or distress warrant is served upon him or her in the same manner as summonses are served in other civil cases, such copies of the judgment, attachment or distress warrant to have endorsed thereon a notice signed by the officer having such document, notifying the debtor that he or she must file a schedule of his or her property within 10 days from the service thereof in order to claim his or her exemption under Part 10 of Article XII of this Act, whereupon the debtor shall make a schedule of all his or her personal property of every kind and character, including money on hand and debts due and owing to the debtor and shall deliver the same to the officer having the certified copy of the judgment, attachment or distress warrant, or file the same in the court which entered the document, which schedule shall be subscribed and sworn to by the debtor, and any property owned by the debtor, and not included in such schedule shall not be exempt, and thereupon the court which entered the judgment or attachment or issued the distress warrant shall summon 3 householders, who, after being duly sworn to fairly and impartially appraise the property of the debtor, shall fix a fair valuation upon each article contained in such schedule, and the debtor shall then select from such schedule the articles he or she may desire to retain, the aggregate value of which shall not exceed the amount exempted, to which he or she may be entitled, and deliver the remainder to the officer having the document; and the officer having such document is authorized to administer the oaths required herein of the debtor and appraisers. In case no schedule is filed, it shall be the duty of the officer to exempt and disregard the articles enumerated in paragraphs (a), (e), (f), (g) and (h) of Section 12–1001 of this Act and the personal property if it is worth not more than the amount the debtor is entitled to have exempted under paragraphs (b), (c) and (d) of Section 12–1001 of this Act and if the personal property is worth more than the amount of the exemption to which the debtor is entitled, the court which entered the judgment or the attachment order or the distress warrant issued shall secure a fair and impartial appraisal of the personal property in the same manner as all the personal property is appraised when a schedule is filed, and after such valuation, such officer shall select and exempt personal property to the amount to which the debtor is entitled to retain. When the judgment debtor has presented a sufficient schedule of all his or her personal estate, the return of such judgment unsatisfied, shall not render it necessary for such judgment debtor, for the purpose of availing himself or herself of the benefits of the exemption laws of this state, to present an additional schedule unless additional property has been acquired, before 90 days from the date of the issuance of the certified copy of the judgment.

P.A. 82–280, § 12–1002, eff. July 1, 1982. Amended by P.A. 82–783, Art. III, § 43, eff. July 13, 1982; P.A. 83–968, § 1, eff. Dec. 2, 1983.

Formerly Ill.Rev.Stat.1991, ch. 110, ¶ 12–1002.

5/12–1003. When family entitled to exemptions

§ 12–1003. When family entitled to exemptions. When the head of a family dies, deserts or does not reside with the same, the family shall be entitled to and receive all the benefit and privileges which are by Part 10 of Article XII of this Act conferred upon the head of a family residing with the same.

P.A. 82–280, § 12–1003, eff. July 1, 1982.

Formerly Ill.Rev.Stat.1991, ch. 110, ¶ 12–1003.

5/12–1004. Judgment for wages

§ 12–1004. Judgment for wages. No personal property shall be exempt from levy of attachment or judgment if the debt or judgment is for the wages of any laborer or employee, providing the court entering judgment finds that the claim sued for is for wages due such person as laborer or employee, which finding shall be expressly stated in the judgment.

P.A. 82–280, § 12–1004, eff. July 1, 1982. Amended by P.A. 83–1362, Art. III, § 16, eff. Sept. 11, 1984.

Formerly Ill.Rev.Stat.1991, ch. 110, ¶ 12–1004.

5/12–1005. Liability for seizing exempt property

§ 12–1005. Liability for seizing exempt property. If any officer by virtue of any judgment or process, or any other person by any right of distress takes or seizes any of the articles of property exempted from levy and sale, as provided in Part 10 of Article XII of this Act, such officer or person shall be liable in a civil action to the party damaged for double the value of the property so illegally taken or seized and costs of the action.

P.A. 82–280, § 12–1005, eff. July 1, 1982. Amended by P.A. 83–707, § 1, eff. Sept. 23, 1983.

Formerly Ill.Rev.Stat.1991, ch. 110, ¶ 12–1005.

5/12–1006. Exemption for retirement plans

§ 12–1006. Exemption for retirement plans. (a) A debtor's interest in or right, whether vested or not, to the assets held in or to receive pensions, annuities, benefits, distributions, refunds of contributions, or other payments under a retirement plan is exempt from judgment, attachment, execution, distress for rent, and seizure for the satisfaction of debts if the plan (i) is intended in good faith to qualify as a retirement plan under applicable provisions of the Internal Revenue Code of 1986, as now or hereafter amended,[1] or (ii) is a public employee pension plan created under the Illinois Pension Code, as now or hereafter amended.[2]

(b) "Retirement plan" includes the following:

(1) a stock bonus, pension, profit sharing, annuity, or similar plan or arrangement, including a retirement plan for self-employed individuals or a simplified employee pension plan;

(2) a government or church retirement plan or contract;

(3) an individual retirement annuity or individual retirement account; and

(4) a public employee pension plan created under the Illinois Pension Code, as now or hereafter amended.

(c) A retirement plan that is (i) intended in good faith to qualify as a retirement plan under the applicable provisions of the Internal Revenue Code of 1986, as now or hereafter amended, or (ii) a public employee pension plan created under the Illinois Pension Code, as now or hereafter amended, is conclusively presumed to be a spendthrift trust under the law of Illinois.

(d) This Section applies to interests in retirement plans held by debtors subject to bankruptcy, judicial, administrative or other proceedings pending on or filed after August 30, 1989.

P.A. 82–280, § 12–1006, added by P.A. 86–393, § 1, eff. Aug. 30, 1989. Amended by P.A. 86–1329, § 1, eff. Jan. 1, 1991.

Formerly Ill.Rev.Stat.1991, ch. 110, ¶ 12–1006.

[1] 26 U.S.C.A. § 1 et seq.
[2] 40 ILCS 5/1–101 et seq.

Validity

Enforcement of judgment provisions concerning exemption for retirement plans has been held unconstitutional as preempted by the federal Bankruptcy Code in the case of In re Kazi, Bkrtcy, 125 B.R. 981 (S.D. Ill. 1991).

PART 11. GARNISHMENT IN VIOLATION OF EXEMPTION

5/12–1101. Sending claim out of State

§ 12–1101. Sending claim out of State. Whoever, whether principal, agent or attorney, with intent thereby to deprive any bona fide resident of the State of Illinois of his or her rights, under the statutes of Illinois on the subject of the exemption of property from levy and sale on a judgment, or in attachment or garnishment, sends, or causes to be sent out of the State of Illinois any claim for a debt to be collected by proceedings in attachment, garnishment, or other process, when the creditor, debtor or person, or corporation owing for the earnings intended to be reached by such proceedings in attachment are each and all within the jurisdiction of the courts of the State of Illinois, shall be guilty of a petty offense and fined for each and every claim so sent in any sum not less than $10 nor more than $50.

P.A. 82–280, § 12–1101, eff. July 1, 1982.

Formerly Ill.Rev.Stat.1991, ch. 110, ¶ 12–1101.

5/12–1102. Assignment or transfer of claim

§ 12–1102. Assignment or transfer of claim. Whoever, either directly or indirectly, assigns or transfers any claim for a debt against a citizen of Illinois, for the purpose of having the same collected by proceedings in attachment, garnishment, or other process, out of the wages or personal earnings of the debtor, in courts outside of the State of Illinois, when the creditor, debtor, person or corporation owing the money intended to be reached by the proceedings in attachment are each and all within the jurisdiction of the courts of the State of Illinois, is guilty of a petty offense.

P.A. 82–280, § 12–1102, eff. July 1, 1982.

Formerly Ill.Rev.Stat.1991, ch. 110, ¶ 12–1102.

PART 12. EXEMPTION IN BANKRUPTCY

5/12–1201. Bankruptcy exemption

§ 12–1201. Bankruptcy exemption. In accordance with the provision of Section 522(b) of the Bankruptcy Code of 1978, (11 U.S.C. 522(b)), residents of this State shall be prohibited from using the federal exemptions provided in Section 522(d) of the Bankruptcy Code of 1978 (11 U.S.C. 522(d)), except as may otherwise be permitted under the laws of Illinois.

P.A. 82–280, § 12–1201, eff. July 1, 1982.

Formerly Ill.Rev.Stat.1991, ch. 110, ¶ 12–1201.

PART 13. INSOLVENT DEBTORS

5/12–1301 to 5/12–1330. §§ 12–1301 to 12–1330. Repealed by P.A. 83–352, § 2, eff. Sept. 14, 1983

PART 14. ORDERS TO TAKE INTO CUSTODY

Section
5/12–1401.   Orders to Take Into Custody.

Date Effective

Part 14 was added by P.A. 84–942, § 1, eff. Sept. 25, 1985.

5/12–1401.   Orders to Take Into Custody

§ 12–1401.   Orders to Take Into Custody. In any civil case where an order issues to take any person into custody for any reason, the order shall contain, if known, the name, date of birth, sex, physical description, and last known address of the person to be taken into custody. It shall also contain a statement of the reason the person is to be taken into custody and the date of issuance. However, nothing herein shall impose a duty upon the court to discern or seek out any of the information relating to the date of birth, sex, physical description, or last known address of the person to be taken into custody which is not provided by a litigant. Moreover, no order is invalid by reason of its failure to contain any of the information specified herein except as otherwise required by law.

P.A. 82–280, § 12–1401, added by P.A. 84–942, § 1, eff. Sept. 25, 1985.

Formerly Ill.Rev.Stat.1991, ch. 110, ¶ 12–1401.

ARTICLE XIII.   LIMITATIONS

Part
1. Real Actions.
2. Personal Actions.

PART 1.   REAL ACTIONS

5/13–101.   Twenty years—Recovery of land

§ 13–101.   Twenty years—Recovery of land. No person shall commence an action for the recovery of lands, nor make an entry thereon, unless within 20 years after the right to bring such action or make such entry first accrued, or within 20 years after he, she or those from, by, or under whom he or she claims, have acquired title or possession of the premises, except as provided in Sections 13–102 through 13–122 of this Act.

P.A. 82–280, § 13–101, eff. July 1, 1982.

Formerly Ill.Rev.Stat.1991, ch. 110, ¶ 13–101.

5/13–102.   Breach of condition subsequent

§ 13–102.   Breach of condition subsequent. No person shall commence an action for the recovery of lands, nor make an entry thereon, by reason of the breach of a condition subsequent, unless within 7 years after the time that condition is first broken. Continuing, successive or recurring breaches shall not extend the time for commencing the action or making the entry. Possession shall be deemed to be adverse and hostile from and after the first breach of a condition subsequent, notwithstanding the occurrence of successive or recurrent breaches.

P.A. 82–280, § 13–102, eff. July 1, 1982.

Formerly Ill.Rev.Stat.1991, ch. 110, ¶ 13–102.

5/13–103.   Termination of estate upon limitation

§ 13–103.   Termination of estate upon limitation. No person shall commence an action for the recovery of lands, nor make an entry thereon, by reason of the termination of an estate upon limitation or of an estate upon conditional limitation, unless within 7 years after the termination.

P.A. 82–280, § 13–103, eff. July 1, 1982.

Formerly Ill.Rev.Stat.1991, ch. 110, ¶ 13–103.

5/13–104.   Under mortgage or lease

§ 13–104.   Under mortgage or lease. Nothing in Sections 13–102 and 13–103 of this Act affects the time for the enforcement of any right under or by virtue of a mortgage or lease.

P.A. 82–280, § 13–104, eff. July 1, 1982.

Formerly Ill.Rev.Stat.1991, ch. 110, ¶ 13–104.

5/13–105.   Twenty years—Computation

§ 13–105.   Twenty years—Computation. If such right or title first accrued to an ancestor or predecessor of the person who brings the action or makes the entry, or to any person from, by, or under whom he or she claims, the 20 years shall be computed from the time when the right or title so first accrued.

P.A. 82–280, § 13–105, eff. July 1, 1982.

Formerly Ill.Rev.Stat.1991, ch. 110, ¶ 13–105.

5/13–106. Accrual of right of entry or to bring action

§ 13–106. Accrual of right of entry or to bring action. The right to make an entry or bring an action to recover land shall be deemed to have first accrued at the times respectively hereinafter provided:

(a) When any person is wrongfully ousted from possession, his or her right of entry or of action shall be deemed to have accrued at the time of such wrongful ouster.

(b) When he or she claims as heir or legatee of an owner in possession who died, his or her right shall be deemed to have accrued at the time of such death, unless there is an estate intervening after the death of such ancestor or testator; in which case his or her right shall be deemed to accrue when such intermediate estate expires, or when it would have expired by its own limitations.

(c) When there is such an intermediate estate, and in all other cases when the party claims by force of any remainder or reversion, his or her right, so far as it is affected by the limitation herein prescribed, shall be deemed to accrue when the intermediate or precedent estate would have expired by its own limitation, notwithstanding any forfeiture thereof for which he or she might have entered at an earlier time.

(d) Paragraph (c) of this Section shall not prevent a person from entering when entitled to do so by reason of any forfeiture or breach of condition; but if he or she claims under such a title, his or her right shall be deemed to have accrued when the forfeiture was incurred or the condition was broken.

(e) In all cases not otherwise specially provided for, the right shall be deemed to have accrued when the claimant, or the person under whom he or she claims, first became entitled to the possession of the premises under the title upon which the entry or the action is founded.

P.A. 82–280, § 13–106, eff. July 1, 1982. Amended by P.A. 84–549, § 22, eff. Sept. 18, 1985.

Formerly Ill.Rev.Stat.1991, ch. 110, ¶ 13–106.

5/13–107. Seven years with possession and record title

§ 13–107. Seven years with possession and record title. Actions brought for the recovery of any lands, tenements or hereditaments of which any person may be possessed by actual residence thereon for 7 successive years, having a connected title, deductible of

record, from this State or the United States, or from any public officer or other person authorized by the laws of this State to sell such land for the nonpayment of taxes, or from any sheriff, marshal, or other person authorized to sell such land for the enforcement of a judgment or under any order or judgment of any court shall be brought within 7 years next after possession is taken, but when the possessor acquires such title after taking such possession, the limitation shall begin to run from the time of acquiring title.

P.A. 82–280, § 13–107, eff. July 1, 1982.

Formerly Ill.Rev.Stat.1991, ch. 110, ¶ 13–107.

5/13–108. Right extended to heirs

§ 13–108. Right extended to heirs. The heirs, legatees and assigns of the person having such title and possession, shall have the same benefit of the preceding section as the person from whom the possession is derived.

P.A. 82–280, § 13–108, eff. July 1, 1982.

Formerly Ill.Rev.Stat.1991, ch. 110, ¶ 13–108.

5/13–109. Payment of taxes with color of title

§ 13–109. Payment of taxes with color of title. Every person in the actual possession of lands or tenements, under claim and color of title, made in good faith, and who for 7 successive years continues in such possession, and also, during such time, pays all taxes legally assessed on such lands or tenements, shall be held and adjudged to be the legal owner of such lands or tenements, to the extent and according to the purport of his or her paper title. All persons holding under such possession, by purchase, legacy or descent, before such 7 years have expired, and who continue such possession, and continue to pay the taxes as above set forth so as to complete the possession and payment of taxes for the term above set forth, are entitled to the benefit of this Section.

P.A. 82–280, § 13–109, eff. July 1, 1982. Amended by P.A. 88–45, Art III, § 3–130.8, eff. July 6, 1993.

Formerly Ill.Rev.Stat.1991, ch. 110, ¶ 13–109.

5/13–110. Vacant land—Payment of taxes with color of title

§ 13–110. Vacant land—Payment of taxes with color of title. Whenever a person having color of title, made in good faith, to vacant and unoccupied land, pays all taxes legally assessed thereon for 7 successive years, he or she shall be deemed and adjudged to be the legal owner of such vacant and unoccupied land, to the extent and according to the purport of his or her paper title. All persons holding under such taxpayer, by purchase, legacy or descent, before such 7 years expired, and who continue to pay the taxes, as above set out, so as to complete the payment of taxes for the term, are entitled to the benefit of this Section. However, if any person, having a better paper title to such vacant and unoccupied land, during the term of 7 years, pays the taxes assessed on such land for any one or more years of the term of 7 years, then such taxpayer, his or her heirs, legatees or assigns, shall not be entitled to the benefit of this Section.

P.A. 82–280, § 13–110, eff. July 1, 1982. Amended by P.A. 83–707, § 1, eff. Sept. 23, 1983; P.A. 98–756, § 725, eff. July 16, 2014.

Formerly Ill.Rev.Stat.1991, ch. 110, ¶ 13–110.

5/13–111. State and United States

§ 13–111. State and United States. Sections 13–109 and 13–110 of this Act shall not extend to lands or tenements owned by the United States or of this State, nor to school and seminary lands, nor to lands held for the use of religious societies, nor to lands held for any public purpose. Nor shall they extend to lands or tenements when there is an adverse title to such lands or tenements, and the holder of such adverse title is a minor, person under legal disability, imprisoned, out of the limits of the United States, and in the employment of the United States or of this State. Such person shall commence an action to recover such lands or tenements so possessed, as above set out, within 3 years after the several disabilities herein enumerated cease to exist, and shall prosecute such action to judgment, or in case of vacant and unoccupied land, shall, within the time last set out, pay to the person or persons who have paid the same, all the taxes, with interest thereon, at the rate of 12% per annum, that have been paid on such vacant and unimproved land.

The exceptions provided in this Section shall not apply to the provisions of Sections 13–118 through 13–121 of this Act.

P.A. 82–280, § 13–111, eff. July 1, 1982.

Formerly Ill.Rev.Stat.1991, ch. 110, ¶ 13–111.

5/13–112. Minors and persons under legal disability

§ 13–112. Minors and persons under legal disability. If, at the time when such right of entry or of action upon or for lands first accrues, the person entitled to such entry or action is a minor, or person under legal disability, imprisoned or absent from the United States in the service of the United States or of this State, such person or any one claiming from, by or under him or her, may make the entry or bring the action at any time within 2 years after such disability is removed, notwithstanding the time before limited in that behalf has expired.

The exceptions provided in this Section shall not apply to the provisions of Sections 13–118 through 13–121 of this Act.

P.A. 82–280, § 13–112, eff. July 1, 1982.

Formerly Ill.Rev.Stat.1991, ch. 110, ¶ 13–112.

5/13–113. Extension to heirs

§ 13–113. Extension to heirs. If the person first entitled to make entry or bring such action dies during the continuance of any of the disabilities mentioned in Section 13–112 of this Act, and no determination or judgment has been had of or upon the title, right or action which accrued to him or her, the entry may be made or the action brought by his or her heirs or any person claiming from, by or under him or her at any time within 2 years after his or her death, notwithstanding the time before limited in that behalf has expired.

The exceptions provided in this Section shall not apply to the provisions of Sections 13–118 through 13–121 of this Act.

P.A. 82–280, § 13–113, eff. July 1, 1982. Amended by P.A. 90–655, § 166, eff. July 30, 1998.

Formerly Ill.Rev.Stat.1991, ch. 110, ¶ 13–113.

5/13–114. Seventy-five year limitation

§ 13–114. Seventy-five year limitation. No deed, will, estate, proof of heirship, plat, affidavit or other instrument or document, or any court proceeding, order or judgment, or any agreement, written or unwritten, sealed or unsealed, or any fact, event, or statement, or any part or copy of any of the foregoing, relating to or affecting the title to real estate in the State of Illinois, which happened, was administered, or was executed, dated, delivered, recorded or entered into more than 75 years prior to July 1, 1872, or such subsequent date as the same is offered, presented, urged, claimed, asserted, or appears against any person hereafter becoming interested in the title to any real estate, or to any agent or attorney thereof, shall adversely to the party or parties hereafter coming into possession of such real estate under claim or color of title or persons claiming under him, her or them, constitute notice, either actual or constructive of any right, title, interest or claim in and to such real estate, or any part thereof, or be, or be considered to be evidence or admissible in evidence or be held or urged to make any title unmarketable in part or in whole, or be required or allowed to be alleged or proved as a basis for any action, or any statutory proceeding affecting directly or indirectly the title to such real estate.

The limitation of this Section, however, shall be deferred from and after the expiration of such 75 year period for an additional period of 10 years, if a claim in writing in and to real estate therein particularly described, incorporating the terms or substance of any such deed, will, estate, proof of heirship, plat, affidavit, or other instrument or document, or any court proceeding, order or judgment or any agreement, written or unwritten, sealed or unsealed, or any fact, event or statement, or any part or copy thereof in such claim, is filed in the office of the recorder in the county or counties in which such real estate is located:

1. within 3 years prior to the expiration of such 75 year period; or

2. after the expiration of such 75 year period, by a minor or a claimant under a legal disability who became under such disability during such 75 year period and within 2 years after the disability of such minor or of the claimant a under legal disability has been removed; or

3. after the expiration of such 75 year period, by a guardian of a minor or person who was determined by a court to be under a legal disability during such 75 year period and within 2 years after such guardian has been appointed for such minor or person under a legal disability.

The provisions of this Section shall not apply to or operate against the United States of America or the State of Illinois or any other state of the United States of America; or as to real estate held for a public purpose by any municipality or other political subdivision of the State of Illinois; or against any person under whom the party or parties in possession during the period herein permitted for reassertion of title claim by lease or other privity of contract; or against any person who during the entire period herein permitted for reassertion of title, or prior thereto, has not had the right to sue for and protect his or her claim, interest or title.

P.A. 82–280, § 13–114, eff. July 1, 1982. Amended by P.A. 83–358, § 76, eff. Sept. 14, 1983; P.A. 83–707, § 1, eff. Sept. 23, 1983; P.A. 83–1362, Art. II, § 109, eff. Sept. 11, 1984; P.A. 99–143, § 915, eff. July 27, 2015.

Formerly Ill.Rev.Stat.1991, ch. 110, ¶ 13–114.

5/13–115. Foreclosure of mortgage

§ 13–115. Foreclosure of mortgage. No person shall commence an action or make a sale to foreclose any mortgage or deed of trust in the nature of a mortgage, unless within 10 years after the right of action or right to make such sale accrues.

P.A. 82–280, § 13–115, eff. July 1, 1982.

Formerly Ill.Rev.Stat.1991, ch. 110, ¶ 13–115.

5/13–116. Lien of mortgage, trust or vendor's lien

§ 13–116. Lien of mortgage, trust or vendor's lien. (a) The lien of every mortgage, trust deed in the nature of a mortgage, and vendor's lien, the due date of which is stated upon the face, or ascertainable from the written terms thereof, filed for record either before or after July 16, 1941, which has not ceased by limitation before July 16, 1941, shall cease by limitation after the expiration of 20 years from the time the last payment on such mortgage, trust deed in the nature of a mortgage, or vendor's lien became or becomes due upon its face and according to its written

terms, unless the owner of such mortgage or vendor's lien, or the owner or trustee of such trust deed in the nature of a mortgage either

(1) Before July 16, 1941, and within such 20 year period has filed or caused to be filed for record an extension agreement showing the time for which the payment of the indebtedness is extended, and the amount remaining unpaid on such indebtedness; or

(2) After July 16, 1941, and within such 20 year period or within one year after July 21, 1947, provided the due date of the instrument was more than 19 years before July 21, 1947, files or causes to be filed for record, either (i) an affidavit executed by himself or herself or by some person on his or her behalf, stating the amount or amounts claimed to be unpaid on the indebtedness secured by such mortgage, trust deed in the nature of a mortgage, or vendor's lien; or (ii) an extension agreement executed as hereinafter provided.

(b) The lien of every mortgage, trust deed in the nature of a mortgage, and vendor's lien, in which no due date is stated upon the face, or is ascertainable from the written terms thereof, shall cease by limitation after the expiration of 30 years from the date of the instrument creating the lien, unless the owner of such mortgage or vendor's lien, or the owner or trustee of such trust deed in the nature of a mortgage, within such 30 year period or within one year after July 21, 1947, provided the date of the instrument was more than 29 years before July 21, 1947, files or causes to be filed for record either (1) an affidavit executed by himself or herself or by some person on his or her behalf, stating the amount or amounts claimed to be unpaid on the indebtedness secured by such mortgage, trust deed in the nature of a mortgage, or vendor's lien; or (2) an extension agreement executed as hereinafter provided.

The filing for record of an affidavit provided for by this Section, within such 20 or 30 year period or one year period, as the case may be, shall extend the lien for a period of 10 years after the date on which such lien would cease if neither an affidavit nor extension agreement were filed, and no more, and a subsequent affidavit filed within the last 10 year period of the lien, as extended, shall extend the lien for an additional 10 year period, and no more, but successive affidavits may be filed, each extending the lien 10 years.

The filing for record of an extension agreement within such 20 or 30 year period or one year period, as the case may be, whether before or after July 16, 1941, shall extend the lien for 10 years from the date the final payment becomes due under such extension agreement, and no more, but subsequent extension agreements filed before the lien, as extended, ceases, shall extend the lien for an additional 10 year period from the date the final payment becomes due under such extension agreement, and no more. The filing of an extension agreement shall not be construed in any way to cause the lien to cease before it would cease if neither an extension agreement nor an affidavit were filed. Affidavits may be followed by extension agreements, and extension agreements may be followed by affidavits.

An extension agreement executed after July 16, 1941, to be effective for the purpose of continuing the lien of any mortgage, trust deed in the nature of a mortgage, or vendor's lien shall show the time for which the payment of the indebtedness secured thereby is extended and the amount remaining unpaid on such indebtedness, and shall be executed and acknowledged by the owner of the mortgage, trust deed in the nature of a mortgage, or vendor's lien, or someone on his or her behalf, and by one or more persons representing himself, herself or themselves to be the then owners of the real estate. The affidavit or extension agreement shall be effective only as to the lands within the county or counties wherein such affidavit or extension agreement, or a copy thereof, is filed for record.

When a corporation is the owner or trustee of any such mortgage, trust deed in the nature of a mortgage, or vendor's lien, the affidavit herein described shall be deemed effective for all purposes under this Section when it has been executed by any officer of such corporation, or by any person authorized by the corporation to execute such affidavit.

The Section shall apply to mortgages, trust deeds in the nature of mortgages, and vendor's liens on both registered and unregistered lands. "Filed for record" or "the filing for record" as used in Article XIII of this Act means filing in the office of the recorder in the county in which the lands are situated, if such lands are unregistered, or in the office of the registrar of titles for such county, if such lands are registered. Nothing herein contained shall be construed to revive the lien of any such instrument which has expired by limitation before July 16, 1941.

P.A. 82–280, § 13–116, eff. July 1, 1982. Amended by P.A. 83–358, § 76, eff. Sept. 14, 1983; P.A. 83–707, § 1, eff. Sept. 23, 1983; P.A. 83–1362, Art. II, § 109, eff. Sept. 11, 1984.

Formerly Ill.Rev.Stat.1991, ch. 110, ¶ 13–116.

5/13–117. Limitation on mortgage

§ 13–117. Limitation on mortgage. The lien of every mortgage or trust deed in the nature of a mortgage of record on July 1, 1915, where more than 20 years have elapsed from the time the indebtedness secured thereby is due according to its written terms, or according to any extension agreement on record on July 1, 1915, is declared to have ceased by limitation unless the holder of the indebtedness secured thereby and the then owner of the real estate within 5 years after July 1, 1915, files in the office of the recorder where the mortgage or trust deed in the nature of a mortgage is recorded, an extension agreement showing the time for which the payment of the indebtedness is extended, the time when the indebtedness will

become due by the terms of the extension agreement and the amount remaining unpaid on the indebtedness, then the mortgage or trust deed in the nature of a mortgage shall continue to be a lien upon the real estate described therein for a period of 10 years from the time the indebtedness will be due as shown by the extension agreement and no longer, unless some further extension agreement is filed of record. Such extension agreements shall be acknowledged and recorded in the same manner as mortgages and trust deeds in the nature of a mortgage are required by law to be acknowledged and recorded.

P.A. 82–280, § 13–117, eff. July 1, 1982.

Formerly Ill.Rev.Stat.1991, ch. 110, ¶ 13–117.

5/13–118. Forty year limitation on claims to real estate

§ 13–118. Forty year limitation on claims to real estate. No action based upon any claim arising or existing more than 40 years before the commencement of such action shall be maintained in any court to recover any real estate in this State or to recover or establish any interest therein or claim thereto, against the holder of the record title to such real estate when such holder of the record title and his or her grantors immediate or remote are shown by the record to have held chain of title to such real estate for at least 40 years before the action is commenced, unless such claimant, by himself or herself, or by his or her attorney or agent, or if he or she is a minor or under legal disability, by his or her guardian, trustee, either parent, or any other person acting in his or her behalf shall within 40 years after the claim upon which such action is based arises, file in the office of the recorder of the county wherein such real estate is situated, a verified statement definitely describing the real estate involved, the nature and extent of the right or interest claimed, and stating the facts upon which the same is based. However, the holder of the record title to such real estate shall not be entitled to the protection of Sections 13–118 through 13–121 of this Act if the real estate is in the adverse possession of another.

For purposes of this Section an unborn or unascertained person may be a claimant and a verified statement may be filed on his or her behalf as provided in this Section.

For the purposes of Sections 13–118 through 13–121 of this Act, any person who holds title to real estate by will or descent from any person who held the title of record to such real estate at the date of his or her death or who holds title by judgment or order of any court, or by deed issued pursuant thereto, i.e., by trustee's, trustee's in bankruptcy, conservator's, guardian's, executor's, administrator's, receiver's, assignee's, master's in chancery, or sheriff's deed shall be deemed to hold chain of title the same as though holding by direct conveyance.

P.A. 82–280, § 13–118, eff. July 1, 1982. Amended by P.A. 83–358, § 76, eff. Sept. 14, 1983.

Formerly Ill.Rev.Stat.1991, ch. 110, ¶ 13–118.

5/13–119. Claim index

§ 13–119. Claim index. All claims filed in the office of the recorder as provided in Section 13–118 of this Act shall be recorded and indexed in the manner provided by law. In counties where the recorder is not required to keep a tract index, he or she shall index such claims in an index labelled "Claimant's Book". Such book shall be indexed under the name of the person filing the claim and under the name of the person against whom the claim is filed, if such person is named in the claim, followed in each instance by the document number of such claim (or the book and page wherein the same is recorded) and a description of the real estate involved.

P.A. 82–280, § 13–119, eff. July 1, 1982. Amended by P.A. 83–358, § 76, eff. Sept. 14, 1983.

Formerly Ill.Rev.Stat.1991, ch. 110, ¶ 13–119.

5/13–120. Limitation on sections

§ 13–120. Limitation on sections. Sections 13–118 through 13–121 of this Act shall not be applied:

1. to bar any lessor or his or her successor as reversioner of his or her right to possession on the expiration of any lease or any lessee or his or her successor of his or her rights in and to any lease; or

2. to bar or extinguish any interest created or held for any public utility purpose; or

3. to bar or extinguish any easement or interest in the nature of an easement, or any rights granted, reserved or excepted by any instrument creating such easement or interest, the existence of which such easement or interest either is apparent from or can be proved by physical evidences of its use, whether or not such physical evidences of its use are visible from the surface; or

4. to bar or extinguish any separate mineral estate or any rights, immunities and interests appurtenant or relating thereto; or

5. to bar any interest of a mortgagee or interest in the nature of that of a mortgagee where the due date of the mortgage is stated on the face, or ascertainable from the written terms thereof and is not barred by Section 13–116 of this Act.

6. to validate any encroachment on any street, highway or public waters.

Nothing contained in Sections 13–118 through 13–121 of this Act shall be construed to extend the period for the beginning of any action or the doing of any other required act under any statutes of limitation nor to affect the operation of any statutes or case law governing the recording or the failure to record any instruments affecting land.

No statement recorded or action filed pursuant to the provisions of Sections 13–118 through 13–121 of this Act shall affect real estate registered under "An Act concerning land titles" approved May 1, 1897, as amended;[1] and real estate heretofore or hereafter registered under "An Act concerning land titles" shall be subject to the terms thereof and all subsequent amendments thereto.

Sections 13–118 through 13–121 of this Act shall not be deemed to affect any right, title or interest of the United States unless the Congress shall assent to its operation in that behalf.

P.A. 82–280, § 13–120, eff. July 1, 1982.

Formerly Ill.Rev.Stat.1991, ch. 110, ¶ 13–120.
  [1] 765 ILCS 35/0.01 et seq.

5/13–121. Construction

§ 13–121. Construction. Sections 13–118 through 13–121 of this Act shall be liberally construed to effect the legislative purpose of simplifying and facilitating land title transactions by allowing persons to rely on a record chain of title as described in Section 13–118 of this Act, subject to such limitations as appear in Section 13–120 of this Act. The claims extinguished by Sections 13–118 through 13–121 of this Act include any and all interests of any nature whatsoever, however er denominated, whether vested or contingent, whether present or future, whether such claims are asserted by a person sui juris or under disability or might be asserted by a person not yet in being, whether such person be within or without the State, and whether such person be natural or corporate, or private or governmental.

Except as otherwise provided in Sections 13–118 through 13–121 of this Act, the rule that the State of Illinois is not bound by acts of limitations shall not apply to Sections 13–118 through 13–121 of this Act, and these Sections shall serve to bar any right, title, interest or lien in land which the State of Illinois or any department, commission or political subdivision thereof would otherwise have.

P.A. 82–280, § 13–121, eff. July 1, 1982.

Formerly Ill.Rev.Stat.1991, ch. 110, ¶ 13–121.

5/13–122. Posting of notice that right of access is by permission and subject to control of owner

§ 13–122. Posting of notice that right of access is by permission and subject to control of owner. No use of any land by any person or by the public generally, no matter how long continued, shall ever ripen into an easement by prescription, or be deemed to be an implied dedication, or be deemed to give rise to any other right, customary or otherwise, to be on, or to engage in activities on, such land, if the owner of such property for a continuous period posts at each entrance to the property or at intervals of not more than 200 feet along the boundary a sign reading substantially as follows: "Right of access by permission, and subject to control of owner".

If the entrances or boundaries of the property sought to be protected are paved, the sign referred to in this Section may be embedded in the pavement, provided that the inscription is legible and in letters at least as large as 24 point type.

The procedure provided in this Section does not constitute the exclusive method of preventing the use of land from creating an easement by prescription, an implied dedication or any other right to be on or to engage in activities on the land, but is in addition to any other methods now or hereafter provided by law. This Section shall not be applied retroactively to events which took place before October 1, 1975.

P.A. 82–280, § 13–122, eff. July 1, 1982.

Formerly Ill.Rev.Stat.1991, ch. 110, ¶ 13–122.

PART 2. PERSONAL ACTIONS

5/13–201. Defamation—Privacy

§ 13–201. Defamation—Privacy. Actions for slander, libel or for publication of matter violating the right of privacy, shall be commenced within one year next after the cause of action accrued.

P.A. 82–280, § 13–201, eff. July 1, 1982.

Formerly Ill.Rev.Stat.1991, ch. 110, ¶ 13–201.

5/13–202. Personal injury—Penalty

§ 13–202. Personal injury—Penalty. Actions for damages for an injury to the person, or for false imprisonment, or malicious prosecution, or for a statutory penalty, or for abduction, or for seduction, or for criminal conversation that may proceed pursuant to subsection (a) of Section 7.1 of the Criminal Conversation Abolition Act, except damages resulting from first degree murder or the commission of a Class X felony and the perpetrator thereof is convicted of such crime, shall be commenced within 2 years next after the cause of action accrued but such an action against a defendant arising from a crime committed by the defendant in whose name an escrow account was established under the "Criminal Victims' Escrow Account Act"[1] shall be commenced within 2 years after the establishment of such account. If the compelling of a confession or information by imminent bodily harm or threat of imminent bodily harm results in whole or in part in a criminal prosecution of the plaintiff, the 2–year period set out in this Section shall be tolled during the time in which the plaintiff is incarcerated, or until criminal prosecution has been finally adjudicated in favor of the above referred plaintiff, whichever is later. However, this provision relating to the compelling of a confession or information shall not apply to units of local government subject to the Local Governmental and Governmental Employees Tort Immunity Act.

P.A. 82–280, § 13–202, eff. July 1, 1982. Amended by P.A. 83–293, § 1, eff. Sept. 14, 1983; P.A. 84–1450, § 8, eff. July 1, 1987; P.A. 94–1113, § 110, eff. Jan. 1, 2008; P.A. 99–90, § 1–5, eff. Jan. 1, 2016.

Formerly Ill.Rev.Stat.1991, ch. 110, ¶ 13–202.
[1] 725 ILCS 145/1 et seq.

5/13–202.1. No limitations on certain actions—Duties of Department of Corrections and State's Attorneys

§ 13–202.1. No limitations on certain actions—Duties of Department of Corrections and State's Attorneys.

(a) Notwithstanding any other provision of law, any action for damages against a person, however the action may be designated, may be brought at any time if—

(1) the action is based upon conduct of a person which constituted the commission of first degree murder, a Class X felony, or a Class 1 felony as these terms are utilized at the time of filing of the action; and

(2) the person was convicted of the first degree murder, Class X felony, or Class 1 felony.

(b) The provisions of this Section are fully applicable to convictions based upon defendant's accountability under Section 5–2 of the Criminal Code of 1961 or the Criminal Code of 2012. [1]

(c) Paragraphs (a) and (b) above shall apply to any cause of action regardless of the date on which the defendant's conduct is alleged to have occurred or of the date of any conviction resulting therefrom. In addition, this Section shall be applied retroactively and shall revive causes of actions which otherwise may have been barred under limitations provisions in effect prior to the enactment and/or effect of P.A. 84–1450.

(d) Whenever there is any settlement, verdict or judgment in excess of $500 in any court against the Department of Corrections or any past or present employee or official in favor of any person for damages incurred while the person was committed to the Department of Corrections, the Department within 14 days of the settlement, verdict or judgment shall notify the State's Attorney of the county from which the person was committed to the Department. The State's Attorney shall in turn within 14 days after receipt of the notice send the same notice to the person or persons who were the victim or victims of the crime for which the offender was committed, at their last known address, along with the information that the victim or victims should contact a private attorney to advise them of their rights under the law.

(e) Whenever there is any settlement, verdict or judgment in excess of $500 in any court against any county or county sheriff or any past or present employee or official in favor of any person for damages incurred while the person was incarcerated in any county jail, the county or county sheriff, within 14 days of the settlement, verdict or judgment shall notify the State's Attorney of the county from which the person was incarcerated in the county jail. The State's Attorney shall within 14 days of receipt of the notice send the same notice to the person or persons who were the victim or victims of the crime for which the offender was committed, at their last known address, along with the information that the victim or victims should contact a private attorney to advise them of their rights under the law.

(f) No civil action may be brought by anyone against the Department of Corrections, a State's Attorney, a County, a county sheriff, or any past or present employee or agent thereof for any alleged violation by any such entity or person of the notification requirements imposed by paragraph (d) or (e).
P.A. 82–280, § 13–202.1, added by P.A. 83–1040, § 1, eff. Jan. 5, 1984. Amended by P.A. 84–1450, § 8, eff. July 1, 1987; P.A. 87–941, § 1, eff. Aug. 28, 1992; P.A. 89–8, Art. 5, § 5–20, eff. March 21, 1995; P.A. 90–655, § 166, eff. July 30, 1998; P.A. 95–975, § 5, eff. Jan. 1, 2009; P.A. 97–1150, § 705, eff. Jan. 25, 2013.

Formerly Ill.Rev.Stat.1991, ch. 110, ¶ 13–202.1.
[1] 720 ILCS 5/5–2.

Validity

Limitations provision added by P.A. 87–941 has been held by the Illinois Supreme Court to violate due process guarantees in the case of Sepmeyer v. Holman, 162 Ill.2d 249, 642 N.E.2d 1242, 205 Ill.Dec. 125 (1994).

5/13–202.2.   Childhood sexual abuse

§ 13–202.2. Childhood sexual abuse.

(a) In this Section:

"Childhood sexual abuse" means an act of sexual abuse that occurs when the person abused is under 18 years of age.

"Sexual abuse" includes but is not limited to sexual conduct and sexual penetration as defined in Section 11–0.1 of the Criminal Code of 2012. [1]

(b) Notwithstanding any other provision of law, an action for damages for personal injury based on childhood sexual abuse must be commenced within 20 years of the date the limitation period begins to run under subsection (d) or within 20 years of the date the person abused discovers or through the use of reasonable diligence should discover both (i) that the act of childhood sexual abuse occurred and (ii) that the injury was caused by the childhood sexual abuse. The fact that the person abused discovers or through the use of reasonable diligence should discover that the act of childhood sexual abuse occurred is not, by itself, sufficient to start the discovery period under this subsection (b). Knowledge of the abuse does not constitute discovery of the injury or the causal relationship between any later- discovered injury and the abuse.

(c) If the injury is caused by 2 or more acts of childhood sexual abuse that are part of a continuing series of acts of childhood sexual abuse by the same abuser, then the discovery period under subsection (b) shall be computed from the date the person abused discovers or through the use of reasonable diligence should discover both (i) that the last act of childhood sexual abuse in the continuing series occurred and (ii) that the injury was caused by any act of childhood sexual abuse in the continuing series. The fact that the person abused discovers or through the use of reasonable diligence should discover that the last act of childhood sexual abuse in the continuing series occurred is not, by itself, sufficient to start the discovery period under subsection (b). Knowledge of the abuse does not constitute discovery of the injury or the causal relationship between any later-discovered injury and the abuse.

(d) The limitation periods under subsection (b) do not begin to run before the person abused attains the age of 18 years; and, if at the time the person abused attains the age of 18 years he or she is under other legal disability, the limitation periods under subsection (b) do not begin to run until the removal of the disability.

(d–1) The limitation periods in subsection (b) do not run during a time period when the person abused is subject to threats, intimidation, manipulation, or fraud perpetrated by the abuser or by any person acting in the interest of the abuser.

(e) This Section applies to actions pending on the effective date of this amendatory Act of 1990 as well as to actions commenced on or after that date. The changes made by this amendatory Act of 1993 shall apply only to actions commenced on or after the effective date of this amendatory Act of 1993. The changes made by this amendatory Act of the 93rd General Assembly apply to actions pending on the effective date of this amendatory Act of the 93rd General Assembly as well as actions commenced on or after that date. The changes made by this amendatory Act of the 96th General Assembly apply to actions commenced on or after the effective date of this amendatory Act of the 96th General Assembly if the action would not have been time barred under any statute of limitations or statute of repose prior to the effective date of this amendatory Act of the 96th General Assembly.

(f) Notwithstanding any other provision of law, an action for damages based on childhood sexual abuse may be commenced at any time; provided, however, that the changes made by this amendatory Act of the 98th General Assembly apply to actions commenced on or after the effective date of this amendatory Act of the 98th General Assembly if the action would not have been time barred under any statute of limitations or statute of repose prior to the effective date of this amendatory Act of the 98th General Assembly.

P.A. 82–280, § 13–202.2, added by P.A. 86–1346, § 1, eff. Jan. 1, 1991. Amended by P.A. 88–127, § 5, eff. Jan. 1, 1994; P.A. 93–356, § 15, eff. July 24, 2003; P.A. 96–1093, § 5, eff. Jan. 1, 2011; P.A. 96–1551, Art. 2, § 1085, eff. July 1, 2011; P.A. 97–1150, § 705, eff. Jan. 25, 2013; P.A. 98–276, § 5, eff. Jan. 1, 2014.

Formerly Ill.Rev.Stat.1991, ch. 110, ¶ 13–202.2.
¹ 720 ILCS 5/11–0.1.

5/13–202.3. Limitation period in Section 13–202

§ 13–202.3. For an action arising out of an injury caused by "sexual conduct" or "sexual penetration" as defined in Section 11–0.1 of the Criminal Code of 2012, the limitation period in Section 13–202 does not run

during a time period when the person injured is subject to threats, intimidation, manipulation, or fraud perpetrated by the perpetrator or by a person the perpetrator knew or should have known was acting in the interest of the perpetrator. This Section applies to causes of action arising on or after the effective date of this amendatory Act of the 95th General Assembly or to causes of action for which the limitation period has not yet expired.

P.A. 82–280, § 13–202.3, added by P.A. 95–589, § 5, eff. Jan. 1, 2008. Amended by P.A. 96–1551, Art. 2, § 1085, eff. July 1, 2011; P.A. 97–1150, § 705, eff. Jan. 25, 2013.

5/13–203. Loss of consortium—Injury to person

§ 13–203. Loss of consortium—Injury to person. Actions for damages for loss of consortium or other actions, including actions for the medical expenses of minors or persons under legal disability, deriving from injury to the person of another, except damages resulting from first degree murder or the commission of a Class X felony, shall be commenced within the same period of time as actions for damages for injury to such other person. Where the time in which the cause of action of the injured person whose injuries give rise to the cause of action brought under this Section is tolled or otherwise extended by any other Section of this Act, including Sections 13–211, 13–212 and 13–215, the time in which the cause of action must be brought under this Section is also tolled or extended to coincide with the period of time in which the injured person must commence his or her cause of action.

P.A. 82–280, § 13–203, eff. July 1, 1982. Amended by P.A. 83–293, § 1, eff. Sept. 14, 1983; P.A. 84–1450, § 8, eff. July 1, 1987; P.A. 85–907, Art. II, § 1, eff. Nov. 23, 1987; P.A. 88–22, § 5, eff. Jan. 1, 1994.

Formerly Ill.Rev.Stat.1991, ch. 110, ¶ 13–203.

5/13–203a. § 13–203a. Renumbered as § 13–203.1 by P.A. 84–1043, § 1, eff. Nov. 26, 1985

5/13–203.1. Loss of means of support or parental relationships

§ 13–203.1. Loss of means of support or parental relationships. Actions for damages for loss of means of support or loss of parental or in loco parentis relationships sustained by a minor resulting from an injury described in Section 13–214.1 may be commenced no later than 10 years after the person who inflicted such injury has completed his sentence therefor.

P.A. 82–280, § 13–203a, added by P.A. 83–293, § 1, eff. Sept. 14, 1983. Renumbered as § 13–203.1 and amended by P.A. 84–1043, § 1, eff. Nov. 26, 1985.

Formerly Ill.Rev.Stat.1991, ch. 110, ¶ 13–203.1.

5/13–204. Contribution and indemnity

§ 13–204. Contribution and indemnity.

(a) In instances where no underlying action seeking recovery for injury to or death of a person or injury or damage to property has been filed by a claimant, no action for contribution or indemnity may be commenced with respect to any payment made to that claimant more than 2 years after the party seeking contribution or indemnity has made the payment in discharge of his or her liability to the claimant.

(b) In instances where an underlying action has been filed by a claimant, no action for contribution or indemnity may be commenced more than 2 years after the party seeking contribution or indemnity has been served with process in the underlying action or more than 2 years from the time the party, or his or her privy, knew or should reasonably have known of an act or omission giving rise to the action for contribution or indemnity, whichever period expires later.

(c) The applicable limitations period contained in subsection (a) or (b) shall apply to all actions for contribution or indemnity and shall preempt, as to contribution and indemnity actions only, all other statutes of limitation or repose, but only to the extent that the claimant in an underlying action could have timely sued the party from whom contribution or indemnity is sought at the time such claimant filed the underlying action, or in instances where no underlying action has been filed, the payment in discharge of the obligation of the party seeking contribution or indemnity is made before any such underlying action would have been barred by lapse of time.

(d) The provisions of this Section, as amended by Public Act 88–538, shall be applied retroactively when substantively applicable, including all pending actions without regard to when the cause of action accrued; provided, however, that this amendatory Act of 1994 shall not operate to affect statutory limitations or repose rights of any party which have fully vested prior to its effective date.

(e) The provisions of this Section shall not apply to any action for damages in which contribution or indemnification is sought from a party who is alleged to have been negligent and whose negligence has been alleged to have resulted in injuries or death by reason of medical or other healing art malpractice.

P.A. 82–280, § 13–204, eff. July 1, 1982. Amended by P.A. 88–538, § 5, eff. Jan. 1, 1995; P.A. 89–626, Art. 3, § 3–39, eff. Aug. 9, 1996.

Formerly Ill.Rev.Stat.1991, ch. 110, ¶ 13–204.

5/13–205. Five year limitation

§ 13–205. Five year limitation. Except as provided in Section 2–725 of the "Uniform Commercial Code", approved July 31, 1961, as amended,[1] and Section 11–13 of "The Illinois Public Aid Code", approved April 11, 1967, as amended,[2] actions on unwritten contracts, expressed or implied, or on awards of arbitration, or to recover damages for an injury done to property, real or personal, or to recover the possession of personal property or damages for the detention or conversion thereof, and all civil actions not otherwise provided for, shall be commenced within 5 years next after the cause of action accrued.

P.A. 82–280, § 13–205, eff. July 1, 1982.

Formerly Ill.Rev.Stat.1991, ch. 110, ¶ 13–205.
[1] 810 ILCS 5/2–725.
[2] 305 ILCS 5/11–13.

5/13–206. Ten year limitation

§ 13–206. Ten year limitation. Except as provided in Section 2–725 of the "Uniform Commercial Code",[1] actions on bonds, promissory notes, bills of exchange, written leases, written contracts, or other evidences of indebtedness in writing and actions brought under the Illinois Wage Payment and Collection Act shall be commenced within 10 years next after the cause of action accrued; but if any payment or new promise to pay has been made, in writing, on any bond, note, bill, lease, contract, or other written evidence of indebtedness, within or after the period of 10 years, then an action may be commenced thereon at any time within 10 years after the time of such payment or promise to pay. For purposes of this Section, with regard to promissory notes dated on or after the effective date of this amendatory Act of 1997, a cause of action on a promissory note payable at a definite date accrues on the due date or date stated in the promissory note or the date upon which the promissory note is accelerated. With respect to a demand promissory note dated on or after the effective date of this amendatory Act of 1997, if a demand for payment is made to the maker of the demand promissory note, an action to enforce the obligation of a party to pay the demand promissory note must be commenced within 10 years after the demand. An action to enforce a demand promissory note is barred if neither principal nor interest on the demand promissory note has been paid for a continuous period of 10 years and no demand for payment has been made to the maker during that period.

P.A. 82–280, § 13–206, eff. July 1, 1982. Amended by P.A. 90–451, § 5, eff. Jan. 1, 1998; P.A. 95–209, § 5, eff. Aug. 16, 2007.

Formerly Ill.Rev.Stat.1991, ch. 110, ¶ 13–206.
[1] 810 ILCS 5/2–725.

5/13–207. Counterclaim or set-off

§ 13–207. Counterclaim or set-off. A defendant may plead a set-off or counterclaim barred by the statute of limitation, while held and owned by him or her, to any action, the cause of which was owned by the plaintiff or person under whom he or she claims, before such set-off or counterclaim was so barred, and not otherwise. This section shall not affect the right of a bona fide assignee of a negotiable instrument assigned before due.

P.A. 82–280, § 13–207, eff. July 1, 1982. Amended by P.A. 83–707, § 1, eff. Sept. 23, 1983.

Formerly Ill.Rev.Stat.1991, ch. 110, ¶ 13–207.

5/13–208. Absence from State

§ 13–208. Absence from State. (a) If, when the cause of action accrues against a person, he or she is out of the state, the action may be commenced within the times herein limited, after his or her coming into or return to the state; and if, after the cause of action accrues, he or she departs from and resides out of the state, the time of his or her absence is no part of the time limited for the commencement of the action.

(b) For purposes of subsection (a) of this Section, no person shall be considered to be out of the State or to have departed from the State or to reside outside of the State during any period when he or she is subject to the jurisdiction of the courts of this State with respect to that cause of action pursuant to Sections 2–208 and 2–209 of this Act, Section 10–301 of "The Illinois Vehicle Code",[1] Section 5.25 of the "Business Corporation Act of 1983",[2] or any other statute authorizing service of process which would subject that person to the jurisdiction of the courts of this State. If a person files an action in a court of this State and attempts to secure service of process upon a defendant pursuant to a statute referred to in the preceding sentence, but does not obtain service of process upon such defendant, such defendant shall not be considered to be subject to the jurisdiction of the courts of this State at the time such action was filed, for purposes of the preceding sentence of this section. This subsection (b) of Section 13–208 of this Act shall apply only to actions commenced after October 1, 1973.

P.A. 82–280, § 13–208, eff. July 1, 1982. Amended by P.A. 83–707, § 1, eff. Sept. 23, 1983; P.A. 83–1362, Art. IV, § 20, eff. Sept. 11, 1984.

Formerly Ill.Rev.Stat.1991, ch. 110, ¶ 13–208.
[1] 625 ILCS 5/10–301.
[2] 805 ILCS 5/5.25.

5/13–209. Death of party

§ 13–209. Death of party.

(a) If a person entitled to bring an action dies before the expiration of the time limited for the commencement thereof, and the cause of action survives:

(1) an action may be commenced by his or her representative before the expiration of that time, or within one year from his or her death whichever date is the later;

(2) if no petition for letters of office for the decedent's estate has been filed, the court may appoint a special representative for the deceased for the purpose of prosecuting the action. The appointment shall be on verified motion of any party who appears entitled to participate in the deceased's estate, reciting the names and last known addresses of all known heirs and the legatees and executor named in any will that has been filed. The court's determination that a person appears entitled to participate in the deceased's estate shall be solely for purposes of this Section and not determinative of rights in final disposition. Within 90 days after appointment, the special representative shall notify the heirs and legatees of the following information by mail: that an appointment has been made, the court in which the case was filed, the caption of the case, and a description of the nature of the case. The special representative shall publish notice to unknown heirs and legatees as provided in the Probate Act of 1975.[1] If a will is filed within 90 days after the appointment of the special representative, the same notice shall be given to any additional executors and legatees named in the will. At any time that an estate is opened with a representative other than the special representative, the court may upon motion substitute the representative for the special representative. In this case, the court shall allow disbursements and fees of the special representative and his or her attorney as a claim against any proceeds received. The proceeds of any judgment or settlement shall be distributed under the provisions of the Probate Act of 1975.

(b) If a person against whom an action may be brought dies before the expiration of the time limited for the commencement thereof, and the cause of action survives, and is not otherwise barred:

(1) an action may be commenced against his or her personal representative after the expiration of the time limited for the commencement of the action, and within 6 months after the person's death;

(2) if no petition has been filed for letters of office for the deceased's estate, the court, upon the motion of a person entitled to bring an action and after the notice to the party's heirs or legatees as the court directs and without opening an estate, may appoint a special representative for the deceased party for the purposes of defending the action. If a party elects to have a special representative appointed under this paragraph (2), the recovery shall be limited to the proceeds of any liability insurance protecting the estate and shall not bar the estate from enforcing any claims that might have been available to it as counterclaims.

(c) If a party commences an action against a deceased person whose death is unknown to the party before the expiration of the time limited for the commencement thereof, and the cause of action survives, and is not otherwise barred, the action may be commenced against the deceased person's personal representative if all of the following terms and conditions are met:

(1) After learning of the death, the party proceeds with reasonable diligence to move the court for leave to file an amended complaint, substituting the personal representative as defendant.

(2) The party proceeds with reasonable diligence to serve process upon the personal representative.

(3) If process is served more than 6 months after the issuance of letters of office, liability of the estate is limited as to recovery to the extent the estate is protected by liability insurance.

(4) In no event can a party commence an action under this subsection (c) unless a personal representative is appointed and an amended complaint is filed within 2 years of the time limited for the commencement of the original action.

P.A. 82–280, § 13–209, eff. July 1, 1982. Amended by P.A. 83–707, § 1, eff. Sept. 23, 1983; P.A. 86–793, § 1, eff. Jan. 1, 1990; P.A. 86–815, § 2, eff. Sept. 7, 1989; P.A. 86–1028, Art. II, § 2–50, eff. Feb. 5, 1990; P.A. 90–111, § 5, eff. July 14, 1997.

Formerly Ill.Rev.Stat.1991, ch. 110, ¶ 13–209.

1 755 ILCS 5/1–1 et seq.

5/13–210. Foreign limitation

§ 13–210. Foreign limitation. When a cause of action has arisen in a state or territory out of this State, or in a foreign country, and, by the laws thereof, an action thereon cannot be maintained by reason of the lapse of time, an action thereon shall not be maintained in this State.

P.A. 82–280, § 13–210, eff. July 1, 1982. Amended by P.A. 83–707, § 1, eff. Sept. 23, 1983.

Formerly Ill.Rev.Stat.1991, ch. 110, ¶ 13–210.

5/13–211. Minors and persons under legal disability

§ 13–211. Minors and persons under legal disability.

(a) If the person entitled to bring an action, specified in Sections 13–201 through 13–210 of this Code, at the time the cause of action accrued, is under the age of 18 years or is under a legal disability, then he or she may bring the action within 2 years after the person attains the age of 18 years, or the disability is removed.

(b) If the person entitled to bring an action specified under Sections 13–201 through 13–210 of this Code is not under a legal disability at the time the cause of action accrues, but becomes under a legal disability before the period of limitations otherwise runs, the period of limitations is stayed until the disability is removed. This subsection (b) does not invalidate any statute of repose provisions contained in Sections 13–201, 13–202, 13–202.1, 13–202.2, 13–202.3, 13–203, 13–203.1, 13–204, 13–207, 13–208, 13–209, and 13–210 of this Code. In no event shall the period of limitations for a cause of action under Sec-

tion 13–205 or 13–206 of this Code be stayed in excess of 10 years from the date of the adjudication of legal disability. This subsection (b) applies to actions commenced or pending on or after the effective date of this amendatory Act of the 98th General Assembly.

P.A. 82–280, § 13–211, eff. July 1, 1982. Amended by P.A. 85–18, § 1, eff. July 20, 1987; P.A. 85–907, Art. II, § 1, eff. Nov. 23, 1987; P.A. 86–1329, § 4, eff. Jan. 1, 1991; P.A. 98–1077, § 5, eff. Jan. 1, 2015.

Formerly Ill.Rev.Stat.1991, ch. 110, ¶ 13–211.

5/13–212. Physician or hospital

§ 13–212. Physician or hospital.

(a) Except as provided in Section 13–215 of this Act, no action for damages for injury or death against any physician, dentist, registered nurse or hospital duly licensed under the laws of this State, whether based upon tort, or breach of contract, or otherwise, arising out of patient care shall be brought more than 2 years after the date on which the claimant knew, or through the use of reasonable diligence should have known, or received notice in writing of the existence of the injury or death for which damages are sought in the action, whichever of such date occurs first, but in no event shall such action be brought more than 4 years after the date on which occurred the act or omission or occurrence alleged in such action to have been the cause of such injury or death.

(b) Except as provided in Section 13–215 of this Act, no action for damages for injury or death against any physician, dentist, registered nurse or hospital duly licensed under the laws of this State, whether based upon tort, or breach of contract, or otherwise, arising out of patient care shall be brought more than 8 years after the date on which occurred the act or omission or occurrence alleged in such action to have been the cause of such injury or death where the person entitled to bring the action was, at the time the cause of action accrued, under the age of 18 years; provided, however, that in no event may the cause of action be brought after the person's 22nd birthday. If the person was under the age of 18 years when the cause of action accrued and, as a result of this amendatory Act of 1987, the action is either barred or there remains less than 3 years to bring such action, then he or she may bring the action within 3 years of July 20, 1987.

(c) If the person entitled to bring an action described in this Section is, at the time the cause of action accrued, under a legal disability other than being under the age of 18 years, then the period of limitations does not begin to run until the disability is removed.

(d) If the person entitled to bring an action described in this Section is not under a legal disability at the time the cause of action accrues, but becomes under a legal disability before the period of limitations otherwise runs, the period of limitations is stayed until the disability is removed. This subsection (d) does not invalidate any statute of repose provisions contained in this Section. This subsection (d) applies to actions commenced or pending on or after the effective date of this amendatory Act of the 98th General Assembly.

P.A. 82–280, § 13–212, eff. July 1, 1982. Amended by P.A. 82–783, Art. III, § 43, eff. July 13, 1982; P.A. 83–235, § 1, eff. Sept. 8, 1983; P.A. 85–18, § 1, eff. July 20, 1987; P.A. 85–907, Art. II, § 1, eff. Nov. 23, 1987; P.A. 86–1329, § 4, eff. Jan. 1, 1991; P.A. 98–1077, § 5, eff. Jan. 1, 2015.

Formerly Ill.Rev.Stat.1991, ch. 110, ¶ 13–212.

5/13–213. Product liability; statute of repose

§ 13–213. Product liability; statute of repose.

(a) As used in this Section, the term:

(1) "alteration, modification or change" or "altered, modified, or changed" means an alteration, modification or change that was made in the original makeup characteristics, function or design of a product or in the original recommendations, instructions and warnings given with respect to a product including the failure properly to maintain and care for a product.

(2) "product" means any tangible object or goods distributed in commerce, including any service provided in connection with the product. Where the term "product unit" is used, it refers to a single item or unit of a product.

(3) "product liability action" means any action based on any theory or doctrine brought against the seller of a product on account of personal injury, (including illness, disease, disability and death) or property, economic or other damage allegedly caused by or resulting from the manufacture, construction, preparation, assembly, installation, testing, makeup, characteristics, functions, design, formula, plan, recommendation, specification, prescription, advertising, sale, marketing, packaging, labeling, repair, maintenance or disposal of, or warning or instruction regarding any product. This definition excludes actions brought by State or federal regulatory agencies pursuant to statute.

(4) "seller" means one who, in the course of a business conducted for the purpose, sells, distributes, leases, assembles, installs, produces, manufactures, fabricates, prepares, constructs, packages, labels, markets, repairs, maintains, or otherwise is involved in placing a product in the stream of commerce.

(b) Subject to the provisions of subsections (c) and (d) no product liability action based on any theory or doctrine shall be commenced except within the applicable limitations period and, in any event, within 12 years from the date of first sale, lease or delivery of possession by a seller or 10 years from the date of first sale, lease or delivery of possession to its initial user, consumer, or other non-seller, whichever period expires earlier, of any product unit that is claimed to have injured or damaged the plaintiff, unless the defendant expressly has warranted or promised the product for a longer period and the action is brought within that period.

(c) No product liability action based on any theory or doctrine to recover for injury or damage claimed to have resulted from an alteration, modification or change of the product unit subsequent to the date of first sale, lease or delivery of possession of the product unit to its initial user, consumer or other non-seller shall be limited or barred by subsection (b) hereof if:

(1) the action is brought against a seller making, authorizing, or furnishing materials for the accomplishment of such alteration, modification or change (or against a seller furnishing specifications or instructions for the accomplishment of such alteration, modification or change when the injury is claimed to have resulted from failure to provide adequate specifications or instructions), and

(2) the action commenced within the applicable limitation period and, in any event, within 10 years from the date such alteration, modification or change was made, unless defendant expressly has warranted or promised the product for a longer period and the action is brought within that period, and

(3) when the injury or damage is claimed to have resulted from an alteration, modification or change of a product unit, there is proof that such alteration, modification or change had the effect of introducing into the use of the product unit, by reason of defective materials or workmanship, a hazard not existing prior to such alteration, modification or change.

(d) Notwithstanding the provisions of subsection (b) and paragraph (2) of subsection (c) if the injury complained of occurs within any of the periods provided by subsection (b) and paragraph (2) of subsection (c), the plaintiff may bring an action within 2 years after the date on which the claimant knew, or through the use of reasonable diligence should have known, of the existence of the personal injury, death or property damage, but in no event shall such action be brought more than 8 years after the date on which such personal injury, death or property damage occurred. In any such case, if the person entitled to bring the action was, at the time the personal injury, death or property damage occurred, under the age of 18 years, or under a legal disability, then the period of limitations does not begin to run until the person attains the age of 18 years, or the disability is removed.

(e) Replacement of a component part of a product unit with a substitute part having the same formula or design as the original part shall not be deemed a sale, lease or delivery of possession or an alteration, modification or change for the purpose of permitting commencement of a product liability action based on any theory or doctrine to recover for injury or damage claimed to have resulted from the formula or design of such product unit or of the substitute part when such action would otherwise be barred according to the provisions of subsection (b) of this Section.

(f) Nothing in this Section shall be construed to create a cause of action or to affect the right of any person to seek and obtain indemnity or contribution.

(g) The provisions of this Section 13–213 of this Act apply to any cause of action accruing on or after January 1, 1979, involving any product which was in or entered the stream of commerce prior to, on, or after January 1, 1979.

(h) This amendatory Act of 1995 applies to causes of action accruing on or after its effective date.

P.A. 82–280, § 13–213, eff. July 1, 1982. Amended by P.A. 83–707, § 1, eff. Sept. 23, 1983; P.A. 85–907, Art. II, § 1, eff. Nov. 23, 1987; P.A. 86–1329, § 4, eff. Jan. 1, 1991; P.A. 89–7, § 15, eff. March 9, 1995.

Formerly Ill.Rev.Stat.1991, ch. 110, ¶ 13–213.

Validity

Public Act 89–7, which amended this section, has been held unconstitutional in its entirety by the Illinois Supreme Court in the case of Best v. Taylor Machine Works, 1997, 689 N.E.2d 1057, 228 Ill.Dec. 636, 179 Ill.2d 367.

P.A. 89–7, in the section heading, added "; statute of repose"; substituted "any theory or doctrine" for "the doctrine of strict liability in tort" in four places; and added the paragraph relating to the applicability of this amendatory Act.

Prior to the amendment by P.A. 89–7, this section read:

"Product liability.

"(a) As used in this Section, the term:

"(1) 'alteration, modification or change' or 'altered, modified, or changed' means an alteration, modification or change that was made in the original makeup characteristics, function or design of a product or in the original recommendations, instructions and warnings given with respect to a product including the failure properly to maintain and care for a product.

"(2) 'product' means any tangible object or goods distributed in commerce, including any service provided in connection with the product. Where the term 'product unit' is used, it refers to a single item or unit of a product.

"(3) 'product liability action' means any action based on the doctrine of strict liability in tort brought against the seller of a product on account of personal injury, (including illness, disease, disability and death) or property, economic or other damage allegedly caused by or resulting from the manufacture, construction, preparation, assembly, installation, testing, makeup, characteristics, functions, design, formula, plan, recommendation, specification, prescription, advertising, sale, marketing, packaging, labeling, repair, maintenance or disposal of, or warning or instruction regarding any product. This definition excludes actions brought by State or federal regulatory agencies pursuant to statute.

"(4) 'seller' means one who, in the course of a business conducted for the purpose, sells, distributes, leases, assembles, installs, produces, manufactures, fabricates, prepares, constructs, packages, labels, markets, repairs, maintains, or otherwise is involved in placing a product in the stream of commerce.

"(b) Subject to the provisions of subsections (c) and (d) no product liability action based on the doctrine of strict liability in tort shall be commenced except within the applicable limitations period and, in any event, within 12 years from the date of first sale, lease or delivery of possession by a seller or 10 years from the date of first sale, lease or delivery of possession to its initial user, consumer, or other non-seller, whichever period expires earlier, of any product unit that is claimed to have injured or damaged the plaintiff, unless the defendant expressly has warranted or promised the product for a longer period and the action is brought within that period.

"(c) No product liability action based on the doctrine of strict liability in tort to recover for injury or damage claimed to have resulted from an alteration, modification or change of the product unit subsequent to the date of first sale, lease or delivery of possession of the product unit to its initial user, consumer or other non-seller shall be limited or barred by subsection (b) hereof if:

"(1) the action is brought against a seller making, authorizing, or furnishing materials for the accomplishment of such alteration, modification or change (or against a seller furnishing specifications or instructions for the accomplishment of such alteration, modification or change when the injury is claimed to have resulted from failure to provide adequate specifications or instructions), and

"(2) the action commenced within the applicable limitation period and, in any event, within 10 years from the date such alteration, modification or change was made, unless defendant expressly has warranted or promised the product for a longer period and the action is brought within that period, and

"(3) when the injury or damage is claimed to have resulted from an alteration, modification or change of a product unit, there is proof that such alteration, modification or change had the effect of introducing into the use of the product unit, by reason of defective materials or workmanship, a hazard not existing prior to such alteration, modification or change.

"(d) Notwithstanding the provisions of subsection (b) and paragraph (2) of subsection (c) if the injury complained of occurs within any of the periods provided by subsection (b) and paragraph (2) of subsection (c), the plaintiff may bring an action within 2 years after the date on which the claimant knew, or through the use of reasonable diligence should have known, of the existence of the personal injury, death or property damage, but in no event shall such action be brought more than 8 years after the date on which such personal injury, death or property damage occurred. In any such case, if the person entitled to bring the action was, at the time the personal injury, death or property damage occurred, under the age of 18 years, or under a legal disability, then the period of limitations does not begin to run until the person attains the age of 18 years, or the disability is removed.

"(e) Replacement of a component part of a product unit with a substitute part having the same formula or design as the original part shall not be deemed a sale, lease or delivery of possession or an alteration, modification or change for the purpose of permitting commencement of a product liability action based on the doctrine of strict liability in tort to recover for injury or damage claimed to have resulted from the formula or design of such product unit or of the substitute part when such action would otherwise be barred according to the provisions of subsection (b) of this Section.

"(f) Nothing in this Section shall be construed to create a cause of action or to affect the right of any person to seek and obtain indemnity or contribution.

"(g) The provisions of this Section 13–213 of this Act apply to any cause of action accruing on or after January 1, 1979, involving any product which was in or entered the stream of commerce prior to, on, or after January 1, 1979."

For applicability of P.A. 89–7, see note following 735 ILCS 5/2–402

Section 995 of P.A. 89–7, approved March 9, 1995, provides:

"Effective date. This Act takes effect upon becoming law, and applies to causes of action as specified in each Section or part of this Act."

5/13–214. Construction—Design management and supervision

§ 13–214. Construction—Design management and supervision. As used in this Section "person" means any individual, any business or legal entity, or any body politic.

(a) Actions based upon tort, contract or otherwise against any person for an act or omission of such person in the design, planning, supervision, observation or management of construction, or construction of an improvement to real property shall be commenced within 4 years from the time the person bringing an action, or his or her privity, knew or should reasonably have known of such act or omission. Notwithstanding any other provision of law, contract actions against a surety on a payment or performance bond shall be commenced, if at all, within the same time limitation applicable to the bond principal.

(b) No action based upon tort, contract or otherwise may be brought against any person for an act or omission of such person in the design, planning, supervision, observation or management of construction, or construction of an improvement to real property after 10 years have elapsed from the time of such act or omission. However, any person who discovers such act or omission prior to expiration of 10 years from the time of such act or omission shall in no event have less than 4 years to bring an action as provided in subsection (a) of this Section. Notwithstanding any other provision of law, contract actions against a surety on a payment or performance bond shall be commenced, if at all, within the same time limitation applicable to the bond principal.

(c) If a person otherwise entitled to bring an action could not have brought such action within the limitation periods herein solely because such person was under the age of 18 years, or a person with a developmental disability or a person with mental illness, then the limitation periods herein shall not begin to run until the person attains the age of 18 years, or the disability is removed.

(d) Subsection (b) shall not prohibit any action against a defendant who has expressly warranted or promised the improvement to real property for a longer period from being brought within that period.

(e) The limitations of this Section shall not apply to causes of action arising out of fraudulent misrepresentations or to fraudulent concealment of causes of action.

(f) Subsection (b) does not apply to an action that is based on personal injury, disability, disease, or death resulting from the discharge into the environment of asbestos.

P.A. 82–280, § 13–214, eff. July 1, 1982. Amended by P.A. 82–783, Art. III, § 43, eff. July 13, 1982; P.A. 83–707, § 1, eff. Sept. 23, 1983; P.A. 84–551, § 54A, eff. Sept. 18, 1985; P.A. 85–887, § 1, eff. Nov. 6, 1987; P.A. 85–907, Art. II, § 1, eff. Nov. 23, 1987; P.A. 85–1209, Art. II, § 2–53, eff. Aug. 30, 1988; P.A. 86–1329, § 4, eff. Jan. 1, 1991; P.A. 88–380, § 125, eff. Aug. 20, 1993; P.A. 98–1131, § 5, eff. June 1, 2015.

Formerly Ill.Rev.Stat.1991, ch. 110, ¶ 13–214.

5/13–214a. § 13–214a. Renumbered as § 13–214.1 by P.A. 84–1043, § 1, eff. Nov. 26, 1985

5/13–214.1. Action for damages involving criminal acts

§ 13–214.1. Action for damages involving criminal acts. Actions for damages for an injury described in Section 13–202 or Section 13–203 arising out of first degree murder or the commission of a Class X felony by the person against whom the action is brought may be commenced no later than 10 years after the person who inflicted such injury has completed his or her sentence therefor.

P.A. 82–280, § 13–214a, added by P.A. 83–293, § 1, eff. Sept. 14, 1983. Renumbered as § 13–214.1 and amended by P.A. 84–1043, § 1, eff. Nov. 26, 1985. Amended by P.A. 84–1450, § 8, eff. July 1, 1987; P.A. 85–293, Art. II, § 14, eff. Sept. 8, 1987.

Formerly Ill.Rev.Stat.1991, ch. 110, ¶ 13–214.1.

5/13–214.2. Public accounting

§ 13–214.2. (a) Actions based upon tort, contract or otherwise against any person, partnership or corporation registered pursuant to the Illinois Public Accounting Act, as amended,[1] or any of its employees, partners, members, officers or shareholders, for an act or omission in the performance of professional services shall be commenced within 2 years from the time the person bringing an action knew or should reasonably have known of such act or omission.

(b) In no event shall such action be brought more than 5 years after the date on which occurred the act or omission alleged in such action to have been the cause of the injury to the person bringing such action against a public accountant. Provided, however, that in the event that an income tax assessment is made or criminal prosecution is brought against a person, that person may bring an action against the public accountant who prepared the tax return within two years from the date of the assessment or conclusion of the prosecution.

(c) If a person entitled to bring the action is, at the time the cause of action accrues, under the age of 18, or under a legal disability, the period of limitations shall not begin to run until the disability is removed.

(d) This Section shall apply to all causes of action which accrue on or after its effective date.

P.A. 82–280, § 13–214.2, added by P.A. 85–655, § 1, eff. Sept. 20, 1987. Amended by P.A. 86–1329, § 4, eff. Jan. 1, 1991.

Formerly Ill.Rev.Stat.1991, ch. 110, ¶ 13–214.2.

[1] 225 ILCS 450/0.01 et seq.

5/13–214.3. Attorneys

§ 13–214.3. Attorneys.

(a) In this Section: "attorney" includes (i) an individual attorney, together with his or her employees who are attorneys, (ii) a professional partnership of attorneys, together with its employees, partners, and members who are attorneys, and (iii) a professional service corporation of attorneys, together with its employees, officers, and shareholders who are attorneys; and "non-attorney employee" means a person who is not an attorney but is employed by an attorney.

(b) An action for damages based on tort, contract, or otherwise (i) against an attorney arising out of an act or omission in the performance of professional services or (ii) against a non-attorney employee arising out of an act or omission in the course of his or her employment by an attorney to assist the attorney in performing professional services must be commenced within 2 years from the time the person bringing the action knew or reasonably should have known of the injury for which damages are sought.

(c) Except as provided in subsection (d), an action described in subsection (b) may not be commenced in any event more than 6 years after the date on which the act or omission occurred.

(d) When the injury caused by the act or omission does not occur until the death of the person for whom the professional services were rendered, the action may be commenced within 2 years after the date of the person's death unless letters of office are issued or the person's will is admitted to probate within that 2 year period, in which case the action must be commenced within the time for filing claims against the estate or a petition contesting the validity of the will of the deceased person, whichever is later, as provided in the Probate Act of 1975.

(e) If the person entitled to bring the action is under the age of majority or under other legal disability at the time the cause of action accrues, the period of limitations shall not begin to run until majority is attained or the disability is removed.

(f) If the person entitled to bring an action described in this Section is not under a legal disability at the time the cause of action accrues, but becomes under a legal disability before the period of limitations otherwise runs, the period of limitations is stayed until the disability is removed. This subsection (f) does not invalidate any statute of repose provisions contained in this Section. This subsection (f) applies to actions commenced or pending on or after the effective date of this amendatory Act of the 98th General Assembly.

(g) This Section applies to all causes of action accruing on or after its effective date.

P.A. 82–280, § 13–214.3, added by P.A. 86–1371, § 1, eff. Jan. 1, 1991. Amended by P.A. 89–7, § 15, eff. March 9, 1995; P.A. 98–1077, § 5, eff. Jan. 1, 2015.

Formerly Ill.Rev.Stat.1991, ch. 110, ¶ 13–214.3.

Validity

Public Act 89–7, which amended this section, has been held unconstitutional in its entirety by the Illinois Supreme Court in the case of Best v. Taylor Machine Works, 1997, 689 N.E.2d 1057, 228 Ill.Dec. 636, 179 Ill.2d 367. Morris v. Margulis, App. 5 Dist.1999, 241 Ill.Dec. 138, 307 Ill.App.3d 1024, 718 N.E.2d 709, rehearing denied, appeal allowed 244 Ill.Dec. 185, 187 Ill.2d 571, 724 N.E.2d 1269, reversed 257 Ill.Dec. 656, 197 Ill.2d 28, 754 N.E.2d 314, provided, in part, that the text of the section prior to amendment by P.A. 89–7 was reinstated. Morris was reversed on other grounds. See Historical and Statutory Notes, post, for the text of this section as it read prior to amendment by P.A. 89–7. The amendment by P.A. 98–1077 was made without the text of changes made by P.A. 89–7, which had been held unconstitutional.

P.A. 89–7 rewrote this section, which prior thereto read: "Attorneys.

"(a) In this Section: 'attorney' includes (i) an individual attorney, together with his or her employees who are attorneys, (ii) a professional partnership of attorneys, together with its employees, partners, and members who are attorneys, and (iii) a professional service corporation of attorneys, together with its employees, officers, and shareholders who are attorneys; and 'non-attorney employee' means a person who is not an attorney but is employed by an attorney.

"(b) An action for damages based on tort, contract, or otherwise (i) against an attorney arising out of an act or omission in the performance of professional services or (ii) against a non-attorney employee arising out of an act or omission in the course of his or her employment by an attorney to assist the attorney in performing professional services must be commenced within 2 years from the time the person bringing the action knew or reasonably should have known of the injury for which damages are sought.

"(c) Except as provided in subsection (d), an action described in subsection (b) may not be commenced in any event more than 6 years after the date on which the act or omission occurred.

"(d) When the injury caused by the act or omission does not occur until the death of the person for whom the professional services were rendered, the action may be commenced within 2 years after the date of the person's death unless letters of office are issued or the person's will is admitted to probate within that 2 year period, in which case the action must be commenced within the time for filing claims against the estate or a petition contesting the validity of the will of the deceased person, whichever is later, as provided in the Probate Act of 1975.

"(e) If the person entitled to bring the action is under the age of majority or under other legal disability at the time the cause of action accrues, the period of limitations shall not begin to run until majority is attained or the disability is removed.

"(f) This Section applies to all causes of action accruing on or after its effective date."

For applicability of P.A. 89–7, see note following 735 ILCS 5/2–402 Section 995 of P.A. 89–7, approved March 9, 1995, provides:

"Effective date. This Act takes effect upon becoming law, and applies to causes of action as specified in each Section or part of this Act."

5/13–214.4. Actions against insurance producers, limited insurance representatives, and registered firms

§ 13–214.4. Actions against insurance producers, limited insurance representatives, and registered firms. All causes of action brought by any person or entity under any statute or any legal or equitable theory against an insurance producer, registered firm, or limited insurance representative concerning the sale, placement, procurement, renewal, cancellation of, or failure to procure any policy of insurance shall be brought within 2 years of the date the cause of action accrues.

P.A. 82–280, § 13–214.4, added by P.A. 89–152, § 5, eff. Jan. 1, 1996.

5/13–215. Fraudulent concealment

§ 13–215. Fraudulent concealment. If a person liable to an action fraudulently conceals the cause of such action from the knowledge of the person entitled thereto, the action may be commenced at any time within 5 years after the person entitled to bring the same discovers that he or she has such cause of action, and not afterwards.

P.A. 82–280, § 13–215, eff. July 1, 1982.

Formerly Ill.Rev.Stat.1991, ch. 110, ¶ 13–215.

5/13–216. Stay of action

§ 13–216. Stay of action. When the commencement of an action is stayed by injunction, order of a court, or statutory prohibition, the time of the continuance of the injunction or prohibition is not part of the time limited for the commencement of the action.

P.A. 82–280, § 13–216, eff. July 1, 1982.

Formerly Ill.Rev.Stat.1991, ch. 110, ¶ 13–216.

5/13–217. Reversal or dismissal

§ 13–217. Reversal or dismissal. In the actions specified in Article XIII of this Act or any other act or contract where the time for commencing an action is limited, if judgment is entered for the plaintiff but reversed on appeal, or if there is a verdict in favor of the plaintiff and, upon a motion in arrest of judgment, the judgment is entered against the plaintiff, or the action is dismissed by a United States District Court for lack of jurisdiction, or the action is dismissed by a United States District Court for improper venue, then, whether or not the time limitation for bringing such action expires during the pendency of such action, the plaintiff, his or her heirs, executors or administrators may commence a new action within one year or within the remaining period of limitation, whichever is greater, after such judgment is reversed or entered against the plaintiff, or the action is dismissed by a United States District Court for lack of jurisdiction, or the action is dismissed by a United States District Court for improper venue. No action which is voluntarily dismissed by the plaintiff or dismissed for want of prosecution by the court may be filed where the time for commencing the action has expired.

This amendatory Act of 1995 applies to causes of action accruing on or after its effective date.

P.A. 82–280, § 13–217, eff. July 1, 1982. Amended by P.A. 87–1252, § 2, eff. Jan. 7, 1993; P.A. 89–7, § 15, eff. March 9, 1995.

Formerly Ill.Rev.Stat.1991, ch. 110, ¶ 13–217.

Validity

Public Act 89–7, which amended this section, has been held unconstitutional in its entirety by the Illinois Supreme Court in the case of Best v. Taylor Machine Works, 1997, 689 N.E.2d 1057, 228 Ill.Dec. 636, 179 Ill.2d 367.

P.A. 89–7, in the paragraph relating to the ability to commence a new action following reversal or dismissal, in the first sentence, deleted "or the action is voluntarily dismissed by the plaintiff, or the action is dismissed for want of prosecution," following "the judgment is entered against the plaintiff," and "or after the action is voluntarily dismissed by the plaintiff, or the action is dismissed for want of prosecution," following "reversed or entered against the plaintiff,", and added the second sentence; and added the paragraph relating to the applicability of this amendatory Act.

Prior to amendment by P.A. 89–7, this section read:

"Reversal or dismissal. In the actions specified in Article XIII of this Act or any other act or contract where the time for commencing an action is limited, if judgment is entered for the plaintiff but reversed on appeal, or if there is a verdict in favor of the plaintiff and, upon a motion in arrest of judgment, the judgment is entered against the plaintiff, or the action is voluntarily dismissed by the plaintiff, or the action is dismissed for want of prosecution, or the action is dismissed by a United States District Court for lack of jurisdiction, or the action is dismissed by a United States District Court for improper venue, then, whether or not the time limitation for bringing such action expires during the pendency of such action, the plaintiff, his or her heirs, executors or administrators may commence a new action within one year or within the remaining period of limitation, whichever is greater, after such judgment is reversed or entered against the plaintiff, or after the action is voluntarily dismissed by the plaintiff, or the action is dismissed for want of prosecution, or the action is dismissed by a United States District Court for lack of jurisdiction, or the action is dismissed by a United States District Court for improper venue."

For applicability of P.A. 89–7, see note following 735 ILCS 5/2–402

Section 995 of P.A. 89–7, approved March 9, 1995, provides:

"Effective date. This Act takes effect upon becoming law, and applies to causes of action as specified in each Section or part of this Act."

5/13–218. Revival of judgment

§ 13–218. Revival of judgment. A petition to revive a judgment, as provided by Section 2–1601 of this Code, may be filed no later than 20 years next after the date of entry of such judgment. The provisions of this amendatory Act of the 96th General Assembly are declarative of existing law.

P.A. 82–280, § 13–218, eff. July 1, 1982. Amended by P.A. 83–1362, Art. IV, § 20, eff. Sept. 11, 1984; P.A. 96–305, § 5, eff. Aug. 11, 2009.

Formerly Ill.Rev.Stat.1991, ch. 110, ¶ 13–218.

5/13–219. Railroads and carriers

§ 13–219. Railroads and carriers. (a) All actions by railroads, motor carriers, common carriers by water, common carriers by air, the Railway Express Agency or freight forwarders for the recovery of their charges, or any part thereof, for the transportation of property moving wholly within the State of Illinois shall be filed within 3 years from the time the cause of action accrues, and not after.

(b) All actions against railroads, motor carriers, common carriers by water, common carriers by air, the Railway Express Agency or freight forwarders for the recovery of any part of transportation charges paid to such carrier for the transportation of property moving wholly within the State of Illinois shall be filed within 3 years from the time the cause of action accrues, and not after.

(c) If on or before the expiration of the 3 year period of limitation in subsection (b) a railroad, motor carrier, common carrier by water, common carrier by air, the Railway Express Agency or a freight forwarder files an action under subsection (a) for recovery of charges in respect of the same transportation service, or, without filing an action, collects charges in respect of that service, the period of limitation shall be extended to include 90 days from the time such action is filed or such charges are collected.

(d) The cause of action in respect of a shipment of property shall, for the purposes of this section, be deemed to accrue upon delivery or tender of delivery thereof by a railroad, motor carrier, common carrier by water, common carrier by air, the Railway Express Agency, or a freight forwarder, and not after.
P.A. 82–280, § 13–219, eff. July 1, 1982.

Formerly Ill.Rev.Stat.1991, ch. 110, ¶ 13–219.

5/13–220. Fraud by decedents

§ 13–220. Fraud by decedents. Actions under Sections 10 to 14, both inclusive, of "An Act to revise the law in relation to frauds and perjuries", approved February 16, 1874, as amended,[1] shall be commenced within 2 years after the death of the person who makes a fraudulent legacy as provided in that Act, or who dies intestate and leaves real estate to his or her heirs to descend according to the laws of this State, unless letters of office are applied for on his or her estate within 2 years after his or her death and the representative has complied with the provisions of Section 18–3 of the Probate Act of 1975, as amended,[2] in regard to the giving of notice to creditors, in which case the action shall be commenced within and not after the time for presenting claims against estates of deceased persons as provided in the Probate Act of 1975, as amended.[3]
P.A. 82–280, § 13–220, eff. July 1, 1982. Amended by P.A. 83–707, § 1, eff. Sept. 23, 1983; P.A. 86–815, § 2, eff. Sept. 7, 1989.

Formerly Ill.Rev.Stat.1991, ch. 110, ¶ 13–220.
[1] 740 ILCS 80/10 to 80/14.
[2] 755 ILCS 5/18–3.
[3] 755 ILCS 5/1–1 et seq.

5/13–221. Contract to make will

§ 13–221. Contract to make will. An action against the representative, heirs and legatees of a deceased person to enforce a contract to make a will, shall be commenced within 2 years after the death of the deceased person unless letters of office are applied for on his or her estate within 2 years after his or her death and the representative has complied with the provisions of Section 18–3 of the Probate Act of 1975, as amended,[1] in regard to the giving of notice to creditors, in which case the action shall be commenced within and not after the time for presenting a claim against the estate of a deceased person as provided in the Probate Act of 1975, as amended.[2]

P.A. 82–280, § 13–221, eff. July 1, 1982. Amended by P.A. 83–707, § 1, eff. Sept. 23, 1983; P.A. 86–815, § 2, eff. Sept. 7, 1989.

Formerly Ill.Rev.Stat.1991, ch. 110, ¶ 13–221.
[1] 755 ILCS 5/18–3.
[2] 755 ILCS 5/1–1 et seq.

5/13–222. Action against land surveyor

§ 13–222. Action against land surveyor.

(a) Registered land surveyor. No action may be brought against a Registered Land Surveyor to recover damages for negligence, errors or omissions in the making of any survey nor for contribution or indemnity related to such negligence, errors or omissions more than 4 years after the person claiming such damages actually knows or should have known of such negligence, errors or omissions. This Section applies to surveys completed after July 26, 1967. This subsection (a) applies only to causes of action accruing before the effective date of this amendatory Act of the 92nd General Assembly.

(b) Professional land surveyor. No action may be brought against a professional land surveyor to recover damages for negligence, errors, omissions, torts, breaches of contract, or otherwise in the making of any survey, nor contribution or indemnity, more than 4 years after the person claiming the damages actually knows or should have known of the negligence, errors, omissions, torts, breaches of contract, or other action.

In no event may such an action be brought if 10 years have elapsed from the time of the act or omission. Any person who discovers the act or omission before expiration of the 10–year period, however, may in no event have less than 4 years to bring an action. Contract actions against a surety on a payment or performance bond must be commenced within the same time limitation applicable to the bond principal.

If the person entitled to bring the action is under the age of 18 or under a legal disability, the period of limitation does not begin to run until the person reaches 18 years of age or the disability is removed.

This subsection (b) applies to causes of action accruing on or after the effective date of this amendatory Act of the 92nd General Assembly.

P.A. 82–280, § 13–222, eff. July 1, 1982. Amended by P.A. 92–265, § 5, eff. Jan. 1, 2002.

Formerly Ill.Rev.Stat.1991, ch. 110, ¶ 13–222.

5/13–223. Inter vivos trusts

§ 13–223. Inter vivos trusts. An action to set aside or contest the validity of a revocable inter vivos trust agreement or declaration of trust to which a legacy is provided by the settlor's will which is admitted to probate, shall be commenced within and not after the time to contest the validity of a will as provided in the Probate Act of 1975 as amended.[1]

P.A. 82–280, § 13–223, eff. July 1, 1982. Amended by P.A. 83–707, § 1, eff. Sept. 23, 1983.

Formerly Ill.Rev.Stat.1991, ch. 110, ¶ 13–223.

[1] 755 ILCS 5/1–1 et seq.

5/13–224. Recovery in Tax Actions

§ 13–224. Recovery in Tax Actions. In any action against the State to recover taxes imposed pursuant to Section 2 of the Messages Tax Act,[1] Section 2 of the Gas Revenue Tax Act,[2] Section 2 of the Public Utilities Revenue Act[3] or Section 2–202 of The Public Utilities Act[4], that were illegally or unconstitutionally collected, or in any action against a municipality to recover taxes imposed pursuant to Section 8–11–2 of the Illinois Municipal Code[5] that were illegally or unconstitutionally collected or in any action against a taxpayer to recover charges imposed pursuant to Sections 9–201 or 9–202 of The Public Utilities Act[6] that were illegally or unconstitutionally collected, the prevailing party shall not be entitled to recover an amount exceeding such taxes or charges paid, plus interest, where applicable, during a period beginning 3 years prior to the date of filing an administrative claim as authorized by statute or ordinance or court complaint, whichever occurs earlier. This provision shall be applicable to all actions filed on or after September 21, 1985.

P.A. 82–280, § 13–224, added by P.A. 84–732, § 1, eff. Sept. 21, 1985. Amended by P.A. 85–1209, Art. III, § 3–69, eff. Aug. 30, 1988.

Formerly Ill.Rev.Stat.1991, ch. 110, ¶ 13–224.

[1] Former Ill.Rev.Stat. ch. 120, ¶ 467.2 (repealed).
[2] 35 ILCS 615/2.
[3] 35 ILCS 620/2 (repealed).
[4] 220 ILCS 5/2–202.
[5] 65 ILCS 5/8–11–2.
[6] 220 ILCS 5/9–201 or 5/9–202.

5/13–225. Predator accountability

§ 13–225. Predator accountability.

(a) In this Section, "sex trade" and "victim of the sex trade" have the meanings ascribed to them in Section 10 of the Predator Accountability Act.

(b) Subject to both subsections (e) and (f) and notwithstanding any other provision of law, an action under the Predator Accountability Act must be commenced within 10 years of the date the limitation period begins to run under subsection (d) or within 10 years of the date the plaintiff discovers or through the use of reasonable diligence should discover both (i) that the sex trade act occurred, and (ii) that the defendant caused, was responsible for, or profited from the sex trade act. The fact that the plaintiff discovers or through the use of reasonable diligence should discover that the sex trade act occurred is not, by itself, sufficient to start the discovery period under this subsection (b).

(c) If the injury is caused by 2 or more acts that are part of a continuing series of sex trade acts by the same defendant, then the discovery period under subsection (b) shall be computed from the date the person abused discovers or through the use of reasonable diligence should discover (i) that the last sex trade act in the continuing series occurred, and (ii) that the defendant caused, was responsible for, or profited from the series of sex trade acts. The fact that the plaintiff discovers or through the use of reasonable diligence should discover that the last sex trade act in the continuing series occurred is not, by itself, sufficient to start the discovery period under subsection (b).

(d) The limitation periods in subsection (b) do not begin to run before the plaintiff attains the age of 18 years; and, if at the time the plaintiff attains the age of 18 years he or she is under other legal disability, the limitation periods under subsection (b) do not begin to run until the removal of the disability.

(e) The limitation periods in subsection (b) do not run during a time period when the plaintiff is subject to threats, intimidation, manipulation, or fraud perpetrated by the defendant or by any person acting in the interest of the defendant.

(f) The limitation periods in subsection (b) do not commence running until the expiration of all limitations periods applicable to the criminal prosecution of the plaintiff for any acts which form the basis of a cause of action under the Predator Accountability Act.

P.A. 82–280, § 13–225, added by P.A. 94–998, § 80, eff. July 3, 2006.

ARTICLE XIV. MANDAMUS

5/14–101. Action commenced by plaintiff

§ 14–101. Action commenced by plaintiff. In all proceedings commenced under Article XIV of this Act the name of the person seeking the relief afforded by this Article shall be set out as plaintiff without the use of the phrase "People ex rel." or "People on the relation of".

P.A. 82–280, § 14–101, eff. July 1, 1982. Amended by P.A. 83–707, § 1, eff. Sept. 23, 1983.

Formerly Ill.Rev.Stat.1991, ch. 110, ¶ 14–101.

5/14–102. Summons to issue

§ 14–102. Summons to issue. Upon the filing of a complaint for mandamus the clerk of the court shall issue a summons, in like form, as near as may be as summons in other civil cases. The summons shall be made returnable within a time designated by the plaintiff not less than 5 nor more than 30 days after the service of the summons.

P.A. 82–280, § 14–102, eff. July 1, 1982. Amended by P.A. 83–357, § 1, eff. Sept. 14, 1983.

Formerly Ill.Rev.Stat.1991, ch. 110, ¶ 14–102.

5/14–103. Defendant to plead

§ 14–103. Defendant to plead. Every defendant who is served with summons shall answer or otherwise plead on or before the return day of the summons, unless the time for doing so is extended by the court. If the defendant defaults, judgment by default may be entered by the court. No matters not germane to the distinctive purpose of the proceeding shall be introduced by joinder, counterclaim or otherwise.

P.A. 82–280, § 14–103, eff. July 1, 1982. Amended by P.A. 90–655, § 166, eff. July 30, 1998.

Formerly Ill.Rev.Stat.1991, ch. 110, ¶ 14–103.

5/14–104. Reply by plaintiff

§ 14–104. Reply by plaintiff. The plaintiff may reply or otherwise plead to the answer, within 5 days after the last day allowed for the filing of the answer, unless the time for doing so is extended and further pleadings may be had as in other civil cases.

P.A. 82–280, § 14–104, eff. July 1, 1982.

Formerly Ill.Rev.Stat.1991, ch. 110, ¶ 14–104.

5/14–105. Judgment—Costs

§ 14–105. Judgment—Costs. If judgment is entered in favor of the plaintiff, the plaintiff shall recover damages and costs. If judgment is entered in favor of the defendant, the defendant shall recover costs.

P.A. 82–280, § 14–105, eff. July 1, 1982.

Formerly Ill.Rev.Stat.1991, ch. 110, ¶ 14–105.

5/14–106. False return

§ 14–106. False return. If damages are recovered against the defendant, the defendant shall not be liable to be sued in any other action or proceeding for making a false return.

P.A. 82–280, § 14–106, eff. July 1, 1982.

Formerly Ill.Rev.Stat.1991, ch. 110, ¶ 14–106.

5/14–107. Successor in office

§ 14–107. Successor in office. The death, resignation or removal from office, by lapse of time or otherwise, of any defendant, shall not have the effect to abate the proceeding, and upon a proper showing, the officer's successor may be made a party thereto, and any relief may be directed against the successor officer.

P.A. 82–280, § 14–107, eff. July 1, 1982.

Formerly Ill.Rev.Stat.1991, ch. 110, ¶ 14–107.

5/14–108. Other remedy—Amendments

§ 14–108. Other remedy—Amendments. The proceedings for mandamus shall not be dismissed nor the relief denied because the plaintiff may have another judicial remedy, even where such other remedy will afford proper and sufficient relief; and amendments may be allowed as in other civil cases.

P.A. 82–280, § 14–108, eff. July 1, 1982.

Formerly Ill.Rev.Stat.1991, ch. 110, ¶ 14–108.

5/14–109. Seeking wrong remedy not fatal

§ 14–109. Seeking wrong remedy not fatal. Where relief is sought under Article XIV of this Act and the court determines, on motion directed to the pleadings, or on motion for summary judgment or upon trial, that the plaintiff has pleaded or established facts which entitle the plaintiff to relief but that the plaintiff has sought the wrong remedy, the court shall permit the pleadings to be amended, on just and reasonable terms, and the court shall grant the relief to which the plaintiff is entitled on the amended pleadings or upon the evidence. In considering whether a proposed amendment is just and reasonable, the court shall consider the right of the defendant to assert additional defenses, to demand a trial by jury, to plead a counterclaim or third party complaint, and to order the plaintiff to take additional steps which were not required under the pleadings as previously filed.

P.A. 82–280, § 14–109, eff. July 1, 1982.

Formerly Ill.Rev.Stat.1991, ch. 110, ¶ 14–109.

ARTICLE XV. MORTGAGE FORECLOSURE

PART 1. IN GENERAL

5/15–101 to 5/15–117. §§ 15–101 to 15–117. Repealed by P.A. 84–1462, § 7, eff. July 1, 1987; P.A. 85–293, Art. II, § 23, eff. Sept. 8, 1987

PART 2. JUDGMENT ON MOTION

5/15–201. § 15–201. Repealed by P.A. 84–1462, § 7, eff. July 1, 1987

PART 3. POSSESSION OF REALTY AFTER DEFAULT

5/15–301 to 5/15–311. §§ 15–301 to 15–311. Repealed by P.A. 84–1462, § 7, eff. July 1, 1987; P.A. 85–293, Art. II, § 23, eff. Sept. 8, 1987

PART 11. GENERAL PROVISIONS

Date Effective

Part 11 was added by P.A. 84–1462, § 2, eff. July 1, 1987.

5/15–1101. Title

§ 15–1101. Title. This Article shall be known, and may be cited, as the Illinois Mortgage Foreclosure Law.

P.A. 82–280, § 15–1101, added by P.A. 84–1462, § 2, eff. July 1, 1987.

Formerly Ill.Rev.Stat.1991, ch. 110, ¶ 15–1101.

5/15–1102. Enforcement

§ 15–1102. Enforcement. The Court has full power to enforce any order entered pursuant to this Article by contempt process or by such other order as may be appropriate.

P.A. 82–280, § 15–1102, added by P.A. 84–1462, § 2, eff. July 1, 1987.

Formerly Ill.Rev.Stat.1991, ch. 110, ¶ 15–1102.

5/15–1103. Jurisdiction

§ 15–1103. Jurisdiction. The authority of the court continues during the entire pendency of the foreclosure and until disposition of all matters arising out of the foreclosure.

P.A. 82–280, § 15–1103, added by P.A. 84–1462, § 2, eff. July 1, 1987. Amended by P.A. 85–907, Art. I, § 1, eff. Nov. 23, 1987.

Formerly Ill.Rev.Stat.1991, ch. 110, ¶ 15–1103.

5/15–1104. Wrongful Inducement of Abandonment

§ 15–1104. Wrongful Inducement of Abandonment. Any person who willfully misrepresents to the Court any fact resulting in a finding of abandonment of mortgaged real estate in connection with subsection (b) of Section 15–1603 or subsection (d) of Section 15–1706 of this Article or who threatens to injure the person or property of occupants of mortgaged real estate, or who knowingly gives such occupants false and misleading information, or who harasses or intimidates such occupants, with the intent of inducing such occupants to abandon the mortgaged premises, in order to obtain a finding of abandonment under subsection (b) of Section 15–1603 or subsection (d) of Section 15–1706 of this Article, shall be guilty of a Class B misdemeanor.

P.A. 82–280, § 15–1104, added by P.A. 84–1462, § 2, eff. July 1, 1987.

Formerly Ill.Rev.Stat.1991, ch. 110, ¶ 15–1104.

5/15–1105. Interpretation

§ 15–1105. Interpretation. (a) "May." The word "may" as used in this Article means permissive and not mandatory.

(b) "Shall." The word "shall" as used in this Article means mandatory and not permissive.

P.A. 82–280, § 15–1105, added by P.A. 84–1462, § 2, eff. July 1, 1987.

Formerly Ill.Rev.Stat.1991, ch. 110, ¶ 15–1105.

5/15–1106. Applicability of Article

§ 15–1106. Applicability of Article. (a) Exclusive Procedure. From and after the effective date of this amendatory Act of 1986, the following shall be foreclosed in a foreclosure pursuant to this Article:

(1) any mortgage created prior to, on or after the effective date of this amendatory Act of 1986;

(2) any real estate installment contract for residential real estate entered into on or after the effective date of this amendatory Act of 1986 and under which (i) the purchase price is to be paid in installments over a period in excess of five years and (ii) the amount unpaid under the terms of the contract at the time of the filing of the foreclosure complaint, including principal and due and unpaid interest, at the rate prior to default, is less than 80% of the original purchase price of the real estate as stated in the contract;

(3) any collateral assignment of beneficial interest made on or after the effective date of this amendatory Act of 1986 (i) which is made with respect to a land trust which was created contemporaneously with the collateral assignment of beneficial interest, (ii) which is made pursuant to a requirement of the holder of the obligation to secure the payment of money or performance of other obligations and (iii) as to which the security agreement or other writing creating the collateral assignment permits the real estate which is the subject of the land trust to be sold to satisfy the obligations.

(b) Uniform Commercial Code. A secured party, as defined in Article 9 of the Uniform Commercial Code,[1] may at its election enforce its security interest in a foreclosure under this Article if its security interest was created on or after the effective date of this amendatory Act of 1986 and is created by (i) a collateral assignment of beneficial interest in a land trust or (ii) an assignment for security of a buyer's interest in a real estate installment contract. Such election shall be made by filing a complaint stating that it is brought under this Article, in which event the provisions of this Article shall be exclusive in such foreclosure.

(c) Real Estate Installment Contracts. A contract seller may at its election enforce in a foreclosure under this Article any real estate installment contract entered into on or after the effective date of this Amendatory Act of 1986 and not required to be fore-
closed under this Article. Such election shall be made by filing a complaint stating that it is brought under this Article, in which event the provisions of this Article shall be exclusive in such foreclosure. A contract seller must enforce its contract under this Article if the real estate installment contract is one described in paragraph (2) of subsection (a) of Section 15–1106.

(d) Effect of Election. An election made pursuant to subsection (b) or (c) of Section 15–1106 shall be binding only in the foreclosure and shall be void if the foreclosure is terminated prior to entry of judgment.

(e) Supplementary General Principles of Law. General principles of law and equity, such as those relating to capacity to contract, principal and agent, marshalling of assets, priority, subrogation, estoppel, fraud, misrepresentations, duress, collusion, mistake, bankruptcy or other validating or invalidating cause, supplement this Article unless displaced by a particular provision of it. Section 9–110 of the Code of Civil Procedure shall not be applicable to any real estate installment contract which is foreclosed under this Article.

(f) Pending Actions. A complaint to foreclose a mortgage filed before July 1, 1987, and all proceedings and third party actions in connection therewith, shall be adjudicated pursuant to the Illinois statutes and applicable law in effect immediately prior to July 1, 1987. Such statutes shall remain in effect with respect to such complaint, proceedings and third party actions notwithstanding the amendment or repeal of such statutes on or after July 1, 1987.

P.A. 82–280, § 15–1106, added by P.A. 84–1462, § 2, eff. July 1, 1987. Amended by P.A. 85–907, Art. I, § 1, eff. Nov. 23, 1987.

Formerly Ill.Rev.Stat.1991, ch. 110, ¶ 15–1106.
   [1] 810 ILCS 5/9–101 et seq.

5/15–1107. Mode of Procedure

§ 15–1107. Mode of Procedure.

(a) Other Statutes. Except as otherwise provided in this Article, the mode of procedure, including the manner of service of pleadings and other papers and service by publication, shall be in accordance with the provisions of Article II of the Illinois Code of Civil Procedure and any other statutes of this State which are from time to time applicable, and with Illinois Supreme Court Rules [1] applicable to actions generally or otherwise applicable. If a mortgage lien is being foreclosed under this Article and one or more non-mortgage liens or encumbrances is being foreclosed or enforced in the same proceedings, then, regardless of the respective priorities of the various liens or encumbrances, the procedures and all other provisions of this Article shall govern such proceedings, and any inconsistent statutory provisions shall not be applicable. Without limiting the foregoing, any provision of Article XII or any other Article of the Code of Civil

Procedure shall apply unless inconsistent with this Article and, in case of such inconsistency, shall not be applicable to actions under this Article.

(b) Mechanics' Liens. Mechanics' liens shall be enforced as provided in the Mechanics Lien Act;[2] provided, however, that any mechanics' lien claimant may assert such lien in a foreclosure under this Article, may intervene in such foreclosure in accordance with this Article and may be made a party in such foreclosure.

(c) Instruments Deemed a Mortgage. For the purpose of proceeding under this Article, any instrument described in paragraph (2) or (3) of subsection (a) of Section 15–1106, or in subsection (b) or (c) of Section 15–1106 which is foreclosed under this Article shall be deemed a mortgage. For such purpose, the real estate installment contract purchaser, the assignor of the beneficial interest in the land trust and the debtor, as appropriate, shall be deemed the mortgagor, and the real estate installment contract seller, the assignee of the beneficial interest in the land trust and the secured party, as appropriate, shall be deemed the mortgagee.

P.A. 82–280, § 15–1107, added by P.A. 84–1462, § 2, eff. July 1, 1987. Amended by P.A. 85–907, Art. I, § 1, eff. Nov. 23, 1987; P.A. 96–328, § 365, eff. Aug. 11, 2009.

Formerly Ill.Rev.Stat.1991, ch. 110, ¶ 15–1107.

[1] S.Ct. Rule 1 et seq.
[2] 770 ILCS 60/0.01 et seq.

5/15–1108. Declaration of policy relating to abandoned residential property

§ 15–1108. Declaration of policy relating to abandoned residential property. The following findings directly relate to the changes made by this amendatory Act of the 97th General Assembly. The General Assembly finds that residential mortgage foreclosures and the abandoned properties that sometimes follow create enormous challenges for Illinois residents, local governments, and the courts, reducing neighboring property values, reducing the tax base, increasing crime, placing neighbors at greater risk of foreclosure, imposing additional costs on local governments, and increasing the burden on the courts of this State; conversely, maintaining and securing abandoned properties stabilizes property values and the tax base, decreases crime, reduces the risk of foreclosure for nearby properties, thus reducing costs for local governments and making a substantial contribution to the operation and maintenance of the courts of this State by reducing the volume of matters which burden the court system in this State. The General Assembly further finds that the average foreclosure case for residential property takes close to 2 years in Illinois; when a property is abandoned, the lengthy foreclosure process harms lien-holders, neighbors, and local governments, and imposes significant and unnecessary burdens on the courts of this State; and an expedited foreclosure process for abandoned residential proper-

ty can also help the courts of this State by decreasing the volume of foreclosure cases and allowing these cases to proceed more efficiently through the court system. The General Assembly further finds that housing counseling has proven to be an effective way to help many homeowners find alternatives to foreclosure; and that housing counseling therefore also reduces the volume of matters which burden the court system in this State and allows the courts to more efficiently handle the burden of foreclosure cases.

P.A. 82–280, § 15–1108, added by P.A. 97–1164, § 15, eff. June 1, 2013.

PART 12. DEFINITIONS

Date Effective

Part 12 was added by P.A. 84–1462, § 2, eff. July 1, 1987.

5/15–1200.5. Abandoned residential property

§ 15–1200.5. Abandoned residential property. "Abandoned residential property" means residential real estate that:

(a) either:

(1) is not occupied by any mortgagor or lawful occupant as a principal residence; or

(2) contains an incomplete structure if the real estate is zoned for residential development, where the structure is empty or otherwise uninhabited and is in need of maintenance, repair, or securing; and

(b) with respect to which either:

(1) two or more of the following conditions are shown to exist:

(A) construction was initiated on the property and was discontinued prior to completion, leaving a building unsuitable for occupancy, and no construction has taken place for at least 6 months;

(B) multiple windows on the property are boarded up or closed off or are smashed through, broken off, or unhinged, or multiple window panes are broken and unrepaired;

(C) doors on the property are smashed through, broken off, unhinged, or continuously unlocked;

(D) the property has been stripped of copper or other materials, or interior fixtures to the property have been removed;

(E) gas, electrical, or water services to the entire property have been terminated;

(F) there exist one or more written statements of the mortgagor or the mortgagor's personal representative or assigns, including documents of conveyance, which indicate a clear intent to abandon the property;

(G) law enforcement officials have received at least one report of trespassing or vandalism or other illegal acts being committed at the property in the last 6 months;

(H) the property has been declared unfit for occupancy and ordered to remain vacant and unoccupied under an order issued by a municipal or county authority or a court of competent jurisdiction;

(I) the local police, fire, or code enforcement authority has requested the owner or other interested or authorized party to secure or winterize the property due to the local authority declaring the property to be an imminent danger to the health, safety, and welfare of the public;

(J) the property is open and unprotected and in reasonable danger of significant damage due to exposure to the elements, vandalism, or freezing; or

(K) there exists other evidence indicating a clear intent to abandon the property; or

(2) the real estate is zoned for residential development and is a vacant lot that is in need of maintenance, repair, or securing.

P.A. 82–280, § 15–1200.5, added by P.A. 97–1164, § 15, eff. June 1, 2013.

5/15–1200.7. Abandoned residential property; exceptions

§ 15–1200.7. Abandoned residential property; exceptions. A property shall not be considered abandoned residential property if: (i) there is an unoccupied building which is undergoing construction, renovation, or rehabilitation that is proceeding diligently to completion, and the building is in substantial compliance with all applicable ordinances, codes, regulations, and laws; (ii) there is a building occupied on a seasonal basis, but otherwise secure; (iii) there is a secure building on which there are bona fide rental or sale signs; (iv) there is a building that is secure, but is the subject of a probate action, action to quiet title, or other ownership dispute; or (v) there is a building that is otherwise secure and in substantial compliance with all applicable ordinances, codes, regulations, and laws.

P.A. 82–280, § 15–1200.7, added by P.A. 97–1164, § 15, eff. June 1, 2013.

5/15–1201. Agricultural Real Estate

§ 15–1201. Agricultural Real Estate. "Agricultural real estate" means real estate which is used primarily (i) for the growing and harvesting of crops, (ii) for the feeding, breeding and management of livestock, (iii) for dairying, or (iv) for any other agricultural or horticultural use or combination thereof, including without limitation, aquaculture, silviculture, and any other activities customarily engaged in by persons engaged in the business of farming.

P.A. 82–280, § 15–1201, added by P.A. 84–1462, § 2, eff. July 1, 1987. Amended by P.A. 95–331, § 1085, eff. Aug. 21, 2007.

Formerly Ill.Rev.Stat.1991, ch. 110, ¶ 15–1201.

5/15–1202. Collateral Assignment of Beneficial Interest

§ 15–1202. Collateral Assignment of Beneficial Interest. "Collateral assignment of beneficial interest" means any pledge or assignment of the beneficial interest in a land trust to any person to secure a debt or other obligation.

P.A. 82–280, § 15–1202, added by P.A. 84–1462, § 2, eff. July 1, 1987.

Formerly Ill.Rev.Stat.1991, ch. 110, ¶ 15–1202.

5/15–1202.5. Dwelling unit

§ 15–1202.5. Dwelling unit. For the purposes of Sections 9–207.5, 15–1224, 15–1225, 15–1506, 15–1508, 15–1508.5, 15–1701, 15–1703, and 15–1704 only, "dwelling unit" means a room or suite of rooms providing complete, independent living facilities for at least one person, including permanent provisions for sanitation, cooking, eating, sleeping, and other activities routinely associated with daily life.

P.A. 82–280, § 15–1202.5, added by P.A. 96–111, § 5, eff. Oct. 29, 2009. Amended by P.A. 97–575, § 5, eff. Aug. 26, 2011; P.A. 98–514, § 5, eff. Nov. 19, 2013.

5/15–1203. Foreclosure

§ 15–1203. Foreclosure. "Foreclosure" means an action commenced under this Article and "to foreclose" means to terminate legal and equitable interests in real estate pursuant to a foreclosure.

P.A. 82–280, § 15–1203, added by P.A. 84–1462, § 2, eff. July 1, 1987.

Formerly Ill.Rev.Stat.1991, ch. 110, ¶ 15–1203.

5/15–1204. Guarantor

§ 15–1204. Guarantor. "Guarantor" means any person who has undertaken to pay any indebtedness or perform any obligation of a mortgagor under a mortgage or of any other person who owes payment or the performance of other obligations secured by the mortgage, which undertaking is made by a guaranty or surety agreement of any kind.

P.A. 82–280, § 15–1204, added by P.A. 84–1462, § 2, eff. July 1, 1987.

Formerly Ill.Rev.Stat.1991, ch. 110, ¶ 15–1204.

5/15–1205. Land Trust

§ 15–1205. Land Trust. "Land trust" means any trust arrangement under which the legal and equitable title to real estate is held by a trustee, the interest of the beneficiary of the trust is personal property and the beneficiary or any person designated in writing by the beneficiary has (i) the exclusive power to direct or control the trustee in dealing with the title to the trust property, (ii) the exclusive control of the management, operation, renting and selling of the trust property and (iii) the exclusive right to the earnings, avails and proceeds of the trust property.

P.A. 82–280, § 15–1205, added by P.A. 84–1462, § 2, eff. July 1, 1987.

Formerly Ill.Rev.Stat.1991, ch. 110, ¶ 15–1205.

5/15–1206. Mechanics' Lien

§ 15–1206. Mechanics' Lien. "Mechanics' lien" or "mechanics' lien claim" means a lien or claim arising under the Mechanics Lien Act.[1]

P.A. 82–280, § 15–1206, added by P.A. 84–1462, § 2, eff. July 1, 1987. Amended by P.A. 96–328, § 365, eff. Aug. 11, 2009.

Formerly Ill.Rev.Stat.1991, ch. 110, ¶ 15–1206.
[1] 770 ILCS 60/0.01 et seq.

5/15–1207. Mortgage

§ 15–1207. Mortgage. "Mortgage" means any consensual lien created by a written instrument which grants or retains an interest in real estate to secure a debt or other obligation. The term "mortgage" includes, without limitation:

(a) mortgages securing "reverse mortgage" loans as authorized by subsection (a) of Section 5 of the Illinois Banking Act;[1]

(b) mortgages securing "revolving credit" loans as authorized by subsection (c) of Section 5 of the Illinois Banking Act,[2] Section 1–6b of the Illinois Savings and Loan Act[3] and Section 46 of the Illinois Credit Union Act;[4]

(c) every deed conveying real estate, although an absolute conveyance in its terms, which shall have been intended only as a security in the nature of a mortgage;

(d) equitable mortgages; and

(e) instruments which would have been deemed instruments in the nature of a mortgage prior to the effective date of this amendatory Act of 1987.

P.A. 82–280, § 15–1207, added by P.A. 84–1462, § 2, eff. July 1, 1987. Amended by P.A. 85–907, Art. I, § 1, eff. Nov. 23, 1987.

Formerly Ill.Rev.Stat.1991, ch. 110, ¶ 15–1207.
[1] Should read "Section 5a". See 205 ILCS 5/5a.
[2] Should read "Section 5d". See 205 ILCS 5/5d.
[3] 205 ILCS 105/1–6b.
[4] 205 ILCS 305/46.

5/15–1208. Mortgagee

§ 15–1208. Mortgagee. "Mortgagee" means (i) the holder of an indebtedness or obligee of a non-monetary obligation secured by a mortgage or any person designated or authorized to act on behalf of such holder and (ii) any person claiming through a mortgagee as successor.

P.A. 82–280, § 15–1208, added by P.A. 84–1462, § 2, eff. July 1, 1987.

Formerly Ill.Rev.Stat.1991, ch. 110, ¶ 15–1208.

5/15–1209. Mortgagor

§ 15–1209. Mortgagor. "Mortgagor" means (i) the person whose interest in the real estate is the subject of the mortgage and (ii) any person claiming through a mortgagor as successor. Where a mortgage is executed by a trustee of a land trust, the mortgagor is the trustee and not the beneficiary or beneficiaries.

P.A. 82–280, § 15–1209, added by P.A. 84–1462, § 2, eff. July 1, 1987. Amended by P.A. 85–907, Art. I, § 1, eff. Nov. 23, 1987.

Formerly Ill.Rev.Stat.1991, ch. 110, ¶ 15–1209.

5/15–1210. Nonrecord Claimant

§ 15–1210. Nonrecord Claimant. "Nonrecord claimant" means any person (i) who has or claims to have an interest in mortgaged real estate, (ii) whose name or interest, at the time a notice of foreclosure is recorded in accordance with Section 15–1503, is not disclosed of record either (1) by means of a recorded notice or (2) by means of a proceeding which under the law as in effect at the time the foreclosure is commenced would afford constructive notice of the existence of such interest and (iii) whose interest falls in any of the following categories: (1) right of homestead, (2) judgment creditor, (3) beneficial interest under any trust other than the beneficial interest of a beneficiary of a trust in actual possession of all or part of the real estate or (4) mechanics' lien claim. Notwithstanding the foregoing, for the purpose of this Article no proceeding shall be deemed to constitute constructive notice of the interest of any nonrecord claimant in the mortgaged real estate unless in the proceeding there is a legal description of the real estate sufficient to identify it with reasonable certainty. The classification of any person as a nonrecord claimant under the foregoing definition shall not be affected by any actual notice or knowledge of or attributable to the mortgagee.

P.A. 82–280, § 15–1210, added by P.A. 84–1462, § 2, eff. July 1, 1987.

Formerly Ill.Rev.Stat.1991, ch. 110, ¶ 15–1210.

5/15–1211. Notice of Foreclosure

§ 15–1211. Notice of Foreclosure. "Notice of foreclosure" means the notice of a foreclosure which is made and recorded in accordance with Section 15–1503 of this Article.

P.A. 82–280, § 15–1211, added by P.A. 84–1462, § 2, eff. July 1, 1987.

Formerly Ill.Rev.Stat.1991, ch. 110, ¶ 15–1211.

5/15–1212. Owner of Redemption

§ 15–1212. Owner of Redemption. "Owner of redemption" means a mortgagor, or other owner or co-owner of the mortgaged real estate.

P.A. 82–280, § 15–1212, added by P.A. 84–1462, § 2, eff. July 1, 1987.

Formerly Ill.Rev.Stat.1991, ch. 110, ¶ 15–1212.

5/15–1213. Real Estate

§ 15–1213. Real Estate. "Real estate" means land or any estate or interest in, over or under land (including minerals, air rights, structures, fixtures and other things which by custom, usage or law pass with a conveyance of land though not described or mentioned in the contract of sale or instrument of conveyance). "Mortgaged real estate" means the real estate which is the subject of a mortgage. "Real Estate" includes a manufactured home as defined in subdivision (53) of Section 9–102 of the Uniform Commercial Code [1] that is real property as defined in the Conveyance and Encumbrance of Manufactured Homes as Real Property and Severance Act. [2]

P.A. 82–280, § 15–1213, added by P.A. 84–1462, § 2, eff. July 1, 1987. Amended by P.A. 98–749, § 10–75, eff. July 16, 2014.

Formerly Ill.Rev.Stat.1991, ch. 110, ¶ 15–1213.
[1] 810 ILCS 5/9–102.
[2] 765 ILCS 170/5–1 et seq.

5/15–1214. Real Estate Installment Contract

§ 15–1214. Real Estate Installment Contract. "Real estate installment contract" means any agreement or contract for a deed under which the purchase price is to be paid in installments with title to the real estate to be conveyed to the buyer upon payment of the purchase price or a specified portion thereof. For the purpose of this definition, an earnest money deposit shall not be considered an installment.

P.A. 82–280, § 15–1214, added by P.A. 84–1462, § 2, eff. July 1, 1987.

Formerly Ill.Rev.Stat.1991, ch. 110, ¶ 15–1214.

5/15–1215. Receiver

§ 15–1215. Receiver. "Receiver" means a receiver appointed pursuant to Section 15–1704 of this Article.

P.A. 82–280, § 15–1215, added by P.A. 84–1462, § 2, eff. July 1, 1987.

Formerly Ill.Rev.Stat.1991, ch. 110, ¶ 15–1215.

5/15–1216. Recorder

§ 15–1216. Recorder. "Recorder" means (i) the Recorder of the county in which the mortgaged real estate is located or (ii) if the mortgaged real estate is registered under the Torrens Act,[1] the Registrar of Titles of the county in which the mortgaged real estate is located. "Recorder" includes any authorized assistant or employee of the Recorder.

P.A. 82–280, § 15–1216, added by P.A. 84–1462, § 2, eff. July 1, 1987.

Formerly Ill.Rev.Stat.1991, ch. 110, ¶ 15–1216.
[1] 765 ILCS 35/1 et seq. (repealed).

5/15–1217. Recording of Instruments

§ 15–1217. Recording of Instruments. "Recording of instruments" or "to record" means to present to the Recorder a document, in recordable form, which is to be recorded in accordance with Section 3–5024 of the Counties Code, [1] together with the required recording fee. The Registrar of Titles shall accept the filing of notices or affidavits required or permitted by this Article without the necessity of the production of evidence of title.

P.A. 82–280, § 15–1217, added by P.A. 84–1462, § 2, eff. July 1, 1987. Amended by P.A. 96–328, § 365, eff. Aug. 11, 2009.

Formerly Ill.Rev.Stat.1991, ch. 110, ¶ 15–1217.
[1] 55 ILCS 5/3–5024.

5/15–1218. Recorded Notice

§ 15–1218. Recorded Notice. "Recorded notice" with respect to any real estate means (i) any instrument filed in accordance with Sections 2–1901 or 12–101 of the Code of Civil Procedure or (ii) any recorded instrument which discloses (a) the names and addresses of the persons making the claim or asserting the interest described in the notice; (b) that such persons have or claim some interest in or lien on the subject real estate; (c) the nature of the claim; (d) the names of the persons against whom the claim is made; (e) a legal description of the real estate sufficient to identify it with reasonable certainty; (f) the name and address of the person executing the notice; and (g) the name and address of the person preparing the notice.

P.A. 82–280, § 15–1218, added by P.A. 84–1462, § 2, eff. July 1, 1987. Amended by P.A. 85–907, Art. I, § 1, eff. Nov. 23, 1987.

Formerly Ill.Rev.Stat.1991, ch. 110, ¶ 15–1218.

5/15–1219. Residential Real Estate

§ 15–1219. Residential Real Estate. "Residential real estate" means any real estate, except a single tract of agricultural real estate consisting of more than 40 acres, which is improved with a single family residence or residential condominium units or a multiple dwelling structure containing single family dwelling units for six or fewer families living independently of each other, which residence, or at least one of which condominium or dwelling units, is occupied as a principal residence either (i) if a mortgagor is an individual, by that mortgagor, that mortgagor's spouse or that mortgagor's descendants, or (ii) if a mortgagor is a trustee of a trust or an executor or administrator of an estate, by a beneficiary of that trust or estate or by such beneficiary's spouse or descendants or (iii) if a mortgagor is a corporation, by persons owning collectively at least 50 percent of the shares of voting stock of such corporation or by a spouse or descendants of such persons. The use of a portion of residential real estate for non-residential purposes shall not affect the characterization of such real estate as residential real estate. For purposes of the definition of the term "abandoned residential property" in Section 15–1200.5 of this Article, "abandoned residential property" shall not include the requirement that the real estate be occupied, or if zoned for residential development, improved with a dwelling structure.

P.A. 82–280, § 15–1219, added by P.A. 84–1462, § 2, eff. July 1, 1987. Amended by P.A. 85–907, Art. I, § 1, eff. Nov. 23, 1987; P.A. 97–1164, § 15, eff. June 1, 2013.

Formerly Ill.Rev.Stat.1991, ch. 110, ¶ 15–1219.

5/15–1220. Statutory Judgment Rate

§ 15–1220. Statutory Judgment Rate. "Statutory judgment rate" means the rate of interest on judgments specified in Section 2–1303 of the Code of Civil Procedure.

P.A. 82–280, § 15–1220, added by P.A. 84–1462, § 2, eff. July 1, 1987.

Formerly Ill.Rev.Stat.1991, ch. 110, ¶ 15–1220.

5/15–1221. Unknown Owner

§ 15–1221. Unknown Owner. "Unknown owner" means the same as "unknown owner" as used in Section 2–413 of the Code of Civil Procedure.

P.A. 82–280, § 15–1221, added by P.A. 84–1462, § 2, eff. July 1, 1987.

Formerly Ill.Rev.Stat.1991, ch. 110, ¶ 15–1221.

5/15–1222. Acts Referred to in this Article

§ 15–1222. Acts Referred to in this Article. Acts referred to by name in this Article shall mean those Acts, as amended from time to time, and, in particular:

(a) "Torrens Act" [1] means "An act concerning land titles", approved May 1, 1897.

(b) (Blank).

(c) "Mechanics Lien Act" means the Mechanics Lien Act, [2] 770 ILCS 60/Act.

P.A. 82–280, § 15–1222, added by P.A. 84–1462, § 2, eff. July 1, 1987. Amended by P.A. 96–328, § 365, eff. Aug. 11, 2009.

Formerly Ill.Rev.Stat.1991, ch. 110, ¶ 15–1222.

[1] 765 ILCS 35/1 et seq. (repealed).
[2] 770 ILCS 60/0.01 et seq.

5/15–1223. Occupant

§ 15–1223. Occupant. "Occupant" means a person in lawful physical possession of all or part of the mortgaged real estate.

P.A. 82–280, § 15–1223, added by P.A. 88–265, § 5, eff. Jan. 1, 1994.

5/15–1224. Bona fide lease

§ 15–1224. Bona fide lease.

(a) For purposes of Sections 9–207.5, 15–1225, 15–1506, 15–1508, and 15–1701 of this Code only, the term "bona fide lease" means a lease of a dwelling unit in residential real estate in foreclosure for which:

(1) the mortgagor or the child, spouse, or parent of the mortgagor is not the tenant;

(2) the lease was the result of an arms-length transaction;

(3) the lease requires the receipt of rent that is not substantially less than fair market rent for the property or the rent is reduced or subsidized pursuant to a federal, State, or local subsidy; and

(4) either (i) the lease was entered into or renewed on or before the date of the filing of the lis pendens on the residential real estate in foreclosure pursuant to Section 2–1901 of this Code or (ii) the lease was entered into or renewed after the date of the filing of the lis pendens on the residential real estate in foreclosure and before the date of the judicial sale of the residential real estate in foreclosure, and the term of the lease is for one year or less.

(b) A written lease for a term exceeding one year that is entered into or renewed after the date of the filing of the lis pendens on the residential real estate in foreclosure pursuant to Section 2–1901 of this Code and before the date of the judicial sale of the residential real estate in foreclosure that otherwise meets the requirements of subsection (a) of this Section shall be deemed to be a bona fide lease for a term of one year.

(c) An oral lease entered into at any time before the date of the judicial sale of the residential real estate in foreclosure that otherwise meets the requirements of subsection (a) of this Section shall be deemed to be a bona fide lease for a month-to-month term, unless the lessee proves by a preponderance of evidence that the oral lease is for a longer term. In no event shall an oral lease be deemed to be a bona fide lease for a term of more than one year.

(d) A written or oral lease entered into on or after the date of the judicial sale of the residential real estate in foreclosure and before the date of the court order confirming the judicial sale that otherwise meets the requirements of subsection (a) of this Section shall be deemed to be a bona fide lease for a month-to-month term.

(e) Notwithstanding paragraph (1) of subsection (a) of this Section, a child, spouse, or parent of the mortgagor may prove by a preponderance of evidence that a written or oral lease that otherwise meets the requirements of subsection (a) of this Section is a bona fide lease.

P.A. 82–280, § 15–1224, added by P.A. 98–514, § 5, eff. Nov. 19, 2013.

5/15–1225. Residential real estate in foreclosure

§ 15–1225. Residential real estate in foreclosure. For purposes of Sections 9–207.5, 15–1224, 15–1506, 15–1508, and 15–1701 of this Code only, the term "residential real estate in foreclosure" means any real estate, except a single tract of agricultural real estate consisting of more than 40 acres, which is improved with a single family residence or residential condominium units or a multiple dwelling structure containing single family dwelling units for one or more families living independently of one another, for which an action to foreclose the real estate: (1) has commenced and is pending; (2) was pending when the bona fide lease was entered into or renewed; or (3) was commenced after the bona fide lease was entered into or renewed.

P.A. 82–280, § 15–1225, added by P.A. 98–514, § 5, eff. Nov. 19, 2013.

PART 13. MORTGAGE LIEN PRIORITIES

Date Effective

Part 13 was added by P.A. 84–1462, § 2, eff. July 1, 1987.

5/15–1301. Lien Created

§ 15–1301. Lien Created. Except as provided in Section 15–1302, from the time a mortgage is recorded it shall be a lien upon the real estate that is the subject of the mortgage for all monies advanced or applied or other obligations secured in accordance with the terms of the mortgage or as authorized by law, including the amounts specified in a judgment of foreclosure in accordance with subsection (d) of Section 15–1603.

P.A. 82–280, § 15–1301, added by P.A. 84–1462, § 2, eff. July 1, 1987.

Formerly Ill.Rev.Stat.1991, ch. 110, ¶ 15–1301.

5/15–1302. Certain Future Advances

§ 15–1302. Certain Future Advances.

(a) Advances Made After Eighteen Months. Except as provided in subsection (b) of Section 15–1302, as to any monies advanced or applied more than 18 months after a mortgage is recorded, the mortgage shall be a lien as to subsequent purchasers and judgment creditors only from the time such monies are advanced or applied. However, nothing in this Section shall affect any lien arising or existing by virtue of the Mechanics Lien Act. [1]

(b) Exceptions.

(1) All monies advanced or applied pursuant to commitment, whenever advanced or applied, shall be a lien from the time the mortgage is recorded. An advance shall be deemed made pursuant to commitment only if the mortgagee has bound itself to make such advance in the mortgage or in an instrument executed contemporaneously with, and referred to in, the mortgage, whether or not a subsequent event of default or other event not within the mortgagee's control has relieved or may relieve the mortgagee from its obligation.

(2) All monies advanced or applied, whenever advanced or applied, in accordance with the terms of a reverse mortgage shall be a lien from the time the mortgage is recorded.

(3) All monies advanced or applied in accordance with the terms of a revolving credit arrangement secured by a mortgage as authorized by law shall be a lien from the time the mortgage is recorded.

(4) All interest which in accordance with the terms of a mortgage is accrued or added to the principal amount secured by the mortgage, whenever added, shall be a lien from the time the mortgage is recorded.

(5) All monies advanced by the mortgagee in accordance with the terms of a mortgage to (i) preserve or restore the mortgaged real estate, (ii) preserve the lien of the mortgage or the priority thereof or (iii) enforce the mortgage, shall be a lien from the time the mortgage is recorded.

P.A. 82–280, § 15–1302, added by P.A. 84–1462, § 2, eff. July 1, 1987. Amended by P.A. 96–328, § 365, eff. Aug. 11, 2009.

Formerly Ill.Rev.Stat.1991, ch. 110, ¶ 15–1302.

1 770 ILCS 60/0.01 et seq.

PART 14. METHODS OF TERMINATING MORTGAGOR'S INTEREST IN REAL ESTATE

Date Effective

Part 14 was added by P.A. 84–1462, § 2, eff. July 1, 1987.

5/15–1401. Deed in Lieu of Foreclosure

§ 15–1401. Deed in Lieu of Foreclosure. The mortgagor and mortgagee may agree on a termination of the mortgagor's interest in the mortgaged real estate after a default by a mortgagor. Any mortgagee or mortgagee's nominee may accept a deed from the mortgagor in lieu of foreclosure subject to any other claims or liens affecting the real estate. Acceptance of a deed in lieu of foreclosure shall relieve from personal liability all persons who may owe payment or the performance of other obligations secured by the mortgage, including guarantors of such indebtedness or obligations, except to the extent a person agrees not to be relieved in an instrument executed contemporaneously. A deed in lieu of foreclosure, whether to the mortgagee or mortgagee's nominee, shall not effect a merger of the mortgagee's interest as mortgagee and the mortgagee's interest derived from the deed in lieu of foreclosure. The mere tender of an executed deed by the mortgagor or the recording of a deed by the mortgagor to the mortgagee shall not constitute acceptance by the mortgagee of a deed in lieu of foreclosure.

P.A. 82–280, § 15–1401, added by P.A. 84–1462, § 2, eff. July 1, 1987. Amended by P.A. 86–974, § 1, eff. July 1, 1990.

Formerly Ill.Rev.Stat.1991, ch. 110, ¶ 15–1401.

5/15–1401.1. Short sale in foreclosure

§ 15–1401.1. Short sale in foreclosure.

(a) For purposes of this Section, "short sale" means the sale of real estate that is subject to a mortgage for an amount that is less than the amount owed to the mortgagee on the outstanding mortgage note.

(b) In a foreclosure of residential real estate, if (i) the mortgagor presents to the mortgagee a bona fide written offer from a third party to purchase the property that is the subject of the foreclosure proceeding, (ii) the written offer to purchase is for an amount which constitutes a short sale of the property, and (iii) the mortgagor makes a written request to the mortgagee to approve the sale on the terms of the offer to purchase, the mortgagee must respond to the mortgagor within 90 days after receipt of the written offer and written request.

(c) The mortgagee shall determine whether to accept the mortgagor's short sale offer. Failure to accept the offer shall not impair or abrogate in any way the rights of the mortgagee or affect the status of the foreclosure proceedings. The 90–day period shall not operate as a stay of the proceedings.

P.A. 82–280, § 15–1401.1, added by P.A. 97–666, § 5, eff. Jan. 13, 2012.

5/15–1402. Consent Foreclosure

§ 15–1402. Consent Foreclosure. **(a) No Objection.** In a foreclosure, the court shall enter a judgment satisfying the mortgage indebtedness by vesting absolute title to the mortgaged real estate in the mortgagee free and clear of all claims, liens (except liens of the United States of America which cannot be foreclosed without judicial sale) and interest of the mortgagor, including all rights of reinstatement and redemption, and of all rights of all other persons made parties in the foreclosure whose interests are subordinate to that of the mortgagee and all nonrecord claimants given notice in accordance with paragraph (2) of subsection (c) of Section 15–1502 if at any time before sale:

(1) the mortgagee offers, in connection with such a judgment, to waive any and all rights to a personal judgment for deficiency against the mortgagor and against all other persons liable for the indebtedness or other obligations secured by the mortgage;

(2) such offer is made either in the foreclosure complaint or by motion upon notice to all parties not in default;

(3) all mortgagors who then have an interest in the mortgaged real estate, by answer to the complaint, response to the motion or stipulation filed with the court expressly consent to the entry of such judgment;

(4) no other party, by answer or by response to the motion or stipulation, within the time allowed for such answer or response, objects to the entry of such judgment; and

(5) upon notice to all parties who have not previously been found in default for failure to appear, answer or otherwise plead.

(b) Objection. If any party other than a mortgagor who then has an interest in the mortgaged real estate objects to the entry of such judgment by consent, the court, after hearing, shall enter an order providing either:

(1) that for good cause shown, the judgment by consent shall not be allowed; or

(2) that, good cause not having been shown by the objecting party and the objecting party not having agreed to pay the amount required to redeem in accordance with subsection (d) of Section 15–1603, title to the mortgaged real estate be vested in the mortgagee as requested by the mortgagee and consented to by the mortgagor; or

(3) determining the amount required to redeem in accordance with subsection (d) of Section 15–1603, finding that the objecting party (or, if more than one party so objects, the objecting party who has the least priority) has agreed to pay such amount and additional interest under the mortgage accrued to the date of payment within 30 days after entry of the order, and declaring that upon payment of such amount within 30 days title to the mortgaged real estate shall be vested in such objecting party. Title so vested shall be free and clear of all claims, liens (except liens of the United States of America which cannot be foreclosed without judicial sale) and interest of the mortgagor and of all rights of other persons made parties in the foreclosure whose interests are subordinate to the interest of the mortgagee and all nonrecord claimants given notice in accordance with paragraph (2) of subsection (c) of Section 15–1502. If any objecting party subject to such an order has not paid the amount required to redeem in accordance with that order within the 30–day period, the court (i) shall order that such title to the mortgaged real estate shall vest in the objecting party next higher in priority (and successively with respect to each other objecting party in increasing order of such party's priority), if any, upon that party's agreeing to pay within 30 days after the entry of such further order, such amount as specified in the original order plus additional interest under the terms of the mortgage accrued to the date of payment, provided that such party pays such amount within the 30–day period, and (ii) may order that the non-paying objecting party pay costs, interest accrued between the start of the preceding 30–day period and the later of the date another objecting party makes the payment, if applicable, or the date such period expired, and the reasonable attorneys' fees incurred by all other parties on account of that party's objection.

(c) Judgment. Any judgment entered pursuant to Section 15–1402 shall recite the mortgagee's waiver of rights to a personal judgment for deficiency and shall bar the mortgagee from obtaining such a deficiency judgment against the mortgagor or any other person liable for the indebtedness or other obligations secured by the mortgage.

P.A. 82–280, § 15–1402, added by P.A. 84–1462, § 2, eff. July 1, 1987. Amended by P.A. 86–974, § 1, eff. July 1, 1990.

Formerly Ill.Rev.Stat.1991, ch. 110, ¶ 15–1402.

5/15–1403. Common Law Strict Foreclosure

§ 15–1403.   Common Law Strict Foreclosure. Nothing in this Article shall affect the right of a mortgagee to foreclose its mortgage by a common law strict foreclosure as in existence in Illinois on the effective date of this Article.

P.A. 82–280, § 15–1403, added by P.A. 84–1462, § 2, eff. July 1, 1987.

Formerly Ill.Rev.Stat.1991, ch. 110, ¶ 15–1403.

5/15–1404. Judicial Foreclosure

§ 15–1404. Judicial Foreclosure. Except as provided in subsection (d) of Section 15–1501, the interest in the mortgaged real estate of (i) all persons made a party in such foreclosure and (ii) all nonrecord claimants given notice in accordance with paragraph (2) of subsection (c) of Section 15–1502, shall be terminated by the judicial sale of the real estate, pursuant to a judgment of foreclosure, provided the sale is confirmed in accordance with this Article.

P.A. 82–280, § 15–1404, added by P.A. 84–1462, § 2, eff. July 1, 1987. Amended by P.A. 85–907, Art. I, § 1, eff. Nov. 23, 1987.

Formerly Ill.Rev.Stat.1991, ch. 110, ¶ 15–1404.

5/15–1405. Power of Sale

§ 15–1405. Power of Sale. No real estate within this State may be sold by virtue of any power of sale contained in a mortgage or any other agreement, and all such mortgages may only be foreclosed in accordance with this Article.

P.A. 82–280, § 15–1405, added by P.A. 84–1462, § 2, eff. July 1, 1987.

Formerly Ill.Rev.Stat.1991, ch. 110, ¶ 15–1405.

PART 15. JUDICIAL FORECLOSURE PROCEDURE

Date Effective

Part 15 was added by P.A. 84–1462, § 2, eff. July 1, 1987.

5/15–1501. Parties

§ 15–1501. Parties.

(a) Necessary Parties. For the purposes of Section 2–405 of the Code of Civil Procedure,[1] only (i) the mortgagor and (ii) other persons (but not guarantors) who owe payment of indebtedness or the performance of other obligations secured by the mortgage and against whom personal liability is asserted shall be necessary parties defendant in a foreclosure. The court may proceed to adjudicate their respective interests, but any disposition of the mortgaged real estate shall be subject to (i) the interests of all other persons not made a party or (ii) interests in the mortgaged real estate not otherwise barred or terminated in the foreclosure.

(b) Permissible Parties. Any party may join as a party any other person, although such person is not a necessary party, including, without limitation, the following:

(1) All persons having a possessory interest in the mortgaged real estate;

(2) A mortgagor's spouse who has waived the right of homestead;

(3) A trustee holding an interest in the mortgaged real estate or a beneficiary of such trust;

(4) The owner or holder of a note secured by a trust deed;

(5) Guarantors, provided that in a foreclosure any such guarantor also may be joined as a party in a separate count in an action on such guarantor's guaranty;

(6) The State of Illinois or any political subdivision thereof, where a foreclosure involves real estate upon which the State or such subdivision has an interest or claim for lien, in which case "An Act in relation to immunity for the State of Illinois", approved December 10, 1971, as amended,[2] shall not be effective;

(7) The United States of America or any agency or department thereof where a foreclosure involves real estate upon which the United States of America or such agency or department has an interest or a claim for lien;

(8) Any assignee of leases or rents relating to the mortgaged real estate;

(9) Any person who may have a lien under the Mechanic's Lien Act;[3] and

(10) Any other mortgagee or claimant.

(c) Unknown Owners. Any unknown owner may be made a party in accordance with Section 2–413 of the Code of Civil Procedure.[4]

(d) Right to Become Party. Any person who has or claims an interest in real estate which is the subject of a foreclosure or an interest in any debt secured by the mortgage shall have an unconditional right to appear and become a party in such foreclosure in accordance with subsection (e) of Section 15–1501, provided, that neither such appearance by a lessee whose interest in the real estate is subordinate to the interest being foreclosed, nor the act of making such lessee a party, shall result in the termination of the lessee's lease unless the termination of the lease or lessee's interest in the mortgaged real estate is specifically ordered by the court in the judgment of foreclosure.

(e) Time of Intervention.

(1) Of Right. A person not a party, other than a nonrecord claimant given notice in accordance with paragraph (2) of subsection (c) of Section 15–1502, who has or claims an interest in the mortgaged real estate may appear and become a party at any time prior to the entry of judgment of foreclosure. A nonrecord claimant given such notice may appear and become a party at any time prior to the earlier of (i) the entry of a judgment of foreclosure or (ii) 30 days after such notice is given.

(2) In Court's Discretion. After the right to intervene expires and prior to the sale in accordance with the judgment, the court may permit a person who has or claims an interest in the mortgaged real estate to appear and become a party on such terms as the court may deem just.

(3) Later Right. After the sale of the mortgaged real estate in accordance with a judgment of foreclosure and prior to the entry of an order confirming the sale, a person who has or claims an interest in the mortgaged real estate, may appear and become a party, on such terms as the court may deem just, for the sole purpose of claiming an interest in the

proceeds of sale. Any such party shall be deemed a party from the commencement of the foreclosure, and the interest of such party in the real estate shall be subject to all orders and judgments entered in the foreclosure.

(4) Termination of Interest. Except as provided in Section 15–1501(d), the interest of any person who is allowed to appear and become a party shall be terminated, and the interest of such party in the real estate shall attach to the proceeds of sale.

(f) Separate Actions. Any mortgagee or claimant, other than the mortgagee who commences a foreclosure, whose interest in the mortgaged real estate is recorded prior to the filing of a notice of foreclosure in accordance with this Article but who is not made a party to such foreclosure, shall not be barred from filing a separate foreclosure (i) as an intervening defendant or counterclaimant in accordance with subsections (d) and (e) of Section 15–1501 if a judgment of foreclosure has not been entered in the original foreclosure or (ii) in a new foreclosure subsequent to the entry of a judgment of foreclosure in the original foreclosure.

(g) Service on the State of Illinois. When making the State of Illinois a party to a foreclosure, summons may be served by sending, by registered or certified mail, a copy of the summons and the complaint to the Attorney General. The complaint shall set forth with particularity the nature of the interest or lien of the State of Illinois. If such interest or lien appears in a recorded instrument, the complaint must state the document number of the instrument and the office wherein it was recorded.

(h) Special Representatives. With respect to the property that is the subject of the action, the court is not required to appoint a special representative for a deceased mortgagor for the purpose of defending the action, if there is a:

(1) living person, persons, or entity that holds a 100% interest in the property, by virtue of being the deceased mortgagor's surviving joint tenant or surviving tenant by the entirety;

(2) beneficiary under a transfer on death instrument executed by the deceased mortgagor prior to death;

(3) person, persons, or entity that was conveyed title to the property by the deceased mortgagor prior to death;

(4) person, persons, or entity that was conveyed title to the property from the deceased mortgagor's probate estate by the administrator or executor; or

(5) trust that was conveyed title to the property by:

(A) the deceased mortgagor prior to death; or

(B) any other person, persons, or entity that is identified in this subsection (h) as being exempt

from the requirement to appoint a special representative.

In no event may a deficiency judgment be sought or entered in the foreclosure case pursuant to subsection (e) of Section 15–1508 against a deceased mortgagor.
P.A. 82–280, § 15–1501, added by P.A. 84–1462, § 2, eff. July 1, 1987. Amended by P.A. 85–907, Art. I, § 1, eff. Nov. 23, 1987; P.A. 86–974, § 1, eff. July 1, 1990; P.A. 88–265, § 5, eff. Jan. 1, 1994; P.A. 98–514, § 5, eff. Nov. 19, 2013; P.A. 99–24, § 5, eff. Jan. 1, 2016.

Formerly Ill.Rev.Stat.1991, ch. 110, ¶ 15–1501.
 1 735 ILCS 5/2–405.
 2 745 ILCS 5/0.01 et seq.
 3 770 ILCS 60/0.01 et seq.
 4 735 ILCS 5/2–413.

5/15–1501.5.　Return from combat stay

§ 15–1501.5. Return from combat stay. In addition to any rights and obligations provided under the federal Servicemembers Civil Relief Act, whenever it is determined in a foreclosure proceeding that the mortgagor defendant is a person who was deployed to a combat or combat support posting while on active military duty and serving overseas within the previous 12 months, the court must stay the proceedings for a period of 90 days upon application to the court by the mortgagor defendant. "Active military duty" means, for purposes of this Section, service on active duty as a member of the Armed Forces of the United States, the Illinois National Guard, or any reserve component of the Armed Forces of the United States.
P.A. 82–280, § 15–1501.5, added by P.A. 96–901, § 5, eff. Jan. 1, 2011. Amended by P.A. 97–333, § 575, eff. Aug. 12, 2011.

5/15–1501.6.　Relief in mortgage foreclosure proceedings for military personnel in military service

§ 15–1501.6. Relief in mortgage foreclosure proceedings for military personnel in military service.

(a) In this Section:

"Military service" means any full-time training or duty, no matter how described under federal or State law, for which a service member is ordered to report by the President, Governor of a state, commonwealth, or territory of the United States, or other appropriate military authority.

"Service member" means a resident of Illinois who is a member of any component of the U.S. Armed Forces or the National Guard of any state, the District of Columbia, a commonwealth, or a territory of the United States.

(b) In an action for foreclosure, a mortgagor who is a service member that has entered military service for a period greater than 29 consecutive days or any member of the mortgagor's family who resides with the mortgagor at the mortgaged premises, if the mortgagor entered into the mortgage agreement before the mortgagor received orders for military service on or after the effective date of this amendatory Act of the 97th General Assembly, may file a motion for relief and the court shall, if the mortgagor's ability to pay the agreed mortgage payments or to defend the foreclosure proceedings is materially affected by the mortgagor's military service, do one or more of the following:

(1) stay the proceedings for a period of 90 days after the mortgagor returns from military service, unless, in the opinion of the court, justice and equity require a longer or shorter period of time; or

(2) adjust the obligation under the mortgage agreement by reducing the monthly payments for a period lasting up to 90 days after the mortgagor returns from military service and extending the term of the mortgage, provided that the adjustment preserves the interest of all parties to it.

(c) In order to be eligible for the benefits granted to a service member under this Section, a service member or a member of the service member's family who resides with the service member at the mortgaged premises must provide the court and the mortgagee with a copy of the orders calling the service member to military service in excess of 29 consecutive days and of any orders further extending the service member's period of service.

(d) If a stay is granted under this Section, the court may grant the mortgagee such relief as equity may require.

(e) The forms of relief available under this Section shall continue to be available up to 90 days after the completion of the service member's military service.

(f) In addition to any sanction available to the court for violation of a stay or order, a violation of this Section constitutes a civil rights violation under the Illinois Human Rights Act. All proceeds from the collection of any civil penalty imposed pursuant to the Illinois Human Rights Act under this subsection shall be deposited into the Illinois Military Family Relief Fund.

P.A. 82–280, § 15–1501.6, added by P.A. 97–913, § 940, eff. Jan. 1, 2013.

5/15–1502. Nonrecord Claimants

§ 15–1502. Nonrecord Claimants. (a) Right to Become Record Claimant. At any time prior to the recording of a notice of foreclosure in accordance with Section 15–1503, a nonrecord claimant or unknown owner may become a record claimant with respect to the foreclosure by recording a notice of such claimant's interest in the mortgaged real estate in accordance with Section 15–1218.

(b) Rights of Nonrecord Claimants After Notice. The interest in the mortgaged real estate of a nonrecord claimant who is given notice of the foreclosure as provided in paragraph (2) of subsection (c) of Section 15–1502 shall be barred and terminated by any judg-ment of foreclosure to the same extent as if such claimant had been a party.

(c) Terminating Rights of Nonrecord Claimants. (1) Contents of Affidavit. A party in a foreclosure seeking to bar and terminate the interest in the mortgaged real estate of nonrecord claimants shall file in the office of the clerk of the court in which such action is pending an affidavit stating (i) the names and respective present or last known places of residence of such nonrecord claimants, or (ii) that the existence, names or the present or last known places of residence, or both, of such nonrecord claimants are unknown as of that time to the party and to the party's attorney. Such affidavit, with respect to names and places of residence, may be made upon information and belief of the affiant. The affidavit need not state that inquiry has been made to ascertain the names or present or last known places of residence of such nonrecord claimants, and no such inquiry need be made.

(2) Notice. At least 30 days prior to the entry of a judgment of foreclosure, any person identified in the affidavit described in paragraph (1) of subsection (c) of Section 15–1502 shall be given a notice of the foreclosure complying with the requirements of Section 15–1503 by the party filing the affidavit. Such notice shall be given in the manner and upon the terms and conditions set forth in Sections 2–206 and 2–207 of the Code of Civil Procedure, except that (i) such notice with respect to nonrecord claimants whose names are not set forth in such affidavit, instead of being addressed to such nonrecord claimants by name, may simply be addressed to "Nonrecord Claimants" and (ii) when the mortgaged real estate is located within a municipality in a county with a population under 2,000,000, publication shall be in a newspaper generally circulated in such municipality. Such notice shall have the same effect with respect to all nonrecord claimants designated therein as though a notice containing their names had been published in accordance with Sections 2–206 and 2–207 of the Code of Civil Procedure and may be combined with any notice published against parties defendant in the same action pursuant to those Sections.

(3) Errors. Any inaccuracy in the affidavit described in paragraph (1) of subsection (c) of Section 15–1502 or the failure to file such affidavit or the failure to give notice in accordance with paragraph (2) of subsection (c) of Section 15–1502 shall not invalidate any sale made pursuant to this Article.

(4) Rights of Barred Nonrecord Claimant. Nothing in paragraph (3) of subsection (c) of Section 15–1502 shall affect the rights, if any, of any nonrecord claimant whose interest in the mortgaged real estate was barred and terminated to bring an action against any party to the foreclosure on whose behalf the affidavit was filed, on account of the filing of an inaccurate affidavit by such party in accordance with paragraph (1) of subsection (c) of Section 15–1502 or the failure

to give notice in accordance with paragraph (2) of subsection (c) of Section 15–1502.

P.A. 82–280, § 15–1502, added by P.A. 84–1462, § 2, eff. July 1, 1987.

Formerly Ill.Rev.Stat.1991, ch. 110, ¶ 15–1502.

5/15–1502.5.   Homeowner protection

§ 15–1502.5.   Homeowner protection.

(a) As used in this Section:

"Approved counseling agency" means a housing counseling agency approved by the U.S. Department of Housing and Urban Development.

"Approved Housing Counseling" means in-person counseling provided by a counselor employed by an approved counseling agency to all borrowers, or documented telephone counseling where a hardship would be imposed on one or more borrowers. A hardship shall exist in instances in which the borrower is confined to his or her home due to medical conditions, as verified in writing by a physician or the borrower resides 50 miles or more from the nearest approved counseling agency. In instances of telephone counseling, the borrower must supply all necessary documents to the counselor at least 72 hours prior to the scheduled telephone counseling session.

"Delinquent" means past due with respect to a payment on a mortgage secured by residential real estate.

"Department" means the Department of Financial and Professional Regulation.

"Secretary" means the Secretary of Financial and Professional Regulation or other person authorized to act in the Secretary's stead.

"Sustainable loan workout plan" means a plan that the mortgagor and approved counseling agency believe shall enable the mortgagor to stay current on his or her mortgage payments for the foreseeable future when taking into account the mortgagor income and existing and foreseeable debts. A sustainable loan workout plan may include, but is not limited to, (1) a temporary suspension of payments, (2) a lengthened loan term, (3) a lowered or frozen interest rate, (4) a principal write down, (5) a repayment plan to pay the existing loan in full, (6) deferred payments, or (7) refinancing into a new affordable loan.

(b) Except in the circumstance in which a mortgagor has filed a petition for relief under the United States Bankruptcy Code, no mortgagee shall file a complaint to foreclose a mortgage secured by residential real estate until the requirements of this Section have been satisfied.

(c) Notwithstanding any other provision to the contrary, with respect to a particular mortgage secured by residential real estate, the procedures and forbearances described in this Section apply only once per subject mortgage.

Except for mortgages secured by residential real estate in which any mortgagor has filed for relief under the United States Bankruptcy Code, if a mortgage secured by residential real estate becomes delinquent by more than 30 days the mortgagee shall send via U.S. mail a notice advising the mortgagor that he or she may wish to seek approved housing counseling. Notwithstanding anything to the contrary in this Section, nothing shall preclude the mortgagor and mortgagee from communicating with each other during the initial 30 days of delinquency or reaching agreement on a sustainable loan workout plan, or both.

No foreclosure action under Part 15 of Article XV of the Code of Civil Procedure shall be instituted on a mortgage secured by residential real estate before mailing the notice described in this subsection (c).

The notice required in this subsection (c) shall state the date on which the notice was mailed, shall be headed in bold 14–point type "GRACE PERIOD NOTICE", and shall state the following in 14–point type: "YOUR LOAN IS MORE THAN 30 DAYS PAST DUE. YOU MAY BE EXPERIENCING FINANCIAL DIFFICULTY. IT MAY BE IN YOUR BEST INTEREST TO SEEK APPROVED HOUSING COUNSELING. YOU HAVE A GRACE PERIOD OF 30 DAYS FROM THE DATE OF THIS NOTICE TO OBTAIN APPROVED HOUSING COUNSELING. DURING THE GRACE PERIOD, THE LAW PROHIBITS US FROM TAKING ANY LEGAL ACTION AGAINST YOU. YOU MAY BE ENTITLED TO AN ADDITIONAL 30 DAY GRACE PERIOD IF YOU OBTAIN HOUSING COUNSELING FROM AN APPROVED HOUSING COUNSELING AGENCY. A LIST OF APPROVED COUNSELING AGENCIES MAY BE OBTAINED FROM THE ILLINOIS DEPARTMENT OF FINANCIAL AND PROFESSIONAL REGULATION."

The notice shall also list the Department's current consumer hotline, the Department's website, and the telephone number, fax number, and mailing address of the mortgagee. No language, other than language substantially similar to the language prescribed in this subsection (c), shall be included in the notice. Notwithstanding any other provision to the contrary, the grace period notice required by this subsection (c) may be combined with a counseling notification required under federal law.

The sending of the notice required under this subsection (c) means depositing or causing to be deposited into the United States mail an envelope with first-class postage prepaid that contains the document to be delivered. The envelope shall be addressed to the mortgagor at the common address of the residential real estate securing the mortgage.

(d) Until 30 days after mailing the notice provided for under subsection (c) of this Section, no legal action shall be instituted under Part 15 of Article XV of the Code of Civil Procedure.

(e) If, within the 30–day period provided under subsection (d) of this Section, an approved counseling agency provides written notice to the mortgagee that the mortgagor is seeking approved counseling services, then no legal action under Part 15 of Article XV of the Code of Civil Procedure shall be instituted for 30 days after the date of that notice. The date that such notice is sent shall be stated in the notice, and shall be sent to the address or fax number contained in the Grace Period Notice required under subsection (c) of this Section. During the 30–day period provided under this subsection (e), the mortgagor or counselor or both may prepare and proffer to the mortgagee a proposed sustainable loan workout plan. The mortgagee will then determine whether to accept the proposed sustainable loan workout plan. If the mortgagee and the mortgagor agree to a sustainable loan workout plan, then no legal action under Part 15 of Article XV of the Code of Civil Procedure shall be instituted for as long as the sustainable loan workout plan is complied with by the mortgagor.

The agreed sustainable loan workout plan and any modifications thereto must be in writing and signed by the mortgagee and the mortgagor.

Upon written notice to the mortgagee, the mortgagor may change approved counseling agencies, but such a change does not entitle the mortgagor to any additional period of forbearance.

(f) If the mortgagor fails to comply with the sustainable loan workout plan, then nothing in this Section shall be construed to impair the legal rights of the mortgagee to enforce the contract.

(g) A counselor employed by a housing counseling agency or the housing counseling agency that in good faith provides counseling shall not be liable to a mortgagee or mortgagor for civil damages, except for willful or wanton misconduct on the part of the counselor in providing the counseling.

(h) There shall be no waiver of any provision of this Section.

(i) It is the General Assembly's intent that compliance with this Section shall not prejudice a mortgagee in ratings of its bad debt collection or calculation standards or policies.

(j) This Section shall not apply, or shall cease to apply, to residential real estate that is not occupied as a principal residence by the mortgagor.

(k) This Section is repealed July 1, 2016.

P.A. 82–280, § 15–1502.5, added by P.A. 95–1047, § 35, eff. April 6, 2009. Amended by P.A. 96–1419, § 15, eff. Oct. 1, 2010; P.A. 98–25, § 5, eff. June 20, 2013.

5/15–1503. Notice of Foreclosure

§ 15–1503. Notice of Foreclosure.

(a) A notice of foreclosure, whether the foreclosure is initiated by complaint or counterclaim, made in accordance with this Section and recorded in the county in which the mortgaged real estate is located shall be constructive notice of the pendency of the foreclosure to every person claiming an interest in or lien on the mortgaged real estate, whose interest or lien has not been recorded prior to the recording of such notice of foreclosure. Such notice of foreclosure must be executed by any party or any party's attorney and shall include (i) the names of all plaintiffs and the case number, (ii) the court in which the action was brought, (iii) the names of title holders of record, (iv) a legal description of the real estate sufficient to identify it with reasonable certainty, (v) a common address or description of the location of the real estate and (vi) identification of the mortgage sought to be foreclosed. An incorrect common address or description of the location, or an immaterial error in the identification of a plaintiff or title holder of record, shall not invalidate the lis pendens effect of the notice under this Section. A notice which complies with this Section shall be deemed to comply with Section 2–1901 of the Code of Civil Procedure and shall have the same effect as a notice filed pursuant to that Section; however, a notice which complies with § 2–1901 shall not be constructive notice unless it also complies with the requirements of this Section.

(b) With respect to residential real estate, a copy of the notice of foreclosure described in subsection (a) of Section 15–1503 shall be sent by first class mail, postage prepaid, to the municipality within the boundary of which the mortgaged real estate is located, or to the county within the boundary of which the mortgaged real estate is located if the mortgaged real estate is located in an unincorporated territory. A municipality or county must clearly publish on its website a single address to which such notice shall be sent. If a municipality or county does not maintain a website, then the municipality or county must publicly post in its main office a single address to which such notice shall be sent. In the event that a municipality or county has not complied with the publication requirement in this subsection (b), then the copy of the notice to the municipality or county shall be sent by first class mail, postage prepaid, to the chairperson of the county board or county clerk in the case of a county, to the mayor or city clerk in the case of a city, to the president of the board of trustees or village clerk in the case of a village, or to the president or town clerk in the case of a town. Additionally, if the real estate is located in a city with a population of more than 2,000,000, regardless of whether that city has complied with the publication requirement in this subsection (b), the party must, within 10 days after filing the complaint or counterclaim: (i) send by first class mail, postage prepaid, a copy of the notice of foreclosure to the alderman for the ward in which the real estate is located and (ii) file an affidavit with the court attesting to the fact that the notice was sent to the alderman for the ward in which the real estate is located. The failure to send a copy of the notice to the alderman or to file an affidavit as required results in the dismissal without prejudice of the complaint or counterclaim on a motion of a party or the court. If, after the complaint or counterclaim has been dismissed without prejudice, the party refiles the complaint or counterclaim, then the party must again comply with the requirements that the party send by first class mail, postage prepaid, the notice to the alderman for the ward in which the real estate is located and file an affidavit attesting to the fact that the notice was sent.

P.A. 82–280, § 15–1503, added by P.A. 84–1462, § 2, eff. July 1, 1987. Amended by P.A. 85–907, Art. I, § 1, eff. Nov. 23, 1987; P.A. 86–974, § 1, eff. July 1, 1990; P.A. 96–856, § 25, eff. March 1, 2010; P.A. 97–1164, § 15, eff. June 1, 2013.

Formerly Ill.Rev.Stat.1991, ch. 110, ¶ 15–1503.

5/15–1504. Pleadings and service

§ 15–1504. Pleadings and service.

(a) Form of Complaint. A foreclosure complaint may be in substantially the following form:

(1) Plaintiff files this complaint to foreclose the mortgage (or other conveyance in the nature of a mortgage) (hereinafter called "mortgage") hereinafter described and joins the following person as defendants: (here insert names of all defendants).

(2) Attached as Exhibit "A" is a copy of the mortgage and as Exhibit "B" is a copy of the note secured thereby.

(3) Information concerning mortgage:

(A) Nature of instrument: (here insert whether a mortgage, trust deed or other instrument in the nature of a mortgage, etc.)

(B) Date of mortgage:

(C) Name of mortgagor:

(D) Name of mortgagee:

(E) Date and place of recording:

(F) Identification of recording: (here insert book and page number or document number)

(G) Interest subject to the mortgage: (here insert whether fee simple, estate for years, undivided interest, etc.)

(H) Amount of original indebtedness, including subsequent advances made under the mortgage:

(I) Both the legal description of the mortgaged real estate and the common address or other information sufficient to identify it with reasonable certainty:

(J) Statement as to defaults, including, but not necessarily limited to, date of default, current unpaid principal balance, per diem interest accruing, and any further information concerning the default:

(K) Name of present owner of the real estate:

(L) Names of other persons who are joined as defendants and whose interest in or lien on the mortgaged real estate is sought to be terminated:

(M) Names of defendants claimed to be personally liable for deficiency, if any:

(N) Capacity in which plaintiff brings this foreclosure (here indicate whether plaintiff is the legal holder of the indebtedness, a pledgee, an agent, the trustee under a trust deed or otherwise, as appropriate):

(O) Facts in support of redemption period shorter than the longer of (i) 7 months from the date the mortgagor or, if more than one, all the mortgagors (I) have been served with summons or by publication or (II) have otherwise submitted to the jurisdiction of the court, or (ii) 3 months from the entry of the judgment of foreclosure, if sought (here indicate whether based upon the real estate not being residential or real estate value less than 90% of amount owed, etc.):

(P) Statement that the right of redemption has been waived by all owners of redemption, if applicable:

(Q) Facts in support of request for attorneys' fees and of costs and expenses, if applicable:

(R) Facts in support of a request for appointment of mortgagee in possession or for appointment of receiver, and identity of such receiver, if sought:

(S) Offer to mortgagor in accordance with Section 15–1402 to accept title to the real estate in satisfaction of all indebtedness and obligations secured by the mortgage without judicial sale, if sought:

(T) Name or names of defendants whose right to possess the mortgaged real estate, after the confirmation of a foreclosure sale, is sought to be terminated and, if not elsewhere stated, the facts in support thereof:

REQUEST FOR RELIEF

Plaintiff requests:

(i) A judgment of foreclosure and sale.

(ii) An order granting a shortened redemption period, if sought.

(iii) A personal judgment for a deficiency, if sought.

(iv) An order granting possession, if sought.

(v) An order placing the mortgagee in possession or appointing a receiver, if sought.

(vi) A judgment for attorneys' fees, costs and expenses, if sought.

(b) Required Information. A foreclosure complaint need contain only such statements and requests called for by the form set forth in subsection (a) of Section 15–1504 as may be appropriate for the relief sought. Such complaint may be filed as a counterclaim, may be joined with other counts or may include in the same count additional matters or a request for any additional relief permitted by Article II of the Code of Civil Procedure. [1]

(c) Allegations. The statements contained in a complaint in the form set forth in subsection (a) of Section 15–1504 are deemed and construed to include allegations as follows:

(1) that, on the date indicated, the obligor of the indebtedness or other obligations secured by the mortgage was justly indebted in the amount of the indicated original indebtedness to the original mortgagee or payee of the mortgage note;

(2) that the exhibits attached are true and correct copies of the mortgage and note and are incorporated and made a part of the complaint by express reference;

(3) that the mortgagor was at the date indicated an owner of the interest in the real estate described in the complaint and that as of that date made, executed and delivered the mortgage as security for the note or other obligations;

(4) that the mortgage was recorded in the county in which the mortgaged real estate is located, on the date indicated, in the book and page or as the document number indicated;

(5) that defaults occurred as indicated;

(6) that at the time of the filing of the complaint the persons named as present owners are the owners of the indicated interests in and to the real estate described;

(7) that the mortgage constitutes a valid, prior and paramount lien upon the indicated interest in the mortgaged real estate, which lien is prior and superior to the right, title, interest, claim or lien of all parties and nonrecord claimants whose interests in the mortgaged real estate are sought to be terminated;

(8) that by reason of the defaults alleged, if the indebtedness has not matured by its terms, the same has become due by the exercise, by the plaintiff or other persons having such power, of a right or power to declare immediately due and payable the whole of all indebtedness secured by the mortgage;

(9) that any and all notices of default or election to declare the indebtedness due and payable or other notices required to be given have been duly and properly given;

(10) that any and all periods of grace or other period of time allowed for the performance of the covenants or conditions claimed to be breached or for the curing of any breaches have expired;

(11) that the amounts indicated in the statement in the complaint are correctly stated and if such statement indicates any advances made or to be made by the plaintiff or owner of the mortgage indebtedness, that such advances were, in fact, made or will be required to be made, and under and

by virtue of the mortgage the same constitute additional indebtedness secured by the mortgage; and

(12) that, upon confirmation of the sale, the holder of the certificate of sale or deed issued pursuant to that certificate or, if no certificate or deed was issued, the purchaser at the sale will be entitled to full possession of the mortgaged real estate against the parties named in clause (T) of paragraph (3) of subsection (a) of Section 15–1504 or elsewhere to the same effect; the omission of any party indicates that plaintiff will not seek a possessory order in the order confirming sale unless the request is subsequently made under subsection (h) of § 15–1701 or by separate action under Article 9 of this Code. [2]

(d) Request for Fees and Costs. A statement in the complaint that plaintiff seeks the inclusion of attorneys' fees and of costs and expenses shall be deemed and construed to include allegations that:

(1) plaintiff has been compelled to employ and retain attorneys to prepare and file the complaint and to represent and advise the plaintiff in the foreclosure of the mortgage and the plaintiff will thereby become liable for the usual, reasonable and customary fees of the attorneys in that behalf;

(2) the plaintiff has been compelled to advance or will be compelled to advance, various sums of money in payment of costs, fees, expenses and disbursements incurred in connection with the foreclosure, including, without limiting the generality of the foregoing, filing fees, stenographer's fees, witness fees, costs of publication, costs of procuring and preparing documentary evidence and costs of procuring abstracts of title, Torrens certificates, foreclosure minutes and a title insurance policy;

(3) under the terms of the mortgage, all such advances, costs, attorneys' fees and other fees, expenses and disbursements are made a lien upon the mortgaged real estate and the plaintiff is entitled to recover all such advances, costs, attorneys' fees, expenses and disbursements, together with interest on all advances at the rate provided in the mortgage, or, if no rate is provided therein, at the statutory judgment rate, from the date on which such advances are made;

(4) in order to protect the lien of the mortgage, it may become necessary for plaintiff to pay taxes and assessments which have been or may be levied upon the mortgaged real estate;

(5) in order to protect and preserve the mortgaged real estate, it may also become necessary for the plaintiff to pay liability (protecting mortgagor and mortgagee), fire and other hazard insurance premiums on the mortgaged real estate, make such repairs to the mortgaged real estate as may reasonably be deemed necessary for the proper preservation thereof, advance for costs to inspect the mortgaged real estate or to appraise it, or both, and advance for premiums for pre-existing private or

governmental mortgage insurance to the extent required after a foreclosure is commenced in order to keep such insurance in force; and

(6) under the terms of the mortgage, any money so paid or expended will become an additional indebtedness secured by the mortgage and will bear interest from the date such monies are advanced at the rate provided in the mortgage, or, if no rate is provided, at the statutory judgment rate.

(e) Request for Foreclosure. The request for foreclosure is deemed and construed to mean that the plaintiff requests that:

(1) an accounting may be taken under the direction of the court of the amounts due and owing to the plaintiff;

(2) the defendants be ordered to pay to the plaintiff before expiration of any redemption period (or, if no redemption period, before a short date fixed by the court) whatever sums may appear to be due upon the taking of such account, together with attorneys' fees and costs of the proceedings (to the extent provided in the mortgage or by law);

(3) in default of such payment in accordance with the judgment, the mortgaged real estate be sold as directed by the court, to satisfy the amount due to the plaintiff as set forth in the judgment, together with the interest thereon at the statutory judgment rate from the date of the judgment;

(4) in the event the plaintiff is a purchaser of the mortgaged real estate at such sale, the plaintiff may offset against the purchase price of such real estate the amounts due under the judgment of foreclosure and order confirming the sale;

(5) in the event of such sale and the failure of any person entitled thereto to redeem prior to such sale pursuant to this Article, the defendants made parties to the foreclosure in accordance with this Article, and all nonrecord claimants given notice of the foreclosure in accordance with this Article, and all persons claiming by, through or under them, and each and any and all of them, may be forever barred and foreclosed of any right, title, interest, claim, lien, or right to redeem in and to the mortgaged real estate; and

(6) if no redemption is made prior to such sale, a deed may be issued to the purchaser thereat according to law and such purchaser be let into possession of the mortgaged real estate in accordance with Part 17 of this Article. [3]

(f) Request for Deficiency Judgment. A request for a personal judgment for a deficiency in a foreclosure complaint if the sale of the mortgaged real estate fails to produce a sufficient amount to pay the amount found due, the plaintiff may have a personal judgment against any party in the foreclosure indicated as being personally liable therefor and the enforcement thereof be had as provided by law.

(g) Request for Possession or Receiver. A request for possession or appointment of a receiver has the meaning as stated in subsection (b) of Section 15–1706.

(h) Answers by Parties. Any party may assert its interest by counterclaim and such counterclaim may at the option of that party stand in lieu of answer to the complaint for foreclosure and all counter complaints previously or thereafter filed in the foreclosure. Any such counterclaim shall be deemed to constitute a statement that the counter claimant does not have sufficient knowledge to form a belief as to the truth or falsity of the allegations of the complaint and all other counterclaims, except to the extent that the counterclaim admits or specifically denies such allegations.

P.A. 82–280, § 15–1504, added by P.A. 84–1462, § 2, eff. July 1, 1987. Amended by P.A. 85–907, Art. I, § 1, eff. Nov. 23, 1987; P.A. 86–974, § 1, eff. July 1, 1990; P.A. 88–265, § 5, eff. Jan. 1, 1994; P.A. 91–357, § 250, eff. July 29, 1999; P.A. 97–1164, § 15, eff. June 1, 2013.

Formerly Ill.Rev.Stat.1991, ch. 110, ¶ 15–1504.

[1] 735 ILCS 5/2–101 et seq.
[2] 735 ILCS 5/9–101 et seq.
[3] 735 ILCS 5/15–1701 et seq.

5/15–1504.1. Filing fee for Foreclosure Prevention Program Fund, Foreclosure Prevention Program Graduated Fund, and Abandoned Residential Property Municipality Relief Fund

§ 15–1504.1. Filing fee for Foreclosure Prevention Program Fund, Foreclosure Prevention Program Graduated Fund, and Abandoned Residential Property Municipality Relief Fund.

(a) Fee paid by all plaintiffs with respect to residential real estate. With respect to residential real estate, at the time of the filing of a foreclosure complaint, the plaintiff shall pay to the clerk of the court in which the foreclosure complaint is filed a fee of $50 for deposit into the Foreclosure Prevention Program Fund, a special fund created in the State treasury. The clerk shall remit the fee collected pursuant to this subsection (a) to the State Treasurer to be expended for the purposes set forth in Section 7.30 of the Illinois Housing Development Act. All fees paid by plaintiffs to the clerk of the court as provided in this subsection (a) shall be disbursed within 60 days after receipt by the clerk of the court as follows: (i) 98% to the State Treasurer for deposit into the Foreclosure Prevention Program Fund, and (ii) 2% to the clerk of the court to be retained by the clerk for deposit into the Circuit Court Clerk Operation and Administrative Fund to defray administrative expenses related to implementation of this subsection (a). Notwithstanding any other law to the contrary, the Foreclosure Prevention Program Fund is not subject to sweeps, administrative charge-backs, or any other fiscal maneuver that would in any way transfer any amounts from the Foreclosure Prevention Program Fund into any other fund of the State.

(a–5) Additional fee paid by plaintiffs with respect to residential real estate.

(1) Until January 1, 2018, with respect to residential real estate, at the time of the filing of a foreclosure complaint and in addition to the fee set forth in subsection (a) of this Section, the plaintiff shall pay to the clerk of the court in which the foreclosure complaint is filed a fee for the Foreclosure Prevention Program Graduated Fund and the Abandoned Residential Property Municipality Relief Fund as follows:

(A) The fee shall be $500 if:

(i) the plaintiff, together with its affiliates, has filed a sufficient number of foreclosure complaints so as to be included in the first tier foreclosure filing category and is filing the complaint on its own behalf as the holder of the indebtedness; or

(ii) the plaintiff, together with its affiliates, has filed a sufficient number of foreclosure complaints so as to be included in the first tier foreclosure filing category and is filing the complaint on behalf of a mortgagee that, together with its affiliates, has filed a sufficient number of foreclosure complaints so as to be included in the first tier foreclosure filing category; or

(iii) the plaintiff is not a depository institution and is filing the complaint on behalf of a mortgagee that, together with its affiliates, has filed a sufficient number of foreclosure complaints so as to be included in the first tier foreclosure filing category.

(B) The fee shall be $250 if:

(i) the plaintiff, together with its affiliates, has filed a sufficient number of foreclosure complaints so as to be included in the second tier foreclosure filing category and is filing the complaint on its own behalf as the holder of the indebtedness; or

(ii) the plaintiff, together with its affiliates, has filed a sufficient number of foreclosure complaints so as to be included in the first or second tier foreclosure filing category and is filing the complaint on behalf of a mortgagee that, together with its affiliates, has filed a sufficient number of foreclosure complaints so as to be included in the second tier foreclosure filing category; or

(iii) the plaintiff, together with its affiliates, has filed a sufficient number of foreclosure complaints so as to be included in the second tier foreclosure filing category and is filing the complaint on behalf of a mortgagee that, together with its affiliates, has filed a sufficient number of foreclosure complaints so as to be included in the first tier foreclosure filing category; or

(iv) the plaintiff is not a depository institution and is filing the complaint on behalf of a mortgagee that, together with its affiliates, has filed a sufficient number of foreclosure complaints so as to be included in the second tier foreclosure filing category.

(C) The fee shall be $50 if:

(i) the plaintiff, together with its affiliates, has filed a sufficient number of foreclosure complaints so as to be included in the third tier foreclosure filing category and is filing the complaint on its own behalf as the holder of the indebtedness; or

(ii) the plaintiff, together with its affiliates, has filed a sufficient number of foreclosure complaints so as to be included in the first, second, or third tier foreclosure filing category and is filing the complaint on behalf of a mortgagee that, together with its affiliates, has filed a sufficient number of foreclosure complaints so as to be included in the third tier foreclosure filing category; or

(iii) the plaintiff, together with its affiliates, has filed a sufficient number of foreclosure complaints so as to be included in the third tier foreclosure filing category and is filing the complaint on behalf of a mortgagee that, together with its affiliates, has filed a sufficient number of foreclosure complaints so as to be included in the first tier foreclosure filing category; or

(iv) the plaintiff, together with its affiliates, has filed a sufficient number of foreclosure complaints so as to be included in the third tier foreclosure filing category and is filing the complaint on behalf of a mortgagee that, together with its affiliates, has filed a sufficient number of foreclosure complaints so as to be included in the second tier foreclosure filing category; or

(v) the plaintiff is not a depository institution and is filing the complaint on behalf of a mortgagee that, together with its affiliates, has filed a sufficient number of foreclosure complaints so as to be included in the third tier foreclosure filing category.

(2) The clerk shall remit the fee collected pursuant to paragraph (1) of this subsection (a–5) to the State Treasurer to be expended for the purposes set forth in Sections 7.30 and 7.31 of the Illinois Housing Development Act and for administrative expenses. All fees paid by plaintiffs to the clerk of the court as provided in paragraph (1) shall be disbursed within 60 days after receipt by the clerk of the court as follows:

(A) 28% to the State Treasurer for deposit into the Foreclosure Prevention Program Graduated Fund;

(B) 70% to the State Treasurer for deposit into the Abandoned Residential Property Municipality Relief Fund; and

(C) 2% to the clerk of the court to be retained by the clerk for deposit into the Circuit Court Clerk Operation and Administrative Fund to defray administrative expenses related to implementation of this subsection (a–5).

(3) Until January 1, 2018, with respect to residential real estate, at the time of the filing of a foreclosure complaint, the plaintiff or plaintiff's representative shall file a verified statement that states which additional fee is due under paragraph (1) of this subsection (a–5), unless the court has established another process for a plaintiff or plaintiff's representative to certify which additional fee is due under paragraph (1) of this subsection (a–5).

(4) If a plaintiff fails to provide the clerk of the court with a true and correct statement of the additional fee due under paragraph (1) of this subsection (a–5), and the mortgagor reimburses the plaintiff for any erroneous additional fee that was paid by the plaintiff to the clerk of the court, the mortgagor may seek a refund of any overpayment of the fee in an amount that shall not exceed the difference between the higher additional fee paid under paragraph (1) of this subsection (a–5) and the actual fee due thereunder. The mortgagor must petition the judge within the foreclosure action for the award of any fee overpayment pursuant to this paragraph (4) of this subsection (a–5), and the award shall be determined by the judge and paid by the clerk of the court out of the fund account into which the clerk of the court deposits fees to be remitted to the State Treasurer under paragraph (2) of this subsection (a–5), the timing of which refund payment shall be determined by the clerk of the court based upon the availability of funds in the subject fund account. This refund shall be the mortgagor's sole remedy and a mortgagor shall have no private right of action against the plaintiff or plaintiff's representatives if the additional fee paid by the plaintiff was erroneous.

(5) This subsection (a–5) is inoperative on and after January 1, 2018.

(b) Not later than March 1 of each year, the clerk of the court shall submit to the Illinois Housing Development Authority a report of the funds collected and remitted pursuant to this Section during the preceding year.

(c) As used in this Section:

"Affiliate" means any company that controls, is controlled by, or is under common control with another company.

"Approved counseling agency" and "approved housing counseling" have the meanings ascribed to those terms in Section 7.30 of the Illinois Housing Development Act.

"Depository institution" means a bank, savings bank, savings and loan association, or credit union chartered, organized, or holding a certificate of authority to do business under the laws of this State, another state, or the United States.

"First tier foreclosure filing category" is a classification that only applies to a plaintiff that has filed 175 or more foreclosure complaints on residential real estate located in Illinois during the calendar year immediately preceding the date of the filing of the subject foreclosure complaint.

"Second tier foreclosure filing category" is a classification that only applies to a plaintiff that has filed at least 50, but no more than 174, foreclosure complaints on residential real estate located in Illinois during the calendar year immediately preceding the date of the filing of the subject foreclosure complaint.

"Third tier foreclosure filing category'" is a classification that only applies to a plaintiff that has filed no more than 49 foreclosure complaints on residential real estate located in Illinois during the calendar year immediately preceding the date of the filing of the subject foreclosure complaint.

(d) In no instance shall the fee set forth in subsection (a–5) be assessed for any foreclosure complaint filed before the effective date of this amendatory Act of the 97th General Assembly.

(e) Notwithstanding any other law to the contrary, the Abandoned Residential Property Municipality Relief Fund is not subject to sweeps, administrative charge-backs, or any other fiscal maneuver that would in any way transfer any amounts from the Abandoned Residential Property Municipality Relief Fund into any other fund of the State.

P.A. 82–280, § 15–1504.1, added by P.A. 96–1419, § 15, eff. Oct. 1, 2010. Amended by P.A. 97–333, § 575, eff. Aug. 12, 2011; P.A. 97–1164, § 15, eff. June 1, 2013; P.A. 98–20, § 15, eff. June 11, 2013.

5/15–1504.5. Homeowner notice to be attached to summons

§ 15–1504.5. Homeowner notice to be attached to summons. For all residential foreclosure actions filed, the plaintiff must attach a Homeowner Notice to the summons. The Homeowner Notice must be in at least 12 point type and in English and Spanish. The Spanish translation shall be prepared by the Attorney General and posted on the Attorney General's website. A notice that includes the Attorney General's Spanish translation in substantially similar form shall be deemed to comply with the Spanish notice requirement in this Section. The Notice must be in substantially the following form:

IMPORTANT INFORMATION FOR HOMEOWNERS IN FORECLOSURE

1. **POSSESSION:** The lawful occupants of a home have the right to live in the home until a judge enters an order for possession.

2. OWNERSHIP: You continue to own your home until the court rules otherwise.

3. REINSTATEMENT: As the homeowner you have the right to bring the mortgage current within 90 days after you receive the summons.

4. REDEMPTION: As the homeowner you have the right to sell your home, refinance, or pay off the loan during the redemption period.

5. SURPLUS: As the homeowner you have the right to petition the court for any excess money that results from a foreclosure sale of your home.

6. WORKOUT OPTIONS: The mortgage company does not want to foreclose on your home if there is any way to avoid it. Call your mortgage company [insert name of the homeowner's current mortgage servicer in bold and 14 point type] or its attorneys to find out the alternatives to foreclosure.

7. PAYOFF AMOUNT: You have the right to obtain a written statement of the amount necessary to pay off your loan. Your mortgage company (identified above) must provide you this statement within 10 business days of receiving your request, provided that your request is in writing and includes your name, the address of the property, and the mortgage account or loan number. Your first payoff statement will be free.

8. GET ADVICE: This information is not exhaustive and does not replace the advice of a professional. You may have other options. Get professional advice from a lawyer or certified housing counselor about your rights and options to avoid foreclosure.

9. LAWYER: If you do not have a lawyer, you may be able to find assistance by contacting the Illinois State Bar Association or a legal aid organization that provides free legal assistance.

10. PROCEED WITH CAUTION: You may be contacted by people offering to help you avoid foreclosure. Before entering into any transaction with persons offering to help you, please contact a lawyer, government official, or housing counselor for advice.

P.A. 82–280, § 15–1504.5, added by P.A. 95–961, § 5, eff. Jan. 1, 2009.

5/15–1505. Real Estate Subject to Senior Liens

§ 15–1505. Real Estate Subject to Senior Liens. During a foreclosure, and any time prior to sale, a mortgagee or any other lienor may pay (i) when due installments of principal, interest or other obligations in accordance with the terms of any senior mortgage, (ii) when due installments of real estate taxes or (iii) any other obligation authorized by the mortgage instrument. With court approval, a mortgagee or any other lienor may pay any other amounts in connection with other liens, encumbrances or interests reasonably necessary to preserve the status of title.

P.A. 82–280, § 15–1505, added by P.A. 84–1462, § 2, eff. July 1, 1987.

Formerly Ill.Rev.Stat.1991, ch. 110, ¶ 15–1505.

5/15–1505.5. Payoff demands

§ 15–1505.5. Payoff demands.

(a) In a foreclosure action subject to this Article, on the written demand of a mortgagor or the mortgagor's authorized agent (which shall include the mortgagor's name, the mortgaged property's address, and the mortgage account or loan number), a mortgagee or the mortgagee's authorized agent shall prepare and deliver an accurate statement of the total outstanding balance of the mortgagor's obligation that would be required to satisfy the obligation in full as of the date of preparation ("payoff demand statement") to the mortgagor or the mortgagor's authorized agent who has requested it within 10 business days after receipt of the demand. For purposes of this Section, a payoff demand statement is accurate if prepared in good faith based on the records of the mortgagee or the mortgagee's agent.

(b) The payoff demand statement shall include the following:

(1) the information necessary to calculate the payoff amount on a per diem basis for the lesser of a period of 30 days or until the date scheduled for judicial sale;

(2) estimated charges (stated as such) that the mortgagee reasonably believes may be incurred within 30 days from the date of preparation of the payoff demand statement; and

(3) the loan number for the obligation to be paid, the address of the mortgagee, the telephone number of the mortgagee and, if a banking organization or corporation, the name of the department, if applicable, and its telephone number and facsimile phone number.

(c) A mortgagee or mortgagee's agent who willfully fails to prepare and deliver an accurate payoff demand statement within 10 business days after receipt of a written demand is liable to the mortgagor for actual damages sustained for failure to deliver the statement. The mortgagee or mortgagee's agent is liable to the mortgagor for $500 if no actual damages are sustained. For purposes of this subsection, "willfully" means a failure to comply with this Section without just cause or excuse or mitigating circumstances.

(d) The mortgagor must petition the judge within the foreclosure action for the award of any damages pursuant to this Section, which award shall be determined by the judge.

(e) Unless the payoff demand statement provides otherwise, the statement is deemed to apply only to the unpaid balance of the single obligation that is named in the demand and that is secured by the mortgage or deed of trust identified in the payoff demand statement.

(f) The demand for and preparation and delivery of a payoff demand statement pursuant to this Section does not change any date or time period that is prescribed in the note or that is otherwise provided by law. Failure to comply with any provision of this Section does not change any of the rights of the parties as set forth in the note, mortgage, or applicable law.

(g) The mortgagee or mortgagee's agent shall furnish the first payoff demand statement at no cost to the mortgagor.

(h) For the purposes of this Section, unless the context otherwise requires, "deliver" or "delivery" means depositing or causing to be deposited into the United States mail an envelope with postage prepaid that contains a copy of the documents to be delivered and that is addressed to the person whose name and address are provided in the payoff demand. "Delivery" may also include transmitting those documents by telephone facsimile to the person or electronically if the payoff demand specifically requests and authorizes that the documents be transmitted in electronic form.

(i) The mortgagee or mortgagee's agent is not required to comply with the payoff demand statement procedure set forth in this Section when responding to a notice of intent to redeem issued under Section 15–1603(e).

P.A. 82–280, § 15–1505.5, added by P.A. 95–961, § 5, eff. Jan. 1, 2009.

5/15–1505.6. Objection to jurisdiction over the person

§ 15–1505.6. Objection to jurisdiction over the person.

(a) In any residential foreclosure action, the deadline for filing a motion to dismiss the entire proceeding or to quash service of process that objects to the court's jurisdiction over the person, unless extended by the court for good cause shown, is 60 days after the earlier of these events: (i) the date that the moving party filed an appearance; or (ii) the date that the moving party participated in a hearing without filing an appearance.

(b) In any residential foreclosure action, if the objecting party files a responsive pleading or a motion (other than a motion for an extension of time to answer or otherwise appear) prior to the filing of a motion in compliance with subsection (a), that party waives all objections to the court's jurisdiction over the party's person.

P.A. 82–280, § 15–1505.6, added by P.A. 97–329, § 5, eff. Aug. 12, 2011.

5/15–1505.8. Expedited judgment and sale procedure for abandoned residential property

§ 15–1505.8. Expedited judgment and sale procedure for abandoned residential property.

(a) Upon motion and notice, the mortgagee may elect to utilize the expedited judgment and sale procedure for abandoned residential property stated in this Section to obtain a judgment of foreclosure pursuant to Section 15–1506. The motion to expedite the judgment and sale may be combined with or made part of the motion requesting a judgment of foreclosure. The notice of the motion to expedite the judgment and sale shall be sent by first-class mail to the last known address of the mortgagor, and the notice required by paragraph (1) of subsection (*l*) of this Section shall be posted at the property address.

(b) The motion requesting an expedited judgment of foreclosure and sale may be filed by the mortgagee at the time the foreclosure complaint is filed or any time thereafter, and shall set forth the facts demonstrating that the mortgaged real estate is abandoned residential real estate under Section 15–1200.5 and shall be supported by affidavit.

(c) If a motion for an expedited judgment and sale is filed at the time the foreclosure complaint is filed or before the period to answer the foreclosure complaint has expired, the motion shall be heard by the court no earlier than before the period to answer the foreclosure complaint has expired and no later than 21 days after the period to answer the foreclosure complaint has expired.

(d) If a motion for an expedited judgment and sale is filed after the period to answer the foreclosure complaint has expired, the motion shall be heard no later than 21 days after the motion is filed.

(e) The hearing shall be given priority by the court and shall be scheduled to be heard within the applicable time period set forth in subsection (c) or (d) of this Section.

(f) Subject to subsection (g), at the hearing on the motion requesting an expedited judgment and sale, if the court finds that the mortgaged real estate is abandoned residential property, the court shall grant the motion and immediately proceed to a trial of the foreclosure. A judgment of foreclosure under this Section shall include the matters identified in Section 15–1506.

(g) The court may not grant the motion requesting an expedited judgment and sale if the mortgagor, an unknown owner, or a lawful occupant appears in the action in any manner before or at the hearing and objects to a finding of abandonment.

(h) The court shall vacate an order issued pursuant to subsection (f) of this Section if the mortgagor or a lawful occupant appears in the action at any time prior to the court issuing an order confirming the sale pursuant to subsection (b–3) of Section 15–1508 and presents evidence establishing to the satisfaction of the court that the mortgagor or lawful occupant has not abandoned the mortgaged real estate.

(i) The reinstatement period and redemption period for the abandoned residential property shall end in accordance with paragraph (4) of subsection (b) of Section 15–1603, and the abandoned residential property shall be sold at the earliest practicable time at a sale as provided in this Article.

(j) The mortgagee or its agent may enter, secure, and maintain abandoned residential property subject to subsection (e–5) of Section 21–3 of the Criminal Code of 2012.

(k) Personal property.

(1) Upon confirmation of the sale held pursuant to Section 15–1507, any personal property remaining in or upon the abandoned residential property shall be deemed to have been abandoned by the owner of such personal property and may be disposed of or donated by the holder of the certificate of sale (or, if none, by the purchaser at the sale). In the event of donation of any such personal property, the holder of the certificate of sale (or, if none, the purchaser at the sale) may transfer such donated property with a bill of sale. No mortgagee or its successors or assigns, holder of a certificate of sale, or purchaser at the sale shall be liable for any such disposal or donation of personal property.

(2) Notwithstanding paragraph (1) of this subsection (k), in the event a lawful occupant is in possession of the mortgaged real estate who has not been made a party to the foreclosure and had his or her interests terminated therein, any personal property of the lawful occupant shall not be deemed to have been abandoned, nor shall the rights of the lawful occupant to any personal property be affected.

(l) Notices to be posted at property address.

(1) The notice set out in this paragraph (1) of this subsection (l) shall be conspicuously posted at the property address at least 14 days before the hearing on the motion requesting an expedited judgment and sale and shall be in boldface, in at least 12 point type, and in substantially the following form:

"NOTICE TO ANY TENANT OR OTHER LAWFUL OCCUPANT OF THIS PROPERTY

A lawsuit has been filed to foreclose on this property, and the party asking to foreclose on this property has asked a judge to find that THIS PROPERTY IS ABANDONED.

The judge will be holding a hearing to decide whether this property is ABANDONED.

IF YOU LAWFULLY OCCUPY ANY PART OF THIS PROPERTY, YOU MAY CHOOSE TO GO TO

THIS HEARING and explain to the judge how you are a lawful occupant of this property.

If the judge is satisfied that you are a LAWFUL OCCUPANT of this property, the court will find that this property is NOT ABANDONED.

This hearing will be held in the courthouse at the following address, date, and time:

Court name: . . . .

Court address: . . . .

Court room number where hearing will be held: . . . .

(There should be a person in this room called a CLERK who can help you. Make sure you know THIS PROPERTY'S ADDRESS.)

Date of hearing: . . . .

Time of hearing: . . . .

MORE INFORMATION

Name of lawsuit: . . . .

Number of lawsuit: . . . .

Address of this property: . . . .

IMPORTANT

This is NOT a notice to vacate the premises. You may wish to contact a lawyer or your local legal aid or housing counseling agency to discuss any rights that you may have.

WARNING

INTENTIONAL REMOVAL OF THIS NOTICE BEFORE THE DATE AND TIME STATED IN THIS NOTICE IS A CLASS B MISDEMEANOR, PUNISHABLE BY UP TO 180 DAYS IN JAIL AND A FINE OF UP TO $1500, UNDER ILLINOIS LAW. 720 ILCS 5/21–3(a).

NO TRESPASSING

KNOWINGLY ENTERING THIS PROPERTY WITHOUT LAWFUL AUTHORITY IS A CLASS B MISDEMEANOR, PUNISHABLE BY UP TO 180 DAYS IN JAIL AND A FINE OF UP TO $1500, UNDER ILLINOIS LAW. 720 ILCS 5/21–3(a).".

(2) The notice set out in this paragraph (2) of this subsection (l) shall be conspicuously posted at the property address at least 14 days before the hearing to confirm the sale of the abandoned residential property and shall be in boldface, in at least 12 point type, and in substantially the following form:

"NOTICE TO ANY TENANT OR OTHER LAWFUL OCCUPANT OF THIS PROPERTY

A lawsuit has been filed to foreclose on this property, and the judge has found that THIS PROPERTY IS

ABANDONED. As a result, THIS PROPERTY HAS BEEN OR WILL BE SOLD.

HOWEVER, there still must be a hearing for the judge to approve the sale. The judge will NOT APPROVE this sale if the judge finds that any person lawfully occupies any part of this property.

IF YOU LAWFULLY OCCUPY ANY PART OF THIS PROPERTY, YOU MAY CHOOSE TO GO TO THIS HEARING and explain to the judge how you are a lawful occupant of this property. You also may appear BEFORE this hearing and explain to the judge how you are a lawful occupant of this property.

If the judge is satisfied that you are a LAWFUL OCCUPANT of this property, the court will find that this property is NOT ABANDONED, and there will be no sale of the property at this time.

This hearing will be held in the courthouse at the following address, date, and time:

Court name: ....

Court address: ....

Court room number where hearing will be held: ....

(There should be a person in this room called a CLERK who can help you. Make sure you know THIS PROPERTY'S ADDRESS.)

Date of hearing: ....

Time of hearing: ....

MORE INFORMATION

Name of lawsuit: ....

Number of lawsuit: ....

Address of this property: ....

IMPORTANT

This is NOT a notice to vacate the premises. You may wish to contact a lawyer or your local legal aid or housing counseling agency to discuss any rights that you may have.

WARNING

INTENTIONAL REMOVAL OF THIS NOTICE BEFORE THE DATE AND TIME STATED IN THIS NOTICE IS A CLASS B MISDEMEANOR, PUNISHABLE BY UP TO 180 DAYS IN JAIL AND A FINE OF UP TO $1500, UNDER ILLINOIS LAW. 720 ILCS 5/21–3(a).

NO TRESPASSING

KNOWINGLY ENTERING THIS PROPERTY WITHOUT LAWFUL AUTHORITY IS A CLASS B MISDEMEANOR, PUNISHABLE BY UP TO 180 DAYS IN JAIL AND A FINE OF UP TO $1500, UNDER ILLINOIS LAW. 720 ILCS 5/21–3(a)."

P.A. 82–280, § 15–1505.8, added by P.A. 97–1164, § 15, eff. June 1, 2013. Amended by P.A. 98–20, § 15, eff. June 11, 2013.

5/15–1506. Judgment

§ 15–1506. Judgment.

(a) Evidence. In the trial of a foreclosure, the evidence to support the allegations of the complaint shall be taken in open court, except:

(1) where an allegation of fact in the complaint is not denied by a party's verified answer or verified counterclaim, or where a party pursuant to subsection (b) of Section 2–610 of the Code of Civil Procedure states, or is deemed to have stated, in its pleading that it has no knowledge of such allegation sufficient to form a belief and attaches the required affidavit, a sworn verification of the complaint or a separate affidavit setting forth such fact is sufficient evidence thereof against such party and no further evidence of such fact shall be required; and

(2) where all the allegations of fact in the complaint have been proved by verification of the complaint or affidavit, the court upon motion supported by an affidavit stating the amount which is due the mortgagee, shall enter a judgment of foreclosure as requested in the complaint.

(b) Instruments. In all cases the evidence of the indebtedness and the mortgage foreclosed shall be exhibited to the court and appropriately marked, and copies thereof shall be filed with the court.

(c) Summary and Default Judgments. Nothing in this Section 15–1506 shall prevent a party from obtaining a summary or default judgment authorized by Article II of the Code of Civil Procedure.

(d) Notice of Entry of Default. When any judgment in a foreclosure is entered by default, notice of such judgment shall be given in accordance with Section 2–1302 of the Code of Civil Procedure.

(e) Matters Required in Judgment. A judgment of foreclosure shall include the last date for redemption and all rulings of the court entered with respect to each request for relief set forth in the complaint. The omission of the date for redemption shall not extend the time for redemption or impair the validity of the judgment.

(f) Special Matters in Judgment. Without limiting the general authority and powers of the court, special matters may be included in the judgment of foreclosure if sought by a party in the complaint or by separate motion. Such matters may include, without limitation:

(1) a manner of sale other than public auction;

(2) a sale by sealed bid;

(3) an official or other person who shall be the officer to conduct the sale other than the one customarily designated by the court;

(4) provisions for non-exclusive broker listings or designating a duly licensed real estate broker nominated by one of the parties to exclusively list the real estate for sale;

(5) the fees or commissions to be paid out of the sale proceeds to the listing or other duly licensed broker, if any, who shall have procured the accepted bid;

(6) the fees to be paid out of the sale proceeds to an auctioneer, if any, who shall have been authorized to conduct a public auction sale;

(7) whether and in what manner and with what content signs shall be posted on the real estate;

(8) a particular time and place at which such bids shall be received;

(9) a particular newspaper or newspapers in which notice of sale shall be published;

(10) the format for the advertising of such sale, including the size, content and format of such advertising, and additional advertising of such sale;

(11) matters or exceptions to which title in the real estate may be subject at the sale;

(12) a requirement that title insurance in a specified form be provided to a purchaser at the sale, and who shall pay for such insurance;

(13) whether and to what extent bids with mortgage or other contingencies will be allowed;

(14) such other matters as approved by the court to ensure sale of the real estate for the most commercially favorable price for the type of real estate involved.

(g) Agreement of the Parties. If all of the parties agree in writing on the minimum price and that the real estate may be sold to the first person who offers in writing to purchase the real estate for such price, and on such other commercially reasonable terms and conditions as the parties may agree, then the court shall order the real estate to be sold on such terms, subject to confirmation of the sale in accordance with Section 15-1508.

(h) Postponement of Proving Priority. With the approval of the court prior to the entry of the judgment of foreclosure, a party claiming an interest in the proceeds of the sale of the mortgaged real estate may defer proving the priority of such interest until the hearing to confirm the sale.

(i) Effect of Judgment and Lien.

(1) Upon the entry of the judgment of foreclosure, all rights of a party in the foreclosure against the mortgagor provided for in the judgment of foreclosure or this Article shall be secured by a lien on the mortgaged real estate, which lien shall have the same priority as the claim to which the judgment relates and shall be terminated upon confirmation of a judicial sale in accordance with this Article.

(2) Upon the entry of the judgment of foreclosure, the rights in the real estate subject to the judgment of foreclosure of (i) all persons made a party in the foreclosure and (ii) all nonrecord claimants given notice in accordance with paragraph (2) of subsection (c) of Section 15-1502, shall be solely as provided for in the judgment of foreclosure and in this Article.

(3) Entry of a judgment of foreclosure does not terminate or otherwise affect a bona fide lease of a dwelling unit in residential real estate in foreclosure, whether or not the lessee has been made a party in the foreclosure.

P.A. 82-280, § 15-1506, added by P.A. 84-1462, § 2, eff. July 1, 1987. Amended by P.A. 85-907, Art. I, § 1, eff. Nov. 23, 1987; P.A. 98-514, § 5, eff. Nov. 19, 2013.

Formerly Ill.Rev.Stat.1991, ch. 110, ¶ 15-1506.

5/15-1507. Judicial Sale

§ 15-1507. Judicial Sale.

(a) In General. Except as provided in Sections 15-1402 and 15-1403, upon entry of a judgment of foreclosure, the real estate which is the subject of the judgment shall be sold at a judicial sale in accordance with this Section 15-1507.

(b) Sale Procedures. Upon expiration of the reinstatement period and the redemption period in accordance with subsection (b) or (c) of Section 15-1603 or upon the entry of a judgment of foreclosure after the waiver of all rights of redemption, except as provided in subsection (g) of Section 15-1506, the real estate shall be sold at a sale as provided in this Article, on such terms and conditions as shall be specified by the court in the judgment of foreclosure. A sale may be conducted by any judge or sheriff.

(c) Notice of Sale. The mortgagee, or such other party designated by the court, in a foreclosure under this Article shall give public notice of the sale as follows:

(1) The notice of sale shall include at least the following information, but an immaterial error in the information shall not invalidate the legal effect of the notice:

(A) the name, address and telephone number of the person to contact for information regarding the real estate;

(B) the common address and other common description (other than legal description), if any, of the real estate;

(C) a legal description of the real estate sufficient to identify it with reasonable certainty;

(D) a description of the improvements on the real estate;

(E) the times specified in the judgment, if any, when the real estate may be inspected prior to sale;

(F) the time and place of the sale;

(G) the terms of the sale;

(H) the case title, case number and the court in which the foreclosure was filed;

(H–1) in the case of a condominium unit to which subsection (g) of Section 9 of the Condominium Property Act applies, the statement required by subdivision (g)(5) of Section 9 of the Condominium Property Act;

(H–2) in the case of a unit of a common interest community to which subsection (g–1) of Section 18.5 of the Condominium Property Act applies, the statement required by subdivision (g–1) of Section 18.5 of the Condominium Property Act; and

(I) such other information ordered by the Court.

(2) The notice of sale shall be published at least 3 consecutive calendar weeks (Sunday through Saturday), once in each week, the first such notice to be published not more than 45 days prior to the sale, the last such notice to be published not less than 7 days prior to the sale, by: (i)(A) advertisements in a newspaper circulated to the general public in the county in which the real estate is located, in the section of that newspaper where legal notices are commonly placed and (B) separate advertisements in the section of such a newspaper, which (except in counties with a population in excess of 3,000,000) may be the same newspaper, in which real estate other than real estate being sold as part of legal proceedings is commonly advertised to the general public; provided, that the separate advertisements in the real estate section need not include a legal description and that where both advertisements could be published in the same newspaper and that newspaper does not have separate legal notices and real estate advertisement sections, a single advertisement with the legal description shall be sufficient; and (ii) such other publications as may be further ordered by the court.

(3) The party who gives notice of public sale in accordance with subsection (c) of Section 15–1507 shall also give notice to all parties in the action who have appeared and have not theretofore been found by the court to be in default for failure to plead. Such notice shall be given in the manner provided in the applicable rules of court for service of papers other than process and complaint, not more than 45 days nor less than 7 days prior to the day of sale. After notice is given as required in this Section a copy thereof shall be filed in the office of the clerk of the court entering the judgment, together with a certificate of counsel or other proof that notice has been served in compliance with this Section.

(4) The party who gives notice of public sale in accordance with subsection (c) of Section 15–1507 shall again give notice in accordance with that Section of any adjourned sale; provided, however, that if the adjourned sale is to occur less than 60 days after the last scheduled sale, notice of any adjourned sale need not be given pursuant to this Section. In the event of adjournment, the person conducting the sale shall, upon adjournment, announce the date, time and place upon which the adjourned sale shall be held. Notwithstanding any language to the contrary, for any adjourned sale that is to be conducted more than 60 days after the date on which it was to first be held, the party giving notice of such sale shall again give notice in accordance with this Section.

(5) Notice of the sale may be given prior to the expiration of any reinstatement period or redemption period.

(6) No other notice by publication or posting shall be necessary unless required by order or rule of the court.

(7) The person named in the notice of sale to be contacted for information about the real estate may, but shall not be required, to provide additional information other than that set forth in the notice of sale.

(d) Election of Property. If the real estate which is the subject of a judgment of foreclosure is susceptible of division, the court may order it to be sold as necessary to satisfy the judgment. The court shall determine which real estate shall be sold, and the court may determine the order in which separate tracts may be sold.

(e) Receipt upon Sale. Upon and at the sale of mortgaged real estate, the person conducting the sale shall give to the purchaser a receipt of sale. The receipt shall describe the real estate purchased and shall show the amount bid, the amount paid, the total amount paid to date and the amount still to be paid therefor. An additional receipt shall be given at the time of each subsequent payment.

(f) Certificate of Sale. Upon payment in full of the amount bid, the person conducting the sale shall issue, in duplicate, and give to the purchaser a Certificate of Sale. The Certificate of Sale shall be in a recordable form, describe the real estate purchased, indicate the date and place of sale and show the amount paid therefor. The Certificate of Sale shall further indicate that it is subject to confirmation by the court. The duplicate certificate may be recorded in accordance with Section 12–121. The Certificate of Sale shall be freely assignable by endorsement thereon.

(g) Interest after Sale. Any bid at sale shall be deemed to include, without the necessity of a court order, interest at the statutory judgment rate on any unpaid portion of the sale price from the date of sale to the date of payment.

P.A. 82–280, § 15–1507, added by P.A. 84–1462, § 2, eff. July 1, 1987. Amended by P.A. 85–907, Art. I, § 1, eff. Nov. 23, 1987; P.A. 85–1298, § 1, eff. Jan. 1, 1989; P.A. 86–974, § 1, eff. July 1, 1990; P.A. 94–1049, § 2, eff. Jan. 1, 2007; P.A. 96–1045, § 5, eff. July 14, 2010.

Formerly Ill.Rev.Stat.1991, ch. 110, ¶ 15–1507.

5/15–1507.1. Judicial sale fee for Abandoned Residential Property Municipality Relief Fund

§ 15–1507.1. Judicial sale fee for Abandoned Residential Property Municipality Relief Fund.

(a) Upon and at the sale of residential real estate under Section 15–1507, the purchaser shall pay to the person conducting the sale pursuant to Section 15–1507 a fee for deposit into the Abandoned Residential Property Municipality Relief Fund, a special fund created in the State treasury. The fee shall be calculated at the rate of $1 for each $1,000 or fraction thereof of the amount paid by the purchaser to the person conducting the sale, as reflected in the receipt of sale issued to the purchaser, provided that in no event shall the fee exceed $300. No fee shall be paid by the mortgagee acquiring the residential real estate pursuant to its credit bid at the sale or by any mortgagee, judgment creditor, or other lienor acquiring the residential real estate whose rights in and to the residential real estate arose prior to the sale. Upon confirmation of the sale under Section 15–1508, the person conducting the sale shall remit the fee to the clerk of the court in which the foreclosure case is pending. The clerk shall remit the fee to the State Treasurer as provided in this Section, to be expended for the purposes set forth in Section 7.31 of the Illinois Housing Development Act.

(b) All fees paid by purchasers as provided in this Section shall be disbursed within 60 days after receipt by the clerk of the court as follows: (i) 98% to the State Treasurer for deposit into the Abandoned Residential Property Municipality Relief Fund, and (ii) 2% to the clerk of the court to be retained by the clerk for deposit into the Circuit Court Clerk Operation and Administrative Fund to defray administrative expenses related to implementation of this Section.

(c) Not later than March 1 of each year, the clerk of the court shall submit to the Illinois Housing Development Authority a report of the funds collected and remitted during the preceding year pursuant to this Section.

(d) Subsections (a) and (b) of this Section shall become inoperative on January 1, 2017. This Section is repealed on March 2, 2017.

P.A. 82–280, § 15–1507.1, added by P.A. 96–1419, § 15, eff. Oct. 1, 2010. Amended by P.A. 98–20, § 15, eff. June 11, 2013; P.A. 99–493, § 5, eff. Dec. 17, 2015.

5/15–1508. Report of Sale and Confirmation of Sale

§ 15–1508. Report of Sale and Confirmation of Sale.

(a) Report. The person conducting the sale shall promptly make a report to the court, which report shall include a copy of all receipts and, if any, certificate of sale.

(b) Hearing. Upon motion and notice in accordance with court rules applicable to motions generally, which motion shall not be made prior to sale, the court shall conduct a hearing to confirm the sale. Unless the court finds that (i) a notice required in accordance with subsection (c) of Section 15–1507 was not given, (ii) the terms of sale were unconscionable, (iii) the sale was conducted fraudulently, or (iv) justice was otherwise not done, the court shall then enter an order confirming the sale. The confirmation order shall include a name, address, and telephone number of the holder of the certificate of sale or deed issued pursuant to that certificate or, if no certificate or deed was issued, the purchaser, whom a municipality or county may contact with concerns about the real estate. The confirmation order may also:

(1) approve the mortgagee's fees and costs arising between the entry of the judgment of foreclosure and the confirmation hearing, those costs and fees to be allowable to the same extent as provided in the note and mortgage and in Section 15–1504;

(2) provide for a personal judgment against any party for a deficiency; and

(3) determine the priority of the judgments of parties who deferred proving the priority pursuant to subsection (h) of Section 15–1506, but the court shall not defer confirming the sale pending the determination of such priority.

(b–3) Hearing to confirm sale of abandoned residential property. Upon motion and notice by first-class mail to the last known address of the mortgagor, which motion shall be made prior to the sale and heard by the court at the earliest practicable time after conclusion of the sale, and upon the posting at the property address of the notice required by paragraph (2) of subsection (l) of Section 15–1505.8, the court shall enter an order confirming the sale of the abandoned residential property, unless the court finds that a reason set forth in items (i) through (iv) of subsection (b) of this Section exists for not approving the sale, or an order is entered pursuant to subsection (h) of Section 15–1505.8. The confirmation order also may address the matters identified in items (1) through (3) of subsection (b) of this Section. The notice required under subsection (b–5) of this Section shall not be required.

(b–5) Notice with respect to residential real estate. With respect to residential real estate, the notice required under subsection (b) of this Section shall be sent to the mortgagor even if the mortgagor has previously been held in default. In the event the mortgagor has filed an appearance, the notice shall be sent to the address indicated on the appearance. In all other cases, the notice shall be sent to the mortgagor at the common address of the foreclosed property. The notice shall be sent by first class mail. Unless the right to possession has been previously terminated by the court, the notice shall include the following language in 12–point boldface capitalized type:

IF YOU ARE THE MORTGAGOR (HOME-OWNER), YOU HAVE THE RIGHT TO RE-MAIN IN POSSESSION FOR 30 DAYS AFTER ENTRY OF AN ORDER OF POSSESSION, IN ACCORDANCE WITH SECTION 15–1701(c) OF THE ILLINOIS MORTGAGE FORECLO-SURE LAW.

(b–10) Notice of confirmation order sent to municipality or county. A copy of the confirmation order required under subsection (b) shall be sent to the municipality in which the foreclosed property is located, or to the county within the boundary of which the foreclosed property is located if the foreclosed property is located in an unincorporated territory. A municipality or county must clearly publish on its website a single address to which a copy of the order shall be sent. If a municipality or county does not maintain a website, then the municipality or county must publicly post in its main office a single address to which a copy of the order shall be sent. In the event that a municipality or county has not complied with the publication requirement in this subsection (b–10), then a copy of the order shall be sent by first class mail, postage prepaid, to the chairperson of the county board or county clerk in the case of a county, to the mayor or city clerk in the case of a city, to the president of the board of trustees or village clerk in the case of a village, or to the president or town clerk in the case of a town.

(b–15) Notice of confirmation order sent to known insurers. With respect to residential real estate, the party filing the complaint shall send a copy of the confirmation order required under subsection (b) by first class mail, postage prepaid, to the last known property insurer of the foreclosed property. Failure to send or receive a copy of the order shall not impair or abrogate in any way the rights of the mortgagee or purchaser or affect the status of the foreclosure proceedings.

(c) Failure to Give Notice. If any sale is held without compliance with subsection (c) of Section 15–1507 of this Article, any party entitled to the notice provided for in paragraph (3) of that subsection (c) who was not so notified may, by motion supported by affidavit made prior to confirmation of such sale, ask the court which entered the judgment to set aside the sale. Any such party shall guarantee or secure by bond a bid equal to the successful bid at the prior sale, unless the party seeking to set aside the sale is the mortgagor, the real estate sold at the sale is residential real estate, and the mortgagor occupies the residential real estate at the time the motion is filed. In that event, no guarantee or bond shall be required of the mortgagor. Any subsequent sale is subject to the same notice requirement as the original sale.

(d) Validity of Sale. Except as provided in subsection (c) of Section 15–1508, no sale under this Article shall be held invalid or be set aside because of any defect in the notice thereof or in the publication of the same, or in the proceedings of the officer conducting the sale, except upon good cause shown in a hearing pursuant to subsection (b) of Section 15–1508. At any time after a sale has occurred, any party entitled to notice under paragraph (3) of subsection (c) of Section 15–1507 may recover from the mortgagee any damages caused by the mortgagee's failure to comply with such paragraph (3). Any party who recovers damages in a judicial proceeding brought under this subsection may also recover from the mortgagee the reasonable expenses of litigation, including reasonable attorney's fees.

(d–5) Making Home Affordable Program. The court that entered the judgment shall set aside a sale held pursuant to Section 15–1507, upon motion of the mortgagor at any time prior to the confirmation of the sale, if the mortgagor proves by a preponderance of the evidence that (i) the mortgagor has applied for assistance under the Making Home Affordable Program established by the United States Department of the Treasury pursuant to the Emergency Economic Stabilization Act of 2008, as amended by the American Recovery and Reinvestment Act of 2009, and (ii) the mortgaged real estate was sold in material violation of the program's requirements for proceeding to a judicial sale. The provisions of this subsection (d–5), except for this sentence, shall become inoperative on January 1, 2016 for all actions filed under this Article after December 31, 2015, in which the mortgagor did not apply for assistance under the Making Home Affordable Program on or before December 31, 2015.

(e) Deficiency Judgment. In any order confirming a sale pursuant to the judgment of foreclosure, the court shall also enter a personal judgment for deficiency against any party (i) if otherwise authorized and (ii) to the extent requested in the complaint and proven upon presentation of the report of sale in accordance with Section 15–1508. Except as otherwise provided in this Article, a judgment may be entered for any balance of money that may be found due to the plaintiff, over and above the proceeds of the sale or sales, and enforcement may be had for the collection of such balance, the same as when the judgment is solely for the payment of money. Such judgment may be entered, or enforcement had, only in cases where personal service has been had upon the persons personally liable for the mortgage indebtedness, unless they have entered their appearance in the foreclosure action.

(f) Satisfaction. Upon confirmation of the sale, the judgment stands satisfied to the extent of the sale price less expenses and costs. If the order confirming the sale includes a deficiency judgment, the judgment shall become a lien in the manner of any other judgment for the payment of money.

(g) The order confirming the sale shall include, notwithstanding any previous orders awarding possession during the pendency of the foreclosure, an award to the purchaser of possession of the mortgaged real estate, as of the date 30 days after the entry of the order, against the parties to the foreclosure whose interests have been terminated.

An order of possession authorizing the removal of a person from possession of the mortgaged real estate shall be entered and enforced only against those persons personally named as individuals in the complaint or the petition under subsection (h) of Section 15–1701. No order of possession issued under this Section shall be entered against a lessee with a bona fide lease of a dwelling unit in residential real estate in foreclosure, whether or not the lessee has been made a party in the foreclosure. An order shall not be entered and enforced against any person who is only generically described as an unknown owner or nonrecord claimant or by another generic designation in the complaint.

Notwithstanding the preceding paragraph, the failure to personally name, include, or seek an award of possession of the mortgaged real estate against a person in the confirmation order shall not abrogate any right that the purchaser may have to possession of the mortgaged real estate and to maintain a proceeding against that person for possession under Article IX of this Code or, if applicable, under subsection (h) of Section 15–1701; and possession against a person who (1) has not been personally named as a party to the foreclosure and (2) has not been provided an opportunity to be heard in the foreclosure proceeding may be sought only by maintaining a proceeding under Article IX of this Code [1] or, if applicable, under subsection (h) of Section 15–1701.

(h) With respect to mortgaged real estate containing 5 or more dwelling units, the order confirming the sale shall also provide that (i) the mortgagor shall transfer to the purchaser the security deposits, if any, that the mortgagor received to secure payment of rent or to compensate for damage to the mortgaged real estate from any current occupant of a dwelling unit of the mortgaged real estate, as well as any statutory interest that has not been paid to the occupant, and (ii) the mortgagor shall provide an accounting of the security deposits that are transferred, including the name and address of each occupant for whom the mortgagor holds the deposit and the amount of the deposit and any statutory interest.

P.A. 82–280, § 15–1508, added by P.A. 84–1462, § 2, eff. July 1, 1987. Amended by P.A. 85–907, Art. I, § 1, eff. Nov. 23, 1987; P.A. 86–974, § 1, eff. July 1, 1990; P.A. 88–265, § 5, eff. Jan. 1, 1994; P.A. 89–203, § 30, eff. July 21, 1995; P.A. 95–826, § 5, eff. Aug. 14, 2008; P.A. 96–265, § 5, eff. Aug. 11, 2009; P.A. 96–856, § 25, eff. March 1, 2010; P.A. 96–1245, § 5, eff. July 23, 2010; P.A. 97–333, § 575, eff. Aug. 12, 2011; P.A. 97–575, § 5, eff. Aug. 26, 2011; P.A. 97–1159, § 5, eff. Jan. 29, 2013; P.A. 97–1164, § 15, eff. June 1, 2013; P.A. 98–514, § 5, eff. Nov. 19, 2013; P.A. 98–605, § 5, eff. Dec. 26, 2013.

Formerly Ill.Rev.Stat.1991, ch. 110, ¶ 15–1508.

[1] 735 ILCS 5/9–101 et seq.

Validity

On November 18, 1999, the Supreme Court of Illinois held that P.A. 89–203 violated the single-subject rule of the Illinois Constitution in the case of People v. Wooters, 1999, 243 Ill.Dec. 33, 188 Ill.2d 500, 722 N.E.2d 1102.

P.A. 98–605 incorporated the amendment by P.A. 98–514.

5/15–1508.5. Notice by holder or purchaser to known occupants of dwelling units of mortgaged real estate

§ 15–1508.5. Notice by holder or purchaser to known occupants of dwelling units of mortgaged real estate.

(a) The holder of the certificate of sale or deed issued pursuant to that certificate or, if no certificate or deed was issued, the purchaser, shall:

(1) following the judicial sale under Section 15–1507, but no later than 21 days after the confirmation of sale under Section 15–1508, make a good faith effort to ascertain the identities and addresses of all occupants of dwelling units of the mortgaged real estate; and

(2) following the order confirming sale under Section 15–1508, but no later than 21 days after the order confirming sale, notify all known occupants of dwelling units of the mortgaged real estate that the holder or purchaser has acquired the mortgaged real estate. The notice shall be in writing and shall:

(i) identify the occupant being served by the name known to the holder or purchaser;

(ii) inform the occupant that the mortgaged real estate at which the dwelling unit is located is the subject of a foreclosure and that control of the mortgaged real estate has changed;

(iii) provide the name, address, and telephone number of an individual or entity whom the occupants may contact with concerns about the mortgaged real estate or to request repairs of that property;

(iv) include the following language, or language that is substantially similar: "This is NOT a notice to vacate the premises. You may wish to contact a lawyer or your local legal aid or housing counseling agency to discuss any rights that you may have.";

(v) include the name of the case, the case number, and the court where the order confirming the sale has been entered; and

(vi) provide instructions on the method of payment of future rent, if applicable.

(b) The written notice required by subsection (a) of this Section shall be served by delivering a copy thereof to the known occupant, or by leaving the same with some person of the age of 13 years or upwards who is residing on or in possession of the premises, or by sending a copy of the notice to the known occupant by first-class mail, addressed to the occupant by the name known to the holder or purchaser.

(c) In the event that the holder or purchaser ascertains the identity and address of an occupant of a dwelling unit of the mortgaged real estate more than 21 days after the confirmation of sale under Section 15–1508, the holder or purchaser shall provide the notice required by subparagraph (2) of subsection (a) within 7 days of ascertaining the identity and address of the occupant.

(d)(i) A holder or purchaser who fails to comply with subsections (a), (b), and (c) may not collect any rent due and owing from a known occupant, or terminate a known occupant's tenancy for non-payment of such rent, until the holder or purchaser has served the notice described in paragraph (2) of subsection (a) of this Section upon the known occupant. After providing such notice, the holder or purchaser may collect any and all rent otherwise due and owing the holder or purchaser from the known occupant and may terminate the known occupant's tenancy for non-payment of such rent if the holder or purchaser otherwise has such right to terminate.

(ii) An occupant who previously paid rent for the current rental period to the mortgagor, or other entity with the authority to operate, manage, and conserve the mortgaged real estate at the time of payment, shall not be held liable for that rent by the holder or purchaser, and the occupant's tenancy shall not be terminated for non-payment of rent for that rental period.

(e) Within 21 days of the confirmation of sale under Section 15–1508, the holder or purchaser shall post a written notice on the primary entrance of each dwelling unit subject to the foreclosure action. This notice shall:

(i) inform occupant that the dwelling unit is the subject of a foreclosure action and that control of the mortgaged real estate has changed;

(ii) include the following language: "This is NOT a notice to vacate the premises.";

(iii) provide the name, address, and telephone number of the individual or entity whom occupants may contact with concerns about the mortgaged real estate or to request repairs of the property; and

(iv) provide instructions on the method of payment of future rent, if applicable.

(f)(i) The provisions of subsection (d) of this Section shall be the exclusive remedy for the failure of a holder or purchaser to provide notice to a known occupant under this Section.

(ii) This Section shall not abrogate any right that a holder or purchaser may have to possession of the mortgaged real estate and to maintain a proceeding against an occupant of a dwelling unit for possession

under Article IX of this Code or subsection (h) of Section 15–1701.

(iii) In the event that the holder or purchaser is a mortgagee in possession of the mortgaged real estate pursuant to Section 15–1703 at the time of the confirmation of sale and has complied with requirements of subsection (a–5) of Section 15–1703, the holder or purchaser is excused from the requirements of subsections (a) and (e) of this Section.

(iv) A holder or purchaser is not required to provide the notice required by this Section to a mortgagor or party against whom an order of possession has been entered authorizing the removal of the mortgagor or party pursuant to subsection (g) of Section 15–1508.

P.A. 82–280, § 15–1508.5, added by P.A. 96–111, § 5, eff. Oct. 29, 2009. Amended by P.A. 98–514, § 5, eff. Nov. 19, 2013.

5/15–1509. Transfer of Title and Title Acquired

§ 15–1509. Transfer of Title and Title Acquired. **(a) Deed.** After (i) confirmation of the sale, and (ii) payment of the purchase price and any other amounts required to be paid by the purchaser at sale, the court (or, if the court shall so order, the person who conducted the sale or such person's successor or some persons specifically appointed by the court for that purpose), shall upon the request of the holder of the certificate of sale (or the purchaser if no certificate of sale was issued), promptly execute a deed to the holder or purchaser sufficient to convey title. Such deed shall identify the court and the caption of the case in which judgment was entered authorizing issuance of the deed. Signature and the recital in the deed of the title or authority of the person signing the deed as grantor, of authority pursuant to the judgment and of the giving of the notices required by this Article is sufficient proof of the facts recited and of such authority to execute the deed, but such deed shall not be construed to contain any covenant on the part of the person executing it. If the deed issues to a grantee prior to the expiration of the period for appealing the confirmation of sale, and the grantee conveys title to another party within that period, that other party will not be deemed a bona fide purchaser unless and until such period expires without an appeal having been filed or, an appeal having been filed, such appeal is denied or withdrawn.

(b) Effect Upon Delivery of Deed. Delivery of the deed executed on the sale of the real estate, even if the purchaser or holder of the certificate of sale is a party to the foreclosure, shall be sufficient to pass the title thereto.

(c) Claims Barred. Any vesting of title by a consent foreclosure pursuant to Section 15–1402 or by deed pursuant to subsection (b) of Section 15–1509, unless otherwise specified in the judgment of foreclosure, shall be an entire bar of (i) all claims of parties to the foreclosure and (ii) all claims of any nonrecord claimant who is given notice of the foreclosure in accordance with paragraph (2) of subsection (c) of Section 15–1502, notwithstanding the provisions of subsection (g) of Section 2–1301 to the contrary. Any person seeking relief from any judgment or order entered in the foreclosure in accordance with subsection (g) of Section 2–1301 of the Code of Civil Procedure may claim only an interest in the proceeds of sale.

P.A. 82–280, § 15–1509, added by P.A. 84–1462, § 2, eff. July 1, 1987. Amended by P.A. 85–907, Art. I, § 1, eff. Nov. 23, 1987; P.A. 86–974, § 1, eff. July 1, 1990.

Formerly Ill.Rev.Stat.1991, ch. 110, ¶ 15–1509.

5/15–1509.5. Notice at time of conveyance

§ 15–1509.5. Notice at time of conveyance. Any deed executed pursuant to this Article or judgment vesting title by a consent foreclosure pursuant to Section 15–1402 shall state the grantee's or mortgagee's name (and the name of a contact person), street and mailing addresses, and telephone number.

P.A. 82–280, § 15–1509.5, added by P.A. 96–110, § 5, eff. July 31, 2009.

5/15–1510. Attorney's Fees and Costs

§ 15–1510. Attorney's Fees and Costs.

(a) The court may award reasonable attorney's fees and costs to the defendant who prevails in a motion, an affirmative defense or counterclaim, or in the foreclosure action. A defendant who exercises the defendant's right of reinstatement or redemption shall not be considered a prevailing party for purposes of this Section. Nothing in this subsection shall abrogate contractual terms in the mortgage or other written agreement between the mortgagor and the mortgagee or rights as otherwise provided in this Article which allow the mortgagee to recover attorney's fees and costs under subsection (b).

(b) Attorneys' fees and other costs incurred in connection with the preparation, filing or prosecution of the foreclosure suit shall be recoverable in a foreclosure only to the extent specifically set forth in the mortgage or other written agreement between the mortgagor and the mortgagee or as otherwise provided in this Article.

P.A. 82–280, § 15–1510, added by P.A. 84–1462, § 2, eff. July 1, 1987. Amended by P.A. 86–974, § 1, eff. July 1, 1990; P.A. 95–961, § 5, eff. Jan. 1, 2009.

5/15–1511. Deficiency

§ 15–1511. Deficiency. Except as expressly prohibited by this Article, foreclosure of a mortgage does not affect a mortgagee's rights, if any, to obtain a personal judgment against any person for a deficiency.

P.A. 82–280, § 15–1511, added by P.A. 84–1462, § 2, eff. July 1, 1987.

Formerly Ill.Rev.Stat.1991, ch. 110, ¶ 15–1511.

5/15–1512. Application of Proceeds of Sale and Surplus

§ 15–1512. Application of Proceeds of Sale and Surplus. The proceeds resulting from a sale of real estate under this Article shall be applied in the following order:

(a) the reasonable expenses of sale;

(b) the reasonable expenses of securing possession before sale, holding, maintaining, and preparing the real estate for sale, including payment of taxes and other governmental charges, premiums on hazard and liability insurance, receiver's and management fees, and, to the extent provided for in the mortgage or other recorded agreement and not prohibited by law, reasonable attorneys' fees, payments made pursuant to Section 15–1505 and other legal expenses incurred by the mortgagee;

(c) if the sale was pursuant to judicial foreclosure, satisfaction of claims in the order of priority adjudicated in the judgment of foreclosure or order confirming the sale; and

(d) remittance of any surplus to be held by the person appointed by the court to conduct the sale until further order of the court. If there is a surplus, such person conducting the sale shall send written notice to all parties to the proceeding advising them of the amount of the surplus, and that the surplus shall be held until a party obtains a court order for its distribution or until, in the absence of an order, the surplus is forfeited to the State.

P.A. 82–280, § 15–1512, added by P.A. 84–1462, § 2, eff. July 1, 1987. Amended by P.A. 85–907, Art. I, § 1, eff. Nov. 23, 1987; P.A. 86–974, § 1, eff. July 1, 1990.

Formerly Ill.Rev.Stat.1991, ch. 110, ¶ 15–1512.

PART 16. REINSTATEMENT AND REDEMPTION

Date Effective

Part 16 was added by P.A. 84–1462, § 2, eff. July 1, 1987.

5/15–1601. Waiver of Rights of Reinstatement and Redemption

§ 15–1601. Waiver of Rights of Reinstatement and Redemption. (a) Residential and Certain Agricultural Real Estate. Except as otherwise provided in this Article, no mortgagor of real estate which is residential real estate at the time of such attempted waiver may waive the mortgagor's rights of reinstatement and redemption, or either of them, and any such waiver shall be void. Except as otherwise provided in subsection (b) of this Section, no mortgagor of real estate which is agricultural real estate at the time of such attempted waiver may waive the mortgagor's rights of reinstatement and redemption, or either of them, and any such waiver shall be void.

(b) Other Real Estate. Any corporation or any corporate trustee of any express trust who is a mortgagor of agricultural real estate may waive the mortgagor's right of redemption (i) by express waiver stated in the mortgage or (ii) by any other waiver in writing which has been acknowledged by the mortgagor and recorded. A mortgagor of real estate other than a mortgagor of residential real estate or other mortgagor who is not otherwise so prohibited by this Article may waive the mortgagor's right of redemption (i) by express waiver stated in the mortgage or (ii) by any other waiver in writing which has been acknowledged by the mortgagor and recorded.

(c) Waiver After Commencement of Foreclosure. After commencement of a foreclosure proceeding under this Article a mortgagor of residential real estate or other mortgagor who is otherwise so prohibited may waive the mortgagor's rights of reinstatement and redemption, or either of them, if (i) the mortgagor expressly consents in writing to the entry of a judgment without such right of reinstatement or redemption, (ii) such written consent is filed with the clerk of the court, and (iii) the mortgagee consents and agrees to waive any and all rights to a deficiency judgment.

(d) Prior Waivers. Nothing contained in this Section shall invalidate any waiver of any right of redemption made pursuant to Section 12–124 or Section 12–125 of the Code of Civil Procedure in effect prior to July 1, 1987 which is contained in any instrument executed prior to July 1, 1987.

P.A. 82–280, § 15–1601, added by P.A. 84–1462, § 2, eff. July 1, 1987. Amended by P.A. 85–907, Art. I, § 1, eff. Nov. 23, 1987.

Formerly Ill.Rev.Stat.1991, ch. 110, ¶ 15–1601.

5/15–1602. Reinstatement

§ 15–1602. Reinstatement. In any foreclosure of a mortgage executed after July 21, 1959, which has become due prior to the maturity date fixed in the mortgage, or in any instrument or obligation secured by the mortgage, through acceleration because of a default under the mortgage, a mortgagor may reinstate the mortgage as provided herein. Reinstatement is effected by curing all defaults then existing, other than payment of such portion of the principal which would not have been due had no acceleration occurred, and by paying all costs and expenses required by the mortgage to be paid in the event of such defaults, provided that such cure and payment are made prior to the expiration of 90 days from the date the mortgagor or, if more than one, all the mortgagors (i) have been served with summons or by publication or (ii) have otherwise submitted to the jurisdiction of the court. When service is made by publication, the first date of publication shall be used for the calculation. Upon such reinstatement of the mortgage, the foreclosure and any other proceedings for the collection or enforcement of the obligation secured by the mortgage shall be dismissed and the mortgage documents shall remain in full force and effect as if no acceleration or default had occurred. The relief granted by this Section shall not be exhausted by a single use thereof, but if the court has made an express written finding that the mortgagor has exercised its right to reinstate pursuant to this Section, such relief shall not be again available to the mortgagor under the same mortgage for a period of five years from the date of the dismissal of such foreclosure. The provisions of Section 9–110 of the Code of Civil Procedure shall be inapplicable with respect to any instrument which is deemed a mortgage under this Article. The court may enter a judgment of foreclosure prior to the expiration of the reinstatement period, subject to the right of the mortgagor to reinstate the mortgage under this Section.

P.A. 82–280, § 15–1602, added by P.A. 84–1462, § 2, eff. July 1, 1987. Amended by P.A. 85–907, Art. I, § 1, eff. Nov. 23, 1987; P.A. 86–974, § 1, eff. July 1, 1990.

Formerly Ill.Rev.Stat.1991, ch. 110, ¶ 15–1602.

5/15–1603. Redemption

§ 15–1603. Redemption. **(a) Owner of Redemption.** Except as provided in subsection (b) of Section 15–1402, only an owner of redemption may redeem from the foreclosure, and such owner of redemption may redeem only during the redemption period specified in subsection (b) of Section 15–1603 and only if the right of redemption has not been validly waived.

(b) Redemption Period.

(1) In the foreclosure of a mortgage of real estate which is residential real estate at the time the foreclosure is commenced, the redemption period shall end on the later of (i) the date 7 months from the date the mortgagor or, if more than one, all the mortgagors (A) have been served with summons or by publication or (B) have otherwise submitted to the jurisdiction of the court, or (ii) the date 3 months from the date of entry of a judgment of foreclosure.

(2) In all other foreclosures, the redemption period shall end on the later of (i) the date 6 months from the date the mortgagor or, if more than one, all the mortgagors (A) have been served with summons or by publication or (B) have otherwise submitted to the jurisdiction of the court, or (ii) the date 3 months from the date of entry of a judgment of foreclosure.

(3) Notwithstanding paragraphs (1) and (2), the redemption period shall end at the later of the expiration of any reinstatement period provided for in Section 15–1602 or the date 60 days after the date the judgment of foreclosure is entered, if the court finds that (i) the value of the mortgaged real estate as of the date of the judgment is less than 90% of the amount specified pursuant to subsection (d) of Section 15–1603 and (ii) the mortgagee waives any and all rights to a personal judgment for a deficiency against the mortgagor and against all other persons liable for the indebtedness or other obligations secured by the mortgage.

(4) Notwithstanding paragraphs (1) and (2), the redemption period shall end on the date 30 days after the date the judgment of foreclosure is entered if the court finds that the mortgaged real estate has been abandoned. In cases where the redemption period is shortened on account of abandonment, the reinstatement period shall not extend beyond the redemption period as shortened.

(c) Extension of Redemption Period.

(1) Once expired, the right of redemption provided for in Sections 15–1603 or 15–1604 shall not be revived. The period within which the right of redemption provided for in Sections 15–1603 or 15–1604 may be exercised runs independently of any action by any person to enforce the judgment of foreclosure or effect a sale pursuant thereto. Neither the initiation of any legal proceeding nor the order of any court staying the enforcement of a judgment of foreclosure or the sale pursuant to a judgment or the confirmation of the sale, shall have the effect of tolling the running of the redemption period.

(2) If a court has the authority to stay, and does stay, the running of the redemption period, or if the redemption period is extended by any statute of the United States, the redemption period shall be extended until the expiration of the same number of days after the expiration of the stay order as the number of days remaining in the redemption period at the time the stay order became effective, or, if later, until the expiration of 30 days after the stay order terminates. If the stay order terminates more than 30 days prior to the expiration of the redemption period, the redemption period shall not be extended.

(d) Amount Required to Redeem. The amount required to redeem shall be the sum of:

(1) The amount specified in the judgment of foreclosure, which shall consist of (i) all principal and accrued interest secured by the mortgage and due as of the date of the judgment, (ii) all costs allowed by law, (iii) costs and expenses approved by the court, (iv) to the extent provided for in the mortgage and approved by the court, additional costs, expenses and reasonable attorneys' fees incurred by the mortgagee, (v) all amounts paid pursuant to Section 15–1505 and (vi) per diem interest from the date of judgment to the date of redemption calculated at the mortgage rate of interest applicable as if no default had occurred; and

(2) The amount of other expenses authorized by the court which the mortgagee reasonably incurs between the date of judgment and the date of redemption, which shall be the amount certified by the mortgagee in accordance with subsection (e) of Section 15–1603.

(e) Notice of Intent to Redeem. An owner of redemption who intends to redeem shall give written notice of such intent to redeem to the mortgagee's attorney of record specifying the date designated for redemption and the current address of the owner of redemption for purposes of receiving notice. Such owner of redemption shall file with the clerk of the court a certification of the giving of such notice. The notice of intent to redeem must be received by the mortgagee's attorney at least 15 days (other than Saturday, Sunday or court holiday) prior to the date designated for redemption. The mortgagee shall thereupon file with the clerk of the court and shall give written notice to the owner of redemption at least three days (other than Saturday, Sunday or court holiday) before the date designated for redemption a certification, accompanied by copies of paid receipts or appropriate affidavits, of any expenses authorized in paragraph (2) of subsection (d) of Section 15–1603. If the mortgagee fails to serve such certification within the time specified herein, then the owner of redemption intending to redeem may redeem on the date designated for redemption in the notice of intent to redeem, and the mortgagee shall not be entitled to payment of any expenses authorized in paragraph (2) of subsection (d) of Section 15–1603.

(f) Procedure for Redemption.

(1) An owner of redemption may redeem the real estate from the foreclosure by paying the amount specified in subsection (d) of Section 15–1603 to the mortgagee or the mortgagee's attorney of record on or before the date designated for redemption pursuant to subsection (e) of Section 15–1603.

(2) If the mortgagee refuses to accept payment or if the owner of redemption redeeming from the foreclosure objects to the reasonableness of the additional expenses authorized in paragraph (2) of subsection (d) of Section 15–1603 and certified in accordance with subsection (e) of Section 15–1603, the owner of redemption shall pay the certified amount to the clerk of the court on or before the date designated for redemption, together with a written statement specifying the expenses to which objection is made. In such case the clerk shall pay to the mortgagee the amount tendered minus the amount to which the objection pertains.

(3) Upon payment to the clerk, whether or not the owner of redemption files an objection at the time of payment, the clerk shall give a receipt of payment to the person redeeming from the foreclosure, and shall file a copy of that receipt in the foreclosure record. Upon receipt of the amounts specified to be paid to the mortgagee pursuant to this Section, the mortgagee shall promptly furnish the mortgagor with a release of the mortgage or satisfaction of the judgment, as appropriate, and the evidence of all indebtedness secured by the mortgage shall be cancelled.

(g) Procedure Upon Objection. If an objection is filed by an owner of redemption in accordance with paragraph (2) of subsection (f) of Section 15–1603, the clerk shall hold the amount to which the objection pertains until the court orders distribution of those funds. The court shall hold a hearing promptly to determine the distribution of any funds held by the clerk pursuant to such objection. Each party shall pay its own costs and expenses in connection with any objection, including attorneys' fees, subject to Section 2–611 of the Code of Civil Procedure.

(h) Failure to Redeem. Unless the real estate being foreclosed is redeemed from the foreclosure, it shall be sold as provided in this Article.

P.A. 82–280, § 15–1603, added by P.A. 84–1462, § 2, eff. July 1, 1987. Amended by P.A. 85–907, Art. I, § 1, eff. Nov. 23, 1987; P.A. 86–974, § 1, eff. July 1, 1990.

Formerly Ill.Rev.Stat.1991, ch. 110, ¶ 15–1603.

5/15–1603.5. Strict foreclosure of an omitted subordinate interest

§ 15–1603.5. Strict foreclosure of an omitted subordinate interest.

(a) As used in this Section, "omitted subordinate interest" means a recorded subordinate interest in real estate where:

(1) the real estate is the subject of a foreclosure action under this Article;

(2) a motion to confirm judicial sale under subsection (b) of Section 15–1508 is either pending or has been granted;

(3) the interest attached to the real estate prior to the filing or recording of any notice in accordance with Sections 2–1901 and 15–1503; and

(4) the person who has the interest was not named in the foreclosure complaint.

(b) The holder of the certificate of sale or any person who acquired title pursuant to Section 15–1509 or any subsequent successor, assignee, transferee, or grantee who discovers an omitted subordinate interest may file a strict foreclosure complaint naming the person who has the omitted subordinate interest as the defendant. A complaint filed under this Section must include substantially the following:

(1) the identity of the plaintiff and how the plaintiff acquired its interest in the property which is the subject of the strict foreclosure;

(2) the docket number of the prior foreclosure action and the recording number and date of the mortgage that was previously foreclosed;

(3) the legal description, common address, and parcel identification number of the real estate which is the subject of the strict foreclosure;

(4) the recording number and a copy of the recorded instrument identifying the person who has the omitted subordinate interest that is named as the defendant;

(5) the amount of the successful bid at the foreclosure sale, as stated in the report of sale in the prior foreclosure action, with a copy of the report of sale attached to the complaint;

(6) an allegation that, due to inadvertence or mistake or such other reason as may be applicable, the person who has the omitted subordinate interest was not made a party defendant in the prior foreclosure action and the omitted subordinate interest was not terminated by the judgment of foreclosure and when the subject property was sold by judicial sale; and

(7) a request for relief setting forth the redemption period as provided in this Section and identifying a contact by name and telephone number who will accept tender of the redemption amount.

(c) Subject to the objection of the defendant, the court shall enter a judgment extinguishing the omitted subordinate interest.

(d) If the defendant objects to the entry of the judgment, the court, after a hearing, shall enter an order providing either:

(1) that the defendant has not agreed to pay the amount required to redeem, in which event the court shall proceed to enter the judgment; or

(2) that the defendant has agreed to pay the amount required to redeem.

(e) The amount required to redeem shall be the sum bid at the prior foreclosure sale plus any costs and fees incurred subsequent to the sale for the payment of taxes, preservation of the property, or any other actions taken by the holder of the certificate of sale to protect its interest in the property. The amount required to redeem shall not include any costs or fees incurred by the plaintiff in the strict foreclosure case filed under this Section.

The order shall state that upon payment of the redemption amount within the redemption period, which shall extend 30 days after the entry of the order, title to the real estate shall vest in the defendant who redeems pursuant to this Section. If the defendant subject to the order has not paid the amount required to redeem within the 30–day redemption period, the interest of the defendant in the property is terminated.

(f) A person whose omitted subordinate interest was not terminated by a prior foreclosure action does not have a right to file a strict foreclosure action.

(g) Notwithstanding that the person's omitted subordinate interest in the real estate has been terminated pursuant to this Section, nothing in this Section shall be construed to extinguish or impair any claim of such person in the surplus proceeds of a sale held or distributed pursuant to subsection (d) of Section 15–1512 of this Code after the confirmation of the sale of the real estate for which such person had an omitted subordinate interest.

P.A. 82–280, § 15–1603.5, added by P.A. 98–1099, § 5, eff. Aug. 26, 2014.

5/15–1604. Special Right to Redeem

§ 15–1604. Special Right to Redeem. **(a) Circumstances.** With respect to residential real estate, if (i) the purchaser at the sale was a mortgagee who was a party to the foreclosure or its nominee and (ii) the sale price was less than the amount specified in subsection (d) of Section 15–1603, then, and only in such circumstances, an owner of redemption as specified in subsection (a) of Section 15–1603 shall have a special right to redeem, for a period ending 30 days after the date the sale is confirmed, by paying to the mortgagee (i) the sale price, (ii) all additional costs and expenses incurred by the mortgagee set forth in the report of sale and confirmed by the court, and (iii) interest at the statutory judgment rate from the date the purchase price was paid or credited as an offset.

(b) Procedure. Upon receipt of such amount, the mortgagee shall assign to the redeeming owner of redemption its certificate of sale or its right to such certificate or to a deed. The mortgagee shall give to the redeeming owner of redemption an executed duplicate of such assignment, marked "Duplicate", which duplicate the owner of redemption shall file with the court. If a deed has been issued to the mortgagee or its nominee, the holder of such deed, or such holder's successor in title, shall execute and deliver a deed conveying the mortgaged real estate to the redeeming owner of redemption subject only to those encumbrances that would normally arise on title if a redemption were made under Section 15–1603, including a deficiency, if any, resulting from the foreclosure sale. Nothing contained herein shall affect the right to a personal or in rem deficiency judgment, and enforcement thereof shall be allowed as provided by law. Any deficiency judgment shall retain the same priority on title as did the mortgage from which it arose. The mortgagee, its nominee or its successors in title shall not permit encumbrances on title arising on or after the date of the deed to the mortgagee or nominee

caused by or relating to the mortgagee or its nominee or its successors in title.

P.A. 82–280, § 15–1604, added by P.A. 84–1462, § 2, eff. July 1, 1987. Amended by P.A. 85–907, Art. I, § 1, eff. Nov. 23, 1987; P.A. 86–974, § 1, eff. July 1, 1990.

Formerly Ill.Rev.Stat.1991, ch. 110, ¶ 15–1604.

5/15–1605. Equitable Right of Redemption

§ 15–1605. Equitable Right of Redemption. No equitable right of redemption shall exist or be enforceable under or with respect to a mortgage after a judicial sale of the mortgaged real estate pursuant to Section 15–1507 or after entry of a judgment of foreclosure pursuant to Sections 15–1402 or 15–1403.

P.A. 82–280, § 15–1605, added by P.A. 84–1462, § 2, eff. July 1, 1987.

Formerly Ill.Rev.Stat.1991, ch. 110, ¶ 15–1605.

PART 17. POSSESSION DURING FORECLOSURE

Section
5/15–1701. Right to possession.
5/15–1702. Specific Rules of Possession.
5/15–1703. Mortgagee in Possession.
5/15–1704. Receivers.
5/15–1705. Bond.
5/15–1706. Possession.

Date Effective

Part 17 was added by P.A. 84–1462, § 2, eff. July 1, 1987.

5/15–1701. Right to possession

§ 15–1701. Right to possession.

(a) General. The provisions of this Article shall govern the right to possession of the mortgaged real estate during foreclosure. Possession under this Article includes physical possession of the mortgaged real estate to the same extent to which the mortgagor, absent the foreclosure, would have been entitled to physical possession. For the purposes of Part 17, real estate is residential real estate only if it is residential real estate at the time the foreclosure is commenced.

(b) Pre–Judgment. Prior to the entry of a judgment of foreclosure:

(1) In the case of residential real estate, the mortgagor shall be entitled to possession of the real estate except if (i) the mortgagee shall object and show good cause, (ii) the mortgagee is so authorized by the terms of the mortgage or other written instrument, and (iii) the court is satisfied that there is a reasonable probability that the mortgagee will prevail on a final hearing of the cause, the court shall upon request place the mortgagee in possession. If the residential real estate consists of more than one dwelling unit, then for the purpose of this

Part residential real estate shall mean only that dwelling unit or units occupied by persons described in clauses (i), (ii) and (iii) of Section 15–1219.

(2) In all other cases, if (i) the mortgagee is so authorized by the terms of the mortgage or other written instrument, and (ii) the court is satisfied that there is a reasonable probability that the mortgagee will prevail on a final hearing of the cause, the mortgagee shall upon request be placed in possession of the real estate, except that if the mortgagor shall object and show good cause, the court shall allow the mortgagor to remain in possession.

(c) Judgment Through 30 Days After Sale Confirmation. After the entry of a judgment of foreclosure and through the 30th day after a foreclosure sale is confirmed:

(1) Subsection (b) of Section 15–1701 shall be applicable, regardless of the provisions of the mortgage or other instrument, except that after a sale pursuant to the judgment the holder of the certificate of sale (or, if none, the purchaser at the sale) shall have the mortgagee's right to be placed in possession, with all rights and duties of a mortgagee in possession under this Article.

(2) Notwithstanding paragraph (1) of subsection (b) and paragraph (1) of subsection (c) of Section 15–1701, upon request of the mortgagee, a mortgagor of residential real estate shall not be allowed to remain in possession between the expiration of the redemption period and through the 30th day after sale confirmation unless (i) the mortgagor pays to the mortgagee or such holder or purchaser, whichever is applicable, monthly the lesser of the interest due under the mortgage calculated at the mortgage rate of interest applicable as if no default had occurred or the fair rental value of the real estate, or (ii) the mortgagor otherwise shows good cause. Any amounts paid by the mortgagor pursuant to this subsection shall be credited against the amounts due from the mortgagor.

(d) After 30 Days After Sale Confirmation. The holder of the certificate of sale or deed issued pursuant to that certificate or, if no certificate or deed was issued, the purchaser, except to the extent the holder or purchaser may consent otherwise, shall be entitled to possession of the mortgaged real estate, as of the date 30 days after the order confirming the sale is entered, against those parties to the foreclosure whose interests the court has ordered terminated, without further notice to any party, further order of the court, or resort to proceedings under any other statute other than this Article. This right to possession shall be limited by the provisions governing entering and enforcing orders of possession under subsection (g) of Section 15–1508. If the holder or purchaser determines that there are occupants of the mortgaged real estate who have not been made parties to the foreclosure and had their interests terminated therein, the holder or purchaser may bring a proceeding under subsection (h) of this Section, if applicable, or under Article IX of this Code to terminate the rights of possession of any such occupants. The holder or purchaser shall not be entitled to proceed against any such occupant under Article IX of this Code until after 30 days after the order confirming the sale is entered.

(e) Termination of Leases. A lease of all or any part of the mortgaged real estate shall not be terminated automatically solely by virtue of the entry into possession by (i) a mortgagee or receiver prior to the entry of an order confirming the sale, (ii) the holder of the certificate of sale, (iii) the holder of the deed issued pursuant to that certificate, or (iv) if no certificate or deed was issued, the purchaser at the sale.

(f) Other Statutes; Instruments. The provisions of this Article providing for possession of mortgaged real estate shall supersede any other inconsistent statutory provisions. In particular, and without limitation, whenever a receiver is sought to be appointed in any action in which a foreclosure is also pending, a receiver shall be appointed only in accordance with this Article. Except as may be authorized by this Article, no mortgage or other instrument may modify or supersede the provisions of this Article.

(g) Certain Leases. Leases of the mortgaged real estate entered into by a mortgagee in possession or a receiver and approved by the court in a foreclosure shall be binding on all parties, including the mortgagor after redemption, the purchaser at a sale pursuant to a judgment of foreclosure and any person acquiring an interest in the mortgaged real estate after entry of a judgment of foreclosure in accordance with Sections 15–1402 and 15–1403.

(h) Proceedings Against Certain Occupants.

(1) The mortgagee-in-possession of the mortgaged real estate under Section 15–1703, a receiver appointed under Section 15–1704, a holder of the certificate of sale or deed, or the purchaser may, at any time during the pendency of the foreclosure and up to 90 days after the date of the order confirming the sale, file a supplemental petition for possession against a person not personally named as a party to the foreclosure. This subsection (h) does not apply to any lessee with a bona fide lease of a dwelling unit in residential real estate in foreclosure.

(2) The supplemental petition for possession shall name each such occupant against whom possession is sought and state the facts upon which the claim for relief is premised.

(3) The petitioner shall serve upon each named occupant the petition, a notice of hearing on the petition, and, if any, a copy of the certificate of sale or deed. The proceeding for the termination of such occupant's possessory interest, including service of the notice of the hearing and the petition, shall in all respects comport with the requirements of Article IX of this Code, except as otherwise

specified in this Section. The hearing shall be no less than 21 days from the date of service of the notice.

(4) The supplemental petition shall be heard as part of the foreclosure proceeding and without the payment of additional filing fees. An order for possession obtained under this Section shall name each occupant whose interest has been terminated, shall recite that it is only effective as to the occupant so named and those holding under them, and shall be enforceable for no more than 120 days after its entry, except that the 120–day period may be extended to the extent and in the manner provided in Section 9–117 of Article IX and except as provided in item (5) of this subsection (h).

(5) In a case of foreclosure where the occupant is current on his or her rent, or where timely written notice of to whom and where the rent is to be paid has not been provided to the occupant, or where the occupant has made good-faith efforts to make rental payments in order to keep current, any order of possession must allow the occupant to retain possession of the property covered in his or her rental agreement (i) for 120 days following the notice of the hearing on the supplemental petition that has been properly served upon the occupant, or (ii) through the duration of his or her lease, whichever is shorter, provided that if the duration of his or her lease is less than 30 days from the date of the order, the order shall allow the occupant to retain possession for 30 days from the date of the order. A mortgagee in possession, receiver, holder of a certificate of sale or deed, or purchaser at the judicial sale, who asserts that the occupant is not current in rent, shall file an affidavit to that effect in the supplemental petition proceeding. If the occupant has been given timely written notice of to whom and where the rent is to be paid, this item (5) shall only apply if the occupant continues to pay his or her rent in full during the 120–day period or has made good-faith efforts to pay the rent in full during that period.

(6) The court records relating to a supplemental petition for possession filed under this subsection (h) against an occupant who is entitled to notice under item (5) of this subsection (h), or relating to a forcible entry and detainer action brought against an occupant who would have lawful possession of the premises but for the foreclosure of a mortgage on the property, shall be ordered sealed and shall not be disclosed to any person, other than a law enforcement officer or any other representative of a governmental entity, except upon further order of the court.

(i) Termination of bona fide leases. The holder of the certificate of sale, the holder of the deed issued pursuant to that certificate, or, if no certificate or deed was issued, the purchaser at the sale shall not terminate a bona fide lease of a dwelling unit in residential real estate in foreclosure except pursuant to Article IX of this Code.

P.A. 82–280, § 15–1701, added by P.A. 84–1462, § 2, eff. July 1, 1987. Amended by P.A. 85–907, Art. I, § 1, eff. Nov. 23, 1987; P.A. 88–21, § 5, eff. July 6, 1993; P.A. 88–265, § 5, eff. Jan. 1, 1994; P.A. 88–670, Art. 2, § 2–67, eff. Dec. 2, 1994; P.A. 89–203, § 30, eff. July 21, 1995; P.A. 95–262, § 5, eff. Jan. 1, 2008; P.A. 95–933, § 5, eff. Aug. 26, 2008; P.A. 96–60, § 5, eff. July 23, 2009; P.A. 96–111, § 5, eff. Oct. 29, 2009; P.A. 96–1000, § 625, eff. July 2, 2010; P.A. 98–514, § 5, eff. Nov. 19, 2013.

Formerly Ill.Rev.Stat.1991, ch. 110, ¶ 15–1701.

Validity

On November 18, 1999, the Supreme Court of Illinois held that P.A. 89–203 violated the single-subject rule of the Illinois Constitution in the case of People v. Wooters, 1999, 243 Ill.Dec. 33, 188 Ill.2d 500, 722 N.E.2d 1102.

5/15–1702. Specific Rules of Possession

§ 15–1702. Specific Rules of Possession. (a) Mortgagee's Rights. No mortgagee shall be required to take possession of the mortgaged real estate, whether upon application made by any other party or otherwise. Whenever a mortgagee entitled to possession so requests, the court shall appoint a receiver. The failure of a mortgagee to request possession or appointment of a receiver shall not preclude a mortgagee otherwise entitled to possession from making such a request at any future time. The appointment of a receiver shall not preclude a mortgagee from thereafter seeking to exercise such mortgagee's right to be placed in possession.

(b) Designation of Receivers. Whenever a receiver is to be appointed, the mortgagee shall be entitled to designate the receiver. If the mortgagor or any other party to the foreclosure objects to any such designation or designations and shows good cause, or the court disapproves the designee, the mortgagee in such instance shall be entitled to make another designation.

(c) Rights of Mortgagee Having Priority. If a mortgagee having priority objects to the proposed possession by a subordinate mortgagee or by a receiver designated by the subordinate mortgagee, upon entry of a finding in accordance with subsection (d) of Section 15–1702 the court shall instead place that objecting mortgagee in possession or, if a receiver is to be designated in accordance with subsection (b) of Section 15–1702, allow the designation of the receiver to be made by that objecting mortgagee.

(d) Removal of Mortgagee in Possession. A mortgagee placed in possession shall not be removed from possession, and no receiver or other mortgagee shall be placed in possession except upon (i) the mortgagee's misconduct, death, legal disability or other inability to act, (ii) appointment of a receiver in accordance with subsection (a) of Section 15–1704 or (iii) a showing of good cause by a mortgagee having priority. A receiver shall not be removed solely on account of being designated by a mortgagee later determined not to have priority.

(e) Determination of Priority. If the court is required to determine priority for the purposes of subsection (c) of Section 15–1702, a new determination shall be made each time a mortgagee is to be placed in possession or a receiver is to be appointed and shall be an interim determination which shall not preclude the court from making a contrary determination later in the foreclosure. If the court subsequently shall make such a contrary determination, a mortgagee in possession or acting receiver shall not be removed except in accordance with Part 17 of this Article.

(f) Rights to Crops. With respect to any crops growing or to be grown on the mortgaged real estate, the rights of a holder of any obligation secured by a collateral assignment of beneficial interest in a land trust, the rights of a mortgagee in possession, or the rights of a receiver, including rights by virtue of an equitable lien, shall be subject to a security interest properly perfected pursuant to Article 9 of the Uniform Commercial Code,[1] where the holder of a collateral assignment, mortgagee in possession, or receiver becomes entitled to crops by obtaining possession on or after the effective date of this Amendatory Act of 1988.

P.A. 82–280, § 15–1702, added by P.A. 84–1462, § 2, eff. July 1, 1987. Amended by P.A. 85–1427, § 5, eff. Dec. 22, 1988.

Formerly Ill.Rev.Stat.1991, ch. 110, ¶ 15–1702.

[1] 810 ILCS 5/9–101 et seq.

5/15–1703. Mortgagee in Possession

§ 15–1703. Mortgagee in Possession.

(a) Powers and Duties. A mortgagee placed in possession of the real estate pursuant to Section 15–1701 or Section 15–1702 shall have:

(1) such power and authority with respect to the real estate and other property subject to the mortgage, including the right to receive the rents, issues and profits thereof, as may have been conferred upon the mortgagee by the terms of the mortgage or other written instrument authorizing the taking of possession;

(2) all other rights and privileges of a mortgagee in possession under law not inconsistent herewith; and

(3) the same powers, duties and liabilities as a receiver appointed for the real estate in accordance with this Article. If an order placing a mortgagee in possession is modified, revoked or set aside, the mortgagee shall not be liable for any damages to the extent such damages arise solely out of the fact that the mortgagor was removed from possession or that the mortgagee was placed in possession.

(a–5) Notice to occupants.

(1) Following the order placing the mortgagee in possession of the mortgaged real estate, but no later than 21 days after the entry of such order, the mortgagee in possession shall make a good faith effort to ascertain the identities and addresses of all occupants of dwelling units of the mortgaged real estate.

(2) Following the order placing the mortgagee in possession of the mortgaged real estate, but no later than 21 days after the entry of such order, the mortgagee in possession shall notify all known occupants of dwelling units of the mortgaged real estate that the mortgagee has taken possession of the mortgaged real estate. The notice shall be in writing and shall:

(i) identify the occupant being served by the name known to the mortgagee in possession;

(ii) inform the occupant that the mortgaged real estate at which the dwelling unit is located is the subject of a foreclosure action and that control of the mortgaged real estate has changed;

(iii) provide the name, address, and telephone number of the individual or entity whom occupants may contact with concerns about the mortgaged real estate or to request repairs of that property;

(iv) include the following language, or language that is substantially similar: "This is NOT a notice to vacate the premises. You may wish to contact a lawyer or your local legal aid or housing counseling agency to discuss any rights that you may have.";

(v) include the name of the case, the case number, and the court where the foreclosure action is pending; and

(vi) provide instructions on the method of payment of future rent, if applicable.

(3) The written notice required by item (2) of this subsection (a–5) shall be served by delivering a copy thereof to the known occupant, or by leaving the same with some person of the age of 13 years or upwards, who is residing on or in possession of the premises; or by sending a copy of the notice to the known occupant by first-class mail, addressed to the occupant by the name known to the mortgagee in possession.

(4) In the event that a mortgagee in possession ascertains the identity and address of an occupant of a dwelling unit of the mortgaged real estate more than 21 days after being placed in possession of the mortgaged real estate pursuant to Section 15–1703, the mortgagee in possession shall provide the notice required by item (2) of this subsection (a–5) within 7 days of ascertaining the identity and address of the occupant.

(5)(i) A mortgagee in possession who fails to comply with items (1), (2), (3), and (4) of this subsection (a–5) may not collect any rent due and owing from a known occupant, or terminate a known occupant's tenancy for non- payment of such rent, until the mortgagee in possession has served the notice described in item (2) of this subsection (a–5) upon the known occupant. After providing such notice, the mortgagee in possession may collect any and all rent otherwise due and owing the mortgagee in possession from the known occupant and may terminate the known occupant's tenancy for non-payment of such rent if the mortgagee in possession otherwise has such right to terminate.

(ii) An occupant who previously paid rent for the current rental period to the mortgagor, or other entity with the authority to operate, manage, and conserve the mortgaged real estate at the time of payment, shall not be held liable for that rent by the mortgagee in possession, and the occupant's tenancy shall not be terminated for non-payment of rent for that rental period.

(6) Within 21 days of the order placing the mortgagee in possession of the mortgaged real estate, the mortgagee in possession shall post a written notice on the primary entrance of each dwelling unit subject to the foreclosure action that informs the occupants that the mortgagee in possession is now operating and managing the mortgaged real estate. This notice shall:

(i) inform occupant that the dwelling unit is the subject of a foreclosure action and that control of the mortgaged real estate has changed;

(ii) include the following language: "This is NOT a notice to vacate the premises.";

(iii) provide the name, address, and telephone number of the individual or entity whom occupants may contact with concerns about the mortgaged real estate or to request repairs of the property; and

(iv) provide instructions on the method of payment of future rent, if applicable.

(7)(i) The provisions of item (5) of this subsection (a–5) shall be the exclusive remedy for the failure of a mortgagee in possession to provide notice to a known occupant under this Section.

(ii) This Section shall not abrogate any right that a mortgagee in possession may have to possession of the mortgaged real estate and to maintain a proceeding against an occupant of a dwelling unit for possession under Article IX of this Code or subsection (h) of Section 15–1701.

(b) Fees and Expenses. A mortgagee in possession shall not be entitled to any fees for so acting, but shall be entitled to reimbursement for reasonable costs, expenses and third party management fees incurred in connection with such possession.

P.A. 82–280, § 15–1703, added by P.A. 84–1462, § 2, eff. July 1, 1987. Amended by P.A. 96–111, § 5, eff. Oct. 29, 2009; P.A. 98–514, § 5, eff. Nov. 19, 2013.

Formerly Ill.Rev.Stat.1991, ch. 110, ¶ 15–1703.

5/15–1704. Receivers

§ 15–1704. Receivers.

(a) Receiver. Notwithstanding the provisions of subsections (b), (c) and (d) of Section 15–1701, and except as provided in Section 15–1702, upon request of any party and a showing of good cause, the court shall appoint a receiver for the mortgaged real estate.

(b) Powers. A receiver appointed pursuant to this Article shall have possession of the mortgaged real estate and other property subject to the mortgage during the foreclosure, shall have full power and authority to operate, manage and conserve such property, and shall have all the usual powers of receivers in like cases. Without limiting the foregoing, a receiver shall have the power and authority to:

(1) secure tenants and execute leases for the real estate, the duration and terms of which are reasonable and customary for the type of use involved, and such leases shall have the same priority as if made by the owner of the real estate; but, unless approved by the Court, the receiver shall not execute oil, gas or other mineral leases, or (even if otherwise allowed by law) leases extending beyond the time of the receiver's possession; provided, however, with respect to residential real estate leased by the receiver, nothing in this Section shall affect the legal rights of any lessee with respect to the safety and habitability of the residential real estate;

(2) collect the rents, issues and profits from the mortgaged real estate;

(3) insure the mortgaged real estate against loss by fire or other casualty;

(4) employ counsel, custodians, janitors and other help; and

(5) pay taxes which may have been or may be levied against the mortgaged real estate.

(c) Duties. A receiver appointed pursuant to this Article must manage the mortgaged real estate as would a prudent person, taking into account the effect of the receiver's management on the interest of the mortgagor. A receiver may, without an order of the court, delegate managerial functions to a person in the business of managing real estate of the kind involved who is financially responsible, not related to the mortgagee or receiver and prudently selected. However, the receiver shall remain responsible to the mortgagor or other persons for the acts or omissions of such management agent. When fees are paid to such a management agent, the receiver's fees may be adjusted to the extent the court deems appropriate. In managing the mortgaged real estate and other property subject to the mortgage, a receiver or receiver's delegate, to the extent the receiver receives sufficient receipts from the mortgaged real estate, such other property or other sources, except to the extent ordered otherwise by the court:

(1) shall maintain the existing casualty and liability insurance required in accordance with the mortgage or applicable to the real estate and other property subject to the mortgage at the time the receiver took possession;

(2) shall use reasonable efforts to maintain the real estate and other property subject to the mortgage in at least as good condition as existed at the time the receiver took possession, excepting reasonable wear and tear and damage by any casualty;

(2.5) shall accept all rental payments from an occupant of the mortgaged property, and any payments from a third party or any rental assistance program in support of an occupant's housing;

(3) shall apply receipts to payment of ordinary operating expenses, including royalties, rents and other expenses of management;

(4) shall pay any shared or common expense assessments due to any association of owners of interests in real estate to the extent that such assessments are or may become a lien against the mortgaged real estate;

(5) may pay the amounts due under any mortgage if the mortgagee thereof is not a party in the foreclosure;

(6) may carry such additional casualty and liability insurance as is reasonably available and reasonable as to amounts and risks covered;

(7) may make other repairs and improvements necessary to comply with building, housing, and other similar codes or with existing contractual obligations affecting the mortgaged real estate;

(8) may hold receipts as reserves reasonably required for the foregoing purposes; and

(9) may take such other actions as may be reasonably necessary to conserve the mortgaged real estate and other property subject to the mortgage, or as otherwise authorized by the court.

(d) Allocation of Receipts. Receipts received from operation of the real estate and other property subject to the mortgage by the receiver shall be applied in the following order of priority.

(1) to reimbursement of the receiver for all reasonable costs and expenses incurred by the receiver or the receiver's delegates;

(2) to payment of insurance premiums authorized in paragraph (1) of subsection (c) of Section 15–1704;

(3) to payment of the receiver's delegates of any reasonable management fees for managing real estate of the type involved;

(4) to payment of receiver's fees allowed by the court;

(5) to payment of expenses authorized in paragraphs (2), (3) and (4) of subsection (c) of Section 15–1704;

(6) to payment of amounts authorized in paragraph (5) of subsection (c) of Section 15–1704;

(7) to payment of expenses authorized in paragraphs (6) and (7) of subsection (c) of Section 15–1704; and

(8) the balance, if any, shall be held or disbursed as ordered by the court.

(e) Non–Liability for Allocations. A receiver shall in no event be liable to any person for the allocation of, or failure to allocate, receipts to possible expenditures within the same priority category.

(f) Notice to occupants.

(1) Following an order appointing a receiver pursuant to Section 15–1704, but no later than 21 days after the entry of such order, the appointed receiver shall make a good faith effort to ascertain the identities and addresses of all occupants of dwelling units of the mortgaged real estate.

(2) Following an order appointing a receiver pursuant to Section 15–1704, but no later than 21 days after the entry of such order, the appointed receiver shall notify all known occupants of dwelling units of the mortgaged real estate that the receiver has been appointed receiver of the mortgaged real estate. Such notice shall be in writing and shall:

(i) identify the occupant being served by the name known to the receiver;

(ii) inform the occupant that the mortgaged real estate at which the dwelling unit is located is the subject of a foreclosure action and that control of the mortgaged real estate has changed;

(iii) provide the name, address, and telephone number of the individual or entity whom occupants may contact with concerns about the mortgaged real estate or to request repairs of that property;

(iv) include the following language, or language that is substantially similar: "This is NOT a notice to vacate the premises. You may wish to contact a lawyer or your local legal aid or housing counseling agency to discuss any rights that you may have.";

(v) include the name of the case, the case number, and the court where the foreclosure action is pending; and

(vi) provide instructions on the method of payment of future rent, if applicable.

(3) The written notice required by item (2) of this subsection (f) shall be served by delivering a copy thereof to the known occupant, or by leaving the same with some person of the age of 13 years or upwards, who is residing on or in possession of the premises; or by sending a copy of the notice to the known occupant by first-class mail, addressed to the occupant by the name known to the receiver.

(4) In the event that a receiver ascertains the identity and address of an occupant of a dwelling

unit of the mortgaged real estate more than 21 days after appointment pursuant to Section 15–1704, the receiver shall provide the notice required by item (2) of this subsection (f) within 7 days of ascertaining the identity and address of the occupant.

(5)(i) A receiver who fails to comply with items (1), (2), (3), and (4) of this subsection (f) may not collect any rent due and owing from a known occupant, or terminate a known occupant's tenancy for non-payment of such rent, until the receiver has served the notice described in item (2) of this subsection (f) upon the known occupant. After providing such notice, the receiver may collect any and all rent otherwise due and owing the receiver from the known occupant and may terminate the known occupant's tenancy for non-payment of such rent if the receiver otherwise has such right to terminate.

(ii) An occupant who previously paid rent for the current rental period to the mortgagor, or other entity with the authority to operate, manage, and conserve the mortgaged real estate at the time of payment, shall not be held liable for that rent by the receiver, and the occupant's tenancy shall not be terminated for non-payment of rent for that rental period.

(6) Within 21 days of appointment, the receiver shall post a written notice on the primary entrance of each dwelling unit subject to the foreclosure action that informs occupants that the receiver has been appointed to operate and manage the property. This notice shall:

(i) inform occupant that the dwelling unit is the subject of a foreclosure action and that control of the mortgaged real estate has changed;

(ii) include the following language: "This is NOT a notice to vacate the premises.";

(iii) provide the name, address, and telephone number of the individual or entity whom occupants may contact with concerns about the mortgaged real estate or to request repairs of the property; and

(iv) provide instructions on the method of payment of future rent, if applicable.

(7)(i) The provisions of item (5) of this subsection (f) shall be the exclusive remedy for the failure of a receiver to provide notice to a known occupant under this Section.

(ii) This Section shall not abrogate any right that a receiver may have to possession of the mortgaged real estate and to maintain a proceeding against an occupant of a dwelling unit for possession under Article IX of this Code or subsection (h) of Section 15–1701.

(g) Increase of rents. Notwithstanding any other provision of this Article, a receiver shall not charge an occupant of the mortgaged real estate a rental amount above that which the occupant had been paying for use and occupancy of the mortgaged real estate prior to the appointment of a receiver without leave of court. The court may allow an increase of rent if, upon motion by the receiver, the court finds by a preponderance of the evidence, that the increase of rent is necessary to operate, manage, and conserve the mortgaged real estate pursuant to this Section. A list of the current rents for each unit in the mortgaged real estate, and a list of the proposed rent increase for each of those units, must be attached to a motion for a rent increase under this subsection (g). All occupants of the mortgaged real estate who may be affected by the motion for a rent increase, if not otherwise entitled to notice, shall be notified in writing of the nature of the motion, the date and time of the motion, and the court where the motion will be heard. Such notice shall be by personal service or first-class mail. In the event that the receiver and an occupant of a dwelling unit agree to a rent increase for that dwelling unit, the receiver is excused from the requirements of this subsection (g) as to that dwelling unit. Nothing in this subsection (g) shall alter the terms of any lease agreement.

(h) Removal. The court may remove a receiver upon a showing of good cause, in which case a new receiver may be appointed in accordance with subsection (b) of Section 15–1702 and subsection (a) of Section 15–1704.

P.A. 82–280, § 15–1704, added by P.A. 84–1462, § 2, eff. July 1, 1987. Amended by P.A. 96–111, § 5, eff. Oct. 29, 2009; P.A. 98–514, § 5, eff. Nov. 19, 2013.

Formerly Ill.Rev.Stat.1991, ch. 110, ¶ 15–1704.

5/15–1705. Bond

§ 15–1705. Bond. (a) Mortgagee in Possession. Upon good cause shown after notice and hearing, the court may require that a mortgagee in possession give bond to other parties to account for what shall come into the mortgagee's possession by virtue of taking possession of the mortgaged real estate and for the acts of such mortgagee. The bond shall be in such reasonable amount, form and with such surety as may be required by the court.

(b) Receiver. When a receiver is appointed, bond may be required in accordance with Section 2–415 of the Code of Civil Procedure.

(c) Corporations. Notwithstanding the provisions of subsections (a) and (b) of Section 15–1705, a corporation qualified to administer trusts in this State that is acting as a mortgagee in possession or receiver shall not be required to give bond other than appeal bonds.

P.A. 82–280, § 15–1705, added by P.A. 84–1462, § 2, eff. July 1, 1987.

Formerly Ill.Rev.Stat.1991, ch. 110, ¶ 15–1705.

5/15–1706. Possession

§ 15–1706. Possession. (a) Request. A request that the mortgagee be placed in possession or that a receiver be appointed may be made by motion, whether or not such request is included in the complaint or other pleading. Any such request shall be supported by affidavit or other sworn pleading.

(b) Meaning of Request. A request in a motion or in the complaint or other pleading that the mortgagee be placed in possession or that a receiver be appointed shall be construed to mean a mortgagee placed in possession or a receiver appointed in accordance with, and with powers and duties specified by, Part 17 of this Article.

(c) Hearing. After reasonable notice has been given to all other parties, the court shall promptly hold a hearing and promptly rule on a request that a mortgagee be placed in possession or that a receiver be appointed, except that, if no objection to the request is made prior to the time specified for the hearing, the court shall rule without a hearing.

(d) Reasonable Notice. For the purposes of subsection (c) of Section 15–1706, notice shall be reasonable if given as much in advance of the hearing as notice of motions generally is required to be given under applicable court rules, and if served in the same manner as motions generally are served; except, if the mortgagor has not been served with the complaint, the mortgagor must be served in the same manner as required for service of process. Notwithstanding anything in the foregoing sentence to the contrary, except with respect to the mortgagor of residential real estate which has not been abandoned, the court may rule without service on a party, if the party is in default or if the party making the request shows good cause by affidavit or other sworn evidence. If the mortgagor is not served prior to the hearing, he shall be given notice of the hearing to the same extent as applicable court rules may provide for post-hearing notice of emergency and ex parte motions.

P.A. 82–280, § 15–1706, added by P.A. 84–1462, § 2, eff. July 1, 1987.

Formerly Ill.Rev.Stat.1991, ch. 110, ¶ 15–1706.

ARTICLE XVI. NE EXEAT

5/16–101. Availability of remedy

§ 16–101. Availability of remedy. Relief by ne exeat republica may be granted, in cases where the debt or claim is not actually due, but exists fairly and bona fide in expectancy at the time of making application, and in cases where the claim is due; and it is not necessary, to authorize the granting of such relief by ne exeat, that the applicant show that his or her debt or claim is purely of an equitable character.

P.A. 82–280, § 16–101, eff. July 1, 1982.

Formerly Ill.Rev.Stat.1991, ch. 110, ¶ 16–101.

5/16–102. In favor of co-obligors or co-debtors

§ 16–102. In favor of co-obligors or co-debtors. In case of joint, or joint and several obligors or debtors, if one or more of them is about to remove outside of the jurisdictional limits of this State, taking their property with them, leaving one or more co-obligors or co-debtors bound with them for the payment of any sum of money, or for the delivery of any article of property, or for the conveyance of land at a certain time, which time has not arrived at the time of such intended removal, such co-obligor or co-debtor who remains is entitled, upon application, to relief by ne exeat, to compel the co-obligor or co-debtor who is about to remove to secure the payment of his or her part of the sum to be paid, or of the delivery of the property, or to convey, or to join in the conveyance of the land. In cases of security, the relief by ne exeat may be granted, on application of a security, against the principal or co-security, when the obligation or debt is not yet due, and the principal or co-security is about removing out of the State.

P.A. 82–280, § 16–102, eff. July 1, 1982.

Formerly Ill.Rev.Stat.1991, ch. 110, ¶ 16–102.

5/16–103. Venue

§ 16–103. Venue. Where ne exeat proceedings are ancillary to any other action or proceeding, the venue shall be the same as that of the main action or proceeding.

P.A. 82–280, § 16–103, eff. July 1, 1982.

Formerly Ill.Rev.Stat.1991, ch. 110, ¶ 16–103.

5/16–104. Complaint or petition—Bond

§ 16–104. Complaint or petition—Bond. No relief by ne exeat shall be granted but upon complaint or petition filed, and affidavit to the truth of the allegation therein contained. Upon the granting of such relief the court shall enter an order stating in what penalty bond and security shall be required of the defendant or respondent. The court shall also require the plaintiff or petitioner, before a certified copy of the ne exeat order is issued by the clerk, bond with good and sufficient surety, in such sum as the court shall deem proper, conditioned that the plaintiff or petitioner will prosecute the complaint or petition with effect, and will reimburse to the defendant or respondent such damages and costs as shall be wrongfully sustained by occasion of the granting of the relief by ne exeat. If any defendant or respondent to any such relief by ne exeat is damaged, he or she may bring an action on such bond; and, if, on trial, it is determined by the court that such relief by ne exeat was applied for without just cause, the person affected shall recover damages, to be assessed as in other cases on penal bonds.

P.A. 82–280, § 16–104, eff. July 1, 1982.

Formerly Ill.Rev.Stat.1991, ch. 110, ¶ 16–104.

5/16–105. Limited to matters which are germane

§ 16–105. Limited to matters which are germane. No matters not germane to the distinctive purpose of the proceeding shall be introduced by joinder, counterclaim or otherwise.

P.A. 82–280, § 16–105, eff. July 1, 1982.

Formerly Ill.Rev.Stat.1991, ch. 110, ¶ 16–105.

5/16–106. Orders returnable

§ 16–106. Orders returnable. All orders for ne exeat shall be returnable to the clerk of the court which entered the orders.

P.A. 82–280, § 16–106, eff. July 1, 1982.

Formerly Ill.Rev.Stat.1991, ch. 110, ¶ 16–106.

5/16–107. Service of order—Bond

§ 16–107. Service of order—Bond. The order for ne exeat shall require the defendant to file his or her answer or otherwise plead within a time designated in the order, and, upon a certified copy of the order being served upon the defendant he or she shall give bond, with surety in the sum specified in such order, conditioned that he or she will not depart the State without leave of the court, and that he or she will render himself or herself to answer any judgment which the court may enter against him or her; and in default of giving such security, he or she may be committed to a penal institution other than the penitentiary, as in other cases, for the want of bail. No temporary departure from the State shall be considered as a breach of the condition of the bond, if he or she returns before personal appearance is necessary to answer or comply with any judgment or order of the court.

P.A. 82–280, § 16–107, eff. July 1, 1982.

Formerly Ill.Rev.Stat.1991, ch. 110, ¶ 16–107.

5/16–108. Surrender of defendant

§ 16–108. Surrender of defendant. The surety in any bond for the defendant may, at any time before the bond is forfeited, surrender the defendant, in exoneration of himself or herself, in the same manner that bail may surrender their principal, and obtain the same discharge.

P.A. 82–280, § 16–108, eff. July 1, 1982.

Formerly Ill.Rev.Stat.1991, ch. 110, ¶ 16–108.

5/16–109. Proceedings after service of order

§ 16–109. Proceedings after service of order. On the return of the order for ne exeat, if it was duly served, the court shall proceed therein as in other cases where equitable relief is sought, if the time of performance of the duty or obligation of the defendant has expired; if not, then the proceedings shall be stayed until it has expired.

P.A. 82–280, § 16–109, eff. July 1, 1982.

Formerly Ill.Rev.Stat.1991, ch. 110, ¶ 16–109.

5/16–110. Vacating order

§ 16–110. Vacating order. Nothing contained in Section 16–109 of this Act shall prevent the court from proceeding at any time to determine whether the order for ne exeat ought not to be vacated.

P.A. 82–280, § 16–110, eff. July 1, 1982.

Formerly Ill.Rev.Stat.1991, ch. 110, ¶ 16–110.

5/16–111. Seeking wrong remedy not fatal

§ 16–111. Seeking wrong remedy not fatal. Where relief is sought under Article XVI of this Act and the court determines, on motion directed to the pleadings, or on motion for summary judgment or upon trial, that the plaintiff or petitioner has pleaded or established facts which entitle him or her to relief but that he or she has sought the wrong remedy, the Court shall permit the pleadings to be amended, on just and reasonable terms, and the Court shall grant the relief to which plaintiff or petitioner is entitled on the amended pleadings or upon the evidence. In considering whether a proposed amendment is just and reasonable, the court shall consider the right of the defendant or respondent to assert additional defenses, to demand a trial by jury, to plead a counterclaim or third party complaint, and to order the plaintiff or petitioner to take additional steps which were not required under the pleadings as previously filed.

P.A. 82–280, § 16–111, eff. July 1, 1982.

Formerly Ill.Rev.Stat.1991, ch. 110, ¶ 16–111.

ARTICLE XVII. PARTITION

5/17–101. Compelling partition

§ 17–101. Compelling partition. When lands, tenements, or hereditaments are held in joint tenancy or tenancy in common or other form of co-ownership and regardless of whether any or all of the claimants are minors or adults, any one or more of the persons interested therein may compel a partition thereof by a verified complaint in the circuit court of the county where the premises or part of the premises are situated. If lands, tenements or hereditaments held in joint tenancy or tenancy in common are situated in 2 or more counties, the venue may be in any one of such counties, and the circuit court of any such county first acquiring jurisdiction shall retain sole and exclusive jurisdiction. Ownership of an interest in the surface of lands, tenements, or hereditaments by a co-owner of an interest in minerals underlying the surface does not prevent partition of the mineral estate. This amendatory Act of the 92nd General Assembly is a declaration of existing law and is intended to remove any possible conflicts or ambiguities, thereby confirming existing law pertinent to the partition of interests in minerals and applies to all actions for the partition of minerals now pending or filed on or after the effective date of this amendatory Act of the 92nd General Assembly. Nothing in this amendatory Act of the 92nd General Assembly shall be construed as allowing an owner of a mineral interest in coal to mine and remove the coal by the surface method of mining without first obtaining the consent of all of the owners of the surface to the mining and removal of coal by the surface method of mining. Ownership of an interest in minerals by a co-owner of an interest in the surface does not prevent the partition of the surface. The ownership of an interest in some, but not all, of the mineral estate by a co-owner of an interest in other minerals does not prevent the partition of the co-owned mineral estate.

P.A. 82–280, § 17–101, eff. July 1, 1982. Amended by P.A. 92–379, § 5, eff. Aug. 16, 2001; P.A. 93–925, § 5, eff. Aug. 12, 2004.

Formerly Ill.Rev.Stat.1991, ch. 110, ¶ 17–101.

5/17–102. Complaint

§ 17–102. Complaint. The verified complaint shall particularly describe the premises sought to be divided, and shall set forth the interests of all parties interested therein, so far as the same are known to the plaintiffs, including tenants for years or for life, and of all persons entitled to the reversion, remainder or inheritance, and of every person who, upon any contingency, may be or become entitled to any beneficial interest in the premises, so far as the same are known to the plaintiffs, and shall ask for the division and partition of the premises according to the respective rights of the parties interested therein, or, if a division and partition of the same cannot be made without manifest prejudice to the owners, that a sale thereof be made and the proceeds divided according to the respective rights of the parties.

P.A. 82–280, § 17–102, eff. July 1, 1982.

Formerly Ill.Rev.Stat.1991, ch. 110, ¶ 17–102.

5/17–103. Parties defendant

§ 17–103. Parties defendant. Every person having any interest, whether in possession or otherwise, who is not a plaintiff shall be made a defendant in such complaint.

P.A. 82–280, § 17–103, eff. July 1, 1982.

Formerly Ill.Rev.Stat.1991, ch. 110, ¶ 17–103.

5/17–104. Unknown parties

§ 17–104. Unknown parties. When there are any persons interested in the premises whose names are unknown, or the share or quantity of interest of any of the parties is unknown to the plaintiff, or such share or interest is uncertain or contingent, or the ownership of the inheritance depends upon an executory devise, or the remainder is contingent, so that such parties cannot be named, it shall be so stated in the verified complaint.

P.A. 82–280, § 17–104, eff. July 1, 1982.

Formerly Ill.Rev.Stat.1991, ch. 110, ¶ 17–104.

5/17–105. Judgment

§ 17–105. Judgment. The court shall ascertain and declare the rights, titles and interest of all the parties in such action, the plaintiffs as well as the defendants, and shall enter judgment according to the rights of the parties. After entry of judgment adjudicating the rights, titles, and interests of the parties, the court upon further hearing shall determine whether or not the premises or any part thereof can be divided among the parties without manifest prejudice to the parties in interest. If the court finds that a division can be made, then the court shall enter further judgment fairly and impartially dividing the premises among the parties with or without owelty. If the court finds that the whole or any part of the premises sought to be partitioned cannot be divided without manifest prejudice to the owners thereof, then the court shall order the premises not susceptible of division to be sold at public sale in such manner and upon such terms and notice of sale as the court directs. If the court orders the sale of the premises or any part thereof, the court shall fix the value of the premises to be sold. No sale may be approved for less than two-thirds of the total amount of the valuation of the premises to be sold. If it appears to the court that any of the premises will not sell for two-thirds of the amount of the valuation thereof, the court upon further hearing may either revalue the premise and approve the sale or order a new sale.

P.A. 82–280, § 17–105, eff. July 1, 1982. Amended by P.A. 93–925, § 5, eff. Aug. 12, 2004.

Formerly Ill.Rev.Stat.1991, ch. 110, ¶ 17–105.

5/17–106. Appointment of commissioner and surveyor

§ 17–106. Appointment of commissioner and surveyor. The court in its discretion, sua sponte, or on the motion of any interested party, may appoint a disinterested commissioner who, subject to direction by the court, shall report to the court in writing under oath as to whether or not the premises are subject to division without manifest prejudice to the rights of the parties and, if so, report how the division may be made. The court may authorize the employment of a surveyor to carry out or assist in the division of the premises. The fees and expenses of the commissioner and of the surveyor and the person making the sale shall be taxed as costs in the proceedings.

P.A. 82–280, § 17–106, eff. July 1, 1982. Amended by P.A. 93–925, § 5, eff. Aug. 12, 2004.

Formerly Ill.Rev.Stat.1991, ch. 110, ¶ 17–106.

5/17–107 to 5/17–111. §§ 17–107 to 17–111. Repealed by P.A. 93–925, § 10, eff. August 12, 2004

5/17–112. Homestead

§ 17–112. Homestead. If any party to the action is entitled to an estate of homestead in the premises, or any part thereof, and the homestead has not been set off, the homestead may be set off by the court; and if the court so directs, the premises so allotted or set off may be partitioned among the claimants, subject thereto.

P.A. 82–280, § 17–112, eff. July 1, 1982. Amended by P.A. 93–925, § 5, eff. Aug. 12, 2004.

Formerly Ill.Rev.Stat.1991, ch. 110, ¶ 17–112.

5/17–113. Election as to shares

§ 17–113. Election as to shares. Several parties interested in the premises may, if they so elect, have their shares set off together or in severalty.

P.A. 82–280, § 17–113, eff. July 1, 1982.

Formerly Ill.Rev.Stat.1991, ch. 110, ¶ 17–113.

5/17–114. Liens

§ 17–114. Liens. A person having a mortgage, attachment, or other lien on the share of a part owner shall be concluded by the judgment of partition so far as it relates to the partition and the assignment of the shares, but his or her lien shall remain in full force upon the part assigned to or left for such part owner.

P.A. 82–280, § 17–114, eff. July 1, 1982.

Formerly Ill.Rev.Stat.1991, ch. 110, ¶ 17–114.

5/17–115. Eviction by person with better title

§ 17–115. Eviction by person with better title. If a person to whom any share has been allotted is evicted by a person who, at the time of the partition, had a title older and better than the title of those who were parties to the action, the person evicted may have a new partition of the residue as if no partition had been made, if such new partition can be justly made, or he or she may have contribution from the others, so as to make his or her share just and proportional with the others, according to the rights in the premises.

P.A. 82–280, § 17–115, eff. July 1, 1982.

Formerly Ill.Rev.Stat.1991, ch. 110, ¶ 17–115.

5/17–116, 5/17–117. Repealed by P.A. 93–925, § 10, effective August 12, 2004

5/17–118. Report of sale—Conveyances

§ 17–118. Report of sale—Conveyances. The officer making such sale shall, within 10 days thereafter, file a report of his or her action in the office of the clerk of the court ordering such sale. The court may approve the report and confirm the sale reported if no objections have been filed or may disapprove the sale and order the real estate to be resold; if objections have been filed to the report, the court may at once proceed to hear such objections and sustain or overrule them.

Upon confirmation of the sale, the person making the sale or some person specially appointed shall execute and deliver to the purchaser proper conveyances, taking in case of sale on credit, security as required by the judgment. These conveyances shall operate as an effectual bar against all parties and privies to the proceedings and all persons claiming under them.

P.A. 82–280, § 17–118, eff. July 1, 1982.

Formerly Ill.Rev.Stat.1991, ch. 110, ¶ 17–118.

5/17–119. Distribution of proceeds

§ 17–119. Distribution of proceeds. Upon the approval of the report by the court, the proceeds of the sale shall be distributed by the person making the sale, as directed by the court, to the persons entitled thereto, according to their interests, or, in appropriate cases, to the persons and in the amounts and manner as now or hereafter provided in the applicable sections of the Probate Act of 1975, as amended,[1] relating to small estates.

P.A. 82–280, § 17–119, eff. July 1, 1982.

Formerly Ill.Rev.Stat.1991, ch. 110, ¶ 17–119.

[1] 755 ILCS 5/1–1 et seq.

5/17–120. Life estate or homestead

§ 17–120. Life estate or homestead. In case of sale the court may, with the consent of the person entitled to an estate for life, or for years, or of homestead, to the whole or any part of the premises, who is a party in the action, sell such estate with the rest. Such consent shall be in writing, signed by such person, and filed in the court wherein the proceedings for partition are pending.

If such persons are incapable of giving consent, the court may determine, taking into consideration the interests of all parties, whether such estate ought to be excluded from the sale or sold.

When such interest is sold, the value thereof may be ascertained and paid over in gross, or the proper proportion of the funds invested, and the income paid over to the party entitled thereto, during the continuance of the estate.

P.A. 82–280, § 17–120, eff. July 1, 1982.

Formerly Ill.Rev.Stat.1991, ch. 110, ¶ 17–120.

5/17–121. Unknown owners

§ 17–121. Unknown owners. If the person entitled to any estate is unknown, the court may determine whether the estate shall be sold or not, as in case of persons under disability, and in the event of sale, make such order for the protection of the rights of such person, in the same manner, as far as may be, as if the person were known and had appeared.

P.A. 82–280, § 17–121, eff. July 1, 1982.

Formerly Ill.Rev.Stat.1991, ch. 110, ¶ 17–121.

5/17–122. Deposit of proceeds of sale

§ 17–122. Deposit of proceeds of sale. When a sale of premises is made, and no person appears to claim such portion of the money as may belong to any non-resident or person whose name is unknown, the court shall require such money to be deposited in the county treasury, subject to the further order of the court. All money so required to be deposited shall be received by the county treasurer and paid upon the order of the court.

P.A. 82–280, § 17–122, eff. July 1, 1982.

Formerly Ill.Rev.Stat.1991, ch. 110, ¶ 17–122.

5/17–123. Application for deposited money

§ 17–123. Application for deposited money. When money is so deposited in the county treasury, the person or persons entitled to the same, may at any time apply to the court making the order of sale and obtain an order for the same upon making satisfactory proof to the court of his or her right thereto.

P.A. 82–280, § 17–123, eff. July 1, 1982.

Formerly Ill.Rev.Stat.1991, ch. 110, ¶ 17–123.

5/17–124. Vesting title

§ 17–124. Vesting title. In all actions for the partition of real estate, the court may: investigate and determine all questions of conflicting or controverted titles, and remove clouds upon the titles to any of the premises sought to be partitioned; vest titles, by its order, in the parties to whom the premises are allotted, without the forms of conveyances by minors or unknown heirs or other parties to the action; order a sale of the premises for the purpose of dividing the premises in proper cases, and by its order, vest the purchaser with title, and apportion incumbrances among the parties to whom the incumbered premises are allotted.

P.A. 82–280, § 17–124, eff. July 1, 1982. Amended by P.A. 84–1308, Art. III, § 46, eff. Aug. 25, 1986.

Formerly Ill.Rev.Stat.1991, ch. 110, ¶ 17–124.

5/17–125. Costs

§ 17–125. Costs. In all proceedings for the partition of real estate, when the rights and interests of all the parties in interest are properly set forth in the complaint, the court shall apportion the costs among the parties in interest in the action, including the necessary expense of procuring such evidence of title to the real estate as is usual and customary for making sales of real estate, and a reasonable fee for plaintiff's attorney, so that each party shall pay his or her equitable portion thereof, unless the defendants, or some of them, interpose a good and substantial defense to the complaint. In such case the party or parties making such substantial defense shall recover their costs against the plaintiff according to justice and equity.

P.A. 82–280, § 17–125, eff. July 1, 1982.

Formerly Ill.Rev.Stat.1991, ch. 110, ¶ 17–125.

5/17–126. Adjustment of rights after judgment

§ 17–126. Adjustment of rights after judgment. In any case where, after judgment of partition, and before division or sale is had (as the case may be), the parties in interest adjust the respective rights among themselves so that further proceedings leading to such actual division or sale become unnecessary, an order shall be entered terminating further proceedings, whereupon the judgment of partition shall remain in full force and effect to determine the rights and interests of the parties as adjudicated therein, and there shall be no judicial division or sale of the premises, rights or interests pursuant to such judgment.

P.A. 82–280, § 17–126, eff. July 1, 1982.

Formerly Ill.Rev.Stat.1991, ch. 110, ¶ 17–126.

5/17–127. Proceedings herein

§ 17–127. Proceedings herein. Proceedings for partition shall be conducted in accordance with the provisions of Article XVII of this Act.

P.A. 82–280, § 17–127, eff. July 1, 1982.

Formerly Ill.Rev.Stat.1991, ch. 110, ¶ 17–127.

ARTICLE XVIII. QUO WARRANTO

Section
5/18–101. Grounds.
5/18–102. Parties.
5/18–103. Pleadings.
5/18–104. Limitation.
5/18–105. Security for costs.
5/18–106. Summons—Appearance.
5/18–107. Seeking wrong remedy not fatal.
5/18–108. Judgment.

5/18–101. Grounds

§ 18–101. Grounds. A proceeding in quo warranto may be brought in case:

(1) Any person usurps, intrudes into, or unlawfully holds or executes any office, or franchise, or any office in any corporation created by authority of this State;

(2) Any person holds or claims to hold or exercise any privilege, exemption or license which has been improperly or without warrant of law issued or granted by any officer, board, commissioner, court, or other person or persons authorized or empowered by law to grant or issue such privilege, exemption or license;

(3) Any public officer has done, or allowed any act which by the provisions of law, works a forfeiture of his or her office;

(4) Any association or number of persons act within this State as a corporation without being legally incorporated;

(5) Any corporation does or omits to do any act which amounts to a surrender or forfeiture of its rights and privileges as a corporation, or exercises powers not conferred by law;

(6) Any railroad company doing business in this State charges an extortionate rate for the transportation of any freight or passenger, or makes any unjust discrimination in the rate of freight or passenger tariff over or upon its railroad.

P.A. 82–280, § 18–101, eff. July 1, 1982.

Formerly Ill.Rev.Stat.1991, ch. 110, ¶ 18–101.

5/18–102. Parties

§ 18–102. Parties. The proceeding shall be brought in the name of the People of the State of Illinois by the Attorney General or State's Attorney of the proper county, either of his or her own accord or at the instance of any individual relator; or by any citizen having an interest in the question on his or her own relation, when he or she has requested the Attorney General and State's Attorney to bring the same, and the Attorney General and State's Attorney have refused or failed to do so, and when, after notice to the Attorney General and State's Attorney, and to the adverse party, of the intended application, leave has been granted by the circuit court.

P.A. 82–280, § 18–102, eff. July 1, 1982.

Formerly Ill.Rev.Stat.1991, ch. 110, ¶ 18–102.

5/18–103. Pleadings

§ 18–103. Pleadings. The People of the State of Illinois shall be deemed the plaintiff and the adverse parties shall be defendants, and the first pleading by the plaintiff shall be designated a complaint. The complaint need not set forth the basis of the challenge, but may in general terms allege that the defendant is exercising the claimed right without lawful authority and call upon the defendant to show by what warrant he, she or it exercises it, and if more than one ground exists they may all be joined in one count.

When the complaint is filed by a citizen on his or her own relation, it shall be alleged therein that his or her requests of the Attorney General and the State's Attorney, respectively, to bring the action, have been refused, or that they have failed to act, as the case may be, and that leave of court to file the complaint has been granted as provided in Article XVIII of this Act.

The several rights of diverse parties to the same office or franchise, privilege, exemption or license, may properly be determined in one action, and all such persons may be joined in the same complaint, in order to try their respective rights to such office, franchise, privilege, exemption or license; but the court, in its discretion, may order separate trials when convenience in the determination of any of such rights so requires. No matters not germane to the distinctive purpose of the proceeding shall be introduced by joinder, counterclaim or otherwise.

If the plaintiff elects to set forth expressly in the complaint the grounds for an attack on the defendant's claimed right, the defendant may answer the complaint or present a motion directed thereto as in other civil actions, but if the complaint is in general terms, as provided in Article XVIII of this Act, the defendant shall by answer disclaim or justify, and, if the defendant justifies, shall set out the facts which show the lawful authority to exercise the right claimed. The plaintiff may reply to the answer or present a motion directed thereto as in other civil cases.

P.A. 82–280, § 18–103, eff. July 1, 1982.

Formerly Ill.Rev.Stat.1991, ch. 110, ¶ 18–103.

5/18–104. Limitation

§ 18–104. Limitation. No action shall be brought by quo warranto, or otherwise, questioning the legality of the organization of any county, city, village, incorporated town, township, school district, park district, road district, drainage district, sanitary district, authority or any other municipal corporation or political subdivision in the State of Illinois after such municipal corporation or political subdivision has been in de facto existence for a period of 3 years.

P.A. 82–280, § 18–104, eff. July 1, 1982.

Formerly Ill.Rev.Stat.1991, ch. 110, ¶ 18–104.

5/18–105. Security for costs

§ 18–105. Security for costs. When the action is brought by any citizen on his or her own relation, as above provided, he or she shall file security for costs to be approved by the clerk, at the time the complaint is filed.

P.A. 82–280, § 18–105, eff. July 1, 1982.

Formerly Ill.Rev.Stat.1991, ch. 110, ¶ 18–105.

5/18–106. Summons—Appearance

§ 18–106. Summons—Appearance. Upon the filing of the complaint, the clerk of court shall issue a summons, in like form, as near as may be, as summons in other civil cases. The summons shall be made returnable within a time designated by the plaintiff not less than 5 nor more than 30 days after the service of the summons. Every defendant who is served with summons shall answer or otherwise appear on or before the return day of the summons, unless the time for doing so is extended by the court. If the defendant fails to do so, judgment may be entered against the defendant. Reply to or motion directed against the answer may be filed by the plaintiff within 5 days after the last day allowed for the filing of the answer, unless the time for doing so is extended by the court.

P.A. 82–280, § 18–106, eff. July 1, 1982. Amended by P.A. 83–357, § 1, eff. Sept. 14, 1983.

Formerly Ill.Rev.Stat.1991, ch. 110, ¶ 18–106.

5/18–107. Seeking wrong remedy not fatal

§ 18–107. Seeking wrong remedy not fatal. Where relief is sought under Article XVIII of this Act and the court determines, on motion directed to the pleadings, or on motion for summary judgment or upon trial, that the plaintiff has pleaded or established facts which entitle the plaintiff to relief but that the plaintiff has sought the wrong remedy, the court shall permit the pleadings to be amended, on just and reasonable terms, and the court shall grant the relief to which plaintiff is entitled on the amended pleadings or upon the evidence. In considering whether a proposed amendment is just and reasonable, the court shall consider the right of the defendant to assert additional defenses, to demand a trial by jury, to plead a counterclaim or third party complaint, and to order the plaintiff to take additional steps which were not required under the pleadings as previously filed.

P.A. 82–280, § 18–107, eff. July 1, 1982.

Formerly Ill.Rev.Stat.1991, ch. 110, ¶ 18–107.

5/18–108. Judgment

§ 18–108. Judgment. The court shall determine and adjudge the rights of all parties to the proceeding. In case any person or corporation against whom such complaint is filed is adjudged guilty as charged in the complaint, the court may enter judgment of ouster against such person or corporation from the office or franchise, and fine such person or corporation, and also enter judgment in favor of the relator for the cost of the prosecution. Instead of entering judgment of ouster from a franchise for an abuse thereof, the court may fine the person or corporation found guilty in any sum not exceeding $25,000.00 for each offense. When judgment is entered in favor of any defendant, such defendant shall recover costs against the relator.

P.A. 82–280, § 18–108, eff. July 1, 1982. Amended by P.A. 83–707, § 1, eff. Sept. 23, 1983.

Formerly Ill.Rev.Stat.1991, ch. 110, ¶ 18–108.

ARTICLE XIX. REPLEVIN

5/19–101. When brought

§ 19–101. When brought. Whenever any goods or chattels have been wrongfully distrained, or otherwise wrongfully taken or are wrongfully detained, an action of replevin may be brought for the recovery of such goods or chattels, by the owner or person entitled to their possession.

P.A. 82–280, § 19–101, eff. July 1, 1982.

Formerly Ill.Rev.Stat.1991, ch. 110, ¶ 19–101.

5/19–102. When not available

§ 19–102. When not available. No action of replevin shall lie on behalf of a defendant against whom a judgment or attachment is in the process of enforcement, to recover goods or chattels seized by virtue thereof, unless such goods and chattels are exempted, by law, from such enforcement of the judgment or attachment; nor shall an action of replevin lie for such goods and chattels at the action of any other person, unless such other person has, at the time, a right to reduce the goods taken to his or her possession.

P.A. 82–280, § 19–102, eff. July 1, 1982.

Formerly Ill.Rev.Stat.1991, ch. 110, ¶ 19–102.

5/19–103. Venue

§ 19–103. Venue. The venue provisions applicable to other civil cases shall apply to actions of replevin; and in addition an action of replevin may be brought in any county in which the goods or chattels or any part of them are located.

P.A. 82–280, § 19–103, eff. July 1, 1982.

Formerly Ill.Rev.Stat.1991, ch. 110, ¶ 19–103.

5/19–104. Complaint

§ 19–104. Complaint. An action of replevin shall be commenced by the filing of a verified complaint which describes the property to be replevied and states that the plaintiff in such action is the owner of the property so described, or that he or she is then lawfully entitled to the possession thereof, and that the property is wrongfully detained by the defendant, and that the same has not been taken for any tax, assessment, or fine levied by virtue of any law of this State, against the property of such plaintiff, or against him or her individually, nor seized under any lawful process against the goods and chattels of such plaintiff subject to such lawful process, nor held by virtue of any order for replevin against such plaintiff.

P.A. 82–280, § 19–104, eff. July 1, 1982.

Formerly Ill.Rev.Stat.1991, ch. 110, ¶ 19–104.

5/19–105. Notice

§ 19–105. Notice. The defendant shall be given 5 days written notice in the manner required by rule of the Supreme Court, of a hearing before the court to contest the entry of an order for replevin. No order for replevin may be entered nor may property be seized pursuant to an order for replevin prior to such notice and hearing except as provided in Section 19–106 of this Act.

As to any particular property, the right to notice and hearing established in this Section may not be waived by any consumer. As used in this Section, a consumer is an individual who obtained possession of the property for personal, family, household, or agricultural purposes.

Any waiver of the right to notice and hearing established in this Section must be in writing and must be given voluntarily, intelligently, and knowingly.

P.A. 82–280, § 19–105, eff. July 1, 1982.

Formerly Ill.Rev.Stat.1991, ch. 110, ¶ 19–105.

5/19–106. Exception to requirement of notice

§ 19–106. Exception to requirement of notice. Notice to the defendant is not required if the plaintiff establishes and the court finds as a matter of record and supported by evidence that summary seizure of the property is justified by reason of necessity to:

(1) protect the plaintiff from an immediately impending harm which will result from the imminent destruction or concealment of the disputed property in derogation of the plaintiff's rights in the property;

(2) protect the plaintiff from an immediately impending harm which will result from the imminent removal of the disputed property from the State, taking into consideration the availability of judicial remedies in the event of such removal;

(3) protect the plaintiff from an immediately impending harm which will result from the perishable nature of the disputed property under the particular circumstances at the time of the action;

(4) protect the plaintiff from an immediately impending harm which will result from the imminent sale, transfer or assignment of the disputed property to the extent such sale, transfer or assignment is

fraudulent or in derogation of the plaintiff's rights in the property;

(5) recover the property from a defendant who has obtained possession by theft.

At an ex parte hearing to determine if notice is not required, the court shall examine the evidence on each element required by this Section or any written waiver of rights presented by the plaintiff. If the court finds that notice is not required, or that the waiver is in accordance with law, it shall order a hearing as soon as practicable on the entry of an order for replevin.

P.A. 82–280, § 19–106, eff. July 1, 1982.

Formerly Ill.Rev.Stat.1991, ch. 110, ¶ 19–106.

5/19–107. Hearing for entry of order

§ 19–107. Hearing for entry of order. At the hearing on the entry of an order for replevin, which may be a hearing to contest pursuant to notice under Section 19–105 of this Act or an ex parte hearing pursuant to a finding under Section 19–106 of this Act, the court shall review the basis of the plaintiff's claim to possession. If the plaintiff establishes a prima facie case to a superior right to possession of the disputed property, and if the plaintiff also demonstrates to the court the probability that the plaintiff will ultimately prevail on the underlying claim to possession, the court shall so find as a matter of record and an order for replevin shall be entered by the court.

P.A. 82–280, § 19–107, eff. July 1, 1982.

Formerly Ill.Rev.Stat.1991, ch. 110, ¶ 19–107.

5/19–108. Direction of order

§ 19–108. Direction of order. The order shall be directed to the sheriff or other proper officer of the proper county, to serve; and for the purpose only of service as summons shall be directed also to any person authorized to serve summons.

P.A. 82–280, § 19–108, eff. July 1, 1982.

Formerly Ill.Rev.Stat.1991, ch. 110, ¶ 19–108.

5/19–109. Order

§ 19–109. Order. The order for replevin shall require the sheriff, or other officer to whom it is directed to take the property, describing it as in the complaint, from the possession of the defendant, and deliver the same to the plaintiff unless such defendant executes a bond and security as hereinafter provided, and to summon the defendant to answer the complaint or otherwise appear in the action, or in case the property or any part thereof is not found and delivered to the sheriff or other officer, to answer to the plaintiff for the value of the same. The order for replevin may be served as a summons for a trial on the merits of the case by any person authorized to serve summons.

P.A. 82–280, § 19–109, eff. July 1, 1982. Amended by P.A. 83–707, § 1, eff. Sept. 23, 1983.

Formerly Ill.Rev.Stat.1991, ch. 110, ¶ 19–109.

5/19–110. Several counties involved

§ 19–110. Several counties involved. Additional certified copies of the order for replevin may be issued by the clerk of court, upon the request of the plaintiff, to be used in several counties.

P.A. 82–280, § 19–110, eff. July 1, 1982.

Formerly Ill.Rev.Stat.1991, ch. 110, ¶ 19–110.

5/19–111. Additional copies of order

§ 19–111. Additional copies of order. When it appears by the return of the officer that any defendant or the property described in the order or any part thereof, is not found, additional certified copies directing the officer to summon such defendant and to take the property from the possession of the defendant and deliver the same to the plaintiff, may be issued by the clerk of court on the request of the plaintiff until such defendant is served or until such property is taken.

P.A. 82–280, § 19–111, eff. July 1, 1982.

Formerly Ill.Rev.Stat.1991, ch. 110, ¶ 19–111.

5/19–112. Replevin bond

§ 19–112. Replevin bond. Before the service of the order for replevin the plaintiff or someone else on his or her behalf shall give to the sheriff or other officer a bond with sufficient security in double the value of the property about to be replevied, conditioned that he or she will prosecute such action to effect and without delay and make return of the property to the defendant if return of the property shall be awarded or will deliver the same to the intervening petitioner should it be found that the property belongs to him or her, and save and keep harmless such sheriff or other officer as the case may be, in replevying such property and further conditioned for the payment of all costs and damages occasioned by wrongfully obtaining out the order for replevin, and if the sureties on such bond at any time before trial becomes insolvent, an order shall be entered requiring good and sufficient replevin bond to be filed, and if the same is not so filed within the time fixed by the court, the action shall be dismissed.

P.A. 82–280, § 19–112, eff. July 1, 1982.

Formerly Ill.Rev.Stat.1991, ch. 110, ¶ 19–112.

5/19–113. Return

§ 19–113. Return. Such officer shall return the bond so taken by the officer, together with the certified copy of the order to the clerk of court who issued such certified copy of the order.

P.A. 82–280, § 19–113, eff. July 1, 1982.

Formerly Ill.Rev.Stat.1991, ch. 110, ¶ 19–113.

5/19–114. Failure to take and return bond

§ 19–114. Failure to take and return bond. If the sheriff or other officer fails to take and return the bond, as required by Article XIX of this Act, or returns in insufficient bond, he or she shall be liable to the party injured for all damages such party may sustain by reason of such neglect, which may be recovered in an action against the sheriff or other officer, or by an action upon the sheriff's or other officer's official bond.

P.A. 82–280, § 19–114, eff. July 1, 1982. Amended by P.A. 83–707, § 1, eff. Sept. 23, 1983.

Formerly Ill.Rev.Stat.1991, ch. 110, ¶ 19–114.

5/19–115. Limitation

§ 19–115. Limitation. No sheriff or other officer shall be liable, under the preceding section, unless the bond was insufficient when taken, nor unless action is commenced against him or her or upon his or her bond, within 3 years after the cause of action accrues.

P.A. 82–280, § 19–115, eff. July 1, 1982.

Formerly Ill.Rev.Stat.1991, ch. 110, ¶ 19–115.

5/19–116. Service of order

§ 19–116. Service of order. Upon the bond being given the sheriff or other proper officer shall forthwith serve the certified copy of the order by seizing the property therein mentioned and by serving such order upon the defendant as summons is served in other civil cases.

The order for replevin issued as provided in Section 19–108 of this Act, may be served as a summons upon defendants wherever they may be found in the State by any person authorized to serve summons in other civil cases; but property may be taken from the possession of a defendant under a replevin order only in the county in which the order is entered and by a proper officer of the county.

The officer serving such certified order having taken the property or any part thereof shall forthwith deliver such property to the plaintiff unless the defendant executes a bond and security approved by such officer, before such property is actually delivered to the plaintiff. Such bond shall be given in an amount double the value of such property and conditioned that the defendant will appear in and defend the action, and will deliver such property in accordance with the order of the court, in as good condition as it was when the action was commenced, and that the defendant will pay only those costs and damages that may be incurred during the time the property is out of the

possession of the officer and back in his or her possession and adjudged against the defendant in such action.

Such bond shall be returned to the court by the officer serving the order on the day such order is returnable.

P.A. 82–280, § 19–116, eff. July 1, 1982. Amended by P.A. 83–707, § 1, eff. Sept. 23, 1983.

Formerly Ill.Rev.Stat.1991, ch. 110, ¶ 19–116.

5/19–117. Service upon defendant

§ 19–117. Service upon defendant. It shall be the duty of the officer having an order for replevin, to serve the same upon the defendant, whether the property is found or delivered to him or her, or not, unless, when none of the property is found, the officer is otherwise directed by the plaintiff or his or her attorney or agent.

If the defendant fails to deliver up to the sheriff the chattel which is the subject of the order for replevin and the plaintiff has a reasonable belief as to where the chattel is sequestered, the court may authorize the sheriff to use reasonable force to enter into the property to recover same upon such terms and conditions as the court may direct.

P.A. 82–280, § 19–117, eff. July 1, 1982; P.A. 95–661, § 5, eff. Jan. 1, 2008.

Formerly Ill.Rev.Stat.1991, ch. 110, ¶ 19–117.

5/19–118. Notice by publication

§ 19–118. Notice by publication. If it appears by affidavit of the plaintiff, his or her attorney or agent, or by the return of the officer, that any defendant in such action is not a resident of this State, or has departed from this State, or on due inquiry cannot be found, or is concealed within this State, so that process cannot be served on him or her, notice may be given as provided by law in cases of attachment, and with like effect.

P.A. 82–280, § 19–118, eff. July 1, 1982.

Formerly Ill.Rev.Stat.1991, ch. 110, ¶ 19–118.

5/19–119. Answer or otherwise appear

§ 19–119. Answer or otherwise appear. The defendant shall answer or otherwise appear as in other civil cases.

P.A. 82–280, § 19–119, eff. July 1, 1982.

Formerly Ill.Rev.Stat.1991, ch. 110, ¶ 19–119.

5/19–120. When property not found

§ 19–120. When property not found. When the property or any part thereof is not found or delivered as above stated, and the defendant is summoned or enters his or her appearance, the plaintiff may proceed, under the original or amended complaint, as in an action for the wrongful taking and detention of such property or so much thereof as is not found and delivered to the sheriff or other officer, and as to the property not found and delivered, the plaintiff, if he or she recovers, shall be entitled to judgment for the value thereof or his or her interest therein, and such damages as he or she has sustained by reason of the wrongful taking and detention.

P.A. 82–280, § 19–120, eff. July 1, 1982.

Formerly Ill.Rev.Stat.1991, ch. 110, ¶ 19–120.

5/19–121. Distress for rent

§ 19–121. Distress for rent. It shall be sufficient for the defendant, in all cases of replevin for distress taken for rent, to allege generally without particularly setting forth the tenure or title to the lands whereon such distress was taken.

P.A. 82–280, § 19–121, eff. July 1, 1982.

Formerly Ill.Rev.Stat.1991, ch. 110, ¶ 19–121.

5/19–122. Seeking wrong remedy not fatal

§ 19–122. Seeking wrong remedy not fatal. Where relief is sought under Article XIX of this Act and the court determines, on motion directed to the pleadings, or on motion for summary judgment or upon trial, that the plaintiff has pleaded or established facts which entitle the plaintiff to relief but that the plaintiff has sought the wrong remedy, the court shall permit the pleadings to be amended, on just and reasonable terms, and the court shall grant the relief to which the plaintiff is entitled on the amended pleadings or upon the evidence. In considering whether a proposed amendment is just and reasonable, the court shall consider the right of the defendant to assert additional defenses, to demand a trial by jury, to plead a counterclaim or third party complaint, and to order the plaintiff to take additional steps which were not required under the pleadings as previously filed.

P.A. 82–280, § 19–122, eff. July 1, 1982.

Formerly Ill.Rev.Stat.1991, ch. 110, ¶ 19–122.

5/19–123. Judgment against plaintiff

§ 19–123. Judgment against plaintiff. If the plaintiff in an action of replevin obtains an order for replevin and the right of property is adjudged against the plaintiff, judgment shall be entered for a return of the property if such property has been delivered to the plaintiff, and damages for the use thereof from the time it was taken until a return thereof is made, unless the plaintiff shall, in the meantime, have become entitled to the possession of the property, in which event judgment may be entered against the plaintiff for costs and such damage as the defendant has sustained; or if the property was held for the payment of any money, the judgment may be in the alternative that the plaintiff pay the amount for which the same was rightfully held, with proper damages, within a given time, or make return of the property in case such property was delivered to the plaintiff.

P.A. 82–280, § 19–123, eff. July 1, 1982; P.A. 95–661, § 5, eff. Jan. 1, 2008.

Formerly Ill.Rev.Stat.1991, ch. 110, ¶ 19–123.

5/19–124. Intervention

§ 19–124. Intervention. In replevin cases pending in circuit courts, any person other than the defendant claiming the property replevied may intervene, verifying the petition by affidavit. The court shall direct a trial of the right of property as in other cases and in case judgment is rendered for the intervening party and it is further found that such party is entitled to the possession of all or any part of the property, judgment shall be entered accordingly and the property to which the claimant is entitled ordered to be delivered to such claimant together with payment of the claimant's costs. In case judgment is entered for the claimant, although he or she is not then entitled to possession of the property, he or she shall be entitled to his or her costs. In case judgment is entered for the plaintiff, the plaintiff shall be entitled to recover the plaintiff's costs from the claimant. If the claimant is a non-resident of the State, he or she shall file security for costs as required of non-resident plaintiffs.

P.A. 82–280, § 19–124, eff. July 1, 1982.

Formerly Ill.Rev.Stat.1991, ch. 110, ¶ 19–124.

5/19–125. Judgment for plaintiff

§ 19–125. Judgment for plaintiff. If judgment is entered in favor of the plaintiff in replevin, the plaintiff shall recover damages for the detention of the property while the same was wrongfully detained by the defendant.

P.A. 82–280, § 19–125, eff. July 1, 1982.

Formerly Ill.Rev.Stat.1991, ch. 110, ¶ 19–125.

5/19–126. Damages

§ 19–126. Damages. In either case provided for in Sections 19–124 and 19–125 of this Act, if the case is tried by a jury, the damages may be assessed by such jury, but if the plaintiff takes a voluntary dismissal or an involuntary dismissal is ordered by the court or judgment is entered for defendant without a trial, the damages may be assessed by the court or by a jury impaneled for that purpose.

P.A. 82–280, § 19–126, eff. July 1, 1982.

Formerly Ill.Rev.Stat.1991, ch. 110, ¶ 19–126.

5/19–127. Action on bond

§ 19–127. Action on bond. If at any time the conditions of the bond required by Section 19–112 of this Act, or of the bond provided for in Section 19–116 of this Act are broken, the sheriff or other officer or plaintiff in the name of the sheriff, for his or her own use, or the defendant or intervening party, as the case may be, may proceed and maintain an action on such bond for the recovery of all damages and costs, as have been sustained in consequence of the breach of such condition.

P.A. 82–280, § 19–127, eff. July 1, 1982.

Formerly Ill.Rev.Stat.1991, ch. 110, ¶ 19–127.

5/19–128. Defense to action on bond

§ 19–128. Defense to action on bond. If the merits of the case have not been determined in the trial of the action in which the bond was given, the defendant in the action upon the replevin bond may plead that fact and his or her title to the property in dispute, in the action of replevin.

P.A. 82–280, § 19–128, eff. July 1, 1982.

Formerly Ill.Rev.Stat.1991, ch. 110, ¶ 19–128.

5/19–129. Mobile homes

§ 19–129. Mobile homes. If the chattel which is the subject of the replevin action is a mobile home and is occupied by the defendant or other persons, the court may issue a forcible order directing the sheriff to remove the personal property of the defendant or occupants from the mobile home provided that the defendants and unknown occupants are given notice of plaintiff's intent to seek a forcible order and that upon entry of said order for possession, the execution is stayed for a reasonable time as determined by the court so as to allow the defendants and unknown occupants to remove their property from the mobile home.

P.A. 82–280, § 19–129, added by P.A. 95–661, § 5, eff. Jan. 1, 2008.

ARTICLE XIX–a. AMENDATORY PROVISIONS

5/19a–101 to 5/19a–103. Conforming amendments and additions [Omitted]

ARTICLE XIX–b. REPEALER

Section
5/19b–101. Repealer.

5/19b–101. Repealer

(Ch. 1, par. 1305) [1]

"An Act to publish, distribute and sell the laws of the territory of Illinois and all the laws and joint resolutions passed prior to January 1, 1917, at all regular and special sessions of the General Assemblies of the State of Illinois, and provide for this admission into evidence and to repeal an Act therein named", approved June 25, 1917, as amended.

(Ch. 11, pars. 1 through 44)

"An Act in regard to attachments", approved December 23, 1871, as amended.

(Ch. 12, pars. 1 through 47)

"An Act to revise the law in relation to attachments of boats, vessels and rafts", approved March 25, 1874, as amended.

(Ch. 33, pars. 1 through 28)

"An Act to revise the law in relation to costs", approved February 11, 1874, as amended.

(Ch. 45, pars. 1 through 62)

"An Act in regard to the practice in actions of ejectments", approved March 20, 1872, as amended.

(Ch. 47, pars. 1 through 16)

"An Act to provide for the exercise of the right of eminent domain", approved April 10, 1872, as amended.

(Ch. 47, par. 17)

"An Act for the further protection of the state institutions", approved March 9, 1867.

(Ch. 51, par. 1 through 48)

"An Act in regard to evidence and depositions", approved March 29, 1872, as amended.

(Ch. 51, par. 48.01)

"An Act to provide for interpreters for deaf-mutes in legal proceedings", approved August 19, 1963.

(Ch. 51, pars. 48a and 48b)

"An Act in relation to judicial notice", approved June 21, 1929, as amended.

(Ch. 51, pars. 48c through 48f)

"An Act concerning the proof of statutes of other jurisdictions and to make uniform the law with reference thereto", approved July 19, 1939.

(Ch. 51, pars. 48g through 48n)

"An Act for the judicial notice of the laws of other jurisdictions and for proof thereof and to make uniform the law with reference thereto", approved July 19, 1939.

(Ch. 51, par. 48.1)

"An Act relating to communications to clergymen and practitioners of religious denominations", approved August 17, 1961.

(Ch. 51, par. 49)

"An Act in regard to proof of deeds and other instruments in writing when attested by subscribing witnesses", approved June 18, 1883.

(Ch. 51, pars. 50 through 52)

"An Act concerning proof of handwriting and to permit proof of handwriting to be made by comparison", approved June 23, 1915.

(Ch. 51, pars. 53 and 54)

"An Act in relation to the mode of proving title to the lands granted to the Illinois Central Railroad Company", approved March 7, 1872.

(Ch. 51, par. 57)

"An Act in relation to the rights of witnesses at proceedings conducted by a court, commission, administrative agency or other tribunal in this state which are televised or broadcast or at which motion pictures are taken", approved July 13, 1953.

(Ch. 51, par. 58)

"An Act regarding claims in relation to work or service on real property and any product incorporated therein to become part thereof", approved October 14, 1969.

(Ch. 51, par. 61)

"An Act in relation to non-admission of liability by providing, paying for, or offering to provide or pay for, medical, surgical, hospital, or rehabilitation services, facilities, or equipment, and restricting the admission in evidence of testimony, writings, records, reports, or information in respect thereto in any court, commission, administrative agency or other tribunal in this State", approved August 14, 1967.

(Ch. 51, pars. 71 through 73a)

"An Act relating to the inspection of hospital and physician records", approved August 20, 1976, as amended.

(Ch. 51, pars. 101 through 105)

"An Act providing for the confidential character of medical studies conducted by the Illinois Department of Public Health, Illinois State Medical Society, allied medical societies and committees of accredited hospitals, and providing a penalty for the violation thereof", approved September 18, 1977, as amended.

(Ch. 51, pars. 111 through 119)

"An Act concerning disclosure of the sources of information obtained by certain persons in the news media", approved September 23, 1971.

(Ch. 52, pars. 1 through 12)

"An Act to exempt the homestead from forced sale, and to provide for setting off the same, and to exempt certain personal property from attachment and sale on execution, and from distress for rent", approved April 30, 1873, as amended.

(Ch. 52, pars. 13 through 17)

"An Act to exempt certain personal property from attachment and sale on execution, and from distress for rent", approved May 24, 1877, as amended.

(Ch. 52, pars. 19, 20)

"An Act to prevent oppressive garnishment and the transferring of claims for the purpose of depriving debtors of their exemption rights", approved June 17, 1891, as amended.

(Ch. 57, pars. 1 through 22)

"An Act in regard to forcible entry and detainer", approved February 16, 1874, as amended.

(Ch. 62, pars. 33 through 52)

"An Act in regard to Garnishment and to repeal certain acts named therein", approved July 22, 1959, as amended.

(Ch. 62, pars. 71 through 88)

"An Act relating to wage deductions for the benefit of creditors and regulating the issuance of deduction orders", approved June 19, 1961, as amended.

(Ch. 65, pars. 1 through 36.2)

"An Act to revise the law in relation to habeas corpus", approved March 2, 1874, as amended.

(Ch. 69, pars. 1 through 27)

"An Act to revise the law in relation to injunction", approved March 25, 1874, as amended.

(Ch. 72. pars. 1 through 34)

"An Act concerning insolvent debtors", approved April 10, 1872, as amended.

(Ch. 74, par. 3 [2])

Section 3 of "An Act in relation to the rate of interest and other charges in connection with sales on credit and the lending of money", approved May 24, 1879, as amended.

(Ch. 77, pars. 1 through 68a)

"An Act in regard to judgments and the manner of enforcing the same, and to provide for redemption of real estate sold under judgment and for the release of liens on real estate by satisfactions of money judgments by the court", approved March 22, 1872, as amended.

(Ch. 77, pars. 69 and 69a)

"An Act to give effect to the acts of congress regulating the liens of judgments and decrees of courts of the United States", approved April 29, 1889, as amended.

(Ch. 77, pars. 70 through 82)

"An Act providing for the trial of the right of property and claims of exemption", approved April 9, 1875, as amended.

(Ch. 77, pars. 86 through 87)

"An Act in regard to redemption by the State of Illinois of real estate sold at judicial or execution sale", filed July 13, 1933, as amended.

(Ch. 77, pars. 88 through 105)

"An Act in relation to the enforcement of judgments, decrees and orders of courts of the United States and of states and territories thereof, and to make uniform the law relating thereto", approved August 2, 1951.

(Ch. 77, par. 111)

"An Act punishing persons hiding or concealing property levied by legal process or held under a distress warrant", approved May 31, 1879, as amended.

(Ch. 77, pars. 121 through 130)

"An Act in relation to the recognition and enforcement of judgments of foreign states and to make uniform the law relating thereto", approved July 15, 1963.

(Ch. 80, pars. 1 through 34)

"An Act to revise the law in relation to landlord and tenant", approved May 1, 1873, as amended.

(Ch. 80, par. 35)

"An Act in relation to landlord and tenant", approved May 21, 1877.

(Ch. 80, par. 36)

"An Act in relation to landlord and tenant", approved June 11, 1897.

(Ch. 83, pars. 1 through 27)

"An Act in regard to limitations", approved April 4, 1872, as amended.

(Ch. 83, pars. 12.1 through 12.4)

"An Act relating to claims to real estate", approved July 14, 1959, as amended.

(Ch. 87, pars. 1 through 13)

"An Act to revise the law in relation to mandamus", approved February 25, 1874, as amended.

(Ch. 95, par. 22b)

"An Act in relation to evidence, proof and practice in the foreclosure of mortgages hereafter executed", approved July 21, 1947, as amended.

(Ch. 95, pars. 22b51 through 22b63)

"An Act in relation to the rights of mortgagees and other persons empowered to take possession of mortgaged real estate after default and the enforcement of such rights by the court of this State", approved August 7, 1961.

(Ch. 95, pars. 23 to 23.11)

"An Act in relation to mortgages and trust deeds and the foreclosure thereof", approved May 7, 1879, as amended.

(Ch. 97, pars. 1 through 14)

"An Act to revise the law in relation to ne exeat", approved March 12, 1874, as amended.

(Ch. 102, pars. 11 through 16)

"An Act in relation to suits to restrain and enjoin the disbursement of public moneys by officers of the state", approved June 27, 1917, as amended.

(Ch. 106, pars. 44 through 72)

"An Act in relation to the partition of real estate, and to repeal an act herein named", approved August 3, 1949, as amended.

(Ch. 110, pars. 1 through 94)

"The Civil Practice Act", approved June 23, 1933, as amended.

(Ch. 100, par. 100)

"An Act concerning physical and mental examination of claimants in litigated cases", approved October 3, 1969.

(Ch. 110, pars. 263a through 263e [3])

"An Act in relation to actions against non-resident owners or operators of aircraft or watercraft", approved July 16, 1951.

(Ch. 110, pars. 264 through 279)

"The Administrative Review Act", approved May 8, 1945, as amended.

(Ch. 110, pars. 355 through 402)

"An Act to regulate the practice of courts in granting equitable relief", approved March 15, 1872, as amended.

(Ch. 110, pars. 407 and 408)

"An Act concerning the appointment and discharge of receivers", approved May 15, 1903.

(Ch. 110, pars. 501 through 536)

"An Act to revise the law in relation to change of venue", approved March 25, 1874, as amended.

(Ch. 110, par. 601)

"An Act in relation to writs", approved July 31, 1978.

(Ch. 112, pars. 9 through 17 [4])

"An Act in relation to practice and procedure in cases of quo warranto", approved July 2, 1937, as amended.

(Ch. 119, pars. 1 through 28)

"An Act to revise the law in relation to replevin", approved February 9, 1874, as amended.

(Public Act 81–1505 [5])

"An Act in relation to exemptions in bankruptcy proceedings, providing that the federal exemptions in Section 522(d) of the Bankruptcy Code of 1978 (11 U.S.C. 522(d)) are not available to persons residing in this State", approved September 22, 1980.

P.A. 82–280, § 19B–101, eff. July 1, 1982.

Formerly Ill.Rev.Stat.1991, ch. 110, ¶ 19B–101.

[1] References herein are to paragraphs and chapter of Illinois Revised Statutes.

[2] Transferred to Ch. 17, par. 6403 (repealed; see, now, 735 ILCS 5/2–1303).

[3] So in enrolled bill. Probably should read Ch. 110, par. 263a to 263c.

[4] Probably should read "pars. 9 through 18". The repealed chapter, as amended, contained ¶¶ 9 through 18.

[5] Chapter 52, ¶ 101.

ARTICLE XIX–c. EFFECTIVE DATE

Section
5/19c–101. Effective date.

5/19c–101. Effective date

§ 19c–101. (a) This Act takes effect July 1, 1982, and shall apply to all cases and proceedings commenced on or after that date.

(b) For cases and proceedings commenced prior to and still pending on July 1, 1982, this Act shall apply only to those proceedings which take place on or after that date.

P.A. 82–280, § 19c–101, eff. July 1, 1982.

Formerly Ill.Rev.Stat.1991, ch. 110, ¶ 19c–101.

ARTICLE XX. RECOVERY OF FRAUDULENTLY OBTAINED PUBLIC FUNDS

Section
5/20–101. Definitions.
5/20–102. Refunds.
5/20–103. Repayment; civil penalties; lien.
5/20–104. Collection; civil recoveries; citizen actions.
5/20–105. Certain rights not affected.

Date Effective

Article XX was added by P.A. 84–1462, § 2, eff. July 1, 1987.

5/20–101. Definitions

§ 20–101. As used in this Article:

(1) "Compensation, benefits or remuneration" includes regular compensation, overtime compensation, vacation compensation, deferred compensation, sick pay, disability pay, sick leave, disability leave, medical, dental, optical or other health benefits, pension or retirement benefits or any other pay, compensation, benefits, or any other remuneration.

(2) "Person" includes any firm, corporation, association, agency, institution or other legal entity, as well as any natural person.

(3) "Local governmental unit" means any unit of local government or school district.

P.A. 82–280, § 20–101, added by P.A. 84–1462, § 2, eff. July 1, 1987.

Formerly Ill.Rev.Stat.1991, ch. 110, ¶ 20–101.

5/20–102. Refunds

§ 20–102. Any person who has received from the State or from any local governmental unit compensation, benefits or remuneration by means of a false or fraudulent record, statement, or claim or other willful misrepresentation, or by his failure to notify the State or local governmental unit of a change in his status as may be required by the State or local governmental unit, or by other fraudulent device, shall be answerable to the State or local governmental unit, as the case may be, for refunding the entire amount of such compensation, benefits or remuneration received. If the refund is not made, it shall be recoverable in a civil action from the person who received the compensation, benefits or remuneration, or from anyone who knowingly aided such person in obtaining the compensation, benefits or remuneration.

P.A. 82–280, § 20–102, added by P.A. 84–1462, § 2, eff. July 1, 1987.

Formerly Ill.Rev.Stat.1991, ch. 110, ¶ 20–102.

5/20–103. Repayment; civil penalties; lien

§ 20–103. Any person who by means of a false record, statement or representation, or by willful concealment of any material fact, or by other fraudulent scheme or device on behalf of himself, his dependents or others, knowingly obtains from the State or local governmental unit compensation, benefits or remuneration to which he is not entitled, or in a greater amount than that to which he is entitled, shall be liable for full repayment of such compensation, benefits or remuneration received to which the person was not entitled. In addition to any other penalties provided by law, the court shall impose civil penalties consisting of interest on the amount of the compensation, benefits or remuneration received to which the person was not entitled at the maximum legal rate for interest on judgments in effect on the date the payment was made to such person for the period beginning on the date upon which payment was made to the date upon which repayment is made; and may impose either of the following penalties: (1) an amount not to exceed 3 times the amount of such compensation, benefits or remuneration to which the person was not entitled; or (2) an amount not to exceed $2,000 for each instance that the person used any fraudulent scheme or device to obtain compensation, benefits or remuneration to which he is not entitled, whichever penalty the court deems more appropriate. Except as provided by Section 20–105, upon entry of a judgment for repayment of such compensation, benefits or remuneration, or for any civil penalties assessed by the court, a lien shall attach to all property and assets of such person until the judgment is satisfied, subject to the exemptions otherwise applying to the real and personal property of judgement debtors.

P.A. 82–280, § 20–103, added by P.A. 84–1462, § 2, eff. July 1, 1987.

Formerly Ill.Rev.Stat.1991, ch. 110, ¶ 20–103.

5/20–104. Collection; civil recoveries; citizen actions

§ 20–104. (a) Before any action is instituted pursuant to this Act, the State or local governmental unit shall make a good faith attempt to collect amounts owed to it by using informal procedures and methods. Civil recoveries provided for in this Article shall be recoverable only: (1) in actions on behalf of the State, by the Attorney General; (2) in actions on behalf of a municipality with a population over 500,000, by the corporation counsel of such municipality; and (3) in actions on behalf of any other local governmental unit, by counsel designated by the local government unit or, if so requested by the local governmental unit and the state's attorney so agrees, by the state's attorney. However, nothing in clause (3) of this subsection (a) shall affect agreements made pursuant to the State's Attorney Appellate Prosecutor's Act, as amended.[1] If the state's attorney of a county brings an action on behalf of another unit of local government pursuant to this Section, the county shall be reimbursed by the unit of local government in an amount mutually agreed upon before the action is initiated.

(b) Notwithstanding any other provision in this Section, any private citizen residing within the boundaries of the governmental unit affected may bring an action to recover the damages authorized in this Article on behalf of such governmental unit if: (a) the citizen has sent a letter by certified mail, return receipt requested, to the appropriate government official stating his intention to file suit for recovery under this Article and (b) the appropriate governmental official has not, within 60 days of the date of delivery on the citizen's return receipt, either instituted an action for recovery or sent notice to the citizen by certified mail, return receipt requested, that the official has arranged for a settlement with the party alleged to have illegally obtained the compensation or that the official intends to commence suit within 60 days of the date of the notice. A denial by the official of the liability of the party alleged liable by the citizen, failure to have actually arranged for a settlement as stated, or failure to commence a suit within the designated period after having stated the intention in the notice to do so shall also permit the citizen to commence the action.

For purposes of this subsection (b), "appropriate government official" shall mean: (1) the Attorney General, where the government unit alleged damaged is the State; (2) the corporation counsel where the government unit alleged damaged is a municipality with a population of over 500,000; and (3) the chief executive officer of any other local government unit where that unit is alleged damaged.

Any private citizen commencing an action in compliance with this subsection which is reasonable and commenced in good faith shall be entitled to recover court costs and litigation expenses, including reasonable attorney's fees, from any defendant found liable under this Article.

P.A. 82–280, § 20–104, added by P.A. 84–1462, § 2, eff. July 1, 1987.

Formerly Ill.Rev.Stat.1991, ch. 110, ¶ 20–104.

[1] 725 ILCS 210/1 et seq.

Validity

Subsection (b) has been held unconstitutional to the extent it purports to confer standing on private citizens to sue in cases where the State is the real party in interest in the case of Lyons v. Ryan, App. 1 Dist. 2001, 324 Ill.App.3d 1094, 756 N.E.2d 396, 258 Ill.Dec. 414.

5/20–105. Certain rights not affected

§ 20–105. Certain rights not affected. No judgment entered pursuant to this Article shall affect the rights of any bona fide purchaser, mortgagee, judgment creditor or other lien holder arising prior to the date on which a transcript, certified copy or memorandum of such judgment is filed in the office of the recorder of deeds or registrar of titles in the county in which real estate subject to the lien is located.

P.A. 82–280, § 20–105, added by P.A. 84–1462, § 2, eff. July 1, 1987.

Formerly Ill.Rev.Stat.1991, ch. 110, ¶ 20–105.

ARTICLE XXI. CHANGE OF NAME

Date Effective

Article XXI was added by P.A. 87–409, Art. 5, § 5–5, eff. Sept. 10, 1991

5/21–101. Proceedings; parties

§ 21–101. Proceedings; parties. If any person who is a resident of this State and has resided in this State for 6 months desires to change his or her name and to assume another name by which to be afterwards called and known, the person may file a petition in the circuit court of the county wherein he or she resides praying for that relief. If it appears to the court that the conditions hereinafter mentioned have been complied with and that there is no reason why the prayer should not be granted, the court, by an order to be entered of record, may direct and provide that the name of that person be changed in accordance with the prayer in the petition. The filing of a petition in accordance with this Section shall be the sole and exclusive means by which any person committed under the laws of this State to a penal institution may change his or her name and assume another name. However, any person convicted of a felony in this State or any other state who has not been pardoned may not file a petition for a name change until 10 years have passed since completion and discharge from his or her sentence. A person who has been convicted of identity theft, aggravated identity theft, felony or misdemeanor criminal sexual abuse when the victim of the offense at the time of its commission is under 18 years of age, felony or misdemeanor sexual exploitation of a child, felony or misdemeanor indecent solicitation of a child, or felony or misdemeanor indecent solicitation of an adult, or any other offense for which a person is required to register under the Sex Offender Registration Act [1] in this State or any other state who has not been pardoned shall not be permitted to file a petition for a name change in the courts of Illinois. A petitioner may include his or her spouse and adult unmarried children, with their consent, and his or her minor children where it appears to the court that it is for their best interest, in the petition and prayer, and the court's order shall then include the spouse and children. Whenever any minor has resided in the family of any person for the space of 3 years and has been recognized and known as an adopted child in the family of that person, the application herein provided for may be made by the person having that minor in his or her family.

An order shall be entered as to a minor only if the court finds by clear and convincing evidence that the change is necessary to serve the best interest of the child. In determining the best interest of a minor child under this Section, the court shall consider all relevant factors, including:

(1) The wishes of the child's parents and any person acting as a parent who has physical custody of the child.

(2) The wishes of the child and the reasons for those wishes. The court may interview the child in chambers to ascertain the child's wishes with respect to the change of name. Counsel shall be present at the interview unless otherwise agreed upon by the parties. The court shall cause a court reporter to be present who shall make a complete record of the interview instantaneously to be part of the record in the case.

(3) The interaction and interrelationship of the child with his or her parents or persons acting as parents who have physical custody of the child, step-parents, siblings, step-siblings, or any other person who may significantly affect the child's best interest.

(4) The child's adjustment to his or her home, school, and community.

P.A. 82–280, § 21–101, added by P.A. 87–409, Art. 5, § 5–5, eff. Sept. 10, 1991. Amended by P.A. 88–25, § 5, eff. July 6, 1993; P.A. 89–192, § 5, eff. Jan. 1, 1996; P.A. 89–462, Art. 3, § 310, eff. May 29, 1996; P.A. 94–944, § 5, eff. Jan. 1, 2007.

Formerly Ill.Rev.Stat.1991, ch. 110, ¶ 21–101.

[1] 730 ILCS 150/1 et seq.

5/21–102. Petition

§ 21–102. Petition. The petition shall set forth the name then held, the name sought to be assumed, the residence of the petitioner, the length of time the petitioner has resided in this State, and the state or country of the petitioner's nativity or supposed nativity. The petition shall be signed by the person petitioning or, in case of minors, by the parent or guardian having the legal custody of the minor. The petition shall be verified by the affidavit of some credible person.

P.A. 82–280, § 21–102, added by P.A. 87–409, Art. 5, § 5–5, eff. Sept. 10, 1991.

Formerly Ill.Rev.Stat.1991, ch. 110, ¶ 21–102.

5/21–103. Notice by publication

§ 21–103. Notice by publication.

(a) Previous notice shall be given of the intended application by publishing a notice thereof in some newspaper published in the municipality in which the person resides if the municipality is in a county with a population under 2,000,000, or if the person does not reside in a municipality in a county with a population under 2,000,000, or if no newspaper is published in the municipality or if the person resides in a county with a population of 2,000,000 or more, then in some newspaper published in the county where the person resides, or if no newspaper is published in that county, then in some convenient newspaper published in this State. The notice shall be inserted for 3 consecutive weeks after filing, the first insertion to be at least 6 weeks before the return day upon which the petition is to be heard, and shall be signed by the petitioner or, in case of a minor, the minor's parent or guardian, and shall set forth the return day of court on which the petition is to be heard and the name sought to be assumed.

(b) The publication requirement of subsection (a) shall not be required in any application for a change of name involving a minor if, before making judgment under this Article, reasonable notice and opportunity to be heard is given to any parent whose parental rights have not been previously terminated and to any person who has physical custody of the child. If any of these persons are outside this State, notice and opportunity to be heard shall be given under Section 21–104.

(c) The Director of State Police or his or her designee may apply to the circuit court for an order directing that the notice and publication requirements of this Section be waived if the Director or his or her designee certifies that the name change being sought is intended to protect a witness during and following a criminal investigation or proceeding.

P.A. 82–280, § 21–103, added by P.A. 87–409, Art. 5, § 5–5, eff. Sept. 10, 1991. Amended by P.A. 91–62, § 5, eff. Jan. 1, 2000; P.A. 94–147, § 5, eff. Jan. 1, 2006.

Formerly Ill.Rev.Stat.1991, ch. 110, ¶ 21–103.

Validity

Subsection (b), which requires notice by publication of a petition to change a minor's name, is unconstitutional as applied to a noncustodial parent who was not given actual notice of a petition by the custodial parent to change their child's surname. In re Petition of Sanjuan–Moeller, 343 Ill. App. 3d 202, 796 N.E.2d 736, 277 Ill.Dec. 650 (2nd Dist. 2003).

5/21–104. Process and notice to persons outside this State

§ 21–104. Process and notice to persons outside this State.

(a) Process in change of name proceedings shall be governed by this Code.

(b) Notice in all change of name proceedings required for the exercise of jurisdiction over a person outside this State shall be given in a manner best calculated to give actual notice and shall be given in one of the following manners:

(1) By personal delivery outside this State in the manner prescribed for service of process within this State.

(2) In the manner prescribed by the law of the place in which the service is made for service of process in that place in an action in any of its courts of general jurisdiction.

(3) By any form of mail addressed to the person to be served and requesting a receipt.

(4) As directed by the court if other means of notification are ineffective.

(c) Notice under this Section shall be served, mailed, or delivered at least 10 days before any hearing in this State.

(d) Proof of service outside this State may be made by affidavit of the individual who made the service or in the manner prescribed by the law of this State, the order pursuant to which the service is made, or the law of the place in which the service is made. If service is made by mail, proof may be a receipt signed by the addressee or other evidence of delivery to the addressee.

P.A. 82–280, § 21–104, added by P.A. 87–409, Art. 5, § 5–5, eff. Sept. 10, 1991.

Formerly Ill.Rev.Stat.1991, ch. 110, ¶ 21–104.

5/21–105. Invalidity of common law name changes

§ 21–105. Invalidity of common law name changes. Common law name changes adopted in this State on or after July 1, 2010 are invalid. All name changes shall be made pursuant to marriage or other legal proceedings.

P.A. 82–280, § 21–105, added by P.A. 96–1231, § 15, eff. July 23, 2010.

ARTICLE XXII. FRIVOLOUS LAWSUITS FILED BY PRISONERS

Section
5/22–105. Frivolous lawsuits filed by prisoners.

Date Effective

Article XXII was added by P.A. 90–505, § 30, eff. August 19, 1997.

5/22–105. Frivolous lawsuits filed by prisoners

§ 22–105. Frivolous lawsuits filed by prisoners.

(a) If a prisoner confined in an Illinois Department of Corrections facility files a pleading, motion, or other filing which purports to be a legal document in a case seeking post-conviction relief under Article 122 of the Code of Criminal Procedure of 1963,[1] pursuant to Section 116–3 of the Code of Criminal Procedure of 1963,[2] in a habeas corpus action under Article X of this Code,[3] in a claim under the Court of Claims Act,[4] or a second or subsequent petition for relief from judgment under Section 2–1401 of this Code or in another action against the State, the Illinois Department of Corrections, or the Prisoner Review Board, or against any of their officers or employees and the Court makes a specific finding that the pleading, motion, or other filing which purports to be a legal document filed by the prisoner is frivolous, the prisoner is responsible for the full payment of filing fees and actual court costs.

On filing the action or proceeding the court shall assess and, when funds exist, collect as a partial payment of any court costs required by law a first time payment of 50% of the average monthly balance of the prisoner's trust fund account for the past 6 months. Thereafter 50% of all deposits into the prisoner's individual account under Sections 3–4–3 and 3–12–5 of the Unified Code of Corrections[5] administered by the Illinois Department of Corrections shall be withheld until the actual court costs are collected in full. The Department of Corrections shall forward any moneys withheld to the court of jurisdiction. If a prisoner is released before the full costs are collected, the Department of Corrections shall forward the amount of costs collected through the date of release. The court of jurisdiction is responsible for sending the Department of Corrections a copy of the order mandating the amount of court fees to be paid. Nothing in this Section prohibits an applicant from filing an action or proceeding if the applicant is unable to pay the court costs.

(b) In this Section, "frivolous" means that a pleading, motion, or other filing which purports to be a legal document filed by a prisoner in his or her lawsuit meets any or all of the following criteria:

(1) it lacks an arguable basis either in law or in fact;

(2) it is being presented for any improper purpose, such as to harass or to cause unnecessary delay or needless increase in the cost of litigation;

(3) the claims, defenses, and other legal contentions therein are not warranted by existing law or by a nonfrivolous argument for the extension, modification, or reversal of existing law or the establishment of new law;

(4) the allegations and other factual contentions do not have evidentiary support or, if specifically so identified, are not likely to have evidentiary support after a reasonable opportunity for further investigation or discovery; or

(5) the denials of factual contentions are not warranted on the evidence, or if specifically so identified, are not reasonably based on a lack of information or belief.

P.A. 82–280, § 22–105, added by P.A. 90–505, § 30, eff. Aug. 19, 1997. Amended by P.A. 95–424, § 5, eff. Jan. 1, 2008.

[1] 725 ILCS 5/122–1 et seq.
[2] 725 ILCS 5/116–3.
[3] 735 ILCS 5/10–101 et seq.
[4] 705 ILCS 505/1 et seq.
[5] 730 ILCS 5/3–4–3 and 5/3–12–5.

ACT 30. EMINENT DOMAIN ACT

ARTICLE 1. GENERAL PROVISIONS

30/1–1–1. Short title

§ 1–1–1. Short title. This Act may be cited as the Eminent Domain Act.

P.A. 94–1055, Art. 1, § 1–1–1, eff. Jan. 1, 2007.

An Act concerning government, which may be referred to as the Equity in Eminent Domain Act. P.A. 94–1055, approved July 28, 2006, effective January 1, 2007.

30/1–1–5. Definitions

§ 1–1–5. Definitions. As used in this Act, except with respect to the acquisition or damaging of property authorized under the O'Hare Modernization Act:

"Acquisition of property", unless the context otherwise requires, includes the acquisition, damaging, or use of property or any right to or interest in property.

"Blighted area", "blight", and "blighted" have the same meanings as under the applicable statute authorizing the condemning authority to exercise the power of eminent domain or, if those terms have no defined meaning under the applicable statute, then the same meanings as under Section 11–74.4–3 of the Illinois Municipal Code.

"Condemning authority" means the State or any unit of local government, school district, or other entity authorized to exercise the power of eminent domain.

P.A. 94–1055, Art. 1, § 1–1–5, eff. Jan. 1, 2007.

ARTICLE 5. GENERAL EXERCISE

30/5–5–5. Exercise of the power of eminent domain; public use; blight

§ 5–5–5. Exercise of the power of eminent domain; public use; blight.

(a) In addition to all other limitations and requirements, a condemning authority may not take or damage property by the exercise of the power of eminent domain unless it is for a public use, as set forth in this Section.

(a–5) Subsections (b), (c), (d), (e), and (f) of this Section do not apply to the acquisition of property under the O'Hare Modernization Act. A condemning authority may exercise the power of eminent domain for the acquisition or damaging of property under the O'Hare Modernization Act as provided for by law in effect prior to the effective date of this Act.

(a–10) Subsections (b), (c), (d), (e), and (f) of this Section do not apply to the acquisition or damaging of property in furtherance of the goals and objectives of an existing tax increment allocation redevelopment plan. A condemning authority may exercise the power of eminent domain for the acquisition of property in furtherance of an existing tax increment allocation redevelopment plan as provided for by law in effect prior to the effective date of this Act.

As used in this subsection, "existing tax increment allocation redevelopment plan" means a redevelopment plan that was adopted under the Tax Increment Allocation Redevelopment Act (Article 11, Division 74.4 of the Illinois Municipal Code) prior to April 15, 2006 and for which property assembly costs were, before that date, included as a budget line item in the plan or described in the narrative portion of the plan as part of the redevelopment project, but does not include (i) any additional area added to the redevelopment project area on or after April 15, 2006, (ii) any subsequent extension of the completion date of a redevelopment plan beyond the estimated completion date established in that plan prior to April 15, 2006, (iii) any acquisition of property in a conservation area for which the condemnation complaint is filed more than 12 years after the effective date of this Act, or (iv) any acquisition of property in an industrial park conservation area.

As used in this subsection, "conservation area" and "industrial park conservation area" have the same meanings as under Section 11–74.4–3 of the Illinois Municipal Code.

(b) If the exercise of eminent domain authority is to acquire property for public ownership and control, then the condemning authority must prove that (i) the acquisition of the property is necessary for a public purpose and (ii) the acquired property will be owned and controlled by the condemning authority or another governmental entity.

(c) Except when the acquisition is governed by subsection (b) or is primarily for one of the purposes specified in subsection (d), (e), or (f) and the condemning authority elects to proceed under one of those subsections, if the exercise of eminent domain authority is to acquire property for private ownership or control, or both, then the condemning authority must prove by clear and convincing evidence that the acquisition of the property for private ownership or control is (i) primarily for the benefit, use, or enjoyment of the public and (ii) necessary for a public purpose.

An acquisition of property primarily for the purpose of the elimination of blight is rebuttably presumed to be for a public purpose and primarily for the benefit, use, or enjoyment of the public under this subsection.

Any challenge to the existence of blighting factors alleged in a complaint to condemn under this subsection shall be raised within 6 months of the filing date of the complaint to condemn, and if not raised within that time the right to challenge the existence of those blighting factors shall be deemed waived.

Evidence that the Illinois Commerce Commission has granted a certificate or otherwise made a finding of public convenience and necessity for an acquisition of property (or any right or interest in property) for private ownership or control (including, without limitation, an acquisition for which the use of eminent domain is authorized under the Public Utilities Act, the Telephone Company Act, or the Electric Supplier Act) to be used for utility purposes creates a rebuttable presumption that such acquisition of that property (or right or interest in property) is (i) primarily for the benefit, use, or enjoyment of the public and (ii) necessary for a public purpose.

In the case of an acquisition of property (or any right or interest in property) for private ownership or control to be used for utility, pipeline, or railroad purposes for which no certificate or finding of public convenience and necessity by the Illinois Commerce Commission is required, evidence that the acquisition

is one for which the use of eminent domain is authorized under one of the following laws creates a rebuttable presumption that the acquisition of that property (or right or interest in property) is (i) primarily for the benefit, use, or enjoyment of the public and (ii) necessary for a public purpose:

(1) the Public Utilities Act,

(2) the Telephone Company Act,

(3) the Electric Supplier Act,

(4) the Railroad Terminal Authority Act,

(5) the Grand Avenue Railroad Relocation Authority Act,

(6) the West Cook Railroad Relocation and Development Authority Act,

(7) Section 4–505 of the Illinois Highway Code,

(8) Section 17 or 18 of the Railroad Incorporation Act,

(9) Section 18c–7501 of the Illinois Vehicle Code.

(d) If the exercise of eminent domain authority is to acquire property for private ownership or control and if the primary basis for the acquisition is the elimination of blight and the condemning authority elects to proceed under this subsection, then the condemning authority must: (i) prove by a preponderance of the evidence that acquisition of the property for private ownership or control is necessary for a public purpose; (ii) prove by a preponderance of the evidence that the property to be acquired is located in an area that is currently designated as a blighted area or conservation area under an applicable statute; (iii) if the existence of blight or blighting factors is challenged in an appropriate motion filed within 6 months after the date of filing of the complaint to condemn, prove by a preponderance of the evidence that the required blighting factors existed in the area so designated (but not necessarily in the particular property to be acquired) at the time of the designation under item (ii) or at any time thereafter; and (iv) prove by a preponderance of the evidence at least one of the following:

(A) that it has entered into an express written agreement in which a private person or entity agrees to undertake a development project within the blighted area that specifically details the reasons for which the property or rights in that property are necessary for the development project;

(B) that the exercise of eminent domain power and the proposed use of the property by the condemning authority are consistent with a regional plan that has been adopted within the past 5 years in accordance with Section 5–14001 of the Counties Code or Section 11–12–6 of the Illinois Municipal Code or with a local land resource management plan adopted under Section 4 of the Local Land Resource Management Planning Act; or

(C) that (1) the acquired property will be used in the development of a project that is consistent with the land uses set forth in a comprehensive redevelopment plan prepared in accordance with the applicable statute authorizing the condemning authority to exercise the power of eminent domain and is consistent with the goals and purposes of that comprehensive redevelopment plan, and (2) an enforceable written agreement, deed restriction, or similar encumbrance has been or will be executed and recorded against the acquired property to assure that the project and the use of the property remain consistent with those land uses, goals, and purposes for a period of at least 40 years, which execution and recording shall be included as a requirement in any final order entered in the condemnation proceeding.

The existence of an ordinance, resolution, or other official act designating an area as blighted is not prima facie evidence of the existence of blight. A finding by the court in a condemnation proceeding that a property or area has not been proven to be blighted does not apply to any other case or undermine the designation of a blighted area or conservation area or the determination of the existence of blight for any other purpose or under any other statute, including without limitation under the Tax Increment Allocation Redevelopment Act (Article 11, Division 74.4 of the Illinois Municipal Code).

Any challenge to the existence of blighting factors alleged in a complaint to condemn under this subsection shall be raised within 6 months of the filing date of the complaint to condemn, and if not raised within that time the right to challenge the existence of those blighting factors shall be deemed waived.

(e) If the exercise of eminent domain authority is to acquire property for private ownership or control and if the primary purpose of the acquisition is one of the purposes specified in item (iii) of this subsection and the condemning authority elects to proceed under this subsection, then the condemning authority must prove by a preponderance of the evidence that: (i) the acquisition of the property is necessary for a public purpose; (ii) an enforceable written agreement, deed restriction, or similar encumbrance has been or will be executed and recorded against the acquired property to assure that the project and the use of the property remain consistent with the applicable purpose specified in item (iii) of this subsection for a period of at least 40 years, which execution and recording shall be included as a requirement in any final order entered in the condemnation proceeding; and (iii) the acquired property will be one of the following:

(1) included in the project site for a residential project, or a mixed-use project including residential units, where not less than 20% of the residential units in the project are made available, for at least 15 years, by deed restriction, long-term lease, regulatory agreement, extended use agreement, or a comparable recorded encumbrance, to low-income households and very low-income households, as defined in Section 3 of the Illinois Affordable Housing Act;

(2) used primarily for public airport, road, parking, or mass transportation purposes and sold or leased to a private party in a sale-leaseback, lease-leaseback, or similar structured financing;

(3) owned or used by a public utility or electric cooperative for utility purposes;

(4) owned or used by a railroad for passenger or freight transportation purposes;

(5) sold or leased to a private party that operates a water supply, waste water, recycling, waste disposal, waste-to-energy, or similar facility;

(6) sold or leased to a not-for-profit corporation whose purposes include the preservation of open space, the operation of park space, and similar public purposes;

(7) used as a library, museum, or related facility, or as infrastructure related to such a facility;

(8) used by a private party for the operation of a charter school open to the general public; or

(9) a historic resource, as defined in Section 3 of the Illinois State Agency Historic Resources Preservation Act, a landmark designated as such under a local ordinance, or a contributing structure within a local landmark district listed on the National Register of Historic Places, that is being acquired for purposes of preservation or rehabilitation.

(f) If the exercise of eminent domain authority is to acquire property for public ownership and private control and if the primary purpose of the acquisition is one of the purposes specified in item (iii) of this subsection and the condemning authority elects to proceed under this subsection, then the condemning authority must prove by a preponderance of the evidence that: (i) the acquisition of the property is necessary for a public purpose; (ii) the acquired property will be owned by the condemning authority or another governmental entity; and (iii) the acquired property will be controlled by a private party that operates a business or facility related to the condemning authority's operation of a university, medical district, hospital, exposition or convention center, mass transportation facility, or airport, including, but not limited to, a medical clinic, research and development center, food or commercial concession facility, social service facility, maintenance or storage facility, cargo facility, rental car facility, bus facility, taxi facility, flight kitchen, fixed based operation, parking facility, refueling facility, water supply facility, and railroad tracks and stations.

(g) This Article is a limitation on the exercise of the power of eminent domain, but is not an independent grant of authority to exercise the power of eminent domain.

P.A. 94-1055, Art. 5, § 5-5-5, eff. Jan. 1, 2007.

ARTICLE 10. GENERAL PROCEDURE

30/10–5–5. Compensation; jury

§ 10–5–5. Compensation; jury.

(a) Private property shall not be taken or damaged for public use without just compensation and, in all cases in which compensation is not made by the condemning authority, compensation shall be ascertained by a jury, as provided in this Act. When compensation is so made by the condemning authority, any party, upon application, may have a trial by jury to ascertain the just compensation to be paid. A demand on the part of the condemning authority for a trial by jury shall be filed with the complaint for condemnation of the condemning authority. When the condemning authority is plaintiff, a defendant desirous of a trial by jury must file a demand for a trial by jury on or before the return date of the summons served on him or her or on or before the date fixed in the publication in case of defendants served by publication. If no party in the condemnation action demands a trial by jury, as provided for by this Section, then the trial shall be before the court without a jury.

(b) The right to just compensation, as provided in this Act, applies to the owner or owners of any lawfully erected off-premises outdoor advertising sign that is compelled to be altered or removed under this Act or any other statute, or under any ordinance or regulation of any municipality or other unit of local government, and also applies to the owner or owners of the property on which that sign is erected. The right to just compensation, as provided in this Act, applies to property subject to a conservation right under the Real Property Conservation Rights Act. The amount of compensation for the taking of the property shall not be diminished or reduced by virtue of the existence of the conservation right. The holder of the conservation right shall be entitled to just compensation for the value of the conservation right.

P.A. 94–1055, Art. 10, § 10–5–5, eff. Jan. 1, 2007.

30/10–5–10. Parties

§ 10–5–10. Parties.

(a) When the right (i) to take private property for public use, without the owner's consent, (ii) to construct or maintain any public road, railroad, plankroad, turnpike road, canal, or other public work or improvement, or (iii) to damage property not actually taken has been or is conferred by general law or special charter upon any corporate or municipal authority, public body, officer or agent, person, commissioner, or corporation and when (i) the compensation to be paid for or in respect of the property sought to be appropriated or damaged for the purposes mentioned cannot be agreed upon by the parties interested, (ii) the owner of the property is incapable of consenting, (iii) the owner's name or residence is unknown, or (iv) the owner is a nonresident of the State, then the party authorized to take or damage the property so required, or to construct, operate, and maintain any public road, railroad, plankroad, turnpike road, canal, or other public work or improvement, may apply to the circuit court of the county where the property or any part of the property is situated, by filing with the clerk a complaint. The complaint shall set forth, by reference, (i) the complainant's authority in the premises, (ii) the purpose for which the property is sought to be taken or damaged, (iii) a description of the property, and (iv) the names of all persons interested in the property as owners or otherwise, as appearing of record, if known, or if not known stating that fact; and shall pray the court to cause the compensation to be paid to the owner to be assessed.

(b) If it appears that any person not in being, upon coming into being, is, or may become or may claim to be, entitled to any interest in the property sought to be appropriated or damaged, the court shall appoint some competent and disinterested person as guardian ad litem to appear for and represent that interest in the proceeding and to defend the proceeding on behalf of the person not in being. Any judgment entered in the proceeding shall be as effectual for all purposes as though the person was in being and was a party to the proceeding.

(c) If the proceeding seeks to affect the property of persons under guardianship, the guardians shall be made parties defendant.

(d) Any interested persons whose names are unknown may be made parties defendant by the same descriptions and in the same manner as provided in other civil cases.

(e) When the property to be taken or damaged is a common element of property subject to a declaration of condominium ownership, pursuant to the Condominium Property Act, or of a common interest community, the complaint shall name the unit owners' association in lieu of naming the individual unit owners and lienholders on individual units. Unit owners, mortgagees, and other lienholders may intervene as parties defendant. For the purposes of this Section, "common interest community" has the same meaning as set forth in subsection (c) of Section 9–102 of the Code of Civil Procedure. "Unit owners' association" or "association" shall refer to both the definition contained in Section 2 of the Condominium Property Act and subsection (c) of Section 9–102 of the Code of Civil Procedure.

(f) When the property is sought to be taken or damaged by the State for the purposes of establishing, operating, or maintaining any State house or State charitable or other institutions or improvements, the complaint shall be signed by the Governor, or the Governor's designee, or as otherwise provided by law.

(g) No property, except property described in Section 3 of the Sports Stadium Act, property to be acquired in furtherance of actions under Article 11, Divisions 124, 126, 128, 130, 135, 136, and 139, of the Illinois Municipal Code, property to be acquired in furtherance of actions under Section 3.1 of the Intergovernmental Cooperation Act, property to be acquired that is a water system or waterworks pursuant to the home rule powers of a unit of local government, and property described as Site B in Section 2 of the Metropolitan Pier and Exposition Authority Act, and property that may be taken as provided in the Public–Private Agreements for the South Suburban Airport Act belonging to a railroad or other public utility subject to the jurisdiction of the Illinois Commerce Commission may be taken or damaged, pursuant to the provisions of this Act, without the prior approval of the Illinois Commerce Commission.

P.A. 94–1055, Art. 10, § 10–5–10, eff. Jan. 1, 2007. Amended by P.A. 95–331, § 1090, eff. Aug. 21, 2007; P.A. 98–109, § 4–70, eff. July 25, 2013.

30/10–5–15. State agency proceedings; information

§ 10–5–15. State agency proceedings; information.

(a) This Section applies only to the State and its agencies, and only to matters arising after December 31, 1991.

(b) Before any State agency initiates any proceeding under this Act, the agency must designate and provide for an appropriate person to respond to requests arising from the notifications required under this Section. The designated person may be an employee of the agency itself or an employee of any other appropriate State agency. The designated person shall respond to property owners' questions about the authority and procedures of the State agency in acquiring property by condemnation and about the property owner's general rights under those procedures. However, the designated person shall not provide property owners with specific legal advice or specific legal referrals.

(c) At the time of first contact with a property owner, whether in person or by letter, the State agency shall advise the property owner, in writing, of the following:

(1) A description of the property that the agency seeks to acquire.

(2) The name, address, and telephone number of the State official designated under subsection (b) to answer the property owner's questions.

(3) The identity of the State agency attempting to acquire the property.

(4) The general purpose of the proposed acquisition.

(5) The type of facility to be constructed on the property, if any.

(d) At least 60 days before filing a petition with any court to initiate a proceeding under this Act, a State agency shall send a letter by certified mail, return receipt requested, to the owner of the property to be taken, giving the property owner the following information:

(1) The amount of compensation for the taking of the property proposed by the agency and the basis for computing it.

(2) A statement that the agency continues to seek a negotiated agreement with the property owner.

(3) A statement that, in the absence of a negotiated agreement, it is the intention of the agency to initiate a court proceeding under this Act.

The State agency shall maintain a record of the letters sent in compliance with this Section for at least one year.

(e) Any duty imposed on a State agency by this Section may be assumed by the Office of the Attorney General, the Capital Development Board, or any other agency of State government that is assisting or acting on behalf of the State agency in the matter.

P.A. 94–1055, Art. 10, § 10–5–15, eff. Jan. 1, 2007.

30/10–5–20. Construction easement

§ 10–5–20. Construction easement. If a taking is for a construction easement only, any structure that has been removed or taken shall be repaired, reestablished or relocated, at the option of the landowner, when the cost of the action does not exceed the just compensation otherwise payable to the landowner.

P.A. 94–1055, Art. 10, § 10–5–20, eff. Jan. 1, 2007.

30/10–5–25. Service; notice

§ 10–5–25. Service; notice. Service of summons and publication of notice shall be made as in other civil cases.

P.A. 94–1055, Art. 10, § 10–5–25, eff. Jan. 1, 2007.

30/10–5–30. Hearing

§ 10–5–30. Hearing. Except as provided in Sections 20–5–10, 20–5–15, 20–5–20, and 20–5–45 of this Act, no cause shall be heard earlier than 20 days after service upon defendant or upon due publication against non-residents.

Any number of separate parcels of property, situated in the same county, may be included in one complaint, and the compensation for each shall be assessed separately by the same or different juries, as the court may direct.

Amendments to the complaint, or to any paper or record in the cause, may be permitted whenever necessary to a fair trial and final determination of the questions involved.

Should it become necessary at any stage of the proceedings to bring in a new party in the litigation, the court has the power to: (i) make any rule or order in relation thereto as may be deemed reasonable and proper; (ii) make all necessary rules and orders for notice to parties of the pendency of the proceedings; and (iii) issue all process necessary to the enforcement of orders and judgments.

P.A. 94–1055, Art. 10, § 10–5–30, eff. Jan. 1, 2007.

30/10–5–35. Challenge of jurors

§ 10–5–35. Challenge of jurors. The plaintiff, and every party interested in the ascertaining of compensation, shall have the same right of challenge of jurors as in other civil cases in the circuit courts.

P.A. 94–1055, Art. 10, § 10–5–35, eff. Jan. 1, 2007.

30/10–5–40. Oath of jury

§ 10–5–40. Oath of jury. When the jury is selected, the court shall cause the following oath to be administered to the jury:

You and each of you do solemnly swear that you will well and truly ascertain and report just compensation to the owner (and each owner) of the property which it is sought to take or damage in this case, and to each person therein interested, according to the facts in the case, as the same may appear by the evidence, and that you will truly report such compensation so ascertained: so help you God.

P.A. 94–1055, Art. 10, § 10–5–40, eff. Jan. 1, 2007.

30/10–5–45. View of premises; jury's report

§ 10–5–45. View of premises; jury's report. The jury shall, at the request of either party, go upon the land sought to be taken or damaged, in person, and examine the same. After hearing the proof offered, the jury shall make its report in writing. The report shall be subject to amendment by the jury, under the direction of the court, so as to clearly set forth and show the compensation ascertained to each person thereto entitled, and the verdict shall thereupon be recorded. However, no benefits or advantages which may accrue to lands or property affected shall be set off against or deducted from such compensation, in any case.

P.A. 94–1055, Art. 10, § 10–5–45, eff. Jan. 1, 2007.

30/10–5–50. Admissibility of evidence

§ 10–5–50. Admissibility of evidence. Evidence is admissible as to: (1) any benefit to the landowner that will result from the public improvement for which the eminent domain proceedings were instituted; (2) any unsafe, unsanitary, substandard, or other illegal condition, use, or occupancy of the property, including any violation of any environmental law or regulation; (3) the effect of such condition on income from or the fair market value of the property; and (4) the reasonable cost of causing the property to be placed in a legal condition, use, or occupancy, including compliance with environmental laws and regulations. Such evidence is admissible notwithstanding the absence of any official action taken to require the correction or abatement of the illegal condition, use, or occupancy.

P.A. 94–1055, Art. 10, § 10–5–50, eff. Jan. 1, 2007.

30/10–5–55. Special benefits

§ 10–5–55. Special benefits. In assessing damages or compensation for any taking or property acquisition under this Act, due consideration shall be given to any special benefit that will result to the property owner from any public improvement to be erected on the property. This Section is applicable to all private property taken or acquired for public use and applies whether damages or compensation are fixed by negotiation, by a court, or by a jury.

P.A. 94–1055, Art. 10, § 10–5–55, eff. Jan. 1, 2007.

30/10–5–60. Value

§ 10–5–60. Value. Except as to property designated as possessing a special use, the fair cash market value of property in a proceeding in eminent domain shall be the amount of money that a purchaser, willing, but not obligated, to buy the property, would pay to an owner willing, but not obliged, to sell in a voluntary sale.

For the acquisition or damaging of property under the O'Hare Modernization Act, the amount shall be determined as of the date of filing the complaint to condemn. For the acquisition of other property, the amount shall be determined and ascertained as of the date of filing the complaint to condemn, except that:

(i) in the case of property not being acquired under Article 20 (quick-take), if the trial commences more than 2 years after the date of filing the complaint to condemn, the court may, in the interest of justice and equity, declare a valuation date no sooner than the date of filing the complaint to condemn and no later than the date of commencement of the trial; and

(ii) in the case of property that is being acquired under Article 20 (quick-take), if the trial commences more than 2 years after the date of filing the complaint to condemn, the court may, in the interest of justice and equity, declare a valuation date no sooner than the date of filing the complaint to condemn and no later than the date on which the condemning authority took title to the property.

In the condemnation of property for a public improvement, there shall be excluded from the fair cash market value of the property any appreciation in value proximately caused by the improvement and any depreciation in value proximately caused by the improvement. However, such appreciation or depreciation shall not be excluded when property is condemned for a separate project conceived independently of and subsequent to the original project.

P.A. 94-1055, Art. 10, § 10-5-60, eff. Jan. 1, 2007.

30/10-5-62.　Relocation costs

§ 10-5-62.　Relocation costs.　Except when federal funds are available for the payment of direct financial assistance to persons displaced by the acquisition of their real property, in all condemnation proceedings for the taking or damaging of real property under the exercise of the power of eminent domain, the condemning authority shall pay to displaced persons reimbursement for their reasonable relocation costs, determined in the same manner as under the federal Uniform Relocation Assistance and Real Property Acquisition Policies Act of 1970, as amended from time to time, and as implemented by regulations promulgated under that Act.　This Section does not apply to the acquisition or damaging of property under the O'Hare Modernization Act.

P.A. 94-1055, Art. 10, § 10-5-62, eff. Jan. 1, 2007.

30/10-5-65.　Reimbursement; inverse condemnation

§ 10-5-65.　Reimbursement; inverse condemnation.　When the condemning authority is required by a court to initiate condemnation proceedings for the actual physical taking of real property, the court rendering judgment for the property owner and awarding just compensation for the taking shall determine and award or allow to the property owner, as part of that judgment or award, further sums as will, in the opinion of the court, reimburse the property owner for the owner's reasonable costs, disbursements, and expenses, including reasonable attorney, appraisal, and engineering fees actually incurred by the property owner in those proceedings.

P.A. 94-1055, Art. 10, § 10-5-65, eff. Jan. 1, 2007.

30/10-5-70.　Judgments

§ 10-5-70.　Judgments.

(a) If the plaintiff is not in possession pursuant to an order entered under the provisions of Section 20-5-15 of this Act, the court, upon the report of the jury under Section 10-5-45 or upon the court's ascertainment and finding of the just compensation when there was no jury, shall proceed to adjudge and make such order as to right and justice shall pertain, ordering that the plaintiff shall enter upon the property and the use of the property upon payment of full compensation as ascertained, within a reasonable time to be fixed by the court.　That order, together with evidence of payment, shall constitute complete justification of the taking of the property.　Thereupon, the court in the same eminent domain proceeding in which the orders have been made shall have exclusive authority to hear and determine all rights in and to just compensation and shall make findings as to the rights of the parties, which shall be paid by the county treasurer out of the respective awards deposited with him or her, as provided in Section 10-5-85 of this Act, except when the parties claimant are engaged in litigation in a court having acquired jurisdiction of the parties with respect to their rights in the property condemned prior to the time of the filing of the complaint to condemn.　Appeals may be taken from any findings by the court as to the rights of the parties in and to the compensation paid to the county treasurer as in other civil cases.

If the plaintiff dismisses the complaint before the entry of the order by the court first mentioned in this subsection (a) or fails to make payment of full compensation within the time named in that order or if the final judgment is that the plaintiff cannot acquire the property by condemnation, the court shall, upon the application of the defendants or any of them, enter an order in the action for the payment by the plaintiff of all costs, expenses, and reasonable attorney fees paid or incurred by the defendant or defendants in defense of the complaint, as upon the hearing of the application shall be right and just, and also for the payment of the taxable costs.

(b) If the plaintiff is in possession pursuant to an order entered under the provisions of Section 20-5-15 of this Act and if Section 20-5-45 of this Act is inapplicable, then the court, upon the jury's report under Section 10-5-45 of this Act or upon the court's determination of just compensation if there was no jury, shall enter an order setting forth the amount of just compensation so finally ascertained and ordering and directing the payment of any amount of just compensation that may remain due to any of the interested parties, directing the return of any excess in the deposit remaining with the clerk of the court, and directing the refund of any excess amount withdrawn from the deposit by any of the interested parties.

P.A. 94-1055, Art. 10, § 10-5-70, eff. Jan. 1, 2007.

30/10-5-75. Intervening petition

§ 10-5-75. Intervening petition. Any person not made a party may become a party by filing an intervening petition setting forth that the petitioner is the owner or has an interest in property that will be taken or damaged by the proposed work. The rights of the petitioner shall thereupon be fully considered and determined.

P.A. 94-1055, Art. 10, § 10-5-75, eff. Jan. 1, 2007.

30/10-5-80. Bond; use of premises

§ 10-5-80. Bond; use of premises. When compensation is ascertained, as provided in this Act, if the party in whose favor the compensation is ascertained appeals the order or judgment ascertaining just compensation, the plaintiff shall, notwithstanding, have the right to enter upon the use of the property upon entering into bond, with sufficient surety, payable to the party interested in the compensation, conditioned for the payment of compensation in the amount finally adjudged in the case and, in case of appeal by the plaintiff, the plaintiff shall enter into like bond with approved surety. The bonds shall be approved by the court in which the proceeding is had and executed and filed within the time fixed by the court. However, if the plaintiff is the State of Illinois, no bond shall be required.

P.A. 94-1055, Art. 10, § 10-5-80, eff. Jan. 1, 2007.

30/10-5-85. Payment to county treasurer

§ 10-5-85. Payment to county treasurer. Payment of the final compensation adjudged, including any balance remaining due because of the insufficiency of any deposit made under Section 20-5-15 of this Act to satisfy in full the amount finally adjudged to be just compensation, may be made in all cases to the county treasurer, who shall receive and disburse the final compensation, subject to an order of the court, as provided in subsection (a) of Section 10-5-70 of this Act or payment may be made to the party entitled or his, her, or their guardian.

P.A. 94-1055, Art. 10, § 10-5-85, eff. Jan. 1, 2007.

30/10-5-90. Distribution of compensation

§ 10-5-90. Distribution of compensation. The amount of just compensation shall be distributed among all persons having an interest in the property according to the fair value of their legal or equitable interests. If there is a contract for deed to the property, the contract shall be abrogated and the amount of just compensation distributed by allowing to the purchaser on the contract for deed: (1) an amount equal to the down payment on the contract; (2) an amount equal to the monthly payments made on the contract, less interest and an amount equal to the fair rental value of the property for the period the purchaser has enjoyed the use of the property under the contract; and (3) an amount equal to amounts expended on improvements to the extent the expenditures increased the fair market value of the property; and by allowing to the seller on the contract for deed the amount of just compensation after allowing for amounts distributed under (1), (2), and (3) of this Section. However, the contract purchaser may pay to the contract seller the amount to be paid on the contract and shall then be entitled to the amount of just compensation paid by the condemnor either through negotiation or awarded in judicial proceedings.

P.A. 94-1055, Art. 10, § 10-5-90, eff. Jan. 1, 2007.

30/10-5-95. Verdict and judgment to be filed of record

§ 10-5-95. Verdict and judgment to be filed of record. The court shall cause the verdict of the jury and the judgment of the court to be filed of record.

P.A. 94-1055, Art. 10, § 10-5-95, eff. Jan. 1, 2007.

30/10-5-100. Lands of State institutions not taken

§ 10-5-100. Lands of State institutions not taken. No part of any land conveyed before, on, or after the effective date of this Act to the State of Illinois, for the use of any benevolent institutions of the State (or to any such institutions), shall be entered upon, appropriated, or used by any railroad or other company for railroad or other purposes, without the previous consent of the General Assembly. No court or other tribunal shall have or entertain jurisdiction of any proceeding instituted or to be instituted for the purpose of appropriating any such land for any of the purposes stated in this Section, without that previous consent.

P.A. 94-1055, Art. 10, § 10-5-100, eff. Jan. 1, 2007.

30/10-5-105. Sale of certain property acquired by condemnation

§ 10-5-105. Sale of certain property acquired by condemnation.

(a) This Section applies only to property that (i) has been acquired after the effective date of this Act by condemnation or threat of condemnation, (ii) was acquired for public ownership and control by the condemning authority or another public entity, and (iii) has been under the ownership and control of the condemning authority or that other public entity for a total of less than 5 years.

As used in this Section, "threat of condemnation" means that the condemning authority has made an offer to purchase property and has the authority to exercise the power of eminent domain with respect to that property.

(b) Any governmental entity seeking to dispose of property to which this Section applies must dispose of that property in accordance with this Section, unless disposition of that property is otherwise specifically authorized or prohibited by law enacted by the General Assembly before, on, or after the effective date of this Act.

(c) The sale or public auction by the State of property to which this Section applies must be conducted in the manner provided in the State Property Control Act for the disposition of surplus property.

(d) The sale or public auction by a municipality of property to which this Section applies must be conducted in accordance with Section 11–76–4.1 or 11–76–4.2 of the Illinois Municipal Code.

(e) The sale or public auction by any other unit of local government or school district of property to which this Section applies must be conducted in accordance with this subsection (e). The corporate authorities of the [1] unit of local government or school district, by resolution, may authorize the sale or public auction of the property as surplus public real estate. The value of the real estate shall be determined by a written MAI-certified appraisal or by a written certified appraisal of a State-certified or State-licensed real estate appraiser. The appraisal shall be available for public inspection. The resolution may direct the sale to be conducted by the staff of the unit of local government or school district; by listing with local licensed real estate agencies, in which case the terms of the agent's compensation shall be included in the resolution; or by public auction. The resolution shall be published at the first opportunity following its passage in a newspaper or newspapers published in the county or counties in which the unit of local government or school district is located. The resolution shall also contain pertinent information concerning the size, use, and zoning of the real estate and the terms of sale. The corporate authorities of the unit of local government or school district may accept any contract proposal determined by them to be in the best interest of the unit of local government or school district by a vote of two-thirds of the members of the corporate authority of the unit of local government or school district then holding office, but in no event at a price less than 80% of the appraised value.

(f) This Section does not apply to the acquisition or damaging of property under the O'Hare Modernization Act.

P.A. 94–1055, Art. 10, § 10–5–105, eff. Jan. 1, 2007. Amended by P.A. 95–331, § 1090, eff. Aug. 21, 2007.

[1] So in enrolled law.

30/10–5–110. Offers of settlement by defendant; attorney's fees and litigation expenses

§ 10–5–110. Offers of settlement by defendant; attorney's fees and litigation expenses.

(a) This Section applies only to proceedings for the acquisition of property for private ownership or control that are subject to subsection (c), (d), (e), or (f) of Section 5–5–5.

(b) At any time between (i) the close of discovery in accordance with Supreme Court Rule 218(c), as now or hereafter amended, or another date set by the court or agreed to by the parties, and (ii) 14 days before the commencement of trial to determine final just compensation, any defendant may serve upon the plaintiff a written offer setting forth the amount of compensation that the defendant will accept for the taking of that defendant's interest in the property. If the defendant does not make such an offer, the defendant shall not be entitled to the attorney's fees and other reimbursement provided under subsection (e) of this Section.

(c) If, within 10 days after service of the offer, the plaintiff serves written notice upon that defendant that the offer is accepted, then either of those parties may file a copy of the offer and a copy of the notice of acceptance together with proof of service of the notice. The court shall then enter judgment.

(d) An offer that is not accepted within the 10-day period is deemed to be withdrawn and evidence of the offer is not admissible at trial.

(e) If a plaintiff does not accept an offer as provided in subsection (c) and if the final just compensation for the defendant's interest is determined by the trier of fact to be equal to or in excess of the amount of the defendant's last written offer under subsection (b), then the court must order the plaintiff to pay to the defendant that defendant's attorney's fees as calculated under subsection (f) of this Section. The plaintiff shall also pay to the defendant that defendant's reasonable costs and litigation expenses, including, without limitation, expert witness and appraisal fees, incurred after the making of the defendant's last written offer under subsection (b).

(f) Any award of attorney's fees under this Section shall be based solely on the net benefit achieved for the property owner, except that the court may also consider any non-monetary benefits obtained for the property owner through the efforts of the attorney to the extent that the non-monetary benefits are specifically identified by the court and can be quantified by the court with a reasonable degree of certainty. "Net benefit" means the difference, exclusive of interest, between the final judgment or settlement and the last written offer made by the condemning authority before the filing date of the condemnation complaint. The award shall be calculated as follows, subject to the Illinois Rules of Professional Conduct:

(1) 33% of the net benefit if the net benefit is $250,000 or less;

(2) 25% of the net benefit if the net benefit is more than $250,000 but less than $1 million; or

(3) 20% of the net benefit if the net benefit is $1 million or more.

(g) This Section does not apply to the acquisition of property under the O'Hare Modernization Act.

P.A. 94–1055, Art. 10, § 10–5–110, eff. Jan. 1, 2007.

30/10–5–115. Eligible costs

§ 10–5–115. Eligible costs. Any cost required to be paid by a condemning authority under this Act, including, but not limited to, relocation costs and attorney's fees, shall be deemed a redevelopment project cost or eligible cost under the statute pursuant to which the condemning authority exercised its power of eminent domain, even if those costs are not identified as such as of the effective date of this Act.

P.A. 94–1055, Art. 10, § 10–5–115, eff. Jan. 1, 2007.

ARTICLE 15. EXPRESS EMINENT DOMAIN POWER

Part
1. General Provisions.
5. List of Eminent Domain Powers.

PART 1. GENERAL PROVISIONS

Section
30/15–1–5. Grants of power in other statutes; this Act controls.

30/15–1–5. Grants of power in other statutes; this Act controls

§ 15–1–5. Grants of power in other statutes; this Act controls. The State of Illinois and its various subdivisions and agencies, and all units of local government, school districts, and other entities, have the powers of condemnation and eminent domain that are (i) expressly provided in this Act or (ii) expressly provided in any other provision of law. Those powers may be exercised, however, only in accordance with this Act. If any power of condemnation or eminent domain that arises under any other provision of law is in conflict with this Act, this Act controls. This Section does not apply to the acquisition or damaging of property under the O'Hare Modernization Act.

P.A. 94–1055, Art. 15, § 15–1–5, eff. Jan. 1, 2007.

PART 5. LIST OF EMINENT DOMAIN POWERS

30/15–5–1. Form and content of list

§ 15–5–1. Form and content of list. The Sections of this Part 5 are intended to constitute a list of the Sections of the Illinois Compiled Statutes that include express grants of the power to acquire property by condemnation or eminent domain.

The list is intended to be comprehensive, but there may be accidental omissions and inclusions. Inclusion in the list does not create a grant of power, and it does not continue or revive a grant of power that has been amended or repealed or is no longer applicable. Omission from the list of a statute that includes an express grant of the power to acquire property by condemnation or eminent domain does not invalidate that grant of power.

The list does not include the grants of quick-take power that are set forth in Article 25 of this Act, nor any other grants of power that are expressly granted under the other provisions of this Act.

Items in the list are presented in the following form: ILCS citation; short title of the Act; condemning authority; brief statement of purpose for which the power is granted.

P.A. 94–1055, Art. 15, § 15–5–1, eff. Jan. 1, 2007.

30/15–5–5. Eminent domain powers in ILCS Chapters 5 through 40

§ 15–5–5. Eminent domain powers in ILCS Chapters 5 through 40. The following provisions of law may include express grants of the power to acquire property by condemnation or eminent domain:

(5 ILCS 220/3.1); Intergovernmental Cooperation Act; cooperating entities; for Municipal Joint Action Water Agency purposes.

(5 ILCS 220/3.2); Intergovernmental Cooperation Act; cooperating entities; for Municipal Joint Action Agency purposes.

(5 ILCS 585/1); National Forest Land Act; United States of America; for national forests.

(15 ILCS 330/2); Secretary of State Buildings in Cook County Act; Secretary of State; for office facilities in Cook County.

(20 ILCS 5/5–675); Civil Administrative Code of Illinois; the Secretary of Transportation, the Director of Natural Resources, and the Director of Central Management Services; for lands, buildings, and grounds for which an appropriation is made by the General Assembly.

(20 ILCS 620/9); Economic Development Area Tax Increment Allocation Act; municipalities; to

achieve the objectives of the economic development project.

(20 ILCS 685/1); Particle Accelerator Land Acquisition Act; Department of Commerce and Economic Opportunity; for a federal high energy BEV Particle Accelerator.

(20 ILCS 835/2); State Parks Act; Department of Natural Resources; for State parks.

(20 ILCS 1110/3); Illinois Coal and Energy Development Bond Act; Department of Commerce and Economic Opportunity; for coal projects.

(20 ILCS 1920/2.06); Abandoned Mined Lands and Water Reclamation Act; Department of Natural Resources; for reclamation purposes.

(20 ILCS 1920/2.08); Abandoned Mined Lands and Water Reclamation Act; Department of Natural Resources; for reclamation purposes and for the construction or rehabilitation of housing.

(20 ILCS 1920/2.11); Abandoned Mined Lands and Water Reclamation Act; Department of Natural Resources; for eliminating hazards.

(20 ILCS 3105/9.08a); Capital Development Board Act; Capital Development Board; for lands, buildings and grounds for which an appropriation is made by the General Assembly.

(20 ILCS 3110/5); Building Authority Act; Capital Development Board; for purposes declared by the General Assembly to be in the public interest.

(40 ILCS 5/15–167); Illinois Pension Code; State Universities Retirement System; for real estate acquired for the use of the System.

P.A. 94–1055, Art. 15, § 15–5–5, eff. Jan. 1, 2007.

30/15–5–10. Eminent domain powers in ILCS Chapter 45 through 65

§ 15–5–10. Eminent domain powers in ILCS Chapters 45 through 65. The following provisions of law may include express grants of the power to acquire property by condemnation or eminent domain:

(45 ILCS 30/3); Quad Cities Interstate Metropolitan Authority Compact Act; Quad Cities Interstate Metropolitan Authority; for the purposes of the Authority.

(45 ILCS 35/40); Quad Cities Interstate Metropolitan Authority Act; Quad Cities Interstate Metropolitan Authority; for metropolitan facilities.

(45 ILCS 110/1); Bi-State Development Powers Act; Bi-State Development Agency; for the purposes of the Bi-State Development Agency.

(50 ILCS 20/14); Public Building Commission Act; public building commissions; for general purposes.

(50 ILCS 30/6.4); Exhibition Council Act; exhibition councils; for council purposes.

(50 ILCS 605/4); Local Government Property Transfer Act; State of Illinois; for the removal of any restriction on land transferred to the State by a municipality.

(55 ILCS 5/5–1095); Counties Code; counties; for easements for community antenna television systems.

(55 ILCS 5/5–1119); Counties Code; any county that is bordered by the Mississippi River and that has a population in excess of 62,000 but less than 80,000; for the operation of ferries.

(55 ILCS 5/5–11001); Counties Code; counties; for motor vehicle parking lots or garages.

(55 ILCS 5/5–15007); Counties Code; counties; for water supply, drainage, and flood control, including bridges, roads, and waste management.

(55 ILCS 5/5–15009); Counties Code; counties; for water supply, drainage, and flood control.

(55 ILCS 5/5–30021); Counties Code; county preservation commissions; for historic preservation purposes.

(55 ILCS 85/9); County Economic Development Project Area Property Tax Allocation Act; counties; for the objectives of the economic development plan.

(55 ILCS 90/60); County Economic Development Project Area Tax Increment Allocation Act of 1991; counties; for the objectives of the economic development project.

(60 ILCS 1/115–20, 1/115–30, 1/115–35, 1/115–40, 1/115–55, and 1/115–120); Township Code; townships with a population over 250,000; for an open space program.

(60 ILCS 1/120–10); Township Code; townships; for park purposes.

(60 ILCS 1/130–5); Township Code; townships; for cemeteries.

(60 ILCS 1/130–30); Township Code; any 2 or more cities, villages, or townships; for joint cemetery purposes.

(60 ILCS 1/135–5); Township Code; any 2 or more townships or road districts; for joint cemetery purposes.

(60 ILCS 1/205–40); Township Code; townships; for waterworks and sewerage systems.

(65 ILCS 5/Art. 9, Div. 2); Illinois Municipal Code; municipalities; for local improvements.

(65 ILCS 5/11–11–1); Illinois Municipal Code; municipalities; for the rehabilitation or redevelopment of blighted areas and urban community conservation areas.

(65 ILCS 5/11–12–8); Illinois Municipal Code; municipalities; for acquiring land for public purposes as designated on proposed subdivision plats.

(65 ILCS 5/11–13–17); Illinois Municipal Code; municipalities; for nonconforming structures under a zoning ordinance and for areas blighted by substandard buildings.

(65 ILCS 5/11–19–10); Illinois Municipal Code; municipalities; for waste disposal purposes.

(65 ILCS 5/11–28–1); Illinois Municipal Code; municipalities; for municipal hospital purposes.

(65 ILCS 5/11–29.3–1); Illinois Municipal Code; municipalities; for senior citizen housing.

(65 ILCS 5/11–42–11); Illinois Municipal Code; municipalities; for easements for community antenna television systems.

(65 ILCS 5/11–45.1–2); Illinois Municipal Code; municipalities; for establishing cultural centers.

(65 ILCS 5/11–48.2–2); Illinois Municipal Code; municipalities; for historical preservation purposes.

(65 ILCS 5/11–52.1–1); Illinois Municipal Code; municipalities; for cemeteries.

(65 ILCS 5/11–52.1–3); Illinois Municipal Code; any 2 or more cities, villages, or townships; for joint cemetery purposes.

(65 ILCS 5/11–61–1); Illinois Municipal Code; municipalities; for municipal purposes or public welfare.

(65 ILCS 5/11–61–1a); Illinois Municipal Code; municipality with a population over 500,000; quick-take power for rapid transit lines (obsolete).

(65 ILCS 5/11–63–5); Illinois Municipal Code; municipalities; for community buildings.

(65 ILCS 5/11–65–3); Illinois Municipal Code; municipalities; for municipal convention hall purposes.

(65 ILCS 5/11–66–10); Illinois Municipal Code; municipalities; for a municipal coliseum.

(65 ILCS 5/11–68–4); Illinois Municipal Code; board of stadium and athletic field commissioners; for a stadium and athletic field.

(65 ILCS 5/11–69–1); Illinois Municipal Code; any 2 or more municipalities with the same or partly the same territory; for their joint municipal purposes.

(65 ILCS 5/11–71–1); Illinois Municipal Code; municipalities; for parking facilities.

(65 ILCS 5/11–71–10); Illinois Municipal Code; municipalities; for the removal of a lessee's interest in the leased space over a municipally-owned parking lot.

(65 ILCS 5/11–74.2–8); Illinois Municipal Code; municipalities; for carrying out a final commercial redevelopment plan.

(65 ILCS 5/11–74.2–9); Illinois Municipal Code; municipalities; for commercial renewal and redevelopment areas.

(65 ILCS 5/11–74.3–3); Illinois Municipal Code; municipalities; for business district development or redevelopment.

(65 ILCS 5/11–74.4–4); Illinois Municipal Code; municipalities; for redevelopment project areas.

(65 ILCS 5/11–74.6–15); Illinois Municipal Code; municipalities; for projects under the Industrial Jobs Recovery Law.

(65 ILCS 5/11–75–5); Illinois Municipal Code; municipalities; for the removal of a lessee's interest in a building erected on space leased by the municipality.

(65 ILCS 5/11–80–21); Illinois Municipal Code; municipalities; for construction of roads or sewers on or under the track, right-of-way, or land of a railroad company.

(65 ILCS 5/11–87–3); Illinois Municipal Code; municipalities; for non-navigable streams.

(65 ILCS 5/11–87–5); Illinois Municipal Code; municipalities; for improvements along re-channeled streams.

(65 ILCS 5/11–92–3); Illinois Municipal Code; municipalities; for harbors for recreational use.

(65 ILCS 5/11–93–1); Illinois Municipal Code; municipalities; for bathing beaches and recreation piers.

(65 ILCS 5/11–94–1); Illinois Municipal Code; municipalities with a population of less than 500,000; for recreational facilities.

(65 ILCS 5/11–97–2); Illinois Municipal Code; municipalities; for driveways to parks owned by the municipality outside its corporate limits.

(65 ILCS 5/11–101–1); Illinois Municipal Code; municipalities; for public airport purposes.

(65 ILCS 5/11–102–4); Illinois Municipal Code; municipalities with a population over 500,000; for public airport purposes.

(65 ILCS 5/11–103–2); Illinois Municipal Code; municipalities with a population under 500,000; for public airport purposes.

(65 ILCS 5/11–110–3); Illinois Municipal Code; municipalities; for drainage purposes.

(65 ILCS 5/11–112–6); Illinois Municipal Code; municipalities; for levees, protective embankments, and structures.

(65 ILCS 5/11–117–1, 5/11–117–4, 5/11–117–7, and 5/11–117–11); Illinois Municipal Code; municipalities; for public utility purposes.

(65 ILCS 5/11–119.1–5, 5/11–119.1–7, and 5/11–119.1–10); Illinois Municipal Code; municipal power agencies; for joint municipal electric power agency purposes.

(65 ILCS 5/11–119.2–5 and 5/11–119.2–7); Illinois Municipal Code; municipal natural gas agencies; for joint municipal natural gas agency purposes.

(65 ILCS 5/11–121–2); Illinois Municipal Code; municipalities; for constructing and operating subways.

(65 ILCS 5/11–122–3); Illinois Municipal Code; municipalities; for street railway purposes.

(65 ILCS 5/1–123–4 and 5/11–123–24); Illinois Municipal Code; municipalities; for harbor facilities.

(65 ILCS 5/11–125–2); Illinois Municipal Code; municipalities; for waterworks purposes.

(65 ILCS 5/11–126–3); Illinois Municipal Code; municipalities; for water supply purposes, including joint construction of waterworks.

(65 ILCS 5/11–130–9); Illinois Municipal Code; municipalities; for waterworks purposes.

(65 ILCS 5/11–135–6); Illinois Municipal Code; municipal water commission; for waterworks purposes, including quick-take power.

(65 ILCS 5/11–136–6); Illinois Municipal Code; municipal sewer or water commission; for waterworks and sewer purposes.

(65 ILCS 5/11–138–2); Illinois Municipal Code; water companies; for pipes and waterworks.

(65 ILCS 5/11–139–12); Illinois Municipal Code; municipalities; for waterworks and sewerage systems.

(65 ILCS 5/11–140–3 and 5/11–140–5); Illinois Municipal Code; municipalities; for outlet sewers and works.

(65 ILCS 5/11–141–10); Illinois Municipal Code; municipalities; for sewerage systems.

(65 ILCS 5/11–148–6); Illinois Municipal Code; municipalities; for sewage disposal plants.

(65 ILCS 20/21–19 and 20/21–21); Revised Cities and Villages Act of 1941; City of Chicago; for municipal purposes or public welfare.

(65 ILCS 100/3); Sports Stadium Act; municipality with a population over 2,000,000; for sports stadium purposes, including quick-take power (obsolete).

(65 ILCS 110/60); Economic Development Project Area Tax Increment Allocation Act of 1995; municipalities; for economic development projects.

P.A. 94–1055, Art. 15, § 15–5–10, eff. Jan. 1, 2007.

30/15–5–15. Eminent domain powers in ILCS Chapter 70 through 75

§ 15–5–15. Eminent domain powers in ILCS Chapters 70 through 75. The following provisions of law may include express grants of the power to acquire property by condemnation or eminent domain:

(70 ILCS 5/8.02 and 5/9); Airport Authorities Act; airport authorities; for public airport facilities.

(70 ILCS 5/8.05 and 5/9); Airport Authorities Act; airport authorities; for removal of airport hazards.

(70 ILCS 5/8.06 and 5/9); Airport Authorities Act; airport authorities; for reduction of the height of objects or structures.

(70 ILCS 10/4); Interstate Airport Authorities Act; interstate airport authorities; for general purposes.

(70 ILCS 15/3); Kankakee River Valley Area Airport Authority Act; Kankakee River Valley Area Airport Authority; for acquisition of land for airports.

(70 ILCS 200/2–20); Civic Center Code; civic center authorities; for grounds, centers, buildings, and parking.

(70 ILCS 200/5–35); Civic Center Code; Aledo Civic Center Authority; for grounds, centers, buildings, and parking.

(70 ILCS 200/10–15); Civic Center Code; Aurora Metropolitan Exposition, Auditorium and Office Building Authority; for grounds, centers, buildings, and parking.

(70 ILCS 200/15–40); Civic Center Code; Benton Civic Center Authority; for grounds, centers, buildings, and parking.

(70 ILCS 200/20–15); Civic Center Code; Bloomington Civic Center Authority; for grounds, centers, buildings, and parking.

(70 ILCS 200/35–35); Civic Center Code; Brownstown Park District Civic Center Authority; for grounds, centers, buildings, and parking.

(70 ILCS 200/40–35); Civic Center Code; Carbondale Civic Center Authority; for grounds, centers, buildings, and parking.

(70 ILCS 200/55–60); Civic Center Code; Chicago South Civic Center Authority; for grounds, centers, buildings, and parking.

(70 ILCS 200/60–30); Civic Center Code; Collinsville Metropolitan Exposition, Auditorium and Office Building Authority; for grounds, centers, buildings, and parking.

(70 ILCS 200/70–35); Civic Center Code; Crystal Lake Civic Center Authority; for grounds, centers, buildings, and parking.

(70 ILCS 200/75–20); Civic Center Code; Decatur Metropolitan Exposition, Auditorium and Office Building Authority; for grounds, centers, buildings, and parking.

(70 ILCS 200/80–15); Civic Center Code; DuPage County Metropolitan Exposition, Auditorium and Office Building Authority; for grounds, centers, buildings, and parking.

(70 ILCS 200/85–35); Civic Center Code; Elgin Metropolitan Exposition, Auditorium and Office Building Authority; for grounds, centers, buildings, and parking.

(70 ILCS 200/95–25); Civic Center Code; Herrin Metropolitan Exposition, Auditorium and Office

Building Authority; for grounds, centers, buildings, and parking.

(70 ILCS 200/110–35); Civic Center Code; Illinois Valley Civic Center Authority; for grounds, centers, buildings, and parking.

(70 ILCS 200/115–35); Civic Center Code; Jasper County Civic Center Authority; for grounds, centers, buildings, and parking.

(70 ILCS 200/120–25); Civic Center Code; Jefferson County Metropolitan Exposition, Auditorium and Office Building Authority; for grounds, centers, buildings, and parking.

(70 ILCS 200/125–15); Civic Center Code; Jo Daviess County Civic Center Authority; for grounds, centers, buildings, and parking.

(70 ILCS 200/130–30); Civic Center Code; Katherine Dunham Metropolitan Exposition, Auditorium and Office Building Authority; for grounds, centers, buildings, and parking.

(70 ILCS 200/145–35); Civic Center Code; Marengo Civic Center Authority; for grounds, centers, buildings, and parking.

(70 ILCS 200/150–35); Civic Center Code; Mason County Civic Center Authority; for grounds, centers, buildings, and parking.

(70 ILCS 200/155–15); Civic Center Code; Matteson Metropolitan Civic Center Authority; for grounds, centers, buildings, and parking.

(70 ILCS 200/160–35); Civic Center Code; Maywood Civic Center Authority; for grounds, centers, buildings, and parking.

(70 ILCS 200/165–35); Civic Center Code; Melrose Park Metropolitan Exposition Auditorium and Office Building Authority; for grounds, centers, buildings, and parking.

(70 ILCS 200/170–20); Civic Center Code; certain Metropolitan Exposition, Auditorium and Office Building Authorities; for general purposes.

(70 ILCS 200/180–35); Civic Center Code; Normal Civic Center Authority; for grounds, centers, buildings, and parking.

(70 ILCS 200/185–15); Civic Center Code; Oak Park Civic Center Authority; for grounds, centers, buildings, and parking.

(70 ILCS 200/195–35); Civic Center Code; Ottawa Civic Center Authority; for grounds, centers, buildings, and parking.

(70 ILCS 200/200–15); Civic Center Code; Pekin Civic Center Authority; for grounds, centers, buildings, and parking.

(70 ILCS 200/205–15); Civic Center Code; Peoria Civic Center Authority; for grounds, centers, buildings, and parking.

(70 ILCS 200/210–35); Civic Center Code; Pontiac Civic Center Authority; for grounds, centers, buildings, and parking.

(70 ILCS 200/215–15); Civic Center Code; Illinois Quad City Civic Center Authority; for grounds, centers, buildings, and parking.

(70 ILCS 200/220–30); Civic Center Code; Quincy Metropolitan Exposition, Auditorium and Office Building Authority; for grounds, centers, buildings, and parking.

(70 ILCS 200/225–35); Civic Center Code; Randolph County Civic Center Authority; for grounds, centers, buildings, and parking.

(70 ILCS 200/230–35); Civic Center Code; River Forest Metropolitan Exposition, Auditorium and Office Building Authority; for grounds, centers, buildings, and parking.

(70 ILCS 200/235–40); Civic Center Code; Riverside Civic Center Authority; for grounds, centers, buildings, and parking.

(70 ILCS 200/245–35); Civic Center Code; Salem Civic Center Authority; for grounds, centers, buildings, and parking.

(70 ILCS 200/255–20); Civic Center Code; Springfield Metropolitan Exposition and Auditorium Authority; for grounds, centers, and parking.

(70 ILCS 200/260–35); Civic Center Code; Sterling Metropolitan Exposition, Auditorium and Office Building Authority; for grounds, centers, buildings, and parking.

(70 ILCS 200/265–20); Civic Center Code; Vermilion County Metropolitan Exposition, Auditorium and Office Building Authority; for grounds, centers, buildings, and parking.

(70 ILCS 200/270–35); Civic Center Code; Waukegan Civic Center Authority; for grounds, centers, buildings, and parking.

(70 ILCS 200/275–35); Civic Center Code; West Frankfort Civic Center Authority; for grounds, centers, buildings, and parking.

(70 ILCS 200/280–20); Civic Center Code; Will County Metropolitan Exposition and Auditorium Authority; for grounds, centers, and parking.

(70 ILCS 210/5); Metropolitan Pier and Exposition Authority Act; Metropolitan Pier and Exposition Authority; for general purposes, including quick-take power.

(70 ILCS 405/22.04); Soil and Water Conservation Districts Act; soil and water conservation districts; for general purposes.

(70 ILCS 410/10 and 410/12); Conservation District Act; conservation districts; for open space, wildland, scenic roadway, pathway, outdoor recreation, or other conservation benefits.

(70 ILCS 503/25); Chanute–Rantoul National Aviation Center Redevelopment Commission Act; Chanute–Rantoul National Aviation Center Redevelopment Commission; for general purposes.

(70 ILCS 507/15); Fort Sheridan Redevelopment Commission Act; Fort Sheridan Redevelopment Commission; for general purposes or to carry out comprehensive or redevelopment plans.

(70 ILCS 520/8); Southwestern Illinois Development Authority Act; Southwestern Illinois Development Authority; for general purposes, including quick-take power.

(70 ILCS 605/4–17 and 605/5–7); Illinois Drainage Code; drainage districts; for general purposes.

(70 ILCS 615/5 and 615/6); Chicago Drainage District Act; corporate authorities; for construction and maintenance of works.

(70 ILCS 705/10); Fire Protection District Act; fire protection districts; for general purposes.

(70 ILCS 750/20); Flood Prevention District Act; flood prevention districts; for general purposes.

(70 ILCS 805/6); Downstate Forest Preserve District Act; certain forest preserve districts; for general purposes.

(70 ILCS 805/18.8); Downstate Forest Preserve District Act; certain forest preserve districts; for recreational and cultural facilities.

(70 ILCS 810/8); Cook County Forest Preserve District Act; Forest Preserve District of Cook County; for general purposes.

(70 ILCS 810/38); Cook County Forest Preserve District Act; Forest Preserve District of Cook County; for recreational facilities.

(70 ILCS 910/15 and 910/16); Hospital District Law; hospital districts; for hospitals or hospital facilities.

(70 ILCS 915/3); Illinois Medical District Act; Illinois Medical District Commission; for general purposes.

(70 ILCS 915/4.5); Illinois Medical District Act; Illinois Medical District Commission; quick-take power for the Illinois State Police Forensic Science Laboratory (obsolete).

(70 ILCS 920/5); Tuberculosis Sanitarium District Act; tuberculosis sanitarium districts; for tuberculosis sanitariums.

(70 ILCS 925/20); Mid-Illinois Medical District Act; Mid-Illinois Medical District; for general purposes.

(70 ILCS 930/20); Mid-America Medical District Act; Mid-America Medical District Commission; for general purposes.

(70 ILCS 935/20); Roseland Community Medical District Act; medical district; for general purposes.

(70 ILCS 1005/7); Mosquito Abatement District Act; mosquito abatement districts; for general purposes.

(70 ILCS 1105/8); Museum District Act; museum districts; for general purposes.

(70 ILCS 1205/7–1); Park District Code; park districts; for streets and other purposes.

(70 ILCS 1205/8–1); Park District Code; park districts; for parks.

(70 ILCS 1205/9–2 and 1205/9–4); Park District Code; park districts; for airports and landing fields.

(70 ILCS 1205/11–2 and 1205/11–3); Park District Code; park districts; for State land abutting public water and certain access rights.

(70 ILCS 1205/11.1–3); Park District Code; park districts; for harbors.

(70 ILCS 1225/2); Park Commissioners Land Condemnation Act; park districts; for street widening.

(70 ILCS 1230/1 and 1230/1–a); Park Commissioners Water Control Act; park districts; for parks, boulevards, driveways, parkways, viaducts, bridges, or tunnels.

(70 ILCS 1250/2); Park Commissioners Street Control (1889) Act; park districts; for boulevards or driveways.

(70 ILCS 1290/1); Park District Aquarium and Museum Act; municipalities or park districts; for aquariums or museums.

(70 ILCS 1305/2); Park District Airport Zoning Act; park districts; for restriction of the height of structures.

(70 ILCS 1310/5); Park District Elevated Highway Act; park districts; for elevated highways.

(70 ILCS 1505/15); Chicago Park District Act; Chicago Park District; for parks and other purposes.

(70 ILCS 1505/25.1); Chicago Park District Act; Chicago Park District; for parking lots or garages.

(70 ILCS 1505/26.3); Chicago Park District Act; Chicago Park District; for harbors.

(70 ILCS 1570/5); Lincoln Park Commissioners Land Condemnation Act; Lincoln Park Commissioners; for land and interests in land, including riparian rights.

(70 ILCS 1801/30); Alexander–Cairo Port District Act; Alexander–Cairo Port District; for general purposes.

(70 ILCS 1805/8); Havana Regional Port District Act; Havana Regional Port District; for general purposes.

(70 ILCS 1810/7); Illinois International Port District Act; Illinois International Port District; for general purposes.

(70 ILCS 1815/13); Illinois Valley Regional Port District Act; Illinois Valley Regional Port District; for general purposes.

(70 ILCS 1820/4); Jackson–Union Counties Regional Port District Act; Jackson–Union Counties Regional Port District; for removal of airport hazards or reduction of the height of objects or structures.

(70 ILCS 1820/5); Jackson–Union Counties Regional Port District Act; Jackson–Union Counties Regional Port District; for general purposes.

(70 ILCS 1825/4.9); Joliet Regional Port District Act; Joliet Regional Port District; for removal of airport hazards.

(70 ILCS 1825/4.10); Joliet Regional Port District Act; Joliet Regional Port District; for reduction of the height of objects or structures.

(70 ILCS 1825/4.18); Joliet Regional Port District Act; Joliet Regional Port District; for removal of hazards from ports and terminals.

(70 ILCS 1825/5); Joliet Regional Port District Act; Joliet Regional Port District; for general purposes.

(70 ILCS 1830/7.1); Kaskaskia Regional Port District Act; Kaskaskia Regional Port District; for removal of hazards from ports and terminals.

(70 ILCS 1830/14); Kaskaskia Regional Port District Act; Kaskaskia Regional Port District; for general purposes.

(70 ILCS 1831/30); Massac–Metropolis Port District Act; Massac–Metropolis Port District; for general purposes.

(70 ILCS 1835/5.10); Mt. Carmel Regional Port District Act; Mt. Carmel Regional Port District; for removal of airport hazards.

(70 ILCS 1835/5.11); Mt. Carmel Regional Port District Act; Mt. Carmel Regional Port District; for reduction of the height of objects or structures.

(70 ILCS 1835/6); Mt. Carmel Regional Port District Act; Mt. Carmel Regional Port District; for general purposes.

(70 ILCS 1837/30); Ottawa Port District Act; Ottawa Port District; for general purposes.

(70 ILCS 1845/4.9); Seneca Regional Port District Act; Seneca Regional Port District; for removal of airport hazards.

(70 ILCS 1845/4.10); Seneca Regional Port District Act; Seneca Regional Port District; for reduction of the height of objects or structures.

(70 ILCS 1845/5); Seneca Regional Port District Act; Seneca Regional Port District; for general purposes.

(70 ILCS 1850/4); Shawneetown Regional Port District Act; Shawneetown Regional Port District; for removal of airport hazards or reduction of the height of objects or structures.

(70 ILCS 1850/5); Shawneetown Regional Port District Act; Shawneetown Regional Port District; for general purposes.

(70 ILCS 1855/4); Southwest Regional Port District Act; Southwest Regional Port District; for removal of airport hazards or reduction of the height of objects or structures.

(70 ILCS 1855/5); Southwest Regional Port District Act; Southwest Regional Port District; for general purposes.

(70 ILCS 1860/4); Tri–City Regional Port District Act; Tri–City Regional Port District; for removal of airport hazards.

(70 ILCS 1860/5); Tri–City Regional Port District Act; Tri–City Regional Port District; for the development of facilities.

(70 ILCS 1863/11); Upper Mississippi River International Port District Act; Upper Mississippi River International Port District; for general purposes.

(70 ILCS 1865/4.9); Waukegan Port District Act; Waukegan Port District; for removal of airport hazards.

(70 ILCS 1865/4.10); Waukegan Port District Act; Waukegan Port District; for restricting the height of objects or structures.

(70 ILCS 1865/5); Waukegan Port District Act; Waukegan Port District; for the development of facilities.

(70 ILCS 1870/8); White County Port District Act; White County Port District; for the development of facilities.

(70 ILCS 1905/16); Railroad Terminal Authority Act; Railroad Terminal Authority (Chicago); for general purposes.

(70 ILCS 1915/25); Grand Avenue Railroad Relocation Authority Act; Grand Avenue Railroad Relocation Authority; for general purposes, including quick-take power (now obsolete).

(70 ILCS 1935/25); Elmwood Park Grade Separation Authority Act; Elmwood Park Grade Separation Authority; for general purposes.

(70 ILCS 2105/9b); River Conservancy Districts Act; river conservancy districts; for general purposes.

(70 ILCS 2105/10a); River Conservancy Districts Act; river conservancy districts; for corporate purposes.

(70 ILCS 2205/15); Sanitary District Act of 1907; sanitary districts; for corporate purposes.

(70 ILCS 2205/18); Sanitary District Act of 1907; sanitary districts; for improvements and works.

(70 ILCS 2205/19); Sanitary District Act of 1907; sanitary districts; for access to property.

(70 ILCS 2305/8); North Shore Sanitary District Act; North Shore Sanitary District; for corporate purposes.

(70 ILCS 2305/15); North Shore Sanitary District Act; North Shore Sanitary District; for improvements.

(70 ILCS 2405/7.9); Sanitary District Act of 1917; Sanitary District of Decatur; for carrying out agreements to sell, convey, or disburse treated wastewater to a private entity.

(70 ILCS 2405/8); Sanitary District Act of 1917; sanitary districts; for corporate purposes.

(70 ILCS 2405/15); Sanitary District Act of 1917; sanitary districts; for improvements.

(70 ILCS 2405/16.9 and 2405/16.10); Sanitary District Act of 1917; sanitary districts; for waterworks.

(70 ILCS 2405/17.2); Sanitary District Act of 1917; sanitary districts; for public sewer and water utility treatment works.

(70 ILCS 2405/18); Sanitary District Act of 1917; sanitary districts; for dams or other structures to regulate water flow.

(70 ILCS 2605/8); Metropolitan Water Reclamation District Act; Metropolitan Water Reclamation District; for corporate purposes.

(70 ILCS 2605/16); Metropolitan Water Reclamation District Act; Metropolitan Water Reclamation District; quick-take power for improvements.

(70 ILCS 2605/17); Metropolitan Water Reclamation District Act; Metropolitan Water Reclamation District; for bridges.

(70 ILCS 2605/35); Metropolitan Water Reclamation District Act; Metropolitan Water Reclamation District; for widening and deepening a navigable stream.

(70 ILCS 2805/10); Sanitary District Act of 1936; sanitary districts; for corporate purposes.

(70 ILCS 2805/24); Sanitary District Act of 1936; sanitary districts; for improvements.

(70 ILCS 2805/26i and 2805/26j); Sanitary District Act of 1936; sanitary districts; for drainage systems.

(70 ILCS 2805/27); Sanitary District Act of 1936; sanitary districts; for dams or other structures to regulate water flow.

(70 ILCS 2805/32k); Sanitary District Act of 1936; sanitary districts; for water supply.

(70 ILCS 2805/32l); Sanitary District Act of 1936; sanitary districts; for waterworks.

(70 ILCS 2905/2–7); Metro–East Sanitary District Act of 1974; Metro–East Sanitary District; for corporate purposes.

(70 ILCS 2905/2–8); Metro–East Sanitary District Act of 1974; Metro–East Sanitary District; for access to property.

(70 ILCS 3010/10); Sanitary District Revenue Bond Act; sanitary districts; for sewerage systems.

(70 ILCS 3205/12); Illinois Sports Facility Authority Act; Illinois Sports Facility Authority; quick-take power for its corporate purposes (obsolete).

(70 ILCS 3405/16); Surface Water Protection District Act; surface water protection districts; for corporate purposes.

(70 ILCS 3605/7); Metropolitan Transit Authority Act; Chicago Transit Authority; for transportation systems.

(70 ILCS 3605/8); Metropolitan Transit Authority Act; Chicago Transit Authority; for general purposes.

(70 ILCS 3605/10); Metropolitan Transit Authority Act; Chicago Transit Authority; for general purposes, including railroad property.

(70 ILCS 3610/3 and 3610/5); Local Mass Transit District Act; local mass transit districts; for general purposes.

(70 ILCS 3615/2.13); Regional Transportation Authority Act; Regional Transportation Authority; for general purposes.

(70 ILCS 3705/8 and 3705/12); Public Water District Act; public water districts; for waterworks.

(70 ILCS 3705/23a); Public Water District Act; public water districts; for sewerage properties.

(70 ILCS 3705/23e); Public Water District Act; public water districts; for combined waterworks and sewerage systems.

(70 ILCS 3715/6); Water Authorities Act; water authorities; for facilities to ensure adequate water supply.

(70 ILCS 3715/27); Water Authorities Act; water authorities; for access to property.

(75 ILCS 5/4–7); Illinois Local Library Act; boards of library trustees; for library buildings.

(75 ILCS 16/30–55.80); Public Library District Act of 1991; public library districts; for general purposes.

(75 ILCS 65/1 and 65/3); Libraries in Parks Act; corporate authorities of city or park district, or board of park commissioners; for free public library buildings.

P.A. 94–1055, Art. 15, § 15–5–15, eff. Jan. 1, 2007. Amended by P.A. 94–1109, § 10, eff. Feb. 23, 2007; P.A. 95–693, § 15, eff. Nov. 5, 2007; P.A. 96–1000, § 630, eff. July 2, 2010; P.A. 97–333, § 580, eff. Aug. 12, 2011; P.A. 97–813, § 675, eff. July 13, 2012; P.A. 98–756, § 730, eff. July 16, 2014.

30/15–5–20. Eminent domain powers in ILCS Chapters 105 through 115

§ 15–5–20. Eminent domain powers in ILCS Chapters 105 through 115. The following provisions of law may include express grants of the power to acquire property by condemnation or eminent domain:

(105 ILCS 5/10–22.35A); School Code; school boards; for school buildings.

(105 ILCS 5/16–6); School Code; school boards; for adjacent property to enlarge a school site.

(105 ILCS 5/22–16); School Code; school boards; for school purposes.

(105 ILCS 5/32–4.13); School Code; special charter school districts; for school purposes.

(105 ILCS 5/34–20); School Code; Chicago Board of Education; for school purposes.

(110 ILCS 305/7); University of Illinois Act; Board of Trustees of the University of Illinois; for general purposes, including quick-take power.

(110 ILCS 325/2); University of Illinois at Chicago Land Transfer Act; Board of Trustees of the University of Illinois; for removal of limitations or restrictions on property conveyed by the Chicago Park District.

(110 ILCS 335/3); Institution for Tuberculosis Research Act; Board of Trustees of the University of Illinois; for the Institution for Tuberculosis Research.

(110 ILCS 525/3); Southern Illinois University Revenue Bond Act; Board of Trustees of Southern Illinois University; for general purposes.

(110 ILCS 615/3); State Colleges and Universities Revenue Bond Act of 1967; Board of Governors of State Colleges and Universities; for general purposes.

(110 ILCS 660/5–40); Chicago State University Law; Board of Trustees of Chicago State University; for general purposes.

(110 ILCS 661/6–10); Chicago State University Revenue Bond Law; Board of Trustees of Chicago State University; for general purposes.

(110 ILCS 665/10–40); Eastern Illinois University Law; Board of Trustees of Eastern Illinois University; for general purposes.

(110 ILCS 666/11–10); Eastern Illinois University Revenue Bond Law; Board of Trustees of Eastern Illinois University; for general purposes.

(110 ILCS 670/15–40); Governors State University Law; Board of Trustees of Governors State University; for general purposes.

(110 ILCS 671/16–10); Governors State University Revenue Bond Law; Board of Trustees of Governors State University; for general purposes.

(110 ILCS 675/20–40); Illinois State University Law; Board of Trustees of Illinois State University; for general purposes.

(110 ILCS 676/21–10); Illinois State University Revenue Bond Law; Board of Trustees of Illinois State University; for general purposes.

(110 ILCS 680/25–40); Northeastern Illinois University Law; Board of Trustees of North-eastern Illinois University; for general purposes.

(110 ILCS 681/26–10); Northeastern Illinois University Revenue Bond Law; Board of Trustees of Northeastern Illinois University; for general purposes.

(110 ILCS 685/30–40); Northern Illinois University Law; Board of Trustees of Northern Illinois University; for general purposes.

(110 ILCS 685/30–45); Northern Illinois University Law; Board of Trustees of Northern Illinois University; for buildings and facilities.

(110 ILCS 686/31–10); Northern Illinois University Revenue Bond Law; Board of Trustees of Northern Illinois University; for general purposes.

(110 ILCS 690/35–40); Western Illinois University Law; Board of Trustees of Western Illinois University; for general purposes.

(110 ILCS 691/36–10); Western Illinois University Revenue Bond Law; Board of Trustees of Western Illinois University; for general purposes.

(110 ILCS 710/3); Board of Regents Revenue Bond Act of 1967; Board of Regents; for general purposes.

(110 ILCS 805/3–36); Public Community College Act; community college district boards; for sites for college purposes.

P.A. 94–1055, Art. 15, § 15–5–20, eff. Jan. 1, 2007. Amended by P.A. 96–328, § 370, eff. Aug. 11, 2009.

30/15–5–25. Eminent domain powers in ILCS Chapters 205 through 430

§ 15–5–25. Eminent domain powers in ILCS Chapters 205 through 430. The following provisions of law may include express grants of the power to acquire property by condemnation or eminent domain:

(220 ILCS 5/8–509); Public Utilities Act; public utilities; for construction of certain improvements.

(220 ILCS 15/1); Gas Storage Act; corporations engaged in the distribution, transportation, or storage of natural gas or manufactured gas; for their operations.

(220 ILCS 15/2 and 15/6); Gas Storage Act; corporations engaged in the distribution, transportation, or storage of natural gas or manufactured gas; for use of an underground geological formation for gas storage.

(220 ILCS 30/13); Electric Supplier Act; electric cooperatives; for general purposes.

(220 ILCS 55/3); Telegraph Act; telegraph companies; for telegraph lines.

(220 ILCS 65/4); Telephone Company Act; telecommunications carriers; for telephone company purposes.

(225 ILCS 435/23); Ferries Act; ferry operators; for a landing, ferryhouse, or approach.

(225 ILCS 440/9); Highway Advertising Control Act of 1971; Department of Transportation; for removal of signs adjacent to highways.

(310 ILCS 5/6 and 5/38); State Housing Act; housing corporations; for general purposes.

(310 ILCS 10/8.3); Housing Authorities Act; housing authorities; for general purposes.

(310 ILCS 10/8.15); Housing Authorities Act; housing authorities; for implementation of conservation plans and demolition.

(310 ILCS 10/9); Housing Authorities Act; housing authorities; for general purposes.

(310 ILCS 20/5); Housing Development and Construction Act; housing authorities; for development or redevelopment.

(310 ILCS 35/2); House Relocation Act; political subdivisions and municipal corporations; for relocation of dwellings for highway construction.

(315 ILCS 5/14); Blighted Areas Redevelopment Act of 1947; land clearance commissions; for redevelopment projects.

(315 ILCS 10/5); Blighted Vacant Areas Development Act of 1949; State of Illinois; for housing development.

(315 ILCS 20/9 and 20/42); Neighborhood Redevelopment Corporation Law; neighborhood redevelopment corporations; for general purposes.

(315 ILCS 25/4 and 25/6); Urban Community Conservation Act; municipal conservation boards; for conservation areas.

(315 ILCS 30/12); Urban Renewal Consolidation Act of 1961; municipal departments of urban renewal; for blighted area redevelopment projects.

(315 ILCS 30/20 and 30/22); Urban Renewal Consolidation Act of 1961; municipal departments of urban renewal; for implementing conservation areas.

(315 ILCS 30/24); Urban Renewal Consolidation Act of 1961; municipal departments of urban renewal; for general purposes.

(415 ILCS 95/6); Junkyard Act; Department of Transportation; for junkyards or scrap processing facilities.

(420 ILCS 35/1); Radioactive Waste Storage Act; Illinois Emergency Management Agency; for radioactive by-product and waste storage.

P.A. 94–1055, Art. 15, § 15–5–25, eff. Jan. 1, 2007.

30/15–5–30. Eminent domain powers in ILCS Chapters 505 through 525

§ 15–5–30. Eminent domain powers in ILCS Chapters 505 through 525. The following provisions of law may include express grants of the power to acquire property by condemnation or eminent domain:

(515 ILCS 5/1–145); Fish and Aquatic Life Code; Department of Natural Resources; for fish or aquatic life purposes.

(520 ILCS 5/1.9); Wildlife Code; Department of Natural Resources; for conservation, hunting, and fishing purposes.

(520 ILCS 25/35); Habitat Endowment Act; Department of Natural Resources; for habitat preservation with the consent of the landowner.

(525 ILCS 30/7.05); Illinois Natural Areas Preservation Act; Department of Natural Resources; for the purposes of the Act.

(525 ILCS 40/3); State Forest Act; Department of Natural Resources; for State forests.

P.A. 94–1055, Art. 15, § 15–5–30, eff. Jan. 1, 2007.

30/15–5–35. Eminent domain powers in ILCS Chapters 605 through 625

§ 15–5–35. Eminent domain powers in ILCS Chapters 605 through 625. The following provisions of law may include express grants of the power to acquire property by condemnation or eminent domain:

(605 ILCS 5/4–501); Illinois Highway Code; Department of Transportation and counties; for highway purposes.

(605 ILCS 5/4–502); Illinois Highway Code; Department of Transportation; for ditches and drains.

(605 ILCS 5/4–505); Illinois Highway Code; Department of Transportation; for replacement of railroad and public utility property taken for highway purposes.

(605 ILCS 5/4–509); Illinois Highway Code; Department of Transportation; for replacement of property taken for highway purposes.

(605 ILCS 5/4–510); Illinois Highway Code; Department of Transportation; for rights-of-way for future highway purposes.

(605 ILCS 5/4–511); Illinois Highway Code; Department of Transportation; for relocation of structures taken for highway purposes.

(605 ILCS 5/5–107); Illinois Highway Code; counties; for county highway relocation.

(605 ILCS 5/5–801); Illinois Highway Code; counties; for highway purposes.

(605 ILCS 5/5–802); Illinois Highway Code; counties; for ditches and drains.

(605 ILCS 5/6–309); Illinois Highway Code; highway commissioners or county superintendents; for township or road district roads.

(605 ILCS 5/6–801); Illinois Highway Code; highway commissioners; for road district or township roads.

(605 ILCS 5/6–802); Illinois Highway Code; highway commissioners; for ditches and drains.

(605 ILCS 5/8–102); Illinois Highway Code; Department of Transportation, counties, and municipalities; for limiting freeway access.

(605 ILCS 5/8–103); Illinois Highway Code; Department of Transportation, counties, and municipalities; for freeway purposes.

(605 ILCS 5/8–106); Illinois Highway Code; Department of Transportation and counties; for relocation of existing crossings for freeway purposes.

(605 ILCS 5/9–113); Illinois Highway Code; highway authorities; for utility and other uses in rights-of-ways.

(605 ILCS 5/10–302); Illinois Highway Code; counties; for bridge purposes.

(605 ILCS 5/10–602); Illinois Highway Code; municipalities; for ferry and bridge purposes.

(605 ILCS 5/10–702); Illinois Highway Code; municipalities; for bridge purposes.

(605 ILCS 5/10–901); Illinois Highway Code; Department of Transportation; for ferry property.

(605 ILCS 10/9); Toll Highway Act; Illinois State Toll Highway Authority; for toll highway purposes.

(605 ILCS 10/9.5); Toll Highway Act; Illinois State Toll Highway Authority; for its authorized purposes.

(605 ILCS 10/10); Toll Highway Act; Illinois State Toll Highway Authority; for property of a municipality or political subdivision for toll highway purposes.

(605 ILCS 115/14); Toll Bridge Act; counties; for toll bridge purposes.

(605 ILCS 115/15); Toll Bridge Act; counties; for the purpose of taking a toll bridge to make it a free bridge.

(605 ILCS 130/80); Public Private Agreements for the Illiana Expressway Act; Department of Transportation; for the Illiana Expressway project.

(610 ILCS 5/17); Railroad Incorporation Act; railroad corporation; for real estate for railroad purposes.

(610 ILCS 5/18); Railroad Incorporation Act; railroad corporations; for materials for railways.

(610 ILCS 5/19); Railroad Incorporation Act; railways; for land along highways.

(610 ILCS 70/1); Railroad Powers Act; purchasers and lessees of railroad companies; for railroad purposes.

(610 ILCS 115/2 and 115/3); Street Railroad Right of Way Act; street railroad companies; for street railroad purposes.

(615 ILCS 5/19); Rivers, Lakes, and Streams Act; Department of Natural Resources; for land along public waters for pleasure, recreation, or sport purposes.

(615 ILCS 10/7.8); Illinois Waterway Act; Department of Natural Resources; for waterways and appurtenances.

(615 ILCS 15/7); Flood Control Act of 1945; Department of Natural Resources; for the purposes of the Act.

(615 ILCS 30/9); Illinois and Michigan Canal Management Act; Department of Natural Resources; for dams, locks, and improvements.

(615 ILCS 45/10); Illinois and Michigan Canal Development Act; Department of Natural Resources; for development and management of the canal.

(620 ILCS 5/72); Illinois Aeronautics Act; Division of Aeronautics of the Department of Transportation; for airport purposes.

(620 ILCS 5/73); Illinois Aeronautics Act; Division of Aeronautics of the Department of Transportation; for removal of airport hazards.

(620 ILCS 5/74); Illinois Aeronautics Act; Division of Aeronautics of the Department of Transportation; for airport purposes.

(620 ILCS 25/33); Airport Zoning Act; Division of Aeronautics of the Department of Transportation; for air rights.

(620 ILCS 40/2 and 40/3); General County Airport and Landing Field Act; counties; for airport purposes.

(620 ILCS 40/5); General County Airport and Landing Field Act; counties; for removing hazards.

(620 ILCS 45/6 and 45/7); County Airport Law of 1943; boards of directors of airports and landing fields; for airport and landing field purposes.

(620 ILCS 50/22 and 50/31); County Airports Act; counties; for airport purposes.

(620 ILCS 50/24); County Airports Act; counties; for removal of airport hazards.

(620 ILCS 50/26); County Airports Act; counties; for acquisition of airport protection privileges.

(620 ILCS 52/15); County Air Corridor Protection Act; counties; for airport zones.

(620 ILCS 55/1); East St. Louis Airport Act; Department of Transportation; for airport in East St. Louis metropolitan area.

(620 ILCS 65/15); O'Hare Modernization Act; Chicago; for the O'Hare modernization program, including quick-take power.

(620 ILCS 75/2–15 and 75/2–90); Public–Private Agreements for the South Suburban Airport Act; Department of Transportation; for South Suburban Airport purposes.

(625 ILCS 5/2–105); Illinois Vehicle Code; Secretary of State; for general purposes.

(625 ILCS 5/18c–7501); Illinois Vehicle Code; rail carriers; for railroad purposes, including quick-take power.

P.A. 94–1055, Art. 15, § 15–5–35, eff. Jan. 1, 2007. Amended by P.A. 97–808, § 10, eff. July 13, 2012; P.A. 98–756, § 730, eff. July 16, 2014.

30/15–5–40. Eminent domain powers in ILCS Chapters 705 through 820

§ 15–5–40. Eminent domain powers in ILCS Chapters 705 through 820. The following provisions of law may include express grants of the power to acquire property by condemnation or eminent domain:

(765 ILCS 230/2); Coast and Geodetic Survey Act; United States of America; for carrying out coast and geodetic surveys.

(765 ILCS 505/1); Mining Act of 1874; mine owners and operators; for roads, railroads, and ditches.

(805 ILCS 25/2); Corporation Canal Construction Act; general corporations; for levees, canals, or tunnels for agricultural, mining, or sanitary purposes.

(805 ILCS 30/7); Gas Company Property Act; consolidating gas companies; for acquisition of stock of dissenting stockholder.

(805 ILCS 120/9); Merger of Not For Profit Corporations Act; merging or consolidating corporations; for acquisition of interest of objecting member or owner.

P.A. 94–1055, Art. 15, § 15–5–40, eff. Jan. 1, 2007. Amended by P.A. 96–863, § 90–33, eff. Jan. 19, 2010.

30/15–5–45. § 15–5–45. Repealed by P.A. 96–1000, § 632, eff. July 2, 2010

30/15–5–46. Eminent domain powers in new Acts

§ 15–5–46. Eminent domain powers in new Acts. The following provisions of law may include express grants of the power to acquire property by condemnation or eminent domain:

(Reserved).

P.A. 94–1055, Art. 15, § 15–5–46, added by P.A. 96–1522, § 185, eff. Feb. 14, 2011; P.A. 97–259, § 90, eff. Aug. 5, 2011. Amended by P.A. 97–813, § 675, eff. July 13, 2012.

30/15–5–47. Eminent domain powers in new Acts

§ 15–5–47. Eminent domain powers in new Acts. The following provisions of law may include express grants of the power to acquire property by condemnation or eminent domain:

(Reserved).

P.A. 94–1055, Art. 15, § 15–5–47, added by P.A. 98–109, § 4–70, eff. July 25, 2013; P.A. 98–564, § 120, eff. Aug. 27, 2013. Amended by P.A. 98–756, § 730, eff. July 16, 2014.

ARTICLE 20.   QUICK—TAKE PROCEDURE

Section

30/20–5–5. Quick-take

§ 20–5–5. Quick-take.

(a) This Section applies only to proceedings under this Article that are authorized in this Article and in Article 25 of this Act.

(b) In a proceeding subject to this Section, the plaintiff, at any time after the complaint has been filed and before judgment is entered in the proceeding, may file a written motion requesting that, immediately or at some specified later date, the plaintiff either: (i) be vested with the fee simple title (or such lesser estate, interest, or easement, as may be required) to the real property, or a specified portion of that property, which is the subject of the proceeding, and be authorized to take possession of and use the property; or (ii) only be authorized to take possession of and to use the property, if possession and use, without the vesting of title, are sufficient to permit the plaintiff to proceed with the project until the final ascertainment of compensation. No land or interests in land now or hereafter owned, leased, controlled, or operated and used by, or necessary for the actual operation of, any common carrier engaged in interstate commerce, or any other public utility subject to the jurisdiction of the Illinois Commerce Commission, shall be taken or appropriated under this Section by the State of Illinois, the Illinois Toll Highway Authority, the sanitary district, the St. Louis Metropolitan Area Airport Authority, or the Board of Trustees of the University of

Illinois without first securing the approval of the Illinois Commerce Commission.

Except as otherwise provided in this Article, the motion for taking shall state: (1) an accurate description of the property to which the motion relates and the estate or interest sought to be acquired in that property; (2) the formally adopted schedule or plan of operation for the execution of the plaintiff's project; (3) the situation of the property to which the motion relates, with respect to the schedule or plan; (4) the necessity for taking the property in the manner requested in the motion; and (5) if the property (except property described in Section 3 of the Sports Stadium Act or property described as Site B in Section 2 of the Metropolitan Pier and Exposition Authority Act) to be taken is owned, leased, controlled, or operated and used by, or necessary for the actual operation of, any interstate common carrier or other public utility subject to the jurisdiction of the Illinois Commerce Commission, a statement to the effect that the approval of the proposed taking has been secured from the Commission, and attaching to the motion a certified copy of the order of the Illinois Commerce Commission granting approval. If the schedule or plan of operation is not set forth fully in the motion, a copy of the schedule or plan shall be attached to the motion. P.A. 94–1055, Art. 20, § 20–5–5, eff. Jan. 1, 2007.

30/20–5–10. Preliminary finding of compensation

§ 20–5–10. Preliminary finding of compensation.

(a) The court shall fix a date, not less than 5 days after the filing of a motion under Section 20–5–5, for the hearing on that motion and shall require due notice to be given to each party to the proceeding whose interests would be affected by the taking requested, except that any party who has been or is being served by publication and who has not entered his or her appearance in the proceeding need not be given notice unless the court so requires, in its discretion and in the interests of justice.

(b) At the hearing, if the court has not previously, in the same proceeding, determined that the plaintiff has authority to exercise the right of eminent domain, that the property sought to be taken is subject to the exercise of that right, and that the right of eminent domain is not being improperly exercised in the particular proceeding, then the court shall first hear and determine those matters. The court's order on those matters is appealable and an appeal may be taken from that order by either party within 30 days after the entry of the order, but not thereafter, unless the court, on good cause shown, extends the time for taking the appeal. However, no appeal shall stay the further proceedings prescribed in this Act unless the appeal is taken by the plaintiff or unless an order staying further proceedings is entered either by the trial court or by the court to which the appeal is taken.

(c) If the foregoing matters are determined in favor of the plaintiff and further proceedings are not stayed, or if further proceedings are stayed and the appeal results in a determination in favor of the plaintiff, the court then shall hear the issues raised by the plaintiff's motion for taking. If the court finds that reasonable necessity exists for taking the property in the manner requested in the motion, then the court shall hear such evidence as it may consider necessary and proper for a preliminary finding of just compensation. In its discretion, the court may appoint 3 competent and disinterested appraisers as agents of the court to evaluate the property to which the motion relates and to report their conclusions to the court; and their fees shall be paid by the plaintiff. The court shall then make a preliminary finding of the amount constituting just compensation.

(d) The court's preliminary finding of just compensation and any deposit made or security provided pursuant to that finding shall not be evidence in the further proceedings to ascertain finally the just compensation to be paid and shall not be disclosed in any manner to a jury impaneled in the proceedings. If appraisers have been appointed, as authorized under this Article, their report shall not be evidence in those further proceedings, but the appraisers may be called as witnesses by the parties to the proceedings. P.A. 94–1055, Art. 20, § 20–5–10, eff. Jan. 1, 2007.

30/20–5–15. Deposit in court; possession

§ 20–5–15. Deposit in court; possession.

(a) If the plaintiff deposits with the county treasurer money in the amount preliminarily found by the court to be just compensation, the court shall enter an order of taking, vesting in the plaintiff the fee simple title (or such lesser estate, interest, or easement, as may be required) to the property, if such vesting has been requested and has been found necessary by the court, at a date the court considers proper, and fixing a date on which the plaintiff is authorized to take possession of and to use the property.

(b) If, at the request of any interested party and upon his or her showing of undue hardship or other good cause, the plaintiff's authority to take possession of the property is postponed for more than 10 days after the date of vesting of title or more than 15 days after the entry of the order of taking when the order does not vest title in the plaintiff, then that party shall pay to the plaintiff a reasonable rental for the property in an amount determined by the court. Injunctive relief or any other appropriate judicial process or procedure shall be available to place the plaintiff in possession of the property on and after the date fixed by the court for the taking of possession and to prevent any unauthorized interference with possession and the plaintiff's proper use of the property. The county treasurer shall refund to the plaintiff the amount deposited prior to October 1, 1973 that is in excess of the amount preliminarily found by the court to be just compensation.

(c) When property is taken by a unit of local government for the purpose of constructing a body of water to be used by a local government-owned "public utility", as defined in Section 11–117–2 of the Illinois Municipal Code, and the unit of local government intends to sell or lease the property to a non-governmental entity, the defendants holding title before the order that transferred title shall be allowed first opportunity to repurchase the property for a fair market value or first opportunity to lease the property for a fair market value.

P.A. 94–1055, Art. 20, § 20–5–15, eff. Jan. 1, 2007.

30/20–5–20. Withdrawal by persons having an interest

§ 20–5–20. Withdrawal by persons having an interest. At any time after the plaintiff has taken possession of the property pursuant to the order of taking, if an appeal has not been and will not be taken from the court's order described in subsection (b) of Section 20–5–10 of this Act, or if such an appeal has been taken and has been determined in favor of the plaintiff, any party interested in the property may apply to the court for authority to withdraw, for his or her own use, his or her share (or any part thereof) of the amount preliminarily found by the court to be just compensation and deposited by the plaintiff, in accordance with the provisions of subsection (a) of Section 20–5–15 of this Act, as that share is determined by the court. The court shall then fix a date for a hearing on the application for authority to withdraw and shall require due notice of the application to be given to each party whose interests would be affected by the withdrawal. After the hearing, the court may authorize the withdrawal requested, or any part thereof as is proper, but upon the condition that the party making the withdrawal shall refund to the clerk of the court, upon the entry of a proper court order, any portion of the amount withdrawn that exceeds the amount finally ascertained in the proceeding to be just compensation (or damages, costs, expenses, or attorney fees) owing to that party.

P.A. 94–1055, Art. 20, § 20–5–20, eff. Jan. 1, 2007.

30/20–5–25. Persons contesting not to be prejudiced

§ 20–5–25. Persons contesting not to be prejudiced. Neither the plaintiff nor any party interested in the property, by taking any action authorized by Sections 20–5–5 through 20–5–20, inclusive, of this Act, or authorized under Article 25 of this Act, shall be prejudiced in any way in contesting, in later stages of the proceeding, the amount to be finally ascertained to be just compensation.

P.A. 94–1055, Art. 20, § 20–5–25, eff. Jan. 1, 2007.

30/20–5–30. Interest payments

§ 20–5–30. Interest payments. The plaintiff shall pay, in addition to the just compensation finally adjudged in the proceeding, interest at the rate of 6% per annum upon:

(1) Any excess of the just compensation finally adjudged, over the amount preliminarily found by the court to be just compensation in accordance with Section 20–5–10 of this Act, from the date on which the parties interested in the property surrendered possession of the property in accordance with the order of taking, to the date of payment of the excess by the plaintiff.

(2) Any portion of the amount preliminarily found by the court to be just compensation and deposited by the plaintiff, to which any interested party is entitled, if the interested party applied for authority to withdraw that portion in accordance with Section 20–5–20 of this Act, and upon objection by the plaintiff (other than on grounds that an appeal under subsection (b) of Section 20–5–10 of this Act is pending or contemplated), authority to withdraw was denied; interest shall be paid to that party from the date of the plaintiff's deposit to the date of payment to that party.

When interest is allowable as provided under item (1) of this Section, no further interest shall be allowed under the provisions of Section 2–1303 of the Code of Civil Procedure or any other law.

P.A. 94–1055, Art. 20, § 20–5–30, eff. Jan. 1, 2007.

30/20–5–35. Refund of excess deposit

§ 20–5–35. Refund of excess deposit. If the amount withdrawn from deposit by any interested party under the provision of Section 20–5–20 of this Act exceeds the amount finally adjudged to be just compensation (or damages, costs, expenses, and attorney fees) due to that party, the court shall order that party to refund the excess to the clerk of the court and, if refund is not made within a reasonable time fixed by the court, shall enter judgment for the excess in favor of the plaintiff and against that party.

P.A. 94–1055, Art. 20, § 20–5–35, eff. Jan. 1, 2007.

30/20–5–40. Dismissal; abandonment

§ 20–5–40. Dismissal; abandonment. After the plaintiff has taken possession of the property pursuant to the order of taking, the plaintiff shall have no right to dismiss the complaint or to abandon the proceeding, as to all or any part of the property so taken, except upon the consent of all parties to the proceeding whose interests would be affected by the dismissal or abandonment.

P.A. 94–1055, Art. 20, § 20–5–40, eff. Jan. 1, 2007.

30/20–5–45. Payment of costs

§ 20–5–45. Payment of costs. If, on an appeal taken under the provisions of Section 20–5–10 of this

Act, the plaintiff is determined not to have the authority to maintain the proceeding as to any property that is the subject of that appeal or if, with the consent of all parties to the proceeding whose interests are affected, the plaintiff dismisses the complaint or abandons the proceedings as to any property that is the subject of the appeal, the trial court then shall enter an order: (i) revesting the title to the property in the parties entitled thereto, if the order of taking vested title in the plaintiff; (ii) requiring the plaintiff to deliver possession of the property to the parties entitled to possession; and (iii) making such provision as is just for the payment of damages arising out of the plaintiff's taking and use of the property and also for costs, expenses, and attorney fees, as provided in Section 10–5–70 of this Act. The court may order the clerk of the court to pay those sums to the parties entitled thereto out of the money deposited by the plaintiff in accordance with the provisions of subsection (a) of Section 20–5–15 of this Act.

P.A. 94–1055, Art. 20, § 20–5–45, eff. Jan. 1, 2007.

30/20–5–50. Construction of Article

§ 20–5–50. Construction of Article. The right to take possession and title prior to the final judgment, as prescribed in this Article and Article 25 of this Act shall be in addition to any other right, power, or authority otherwise conferred by law and shall not be construed as abrogating, limiting, or modifying any other right, power, or authority.

P.A. 94–1055, Art. 20, § 20–5–50, eff. Jan. 1, 2007.

ARTICLE 25.   EXPRESS QUICK—
TAKE POWERS

Part
5.   **New Quick--Take Powers.**
7.   **Existing Quick--Take Powers.**

PART 5.   NEW QUICK—TAKE POWERS

30/25–5–5.   Quick–take;   Village of Skokie

§ 25–5–5. Quick-take; Village of Skokie. Quick-take proceedings under Article 20 may be used for a period of 12 months after the effective date of this amendatory Act of the 95th General Assembly by the Village of Skokie for the acquisition of property to be used for pedestrian egress and ingress, drop-off and pick-up areas, taxi waiting areas, and a bus connection stop to support a rail transit station, and for improvements to Skokie Boulevard and Searle Parkway to accommodate traffic signals, improved turning radii, and lane widening, as follows:

8116 Skokie Boulevard

Index Number (PIN) 10–21–501–011–0000

ALL THAT PART OF BLOCK 4 IN THE SUBDIVISION OF LOT 2 OF THE SUBDIVISION OF THE SOUTH 105 ACRES OF THE SOUTHEAST ¼ OF SECTION 21, TOWNSHIP 41 NORTH, RANGE 13, EAST OF THE THIRD PRINCIPAL MERIDIAN, LYING EASTERLY OF A LINE DRAWN 135.0 FEET EASTERLY OF PARALLEL TO THE RIGHT OF WAY OF THE CHICAGO AND NORTHWESTERN RAILWAY COMPANY, MEASURED AT RIGHT ANGLES THERETO (EXCEPT THAT PART TAKEN FOR STREETS) IN COOK COUNTY, ILLINOIS.

8156–8200 Skokie Boulevard

Index Number (PIN) 10–21–402–077–0000

THAT PART OF LOT 1 LYING EASTERLY OF THE LINE DRAWN PARALLEL IN DISTANCE 135 FEET AT RIGHT ANGLES IN AN EASTERLY DIRECTION FROM THE EAST LINE OF THE RIGHT–OF–WAY OF THE CHICAGO AND NORTHWESTERN RAILROAD COMPANY AND SOUTHERLY OF A LINE PARALLEL TO AND 353 FEET SOUTHERLY OF THE NORTH LINE OF BLOCK 1 IN BLAMEUSER'S SUBDIVISION OF THE SOUTH 105 ACRES OF THE SOUTHEAST ¼ OF SECTION 21, TOWNSHIP 41 NORTH, RANGE 13, EAST OF THE THIRD PRINCIPAL MERIDIAN, IN COOK COUNTY, ILLINOIS.

P.A. 94–1055, Art. 25, § 25–5–5, added by P.A. 95–706, § 5, eff. Jan. 8, 2008.

30/25–5–10.   Quick-take; City of Champaign, Village of Savoy and County of Champaign

§ 25–5–10. Quick-take; City of Champaign, Village of Savoy and County of Champaign. Quick-take proceedings under Article 20 may be used for a period of no more than one year after the effective date of this amendatory Act of the 95th General Assembly by the City of Champaign, the Village of Savoy, and the County of Champaign, for the acquisition of the following described properties for the purpose of road construction right-of- way, permanent easements, and temporary easements:

Alexander C. Lo, as Trustee—Parcel 040

Right-of-Way:

A part of the South Half of Section 26, and the North Half of Section 35, Township 19 North, Range 8 East of the Third Principal Meridian, Champaign County, Illinois with bearing datum based on Illinois State Plane Coordinate System, East Zone;

Beginning at the southwest corner of Section 26, Township 19 North, Range 8 East of the Third Principal Meridian; thence along the west line of said Section 26, North 00 degrees 50 minutes 27 seconds West 887.52 feet; thence North 89 degrees 09 minutes 33 seconds East 45.00 feet; thence South 00 degrees 50 minutes 27 seconds East 50.00 feet; thence South 03 degrees 42 minutes 12 seconds East 300.37 feet; thence along a line parallel to and 60.00 feet offset easterly from said west line of Section 26, South 00 degrees 50 minutes 27 seconds East 200.00 feet; thence South 06 degrees 25 minutes 24 seconds East 185.04 feet; thence along a line parallel to and 155.00 feet offset northerly from the south line of said Section 26, South 89 degrees 36 minutes 45 seconds East 349.35 feet; thence South 86 degrees 45 minutes 01 seconds East 100.12 feet; thence along a line parallel to and 150.00 feet offset northerly from said south line of Section 26, South 89 degrees 36 minutes 45 seconds East 850.00 feet; thence South 85 degrees 56 minutes 46 seconds East 703.70 feet; thence along a line parallel to and 105.00 feet offset northerly from said south line of Section 26, South 89 degrees 36 minutes 45 seconds East 322.03 feet; thence South 00 degrees 23 minutes 15 seconds West 22.00 feet; thence along a line parallel to and 83.00 feet offset northerly from said south line of Section 26, South 89 degrees 36 minutes 45 seconds East 237.29 feet; thence North 00 degrees 38 minutes 43 seconds West 30.00 feet; thence along a line parallel to and 113.00 feet offset northerly from said south line of Section 26, South 89 degrees 36 minutes 56 seconds East 88.24 feet; thence South 87 degrees 19 minutes 30 seconds East 300.24 feet; thence along a line parallel to and 101.00 feet offset northerly from said south line of Section 26, South 89 degrees 36 minutes 56 seconds East 700.00 feet; thence South 87 degrees 54 minutes 06 seconds East 228.20 feet, to the east line of the west half of the southeast Quarter of aforesaid Section 26; thence along said east line, South 00 degrees 39 minutes 19 seconds East 94.19 feet, to the south line of said Section 26; thence along said south line of Section 26, South 89 degrees 36 minutes 56 seconds East 1316.02 feet, to a point being the southeast corner of said Section 26, said point also being the northeast corner of Section 35, Township 19 North, Range 8 East of the Third Principal Meridian; thence along the east line of said Section 35, South 00 degrees 27 minutes 33 seconds East 920.45 feet; thence South 89 degrees 32 minutes 27 seconds West 275.00 feet; thence North 00 degrees 27 minutes 33 seconds West 600.00 feet; thence North 89 degrees 32 minutes 27 seconds East 235.00 feet; thence along a line parallel to and 40.00 feet offset westerly from aforesaid east line of Section 35, North 00 degrees 27 minutes 33 seconds West 218.02 feet; thence along a line parallel to and 103.00 feet offset southerly from the north line of said Section 35, North 89 degrees 36 minutes 56 seconds West 158.05 feet; thence North 87 degrees 19 minutes 30 seconds West 150.12 feet; thence along a line parallel to and 97.00 feet offset southerly from said north line of Section 35, North 89 degrees 36 minutes 56 seconds West 401.25 feet; thence North 85 degrees 58 minutes 01 seconds West 502.84 feet; thence North 88 degrees 27 minutes 19 seconds West 296.29 feet; thence along a line parallel to and 59.00 feet offset southerly from said north line of Section 35, North 89 degrees 36 minutes 56 seconds West 700.00 feet; thence South 88 degrees 28 minutes 31 seconds West 300.17 feet; thence along a line parallel to and 69.00 feet offset southerly from said north line of Section 35, North 89 degrees 36 minutes 56 seconds West 85.23 feet, to the west line of the northeast Quarter of said Section 35; thence along a line parallel to and 69.00 feet offset southerly from said north line of Section 35, North 89 degrees 36 minutes 45 seconds West 114.77 feet; thence North 87 degrees 54 minutes 07 seconds West 804.04 feet; thence along a line parallel to and 45.00 feet offset southerly from said north line of Section 35, North 89 degrees 36 minutes 45 seconds West 397.76 feet; thence North 00 degrees 20 minutes 35 seconds West 45.00 feet, to the northerly line of said Section 35; thence along said northerly line of Section 35, North 89 degrees 36 minutes 45 seconds West 1315.81 feet, to the Point of Beginning, situated in Champaign County, Illinois and containing 22.351 acres, more or less (Part of PIN #03-20-26-300-020; Part of PIN #03-20-26-300-021; Part of PIN #03-20-26-400-001; Part of PIN #03-20-35-100-002 and Part of PIN #03-20-35-200-001)

Permanent Easement #1:

A part of the southeast quarter of the southwest quarter of Section 26, Township 19 North, Range 8 East of the Third Principal Meridian, Champaign County, Illinois with bearing datum based on Illinois State Plane Coordinate System, East Zone;

Commencing at the southeast corner or the southwest quarter of Section 16, Township 19 North, Range 8 East of the Third Principal Meridian; thence along the easterly line of said southwest quarter of Section 26, North 00 degrees 38 minutes 43 seconds West 83.01 feet, to the Point of Beginning; thence North 89 degrees 36 minutes 45 seconds West 237.29 feet; thence North 00 degrees 23 minutes 15 seconds East 15.00 feet; thence South 89 degrees 36 minutes 45 seconds East 237.02 feet; thence South 00 degrees 38 minutes 43 seconds East 15.00 feet, to the Point of Beginning, situated in Champaign County, Illinois and containing 0.082 of an acre, more or less (Part of PIN #03-20-26-300-021)

Permanent Easement #2:

A part of the west half of the southwest quarter of Section 26, and a part of the west half of the northwest quarter of Section 26, Township 19 North, Range

8 East of the Third Principal Meridian, Champaign County, Illinois with bearing datum based on Illinois State Plane Coordinate System, East Zone;

Commencing at the southwest corner of Section 26, Township 19 North, Range 8 East of the Third Principal Meridian; thence along the southerly line of said Section 26, South 89 degrees 36 minutes 45 seconds East 1166.28 feet; thence North 00 degrees 23 minutes 15 seconds East 150.00 feet, to the Point of Beginning; thence along a curve to the left having a radius of 300.00 feet, an arc length of 49.50 feet, a chord bearing of North 11 degrees 23 minutes 05 seconds West and a chord length of 49.45 feet; thence North 16 degrees 06 minutes 44 seconds West 1098.24 feet; thence along a curve to the right having a radius of 840.00 feet, an arc length of 285.88 feet, a chord bearing of North 06 degrees 21 minutes 44 seconds West and a chord length of 284.51 feet; thence North 03 degrees 23 minutes 16 seconds East 1031.54 feet; thence along a curve to the left having a radius of 760.00 feet, an arc length of 134.77 feet, a chord bearing of North 01 degrees 41 minutes 32 seconds West and a chord length of 134.59 feet; thence South 89 degrees 42 minutes 45 seconds East 80.55 feet; thence along a curve to the right having a radius of 840.00 feet, an arc length of 139.06 feet, a chord bearing of South 01 degrees 21 minutes 17 seconds East and a chord length of 138.90 feet; thence South 03 degrees 23 minutes 16 seconds West 1031.54 feet; thence along a curve to the left having a radius of 760.00 feet, an arc length of 258.66 feet, a chord bearing of South 06 degrees 21 minutes 44 seconds East and a chord length of 257.41 feet; thence South 16 degrees 06 minutes 44 seconds East 1098.24 feet; thence along a curve to the right having a radius of 380.00 feet, an arc length of 72.58 feet, a chord bearing of South 10 degrees 38 minutes 26 seconds East and a chord length of 72.47 feet; thence North 89 degrees 36 minutes 45 seconds West 80.48 feet, to the Point of Beginning, situated in Champaign County, Illinois and containing 4.775 acres or 208,000 square feet, more or less. (Part of PIN #03–20–26–300–019 and #03–20–26–300–020)

Temporary Easement #1:

A part of Section 26, Township 19 North, Range 8 East of the Third Principal Meridian, Champaign County, Illinois with bearing datum based on Illinois State Plane Coordinate System, East Zone;

Beginning at a point being 91.50 feet normally offset northerly from FAP Route 807 (Curtis Road) centerline station 112 + 31.76; thence North 89 degrees 36 minutes 56 seconds West 20.00 feet; thence South 00 degrees 38 minutes 43 seconds East 15.00 feet; thence North 89 degrees 36 minutes 45 seconds West 137.02 feet; thence North 00 degrees 31 minutes 33 seconds West 113.51 feet; thence North 89 degrees 36 minutes 45 seconds West 80.00 feet; thence South 00 degrees 23 minutes 15 seconds West 10.00 feet; thence North 89 degrees 36 minutes 45 seconds West 50.00 feet;

thence North 00 degrees 23 minutes 15 seconds East 60.00 feet; thence South 89 degrees 36 minutes 45 seconds East 50.00 feet; thence South 00 degrees 23 minutes 15 seconds West 10.00 feet; thence South 89 degrees 36 minutes 45 seconds East 236.07 feet; thence South 00 degrees 38 minutes 43 seconds East 138.52 feet, to the Point of Beginning, situated in Champaign County, Illinois and containing 0.688 of an acre or 29,966 square feet, more or less. (Part of PIN #03–20–26–300–021)

Temporary Easement #2:

A part of Section 26, Township 19 North, Range 8 East of the Third Principal Meridian, Champaign County, Illinois with bearing datum based on Illinois State Plane Coordinate System, East Zone;

Beginning at a point being 102.49 feet normally offset northerly from FAP Route 807 (Curtis Road) centerline station 87 + 50.00; thence North 00 degrees 23 minutes 16 seconds East 46.18 feet; thence South 89 degrees 09 minutes 33 seconds West 99.13 feet; thence North 06 degrees 25 minutes 24 seconds West 90.43 feet; thence North 89 degrees 09 minutes 33 seconds East 210.11 feet; thence South 00 degrees 34 minutes 28 seconds West 70.84 feet; thence South 89 degrees 36 minutes 44 seconds East 100.00 feet; thence South 00 degrees 23 minutes 16 seconds West 67.51 feet; thence North 89 degrees 36 minutes 45 seconds West 200.00 feet, to the Point of Beginning, situated in Champaign County, Illinois and containing 0.686 of an acre or 29,891 square feet more or less. (Part of PIN #03–20–26–300–020)

Temporary Easement #3:

A part of Section 26, Township 19 North, Range 8 East of the Third Principal Meridian, Champaign County, Illinois with bearing datum based on Illinois State Plane Coordinate System, East Zone;

Beginning at a point being 97.50 feet normally offset northerly from FAP Route 807 (Curtis Road) centerline station 97 + 00.00; thence North 35 degrees 20 minutes 49 seconds East 57.33 feet; thence North 16 degrees 06 minutes 44 seconds West 1098.24 feet; thence along a curve to the right having a radius of 845.00 feet, an arc length of 287.59 feet, a chord bearing of North 06 degrees 21 minutes 44 seconds West and a chord length of 286.20 feet; thence North 03 degrees 23 minutes 16 seconds East 1031.54 feet; thence along a curve to the left having a radius of 755.00 feet, an arc length of 134.50 feet, a chord bearing of North 01 degrees 42 minutes 57 seconds West and a chord length of 134.33 feet; thence South 89 degrees 42 minutes 45 seconds East 5.04 feet; thence along a curve to the right having a radius of 760.00 feet, an arc length of 134.77 feet, a chord bearing of South 01 degrees 41 minutes 32 seconds East and a chord length of 134.59 feet; thence South 03 degrees 23 minutes 16 seconds West 1031.54 feet; thence along a curve to the left having a radius of 840.00 feet, an arc length of 285.88 feet, a chord bearing of South 06 degrees 21 minutes 44 seconds East and a chord length of 284.51 feet; thence South 16 degrees 06 minutes 44 seconds East 1098.24 feet; thence along a curve to the right having a radius of 300.00 feet, an arc length of 49.50 feet, a chord bearing of South 11 degrees 23 minutes 05 seconds East and a chord length of 49.45 feet; thence North 89 degrees 36 minutes 45 seconds West 47.73 feet, to the Point of Beginning, situated in Champaign County, Illinois and containing 0.322 acres or 14,034 square feet, more or less. (Part of PIN 03–20–26–300–019 & 03–20–26–300–020)

Temporary Easement #4:

A part of Sections 26 and 35, Township 19 North, Range 8 East of the Third Principal Meridian, Champaign County, Illinois with bearing datum based on Illinois State Plane Coordinate System, East Zone

Beginning at a point being 97.50 feet normally offset northerly from FAP Route 807 (Curtis Road) centerline station 98 + 75.00; thence North 89 degrees 36 minutes 45 seconds West 46.79 feet; thence along a curve to the left having a radius of 380.00 feet, an arc length of 72.58 feet, a chord bearing of North 10 degrees 38 minutes 26 seconds West and a chord length of 72.47 feet; thence North 16 degrees 06 minutes 44 seconds West 1098.24 feet; thence along a curve to the right having a radius of 760.00 feet, an arc length of 258.66 feet, a chord bearing of North 06 degrees 21 minutes 44 seconds West and a chord length of 257.41 feet; thence North 03 degrees 23 minutes 16 seconds East 1031.54 feet; thence along a curve to the left having a radius of 840.00 feet, an arc length of 139.06 feet, a chord bearing of North 01 degrees 21 minutes 17 seconds West and a chord length of 138.90 feet; thence South 89 degrees 42 minutes 45 seconds East 5.03 feet; thence along a curve to the right having a radius of 845.00 feet, an arc length of 139.33 feet, a chord bearing of South 01 degrees 20 minutes 08 seconds East and a chord length of 139.17 feet; thence South 03 degrees 23 minutes 16 seconds West 1031.54 feet; thence along a curve to the left having a radius of 755.00 feet, an arc length of 256.96 feet, a chord bearing of South 06 degrees 21 minutes 44 seconds East and a chord length of 255.72 feet; thence South 16 degrees 06 minutes 44 seconds East 1098.24 feet; thence South 37 degrees 12 minutes 15 seconds East 91.56 feet, to the Point of Beginning, situated in Champaign County, Illinois and containing 0.331 acres or 14,428 square feet, more or less. (Part of PIN 03–20–26–300–019 & 03–20–26–300–020)

Temporary Easement #5:

A part of Sections 26 and 35, Township 19 North, Range 8 East of the Third Principal Meridian, Champaign County, Illinois with bearing datum based on Illinois State Plane Coordinate System, East Zone;

Beginning at a point being 94.00 feet normally offset southerly from FAP Route 807 (Curtis Road) center-

line station 137 + 93.04: thence South 00 degrees 27 minutes 33 seconds East 218.80 feet; thence North 89 degrees 32 minutes 27 seconds East 15.00 feet; thence North 00 degrees 27 minutes 33 seconds West 208.58 feet; thence North 45 degrees 02 minutes 15 seconds West 14.25 feet; thence North 89 degrees 36 minutes 56 seconds West 5.00 feet, to the Point of Beginning, situated in Champaign County, Illinois and containing 0.074 of an acre or 3230 square feet, more or less. (Part of PIN #03–20–35–200–001)

Adolf M. Lo—Parcel 041

Permanent Easement:

A part of Sections 26 and 35, Township 19 North, Range 8 East of the Third Principal Meridian, Champaign County, Illinois with bearing datum based on Illinois State Plane Coordinate System, East Zone;

Beginning at a point being 94.00 feet normally offset southerly from FAP Route 807 (Curtis Road) centerline station 137 + 93.04: thence South 00 degrees 27 minutes 33 seconds East 218.80 feet; thence North 89 degrees 32 minutes 27 seconds East 15.00 feet; thence North 00 degrees 27 minutes 33 seconds West 208.58 feet; thence North 45 degrees 02 minutes 15 seconds West 14.25 feet; thence North 89 degrees 36 minutes 56 seconds West 5.00 feet, to the Point of Beginning, situated in Champaign County, Illinois and containing 0.074 of an acre or 3230 square feet, more or less. (Part of PIN #03–20–35–200–001)

Temporary Easement #1:

A part of Section 26, Township 19 North, Range 8 East of the Third Principal Meridian, Champaign County, Illinois with bearing datum based on Illinois State Plane Coordinate System, East Zone;

Commencing at the southwest corner of the northwest quarter of Section 26, Township 19 North, Range 8 East of the Third Principal Meridian; thence along the west line of said northwest quarter, North 00 degrees 32 minutes 29 seconds West 60.01 feet; thence along the north line of the south 60 feet of the south half of the southwest quarter of the northwest quarter of said Section 26, South 89 degrees 42 minutes 45 seconds East 917.47 feet, to the Point of Beginning; thence along a curve to the left having a radius of 760.00 feet, an arc length of 57.56 feet, a chord bearing of North 08 degrees 56 minutes 32 seconds West and a chord length of 57.55 feet; thence North 11 degrees 06 minutes 44 seconds West 466.55 feet; thence along a curve to the left having a radius of 760.00 feet, an arc length of 93.84 feet, a chord bearing of North 14 degrees 38 minutes 58 seconds West and a chord length of 93.78 feet, to the north line of the south half of the southwest quarter of the northwest quarter of aforesaid Section 26; thence along said north line, North 89 degrees 49 minutes 23 seconds West 5.27 feet; thence along a curve to the right having a radius of 755.00 feet, an arc length of 94.89 feet, a chord bearing of South 14 degrees 42

Point of Beginning; thence North 89 degrees 27 minutes 54 seconds West 282.46 feet; thence South 89 degrees 53 minutes 41 seconds West 89.50 feet, to the westerly line of said Lot 401; thence along said westerly line, South 45 degrees 02 minutes 16 seconds West 11.22 feet; thence South 89 degrees 27 minutes 54 seconds East 277.36 feet; thence South 00 degrees 32 minutes 06 seconds West 10.00 feet; thence South 89 degrees 27 minutes 54 seconds East 102.44 feet, to aforesaid easterly line of Lot 401; thence along said easterly line, North 00 degrees 35 minutes 41 seconds East 19.00 feet, to the Point of Beginning, containing 0.100 acres or 4359 square feet, more or less.

PROSPECT POINT LLC—PARCEL 54

Right of Way

A part of Lot 402 of the Arbour Subdivision No. 4, as per plat recorded as Document Number 92R37248, Champaign County, Illinois, with bearing datum based on Illinois State Plane Coordinate System, East Zone;

Beginning at the northeast corner of the above described Lot 402 of Arbour Subdivision No. 4, thence along the easterly line of said Lot 402, South 00 degrees 31 minutes 44 seconds West 40.00 feet; thence North 23 degrees 44 minutes 15 seconds West 28.52 feet; thence North 83 degrees 07 minutes 30 seconds West 27.17 feet; thence along a line being parallel to and 11.00 feet offset southerly from the northerly line of said Lot 402, North 89 degrees 27 minutes 54 seconds West 242.54 feet, to the westerly line of said Lot 402; thence along said westerly line, North 00 degrees 35 minutes 41 seconds East 11.00 feet, to the northwest corner of said Lot 402; thence along the northerly line of said Lot 402, South 89 degrees 27 minutes 54 seconds East 281.25 feet, to the Point of Beginning, containing 0. 076 of an acre or 3322 square feet, more or less.

Temporary Easement

A part of Lot 402 of the Arbour Meadows Subdivision No. 4, as per plat recorded as Document Number 92R37248, Champaign County, Illinois, with bearing datum based on Illinois State Plane Coordinate System, East Zone:

TE–1

Beginning at the northeast corner of the above described Lot 402; thence along the easterly line of said Lot 402, South 00 degrees 35 minutes 44 seconds West 40.00 feet, to the Point of Beginning; thence North 23 degrees 44 minutes 15 seconds West 28.52 feet; thence North 83 degrees 07 minutes 30 seconds West 27.17 feet; thence North 89 degrees 27 minutes 54 seconds West 242.54 feet, to the westerly line of aforesaid Lot 402; thence along said westerly line, South 00 degrees 35 minutes 41 seconds West 19.00 feet; thence South 89 degrees 27 minutes 54 seconds East 17.56 feet; thence North 00 degrees 32 minutes 06 seconds East 10.00 feet; thence South 89 degrees 27 minutes 54 seconds East 250.00 feet; thence South 00 degrees 32 minutes 06 seconds West 24.00 feet; thence South 89 degrees 27 minutes 54 seconds East 13.72 feet, to the aforesaid easterly line of Lot 402; thence along said easterly line, North 00 degrees 31 minutes 44 seconds East 4.00 feet, to the Point of Beginning, containing 0.064 of an acre or 2808 square feet, more or less.

TE–2

Beginning at a point on the easterly line of the above described Lot 402, said point being offset 196.00 feet normally distant southerly from FAP Route 807 (Curtis Road) centerline; thence along said easterly line of Lot 402, South 00 degrees 31 minutes 44 seconds West 40.00 feet; thence North 89 degrees 28 minutes 16 seconds West 60.00 feet; thence North 00 degrees 31 minutes 44 seconds East 40.00 feet; thence South 89 degrees 28 minutes 16 seconds East 60.00 feet, to the Point of Beginning, containing 0.055 of an acre or 2400 square feet, more or less.

Tracts TE–1 and TE–2 totaling 0.119 of an acre or 5208 square feet, more or less.

MAIN STREET BANK, TRUSTEE—PARCEL 55

Right of Way

All of the Commons area of the Arbour Meadows Subdivision No. 4, as per plat recorded December 24, 1992 in Book "BB" at Page 213 as Document 92R 37248, in the Village of Savoy, Champaign County, Illinois, containing 0.529 of an acre, more or less.

PROSPECT POINT EAST, LLC—PARCEL 56

Temporary Easement

A part of Lot 201 of the Arbour Meadows Subdivision No. 2, as per plat recorded in Plat Book "AA" at Page 251, Champaign County, Illinois, with bearing datum based on Illinois State Plane Coordinate System, East Zone:

Beginning at the northwest corner of the above described Lot 201 of the Arbour Meadows Subdivision No. 2; thence along the northerly line of said Lot 201, South 89 degrees 27 minutes 54 seconds East 15.11 feet; thence South 45 degrees 44 minutes 50 seconds West 21.29 feet, to the westerly line of said Lot 201; thence along said westerly line, North 00 degrees 31 minutes 44 seconds East 15.00 feet, to the Point of Beginning, containing 0.003 of an acre or 113 square feet, more or less.

P.A. 94–1055, Art. 25, § 25–7–103.150, added by P.A. 95–611, § 5, eff. Sept. 11, 2007. Renumbered § 25–5–10 by P.A. 95–876, § 370, eff. Aug. 21, 2008.

This section was renumbered as § 25–5–10 by P.A. 95–876, § 370, eff. Aug. 21, 2008 from § 25–7–103.150 as added by P.A. 95–611, § 5, eff. Sept. 11, 2007.

30/25–5–15. Quick-take; Village of Lake in the Hills

§ 25–5–15.   Quick-take; Village of Lake in the Hills.   Quick-take proceedings under Article 20 may be used for a period of no more than one year after the effective date of this amendatory Act of the 95th General Assembly by the Village of Lake in the Hills for the acquisition of the following described property for runway purposes at the Lake in the Hills Airport:

PART OF THE NORTHEAST QUARTER OF SECTION 17, TOWNSHIP 43 NORTH, RANGE 8, EAST OF THE THIRD PRINCIPAL MERIDIAN AND MORE PARTICULARLY DESCRIBED AS FOLLOWS:

COMMENCING AT THE NORTHEAST COR-NER OF SAID NORTHEAST QUARTER, THENCE SOUTH 00 DEGREES 37 MINUTES 09 SECONDS EAST ALONG THE EAST LINE OF SAID NORTHEAST QUARTER, 1144.93 FEET TO THE POINT OF BEGINNING; THENCE CONTINUING SOUTH 00 DEGREES 37 MINUTES 09 SECONDS EAST ALONG THE EAST LINE OF SAID NORTHEAST QUARTER, 105.12 FEET TO THE SOUTH LINE OF THE PARCEL DESCRIBED IN DOCUMENT NUM-BER 95R011851 AS RECORDED IN THE MCHENRY COUNTY RECORDER'S OFFICE; THENCE SOUTH 89 DEGREES 22 MINUTES 51 SECONDS WEST ALONG THE SOUTH LINE OF THE PARCEL DESCRIBED IN DOCU-MENT NUMBER 95R011851, 593.00 FEET TO THE WEST LINE OF THE PARCEL DE-SCRIBED IN DOCUMENT NUMBER 95R011851; THENCE NORTH 00 DEGREES 37 MINUTES 09 SECONDS WEST, ALONG THE WEST LINE OF THE PARCEL DESCRIBED IN DOCUMENT NUMBER 95R011851, 3.99 FEET; THENCE 79 DEGREES 42 MINUTES 11 SECONDS EAST ALONG A LINE 306.00 FEET NORTHWESTERLY OF AND PARALLEL WITH THE CENTERLINE OF RUNWAY NUM-BER ⁹⁄₂₆, 601.56 FEET TO THE POINT OF BE-GINNING AND CONTAINING 32,351 SQUARE FEET OR 0.743 ACRES MORE OR LESS, ALL IN MCHENRY COUNTY, ILLINOIS, AND EX-CEPTING THAT PART USED FOR ROADWAY PURPOSES.

P.A. 94–1055, Art. 25, § 25–5–15, added by P.A. 95–929, § 5, eff. Aug. 26, 2008. Amended by P.A. 96–328, § 370, eff. Aug. 11, 2009.

P.A. 96–328, § 370, effective August 11, 2009 renumbered another § 25–5–15 relating to Quick-take; City of Champaign as § 25–5–20.

30/25–5–20. Quick-take; City of Champaign

§ 25–5–20. Quick-take; City of Champaign. Quick-take proceedings under Article 20 may be used for a period of no more than one year after the effective date of this amendatory Act of the 95th General Assembly by the City of Champaign for the acquisition of the following properties for the purpose of drainage and other improvements related to the Boneyard Creek Project, including right of way, per-manent easements, and temporary easements:

Parcel A—(PIN 46–21–07–351–014) 112 East Clark Street

Lot 12 in Block 1 of Campbell and Kirkpatrick's Addition to Urbana, now a part of the City of Champaign, as per Plat recorded in Deed Record "E" at Page 352, situated in Champaign County, Illinois.

Parcel B—(PIN 46–21–07–353–005) 111 East White Street

The East 34 feet of Lot 2 of a Subdivision of Block 1 of J. C. Kirkpatrick's Second Addition to the Town of West Urbana, now City of Champaign, as per plat recorded in Deed Record 8 at page 232, in Champaign County, Illinois.

Parcel D—(PIN 46–21–07–353–010) 108 East Stoughton Street

Lot 10 of a Subdivision of Block 1 of J. C. Kirkpat-rick's Second Addition to the Town of West Urbana, now City of Champaign, as per plat recorded in Deed Record 8 at Page 232, in Champaign County, Illinois.

Parcel G (PIN 46–21–07–355–002) 201–½ East Uni-versity Avenue

Tract I—Beginning at the Northeast corner of Lot 6 in Block 2 in Campbell & Kirkpatrick's Addition to Urbana (now a part of the City of Champaign) running thence West 20 feet; thence South 80 feet; thence East 20 feet; thence North 80 feet to the point of beginning, situated in Champaign County, Illinois. Tract II—The West 8 feet of the East 28 feet of the North 80 feet of Lot 6 in Block 2 in Campbell & Kirkpatrick's Addition to Urbana (now a part of the City of Champaign), in Champaign County, Illinois.

Parcel H (PIN 46–21–07–355–001) 201 East Univer-sity Avenue

The West 38 feet of the North 80 feet of Lot 6 in Block 2 of Campbell and Kirkpatrick's Addition to Urbana, now a part of the City of Champaign, as per Plat recorded in Deed Record "E" at page 352, situated in Champaign County, Illinois.

P.A. 94–1055, Art. 25, § 25–5–15, added by P.A. 95–974, § 5, eff. Sept. 22, 2008. Renumbered § 25–5–20 by P.A. 96–328, § 370, eff. Aug. 11, 2009

This section was renumbered as § 25–5–20 by P.A. 96–328, § 370, eff. Aug. 11, 2009 from § 25–5–15 as added by P.A. 95–974, § 5, eff. Sept. 22, 2008.

30/25–5–25. Quick-take; Village of Johnsburg

§ 25–5–25. Quick-take; Village of Johnsburg. Quick-take proceedings under Article 20 may be used for a period of no more than one year after the effective date of this amendatory Act of the 96th General Assembly by the Village of Johnsburg, McHenry County for the acquisition of the following described property for the purpose of constructing a METRA rail station and rail storage yard:

PARCEL 1:

That part of the of the Southwest Quarter, part of the Southeast Quarter of Section 15 and part of the Northeast Quarter of Section 22, Township 45 North, Range 8 East of the Third Principal Meridian, McHenry County, Illinois more particularly described as follows: Beginning at the intersection of the North line of the said Southwest Quarter and the westerly line of the Chicago and Northwestern Railroad; thence southerly along said westerly line to the intersection of the East line of said Southwest Quarter and said westerly line; thence continuing southerly along said westerly line to the intersection of the South line of said Southeast Quarter and said westerly line; thence continuing southerly along said westerly line to the northerly line of F.A.P. Route 420; thence northwesterly along said northerly line to a line lying 530.00 feet westerly of and parallel with the said westerly line of the Chicago and Northwestern Railroad; thence northerly along said parallel line to a line lying 392.00 feet southerly of and parallel with the said North line of the Southwest Quarter; thence northerly along a line which intersects with the said North line of said Southwest Quarter and a line lying 412.05 feet westerly of and parallel with the said westerly line of the Chicago and Northwestern Railroad; thence easterly along said North line to the point of beginning.

PARCEL 2:

That part of the Northwest Quarter of Section 15, Township 45 North, Range 8 East of the Third Principal Meridian, McHenry County, Illinois more particularly described as follows: Beginning at the intersection of the North line of the South Half of said Northwest Quarter and the westerly line of the Chicago and Northwestern Railroad; thence southerly along said westerly line to the South line of the said Northwest Quarter; thence westerly along said South line to a line lying 412.05 feet westerly of and parallel with the said westerly line of the Chicago and Northwestern Railroad; thence northerly along said parallel line to said North line of the said South Half; thence easterly along said North line of said South Half to the point of beginning.

P.A. 94–1055, Art. 25, § 25–5–25, added by P.A. 96–709, § 5, eff. Aug. 25, 2009.

30/25–5–30. Quick-take; Village of Johnsburg

§ 25–5–30. Quick-take; Village of Johnsburg. Quick-take proceedings under Article 20 may be used for a period of no longer than one year after the effective date of this amendatory Act of the 96th General Assembly, by the Village of Johnsburg, McHenry County for the acquisition of the following described property for the purpose of constructing a METRA rail station and rail storage yard:

LEGAL DESCRIPTION

THAT PART OF SECTION 15 AND 22, IN TOWNSHIP 45 NORTH, RANGE 8 EAST OF THE THIRD PRINCIPAL MERIDIAN, DESCRIBED AS FOLLOWS: BEGINNING AT THE INTERSECTION OF THE WESTERLY RIGHT–OF–WAY LINE OF THE UNION PACIFIC RAILROAD (FORMERLY THE CHICAGO AND NORTHWESTERN RAILWAY) AND THE NORTHEASTERLY RIGHT–OF–WAY LINE OF FEDERAL AID ROUTE 420 (ALSO KNOWN AS FEDERAL AID ROUTE 201); THENCE NORTH 61 DEGREES 54 MINUTES 08 SECONDS WEST (BEARINGS BASED ON ILLINOIS STATE PLANE COORDINATES EAST ZONE 1983 DATUM) ALONG SAID NORTHEASTERLY RIGHT–OF–WAY LINE, A DISTANCE OF 503.21 FEET TO A BEND POINT IN SAID NORTHEASTERLY RIGHT–OF–WAY LINE; THENCE NORTH 63 DEGREES 49 MINUTES 56 SECONDS WEST ALONG SAID NORTHEASTERLY RIGHT–OF–WAY LINE, A DISTANCE OF 837.29 FEET TO A BEND POINT IN SAID NORTHEASTERLY RIGHT–OF–WAY LINE; THENCE NORTH 64 DEGREES 23 MINUTES 38 SECONDS WEST ALONG SAID NORTHEASTERLY RIGHT–OF–WAY LINE, A DISTANCE OF 81.77 FEET; THENCE NORTH 11 DEGREES 48 MINUTES 49 SECONDS WEST, A DISTANCE OF 737.72 FEET; THENCE NORTH 35 DEGREES 16 MINUTES 32 SECONDS WEST, A DISTANCE OF 1001.50 FEET; THENCE NORTH 33 DEGREES 34 MINUTES 33 SECONDS WEST, A DISTANCE OF 1019.96 FEET TO A POINT OF CURVATURE; THENCE NORTHERLY ALONG A CURVE, CONCAVE TO THE EAST, HAVING A RADIUS OF 600.00 FEET, AN ARC LENGTH OF 346.77 FEET TO A POINT OF TANGENCY, THE CHORD OF SAID CURVE HAVING A LENGTH OF 341.97 FEET AND A BEARING OF NORTH 17 DEGREES 01 MINUTES 07 SECONDS WEST; THENCE NORTH 00 DEGREES 27 MINUTES 41 SECONDS WEST, A DISTANCE OF 518.80 FEET TO THE POINT OF INTERSECTION WITH A LINE 80.00 FEET SOUTH OF AND PARALLEL WITH THE NORTH LINE OF THE SOUTH HALF OF THE NORTHWEST QUARTER OF SAID SECTION 15; THENCE SOUTH 89 DEGREES 04 MINUTES 23 SECONDS EAST ALONG SAID LINE 80.00 FEET SOUTH OF AND PARALLEL WITH THE NORTH LINE OF THE SOUTH HALF OF THE NORTHWEST QUARTER OF SAID SECTION 15, A DISTANCE OF 323.79 FEET; THENCE SOUTH 00 DEGREES 27 MINUTES 41 SECONDS EAST, A DISTANCE OF 545.39 FEET; THENCE SOUTH 33 DEGREES 34 MINUTES 33 SECONDS EAST, A DISTANCE OF

563.07 FEET; THENCE SOUTH 86 DEGREES 02 MINUTES 35 SECONDS EAST, A DISTANCE OF 289.88 FEET; THENCE SOUTH 3 DEGREES 57 MINUTES 25 SECONDS WEST, A DISTANCE OF 242.15 FEET; THENCE SOUTH 51 DEGREES 02 MINUTES 02 SECONDS EAST, A DISTANCE OF 159. 41 FEET; THENCE NORTH 88 DEGREES 00 MINUTES 32 SECONDS EAST, A DISTANCE OF 750.85 FEET TO THE POINT OF INTERSECTION WITH SAID WESTERLY RIGHT–OF–WAY LINE OF THE UNION PACIFIC RAILROAD; THENCE SOUTH 19 DEGREES 11 MINUTES 49 SECONDS EAST ALONG SAID WESTERLY RIGHT–OF–WAY LINE, A DISTANCE OF 2677.76 FEET TO THE POINT OF BEGINNING, IN McHENRY COUNTY, ILLINOIS.

P.A. 94–1055, Art. 25, § 25–5–30, added by P.A. 96–1525, § 5, eff. Feb. 14, 2011. Amended by P.A. 97–813, § 675, eff. July 13, 2012.

30/25–5–35. Quick-take; City of Country Club Hills

§ 25–5–35. Quick-take; City of Country Club Hills. Quick-take proceedings under Article 20 may be used for a period of no longer than one year from the effective date of this amendatory Act of the 96th General Assembly by the City of Country Club Hills for the acquisition of the following described property for the purpose of building streets, roadways, or other public improvements to serve the City's I–57/I–80 Tax Increment Financing District:

That part of Lots 2, 4 through 10 (both inclusive) and 16 in Gatling Country Club Hills Resubdivision being a Resubdivision of part of Gatling Country Club Hills Subdivision in the Northeast Quarter of Section 27, Township 36 North, Range 13 East of the Third Principal Meridian, South of the Indian Boundary Line, according to the plat thereof recorded June 9, 2004 as Document No. 0416145163, taken as a tract and described as follows:

Beginning at the Northwesterly corner of said Lot 10; thence North 89 Degrees 58 Minutes 52 Seconds West along the North line of said Lot 16, 100.47 feet to the Northeast corner of said Lot 16; thence South 00 Degrees 01 Minute 08 Seconds West along the West line of Lot 16, 24.00 feet; thence North 89 Degrees 58 Minutes 52 Seconds West, 12.20 Feet; thence South 11 Degrees 27 Minutes 13 Seconds East, 46.94 feet; thence South 00 Degrees 00 Minutes 31 Seconds East, 132.33 feet to a point of curve; thence Southerly along a curve concave Westerly having a radius of 37.73 feet and a central angle of 50 Degrees 50 Minutes 17 Seconds a distance of 30.81 feet to a point of tangency, thence South 50 Degrees 05 Minutes 28 Seconds West, 30.65 feet; thence South 90 Degrees 00 Minutes 00 Seconds West, 1177.04 feet to the West line of said Resubdivision; thence South 00 Degrees 00

Minutes 00 Seconds West along said last described line, 45.00 feet; thence South 90 Degrees 00 Minutes 00 Seconds East, 1192.95 feet; thence South 45 Degrees 00 Minutes 00 Seconds East, 54.13 feet; thence South 00 Degrees 03 Minutes 38 Seconds East, 18.73 feet; thence North 89 Degrees 56 Minutes 22 Seconds East, 45.00 feet; thence North 00 Degrees 03 Minutes 38 Seconds West, 20.23 feet; thence North 45 Degrees 00 Minutes 00 Seconds, 43.46 feet; thence North 90 Degrees 00 Minutes 00 Seconds East, 163.27 feet; thence North 00 Degrees 00 Minutes 00 Seconds West, 50.00 feet; thence North 89 Degrees 59 Minutes 59 Seconds West, 69.27 feet; thence North 85 Degrees 04 Minutes 24 Seconds West, 51.65 feet; thence North 74 Degrees 17 Minutes 00 Seconds West, 26.77 feet; thence North 00 Degrees 00 Minutes 00 Seconds East, 8.29 feet; thence North 45 Degrees 00 Minutes 00 Seconds West, 43.54 feet; thence North 00 Degrees 00 Minutes 00 Seconds East, 133.54 feet; thence North 19 Degrees 33 Minutes 58 Seconds East, 69.77 feet to the point of beginning, all in Cook County, Illinois.

P.A. 94–1055, Art. 25, § 25–5–30, added by P.A. 96–1537, § 5, eff. March 4, 2011. Renumbered as § 25–5–35 by P.A. 97–813, § 675, eff. July 13, 2012.

30/25–5–40. Quick-take; Will County

§ 25–5–40. Quick-take; Will County. Quick-take proceedings under Article 20 may be used for a period of one year after the effective date of this amendatory Act of the 97th General Assembly by Will County for the acquisition of property to be used for the reconstruction of the Weber Road (County Highway 88) and Renwick Road (County Highway 36) intersection, as follows:

PARCEL 0001

The east 30.00 feet of that part of Lot 6 in McGilvray Acres, being a subdivision of part of the Northeast Quarter of Section 19, Township 36 North, Range 10 East of the Third Principal Meridian, according to the plat thereof recorded December 15, 1965, as Document No. R65–11631, lying southerly of a line described as follows: Beginning at a point on the west line of Lot 6, said point being 110.00 feet south of the north line of said lot; thence southeasterly to a point on the east line of said lot, said point being 114.00 feet south of the north line of said Lot 6

Together with

That part of the east half of the Northeast Quarter of Section 19, Township 36 North, Range 10 East of the Third Principal Meridian lying south of the south line (and easterly projection thereof) of aforementioned Lot 6 in McGilvray Acres, lying northerly of the north line of McGilvray Drive, and lying east of the east line of McGilvray Acres Unit No. 3, according to the plat thereof recorded May 25, 1973, as Document No. R73–14934 bounded by a line described as follows, to wit: Beginning at the intersection of the west line of

Weber Road as dedicated by Document No. R78–19275, recorded May 25, 1978 with the north line of McGilvray Drive as dedicated by Document No. R69–20184, recorded October 30, 1969; thence South 89 Degrees 25 Minutes 29 Seconds West, (on an assumed bearing) along the north line of said McGilvray Drive, 70.00 feet; thence North 44 Degrees 42 Minutes 59 Seconds East, 71.07 feet to a point in the west line of the east 70.00 feet of the Northeast Quarter of aforesaid Section 19; thence North 00 Degrees 00 Minutes 29 Seconds East, along said west line, 46.02 to a point in the south line of aforementioned Lot 6 in McGilvray Acres; thence North 89 Degrees 39 Minutes 49 Seconds East, along said south line, 20.00 feet to a point in the aforementioned west line of Weber Road; thence South 00 Degrees 00 Minutes 29 Seconds West, along said west line, 95.94 feet to the point of beginning. All situated in Will County, Illinois.

Said parcel containing 6,686 square feet, (0.154 acres) of land, more or less.

PARCEL 0002

The east 30.00 feet of the north 114.00 feet of Lot 6 in McGilvray Acres, being a subdivision of part of the Northeast Quarter of Section 19, Township 36 North, Range 10 East of the Third Principal Meridian, according to the plat thereof recorded December 15, 1965, as Document No. R65–11631, in Will County, Illinois, excepting therefrom that part of the north 114.00 feet of said Lot 6 described as beginning at a point on the west line of said Lot 6, said point being 110 feet south of the north line of said lot; thence southeasterly to a point on the east line of said lot, said point being 114 feet south of the north line of said lot; thence west parallel to the north line of said lot, 290 feet to the west line of said lot; thence north 4 feet to the point of beginning. Situated in the County of Will and State of Illinois.

Said parcel containing 3,414 square feet, (0.078 acres) of land, more or less.

PARCEL 0004

The east 30.00 feet of Lot 4 in McGilvray Acres, being a subdivision of part of the Northeast Quarter of Section 19, Township 36 North, Range 10 East of the Third Principal Meridian, according to the plat thereof recorded December 15, 1965, as Document No. R65–11631. Situated in Will County, Illinois.

Said parcel containing 3,960 square feet, (0.091 acres) of land, more or less.

PARCEL 0005

The east 30.00 feet of Lot 3 in McGilvray Acres, being a subdivision of part of the Northeast Quarter of Section 19, Township 36 North, Range 10 East of the Third Principal Meridian, according to the plat thereof recorded December 15, 1965, as Document No. R65–11631. Situated in Will County, Illinois.

Said parcel containing 3,960 square feet, (0.091 acres) of land, more or less.

PARCEL 0006

The east 30.00 feet of Lot 2 in McGilvray Acres, being a subdivision of part of the Northeast Quarter of Section 19, Township 36 North, Range 10 East of the Third Principal Meridian, according to the plat thereof recorded December 15, 1965, as Document No. R65–11631. Situated in Will County, Illinois.

Said parcel containing 3,960 square feet, (0.091 acres) of land, more or less.

PARCEL 0007

The east 30.00 feet of Lot 1 in McGilvray Acres, being a subdivision of part of the Northeast Quarter of Section 19, Township 36 North, Range 10 East of the Third Principal Meridian, according to the plat thereof recorded December 15, 1965, as Document No. R65–11631. Situated in Will County, Illinois.

Said parcel containing 3,960 square feet, (0.091 acres) of land, more or less.

PARCEL 0007 T.E.

The south 50.00 feet of the north 64.00 feet of the west 10.00 feet of the east 40.00 feet of Lot 1 in McGilvray Acres, being a subdivision of part of the Northeast Quarter of Section 19, Township 36 North, Range 10 East of the Third Principal Meridian, according to the plat thereof recorded December 15, 1965, as Document No. R65–11631. Situated in Will County, Illinois.

Said parcel containing 500 square feet, (.011 Acres) of land, more or less.

PARCEL 0008

The west 20.00 feet of the east 70.00 feet of the south 132.00 feet of the north 1,056.00 feet of the east 330.00 feet of the Northeast Quarter of Section 19, Township 36 North, Range 10 East of the Third Principal Meridian, in Will County, Illinois. Said parcel containing 2,640 square feet, (0.061 acres) of land, more or less.

PARCEL 0008 T.E.

That part of the south 132.00 feet of the north 1,056.00 feet of the Northeast Quarter of Section 19, Township 36 North, Range 10 East of the Third Principal Meridian, bounded by a line described as follows, to wit: Commencing at the intersection of the south line of the north 1,056.00 feet of the aforesaid Northeast Quarter with the west line of Weber Road according to Document Numbers R83–13447 and R85–05784, said line also being the west line of the east 50.00 feet of said Northeast Quarter; thence South 89 Degrees 39 Minutes 49 Seconds West, along the south line of the north 1,056.00 feet of said Northeast Quarter, 20.00 feet; thence North 00 Degrees 00 Minutes 29 Seconds East, parallel with the east line of said Northeast Quarter, 5.00 feet to the Point of Beginning; thence South 89 Degrees 39 Minutes 49 Seconds West, parallel with the north line of said Northeast

Quarter, 10.00 feet; thence North 00 Degrees 00 Minutes 29 Seconds East, parallel with the east line of said Northeast Quarter, 50.00 feet; thence North 89 Degrees 39 Minutes 49 Seconds East, parallel with the north line of said Northeast Quarter, 10.00 feet; thence South 00 Degrees 00 Minutes 29 Seconds West, parallel with the east line of said Northeast Quarter, 50.00 feet to the Point of Beginning, in Will County, Illinois. Said parcel containing 500 square feet, (0.011 Acres) of land, more or less.

PARCEL 0009

The west 20.00 feet of the east 70.00 feet of the south 132.00 feet of the north 924.00 feet of the east 330.00 feet of the Northeast Quarter of Section 19, Township 36 North, Range 10 East of the Third Principal Meridian, in Will County, Illinois. Said parcel containing 2,640 square feet, (0.061 acres) of land, more or less.

PARCEL 0010

The west 20.00 feet of the east 70.00 feet of the south 120.00 feet of the north 792.00 feet of the east 330.00 feet of the Northeast Quarter of Section 19, Township 36 North, Range 10 East of the Third Principal Meridian, in Will County, Illinois. Said parcel containing 2,400 square feet, (0.055 acres) of land, more or less.

PARCEL 0011

The west 20.00 feet of the east 70.00 feet of the south 132.00 feet of the north 672.00 feet of the east 330.00 feet of the Northeast Quarter of Section 19, Township 36 North, Range 10 East of the Third Principal Meridian, in Will County, Illinois. Said parcel containing 2,640 square feet, (0.061 acres) of land, more or less.

PARCEL 0012

The west 20.00 feet of the east 70.00 feet of the south 144.00 feet of the north 540.00 feet of the east 330.00 feet of the Northeast Quarter of Section 19, Township 36 North, Range 10 East of the Third Principal Meridian, in Will County, Illinois. Said parcel containing 2,880 square feet, (0.066 acres) of land, more or less.

PARCEL 0013

The west 20.00 feet of the east 70.00 feet of the south 132.00 feet of the north 396.00 feet of the east 330.00 feet of the Northeast Quarter of Section 19, Township 36 North, Range 10 East of the Third Principal Meridian, in Will County, Illinois. Said parcel containing 2,640 square feet, (0.061 acres) of land, more or less.

PARCEL 0014

That part of the North 264.00 feet of the East 330.00 feet of the Northeast Quarter of Section 19, Township 36 North, Range 10 East of the Third Principal Meridian, bounded by a line described as follows: Beginning at the point of intersection of the south line of the north 264.00 feet of the East 330.00 feet of said Northeast Quarter with the west line of the East 50.00 feet of said Northeast Quarter, said line being the west line of Weber Road according to Document R78–31739; thence South 89 Degrees 39 Minutes 49 Seconds West, on an assumed bearing, along the south

line of the North 264.00 feet of said Northeast Quarter, 20.00 feet to a point in the west line of the East 70.00 feet of said Northeast Quarter; thence North 0 Degrees 00 Minutes 29 Seconds East, along the west line of the East 70.00 feet of said Northeast Quarter, 188.23 feet; thence North 45 Degrees 12 Minutes 33 Seconds West, 37.07 feet to a point in the south line of Renwick Road, according to Document No. 538055; thence South 89 Degrees 34 Minutes 24 Seconds West, along said south line, 233.70 feet to the west line of the East 330.00 feet of said Northeast Quarter; thence North 0 Degrees 00 Minutes 29 Seconds East, along said line, 49.87 feet to the north line of the Northeast Quarter of said Section 19; thence North 89 Degrees 39 Minutes 49 Seconds East, along said north line, 280.01 feet to the aforementioned west line of Weber Road; thence South 0 Degrees 00 Minutes 29 Seconds West, along said west line, 264.00 feet to the point of beginning, all in Will County, Illinois.

Said parcel containing 0.426 Acres of land, more or less, of which 0.319 Acres of land, more or less has been previously dedicated for roadway purposes by Document No. 538055.

PARCEL 0014 T.E.

That part of the North 264.00 feet of the East 330.00 feet of the Northeast Quarter of Section 19, Township 36 North, Range 10 East of the Third Principal Meridian, bounded by a line described as follows: Commencing at the intersection of the west line of the East 330.00 feet of said Northeast Quarter with the north line of said Northeast Quarter; thence, on an assumed bearing, South 00 Degrees 00 Minutes 29 Seconds West, along the west line of the East 330.00 of said Northeast Quarter, 49.87 feet to a point in the south line of Renwick Road according to Document No. 538055; thence North 89 Degrees 34 Minutes 24 Seconds East, along the south line of Renwick Road aforesaid, 50.00 feet to the point of beginning; thence continuing North 89 Degrees 34 Minutes 24 Seconds East, along the south line of Renwick Road aforesaid, 65.00 feet; thence South 00 Degrees 25 Minutes 36 Seconds East, perpendicular to the last described course, 10.00 feet; thence South 89 Degrees 34 Minutes 24 Seconds West, parallel with the south line of Renwick Road aforesaid, 65.00 feet; thence North 00 Degrees 25 Minutes 36 Seconds West, perpendicular to the last described course, 10.00 feet to the Point of Beginning, in Will County, Illinois.

Said parcel containing 650 square feet, (0.015 Acres) of land, more or less.

PARCEL 0014 T.E.–A

That part of the North 264.00 feet of the East 330.00 feet of the Northeast Quarter of Section 19, Township 36 North, Range 10 East of the Third Principal Meridian, bounded by a line described as follows: Beginning at the intersection of the south line of the North 264.00 feet of the East 330.00 feet of said Northeast Quarter with the west line of the East 70.00 feet of said Northeast Quarter; thence South 89 Degrees 39 Minutes 49 Seconds West, along the south line of said North 264.00 feet of said Northeast Quarter, 10.00 feet; thence North 00 Degrees 00 Minutes 29 Seconds East, along the west line of the East 80.00 feet of said Northeast Quarter, 65.00 feet; thence North 89 Degrees 39 Minutes 49 Seconds East, perpendicular to the last described course, 5.00 feet; thence North 00 Degrees 00 Minutes 29 Seconds East, along the west line of the East 75.00 feet of said Northeast Quarter, 121.18 feet; thence North 45 Degrees 12 Minutes 33 Seconds West, 39.95 feet to a point in the south line of Renwick Road according to Document No. 538055; thence North 89 Degrees 34 Minutes 24 Seconds East, along said south line of Renwick Road, 7.04 feet; thence South 45 Degrees 12 Minutes 33 Seconds East, 37.07 feet to a point in the west line of the East 70.00 feet of the aforesaid Northeast Quarter of said Section 19; thence South 00 Degrees 00 Minutes 29 Seconds West, along said west line, 188.23 feet to the point of beginning, in Will County, Illinois.

Said parcel containing 1,454 square feet (0.033 Acres) of land, more or less.

PARCEL 0022

The south 65.00 feet of the west 60.00 feet of the East Half of the Southwest Quarter of Section 17, Township 36 North, Range 10 East of the Third Principal Meridian. All situated in Will County, Illinois.

Said parcel containing 0.089 acres, more or less of which 0.069 acres, more or less, has been previously dedicated for roadway purposes by Document No.'s 538058 and 538059.

PARCEL 0023

The south 65.00 feet of the east 440.00 feet of the west 500.00 feet of the East Half of the Southwest Quarter of Section 17, Township 36 North, Range 10 East of the Third Principal Meridian. All situated in Will County, Illinois.

Said parcel containing 0.657 acres, more or less of which 0.509 acres, more or less, has been previously dedicated for roadway purposes by Document No.'s 538058 and 538059.

PARCEL 0024

That part of Lot C in Lakewood Falls Unit 7C being a subdivision of part of the Southeast Quarter of Section 18, Township 36 North, Range 10 East of the Third Principal Meridian, according to the plat thereof recorded August 26, 2002 as Document Number R2002–138021 bounded by a line described as follows, to wit: Beginning at the southwest corner of said Lot C; thence North 0 Degrees 25 Minutes 36 Seconds West (assumed)(North 02 Degrees 04 Minutes 21 Seconds West, record) along the west line of said Lot C, also being the east line of Zachary Drive, 31.21 feet; thence northerly along the arc of a curve right, tangent to the last described course and having a radius of 470.00 feet, the chord of which bears North

01 Degrees 19 Minutes 45 seconds East, an arc distance of 28.81 feet; thence South 44 Degrees 54 Minutes 59 Seconds East, 70.09 feet to a point in the north line of the south 10.00 feet of said Lot C; thence North 89 Degrees 34 Minutes 24 Seconds East (North 87 Degrees 55 Minutes 39 Seconds East, record), parallel with the north line of Renwick Road, as dedicated by aforementioned Document Number R2002–138021, a distance of 225.90 feet to a point in the east line of said Lot C; thence South 0 Degrees 00 Minutes 11 Seconds East (South 1 Degree 38 Minutes 56 Seconds East, record) along said east line, 10. 00 feet to the southeast corner of said Lot C, also being the north line of Renwick Road, aforesaid; thence South 89 Degrees 34 Minutes 24 Seconds West (South 87 Degrees 55 Minutes 39 Seconds West, record), along said north line of Renwick Road, 275.82 feet to the point of beginning. All situated in Will County, Illinois.

Said parcel containing 4,022 Sq. Ft., (0.092 acres) of land, more or less.

PARCEL 0025

That part of Lot B in Lakewood Falls Unit 7C being a subdivision of part of the Southeast Quarter of Section 18, Township 36 North, Range 10 East of the Third Principal Meridian, according to the plat thereof recorded August 26, 2002 as Document Number R2002–138021 bounded by a line described as follows, to wit: Beginning at the southeast corner of said Lot B; thence South 89 Degrees 34 Minutes 24 Seconds West (assumed bearing)(South 87 Degrees 55 Minutes 39 Seconds West, record), along the south line of said Lot B, also being the north line of Renwick Road, 206.11 feet; thence North 0 Degrees 25 Minutes 36 Seconds West, perpendicular to the last described course, 10.00 feet to the north line of the south 10.00 feet of said Lot B; thence North 89 Degrees 34 Minutes 24 Seconds East, parallel with the north line of Renwick Road, aforesaid, 156.11 feet; thence North 45 Degrees 01 Minutes 05 Seconds East, 71.27 feet to a point in the east line of said Lot B, also being the west line of Zachary Drive; thence southerly along the arc of a curve left, along the West line of said Zachary Drive, not tangent to the last described course, having a radius of 530.00 feet, the chord of which bears South 01 Degrees 07 Minutes 49 Seconds West, an arc distance of 28.80 feet; thence South 0 Degrees 25 Minutes 36 Seconds East, tangent to the last described curve, continuing along said west line of Zachary Drive, 31.21 feet to the point of beginning. All situated in Will County, Illinois.

Said parcel containing 3,299 Sq. Ft., (0.076 acres) of land, more or less

PARCEL 0026

That part of the north 258.71 feet of the west 259.71 feet of the Northwest Quarter of Section 20, Township 36 North, Range 10 East of the Third Principal Meridian, bounded by a line described as follows: Beginning at the point intersection of the south line of Renwick Road as dedicated by Document Number 538061, recorded January 15, 1941 with the east line of the west 259.71 feet of said Northwest Quarter, said point being 49.40 feet south from the north line of said Northwest Quarter when measured along the east line of the west 259.71 feet of said Northwest Quarter; thence South 00 Degrees 00 Minutes 29 Seconds West, on an assumed bearing, parallel with the west line of said Northwest Quarter, along the east line of the west 259.71 feet of said Northwest Quarter, 10.60 feet to a point in the south line of the north 60.00 feet of said Northwest Quarter; thence South 89 Degrees 31 Minutes 14 Seconds West, parallel with the north line of said Northwest Quarter, along the south line of the north 60.00 feet of said Northwest Quarter, 167.59 feet; thence South 44 Degrees 45 Minutes 52 Seconds West, 31.43 feet to a point in the east line of the west 70.00 feet of said Northwest Quarter; thence South 00 Degrees 00 Minutes 29 Seconds West, parallel with the west line of said Northwest Quarter, along the east line of the west 70.00 feet of said Northwest Quarter, 176.59 feet to a point in the south line of the north 258.71 feet of said Northwest Quarter; thence South 89 Degrees 31 Minutes 14 Seconds West, parallel with the north line of said Northwest Quarter, along the south line of the north 258.71 feet of said Northwest Quarter, 10.00 feet to a point in the east line of the west 60.00 feet of said Northwest Quarter said line being the east line of Weber Road according to the Plat of Dedication to the Will County Highway Department recorded October 28, 1996 as Document R96–096956; thence North 00 Degrees 00 Minutes 29 Seconds East, along said east line, 174.35 feet (173.72 feet record); thence North 44 Degrees 46 Minutes 10 Seconds East, along the southeasterly line of Weber Road according to aforementioned Document R96–0969056, a distance of 49.71 feet to a point in the south line of Renwick Road according to aforementioned Document Number 538061; thence South 89 Degrees 31 Minutes 52 Seconds West, along said line, 45.00 feet to the east line of the west 50.00 feet of said Section 20, also being the east line of Weber Road according to Condemnation Proceedings No. 81ED22 in the Circuit Court of the 12th Judicial District, Will County as adjudicated on February 18, 1983; thence North 00 Degrees 00 Minutes 29 Seconds East, along said line, 49.36 feet to the North line of the Northwest Quarter of said Section 20; thence North 89 Degrees 31 Minutes 14 Seconds West, along said north line, 209.72 feet to the east line of the west 259.71 feet of the Northwest Quarter of said Section 20; thence South 00 Degrees 00 Minutes 29 Seconds West, along said line, 49.40 feet to the point of beginning. All situated in Will County, Illinois.

Said parcel containing 0.324 acres of land more or less, of which 0.238 acres, more or less, has been previously dedicated for roadway purposes by Document No. 538061.

PARCEL 0026 T.E.

That part of the north 258.71 feet of the west 259.71 feet of the Northwest Quarter of Section 20, Township 36 North, Range 10 East of the Third Principal Meridian, bounded by a line described as follows: Commencing at the point intersection of the south line of the north 258.71 feet of said Northwest Quarter with the east line of the west 70.00 feet of said Northwest Quarter, when measured perpendicular to the north and west lines thereof; thence North 00 Degrees 00 Minutes 29 Seconds East, along the east line of the west 70.00 feet of said Northwest Quarter, 25.48 feet to the point of beginning; thence South 89 Degrees 59 Minutes 31 Seconds East, perpendicular to the last described course, 10.00 feet, thence North 00 Degrees 00 Minutes 29 Seconds East, along the east line of the west 80.00 feet of said Northwest Quarter, 65.00 feet; thence North 89 Degrees 59 Minutes 31 Seconds West, perpendicular to the last described course, 5.00 feet to a point in the east line of the west 75.00 feet of said Northwest Quarter; thence North 00 Degrees 00 Minutes 29 Seconds East, along the east line of the west 75.00 feet of said Northwest Quarter, 84.04 feet; thence North 44 Degrees 45 Minutes 52 Seconds East, 27.31 feet to a point in the south line of the north 65.00 feet of said Northwest Quarter of said Section 20; thence North 89 Degrees 31 Minutes 14 Seconds East, along said line, 45.10 feet; thence South 00 Degrees 28 Minutes 46 Seconds East, perpendicular to the last described course, 5.00 feet; thence North 89 Degrees 31 Minutes 14 Seconds East, perpendicular to the last described course, 65.00 feet; thence North 00 Degrees 28 Minutes 46 Seconds West, perpendicular to the last described course, 5.00 feet to a point in the south line of the north 65.00 feet of said Northwest Quarter of said Section 20; thence North 89 Degrees 31 Minutes 14 Seconds East, along said line, 55.38 feet to a point in the east line of the west 259.71 feet of said Northwest Quarter of said Section 20; thence North 00 Degrees 00 Minutes 29 Seconds East, along said east line, 5.00 feet to a point in the south line of the north 60.00 feet of said Northwest Quarter of said Section 20; thence South 89 Degrees 31 Minutes 14 Seconds West, along said south line of the north 60.00 feet of said Northwest Quarter of said Section 20, a distance of 167.59 feet; thence South 44 Degrees 45 Minutes 52 Seconds West, 31.43 feet to a point in the east line of the west 70.00 feet of said Northwest Quarter of said Section 20; thence South 00 Degrees 00 Minutes 29 Seconds West, along said east line of the west 70.00 feet of said Northwest Quarter of said Section 20, a distance of 151.11 feet to the point of beginning. All situated in Will County, Illinois.

Said parcel containing 2,380 square feet, (0.055 acres) of land more or less

PARCEL 0028

The north 60.00 feet of the west 80.00 feet of the East Half of the Northwest Quarter and the north 60.00 feet of the east 20.00 feet of the West Half of the

Northwest Quarter of Section 20, Township 36 North, Range 10 East of the Third Principal Meridian. All situated in Will County, Illinois. Said parcel containing 0.138 acres, more or less of which 0.114 acres, more or less, has been previously dedicated for roadway purposes by Document No. 538061.

PARCEL 0029

That part of the north 60.00 feet of the East Half of the Northwest Quarter of Section 20, except the west 80.00 feet thereof, Township 36 North, Range 10 East of the Third Principal Meridian, bounded by a line described as follows: Beginning at the point intersection of the south line of north 60.00 feet of said Northwest Quarter with the east line of the west 80.00 feet of the East Half of said Northwest Quarter; thence North 00 Degrees 00 Minutes 42 Seconds West, on an assumed bearing along the east line of the west 80.00 feet of the East Half of said Northwest Quarter, a distance of 60.00 feet to the north line of the Northwest Quarter of said Section 20; thence North 89 Degrees 31 Minutes 14 Seconds East, along said north line, 106.52 feet; thence South 0 Degrees 28 Minutes 46 Seconds East, perpendicular to the north line of said Northwest Quarter, 60.00 feet to a point of intersection with a line 60.00 feet south from and parallel with the north line of said Northwest Quarter when measured perpendicular thereto; thence South 89 Degrees 31 Minutes 14 Seconds West, along said parallel line, perpendicular to the last described course, 107.01 feet to the point of beginning. All situated in Will County, Illinois.

Said parcel containing 0.148 acres, more or less of which 0.122 Acres, more or less, has been previously dedicated for roadway purposes by Document No. 538061.

PARCEL 0030 T.E.

That part of Lot 6 in Crest Hill Business Center being a subdivision of part of the Northwest Quarter of Section 20, Township 36 North, Range 10 East of the Third Principal Meridian, according to the plat thereof recorded July 25, 2005 as Document No. R2005124097, bounded by a line described as follows: Beginning at the Northeast corner of Lot 6, thence South 00 Degrees 28 Minutes 09 Seconds East (South 02 Degrees 06 Minutes 31 Seconds East record), along the east line of said Lot 6 a distance of 65.00 feet; thence South 89 Degrees 31 Minutes 14 Seconds West, parallel with the north line of said Lot 6, a distance of 44.46 feet; thence North 00 Degrees 28 Minutes 09 Seconds West, parallel with the east line of said Lot 6, a distance of 65.00 feet to the north line of said Lot 6, also being the south line of Renwick Road as dedicated by aforementioned Document No. R2005124097; thence North 89 Degrees 31 Minutes 14 Seconds East (North 87 Degrees 53 Minutes 29 Seconds East record), along the north line of said Lot 6, also being the south line of Renwick Road, 44.46 feet to the point of beginning. All situated in Will County, Illinois.

Said parcel containing 2,890 square feet, (0.066 acres) of land more or less

PARCEL 0031 T.E.

That part of Lot 7 in Crest Hill Business Center being a subdivision of part of the Northwest Quarter of Section 20, Township 36 North, Range 10 East of the Third Principal Meridian, according to the plat thereof recorded July 25, 2005 as Document No. R2005124097, bounded by a line described as follows: Beginning at the Northwest corner of Lot 7, thence South 00 Degrees 28 Minutes 09 Seconds East (South 02 Degrees 06 Minutes 31 Seconds East record), along the west line of said Lot 7 a distance of 65.00 feet; thence North 89 Degrees 31 Minutes 14 Seconds East, parallel with the north line of said Lot 7, a distance of 30.54 feet; thence North 00 Degrees 28 Minutes 09 Seconds West, parallel with the west line of said Lot 7, a distance of 65.00 feet to the north line of said Lot 7, also being the south line of Renwick Road as dedicated by aforementioned Document No. R2005124097; thence South 89 Degrees 31 Minutes 14 Seconds West (South 87 Degrees 53 Minutes 29 Seconds West, record), along the north line of said Lot 7, also being the south line of Renwick Road, 30.54 feet to the point of beginning. All situated in Will County, Illinois.

Said parcel containing 1,985 square feet, (0.046 acres) of land more or less

PARCEL 0032 T.E.

That part of Outlot A of Rose Subdivision, being a subdivision of part of the Southeast Quarter of Section 18, Township 36 North, Range 10 East of the Third Principal Meridian, according to the plat thereof recorded on March 9, 2005 as Document No. R2005040528 as corrected by Certificate of Correction recorded December 28, 2005 as Document R2005228067 as further corrected by Certificate of Correction recorded December 18, 2006 as Document R2006208515 bounded by a line described as follows: Beginning at the easterly most southeast corner of said Outlot A located on the west line of Weber Road (County Highway 88) as dedicated by Document No. R2003016054, recorded January 23, 2003; thence North 53 Degrees 23 Minutes 42 Seconds West (North 55 Degrees 02 Minutes 09 Seconds, record), along a southerly line of said Outlot A, 23.96 feet; thence South 89 Degrees 35 Minutes 27 Seconds West (South 87 Degrees 57 Minutes 00 Seconds West, record) along a south line of said Outlot A, 50.77 feet; thence North 00 Degrees 00 Minutes 29 Seconds West, parallel with the east line of said Outlot A, 33.86 feet to a point on a north line of said Outlot A, thence North 89 Degrees 35 Minutes 27 Seconds East, along said north line, 50.00 feet; thence North 56 Degrees 37 Minutes 56 Seconds East (North 45 Degrees 37 Minutes 22 Seconds East, record), along a northerly line of said Outlot A, 23.95 feet to a point on an east line of said Outlot A, also being the west line of Weber Road aforesaid; thence South 00 Degrees 00 Minutes 29 Seconds East (South 01 Degrees 38 Minutes 56 Seconds East, record), along the west line of said Weber Road, 61.32 feet to the point of beginning, in Will County, Illinois.

Said parcel containing 2,640 square feet, (0.060 acres) of land, more or less.

PARCEL 0033 T.E.

That part of Lot 2 of Rose Resubdivision, being a resubdivision of Lots 1 through 4 (both inclusive) along with part of Outlot A all in Rose Subdivision, being a resubdivision of the Southeast Quarter of Section 18, Township 36 North, Range 10 East of the Third Principal Meridian, according to the plat of said Rose Resubdivision recorded on November 1, 2005 as Document No. R2005–191530 bounded by a line described as follows: Beginning at the southerly most southeast corner of said Lot 2; thence South 89 Degrees 35 Minutes 27 Seconds West (South 87 Degrees 57 Minutes 00 Seconds West, record) along the south line of said Lot 2 a distance of 50.00 feet; thence North 00 Degrees 00 Minutes 29 Seconds West, parallel with the east line of said Lot 2 a distance of 10.00 feet; thence North 89 Degrees 35 Minutes 27 Seconds East (North 87 Degrees 57 Minutes 00 Seconds East, record), parallel with the south line of said Lot 2, a distance of 65.35 feet to a point in the southeasterly line of said Lot 2; thence South 56 Degrees 37 Minutes 56 Seconds West (South 55 Degrees 00 Minutes 31 Seconds West, record) along said southeasterly line, 18.38 feet to the point of beginning, in Will County, Illinois.

Said parcel containing 577 square feet, (0.013 acres) of land, more or less.

PARCEL 0034DED

The west 25.00 feet of Lot 2 in E.M.S. Subdivision (being a subdivision of part of the Southwest Quarter of Section 17, Township 36 North, Range 10 East of the Third Principal Meridian) as per plat thereof recorded December 7, 1989 as document number R89–64001, in Will County, Illinois.

Said parcel containing 0.034 acres more or less.

PARCEL 0035DED

The west 25.00 feet of Lot 1 in E.M.S. Subdivision (being a subdivision of part of the Southwest Quarter of Section 17, Township 36 North, Range 10 East of the Third Principal Meridian) as per plat thereof recorded December 7, 1989 as document number R89–64001, in Will County, Illinois.

Said parcel containing 0.060 acres more or less.

PARCEL 0037DED

A part of the West Half of the Northwest Quarter of Section 17, Township 36 North, Range 10 East of the Third Principal Meridian, described as follows: the east 25.00 feet of the west 75.00 feet of the south 50.00 feet of the West Half of the Northwest Quarter of said Section 17, in Will County, Illinois.

Said parcel containing 0.029 acres more or less.

PARCEL 0038DED

That part of Lot 1 in Grand Haven Retail Development (being a subdivision in the Southeast Quarter of Section 18, Township 36 North, Range 10 East of the Third Principal Meridian) as per plat thereof recorded December 15, 2003 as document number R2003302173 described as follows: Beginning at a southeast corner of said Lot 1, said southeast corner bears South 01 degrees 38 minutes 41 seconds East (South 01 degrees 38 minutes 56 seconds East, record), 184.08 feet (184.18 feet Record) from the northeast corner of said Lot 1; thence South 43 degrees 15 minutes 40 seconds West, along the southeast line of said Lot 1, 56.66 feet, to a south line of said Lot 1; thence South 88 degrees 10 minutes 49 seconds West, along said south line, 28.32 feet, to a line 20.00 feet northwest of and parallel to the southeast line of said Lot 1; thence North 43 degrees 15 minutes 40 seconds East, along said parallel line, 96.78 feet, to the east line of said Lot 1; thence South 01 degrees 38 minutes 41 seconds East, along said east line, 28.33 feet, to the Point of Beginning, in Will County, Illinois.

Said parcel containing 0.035 acres more or less.

PARCEL 0039DED

That part of the Northeast Quarter of Section 18, Township 36 North, Range 10 East of the Third Principal Meridian described as follows: Commencing at the southeast corner of said Northeast Quarter; thence North 01 degrees 40 minutes 43 seconds West, along the east line of said Section 18, a distance of 456.50 feet; thence South 68 degrees 19 minutes 17 seconds West, in a southwesterly direction at an angle of 70 degrees, 63.85 feet to the west line of the east 60.00 feet of said Northeast Quarter and the Point of Beginning; thence continuing South 68 degrees 19 minutes 17 seconds West, along the last described line, 15.96 feet to the west line of the east 75.00 feet of said Northeast Quarter; thence South 01 degrees 40 minutes 43 seconds East, along said west line, 74.54 feet; thence North 88 degrees 19 minutes 17 seconds East, at right angles to the last described line, 15.00 feet, to the west line of the east 60.00 feet of said Northeast Quarter; thence North 01 degrees 40 minutes 43 seconds West, along said west line, 80.00 feet to the Point of Beginning, all in Will County, Illinois.

Said parcel containing 0.027 acres more or less.

PARCEL 0039TEA

That part of the Northeast Quarter of Section 18, Township 36 North, Range 10 East of the Third Principal Meridian described as follows: Commencing at the southeast corner of said Northeast Quarter; thence North 01 degrees 40 minutes 43 seconds West, along the east line of said Section 18, a distance of 456.50 feet; thence South 68 degrees 19 minutes 17 seconds West, in a southwesterly direction at an angle of 70 degrees, 79.81 feet, to the west line of the east 75.00 feet of said Northeast Quarter; thence South 01 degrees 40 minutes 43 seconds East, along said west line, 74.54 feet; thence North 88 degrees 19 minutes 17 seconds East, at right angles to the last described line, 5.00 feet, to the west line of the east 70.00 feet of said Northeast Quarter, and the Point of Beginning; thence continuing North 88 degrees 19 minutes 17 seconds East, 10.00 feet, to the west line of the east 60.00 feet of said Northeast Quarter; thence South 01 degrees 40 minutes 43 seconds East, along said west line, 304.88 feet, to the north line of the south 50.00 feet of said Northeast Quarter; thence South 88 degrees 07 minutes 04 seconds West, along said north line, 10.00 feet, to the west line of the east 70.00 feet of said Northeast Quarter; thence North 01 degrees 40 minutes 43 seconds West, along said west line, 304.91 feet to the Point of Beginning, all in Will County, Illinois.

Said parcel containing 0.070 acres more or less.

PARCEL 0039TEB

That part of the Northeast Quarter of Section 18, Township 36 North, Range 10 East of the Third Principal Meridian described as follows: Commencing at the southeast corner of said Northeast Quarter; thence North 01 degrees 40 minutes 43 seconds West, along the east line of said Section 18, a distance of 456.50 feet; thence South 68 degrees 19 minutes 17 seconds West, in a southwesterly direction at an angle of 70 degrees, 79.81 feet, to the west line of the east 75.00 feet of said Northeast Quarter, and the Point of Beginning; thence continuing South 68 degrees 19 minutes 17 seconds West, along the last described line, 42.57 feet, to the west line of the east 115.00 feet of said Northeast Quarter; thence South 01 degrees 40 minutes 43 seconds East, along said west line, 48.60 feet; thence North 88 degrees 19 minutes 17 seconds East, at right angles to the last described line, 40.00 feet, to the west line of the east 75.00 feet of said Northeast Quarter; thence North 01 degrees 40 minutes 43 seconds West, along said west line, 63.16 feet, to the Point of Beginning, all in Will County, Illinois.

Said parcel containing 0.051 acres more or less.

PARCEL 0040TE

The south 59.00 feet of the north 328.45 feet of the east 25.00 feet of the west 100.00 feet of the West Half of the Southwest Quarter of Section 17, Township 36 North, Range 10 East of the Third Principal Meridian, Will County, Illinois.

Said parcel containing 0.033 acres more or less.

PARCEL 0042TE

That part of Lot 3 in Grand Haven Retail Development (being a subdivision in the Southeast Quarter of Section 18, Township 36 North, Range 10 East of the Third Principal Meridian) as per plat thereof recorded December 15, 2003 as document number R2003302173 described as follows: Beginning at the northeast corner of said Lot 3; thence South 01 degrees 38 minutes 41 seconds East, along the east line of said Lot 3, 40.15 feet; thence South 88 degrees 21 minutes 19

seconds West, at right angles to the last described line, 40.00 feet; thence North 01 degrees 38 minutes 41 seconds West, at right angles to the last described line, 20.00 feet; thence South 88 degrees 21 minutes 19 seconds West, at right angles to the last described line, 25.00 feet; thence North 01 degrees 38 minutes 41 seconds West, at right angles to the last described line, 20.15 feet, to the north line of said Lot 3; thence North 88 degrees 21 minutes 19 seconds East, along said north line, 65.00 feet, to the Point of Beginning.

Said parcel containing 0.048 acres more or less.

PARCEL 0044DED

The West 10.00 feet of the East 70.00 feet of the South 50.00 feet of the Northeast Quarter of Section 18, Township 36 North, Range 10 East of the Third Principal Meridian, in Will County, Illinois.

Said parcel containing 0.011 acres more or less.

P.A. 94–1055, Art. 25, § 25–5–30, added by P.A. 97–458, § 5, eff. Aug. 19, 2011. Renumbered as § 25–5–40 by P.A. 97–813, § 675, eff. July 13, 2012.

30/25–5–45. Quick-take; South Suburban Airport

§ 25–5–45. Quick-take; South Suburban Airport. Quick-take proceedings under Article 20 may be used by the Department of Transportation for the purpose of development of the South Suburban Airport within the boundaries designated on the map filed with the Secretary of State on May 28, 2013 and known as file number 98–GA–D01.

P.A. 94–1055, Art. 25, § 25–5–45, added by P.A. 98–109, § 4–70, eff. July 25, 2013. Amended by P.A. 98–756, § 730, eff. July 16, 2014.

30/25–5–50. Quick-take; McHenry County

§ 25–5–50. Quick-take; McHenry County. Quick-take proceedings under Article 20 may be used for a period of no longer than one year from the effective date of this amendatory Act of the 98th General Assembly by McHenry County for the acquisition of the following described property for the purpose of public improvements to serve McHenry County:

Route: F.A.U. 168 (Johnsburg Road)

Section: 05–00314–00–WR

County: McHenry Job No.: R–91–005–06

Parcel: 1HK0045

Sta. 58 + 07.09 To Sta. 58 + 31.89

Sta. 176 + 10.72 To Sta. 177 + 36.15

Owner: JNL–Johnsburg Properties, Inc.

Index No. 09–13–277–001

09–13–277–002

That part of Sub Lot 2 of Lot 28 in Plat Number 3 McHenry, County Clerk's Plat of Section 13, Township 45 North, Range 8 East of the Third Principal Meridian, according to the plat thereof recorded May

6, 1902 as document number 14079, in McHenry County, Illinois, described as follows:

Commencing at the southeast corner of the Northeast Quarter of said Section 13; thence on an assumed bearing of South 89 degrees 15 minutes 13 seconds West along the south line of the Northeast Quarter of said Section 13, as monumented and occupied, a distance of 824.94 feet (825.2 feet, recorded) (826.0 feet, recorded) to a point of intersection with the Southerly extension of the east line of the grantor; thence North 1 degree 20 minutes 53 seconds East along the said Southerly extension of the east line of the grantor, a distance of 132.49 feet to the northeasterly right of way line of Chapel Hill Road recorded January 26, 1932 as document number 100422, being also the southeast corner of the grantor; thence North 46 degrees 56 minutes 58 seconds West along the said northeasterly right of way line of Chapel Hill Road and along the northeasterly right of way line of Chapel Hill Road recorded January 26, 1932 as document number 100421, a distance of 261.08 feet to the point of beginning; thence continuing North 46 degrees 56 minutes 58 seconds West along the northeasterly right of way line of Chapel Hill Road recorded as document number 100421, a distance of 14.94 feet to the east right of way line of Chapel Hill Road recorded January 26, 1932 as document number 100420; thence North 2 degrees 09 minutes 50 seconds East along the said east right of way line of Chapel Hill Road and the Northerly extension thereof, a distance of 64.92 feet (64.91 feet, more or less, recorded) to the center line of Johnsburg Road; thence North 87 degrees 42 minutes 53 seconds East along the said center line of Johnsburg Road, a distance of 123.08 feet; thence South 2 degrees 17 minutes 07 seconds East, a distance of 30.00 feet to the south right of way line of Johnsburg Road according to a Plat of Survey by the County Surveyor dated October 21, 1952 in Surveyor Book Number 5, page 204; thence South 2 degrees 48 minutes 02 seconds East, a distance of 1.05 feet; thence westerly 59.83 feet along a curve to the left having a radius of 987.47 feet, the chord of said curve bears South 85 degrees 27 minutes 49 seconds West, 59.82 feet; thence South 70 degrees 14 minutes 11 seconds West, a distance of 47.08 feet; thence South 22 degrees 40 minutes 19 seconds West, a distance of 30.69 feet to the point of beginning.

Said parcel containing 0.117 acre, more or less, of which 0.086 acre, more or less, was previously dedicated or used for highway purposes.

P.A. 94–1055, Art. 25, § 25–5–45, added by P.A. 98–229, § 5, eff. Aug. 9, 2013. Renumbered as § 25–5–50 by P.A. 98–756, § 730, eff. July 16, 2014.

30/25–5–55.　Quick-take; McHenry County

§ 25–5–55.　Quick-take; McHenry County. Quick-take proceedings under Article 20 may be used for a period of no longer than one year from the effective date of this amendatory Act of the 98th General Assembly by McHenry County for the acquisition of the following described property for the purpose of reconstruction of the intersection of Miller Road and Illinois Route 31:

Route: Illinois State Route 31

Section: Section 09–00372–00–PW

County: McHenry County

Job No.: R–91–020–06

Parcel: 0003

Sta. 119 + 70.41 To Sta. 136 + 74.99

Owner: Parkway Bank and Trust

Company as Trustee under Trust

Agreement dated October 25, 1988

known as trust No. 9052

Index No. 14–02–100–002, 14–02– 100–051

A part of the Northwest Quarter of Section 2, Township 44 North, Range 8 East of the Third Principal Meridian, in McHenry County, Illinois, described as follows:

Commencing at the southwest corner of said Northwest Quarter; thence North 0 degrees 40 minutes 30 seconds East, (bearings based on Illinois State Plane Coordinates East Zone 1983 Datum) along the west line of said Northwest Quarter, 33.01 feet; thence North 89 degrees 27 minutes 02 seconds East along a line parallel with and 33.00 feet north of the south line of said Northwest Quarter, 633.53 feet to the Point of Beginning; thence North 47 degrees 43 minutes 11 seconds East, 76.04 feet; thence Northeasterly 892.04 feet along a curve to the left having a radius of 5900.00 feet, the chord of said curve bears North 03 degrees 13 minutes 38 seconds East, a chord distance of 891.20 feet; thence North 01 degrees 06 minutes 15 seconds West, 737.81 feet; thence North 88 degrees 52 minutes 57 seconds East, 60.00 feet to a point on the westerly line of Illinois State Route 31 as dedicated per Book 12 of Miscellaneous Records, pages 200, 201 and 203; thence South 01 degrees 06 minutes 15 seconds East along said westerly line, 405.84 feet; thence South 01 degrees 00 minutes 45 seconds West along said westerly line, 135.20 feet; thence South 02 degrees 50 minutes 15 seconds East along said westerly line, 165.10 feet; thence South 01 degrees 06 minutes 15 seconds East along said westerly line, 407.00 feet; thence Southwesterly 567.07 feet along said westerly line, said line being a curve to the right having a radius of 3779.83 feet, the chord of said curve bears South 03 degrees 11 minutes 37 seconds West, a chord distance of 566.54 feet to point on a line parallel with and 33.00 feet north of the south line of said Northwest Quarter; thence South 89 degrees 27 minutes 02 seconds West along a line parallel with and 33.00 feet north of the south line of said Northwest Quarter, 142.09 feet to the Point of Beginning in McHenry County, Illinois.

Said parcel containing 116,716 square feet (2.679 acres) more or less.

Route: Bull Valley Road

Section: Section 09–00372–00–PW

County: McHenry County

Job No.: R–91–020–06

Parcel: 0003TE

Sta. 531 + 73.39 To Sta. 532 + 82.90

Owner: Parkway Bank and Trust

Company as Trustee under Trust

Agreement dated October 25, 1988

known as trust No. 9052

Index No. 14–02–100–002

A part of the Southwest Quarter of the Northwest Quarter of Section 2, Township 44 North, Range 8 East of the Third Principal Meridian, in McHenry County, Illinois, described as follows:

Commencing at the southwest corner of said Southwest Quarter; thence North 00 degrees 40 minutes 30 seconds East, (bearings based on Illinois State Plane Coordinates East Zone 1983 Datum) along the west line of said Southwest Quarter, 33.01 feet; thence North 89 degrees 27 minutes 02 seconds East along a line parallel with and 33.00 feet north of the south line of said Southwest Quarter, 540.42 feet to the Point of Beginning; thence North 00 degrees 33 minutes 06 seconds West, 14.95 feet; thence North 89 degrees 26 minutes 54 seconds East, 109.87 feet; thence South 47 degrees 43 minutes 11 seconds West, 22.47 feet to a point on a line parallel with and 33.00 feet north of the south line of said Southwest Quarter; thence South 89 degrees 27 minutes 02 seconds West along said line parallel with and 33.00 feet north of the south line of said Southwest Quarter, 93.10 feet to the Point of Beginning in McHenry County, Illinois.

Said parcel containing 1,518 square feet (0.035 acres) more or less.

Route: Illinois State Route 31

Section: Section 09–00372–00–PW

County: McHenry County

Job No.: R–91–020–06

Parcel: 0011

Sta. 124 + 14.14 To Sta. 124 + 35.35

Owner: Trapani, LLC, an Illinois

limited liability company

Index No. 14–02–100–050

A part of the Southwest Quarter of the Northwest Quarter of Section 2, Township 44 North, Range 8 East of the Third Principal Meridian, in McHenry County, Illinois, described as follows:

Commencing at the northwest corner of Lot 1 in McDonalds Subdivision, being a subdivision of part of the Northwest Quarter of Section 2, Township 44

North, Range 8 East of the Third Principal Meridian, according to the plat thereof recorded December 22, 1993 as Document No. 93R80090, in McHenry County, Illinois; thence Northeasterly along the easterly line of Illinois State Route 31 as dedicated per Book 12 of Miscellaneous Records, pages 200, 201 and 203, 206.43 feet along a curve to the left having a radius of 3859.83 feet, the chord of said curve bears North 2 degrees 41 minutes 29 seconds East, (bearings based on Illinois State Plane Coordinates East Zone 1983 Datum) a chord distance of 206.41 feet to the Point of Beginning; thence continuing Northeasterly along said easterly line, 21.36 feet, said line being a curve to the left having a radius of 3859.83 feet, the chord of said curve bears North 1 degrees 00 minutes 02 seconds East, a chord distance of 21.36 feet to a point the south line of a parcel of land per deed recorded February 10, 2003 as Document No. 2003R0017053; thence North 89 degrees 22 minutes 29 seconds East along said south line, 1.04 feet; thence Southwesterly 21.41 feet along a curve to the right having a radius of 6060.00 feet, the chord of said curve bears South 03 degrees 47 minutes 21 seconds West, a chord distance of 21.41 feet to the Point of Beginning in McHenry County, Illinois.

Said parcel containing 11 square feet (0.000 acres) more or less.

Route: Illinois State Route 31

Section: Section 09–00372–00–PW

County: McHenry County

Job No.: R–91–020–06

Parcel: 0011TE–1

Sta. 123 + 50.48 To Sta. 124 + 26.94

Owner: Trapani, LLC, an Illinois

limited liability company

Index No. 14–02–100–050

A part of the Southwest Quarter of the Northwest Quarter of Section 2, Township 44 North, Range 8 East of the Third Principal Meridian, in McHenry County, Illinois, described as follows:

Commencing at the northwest corner of Lot 1 in McDonalds Subdivision, being a subdivision of part of the Northwest Quarter of Section 2, Township 44 North, Range 8 East of the Third Principal Meridian, according to the plat thereof recorded December 22, 1993 as Document No. 93R80090, in McHenry County, Illinois; thence Northeasterly along the easterly line of Illinois State Route 31 as dedicated per Book 12 of Miscellaneous Records, pages 200, 201 and 203, 142.05 feet along a curve to the left having a radius of 3859.83 feet, the chord of said curve bears North 3 degrees 10 minutes 09 seconds East, (bearings based on Illinois State Plane Coordinates East Zone 1983 Datum) a chord distance of 142.05 feet to the Point of Beginning; thence continuing Northeasterly along said easterly line, 64.39 feet, said line being a curve to the left having a radius of 3859.83 feet, the chord of said curve bears North 1 degrees 38 minutes 13 seconds East, a chord distance of 64.38 feet; thence Northeasterly 12.69 feet along a curve to the left having a radius of 6060.00 feet, the chord of said curve bears North 03 degrees 49 minutes 49 seconds East, a chord distance of 12.69 feet; thence South 89 degrees 01 minutes 32 seconds East, 4.46 feet; thence Southwesterly 77.18 feet along a curve to the right having a radius of 3864.83 feet, the chord of said curve bears South 01 degrees 32 minutes 47 seconds West, a chord distance of 77.17 feet; thence North 87 degrees 52 minutes 53 seconds West, 5.07 feet to the Point of Beginning in McHenry County, Illinois.

Said parcel containing 387 square feet (0.009 acres) more or less.

Route: Charles J. Miller Road

Section: Section 09–00372–00–PW

County: McHenry County

Job No.: R–91–020–06

Parcel: 0011TE–2

Sta. 537 + 44.77 To Sta. 538 + 37.59

Owner: Trapani, LLC, an Illinois

limited liability company

Index No. 14–02–100–050

A part of Lot 2, in McDonald's Subdivision, being a subdivision of part of the Northwest Quarter of Section 2, Township 44 North, Range 8 East of the Third Principal Meridian, according to the plat thereof recorded December 22, 1993 as Document No. 93R80090, in McHenry County, Illinois, described as follows:

Beginning at the southeast corner of said Lot 2; thence South 89 degrees 27 minutes 02 seconds West (bearings based on Illinois State Plane Coordinates East Zone 1983 Datum) along the south line of said Lot 2, 92.83 feet; thence North 00 degrees 33 minutes 02 seconds West, 33.91 feet; thence North 89 degrees 36 minutes 46 seconds East, 93.43 feet to a point on the east line of said Lot 2; thence South 00 degrees 28 minutes 57 seconds West along said east line, 33.66 feet to the Point of Beginning in McHenry County, Illinois.

Said parcel containing 3,146 square feet (0.072 acres) more or less.

Route: Charles J. Miller Road

Section: Section 09–00372–00–PW

County: McHenry County

Job No.: R–91–020–06

Parcel: 0016

Sta. 538 + 37.74 To Sta. 539 + 63.26

Owner: Marion R. Reinwall Hoak

as Trustee of the Marion R.

Reinwall Hoak Living trust dated

September 15, 1998

Index No. 14–02–100–022

A part of the West Half of Government Lot 1 in the Northwest Quarter of Section 2, Township 44 North, Range 8 East of the Third Principal Meridian in McHenry County, Illinois, described as follows:

Beginning at the southeast corner of said West Half of Government Lot 1; thence South 89 degrees 27 minutes 02 seconds West (bearings based on Illinois State Plane Coordinates East Zone 1983 Datum) along the south line of said West Half of Government Lot 1, 115.35 feet to the point of intersection with the east line of Lot 2 in McDonald's Subdivision, being a subdivision of part of the Northwest Quarter of Section 2, Township 44 North, Range 8 East of the Third Principal Meridian, according to the plat thereof recorded December 22, 1993 as Document No. 93R80090, in McHenry County, Illinois extended southerly; thence North 00 degrees 28 minutes 57 seconds East along said east line extended southerly and along said east line, 48.01 feet; thence North 89 degrees 27 minutes 02 seconds East, 115.36 feet to a point on the east line of said West Half of Government Lot 1; thence South 00 degrees 29 minutes 41 seconds West along said east line, 48.01 feet to the Point of Beginning in McHenry County, Illinois.

Said parcel containing 5,537 square feet (0.127 acres) more or less, of which 0.087 acres more or less, has been previously used or dedicated.

Route: Illinois State Route 31

Section: Section 09–00372–00–PW

County: McHenry County

Job No.: R–91–020–06

Parcel: 0017

Sta. 536 + 90.86 To Sta. 539 + 43.61

Owner: Alliance Bible Church of

the Christian and Missionary

Alliance, an Illinois not for profit

corporation

Index No. 14–02–302–005; 14–02–302–004; 14–02–302–002

A part of Lots 4 and 5, in Smith First Addition being a subdivision of the North 473.90 feet of the Northwest Quarter of the Southwest Quarter of Section 2, Township 44 North, Range 8 East of the Third Principal Meridian, lying easterly of the easterly right-of-way of State Route 31, according to the plat thereof recorded in the recorder's office of McHenry County, Illinois on February 16, 1973, as Document No. 586905 in McHenry County, Illinois, described as follows:

Beginning at the northeast corner of said Lot 5; thence South 00 degrees 08 minutes 56 seconds West (bearings based on Illinois State Plane Coordinates East Zone 1983 Datum) along the east line of said Lot 5, 33.94 feet; thence Southwesterly 106.41 feet along a curve to the right having a radius of 795.00 feet, the chord of said curve bears South 85 degrees 36 minutes 55 seconds West, a chord distance of 106.34 feet; thence South 89 degrees 26 minutes 58 seconds West, 154.36 feet to a point on the west line of said Lot 4; thence North 00 degrees 10 minutes 27 seconds East along said west line, 41.06 feet to the northwest corner of said Lot 4; thence North 89 degrees 27 minutes 02 seconds East along the north line of said Lots 4 and 5, 260.35 feet to the Point of Beginning in McHenry County, Illinois.

Said parcel containing 10,438 square feet (0.240 acres) more or less.

P.A. 94–1055, Art. 25, § 25–5–55, added by P.A. 98–852, § 5, eff. Aug. 1, 2014. Amended by P.A. 99–78, § 540, eff. July 20, 2015.

30/25–5–60. Quick-take; Village of Mundelein

§ 25–5–60. Quick-take; Village of Mundelein. Quick-take proceedings under Article 20 may be used for a period of no longer than one year after the effective date of this amendatory Act of the 98th General Assembly by the Village of Mundelein in Lake County for the acquisition of property and easements, legally described below, for the purpose of widening and reconstructing Hawley Street from Midlothian Road to Seymour Avenue, and making other public utility improvements including the construction of a bike path:

PIN: 10–24–423–010

That part of Lot 11 (as originally platted), in Western Slope Subdivision of Mundelein, being a Subdivision of part of the Southeast Quarter of Section 24, and of the Northeast Quarter of Section 25, Township 44 North, Range 10, East of the Third Principal Meridian, according to the plat thereof recorded May 9, 1925 as Document 257151, in Book "N" of Plats, Page 98, described as follows: beginning at the Southeast corner of Lot 11; thence West along the South line of said Lot, 99.95 (meas.) 100.00 feet (rec.) to the Southwest corner of said Lot; thence North along the West line of said Lot, 10.00 feet; thence Southeasterly 8.51 feet to a point 6.00 feet East of and 4.00 feet North of the Southwest corner of said Lot; thence East parallel with the South line of said Lot, 93.97 feet to the East line of said Lot; thence South along said last described line, 4.00 feet to the point of beginning, Lake County, Illinois. 417.50 sq. ft.

Temporary easement:

That part of Lot 11 (as originally platted), in Western Slope Subdivision of Mundelein, being a Subdivision of part of the Southeast Quarter of Section 24, and of the Northeast Quarter of Section 25, Township 44 North, Range 10, East of the Third Principal Meridian, according to the plot thereof recorded May 9, 1925 as Document 257151, in Book "N" of Plats, Page 98, described as follows: commencing at the Southwest corner of said Lot 11; thence North along the West

line of said Lot, 10.00 feet to the point of beginning; thence continuing North along said last described line, 35.00 feet; thence East parallel with the South line of said Lot, 10.00 feet; thence South parallel with the West line of said Lot, 25.00 feet to a line 20.00 feet North of and parallel with the South line of said Lot; thence East along said last described line, 20.00 feet; thence South parallel with the West line of said Lot, 16.00 feet to a line 4.00 feet North of and parallel with the South line of said Lot; thence West along said last described line, 24.00 feet to a point 6.00 feet East of the West line of said Lot; thence Northwesterly, 8.51 feet to the point of beginning, in Lake County, Illinois. Containing 712.00 sq. ft.

PIN: 10–24–423–011

The South 4.00 feet of Lot 10 (as originally platted), in Western Slope Subdivision of Mundelein, being a Subdivision of part of the Southeast Quarter of Section 24, and of the Northeast Quarter of Section 25, Township 44 North, Range 10, East of the Third Principal Meridian, according to the plat thereof recorded May 9, 1925 as Document 257151, in Book "N" of Plats, Page 98, Lake County, Illinois. 400.00 sq. ft.

PIN: 10–24–423–013

The South 4.00 feet of Lot 8 (as originally platted), in Western Slope Subdivision of Mundelein, being a Subdivision of part of the Southeast Quarter of Section 24, and of the Northeast Quarter of Section 25, Township 44 North, Range 10, East of the Third Principal Meridian, according to the plat thereof recorded May 9, 1925 as Document 257151, in Book "N" of Plats, Page 98, Lake County, Illinois. 400.00 sq. ft.

PIN: 10–24–423–016

The South 7.00 feet of Lot 5 (as originally platted), in Western Slope Subdivision of Mundelein, being a Subdivision of part of the Southeast Quarter of Section 24, and of the Northeast Quarter of Section 25, Township 44 North, Range 10, East of the Third Principal Meridian, according to the plat thereof recorded May 9, 1925 as Document 257151, in Book "N" of Plats, Page 98, Lake County, Illinois. 700.00 sq. ft.

Temporary Easement:

That part of Lot 5 (as originally platted), in Western Slope Subdivision of Mundelein, being a Subdivision of part of the Southeast Quarter of Section 24, and of the Northeast Quarter of Section 25, Township 44 North, Range 10, East of the Third Principal Meridian, according to the plat thereof recorded May 9, 1925 as Document 257151, in Book "N" of Plats, Page 98, described as follows: commencing at the Southeast corner of said Lot 5; thence North along the East line of said Lot, 7.00 feet to the point of beginning; thence West parallel with the South line of said Lot, 100.00 feet to the West line of said Lot; thence North along said last described line, 5.00 feet; thence East parallel with the South line of said Lot, 52.00 feet; thence North parallel with the West line of said Lot, 22.50 feet; thence East parallel with the South line of said

Lot, 14.50 feet; thence North parallel with the West line of said Lot, 5.20 feet; thence East parallel with the South line of said Lot, 33.50 feet to the East line of said Lot; thence South along the last described line, 32.70 feet to the point of beginning, in Lake County, Illinois. 1754.20 sq. ft.

PIN: 10–24–423–018

The South 13.50 feet of Lot 3 (as originally platted), in Western Slope Subdivision of Mundelein, being a Subdivision of part of the Southeast Quarter of Section 24, and of the Northeast Quarter of Section 25, Township 44 North, Range 10, East of the Third Principal Meridian, according to the plat thereof recorded May 9, 1925 as Document 257151, in Book "N" of Plats, Page 98, Lake County, Illinois. 1350.00 sq. ft.

Temporary Easement:

That part of Lot 3 (as originally platted), in Western Slope Subdivision of Mundelein, being a Subdivision of part of the Southeast Quarter of Section 24, and of the Northeast Quarter of Section 25, Township 44 North, Range 10, East of the Third Principal Meridian, according to the plat thereof recorded May 9, 1925 as Document 257151, in Book "N" of Plats, Page 98, described as follows: commencing at the Southeast corner of said Lot 3; thence North along the East line of said Lot, 13.50 feet to the point of beginning; thence West parallel with the South line of said Lot, 100.00 feet to the West line of said Lot; thence North along said last described line, 10.00 feet; thence East parallel with the South line of said Lot, 45.00 feet; thence North parallel with the West line of said Lot, 30.00 feet; thence East parallel with the South line of said Lot, 34.00 feet; thence South parallel with the West line of said Lot, 30.00 feet; thence East parallel with the South line of said Lot, 21.00 feet to the East line of said Lot; thence South along the last described line, 10.00 feet to the point of beginning, in Lake County, Illinois. 2020.00 sq. ft.

PIN: 10–24–423–019

The South 13.50 feet of Lot 2 (as originally platted), in Western Slope Subdivision of Mundelein, being a Subdivision of part of the Southeast Quarter of Section 24, and of the Northeast Quarter of Section 25, Township 44 North, Range 10, East of the Third Principal Meridian, according to the plat thereof recorded May 9, 1925 as Document 257151, in Book "N" of Plats, Page 98, Lake County, Illinois. 1350.00 sq. ft.

PIN: 10–24–423–021

The South 13.50 feet of a tract of land described as Lot 1 (as originally platted), (except that part taken for highway per Document No. 2242325 and 2242326), in Western Slope Subdivision of Mundelein, being a Subdivision of part of the Southeast Quarter of Section 24, and of the Northeast Quarter of Section 25, Township 44 North, Range 10, East of the Third Principal Meridian, according to the plat thereof recorded May 9, 1925 as Document 257151, in Book "N" of Plats, Page 98, Lake County, Illinois. 1040.30 sq. ft.

PIN: 10–25–205–003

Temporary Easement:

That part of Lot 44 (as originally platted), in Western Slope Subdivision of Mundelein, being a Subdivision of part of the Southeast Quarter of Section 24, and of the Northeast Quarter of Section 25, Township 44 North, Range 10, East of the Third Principal Meridian, according to the plat thereof recorded May 9, 1925 as Document 257151 in Book "N" of Plats, Page 98, described as follows: commencing at the Northeast corner of said Lot 44; thence South along the East line of said Lot, 5.00 feet; thence West parallel with the North line of said Lot, 34.00 feet; thence South parallel with the East line of said Lot, 5.00 feet; thence West parallel with the North line of said Lot, 16.00 feet to the West line of said Lot; thence North along said last described Lot, 10.00 feet to the Northwest corner of said lot; thence East along the North line of said lot, 50.00 feet to the point of beginning, in Lake County, Illinois. Containing 331.00 sq. ft.

PIN: 10–25–205–004

Temporary Easement:

The North 10.00 feet (except the South 5.00 feet of the West 24.00 feet and the South 5.00 feet of the East 3.00 feet thereof) of Lot 45 (as originally platted), in Western Slope Subdivision of Mundelein, being a Subdivision of part of the Southeast Quarter of Section 24, and of the Northeast Quarter of Section 25, Township 44 North, Range 10, East of the Third Principal Meridian, according to the plat thereof recorded May 9, 1925 as Document 257151, in Book "N" of Plats, Page 98, Lake County, Illinois. Containing 365.40 sq. ft.

PIN: 10–25–205–005

Temporary Easement:

The North 5.00 feet of Lot 46 (as originally platted), in Western Slope Subdivision of Mundelein, being a Subdivision of part of the Southeast Quarter of Section 24, and of the Northeast Quarter of Section 25, Township 44 North, Range 10, East of the Third Principal Meridian, according to the plat thereof recorded May 9, 1925 as Document 257151, in Book "N" of Plats, Page 98, Lake County, Illinois. 250.00 sq. ft.

PIN: 10–25–206–003

Temporary Easement:

The North 5.00 feet of Lot 60 (as originally platted), in Western Slope Subdivision of Mundelein, being a Subdivision of part of the Southeast Quarter of Section 24, and of the Northeast Quarter of Section 25, Township 44 North, Range 10, East of the Third Principal Meridian, according to the plat thereof recorded May 9, 1925 as Document 257151, in Book "N" of Plats, Page 98, in Lake County, Illinois. 250.00 sq. ft.

PIN: 11–30–101–004

Temporary Easement:

The North 5.00 feet of the East 30.00 feet of a tract of land described as the West 75.00 feet of Lots 1 and 2, in Block 1 of Hammond's Addition to Rockefeller, being a Subdivision of part of Lot 2 of the Northwest Quarter of Section 30, Township 44 North, Range 11 East of the Third Principal Meridian, according to the plat thereof recorded April 2, 1895 as Document No. 61511, in Book "D" of Plats, Page 24,in Lake County, Illinois. 150.00 sq. ft.

PIN: 11–30–120–001

That part of Lot 1 in Hawley Commons, being a subdivision of part of the Northwest Quarter of Section 30, Township 44 North, Range 11 East, of the Third Principal Meridian according to the plat thereof recorded October 8, 1999 as Document No. 4432301, and described as follows: Beginning at the Northwest corner of Lot 1; thence South along the West line of said Lot 1, 17.00 feet; thence Northeasterly 23.91 feet to a point 17.00 feet East of the point of beginning and on the North line of said Lot 1; thence West along the North line of Lot 1, 17.00 feet to the point of beginning, in Lake County, Illinois. Containing 144.50 sq. ft.

PIN: 10–24–314–036

That part of Lot 14 in Block 2 in Mundelein Home Crest Subdivision of the Northeast Quarter of the Northwest Quarter of Section 25 and part of the East Half of the Southwest Quarter of Section 24, all in Township 44 North, Range 10 East of the Third Principal Meridian, according to the plat thereof recorded June 4, 1926 as Document No. 280148 in Book "P" of Plats, Pages 62 and 63, described as lying Southeasterly of a curve concave Northwesterly having a radius of 45.00 feet and being tangent to the East and South lines of said Lot 14, in Lake County, Illinois. 445.10 sq. ft.

P.A. 94–1055, Art. 25, § 25–5–55, added by P.A. 98–1070, § 5, eff. Aug. 26, 2014. Renumbered as § 25–5–60, by P.A. 99–78, § 540, eff. July 20, 2015.

PART 7. EXISTING QUICK—TAKE POWERS

30/25–7–103.1.   Quick-take; highway purposes

§ 25–7–103.1. Quick-take; highway purposes. Quick-take proceedings under Article 20 may be used by the State of Illinois, the Illinois Toll Highway Authority or the St. Louis Metropolitan Area Airport Authority for the acquisition of land or interests therein for highway purposes.

P.A. 94–1055, Art. 25, § 25–7–103.1, eff. Jan. 1, 2007.

30/25–7–103.3.   Quick-take; coal development purposes

§ 25–7–103.3. Quick-take; coal development purposes. Quick-take proceedings under Article 20 may be used by the Department of Commerce and Economic Opportunity for the purpose specified in the Illinois Coal Development Bond Act.

P.A. 94–1055, Art. 25, § 25–7–103.3, eff. Jan. 1, 2007. Amended by P.A. 95–331, § 1090, eff. Aug. 21, 2007.

30/25–7–103.5.   Quick-take; St. Louis Metropolitan Area Airport Authority purposes

§ 25–7–103.5. Quick-take; St. Louis Metropolitan Area Airport Authority purposes. Quick-take proceedings under Article 20 may be used for the purpose specified in the St. Louis Metropolitan Area Airport Authority Act.

P.A. 94–1055, Art. 25, § 25–7–103.5, eff. Jan. 1, 2007.

30/25–7–103.6.   Quick-take; Southwestern Illinois Development Authority Purposes

§ 25–7–103.6. Quick-take; Southwestern Illinois Development Authority purposes. Quick-take proceedings under Article 20 may be used for a period of 24 months after May 24, 1996, by the Southwestern Illinois Development Authority pursuant to the Southwestern Illinois Development Authority Act.

P.A. 94–1055, Art. 25, § 25–7–103.6, eff. Jan. 1, 2007.

30/25–7–103.7.   Quick-take; Quad Cities Regional Economic Development Authority purposes

§ 25–7–103.7. Quick-take; Quad Cities Regional Economic Development Authority purposes. Quick-take proceedings under Article 20 may be used for a period of 3 years after December 30, 1987, by the Quad Cities Regional Economic Development Authority (except for the acquisition of land or interests therein that is farmland, or upon which is situated a farm dwelling and appurtenant structures, or upon which is situated a residence, or which is wholly within an area that is zoned for residential use) pursuant to the Quad Cities Regional Economic Development Authority Act.

P.A. 94–1055, Art. 25, § 25–7–103.7, eff. Jan. 1, 2007.

30/25–7–103.8. Quick-take; Metropolitan Water Reclamation District purposes

§ 25–7–103.8. Quick-take; Metropolitan Water Reclamation District purposes. Quick-take proceedings under Article 20 may be used by a sanitary district created under the Metropolitan Water Reclamation District Act for the acquisition of land or interests therein for purposes specified in that Act.

P.A. 94–1055, Art. 25, § 25–7–103.8, eff. Jan. 1, 2007.

30/25–7–103.9. Quick-take; rail carriers

§ 25–7–103.9. Quick-take; rail carriers. Quick-take proceedings under Article 20 may be used by a rail carrier within the time limitations and subject to the terms and conditions set forth in Section 18c–7501 of the Illinois Vehicle Code.

P.A. 94–1055, Art. 25, § 25–7–103.9, eff. Jan. 1, 2007.

30/25–7–103.10. Quick-take; water commissions

§ 25–7–103.10. Quick-take; water commissions. Quick-take proceedings under Article 20 may be used for a period of 18 months after January 26, 1987, for the purpose specified in Division 135 of Article 11 of the Illinois Municipal Code, by a commission created under Section 2 of the Water Commission Act of 1985.

P.A. 94–1055, Art. 25, § 25–7–103.10, eff. Jan. 1, 2007.

30/25–7–103.11. Quick-take; refuse-derived fuel system purposes

§ 25–7–103.11. Quick-take; refuse-derived fuel system purposes. Quick-take proceedings under Article 20 may be used by a village containing a population of less than 15,000 for the purpose of acquiring property to be used for a refuse derived fuel system designed to generate steam and electricity, and for industrial development that will utilize such steam and electricity, pursuant to Section 11–19–10 of the Illinois Municipal Code.

P.A. 94–1055, Art. 25, § 25–7–103.11, eff. Jan. 1, 2007.

30/25–7–103.12. Quick-take; certain municipal purposes

§ 25–7–103.12. Quick-take; certain municipal purposes. Quick-take proceedings under Article 20 may be used after receiving the prior approval of the City Council, by a municipality having a population of more than 500,000 for the purposes set forth in Section 11–61–1a and Divisions 74.2 and 74.3 of Article 11 of the Illinois Municipal Code, and for the same purposes when established pursuant to home rule powers.

P.A. 94–1055, Art. 25, § 25–7–103.12, eff. Jan. 1, 2007.

30/25–7–103.13. Quick-take; enterprise zone purposes

§ 25–7–103.13. Quick-take; enterprise zone purposes. Quick-take proceedings under Article 20 may be used by a home rule municipality, after a public hearing held by the corporate authorities or by a committee of the corporate authorities and after approval by a majority of the corporate authorities, within an area designated as an enterprise zone by the municipality under the Illinois Enterprise Zone Act.

P.A. 94–1055, Art. 25, § 25–7–103.13, eff. Jan. 1, 2007.

30/25–7–103.14. Quick-take; Illinois Sports Facilities Authority purposes

§ 25–7–103.14. Quick-take; Illinois Sports Facilities Authority purposes. Quick-take proceedings under Article 20 may be used by the Illinois Sports Facilities Authority for the purpose specified in Section 12 of the Illinois Sports Facilities Authority Act.

P.A. 94–1055, Art. 25, § 25–7–103.14, eff. Jan. 1, 2007.

30/25–7–103.15. Quick-take; sports stadium purposes

§ 25–7–103.15. Quick-take; sports stadium purposes. Quick-take proceedings under Article 20 may be used by a municipality having a population of more than 2,000,000 for the purpose of acquiring the property described in Section 3 of the Sports Stadium Act.

P.A. 94–1055, Art. 25, § 25–7–103.15, eff. Jan. 1, 2007.

30/25–7–103.16. Quick-take; University of Illinois

§ 25–7–103.16. Quick-take; University of Illinois. Quick-take proceedings under Article 20 may be used for a period of 18 months after July 29, 1986, in any proceeding by the Board of Trustees of the University of Illinois for the acquisition of land in Champaign County or interests therein as a site for a building or for any educational purpose.

P.A. 94–1055, Art. 25, § 25–7–103.16, eff. Jan. 1, 2007.

30/25–7–103.17. Quick-take; industrial harbour port

§ 25–7–103.17. Quick-take; industrial harbour port. Quick-take proceedings under Article 20 may be used for a period of 2 years after July 1, 1990, by a home rule municipality and a county board, upon approval of a majority of the corporate authorities of both the county board and the municipality, within an area designated as an enterprise zone by the municipality and the county board through an intergovernmental agreement under the Illinois Enterprise Zone Act, when the purpose of the condemnation proceeding is to acquire land for the construction of an industrial harbor port, and when the total amount of land to be acquired for that purpose is less than 75 acres and is adjacent to the Illinois River.

P.A. 94–1055, Art. 25, § 25–7–103.17, eff. Jan. 1, 2007.

30/25–7–103.18. Quick-take; airport authority purposes

§ 25–7–103.18. Quick-take; airport authority purposes. Quick-take proceedings under Article 20 may be used by an airport authority located solely within the boundaries of Madison County, Illinois, and which is organized pursuant to the provisions of the Airport Authorities Act, (i) for the acquisition of 160 acres, or less, of land or interests therein for the purposes specified in that Act which may be necessary to extend, mark, and light runway 11/29 for a distance of 1600 feet in length by 100 feet in width with parallel taxiway, to relocate and mark County Highway 19, Madison County, known as Moreland Road, to relocate the instrument landing system including the approach lighting system and to construct associated drainage, fencing and seeding required for the foregoing project and (ii) for a period of 6 months after December 28, 1989, for the acquisition of 75 acres, or less, of land or interests therein for the purposes specified in that Act which may be necessary to extend, mark and light the south end of runway 17/35 at such airport.

P.A. 94–1055, Art. 25, § 25–7–103.18, eff. Jan. 1, 2007.

30/25–7–103.19. Quick-take; Little Calumet River

§ 25–7–103.19. Quick-take; Little Calumet River. Quick-take proceedings under Article 20 may be used by any unit of local government for a permanent easement for the purpose of maintaining, dredging or cleaning the Little Calumet River.

P.A. 94–1055, Art. 25, § 25–7–103.19, eff. Jan. 1, 2007.

30/25–7–103.20. Quick-take; Salt Creek

§ 25–7–103.20. Quick-take; Salt Creek. Quick-take proceedings under Article 20 may be used by any unit of local government for a permanent easement for the purpose of maintaining, dredging or cleaning the Salt Creek in DuPage County.

P.A. 94–1055, Art. 25, § 25–7–103.20, eff. Jan. 1, 2007.

30/25–7–103.21. Quick-take; Scott Air Force Base

§ 25–7–103.21. Quick-take; Scott Air Force Base. Quick-take proceedings under Article 20 may be used by St. Clair County, Illinois, for the development of a joint use facility at Scott Air Force Base.

P.A. 94–1055, Art. 25, § 25–7–103.21, eff. Jan. 1, 2007.

30/25–7–103.22. Quick-take; Village of Summit

§ 25–7–103.22. Quick-take; Village of Summit. Quick-take proceedings under Article 20 may be used by the Village of Summit, Illinois, to acquire land for a waste to energy plant.

P.A. 94–1055, Art. 25, § 25–7–103.22, eff. Jan. 1, 2007.

30/25–7–103.23. Quick-take; Chanute Air Force Base

§ 25–7–103.23. Quick-take; Chanute Air Force Base. Quick-take proceedings under Article 20 may be used for a period of 15 months after September 7, 1990, by the Department of Transportation or by any unit of local government under the terms of an intergovernmental cooperation agreement between the Department of Transportation and the unit of local government for the purpose of developing aviation facilities in and around Chanute Air Force Base in Champaign County, Illinois.

P.A. 94–1055, Art. 25, § 25–7–103.23, eff. Jan. 1, 2007.

30/25–7–103.24. Quick-take; Morris Municipal Airport

§ 25–7–103.24. Quick-take; Morris Municipal Airport. Quick-take proceedings under Article 20 may be used for a period of 1 year after December 12, 1990, by the City of Morris for the development of the Morris Municipal Airport.

P.A. 94–1055, Art. 25, § 25–7–103.24, eff. Jan. 1, 2007.

30/25–7–103.25. Quick-take; Greater Rockford Airport Authority

§ 25–7–103.25. Quick-take; Greater Rockford Airport Authority. Quick-take proceedings under Article 20 may be used for a period of 1 year after June 19, 1991, by the Greater Rockford Airport Authority for airport expansion purposes.

P.A. 94–1055, Art. 25, § 25–7–103.25, eff. Jan. 1, 2007.

30/25–7–103.26. Quick-take; Aurora Municipal Airport

§ 25–7–103.26. Quick-take; Aurora Municipal Airport. Quick-take proceedings under Article 20 may be used for a period of 24 months after June 30, 1991, by the City of Aurora for completion of an instrument landing system and construction of an east-west runway at the Aurora Municipal Airport.

P.A. 94–1055, Art. 25, § 25–7–103.26, eff. Jan. 1, 2007.

30/25–7–103.27. Quick-take; Metropolitan Pier and Exposition Authority purposes

§ 25–7–103.27. Quick-take; Metropolitan Pier and Exposition Authority purposes. Quick-take proceedings under Article 20 may be used for the acquisition by the Metropolitan Pier and Exposition Authority of property described in subsection (f) of Section 5 of the

Metropolitan Pier and Exposition Authority Act for the purposes of providing additional grounds, buildings, and facilities related to the purposes of the Metropolitan Pier and Exposition Authority.

P.A. 94–1055, Art. 25, § 25–7–103.27, eff. Jan. 1, 2007.

30/25–7–103.28. Quick-take; road realignment

§ 25–7–103.28. Quick-take; road realignment. Quick-take proceedings under Article 20 may be used for a period of 24 months after March 1, 1992, by the Village of Wheeling and the City of Prospect Heights, owners of the Palwaukee Municipal Airport, to allow for the acquisition of right of way to complete the realignment of Hintz Road and Wolf Road.

P.A. 94–1055, Art. 25, § 25–7–103.28, eff. Jan. 1, 2007.

30/25–7–103.29. Quick-take; Bloomington-Normal Airport Authority

§ 25–7–103.29. Quick-take; Bloomington–Normal Airport Authority. Quick-take proceedings under Article 20 may be used for a period of one year from the effective date of this amendatory Act of 1992, by the Bloomington–Normal Airport Authority for airport expansion purposes.

P.A. 94–1055, Art. 25, § 25–7–103.29, eff. Jan. 1, 2007.

30/25–7–103.30. Quick-take; Lake-Cook Road

§ 25–7–103.30. Quick-take; Lake–Cook Road. Quick-take proceedings under Article 20 may be used for a period of 24 months after September 10, 1993, by the Cook County Highway Department and Lake County Department of Transportation to allow for the acquisition of necessary right-of-way for construction of underpasses for Lake–Cook Road at the Chicago Northwestern Railroad crossing, west of Skokie Boulevard, and the Chicago, Milwaukee, St. Paul and Pacific Railroad crossing, west of Waukegan Road.

P.A. 94–1055, Art. 25, § 25–7–103.30, eff. Jan. 1, 2007.

30/25–7–103.31. Quick-take; Arcola/Tuscola Water Transmission Pipeline Project

§ 25–7–103.31. Quick-take; Arcola/Tuscola Water Transmission Pipeline Project. Quick-take proceedings under Article 20 may be used for a period of one year after December 23, 1993, by the City of Arcola and the City of Tuscola for the development of the Arcola/Tuscola Water Transmission Pipeline Project pursuant to the intergovernmental agreement between the City of Arcola and the City of Tuscola.

P.A. 94–1055, Art. 25, § 25–7–103.31, eff. Jan. 1, 2007.

30/25–7–103.32. Quick-take; Bensenville Ditch

§ 25–7–103.32. Quick-take; Bensenville Ditch. Quick-take proceedings under Article 20 may be used for a period of 24 months from December 23, 1993, by the Village of Bensenville for the acquisition of prop-erty bounded by Illinois Route 83 to the west and O'Hare International Airport to the east to complete a flood control project known as the Bensenville Ditch.

P.A. 94–1055, Art. 25, § 25–7–103.32, eff. Jan. 1, 2007.

30/25–7–103.33. Quick-take; Medical Center Commission

§ 25–7–103.33. Quick-take; Medical Center Commission. Quick-take proceedings under Article 20 may be used for a period of 9 months after November 1, 1993, by the Medical Center Commission for the purpose of acquiring a site for the Illinois State Police Forensic Science Laboratory at Chicago, on the block bounded by Roosevelt Road on the north, Wolcott Street on the east, Washburn Street on the south, and Damen Avenue on the west in Chicago, Illinois.

P.A. 94–1055, Art. 25, § 25–7–103.33, eff. Jan. 1, 2007.

30/25–7–103.34. Quick-take; White County

§ 25–7–103.34. Quick-take; White County. Quick-take proceedings under Article 20 may be used for a period of 36 months after July 14, 1995, by White County for the acquisition of a 3 ½ mile section of Bellaire Road, which is described as follows: Commencing at the Northwest Corner of the Southeast ¼ of Section 28, Township 6 South, Range 10 East of the 3rd Principal Meridian; thence South to a point at the Southwest Corner of the Southeast ¼ of Section 9, Township 7 South, Range 10 East of the 3rd Principal Meridian.

P.A. 94–1055, Art. 25, § 25–7–103.34, eff. Jan. 1, 2007.

30/25–7–103.35. Quick-take; Indian Creek Flood Control Project

§ 25–7–103.35. Quick-take; Indian Creek Flood Control Project.

(a) Quick-take proceedings under Article 20 may be used for a period of one year after July 14, 1995, by the City of Aurora for permanent and temporary easements except over land adjacent to Indian Creek and west of Selmarten Creek located within the City of Aurora for the construction of Phase II of the Indian Creek Flood Control Project.

(b) Quick-take proceedings under Article 20 may be used for a period beginning June 24, 1995 (the day following the effective date of Public Act 89–29) and ending on July 13, 1995 (the day preceding the effective date of Public Act 89–134), by the City of Aurora for permanent and temporary easements for the construction of Phase II of the Indian Creek Flood Control Project.

P.A. 94–1055, Art. 25, § 25–7–103.35, eff. Jan. 1, 2007.

30/25–7–103.36. Quick-take; Grand Avenue Railroad Relocation Authority

§ 25–7–103.36. Quick-take; Grand Avenue Railroad Relocation Authority. Quick-take proceedings under Article 20 may be used for a period beginning July 14, 1995, and ending one year after the effective date of this amendatory Act of the 93rd General Assembly, by the Grand Avenue Railroad Relocation Authority for the Grand Avenue Railroad Grade Separation Project within the Village of Franklin Park, Illinois.

P.A. 94–1055, Art. 25, § 25–7–103.36, eff. Jan. 1, 2007.

30/25–7–103.37. Quick-take; 135th Street Bridge Project

§ 25–7–103.37. Quick-take; 135th Street Bridge Project.

(a) Quick-take proceedings under Article 20 may be used for a period of 3 years after July 14, 1995, by the Village of Romeoville for the acquisition of rights-of-way for the 135th Street Bridge Project, lying within the South ½ of Section 34, Township 37 North, Range 10 East and the South ½ of Section 35, Township 37 North, Range 10 East of the Third Principal Meridian, and the North ½ of Section 2, Township 36 North, Range 10 East and the North ½ of Section 3, Township 36 North, Range 10 East of the 3rd Principal Meridian, in Will County, Illinois.

(b) Quick-take proceedings under Article 20 may be used for a period of 3 years after June 23, 1995, by the Illinois Department of Transportation for the acquisition of rights-of-way for the 135th Street Bridge Project between the Des Plaines River and New Avenue lying within the South ½ of Section 35, Township 37 North, Range 10 East of the Third Principal Meridian and the North ½ of Section 2, Township 36 North, Range 10 East of the 3rd Principal Meridian, in Will County, Illinois.

P.A. 94–1055, Art. 25, § 25–7–103.37, eff. Jan. 1, 2007.

30/25–7–103.38. Quick-take; Anna-Jonesboro Water Commission

§ 25–7–103.38. Quick-take; Anna–Jonesboro Water Commission. Quick-take proceedings under Article 20 may be used for a period beginning June 24, 1995 (the day after the effective date of Public Act 89–29) and ending 18 months after July 14, 1995 (the effective date of Public Act 89–134), by the Anna–Jonesboro Water Commission for the acquisition of land and easements for improvements to its water treatment and storage facilities and water transmission pipes.

P.A. 94–1055, Art. 25, § 25–7–103.38, eff. Jan. 1, 2007.

30/25–7–103.39. Quick-take; City of Effingham

§ 25–7–103.39. Quick-take; City of Effingham. Quick-take proceedings under Article 20 may be used for a period of 36 months after July 14, 1995, by the City of Effingham for the acquisition of property which is described as follows:

Tract 1:

Lots 26 and 27 in Block 4 in RAILROAD ADDITION TO THE TOWN (NOW CITY) OF EFFINGHAM (reference made to Plat thereof recorded in Book "K", Page 769, in the Recorder's Office of Effingham County), situated in the City of Effingham, County of Effingham and State of Illinois.

Tract 2:

The alley lying South and adjoining Tract 1, as vacated by Ordinance recorded on July 28, 1937 in Book 183, Page 465, and all right, title and interest in and to said alley as established by the Contract for Easement recorded on August 4, 1937 in Book 183, Page 472.

P.A. 94–1055, Art. 25, § 25–7–103.39, eff. Jan. 1, 2007.

30/25–7–103.40. Quick-take; Village of Palatine

§ 25–7–103.40. Quick-take; Village of Palatine. Quick-take proceedings under Article 20 may be used for a period of one year after July 14, 1995, by the Village of Palatine for the acquisition of property located along the south side of Dundee Road between Rand Road and Hicks Road for redevelopment purposes.

P.A. 94–1055, Art. 25, § 25–7–103.40, eff. Jan. 1, 2007.

30/25–7–103.41. Quick-take; Medical Center District

§ 25–7–103.41. Quick-take; Medical Center District. Quick-take proceedings under Article 20 may be used for a period of 6 years after July 1, 1995, for the acquisition by the Medical Center District of property described in Section 3 of the Illinois Medical District Act within the District Development Area as described in Section 4 of that Act for the purposes set forth in that Act.

P.A. 94–1055, Art. 25, § 25–7–103.41, eff. Jan. 1, 2007.

30/25–7–103.41a. Quick-take; South Raney Street Improvement Project Phase I

§ 25–7–103.41a. Quick-take; South Raney Street Improvement Project Phase I. Quick-take proceedings under Article 20 may be used for a period of 24 months after June 21, 1996 by the City of Effingham, Illinois for acquisition of property for the South Raney Street Improvement Project Phase I.

P.A. 94–1055, Art. 25, § 25–7–103.41a, eff. Jan. 1, 2007.

30/25–7–103.42. Quick-take; Village of Deerfield

§ 25–7–103.42. Quick-take; Village of Deerfield. Quick-take proceedings under Article 20 may be used for a period of 3 years after June 21, 1996, by the Village of Deerfield for the acquisition of territory within the Deerfield Village Center, as designated as of that date by the Deerfield Comprehensive Plan, with the exception of that area north of Jewett Park

Drive (extended) between Waukegan Road and the Milwaukee Railroad Tracks, for redevelopment purposes.

P.A. 94–1055, Art. 25, § 25–7–103.42, eff. Jan. 1, 2007.

30/25–7–103.43. Quick-take; City of Harvard

§ 25–7–103.43. Quick-take; City of Harvard. Quick-take proceedings under Article 20 may be used for a period of 12 months after June 21, 1996, by the City of Harvard for the acquisition of property lying west of Harvard Hills Road of sufficient size to widen the Harvard Hills Road right of way and to install and maintain city utility services not more than 200 feet west of the center line of Harvard Hills Road.

P.A. 94–1055, Art. 25, § 25–7–103.43, eff. Jan. 1, 2007.

30/25–7–103.44. Quick-take; Village of River Forest

§ 25–7–103.44. Quick-take; Village of River Forest. Quick-take proceedings under Article 20 may be used for a period of 5 years after June 21, 1996, by the Village of River Forest, Illinois, within the area designated as a tax increment financing district when the purpose of the condemnation proceeding is to acquire land for any of the purposes contained in the River Forest Tax Increment Financing Plan or authorized by the Tax Increment Allocation Redevelopment Act, provided that condemnation of any property zoned and used exclusively for residential purposes shall be prohibited.

P.A. 94–1055, Art. 25, § 25–7–103.44, eff. Jan. 1, 2007.

30/25–7–103.45. Quick-take; Village of Schaumburg

§ 25–7–103.45. Quick-take; Village of Schaumburg. Quick-take proceedings under Article 20 may be used for a period of 18 months after June 28, 1996, by the Village of Schaumburg for the acquisition of land, easements, and aviation easements for the purpose of a public airport in Cook and DuPage Counties; provided that if any proceedings under the provisions of this Article are pending on that date, "quick-take" may be utilized by the Village of Schaumburg.

P.A. 94–1055, Art. 25, § 25–7–103.45, eff. Jan. 1, 2007.

30/25–7–103.46. Quick-take; City of Pinckneyville

§ 25–7–103.46. Quick-take; City of Pinckneyville. Quick-take proceedings under Article 20 may be used for a period of one year after June 28, 1996, by the City of Pinckneyville for the acquisition of land and easements to provide for improvements to its water treatment and storage facilities and water transmission pipes, and for the construction of a sewerage treatment facility and sewerage transmission pipes to serve the Illinois Department of Corrections Pinckneyville Correctional Facility.

P.A. 94–1055, Art. 25, § 25–7–103.46, eff. Jan. 1, 2007.

30/25–7–103.47. Quick-take; City of Streator

§ 25–7–103.47. Quick-take; City of Streator. Quick-take proceedings under Article 20 may be used for a period of 6 months after June 28, 1996, by the City of Streator for the acquisition of property described as follows for a first flush basin sanitary sewer system:

Tract 5: That part of lots 20 and 21 in Block 6 in Moore and Plumb's addition to the city of Streator, Illinois, lying south of the right of way of the switch track of the Norfolk and Western Railroad (now abandoned) in the county of LaSalle, state of Illinois;

Tract 6: That part of lots 30, 31 and 32 in Block 7 in Moore and Plumb's Addition to the city of Streator, Illinois, lying north of the centerline of Coal Run Creek and south of the right of way of the switch track of the Norfolk and Western Railroad (now abandoned) in the county of LaSalle, state of Illinois.

P.A. 94–1055, Art. 25, § 25–7–103.47, eff. Jan. 1, 2007.

30/25–7–103.48. Quick-take; MetroLink Light Rail System

§ 25–7–103.48. Quick-take; MetroLink Light Rail System. Quick-take proceedings under Article 20 may be used for a period of 48 months after January 16, 1997, by the Bi-State Development Agency of the Missouri–Illinois Metropolitan District for the acquisition of rights of way and related property necessary for the construction and operation of the MetroLink Light Rail System, beginning in East St. Louis, Illinois, and terminating at Mid America Airport, St. Clair County, Illinois.

P.A. 94–1055, Art. 25, § 25–7–103.48, eff. Jan. 1, 2007.

30/25–7–103.49. Quick-take; Village of Schaumburg

§ 25–7–103.49. Quick-take; Village of Schaumburg. Quick-take proceedings under Article 20 may be used for a period of 2 years after January 16, 1997, by the Village of Schaumburg for the acquisition of rights-of-way, permanent easements, and temporary easements for the purpose of improving the Roselle Road/Illinois Route 58/ Illinois Route 72 corridor, including rights-of-way along Roselle Road, Remington Road, Valley Lake Drive, State Parkway, Commerce Drive, Kristin Circle, and Hillcrest Boulevard, a permanent easement along Roselle Road, and temporary easements along Roselle Road, State Parkway, Valley Lake Drive, Commerce Drive, Kristin Circle, and Hillcrest Boulevard, in Cook County.

P.A. 94–1055, Art. 25, § 25–7–103.49, eff. Jan. 1, 2007.

30/25–7–103.51. Quick-take; Village of Bloomingdale

§ 25–7–103.51. Quick-take; Village of Bloomingdale. Quick-take proceedings under Article 20 may be used for a period of 12 months after July 25, 1997, by the Village of Bloomingdale for utility relocations necessitated by the Lake Street Improvement Project on Lake Street between Glen Ellyn Road and Springfield Drive in the Village of Bloomingdale.

P.A. 94–1055, Art. 25, § 25–7–103.51, eff. Jan. 1, 2007.

30/25–7–103.52. Quick-take; City of Freeport

§ 25–7–103.52. Quick-take; City of Freeport. Quick-take proceedings under Article 20 may be used for a period of 36 months after July 25, 1997, by the City of Freeport, owners of the Freeport Albertus Municipal Airport, to allow for acquisition of any land, rights, or other property lying between East Lamm Road and East Borchers Road to complete realignment of South Hollywood Road and to establish the necessary runway safety zone in accordance with Federal Aviation Administration and Illinois Department of Transportation design criteria.

P.A. 94–1055, Art. 25, § 25–7–103.52, eff. Jan. 1, 2007.

30/25–7–103.53. Quick-take; Village of Elmwood Park

§ 25–7–103.53. Quick-take; Village of Elmwood Park. Quick-take proceedings under Article 20 may be used for a period of 3 years after July 1, 1997, by the Village of Elmwood Park to be used only for the acquisition of commercially zoned property within the area designated as the Tax Increment Redevelopment Project Area by ordinance passed and approved on December 15, 1986, as well as to be used only for the acquisition of commercially zoned property located at the northwest corner of North Avenue and Harlem Avenue and commercially zoned property located at the southwest corner of Harlem Avenue and Armitage Avenue for redevelopment purposes, as set forth in Division 74.3 of Article 11 of the Illinois Municipal Code.

P.A. 94–1055, Art. 25, § 25–7–103.53, eff. Jan. 1, 2007.

30/25–7–103.54. Quick-take; Village of Oak Park

§ 25–7–103.54. Quick-take; Village of Oak Park.

(a) Quick-take proceedings under Article 20 may be used for a period of 3 years after July 25, 1997, by the Village of Oak Park for the acquisition of property located along the south side of North Avenue between Austin Boulevard and Harlem Avenue or along the north and south side of Harrison Street between Austin Boulevard and Elmwood Avenue, not including residentially zoned properties within these areas, for commercial redevelopment goals.

(b) Quick-take proceedings under Article 20 may be used for a period of 3 years after August 14, 1997, by the Village of Oak Park for the acquisition of property within the areas designated as the Greater Downtown Area Tax Increment Financing District, the Harlem/Garfield Tax Increment Financing District, and the Madison Street Tax Increment Financing District, not including residentially zoned properties within these areas, for commercial redevelopment goals.

(c) Quick-take proceedings under Article 20 may be used for a period of 3 years after August 14, 1997, by the Village of Oak Park for the acquisition of property within the areas designated as the North Avenue Commercial Strip and the Harrison Street Business Area, not including residentially zoned properties within these areas, for commercial redevelopment goals.

P.A. 94–1055, Art. 25, § 25–7–103.54, eff. Jan. 1, 2007.

30/25–7–103.55. Quick-take; Village of Morton Grove

§ 25–7–103.55. Quick-take; Village of Morton Grove. Quick-take proceedings under Article 20 may be used for a period of 3 years after August 14, 1997 by the Village of Morton Grove, within the area designated as the Waukegan Road Tax Increment Financing District to be used only for acquiring commercially zoned properties located on Waukegan Road for tax increment redevelopment projects contained in the redevelopment plan for the area.

P.A. 94–1055, Art. 25, § 25–7–103.55, eff. Jan. 1, 2007.

30/25–7–103.56. Quick-take; Village of Rosemont

§ 25–7–103.56. Quick-take; Village of Rosemont. Quick-take proceedings under Article 20 may be used for a period of 2 years after August 14, 1997, by the Village of Rosemont for the acquisition of the property described as Tract 1, and the acquisition of any leasehold interest of the property described as Tract 2, both described as follows:

Tract 1

PARCEL 1:

THAT PART OF THE SOUTHWEST ¼ OF SECTION 33, TOWNSHIP 41 NORTH, RANGE 12, EAST OF THE THIRD PRINCIPAL MERIDIAN, DESCRIBED AS FOLLOWS:

COMMENCING AT THE INTERSECTION OF A LINE 50.00 FEET, AS MEASURED AT RIGHT ANGLES, NORTH OF AND PARALLEL WITH THE SOUTH LINE OF SAID SOUTHWEST ¼ WITH A LINE 484.69 FEET, AS MEASURED AT RIGHT ANGLES, EAST OF AND PARALLEL WITH THE WEST LINE OF SAID SOUTHWEST ¼ (THE WEST LINE OF SAID SOUTHWEST ¼ HAVING AN ASSUMED BEARING OF NORTH 00 DEGREES 00 MINUTES 00 SECONDS EAST FOR THIS LEGAL DESCRIPTION); THENCE NORTH 00 DEGREES 00 MINUTES 00 SECONDS EAST ALONG SAID LAST DESCRIBED PARALLEL LINE, 427.26 FEET TO A POINT FOR A PLACE OF BEGIN-

NING; THENCE CONTINUING NORTH 00 DEGREES 00 MINUTES 00 SECONDS EAST ALONG SAID LAST DESCRIBED PARALLEL LINE, 251.92 FEET; THENCE NORTH 45 DEGREES 00 MINUTES 00 SECONDS EAST, 32.53 FEET; THENCE NORTH 90 DEGREES 00 MINUTES 00 SECONDS EAST, 53.70 FEET; THENCE SOUTH 72 DEGREES 34 MINUTES 18 SECONDS EAST, 149.63 FEET; THENCE SOUTH 00 DEGREES 00 MINUTES 00 SECONDS WEST, 230.11 FEET; THENCE SOUTH 90 DEGREES 00 MINUTES 00 SECONDS WEST, 219.46 FEET, TO THE POINT OF BEGINNING IN COOK COUNTY, ILLINOIS.

PARCEL 2:

THAT PART OF THE SOUTHWEST ¼ OF SECTION 33, TOWNSHIP 41 NORTH, RANGE 12, EAST OF THE THIRD PRINCIPAL MERIDIAN, DESCRIBED AS FOLLOWS:

COMMENCING AT THE INTERSECTION OF A LINE 50.00 FEET, AS MEASURED AT RIGHT ANGLES, NORTH OF AND PARALLEL WITH THE SOUTH LINE OF SAID SOUTHWEST ¼ WITH A LINE 484.69 FEET, AS MEASURED AT RIGHT ANGLES, EAST OF AND PARALLEL WITH THE WEST LINE OF SAID SOUTHWEST ¼ (THE WEST LINE OF SAID SOUTHWEST ¼ HAVING AN ASSUMED BEARING OF NORTH 00 DEGREES, 00 MINUTES, 00 SECONDS EAST FOR THIS LEGAL DESCRIPTION); THENCE NORTH 00 DEGREES, 00 MINUTES, 00 SECONDS EAST ALONG SAID LAST DESCRIBED PARALLEL LINE, 153.00 FEET; THENCE NORTH 90 DEGREES, 00 MINUTES, 00 SECONDS EAST, 89.18 FEET; THENCE NORTH 00 DEGREES, 00 MINUTES, 00 SECONDS EAST, 48.68 FEET; THENCE NORTH 90 DEGREES, 00 MINUTES, 00 SECONDS EAST, 43.53 FEET; THENCE SOUTH 00 DEGREES, 00 MINUTES, 00 SECONDS EAST, 8.00 FEET; THENCE NORTH 90 DEGREES, 00 MINUTES, 00 SECONDS EAST, 44.23 FEET; THENCE NORTH 45 DEGREES, 00 MINUTES, 00 SECONDS EAST, 60.13 FEET; THENCE NORTH 00 DEGREES, 00 MINUTES, 00 SECONDS EAST, 141.06 FEET TO A POINT FOR A PLACE OF BEGINNING, SAID POINT BEING 447.18 FEET NORTH AND 704.15 FEET EAST OF THE SOUTHWEST CORNER OF THE SOUTHWEST ¼ OF SAID SECTION 33, AS MEASURED ALONG THE WEST LINE OF SAID SOUTHWEST ¼ AND ALONG A LINE AT RIGHT ANGLES THERETO; THENCE NORTH 00 DEGREES, 00 MINUTES, 00 SECONDS EAST, 280.11 FEET; THENCE NORTH 72 DEGREES, 34 MINUTES, 18 SECONDS WEST, 149.63 FEET; THENCE SOUTH 90 DEGREES, 00 MINUTES, 00 SECONDS WEST, 53.70 FEET; THENCE SOUTH 45 DEGREES, 00 MINUTES, 00 SECONDS WEST, 32.53 FEET TO A POINT

ON A LINE 484.69 FEET, AS MEASURED AT RIGHT ANGLES, EAST OF AND PARALLEL WITH THE WEST LINE OF SAID SOUTHWEST ¼, SAID POINT BEING 679.18 FEET, AS MEASURED ALONG SAID PARALLEL LINE, NORTH OF THE AFOREDESCRIBED POINT OF COMMENCEMENT; THENCE NORTH 00 DEGREES, 00 MINUTES, 00 SECONDS EAST ALONG SAID LAST DESCRIBED PARALLEL LINE, 158.10 FEET; THENCE NORTH 39 DEGREES, 39 MINUTES, 24 SECONDS EAST, 27.09 FEET TO AN INTERSECTION WITH THE SOUTHERLY LINE OF HIGGINS ROAD, BEING A LINE 50.00 FEET, AS MEASURED AT RIGHT ANGLES, SOUTHERLY OF AND PARALLEL WITH THE CENTER LINE OF SAID ROAD; THENCE SOUTH 72 DEGREES, 34 MINUTES, 18 SECONDS EAST ALONG SAID LAST DESCRIBED SOUTHERLY LINE, 382.55 FEET TO AN INTERSECTION WITH THE WESTERLY RIGHT OF WAY LINE OF THE MINNEAPOLIS, ST. PAUL AND SAULT STE. MARIE RAILROAD (FORMERLY THE CHICAGO AND WISCONSIN RAILROAD); THENCE SOUTH 14 DEGREES, 51 MINUTES, 36 SECONDS EAST ALONG SAID LAST DESCRIBED WESTERLY LINE, 378.97 FEET; THENCE SOUTH 90 DEGREES, 00 MINUTES, 00 SECONDS WEST, 260.00 FEET TO THE PLACE OF BEGINNING, IN COOK COUNTY, ILLINOIS.

Generally comprising approximately 3.8 acres along the south side of Higgins Road, East of Mannheim Road.

Tract 2

PARCEL 1:

Any leasehold interest of any portion of the property legally described as follows:

THAT PART OF THE EAST 8 ACRES OF LOT 2 IN FREDERICK JOSS'S DIVISION OF LAND IN SECTION 9, TOWNSHIP 40 NORTH, RANGE 12 EAST OF THE THIRD PRINCIPAL MERIDIAN (EXCEPT THE NORTH 500 FEET THEREOF AS MEASURED ON THE EAST LINE) LYING EASTERLY OF THE FOLLOWING DESCRIBED LINE: BEGINNING AT A POINT ON THE NORTH LINE OF SAID LOT 2, 19.07 FEET WEST OF THE NORTHEAST CORNER THEREOF; THENCE SOUTHWESTERLY ALONG A LINE FORMING AN ANGLE OF 73 DEGREES 46 MINUTES 40 SECONDS (AS MEASURED FROM WEST TO SOUTHWEST) WITH THE AFORESAID NORTH LINE OF LOT 2, A DISTANCE OF 626.69 FEET TO A POINT; THENCE SOUTHEASTERLY ALONG A LINE FORMING AN ANGLE OF 20 DEGREES 58 MINUTES 25 SECONDS (AS MEASURED TO THE LEFT) WITH A PROLONGA-

TION OF THE LAST DESCRIBED COURSE A DISTANCE OF 721.92 FEET TO A POINT IN THE SOUTH LINE OF SAID LOT WHICH IS 85.31 FEET WEST OF THE SOUTHEAST CORNER OF SAID LOT 2, EXCEPTING THEREFROM THE FOLLOWING DESCRIBED PREMISES: THE SOUTH 50 FEET OF LOT 2 LYING EAST OF THE FOLLOWING DESCRIBED LINE; BEGINNING AT A POINT IN THE SOUTH LINE OF LOT 2, WHICH IS 85.31 FEET WEST OF THE SOUTHEAST CORNER OF SAID LOT; THENCE NORTHERLY ON A LINE WHICH FORMS AN ANGLE OF 85 DEGREES 13 MINUTES 25 SECONDS IN THE NORTHWEST ¼ WITH SAID LAST DESCRIBED LINE IN FREDERICK JOSS'S DIVISION OF LANDS IN THE NORTHEAST ¼ OF SECTION 9, TOWNSHIP 40 NORTH, RANGE 12 EAST OF THE THIRD PRINCIPAL MERIDIAN.

PARCEL 2:

Plus any rights of ingress and egress which the said holder of the leasehold interest may have pursuant to the following described easement:

GRANT OF EASEMENT FOR THE BENEFIT OF PARCEL 1 AS CREATED BY GRANT FROM FRACAP SHEET METAL MANUFACTURING COMPANY, INC. TO JUNE WEBER POLLY DATED NOVEMBER 16, 1970 AND RECORDED APRIL 7, 1971 AS DOCUMENT 21442818 FOR PASSAGEWAY OVER THE EAST 20 FEET AS MEASURED AT RIGHT ANGLES TO THE EAST LINE THEREOF OF THE NORTH 500 FEET OF THAT PART OF THE EAST 8 ACRES OF LOT 2 IN FREDERICK JOSS'S DIVISION OF LAND IN SECTION 9, TOWNSHIP 40 NORTH, RANGE 12 EAST OF THE THIRD PRINCIPAL MERIDIAN, LYING EASTERLY OF THE FOLLOWING DESCRIBED LINE: BEGINNING AT A POINT ON THE NORTH LINE OF SAID LOT 2, 19.07 FEET WEST OF THE NORTHEAST CORNER THEREOF; THENCE SOUTHWESTERLY ALONG A LINE FORMING AN ANGLE OF 73 DEGREES 46 MINUTES 40 SECONDS (AS MEASURED FROM WEST TO SOUTHWEST) WITH THE AFORESAID NORTH LINE OF LOT 2, A DISTANCE OF 626.69 FEET TO A POINT; THENCE SOUTHEASTERLY ALONG A LINE FORMING AN ANGLE OF 20 DEGREES 58 MINUTES 25 SECONDS (AS MEASURED TO THE LEFT) WITH A PROLONGATION OF THE LAST DESCRIBED COURSE A DISTANCE OF 721.92 FEET TO A POINT IN THE SOUTH LINE OF SAID LOT 2, WHICH IS 85.31 FEET WEST OF THE SOUTHEAST CORNER OF SAID LOT 2, IN COOK COUNTY, ILLINOIS.

P.A. 94–1055, Art. 25, § 25–7–103.56, eff. Jan. 1, 2007.

30/25–7–103.57. Quick-take; City of Champaign

§ 25–7–103.57. Quick-take; City of Champaign. Quick-take proceedings under Article 20 may be used for a period of 24 months from August 14, 1997, by the City of Champaign for the acquisition of land and easements in and adjacent to the City of Champaign for the improvement of Windsor Road and Duncan Road and for the construction of the Boneyard Creek Improvement Project.

P.A. 94–1055, Art. 25, § 25–7–103.57, eff. Jan. 1, 2007.

30/25–7–103.58. Quick-take; City of Rochelle

§ 25–7–103.58. Quick-take; City of Rochelle. Quick-take proceedings under Article 20 may be used for a period of 24 months from July 30, 1998, by the City of Rochelle, to allow the acquisition of easements for the construction and maintenance of overhead utility lines and poles along a route within and adjacent to existing roadway easements on Twombley, Mulford, and Paw Paw roads in Ogle and Lee counties.

P.A. 94–1055, Art. 25, § 25–7–103.58, eff. Jan. 1, 2007.

30/25–7–103.59. Quick-take; Village of Bolingbrook

§ 25–7–103.59. Quick-take; Village of Bolingbrook. Quick-take proceedings under Article 20 may be used for a period of 3 years after July 30, 1998, by the Village of Bolingbrook for acquisition of property within a Regional Stormwater Detention Project Area, when the purpose of the condemnation proceeding is to acquire land for one or more of the following public purposes: drainage, stormwater management, open space, recreation, improvements for water service and related appurtenances, or wetland mitigation and banking; the project area is in Wheatland Township, Will County, bounded generally by Essington Road, 127th Street, and Kings Road and is more particularly described as follows: That part of Section 25 Township 37 N Range 9 E of the 3rd Principal Meridian all in Wheatland Township, Will County, except the Northeast Quarter; the North ½ of the Northwest Quarter; and the Southwest Quarter of the Southwest Quarter.

P.A. 94–1055, Art. 25, § 25–7–103.59, eff. Jan. 1, 2007.

30/25–7–103.60. Quick-take; Village of Franklin Park

§ 25–7–103.60. Quick-take; Village of Franklin Park. Quick-take proceedings under Article 20 may be used for a period of 36 months after July 1, 1998, by the Village of Franklin Park, for the acquisition for school purposes, including, but not limited to, school parking lot purposes, of property bounded on the west by Rose Street, on the north by Nerbonne Street, on the east by Pearl Street extended north on Nerbonne Street, and on the south by King Street, except that no portion used for residential purposes shall be taken.

P.A. 94–1055, Art. 25, § 25–7–103.60, eff. Jan. 1, 2007.

30/25–7–103.61.   Quick-take; Village of Melrose Park

§ 25–7–103.61.   Quick-take; Village of Melrose Park.   Quick-take proceedings under Article 20 may be used for a period of 5 years after June 1, 1998 by the Village of Melrose Park to acquire the following described property, for the purpose of redeveloping blighted areas:

Golfland

That part of the North half of the South East Quarter of the South West quarter of Section 35, Township 40 North, Range 12, East of the Third Principal Meridian, lying Northeast of the Northeasterly right-of-way line of the Minneapolis, St. Paul and Sault Ste. Marie Railroad; lying South of a line 443.00 feet North of and parallel to the South line of the North half of the South East Quarter of the South West Quarter of Section 35, aforesaid; and lying west of the West line of the East 490 feet of the North half of the South East Quarter of the South West Quarter of Section 35, aforesaid (excepting therefrom the East 50 feet of the North 80 feet thereof and except that part taken and dedicated for 5th Avenue);

ALSO

That part of the South half of the South East Quarter of the South West Quarter of Section 35, Township 30 North, Range 12, East of the Third Principal Meridian, lying Northeast of the Northeasterly right-of-way line of the Minneapolis, St. Paul and Sault Ste. Marie Railroad, described as follows: commencing at the intersection of the West line of the South East Quarter of the South West Quarter of Section 35, aforesaid, with the North line of the South half of the South East Quarter of the South West Quarter of said Section 35; thence East along the aforementioned North line 67.91 Feet to the point of beginning of land herein described; thence continue East along said North line 297.59 feet; thence Southwesterly along a line forming an angle of 17 degrees 41 minutes 34 seconds, measured from West to South West with last described course, from a distance of 240.84 feet to a point 100 feet Southeasterly of the point of beginning; thence Northwesterly 100 feet to the point of beginning; all in Cook County.

P.A. 94–1055, Art. 25, § 25–7–103.61, eff. Jan. 1, 2007.

30/25–7–103.62.   Quick-take; Village of Melrose Park

§ 25–7–103.62.   Quick-take; Village of Melrose Park.   Quick-take proceedings under Article 20 may be used for a period of 3 years after June 1, 1998, by the Village of Melrose Park to acquire property described as follows for the purpose of redeveloping blighted areas:

THAT PART OF THE WEST 340 FEET OF THE EAST 1360 FEET OF THE NORTH HALF OF THE NORTHEAST QUARTER OF SECTION 2, TOWNSHIP 39 NORTH, RANGE 12, EAST OF THE THIRD PRINCIPAL MERIDIAN, LYING NORTH OF THE CENTERLINE OF DES PLAINES RIVER (EXCEPT THAT PART OF THE WEST 340 FEET OF THE EAST 1360 FEET OF THE NORTH HALF OF THE NORTHEAST QUARTER OF SECTION 2, TOWNSHIP 39 NORTH, RANGE 12, EAST OF THE THIRD PRINCIPAL MERIDIAN, LYING NORTH OF THE CENTERLINE OF DES PLAINES RIVER AND LYING SOUTH OF A LINE DESCRIBED AS COMMENCING ON THE EAST LINE OF SAID TRACT 880 FEET SOUTH OF THE NORTH LINE OF SAID SECTION 2 RUNNING WESTERLY TO A POINT IN THE WEST LINE OF SAID TRACT WHICH IS 976 FEET SOUTH OF THE NORTH LINE OF SAID SECTION AND EXCEPT THE NORTH 99.2 FEET AS MEASURED ON THE WEST LINE AND BY 99.6 FEET AS MEASURED ON THE EAST LINE OF SAID WEST 340 FEET AND DEDICATED AND CONVEYED TO STATE OF ILLINOIS FOR ROAD OR PUBLIC HIGHWAY PURPOSES), IN COOK COUNTY, ILLINOIS.

THAT PART OF THE WEST 170 FEET OF THE EAST 1530 FEET OF THE NORTH ½ OF THE NORTHEAST ¼ OF SECTION 2, TOWNSHIP 39 NORTH, RANGE 12, EAST OF THE THIRD PRINCIPAL MERIDIAN, LYING NORTH OF THE CENTER LINE OF DES PLAINES RIVER. (EXCEPT THAT PART OF THE WEST 170 FEET OF THE EAST 1530 FEET OF THE NORTH ½ OF THE NORTHEAST ¼ OF SECTION 2, TOWNSHIP 39 NORTH, RANGE 12, EAST OF THE THIRD PRINCIPAL MERIDIAN, LYING NORTH OF THE CENTER LINE OF DES PLAINES RIVER AND LYING SOUTH OF A LINE DESCRIBED AS COMMENCING ON THE EAST LINE OF SAID TRACT 976 FEET SOUTH OF THE NORTH LINE OF SAID SECTION 2, RUNNING WESTERLY TO A POINT IN THE WEST LINE OF SAID TRACT WHICH IS 1095.50 FEET SOUTH OF THE NORTH LINE OF SAID SECTION AND EXCEPT THE NORTH 100.00 FEET AS MEASURED ON THE WEST LINE AND BY 99.2 FEET AS MEASURED ON THE EAST

LINE OF SAID WEST 170 FEET AND DEDI-
CATED AND CONVEYED TO THE STATE OF
ILLINOIS FOR ROAD OR PUBLIC HIGHWAY
PURPOSES), IN COOK COUNTY, ILLINOIS.

P.A. 94–1055, Art. 25, § 25–7–103.62, eff. Jan. 1, 2007.

30/25–7–103.63. Quick–take; City of Peru

§ 25–7–103.63. Quick–take; City of Peru. Quick-
take proceedings under Article 20 may be used for a
period of 24 months after July 30, 1998 by the City of
Peru for removal of existing residential deed restrictions on the use of property, and the rights of other
property owners in the subdivision to enforce those
restrictions, as they apply to lots 10, 11, 12, 13, 14, 15,
and 16 in Urbanowski's Subdivision to the City of
Peru, all of which are owned by the Illinois Valley
Community Hospital and adjacent to the existing hospital building, for the limited purpose of allowing the
Illinois Valley Community Hospital to expand its hospital facility, including expansion for needed emergency room and outpatient services; under this Section
compensation shall be paid to those other property
owners for the removal of their rights to enforce the
residential deed restrictions on property owned by the
Illinois Valley Community Hospital, but no real estate
owned by those other property owners may be taken.

P.A. 94–1055, Art. 25, § 25–7–103.63, eff. Jan. 1, 2007.
Amended by P.A. 95–331, § 1090, eff. Aug. 21, 2007.

30/25–7–103.64. Quick–take; Village of South Barrington

§ 25–7–103.64. Quick–take; Village of South Barrington. Quick–take proceedings under Article 20
may be used for a period of 3 years after July 30,
1998, by the Village of South Barrington for the
acquisition of land and temporary and permanent
easements for the purposes of construction and maintenance of sewerage facilities and sewerage transmission pipes along an area not to exceed 100 feet north
of the Northwest Tollway between Barrington Road
and Route 72.

P.A. 94–1055, Art. 25, § 25–7–103.64, eff. Jan. 1, 2007.

30/25–7–103.65. Quick–take; Village of North-lake

§ 25–7–103.65. Quick–take; Village of Northlake.
Quick–take proceedings under Article 20 may be used
for a period of 18 months after July 30, 1998, by the
Village of Northlake for the acquisition of the following described property for stormwater management
and public recreation purposes:

LOT 10 IN BLOCK 7 IN TOWN MANOR SUB-
DIVISION OF THE NORTH 100 ACRES OF
THE NORTH EAST ¼ OF SECTION 5, TOWN-
SHIP 39 NORTH, RANGE 12, EAST OF THE
THIRD PRINCIPAL MERIDIAN, IN COOK
COUNTY, ILLINOIS.

Commonly known as 315 E. Morse Drive, Northlake, Illinois, 60164;

LOT 17 IN BLOCK 2 IN MIDLAND DEVEL-
OPMENT COMPANY'S NORTHLAKE VIL-
LAGE, A SUBDIVISION OF THE NORTH
HALF OF THE NORTHWEST QUARTER OF
SECTION 5, TOWNSHIP 39 NORTH, RANGE 12,
EAST OF THE THIRD PRINCIPAL MERIDIAN
(EXCEPT THE SOUTH 208.7 FEET OF THE
WEST 208.7 FEET EAST OF WOLF ROAD OF
THE NORTH HALF OF THE NORTHWEST
QUARTER, AFORESAID), IN COOK COUNTY,
ILLINOIS.

PIN: 15–05–115–001

Commonly known as 101 S. Wolf Road, Northlake, Illinois, 60164.

P.A. 94–1055, Art. 25, § 25–7–103.65, eff. Jan. 1, 2007.

30/25–7–103.66. Quick–take; City of Carbon-dale

§ 25–7–103.66. Quick–take; City of Carbondale.
Quick–take proceedings under Article 20 may be used
for a period of 48 months after July 30, 1998, by the
City of Carbondale, for the acquisition of property
bounded by the following lines for the Mill Street
Underpass Project (which is part of the Carbondale
Railroad Relocation Project): a line 300 feet west of
the centerline of Thompson Street; a line 100 feet
east of the centerline of Wall Street; a line 700 feet
north of the centerline of College Street; and the
centerline of Grand Avenue.

P.A. 94–1055, Art. 25, § 25–7–103.66, eff. Jan. 1, 2007.

30/25–7–103.67. Quick–take; Village of Round Lake Park

§ 25–7–103.67. Quick–take; Village of Round Lake
Park. Quick–take proceedings under Article 20 may
be used for a period of 3 years after July 30, 1998, by
the Village of Round Lake Park in Lake County for
acquisition of temporary construction easements and
permanent easement corridors for providing off-site
water and sewer service for the Alter Business Park,
generally described as follows:

Commencing at the Joint Action Water Agency
(JAWA) facility on the south side of Winchester
Road (County Route A34) and west of Midlothian
Road, the proposed public water line will be located
in the Winchester Road (County Route A34) right-
of-way or immediately adjacent to the right-of-way
from the JAWA facility west to Illinois State Route
83. The water line will then extend under Illinois
State Route 83 and continue in the Winchester
Road (County Route A34) right-of-way or immediately adjacent to the right-of-way as it extends
westerly from Illinois State Route 83 to the proposed pump station and delivery structure at the
most southerly west property line of the Alter property located south of Peterson Road (County Route
A33) and west of Illinois State Route 83. Also, the

proposed public water line will be located in the Peterson Road (County Route A33) right-of-way or immediately adjacent to the right-of-way from Illinois State Route 83 west to the westerly property line of the Alter property, which property line lies approximately 2600′ west of Alleghany Road (County Route V68).

The proposed sanitary sewer route will commence at a location on Fairfield Road (County Route V61) north of Illinois State Route 134 at the Lake County Interceptor (which ultimately extends into the Fox Lake Sanitary District System); the route of the sanitary sewer will continue south of Illinois State Route 134 in the right-of-way of Fairfield Road (County Route V61) or immediately adjacent thereto from its extension north of Illinois State Route 134 to its intersection with Townline Road. The sanitary sewer will then extend east in the right-of-way of Townline Road or immediately adjacent thereto to its intersection with Bacon Road. The sanitary sewer will then extend in the Bacon Road right-of-way line or immediately adjacent thereto continuing in a southeasterly direction until its intersection with Illinois State Route 60. The sanitary line will then extend in the Illinois State Route 60 right-of-way by permit or immediately adjacent thereto continuing easterly along said right-of-way to the point of intersection with Peterson Road (County Route A33). The sanitary line will then continue easterly in the right-of-way of Peterson Road (County Route A33) or immediately adjacent thereto to the point of intersection with Alleghany Road (County Route V68) and then will extend within the Alter property.

P.A. 94–1055, Art. 25, § 25–7–103.67, eff. Jan. 1, 2007.

30/25–7–103.68. Quick-take; Village of Rosemont

§ 25–7–103.68. Quick-take; Village of Rosemont. Quick-take proceedings under Article 20 may be used for a period of 3 years after July 30, 1998, by the Village of Rosemont for redevelopment purposes, including infrastructure improvements, construction of streets, stormwater facilities, and drainage areas, and flood plain improvements, for the acquisition of property described as follows:

That part of the Northwest Quarter and that part of the Southwest Quarter of Section 3, Township 40 North, Range 12, East of the Third Principal Meridian, and being more particularly described as follows:

Beginning at the point of intersection of the west right-of-way line of River Road (as shown on the plat of subdivision for Gerhart Huehl Estates Division per document number 4572711) and the southerly line of Lot 7 in said Gerhart Huehl Estates Division; thence north 14 degrees 38 minutes 19 seconds west, along the aforesaid west right-of-way of River Road, to the point of intersection with a line drawn 490.0 feet south of and parallel to the north line of Lot 3 in the said Gerhart Huehl Estates Division; thence north 89 degrees 07 minutes 41 seconds west, along the previously described parallel line 554.77 feet to the point, said point being 540.00 feet east of the easterly right-of-way line of Schafer Court (Schafer Court being an unrecorded roadway); thence, north 0 degrees 00 minutes 00 seconds east, 284.12 feet to the point of intersection with south line of the aforesaid Lot 3 (said south line also being the north line of Lot 6 in Gerhart Huehl Estates Division); thence north 89 degrees 04 minutes 45 seconds west, along the said south line of Lot 3, 478.29 feet to the point of intersection with the aforesaid easterly right-of-way line of Schafer Court; thence south 12 degrees 16 minutes 34 seconds west, along the said easterly right-of-way line, 312.83 feet; thence south 18 degrees 09 minutes 05 seconds west, continuing along the said easterly right-of-way line, 308.16 feet to the point of intersection with the northerly right-of-way line of Higgins Road as dedicated per document number 11056708; thence, north 66 degrees 43 minutes 09 seconds west along said northerly right-of-way line of Higgins Road to the easterly right-of-way of the Northwest Toll Road; thence southerly along said easterly right-of-way of the Northwest Toll Road to the southerly right-of-way of Maple Avenue extended westerly; thence easterly along said southerly right-of-way line of Maple Avenue (recorded as Bock Avenue) to the easterly right-of-way line of Gage Street; thence northerly along said easterly right-of-way line of Gage Street to the southerly line of Lot 2 in River Rose Subdivision Unit 2 per document number 19594706; thence easterly along the southerly line of said Lot 2 in River Rose Subdivision Unit Number 2 and said southerly line extended easterly to the easterly right-of-way line of Glen Lake Drive (as dedicated in River Rose Subdivision per Document Number 19352146 and dedicated as Willow Creek Drive); thence southwesterly along said easterly right-of-way line to the northwest corner of Lot 1 in said River Rose Subdivision; thence south 59 degrees 08 minutes 47 seconds east, along the northerly lines of Lots 1 through 13 (both inclusive) in the said River Rose subdivision, 757.48 feet to the most northeasterly corner of said Lot 13; thence south 11 degrees 05 minutes 25 seconds west, along the easterly line of said lot 13 in said River Rose Subdivision, 14.08 feet to the northerly line of Glen J. Nixon's subdivision as per document 19753046; thence easterly along said northerly line, 237.43 feet to the westerly right-of-way of said Des Plaines River Road;

Thence southerly along said westerly right-of-way of Des Plaines River Road to the southerly line of the Northerly 90 feet of Lot 2 in said Glen J. Nixon's subdivision; thence westerly along said southerly line to the westerly line of said Glen J. Nixon's subdivision; thence southerly along the said westerly line of Glen J. Nixon's subdivision to the southerly right-of- way of an unrecorded roadway; thence south 70 degrees 43 minutes 16 seconds west, along the southerly line of the unrecorded roadway, 108.23 feet; thence continuing along the southerly right-of-way of the unrecorded roadway, 95.34 feet along an arc of a circle whose radius is 110.00 feet and being convex to the south; thence north 56 degrees 32 minutes 25 seconds west, continuing along the southerly right-of-way of the said unrecorded roadway, 216.00 feet to the southwest corner of said Glen Lake Drive as dedicated in the aforesaid River Rose subdivision; thence north 59 degrees 10 minutes 12 seconds west, along the southerly right-of-way of said Glen Lake Drive, 327.48 feet, to the point of intersection with east line of Lot 8 in Block 1 in Higgins Road Ranchettes Subdivision per Document Number 13820089; thence northerly along the east line of said Lot 8, 97.24 feet to a point; said point being 66.00 feet south of the northeast corner of said Lot 8; thence north 89 degrees 36 minutes 54 seconds west, along a line which is 66.00 feet south of and parallel to the north line of Lots 3, 4, 5, 6, 7, and 8 in said Higgins Road Ranchettes Subdivision (said parallel line also being the south line of an unrecorded street known as Glenlake Street), 621.61 feet to the point of intersection with the northeasterly right-of-way line of Toll Road; the next four courses being along the said northeasterly right-of-way line of the Toll Road; thence south 21 degrees 28 minutes 12 seconds east, 219.81 feet; thence south 34 degrees 29 minutes 34 seconds east, 261.77 feet; thence south 52 degrees 02 minutes 04 seconds east, 114.21 feet; thence south 52 degrees 07 minutes 21 seconds east to the westerly line (extended northerly) of Lots 83 through 87 inclusive in Frederick H. Bartlett's River View Estates recorded as Document Number 853426 in Cook County; thence southerly along said westerly line to the southerly right-of-way line of Thorndale Avenue; thence easterly along said southerly right-of-way line of Thorndale Avenue 14.65 feet; thence southerly along a line parallel with the said westerly line of Lots 83 through 87 inclusive and 14.38 feet easterly, 139.45 feet; thence southwesterly along a line which ends in the southerly line of said Lot 84 extended westerly, 85.35 feet westerly from the southwest corner of said Lot 84; thence easterly along said southerly line to the westerly right-of-way of Des Plaines River Road; thence northerly along said westerly right-of-way line to the said northerly line of the Toll Road; thence south 52 degrees 07 minutes 21 seconds east, along said right-of-way to the centerline of said Des Plaines River Road; thence south 11 degrees 06 minutes 48 seconds west, along said centerline, 1.47 feet; thence south 55 degrees 56 minutes 09 seconds east, continuing along the said northeasterly right-of-way line of the Toll Road (said line also being the south line of Lot 1 in Rosemont Industrial

Center per Document Number 20066369), 411.98 feet; thence south 61 degrees 51 minutes 06 seconds east, continuing along the said northeasterly right-of-way line of the Toll Road (said line also being along the south line of Lots 1, 2, and 5 in said Rosemont Industrial Center), 599.13 feet to the southeast corner of said Lot 5; thence north 12 degrees 45 minutes 47 seconds east, along the east lines of Lots 3 and 5 in said Rosemont Industrial Center, 424.40 feet; thence north 33 degrees 51 minutes 39 seconds east, along the east lines of Lots 3 and 4 in the said Rosemont Industrial Center, 241.42 feet to the northeast corner of said Lot 4; thence north 33 degrees 51 minutes 40 seconds east, 189.38 feet to the center of said Section 3; thence north 2 degrees 42 minutes 55 seconds east, along the east line of the northwest quarter of said Section 3, 375.90 feet to the point of intersection with the south line of Higgins Road, as widened per Document Number 11045055; the next three courses being along the said south right-of-way line of Higgins Road; thence north 64 degrees 30 minutes 51 seconds west, 53.65 feet; thence northwesterly, 436.47 feet along an arc of a circle whose radius is 1,482.69 feet and being convex to the southwest; thence north 47 degrees 57 minutes 51 seconds west, 73.57 feet; thence northeasterly, along an arc of a circle whose radius is 5,679.65 feet and being convex to the northeast, to a point of intersection of said southerly right-of-way of Higgins Road and the southeasterly line of the land conveyed to James H. Lomax by Document Number 1444990; thence northeasterly along said southeasterly line extended, 197 feet to the center line of the Des Plaines River; thence north 49 degrees 11 minutes 20 seconds west 325.90 feet; thence continuing in the said center line of the Des Plaines River, north 27 degrees 56 minutes 17 seconds west 370.53 feet; thence north 12 degrees 10 minutes 40 seconds east, 16.0 feet; thence southwesterly along said southeasterly line of Lot 7 extended in Gerhart Huehl Estates Division, to said place of beginning;

Plus,

That part of the West half of the Northwest quarter of Section 3, Township 40 North, Range 12 East of the Third Principal Meridian, in Cook County, Illinois, described as follows:

Beginning at the intersection of the South line of Devon Avenue with the East line of Shafer Court being a point 281.01 feet East of the West line of the aforementioned West half of the Northwest quarter of Section 33; thence Southerly along the East line of said Shafer Court, 193.91 feet to the South line of Lot 3 in Gerhart Huehl Estate Division according to the plat thereof recorded June 3, 1910, as Document 4572711, being a point 241.74 feet East of the aforementioned West half of the Northwest quarter of Section 33; thence East along the South line of said Lot 3, a distance of 508.5 feet to a point 487.69 feet West of the centerline of River Road; thence continuing easterly along the last described line as extended to the west line of River Road; thence northerly along the west line of River Road to the South line of Devon Avenue; thence westerly along the south line of Devon Avenue to the point of beginning;

Plus,

That part of the Southwest quarter of Section 3, Township 40 North, Range 12 East of the Third Principal Meridian, in Cook County, Illinois, described as follows:

Beginning at the Southeast corner of Rosemont Industrial Center, being a subdivision recorded February 17, 1967 as Document 20066369; thence Northwesterly along the South line of Rosemont Industrial Center aforesaid, and said South line extended to the Westerly line of River Road to the South; thence Southwesterly along said Westerly line, to the North line of Interstate 290; thence Easterly along said North line, to the West line of property owned by the Forest Preserve; thence along and then Northerly along the irregular West line of property owned by the Forest Preserve and extended across the Interstate 290 right-of-way, to the point of beginning;

Plus,

The Northerly 90 feet of Lot 2 in Glen J. Nixon's Subdivision of part of Lot 15 in Assessor's Division of part of Section 3, Township 40 North, Range 12, East of the Third Principal Meridian, according to the plat thereof recorded March 1, 1966 as Document 19753046, in Cook County, Illinois, (except therefrom that part used for River Road), all in Cook County.

PLUS,

THAT PART OF THE NORTHWEST QUARTER OF SECTION 3 TOWNSHIP 40 NORTH, RANGE 12, EAST OF THE THIRD PRINCIPAL MERIDIAN, AND BEING MORE PARTICULARLY DESCRIBED AS FOLLOWS:

BEGINNING AT THE POINT OF INTERSECTION OF THE EASTERLY RIGHT-OF-WAY LINE OF THE NORTHWEST TOLL ROAD AND THE SOUTHERLY RIGHT-OF-WAY LINE OF MAPLE AVENUE EXTENDED WESTERLY; THENCE EASTERLY ALONG SAID SOUTHERLY RIGHT-OF-WAY LINE OF MAPLE AVENUE (RECORDED AS BOCK AVENUE) TO THE EASTERLY RIGHT-OF-WAY LINE OF GAGE STREET; THENCE NORTHERLY ALONG SAID EASTERLY RIGHT-OF-WAY LINE OF GAGE STREET TO THE SOUTHERLY LINE OF LOT 2 IN RIVER ROSE SUBDIVISION UNIT 2 PER DOCUMENT NUMBER 19594706; THENCE EASTERLY ALONG THE SOUTHERLY LINE OF SAID LOT 2 IN RIVER ROSE SUBDIVISION UNIT NUMBER 2 AND

SAID SOUTHERLY LINE EXTENDED EASTERLY TO THE EASTERLY RIGHT-OF-WAY LINE OF GLEN LAKE DRIVE (AS DEDICATED IN RIVER ROSE SUBDIVISION PER DOCUMENT NUMBER 19352146 AND DEDICATED AS WILLOW CREEK DRIVE); THENCE SOUTHWESTERLY ALONG SAID EASTERLY RIGHT-OF-WAY LINE TO THE NORTHWEST CORNER OF LOT 1 IN SAID RIVER ROSE SUBDIVISION; THENCE SOUTHEASTERLY ALONG THE NORTHERLY LINE OF SAID LOT 1 IN SAID RIVER ROSE SUBDIVISION, 86.0 FEET TO THE NORTHEAST CORNER OF SAID LOT 1; THENCE SOUTHWESTERLY ALONG THE EASTERLY LINE OF SAID LOT 1, 120.0 FEET TO THE SOUTHEAST CORNER OF SAID LOT 1; THENCE NORTHWESTERLY ALONG THE SOUTHERLY LINE OF SAID LOT 1 AND THE NORTHERLY RIGHT-OF-WAY LINE OF RIVER ROSE STREET (AS DEDICATED IN RIVER ROSE SUBDIVISION PER DOCUMENT NUMBER 19352146), 34.3 FEET TO THE INTERSECTION OF THE NORTHERLY RIGHT-OF-WAY LINE OF SAID RIVER ROSE STREET AND THE EASTERLY LINE OF SAID WILLOW CREEK DRIVE, ALSO BEING THE SOUTHWEST CORNER OF SAID LOT 1; THENCE SOUTHEASTERLY ALONG THE EASTERLY RIGHT-OF-WAY LINE OF SAID WILLOW CREEK DRIVE TO THE MOST SOUTHWESTERLY CORNER OF LOT 27 IN SAID RIVER ROSE SUBDIVISION; THENCE SOUTHWESTERLY TO THE INTERSECTION OF THE NORTHWESTERLY CORNER OF LOT "B" IN SAID RIVER ROSE SUBDIVISION WITH THE EAST LOT LINE OF LOT 8 IN BLOCK 1 IN HIGGINS ROAD RANCHETTES SUBDIVISION PER DOCUMENT NUMBER 13820089; THENCE NORTHERLY ALONG THE EAST LINE OF SAID LOT 8, 97.24 FEET TO A POINT; SAID POINT BEING 66.00 FEET SOUTH OF THE NORTHEAST CORNER OF SAID LOT 8; THENCE WESTERLY, ALONG A LINE WHICH IS 66.00 FEET SOUTH OF AND PARALLEL TO THE NORTH LINE OF LOTS 3, 4, 5, 6, 7, AND 8 IN SAID HIGGINS ROAD RANCHETTES SUBDIVISION AND THEN WESTERLY THEREOF (SAID PARALLEL LINE ALSO BEING THE SOUTH LINE OF AN UNRECORDED STREET KNOWN AS GLEN-LAKE STREET), TO THE POINT OF INTERSECTION WITH THE EASTERLY RIGHT-OF-WAY LINE OF THE AFORESAID NORTHWEST TOLL ROAD; THENCE NORTHWESTERLY ALONG THE EASTERLY RIGHT-OF-WAY LINE OF SAID NORTHWEST TOLL ROAD TO THE POINT OF BEGINNING;

AREA 1:

That part of the South West Quarter of Section 33, Township 41 North, Range 12 East of the third

Principal Meridian, lying North of a line 575 feet north (measured at 90 degrees) of the South line of said South West Quarter, lying West of a line 451.45 feet East (measured at 90 degrees) of the West line of said South West Quarter and South of the center line of Higgins Road (except parts taken or used for highway purposes, including the land taken by condemnation in Case No. 65 L 8179 Circuit Court of Cook County, Illinois, described as follows: That part of the South West Quarter of Section 33, Township 41 North, Range 12 East of the Third Principal Meridian, bounded and described as follows: Beginning at a point of intersection of the center line of Higgins Road, as now located and established with the West line of the South West Quarter of said Section 33; thence South along said West line of the South West Quarter of said Section, a distance of 560.2 feet to a point in the North line of the South 575.0 feet of said South West Quarter of said Section 33; thence East along said North line of the South 575.0 feet of the South West Quarter of said Section 33, a distance of 45.0 feet to a point; thence Northeasterly in a straight line a distance of 179.27 feet to a point, distance 50.0 feet East, measured at right angles from the West line of the South West Quarter of said Section 33; thence Northeasterly in a straight line a distance of 187.38 feet to a point, distant 62.0 feet East, measured at right angles from said West line of the South West Quarter of said Section 33; thence North parallel with the said West line of the South West Quarter of said Section 33 a distance of 44.74 feet to a point of curvature; thence Northeasterly along a curved line, concave to the Southeast, having a radius of 50.0 feet and a central angle of 107 degrees 28 minutes, a distance of 93.73 feet to a point of tangency, distant 50.0 feet Southwest measured at right angles from the center line of Higgins Road; thence Southeasterly parallel with the center line of Higgins Road, a distance of 345.09 feet to a point on a line distant, 16.0 feet west of the east line of the west 467.34 feet of the South West Quarter of said Section 33; thence North in a straight line a distance of 58.71 feet to a point on said center line of Higgins Road; thence Northwesterly along said center line of Higgins Road a distance of 478.23 feet to the place of beginning) in Cook County, Illinois.

AREA 2:

That part of the South West ¼ of Section 33, Township 41 North, Range 12, East of the Third Principal Meridian, lying West of the West Right of Way Line of the Minneapolis, St. Paul and Sault Ste. Marie Railroad (formerly the Chicago and Wisconsin Railroad) and South of the center line of Higgins Road (except therefrom the South 200 feet of the West 467.84 feet of said South West ¼ and also excepting therefrom that part of said South West ¼ lying North of the North line of the South 575 feet of said South West ¼ and West of a line 16 feet West of and parallel with the West line of the

Tract of land described in a Deed dated May 22, 1929, and recorded July 9, 1929, as Document Number 10422646 (the Tract described in said Deed being the East 10 acres of that part of the South West ¼ of Section 33, Township 41 North, Range 12, East of the Third Principal Meridian, lying South of the Center line of Higgins Road and West of the West line extended North to the center of said Higgins Road of the East 20.62 chains of the North West ¼ of Section 4, Township 40 North, Range 12, East of the Third Principal Meridian (excepting therefrom the right of way of the Minneapolis, St. Paul and Sault Ste. Marie Railroad, formerly the Chicago and Wisconsin Railroad) and also excepting the South 50 feet of the said South West ¼ lying East of the West 467.84 feet thereof) and also excepting that portion of the land condemned for the widening of Higgins Road and Mannheim Road in Case Number 65 L7109, in Cook County, Illinois.

AREA 3:

The North 150 feet of the South 200 feet of that part of the South West ¼ of Section 33, Township 41 North, Range 12 East of the Third Principal Meridian (except the East 10 acres conveyed by George Deamantopulas and others, to Krowka by Document 10422646) lying South of the Center of Higgins Road (so called) and West of the West line extended North to center of Higgins Road of East 20.62 chains in the North West ¼ of Section 4, Township 40 North, Range 12 East of the Third Principal Meridian (except the Right of Way of Chicago and Wisconsin Railroad) in Cook County, Illinois.

AREA 4:

That part of the Southwest quarter of Section 33, Township 41 North, Range 12 East of the Third Principal Meridian, in Cook County, Illinois, described as follows:

Beginning at the intersection of the South line of the Southwest quarter of Section 33 aforesaid with the West line, extended South, of Lot 7 in Frederick H. Bartlett's Higgins Road Farms, being a subdivision recorded December 8, 1938 as Document 12246559; thence North along the aforementioned West line of Lot 7, to the center line of Higgins Road; thence Westerly along the center line of Higgins Road, to the Westerly right-of-way line of the Minneapolis, St. Paul and Sault Ste. Marie Railroad; thence Southerly along said Westerly right-of-way line, to the South line of the Southwest quarter of Section 33 aforesaid; thence East along said South line to the point of beginning.

Area 5

The North 195.00 feet of the west 365.67 feet of the West ½ of the Northeast ¼ of Section 4, Township 40 North, Range 12 East of the Third Principal Meridian.

And also

The north 50.00 feet of the East ½ of the Northwest ¼ of said Section 4 (except that part lying westerly of the easterly right-of-way line of the Wisconsin Central Railroad, formerly known as the Minneapolis, St. Paul and Sault Ste. Marie Railroad), the east 40.00 feet of the north 195.00 feet except the north 50.00 feet thereof of said East ½, and all that part of said East ½ described as follows: Beginning at the northwest corner of Origer and Davis' Addition to Rosemont, being a subdivision of part of said ¼ Section according to the plat thereof recorded May 27, 1963 as Document Number 18807143, in Cook County, Illinois; thence westerly along the northerly line of said Subdivision extended westerly to said easterly Railroad right-of-way line; thence northwesterly along said right-of-way line to the southerly line of north 50.00 feet of said ¼ Section; thence easterly along said southerly line to the easterly right-of-way line of Kirschoff Avenue; thence southerly along said right-of-way line to its intersection with the southerly line of Schullo's Resubdivision extended easterly, said Resubdivision being a Resubdivision of part of said ¼ section according to the plat thereof recorded June 17, 1960 as Document Number 17885160 in Cook County, Illinois; thence westerly along said southerly line extended and said southerly line to the southwest corner of said Resubdivision; thence northwesterly along the westerly line of said Resubdivision to the northwest corner thereof; thence westerly along the northerly line of said Resubdivision extended westerly to a line parallel with and 40.00 feet easterly of the easterly right-of-way line of said Railroad; thence northwesterly along said parallel line to said point of beginning.

And also

That part of the Southwest ¼ of Section 33, Township 41 North, Range 12 East of the Third Principal Meridian lying southerly of the centerline of Higgins Road and easterly of a north line parallel to the south line of said ¼ Section, beginning 565.84 feet west of the northeast corner of the Northwest ¼ of Section 4, Township 40 North, Range 12 East of the Third Principal Meridian all in Cook County, Illinois.

That part of the Southwest quarter of Section 3, the Southeast quarter of Section 4, the Northeast quarter of Section 9, and the Northwest quarter of Section 10, Township 40 North, Range 12 East of the Third Principal Meridian, in the Village of Rosemont, Cook County, Illinois, described as follows:

Beginning in the West half of the Northeast quarter of Section 9 aforesaid, at the intersection of the South line of 61st Street with the Easterly right of way line of the Minneapolis, St. Paul and Sault Ste. Marie Railroad right-of-way; thence East along the South line of 61st Street and its Easterly extension, to the East line of Pearl Street; thence North along the East line of Pearl Street to the

South line of 62nd Street; thence East along the South line of 62nd Street to the Westerly right-of-way line of the Illinois State Toll Road; thence Southerly along the Westerly right-of-way line of the Toll Road to a point on a Westerly extension of the South line of Allen Avenue; thence East along said Westerly extension, and along the South line of Allen Avenue to the West line of Otto Avenue; thence South along the West line of Otto Avenue to a point on a Westerly extension of the North line of the South 30 feet of Lot 12 in First Addition to B.L. Carlsen's Industrial Subdivision, being a Resubdivision in the Northeast quarter of Section 9 aforesaid, according to the plat thereof recorded March 5, 1962 as Document 18416079; thence East along said Westerly extension, and along the aforementioned North line of the South 30 feet of Lot 12, to the East line of Lot 12; thence North along the East line of Lot 12, being also the East line of the Northeast quarter of Section 9, to the North line of Owner's Division of parts of Lots 4 and 5 of Henry Hachmeister's Division, in the Northwest quarter of Section 10, aforesaid, according to the plat thereof recorded April 25, 1949 as Document 14539019; thence East along the North line of said Owner's Division to the West line of Lot 3 in said Owner's Division; thence South along the West line of Lot 3 to the Southwest corner thereof; thence East along the South line of Lot 3 to the Northwest corner of Lot 4 in said Owner's Division; thence South along the West line of Lot 4 to the Southwest corner thereof; thence East along the South line of Lot 4, and said South line extended Easterly, to the Easterly right of way line of River Road; thence Northerly along the Easterly line of River Road to the South line of Crossroads Industrial Park, being a Subdivision in the Northwest quarter of Section 10 aforesaid, according to the plat thereof recorded August 8, 1957 as Document 16980725; thence East along the South line of said Crossroads Industrial Park to the Southeast corner thereof; thence Northeasterly along the Easterly line of said Crossroads Industrial Park, and said Easterly line extended, to the North line of Bryn Mawr Avenue, in the Southwest quarter of Section 3 aforesaid; thence Northerly along the Westerly line of the Forest Preserve District of Cook County, to the Southerly right-of-way line of the Kennedy Expressway, thence west along and following the southerly right-of-way line of the Kennedy Expressway to the Easterly right-of-way line of the Minneapolis, St. Paul, and Sault Ste. Marie Railroad right-of-way; thence Southeasterly along said Easterly right-of-way line to the point of beginning;

AND ALSO, THAT PART OF THE NORTHEAST QUARTER OF SECTION 9 AND THE NORTHWEST QUARTER OF SECTION 10, TOWNSHIP 40 NORTH, RANGE 12 EAST OF THE THIRD PRINCIPAL MERIDIAN, IN THE

VILLAGE OF ROSEMONT, COOK COUNTY, ILLINOIS, DESCRIBED AS FOLLOWS:

BEGINNING IN THE WEST HALF OF THE NORTHEAST QUARTER OF SECTION 9 AFORESAID, AT THE INTERSECTION OF THE SOUTH LINE OF 61ST STREET WITH THE EASTERLY RIGHT-OF-WAY LINE OF THE MINNEAPOLIS, ST. PAUL AND ST. STE. MARIE RAILROAD RIGHT-OF-WAY; THENCE EAST ALONG THE SOUTH LINE OF 61ST STREET AND ITS EASTERLY EXTENSION, TO THE EAST LINE OF PEARL STREET; THENCE NORTH ALONG THE EAST LINE OF PEARL STREET TO THE SOUTH LINE OF 62ND STREET; THENCE EAST ALONG THE SOUTH LINE OF 62ND STREET TO THE WESTERLY RIGHT-OF-WAY LINE OF THE ILLINOIS STATE TOLL ROAD; THENCE SOUTHERLY, ALONG THE WESTERLY RIGHT-OF-WAY LINE OF THE TOLL ROAD TO A POINT ON A WESTERLY EXTENSION OF THE SOUTH LINE OF ALLEN AVENUE; THENCE EAST ALONG SAID WESTERLY EXTENSION, AND ALONG THE SOUTH LINE OF ALLEN AVENUE TO THE WEST LINE OF OTTO AVENUE; THENCE SOUTH ALONG THE WEST LINE OF OTTO AVENUE TO A POINT ON A WESTERLY EXTENSION OF THE NORTH LINE OF THE SOUTH 30 FEET OF LOT 12 IN FIRST ADDITION TO B.L. CARLSEN'S INDUSTRIAL SUBDIVISION, BEING A RESUBDIVISION IN THE NORTHEAST QUARTER OF SECTION 9 AFORESAID, ACCORDING TO THE PLAT THEREOF RECORDED MARCH 5, 1962 AS DOCUMENT 18416079; THENCE EAST ALONG SAID WESTERLY EXTENSION, AND ALONG THE AFOREMENTIONED NORTH LINE OF THE SOUTH 30 FEET OF LOT 12, TO THE EAST LINE OF LOT 12; THENCE NORTH ALONG THE EAST LINE OF LOT 12, BEING ALSO THE EAST LINE OF THE NORTHEAST QUARTER OF SECTION 9, TO THE NORTH LINE OF OWNER'S DIVISION OF PARTS OF LOTS 4 AND 5 OF HENRY HACHMEISTER'S DIVISION, IN THE NORTHWEST QUARTER OF SECTION 10, AFORESAID, ACCORDING TO THE PLAT THEREOF RECORDED APRIL 25, 1949 AS DOCUMENT 14539019; THENCE EAST ALONG THE NORTH LINE OF SAID OWNER'S DIVISION TO THE WEST LINE OF LOT 3 IN SAID OWNER'S DIVISION; THENCE SOUTH ALONG THE WEST LINE OF LOT 3 TO THE SOUTHWEST CORNER THEREOF; THENCE EAST ALONG THE SOUTH LINE OF LOT 3 TO THE NORTHWEST CORNER OF LOT 4 IN SAID OWNER'S SUBDIVISION; THENCE SOUTH ALONG THE WEST LINE OF LOT 4 TO THE SOUTHWEST CORNER THEREOF; THENCE EAST ALONG THE SOUTH LINE OF LOT 4, AND SAID SOUTH LINE EXTENDED EASTERLY, TO THE EASTERLY RIGHT-OF-WAY LINE OF RIVER ROAD; THENCE SOUTHEASTERLY ALONG THE EASTERLY RIGHT-OF-WAY LINE OF SAID RIVER ROAD TO A POINT BEING 198.00 FEET NORTH OF AND PARALLEL TO THE SOUTH LINE OF LOT 5 EXTENDED EASTERLY, IN HENRY HACHMEISTER'S DIVISION PER DOCUMENT NUMBER 4183101; THENCE WESTERLY, ALONG A LINE WHICH IS 198.00 FEET NORTH OF AND PARALLEL TO THE SOUTH LINE OF SAID LOT 5 IN HENRY HACHMEISTER'S DIVISION, TO THE NORTHWEST CORNER OF LOT 6 IN B.L. CARLSEN'S INDUSTRIAL SUBDIVISION PER DOCUMENT NUMBER 1925132; THENCE NORTHERLY TO A POINT BEING THE NORTHEAST CORNER OF A PARCEL BEING DESCRIBED PER DOCUMENT T1862127, SAID POINT BEING 293.73 FEET NORTH OF AND PARALLEL TO THE SOUTH LINE OF SAID LOT 5 IN HENRY HACHMEISTER'S DIVISION; THENCE WESTERLY ALONG A LINE, 293.73 FEET NORTH OF AND PARALLEL TO THE SOUTH LINE OF SAID LOT 5, 91.50 FEET TO THE NORTHWEST CORNER OF SAID PARCEL PER DOCUMENT T1862127; THENCE SOUTHERLY ALONG A LINE BEING THE EAST LINE OF THE WEST 200.00 FEET OF SAID LOT 5, 71.88 FEET TO THE SOUTHEAST CORNER OF A PARCEL BEING DESCRIBED PER DOCUMENT T2257298; THENCE WESTERLY ALONG THE SOUTH LINE AND THE SOUTH LINE EXTENDED WESTERLY OF SAID PARCEL, 233 FEET TO THE POINT OF INTERSECTION WITH THE WEST LINE OF MICHIGAN AVENUE RIGHT-OF-WAY; THENCE NORTHERLY ALONG SAID WEST RIGHT-OF-WAY LINE OF MICHIGAN AVENUE TO THE NORTHEAST CORNER OF LOT 1, BLOCK 12 IN J. TAYLOR'S ADD. TO FAIRVIEW HEIGHTS PER DOCUMENT NUMBER 1876526, SAID POINT ALSO BEING ON THE SOUTH RIGHT-OF-WAY LINE OF 60TH STREET; THENCE WESTERLY ALONG SAID SOUTH RIGHT-OF-WAY LINE OF 60TH STREET TO A POINT OF INTERSECTION WITH THE EASTERLY RIGHT-OF-WAY LINE OF THE AFORESAID MINNEAPOLIS, ST. PAUL AND ST. STE. MARIE RAILROAD RIGHT-OF-WAY; THENCE NORTHWESTERLY ALONG SAID EASTERLY RIGHT-OF-WAY LINE TO THE POINT OF BEGINNING.

P.A. 94–1055, Art. 25, § 25–7–103.68, eff. Jan. 1, 2007.

30/25–7–103.69. Quick-take; City of Evanston

§ 25–7–103.69. Quick-take; City of Evanston. Quick-take proceedings under Article 20 may be used for a period of one year after July 30, 1998, by the

City of Evanston for the acquisition for redevelopment purposes of the real property legally described as:

Lots 5 and 6 in Dempster's Subdivision of Block 66 in the Village (now City) of Evanston in the South West ¼ of Section 18, Township 41 North, Range 14 East of the Third Principal Meridian, in Cook County, Illinois and commonly known as 906-08 Church Street, Evanston, Illinois; and

Lots 7, 8, 9, 10, 11, and 12 in Dempster's Subdivision of Block 66 in Village (now City) of Evanston, in the South West ¼ of Section 18, Township 41 North, Range 14 East of the Third Principal Meridian, in Cook County, Illinois and commonly known as 910-926 Church Street, Evanston, Illinois.

P.A. 94-1055, Art. 25, § 25-7-103.69, eff. Jan. 1, 2007.

30/25-7-103.70. Quick-take; Southwestern Illinois Development Authority

§ 25-7-103.70. Quick-take; Southwestern Illinois Development Authority. Quick-take proceedings under Article 20 may be used for a period from August 30, 2003 to August 30, 2005 by the Southwestern Illinois Development Authority pursuant to the Southwestern Illinois Development Authority Act for a project as defined in Section 3 of that Act.

P.A. 94-1055, Art. 25, § 25-7-103.70, eff. Jan. 1, 2007.

30/25-7-103.71. Quick-take; Village of Franklin Park

§ 25-7-103.71. Quick-take; Village of Franklin Park. Quick-take proceedings under Article 20 may be used for a period of 3 years after December 1, 1998, by the Village of Franklin Park, for the redevelopment of blighted areas, for the acquisition of property within the area legally described as:

BEGINNING AT THE NORTHEAST CORNER OF SAID TRACT NO. 2 (SAID CORNER BEING 50.0 FEET WEST OF THE CENTERLINE OF MANNHEIM ROAD); THENCE SOUTH ALONG THE EAST LINE OF SAID TRACT NO. 2, A DISTANCE OF 305.46 FEET; THENCE WEST, PARALLEL WITH THE NORTH LINE OF SAID TRACT NO. 2, A DISTANCE OF 175.0 FEET; THENCE SOUTH, PARALLEL WITH THE EAST LINE OF SAID TRACT NO. 2, A DISTANCE OF 164.46 FEET TO THE SOUTHERLY LINE OF SAID TRACT NO. 2 (SAID LINE BEING 50.0 FEET NORTHERLY OF THE CENTERLINE OF GRAND AVENUE); THENCE WESTERLY ALONG SAID LINE, 672.75 FEET; THENCE NORTH ALONG A LINE THAT IS 227.30 FEET EAST OF (AS MEASURED AT RIGHT ANGLES) AND PARALLEL WITH THE EAST LINE OF MIKE LATORIA SR. INDUSTRIAL SUBDIVISION, 429.87 FEET TO THE NORTH LINE OF SAID TRACT NO. 2; THENCE EAST ALONG SAID NORTH

LINE, 845.71 FEET TO THE POINT OF BEGINNING, IN OWNER'S DIVISION OF THAT PART OF THE EAST HALF OF THE NORTHEAST QUARTER OF SECTION 29, TOWNSHIP 40 NORTH, RANGE 12 EAST OF THE THIRD PRINCIPAL MERIDIAN, ACCORDING TO THE PLAT THEREOF RECORDED AUGUST 16, 1929 AS DOCUMENT 10456788 AND FILED IN THE REGISTRAR'S OFFICE ON AUGUST 23, 1929 AS DOCUMENT LR474993, IN COOK COUNTY, ILLINOIS.

P.A. 94-1055, Art. 25, § 25-7-103.71, eff. Jan. 1, 2007.

30/25-7-103.72. Quick-take; Village of Franklin Park

§ 25-7-103.72. Quick-take; Village of Franklin Park. Quick-take proceedings under Article 20 may be used for a period of 3 years after December 1, 1998, by the Village of Franklin Park, for the redevelopment of blighted areas, for the acquisition of the property legally described as:

Lots 19, 20, 21, 22, 23, 24, 25, 26 and 27 of the Salerno-Kaufman Subdivision of part of Tract No. 1 in Owner's Division of part of the East ½, Northeast ¼, Section 29, Township 40, Range 12, East of the Third Principal Meridian, in Cook County, Illinois; and

That part of the South 117.64 feet of tract number 1 lying East of a line 235 feet West of and parallel with West line of Mannheim Road in Owner's Division of part of the East half of the Northeast quarter of Section 29, Township 40 North, Range 12, East of the Third Principal Meridian, according to the Plat thereof recorded August 16, 1929 as Document number 10456788, in Cook County, Illinois.

P.A. 94-1055, Art. 25, § 25-7-103.72, eff. Jan. 1, 2007.

30/25-7-103.73. Quick-take; City of Taylorville

§ 25-7-103.73. Quick-take; City of Taylorville. Quick-take proceedings under Article 20 may be used for a period of 2 years following July 30, 1999, by the City of Taylorville for the acquisition of land used for the construction of the second silt dam on Lake Taylorville; the project area is limited to the townships of Greenwood, Johnson, and Locust in southern Christian County.

P.A. 94-1055, Art. 25, § 25-7-103.73, eff. Jan. 1, 2007.

30/25-7-103.74. Quick-take; City of Effingham

§ 25-7-103.74. Quick-take; City of Effingham. Quick-take proceedings under Article 20 may be used for a period of 6 months following July 30, 1999 by the City of Effingham for the acquisition of all the right of way needed for the subject project starting at Wernsing Avenue and running northerly to Fayette Avenue, including the right of way for a structure over the CSX rail line and U.S. Route 40.

P.A. 94–1055, Art. 25, § 25–7–103.74, eff. Jan. 1, 2007.

30/25–7–103.75. Quick-take; City of Effingham

§ 25–7–103.75.   Quick-take; City of Effingham. Quick-take proceedings under Article 20 may be used for a period of one year following July 30, 1999 by the City of Effingham for the acquisition of property for the construction of South Raney Street Project Phase II, including a grade separation over Conrail and U. S. Route 40 in the City of Effingham, from the intersection of South Raney Street and West Wernsing Avenue northerly to the intersection of South Raney Street and West Fayette Avenue.

P.A. 94–1055, Art. 25, § 25–7–103.75, eff. Jan. 1, 2007.

30/25–7–103.76. Quick-take; Village of Lincolnshire

§ 25–7–103.76.   Quick-take; Village of Lincolnshire. Quick-take proceedings under Article 20 may be used for a period of 2 years following July 30, 1999, by the Village of Lincolnshire, for the purpose of redevelopment within the downtown area, for the acquisition of property within that area legally described as follows:

THAT PART OF SECTIONS 15 AND 22, TOWNSHIP 43 NORTH, RANGE 11 EAST OF THE THIRD PRINCIPAL MERIDIAN DESCRIBED AS FOLLOWS: BEGINNING AT THE INTERSECTION OF THE EAST LINE OF THE PROPERTY DESCRIBED IN DOCUMENT NUMBER 2297085 AND THE NORTHERLY LINE OF HALF DAY ROAD; THENCE NORTHEASTERLY ALONG SAID NORTHERLY LINE OF SAID HALF DAY ROAD TO THE INTERSECTION WITH THE WEST LINE OF STATE ROUTE NO. 21 (ALSO KNOWN AS MILWAUKEE AVENUE); THENCE NORTHERLY ALONG SAID WEST LINE OF STATE ROUTE NO. 21 TO THE NORTH LINE OF THE SOUTH 452.20 FEET OF THE NORTHEAST QUARTER OF THE AFORESAID SECTION 15; THENCE EAST ALONG THE SAID NORTH LINE OF THE SOUTH 452.20 FEET TO THE EAST LINE OF THE NORTHEAST QUARTER OF SAID SECTION 15; THENCE SOUTH ALONG THE SAID EAST LINE TO THE SOUTHEAST CORNER OF THE NORTHEAST QUARTER THEREOF; THENCE WEST ALONG THE SOUTH LINE OF THE SAID NORTHEAST QUARTER TO AN EAST LINE OF VERNON CEMETERY AS DESCRIBED IN DOCUMENT NUMBER 263584; THENCE NORTH 37.20 FEET ALONG AFORESAID EAST LINE OF CEMETERY TO THE NORTH EAST CORNER THEREOF; THENCE WEST 297.00 FEET ALONG THE NORTH LINE OF THE AFORESAID CEMETERY, SAID LINE IS THE MOST

NORTHERLY LINE OF CEMETERY ROAD AS OCCUPIED AND EXTENDED TO A WEST LINE OF AFORESAID VERNON CEMETERY EXTENDED NORTH; THENCE SOUTH ALONG THE EXTENSION AND WEST LINE OF THE AFORESAID CEMETERY TO THE SOUTHWEST CORNER THEREOF, SAID SOUTHWEST CORNER IS 296.61 FEET SOUTH OF THE SOUTH LINE OF CEMETERY ROAD AS OCCUPIED; THENCE EAST ALONG THE SOUTH LINE OF VERNON CEMETERY TO THE SOUTH EAST CORNER THEREOF, SAID SOUTHEAST CORNER ALSO BEING A POINT ON THE WEST LINE OF PROPERTY DESCRIBED BY DOCUMENT NUMBER 2012084; THENCE SOUTH ALONG AFORESAID WEST LINE TO THE NORTH LINE OF HALF DAY ROAD; THENCE EAST ALONG LAST SAID NORTH LINE TO A POINT IN THE WEST LINE (EXTENDED) OF INDIAN CREEK SUBDIVISION (RECORDED AS DOCUMENT NUMBER 2084U19); THENCE SOUTH ALONG THE WEST LINE AND AN EXTENSION THEREOF OF INDIAN CREEK CONDOMINIUM SUBDIVISION TO THE SOUTHWEST CORNER THEREOF; THENCE SOUTHEASTERLY ALONG A SOUTH LINE OF INDIAN CREEK CONDOMINIUM SUBDIVISION 130.47 FEET TO THE MOST SOUTHERLY CORNER IN THE AFORESAID SUBDIVISION SAID POINT BEING IN THE NORTH LINE OF RELOCATED ILLINOIS STATE ROUTE 22; THENCE NORTHEASTERLY ALONG A SOUTH LINE OF INDIAN CREEK CONDOMINIUM SUBDIVISION 209.56 FEET, SAID LINE BEING ALSO THE NORTH LINE OF RELOCATED ILLINOIS STATE ROUTE 22, TO THE SOUTHEAST CORNER OF INDIAN CREEK CONDOMINIUM SUBDIVISION; THENCE NORTH ALONG THE EAST LINE OF INDIAN CREEK SUBDIVISION AND AN EXTENSION THEREOF TO THE NORTH LINE OF HALF DAY ROAD; THENCE EAST ALONG THE NORTH LINE OF HALF DAY ROAD TO THE EAST LINE OF THE SOUTHEAST QUARTER OF SAID SECTION 15 TO THE SOUTHEAST CORNER OF THE SOUTHEAST QUARTER OF SECTION 15 AFORESAID; THENCE SOUTHERLY ALONG AN EASTERLY LINE OF THE HAMILTON PARTNERS PROPERTY DESCRIBED AS FOLLOWS, BEGINNING AT THE NORTHEAST CORNER OF THE NORTHEAST QUARTER OF SAID SECTION 22 (THE EAST LINE OF THE NORTHEAST QUARTER OF SAID SECTION 22 HAVING AN ASSUMED BEARING OF SOUTH 00 DEGREES 00 MINUTES 00 SECONDS EAST FOR THIS LEGAL DESCRIPTION); THENCE SOUTH 13 DEGREES 57 MINUTES 09 SECONDS WEST, 519.43 FEET TO A POINT DESCRIBED AS BEARING NORTH 51 DEGREES

41 MINUTES 30 SECONDS WEST, 159.61 FEET FROM A POINT OF THE EAST LINE OF THE NORTHEAST QUARTER OF SECTION 22 AFORESAID, 603.05 FEET, AS MEASURED ALONG SAID EAST LINE, SOUTH OF THE NORTHEAST CORNER OF SAID NORTHEAST QUARTER; THENCE SOUTH 05 DEGREES 08 MINUTES 04 SECONDS EAST, 232.01 FEET TO THE MOST NORTHERLY NORTHEAST CORNER OF MARIOTT DRIVE, ACCORDING TO THE PLAT OF DEDICATION RECORDED AS DOCUMENT NUMBER 1978811; THENCE SOUTH 42 DEGREES 08 MINUTES 46 SECONDS WEST (RECORD SOUTH 42 DEGREES 09 MINUTES 23 SECONDS WEST) ALONG THE NORTHWESTERLY LINE OF SAID MARIOTT DRIVE, 40.70 FEET (RECORD 40.73 FEET) TO AN ANGLE POINT IN THE NORTH LINE OF SAID MARIOTT DRIVE; THENCE SOUTH PERPENDICULAR TO AFOREMENTIONED MARIOTT DRIVE TO A POINT ON THE SOUTH LINE THEREOF; THENCE WEST ALONG THE SOUTH LINE OF MARIOTT DRIVE TO A POINT PERPENDICULAR TO A POINT IN THE NORTH LINE OF MARIOTT DRIVE THAT IS ON A LINE, THE EXTENSION OF WHICH IS THE EASTERLY LINE OF LOTS 1 AND 2 IN INDIAN CREEK RESUBDIVISION; THENCE NORTH PERPENDICULAR TO MARIOTT DRIVE TO THE AFOREMENTIONED POINT ON THE NORTH LINE; THENCE NORTHWESTERLY ON THE EASTERLY LINE & EXTENSION THEREOF OF AFOREMENTIONED LOTS 1 AND 2 TO THE NORTHEAST CORNER OF LOT 2; THENCE WEST ALONG THE NORTH LINE OF LOT 2 TO THE NORTHWEST CORNER THEREOF; THENCE SOUTHWESTERLY PERPENDICULAR TO ILLINOIS ROUTE 21 (MILWAUKEE AVENUE DEDICATED BY DOCUMENT NUMBER 2129168) TO THE WEST LINE THEREOF; THENCE NORTH ALONG THE WEST LINE OF AFOREMENTIONED ILLINOIS ROUTE 21 TO THE NORTHEAST CORNER OF LOT 1 IN MCDONALD'S—KING'S SUBDIVISION; THENCE WEST ALONG THE NORTH LINE OF THE LAST MENTIONED LOT 1, 218.50 FEET TO A JOG IN THE NORTH LINE THEREOF; THENCE NORTHERLY ALONG A WESTERLY LINE OF SAID LOT 1, 20.22 FEET TO A JOG IN THE NORTH LINE; THENCE WEST ALONG THE NORTH LINE OF LOT 1 AFORESAID 150.42 FEET TO THE NORTHWEST CORNER OF THEREOF; THENCE SOUTH 205.94 FEET ALONG THE WEST LINE OF AFOREMENTIONED LOT 1 TO A JOG IN THE WEST LINE THEREOF; THENCE EAST ALONG A SOUTH LINE OF LOT 1 TO A JOG IN THE WEST LINE THEREOF 3.45 FEET; THENCE SOUTH 91.22 FEET ALONG THE WEST LINE LOT 1 TO THE SOUTHWEST CORNER LOT 1 AFOREMENTIONED; THENCE SOUTHERLY RADIAL TO RELOCATED ILLINOIS STATE ROUTE 22 TO THE SOUTH LINE THEREOF; THENCE WEST ALONG THE SOUTH LINE OF RELOCATED ILLINOIS STATE ROUTE 22 TO A POINT PERPENDICULAR TO A POINT AT THE SOUTHWEST CORNER OF THE OLD HALF DAY SCHOOL PARCEL; THENCE NORTHWESTERLY 51.41 FEET ALONG A WEST LINE OF AFORESAID SCHOOL PARCEL TO A CORNER THEREOF; THENCE NORTHEASTERLY 169.30 FEET ALONG A NORTHERLY LINE OF AFORESAID SCHOOL PARCEL TO A CORNER THEREOF; THENCE NORTHWESTERLY 242.80 FEET ALONG A WEST LINE TO THE CENTER LINE OF HALF DAY ROAD; THENCE NORTHWESTERLY NORMAL TO THE AFORESAID ROAD TO THE NORTHERLY RIGHT OF WAY LINE THEREOF; THENCE EAST ALONG THE NORTH LINE OF HALF DAY ROAD TO A POINT SAID POINT IS A BEND IN THE WEST LINE OF PROPERTY DESCRIBED BY DOCUMENT NUMBER 2600952; THENCE NORTHWESTERLY 7.82 CHAINS ALONG THE WEST LINE AFOREMENTIONED TO THE NORTHWEST CORNER THEREOF; THENCE SOUTHEASTERLY 2.39 CHAINS TO THE NORTHEAST CORNER OF THE SAID PROPERTY; THENCE SOUTHEASTERLY ALONG THE EASTERLY LINE OF AFORESAID PROPERTY TO THE NORTHWEST CORNER OF PROPERTY DESCRIBED IN DOCUMENT NUMBER 2297085; THENCE EAST 2.27 CHAINS ALONG THE NORTH LINE OF AFOREMENTIONED PROPERTY TO THE NORTHEAST CORNER THEREOF; THENCE SOUTH ALONG THE EAST LINE OF THE AFOREMENTIONED PROPERTY TO THE PLACE OF BEGINNING, (EXCEPT THEREFROM THE TRACT OF LAND AS DESCRIBED BY DOCUMENT NUMBER 1141157 AND MILWAUKEE AVE. ADJACENT THERETO) ALL IN LAKE COUNTY, ILLINOIS.

P.A. 94–1055, Art. 25, § 25–7–103.76, eff. Jan. 1, 2007.

30/25–7–103.77. Quick-take; City of Marion

§ 25–7–103.77. Quick-take; City of Marion. Quick-take proceedings under Article 20 may be used for a period of 18 months after July 30, 1999, by the City of Marion for the acquisition of property and temporary construction easements bounded by the following lines for improvement of the Pentecost Road project:

A variable width strip of land lying parallel with and contiguous to the existing east and west Right-of-Way lines of Pentecost Road in the following quarter-quarter section:

the NW¼ NW¼, Section 16; NE¼ NE¼, Section 17; NW¼ SW¼, Section 16; SW¼ SW¼, Section 16; NE ¼ SE¼, Section 17; and the SE¼ SE¼, Section 17, all located in Township 9 South, Range 2 East of the Third Principal Meridian; Williamson County, Illinois.

P.A. 94–1055, Art. 25, § 25–7–103.77, eff. Jan. 1, 2007.

30/25–7–103.78. Quick-take; City of Geneva

§ 25–7–103.78. Quick-take; City of Geneva. Quick-take proceedings under Article 20 may be used for a period of 6 months following July 30, 1999, by the City of Geneva, for the Prairie and Wetland Restoration Project, for the acquisition of property described as follows:

PARCEL ONE: THE SOUTH ½ OF THE NORTHEAST ¼ OF SECTION 6, TOWNSHIP 39 NORTH, RANGE 8 EAST OF THE THIRD PRINCIPAL MERIDIAN, IN THE TOWNSHIP OF GENEVA, KANE COUNTY, ILLINOIS.

PARCEL TWO: THE SOUTH HALF OF THE NORTHWEST FRACTIONAL QUARTER OF SECTION 6, TOWNSHIP 39 NORTH, RANGE 8 EAST OF THE THIRD PRINCIPAL MERIDIAN, IN THE TOWNSHIP OF GENEVA, KANE COUNTY, ILLINOIS.

PARCEL THREE: THAT PART OF THE SOUTH ½ OF THE NORTHEAST ¼ OF SECTION 1, TOWNSHIP 39 NORTH, RANGE 7 EAST OF THE THIRD PRINCIPAL MERIDIAN LYING EAST OF THE FOLLOWING TRACT: (A STRIP OF LAND 60 FEET IN WIDTH EXTENDING OVER AND ACROSS THE SOUTH EAST ¼ OF THE NORTHEAST ¼ OF SECTION 1, TOWNSHIP 39 NORTH, RANGE 7 EAST OF THE THIRD PRINCIPAL MERIDIAN, SAID STRIP OF LAND BEING THAT CERTAIN STRIP OF LAND AS CONVEYED BY CHARLES W. PEMBLETON AND WIFE TO THE CHICAGO AND NORTH WESTERN RAILWAY COMPANY (NOW THE CHICAGO AND NORTH WESTERN TRANSPORTATION COMPANY) BY WARRANTY DEED DATED JUNE 29, 1903 AND RECORDED AS DOCUMENT 64790 IN BOOK 430 ON PAGE 337 IN THE OFFICE OF THE REGISTRAR OF DEEDS FOR KANE COUNTY, ILLINOIS) IN THE TOWNSHIP OF BLACKBERRY, KANE COUNTY, ILLINOIS.

P.A. 94–1055, Art. 25, § 25–7–103.78, eff. Jan. 1, 2007.

30/25–7–103.79. Quick-take; City of Arcola

§ 25–7–103.79. Quick-take; City of Arcola. Quick-take proceedings under Article 20 may be used for a period of 2 years after July 30, 1999, by the City of Arcola for the purpose of acquiring property in con-

nection with a project to widen Illinois Route 133 east of Interstate 57.

P.A. 94–1055, Art. 25, § 25–7–103.79, eff. Jan. 1, 2007.

30/25–7–103.80. Quick-take; County of Lake

§ 25–7–103.80. Quick-take; County of Lake. Quick-take proceedings under Article 20 may be used for a period of 24 months after July 30, 1999, by the County of Lake, for the acquisition of necessary right-of-way to complete the improvement of the intersection of County Highway 47 (9th Street) and County Highway 27 (Lewis Avenue).

P.A. 94–1055, Art. 25, § 25–7–103.80, eff. Jan. 1, 2007.

30/25–7–103.81. Quick-take; County of Lake

§ 25–7–103.81. Quick-take; County of Lake. Quick-take proceedings under Article 20 may be used for a period of 24 months after July 30, 1999, by the County of Lake, for the acquisition of necessary right-of-way to complete the improvement of the various intersections and roadways involved in the project to improve County Highway 70 (Hawley Street), County Highway 26 (Gilmer Road), and County Highway 62 (Fremont Center Road) at and near Illinois Route 176.

P.A. 94–1055, Art. 25, § 25–7–103.81, eff. Jan. 1, 2007.

30/25–7–103.82. Quick-take; County of Winnebago

§ 25–7–103.82. Quick-take; County of Winnebago. Quick-take proceedings under Article 20 may be used for a period of 30 months after July 30, 1999, by the County of Winnebago to allow for the acquisition of right-of-way for the construction of the Harrison Avenue Extension project from Montague Road to West State Street lying within Section 20, the east ½ of Section 29, and the northeast ¼ of Section 32, Township 44W, Range 1 East of the 3rd Principal Meridian, in Winnebago County.

P.A. 94–1055, Art. 25, § 25–7–103.82, eff. Jan. 1, 2007.

30/25–7–103.83. Quick-take; Village of Schiller Park

§ 25–7–103.83. Quick-take; Village of Schiller Park. Quick-take proceedings under Article 20 may be used for a period of 2 years after July 30, 1999, by the Village of Schiller Park, for the acquisition of the following described property for purposes of redevelopment of blighted areas:

The following parcel of property lying within the East Half of the Southeast Quarter of Section 17, Township 40 North, Range 12 East of the Third Principal Meridian and the N East Half of the Southwest Quarter of Section 16, Township 40 North, Range 12 East of the Third Principal Meridian all in Cook County, Illinois:

Commencing at the intersection of the center line of Irving Park Road with the west line of Mannheim Road; thence, southwesterly along the westerly line of Mannheim Road to its intersection with the south line of Belle Plaine Avenue, as extended from the east; thence, easterly along the south line of Belle Plaine Avenue to its intersection with the west line, as extended from the North, of Lot 7 in the Subdivision of the West Half of the Southwest Quarter of Section 16, Township 40 North, Range 12 East of the Third Principal Meridian (except that part lying Northerly of Irving Park Road), recorded April 14, 1921 as document no. 7112572; thence, northerly along the west line, as extended from the north, of Lot 7 of the aforecited Subdivision to its intersection with the north line of Belle Plaine Avenue; thence, northeasterly along the northwesterly line of the property acquired by The Illinois State Toll Highway Authority to its intersection with the east line of Lot 7 of the aforecited Subdivision; thence, northerly along the east line of Lot 7 of the aforecited Subdivision to its intersection with the south line of Lot 2 in the aforecited Subdivision; thence, westerly along the south line of Lot 2 of the aforecited Subdivision to its intersection with the west line of Lot 2 of the aforecited Subdivision; thence, northerly along the west line of Lot 2 of the aforecited Subdivision and the extension of the west line of Lot 2 to its intersection with the center line of Irving Park Road; thence, westerly along the center line of Irving Park Road to the point of beginning.

Notwithstanding the property description contained in this Section, the Village of Schiller Park may not acquire, under the authority of this Section, any property that is owned by any other unit of local government.

P.A. 94–1055, Art. 25, § 25–7–103.83, eff. Jan. 1, 2007.

30/25–7–103.84. Quick-take; City of Springfield

§ 25–7–103.84. Quick-take; City of Springfield. Quick-take proceedings under Article 20 may be used for a period of 2 years after July 30, 1999, by the City of Springfield, for the acquisition of (i) the property located in the City of Springfield and bounded on the north by Mason Street, on the west by Fifth Street, on the south by Jefferson Street, and on the east by Sixth Street and (ii) the property located in the City of Springfield and bounded on the north by Madison Street, on the west by Sixth Street, on the south by Washington Street, and on the east by Seventh Street, for the Abraham Lincoln Presidential Library.

P.A. 94–1055, Art. 25, § 25–7–103.84, eff. Jan. 1, 2007.

30/25–7–103.85. Quick-take; McLean County

§ 25–7–103.85. Quick-take; McLean County. Quick-take proceedings under Article 20 may be used for a period of 24 months after July 30, 1999, by McLean County, for the acquisition of property necessary for the purpose of construction with respect to the Towanda–Barnes Road from Route 150 to Ft. Jesse Road.

P.A. 94–1055, Art. 25, § 25–7–103.85, eff. Jan. 1, 2007.

30/25–7–103.86. Quick-take; Pike County

§ 25–7–103.86. Quick-take; Pike County. Quick-take proceedings under Article 20 may be used for a period of 12 months after July 30, 1999, by Pike County, for the acquisition of property necessary for the purpose of construction with respect to F.A.S. 1591, commonly known as Martinsburg Road, from one mile north of Martinsburg to 0.25 mile north of Martinsburg.

P.A. 94–1055, Art. 25, § 25–7–103.86, eff. Jan. 1, 2007.

30/25–7–103.87. Quick-take; Fox Metro Water Reclamation District

§ 25–7–103.87. Quick-take; Fox Metro Water Reclamation District. Quick-take proceedings under Article 20 may be used for a period of 12 months after July 30, 1999, by the Fox Metro Water Reclamation District, for the acquisition of the following described property for the purpose of extending the collector system and construction of facilities for treatment of effluent:

THAT PART OF LOTS 2 AND 3 OF LARSON'S SUBDIVISION DESCRIBED AS FOLLOWS: COMMENCING AT THE NORTHWEST CORNER OF SAID LOT 3 BEING ON THE CENTER LINE OF STATE ROUTE NO. 31; THENCE SOUTH 7 DEGREES 01 MINUTES WEST ALONG SAID CENTER LINE 46.58 FEET FOR THE POINT OF BEGINNING; THENCE NORTH 7 DEGREES 01 MINUTES EAST ALONG SAID CENTER LINE 91.58 FEET; THENCE SOUTH 88 DEGREES 31 MINUTES EAST PARALLEL WITH THE NORTH LINE OF SAID LOT 3, 781.87 FEET TO THE EASTERLY LINE OF SAID LOT 2; THENCE SOUTH 19 DEGREES 40 MINUTES WEST ALONG THE EASTERLY LINES OF LOTS 2 AND 3 106.9 FEET; THENCE SOUTH 9 DEGREES 39 MINUTES EAST ALONG THE EASTERLY LINE OF SAID LOT 3, 70.83 FEET TO A LINE DRAWN SOUTH 82 DEGREES 36 MINUTES EAST, PARALLEL WITH THE SOUTHERLY LINE OF SAID LOT 3, FROM THE PLACE OF BEGINNING; THENCE NORTH 82 DEGREES 36 MINUTES WEST ALONG SAID PARALLEL LINE 775.16 FEET TO THE PLACE OF BEGINNING, IN THE TOWNSHIP OF OSWEGO, KENDALL COUNTY, ILLINOIS.

ALSO:

THAT PART OF THE SOUTHWEST ¼ OF SECTION 5, TOWNSHIP 37 NORTH, RANGE 8 EAST OF THE THIRD PRINCIPAL MERID-

IAN, DESCRIBED AS FOLLOWS: COMMENCING AT THE NORTHWEST CORNER OF THE SOUTHWEST FRACTIONAL QUARTER OF SECTION 6, TOWNSHIP AND RANGE AFORESAID; THENCE SOUTH ALONG THE WEST LINE OF SAID SECTION 6, 1363.34 FEET; THENCE SOUTH 82 DEGREES 36 MINUTES EAST 5298.7 FEET TO THE WESTERLY BANK OF FOX RIVER; THENCE NORTH 18 DEGREES 46 MINUTES WEST ALONG SAID WESTERLY BANK 192.5 FEET FOR THE POINT OF BEGINNING; THENCE NORTH 18 DEGREES 46 MINUTES WEST ALONG SAID WESTERLY BANK 44.35 FEET; THENCE NORTH 37 DEGREES 16 MINUTES WEST ALONG SAID WESTERLY BANK 227.8 FEET; THENCE NORTH 82 DEGREES 36 MINUTES WEST 867.3 FEET TO THE CENTER LINE OF THE ORIGINAL ROAD; THENCE SOUTHERLY ALONG SAID CENTER LINE 200 FEET TO A LINE DRAWN NORTH 82 DEGREES 36 MINUTES WEST FROM THE POINT OF BEGINNING; THENCE SOUTH 82 DEGREES 36 MINUTES EAST 1014.21 FEET TO THE POINT OF BEGINNING, IN THE TOWNSHIP OF OSWEGO, KENDALL COUNTY, ILLINOIS.

ALSO:

PARCEL ONE:
LOT 5 OF LARSON'S SUBDIVISION, TOWNSHIP OF OSWEGO, KENDALL COUNTY, ILLINOIS.
PARCEL TWO:
THAT PART OF THE SOUTHWEST ¼ OF SECTION 5, TOWNSHIP 37 NORTH, RANGE 8 EAST OF THE THIRD PRINCIPAL MERIDIAN DESCRIBED AS FOLLOWS: COMMENCING AT THE INTERSECTION OF THE SOUTH LINE OF SAID SECTION 5 WITH THE CENTER LINE OF ILLINOIS STATE ROUTE NUMBER 31; THENCE NORTH 6 DEGREES 44 MINUTES EAST ALONG SAID CENTER LINE 745.75 FEET; THENCE SOUTH 82 DEGREES 30 MINUTES EAST 100 FEET TO THE POINT OF BEGINNING; THENCE SOUTHWESTERLY AT RIGHT ANGLES WITH THE LAST DESCRIBED COURSE, 110 FEET; THENCE SOUTH 83 DEGREES 30 MINUTES EAST TO THE CENTER THREAD OF THE FOX RIVER; THENCE NORTHERLY ALONG SAID CENTER THREAD TO A LINE DRAWN SOUTH 82 DEGREES 30 MINUTES EAST FOR THE POINT OF BEGINNING; THENCE NORTH 82 DEGREES 30 MINUTES WEST TO THE POINT OF BEGINNING; IN THE TOWNSHIP OF OSWEGO, KENDALL COUNTY, ILLINOIS.

ALSO:

THAT PART OF THE SOUTH ½ OF THE WEST PART OF SECTION 5, TOWNSHIP 37 NORTH, RANGE 8 EAST OF THE THIRD PRINCIPAL MERIDIAN WHICH LIES EAST OF THE CENTER LINE OF STATE ROUTE NO. 31 AND SOUTH OF A LINE EXTENDING SOUTH 82 DEGREES 30 MINUTES EAST FROM A POINT IN THE SAID CENTER LINE OF SAID HIGHWAY THAT IS NORTH 6 DEGREES 44 MINUTES EAST 745.75 FEET FROM THE SOUTH LINE OF SAID SECTION TO THE CENTER THREAD OF THE FOX RIVER (EXCEPT THE RIGHT OF WAY OF THE SAID STATE ROUTE NO. 31 AND A STRIP IN THE NORTHWEST CORNER 67 FEET WIDE AND 325 FEET LONG MEASURED ALONG THE EASTERLY LINE OF SAID HIGHWAY, USED FOR CEMETERY PURPOSES, AND ALSO EXCEPT THAT PART LYING SOUTH OF THE NORTH LINE OF PREMISES CONVEYED TO THE COMMONWEALTH EDISON COMPANY BY WARRANTY DEED RECORDED OCTOBER 9, 1959 AS DOCUMENT 127020 AND ALSO EXCEPT THAT PART DESCRIBED AS FOLLOWS: COMMENCING AT THE INTERSECTION OF THE SOUTH LINE OF SAID SECTION 5 WITH THE CENTER LINE OF ILLINOIS STATE ROUTE NO. 31; THENCE NORTH 6 DEGREES 44 MINUTES EAST ALONG SAID CENTER LINE 745.75 FEET; THENCE SOUTH 82 DEGREES 30 MINUTES EAST 100 FEET FOR THE POINT OF BEGINNING; THENCE SOUTHWESTERLY AT RIGHT ANGLES WITH THE LAST DESCRIBED COURSE, 110 FEET; THENCE SOUTH 82 DEGREES 30 MINUTES EAST TO THE CENTER THREAD OF THE FOX RIVER; THENCE NORTHERLY ALONG SAID CENTER THREAD TO A LINE DRAWN SOUTH 82 DEGREES 30 MINUTES EAST FROM THE POINT OF BEGINNING; THENCE NORTH 82 DEGREES 30 MINUTES WEST TO THE POINT OF BEGINNING), IN THE TOWNSHIP OF OSWEGO, KENDALL COUNTY, ILLINOIS.

P.A. 94-1055, Art. 25, § 25-7-103.87, eff. Jan. 1, 2007.

30/25-7-103.88. Quick-take; St. Clair County

§ 25-7-103.88. Quick-take; St. Clair County. Quick-take proceedings under Article 20 may be used for a period of 12 months after July 30, 1999, by St. Clair County, for the acquisition of property necessary for the purpose of the following county road improvements in the City of O'Fallon and the Village of Shiloh: Section 95-00301-02-PV, Hartman Lane to Shiloh-O'Fallon Road, 2.45 miles of concrete pavement, 24 feet wide, 10-foot shoulders, a 95-foot single-span bridge, earthwork, and traffic signals.

P.A. 94–1055, Art. 25, § 25–7–103.88, eff. Jan. 1, 2007.

30/25–7–103.89. Quick-take; St. Clair County

§ 25–7–103.89. Quick-take; St. Clair County. Quick-take proceedings under Article 20 may be used for a period of 12 months after July 30, 1999, by St. Clair County, for the acquisition of property necessary for the purpose of the following county road improvements in the City of Fairview Heights: Section 97-00301-04-PV, Metro-Link Station to Illinois Route 159, 2.04 miles of concrete pavement, 24 feet wide, 10-foot shoulders, earthwork, and traffic signals.

P.A. 94–1055, Art. 25, § 25–7–103.89, eff. Jan. 1, 2007.

30/25–7–103.90. Quick-take; St. Clair County

§ 25–7–103.90. Quick-take; St. Clair County. Quick-take proceedings under Article 20 may be used for a period of 12 months after July 30, 1999, by St. Clair County, for the acquisition of property necessary for the purpose of the following county road improvements in the City of O'Fallon: Section 97-03080-05-PV, Jennifer Court to Station 122+50, 1.52 miles of concrete pavement, 24 to 40 feet wide, 10-foot shoulders, earthwork, storm sewers, curbs, and gutters.

P.A. 94–1055, Art. 25, § 25–7–103.90, eff. Jan. 1, 2007.

30/25–7–103.91. Quick-take; Madison County

§ 25–7–103.91. Quick-take; Madison County. Quick-take proceedings under Article 20 may be used for a period of 12 months after July 30, 1999, by Madison County, for the acquisition of property necessary for the purpose of approximately 2.4 miles of roadwork commencing at the intersection of Illinois Route 143 northerly over, adjacent to, and near the location of County Highway 19 (locally known as Birch Drive) to the intersection of Buchts Road, traversing through land sections 19, 20, 29, 30, and 31 of Ft. Russell Township, the work to consist of excavation, fill placement, concrete structures, and an aggregate and bituminous base with bituminous binder and surfacing.

P.A. 94–1055, Art. 25, § 25–7–103.91, eff. Jan. 1, 2007.

30/25–7–103.92. Quick-take; Lake County

§ 25–7–103.92. Quick-take; Lake County. Quick-take proceedings under Article 20 may be used for a period of 2 years after July 30, 1999, by Lake County, for the acquisition of property necessary for the purpose of improving County Highway 70 (Hawley Street) from Chevy Chase Road to County Highway 26 (Gilmer Road).

P.A. 94–1055, Art. 25, § 25–7–103.92, eff. Jan. 1, 2007.

30/25–7–103.93. Quick-take; Kendall County

§ 25–7–103.93. Quick-take; Kendall County. Quick-take proceedings under Article 20 may be used for a period of 12 months after July 30, 1999, by Kendall County, for the acquisition of the following described property for the purpose of road construction or improvements, including construction of a bridge and related improvements:

THAT PART OF THE EAST ½ OF SECTION 24, TOWNSHIP 37 NORTH, RANGE 7 EAST OF THE THIRD PRINCIPAL MERIDIAN, KENDALL COUNTY, ILLINOIS DESCRIBED AS FOLLOWS: COMMENCING AT THE NORTHEAST CORNER OF LOT 4 OF CHRISTIE C. HERREN'S 2ND SUBDIVISION; THENCE ON AN ASSUMED BEARING NORTH 89 DEGREES 32 MINUTES 05 SECONDS EAST, 33.00 FEET ALONG THE EASTERLY EXTENSION OF THE NORTH LINE OF SAID LOT 4 TO THE CENTER LINE OF MINKLER ROAD; THENCE NORTH 0 DEGREES 27 MINUTES 55 SECONDS WEST, 1,585.91 FEET ALONG THE CENTER LINE OF MINKLER ROAD TO THE CENTER LINE OF ILLINOIS ROUTE 71; THENCE NORTH 0 DEGREES 53 MINUTES 06 SECONDS WEST, 1,084.14 FEET ALONG THE CENTER LINE OF MINKLER ROAD AND THE NORTHERLY EXTENSION THEREOF TO THE NORTH RIGHT-OF-WAY LINE OF THE BURLINGTON NORTHERN SANTA FE RAILROAD FOR THE POINT OF BEGINNING; THENCE CONTINUING NORTH 0 DEGREES 53 MINUTES 06 SECONDS WEST, 12.95 FEET TO THE SOUTH BANK OF THE FOX RIVER; THENCE NORTH 84 DEGREES 02 MINUTES 18 SECONDS EAST, 192.09 FEET ALONG SAID SOUTH BANK; THENCE SOUTH 23 DEGREES 08 MINUTES 48 SECONDS EAST, 4.22 FEET TO THE NORTH RIGHT-OF-WAY LINE OF THE BURLINGTON NORTHERN SANTA FE RAILROAD; THENCE SOUTHWESTERLY, 194.71 FEET ALONG A 3,956.53 FOOT RADIUS CURVE TO THE LEFT WHOSE CHORD BEARS SOUTH 81 DEGREES 25 MINUTES 34 SECONDS WEST, 194.69 FEET TO THE POINT OF BEGINNING.

AND:

THAT PART OF THE EAST ½ OF SECTION 24, TOWNSHIP 37 NORTH, RANGE 7 EAST OF THE THIRD PRINCIPAL MERIDIAN, KENDALL COUNTY, ILLINOIS DESCRIBED AS FOLLOWS: COMMENCING AT THE NORTHEAST CORNER OF LOT 4 OF CHRISTIE C. HERREN'S 2ND SUBDIVISION; THENCE ON AN ASSUMED BEARING NORTH 89 DEGREES 32 MINUTES 05 SECONDS EAST, 33.00 FEET ALONG THE EASTERLY EXTENSION OF THE NORTH LINE OF SAID LOT 4 TO THE CENTER LINE OF MINKLER ROAD;

THENCE NORTH 0 DEGREES 27 MINUTES 55 SECONDS WEST, 1,585.91 FEET ALONG THE CENTER LINE OF MINKLER ROAD TO THE CENTER LINE OF ILLINOIS ROUTE 71 FOR THE POINT OF BEGINNING; THENCE NORTH 0 DEGREES 53 MINUTES 06 SECONDS WEST, 52.33 FEET ALONG THE CENTER LINE OF MINKLER ROAD; THENCE NORTH 72 DEGREES 01 MINUTES 36 SECONDS EAST, 130.87 FEET ALONG THE NORTH RIGHT-OF-WAY LINE OF ILLINOIS ROUTE 71; THENCE NORTH 18 DEGREES 09 MINUTES 27 SECONDS WEST, 111.00 FEET; THENCE NORTH 74 DEGREES 41 MINUTES 24 SECONDS EAST, 40.24 FEET; THENCE NORTH 3 DEGREES 05 MINUTES 16 SECONDS WEST, 239.00 FEET; THENCE SOUTH 89 DEGREES 29 MINUTES 13 SECONDS WEST, 69.62 FEET; THENCE SOUTH 43 DEGREES 09 MINUTES 14 SECONDS WEST, 46.47 FEET; THENCE SOUTH 89 DEGREES 06 MINUTES 54 SECONDS WEST, 20.00 FEET TO THE CENTER LINE OF MINKLER ROAD; THENCE NORTH 0 DEGREES 53 MINUTES 06 SECONDS WEST, 595.48 FEET ALONG SAID CENTER LINE AND SAID CENTER LINE EXTENDED NORTHERLY TO THE SOUTH RIGHT-OF-WAY LINE OF THE BURLINGTON NORTHERN SANTA FE RAILROAD; THENCE EASTERLY, 222.77 FEET ALONG A 3,881.53 FOOT RADIUS CURVE TO THE RIGHT WHOSE CHORD BEARS NORTH 81 DEGREES 28 MINUTES 59 SECONDS EAST, 222.74 FEET; THENCE SOUTH 20 DEGREES 43 MINUTES 16 SECONDS EAST, 119.40 FEET; THENCE SOUTHERLY, 237.80 FEET ALONG A 717.37 FEET RADIUS CURVE TO THE RIGHT WHOSE CHORD BEARS SOUTH 11 DEGREES 13 MINUTES 29 SECONDS EAST, 236.71 FEET; THENCE SOUTH 1 DEGREES 43 MINUTES 42 SECONDS EAST, 471.58 FEET; THENCE SOUTH 55 DEGREES 31 MINUTES 50 SECONDS EAST, 63.07 FEET; THENCE NORTH 72 DEGREES 01 MINUTES 36 SECONDS EAST, 86.50 FEET; THENCE SOUTH 17 DEGREES 58 MINUTES 24 SECONDS EAST, 20.00 FEET TO THE EXISTING NORTH RIGHT-OF-WAY LINE OF ILLINOIS ROUTE 71; THENCE NORTH 72 DEGREES 01 MINUTES 36 SECONDS EAST, 350.00 FEET ALONG SAID NORTH RIGHT-OF-WAY LINE OF ILLINOIS ROUTE 71; THENCE SOUTH 17 DEGREES 58 MINUTES 24 SECONDS EAST, 50.00 FEET TO THE CENTER LINE OF ILLINOIS ROUTE 71; THENCE SOUTH 72 DEGREES 01 MINUTES 36 SECONDS WEST, 836.88 FEET ALONG SAID CENTER LINE TO THE POINT OF BEGINNING. AND:

THAT PART OF THE EAST ½ OF SECTION 24, TOWNSHIP 37 NORTH, RANGE 7 EAST OF THE THIRD PRINCIPAL MERIDIAN, KENDALL COUNTY, ILLINOIS, DESCRIBED AS FOLLOWS: COMMENCING AT THE NORTHEAST CORNER OF LOT 4 OF CHRISTIE C. HERREN'S 2ND SUBDIVISION; THENCE ON AN ASSUMED BEARING NORTH 89 DEGREES 32 MINUTES 05 SECONDS EAST, 33.00 FEET ALONG THE EASTERLY EXTENSION OF THE NORTH LINE OF SAID LOT 4 TO THE CENTER LINE OF MINKLER ROAD; THENCE NORTH 0 DEGREES 27 MINUTES 55 SECONDS WEST, 1,585.91 FEET ALONG SAID CENTER LINE TO THE CENTER LINE OF ILLINOIS ROUTE 71 FOR THE POINT OF BEGINNING; THENCE NORTH 72 DEGREES 01 MINUTES 36 SECONDS EAST, 836.88 FEET ALONG THE CENTER LINE OF ILLINOIS ROUTE 71; THENCE SOUTH 17 DEGREES 58 MINUTES 24 SECONDS EAST, 50.00 FEET TO THE SOUTH RIGHT-OF-WAY LINE OF ILLINOIS ROUTE 71; THENCE SOUTH 64 DEGREES 54 MINUTES 06 SECONDS WEST, 201.56 FEET; THENCE SOUTH 72 DEGREES 01 MINUTES 36 SECONDS WEST, 331.43 FEET; THENCE SOUTH 1 DEGREES 55 MINUTES 17 SECONDS WEST, 144.09 FEET; THENCE SOUTHERLY 327.44 FEET ALONG AN 853.94 FOOT RADIUS CURVE TO THE RIGHT WHOSE CHORD BEARS SOUTH 12 DEGREES 54 MINUTES 22 SECONDS WEST, 325.44 FEET; THENCE SOUTH 23 DEGREES 53 MINUTES 28 SECONDS WEST, 211.52 FEET; THENCE SOUTHERLY 289.43 FEET ALONG A 673.94 FOOT RADIUS CURVE TO THE LEFT WHOSE CHORD BEARS SOUTH 11 DEGREES 35 MINUTES 17 SECONDS WEST, 287.21 FEET; THENCE SOUTH 0 DEGREES 42 MINUTES 55 SECONDS EAST, 135.43 FEET; THENCE SOUTH 89 DEGREES 17 MINUTES 05 SECONDS WEST, 85.98 FEET TO THE CENTER LINE OF MINKLER ROAD; THENCE NORTH 0 DEGREES 27 MINUTES 55 SECONDS WEST, 459.31 FEET ALONG SAID CENTER LINE; THENCE NORTH 21 DEGREES 25 MINUTES 47 SECONDS EAST, 232.86 FEET; THENCE NORTHERLY 266.09 FEET ALONG A 693.94 FOOT RADIUS CURVE TO THE LEFT WHOSE CHORD BEARS NORTH 12 DEGREES 54 MINUTES 22 SECONDS EAST, 264.46 FEET; THENCE NORTH 1 DEGREES 55 MINUTES 17 SECONDS EAST, 64.92 FEET; THENCE NORTH 53 DEGREES 01 MINUTES 20 SECONDS WEST, 30.54 FEET; THENCE SOUTH 72 DEGREES 01 MINUTES 36 SECONDS WEST, 132.59 FEET TO THE CENTER LINE OF MINKLER ROAD; THENCE NORTH 0 DEGREES 27 MINUTES 55 SECONDS WEST, 73.38 FEET ALONG SAID CENTER LINE TO THE POINT OF BEGINNING.

P.A. 94–1055, Art. 25, § 25–7–103.93, eff. Jan. 1, 2007.

30/25-7-103.94. Quick-take; DU-COMM at Cloverdale, Illinois

§ 25-7-103.94. Quick-take; DU-COMM at Cloverdale, Illinois. Quick-take proceedings under Article 20 may be used for a period of 2 years after July 30, 1999, by DuPage Public Safety Communications (DU-COMM), a unit of intergovernmental cooperation, for the acquisition of property including land, buildings, towers, fixtures, and other improvements located at Cloverdale, Illinois and described as follows:

A tract or parcel of land situated in the Southeast Quarter (SE ¼) of Section Twenty-one (21), Township Forty (40) North, Range Ten (10) East of the Third Principal Meridian, more particularly described as follows:

Commencing at the Southwest corner of the Southeast Quarter (SE ¼) of said Section Twenty-one (21), measure North, along the West line of the Southeast Quarter (SE ¼) of said Section Twenty-one (21) 1287.35 feet, then East at right angles to the said West line of the Southeast Quarter (SE ¼) of said Section Twenty-one (21), 292.57 feet to the point of beginning;

Thence East along the last described course 208.71 feet, thence South at right angles to the last described course 208.71 feet, thence West at right angles to the last described course 208.71 feet, thence North in a direct line 208.71 feet to the point of beginning; also

A right of way and easement thirty-three (33) feet in width for the construction, maintenance, and use of (a) a roadway suitable for vehicular traffic, and (b) such aerial or underground electric power and communication lines as said Company may from time to time desire, consisting of poles, wires, cables, conduits, guys, anchors, and other fixtures and appurtenances, the center line of which right of way and easement is described as follows:

Commencing at a point on the West line of the tract or parcel of land above described, distant Southerly 16.5 feet from the Northwest corner of said tract or parcel, thence Westerly at right angles to the West line of the Southeast Quarter (SE ¼) of said Section Twenty-one (21), 293 feet more or less to the public road situated on the West line of the Southeast Quarter (SE ¼) of said Section Twenty-one (21), Township and Range aforesaid.

P.A. 94-1055, Art. 25, § 25-7-103.94, eff. Jan. 1, 2007.

30/25-7-103.95. Quick-take; City of Crest Hill

§ 25-7-103.95. Quick-take; City of Crest Hill. Quick-take proceedings under Article 20 may be used for a period of 3 years after July 30, 1999, (in the case of the permanent easements described in items (A) and (C)), by the City of Crest Hill, for acquisition of the following easements:

(A) Permanent easement for the purposes of installation, maintenance, and use of water or sewer, or both water and sewer, lines in, along, through, and under the following legally described property:

The East 70 feet of the North half of the North half of the Southeast Quarter of Section 30, Township 36 North, and in Range 10, East of the Third Principal Meridian (Except therefrom the North 12 Rods of the East 13 ½ Rods thereof, and also except the South 99 feet of the East 440 feet thereof), in Will County, Illinois.

(B) Temporary easement for purposes of initial construction of the water or sewer, or both water and sewer, lines in, along, through, and under the permanent easement described in item (A). The temporary easement herein shall arise on September 1, 1999 and shall cease on August 31, 2001 and is legally described as follows:

The East 100 feet of the North half of the North half of the Southeast Quarter of Section 30, Township 36 North, and in Range 10, East of the Third Principal Meridian (Except therefrom the North 12 Rods of the East 13 ½ Rods thereof, and also except the South 99 feet of the East 440 feet thereof), in Will County, Illinois.

(C) Permanent easement for the purposes of installation, maintenance, and use of water or sewer, or both water and sewer, lines in, along, through, and under the following legally described property:

The East 70 feet of the West 120 feet of the South half of the Southeast Quarter of Section 30, in township 36 North, and in Range 10 East of the Third Principal Meridian, in Will County, Illinois, excepting therefrom the following described tracts:

Exception 1: That part of said South half lying Southwesterly of the Northeasterly right-of-way line of the Elgin, Joliet and Eastern Railway Company, in Will County, Illinois.

Exception 2: The West 200 feet of said South half, in Will County, Illinois.

Exception 3: That part of the South half of the Southeast Quarter of Section 30, Township 36 North, and in Range 10 East of the Third Principal Meridian, described as follows: Beginning at a point 250 feet East of the West line of said South half of the Southeast Quarter and 180.58 feet North of the South line of said South half of the Southeast Quarter; thence North along a line 250 feet East of and parallel with the West line of said Southeast Quarter a distance of 1004.55 feet to a point; thence Northwesterly along a diagonal line 65.85 feet to its intersection with a line drawn 200 feet East of and parallel to the West line of said Southeast Quarter, said point also being 100.75 feet South of the North line of the South half of said Southeast Quarter, as measured along said parallel line; thence South along the last described parallel line a distance of 1045.02 feet to a point 50 feet West of the point of beginning and 180.58 feet North of the South line of said Southeast Quarter; thence East 50 feet to the point of beginning, in Will County, Illinois.

Exception 4: Beginning at the Southeast corner of the Southeast Quarter of Section 30, Township 36 North, and in Range 10 East of the Third Principal Meridian, thence Northerly along the East line of said Section for a distance of 346.5 feet; thence Westerly along a line 346.5 feet distant from and parallel with the South line of said Section for a distance of 297 feet; thence Southerly along a line 297 feet distant from and parallel with the East line of said Section for a distance of 346.5 feet to a point, said point being on the South line of said Section; thence Easterly along said South line of said Section 297 feet to the point of beginning, in Will County, Illinois.

Exception 5: That part dedicated for highway purposes in instrument recorded January 28, 1986 as Document No. R86-03205 described as follows: That part of the South half of the Southeast Quarter of Section 30, Township 36 North, and in Range 10 East of the Third Principal Meridian bounded and described as follows: Beginning at the point of intersection of the Northeasterly right-of-way line of the Elgin, Joliet and Eastern Railway Company with the South line of said Southeast Quarter, thence on an assumed bearing of North 90.00 degrees 00 minutes 00 seconds East along said South line a distance of 288.02 feet; thence North 00 degrees 00 minutes 00 seconds East a distance of 33.0 feet; thence North 86 degrees 25 minutes 22 seconds West a distance of 352.57 feet to the Northeasterly right-of-way line of said railway company; thence South 49 degrees 15 minutes 53 seconds East along said Northeasterly right-of-way line, a distance of 84.28 feet to the point of beginning, in Will County, Illinois.

Exception 6: The North 850 feet of the East 1025 feet of the South half of the Southeast Quarter of Section 30, Township 36 North, and in Range 10 East of the Third Principal Meridian, in Will County, Illinois.

(D) Temporary easement for purposes of initial construction of the water or sewer, or both water and sewer, lines in, along, through, and under the permanent easement described in item (C). The temporary easement herein shall arise on September 1, 1999 and shall cease on August 31, 2001 and is legally described as follows:

The East 100 feet of the West 150 feet of the South half of the Southeast Quarter of Section 30, in Township 36 North, and in Range 10 East of the Third Principal Meridian, in Will County, Illinois, excepting therefrom the following described tracts:

Exception 1: That part of said South half lying Southwesterly of the Northeasterly right-of-way line of the Elgin, Joliet and Eastern Railway Company, in Will County, Illinois.

Exception 2: The West 200 feet of said South half, in Will County, Illinois.

Exception 3: That part of the South half of the Southeast Quarter of Section 30, Township 36 North, and in Range 10 East of the Third Principal Meridian, described as follows: Beginning at a point 250 feet East of the West line of said South half of the Southeast Quarter and 180.58 feet North of the South line of said South half of the Southeast Quarter; thence North along a line 250 feet East of and parallel with the West line of said southeast Quarter a distance of 1004.55 feet to a point; thence Northwesterly along a diagonal line 65.85 feet to its intersection with a line drawn 200 feet East of and parallel to the West line of said Southeast Quarter, said point also being 100.75 feet South of the North line of the South half of said Southeast Quarter, as measured along said parallel line; thence South along the last described parallel line a distance of 1045.02 feet to a point 50 feet West of the point of beginning and 180.58 feet North of the South line of said Southeast Quarter; thence East 50 feet to the point of beginning, in Will County, Illinois.

Exception 4: Beginning at the Southeast corner of the Southeast Quarter of Section 30, Township 36 North, and in Range 10 East of the Third Principal Meridian, thence Northerly along the East line of said Section for a distance of 346.5 feet; thence Westerly along a line 346.5 feet distant from and parallel with the South line of said Section for a distance of 297 feet; thence Southerly along a line 297 feet distant from and parallel with the East line of said Section for a distance of 346.5 feet to a point, said point being on the South line of said Section; thence Easterly along said South line of said Section 297 feet to the point of beginning, in Will County, Illinois.

Exception 5: That part dedicated for highway purposes in instrument recorded January 28, 1986 as Document No. R86-03205 described as follows: That part of the South half of the Southeast Quarter of Section 30, Township 36 North, and in Range 10 East of the Third Principal Meridian bounded and described as follows: Beginning at the point of intersection of the Northeasterly right-of-way line of the Elgin, Joliet and Eastern Railway Company with the South line of said Southeast Quarter; thence on an assumed bearing of North 90.00 degrees 00 minutes 00 seconds East along said South line a distance of 288.02 feet; thence North 00 degrees 00 minutes 00 seconds East a distance of 33.0 feet; thence North 86 degrees 25 minutes 22 seconds West a distance of 352.57 feet to the Northeasterly right-of-way line of said railway company; thence South 49 degrees 15 minutes 53 seconds East along said Northeasterly right-of-way line, a distance of 84.28 feet to the point of beginning, in Will County, Illinois.

Exception 6: The North 850 feet of the East 1025 feet of the South half of the Southeast Quarter of Section 30, Township 36 North, and in Range 10 East of the Third Principal Meridian, in Will County, Illinois.

P.A. 94–1055, Art. 25, § 25–7–103.95, eff. Jan. 1, 2007.

30/25–7–103.96.   Quick-take; Village of Palatine

§ 25–7–103.96.   Quick-take; Village of Palatine. Quick-take proceedings under Article 20 may be used for a period of 4 years after July 30, 1999, by the Village of Palatine, for the acquisition of the following described property for the purpose of revitalizing the downtown business area:

Lots 1 through 3 in Block D of the Subdivision of the North 24.60 acres in the NE ¼ of the NE ¼ of Section 22, Township 42, Range 10 East of the Third Principal Meridian, in Cook County, IL;

Property bounded by Bothwell Street, Railroad right-of-way, Plum Grove Road and Chicago Avenue in the Village of Palatine;

Lots 1 through 8 in Block K, of the Town of Palatine, a subdivision of the West 16 ⅔ acres of the South 31 acres of the West ½ of the Southwest ¼ of Section 14 and the Southeast 24.12 acres of the South 31 acres of the East ½ of the Southeast ¼ of Section 15, Township 42 North, Range 10, East of the Third Principal Meridian, Ante-Fire, Re-recorded April 10, 1877 as Document 129579, in Cook County, Illinois;

Property bounded by Wilson Street, Plum Grove Road, Slade Street, Railroad right-of-way and Bothwell Street in the Village of Palatine;

Lots 1 through 8 in Block 8 of the Subdivision of part of the East ½ of the SE ¼ Section, Ante-Fire, Re-recorded on April 10, 1877 as Document Number 129579;

Lots 20 and 21 and the West 71.25 feet of Lot 24 of Arthur T. McIntosh and Company's Palatine Farms, being a subdivision of Section 16, Township 42, Range 10 East of the Third Principal Meridian, in Cook County, IL, recorded on June 16, 1919;

Lots 1 through 3 of Millin's Subdivision of the SE ¼ of Section 15, Township 42, Range 10 East of the Third Principal Meridian, in Cook County, IL;

Property bounded by Colfax Street, Smith Street and Millin's Subdivision of the SE ¼ of Section 15, Township 42, Range 10 East of the Third Principal Meridian, in Cook County, IL;

Property bounded by Wood Street, Brockway Street and Railroad right-of-way in the Village of Palatine;

Lots 45 through 50 and 58 through 64 of Arthur T. McIntosh and Company's Palatine Farms, being a

subdivision of Section 16, Township 42, Range 10 East of the Third Principal Meridian, in Cook County, IL, recorded on June 16, 1919; and Property bounded by Railroad right-of-way, Brockway Street and Slade Street in the Village of Palatine.

P.A. 94–1055, Art. 25, § 25–7–103.96, eff. Jan. 1, 2007.

30/25–7–103.97.   Quick-take; Village of Baylis

§ 25–7–103.97.   Quick-take; Village of Baylis. Quick-take proceedings under Article 20 may be used for a period of 12 months after the effective date of this amendatory Act of the 92nd General Assembly by the Village of Baylis for the acquisition of the following described property for the purpose of constructing a sewer project:

A part of the North One-Half of the Northwest Quarter of the Southeast Quarter of Section Seven (7), Township Four (4) South, Range Four (4) West of the New Salem Township, Pike County, Illinois specifically described as follows:

COMMENCING: At a point of beginning 540.35 feet South 00 degrees 33 minutes 30 seconds West of center of Section Seven (7), Township Four (4) South, Range Four (4) West of the New Salem Township, Pike County, Illinois, Thence 1,481.74 feet North 64 degrees 56 minutes 58 seconds East Thence 800.0 feet North 90 degrees 00 minutes 00 seconds West Thence 172.61 feet North 00 degrees 33 minutes 30 seconds East to the point of beginning, said area to contain 15.00 acres.

PROPOSED ACCESS RIGHT OF WAY: Fifty (50) feet wide by Three hundred eighty six and 77 hundreds feet, said area containing 0.44 Acres more or less.

P.A. 94–1055, Art. 25, § 25–7–103.97, eff. Jan. 1, 2007.

30/25–7–103.98.   Quick-take; County of Lake

§ 25–7–103.98.   Quick-take; County of Lake. Quick-take proceedings under Article 20 may be used for a period of 12 months after the effective date of this amendatory Act of the 92nd General Assembly, by the County of Lake, for the acquisition of the following described property as necessary right-of-way to complete the improvement of County Highway 45 (Washington Street) from Route 45 to Hunt Club Road:

PARCEL 014

THAT PART OF COMMON ELEMENT IN THE TOWN HOMES OF WOODLAND HILLS CONDOMINIUM, PHASE 1B, AS DELINEATED ON THE SURVEY OF PART OF THE WEST HALF OF THE SOUTHEAST QUARTER OF SECTION 20, TOWNSHIP 45 NORTH, RANGE 11, EAST OF THE THIRD PRINCIPAL MERIDIAN, IN LAKE COUNTY, ILLINOIS, DESCRIBED AS FOLLOWS:

COMMENCING AT THE SOUTHEAST CORNER OF THE WIDENING OF WASHINGTON

STREET RECORDED APRIL 15, 1985 AS DOC-
UMENT NO. 2348877, BEING ALSO THE POINT
OF INTERSECTION OF A LINE DRAWN 15.240
METERS (50.00 FEET) SOUTH OF AND PAR-
ALLEL WITH THE EAST-WEST CENTER-
LINE OF SAID SECTION 20, WITH THE EAST
LINE OF SAID WEST HALF OF THE SOUTH-
EAST QUARTER OF SECTION 20; THENCE
WEST ALONG SAID PARALLEL LINE, ON AN
ASSUMED BEARING OF NORTH 89 DEGREES
49 MINUTES 09 SECONDS WEST, A DIS-
TANCE OF 151.292 METERS (493.08 FEET) TO
THE POINT OF BEGINNING; THENCE CON-
TINUING NORTH 89 DEGREES 49 MINUTES
09 SECONDS WEST, A DISTANCE OF 73.395
METERS (240.80 FEET); THENCE ON THE
ARC OF A CURVE TO THE LEFT, SAID
CURVE HAVING A RADIUS OF 7.620 METERS
(25.00 FEET) AND THE CHORD BEARING OF
SOUTH 45 DEGREES 10 MINUTES 51 SEC-
ONDS WEST, AN ARC DISTANCE OF 11.969
METERS (39.27 FEET); THENCE SOUTH 00
DEGREES 10 MINUTES 51 SECONDS WEST, A
DISTANCE OF 6.614 METERS (21.70 FEET);
THENCE ON THE ARC OF A CURVE TO THE
LEFT, SAID CURVE HAVING A RADIUS OF
63.514 METERS (208.38 FEET) AND THE
CHORD BEARING OF SOUTH 11 DEGREES 55
MINUTES 52 SECONDS EAST, AN ARC DIS-
TANCE OF 26.853 METERS (88.10 FEET) TO
THE POINT OF REVERSE CURVATURE;
THENCE ON THE ARC OF A CURVE TO THE
RIGHT, SAID CURVE HAVING A RADIUS OF
241.176 METERS (791.26 FEET) AND THE
CHORD BEARING OF SOUTH 22 DEGREES 33
MINUTES 41 SECONDS EAST, AN ARC DIS-
TANCE OF 12.473 METERS (40.92 FEET);
THENCE SOUTH 89 DEGREES 49 MINUTES
30 SECONDS EAST, A DISTANCE OF 70.607
METERS (231.65 FEET); THENCE NORTH 00
DEGREES 10 MINUTES 30 SECONDS EAST, A
DISTANCE OF 51.789 METERS (169.91 FEET)
TO THE POINT OF BEGINNING.

SAID PARCEL CONTAINING 0.4043 HECTARE
(0.999 ACRE), MORE OR LESS.

PERMANENT INDEX NUMBER: 07-20-400-032
THRU -049.

PARCEL 017

THE SOUTH 18.288 METERS (60.00 FEET) OF
THE EAST HALF (EXCEPT THE EAST 203.912
METERS (669.00 FEET) OF THE NORTHEAST
QUARTER SECTION) OF THE FOLLOWING
PARCEL (TAKEN AS A TRACT): THE NORTH-
EAST QUARTER (EXCEPT EAST 22 RODS
AND THE WEST 60 RODS THEREOF) OF SEC-
TION 20, TOWNSHIP 45 NORTH, RANGE 11,
EAST OF THE THIRD PRINCIPAL MERIDI-
AN, IN LAKE COUNTY, ILLINOIS.

SAID PARCEL CONTAINING 0.2206 HECTARE
(0.545 ACRE), MORE OR LESS, OF WHICH
0.1471 HECTARE (0.363 ACRE), MORE OR
LESS, WAS PREVIOUSLY USED FOR HIGH-
WAY PURPOSES.

PERMANENT INDEX NUMBER: 07-20-200-003.

PARCEL 019

THE SOUTH 18.288 METERS (60.00 FEET) OF
THE EAST 155.144 METERS (509.00 FEET) (EX-
CEPT EAST 22 RODS THEREOF) OF THE
NORTHEAST QUARTER OF SECTION 20,
TOWNSHIP 45 NORTH, RANGE 11, EAST OF
THE THIRD PRINCIPAL MERIDIAN, IN
LAKE COUNTY, ILLINOIS.

SAID PARCEL CONTAINING 0.0814 HECTARE
(0.201 ACRE), MORE OR LESS, OF WHICH
0.0546 HECTARE (0.135 ACRE), MORE OR
LESS, WAS PREVIOUSLY USED FOR HIGH-
WAY PURPOSES.

PERMANENT INDEX NUMBER: 07-20-200-003.

P.A. 94–1055, Art. 25, § 25–7–103.98, eff. Jan. 1, 2007.

30/25–7–103.99.   Quick-take;   Village of Bart-lett

§ 25–7–103.99.   Quick-take; Village of Bartlett.
Quick-take proceedings under Article 20 may be used
for a period of 12 months after the effective date of
this amendatory Act of the 92nd General Assembly by
the Village of Bartlett for the acquisition of the following described easements for the purpose of the construction of an asphalt bicycle and multi-purpose public path:

1. PERMANENT EASEMENT. A permanent
easement appurtenant, 20 feet to 30 feet in width,
over, upon, across, through and under that portion
of the Alperin Property legally described as follows:

Parcel 1:

That part of the East Half of the Northwest Quarter of Section Thirty-Three, Township Forty-One
North, Range Nine, East of the Third Principal
Meridian, bounded and described as follows: Commencing at the Southwest corner of the East Half
of the Northwest Quarter of said Section Thirty-
Three; thence North 00 degrees 26 minutes 35
seconds East, being an assumed bearing on the
West line of the East Half of the Northwest Quarter of said Section Thirty-Three, a distance of
1273.66 feet; thence South 89 degrees 33 minutes
25 seconds East, perpendicular to the last described
West line, a distance of 40.0 feet to the point of
beginning; thence continuing South 89 degrees 33
minutes 25 seconds East, on said perpendicular line,
a distance of 20.0 feet; thence South 00 degrees 26
minutes 35 seconds West, on a line 60.0 feet East of
and parallel with the West line of the East Half of
the Northwest Quarter of said Section Thirty-
Three, a distance of 949.0 feet; thence South 89
degrees 33 minutes 25 seconds East, perpendicular

to the last described West line, a distance of 10.0 feet; thence South 00 degrees 26 minutes 35 seconds West, on a line 70.0 feet East of and parallel with the West line of the East Half of the Northwest Quarter of said Section Thirty-Three, a distance of 323.28 feet to the South line of the East Half of the Northwest Quarter of said Section Thirty-Three; thence South 89 degrees 18 minutes, 39 seconds West, on the last described South line, a distance of 30.01 feet; thence North 00 degrees 26 minutes 35 seconds East, on a line 40.0 feet East of and parallel with West line of the East Half of the Northwest Quarter of said Section Thirty-Three, a distance of 1272.87 feet to the point of beginning, all in Cook County, Illinois.

Parcel 2:

That part of the East Half of the Northwest Quarter of Section Thirty-Three, Township Forty-One North, Range Nine, East of the Third Principal Meridian, bounded and described as follows: Commencing at the Northwest corner of the East Half of the Northwest Quarter of said Section Thirty-Three; thence North 89 degrees 23 minutes 39 seconds East, being an assumed bearing on the North line of the East Half of the Northwest Quarter of said Section Thirty-Three, a distance of 40.0 feet to the point of beginning; thence continuing North 89 degrees 23 minutes 39 seconds East, on the last described North line, a distance of 20.0 feet; thence South 00 degrees 26 minutes 35 seconds West, on a line 60.0 feet East of and parallel with the West line of the East Half of the Northwest Quarter of said Section Thirty-Three, a distance of 1392.66 feet; thence North 89 degrees 33 minutes 25 seconds West, perpendicular to the last described West line, a distance of 20.0 feet; thence North 00 degrees 26 minutes 35 seconds East, on a line 40.0 feet East of and parallel with the West line of the East Half of the Northwest Quarter of said Section Thirty-Three, a distance of 1392.29 feet to the point of beginning, excepting therefrom that part described as follows: Commencing at the Northwest corner of the East Half of the Northwest Quarter of said Section Thirty-Three; thence South 00 degrees 26 minutes 35 seconds West, on the West line of the East Half of the Northwest Quarter of said Section Thirty-Three, a distance of 453.71 feet to the North right-of-way line of the Chicago, Milwaukee, St. Paul and Pacific Railroad; thence South 79 degrees 38 minutes 52 seconds East, on said North railroad right-of-way line, a distance of 40.61 feet to the point of beginning for said exception; thence continuing South 79 degrees 38 minutes 52 seconds East, on said North railroad right-of-way line, a distance of 20.30 feet; thence South 00 degrees 26 minutes 35 seconds West, on a line 60.0 feet East of and parallel with the West line of the East Half of the Northwest Quarter of said Section Thirty-Three, a distance of 101.51 feet to the South right-of-way line of said railroad; thence

North 79 degrees 38 minutes 52 seconds West, on said South railroad right-of-way line, a distance of 20.30 feet; thence North 00 degrees 26 minutes 35 seconds East, on a line 40.0 feet East of and parallel with the West line of the East Half of the Northwest Quarter of said Section Thirty-Three, a distance of 101.51 feet to the point of beginning, all in Cook County, Illinois.

(the "Permanent Easement Parcels") for the purpose of constructing, maintaining, repairing, replacing, gaining access to and use by the public of a 12 foot +/− wide, asphalt multi-purpose path.

2. ACCESS EASEMENT. A non-exclusive easement appurtenant, 25 feet to 27 feet in width, over, upon and across that portion of the Alperin Property legally described as follows:

Parcel 1:

That part of the East Half of the Northwest Quarter of Section Thirty-Three, Township Forty-One North, Range Nine, East of the Third Principal Meridian, bounded and described as follows: Commencing at the Southwest corner of the East Half of the Northwest Quarter of said Section Thirty-Three; thence North 00 degrees 26 minutes 35 seconds East, being an assumed bearing on the West line of the East Half of the Northwest Quarter of said Section Thirty-Three, a distance of 1273.66 feet; thence South 89 degrees 33 minutes 25 seconds East, perpendicular to the last described West line, a distance of 13.11 feet to the point of beginning; thence continuing South 89 degrees 33 minutes 25 seconds East, on said perpendicular line, a distance of 26.89 feet; thence South 00 degrees 26 minutes 35 seconds West, on a line 40.0 feet East of and parallel with the West line of the East Half of the Northwest Quarter of said Section Thirty-Three, a distance of 1243.53 feet to a point on a curve concave to the Northeast and having a radius of 45.87 feet; thence Northwesterly 43.45 feet on the arc of the aforementioned curve, having a chord bearing of North 26 degrees 46 minutes 35 seconds West and a chord distance of 41.84 feet; thence North 00 degrees 21 minutes 44 seconds East, a distance of 310.0 feet; thence North 1 degree 18 minutes 37 seconds West, a distance of 238.87 feet; thence North 00 degrees 26 minutes 07 seconds East, a distance of 383.83 feet; thence North 00 degrees 27 minutes 07 seconds East, a distance of 273.74 feet to the point of beginning, all in Cook County, Illinois.

Parcel 2:

That part of the East Half of the Northwest Quarter of Section Thirty-Three, Township Forty-One North, Range Nine, East of the Third Principal Meridian, bounded and described as follows: Commencing at the Northwest corner of the East Half of the Northwest Quarter of said Section Thirty-Three; thence North 89 degrees 23 minutes 39 seconds East, being an assumed bearing on the

North line of the East Half of the Northwest Quarter of said Section Thirty-Three, a distance of 40.0 feet to the point of beginning; thence South 00 degrees 26 minutes 35 seconds West, on a line 40.0 feet East of and parallel with the West line of the East Half of the Northwest Quarter of said Section Thirty-Three, a distance of 1392.29 feet; thence North 89 degrees 33 minutes 25 seconds West, perpendicular to the last described West line, a distance of 26.89 feet; thence North 00 degrees 27 minutes 07 seconds East, a distance of 9.53 feet; thence North 00 degrees 10 minutes 41 seconds East, a distance of 216.59 feet; thence North 00 degrees 51 minutes 33 seconds East, a distance of 154.56 feet; thence North 00 degrees 24 minutes 25 seconds East, a distance of 260.39 feet; thence North 00 degrees 21 minutes 48 seconds East, a distance of 144.80 feet; thence North 00 degrees 04 minutes 10 seconds West, a distance of 21.74 feet; thence North 00 degrees 41 minutes 33 seconds East, a distance of 50.42 feet; thence North 00 degrees 03 minutes 26 seconds East, a distance of 44.54 feet; thence North 00 degrees 51 minutes 20 seconds East, a distance of 84.53 feet; thence North 1 degree 41 minutes 45 seconds East, a distance of 291.25 feet; thence North 00 degrees 56 minutes 03 seconds East, a distance of 113.65 feet to the North line of the East Half of the Northwest Quarter of said Section Thirty-Three; thence North 89 degrees 23 minutes 39 seconds East, on the last described North line, a distance of 19.47 feet to the point of beginning, excepting therefrom that part falling within the 100.0 foot wide right-of-way of the Chicago, Milwaukee, St. Paul and Pacific Railroad, all in Cook County, Illinois.

(the "Access Easement Parcels") for the purpose of providing access to the public from the center of Naperville Road to the bicycle/multi-purpose asphalt path that will be constructed on the Permanent Easement.

3. CONSTRUCTION EASEMENT. A temporary construction easement, 57 feet to 67 feet in width, over, upon, across, through and under that portion of the Alperin Property legally described as follows:

Parcel 1:

That part of the East Half of the Northwest Quarter of Section Thirty-Three, Township Forty-One North, Range Nine, East of the Third Principal Meridian, bounded and described as follows: Commencing at the Southwest corner of the East Half of the Northwest Quarter of said Section Thirty-Three; thence North 00 degrees 26 minutes 35 seconds East, being an assumed bearing on the West line of the East Half of the Northwest Quarter of said Section Thirty-Three, a distance of 1273.66 feet; thence South 89 degrees 33 minutes 25 seconds East, perpendicular to the last described West line, a distance of 13.11 feet to the point of beginning; thence continuing South 89 degrees 33

minutes 25 seconds East, on said perpendicular line, a distance of 56.89 feet; thence South 00 degrees 26 minutes 35 seconds West, on a line 70.0 feet East of and parallel with the West line of the East Half of the Northwest Quarter of said Section Thirty-Three, a distance of 939.0 feet; thence South 89 degrees 33 minutes 25 seconds East, perpendicular to the last described West line, a distance of 10.0 feet; thence South 00 degrees 26 minutes 35 seconds West, on a line 80.0 feet East of and parallel with the West line of the East Half of the Northwest Quarter of said Section Thirty-Three, a distance of 313.12 feet; thence North 89 degrees 33 minutes 25 seconds West, a distance of 13.27 feet to a point of curve; thence Northwesterly 71.99 feet on the arc of a curve, concave to the Northeast, having a radius of 45.87 feet with a chord bearing of North 44 degrees 35 minutes 51 seconds West and a chord distance of 64.82 feet; thence North 00 degrees 21 minutes 44 seconds East, a distance of 310.0 feet; thence North 1 degree 18 minutes 37 seconds West, a distance of 238.87 feet; thence North 00 degrees 26 minutes 07 seconds East, a distance of 383.83 feet; thence North 00 degrees 27 minutes 07 seconds East, a distance of 273.74 feet to the point beginning, all in Cook County, Illinois.

Parcel 2:

That part of the East Half of the Northwest Quarter of Section Thirty-Three, Township Forty-One North, Range Nine, East of the Third Principal Meridian, bounded and described as follows: Commencing at the Northwest corner of the East Half of the Northwest Quarter of said Section Thirty-Three; thence North 89 degrees 23 minutes 39 seconds East, being an assumed bearing on the North line of the East Half of the Northwest Quarter of said Section Thirty-Three, a distance of 70.0 feet to the point of beginning; thence South 00 degrees 26 minutes 35 seconds West, on a line 70.0 feet East of and parallel with the West line of the East Half of the Northwest Quarter of said Section Thirty-Three, a distance of 1392.84 feet; thence North 89 degrees 33 minutes 25 seconds West, perpendicular to the last described West line, a distance of 56.89 feet; thence North 00 degrees 27 minutes 07 seconds East, a distance of 9.53 feet; thence North 00 degrees 10 minutes 41 seconds East, a distance of 216.59 feet; thence North 00 degrees 51 minutes 33 seconds East, a distance of 154.56 feet; thence North 00 degrees 24 minutes 25 seconds East, a distance of 260.39 feet; thence North 00 degrees 21 minutes 48 seconds East, a distance of 144.80 feet; thence North 00 degrees 04 minutes 10 seconds West, a distance of 21.74 feet; thence North 00 degrees 41 minutes 33 seconds East, a distance of 50.42 feet; thence North 00 degrees 03 minutes 26 seconds East, a distance of 44.54 feet; thence North 00 degrees 51 minutes 20 seconds East, a distance of 84.53 feet; thence North 1 degree 41 minutes 45 seconds East, a distance of

291.25 feet; thence North 00 degrees 56 minutes 03 seconds East, a distance of 113.65 feet to the North line of the East Half of the Northwest Quarter of said Section Thirty-Three; thence North 89 degrees 23 minutes 39 seconds East, on the last described North line, a distance of 49.47 feet to the point of beginning, excepting therefrom that part falling within the 100.0 foot wide right-of-way of the Chicago, Milwaukee, St. Paul and Pacific Railroad, all in Cook County, Illinois.

(the "Temporary Construction Easement Parcels") for the construction and installation of an asphalt, bicycle/multi-purpose path and the restoration of all areas affected and disturbed by said construction as soon as reasonably practical and weather permitting, but in all events all such work shall be completed within 364 days after said easement is granted by court order or decree.

P.A. 94–1055, Art. 25, § 25–7–103.99, eff. Jan. 1, 2007.

30/25–7–103.100. Quick-take; Illinois Department of Natural Resources

§ 25–7–103.100. Quick-take; Illinois Department of Natural Resources.

(a) Quick-take proceedings under Article 20 may be used for a period of 24 months after the effective date of this amendatory Act of the 92nd General Assembly by the Illinois Department of Natural Resources for the acquisition of the following described property for the purpose of flood control:

NINE (9) TRACTS OF LAND, HEREINAFTER DESCRIBED AS PARCELS, BEING ONE PARCEL FOR FEE SIMPLE TITLE AND EIGHT (8) PARCELS FOR PERMANENT EASEMENTS, ALL BEING LOCATED IN SECTIONS 28 AND 29, T17N-R8W OF THE 3RD PRINCIPAL MERIDIAN AND ALL BEING DESCRIBED AS FOLLOWS:

PARCEL A (FEE SIMPLE TITLE)

COMMENCING AT AN EXISTING STONE BEING THE NORTHEAST CORNER OF SECTION 29, T17N-R8W OF THE 3RD PRINCIPAL MERIDIAN; THENCE, S00°17′58″E BEING THE EAST LINE OF SAID SECTION 29, A DISTANCE OF 2456.35 FEET TO A PK NAIL DRIVEN IN THE PAVEMENT; THENCE, N89°48′00″E A DISTANCE OF 32.99 FEET TO THE INTERSECTION WITH A CONCRETE HIGHWAY R.O.W. MONUMENT (DAMAGED) LYING ON THE EASTERLY R.O.W. LINE OF 3 MILE LANE TO BE HEREINAFTER KNOWN AS THE POINT OF BEGINNING OF PARCEL A; THENCE, S51°22′44″E A DISTANCE OF 33.50 FEET TO AN IRON PIN; THENCE, N89°04′24″E A DISTANCE OF 1025.09 FEET TO AN IRON PIN; THENCE, S87°13′56″E A DISTANCE OF 306.24 FEET TO AN IRON PIN;

THENCE, S79°29′07″E A DISTANCE OF 311.29 FEET TO AN IRON PIN LYING ON THE INTERSECTION WITH THE NORTHERLY R.O.W. LINE OF IL. RTE. 125; THENCE, N81°59′11″W ALONG THE NORTHERLY R.O.W. LINE OF IL. RTE. 125 A DISTANCE OF 243.13 FEET TO AN IRON PIN; THENCE, S89°48′00″W ALONG SAID NORTHERLY R.O.W. LINE OF IL. RTE. 125 A DISTANCE OF 1396.06 FEET TO AN IRON PIN; THENCE, N29°15′08″W ALONG THE NORTHERLY R.O.W. LINE OF IL. RTE. 125 A DISTANCE OF 53.76 FEET TO THE POINT OF BEGINNING, SAID PARCEL A CONTAINING 1.046 ACRES, MORE OR LESS; ALSO

PARCEL B (PERMANENT EASEMENT)

COMMENCING AT AN EXISTING STONE BEING THE NORTHEAST CORNER OF SECTION 29, T17N-R8W OF THE 3RD PRINCIPAL MERIDIAN; THENCE, S00°17′58″E BEING THE EAST LINE OF SAID SECTION 29, A DISTANCE OF 2456.35 FEET TO A PK NAIL DRIVEN IN THE PAVEMENT; THENCE, N89°48′00″E A DISTANCE OF 32.99 FEET TO THE INTERSECTION WITH A CONCRETE HIGHWAY R.O.W. MONUMENT (DAMAGED) LYING ON THE EASTERLY R.O.W. LINE OF 3 MILE LANE TO BE HEREINAFTER KNOWN AS THE POINT OF BEGINNING OF PARCEL B; THENCE, S51°22′44″E A DISTANCE OF 33.50 FEET TO AN IRON PIN; THENCE, N89°04′24″E A DISTANCE OF 112.73 FEET TO AN IRON PIN; THENCE, N44°49′15″E A DISTANCE OF 343.99 FEET TO AN IRON PIN; THENCE N17°37′15″W A DISTANCE OF 223.84 FEET TO AN IRON PIN; THENCE, S47°06′00″W A DISTANCE OF 428.80 FEET TO AN IRON PIN LOCATED AT THE INTERSECTION WITH THE EASTERLY R.O.W. LINE OF 3 MILE LANE; THENCE, S00°12′00″E ALONG THE EASTERLY R.O.W. LINE OF 3 MILE LANE A DISTANCE OF 146.36 FEET TO THE POINT OF BEGINNING, SAID PARCEL B CONTAINING 2.108 ACRES, MORE OR LESS; ALSO

PARCEL C (PERMANENT EASEMENT)

COMMENCING AT AN EXISTING STONE BEING THE NORTHEAST CORNER OF SECTION 29, T17N-R8W OF THE 3RD PRINCIPAL MERIDIAN; THENCE, S00°17′58″E BEING THE EAST LINE OF SAID SECTION 29, A DISTANCE OF 2456.35 FEET TO A PK NAIL DRIVEN IN THE PAVEMENT; THENCE S89°48′00″W A DISTANCE OF 27.01 FEET TO THE INTERSECTION WITH A CONCRETE HIGHWAY R.O.W. MONUMENT LYING ON THE WESTERLY R.O.W. LINE OF 3 MILE LANE TO BE HEREINAFTER KNOWN AS THE POINT OF BEGINNING FOR PARCEL C;

THENCE, N00°12′00″W ALONG THE WESTERLY R.O.W. LINE OF 3 MILE LANE A DISTANCE OF 16.25 FEET TO AN IRON PIN; THENCE, N46°47′54″W A DISTANCE OF 84.98 FEET TO AN IRON PIN; THENCE, S47°52′31″W A DISTANCE OF 73.09 FEET TO AN IRON PIN; THENCE, S29°59′17″E A DISTANCE OF 72.48 FEET TO THE INTERSECTION WITH AN IRON PIN ON THE NORTHERLY R.O.W. LINE OF IL. RTE. 125; THENCE, N64°57′00″E ALONG THE NORTHERLY R.O.W. LINE OF IL. RTE. 125 A DISTANCE OF 88.29 FEET TO THE POINT OF BEGINNING, SAID PARCEL C CONTAINING 0.166 ACRES, MORE OR LESS; ALSO

PARCEL D (PERMANENT EASEMENT)

COMMENCING AT AN EXISTING STONE BEING THE NORTHEAST CORNER OF SECTION 29, T17N-R8W OF THE 3RD PRINCIPAL MERIDIAN; THENCE, S00°17′58″E ALONG THE EAST LINE OF SECTION 29 A DISTANCE OF 2633.53 FEET TO A PK NAIL DRIVEN INTO THE PAVEMENT BEING AN INTERSECTION WITH THE SOUTH R.O.W. LINE, AS EXTENDED, OF IL. RTE. 125; THENCE, S89°48′00″W ALONG THE SOUTH R.O.W. LINE OF SAID IL. RTE. 125 A DISTANCE OF 107.69 FEET TO AN IRON PIN TO BE HEREINAFTER KNOWN AS THE EASTERLY PERMANENT EASEMENT LINE AND THE POINT OF BEGINNING FOR PARCEL D; THENCE S89°48′00″W ALONG THE SOUTH R.O.W. LINE OF IL. RTE. 125 A DISTANCE OF 81.06 FEET TO A POINT LOCATED AT THE INTERSECTION WITH THE CENTERLINE OF AN EXISTING DITCH; THENCE, S55°58′52″W ALONG THE CENTERLINE OF THE DITCH A DISTANCE OF 209.47 FEET TO A POINT; THENCE, S53°45′52″W ALONG THE CENTERLINE OF THE DITCH A DISTANCE OF 365.47 FEET TO A POINT; THENCE, S65°19′43″W ALONG THE CENTERLINE OF THE DITCH A DISTANCE OF 113.11 FEET TO A POINT; THENCE, S30°34′40″W ALONG THE CENTERLINE OF THE DITCH A DISTANCE OF 75.27 FEET TO A POINT; THENCE, S12°53′03″W ALONG THE CENTERLINE OF THE DITCH A DISTANCE OF 116.75 FEET TO A POINT; THENCE, S08°04′16″E ALONG THE CENTERLINE OF THE DITCH A DISTANCE OF 168.20 FEET TO A POINT; THENCE, S27°51′33″W ALONG THE CENTERLINE OF THE DITCH A DISTANCE OF 46.96 FEET TO A POINT; THENCE, S65°24′06″W ALONG THE CENTERLINE OF THE DITCH A DISTANCE OF 67.97 FEET TO A POINT; THENCE, S36°00′49″W ALONG THE CENTERLINE OF THE DITCH A DISTANCE OF 59.69 FEET TO A POINT; THENCE, S85°46′17″W ALONG THE CENTERLINE OF THE DITCH A DISTANCE OF 69.25 FEET TO A POINT;

THENCE, S54°45′52″W ALONG THE CENTERLINE OF THE DITCH A DISTANCE OF 98.13 FEET TO A POINT; THENCE, S87°00′39″W ALONG THE CENTERLINE OF THE DITCH A DISTANCE OF 40.02 FEET TO A POINT; THENCE, S28°51′55″W ALONG THE CENTERLINE OF THE DITCH A DISTANCE OF 21.60 FEET TO A POINT ALSO BEING THE INTERSECTION WITH THE NORTHERLY R.O.W. LINE OF FREMONT STREET; THENCE, S73°36′39″E ALONG THE NORTHERLY R.O.W. LINE OF FREMONT STREET A DISTANCE OF 66.26 FEET TO AN IRON PIN, ALSO BEING THE INTERSECTION WITH THE EASTERLY EASEMENT LINE; THENCE, N69°11′51″E ALONG THE EASTERLY EASEMENT LINE A DISTANCE OF 259.39 FEET TO AN IRON PIN; THENCE, N29°51′00″E ALONG THE EASTERLY EASEMENT LINE A DISTANCE OF 206.51 FEET TO AN IRON PIN; THENCE, N13°03′29″W ALONG THE EASTERLY EASEMENT LINE A DISTANCE OF 222.40 FEET TO AN IRON PIN; THENCE, N54°58′36″E ALONG THE EASTERLY EASEMENT LINE A DISTANCE OF 797.16 FEET TO THE POINT OF BEGINNING, SAID PARCEL D CONTAINING 1.878 ACRES, MORE OR LESS; ALSO

PARCEL E (PERMANENT EASEMENT)

COMMENCING AT A PK NAIL DRIVEN INTO THE PAVEMENT BEING AN INTERSECTION WITH THE SOUTH R.O.W. LINE OF SAID IL. RTE. 125, AS EXTENDED, AS PREVIOUSLY DESCRIBED IN PARCEL D; THENCE, S89°48′00″W ALONG THE SOUTH R.O.W. LINE OF IL. RTE. 125 A DISTANCE OF 280.19 FEET TO AN IRON PIN ALSO BEING THE INTERSECTION WITH THE WESTERLY EASEMENT LINE TO BE HEREINAFTER KNOWN AS THE POINT OF BEGINNING FOR PARCEL E; THENCE, S61°41′32″W ALONG THE WESTERLY EASEMENT LINE A DISTANCE OF 544.25 FEET TO AN IRON PIN; THENCE, S27°23′57″W ALONG THE WESTERLY EASEMENT LINE A DISTANCE OF 309.17 FEET TO AN IRON PIN; THENCE, S10°40′01″E ALONG THE WESTERLY EASEMENT LINE A DISTANCE OF 197.30 FEET TO AN IRON PIN; THENCE, S56°43′56″W ALONG THE WESTERLY EASEMENT LINE A DISTANCE OF 78.07 FEET TO AN IRON PIN; THENCE, N59°23′46″W ALONG THE WESTERLY EASEMENT LINE A DISTANCE OF 124.54 FEET TO AN IRON PIN; THENCE, S38°40′25″W ALONG THE WESTERLY EASEMENT LINE A DISTANCE OF 253.15 FEET TO AN IRON PIN LOCATED AT THE NORTHERLY R.O.W. LINE OF FREMONT STREET; THENCE, S73°36′39″E ALONG THE NORTHERLY R.O.W. LINE OF FREMONT STREET A DISTANCE OF 79.92 FEET TO A POINT LOCATED AT THE INTER-

SECTION WITH THE CENTERLINE OF AN EXISTING DITCH; THENCE, N28°51′55″E ALONG THE CENTERLINE OF THE DITCH A DISTANCE OF 21.60 FEET TO A POINT; THENCE, N87°00′39″E ALONG THE CENTERLINE OF THE DITCH A DISTANCE OF 40.02 FEET TO A POINT; THENCE, N54°45′52″E ALONG THE CENTERLINE OF THE DITCH A DISTANCE OF 98.13 FEET TO A POINT; THENCE, N85°46′17″E ALONG THE CENTERLINE OF THE DITCH A DISTANCE OF 69.25 FEET TO A POINT; THENCE, N36°00′49″E ALONG THE CENTERLINE OF THE DITCH A DISTANCE OF 59.69 FEET TO A POINT; THENCE, N65°24′06″E ALONG THE CENTERLINE OF THE DITCH A DISTANCE OF 67.97 FEET TO A POINT; THENCE, N27°51′33″E ALONG THE CENTERLINE OF THE DITCH A DISTANCE OF 46.96 FEET TO A POINT; THENCE, N08°04′16″W ALONG THE CENTERLINE OF THE DITCH A DISTANCE OF 168.20 FEET TO A POINT; THENCE, N12°53′03″E ALONG THE CENTERLINE OF THE DITCH A DISTANCE OF 116.75 FEET TO A POINT; THENCE, N30°34′40″E ALONG THE CENTERLINE OF THE DITCH A DISTANCE OF 75.27 FEET TO A POINT; THENCE, N65°19′43″E ALONG THE CENTERLINE OF THE DITCH A DISTANCE OF 113.11 FEET TO A POINT; THENCE, N53°45′52″E ALONG THE CENTERLINE OF THE DITCH A DISTANCE OF 365.47 FEET TO A POINT; THENCE, N55°58′52″E ALONG THE CENTERLINE OF THE DITCH A DISTANCE OF 209.47 FEET TO A POINT LOCATED AT THE INTERSECTION WITH THE SOUTH R.O.W. LINE OF IL. RTE. 125; THENCE, S89°48′00″W ALONG SAID SOUTH R.O.W. LINE OF IL. RTE. 125 A DISTANCE OF 91.44 FEET TO THE POINT OF BEGINNING, SAID PARCEL E CONTAINING 2.628 ACRES, MORE OR LESS; ALSO

PARCEL F (PERMANENT EASEMENT)

COMMENCING AT AN IRON PIN BEING THE INTERSECTION OF THE NORTH R.O.W. LINE OF FREMONT STREET AND THE WEST EASEMENT LINE, AS PREVIOUSLY DESCRIBED IN PARCEL E; THENCE S15°35′22″W ACROSS SAID FREMONT STREET A DISTANCE OF 60.01 FEET TO AN IRON PIN BEING THE INTERSECTION OF THE WESTERLY PERMANENT EASEMENT LINE AND THE SOUTHERLY R.O.W. LINE OF FREMONT STREET TO BE HEREINAFTER KNOWN AS THE POINT OF BEGINNING OF PARCEL F; THENCE, S19°32′27″W ALONG THE EASEMENT LINE A DISTANCE OF 316.50 FEET TO AN IRON PIN; THENCE, S13°42′05″W ALONG THE EASEMENT LINE A DISTANCE OF 424.35 FEET TO AN IRON PIN; THENCE, S12°12′06″W ALONG THE EASEMENT LINE A

DISTANCE OF 53.67 FEET TO AN IRON PIN; THENCE, S06°54′45″E ALONG THE EASEMENT LINE A DISTANCE OF 270.76 FEET TO AN IRON PIN; THENCE, S29°05′13″E ALONG THE EASEMENT LINE A DISTANCE OF 140.63 FEET TO AN IRON PIN; THENCE, S44°58′33″W ALONG THE EASEMENT LINE A DISTANCE OF 268.58 FEET TO AN IRON PIN; THENCE, S05°01′56″E ALONG THE EASEMENT LINE A DISTANCE OF 228.73 FEET TO AN IRON PIN; THENCE, S65°36′08″W ALONG THE EASEMENT LINE A DISTANCE OF 79.03 FEET TO AN IRON PIN; THENCE, S01°45′38″W ALONG THE EASEMENT LINE A DISTANCE OF 67.29 FEET TO AN IRON PIN LOCATED AT THE INTERSECTION WITH THE NORTH R.O.W. LINE OF CEMETERY ROAD; THENCE, S89°54′53″E ALONG THE NORTHERLY R.O.W. LINE A DISTANCE OF 153.89 FEET TO AN IRON PIN; THENCE, N11°39′38″E ALONG THE EASTERLY EASEMENT LINE A DISTANCE OF 391.73 FEET TO AN IRON PIN; THENCE, N44°53′07″E ALONG THE EASEMENT LINE A DISTANCE OF 130.86 FEET TO AN IRON PIN; THENCE, N00°00′11″E A DISTANCE OF 131.73 FEET TO AN EXISTING REINFORCEMENT BAR; THENCE, N00°00′11″E A DISTANCE OF 148.55 FEET TO AN IRON PIN; THENCE, N08°44′27″W ALONG THE EASEMENT LINE A DISTANCE OF 266.45 FEET TO AN IRON PIN; THENCE, N08°13′22″E ALONG THE EASEMENT LINE A DISTANCE OF 305.08 FEET TO AN IRON PIN; THENCE, N24°29′54″E ALONG THE EASEMENT LINE A DISTANCE OF 202.57 FEET TO AN IRON PIN; THENCE, S73°35′10″E ALONG THE EASEMENT LINE A DISTANCE OF 158.04 FEET TO AN IRON PIN; THENCE, N20°27′57″E ALONG THE EASEMENT LINE A DISTANCE OF 58.70 FEET TO AN IRON PIN; THENCE, N65°18′27″W ALONG THE EASEMENT LINE A DISTANCE OF 138.22 FEET TO AN IRON PIN; THENCE, N19°41′58″E ALONG THE EASEMENT LINE A DISTANCE OF 66.62 FEET TO AN IRON PIN BEING THE INTERSECTION WITH THE SOUTHERLY R.O.W. LINE OF FREMONT STREET; THENCE, N73°36′39″W ALONG THE SOUTHERLY R.O.W. LINE OF FREMONT STREET A DISTANCE OF 126.11 FEET TO THE POINT OF BEGINNING, SAID PARCEL F CONTAINING 5.060 ACRES, MORE OR LESS; ALSO

PARCEL G (PERMANENT EASEMENT)

COMMENCING AT AN EXISTING REINFORCEMENT BAR LOCATED AT S00°00′11″W A DISTANCE OF 30.00 FEET FROM THE SOUTHWEST CORNER OF LOT 4 IN BLOCK 3 OF THE NORTHWEST ADDITION TO THE VILLAGE OF ASHLAND; THENCE,

N89°59′49″W A DISTANCE OF 331.32 FEET TO AN EXISTING REINFORCEMENT BAR; THENCE, N00°00′11″E A DISTANCE OF 157.00 FEET TO AN EXISTING REINFORCEMENT BAR TO BE HEREINAFTER KNOWN AS THE POINT OF BEGINNING OF PARCEL G; THENCE, S89°59′49″E A DISTANCE OF 29.56 FEET TO AN IRON PIN AT THE INTERSECTION WITH THE EASEMENT LINE; THENCE, N13°10′52″W ALONG THE EASEMENT LINE A DISTANCE OF 85.69 FEET TO AN IRON PIN; THENCE, N08°44′27″W ALONG THE EASEMENT LINE A DISTANCE OF 65.89 FEET TO AN IRON PIN; THENCE, S00°00′11″W A DISTANCE OF 148.55 FEET TO THE POINT OF BEGINNING, SAID PARCEL G CONTAINING 0.045 ACRES, MORE OR LESS; ALSO

PARCEL H (PERMANENT EASEMENT)

COMMENCING AT AN EXISTING REINFORCEMENT BAR LOCATED AT S00°00′11″W A DISTANCE OF 30.00 FEET FROM THE SOUTHWEST CORNER OF LOT 4 IN BLOCK 3 OF THE NORTHWEST ADDITION TO THE VILLAGE OF ASHLAND; THENCE, N89°59′49″W A DISTANCE OF 331.32 FEET TO AN EXISTING REINFORCEMENT BAR; THENCE, N00°00′11″E A DISTANCE OF 157.00 FEET TO AN EXISTING REINFORCEMENT BAR TO BE HEREINAFTER KNOWN AS THE POINT OF BEGINNING OF PARCEL H; THENCE, S89°59′49″E A DISTANCE OF 29.56 FEET TO AN IRON PIN BEING THE INTERSECTION OF THE EASEMENT LINE; THENCE, S12°39′02″W ALONG THE EASEMENT LINE A DISTANCE OF 135.01 FEET TO AN IRON PIN; THENCE, N00°00′11″E A DISTANCE OF 131.73 FEET TO THE POINT OF BEGINNING, SAID PARCEL H CONTAINING 0.045 ACRES, MORE OR LESS; ALSO

PARCEL I (PERMANENT EASEMENT)

COMMENCING AT AN EXISTING IRON PIN DESCRIBED ABOVE IN PARCEL F BEING THE INTERSECTION OF THE NORTH R.O.W. LINE OF CEMETERY ROAD WITH THE WESTERLY EASEMENT LINE; THENCE, S18°00′15″E ACROSS CEMETERY ROAD A DISTANCE OF 63.12 FEET TO AN IRON PIN LOCATED AT THE INTERSECTION WITH THE SOUTH R.O.W. LINE OF CEMETERY ROAD, TO BE HEREINAFTER KNOWN AS THE POINT OF BEGINNING OF PARCEL I; THENCE, S38°53′00″W ALONG THE EASEMENT LINE A DISTANCE OF 78.50 FEET TO AN IRON PIN; THENCE, S71°07′03″E ALONG THE EASEMENT LINE A DISTANCE OF 98.61 FEET TO AN IRON PIN; THENCE, N30°48′26″E ALONG THE EASEMENT LINE A DISTANCE OF 108.13 FEET TO AN IRON PIN

LOCATED AT THE INTERSECTION WITH THE SOUTH R.O.W. LINE OF CEMETERY ROAD; THENCE, N89°54′52″W ALONG THE SOUTH R.O.W. LINE OF CEMETERY ROAD A DISTANCE OF 99.40 FEET TO THE POINT OF BEGINNING OF PARCEL I, SAID PARCEL CONTAINING 0.190 ACRES, MORE OR LESS.

P.A. 94–1055, Art. 25, § 25–7–103.100, eff. Jan. 1, 2007.

30/25–7–103.101. Quick-take; County of Monroe

§ 25–7–103.101. Quick-take; County of Monroe. Quick-take proceedings under Article 20 may be used for a period of 12 months after the effective date of this amendatory Act of the 92nd General Assembly, by the County of Monroe, to acquire right-of-way for the proposed Rogers Street Extension project as follows:

A part of Tax lots 3-A and 3-B of U.S. Survey 720, Claim 516, in Township 2 South, Range 9 West of the 3rd Principal Meridian, Monroe County, Illinois, as shown at page 122 of the Surveyor's Official Plat Record "A" in the Recorder's office of Monroe County, Illinois, and being more particularly described as follows, to wit:

BEGINNING at the Southwest corner of Tax Lot 7 of U.S. Survey 641, Claim 1645, Township 2 South, Range 9 West of the 3rd Principal Meridian, Monroe County, Illinois, as shown at page 115 of the Surveyor's Official Plat Record "A" in the Recorder's office of Monroe County, Illinois; thence South 89 degrees 41 minutes 50 seconds East, an assumed bearing along the South line of U.S. Survey 641, Claim 1645 (said line also being the North line of U.S. Survey 720, Claim 516), a distance of 80.00 feet to a point; thence South 00 degrees 10 minutes 08 seconds West, a distance of 72.49 feet to a point; thence South 00 degrees 49 minutes 52 seconds East, a distance of 103.44 feet to a point; thence North 89 degrees 10 minutes 08 seconds East, a distance of 10.00 feet to a point; thence South 00 degrees 49 minutes 52 seconds East, a distance of 140.00 feet to a point; thence North 89 degrees 10 minutes 08 seconds East, a distance of 10.00 feet to a point; thence South 00 degrees 49 minutes 52 seconds East, a distance of 40.00 feet to a point; thence South 89 degrees 10 minutes 08 seconds West, a distance of 10.00 feet to a point; thence South 00 degrees 49 minutes 52 seconds East, a distance of 120.00 feet to a point; thence North 89 degrees 10 minutes 08 seconds East, a distance of 5.00 feet to a point; thence South 00 degrees 49 minutes 52 seconds East, a distance of 25.00 feet to a point; thence North 89 degrees 10 minutes 08 seconds East, a distance of 10.00 feet to a point; thence South 00 degrees 49 minutes 52 seconds East, a distance of 40.00 feet to a point; thence South 89 degrees 10 minutes 08 seconds West, a distance of 10.00 feet to a point; thence South 00 degrees 49 minutes 52 seconds East, a distance of 85.00 feet to a point; thence South 89 degrees 10 minutes 08 seconds West, a distance of 5.00 feet to a point; thence South 00 degrees 49 minutes 52 seconds East, a distance of 700.00 feet to a point; thence South 89 degrees 10 minutes 08 seconds West, a distance of 10.00 feet to a point; thence South 00 degrees 49 minutes 52 seconds East, a distance of 228.94 feet to a point; thence Southeasterly, along a curve to the left having a radius of 19,097.61 feet, a delta of 01 degrees 29 minutes 50 seconds, an arc length of 499.06 feet, and a chord which bears South 01 degrees 34 minutes 48 seconds East, a chord distance of 499.05 feet to a point; thence South 02 degrees 19 minutes 43 seconds East, a distance of 60.17 feet to a point; thence South 18 degrees 45 minutes 15 seconds East, a distance of 58.28 feet to a point on the Northerly right-of-way line of Hamacher Street (45.00 feet left of station 15+80.12) as shown on the PLAT OF RIGHT-OF-WAY for Hamacher Street, City of Waterloo, in Envelope 195-B in the Recorder's office of Monroe County, Illinois; thence Southwesterly along said Northerly right-of-way line of Hamacher Street along a curve to the right having a radius of 3072.40 feet, a delta of 02 degrees 00 minutes 54 seconds, an arc length of 108.05 feet, and a chord which bears South 77 degrees 54 minutes 14 seconds West, a chord distance of 108.05 feet to a point (45.00 feet left of station 14+70.48); thence leaving said Northerly right-of-way line of Hamacher Street, North 02 degrees 19 minutes 43 seconds West, a distance of 134.41 feet to a point; thence Northwesterly, along a curve to the right having a radius of 19,187.61 feet, a delta of 01 degrees 29 minutes 50 seconds, an arc length of 501.41 feet, and a chord which bears North 01 degrees 34 minutes 48 seconds West, a chord distance of 501.40 feet to a point; thence North 00 degrees 49 minutes 52 seconds West, a distance of 978.94 feet to a point; thence South 89 degrees 10 minutes 08 seconds West, a distance of 10.00 feet to a point; thence North 00 degrees 49 minutes 52 seconds West, a distance of 40.00 feet to a point; thence North 89 degrees 10 minutes 08 seconds East, a distance of 10.00 feet to a point; thence North 00 degrees 49 minutes 52 seconds West, a distance of 190.00 feet to a point; thence South 89 degrees 10 minutes 08 seconds West, a distance of 10.00 feet to a point; thence North 00 degrees 49 minutes 52 seconds West, a distance of 40.00 feet to a point; thence North 89 degrees 10 minutes 08 seconds East, a distance of 10.00 feet to a point; thence North 00 degrees 49 minutes 52 seconds West, a distance of 30.00 feet to a point; thence North 89 degrees 10 minutes 08 seconds East, a distance of 10.00 feet to a point; thence North 00 degrees 49 minutes 52 seconds West, a distance of 204.14 feet to a point; thence North 00 degrees 10 minutes 08 seconds East, a distance of 73.37 feet to the POINT OF

BEGINNING, containing 208,032 square feet more or less, or 4.776 acres, more or less.

P.A. 94–1055, Art. 25, § 25–7–103.101, eff. Jan. 1, 2007.

30/25–7–103.102. Quick-take; Lake County

§ 25–7–103.102. Quick-take; Lake County. Quick-take proceedings under Article 20 may be used for a period of 2 years after the effective date of this amendatory Act of the 93rd General Assembly by Lake County for the acquisition of property necessary for the purpose of improving County Highway 31 (Rollins Road) from Illinois Route 83 to U.S. Route 45.

P.A. 94–1055, Art. 25, § 25–7–103.102, eff. Jan. 1, 2007.

30/25–7–103.103. Quick-take; Lake County

§ 25–7–103.103. Quick-take; Lake County. Quick-take proceedings under Article 20 may be used for a period of 2 years after the effective date of this amendatory Act of the 93rd General Assembly by Lake County for the acquisition of property necessary for the purpose of improving County Highway 45 (Washington Street) from Illinois Route 83 to U.S. Route 45.

P.A. 94–1055, Art. 25, § 25–7–103.103, eff. Jan. 1, 2007.

30/25–7–103.104. Quick-take; County of La Salle

§ 25–7–103.104. Quick-take; County of La Salle. Quick-take proceedings under Article 20 may be used for a period of 12 months after the effective date of this amendatory Act of the 93rd General Assembly by the County of La Salle for highway purposes for the acquisition of property described as follows:

County Highway 3 (F.A.S. Route 259) over the Fox River north of the Village of Sheridan, Illinois, BEGINNING at Station -(3+00) on County Highway 3 south of the intersection of Bushnell Street, according to the "Right-of-Way Plans for proposed Federal Aid Highway, F.A.S. Route 259 (C.H. 3), Section 98-00545-00-BR, La Salle County," and extending 3,696.07 feet northerly along the survey centerline for said route to Station 33+96.07 at the intersection of County Highway 3 and North 42nd Road; AND BEGINNING at Station 497+00 on the survey centerline of North 42nd Road and extending 500.00 feet easterly along said centerline to Station 502+00; the net length for land acquisition and authorization being 4,196.07 feet (0.795 miles) all located in Section 5, Township 35 North, Range 5 East of the Third Principal Meridian, La Salle County, Illinois.

P.A. 94–1055, Art. 25, § 25–7–103.104, eff. Jan. 1, 2007.

30/25–7–103.105. Quick-take; Village of Buffalo Grove

§ 25–7–103.105. Quick-take; Village of Buffalo Grove. Quick-take proceedings under Article 20 may be used for a period of 2 years after the effective date of this amendatory Act of the 93rd General Assembly by the Village of Buffalo Grove for the acquisition of the following described property necessary for the purpose of improving the intersection of Port Clinton Road and Prairie Road:

OUTLOT "A" OF EDWARD SCHWARTZ'S INDIAN CREEK OF BUFFALO GROVE, BEING A SUBDIVISION OF PART OF THE NORTHWEST ¼ OF SECTION 16, TOWNSHIP 43 NORTH, RANGE 11, EAST OF THE THIRD PRINCIPAL MERIDIAN, ACCORDING TO THE PLAT THEREOF RECORDED JANUARY 7, 1994, AS DOCUMENT 3467875, IN LAKE COUNTY, ILLINOIS.

And,

THAT PART OF LOT 30, OF SCHOOL TRUSTEES SUBDIVISION, ALSO KNOWN AS THE NORTHWEST ¼ OF THE SOUTHEAST ¼ OF SECTION 16, TOWNSHIP 43 NORTH, RANGE 11 EAST OF THE THIRD PRINCIPAL MERIDIAN BOUNDED AND DESCRIBED AS FOLLOWS; (COMMENCING AT THE NORTHWEST CORNER OF THE SOUTHEAST ¼ OF SAID SECTION 16 AS THE PLACE OF BEGINNING OF THIS CONVEYANCE; THENCE NORTH 89 DEGREES-44'-35" EAST, ALONG THE NORTH LINE OF THE SOUTHEAST ¼ AFORESAID, A DISTANCE OF 397.96 FEET; THENCE SOUTH 0 DEGREES-00'-00" EAST, A DISTANCE OF 48.00 FEET; THENCE SOUTH 89 DEGREES-44'-35" WEST, ALONG A LINE DRAWN PARALLEL TO AND 48.0 FEET SOUTHERLY OF THE NORTH LINE OF THE SOUTHEAST ¼ AFORESAID, A DISTANCE OF 325.28 FEET; THENCE SOUTH 44 DEGREES-52'-15" WEST, A DISTANCE OF 39.23 FEET, TO A POINT WHICH IS 45.0 FEET EASTERLY OF THE WEST LINE OF THE SOUTHEAST ¼ AFORESAID; THENCE SOUTH 0 DEGREES-00'-00" EAST, ALONG A LINE DRAWN PARALLEL TO AND 45.0 FEET EASTERLY OF THE WEST LINE OF THE SOUTHEAST ¼ AFORESAID, A DISTANCE OF 269.10 FEET; THENCE SOUTH 89 DEGREES-44'-35" WEST, A DISTANCE OF 45.0 FEET, TO THE WEST LINE OF THE SOUTHEAST ¼ AFORESAID; THENCE NORTH 0 DEGREES-00'-00" EAST, ALONG THE WEST LINE OF THE SOUTHEAST ¼ AFORESAID, A DISTANCE OF 344.78 FEET, TO THE NORTHWEST CORNER OF THE SAID SOUTHEAST ¼ AFORESAID, AND THE PLACE OF BEGINNING OF THIS CONVEYANCE, ALL IN LAKE COUNTY, ILLINOIS.).

P.A. 94–1055, Art. 25, § 25–7–103.105, eff. Jan. 1, 2007.

30/25–7–103.107. Quick-take; Village of Clarendon Hills

§ 25–7–103.107. Quick-take; Village of Clarendon Hills. Quick-take proceedings under Article 20 may be used for a period of one year after the effective date of this amendatory Act of the 93rd General Assembly by the Village of Clarendon Hills for the acquisition of the following described property for a law enforcement facility and related improvements:

ALL OF LOT 8 AND LOT 9 (EXCEPT THE WESTERLY 120 FEET THEREOF) IN BLOCK 11 IN CLARENDON HILLS, BEING A RESUBDIVISION IN THE EAST ½ OF SECTION 10 AND IN THE WEST ½ OF SECTION 11, TOWNSHIP 38 NORTH, RANGE 11, EAST OF THE THIRD PRINCIPAL MERIDIAN, ACCORDING TO THE PLAT OF SAID RESUBDIVISION RECORDED NOVEMBER 4, 1873 AS DOCUMENT 17060, IN DUPAGE COUNTY, ILLINOIS.

P.I.N.'S: 09-10-400-002 AND 006.

Common Address: 448 Park Avenue, Clarendon Hills, Illinois 60514.

P.A. 94–1055, Art. 25, § 25–7–103.107, eff. Jan. 1, 2007.

30/25–7–103.108. Quick-take;   Governors' Parkway Project

§ 25–7–103.108. Quick-take; Governors' Parkway Project. Quick-take proceedings under Article 20 may be used for a period of 24 months after the effective date of this amendatory Act of the 93rd General Assembly by Madison County for the acquisition of property necessary for the construction of Governors' Parkway between Illinois Route 159 and Illinois 143.

P.A. 94–1055, Art. 25, § 25–7–103.108, eff. Jan. 1, 2007.

30/25–7–103.109. Quick-take; Forest Park

§ 25–7–103.109. Quick-take; Forest Park. Quick-take proceedings under Article 20 may be used for a period of 24 months after the effective date of this amendatory Act of the 93rd General Assembly by the Village of Forest Park for acquisition of property for public building construction purposes:

THE WEST 85.00 FEET OF LOTS 34 THRU 48, INCLUSIVE, IN BLOCK 12; THE EAST HALF OF VACATED HANNAH AVENUE LYING WEST OF AND ADJOINING SAID LOTS 34 THRU 48, INCLUSIVE; THE SOUTH 28.00 FEET OF THE EAST HALF OF VACATED HANNAH AVENUE LYING WEST OF AND ADJOINING A LINE DRAWN FROM THE NORTHWEST CORNER OF LOT 48, IN BLOCK 12 TO THE SOUTHWEST CORNER OF LOT 25 IN BLOCK 5; ALSO THE SOUTH 28.00 FEET OF VACATED 14TH STREET LYING NORTH OF AND ADJOINING THE WEST 85.00 FEET OF SAID LOT 48 IN BLOCK 12 IN BRADISH & MIZNER'S ADDITION TO RIVERSIDE, BEING A SUBDIVISION OF THE EAST HALF OF THE NORTHEAST QUARTER OF SECTION 24, TOWNSHIP 39 NORTH, RANGE 12 EAST OF THE THIRD PRINCIPAL MERIDIAN, IN COOK COUNTY, ILLINOIS.

P.A. 94–1055, Art. 25, § 25–7–103.109, eff. Jan. 1, 2007.

30/25–7–103.110. Quick-take; Urbana–Champaign Sanitary District

§ 25–7–103.110. Quick-take; Urbana–Champaign Sanitary District. Quick-take proceedings under Article 20 may be used for a period of 24 months after the effective date of this amendatory Act of the 93rd General Assembly by the Urbana–Champaign Sanitary District for the acquisition of permanent and temporary easements for the purpose of implementing phase 2 of the Curtis Road–Windsor Road sanitary interceptor sewer project and constructing and operating the proposed sewers.

P.A. 94–1055, Art. 25, § 25–7–103.110, eff. Jan. 1, 2007.

30/25–7–103.111. Quick-take; Village of Palatine

§ 25–7–103.111. Quick-take; Village of Palatine. Quick-take proceedings under Article 20 may be used for a period of 60 months after the effective date of this amendatory Act of the 93rd General Assembly by the Village of Palatine for the acquisition of property for the purposes of the Downtown Tax Increment Redevelopment Project Area, bounded generally by Plum Grove Road on the East, Palatine Road on the South, Cedar Street on the West, and Colfax Street on the North, and the Rand Corridor Redevelopment Project Area, bounded generally by Dundee Road on the South, Lake-Cook Road on the North, and on the East and West by Rand Road, in the Village of Palatine more specifically described in the following ordinances adopted by the Village of Palatine:

Village ordinance 0–224–99, adopted December 13, 1999;

Village ordinance 0–225–99, adopted December 13, 1999;

Village ordinance 0–226–99, adopted December 13, 1999;

Village ordinance 0–13–00, adopted January 24, 2000, correcting certain scrivener's errors and attached as exhibit A to the foregoing legal descriptions;

Village ordinance 0–23–03, adopted January 27, 2003;

Village ordinance 0–24–03, adopted January 27, 2003; and

Village ordinance 0–25–03, adopted January 27, 2003.

P.A. 94–1055, Art. 25, § 25–7–103.111, eff. Jan. 1, 2007.

30/25–7–103.112. Quick-take; Bi-State Development Agency; MetroLink Light Rail System

§ 25–7–103.112. Quick-take; Bi-State Development Agency; MetroLink Light Rail System. Quick-take proceedings under Article 20 may be used for a period from September 1, 2003 through September 1, 2004 by the Bi-State Development Agency of the Missouri–Illinois Metropolitan District for station area development, transit oriented development and economic development initiatives in support of the MetroLink Light Rail System, beginning in East St. Louis, Illinois, and terminating at MidAmerica Airport, St. Clair County, Illinois.

P.A. 94–1055, Art. 25, § 25–7–103.112, eff. Jan. 1, 2007.

30/25–7–103.113. Quick-take; Village of Bridgeview

§ 25–7–103.113. Quick-take; Village of Bridgeview. Quick-take proceedings under Article 20 may be used for a period of 12 months after the effective date of this amendatory Act of the 93rd General Assembly by the Village of Bridgeview for the purpose of acquiring property for a municipal sports stadium and parking areas, team practice facilities, and other related uses as follows:

Parcel 1:

That part of the West half of the Southwest Quarter of Section 30, Township 38 North, Range 13 East of the Third Principal Meridian, described as follows:

Beginning on the East line of the West half of the Southwest quarter with the North line of M.S.A. Bridgeview Court Subdivision recorded on June 8, 1988, as Document Number 88246171, also being the South line of the North 1090 feet of the said Southwest quarter of Section 30; thence South 89 degrees 49 minutes 10 seconds West along said line 33.00 feet; thence North 16 degrees 00 minutes 23 seconds West 70.00 feet; thence South 88 degrees 47 minutes 22 seconds West 444.48 feet; thence South 47 degrees 23 minutes 28 seconds West 65.00 feet to the North line of said M.S.A. Bridgeview Court Subdivision, also being the South line of the North 1090 feet of the Southwest quarter of Section 30; thence South 89 degrees 49 minutes 10 seconds East along said lines to the point of beginning,

ALSO

That part of the West half of the Southwest Quarter of Section 30, Township 38 North, Range 13 East of the Third Principal Meridian, described as follows:

Beginning at the intersection of the South line of the North 1090 feet of said Southwest quarter also being the North line of M.S.A. Bridgeview Court and the West line of Harlem Avenue as dedicated, being 50 feet East of the West of said Southwest quarter; thence North 0 degrees 16 minutes 38 seconds West 349.88 feet along the said East line of Harlem Avenue to the Southwest corner of the land conveyed by Document 0333942009; thence North 89 degrees 46 minutes 35 seconds East to the Northwest corner of the land conveyed by document 99855126; thence South along the West line of the land conveyed by said Document 99855126, 350 feet to the South line of the North 1090 feet also being the North line of M.S.A. Bridgeview Court; thence West along said line to the point of beginning, in Cook County, Illinois.

Parcel 2:

Lots 1, 2, 4, 6, 7 and 8, in M.S.A. Bridgeview Court, being a Subdivision of part of the West half of the southwest quarter of Section 30, Township 38 North, Range 13 East of the Third Principal Meridian, recorded June 7, 1988 as Document 88246171, except that part of Lot 1 conveyed by Deed recorded as document No. 99016579, except that part of Lot 6 conveyed by Deed recorded as Document No. 93589062, except that part of Lot 7 conveyed in Deed recorded as Document No. 91540434, and except that part of Lot 8 recorded as Document No. 0010326872, in Cook County, Illinois.

Parcel 3:

Easement appurtenant to Parcel 2 for ingress, egress, access, parking, deposit and retention of storm water over the common areas as described and set forth in Construction, Operation and Reciprocal Easement Agreement made by and between Bridgeview Associates, the May Department Stores Company, and Midfield, Inc., dated July 25, 1988 and recorded July 29, 1988 as Document No. 88340706.

P.A. 94-1055, Art. 25, § 25-7-103.113, eff. Jan. 1, 2007.

30/25-7-103.114. Quick-take; City of Ottawa

§ 25-7-103.114.   Quick-take;   City of Ottawa. Quick-take proceedings under Article 20 may be used for a period of 12 months after the effective date of this amendatory Act of the 93rd General Assembly by the City of Ottawa for the acquisition of property for the purpose of immediate eradication of a blighted area resulting from the destruction of most improvements because of fire as follows:

All lots in Block 18 in the Original Town of Ottawa, now the City of Ottawa, in LaSalle County, Illinois.
P.A. 94-1055, Art. 25, § 25-7-103.114, eff. Jan. 1, 2007.

30/25-7-103.115. Quick-take; City of Ottawa

§ 25-7-103.115.   Quick-take;   City of Ottawa. Quick-take proceedings under Article 20 may be used for a period of 12 months after the effective date of this amendatory Act of the 93rd General Assembly by the City of Ottawa for the acquisition of property for the purpose of installation of public utilities as follows:

That part of the Southeast Quarter of Section 8, Township 33 North, Range 4 East of the Third Principal Meridian described as follows:

Commencing at the Northwest corner of the Southeast Quarter of said Section 8; thence South 89 degrees 41 minutes 32 seconds East 48.60 feet along the North line of the said Southeast Quarter to the intersection of said North line and the North Right of Way line of the CSX Railroad which point is also the Point of Beginning; thence continuing South 89 degrees 41 minutes 32 seconds East 1303.50 feet along said North line to the Northeast corner of the West Half of the Southeast Quarter of said Section 8; thence Southeasterly on a 573.75 foot radius

curve to the right 564.56 feet, whose chord bears South 33 degrees 50 minutes 57 seconds East 542.06 feet to a point on the North Right of Way line of the CSX railroad; thence North 74 degrees 06 minutes 16 seconds West 1669.24 feet to the Point of Beginning containing 6.140 acres more or less and all situated in LaSalle County, Illinois.

P.A. 94-1055, Art. 25, § 25-7-103.115, eff. Jan. 1, 2007.

30/25-7-103.116. Quick-take; City of Ottawa

§ 25-7-103.116.   Quick-take;   City of Ottawa. Quick-take proceedings under Article 20 may be used for a period of 12 months after the effective date of this amendatory Act of the 93rd General Assembly by the City of Ottawa for the acquisition of property for the purpose of installing a rail spur as follows:

That Portion of the East Half of the Northeast Quarter of Section 8, Township 33 North, Range 4 East of the Third Principal Meridian lying South of the public highway between Ottawa and Marseilles which crosses the said East Half of the Northeast Quarter aforesaid on the northeast portion thereof; ALSO that portion of the Southeast Quarter of Section 8, Township 33 North, Range 4 East of the Third Principal Meridian lying North of the right of way of the Chicago, Rock Island & Pacific Railroad Company; EXCEPTING therefrom that part conveyed to the State of Illinois for highway purposes by deed recorded as Document #558356, all situated in LaSalle County, Illinois.

P.A. 94-1055, Art. 25, § 25-7-103.116, eff. Jan. 1, 2007.

30/25-7-103.117. Quick-take; City of Oakbrook Terrace

§ 25-7-103.117.   Quick-take;   City of Oakbrook Terrace.   Quick-take proceedings under Article 20 may be used for a period of 12 months after the effective date of this amendatory Act of the 93rd General Assembly by the City of Oakbrook Terrace for the acquisition of property for the purpose of water main construction as follows:

Beginning at a point on the east line of the southeast ¼ of Section 21-39-11, located a distance of 520 feet north of the point of intersection of the east line of the southeast ¼ of Section 21 with the present northerly right of way line of Butterfield Road; Thence westerly along a line which forms an angle of 90 degrees 00 minutes 00 seconds to the east line of the southeast ¼ of Section 21, a distance of 340 feet, to an angle point; Thence southwesterly from said angle point along a line which forms an angle of 137 degrees 49 minutes 39 seconds as measured clockwise from west to south, a distance of 297 feet, to a point located 30 feet southwest and perpendicular to the south edge of the existing private road; Thence northwesterly along a curved line located 30 feet south of and parallel to the south edge of the existing private road, through an internal angle of 101 degrees 2 minutes 40 seconds, measured counterclockwise from the northeast to the northwest, a distance of 441.7 feet, to a point located 30 feet southeast and perpendicular to the south edge of the existing private road; Thence, northwesterly along a straight line perpendicular to the existing private road, a distance of 30 feet to a point on the south edge of the existing private road; Thence northeasterly and southeasterly along the curved south edge of the existing private road, a distance of 461.5 feet, to a point on the south edge of the existing private road; Thence northeasterly along a straight line and perpendicular to the south edge of the existing private road, a distance of 277 feet, to an angle point (iron pipe); Thence easterly along a straight line, from said angle point, which forms an angle of 137 degrees 49 minutes 39 seconds as measured counterclockwise from south to east, a distance of 350 feet to a point located on the east line of the southeast ¼ of Section 21–39–11 a distance of 30 feet to the point of beginning.

P.A. 94–1055, Art. 25, § 25–7–103.117, eff. Jan. 1, 2007.

30/25–7–103.118. Quick-take; Ogle County

§ 25–7–103.118. Quick-take; Ogle County. Quick-take proceedings under Article 20 may be used for a period of 12 months after the effective date of this amendatory Act of the 93rd General Assembly by Ogle County for the acquisition of property for the purpose of the construction of a railroad overpass as follows:

A tract of land in the Northeast Quarter in Section 32, Township 40 North, Range 1 East of the Third Principal Meridian, the Township of Flagg, the County of Ogle and the State of Illinois, bounded and described as follows:

Commencing at the Southeast Corner of the Northeast Quarter of said Section 32; thence North 0 degrees 37 minutes 41 seconds West along the East line of said Northeast Quarter, a distance of 420.21 feet to the intersection of said East Line and the Northwesterly Right-of-Way Line of the Union Pacific Railroad, said point being the Point of Beginning of the hereinafter described tract of land; thence continuing North 0 degrees 37 minutes 41 seconds West along said East Line, a distance of 1466.85 feet; thence South 89 degrees 22 minutes 02 seconds West, a distance of 32.74 feet to the existing Westerly Right-of-Way Line of a public road designated Thorpe Road; thence South 2 degrees 41 minutes 56 seconds West, a distance of 67.11 feet; thence South 42 degrees 09 minutes 09 seconds West, a distance of 34.04 feet to the beginning of a curve; thence Southwesterly along a line being curved to the left, having a radius of 183.00 feet a central angle of 90 degrees 00 minutes 00 seconds, a chord bearing of South 44 degrees 22 minutes 02 seconds West and an arc distance of 287.46 feet to the termination of said curve; thence South 0 degrees 37 minutes 58 seconds East paral-

lel with the Centerline of said Thorpe Road, a distance of 949.35 feet to the beginning of a curve; thence Southwesterly a line being curved to the right, having a radius of 487.87 feet a central angle of 62 degrees 20 minutes 35 seconds, a chord bearing of South 30 degrees 32 minutes 20 seconds West and an arc distance of 330.95 feet to the Northwesterly Right-of-Way Line of a public road designated Titus Road; thence South 28 degrees 17 minutes 23 seconds East, a distance of 66.00 to the Northwesterly Right-of-Way Line of the Union Pacific Railroad; thence Northeasterly along a line being curved to the left, Having a radius of 602.66 feet, a central angle of 62 degrees 20 minutes 35 seconds, a chord bearing of North 30 degrees 32 minutes 20 seconds East and an arc distance of 602.66 to the termination of said curve; thence North 0 degrees 37 minutes 58 seconds, West parallel with the Centerline of said Thorpe Road, a distance of 949.35 feet to the beginning of a curve; thence Northeasterly along a line being curved to the right, having a radius of 117.00 feet, a central angle of 90 degrees; 00 minutes 00 seconds, a chord bearing of North 44 degrees 22 minutes 02 seconds East and an arc distance of 183.79 Feet to the termination of said curve; thence South 33 degrees 48 minutes 48 seconds East, a distance of 29.87 feet to the Westerly Right-of-Way Line of said Thorpe Road; thence South 2 degrees 41 minutes 56 seconds West, a distance of 1141.69 feet; thence South 0 degrees 37 minutes 58 seconds East parallel with the Centerline of said Thorpe Road, a distance of 201.54 feet to the Northwesterly Right-of-Way Line of the Union Pacific Railroad; thence North 61 degrees 42 minutes 17 seconds East along said Northwesterly Right-of-Way Line, a distance of 123.77 feet to the Point of Beginning.

Containing 5.292 acres, more or less.

P.A. 94–1055, Art. 25, § 25–7–103.118, eff. Jan. 1, 2007.

30/25–7–103.119. Quick-take;   Village   of Plainfield

§ 25–7–103.119. Quick-take; Village of Plainfield. Quick-take proceedings under Article 20 may be used for the period of 12 months after the effective date of this amendatory Act of the 93rd General Assembly by the Village of Plainfield for the acquisition of the following described property for the purposes of water, sewer, and roadway extensions:

That part of Outlot "A" in Indian Oaks Estates Unit Six, a subdivision of part of the Southeast Quarter of Section 17 in Township 36 North and Range 9 East of the Third Principal Meridian, in Will County, Illinois, according to the plat thereof recorded April 6, 1989 as Document Number R89-15582, described as follows:

Beginning at the southeasterly corner of Outlot A, thence South 45 degrees 31 minutes 50 seconds West along the south line of the aforesaid Outlot

147.49 feet to the southwesterly corner of the aforesaid Outlot; thence North 0 degrees 0 minutes 26 seconds East along the west line of the aforesaid Outlot 221.82 feet; thence on a northwesterly bearing 134.05 feet to a point on the east line of the aforesaid Outlot that is 201.53 feet north of the southeasterly corner; thence southerly along the east line of the aforesaid Outlot 201.53 feet to the point of beginning; containing 0.511 acres, more or less, all in Will County, Illinois.

Pin No: 03-17-408-023-0000

P.A. 94–1055, Art. 25, § 25–7–103.119, eff. Jan. 1, 2007.

30/25–7–103.120. Quick-take; Village of Plainfield

§ 25–7–103.120. Quick-take; Village of Plainfield. Quick-take proceedings under Article 20 may be used for the period of 12 months after the effective date of this amendatory Act of the 93rd General Assembly by the Village of Plainfield for the acquisition of the following described property for the purposes of roadway extensions and traffic signal installation:

Beginning at a P.K. Nail marking the southwest corner of said Section 33; thence on an assumed bearing of North 00 degrees 30 minutes 36 seconds West 523.00 feet along the west line of the Southwest Quarter of said Section 33; thence North 89 degrees 29 minutes 19 seconds East 40.00 feet; thence South 00 degrees 30 minutes 36 seconds East 379.66 feet along a line 40.00 feet easterly of and parallel to the west line of the Southwest Quarter of said Section 33; thence South 26 degrees 12 minutes 37 seconds East 115.56 feet to a point on the northerly existing right of way line of 135th Street (Pilcher Road); thence South 00 degrees 00 minutes 24 seconds East 40.00 feet to a point on the south line of the Southwest Quarter of said Section 33; thence South 89 degrees 59 minutes 36 seconds West 89.76 feet along the south line of the Southwest Quarter of said Section 33 to the Point of Beginning.

Pin No: 01-33-300-008

P.A. 94–1055, Art. 25, § 25–7–103.120, eff. Jan. 1, 2007.

30/25–7–103.121. Quick-take; Rochester Road District

§ 25–7–103.121. Quick-take; Rochester Road District. Quick-take proceedings under Article 20 may be used for a period of 12 months from the effective date of this amendatory Act of the 93rd General Assembly by Rochester Road District, for the purpose of road construction and maintenance, for the acquisition of property legally described as:

Parcel No. 3

A part of the East Half of the Southwest Quarter of Section 6, Township 15 North, Range 4 West of the Third Principal Meridian, Sangamon County, Illinois, described as follows:

Commencing at the Northeast corner of the Southwest Quarter of said Section 6; thence South 0 degrees 44 minutes 49 seconds East along the east line of the Southwest Quarter of said Section 6, a distance of 326.11 feet to the point of beginning; thence continuing South 0 degrees 44 minutes 49 seconds East, 359.27 feet; thence North 86 degrees 59 minutes 03 seconds West, 35.08 feet; thence North 0 degrees 44 minutes 49 seconds West, 359.27 feet; thence South 86 degrees 59 minutes 03 seconds East, 35.08 feet to the point of beginning.

All of the above excludes that portion now in use as a public road, said tract to be conveyed containing 0.124 acres, more or less. Said tract being shown by the plat hereto attached and considered a part hereof.

Parcel No. 6

A part of the East Half of the Southwest Quarter of Section 6, Township 15 North, Range 4 West of the Third Principal Meridian, Sangamon County, Illinois, described as follows:

Commencing at the Northeast corner of the Southwest Quarter of said Section 6; thence South 0 degrees 44 minutes 49 seconds East along the east line of the Southwest Quarter of said Section 6, a distance of 276.00 feet to the point of beginning; thence continuing South 0 degrees 44 minutes 49 seconds East, 50.11 feet; thence North 86 degrees 59 minutes 03 seconds West, 35.08 feet; thence North 0 degrees 44 minutes 49 seconds West, 50.11 feet; thence South 86 degrees 59 minutes 03 seconds East, 35.08 feet to the point of beginning.

All of the above excludes that portion now in use as a public road, said tract to be conveyed containing 0.017 acres, more or less. Said tract being shown by the plat hereto attached and considered a part hereof.

Parcel No. 9

A part of the East Half of the Southwest Quarter of Section 6, Township 15 North, Range 4 West of the Third Principal Meridian, Sangamon County, Illinois, described as follows:

Beginning at the Northeast corner of the Southwest Quarter of said Section 6; thence South 0 degrees 44 minutes 49 seconds East along the east line of the Southwest Quarter of said Section 6, a distance of 276.00 feet; thence North 86 degrees 59 minutes 03 seconds West, 35.08 feet; thence North 0 degrees 44 minutes 49 seconds West, 224.01 feet; thence South 89 degrees 15 minutes 11 seconds West, 5.00 feet; thence North 0 degrees 44 minutes 49 seconds West, 49.07 feet to the north line of the Southwest Quarter of said Section 6; thence North 88 degrees 22 minutes 11 seconds East, 40.00 feet to the point of beginning.

All of the above excludes that portion now in use as a public road, said tract to be conveyed containing 0.100 acres, more or less. Said tract being shown by the plat hereto attached and considered a part hereof.

P.A. 94-1055, Art. 25, § 25-7-103.121, eff. Jan. 1, 2007.

30/25-7-103.122. Quick-take; Village of Skokie

§ 25-7-103.122. Quick-take; Village of Skokie. Quick-take proceedings under Article 20 may be used for a period of 12 months after the effective date of this amendatory Act of the 93rd General Assembly by the Village of Skokie for the acquisition of property for the purpose of open space and the development of a park as follows:

8148 Lincoln Avenue

Index Numbers (PINS): 10-21-409-002-0000 and 10-21-409-003-0000

Lot 2 and the North ½ of Lot 3 in the Subdivision of Lot 28 in the Subdivision of the South 105 acres of the Southeast ¼ of Section 21, Township 41 North, Range 13, East of the Third Principal Meridian, in Cook County, Illinois.

8158 Lincoln Avenue

Index Number (PIN) 10-21-409-001-0000

Lot 1 in the Subdivision of Lot 28 in the Subdivision of the South 105 acres of the Southeast ¼ of Section 21, Township 41 North, Range 13, East of the Third Principal Meridian, in Cook County, Illinois.

P.A. 94-1055, Art. 25, § 25-7-103.122, eff. Jan. 1, 2007.

30/25-7-103.123. Quick-take; Dewitt County

§ 25-7-103.123. Quick-take; Dewitt County. Quick-take proceedings under Article 20 may be used for a period of 12 months after the effective date of this amendatory Act of the 94th General Assembly for road improvement purposes for the acquisition of the following described real property:

PARCEL 1

A part of the Southeast Quarter of Section 35, Township 19 North, Range 3 East of the Third Principal Meridian, described as follows:

Beginning at the Southeast corner of said Section 35; thence South 88 degrees 49 minutes 30 seconds West, a distance of 85.50 feet along the south line of the Southeast Quarter of said Section 35; thence North 1 degree 09 minutes 40 seconds West, 16.57 feet to the north right of way line of a township road; thence North 55 degrees 46 minutes 40 seconds East, 56.79 feet; thence northerly 357.19 feet along a curve to the left having a radius of 8564.37 feet, the chord of said curve bears North 2 degrees 12 minutes 30 seconds East, 357.16 feet; thence North 1 degree 00 minutes 50 seconds East, 496.06 feet; thence North 1 degree 06 minutes 30 seconds East, 599.97 feet; thence North 0 degrees 55 minutes 00 seconds East, 299.96 feet; thence North 0 degrees 55 minutes 50 seconds East, 598.18 feet; thence North 1 degree 16 minutes 00 seconds East,

254.87 feet to the north line of the Southeast Quarter of said Section 35; thence North 88 degrees 58 minutes 30 seconds East along said line, 30.02 feet to the east line of the Southeast Quarter of said Section 35; thence South 0 degrees 58 minutes 50 seconds West along said line, a distance of 2653.24 feet to the point of beginning, including that portion containing 1.717 acres, more or less, which exists as public road right-of-way, said perpetual right-of-way easement containing 1.967 acres, more or less.

ALSO

A part of the Southwest Quarter of Section 36, Township 19 North, Range 3 East of the Third Principal Meridian, described as follows:

A tract of land 5 feet in width lying between Station 23 + 15.00 and Station 23 + 28.73 a distance of 13.73 feet along the east side of the proposed east right of way line of a highway designated as Construction Section 85-00043-00-RS, as surveyed and staked out under the direction of the Dewitt County Highway Department.

PARCEL 2

A part of the Southwest Quarter of Section 36, Township 19 North, Range 3 East of the Third Principal Meridian, described as follows:

Beginning at the Southwest corner of said Section 36; thence North 0 degrees 58 minutes 50 seconds East along the west line of the Southwest Quarter of said Section 36, a distance of 1326.62 feet; thence North 88 degrees 58 minutes 00 seconds East, 29.24 feet; thence South 1 degree 06 minutes 30 seconds West, 428.52 feet; thence South 1 degree 00 minutes 50 seconds West, 496.01 feet; thence southerly 358.88 feet along a curve to the right having a radius of 8624.37 feet, the chord of said curve bears South 2 degrees 12 minutes 20 seconds West, 358.85 feet; thence South 65 degrees 33 minutes 40 seconds East, 47.95 feet to the north right of way line of a township road; thence South 1 degree 00 minutes 10 seconds East, 23.03 feet to the south line of the Southwest Quarter of said Section 36; thence South 89 degrees 00 minutes 30 seconds West along said south line, a distance of 65.15 feet to the point of beginning, including that portion containing 0.741 acres, more or less, which exists as public road right-of-way, said perpetual right-of-way easement containing 0.867 acres, more or less.

PARCEL 3A

A part of the Northwest Quarter of the Southwest Quarter of Section 36, Township 19 North, Range 3 East of the Third Principal Meridian, described as follows:

Beginning at the Northwest Corner of the Southwest Quarter of said Section 36; thence North 88 degrees 55 minutes 30 seconds East, a distance of 30.02 feet; thence South 1 degree 16 minutes 00 seconds West, 257.12 feet; thence South 0 degrees 55 minutes 50 seconds West, 598.00 feet; thence

South 0 degrees 55 minutes 00 seconds West, 300.05 feet; thence South 1 degree 06 minutes 30 seconds West, 171.50 feet to the south line of the Northwest Quarter of the Southwest Quarter of said Section 36; thence South 88 degrees 58 minutes 00 seconds West along said line, 29.24 feet to the west line of the Southwest Quarter of said Section 36; thence North 0 degrees 58 minutes 50 seconds East, a distance of 1326.62 feet to the point of beginning, including that portion containing 0.761 acres, more or less, which exists as public road right-of-way, said perpetual right-of-way easement containing 0.890 acres, more or less.

ALSO

A part of the Southwest Quarter of Section 36, Township 19 North, Range 3 East of the Third Principal Meridian, described as follows:

A tract of land 5 feet in width lying between Station 23 + 28.54 and Station 23 + 50.00 a distance of 21.46 feet along the east side of the proposed east right of way line of a highway designated as Construction Section 85-00043-00-RS, as surveyed and staked out under the direction of the Dewitt County Highway Department.

PARCEL 3B

A part of the Southwest Quarter of the Northwest Quarter of Section 36, Township 19 North, Range 3 East of the Third Principal Meridian, described as follows:

Beginning at the Southwest Corner of the Northwest Quarter of said Section 36; thence North 0 degrees 48 minutes 30 seconds East along the west line of the Northwest Quarter of said Section 36, a distance of 1327.69 feet; thence North 88 degrees 54 minutes 10 seconds East, 31.20 feet; thence South 0 degrees 45 minutes 40 seconds West, 381.76 feet; thence South 0 degrees 47 minutes 50 seconds West, 601.02 feet; thence South 1 degree 04 minutes 50 seconds West, 344.97 feet to the south line of the Northwest Quarter of said Section 36; thence South 88 degrees 55 minutes 30 seconds West along said line, a distance of 30.02 feet to the point of beginning, including that portion containing 0.762 acres, more or less, which exists as public road right-of-way, said perpetual right-of-way easement containing 0.955 acres, more or less.

PARCEL 4

A part of the Northeast Quarter of Section 35, Township 19 North, Range 3 East of the Third Principal Meridian, described as follows:

Beginning at the Southeast corner of the Northeast Quarter of said Section 35; thence North 0 degrees 48 minutes 30 seconds East along the east line of said Section 35, a distance of 1327.69 feet to the north line of the Southeast Quarter of the Northeast Quarter of said Section 35; thence South 89 degrees 10 minutes 50 seconds West along the said north line, 28.83 feet; thence South 0 degrees 45

minutes 40 seconds West, 379.93 feet; thence South 0 degrees 47 minutes 50 seconds West, 600.85 feet; thence South 1 degree 04 minutes 50 seconds West, 347.05 feet to the south line of the Northeast Quarter of said Section 35; thence North 88 degrees 58 minutes 30 seconds East along said south line, a distance of 30.02 feet to the point of beginning, including that portion containing 0.852 acres, more or less, which exists as public road right-of-way, said perpetual right-of-way easement containing 0.874 acres, more or less.

PARCEL 6

A part of the Northwest Quarter of Section 36, Township 19 North, Range 3 East of the Third Principal Meridian, described as follows:

Beginning at the Northwest corner of said Section 36; thence South 0 degrees 48 minutes 30 seconds West along the west line of said Section 36, a distance of 1327.69 feet to the south line of the Northwest Quarter of the Northwest Quarter of said Section 36; thence North 88 degrees 54 minutes 10 seconds East along the said south line, 31.20 feet; thence North 0 degrees 45 minutes 40 seconds East, 217.18 feet; thence North 0 degrees 56 minutes 50 seconds East, 300.01 feet; thence North 0 degrees 41 minutes 10 seconds East, 761.94 feet; thence North 42 degrees 26 minutes 10 seconds East, 30.04 feet to the south right of way line of a township road; thence North 0 degrees 40 minutes 00 seconds East, 26.76 feet to the north line of said Section 36; thence South 88 degrees 53 minutes 00 seconds West along said north line, a distance of 50.02 feet to the point of beginning, including that portion containing 0.777 acres, more or less, which exists as public road right-of-way, said perpetual right-of-way easement containing 0.963 acres, more or less.

ALSO

A part of the Northwest Quarter of Section 36, Township 19 North, Range 3 East of the Third Principal Meridian, described as follows:

A tract of land 5 feet in width lying between Station 50 + 30.00 and Station 50 + 75.00 a distance of 45.00 feet along the east side of the proposed east right of way line of a highway designated as Construction Section 85-00043-00-RS, as surveyed and staked out under the direction of the Dewitt County Highway Department.

PARCEL 7

A part of the Southeast Quarter of Section 26, Township 19 North, Range 3 East of the Third Principal Meridian, described as follows:

Beginning at the Southeast corner of the Southeast Quarter of said Section 26; thence North 0 degrees 58 minutes 30 seconds East along the east line of said Section 26, a distance of 1331.43 feet to the north line of the Southeast Quarter of the Southeast Quarter of said Section 26; thence South 89 degrees

16 minutes 30 seconds West along said north line, 29.65 feet; thence South 0 degrees 58 minutes 20 seconds West, 339.94 feet; thence South 1 degree 13 minutes 40 seconds West, 600.09 feet; thence South 0 degrees 38 minutes 50 seconds West, 343.24 feet; thence South 42 degrees 37 minutes 30 seconds West, 29.90 feet to the north right of way line of a township road; thence South 0 degrees 40 minutes 00 seconds West, 26.33 feet to the south line of said Section 26; thence North 89 degrees 23 minutes 00 East along said south line, a distance of 50.02 feet to the point of beginning, including that portion containing 0.792 acres, more or less, which exists as public road right-of-way, said perpetual right-of-way easement containing 0.954 acres, more or less.

PARCEL 8

A part of the Southwest Quarter of Section 25, Township 19 North, Range 3 East of the Third Principal Meridian, described as follows:

Beginning at the Southwest corner of the Southwest Quarter of said Section 25; thence North 0 degrees 58 minutes 30 seconds East along the west line of said Section 25, a distance of 2662.85 feet to the north line of the Southwest Quarter of said Section 25; thence North 89 degrees 04 minutes 40 seconds East along said north line, 28.37 feet; thence South 0 degrees 49 minutes 50 seconds West, 773.22 feet; thence South 0 degrees 58 minutes 20 seconds West, 900.10 feet; thence South 1 degree 13 minutes 40 seconds West, 599.92 feet; thence South 0 degrees 38 minutes 50 seconds West, 343.01 feet; thence South 40 degrees 45 minutes 00 seconds East, 30.24 feet to the north right of way line of a township road; thence South 0 degrees 40 minutes 00 seconds West, 23.16 feet to the south line of said Section 25; thence South 88 degrees 53 minutes 00 seconds West along said south line, a distance of 50.02 feet to the point of beginning, including that portion containing 1.492 acres, more or less, which exists as public road right-of-way, said perpetual right-of-way easement containing 1.823 acres, more or less.

PARCEL 11

A part of the Northwest Quarter of Section 25, Township 19 North, Range 3 East of the Third Principal Meridian, described as follows:

Beginning at the Southwest corner of the Northwest Quarter of said Section 25; thence North 0 degrees 39 minutes 50 seconds East along the west line of said Section 25, a distance of 285.00 feet to the north property line; thence North 89 degrees 04 minutes 40 seconds East along said north line, a distance of 29.52 feet; thence South 0 degrees 53 minutes 40 seconds West, a distance of 285.03 feet to the south line of the Northwest Quarter of said Section 25; thence South 89 degrees 04 minutes 40 seconds West along said south line, a distance of 28.37 feet to the point of beginning, including that

portion containing 0.153 acres, more or less, which exists as public road right-of-way, said perpetual right-of-way easement containing 0.189 acres, more or less.

PARCEL 12

A part of the Northwest Quarter of Section 25, Township 19 North, Range 3 East of the Third Principal Meridian, described as follows:

Commencing at the Southwest Corner of said Section 25; thence North 0 degrees 39 minutes 50 seconds East along the west line of said Section 25, a distance of 285.00 feet to the south property line and the point of beginning; thence continuing North 0 degrees 39 minutes 50 seconds East along said west line, a distance of 1043.42 feet to the north line of the South Half of the Northwest Quarter of said Section 25; thence North 89 degrees 06 minutes 10 seconds East along said north line, a distance of 31.28 feet; thence South 0 degrees 49 minutes 00 seconds West, a distance of 101.59 feet; thence South 0 degrees 33 minutes 40 seconds West, a distance of 400.04 feet; thence South 0 degrees 53 minutes 50 seconds West, 541.83 feet to the south property line; thence South 89 degrees 04 minutes 40 seconds West along the said south line, a distance of 29.52 feet to the point of beginning, including that portion containing 0.571 acres, more or less, which exists as public road right-of-way, said perpetual right-of-way easement containing 0.741 acres, more or less.

PARCEL 14

A part of the Northeast Quarter of Section 26, Township 19 North, Range 3 East of the Third Principal Meridian, described as follows:

Beginning at the Northeast Corner of said Section 26; thence South 0 degrees 39 minutes 50 seconds West along the east line of the Northeast Quarter of said Section 26, a distance of 1130.32 feet to the south monumented parcel line; thence North 89 degrees 13 minutes 10 seconds West along said south monumented parcel line, 28.20 feet; thence North 0 degrees 49 minutes 00 seconds East, 201.20 feet; thence North 0 degrees 53 minutes 30 seconds East, 875.01 feet; thence North 29 degrees 29 minutes 30 seconds West, 39.54 feet to the south right of way line of a township road; thence North 0 degrees 52 minutes 30 seconds East, 18.75 feet to the north line of the Northeast Quarter of said Section 26; thence North 89 degrees 12 minutes 20 seconds East along said north line, 44.01 feet to the point of beginning, including that portion containing 0.588 acres, more or less, which exists as public road right-of-way, said perpetual right-of-way easement containing 0.696 acres, more or less.

ALSO

A part of the Northeast Quarter of Section 26, Township 19 North, Range 3 East of the Third Principal Meridian, described as follows:

A tract of land 5 feet in width lying between Station 105 + 00.00 and Station 105 + 40.00 a distance of 40.00 feet along the west side of the proposed west right of way line of a highway designated as Construction Section 85-00043-00-RS, as surveyed and staked out under the direction of the Dewitt County Highway Department.

PARCEL 22

A part of the Southeast Quarter of Section 14, Township 19 North, Range 3 East of the Third Principal Meridian, described as follows:

Beginning at the Southeast Corner of said Section 14; thence South 89 degrees 21 minutes 00 seconds West along the south line of the Southeast Quarter of said Section 14, a distance of 36.03 feet; thence North 1 degree 06 minutes 30 seconds East, 31.02 feet to the north right of way line of County Highway 15; thence North 11 degrees 32 minutes 30 seconds East, 54.77 feet; thence North 1 degree 01 minute 40 seconds East, 469.47 feet; thence North 0 degrees 51 minutes 40 seconds East, 750.02 feet; thence North 1 degree 05 minutes 10 seconds East, 25.08 feet to the north line of the south half of the Southeast Quarter of said Section 14; thence North 89 degrees 25 minutes 00 seconds East, 28.95 feet to the east line of the Southeast Quarter of said Section 14; thence South 1 degree 03 minutes 40 seconds West along said line, a distance of 1329.19 feet to the point of beginning, including that portion containing 0.725 acres, more or less, which exists as public road right-of-way, said perpetual right-of-way easement containing 0.838 acres, more or less.

PARCEL 24

A part of the Southeast Quarter of Section 14, Township 19 North, Range 3 East of the Third Principal Meridian, described as follows:

Beginning at the Northeast Corner of the Southeast Quarter of said Section 14; thence South 1 degree 03 minutes 40 seconds West along the east line of said Southeast Quarter, a distance of 1329.19 feet to the south line of the Northeast Quarter of the Southeast Quarter of said Section 14; thence South 89 degrees 25 minutes 00 seconds West, 28.95 feet; thence North 1 degree 05 minutes 20 seconds East, 925.01 feet; thence North 1 degree 11 minutes 50 seconds East, 404.25 feet to the north line of said Southeast Quarter; thence North 89 degrees 28 minutes 50 seconds East along said line, a distance of 27.57 feet to the point of beginning, including that portion containing 0.775 acres, more or less, which exists as public road right-of-way, said perpetual right-of-way easement containing 0.870 acres, more or less.

PARCEL 26

A part of the Southwest Quarter of Section 13, Township 19 North, Range 3 East of the Third Principal Meridian, described as follows:

Beginning at the Northwest Corner of the Southwest Quarter of said Section 13; thence South 1 degree 03 minutes 40 seconds West, along the west line of the Southwest Quarter of said Section 13, a distance of 440.13 feet to the south parcel line; thence North 89 degrees 10 minutes 40 seconds East along said parcel line, 31.50 feet; thence North 1 degree 05 minutes 20 seconds East, 34.00 feet; thence North 1 degree 11 minutes 55 seconds East, 400.01 feet; thence North 1 degree 03 minutes 00 seconds East, 6.15 feet to the north line of the Southwest Quarter of said Section 13; thence South 89 degrees 11 minutes 10 seconds West along said north line, 32.46 feet to the point of beginning, including that portion containing 0.247 acres, more or less, which exists as public road right-of-way, said perpetual right-of-way easement containing 0.323 acres, more or less.

PARCEL 27

A part of the Northeast Quarter of Section 14, Township 19 North, Range 3 East of the Third Principal Meridian, described as follows:

Beginning at the Southeast Corner of the Northeast Quarter of said Section 14; thence North 0 degrees 58 minutes 50 seconds East along the east line of the Northeast Quarter of said Section 14, a distance of 316.77 feet to the north parcel line; thence South 89 degrees 28 minutes 50 seconds West along said line, 27.18 feet; thence South 1 degree 03 minutes 00 seconds West, 316.78 feet to the south line of the Northeast Quarter of said Section 14; thence North 89 degrees 28 minutes 50 seconds East along said line, 27.57 feet to the point of beginning, including that portion containing 0.176 acres, more or less, which exists as public road right-of-way, said perpetual right-of-way easement containing 0.199 acres, more or less.

PARCEL 29

A part of the Northeast Quarter of Section 14, Township 19 North, Range 3 East of the Third Principal Meridian, described as follows:

Beginning at the Northeast Corner of said Section 14; thence South 0 degrees 58 minutes 50 seconds West along the east line of the Northeast Quarter of said Section 14, a distance of 2342.88 feet to the south parcel line; thence South 89 degrees 29 minutes 00 seconds West, 27.18 feet; thence North 1 degree 03 minutes 00 seconds East, 878.86 feet; thence North 0 degrees 50 minutes 10 seconds East, 1399.89 feet; thence North 0 degrees 44 minutes 30 seconds East, 22.44 feet; thence North 40 degrees 31 minutes 30 seconds West, 30.32 feet to the existing south right of way line of a township road; thence North 0 degrees 44 minutes 30 seconds East, 18.43 feet to the north line of said Northeast Quarter; thence North 89 degrees 31 minutes 50 seconds East along said line, 49.89 feet to the point of beginning, including that portion containing 1.238 acres, more or less, which exists as public road right-of-way, said perpetual right-of-way easement containing 1.490 acres, more or less.

PARCEL 30

A part of the Northwest Quarter of Section 13, Township 19 North, Range 3 East of the Third Principal Meridian, described as follows:

Beginning at the Northwest Corner of said Section 13; thence South 0 degrees 58 minutes 50 seconds West along the west line of the Northwest Quarter of said Section 13, a distance of 1329.82 feet to the south parcel line; thence North 89 degrees 09 minutes 50 seconds East along said line, 33.58 feet; thence North 0 degrees 50 minutes 10 seconds East, 1264.13 feet; thence North 0 degrees 44 minutes 30 seconds East, 22.64 feet; thence North 42 degrees 44 minutes 20 seconds East, 29.90 feet to the existing south right of way line of a township road; thence North 0 degrees 44 minutes 40 seconds East, 21.30 feet to the north line of said Northwest Quarter; thence South 89 degrees 08 minutes 50 seconds West along said line, 50.15 feet to the point of beginning, including that portion containing 0.830 acres, more or less, which exists as public road right-of-way, said perpetual right-of-way easement containing 0.989 acres, more or less.

PARCEL 31

A part of the Southwest Quarter of Section 12, Township 19 North, Range 3 East of the Third Principal Meridian, described as follows:

Beginning at the Southwest Corner of said Section 12; thence North 0 degrees 48 minutes 30 seconds East along the west line of the Southwest Quarter of said Section 12, a distance of 2580.09 feet to the north parcel line; thence North 89 degrees 22 minutes 40 seconds East, 31.05 feet; thence South 0 degrees 52 minutes 40 seconds West, 245.61 feet; thence South 0 degrees 45 minutes 00 seconds West, 1099.99 feet; thence South 0 degrees 57 minutes 50 seconds West, 800.03 feet; thence South 0 degrees 44 minutes 30 seconds West, 392.46 feet; thence South 40 degrees 26 minutes 10 seconds East, 30.38 feet to the existing north right of way line of a township road; thence South 0 degrees 44 minutes 40 seconds West, 18.47 feet to the south line of said Southwest Quarter; thence South 89 degrees 08 minutes 50 seconds West along said line, 50.15 feet to the point of beginning, including that portion containing 1.493 acres, more or less, which exists as public road right-of-way, said perpetual right-of-way easement containing 1.840 acres, more or less.

ALSO

A part of the Southwest Quarter of Section 12, Township 19 North, Range 3 East of the Third Principal Meridian, described as follows:

A tract of land 5 feet in width lying between Station 235+40.00 and Station 235+70.00 a distance of 30.00 feet along the east side of the proposed east right of way line of a highway designated as Construction Section8 5-00043-00-RS, as surveyed and staked out under the direction of the Dewitt County Highway Department.

PARCEL 33

A part of the Southeast Quarter of Section 11, Township 19 North, Range 3 East, Third Principal Meridian, described as follows:

Commencing at the Northeast corner of the Southeast Quarter of said Section 11; thence South 0 degrees 48 minutes 30 seconds West along the east line of the Southeast Quarter of said Section 11, a distance of 13.79 feet to the north parcel line and the point of beginning; thence continuing South 0 degrees 48 minutes 30 seconds West, 70.01 feet to the south parcel line; thence South 89 degrees 56 minutes 00 seconds West along said parcel line, 28.95 feet; thence North 0 degrees 52 minutes 40 seconds East, 70.01 feet to the north parcel line; thence North 89 degrees 56 minutes 00 seconds East, 28.86 feet to the point of beginning, including that portion containing 0.040 acres, more or less, which exists as public road right-of-way, said perpetual right-of-way easement containing 0.046 acres, more or less.

PARCEL 34

A part of the Southwest Quarter of Section 12, Township 19 North, Range 3 East, Third Principal Meridian, described as follows:

Beginning at the Northwest corner of the Southwest Quarter of said Section 12; thence North 89 degrees 22 minutes 40 seconds East along the north line of the Southwest Quarter of said Section 12, a distance of 31.17 feet; thence South 0 degrees 52 minutes 40 seconds West, 100.03 feet to the south parcel line; thence South 89 degrees 22 minutes 40 seconds West along said parcel line, 31.05 feet; thence North 0 degrees 48 minutes 30 seconds East, 100.03 feet to the point of beginning, including that portion containing 0.057 acres, more or less, which exists as public road right-of-way, said perpetual right-of-way easement containing 0.071 acres, more or less.

PARCEL 38

A part of the Northwest Quarter of Section 12, Township 19 North, Range 3 East of the Third Principal Meridian, described as follows:

Beginning at the Southwest corner of the Northwest Quarter of said Section 12; thence North 89 degrees 22 minutes 40 seconds East along the south line of the Northwest Quarter of said Section 12, a distance of 31.17 feet; thence North 0 degrees 52 minutes 40 seconds East, 154.41 feet; thence North 0 degrees 39 minutes 40 seconds East, 500.00 feet; thence North 0 degrees 46 minutes 30 seconds East, 199.96 feet; thence North 2 degrees 34 minutes 30 seconds East, 400.20 feet; thence North 2 degrees 41 minutes 10 seconds East, 107.55 feet to the south line of the north 80 acres of the Northwest Quarter of said Section 12; thence South 89 degrees 34 minutes 20 seconds West along said south line, 45.86 feet to the west line of the Northwest Quarter of said Section 12; thence South 0 degrees 48 minutes 30 seconds West along the west line of the Northwest Quarter of said Section 12, a distance of 1361.66 feet to the point of beginning including that portion containing 0.758 acres, more or less, which exists as public road right-of-way, said perpetual right-of-way easement containing 1.042 acres, more or less.

P.A. 94–1055, Art. 25, § 25–7–103.123, eff. Jan. 1, 2007.

30/25–7–103.124.   Quick-take;   Williamson County

§ 25–7–103.124.   Quick-take; Williamson County. The corporate authorities of Williamson County are hereby authorized to acquire, singularly or jointly with other parties, by gift, purchase, condemnation, or otherwise, any land or interest in land, necessary for the construction and development of a coal mine or transportation facilities to serve a coal mine, to improve or arrange for the improvement of the land and, if deemed to be in the public interest, to convey such land, or interest in land, so acquired and improved to a railroad or company developing the coal mine for fair market value. In addition, quick-take proceedings under Article 20 may be used for a period of 12 months after the effective date of this amendatory Act of the 94th General Assembly by Williamson County for the acquisition of the following described property for the purpose of constructing a railroad spur line:

PARCEL 1

As described by deed record book 162, page 337: A triangular tract of land located in the Northwest Quarter of the Southeast Quarter of Section 7, Township 8 South, Range 3 East of the 3rd Principal Meridian bounded and described as follows:

Beginning at the Southwest corner of said Northwest Quarter of the Southeast Quarter and running thence north, along the west line of said land, two hundred forty (240) feet more or less, to a point sixty-five (65) feet northwesterly from the located center line of the track to the Lake Creek Mine, measured at right angle thereto. Thence south fifty-seven (57) degrees east magnetic bearing, parallel to said center line four hundred (400) feet more or less, to a point in the south line of said land, thence west along said south line three hundred twenty (320) feet more or less, to a point of beginning, containing eighty-eight (0.88) of an acre more or less, excepting the coal underlying same which has heretofore been disposed of.

Parcel 1: Containing an estimated 0.88 Acres.

PARCEL 2

As described by deed record book 162, page 336:

A strip of land one hundred thirty (130) feet wide, extending over and across the north half of the Southwest Quarter of the Southeast Quarter of Section Seven (7), Township Eight (8) South, Range Three (3) East of the Third (3rd) Principal Meridian, said strip of land being sixty-five (65) feet in width on each side of the located center line of the track to Lake Creek Mine. Said located center line intersects the north line of said land, at a point two hundred ten (210) feet east of the northwest corner of said land and run thence south fifty-seven (57) degrees east, magnetic bearing, eleven hundred fifty-three (1153) feet more or less, to a point in the south line of said land one hundred eighty-nine (189) feet west of the southeast corner of said land. Said strip of land contains three and forty-five hundredths (3.45) acres more or less.

Parcel 2: Containing an estimated 3.45 Acres.

PARCEL 3

As described by deed record book 162, page 339:

A triangular tract of land located in the South Half of the Southwest Quarter of the Southeast Quarter of Section Seven (7), Township Eight (8) South, Range Three (3) East of the Third (3rd) Principal Meridian, bounded and described as follows:

Beginning at the northeast corner of said land, and running thence west two hundred seventy (270) feet more or less, to a point fifty (50) feet southwesterly from the located center line to the track to Lake Creek Mine, thence south fifty-seven (57) degrees east, magnetic bearing, parallel to said center line, three hundred thirty (330) feet more or less, to the point of beginning, containing sixty-three hundredths (0.63) of an acre more or less; excepting the coal underlying same which has heretofore been disposed of.

Parcel 3: Containing an estimated 0.63 Acres.

PARCEL 4

A parcel of land to the extent owned one hundred and thirty-five (135) feet wide located in and running across the South Half (S ½) of the Southeast Quarter (SE ¼) of Section Seven (7), Township Eight (8) South, Range Three (3) East of the Third (3rd) Principal Meridian, bounded and described as follows:

Beginning at the northwest corner of said South Half (S ½) of the Southeast Quarter (SE ¼) of Section Seven (7), Township Eight (8) South, Range Three (3) East and running thence south along the west line of said land fifty-three (53) feet more or less to the point of beginning, thence south along the west line of the said land one hundred and fifty nine (159) feet thence south fifty-seven degrees (57) east, magnetic bearing eight hundred (800) feet more or less to a point on the south line of Section Seven (7), Township Eight (8) South, Range Three (3) East; said point being six hundred seventy (670) feet east of the southeast corner of said Section

Seven (7), thence east along the south line of said Section Seven (7) two hundred twenty-three (223) feet to a point being four hundred and forty-seven (447) feet east of the southeast corner of said Section Seven (7) thence north fifty-seven (57) degrees west one thousand and sixty-four (1064) feet more or less to the point of beginning; containing 1.48 acres more or less.

Parcel 4: Containing an estimated 1.48 Acres.

P.A. 94–1055, Art. 25, § 25–7–103.124, eff. Jan. 1, 2007.

30/25–7–103.125. Quick-take; City of Mount Vernon

§ 25–7–103.125. Quick-take; City of Mount Vernon. Quick-take proceedings under Article 20 may be used for a period of 12 months after the effective date of this amendatory Act of the 94th General Assembly by the City of Mount Vernon for roadway extension purposes for acquisition of the property described in Parcel 4, Parcel 10, and Parcel 12, and for the acquisition of an easement in the property described as Parcel 12TE, each described as follows:

PARCEL 4

A part of the Southwest Quarter of Section 36, Township 2 South, Range 2 East of the Third Principal Meridian, Jefferson County, Illinois, more particularly described as follows:

Commencing at the northwest corner of Lot 5 in Parkway Pointe Subdivision, thence South 00 degrees 44 minutes 12 seconds West along the west line of Lot 5, a distance of 13.84 feet to the Point of Beginning; thence South 03 degrees 01 minutes 34 seconds East, 323.26 feet; thence South 12 degrees 21 minutes 36 seconds East, 177.55 feet; thence South 42 degrees 33 minutes 50 seconds East, 65.08 feet; thence South 84 degrees 41 minutes 25 seconds East, 200.97 feet; thence South 88 degrees 53 minutes 09 seconds East, 475.09 feet; thence South 77 degrees 33 minutes 00 seconds East, 127.43 feet; thence South 87 degrees 51 minutes 48 seconds East, 290.09 feet to a point of the existing north right-of-way of Veteran's Memorial Drive; thence South 01 degree 03 minutes 41 seconds West along the existing north right-of-way line, 5.00 feet; thence North 88 degrees 56 minutes 19 seconds West along the existing north right-of-way line, 1,055.47 feet to the southeast corner of Lot 8 in Parkway Pointe Subdivision; thence continuing North 88 degrees 56 minutes 19 seconds West along the existing north right-of-way line and the south line of Lot 8, a distance of 69.90 feet; thence North 44 degrees 02 minutes 40 seconds West along the existing north right-of-way line and the south line of Lot 8, a distance of 99.52 feet to the existing east right-of-way line of South 42nd Street and the Southwest corner of Lot 8; thence North 00 degrees 44 minutes 11 seconds East along the east right-of-way line of South 42nd Street and the west line of Lots 5, 6, 7 and 8, a distance of 523.73 feet to the Point of Beginning, containing 1.11 acres (48,299 square feet), more or less.

PARCEL 10

A part of Lot 9 in the Division of Lands of Paulina E. Davidson, located in the Northwest Quarter of Section 1, Township 3 South, Range 2 East of the Third Principal Meridian and more particularly described as follows:

Beginning at the northwest corner of Lot 9 in the Division of Lands of Paulina E. Davidson; thence South 89 degrees 22 minutes 46 seconds East along the north line of Lot 9, a distance of 220.27 feet to the west right-of-way line of Interstates 57 and 64; thence South 18 degrees 17 minutes 35 seconds East along the west right-of-way line, 198.37 feet; thence South 87 degrees 01 minute 47 seconds West, 234.54 feet; thence North 87 degrees 56 minutes 05 seconds East, 49.82 feet to the west line of Lot 9 in the Division of Lands of Paulina E. Davidson; thence North 00 degrees 25 minutes 29 seconds East, 201.09 feet to the Point of Beginning, containing 1.14 acres (49,727 square feet), more or less.

PARCEL 12

A part of Lot 1 in Charles Starrett Subdivision in the Southeast Quarter of Section 35, Township 2 South, Range 2 East of the Third Principal Meridian, Jefferson County, Illinois and more particularly described as follows:

Beginning at the Southwest corner of Lot 1 in Charles Starrett Subdivision; thence North 00 degrees 37 minutes 30 seconds East along the west line of Lot 1, a distance of 22.91 feet; thence North 83 degrees 02 minutes 40 seconds East, 131.58 feet; thence North 88 degrees 15 minutes 04 seconds East, 198.71 feet to the west right-of-way line of Interstates 57 and 64; thence South 18 degrees 00 minutes 35 seconds East along the west right-of-way line, 29.32 feet to the South line of Lot 1 in Charles Starrett Subdivision; thence North 89 degrees 31 minutes 48 seconds West along the south line of Lot 1, a distance of 207.89 feet; thence South 00 degrees 02 minutes 53 seconds East along the south line of Lot 1, a distance of 19.80 feet; thence North 89 degrees 31 minutes 54 seconds West along the south line of Lot 1, a distance of 130.68 feet to the Point of Beginning, containing 0.21 acres (8,988 square feet), more or less.

PARCEL 12 TE (Easement)

A part of Lot 1 in Charles Starrett Subdivision in the Southeast Quarter of Section 35, Township 2 South, Range 2 East of the Third Principal Meridian, Jefferson County, Illinois and more particularly described as follows:

Beginning at the Southwest corner of Lot 1 in Charles Starrett Subdivision; thence North 00 degrees 37 minutes 32 seconds East along the west line of Lot 1, a distance of 212.31 feet to the Point of

Beginning; thence continuing North 00 degrees 37 minutes 32 seconds East along the west line of Lot 1, a distance of 105.00 feet to the northwest corner of Lot 1; thence South 89 degrees 29 minutes 58 seconds East along the north line of Lot 1, a distance of 25.38 feet; thence South 05 degrees 26 minutes 16 seconds West, 105.39 feet; thence North 89 degrees 29 minutes 58 seconds West, 16.54 feet to the Point of Beginning, containing 0.05 acres (2,200 square feet), more or less.

P.A. 82–280, § 7–103.113, added by P.A. 94–898, § 5, eff. June 22, 2005. Renumbered as § 25–7–103.125 and amended by P.A. 95–331, § 1090, eff. Aug. 21, 2007.

30/25–7–103.139.   Quick-take; Village of Lincolnwood

§ 25–7–103.139.   Quick-take;   Village of Lincolnwood.

(a) Quick-take proceedings under Article 20 may be used for a period of 12 months after the effective date of this amendatory Act of the 92nd General Assembly for the purpose of a municipal parking lot in the Touhy Crawford Business District by the Village of Lincolnwood for the acquisition of a portion of the following properties:

(1) PIN 10-26-316-021;

(2) PIN 10-26-316-022;

(3) PIN 10-26-316-023; and

(4) PIN 10-26-316-024.

(b) Quick-take proceedings under Article 20 may be used for a period of 12 months following the effective date of this amendatory Act of the 92nd General Assembly for the purpose of the construction of the planned East West Connector Road running within its corporate limits by the Village of Lincolnwood for the acquisition of a portion of the following properties:

(1) PIN 10-35-204-002;

(2) PIN 10-35-204-003;

(3) PIN 10-35-204-004;

(4) PIN 10-35-204-005;

(5) PIN 10-35-204-006;

(6) PIN 10-35-204-007;

(7) PIN 10-35-204-008;

(8) PIN 10-35-204-016;

(9) PIN 10-35-136-005;

(10) PIN 10-35-136-008;

(11) PIN 10-35-203-007;

(12) PIN 10-35-135-004;

(13) PIN 10-35-107-002;

(14) PIN 10-35-107-008;

(15) PIN 10-35-500-010;

(16) PIN 10-35-500-012;

(17) PIN 10-35-107-016; and

(18) A 60 foot strip of land across that part of the Chicago and Northwestern Railroad (Union Pacific) railroad property lying in the north ½ of section 35, township 41 north, range 13 east of the third principal meridian in Cook County, Illinois.

(c) Quick-take proceedings under Article 20 may be used for a period of 12 months following the effective date of this amendatory Act of the 92nd General Assembly by the Village of Lincolnwood for the acquisition of the property PIN 10-35-200-039 for the purpose of public works usage and storage within the Touhy Lawndale Tax Increment Financing District and the Northeast Industrial Tax Increment Financing District.

P.A. 94–1055, Art. 25, § 25–7–103.139, eff. Jan. 1, 2007.

30/25–7–103.140.   Quick-take; Village of Bolingbrook

§ 25–7–103.140.   Quick-take;   Village of Bolingbrook.   Quick-take proceedings under Article 20 may be used for a period of 12 months after the effective date of this amendatory Act of the 92nd General Assembly by the Village of Bolingbrook for the acquisition of the following described property for the purpose of roadway extension:

PARCEL 1:

That part of parcel 02-30-200-002 located in the Northeast Quarter of Section 30, Township 37 North, Range 10 East of the Third Principal Meridian lying westerly of Weber Road in Will County, Illinois, more particularly described as follows:

Commencing at the Northeast Corner of said Northeast Quarter; thence S 1 deg. 19 min. 22 sec. E along the east line of said Northeast Quarter a distance of 2047.60 feet to the point of intersection of the centerline of the extension of Remington Boulevard; thence S 88 deg. 40 min. 35 sec. W along said centerline of the extension of Remington Boulevard a distance of 50.00 feet to the intersection of said centerline of Remington Boulevard and the west line of Weber Road at the point of beginning of this description;

1.) thence N 1 deg. 19 min. 22 sec. W along said west line of Weber Road a distance of 519.11 feet;

2.) thence S 88 deg. 14 min. 37 sec. W along north line of said parcel 02-30-200-002 a distance of 20.00 feet;

3.) thence S 1 deg. 19 min. 22 sec. E along a line 20.00 feet parallel to the west line of Weber Road a distance of 418.96 feet;

4.) thence S 43 deg. 40 min. 37 sec. W a distance of 63.64 feet;

5.) thence S 88 deg. 40 min. 35 sec. W a distance of 70.00 feet;

6.) thence S 1 deg. 19 min. 04 sec. E a distance of 5.00 feet;

7.) thence S 88 deg. 40 min. 35 sec. W a distance of 175.00 feet;

8.) thence west a distance of 227.70 feet along a tangential curve concave south having a radius of 686.62 feet and a cord bearing of S 79 deg. 10 min. 35 sec. W;

9.) thence S 67 deg. 10 min. 30 sec. W a distance of 229.11 feet;

10.) thence S 69 deg. 40 min. 35 sec. W a distance of 352.08 feet;

11.) thence west a distance of 559.79 feet; along a tangential curve concave south having a radius of 676.62 feet and a cord bearing of S 45 deg. 58 min. 31 sec. W;

12.) thence south a distance of 55.38 feet along a tangential curve concave east having a radius of 995.00 feet and a cord bearing of S 20 deg. 40 min. 49 sec. W to a point on the south line of said parcel 02-30-200-002;

13.) thence N 88 deg. 14 min. 38 sec. E along said south line of parcel 02-30-200-002 a distance of 42.93 feet to the point of intersection of said south line of parcel 02-30-200-002 and said centerline of the extension of Remington Boulevard;

14.) thence N 88 deg. 14 min. 38 sec. E along said south line of parcel 02-30-200-002 a distance of 43.22 feet;

15.) thence north a distance of 20.27 feet along a non-tangential curve concave east having a radius of 915.00 feet and a cord bearing of N 21 deg. 38 min. 17 sec. E;

16.) thence north a distance of 493.60 feet along a tangential curve concave east having a radius of 596.62 feet and a cord bearing of N 45 deg. 58 min. 31 sec. E;

17.) thence N 69 deg. 40 min. 35 sec. E a distance of 352.08 feet;

18.) thence N 72 deg. 10 min. 40 sec. E a distance of 229.11 feet;

19.) thence east a distance of 194.53 feet along a non-tangential curve concave south having a radius of 586.62 feet and a cord bearing of N 79 deg. 10 min. 36 sec. E;

20.) thence N 88 deg. 40 min. 35 sec. E a distance of 240.00 feet;

21.) thence S 46 deg. 19 min. 23 sec E a distance of 84.85 feet;

22.) thence S 1 deg. 19 min. 22 sec. E along a line 10.00 feet parallel to the west line of Weber Road a distance of 485.00 feet;

23.) thence N 88 deg. 13 min. 38 sec. E along said south line of parcel 02-30-200-002 a distance of 10.00 feet;

24.) thence N 1 deg. 19 min. 22 sec. W along said west line of Weber Road a distance of 594.92 feet to

the point of beginning, in Will County, Illinois, said parcel containing 3.77 acres, more or less.

P.A. 94–1055, Art. 25, § 25–7–103.140, eff. Jan. 1, 2007.

30/25–7–103.141.   Quick-take;   Village   of Downers Grove

§ 25–7–103.141. Quick-take; Village of Downers Grove. Quick-take proceedings under Article 20 may be used for a period of 12 months after the effective date of this amendatory Act of the 92nd General Assembly by the Village of Downers Grove within the area of the Downers Grove Central Business District Tax Increment Financing District described below, to be used only for acquiring properties for providing off-street parking facilities:

THAT PART OF THE SOUTHWEST QUARTER OF SECTION 8, TOWNSHIP 38 NORTH, RANGE 11 EAST OF THE THIRD PRINCIPAL MERIDIAN, DESCRIBED AS BEGINNING AT THE INTERSECTION OF THE SOUTH LINE OF THE NORTH 21.12 FEET OF LOTS 18 AND 19 OF ASSESSOR'S SUBDIVISION, A SUBDIVISION IN SECTIONS 7 AND 8 IN AFORESAID TOWNSHIP 38 NORTH, RANGE 11 EAST, RECORDED AS DOCUMENT NO. 14481 AND THE EAST LINE OF MAIN STREET, AND RUNNING THENCE EASTERLY, ALONG SAID SOUTH LINE, TO THE WEST LINE OF LOT 16, OF AFORESAID ASSESSOR'S SUBDIVISION; THENCE NORTHWESTERLY, ALONG THE WEST LINE OF AFORESAID LOT 16, TO THE SOUTHEAST CORNER OF LOT 17 OF AFORESAID ASSESSOR'S SUBDIVISION; THENCE NORTHERLY, ALONG THE EAST LINE OF AFORESAID LOT 17, TO THE SOUTH LINE OF LOT 52 OF AFORESAID ASSESSOR'S SUBDIVISION; THENCE EASTERLY, ALONG THE SOUTH LINE OF AFORESAID LOT 52 AND THE EASTERLY EXTENSION THEREOF, TO THE WEST LINE OF WASHINGTON STREET; THENCE NORTHERLY, ALONG THE WEST LINE OF WASHINGTON STREET, TO A POINT THAT IS 94.80 FEET SOUTH FROM THE SOUTHEAST CORNER OF LOT 1 IN BLOCK 4 OF CURTISS ADDITION TO DOWNERS GROVE, ACCORDING TO THE PLAT THEREOF RECORDED AS DOCUMENT NO. 7317; THENCE WESTERLY, PARALLEL WITH THE NORTH LINE OF LOT 15 IN AFORESAID ASSESSOR'S SUBDIVISION, TO THE WEST LINE OF SAID LOT 15; THENCE NORTHERLY, ALONG THE WEST LINE OF SAID LOT 15, TO THE NORTH LINE THEREOF, SAID LINE BEING THE SOUTH LINE OF BLOCK 4 IN AFORESAID CURTISS ADDITION TO DOWNERS GROVE; THENCE EASTERLY, ALONG SAID NORTH LINE, TO THE WEST LINE OF WASHINGTON STREET; THENCE NORTHERLY, ALONG SAID WEST LINE,

SAID LINE ALSO BEING THE EAST LINE OF AFORESAID BLOCK 4 IN CURTISS ADDITION TO DOWNERS GROVE, TO THE SOUTH LINE OF CURTISS STREET, SAID LINE BEING THE NORTH LINE OF AFORESAID BLOCK 4; THENCE WESTERLY, ALONG SAID SOUTH LINE TO A POINT THAT IS 32.0 FEET, EASTERLY, AS MEASURED ON THE NORTH LINE OF LOT 8 IN BLOCK 4 OF AFORESAID CURTISS SUBDIVISION; THENCE SOUTHERLY, ALONG THE WEST FACE OF A BRICK BUILDING AND THE SOUTHERLY EXTENSION THEREOF, ON A STRAIGHT LINE, TO AN INTERSECTION WITH A LINE DESCRIBED AS BEGINNING 23 LINKS (15.18 FEET) SOUTH, AS MEASURED ON THE EAST LINE OF MAIN STREET, OF THE SOUTHWEST CORNER OF LOT 10 IN BLOCK 4 OF AFORESAID CURTISS SUBDIVISION AND RUNNING THENCE SOUTHEASTERLY 1.98 CHAINS (130.68 FEET), TO A POINT 32 LINKS (21.12 FEET) SOUTH OF THE SOUTH LINE OF AFORESAID LOT 8, THENCE EASTERLY 86 LINKS, (56.76 FEET), TO THE END OF THE HEREIN DESCRIBED LINE; THENCE WESTERLY, FOLLOWING ALONG SAID PREVIOUSLY DESCRIBED LINE, FROM THE INTERSECTION REFERENCED HEREIN, TO THE EAST LINE OF MAIN STREET; THENCE SOUTHERLY, ALONG SAID EAST LINE OF MAIN STREET, TO THE POINT OF BEGINNING, ALL DUPAGE COUNTY, ILLINOIS.

P.A. 94–1055, Art. 25, § 25–7–103.141, eff. Jan. 1, 2007.

30/25–7–103.142. Quick-take; Village of Mount Prospect

§ 25–7–103.142. Quick-take; Village of Mount Prospect. Quick-take proceedings under Article 20 may be used for a period of 12 months after the effective date of this amendatory Act of the 92nd General Assembly by the Village of Mount Prospect for the acquisition of the following described property for the purpose of constructing a new village hall and public parking facility:

PARCEL 1: THE EAST 50 FEET OF LOT 12 IN BLOCK 4 OF BUSSE AND WILLE'S RESUBDIVISION IN MOUNT PROSPECT IN THE WEST ½ OF SECTION 12, TOWNSHIP 41 NORTH, RANGE 11, EAST OF THE THIRD PRINCIPAL MERIDIAN, IN COOK COUNTY, ILLINOIS.

PARCEL 2: THE SOUTH 32 FEET OF LOT 13 (EXCEPT THE WEST 96 FEET THEREOF) IN BLOCK 4 IN BUSSE AND WILLE'S RESUBDIVISION IN MOUNT PROSPECT IN THE WEST ½ OF SECTION 12, TOWNSHIP 41 NORTH, RANGE 11, EAST OF THE THIRD PRINCIPAL MERIDIAN, ACCORDING TO THE PLAT THEREOF RECORDED MARCH 31, 1906 AS

DOCUMENT 3839591, IN COOK COUNTY, ILLINOIS.

TAX I.D. NUMBERS: 08-12-103-019 AND 08-12-103-027.

and ALL RIGHTS, TITLE, EASEMENTS, LICENSES OR INTERESTS WHATSOEVER FOR INGRESS, EGRESS AND PARKING OVER, UPON AND ACROSS THE REAL PROPERTY IDENTIFIED BELOW:

PARCEL 1: LOT 13 (EXCEPT THE SOUTH 65 FEET THEREOF) IN BLOCK 4 IN BUSSE AND WILLE'S RESUBDIVISION OF MOUNT PROSPECT IN THE WEST ½ OF SECTION 12, TOWNSHIP 41 NORTH, RANGE 11 EAST OF THE THIRD PRINCIPAL MERIDIAN, ACCORDING TO THE PLAT THEREOF RECORDED MARCH 31, 1906 AS DOCUMENT NUMBER 3839591 IN COOK COUNTY, ILLINOIS.

PARCEL 2: THE NORTH 33 FEET OF THE SOUTH 65 FEET OF LOT 13 IN BLOCK 4 IN BUSSE AND WILLE'S RESUBDIVISION OF MOUNT PROSPECT IN THE WEST ½ OF SECTION 12, TOWNSHIP 41 NORTH, RANGE 11 EAST OF THE THIRD PRINCIPAL MERIDIAN, IN COOK COUNTY, ILLINOIS.

PARCEL 3: LOT 8, 9, 10 AND 11 BLOCK 4 IN BUSSE AND WILLE'S RESUBDIVISION IN MOUNT PROSPECT IN WEST ½ OF SECTION 12, TOWNSHIP 41 NORTH, RANGE 11 EAST OF THE THIRD PRINCIPAL MERIDIAN, IN COOK COUNTY, ILLINOIS.

PARCEL 4: THE WEST 96 FEET OF THE SOUTH 32 FEET OF LOT 13 BLOCK 4 IN BUSSE AND WILLE'S RESUBDIVISION IN MOUNT PROSPECT IN WEST ½ OF SECTION 12, TOWNSHIP 41 NORTH, RANGE 11 EAST OF THE THIRD PRINCIPAL MERIDIAN, IN COOK COUNTY, ILLINOIS.

PARCEL 5: LOT 12, (EXCEPT THE EAST 50 FEET THEREOF) BLOCK 4 IN BUSSE AND WILLE'S RESUBDIVISION IN MOUNT PROSPECT IN WEST ½ OF SECTION 12, TOWNSHIP 41 NORTH, RANGE 11 EAST OF THE THIRD PRINCIPAL MERIDIAN, IN COOK COUNTY, ILLINOIS.

TAX I.D. NUMBERS: 08-12-103-020, 08-12-103-021, 08-12-103-025, 08-12-103-026, 08-12-103-014, 08-12-103-017, 08-12-103-032, and 08-12-103-031.

P.A. 94–1055, Art. 25, § 25–7–103.142, eff. Jan. 1, 2007.

30/25–7–103.143. Quick-take; City of Neoga

§ 25–7–103.143. Quick-take; City of Neoga. Quick-take proceedings under Article 20 may be used for a period of 12 months after the effective date of this amendatory Act of the 92nd General Assembly by the City of Neoga for the acquisition of temporary and permanent easements across a portion of the following described property for the purpose of extending the municipal water works system:

1. BEGINNING AT THE POINT OF INTERSECTION OF THE SOUTH LINE OF THE SOUTH ½ OF THE NORTH ½ OF THE SE ¼ OF SEC. 18, T. 10 N., R. 7 E. OF THE 3RD P.M., AND THE EASTERLY RIGHT-OF-WAY LINE OF STATE ROUTE NO. 45; THENCE EAST 300 FEET; THENCE NORTHERLY, 275 FEET, PARALLEL WITH THE EASTERLY RIGHT-OF-WAY LINE OF SAID STATE ROAD; THENCE WEST 300 FEET; THENCE SOUTHERLY, ALONG SAID EAST RIGHT-OF-WAY LINE TO THE POINT OF BEGINNING CONTAINING 2 ACRES, MORE OR LESS, ALL SITUATED IN THE COUNTY OF CUMBERLAND AND STATE OF ILLINOIS.

2. A PART OF THE NE ¼ OF SEC. 19, T. 10 N., R. 7 E. OF THE 3RD P.M., MORE PARTICULARLY DESCRIBED AS FOLLOWS: BEGINNING AT THE INTERSECTION OF THE EAST RIGHT-OF-WAY LINE OF U.S. ROUTE NO. 45 AND THE NORTH LINE OF SEC. 19, T. 10 N., R. 7 E. OF THE 3RD P.M., BEING AN IRON PIN; THENCE S. 90° 42'02″ E., ASSUMED, ALONG THE NORTH LINE OF SAID SECTION 19, A DISTANCE OF 485.09 FEET TO AN IRON PIN; THENCE S. 00° 12'50″ E., A DISTANCE OF 503.64 FEET TO AN IRON PIN; THENCE N. 89° 42'02″ W., PARALLEL WITH THE NORTH LINE OF SAID SECTION 19 TO THE EAST RIGHT-OF-WAY LINE OF U.S. ROUTE NO. 45, A DISTANCE OF 671.23 FEET TO AN IRON PIN; THENCE N. 20° 07'52″ E., ALONG THE EAST LINE OF U.S. ROUTE NO. 45, A DISTANCE OF 535.37 FEET TO THE POINT OF BEGINNING, ALL SITUATED IN THE COUNTY OF CUMBERLAND AND STATE OF ILLINOIS.

3. ALL THAT PART OF THE SOUTH ½ OF THE SE ¼ OF SEC. 18, T. 10 N., R. 7 E. OF THE 3RD P.M., THAT LIES EAST OF THE RIGHT-OF-WAY OF THE ILLINOIS CENTRAL RAILROAD COMPANY, CONTAINING 60 ACRES MORE OR LESS, AND ALSO, THE SOUTH ½ OF THE NORTH ½ OF THE SE ¼ OF SEC. 18, T. 10 N., R. 7 E. OF THE 3RD P.M., LYING EAST OF THE RIGHT-OF-WAY OF THE ILLINOIS CENTRAL RAILROAD, CONTAINING 22 ½ ACRES MORE OR LESS, EXCEPT BEGINNING AT THE POINT OF INTERSECTION OF THE SOUTH LINE OF THE SOUTH ½ OF THE NORTH ½ OF THE SE ¼ OF SEC. 18, T. 10 N., R. 7 E. OF THE 3RD P.M. AND THE EASTERLY RIGHT-OF WAY LINE OF STATE ROUTE NO. 45; THENCE EAST 300 FEET; THENCE NORTHERLY 275 FEET PARALLEL WITH THE EASTERLY RIGHT-OF-WAY LINE OF SAID STATE ROAD; THENCE WEST 300

FEET; THENCE SOUTHERLY, ALONG SAID EAST RIGHT-OF-WAY LINE TO THE POINT OF BEGINNING CONTAINING 2 ACRES, MORE OR LESS,

ALL SITUATED IN THE COUNTY OF CUMBERLAND AND STATE OF ILLINOIS.

4. ALL THAT PART OF THE SW ¼ OF SEC. 19, T. 10 N., R. 7 E. OF THE 3RD P.M., LYING EAST OF THE RIGHT-OF WAY-OF THE ILLINOIS CENTRAL RAILROAD, CONTAINING 70 ACRES, MORE OR LESS,

ALL SITUATED IN THE COUNTY OF CUMBERLAND AND STATE OF ILLINOIS.

5. ALL THAT PART OF THE NORTH ½ OF SEC. 19, LYING EAST OF THE ILLINOIS CENTRAL RAILROAD COMPANY RIGHT-OF-WAY, T. 10 N., R. 7 E. OF THE 3RD P.M., EXCEPT, BEGINNING AT THE INTERSECTION OF THE EAST RIGHT-OF-WAY LINE OF U.S. ROUTE NO. 45 AND THE NORTH LINE OF SEC. 19, T. 10 N., R. 7 E. OF THE 3RD P.M. BEING AN IRON PIN THENCE S. 90° 42'02″ E., ASSUMED, ALONG THE NORTH LINE SAID SECTION 19. A DISTANCE OF 485.09 FEET TO AN IRON PIN; THENCE S. 00° 12'50″ E., A DISTANCE OF 503.64 FEET TO AN IRON PIN; THENCE N. 89° 42'02″ W. PARALLEL WITH THE NORTH LINE OF SAID SECTION 19. TO THE EAST RIGHT-OF-WAY LINE OF U.S. ROUTE NO. 45. A DISTANCE OF 671.23 FEET TO AN IRON PIN; THENCE N. 20° 07'52″ E., ALONG THE EAST LINE OF U.S. ROUTE NO. 45, A DISTANCE OF 535.37 FEET TO THE POINT OF BEGINNING.

SUBJECT TO CONVEYANCE FOR FAI ROUTE 57. ALL SITUATED IN THE COUNTY OF CUMBERLAND IN THE STATE OF ILLINOIS.

P.A. 94–1055, Art. 25, § 25–7–103.143, eff. Jan. 1, 2007.

30/25–7–103.144. Quick-take; Village of Plainfield

§ 25–7–103.144. Quick-take; Village of Plainfield. Quick-take proceedings under Article 20 may be used for a period of 12 months after the effective date of this amendatory Act of the 92nd General Assembly by the Village of Plainfield for the acquisition of the following described property for the purpose of making public improvements to construct road, water, sewer, and drainage systems to serve existing and planned park and school sites:

Parcel #1: THE NORTH 30.00 FEET OF THAT PART OF THE NORTHEAST QUARTER OF SECTION 32, TOWNSHIP 37 NORTH, RANGE 9, EAST OF THE THIRD PRINCIPAL MERIDIAN LYING WESTERLY AND SOUTHERLY OF THE HIGHWAY KNOWN AS LINCOLN HIGHWAY OR UNITED STATES ROUTE 30; AND ALSO THAT PART OF THE WEST HALF OF

THE NORTHEAST QUARTER OF SAID QUARTER SECTION LYING EASTERLY AND NORTHERLY OF THE ELGIN, JOLIET AND EASTERN RAILWAY COMPANY, EXCEPTING THEREFROM THAT PART THEREOF CONVEYED TO PUBLIC SERVICE COMPANY OF NORTHERN ILLINOIS BY DEED DOCUMENT 402715, RECORDED JANUARY 22, 1927; AND ALSO EXCEPTING THEREFROM THAT PART THEREOF CONVEYED TO COMMONWEALTH EDISON COMPANY, A CORPORATION OF ILLINOIS BY WARRANTY DEED RECORDED OCTOBER 16, 1962 AS DOCUMENT 968125 IN WILL COUNTY, ILLINOIS. PIN #01-32-200-001.

Parcel #2: THE NORTH 30.00 FEET OF A STRIP OF LAND LYING BETWEEN THE SOUTHWESTERLY RIGHT OF WAY LINE OF THE ELGIN, JOLIET AND EASTERN RAILROAD AND THE NORTHEASTERLY RIGHT OF WAY LINE OF U.S. ROUTE 30 IN THE NORTHEAST QUARTER OF SECTION 32, TOWNSHIP 37 NORTH, RANGE 9, EAST OF THE THIRD PRINCIPAL MERIDIAN, IN WILL COUNTY, ILLINOIS. PIN #01-32-200-002.

Parcel #3: THE NORTH 30.00 FEET OF THAT PART THE WEST HALF OF THE NORTHEAST QUARTER OF SECTION 32, TOWNSHIP 37 NORTH, RANGE 9, EAST OF THE THIRD PRINCIPAL MERIDIAN LYING SOUTHWESTERLY OF AND COINCIDENT WITH LANDS CONVEYED TO PUBLIC SERVICE COMPANY OF NORTHERN ILLINOIS BY WARRANTY DEED RECORDED JANUARY 22, 1927 AS DOCUMENT 402715, AND LYING NORTHEASTERLY OF AND COINCIDENT WITH LANDS CONVEYED TO SADDLE SIGNS, INC. BY QUIT CLAIM DEED RECORDED AUGUST 14, 1998 AS DOCUMENT R98–094655, IN WILL COUNTY, ILLINOIS. PIN #01-32-500-001.

Parcel #4: THE NORTH 30 FEET OF THE FOLLOWING DESCRIBED PROPERTY: THAT PART OF THE WEST HALF OF THE NORTHEAST QUARTER OF SECTION 32, TOWNSHIP 37 NORTH, RANGE 9, EAST OF THE THIRD PRINCIPAL MERIDIAN, LYING EASTERLY OF AND IMMEDIATELY ADJACENT TO THE EASTERLY RIGHT-OF-WAY LINE OF LAND CONVEYED TO COMMONWEALTH EDISON COMPANY, SUCCESSOR BY MERGER OF PUBLIC SERVICE COMPANY OF NORTHERN ILLINOIS, BY WARRANTY DEED RECORDED JANUARY 22, 1927, AS DOCUMENT NO. 402715, AND LYING WESTERLY OF A LINE 40 FEET EASTERLY OF MEASURED AT RIGHT ANGLES TO AND PARALLEL WITH SAID EASTERLY RIGHT-OF-WAY LINE, IN WILL COUNTY, ILLINOIS, AND ALSO THE NORTH 30 FEET OF THE FOLLOWING DESCRIBED

PROPERTY: A PARCEL OF LAND IN THE WEST HALF OF THE NORTHEAST QUARTER OF SECTION 32, TOWNSHIP 37 NORTH, RANGE 9 EAST OF THE THIRD PRINCIPAL MERIDIAN, BOUNDED AND DESCRIBED AS FOLLOWS: BEGINNING AT THE INTERSECTION OF THE NORTHEASTERLY RIGHT-OF-WAY LINE OF THE ELGIN, JOLIET AND EASTERN RAILWAY COMPANY WITH THE EAST LINE OF THE WEST HALF OF THE NORTHEAST QUARTER OF SAID SECTION; THENCE NORTHWESTERLY ALONG THE NORTHEASTERLY RIGHT-OF-WAY LINE OF SAID RAILWAY COMPANY TO A POINT IN THE NORTH SECTION LINE OF SAID SECTION WHICH IS 825.52 FEET EAST OF THE NORTHWEST CORNER OF THE NORTHEAST QUARTER OF SAID SECTION; THENCE EAST ALONG THE NORTH SECTION LINE OF SAID SECTION, 167.34 FEET; THENCE SOUTHEASTERLY ALONG A LINE PARALLEL WITH THE NORTHEASTERLY RIGHT-OF-WAY LINE OF SAID RAILWAY COMPANY TO A POINT IN THE EAST LINE OF THE WEST HALF OF NORTHEAST QUARTER OF SAID SECTION WHICH IS 347.07 FEET NORTH OF THE POINT OF BEGINNING: THENCE SOUTH TO THE POINT OF BEGINNING, IN WILL COUNTY, ILLINOIS. PIN # 01-32-200-003.

Parcel #5: THE NORTH 30 FEET OF THAT PART OF THE EAST HALF OF THE NORTHEAST QUARTER OF SECTION 32, TOWNSHIP 37 NORTH, RANGE 9 EAST OF THE THIRD PRINCIPAL MERIDIAN, LYING NORTHEASTERLY OF THE NORTHEASTERLY LINE OF LAND CONVEYED TO COMMONWEALTH EDISON COMPANY, A CORPORATION OF ILLINOIS BY WARRANTY DEED RECORDED NOVEMBER 13, 1952 AS DOCUMENT NO. 970766, IN WILL COUNTY, ILLINOIS. PIN #01-32-200-005.

Parcel #6: THE NORTH 30 FEET OF THE NORTHWEST QUARTER OF SECTION 33, TOWNSHIP 37 NORTH, RANGE 9 EAST OF THE THIRD PRINCIPAL MERIDIAN, WILL COUNTY, ILLINOIS. PIN #01-33-100-006.

Parcel #7: THE WEST 50 FEET OF THE SOUTH 670 FEET OF THE NORTHEAST QUARTER OF SECTION 33, TOWNSHIP 37 NORTH, RANGE 9 EAST OF THE THIRD PRINCIPAL MERIDIAN. PIN #01-33-200-002.

Parcel #8: THE WEST 160.00 FEET OF THE SOUTHWEST QUARTER OF THE SOUTHEAST QUARTER OF SECTION 8, TOWNSHIP 36 NORTH, RANGE 9 EAST OF THE THIRD PRINCIPAL MERIDIAN, (EXCEPTING THEREFROM THAT PART CONVEYED FOR ROADWAY PURPOSES BY DOCUMENT NUM-

BER 484643, RECORDED APRIL 23, 1935), IN WILL COUNTY, ILLINOIS. PIN #03-08-400-006.

P.A. 94–1055, Art. 25, § 25–7–103.144, eff. Jan. 1, 2007.

30/25–7–103.145. Quick-take; City of Champaign and Champaign County

§ 25–7–103.145. Quick-take; City of Champaign and Champaign County. Quick-take proceedings under Article 20 may be used to acquire real property, including fee simple and temporary and permanent easements, for the Olympian Drive construction and reconstruction project for a period of 12 months after the effective date of this amendatory Act of the 92nd General Assembly by the City of Champaign or by the County of Champaign for acquisition of any portion of the following described property:

Land lying within a corridor bounded by a line 200 feet on either side of the existing line of Olympian Drive (also known as TR151) between Mattis Avenue and Market Avenue in Hensley Township in Champaign County; and also land lying within a corridor bounded by a line 200 feet on either side of the center line of Mattis Avenue, Farber Drive, Prospect Avenue, Neil Street (extended), and Market Street for a distance of 1,000 feet north and south of the right-of-way lines of Olympian Drive on each of the named roadways, all located within Hensley Township in Champaign County.

P.A. 94–1055, Art. 25, § 25–7–103.145, eff. Jan. 1, 2007.

30/25–7–103.146. Quick-take; Village of Plainfield

§ 25–7–103.146. Quick-take; Village of Plainfield. Quick-take proceedings under Article 20 may be used by the Village of Plainfield for a period of 12 months after the effective date of this amendatory Act of the 92nd General Assembly to acquire any portion of the following described property for a 30-foot sanitary sewer easement:

THAT PART OF THE FRACTIONAL SOUTHEAST QUARTER OF FRACTIONAL SECTION 8, & TOWNSHIP 36 NORTH, RANGE 9 EAST OF THE THIRD PRINCIPAL MERIDIAN, LYING NORTH OF THE INDIAN BOUNDARY LINE, DESCRIBED AS COMMENCING AT THE SOUTHWEST CORNER OF SAID SOUTHEAST QUARTER; THENCE SOUTH 89 DEGREES 35 MINUTES 10 SECONDS EAST, ON SAID SOUTH LINE, 1941.46 FEET, TO THE WEST LINE OF PARCEL A PER CONDEMNATION CASE W66G730H; THENCE NORTH 01 DEGREE 06 MINUTES 43 SECONDS WEST, ON SAID WEST LINE, 61.62 FEET, TO THE NORTHERLY RIGHT-OF-WAY LINE OF ILLINOIS ROUTE 126. PER DOCUMENT NO. 484643, FOR THE POINT OF BEGINNING; THENCE CONTINUING NORTH 01 DEGREE 06 MINUTES 43 SECONDS WEST, 30.00 FEET, TO A POINT 30.00 FEET NORTH OF, AS MEASURED PERPENDICULAR TO, SAID NORTH RIGHT-OF-WAY; THENCE SOUTH 89 DEGREES 29 MINUTES 41 SECONDS WEST, PARALLEL WITH SAID NORTH RIGHT-OF-WAY, 482.39 FEET, TO A POINT 30.00 FEET NORTH OF AN ANGLE POINT IN SAID RIGHT-OF-WAY; THENCE NORTH 89 DEGREES 55 MINUTES 28 SECONDS WEST, PARALLEL WITH SAID NORTH RIGHT-OF-WAY, 1297.00 FEET, TO THE EAST LINE OF THE WEST 160.00 FEET OF THE SOUTHWEST QUARTER OF SAID SOUTHEAST QUARTER; THENCE SOUTH 00 DEGREES 11 MINUTES 55 SECONDS WEST, ON SAID EAST LINE, 30.00 FEET, TO THE NORTH RIGHT-OF-WAY AFORESAID; THENCE SOUTH 89 DEGREES 55 MINUTES 28 SECONDS EAST, ON SAID NORTH RIGHT-OF-WAY, 1297.22 FEET, TO AN ANGLE POINT IN SAID RIGHT-OF-WAY; THENCE NORTH 89 DEGREES 29 MINUTES 41 SECONDS EAST, ON SAID NORTH RIGHT-OF-WAY, 482.86 FEET, TO THE POINT OF BEGINNING, ALL IN WILL COUNTY, ILLINOIS. PIN NO. 03-08-400-005.

P.A. 94–1055, Art. 25, § 25–7–103.146, eff. Jan. 1, 2007.

30/25–7–103.147. Quick-take; City of West Chicago

§ 25–7–103.147. Quick-take; City of West Chicago. Quick-take proceedings under Article 20 may be used for a period of 12 months after the effective date of this amendatory Act of the 92nd General Assembly by the City of West Chicago for the acquisition of the following described property for the purpose of constructing a water treatment plant:

Lots 1 and 2 in Owen Larson's subdivision, of part of the northwest ¼ of Section 5, Township 39 North, Range 9, East of the Third Principal Meridian, According to the Plat thereof Recorded November 10, 1992 as Document R92-217425, in DuPage County, Illinois. Permanent Parcel Numbers 04-05-200-036 and 04-05-200-037.

P.A. 94–1055, Art. 25, § 25–7–103.147, eff. Jan. 1, 2007.

30/25–7–103.148. Quick-take; Village of Melrose Park

§ 25–7–103.148. Quick-take; Village of Melrose Park. Quick-take proceedings under Article 20 may be used for a period of 12 months after the effective date of this amendatory Act of the 92nd General Assembly by the Village of Melrose Park for the acquisition of the following described property for the purpose of constructing a parking facility and training facility for use by the Village of Melrose Park Fire Prevention Bureau and Fire Station:

LOT 8 (EXCEPT THE NORTH 51.0 FEET THEREOF) IN HEATH'S RESUBDIVISION OF

LOTS H, K, R AND S OF BLOCK 7 IN HENRY SOFFEL'S THIRD ADDITION TO MELROSE PARK IN THE EAST ½ OF SECTION 4, TOWNSHIP 39 NORTH, RANGE 12, EAST OF THE THIRD PRINCIPAL MERIDIAN, IN COOK COUNTY, ILLINOIS. REAL ESTATE TAX NUMBER 15-04-303-058.

P.A. 94–1055, Art. 25, § 25–7–103.148, eff. Jan. 1, 2007.

30/25–7–103.149.   Quick-take; O'Hare Modernization Program purposes

§ 25–7–103.149. Quick-take; O'Hare Modernization Program purposes. Quick-take proceedings under Article 20 may be used by the City of Chicago for the purpose of acquiring property within the area bounded on the north, between Carmen Drive and the Union Pacific/Canadian Pacific Railroad, by Old Higgins Road, and between Old Higgins Road and Touhy Avenue, by the Union Pacific/Canadian Pacific Railroad, and east of the Union Pacific/Canadian Pacific Railroad by the northern boundary of O'Hare existing on January 1, 2003; on the east by the eastern boundary of O'Hare existing on January 1, 2003; on the southeast by the southeastern boundary of O'Hare existing on January 1, 2003; on the south between the eastern boundary of O'Hare and the Union Pacific Railroad by the southern boundary of O'Hare existing on January 1, 2003; on the south, between the Union Pacific Railroad and the east boundary of York Road by the Canadian Pacific railroad yard; on the west, between the Canadian Pacific Railroad Yard and the railroad spur intersecting York Road between Arthur and Pratt Avenues, by the east boundary of York Road; and on the northwest, between York Road and the Union Pacific/Canadian Pacific Railroad, by the railroad spur, and between the railroad spur and the point at which the extended eastern boundary of Carmen Drive intersects the Union Pacific/Canadian Pacific Railroad, by the Union Pacific/Canadian Pacific Railroad, and between the Union Pacific/Canadian Pacific Railroad and Old Higgins Road, by the extended eastern boundary of Carmen Drive and by Carmen Drive, for the O'Hare Modernization Program as defined in Section 10 of the O'Hare Modernization Act.

P.A. 94–1055, Art. 25, § 25–7–103.149, eff. Jan. 1, 2007.

30/25–7–103.150.   Renumbered as § 25–5–10 by P.A. 95–876, § 370, eff. Aug. 21, 2008

ARTICLE 90. MISCELLANEOUS PROVISIONS

30/90–5–5.   Applicability

§ 90–5–5. Applicability. This Act applies only to complaints to condemn that are filed on or after its effective date.

P.A. 94–1055, Art. 90, § 90–5–5, eff. Jan. 1, 2007.

30/90–5–10.   Continuation of prior statutes

§ 90–5–10. Continuation of prior statutes. The provisions of this Act, insofar as they are the same or substantially the same as those of any prior statute, shall be construed as a continuation of that prior statute and not as a new enactment, except as those provisions may be limited by other provisions of this Act.

P.A. 94–1055, Art. 90, § 90–5–10, eff. Jan. 1, 2007.

30/90–5–15.   Strict construction

§ 90–5–15. Strict construction. This Act shall be strictly construed as a limitation on the exercise of eminent domain powers.

P.A. 94–1055, Art. 90, § 90–5–15, eff. Jan. 1, 2007.

30/90–5–20.   Home rule

§ 90–5–20. Home rule. The authorization of the use of eminent domain proceedings to take or damage property is an exclusive power and function of the State. No condemning authority, including a home rule unit, may exercise the power of eminent domain otherwise than as provided in this Act. This Act is a denial and limitation of home rule powers and functions under subsection (h) of Section 6 of Article VII of the Illinois Constitution.

P.A. 94–1055, Art. 90, § 90–5–20, eff. Jan. 1, 2007.

30/90–5–90.   Formatting in Senate Bill 3086

§ 90–5–90. Formatting in Senate Bill 3086. Most of the provisions of Articles 10, 20, and 25 of this Act are derived from Article VII of the Code of Civil Procedure. In the Bill creating this Act, the provisions so derived have been shown in amendatory format, that is, (i) the changes made to those provisions, as they existed in the Code of Civil Procedure on the date that the Bill was prepared, have been shown with striking and underscoring in the manner commonly used in amendatory Acts; (ii) the Section of the Code of Civil Procedure from which the material is derived is shown in the "was" citation at the beginning of the Section; and (iii) the Source information from the Code of Civil Procedure has been retained at the end of the Section. Sections not shown in amendatory format are new.

P.A. 94–1055, Art. 90, § 90–5–90, eff. Jan. 1, 2007.

ARTICLE 99. EFFECTIVE DATE

30/99–5–5. Effective date

§ 99–5–5. Effective date. This Act takes effect on January 1, 2007.

P.A. 94–1055, Art. 99, § 99–5–5, eff. Jan. 1, 2007.

ACT 35.   UNIFORM INTERSTATE DEPOSITIONS AND DISCOVERY ACT

35/1.   Short title

§ 1.   Short title.   This Act may be cited as the Uniform Interstate Depositions and Discovery Act.

P.A. 99–79, § 1, eff. Jan. 1, 2016.

An Act concerning civil law. P.A. 99–79, approved July 20, 2015, effective Jan. 1, 2016.

35/2.   Definitions

§ 2.   Definitions.   In this Act:

(1) "Foreign jurisdiction" means a state other than this State.

(2) "Foreign subpoena" means a subpoena issued under authority of a court of record of a foreign jurisdiction.

(3) "Person" means an individual, corporation, business trust, estate, trust, partnership, limited liability company, association, joint venture, public corporation, government, or governmental subdivision, agency or instrumentality, or any other legal or commercial entity.

(4) "State" means a state of the United States, the District of Columbia, Puerto Rico, the United States Virgin Islands, a federally recognized Indian tribe, or any territory or insular possession subject to the jurisdiction of the United States.

(5) "Subpoena" means a document, however denominated, issued under authority of a court of record requiring a person to:

(A) attend and give testimony at a deposition;

(B) produce and permit inspection and copying of designated books, documents, records, electronically stored information, or tangible things in the possession, custody, or control of the person; or

(C) permit inspection of premises under the control of the person.

P.A. 99–79, § 2, eff. Jan. 1, 2016.

35/3.   Issuance of subpoena

§ 3.   Issuance of subpoena.

(a) To request issuance of a subpoena under this Section, a party must submit a foreign subpoena to a clerk of court in the county in which discovery is sought to be conducted in this State. A request for the issuance of a subpoena under this Act does not constitute an appearance in the courts of this State.

(b) When a party submits a foreign subpoena to a clerk of court in this State, the clerk, in accordance with that court's procedure, shall promptly issue a subpoena for service upon the person to which the foreign subpoena is directed.

(c) A subpoena under subsection (b) must:

(A) incorporate the terms used in the foreign subpoena; and

(B) contain or be accompanied by the names, addresses, and telephone numbers of all counsel of record in the proceeding to which the subpoena relates and of any party not represented by counsel.

P.A. 99–79, § 3, eff. Jan. 1, 2016.

35/4.   Service of subpoena

§ 4.   Service of subpoena.   A subpoena issued by a clerk of court under Section 3 must be served in compliance with Illinois Supreme Court Rules 204 and 237 and Section 2–1101 of the Code of Civil Procedure.

P.A. 99–79, § 4, eff. Jan. 1, 2016.

35/5.   Deposition, production, and inspection

§ 5.   Deposition, production, and inspection.   With respect to depositions, production of documents or other tangible items, or inspections of premises, Illinois Supreme Court Rules 204 and 237 and Section 2–1101 of the Code of Civil Procedure apply to subpoenas issued under Section 3.

P.A. 99–79, § 5, eff. Jan. 1, 2016.

35/6.   Application to court

§ 6.   Application to court.   An application to the court for a protective order or to enforce, quash, or modify a subpoena issued by a clerk of court under

Section 3 must comply with the rules or statutes of this State and be submitted to the court in the county in which discovery is to be conducted.

P.A. 99–79, § 6, eff. Jan. 1, 2016.

35/7. Uniformity of application and construction

§ 7. Uniformity of application and construction. In applying and construing this uniform Act, consideration must be given to the need to promote uniformity of the law with respect to its subject matter among states that enact it.

P.A. 99–79, § 7, eff. Jan. 1, 2016.

35/8. Application to pending actions

§ 8. Application to pending actions. This Act applies to requests for discovery in cases pending on the effective date of this Act.

P.A. 99–79, § 8, eff. Jan. 1, 2016.

35/9. Blank

§ 9. (Blank).

P.A. 99–79, § 9, eff. Jan. 1, 2016.

35/9.5. Limitation

§ 9.5. Limitation. A subpoena issued under this Act may not require compliance outside a deponent's county of residence in the State of Illinois.

P.A. 99–79, § 9.5, eff. Jan. 1, 2016.

ACT 105. CHOICE OF LAW AND FORUM ACT

105/5–1. Short title

§ 5–1. Short title. This Article may be cited as the Choice of Law and Forum Act.

P.A. 90–421, Art. 5, § 5–1, eff. Jan. 1, 1998.

An Act concerning business. P.A. 90–421, approved Aug. 15, 1997, eff. Jan. 1, 1998.

105/5–5. Choice of law

§ 5–5. Choice of law. The parties to any contract, agreement, or undertaking, contingent or otherwise, in consideration of or relating to any obligation arising out of a transaction covering in the aggregate not less than $250,000, including a transaction otherwise covered by subsection (1) of Section 1–105 of the Uniform Commercial Code,[1] may agree that the law of this State shall govern their rights and duties in whole or in part, whether or not the contract, agreement, or undertaking bears a reasonable relation to this State. This Section shall not apply to any contract, agreement, or undertaking (i) for labor or personal services, (ii) relating to any transaction for personal, family, or household services, or (iii) to the extent provided to the contrary in subsection (2) of Section 1–105 of the Uniform Commercial Code. Nothing contained in this Section shall be construed to limit or deny the en-forcement of any provision respecting choice of law in any other contract, agreement, or undertaking.

P.A. 90–421, Art. 5, § 5–5, eff. Jan. 1, 1998.

[1] 810 ILCS 5/1–105.

105/5–10. Choice of forum

§ 5–10. Choice of forum. Any person may maintain an action or proceeding against a foreign corporation, non-resident, or foreign state if the action or proceeding arises out of or relates to any contract, agreement, or undertaking for which a choice of Illinois law has been made in whole or in part pursuant to Section 5–5 and that (i) is a contract, agreement, or undertaking, contingent or otherwise, in consideration of or relating to any obligation arising out of a transaction covering in the aggregate not less than $500,000 and (ii) contains a provision or provisions under which the foreign corporation or non-resident agrees to submit to the jurisdiction of the courts of this State. Nothing contained in this Section shall be construed to affect the enforcement of any provision respecting choice of forum in any contract, agreement, or under-taking.

P.A. 90–421, Art. 5, § 5–10, eff. Jan. 1, 1998.

105/99–5. Effective date

§ 99–5. Effective date. This Act takes effect January 1, 1998.

P.A. 90–421, Art. 99, § 99–5, eff. Jan. 1, 1998.

ACT 110. CITIZEN PARTICIPATION ACT

110/1. Short title

§ 1. Short title. This Act may be cited as the Citizen Participation Act.

P.A. 95–506, § 1, eff. Aug. 28, 2007.

An Act concerning citizen participation. P.A. 95–506, approved and effective August 28, 2007.

110/5. Public policy

§ 5. Public policy. Pursuant to the fundamental philosophy of the American constitutional form of government, it is declared to be the public policy of the State of Illinois that the constitutional rights of citizens and organizations to be involved and participate freely in the process of government must be encouraged and safeguarded with great diligence. The information, reports, opinions, claims, arguments, and other expressions provided by citizens are vital to effective law enforcement, the operation of government, the making of public policy and decisions, and the continuation of representative democracy. The laws, courts, and other agencies of this State must provide the utmost protection for the free exercise of these rights of petition, speech, association, and government participation.

Civil actions for money damages have been filed against citizens and organizations of this State as a result of their valid exercise of their constitutional rights to petition, speak freely, associate freely, and otherwise participate in and communicate with government. There has been a disturbing increase in lawsuits termed "Strategic Lawsuits Against Public Participation" in government or "SLAPPs" as they are popularly called.

The threat of SLAPPs significantly chills and diminishes citizen participation in government, voluntary public service, and the exercise of these important constitutional rights. This abuse of the judicial process can and has been used as a means of intimidating, harassing, or punishing citizens and organizations for involving themselves in public affairs.

It is in the public interest and it is the purpose of this Act to strike a balance between the rights of persons to file lawsuits for injury and the constitutional rights of persons to petition, speak freely, associate freely, and otherwise participate in government; to protect and encourage public participation in government to the maximum extent permitted by law; to establish an efficient process for identification and adjudication of SLAPPs; and to provide for attorney's fees and costs to prevailing movants.

P.A. 95–506, § 5, eff. Aug. 28, 2007.

110/10. Definitions

§ 10. Definitions. In this Act:

"Government" includes a branch, department, agency, instrumentality, official, employee, agent, or other person acting under color of law of the United States, a state, a subdivision of a state, or another public authority including the electorate.

"Person" includes any individual, corporation, association, organization, partnership, 2 or more persons having a joint or common interest, or other legal entity.

"Judicial claim" or "claim" include any lawsuit, cause of action, claim, cross-claim, counterclaim, or other judicial pleading or filing alleging injury.

"Motion" includes any motion to dismiss, for summary judgment, or to strike, or any other judicial pleading filed to dispose of a judicial claim.

"Moving party" means any person on whose behalf a motion described in subsection (a) of Section 20 is filed seeking dismissal of a judicial claim.

"Responding party" means any person against whom a motion described in subsection (a) of Section 20 is filed.

P.A. 95–506, § 10, eff. Aug. 28, 2007.

110/15. Applicability

§ 15. Applicability. This Act applies to any motion to dispose of a claim in a judicial proceeding on the grounds that the claim is based on, relates to, or is in response to any act or acts of the moving party in furtherance of the moving party's rights of petition, speech, association, or to otherwise participate in government.

Acts in furtherance of the constitutional rights to petition, speech, association, and participation in government are immune from liability, regardless of intent or purpose, except when not genuinely aimed at procuring favorable government action, result, or outcome.

P.A. 95–506, § 15, eff. Aug. 28, 2007.

110/20. Motion procedure and standards

§ 20. Motion procedure and standards.

(a) On the filing of any motion as described in Section 15, a hearing and decision on the motion must occur within 90 days after notice of the motion is given to the respondent. An appellate court shall expedite any appeal or other writ, whether interlocutory or not, from a trial court order denying that motion or from a trial court's failure to rule on that motion within 90 days after that trial court order or failure to rule.

(b) Discovery shall be suspended pending a decision on the motion. However, discovery may be taken, upon leave of court for good cause shown, on the issue of whether the movants acts are not immunized from, or are not in furtherance of acts immunized from, liability by this Act.

(c) The court shall grant the motion and dismiss the judicial claim unless the court finds that the responding party has produced clear and convincing evidence that the acts of the moving party are not immunized from, or are not in furtherance of acts immunized from, liability by this Act.

P.A. 95–506, § 20, eff. Aug. 28, 2007.

110/25. Attorney's fees and costs

§ 25. Attorney's fees and costs. The court shall award a moving party who prevails in a motion under this Act reasonable attorney's fees and costs incurred in connection with the motion.

P.A. 95–506, § 25, eff. Aug. 28, 2007.

110/30. Construction of Act

§ 30. Construction of Act.

(a) Nothing in this Act shall limit or preclude any rights the moving party may have under any other constitutional, statutory, case or common law, or rule provisions.

(b) This Act shall be construed liberally to effectuate its purposes and intent fully.

P.A. 95–506, § 30, eff. Aug. 28, 2007.

110/35. Severability

§ 35. Severability. The provisions of this Act are severable under Section 1.31 of the Statute on Statutes.

P.A. 95–506, § 35, eff. Aug. 28, 2007.

110/99. Effective date

§ 99. Effective date. This Act takes effect upon becoming law.

P.A. 95–506, § 99, eff. Aug. 28, 2007.

COURT RULES

ILLINOIS SUPREME COURT RULES

Including Amendments Received Through April 1, 2016

Effective January 1, 1967

Explanatory Notes

The Supreme Court of Illinois on November 28, 1966, adopted Revised Supreme Court Rules governing trial and appellate procedure in both civil and criminal proceedings, effective January 1, 1967. The Revised Rules are incorporated herein.

The Supreme Court of Illinois on October 26, 1967, adopted Revised Rules relating to procedures in traffic cases, quasi-criminal cases and certain misdemeanors, effective January 1, 1968. These Rules are incorporated as Rule 501 et seq. They are designated as Article V of the Supreme Court Rules, which were adopted on November 8, 1966.

ARTICLE I.   GENERAL RULES

CODE OF JUDICIAL CONDUCT

MANDATORY ARBITRATION

EXPEDITED CHILD SUPPORT RULES

Rule 1. Applicability

General rules apply to both civil and criminal proceedings. The rules on proceedings in the trial court, together with the Civil Practice Law [1] and the Code of Criminal Procedure,[2] shall govern all proceedings in the trial court, except to the extent that the procedure in a particular kind of action is regulated by a statute other than the Civil Practice Law. The rules on appeals shall govern all appeals.

Amended Oct. 21, 1969, eff. Jan. 1, 1970; Feb. 19, 1982, eff. April 1, 1982; May 28, 1982; July 1, 1982.

Formerly Ill.Rev.Stat.1991, ch. 110A, ¶ 1.

[1] 735 ILCS 5/2–101 et seq.
[2] 725 ILCS 5/100–1 et seq.

Committee Comments
(Revised July 1, 1971)

This rule changed former Rule 1, in effect until January 1, 1967, which provided that the rules applied only to civil proceedings unless the rules or their context indicated otherwise. In the revised rules, separate articles contain the rules applicable to civil proceedings (articles II and III) and those applicable to criminal proceedings (articles IV and VI). Certain general provisions (article I) apply to both.

The second sentence of Rule 1 establishes for trial court proceedings the same standard for determining applicability that appears in section 1 of the Civil Practice Act.

The third sentence was revised in 1969 when the appeals rules were broadened to cover all appeals. The authority for supersedure of inconsistent statutes is found in the provision of the Judicial Article, effective January 1, 1964 (former Illinois Const. art. VI, § 7), repeated in the new constitution effective July 1, 1971 (art. VI, § 16), that directs the Supreme Court to "provide by rule for expeditious and inexpensive appeals." See Committee Comments to Civil Appeals Rules and Rule 601, *infra.*

Supersedure by the criminal appeals rules (Rule 601 et seq.) of the appeals provisions of the Code of Criminal Procedure of 1963 is covered by Rule 601.

The effective date of the revised rules and their applicability to pending proceedings are covered in the order adopting the rules.

Rule 2. Construction

(a) Standards. These rules are to be construed in accordance with the appropriate provisions of the Statute on Statutes (5 ILCS 70/0.01 *et seq.*), and in accordance with the standards stated in section 1–106 of the Code of Civil Procedure (735 ILCS 5/1–106).

(b) Definitions. The following meanings are to be given terms used in these rules:

(1) "Judge" also includes associate judge and justice.

(2) "Judgment" also includes decree, determination, decision, order, or portion thereof.

(3) "Document" means pleading, motion, notice, affidavit, memorandum, brief, petition, or other document or combination of documents required or permitted to be filed.

Amended effective July 1, 1971; May 28, 1982, effective July 1, 1982; May 30, 2008, effective immediately; Jan. 4, 2013, eff. immediately.

Formerly Ill.Rev.Stat.1991, ch. 110A, ¶ 2.

Committee Comments
(Revised July 1, 1971)

This rule was adopted effective January 1, 1967.

Paragraph (a) makes it clear that the same principles that govern the construction of statutes are applicable to the rules.

Paragraph (b) defines terms that appear frequently in the rules. Like the article VI of the Illinois Constitution the rules use the single word "judgment," instead of "judgment, decree," etc.

Subparagraph (b)(1) was amended in 1971 to delete the reference to "magistrate," consistent with the abolition of the office of magistrate by the Illinois Constitution of 1970.

Rule 3. Rulemaking Procedures

(a) Purpose and Applicability.

(1) These procedures are adopted to provide for the orderly and timely review of proposed rules and proposed amendments to existing rules of the Supreme Court; to provide an opportunity for comments and suggestions by the public, the bench, and the bar; to aid the Supreme Court in discharging its rulemaking responsibilities; to make a public record of all such proposals; and to provide for public access to an annual report concerning such proposals.

(2) The Supreme Court reserves the prerogative of departing from the procedures of this rule. An order of the Supreme Court adopting any rule or amendment shall constitute an order modifying these procedures to the extent, if any, they have not been complied with in respect to that proposal.

(b) Supreme Court Rules Committee. There shall be a Rules Committee which shall be appointed by the Supreme Court. The Administrative Office of the Illinois Courts shall serve as secretary of the Rules Committee. The Rules Committee shall have the following responsibilities:

(1) To implement rulemaking procedures, as provided in paragraph (d) of this rule, for proposed rules or amendments to existing rules received from the Administrative Office.

(2) To periodically review rules in areas which no other committee is specifically charged with the responsibility for reviewing to ensure that such rules facilitate the administration of justice.

(3) To conduct public hearings and submit the annual report as required by administrative order of the Supreme Court. The annual report shall be a public record.

(c) Initiation of Proposal.

Proposed rules and proposed amendments to existing rules of the Supreme Court should be forwarded to the Administrative Office of the Illinois Courts, c/o Secretary—Supreme Court Rules Committee, 222 N. LaSalle Street, 13th Floor, Chicago, Illinois 60601. All proposals shall offer specific language for the proposed rule or amendment, as well as a concise explanation of the proposal.

(d) Procedures for Proposed Rules and Rule Amendments.

(1) If the substance of a proposal received under paragraph (c) of this rule is within the scope of a Supreme Court committee or Judicial Conference committee, the Administrative Office shall forward the proposal to the appropriate committee for review and recommendation.

The Administrative Office also shall forward a copy of the proposal to the Rules Committee, along with notice of the Supreme Court or Judicial Conference committee to which the proposal has been forwarded.

The Rules Committee shall forward a copy of the proposal to the Clerk of the Supreme Court where it will be given a number and placed upon the docket of the Clerk of the Supreme Court.

The committee to which the proposal has been forwarded shall review the proposal for content and style. Within 12 months of the transmission of the proposal from the Administrative Office, the committee to which the proposal has been forwarded shall advise the Administrative Office whether the proposal is recommended for adoption by the Supreme Court. If the proposal is recommended for adoption, the Rules Committee shall place the proposal on the agenda for the next public hearing. In its annual report to the Supreme Court, the Rules Committee shall report the docket number, the content of the proposal, any report submitted by the Supreme Court committee or Judicial Conference committee (including a minority report), the response to the proposal, any comments or revisions submitted by the Supreme Court committee or Judicial Conference committee, the Rules Committee's recommendation, and any alternative proposal the Rules Committee developed in response to public comment.

If the committee to which the proposal has been forwarded does not recommend the proposal for adoption by the Supreme Court, the Rules Committee shall not place the proposal on the agenda for public hearing, but shall report the nonrecommended status to the Clerk of the Supreme Court and the Supreme Court in its annual report.

(2) If the substance of a proposal received under paragraph (c) is in an area where no other committee is specifically charged with responsibility, the Administrative Office shall forward the proposal to the Rules Committee for review of content and style.

The Rules Committee shall forward a copy of the proposal to the Clerk of the Supreme Court where it will be given a number and placed upon the docket of the Clerk of the Supreme Court. If, after review, the Rules Committee determines that the proposal is recommended for adoption by the Supreme Court, the Rules Committee shall place the proposal on the agenda for the next public hearing. In its annual report to the Supreme Court, the Rules Committee shall report the docket number, the content of the proposal, the response to the proposal, the Rules Committee's recommendation, and any alternative proposal the Rules Committee developed in response to public comment.

If the proposal submitted does not have substantial merit, is duplicative of pending proposals, or is not within the Supreme Court's rulemaking authority, the Rules Committee shall not place the proposal on the agenda for public hearing. However, the Rules Committee shall report the proposal as not recommended in its annual report to the Supreme Court.

(3) If a proposed rule or an amendment to an existing rule is submitted under paragraph (c) by a Supreme Court committee or a Judicial Conference committee, the Administrative Office shall forward the proposal to the Rules Committee. The Rules Committee shall forward a copy of the proposal to the Clerk of the Supreme Court where it will be given a number and placed upon the docket of the Clerk of the Supreme Court. The Rules Committee shall not review the proposal.

The Rules Committee shall place the proposal on the agenda for the next public hearing. In its annual report to the Supreme Court, the Rules Committee shall report the docket number, the content of the proposal, any report submitted by the Supreme Court committee or Judicial Conference committee (including a minority report), the response to the proposal, any comments or revisions submitted by the Supreme Court committee or Judicial Conference committee,

the Rules Committee's recommendation, and any alternative proposal the Rules Committee developed in response to public comment.

(e) Responsibilities of Other Committees. Each committee appointed by the Supreme Court, other than the Rules Committee, shall have the following responsibilities:

(1) To periodically review the entire body of rules for which the Supreme Court has indicated the committee is responsible to ensure that those rules continue to facilitate the administration of justice.

(2) To review proposed amendments to existing rules or proposals for new rules transmitted to the committee pursuant to paragraph (c) of this rule. Within 12 months of the transmission of the proposal from the Administrative Office, the committee shall advise the Administrative Office whether the proposal is recommended or not recommended for adoption by the Supreme Court.

If the committee determines that a proposal that has been forwarded to it by the Administrative Office should be adopted, it shall so inform the Administrative Office and provide the Administrative Office with the original proposal and a statement of the committee's reasoning.

If the committee determines that a proposal that has been forwarded to it by the Administrative Office should not be adopted, it shall so inform the Administrative Office and provide the Administrative Office with the original proposal and a statement of the committee's reasoning.

(3) To designate the committee chair, or another member, to represent the committee at any Rules Committee public hearing where a proposal recommended by the committee is scheduled to be held out for public comment. The committee chair, or his or her designee, may sit with the Rules Committee for purposes of answering questions or addressing testimony from individuals offering public comment on the committee's proposal.

(4) Nothing in this rule shall preclude a Supreme Court or Judicial Conference committee from holding a public hearing independently of the Rules Committee, with prior approval of the Supreme Court.

(f) Submissions Other Than Annual Report. When the Rules Committee makes a submission of a proposed rule or amendment separate from its annual report, the committee shall, to the degree practicable, comply with the content requirements of the Supreme Court's administrative order concerning notice and hearing and shall accompany the submission with a statement of:

(1) its reasons for believing that the Court should take action on its proposal prior to the time for action on the next annual submission, and

(2) describe the steps taken by the committee to comply with the Supreme Court's administrative order

regarding public notice, opportunity for comment, and public hearing.

(g) Distribution of New Rules or Amendments. Following the adoption of new rules or amendments, the Clerk of the Supreme Court shall promptly cause copies thereof to be distributed.

(h) Effective Date of Rule Changes. The effective date of all new rules or amendments shall be as ordered by the Supreme Court. If an effective date is not ordered, the new rule or amendment shall take effect on the following July 1.

Adopted Sept. 28, 1994, eff. Oct. 1, 1994. Amended Dec. 3, 1997, eff. Jan. 1, 1998; Oct. 5, 2000, eff. Nov. 1, 2000; May 24, 2006, eff. immediately; amended Mar. 22, 2010, eff. immediately.

Formerly Ill.Rev.Stat.1991, ch. 110A, ¶ 3.

IN THE
SUPREME COURT
OF
THE STATE OF ILLINOIS
MR No. 10549.
ADMINISTRATIVE ORDER

Administrative Order adopted September 28, 1994, effective October 1, 1994; Order amended December 3, 1997, effective January 1, 1998; October 5, 2000, effective November 1, 2000.

(a) Public Meetings.

(1) Except as otherwise provided in Rule 3, no rule shall be presented to the Court for adoption without first having been held out for public comment by the bench, bar and public at a public meeting of the Rules Committee.

(2) All proposals for which the Rules Committee has completed its style and content review and those proposals submitted to the Rules Committee by other Supreme Court committees and Judicial Conference committees recommended for adoption by the Supreme Court shall be considered at the next public meeting. Any proposal on which the Rules Committee has not completed its content review or any proposal which a Supreme Court committee or Judicial Conference committee has not forwarded to the Rules Committee for placement on the public meeting agenda will not be considered at the next public meeting.

(3) A public hearing may be scheduled when either the significance of a particular proposal or the number of proposals ready for public comment would justify holding such a hearing. At least 60 days prior to the date designated for the public hearing, the Rules Committee shall cause notice of the public meeting and an invitation for comments to be distributed by the most economical means, including notification through the Illinois Court's electronic messaging services, such as list mail or Twitter broadcasts. Additionally, a hard copy of the notice shall be mailed to each clerk of the court to be posted in a conspicuous place. The text of the proposed rules or amendments shall be posted on the Court's Web site, with hard copies available by request from the Administrative Office of the Illinois Courts.

(4) Each committee of the Supreme Court may within 21 days following the public meeting respond to public comments received at the meeting by submitting to the Rules Committee:

(i) any revision to a proposal that was recommended by the committee, or

(ii) responsive comments of the committee.

(5) A committee of the Judicial Conference may within 21 days following the public meeting respond to public comments received at the meeting in the following manner. The committee may submit to the Conference (or the Executive Committee acting in its stead) for approval any revision to a proposal that was recommended by the committee or any responsive comment. The revised rule or response to public comments shall be included in the annual report on proposed rules and amendments unless the Conference instructs otherwise within 21 days of its receipt of the submission.

(b) Annual Report on Proposed Rules and Amendments

(1) The Rules Committee shall submit its annual report on rules to the Chief Justice and file it with the Clerk of the Supreme Court.

(2) The report shall include for each proposal: the docket number, the content of the proposal, any report submitted by the Supreme Court committee or Judicial Conference committee (if applicable) including any minority report, the response to the proposal, any comments or revisions submitted by the Supreme Court committee or Judicial Conference committee (if applicable), the Rules Committee's recommendation, and any alternative proposal the Rules Committee developed in response to public comment.

(3) The annual report shall be a public record.

(4) Whenever a lengthy rule or amendment is recommended, the Rules Committee shall prepare and submit a summary thereof for distribution. Whenever the Administrative Office distributes such a summary, the Office shall make provision for supplying the full text of the recommended rule or amendment to any interested person upon reasonable request.

Adopted Sept. 28, 1994, eff. Oct. 1, 1994. Amended Dec. 3, 1997, eff. Jan. 1, 1998; Oct. 5, 2000, eff. Nov. 1, 2000; amended Mar. 22, 2010, eff. immediately.

Rules 4, 5. Reserved

Rule 6. Citations

Citation of Illinois cases filed prior to July 1, 2011, and published in the Illinois Official Reports shall be to the Official Reports, but the citation to the North Eastern Reporter and/or the Illinois Decisions may be added. For Illinois cases filed on or after July 1, 2011, and for any case not published in the Illinois Official Reports prior to that date and for which a public-domain citation has been assigned, the public-domain citation shall be given and, where appropriate, pinpoint citations to paragraph numbers shall be given; a citation to the North Eastern Reporter and/or the Illinois Decisions may be added but is not required. Citation of cases from other jurisdictions that do not utilize a public-domain citation shall include the date and may be to either the official state reports or the National Reporter System, or both. If only the National Reporter System citation is used, the court rendering the decision shall also be identified. For other jurisdictions that have adopted a public-domain system of citation, that citation shall be given along with, where appropriate, pinpoint citations to paragraph numbers; a parallel citation to an additional case reporter may be given but is not required. Textbook citations shall include the date of publication and the edition. Illinois statutes shall generally be cited to the Illinois Compiled Statutes (ILCS) but citations to the session laws of Illinois or to the Illinois Revised Statutes shall be made when appropriate.

Adopted eff. Jan. 20, 1993. Amended May 31, 2011, eff. July 1, 2011.

Commentary

(May 31, 2011)

Background

The system of case citation that has historically prevailed in the United States relies upon the elements of printed case reporters, that is, volume number, case name, beginning and pinpoint page numbers, and year of filing. In Illinois, citations have been made to our state's official reporters (Illinois Reports and Illinois Appellate Reports), with parallel citations to the appropriate West regional reporter (North East Reporter and/or Illinois Decisions) also allowed. But reliance upon printed reports for access to the courts' opinions has diminished with the rise of electronic databases, such as those found on the Court's own Internet website, Westlaw and Lexis–Nexis, and various CD–ROMs. In this state, the Illinois Supreme and Appellate Courts' opinions have been made available on the judiciary's website since 1996. However, the requirement that case citations be made to printed reporters has prevented direct citation of those opinions, even though they are now widely available on various electronic databases.

To remedy this situation, the Illinois Supreme Court has amended Supreme Court Rule 23, and has entered an administrative order in relation to Rule 23, to direct Illinois reviewing courts to assign, at the time of filing, public-domain case designator numbers (*e.g.*, "2011 IL 102345"), as well as internal paragraph numbers, to all opinions and Rule 23 orders filed after July 1, 2011. Further, any opinions that were filed prior to July 1, 2011, but not released for publication until a later date will be assigned a public-domain case designator number and internal paragraph numbers by the Reporter of Decisions. All opinions that have been assigned public-domain case designators and paragraph numbers will be posted to the Illinois judiciary's website.

Additionally, Rule 6 has been amended to require the use of public-domain case citations for all Illinois reviewing court opinions filed or released for publication after July 1, 2011. The amendments to Rules 6 and 23 will thus introduce a new system of case citations to Illinois law based directly on the decisions of the courts. It should be noted, though, that while amended Rule 6 requires a citation to the courts' public-domain numbering and paragraphing scheme in lieu of an Illinois Official Reports citation, the rule continues to allow citations to the unofficial regional reporters.

Citations

A public-domain case designators is unique to each opinion and is comprised of the year of decision, the court abbreviation, and a unique identifier number derived from the docket number. A public-domain citation shall include the designator preceded by the case title and will be in accord with the following examples:

Supreme Court

People v. Doe, 2011 IL 102345

Appellate Court Districts

People v. Doe, 2011 IL App (1st) 101234

People v. Doe, 2011 IL App (2d) 101234

People v. Doe, 2011 IL App (3d) 101234

People v. Doe, 2011 IL App (4th) 101234

People v. Doe, 2011 IL App (5th) 101234

Appellate Court Workers' Compensation Division

Doe v. Illinois Workers' Compensation Comm'n, 2011 IL App (1st) 101234WC

In the above, a citation to *People v. Doe*, 2011 IL 102345, shows *People v. Doe* as the case name; 2011 as the year of decision; the Illinois Supreme Court as the court of decision; and 102345 as the court-assigned identifier number, which, in the Supreme Court, is the docket number and, in the Appellate Court, is the last six digits of the docket number.

Where a subsequent opinion is filed under the same docket number, such as upon reconsideration of the cause after remand, a sequential capital letter will be appended to the unique-identifier number, regardless of the year-designation portion of the citation:

People v. Doe, 2011 IL App (1st) 101236

People v. Doe, 2012 IL App (1st) 101236–B

Orders filed under Illinois Supreme Court Rule 23 will have the letter "U" appended to the unique-identifier number:

People v. Roe, 2011 IL App (5th) 101237–U

Additionally, Illinois reviewing court opinions will include internally numbered paragraphs. Where a pinpoint citation to an opinion is appropriate, the citation shall include the public-domain citation followed by the pinpoint paragraph or paragraphs of the opinion. *E.g.*:

People v. Doe, 2011 IL App (1st) 101234, ¶ 15

People v. Doe, 2011 IL App (1st) 101234, ¶¶ 21–23

People v. Doe, 2011 IL App (1st) 101234, ¶¶ 57, 68

For those opinions filed prior to July 1, 2011, but not released by the filing court for publication until after that date, the Reporter of Decisions office will add internal paragraph numbers, as well as the public-domain designator numbers.

Rules 7 to 9. Reserved

Rule 10. Size of Documents Filed in the Illinois Courts

Except as otherwise provided in these rules, all documents filed in all courts of this State shall be 8½ inches by 11 inches. The court encourages use of recycled paper if the filing is in paper form.

Adopted Jan. 5, 1981, eff. Jan. 1, 1982. Amended June 25, 1990, eff. July 1, 1990; Oct. 24, 2012, eff. Jan. 1, 2013.

Formerly Ill.Rev.Stat.1991, ch. 110A, ¶ 10.

Committee Comments
Rule 10 was added in 1981.

Rule 11. Manner of Serving Documents Other Than Process and Complaint on Parties Not in Default in the Trial and Reviewing Courts

(a) On Whom Made. If a party is represented by an attorney of record, service shall be made upon the attorney. Otherwise service shall be made upon the party.

(b) Method. Documents shall be served by any one of the following alternative methods:

(1) *Personal Service.* Delivering them to the attorney or party personally;

(2) *Delivery to Attorney's Office or Unrepresented Party's Residence.* Leaving them in the office of the attorney with the attorney's clerk, or with a person in charge of the office; or if a party is not represented by counsel, by leaving them at the party's residence with a family member of the age of 13 years or upwards;

(3) *United States Mail.* Depositing them in a United States post office or post office box, enclosed in an envelope, plainly addressed to the attorney at the attorney's business address, or to the party at the party's business address or residence, with postage fully prepaid; or

(4) *Third–Party Commercial Carrier.* Delivering them to a third-party commercial carrier—including deposit in the carrier's pick-up box or drop off with the carrier's designated contractor—enclosed in a package, plainly addressed to the attorney at the attorney's business address, or to the party at the party's business address or residence, with delivery charge fully prepaid;

(5) *Facsimile Transmission.* Transmitting them via facsimile machine to the office of the attorney or party, who has consented to receiving service by facsimile transmission. Briefs filed in reviewing courts shall not be served by facsimile transmission;

(i) A party or attorney electing to serve pleadings by facsimile must include on the certificate of service transmitted the telephone number of the sender's facsimile transmitting device. Use of service by facsimile shall be deemed consent by that party or attorney to receive service by facsimile transmission. Any party may rescind consent of service by facsimile transmission in a case by filing with the court and serving a notice on all parties or their attorneys who have filed appearances that facsimile service will not be accepted. A party or attorney who has rescinded consent to service by facsimile transmission in a case may not serve another party or attorney by facsimile transmission in that case.

(ii) Each page of notices and documents transmitted by facsimile pursuant to this rule should bear the circuit court number, the title of the document, and the page number.

(6) *E–mail Transmission.* Transmitting them via e-mail to all primary and secondary e-mail addresses of record designated by the attorney or unrepresented party in conformance with Rule 131 (d); or

(7) *Electronic In-box.* Transmission through a service provider that provides an electronic in-box for those parties registered to use the service.

(c) Multiple Parties or Attorneys. In cases in which there are two or more plaintiffs or defendants who appear by different attorneys, service of all documents shall be made on the attorney for each of the parties. If one attorney appears for several parties, that attorney is entitled to only one copy of any document served upon the attorney by the opposite side. When more than one attorney appears for a party, service of a copy upon one of them is sufficient.

(d) E–mail Address. An attorney must include on the appearance and on all pleadings filed in court an e-mail address to which documents may be served in conformance with Rule 131(d).

(e) Limited Scope Appearance. After an attorney files a Notice of Limited Scope Appearance in accordance with Rule 13(c)(6), service of all documents shall be made on both the attorney and the party represented on a limited scope basis until: (1) the court enters an order allowing the attorney to withdraw under Rule 13(c) or (2) the attorney's representation automatically terminates under Rule 13(c)(7)(ii).

Amended April 8, 1980, eff. May 15, 1980; April 10, 1987, eff. Aug. 1, 1987; Oct. 30, 1992, eff. Nov. 15, 1992; eff. Dec. 29, 2009; Oct. 24, 2012, eff. Jan. 1, 2013; Dec. 21, 2012, eff. Jan. 1, 2013; June 14, 2013, eff. July 1, 2013; Dec. 9, 2015, eff. Jan. 1, 2016.

Formerly Ill.Rev.Stat.1991, ch. 110A, ¶ 11.

Committee Comment
(December 9, 2015)

In amending Rule 11 to provide for e-mail service, the Committee considered whether special additional rules should apply to documents served by e-mail, *e.g.*, specified file formats, scan resolutions, electronic file size limitations, etc. The Committee rejected such requirements in favor of an approach which provides flexibility to adapt to evolving technology and developing practice. The Committee further anticipates good faith cooperation by practitioners. For example, if an attorney serves a motion in a format which cannot be read by the recipient, the Committee expects the recipient to contact the sender to request an alternative electronic format or a paper copy.

Committee Comment

(December 21, 2012)

New subparagraphs (b)(6) and (7) were created to allow for service of documents electronically. The amendments facilitate electronic communications among the court, parties, and counsel and complement the expansion of e-filing in the trial courts. However, electronic service may not be appropriate in all instances. For example, absent a secure method for electronic service of documents, other service options should be used for cases or documents filed confidentially.

Committee Comments

(December 29, 2009)

The rules on service and filing have been revised to provide for sending documents via third-party commercial carrier. Under these rules, the term "delivery" refers to all the carrier's standard pick-up methods, such as dropping a package in a UPS or FedEx box or with a UPS or FedEx contractor.

Rule 12.　Proof of Service in the Trial and Reviewing Courts; Effective Date of Service

(a) Filing. When service of a document is required, proof of service shall be filed with the clerk.

(b) Manner of Proof. Service is proved:

(1) by written acknowledgment signed by the person served;

(2) in case of service by personal delivery, by certificate of the attorney, or affidavit of a person, other than an attorney, who made delivery;

(3) in case of service by mail or by delivery to a third-party commercial carrier, by certificate of the attorney, or affidavit of a person other than the attorney, who deposited the document in the mail or delivered the document to a third-party commercial carrier, stating the time and place of mailing or delivery, the complete address which appeared on the envelope or package, and the fact that proper postage or the delivery charge was prepaid; or

(4) in case of service by mail by a *pro se* petitioner from a correctional institution, by affidavit, or by certification as provided in section 1–109 of the Code of Civil Procedure (735 ILCS 5/1–109 (West 2012)) of the person who deposited the document in the institutional mail, stating the time and place of deposit and the complete address to which the document was to be delivered;

(5) in case of service by facsimile transmission, by certificate of the attorney or affidavit of a person other than the attorney, who transmitted the document via facsimile machine, stating the time and place of transmission, the telephone number to which the transmission was sent, and the number of pages transmitted.

(6) in case of service by e-mail, by certificate of the attorney or affidavit of a person other than the attorney who transmitted the document via e-mail, stating the time and place of transmission to a designated e-mail address of record.

(c) Effective Date of Service by Mail. Service by mail is complete four days after mailing.

(d) Effective Date of Service by Delivery to Third–Party Commercial Carrier. Service by delivery to a third-party commercial carrier is complete on the third business day after delivery of the package to the third-party carrier.

(e) Effective Date of Service by Facsimile Transmission. Service by facsimile machine is complete on the first court day following transmission.

(f) Effective Date of Service by E–mail. Service by e-mail is complete on the first court day following transmission.

(g) Effective Date of Service by Electronic In-box. Service by electronic in-box under Rule 11(b)(7) is complete on the first court day following transmission.

Amended eff. July 1, 1971; July 1, 1975; Oct. 30, 1992, eff. Nov. 15, 1992; Dec. 29, 2009, eff. immediately; Dec. 21, 2012, eff. Jan. 1, 2013; Jan. 4, 2013, eff. immediately; Sept. 19, 2014, eff. immediately; Dec. 9, 2015, eff. Jan. 1, 2016.

Formerly Ill.Rev.Stat.1991, ch. 110A, ¶ 12.

Committee Comments

(December 29, 2009)

The rules on service and filing have been revised to provide for sending documents via third-party commercial carrier. Under these rules, the term "delivery" refers to all the carrier's standard pick-up methods, such as dropping a package in a UPS or FedEx box or with a UPS or FedEx contractor.

Rule 13.　Appearances—Time to Plead—Withdrawal

(a) Written Appearances. If a written appearance is filed, copies of the appearance shall be served in the manner required for the service of copies of pleadings.

(b) Time to Plead. A party who appears without having been served with summons is required to plead within the same time as if served with summons on the day he appears.

(c) Appearance and Withdrawal of Attorneys.

(1) *Addressing the Court.* An attorney shall file his written appearance or other pleading before he

addresses the court unless he is presenting a motion for leave to appear by intervention or otherwise.

(2) *Notice of Withdrawal.* An attorney may not withdraw his appearance for a party without leave of court and notice to all parties of record, and, unless another attorney is substituted, he must give reasonable notice of the time and place of the presentation of the motion for leave to withdraw, by personal service, certified mail, or a third-party carrier, directed to the party represented by him at his last known business or residence address. Such notice shall advise said party that to insure notice of any action in said cause, he should retain other counsel therein or file with the clerk of the court, within 21 days after entry of the order of withdrawal, his supplementary appearance stating therein an address at which service of notices or other documents may be had upon him.

(3) *Motion to Withdraw.* The motion for leave to withdraw shall be in writing and, unless another attorney is substituted shall state the last known address of the party represented. The motion may be denied by the court if the granting of it would delay the trial of the case, or would otherwise be inequitable.

(4) *Copy to be Served on Party.* If the party does not appear at the time the motion for withdrawal is granted, either in person or by substitute counsel, then, within three days of the entry of the order of withdrawal, a copy thereof shall be served upon the party by the withdrawing attorney in the manner provided in paragraph (c)(2) of this rule, and proof of service shall be made and filed.

(5) *Supplemental Appearance.* Unless another attorney is, at the time of such withdrawal, substituted for the one withdrawing, the party shall file in the case within 21 days after entry of the order of withdrawal a supplementary appearance, stating therein an address at which the service of notices or other documents may be had upon him. In case of his failure to file such supplementary appearance, notice, if by mail or by third-party carrier, shall be directed to him at his last known business or residence address.

(6) *Limited Scope Appearance.* An attorney may make a limited scope appearance on behalf of a party in a civil proceeding pursuant to Rule of Professional Conduct 1.2(c) when the attorney has entered into a written agreement with that party to provide limited scope representation. The attorney shall file a Notice of Limited Scope Appearance in the form attached to this rule, identifying each aspect of the proceeding to which the limited scope appearance pertains.

An attorney may file a Notice of Limited Scope Appearance more than once in a case. An attorney must file a new Notice of Limited Scope Appearance before any additional aspect of the proceeding

in which the attorney intends to appear. A party shall not be required to pay more than one appearance fee in a case.

(7) *Withdrawal Following Completion of Limited Scope Representation.* Upon completing the representation specified in the Notice of Limited Scope Appearance filed pursuant to paragraph (6), the attorney shall withdraw by oral motion or written notice as provided in parts (i)–(ii) of this paragraph. A withdrawal for any reason other than completion of the representation shall be requested by motion under paragraphs (c)(2) and (c)(3).

(i) If the attorney completes the representation at or before a court hearing attended by the party the attorney represents, the attorney may make an oral motion for withdrawal without prior notice to the party the attorney represents or to other parties. The court must grant the motion unless the party objects on the ground that the attorney has not completed the representation. The order granting the withdrawal may require the attorney to give written notice of the order to parties who were neither present nor represented at the hearing. If the party objects that the attorney has not completed the representation, the court must hold an evidentiary hearing on the objection, either immediately or on a specified later date. After hearing the evidence, the court must grant the motion to withdraw unless the court expressly finds that the attorney has not completed the representation specified in the Notice of Limited Scope Appearance.

(ii) An attorney also may withdraw by filing a Notice of Withdrawal of Limited Scope Appearance in the form attached to this rule. The attorney must serve the Notice on the party the attorney represents and must also serve it on other counsel of record and other parties not represented by counsel, unless the court by order excuses service on other counsel and other parties. The attorney must also serve the Notice on the judge then presiding over the case. The attorney must file proof of service in compliance with this paragraph. Within 21 days after the service of the Notice, the party may file an Objection to Withdrawal of Limited Scope Appearance in the form attached to this rule. The party must serve the Objection on the attorney and must also serve it on other counsel of record and other parties not represented by counsel unless the court by order excuses service on other counsel and other parties. If no timely Objection is filed, the attorney's limited scope appearance automatically terminates, without entry of a court order when the 21–day period expires. If a timely Objection is filed, however, the attorney must notice a hearing on the Objection. If the ground for the Objection is that the attorney has not completed the representation specified in the Notice of Limited Scope Appearance, the court must hold an evidentiary hearing. After the requisite hearing, the court must enter an order allowing the attorney to withdraw unless the court expressly finds that the attorney has not completed the representation specified in the Notice of Limited Scope Appearance.

Adopted June 15, 1982, eff. July 1, 1982. Amended eff. Feb. 16, 2011; Jan. 4, 2013, eff. immediately; June 14, 2013, eff. July 1, 2013.

Formerly Ill.Rev.Stat.1991, ch. 110A, ¶ 13.

Committee Comments
(rev. June 14, 2013)

Rule 13 was added in 1982. It was patterned after Proposed Uniform Circuit Court Rule III, which was prepared by a special committee of the Illinois State Bar Association and approved by the ISBA Board of Governors on June 22, 1976. Under paragraph (c) of this rule, an attorney's written appearance on behalf of a client before any court in this State binds the attorney to continue to represent that client in that cause until the court, after notice and motion, grants leave for the attorney to withdraw. See Rule of Professional Conduct 1.16(c).

(June 14, 2013)

Paragraph (c)(6) addresses the provision of limited scope representation to clients under Rule of Professional Conduct 1.2(c). The paragraph is not intended to regulate or impede appearances made pursuant to other types of limited engagements by attorneys, who may appear and withdraw as otherwise provided by Rule 13.

An attorney making a limited scope appearance in a civil proceeding must first enter into a written agreement with the party disclosing the limited nature of the representation. The limited appearance is then effected by using the form Notice of Limited Scope Appearance appended to this Rule. Utilizing this standardized form promotes consistency in the filing of limited scope appearances, makes the notices easily recognizable to judges and court personnel, and helps ensure that the scope of the representation is identified with specificity.

A party on whose behalf an attorney has filed a Notice of Limited Scope Appearance remains responsible, either personally or through an attorney who represents the party, for all matters not specifically identified in the Notice of Limited Scope Appearance.

Paragraph (c)(6) does not restrict (1) the number of limited scope appearances an attorney may make in a case, (2) the aspects of the case for which an attorney may file a limited scope appearance such as, for example, specified court proceedings, depositions, or settlement negotiations, or (3) the purposes for which an attorney may file a limited scope appearance. Notwithstanding the absence of numeric or subject matter restrictions on filing limited scope appearances, nothing in the Rule restricts the ability of a court to manage the cases before it, including taking appropriate action in response to client or lawyer abuse of the limited scope representation procedures.

Paragraph (c)(7) provides two alternative ways for an attorney to withdraw when the representation specified in the Notice of Limited Scope Appearance has been completed. The first method—an oral motion—can be used whenever the representation is completed at or before a hearing attended by the party the attorney represents. Prior notice of such a hearing is not required. The attorney should use this method whenever possible, because its use ensures that withdrawal occurs as soon as possible and that the court knows of the withdrawal.

The second method—filing a Notice of Withdrawal of Limited Scope Appearance—enables the attorney to withdraw easily in other situations, without having to make a court appearance, except when there is a genuine dispute about the attorney's completion of the representation. The Notice must be served on the party represented and on other counsel of record and other parties not represented by counsel unless the court excuses service on other counsel of record and other parties not represented by counsel. The Notice must also be served on the judge then presiding over the case to ensure that the judge is made aware that the limited scope representation has been completed, subject to the client's right to object. The attorney's withdrawal is automatic, without entry of a court order, unless the client files a timely Objection to Withdrawal of Limited Scope Appearance.

If the attorney makes an oral motion to withdraw pursuant to paragraph (c)(7)(i), with or without client objection, or if the client files a timely Objection to Withdrawal of Limited Scope Appearance pursuant to paragraph (c)(7)(ii), the court must allow the attorney to withdraw unless the court expressly finds that the attorney has not completed the representation specified in the Notice of Limited Scope Appearance. An evidentiary hearing is required if the client objects to the attorney's withdrawal based on the attorney's failure to complete the representation. A nonevidentiary hearing is required if the client objects on a ground other than the attorney's failure to complete the representation, although the primary function of such a hearing is to explain to the client that such an objection is not well-founded. A court's refusal to permit withdrawal of a completed limited scope representation, or even its encouragement of the attorney to extend the representation, would disserve the interests of justice by discouraging attorneys from undertaking limited scope representations out of concern that agreements with clients for such representations would not be enforced.

A limited scope appearance under the rule is unrelated to "special and limited" appearances formerly used to object to the lack of personal jurisdiction. The use of such appearances ended with the adoption of Public Act 91–145, which amended section 2–301 of the Code of Civil Procedure (735 ILCS 5/02–301) effective January 1, 2000.

Form for Limited Scope Appearance in Civil Action

IN THE CIRCUIT COURT OF THE _____
JUDICIAL CIRCUIT
_____ COUNTY, ILLINOIS
(OR, IN THE CIRCUIT COURT OF COOK COUN-
TY, ILLINOIS)

_____)
Plaintiff/Petitioner   )
)
v.   ) No.
)
)
_____)
Defendant/Respondent   )

NOTICE OF LIMITED SCOPE APPEARANCE

1. The attorney, _____,
   and the Party, _____, have entered into a written agreement dated
   _____ providing that the attorney will
   provide limited scope representation to the Party
   in the above-captioned matter in accordance with
   Paragraphs 3 and 4, below.

2. The Party is Plaintiff Petitioner Defendant Respondent in this matter. (Circle one)

3. The attorney appears pursuant to Supreme Court
   Rule 13(c)(6).   This appearance is limited in
   scope to the following matter(s) in which the
   attorney will represent the Party (check and complete all that apply):

☐ In the court proceeding (identify) on the following
  date: _____

☐ And in any continuance of that proceeding

☐ At the trial on the following date: _____

☐ And in any continuance of that trial

☐ And until judgment

☐ At the following deposition(s): _____

☐ If a family law matter, specify the scope and
  limits of representation:
  _____

☐ Other (specify the scope and limits of representation):
  _____

4. If this appearance does not extend to all matters
   to be considered at the proceeding(s) above, identify the discrete issues within each proceeding
   covered by this appearance: _____
   _____

5. The attorney may withdraw following completion
   of the limited scope representation specified in
   this appearance as follows:

a. orally move to withdraw at a hearing attended by the Party, at which the Party may object to
   withdrawal if the Party contends that the limited
   scope representation specified in this appearance
   has not been completed; or

b. file a Notice of Withdrawal of Limited Scope
   Representation in the form attached to Supreme
   Court Rule 13. If the attorney files such a
   Notice, the attorney shall serve it upon the Party
   and upon all counsel of record and other parties
   not represented by counsel unless the court excuses service upon other counsel and other unrepresented parties, and upon the judge then presiding over this case. The method of service shall
   be as provided in Supreme Court Rule 11 unless
   the court orders otherwise. If the Party objects
   to the withdrawal, the Party may, within 21 days
   after the date of the attorney's service of the
   Notice of Withdrawal of Limited Scope Appearance, file an Objection to Withdrawal of Limited
   Scope Appearance in the form attached to Supreme Court Rule 13. The attorney will provide
   a copy of the form of Objection to the Party with
   the attorney's Notice, including instructions for
   filing and service of an Objection. If the Party
   timely serves an Objection, the attorney shall
   notice the matter for hearing to rule on the
   Objection.

6. Service of pleadings on the attorney and party
   named above shall be made in accordance with
   Supreme Court Rule 11(e).

7. By signing below, the Party being represented
   under this Limited Scope Appearance:

a. agrees to the delivery of all court papers to
   the addresses specified below; and

b. agrees to inform the court, all counsel of
   record, and all parties not represented by counsel
   of any changes to the Party's address information
   listed below during the limited scope representation.

_____   _____
Signature of Attorney   Name of Attorney

_____   _____

Attorney's Address   Attorney's   Telephone Number

_____   _____

Attorney's E–Mail Address   Attorney Number

_____   _____

Signature of Party   Name of Party

_____   _____

Party's Address   Party's Telephone Number

_____

Party's E–Mail Address

_____

Date

Form for Limited Scope Appearance in Civil Action

IN THE CIRCUIT COURT OF THE _____
JUDICIAL CIRCUIT
_____ COUNTY, ILLINOIS
(OR, IN THE CIRCUIT COURT OF COOK COUNTY, ILLINOIS)

_____)
Plaintiff/Petitioner   )
)
v.   ) No.
)
)
_____)
Defendant/Respondent   )

NOTICE OF WITHDRAWAL OF LIMITED SCOPE APPEARANCE

I withdraw my Notice of Limited Scope Appearance for _____[party], pursuant to Supreme Court Rule 13(c)(7).

I have completed all services within the scope of the Notice of Limited Scope Appearance, and I have completed all acts ordered by the court within the scope of that appearance.

Service of documents upon me under Supreme Court Rule 11(e) will no longer be required upon the later of: (a) 21 days after service of this Notice or, (b) if _____ [party] files and serves an Objection to Withdrawal of Limited Scope Appearance within 21 days after service of this Notice, entry of a court order allowing my withdrawal. Service of documents on _____ [party] continues to be required.

NOTICE TO _____ **[party]:** You have the right to object to my withdrawal as your lawyer if you believe that I have not finished everything that I had agreed to do. To object, you must:

1. Fill in the blanks in the attached form of Objection to Withdrawal of Limited Scope Appearance, including the Certificate of Service and sign where indicated.

2. File the original Objection with the court by _____ ___, _____, [date to be filled in by lawyer] which is 21 days after the date that I am filing and serving this Notice.

3. On the same day that you file the Objection with the court, send copies of it to me and to the other persons listed in the Certificate of Service attached to the Objection. Also, check the boxes in the Certificate of Service to show how you sent the copy to each person.

If you file and serve an Objection within the 21–day period, I will arrange to have a hearing date set by the court. I will send you notice of the date. You must appear at the hearing and explain to the judge why you believe that I have not finished everything that I had agreed to do for you.

_____   _____

Signature of Attorney   Name of Attorney

_____   _____

Attorney's Address   Attorney's   Telephone Number

_____   _____

Attorney's E–Mail Address   Attorney Number

_____

Date

Proof of Filing and Service

I certify that this Notice has been filed with the court on the ___ day of _____, 20 ___, and on the same day I served this Notice on the following, including the Party that I represented, all counsel of record and parties not represented by counsel, and the judge now presiding over this case, by the method checked below for each.

[List Name and Address of Each]

The Honorable _____

_____

_____

[Client] _____

_____

_____

_____

[Repeat Same Information for Each Other Counsel of Record and Unrepresented Party]

Signature of Attorney

[Check Method of Service

[ ] US Mail, Postage Prepaid
[ ] Messenger

[ ] Personal Delivery
[ ] Facsimile

[ ] Email

[ ] US Mail, Postage Prepaid
[ ] Messenger

[ ] Personal Delivery [ ] Facsimile

[ ] Email

****

Form for Objection To Withdrawal of Limited Scope Appearance

[To Withdrawing Attorney: On the Copy of This Form Sent to the Client, List the Parties and Addresses in the Certificate of Service and Complete All Parts of the Form Except the Statement of Grounds, the Signature Block Information, the Date of Filing and Service of the Objection, the Client's Method of Service, and the Client's Signatures]

****

IN THE CIRCUIT COURT OF THE _____ JUDICIAL CIRCUIT
_____ COUNTY, ILLINOIS
(OR, IN THE CIRCUIT COURT OF COOK COUNTY, ILLINOIS)

_____)
Plaintiff/Petitioner   )
)
v.   )   No. _____
)
)
)
_____)
Defendant/Respondent   )

OBJECTION TO WITHDRAWAL OF LIMITED SCOPE APPEARANCE

I, _____, object to my attorney's Notice of Withdrawal of Limited Scope Appearance filed on _____.

My attorney has not finished everything he or she had agreed to do in the Notice of Limited Scope Appearance. I understand this is the only basis for me to present a valid objection to my attorney's notice of withdrawal. The specific services that my attorney has not completed are:

_____

_____

I understand that my objection will be set for a court hearing and I will be required to appear at that hearing and explain to a judge what services my attorney has not completed that he or she had agreed to do for me.

_____   _____
Signature of Party   Name of Party

_____   _____
Party's Address Party's   Telephone Number

_____
Party's E–Mail Address

_____
Date

Proof of Filing and Service

I certify that this Objection has been filed with the court on the ___ day of _____, ___, and on the same day I served this Objection on the following by the method checked below for each.

[List Name and Address of Each]

[Attorney Who Represented Client]

_____

_____

_____

[Check Method of Service

[ ] US Mail, Postage Prepaid

[ ] Messenger

[ ] Personal Delivery [ ] Facsimile

[ ] Email

[Repeat Same Information for Each Other Counsel of Record and Unrepresented Party]

_____
Signature of Party

Rule 14.   Reserved

Rule 15.   Social Security Numbers in Pleadings and Related Matters

(a) Applicability. This rule applies to all documents filed with the court in all cases except civil cases. The confidential treatment of an individual's Social Security number in civil case court filings is separately provided for in Rule 138.

(b) Unless otherwise required by law or ordered by the court, parties shall not include Social Security numbers in documents filed with the court, including exhibits thereto, whether filed electronically or in paper. If disclosure of an individual's Social Security number is required for a particular filing, only the last four digits of that number shall be used. The filing must be accompanied by a confidential information form in substantial compliance with the attached **NOTICE OF CONFIDENTIAL INFORMATION WITHIN COURT FILING**, which shall identify the full Social Security number and shall remain confidential, except as to the parties or as the court may direct.

(c) Neither the court, nor the clerk, will review each pleading for compliance with this rule. If a pleading is filed without redaction, a party or identified person may move the court to order redaction. If the court finds the inclusion of the Social Security number was willful, the court may award the prevailing party reasonable expenses, including attorney fees and court costs, incurred in making or opposing the motion.

(d) This rule does not require any party, attorney, clerk or judicial officer to redact information from a court record that was filed prior to the adoption of this rule; provided, however, that a party may request that a Social Security number be redacted in a matter that preceded the adoption of this rule.

Former Rule 138 adopted Oct. 4, 2011, eff. Jan. 1, 2012. Renumbered as Rule 15 April 16, 2012, eff. immediately. Amended Dec. 24, 2013, eff. Jan. 1, 2014.

Committee Comment

(October 4, 2011)

This rule was adopted pursuant to section 40 of the Identity Protection Act (5 ILCS 179/40 (West 2010)).

[Appendix]
(Revised July 25, 2012)

In the Circuit Court of the _____ Judicial Circuit,
_____ County, Illinois
(Or, In the Circuit Court of Cook County, Illinois)

In the Circuit Court of the _____ Judicial Circuit,
_____ County, Illinois
(Or, In the Circuit Court of Cook County, Illinois)

_____	)
Plaintiff/Petitioner,	)
	)
v.	) Case No. _____
	)
_____	)
Defendant/Respondent	)

NOTICE OF CONFIDENTIAL INFORMATION WITHIN COURT FILING

Pursuant to Illinois Supreme Court Rule 15, the filer of a court record at the time of filing shall include a confidential information form which identifies the full social security numbers for any individuals whose social security numbers are redacted within the filing. **This information will not be available to the public and this document will be stored in a separate location from the case file.**

Party/Individual Information:

1. Name: _____
   Address: _____
   _____
   Phone: _____
   SSN: _____

2. Name: _____
   Address: _____
   _____
   Phone: _____
   SSN: _____

(Attach additional pages, if necessary.)

Rules 16, 17. Reserved

Rule 18. Findings of Unconstitutionality

A court shall not find unconstitutional a statute, ordinance, regulation or other law, unless:

(a) the court makes the finding in a written order or opinion, or in an oral statement on the record that is transcribed;

(b) such order or opinion clearly identifies what portion(s) of the statute, ordinance, regulation or other law is being held unconstitutional;

(c) such order or opinion clearly sets forth the specific ground(s) for the finding of unconstitutionality, including:

(1) the constitutional provision(s) upon which the finding of unconstitutionality is based;

(2) whether the statute, ordinance, regulation or other law is being found unconstitutional on its face, as applied to the case *sub judice*, or both;

(3) that the statute, ordinance, regulation or other law being held unconstitutional cannot reasonably be construed in a manner that would preserve its validity;

(4) that the finding of unconstitutionality is necessary to the decision or judgment rendered, and that such decision or judgment cannot rest upon an alternative ground; and

(5) that the notice required by Rule 19 has been served, and that those served with such notice have been given adequate time and opportunity under the circumstances to defend the statute, ordinance, regulation or other law challenged.

Adopted July 27, 2006, effective September 1, 2006.

Committee Comment

(July 27, 2006)

This rule is intended to implement the principles encapsulated in *People v. Cornelius*, 213 Ill. 2d 178 (2004), and *In re Parentage of John M.*, 212 Ill. 2d 253 (2004), concerning the duties incumbent upon the circuit court when declaring state statutes to be unconstitutional.

Rule 19. Notice of Claim of Unconstitutionality or Preemption by Federal Law

(a) Notice Required. In any cause or proceeding in which the constitutionality or preemption by federal law of a statute, ordinance, administrative regulation, or other law affecting the public interest is raised, and to which action or proceeding the State or the political subdivision, agency, or officer affected is not already a party, the litigant raising the constitutional or preemption issue shall serve an appropriate notice thereof on the Attorney General, State's Attorney, municipal counsel or agency attorney, as the case may be.

(b) Contents and Time for Filing Notice. The notice shall identify the particular statute, ordinance, regulation, or other law, and shall briefly describe the nature of the constitutional or preemption challenge. The notice shall be served at the time of suit, answer or counterclaim, if the challenge is raised at that level, or promptly after the constitutional or preemption question arises as a result of a circuit or reviewing court ruling or judgment.

(c) Purpose of Notice. The purpose of such notice shall be to afford the State, political subdivision, agency or officer, as the case may be, the opportunity, but not the obligation, to intervene in the cause or proceeding for the purpose of defending the law or regulation challenged. The election to intervene shall be subject to applicable provisions of law governing intervention or impleading of interested parties.

Adopted Feb. 21, 1986, eff. Aug. 1, 1986; amended July 27, 2006, eff. Sept.1, 2006.

Formerly Ill.Rev.Stat.1991, ch. 110A, ¶ 19.

Committee Comments

(February 21, 1986)

Rule 19 was adopted effective August 1, 1986. The procedure established by this rule parallels the procedure prescribed for the Federal system under 28 U.S.C. section 2403 (1982). A representative of an appropriate governmental agency, upon receiving notice that a litigant has drawn into question the constitutionality of a statute, ordinance or administrative regulation affecting the public interest, may apply for leave to intervene, as provided by section 2–408(d) of the Code of Civil Procedure (Ill.Rev. Stat.1983, ch. 110, par. 2–408(d)), but the representative is not obliged to do so.

Rule 20. Certification of Questions of State Law from Certain Federal Courts

(a) Certification. When it shall appear to the Supreme Court of the United States, or to the United States Court of Appeals for the Seventh Circuit, that there are involved in any proceeding before it questions as to the law of this State, which may be determinative of the said cause, and there are no controlling precedents in the decisions of this court, such court may certify such questions of the laws of this State to this court for instructions concerning such questions of State law, which certificate this court, by written opinion, may answer.

(b) Contents of Certification Order. A certification order shall contain:

(1) the questions of law to be answered; and

(2) a statement of all facts relevant to the questions certified and showing fully the nature of the controversy in which the questions arose.

(c) Record Before Certifying Court. This court may require the original or copies of all or of any portion of the record before the certifying court to be filed with it, if, in the opinion of this court, the record or a portion thereof may be necessary in answering the questions.

(d) Briefs and Argument. Proceedings in this court shall be those provided in these rules governing briefs and oral arguments, except that the time for filing briefs specified in Rule 343 begins to run from the day this court agrees to answer the certified question of law, and the parties retain the same designation as they have in the certifying court.

(e) Costs of Certification. Fees and costs shall be the same as in civil appeals docketed before this court and shall be equally divided between the parties unless otherwise ordered by the certifying court.

Adopted Aug. 30, 1983, eff. Oct. 1, 1983. Amended April 1, 1992, eff. Aug. 1, 1992.

Formerly Ill.Rev.Stat.1991, ch. 110A, ¶ 20.

Committee Comments

This rule permits the Supreme Court of the United States or the United States Court of Appeals for the Seventh Circuit to certify a question of Illinois law to the Supreme Court of Illinois, which question may be controlling in an action pending before said court and upon which no controlling Illinois authority exists.

The Court of Appeals for the Seventh Circuit has a rule which encourages certification in jurisdictions that have a rule similar to the one provided herein. See Rule 13 of the Rules of the United States Court of Appeals for the Seventh Circuit.

Subparagraph (a) establishes the standard for certification and also makes the acceptance of certification by the Supreme Court of Illinois discretionary.

Subparagraph (b) establishes the contents of a certification order.

Subparagraph (c) provides that the Supreme Court of Illinois may require the original or copies of all or any portions of the record before the certifying court.

Subparagraph (d) provides that briefs and arguments are to be governed by the Supreme Court of Illinois rules dealing with briefs and oral arguments. Amended in 1992 to provide that the time schedule for briefs will not begin to run until the court decides that it will answer the certified question.

Subparagraph (e) of the rule provides for fees and costs in the Supreme Court of Illinois.

Rule 21. Circuit Court Rules and Filing of Rules; Administrative Authority; General Orders

(a) **Circuit Court Rules.** A majority of the circuit judges in each circuit may adopt rules governing civil and criminal cases which are consistent with these rules and the statutes of the State, and which, so far as practicable, shall be uniform throughout the State. All rules of court shall be filed with the Administrative Director within 10 days after they are adopted.

(b) **Administrative Authority.** Subject to the overall authority of the Supreme Court, the chief circuit judge shall have the authority to determine, among other things, the hours of court, available leave time to which a judge is entitled, and to instruct the way in which a judge on the bench is expected to behave. In the exercise of this general administrative authority, the chief judge shall take or initiate appropriate measures to address the persistent failure of any judge to perform his or her judicial duties.

(c) **General Orders.** The chief judge of each circuit may enter general orders in the exercise of his or her general administrative authority, including orders providing for assignment of judges, general or specialized divisions, and times and places of holding court.

(d) **Proceedings to Compel Compliance With Certain Orders Entered by a Chief Circuit Judge.** Any proceeding to compel a person or agency other than personnel of the circuit court to comply with an administrative order of the chief circuit judge shall be commenced by filing a complaint and summons and shall be tried without a jury by a judge from a circuit other than the circuit in which the complaint was filed. The proceedings shall be held as in other civil cases.

Amended Aug. 9, 1983, eff. Oct. 1, 1983; amended, eff. Dec. 1, 2008.

FormerlyIll.Rev.Stat.1991, ch. 110A, ¶ 21.

Committee Comments

This rule consists of paragraphs (2), (3), and (4) of former Rule 1, which was revised effective January 1, 1964.

New paragraph (b) was adopted December 1, 2008, to clarify that a chief circuit judge's administrative role includes the authority, and the responsibility, to address the persistent failure of any judge to perform his or her judicial duties. Such failure may be due to, among other things, professional incompetence, poor case load management, or chronic absenteeism. Depending on the facts involved, the expectation is that the chief circuit judge will take or initiate appropriate action to remedy the situation. It shall be the duty of the chief judge to provide counseling, if deemed necessary or appropriate, and to report violations of the Canons to the Judicial Inquiry Board. In circumstances where there is uncertainty as to whether the conduct at issue is violative of the Canons, the chief judge shall report the conduct, with substantial particularity, to the Supreme Court.

Rule 22. Appellate Court Organization; Administrative Authority; Appellate Court Rules

(a) **Divisions–Appellate Districts.**

(1) Each district of the Appellate Court shall consist of one division unless the Supreme Court provides otherwise by order. The First District shall sit in the city of Chicago. The Second District shall sit in the city of Elgin. The Third District shall sit in the city of Ottawa. The Fourth District shall sit in the city of Springfield. The Fifth District shall sit in the city of Mount Vernon. With the approval of the chief justice of the Supreme Court, a division may sit at any place in the State. The Appellate Court in each district shall be in session throughout the year, and each division shall sit periodically as its judicial business requires. Each division shall sit in panels of three judges as hereinafter provided.

(2) Oral arguments in the appellate court will normally be held in the courthouse provided for that purpose in the appropriate city designated in subparagraph (a)(1). However, with the approval of all the parties and the chief justice, a panel of the appellate court may, on occasion, agree to set an oral argument to be held in a suitable, alternative location but outside the courthouse in which the panel would otherwise normally preside.

(b) **Assignment to Divisions–Designation of Panels.** The Supreme Court shall assign judges to the various divisions. The presiding judge of a division shall designate judges serving in that division to sit in panels of three. Such a three-judge panel shall constitute the division for purposes of rendering a decision in a case. The Executive Committee of the First District, upon request of a division of that district, may designate any Appellate Court judge of that district to sit in the place of a judge of the requesting division for such case or cases as may be designated in the request.

(c) Decisions. Three judges must participate in the decision of every case, and the concurrence of two shall be necessary to a decision. One judge may decide motions of course.

(d) Divisions–Presiding Judge. The judges of each division shall select one of their number to serve as presiding judge of that division for a term of one year.

(e) Executive Committee of the Appellate Court of Illinois. The presiding judges of the Second, Third, Fourth, and Fifth Districts and the members of the Executive Committee of the First District shall constitute the Executive Committee of the Appellate Court of Illinois. Meetings of the executive committee may be called by any three of its members, and meetings of the Appellate Court may be called by the executive committee.

(f) Executive Committee of the Appellate Court in the First Appellate District. There shall be an Executive Committee of the First District composed of one member of each division, which committee shall exercise general administrative authority. The executive committee shall select one of its number as chairman.

(g) Administrative Authority. Subject to the overall authority of the Supreme Court, the presiding judge of each district, and the chairman of the Executive Committee in the First District, shall have the authority to determine, among other things, the hours of court, available leave time to which a judge is entitled, and to instruct the way in which a judge on the bench is expected to behave. In the exercise of this general administrative authority, the presiding judge of each judicial district and the chairman of the Executive Committee in the First District shall take or initiate appropriate measures to address the persistent failure of any judge to perform his or her judicial duties.

(h) Appellate Court Rules. A majority of the appellate court judges in each district may adopt rules governing civil and criminal cases which are consistent with these rules and the statutes of the state, and which, so far as practicable, shall be uniform throughout the state. All rules of court shall be filed with the Administrative Director within 10 days after they are adopted.

(i) Workers' Compensation Commission Appeals. A five- judge panel of the Appellate Court will sit as the Workers' Compensation Commission division of each district of the Appellate Court. The Workers' Compensation Commission division will hear and decide all appeals involving proceedings to review orders of the Workers' Compensation Commission. The division will sit, periodically, as its judicial business requires, at any place in the State it chooses. Five judges must participate in the decisions of the Workers' Compensation Commission division, and the concurrence of three shall be necessary to a decision. If

a judge designated to serve on this panel cannot participate, the alternate designated by the Supreme Court shall participate. Motions of course may be decided by one judge.

Amended eff. July 1, 1971; Dec. 9, 1974; amended July 30, 1979, eff. Oct. 15, 1979; amended eff. Feb. 1, 1984, with Justice Moran dissenting (see *Yellow Cab Co. v. Jones* (1985), 108 Ill.2d 330, 342); amended April 10, 1987, eff. Aug. 1, 1987; amended eff. Nov. 20, 1991; amended Oct. 15, 2004, eff. Jan. 1, 2005; amended May 23, 2005, eff. immediately; amended, eff. Dec. 1, 2008.

Formerly Ill.Rev.Stat.1991, ch. 110A, ¶ 22.

Committee Comments
(Revised February 1, 1984)

As originally adopted, Rule 22 was derived from former Rule 56–2, effective January 1, 1964, and modified June 24, 1965, without change in substance.

Paragraph (a)

As originally adopted, paragraph (a) provided that the Appellate Court should sit in divisions and specified the number of divisions in each of the five districts, four in the First, and one in each of the other districts. It was amended in 1971 to reflect the creation of a fifth division in the First District, and again in 1974, to authorize the creation of a second division in the Second District.

In 1979, the paragraph was amended. Under the paragraph, as amended, each district constitutes a single division unless the Supreme Court provides otherwise by order. A division may consist of four, five, or six judges. Cases are assigned to panels of three judges. The concurrence of two is necessary for a decision.

Paragraph (b)

In 1979, paragraph (b) was amended to permit the presiding judges to designate judges within their division to sit in panels. The authority of the Executive Committee of the First District to make designations on request of a division was retained.

Paragraph (c)

Paragraph (c) provides that three judges must participate in the decision of every case, and that two shall be necessary to a decision, other than a ruling on a motion of course. The 1979 amendments to the rule made no change in paragraph (c). Thus, though a division may consist of more than three judges, it sits in panels of three.

Paragraph (d)

The 1979 amendment retained the one year term for the presiding judges, but eliminated the provision in the pre–1979 text requiring that the position of presiding judge be rotated among the judges of the division.

Paragraph (e)

Until 1979, paragraph (e) provided that the presiding judge of each division should be a member of the Executive Committee of the Appellate Court of Illinois. In that year it was amended to provide that the presiding judges of the Second, Third, Fourth, and Fifth Districts, together with the members of the Executive Committee of the Appellate Court in the First Appellate District, shall constitute the Executive Committee of the Appellate Court of Illinois. The 1979 amendment makes some change in the First District representation on the Executive Committee, since the members of the Executive Committee of the Appellate Court in the First Appellate District are not necessarily the presiding judges of the divisions of the First District.

Paragraph (f)

Paragraph (f) was amended in 1979 to reflect the deletion from paragraph (a) of the specific provision setting out the number of divisions in each district. There was no change in substance.

Paragraph (g)

Paragraph (g) was added in 1984 to provide for the creation of the Industrial Commission division of the Appellate Court. A single panel of five appellate judges, one from each district (or alternates designated by the Supreme Court), will hear and decide all cases involving proceedings to review orders of the Industrial Commission. The procedure is adopted to relieve the Supreme Court of the growing burden of hearing all such appeals (see amended Rule 302(a)), and to insure that such appeals will continue to enjoy the traditional benefits of speedy consideration and uniform application of the law, the need for which was considered the original justification for giving such cases preferred status in the first place.

Notices of appeal from trial court orders disposing of cases involving review of Industrial Commission orders will be filed in the circuit court in accordance with Rule 303, and copies thereof will be sent to the clerk of the Appellate Court, as required in Rule 303(a)(4).

New paragraph (g) was adopted December 1, 2008, to clarify that a presiding judge's administrative role includes the authority, and the responsibility, to address the persistent failure of any judge to perform his or her judicial duties. Such failure may be due to, among other things, professional incompetence, poor case load management, or chronic absenteeism. Depending on the facts involved, the expectation is that the presiding judge will take or initiate appropriate action to remedy the situation. It shall be the duty of the presiding judge to provide counseling, if deemed necessary and appropriate, and to report violations of the Canons to the Judicial Inquiry Board. In circumstances where there is uncertainty as to whether the conduct at issue is violative of the Canons, the presiding judge shall report the conduct, with substantial particularity, to the Supreme Court.

Rule 23. Disposition of Cases in the Appellate Court

The decision of the Appellate Court may be expressed in one of the following forms: a full opinion, a concise written order, or a summary order conforming to the provisions of this rule. All dispositive opinions and orders shall contain the names of the judges who rendered the opinion or order.

(a) Opinions. A case may be disposed of by an opinion only when a majority of the panel deciding the case determines that at least one of the following criteria is satisfied:

(1) the decision establishes a new rule of law or modifies, explains or criticizes an existing rule of law; or

(2) the decision resolves, creates, or avoids an apparent conflict of authority within the Appellate Court.

(b) Written Order. Cases which do not qualify for disposition by opinion may be disposed of by a concise written order which shall succinctly state:

(1) in a separate introductory paragraph, a concise syllabus of the court's holding(s) in the case;

(2) the germane facts;

(3) the issues and contentions of the parties when appropriate;

(4) the reasons for the decision; and

(5) the judgment of the court.

(c) Summary Order. In any case in which the panel unanimously determines that any one or more of the following dispositive circumstances exist, the decision of the court may be made by summary order. A summary order may be utilized when:

(1) the Appellate Court lacks jurisdiction;

(2) the disposition is clearly controlled by case law precedent, statute, or rules of court;

(3) the appeal is moot;

(4) the issues involve no more than an application of well-settled rules to recurring fact situations;

(5) the opinion or findings of fact and conclusions of law of the trial court or agency adequately explain the decision;

(6) no error of law appears on the record;

(7) the trial court or agency did not abuse its discretion; or

(8) the record does not demonstrate that the decision of the trier of fact is against the manifest weight of the evidence.

When a summary order is issued it shall contain:

(i) a statement describing the nature of the case and the dispositive issues without a discussion of the facts;

(ii) a citation to controlling precedent, if any; and

(iii) the judgment of the court and a citation to one or more of the criteria under this rule which supports the judgment, *e.g.*, "Affirmed in accordance with Supreme Court Rule 23(c)(1)."

The court may dispose of a case by summary order at any time after the case is docketed in the Appellate Court. The disposition may provide for dismissal, affirmance, remand, reversal or any combination thereof as appropriate to the case. A summary order may be entered after a dispositive issue has been fully briefed, or if the issue has been raised by motion of a party or by the court, *sua sponte*, after expiration of the time for filing a response to the motion or rule to show cause issued by the court.

(d) Captions. All opinions and orders entered under this rule shall bear a caption substantially conforming to the requirements of Rule 330. Additionally, an opinion or order entered under subpart (a) or (b) of this rule must clearly show the date of filing on its initial page.

(e) Effect of Orders.

(1) An order entered under subpart (b) or (c) of this rule is not precedential and may not be cited by any party except to support contentions of double jeopardy, *res judicata*, collateral estoppel or law of the case. When cited for these purposes, a copy of the order shall be furnished to all other counsel and the court.

(2) An order entered under subpart (b) of this rule must contain on its first page a notice in substantially the following form:

NOTICE: This order was filed under Supreme Court Rule 23 and may not be cited as precedent by any party except in the limited circumstances allowed under Rule 23(e)(1).

(f) Motions to Publish. If an appeal is disposed of by order, any party may move to have the order published as an opinion. The motion shall set forth the reasons why the order satisfies the criteria for disposition as an opinion and shall be filed within 21 days of the entry of the order.

(g) Electronic Publication. In order to make available to the public all opinions and orders entered under subparts (a) and (b) of this rule, the clerks of the Appellate Court shall transmit an electronic copy of each opinion or order filed in his or her district to the webmaster of the Illinois Supreme and Appellate Courts' Web site on the day of filing. No opinion or order may be posted to the Web site that does not substantially comply with the Style Manual for the Supreme and Appellate Courts.

(h) Public–Domain Case Designators

An opinion or order entered under subpart (a) or (b) of this rule must be assigned a public-domain case designator and internal paragraph numbers, as set forth in the accompanying administrative order.

Adopted eff. Jan. 31, 1972. Amended eff. July 1, 1975; Feb. 19, 1982, eff. April 1, 1982; May 18, 1988, eff. Aug. 1, 1988; Nov. 21, 1988, eff. Jan. 1, 1989; amended and Commentary and Administrative Order adopted June 27, 1994, eff. July 1, 1994; amended May 30, 2008, eff. immediately; Sept. 13, 2010, eff. Jan. 1, 2011; May 31, 2011, eff. July 1, 2011.

M.R. No. 10343
(Amended October 4, 2011)

Under the general administrative and supervisory authority granted the Illinois Supreme Court over the courts of this state (Ill. Const. 1970, art. VI, § 16), the order entered under Supreme Court Rule 23, dated May 31, 2011, is amended as follows:

(A) Assignment of Public–Domain Case Designators.

The Districts of the Illinois Appellate Court shall assign a public-domain case designator to those opinions filed on or after July 1, 2011. This designator number for an opinion must be unique to that opinion and shall include the year of decision, the court abbreviation, and an identifier number comprised of the final six digits of the docket number, or the final six digits of the initial docket number in a consolidated appeal, without use of the hyphen. In the case of opinions by the Workers' Compensation Commission Division of the Appellate Court, the letters "WC" shall be added as a suffix. The public-domain identifier shall appear at top of the first page of an opinion and shall be in the following form:

[year] IL App (1st) [no.]
[year] IL App (2d) [no.]
[year] IL App (3d) [no.]
[year] IL App (4th) [no.]
[year] IL App (5th) [no.]
Workers' Compensation Commission Division
2011 IL App ([dist.]) [no.]WC

By way of example, should the First District file an opinion in cause No. 1–10–1234 in 2011, the public-domain case designator will be "2011 IL App (1st) 101234."

Where a second opinion is filed under the same docket number after remand, a capital letter "B" will be appended to the case-designator number, regardless of the year-designator portion of the citation:

2011 IL App (1st) 101159
2012 IL App (1st) 101159–B

Any further opinions arising from the same appeal shall be assigned an alphabetic letter consecutive to the preceding opinion.

However, where an opinion is withdrawn while jurisdiction has been retained by the issuing court, the new opinion or order in the matter shall be given the same case-designator number as the withdrawn opinion without the addition of a sequential alphabetic designator.

Orders filed under Illinois Supreme Court Rule 23(b) shall have the letter "U," preceded by a hyphen, appended to the case-designator number:

2011 IL App (5th) 101160–U

A subsequently filed unpublished order in the same cause of action will result in use of both a "U" and an alphabetic designator:

2011 IL App (5th) 101160–UB

Use of the "U" designator for unpublished decisions and use of an alphabetic designator ("B," "C," *etc.*) for a subsequent opinion or order are independent elements of the case-designator number:

2011 IL App (5th) 101160–U [unpublished; initial decision]
2011 IL App (5th) 101160–B [published; decision after remand]
2011 IL App (5th) 101160–UC [unpublished; decision after second remand]

Should an unpublished order under Supreme Court Rule 23 be converted to a published opinion, the "U" designation shall be deleted.

(B) Internal Paragraphing of Opinions.

Illinois reviewing court opinions shall include internally numbered paragraphs as directed below. Use of internal paragraph numbers allows a pinpoint citation to the appropriate portions of an opinion when cited for a specific proposition. Such a citation will include the case name, the public-domain designator number, and the specific, or pinpoint, paragraph or paragraph numbers within the opinion:

People v. Doe, 2011 IL App (1st) 101157, ¶ 15

People v. Doe, 2011 IL App (1st) 101157, ¶¶ 21–23

People v. Doe, 2011 IL App (1st) 101157, ¶¶ 57, 68

Except for the materials denoted in paragraph below, each paragraph of text is to be numbered consecutively beginning after the heading "OPINION" or "ORDER" (including the lead-in line to a separate opinion and any joiner lines thereto).

(2) The numbering of paragraphs within a separate opinion shall be consecutive to the final paragraph number of the opinion that precedes it, beginning with the lead-in line to the separate opinion, as shown in the example below:

¶ 43 CONCLUSION

¶ 44 For the reason stated, the judgment of the circuit court is reversed and the cause is remanded to that court for further proceedings.

¶ 45 Judgment reversed;

¶ 46 cause remanded.

¶ 47 JUSTICE DOE, dissenting:

¶ 48 Because I believe the circuit court correctly resolved the issues presented in the motion to suppress, I would affirm.

The following portions of an opinion do not constitute new paragraphs and shall not be numbered:

(a) indented (blocked) text, regardless of the nature material (e.g., quotation, listing of issues, etc.) or the length of the material;

(b) text immediately following indented text, unless such text begins a new paragraph;

(c) text within footnotes;

(d) appendices or other attachments.

If quoted text, including indented quotations, is derived from a source that uses numbered paragraphs under a public-domain system of citation, the numbers from the original source shall not be shown in the quoted material but in the citation only.

If a supplemental document is filed, the paragraph numbering in the original document shall be continued into the supplemental document, including any lead-in lines and document headings (e.g., "Supplemental Opinion"; "Dissent Upon Denial of Rehearing").

Where revisions are made to an opinion following filing that result in the addition of a new paragraph or paragraphs, the new paragraph(s) shall be denoted by use of the paragraph number that preceded the new materials, plus the addition of consecutive, alphabetical letters (e.g., ¶ 11b, ¶ 11c, etc.)

Each paragraph number shall be shown using the paragraph symbol, followed by a space, and then the number (e.g., ¶ 1). The paragraph number is placed at the left margin, followed by a tab that indents the paragraphed text, as follows:

¶ 23 The appellate court found that Grant supported its conclusion that the designation of the NAF in the agreement to arbitrate was integral to the agreement. Specifically, citing Grant, the court noted:

"[The NAF] has a very specific set of rules and procedures that has implications for every aspect of the arbitration process."

Thus the court found that section 5 of the Arbitration Act could not be used to reform the arbitration provision.

¶ 24 The defendant argues that the appellate court erroneously determined there is a split in federal case law as to the proper application of section 5 of the Act.

Order entered December 18, 2006.

A December 18, 2006 Supreme Court Order, effective January 1, 2007, vacated Administrative Order No. M.R. 10343. The order provided:

"In re Administrative Order No. M.R. 10343

"On the court's own motion, effective January 1, 2007, the administrative order entered in M.R. No. 10343, on June 27, 1994, is hereby vacated."

Administrative Order No. M.R. 10343 had read:

"IN THE
SUPREME COURT
OF
THE STATE OF ILLINOIS
"ADMINISTRATIVE ORDER
"MR No. 10343

"Order entered June 27, 1994.

"Under the general administrative and supervisory authority granted the Illinois Supreme Court over the courts of this State (Ill. Const.1970, art. VI, § 16), it is ordered that the districts of the Appellate Court shall be limited in the number of opinions each may file annually commencing July 1, 1994, as follows:

"First District: 750

"Second District: 250

"Third District: 150

"Fourth District: 150

"Fifth District: 150

"The Executive Committee of the First District and the presiding justice of the other districts shall establish a procedure to determine those cases that will be disposed of by opinion, rather than by order under Supreme Court Rule 23, in his or her respective district.

"Further, it is ordered that opinions shall be produced on paper 8½ by 11 inches, with the text of the opinion double spaced and in type not smaller than 10 point, or standard elite type, and not to exceed 6½ by 9 inches. Opinions shall not exceed 20 pages in length, excluding any concurring or dissenting opinions, which shall not exceed 5 pages in length. In order to comply with this page limitation, nonprecedential issues raised by an appeal may be designated as nonpublishable material within the disposition.

"CHIEF JUSTICE BILANDIC, writing in support:

"The avalanche of opinions emanating from our Appellate Court has taxed the capacity of the members of that court to read the opinions filed in all of the appellate districts. If the Justices who author these opinions are burdened, then consider the plight of the members of the bar. With their busy practices, it is almost impossible to keep up with the Appellate Court output.

"Our research has revealed that a great majority of State courts which have an intermediate court of appeals, and all Federal courts of appeal, permit some form of summary disposition at the intermediate appellate level. This amendment to Rule 23 and administrative order are long overdue.

"The only other logical alternative is to return to the pre–1935 practice when Appellate Court opinions were not binding authority. The only binding authority were the opinions of the Supreme Court of this State. Chicago Title & Trust Co. v. Vance (1988), 175 Ill.App.3d 600, 606.

"In all other respects, I join in the supporting opinion of Justice Heiple.

"JUSTICE HEIPLE joins in this supporting opinion.

"JUSTICE HEIPLE, also writing in support:

"In 1993, the Appellate Court of Illinois published 2,195 opinions. Many of these published opinions were redundant and lacking in precedential value. The problem here, it should be noted, is greater than merely the filling up of book shelves and the loss of forests. The more serious problem is that legal research is being rendered unnecessarily burdensome, difficult and costly by the publication of multiple opinions expounding the same point of law.

"In addition to the sheer number of opinions, it is also to be observed that many appellate authors are unwilling to state their findings in a few pages. In short, they are too long. Legal researchers must read through many opinions and many pages of many opinions in order to locate the essence of a single point of law. This is unnecessarily tedious and wasteful of time and effort. It drives up the cost of legal research and the litigation expenses of the client.

"The judicial process serves two basic functions. It decides controversies and it offers guidance for future conduct. The purpose of a published opinion is to offer guidance. If an opinion merely settles a controversy between the parties and lacks precedential value, there is no reason to publish it in the case books.

"The new Supreme Court Rule 23 and this accompanying order are modest efforts to curtail the publication of unnecessary opinions and to render those opinions that are published to be of readable length. The majority of this court, consisting entirely of former appellate court justices, believes that both goals are desirable and attainable. They further believe that adherence to the revised Rule 23 and this order will benefit the general public and the practicing bar and that it will elevate the significance of both the appellate court as an institution and its opinions as precedential authority.

"CHIEF JUSTICE BILANDIC and JUSTICES HARRISON and NICKELS join in this supporting opinion.

"JUSTICE MILLER, dissenting:

"Unlike my colleagues, I do not see the wisdom in imposing numerical limits either on the quantity of opinions published by the various districts of the appellate court or on the length of each published opinion, concurrence, or dissent. Granted, certain appellate court cases are being disposed of by published opinion when an unpublished order would be more appropriate, and other opinions (and concurrences and dissents) are unnecessarily long. The majority's solution, in the present order, limiting the quantity and length of appellate court opinions, however, is simply a mechanical, arbitrary exercise, demeaning to the appellate court, and to the public it serves. Some districts might find that they have produced more than the prescribed number of publishable opinions in a year; some published cases will require more than 20 pages of explanation and analysis.

"Apart from the administrative order, our newly amended Rule 23, in which I concur, provides a more flexible approach to these problems, narrowing the criteria under which publication is appropriate and permitting cases to be disposed of by summary order. In its zeal to reduce the volume of published cases and to promote brevity over verbosity, the majority has lost sight of the purposes of our courts, and of the nature of the judicial process.

"JUSTICE McMORROW joins in this dissent."

Committee Comments

Rule 23 was adopted in 1972, and its original text provided for disposition of cases in the appellate court by memorandum opinion in a limited number of categories—where no error of law appears, an opinion would have no precedential value, and one or more of the following circumstances exists: (a) that a judgment in a civil case is not against the manifest weight of the evidence, (b) that a judgment in a civil case entered upon allowance of a motion for directed verdict should be affirmed because all of the evidence, when viewed in the light most favorable to the appellant, so overwhelmingly favors the appellee that no contrary verdict based on that evidence could ever stand, (c) that in a criminal case the evidence is not so unsatisfactory as to leave a reasonable doubt as to defendant's guilt, or (d) that the decision of an administrative body or agency reviewed under the provisions of the Administrative Review Act and confirmed by the circuit court is not against the manifest weight of the evidence. The rule also provided the minimum necessities of a memorandum decision. Limited, as it was, in application, and even where applicable in its departure from the normal requirements of an opinion, Rule 23 was seldom applied. In 1975, it was amended to broaden considerably the power of the appellate court to dispose of cases without opinion. It still requires, however, that in every case disposed of the litigants be given some statement of reasons. The length of such a statement will, perforce, vary with the circumstances of the case. In a case, for example, in which the issue involved is clearly covered by binding precedent, it would suffice to cite the authority held to be dispositive.

(June 27, 1994)

By this amendment, Rule 23 creates a presumption against disposing of Appellate Court cases by full, published opinions and authorizes a third type of disposition by summary order in select circumstances. The concept of the traditional "Rule 23 order" remains, but conciseness is encouraged. Disposition by order rather than by opinion reflects the precedential value of a case, not necessarily its merits.

Two of the criteria upon which a case could qualify for disposition by opinion and the preference for publishing cases which include concurring and/or dissenting opinions have been eliminated consistent with the presumption against publication.

An administrative order which complements these changes has been entered simultaneously with the amendment of Rule 23.

Rule 24. Research Department in Each District of the Appellate Court

In each Appellate Court district there shall be a research department supervised by a director of research and staffed by such number of staff attorneys as the Supreme Court may from time to time determine. The research department in each district shall perform such duties as may be assigned to it by the presiding judge of the district or, in the First District, by the Executive Committee. The research departments of the various districts shall coordinate their activities, exchange information, and publish and maintain a manual of procedures for the research staff. An assistant to the Supreme Court may be assigned by that court to coordinate the activities of the research departments hereby created. The director of research and all staff attorneys employed in any research department shall be graduates of law schools approved by the American Bar Association. Adopted July 30, 1979, eff. Oct. 15, 1979. Amended April 10, 1987, eff. Aug. 1, 1987.

Formerly Ill.Rev.Stat.1991, ch. 110A, ¶ 24.

Committee Comments

Rule 24 is new. It recedes from the recommendation of the 1972 committee report for a statewide research department and incorporates the development of research departments in each district with a coordination of the activities of those departments by an assistant to the Supreme Court.

Rules 25 to 29. Reserved

Rule 30. Administrative Duties of the Chief Justice and the Administrative Director

(a) **The Chief Justice.** The chief justice of the Supreme Court shall be responsible for the administration of all courts in the State. To assist him, the court shall appoint an Administrative Director to serve at its pleasure, who shall report directly to the chief justice. If there is a vacancy in the office of the chief justice, the senior justice shall serve temporarily as acting chief justice. Seniority shall be determined as provided in Rule 31. If the chief justice is absent or unable to serve, the senior justice shall serve temporarily as acting chief justice.

(b) The Administrative Director. The Administrative Director of the courts shall be generally responsible for the enforcement of the rules, orders, policies and directives of the Supreme Court and the chief justice relating to matters of administration. At the direction of the chief justice and the Supreme Court, the Administrative Director shall develop, compile and promulgate administrative rules and directives relating to case processing, records and management information services, personnel, budgeting and such other matters as the chief justice and the Supreme Court shall direct. The Administrative Director also shall perform such other functions and duties as may be assigned by the chief justice or by the Supreme Court.

Adopted Nov. 21, 1988, eff. Jan. 1, 1989.

Formerly Ill.Rev.Stat.1991, ch. 110A, ¶ 30.

Rule 31. Seniority in Supreme Court

Seniority among the judges of the Supreme Court shall be determined by length of continuous service, but if the terms of two or more judges begin at the same time they shall determine the seniority as between or among themselves by lot, unless they are able to determine it by agreement.

Formerly Ill.Rev.Stat.1991, ch. 110A, ¶ 31.

Committee Comments

This is former Rule 56 without change of substance.

Rule 32. Repealed eff. Oct. 1, 1971

Rule 33. Library of Supreme Court

The librarian of the library of the Supreme Court shall not permit any person except judges of the court to take any book from the library without the consent of the court or the chief justice. No books shall be marked or underlined, nor shall the pages of any book be folded down. Any person who offends against the provisions of this rule is in contempt of the Supreme Court.

Formerly Ill.Rev.Stat.1991, ch. 110A, ¶ 33.

Committee Comments

This is former Rule 55 with minor language changes.

Rules 34 to 38. Reserved

Rule 39. Appointment of Associate Judges

(a) Terms.

(1) The terms of all associate judges in office shall expire on June 30th of every fourth year subsequent to 1975, regardless of the date on which any judge is appointed. Notwithstanding the provisions for conditional notices of vacancy as contained in paragraph (a)(2) of this rule, the office of an associate judge shall be vacant upon his or her death, resignation, retirement, or removal, or upon the expiration of his or her term without his or her reappointment. When a sitting associate judge submits in writing his or her resignation, the chief judge of the circuit may, no sooner than 120 days before the effective date of such resignation, cause notice of the vacancy to be given pursuant to subpart (b) of this rule, provided that the candidate appointed to fill the vacancy shall not take office before the effective date of such resignation.

(2) In those instances where a sitting associate judge is running unopposed or where two or more associate judges are the only candidates opposing one another in the general election and an associate judge vacancy therefore can be anticipated, the Administrative Director may, upon the chief judge's request, approve posting of a conditional notice of vacancy not more than 30 days prior to the general election and absent a letter of resignation from a sitting associate judge. The conditional notice of vacancy shall clearly advise potential associate judge candidates that the vacancy is contingent upon certification by the Illinois Board of Elections of general election results declaring a sitting associate judge the winner. Prior to the distribution of ballots provided for in paragraph (b)(4), the Director shall await the Illinois Board of Elections' certification of the general election results.

(b) Filling Vacancies. Vacancies in the office of associate judge shall be filled in the following manner:

(1) *Notice of Vacancy.* Upon approval of the Director of the Administrative Office of the Illinois Courts, the chief judge of the circuit shall, after forwarding a copy of the notice to the Director, cause notice to be given to the bar of the circuit, in the same manner as notice of matters of general interest to the bar is customarily given in the circuit, that the vacancy exists and will be filled by the judges of the circuit. The notice of vacancy shall be given as soon as practicable, but no later than 30 days after the accumulation of five consecutive vacancies for which notice has not been given. If the chief judge of the circuit fails to give notice within the time period prescribed by this provision, the Chief Justice of the Supreme Court may direct the Director of the Administrative Office of the Illinois Courts to give notice of the vacancies in the manner prescribed by this rule.

(2) *Applications and Certification.* Any attorney who seeks appointment to the office of associate judge must be a United States citizen, licensed to practice law in this state, and a resident of the unit

from which he/she seeks appointment. Applicants shall have 30 days after the notice of vacancy is given within which to electronically file with the Director of the Administrative Office of the Illinois Courts a signed application on the form prescribed and furnished by the Director. If an applicant is not able to submit an application electronically, an applicant shall have 30 days after the notice of vacancy is given within which to file with the Director of the Administrative Office of the Illinois Courts two signed originals of an application on the form prescribed and furnished by the Director. Applications must be received by the Director within the 30–day period. Applications transmitted via facsimile will not be accepted. At the close of the application process, the Director shall certify to the chief judge a list of those applicants who have timely filed and provide a copy of those applications.

(3) *Nomination.* In judicial circuits having a population of more than 500,000, the chief judge of each circuit and at least two but not more than 10 additional circuit judges selected by their fellow circuit judges shall serve as a nominating committee for candidates for appointment to the office of associate judge of their circuit. If there are fewer than 20 circuit judges in a circuit, all of the circuit judges may sit as a nominating committee. When one or more vacancies in the office of associate judge are to be filled, the nominating committee shall select from the applications filed twice as many names of qualified candidates as there are vacancies to be filled.

(4) *Distribution of Ballots and Related Materials.*

(i) In judicial circuits having a population of more than 500,000, the chief judge shall notify the Director of the names of those candidates selected by the nominating committee and request that the Director initiate the balloting process. Within 14 days after the chief judge's notification, the Director shall place the name of each candidate on a ballot in alphabetical order. The ballot shall also contain blank spaces equal in number to the number of vacancies to be filled, in which spaces may be written the name of any qualified applicant whose name does not appear on the ballot as a candidate.

(ii) In judicial circuits having a population of less than 500,000, the chief judge shall request that the Director initiate the balloting process. Within 14 days after the chief judge's request, the Director shall place the name of each candidate on a ballot in alphabetical order.

(iii) A ballot and a brief biographical synopsis of each candidate shall be mailed to each circuit judge in the circuit. Each ballot shall also be accompanied by a stamped, addressed return envelope, an envelope marked "For Ballot Only," and a signature card. Upon request, any circuit judge may obtain a copy of the complete application of any applicant.

(5) *Balloting.* Each circuit judge shall complete his or her ballot by voting for one candidate for each vacancy to be filled, enclose the ballot in the envelope marked "For Ballot Only," seal the envelope, sign the signature card, and enclose that envelope and signature card in the stamped, addressed return envelope, which shall be delivered to the Director within 14 days of the date the ballots were distributed. The Director shall count the ballots which are accompanied by a signed signature card, tabulate the results and certify them to the chief judge, maintaining the secrecy of the ballots.

(6) *Results of Balloting; Runoffs.*

(i) In judicial circuits having a population of more than 500,000 the candidates receiving the most votes shall be declared to be appointed to fill the vacancies. Where a tie prevents a winner from being declared, reballoting shall proceed in the manner provided above for the first balloting except that ballots shall include only the names of those candidates whose tied votes prevented a winner from being declared.

(ii) In judicial circuits having a population of less than 500,000 the candidates receiving votes from a majority of the circuit judges who have voted shall be declared to be appointed to fill the vacancies. If there are not enough candidates receiving majorities to fill all the vacancies, the Director shall list alphabetically on a runoff ballot the remaining candidates, in number equal to twice the number of remaining vacancies, who received the most votes in the first balloting (or twice that number plus any who are tied with the candidate in the list who received the least number of votes). The candidates receiving the most votes in the runoff balloting shall be declared to be appointed to vacancies not filled as a result of the first balloting. Where a tie prevents a winner from being declared, reballoting shall proceed in the manner provided above for the first balloting except that ballots shall include only the names of those candidates whose tied votes prevented a winner from being declared.

(c) Reappointment of Associate Judges Upon Expiration of Their Terms.

(1) *Request for Reappointment.* An associate judge may file a request for reappointment with the chief judge of the circuit at least three months but not more than six months before the expiration of his or her term. At least 63 days before the expiration of the terms of associate judges, each chief judge shall certify to the Director the names of the associate judges in the circuit who have requested reappointment.

(2) *Distribution of Ballots.* At least 40 days before the expiration of the terms of associate

judges, the Director shall prepare and distribute ballots on which each circuit judge shall vote on the question whether each associate judge who has requested reappointment shall be reappointed for another term. Each ballot shall be accompanied by a stamped, addressed return envelope, an envelope marked "For Ballot Only," and a signature card.

(3) *Balloting.* Each circuit judge shall complete his or her ballot, enclose it in the envelope marked "For Ballot Only," seal the envelope, sign the signature card, and enclose the sealed envelope and signature card in the stamped, addressed return envelope, which shall be delivered to the Director within 14 days after it was distributed. The Director shall count the ballots which are accompanied by a signed signature card, tabulate the results and certify them to the chief judge, maintaining the secrecy of the ballots. If three fifths of the circuit judges voting on the question vote in favor of reappointment of an associate judge, he or she shall be declared reappointed for another term.

(d) Definition of "Circuit Judge." For the purposes of this rule, "circuit judge" shall include a circuit judge elected or appointed to a term of office within a circuit (or a unit defined by law which is smaller than the circuit), including a circuit judge who is assigned to the Supreme or the Appellate Court (whether relieved of judicial duties on the circuit court or not), and a circuit judge temporarily recalled from retirement and assigned to judicial duty as a circuit judge in the circuit from which the circuit judge had been elected or appointed, but shall not include a circuit judge who was elected or appointed in another circuit but is temporarily assigned to a circuit which is in the process of selecting or retaining an associate judge. A circuit judge appointed to office during the balloting period may vote to fill associate judge vacancies in his or her circuit if the circuit judge has been sworn in and has provided a copy of his or her signed oath of office to the Director. The newly appointed circuit judge must complete and deliver his or her ballot to the Director within the same 14–day period that the ballots were distributed to the circuit judges under paragraph (b)(5). In no instance will the 14–day period specified in paragraph (b)(5) be extended for those circuit judges appointed to office during the balloting period.

Adopted June 25, 1971, eff. July 1, 1971. Amended eff. Oct. 14, 1971; April 1, 1992, eff. Aug. 1, 1992; Dec. 3, 1997, eff. Jan. 1, 1998; Dec. 17, 1999, eff. immediately; March 16, 2001, eff. immediately; Nov. 27, 2002, eff. immediately; May 28, 2003, eff. immediately; Jan. 25, 2007, corrected January 26, 2007, eff. Feb. 1, 2007; April 23, 2009, eff. July 1, 2009; Oct. 30, 2012, eff. immediately; Dec. 28, 2012, eff. immediately; Jan. 29, 2015, eff. immediately; Aug. 10, 2015, eff. Sept. 1, 2015; Oct. 15, 2015, eff. immediately.

Formerly Ill.Rev.Stat.1991, ch. 110A, ¶ 39.

Committee Comments

(July 1, 1971)

This rule implements section 8 of article VI of the new Illinois Constitution, which provides, "Associate Judges shall be appointed by the Circuit Judges in each circuit as the Supreme Court shall provide by rule."

Rule 40. Marriage and Civil Union Divisions

(a) Creation. The chief judge of any judicial circuit may, by administrative order, establish a marriage and civil union division in any county in the circuit and specify the times and places at which those judges willing to perform marriage solemnizations and civil union certifications will normally be available to do so. A marriage and civil union fund may be established on a circuitwide basis rather than a county-by-county basis when the chief judge, along with the majority of circuit judges, determines that the circuit's judicial needs are best served by a circuitwide fund.

(b) Clerk–Fee. The chief judge may provide that the clerk of the circuit court or someone designated by the clerk shall attend each regular session of each marriage and civil union division to assist the judge assigned thereto. The chief judge may set a fee to be collected by the clerk in an amount not to exceed $10 for each marriage solemnization or civil union certification performed. No additional fee or gratuity will be solicited or accepted.

(c) Trust Account. The fees received shall be deposited in a federally insured or fully collateralized bank account in the name of the "Marriage and Civil Union Fund of the Circuit Court of _____ County" or the "Marriage and Civil Union Fund of the _____ Circuit Court." The trustees of the account shall be three in number, consisting of the chief judge, the administrative secretary to the chief judge, and a resident circuit judge of the county. If there is no administrative secretary to the chief judge, or if there is no resident circuit judge of the county, the chief judge shall designate one or two fellow circuit judges as his or her co-trustees. Money in a marriage and civil union fund may be spent in furtherance of the administration of justice for the following items:

bank charges;

business meal costs when an agenda is prepared for the meeting;

courtroom and judicial office improvements;

electronic legal research services;

equipment-purchase, repair, and service;

judicial robes-purchase, repair, and cleaning;

jury room supplies and equipment;

legal publications;

membership dues for legal and judicial associations;

name plates for judges;

office supplies;

pictures, plaques, and frames for the courthouse;

public education/awareness program materials;

training courses approved by the judicial education committee;

training and professional education programs for nonjudicial employees of the judicial branch; and

travel for judicial business, not to exceed reimbursement levels consistent with the Supreme Court's travel reimbursement guidelines for judicial and nonjudicial members of the judicial branch.

Payment of a reasonable per diem fee to the clerk, or person designated by the clerk, who attends the marriage and civil union division on a day other than a regular working day may be made from the fund.

(d) Reporting and Auditing Requirements.

(1) Funds with Balances Under $50,000 at the end of the State Fiscal Year. For marriage and civil union funds that reflect a balance under $50,000 at the end of each State Fiscal Year (June 30), the chief judge of the circuit shall file, quarterly in the next fiscal year, reports with the Administrative Director of the Illinois Courts. The reports shall be filed not later than the fifteenth of each October, January, April and July. The report shall contain (i) the name of the marriage and civil union fund; (ii) the quarter end date; (iii) the balance on hand at the beginning of the quarter; (iv) the total income, including a detailed list of any income other than marriage and civil union fees for the quarter; (v) the total expenses for the quarter with a detailed list including the name of the vendor paid, description of the goods or services purchased, and the amount of each expense, and (vi) such other information as deemed necessary by the Administrative Director. The report shall be in a format prescribed by the Administrative Office. These reports shall be prepared by the administrative secretary or the resident judge and approved by the chief circuit judge.

(2) Funds with Balances of $50,000 and over at the end of the State Fiscal Year. On an annual basis, and not later than September 30, the chief judge of the circuit shall file with the Administrative Director of the Illinois Courts a professional, independent audit conducted by an accredited audit firm for each marriage and civil union fund in his or her circuit reflecting a balance of $50,000 and over at the end of the prior State fiscal year. The content of the annual audit shall be consistent with the reporting requirements contained in paragraphs (d)(1)(i) through (d)(1)(vi) of this rule.

(3) Records relating to the revenue and expenses of the marriage and civil union funds shall be retained in either paper or electronic format for the current State Fiscal Year plus five (5) prior fiscal years.

(e) Excess Funds to County Treasurer. The trustees for all marriage and civil union funds shall pay into the county general fund or other judicial-related county funds such amounts as in their judgment may be appropriate.

Adopted eff. April 1, 1974. Amended Jan. 7, 2002, eff. March 1, 2002; Oct. 29, 2004, eff. Jan. 1, 2005; May 24, 2006, eff. immediately; Dec. 6, 2006, eff. Jan. 1, 2007; Dec. 17, 2007, eff. Jan. 1, 2008; May 26, 2011, eff. immediately; Oct. 1, 2014, eff. immediately.

Formerly Ill.Rev.Stat.1991, ch. 110A, ¶ 40.

JUSTICE FREEMAN, dissenting [March 1, 2002 amendment]:

I would quickly join the court in adopting the March 1, 2002, amendments to Supreme Court Rule 40 (134 Ill. 2d R. 40), which increase auditing and spending accountability, but for my fundamental constitutional concern with certain parts of the rule itself. Notwithstanding the amendments, the collection and disbursement of marriage fees is simply beyond this court's constitutional authority. So, while I commend the efforts taken today by my colleagues, I must dissent because the provisions amended are themselves invalid under the separation of powers doctrine.

Although there is no question that the Illinois Constitution provides this court with the authority to create, within the circuit courts, marriage divisions such as those provided for in Rule 40(a), our Constitution gives to the General Assembly-not this court-the power to set and control the deposit and disbursement of fees. The Constitution states that "[f]ees may be collected as provided *by law and by ordinance* and shall be deposited upon receipt with the treasury of the unit." (Emphasis added.) Ill. Const. 1970, art. VII, § 9. The phrase "by law," as used in our Constitution, means the General Assembly's entire lawmaking process and encompasses the "normal legislative manner." *Quinn v. Donnewald*, 107 Ill. 2d 179, 186–87 (1985). This court has recognized that the normal legislative manner consists of the vote of a majority of both houses of the General Assembly, with presentment to the Governor for his or her action, bills that successfully passed each house of the legislature. *Quinn*, 107 Ill. 2d at 186–87. In defining the phrase "by law," this court specifically relied on the drafters' meaning of the phrase as was recorded at the Constitutional Convention. *Quinn*, 107 Ill. 2d at 186. In particular, the court noted the remarks of Delegate Wayne W. Whalen, who stated that

" '[t]he reason for the addition of the words "by law" was to point out to you that it was not the intent of the Committee of the Whole or the Substantive Committee that the General Assembly could act in any other way than the lawmaking process. As you know, the General Assembly can act by rule, it can act by resolution; that was not the intent. The intent was to use the entire law-making progress as sent out in the constitution, so to clarify this ambiguity we added the term "by law" ***.' " *Quinn*, 107 Ill. 2d at 186, quoting 3 Record of Proceedings, Sixth Illinois Constitutional Convention 2180 (statements of Delegate Whalen).

Delegate Whalen's construction of the phrase is faithful to its commonly understood legal meaning–Black's Law Dictionary notes that the phrase "provided by law" when used in a constitution or statute generally means "prescribed or provided by some statute" (Black's Law Dictionary 1102 (5th ed. 1979)), and his construction was understood by the delegates to be the meaning of the phrase throughout the entire constitutional document. See 4 Record of Proceedings, Sixth Illinois Constitutional Convention 3416 (comments of Delegate Netsch, stating "the Style and Drafting Committee has adopted a practice *** whereby the expression 'by law' refers only to laws enacted by the General Assembly"); see also 4 Record of Proceedings, Sixth Illinois Constitutional Convention 2629 (comments of Delegate Nudelman). In short, the constitutional provision "as provided by law" means "as by provided by statute." In other words, the Constitution means to exclude, as the source of fee provisions, any rulemaking authority, judicial or otherwise.

Any doubt about this construction is dispelled by the fact that the Constitution provided, in juxtaposition, that fees might also be collected by municipal ordinances. An "ordinance" is defined as "a local rule enacted by a unit of government pursuant to authority delegated by the State." *City of Peoria v. Toft*, 215 Ill. App. 3d 440, 443 (1991). In light of the phrase "by law or ordinance," the Constitution demands that fees be enacted through the legislative process, on a statewide basis or on a local government basis, as opposed to any judicial rulemaking process.

Pursuant to this constitutional grant of authority, our General Assembly has set out an extensive fee schedule in the Clerks of Courts Act (705 ILCS 105/0.01 *et seq.* (West 1998)), which is arranged according to county population. See 705 ILCS 105/27.1 (West 1998) (pertaining to counties of 180,000 or less); 705 ILCS 105/27.1a (West 1998) (pertaining to counties over 180,000, but not more than 650,000); 705 ILCS 105/27.2 (West 1998) (pertaining to counties over 650,000, but less than 3 million); 705 ILCS 105/27.2a (West 1998) (pertaining to counties of 3 million or more). The Act sets a $10 fee for all in-court marriages in counties having populations of not more than 650,000. See 705 ILCS 105/27.1(b)(3), 27.1a(a–1) (West 1998). The legislature has not expressly provided a fee amount for in-court marriages performed in counties having populations greater than 650,000. In these counties, the legislature has provid-

ed that "[a]ny fees not covered in this Section shall be set by rule or administrative order of the Circuit Court with the approval of the Administrative Office of the Illinois Courts." 705 ILCS 105/27.2(r), 27.2a(r) (West 1998). Thus, we, as a court, have been given authority by the legislature to set a fee for in-court marriages performed in counties having populations of over 650,000. Rule 40(b), which provides for a $10 marriage fee, is only constitutional in those counties where the legislature has not expressly provided for an in-court marriage fee.

This court's authority to direct the deposit and disbursement of the fees collected by the clerks of the circuit courts is also governed by our Constitution. Section 9(a) states:

"Compensation of officers and employees and the office expenses of units of local government shall not be paid from fees collected. Fees may be collected as provided by law and by ordinance and shall be deposited upon receipt with the treasurer of the unit. Fees shall not be based upon funds disbursed or collected, nor upon the levy or extension of taxes." Ill. Const. 1970, art. VII, § 9(a).

In order to implement this constitutional ban on fee offices within units of local government and the judicial system, the General Assembly enacted the Fee Deposit Act in 1972. *Kaden v. Kagann*, 260 Ill. App. 3d 256, 265 (1994). Section 2 of the Fee Deposit Act mandates

"All elected or appointed officials of units of local government, and clerks of the circuit courts, authorized by law to collect fees which collection is not prohibited by Section 9 of Article VII of the Constitution, shall deposit all such collected fees upon receipt with the county treasurer or treasurer of such other unit of local government, as the case may be, except as otherwise provided by law; and except that such officials may maintain overpayments, tax redemptions, trust funds and special funds as provided for by law or local ordinance." 50 ILCS 315/2 (West 1998).

Section 2 of the Fee Deposit Act requires that, except as "provided by law" to the contrary, monies collected by the clerks of the circuit court cannot be deposited with any entity other than the county treasurer. As noted above, the phrase "provided by law" means a statute-not judicial rulemaking. Furthermore, section 2's reference to "trust funds" does not mean trust funds provided by judicial rule, but rather those "provided for by law or local ordinance." The trust fund established in Rule 40(c) does not fall within the ambit of this exception. Indeed, my research has not revealed the "law or local ordinance" by which the in-court marriage fees collected under Rule 40 may be excepted from deposit with the county treasurer and, instead, placed in a trust fund. The General Assembly, by way of the Fee Deposit Act, has expressly directed that all fees collected by the clerks of the circuit court be deposited with the treasurer of the county in which the court sits. To the extent that this court, through Rule 40, directs otherwise, it would appear that this court is improperly acting in an area wholly reserved, by constitutional fiat, to our legislature.

Our Constitution is silent as to the disposition or disbursement of fees. Our appellate court has recognized that the drafters of the 1970 Constitution, in contemplating the inclusion of a provision in the Constitution that would direct the disposition of fees, believed the issue was a matter for the General Assembly. *Kaden*, 260 Ill. App. 3d at 261 (acknowledging that it was "clear from this debate *** the drafters intended that the General Assembly determine where such fees should be deposited"). I would point out the comments of Delegate Fay: "I must respectfully urge the defeat of this proposed amendment, and the reason I do so is because *** the legislature could take care of this matter, and I think that we should let them do so rather than engraft this in the constitution where it is not needed." 4 Record of Proceedings, Sixth Illinois Constitutional Convention 2632–33 (statements of Delegate Fay). These statements led the appellate court to conclude that the Constitution left the matter of fee disbursement to the authority of our legislative branch of government and that neither the state nor the counties have a constitutional right to fees collected by the circuit court clerks. *Kaden*, 260 Ill. App. 3d at 260–61.

In the absence of an express constitutional provision on a subject, the legislature is free to act. *County of Stark v. County of Henry*, 326 Ill. 535, 538 (1927). The General Assembly has comprehensively provided for the disbursement of clerks' fees in the Clerks of Courts Act. Section 27.5 of that Act states that

"All *fees*, fines, costs, additional penalties, bail balances assessed or forfeited, and any other amount paid by a person to the circuit clerk *that equals an amount less than $55*, except restitution under Section 5–5–6 of the Unified Code of Corrections, reimbursement for the costs of an emergency response as provided under Section 5–5–3 of the Unified Code of Corrections, any fees collected for attending a traffic safety program under paragraph (c) of Supreme Court Rule 529, any fee collected on behalf of a State's Attorney under Section 4–2002 of the Counties Code or a sheriff under Section 4–5001 of the Counties Code, or any cost imposed under Section 124A–5 of the Code of Criminal Procedure of 1963, for convictions, orders of supervision, or any other disposition for a violation of Chapters 3, 4, 6, 11, and 12 of the Illinois Vehicle Code, or a similar provision of a local ordinance, and any violation of the Child Passenger Protection Act, or a similar provision of a local ordinance, *shall be disbursed within 60 days after receipt by the circuit clerk as follows*: 47% shall be disbursed to the entity authorized by law to receive the fine imposed in the case; 12% shall be disbursed to the State

Treasurer; and 41% shall be disbursed to the county's general corporate fund. Of the 12% disbursed to the State Treasurer, 1/6 shall be deposited by the State Treasurer into the Violent Crime Victims Assistance Fund, 1/2 shall be deposited into the Traffic and Criminal Conviction Surcharge Fund, and 1/3 shall be deposited into the Drivers Education Fund. For fiscal years 1992 and 1993, amounts deposited into the Violent Crime Victims Assistance Fund, the Traffic and Criminal Conviction Surcharge Fund, or the Drivers Education Fund shall not exceed 110% of the amounts deposited into those funds in fiscal year 1991. Any amount that exceeds the 110% limit shall be distributed as follows: 50% shall be disbursed to the county's general corporate fund and 50% shall be disbursed to the entity authorized by law to receive the fine imposed in the case. Not later than March 1 of each year the circuit clerk shall submit a report of the amount of funds remitted to the State Treasurer under this Section during the preceding year based upon independent verification of fines and fees. All counties shall be subject to this Section, except that counties with a population under 2,000,000 may, by ordinance, elect not to be subject to this Section. For offenses subject to this Section, judges shall impose one total sum of money payable for violations. The circuit clerk may add on no additional amounts except for amounts that are required by Sections 27.3a and 27.3c of this Act, unless those amounts are specifically waived by the judge. With respect to money collected by the circuit clerk as a result of forfeiture of bail, ex parte judgment or guilty plea pursuant to Supreme Court Rule 529, the circuit clerk shall first deduct and pay amounts required by Sections 27.3a and 27.3c of this Act. This Section is a denial and limitation of home rule powers and functions under subsection (h) of Section 6 of Article VII of the Illinois Constitution." (Emphases added.) 705 ILCS 105/27.5 (West 1998).

The comprehensive treatment could not more strongly demonstrate the legislature's intention that *all* fees covered by the law, except those the legislature wanted to exempt, were to be disbursed in the manner described. In fact, the reference to our Rule 529 shows that when the General Assembly wanted to refer to monies collected by way of this court's rules, it expressly so provided. Moreover, the fact that the General Assembly specifically referred to this section as a "denial and limitation" on the home rule power provides further proof of the intention that the General Assembly *itself* solely provide for the disbursement of fees collected by the clerks of our courts. The disbursement provisions contained in Rule 40 are at odds with the statutory provisions mandated by our legislature. Because our Constitution intends for this matter to be left to the legislature and not this court, I believe that the conflict must be resolved in favor of the legislature.

In sum, the Constitution mandates that fees must be collected by statute (or ordinance) and not by judicial rule. The legislature has expressly provided for the collection of fees in the Clerks of Courts Act and has further provided that any fees not covered specifically in that Act shall be set by rule or administrative order of the circuit court with the approval of the Administrative Office of the Illinois Courts. So it is by legislative enactment that the court may, by rule, set those fees not otherwise provided by law. Our Constitution also mandates that fees collected be deposited with the treasurer of the unit. There is no complementary constitutional provision which mandates the manner in which fees collected by clerks of the courts shall be disbursed; rather the matter is left to legislative authority. The General Assembly has implemented the constitutional mandate regarding fee deposits through enactment of the Fee Deposit Act and has provided for fee disbursements through enactment of the Clerks of Courts Act. Neither of these pieces of legislation grant to this court any authority whatsoever to direct either the deposit or disposition of fees.

Other observations support this conclusion. I refer specifically to the duty given by the legislature to the county boards to provide for court facilities. See 55 ILCS 5/5–1106 (West 1998). Section 5–1106 of the Counties Code mandates that the county board of each county provide reasonable and necessary expenses for the use of, *inter alios*, judges and clerks of the courts. The Code further mandates each county board to provide for proper rooms and offices for the accommodation of the circuit court of the county and to provide "suitable furnishings for such rooms and offices. *** The court rooms and furnishings thereof shall meet with reasonable minimum standards prescribed by the Supreme Court of Illinois. Such standards shall be substantially the same as those generally accepted in court rooms as to general furnishings, arrangement of bench, tables and chairs, cleanliness, convenience to litigants, decorations, lighting and other such matters relating to the physical appearance of the court room." 55 ILCS 5/5–1106 (West 1998). These mandates from the General Assembly are in harmony with the fee deposit and disbursement system established by the legislature-the fees revert directly to the county, which is charged with the responsibility of providing the upkeep of its courts.

The only conclusion that can be reached in light of the foregoing is that this court simply lacks the authority to create marriage trust funds in the manner prescribed in Rule 40. The Illinois Attorney General reached the same conclusion in 1977, when he issued an opinion finding that Rule 40 was inoperative insofar as it authorized deposits and disbursements of fees in contravention of statute. See 1977 Ill. Att'y Gen. Op. 159. Again, the fact that the amendments are well-intended and commendable must be separated from the fact that the collection and disbursement provisions of Rule 40 violate the separation of powers doctrine. This is no small concern. We, as an institution charged with the solemn authority to measure the constitutionality of legislative acts, must also be diligent to circumscribe our conduct to what is constitutionally permissive. Unfortunately, that has not occurred with respect to Rule 40. For these reasons, I respectfully dissent.

Committee Comment

(May 24, 2006)

Rule 40 provides that marriage funds may be expended to support judicial "training courses approved by the judicial education committee." Under this provision, marriage funds may be expended for only those judicial education programs which have been approved for the award of continuing judicial education credit, pursuant to the Supreme Court's Comprehensive Judicial Education Plan for Illinois Judges. The role of the Illinois Judicial Conference Committee on Education, under Rule 40, is limited to review and recommendation to the Supreme Court regarding the award of judicial education credit. The authority to expend marriage funds for those courses approved by the Court for the award of judicial education credit rests with the chief circuit judges.

Rule 41. Judicial Conference

(a) Duties. There shall be a Judicial Conference to consider the work of the courts, to suggest improvements in the administration of justice, and to make recommendations for the improvement of the courts.

(b) Membership.

(1) The membership of the Judicial Conference shall consist of:

(A) The Chief Justice of the Supreme Court of Illinois, who shall preside over the conference;

(B) The other members of the Supreme Court, who shall be *ex officio* members of the conference, and the Director of the Administrative Office of the Illinois Courts, who shall also be an *ex officio* member;

(C) The chairperson of the Executive Committee of the Appellate Court of the First Judicial District and the presiding judge of the appellate court in each judicial district other than the First Judicial District;

(D) Thirty judges from the First Judicial District, including the chief circuit judge;

(E) Ten judges from each judicial district other than the First Judicial District, including at least one chief circuit judge from each judicial district.

(F) The Supreme Court may appoint any judge, lawyer, or person involved with the judicial branch or administration of justice as an advisor to the Judicial Conference.

(2)(A) All members designated in subparagraphs (1)(D), (E) and (F) shall be appointed by the Supreme Court.

(B) One–third of the initial members appointed by the Court from the First Judicial District shall serve until January 1, 1994; one–third shall serve until January 1, 1995; and one-third shall serve until January 1, 1996, or until their successors are appointed. In each of the other judicial districts, four of the initial members appointed by the Court shall serve until January 1, 1994; three shall serve until January 1, 1995; and three shall serve until January 1, 1996, or until their successors are appointed. Each term thereafter shall be for three years subject to the discretion of the Supreme Court, and no member or advisor may be appointed to more than two full consecutive terms (six years) subject to the discretion of the Supreme Court.

(c) Executive Committee.

(1) The Supreme Court shall appoint six members of the conference from the First Judicial District and two members from each of the other districts to serve on the Executive Committee, which shall act on behalf of the conference when the conference is not in session.

(2) The Chief Justice shall serve as chairperson of the committee, and shall convene the committee as necessary to attend to the business of the conference.

(3) At least 60 days prior to the date on which the Judicial Conference is to be convened the committee shall submit to the Supreme Court a suggested agenda for the annual meeting.

(d) Other Committees. The Supreme Court shall appoint such other committees as are necessary to further the work of the conference. The Executive Committee shall annually receive from each committee a recommendation as to whether that committee should be maintained or abolished and make appropriate recommendations to the Supreme Court. Each recommendation shall be accompanied by a justification for the recommendation.

(e) Meetings of Conference. The conference shall meet at least once annually at a place and on a date to be designated by the Supreme Court.

(f) Secretary. The Administrative Office of the Illinois Courts shall be secretary of the conference.

Amended eff. July 1, 1971; March 1, 1993, eff. immediately; Sept. 23, 2008, eff. immediately; Oct. 11, 2012, eff. immediately; Oct. 4, 2013, eff. Nov. 1, 2013; Dec. 9, 2014, eff. Oct. 1, 2014 *nunc pro tunc.*

Formerly Ill.Rev.Stat.1991, ch. 110A, ¶ 41.

Committee Comments
(Revised July 1, 1971)

This is former Rule 56–1, as amended January 25, 1966, with minor language changes.

Subparagraph (b) was amended in 1971 to delete the reference to "associate judges" of the circuit courts. Prior to the adoption of the 1970 constitution, associate judges of the circuit court, as elected judges, were members of the Judicial Conference, but magistrates were not. Under the 1970 constitution all elected judicial officers are called judges, and appointive judicial officers formerly called "magistrates" are called "associate judges." The 1971 amendment reflects this change in terminology.

Rule 42. Conference of Chief Circuit Judges

(a) Responsibilities. A conference of the chief circuit judges shall meet regularly to consider problems relating to the administration of the circuit courts and such other matters as may from time to time be referred to the conference by this court.

(b) Membership, Officers. The duly elected chief judge of each judicial circuit shall be a member of the conference of chief circuit judges. The chief judges shall select one of their number to serve as chairman of the conference and another to serve as vice-chairman. The chairman and vice-chairman shall serve two-year terms, beginning on January 1 of each even-numbered year and ending on December 31 of each odd-numbered year.

(c) Meetings. The conference shall meet at such times and places as may be designated by the members.

(d) Secretary. The Administrative Office of the Illinois Courts shall be secretary of the conference.

Adopted Sept. 29, 1978, eff. Nov. 1, 1978. Amended June 15, 1982, eff. July 1, 1982.

Formerly Ill.Rev.Stat.1991, ch. 110A, ¶ 42.

Rules 43 to 45. Reserved

Rule 46. Official Record of Court Proceedings

(a) Taking of the Record. The record of court proceedings may be taken by stenographic means or by an electronic recording system approved by the Supreme Court. All transcripts prepared as the official record of court proceedings shall be prepared pursuant to applicable supreme court rules.

(b) Security of the Record. The confidentiality of court proceedings and the retention and safekeeping of notes and electronic recordings shall be maintained consistent with standards established by the Supreme Court through its Administrative Office.

(c) Court Reporting Personnel. For purposes of this rule and other supreme court rules regarding the official record, "court reporting personnel" shall include:

(1) court reporters as defined by the Court Reporters Act (705 ILCS 70/1);

(2) court personnel who have fulfilled the training and certification standards promulgated by the Supreme Court and consistent with paragraph (d) of this rule; and

(3) certified shorthand reporters hired through an agency or as an independent contractor by a private party or parties to take a stenographic record in court proceedings.

(d) Electronic Recording of Court Proceedings.

(1) The Supreme Court shall provide for and prescribe the types of electronic recording equipment that may be used in the circuit courts. Those jurisdictions with electronic recording systems installed are required to properly utilize and staff such equipment in order to produce a reliable verbatim record of the proceedings.

(2) Court reporting personnel, including court reporters as defined by the Court Reporters Act (705 ILCS 70/1), must successfully complete training and certification designed to qualify them to operate electronic recording equipment, prepare transcripts from such proceedings, and certify the record on appeal. Such training and certification shall be consistent with standards established by the Supreme Court, through its Administrative Office.

(3) Electronic recordings of proceedings shall remain under the control of the court having custody of them. The chief judges shall provide for the storage and safekeeping of such recordings consistent with the standards referenced in paragraph (b) of this rule.

(4) The Administrative Office shall monitor the operation of electronic recording equipment, the security of the electronic recordings, and the training of court reporting personnel to assure that each county is in compliance with this rule.

Adopted December 13, 2005, effective immediately.

Rules 47 to 50. Reserved

Rule 51. Rescinded eff. July 1, 1971

Rules 52 to 55. Reserved

Rule 56. Temporary Assignment to Other Duties

(a) Policy. In order to promote public confidence in the integrity and impartiality of the judiciary, and taking into consideration the nature and severity of any charges against or implications of improper conduct by a judge, a chief judge of the circuit court, or the presiding judge in the appellate court, whichever the case may be, may temporarily assign a judge to restricted duties or duties other than judicial duties. A chief circuit judge, or the presiding appellate judge, whichever the case may be, shall enter a written administrative order setting out the reasons for such assignments. The reasons for such assignments may include, but need not be limited to, the following:

(1) the judge has been formally charged with the commission of a crime which involves moral turpitude or reflects adversely upon the judge's fitness to serve; or

(2) a complaint has been filed with the Courts Commission by the Judicial Inquiry Board or a judge has allegedly committed a violation of the Code of Judicial Conduct which involves fraud, or moral turpitude, persistent nonperformance of judicial duties or threatens irreparable injury to the public, to the judicial branch of government, or to the orderly administration of justice;

(3) a judge has been publicly implicated in conduct which, if true, would constitute impropriety or an appearance of impropriety which involves moral turpitude or threatens irreparable injury to the public, to the judicial branch of government, or to the orderly administration of justice; or

(4) There is reasonable cause to believe that a medical examination would reveal that a judge is mentally incompetent or physically unable to perform his or her duties, whether the impairment is caused by injury, infirmity, a chemical dependency, other disease, or by any other cause whatever, and it appears that the incompetence is or may be permanent or will likely be of such duration that the judge's continued assignment to judicial duties could result in irreparable injury to the public, impede the orderly administration of justice, or bring dishonor on the judicial system. Determinations as to a judge's mental or physical ability to perform his or her duties shall be in compliance with all applicable federal and state disability laws.

(b) Form and Service of Order. The chief judge's order shall be served personally upon the judge. If the judge is unavailable or the judge's whereabouts are unknown, the order shall be served by mailing a copy of the order by ordinary mail to the judge's last known address.

(c) Petition for Return to Full Assignment. Any judge temporarily assigned pursuant to this rule may request that the chief judge vacate the order. In the alternative the judge may, at any time, petition the Supreme Court for a return to full-duty assignment. A petition filed with the Supreme Court shall be in accordance with procedures outlined in Rule 383.

Adopted Nov. 29, 1990, eff. Dec. 1, 1990; amended, eff. Dec. 1, 2008.

Formerly Ill.Rev.Stat.1991, ch. 110A, ¶ 56.

Committee Comments

Each judge is elected or appointed to a term of office specified by section 10 of article VI of the Illinois Constitution. During such tenure, a judge is vested with the full jurisdiction of the court to which elected or appointed. However, the matters over which the judge may exercise that jurisdiction on a day-to-day basis is determined in large measure by the judge's *assignment* and is subject to the chief judge's general administrative authority. (Supreme Court Rule 21(b); see *People v. Joseph* (1986), 113 Ill.2d 36.) The chief circuit judge may assign any judge serving in the circuit to any judicial duty. Assignment of a judge to restricted duties or to duties other than judicial duties (or assignment to no duties) is not expressly dealt with in the Illinois Constitution, but the Committee believes that power falls within the general administrative powers granted to the chief judge by our constitution.

While not normally considered a binding authority on the interpretation of the Illinois Constitution, the Illinois Courts Commission appears to confirm that, in its opinion, the chief circuit judge does possess such power.

In *In re Murphy* (1968), 1 Ill. Cts. Com. 3, the courts Commission found that Chief Circuit Judge Boyle had acted properly (and, presumably, within the scope of his constitutional powers) when he relieved the respondent of his duties both before the investigation commenced and during the pendency of proceedings before the Commission:

"[T]his Commission finds:

(1) That the action of Chief Judge Boyle in relieving this respondent of his duties and his letter suggesting to the Supreme Court that an investigation should be made by the Commission was a proper action;

* * * * * * *

(6) That the action of Chief Judge Boyle in relieving the respondent of his duties during the pendency of this hearing was proper."

This rule suggests circumstances which might warrant assignment of judges to restricted duties or to duties other than judicial duties and provides a procedure by which a chief circuit judge may temporarily assign judges to restricted duties or to duties other than judicial duties. This rule is modeled, in part, on Rule 774, Interim Suspension, under which the Supreme Court, on its own motion or on motion of the ARDC Administrator, may temporarily suspend an attorney from the practice of law, pending the outcome of prosecutions or investigations.

A judge assigned under this rule may seek relief either by asking the chief judge to vacate the order or by petitioning the Supreme Court for a return to a full-duty assignment. If the judge believes that a request directed to the chief judge would be unavailing, the judge is not bound to exhaust that possible remedy before filing his petition with the Supreme Court.

Assignments under this rule do not affect a judge's right to salary or to any of the emoluments of office, and are not disciplinary in nature. (*Cf. In re Kaye* (1974), 1 Ill. Cts. Com. 36.) If a judge is to be removed from office, suspended without pay, censured or reprimanded for any misconduct, or if a judge is to be suspended, with or without pay, or

retired for being either physically or mentally unable to perform his or her duties, the Judicial Inquiry Board and the Courts Commission are responsible for conducting hearings and proceedings and imposing whatever remedy may be appropriate.

Rule 57. Reserved

Rule 58. Judicial Performance Evaluation

(a) **Definitions.**

(1) Whenever the word "judge" is used in this rule, it includes only circuit and associate judges.

(2) Whenever the pronoun "he" is used in this rule, it includes the feminine as well as the masculine form.

(b) **Preamble.** The courts, the public and the bar have a vital interest in a responsive and respected judiciary. In its supervisory role and pursuant to its power over the court system and judges, the court has determined that the periodic evaluation of a judge's performance is a reliable method to promote judicial excellence and competence. Accordingly, the court has authorized a program of mandatory judicial performance evaluation. The program shall be supervised by the court and shall be implemented and monitored by a committee appointed by the court designated as the Judicial Performance Evaluation Committee, which shall establish procedures to implement this program.

(c) **Purpose.** There shall be a mandatory program of judicial performance evaluation for the purpose of achieving excellence in the performance of individual judges and the improvement of the judiciary as a whole.

(d) **Confidentiality.** The program must be conducted candidly and in strict confidence so that evaluations may be based on objective criteria and the areas for improvement determined fairly. The disclosure of evaluation information would be counterproductive to the goals of the evaluation program, reduce the free flow of comment, and result in the termination of the program. The following rules of confidentiality are essential to the successful implementation of the judicial evaluation program.

(1) *Information Obtained.* All information, questionnaires, notes, memoranda, electronic and computer data, and any other data obtained and used in the course of any judicial performance evaluation shall be privileged and strictly confidential. For the purpose of self-improvement, only the individual judge evaluated and the agents assigned to present the data to the judge will be permitted to know to which judge particular information applies. The information, in summary form only and without disclosing the names of individual judges, may also be used by the Supreme Court and its designated agents for the purposes of improvement of the judiciary, and for use in administering the courts

and for the development of judicial education programs. The identity of any person who provides information shall be privileged and held confidential and shall not be made available to any person. Notwithstanding the foregoing, information disclosing a criminal act may be provided to law enforcement authorities at the direction of the Supreme Court. Requests for such information shall be made by written petition setting forth in particularity the need for such information. All information and data provided to law enforcement authorities pursuant to this paragraph shall no longer be deemed privileged and confidential. As to all information and data obtained in the operation of the program for judicial performance evaluation, the members of the Oversight Committee are hereby exempted from the requirements of the following rules of this court: Article I, Rule 63B(3) (Code of Judicial Conduct), and Article VIII, Rule 8.3 (Illinois Rules of Professional Conduct), except as herein provided.

(2) *Admissibility as Evidence.* Except as disclosed pursuant to paragraph (d)(1) hereof, all information, questionnaires, notes, memoranda or other data declared to be privileged and confidential hereby shall not be admissible as evidence, nor discoverable in any action of any kind in any court or before any tribunal, board, agency or person.

Adopted Sept. 30, 1988, eff. Oct. 1, 1988. Amended April 1, 1992, eff. Aug. 1, 1992; amended March 1, 2011, effective immediately.

Formerly Ill.Rev.Stat.1991, ch. 110A, ¶ 58.

Rules 59, 60.   Reserved

CODE OF JUDICIAL CONDUCT

Committee Commentary

Preface

Prior to 1964, Illinois let the matter of judicial ethics to the individual conscience of the judge, subject to the impeachment power of the General Assembly and the requirement that each judge run for reelection at the expiration of his term of office. On January 1, 1964, the effective date of the amendment to the judicial article of the 1870 Constitution, the Courts Commission was established to investigate, prosecute and adjudicate complaints of judicial misconduct against judicial officers. Concomitantly, the Illinois Judicial Conference adopted advisory Canons of Judicial Ethics.

In January 1970, the Illinois Supreme Court adopted the first rules of judicial conduct, effective March 15 of that year. With the adoption of the 1970 Constitution of Illinois, the present system for the enforcement of judicial ethics through the Judicial Inquiry Board and the Courts Commission was established. This first judicial code was based on the efforts of the Supreme Court Committee on Judicial Ethics. The report recommended that the matter be kept under constant surveillance, particularly "in view of the current work of the American Bar Association in this area and the approaching Constitutional Convention in the state."

With the adoption of a new code of judicial ethics by the American Bar Association in 1972, a joint Illinois State Bar Association and Chicago Bar Association committee submitted a report recommending that the new ABA Code be made the basis of a new Illinois code of judicial ethics. This report was studied by a committee of the Illinois Judicial Conference, whose report in 1975 led to several amendments to the Illinois code in 1976.

The initial determination of the present committee was to propose the adoption of a new code based on the ABA canons. There was general agreement that revisions of the existing code would be sufficient to keep Illinois in the forefront of the modern movement toward full but fair regulation of judicial ethics. Indeed, the comprehensiveness and wisdom of that code is reflected in the fact that it was the committee's conclusion that the adoption of the ABA canons would work no significant substantive changes in the existing law. The unanimous decision of the committee to recommend that the ABA canons be adopted as the foundation of the Illinois rules was primarily predicated on two interrelated factors: the desire for uniformity with rules governing judicial officers in other States and the need for a body of interpretative decisions to guide judicial officers when the application of a rule in a particular factual situation is not clear. With regard to the latter problem, an additional benefit lies in the fact that the ABA has established a Standing Committee on Ethics and Professional Responsibility which renders opinions on matters of proper professional or judicial conduct.

It was, of course, not feasible to recommend that the ABA canons be adopted verbatim. Specific provisions of the Illinois Constitution and statutes as well as circumstances unique to Illinois required that the canons be modified in accord with any superseding legal requirements and extraordinary circumstances. The committee commentary is primarily concerned with these modifications; however, wherever appropriate, the ABA commentary has been incorporated into the committee commentary. For an excellent background commentary on the ABA canons themselves see Thode, *Reporter's Notes to Code of Judicial Conduct* (ABA 1973).

Preamble

Our legal system is based on the principle that an independent, fair and competent judiciary will interpret and apply the laws that govern us. The role of the judiciary is central to American concepts of justice and the rule of law. Intrinsic to all provisions of this code are precepts that judges, individually and collectively, must respect and honor the judicial office as a public trust and strive to enhance and maintain confidence in our legal system. The judge is an arbiter of facts and law for the resolution of disputes and a highly visible symbol of government under the rule of law.

The Code of Judicial Conduct is intended to establish standards for ethical conduct of judges. It consists of broad statements called canons, specific rules set forth in lettered subsections under each canon, and Committee Commentary. The text of the canons and the rules is authoritative. The Committee Commentary, by explanation, and example, provides guidance with respect to the purpose and meaning of the canons and rules. The Commentary is not intended as a statement of additional rules.

The canons and rules are rules of reason. They should be applied consistent with constitutional requirements, statutes, other court rules and decisional law and in the context of all relevant circumstances. The Code is to be construed so as not to impinge on the essential independence of judges in making judicial decisions.

The Code is designed to provide guidance to judges and candidates for judicial office and to provide a structure for regulating conduct through disciplinary agencies. It is not designed or intended as a basis for civil liability or criminal prosecution. Furthermore, the purpose of the Code would be subverted if the Code were invoked by lawyers for mere tactical advantage in a proceeding.

The canons are not standards of discipline in themselves, but express the policy considerations underlying the rules contained within the canons. The text of the rules is intended to govern conduct of judges and to be binding upon them. It is not intended, however, that every transgression will result in disciplinary action. Whether disciplinary action is appropriate, and the degree of discipline to be imposed, should be determined through a reasonable and reasoned application of the text of the rules and should depend on such factors as the seriousness of the transgression, whether there is a pattern of improper activity and the effect of the improper activity on others or on the judicial system.

The Code of Judicial Conduct is not intended as an exhaustive guide for the conduct of judges. They should also be governed in their judicial and personal conduct by general ethical standards. The Code is intended, however, to state basic standards which should govern the conduct of all judges and to provide guidance to assist judges in establishing and maintaining high standards of judicial and personal conduct.

Adopted eff. Aug. 6, 1993.

Terminology

"Candidate." A candidate is a person seeking public election for or public retention in judicial office. A person becomes a candidate for judicial office as soon as he or she makes a public announcement of candidacy, declares or files as a candidate with the election authority, or authorizes solicitation or acceptance of contributions or support.

"Court personnel" does not include the lawyers in a proceeding before a judge.

"*De minimis*" denotes an insignificant interest that could not raise reasonable question as to a judge's impartiality.

"Economic interest" denotes ownership of a more than *de minimis* legal or equitable interest, or a relationship as officer, director, advisor or other active participant in the affairs of a party, except that:

(i) ownership of an interest in a mutual or common investment fund that holds securities is not an economic interest in such securities unless the judge participates in the management of the fund or a proceeding pending or impending before the judge could substantially affect the value of the interest;

(ii) service by a judge as an officer, director, advisor or other active participant in an educational, religious, charitable, fraternal or civic organization, or service by a judge's spouse, parent or child as an officer, director, advisor or other active participant in any organization does not create an economic interest in securities held by that organization;

(iii) a deposit in a financial institution, the proprietary interest of a policyholder in a mutual insurance company, of a depositor in a mutual savings association or of a member in a credit union, or a similar proprietary interest, is not an economic interest in the organization unless a proceeding pending or impending before the judge could substantially affect the value of the interest;

(iv) ownership of government securities is not an economic interest in the issuer unless a proceeding pending or impending before the judge could substantially affect the value of the securities.

"Fiduciary" includes such relationships as executor, administrator, trustee, and guardian.

"He." Whenever this pronoun is used it includes the feminine as well as the masculine form.

"Judge" includes circuit and associate judges and judges of the appellate and supreme court.

"Knowingly," "knowledge," "known" or "knows" denotes actual knowledge of the fact in question. A person's knowledge may be inferred from circumstances.

"Law" denotes court rules as well as statutes, constitutional provisions and decisional law.

"Member of a candidate's/judge's family" denotes a spouse, child, grandchild, parent, grandparent or other relative or person with whom the candidate maintains a close familial relationship.

"Member of the judge's family residing in the judge's household" denotes any relative of a judge by blood or marriage, or a person treated by a judge as a member of the judge's family, who resides in the judge's household.

"Political organization" denotes a political party or other group, the principal purpose of which is to further the election or appointment of candidates to political office.

"Public election." This term includes primary and general elections; it includes partisan elections, non-partisan elections and retention elections.

"Require." The rules prescribing that a judge "require" certain conduct of others are, like all of the rules in this Code, rules of reason. The use of the term "require" in that context means a judge is to exercise reasonable direction and control over the conduct of those persons subject to the judge's direction and control.

"Third degree of relationship." The following persons are relatives within the third degree or relationship: great-grandparent, grandparent, parent, uncle, aunt, brother, sister, child, grandchild, great-grandchild, nephew or niece.

Adopted eff. Aug. 6, 1993.

Rule 61. [A Judge Should Uphold the Integrity and Independence of the Judiciary]

CANON 1

A Judge Should Uphold the Integrity and Independence of the Judiciary

An independent and honorable judiciary is indispensable to justice in our society. A judge should participate in establishing, maintaining, and enforcing, and should personally observe, high standards of conduct so that the integrity and independence of the judiciary may be preserved. The provisions of this Code should be construed and applied to further that objective.

Adopted Dec. 2, 1986, eff. Jan. 1, 1987. Amended eff. Aug. 6, 1993; Oct. 15, 1993.

Formerly Ill.Rev.Stat.1991, ch. 110A, ¶ 61.

Committee Commentary

This canon is substantially identical to the 1972 version of the ABA canon.

Rule 62. [A Judge Should Avoid Impropriety and the Appearance of Impropriety in All of the Judge's Activities]

CANON 2

A Judge Should Avoid Impropriety and the Appearance of Impropriety in All of the Judge's Activities

A. A judge should respect and comply with the law and should conduct himself or herself at all times in a manner that promotes public confidence in the integrity and impartiality of the judiciary.

B. A judge should not allow the judge's family, social, or other relationships to influence the judge's judicial conduct or judgment. A judge should not lend the prestige of judicial office to advance the private interests of others; nor should a judge convey or permit others to convey the impression that they are in a special position to influence the judge. A judge should not testify voluntarily as a character witness.

Adopted Dec. 2, 1986, eff. Jan. 1, 1987. Amended eff. Oct. 15, 1993.

Formerly Ill.Rev.Stat.1991, ch. 110A, ¶ 62.

Committee Commentary

This Canon is substantially identical to ABA Canon 2. Public confidence in the judiciary is eroded by irresponsible or improper conduct by judges. A judge must avoid all impropriety and appearance of impropriety. A judge must expect to be the subject of constant public scrutiny. A judge must therefore accept restrictions on his or her conduct that might be viewed as burdensome by the ordinary citizen and should do so freely and willingly.

The testimony of a judge as a character witness injects the prestige of judicial office into the proceeding in which the judge testifies and may be misunderstood to be an official testimonial. This canon, however, does not afford a judge a privilege against testifying in response to an official summons.

Rule 63. [A Judge Should Perform the Duties of Judicial Office Impartially and Diligently]

CANON 3

A Judge Should Perform the Duties of Judicial Office Impartially and Diligently

The judicial duties of a judge take precedence over all the judge's other activities. The judge's judicial duties include all the duties of the judge's office prescribed by law. In the performance of these duties, the following standards apply:

A. Adjudicative Responsibilities.

(1) A judge should be faithful to the law and maintain professional competence in it. A judge should be unswayed by partisan interests, public clamor, or fear of criticism.

(2) A judge should maintain order and decorum in proceedings before the judge.

(3) A judge should be patient, dignified, and courteous to litigants, jurors, witnesses, lawyers, and others with whom the judge deals in an official capacity, and should require similar conduct of law-

yers, and of staff, court officials, and others subject to the judge's direction and control.

(4) A judge shall accord to every person who has a legal interest in a proceeding, or that person's lawyer, the right to be heard according to law. A judge may make reasonable efforts, consistent with the law and court rules, to facilitate the ability of self-represented litigants to be fairly heard.

(5) A judge shall not initiate, permit, or consider *ex parte* communications, or consider other communications made to the judge outside the presence of the parties concerning a pending or impending proceeding except that:

(a) Where circumstances require, *ex parte* communications for scheduling, administrative purposes or emergencies that do not deal with substantive matters or issues on the merits are authorized; provided:

(i) the judge reasonably believes that no party will gain a procedural or tactical advantage as a result of the *ex parte* communication, and

(ii) the judge makes provision promptly to notify all other parties of the substance of the *ex parte* communication and allows an opportunity to respond.

(b) A judge may consult with court personnel whose function is to aid the judge in carrying out the judge's adjudicative responsibilities or with other judges.

(c) A judge may, with the consent of the parties, confer separately with the parties and their lawyers in an effort to mediate or settle matters pending before the judge.

(d) A judge may initiate or consider any *ex parte* communications when expressly authorized by law to do so.

(e) A judge may consult with members of a Problem Solving Court Team when serving as a Judge in a certified Problem Solving Court as defined in the Supreme Court "Problem Solving Court Standards."

(6) A judge shall devote full time to his or her judicial duties, and should dispose promptly of the business of the court.

(7) A judge should abstain from public comment about a pending or impending proceeding in any court, and should require similar abstention on the part of court personnel subject to the judge's direction and control. This paragraph does not prohibit judges from making public statements in the course of their official duties or from explaining for public information the procedures of the court.

(8) Proceedings in court should be conducted with fitting dignity, decorum, and without distraction. The taking of photographs in the courtroom during sessions of the court or recesses between proceedings, and the broadcasting or televising of court proceedings is permitted only to the extent authorized by order of the Supreme Court. This rule is not intended to prohibit local circuit courts from using security cameras to monitor courtrooms, provided that cameras are controlled by designated court personnel. For the purposes of this rule, the use of the terms "photographs," "broadcasting," and "televising" include the audio or video transmissions or recordings made by telephones, personal data assistants, laptop computers, and other wired or wireless data transmission and recording devices.

(9) A judge shall perform judicial duties without bias or prejudice. A judge shall not, in the performance of judicial duties, by words or conduct manifest bias or prejudice, including but not limited to bias or prejudice based upon race, sex, religion, national origin, disability, age, sexual orientation or socioeconomic status, and shall not permit staff, court officials and others subject to the judge's direction and control to do so.

(10) Proceedings before a judge shall be conducted without any manifestation, by words or conduct, of prejudice based upon race, sex, religion, national origin, disability, age, sexual orientation or socioeconomic status, by parties, jurors, witnesses, counsel, or others. This section does not preclude legitimate advocacy when these or similar factors are issues in the proceedings.

B. Administrative Responsibilities.

(1) A judge should diligently discharge the judge's administrative responsibilities, maintain professional competence in judicial administration, and facilitate the performance of the administrative responsibilities of other judges and court officials.

(2) A judge should require staff, court officials and others subject to the judge's direction and control to observe the standards of fidelity and diligence that apply to the judge.

(3)(a) A judge having knowledge of a violation of these canons on the part of a judge or a violation of Rule 8.4 of the Rules of Professional Conduct on the part of a lawyer shall take or initiate appropriate disciplinary measures.

(b) Acts of a judge in mentoring a new judge pursuant to M.R. 14618 (Administrative Order of February 6, 1998, as amended June 5, 2000) and in the discharge of disciplinary responsibilities required or permitted by Canon 3 or article VIII of the Rules of Professional Conduct are part of a judge's judicial duties and shall be absolutely privileged.

(c) Except as otherwise required by the Supreme Court rules, information pertaining to the new judge's performance which is obtained by the mentor in the course of the formal mentoring relationship shall be held in confidence by the mentor.

(4) A judge should not make unnecessary appointments. A judge should exercise the power of

appointment on the basis of merit, avoiding nepotism and favoritism. A judge should not approve compensation of appointees beyond the fair value of services rendered.

(5) A judge should refrain from casting a vote for the appointment or reappointment to the office of associate judge, of the judge's spouse or of any person known by the judge to be within the third degree of relationship to the judge or the judge's spouse (or the spouse of such a person).

C. Disqualification.

(1) A judge shall disqualify himself or herself in a proceeding in which the judge's impartiality might reasonably be questioned, including but not limited to instances where:

(a) the judge has a personal bias or prejudice concerning a party or a party's lawyer, or personal knowledge of disputed evidentiary facts concerning the proceeding;

(b) the judge served as a lawyer in the matter in controversy, or a lawyer with whom the judge previously practiced law served during such association as a lawyer concerning the matter, or the judge has been a material witness concerning it;

(c) the judge was, within the preceding three years, associated in the private practice of law with any law firm or lawyer currently representing any party in the controversy (provided that referral of cases when no monetary interest was retained shall not be deemed an association within the meaning of this subparagraph) or, for a period of seven years following the last date on which the judge represented any party to the controversy while the judge was an attorney engaged in the private practice of law;

(d) the judge knows that he or she, individually or as a fiduciary, or the judge's spouse, parent or child wherever residing, or any other member of the judge's family residing in the judge's household, has an economic interest in the subject matter in controversy or in a party to the proceeding, or has any other more than *de minimis* interest that could be substantially affected by the proceeding; or

(e) the judge or the judge's spouse, or a person within the third degree of relationship to either of them, or the spouse of such a person:

(i) is a party to the proceeding, or an officer, director, or trustee of a party;

(ii) is acting as a lawyer in the proceeding;

(iii) is known by the judge to have a more than *de minimis* interest that could be substantially affected by the proceeding; or,

(iv) is to the judge's knowledge likely to be a material witness in the proceeding.

(2) A judge shall keep informed about the judge's personal and fiduciary economic interests, and make a reasonable effort to keep informed about the personal economic interests of the judge's spouse and minor children residing in the judge's household.

D. Remittal of Disqualification.

A judge disqualified by the terms of Section 3C may disclose on the record the basis of the judge's disqualification and may ask the parties and their lawyers to consider, out of the presence of the judge, whether to waive disqualification. If following disclosure of any basis for disqualification other than personal bias or prejudice concerning a party, the parties and lawyers, without participation by the judge, all agree that the judge should not be disqualified, and the judge is then willing to participate, the judge may participate in the proceeding. This agreement shall be incorporated in the record of the proceeding.

Adopted Dec. 2, 1986, eff. Jan. 1, 1987. Amended June 12, 1987, eff. Aug. 1, 1987; eff. Nov. 25, 1987; Aug. 6, 1993; Oct. 15, 1993; eff. March 26, 2001; April 1, 2003, eff. immediately; Dec. 5, 2003, eff. immediately; April 16, 2007, eff. immediately; June 18, 2013, eff. July 1, 2013; Dec. 8, 2015, eff. Jan. 1, 2016.

Formerly Ill.Rev.Stat.1991, ch. 110A, ¶ 63.

IN THE
SUPREME COURT
OF
THE STATE OF ILLINOIS
MR No. 2634.
In re PHOTOGRAPHING, BROADCASTING, AND TELEVISING PROCEEDINGS IN THE COURTS OF ILLINOIS

Order entered April 16, 2007.

Any security cameras installed in the courtrooms in the various circuits shall be in accordance with the following standards; (1) security cameras are to be placed in areas of the courtroom such that there is no video recording of the jury or witnesses; (2) audio recordings of the proceedings are prohibited in connection with security cameras; (3) use of such cameras is limited to security purposes and any video tape produced therefrom shall remain the property of the court and may not be used for evidentiary purposes by the parties or included in the record on appeal; (4) security cameras shall be monitored by designated court personnel only; and (5) signs shall be posted in and outside of the courtroom notifying those present of the existence of the court surveillance.

Order entered March 13, 1987.

As a result of the adoption of the new Code of Judicial Conduct effective January 1, 1987, the provision formerly contained in Supreme Court Rule 61(c)(24) permitting the photographing, broadcasting or televising of court proceedings only to the extent authorized by order of the supreme court is now contained in Supreme Court Rule 63(A)(7). In view of this, the orders authorizing the photographing, broadcasting and televising of proceedings in the supreme and appellate courts of this State on an experimental basis on November 29, 1983, and on a permanent basis on January 22, 1985, are hereby made applicable to Rule 63(A)(7).

Order entered January 22, 1985.

The supplemental petition for modification of Supreme Court Rule 61(c)(24), by the Illinois News Broadcasters Association *et al.*, is allowed in part. It is hereby ordered that the photographing, broadcasting, and televising of proceedings in the supreme and appellate courts of this State, authorized on an experimental basis by order of this court in this cause on November 29, 1983, is adopted on a permanent basis, subject to the conditions enumerated in the order of November 29, 1983. Extended coverage of circuit court proceedings is not authorized. To the extent our Rule 61(c)(24) is inconsistent herewith, this order and the conditions enumerated in the order of November 29, 1983, shall control until Rule 61(c)(24) has been formally amended to permit the extended coverage authorized by this order.

Chief Justice Clark, Justice Moran and Justice Simon dissent from the portion of this order prohibiting extended coverage of circuit court proceedings for the reasons expressed in their opinions concurring in part and dissenting in part from the order of November 29, 1983.

Order entered November 29, 1983.

The court has considered petitions urging the amendment of Supreme Court Rule 61(c)(24) (87 Ill.2d R. 61(c)(24)) to allow photographing, broadcasting and televising of court proceedings, which is hereafter referred to as extended coverage. The question is one that has been widely discussed. The petitions allege that extended coverage will be in the public interest. These claims are set out in part in the partly concurring and partly dissenting opinions filed with this order. The specially concurring opinions which are also filed today state some of the perceived dangers if extended coverage were to be allowed, and in particular if extended coverage were to be permitted of trial proceedings.

We have given long and full consideration to the question, balancing the asserted dangers and advantages of extended coverage. Our conclusion is that extended coverage should be allowed on an experimental basis in the supreme and appellate courts, subject to conditions hereafter stated, and that extended coverage of trial court proceedings should not be authorized.

Extended coverage is allowed upon various terms and court levels in some jurisdictions; in others it is not permitted. Extended coverage is prohibited in the Supreme Court of the United States and in all other Federal courts. In some of the jurisdictions which allow extended coverage, coverage is permitted at trial court and at appellate court levels; in other jurisdictions it is allowed only at appellate levels. New York, the center of the television industry, is one of the States which allows extended coverage only at the appellate level. Some of the jurisdictions which authorize extended coverage only at the appellate level restrict this coverage to proceedings in their highest courts. Texas considered and refused to allow audio recording only at the appellate court level, maintaining its complete ban on extended coverage. In practically all of the jurisdictions permitting extended coverage, it has been introduced on an experimental basis.

The purpose of courts is to administer justice. Basically, courts adjudicate disputes. They insure that civil and criminal proceedings are conducted according to the requirements of law. Courts have the responsibility of safeguarding individual liberties and insuring the freedom to exercise legally assured rights. The function of a court is to do justice in cases that come before it. It is not its role to be a teaching or informational instrument, though, of course, court proceedings, including trials, are public. Judicial proceedings are open to and are attended by members of the public and representatives of the communications media. It is obvious that openness in government is entirely a different subject and is not a question involved in the petitions before the court.

The court recognizes that there have been substantial technological improvements in the communications industry which have eliminated or reduced some of the earlier concerns regarding courtroom photography. The serious concerns pointed out in the specially concurring opinions, however, persist. A trial is a complex proceeding involving human factors difficult to measure or explicate. There are inherent problems in any trial proceeding which would be exacerbated by the presence of extended coverage. They often involve psychological factors which cannot be reached by rules of court attempting to govern extended coverage of a trial. Trials are too sensitive and important to admit approval of factors that may expose them to prejudicial influences.

We consider that the more acute concerns regarding extended coverage which we have expressed and which are described in the specially concurring opinions would not be present in cases of extended coverage of appellate court proceedings. A court of review considers only questions of law. There is no jury, and witnesses do not appear before the court.

Enforcement of the following rules shall be the responsibility of the judicial officer presiding at the proceeding covered.

(A) Applicability

Effective January 1, 1984, and terminating December 31, 1984, unless terminated earlier at the discretion of this court, this order governs photographing, broadcasting, and televising of proceedings in the supreme and appellate courts. To the extent our Rule 61(c)(24) is inconsistent herewith, this order shall control during its effective period.

(B) Definitions

As used in this order, unless the context otherwise requires:

(1) "Proceeding" means any public session of the full supreme court or a panel of the appellate court while sitting in open court.

(2) "Extended coverage" means any media recording or broadcasting of proceedings by the use of television, radio, photographic, or recording equipment.

(3) "Presiding judge" means the presiding judge of the Second, Third, Fourth, or Fifth Judicial District in which extended coverage of an appellate court proceeding is occurring or sought.

(4) "Executive committee" means the executive committee of the Appellate Court for the First Judicial District and the chairperson thereof.

(5) "Chief justice" means the chief justice of the Supreme Court of Illinois.

(6) "Marshal" means the marshal of the Supreme Court of Illinois.

(7) "Clerk of court" means the clerk of the court in which extended coverage of a proceeding is occurring or sought.

(8) "Media" means any recognized news-gathering or news-reporting agency and the individual persons involved, and includes newspapers, radio, television, radio and television networks, news services, magazines, trade papers, in-house publications, professional journals, or other news-reporting or news-gathering agency whose function it is to inform the public or some segment thereof.

(9) "Administrative director" means the director of the Administrative Office of the Illinois Courts.

(10) "Court days" means the days of a calendar week, excluding Saturday, Sunday, and court holidays.

(11) "Pooling arrangements" means media cooperative agreements to request extended coverage.

(C) General provisions and exclusions

(1) Nothing in this order is intended to alter, modify, or change any provisions of the Rules of Professional Conduct contained in article VIII of the supreme court rules or supreme court rules governing the conduct of judges, except as provided in this order.

(2) Nothing in this order is intended to limit or restrict the power of a presiding judicial officer to control the conduct of any proceeding, except as herein provided.

(3) No proceeding shall be commenced, delayed or continued to allow for extended coverage.

(4) A decision by a presiding judicial officer to deny, limit or terminate extended coverage is not appealable.

(5) Extended coverage shall be conducted so as not to be distracting and not to interfere with the solemnity, decorum, and dignity which must attend the making of decisions that affect the life, liberty, or property of citizens. The attire of media personnel shall not be inappropriate to the occasion.

(6) Unless otherwise ordered, extended coverage of appellate argument is permitted only in the supreme court courtrooms in Springfield and Chicago; and in the appellate court courtrooms in Chicago, Elgin, Ottawa, Springfield, and Mt. Vernon.

(7) No consent is required for extended coverage of appellate argument; however, the chief justice, presiding judge of the judicial district in which extended coverage is contemplated, or the chairperson of the executive committee of the First District of the Appellate Court, as the case may be, may prohibit extended coverage of a particular appellate argument.

(8) During appellate argument proceedings, there shall be no extended coverage of bench conferences among the members of the supreme court, among the members of the appellate court panel, or among appellate counsel and his or her client or clients.

(9) The judicial officer presiding at the proceeding may, for good cause, terminate extended coverage at any time.

(D) Procedure for extended coverage

413

(1) When extended coverage of an argument before the supreme court is sought, the media representative shall notify the marshal, in writing, not less than five court days prior to the date the appellate argument is scheduled. The marshal shall promptly advise the chief justice of such request. The notice shall contain:

(a) the title and docket number of the case to be argued, and the date and time, if available, the case is to be argued; and

(b) the name, address and telephone number of the media representative making the request, the representative's employer, and the kind of extended coverage to be used.

The marshal shall, as soon as practicable, acknowledge receipt of the notice. All arrangements for the extended coverage shall be coordinated through the marshal's office, including but not limited to kind and location of extended coverage equipment.

(2) Except in the First and Fourth Districts of the Appellate Court, when extended coverage of an appellate argument in the appellate court is sought, the media representative shall, not less than five court days prior to the date the appellate argument is scheduled, notify, in writing, the clerk of the appellate court, who shall promptly advise the presiding judge. The notice shall contain the information specified in preceding sections (1)(a) and (b), and the clerk shall perform the same functions assigned to the marshal in preceding section (1).

(3) In the Fourth District of the Appellate Court, the procedure specified in preceding section (2) shall be followed, except the supreme court marshal is substituted for the clerk. In the First District of the Appellate Court, the procedure specified in preceding section (2) shall be followed, except (a) the notice shall also contain the division of that court before which the case is to be argued, (b) the notice shall be directed to that court's administrative assistant, who shall promptly advise the chairperson of the executive committee and presiding judge of the appropriate division, and (c) the administrative assistant is substituted for the clerk.

(E) Extended coverage media standards and "pooling" applicable

(1) Equipment and personnel

(a) Equipment from only one television station or network (the pooling station or network) shall be permitted in a proceeding subject to extended coverage. The pooling station or network shall use only television cameras which are silent videotape electronic cameras or, in the absence of such equipment, silent 16mm sound on film (self-blimped) cameras. One television camera, operated by one camera person, shall be admitted to record a proceeding.

(b) Only one audio system for broadcast shall be permitted in a proceeding subject to extended coverage. Where possible, audio for all media shall be from any existing audio system present in the courtroom. If no technically suitable audio system exists, microphones, wiring, and recording equipment shall be furnished and temporarily installed by the extended-coverage media without public expense, shall be unobtrusive, shall not interfere with the sound quality of any existing courtroom audio system, shall be operated by one person, and shall be located in places designated in advance by the marshal, clerk of the appellate court, or the appellate court administrative assistant, as the case may be.

(c) Only one still photographer, using not more than two still cameras with not more than two lenses for each camera, shall be permitted in a proceeding subject to extended coverage.

(d) Sufficient video and audio tape capacities should be provided to obviate tape changes except during court recess.

(e) No equipment or clothing of any extended-coverage personnel shall bear any insignia or identification of the individual medium or network involved in extended coverage.

(f) No extended-coverage equipment or personnel shall impede pedestrian traffic movement in, to, or from the courthouse, including but not limited to courthouse corridors and courtroom entrances and exits.

(2) Sound and light criteria

(a) Artificial lighting devices shall not be used in connection with any equipment employed to cover proceedings. Only equipment that does not produce distracting sound or light shall be employed to cover proceedings. Specifically, video and audio equipment shall produce no greater sound than the equipment designated in schedule A (annexed hereto) when the same is in good working order; still camera equipment shall produce no greater sound than the camera equipment designated in schedule B (annexed hereto) when the same is in good working order. No motorized drives shall be permitted.

(b) It shall be the affirmative duty of extended-coverage personnel, when requested, to demonstrate to the marshal, clerk of the appellate court, or appellate court administrative assistant, as the case may be, adequately in advance of any proceeding, that the equipment sought to be used meets the established sound and light criteria.

(c) No light or signal visible or audible to participants in the appellate proceeding shall be used on any equipment during extended coverage to indicate whether it is operating.

(3) Position and movement during proceedings

(a) Extended-coverage personnel and equipment shall be positioned so as to provide reasonable coverage in such location in the court facility as shall be designated by the marshal, clerk of the appellate court, or appellate court administrative assistant, as the case may be. Necessary equipment that is not a component part of a television camera, and video and sound recording equipment, shall be located outside the courthouse where practicable or, if not practicable, outside the courtroom, unless other arrangements are approved in advance by the marshal, clerk of the appellate court, or appellate court administrative assistant, as the case may be.

(b) Extended-coverage equipment shall not be placed in or removed from the courtroom except prior to or after proceedings each day, or during a recess. Such equipment shall not be stored in the courthouse.

(c) All extended-coverage-equipment operators shall act in a manner so as not to call undue attention to their presence or activities. Extended-coverage-equipment operators shall not be permitted to move about within the courtroom during the court session.

(4) Pooling

(a) If it is necessary to limit the number of media personnel or equipment in the courtroom in order to comply with this order, pooling arrangements shall be instituted by the media to insure that all media seeking extended coverage are provided with access to extended coverage. If the number of timely notices for a particular kind of extended coverage would, if permitted, exceed the number limitations allowed for extended coverage of a particular proceeding as set forth in preceding section (1), the marshal, clerk of the appellate court, or appellate court administrative assistant, as the case may be, shall promptly notify the appropriate media representatives.

(b) Pooling arrangements among members of the media shall be the sole responsibility of the media and no judicial officer or other court personnel shall mediate disputes. In the absence of agreement or in the event of unresolved disputes relating to pooling arrangements, the kind of extended coverage sought shall be prohibited and excluded from the proceeding.

(F) Reporting requirements

In proceedings for which extended coverage was sought, the marshal, clerk of court, or appellate court administrative assistant, as the case may be, shall file a semi-annual written report on July 1, 1984, and six months thereafter, with the administrative director, with a copy to the chief justice, presiding judge or chairperson of the executive committee, as the case may be. The report shall contain the following information: the caption of the case, whether requested extended coverage did or did not take place, the kind of extended coverage, the date, time and place of the proceeding covered, a statement of any problems encountered, and any other information relevant to the extended coverage of the proceeding. All reports shall be confidential and may contain the reporting person's observations, comments, or recommendations concerning extended coverage. The report may be supplemented with the observations, comments, and recommendations of the chief justice, presiding judge, or chairperson of the executive committee.

SCHEDULE A

SCHEDULE A

FILM CAMERAS	16mm Sound on(self-blimped) Film	
1. CINEMA PRODUCTS	CP–16A–R	Sound Camera
2. ARRIFLEX	16mm–16BL Model	Sound Camera
3. FREZZOLINI	16mm(LW 16)	Sound on Film Camera
4. AURICON	"Cini-Voice"	Sound Camera
5. AURICON	"Pro–600"	Sound Camera
6. GENERAL CAMERA	SS III	Sound Camera
7. ECLAIR	Model ACL	Sound Camera
8. GENERAL CAMERA	DGX	Sound Camera
9. WILCAM FLEX	RE-16mm	Sound Camera

VIDEO TAPE ELECTRONIC CAMERAS

1.	Ikegami	HL–77 HL–33 HL–35 HL–34 HL–5
2.	RCA	TK–76
3.	Sony	DXC–1600 Trinicon
3a.	ASACA	ACC–2006
4.	Hitachi	SK80 SK90
5.	Hitachi	FP–3030
6.	Philips	LDK–25
7.	Sony BVP–200	ENG Camera
8.	Fornseh	Video Camera
9.	JVC–8800 u	ENG Camera
10.	AKAI	CVC–150 VTS–150
11.	Panasonic	WV–3085 NV–3085
12.	JVC	GC–4800u

VIDEO TAPE RECORDERS/used with video cameras

1.	Ikegami	3800
2.	Sony	3800
3.	Sony	BVU–100
4.	Ampex	Video Recorder
5.	Panasonic	1-inch Video Recorder
6.	JVC	4400
7.	Sony	3800H

SCHEDULE B

Rangefinder
Leica M42
Single Lens Reflex
Nikon FM
Nikon FE
Canon A1
Canon AE1
Canon AT1
Minolta XD11
Pentax MX
Olympus OM–I

Committee Commentary
(April 1, 2003)

New subpart (B)(3)(b) is a modified version of the ABA Model Code of Judicial Conduct, Canon 3D(3) (1990).

New subpart (B)(3)(c) is the identical language currently contained in M.R. 14618 (Administrative Order of February 6, 1998, as amended June 5, 2000) subparagraph (b)(4) on confidentiality.

Committee Commentary

The provisions of this canon relate to judicial performance of adjudicative responsibilities, judicial performance of administrative responsibilities and the circumstances and procedure for judicial disqualification.

Paragraph A(4) and subsections C and D were amended, effective August 6, 1993, to incorporate the provisions of the Model Code of Judicial Conduct adopted by the ABA in 1990.

Paragraphs A(1) through A(3). The duty to hear all proceedings fairly and with patience is not inconsistent with the duty to dispose promptly of the business of the court. Courts can be efficient and business-like while being patient and deliberate.

Paragraph A(4). This paragraph was amended, effective August 6, 1993, to adopt the provisions of Canon 3B(7) of the 1990 ABA Model Code of Judicial Conduct relating to *ex parte* communications. Paragraph A(4) differs in that it modifies ABA Canon 3B(7) by deleting the sentence which provides: "A judge may obtain the advice of a disinterested expert on the law applicable to a proceeding before the judge if the judge gives notice to the parties of the person consulted and the substance of the advice, and affords the parties reasonable opportunity to respond." The committee believed that such a procedure would be too close to the former practice of using masters in chancery which was abolished by the 1962 amendment of the judicial article. Furthermore both bar association committees were concerned with the possibility of a judge seeking advice from a law professor. The committee does not believe that the deletion of this provision affects the obligation of a judge to disclose any extrajudicial communication concerning a case pending before the judge to the parties or their attorneys. The proscription against communications concerning a proceeding includes communications from lawyers, law teachers, and other persons who are not participants in the proceeding.

To the extent reasonably possible, all parties or their lawyers shall be included in communications with a judge.

Whenever presence of a party or notice to a party is required by paragraph A(4), it is the party's lawyer, or if the party is unrepresented the party, who is to be present or to whom notice is to be given.

Certain *ex parte* communication is approved by paragraph A(4) to facilitate scheduling and other administrative purposes and to accommodate emergencies. In general, however, a judge must discourage *ex parte* communication and allow it only if all the criteria stated in paragraph A(4) are clearly met. A judge must disclose to all parties all *ex parte* communications described in subparagraph A(4)(a) regarding a proceeding pending or impending before the judge.

A judge must not independently investigate facts in a case and must consider only the evidence presented.

A judge may request a party to submit proposed findings of fact and conclusions of law, so long as the other parties are apprised of the request and are given an opportunity to respond to the proposed findings and conclusions.

A judge must make reasonable efforts, including the provision of appropriate supervision, to ensure that paragraph A(4) is not violated through law clerks or other personnel on the judge's staff.

Paragraph A(5). The ABA 1972 canon provides that "[a] judge should dispose promptly of the business of the court." The committee agreed with the ISBA/CBA joint committee recommendation that the language of the Illinois Constitution (art. VI, § 13(b)) which requires that a judge should devote full time to his or her judicial duties should be incorporated into this paragraph. Prompt disposition of the court's business requires a judge to devote adequate time to judicial duties, to be punctual in attending court and expeditious in determining matters under submission, and to insist that court officials, litigants and their lawyers cooperate with the judge to that end.

Paragraph A(6). ABA Canon 3A(6) is adopted without substantive change. It was the view of the committee that, with regard to matters pending before the judge, a judicial officer should discuss only matters of public record, such as the filing of documents, and should not comment on a controversy not pending before the judge but which could come before the judge. "Court personnel" does not include the lawyers in a proceeding before a judge. The conduct of lawyers is governed by Rule 3.6 of the Illinois Rules of Professional Conduct.

Paragraph A(7). The Illinois Supreme Court allows extended media coverage of proceedings in the supreme and appellate courts subject to certain specified conditions. Except to the extent so authorized, however, the existing prohibition of the taking of photographs in the courtroom during sessions of the court or recesses between proceedings, and the broadcasting or televising of court proceedings, other than those of a ceremonial nature, is retained. While this prohibition does not extend to areas immediately adjacent to the courtroom, it does not preclude orders regulating or restricting the use of those areas by the media where the circumstances so warrant.

Paragraph A(8). A judge must refrain from speech, gestures or other conduct that could reasonably be perceived as sexual harassment and must require the same standard of conduct of others subject to the judge's direction and control.

A judge must perform judicial duties impartially and fairly. A judge who manifests bias on any basis in a proceeding impairs the fairness of the proceeding and brings the judiciary into disrepute. A judge must be alert to avoid behavior that may be perceived as prejudicial.

Paragraph B(3). A modified version of the ABA canon was recommended even though Illinois Supreme Court Rule 61(c)(10) only referred to an obligation to refer an attorney's unprofessional conduct in matters before the judge to the proper authorities. Thus the rule here is broader, in that it is not limited to matters before the judge, and in that it extends the obligation to unprofessional conduct of other judges. In the case of misconduct by lawyers, the Rules of Professional Conduct, Rule 8.4, contains the circumstances of misconduct that are covered by paragraph B(3). This canon requires a judge to take or initiate appropriate disciplinary measures where he or she has knowledge of a violation of Rule 8.4. Where misconduct by an attorney is involved, a finding of contempt may, in appropriate circumstances, constitute the initiation of appropriate disciplinary measures. Furthermore, in both cases, the rule does not preclude a judge from taking or initiating more than a single appropriate disciplinary measure. Additionally, a judge may have a statutory obligation to report unprofessional conduct which is also criminal to an appropriate law enforcement official.

Paragraph B(4). It is the position of the committee that this ABA canon implicitly includes the provision of Illinois Supreme Court Rule 61(c)(11) that a judge "should not offend against the spirit of this standard by interchanging appointments with other judges, or by any other device." Appointees of the judge include officials such as receivers and guardians, and personnel such as clerks, secretaries, and bailiffs. Consent by the parties to an appointment or an award of compensation does not relieve the judge of the obligation prescribed by this paragraph.

Paragraphs C(1)(a) through C(*l*)(c). When originally adopted on December 2, 1986, the existing ABA canon was modified in two ways. The words "or his lawyer" were added to paragraph C(*l*)(a) to expressly mandate disqualification in the case of personal bias or prejudice toward an attorney rather than a party. This modification was later incorporated by the ABA into its 1990 revision. More significantly a new subparagraph, C(1)(c), was added in 1986 regulating disqualifications when one of the parties is represented by an attorney with whom the judge was formerly associated and when one of the parties was a client of the judge. These modifications were in substantial accord with the joint committee recommendations. Hence ABA subparagraphs (c) and (d) were renumbered and are now subparagraphs (d) and (e) respectively.

Paragraphs C(1)(d) and (1)(e). The fact that a lawyer in a proceeding is affiliated with a law firm with which a relative of the judge is affiliated does not of itself disqualify the judge. Under appropriate circumstances, the fact that "the judge's impartiality might reasonably be questioned" under Canon 3C(1), or that the relative is known by the judge to have an interest, or its equivalent, in the law firm that could be "substantially affected by the outcome of the proceeding" under Canon 3C(*l*)(e)(iii) may require the judge's disqualification.

Paragraph D. A remittal procedure provides the parties an opportunity to proceed without delay if they wish to waive the disqualification. To assure that consideration of the question of remittal is made independently of the judge, a judge must not solicit, seek or hear comment on possible remittal or waiver of the disqualification unless the lawyers jointly propose remittal after consultation as provided in the rule. A party may act through counsel if counsel represents on the record that the party has been consulted and consents. As a practical matter, a judge may wish to have all parties and their lawyers sign the remittal agreement.

Rule 64. [A Judge May Engage in Activities to Improve the Law, the Legal System, and the Administration of Justice]

CANON 4

A Judge May Engage in Activities to Improve the Law, the Legal System, and the Administration of Justice

A judge, subject to the proper performance of his or her judicial duties, may engage in the following law-related activities, if in doing so the judge does not cast doubt on his or her capacity to decide impartially any issue that may come before him or her.

A. A judge may speak, write, lecture, teach (with the approval of the judge's supervising, presiding, or chief judge), and participate in other activities concerning the law, the legal system, and the administration of justice.

B. A judge may appear at a public hearing before an executive or legislative body or official on matters concerning the law, the legal system, and the administration of justice, and he or she may otherwise consult with an executive or legislative body or official, but only on matters concerning the administration of justice.

C. A judge may serve as a member, officer, or director of a bar association, governmental agency, or other organization devoted to the improvement of the law, the legal system, or the administration of justice. He or she may assist such an organization in planning fund-raising activities; may participate in the management and investment of the organization's funds; and may appear at, participate in, and allow his or her title to be used in connection with a fund-raising event for the organization. Under no circumstances, however, shall a judge engage in direct, personal solicitation of funds on the organization's behalf. Inclusion of a judge's name on written materials used by the organization for fund-raising purposes is permissible under this rule so long as the materials do not purport to be from the judge and list only the judge's name, office or other position in the organization and, if comparable designations are listed for other persons holding a similar position, the judge's judicial title.

D. A judge may make recommendations to public and private fund-granting agencies on projects and programs concerning the law, the legal system, and the administration of justice.

CHIEF JUSTICE MILLER, specially concurring [June 4, 1991 amendment]:

I concur in the amendments made to Supreme Court Rules 64 and 66 by order of this court entered June 4, 1991, and effective August 1, 1991. I write to explain the basis for my agreement with the court's action.

The present amendments to Rules 64 and 66, which are canons 4 and 6 of the Code of Judicial Conduct, draw their authority from the judicial article of the Illinois Constitution and are intended to give effect to certain requirements imposed by those provisions. Recently, it had become evident to the court that uncertainty may exist among members of the branches of State government, as well as among members of the public at large, regarding the scope of the constitutional provisions restricting the performance by judges of extrajudicial, law-related activities. The constitutional provisions are not self-executing, and canons 4 and 6 are being amended now so that they will provide greater guidance concerning the requirements of the judicial article. At the same time, it should be clear that the present amendments are not intended to embody the entire corpus of law on judicial conduct; the amendments make no pretense of providing a restatement, or catalogue, of all prohibited activities. For more complete direction, reference must be had to the remaining provisions of the Code.

As amended, canons 4 and 6 of the Code of Judicial Conduct restrict the hours during which a judge may conduct a regular course of outside teaching, prohibit the receipt by a judge of compensation for extrajudicial, law-related activities, and limit the honoraria a judge may accept for those activities. That these amendments simply effectuate the provisions of the judicial article is demonstrated by a review of the relevant constitutional provisions, and of their progress through the proceedings of the 1970 constitutional convention.

Article VI, section 13(a), of the Illinois Constitution expressly directs this court to "adopt rules of conduct for Judges and Associate Judges." (Ill. Const.1970, art. VI, § 13(a).) In addition, section 13(b) provides:

"Judges and Associate Judges shall devote full time to judicial duties. They shall not practice law, hold a position of profit, hold office under the United States or this State or unit of local government or school district or in a political party. Service in the State militia or armed forces of the United States for periods of time permitted by rule of the Supreme Court shall not disqualify a person from serving as a Judge or Associate Judge." (Ill. Const.1970, art. VI, § 13(b).)

Of particular significance here are the requirements that judges devote full time to their judicial duties and the prohibition of positions of profit. The former provision appeared in the preceding constitution; the latter provision was added in 1970.

As amended by the 1964 revisions to the judicial article, the corresponding section of the prior State constitution required judges to devote full time to their official duties and prohibited judges from practicing law, from holding any other public office, and from holding office in any political party; the prior constitution did not otherwise restrict judges in their private employment. (Ill. Const.1870, art. VI (1964), § 16.) In formulating a new judicial article for the 1970 constitutional convention, the judiciary committee proposed, in what was then designated section 16, to retain the existing provisions and to add one further restriction, which would prohibit judges from serving "as an officer or director of any for-profit corporation." (See 6 Record of Proceedings, Sixth Illinois Constitutional Convention 830–34 (text and committee commentary) (Proceedings).) This additional provision was derived from a recently enacted statute (see Ill.Rev.Stat.1969, ch. 37, par. 160.11),[1] and the committee proposed to include the statutory language in the new judicial article.

When the judiciary committee's work was presented to the convention on first reading, the delegates considered and adopted a broader restriction on judges' extrajudicial activities. Delegate Peter Tomei introduced an amendment that sought to replace the prohibition concerning officerships and directorships in for-profit corporations with a much broader provision, one that would preclude a judge from holding "any position of profit" apart from the judge's official employment. 2 Proceedings 954.

The delegates discussed at length the scope and meaning of the proposed amendment. The sponsor explained that his proposal was designed to ensure that members of the judiciary were not employed in other positions. Introducing the amendment, Delegate Tomei stated:

"My language, 'positions of profit,' very briefly, is—it contemplates officerships, directorships, or employment status of any kind where there is compensation—something other than mere reimbursement for expenses—something other than simply an honorary position that many judges have and probably will continue to have. For instance, it would not prohibit a judge from serving as a member of a corporation of a university or institution of higher learning if it were not a compensated position and he only received reimbursement for his expenses. So it is intended to reach employment situations. It does not get into the question—nor do I think it should—of writing books or things of that nature, but it does reach the employment area. And I do think it is in the employment area where, if we expect our judges to work full time and pay them to work full time, we can expect that of them." 2 Proceedings 954.

Later, in responding to a question concerning the scope of the proposed language, Delegate Tomei repeated the substance of his earlier remarks. (2 Proceedings 955 (" 'Position,' as I indicated before, * * * mean[s] some sort of employment relationship"; "[p]osition[ ] * * * would include officerships, directorships, or employment—continuing employment relationships").) Delegate Tomei distinguished positions of profit from economic holdings, such as financial assets and real estate, which, he stated, would not fall within the scope of his proposed amendment. (2 Proceedings 955, 958.) Following further debate, the convention delegates adopted the Tomei amendment. (2 Proceedings 959–60.) Through subsequent, nonsubstantive revisions, the judiciary committee's draft proposal, as amended, metamorphosed into the provisions contained in article VI, section 13, which were ultimately approved by the convention delegates and later ratified by the voters of this State.

Thus, not only did the convention delegates choose to require that judges devote full time to their judicial duties, they also decided to expressly forbid judges to hold other positions of employment or profit, whether of a public or private nature. In the court's view, a compensated teaching position that requires a judge's regular attendance during normal business hours falls within the terms of those constitutional proscriptions. By permitting judges to teach only during non-business hours and to receive only limited honoraria for that activity, the present amendments to canons 4 and 6 of the Code of Judicial Conduct are designed to provide more explicit guidance with respect to the scope of the constitutional requirements. And by making the same financial guidelines applicable to all extrajudicial, law-related activities, the court intends to give effect to the considerations animating the constitutional commands while preserving society's interest in seeing judicial expertise applied to pursuits carried on outside a judge's chambers or courtroom.

No judge is excepted from the provisions contained in the judicial article. Although, as some would suggest, differences might exist in the schedules of trial and reviewing court judges, section 13(b) draws no distinction among judges on the basis of their position or assignment. Rather, all members of the judiciary are subject to the same requirements; the Illinois Constitution does not prescribe one rule for one set of judges and a different rule for a different set of judges. The amended canons, of uniform application, will help accomplish the clearly stated goals of the constitution's drafters.

Classroom teaching, like other extrajudicial, law-related activities, is capable of producing a wide range of benefits to the participants and to the public at large. The amendments will strike an appropriate balance between those benefits and the concerns expressed in the constitution. The drafters of the constitution made clear that judicial service is full-time employment, and that extrajudicial activities cannot be allowed to intrude on a judge's official responsibilities. The drafters also recognized, however, that judicial service, as full-time employment, must be compensated on that basis. Accordingly, adequate compensation should be provided so that judges do not find it necessary to rely on extrajudicial, law-related activities as a supplemental source of income.

JUSTICES MORAN, FREEMAN and CUNNINGHAM join in this special concurrence [June 4, 1991 amendment].

JUSTICE BILANDIC, dissenting [June 4, 1991 amendment]:

I respectfully dissent because the well-intentioned reforms adopted by the majority in the amendments to Rules 64 and 66 are unconstitutional.

I

The restrictions placed on writing and lecturing violate section 13 of the Judicial Article of the 1970 Constitution. (Ill. Const.1970, Art. VI, § 13(b).) Article VI, section 13, of the Illinois Constitution of 1970 provides:

"Prohibited Activities.

* * *

(b) Judges and Associate Judges shall devote full time to judicial duties. They shall not practice law, hold a position of profit, hold office under the United States or this State or unit of local government or school district or in a political party." Ill. Const.1970, art. VI, § 13(b).

When section 13 was adopted, there was some discussion among the delegates to the Constitutional Convention regarding the meaning of "position of profit." Delegate Tomei, who sponsored the amendment that offered the words "position of profit," said: "It does not get into the question—nor do I think it should—of writing books or things of that nature, but it does reach the employment area." (2 Record of Proceedings, Sixth Illinois Constitutional Convention 954.) In closing the debate on his amendment offering the words "position of profit," Delegate Tomei concluded: "[W]e wouldn't prevent judges from writing books or making lectures or what have you. * * * [Y]ou don't want a judge on somebody else's payroll. And that is what 'position of profit' is all about." (2 Record of Proceedings, Sixth Illinois Constitutional Convention 958.) To the extent that restrictions are placed on writing and lecturing the rules adopted by the majority violate article VI, section 13, of the 1970 Constitution because these activities *are not prohibited* and do not constitute holding a "position of profit."

II

The prohibition of compensation, limitation of honoraria and time restrictions constitute a "prior restraint" and run afoul of the rights of teaching judges, law schools, law students and the general public to exercise and benefit from constitutional protections afforded by the first amendment to the United States Constitution (U.S. Const., amend. I). The first amendment provides, in pertinent part:

"Congress shall make no law * * * abridging the freedom of speech or of the press." (U.S. Const., amend. I.)

By operation of the due process clause of the fourteenth amendment of the United States Constitution, the liberties guaranteed by the first amendment cannot be circumscribed by State action. (*Joseph Burstyn, Inc. v. Wilson* (1952), 343 U.S. 495, 500, 96 L.Ed.2d 1098, 1105, 72 S.Ct. 777, 779.) Acts of this court constitute State action and, thus, cannot violate the first amendment.

My colleagues, in their zeal to correct certain alleged excesses by a few teaching judges, adopted the amendments to Rules 64 and 66, although I believe other remedies are available. I applaud their motives but disagree with their methods which unintentionally violate constitutional rights. As the United States Supreme Court has stated:

"It is characteristic of the freedoms of expression in general that they are vulnerable to gravely damaging yet barely visible encroachments." (*Bantam Books v. Sullivan* (1963), 372 U.S. 58, 66, 9 L.Ed.2d 584, 590, 83 S.Ct. 631, 637.)

That Court has further stated that:

"[T]he people of this nation have ordained in the light of history, that, in spite of the probability of excesses and abuses, these liberties are, in the long view, essential to enlightened opinion and right conduct on the part of the citizens of a democracy." *New York Times Co. v. Sullivan* (1964), 376 U.S. 254, 271, 11 L.Ed.2d 686, 701, 84 S.Ct. 710, 721.

It is undisputed that a full-time teaching position held by a judge would be a prohibited activity because it would require the judge to be on the payroll of an educational institution and would be a "position of profit." When teaching is limited, we reach a grey area. Based on comparable compensation for law school faculty who are not judges, we must determine at what point the remuneration of faculty members who are judges becomes a "position of profit." The rules adopted by the majority constitute a "prior restraint." The question that is begging for an answer is whether this "prior restraint" offends the first amendment. Reconsideration would provide the opportunity for a more reasonable exercise of "prior restraint" which "has been recognized only in exceptional cases." *Joseph Burstyn, Inc. v. Wilson* (1952),

343 U.S. 495, 503–04, 96 L.Ed.2d 1098, 1107, 72 S.Ct. 777, 781.

It may be advisable to revisit the position of the United States Supreme Court on the subject of prior restraint:

"Prior restraint upon speech suppresses the precise freedom which the First Amendment sought to protect against abridgment.

* * *

* * * An order issued in the area of First Amendment rights must be couched in the narrowest terms that will accomplish the pin-pointed objectives permitted by constitutional mandate and the essential needs of the public order. In this sensitive field, the State may not employ 'means that broadly stifle fundamental personal liberties when the end can be more narrowly achieved.' [Citation.] In other words, the order must be tailored as precisely as possible to the exact needs of the case. The participation of both sides is necessary for this purpose. Certainly, the failure to invite participation of the party seeking to exercise First Amendment rights reduces the possibility of a narrowly drawn order, and substantially imperils the protection which the Amendment seeks to assure." (*Carroll v. President & Commissioners of Princess Anne* (1968), 393 U.S. 175, 181, 183–84, 21 L.Ed.2d 325, 331, 332–33, 89 S.Ct. 347, 351, 353.)

The majority, in its noble pursuit, has exceeded constitutional bounds and then compounds that error by denying a rehearing.

JUSTICE HEIPLE, dissenting [June 4, 1991 amendment]:

The Illinois Constitution provides that judges shall devote full time to judicial duties and shall not otherwise hold positions of profit. It further provides that the Supreme Court shall adopt rules of conduct for judges. (Ill. Const.1970, art. VI, § 13.) Grounded on that constitutional authority, the court on December 2, 1986, adopted the Code of Judicial Conduct with its seven canons of judicial ethics. (134 Ill.2d Rules 61 through 67.) Canon 4 provided that a judge might engage in activities to improve the law, the legal system, and the administration of justice. (134 Ill.2d R. 64.) Canon 6 provided that a judge might receive certain nonjudicial compensation. 134 Ill.2d R. 66.

For as long as anyone is aware, judges have taught classes, lectured and written on subjects both legal and nonlegal. They have served as part-time lecturers and adjunct professors in numerous law schools and colleges. They have also engaged in writing and speaking activities on a wide variety of subjects. That the public has benefited from these activities is unquestioned. Neither the Illinois Constitution of 1970 nor the Code of Judicial Conduct of 1986 effected any observable change in this longstanding practice.

Now, however by restrictive amendments to canons 4 and 6 of the Code of Judicial Conduct, the court has severely crippled the utilization of Illinois judges as teachers, lecturers and writers.

The amendment to canon 4 imposes something entirely new. A daytime judicial curfew. No judge may teach before 5:30 p.m. What the amendment does not say, however, is as interesting as what the amendment does say. It does not restrict the judge from the daytime playing of tennis or sailboating. It does not preclude the judge from taking a two-hour lunch. It does not enjoin him to arrive at the courthouse before a certain hour. Indeed, it does not require him to come to the courthouse at all. He may, in fact, *take* daytime classes. But, he may not *teach* them. Presumably, however, the public can now breathe easier. Judges will not be going about teaching in broad daylight.

The amendment to canon 6 takes away the judge's right to "compensation" for any and all nonjudicial activities but then allows him the right to receive an "honorarium" not to exceed $2,000 in any six-month period. Webster defines an honorarium as "an honorary payment or reward usually given as compensation for services on which custom or propriety forbids any fixed business price to be set or for which no payment can be enforced at law." (Webster's Third New International Dictionary 1087 (1986).) In other words, the judge may not contract to receive payment for nonjudicial services but he may accept a voluntary reward. That is to say, the party benefited may, in effect, throw the cash through the open transom of the judge's office or slip it under the door. As long as the total sum is limited to $2,000 every six months and is unsolicited, it is OK.

I have some fundamental objections to these amendments. The first is that the legal profession, the law schools, the colleges and the public will lose the services of judges as teachers, lecturers and writers. Most people attend classes in the daytime and judges are now precluded from teaching in the daytime. Additionally, since judges cannot be paid for their teaching, lecturing and writing, the time devoted to these activities will be substantially diminished in many cases and totally stopped in others. That there are selfless or otherwise driven individuals who will pursue their teaching, lecturing and writing absent financial reward is to be expected. Financial reward, although a major incentive to productive effort, is not the only one. That the removal of a financial incentive will severely deter these activities, however, cannot be doubted. Few judges question the proposition that low or inadequate judicial salaries deter people from entering in or staying with the judicial profession. The principle is of universal application.

The rationale for these restrictive amendments is that since judges are commanded by the constitution to devote full time to their judicial duties and are further proscribed from holding positions of profit, they therefore should not be permitted to teach during the daytime or to be paid for teaching even at night. The rule goes even further by denying payment for writing books or articles, and for lecturing or public speaking. These latter endeavors are, of course, wholly outside the proscriptions of the constitution and the limitations imposed thereon are without any basis in law or reason. Why should not a judge write, publish, and lecture on his own time and without interference with his judicial duties? Why should he not teach and be paid for teaching so long as it does not interfere with his judicial duties? My opinion is that the judges should be encouraged in these activities. Instead, the amended canons are designed to stop them.

Reference to the various comments at the constitutional convention discloses no meeting of the minds on the term "position of profit." That was left for the court to define by rule. (2 Record of Proceedings, Sixth Illinois Constitutional Convention 951–61.) It is clear, however, that writing and lecturing are not positions. What the delegates to the convention were really aiming at was the posture of a judge on a public or private payroll that would interfere with or influence his judicial conduct. A rule of reason might have defined that term in relation to a percentage of the judicial salary. That is, payment for teaching in a sum not to exceed a stated percentage of the judicial salary would not be deemed a position of profit but that a sum in excess of that percentage would be so construed. If teaching compensation, for instance, did not exceed 10 or 15% of the judge's salary and if the work did not conflict with his judicial duties, few could reasonably complain.

The facts of judicial employment are that a trial judge would not normally be available for any nonjudicial matter during regular business days. With limited exceptions, trial courts generally sit during the day. What is true for trial courts, however, is not true for the courts of appeal. Appellate and supreme court judges would ordinarily not be in the courtroom and on the bench for even as many as 50 days out of the year. This is so because their work is principally done in their chambers throughout the day and often on evenings and weekends. The working schedule of an appeals court judge, while demanding, is quite flexible. Thus, it would be quite possible for an appellate or a supreme court judge to teach a daytime class on one, two or three days out of a week without conflicting with a full complement of judicial duties.

The amended rules have gone much further than was either necessary or desirable. They have denied "compensation" altogether and have resorted to the use of a euphemism, namely "honorarium," in its place. This deflective tactic merely clouds the issue and renders the whole change intellectually objectionable.

Finally, one must ask, why is the court doing this? What circumstance has occurred since 1970 when the Illinois Constitution was adopted to bring this about? What circumstance has occurred since the Judicial Code of Conduct was adopted in 1986 to bring this about? The answer, of course, is that, except for the passage of time and the change of personnel, no circumstance has changed.

Historically, it is significant that no complaints have ever been filed with the Illinois Courts Commission charging a judge with neglecting his judicial duties due to teaching activities or with violating the rule as to position of profit for teaching. If a problem were to arise in this area, certainly, it could be dealt with through the mechanism of the judicial disciplinary system on a case-by-case basis. The fact that no complaints have been filed indicates, however, the sensitivity and awareness of the judiciary as to the limits of their teaching activities. The current rule change thus flies in the face of that ancient caveat, "If it ain't broke, don't fix it!"

I must add that no public hearings were held on this proposed change. It was not referred to any committee of the court for study and recommendation. No input was solicited from colleges, teachers, bar associations, judges' associations or any interested parties. The rule changes were simply adopted in closed session and presented as an accomplished fact.

For the reason that I deem the rule changes to be deleterious to the public good, I respectfully dissent.

Adopted December 2, 1986, eff. Jan. 1, 1987. Amended June 4, 1991, eff. Aug. 1, 1991. Committee Commentary amended Oct. 15, 1993, eff. immediately. Rule amended Sept. 30, 2002, eff. immediately; May 24, 2006, eff. immediately. Committee Commentary amended Dec. 19, 2014, eff. immediately.

Formerly Ill.Rev.Stat.1991, ch. 110A, ¶ 64.
[1] 705 ILCS 60/1.

Committee Commentary

A judge may serve on a committee that includes other judges, attorneys and members of the community for the purpose of developing programs or initiatives aimed at improving the outcomes for juveniles involved in the juvenile court system, or adults in the criminal court system. Such programs may include diversion, restorative justice and problem-solving court programs, among others.

This canon regulates the permissible scope of a judicial officer's law-related activities. As a judicial officer and person specially learned in the law, a judge is in a unique position to contribute to the improvement of the law, the legal system, and the administration of justice, including revision of substantive and procedural law and improvement of criminal and juvenile justice. To the extent that the judge's time permits, he or she is encouraged to do so through appropriate channels.

Extrajudicial activities are governed by Canon 5.

For the distinction between those organizations devoted to the improvement of the law, the legal system, and the administration of justice referred to in paragraph C and other civic or charitable organizations, see Thode at page 76.

Rule 65. [A Judge Should Regulate His or Her Extrajudicial Activities to Minimize the Risk of Conflict With the Judge's Judicial Duties]

CANON 5

A Judge Should Regulate His or Her Extrajudicial Activities to Minimize the Risk of Conflict With the Judge's Judicial Duties

A. Avocational Activities. A judge may write, lecture, teach, and speak on nonlegal subjects, and engage in the arts, sports, and other social and recreational activities, if such avocational activities do not detract from the dignity of the judge's office or interfere with the performance of the judge's judicial duties.

B. Civic and Charitable Activities. A judge may participate in civic and charitable activities that do not reflect adversely upon the judge's impartiality or interfere with the performance of the judge's judicial duties. A judge may serve as an officer, director, trustee, or nonlegal advisor of an educational, religious, charitable, fraternal, or civic organization not conducted for the economic or political advantage of its members, subject to the following limitations:

(1) A judge should not serve if it is likely that the organization will be engaged in proceedings that would ordinarily come before the judge or will be regularly engaged in adversary proceedings in any court.

(2) A judge should not solicit or permit his or her name to be used in any manner to solicit funds or other assistance for any such organization. A judge should not allow his or her name to appear on the letterhead of any such organization where the stationery is used to solicit funds and should not permit the judge's staff, court officials or others subject to the judge's direction or control to solicit on the judge's behalf for any purpose, charitable or otherwise. However, a judge may be a speaker or the guest of honor at an organization's fund-raising events and may allow event-related promotional materials, invitations, and other communications to mention such participation by the judge.

C. Financial Activities.

(1) A judge should refrain from financial and business dealings that tend to reflect adversely on the judge's impartiality, interfere with the proper performance of the judge's judicial duties, exploit the judge's judicial position, or involve the judge in frequent transactions with lawyers or persons likely to come before the court on which the judge serves.

(2) Subject to the requirements of subsection (1), a judge may hold and manage investments, including real estate, and engage in the activities usually incident to the ownership of such investments, but a judge should not assume an active role in the management or serve as an officer, director, or employee of any business.

(3) A judge should manage his or her investments and other financial interests to minimize the number of cases in which the judge is disqualified. As soon as the judge can do so without serious financial detriment, the judge should divest himself or herself of investments and other financial interests that might require frequent disqualification.

(4) Neither a judge nor a member of the judge's family residing in the judge's household should accept a gift, bequest, favor, or loan from anyone except as follows:

(a) a judge may accept a gift incident to a public testimonial to the judge; books supplied by publishers on a complimentary basis for official use; or an invitation to the judge and the judge's spouse to attend a bar-related function or activity devoted to the improvement of the law, the legal system, or the administration of justice;

(b) a judge or a member of the judge's family residing in the judge's household may accept ordinary social hospitality; a gift, bequest, favor, or loan from a relative; a wedding or engagement gift; a loan from a lending institution in its regular course of business on the same terms generally available to persons who are not judges; or a scholarship or fellowship awarded on the same terms applied to other applicants;

(c) a judge or a member of the judge's family residing in the judge's household may accept any other gift, bequest, favor, or loan only if the donor is not a party or other person whose interests have come or are likely to come before the judge, including lawyers who practice or have practiced before the judge.

(5) Information acquired by a judge in the judge's judicial capacity should not be used or disclosed by the judge in financial dealings or for any other purpose not related to the judge's judicial duties.

D. Fiduciary Activities. A judge should not serve as the executor, administrator, trustee, guardian, or other fiduciary, except for the estate, trust, or person of a member of the judge's family, and then only if such service will not interfere with the proper performance of the judge's judicial duties. As a family fiduciary a judge is subject to the following restrictions:

(1) The judge should not serve if it is likely that as a fiduciary the judge will be engaged in proceedings that would ordinarily come before the judge, or if the estate, trust, or ward becomes involved in adversary proceedings in the court on which the judge serves or one under its appellate jurisdiction.

(2) While acting as a fiduciary a judge is subject to the same restrictions on financial activities that apply to the judge in his or her personal capacity.

E. Arbitration. A judge should not act as an arbitrator or mediator.

F. Practice of Law. A judge should not practice law.

G. Extrajudicial Appointments. A judge should not accept appointment to a governmental committee, commission, or other position that is concerned with issues of fact or policy on matters other than the improvement of the law, the legal system, or the administration of justice. A judge, however, may represent his or her country, State, or locality on ceremonial occasions or in connection with historical, educational, and cultural activities.

Adopted Dec. 2, 1986, eff. Jan. 1, 1987. Amended Oct. 15, 1993, eff. immediately; May 24, 2006, effective immediately; Dec. 7, 2011, eff. immediately.

Committee Commentary

This canon governs the permissible scope of a judicial officer's extrajudicial activities. Avocational, civic and charitable, financial, and fiduciary activities are regulated as well as practice as an arbitrator or lawyer and the propriety of accepting extrajudicial appointments. ABA Canon 5(C)(6), which provides that "[a] judge is not required by this Code to disclose his income, debts, or investments except as provided in this Canon and Canons 3 and 6," was deleted as inconsistent with the present Illinois disclosure requirements which are retained in this code. The remaining subparagraphs were renumbered. In adapting the ABA canons to Illinois, certain adjustments were required in this canon because of the impact of article VI, section 13(b), of the Illinois Constitution, which prohibits a judicial officer from holding "a position of profit."

Paragraph (A). Complete separation of a judge from extrajudicial activities is neither possible nor wise; he should not become isolated from the society in which he lives.

Paragraph (B)(1). The changing nature of some organizations and of their relationship to the law makes it necessary for a judge regularly to reexamine the activities of each organization with which the judge is affiliated to determine if it is proper for the judge to continue the judge's relationship with it. For example, in many jurisdictions charitable hospitals are now more frequently in court than in the past. Similarly, the boards of some legal aid organizations now make policy decisions that may have political significance or imply commitment to causes that may come before the courts for adjudication.

Paragraph (B)(2). This subparagraph is largely based on Illinois Supreme Court Rule 64. The major difference is that the ABA canon would allow a judicial officer to be listed on the letterhead of such an association as an officer, director or trustee. This canon will not allow that where the letterhead is used to solicit funds. The provision prohibiting a judge from allowing judicial staff to solicit on the judge's behalf for any purpose, charitable or otherwise is a replacement for the provision of the ABA canon that provides that the judge should not use or permit the use of "the prestige of his office for that purpose."

Paragraph (C)(2). This subparagraph retains the language of Illinois Supreme Court Rule 63. See also 705 ILCS 60/1.

Paragraph (C)(3). This is ABA Canon 5(C)(3). The committee noted that this canon requires divestment of an investment only when it would cause frequent disqualification, and, even in that case, the divestment need not be made until the asset can be disposed of without serious financial detriment.

Paragraph (C)(4). This subparagraph combines ABA Canon 5(C)(4)(c) and the requirements of present Illinois Supreme Court Rule 61(c)(22). The ABA provisions regarding reporting are deleted since that is covered by Canon 6 of this code and by the Illinois Governmental Ethics Act (5 ILCS 420/1–101 *et seq.*).

Paragraph (D)(2). A judge's obligation under this canon and his or her obligation as a fiduciary may come into conflict. For example, a judge should resign as trustee if it would result in detriment to the trust to divest it of holdings whose retention would place the judge in violation of Canon 5(C)(3).

Paragraphs (E), (F) and (G). Valuable services have been rendered in the past to the States and the nation by judges appointed by the executive to undertake important extrajudicial assignments. The appropriateness of conferring these assignments on judges must be reassessed, however, in light of the demands on judicial manpower created by today's crowded dockets and the need to protect the courts from involvement in extrajudicial matters that may prove to be controversial. Judges should not be expected or permitted to accept governmental appointments that could interfere with the effectiveness and independence of the judiciary.

Rule 66. [Nonjudicial Compensation and Annual Statement of Economic Interests]

CANON 6

Nonjudicial Compensation and Annual Statement of Economic Interests

A judge may receive compensation for the law-related and extrajudicial activities permitted by this Code if the source of such payments does not give the appearance of influencing the judge in his or her judicial duties or otherwise give the appearance of impropriety subject to the following restrictions:

A. Compensation. Compensation should not exceed a reasonable amount nor should it exceed what a person who is not a judge would receive for the same activity.

B. Expense Reimbursement. Expense reimbursement shall be limited to the actual cost of travel, food, and lodging reasonably incurred by the judge and, where appropriate to the occasion, by the judge's spouse. Any payment in excess of such an amount is compensation.

C. Annual Declarations of Economic Interests.
A judge shall file a statement of economic interests as required by Rule 68, as amended effective August 1, 1986, and thereafter.

CHIEF JUSTICE MILLER, joined by JUSTICES MORAN, FREEMAN and CUNNINGHAM, specially concurring

[See special concurrence to amendment of S. Ct. Rule 64]

JUSTICE BILANDIC, dissenting

[see dissent to amendment of S. Ct. Rule 64]

JUSTICE HEIPLE, dissenting

[see dissent to amendment of S. Ct. Rule 64]

Adopted December 2, 1986, effective January 1, 1987; amended June 4, 1991, effective August 1, 1991; amended April 1, 1992, effective August 1, 1992; amended October 15, 1993, effective immediately; amended December 13, 1996, effective immediately; amended September 30, 2002, effective immediately.

Formerly Ill.Rev.Stat.1991, ch. 110A, ¶ 66.

Rule 67. [A Judge or Judicial Candidate Shall Refrain from Inappropriate Political Activity]

CANON 7

A Judge or Judicial Candidate Shall Refrain From Inappropriate Political Activity

A. All Judges and Candidates.

(1) Except as authorized in subsections B(1)(b) and B(3), a judge or a candidate for election to judicial office shall not:

(a) act as a leader or hold an office in a political organization;

(b) publicly endorse or publicly oppose another candidate for public office;

(c) make speeches on behalf of a political organization;

(d) solicit funds for, or pay an assessment to a political organization or candidate.

(2) A judge shall resign from judicial office upon becoming a candidate for a non-judicial office either in a primary or in a general election.

(3) A candidate for a judicial office:

(a) shall maintain the dignity appropriate to judicial office and act in a manner consistent with the integrity and independence of the judiciary, and shall encourage members of the candidate's family to adhere to the same standards of political conduct in support of the candidate as apply to the candidate;

(b) shall prohibit employees and officials who serve at the pleasure of the candidate, and shall discourage other employees and officials subject to the candidate's direction and control from doing on the candidate's behalf what the candidate is prohibited from doing under the provisions of this Canon;

(c) except to the extent permitted by subsection B(2), shall not authorize or knowingly permit any other person to do for the candidate what the candidate is prohibited from doing under the provisions of this Canon;

(d) shall not:

(i) make statements that commit or appear to commit the candidate with respect to cases, controversies or issues within cases that are likely to come before the court; or

(ii) knowingly misrepresent the identity, qualifications, present position or other fact concerning the candidate or an opponent; and

(e) may respond to personal attacks or attacks on the candidate's record as long as the response does not violate subsection A(3)(d).

B. Authorized Activities for Judges and Candidates.

(1) A judge or candidate may, except as prohibited by law:

(a) at any time

(i) purchase tickets for and attend political gatherings;

(ii) identify himself or herself as a member of a political party; and

(iii) contribute to a political organization;

(b) when a candidate for public election

(i) speak to gatherings on his or her own behalf;

(ii) appear in newspaper, television and other media advertisements supporting his or her candidacy;

(iii) distribute pamphlets and other promotional campaign literature supporting his or her candidacy; and

(iv) publicly endorse or publicly oppose other candidates in a public election in which the judge or judicial candidate is running.

(2) A candidate shall not personally solicit or accept campaign contributions. A candidate may establish committees of responsible persons to conduct campaigns for the candidate through media advertisements, brochures, mailings, candidate forums and other means not prohibited by law. Such committees may solicit and accept reasonable campaign contributions, manage the expenditure of funds for the candidate's campaign and obtain public statements of support for his or her candidacy. Such committees are not prohibited from soliciting

and accepting reasonable campaign contributions and public support from lawyers. A candidate's committees may solicit contributions and public support for the candidate's campaign no earlier than one year before an election and no later than 90 days after the last election in which the candidate participates during the election year. A candidate shall not use or permit the use of campaign contributions for the private benefit of the candidate or others.

(3) Except as prohibited by law, a candidate for judicial office in a public election may permit the candidate's name: (a) to be listed on election materials along with the names of other candidates for elective public office, and (b) to appear in promotions of the ticket.

C. Incumbent Judges. A judge shall not engage in any political activity except (i) as authorized under any other provision of this Code, (ii) on behalf of measures to improve the law, the legal system or the administration of justice, or (iii) as expressly authorized by law.

D. Applicability. Canon 7 generally applies to all incumbent judges and judicial candidates. A successful candidate, whether or not an incumbent, is subject to judicial discipline for his or her campaign conduct; an unsuccessful candidate who is a lawyer is subject to lawyer discipline for his or her campaign conduct. A lawyer who is a candidate for judicial office is subject to Rule 8.2(b) of the Rules of Professional Conduct.

JUSTICE HEIPLE, concurring [August 6, 1993 amendment]:

First and foremost, Rule 67 and these canons of judicial ethics are intended as a working guide of conduct for judges and judicial candidates. They indicate areas of activity that are deemed to be within and without proper limits of judicial conduct. In between, of course, are uncertain areas which lack definition. What the canons seek is judicial conduct that is in keeping with the high calling of judicial office. They are not intended to facilitate the filing of casual or vindictive charges against judges or judicial candidates.

The application of these canons require a high measure of common sense and good judgment. Matters that are either minor in nature or susceptible to differing interpretations ought not result in charges being filed. Charges of misconduct should be limited to matters that are both clearly defined and commonly accepted as serious.

The canons have attempted to recognize that Illinois has an elective judiciary. As a practical matter, the Illinois judge must involve himself in matters political. That is to say, the judge or candidate must be a participant in the system. A corollary of this activity is the public's right to know whom they are voting for. Realistically speaking, it is not enough for the judge

or candidate to merely give name, rank and serial number as though he were a prisoner of war. Rather, the public has a right to know the candidate's core beliefs on matters of deep conviction and principle. While the candidate is not required to disclose these beliefs, he should neither be deterred nor penalized for doing so. In so doing, however, the judge or judicial candidate ought to refrain from stultifying himself as to his evenhanded participation in future cases. Rule 67 attempts to make that clear.

What fair-minded people seek in a judge is a person who will be fair and impartial and who will follow the law. Those considerations overshadow matters of nonjudicial ideology such as socialism, anti-vivisection, membership in the Flat Earth Society, an obsession with gender neutral language, or whatever. The matter of nonjudicial ideology is of direct and primary concern, of course, when judges begin to act as legislators rather than jurists. Judges who adhere to the rule that their conscience is their guide and that the law must accommodate their conscience are especially deserving of close scrutiny and concern. Under our Illinois constitutional scheme, however, it is the voters who are to make that call, not a governmental prosecutorial body or an association of lawyers.

JUSTICE McMORROW, dissenting [August 6, 1993]:

I dissent from the adoption of certain portions of new Rule 67 of the Code.

At the time of this writing, Illinois elects its judges. Irrespective of the merits or demerits of the elective process, it is essential to the justice system that judges be "independent, fair, and competent" so as to honor the public trust placed in them by virtue of their position. The purposes of the Code of Judicial Conduct are set forth in the Preamble to the Code. That Preamble, as amended, *inter alia*, provides:

"Our legal system is based on the principle that an independent, fair and competent judiciary will interpret and apply the laws that govern us. The role of the judiciary is central to American concepts of justice and the rule of law. Intrinsic to all provisions of this code are precepts that judges, individually and collectively, must respect and honor the judicial office as a public trust and strive to enhance and maintain confidence in our legal system."

In this Code of Judicial Conduct, the Supreme Court of Illinois has set the standard by which judges are to be guided in their professional conduct. In my opinion, these standards should be high, and should be in keeping with the principles espoused in the Preamble. They are the guidelines which tell judges in this State in what activities they may or may not participate. The primary goal of the Code should be the attainment of a fair and impartial judiciary.

Today, in adopting certain amendments to Rule 67, the majority apparently wishes to accommodate the elective process to which judges are presently subjected. In so doing, the majority has substantially broadened the political activity in which judges may participate. For example, by deleting certain prohibitions which appeared in Rule 67 prior to the amendments, a judge may now *at any time* attend political gatherings, may make unlimited contributions to a political organization, may identify himself or herself as a member of a political party, or may purchase tickets for political dinners or other functions. Rules 67(B)(1)(a)(i), (B)(1)(a)(ii), (B)(1)(a)(iii).

However, our prior Rule 67 was not unduly restrictive. Indeed, no hardship to judges under the former rule has been demonstrated, nor has there been any hue or cry for the changes which have been adopted. I am unaware of any need for judges to make unlimited contributions to a political party, to attend political gatherings, or to identify their political party allegiance. On the contrary, upon election to judicial office, judges are to be impartial; they are to be unbiased with respect to race, gender, and political party affiliation. Upon election, judges should no longer be Democrats or Republicans. Rather, judges are elected to apply the rule of law without respect to political organization affiliation. Although I recognize the need to solicit political organizational support at the time a candidate is seeking election to the judiciary, or at such time as a judge is seeking retention, I am particularly disturbed by the amendments' allowance of a judge to engage in the political activities permitted by these amendments *at any time.*

I submit that the new rule "abandon[s] several important ethical standards that uphold the independence and dignity of judicial office" and will surely cause severe problems in the public perception of judicial candidates. (Report of the Committee on Judicial Performance and Conduct of the Lawyers' Conference of the Judicial Administration Division of the American Bar Association on the Final Draft of the Model Code of Judicial Conduct 28 (1990) (hereinafter Report of the Committee on Judicial Performance).) In my view, the new standards of the rule are too permissive with respect to the political activities of judicial candidates. The increased permissiveness in judicial candidates' political activities fosters a misguided over-politicization of the judicial election process in this State. In my judgment the time and efforts of the Illinois Supreme Court might be better expended by addressing the myriad of problems confronting the justice system, rather than considering and adopting amendments which allow judges to participate in additional political activity. I dissent from the adoption of these amendments because they are imprudent, unnecessary, and lend themselves to abuse.

In addition, I cannot agree with the majority's new view of the appropriate scope of a judicial candidate's public comment on matters that may or are likely to come before the court, provided the candidate does not "make statements that commit or appear to commit the candidate with respect to cases, controversies or issues within cases that are likely to come before the court." (Rule 67(A)(3)(d)(i).) Ultimately, the new Rule is short-sighted because it places candidates for judicial office in an unseemly position where they may feel compelled to "pander" for votes by publicly adopting views which appear popular to the electorate. See Report of the Committee on Judicial Performance at 31.

The Commentary indicates that this amendment was adopted in response to the decision of the Federal court in *Buckley v. Illinois Judicial Inquiry Board* (7th Cir.1993), ____ F.2d ____ (Nos. 92–3279, 92–3291 and 92–3283) (filed June 10, 1993). In that case, the Seventh Circuit Court of Appeals held unconstitutional the portion of our rule that forbids a judicial candidate from "announc[ing] his views on disputed legal or political issues." (134 Ill.2d R. 67(B)(1)(c).) The Federal court concluded that this "announcement" prohibition invaded a candidate's constitutional rights, because it "reache[d] far beyond speech that could reasonably be interpreted as committing the candidate in a way that would compromise his impartiality should he be successful in the election." *Buckley,* slip op. at 8.

It is indisputable that the constitutional guarantee of freedom of speech must be balanced against the right of the public to a judiciary which will decide the issues presented to it in the courtroom setting, on the basis of the facts and applicable law. A judicial candidate's right to free speech may be restricted where a compelling State interest is present which counterbalances the candidate's ability to speak freely. The integrity and impartiality and independence of the judiciary is, in my opinion, such a compelling State interest to which deference should be paid.

The key words in the amendment which now appear in Rule 67(A)(3)(d)(i) are "commit or appear to commit." These words are subject to varying interpretations and, I submit, are unnecessarily too broad to cure the fault found by the Federal court in the *Buckley* case. I question whether the amendment permitting a judge to speak on issues which may come before the court, provided the judge uses the magic words that the judge "is not committing" will be more problematic than the rule was prior to this amendment.

I also find disturbing the Commentary to the amendments to the effect that a judge or judicial candidate may respond to "false information concerning a judicial candidate [that] is made public." (Rule 67, Committee Commentary). The Report of the Committee on Judicial Performance stated the following with regard to this provision:

"This new expansion of free speech for judges who might be tempted to come to the aid of another judge or judicial candidate who has been the subject of criticism in a political campaign is totally without merit. There is no reason for a judge to become involved as a spokesperson or in any other capacity for another judge who has been publicly maligned. Publicly 'correcting' what the judge regards as a misstatement of fact in a judicial campaign is one of the acts presently prohibited by the existing Code, and it should continue to be prohibited.

Most issues of 'fact' in the context of judicial elections are, at best, mixed issues of fact and opinion and at worst are pure issues of opinion. Thus, the 'narrow' exception anticipated by the draftspersons would, in reality, become a large loophole.

The new provision would put enormous pressure on judges to become actively involved in campaigns of other judges or candidates." Report of the Committee on Judicial Performance at 5–6.

I agree with these comments from the Report of the Committee on Judicial Performance regarding this new amendment to Rule 67.

In my opinion, public perception of a fair and impartial judiciary is diminished by adoption of the amendments to which I have made reference. Because the majority permits potential further politicization of the Illinois judiciary by adoption of the above-referenced amendments, I respectfully dissent.

Adopted Dec. 2, 1986, eff. Jan. 1, 1987. Amended April 20, 1987, eff. Aug. 1, 1987; amended eff. Aug. 6, 1993; March 24, 1994.

Formerly Ill.Rev.Stat.1991, ch. 110A, ¶ 67.

Committee Commentary

This canon regulates the extent to which a judicial officer may engage in political activity.

Canon 7 adopts as its foundation the provisions of Canon 5 of the ABA Model Code of Judicial Conduct, which was adopted by the ABA in 1990.

Paragraph 7(A)(1). A judge or candidate for judicial office retains the right to participate in the political process as a voter.

Where false information concerning a judicial candidate is made public, a judge or another judicial candidate having knowledge of the facts is not prohibited by paragraph 7A(1) from making the facts public.

Subparagraph 7A(1)(a) does not prohibit a candidate for elective judicial office from retaining during candidacy a public office such as State's Attorney, which is not "an office in a political organization."

Subparagraph 7A(1)(b) does not prohibit a judge or judicial candidate from privately expressing his or her views on judicial candidates or other candidates for public office.

A candidate does not publicly endorse another candidate for public office by having that candidate's name on the same ticket.

Subparagraph 7A(1)(d). The ABA provisions that prohibit the following activities were deleted: attending political gatherings (5A(1)(d) of ABA), making contributions to political organizations or candidates (5A(1)(e)), and purchasing tickets for political party dinners or other functions (5A(1)(e)). These provisions were deleted because the ABA provisions adopted in subparagraph 7B(1)(a) were modified to authorize all judges and candidates to engage in such activities at any time. However, the prohibition on the solicitation of funds for, or paying an assessment to, a political organization or candidate, is adopted and renumbered as subparagraph (d).

Subparagraph 7A(3)(a). Although a judicial candidate must encourage members of his or her family to adhere to the same standards of political conduct in support of the candidate that apply to the candidate, family members are free to participate in other political activity.

Subparagraph 7A(3)(d). The ABA clause prohibiting "pledges and promises of conduct in office," found in Canon 5A(3)(d) of the Model Code (which was similar to the language of Canon 7B(1)(c) of our previous rules on political conduct) was deleted. This change was made to clarify the limitations of the rule, see *In re Buckley* (Ill.Cts.Comm'n Oct. 25, 1991), No. 91–CC–1 slip. op., which gave a broader construction to the rule. Subparagraph 7A(3)(d) prohibits a candidate for judicial office from making statements that commit or appear to commit the candidate with respect to cases, controversies or issues within cases that are likely to come before the court. However, as a corollary, a candidate should emphasize in any public statement the candidate's duty to uphold the law regardless of his or her personal views. See also paragraph 3A(6), the general rule on public comment by judges. Subparagraph 7A(3)(d) does not prohibit a candidate from making pledges or promises respecting improvements in court administration. Nor does this provision prohibit an incumbent judge from making private statements to other judges or court personnel in the performance of judicial duties. This subparagraph applies to any statement made in the process of securing judicial office. See also Rule 8.2 of the Rules of Professional Conduct.

The ABA Model Code of 1990 was modified to remove the provisions pertaining to candidates seeking appointment to judicial or other governmental office that are found in subsection B of Canon 5. Hence ABA subsections C, D and E were renumbered and are now subsections B, C and D of our Canon 7.

Paragraph 7B(1). This paragraph permits judges at any time to be involved in limited political activity. Subsection 7C, applicable solely to judges, would otherwise bar this activity.

Paragraph 7B(2). This paragraph is substantially identical to the Section 5C(2) of the 1990 ABA Model Code. The one difference is that the language prohibiting the candidates from personally soliciting publicly stated support is omitted to allow judicial candidates to appear before editorial boards of newspapers and other organizations. Paragraph 7B(2) permits a candidate to solicit publicly stated support, and to establish campaign committees to solicit and accept public support and reasonable financial contributions. At the start of the campaign, the candidate must instruct his or her campaign committees to solicit or accept only contributions that are reasonable under the circumstances. Though not prohibited, campaign contributions of which a judge has knowledge, made by lawyers or others who appear before the judge, may be relevant to disqualification under subsection C of Canon 3.

Campaign committees established under Section 7B(2) should manage campaign finances responsibly; avoiding deficits that might necessitate post-election fund-raising, to the extent possible.

Paragraph 7B(3). This paragraph provides a limited exception to the restrictions imposed by paragraph 7A(1).

Subsection 7C. Neither subsection 7C nor any other section of the Code prohibits a judge in the exercise of administrative functions from engaging in planning and other official activities with members of the executive and legislative branches of government.

Rule 68. [Declaration of Economic Interests]

A judge shall file annually with the Clerk of the Illinois Supreme Court (the Clerk) a verified written statement of economic interests and relationships of the judge and members of the judge's immediate family (the statement).

As statements are filed in the Clerk's office, the Clerk shall cause the fact of that filing to be indicated on an alphabetical listing of judges who are required to file such statements. Blank statement forms shall be furnished to the Clerk by the Director of the Administrative Office of the Illinois Courts (the Director).

Any person who files or has filed a statement under this rule shall receive from the Clerk a receipt indicating that the person has filed such a statement and the date of such filing.

All statements filed under this rule shall be available for examination by the public during business hours in the Clerk's office in Springfield or in the satellite office of the Clerk in Chicago. Original copies will be maintained only in Springfield, but requests for examination submitted in Chicago will be satisfied promptly. Each person requesting examination of a statement or portion thereof must first fill out a form prepared by the Director specifying the statement requested, identifying the examiner by name, occupation, address and telephone number, and listing the date of the request and the reason for such request. The Director shall supply such forms to the Clerk and replenish such forms upon request. Copies of statements or portions of statements will be supplied to persons ordering them upon payment of such reasonable fee per page as is required by the Clerk. Payment may be by check or money order in the exact amount due.

The Clerk shall promptly notify each judge required to file a statement under this rule of each instance of an examination of the statement by sending the judge a copy of the identification form filled out by the person examining the statement.

The contents of the statement required by this rule shall be as specified by administrative order of this court.

Adopted eff. March 15, 1970. Amended April 1, 1986, eff. Aug. 1, 1986.

Formerly Ill.Rev.Stat.1991, ch. 110A, ¶ 68.

IN THE SUPREME COURT OF THE STATE OF ILLINOIS

ADMINISTRATIVE ORDER

Order entered April 1, 1986; amended Sept. 23, 2005:

The verified statements of economic interests and relationships referred to in our Rule 68, as amended effective August 1, 1986, shall be filed by all judges on or before April 30, 1987, and on or before April 30, annually thereafter. Such statements shall also be filed by every person who becomes a judge, within 45 days after assuming office. However, judges who assume office on or after December 1 and who file the statement before the following April 30 shall not be required to file the statement due on April 30. The form of such statements shall be as provided by the Administrative Director of the Illinois Courts, and they shall include all information required by Rule 68 and this order, including:

1. Current economic interests of the judge and members of the judge's immediate family (spouse and minor children residing with the judge) whether in the form of stock, bond, dividend, interest, trust, realty, rent, certificate of deposit, deposit in any financial institution, pension plan, Keogh plan, Individual Retirement Account, equity or creditor interest in any corporation, proprietorship, partnership, instrument of indebtedness or otherwise. Every source of noninvestment income in the form of a fee, commission, compensation, compensation for personal service, royalty, pension, honorarium or otherwise must also be listed. No reimbursement of expenses by any unit of government and no interest in deferred compensation under a plan administered by the State of Illinois need be listed. No amounts or account numbers need be listed in response to this paragraph 1. In listing his or her personal residence(s) in response to this paragraph 1, the judge shall not state the address(es). Current economic interests shall be as of a date within 30 days preceding the date of filing the statement.

2. Former economic interests of the type required to be disclosed in response to numbered paragraph 1 which were held by the judge or any member of the judge's immediate family (spouse and minor children residing with the judge) during the year preceding the date of verification. Current economic interests listed in response to numbered paragraph 1 need not be listed. No amounts or account numbers need be listed in response to this paragraph 2. In listing his or her personal residence(s) in response to this paragraph 2, the judge shall not state the address(es).

3. The names of all creditors to whom amounts in excess of $500 are owed by the judge or members of the judge's immediate family (spouse and minor children residing with the judge) or were owed during the year preceding the date of verification. For each such obligation there is to be listed the category for the amount owed as of the date of verification and the maximum category for the amount of each such obligation during the year preceding the date of verification of the statement. The categories for reporting the amount of each such obligation are as follows:

(a) not more than $5,000;

(b) greater than $5,000 but not more than $15,000;

(c) greater than $15,000 but not more than $50,000;

(d) greater than $50,000 but not more than $100,000;

(e) greater than $100,000 but not more than $250,000; and

(f) greater than $250,000.

Excluded from this requirement are obligations consisting of revolving charge accounts, with an outstanding liability equal to or less than $5,000.

4. The name of any individual personally known by the judge to be licensed to practice law in Illinois who is a co-owner with the judge or members of the judge's immediate family (spouse and minor children residing with the judge) of any of the economic interests disclosed in paragraphs 1 and 2, and the name of any person who has acted as a surety or guarantor of any of the obligations required to be disclosed in paragraph 3.

5. A list of every office, directorship and salaried employment of the judge and members of the judge's immediate family (spouse and minor children residing with the judge). Exclude unsalaried positions in religious, social or fraternal organizations, and honorary positions.

6. Pending cases in which the judge or members of the judge's immediate family (spouse and minor children residing with the judge) are parties in interest and, to the extent personally known to the judge, pending cases in which a party is an economic entity in which the judge or any member of the judge's immediate family has an interest. Cases in which a judge has been sued in the judge's official capacity shall not be included.

7. Any fiduciary position, including executorships and trusteeships of the judge or members of the judge's immediate family (spouse or minor children residing with the judge).

8. The name of the donor and a brief description of any gifts received by the judge or members of the judge's immediate family (spouse and minor children residing with the judge). Gifts of transportation, food, lodging or entertainment having a value in excess of $250 must be reported. All other gifts having a value in excess of $100 must be reported. Gifts between the judge and the judge's spouse, children, or parents shall not be reported.

9. Any other economic interest or relationship of the judge or of members of the judge's immediate family (spouse and minor children residing with the judge) which could create a conflict of interest for the judge in the judge's judicial capacity, other than those listed in numbered paragraphs 1 to 8 hereof.

Prior to the first Monday in March of each year the Director shall inform each judge by letter of the requirements of this amended rule. The Director shall similarly inform by letter each person who becomes a judge of the requirements of the rule within 10 days of such person assuming office. The Director shall include with such letter instructions concerning the required statements, two sets of the statement forms, and one mailing envelope preaddressed to the Clerk. The Clerk shall redact personal residence addresses contained in any statement filed pursuant to Supreme Court Rule 68. The letter, instructions, and statements shall be in substantially the form set forth below:

[Letterhead of Administrative Office of the Illinois Courts]

——————, 20 ——

TO: MEMBERS OF THE JUDICIARY OF THE STATE OF ILLINOIS

RE: Compliance with Supreme Court Rule 68

As a member of the judiciary, you are required to file an annual statement of economic interests pursuant to Supreme Court Rule 68. Enclosed are the necessary forms and envelopes to be used in complying with Rule 68 on or before ——————, 20 ——.

In this packet are:

(A) One copy of "Instructions Concerning Required Statement for Members of the Judiciary of the State of Illinois."

(B) Two copies of the form entitled "Statement Required of Members of the Judiciary of the State of Illinois." [One copy to be filed with the Clerk of the Supreme Court; one copy to be retained for your records.]

(C) One 9 x 12 mailing envelope preaddressed to the Clerk of the Supreme Court.

The Supreme Court requests you follow these instructions carefully and asks that you be certain to return the original of your statement in the mailing envelope furnished herewith preaddressed to the Clerk of the Supreme Court.

Forms for compliance with Public Act 77–1806, "Illinois Governmental Ethics Act," will be mailed to you under separate cover and must be filed separately with the Secretary of State.

Very truly yours,

Director

INSTRUCTIONS CONCERNING REQUIRED STATEMENT FOR MEMBERS OF THE JUDICIARY OF THE STATE OF ILLINOIS

On or before April 30, 1987, and on or before April 30, annually thereafter, every judge of the Supreme Court, the Appellate Court, and every judge and associate judge of the Circuit Court shall file a verified written statement (the statement) of economic interests and relationships which may create conflicts of interest, with the Clerk of the Illinois Supreme Court. Such statements shall be filed by every person who becomes a judge or associate judge within 45 days after assuming office and on or before each April 30 thereafter. However, judges who assume office on or after December 1 and who file the statement before the following April 30 shall not be required to file the statement due on April 30.

The statements required shall include the following information which, except where noted, shall include information as of the date of verification of the statement.

1. Current economic interests of the judge and members of the judge's immediate family (spouse and minor children residing with the judge) whether in the form of stock, bond, dividend, interest, trust, realty, rent, certificate of deposit, deposit in any financial institution, pension plan, Keogh plan, Individual Retirement Account, equity or creditor interest in any corporation, proprietorship, partnership, instrument of indebtedness or otherwise. Every source of noninvestment income in the form of a fee, commission, compensation, compensation for personal service, royalty, pension, honorarium or otherwise must also be listed. No reimbursement of expenses by any unit of government and no interest in deferred compensation under a plan administered by the State of Illinois need be listed. No amounts or account numbers need be listed in response to this paragraph 1. In listing his or her personal residence(s) in response to this paragraph 1, the judge shall not state the address(es). Current economic interests shall be as of a date within 30 days preceding the date of filing the statement.

2. Former economic interests of the type required to be disclosed in response to numbered paragraph 1 which were held by the judge or any member of the judge's immediate family (spouse and minor children residing with the judge) during the year preceding the date of verification. Current economic interests listed in response to numbered paragraph 1 need not be listed. No amounts or account numbers need be listed in response to this paragraph 2. In listing his or her personal residence(s) in response to this paragraph 2, the judge shall not state the address(es).

3. The names of all creditors to whom amounts in excess of $500 are owed by the judge or members of the judge's immediate family (spouse and minor children residing with the judge) or were owed during the year preceding the date of verification. For each such obligation there is to be listed the category for the amount owed as of the date of verification and the maximum category for the amount of each such obligation during the year preceding the date of verification of the statement. The categories for reporting the amount of each such obligation are as follows:

(a) not more than $5,000;

(b) greater than $5,000 but not more than $15,000;

(c) greater than $15,000 but not more than $50,000;

(d) greater than $50,000 but not more than $100,000;

(e) greater than $100,000 but not more than $250,000; and

(f) greater than $250,000.

Excluded from this requirement are obligations consisting of revolving charge accounts, with an outstanding liability equal to or less than $5,000.

4. The name of any individual personally known by the judge to be licensed to practice law in Illinois who is a co-owner with the judge or members of the judge's immediate family (spouse and minor children residing with the judge) of any of the economic interests disclosed in paragraphs 1 and 2, and the name of any person who has acted as a surety or guarantor of any of the obligations required to be disclosed in paragraph 3.

5. A list of every office, directorship and salaried employment of the judge and members of the judge's immediate family (spouse and minor children residing with the judge). Exclude unsalaried positions in religious, social or fraternal organizations, and honorary positions.

6. Pending cases in which the judge or members of the judge's immediate family (spouse and minor children residing with the judge) are parties in interest, and, to the extent personally known to the judge, pending cases in which a party is an economic entity in which the judge or any member of the judge's immediate family has an interest. Cases in which a judge has been sued in the judge's official capacity shall not be included.

7. Any fiduciary position, including executorships and trusteeships of the judge and members of the judge's immediate family (spouse and any minor child residing with the judge).

8. The name of the donor and a brief description of any gifts received by the judge or members of the judge's immediate family (spouse and minor children residing with the judge). Gifts of transportation, food, lodging, or entertainment having a value in excess of $250 must be reported. All other gifts having a value in excess of $100 must be reported. Gifts between the judge and the judge's spouse, children or parents shall not be reported.

9. Any other economic interest or relationship of the judge or of members of the judge's immediate family (spouse and minor children residing with the judge) which could create a conflict of interest for the judge in the judge's judicial capacity other than those listed in numbered paragraphs 1 to 8 hereof.

The Statement required herein shall be in substantially the form titled "STATEMENT REQUIRED OF MEMBERS OF THE JUDICIARY OF THE STATE OF ILLINOIS," which is attached hereto as Exhibit A.

(SAMPLE)

EXHIBIT A

STATEMENT REQUIRED OF MEMBERS OF THE JUDICIARY OF THE STATE OF ILLINOIS

1. My current economic interests and the current economic interests of my immediate family (spouse and minor children residing with me) are as follows:

(Here list current economic interests specified in numbered paragraph 1 of the instructions setting forth the date (within 30 days of the date of filing) as of which said interests are being reported.)

2. My former economic interests and the former economic interests of my immediate family (spouse and minor children residing with me) held during the year preceding the date of verification:

(Here list former economic interests specified in numbered paragraph 2 of the instructions.)

3. Creditors to whom amounts in excess of $500 are owed as of the date of verification or were owed during the year preceding the date of verification by me or members of my immediate family (spouse and minor children residing with me), exclusive of revolving charge accounts with an outstanding liability equal to or less than $5,000, the amount of each such obligation outstanding as of the date of verification and the maximum amount of each such obligation during such preceding year within the categories set forth in numbered paragraph 3 of the instructions:

(Here list in accordance with numbered paragraph 3 of the instructions.)

4. The name of any individual personally known by me to be licensed to practice law in Illinois who is a co-owner with me or members of my immediate family (spouse and minor children residing with me) of any of the economic interests disclosed in paragraphs 1 and 2, and the name of any person who has acted as a surety or guarantor of any of the obligations required to be disclosed in paragraph 3.

(Here list in accordance with numbered paragraph 4 of the instructions.)

5. My offices, directorships, and salaried employments and the offices, directorships and salaried employments of my immediate family (spouse and minor children residing with me) are as follows:

(Here list in accordance with numbered paragraph 5 of the instructions.)

6. Pending cases in which I or members of my immediate family (spouse and minor children residing with me) have an interest are as follows:

(Here list pending cases in which you or members of your immediate family are parties in interest, or an economic entity in which you or they have an interest is a party, in accordance with numbered paragraph 6 of the instructions.)

7. My fiduciary positions, including executorships and directorships, and the fiduciary positions of the members of my immediate family (my spouse and minor children residing with me) are as follows:

(Here list fiduciary positions in accordance with numbered paragraph 7 of the instructions.)

8. The name of the donor of gifts received by me or members of my immediate family (spouse and minor children residing with me) during the year preceding the date of verification, are as follows:

(Here list gifts in accordance with numbered paragraph 8 of the instructions.)

9. My economic interests and relationships and those of my immediate family (spouse and minor children residing with me), other than those listed in numbered paragraphs 1 to 8 hereof, which could create conflicts of interest for me in my judicial capacity are as follows:

(Here insert any economic interest or relationship which might or could create a substantial conflict of interest.)

VERIFICATION

Pursuant to Supreme Court Rule 68, I declare that this statement of economic interest, including any accompanying schedules and statements, as it relates to me and members of my immediate family, has been examined by me and to the best of my knowledge and belief is true, correct and complete.

_____

Judge's Signature

_____

Date

Order adopted April 1, 1986; order amended April 20, 1987, eff. Aug. 1, 1987; order amended Dec. 30, 1993, eff. Jan. 1, 1994; order amended eff. Dec. 1, 1995, effective immediately; order amended September 23, 2005, effective immediately.

Rules 69, 70. Reserved

Rule 71. [Violation of Rules]

A judge who violates Rules 61 through 68 may be subject to discipline by the Illinois Courts Commission.

Adopted Jan. 30, 1970, eff. March 15, 1970. Amended eff. Oct. 1, 1971; amended June 24, 1976, eff. July 15, 1976; Dec. 2, 1986, eff. Jan. 1, 1987.

Formerly Ill.Rev.Stat.1991, ch. 110A, ¶ 71.

Rules 72 to 75. Reserved

Rule 76. [Military Service of Judges]

(a) Military Service During War. A judge or associate judge may serve for a period of no more than 12 months in the state militia or the armed forces of the United States when called into active military service during war between the United States and a foreign government. The judge or associate judge's military pay may be supplemented for the first 30 days with full pay and, thereafter, in an amount necessary to bring his or her total salary, inclusive of base military pay, to the level earned at the time he or she was called to service. After the 12–month period, a judge or associate judge who remains on active duty may request from the Supreme Court of Illinois an extension of the 12–month period.

(b) Reserve or Guard Training. A judge or associate judge who is a commissioned reserve officer or a reserve enlisted in the United States military or naval service or a member of the National Guard may serve on all days during which they are engaged in training ordered under the provisions of the United States military or naval training regulations for such personnel when assigned to active or inactive duty. Training shall be with full pay, not to exceed 30 days in each year.

(c) Benefits During Military Service. During periods of active military service, a judge or associate judge may be entitled to continued health insurance and other existing benefits, including retirement privileges. For purposes of computing whether a judge or associate judge may be entitled to retirement, a period of active military service shall be deemed continuous service in the office of said judge or associate judge.

(d) Resumption of Judicial Duties. A judge or associate judge terminating active military service shall immediately enter upon his or her judicial duties for the unexpired portion of the term for which he or she was elected or appointed.

(e) Term of Office. In the event that the term of office of a judge or associate judge shall expire during such period of active military service, the office shall be filled by election or appointment as may be required by law; provided, however, that a supreme, appellate or circuit judge in active military service shall have the right to file a declaration of candidacy and run for retention of his or her judicial seat, and an associate judge in active military service shall have the right to file a request for reappointment to his or her judicial seat.

(f) Definitions.

(1) The term "active military service" as used in this rule shall signify active duty in the Illinois defense force or federal service in training or on active duty with any branch of the Army of the United States, the United States Navy, the United States Air Force, the Marine Corps of the United States, the Coast Guard of the United States, and service of all officers of the United States Public Health Service detailed by proper authority for duty either with the army or the navy, and shall include the period during which a judge or associate judge in military service is absent from duty on account of sickness, wounds, leave, or other lawful causes.

(2) The term "period of active military service" as used in this rule shall begin with the date of entering upon active military service and shall terminate with death or the date immediately next succeeding the date of release or discharge from active military service or upon return from active military service, whichever shall occur first.

Adopted June 25, 1971, eff. July 1, 1971; amended May 28, 2003, eff. immediately; June 6, 2003, eff. immediately.

Formerly Ill.Rev.Stat.1991, ch. 110A, ¶ 76.

Committee Comments

(July 1, 1971)

This rule was adopted pursuant to the authority granted in section 13(b) of article VI of the new Illinois Constitution to prescribe the periods of time that a judge or associate judge may serve in the State militia or armed forces of the United States without becoming disqualified from serving as a judge or associate judge.

Rules 77 to 85. Reserved

MANDATORY ARBITRATION

Introductory Comments

Objectives

The Committee, from its inception, was duly aware of the formidability of its undertaking in the light of the novelty to the Illinois bar of the concept as well as the procedure for the conduct of nonbinding court-annexed arbitration as a method for dispute resolution. It finds, even at this date, approximately one year after the effective date of the enabling legislation, after the publication of numerous articles, the consideration of proposed rules by three major bar associations and public hearings, that the vast majority of the Illinois bar is unaware of the existence of this act and the imminence of this procedure as an integral part of the State judicial system.

The clarity, the reasonableness and the fairness of the rules to be recommended were a foremost consideration by the Committee to address both the fact of the foregoing novelty as well as the apprehension usually attendant to the introduction of a new procedure to be learned and put into practice. Equally, if not more so, was the Committee dedicated to achieving a product worthy of acceptance and promulgation by this court.

At the time of our appointment, there were in effect in approximately 16 jurisdictions rules for the conduct of mandatory arbitration programs, any set of which conceivably could have served as a viable model for adoption and use in Illinois. However, the focus of our effort in relation to a set of specific rules was to recommend that which would induce support from all affected sectors of the bar and the public, and which would manifest itself as a feasible vehicle for an early, economical and fair resolution of monetary disputes.

Toward these ends, it was our intention in the conduct and course of deliberations to obtain a product refined from the use and experience of the full panoply of models in existence and that of Pennsylvania in particular.

Background and Sources

When the Committee began its deliberations, there were among its members four judges who had previously served on a Judicial Conference Study Committee, whose recommendations served as the basis for the present mandatory Arbitration Act. These four judges, as a result of the prior study, had available to them for use in the work of this Committee a considerable bank of knowledge of existing arbitration systems. A national conference on mandatory arbitration sponsored by the National Institute for Dispute Resolution held in Washington, D.C., May 29–31, 1985, provided the chair of this Committee with a further opportunity to discuss the development of these programs with representatives of other jurisdictions.

To enable those members of this Committee who had not served on the Study Committee to become equally informed, a visit was arranged for them to attend and observe the operation of the mandatory arbitration program at Philadelphia, Pennsylvania, and to meet with judicial and administrative personnel so engaged. For two days—December 9 and 10, 1985—several members of the Committee, State Senator Arthur Berman and four members of the Chicago bar, knowledgeable in the field of voluntary arbitration, attended actual hearings being conducted at the Arbitration Center and meetings with supervisory judges and administrators. On December 10 a round-table discussion was arranged for our contingent with 14 practitioners of Philadelphia, representing plaintiff and defense bars, insurance carriers and the metropolitan transit system. Without exception those members of the Committee who had not previously been knowledgeable of this process, as well as the other attendees from Illinois, were imbued with enthusiasm for the prospect of a similar program available to Illinois and immensely impressed with the apparent effectiveness as well as the wide-scale acceptance of this procedure in Philadelphia.

In addition to the Philadelphia on-site study by members of this Committee, its chair and member Judge Harris Agnew, accompanied by staff attorney

James Woodward, on a later occasion visited four other less populous counties of Pennsylvania to study the use and operation of their mandatory arbitration programs. These visits provided models of local rules and the opportunity to interview judges and practitioners involved as well as to learn their evaluations of the effectiveness of rules in place.

The Committee's chair met with the supervising judge, the administrator and attorney practitioners in the arbitration program at Passaic County, New Jersey, and then repeated this scenario at Pittsburgh. On a later occasion the chair visited with the administrator of the King County (Seattle), Washington, arbitration program and one of its leading practitioners to discuss the effectiveness of their local and statewide rules.

It was uniformly reported to this Committee, from those thoroughly experienced with this procedure, that a full hearing necessary to arrive at award could be achieved in less than three hours. Reports from several jurisdictions were that a full hearing usually required even less than two hours to completion. It was feasible to expect completion of a three-day, 12–person jury trial within that time via the arbitration procedure under similar rules.

The fairness of the rules governing these hearings is evidenced by the high rate of acceptance by litigants, the steady increase in the number of jurisdictions initiating these programs, and their proliferation among judicial districts within a jurisdiction once it has been initiated. The reliability and durability of existing programs are further evidenced by the relatively few amendments to the rules that have been adopted since their inception. When there has been amendment, it usually consisted of an increase in the monetary limit for arbitrability, which in itself attests to the acknowledgment of the effectiveness of their rules and this mechanism for dispute resolution.

By late summer of 1986, the Committee had reached a consensus for proposed rules for consideration by the general bar and interested members of the private and public sectors. A draft of these proposed rules was widely distributed and responses invited. The Illinois State Bar Association, the Chicago Bar Association and the Chicago Council of Lawyers were specially requested to invite appropriate committees of those associations to consider these rules and formulate responses. The Committee arranged and conducted two hearings, one in Chicago and the other in Springfield. At those hearings, representatives of these bar groups, of the judiciary, and of major insurance carrier trade associations representing the membership of several hundred companies appeared to present their views relative to the draft.

Review of this draft by respected authorities among the judiciary in Philadelphia who served in supervisory positions relative to their arbitrary programs was supportive and complimentary.

Altogether, the review of the proposed draft and the responses received were highly supportive for its acceptance in that form. Nevertheless, the Committee saw fit to consider incorporating, in the rules, recommendations that appeared to have merit and to seek to clarify those provisions that seemed to elicit misunderstanding or confusion.

The last major inquiry by the Committee consisted of a meeting on December 12 sponsored by the National Institute for Dispute Resolution, with eight distinguished attorneys selected by the Committee, from out of State, and well informed in the conduct of mandatory arbitration proceedings in their jurisdictions. The inquiry at the meeting centered on the conduct of the hearing itself in an effort to refine the rules to the extent and in such form as would provide the broadest acceptance by all affected thereby.

Not the least of the Committee's efforts were the many meetings attended and the hundreds of hours of discussion and deliberation devoted to this undertaking.

As knowledgeable on this subject, if not more so, than any member of the Committee, Supreme Court Justice Howard C. Ryan, Liaison to the Committee, shared his knowledge and wisdom with us throughout the course of our deliberations. Constantly etched in our minds were his astute recommendations that we pay particular heed to the effectiveness of the Pennsylvania rules in the use of general guideline principles, leaving to the circuits the development of more detailed guidelines for local needs.

In aid of the objectives stated and from the foregoing sources, the following recommendations evolved.

Rule 86. Actions Subject to Mandatory Arbitration

(a) **Applicability to Circuits.** Mandatory arbitration proceedings shall be undertaken and conducted in those judicial circuits which, with the approval of the Supreme Court, elect to utilize this procedure and in such other circuits as may be directed by the Supreme Court.

(b) **Eligible Actions.** A civil action shall be subject to mandatory arbitration if each claim therein is exclusively for money in an amount or of a value not in excess of the monetary limit authorized by the Supreme Court for that circuit or county within that circuit, exclusive of interest and costs.

(c) **Local Rules.** Each judicial circuit court may adopt rules for the conduct of arbitration proceedings which are consistent with these rules and may determine which matters within the general classification of eligible actions shall be heard in arbitration.

(d) **Assignment from Pretrials.** Cases not assigned to an arbitration calendar may be ordered to arbitration at a status call or pretrial conference when it appears to the court that no claim in the action has a value in excess of the monetary limit authorized by the Supreme Court for that circuit or county within that circuit, irrespective of defenses.

(e) **Applicability of Code of Civil Procedure and Rules of the Supreme Court.** Notwithstanding that any action, upon filing, is initially placed in an arbitration track or is thereafter so designated for hearing, the provisions of the Code of Civil Procedure and the rules of the Supreme Court shall be applicable to its proceedings except insofar as these rules otherwise provide.

Adopted May 20, 1987, eff. June 1, 1987. Amended Dec. 30, 1993, eff. Jan. 1, 1994.

Formerly Ill.Rev.Stat.1991, ch. 110A, ¶ 86.

Committee Comments

Paragraph (a)

It is implicit from the authority granted to it by the enabling legislation and appropriate to its responsibility for the effective operation of the courts that the Supreme Court shall decide which, if any, circuit should undertake a mandatory arbitration program. Where available resources permit, and the benefits anticipated are determined, any other circuit, with the approval of the Supreme Court and by virtue of the authority of this rule, can elect to institute such program.

Paragraphs (b) and (c)

Examination of existing statutes and rules in jurisdictions with mandatory arbitration reveals that claims for a specific sum of money or money damages are the cornerstone for this form of disposition. Pennsylvania, by statute, limits this remedy to such civil matters or issues where the amount in controversy, exclusive of interest and costs, does not exceed a certain value and which do not involve title to real property. Within that broad spectrum, further limitation is authorized by rule of court. Most jurisdictions expressly exclude actions involving title to real property or equitable issues.

It was the consensus of the Committee that arbitrable actions should be limited by rule only to those matters involving a claim exclusively for money. Eligibility for arbitration, by the terms of the Act, could be more broadly interpreted. The less complex the issues, the less concern there need be for the level of experience or specialized practice of the arbitrators.

The present volume of cases in litigation potentially arbitrable under this rule, in many of the circuits, could quickly exhaust the resources that would be available to administer the program for all. For this reason, each circuit should be authorized, as is herein permitted, to further limit and define that class of cases, within the general class of arbitrability, that it may wish to submit to this program.

It could prove to be appropriate, in some circuits, until its requirements and resources dictate otherwise, to limit its program solely to actions within the monetary limit, in which jury demands have been filed. Obviously, considerable cost savings could be achieved if such matters could be resolved at a two or three hour hearing as compared to a two- or three-day trial to a jury.

The initial draft of the Committee excluded from eligible actions small claims as defined by Rule 281.

The exclusion of such actions of insubstantial amounts is not unusual in arbitration jurisdictions. Although their inclusion in the conduct of hearings would appear to be an indiscriminate use of manpower and funding resources, the Committee considers that such discretion best be left to the circuit. That court may determine that those small claims cases with jury demands should be arbitrable and thus susceptible to quick and early resolution.

If the amount of claimed interest and costs is determinable by the time of filing and constitutes an integral part of the claim, the amount of the demand, including such items, would determine eligibility for arbitration. If, however, interest and costs are determined by the arbitrators to be includable, and due and owing as of the date of the award, then the amount thereof may be added to the award even though by such addition the arbitrable limit is exceeded.

Paragraph (d)

This paragraph of the rule enables the court to order the matter to hearing in arbitration when it reasonably appears to the court that the claim has a value not in excess of the arbitrable limit although the prayer is for an amount or of a claimed value in excess thereof. Early skepticism on the part of the bar relative to the merits of this form of dispute resolution could serve to cause demands in an amount that would avoid assignment of the claim to an arbitration hearing. Some jurisdictions provide for an early conference call on all civil matters at which time arbitrability would be determined.

Philadelphia County enables the claim to be placed in the arbitration track at time of filing, at which time the date and time of hearing is assigned. The hearing date given is eight months from date of filing. Although the court in Philadelphia County may divert a case from the major case trial track to arbitration, that event is altogether infrequent. The Philadelphia bar has long recognized the benefits and advantages available in its arbitration program and do not see fit to avoid its process.

An undervaluation of the claim at the time of filing or by the court in diverting the claim to arbitration as a result of its undervaluation does not preclude the claimant from the opportunity to eventually realize its potential value. No party need accept as final the award of the arbitrators and any may reject the award and proceed on to trial in which no monetary limit would apply.

A claimant who believes he has a reasonable basis for having the matter removed from an arbitration track may move the court for such relief prior to hearing. Where there are multiple claims in the action, the court may exercise its discretion to determine whether all meet the requirements of eligibility for arbitration and if not whether a severance could be made of any or several without prejudice to the parties.

Paragraph (e)

The concern expressed by some reviewers in response to the initial draft as to whether or not the Code of Civil Procedure and the rules of the Supreme Court would apply to matters that are to be arbitrated caused the Committee to realize that some perceived this procedure as essentially *sui generis*. What we thought apparently went without saying, did not. To avoid any misconception in that regard, the Committee has adopted this part to the rule.

Rule 87. Appointment, Qualification and Compensation of Arbitrators

(a) List of Arbitrators. A list of arbitrators shall be prepared in the manner prescribed by a circuit rule. The list shall consist of a sufficient number of members of the bar engaged in the practice of law and retired judges within the circuit in which the court is situated.

(b) Panel. The panel of arbitrators shall consist of three members of the bar, or such lesser number as may be agreed upon by the parties, appointed from the list of available arbitrators, as prescribed by circuit rule, and shall be chaired by a member of the bar who has engaged in trial practice for at least three years or by a retired judge. Not more than one member or associate of a firm or office association of attorneys shall be appointed to the same panel.

(c) Disqualification. Upon appointment to a case, an arbitrator shall notify the court and withdraw from the case if any grounds appear to exist for disqualification pursuant to the Code of Judicial Conduct.

(d) Oath of Office. Each arbitrator shall take an oath of office in each county or circuit in which the arbitrator intends to serve on an arbitration panel. The oath shall be in conformity with the form provided in Rule 94 herein and shall be executed by the arbitrator when such arbitrator's name is placed on the list of arbitrators.

Arbitrators previously listed as arbitrators shall be relisted on taking the oath provided in Rule 94.

(e) Compensation. Each arbitrator shall be compensated in the amount of $100 per hearing.

Adopted May 20, 1987, eff. June 1, 1987. Amended Dec. 3, 1997, eff. Jan. 1, 1998; eff. March 1, 2001; Jan. 25, 2007, corrected Jan. 26, 2007, eff. Feb. 1, 2007.

Formerly Ill.Rev.Stat.1991, ch. 110A, ¶ 87.

Committee Comments
Paragraph (a)

Paragraph (a) is substantially modeled after Pennsylvania Rule 1302. The Committee, in its investigation of several programs in that jurisdiction, found that there were some, particularly at Pittsburgh and Philadelphia, where the arbitration lists were adequately filled by volunteers. In other counties, either by reason of the lack of enough volunteers or the view that this was an essential public service, all members of the bar were listed for such service. It is the Committee's recommendation that each circuit engaged in an arbitration program can best determine its method of utilizing its attorney resources. Retired judges are often interested and available for such service and should be considered eligible even though not then engaged in the practice of law.

Paragraph (b)

The Committee has learned of several methods extant for the appointment of arbitrators to hearing panels. Most frequently recommended is the method of random selection. Other methods include: appointment from the list in alphabetical order or in the order of arrival on signing-in on the hearing date. One jurisdiction selects three members with a combined experience of 10 years. The Committee believes that each circuit should determine its own method of appointment.

There also exist variations for the appointment of chairpersons for each panel. In some jurisdictions and districts, the member with the longest number of years in practice becomes the chairperson. In Allegheny County (Pittsburgh) a special list is maintained as the roster for appointment of the chairperson of the panel. This list consists of those who are determined by the arbitration administrator to have the longest and most pertinent experience in the practice. Here again, rather than by specific rule, the Committee recommends that this subject be determined by the circuit.

The qualification for members of the panel other than the chairperson consists of their then being engaged in the practice of law or if the retired judge does not see fit to act as chairperson, he is otherwise eligible to serve as another member of the panel.

In our initial draft of proposed rules, we adopted the phrase "actively engaged in the practice of law." At the hearings held by the Committee, representatives of the Illinois bar raised questions as to the intended meaning of the words "actively engaged." Although Pennsylvania uses those terms as a condition of eligibility and for service, its rules and reports offer no interpretation of what would constitute active engagement in the practice and leaves the interpretation to each judicial district.

The meetings held with out-of-State attorney practitioners has produced the universal recommendation from them that we avoid wherever possible imprecise terms. They called to our attention that there will always be members of the bar whom they refer to as "technocrats," inclined to demand a precise as opposed to a reasonable interpretation. Accordingly and to avoid difficulty in the interpretation of what constitutes "actively engaged" we have omitted the word "actively" in the firm belief it adds nothing substantive to the purpose intended. Leading members of the Philadelphia and Pittsburgh bars fully endorse minimal requirements for qualification to serve on the panel other than that for the chairperson.

The Pennsylvania statewide rule requires that the chairperson be admitted to practice for a minimum of three years. We have determined to add the additional requirement of trial experience. Trial experience brings with it an understanding of the role of the arbiter in a trial setting as well as

knowledge of the rules of evidence. Interviews conducted, and hearings held, disclose a prevalent and seemingly valid concern on the part of the practicing bar that arbitrators, particularly the chairperson, be fully conversant with established rules of evidence. This knowledge is more likely to facilitate an expedited hearing and acceptable results. By reason of their experience in this regard, retired judges would seemingly fit this requirement.

President Judge Michael J. O'Malley, at Pittsburgh responding to an inquiry, expressed the following view.

"Experienced trial attorneys serving as arbitrators are extremely valuable. Indeed, we attempt in Pittsburgh to have the chair of each three-member panel be an experienced lawyer. It would be even better if all three had extensive trial experience but it is not an absolute necessity." (Letter to Judge Lerner dated April 22, 1986.)

The majority of jurisdictions utilizing a single arbitrator require, as a minimum, five years' admission to the bar.

The following minimal qualifications for years of admission to practice for chairpersons were adopted in the counties, other than Philadelphia, visited by the Committee: Allegheny 5, Bucks 4, Northampton 5, Lancaster 5 and Chester 10.

Although there were members of the Committee who preferred a five-year trial experience qualification for the chairperson, the concern expressed by some that certain circuits might be hard pressed to obtain sufficient volunteers brought about the three-year minimum stated in the rule.

The qualifications stated in this rule are intended to be minimal. Each circuit may opt to enlarge upon those stated herein both as to chairpersons and other members of the panel.

Paragraph (c)

No provision is made in these rules for a substitution of arbitrators or change of venue from the panel or any of its members. The remedy of rejection of an award and the right to proceed to trial is determined to be the appropriate response to perceived bias or prejudice on the part of any member of the panel or error by the panel in the determination of its award. Subdivision (c) requires an attorney who has been appointed to serve as arbitrator to disqualify himself or herself on a particular case if circumstances relating to the parties, their counsel, or the matter in controversy would appear to be grounds for such recusal under the Code of Judicial Conduct. A motion on that basis could be presented to the court to determine the existence of any basis for disqualification and for reassignment to another panel or the substitution of another panelist. Where one of the counsel has raised the question of bias or prejudice of a member of the panel, if that panelist is not replaced or a new panel made available, an award adverse to that counsel will likely be rejected.

Paragraph (d)

As is the case with Pennsylvania, we recommend an official form for this purpose, similar to that of the Pennsylvania rules.

Paragraph (e)

The fee recommended in this rule to be paid to arbitrators is consistent with the amounts now being paid as arbitrators' fees in other jurisdictions. It was the view of the Committee that the fee be standard throughout the circuits utilizing these services; the same level of competency and performance should be expected.

Rule 88. Scheduling of Hearings

The procedure for fixing the date, time and place of a hearing before a panel of arbitrators shall be prescribed by circuit rule provided that not less than 60 days' notice in writing shall be given to the parties or their attorneys of record. The hearing shall be held on the scheduled date and within one year of the date of filing of the action, unless continued by the court upon good cause shown. The hearing shall be held at a location provided or authorized by the court.

Adopted May 20, 1987, eff. June 1, 1987.

Formerly Ill.Rev.Stat.1991, ch. 110A, ¶ 88.

Committee Comments

Each circuit engaged in a mandatory arbitration program is best suited to determine the scheduling of hearings to accommodate its case-flow needs and the availability of arbitrator personnel.

The Philadelphia program is eminently successful in achieving an efficient program—at the time it is filed, a case in the arbitration track is assigned a hearing date eight months from the date of filing. Philadelphia has a central facility styled "Arbitration Center," in an office building in the city center, a short distance from most other court facilities. The eight-month period has proved to be sufficient to enable the parties to complete their discovery and preparation for hearing. Most matters scheduled for arbitration are settled prior to hearing.

The time within which matters in arbitration should be heard is not intended to be a period of limitations but rather a reasonable expectation. Every jurisdiction studied, many with higher monetary limits for arbitrability, have reported that these cases can be heard within the period of one year without prejudice to the parties.

Experience dictates that the use of courthouse facilities provides a desirable quasi-judicial atmosphere and a ready access to the court for timely rulings. A centralized operation of the program provides greater efficiency in the use of arbitrator's and attorney's time. A central facility also results in better monitoring of the progress of a case diverted to arbitration.

Rule 89. Discovery

Discovery may be conducted in accordance with established rules and shall be completed prior to the hearing in arbitration. However, such discovery shall be conducted in accordance with Rule 222, except that the timelines may be shortened by local rule. No discovery shall be permitted after the hearing, except upon leave of court and good cause shown.

Adopted May 20, 1987, eff. June 1, 1987. Amended eff. March 26, 1996.

Formerly Ill.Rev.Stat.1991, ch. 110A, ¶ 89.

Committee Comments

The rules for discovery are intended to provide the means to obtain fair and full disclosure of the facts; they are not intended to provide a weapon for abusive tactics. The Committee anticipates a good faith effort on the part of the bar to utilize discovery to an extent and in a manner consistent with the value and complexity of arbitrable claims.

If the amount of the claim is stated to have a value not in excess of $50,000, Supreme Court Rule 222 would apply. Note that the timelines provided in Supreme Court Rule 222(c) for full compliance may be amended by a local arbitration rule. Relief from any undue restrictions under the rule should readily be forthcoming from the court; preferably counsel will cooperate to meet their recognized requirements in that regard.

Our study has disclosed relatively little use of depositions for discovery and preparation for the mandatory arbitration hearing. Rather, there has been a more extensive use of interrogatories. We are not aware of the requirement of disclosure statements in the other jurisdictions as are required under our Rule 222. It may be that the content of the disclosure statements, if fully and fairly revealed, may make sufficient the limited number of interrogatories permitted. If the allowance of more interrogatories would obviate the need for taking one or more depositions, the cost savings alone would justify such alternative.

An early and timely disposition of arbitrable matters must be doomed by courts that are tolerant of late attention to discovery. Firmness of the courts in the implementation of this rule will help to insure the successful results that are available from this procedure.

Prohibiting discovery after award places a premium on as early, and as thorough, a degree of preparation as is necessary to achieve a full hearing on the merits of the controversy. Neither side should be encouraged to use this proceeding, *i.e.*, the hearing itself, merely as an opportunity to discover the adversary's case en route to an eventual trial.

If the lapse of time between an award and a requested trial is substantial or if in that period there has been a change in the circumstances at issue, additional discovery would appear to be appropriate and should be granted.

Rule 90. Conduct of the Hearings

(a) **Powers of Arbitrators.** The arbitrators shall have the power to administer oaths and affirmations to witnesses, to determine the admissibility of evidence and to decide the law and the facts of the case. Rulings on objections to evidence or on other issues which arise during the hearing shall be made by the chairperson of the panel.

(b) **Established Rules of Evidence Apply.** Except as prescribed by this rule, the established rules of evidence shall be followed in all hearings before arbitrators.

(c) **Documents Presumptively Admissible.** All documents referred to under this provision shall be accompanied by a summary cover sheet listing each item that is included detailing the money damages incurred by the categories as set forth in this rule and specifying whether each bill is paid or unpaid. If at least 30 days' written notice of the intention to offer the following documents in evidence is given to every other party, accompanied by a copy of the document, a party may offer in evidence, without foundation or other proof:

(1) bills (specified as paid or unpaid), records and reports of hospitals, doctors, dentists, registered nurses, licensed practical nurses and physical therapists, or other health-care providers;

(2) bills for drugs, medical appliances and prostheses (specified as paid or unpaid);

(3) property repair bills or estimates, when identified and itemized setting forth the charges for labor and material used or proposed for use in the repair of the property;

(4) a report of the rate of earnings and time lost from work or lost compensation prepared by an employer;

(5) the written statement of any expert witness, the deposition of a witness, the statement of a witness which the witness would be allowed to express if testifying in person, if the statement is made by affidavit or by certification as provided in section 1–109 of the Code of Civil Procedure; [1]

(6) any other document not specifically covered by any of the foregoing provisions, and which is otherwise admissible under the rules of evidence.

The pages of any Rule 90(c) package submitted to the arbitrators should be numbered consecutively from the first page to the last page of the package in addition to any separate numbering of the pages of individual documents comprising such package.

(d) **Opinions of Expert Witnesses.** A party who proposes to use a written opinion of any expert witness or the testimony of any expert witness at the hearing may do so provided a written notice of such intention is given to every other party not less than 30 days prior to the date of hearing, accompanied by a statement containing the identity of the expert witness, the expert's qualifications, the subject matter, the basis of the expert's conclusions, and the expert's opinion as well as any other information required by Rule 222(d)(6).

(e) **Right to Subpoena Maker of the Document.** Any other party may subpoena the author or maker of a document admissible under this rule, at that party's expense, and examine the author or maker as if under cross-examination. The provisions of the Code of Civil Procedure relative to subpoenas, section 2–1101,[2] shall be applicable to arbitration hearings and it shall be the duty of a party requesting the subpoena to modify the form to show that the appearance is set before an arbitration panel and to give the time and place set for the hearing.

(f) **Adverse Examination of Parties or Agents.** The provisions of the Code of Civil Procedure relative to the adverse examination of parties or agents, section 2–1102,[3] shall be applicable to arbitration hearings as upon the trial of a case.

(g) **Compelling Appearance of Witness at Hearing.** The provisions of Rule 237, herein, shall be equally applicable to arbitration hearings as they are to trials. The presence of a party may be waived by stipulation or excused by court order for good cause shown not less than seven days prior to the hearing. Remedies upon a party's failure to comply with notice pursuant to Rule 237(b) may include an order debarring that party from rejecting the award.

(h) **Prohibited Communication.** Until the arbitration award is issued and has become final by either acceptance or rejection, an arbitrator may not be contacted *ex parte*, nor may an arbitrator publicly comment or respond to questions regarding a particular arbitration case heard by that arbitrator. Discussions between an arbitrator and judge regarding an infraction or impropriety during the arbitration process are not prohibited by this rule. Nothing in this rule shall be construed to limit or expand judicial review of an arbitration award or limit or expand the testimony of an arbitrator at judicial hearing to clarify a mistake or error appearing on the face of an award.

[Rule 90(c) Cover Sheet]

IN THE CIRCUIT OF   COUNTY, ILLINOIS

Plaintiff	)
	)
	) No.
	)
v.	)
	)
	)
	)
Defendant	)
	)

NOTICE OF INTENT PURSUANT TO SUPREME COURT RULE 90(C)

Pursuant to Supreme Court Rule 90(c), the plaintiff(s) intend(s) to offer the following documents that are attached into evidence at the arbitration proceeding:

I.   Healthcare Provider Bills   Amount Paid   Amount Unpaid

    1.
    2.
    3.
    4.
    5.
    6.
    7.
    8.
    9.
    10.

II.   Other Items of Compensable Damages

    1.
    2.
    3.
    4.
    5.

_____

Attorney for Plaintiff

Adopted May 20, 1987, effective June 1, 1987; amended April 7, 1993, effective June 1, 1993; amended March 26, 1996, effective immediately; amended March 28, 2002, effective July 1, 2002; amended December 5, 2003, effective January 1, 2004; amended October 14, 2005, effective January 1, 2006; amended June 4, 2008, effective July 1, 2008.

Formerly Ill.Rev.Stat.1991, ch. 110A, ¶ 90.

[1] 735 ILCS 5/1–109.
[2] 735 ILCS 5/2–1101.
[3] 735 ILCS 5/2–1102.

Committee Comments

The conduct of the hearings, the outcome included, will substantially determine the regard and acceptance to be held by the legal community for this procedure as an effective method of dispute resolution for achieving a fair, early, economical and final result. For this reason, more perhaps than for any other of these rules, has the Committee devoted its attention to this rule. Meetings and interviews with out-of-State practitioners, judges and administrators were conducted with the greatest emphasis on the evidentiary aspect of the hearings.

Paragraph (a)

The authority and power of the arbitrators exist only in relation to the conduct of the hearing at the time it is held. Issues that may arise in the proceedings of the case prior, ancillary or subsequent to the hearing must be resolved by the court.

In some jurisdictions, including Pennsylvania, rulings on the evidence are to be made by a majority of the panel. Ohio has recently amended its rule to permit the chairperson to make such rulings. Practitioners, familiar with the practice in multiple-person panels, recommend that the ultimate authority reside with the chairperson. In practice one could reasonably expect the chairperson to consult with other members of the panel on difficult questions of admissibility.

Paragraph (b)

Several jurisdictions do not require hearings to be conducted according to the established rules of evidence.

New Jersey provides: "The arbitrator shall admit all relevant evidence and shall not be bound by the rules of evidence."

Ohio's statewide rules make no reference to the nature of the evidence admissible in mandatory arbitration hearings. Cuyahoga County (Cleveland), Hamilton County (Cincinnati) and Stark County (Canton) by local rules provide that the arbitrators shall be the judges of the relevancy and materiality of the evidence and "conformity to legal rules of evidence shall not be necessary."

The State of Washington rules leave to the discretion of the arbitrator the extent to which the rules of evidence will apply.

The States of Arizona, California, Minnesota, New York and Pennsylvania provide, as does this rule, for the application of the established rules of evidence with exceptions similar to those stated under paragraph (c).

It is the view of the Committee that the Illinois practitioner will enjoy a sense of security in that the established rules of evidence will apply to these hearings.

Paragraph (c)

All jurisdictions utilizing court-annexed arbitration have adopted rules substantially and conceptually similar to the provisions at paragraph (c) of this rule. The purpose for allowing presumptive admissibility of documents is to enable the parties to achieve the economy of time and expense available for the conduct of the hearing. The emphasis should be placed on substance and not form; the integrity of the evidence should be more meaningful than its formal method of introduction. The documents described in (c) are generally considered reliable and trustworthy for the purpose of admission. The documents that could be admitted under the general classification in (c)(6) could be photos, maps, drawings and blueprints, weather reports, business records and communications, and the like, so as to relieve the requirements of a foundational predicate for their admission.

The practice of the presumptive admission of documents of the type and nature described in the rule has stood the test of time and of experience in many thousands of hearings; one encounters no reported criticism or suggestion for change.

Regardless of the presumptive admissibility of the documents, the arbitrators will be required to apply the tests under established rules of evidence otherwise relating to admissibility and credibility and to determine, fairly, the weight to be given such evidence. Otherwise, the purpose of this procedure to achieve a fair, economical and early disposition of the controversy must ultimately fail by virtue of the lack of an essential integrity to the hearing itself.

Practitioners may not assume that practice will tolerate the blanket submission of voluminous records, charts or entire depositions with the expectation that the panel must pore over these documents and attempt to sort out that part which may be relevant or material to the issues at hand. Nor should such burden be placed on opposing counsel when such documents have been provided by notice. It would not be inappropriate or unreasonable, on the part of the panel, if it were to reject such blanket submissions unless proffering counsel specifies the entries or statements therein having relevancy and materiality.

None of the documents eligible for admission without foundation may be so offered unless the intention to do so, and a copy thereof, has been provided to opposing counsel not less than 30 days prior to the hearing. That length of time should be sufficient to enable counsel to verify the authenticity of the document, if prior discovery has not already accomplished that purpose. The Committee is recommending a period of notice longer than any of the arbitration jurisdictions; many provide a 20–day notice and some as few as seven days. We recommend the longer period so that there is less reason for the parties to request a continuance.

If the period of notice given for the submission of documents for presumptive admission is the minimum provided by this rule, and opposing counsel, in the exercise of prudent practice finds need to submit a document in rebuttal, he should apply to the court for leave to do so, unless his adversary will stipulate to a submission in less time than is required by this rule. Under such circumstances the court, in its ruling, should be guided by the degree of diligence and preparation previously undertaken by both counsel.

Whenever possible, counsel should endeavor to avoid delay and needless expense by stipulating to the admission of documents where there is no reasonable basis for believing they will not and should not be admitted.

Paragraph (d)

It is intended under this paragraph to require disclosure of the identity of an opinion witness whose written opinion will be offered under the provisions of paragraph (c)(5) herein, or who will testify at the hearings; and to the extent required under Rule 222, his qualifications, the subject matter of his testimony, and the basis of conclusions and opinions as well as any other information required by Rule 222(d)(6). This information must be provided not less than 30 days prior to the scheduled date of hearing. The longer the period of notice provided to one's adversary, the less justification there would be to delay the hearing by reason of a late and unexpected disclosure.

Paragraph (e)

Although existing practice in other jurisdictions indicates that the option provided under (e) is rarely exercised, opposing counsel is given the right to subpoena the maker of the document as an adverse witness, and examine that witness as if under cross-examination. This provision is not intended to act as a substitute for the right, under Rule 237, to require the production of a party at the hearing. In the event the maker sought to be served is not amenable to service of a subpoena, and provided further that counsel has been diligent in attempting to obtain such service, it would be incumbent on counsel to seek to bar its admissibility. Such motion should be made well in advance of the hearing date.

The Explanatory Note to Pennsylvania Rule 1305 states that if a member or author of the document is not subject to the jurisdiction of the court and cannot be subpoenaed, that document would not be presumptively admissible. The use of subpoena under this provision of the rule is rare and this problem does not appear to be one that has been bothersome to the practitioners. The Committee does not believe that there should be a hard and fast rule if such issue should arise but rather that it be decided on a case-by-case basis. This seems to be the prevalent view among practitioners of other jurisdictions. The materiality of the document to the issues should be a significant matter. The courts should also be alert to prevent the attempted use of this process by opposing counsel as an abusive tactic for delay and harassment.

Paragraphs (f) and (g)

Although these provisions of the Code of Civil Procedure and Supreme Court Rule 237 apply to trials, they should be equally applicable to hearings in arbitration. The Committee is advised that in actual practice it has been customary for counsel to arrange for the appearance of such witnesses by agreement.

A party who fails to comply with a Rule 237(b) notice to appear at a trial is subject to sanctions pursuant to Rule 219(c). Those sanctions may include an order debarring that party from maintaining a claim, counterclaim, etc. The 1993 amendment to Rule 90(g) is to make clear that a Rule 237(b) notice to appear at an arbitration hearing carries equivalent importance, such that a court may, in an appropriate case, debar a party who fails to comply from rejecting the award. The amendments also allow a party who received a notice to appear an opportunity to be excused in advance from appearing for good cause or by stipulation. For example, in a case where the party is willing to stipulate to the issue of liability and the only question which remains is damages, the party served with a Rule 237 notice may be excused by stipulation of the parties.

(March 28, 2002)

This rule is amended to conform to the changes in terminology made in Supreme Court Rule 213.

(January 1, 2006)

Paragraph (h) is directed toward eliminating the problem of party or attorney use of information/feedback obtained during posthearing *ex parte* communication. Such communication could hinder the program goal of parties participating in good faith and could possibly influence the decision of the parties to accept or reject an award. This rule is not intended to restrict the ability of a party to communicate *ex parte* with a nonneutral party-arbitrator when used outside of court-annexed mandatory arbitration.

Rule 91. Absence of Party at Hearing

(a) Failure to be Present at Hearing. The arbitration hearing shall proceed in the absence of any party who, after due notice, fails to be present. The panel shall require the other party or parties to submit such evidence as the panel may require for the making of an award. The failure of a party to be present, either in person or by counsel, at an arbitration hearing shall constitute a waiver of the right to reject the award and a consent to the entry by the court of a judgment on the award. In the event the party who fails to be present thereafter moves, or files a petition to the court, to vacate the judgment as provided therefor under the provisions of the Code of Civil Procedure for the vacation of judgments by default, sections 2–1301 and 2–1401,[1] the court, in its discretion, in addition to vacating the judgment, may order the matter for rehearing in arbitration, and may also impose the sanction of costs and fees as a condition for granting such relief.

(b) Good–Faith Participation. All parties to the arbitration hearing must participate in the hearing in good faith and in a meaningful manner. If a panel of arbitrators unanimously finds that a party has failed to participate in the hearing in good faith and in a meaningful manner, the panel's finding and factual basis therefor shall be stated on the award. Such award shall be *prima facie* evidence that the party failed to participate in the arbitration hearing in good faith and in a meaningful manner and a court, when presented with a petition for sanctions or remedy therefor, may order sanctions as provided in Rule 219(c), including, but not limited to, an order debarring that party from rejecting the award, and costs and attorney fees incurred for the arbitration hearing and in the prosecution of the petition for sanctions, against that party.

Adopted May 20, 1987, eff. June 1, 1987. Amended April 7, 1993, eff. June 1, 1993.

Formerly Ill.Rev.Stat.1991, ch. 110A, ¶ 91.
[1] 735 ILCS 5/2–1301, 5/2–1401.

Committee Comments
Paragraph (a)

There is precedent for such a rule and its consequence in the rules of other jurisdictions. Cuyahoga County (Cleveland), Ohio, has long had a rule which provides that the failure of a party to appear at the hearing either in person or by counsel constitutes a waiver of his right to reject the award and demand trial and further operates as a consent to the entry of judgment on the award.

The Washington rules provide that a party who fails to participate at the hearing without good cause waives the right to a trial.

The court administrator of the Philadelphia Court of Common Pleas, Judge Harry A. Takiff, upon reviewing our initial draft, applauded the inclusion of this rule. Judge Takiff proposed to recommend the adoption of a like rule for the Pennsylvania arbitration programs.

The enactment, by the legislature, establishing the procedure of mandatory court-annexed arbitration as an integral part of the juridical process of dispute resolution and the promulgation of these rules to implement such legislation compels the conclusion that its process must be utilized in arbitrable matters either to finally resolve the dispute or as the obligatory step prior to resolution by trial. To permit any party or counsel to ignore the arbitration hearing or to exhibit an indifference to its conduct would permit a mockery of this deliberate effort on behalf of the public, the bar and judiciary to attempt to achieve an expeditious and less costly resolution of private controversies.

A party who knowingly fails to attend the scheduled hearing, either in person or by counsel, must be deemed to have done so with full knowledge of the consequences that inhere with this rule. Where the failure to attend was inadvertent, relief may be available to the party under the provisions of the Code of Civil Procedure, sections 2–1301 or 2–1401, upon such terms and conditions as shall be reasonable. See Ill.Ann.Stat., ch. 110, pars. 2–1301, 2–1401, Historical & Practice Notes (Smith–Hurd 1983); also *Braglia v. Cephus* (1986), 146 Ill.App.3d 241, 496 N.E.2d 1171.

Paragraph (b)

Prior to the adoption of these sanctions, there were complaints by arbitrators that some parties and lawyers would merely attend but refuse to participate in arbitration. This paragraph was adopted to discourage such misconduct.

The arbitration process, and this rule in particular, was not intended to force parties to settle cases. Settlement, by definition, must be voluntary and not compelled. However, mandatory arbitration is a dispute resolution process under the auspices of the court. Parties and lawyers must not be allowed to abuse the arbitration process so as to make it meaningless.

Arbitration must not be perceived as just another hurdle to be crossed in getting the case to trial. Good-faith participation, as required by this rule, was therefore intended to assure the integrity of the arbitration process.

In drafting Rule 91(b), the committee surveyed the experience of other States, drawing particularly on similar requirements for good-faith participation in the mandatory arbitration rules of Arizona, California and South Carolina.

Rule 92. Award and Judgment on Award

(a) **Definition of Award.** An award is a determination in favor of a plaintiff or defendant.

(b) **Determining an Award.** The panel shall make an award promptly upon termination of the hearing. The award shall dispose of all claims for relief. The award may not exceed the monetary limit authorized by the Supreme Court for that circuit or county within that circuit, exclusive of interest and costs. The award shall be signed by the arbitrators or the majority of them. A dissenting vote without further comment may be noted. Thereafter, the award shall be filed immediately with the clerk of the court, who shall serve notice of the award, and the entry of the same on the record, to other parties, including any in default.

(c) **Judgment on the Award.** In the event none of the parties files a notice of rejection of the award and requests to proceed to trial within the time required herein, any party thereafter may move the court to enter judgment on the award.

(d) **Correction of Award.** Where the record and the award disclose an obvious and unambiguous error in mathematics or language, the court, on application of a party within the 30–day period allowed for rejection of an award, may correct the same. The filing of such an application shall stay all proceedings, including the running of the 30–day period for rejection of the award, until disposition of the application by the court.

Adopted May 20, 1987, eff. June 1, 1987. Amended Dec. 30, 1993, eff. Jan. 1, 1994.

Formerly Ill.Rev.Stat.1991, ch. 110A, ¶ 92.

Committee Comments

Paragraph (b)

The most efficient use of panels would require that a sufficient number of matters for hearing be assigned to them for the date of service. It has been the experience at Philadelphia, and other counties of Pennsylvania, that their panels will conduct two or more full hearings on the assigned date of service. The form of the award proposed in Rule 94 is modeled after the official form of Pennsylvania, in its Rule 1312. The Committee recommends that no findings of fact or conclusions of law be required of the panel to be stated in its award. This is the accepted practice in Pennsylvania.

Paragraph (c)

Only the court may enter the judgment in a pending action. Unless the parties stipulate to dismiss the cause after the hearing and award, it is incumbent on a party to move the court to enter judgment after the 30–day period allowed for rejection at Rule 93 herein.

Rule 93. Rejection of Award

(a) **Rejection of Award and Request for Trial.** Within 30 days after the filing of an award with the clerk of the court, and upon payment to the clerk of the court of the sum of $200 for awards of $30,000 or less or $500 for awards greater than $30,000, any party who was present at the arbitration hearing, either in person or by counsel, may file with the clerk a written notice of rejection of the award and request to proceed to trial, together with a certificate of service of such notice on all other parties. The filing of a single rejection shall be sufficient to enable all parties except a party who has been debarred from rejecting the award to proceed to trial on all issues of the case without the necessity of each party filing a separate rejection. The filing of a notice of rejection shall not be effective as to any party who is debarred from rejecting an award.

(b) **Arbitrator May Not Testify.** An arbitrator may not be called to testify as to what transpired before the arbitrators and no reference to the fact of the conduct of the arbitration hearing may be made at trial.

(c) **Waiver of Costs.** Upon application of a poor person, pursuant to Rule 298, herein, the sum required to be paid as costs upon rejection of the award may be waived by the court.

Adopted May 20, 1987, eff. June 1, 1987. Amended April 7, 1993, eff. June 1, 1993; Dec. 3, 1996, eff. Jan. 1, 1997.

Formerly Ill.Rev.Stat.1991, ch. 110A, ¶ 93.

Committee Comments

Paragraph (a)

Delaware and New Jersey rules relative to arbitration programs expressly provide that the sole remedy of a party unwilling to accept the arbitration award is to file a rejection and to proceed on to trial. It is the Committee's view that this should be the interpretation applied by the courts with regard to proceedings after award.

Even under the Illinois Uniform Arbitration Act, section 112, it has been interpreted by the Illinois Supreme Court that an arbitration award may not be set aside, upon application to a court, for the arbitrator's errors in judgment or mistakes of law or fact. (*Garner v. Ferguson* (1979), 76 Ill.2d 1, 389 N.E.2d 1181.) Under this section of the U.A.A., a party may apply to the court to vacate the award where the award was procured by corruption, fraud or other undue means; or that an arbitrator was guilty of misconduct prejudicing the rights of any party; or the arbitrators exceeded their powers. The Committee urges the interpretation that such alleged conduct should be addressed to the court for redress in a petition independent of the course of the proceedings in the action subsequent to the award; that the sole remedy in relation to the award, as an intermediate mechanism to resolve the dispute, should be to avail oneself of the right to a trial. The enabling act of Illinois expressly provides that the Illinois Uniform Arbitration Act shall not apply to these mandatory arbitration proceedings.

The 1981 official Explanatory Note to Pennsylvania Rule 1308 states:

"The Rules do not continue the practice of petitioning to set aside an award for corruption or misbehavior. Hearings or depositions on the petition proceedings could delay the proceedings. Rule 1311(b) creates quasi-judicial immunity for the arbitrators with respect to their official actions and they cannot be called to testify. As a practical matter, if the fraud or corruption were proved, remand and the appointment of a new panel could be the only relief. *Trial de novo is preferable since it expedites the proceedings. The court would of course have the power to punish the attorney-arbitrators involved for any professional misconduct that could be proved.*" (Emphasis added.) (Our recommended Rule 93(b) incorporates the exact language of Pennsylvania Rule 1311(b).)

Only a party who has attended the hearing in person or by counsel shall have the right to reject the award without regard to the basis for such rejection. The filing of a rejection and request for trial will permit any other party, whose interest has not been otherwise adjudicated, to participate in the trial.

A party who fails to appear at the hearing, although thereby deemed to have waived the right to reject the award, may nevertheless participate in a trial of the cause upon rejection of the award by any other party, provided a judgment has not been entered against him on the award and the judgment has not been vacated.

The assessment of the fee of $200 on the party who files the rejection is an item of cost consistent with the authorization provided therefor by the enabling legislation and is consistent with similar costs imposed in other jurisdictions in relation to the right to proceed further to a trial. This sum amounts to a small measure of the concomitant cost to the public for the conduct of the trial itself and would appear appropriate as an imposition on a party who has already been provided with a full hearing forum to resolve the dispute.

The Committee is unable to reach a consensus on the question of recommending a specific rule on whether or not the $200 fee should be recoverable as a taxable cost. Pennsylvania, as does New York and Ohio, provides by rule that the costs assessed on the rejecting party shall apply to the cost of arbitrators fees and shall not be taxed as costs or be recoverable in any proceeding. The sum of $200 is the same amount imposed by Philadelphia County's rule on a party requesting trial after an award. Other jurisdictions, on the other hand, provide that such fee is recoverable and may be taxed as costs. If clarity in this regard requires a definitive rule, it is the Committee's preference that the rule be stated similarly to that of Pennsylvania; to wit, the sum so paid to the clerk shall not be taxed as costs or recoverable in any proceeding.

Many jurisdictions authorize fee and cost sanctions to be imposed on parties who fail to improve their positions at the trial after hearing. It is hoped that the quality of the arbitrators, the integrity of the hearings and the fairness of the awards will keep, to a minimum, the number of rejections. Both the Pittsburgh and Philadelphia programs, in Pennsylvania, are prime examples of effective arbitration systems without the use of cost and fee sanctions. Until such time as it becomes evident that there is an abusive use of the right of rejection, the Committee proposes to rely on the integrity of practitioners and their clients to abide a fair decision of the arbitrators. Abuse of this process may be dealt with under existing disciplinary and remedial measures.

In *Campbell v. Washington* (1991), 223 Ill.App.3d 283, the court interpreted Rule 93 as providing that a party's right to reject an award is preserved when either the party or its attorney appears at the arbitration hearing. Therefore, the court held a trial court could not enter an order requiring forfeiture of the right of rejection as a sanction for failure of a party to appear pursuant to notice. The 1993 amendment to Rule 93 makes this rule consistent with other rules (for example, Rules 90(g) and 91(b)) that allow a court to enter an order debarring a party from rejecting the award. The filing of a rejection by a party who is or has been debarred from rejecting is ineffective even if the party was present at the arbitration hearing in person or by counsel.

Paragraph (b)

The majority of jurisdictions prohibit any reference in a subsequent trial to the fact that an arbitration proceeding was held or that an award was made; arbitrators are not permitted to testify regarding the conduct at the hearing. In addition, several of the jurisdictions, California and New Jersey in particular, prohibit recording of the arbitration proceedings or the use of any testimony taken at the hearing at a subsequent trial. However, where a recording of testimony at the hearing is not prohibited such testimony could be used at trial if otherwise admissible under the established rules of evidence of that jurisdiction.

Paragraph (c)

In some jurisdictions where costs such as herein imposed are waived, it is provided in their rules that such costs may be imposed thereafter as an offset in the event a sufficient sum is recovered by the indigent party upon the trial of the cause.

Rule 94. Form of Oath, Award and Notice of Award

The oath, award of arbitrators, and notice of award shall be in substantially the following form:

In the Circuit Court of the _____ Judicial Circuit, _____ County, Illinois.

(Or, in the Circuit Court of Cook County, Illinois)

OATH

I do solemnly swear (or affirm) that I will support, obey, and defend the Constitution of the United States and the Constitution of the State of Illinois and that I will faithfully discharge the duties of my office.

_____
Name of Arbitrator   Date

AWARD OF ARBITRATORS

In the Circuit Court of the _____ Judicial Circuit, _____ County, Illinois.

(Or, in the Circuit Court of Cook County, Illinois)

A.B., C.D., etc.	)
(naming all plaintiffs),	)
Plaintiffs	)
v.	) No. _____
H.J., K.L., etc.	) Amount Claimed _____
(naming all defendants),	)
Defendants	)

☐ All parties participated in good faith.
☐ did NOT participate in good faith based upon the following findings.

Findings:

_____
_____
_____
_____
_____
_____
_____
_____
_____
_____
_____
_____
_____

We, the undersigned arbitrators, having been duly appointed and sworn (or affirmed), make the following award:

_____
_____
_____
_____
_____

_____
_____
_____
_____
_____
_____
_____

_____ Dissents as to the Award

Date of Award: _____

NOTICE OF AWARD

In the Circuit Court of the _____ Judicial Circuit, _____ County, Illinois.

(Or, in the Circuit Court of Cook County, Illinois)

A.B., C.D., etc.	)
(naming all plaintiffs),	)
Plaintiffs	)
v.	) No. _____
H.J., K.L., etc.	) Amount Claimed _____
(naming all defendants),	)
Defendants	)

On the ___ day of _____, 20 ___, the award of the arbitrators dated ___ _____, 20 ___, a copy of which is attached hereto, was filed and entered of record in this Cause. A copy of this NOTICE has on this date been sent by regular mail, postage prepaid, addressed to each of the parties appearing herein, at their last known address, or to their attorney of record.

Dated this ___ day of _____, 20 ___.

_____
Clerk of the Circuit Court

Adopted May 20, 1987, eff. June 1, 1987; amended eff. March 1, 2001; amended Oct. 20, 2003, eff. Dec. 1, 2003.

Formerly Ill.Rev.Stat.1991, ch. 110A, ¶ 94.

Rule 95. Form of Notice of Rejection of Award

The notice of rejection of the award shall be in substantially the following form:

In the Circuit Court of the _____ Judicial Circuit, _____ County, Illinois.

(Or, in the Circuit Court of Cook County, Illinois.)

A.B., C.D. _etc._	)
(naming all plaintiffs),	)
Plaintiffs	)
v.	) No. _____
H.J., K.L. _etc._	) Amount Claimed _____
(naming all defendants),	)
Defendants	)

NOTICE OF REJECTION OF AWARD

To the Clerk of the Circuit Court:

Notice is given that _____
rejects the award of the arbitrators entered in this
cause on _____,
and hereby requests a trial of this action.

By: _____

(Certificate of Notice of Attorney)

Adopted May 20, 1987, eff. June 1, 1987.

Formerly Ill.Rev.Stat.1991, ch. 110A, ¶ 95.

Rules 96 to 98. Reserved

Rule 99. Mediation Programs

(a) Applicability to Circuits. Mediation programs
may be undertaken and conducted in those judicial
circuits which, with the approval of the Supreme
Court, elect to utilize this procedure and in such other
circuits as directed by the Supreme Court.

(b) Local Rules.

(1) Each judicial circuit electing to establish a
mediation program shall adopt rules for the conduct
of the mediation proceedings. A person approved
by the circuit to act as a mediator under these rules
shall have judicial immunity in the same manner
and to the same extent as a judge. Prior to the
establishment of such a program, the Chief Judge of
the circuit shall submit to the Supreme Court for its
review and approval, through its Administrative
Office, rules governing the operation of the circuit's
program. A circuit operating a mediation program
on the effective date of this Rule may continue the
program for one year after the effective date of this
Rule, but must, within 90 days of the effective date
of this Rule, submit for the Supreme Court's review
and approval the rules under which the mediation
program is operating. Any amendments to approved local rules must be submitted to the Administrative Office for review and approval prior to
implementation.

(2) At a minimum, the local circuit court rules
shall address:

(i) Actions eligible for referral to mediation;

(ii) Appointment, qualifications and compensation of the mediators;

(iii) Scheduling of the mediation conferences;

(iv) Conduct of the conferences;

(v) Discovery;

(vi) Absence of party at the conference and
sanctions;

(vii) Termination and report of mediation conference;

(viii) Finalization of agreement;

(ix) Confidentiality;

(x) Reporting to the Supreme Court for each
approved mediation program shall be conducted
in a manner and method as prescribed by the
Administrative Office of the Illinois Courts.

Adopted April 11, 2001, eff. immediately. Amended Oct. 10,
2001, eff. immediately; Oct. 15, 2015, eff. immediately.

Rule 99.1. Mortgage Foreclosure Mediation Programs

(a) Mortgage foreclosure specific mediation programs implemented by any judicial circuit must adhere to the requirements set forth in Rule 99 and this
rule.

(b) Each judicial circuit that currently has approved
local rules for a mediation program in place in accordance with Rule 99 may apply that program to mortgage foreclosure cases if applicable. Local rules
amended or created to accommodate mortgage foreclosure cases consistent with this rule must be submitted to the Administrative Office of the Illinois Courts
for review and approval prior to implementation.

(c) Each judicial circuit electing to establish a new
mortgage foreclosure mediation program shall adopt
rules for the conduct of the mortgage foreclosure
mediation proceedings. If a judicial circuit elects to
establish a new mortgage foreclosure mediation program, the judicial circuit shall establish a plan for
starting a mortgage foreclosure mediation program
that demonstrates the mediation program can be implemented for that particular county or counties at the
time of submission of the local rules for approval by
the Administrative Office.

(d) Based on the plan established pursuant to paragraph (c), the local circuit rules shall address:

(i) the requirements set forth in Rule 99;

(ii) resources to provide meaningful access to
HUD-certified housing counseling services for eligible homeowners;

(iii) resources to provide meaningful access to *pro
bono* legal representation for eligible homeowners;

(iv) resources to provide meaningful language access for program participants;

(v) any costs charged to any participant in the
mortgage foreclosure case;

(vi) a sustainability plan that includes a long-term
funding plan; and

(vii) training of judges, key court personnel and
volunteers on mortgage foreclosure mediation.

Adopted Feb. 22, 2013, eff. Mar. 1, 2013.

Committee Comments
(March 1, 2013)

The creation of Rule 99.1 resulted from the drastic increase in mortgage foreclosure cases and the
resultant burden on judicial circuits throughout the
state. Each judicial circuit faced a foreclosure crisis and began adapting its court procedures to most

effectively administer the foreclosure proceedings. As a result, the judicial circuits began applying to the Illinois Supreme Court under Rule 99 for approval of mortgage foreclosure specific mediation programs. These programs varied widely in scope, capacity, and structure. To more fully understand the needs of mortgage foreclosure specific mediation, the Illinois Supreme Court appointed a committee to study and hold public hearings to address the need for uniformity among mediation programs. The Special Supreme Court Committee on Mortgage Foreclosures concluded that there was no one model that would work well for each judicial circuit but certain elements must be present to provide equal accessibility and assistance throughout the state. The intention of this rule is to incorporate more consistent elements in programs throughout the state while also allowing flexibility for changing conditions with mortgage foreclosure filings in the future.

The plan required in paragraph (c) recognizes the Supreme Court's need to understand the extent of the mortgage foreclosure problem in the county or counties in each judicial circuit applying for approval. The Supreme Court should be provided the history of the mortgage foreclosure filings in the judicial circuit, the available resources, and the staffing scope of the judicial circuit that shows that the mortgage foreclosure program is realistically attainable for the judicial circuit. The judicial circuit applying for approval should provide a plan that is comparable in scope, size and capacity to the mortgage foreclosure problem facing that circuit. Additionally, the plan should include information about available resources for qualified homeowners

that will contribute to the successful implementation of such a program.

Paragraph (d) sets forth requirements specific to mortgage foreclosure mediation programs in addition to the requirements articulated in Rule 99. The Committee concluded that for residential mortgage foreclosures where a defendant was actively living in the home and facing foreclosure, access to a HUD-certified housing counselor and *pro bono* legal representation is beneficial. However, the Committee also recognized that the availability of those resources may differ from circuit to circuit in the state. As a result, any program proposal submitted for approval shall detail the access the program will be able to provide to eligible homeowners to HUD–certified housing counseling services and *pro bono* legal representation. Lack of availability of particular resources due to financial or geographic constraints shall not preclude approval of a mediation program.

The Committee also recognized that the implementation of a mortgage foreclosure mediation program can drain a court's resources both financially and in staffing capacity. As a result, paragraphs (d)(v) and (vi) require any new mortgage foreclosure mediation program to set forth any costs charged to the parties in the litigation, as well as the sustainability funding plan. The fees charged may include, but are not limited to, mediator fees for mediation sessions and dedicated filing-fee add-ons. A sustainability plan may include those costs charged to litigants or another identifiable source of funding.

Rule 100.   Reserved

EXPEDITED CHILD SUPPORT RULES

Rule 100.1. Implementation of Expedited Child Support System

(a) Applicability to Circuits. An Expedited Child Support System may be established in those judicial circuits which, with the approval of the Supreme Court, elect to implement the System and in such other judicial circuits as may be directed by the Supreme Court.

(b) Submission of a Plan. The chief judge of a judicial circuit which elects to create a System must submit a Plan of Implementation. The Plan may establish a circuit-wide system, a system in each county within the circuit or a system in any county in the circuit. The chief judges of two or more contiguous judicial circuits may submit a Plan for the creation of a single system encompassing those judicial circuits or encompassing contiguous counties within the judicial circuits.

(c) The Plan. Each Plan must:

(1) describe how the Plan will ensure that support orders will be expedited, setting forth the time frames and the mechanism for expediting matters

eligible for a hearing before an administrative hearing officer;

(2) describe how the System will comply with the Federal time frames established for the IV–D program in regulations promulgated by the United States Department of Health and Human Services Office of Child Support Enforcement (codified at 45 C.F.R. 303), for the disposition of parentage and child support cases, and how compliance information shall be provided with respect to IV–D and non–IV–D cases;

(3) indicate whether the System is to be made available to nonparticipants in the IV–D program as specified in subsection (d) below;

(4) indicate which of the actions eligible for a hearing under Rule 100.3 will be subject to a hearing before an administrative hearing officer;

(5) designate the number of administrative hearing officers to be employed, and whether they will be employed full-time or part-time;

(6) indicate the compensation to be paid to each administrative hearing officer;

(7) describe the personnel policies applicable to employees of the System;

(8) describe the facilities and security arrangements to be used for hearings, including the days and hours of availability;

(9) describe the procedures for training administrative hearing officers;

(10) describe the documentation and forms required for an expedited child support hearing in addition to those required by the Supreme Court;

(11) describe the procedure for transmittal to a judge of contested prehearing motions, other matters that require a court order, recommended orders, and any other matters that require transfer or should be referred to a judge;

(12) describe the procedure for transfer of matters from a judge to an administrative hearing officer; and

(13) describe the procedure for action by a judge on an administrative hearing officer's recommendations.

(d) Availability of System to Non–IV–D Participants. A Plan may provide that the System is available in cases where both parties are non–IV–D participants and request access to the System. If the System is available to non–IV–D participants, administrative expenses must be appropriated by the county board and a plan for cost-sharing must be approved as provided in subsection (g) below.

(e) Establishment of Demonstration Programs. The Illinois Department of Public Aid may notify the Supreme Court of its desire to establish a demonstration program in one or more circuits or counties. Any such program shall be available to IV–D participants. Upon receipt of such notification, the Supreme Court will notify the chief judge of each judicial circuit of the Department's desire to establish a demonstration program. Each chief judge may submit a demonstration Plan to the Supreme Court which, upon approval, will submit the Plan to the Department. The Department may select one or more circuits or counties to participate in the demonstration program after reviewing the submitted Plans. The Department shall notify the Supreme Court of its decision. The submitted demonstration Plan shall include each element listed in subsection (c) above. In addition, each demonstration Plan shall include a projected budget for operation of the System. The demonstration Plan shall specify whether it is available to non–IV–D participants, and if so, shall provide that the portion of the administrative costs attributable to use by non–IV–D participants has been appropriated by the demonstration county and meets the requirements of subsection (g) below.

(f) Supreme Court Review and Approval. The Supreme Court shall review and approve or request that the chief judge modify any submitted Plan or demonstration Plan for compliance with the Act, these rules and, to the extent Federal reimbursement is sought, the rules of the IV–D program. Upon Supreme Court approval of a Plan, any nondemonstration county, circuit, multicircuit area or multicounty area may establish a System. Approved demonstration Plans will be submitted to the Department of Public Aid for review based on Department standards.

(g) Funding. Before establishment of a System according to a Supreme Court approved Plan, each participating nondemonstration county board or boards must appropriate the administrative expenses incurred to establish and maintain the non–IV–D portion of the System and the IV–D portion that is not subject to Federal reimbursement. A Plan for cost-sharing must be submitted to the Department of Public Aid for approval. Each chief judge shall be responsible for documenting and recording the number of IV–D and non–IV–D cases pending and disposed of in the System each month, and the portion of administrative expenses eligible for Federal reimbursement under the IV–D program, in such a manner as to insure Federal reimbursement. Information necessary for Federal reimbursement shall be submitted to the Department of Public Aid 14 days after the end of each month. The chief judge shall also submit copies of such information to the Supreme Court. The Illinois Department of Public Aid shall forward all reimbursement to the county in which the Plan is approved. The Supreme Court shall remain a signatory to the contract and shall maintain general supervisory oversight.

(h) Administration. Pursuant to rule, the chief judge of each judicial circuit shall be responsible for administering the System on a day-to-day basis, shall employ and terminate administrative hearing officers and other necessary staff, and shall review and evaluate the performance of each administrative hearing officer. Reviews shall be conducted quarterly in the first year of employment, and annually thereafter.

(i) Reporting of Data. The chief judge shall file a report with the Supreme Court within 35 days of the end of each State fiscal year detailing the number of:

(1) matters initially assigned to an administrative hearing officer;

(2) matters transferred to an administrative hearing officer;

(3) matters returned to an administrative hearing officer from a judge;

(4) matters submitted to a judge from an administrative hearing officer with recommendation for a court order;

(5) recommended court orders entered by a judge;

(6) recommended court orders rejected by a judge;

(7) matters submitted by an administrative hearing officer to a judge for hearings;

(8) IV–D and non–IV–D matters pending and disposed of in the System; and

(9) matters which complied or failed to comply with Federal time frames. The above data shall be reported for each fiscal year with respect to each administrative hearing office and for the System as a whole.

(j) Local Rules. Each judicial circuit may adopt rules for the conduct of expedited child support hearings which are consistent with these rules and may determine which matters within the general classification of eligible actions shall be heard by administrative hearing officers.

(k) Applicability of Other Acts, the Code of Civil Procedure and Rules of the Supreme Court. The provisions of the Illinois Marriage and Dissolution of Marriage Act,[1] the Illinois Parentage Act of 1984,[2] the Illinois Public Aid Code,[3] the Revised Uniform Reciprocal Enforcement of Support Act,[4] the Nonsupport of Spouse and Children Act,[5] the State Mandates Act,[6] the Code of Civil Procedure[7] and the rules of the Supreme Court shall be applicable to expedited child support hearings except insofar as these rules otherwise provide.

Adopted eff. April 1, 1992. Amended March 19, 1997, eff. April 15, 1997.

Formerly Ill.Rev.Stat.1991, ch. 110A, ¶ 100.1.

[1] 750 ILCS 5/101 et seq.
[2] 750 ILCS 45/1 et seq.
[3] 305 ILCS 5/1–1 et seq.
[4] 750 ILCS 20/1 et seq.
[5] 750 ILCS 15/1 et seq.
[6] 30 ILCS 805/1 et seq.
[7] 735 ILCS 5/1–101 et seq.

Committee Comments

Rule 100.1 provides for the creation of an Expedited Child Support System in judicial circuits. It specifies that each judicial circuit which elects to create such a System must submit a Plan of Implementation to the Supreme Court for approval, identifies the matters which must be set forth in the Plan, and provides for Supreme Court review and approval. The rule addresses the availability of the System to various classes of participants, the use of demonstration programs, and funding of Systems. The rule makes judicial circuits responsible for administration of the System and reporting of data relative to the System. The rule also provides for the establishment of local rules to accompany these rules and specifies those other rules, acts and codes which apply to the conduct of the System.

Rule 100.2. Appointment, Qualification and Compensation of Administrative Hearing Officers

(a) Appointment. Administrative hearing officers shall be hired by the chief judge of each judicial circuit, after satisfying the qualifications set by the Supreme Court. Candidates for the position of administrative hearing officer must apply for appointment with the chief judge of each judicial circuit.

(b) Qualifications. Administrative hearing officers must be licensed to practice law in Illinois and must have been engaged in the active practice of law for a minimum of three years.

(c) Disqualification. A full-time administrative hearing officer shall not practice law before any court. A part-time administrative hearing officer shall not practice law in any domestic relations matter or other matter which would qualify for an expedited hearing before an administrative hearing officer without the written consent of both parties. Upon appointment to a case, an administrative hearing officer shall notify the judge and withdraw from the case if any grounds appear to exist for disqualification under Supreme Court Rules 61 through 67.

(d) Oath of Office. Each administrative hearing officer shall take an oath of office similar to a judicial oath.

(e) Compensation. Each administrative hearing officer shall be compensated as provided in the Plan.

(f) Communications with Attorneys. Disciplinary rules governing the conduct of attorneys before a court remain applicable in expedited child support hearings. Disciplinary rules governing communications between an attorney and a judge govern communications between attorneys and administrative hearing officers.

Adopted eff. April 1, 1992.

Formerly Ill.Rev.Stat.1991, ch. 110A, ¶ 100.2.

Committee Comments

Rule 100.2 provides for the appointment, qualification, disqualification and compensation of administrative hearing officers. The rule specifies that administrative hearing officers take an oath of office and conduct hearings according to applicable disciplinary rules.

Rule 100.3. Actions Subject to Expedited Child Support Hearings

(a) Eligible Actions. The following actions, if so provided for in the Plan, are eligible to be heard by an administrative hearing officer:

(1) actions pursuant to the Illinois Public Aid Code, as amended,[1] to establish temporary and final child support and medical support, and to enforce or modify existing orders of child support and medical support;

(2) actions pursuant to the Illinois Parentage Act of 1984, as amended,[2] to establish a parent and child relationship; to establish child support and medical support after parentage has been acknowledged or established, whether or not these issues were re-

served at the time judgment was entered; and to enforce or modify existing child support and medical support orders;

(3) actions pursuant to the Illinois Marriage and Dissolution of Marriage Act, as amended,[3] to establish temporary and final child support and medical support, whether or not these issues were reserved or could not be ordered at the time judgment was entered because the court lacked personal jurisdiction over the obligor; and to enforce or modify existing orders of child support and medical support;

(4) actions pursuant to the Nonsupport of Spouse and Children Act[4] to establish temporary child support and to enforce and modify such orders;

(5) actions pursuant to the Revised Uniform Reciprocal Enforcement of Support Act[5] to establish temporary and final child support and medical support, whether or not these issues were reserved or could not be ordered at the time judgment was entered because the court lacked personal jurisdiction over the obligor; and to enforce and modify existing child support and medical support orders; and

(6) any other child support or medical support matter.

(b) Other Eligible Prejudgment Proceedings. If provided for in the Plan, the System may be available in prejudgment proceedings for dissolution of marriage, declaration of invalidity of marriage and legal separation.

Adopted eff. April 1, 1992.

Formerly Ill.Rev.Stat.1991, ch. 110A, ¶ 100.3.

[1] 305 ILCS 5/1–1 et seq.
[2] 750 ILCS 45/1 et seq.
[3] 750 ILCS 5/101 et seq.
[4] 750 ILCS 15/1 et seq.
[5] 750 ILCS 20/1 et seq.

Committee Comments

Rule 100.3 lists those actions which are eligible to be heard by an administrative hearing officer if so specified in the judicial circuit's Plan of Implementation.

Rule 100.4. Authority of Administrative Hearing Officers

(a) Powers of Administrative Hearing Officers. Administrative hearing officers shall have the authority to conduct child support hearings, to administer oaths and affirmations, to take testimony under oath or affirmation, to determine the admissibility of evidence, to propose findings of fact, and to recommend orders to the judge based on such evidence as prescribed by the Act.

(b) Accept Voluntary Agreements of Parties. Administrative hearing officers may accept stipulations of fact and voluntary agreements of the parties

setting the amount of child support to be paid or medical support liability and to recommend to the judge the entry of orders incorporating such agreements.

(c) Accept Voluntary Acknowledgments of Parentage. Administrative hearing officers may accept voluntary orders of parentage and recommend to the judge the entry of orders based on such acknowledgments. Prior to accepting an acknowledgment of parentage, administrative hearing officers shall advise the putative father of his rights and obligations.

(d) Discovery. Administrative hearing officers shall manage all stages of discovery, including hearings on citations to discover assets and setting deadlines for the completion of discovery, and to direct the submission to tests pursuant to section 11 of the Illinois Parentage Act of 1984[1] and Rule 100.5 below. Administrative hearing officers may not enter orders with respect to disputed discovery matters though they may recommend the entry of such orders to a judge. Discovery shall be conducted in accordance with these rules and shall be completed prior to the expedited child support hearing. No discovery shall be permitted after the hearing, except upon leave of court and good cause shown.

(e) Compelling Appearance of the Obligor. The person designated in the Plan may recommend that the judge issue a notice requiring the obligor to appear before the administrative hearing officer or in court.

(f) Recommend Default Orders. Administrative hearing officers may recommend that the judge issue a default order to absent parties who fail to respond to a notice to appear before the administrative hearing officer or such other orders as are specified in Rule 100.11(d).

(g) Authority over Unemployed Obligor. Administrative hearing officers may recommend that an unemployed obligor who is not making child support payments or who is unable to provide support be ordered to seek employment and may recommend that the obligor be required to submit periodic reports as to such efforts. Administrative hearing officers may recommend that the obligor be ordered to report to the appropriate agency to participate in job search, training or work programs.

(h) Foreign Support Matters. Administrative hearing officers may recommend that foreign support judgments or orders be registered as Illinois judgments or orders.

(i) Non–IV–D Obligees. Administrative hearing officers shall inform non–IV–D obligees of the existence and services of the IV–D program and provide applications if requested. Administrative hearing officers shall also inform such obligees that payment may be requested through the clerk of the circuit court. Any such request that payment be made through the clerk shall be noted in the recommended order to the judge.

Adopted eff. April 1, 1992.

Formerly Ill.Rev.Stat.1991, ch. 110A, ¶ 100.4.

[1] 750 ILCS 45/1 et seq.

Committee Comments

Rule 100.4 specifies the powers of administrative hearing officers relative to the conduct of child support hearings, management of discovery, authority over parties, and resolution of matters.

Rule 100.5. Blood Tests

(a) [1]**Order to Submit to Tests.** Administrative hearing officers may recommend, upon the request of a party, that the judge order the mother, child and alleged father to submit to appropriate tests to determine inherited characteristics including, but not limited to, blood types and genetic markers such as those found by Human Leucocyte Antigen (HLA) tests. The judge shall determine the appropriate tests to be conducted and appoint an expert to determine the testing procedures and conduct the tests.

Adopted eff. April 1, 1992.

Formerly Ill.Rev.Stat.1991, ch. 110A, ¶ 100.5.

[1] There is no subsec. (b) in Rule 100.5.

Committee Comments

Rule 100.5 provides the administrative hearing officers with authority to recommend submission to blood tests. The rule provides for the admissibility of blood test results, a party's objections to matters involving blood tests, the evidentiary value of blood tests and the cost of blood tests in matters before an administrative hearing officer.

Rule 100.6. Scheduling of the Hearings

(a) **Assignment of Hearing Date.** If an action or a motion filed by a IV–D participant qualifies as an action over which an administrative hearing officer has authority, the person designated in the Plan shall assign a hearing date before an administrative hearing officer. Non–IV–D participants may request that the clerk assign eligible actions a hearing date before an administrative hearing officer. The procedure for fixing the date, time and place of a hearing before an administrative hearing officer shall be prescribed by circuit rule provided that not less than seven days' notice in writing shall be given to the parties or their attorneys of record. In cases in which the court has previously acquired jurisdiction over the responding party, the hearing shall be held on the scheduled date and not less than 21 days or more than 35 days of the date of filing of the action, unless continued by the administrative hearing officer or court upon good cause shown. In cases in which the court has not previously acquired jurisdiction over the responding party, the hearing shall be held on the scheduled date and not less than 21 days or more than 45 days of the

date of filing of the action, unless continued by the administrative hearing officer or court upon good cause shown. The hearing shall be held at a location provided or authorized by the chief judge of the circuit.

(b) **Providing Notice of Hearing Date.** The person designated in the Plan shall serve notice of the action and the hearing date on respondent by regular mail to his or her last known address, unless the action is one over which no court has previously acquired personal jurisdiction, in which case service will be in the same manner as summonses are served in other civil proceedings. If service is made by mail, the person serving notice shall prepare a certificate of mailing to be included in the file.

(c) **Subpoenas.** The clerk of the circuit court may issue subpoenas upon, or prior to, the filing of a petition if the court has previously acquired jurisdiction over the subject matter of the underlying action.

(d) **Affidavit of Income and Expenses.** A form affidavit of income and expenses, in such form as the Supreme Court shall prescribe, may be served on the respondent with the petition initiating the proceedings before the administrative hearing officer. Each party should be requested to complete the form prior to the first appearance before the administrative hearing officer.

Adopted eff. April 1, 1992.

Formerly Ill.Rev.Stat.1991, ch. 110A, ¶ 100.6.

Committee Comments

Rule 100.6 sets forth the procedure for assignment of a hearing date before an administrative hearing officer, the time period in which a hearing must be held, and the procedure for providing notice to the responding party.

Rule 100.7. Conduct of the Hearing

(a) **Established Rules of Evidence Apply.** Except as provided by this rule, the rules of evidence shall be liberally construed in all expedited child support hearings.

(b) **Documents Presumptively Admissible.** A party may offer in evidence, without foundation or other proof:

(1) the obligor's pay stubs or other employer-provided statement of gross income, deductions and net income or other records prepared by the employer in the usual course of business.

(2) documents provided by the obligor's insurance company which describe the dependent care coverage available to the obligor; and

(3) records kept by the clerk of the circuit court as to payment of child support.

If at least seven days written notice of the intention to offer the following documents in evidence is given to every other party, accompanied by a copy of the document, or if at the expedited child support hearing the other party does not object, a party may offer in evidence without foundation or other proof:

(1) the deposition of a witness, the statement of a witness which the witness would be allowed to express if testifying in person, if the statement is made by affidavit or by certification as provided in section 1–109 of the Code of Civil Procedure;[1]

(2) computer-generated documents and records, unless objected to by a party; and

(3) any other document not specifically covered by any of the foregoing provisions, and which is otherwise admissible under the rules of evidence.

(c) Opinions of Expert Witnesses. Notwithstanding the provisions of Rule 220, a party who proposes to use a written opinion of an expert witness or the testimony of an expert witness at the hearing may do so provided a written notice of such intention is given to every other party not less than seven days prior to the date of hearing, accompanied by a statement containing the identity of the expert, his qualifications, the subject matter, the basis of his conclusions, and his opinion.

(d) Right to Subpoena Maker of a Document. Any other party may subpoena the author or maker of a document admissible under this rule, at that party's expense, and examine the author or maker as if under cross-examination. The provisions of the Code of Civil Procedure relative to subpoenas, section 2–1101,[2] shall be applicable to expedited child support hearings and it shall be the duty of the party requesting the subpoena to modify the form to show that the appearance is set before an administrative hearing officer and to give the time and place set for the hearing.

(e) Adverse Examination of Parties or Agents. The provisions of the Code of Civil Procedure relative to the adverse examination of parties or agents, section 2–1102,[3] shall be applicable to expedited child support hearings as upon the trial of a case.

(f) Compelling Appearance of Witness at Hearing. The provisions of Supreme Court Rule 237 shall be equally applicable to expedited child support hearings as they are to trials.

Adopted eff. April 1, 1992.

Formerly Ill.Rev.Stat.1991, ch. 110A, ¶ 100.7.
[1] 735 ILCS 5/1–109.
[2] 735 ILCS 5/2–1101.
[3] 735 ILCS 5/2–1102.

Committee Comments

Rule 100.7 governs the conduct of expedited child support hearings and specifies that the rules of evidence apply to such hearings. The rule prescribes the circumstances under which certain specified documents are presumptively admissible in evidence. The rule sets forth the procedure for offering expert testimony and a party's right to subpoena the maker of admissible documents and

to cross-examine parties and their agents. The rule also provides for compelling the appearance of a witness at an expedited child support hearing.

Rule 100.8.   Absence of Party at Hearing

(a) Failure to be Present at Hearing. The expedited child support hearing may proceed in the absence of the responding party if service has been made and the petitioning party and/or his or her attorney is present. Based upon the testimony of the petitioning party and any other evidence that may have been presented, the administrative hearing officer shall recommend that the judge enter an appropriate order. If the petitioning party does not agree to the recommended order, the administrative hearing officer shall immediately schedule a judicial hearing, record the date, time and place of the hearing upon a notice and provide such notice to the petitioning party at the expedited hearing. Such notice shall be sent to the nonappearing party by regular mail. If the petitioning party agrees to and signs the order, a copy of the signed order and a notification of the right to object to the order shall be served upon the nonappearing party as directed in subsection (b) below. If the petitioning party is not present, either in person or through an attorney, the administrative hearing officer may continue the matter or may strike the matter with leave to reinstate. Notification of such action shall be served upon the petitioning party by regular mail.

(b) Service of Recommended Order and Notice. If service to commence the hearing before the administrative hearing officer was made by regular mail, the notice and recommended order shall be served in the same manner as summonses are served in other civil proceedings or by certified mail, return receipt requested, mailed to the nonappearing party's last known address. If service to commence the hearing was as provided in the Code of Civil Procedure,[1] the notice and recommended order shall be served by regular mail to the nonappearing party's last known address.

(c) Objections. The nonappearing party may file with the judge a written objection to the entry of the recommended order within 14 days after the order was mailed. If no objection is filed within 14 days, the nonappearing party is deemed to have accepted the recommended order. The judge may then enter the order, refer the case back to the administrative hearing officer for further proceedings, or conduct a judicial hearing. If a timely objection is filed, the judge must hold a judicial hearing and shall enter an appropriate order.

Adopted eff. April 1, 1992.

Formerly Ill.Rev.Stat.1991, ch. 110A, ¶ 100.8.
[1] 735 ILCS 5/1–101 et seq.

Committee Comments

Rule 100.8 governs the conduct of the expedited child support hearing in the absence of a party, the service of the recommended order and notice upon an absent party, and the filing of objections by an absent party.

Rule 100.9.   Transfers for Judicial Hearings

(a) Domestic Relations Matters Other than Child Support and Parentage. Any domestic relations matter other than child support and parentage, including but not limited to petitions for visitation, custody, distribution of property, petitions pursuant to section 513 of the Illinois Marriage and Dissolution of Marriage Act,[1] and spousal maintenance shall be transferred according to the judicial circuit's Plan to a judge for a judicial hearing. The administrative hearing officer shall proceed as scheduled with matters relative to child support or parentage. In actions to establish parentage where the putative father voluntarily acknowledges paternity, the recommended order shall include provisions for custody of the child in the mother and reasonable visitation for the father if both parties agree. If either party wishes to contest custody or visitation, the recommended order will be silent on those issues, but the contest will not delay the entry of the order establishing parentage and child support.

(b) Prehearing Motions and Other Matters that Require a Court Order. All prehearing motions and other matters that require a court order or judicial hearing, as defined in the Act and in these rules, shall be transferred to a judge for resolution in an expeditious manner. However, if the parties are in agreement as to the prehearing motion or other such matters, the administrative hearing officer shall transmit a recommended order, signed by both parties to a judge.

(c) Matters Requiring Judicial Hearing. All other matters requiring a judicial hearing, as provided for in the Act and in these rules, shall be immediately transferred according to the judicial circuit's Plan to a judge for a judicial hearing.

(d) Service of Orders of Withholding Pending Judicial Hearing. Whenever the parties disagree with part of the administrative hearing officer's recommendations, but do agree as to the existing obligation and no order for withholding was previously served upon the obligor's employer, the order for withholding shall be served upon the obligor's employer as to the existing support obligation pending judicial hearing on the contested matter.

Adopted eff. April 1, 1992.

Formerly Ill.Rev.Stat.1991, ch. 110A, ¶ 100.9.
[1] 750 ILCS 5/513.

Committee Comments

Rule 100.9 lists those matters which must be transferred to a judge for a judicial hearing or court order.

Rule 100.10.   Submission of Recommendations to the Court

(a) Notice to Parties. The administrative hearing officer shall present each party with a copy of the recommended order to be submitted to a judge. The administrative hearing officer shall also present each party with a written notice informing the parties of their right to request a judicial hearing and the procedures for so doing. The recommended order and notice shall be presented to each party at the conclusion of the hearing. If either party is not present at the conclusion of the hearing, either in person or through an attorney, the recommendation and order shall be mailed by regular mail to the party's last known address.

(b) Acceptance of Recommended Order. If both parties are present at the hearing and agree to the recommended order, they shall sign the recommended order. The administrative hearing officer shall transmit the signed recommended order to a judge as provided for in the Plan of Implementation.

(c) Rejection of Recommended Order. If either party does not agree to the recommended order or any part thereof, the administrative hearing officer shall immediately request a judicial hearing to resolve the contested matter. The administrative hearing officer shall record the date, time and place of such judicial hearing on a notice which shall be presented to the parties at the conclusion of the hearing. Notice shall be sent to nonappearing parties by regular mail. The administrative hearing officer shall transmit to a judge a written statement indicating those issues to which the parties agree and disagree, all documentary evidence and all schedules presented at the expedited child support hearing.

(d) Administrative Hearing Officer May Not Testify. An administrative hearing officer may not be called or compelled to testify as to what transpired before the administrative hearing officer with respect to contested matters.

Adopted eff. April 1, 1992.

Formerly Ill.Rev.Stat.1991, ch. 110A, ¶ 100.10.

Committee Comments

Rule 100.10 sets forth the procedure for submission of recommendations to a judge upon acceptance of a recommended order by both parties, and the presentation of the recommended order and of a written notice of the right to a judicial hearing to each party. The rule sets forth the procedure for scheduling a judicial hearing upon rejection of the recommended order by either party, notice to the parties of such hearing, and transmittal to the judge of a written statement indicating the issues to which the parties agree and those to which they disagree and of all documentary evidence presented at the expedited child support hearing.

Rule 100.11. Authority Retained by the Court

(a) Review Recommendations of Administrative Hearing Officers. The judge shall review all recommended orders of an administrative hearing officer upon which parties agree and enter such orders as are appropriate as to all or part of the matters indicated on the recommended order.

(b) Conduct Judicial Hearings. The judge shall conduct judicial hearings on all prehearing motions the parties disagree with, the recommended order of the administrative hearing officer on any domestic relations matters other than uncontested child support and parentage matters, on objections to the entry of orders as provided for in Rule 100.6 and section 10 of the Act,[1] and on any other matters properly before the court.

(c) Hear Contested Parentage Matters. Only the judge may conduct trials in contested parentage cases.

(d) Issue Special Orders. Only the judge may issue body attachment orders, rules to show cause, or conduct contempt proceedings. The judge shall impose sanctions or relief in such cases as are appropriate.

(e) Impose Sanctions. Only the judge may impose sanctions pursuant to Supreme Court Rule 137.

Adopted eff. April 1, 1992.

Formerly Ill.Rev.Stat.1991, ch. 110A, ¶ 100.11.

[1] 750 ILCS 25/10.

Committee Comments

Rule 100.11 sets forth the judge's authority to review recommendations of administrative hearing officers, to conduct judicial hearings, to hear contested parentage actions, to issue special orders and to impose sanctions.

Rule 100.12. Judicial Hearings

(a) Recommended Orders Agreed Upon by the Parties. The judge shall review the recommended orders of administrative hearing officers in a timely fashion. The judge (1) may enter an order consistent with the recommended order, (2) may reject all or part of the recommended order and refer the matter to the administrative hearing officer for further proceedings, or (3) may conduct judicial hearings as are necessary. The judge shall provide the administrative hearing officer with a copy of the entered order and may inform the administrative hearing officer if a recommended order was not accepted by the judge and the reasons for the changes or rejection. If the judge enters an order consistent with a recommended order, the effective date of the order shall be (1) the date on which the recommended order was signed by both parties, or (2) if the respondent party failed to

appear and failed to file a timely objection to the recommended order pursuant to Rule 100.8(c), the date the recommended order was signed by the petitioning party. The order may specify the date payments of support are to begin, which may be different from the effective date of the order.

(b) Recommended Orders Rejected by the Parties. Upon receipt of a statement from the administrative hearing officer that the parties do not agree to all or part of a recommended order, the judge shall promptly conduct a judicial hearing to resolve any contested matters and shall enter an appropriate order.

(c) Presentation of Order to the Parties. The clerk of the circuit court shall mail a copy of all orders to the parties within five days of entry. If the parties are present in court at the time the order is entered, a copy shall be given to both parties in open court. If an order sets forth an amount for support, an immediate withholding order shall be specially certified and mailed to the obligee or his or her attorney for service.

Adopted eff. April 1, 1992.

Formerly Ill.Rev.Stat.1991, ch. 110A, ¶ 100.12.

Committee Comments

Rule 100.12 governs the procedure whereby a judge reviews recommended orders and enters judicial orders based thereon. The rule sets forth the conduct of further judicial hearings and the resolution of contested matters. The rule also provides for the presentation of orders to the parties.

Rule 100.13. Definitions

For purposes of these rules, the following terms shall have the following meanings:

(a) "Act" shall mean the Expedited Child Support Act of 1990.[1]

(b) "Administrative hearing officer" shall mean the person employed by the chief judge of the circuit court of each circuit, county, multicounty area or multicircuit area establishing an expedited child support system for the purpose of hearing child support and parentage matters and recommending orders.

(c) "Expedited child support hearing" shall mean a hearing before an administrative hearing officer pursuant to the Act and these rules.

(d) "Plan" shall mean the plan submitted by the chief judge of a judicial circuit to the Supreme Court for the creation of an expedited child support system in such circuit pursuant to the Act and these rules.

(e) "System" shall mean the procedures and personnel created by the Act and these rules for the expedited establishment, modification, and enforcement of child support orders, and for the expedited establishment of parentage.

(f) "IV–D program" shall mean the Child Support Enforcement Program established pursuant to Title IV, Part D, of the Social Security Act (42 U.S.C.

§ 651 et seq.) as administered by the Illinois Department of Public Aid.

Adopted eff. April 1, 1992.

Formerly Ill.Rev.Stat.1991, ch. 110A, ¶ 100.13.
[1] 750 ILCS 25/1 et seq.

Committee Comments

Rule 100.13 defines certain terms, in accordance with the Expedited Child Support Act, as used throughout the Expedited Child Support Rules.

ARTICLE II. RULES ON CIVIL PROCEEDINGS IN THE TRIAL COURT

PART G. ENTRY OF ORDERS AND JUDGMENTS

PART H. POST–JUDGMENT PROCEEDINGS

PART I. SMALL CLAIMS

PART J. MISCELLANEOUS

PART A. PROCESS AND NOTICE

Rule 101. Summons and Original Process–Form and Issuance

(a) **General.** The summons shall be issued under the seal of the court, tested in the name of the clerk, and signed with his name. It shall be dated on the date it is issued, shall be directed to each defendant, and shall bear the information required by Rule 131(d) for the plaintiff's attorney or the plaintiff if not represented by an attorney.

(b) **Summons Requiring Appearance on Specified Day.**

(1) In an action for money not in excess of $50,000, exclusive of interest and costs, or in any action subject to mandatory arbitration where local rule prescribes a specific date for appearance, the summons shall require each defendant to appear on a day specified in the summons not less than 21 or more than 40 days after the issuance of the summons (see Rule 181(b)), and shall be in substantially the following form:

In the Circuit Court of the _____ Judicial Circuit, _____ County, Illinois (Or, In the Circuit Court of Cook County, Illinois)

A.B., C.D., *etc.*
(naming all plaintiffs),
    Plaintiffs,

v.   No. _____

                      Amount Claimed _____

H.J., K.L. *etc.*,
(naming all defendants),
    Defendants

SUMMONS

To each defendant:

You are hereby summoned and required to appear before this court at _____ at _____ o'clock _____ M., on _____ 20 ___, to answer the complaint in this case, a copy of which is hereto attached. If you fail to do so, a judgment by default may be entered against you for the relief asked in the complaint.

To the officer:

This summons must be returned by the officer or other person to whom it was given for service, with indorsement of service and fees, if any, immediately after service. If service cannot be made, this summons shall be returned so indorsed.

This summons may not be served later than 30 days after its date.

                    Witness _____

(Seal of Court)

_____
                    Clerk of Court

Plaintiff's Attorney (or plaintiff, if he is not represented by attorney)

_____

Address _____

Telephone No. _____

Facsimile Telephone No. _____

E–mail Address _____

(If service by facsimile transmission will be accepted, the telephone number of the plaintiff or plaintiff's attorney's facsimile machine is additionally required.)

Date of service _____, 20 ___ (to be inserted by officer on copy left with defendant or other person).

NOTICE TO DEFENDANTS

[Here simple and specific instructions, conforming to local practice, shall be set out outlining procedure for appearance and trial of the type of case covered by the summons.]

(2) In any action for forcible detainer or for recovery of possession of tangible personal property, the summons shall be in the same form, but shall require each defendant to appear on a day specified in the summons not less than seven or more than 40 days after the issuance of summons.

(3) If service is to be made under section 2–208 of the Code of Civil Procedure the return day shall be not less than 40 days or more than 60 days after the issuance of summons, and no default shall be taken until the expiration of 30 days after service.

(c) Summons in Certain Other Cases in Which Specific Date for Appearance is Required. In all proceedings in which the form of process is not otherwise prescribed and in which a specific date for appearance is required by statute or by rules of court, the form of summons shall conform as nearly as may be to the form set forth in paragraph (b) hereof.

(d) Summons Requiring Appearance Within 30 Days After Service. In all other cases the summons shall require each defendant to file his answer or otherwise file his appearance within 30 days after service, exclusive of the day of service (see Rule 181(a)), and shall be in substantially the following form:

In the Circuit Court of the _____ Judicial Circuit, _____ County, Illinois (Or, In the Circuit Court of Cook County, Illinois)
A.B., C.D., *etc.*
(naming all plaintiffs),
    Plaintiffs,
v.   No. _____

H.J., K.L. *etc.*,
(naming all defendants),
    Defendants

SUMMONS

To each defendant:

You are summoned and required to file an answer to the complaint in this case, a copy of which is hereto attached, or otherwise file your appearance, in the office of the clerk of this court within 30 days after service of this summons, not counting the day of service. If you fail to do so, a judgment by default may be entered against you for the relief asked in the complaint.

To the officer:

This summons must be returned by the officer or other person to whom it was given for service, with indorsement of service and fees, if any, immediately after service. If service cannot be made, this summons shall be returned so indorsed.

This summons may not be served later than 30 days after its date.

Witness _____

(Seal of Court)

_____
                 Clerk of Court

Plaintiff's Attorney (or plaintiff, if he is not represented by attorney)

_____

Address _____
Telephone No. _____
Facsimile Telephone No. _____
E–mail Address _____

(If service by facsimile transmission will be accepted, the telephone number of the plaintiff or plaintiff's attorney's facsimile machine is additionally required.)

Date of service _____, 20 ___ (to be inserted by officer on copy left with defendant or other person).

(e) Summons in Cases under the Illinois Marriage and Dissolution of Marriage Act. In all proceedings under the Illinois Marriage and Dissolution of Marriage Act, the summons shall include a notice on its reverse side referring to a dissolution action stay being in effect on service of summons, and shall state that any person who fails to obey a dissolution action stay may be subject to punishment for contempt, and shall include language:

(1) restraining both parties from physically abusing, harassing, intimidating, striking, or interfering with the personal liberty of the other party or the minor children of either party; and

(2) restraining both parties from removing any minor child of either party from the State of Illinois or from concealing any such child from the other party, without the consent of the other party or an order of the court.

(f) Waiver of Service of Summons. In all cases in which a plaintiff notifies a defendant of the commencement of an action and requests that the defendant waive service of summons under section 2–213 of the Code of Civil Procedure, the request shall be in writing in the following form:

In the Circuit Court of the _____ Judicial Circuit, _____ County, Illinois (Or, In the Circuit Court of Cook County, Illinois)

A.B., C.D., *etc.*
(naming all plaintiffs),
    Plaintiffs,
    v.   No. _____
            Amount Claimed _____

H.J., K.L. *etc.*,
(naming all defendants),
    Defendants

Notice and Acknowledgment of Receipt of Summons and Complaint

NOTICE

To: (Insert the name and address of the person to be served)

The enclosed summons and complaint are served pursuant to section 2–213 of the Code of Civil Procedure.

You must complete the acknowledgment part of this form and return one copy of the completed form to the sender within _____ * days.

You must sign and date the acknowledgment. If you are served on behalf of a corporation, unincorporated association (including a partnership), or other entity, you must indicate under your signature your relationship to that entity. If you are served on behalf of another person and you are authorized to receive process, you must indicate under your signature your authority.

If you do not complete and return the form to the sender within _____ * days, you (or the party on whose behalf you are being served) may be served a summons and complaint in any other manner permitted by law.

If you do complete and return this form, you (or the party on whose behalf you are being served) must answer the complaint within _____ ** days. If you fail to do so, judgment by default will be taken against you for the relief demanded in the complaint.

I declare, under penalty of perjury, that this notice and acknowledgment of receipt of summons and complaint will have been mailed on _____. (Insert Date)

Signature _____

Date of Signature _____

ACKNOWLEDGMENT OF RECEIPT OF SUMMONS AND COMPLAINT

I declare, under penalty of perjury, that I received a copy of the summons and of the complaint in the above-captioned matter at (inset address).

PRINT or TYPE Name _____

Relationship to Entity/Authority to Receive Service of Process

_____

(Not Applicable if you are the named Defendant or Respondent)

Signature _____

Date of Signature _____

*(To be completed by the person sending the notice.) Date for return of waiver must be at least 30 days from the date on which the request is sent, or 60 days if the defendant is addressed outside the United States.

**(To be completed by the person sending the notice.) Date for answering complaint must be at least 60 days from the date on which the request is sent, or 90 days if the defendant is addressed outside the United States.

(g) Use of Wrong Form of Summons. The use of the wrong form of summons shall not affect the jurisdiction of the court.

Amended effective August 3, 1970; July 1, 1971; September 1, 1974; amended May 28, 1982, effective July 1, 1982; October 30, 1992, effective November 15, 1992; amended January 20, 1993, effective immediately; amended December 30, 1993, effective January 1, 1994; amended February 1, 1996, effective immediately; amended May 30, 2008, effective immediately; Dec. 9, 2015, eff. Jan. 1, 2016.

Formerly Ill.Rev.Stat.1991, ch. 110A, ¶ 101.

Committee Comments
(Revised September 1, 1974)

As adopted in 1967, Rule 101 was derived from former Rule 2, with changes in paragraph (b). Paragraph (b) was inserted in former Rule 2, effective January 1, 1964, to provide, for relatively small cases, the form of summons that had been in use in the Municipal Court of Chicago prior to that date. In cases up to $10,000, the time was changed to not less than 21 or more than 40 days. Effective August 3, 1970, the $10,000 limit was changed to $15,000. The appearance day in small claims is covered by Rule 283.

The appearance day in forcible entry and detainer cases was left at not less than seven or more than 40 days. To conform the practice to the requirements of notice in actions seeking restoration of property wrongfully detained, set forth by the Supreme Court of the United States in *Fuentes v. Shevin* (1972), 407 U.S. 67, subparagraph (b)(2) of the rule was amended in 1974 to provide for a summons in such cases returnable on a day specified in the summons, not less than seven or more than 40 days from issuance, as in forcible entry and detainer cases. Under the rule as amended, independent of the statutory remedy of replevin, a party seeking return of personal property may proceed in an action in the nature of an action in detinue at common law, and serve process in the manner provided.

Subparagraph (b)(3), added to former Rule 2 in 1964 and carried forward into Rule 101 in 1967, set 40 days as the return day on service made under section 16 of the Civil Practice Act. Effective July 1, 1971, this provision was amended to substitute for "40 days" the somewhat more flexible provision "not less than 40 days or more than 60 days."

The provision of paragraph (b) of this rule permitting specific instructions under the heading "Notice to Defendant" has probably not been adequately implemented by the judges of the trial courts. It is the committee's view that the summons should give as much specific information to the defendant as possible. For instance, the particular court room number and place of holding court ought to be given. Instructions regarding the method of entering an appearance and a statement whether an answer must be filed with the appearance, or the date for filing an answer after an appearance, can be stated in the "Notice to Defendant." Rule 181, relating to appearance, expressly recognizes that the "Notice to Defendant" under Rule 101(b) is controlling.

In 1974, paragraph (d) was amended to insert in the specimen summons reference to the fact that a copy of the complaint is attached, thus conforming the language of the summons under paragraph (d) in this respect to the language in the summons under paragraph (b).

Rule 102. Service of Summons and Complaint; Return

(a) Placement for Service. Promptly upon issuance, summons (together with copies of the complaint as required by Rule 104), shall be placed for service with the sheriff or other officer or person authorized to serve process.

(b) When Service Must Be Made. No summons in the form provided in paragraph (d) of Rule 101 may be served later than 30 days after its date. A summons in the form provided in paragraph (b) of Rule 101 may not be served later than three days before the day for appearance.

(c) Indorsement Showing Date of Service. The officer or other person making service of summons shall indorse the date of service upon the copy left with the defendant or other person. Failure to indorse the date of service does not affect the validity of service.

(d) Return. The officer or person making service shall make a return by filing proof of service immediately after service on all defendants has been had, and, in any event, shall make a return: (1) in the case of a summons bearing a specific return day or day for appearance, not less than 3 days before that day; (2) in other cases, immediately after the last day fixed for service. If there is more than one defendant, the proof of service shall, at the request of the plaintiff or his attorney, be made immediately after service on each defendant. In that case, the proof of service to be filed may be indorsed upon a copy of the summons

and the original retained until service is had upon all defendants or until expiration of the time provided for service. The proof of service need not state whether a copy of the complaint was served. The officer or other person serving the summons may file proof of service by mail. Failure of the officer or other person to return the summons or file proof of service does not invalidate the summons or the service thereof, if had.

(e) Post Card Notification to Plaintiff. If the plaintiff furnishes a post card, the officer or other person making service of the summons, immediately upon return of the summons, shall mail to the plaintiff or his attorney the post card indicating whether or not service has been had, and if so on what date.

Formerly Ill.Rev.Stat.1991, ch. 110A, ¶ 102.

Committee Comments

(Revised July 1, 1971)

This is former Rule 3, as it existed prior to January 1, 1964, without change of substance, except for the deletion of the last paragraph, which provided for writs made returnable to justices of the peace, etc., during the transition into practice under the 1964 Judicial Article and is no longer necessary.

Rule 103. Alias Summons; Dismissal for Lack of Diligence

(a) Alias Summonses. On request of any party, the clerk shall issue successive alias summonses, regardless of the disposition of any summons or alias summons previously issued.

(b) Dismissal for Lack of Diligence. If the plaintiff fails to exercise reasonable diligence to obtain service on a defendant prior to the expiration of the applicable statute of limitations, the action as to that defendant may be dismissed without prejudice. If the failure to exercise reasonable diligence to obtain service on a defendant occurs after the expiration of the applicable statute of limitations, the dismissal shall be with prejudice as to that defendant only and shall not bar any claim against any other party based on vicarious liability for that dismissed defendant's conduct. The dismissal may be made on the application of any party or on the court's own motion. In considering the exercise of reasonable diligence, the court shall review the totality of the circumstances, including both lack of reasonable diligence in any previous case voluntarily dismissed or dismissed for want of prosecution, and the exercise of reasonable diligence in obtaining service in any case refiled under section 13–217 of the Code of Civil Procedure.

(c) Summonses for Additional Parties. On request, the clerk shall issue summonses for third-party defendants and for parties added as defendants by order of court or otherwise.

Amended Oct. 21, 1969, eff. Jan. 1, 1970; May 28, 1982, eff. July 1, 1982; May 20, 1997, eff. July 1, 1997; June 5, 2007, eff. July 1, 2007.

Formerly Ill.Rev.Stat.1991, ch. 110A, ¶ 103.

Committee Comments

(Revised May 1997)

This rule, except for paragraph (b), is former Rule 4, as it existed prior to 1967.

Paragraph (b) was changed in the 1967 revision to provide that the dismissal may be with prejudice, and was further revised in 1969 to provide that a dismissal with prejudice shall be entered only when the failure to exercise due diligence to obtain service occurred after the expiration of the applicable statute of limitations. Prior to the expiration of the statute, a delay in service does not prejudice a defendant.

The 1997 amendment eliminates the power to dismiss an entire action based on a delay in serving some of the defendants if the plaintiff has exercised reasonable diligence with respect to other defendants. The amendment also eliminates the *res judicata* effect (but not the statute of limitation effect) of a Rule 103(b) dismissal. Rule 4(m) of the Federal Rules of Civil Procedure has similar provisions regarding dismissals for delay in serving process in federal court actions.

Because a Rule 103(b) dismissal will be "without prejudice" for *res judicata* purposes, the dismissal will not extinguish any claims that the plaintiff might have against an undismissed defendant. Whether the dismissal will extinguish the plaintiff's claims against the dismissed defendant will depend on whether the dismissal occurs before or after the statute of limitation has run. If before, the plaintiff will be able to refile; if after, the plaintiff will be unable to refile because the claims will be time-barred.

(June 5, 2007)

The 2007 amendment clarified that a Rule 103(b) dismissal which occurred after the expiration of the applicable statute of limitations shall be made with prejudice as to that defendant if the failure to exercise reasonable diligence to obtain service on the defendant occurred after the expiration of the applicable statute of limitations. However, even a dismissal with prejudice would not bar any claim against any other party based on vicarious liability for that dismissed defendant's conduct.

Further, the last sentence of Rule 103(b) addresses situations where the plaintiff has refiled a complaint under section 13–217 of the Code of Civil Procedure within one year of the case either being voluntarily dismissed pursuant to section 2–1009 or being dismissed for want of prosecution. If the statute of limitations has run prior to the plaintiff's refiled complaint, the trial court has the discretion to dismiss the refiled case if the plaintiff failed to exercise reasonable diligence in obtaining service. The 2007 amendment applies the holding in *Martinez v. Erickson*, 127 Ill. 2d 112, 121–22 (1989), requiring a trial judge "to consider service after refiling in the light of the entire history of the case" including reasonable diligence by plaintiff after refiling.

Because public policy favors the determination of controversies according to the substantive rights of the parties, Rule 103(b) should not be used by the trial courts to simply clear a crowded docket, nor should they delay ruling on a defendant's dismissal motion until after the statute of limitations has run. See *Kole v. Brubaker*, 325 Ill. App. 3d 944, 954 (2001).

Rule 104. Service of Pleadings and Other Documents; Filing

(a) Delivery of Copy of Complaint. Every copy of a summons used in making service shall have attached thereto a copy of the complaint, which shall be furnished by plaintiff.

(b) Filing of Documents and Proof of Service. Pleadings subsequent to the complaint, written motions, and other documents required to be filed shall be filed with the clerk with a certificate of counsel or other proof that copies have been served on all parties who have appeared and have not theretofore been found by the court to be in default for failure to plead.

(c) Excusing Service. For good cause shown on *ex parte* application, the court or any judge thereof may excuse the delivery or service of any complaint, pleading, or written motion or part thereof on any party, but the attorney filing it shall furnish a copy promptly and without charge to any party requesting it.

(d) Failure to Serve Copies. Failure to deliver or serve copies as required by this rule does not in any way impair the jurisdiction of the court over the person of any party, but the aggrieved party may obtain a copy from the clerk and the court shall order the offending party to reimburse the aggrieved party for the expense thereof.

Amended eff. Jan. 1, 1970; Jan. 4, 2013, eff. immediately.

Formerly Ill.Rev.Stat.1991, ch. 110A, ¶ 104.

Committee Comments

This is former Rule 5 without change of substance.

Rule 105. Additional Relief Against Parties in Default—Notice

(a) Notice—Form and Contents. If new or additional relief, whether by amendment, counterclaim, or otherwise, is sought against a party not entitled to notice under Rule 104, notice shall be given him as herein provided. The notice shall be captioned and numbered in the case and directed to the party. It shall state that a pleading seeking new or additional relief against him has been filed and that a judgment by default may be taken against him for the new or additional relief unless he files an answer or otherwise files an appearance in the office of the clerk of the court within 30 days after service, receipt by certified or registered mail, or the first publication of the notice, as the case may be, exclusive of the day of service, receipt or first publication. Except in case of publication, a copy of the new or amended pleading shall be attached to the notice, unless excused by the court for good cause shown on *ex parte* application.

(b) Service. The notice may be served by any of the following methods:

(1) By any method provided by law for service of summons, either within or without this State. Service may be made by an officer or by any person over 18 years of age not a party to the action. Proof of service by an officer may be made by return as in the case of a summons. Otherwise proof of service shall be made by affidavit of the server, stating the time, manner, and place of service. The court may consider the affidavit and any other competent proofs in determining whether service has been properly made.

(2) By prepaid certified or registered mail addressed to the party, return receipt requested, showing to whom delivered and the date and address of delivery. The notice shall be sent "restricted delivery" when service is directed to a natural person. Service is not complete until the notice is received by the defendant, and the registry receipt is *prima facie* evidence thereof.

(3) By publication, upon the filing of an affidavit as required for publication of notice of pendency of the action in the manner of but limited to the cases provided for, and with like effect as, publication of notice of pendency of the action.

Amended Sept. 29, 1978, eff. Nov. 1, 1978; May 28, 1982, eff. July 1, 1982; Nov. 21, 1988, eff. Jan. 1, 1989.

Formerly Ill.Rev.Stat.1991, ch. 110A, ¶ 105.

Committee Comments

Rule 105, as adopted in 1967, carried forward former Rule 7–1 without change. Subparagraph (b)(2) was amended in 1978 to permit service by "certified or registered mail addressed to the party, restricted delivery, return receipt requested showing to whom, date and address of delivery," instead of "registered mail addressed to the party, return receipt requested, delivery limited to addressee only," the latter class of postal service having been discontinued.

Rule 106. Notice of Petitions Filed for Relief From, or Revival of, Judgments

Notice of the filing of a petition under section 2–1401, section 2–1601 or section 12–183(g) of the Code of Civil Procedure [1] shall be given by the same methods provided in Rule 105 for the giving of notice of additional relief to parties in default.

Amended eff. July 1, 1971; amended May 28, 1982, eff. July 1, 1982; July 1, 1985, eff. Aug. 1, 1985.

Formerly Ill.Rev.Stat.1991, ch. 110A, ¶ 106.

[1] 735 ILCS 5/2–1401, 5/2–1601, 5/12–183.

Committee Comments

(July 1, 1985)

This is former Rule 7–2, as it existed prior to 1964, without change of substance. In 1971, it was amended to insert cross-references to section 72 of the Civil Practice Act and Rule 105.

This rule was amended in 1985 to provide a specific requirement for notice in both revival-of-judgment proceedings and release-of-judgment proceedings, as well as in cases involving petitions seeking relief from certain final judgments.

Rule 107. Notice of Hearing for an Order of Replevin

(a) Form of Notice. A notice for an order of replevin (see 735 ILCS 5/19–105) shall be substantially in the following form:

In the Circuit Court of the _____ Judicial Circuit, _____ County, Illinois (Or, In the Circuit Court of Cook County, Illinois) A.B., C.D., *etc.* (naming all plaintiffs),

            Plaintiffs,

v.   No. _____

H.J., K.L., *etc.* (naming all defendants),

            Defendants

To each defendant:

You are hereby notified that on _____, 20 _____, a complaint, a copy of which is attached, was filed in the above court seeking an order of replevin. Pursuant to law a hearing will be held to determine whether such an order shall be entered in this case. If you wish to contest the entry of such order, you must appear at this hearing at _____, at _____ o'clock _____ M., on _____, 20 ___.

             _____

              Attorney for the Plaintiff

Address _____

Telephone No. _____

Facsimile Telephone No. _____

E–mail Address _____

(If service by facsimile transmission will be accepted, the telephone number of the plaintiff or plaintiff's attorney's facsimile machine is required.)

(b) Service. Notice of the hearing shall be served not less than five days prior to the hearing in accordance with sections 2–202 through 2–205 of the Code of Civil Procedure,[1] or by mail in the manner prescribed in Rule 284.

Adopted June 28, 1974, effective September 1, 1974. Amended May 28, 1982, effective July 1, 1982; October 30, 1992, effective November 15, 1992; May 30, 2008, effective immediately; Dec. 9, 2015, eff. Jan. 1, 2016.

Formerly Ill.Rev.Stat.1991, ch. 110A, ¶ 107.

[1] 735 ILCS 5/2–202, 5/2–205.

Committee Comments

In 1973, the Illinois Replevin Act (Ill. Rev. Stat. 1973, ch. 119) was amended to provide for a notice and hearing prior to the issuance of the writ in conformity with the decision of the United States Supreme Court in *Fuentes v. Shevin* (1972), 407 U.S. 67. Section 4(a) of the statute, as amended, provides that five days' notice of a hearing on the question of the issuance of a writ of replevin be given "in the manner required by Rule of the Supreme Court." Rule 107 provides the form and manner of service of such notice.

Rule 108. Explanation of Rights of Heirs and Legatees When Will Admitted or Denied Probate

(a) Wills Originally Proved. When a will is admitted or denied admission to probate under section 6–4 or section 7–4 of the Probate Act of 1975, as amended,[1] the information mailed to each heir and legatee under section 6–10[2] shall include an explanation of the rights of interested persons in substantially the following form (Form 1 should be used when the will is admitted to probate and Form 2 when probate is denied):

Form 1

Notice to Heirs and Legatees

Attached to this notice are copies of a petition to probate a will and an order admitting the will to probate. You are named in the petition as an heir or legatee of the decedent.

Within 42 days after the effective date of the original order of admission, you may file a petition with the court to require proof of the will by testimony of the witnesses to the will in open court or other evidence, as provided in section 6–21 of the Probate Act of 1975 (755 ILCS 5/6–21).

You also have the right under section 8–1 of the Probate Act of 1975 (755 ILCS 5/8–1) to contest the validity of the will by filing a petition with the court within 6 months after admission of the will to probate.

Form 2

Notice to Heirs and Legatees

Attached to this notice are copies of a petition to probate a will and an order denying admission of the will to probate. You are named in the petition as an heir or legatee of the decedent.

You have the right under section 8–2 of the Probate Act of 1975 (755 ILCS 5/8–2) to contest the denial of admission by filing a petition with the court within 6 months after entry of the order of denial.

When a will is admitted or denied admission to probate under section 6–4 or section 7–4 of the Probate Act of 1975, as amended, and where notice under section 6–10 is given by publication, such notice shall be in substantially the following form (Form 3 should be used when the will is admitted to probate and Form 4 when probate is denied):

Form 3

Notice to Heirs and Legatees

Notice is given to _____ (names), who are heirs or legatees in the above proceeding to probate a will and whose name or address is not stated in the petition to admit the will to probate, that an order was entered by the court on _____, admitting the will to probate.

Within 42 days after the effective date of the original order of admission you may file a petition with the court to require proof of the will by testimony of the witnesses to the will in open court or other evidence, as provided in section 6–21 of the Probate Act of 1975 (755 ILCS 5/6–21).

You also have the right under section 8–1 of the Probate Act of 1975 (755 ILCS 5/8–1) to contest the validity of the will by filing a petition with the court within 6 months after admission of the will to probate.

Form 4

Notice to Heirs and Legatees

Notice is given to _____ (names), who are heirs or legatees in the above proceeding to probate a will and whose name or address is not stated in the petition to admit the will to probate, that an order was entered by the court on _____, denying admission of the will to probate.

You have the right under section 8–2 of the Probate Act of 1975 (755 ILCS 5/8–2) to contest the denial of admission by filing a petition with the court within 6 months after entry of the order of denial.

(b) Foreign Wills Proved by Copy. When a will is admitted or denied admission to probate under section 7–3 of the Probate Act of 1975, as amended[3] ("Proof of foreign will by copy"), the information mailed to each heir and legatee under section 6–10 of the Probate Act of 1975, as amended, shall include an explanation of the rights of interested persons in substantially the following form (Form 1 should be used when the will is admitted to probate and Form 2 when probate is denied):

Form 1

Notice to Heirs and Legatees

Attached to this notice are copies of a petition to probate a foreign will and an order admitting the foreign will to probate. You are named in the petition as an heir or legatee of the decedent.

You have the right under section 8–1 of the Probate Act of 1975 (755 ILCS 5/8–1) to contest the validity of the foreign will by filing a petition with the court within 6 months after admission of the foreign will to probate.

Form 2

Notice to Heirs and Legatees

Attached to this notice are copies of a petition to probate a foreign will and an order denying admission of that foreign will to probate. You are named in the petition as an heir or legatee of the decedent.

You have the right under section 8–2 of the Probate Act of 1975 (755 ILCS 5/8–2) to contest the denial of admission by filing a petition with the court within 6 months after entry of the order of denial.

When a will is admitted or denied probate under section 7–3 of the Probate Act of 1975, as amended ("Proof of foreign will by copy"), and where notice under section 6–10 is given by publication, such notice shall be in substantially the following form (Form 3 should be used when the will is admitted to probate and Form 4 when probate is denied):

Form 3

Notice to Heirs and Legatees

Notice is given to _____ (names), who are heirs or legatees in the above proceeding to probate a foreign will and whose name or address is not stated in the petition to admit the foreign will to probate, that an order was entered by the court on _____, admitting the foreign will to probate.

You have the right under section 8–1 of the Probate Act of 1975 (755 ILCS 5/8–1) to contest the validity of the foreign will by filing a petition with the court within 6 months after admission of the foreign will to probate.

Form 4

Notice to Heirs and Legatees

Notice is given to _____ (names), who are heirs or legatees in the above proceeding to probate a foreign will and whose name or address is not stated in the petition to admit the foreign will to probate, that an order was entered by the court on _____, denying admission of the foreign will to probate.

You have the right under section 8–2 of the Probate Act of 1975 (755 ILCS 5/8–2) to contest the denial of admission by filing a petition with the court within 6 months after entry of the order of denial.

Adopted February 1, 1980, effective March 1, 1980; amended August 9, 1983, effective October 1, 1983; amended April 1, 1992, effective August 1, 1992; amended May 30, 2008, effective immediately.

[1] 755 ILCS 5/6–4 or 5/7–4.
[2] 755 ILCS 5/6–10.
[3] 755 ILCS 5/7–3.

Committee Comments
(February 1980)

This rule was adopted pursuant to amended section 6–10(a) of the Probate Act of 1975, effective January 1, 1980. The first blank in forms 3 and 4 is for the names of heirs and legatees whose addresses are unknown and for insertion of "unknown heirs" if unknown heirs are referred to in the petition.

Rule 109. Reserved

Rule 110. Explanation of Rights in Independent Administration; Form of Petition to Terminate

When independent administration is granted in accordance with section 28–2 of the Probate Act of 1975, as amended,[1] the notice required to be mailed to heirs and legatees under section 6–10[2] or section 28–2(c) of that act shall be accompanied by an explanation of the rights of interested persons in substantially the following form:

Rights of Interested Persons During Independent Administration; Form of Petition to Terminate Administration

A copy of an order is enclosed granting independent administration of decedent's estate. This means that the executor or administrator will not have to obtain court orders or file estate documents in court during probate. The estate will be administered without court supervision, unless an interested person asks the court to become involved.

Under section 28–4 of the Probate Act of 1975 (755 ILCS 5/28–4) any interested person may terminate independent administration at any time by mailing or delivering a petition to terminate to the clerk of the court. However, if there is a will which directs independent administration, independent administration will be terminated only if the court finds there is good cause to require supervised administration; and if the petitioner is a creditor or nonresiduary legatee, independent administration will be terminated only if the court finds that termination is necessary to protect the petitioner's interest.

A petition in substantially the following form may be used to terminate independent administration:

In the Circuit Court of the _____ Judicial Circuit,
_____ County, Illinois
(Or, In the Circuit Court of Cook County, Illinois)
In re Estate of _____,Deceased
(name of decedent)

No. _____
Petition to Terminate Independent Administration
_____, on oath states:

1. On _____ ____, 20 ___, an order was entered granting independent administration to _____ as independent _____

       (executor) (administrator)

2. I am an interested person in this estate as _____

(heir) (nonresiduary legatee) (residuary legatee) (creditor) (representative)

*3. The will _____ direct independent administration.
       (does) (does not)

4. I request that independent administration be terminated.

                        _____
                           (Signature of petitioner)

                        Signed and sworn to before me

                        _____, 20 _____

                        _____
                                Notary Public

*Strike if no will.

In addition to the right to terminate independent administration, any interested person may petition the court to hold a hearing and resolve any particular question that may arise during independent administration, even though supervised administration has not been requested (755 ILCS 5/28–5). The independent representative must mail a copy of the estate inventory and final account to each interested person and must send notice to or obtain the approval of each interested person before the estate can be closed (755 ILCS 5/28–6, 28–11). Any interested person has the right to question or object to any item included in or omitted from an inventory or account or to insist on a full court accounting of all receipts and disbursements with prior notice, as required in supervised administration (755 ILCS 5/28–11).

Adopted February 1, 1980, effective March 1, 1980; amended May 30, 2008, effective immediately; Jan. 4, 2013, eff. immediately.

Formerly Ill.Rev.Stat.1991, ch. 110A, ¶ 110.

1 755 ILCS 5/28–2.

2 755 ILCS 5/6–10.

Committee Comments

(February 1980)

This rule was adopted pursuant to new section 28–2(a) of the Probate Act of 1975, effective January 1, 1980.

Rules 111 to 112. Reserved

Rule 113. Practice and Procedure in Mortgage Foreclosure Cases

(a) **Applicability of the Rule**. The requirements of this rule supplement, but do not replace, the requirements set forth in the Illinois Mortgage Foreclosure Law (735 ILCS 5/15–1101 *et seq.*) and are applicable only to those foreclosure actions filed on or after the effective date of May 1, 2013.

(b) **Supporting Documents for Complaints.** In addition to the documents listed in section 15–1504 of the Illinois Mortgage Foreclosure Law (735 ILCS 5/15–1504), a copy of the note, as it currently exists, including all indorsements and allonges, shall be attached to the mortgage foreclosure complaint at the time of filing.

(c) **Prove–up Affidavits.**

(1) Requirement of Prove-up Affidavits. All plaintiffs seeking a judgment of foreclosure, under section 15–1506 of the Illinois Mortgage Foreclosure Law (735 ILCS 5/15–1506), by default or otherwise, shall be required to submit an affidavit in support of the amounts due and owing under the note when they file any motion requesting a judgment of default against a mortgagor or a judgment of foreclosure.

(2) Content of Prove-up Affidavits. All affidavits submitted in support of entry of a judgment of foreclosure, default or otherwise, shall contain, at a minimum, the following information:

(i) The identity of the affiant and an explanation as to whether the affiant is a custodian of records or a person familiar with the business and its mode of operation. If the affiant is a person familiar with the business and its mode of operation, the affidavit shall explain how the affiant is familiar with the business and its mode of operation.

(ii) An identification of the books, records, and/or other documents in addition to the payment history that the affiant reviewed and/or relied upon in drafting the affidavit, specifically including records transferred from any previous lender or servicer. The payment history must be attached to the affidavit in only those cases where the defendant(s) filed an appearance or responsive pleading to the complaint for foreclosure.

(iii) The identification of any computer program or computer software that the entity relies on to record and track mortgage payments. Identification of the computer program or computer software shall also include the source of the information, the method and time of preparation of the record to establish that the computer program produces an accurate payment history, and an explanation as to why the records should be considered "business records" within the meaning of the law.

(3) Additional Evidence. The affidavit shall contain any additional evidence, as may be necessary, in connection with the party's right to enforce the instrument of indebtedness.

(4) Form of Prove-up Affidavits. The affidavit prepared in support of entry of a judgment of foreclosure, by default or otherwise, shall not have a stand-alone signature page if formatting allows the signature to begin on the last page of the affiant's statements. The affidavit prepared shall, at a minimum, be in substantially the following form:

Form 1

IN THE CIRCUIT COURT OF THE ____ JUDICIAL
CIRCUIT
FOR _____ COUNTY, ILLINOIS

_____)	
Plaintiff(s))	
v.)	Case. No. _____
_____)	
Defendant(s))	

AFFIDAVIT OF AMOUNTS DUE AND OWING

I, _____, am a
_____ of _____. I
have authority to make this statement on its behalf
because _____ (identify whether you
are a custodian of records or a person familiar with
the business and its mode of operation; if you are a
person familiar with the business and its mode of
operation, explain how you are familiar with the business and its mode of operation). If called to testify at
the trial of this matter, I could competently testify as
to the facts contained in this affidavit.

[If the loan was previously serviced by another
entity, the affidavit should provide as follows for the
most recent transfer of servicing rights: _____
(name of the bank) acquired the servicing rights for
the Defendant's loan on ___ (date) from _____
(name of the prior institution). At the time of this
transfer, the Defendant's loan was ___ (current, or
state the amount by which the loan was in default at
the time of the transfer).]

The amount due is based on my review of the
following records: _____. A true
and accurate copy of the payment history and any
other document I reviewed when making this calculation is attached to this affidavit (this sentence would
only be included if applicable).

_____ (name of the bank) uses _____
(name of the computer program/software) to automatically record and track mortgage payments. This type
of tracking and accounting program is recognized as
standard in the industry. When a mortgage payment
is received, the following procedure is used to process
and apply the payment, and to create the records I
reviewed: _____ (include the source
of the information, method and time of preparation of
the record to establish that the computer program
produces an accurate record). The record is made in
the regular course of _____'s (name of bank)
business. In the case at bar, the entries reflecting the
Defendant's payments were made in accordance with
the procedure detailed above, and these entries were
made at or near the time that the payment was
received. _____ (name of the computer pro-
gram/software) accurately records mortgage pay-

ments when properly operated. In the case at bar,
_____ (name of the computer program/software)
was properly operated to accurately record the Defendant's mortgage payments.

Based on the foregoing, _____ failed to pay
amounts due under the Note, and the amount due and
owing as of _____ is:

Principal	$_____
Interest	$_____
Pro Rata MIP/PMI	$_____
Escrow Advance	$_____
Late Charges	$_____
NSF Charges	$_____
Property Maintenance	$_____
Property Inspections	$_____
BPO	$_____
GROSS AMOUNT DUE	$_____
Less/Plus balance in reserve ac-counts	$_____
NET AMOUNT DUE	$_____

AFFIANT STATES NOTHING MORE.

BY: _____

Affiant

Subscribed and sworn to before me this ___ day of
_____, _____

By _____

_____

Notary Public

State of [   ]

My Commission expires: _____, _____

Personally Known ___ OR Produced Identification
___.

Type of identification produced:
_____.

If executed within the boundaries of Illinois, the
affidavit may be signed pursuant to section 1–109 of
the Illinois Code of Civil Procedure (735 ILCS
5/01–109) rather than being notarized.

(d) Defaults.

(1) Notice Required. In all mortgage foreclosure
cases where the borrower is defaulted by court
order, a notice of default and entry of judgment of
foreclosure shall be prepared by the attorney for
plaintiff and shall be mailed by the Clerk of the
Circuit Court for each judicial circuit. The attorney
for plaintiff shall prepare the notice in its entirety

and deliver to the Clerk of the Circuit Court one copy for filing and one copy for mailing within two business days after the entry of default. The Clerk of the Circuit Court shall mail within five business days after the entry of default, by United States Postal Service, a copy of the notice of default and entry of judgment of foreclosure to the address(es) provided by the attorney for the plaintiff in an envelope bearing the return address of the Clerk of the Circuit Court and file proof thereof. The notice shall be mailed to the property address or the address on any appearance or other document filed by any defendant. Any notices returned by the United States Postal Service as undeliverable shall be filed in the case file maintained by the Clerk of the Circuit Court.

(2) Form of Notice. The notice of default and entry of judgment of foreclosure shall be in substantially the following form:

Form 2

IN THE CIRCUIT COURT OF THE ___ JUDICIAL CIRCUIT
FOR _____ COUNTY, ILLINOIS

_____	)
Plaintiff(s)	)
v.	) Case. No. _____
_____	)
Defendant(s)	)

NOTICE OF ENTRY OF DEFAULT AND JUDGMENT OF FORECLOSURE

To: _____

_____

_____

This notice is to advise you of recent activity in the mortgage foreclosure lawsuit now pending in the Circuit Court. DO NOT IGNORE THIS NOTICE. YOU SHOULD ACT IMMEDIATELY.

The Circuit Court has entered an Order of Default and a Judgment of Foreclosure and Sale against you in your case concerning the property located at [insert address].

You may be entitled to file a Motion to Vacate this order. Any such motion should be filed as soon as possible.

[If applicable] You may redeem the property from foreclosure by paying $ _____, which is the total amount due plus fees and costs, by [insert day].

[If applicable] If you need legal advice, you may contact _____ for free legal advice.

[NAME OF CLERK]

Clerk of the Circuit Court
of ___ County
[Contact information]

(e) Effect on Judgment and Orders. Neither the failure to send the notice required by paragraph (d)(i) nor any errors in preparing or sending the notice shall affect the legal validity of the order of default, the judgment of foreclosure, or any other orders entered pursuant to the Illinois Mortgage Foreclosure Law (735 ILCS 5/15–1101 *et seq.*) and cannot be the basis for vacating an otherwise validly entered order.

(f) Judicial Sales. In addition to the requirements for judicial sales set forth in sections 15–1506 and 15–1507 of the Illinois Mortgage Foreclosure Law (735 ILCS 5/15–1506, 15–1507) the following will apply to mortgage foreclosure sales:

(1) Notice of Sale. Not fewer than 10 business days before the sale, the attorney for the plaintiff shall send notice by mail to all defendants, including defendants in default, of the foreclosure sale date, time, and location of the sale.

(2) Selling Officers. Any foreclosure sale held pursuant to section 15–1507 may be conducted by a private selling officer who is appointed in accordance with section 15–1506(f)(3).

(3) Surplus Funds. If a judicial foreclosure sale held pursuant to Section 15–1507 of the Illinois Mortgage Foreclosure Law (735 ILCS 5/15–1507) results in the existence of a surplus of funds exceeding the amount due and owing as set forth in the judgment of foreclosure, the attorney for the plaintiff shall send a special notice to the mortgagors advising them of the surplus funds and enclosing a form for presentment of the motion to the court for the funds.

(g) Special Notice of Surplus Funds. The special notice shall be mailed and shall be in substantially the following form:

Form 3

IN THE CIRCUIT COURT OF THE _____ JUDICIAL CIRCUIT
FOR ___ COUNTY, ILLINOIS

_____	)
Plaintiff(s)	)
v.	) Case. No. _____
_____	)
Defendant(s)	)

SPECIAL NOTICE OF SURPLUS FUNDS

To: _____

_____

_____

There is $ ___ remaining after the sale of your property at [insert address of property sold]. You may be entitled to this money.

If you want to obtain this money, you need to:

(1) Complete the enclosed form.

(2) Take the completed form to the Clerk of the Circuit Court [insert the information for the Clerk of the Circuit Court in which the case is pending].

(3) Schedule a date to present the paperwork to the judge.

(4) Mail a copy of the completed form, at least five business days before the date with the judge, to: [insert service list].

(h) Petition for Turnover of Surplus Funds. Each judicial circuit shall make readily available a form petition for turnover of surplus funds to be included in the Special Notice of Surplus Funds required to be mailed by the attorney for plaintiffs. The petition shall be in substantially the following form:

Form 4

IN THE CIRCUIT COURT OF THE _____ JUDICIAL CIRCUIT
FOR _____ COUNTY, ILLINOIS

_____)	
Plaintiff(s))	
v.)	Case. No. _____
_____)	
Defendant(s))	

NOTICE OF MOTION AND PETITION FOR TURNOVER OF SURPLUS FUNDS

TO: _____

_____

_____

On _____, _____, at _____ a.m./p.m. or as soon thereafter as counsel may be heard, I shall appear before the Honorable _____ or any Judge sitting in that Judge's stead, in the courtroom usually occupied by him/her, located at _____, Illinois, and present:

PETITION FOR TURNOVER OF SURPLUS FUNDS

(with Appearance)

Now come(s) _____, and move(s) this Court for entry of an order turning over the surplus proceeds from the foreclosure sale. In support of this Petition, Petitioner(s) state(s) as follows:

(1) All parties to this proceeding have been given notice of this Petition.

(2) The subject property was sold at a foreclosure sale for more than the amount owed the mortgage company and the sale was approved by the Court on ___ / ___ / ___.

(3) There is a surplus remaining after all sums are paid in the amount of $ _____.

(4) Petitioner(s) is/are a party/parties to the foreclosure case and has/have filed an appearance in the case.

(5) Petitioner's/Petitioners' interest in the property is (select one, and attach any supporting documents): Owner(s)/Mortgagor(s); Judgment Creditor; Lien Holder; Other (please specify): _____.

(6) If Petitioner(s) is/are not the Mortgagor(s), judgment for the Petitioner(s) has been proved up in the amount of $ _____.

(7) Pick one:

- Petitioner(s) has/have a bankruptcy case pending in Bankruptcy Court and has/have ATTACHED a copy of the order from the Bankruptcy Court allowing receipt of the surplus funds ("Order Authorizing Distribution of Surplus Funds").

- Petitioner(s) DOES NOT/DO NOT have a bankruptcy case pending in Bankruptcy Court. Wherefore, the Petitioner(s), _____, move this Court to turn over to him/her/them the surplus from the foreclosure sale.

I/We, _____, enter my/our appearance(s), *pro se*:

Signature _____

Signature _____

VERIFICATION AND PROOF OF SERVICE

I/We certify under penalty of perjury as provided by law pursuant to section 1–109 of the Illinois Code of Civil Procedure, that I/we have read the foregoing Verified Petition for Turnover of Surplus Funds and the statements set forth therein are true and correct and that I sent a copy of this Appearance and Answer by United States mail to the Plaintiff's attorney and any other parties who have appeared and have not heretofore been found by the Court to be in default, on _____, 20 ___.

Signature _____

Signature _____

(i) Deceased Mortgagors. In all mortgage foreclosure cases where the mortgagor or mortgagors is or are deceased, and no estate has been opened for the deceased mortgagor(s), the court shall, on motion of a party, appoint a special representative to stand in the place of the deceased mortgagor(s) who shall act in a manner similar to that provided by section 13–209 of the Illinois Code of Civil Procedure (735 ILCS 5/13–209).

Adopted Feb. 22, 2013, eff. May 1, 2013. Amended April 8, 2013, eff. May 1, 2013.

Committee Comments

(February 22, 2013)

On April 11, 2011, the Illinois Supreme Court created the Special Supreme Court Committee on Mortgage Foreclosures and charged it with the following tasks: investigating the procedures used throughout the State of Illinois in mortgage foreclosure proceedings; studying relevant Illinois Supreme Court Rules and local rules that directly or indirectly affect such proceedings; analyzing the procedures adopted in other states in response to the unprecedented number of foreclosure filings nationwide; and reviewing legislative proposals pending in the Illinois General Assembly that may impact the mortgage foreclosure rules for the state. To meet this charge, the Committee established subcommittees, one of which was the Practice and Procedures Subcommittee. The Practice and Procedures Subcommittee submitted proposals for changes to the practice and procedures for mortgage foreclosure cases for discussion at a public hearing held on April 27, 2012. After consideration of comments and discussion at the public hearing, the Committee proposed this new rule governing mortgage foreclosure practice and procedure.

Paragraph (b) is derived from the need to address evidentiary issues that often arise during the course of a mortgage foreclosure. The new requirement to attach a copy of the note, as it currently exists with all indorsements and allonges, supplements the Illinois Mortgage Foreclosure Law to provide this necessary document to the defendant and the court at the outset. Including this additional document will prevent unnecessary delays caused by motion practice and discovery often used by defendants.

In drafting this section of the rule, the Committee took into consideration the positions of both the judiciary and comments provided at the public hearing regarding attaching a copy of all assignments to the complaint. The Committee members recognized that with the increase in transfers of mortgages and notes, Illinois courts have seen a dramatic increase in assertions by mortgagors that the mortgagee lacks standing to bring the foreclosure complaint. Quite often, mortgagors who ignore the judicial process until after a foreclosure or sale has occurred have raised standing issues as a defense, but have been told that their claim was forfeited by the failure to raise it in a timely manner. The Committee considered that as a matter of judicial economy, requiring that all executed assignments of the mortgage be attached at the time of filing could provide current documentation at the outset to all defendants and the circuit court demonstrating how the plaintiff has standing to file the complaint. However, due to industry changes in the documentation requirements for mortgage assignments over the past two decades, a requirement to attach all copies of assignments to the complaint at the time of filing proved to be impractical and overly burden-

some for practitioners given the current volume of foreclosures statewide. This rule does not prohibit the attachment of such assignments should a plaintiff choose to do so. This rule also does not preclude the requirement of submission of all assignments at a later date in the litigation should the appropriate issues present themselves and presentation of the documents to the court and litigants becomes necessary.

Paragraph (c) addresses some of the many issues that arise from document handling procedures by lenders and servicers. Illinois courts, along with courts nationwide, have faced issues relating to "robo-signing" practices at major lenders, where affidavits were not properly notarized or where the affiant did not actually review any of the pertinent loan records. In addition to questionable document handling procedures, circuit courts have dealt with prove-up affidavits that come in varied forms, many of which do not properly address the foundational requirements necessary for establishing the accuracy of computerized business records nor the correct amount due and owing under the mortgage and note. Paragraph (c)(2) identifies the minimum requirements necessary for a prove-up affidavit submitted by the mortgagee for entry of a judgment of foreclosure and Form 1 gives a form affidavit that should be used.

No judgment of foreclosure will be entered without compliance with Paragraph (c). However, Form 1 establishes only the amounts due and owing on the borrower's loan. Paragraph (c)(2) and Form 1 do not relieve the foreclosing party from establishing other evidentiary requirements, as necessary, in connection with proving the allegations contained in its complaint including, but not limited to, the party's right to enforce the instrument of indebtedness, if applicable.

Paragraph (d) addresses the desire of the Illinois courts to have adequate assurance that the mortgagor is sufficiently notified when an order of default and a judgment of foreclosure are entered against the mortgagor. Many mortgagors ignore court notices, believing that they are in error because their lender is negotiating with them for a loan modification. Other mortgagors have been told by servicers that their foreclosure case is on hold, but the servicer has not told the plaintiff's attorneys to place the file on hold. Currently, many circuit court clerks send a generic postcard that notifies any defendant, who has an appearance on file, of entry of a default order. Thus, if the mortgagor has not filed an appearance, the mortgagor may not receive notice of the default order from the clerk. The post card may not contain any helpful information that the defendant can understand. Likewise, notice of the default order is not mailed to the property address as a matter of course. While section 2–1302 of the Illinois Code of Civil Procedure (735 ILCS 5/2–1302) requires that a plaintiff give notice of entry of a default order to be sent to all parties against whom the order applies, failure to give such notice does not affect the validity of the order. As a result, a mortgagor may not receive notice of entry of the default order from either the Clerk of the Circuit Court or the mortgagee's counsel.

Paragraph (d) addresses this deficiency in the notification process and requires the mortgagee's counsel to prepare a specific "Notice of Entry of Default and Judgment of Foreclosure" (Form 2). Counsel for the plaintiff must prepare this notice for the property address or any other address where the defendant is most likely to receive it. A defendant may have filed an appearance or another court paper that would indicate an address that may be different from the address of service of summons and different from the property address. By preparing this notice, and having the Clerk of the Circuit Court mail the notices, any undeliverable mail will remain in the court file and defaulted mortgagors will receive a clearer notice of the order and the judgment of foreclosure than they do currently.

Paragraph (f) addresses two issues relating to judicial sales that have become substantial problems throughout the state. Paragraph (f)(1) attempts to provide adequate notice to those mortgagors who are about to lose their home. Currently, the Illinois Mortgage Foreclosure Law does not specify that a separate notice of the sale be sent to defaulted defendants, and assumes that the publication requirements are adequate for those that have not otherwise participated in the foreclosure proceedings. See 735 ILCS 5/15–1507(c)(3) (lacking a specific requirement that a separate notice of sale be sent to a defaulted mortgagor). However, in many residential cases, a lack of participation, for any reason, results in a lack of notice of the sale to the mortgagor living in the property being foreclosed. That lack of notice often results in the mortgagor learning about the sale on the eve of the sale and filing an emergency motion to stay the sale. In cases where the mortgagor finds out about the sale from a notice of confirmation of sale or through the sheriff's notice of eviction, the courts then must hear motions to vacate the sale and motions to stay possession. See 735 ILCS 5/15–1508(b–5) (requiring notice of confirmation of sale be sent to a defaulted mortgagor). Many of these motions could be avoided and judicial efficiency increased if all parties, including defaulted parties, are given notice of the sale. Accordingly, paragraph (f)(1) implements a new notice requirement to supplement section 15–1507(c)(3) by mandating a separate notice to a defaulted mortgagor presale while also complementing section 15–1508(b–5) that requires notice postsale for confirmation.

Paragraph (f)(2) addresses the selling officer. Currently, section 15–1506(f)(3) of the Illinois Mortgage Foreclosure Law (735 ILCS 5/15–1506(f)(3)) allows, by special motion, an official other than the one customarily designated by a court to be appointed to conduct judicial sales. The Committee recognized that the customarily appointed selling officer is the sheriff in many counties statewide, section 15–1506 allows a court to appoint a private selling officer upon motion. Given the high volume of foreclosures throughout the state, many sales are being held nearly a year after the expiration of the redemption period. In some cases, this is due to the failure of the sheriff to promptly obey the court order commanding him to sell the property at auc-

tion. Accordingly, the loan accrues late fees and increased interest charges. These additional charges do not benefit any party to the foreclosure and do not help the communities if the property remains vacant during that idle period. In order to correct these deficiencies in the process, the Committee recommended that a rule be enacted that expressly allows the use of private selling officers throughout the state. In many instances, private selling officers have lower costs with the capacity and ability to conduct a sale in a timely manner that prevents the accrual of additional fees and facilitates the rehabilitation of properties into valuable components of neighborhoods.

Paragraph (g) implements a specific notification process for informing mortgagors about the existence of surplus funds resulting from a judicial sale. Currently, many clerks of the circuit courts are holding unclaimed surplus funds from judicial sales. Due to the lack of notice, these funds remain unclaimed. Paragraph (g) implements a specific "Special Notice of Surplus Funds" (Form 3) that the plaintiff's counsel must send to the mortgagors and paragraph (h) includes a specific motion (Form 4) that can be completed by the mortgagors for presentment to the court without an attorney. This paragraph is intended to facilitate the ability of mortgagors to claim those funds to which they may be entitled.

Paragraph (i) addresses the issue of a deceased mortgagor and the subject matter jurisdiction issues addressed in *ABN Amro Mortgage Group, Inc. v. McGahan*, 237 Ill. 2d 526 (2010), which have not been specifically addressed by remedial legislation.

Rule 114. Loss Mitigation Affidavit

(a) **Loss Mitigation.** For all actions filed under the Illinois Mortgage Foreclosure Law, and where a mortgagor has appeared or filed an answer or other responsive pleading, Plaintiff must, prior to moving for a judgment of foreclosure, comply with the requirements of any loss mitigation program which applies to the subject mortgage loan.

(b) **Affidavit Prior to or at the Time of Moving for a Judgment of Foreclosure.** In order to document the compliance required by paragraph (a) above, Plaintiff, prior to or at the time of moving for a judgment of foreclosure, must file an affidavit specifying:

(1) Any type of loss mitigation which applies to the subject mortgage;

(2) What steps were taken to offer said type of loss mitigation to the mortgagor(s); and

(3) The status of any such loss mitigation efforts.

(c) **Form of Affidavit.** The form of the affidavit shall be as set forth below in Form 1, or shall be in a form specified by amendment to this rule, but, in any case, shall contain the information set forth in paragraph (b) above.

Form 1

IN THE CIRCUIT COURT OF THE ____ JUDICIAL
CIRCUIT
FOR _____ COUNTY, ILLINOIS

_____)
Plaintiff(s)   )
      v.   )   Case. No. _____
_____)
Defendant(s)   )

LOSS MITIGATION AFFIDAVIT

I, ___ [name] ___ , hereby state as follows:

(1) I am employed as ___ [job title] ___ of [name] , the mortgagee as defined in section 15–1208 of the Illinois Mortgage Foreclosure Law for the residential mortgage loan that is the subject of the pending foreclosure case, and I am authorized to act on behalf of plaintiff.

(2) With respect to the subject mortgage loan, my employer is the appropriate entity to extend loss mitigation, if any, to the mortgagor(s), as defined in Section 15–1209 of the Illinois Mortgage Foreclosure Law.

(3) I have performed or caused to be performed a review of the records maintained in the ordinary course of the business of my employer relating to the subject mortgage loan, and based upon that review:

(a) The subject mortgage loan is eligible for the following loss mitigation programs:[1]

_____

_____

(b) For each of the programs listed above in 3(a), the following steps have been taken by the mortgagee to comply with its obligations under such program:

_____

_____

(c) For each of the programs listed above in 3(a), the current status of loss mitigation effort is as follows:

_____

_____

(4) The above is true and accurate to the best of my personal knowledge and based upon my review of the records as set forth above.

Affiant states nothing more.

BY: _____

    AFFIANT

Subscribed and sworn to before me this _____ day of _____, 20 ___ by _____.

Notary Public

State of [name]

My Commission expires: _____, 20 ___

Personally Known ___ **OR** Produced Identification ___.

Type of Identification Produced: _____.

(d) Enforcement. The court may, either *sua sponte* or upon motion of a mortgagor, stay the proceedings or deny entry of a foreclosure judgment if Plaintiff fails to comply with the requirements of this rule.

Adopted Feb. 22, 2013, eff. May 1, 2013. Amended April 8, 2013, eff. May 1, 2013.

[1] Identify here all applicable loss mitigation programs including but not limited to those available under the Making Home Affordable Program, the 2012 National Attorney General Settlement, or the FHA, VA, or USDA insured-loan programs. Also identify any "in-house" loss mitigation regularly provided by the mortgagee for a mortgage loan of this type. "Eligible" means the loan is eligible to be considered under such programs because it meets the threshold requirements; eligible does not mean that a loss mitigation alternative to foreclosure is guaranteed.

Committee Comments
(April 8, 2013)

The context out of which Rule 114 arises is the huge increase in the number of foreclosure cases filed in the Illinois state courts. It is recognized by all members of the Committee that, wherever possible, it is in the best interests of all parties, the courts, and the local communities to avoid a foreclosure sale in favor of a workable loss mitigation alternative. Toward this end, Rule 114 requires the plaintiff to file an affidavit to document compliance with any loss mitigation program applicable to the mortgage loan at issue. The affidavit must be filled out and filed prior to or at the time of moving for a judgment of foreclosure. As such, the intended purpose of the rule is to prevent the entry of a judgment of foreclosure where the plaintiff has theretofore failed to comply with applicable loss mitigation requirements, be they local, state, or federal. The filing of the affidavit allows the court to review the plaintiff's level of compliance with applicable loss mitigation requirements, and, if necessary, to deny a motion for judgment of foreclosure if said compliance is lacking.

Specific procedures for filing and presenting the affidavit to the court may differ from county to county. Where counties have mediation programs in place, it is advisable that the county adopt procedures to incorporate the loss mitigation affidavit into the mediation process. Where no mediation program is in place, or where an individual case is not subject to mediation, the county and individual courts should consider appropriate local procedures to facilitate the use of the affidavit in achieving its intended purpose. The affidavit requirement is intended to apply to all judgments on or after the effective date of the rule, no matter the foreclosure filing date. Because the affidavit must be filed prior to the entry of a foreclosure judgment, the effective date requires application to any case where a judgment of foreclosure has not yet been entered. Thus, although a case may already have been filed prior to the effective date of Rule 114, the Rule would apply if a judgment of foreclosure has not yet been entered.

Rules 115 to 130.   Reserved

PART B.   PLEADINGS AND OTHER DOCUMENTS

Rule 131.   Form of Documents

(a) Legibility. All documents and copies thereof for filing and service shall be legibly written, typewritten, printed, or otherwise duplicated. The clerk shall not file any which do not conform to this rule.

(b) Titles. All documents shall be entitled in the court and cause, and the plaintiff's name shall be placed first.

(c) Multiple Parties. In cases in which there are two or more plaintiffs or two or more defendants, it is sufficient in entitling documents, except a summons, to name the first-named plaintiff and the first-named defendant with the usual indication of other parties, provided there be added the official number of the cause.

(d) Name, Address, Telephone Number, Facsimile Number and E–mail Address.

(1) **Attorneys.** All documents filed or served in any cause by an attorney upon another party shall bear the attorney's name, business address, e–mail address, and telephone number. The attorney must designate a primary e-mail address and may designate no more than two secondary e-mail addresses.

(2) **Unrepresented Parties.** All documents filed or served in any cause by an unrepresented party upon another party shall bear the unrepresented party's mailing address and telephone number. Additionally, an unrepresented party may designate a single e-mail address to which service may be directed under Rule 11(b)(6). If an unrepresented party does not designate an e-mail address, then service upon and by that party must be made by a method specified in Rule 11 other than e-mail transmission under Rule 11(b)(6).

(3) **All parties.** If the attorney or unrepresented party will accept service by facsimile transmission, then the document shall also bear the statement "Service by facsimile transmission will be accepted at [facsimile telephone number]."

Amended Feb. 19, 1981, eff. April 1, 1982; Oct. 30, 1992, eff. Nov. 15, 1992; Dec. 21, 2012, eff. Jan. 1, 2013; Jan. 4, 2013, eff. immediately; Dec. 9, 2015, eff. Jan. 1, 2016.

Formerly Ill.Rev.Stat.1991, ch. 110A, ¶ 131.

Committee Comments

(Revised February 1982)

In 1982 the rule, which was former Rule 6 without change of substance, was amended to require that all papers filed or served had to bear the name, as well as the address and telephone number, of the responsible attorney or attorneys and law firm filing them.

Rule 132.   Designation of Cases

Every complaint or other document initiating any civil action or proceeding shall contain in the caption the words "at law," "in chancery," "in probate," "small claim," or other designation conforming to the organization of the circuit court into divisions. Misdesignation shall not affect the jurisdiction of the court. Amended Jan. 4, 2013, eff. immediately.

Formerly Ill.Rev.Stat.1991, ch. 110A, ¶ 132.

Committee Comments

This is former Rule 9(1) without change of substance.

Rule 133.   Pleading Breach of Statutory Duty; Judgment or Order; Breach of Condition Precedent

(a) Statutory Duty. If a breach of statutory duty is alleged, the statute shall be cited in connection with the allegation.

(b) Judgment or Order. In pleading a judgment or order of any State or Federal court or the decision of any State or Federal officer or board of special jurisdiction, it is sufficient to state the date of its entry, and describe its general nature and allege generally that the judgment or decision was duly given or made.

(c) Condition Precedent. In pleading the performance of a condition precedent in a contract, it is sufficient to allege generally that the party performed all the conditions on his part; if the allegation be denied, the facts must be alleged in connection with the denial showing wherein there was a failure to perform.

Formerly Ill.Rev.Stat.1991, ch. 110A, ¶ 133.

Committee Comments

This is former Rule 13 without change of substance.

Rule 134.   Incorporation of Pleadings by Reference

If facts are adequately stated in one part of a pleading, or in any one pleading, they need not be repeated elsewhere in the pleading, or in the pleadings, and may be incorporated by reference elsewhere or in other pleadings.

Formerly Ill.Rev.Stat.1991, ch. 110A, ¶ 134.

Committee Comments

This is former Rule 11–1.

Rule 135. Pleading Equitable Matters

(a) Single Equitable Cause of Action. Matters within the jurisdiction of a court of equity, whether directly or as an incident to other matters before it, or which an equity court can hear so as to do complete justice between the parties, may be regarded as a single equitable cause of action and when so treated as a single cause of action shall be pleaded without being set forth in separate counts and without the use of the term "count."

(b) Joinder of Legal and Equitable Matters. When actions at law and in chancery that may be prosecuted separately are joined, the party joining the actions may, if he desires to treat them as separate causes of action, plead them in distinct counts, marked respectively "separate action at law" and "separate action in chancery." This paragraph applies to answers, counterclaims, third-party claims, and any other pleadings wherever legal and equitable matters are permitted to be joined under the Civil Practice Law [1].
Amended May 28, 1982, eff. July 1, 1982.

Formerly Ill.Rev.Stat.1991, ch. 110A, ¶ 135.
[1] 735 ILCS 5/2–101 et seq.

Committee Comments

This rule contains the pleading provisions of former Rules 10 and 11 without change in substance. The provisions of those rules relating to trial appear in new Rule 232.

Rule 136. Denials

(a) Form of Denials. If a pleader can in good faith deny all the allegations in a paragraph of the opposing party's pleading, or all the allegations in the paragraph that are not specifically admitted, he may do so without paraphrasing or separately describing each allegation denied.

(b) Pleadings After Reply. Unless the court orders otherwise, no response to a reply or subsequent pleading is required and any new matter in a reply or subsequent pleading shall be taken as denied.

Formerly Ill.Rev.Stat.1991, ch. 110A, ¶ 136.

Committee Comments

Paragraph (a)

This provision is new. It is designed to clarify section 40 of the Illinois Civil Practice Act.

When several allegations in a paragraph are to be denied, the responsive pleading may be more intelligible if they are identified without a paraphrase or separate description of each one. Doubt has been cast on this method of pleading by Johnson v. Schuberth, 40 Ill.App.2d 467, 189 N.E.2d 768 (1st Dist.1963). Compare, however, Dennehy v. Wood

Co., 285 Ill.App. 598, 2 N.E.2d 586 (2d Dist. Abst.Op.1936).

The new rule permits pleading substantially as in the following illustration:

"5. Defendant denies the allegations of paragraph 5 of the complaint and each of them."

Or, if some of the allegations of a paragraph are to be admitted and some denied, the pleader may state substantially as follows:

"5. Defendant admits [stating facts admitted] and denies the remaining allegations of paragraph 5 and each of them."

The new rule is based in part upon provisions in Rule 8(b) of the Federal Rules of Civil Procedure. See also 2 Moore, Federal Practice, par. 8.23 (2d ed. 1965). Unlike the Federal rule, however, the new rule does not permit a general denial of an entire pleading, even in the very unusual case in which such a denial would be appropriate. Not only does section 40 of the Civil Practice Act forbid this result, but the disciplinary effect of requiring the pleader to address himself separately to each paragraph and allegation therein is highly desirable and should be preserved.

Paragraph (b)

Paragraph (b), an express statement of what the Committee believes to be the existing rule, is based upon Rule 8(d) of the Federal Rules of Civil Procedure.

Rule 137. Signing of Pleadings, Motions and Other Documents—Sanctions

(a) Signature requirement/certification. Every pleading, motion and other document of a party represented by an attorney shall be signed by at least one attorney of record in his individual name, whose address shall be stated. A party who is not represented by an attorney shall sign his pleading, motion, or other document and state his address. Except when otherwise specifically provided by rule or statute, pleadings need not be verified or accompanied by affidavit. The signature of an attorney or party constitutes a certificate by him that he has read the pleading, motion or other document; that to the best of his knowledge, information, and belief formed after reasonable inquiry it is well grounded in fact and is warranted by existing law or a good-faith argument for the extension, modification, or reversal of existing law, and that it is not interposed for any improper purpose, such as to harass or to cause unnecessary delay or needless increase in the cost of litigation. If a pleading, motion, or other document is not signed, it shall be stricken unless it is signed promptly after the omission is called to the attention of the pleader or movant. If a pleading, motion, or other document is signed in violation of this rule, the court, upon motion or upon its own initiative, may impose upon the person who signed it, a represented party, or both, an appropriate sanction, which may include an order to pay to the other party or parties the amount of reasonable expenses incurred because of the filing of the pleading, motion or other document, including a reasonable attorney fee.

(b) Procedure for Alleging Violations of This Rule. All proceedings under this rule shall be brought within the civil action in which the pleading, motion or other document referred to has been filed, and no violation or alleged violation of this rule shall give rise to a separate civil suit, but shall be considered a claim within the same civil action. Motions brought pursuant to this rule must be filed within 30 days of the entry of final judgment, or if a timely post-judgment motion is filed, within 30 days of the ruling on the post-judgment motion.

(c) Applicability to State Entities and Review of Administrative Determinations. This rule shall apply to the State of Illinois or any agency of the State in the same manner as any other party. Furthermore, where the litigation involves review of a determination of an administrative agency, the court may include in its award for expenses an amount to compensate a party for costs actually incurred by that party in contesting on the administrative level an allegation or denial made by the State without reasonable cause and found to be untrue.

(d) Required Written Explanation of Imposition of Sanctions. Where a sanction is imposed under this rule, the judge shall set forth with specificity the reasons and basis of any sanction so imposed either in the judgment order itself or in a separate written order.

(e) Attorney Assistance Not Requiring an Appearance or Signature. An attorney may assist a self-represented person in drafting or reviewing a pleading, motion, or other paper without making a general or limited scope appearance. Such assistance does not constitute either a general or limited scope appearance by the attorney. The self-represented person shall sign the pleading, motion, or other paper. An attorney providing drafting or reviewing assistance may rely on the self-represented person's representation of facts without further investigation by the attorney, unless the attorney knows that such representations are false.

Adopted June 19, 1989, eff. Aug. 1, 1989. Amended Dec. 17, 1993, eff. Feb. 1, 1994; Jan. 4, 2013, eff. immediately; June 14, 2013, eff. July 1, 2013.

Formerly Ill.Rev.Stat.1991, ch. 110A, ¶ 137.

Committee Comments

(August 1, 1989)

The Supreme Court has adopted Rule 137, effective August 1, 1989. Rule 137 will require all pleadings and papers to be signed by an attorney of record or by a party, if the party is not represented by an attorney, and (treating such signature as a certification that the paper has been read, that after reasonable inquiry it is well-grounded in fact and law, and that it is not interposed for any improper

purpose, *etc.*) the rule authorizes the trial courts to impose certain sanctions for violations of the rule. Rule 137 preempts all matters sought to be covered by section 2–611 of the Code of Civil Procedure. Unlike section 2–611, Rule 137 allows but does not require the imposition of sanctions. Unlike section 2–611, Rule 137 requires a trial judge who imposes sanctions to set forth with specificity the reasons and basis of any sanction in a separate written order. Unlike section 2–611, Rule 137 does not make special provisions concerning the potential exposure to sanctions of insurance companies that might employ attorneys.

(December 17, 1993)

The rule is modified to clarify when motions for sanctions must be filed.

(June 14, 2013)

Under Illinois Rule of Professional Conduct 1.2(c), an attorney may limit the scope of a representation if the limitation is reasonable under the circumstances and the client gives informed consent. Such a limited scope representation may include providing advice to a party regarding the drafting of a pleading, motion or other paper, or reviewing a pleading, motion or other paper drafted by a party, without filing a general or limited scope appearance. In such circumstances, an attorney is not required to sign or otherwise note the attorney's involvement and the certification requirements in Rule 137 are inapplicable. Moreover, even if an attorney is identified in connection with such a limited scope representation, the attorney will not be deemed to have made a general or limited scope appearance.

Consistent with the limited scope of services envisioned under this drafting and reviewing function, attorneys may rely on the representation of facts provided by the self-represented person. This rule applies, for example, to an attorney who advises a caller to a legal aid telephone hotline regarding the completion of a form pleading, motion or other paper or an attorney providing information at a pro bono clinic.

All obligations under Rule 137 with respect to signing pleadings and certifications apply fully in those limited scope representations where an attorney has filed a general or limited scope appearance. Drafting a pleading, motion or other paper, or reviewing a pleading, motion or paper drafted by a party does not establish any independent responsibility not already applicable under current law.

Rule 138. Personal Identity Information

(a) Applicability.

(1) In civil cases, personal identity information shall not be included in documents or exhibits filed with the court except as provided in paragraph (c). This rule applies to paper and electronic filings.

(2) This rule does not apply to cases filed confidentially and not available for public inspection.

(b) Personal identity information, for purposes of this rule, is defined as follows:

(1) Social Security and individual taxpayer-identification numbers;

(2) driver's license numbers;

(3) financial account numbers; and

(4) debit and credit card numbers.

A court may order other types of information redacted or filed confidentially, consistent with the purpose and procedures of this rule.

(c) A redacted filing of personal identity information for the public record is permissible and shall only include:

(1) the last four digits of the Social Security or individual taxpayer-identification number;

(2) the last four digits of the driver's license number;

(3) the last four digits of the financial account number; and

(4) the last four digits of the debit and credit card number.

When the filing of personal identity information is required by law, ordered by the court, or otherwise necessary to effect disposition of a matter, the party shall file a form in substantial compliance with the appended "Notice Of Confidential Information Within Court Filing." This document shall contain the personal identity information in issue, and shall be impounded by the clerk immediately upon filing. Thereafter, the document and any attachments thereto shall remain impounded and be maintained as confidential, except as provided in paragraph (d) or as the court may order.

After the initial impounded filing of the personal identity information, subsequent documents filed in the case shall include only redacted personal identity information with appropriate reference to the impounded document containing the personal identity information.

If any of the impounded personal identity information in the initial filing subsequently requires amendment or updating, the responsible party shall file the amended or additional information by filing a separate "Notice Of Confidential Information Within Court Filing" form.

(d) The information provided with the "Notice of Confidential Information Within Court Filing" shall be available to the parties, to the court, and to the clerk in performance of any requirement provided by law, including the transfer of such information to appropriate justice partners, such as the sheriff, guardian *ad litem*, and the State Disbursement Unit (SDU), the Secretary of State or other governmental agencies, and legal aid agencies or bar association *pro bono* groups. In addition, the clerk, the parties, and the parties' attorneys may prepare and provide copies of documents without redaction to financial institutions and other entities or persons which require such documents.

(e) Neither the court nor the clerk is required to review documents or exhibits for compliance with this rule. If the clerk becomes aware of any noncompliance, the clerk may call it to the court's attention. The court, however, shall not require the clerk to review documents or exhibits for compliance with this rule.

(f)(1) If a document or exhibit is filed containing personal identity information, a party or any other person whose information has been filed may move that the court order redaction and confidential filing as provided in paragraph (b). The motion shall be impounded, and the clerk shall remove the document or exhibit containing the personal identity information from public access pending the court's ruling on the substance of the motion. A motion requesting redaction of a document in the court file shall have attached a copy of the redacted version of the document. If the court allows the motion, the clerk shall retain the unredacted copy under impoundment and the redacted copy shall become part of the court record.

(2) If the court finds the inclusion of personal identity information in violation of this rule was willful, the court may award the prevailing party reasonable expenses, including attorney fees and court costs.

(g) This rule does not require any clerk or judicial officer to redact personal identity information from the court record except as provided in this rule.

Adopted Oct. 24, 2012, eff. July 1, 2013. Amended June 3, 2013, eff. July 1, 2013; June 27, 2013, eff. July 1, 2013; Dec. 24, 2013, eff. Jan. 1, 2014; May 29, 2014, eff. immediately; Nov. 21, 2014, eff. immediately.

Committee Comments
October 24, 2012
(Revised June 3, 2013)
(Revised December 24, 2013)
(Revised May 29, 2014)
Paragraph (a)

Supreme Court Rule 138, adopted October 24, 2012, prohibits the filing of personal identity information that could be used for identity theft. For instance, financial disclosure statements used in family law cases typically contain a variety of personal information that shall remain confidential to protect privacy concerns.

Paragraph (b)

While paragraph (b) defines the most common types of personal identity information, it further allows the court to order redaction or confidential filing of other types of information as necessary to prevent identity theft.

Paragraph (c)

The procedures in paragraph (c) address the filing of personal identity information in redacted form for the public record. Where the personal identity information is required by law, ordered by the court, or otherwise necessary to effect a disposition of a matter, the litigant shall file the document in redacted form and separately file the subject personal identity information in a protected document titled a "Notice of Confidential Information Within Court Filing," using the appended form. The filing of a separate document without redaction is not necessary or required because the personal identity information will be available to authorized persons by referring to the "Notice of Confidential Information Within Court Filing" form.

Paragraph (d)

The clerk of court can utilize personal identity information and share that information with other agencies, entities and individuals, as provided by law.

[Appendix]

In the Circuit Court of the _____ Judicial Circuit, ___ County, Illinois

(Or, In the Circuit Court of Cook County, Illinois)

_____)	
Plaintiff/Petitioner,)	
)	
v.)	Case No. _____
)	
_____)	
Defendant/Respondent)	

NOTICE OF CONFIDENTIAL INFORMATION WITHIN COURT FILING

Pursuant to Illinois Supreme Court Rule 138(c), the filer of a document containing personal identity information required by law, ordered by the court, or otherwise necessary to effect disposition of a matter shall, at the time of such filing, include this confidential information form which identifies the personal identity information redacted from such filing pursuant to Rule 138(c), and which will be redacted from future filings to protect the subject personal identity information. **This personal identity information will not be available to the public and this document will be stored in a separate location from the case file.**

Party/Individual Information:

1. Name: _____

    Address: _____

    _____

    Phone: _____
    SSN: _____

    Other personal identity information as defined in Rule 138(b), to the extent applicable:

2. Name: _____

    Address: _____

    _____

    Phone: _____
    SSN: _____

    Other personal identity information as defined in Rule 138(b), to the extent applicable:

(Attach additional pages, if necessary.)

Rules 139 to 180. Reserved

PART C. APPEARANCES AND TIME FOR ANSWERS, REPLIES, AND MOTIONS

Rule 181. Appearances–Answers–Motions

(a) When Summons Requires Appearance Within 30 Days After Service. When the summons requires appearance within 30 days after service, exclusive of the day of service (see Rule 101(d)), the 30–day period shall be computed from the day the copy of the summons is left with the person designated by law and not from the day a copy is mailed, in case mailing is also required. The defendant may make his or her appearance by filing a motion within the 30–day period, in which instance an answer or another appropriate motion shall be filed within the time the court directs in the order disposing of the motion. If the defendant's appearance is made in some other manner, nevertheless his or her answer or appropriate motion shall be filed on or before the last day on which he or she was required to appear.

(b) When Summons Requires Appearance on Specified Day.

(1) *Actions for Money.* Unless the "Notice to Defendant" (see Rule 101(b)) provides otherwise, an appearance in a civil action for money in which the summons requires appearance on a specified day may be made by appearing in person or by attorney at the time and place specified in the summons and making the appearance known to the court, or before the time specified for appearance by filing a written appearance, answer, or motion, in person or by attorney. The written appearance, answer, or motion shall state with particularity the address where service of notice or documents may be made upon the party or attorney so appearing. When a defendant appears in open court, the court shall require him to enter an appearance in writing. When an appearance is made in writing otherwise than by filing an answer or motion, the defendant shall be allowed 10 days after the day for appearance within which to file an answer or motion, unless the court, by rule or order, otherwise directs.

(2) *Forcible Detainer Actions.* In actions for forcible detainer (see Rule 101(b)), the defendant must appear at the time and place specified in the summons. If the defendant appears, he or she need not file an answer unless ordered by the court; and when no answer is ordered, the allegations of the

complaint will be deemed denied, and any defense may be proved as if it were specifically pleaded.

(3) *Small Claims.* Appearances in small claims (actions for money not in excess of $10,000) are governed by Rule 286.

Amended Oct. 21, 1969, eff. Jan. 1, 1970; Dec. 3, 1996, eff. Jan. 1, 1997; Feb. 10, 2006, eff. immediately; Jan. 4, 2013, eff. immediately.

Formerly Ill.Rev.Stat.1991, ch. 110A, ¶ 181.

Committee Comments

This rule consists of paragraphs (1) and (2) of former Rule 8 without change of substance.

Rule 182. Time for Pleadings and Motions Other than those Directed to Complaint

(a) **Replies.** Replies to answers shall be filed within 21 days after the last day allowed for the filing of the answer. Any subsequent pleadings allowed or ordered shall be filed at such time as the court may order.

(b) **Responding to Counterclaims.** Answers to and motions directed against counterclaims shall be filed by parties already before the court within 21 days after the last day allowed for the filing of the counterclaim.

(c) **Motions.** A motion attacking a pleading other than the complaint must be filed within 21 days after the last day allowed for the filing of the pleading attacked.

Formerly Ill.Rev.Stat.1991, ch. 110A, ¶ 182.

Committee Comments

This rule consists of paragraphs (3) and (4) of former Rule 8 divided into three paragraphs. Twenty days is changed to 21 days.

Rule 183. Extensions of Time

The court, for good cause shown on motion after notice to the opposite party, may extend the time for filing any pleading or the doing of any act which is required by the rules to be done within a limited period, either before or after the expiration of the time.

Corrected eff. Feb. 16, 2011.

Formerly Ill.Rev.Stat.1991, ch. 110A, ¶ 183.

Committee Comments

This is paragraph (5) of former Rule 8 without change in substance.

Rule 184. Hearings on Motions

No provision in these rules or in the Civil Practice Law [1] prescribing a period for filing a motion requires that the motion be heard within that period. Either party may call up the motion for disposition before or after the expiration of the filing period.

Amended May 28, 1982, eff. July 1, 1982.

Formerly Ill.Rev.Stat.1991, ch. 110A, ¶ 184.
[1] 735 ILCS 5/2–101 et seq.

Committee Comments

This is a revision of paragraph (6) of former Rule 8 without change except for the specific reference to the Civil Practice Act.

Rule 185. Telephone Conferences

Except as may be otherwise provided by rule of the circuit court, the court may, at a party's request, direct argument of any motion or discussion of any other matter by telephone conference without a court appearance. The court may further direct which party shall pay the cost of the telephone calls.

Adopted April 1, 1992, eff. Aug. 1, 1992.

Formerly Ill.Rev.Stat.1991, ch. 110A, ¶ 185.

Committee Comments

This rule was adopted as part of a package of measures to increase the use of electronic and telephonic technology and to simplify and make more efficient motion and conference practices. The availability of this alternative procedure may be modified by local rule, inasmuch as telephone conferencing may not be the most efficient way to handle motions, etc., in some circuits or counties.

Rule 186. Reserved

Rule 187. Motions on Grounds of Forum Non Conveniens

(a) **Time for Filing.** A motion to dismiss or transfer the action under the doctrine of *forum non conveniens* must be filed by a party not later than 90 days after the last day allowed for the filing of that party's answer.

(b) **Proceedings on motions.** Hearings on motions to dismiss or transfer the action under the doctrine of *forum non conveniens* shall be scheduled so as to allow the parties sufficient time to conduct discovery on issues of fact raised by such motions. Such motions may be supported and opposed by affidavit. In determining issues of fact raised by affidavits, any competent evidence adduced by the parties shall also be considered. The determination of any issue of fact in connection with such a motion does not constitute a determination of the merits of the case or any aspect thereof.

(c) **Proceedings upon granting of motions.**

(1) *Intrastate transfer of action.* The clerk of the court from which a transfer is granted to another circuit court in this State on the ground of *forum non conveniens* shall immediately certify and trans-

mit to the clerk of the court to which the transfer is ordered the originals of all documents filed in the case together with copies of all orders entered therein. In the event of a severance, certified copies of documents filed and orders entered shall be transmitted. The clerk of the court to which the transfer is ordered shall file the documents and transcript transmitted to him or her and docket the case, and the action shall proceed and be determined as if it had originated in that court. The costs attending a transfer shall be taxed by the clerk of the court from which the transfer is granted, and, together with the filing fee in the transferee court, shall be paid by the party or parties who applied for the transfer.

(2) *Dismissal of action.* Dismissal of an action under the doctrine of *forum non conveniens* shall be upon the following conditions:

(i) if the plaintiff elects to file the action in another forum within six months of the dismissal order, the defendant shall accept service of process from that court; and

(ii) if the statute of limitations has run in the other forum, the defendant shall waive that defense.

If the defendant refuses to abide by these conditions, the cause shall be reinstated for further proceedings in the court in which the dismissal was granted. If the court in the other forum refuses to accept jurisdiction, the plaintiff may, within 30 days of the final order refusing jurisdiction, reinstate the action in the court in which the dismissal was granted. The costs attending a dismissal may be awarded in the discretion of the court.

Adopted Feb. 21, 1986, eff. Aug. 1, 1986. Amended Jan. 4, 2013, eff. immediately.

Formerly Ill.Rev.Stat.1991, ch. 110A, ¶ 187.

Committee Comments
(February 21, 1986)

Rule 187 was adopted, effective August 1, 1986, to provide for the timely filing of motions on *forum non conveniens* grounds (see *Bell v. Louisville & Nashville R.R. Co.* (1985), 106 Ill.2d 135), and to standardize the procedure governing interstate and intrastate *forum non conveniens* motions.

Paragraph (a)

Paragraph (a) calculates the period for filing a *forum non conveniens* motion from the last day allowed for the filing of that party's answer. (Compare Rule 182(a).) Paragraph (a) refers to "*that party's* answer" to insure that a later-joined defendant is not foreclosed from filing a *forum non conveniens* motion by the failure of another defendant to do so in a timely manner.

Paragraph (b)

Paragraph (b) requires that hearings on *forum non conveniens* motions be scheduled to allow the

parties sufficient time to conduct discovery on factual issues raised by such motions. The trial court should exercise its discretion in determining how much time is sufficient.

Paragraph (c)

Paragraph (c)(1) establishes the procedure to be followed when a transfer to another Illinois county on *forum non conveniens* grounds is granted. The procedures to be followed by the clerks of the transferee and transferor courts are similar to those in cases of transfer for wrong venue. See Section 2–106(b) of the Code of Civil Procedure. Attorney fees may not be awarded under this subparagraph.

Paragraph (c)(2) establishes two mandatory conditions to be placed on all dismissals on *forum non conveniens* grounds. If a defendant does not abide by those conditions, the cause is to be reinstated in the court in which the dismissal was granted. If the court in an appropriate forum refuses jurisdiction, the plaintiff has 30 days from the final order refusing jurisdiction to refile the action in the court in which the dismissal was granted. The awarding of costs is discretionary with the trial court. Attorney fees may not be awarded under this subparagraph.

Rules 188 to 190. Reserved

PART D. MOTIONS FOR SUMMARY JUDGMENTS AND EVIDENTIARY AFFIDAVITS

Part D heading was amended eff. July 1, 1971.

Rule 191. Proceedings Under Sections 2–1005, 2–619 and 2–301(b) of the Code of Civil Procedure

(a) Requirements. Motions for summary judgment under section 2–1005 of the Code of Civil Procedure [1] and motions for involuntary dismissal under section 2–619 of the Code of Civil Procedure [2] must be filed before the last date, if any, set by the trial court for the filing of dispositive motions. Affidavits in support of and in opposition to a motion for summary judgment under section 2–1005 of the Code of Civil Procedure, affidavits submitted in connection with a motion for involuntary dismissal under section 2–619 of the Code of Civil Procedure, and affidavits submitted in connection with a motion to contest jurisdiction over the person, as provided by section 2–301 of the Code of Civil Procedure, [3] shall be made on the personal knowledge of the affiants; shall set forth with particularity the facts upon which the claim, counterclaim, or defense is based; shall have attached thereto sworn or certified copies of all documents upon which the affiant relies; shall not consist of conclusions but of facts admissible in evidence; and shall affirmatively show that the affiant, if sworn as a witness, can testify competently thereto. If all of the facts to be shown are not within the personal knowledge of one person, two or more affidavits shall be used.

(b) When Material Facts Are Not Obtainable by Affidavit. If the affidavit of either party contains a statement that any of the material facts which ought to appear in the affidavit are known only to persons whose affidavits affiant is unable to procure by reason of hostility or otherwise, naming the persons and showing why their affidavits cannot be procured and what affiant believes they would testify to if sworn, with his reasons for his belief, the court may make any order that may be just, either granting or refusing the motion, or granting a continuance to permit affidavits to be obtained, or for submitting interrogatories to or taking the depositions of any of the persons so named, or for producing documents in the possession of those persons or furnishing sworn copies thereof. The interrogatories and sworn answers thereto, depositions so taken, and sworn copies of documents so furnished, shall be considered with the affidavits in passing upon the motion.

Amended eff. July 1, 1971; May 28, 1982, eff. July 1, 1982; April 1, 1992, eff. Aug. 1, 1992; March 28, 2002, eff. July 1, 2002; Jan. 4, 2013, eff. immediately.

Formerly Ill.Rev.Stat.1991, ch. 110A, ¶ 191.

1 735 ILCS 5/2–1005.
2 735 ILCS 5/2–619.
3 735 ILCS 5/2–301.

Committee Comments

This is former Rule 15, as it existed before 1964, without change in substance. Note that a discovery deposition or an answer to an interrogatory may be used as if it were an affidavit. (See Rules 212(a)(4) and 213(f).) Paragraph (a) of Rule 191 was amended in 1971 to make the rule applicable to affidavits submitted in connection with special appearances under section 20(2) of the Civil Practice Act to contest jurisdiction over the person.

Sections 2–1005(a) and 2–1005(b) of the Code of Civil Procedure (Ill.Rev.Stat.1989, ch. 110, par. 2–1005) set time limits within which a plaintiff or a defendant may file motions for summary judgment. In 1992, paragraph (a) was amended to require that motions for summary judgment and motions for involuntary dismissal must be filed not later than the last date, if any, set by the court for the filing of dispositive motions.

(March 28, 2002)

The words "special appearance," which formerly appeared in paragraph (a) of Rule 191, were replaced in 2002 with the word "motion" in order to conform to changes in terminology in section 2–301 of the Code of Civil Procedure (735 ILCS 5/2–301 (West 1998)).

Rule 192. Summary Judgments—Multiple Issues

When the entry of a summary judgment will not dispose of all the issues in the case, the court may, as the justice of the case shall require, either (1) allow the motion and postpone the entry of judgment thereon; (2) allow the motion and enter judgment thereon; or (3) allow the motion, enter judgment thereon, and stay the enforcement pending the determination of the remaining issues in the case. If a party resisting the entry of a summary judgment relies upon an affirmative demand against the moving party for an amount less than the latter's demand, judgment for the difference may be entered and enforced.

Formerly Ill.Rev.Stat.1991, ch. 110A, ¶ 192.

Committee Comments

This is former Rule 16 without change in substance.

Rules 193 to 200. Reserved

PART E. DISCOVERY, REQUESTS FOR ADMISSION, AND PRETRIAL PROCEDURE

Rule 201. General Discovery Provisions

(a) Discovery Methods. Information is obtainable as provided in these rules through any of the following discovery methods: depositions upon oral examination or written questions, written interrogatories to parties, discovery of documents, objects or tangible things, inspection of real estate, requests to admit and physical and mental examination of persons. Duplication of discovery methods to obtain the same information and discovery requests that are disproportionate in terms of burden or expense should be avoided.

(b) Scope of Discovery.

(1) *Full Disclosure Required.* Except as provided in these rules, a party may obtain by discovery full disclosure regarding any matter relevant to the subject matter involved in the pending action, whether it relates to the claim or defense of the party seeking disclosure or of any other party, including the existence, description, nature, custody, condition, and location of any documents or tangible things, and the identity and location of persons having knowledge of relevant facts. The word "documents," as used in Part E of Article II, includes, but is not limited to, papers, photographs, films, recordings, memoranda, books, records, accounts, communications and electronically stored information as defined in Rule 201(b)(4).

(2) *Privilege and Work Product.* All matters that are privileged against disclosure on the trial, including privileged communications between a party or his agent and the attorney for the party, are privileged against disclosure through any discovery procedure. Material prepared by or for a party in preparation for trial is subject to discovery only if it does not contain or disclose the theories, mental impressions, or litigation plans of the party's attorney. The court may apportion the cost involved in

originally securing the discoverable material, including when appropriate a reasonable attorney's fee, in such manner as is just.

(3) *Consultant.* A consultant is a person who has been retained or specially employed in anticipation of litigation or preparation for trial but who is not to be called at trial. The identity, opinions, and work product of a consultant are discoverable only upon a showing of exceptional circumstances under which it is impracticable for the party seeking discovery to obtain facts or opinions on the same subject matter by other means.

(4) *Electronically Stored Information.* ("ESI") shall include any writings, drawings, graphs, charts, photographs, sound recordings, images, and other data or data compilations in any medium from which electronically stored information can be obtained either directly or, if necessary, after translation by the responding party into a reasonably usable form.

(c) Prevention of Abuse.

(1) *Protective Orders.* The court may at any time on its own initiative, or on motion of any party or witness, make a protective order as justice requires, denying, limiting, conditioning, or regulating discovery to prevent unreasonable annoyance, expense, embarrassment, disadvantage, or oppression.

(2) *Supervision of Discovery.* Upon the motion of any party or witness, on notice to all parties, or on its own initiative without notice, the court may supervise all or any part of any discovery procedure.

(3) *Proportionality.* When making an order under this Section, the court may determine whether the likely burden or expense of the proposed discovery, including electronically stored information, outweighs the likely benefit, taking into account the amount in controversy, the resources of the parties, the importance of the issues in the litigation, and the importance of the requested discovery in resolving the issues.

(d) Time Discovery May Be Initiated. Prior to the time all defendants have appeared or are required to appear, no discovery procedure shall be noticed or otherwise initiated without leave of court granted upon good cause shown.

(e) Sequence of Discovery. Unless the court upon motion, for the convenience of parties and witnesses and in the interests of justice, orders otherwise, methods of discovery may be used in any sequence, and the fact that a party is conducting discovery shall not operate to delay any other party's discovery.

(f) Diligence in Discovery. The trial of a case shall not be delayed to permit discovery unless due diligence is shown.

(g) Discovery in Small Claims. Discovery in small claims cases is subject to Rule 287.

(h) Discovery in Ordinance Violation Cases. In suits for violation of municipal ordinances where the penalty is a fine only no discovery procedure shall be used prior to trial except by leave of court.

(i) Stipulations. If the parties so stipulate, discovery may take place before any person, for any purpose, at any time or place, and in any manner.

(j) Effect of Discovery Disclosure. Disclosure of any matter obtained by discovery is not conclusive, but may be contradicted by other evidence.

(k) Reasonable Attempt to Resolve Differences Required. The parties shall facilitate discovery under these rules and shall make reasonable attempts to resolve differences over discovery. Every motion with respect to discovery shall incorporate a statement that counsel responsible for trial of the case after personal consultation and reasonable attempts to resolve differences have been unable to reach an accord or that opposing counsel made himself or herself unavailable for personal consultation or was unreasonable in attempts to resolve differences.

(*l*) Discovery Pursuant to Personal Jurisdiction Motion.

(1) While a motion filed under section 2–301 of the Code of Civil Procedure is pending, a party may obtain discovery only on the issue of the court's jurisdiction over the person of the defendant unless: (a) otherwise agreed by the parties; or (b) ordered by the court upon a showing of good cause by the party seeking the discovery that specific discovery is required on other issues.

(2) An objecting party's participation in a hearing regarding discovery, or in discovery as allowed by this rule, shall not constitute a waiver of that party's objection to the court's jurisdiction over the person of the objecting party.

(m) Filing Materials with the Clerk of the Circuit Court. No discovery may be filed with the clerk of the circuit court except by order of court. Local rules shall not require the filing of discovery. Any party serving discovery shall file a certificate of service of discovery document. Service of discovery shall be made in the manner provided for service of documents in Rule 11.

(n) Claims of Privilege. When information or documents are withheld from disclosure or discovery on a claim that they are privileged pursuant to a common law or statutory privilege, any such claim shall be made expressly and shall be supported by a description of the nature of the documents, communications or things not produced or disclosed and the exact privilege which is being claimed.

(*o*) Filing of Discovery Requests to Nonparties. Notwithstanding the foregoing, a copy of any discovery request under these rules to any nonparty shall be filed with the clerk in accord with Rule 104(b).

(p) Asserting Privilege or Work Product Following Discovery Disclosure. If information inadvertently produced in discovery is subject to a claim of privilege or of work-product protection, the party making the claim may notify any party that received the information of the claim and the basis for it. After being notified, each receiving party must promptly return, sequester, or destroy the specified information and any copies; must not use or disclose the information until the claim is resolved; must take reasonable steps to retrieve the information if the receiving party disclosed the information to third parties before being notified; and may promptly present the information to the court under seal for a determination of the claim. The producing party must also preserve the information until the claim is resolved.

Amended eff. Sept. 1, 1974; Sept. 29, 1978, eff. Nov. 1, 1978; Jan. 5, 1981, eff. Feb. 1, 1981; May 28, 1982, eff. July 1, 1982; June 19, 1989, eff. Aug. 1, 1989; June 1, 1995, eff. Jan. 1, 1996; March 28, 2002, eff. July 1, 2002; Oct. 24, 2012, eff. Jan. 1, 2013; Nov. 28, 2012, eff. Jan. 1, 2013; May 29, 2014, eff. July 1, 2014; July 30, 2014, corrected *nunc pro tunc* May 29, 2014.

Formerly Ill.Rev.Stat.1991, ch. 110A, ¶ 201.

Committee Comments
(Revised May 29, 2014)
Paragraph (b)

Paragraph (b), subparagraph (1) was amended to conform with the definition in newly added paragraph (b), subparagraph (4) and complies with the Federal Rules of Civil Procedure.

Paragraph (b), subparagraph (4) was added to provide a definition of electronically stored information that comports with the Federal Rule of Civil Procedure 34(a)(1)(a) and is intended to be flexible and expansive as technology changes.

Paragraph (c)

Subparagraph (3) was added to address the production of materials when benefits do not outweigh the burden of producing them, especially in the area of electronically stored information ("ESI").

The proportionality analysis called for by subparagraph (3) often may indicate that the following categories of ESI should not be discoverable; (A) "deleted," "slack," "fragmented," or "unallocated" data on hard drives; (B) random access memory ("RAM") or other ephemeral data; (C) on-line access data; (D) data in metadata fields that are frequently updated automatically; (E) backup data that is substantially duplicative of data that is more accessible elsewhere; (F) legacy data; (G) information whose retrieval cannot be accomplished without substantial additional programming or without transforming it into another form before search and retrieval can be achieved; and (H) other forms of ESI whose preservation or production requires extraordinary affirmative measures. *See* Seventh Circuit Electronic Discovery Committee, "Principles Relating to the Discovery of Electronically Stored

Information," Principle 2.04(d). In other cases, however, the proportionality analysis may support the discovery of some of the types of ESI on this list. Moreover, this list is not static, since technological changes eventually might reduce the cost of producing some of these types of ESI. Subparagraph (3) requires a case-bycase analysis. If any party intends to request the preservation or production of potentially burdensome categories of ESI, then that intention should be addressed at the initial case management conference in accordance with Supreme Court Rule 218(a)(10) or as soon thereafter as practicable.

Paragraph (p)

This provision is referred to as the "clawback" provision and comports with the new Code of Ethics requirement that if an attorney receives privileged documents, he or she must notify the other side.

Committee Comments
(October 24, 2012)

Paragraph (m) was amended in 2012 to eliminate the filing of discovery with the clerk of the circuit court absent leave of court granted in individual cases based on limited circumstances. The rule is intended to minimize any invasion of privacy that a litigant may have by filing discovery in a public court file.

Committee Comments
(March 28, 2002)
Paragraph (*l*)

The words "special appearance," which formerly appeared in paragraph (1) of Rule 201(*l*), were replaced in 2002 with the word "motion" in order to conform to changes in terminology in section 2–301 of the Code of Civil Procedure (735 ILCS 5/2–301 (West 1998)).

Since the amendment to section 2–301 allows a party to file a combined motion, it is possible that discovery could proceed on issues other than the court's jurisdiction over a party's person prior to the court ruling on the objection to jurisdiction. While the court may allow discovery on issues other than the court's jurisdiction over the person of the defendant prior to a ruling on the defendant's objection to jurisdiction, it is expected that in most cases discovery would not be expanded by the court to other issues until the jurisdictional objection is ruled upon. It sometimes may be logical for the court to allow specific, requested discovery on other issues, for example, where a witness is about to die or leave the country, when the party requesting the additional discovery makes a prima facie showing that the party will suffer substantial injustice if the requested discovery is not allowed.

Paragraph (2) recognizes that discovery may proceed on other than jurisdictional issues before the court rules on the objecting party's motion objecting to jurisdiction. Participation in discovery by the objecting party does not constitute a waiver by the objecting party's challenge to jurisdiction.

Committee Comments
(Revised June 1, 1995)
Paragraph (a)

Paragraph (a) of this rule sets forth the four discovery methods provided for and cautions against duplication. The committee considered and discarded a provision requiring leave of court before a party could request by one discovery method information already obtained through another. The committee concluded that there are circumstances in which it is justifiable to require answers to the same or related questions by different types of discovery procedures but felt strongly that the rules should discourage time-wasting repetition; hence the provision that duplication should be avoided. This language is precatory but in the application of the medical examination rule, and in the determination of what is unreasonable annoyance under paragraph (c) of this rule, dealing with prevention of abuse, such a phrase has the beneficial effect of drawing particular attention to the question whether the information sought has already been made available to the party seeking it so that further discovery should be curtailed.

Paragraph (b)

Paragraph (b), subparagraph (1), sets forth generally the scope of discovery under the rules. The language "any matter relevant to the subject matter involved in the pending action" is the language presently employed in Federal Rule 26. The Federal rule also contains the sentence: "It is not ground for objection that the testimony will be inadmissible at the trial if the information sought appears reasonably calculated to lead to the discovery of admissible evidence." The Joint Committee Comments that accompanied former Illinois Rule 19–4 indicate that a similar sentence appearing in the pre–1970 Federal rule was deliberately omitted from the Illinois rule and suggest that perhaps the language "relating to the merits of the matter in litigation" was intended to limit discovery to evidence. This language was not construed in this restrictive fashion, however. (See *Monier v. Chamberlain*, 31 Ill. 2d 400, 202 N.E.2d 15 (1964), 66 Ill. App. 2d 472, 213 N.E.2d 425 (3d Dist. 1966), aff'd, 35 Ill. 2d 351, 221 N.E.2d 410 (1966); *People ex rel. Terry v. Fisher*, 12 Ill. 2d 231, 145 N.E.2d 588 (1957); *Krupp v. Chicago Transit Authority*, 8 Ill. 2d 37, 132 N.E.2d 532 (1956).) The only other effect the term "merits" could have would be to prevent discovery of information relating to jurisdiction, a result the committee thought undesirable. Accordingly, the phrase "relevant to the subject matter" was substituted for "relating to the merits of the matter in litigation" as more accurately reflecting the case law.

The phrase "identity and location of persons having knowledge of relevant facts," which appears in both former Rule 19–4 and Federal Rule 26, was retained. This language has been interpreted to require that the interrogating party frame his request in terms of some stated fact rather than simply in the language of the rule, because the use of the broad term "relevant facts" places on the answering party the undue burden of determining relevancy. See *Reske v. Klein*, 33 Ill. App. 2d 302, 305–06, 179 N.E.2d 415 (1st Dist. 1962); *Fedors v. O'Brien*, 39 Ill. App. 2d 407, 412–13, 188 N.E.2d 739 (1st Dist. 1963); *Nelson v. Pals*, 51 Ill. App. 2d 269, 273–75, 201 N.E.2d 187 (1st Dist. 1964); *Grant v. Paluch*, 61 Ill. App. 2d 247, 210 N.E.2d 35 (1st Dist. 1965).

The definition of "documents" in subparagraph (b)(1) has been expanded to include "all retrievable information in computer storage." This amendment recognizes the increasing reliability on computer technology and thus obligates a party to produce on paper those relevant materials which have been stored electronically.

The first sentence of subparagraph (b)(2) is derived from the first sentence of former Rule 19–5(1). The second sentence was new. It constituted a restatement of the law on the subject of work product as it had developed in the cases decided over the previous decade. See *Monier v. Chamberlain*, 35 Ill. 2d 351, 221 N.E.2d 410 (1966), aff'g 66 Ill. App. 2d 472, 213 N.E.2d 425 (3d Dist. 1966); *Stimpert v. Abdnour*, 24 Ill. 2d 26, 179 N.E.2d 602 (1962); *Day v. Illinois Power Co.*, 50 Ill. App. 2d 52, 199 N.E.2d 802 (5th Dist. 1964); *Oberkircher v. Chicago Transit Authority*, 41 Ill. App. 2d 68, 190 N.E.2d 170 (1st Dist. 3d Div. 1963); *Haskell v. Siegmund*, 28 Ill. App. 2d 1, 170 N.E.2d 393 (3d Dist. 1960); see also *City of Chicago v. Harrison–Halsted Building Corp.*, 11 Ill. 2d 431, 435, 143 N.E.2d 40 (1957), and *City of Chicago v. Shayne*, 46 Ill. App. 2d 33, 40, 196 N.E.2d 521 (1st Dist. 1964). The final sentence of this subparagraph was new and is intended to prevent penalizing the diligent and rewarding the slothful.

Discovery of consultants as provided by Rule 201(b)(3) will be proper only in extraordinary cases. In general terms, the "exceptional circumstances" provision is designed to permit discovery of consultants only when it is "impracticable" for a party to otherwise obtain facts or opinions on the same subject. Discovery under the corresponding Federal provision, Rule 26(b)(4)(B) of the Federal Rules of Civil Procedure, has generally been understood as being appropriate, for example, in cases in which an item of physical evidence is no longer available because of destructive testing and the adversary's consultant is the only source of information about the item, or in cases in which all the experts in a field have been retained by other parties and it is not possible for the party seeking discovery to obtain his or her own expert.

Paragraph (c)

Subparagraph (c)(1) covers the substance of former Rule 19–5(2). That rule listed a number of possible protective orders, ending with the catchall phrase, "or *** any other order which justice requires to protect party or deponent from annoyance, embarrassment, or oppression." Subparagraph (c)(2) substitutes the language "denying, limiting, conditioning, or regulating discovery to prevent unreasonable annoyance, expense, embarrassment, disadvantage, or oppression." The list of possible discovery orders was deleted as unnecessary in view of the broader language of the new rule. The change in language is by way of clarification and was not intended to effect any change in the broad discretion to make protective orders that was provided by former Rule 19–5(2). See *Stowers v. Carp*, 29 Ill. App. 2d 52, 172 N.E.2d 370 (2d Dist. 1961).

Subparagraph (c)(2), like subparagraph (c)(1), is designed to clarify rather than change the Illinois practice. The committee was of the opinion that under certain circumstances it might be desirable for the trial court to direct that discovery proceed under its direct supervision, and that this practice might be unusual enough to call for special mention in the rule. The language was taken from section 3104 of the New York Civil Practice Act.

Paragraph (d)

Paragraph (d) of this rule makes it clear that except by order of court discovery procedures may not be initiated before the defendants have appeared or are required to appear. Former Rule 19–1 provided that depositions could not be taken before the defendants had appeared or were required to appear, and former Rule 19–11 made the time requirements for taking depositions applicable to the serving of interrogatories. The former rules, however, left the plaintiff free to serve notice at any time after the commencement of the action of the taking of a deposition, just as long as the taking was scheduled after the date on which the defendants were required to appear, a practice which the bar has found objectionable.

Paragraph (e)

Paragraph (e), as adopted in 1967, provided that unless otherwise ordered "depositions and other discovery procedures shall be conducted in the sequence in which they are noticed or otherwise initiated." The effect of this provision was to give the last defendant served priority in discovery, since he could determine the date of his appearance. In 1978, this paragraph was amended to adopt the practice followed in the Federal courts since 1970, permitting all parties to proceed with discovery simultaneously unless the court orders otherwise. While empirical studies conducted preliminary to the proposals for amendment of the Federal discovery rules adopted in 1970 indicate that both defendants and plaintiffs are so often dilatory in beginning their discovery that a race for priority does not occur very frequently, affording a priority based on first notice in some cases can result in postponing the other parties' discovery for a very long time. (See Advisory Committee Note to Fed. R. Civ. P. 26.) In most cases it appears more efficient to permit each party to proceed with its discovery, whether by deposition or otherwise, unless in the interests of justice the establishment of priority seems to be called for. The amended rule reserves to the court the power to make such an order. In most instances, however, problems of timing should be worked out between counsel. See paragraph (k).

Paragraph (f)

Paragraph (f) of this rule is derived from the last sentence of former Rule 19–1. The language is unchanged except that it is made applicable to all discovery proceedings.

Paragraph (g)

Paragraph (g) of this rule is a cross-reference to Rule 287, which provides that discovery is not permitted without leave of court in small claims cases, defined in Rule 281 as actions for money not in excess of $2,500, or for the collection of taxes not in excess of that amount.

Paragraph (h)

Rule 201 was amended in 1974 to add paragraph (h) and to reletter former paragraphs (h) and (i) as (i) and (j). Paragraph (h) extends to ordinance violation cases the principle applicable to small claims that discovery procedures under the rules may not be used without leave of court.

Paragraph (i)

Paragraph (i) of this rule makes the provisions of former Rule 19–3, dealing with stipulations for the taking of depositions, applicable to discovery in general. As originally adopted this paragraph was (h). It was relettered (i) in 1974, when the present paragraph (h) was added.

Paragraph (j)

Paragraph (j) of this rule is derived from the last sentence of former Rule 20. The language is unchanged. As originally adopted, this was paragraph (i). It was relettered (j) when present paragraph (h) was added in 1974.

Paragraph (k)

Paragraph (k) was added in 1974. Patterned after the practice in the United States District Courts for the Eastern and Northern Districts of Illinois, it is designed to curtail undue delay in the administration of justice and to discourage motions of a routine nature.

Paragraph (k) was amended to remedy several problems associated with discovery. Language has been added to encourage attorneys to try and resolve discovery differences on their own. Also, committee members cited the problem of junior attorneys, who are not ultimately responsible for cases, perpetuating discovery disagreements. It was agreed that many discovery differences could be eliminated if the attorneys responsible for trying the case were involved in attempts to resolve discovery differences. Reasonable attempts must be made to resolve discovery disputes prior to bringing a motion for sanctions. Counsel responsible for the trial of a case are required to have or attempt a personal consultation before a motion with respect to discovery is initiated. The last sentence of paragraph (k) has been deleted, as the consequences of failing to comply with discovery are discussed in Rule 219.

Paragraph (*l*)

Paragraph (*l*) was added in 1981 to negate any possible inference from the language of section 20 of the Civil Practice Act that participation in discovery proceedings after making a special appearance to contest personal jurisdiction constitutes a general appearance and waives the jurisdictional objection, so long as the discovery is limited to the issue of personal jurisdiction.

Paragraph (m)

Paragraph (m) was added in 1989. The new paragraph allows the circuit courts to adopt local rules to regulate or prohibit the filing of designated discovery materials with the clerk. The identity of the affected materials should be designated in the local rules, as should any procedures to compel the filing of materials that would otherwise not be filed under the local rules.

Paragraphs (n) and (o)

Regarding paragraph (n), any claim of privilege with respect to a document must be stated specifically pursuant to this rule. Pursuant to paragraph (o), all discovery filed upon a nonparty shall be filed with the clerk of the court.

Rule 202. Purposes for Which Depositions May be Taken in a Pending Action

Any party may take the testimony of any party or person by deposition upon oral examination or written questions for the purpose of discovery or for use as evidence in the action. The notice, order, or stipulation to take a deposition shall specify whether the deposition is to be a discovery deposition or an evidence deposition. In the absence of specification a deposition is a discovery deposition only. If both discovery and evidence depositions are desired of the same witness they shall be taken separately, unless the parties stipulate otherwise or the court orders otherwise upon notice and motion. If the evidence deposition of a witness is to be taken within 21 days of trial, a discovery deposition is not permitted unless the parties stipulate otherwise or the court orders otherwise upon notice and motion.

Amended June 1, 1995, eff. Jan. 1, 1996.

Formerly Ill.Rev.Stat.1991, ch. 110A, ¶ 202.

Committee Comments

This rule is former Rule 19 with minor language changes but no changes of substance. The rule preserves the distinction that has been made in Illinois between a deposition taken for discovery purposes and one taken for evidence. See Rule 212, dealing with the use of discovery depositions and evidence depositions at the trial.

Pursuant to the amended language of this rule, an evidence deposition may be taken within 21 days of trial without a discovery deposition. This change is to ensure that there will no longer be delays in commencing a trial because an attorney wanted a separate discovery deposition prior to taking an evidence deposition shortly before trial without leave of court or stipulation.

Rule 203. Where Depositions May be Taken

Unless otherwise agreed, depositions shall be taken in the county in which the deponent resides or is employed or transacts business in person, or, in the case of a plaintiff-deponent, in the county in which the action is pending. However, the court, in its discretion, may order a party or a person who is currently an officer, director, or employee of a party to appear at a designated place in this State or elsewhere for the purpose of having the deposition taken. The order designating the place of a deposition may impose any terms and conditions that are just, including payment of reasonable expenses.

Amended June 26, 1987, eff. Aug. 1, 1987; June 1, 1995, eff. Jan. 1, 1996.

Formerly Ill.Rev.Stat.1991, ch. 110A, ¶ 203.

Committee Comments
(Revised June 1, 1995)

This rule is derived from former Rule 19—8(3). There is one change of substance. The phrase "or a nonresident for whose benefit the action is brought" has been added to require that not only the nominal plaintiff but the person for whose benefit the action is brought must present himself for the taking of his deposition.

Supreme Court Rule 203 was amended contemporaneously with the change in 206(a) in 1987 to protect nonparty witnesses from unwarranted interference with their business and/or personal lives which might otherwise occur when Rule 206(a) is employed.

The only revision which has been made to this rule is one of form, which makes the rule gender-neutral.

Rule 204. Compelling Appearance of Deponent

(a) Action Pending in This State.

(1) *Subpoenas.* Except as provided in paragraph (c) hereof: (i) the clerk of the court shall issue subpoenas on request; or (ii) subpoenas may be issued by an attorney admitted to practice in the State of Illinois who is currently counsel of record in the pending action. The subpoena may command the person to whom it is directed to produce documents or tangible things which constitute or contain evidence relating to any of the matters within the scope of the examination permitted under these rules subject to any limitations imposed under Rule 201(c).

(2) *Service of Subpoenas.* A deponent shall respond to any lawful subpoena of which the deponent has actual knowledge, if payment of the fee and mileage has been tendered. Service of a subpoena by mail may be proved prima facie by a return receipt showing delivery to the deponent or his

authorized agent by certified or registered mail at least seven days before the date on which appearance is required and an affidavit showing that the mailing was prepaid and was addressed to the deponent, restricted delivery, return receipt requested, showing to whom, date and address of delivery, with a check or money order for the fee and mileage enclosed.

(3) *Notice to Parties, et al.* Service of notice of the taking of the deposition of a party or person who is currently an officer, director, or employee of a party is sufficient to require the appearance of the deponent and the production of any documents or tangible things listed in the notice.

(4) *Production of Documents in Lieu of Appearance of Deponent.* The notice, order or stipulation to take a deposition may specify that the appearance of the deponent is excused, and that no deposition will be taken, if copies of specified documents or tangible things are served on the party or attorney requesting the same by a date certain. That party or attorney shall serve all requesting parties of record at least three days prior to the scheduled deposition, with true and complete copies of all documents, and shall make available for inspection tangible things, or other materials furnished, and shall file a certificate of compliance with the court. Unless otherwise ordered or agreed, reasonable charges by the deponent for production in accordance with this procedure shall be paid by the party requesting the same, and all other parties shall pay reasonable copying and delivery charges for materials they receive. A copy of any subpoena issued in connection with such a deposition shall be attached to the notice and immediately filed with the court, not less than 14 days prior to the scheduled deposition. The use of this procedure shall not bar the taking of any person's deposition or limit the scope of same.

(b) Action Pending in Another State, Territory, or Country. Any officer or person authorized by the laws of another State, territory, or country to take any deposition in this State, with or without a commission, in any action pending in a court of that State, territory, or country may petition the circuit court in the county in which the deponent resides or is employed or transacts business in person or is found for a subpoena to compel the appearance of the deponent or for an order to compel the giving of testimony by the deponent. The court may hear and act upon the petition with or without notice as the court directs.

(c) Depositions of Physicians. The discovery depositions of nonparty physicians being deposed in their professional capacity may be taken only with the agreement of the parties and the subsequent consent of the deponent or under a subpoena issued upon order of court. A party shall pay a reasonable fee to a physician for the time he or she will spend testifying at any such deposition. Unless the physician was

retained by a party for the purpose of rendering an opinion at trial, or unless otherwise ordered by the court, the fee shall be paid by the party at whose instance the deposition is taken.

(d) Noncompliance by Nonparties: Body Attachment.

(1) An order of body attachment upon a nonparty for noncompliance with a discovery order or subpoena shall not issue without proof of personal service of the rule to show cause or order of contempt upon the nonparty.

(2) The service of the rule to show cause or order of contempt upon the nonparty, except when the rule or order is initiated by the court, shall include a copy of the petition for rule and the discovery order or subpoena which is the basis for the petition for rule.

(3) The service of the rule to show cause or order of contempt upon the nonparty shall be made in the same manner as service of summons provided for under sections 2–202, 2–203(a)(1) and 2–203.1 of the Code of Civil Procedure.

Amended eff. June 23, 1967; amended Oct. 21, 1969, eff. Jan. 1, 1970; Sept. 29, 1978, eff. Nov. 1, 1978; July 1, 1985, eff. Aug. 1, 1985; Nov. 21, 1988, eff. Jan. 1, 1989; June 19, 1989, eff. Aug. 1, 1989; amended June 1, 1995, eff. Jan. 1, 1996; amended, eff. June 11, 2009; amended, eff. Dec. 16, 2010; May 29, 2014, eff. July 1, 2014.

Formerly Ill.Rev.Stat.1991, ch. 110A, ¶ 204.

Committee Comments
(Revised June 1, 1995)

Paragraph (a) of this rule was revised effective June 23, 1967, to divide it into three subparagraphs and add the material contained in subparagraph (a)(2), dealing with service of subpoenas.

The first sentence of the subparagraph (a)(2) states existing law. (*Chicago and Aurora R.R. Co. v. Dunning* (1857), 18 Ill. 494.) The second sentence simplifies proof of actual notice when service is made by certified or registered mail. It was amended in 1978 to conform its requirements to presently available postal delivery service. See Committee Comments to Rule 105.

Subparagraphs (a)(1) and (a)(3), without their present subtitles, appeared as paragraph (a) of Rule 204(a) as adopted effective January 1, 1967. New at that time was the provision now in subparagraph (a)(1) making an order of the court a prerequisite to the issuance of subpoena for the discovery deposition of a physician or surgeon. Also new in the 1967 rule was the use of the term "employee" instead of the former "managing agent" in what is now subparagraph (a)(3). The phrase "and no subpoena is necessary" which appeared in former Rule 19—8(1) (effective January 1, 1956), on which Rule 204(a) was based, was placed there to emphasize a change in practice to which the bar had been accustomed by 1967, and it was deleted in the 1967 revision as no longer needed.

Subparagraph (4) of paragraph (a) sets forth the procedures to be followed in those instances where the production of documents or tangible things by an individual may obviate the need for taking that person's deposition. The rule recognizes that subpoenas must be directed to individuals, not inanimate objects. Existing law regarding privilege and permissible discovery in a given case is unaffected by the rule. (See *Lewis v. Illinois Central R.R. Co.*, 234 Ill. App. 3d 669 (5th Dist. 1992).) The rule requires disclosure to all parties with prompt and complete production of all materials received, regardless of whether materials in addition to those specified are furnished by the deponent.

Paragraph (b) was not affected by the June 23, 1967, amendment. It was derived from former Rule 19—8(2) as it stood before 1967.

In 1985 paragraph (a) was amended and paragraph (c) was added to regulate the practice of compelling physicians and surgeons to appear to be deposed in their professional capacity and to set guidelines concerning professional fees which may, by agreement, be paid to physicians and surgeons for attending such depositions. Traditionally, expert witnesses are in the same position as other witnesses with respect to their fees. (*In re Estate of James* (1956), 10 Ill. App. 2d 232.) Physicians and other experts subpoenaed to testify may not refuse to do so on the ground that they are entitled to be paid some additional fee on the basis of being an expert. (*Dixon v. People* (1897), 168 Ill. 179.) Expert witnesses, like other witnesses, normally are entitled only to $20 per day and 20 cents per mile of necessary travel. (*Falkenthal v. Public Building Com.* (1983), 111 Ill. App. 3d 703.) As a practical matter, however, physicians and surgeons usually do request a professional fee, in addition to the statutory witness fee, to reimburse them for the time they spend testifying at depositions, and the party at whose instance the physician or surgeon is subpoenaed is normally loathe to refuse. This rule is intended to regulate this practice. A party may agree to pay a reasonable professional fee to a physician or surgeon for the time he or she will spend testifying at any deposition. The fee should be paid only after the doctor has testified, and it should not exceed an amount which reasonably reimburses the doctor for the time he or she actually spent testifying at deposition. Unless the doctor was retained for the purpose of rendering an expert opinion at trial, or unless otherwise ordered by the court, the party at whose instance the deposition is being taken would be responsible for paying the professional fee, as well as other fees and expenses provided for in Rule 208.

Rule 204(c) implies that the trial court will exercise discretion in ordering the issuance of a subpoena upon a physician or surgeon and will refuse to do so unless there is some preliminary showing of good cause, regardless of whether there has been an objection by opposing counsel. At a minimum the moving party must be able to show that he has received the medical records available in the case and nevertheless has good reason to believe that a deposition is necessary. If appropriate, the court may require that such a showing of good cause be accomplished by an affidavit accompanying the motion.

Paragraph (c) was amended in 1989 to provide that a party "shall pay," rather than "may agree to pay," a reasonable fee to a physician or surgeon for the time the physician or surgeon will spend testifying at any such deposition. This change will clarify the responsibility of parties to not intrude on the time of physicians and surgeons without seeing to it that the physicians or surgeons receive reasonable compensation for the time they spend undergoing questioning on deposition.

The reference in paragraph (c) to "surgeons" has been stricken because it is redundant. Moreover, paragraph (c) is made applicable only to "nonparty" physicians. The protection afforded a physician by paragraph (c), including the payment of a fee for time spent, has no application to a physician who is a party to the suit. Such protection should likewise be unavailable to nonparty physicians who are closely associated with a party, such as physicians who are stockholders in or officers of a professional corporation named as a defendant, or a physician who is a respondent in discovery.

Rule 205. Persons Before Whom Depositions May Be Taken

(a) Within the United States. Within the United States or within a territory or insular possession subject to the dominion of the United States, depositions shall be taken (1) before an officer authorized to administer oaths by the laws of this State or of the United States or of the place where the examination is held, or (2) before a person appointed by the court. The officer or person is empowered to administer oaths and take testimony. Whenever the term "officer" is used in these rules, it includes a person appointed by the court unless the context indicates otherwise.

(b) In Foreign Countries. In a foreign state or country depositions shall be taken (1) before a secretary of embassy, consul general, consul, vice-consul, or consular agent of the United States, or any officer authorized to administer oaths under the laws of this State, or of the United States, or of the place where the examination is held, or (2) before a person appointed by the court. The officer or person is empowered to administer oaths and take testimony.

(c) Issuance of Commissions and Letters Rogatory. A commission, dedimus potestatem, or letter rogatory is not required but if desired shall be issued by the clerk without notice. An officer may be designated in a commission either by name or descriptive title and a letter rogatory may be addressed "To the Appropriate Authority in (here name the country)."

(d) Disqualification for Interest. No deposition shall be taken before a person who is a relative of or attorney for any of the parties, a relative of the attorney, or financially interested in the action.

Formerly Ill.Rev.Stat.1991, ch. 110A, ¶ 205.

Committee Comments
Paragraphs (a) and (b)

Paragraphs (a) and (b) of this rule are derived from former Rule 19—2(1), (2), and (3) with minor language changes, but no changes of substance.

Paragraph (c)

Paragraph (c) is derived from former Rule 19—2(4). The reference to letters rogatory was added because, though requests for them may be rare in State practice, there may be occasional situations in which they are required. See N.Y. CPA § 3113(a)3 and Rule 28(b) of the Federal Rules of Civil Procedure.

Paragraph (d)

Paragraph (d) is former Rule 19—2(5) with minor language changes.

Rule 206. Method of Taking Depositions on Oral Examination

(a) Notice of Examination; Time and Place. A party desiring to take the deposition of any person upon oral examination shall serve notice in writing a reasonable time in advance on the other parties. The notice shall state the time and place for taking the deposition; the name and address of each person to be examined, if known, or, if unknown, information sufficient to identify the deponent; and whether the deposition is for purposes of discovery or for use in evidence.

(1) *Representative Deponent.* A party may in the notice and in a subpoena, if required, name as the deponent a public or private corporation or a partnership or association or governmental agency and describe with reasonable particularity the matters on which examination is requested. In that event, the organization so named shall designate one or more officers, directors, or managing agents, or other persons to testify on its behalf, and may set forth, for each person designated, the matters on which that person will testify. The subpoena shall advise a nonparty organization of its duty to make such a designation. The persons so designated shall testify as to matters known or reasonably available to the organization.

(2) *Audio–Visual Recording to be Used.* If a party serving notice of deposition intends to record the deponent's testimony by use of an audio-visual recording device, the notice of deposition must so advise all parties to the deposition. If any other party intends to record the testimony of the witness by use of an audiovisual recording device, notice of that intent must likewise be served upon all other parties a reasonable time in advance. Such notices shall contain the name of the recording-device operator. After notice is given that a deposition will be recorded by an audio-visual recording device, any party may make a motion for relief in the form of a protective order under Rule 201. If a hearing is not held prior to the taking of the deposition, the recording shall be made subject to the court's ruling at a later time.

If the deposition is to be taken pursuant to a subpoena, a copy of the subpoena shall be attached to the notice. On motion of any party upon whom the notice is served, the court, for cause shown, may extend or shorten the time. Unless otherwise agreed by the parties or ordered by the court, depositions shall not be taken on Saturdays, Sundays, or court holidays.

(b) Any Party Entitled to Take Deposition Pursuant to a Notice. When a notice of the taking of a deposition has been served, any party may take a deposition under the notice, in which case the party shall pay the fees and charges payable by the party at whose instance a deposition is taken.

(c) Scope and Manner of Examination and Cross–Examination.

(1) The deponent in a discovery deposition may be examined regarding any matter subject to discovery under these rules. The deponent may be questioned by any party as if under cross-examination.

(2) In an evidence deposition the examination and cross-examination shall be the same as though the deponent were testifying at the trial.

(3) Objections at depositions shall be concise, stating the exact legal nature of the objection.

(d) Duration of Discovery Deposition. No discovery deposition of any party or witness shall exceed three hours regardless of the number of parties involved in the case, except by stipulation of all parties or by order upon showing that good cause warrants a lengthier examination.

(e) Motion to Terminate or Limit Examination. At any time during the taking of the deposition, on motion of any party or of the deponent and upon a showing that the examination is being conducted in bad faith or in any manner that unreasonably annoys, embarrasses, or oppresses the deponent or party, the court may order that the examination cease forthwith or may limit the scope and manner of taking the examination as provided by these rules. An examination terminated by the order shall be resumed only upon further order of the court. Upon the demand of the objecting party or deponent, the taking of the deposition shall be suspended for the time necessary to present a motion for an order. The court may require any party, attorney or deponent to pay costs or expenses, including reasonable attorney fees, or both, as the court may deem reasonable.

(f) Record of Examination; Oath; Objections. The officer before whom the deposition is to be taken shall put the witness on oath and shall personally, or by someone acting under the officer's direction and in his or her presence, record the testimony of the witness. The testimony shall be taken stenographically, by sound-recording device, by audio-visual recording device, or by any combination of all three. The testimony shall be transcribed at the request of any party. Objections made at the time of the examination to the qualifications of the officer taking the deposition, to the manner of taking it, to the evidence presented, or to the conduct of any person, and any other objection to the proceedings, shall be included in the deposition. Evidence objected to shall be taken subject to the objection. In lieu of participating in the oral examination, parties served with notice of taking a deposition may transmit written questions to the officer, who shall propound them to the witness and record the answers verbatim.

(g) Videotaped Depositions. Except as otherwise provided in this rule, the rules governing the practice, procedures and use of depositions shall apply to videotaped depositions.

(1) Depositions which are to be recorded on an audio-visual recording device shall begin by the operator of the device stating, on camera, (1) the operator's name and address, (2) the date, time and place of the deposition, (3) the caption of the case, (4) the name of the witness, (5) the party on whose behalf the deposition is being taken, and (6) the party at whose instance the deposition is being recorded on an audio-visual recording device. The officer before whom the deposition is being taken shall identify himself or herself and swear the witness on camera. At the conclusion of the deposition the operator shall state on camera that the deposition is concluded. If the deposition requires the use of more than one videotape, the end of each videotape and the beginning of each succeeding tape shall be announced on camera by the operator.

(2) The operator shall initially take custody of the videotape of the deposition and shall run through the videotape to determine the exact length of time of the deposition. The operator shall sign an affidavit stating the length of time of the deposition and shall certify that the videotape is a true record of the deposition and shall certify that the operator has not edited or otherwise altered the videotape. A deposition so certified requires no further proof of authenticity. If requested by any party at the conclusion of the taking of the deposition, the operator shall make a copy of the videotape and deliver it to the party requesting it at the cost of that party.

(3) A videotape of a deposition for purposes of discovery only shall be returned to the attorney for the party at whose instance the deposition was videotaped. Said attorney is responsible for the safeguarding of the videotape and shall permit the viewing of and shall provide a copy of the videotape upon the request and at the cost of any party. A videotape of a discovery deposition shall not be filed with the court except by leave of court for good cause shown.

(4) A videotape of a deposition for use in evidence shall be securely sealed by the operator, in an envelope bearing the title and number of the action, and marked "Deposition(s) of (here insert name(s) of deponent(s))," and promptly filed or sent by certified mail to the clerk of the court for filing. Upon payment of reasonable charges therefor, the operator shall furnish a copy of the videotape to any party or the deponent.

(5) The party at whose instance the videotaped deposition is taken shall pay the charges of the videotape operator for attending and shall pay any charges for filing the videotape of an evidence deposition.

(6) The videotape of a deposition may be presented at trial in lieu of reading from the stenographic transcription of the deposition.

(h) Remote Electronic Means Depositions. Any party may take a deposition by telephone, videoconference, or other remote electronic means by stating in the notice the specific electronic means to be used for the deposition, subject to the right to object. For the purposes of Rule 203, Rule 205, and this rule, such a deposition is deemed taken at the place where the deponent is to answer questions. Except as otherwise provided in this paragraph (h), the rules governing the practice, procedures and use of depositions shall apply to remote electronic means depositions.

(1) The deponent shall be in the presence of the officer administering the oath and recording the deposition, unless otherwise agreed by the parties.

(2) Any exhibits or other demonstrative evidence to be presented to the deponent by any party at the deposition shall be provided to the officer administering the oath and all other parties within a reasonable period of time prior to the deposition.

(3) Nothing in this paragraph (h) shall prohibit any party from being with the deponent during the deposition, at that party's expense; provided, however, that a party attending a deposition shall give written notice of that party's intention to appear at the deposition to all other parties within a reasonable time prior to the deposition.

(4) The party at whose instance the remote electronic means deposition is taken shall pay all costs of the remote electronic means deposition, unless otherwise agreed by the parties.

Amended Sept. 8, 1975, eff. Oct. 1, 1975; Jan. 5, 1981, eff. Feb. 1, 1981; July 1, 1985, eff. Aug. 1, 1985; June 26, 1987, eff. Aug. 1, 1987; amended June 1, 1995, eff. Jan. 1, 1996; Oct. 22, 1999, eff. Dec. 1, 1999; amended eff. Feb. 16, 2011.

Formerly Ill.Rev.Stat.1991, ch. 110A, ¶ 206.

Committee Comments
(Revised October 22, 1999)

Paragraph (a)

Paragraph (a) of this rule is derived from former Rule 19–6(1). The requirement that the notice state the name or title of the person before whom a deposition is to be taken has been eliminated, and the phrase "if the name is not known, a general description" changed to "if unknown, information." The penultimate sentence is new. "Subpoena," of course, includes a subpoena *duces tecum.*

In 1985, Rule 206 was amended to allow audio-visual recordation of depositions upon notice, without a requirement that the parties obtain leave of court.

Paragraph (a) was amended in 1985 to bar depositions from being taken on Saturday, Sunday or court holidays, unless otherwise ordered by the court.

Paragraph (a) was amended in 1987 to add paragraph (a)(1) on representative deponents. The procedure is substantially similar to the procedure set forth in Federal Rule of Civil Procedure 30(b). The intent of the rule is to provide a mechanism for obtaining information without representative depositions. Failure to comply with the rules should call for appropriate sanctions.

Supreme Court Rule 203 was amended contemporaneously with the change in 206(a) in 1987. The elimination of the court's discretion to order depositions "in any other place designated by an order of the court" in old Rule 203 was to protect nonparty witnesses from unwarranted interference with their business and/or personal lives which might otherwise occur when 206(a) is employed.

The amendment to Rule 206(a) is not intended to expand the court's subpoena power in any way. A nonparty, nonresident witness is subject to the court's subpoena power only to the extent authorized by law.

Paragraph (b)

Paragraph (b) is new. It covers the situation in which one party serves a notice to take the discovery and evidence depositions of a deponent and after taking the discovery deposition decides not to take the deposition for evidence. The new provision permits the opposing party to proceed to take the evidence deposition without the necessity of serving a new notice.

Paragraph (c)

Paragraph (c) covers part of the subject matter covered by former Rule 19–4. The provision dealing with general scope of discovery appearing in former Rule 19–4 has been deleted, since that subject is covered in Rule 201(b). The first sentence of paragraph (c) of this rule is simply a cross-reference to that provision. The second sentence effects a change in Illinois practice. Under former Rule 19–4, a party was permitted to question a deponent as if under cross-examination in a discovery deposition only if the witness was hostile. The prevailing practice appeared to be to examine witnesses as if under cross-examination whether or not they were hostile. Therefore, the committee deleted the requirement of hostility to conform the language of the rule to the actual practice. In subparagraph (c)(2) of this rule, the requirement that examination and cross-examination in the taking of an evidence deposition shall be the same as though the deponent were testifying at the trial is retained.

Subparagraph (c)(3) has been added to eliminate speaking objections.

Paragraph (d)

The Committee is of the opinion that the vast majority of all discovery depositions can easily be concluded within three hours. (For further comment on this issue, see committee comments to Rule 218.)

Paragraphs (e) and (f)

Paragraphs (e) and (f) of this rule are derived from former Rules 19—6(3) and (2), respectively, with minor language changes, but no changes in substance.

Paragraph (f) was amended in 1975 to provide for the recording of depositions by audio-visual as well as sound-recording devices.

Paragraph (g)

The precautions built into paragraph (g), "Video-taped Depositions," are intended to insure that strict adherence to accepted procedures found in other States that allow videotaping will avoid any problems if videotaping of depositions becomes a widespread practice.

Paragraph (h)

The committee is of the opinion that telephonic and other remote electronic means depositions should be allowed by a specific paragraph of Rule 206. It is meant to reduce unnecessary discovery costs. The committee recommends that all other demonstrative evidence to be presented to the deponent be premarked before being provided to the officer administering the oath and the other parties. The parties may agree pursuant to Rule 201(i) to amend or waive any conditions of paragraph (h).

(February 16, 2011)

Paragraph (h)

The Committee is of the opinion that the apparent acceptance and utilization of telephonic and other remote electronic means depositions demonstrate that there is no need to require a party to obtain an order on motion to proceed with such depositions absent a written stipulation. Therefore, the Committee recommended the elimination of such a requirement so that the depositions may proceed by notice.

Rule 207. Signing and Filing Depositions

(a) Submission to Deponent; Changes; Signing. Unless signature is waived by the deponent, the officer shall instruct the deponent that if the testimony is transcribed the deponent will be afforded an opportunity to examine the deposition at the office of the officer or reporter, or elsewhere, by reasonable arrangement at the deponent's expense, and that corrections based on errors in reporting or transcription which the deponent desires to make will be entered upon the deposition with a statement by the deponent that the reporter erred in reporting or transcribing the answer or answers involved. The deponent may not otherwise change either the form or substance of his or her answers. The deponent shall provide the officer with an address to which notice is to be sent when the transcript is available for examination and signing. When the deposition is fully transcribed, the officer shall mail to the deponent, at the address last supplied, notice that it is available and may be examined at a stated place at stated times, or pursuant to arrangement. After the deponent has examined the deposition, the officer shall enter upon it any changes the deponent desires to make, with the reasons the deponent gives for making them. If the deponent does not appear at the place specified in the notice within 28 days after the mailing of the notice, or within the same 28 days make other arrangements for examination of the deposition, or after examining the deposition refuses to sign it, or after it has been made available to the deponent by arrangement it remains unsigned for 28 days, the officer's certificate shall state the reason for the omission of the signature, including any reason given by the deponent for a refusal to sign. The deposition may then be used as fully as though signed, unless on a motion to suppress under Rule 211(d) the court holds that the reasons given by the deponent for a refusal to sign require rejection of the deposition in whole or in part.

(b) Certification, Filing, and Notice of Filing.

(1) If the testimony is transcribed, the officer shall certify on the deposition that the deponent was duly sworn by him and that the deposition is a true record of the testimony given by the deponent. A deposition so certified requires no further proof of authenticity. At the request of any party, the officer shall then securely seal the deposition, together with all exhibits, or copies thereof, in an envelope bearing the title and number of the action and marked "Deposition(s) of (here insert name(s) of deponent(s))" and promptly file it or send it by registered or certified mail to the clerk of the court for filing.

(2) The party causing a deposition to be filed shall promptly serve notice thereof on the other parties.

Amended Jan. 5, 1981, eff. Feb. 1, 1981; June 1, 1995, eff. Jan. 1, 1996.

Formerly Ill.Rev.Stat.1991, ch. 110A, ¶ 207.

Committee Comments
(Revised June 1, 1995)

Paragraph (a)

Paragraph (a), as adopted in 1967, was derived from former Rule 19–6(4), with some changes. For-

mer Rule 19–6(4) contemplated that all depositions would be transcribed, that unless reading was waived by the parties and the deponent all depositions would be read to or by the deponent, and that all depositions would be signed by the deponent unless signature was waived, or the deponent was ill or could not be found, or refused to sign. Paragraph (a) of the rule as adopted in 1967 contemplated that the contents of a deposition will not always warrant the expense of having it transcribed. It provided that if the deposition were transcribed, it had to be made available to the deponent for examination and changes, if any, unless the parties and deponent waived signature. Thus the new rule substituted a single waiver for the two provided in former Rule 19–6(4).

The procedure was further simplified in 1981 when the paragraph was amended to eliminate the requirement that the deponent sign the deposition unless he is ill, cannot be found, or refuses to sign, or unless signature is waived by the parties and by the deponent. Under the paragraph as amended, if the deposition is transcribed, the officer must notify the deponent that it is available for his inspection, and that after inspecting it he may make such changes as he wishes. If the deponent does not appear or make arrangements to inspect the deposition, after four weeks the officer will certify the deposition and it will be useable as if it had been inspected and signed by the deponent.

Supreme Court Rule 207(a) currently permits a deponent to make changes in both the form and substance of the answers which he or she gives under oath at the time of a deposition. The potential for testimonial abuse has become increasingly evident as witnesses submit lengthy errata sheets in which their testimony is drastically altered, including changing affirmative responses to negative and the reverse. *LaSalle National Bank v. 53rd–Ellis Currency Exchange, Inc.,* 249 Ill.App.3d 415, 433–36 (1st Dist.1993).

This rule has been amended to permit "corrections" only under circumstances where the deponent believes the court reporter has inaccurately reported or transcribed an answer or answers. Testimony accurately reported and transcribed at a deposition may not be subsequently revised by the deponent. No change is made regarding existing law as to the uses of deposition testimony at trial or hearing for impeachment, as an evidentiary or judicial admission, or for any other permitted purpose. See Rule 212; *Hansen v. Ruby Construction Co.,* 155 Ill.App.3d 475, 480–82 (1st Dist.1987); *Caponi v. Larry's 66,* 236 Ill.App.3d 660, 665–67, 671–73 (2d Dist.1992).

Paragraph (b)

Paragraph (b) of this rule does away with the requirement of former Rule 19–6(5)(a) that all evidence depositions be transcribed and filed. When no party cares to have the deposition transcribed and filed, there is no reason for requiring the party taking the deposition to undergo the expense of transcription and filing. Certification, rather than certification *and filing,* establishes authenticity under the new provision. Otherwise the language of former Rule 19–6(5)(a) is unchanged. Subparagraph (b)(2) is derived from former Rule 19–6(5)(b). The language is unchanged.

Rule 208.   Fees and Charges; Copies

(a) Who Shall Pay. Except as provided in paragraph (e), the party at whose instance the deposition is taken shall pay the fees of the witness and of the officer and the charges of the recorder or stenographer for attending. The party at whose request a deposition is transcribed and filed shall pay the charges for transcription and filing. The party at whose request a tape-recorded deposition is filed without having been transcribed shall pay the charges for filing, and if such deposition is subsequently transcribed the party requesting it shall pay the charges for such transcription. If, however, the scope of the examination by any other party exceeds the scope of examination by the party at whose instance the deposition is taken, the fees and charges due to the excess shall be summarily taxed by the court and paid by the other party.

(b) Amount. The officer taking and certifying a deposition is entitled to any fees provided by statute, together with the reasonable and necessary charges for a recorder or stenographer for attending and transcribing the deposition. Every witness attending before the officer is entitled to the fees and mileage allowance provided by statute for witnesses attending courts in this State.

(c) Copies. Upon payment of reasonable charges therefor, the officer shall furnish a copy of the deposition to any party or to the deponent.

(d) Taxing as Costs. The fees and charges provided for in paragraphs (a) through (c) may, in the discretion of the trial court, be taxed as costs.

(e) Controlled Expert Witness Fees. Each party shall, unless manifest injustice would result, bear the expense of all fees charged by his or her Rule 213(f)(3) controlled expert witness or witnesses.
Amended Sept. 8, 1975, eff. Oct. 1, 1975; Oct. 4, 2011, eff. Nov. 1, 2011.

Formerly Ill.Rev.Stat.1991, ch. 110A, ¶ 208.

Committee Comments
Paragraph (a)

Paragraph (a) of this rule is derived from former Rule 19–6(5)(c). Under the latter provision the cost of transcribing and filing a deposition taken for discovery purposes was charged to the party at whose request it was filed, while the cost of transcribing and filing a deposition taken for purposes of evidence was charged in all cases to the person at whose instance it was taken. This reflected the fact that all evidence depositions were required to be transcribed and filed. Since under paragraph (b) of Rule 207, *supra*, the evidence deposition, like the discovery deposition, is transcribed and filed only if one of the parties requests it, the rule has been

changed to place the cost of transcription and filing on the party making the request. The last sentence of former Rule 19–6(5)(c) is paragraph (c) of the new rule. Otherwise the provisions of former Rule 19–6(5)(c) appear without change in paragraph (a) of this rule.

Paragraph (a) was amended in 1975, to make it plain that the party at whose instance a deposition is taken shall pay the charges for the recorder when the deposition is recorded by sound or audio-visual means, that when such a deposition is filed without being transcribed, the party at whose instance it is filed shall pay the charges for filing, and that if subsequently transcribed, the party requesting it shall pay the charges for such transcription.

Paragraph (b)

Paragraph (b) of this rule is derived from former Rule 19–6(5)(d). The language is unchanged except for the deletion of the reference to masters in chancery made necessary by the provision of the Judicial Article abolishing that office. The rule provides simply that the fees shall be set by statute.

Paragraph (b) was amended in 1975 to make it plain that when a deposition is recorded by sound or audio-visual device, the officer taking and certifying the deposition is entitled to the reasonable and necessary charges for a recorder.

Paragraph (c)

This is the last sentence of former Rule 19–6(5)(c).

Paragraph (d)

Paragraph (d) is derived from former Rule 19–6(5)(e). The words "as in equity cases" have been deleted.

Rule 209.   Failure to Attend or Serve Subpoena; Expenses

(a) Failure to Attend or to Proceed; Expenses. If the party serving notice of the taking of a deposition fails to attend or to proceed therewith and another party attends in person or by attorney pursuant to the notice, the court may order the party serving the notice to pay to the other party the amount of the reasonable expenses incurred by him and his attorney in so attending, including reasonable attorney's fees.

(b) Failure to Serve Subpoena or Notice; Expenses. If the party serving notice of the taking of a deposition fails to serve a subpoena or notice, as may be appropriate, requiring the attendance of the deponent and because of that failure the deponent does not attend, and if another party attends in person or by attorney because he expects the deposition of that deponent to be taken, the court may order the party serving the notice to pay to the other party the amount of the reasonable expenses incurred by him and his attorney in attending, including reasonable attorney's fees.

Formerly Ill.Rev.Stat.1991, ch. 110A, ¶ 209.

Committee Comments

Paragraphs (a) and (b) of this rule are former Rule 19–6(6), with a language revision in paragraph (b), but no change of substance.

Rule 210. Depositions on Written Questions

(a) Serving Questions; Notice. A party desiring to take the deposition of any person upon written questions shall serve them upon the other parties with a notice stating the name and address of the person who is to answer them if known, or, if the name is not known, a general description sufficient to identify him, and the name or descriptive title and address of the officer before whom the deposition is to be taken. Within 14 days thereafter a party so served may likewise serve cross-questions. Within 7 days after being served with cross-questions a party may likewise serve redirect questions. Within 7 days after being served with redirect questions, a party may likewise serve re-cross-questions.

(b) Officer to Take Responses and Prepare Record. The party at whose instance the deposition is taken shall transmit a copy of the notice and copies of the initial and subsequent questions served to the officer designated in the notice, who shall proceed promptly, in the manner provided by Rules 206 (f) and 207, to take the testimony of the deponent in response to the questions and to prepare, certify, and file or mail the deposition, attaching thereto the copy of the notice and the questions received by him. No party, attorney, or person interested in the event of the action (unless he is the deponent) shall be present during the taking of the deposition or dictate, write, or draw up any answer to the questions.

(c) Notice of Filing. The party causing a deposition to be filed shall promptly serve notice thereof on the other parties.

Amended eff. Jan. 12, 1967; amended October 17, 2006, effective immediately.

Formerly Ill.Rev.Stat.1991, ch. 110A, ¶ 210.

Committee Comments

Paragraph (a)

Paragraph (a) of this rule is derived from former Rule 19–7(1). The language is unchanged except that the phrase, "if known, or, if the name is not known, a general description sufficient to identify him," has been inserted to make the requirements for notices to take depositions upon written questions and upon oral examination the same. See Rule 206(a), *supra.*

Paragraphs (b) and (c)

Paragraphs (b) and (c) are derived from former Rule 19–7(2) and (3), respectively. There are no changes of substance.

Rule 211. Effect of Errors and Irregularities in Depositions; Objections

(a) As to Notice. All errors and irregularities in the notice for taking a deposition are waived unless written objection is promptly served upon the party giving the notice.

(b) As to Disqualification of Officer or Person. Objection to taking a deposition because of disqualification of the officer or person before whom it is to be taken is waived unless made before the taking of the deposition begins or as soon thereafter as the disqualification becomes known or could have been discovered with reasonable diligence.

(c) As to Competency of Deponent; Admissibility of Testimony; Questions and Answers; Misconduct; Irregularities. (1) Grounds of objection to the competency of the deponent or admissibility of testimony which might have been corrected if presented during the taking of the deposition are waived by failure to make them at that time; otherwise objections to the competency of the deponent or admissibility of testimony may be made when the testimony is offered in evidence.

(2) Objections to the form of a question or answer, errors and irregularities occurring at the oral examination in the manner of taking the deposition, in the oath or affirmation, or in the conduct of any person, and errors and irregularities of any kind which might be corrected if promptly presented, are waived unless seasonable objection thereto is made at the taking of the deposition.

(3) Objections to the form of written questions are waived unless served in writing upon the party propounding them within the time allowed for serving succeeding questions and, in the case of the last questions authorized, within 7 days after service thereof.

(4) A motion to suppress is unnecessary to preserve an objection seasonably made. Any party may, but need not, on notice and motion obtain a ruling by the court on the objections in advance of the trial.

(d) As to Completion and Return of Deposition. Errors and irregularities in the manner in which the testimony is transcribed or the deposition is prepared, signed, certified, sealed, indorsed, transmitted, filed, or otherwise dealt with by the officer are waived unless a motion to suppress the deposition or some part thereof is made with reasonable promptness after the defect is, or with due diligence might have been, ascertained.

Formerly Ill.Rev.Stat.1991, ch. 110A, ¶ 211.

Committee Comments

This rule is derived from former Rule 19–9. The language is unchanged except that the period for filing objections to the form of written questions has been extended to seven days in subparagraph (c)(3) in keeping with the Committee's policy of measuring time periods in multiples of seven days.

Rule 212. Use of Depositions

(a) Purposes for Which Discovery Depositions May Be Used. Discovery depositions taken under the provisions of this rule may be used only:

(1) for the purpose of impeaching the testimony of the deponent as a witness in the same manner and to the same extent as any inconsistent statement made by a witness;

(2) as an admission made by a party or by an officer or agent of a party in the same manner and to the same extent as any other admission made by that person;

(3) if otherwise admissible as an exception to the hearsay rule;

(4) for any purpose for which an affidavit may be used; or

(5) upon reasonable notice to all parties, as evidence at trial or hearing against a party who appeared at the deposition or was given proper notice thereof, if the court finds that the deponent is not a controlled expert witness, the deponent's evidence deposition has not been taken, and the deponent is unable to attend or testify because of death or infirmity, and if the court, based on its sound discretion, further finds such evidence at trial or hearing will do substantial justice between or among the parties.

(b) Use of Evidence Depositions. The evidence deposition of a physician or surgeon may be introduced in evidence at trial on the motion of either party regardless of the availability of the deponent, without prejudice to the right of either party to subpoena or otherwise call the physician or surgeon for attendance at trial. All or any part of other evidence depositions may be used for any purpose for which a discovery deposition may be used, and may be used by any party for any purpose if the court finds that at the time of the trial:

(1) the deponent is dead or unable to attend or testify because of age, sickness, infirmity or imprisonment;

(2) the deponent is out of the county, unless it appears that the absence was procured by the party offering the deposition, provided, that a party who is not a resident of this State may introduce his own deposition if he is absent from the county; or

(3) the party offering the deposition has exercised reasonable diligence but has been unable to procure the attendance of the deponent by subpoena; or finds, upon notice and motion in advance of trial, that exceptional circumstances exist which make it desirable, in the interest of justice and with due regard for the importance of presenting the testimony of witnesses orally in open court, to allow the deposition to be used.

(c) Partial Use. If only a part of a deposition is read or used at the trial by a party, any other party may at that time read or use or require him to read any other part of the deposition which ought in fairness to be considered in connection with the part read or used.

(d) Use After Substitution, Dismissal, or Remandment. Substitution of parties does not affect the right to use depositions previously taken. If any action in any court of this or any other jurisdiction of the United States is dismissed and another action involving the same subject matter is afterward brought between the same parties or their representatives or successors in interest, or if any action is remanded by a court of the United States to a court of this State, all depositions lawfully taken and duly filed in the former action, or before remandment, may be used as if taken in the later action, or after remandment.

Amended Feb. 19, 1982, eff. April 1, 1982; May 28, 1982, eff. July 1, 1982; eff. March 1, 2001; March 28, 2002, eff. July 1, 2002; Dec. 8, 2010, eff. Jan. 1, 2011.

Formerly Ill.Rev.Stat.1991, ch. 110A, ¶ 212.

Committee Comments
(Revised March 1, 2001)

Paragraphs (a), (b) and (c)

Paragraphs (a), (b), and (c), of this rule are derived from former Rule 19—10. The language is unchanged except that in subparagraph (a)(4) the rule codifies the prevailing practice that permits use of discovery depositions for any purpose for which an affidavit may be used, and paragraph (b) was amended in 1982 to include the provision regarding the use of evidence depositions of physicians and surgeons.

Subparagraph (a)(5) was added in 2001 to permit a discovery deposition to be introduced in evidence at trial or hearing under specified circumstances.

Paragraph (d)

Paragraph (d) of this rule is derived from former Rule 19—10(5). The language has been changed to make it clear that depositions taken in the Federal court prior to remandment are to be treated in the same fashion as depositions taken in the Federal court in a case dismissed in that court and subsequently filed in the State court.

(March 28, 2002)

This rule is amended to conform to the changes in terminology made in Supreme Court Rule 213.

(January 1, 2011)

Paragraph (a)

The Committee was prompted to examine this issue by the decision in *Berry v. American Standard, Inc.*, 382 Ill. App. 3d 895 (5th Dist. 2008). The Committee believes that a trial court should have the discretion under subparagraph (a)(5) to permit the use of a party's discovery deposition at trial. It appears that there may be rare, but compelling, circumstances under which a party's discovery deposition should be permitted to be used. In the Committee's view, *Berry* presents such circumstances. Given that in most cases counsel will have the opportunity to preserve a party's testimony via an evidence deposition, it is expected that the circumstances that would justify use of a discovery deposition would be extremely limited.

This amendment applies to cases filed on or after the effective date.

Rule 213. Written Interrogatories to Parties

(a) Directing Interrogatories. A party may direct written interrogatories to any other party. A copy of the interrogatories shall be served on all other parties entitled to notice.

(b) Duty of Attorney. It is the duty of an attorney directing interrogatories to restrict them to the subject matter of the particular case, to avoid undue detail, and to avoid the imposition of any unnecessary burden or expense on the answering party.

(c) Number of Interrogatories. Except as provided in subparagraph (j), a party shall not serve more than 30 interrogatories, including sub-parts, on any other party except upon agreement of the parties or leave of court granted upon a showing of good cause. A motion for leave of court to serve more than 30 interrogatories must be in writing and shall set forth the proposed interrogatories and the reasons establishing good cause for their use.

(d) Answers and Objections. Within 28 days after service of the interrogatories upon the party to whom they are directed, the party shall serve a sworn answer or an objection to each interrogatory, with proof of service upon all other parties entitled to notice. Any objection to an answer or to the refusal to answer an interrogatory shall be heard by the court upon prompt notice and motion of the party propounding the interrogatory. The answering party shall set forth in full each interrogatory being answered immediately preceding the answer. Sworn answers to interrogatories directed to a public or private corporation, or a partnership or association shall be made by an officer, partner, or agent, who shall furnish such information as is available to the party.

(e) Option to Produce Documents. When the answer to an interrogatory may be obtained from documents in the possession or control of the party on whom the interrogatory was served, it shall be a sufficient answer to the interrogatory to produce those documents responsive to the interrogatory. When a party elects to answer an interrogatory by the production of documents, that production shall comply with the requirements of Rule 214.

(f) Identity and Testimony of Witnesses. Upon written interrogatory, a party must furnish the identities and addresses of witnesses who will testify at trial and must provide the following information:

(1) *Lay Witnesses.* A "lay witness" is a person giving only fact or lay opinion testimony. For each lay witness, the party must identify the subjects on which the witness will testify. An answer is sufficient if it gives reasonable notice of the testimony, taking into account the limitations on the party's knowledge of the facts known by and opinions held by the witness.

(2) *Independent Expert Witnesses.* An "independent expert witness" is a person giving expert testimony who is not the party, the party's current employee, or the party's retained expert. For each independent expert witness, the party must identify the subjects on which the witness will testify and the opinions the party expects to elicit. An answer is sufficient if it gives reasonable notice of the testimony, taking into account the limitations on the party's knowledge of the facts known by and opinions held by the witness.

(3) *Controlled Expert Witnesses.* A "controlled expert witness" is a person giving expert testimony who is the party, the party's current employee, or the party's retained expert. For each controlled expert witness, the party must identify: (i) the subject matter on which the witness will testify; (ii) the conclusions and opinions of the witness and the bases therefor; (iii) the qualifications of the witness; and (iv) any reports prepared by the witness about the case.

(g) Limitation on Testimony and Freedom to Cross–Examine. The information disclosed in answer to a Rule 213(f) interrogatory, or in a discovery deposition, limits the testimony that can be given by a witness on direct examination at trial. Information disclosed in a discovery deposition need not be later specifically identified in a Rule 213(f) answer, but, upon objection at trial, the burden is on the proponent of the witness to prove the information was provided in a Rule 213(f) answer or in the discovery deposition. Except upon a showing of good cause, information in an evidence deposition not previously disclosed in a Rule 213(f) interrogatory answer or in a discovery deposition shall not be admissible upon objection at trial.

Without making disclosure under this rule, however, a cross-examining party can elicit information, including opinions, from the witness. This freedom to cross-examine is subject to a restriction that applies in actions that involve multiple parties and multiple representation. In such actions, the cross-examining party may not elicit undisclosed information, including opinions, from the witness on an issue on which its position is aligned with that of the party doing the direct examination.

(h) Use of Answers to Interrogatories. Answers to interrogatories may be used in evidence to the same extent as a discovery deposition.

(i) Duty to Supplement. A party has a duty to seasonably supplement or amend any prior answer or response whenever new or additional information subsequently becomes known to that party.

(j) The Supreme Court, by administrative order, may approve standard forms of interrogatories for different classes of cases.

(k) Liberal Construction. This rule is to be liberally construed to do substantial justice between or among the parties.

Amended eff. Jan. 1, 1967; July 1, 1985, eff. Aug. 1, 1985; June 1, 1995, eff. Jan. 1, 1996; April 3, 1997, eff. May 1, 1997; March 28, 2002, eff. July 1, 2002; May 14, 2005, eff. June 2, 2005; Dec. 6, 2006, eff. Jan. 1, 2007.

Formerly Ill.Rev.Stat.1991, ch. 110A, ¶ 213.

Committee Comments

(Revised June 1, 1995)

Paragraph (a)

The provision of former Rule 19–11(1) as to who is to answer interrogatories served on corporations, partnerships, and associations appears in paragraph (d) of this rule. The provisions of former Rule 19–11(1) stating that both interrogatories and depositions could be employed and that the court may issue protective orders were deleted because these matters are covered in Rules 201(a) and (c). A prior requirement that the written interrogatories be spaced so as to permit the answering party to answer upon the interrogatory served upon him has been amended to eliminate the spacing requirement, primarily because of the practical and customary way in which interrogatories are answered.

Paragraph (b)

Like paragraph (a) of Rule 201, which cautions against duplication, this provision states the general policy of the rules for the guidance for the court when it is called upon to frame protective orders or dispose of objections to interrogatories as provided in paragraph (d) of Rule 213.

Paragraph (c)

Paragraph (c) is new. Because of widespread complaints that some attorneys engage in the practice of submitting needless, repetitious, and burdensome interrogatories, paragraph (c) limits the number of all interrogatories, regardless of when propounded, to 30 (including subparts), unless "good cause" requires a greater number.

Paragraph (d)

Paragraph (d) is derived from former Rules 19–11(2) and (3). This paragraph embodies a number of changes in the present practice. The time for answering interrogatories is fixed at 28 days instead of 30 (as in former Rule 19–11(2)), consistent with the committee's general policy of establishing time periods that are multiples of seven days. Under former Rule 19–11(3), the time for making objections is 15 days. Paragraph (d) increases this to 28 days, making the time limit for answering and objecting the same. The other change in Illinois practice effected by paragraph (d) is the requirement that motions to hear objections to interrogatories must be noticed by the party seeking to have the interrogatories answered. Under former Rule 19–11(3) the objection must be noticed by the party making it. This change was made because the committee believes the party seeking the information should have the burden of seeking a disposition of the objection, and that this will tend to reduce the number of rulings that are necessary by automatically suspending interrogatories which a party is not seriously interested in pursuing. The last phrase provides that the person answering must furnish such information as is available to the party. This phrase was added, as was the same provision to Federal Rule 33 in 1946, to make certain that a corporation, partnership, or association may not avoid answering an interrogatory by disclaiming personal knowledge of the matter on the part of the answering official.

Paragraph (e)

Paragraph (e) has been amended to require a party who elects to answer an interrogatory by referring to documents, to produce the responsive documents as part of the party's answer. When a party elects to respond to an interrogatory by the production of documents, that production must comply with the requirements of Rule 214.

Paragraph (f)

Paragraph (f) now requires a party to serve the identity and location of witnesses who will testify at trial, together with the subject of their testimony. This is a departure from the previously recognized law. This paragraph, as well as others contained in these rules, imposes a "seasonable" duty to supplement.

Paragraph (g)

In light of the elimination of former Supreme Court Rule 220, the definition of an opinion witness is now a person who will offer "any" opinion testimony. It is the Committee's belief that in order to avoid surprise, the subject matter of all opinions must be disclosed pursuant to this rule and Supreme Court Rule 218, and that no new or additional opinions will be allowed unless the interests of justice require otherwise. For purposes of this paragraph, there is no longer a distinction between retained and nonretained experts. Further, upon written interrogatories, a party must state the subject matter to be testified to, the conclusions, opinions and qualifications of opinion witnesses, and provide all reports of opinion witnesses.

Paragraph (h)

Paragraph (h) is derived from former Rule 19–11(4), which provided that answers to interrogatories could be used to the same extent as the deposition of an adverse party. Under former Rule 19–11(1), interrogatories can be directed only to adverse parties; hence the provision in former Rule 19–11(4) to the effect that the answers could be used as could a deposition of an adverse party.

Paragraph (a) of the new rule provides that interrogatories can be directed to any party. Accordingly, paragraph (h) of the new rule provides that the answers can be used to the same extent as a discovery deposition. Former Rule 19–11(4) also contained a statement on the scope of interrogatories, equating the permissible scope of inquiry to that permitted in the taking of a deposition. This provision was deleted as unnecessary in view of the provisions of Rule 201(b)(1).

Paragraph (i)

With regard to paragraph (i), the new rule imposes a "seasonable" duty to supplement or amend prior answers when new or additional information becomes known to that party. This is a change from previous discovery requirements and thus eliminates the need for supplemental interrogatories unless different information is sought. The Committee believes that the definition of "seasonable" varies by the facts of each case and by the type of case, but in no event should it allow a party or an attorney to fail to comply with the spirit of this rule by either negligent or wilful noncompliance.

Paragraph (j)

In an effort to avoid discovery disputes, the practitioner is encouraged to utilize interrogatories approved by the Supreme Court pursuant to paragraph (j) whenever possible.

(March 28, 2002)

Paragraph (f)

The purpose of this paragraph is to prevent unfair surprise at trial, without creating an undue burden on the parties before trial. The paragraph divides witnesses into three categories, with separate disclosure requirements for each category.

"Lay witnesses" include persons such as an eyewitness to a car accident. For witnesses in this category, the party must identify the "subjects" of testimony—meaning the topics, rather than a summary. An answer must describe the subjects sufficiently to give "reasonable notice" of the testimony, enabling the opposing attorney to decide whether to depose the witness, and on what topics. In the above example, a proper answer might state that the witness will testify about: "(1) the path of travel and speed of the vehicles before impact, (2) a description of the impact, and (3) the lighting and weather conditions at the time of the accident." The answer would not be proper if it said only that the witness will testify about: "the accident." Requiring disclosure of only the subjects of lay witness testimony represents a change in the former rule, which required detailed disclosures regarding the subject matter, conclusions, opinions, bases and qualifications of any witness giving any opinion testimony, including lay opinion testimony. Experience has shown that applying this detailed-disclosure requirement to lay witnesses creates a serious burden without corresponding benefit to the opposing party.

"Independent expert witnesses" include persons such as a police officer who gives expert testimony based on the officer's investigation of a car accident, or a doctor who gives expert testimony based on the doctor's treatment of the plaintiff's injuries. For witnesses in this category, the party must identify the "subjects" (meaning topics) on which the witness will testify and the "opinions" the party expects to elicit. The limitations on the party's knowledge of the facts known by and opinions held by the witness often will be important in applying the "reasonable notice" standard. For example, a treating doctor might refuse to speak with the plaintiff's attorney, and the doctor cannot be contacted by the defendant's attorney, so the opinions set forth in the medical records about diagnosis, prognosis, and cause of injury might be all that the two attorneys know about the doctor's opinions. In these circumstances, the party intending to call the doctor need set forth only a brief statement of the opinions it expects to elicit. On the other hand, a party might know that a treating doctor will testify about another doctor's compliance with the standard of care, or that a police officer will testify to an opinion based on work done outside the scope of the officer's initial investigation. In these examples, the opinions go beyond those that would be reasonably expected based on the witness' apparent involvement in the case. To prevent unfair surprise in circumstances like these, an answer must set forth a more detailed statement of the opinions the party expects to elicit. Requiring disclosure of only the "subjects" of testimony and the "opinions" the party expects to elicit represents a change in the former rule, which required detailed disclosures about the subject matter, conclusions, opinions, bases, and qualifications of all witnesses giving opinion testimony, including expert witnesses over whom the party has no control. Experience has shown that the detailed-disclosure requirement is too demanding for independent expert witnesses.

"Controlled expert witnesses" include persons such as retained experts. The party can count on full cooperation from the witnesses in this category, so the amended rule requires the party to provide all of the details required by the former rule. In particular, the requirement that the party identify the "subject matter" of the testimony means that the party must set forth the gist of the testimony on each topic the witness will address, as opposed to setting forth the topics alone.

A party may meet its disclosure obligation in part by incorporating prior statements or reports of the witness. The answer to the Rule 213(f) interrogatories served on behalf of a party may be sworn to by the party or the party's attorney.

Paragraph (g)

Parties are to be allowed a full and complete cross-examination of any witness and may elicit additional undisclosed opinions in the course of cross-examination. This freedom to cross-examine is subject to a restriction that, for example, prevents a party from eliciting previously undisclosed contributory negligence opinions from a coparty's expert.

Note that the exception to disclosure described in this paragraph is limited to the cross-examining party. It does not excuse the party calling the witness from the duty to supplement described in paragraph (i).

Paragraph (i)

The material deleted from this paragraph now appears in modified form in paragraph (g).

Paragraph (k)

The application of this rule is intended to do substantial justice between the parties. This rule is intended to be a shield to prevent unfair surprise but not a sword to prevent the admission of relevant evidence on the basis of technicalities. The purpose of the rule is to allow for a trial to be decided on the merits. The trial court should take this purpose into account when a violation occurs and it is ordering appropriate relief under Rule 219(c).

The rule does not apply to demonstrative evidence that is intended to explain or convey to the trier of fact the theories expressed in accordance with this rule.

STANDARD INTERROGATORIES UNDER SUPREME COURT RULE 213(J)

Filed December 31, 1998

Under Supreme Court Rule 213(j), "[t]he Supreme Court, by administrative order, may approve standard forms of interrogatories for different classes of cases." The committee comments to this rule state, "In an effort to avoid discovery disputes, the practitioner is encouraged to utilize interrogatories approved by the Supreme Court pursuant to paragraph (j) whenever possible." The following interrogatories are hereby approved pursuant to that rule. A party may use one or more interrogatories which are part of a form set of interrogatories. Any such interrogatory so used shall be counted as one interrogatory in determining the total number of interrogatories propounded, regardless of any subparts or multiple inquiries therein. A party may combine form interrogatories with other interrogatories, subject to applicable limitations as to number. A party shall avoid propounding a form interrogatory which has no application to the case.

Counsel should note other provisions of Rule 213 that are reflected in these standard interrogatories, and which are applicable to nonstandard interrogatories as well. As the committee comments to Rule 213(a) indicate, "[the] prior requirement that the written interrogatories be spaced so as to permit the answering party to answer upon the interrogatory served upon him has been amended to eliminate the spacing requirement, primarily because of the practical and customary way in which interrogatories are answered." Although the proponent of interrogatories may still use spacing between his or her interrogatories, these standard interrogatories do not.

Also, Rule 213(d) retains the requirement that "[w]ithin 28 days after service of the interrogatories

upon the party to whom they are directed, the party shall serve a *sworn answer* or an objection to each interrogatory, with proof of service upon all other parties entitled to notice. *** The answering party shall set forth in full each interrogatory being answered immediately preceding the answer." (Emphasis added.) While the supreme court envisions that parties will continue with the practice of creating a new document in response to interrogatories, and it is the duty of the respondent to interrogatories to attest to the truthfulness of his or her answers, these standard interrogatories include sample attestation clauses.

Finally, under Supreme Court Rule 213(i), a party has a duty to seasonably supplement or amend any prior answer or response whenever new or additional information subsequently becomes known to that party. The proponent of the interrogatories may wish to include a remainder of this duty in the interrogatories.

AMENDED INTERROGATORIES UNDER RULE 213(J)

(eff. June 2, 2005)

MOTOR VEHICLE INTERROGATORIES TO PLAINTIFFS

1. State your full name, as well as your current residence address, date of birth, marital status, driver's license number and issuing state, and the last four digits of your social security number.

2. State the full name and current residence address of each person who witnessed or claims to have witnessed the occurrence that is the subject of the suit (hereinafter referred to simply as the occurrence).

3. State the full name and current residence address of each person, not named in interrogatory No. 2 above, who was present and/or claims to have been present at the scene immediately before, at the time of, and/or immediately after the occurrence.

4. As a result of the occurrence, were you made a defendant in any criminal or traffic case? If so, state the court, the caption, the case number, the charge or charges filed against you, whether you pleaded guilty thereto and the final disposition.

5. Describe the personal injuries sustained by you as a result of the occurrence.

6. With regard to your injuries, state:

(a) The name and address of each attending physician and/or health care professional;

(b) The name and address of each consulting physician and/or other health care professional;

(c) The name and address of each person and/or laboratory taking any X ray, MRI and/or other radiological tests of you;

(d) The date or inclusive dates on which each of them rendered you service;

(e) The amounts to date of their respective bills for services; and

(f) From which of them you have written reports.

7. As the result of your personal injuries, were you a patient or outpatient in any hospital and/or clinic? If so, state the names and addresses of all hospitals and/or clinics, the amounts of their respective bills and the date or inclusive dates of their services.

8. As the result of your personal injuries, were you unable to work? If so, state:

(a) The name and address of your employer, if any, at the time of the occurrence, your wage and/or salary, and the name of your supervisor and/or foreperson;

(b) The date or inclusive dates on which you were unable to work;

(c) The amount of wage and/or income loss claimed by you; and

(d) The name and address of your present employer and your wage and/or salary.

9. State any and all other expenses and/or losses you claim as a result of the occurrence. As to each expense and/or loss, state the date or dates it was incurred, the name of the person, firm and/or company to whom such amounts are owed, whether the expense and/or loss in question has been paid and, if so, by whom it was so paid, and describe the reason and/or purpose for each expense and/or loss.

10. Had you suffered any personal injury or prolonged, serious and/or chronic illness prior to the date of the occurrence? If so, state when and how you were injured and/or ill, where you were injured and/or ill, describe the injuries and/or illness suffered, and state the name and address of each physician, or other health care professional, hospital and/or clinic rendering you treatment for each injury and/or chronic illness.

11. Are you claiming any psychiatric, psychological and/or emotional injuries as a result of this occurrence? If so, state:

(a) The name of any psychiatric, psychological and/or emotional injury claimed, and the name and address of each psychiatrist, physician, psychologist, therapist or other health care professional rendering you treatment for each injury;

(b) Whether you had suffered any psychiatric, psychological and/or emotional injury prior to the date of the occurrence; and

(c) If (b) is in the affirmative, please state when and the nature of any psychiatric, psychological and/or emotional injury, and the name and address of each psychiatrist, physician, psychologist, therapist or other health care professional rendering you treatment for each injury.

12. Have you suffered any personal injury or prolonged, serious and/or chronic illness since the date of the occurrence? If so, state when you were injured and/or ill, where and how you were injured and/or ill, describe the injuries and/or the illness suffered, and state the name and address of each physician or other health care professional, hospital and/or clinic rendering you treatment for each injury and/or chronic illness.

13. Have you ever filed any other suits for your own personal injuries? If so, state the nature of the injuries claimed, the courts and the captions in which filed, the years filed, and the titles and docket numbers of the suits.

14. Have you ever filed a claim for and/or received any workers' compensation benefits? If so, state the name and address of the employer against whom you filed for and/or received benefits, the date of the alleged accident or accidents, the description of the alleged accident or accidents, the nature of your injuries claimed and the name of the insurance company, if any, who paid any such benefits.

15. Were any photographs, movies and/or videotapes taken of the scene of the occurrence or of the persons and/or vehicles involved? If so, state the date or dates on which such photographs, movies and/or videotapes were taken, the subject thereof, who now has custody of them, and the name, address, occupation and employer of the person taking them.

16. Have you (or has anyone acting on your behalf) had any conversations with any person at any time with regard to the manner in which the occurrence complained of occurred, or have you overheard any statements made by any person at any time with regard to the injuries complained of by plaintiff or to the manner in which the occurrence complained of occurred? If the answer to this interrogatory is in the affirmative, state the following:

(a) The date or dates of such conversations and/or statements;

(b) The place of such conversations and/or statements;

(c) All persons present for the conversations and/or statements;

(d) The matters and things stated by the person in the conversations and/or statements;

(e) Whether the conversation was oral, written and/or recorded; and

(f) Who has possession of the statement if written and/or recorded.

17. Do you know of any statements made by any person relating to the occurrence? If so, give the name and address of each such witness, the date of the statement, and state whether such statement was written and/or oral.

18. Had you consumed any alcoholic beverage within 12 hours immediately prior to the occurrence? If so, state the names and addresses of those from whom it was obtained, where it was consumed, the particular kind and amount of alcoholic beverage so consumed by you, and the names and current residence addresses of all persons known by you to have knowledge concerning the consumption of alcoholic beverages.

19. Have you ever been convicted of a misdemeanor involving dishonesty, false statement or a felony? If so, state the nature thereof, the date of the conviction, and the court and the caption in which the conviction occurred. For the purpose of this interrogatory, a plea of guilty shall be considered as a conviction.

20. Had you used any drugs or medications within 24 hours immediately prior to the occur-

rence? If so, state the names and addresses of those from whom it was obtained, where it was used, the particular kind and amount of drug or medication so used by you, and the names and current residence addresses of all persons known by you to have knowledge concerning the use or said drug or medication.

21. Have you received any payment and/or other consideration from any source in compensation for the injuries alleged in your complaint? If your answer is in the affirmative, state:

(a) The amount of such payment and/or other consideration received;

(b) The name of the person, firm, insurance company and/or corporation making such payment or providing other consideration and the reason for the payment and/or other consideration; and

(c) Whether there are any documents evidencing such payment and/or other consideration received.

22. State the name and address of the registered owner of each vehicle involved in the occurrence.

23. Were you the owner and/or driver of the vehicle involved in the occurrence? If so, state whether the vehicle was repaired and, if so, state when, where, by whom, and the cost of the repairs.

24. What was the purpose and/or use for which the vehicle was being operated at the time of the occurrence?

25. State the names and addresses of all persons who have knowledge of the purpose for which the vehicle was being used at the time of the occurrence.

26. Pursuant to Illinois Supreme Court Rule 213(f), provide the name and address of each witness who will testify at trial and all other information required for each witness.

27. List the names and addresses of all other persons (other than yourself and persons heretofore listed) who have knowledge of the facts of the occurrence and/or the injuries and damages claimed to have resulted therefrom.

28. Identify any statements, information and/or documents known to you and requested by any of the foregoing interrogatories which you claim to be work product or subject to any common law or statutory privilege, and with respect to each interrogatory, specify the legal basis for the claim as required by Illinois Supreme Court Rule 201(n).

ATTESTATION

STATE OF ILLINOIS   )

) SS.

COUNTY OF _____)

_____, being first duly sworn on oath, deposes and states that he/she is a plaintiff in the above-captioned matter; that he/she has read the foregoing document, and the answers made herein are true, correct and complete to the best of his/her knowledge and belief.

SIGNATURE

SUBSCRIBED and SWORN to before me this ___ day of _____, 19 ___.

_____

NOTARY PUBLIC

MOTOR VEHICLE INTERROGATORIES TO DEFENDANTS

1. State the full name of the defendant answering, as well as your current residence address, date of birth, marital status, driver's license number and issuing state, and the last four digits of your social security number, and if different give the full name, as well as the current residence address, date of birth, marital status, driver's license number and issuing state, and the last four digits of the social security number of the individual signing these answers.

2. State the full name and current residence address of each person who witnessed or claims to have witnessed the occurrence that is the subject of this suit.

3. State the full name and current residence address of each person not named in interrogatory No. 2 above who was present and/or claims to have been present at the scene immediately before, at the time of, and/or immediately after the occurrence.

4. As a result of the occurrence, were you made a defendant in any criminal or traffic case? If so, state the court, the caption, the case number, the charge or charges filed against you, whether you pleaded guilty thereto and the final disposition.

5. Were you the owner and/or driver of the vehicle involved in the occurrence? If so, state whether the vehicle was repaired and, if so, state when, where, by whom, and the cost of the repairs.

6. Were you the owner and/or driver of any vehicle involved in the occurrence? If so, state whether you were named or covered under any policy, or policies, of liability insurance effective on the date of the occurrence and, if so, state the name of each such company or companies, the policy number or numbers, the effective period(s) and the maximum liability limits for each person and each occurrence, including umbrella or excess insurance coverage, property damage and medical payment coverage.

7. Do you have any information:

(a) That any plaintiff was, within the five years immediately prior to the occurrence, confined in a hospital and/or clinic, treated by a physician and/or other health professional, or x-rayed for any reason other than personal injury? If so, state each plaintiff so involved, the name and address of each such hospital and/or clinic, physician, technician and/or other health care professional, the approximate date of such confinement or service and state the reason for such confinement or service;

(b) That any plaintiff has suffered any serious personal injury and/or illness prior to the date of the occurrence? If so, state the name of each plaintiff so involved and state when, where and how he or she was injured and/or ill and describe the injuries and/or illness suffered;

(c) That any plaintiff has suffered any serious personal injury and/or illness since the date of the occurrence? If so, state the name of each plaintiff so involved and state when, where and how he or she was injured and/or ill and describe the injuries and/or illness suffered;

(d) That any plaintiff has ever filed any other suit for his or her own personal injuries? If so, state the name of each plaintiff so involved and state the court and caption in which filed, the year filed, the title and docket number of the case.

8. Were any photographs, movies and/or videotapes taken of the scene of the occurrence or of the persons and/or vehicles involved? If so, state the date or dates on which such photographs, movies and/or videotapes were taken, the subject thereof, who now has custody of them, and the name, address and occupation and employer of the person taking them.

9. Have you (or has anyone acting on your behalf) had any conversations with any person at any time with regard to the manner in which the occurrence complained of occurred, or have you overheard any statements made by any person at any time with regard to the injuries complained of by plaintiff or the manner in which the occurrence complained of occurred? If the answer to this interrogatory is in the affirmative, state the following:

(a) The date or dates of such conversations and/or statements;

(b) The place of such conversations and/or statements;

(c) All persons present for the conversations and/or statements;

(d) The matters and things stated by the person in the conversations and/or statements;

(e) Whether the conversation was oral, written and/or recorded; and

(f) Who has possession of the statement if written and/or recorded.

10. Do you know of any statements made by any person relating to the occurrence complained of by the plaintiff? If so, give the name and address of each such witness and the date of the statement, and state whether such statement was written and/or oral.

11. Had you consumed any alcoholic beverage within 12 hours immediately prior to the occurrence? If so, state the names and addresses of those from whom it was obtained, where it was consumed, the particular kind and amount of alcoholic beverage so consumed by you, and the names and current residence addresses of all persons known by you to have knowledge concerning the consumption of the alcoholic beverages.

12. Have you ever been convicted of a misdemeanor involving dishonesty, false statement or a felony? If so, state the nature thereof, the date of the conviction, and the court and the caption in which the conviction occurred. For the purpose of this interrogatory, a plea of guilty shall be considered as a conviction.

13. Had you used any drugs or medications within 24 hours immediately prior to the occurrence? If so, state the names and addresses of those from whom it was obtained, where it was used, the particular kind and amount of drug or medication so used by you, and the names and current residence addresses of all persons known by you to have knowledge concerning the use of the drug or medication.

14. Were you employed on the date of the occurrence? If so, state the name and address of your employer, and the date of employment and termination, if applicable. If your answer is in the affirmative, state the position, title and nature of your occupational responsibilities with respect to your employment.

15. What was the purpose and/or use for which the vehicle was being operated at the time of the occurrence?

16. State the names and addresses of all persons who have knowledge of the purpose for which the vehicle was being used at the time of the occurrence.

17. State the name and address of the registered owner of each vehicle involved in the occurrence.

18. Have you ever had your driver's license suspended or revoked? If so, state whether it was suspended or revoked, the date it was suspended or revoked, the reason for the suspension or revocation, the period of time for which it was suspended or revoked, and the state that issued the license.

19. Do you have or have you had any restrictions on your driver's license? If so, state the nature of the restrictions.

20. Do you have any medical and/or physical condition which required a physician's report and/or letter of approval in order to drive? If so, state the nature of the medical and/or physical condition, the physician or other health care professional who issued the letter and/or report, and the names and addresses of any physician or other health care professional who treated you for this condition prior to the occurrence.

21. State the name and address of any physician, ophthalmologist, optician or other health care professional who performed any eye examination of you within the last five years and the dates of each such examination.

22. State the name and address of any physician or other health care professional who examined and/or treated you within the last 10 years and the reason for such examination and/or treatment.

23. Pursuant to Illinois Supreme Court Rule 213(f), provide the name and address of each witness who will testify at trial and all other information required for each witness.

24. List the names and addresses of all other persons (other than yourself and persons heretofore listed) who have knowledge of the facts of the occurrence and/or of the injuries and damages claimed to have resulted therefrom.

25. Identify any statements, information and/or documents known to you and requested by any of

the foregoing interrogatories which you claim to be work product or subject to any common law or statutory privilege, and with respect to each interrogatory, specify the legal basis for the claim as required by Illinois Supreme Court Rule 201 (n).

ATTESTATION

STATE OF ILLINOIS   )
) SS.
COUNTY OF _____   )

_____, being first duly sworn on oath, deposes and states that he/she is a defendant in the above-captioned matter, that he/she has read the foregoing document, and the answers made herein are true, correct and complete to the best of his/her knowledge and belief.

_____

SIGNATURE

SUBSCRIBED and SWORN to before me this ___ day of _____, 19 ___.

_____

NOTARY PUBLIC

MATRIMONIAL INTERROGATORIES

1. State your full name, current address, date of birth and the last four digits of your social security number.

2. List all employment held by you during the preceding three years and with regard to each employment state:

(a) The name and address of each employer;

(b) Your position, job title or description;

(c) If you had an employment contract;

(d) The date on which you commenced your employment and, if applicable, the date and reason for the termination of your employment;

(e) Your current gross and net income per pay period;

(f) Your gross income as shown on the last W–2 tax and wage statement received by you, your social security wages as shown on the last W–2 tax and wage statement received by you, and the amounts of all deductions shown thereon; and

(g) All additional benefits or perquisites received from your employment stating the type and value thereof.

3. During the preceding three years, have you had any source of income other than from your employment listed above? If so, with regard to each source of income, state the following:

(a) The source of income, including the type of income and name and address of the source;

(b) The frequency in which you receive income from the source;

(c) The amount of income received by you from the source during the immediately preceding three years; and

(d) The amount of income received by you from the source for each month during the immediately preceding three years.

4. Do you own any interest in real estate? If so, with regard to each such interest state the following:

(a) The size and description of the parcel of real estate, including improvements thereon;

(b) The name, address and interest of each person who has or claims to have an ownership interest in the parcel of real estate;

(c) The date your interest in the parcel of real estate was acquired;

(d) The consideration you transferred or paid for your interest in the parcel of real estate;

(e) Your estimate of the current fair market value of the parcel of real estate and your interest therein; and

(f) The amount of any indebtedness owed on the parcel of real estate and to whom.

5. For the preceding three years, list the names and addresses of all associations, partnerships, corporations, enterprises or entities in which you have an interest or claim any interest, the nature of your interest or claim of interest therein the amount of percentage of your interest or claim of interest therein, and an estimate of the value of your interest therein.

6. During the preceding three years, have you had any account or investment in any type of financial institution, individually or with another or in the name of another, including checking accounts, savings accounts, certificates of deposit and money market accounts? If so, with regard to each such account or investment, state the following:

(a) The type of account or investment;

(b) The name and address of the financial institution;

(c) The name and address of each person in whose name the account is held; and

(d) Both the high and the low balance of the account or investment, stating the date of the high balance and the date of the low balance.

7. During the preceding three years, have you been the holder of or had access to any safety deposit boxes? If so, state the following:

(a) The name of the bank or institution where such box is located;

(b) The number of each box;

(c) A description of the contents of each box during the immediately preceding three years and as of the date of the answer; and

(d) The name and address of any joint or co-owners of such safety deposit box or any trustees holding the box for your benefit.

8. During the immediately preceding three years, has any person or entity held cash or property on your behalf? If so, state:

(a) The name and address of the person or entity holding the cash or property; and

(b) The type of cash or property held and the value thereof.

9. During the preceding three years, have you owned any stocks, bonds, securities or other investments, including savings bonds? If so, with regard

to each such stock, bond, security or investment state:

    (a) A description of the stock, bond, security or investment;

    (b) The name and address of the entity issuing the stock, bond, security or investment;

    (c) The present value of such stock, bond, security or investment;

    (d) The date of acquisition of the stock, bond, security or investment;

    (e) The cost of the stock, bond, security or investment;

    (f) The name and address of any other owner or owners in such stock, bond, security or investment; and

    (g) If applicable, the date sold and the amount realized therefrom.

10. Do you own or have any incidents of ownership in any life, annuity or endowment insurance policies? If so, with regard to each such policy state:

    (a) The name of the company;

    (b) The number of the policy;

    (c) The face value of the policy;

    (d) The present value of the policy;

    (e) The amount of any loan or encumbrance on the policy;

    (f) The date of acquisition of the policy; and

    (g) With regard to each policy, the beneficiary or beneficiaries.

11. Do you have any right, title, claim or interest in or to a pension plan, retirement plan or profit sharing plan, including, but not limited to, individual retirement accounts, 401(k) plans and deferred compensation plans? If so, with regard to each such plan state:

    (a) The name and address of the entity providing the plan;

    (b) The date of your initial participation in the plan; and

    (c) The amount of funds currently held on your behalf under the plan.

12. Do you have any outstanding indebtedness or financial obligations, including mortgages, promissory notes, or other oral or written contracts? If so, with regard to each obligation state the following:

    (a) The name and address of the creditor;

    (b) The form of the obligation;

    (c) The date the obligation was initially incurred;

    (d) The amount of the original obligation;

    (e) The purpose or consideration for which the obligation was incurred;

    (f) A description of any security connected with the obligation;

    (g) The rate of interest on the obligation;

    (h) The present unpaid balance of the obligation;

    (i) The dates and amounts of installment payments; and

    (j) The date of maturity of the obligation.

13. Are you owed any money or property? If so, state:

    (a) The name and address of the debtor;

    (b) The form of the obligation;

    (c) The date the obligation was initially incurred;

    (d) The amount of the original obligation;

    (e) The purpose or consideration for which the obligation was incurred;

    (f) The description of any security connected with the obligation;

    (g) The rate of interest on the obligation;

    (h) The present unpaid balance of the obligation;

    (i) The dates and amounts of installment payments; and

    (j) The date of maturity of the obligation.

14. State the year, make and model of each motor or motorized vehicle, motor or mobile home and farm machinery or equipment in which you have an ownership, estate, interest or claim of interest, whether individually or with another, and with regard to each item state:

    (a) The date the item was acquired;

    (b) The consideration paid for the item;

    (c) The name and address of each other person who has a right, title, claim or interest in or to the item;

    (d) The approximate fair market value of the item; and

    (e) The amount of any indebtedness on the item and the name and address of the creditor.

15. Have you purchased or contributed towards the payment for or provided other consideration or improvement with regard to any real estate, motorized vehicle, financial account or securities, or other property, real or personal, on behalf of another person or entity other than your spouse during the preceding three years. If so, with regard to each such transaction state:

    (a) The name and address of the person or entity to whom you contributed;

    (b) The type of contribution made by you;

    (c) The type of property to which the contribution was made;

    (d) The location of the property to which the contribution was made;

    (e) Whether or not there is written evidence of the existence of a loan; and

    (f) A description of the written evidence.

16. During the preceding three years, have you made any gift of cash or property, real or personal, to any person or entity not your spouse? If so, with regard to each such transaction state:

    (a) A description of the gift;

    (b) The value of the gift;

    (c) The date of the gift;

    (d) The name and address of the person or entity receiving the gift;

    (e) Whether or not there is written evidence of the existence of a gift; and

    (f) A description of the written evidence.

17. During the preceding three years, have you made any loans to any person or entity not your spouse and, if so, with regard to each such loan state:

    (a) A description of the loan;

    (b) The value of the loan;

    (c) The date of the loan;

    (d) The name and address of the person or entity receiving the loan;

    (e) Whether or not there is written evidence of the existence of a loan; and

    (f) A description of the written evidence.

18. During the preceding three years, have you sold, transferred, conveyed, encumbered, concealed, damaged or otherwise disposed of any property owned by you and/or your spouse individually or collectively? If so, with regard to each item of property state:

    (a) A description of the property;

    (b) The current location of the property;

    (c) The purpose or reason for the action taken by you with regard to the property;

    (d) The approximate fair market value of the property;

    (e) Whether or not there is written evidence of any such transaction; and

    (f) A description of the written evidence.

19. During the preceding three years, have any appraisals been made with regard to any of the property listed by you under your answers to these interrogatories? If so, state:

    (a) The name and address of the person conducting each such appraisal;

    (b) A description of the property appraised;

    (c) The date of the appraisal; and

    (d) The location of any copies of each such appraisal.

20. During the preceding three years, have you prepared or has anyone prepared for you any financial statements, net worth statements or lists of assets and liabilities pertaining to your property or financial affairs? If so, with regard to each such document state:

    (a) The name and address of the person preparing each such document;

    (b) The type of document prepared;

    (c) The date the document was prepared; and

    (d) The location of all copies of each such document.

21. State the name and address of any accountant, tax preparer, bookkeeper and other person, firm or entity who has kept or prepared books, documents and records with regard to your income, property, business or financial affairs during the course of this marriage.

22. List all nonmarital property claimed by you, identifying each item of property as to the type of property, the date received, the basis on which you claim it is nonmarital property, its location, and the present value of the property.

23. List all marital property of this marriage, identifying each item of property as to the type of property, the basis on which you claim it to be marital property, its location, and the present value of the property.

24. What contribution or dissipation has your spouse made to the marital estate, including but not limited to each of the items or property identified in response to interrogatories No. 22 and No. 23 above, citing specifics, if any, for each item of property?

25. Pursuant to Illinois Supreme Court Rule 213(f), provide the name and address of each witness who will testify at trial and all other information required for each witness.

26. Are you in any manner incapacitated or limited in your ability to earn income at the present time? If so, define and describe such incapacity or limitation, and state when such incapacity or limitation commenced and when it is expected to end.

27. Identify any statements, information and/or documents known to you and requested by any of the foregoing interrogatories which you claim to be work product or subject to any common law or statutory privilege, and with respect to each interrogatory, specify the legal basis for the claim as required by Illinois Supreme Court Rule 201 (n).

ATTESTATION

STATE OF ILLINOIS   )

) SS.

COUNTY OF _____)

_____, being first duly sworn on oath, deposes and states that he/she is a _____ in the above-captioned matter, that he/she has read the foregoing document, and the answers made herein are true, correct and complete to the best of his/her knowledge and belief.

_____

SIGNATURE

SUBSCRIBED and SWORN to before me this ___ day of _____, 19 ___.

_____

NOTARY PUBLIC

MEDICAL MALPRACTICE INTERROGATORIES

TO PLAINTIFF

1. State your full name, as well as your current residence address, the last four digits of your social security number, date and place of birth, and any other name by which you have ever been known.

2. Describe the acts and/or omissions of the defendant(s), *i.e.*, the specific diagnosis, procedure, test, therapy, treatment or other type of healing arts ministration which you claim caused or contributed to the injuries for which you seek damages and, as to each, state:

    (a) The date or dates thereof;

    (b) The name and address of each witness;

    (c) The names and addresses of all other persons having knowledge thereof and as to each such person the basis for his or her knowledge; and

(d) The location of any and all documents, including without limitation, hospital and medical records reflecting such acts and/or omissions.

3. State the full name, last known address, telephone number, occupation and/or profession, employer or business affiliation, and relationship to you of each person who has or claims to have knowledge that the defendant(s) deviated from any applicable standard of care in relation to you. As to each such person, state:

(a) The nature of such knowledge;

(b) The manner whereby it was acquired;

(c) The date or dates upon which such knowledge was acquired; and

(d) The identity and location of any and all documents reflecting such deviation.

4. Please state the name, address and specialty, if any, of all treating physicians, nurses, medical technicians or other persons practicing the healing arts in any of its branches with whom you or your attorneys have discussed any of the following:

(a) The standard of care owed to you by the defendant(s);

(b) The negligent acts and/or omissions described in your Complaint;

(c) The nature and extent of any injuries suffered by you; and

(d) The relationship between acts and/or omissions on the part of the defendant(s) and such injuries.

5. Do you know of any statements made by any person relating to the care and treatment or the damages alleged in the Complaint? If so, give the name and address of each such witness and the date of the statement, and state whether such statement was written or oral and if written the present location of each such statement.

6. State the name, author, publisher, title, and date of publication and specific provision of all medical texts, books, journals or other medical literature which you or your attorney intend to use as authority or reference in proving any of the allegations set forth in the Complaint.

7. Identify each and every rule, regulation, by-law, protocol, standard or writing of whatsoever nature by any professional group, association, credentialing body, accrediting authority or governmental agency which you, or your attorney, may use at trial to establish the standard of care owed by the defendant(s), or the breach thereof.

8. Please identify and state the location of any of the following documents relating to the issues in this case which either bear the name, handwriting and/or signature of the defendant(s):

(a) Publications and/or professional literature authored by the defendant(s), including publication source and reference;

(b) Correspondence, records, memoranda or other writings prepared by they defendant(s) regarding your diagnosis, care and treatment, other than medical and hospital records in this case; and

(c) Documents prepared by persons other than you or your attorneys which contain the name of the defendant(s).

9. Describe the personal injuries sustained by you as the result of the negligent act or omissions described in your Complaint.

10. With regard to your injuries, state:

(a) The name and address of each attending physician and/or health care professional;

(b) The name and address of each consulting physician and/or other health care professional;

(c) The name and address of each person and/or laboratory taking any X ray, MRI and/or other radiological tests of you;

(d) The date or inclusive dates on which each of them rendered you service;

(e) The amounts to date of their respective bills for service; and

(f) From which of them you have written reports.

11. As the result of your personal injuries, were you a patient or outpatient in any hospital and/or clinic? If so, state the names and addresses of all hospitals and/or clinics, the amounts of their respective bills and the date or inclusive dates of their services.

12. As the result of your personal injuries, were you unable to work? If so, state:

(a) The name and address of your employer, if any, at the time of the acts and/or omissions described in the Complaint, your wage and/or salary, and the name of your supervisor and/or foreperson.

(b) The date or inclusive dates on which you were unable to work;

(c) The amount of wage and/or income loss claimed by you; and

(d) The name and address of your present employer and your wage and/or salary.

13. State any and all other expenses and/or losses you claim as a result of the acts and/or omissions described in the complaint. As to each expense and/or loss, state the date or dates it was incurred, the name of the person, firm and/or company to whom such amounts are owed, whether the expense and/or loss in question has been paid and, if so, by whom it was so paid, and describe the reason and/or purpose for each expense and/or loss.

14. Had you suffered any personal injury or prolonged, serious and/or chronic illness within ten (10) years prior to the date of the acts and/or omissions described in your complaint? If so, state when and how you were injured and/or ill, where you were injured and/or ill, describe the injuries and/or illness suffered, and state the name and address of each physician, or other health care professional, hospital and/or clinic rendering you treatment for each injury and/or chronic illness.

For each physician, or other health care professional, hospital and/or clinic identified in the preceding paragraph, state the name and address of each insurance company or other entity (health maintenance organization, governmental public assistance program, *etc.*) which provided to you indemnity, reimbursement or other payment for the medical services received by you and as to each such payor, state the policy number, group number and/or identification number under which you were able to obtain such medical services.

15. Have you suffered any personal injury or prolonged, serious and/or chronic illness since the date of the negligent act or omission alleged in your complaint? If so, state when you were injured and/or ill, where and how you were injured and/or ill, describe the injuries and/or illness suffered, and state the name and address of each physician or other health care professional, hospital and/or clinic rendering you treatment for each injury and/or chronic illness.

16. Have any other suits been filed for your personal injuries preceding the filing of this lawsuit? If so, state the nature of the injuries claimed, the courts and the captions in which filed, the years filed, and the titles and docket numbers of the suits.

17. Have you filed a claim for and/or received workers' compensation benefits? If so, state the name and address of the employer, the date(s) of the accident(s), the identity of the insurance company that paid any such benefits and the case number(s) and jurisdiction(s) where filed.

18. Did defendant(s) or anyone associated with defendant(s) give you information or discuss with you the risks involved in the treatment to be given you? If so, state the date(s) and place(s) such information was given, the name(s) of the person(s) providing such information or engaging you in the discussion, and give a description of the information provided or discussed with you.

19. Are you claiming any psychiatric, psychological and/or emotional injuries as a result of the acts and/or omissions described in the complaint? If so, state:

(a) The name of any psychiatric, psychological and/or emotional injury claimed, and the name and address of each psychiatrist, physician, psychologist, therapist or other health care professional rendering you treatment for each injury;

(b) Whether you had suffered any psychiatric, psychological and/or emotional injury prior to the date of the acts and/or omissions described in the complaint; and

(c) If (b) is in the affirmative, please state when and the nature of any psychiatric, psychological and/or emotional injury, and the name and address of each psychiatrist, physician, psychologist, therapist or other health care professional rendering you treatment for each injury.

20. Pursuant to Illinois Supreme Court Rule 213(f), provide the name and address of each witness who will testify at trial and all other information required for each witness.

21. Do you have any photographs, movies and/or videotapes relating to the acts and/or omissions which are described in your complaint and/or the nature and extent of any injuries for which recovery is sought? If so, state the date or dates on which such photographs, movies and/or videotapes were taken, who was displayed therein, who now has custody of them, and the name, address, occupation and employer of the person taking them.

22. Have you (or has anyone acting on your behalf) had any conversations with any person at any time with regard to the manner in which the care and treatment described in your complaint was provided, or have you overheard any statement made by any person at any time with regard to the injuries complained of by plaintiff or the manner in which the care and treatment alleged in the complaint was provided? It so, state:

(a) The date or dates of such conversation(s) and/or statement(s);

(b) The place of such conversation(s) and/or statement(s);

(c) All persons present for the conversation(s) and/or statement(s);

(d) The matters and things stated by the person in the conversation(s) and/or statement(s);

(e) Whether the conversation(s) was oral, written and/or recorded; and

(f) Who has possession of the statement(s) if written and/or recorded.

23. Have you received any payment and/or other consideration from any source in compensation for the injuries alleged in your complaint? If your answer is in the affirmative, state:

(a) The amount of such payment and/or other consideration received;

(b) The name of the person, firm, insurance company and/or corporation making such payment or providing other consideration and the reason for the payment and/or other consideration; and

(c) Whether there are any documents evidencing such payment and/or other consideration received.

24. Identify any statements, information and/or documents known to you and requested by any of the foregoing interrogatories which you claim to be work product or subject to any common law or statutory privilege, and with respect to each interrogatory, specify the legal basis for the claim as required by Illinois Supreme Court Rule 201(n).

25. List the names and addresses of all persons (other than yourself and persons heretofore listed) who have knowledge of the facts regarding the care and treatment complained of in the complaint filed herein and/or of the injuries claimed to have resulted therefrom.

ATTESTATION

STATE OF ILLINOIS   )
) SS.
COUNTY OF _____)

_____, being first duly sworn on oath, deposes and states that he/she is a _____ in the above-captioned matter, that he/she has read the foregoing document, and the answers made herein are true, correct and complete to the best of his/her knowledge and belief.

_____

SIGNATURE

SUBSCRIBED and SWORN to before me this ___ day of _____, 19 ___.

_____

NOTARY PUBLIC

MEDICAL MALPRACTICE INTERROGATORIES
TO DEFENDANT DOCTOR

1. State your full name, professional and residence addresses, and attach a current copy of your *curriculum vitae* (CV). In the event you do not have a CV, state in detail your professional qualifications, including your education by identifying schools from which you graduated and the degrees granted and dates thereof, your medical internships and residencies, fellowships and a bibliography of your professional writing(s).

2. State whether you have held any position on a committee or with an administrative body at any hospital. If so, state when you held such position(s) and the duties and responsibilities involved in such position(s).

3. Have you ever been named as a defendant in a lawsuit arising from alleged malpractice or professional negligence? If so, state the court, the caption and the case number for each lawsuit.

4. Since the institution of this action, have you been asked to appear before or attend any meeting of a medical committee or official board of any medical society or other entity for the purpose of discussing this case? If so, state the date(s) of each such meeting and the name and address of the committee, society or other entity conducting each meeting.

5. Have you ever testified in court in a medical malpractice case? If so, state the court, the caption and the case number of each such case, the approximate date of your testimony, whether you testified as a treating physician or expert and whether you testified on your own behalf or on behalf of the defendant or the plaintiff.

6. Has your license to practice medicine ever been suspended or has any disciplinary action ever been taken against you in reference to your license? If so, state the specific disciplinary action taken, the date of the disciplinary action, the reason for the disciplinary action, the period of time for which the disciplinary action was effective and the name and address of the disciplinary entity taking the action.

7. State the exact dates and places on and at which you saw the plaintiff for the purpose of providing care or treatment.

8. State the name, author, publisher, title, date of publication and specific provision of all medical texts, books, journals or other medical literature which you or your attorney intend to use as authority or reference in defending any of the allegations set forth in the complaint.

9. Were you named or covered under any policy or policies of liability insurance at the time of the care and treatment alleged in the complaint? If so, state for each policy:

    a. The name of the insurance company;

    b. The policy number;

    c. The effective policy period;

    d. The maximum liability limits for each person and each occurrence, including umbrella and excess liability coverage; and

    e. The named insured(s) under the policy.

10. Are you incorporated as a professional corporation? If so, state the legal name of your corporation and the name(s) and address(es) for all shareholders.

11. If you are not incorporated as a professional corporation, state whether you were affiliated with a corporate medical practice or partnership in any manner on the date of the occurrence alleged in the complaint. If so, state the name of the corporate medical practice or partnership, the nature of your affiliation and the dates of your affiliation.

12. Were you at any time an employee, agent, servant, shareholder or partner of [NAME OF HOSPITAL]? If so, state the date(s) and nature of your relationship.

13. State whether there were any policies, procedures, guidelines, rules or protocols for [THE PROCEDURE COMPLAINED OF] that were in effect at [NAME OF THE HOSPITAL WHERE PROCEDURE WAS PERFORMED] at the time of the care and/or treatment alleged in the complaint. If so, state:

    a. Whether such policies, guidelines, rules or protocols are published and by whom;

    b. The effective date of said policies, guidelines, rules or protocols;

    c. Which medical professionals are bound by said policies, guidelines, rules or protocols;

    d. Who is the administrator of any such policies, procedures, guidelines, rules and/or protocols; and

    e. Whether the policies, guidelines, rules or protocols in effect at the time of the occurrence alleged in the complaint have been changed, amended, or altered since the occurrence. If so, state the change(s) and the date(s) of any such change(s).

14. Were any photographs, movies and/or videotapes taken of the plaintiff or of the procedures complained of? If so, state the date(s) on which such photographs, movies and/or videotapes were taken, who is displayed therein, who now has custody of them, and the name, address, occupation and employer of the person taking them.

15. Do you know of any statements made by any person relating to the care and treatment or the damages described in the complaint? If so, give the name and address of each such witness and the date of the statement, and state whether such statement was written or oral and if written the present location of each such statement.

16. Do you have any information:

    a. That any plaintiff was, within the 10 years immediately prior to the care and treatment described in the complaint, confined in a hospital and/or clinic, treated by a physician and/or other health professional, or x-rayed for any reason other than personal injury? If so, state the name of each plaintiff so involved, the name and address of each such hospital and/or clinic, physician, technician and/or health-care professional, the approximate date of such confinement or service and state the reason for such confinement or service.

b. That any plaintiff has suffered any serious personal injury and/or illness within 10 years prior to the date of the occurrence? If so, state the name of each plaintiff so involved and state when, where and how he or she was injured and/or ill and describe the injuries and/or illness suffered.

c. That any plaintiff has suffered any serious personal injury and/or illness since the date of the occurrence? If so, state the name of each plaintiff so involved and state when, where and how he or she was injured and/or ill and describe the injuries and/or illness suffered.

d. That any other suits have been filed for any plaintiff's personal injuries? If so, state the name of each plaintiff involved, the nature of the injuries claimed, the court(s) and caption(s) in which filed, the year(s) filed, and the title(s) and docket number(s) of the suit(s).

e. That any claim for workers' compensation benefits has been filed for any plaintiff? If so, state the name and address of the employer, the date(s) of the accident(s), the identity of the insurance company that paid any such benefits and the case number(s) and jurisdiction(s) where filed.

17. Have you (or has anyone acting on your behalf) had any conversations with any person at any time with regard to the manner in which the care and treatment described in the complaint was provided, or have you overheard any statement made by any person at any time with regard to the injuries complained of by the plaintiff or the manner in which the care and treatment described in the complaint was provided? If so, state the following:

a. The date or dates of such conversation(s) and/or statement (s);

b. The place of such conversation(s) and/or statements(s);

c. All persons present for the conversation(s) and/or statement(s);

d. The matters and things stated by the person in the conversation(s) and/or statement(s);

e. Whether the conversation(s) was oral, written and/or recorded; and

f. Who has possession of the statement(s) if written and/or recorded.

18. Pursuant to Illinois Supreme Court Rule 213(f), provide the name and address of each witness who will testify at trial and all other information required for each witness.

19. Identify any statements, information and/or documents known to you and requested by any of the foregoing interrogatories which you claim to be work product or subject to any common law or statutory privilege, and with respect to each interrogatory, specify the legal basis for the claim as required by Illinois Supreme Court Rule 201 (n).

20. List the name and addresses of all persons (other than yourself and persons heretofore listed) who have knowledge of the facts regarding the care and treatment complained of in the complaint filed

herein and/or of the injuries claimed to have resulted therefrom.

ATTESTATION

STATE OF ILLINOIS   )
) SS.
COUNTY OF _____   )

_____, being first duly sworn on oath, deposes and states that he/she is a plaintiff in the above-captioned matter; that he/she has read the foregoing document, and the answers made herein are true, correct and complete to the best of his/her knowledge and belief.

_____
SIGNATURE

SUBSCRIBED and SWORN to before me this ___ day of _____, 19 ___.

_____
NOTARY PUBLIC

MEDICAL MALPRACTICE INTERROGATORIES TO DEFENDANT HOSPITAL

1. State the full name and address of the person answering and, if different, the full name and address of the individual signing the answers.

2. Do you know of any statements made by any person relating to the care and treatment of the plaintiff or the damages alleged of in the complaint? If so, give the name and address of each such witness and the date of the statement, and state whether such statement was written or oral and if written the present location of each such statement.

3. Has the [NAME OF DEFENDANT HOSPITAL] been named as a defendant in a lawsuit arising from alleged malpractice or professional negligence during the 8 year period preceding the filing of this lawsuit? If so, state the court, the caption and the case number for such lawsuit.

4. State whether [NAME OF DEFENDANT HOSPITAL] was named or covered under any policy or policies of medical liability insurance at the time of the care or treatment alleged in the complaint? If so, state for each policy:

a. The name of the insurance company;

b. The policy number;

c. The effective policy period;

d. The maximum liability limits for each person and each occurrence, including umbrella and excess liability coverage; and

e. The named insured(s) under each policy.

5. State whether any hearing dealing with mortality or morbidity was held regarding the care and treatment of the plaintiff alleged in the Complaint.

6. State the name, author, publisher, title, date of publication and specific provision of all medical texts, books, journals or other medical literature which you or your attorney intend to use as authority or reference in defending any of the allegations set forth in the Complaint.

7. Identify each and every rule, regulation, by-law or other document of any hospital, association, licensing authority, accrediting authority or other

private body which you, or your attorneys, may use at trial in defense of the allegations contained in the Complaint.

8. State whether there were any policies, procedures, guidelines, rules or protocols for [PROCEDURE COMPLAINED OF] in effect at [DEFENDANT HOSPITAL] at the time of the care and/or treatment of the plaintiff alleged in the Complaint. If so, state:

a. Whether such policies, procedures, opinions, rules or protocols are published and by whom;

b. The effective date of said policies, procedures, guidelines, rules or protocols;

c. Which medical professionals are bound by said policies, procedures, guidelines, rules or protocols;

d. Who is the administrator of any such policies, procedures, guidelines, rules or protocols; and

e. Whether the policies, procedures, guidelines, rules or protocols in effect at the time of the occurrence alleged in the Complaint have been changed, amended or altered after the occurrence. If so, state the change(s) and the date(s) of any such change(s).

9. Was [DEFENDANT DOCTOR] an employee, agent, servant, shareholder or partner of [DEFENDANT HOSPITAL] at the time of the care or treatment of the plaintiff alleged in the Complaint? If so, state with specificity the nature of the relationship.

10. State for each person who directly or indirectly was involved in the care or treatment of the plaintiff alleged in the Complaint:

a. That person's full name and current residence address;

b. The name and current address of that person's employer;

c. The employment relationship of that person with [DEFENDANT HOSPITAL];

d. The date(s) of such person's care or treatment, including a description of the care or treatment; and

e. The name and current address of any other individual present when the care or treatment was rendered.

11. Were any photographs, movies and/or videotapes taken of the plaintiff or of the procedures complained of? If so, state the date(s) on which such photographs, movies and/or videotapes were taken, who is displayed therein, who now has custody of them, and the name, address, occupation and employer of the person taking them.

12. Have you (or has anyone acting on your behalf) had any conversations with any person at any time with regard to the manner in which the care and treatment alleged in the complaint was provided, or have you overheard any statement made by any persons at any time with regard to the injuries complained of by the plaintiff or the manner in which the care and treatment alleged in the complaint was provided? If so, state:

a. The date or dates of such conversation(s) and/or statements(s);

b. The place of such conversation(s) and/or statement(s);

c. All persons present for the conversation(s) and/or statement(s);

d. The matters and things stated by the person in the conversation(s) and/or statement(s);

e. Whether the conversation(s) was oral, written and/or recorded; and

f. Who has possession of the statement(s) if written and/or recorded.

13. Do you have any information:

a. That any plaintiff was, within the 10 years immediately prior to the care and treatment alleged in the complaint, confined in a hospital and/or clinic, treated by a physician and/or other health professional, or x-rayed for any reason other than personal injury? If so, state the name of each plaintiff so involved, the name and address of each such hospital and/or clinic, physician, technician and/or other health care professional, the approximate date of such confinement or service and state the reason for such confinement or service.

b. That any plaintiff has suffered any serious personal injury and/or illness within 10 years prior to the date of the occurrence? If so, state the name of each plaintiff so involved and state when, where and how he or she was injured and/or ill and describe the injuries and/or illness suffered.

c. That any plaintiff has suffered any serious personal injury and/or illness since the date of the occurrence? If so, state the name of each plaintiff so involved and state when, where and how he or she was injured and/or ill and describe the injuries and/or illness suffered.

d. That any other suit has been filed for any plaintiff's personal injuries? If so, state the name of each plaintiff involved, the nature of the injuries claimed, the court(s) and caption(s) in which filed, the year(s) filed, and the title(s) and docket number(s) of the suit(s).

e. That any claim for workers' compensation benefits has been filed for any plaintiff? If so, state the name and address of the employer, the date(s) of the accident(s), the identity of the insurance company that paid any such benefits and the case number(s) and jurisdiction(s) where filed.

14. Pursuant to Illinois Supreme Court Rule 213(f), provide the name and address of each witness who will testify at trial and all other information required for each witness.

15. Identify any statements, information and/or documents known to you and requested by any of the foregoing interrogatories which you claim to be work product or subject to any common law or statutory privilege, and with respect to each interrogatory, specify the legal basis for the claim as required by Illinois Supreme Court Rule 201 (n).

16. List the name and address of all persons (other than yourself and persons heretofore listed) who have knowledge of the facts of the care and treatment complained of in the complaint filed here-

in and/or of the injuries claimed to have resulted therefrom.

ATTESTATION

STATE OF ILLINOIS   )
) SS.
COUNTY OF _____)

_____, being first duly sworn on oath, deposes and states that he/she is a defendant in the above-captioned matter, that he/she has read the foregoing document, and the answers made herein are true, correct and complete to the best of his/her knowledge and belief.

_____
SIGNATURE
SUBSCRIBED and SWORN to before me this ___ day of _____, 19 ___.

_____
NOTARY PUBLIC

Rule 214. Discovery of Documents, Objects, and Tangible Things—Inspection of Real Estate

(a) Any party may by written request direct any other party to produce for inspection, copying, reproduction photographing, testing or sampling specified documents, including electronically stored information as defined under Rule 201(b)(4), objects or tangible things, or to permit access to real estate for the purpose of making surface or subsurface inspections or surveys or photographs, or tests or taking samples, or to disclose information calculated to lead to the discovery of the whereabouts of any of these items, whenever the nature, contents, or condition of such documents, objects, tangible things, or real estate is relevant to the subject matter of the action. The request shall specify a reasonable time, which shall not be less than 28 days except by agreement or by order of court, and the place and manner of making the inspection and performing the related acts.

(b) With regard to electronically stored information as defined in Rule 201(b)(4), if a request does not specify a form for producing electronically stored information, a party must produce it in a form or forms in which it is ordinarily maintained or in a reasonably usable form or forms.

(c) One copy of the request shall be served on all other parties entitled to notice. A party served with the written request shall (1) identify all materials in the party's possession responsive to the request and copy or provide reasonable opportunity for copying or inspections. Production of documents shall be as they are kept in the usual course of business or organized and labeled to correspond with the categories in the request, or (2) serve upon the party so requesting written objections on the ground that the request is improper in whole or in part. If written objections to a part of the request are made, the remainder of the request shall be complied with. A party may object to a request on the basis that the burden or expense of producing the requested materials would be disproportionate to the likely benefit, in light of the factors set out in Rule 201(c)(3). Any objection to the request or the refusal to respond shall be heard by the court upon prompt notice and motion of the party submitting the request. If the party claims that the item is not in his or her possession or control or that he or she does not have information calculated to lead to the discovery of its whereabouts, the party may be ordered to submit to examination in open court or by deposition regarding such claim. The producing party shall furnish an affidavit stating whether the production is complete in accordance with the request. Copies of identifications, objections and affidavits of completeness shall be served on all parties entitled to notice.

(d) A party has a duty to seasonably supplement any prior response to the extent of documents, objects or tangible things which subsequently come into that party's possession or control or become known to that party.

(e) This rule does not preclude an independent action against a person not a party for production of documents and things and permission to enter upon real estate.

Amended June 28, 1974, eff. Sept. 1, 1974; Sept. 28, 1976, eff. Nov. 15, 1976; June 1, 1995, eff. Jan. 1, 1996; May 29, 2014, eff. July 1, 2014.

Formerly Ill.Rev.Stat.1991, ch. 110A, ¶ 214.

Committee Comments
(Revised May 29, 2014)
Paragraphs (a) and (b)

The Committee reorganized Rule 214 as well as creating new paragraph (b), which is modeled after Federal Rule of Civil Procedure 34(b).

Paragraph (c)

The Committee's intent was to assist in the area of electronically stored information by allowing for identification of materials.

Committee Comments
(Revised June 1, 1995)

As originally promulgated Rule 214 was patterned after former Rule 17. It provided for discovery of documents and tangible things, and for entry upon real estate, in the custody or control of any "party or other person," by moving the court for an order compelling such discovery. In 1974, the rule was amended to eliminate the requirement of a court order. Under the amended rule a party seeking production of documents or tangible things or entry on real estate in the custody or control of any other party may serve the party with a request for the production of the documents or things, or for permission to enter upon the real estate. The party receiving the request must comply with it or serve objections. If objections are served, the party seeking the discovery may serve a notice of hearing on the objections, or in case of failure to respond to the request may move the court for an order under Rule 219(a).

The request procedure may be utilized only when discovery is sought from a party to the action. Discovery of documents and tangible things in the custody or control of a person not a party may be obtained by serving him with a subpoena *duces tecum* for the taking of his deposition. The last paragraph of the rule was added to indicate that the rule is not preemptive of an independent action for discovery in the nature of a bill in equity. Such an action can be employed, then, in the occasional case in which a party seeks to inspect real estate that is in the custody or control of a person not a party to the main action.

The first paragraph has been revised to require a party producing documents to produce those documents organized in the order in which they are kept in the usual course of business, or organized and labeled to correspond with the categories in the request. This revision requires the party producing documents and that party's attorney to make a good-faith review of documents produced to ensure full compliance with the request, but not to burden the requesting party with nonresponsive documents.

The failure to organize the requested documents as required by this rule, or the production of nonresponsive documents intermingled among the requested documents, constitutes a discovery abuse subject to sanctions under Rule 219.

The first paragraph has also been amended to require a party to include in that party's production response all responsive information in computer storage in printed form. This change is intended to prevent parties producing information from computer storage on storage disks or in any other manner which tends to frustrate the party requesting discovery from being able to access the information produced.

Rule 201(b) has also been amended to include in the definition of "documents" all retrievable information in computer storage, so that there can be no question but that a producing party must search its computer storage when responding to a request to produce documents pursuant to this rule.

The last sentence of the first paragraph has also been revised to make mandatory the requirement that the party producing documents furnish an affidavit stating whether the production is complete in accordance with the request. Previously, the party producing documents was not required to furnish such an affidavit unless requested to do so.

The second paragraph is new. This paragraph parallels the similar requirement in Rule 213 that a party must seasonably supplement any prior response to the extent that documents, objects or tangible things subsequently come into that party's possession or control or become known to that party. A party who has knowledge of documents, objects or tangible things responsive to a previously served request must disclose that information to the requesting party whether or not the actual documents, objects or tangible things are in the posses-

sion of the responding party. To the extent that responsive documents, objects or tangible things are not in the responding party's possession, the compliance affidavit requires the producing party to identify the location and nature of such responsive documents, objects or tangible things. It is the intent of this rule that a party must produce all responsive documents, objects or tangible things in its possession, and fully disclose the party's knowledge of the existence and location of responsive documents, objects or tangible things not in its possession so as to enable the requesting party to obtain the responsive documents, objects or tangible things from the custodian.

Rule 215. Physical and Mental Examination of Parties and Other Persons

(a) Notice; Motion; Order. In any action in which the physical or mental condition of a party or of a person in the party's custody or legal control is in controversy, the court, upon notice and on motion made within a reasonable time before the trial, may order such party to submit to a physical or mental examination by a licensed professional in a discipline related to the physical or mental condition which is involved. The motion shall suggest the identity of the examiner and set forth the examiner's specialty or discipline. The court may refuse to order examination by the examiner suggested but in that event shall permit the party seeking the examination to suggest others. A party or person shall not be required to travel an unreasonable distance for the examination. The order shall fix the time, place, conditions, and scope of the examination and designate the examiner. The party calling an examiner to testify at trial shall disclose the examiner as a controlled expert witness in accordance with these rules.

(b) Examiner's Fee and Compensation for Loss of Earnings. The party requesting the examination shall pay the fee of the examiner and compensation for any loss of earnings incurred or to be incurred by the party or person to be examined in complying with the order for examination, and shall advance all reasonable expenses incurred or to be incurred by the party or person in complying with the order.

(c) Examiner's Report. Within 21 days after the completion of the examination, the examiner shall prepare and mail or deliver to the attorneys for the party requesting the examination and the party examined duplicate originals of a written report of the examination, setting out the examiner's findings, results of all tests made, and the examiner's diagnosis and conclusions. The court may enforce compliance with this requirement. If the report is not delivered or mailed to the attorney for the party examined within the time herein specified or within any extensions or modifications thereof granted by the court, neither the examiner's report, the examiner's testimony, the examiner's findings, X-ray films, nor the results of any tests the examiner has made may be received in evidence except at the instance of the party examined or who produced the person examined. No examiner under this rule shall be considered a consultant.

(d) Impartial Medical Examiner.

(1) *Examination Before Trial.* A reasonable time in advance of the trial, the court may on its own motion or that of any party, order an impartial physical or mental examination of a party where conflicting medical testimony, reports or other documentation has been offered as proof and the party's mental or physical condition is thereby placed in issue, when in the court's discretion it appears that such an examination will materially aid in the just determination of the case. The examination shall be made by a member or members of a panel of physicians chosen for their special qualifications by the Administrative Office of the Illinois Courts.

(2) *Examination During Trial.* Should the court at any time during the trial find that compelling considerations make it advisable to have an examination and report at that time, the court may in its discretion so order.

(3) *Copies of Report.* A copy of the report of examination shall be given to the court and to the attorneys for the parties.

(4) *Testimony of Examining Physician.* Either party or the court may call the examining physician or physicians to testify. Any physician so called shall be subject to cross-examination.

(5) *Costs and Compensation of Physician.* The examination shall be made, and the physician or physicians, if called, shall testify without cost to the parties. The court shall determine the compensation of the physician or physicians.

(6) *Administration of Rule.* The Administrative Director and the Deputy Administrative Director are charged with the administration of the rule.

Amended June 1, 1995, eff. Jan. 1, 1996; March 28, 2002, eff. July 1, 2002; amended, eff. March 28, 2011.

Formerly Ill.Rev.Stat.1991, ch. 110A, ¶ 215.

Committee Comments
(Revised June 1, 1995)

This rule is derived from former Rules 17–1 and 17–2. The language of Rule 17–1 was not changed except that the time in which the examining physician shall present his findings has been extended to 21 days in paragraph (c) of Rule 215. Under former Rule 17–1(3) that period was 20 days. Paragraph (c) of the new rule also requires that the physician present his report 14 days before trial. Former Rule 17–1(3) required the physician to present his findings not later than 10 days before trial. These changes are consistent with the committee's general policy of establishing time periods in multiples of seven days.

Former Rule 17–2 has been revised as paragraph (d) of the new rule, but the substance is not

changed, except that the provision is no longer limited to personal injury cases.

This rule is intended to provide an orderly procedure for the examination of civil litigants whose physical or mental condition is in controversy. Originally, the rule concerned only physicians. The new rule recognizes that a number of professionals in other health-related disciplines are licensed to perform physical and mental examinations and therefore the designation "licensed professional" is substituted for "physician." The new language was adopted to effectuate the objectives of the rule with minimal judicial involvement. The requirement of "good cause" was therefore eliminated as grounds for seeking an examination.

Timing is the critical consideration. Examining professionals under the rule fall within the classification of opinion witnesses under Supreme Court Rule 213(g) as opposed to consultants under Supreme Court Rule 201(b)(3). Consequently, the rule has been amended to require that the examination be scheduled in order that the report contemplated by subsection (c) is provided in accordance with the deadlines imposed by Supreme Court Rule 218(c). In addition, the failure to provide the attorney for the party who was examined with a copy of the examiner's report within the 21–day period specified by paragraph (c) will result in exclusion of the examiner's testimony, opinions, and the results of any tests or X-rays that were performed.

Supreme Court Rule 215 is the compilation of rules previously and independently suggested by the Illinois Judicial Conference Committee on Discovery Procedures and the Supreme Court Rules Committee. The new rule allows for physical and mental examinations of "licensed professionals" and not merely physicians. The contemplated circumstances include sociologists, psychologists or other licensed professionals in juvenile, domestic relations and child custody cases. The Committee feels that this will aid not only in the previously designated cases but in other circumstances where it may become necessary for such a "professional" to be utilized. In particular, smaller counties have had difficulty in finding psychiatrists because of their limited number and lack of availability. This rule should help to alleviate this problem. The requirement of "good cause" for seeking such an examination was eliminated from the rule. In addition, the reference to the Illinois State Medical Society has been stricken, and the Administrative Office of the Illinois Courts has been substituted in its place.

(March 28, 2002)

This rule is amended to conform to the changes in terminology made in Supreme Court Rule 213.

(March 28, 2011)

Paragraph (d) provides that a trial court may order impartial medical examinations only where the parties have presented conflicting medical testimony, reports or other such documentation which places a party's mental or physical condition "in issue" and, in the court's discretion, it appears that the examination will materially aid in the just determination of the case. Mere allegations are insufficient to place a party's mental or physical condition "in issue."

The impartial medical examiner cannot answer the ultimate legal issues in the case; rather, the examiner can render a medical opinion which can assist in the resolution of those issues.

Rule 216. Admission of Fact or of Genuineness of Documents

(a) Request for Admission of Fact. A party may serve on any other party a written request for the admission by the latter of the truth of any specified relevant fact set forth in the request. A copy of the request for admission shall be served on all parties entitled to notice.

(b) Request for Admission of Genuineness of Document. A party may serve on any other party a written request for admission of the genuineness of any relevant documents described in the request. Copies of the documents shall be served with the request unless copies have already been furnished.

(c) Admission in the Absence of Denial. Each of the matters of fact and the genuineness of each document of which admission is requested is admitted unless, within 28 days after service thereof, the party to whom the request is directed serves upon the party requesting the admission either (1) a sworn statement denying specifically the matters of which admission is requested or setting forth in detail the reasons why the party cannot truthfully admit or deny those matters or (2) written objections on the ground that some or all of the requested admissions are privileged or irrelevant or that the request is otherwise improper in whole or in part. If written objections to a part of the request are made, the remainder of the request shall be answered within the period designated in the request. A denial shall fairly meet the substance of the requested admission. If good faith requires that a party deny only a part, or requires qualification, of a matter of which an admission is requested, the party shall specify so much of it as is true and deny only the remainder. Any objection to a request or to an answer shall be heard by the court upon prompt notice and motion of the party making the request. The response to the request, sworn statement of denial, or written objection, shall be served on all parties entitled to notice.

(d) Public Records. If any public records are to be used as evidence, the party intending to use them may prepare a copy of them insofar as they are to be used, and may seasonably present the copy to the adverse party by notice in writing, and the copy shall thereupon be admissible in evidence as admitted facts in the case if otherwise admissible, except insofar as its inaccuracy is pointed out under oath by the adverse party in an affidavit filed and served within 28 days after service of the notice.

(e) Effect of Admission. Any admission made by a party pursuant to request under this rule is for the purpose of the pending action and any action commenced pursuant to the authority of section 13–217 of the Code of Civil Procedure (735 ILCS 5/13–217) only. It does not constitute an admission by him for any other purpose and may not be used against him in any other proceeding.

(f) Number of Requests. The maximum number of requests for admission a party may serve on another party is 30, unless a higher number is agreed to by the parties or ordered by the court for good cause shown. If a request has subparts, each subpart counts as a separate request.

(g) Special Requirements. A party must: (1) prepare a separate document which contains only the requests and the documents required for genuine document requests; (2) serve this document separate from other documents; and (3) put the following warning in a prominent place on the first page in 12–point or larger boldface type: **"WARNING: If you fail to serve the response required by Rule 216 within 28 days after you are served with this document, all the facts set forth in the requests will be deemed true and all the documents described in the requests will be deemed genuine."**

Amended July 1, 1985, eff. Aug. 1, 1985; May 30, 2008, eff. immediately; Oct. 1, 2010, eff. Jan. 1, 2011; Jan. 4, 2013, eff. immediately; March 15, 2013, eff. May 1, 2013; May 29, 2014, eff. July 1, 2014.

Formerly Ill.Rev.Stat.1991, ch. 110A, ¶ 216.

Committee Comment
(October 1, 2010)

Paragraphs (f) and (g) are designed to address certain problems with Rule 216, including the service of hundreds of requests for admission. For the vast majority of cases, the limitation to 30 requests now found in paragraph (f) will eliminate this abusive practice. Other noted problems include the bundling of discovery requests to form a single document into which the requests to admit were intermingled. This practice worked to the disadvantage of certain litigants, particularly pro se litigants, who do not understand that failure to respond within the time allowed results in the requests being deemed admitted. Paragraph (g) provides for requests to be contained in a separate paper containing a boldface warning regarding the effect of the failure to respond within 28 days. *Consistent with Vision Point of Sale Inc. v. Haas,* 226 Ill.2d 334 (2007), trial courts are vested with discretion with respect to requests for admission.

Committee Comments
(Revised July 1, 1985)

This rule is derived from former Rule 18. Despite the usefulness of requests for admission of facts in narrowing issues, such requests seem to have been used very little in Illinois practice. The committee was of the opinion that perhaps this has resulted in part from the fact that they are provided for in the text of a rule that reads as if it relates primarily to admission of the genuineness of documents. Accordingly, it has rewritten the rule to place the authorization for request for admission of facts in a separate paragraph. No change in the substance of former Rule 18 was intended.

Subparagraph (e) was amended in 1985 to resolve an apparent conflict about whether admissions are carried over into subsequent cases between the same parties, involving the same subject matter, as are the fruits of other discovery activities (see Rule 212(d)). Relief from prior admissions is available to the same extent in the subsequent action as in the case which was dismissed or remanded.

Rule 217. Depositions for the Purpose of Perpetuating Testimony

(a) Before Action.

(1) *Petition.* A person who desires to perpetuate his own testimony or that of another person regarding any matter that is or may be cognizable in any court or proceeding may file a verified petition in the court of the county in which the action or proceeding might be brought or had or in which one or more of the persons to be examined reside. The petition shall be entitled in the name of the petitioner as petitioner and against all other expected parties or interested persons, including unknown owners, as respondents and shall show: (i) the facts which he desires to establish by the proposed testimony and his reasons for desiring to perpetuate it, (ii) the names or a description of the persons interested or whom he expects will be adverse parties and their addresses so far as known, and (iii) the names and addresses of the persons to be examined, and shall ask for an order authorizing the petitioner to take the depositions of the persons to be examined named in the petition for the purpose of perpetuating their testimony.

(2) *Notice and Service.* The petitioner shall serve upon each person named or described in the petition as respondent a copy of the petition, together with a notice stating that the petitioner will apply to the court, at a time and place designated in the notice, for the order described in the petition. Unless a shorter period is fixed by the court, the notice shall be served either within or without the State at least 21 days before the date of hearing, in the manner provided for service of summons. If service cannot with due diligence be made upon any respondent named or described in the petition, the court may by order provide for service by publication or otherwise. For persons not personally served and not otherwise represented, the court shall appoint an attorney who shall represent them and cross-examine the deponent. If any respondent is a minor or a person under legal disability or not yet in being, a guardian *ad litem* shall be appointed to represent his interests. The fees and costs of a court-appointed attorney or guardian *ad litem* shall be borne by the petitioner.

(3) *Order and Examination.* If the court is satisfied that the perpetuation of the testimony may prevent a failure or delay of justice, it shall make an order designating or describing the persons whose depositions may be taken, specifying the subject matter of the examination and whether the depositions shall be taken upon oral examination or written questions, and fixing the time, place, and conditions of the examination.

(b) Pending Appeal. If an appeal has been taken from the judgment of a trial court, or before the taking of an appeal if the time therefor has not expired, the court in which the judgment was rendered may on motion and for good cause shown allow the taking of depositions of witnesses to perpetuate their testimony for use in the event of further proceedings in that court.

Amended May 28, 1982, eff. July 1, 1982.

Formerly Ill.Rev.Stat.1991, ch. 110A, ¶ 217.

Committee Comments

This rule is derived from former Rule 21. The language is substantially unchanged except that, in keeping with the Committee's general policy, subparagraph (a)(2) requires notice to be given at least 21 days before date of the hearing, as opposed to 20 days under former Rule 21(1)(b); and that subparagraph (a)(2) adds the requirement that petitioner pay the expenses of a court appointed attorney or guardian ad litem.

Rule 218. Pretrial Procedure

(a) Initial Case Management Conference. Except as provided by local circuit court rule, which on petition of the chief judge of the circuit has been approved by the Supreme Court, the court shall hold a case management conference within 35 days after the parties are at issue and in no event more than 182 days following the filing of the complaint. At the conference counsel familiar with the case and authorized to act shall appear and the following shall be considered:

(1) the nature, issues, and complexity of the case;

(2) the simplification of the issues;

(3) amendments to the pleadings;

(4) the possibility of obtaining admissions of fact and of documents which will avoid unnecessary proof;

(5) limitations on discovery including:

(i) the number and duration of depositions which may be taken;

(ii) the area of expertise and the number of expert witnesses who may be called; and

(iii) deadlines for the disclosure of witnesses and the completion of written discovery and depositions;

(6) the possibility of settlement and scheduling of a settlement conference;

(7) the advisability of alternative dispute resolution;

(8) the date on which the case should be ready for trial;

(9) the advisability of holding subsequent case management conferences; and

(10) any other matters which may aid in the disposition of the action including but not limited to issues involving electronically stored information and preservation.

(b) Subsequent Case Management Conferences. At the initial and any subsequent case management conference, the court shall set a date for a subsequent management conference or a trial date.

(c) Order. At the case management conference, the court shall make an order which recites any action taken by the court, the agreements made by the parties as to any of the matters considered, and which specifies as the issues for trial those not disposed of at the conference. The order controls the subsequent course of the action unless modified. All dates set for the disclosure of witnesses, including rebuttal witnesses, and the completion of discovery shall be chosen to ensure that discovery will be completed not later than 60 days before the date on which the trial court reasonably anticipates that trial will commence, unless otherwise agreed by the parties. This rule is to be liberally construed to do substantial justice between and among the parties.

(d) Calendar. The court shall establish a pretrial calendar on which actions shall be placed for consideration, as above provided, either by the court on its own motion or on the motion of any party.

Amended June 1, 1995, effective January 1, 1996; amended May 31, 2002, effective July 1, 2002; amended October 4, 2002, effective immediately; May 29, 2014, eff. July 1, 2014.

Formerly Ill.Rev.Stat.1991, ch. 110A, ¶ 218.

Committee Comment
(Revised May 29, 2014)
Paragraph (a)

Paragraph (a), subparagraph (10) is intended to encourage parties to use the case management conference to resolve issues concerning electronically stored information early in the case.

Committee Comment
(October 4, 2002)

The rule is amended to clarify that case management orders will set dates for disclosure of rebuttal witnesses, if any, and that parties may agree to waive or modify the 60–day rule without altering the trial date.

Committee Comment
(May 31, 2002)

This rule is amended to conform to the changes in terminology made in Supreme Court Rule 213.

Committee Comments
(Revised June 1, 1995)

This rule is former Rule 22.

Rule 218 has been substantially modified to implement the objective of early and ongoing differential case management. The former rule contemplated a single pretrial conference which could be held at the discretion of the court. The new rule mandates an initial case management conference which must be held within 35 days after the parties are at issue or in any event not later than 182 days after the complaint is filed. The principal goal of the initial case management conference is to tailor the future course of the litigation to reflect the singular characteristics of the case.

The new rule recognizes that each case is a composite of variable factors including the nature, number and complexity of the substantive and procedural issues which are involved, the number of parties and potential witnesses as well as the type and economic value of the relief sought. Less complex cases with limited damages and fewer parties require less discovery and involve less time to prepare than do cases with multiple complex issues involving numerous parties and damages or other remedies of extraordinary economic consequence. By focusing upon each case within six months after it is filed, the court and the parties are able to formulate a case management plan which avoids both the potential abuses and injustices that are inherent in the previous "cookie cutter" approach.

At the initial case management conference the court and counsel will consider the specific matters which are enumerated in subparagraphs (a)(1) through (a)(10). Chief among these are those which require early recognition of the complexity of the claim in order to regulate the type of discovery which will follow and the amount of time which the court and counsel believe will be required before the case can be tried. In less complex cases, subparagraphs (a)(5)(i) and (a)(5)(ii) contemplate limitations on the number and duration of depositions and restriction upon the type and number of opinion witnesses which each side may employ. This type of management eliminates discovery abuse in smaller cases without inflexibly inhibiting the type of preparation which is required in more complex litigation.

The new rule also recognizes a number of the uncertainties and problems which existed under the prior scheduling provision of former Rule 220. It attempts to eliminate those difficulties by requiring the court, at the initial management conference, to set deadlines for the disclosure of opinion witnesses as well as for the completion of written discovery and depositions. Amendments to Supreme Court Rules 213 and 214 impose a continuing obligation to supplement discovery responses, including the identification of witnesses who will testify at trial and the subject matter of their testimony. Consequently, the trial of cases should not be delayed by the late identification of witnesses, including opinion witnesses, or by virtue of surprise because the nature of their testimony and opinions is unknown. In this regard, paragraph (c) provides that deadlines established by the court must take into account the completion of discovery not later than 60 days before it is anticipated that trial will commence. For example, opinion witnesses should be disclosed, and their opinions set forth pursuant to interrogatory answer, at such time or times as will permit their depositions to be taken more than 60 days before trial.

Paragraph (a) also enumerates the other matters which the court and counsel are to consider, including the elimination of nonmeritorious issues and defenses and the potential for settlement or alternative dispute resolution. Except in instances where the case is sufficiently simple to permit trial to proceed without further management, the rule contemplates that subsequent case management conferences will be held. The Committee believes that useless or unnecessary depositions should not take place during the discovery process and that no deposition should be longer than three hours unless good cause is shown. Circuits which adopt a local circuit court rule should accomplish the purpose and goals of this proposal. Any local circuit court rule first must be approved by the Supreme Court.

Paragraph (b) reflects the belief that case management is an ongoing process in which the court and counsel will periodically review the matters specified in subparagraphs (a)(1) through (a)(10). As additional parties are added, or amendments are made to the complaint or defenses, it may be necessary to increase or further limit the type of discovery which is required. Consequently, paragraph (c) provides that at the conclusion of each case management conference, the court shall enter an order which reflects the action which was taken. That order will control the course of litigation unless and until it is modified by a subsequent case management order. A separate road map will chart the course of each case from a point within six months from the date on which the complaint is filed until it is tried. By regulating discovery on a case-specific basis, the trial court will keep control of the litigation and thereby prevent the potential for discovery abuse and delay which might otherwise result.

Paragraph (c) controls the subsequent course of action of the litigation unless modified and should ensure that the disclosure of opinion witnesses and discovery will be completed no later than 60 days before the date on which the matter is set for trial.

Rule 219. Consequences of Refusal to Comply with Rules or Order Relating to Discovery or Pretrial Conferences

(a) Refusal to Answer or Comply with Request for Production. If a party or other deponent refuses to answer any question propounded upon oral examination, the examination shall be completed on other matters or adjourned, as the proponent of the question may prefer. Thereafter, on notice to all persons affected thereby, the proponent of the question may move the court for an order compelling an answer. If a party or other deponent refuses to answer any written question upon the taking of his or her deposition or if a party fails to answer any interrogatory

served upon him or her, or to comply with a request for the production of documents or tangible things or inspection of real property, the proponent of the question or interrogatory or the party serving the request may on like notice move for an order compelling an answer or compliance with the request. If the court finds that the refusal or failure was without substantial justification, the court shall require the offending party or deponent, or the party whose attorney advised the conduct complained of, or either of them, to pay to the aggrieved party the amount of the reasonable expenses incurred in obtaining the order, including reasonable attorney's fees. If the motion is denied and the court finds that the motion was made without substantial justification, the court shall require the moving party to pay to the refusing party the amount of the reasonable expenses incurred in opposing the motion, including reasonable attorney's fees.

(b) Expenses on Refusal to Admit. If a party, after being served with a request to admit the genuineness of any documents or the truth of any matters of fact, serves a sworn denial thereof, and if the party requesting the admissions thereafter proves the genuineness of the document or the truth of the matter of fact, the requesting party may apply to the court for an order requiring the other party to pay the requesting party the reasonable expenses incurred in making the proof, including reasonable attorney's fees. Unless the court finds that there were good reasons for the denial or that the admissions sought were of no substantial importance, the order shall be made.

(c) Failure to Comply with Order or Rules. If a party, or any person at the instance of or in collusion with a party, unreasonably fails to comply with any provision of part E of article II of the rules of this court (Discovery, Requests for Admission, and Pretrial Procedure) or fails to comply with any order entered under these rules, the court, on motion, may enter, in addition to remedies elsewhere specifically provided, such orders as are just, including, among others, the following:

(i) That further proceedings be stayed until the order or rule is complied with;

(ii) That the offending party be debarred from filing any other pleading relating to any issue to which the refusal or failure relates;

(iii) That the offending party be debarred from maintaining any particular claim, counterclaim, third-party complaint, or defense relating to that issue;

(iv) That a witness be barred from testifying concerning that issue;

(v) That, as to claims or defenses asserted in any pleading to which that issue is material, a judgment by default be entered against the offending party or that the offending party's action be dismissed with or without prejudice;

(vi) That any portion of the offending party's pleadings relating to that issue be stricken and, if thereby made appropriate, judgment be entered as to that issue; or

(vii) That in cases where a money judgment is entered against a party subject to sanctions under this subparagraph, order the offending party to pay interest at the rate provided by law for judgments for any period of pretrial delay attributable to the offending party's conduct.

In lieu of or in addition to the foregoing, the court, upon motion or upon its own initiative, may impose upon the offending party or his or her attorney, or both, an appropriate sanction, which may include an order to pay to the other party or parties the amount of reasonable expenses incurred as a result of the misconduct, including a reasonable attorney fee, and when the misconduct is wilful, a monetary penalty. When appropriate, the court may, by contempt proceedings, compel obedience by any party or person to any subpoena issued or order entered under these rules. Notwithstanding the entry of a judgment or an order of dismissal, whether voluntary or involuntary, the trial court shall retain jurisdiction to enforce, on its own motion or on the motion of any party, any order imposing monetary sanctions, including such orders as may be entered on motions which were pending hereunder prior to the filing of a notice or motion seeking a judgment or order of dismissal.

Where a sanction is imposed under this paragraph (c), the judge shall set forth with specificity the reasons and basis of any sanction so imposed either in the judgment order itself or in a separate written order.

(d) Abuse of Discovery Procedures. The court may order that information obtained through abuse of discovery procedures be suppressed. If a party wilfully obtains or attempts to obtain information by an improper discovery method, wilfully obtains or attempts to obtain information to which that party is not entitled, or otherwise abuses these discovery rules, the court may enter any order provided for in paragraph (c) of this rule.

(e) Voluntary Dismissals and Prior Litigation. A party shall not be permitted to avoid compliance with discovery deadlines, orders or applicable rules by voluntarily dismissing a lawsuit. In establishing discovery deadlines and ruling on permissible discovery and testimony, the court shall consider discovery undertaken (or the absence of same), any misconduct, and orders entered in prior litigation involving a party. The court may, in addition to the assessment of costs, require the party voluntarily dismissing a claim to pay an opposing party or parties reasonable expenses incurred in defending the action including but not limited to discovery expenses, expert witness fees,

reproduction costs, travel expenses, postage, and phone charges.

Amended eff. Sept. 1, 1974; May 28, 1982, eff. July 1, 1982; July 1, 1985, eff. Aug. 1, 1985; June 1, 1995, eff. Jan. 1, 1996; March 28, 2002, eff. July 1, 2002.

Formerly Ill.Rev.Stat.1991, ch. 110A, ¶ 219.

Committee Comment
(Revised May 29, 2014)

The Committee believes that the rule is sufficient to cover sanction issues as they relate to electronic discovery. The rulings in *Shimanovsky v. GMC*, 181 Ill. 2d 112 (1998) and *Adams v. Bath and Body Works*, 358 Ill.App.3d 387 (1st Dist. 2005) contain detailed discussion of sanctions for discovery violations for the loss or destruction of relevant evidence and for the separate and distinct claim for the tort of negligent spoliation of evidence.

Administrative Order

In re Discovery Rules

The order entered March 28, 2002, amending various rules and effective July 1, 2002, shall apply to all cases filed after such effective date as well as all cases pending on such effective date, provided that any discovery order entered in any such case prior to July 1, 2002, shall remain in effect unless and until amended by the trial court.

Order entered November 27, 2002, effective immediately.

Committee Comment
(March 28, 2002)

This rule is amended to conform to the changes in terminology made in Supreme Court Rule 213.

Committee Comments
(Revised June 1, 1995)
Paragraphs (a) and (b)

Paragraphs (a) and (b) of this rule were derived from former Rules 19—12(1) and (2). In 1974, Rule 214 was amended to provide for a request procedure in the production of documents and tangible things and inspection of real estate, eliminating the requirement that the party seeking such discovery obtain an order of court. Paragraph (a) of Rule 219 was amended at the same time to extend its coverage to cases in which a party refuses to comply with a request under amended Rule 214.

Paragraph (c)

Paragraph (c) is derived from former Rule 19—12(3). The paragraph has been changed to permit the court to render a default judgment against either party. This is consistent with Federal Rule 37(b)(iii), and makes effective the remedy against a balky plaintiff. The remedy was previously limited to dismissal (although it is to be noted that in former Rule 19—12(3) nonsuit and dismissal were both mentioned), and the plaintiff could presumably bring his action again, while in case of the defendant the answer could be stricken and the case decided on the complaint alone. The sanctions imposed must relate to the issue to which the misconduct relates and may not extend to other issues in the case.

Subparagraph (c) was amended in 1985 to make it clear that the sanctions provided for therein applied to violations of new Rules 220 and 222, as well as any discovery rules that may be enacted in the future. Subparagraph (c) was further amended in 1985 to recognize the trial court's continuing jurisdiction to enforce any monetary sanctions imposed thereunder for any abuse of discovery in any case in which an order prescribing such sanctions was entered before any judgment or order of dismissal, whether voluntary or involuntary (see *North Park Bus Service, Inc. v. Pastor* (1976), 39 Ill. App. 3d 406), or to order such monetary sanctions, and enforce them, in any case in which a motion for sanctions was pending before the trial court prior to the filing of a notice or motion seeking a judgment or order of dismissal, whether voluntary or involuntary. This change in no way compromises a plaintiff's right to voluntarily dismiss his action under section 2—1009 of the Code of Civil Procedure (Ill. Rev. Stat. 1983, ch. 110, par. 2–1009). It simply makes it clear that a party may not avoid the consequences of an abuse of the discovery process by filing a notice of voluntary dismissal.

Paragraph (c) has been expanded to provide: (1) for the imposition of prejudgment interest in those situations where a party who has failed to comply with discovery has delayed the entering of a money judgment; (2) the imposition of a monetary penalty against a party or that party's attorney for a wilful violation of the discovery rules; and (3) for other appropriate sanctions against a party or that party's attorney including the payment of reasonable expenses incurred as a result of the misconduct together with a reasonable attorney fee.

Paragraph (c) is expanded first by adding subparagraph (vii), which specifically allows the trial court to include in a judgment, interest for any period of pretrial delay attributable to discovery abuses by the party against whom the money judgment is entered.

Paragraph (c) has also been expanded to provide for the imposition of a monetary penalty against a party or that party's attorney as a result of a wilful violation of the discovery rules. See *Safeway Insurance Co. v. Graham*, 188 Ill. App. 3d 608 (1st Dist. 1989). The decision as to whom such a penalty may be payable is left to the discretion of the trial court based on the discovery violation involved and the consequences of that violation. This language is intended to put to rest any doubt that a trial court has the authority to impose a monetary penalty against a party or that party's attorney. See *Transamerica Insurance Group v. Lee*, 164 Ill. App. 3d 945 (1st Dist. 1988) (McMorrow, J., dissenting).

The last full paragraph of paragraph (c) has also been amended to give greater discretion to the trial court to fashion an appropriate sanction against a party who has violated the discovery rules or orders. The amended language parallels that used in Rule 137. This paragraph has also been amended

to require a judge who imposes a sanction under paragraph (c) to specify the reasons and basis for the sanction imposed either in the judgment order itself or in a separate written order. This language is the same as that now contained in Rule 137.

Paragraph (d)

Paragraph (d) is new. It extends the sanctions provided for in the new rule to general abuse of the discovery rules.

Paragraph (e)

Paragraph (e) addresses the use of voluntary dismissals to avoid compliance with discovery rules or deadlines, or to avoid the consequences of discovery failures, or orders barring witnesses or evidence. This paragraph does not change existing law regarding the right of a party to seek or obtain a voluntary dismissal. However, this paragraph does clearly dictate that when a case is refiled, the court shall consider the prior litigation in determining what discovery will be permitted, and what witnesses and evidence may be barred. The consequences of noncompliance with discovery deadlines, rules or orders cannot be eliminated by taking a voluntary dismissal. Paragraph (e) further authorizes the court to require the party taking the dismissal to pay the out-of-pocket expenses actually incurred by the adverse party or parties. This rule reverses the holdings in *In re Air Crash Disaster at Sioux City, Iowa, on July 19, 1989*, 259 Ill. App. 3d 231, 631 N.E.2d 1302 (1st Dist. 1994), and *Galowich v. Beech Aircraft Corp.*, 209 Ill. App. 3d 128, 568 N.E.2d 46 (1st Dist. 1991). Paragraph (e) does not provide for the payment of attorney fees when an action is voluntarily dismissed.

Rules 220, 221. Reserved

Rule 222. Limited and Simplified Discovery in Certain Cases

(a) Applicability. This rule applies to all cases subject to mandatory arbitration, civil actions seeking money damages not in excess of $50,000 exclusive of interest and costs, and to cases for the collection of taxes not in excess of $50,000. This rule does not apply to small claims, ordinance violations, actions brought pursuant to 750 ILCS (FAMILIES), and actions seeking equitable relief. Except as otherwise specifically provided by this rule, the general rules governing discovery procedures remain applicable to cases governed by this rule.

(b) Affidavit *re* Damages Sought. Any civil action seeking money damages shall have attached to the initial pleading the party's affidavit that the total of money damages sought does or does not exceed $50,000. If the damages sought do not exceed $50,000, this rule shall apply. Any judgment on such claim which exceeds $50,000 shall be reduced posttrial to an amount not in excess of $50,000. Any such affidavit may be amended or superseded prior to trial pursuant to leave of court for good cause shown, and only if it is clear that no party will suffer any prejudice as a result of such amendment. Any affidavit filed pursuant hereto shall not be admissible in evidence at trial.

(c) Time for Disclosure; Continuing Duty. The parties shall make the initial disclosure required by this rule as fully as then possible in accordance with the time lines set by local rule, provided however that if no local rule has been established pursuant to Rule 89 then within 120 days after the filing of a responsive pleading to the complaint, counter-complaint, third-party complaint, *etc.*, unless the parties otherwise agree, or for good cause shown, if the court shortens or extends the time. Upon service of a disclosure, a notice of disclosure shall be promptly filed with the court. The duty to provide disclosures as delineated in this rule and its subsections shall be a continuing duty, and each party shall seasonably supplement or amend disclosures whenever new or different information or documents become known to the disclosing party.

All disclosures shall include information and data in the possession, custody and control of the parties as well as that which can be ascertained, learned or acquired by reasonable inquiry and investigation.

(d) Prompt Disclosure of Information. Within the times set forth in section (c) above, each party shall disclose in writing to every other party:

(1) The factual basis of the claim or defense. In the event of multiple claims or defenses, the factual basis for each claim or defense.

(2) The legal theory upon which each claim or defense is based including, where necessary for a reasonable understanding of the claim or defense, citations of pertinent legal or case authorities.

(3) The names, addresses, and telephone numbers of any witnesses whom the disclosing party expects to call at trial with a designation of the subject matter about which each witness might be called to testify.

(4) The names, addresses, and telephone numbers of all persons whom the party believes may have knowledge or information relevant to the events, transactions, or occurrences that gave rise to the action, and the nature of the knowledge or information each such individual is believed to possess.

(5) The names, addresses, and telephone numbers of all persons who have given statements, whether written or recorded, signed or unsigned, and the custodian of the copies of those statements.

(6) The identity and address of each person whom the disclosing party expects to call as an expert witness at trial, plus the information called for by Rule 213(f).

(7) A computation and the measure of damages alleged by the disclosing party and the document or testimony on which such computation and measure are based and the names, addresses, and telephone numbers of all damage witnesses.

(8) The existence, location, custodian, and general description of any tangible evidence or documents that the disclosing party plans to use at trial and relevant insurance agreements.

(9) A list of the documents or, in the case of voluminous documentary information, a list of the categories of documents, known by a party to exist whether or not in the party's possession, custody or control and which that party believes may be relevant to the subject matter of the action, and those which appear reasonably calculated to lead to the discovery of admissible evidence, and the dates(s) upon which those documents will be made, or have been made, available for inspection and copying. Unless good cause is stated for not doing so, a copy of each document listed shall be served with the disclosure. If production is not made, the name and address of the custodian of the document shall be indicated. A party who produces documents for inspection shall produce them as they are kept in the usual course of business.

(e) Affidavit *re* Disclosure. Each disclosure shall be made in writing, accompanied by the affidavit of an attorney or a party which affirmatively states that the disclosure is complete and correct as of the date of the disclosure and that all reasonable attempts to comply with the provisions of this rule have been made.

(f) Limited and Simplified Discovery Procedures. Except as may be ordered by the trial court, upon motion and for good cause shown, the following limited and simplified discovery procedures shall apply:

(1) Each party may propound to any other party a total of 30 interrogatories and supplemental interrogatories in the aggregate, including subsections. Interrogatories may require the disclosure of facts upon which a party bases a claim or defense, the enumeration, with proper identification, of all persons having knowledge of relevant facts, and the identification of trial witnesses and trial exhibits.

(2) *Discovery Depositions.* No discovery deposition shall exceed three hours, absent agreement among the parties. Except as otherwise ordered by court, the only individuals whose discovery depositions may be taken are the following:

(a) *Parties.* The discovery depositions of parties may be taken. With regard to corporations, partnerships, voluntary associations, or any other groups or entities, one representative deponent may be deposed.

(b) *Treating Physicians and Expert Witnesses.* Treating physicians and expert witnesses may be deposed, but only if they have been identified as witnesses who will testify at trial. The provisions of Rule 204(c) do not apply to treating physicians who are deposed under this Rule 222. The party at whose instance the deposition is taken shall pay a reasonable fee to the deponent, unless the deponent was retained by a party to testify at trial or unless otherwise ordered by the court.

(3) *Evidence Depositions.* No evidence depositions shall be taken except pursuant to leave of court for good cause shown. Leave of court shall not be granted unless it is shown that a witness is expected to testify on matters material to the issues and it is unlikely that the witness will be available for trial, or other exceptional circumstances exist. Motions requesting the taking of evidence depositions shall be supported by affidavit. Evidence depositions shall be taken to secure trial testimony, not as a substitute for discovery depositions.

(4) Requests pursuant to Rules 214 and 215 are permitted, as are notices pursuant to Rule 237.

(5) Requests pursuant to Rule 216 are permitted except that no request may be filed less than 60 days prior to the scheduled trial date or, if within said 60 days, only by order of court.

(g) Exclusion of Undisclosed Evidence. In addition to any other sanction the court may impose, the court shall exclude at trial any evidence offered by a party that was not timely disclosed as required by this rule, except by leave of court for good cause shown.

(h) Claims of Privilege. When information or documents are withheld from disclosure or discovery on a claim that they are privileged pursuant to a common law or statutory privilege, any such claim shall be made expressly and shall be supported by a description of the nature of the documents, communications or things not produced or disclosed and the exact privilege which is being claimed.

(i) Affidavits Wrongly Filed. The court shall enter an appropriate order pursuant to Rule 219(c) against any party or his or her attorney, or both, as a result of any affidavit filed pursuant to (b) or (e) above which the court finds was (a) false; (b) filed in bad faith; or (c) was without reasonable factual support.

(j) Applicability Pursuant to Local Rule. This rule may be made applicable to additional categories of cases pursuant to local rules enacted in any judicial circuit.

Adopted June 1, 1995, effective January 1, 1996; amended March 28, 2002, effective July 1, 2002; amended February 10, 2006, effective July 1, 2006; amended October 1, 2010, effective January 1, 2011.

Committee Comments

Neither this rule nor any other proposed amendment modifies existing Illinois law regarding information or documents which are privileged from disclosure. Moreover, the scope of discovery remains unchanged, except for the identity of trial witnesses and trial documents. See Supreme Court Rule 201(b).

Dissolution of marriage and other family law proceedings provided for in 750 ILCS have been exempted. Those proceedings are already becoming too expensive for many parties. Mandatory disclo-

sure might impose an unnecessary and inappropriate burden in many such proceedings.

This rule sets forth reforms in the discovery process in cases seeking money damages not in excess of $50,000. Two major elements of reform are imposed: (1) mandatory disclosure, and (2) limits on discovery.

The mandatory disclosure provisions are contained in paragraph (d). A continuing duty to disclose is imposed under paragraph (c).

Violations of the mandatory disclosure requirements should ordinarily result in sanctions, including the exclusion of evidence.

Under paragraph (f), the number of interrogatories is limited to 30, including subsections, and only the discovery depositions of parties and experts who have been identified as trial witnesses may be taken without leave of court. Evidence depositions can only be taken pursuant to leave of court. The requirement of a court order, upon good cause shown, is designed to encourage judicial involvement in limiting the number of depositions taken. The appropriate exercise of judicial authority will ensure that evidence depositions are not used as a substitute for discovery depositions or for other discovery procedures. The time limit of three hours should be adequate for the majority of discovery depositions.

The limited and simplified discovery procedures are triggered by the filing of an appropriate affidavit as set forth in paragraph (b). For good cause shown, the court can permit the affidavit to be amended or superseded, thereby making this rule no longer applicable. Affidavits must also be filed with the mandatory disclosures required by the rule. Affidavits wrongly filed should be sanctioned in accordance with paragraph (i).

The cases to which this rule applies may be expanded by local rule of court. (Paragraph (j).) Experience under the rule may prompt the Supreme Court or some circuits to expand the applicability of the rule.

The general provisions of Supreme Court Rule 201(i) remain applicable to this rule.

(March 28, 2002)

This rule is amended to conform to the changes in terminology made in Supreme Court Rule 213.

(February 10, 2006)

The change to paragraph (c) is intended to require practitioners to follow the dictates of local rule. The Committee's intention is to refer practitioners to the rule(s) prescribed by local jurisdictions thereby eliminating confusion and the ability of noncomplying counsel to state that they agreed to extend the time for disclosure without court approval.

(October 1, 2010)

Subparagraph (f)(5) has been added to provide a time frame for the issuance in anticipation of a trial date.

Rule 223.   Reserved

Rule 224.   Discovery Before Suit to Identify Responsible Persons and Entities

(a) Procedure.

(1) *Petition.*

(i) A person or entity who wishes to engage in discovery for the sole purpose of ascertaining the identity of one who may be responsible in damages may file an independent action for such discovery.

(ii) The action for discovery shall be initiated by the filing of a verified petition in the circuit court of the county in which the action or proceeding might be brought or in which one or more of the persons or entities from whom discovery is sought resides. The petition shall be brought in the name of the petitioner and shall name as respondents the persons or entities from whom discovery is sought and shall set forth: (A) the reason the proposed discovery is necessary and (B) the nature of the discovery sought and shall ask for an order authorizing the petitioner to obtain such discovery. The order allowing the petition will limit discovery to the identification of responsible persons and entities and where a deposition is sought will specify the name and address of each person to be examined, if known, or, if unknown, information sufficient to identify each person and the time and place of the deposition.

(2) *Summons and Service.* The petitioner shall serve upon the respondent or respondents a copy of the petition together with a summons in a form substantially as follows:

In the Circuit Court of the _____ Judicial Circuit, _____ County, Illinois

(Or, In the Circuit Court of Cook County, Illinois)

A.B., C.D., *et al.*
(naming all petitioners),
    Petitioners,

    v.   No. _____

H.J., K.L. *et al.*
(naming all respondents),
    Respondents.

SUMMONS FOR DISCOVERY

TO EACH RESPONDENT:

You are hereby notified that on _____ ___, 20 ___, a petition, a copy of which is attached, was filed in the above court seeking an order of discovery. Pursuant to law a hearing will be held to determine whether such an order shall be entered in this case. If you wish to contest the entry of such order, you must

appear at this hearing at _____, at ___ o'clock ___ M., on _____, _____ ___, 20 ___.

_____
Clerk of the Circuit Court

Unless a shorter period is fixed by the court, the summons shall be served at least 14 days before the date of hearing, in the manner provided for service of summons in other civil cases. If service cannot with due diligence be made upon the respondent(s), the court may by order provide for service by publication or otherwise.

(b) Expiration and Sanctions. Unless extended for good cause, the order automatically expires 60 days after issuance. The sanctions available under Supreme Court Rule 219 may be utilized by a party initiating an action for discovery under this rule or by a respondent who is the subject of discovery under this rule.

(c) Expenses of Complying. The reasonable expenses of complying with the requirements of the Order of Discovery shall be borne by the person or entity seeking the discovery.

Adopted June 19, 1989, effective August 1, 1989. Amended May 30, 2008, effective immediately.

Formerly Ill.Rev.Stat.1991, ch. 110A, ¶ 224.

Committee Comments
(August 1, 1989)

New Rule 224 was adopted effective August 1, 1989. This rule provides a tool by which a person or entity may, with leave of court, compel limited discovery before filing a lawsuit in an effort to determine the identity of one who may be liable in damages. The rule is not intended to modify in any way any other rights secured or responsibilities imposed by law. It provides a mechanism for plaintiffs to ascertain the identity of potential defendants in a variety of civil cases, including Structural Works Act, products liability, malpractice and negligence claims. The rule will be of particular benefit in industrial accident cases where the parties responsible may be known to the plaintiff's employer, which may immunize itself from suit. The rule facilitates the identification of potential defendants through discovery depositions or through any of the other discovery tools set forth in Rules 201 through 214. The order allowing the petition will limit discovery to the identification of responsible persons and entities. Therefore, Supreme Court Rule 215, dealing with mental and physical exams, and Supreme Court Rule 216, dealing with requests to admit, are not included as means of discovery under this rule.

Rules 225 to 230.   Reserved

PART F.   TRIALS

Rule 231.   Motions for Continuance

(a) Absence of Material Evidence. If either party applies for a continuance of a cause on account of the absence of material evidence, the motion shall be supported by the affidavit of the party so applying or his authorized agent. The affidavit shall show (1) that due diligence has been used to obtain the evidence, or the want of time to obtain it; (2) of what particular fact or facts the evidence consists; (3) if the evidence consists of the testimony of a witness, his place of residence, or if his place of residence is not known, that due diligence has been used to ascertain it; and (4) that if further time is given the evidence can be procured.

(b) When Continuance Will Be Denied. If the court is satisfied that the evidence would not be material, or if the other party will admit the affidavit in evidence as proof only of what the absent witness would testify to if present, the continuance shall be denied unless the court, for the furtherance of justice, shall consider a continuance necessary.

(c) Other Causes for Continuance. It is sufficient cause for the continuance of any action: (1) that in time of war or insurrection, a party whose presence is necessary for the full and fair prosecution or defense of the action is in the military service of the United States or of this State and that his military service materially impairs his ability to prosecute or defend the action; or (2) that the party applying therefor or his attorney is a member of either house of the General Assembly during the time the General Assembly is in session, if the presence of that party is necessary for the full and fair trial of the action, and in the case of the attorney, if the attorney was retained by the party prior to the time the cause was set for trial.

(d) Amendment as Cause. No amendment is cause for continuance unless the party affected thereby, or his agent or attorney, shall make affidavit that, in consequence thereof, he is unprepared to proceed to or with the trial. If the cause thereof is the want of material evidence, a continuance shall be granted only on a further showing as may be required for continuance for that cause.

(e) Court's Own Motion. The court may on its own motion, or with the consent of the adverse party, continue a cause for trial to a later day.

(f) Time for Motion. No motion for the continuance of a cause made after the cause has been reached for trial shall be heard, unless a sufficient excuse is shown for the delay.

(g) Taxing of Costs. When a continuance is granted upon payment of costs, the costs may be taxed summarily by the court, and on being taxed shall be paid on demand of the party, his agent, or his attorney, and, if not so paid, on affidavit of the fact, the continuance may be vacated, or the court may enforce the payment with the accruing costs, by contempt proceedings.

Amended Oct. 21, 1969, eff. Jan. 1, 1970.

Formerly Ill.Rev.Stat.1991, ch. 110A, ¶ 231.

Committee Comments

(Revised October, 1969)

This rule, as adopted effective January 1, 1967, was former Rule 14 without change in substance.

Paragraph (c) of the rule was amended in 1969 to conform with the 1967 amendment of section 59 of the Civil Practice Act. Laws 1967, p. 326.

Rule 232. Trial of Equitable and Legal Matters

(a) Trial of a Single Equitable Cause of Action. When matters are treated as a single equitable cause of action as provided in Rule 135(a), they shall be heard and determined in the manner heretofore practiced in courts of equity. When legal and equitable matters that may be asserted separately are pleaded as provided in Rule 135, the court shall first determine whether the matters joined are properly severable, and, if so, whether they shall be tried together or separately and in what order.

(b) Trial of Joined Equitable and Legal Matters. If the court determines that the matters are severable, the issues formed on the law counts shall be tried before a jury when a jury has been properly demanded, or by the court when a jury has not been properly demanded. The equitable issues shall be heard and decided in the manner heretofore practiced in courts of equity.

Formerly Ill.Rev.Stat.1991, ch. 110A, ¶ 232.

Committee Comments

This is a revision of the trial provisions of former Rules 10 and 11, without change in substance. The pleading provisions appear as Rule 135.

Rule 233. Parties' Order of Proceeding

The parties shall proceed at all stages of the trial, including the selection of prospective jurors as specified in Rule 234, opening and closing statements, the offering of evidence, and the examination of witnesses, in the order in which they appear in the pleadings unless otherwise agreed by all parties or ordered by the court. In consolidated cases, third-party proceedings, and all other cases not otherwise provided for, the court shall designate the order.

Amended eff. July 1, 1975.

Formerly Ill.Rev.Stat.1991, ch. 110A, ¶ 233.

Committee Comments

(Revised July 1, 1975.)

This is Rule 6.2 of the Uniform Rules for the Circuit Courts of Illinois.

The phrase "as specified in Rule 234" was added in 1975 to reflect changes in the procedure for conduct of the voir dire examination of prospective jurors, effected at the same time by amendments to Rule 234.

Rule 234. Voir Dire Examination of Jurors and Cautionary Instructions

The court shall conduct the voir dire examination of prospective jurors by putting to them questions it thinks appropriate touching upon their qualifications to serve as jurors in the case on trial. The court may permit the parties to submit additional questions to it for further inquiry if it thinks they are appropriate, and shall permit the parties to supplement the examination by such direct inquiry as the court deems proper for a reasonable period of time depending upon the length of examination by the court, the complexity of the case, and the nature and extent of the damages. Questions shall not directly or indirectly concern matters of law or instructions. The court shall acquaint prospective jurors with the general duties and responsibilities of jurors.

Amended eff. July 1, 1975; amended Aug. 9, 1983, eff. Oct. 1, 1983; April 3, 1997, eff. May 1, 1997.

Formerly Ill.Rev.Stat.1991, ch. 110A, ¶ 234.

Committee Comments
(Revised July 1, 1975.)

[This is former Rule 24–1 without change in substance.]

Rule 234 was amended in 1975 to emphasize the duty of the court to manage the voir dire examination. Under the rule as amended the court must put to the prospective jurors such questions as it thinks necessary and then may either permit the attorneys or the parties to supplement the examination by putting questions directly to the prospective jurors or may require them to submit the questions to him, in which event he will put such of the questions submitted as he thinks proper.

Rule 235. Opening Statements

As soon as the jury is empaneled the attorney for the plaintiff may make an opening statement. The attorney for the defendant may immediately follow with an opening statement. An opening statement may not be made at any other time, except in the discretion of the trial court.

Formerly Ill.Rev.Stat.1991, ch. 110A, ¶ 235.

Committee Comments

This is a revision of Rule 6.4 of the Uniform Rules for the Circuit Courts of Illinois.

Rule 236. Admission of Business Records in Evidence

(a) Any writing or record, whether in the form of any entry in a book or otherwise, made as a memorandum or record of any act, transaction, occurrence, or event, shall be admissible as evidence of the act, transaction, occurrence, or event, if made in the regular course of any business, and if it was the regular course of the business to make such a memorandum or record at the time of such an act, transaction, occurrence, or event or within a reasonable time thereafter. All other circumstances of the making of the writing or record, including lack of personal knowledge by the entrant or maker, may be shown to affect its weight, but shall not affect its admissibility. The term "business," as used in this rule, includes business, profession, occupation, and calling of every kind.

(b) Although police accident reports may otherwise be admissible in evidence under the law, subsection (a) of this rule does not allow such writings to be admitted as a record or memorandum made in the regular course of business.

Amended Aug. 9, 1983, eff. Oct. 1, 1983; April 1, 1992, eff. Aug. 1, 1992.

Formerly Ill.Rev.Stat.1991, ch. 110A, ¶ 236.

Committee Comments
Paragraph (a)

Paragraph (a) of this rule is a revision without change in substance of subsection 1732(a) of Title 28 of U.S.C., generally known as the Federal Business Records Act. This act reflects the modern approach to the admissibility of business records as evidence.

As early as the 1600's the common law had developed as an exception to the hearsay rule the practice of admitting shop-books in evidence, whether kept by the party himself or a clerk, and whether the entrant was living or dead. The custom was abused, however, and was restricted by statute in 1609. Colonial practice in this country adopted the limitations on the exception, and these historical boundaries have continued to restrict the admission of business records in many states until modern times. 5 Wigmore, Evidence 346, 347–361 (3d ed. 1940). "The gross result," Professor Wigmore declares, "is a mass of technicalities which serve no useful purpose in getting at the truth." 5 Wigmore, Evidence 346, 361 (3d ed. 1940).

In 1927 the Commonwealth Fund of New York appointed a committee of experts to restate the law in the form of a single rule, broad and flexible enough to correspond to contemporary business practices, while safeguarding fundamental requirements. The result was a model act similar in substance to paragraph (a) of Rule 236. In 1936 the National Conference of Commissioners on Uniform State Laws approved a recommended uniform act on business records, which revised the 1927 rule. On the basis of this revised proposal, Congress adopted subsection 1732(a) of Title 28 of the U.S.C. on June 20, 1936.

In Illinois the trend has been similar. In People v. Small, 319 Ill. 437, 477, 150 N.E. 435 (1926), the Supreme Court held bank records admissible on the basis of a foundation laid by the officers in charge of the records, stating, "The business of this great commercial country is transacted on records kept in the usual course of business and vouched for by the supervising officer, and such evidence ought to be competent in a court of justice. Modern authority sustains this view."

The Municipal Court of Chicago adopted the principles of the rule prepared by the Commonwealth Fund of New York as Municipal Court Rule 70. Later the Municipal Court modified the rule by following the language of 28 U.S.C. § 1732(a). In Secco v. Chicago Transit Authority, 6 Ill.App.2d 266, 269–70, 127 N.E.2d 266 (1st Dist.1955) rule 70 was held valid, with the following comments (6 Ill.App.2d at 269–270):

"Rule 70's general purpose is to liberalize the rules of evidence pertaining to regular business entries. (Bell v. Bankers Life & Casualty Co., 327 Ill.App. 321 (1945).) Abandoned are the anachronisms of an older day whose influence is felt even today in many of those jurisdictions which have legislatively adopted Rule 70. It was intended to make unnecessary the original entrants' production at the trial because of their numbers or anonymity, or for reasons which made their production impracticable. It was also intended to make unnecessary the production of the original entrant although he alone and without the aid of others made the entries. The routine character of a business is reflected in its records accumulating instance upon instance of some particular transaction or event, and because of this it was felt that the original entrant would have no present recollection of the various details lost within the mass of recorded entries. ... It was intended to be sufficient, if the custodian of the records or some person familiar with the business and its mode of operation, would testify at the trial as to the manner in which the record was prepared, the objective being that the principle of an absent witness' unavailability should not be applied with identical logical narrowness of an earlier day, and to bring it nearer to standards accepted in reasonable action outside the courts. 5 Wigmore on Evidence (3d ed. 1940) p. 391."

The language of paragraph (a) of Rule 236 is that of the federal statute and Chicago Municipal Court rule with only minor language changes. The Committee believes that it is desirable to retain this often-interpreted language without substantial change in the interest of having established judicial construction to work with.

A portion of the Federal statute (28 U.S.C. § 1732(b)) is a provision permitting the retention of microfilm records in lieu of the originals, which is a desirable complement to the business records act. However, it is not included in Rule 236 because this subject is already covered by the Evidence Act (Ill.Rev.Stat.1965, ch. 51, § 3).

Paragraph (b)

Paragraph (b) of Rule 236 provides that the law governing admissibility of police accident reports is not affected by this rule. The rule was amended in 1992 to allow medical records to be treated as any other business record under paragraph (a).

Rule 237. Compelling Appearances of Witnesses at Trial

(a) **Service of Subpoenas.** Any witness shall respond to any lawful subpoena of which he or she has actual knowledge, if payment of the fee and mileage has been tendered. Service of a subpoena by mail may be proved *prima facie* by a return receipt showing delivery to the witness or his or her authorized agent by certified or registered mail at least seven days before the date on which appearance is required and an affidavit showing that the mailing was prepaid and was addressed to the witness, restricted delivery, with a check or money order for the fee and mileage enclosed.

(b) **Notice of Parties *et al.* at Trial or Other Evidentiary Hearings.** The appearance at the trial or other evidentiary hearing of a party or a person who at the time of trial or other evidentiary hearing is an officer, director, or employee of a party may be required by serving the party with a notice designating the person who is required to appear. The notice also may require the production at the trial or other evidentiary hearing of the originals of those documents or tangible things previously produced during discovery. If the party or person is a nonresident of the county, the court may order any terms and conditions in connection with his or her appearance at the trial or other evidentiary hearing that are just, including payment of his or her reasonable expenses. Upon a failure to comply with the notice, the court may enter any order that is just, including any sanction or remedy provided for in Rule 219(c) that may be appropriate.

(c) **Notice of Parties at Expedited Hearings in Domestic Relations Cases.** In a domestic relations case, the appearance at an expedited hearing of a party who has been served with process or appeared may be required by serving the party with a notice designating the party who is required to appear. The notice may also require the production at the hearing of the original documents or tangible things relevant to the issues to be addressed at the hearing. If the party is a nonresident of the county, the court may order any terms and conditions in connection with his or her appearance at the hearing that are just, including payment of his or her reasonable expenses. Upon a failure to comply with the notice, the court may enter any order that is just, including any sanction or remedy provided for in Rule 219(c) that may be appropriate.

Amended June 19, 1968, and amended October 21, 1969, effective January 1, 1970; amended September 29, 1978, effective November 1, 1978; amended June 1, 1995; effective January 1, 1996; amended February 1, 2005, effective July 1, 2005.

Formerly Ill.Rev.Stat.1991, ch. 110A, ¶ 237.

Committee Comments

(Revised June 1, 1995)

This rule conforms substantially with Rule 204(a), which deals with compelling the appearance of witnesses for depositions.

Rule 237 contains no counterpart to Rule 204(a)(1), because the authority for the issuance of subpoenas is provided by section 62 of the Civil Practice Act (Ill.Rev.Stat.1977, ch. 110, par. 62).

Paragraph (a) of Rule 237 was added to the rule in 1969. It is identical with Rule 204(a)(2) except for the substitution of "witness" for "deponent." Together with Rule 204 it was amended in 1978 to conform its requirements to presently available postal delivery service. See the committee comments to Rule 105.

Paragraph (a) formerly provided that proof of service of a subpoena by mail may be proved by a return receipt and an affidavit of mailing. In the new rule, such proof is described as "*prima facie*" to make it clear that such proof may be rebutted. This effects no substantive change.

Paragraph (b) of this rule, except for the last sentence, which was added by amendment in 1968, was Rule 237 as adopted effective January 1, 1967. Comparable provisions applicable to depositions had been in effect since January 1, 1956, but prior to the adoption of Rule 237 it was necessary to serve a subpoena to assure the attendance of the opposing party at the trial. There was obviously no reason for such a distinction.

Paragraph (b) has been revised to clarify the fact that Rule 237(b) is not a discovery option to be used on the eve of trial in lieu of a timely request for the production of documents, objects and tangible things pursuant to Rule 214. Discovery of relevant documents, objects and tangible things should be diligently pursued before trial pursuant to Rule 214. Under the new paragraph, a Rule 237(b) request to produce at trial will be expressly limited to those documents, objects and tangible things produced during discovery. This revision will effect a change in current practice, under which a Rule 237(b) request to produce at trial is often utilized as a major discovery tool by nondiligent litigants, a practice that often causes trial delay. It is the intent of this revision to establish that due diligence for the purposes of a motion to delay the trial cannot be shown by a party who first attempts to discover documents, objects or tangible things by serving a request under Rule 237(b). See *Campen v. Executive House Hotel, Inc.*, 105 Ill.App.3d 576, 434 N.E.2d 511 (1st Dist.1982).

(February 1, 2005)

Paragraph (c) was added to the rule effective July 1, 2005. Because of the important issues decided in expedited hearings in domestic relations cases, including temporary family support, temporary child custody, and temporary restraining orders, a trial court should have the benefit of the attendance of individuals and production of documents and tangible things on an expedited basis.

Rule 238. Impeachment of Witnesses; Hostile Witnesses

(a) The credibility of a witness may be attacked by any party, including the party calling the witness.

(b) If the court determines that a witness is hostile or unwilling, the witness may be examined by the party calling the witness as if under cross-examination.

Amended Feb. 19, 1982, eff. April 1, 1982; amended eff. April 11, 2001.

Formerly Ill.Rev.Stat.1991, ch. 110A, ¶ 238.

Committee Comments

This rule is new. It extends the provision of section 60 of the Civil Practice Act authorizing cross examination to any witness who proves hostile or unwilling and the provision authorizing impeachment by prior inconsistent statements to any occurrence witness who surprises the party calling him by testimony on a material matter that is inconsistent with a prior statement made by him.

Under existing law, a witness not called under section 60 who proves hostile or unwilling can, in the discretion of the trial court, be asked leading questions. Bradshaw v. Combs, 102 Ill. 428, 434 (1882); People v. Gallery, 336 Ill. 580, 584–85, 168 N.E. 650, 651 (1929). A number of Illinois decisions hold that a witness who unexpectedly gives testimony against the party calling him inconsistent with prior statements may be examined by that party concerning the prior inconsistent statements for the purpose of refreshing the witness' recollection or awakening his conscience. People v. Michaels, 335 Ill. 590, 592, 167 N.E. 857, 858 (1929); People v. O'Gara, 271 Ill. 138, 143, 110 N.E. 828, 829 (1915); People v. Lukoszus, 242 Ill. 101, 107, 89 N.E. 749, 751 (1909); Chicago City Ry. Co. v. Gregory, 221 Ill. 591, 598, 77 N.E. 1112, 1114 (1906).

The new rule establishes the more straightforward practice of permitting the party calling such a witness to impeach him by proof of prior inconsistent statements. This provision is consistent with the views of modern authorities in this field. 3 Wigmore, Evidence 383, 389 (3d ed. 1940); Morgan, Basic Problems in Evidence, vol. 1, pp. 64–65 (Committee on Continuing Legal Education, American Law Institute, 1954); Tracy, Handbook of the Law of Evidence 193 (1953); Maguire, Evidence—Common Sense and Common Law 43 (1947); Ladd, Impeachment of One's Own Witness—New Developments, 4 Univ. of Chi.L.Rev. 69 (1936); American Law Institute, Model Code of Evidence, Rule 106. The provision is limited to occurrence witnesses in order to forestall possible abuses in the area of expert witnesses.

A number of States permit impeachment of any witness by proof of prior inconsistent statements. *E.g.*, Calif.Code Civ.Proc. § 2049; Burns' Ind.Stat., Ch. 2, § 1726; Mass.Ann.Laws, Ch. 233, § 23; N.Y.Civ.Prac. Act § 343–a (limited to writings and to statements under oath); Ore.Rev.Stat. § 45–590 (no limitation on method of impeachment in case of adverse party).

Rule 239. Instructions

(a) **Use of IPI Instruction; Requirements of Other Instructions.** Whenever Illinois Pattern Jury Instructions (IPI), Civil, contains an instruction applicable in a civil case, giving due consideration to the facts and the prevailing law, and the court determines that the jury should be instructed on the subject, the IPI instruction shall be used, unless the court determines that it does not accurately state the law. The most current version of the IPI Civil instructions is maintained on the Supreme Court website. Whenever IPI does not contain an instruction on a subject on which the court determines that the jury should be instructed, the instruction given in that subject should be simple, brief, impartial, and free from argument.

(b) Court's Instructions. At any time before or during the trial, the court may direct counsel to prepare designated instructions. Counsel shall comply with the direction, and copies of instructions so prepared shall be marked "Court's Instruction." Counsel may object at the conference on instructions to any instruction prepared at the court's direction, regardless of who prepared it, and the court shall rule on these objections as well as objections to other instructions. The grounds of the objections shall be particularly specified.

(c) Procedure. Each instruction shall be accompanied by a copy, and a copy shall be delivered to opposing counsel. In addition to numbering the copies and indicating who tendered them, as required by section 2–1107 of the Code of Civil Procedure, the copy shall contain a notation substantially as follows:

"IPI No. ___" or "IPI No. ___ Modified" or "Not in IPI"

as the case may be. All objections made at the conference and the rulings thereon shall be shown in the report of proceedings. The original instructions given by the court to the jury shall be taken by the jury to the jury room.

(d) Instructions Before Opening Statements. After the jury is selected and before opening statements, the court may orally instruct the jury as follows:

    (i) On cautionary or preliminary matters, including, but not limited to, the burden of proof, the believability of witnesses, and the receipt of evidence for a limited purpose.

    (ii) On the substantive law applicable to the case, including, but not limited to, the elements of the claim or affirmative defense.

(e) Instructions After the Close of Evidence. After the close of evidence, the court shall repeat any applicable instructions given to the jury before opening statements and instruct the jury on procedural issues and the substantive law applicable to the case, including, but not limited to, the elements of the claim or affirmative defense. The court may, in its discretion, read the instructions to the jury prior to closing argument. Whether or not the instructions are read prior to closing argument, the court shall read the instructions to the jury following closing argument and may, in its discretion, distribute a written copy of the instructions to each juror. Jurors shall not be

given a written copy of the jury instructions prior to counsel concluding closing argument.

(f) Instructions During Trial. Nothing in this rule is intended to restrict the court's authority to give any appropriate instruction during the course of the trial.

Amended May 28, 1982, eff. July 1, 1982; Oct. 1, 1998, eff. Jan. 1, 1999; June 11, 2009, eff. Sept. 1, 2009; Dec. 16, 2010, eff. Jan. 1, 2011; April 8, 2013, eff. immediately.

Formerly Ill.Rev.Stat.1991, ch. 110A, ¶ 239.

Committee Comments

This is former Rule 25–1 without change in substance.

Rule 240.   Directed Verdicts

The order of the court granting a motion for a directed verdict is effective without any assent of the jury.

Formerly Ill.Rev.Stat.1991, ch. 110A, ¶ 240.

Committee Comments

This new rule, taken from Rule 50(a) of the Federal Rules of Civil Procedure, as amended in 1963, eliminates an archaic and futile ceremony. See Kaplan, Amendments of the Federal Rules of Civil Procedure, 1961–63(II), 77 Harv.L.Rev. 801, 823 (1964).

Rule 241.   Use of Video Conference Technology in Civil Cases

The court may, for good cause shown in compelling circumstances and upon appropriate safeguards, permit presentation of testimony in open court by contemporaneous transmission from a different location.

Adopted Oct. 4, 2011, eff. immediately.

Committee Comments

The presentation of live testimony in court remains of utmost importance. As such, showings of good cause and compelling circumstances are likely to arise when a witness is unable to attend trial for unexpected reasons, such as accident or illness, but is able to testify from a remote location. Advance notice should be given to all parties of foreseeable circumstances that may lead the proponent to offer testimony by contemporaneous transmission.

Good cause and compelling circumstances may be established if all parties agree that testimony should be presented by contemporaneous transmission; however, the court is not bound by a stipulation and can insist on live testimony.

Adequate safeguards are necessary to ensure accurate identification of the witness and protect against influences by persons present with the witness. Accurate transmission must also be assured.

Rule 242.   Reserved

Rule 243.   Written Juror Questions Directed to Witnesses

(a) Questions Permitted. The court may permit jurors in civil cases to submit to the court written questions directed to witnesses.

(b) Procedure. Following the conclusion of questioning by counsel, the court shall determine whether the jury will be afforded the opportunity to question the witness. Regarding each witness for whom the court determines questions by jurors are appropriate, the jury shall be asked to submit any question they have for the witness in writing. No discussion regarding the questions shall be allowed between jurors at this time; neither shall jurors be limited to posing a single question nor shall jurors be required to submit questions. The bailiff will then collect any questions and present the questions to the judge. Questions will be marked as exhibits and made a part of the record.

(c) Objections. Out of the presence of the jury, the judge will read the question to all counsel, allow counsel to see the written question, and give counsel an opportunity to object to the question. If any objections are made, the court will rule upon them at that time and the question will be either admitted, modified, or excluded accordingly. The limitations on direct examination set forth in Rule 213(g) apply to juror-submitted questions.

(d) Questioning of the Witness. The court shall instruct the witness to answer only the question presented, and not exceed the scope of the question. The court will ask each question; the court will then provide all counsel with an opportunity to ask follow-up questions limited to the scope of the new testimony.

(e) Admonishment to Jurors. At times before or during the trial that it deems appropriate, the court shall advise the jurors that they shall not concern themselves with the reason for the exclusion or modification of any question submitted and that such measures are taken by the court in accordance with the rules of evidence that govern the case.

Adopted April 3, 2012, eff. July 1, 2012. Amended May 29, 2014, eff. July 1, 2014.

Committee Comments
(April 3, 2012)

This rule gives the trial judge discretion in civil cases to permit jurors to submit written questions to be directed to witnesses—a procedure which has been used in other jurisdictions to improve juror comprehension, attention to the proceedings, and satisfaction with jury service. The trial judge may discuss with the parties' attorneys whether the procedure will be helpful in the case, but the decision whether to use the procedure rests entirely with the trial judge. The rule specifies some of the procedures the trial judge must follow, but it leaves other details to the trial judge's discretion.

Rules 244 to 270.   Reserved

PART G.   ENTRY OF ORDERS AND JUDGMENTS

Rule 271.   Orders on Motions

When the court rules upon a motion other than in the course of trial, the attorney for the prevailing party shall prepare and present to the court the order or judgment to be entered, unless the court directs otherwise.

Formerly Ill.Rev.Stat.1991, ch. 110A, ¶ 271.

Committee Comments

This is a revision of Rule 7.1 of the Uniform Rules for the Circuit Courts of Illinois.

Rule 272.   When Judgment is Entered

If at the time of announcing final judgment the judge requires the submission of a form of written judgment to be signed by the judge or if a circuit court rule requires the prevailing party to submit a draft order, the clerk shall make a notation to that effect and the judgment becomes final only when the signed judgment is filed. If no such signed written judgment is to be filed, the judge or clerk shall forthwith make a notation of judgment and enter the judgment of record promptly, and the judgment is entered at the time it is entered of record.

Amended Oct. 25, 1990, eff. Nov. 1, 1990.

Formerly Ill.Rev.Stat.1991, ch. 110A, ¶ 272.

Committee Comments

The purpose of this rule is to remove any doubt as to the date a judgment is entered. It applies to both law and equity, and the distinction stated in *Freeport Motor Casualty Co. v. Tharp*, 406 Ill. 295, 94 N.E.2d 139 (1950), as to the effective dates of a judgment at law and a decree in equity is abolished. In 1990 the rule was amended to provide that in those cases in which, by circuit court rule, the prevailing party is required to submit a draft order, a judgment becomes final only after the signed judgment is filed. The 1990 amendment was intended to negate the ruling in *Davis v. Carbondale Elementary School District No. 95* (1988), 170 Ill. App.3d 687, 525 N.E.2d 135.

Rule 273.   Effect of Involuntary Dismissal

Unless the order of dismissal or a statute of this State otherwise specifies, an involuntary dismissal of an action, other than a dismissal for lack of jurisdiction, for improper venue, or for failure to join an indispensable party, operates as an adjudication upon the merits.

Formerly Ill.Rev.Stat.1991, ch. 110A, ¶ 273.

Committee Comments

This rule is new. It is based upon Rule 41(b) of the Federal Rules of Civil Procedure and sets to rest the question of the effect of an involuntary dismissal other than those excepted by the rule. Cf. Lurie v. Rupe, 51 Ill.App.2d 164, 176, 201 N.E.2d 158 (1st Dist.1964).

Rule 274. Multiple Final Orders and Post-judgment Motions

A party may make only one postjudgment motion directed at a judgment order that is otherwise final. If a final judgment order is modified pursuant to a postjudgment motion, or if a different final judgment or order is subsequently entered, any party affected by the order may make one postjudgment motion directed at the superseding judgment or order. Until disposed, each timely postjudgment motion shall toll the finality and appealability of the judgment or order at which it is directed. The pendency of a Rule 137 claim does not affect the time in which postjudgment motions directed at final underlying judgments or orders must be filed, but may toll the appealability of the judgment under Rule 303(a)(1). A postjudgment motion directed at a final order on a Rule 137 claim is also subject to this rule.

Adopted October 14, 2005; effective January 1, 2006.

Committee Comments

(January 1, 2006)

New Rule 274 clarifies the status of successive (superseding) final judgments, and of postjudgment motions directed at each final judgment, allowing one such motion per party per final judgment, Rule 274 further clarifies that a timely postjudgment motion directed at any final judgment, including a later superseding judgment, tolls the appeal time. See Rule 303. Rule 274 codifies *Gibson v. Belvidere National Bank & Trust Co.*, 326 Ill. App. 3d 45 (2002), *appeal denied*, 198 Ill.2d 614 (2002) (table). Rule 274 also clarifies that Rule 137 proceedings do not affect the postjudgment motion procedures on the underlying substantive judgments in the case.

Rule 275. Reserved

PART H. POST–JUDGMENT PROCEEDINGS

Rule 276. Opening of Judgment by Confession

A motion to open a judgment by confession shall be supported by affidavit in the manner provided by Rule 191 for summary judgments, and shall be accompanied by a verified answer which defendant proposes to file. If the motion and affidavit disclose a *prima facie* defense on the merits to the whole or a part of the plaintiff's claim, the court shall set the motion for hearing. The plaintiff may file counteraffidavits. If, at the hearing upon the motion, it appears that the defendant has a defense on the merits to the whole or a part of the plaintiff's claim and that he has been diligent in presenting his motion to open the judgment, the court shall sustain the motion either as to the whole of the judgment or as to any part thereof as to which a good defense has been shown, and the case shall thereafter proceed to trial upon the complaint, answer, and any further pleadings which are required or permitted. If an order is entered opening the judgment, defendant may assert any counterclaim, and plaintiff may amend his complaint so as to assert any other claims, including claims which have accrued subsequent to the entry of the original judgment. The issues of the case shall be tried by the court without a jury unless the defendant or the plaintiff demands a jury and pays the proper fee (if one is required by law) to the clerk at the time of the entry of the order opening the judgment. The original judgment stands as security, and all further proceedings thereon are stayed until the further order of the court, but if the defense is to a part only of the original judgment, the judgment stands as to the balance and enforcement may be had thereon. If a defendant files a motion supported by affidavit which does not disclose a defense to the merits but discloses a counterclaim against the plaintiff, and defendant has been diligent in presenting his motion, the trial court may permit the filing of the counterclaim and to the extent justice requires may stay proceedings on the judgment by confession until the counterclaim is disposed of.

Amended May 28, 1982, eff. July 1, 1982.

Formerly Ill.Rev.Stat.1991, ch. 110A, ¶ 276.

Committee Comments

This is former Rule 23 with the language of the last sentence changed to clarify the right of the trial court to stay or refuse to stay proceedings in whole or in part until the counterclaim is disposed of.

Rule 277. Supplementary Proceedings

(a) **When Proceeding May be Commenced and Against Whom; Subsequent Proceeding Against Same Party.** A supplementary proceeding authorized by section 2–1402 of the Code of Civil Procedure [1] may be commenced at any time with respect to a judgment which is subject to enforcement. The proceeding may be against the judgment debtor or any third party the judgment creditor believes has property of or is indebted to the judgment debtor. If there has been a prior supplementary proceeding with respect to the same judgment against the party, whether he is the judgment debtor or a third party, no further proceeding shall be commenced against him except by leave of court. The leave may be granted upon *ex parte* motion of the judgment creditor, but only upon a finding of the court, based upon affidavit of the judgment creditor or some other person, having personal knowledge of the facts, (1) that there is reason to believe the party against whom the proceeding is sought to be commenced has property or income the creditor is entitled to reach, or, if a third party, is indebted to the judgment debtor, (2) that the existence of the property, income or indebtedness was not known to the judgment creditor during the pendency of any prior supplementary proceeding, and (3) that the additional supplementary proceeding is sought in good faith to discover assets and not to harass the judgment debtor or third party.

(b) How Commenced. The supplementary proceeding shall be commenced by the service of a citation on the party against whom it is brought. The clerk shall issue a citation upon oral request. In cases in which an order of court is prerequisite to the commencement of the proceeding, a copy of the order shall be served with the citation.

(c) Citation—Form, Contents, and Service. The citation by which a supplementary proceeding is commenced:

(1) shall be captioned in the cause in which the judgment was entered;

(2) shall state the date the judgment was entered or revived, and the amount thereof remaining unsatisfied;

(3) shall require the party to whom it is directed, or if directed to a corporation or partnership, a designated officer or partner thereof, to appear for examination at a time (not less than 5 days from the date of service of the citation) and place to be specified therein, concerning the property or income of or indebtedness due the judgment debtor; and

(4) may require, upon reasonable specification thereof, the production at the examination of any books, documents, or records in his or its possession or control which have or may contain information concerning the property or income of the debtor.

The citation shall be served and returned in the manner provided by rule for service, otherwise than by publication, of a notice of additional relief upon a party in default.

(d) When Proceeding May Be Commenced. A supplementary proceeding against the judgment debtor may be commenced in the court in which the judgment was entered. A supplementary proceeding against a third party must, and against the judgment debtor may, be commenced in a county of this State in which the party against whom it is brought resides, or, if an individual, is employed or transacts business in person, upon the filing of a transcript of the judgment in the court in that county. If the party to be cited neither resides nor is employed nor transacts his business in person in this State, the proceeding may be commenced in any county in the State, upon the filing of a transcript of the judgment in the court in the county in which the proceeding is to be commenced.

(e) Hearing. The examination of the judgment debtor, third party or other witnesses shall be before the court, or, if the court so orders, before an officer authorized to administer oaths designated by the court, unless the judgment creditor elects, by so indicating in the citation or subpoena served or by requesting the court to so order, to conduct all or a part of the hearing by deposition as provided by the rules of this court for discovery depositions. The court at any time may terminate the deposition or order that proceedings be conducted before the court or officer designated by the court, and otherwise control and direct the proceeding to the end that the rights and interests of all parties and persons involved may be protected and harassment avoided. Any interested party may subpoena witnesses and adduce evidence as upon the trial of any civil action. Upon the request of either party or the direction of the court, the officer before whom the proceeding is conducted shall certify to the court any evidence taken or other proceedings had before him.

(f) When Proceeding Terminated. A proceeding under this rule continues until terminated by motion of the judgment creditor, order of the court, or satisfaction of the judgment, but terminates automatically 6 months from the date of (1) the respondent's first personal appearance pursuant to the citation or (2) the respondent's first personal appearance pursuant to subsequent process issued to enforce the citation, whichever is sooner. The court may, however, grant extensions beyond the 6 months, as justice may require. Orders for the payment of money continue in effect notwithstanding the termination of the proceedings until the judgment is satisfied or the court orders otherwise.

(g) Concurrent and Consecutive Proceedings. Supplementary proceedings against the debtor and third parties may be conducted concurrently or consecutively. The termination of one proceeding does not affect other pending proceedings not concluded.

(h) Sanctions. Any person who fails to obey a citation, subpoena, or order or other direction of the court issued pursuant to any provision of this rule may be punished for contempt. Any person who refuses to obey any order to deliver up or convey or assign any personal property or in an appropriate case its proceeds or value or title to lands, or choses in action, or evidences of debt may be committed until he has complied with the order or is discharged by due course of law. The court may also enforce its order against the real and personal property of that person.

(i) Costs. The court may tax as costs a sum for witness', stenographer's, and officer's fees, and the fees and outlays of the sheriff, and direct the payment thereof out of any money which may come into the hands of the sheriff or the judgment creditor as a result of the proceeding. If no property applicable to the payment of the judgment is discovered in the course of the proceeding, the court may tax as costs a sum for witness', stenographer's, and officer's fees incurred by any person subpoenaed, to be paid to him by the person who subpoenaed him, and unless paid within the time fixed, enforcement may be had in the manner provided by law for the collection of a judgment for the payment of money.

Amended Oct. 1, 1976, eff. Nov. 15, 1976; Sept. 29, 1978, eff. Nov. 1, 1978; May 28, 1982, eff. July 1, 1982; Jan. 4, 2013, eff. immediately.

Formerly Ill.Rev.Stat.1991, ch. 110A, ¶ 277.
1 735 ILCS 5/2–1402.

Committee Comments
(Revised September 29, 1978)

This is former Rule 24 without change in substance, except for changing 30 days to 28 days in paragraph (f), in accordance with the policy of establishing time periods in multiples of seven. The last sentence has been added to paragraph (f) to make it clear that an order for the payment of money entered in the proceeding is not automatically vacated at the end of the six months' period.

In 1978, Rule 277 was amended to delete the words "or decree." This change effected no change in substance. See Rule 2(b)(2).

Rules 278 to 280.   Reserved

PART I.   SMALL CLAIMS

Rule 281.   Definition of Small Claim

For the purpose of the application of Rules 281 through 288, a small claim is a civil action based on either tort or contract for money not in excess of $10,000, exclusive of interest and costs, or for the collection of taxes not in excess of that amount.

The order entered December 6, 2005, amending Rule 281 and effective January 1, 2006, shall apply only to cases filed after such effective date.

Amended effective December 15, 1966; amended May 27, 1969, effective July 1, 1969; amended January 5, 1981, effective February 1, 1981; amended December 3, 1996, effective January 1, 1997; amended December 6, 2005, effective January 1, 2006.

Formerly Ill.Rev.Stat.1991, ch. 110A, ¶ 281.

Committee Comments
(Revised December 6, 2005)

This rule was based on paragraph A of former Rule 9–1 which was in effect from January 1, 1964, to January 1, 1967. The only changes of substance made by the 1967 revision were increasing the upper limit of a small claim from $200 to $500, including tax-collection cases in the definition, and adding the phrase "based on either tort or contract." The limit was further increased to $1,000 by the 1969 amendment, and to $2,500 by amendment in 1981.

Rule 281 was amended in 2005 to increase the jurisdictional limit from $5,000 to $10,000. As the

change will require a modification to the allocation of judicial resources, the change was made applicable only to new cases and does not apply to pending cases.

Rule 282.   Commencement of Action—Representation of Corporations

(a) **Commencement of Actions.** An action on a small claim may be commenced by paying to the clerk of the court the required filing fee and filing a short and simple complaint setting forth (1) plaintiff's name, residence address, and telephone number, (2) defendant's name and place of residence, or place of business or regular employment, and (3) the nature and amount of the plaintiff's claim, giving dates and other relevant information. If the claim is based upon a written instrument, a copy thereof or of so much of it as is relevant must be copied in or attached to the original and all copies of the complaint, unless the plaintiff attaches to the complaint an affidavit stating facts showing that the instrument is unavailable to him.

(b) **Representation of Corporations.** No corporation may appear as claimant, assignee, subrogee or counterclaimant in a small claims proceeding, unless represented by counsel. When the amount claimed does not exceed the jurisdictional limit for small claims, a corporation may defend as defendant any small claims proceeding in any court of this State through any officer, director, manager, department manager or supervisor of the corporation, as though such corporation were appearing in its proper person. For the purposes of this rule, the term "officer" means the president, vice-president, registered agent or other person vested with the responsibility of managing the affairs of the corporation.

Amended June 12, 1987, eff. Aug. 1, 1987; May 20, 1997, eff. July 1, 1997.

Formerly Ill.Rev.Stat.1991, ch. 110A, ¶ 282.

Committee Comments

Paragraph (a) of this rule is paragraph B of former Rule 9–1, effective January 1, 1964, with the last sentence conformed to section 36 of the Civil Practice Act (now section 2–606 of the Code of Civil Procedure). Paragraph (b) was added, effective August 1, 1987, to allow corporate officers to appear and defend small claims actions, as though such corporation were appearing in its own proper person, in any case in which the amount claimed does not exceed $1,500.

Rule 283.   Form of Summons

Summons in small claims shall require each defendant to appear on a day specified in the summons not less than 14 or more than 40 days after issuance of the summons (see Rule 181(b)) and shall be in the form provided for in Rule 101(b) in actions for money not in excess of $50,000.

Amended eff. Aug. 3, 1970; Dec. 3, 1996.

Formerly Ill.Rev.Stat.1991, ch. 110A, ¶ 283.

Committee Comments

This is derived from paragraph C of former Rule 9–1, effective January 1, 1964. The earliest return day is increased from seven to 14. See also the comments to Rules 101(b) and 286, which deal with the right of the court to control the return day, manner of appearance, and related matters.

Rule 284. Service by Certified or Registered Mail

Unless otherwise provided by circuit court rule, at the request of the plaintiff and in lieu of personal service, service in small claims may be made within the state as follows:

(a) For each defendant to be served the plaintiff shall pay to the clerk of the court a fee of $2, plus the cost of mailing, and furnish to the clerk an original and one copy of a summons containing an affidavit setting forth the defendant's last known mailing address, and a copy of the complaint in addition to the original. The original summons shall be retained by the clerk.

(b) The clerk forthwith shall mail to the defendant, at the address appearing in the affidavit, the copy of the summons and complaint, certified or registered mail, return receipt requested, showing to whom delivered and the date and address of delivery. The summons and complaint shall be mailed on a "restricted delivery" basis when service is directed to a natural person. The envelope and return receipt shall bear the return address of the clerk, and the return receipt shall be stamped with the docket number of the case. The receipt for certified or registered mail shall state the name and address of the addressee, and the date of mailing, and shall be attached to the original summons.

(c) The return receipt, when returned to the clerk, shall be attached to the original summons, and, if it shows delivery at least 3 days before the day for appearance, shall constitute proof of service.

(d) The clerk shall note the fact of service in a permanent record.

Amended Oct. 1, 1976, eff. Nov. 15, 1976; Sept. 29, 1978, eff. Nov. 1, 1978; Feb. 15, 1979, eff. March 1, 1979; July 1, 1985, eff. Aug. 1, 1985; Nov. 21, 1988, eff. Jan. 1, 1989; eff. April 11, 2001.

Formerly Ill.Rev.Stat.1991, ch. 110A, ¶ 284.

Committee Comments

This is paragraphs D(1), (2), (3), and (4) of former Rule 9–1, effective January 1, 1964, Paragraph (b) was amended in 1978 to require mailing by certified or registered mail, "restricted delivery, return re-ceipt requested, showing to whom, date and address of delivery." Prior to 1978, this subparagraph required that process be mailed "certified mail, return receipt requested." In this respect it differed from Rules 105, 204, and 237, which required mailing "addressee only." In 1978, this class of delivery having been discontinued by the Postal Service, Rules 105, 204, and 237 were amended to require mailing "restricted delivery, return receipt requested, showing to whom, date and address of delivery," the most restricted delivery provided for in current postal regulations. At the same time Rule 284(b) was amended to require the same class delivery, thus making the requirement uniform. See Committee Comment to Rule 105.

The amendment effective August 1, 1985, changed the fee for mailing from $3 to $2 plus the cost of mailing. This amendment insulates the rule from further change by making the "cost of mailing" an element of the fee charged by the clerk.

Rule 285. Jury Demands

A small claim shall be tried by the court unless a jury demand is filed by the plaintiff at the time the action is commenced or by the defendant not later than the date he is required to appear. There shall be 6 jurors unless either party demands 12. A party demanding a jury shall pay a fee of $12.50 unless he demands a jury of 12, in which case he shall pay a fee of $25.00, or, if another party has previously paid a fee for a jury of 6, $12.50.

Formerly Ill.Rev.Stat.1991, ch. 110A, ¶ 285.

Committee Comments

This is paragraph E of former Rule 9–1, effective January 1, 1964, without change.

Rule 286. Appearance and Trial

(a) Unless the "Notice to Defendant" (see Rule 101(b)) provides otherwise, the defendant in a small claim must appear at the time and place specified in the summons and the case shall be tried on the day set for appearance unless otherwise ordered. If the defendant appears, he need not file an answer unless ordered to do so by the court; and when no answer is ordered the allegations of the complaint will be considered denied and any defense may be proved as if it were specifically pleaded.

(b) Informal Hearings in Small Claims Cases. In any small claims case, the court may, on its own motion or on motion of any party, adjudicate the dispute at an informal hearing. At the informal hearing all relevant evidence shall be admissible and the court may relax the rules of procedure and the rules of evidence. The court may call any person present at the hearing to testify and may conduct or participate in direct and cross-examination of any witness or party. At the conclusion of the hearing the court shall render judgment and explain the reasons therefor to all parties.

Amended June 12, 1987, eff. Aug. 1, 1987; April 1, 1992, eff. Aug. 1, 1992.

Formerly Ill.Rev.Stat.1991, ch. 110A, ¶ 286.

Committee Comments

This is paragraph F of former Rule 9–1, effective January 1, 1964, with a caveat that the trial court may by "Notice to Defendant" on the summons mentioned in Rule 101(b) adopt the procedure best suited to local conditions in the handling of small claims. By the notice of the summons, the defendant should be given explicit directions where to appear, whether he must appear ready for trial on the day for appearance, or whether by filing a written appearance or giving appropriate notice to the plaintiff he will be excused from going to trial at that time. If by entry of a written appearance or by personal appearance of the defendant the case is automatically set over for trial on a specified later date, the notice to defendant should so state. These suggestions are only illustrative. See also the Committee Comments to Rule 101(b).

Paragraph (b) was added effective August 1, 1987. The rule authorizes the court on its own motion or on motion of any party to conduct an informal hearing to decide small claims cases where the amount claimed by any party does not exceed $1,000. Amended in 1992 to delete the condition setting an upper limit on the value of cases in which an informal hearing may be had.

Rule 287. Depositions, Discovery and Motions

(a) No depositions shall be taken or interrogatories or other discovery proceeding or requests to admit be used prior to trial in small claims except by leave of court.

(b) Motions. Except as provided in sections 2–619 and 2–1001 of the Code of Civil Procedure,[1] no motion shall be filed in small claims cases, without prior leave of court.

Amended June 12, 1987, eff. Aug. 1, 1987; April 1, 1992, eff. Aug. 1, 1992.

Formerly Ill.Rev.Stat.1991, ch. 110A, ¶ 287.
[1] 735 ILCS 5/2–619 and 5/2–1001.

Committee Comments

Paragraph (a) is substantially paragraph G of former Rule 9–1, effective January 1, 1964. The restriction on discovery proceedings obviously does not apply to interrogatories in garnishment or to supplementary proceedings under Rule 277. Amended in 1992 to provide that a request to admit under Rule 216 is not to be used in small claims cases, except upon leave of court.

Paragraph (b) was added in August of 1987. The basic purposes of the Supreme Court Rules applicable to small claims cases are to simplify procedures and reduce the cost of litigation. In keeping with these objectives, motions in such cases should only be permitted to the extent that the motion may be dispositive of the claim and to the extent that the trial judge, in his discretion, may allow in the interests of justice.

Rule 288. Installment Payment of Judgments

The court may order that the amount of a small claim judgment shall be paid to the prevailing party on a certain date or in specified installments, and may stay the enforcement of the judgment and other supplementary process during compliance with such order. The stay may be modified or vacated by the court, but the installment payments of small claims judgments shall not extend over a period in excess of three years duration.

Amended eff. Jan. 21, 1969; amended May 28, 1982, eff. July 1, 1982.

Formerly Ill.Rev.Stat.1991, ch. 110A, ¶ 288.

Committee Comments
(Revised October, 1969)

As adopted effective January 1, 1967, this rule was paragraph H of former Rule 9–1, effective January 1, 1964, without change.

The provision in the last sentence that installment payments shall not extend over a period of more than three years was added by amendment January 21, 1969, in view of the provision in the Supreme Court Recordkeeping Order that Small Claims files are to be destroyed three years after the date of judgment, unless otherwise ordered by the trial court.

Rule 289. Service of Process in Proceedings to Confirm a Judgment by Confession or to Collect a Judgment for $10,000 or Less

In proceedings to confirm a judgment by confession or to collect a judgment for money, in which the judgment is for $10,000 or less, exclusive of interest and costs, process may be served in the manner provided in Rule 284.

Adopted Jan. 5, 1981, eff. Feb. 1, 1981. Amended Dec. 3, 1996, eff. Jan. 1, 1997; March 8, 2007, eff. April 1, 2007.

Formerly Ill.Rev.Stat.1991, ch. 110A, ¶ 289.

Committee Comments
(Revised March 8, 2007)

Rule 289 was added in 1981 to permit service by mail in proceedings to confirm a judgment by confession and in proceedings to collect a judgment, e.g., wage deductions and garnishment, when the amount of the judgment is $2,500 or less, the figure used to define a small claim in Rule 281.

In 2007 the rule was amended to reflect the increased jurisdictional limit from $5,000 to $10,000 for small-claims actions under Rule 281.

Rule 290. Reserved

PART J. MISCELLANEOUS

Rule 291. Proceedings Under the Administrative Review Law

(a) Form of Summons. The summons in proceedings under the Administrative Review Law [1] shall be drawn in substantially the following form:

In the Circuit Court of the _____ Judicial Circuit
_____ County, Illinois
(Or, In the Circuit Court of Cook County, Illinois)
A.B., C.D., *etc.* (naming all plain-
    tiffs),
                        Plaintiffs,
        v.   No. _____

First the Agency appealed from,
    and the defendants, and parties
    not appealing,
                        Defendants.

To each of the above-named defendants:

You are hereby summoned and required to file an answer in this case or otherwise file your appearance in the office of the clerk of this court within 35 days after the date of this summons.

This summons is served upon you by registered or certified mail pursuant to the provisions of the Administrative Review Law.

                              Witness _____, 20 _____
(Seal of Court)   _____
                                      Clerk of Court

Plaintiff's Attorney (or plaintiff, if he is not represented by attorney) _____

Address _____

Telephone No. _____

Facsimile Telephone No. _____

E–Mail Address _____

(If service by facsimile transmission will be accepted, the telephone number of the plaintiff or plaintiff's attorney's facsimile machine is additionally required.)

(b) Service. The clerk shall promptly serve each defendant by mailing a copy of the summons by registered or certified mail as provided in the Administrative Review Law. Not later than 5 days after the mailing of copies of the summons, the clerk shall file a certificate showing that he served the defendants by registered or certified mail pursuant to the provisions of the Administrative Review Law.

(c) Appearance. The defendant shall appear not later than 35 days after the date the summons bears.

(d) Other Rules Applicable. Rules 181(b), 182(b), 183, and 184 shall apply to proceedings under the Administrative Review Law.

(e) Record on Appeal. The original copy of the answer of the administrative agency, consisting of the record of proceedings (including the evidence and exhibits, if any) had before the administrative agency, shall be incorporated in the record on appeal unless the parties stipulate to less, or the trial court after notice and hearing, or the reviewing court, orders less.

Amended July 30, 1979, effective October 15, 1979; May 28, 1982, effective July 1, 1982; April 27, 1984, effective July 1, 1984; October 30, 1992, effective November 15, 1992; May 30, 2008, effective immediately; Dec. 9, 2015, eff. Jan. 1, 2016.

Formerly Ill.Rev.Stat.1991, ch. 110A, ¶ 291.
[1] 735 ILCS 5/3–101 et seq.

Committee Comments

(Revised 1984)

As originally adopted, Rule 291 carried forward the provisions of former Rule 71 without substantial change. Paragraphs (a) through (d) remain as originally adopted. In 1979, paragraph (e) was amended in four respects. First, language was added to make it clear that the exhibits, as well as any other "evidence," constitute a part of the record of proceedings had before the administrative agency. Second, it was provided that the parties may stipulate for inclusion in the record on appeal of less than the full record of proceedings. Third, it was provided that, if the trial court orders less, it must do so after notice and hearing. Fourth, it was provided that the reviewing court, without notice and hearing, may order less.

Section 3–105 of the Code of Civil Procedure was amended, effective July 13, 1982, and, in 1984, paragraph (b) of this rule was amended to allow service of summons by certified mail, as well as registered mail.

Rule 292. Form of Summons in Proceedings to Review Orders of the Illinois Workers' Compensation Commission

Upon the filing of a written request to commence a proceeding to review an order of the Illinois Workers' Compensation Commission under either the Workers' Compensation Act, approved July 9, 1951, as amended,[1] or the Workers' Occupational Diseases Act, approved July 9, 1951, as amended,[2] the clerk of the circuit court shall issue a summons in substantially the following form to the Commission and all other parties in interest:

In the Circuit Court of the _____ Judicial Circuit, _____ County, Illinois.

(Or, In the Circuit Court of Cook County, Illinois.)

_____,
    Petitioner,

v.   No. _____

The Illinois Workers' Compensation Commission
and _____

————————

————————,

Respondents.

SUMMONS

To each respondent:

You are hereby summoned and required to file your appearance on or before _____, 20 ___, in the above entitled proceeding, in the office of the clerk of this court; and the Illinois Workers' Compensation Commission shall, on or before _____, 20 ___, certify and file, in the above-entitled proceeding, in the office of the clerk of this court, a transcript of the proceedings had before the Commission, in Illinois Workers' Compensation Commission No. ___, in which a decision or award was rendered on _____, 20 ___, by the Illinois Workers' Compensation Commission for _____ and against _____.

Witness _____, 20 ___

(Seal of Court)

————————————————

Clerk of the Circuit Court

Name _____

Attorney for _____

Address _____

Telephone No. _____

Note: Pursuant to law, proceedings for judicial review shall be commenced within 20 days of the receipt of notice of the decision of the Commission. The summons shall be issued by the clerk of such court upon written request, returnable on a designated return day, not less than 10 nor more than 60 days from the date of issuance thereof.

On _____, 20 ___, in accordance with law, I mailed a copy of this summons, postage prepaid, to the office of the Illinois Workers' Compensation Commission and to the following parties in interest or their attorney or attorneys of record:

Respondent _____

Address _____

Dated _____, 20 ___

————————————————

Clerk of Court

Adopted April 27, 1984, eff. July 1, 1984. Amended Oct. 9, 1984, eff. Nov. 1, 1984; amended Oct. 15, 2004, eff. Jan. 1, 2005.

Formerly Ill.Rev.Stat.1991, ch. 110A, ¶ 292.

1 820 ILCS 305/1 et seq.

2 820 ILCS 310/1 et seq.

Committee Comments

Rule 292 was adopted in 1984 in order to insure uniform adherence to the requirements of Public Act 83–360 and Public Act 83–361, which make

summons, rather than writ of *certiorari*, the proper device for the commencement of review of Industrial Commission orders. The proceedings must be commenced within 20 days of the receipt of notice of the decision of the Commission. The summons shall be issued by the clerk of the circuit court upon written request, returnable on a designated return day, not less than 10 nor more than 60 days from the date of issuance of the summons.

Rules 293, 294. Reserved

Rule 295. Matters Assignable to Associate Judges

The Chief Judge of each circuit or any circuit judge designated by him may assign an associate judge to hear and determine any matters except the trial of criminal cases in which the defendant is charged with an offense punishable by imprisonment for more than one year. Upon a showing of need presented to the supreme court by the chief judge of a circuit, the supreme court may authorize the chief judge to make temporary assignments of individual associate judges to conduct trials of criminal cases in which the defendant is charged with an offense punishable by imprisonment for more than one year.

Amended June 26, 1970, eff. July 1, 1970; amended eff. Oct. 7, 1970; April 1, 1971; July 1, 1971; May 28, 1975.

Formerly Ill.Rev.Stat.1991, ch. 110A, ¶ 295.

Committee Comments

(Revised July 1, 1971)

Section 8 of article VI of the new Illinois Constitution provides, "The Supreme Court shall provide by rule for matters to be assigned to Associate Judges." Accordingly, a new rule 295 was drafted to replace the statute dealing with assignments to magistrates (Ill.Rev.Stat.1969, ch. 37, ¶ 621 et seq.) and former Rule 295, which supplemented the statute.

The new rule leaves it to the Chief Judge of each circuit, who will know the capabilities of the associate judges in his circuit and the requirements for disposition of judicial business, to determine the kinds of matters other than the trial of major criminal cases that may be assigned to an associate judge. The restriction against assignment of the trial of major criminal cases does not prevent assignment of an associate judge to conduct proceedings other than the trial in such cases.

Rule 296. Reserved

Adopted February 1, 1989, effective immediately. Amended May 30, 2008, effective September 1, 2008. Repealed and reserved October 1, 2010, effective immediately.

Formerly Ill.Rev.Stat.1991, ch. 110A, ¶ 296.

Rule 297. Reserved

Rule 298. Application for Waiver of Court Fees

(a) **Contents.** An Application for Waiver of Court Fees in a civil action pursuant to 735 ILCS 5/5–105 shall be in writing and signed by the applicant or, if the applicant is a minor or an incompetent adult, by another person having knowledge of the facts.

(1) The contents of the Application must be sufficient to allow a court to determine whether an applicant qualifies for waiver of fees pursuant to 735 ILCS 5/5–105, and shall include information regarding the applicant's household composition; receipt of need-based public benefits; income; expenses; and nonexempt assets.

(2) The court shall provide and applicants shall be required to use a standardized form expressly titled "Application for Waiver of Court Fees" adopted by the Illinois Supreme Court Access to Justice Commission.

(b) **Ruling.** The court shall either enter a ruling on the Application or shall set the Application for a hearing requiring the applicant to personally appear in a timely manner. The court may order the applicant to produce copies of certain documents in support of the Application at the hearing. The court's ruling on an Application for Waiver of Court Fees shall be made according to standards set forth in 735 ILCS 5/5–105. If the Application is denied, the court shall enter an order to that effect stating the specific reason for the denial. If the Application is granted, the court shall enter an order permitting the applicant to sue or defend without payment of fees, costs or charges.

(c) **Filing.** No fee may be charged for filing an Application for Waiver of Court Fees. The clerk must allow an applicant to file an Application for Waiver of Court Fees in the court where his case will be heard.

(d) **Cases involving representation by civil legal services provider or lawyer in court-sponsored pro bono program.** In any case where a party is represented by a civil legal services provider or attorney in a court-sponsored pro bono program as defined in 735 ILCS 5/5–105.5, the attorney representing that party shall file a certification with the court in the form attached to this rule and that party shall be allowed to sue or defend without payment of fees, costs or charges as defined in 735 ILCS 5/5–105(a)(1) without necessity of an Application under this rule.

RULE 298 CERTIFICATION FOR WAIVER OF FEES REPRESENTATION BY CIVIL LEGAL SERVICES PROVIDER OR COURT–SPONSORED PRO BONO PROGRAM

Pursuant to Supreme Court Rule 298, the undersigned counsel hereby certifies that he/she is an attorney for _____ (*name of organization or court program*), a civil legal services provider or court-sponsored pro bono program as defined in 735 ILCS 5/5–105.5(a), and that _____ (*name of organization or court program*) has made the determination that _____ (*name of party*) has income of 125% or less of the current official poverty guidelines or is otherwise eligible to receive services under the eligibility guidelines of the civil legal services provider or court-sponsored pro bono program. As a result, under Supreme Court Rule 298, _____ (*name of party*) is eligible to sue or defend without payment of fees, costs or charges as defined at 735 ILCS 5/5–105(a)(1).

———————————

Attorney Certification

Name of Organization or Court Program: _____

Attorney Name _____

Attorney No. _____

Address _____

City, State, Zip _____

Telephone _____

Amended Oct. 20, 2003, eff. Nov. 1, 2003; Sept. 25, 2014, eff. immediately

Formerly Ill.Rev.Stat.1991, ch. 110A, ¶ 298.

Rule 299. Compensation for Attorneys Appointed to Represent Indigent Parties

(a) Attorneys who are appointed by the courts of this state to represent indigent parties shall be entitled to receive a reasonable fee for their services. In arriving at a reasonable fee for appointed counsel's services, the appointing court should consider: (1) the time spent and the services rendered; (2) the attorney's skill and experience; (3) the complexity of the case; (4) the overhead costs and the burden on the attorney's practice; (5) the rate of compensation for comparable services in the locality; (6) the reduction of the comparable fee by a *pro bono* factor; (7) the number of appointments given to the attorney; and (8) the availability of public funds. No single factor is determinative in establishing a reasonable fee.

(b) **Hourly Rate.** An attorney appointed by a court in this state to represent an indigent party may be compensated at a rate set by local rule, but not less than $75 per hour for time expended in court and $50 per hour for time reasonably expended out of court.

(c) **Maximum Amount.** Maximum compensation is limited as follows:

For representation of an indigent defendant charged with a misdemeanor, $750.

For indigent persons: (1) charged with one or more felonies; (2) whose parental rights are sought to be terminated pursuant to the Adoption Act (750 ILCS 50/8) or the Juvenile Court Act (705 ILCS 405/1 through 5); (3) whom the State is seeking to commit as a sexually dangerous person pursuant to the Sexually Dangerous Persons Act (725 ILCS 205/0.01 *et seq.*) or as a sexually violent person pursuant to the Sexually Violent Persons Commitment Act (725 ILCS 207/1 *et seq.*); (4) who have an absolute right to appeal from determinations concerning categories (1), (2) and (3) above, the compensation to be paid to an attorney shall not exceed $5,000.

(d) Waiving Maximum Amounts. Payment in excess of any maximum amount provided in paragraph (c) may be made for extended or complex representation only when the court making the appointment makes an express, written finding that good cause and exceptional circumstances exist and that the amount of the excess payment is necessary to provide fair compensation and the chief judge of the circuit or the presiding judge of the applicable division of the circuit court of Cook County approves the excess payment. All petitions to exceed the maximum fee guidelines must be approved prior to the guidelines being exceeded.

Adopted February 10, 2006, effective July 1, 2006.

Committee Comments

(February 10, 2006)

Section 113–3 of the Code of Civil Procedure (725 ILCS 5/113–3) provides: "In all cases, except where the penalty is a fine only, if the court determines that the defendant is indigent and desires counsel the Public Defender shall be appointed as counsel. Section 113–3 also provides under which circumstances counsel other than a public defender may be appointed.

The Juvenile Court Act provides for counsel to be appointed to all indigent parents threatened with the loss of parental rights (705 ILCS 405/1–5(1)). In *In re Adoption of L.T.M.*, 214 Ill. 2d 60 (2005), the supreme court held that the equal protection clause of the fourteenth amendment to the United States Constitution mandated that indigent parents threatened with the loss of parental rights under the Adoption Act (750 ILCS 50/8) are also entitled to appointed counsel.

Section 5 of the Sexually Dangerous Persons Act (725 ILCS 205/5) provides that persons whom the State seeks to confine pursuant to the Act are entitled to be represented by counsel. Section 30(e) of the Sexually Violent Persons Commitment Act (725 ILCS 207/30(e)) provides that the court shall appoint counsel if the person named in the petition claims or appears to be indigent.

In setting the hourly rate and total compensation, the Committee took into consideration the fact that section 113–3(c)'s provisions of $40 for time spent in court and $30 for all other time, applicable only to Cook County, had not been changed in more than 20 years. Section 10(b) of the Capital Crimes Litigation Act (725 ILCS 124/10(b)) provides that trial counsel appointed to represent indigents who are charged in capital cases may be paid a "reasonable rate not to exceed $125 per hour. The Committee also considered 18 U.S.C. § 3006A ("Adequate Representation of Defendants), which gives the federal Judicial Conference the authority to set a rate of $90 per hour for time expended in court or for time expended out of court. Section 3006A also sets $7,000 as a maximum fee in felony cases, $2,000 in misdemeanor cases and $5,000 in appellate cases.

Rule 300. Reserved

ARTICLE III. CIVIL APPEALS RULES

Revision

Order entered December 17, 1993, provides:

"After careful consideration of the Report and Proposal for Changes to the Rules Cov-ering Civil Appellate Procedure submitted by this court's Rules Committee and having used that report to focus the court's review of the rules, the Supreme Court has made the appropriate changes to its rules governing appellate practice. The court emphasizes that development of a cohesive set of procedural rules is an ongoing, evolutionary process and that continuing consideration is being given to a number of proposals which are not reflected in the changes the court has adopted at this time. The changes that the court has adopted are substantive and stylistic. Obsolete provisions have been deleted; some rules have been reorganized to promote ease of use; and language has been made gender neutral.

"The Supreme Court thanks the members of the Rules Committee and its subcommittee on civil appeals for devoting their time and effort to a most ambitious project and acknowledges that the Committee has dedicated its work to the memory of member Sidney Z. Karasik, who served on the Committee for 14 years."

PART A.   APPEALS FROM THE CIRCUIT COURT

Rule 301.   Method of Review

Every final judgment of a circuit court in a civil case is appealable as of right. The appeal is initiated by filing a notice of appeal. No other step is jurisdictional. An appeal is a continuation of the proceeding.

Amended Dec. 17, 1993, eff. Feb. 1, 1994.

Formerly Ill.Rev.Stat.1991, ch. 110A, ¶ 301.

Committee Comments

(Revised July 1, 1971)

This rule, adopted pursuant to the authority given the Supreme Court by the Judicial Article effective January 1, 1964, former article VI, § 7, present article VI, § 16, prescribes the method of review of final judgments. The rule was primarily based upon and replaced former sections 74, 76(2), and 80 of the Civil Practice Act. The next to last sentence of the proposed rule was intended to incorporate and restate the provisions of the last two sentences of former section 74(1).

Supersedure of statutory provisions relating to appeals is covered by Rule 1.

(December 17, 1993)

The last two sentences concerning a writ of error have been deleted because they are outdated. The notice of appeal preserves for review all judgments and orders specified therein.

Rule 302. Direct Appeals to the Supreme Court

(a) Cases Directly Appealable. Appeals from final judgments of circuit courts shall be taken directly to the Supreme Court (1) in cases in which a statute of the United States or of this state has been held invalid, and (2) in proceedings commenced under Rule 21(d) of this court. For purposes of this rule, invalidity does not include a determination that a statute of this state is preempted by federal law.

(b) Cases in Which the Public Interest Requires Expeditious Determination. After the filing of the notice of appeal to the Appellate Court in a case in which the public interest requires prompt adjudication by the Supreme Court, the Supreme Court or a justice thereof may order that the appeal be taken directly to it. Upon the entry of such an order any documents already filed in the Appellate Court shall be transmitted by the clerk of that court to the clerk of the Supreme Court. From that point the case shall proceed in all respects as though the appeal had been taken directly to the Supreme Court.

(c) Summary Disposition.

(1) The Supreme Court, after the briefs have been filed, may dispose of any case without oral argument or opinion if no substantial question is presented or if jurisdiction is lacking.

(2) The Supreme Court, on its own motion or upon the motion of a party, before or after any brief has been filed or oral argument held, may summarily vacate and remand a judgment of the circuit court for noncompliance with Rule 18. Such vacatur shall not constitute a determination on the merits of the constitutional question presented.

Amended eff. July 1, 1971. (An amendment of June 29, 1978, was to have abolished direct appeals in proceedings to review orders of the Industrial Commission. The amendment was to have been effective January 1, 1979. On December 1, 1978, the effective date of the amendment was postponed until July 1, 1979. On June 1, 1979, the amendment was rescinded.) Amended Aug. 9, 1983, eff. Oct. 1, 1983; Feb. 1, 1984, eff. Feb. 1, 1984, with Justice Moran dissenting (see *Yellow Cab Co. v. Jones* (1985), 108 Ill. 2d 330, 342); July 27, 2006, eff. Sept. 1, 2006; Oct. 4, 2011, eff. immediately.

Formerly Ill.Rev.Stat.1991, ch. 110A, ¶ 302.

Committee Comments

(Revised February 1, 1984)

When adopted effective January 1, 1967, this rule was the same as former Rule 28–1, which was effective between January 1, 1964 and January 1, 1967, except for the transfer to new Rule 365 of the paragraph providing that the taking of an appeal to the wrong court is not a waiver of the right to present any issue to the appropriate court, and the transfer to new Rule 603 of the provision for direct appeals in capital cases. Although former Rule 28–1 was new in 1964, the same subject had been partly covered by section 75 of the Civil Practice Act, which was repealed, part on January 1, 1964,

and the remainder on August 4, 1965. Laws of 1963, p. 2691, and Laws of 1965, p. 3543.

The 1971 revision of paragraphs (a) and (b) of this rule was made in light of the new Illinois Constitution effective July 1, 1971, which eliminated the mandatory direct appellate jurisdiction of the Supreme Court in all cases except those in which a sentence of death has been imposed. The revised rule is based upon the principle that the Supreme Court of Illinois should have a role in the State judicial system similar to that of the Supreme Court of the United States in the Federal system; that is, the Supreme Court should be the forum for the decision of important questions which affect the public interest or are otherwise of importance and general applicability and should exercise supervisory jurisdiction over the State judicial system. Accordingly, the Supreme Court's mandatory direct appellate jurisdiction is reduced and its appellate jurisdiction is made largely discretionary.

Paragraph (a)

Paragraph (a) was accordingly revised effective July 1, 1971, to limit direct appeals from the circuit courts to the Supreme Court to two classes of cases: cases in which a statute of the United States or Illinois has been held invalid, and proceedings to review orders of the Industrial Commission. Paragraph (a) was amended in 1978 to eliminate direct appeals in workmen's compensation cases, but the amendment was rescinded before it became effective. Mr. Justices Clark and Moran dissented from the rescission of the amendment. When a circuit court holds a statute unconstitutional, that decision should be reviewed and the issue presented resolved as promptly as possible. (See 28 U.S.C. §§ 1252 and 1257.)

In 1984, paragraph (a) was amended to eliminate direct review of orders of the Industrial Commission by the Supreme Court. See Comment to Rule 22(g).

Paragraph (b)

Paragraph (b) is based upon former paragraph (d). Its language was revised in 1971 to liberalize the description of the kinds of cases which, after the filing of a notice of appeal to the Appellate Court, may be brought directly to the Supreme Court, thereby allowing the Supreme Court to choose cases appropriate for its direct review.

Paragraph (c)

This paragraph is meant to advise the bar that the Supreme Court may summarily dispose of any appeal without allowing oral argument if, on the face of the briefs, jurisdiction is lacking or no substantial question is presented. The United States Supreme Court has long followed a somewhat similar practice to avoid wasting unnecessary time on appeals that lack substance.

(July 27, 2006)

The amendment to Rule 302(c) recognizes that the Supreme Court may summarily vacate and remand any circuit court judgment that fails to comply with Rule 18.

Rule 303. Appeals from Final Judgments of the Circuit Court in Civil Cases

(a) Time; Filing; Transmission of Copy.

(1) The notice of appeal must be filed with the clerk of the circuit court within 30 days after the entry of the final judgment appealed from, or, if a timely posttrial motion directed against the judgment is filed, whether in a jury or a nonjury case, within 30 days after the entry of the order disposing of the last pending postjudgment motion directed against that judgment or order, irrespective of whether the circuit court had entered a series of final orders that were modified pursuant to postjudgment motions. A judgment or order is not final and appealable while a Rule 137 claim remains pending unless the court enters a finding pursuant to Rule 304(a). A notice of appeal filed after the court announces a decision, but before the entry of the judgment or order, is treated as filed on the date of and after the entry of the judgment or order. The notice of appeal may be filed by any party or by any attorney representing the party appealing, regardless of whether that attorney has filed an appearance in the circuit court case being appealed.

(2) When a timely postjudgment motion has been filed by any party, whether in a jury case or a nonjury case, a notice of appeal filed before the entry of the order disposing of the last pending postjudgment motion, or before the final disposition of any separate claim, becomes effective when the order disposing of said motion or claim is entered. A party intending to challenge an order disposing of any postjudgment motion or separate claim, or a judgment amended upon such motion, must file a notice of appeal, or an amended notice of appeal within 30 days of the entry of said order or amended judgment, but where a postjudgment motion is denied, an appeal from the judgment is deemed to include an appeal from the denial of the postjudgment motion. No request for reconsideration of a ruling on a postjudgment motion will toll the running of the time within which a notice of appeal must be filed under this rule.

(3) If a timely notice of appeal is filed and served by a party, any other party, within 10 days after service upon him or her, or within 30 days from the entry of the judgment or order being appealed, or within 30 days of the entry of the order disposing of the last pending postjudgment motion, whichever is later, may join in the appeal, appeal separately, or cross-appeal by filing a notice of appeal, indicating which type of appeal is being taken.

(4) Within five days after the filing of a notice of appeal, or an amendment of a notice of appeal filed in the circuit court pursuant to subparagraph (b)(45) of this rule, the clerk of the circuit court shall transmit to the clerk of the court to which the appeal is being taken a copy of the notice of appeal or of the amendment.

(b) Form and Contents of Notice of Appeal.

(1) The notice of appeal shall be captioned as follows:

(i) At the top shall appear the statement "Appeal to the _____ Court," naming the court to which the appeal is taken, and below this shall be the statement "From the Circuit Court of _____," naming the court from which the appeal is taken.

(ii) It shall bear the title of the case, naming and designating the parties in the same manner as in the circuit court and adding the further designation "appellant" or "appellee," *e.g.*, "Plaintiff–Appellee."

(iii) It shall be designated "Notice of Appeal," "Joining Prior Appeal," "Separate Appeal," or "Cross–Appeal," as appropriate.

(2) It shall specify the judgment or part thereof or other orders appealed from and the relief sought from the reviewing court.

(3) A notice of appeal filed pursuant to Rule 302(a)(1) from a judgment of a circuit court holding unconstitutional a statute of the United States or of this state shall have appended thereto a copy of the court's findings made in compliance with Rule 18.

(4) It shall contain the signature and address of each appellant or appellant's attorney.

(5) The notice of appeal may be amended without leave of court within the original 30–day period to file the notice as set forth in paragraph (a) above. Thereafter it may be amended only on motion, in the reviewing court, pursuant to paragraph (d) of this rule. Amendments relate back to the time of the filing of the notice of appeal.

(c) Service of Notice of Appeal.
The party filing the notice of appeal or an amendment as of right, shall, within 7 days, file a notice of filing with the reviewing court and serve a copy of the notice of appeal upon every other party and upon any other person or officer entitled by law to notice. Proof of service, as provided by Rule 12, shall be filed with the notice.

(d) Extension of Time in Certain Circumstances.
On motion supported by a showing of reasonable excuse for failure to file a notice of appeal on time, accompanied by the proposed notice of appeal and the filing fee, filed in the reviewing court within 30 days after expiration of the time for filing a notice of appeal, the reviewing court may grant leave to appeal and order the clerk to transmit the notice of appeal to the trial court for filing. If the reviewing court allows leave to file a late notice of appeal, any other party may, within 10 days of the order allowing the filing of the late notice, join in the appeal separately or cross-appeal as set forth in Rule 303(a)(3).

(e) Docketing. Upon receipt of the copy of the notice of appeal transmitted to the reviewing court pursuant to paragraph (a) of this rule, or receipt of a motion for leave to appeal under paragraph (d) of this rule, the clerk of the reviewing court shall enter the appeal upon the docket.

Amended eff. Jan. 12, 1967; Jan. 1, 1970; Oct. 21, 1969, eff. Jan. 1, 1970; July 1, 1971; Sept. 1, 1974; Oct. 1, 1976, eff. Nov. 15, 1976; July 30, 1979, eff. Oct. 15, 1979; Aug. 9, 1983, eff. Oct. 1, 1983; April 27, 1984, eff. July 1, 1984; Dec. 17, 1993, eff. Feb. 1, 1994. Corrected March 18, 2005, eff. immediately. Amended Oct. 14, 2005, eff. Jan. 1, 2006; July 27, 2006, eff. Sept. 1, 2006; March 16, 2007, eff. May 1, 2007; May 30, 2008, eff. immediately. Corrected June 4, 2008, eff. immediately. Amended Dec. 11, 2014, eff. Jan. 1, 2015.

Formerly Ill.Rev.Stat.1991, ch. 110A, ¶ 303.

Committee Comments

(Revised December 17, 1993)

The term "post-judgment" motion is substituted, when appropriate, in this and other rules for the term "post-trial" motion because it more accurately describes trial practice. Many final judgments which are subject to post-judgment motions which toll the time for filing an appeal are not preceded by trials. See *Anderson v. Resource Economics Corp.* (1990), 133 Ill.2d 342.

Paragraph (b)(4) is revised to eliminate wordiness and redundancy.

Paragraph (c) concerning service of the notice of appeal is modified to require that service is to be filed with the reviewing court rather than the trial court. This permits the reviewing court to immediately ascertain the identity of all parties to the appeal and serves as a cross-check in the event that the notice of appeal has not been timely forwarded to the reviewing court by a circuit clerk.

The docketing statement has been removed to a new rule.

(Revised 1979)

Paragraph (a)

The requirement that a notice of appeal be filed within 30 days after the entry of the judgment appealed from carried into the rules the provision of former section 76 of the Civil Practice Act as amended in 1966. The rules eliminated, however, a provision of former section 76 for an appeal within one year by order of the reviewing court entered within 14 months. The circumstances that were thought to justify the provision for delayed appeal under former section 76 are cared for by the provisions of paragraph (e) of the rule, permitting the reviewing court to grant leave to appeal upon motion made within 30 days after the expiration of the normal time for appeal on a showing of reasonable excuse for the failure to file a notice of appeal within the prescribed time. See the comments to paragraph (e).

The second sentence of paragraph (a), adopted in 1967 as then paragraph (b) of this rule, replaced the unnecessarily elaborate provisions of former Rule 35, dealing with joinder in appeals, separate ap-

peals, and cross appeals. The express statement in paragraph (3) of former Rule 35 that parties not taking a timely appeal, separate appeal, or cross appeal are thereafter barred from appealing was omitted as unnecessary, since the same result follows inevitably from the absence of any provision for an appeal by a party who fails to follow the time schedule set out in the rule. The phrase "indicating which type of appeal is being taken," was added in 1974. It is designed to make such that the appellee is on notice of any separate appeals that will affect the schedule for filing briefs. See Rule 343(b)(ii).

The requirement of the second paragraph of paragraph (a), that upon the filing of a notice of appeal the clerk of the circuit court shall transmit a copy to the clerk of the reviewing court, was added in 1976 and expanded in 1979 to include amendments to a notice of appeal. It was designed to give the reviewing court early notice of the pendency of appeals, as an aid to the efficient management of its docket. This move toward early control of appeals by the reviewing court was implemented in 1979 by provision for docketing the appeal in the reviewing court on receipt of the copy of the notice of appeal rather than upon the filing of the record as previously provided. See the comments to paragraph (f), below, and Rule 327.

Paragraph (b)

Paragraph (b) was inserted in the rule in 1969 as part of a revision designed to make the Supreme Court Rules applicable to appeals formerly governed in whole or in part by special statutes. The authority for comprehensive rules governing appeals was the provision in the 1964 judicial article (art. VI, sec. 7), now section 16 of article VI of the 1970 Constitution, that directs the Supreme Court to "provide by rule for expeditious and inexpensive appeals." As adopted in 1969, paragraph (b) included provisions incorporating by reference the statutory provisions for appeal in forcible entry and detainer cases and local improvement cases. In 1971, it was amended to add drainage cases. In 1974, it was amended to delete the reference to forcible entry and detainer cases, leaving such cases governed by the general rules governing appeals except for the special provision for summons in such cases found in Rule 101(b)(2).

The special statutory proceedings in local improvement and drainage cases have peculiar characteristics, arising from the nature of the problems with which they deal, which require that trial and appellate procedures be closely integrated, as they are in the statutes. The appeal provisions in these statutes have been carefully worked out and have proved satisfactory. Appeals in these cases are not of such frequency as to warrant burdening the rules with detailed provisions on these subjects. The rule recognizes the constitutional authority of the Supreme Court over all appellate procedures.

Paragraph (c)

Subparagraphs (1) through (3) of paragraph (c) made no substantive change in the provisions of former Rule 33, in effect until 1967.

Subparagraph (4), however, eliminated the requirement of an order of court for amendment of a notice of appeal in which the amendment is made within 30 days after the entry of the judgment, and reduced from 60 days to 30 days the period during which an appeal may be taken by amendment of the notice of appeal to specify a part of the judgment not specified in the original notice of appeal. This latter change reflected the reduction from 60 days to 30 days of the time for filing the notice of appeal. But the 30 days may be enlarged by a motion pursuant to paragraph (e).

Paragraph (c) was amended in 1969 to insert the "or" clause in the first sentence, applicable when a timely posttrial motion is filed. This language was inadvertently omitted from the rule as originally adopted, and its addition effected no change in substance.

As originally adopted, paragraph (c)(4) provided that a motion to amend a notice of appeal should be made in the circuit court if the appeal had not been docketed in the Appellate Court, but in the Appellate Court if the appeal had been docketed. At that time, docketing took place after the filing of the record in the Appellate Court. In 1979 the practice was changed to provide for docketing at an earlier point. (See the comments to paragraph (f), below.) To conform the practice to this change, paragraph (c)(4) was amended to require that a motion to amend the notice of appeal more than 30 days after the entry of the judgment must be made in the Appellate Court.

Paragraph (d)

Paragraph (d) simplified the provisions of former Rule 34, which governed service of a notice of appeal, by adopting by express reference the methods of service provided in Rule 11. Because an appeal is the continuation of the same cause, these methods are more appropriate to the service of a notice of appeal than those provided in the elaborate provisions in former Rule 34. Rule 34 was plainly influenced by the former writ of error practice, in which the issuance of a writ of error constituted the commencement of a new suit.

Paragraph (e)

Paragraph (e), patterned to some extent on former Rule 73(a) of the Federal Rules of Civil Procedure (presently Rule 4(a) of the Federal Rules of Appellate Procedure), provides a 30-day "safety valve" for cases in which the party seeking to appeal can demonstrate a reasonable excuse for failure to file a notice of appeal within the 30 days prescribed by paragraph (a). This replaced the provision in former section 76 of the Civil Practice Act for a delayed appeal on motion made to the reviewing court within a year and granted within 14 months. The special circumstances that would warrant the granting of leave to file an appeal after the time has expired, such as illness of counsel, unpredictable delay in the mails, etc., in almost all cases will require no more than an additional 30 days, which the rule provides. Under the previous practice no one could be certain that any judgment was final for a year, even if no notice of appeal had been filed. This delay in the finality of judgments was more harmful than could be justified by the speculation of injustice that might result from a "safety valve" of 30 days rather than a year.

It is also to be noted that, by the language of paragraph (c), amendment of a notice of appeal to include a part of a judgment not specified in the original notice of appeal is governed by paragraph (e).

In 1979, paragraph (e) was amended to require that a motion for leave to appeal after the expiration of the 30 days prescribed by paragraph (a) must be accompanied by a filing fee of $25. This reflects the changes in the rules in that year to provide for the docketing of an appeal upon receipt of a copy of the notice of appeal transmitted to the reviewing court as provided by paragraph (a). (See comments to paragraph (f), below.) Until 1979, the appellant was required to pay a docketing fee at the time the record was filed.

Paragraph (f)

Paragraph (f) was added in 1979. Prior to that time, under Rule 327, an appeal was docketed in the reviewing court after the filing of the record, a short record, or a certificate in lieu of the record, and after the payment of a docket fee. The 1979 amendments were designed to afford the Appellate Court a greater measure of authority to supervise the progress of an appeal, and paragraph (f) is an important feature of the new practice. Under paragraph (a), within 5 days after the filing of a notice of appeal the clerk of the circuit court will transmit to the clerk of the Appellate Court a copy of the notice of appeal. Under paragraph (f), as soon as the clerk receives this copy he will enter the appeal on the docket. Except as provided in paragraph (g), all fees will be paid at the time the notice of appeal is filed. Thus the general control of the appeal will be placed in the Appellate Court from almost the beginning. Appropriate amendment was made to Rule 327. To provide the Appellate Court with the information necessary in its new management function, paragraph (g) was added, requiring the appellant to file a docketing statement within 14 days after the filing of the notice of appeal. See paragraph (g), above.

Paragraph (g)

Paragraph (g), requiring the filing of a docketing statement and payment of the docket fee in the Appellate Court within 14 days after the filing of a notice of appeal, and setting forth the contents and form of such a statement, is designed to provide the Appellate Court with information about the cases docketed in the court under paragraph (f) as an aid in the efficient handling of its docket. Having such information will enable it, through its staff or otherwise, to take an active part in supervising the progress of the appeal.

(March 16, 2007)

Rule 303(a)(2) is intended to address concerns raised in cases such as *John G. Phillips & Assoc. v. Brown*, 197 Ill. 2d 337 (2001). Subparagraph (a)(2) protects the rights of an appellant who has filed a "premature" notice of appeal by making the notice of appeal effective when the order denying a post-judgment motion or resolving a still-pending separate claim is entered. See Fed. R. App. P. 4(a)(4)(E)(i), (a)(4)(E)(ii). The question whether a particular "claim" is a separate claim for purposes of Rule 304(a) is often a difficult one. See *Dewan v. Ford Motor Co.*, 343 Ill. App. 3d 1062 (2003); *In re Marriage of King*, 208 Ill. 2d 332 (2003); *Marsh v. Evangelical Covenant Church of Hinsdale*, 138 Ill. 2d 458 (1990); *Physicians Insurance Exchange v. Jennings*, 316 Ill. App. 3d 443 (2000); *F.H. Prince & Co., Inc. v. Towers Financial Corp.*, 266 Ill. App. 3d 977 (1994); *Servio v. Paul Roberts Auto Sales, Inc.*, 211 Ill. App. 3d 751 (1991). Subparagraph (a)(2) protects the appellant who files a notice of appeal prior to the resolution of a still-pending claim that is determined to be a separate claim under Rule 304(a). Note that under Subparagraph (a)(2), there is no need to file a second notice of appeal where the postjudgment order simply denies the appellant's postjudgment motion. However, where the postjudgment order grants new or different relief than the judgment itself, or resolves a separate claim, a second notice of appeal is necessary to preserve an appeal from such order.

Order entered May 24, 2006—M.R. 20959

By order (M.R. 20959) of the Supreme Court concerning appellate briefs (order entered May 24, 2006, effective immediately), the Court provided:

"In re Appellate Briefs

The clerks of the reviewing courts are directed, to the extent practicable, to refuse to file any brief that does not comply with the rules of this court specifying, inter alia, the form and length of a brief on appeal."

Rule 303A. Expedited and Confidential Proceedings Under the Parental Notification of Abortion Act

(a) Entry of Judgment in the Circuit Court. Upon the filing of a petition in the circuit court for judicial waiver of notice under the Parental Notification of Abortion Act, the circuit court shall rule and issue written findings of fact and conclusions of law within 48 hours of the time that the petition is filed with weekends and holidays excluded, except that the 48-hour limitation may be extended at the request of the minor or incompetent person. The court shall endeavor to rule at the conclusion of any hearing on the petition, but in any event shall rule within 48 hours of the filing of the petition, weekends and holidays excluded, except that the time period for ruling may be extended at the request of the minor or the incompetent person. If the decision is not rendered immediately following a hearing, then the petitioner shall be responsible for contacting the clerk of the court for notification of the decision. All notifications pursuant to this procedure may be informal and shall be confidential. If the court fails to rule within

the 48-hour period and an extension is not requested, then the petition shall be deemed to have been granted and the notice requirement shall be waived. A decision denying a judicial waiver of notice is a final and appealable order, which is appealable in the manner provided in the following paragraphs of this rule.

(b) Review to the Appellate Court as a Matter of Right. In accordance with the provisions of this rule, a minor or incompetent person shall be entitled to an appeal to the Appellate Court as a matter of right when the circuit court denies her a waiver of notice under the Parental Notification of Abortion Act.

(c) Review in the Appellate Court. Review of the denial of a waiver of notice under the Parental Notice of Abortion Act shall be by petition filed in the Appellate Court. The petition shall be in writing, state the relief requested and the grounds for the relief requested, and filed within two days, weekends and holidays excluded, of entry of the denial from which review is being sought, except that the two-day period may be extended at the request of the minor or incompetent person. An appropriate supporting record shall accompany the petition, including a record of proceedings, a copy of the petition filed in the circuit court, the decision of the circuit court, including the specific findings of fact and legal conclusions supporting the decision, and any other supporting documents or matters of record necessary to the petition. The supporting record must be authenticated by the certificate of the circuit court clerk or by the affidavit of the attorney or party filing it.

(d) Appointment of Counsel. The Appellate Court shall appoint counsel to assist the petitioner if she so requests.

(e) Statement of Facts and Memoranda of Law. The minor or incompetent petitioner may file a brief statement of facts and memorandum of law supporting her petition, which together shall not exceed 15 typewritten pages and which also must be filed within two days, excluding weekends and holidays, of the entry of the order being appealed under paragraph (a) of this Rule.

(f) Confidentiality. All proceedings under this rule shall be confidential. The petitioner shall be identified in the petition and any supporting memorandum in the method provided under Rule 660(c), as in appeals in cases arising under the Juvenile Court Act. Alternatively, the petitioner may use a pseudonym if she so requests. All documents relating to proceedings shall be impounded and sealed subject to review only by the minor, her attorney and guardian *ad litem*, the respective judges and their staffs charged with reviewing the case and the respective court clerks and their staffs. After entry of an order by the Appellate Court, the clerk of the Appellate Court shall review the proceedings. If leave to appeal is not sought by the petitioner, the clerk of the Appellate Court shall seal the record on appeal before returning it to the clerk of the circuit court. Any appellate court file shall also be sealed. If leave to appeal to the Supreme Court is sought, the petition for leave to appeal and all supporting documents shall identify the petitioner in manner provided under Rule 660(c). The file in the Supreme Court shall also be sealed and impounded following the decision of the Supreme Court. All notifications of court rulings under this rule may be informal and shall be confidential.

(g) Time for Decision; No Oral Argument. After the petitioner has filed the petition for review in the Appellate Court, along with a supporting record and any memorandum, the Appellate Court shall consider, decide the petition and issue a confidential written order within three days, excluding weekends and holidays. The petitioner shall be responsible for contacting the clerk of the Appellate Court for notification of the decision. Oral argument on the petition will not be heard.

(h) Supreme Court Review. If the Appellate Court affirms the denial of a waiver of notice, the petitioner may file a petition for leave to appeal with the Supreme Court within two days, excluding weekends and holidays, of the Appellate Court's decision to affirm the denial of a waiver of notice, except that the two-day period may be extended at the request of the minor or incompetent person. The petition for leave to appeal to the Supreme Court shall contain (1) a statement of issues presented for review and how those issues were decided by the circuit and appellate courts, (2) a brief statement explaining the reason for appeal to the Supreme Court, (3) any memorandum and statement of facts presented to the appellate court, and (4) the written orders of the circuit and appellate courts. The Supreme Court shall decide whether to allow leave to appeal within three days, excluding weekends and holidays, of the filing of the leave to appeal. In deciding whether to allow leave to appeal, the Supreme Court's discretion shall be guided by the criteria listed in Rule 315(a). The confidentiality of the proceedings shall be maintained in the manner described in paragraph (f) of this rule. If leave to appeal is allowed, the petitioner must then file the record from the proceedings in the circuit court with the clerk the Supreme Court within two days, excluding weekends and holidays, of the date that leave to appeal is allowed, except that the two day period may be extended at the request of the minor or incompetent person. Oral argument in the case will not be heard. The Supreme Court shall then issue a confidential written decision within five days, excluding weekends and holidays, of the date it allowed the petition for leave to appeal. The Supreme Court shall render its decision based on the record from the circuit court, and the petition for leave to appeal and any supporting documentation filed in conjunction with the petition for leave to appeal. The petitioner shall be responsible for contacting the clerk of the Supreme Court for notification of any decisions made by the Supreme Court on either the petition for leave

to appeal or the ultimate disposition of the case by the Supreme Court. All notifications of court rulings under this rule may be informal and shall be confidential.

Adopted September 20, 2006, effective immediately.

Rule 304. Appeals from Final Judgments that do not Dispose of an Entire Proceeding

(a) Judgments As To Fewer Than All Parties or Claims–Necessity for Special Finding. If multiple parties or multiple claims for relief are involved in an action, an appeal may be taken from a final judgment as to one or more but fewer than all of the parties or claims only if the trial court has made an express written finding that there is no just reason for delaying either enforcement or appeal or both. Such a finding may be made at the time of the entry of the judgment or thereafter on the court's own motion or on motion of any party. The time for filing a notice of appeal shall be as provided in Rule 303. In computing the time provided in Rule 303 for filing the notice of appeal, the entry of the required finding shall be treated as the date of the entry of final judgment. In the absence of such a finding, any judgment that adjudicates fewer than all the claims or the rights and liabilities of fewer than all the parties is not enforceable or appealable and is subject to revision at any time before the entry of a judgment adjudicating all the claims, rights, and liabilities of all the parties.

(b) Judgments and Orders Appealable Without Special Finding. The following judgments and orders are appealable without the finding required for appeals under paragraph (a) of this rule:

(1) A judgment or order entered in the administration of an estate, guardianship, or similar proceeding which finally determines a right or status of a party.

(2) A judgment or order entered in the administration of a receivership, rehabilitation, liquidation, or other similar proceeding which finally determines a right or status of a party and which is not appealable under Rule 307(a).

(3) A judgment or order granting or denying any of the relief prayed in a petition under section 2–1401 of the Code of Civil Procedure.

(4) A final judgment or order entered in a proceeding under section 2–1402 of the Code of Civil Procedure.

(5) An order finding a person or entity in contempt of court which imposes a monetary or other penalty.

(6) A custody or allocation of parental responsibilities judgment or modification of such judgment entered pursuant to the Illinois Marriage and Dissolution of Marriage Act (750 ILCS 5/101 *et seq.*) or Illinois Parentage Act of 2015 (750 ILCS 46/101 *et seq.*).

The time in which a notice of appeal may be filed from a judgment or order appealable under this Rule 304(b) shall be as provided in Rule 303.

Amended Oct. 21, 1969, eff. Jan. 1, 1970; May 28, 1982, eff. July 1, 1982; April 27, 1984, eff. July 1, 1984; Nov. 21, 1988, eff. Jan. 1, 1989; Dec. 17, 1993, eff. Feb. 1, 1994; Oct. 14, 2005, eff. Jan. 1, 2006; Feb. 26, 2010, eff. immediately; March 8, 2016, eff. immediately.

Formerly Ill.Rev.Stat.1991, ch. 110A, ¶ 304.

Committee Comments
(March 8, 2016)
Special Supreme Court Committee on Child Custody Issues

The Illinois Marriage and Dissolution of Marriage Act, Pub. Act 99–90 (eff. Jan. 1, 2016) (amending 750 ILCS 5/101 *et seq.*), has changed the terms "Custody," "Visitation" (as to parents) and "Removal" to "Allocation of Parental Responsibilities," "Parenting Time" and "Relocation." These rules are being amended to reflect those changes. The rules utilize both "custody" and "allocation of parental responsibilities" in recognition that some legislative enactments covered by the rules utilize the term "custody" while the Illinois Marriage and Dissolution of Marriage Act and the Illinois Parentage Act of 2015 utilize the term "allocation of parental responsibilities." The Special Committee has attempted to adhere to the usage found in the applicable legislative enactments.

Committee Comments
(February 26, 2010)
Paragraph (b)

The term "custody judgment" comes from section 610 of the Illinois Marriage and Dissolution of Marriage Act (750 ILCS 5/610), where it is used to refer to the trial court's permanent determination of custody entered incident to the dissolution of marriage, as distinguished from any temporary or interim orders of custody entered pursuant to section 603 of the Act (750 ILCS 5/603) and any orders modifying child custody subsequent to the dissolution of a marriage pursuant to section 610 of the Act (750 ILCS 5/610). The Illinois Parentage Act of 1984 also uses the term "judgment" to refer to the order which resolves custody of the subject child. See 750 ILCS 45/14.

Subparagraph (b)(6) is adopted pursuant to the authority given to the Illinois Supreme Court by article VI, sections 6 and 16, of the Illinois Constitution of 1970. The intent behind the addition of subparagraph (b)(6) was to supersede the supreme court's decision in *In re Marriage of Leopando*, 96 Ill. 2d 114, 119 (1983). In *Leopando*, the court held that the dissolution of marriage comprises a single, indivisible claim and that, therefore, a child custody determination cannot be severed from the rest of the dissolution of the marriage and appealed on its own under Rule 304(a). Now, a child custody judgment, even when it is entered prior to the resolution of other matters involved in the dissolution proceeding such as property distribution and support, shall be treated as a distinct claim and shall be appealable without a special finding. A custody judgment entered pursuant to section 14 of the Illinois Parentage Act of 1984 shall also be appealable without a special finding. The goal of this amendment is to promote stability for affected families by providing a means to obtain swifter resolution of child custody matters.

Commentary
(December 17, 1993)

Paragraph (a) is amended to clarify that the trial court's order does not have to make reference to both the enforceability and the appealability of a judgment to render that judgment appealable. See *In re Application of Du Page County Collector* (1992), 152 Ill. 2d 545.

Contempt orders are added to the list of judgments appealable under paragraph (b) without a special finding. This change reflects current practice. See *People ex rel. Scott v. Silverstein* (1981), 87 Ill. 2d 167.

Committee Comments
(Revised September 1988)
Paragraph (a)

Paragraph (a) of this rule was adopted as Rule 304, effective January 1, 1967, to supplant former paragraph (2) of section 50 of the Civil Practice Act without change of substance but with some amplification. The supplanted statutory provision, originally adopted in 1955 (Laws of 1955, p. 2238, § 1) to provide an easy method of determining when certain orders were appealable (and which orders had to be appealed at the peril of the loss of a later right of appeal), proved to be anything but easy. Because this statutory paragraph was the subject of many judicial decisions (see 1965 Supplement to Historical and Practice Notes, S.H. Ill. Ann. Stats., ch. 110, par. 50), the committee concluded that it was unwise to amend the language in any substantial fashion. In moving the provision to the rules, the committee revised the language slightly, however, to emphasize the fact that it is not the court's finding that makes the judgment final, but it is the court's finding that makes this kind of a final judgment appealable. This did not change the law. The second and third sentences, which were new in 1967, codified existing practice.

Rule 304(a) was amended in 1988 to cure the defect that compelled the Supreme Court, in *Elg v. Whittington* (1987), 119 Ill. 2d 344, to hold that the filing of post-trial motions in the trial court do not toll the time for filing a notice of appeal under Rule 304, as it does under Rule 303. This amendment clarifies Rule 304 and makes it clear that the time for filing a notice of appeal under Rule 304 is governed by the provisions of Rule 303 and that the date on which the trial court enters its written finding that there is no just reason for delaying enforcement or appeal shall be treated as the date of the entry of final judgment for purposes of calculating when the notice of appeal must be filed.

Paragraph (b)

Paragraph (b), added in 1969, lists several kinds of judgments and orders that have been appealable without a finding that there is no just reason for delaying enforcement or appeal even though they may not dispose of the entire proceeding in which they have been entered or to which they may be related. This paragraph is intended to be declaratory of existing law and, in certain instances, to remove any doubt or room for argument as to whether the finding provided for in paragraph (a) may be necessary. It is not the intention of the committee to eliminate or restrict appeals from judgments or orders heretofore appealable.

Subparagraph (1) applies to orders that are final in character although entered in comprehensive proceedings that include other matters. Examples are an order admitting or refusing to admit a will to probate, appointing or removing an executor, or allowing or disallowing a claim.

In 1984 paragraph (b)(1) was amended to eliminate the reference to "conservatorship," inasmuch as the office of conservator has been eliminated.

Subparagraph (2) is comparable in scope to subparagraph (1) but excepts orders that are appealable as interlocutory orders under Rule 307. Examples of orders covered by subparagraph (2) are an order allowing or disallowing a claim and an order for the payment of fees.

Subparagraph (3) is derived from paragraph (6) of section 72 of the Civil Practice Act (Ill. Rev. Stat. 1967, ch. 110, par. 72(6)), which deals with relief from judgments after 30 days.

Subparagraph (4) is derived from paragraph (7) of section 73 of the Civil Practice Act (Ill. Rev. Stat. 1967, ch. 110, par. 73(7)), which deals with supplementary proceedings.

Judgments imposing sanctions for contempt of court are not included in the listing in paragraph (b), because a contempt proceeding is "an original special proceeding, collateral to, and independent of, the case in which the contempt arises," and a judgment imposing a fine or sentence of imprisonment for contempt is therefore final and appealable. (*People ex rel. General Motors Corp. v. Bua* (1967), 37 Ill. 2d 180, 191, 226 N.E.2d 6, 13.) The judgment thus disposes of the entire independent contempt proceeding.

Rule 305. Stay of Judgments Pending Appeal

(a) Stay of Enforcement of Money Judgments. The enforcement of a judgment for money only, or any portion of a judgment which is for money, shall be stayed if a timely notice of appeal is filed and an appeal bond or other form of security, including, but not limited to, letters of credit, escrow agreements, and certificates of deposit, is presented to, approved by, and filed with the court within the time for filing the notice of appeal or within any extension of time granted under paragraph (c) of this rule. Notice of the presentment of the bond or other form of security shall be given by the judgment debtor to all parties. The bond or other form of security ordinarily shall be in an amount sufficient to cover the amount of the judgment and costs plus interest reasonably anticipated to accrue during the pendency of the appeal. If a form of security other than an appeal bond is presented, the appellant shall have the burden of demonstrating the adequacy of such other security. If the court, after weighing all the relevant circumstances, including the amount of the judgment, anticipated interest and costs, the availability and cost of a bond or other form of security, the assets of the judgment debtor and of the judgment debtor's insurers and indemnitors, if any, and any other factors the court may deem relevant, determines that a bond or other form of security in the amount of the judgment plus anticipated interest and costs is not reasonably available to the judgment debtor, the court may approve a bond or other form of security in the maximum amount reasonably available to the judgment debtor. In the event that the court approves a bond or other form of security in an amount less than the amount of the judgment plus anticipated interest and costs, the court shall impose additional conditions on the judgment debtor to prevent dissipation or diversion of the judgment debtor's assets during the appeal.

(b) Stays of Enforcements of Nonmoney Judgments and Other Appealable Orders. Except in cases provided for in paragraph (e) of this rule, on notice and motion, and an opportunity for opposing parties to be heard, the court may also stay the enforcement of any judgment, other than a judgment, or portion of a judgment, for money, or the enforcement, force and effect of appealable interlocutory orders or any other appealable judicial or administrative order. The stay shall be conditioned upon such terms as are just. A bond or other form of security may be required in any case, and shall be required to protect an appellee's interest in property.

(c) Extensions of Time. On motion made within the time for filing the notice of appeal or within any extension granted pursuant to this paragraph, the time for the filing and approval of the bond or other form of security may be extended by the circuit court or by the reviewing court or a judge thereof, but the extensions of time granted by the circuit court may not aggregate more than 45 days unless the parties stipulate otherwise. A motion in the reviewing court for any extension of time for the filing and approval of the bond or other form of security in the circuit court must be supported by affidavit and accompanied by a supporting record (Rule 328), if the record on appeal has not been filed.

(d) Stays by the Reviewing Court. Except in cases provided for in paragraph (e) of this rule, application for a stay ordinarily must be made in the first instance to the circuit court. A motion for a stay may be made to the reviewing court, or to a judge thereof, but such a motion must show that application to the circuit court is not practical, or that the circuit court has denied an application or has failed to afford the relief that the applicant has requested, and must be accompanied by suggestions in support of the motion and a supporting record (Rule 328), if the record on appeal has not been filed. If a stay is granted by the reviewing court or a judge thereof, the clerk shall notify the parties and transmit to the clerk of the circuit court or administrative agency a certified copy of the order granting the stay.

(e) Automatic Stay Pending Appeal of Termination of Parental Rights.

(1) An order terminating the parental rights of any person that is entered in a proceeding initiated under the Juvenile Court Act of 1987 shall be automatically stayed for 60 days after entry of the order of termination. If notice of appeal is filed with respect to the termination order within the 60 days, the automatic stay shall continue until the appeal is complete or the stay is lifted by the reviewing court. If notice of appeal is not filed within the 60 days, the automatic stay shall expire.

(2) The automatic stay under this rule shall stay the termination order to the extent that it would permit entry of an order of adoption without the parent's consent or surrender, and shall also operate to stay the termination order with respect to any power granted to a person or agency to consent to an adoption. In all other respects the termination order shall be unaffected. For the purposes of proceedings under the Adoption Act, a person appealing the termination of his or her rights shall be treated as a person whose parental rights have been terminated, except as provided in the first sentence of this paragraph. Neither the appeal nor the automatic stay of the termination order shall affect the trial court's continuing jurisdiction over the care, custody, visitation and support of the child, and a guardian of the child may take any authorized action other than consenting to the child's adoption.

(3) No bond shall be required with respect to a stay of adoption pending appeal of termination of parental rights.

(4)(A) A party to the Juvenile Court Act proceeding in which a termination order was entered or a party to an adoption proceeding delayed by the effect of this rule may file a motion with the reviewing court to lift the automatic stay of a termination order. The stay of an order terminating parental rights may be lifted when it is clearly in the best interests of the child on motion or by the court *sua sponte.*

(B) Motions to lift an automatic stay must be accompanied by suggestions in support of the motion and shall be served on all parties to the Juvenile Court Act proceeding and the parties to any related Adoption Act proceeding, if known. If the movant is a party to an adoption proceeding, the motion must include the caption and case number of

the adoption proceeding and identify the court in which the action is pending.

(C) Motions to lift an automatic stay must be accompanied by a supporting record as provided in Rule 328. If the movant was not a party to the Juvenile Court Act proceeding and is unable to provide the supporting record, a decision on the motion shall be deferred until after the record on appeal is filed.

(D) If a stay is lifted by the reviewing court or a judge thereof, the clerk shall notify the parties and transmit to the clerk of the trial court a certified copy of the order lifting the stay. In the case of a motion filed by a party to an adoption proceeding, the clerk shall also send a certified copy of the order lifting the stay to the trial judge in the adoption proceeding.

(f) When Notice of Appeal Is Amended. If a notice of appeal is amended to specify parts of the judgment not specified in the original notice of appeal, the stay of the judgment described in the original notice of appeal does not extend to any added part of the judgment, but a stay of the added part may be obtained under the same conditions and by the same procedure set forth above.

(g) Condition of the Bond. If an appeal is from a judgment for money, the condition of the bond or other form of security shall be for the prosecution of the appeal and the payment of the judgment, interest, and costs in case the judgment is affirmed or the appeal dismissed unless other terms are approved by the court as provided in paragraph (a) above, except that the bond of an executor or administrator shall be conditioned upon payment in due course of administration and that the bond of a guardian for a minor or a person under legal disability shall be conditioned on payment as the guardian has funds therefor. In all other cases, the condition shall be fixed with reference to the character of the judgment.

(h) Changing the Amount, Terms, and Security of the Bond or Other Form of Security After the Appeal is Docketed. After the case is docketed in the reviewing court, that court or a judge thereof upon motion may, consistent with the provisions of paragraph (a) above, change the amount, terms or security of the bond or other form of security, whether fixed by it or by the circuit court, and failure to comply with the order of the reviewing court or judge shall terminate the stay.

(i) Appeals by Public Agencies. If an appeal is prosecuted by a public, municipal, governmental, or quasi-municipal corporation, or by a public officer in that person's official capacity for the benefit of the public, the circuit court, or the reviewing court or a judge thereof, may stay the judgment pending appeal without requiring that any bond or other form of security be given.

(j) Insurance Policy as Bond. The filing of an insurance policy pursuant to section 392.1 of the Illinois Insurance Code (215 ILCS 5/392.1) shall be considered the filing of a bond for purposes of this rule.

(k) Failure to Obtain Stay; Effect on Interests in Property. If a stay is not perfected within the time for filing the notice of appeal, or within any extension of time granted under subparagraph (c) of this rule, the reversal or modification of the judgment does not affect the right, title, or interest of any person who is not a party to the action in or to any real or personal property that is acquired after the judgment becomes final and before the judgment is stayed; nor shall the reversal or modification affect any right of any person who is not a party to the action under or by virtue of any certificate of sale issued pursuant to a sale based on the judgment and before the judgment is stayed. This paragraph applies even if the appellant is a minor or a person under legal disability or under duress at the time the judgment becomes final.

(*l*) Land Trust Bond. The filing of a bond or other form of security by a beneficiary under a land trust where the land trust is a party shall be considered filing of a bond for purposes of this rule.

(m) Filing with the Circuit Court Clerk. All original appeal bonds or other forms of security, whether approved by the circuit court or the reviewing court, shall be filed with the clerk of the circuit court in which the case was filed.

Amended October 21, 1969, effective January 1, 1970, and amended effective July 1, 1971; amended September 20, 1979, effective October 15, 1979; amended January 5, 1981, effective February 1, 1981; amended May 28, 1982, effective July 1, 1982; amended December 17, 1993, effective February 1, 1994; amended December 5, 2003, effective January 1, 2004; amended June 15, 2004, effective July 1, 2004.

Formerly Ill.Rev.Stat.1991, ch. 110A, ¶ 305.

Commentary

(Revised January 5, 1981)

In 1966, when pursuant to the authority conferred by the 1964 amendment of the Judicial Article of the Illinois Constitution the Supreme Court adopted comprehensive rules governing practice on appeal, a number of provisions previously scattered among the Supreme Court Rules (former Rules 31(3) and 37) and the statutes (former §§ 76 and 82 of the Civil Practice Act and §§ 21 and 22 of the Injunction Act) were consolidated in Rule 305. The rule preserved the Illinois supersedeas practice under which the enforcement of a judgment could be stayed by filing a bond in either the trial or reviewing court, and provided that upon the filing of a bond by the appellant the trial court could stay the force and effect of a permanent injunction or an order appealable under Rule 307 for ten days to permit application to the reviewing court for a stay pending appeal. The reviewing court or a judge thereof was empowered to grant such a stay on motion and after the filing of a bond.

In 1969, the rule was amended to provide that the trial court might stay the force and effect of any "final or interlocutory judgment or judicial or administrative order granting relief other than money" on "such terms as are just," which "may include a bond." As before, the power of the trial court was limited to the grant of a stay not to exceed ten days, and application for a stay of longer duration was available only by motion in the reviewing court. Special provision was made for orders appealable under section 276 of the Probate Act (Ill.Rev.Stat. 1969, ch. 22, ¶ 276), requiring that any stay of such an order must be sought from the reviewing court or a judge thereof.

The 1971 amendments to the rule abandoned the use of the term "supersedeas," while preserving the distinction, introduced in 1969, between judgments for money only, the enforcement of which is stayed upon the filing of an approved bond, and other judgments and orders, the force and effect of which may be stayed by order of the court. The procedure for obtaining a stay was simplified by requiring that all applications for a stay shall normally be filed in the first instance in the trial court.

Paragraph (a)

Under this paragraph, a party appealing from a judgment for money only who has filed a timely notice of appeal as provided in Rule 303(a) may obtain a stay of enforcement of the judgment by filing a bond approved by the trial court within the same time or within any extensions of time granted under subparagraph (2) below. If the appeal is taken after 30 days, pursuant to Rule 303(e), or if a bond is not approved and filed within 30 days after entry of the judgment, enforcement of the judgment may proceed unless stayed by the court pursuant to paragraph (b) below. This represents no change in the pre-existing practice. Subparagraph (a)(2) was amended in 1980 to delete reference to a "short record" and substitute "such parts of [the record] as are relevant." This change was made necessary by the elimination in 1979 of the definition of a "short record" in former Rule 328.

Paragraph (b)

Subparagraph (1) of paragraph (b) empowers the trial or reviewing court, or a judge of the reviewing court, upon notice and motion, to stay pending appeal the enforcement of a judgment for money not stayed under paragraph (a) above, or to stay the force and effect of any other judgments or judicial or administrative orders pending appeal. This represents a change in the previous practice under which stays of such judgments and orders granted by the trial court were limited to a maximum of ten days.

The provision permitting the court to stay administrative as well as judicial orders was added in 1969 to permit stay of an administrative order such as the revocation of a license pending appeal from a judgment of the circuit court upholding the order. Prior to this amendment there was no provision in either the rules or the statutes for such an order pending appeal, though there was statutory authority for stay pending disposition of the case by the circuit court. See Ill.Rev.Stat.1967, ch. 110, ¶ 275(1).

Subparagraph (2) changes the previous practice by requiring that normally all stay applications be made first in the trial court. It is patterned after Rule 8 of the Federal Rules of Appellate Procedure.

Subparagraph (3) requires that the terms of a stay of a money judgment, or a stay having the effect of extending *lis pendens* during the pendency of an appeal, must include a bond, but in other cases leaves the terms to the discretion of the court.

Subparagraph (4), added to the rule in 1969, supersedes sections 21 and 22 of the Injunction Act (Ill.Rev.Stat.1967, ch. 69, ¶¶ 21 and 22) and eliminates certain time limitations which are unnecessary because the appeal from an order dissolving an injunction does not continue the injunction in force unless and until the order permitted in subparagraph (4) is entered.

Subparagraph (5) is a simplified revision of former Rule 37. Prior to 1971, it appeared in Rule 305 as subparagraph (b)(3). The language was revised in 1971 to substitute the term "stay" for the term "supersedeas."

Paragraph (c)

Paragraph (c) is a revision of paragraph (6) of former Rule 37, without change in substance. In 1971, the language was changed to substitute the term "stay" for the term "supersedeas".

Paragraph (d)

As adopted in 1967, this paragraph was derived from the fourth and fifth sentences of former section 82(1) of the Civil Practice Act, as amended, without change in substance. The "except" clause applicable to the bond of an executor or an administrator was added in 1969 and is derived from section 334 of the Probate Act (Ill.Rev.Stat.1967, ch. 3, ¶ 334).

Paragraph (e)

This is former section 82(2) of the Civil Practice Act, as amended, with the words "or judge" inserted.

Paragraph (f)

This is a revision of the sixth sentence of former section 82(1) of the Civil Practice Act, as amended, without change in substance.

Paragraph (g)

This is a revision of the sixth sentence of former section 82(3) of the Civil Practice Act, as amended, without change in substance. The term "stay" was substituted for the term "supersedeas" in 1971.

Paragraph (h)

This provision, which prior to the 1971 amendments was lettered (i), was added to the rule to make it clear that the filing of an insurance policy under the statute referred to is to be treated as a bond for all purposes. Thus, for example, an extension of time may be granted under subparagraph (a)(2) for filing the insurance policy as it can be for the filing of a bond.

Paragraph (i)

This is a revision of the second paragraph of former section 76(1) of the Civil Practice Act, as amended. The evident purpose of section 76(1) was to limit the application of the *lis pendens* statute (Ill.Rev.Stat.1969, ch. 22, ¶ 53) in view of the extension of the time for appeal under the Civil Practice Act of 1933. See Cairo Lumber Co. v. Corwin, 325 Ill.App. 319 (1945); Sanders v. Strauss, 332 Ill.App. 314 (1947). Prior to 1933, appeal could be taken only during term time (generally 30 days), and one step in the perfection of the appeal was the filing of a bond. Since an appeal was looked upon as a continuation of the original proceeding, the effect of *lis pendens* continued during its pendency. If no appeal was taken, however, the effect of *lis pendens* ended with the judgment, as review by writ of error was viewed as a new proceeding. If a writ of error was obtained, *lis pendens* could be revived by obtaining a supersedeas in the reviewing court, but intervening rights would be unaffected. Former section 76(1) merely preserved the previous practice insofar as it related to the application of the *lis pendens* statute after judgment in the trial court.

While the intention was thus plain to permit the appellant to protect himself against transfer of the property which was the subject of the action by obtaining a stay of the judgment on the posting of a bond, the use of the term "supersedeas" in the statute created some doubt as to whether it was applicable to cases in which the judgment was self-executing, since in such cases supersedeas is inappropriate. See Gumberts v. East Oak Street Hotel Co., 404 Ill. 386 (1949). This doubt, left unresolved in 1967 when the substance of the second paragraph of former section 76(1) was carried forward as part of Rule 305, is eliminated by the 1971 amendments to the rule. Under subparagraph (b)(1), the court is empowered to stay the force and effect of a self-executing judgment. Under subparagraph (b)(3), an appellant seeking a stay to protect his asserted interest in property against transfer of the property during the pendency of an appeal must give a bond. Under paragraph (i), if a stay is not obtained, the rights of the transferee are protected.

Committee Comments

(Revised December 17, 1993)

This rule has been reorganized to provide greater clarity to the practice of obtaining a stay of the trial court judgment. Paragraph (a) makes clear that the bond in a money judgment case must be sufficient to cover the entire amount of the judgment, interest and costs.

A certified copy of the reviewing court stay order transmitted to the trial court or administrative agency is substituted for the antiquated reviewing court clerk certificate, and the clerk's authority to approve security is removed.

Commentary

(June 15, 2004)

Paragraph (a)

The amendment is designed to preserve the right of appeal. The traditional method of securing a judgment is to require an appeal bond in the amount of the judgment plus anticipated interest and costs. In recent years, changes in the insurance market have made appeal bonds costly in many cases and unavailable in some cases. When an alternative type of security (*e.g.*, letters of credit, escrow agreement, certificate of deposit) offers comparable assurance of payment at lower cost, requiring an appeal bond needlessly increases the cost of appeal. When seeking to file a form of security other than an appeal bond, it is the judgment debtor's burden to demonstrate that the other form of security is an adequate substitute.

It is anticipated that the amount of the bond or other form of security will normally be in an amount sufficient to cover the judgment, interest, and costs. In some limited instances, however, the appeal bond requirement may be so onerous that it creates an artificial barrier to appeal, forcing a party to settle a case or declare bankruptcy. See, *e.g.*, *Price v. Philip Morris, Inc.*, 341 Ill. App. 3d 941 (2003), *vacated by supervisory order* No. 96644 (September 16, 2003). Thus, the amended rule gives the court discretion in a money judgment case to approve a bond or other form of security that covers less than the entire amount of the judgment plus anticipated interest and costs. This does not lessen the judgment debtor's obligation on the judgment, but simply allows the judgment debtor to obtain a stay of execution on the judgment pending appeal. In such a case, the last sentence of the amended rule makes clear that appropriate conditions shall be imposed to prevent the judgment debtor from dissipating assets that would otherwise be available for payment of the judgment if the appeal is unsuccessful. Thus, depending on the circumstances, a business may be precluded from selling or otherwise disposing of any of its assets outside the ordinary course of its business, or an individual might be prohibited from spending any sums other than are required for ordinary living expenses.

Paragraph (b)

This paragraph has been amended to clarify that it is inapplicable to appeals from judgments for money.

Paragraph (g)

This paragraph has been amended to be consistent with the provisions of paragraph (a) permitting, under certain circumstances, the filing of an appeal bond or other form of security in an amount less than the full amount of the judgment plus anticipated interest and costs.

Paragraph (h)

This paragraph has been amended to clarify that a motion to change the terms or the amount of the

bond must be consistent with the provisions of paragraph (a).

Paragraph (m)

This paragraph has been added because the appellate court clerks may not have appropriate facilities for keeping original bonds or other forms of security.

Rule 306. Interlocutory Appeals by Permission

(a) Orders Appealable by Petition. A party may petition for leave to appeal to the Appellate Court from the following orders of the trial court:

(1) from an order of the circuit court granting a new trial;

(2) from an order of the circuit court allowing or denying a motion to dismiss on the grounds of *forum non conveniens*, or from an order of the circuit court allowing or denying a motion to transfer a case to another county within this State on such grounds;

(3) from an order of the circuit court denying a motion to dismiss on the grounds that the defendant has done nothing which would subject defendant to the jurisdiction of the Illinois courts;

(4) from an order of the circuit court granting or denying a motion for a transfer of venue based on the assertion that the defendant is not a resident of the county in which the action was commenced, and no other legitimate basis for venue in that county has been offered by the plaintiff;

(5) from interlocutory orders affecting the care and custody of or the allocation of parental responsibilities for unemancipated minors, if the appeal of such orders is not otherwise specifically provided for elsewhere in these rules;

(6) from an order of the circuit court which remands the proceeding for a hearing *de novo* before an administrative agency; or

(7) from an order of the circuit court granting a motion to disqualify the attorney for any party;

(8) from an order of the circuit court denying or granting certification of a class action under section 2–802 of the Code of Civil Procedure (735 ILCS 5/2–802); or

(9) from an order of the circuit court denying a motion to dispose under the Citizen Participation Act (735 ILCS 110/1 *et seq.*)

If the petition for leave to appeal an order granting a new trial is granted, all rulings of the trial court on the posttrial motions are before the reviewing court without the necessity of a cross-petition.

(b) Procedure for Petitions Under Subparagraph (a)(5).

(1) *Petition; Service; Record.* Unless another form is ordered by the Appellate Court, review of an order affecting the care and custody of or the

allocation of parental responsibilities for an un-emancipated minor as authorized in paragraph (a)(5) shall be by petition filed in the Appellate Court. The petition shall be in writing and shall state the relief requested and the grounds for the relief requested. An appropriate supporting record shall accompany the petition, which shall include the order appealed from or the proposed order, and any supporting documents or matters of record necessary to the petition. The supporting record must be authenticated by the certificate of the clerk of the trial court or by the affidavit of the attorney or party filing it. The petition, supporting record and the petitioner's legal memorandum, if any, shall be filed in the Appellate Court within 14 days of the entry or denial of the order from which review is being sought, with proof of personal, e-mail or facsimile service as provided in Rule 11. A copy of the petition for leave to appeal must also be served upon the trial court judge who entered the order from which leave to appeal is sought.

(2) *Legal Memoranda.* The petitioner may file a memorandum, not exceeding 15 typewritten pages, with the petition. The respondent or any other party or person entitled to be heard in the case may file, with proof of personal, e-mail or facsimile service as provided in Rule 11, a responding memorandum within five business days following service of the petition and petitioner's memorandum. A memorandum by the respondent or other party may not exceed 15 typewritten pages.

(3) *Replies; Extensions of Time.* Except by order of court, no replies will be allowed and no extension of time will be allowed.

(4) *Variations by Order of Court.* The Appellate Court may, if it deems it appropriate, order a different schedule, or order that no memoranda be filed, or order that other materials need not be filed.

(5) *Procedure if Leave to Appeal Is Granted.* If leave to appeal is granted, the circuit court and the opposing parties shall be served with copies of the order granting leave to appeal. All proceedings shall then be subject to the expedited procedures set forth in Rule 311(a). A party may allow his or her petition or answer to stand as his or her brief or may elect to file a new brief. In order to allow a petition or answer to stand as a brief, the party must notify the other parties and the Clerk of the Appellate Court on or before the due date of the brief.

(c) Procedure for All Other Petitions Under This Rule.

(1) *Petition.* The petition shall contain a statement of the facts of the case, supported by reference to the supporting record, and of the grounds for the appeal. An original and three copies of the petition (or original and five copies in workers' compensation cases arising under Rule 22(g)) shall

be filed in the Appellate Court in accordance with the requirements for briefs within 30 days after the entry of the order. A supporting record conforming to the requirements of Rule 328 shall be filed with the petition.

(2) *Answer.* Any other party may file an original and three copies of an answer (or original and five copies in workers' compensation cases arising under Rule 22(g)) within 21 days of the filing of the petition, together with a supplementary supporting record conforming to Rule 328 consisting of any additional parts of the record the party desires to have considered by the Appellate Court. No reply will be received except by leave of court or a judge thereof.

(3) *Appendix to Petition; Abstract.* The petition shall include, as an appendix, a copy of the order appealed from, and of any opinion, memorandum, or findings of fact entered by the trial judge, and a table of contents of the record on appeal in the form provided in Rule 342(a). If the Appellate Court orders that an abstract of the record be filed, it shall be in the form set forth in Rule 342(b) and shall be filed within the time fixed in the order.

(4) *Extensions of Time.* The above time limits may be extended by the reviewing court or a judge thereof upon notice and motion, accompanied by an affidavit showing good cause, filed before expiration of the original or extended time.

(5) *Stay; Notice of Allowance of Petition.* If the petition is granted, the proceedings in the trial court are stayed. Upon good cause shown, the Appellate Court or a judge thereof may vacate or modify the stay, and may require the petitioner to file an appropriate bond. Within 48 hours after the granting of the petition, the clerk shall send notice thereof to the clerk of the circuit court.

(6) *Additional Record.* If leave to appeal is allowed, any party to the appeal may request that additional portions of the record on appeal be prepared as provided in Rule 321 *et seq.*, or the court may order the appellant to file the record, which shall be filed within 35 days of the date on which such leave was allowed. The filing of an additional record shall not affect the time for filing briefs under this rule.

(7) *Briefs.* A party may allow his or her petition or answer to stand as his or her brief or may file a further brief in lieu of or in addition thereto. If a party elects to allow a petition or answer to stand as a brief, he or she must notify the other parties and the Clerk of the Appellate Court on or before the due date of the brief and supply the court with the requisite number of briefs required by Rule 341(e). If the appellant elects to file a further brief, it must be filed within 35 days from the date on which leave to appeal was granted. The appellant's brief, and other briefs if filed, shall conform to the schedule

and requirements as provided in Rules 341 through 343. Oral argument may be requested as provided in Rule 352(a).

Amended Oct. 21, 1969, eff. Jan. 1, 1970, and eff. Sept. 1, 1974; July 30, 1979, eff. Oct. 15, 1979; Feb. 19, 1982, eff. April 1, 1982; May 28, 1982, eff. July 1, 1982; June 15, 1982, eff. July 1, 1982; Aug. 9, 1983, eff. Oct. 1, 1983; Sept. 16, 1983, eff. Oct. 1, 1983; Dec. 17, 1993, eff. Feb. 1, 1994; Mar. 26, 1996, eff. immediately; Dec. 31, 2002, eff. Jan. 1, 2003; Dec. 5, 2003, eff. Jan. 1, 2004; May 24, 2006, eff. Sept. 1, 2006; Feb. 26, 2010, eff. immediately; Feb. 16, 2011, eff. immediately; May 29, 2014, eff. July 1, 2014; Dec. 9, 2015, eff. Jan. 1, 2016; Mar. 8, 2016, eff. immediately.

Formerly Ill.Rev.Stat.1991, ch. 110A, ¶ 306.

Explanatory Note

An Order entered December 31, 2002, provided:

"Effective immediately, that part of the order entered November 27, 2002, amending Supreme Court Rule 307, effective January 1, 2003, is vacated. Effective January 1, 2003, Supreme Court Rule 306 is amended. The amendment of Rule 306(a) to include paragraph (8) applies only to cases filed in the circuit court on or after the effective date of the amendment, i.e. January 1, 2003."

Committee Comment

(March 8, 2016)

Special Supreme Court Committee on Child Custody Issues

The Illinois Marriage and Dissolution of Marriage Act, Pub. Act 99–90 (eff. Jan. 1, 2016) (amending 750 ILCS 5/101 *et seq.*), has changed the terms "Custody," "Visitation" (as to parents) and "Removal" to "Allocation of Parental Responsibilities," "Parenting Time" and "Relocation." These rules are being amended to reflect those changes. The rules utilize both "custody" and "allocation of parental responsibilities" in recognition that some legislative enactments covered by the rules utilize the term "custody" while the Illinois Marriage and Dissolution of Marriage Act and the Illinois Parentage Act of 2015 utilize the term "allocation of parental responsibilities." The Special Committee has attempted to adhere to the usage found in the applicable legislative enactments.

Committee Comment

(May 29, 2014)

Subparagraph (c)(5)

In exceptional circumstances or by agreement of the parties, it may be appropriate for the parties to continue with certain aspects of the case (such as discovery, for example), provided that such continuation does not interfere with appellate review or otherwise offend the notions of substantial justice. If the stay is vacated or modified, the trial court remains (as with any interlocutory appeal) restrained from entering an order which interferes with the appellate review, such as modifying the trial court order that is the subject of the appeal.

Committee Comments

(February 26, 2010)

In 2010, this rule was reorganized and renumbered for the sake of clarity. No substantive changes were made in this revision.

Paragraph (b)

Paragraph (b) was added to Rule 306 in 2004 to provide a special, expedited procedure to be followed in petitioning for leave to appeal from interlocutory orders affecting the care and custody of unemancipated minors. This procedure applies only to petitions for leave to appeal filed pursuant to subparagraph (a)(5) of this rule. The goal of this special procedure is to provide a faster means for achieving permanency for not only abused or neglected children, but also children whose custody is at issue in dissolution of marriage, adoption, and other proceedings.

Paragraph (c)

Paragraph (c) sets forth the procedures to be followed in petitioning for leave to appeal pursuant to any subparagraph of paragraph (a) except subparagraph (a)(5).

Subparagraph (c)(1)

This subparagraph was amended in 1979 to reflect changes in Rule 321 that eliminated the requirement that a praecipe for the record be filed.

Subparagraph (c)(2)

Subparagraph (c)(2) permits answers to the petition to be filed within 21 days after the due date of the petition instead of "within 15 days after the petition is served upon him." They are not required to be printed as formerly, but may also be otherwise duplicated as are briefs. Former Rule 30 was silent as to a reply. Subparagraph (c)(2) provides that there shall be no reply except by leave.

Subparagraph (c)(3)

As originally promulgated, and as amended in 1974, this subparagraph provided that "excerpts from record" or an abstract should be filed. This represented a change from former Rule 30, which required the filing of a printed abstract of record. It was amended in 1979 to delete reference to "excerpts from record" to reflect the changes made in that year to provide for the hearing of most appeals on the original record, thus dispensing with the reproduction of "excerpts" from the record, and with an abstract as well, unless the court orders that one must be prepared. See the committee comments to Rule 342.

Subparagraph (c)(4)

Subparagraph (c)(4) is a general provision for extensions of time and does not change the practice in existence at the time of the adoption of the rule. In 1982, this subparagraph was reworded but not changed in substance.

Subparagraph (c)(5)

Subparagraph (c)(5) provides that the granting of the appeal from an order allowing a new trial *ipso facto* operates as a stay. The former rule required the giving of some kind of a bond to make a stay effective. A bond is not always appropriate. Subparagraph (c)(5) requires a bond only after a showing of good cause.

Subparagraph (c)(6)

As originally adopted Rule 343 provided that in cases in which a reviewing court grants leave to appeal, or allows an appeal as a matter of right, the appellant must file his brief within 35 days of the order allowing the appeal, and that in cases in which a party allows his petition for leave to appeal or his answer to such a petition to stand as his brief, he must notify the other parties and the clerk of the reviewing court. These provisions were applicable to all cases in which leave to appeal was required, whether to the Appellate Court or the Supreme Court. Rules 306(c)(6), 308(d), and 315(g) provided for the briefing schedule by cross-reference to Rule 343. In 1974, Rule 315(g), dealing with briefs in appeals to the Supreme Court from the Appellate Court, was amended to provide in detail for the filing of briefs, leaving the general language in Rule 343(a) relating to the filing of the appellant's brief in cases taken on motion for leave to appeal applicable only to appeals under Rules 306 and 308, and the provision for notice of intention to let the petition or answer stand as a brief applicable only to appeals under Rule 306. In the interest of clarity these provisions were placed in Rules 306(c)(6) and 308(d) and the general language deleted from Rule 343(a). This represents no change in practice. The briefing schedule after the due date of the appellant's brief (35 days for the appellee's brief and 14 days for a reply brief) remains governed by Rule 343(a).

Subparagraph (c)(7)

Former Rule 30 provided that after allowance of the appeal and the filing of the stay bond, "The case is then pending on appeal." This obvious fact was omitted from Rule 306 as unnecessary. Subparagraph (c)(7) does provide that if the appeal is granted oral argument may be requested as provided in Rule 352.

Committee Comments

(Revised September 1983)

This rule replaced former Rule 30, which was in effect from January 1, 1964, to December 31, 1966, and which in turn was derived from former section 77(2) of the Civil Practice Act, repealed effective January 1, 1964 (Laws of 1963, p. 2691, § 2). The Judicial Article of the new Illinois constitution (art. VI, § 6) contains substantially the same language on interlocutory appeals that appeared in the 1964 Judicial Amendment, and authorizes this rule in the following language:

"The Supreme Court may provide by rule for appeals to the Appellate Court from other than final judgments of the Circuit Courts."

Paragraph (a)

Paragraph (a), as originally adopted, made no change in the prior rule except to permit the petition to be duplicated in the same manner as a brief (see Rule 344) instead of always being printed. The petition is to be filed within 30 days, subject to an extension of time under paragraph (e).

Paragraph (a) was amended in 1969 by adding subparagraph (2), denominating as subparagraph (1) what was formerly entire paragraph (a), and making appropriate changes in the headings. Subparagraph (2), together with Rule 366(b)(2)(v), also added in 1969, abrogates the ruling in *Keen v. Davis*, 108 Ill. App. 2d 55, 63–64 (5th Dist. 1969), denying reviewability, on appeal from an order allowing a new trial, of questions raised by other rulings of the trial court on the post-trial motion. Revised Rule 366(b)(2)(v) makes it clear that the absence of a final judgment is not a bar to review of all the rulings of the trial court on the post-trial motions. See the Committee Comments to that rule.

In 1982, paragraph (a)(1) was amended by adding subparagraphs (i), (ii), (iii), and (iv), expanding the instances in which appeals could be sought in the appellate court. Also in 1982, subparagraph (a)(2) was amended to make it clear that post-trial motions are before the reviewing court without the necessity of filing a cross-appeal only when the appellate court has granted a petition for leave to appeal an order granting a new trial.

In 1983, paragraph (a)(1)(ii) was amended to permit a party to seek leave to appeal from a circuit court order allowing or denying a motion to transfer a case to another county within Illinois on the grounds of *forum non conveniens*. See *Torres v. Walsh* (1983), 97 Ill. 2d 338; *Mesa v. Chicago & North Western Transportation Co.* (1933), 97 Ill. 2d 356.

Paragraph (b)

Paragraph (b) was amended in 1979 to reflect changes in Rule 321 that eliminated the requirement that a praecipe for record be filed.

Paragraph (c)

Paragraph (c) permits answers to the petition to be filed within 21 days after the due date of the petition instead of "within 15 days after the petition is served upon him." They are not required to be printed as formerly, but may also be otherwise duplicated as are briefs. Former Rule 30 was silent as to a reply. Paragraph (c) provides that there shall be no reply except by leave.

Paragraph (d)

As originally promulgated, and as amended in 1974, paragraph (d) provided that "excerpts from record" or an abstract should be filed. This represented a change from former Rule 30, which required the filing of a printed abstract of record. It was amended in 1979 to delete reference to "excerpts from record" to reflect the changes made in that year to provide for the hearing of most appeals on the original record, thus dispensing with the reproduction of "excerpts" from the record, and with an abstract as well, unless the court orders that one must be prepared. See the committee comments to Rule 342.

Paragraph (e)

Paragraph (e) is a general provision for extensions of time and does not change the practice in existence at the time of the adoption of the rule. In 1982, this paragraph was reworded but not changed in substance.

Paragraph (f)

Paragraph (f) provides that the granting of the appeal from an order allowing a new trial *ipso facto* operates as a stay. The former rule required the giving of some kind of a bond to make a stay effective. A bond is not always appropriate. Paragraph (f) requires a bond only after a showing of good cause.

Paragraph (g)

As originally adopted Rule 343 provided that in cases in which a reviewing court grants leave to appeal, or allows an appeal as a matter of right, the appellant must file his brief within 35 days of the order allowing the appeal, and that in cases in which a party allows his petition for leave to appeal or his answer to such a petition to stand as his brief, he must notify the other parties and the clerk of the reviewing court. These provisions were applicable to all cases in which leave to appeal was required, whether to the Appellate Court or the Supreme Court. Rules 306(g), 308(d), and 315(g) provided for the briefing schedule by cross-reference to Rule 343. In 1974, Rule 315(g), dealing with briefs in appeals to the Supreme Court from the Appellate Court, was amended to provide in detail for the filing of briefs, leaving the general language in Rule 343(a) relating to the filing of the appellant's brief in cases taken on motion for leave to appeal applicable only to appeals under Rules 306 and 308, and the provision for notice of intention to let the petition or answer stand as a brief applicable only to appeals under Rule 306. In the interest of clarity these provisions were placed in Rules 306(g) and 308(d) and the general language deleted from Rule 343(a). This represents no change in practice. The briefing schedule after the due date of the appellant's brief (35 days for the appellee's brief and 14 days for a reply brief) remains governed by Rule 343(a).

Paragraph (h)

Former Rule 30 provided that after allowance of the appeal and the filing of the stay bond, "The case is then pending on appeal." This obvious fact was omitted from Rule 306 as unnecessary. Paragraph (h) does provide that if the appeal is granted oral argument may be requested as provided in Rule 352.

Rule 306A.   Reserved

Comment

(February 26, 2010)

In 2010, Rule 306A was reserved and its provisions, as modified, were incorporated into Rule 311(a).

Rule 307.   Interlocutory Appeals as of Right

(a) **Orders Appealable; Time.** An appeal may be taken to the Appellate Court from an interlocutory order of court:

(1) granting, modifying, refusing, dissolving, or refusing to dissolve or modify an injunction;

(2) appointing or refusing to appoint a receiver or sequestrator;

(3) giving or refusing to give other or further powers or property to a receiver or sequestrator already appointed;

(4) placing or refusing to place a mortgagee in possession of mortgaged premises;

(5) appointing or refusing to appoint a receiver, liquidator, rehabilitator, or other similar officer for a bank, savings and loan association, currency exchange, insurance company, or other financial institution, or granting or refusing to grant custody of the institution or requiring turnover of any of its assets;

(6) terminating parental rights or granting, denying or revoking temporary commitment in adoption proceedings commenced pursuant to section 5 of the Adoption Act (750 ILCS 50/5);

(7) determining issues raised in proceedings to exercise the right of eminent domain under section 20–5–10 of the Eminent Domain Act, but the procedure for appeal and stay shall be as provided in that section.

Except as provided in paragraph (b) and (d), the appeal must be perfected within 30 days from the entry of the interlocutory order by filing a notice of appeal designated "Notice of Interlocutory Appeal" conforming substantially to the notice of appeal in other cases. The record must be filed in the Appellate Court within the same 30 days unless the time for filing the record is extended by the Appellate Court or any judge thereof.

(b) **Motion to Vacate.** If an interlocutory order is entered on *ex parte* application, the party intending to take an appeal therefrom shall first present, on notice, a motion to the trial court to vacate the order. An appeal may be taken if the motion is denied, or if the court does not act thereon within 7 days after its presentation. The 30 days allowed for taking an appeal and filing the record begins to run from the day the motion is denied or from the last day for action thereon.

(c) **Time for Briefs and Abstract if an Abstract Is Required.** Unless the Appellate Court orders a different schedule or orders that no briefs be filed, the schedule for filing briefs shall be as follows: The brief of appellant shall be filed in the Appellate Court, with proof of service, within 7 days from the filing of the record on appeal. Within 7 days from the date appellant's brief is filed, the appellee shall file his brief in the Appellate Court with proof of service. Within 7 days from the date appellee's brief is filed, appellant may serve and file a reply brief. The briefs shall otherwise conform to the requirements of Rules 341 through 344. If the Appellate Court so orders, an abstract shall be prepared and filed as provided in Rule 342.

(d) Appeals of Temporary Restraining Orders; Time; Memoranda.

(1) *Petition; Service; Record.* Unless another form is ordered by the Appellate Court, review of the granting or denial of a temporary restraining order or an order modifying, dissolving, or refusing to dissolve or modify a temporary restraining order as authorized in paragraph (a) shall be by petition filed in the Appellate Court, but notice of interlocutory appeal as provided in paragraph (a) shall also be filed, within the same time for filing the petition. The petition shall be in writing, state the relief requested and the grounds for the relief requested, and shall be filed in the Appellate Court, with proof of personal, e-mail or facsimile service as provided in Rule 11, within two days of the entry or denial of the order from which review is being sought. An appropriate supporting record shall accompany the petition, which shall include the notice of interlocutory appeal, the temporary restraining order or the proposed temporary restraining order, the complaint, the motion requesting the granting of the temporary restraining order, and any supporting documents or matters of record necessary to the petition. The supporting record must be authenticated by the certificate of the clerk of the trial court or by the affidavit of the attorney or party filing it.

(2) *Legal Memoranda.* The petitioner may file a memorandum supporting the petition which shall not exceed 15 typewritten pages and which must also be filed within two days of the entry of the order that is being appealed under paragraph 1 of this section. The respondent shall file, with proof of personal, e-mail or facsimile service as provided in Rule 11, any responding memorandum within two days following the filing of the petition, supporting record, and any memorandum which must be personally served upon the respondent. The respondent's memorandum may not exceed 15 typewritten pages and must also be personally served upon the petitioner.

(3) *Replies; Extensions of Time.* Except by order of court, no replies will be allowed and no extension of time will be allowed.

(4) *Time for Decision; Oral Argument.* After the petitioner has filed the petition, supporting record, and any memorandum and the time for filing any responding memorandum has expired, the Appellate Court shall consider and decide the petition within five days thereafter. Oral argument on the petition will not be heard.

(5) *Variations by Order of Court.* The Appellate Court may, if it deems it appropriate, order a different schedule, or order that no memoranda be filed, or order the other materials need not be filed.

Amended October 21, 1969, eff. January 1, 1970; amended July 30, 1979, eff. October 15, 1979; amended May 28, 1982, eff. July 1, 1982; amended November 21, 1988, eff. January 1, 1989; amended June 19, 1989, eff. August 1, 1989; amended December 17, 1993, eff. February 1, 1994; amended December 1, 1995, eff. immediately; amended July 6, 2000, eff. immediately; amended November 27, 2002, eff. January 1, 2003; amendment of November 27, 2002, vacated December 31, 2002; amended March 20, 2009, eff. immediately; amended Feb. 26, 2010, eff. immediately; Dec. 9, 2015, eff. Jan. 1, 2016.

Formerly Ill.Rev.Stat.1991, ch. 110A, ¶ 307.

Explanatory Note

An Order entered December 31, 2002 provided:

"Effective immediately, that part of the order entered November 27, 2002, amending Supreme Court Rule 307, effective January 1, 2003, is vacated. Effective January 1, 2003, Supreme Court Rule 306 is amended. The amendment of Rule 306(a) to include paragraph (8) applies only to cases filed in the circuit court on or after the effective date of the amendment, i.e. January 1, 2003."

Committee Comments

(Revised 1979)

This rule replaced former Rule 31, effective January 1, 1964, and in effect until January 1, 1967. That rule supplanted former section 78 of the Civil Practice Act, repealed effective January 1, 1964 (Laws of 1963, p. 2691, § 1), section 7 of the 1964 judicial article (now section 6 of new article VI) having given the Supreme Court power to provide by rule for interlocutory appeals to the Appellate Court. The word "order" is substituted for "order or decree" throughout the rule, without change of meaning. (See Rule 2.)

Stays pending appeal are governed by Rule 305.

Paragraph (a)

Paragraph (a) provides for a designation—"Notice of Interlocutory Appeal"—on the notice of appeal, and continues the theory that the filing of the notice of appeal and not the filing of a bond perfects the appeal. The paragraph was amended in 1969 by adding items (5) through (7) to the list of appealable interlocutory orders. The amendment carries out the policy of covering all interlocutory appeals in the Supreme Court rules, as contemplated by section 7 of the 1964 judicial article (now section 6 of new article VI). The procedure provided in the Eminent Domain Act for appeal and stay in quick-take cases (Ill.Rev.Stat.1967, ch. 47, par. 2.2(b)) is incorporated by reference in item (7), in lieu of detailed coverage of these matters in the rules, because of the peculiar problems in an appeal of this kind and its relationship to the condemnation proceeding as a whole.

Paragraph (a) was amended in 1979 to reflect changes in Rule 321 that eliminated the requirement that a praecipe for record be filed.

Paragraph (b)

Paragraph (b) is the same as former Rule 31(2) with slight verbal changes.

Paragraph (c)

Paragraph (c), establishing the briefing schedule as 7 days for appellant, 7 days for appellee, and 7 days for the reply brief, all dating from the filing of the record and the filing of the preceding brief (instead of from the due dates thereof), replaces the schedules in Rule 5 of the First District Appellate Court and Rule 23 of the other appellate districts (former Uniform Appellate Court Rule 23). The paragraph gives the court the right to order a different briefing schedule, or to dispense with briefs altogether. Until 1979, it was generally required that an abstract of the record or a reproduction of excerpts from the record be filed in the reviewing court in addition to the record and the briefs. Paragraph (d) provided that where the appellant elected to file excerpts from the record instead of an abstract the excerpts had to be filed within 7 days after the filing of the reply brief. The rules were amended in 1979 to provide that unless the Appellate Court orders that an abstract be prepared and filed, all cases will be heard on the original record and the briefs, the appellant's brief to include an appendix described in Rule 342. Appropriate changes were made in Rule 307(c) to reflect this change in the practice.

Rule 308. Certified Questions

(a) Requests. When the trial court, in making an interlocutory order not otherwise appealable, finds that the order involves a question of law as to which there is substantial ground for difference of opinion and that an immediate appeal from the order may materially advance the ultimate termination of the litigation, the court shall so state in writing, identifying the question of law involved. Such a statement may be made at the time of the entry of the order or thereafter on the court's own motion or on motion of any party. The Appellate Court may thereupon in its discretion allow an appeal from the order.

(b) How Sought. The appeal will be sought by filing an application for leave to appeal with the clerk of the Appellate Court within 30 days after the entry of the order in the trial court or the making of the prescribed statement by the trial court, whichever is later. An original and three copies of the application shall be filed.

(c) Application; Answer. The application shall contain a statement of the facts necessary to an understanding of the question of law determined by the order of the trial court; a statement of the question itself; and a statement of the reasons why a substantial basis exists for a difference of opinion on the question and why an immediate appeal may materially advance the termination of the litigation. The application shall be accompanied by an original supporting record (Rule 328), containing the order appealed from and other parts of the trial court record necessary for the determination of the application for permission to appeal. Within 21 days after the due date of the application, an adverse party may file an answer in opposition, with copies in the number required for the application, together with an original of a supplementary supporting record containing any additional parts of the record the adverse party desires to have considered by the Appellate Court. The application and answer shall be submitted without oral argument unless otherwise ordered.

(d) Record; Briefs. If leave to appeal is allowed, any party may request that an additional record on appeal be prepared as provided in Rule 321 *et seq.*, or the court may order the appellant to file the record, which shall be filed within 35 days of the date on which such leave was allowed. The appellant shall file a brief in the reviewing court within the same 35 days. Otherwise the schedule and requirements for briefs shall be as provided in Rules 341 through 344. If the reviewing court so orders, an abstract shall be prepared and filed as provided in Rule 342.

(e) Stay. The application for permission to appeal or the granting thereof shall not stay proceedings in the trial court unless the trial court or the Appellate Court or a judge thereof shall so order.

Amended June 28, 1974, eff. Sept. 1, 1974; Oct. 15, 1979; Dec. 17, 1993, eff. Feb. 1, 1994; Feb. 26, 2010, eff. immediately; Dec. 11, 2014, eff. Jan. 1, 2015; Oct. 15, 2015, eff. Jan. 1, 2016.

Formerly Ill.Rev.Stat.1991, ch. 110A, ¶ 308.

Committee Comments
(Revised 1979)

This rule was new in 1967. Prior to that time appeals from interlocutory orders had been permitted in Illinois only in a few specified classes of cases. (See former Rule 31 and its predecessor, former section 78 of the Civil Practice Act (Ill. Rev. Stat. 1961, ch. 110, par. 78).) This was also generally true in the Federal courts. In 1958, however, Congress adopted what is now 28 U.S.C. § 1292(b), which permits an interlocutory appeal from other than final orders when the trial court "shall be of the opinion that such order involves a controlling question of law as to which there is substantial ground for difference of opinion and that immediate appeal from the order may materially advance the ultimate termination of the litigation." The court of appeals may then "in its discretion" permit the appeal to be taken. Thus, this type of interlocutory appeal is allowed when both the trial and appellate courts agree that an appeal will expedite the disposition of the litigation, and also that there is a substantial question of law to be decided. The appellate courts themselves can insure that this authority to allow interlocutory appeals is not abused. This power has been sparingly exercised in the Federal courts, but it has proved valuable.

This rule establishes a similar procedure for Illinois. One change from the Federal rule is to eliminate the requirement that the question raised be a "controlling" one. The meaning of "controlling" has not been clear, despite many cases on the point. and experience has shown that sometimes an important question of law that only arguably could be said to be controlling should be heard on appeal without awaiting final judgment.

The 1964 judicial article authorized the Supreme Court to provide by rule for appeals to the Appellate Court of other than final judgments of the circuit court. Arguably, however, it made no provision for rules permitting direct appeal to the Supreme Court except in the case of final judgments. Accordingly, Rule 308 was made applicable only to appeals to the Appellate Court, but it permits the Appellate Court to allow interlocutory appeals in classes of cases in which the *final* judgment is appealable only to the Supreme Court. Though the reference to "final judgments" in section 5 of the 1964 judicial article was not carried forward into article VI, section 4 of the new constitution, direct appeals to the Supreme Court remain limited to appeals from final judgments. See Rule 302.

Normally the interlocutory appeal will not stay proceedings in the trial court. The case may proceed in that court unless the trial court or the Appellate Court or a judge thereof otherwise orders. This will discourage an attempt to take an interlocutory appeal with a motive of delay.

In 1974, paragraph (b) was amended to substitute the word "application" appearing in the last sentence of the paragraph for the word "petition" to make the terminology uniform. At the same time paragraph (d) was amended to insert the clause "the appellant shall file his brief in the reviewing court within 35 days of the date on which such leave was allowed." This requirement formerly appeared in Rule 343(a). See the committee comments to Rule 306, paragraph (g).

Until 1979, paragraph (d) provided that, if appeal were allowed, "[e]xcerpts from record or an abstract shall be prepared and filed as provided in Rule 342." In that year Rule 342 was amended to eliminate altogether the practice of duplicating and filing excerpts from the record and to provide that no abstract shall be filed unless by order of the reviewing court. Accordingly, paragraph (d) was amended to reflect this change. See the committee comments to Rule 342.

Rule 309. Dismissal of Appeals by the Trial Court

Before the record on appeal is filed in the reviewing court, the trial court may dismiss the appeal of any party (1) on motion of that party or (2) on stipulation of the parties. A copy of the order of dismissal filed in the trial court shall be forwarded by the clerk to the reviewing court within 5 days after the entry of such order.

Amended July 30, 1979, eff. Oct. 15, 1979; Sept. 20, 1979, eff. Oct. 15, 1979; Jan. 5, 1981, eff. Feb. 1, 1981.

Formerly Ill.Rev.Stat.1991, ch. 110A, ¶ 309.

Committee Comments
(Revised January 5, 1981)

This rule is based upon former Rule 36(1)(e). The provision permitting the trial court to dismiss on motion of the appealing party was new in 1969. The last sentence was added in 1979 in view of the change in the practice in that year calling for immediate docketing of the appeal in the reviewing court upon receipt of the copy of the notice of appeal transmitted by the clerk of the circuit court. (See the committee comments to paragraph (f) of Rule 303.) For the same reasons the first sentence was amended in 1981 to limit the power of the circuit court to dismiss to the period before the record on appeal is filed, rather than the period before the case is docketed, as provided in the original text.

Rule 310. Prehearing Conference in the Appellate Court

In an appeal pending in the Appellate Court, the court or a judge thereof, on its own motion or on the request of a party, may order a prehearing conference to consider the simplification of the issues and any other matters that may aid in the disposition of the appeal. Unless otherwise agreed by the parties, a judge who will not participate in the decision of the case shall preside at the conference. The judge may enter an order which recites the action taken at the conference and the agreements made by the parties as to any of the matters considered and which limits the issues to those not disposed of by admissions or agreements of counsel. The order controls the subsequent course of the proceeding, unless modified to prevent manifest injustice.

Added June 25, 1971, eff. July 1, 1971. Amended Sept. 8, 1975, eff. Oct. 1, 1975; June 19, 1989, eff. Aug. 1, 1989.

Formerly Ill.Rev.Stat.1991, ch. 110A, ¶ 310.

Committee Comments
(July 1, 1971)

This rule is based upon Rule 33 of the Federal Rules of Appellate Procedure. The provision that a judge who will not participate in the decision of the case shall preside at the conference does not appear in the Federal rule.

Rule 310.1. Appellate Settlement Conference Program

(a) **Program Purpose and Goals.** The purpose of the Appellate Settlement Conference Program (Program) is to provide an alternative means for resolving certain civil appeals in the Illinois Appellate Court. The Program is intended to give parties to an appeal an opportunity and forum to discuss their case, simplify and/or limit the issues, negotiate settlement, and consider any matters that may aid in disposition of the appeal or resolution of the action or proceeding.

The Supreme Court may authorize appellate districts to undertake and conduct settlement conference programs. Such programs shall be provided at no additional court costs to the parties beyond the appellate filing fees as established by the Supreme Court.

(b) Applicability. Only civil appeals are eligible for assignment to the Program. However, appeals from judgments or orders entered in the following types of proceedings or actions are ineligible for inclusion in the Program: juvenile court proceedings, adoption proceedings, paternity proceedings, actions where the custody of or allocation of parental responsibilities for a minor is the sole issue, actions where the mental capacity of a party is at issue, contempt, petitions for extraordinary relief such as *mandamus*, petitions for writs of *habeas corpus*, actions for judicial review of decisions of the Illinois Workers' Compensation Commission, and election contests. Also ineligible are appeals from a judgment or order imposing sanctions upon a litigant or attorney or incarcerating a party.

(c) Local Rules.

(1) Each appellate district conducting a settlement conference program shall adopt local rules for the conduct of such a program. Local rules are to be consistent with the provisions of this rule. Prior to the establishment of a settlement conference program, the presiding judge of the appellate district, or the chairman of the executive committee in the case of the First District, shall submit to the Supreme Court for its review and approval, through its Administrative Office, rules governing the operation of the district's program.

(2) At a minimum, the rules adopted by an appellate district conducting a settlement conference program shall address:

(i) Actions eligible for inclusion in the program consistent with paragraph (b) of this rule;

(ii) Appointment, qualifications and compensation of the mediators;

(iii) Selection of cases for referral to a mediator consistent with paragraphs (e) and (f) of this rule;

(iv) Scheduling of the mediation conferences;

(v) Conduct of the conference and role of the appellate mediator;

(vi) Absence of a party at the conference and sanctions;

(vii) Termination and report of mediation conference;

(viii) Finalization of agreement;

(ix) Confidentiality;

(x) Mechanism for reporting to the Supreme Court on the settlement conference program.

(d) Administration. The Program shall be administered in each appellate district by a mediation committee consisting of two or more judges appointed under that district's rules governing operation of the Program. The mediation committee may be assisted in its duties by a settlement administrator, who may be the clerk of court. The clerk may also be a member of the mediation committee.

(e) Case Selection. Cases may be selected for the Program as follows:

(1) *Settlement Status Report.* Any party may file with the clerk of the court in the district in which the case was filed a "Settlement Status Report." Each appellate district may decide whether the filing of a "Settlement Status Report" shall be mandatory or voluntary. Notice of the filing of a "Settlement Status Report," along with a copy of same, shall be served upon all parties in accordance with the provisions of Supreme Court Rule 11.

(2) *Motions for Assignment to the Settlement Conference Program.* On his or her own motion or on motion of any party, the presiding judge of the appellate district to which a case is assigned, or the presiding judge of the division to which a case is assigned in the case of the First District, may with the approval of the judge to whom the case has been assigned for dispositional purposes, if any, recommend to the mediation committee that a civil appeal be assigned to the Program. Upon receipt of the "Settlement Status Report" or recommendation from a presiding judge, the mediation committee shall evaluate the case to determine if the case is eligible for assignment to the Program. If no objection is filed, and the case is otherwise eligible, an order shall be entered which assigns the case to the Program, transfers it to a settlement docket, and stays the filing of the record and/or briefs pending further order of court.

(f) Objection to Assignment. Any party to an appeal may object to the case being assigned to the Program. Such objections shall be in accordance with the local rules of the appellate district in which the case was filed. Upon receipt of any such objection, the settlement administrator shall send a written notice to all parties and the appellate mediator, informing them that an objection has been received and that the case will be removed from the Program.

(g) Dismissal; Agreement to Narrow Issues.

(1) If the settlement conference results in the settlement of the case and the parties agree to dismiss the appeal, an order dismissing the appeal shall be entered in the manner specified by the rules for that particular district.

(2) If the settlement conference does not result in settlement but the parties agree to narrow the issues on appeal, an order shall be prepared reciting the agreed terms. The order entered shall be binding upon the parties unless modified by subsequent order of the court. An order shall be entered removing the case from the Program, reassigning the case, and reestablishing the filing of the record and/or briefing schedule.

(h) Confidentiality. The settlement conference and all documents prepared by the parties, the appellate mediator, and the settlement administrator shall be confidential. No transcript or recording shall be made of any settlement conference and no mention of the settlement discussions shall be made in any brief filed with this court or in oral argument. Except for orders entered by the appellate court of the district in which the appeal was filed and written stipulations and agreements entered into by the parties, documents prepared by the parties and received by the appellate mediator or the settlement administrator as part of the Program shall not be filed of record with the clerk of the appellate court of that district and, upon dismissal of the case or its removal from the Program, whichever is first to occur, shall be destroyed by the settlement administrator.

(i) Sanctions. Failure of the parties or their authorized representatives to participate in a settlement conference in good faith, failure to attend a regularly scheduled settlement conference, or failure to comply with the rules applicable to settlement conferences adopted by the district in which the case was filed may subject a party to the imposition of sanctions under Supreme Court Rule 375.

(j) Statistical Reporting. The settlement administrator shall maintain statistics as to the number and type of cases which are (1) considered by the mediation committee for inclusion in the Program, (2) assigned to the Program, (3) removed from the program on the objection of a party, (4) removed from the Program without any settlement having been reached, (5) dismissed by agreement of the parties while assigned to the Program, and (6) removed from the Program after the entry of an order narrowing the issues on appeal. The settlement administrator shall report such statistics to the mediation committee in accordance with the local rules in his or her appellate district and annually to the Director of the Administrative Office of the Illinois Courts.

Adopted October 29, 2004, effective January 1, 2005. Amended Mar. 8, 2016, eff. immediately.

Committee Comments

(March 8, 2016)

Special Supreme Court Committee
on Child Custody Issues

The Illinois Marriage and Dissolution of Marriage Act, Pub. Act 99–90 (eff. Jan. 1, 2016) (amending 750 ILCS 5/101 *et seq.*), has changed the terms "Custody," "Visitation" (as to parents) and "Removal" to "Allocation of Parental Responsibilities," "Parenting Time" and "Relocation." These rules are being amended to reflect those changes. The rules utilize both "custody" and "allocation of parental responsibilities" in recognition that some legislative enactments covered by the rules utilize the term "custody" while the Illinois Marriage and Dissolution of Marriage Act and the Illinois Parentage Act of 2015 utilize the term "allocation of parental

responsibilities." The Special Committee has attempted to adhere to the usage found in the applicable legislative enactments.

Rule 311.   Accelerated Docket

(a) Mandatory Accelerated Disposition of Child Custody or Allocation of Parental Responsibilities Appeals. The expedited procedures in this subpart shall apply to appeals from final orders in child custody or allocation of parental responsibilities cases and to interlocutory appeals in child custody or allocation of parental responsibilities cases from which leave to appeal has been granted pursuant to Rule 306(a)(5). If the appeal is taken from a judgment or order affecting other matters, such as support, property issues or decisions affecting the rights of persons other than the child, the reviewing court may handle all pending issues using the expedited procedures in this rule, unless doing so will delay decision on the child custody or allocation of parental responsibilities appeal.

(1) *Special Caption.* The notice of appeal or petition for leave to appeal, docketing statement, briefs and all other notices, motions and pleadings filed by any party in relation to an appeal involving child custody or allocation of parental responsibilities shall include the following statement in bold type on the top of the front page: THIS APPEAL INVOLVES A QUESTION OF CHILD CUSTODY, ALLOCATION OF PARENTAL RESPONSIBILITIES, ADOPTION, TERMINATION OF PARENTAL RIGHTS OR OTHER MATTER AFFECTING THE BEST INTERESTS OF A CHILD.

(2) *Service Upon the Circuit Court.* In addition to the service required by Rule 303(c), a party filing notice of appeal in a child custody or allocation of parental responsibilities case shall, within seven days, serve copies of the same on the trial judge who entered the judgment or order appealed and the office of the chief judge of the circuit in which the judgment or order on appeal was entered. Where leave to appeal has been granted pursuant to Rule 306(a)(5), the appellant shall, within seven days, serve copies of the order granting leave to appeal upon the trial judge who entered the judgment or order appealed from and the office of the chief judge of the circuit in which the judgment or order on appeal was entered.

(3) *Status Hearing in Circuit Court.* On receipt of the notice of appeal or order granting leave to appeal under Rule 306(a)(5) in a child custody or allocation of parental responsibilities case, the trial judge shall set a status hearing within 30 days of the date of filing of the notice of appeal or order granting leave to appeal to determine the status of the case, including payments of required fees to the clerk of the circuit court and court reporting personnel as defined in Rule 46 for the preparation of

the transcript of proceedings, and take any action necessary to expedite preparation of the record on appeal and the transcript of the proceedings. The trial court shall have continuing jurisdiction for the purpose of enforcing the rules for preparation of the record and transcript. The trial court may request the assistance of the chief judge to resolve filing delays, and the chief judge shall assign or reassign the court reporting personnel's work as necessary to ensure compliance with the filing deadlines.

(4) *Record.* The record on appeal and the transcript of proceedings in a child custody or allocation of parental responsibilities case shall be filed no later than 35 days after the filing of the notice of appeal or granting of leave to appeal pursuant to Rule 306(a)(5). Any request for extension of the time for filing shall be accompanied by an affidavit of the court clerk or court reporting personnel stating the reason for the delay, and shall be served on the trial judge and the chief judge of the circuit. Lack of advance payment shall not be a reason for noncompliance with filing deadlines for the record or transcript. Any subsequent request for continuance shall be made to the appellate court by written notice and motion to all parties in accordance with rules.

(5) *Deadline for Decision.* Except for good cause shown, the appellate court shall issue its decision within 150 days after the filing of the notice of appeal or granting of leave to appeal pursuant to Rule 306(a)(5).

(6) *Local Rules.* The appellate court of each district shall by administrative order or rule adopt mandatory procedures to ensure completion of child custody or allocation of parental responsibilities appeals within the time specified in paragraph (5). The order or rule may include provisions regarding the use of memoranda in lieu of briefs, expedited schedules and deadlines, provisions for the separation of child custody or allocation of parental responsibilities issues from other issues on appeal and any other procedures necessary to a fair and timely disposition of the case. The clerk of the appellate court shall be responsible for seeing that the accelerated docket is maintained and for advising the court of any noncompliance with the rules of the court concerning timely filing.

(7) *Continuances Disfavored.* Requests for continuance are disfavored and shall be granted only for compelling circumstances. The appellate court may require personal appearance by the attorney or party requesting the continuance as provided by local rule.

(8) *Effective Date.* This rule shall apply to all orders in which a notice of appeal is filed after its effective date.

(b) Discretionary Acceleration of Other Appeals. Any time after the docketing statement is filed in the reviewing court, the court, on its own motion, or on the motion of any party, for good cause shown, may place the case on an accelerated docket. The motion shall be supported by an affidavit stating reasons why the appeal should be expedited. If warranted by the circumstances, the court may enter an order accepting a supporting record prepared pursuant to Rule 328, consisting of those lower court pleadings, reports of proceedings or other materials that will fully present the issues. In its discretion the court may accept memoranda in lieu of formal briefs. The court may then enter an order setting forth an expedited schedule for the disposition of the appeal.

Added June 15, 1982, eff. July 1, 1982. Amended June 19, 1989, eff. Aug. 1, 1989; Dec. 17, 1993, eff. Feb. 1, 1994; Feb. 26, 2010, eff. immediately; Mar. 8, 2016, eff. immediately

Formerly Ill.Rev.Stat.1991, ch. 110A, ¶ 311.

Committee Comments
(March 8, 2016)

Special Supreme Court Committee
on Child Custody Issues

The Illinois Marriage and Dissolution of Marriage Act, Pub. Act 99–90 (eff. Jan. 1, 2016) (amending 750 ILCS 5/101 et seq.), has changed the terms "Custody," "Visitation" (as to parents) and "Removal" to "Allocation of Parental Responsibilities," "Parenting Time" and "Relocation." These rules are being amended to reflect those changes. The rules utilize both "custody" and "allocation of parental responsibilities" in recognition that some legislative enactments covered by the rules utilize the term "custody" while the Illinois Marriage and Dissolution of Marriage Act and the Illinois Parentage Act of 2015 utilize the term "allocation of parental responsibilities." The Special Committee has attempted to adhere to the usage found in the applicable legislative enactments.

Committee Comments
(February 26, 2010)

Paragraph (a)

Paragraph (a) was originally enacted as Rule 306A in 2004 to expedite the resolution of appeals affecting the care and custody of children. In 2010, Rule 306A was moved to paragraph (a) of this rule. The purpose of this amendment was to streamline the wording of the rule and facilitate its use. The amendment was also intended to clarify that the rule addresses only the procedures to be followed in order to expedite disposition of child custody appeals. Importantly, this rule does not confer any new appeal rights or affect finality for purposes of appellate jurisdiction. The appealability of any order affecting child custody is governed principally by Rules 301, 304, 303, and 306. The expedited procedures set forth in paragraph (a) apply to all child custody appeals, whether they have been taken from final orders appealable as of right or interlocutory orders from which the court has granted leave to appeal. The goal of paragraph (a) remains to promote stability for not only abused and neglected children, but also children whose custody is an issue in dissolution of marriage, adoption, and other proceedings, by mandating swifter disposition of these appeals.

Paragraph (b)

Paragraph (b) encompasses the pre–2010 amendment version of Rule 311, which permits the expedited resolution of any appeal upon the request of any party and at the discretion of the appellate court.

Committee Comments

(August 1, 1989)

Amended in 1989 to give the Appellate Court discretion, for good cause shown, to order cases to an accelerated docket on its own motion or on the motion of a party, rather than requiring that all parties agree to such action.

Rule 312. Docketing Statement

(a) **Appellant's Docketing Statement.** All appellants, including cross-appellants and separate appellants, whether as a matter of right or as a matter of the court's discretion, shall file a docketing statement with the clerk of the reviewing court. In the case of an appeal as of right, the appellant shall file the statement within 14 days after filing the notice of appeal or petition for review of an administrative order or the date upon which a motion to file late notice of appeal is allowed. In the case of a discretionary appeal pursuant to Rule 306 or Rule 308, the statement shall be due at the time that the appellant files his or her Rule 306 petition or Rule 308 application. In cases of appeal pursuant to Rule 307(a), the docketing statement shall be filed within 7 days from the filing of the notice of appeal. The docketing statement shall be accompanied by the required reviewing court filing fee if it has not been previously paid. The docketing statement shall be accompanied by any written requests to the circuit clerk or court reporting personnel as defined in Rule 46 for preparation of their respective portions of the record on appeal and be served on all parties to the case with proof of service attached. Within 7 days thereafter, appellee, if it is deemed necessary, may file a short responsive statement with the clerk of the reviewing court with proof of service on all parties.

The form and contents of the docketing statement shall be as follows:

Docket Number in the Reviewing Court

Case Title (Complete))   Appeal from _____
                            County
)   Circuit Number _____
)   Trial Judge _____
)   Date of Notice of Appeal _____
)   Date of Judgment _____
)   Date of Postjudgment Motion Order

)   Supreme court rule which confers jurisdiction upon the reviewing court _____

DOCKETING STATEMENT
(Civil)

1. Is this a cross-appeal, separate appeal, joining in a prior appeal, or related to another appeal which is currently pending or which has been disposed of by this court? _____

If so, state the docket number(s) of the other appeal(s):

_____

2. If any party is a corporation or association, identify any affiliate, subsidiary, or parent group:

_____

3. Full name and complete address of appellant(s) filing this statement:

Name: _____

Address: _____

Telephone: _____

Email address: _____

*use additional page if multiple appellants.

Counsel on Appeal for appellant(s) filing this statement:

Name: _____ ARDC # _____

Address: _____

Telephone: _____

Email address: _____

Fax: _____

4. Full name and complete address of appellee(s): (Use additional page for multiple appellees.)

Name: _____

Address: _____

Telephone: _____

Counsel on Appeal for appellee(s): (Use additional page for multiple appellees.)

Name: _____

Address: _____

Telephone: _____

Email address: _____

Fax: _____

5. Court reporting personnel: (If more space is needed, use other side.)

Name: _____

Address: _____

Telephone: _____

Email address: _____

6. Is this appeal from a final order in a matter involving child custody or allocation of parental responsibility pursuant to Illinois Supreme Court Rule 311(a) which requires **Mandatory Accelerated Disposition of Child Custody or Allocation of Parental Responsibilities Appeals?**

Yes: _____   No: _____

*If yes, this docketing statement, briefs and all other notices, motions and pleadings filed by any party shall include the following statement in bold type on the top of the front page:

THIS APPEAL INVOLVES A QUESTION OF CHILD CUSTODY, ALLOCATION OF PARENTAL RESPONSIBILITIES, ADOPTION, TERMINATION OF PARENTAL RIGHTS OR OTHER MATTER AFFECTING THE BEST INTERESTS OF A CHILD.

7. State the general issues proposed to be raised (failure to include an issue in this statement will not result in the waiver of the issue on appeal):

_____

_____

_____

_____

As ____ attorney for the appellant _____ *Pro Se* appellant, I hereby certify that on the ____ day of _____, 20 ____, I asked / made a written request to the clerk of the circuit court to prepare the record on appeal, and on the ____ day of _____, 20 ____, I made a written request to the court reporting personnel to prepare the transcript(s).

_____   _____   _____
Date   Appellant's Attorney   *Pro Se* Appellant

In lieu of court reporting personnel's signature I have attached the written request to the court reporting personnel to prepare the transcript(s).

_____   _____   _____
Date   Appellant's Attorney   *Pro Se* Appellant

I hereby acknowledge receipt of an order for the preparation of a report of proceedings.

_____   _____
Date   Court Reporting Personnel or Supervisor

*If the other parties of record are numerous, they may be listed on a separate page instead of in the caption.

Adopted Dec. 17, 1993, eff. Feb. 1, 1994. Amended Dec. 13, 2005, eff. immediately; corrected Feb. 10, 2006, eff. immediately; amended Dec. 12, 2012, eff. Jan. 1, 2013; Jan. 17, 2013, eff. immediately; Mar. 8, 2016, eff. immediately

Committee Comments
(March 8, 2016)

Special Supreme Court Committee
on Child Custody Issues

The Illinois Marriage and Dissolution of Marriage Act, Pub. Act 99–90 (eff. Jan. 1, 2016) (amending 750 ILCS 5/101 *et seq.*), has changed the terms "Custody," "Visitation" (as to parents) and "Removal" to "Allocation of Parental Responsibilities,"

"Parenting Time" and "Relocation." These rules are being amended to reflect those changes. The rules utilize both "custody" and "allocation of parental responsibilities" in recognition that some legislative enactments covered by the rules utilize the term "custody" while the Illinois Marriage and Dissolution of Marriage Act and the Illinois Parentage Act of 2015 utilize the term "allocation of parental responsibilities." The Special Committee has attempted to adhere to the usage found in the applicable legislative enactments.

Committee Comments
(December 17, 1993)

Docketing statements are accorded a separate rule because they now apply to every type of appeal and to every party who files a notice of appeal or petitions for interlocutory review. Separate deadlines for filing the docketing statement, depending upon the type of appeal, are provided in paragraph (a).

In addition to the information sought under current practice, the appellant filing the docketing statement must be specifically identified under Items 1 and 3 and must demonstrate appellate jurisdiction under Item 6.

An alternative to securing the actual signature of a court reporter is provided by permitting the attorney or party to attach the written request to the court reporter for preparation of transcripts to the docketing statement.

Rule 313.   Fees in the Reviewing Court

Text of rule effective until July 1, 2016. See, also, rule effective July 1, 2016.

Unless excused by law, in all cases docketed in the reviewing court all appellants or petitioners shall pay a filing fee of $50.00, and all other parties upon entry of appearance or filing any paper shall pay a $30.00 fee.

Adopted Dec. 17, 1993, eff. Feb. 1, 1994. Amended Jan. 23, 2014, eff. Jan. 1, 2015.

Committee Comments
(December 17, 1993)

Because the authority for collecting reviewing court fees is contained in statutory provisions (see 30 ILCS 220/12 (West 1992); 705 ILCS 25/3 (West 1992)), a fee rule is provided for informational purposes.

Rule 313.   Fees in the Reviewing Court

Text of rule effective July 1, 2016. See, also, rule effective until July 1, 2016.

(a) Docket Fees. Unless excused by law, in all cases docketed in the reviewing court all appellants or petitioners shall pay a filing fee of $50.00, and all other parties upon entry of appearance or filing any paper shall pay a $30.00 fee. Any non party in a case filing any paper, including a motion for leave to file a

brief *amicus curiae* pursuant to Rule 345, shall pay a
$30 fee.

(b) Copy Fees. The clerks of the reviewing courts
shall charge a fee of 25 cents per page for making
copies of papers in their respective offices, except that
the clerks shall furnish without cost copies of opinions
or orders to parties in interest or their attorneys of
record and, in furtherance of the public interest, may
furnish without cost copies of opinions or orders to
other individuals or entities. The clerks shall charge
no fee for copies of papers made, with the clerk's prior
permission, using personal equipment such as a portable scanner or camera. When considering such requests, the clerk shall determine whether the equipment is likely to cause damage to the papers and
whether the equipment and/or request will interfere
with the clerk's office operations. Automatic feed
features or stack feeders are not permitted.

(c) Certificate and Seal. The fee for each official
certificate and seal is $5.

(d) Law License. In the Supreme Court, the fee
for preparing a law license, certifying it with the seal,
administering the oath, and transcribing the name on
the roll of attorneys is $50. The fee for a replacement
law license shall be $25.

(e) Attorney Certificates of Good Standing. In
the Supreme Court, the fee for an attorney certificate
of good standing shall be $15. If multiple copies are
requested, each additional certificate shall be $5.

Adopted Dec. 17, 1993, eff. Feb. 1, 1994. Amended Jan. 23,
2014, eff. Jan. 1, 2015; Dec. 7, 2015, eff. July 1, 2016.

Commentary

(December 17, 1993)

Because the authority for collecting reviewing
court fees is contained in statutory provisions (see
30 ILCS 220/12 (West 1992); 705 ILCS 25/3 (West
1992)), a fee rule is provided for informational purposes.

Rule 314. Reserved

PART B. APPEALS FROM THE APPELLATE COURT TO THE SUPREME COURT

Rule 315. Leave to Appeal From the Appellate Court to the Supreme Court

(a) Petition for Leave to Appeal; Grounds. Except as provided below for appeals from the Illinois
Workers' Compensation Commission division of the
Appellate Court, a petition for leave to appeal to the
Supreme Court from the Appellate Court may be filed
by any party, including the State, in any case not
appealable from the Appellate Court as a matter of
right. Whether such a petition will be granted is a
matter of sound judicial discretion. The following,
while neither controlling nor fully measuring the
court's discretion, indicate the character of reasons
which will be considered: the general importance of
the question presented; the existence of a conflict
between the decision sought to be reviewed and a
decision of the Supreme Court, or of another division
of the Appellate Court; the need for the exercise of
the Supreme Court's supervisory authority; and the
final or interlocutory character of the judgment
sought to be reviewed.

No petition for leave to appeal from a judgment of
the five-judge panel of the Appellate Court designated
to hear and decide cases involving review of Illinois
Workers' Compensation Commission orders shall be
filed, unless two or more judges of that panel join in a
statement that the case in question involves a substantial question which warrants consideration by the Supreme Court. A motion asking that such a statement
be filed may be filed as a prayer for alternative relief
in a petition for rehearing, but must, in any event, be
filed within the time allowed for filing a petition for
rehearing.

(b) Time.

(1) Published Decisions. Unless a timely petition
for rehearing is filed in the Appellate Court, a party
seeking leave to appeal must file the petition for
leave in the Supreme Court within 35 days after the
entry of such judgment. If a timely petition for
rehearing is filed, the party seeking review must file
the petition for leave to appeal within 35 days after
the entry of the order denying the petition for
rehearing. If a petition is granted, the petition for
leave to appeal must be filed within 35 days of the
entry of the judgment on rehearing. The Supreme
Court, or a judge thereof, on motion, may extend
the time for petitioning for leave to appeal, but such
motions are not favored and will be allowed only in
the most extreme and compelling circumstances.

(2) Rule 23 Orders. The time for filing a petition
for leave to appeal a Rule 23 order shall be the
same as for published opinions, except that if the
party who prevailed on an issue in the appellate
court timely files a motion to publish a Rule 23
order pursuant to Rule 23(f), and if the motion is
granted, a nonmoving party may file a petition for
leave to appeal within 35 days after the filing of the
published opinion. The filing of a Rule 23(f) publication motion shall not invalidate a previously filed
petition for leave to appeal.

(c) Contents. The petition for leave to appeal shall
contain, in the following order:

(1) a prayer for leave to appeal;

(2) a statement of the date upon which the judgment was entered; whether a petition for rehearing
was filed and, if so, the date of the denial of the
petition or the date of the judgment on rehearing;

(3) a statement of the points relied upon in asking the Supreme Court to review the judgment of
the Appellate Court;

(4) a fair and accurate statement of the facts, which shall contain the facts necessary to an understanding of the case, without argument or comment, with appropriate references to the pages of the record on appeal, *e.g.*, R. C7 or R. 7, or to the pages of the abstract, if one has been filed, *e.g.*, A. 7. Exhibits may be cited by references to pages of the record on appeal, or of the abstract, or by exhibit number followed by the page number within the exhibit, *e.g.*, Pl. Ex. 1, p. 6;

(5) a short argument (including appropriate authorities) stating why review by the Supreme Court is warranted and why the decision of the Appellate Court should be reversed or modified; and

(6) an appendix which shall include a copy of the opinion or order of the Appellate Court and any documents from the record which are deemed necessary to the consideration of the petition.

(d) Format; Service; Filing. The petition shall otherwise be prepared, duplicated, served, and filed in accordance with the requirements for briefs as set forth in Rules 341 through 343, except that it shall be limited to 20 pages, or alternatively 7,000 words, excluding only the appendix.

(e) Records; Abstracts. If an abstract has been filed in the Appellate Court, the petitioner shall file two or, if available, eight copies thereof in the Supreme Court, and for that purpose the clerk of the Appellate Court, when requested, shall release to the petitioner any available copies thereof. The clerk of the Supreme Court shall send notice of the filing of the petition to the clerk of the Appellate Court, who, upon request of the clerk of the Supreme Court made either before or after the petition is acted upon and at the expense of the petitioner, shall transmit to the clerk of the Supreme Court the record on appeal that was filed in the Appellate Court and a certified copy of the Appellate Court record. If leave to appeal is not granted, any certified papers and, to the extent available, copies of abstracts shall be returned forthwith to the clerk of the Appellate Court.

(f) Answer. The respondent need not but may file an answer, with proof of service, within 21 days after the expiration of the time for the filing of the petition, or within such further time as the Supreme Court or a judge thereof may grant within such 21–day period. An answer shall set forth reasons why the petition should not be granted, and shall conform, to the extent appropriate, to the form specified in this rule for the petition, omitting the items (1), (2), (3), (4) and (6) set forth in paragraph (c) except to the extent that correction of the petition is considered necessary. The answer shall be prepared, duplicated, served, and filed in accordance with the requirements for briefs except that it shall be limited to 20 pages, or alternatively 7,000 words, excluding only the appendix. No reply to the answer shall be filed. If the respondent does not file an answer or otherwise appear but wants notice of the disposition of the petition for leave to appeal, a letter requesting such notice should be directed to the clerk in Springfield.

(g) Abstracts; Transmittal of Trial Court Record if Petition Is Granted. If the petition is granted, and to the extent that copies have not already been filed, the appellant shall file 20 copies of the abstract, as filed in the Appellate Court, within the time for the filing of his or her brief. If no abstract was filed in the Appellate Court, but the Supreme Court so orders, an abstract shall be prepared and filed in accordance with Rule 342. Upon the request of any party made at any time before oral argument or upon direction of the Supreme Court, the clerk of the Appellate Court, at the expense of the petitioner, shall transmit to the Supreme Court the record on appeal that was filed in the Appellate Court and the Appellate Court record, if not already filed in the Supreme Court.

(h) Briefs. If leave to appeal is allowed, the appellant may allow his or her petition for leave to appeal to stand as the brief of appellant, or may file a brief in lieu of or supplemental thereto. Within 14 days after the date on which leave to appeal was allowed, appellant shall serve on all counsel of record a notice of election to allow the petition for leave to appeal to stand as the brief of appellant, or to file an additional brief, and within the same time shall file a copy of the notice with the clerk of the Supreme Court. If appellant elects to allow the petition for leave to appeal to stand as his or her brief, appellant shall file with the notice a complete table of contents, with page references, of the record on appeal and a statement of the applicable standard of review for each issue, with citation to authority, in accordance with Rule 341(h)(3). If appellant elects to file an additional brief, it shall be filed within 35 days from the date on which leave to appeal was allowed. Motions to extend the time for filing an additional brief are not favored and will be allowed only in the most extreme and compelling circumstances.

The appellee may allow his or her answer to the petition for leave to appeal to stand as the brief of appellee, or may file a brief in lieu of or supplemental thereto. If the appellant has elected to allow the petition for leave to appeal to stand as the brief of appellant, within 14 days after the due date of appellant's notice the appellee shall serve on all counsel of record a notice of election to let the answer stand as the brief of appellee, or to file an additional brief, and within the same time shall file a copy of the notice with the clerk of the Supreme Court. If the appellee elects to file an additional brief, such brief shall be filed within 35 days of the due date of appellant's notice of election to let the petition for leave to appeal stand as the brief of appellant.

If the appellant has elected to file an additional brief, within 14 days after the due date of appellant's brief the appellee shall serve on all counsel of record a notice of election to let his or her answer stand as the brief of appellee, or to file an additional brief, and within the same time shall file a copy of the notice with the clerk of the Supreme Court. If appellee elects to file an additional brief it shall be filed within 35 days of the due date of appellant's brief.

If an appellee files a brief, the appellant may file a reply brief within 14 days of the due date of appellee's brief. If the brief of appellee contains arguments in support of cross-relief, the appellant's arguments in opposition shall be included in the reply brief and the appellee may file a reply brief confined strictly to those arguments within 14 days of the due date of appellant's reply brief. If the brief of the appellee contains arguments in support of cross-relief, the cover of the brief shall be captioned: "Brief of Appellee. Cross–Relief Requested."

Briefs, pleadings and other documents filed with the Supreme Court in cases covered by this rule shall, to the extent appropriate, conform to Rules 341 through 343.

In cases involving more than one appellant or appellee, including cases consolidated for purposes of the appeal, any number of either may join in a single brief, and any appellant or appellee may adopt by reference any part of the brief of another. Parties may similarly join in reply briefs.

(i) Child custody cases. A petition for leave to appeal in a child custody or allocation of parental responsibilities case, as defined in Rule 311, and any notice, motion, or pleading related thereto, shall include the following statement in bold type on the top of the front page: THIS APPEAL INVOLVES A QUESTION OF CHILD CUSTODY, ALLOCATION OF PARENTAL RESPONSIBILITIES, ADOPTION, TERMINATION OF PARENTAL RIGHTS OR OTHER MATTER AFFECTING THE BEST INTERESTS OF A CHILD.

(j) Delinquent minor cases. A petition for leave to appeal in a delinquent minor case, as provided for in Rule 660A, and any notice, motion, or pleadings related thereto, shall include the following statement in bold type on the top of the front page: THIS APPEAL INVOLVES A DELINQUENT MINOR PROCEEDING UNDER THE JUVENILE COURT ACT.

(k) Oral Argument. Oral argument may be requested as provided in Rule 352(a).

Amended eff. Nov. 30, 1972; eff. Sept. 1, 1974; Oct. 1, 1976, eff. Nov. 15, 1976; Sept. 29, 1978, eff. Nov. 1, 1978; July 30, 1979, eff. Oct. 15, 1979; Feb. 19, 1982, eff. April 1, 1982; May 28, 1982, eff. July 1, 1982; Feb. 1, 1984, eff. Feb. 1, 1984, with Justice Moran dissenting (see *Yellow Cab Co. v. Jones* (1985), 108 Ill. 2d 330, 342); April 27, 1984, eff. July 1, 1984; Feb. 21, 1986, eff. August 1, 1986; Feb. 27, 1987, eff. April 1, 1987; April 7, 1993, eff. June 1, 1993; Dec. 17, 1993, eff. Feb. 1, 1994; Sept. 23, 1996, eff. immediately; Sept. 22, 1997, eff. Oct. 1, 1997; March 19, 2003, eff. May 1, 2003; Dec. 5, 2003, eff. immediately; Oct. 15, 2004, eff. Jan. 1, 2005; Feb. 10, 2006, effective July 1, 2006; May 24, 2006, eff. Sept. 1, 2006; Aug. 15, 2006, eff. immediately; Oct. 2, 2006, eff. immediately; Sept. 25, 2007, eff. Oct. 15, 2007; eff. Feb. 26, 2010; March 15, 2013, eff. May 1, 2013; May 23, 2013, eff. July 1, 2013; Dec. 11, 2014, eff. Jan. 1, 2015; Mar. 15, 2016, eff. immediately.

Formerly Ill.Rev.Stat.1991, ch. 110A, ¶ 315.

Committee Comments
(Revised April 27, 1984)

This rule and Rules 316–318 are a revision of former Rule 32, effective January 1, 1964, which in itself was a revision of an earlier Rule 32. Appeals by leave of the Supreme Court, by certificate of the Appellate Court, and as of right are treated separately in this rule and Rules 316 and 317. Rule 318 contains general provisions governing all appeals from the Appellate Court to the Supreme Court, taken from former Rules 32 and 39(2).

This rule deals with the usual situation in which review of decisions of the Appellate Court is discretionary with the Supreme Court. The rule makes explicit the considerations which normally will govern the granting of leave to appeal—the importance of the question, conflict with a decision of another Appellate Court or of the Supreme Court, or the need for the exercise of the Supreme Court's supervisory authority, and also whether the judgment is interlocutory or final. The practice is similar to the certiorari procedure in the United States Supreme Court, and the considerations are in the main the same, though adapted to the needs of the State court.

In 1984 paragraph (a) was amended to restrict the filing of petitions for leave to appeal from decisions of the five-judge division of the Appellate Court which hears and decides Industrial Commission cases. (See Comment to Rule 22(g).)

Paragraph (b), as adopted in 1967, changed slightly the time for filing the petition for leave to appeal, measuring the periods in multiples of seven and, in the cases in which no petition for rehearing is filed, from entry of the judgment appealed from rather than from the expiration of the time within which rehearing may be sought. Until 1982, 56 days were allowed if no petition for rehearing was filed and, in cases in which such a petition was filed, 35 days after the denial of the petition or the entry of judgment after rehearing. In that year the paragraph was amended to provide 35 days in each case. In prescribing the contents of the petition, it makes clear that the purpose is to state why the Supreme Court should take the case, and not merely to argue the case on the merits, though a statement as to why the decision below should be reversed is usually pertinent to the former question as well as the latter, as with the petition for certiorari in the United States Supreme Court. The court desires such petitions to be short documents that will enable it to decide whether to entertain the appeal. If such petitions were as long as full briefs on the merits, the purpose of the preliminary sifting procedure would be in substantial part defeated. It is expected that usually 10 or 15 pages will suffice and that more than 20 or 25 pages will seldom be necessary. Paragraph (b) was also amended in 1982 to permit a single justice of the Supreme Court to grant motions for extension of time.

In 1984 paragraph (d) was amended to eliminate a provision that allowed any party to request that the record on appeal be transmitted to the Supreme

Court. It appeared that many petitioners routinely asked that the record in the Appellate Court be forwarded to the Supreme Court at the time they filed their petition for leave to appeal. The trouble of transporting records which are not requested by the Supreme Court and the delays which have been experienced getting them returned to the Appellate Court suggested that only those records asked for by the clerk of the Supreme Court should be sent to the Supreme Court prior to the Court's granting the petition for leave to appeal. Paragraph (f) deals with transmittal of the record if the petition is granted.

The revision of paragraph (e) makes it clear that the respondent need not answer the petition for leave to appeal. Failure to answer will not be construed as a default.

Petitions for leave to appeal and answers thereto need no longer be printed. They may be reproduced in other clearly legible forms, as is provided for briefs in Rule 344. If eight copies of the excerpts or abstract in the form filed in the Appellate Court are available, they are to be filed with the fifteen copies of the petition for leave to appeal. This will enable each judge of the Supreme Court to have a copy at the time he reads the petition. In any event, at least two copies of the excerpts or abstracts must be filed with the petition. In order to prevent unnecessary and costly reproduction, the clerk of the Appellate Court should provide any party, on request, with copies of the excerpts or abstract filed in that court that are no longer needed there.

No copy of the trial court record or the Appellate Court record need be filed unless the Supreme Court calls for it, or one of the parties requests that it be filed.

When the rule was adopted in 1967, paragraph (g) referred to Rule 343 for the schedule for filing of briefs. In 1974, this paragraph was revised to set forth the schedule for the filing of notice of election to let the petition for leave to appeal or the answer stand as a brief, or to file a brief, and the schedule for the filing of the briefs. Under its provisions a party may elect to let his petition for leave to appeal or his answer thereto stand as his brief, or he may file a brief in compliance with Rule 341(e) and (f), or may file a brief supplementing the petition or answer in compliance with Rule 341(i), but must serve notice of his election upon the other parties and file a copy of the notice with the clerk. The appellant's notice must be served and the copy filed within 14 days after the date on which leave was allowed. If he elects to file a brief, it must be filed within 35 days of the date on which leave was allowed. In this circumstance the appellee must serve and file his notice of his election to let his answer stand as his brief, or to file a brief, within 14 days after the due date of appellant's brief, and if he elects to file a brief, must file it within 35 days after the due date of appellant's brief.

If the appellant elects to let his petition stand as his brief, the appellee must serve and file notice of his election to let his answer stand as his brief, or to file a brief, within 14 days after the due date of appellant's notice (28 days after the date on which leave was allowed), and if he elects to file a brief, he must file it within 35 days after the due date of appellant's notice (49 days after the date on which leave was allowed). Paragraph (g) was amended in 1982 to require that if the petitioner elects to allow his petition for leave to appeal to stand as his brief, he shall file with his notice of intention to do so a table of contents of the record on appeal such as would be included in the appendix to his brief. (See Rule 342(a).) If the appellee files a brief in addition to his answer, appellant may file a reply brief within 14 days after the due date of appellee's brief. If appellant wishes to respond to arguments in the answer to the petition, he should elect to file a brief in addition to his petition, since, if he does not and appellee elects to let his answer stand as his brief, no reply brief will be permitted.

The extension or shortening of the times set forth in paragraph (g) is governed by Rule 343(c). The provision for a stay of leave to appeal is granted, formerly in Rule 32(1)(h), is covered by Rule 368.

The penultimate paragraph of paragraph (g) was added in 1978 to make it clear that, to the extent appropriate, Rules 341 and 344 apply to briefs filed under Rule 315. This change effected no change in the practice.

In 1979, Rule 342 and related rules were amended to eliminate the requirement that an abstract or excerpts from the record be prepared and filed, but to preserve the authority of the reviewing court to order the preparation and filing of an abstract. Appropriate changes were made in Rule 315. (See the committee comments to Rule 342.) Because an inadequate statement of facts may require search in the record, of which, normally, there will be only one copy, Rule 315(b)(4) was amended to emphasize the duty of the parties to state the facts in their briefs fairly and accurately. A similar change was made in Rule 341(e)(6).

(December 17, 1993)

Paragraph (b) is amended to require the filing of an affidavit of intent within 21 days of the Appellate Court judgment on rehearing or the Appellate Court order denying a petition for rehearing in order to have 35 days to file the petition for leave to appeal in the Supreme Court. Previously an affidavit of intent was not required to obtain a 35–day period when a petition for rehearing was filed in the Appellate Court.

Paragraphs (c) and (e) were amended to limit petitions for leave to appeal and answers, excluding appendices, to 20 pages.

(September 23, 1996)

Paragraph (b) is amended to clarify that an affidavit of intent is filed with the Appellate Court.

(March 19, 2003)

Paragraph (b) is amended to require that the appendix of the petition for leave to appeal contain a copy of the affidavit of intent to seek review filed with the Appellate Court. This information will enable the Supreme Court to determine at the time a petition is submitted whether a properly executed affidavit was filed with the Appellate Court. See *Roth v. Illinois Farmers Insurance Co.*, 202 Ill. 2d 490 (2002).

(December 5, 2003)

Paragraph (b) is amended to include, as an alternative to a properly executed affidavit, a verification by certification under Section 1–109 of the Code of Civil Procedure of intent to file a petition for leave to appeal.

(February 10, 2006)

Paragraph (b) is amended to dispense with the requirement of filing an affidavit of intent to file a petition for leave to appeal or a certificate of intent to file a petition for leave to appeal. This amendment is consistent with the public policy of this state as evinced by the Code of Civil Procedure, which favors resolution on the merits: "This Act shall be liberally construed, to the end that controversies may be speedily and finally determined according to the substantive rights of the parties. 735 ILCS 5/1–106.

The amendment also addresses the concerns addressed in *A.J. Maggio Co. v. Willis*, 197 Ill. 2d 397 (2001), *Roth v. Illinois Farmers Insurance Co.*, 202 Ill. 2d 490 (2002), and *Wauconda Fire Prevention District v. Stonewall Orchards, LLP*, 214 Ill. 2d 417 (2005), all of which dealt with the rather unclear requirements of Rule 315, which had been amended in 1993 to require the filing of an affidavit of intent within 21 days in order to have 35 days in which to file a petition for leave to appeal.

Paragraph (b) is further amended to separate the provision on the time for filing a petition for leave to appeal, which remains in paragraph (b), from the provision on the content of the petition, which becomes a new paragraph (c). The subsequent paragraphs are relettered accordingly.

Paragraph (b) is also amended to allow a party that may not have sought Supreme Court review of an adverse disposition under Rule 23(b) or (c) the opportunity to seek review of that disposition after the Appellate Court grants a motion to publish it.

The May 23, 2013 amendment added par. (j), and renumbered former par. (j) as present par. (k).

Rule 316. Appeals from Appellate Court to Supreme Court on Certificate

Appeals from the Appellate Court shall lie to the Supreme Court upon the certification by the Appellate Court that a case decided by it involves a question of such importance that it should be decided by the Supreme Court. Application for a certificate of importance may be included in a petition for rehearing or may be made by filing four copies of a petition, clearly setting forth the grounds relied upon, with the clerk of the Appellate Court within 35 days after the entry of the judgment appealed from if no petition for rehearing is filed or, if a petition for rehearing is filed, within 14 days after the denial of the petition or the entry of the judgment on rehearing. An application for a certificate of importance does not extend the time for filing a petition for leave to appeal to the Supreme Court.

When the Appellate Court has granted a certificate of importance, the clerk of that court shall transmit to the clerk of the Supreme Court the record on appeal that was filed in the Appellate Court, with a certified copy of the Appellate Court record and opinions appended thereto, and the certificate of importance of the Appellate Court. The Appellate Court may require bond as a condition of granting a certificate of importance. The record shall be transmitted to the office of the clerk of the Supreme Court not later than 14 days from the date the certificate of importance is granted. Briefs shall be filed as provided in Rules 341 through 344. The appellant's brief shall contain a copy of the Appellate Court opinion. If an abstract was filed in the Appellate Court, 20 copies of the abstract shall be filed with the briefs, or if the Supreme Court so orders an abstract shall be prepared and filed in accordance with Rule 342.

Amended eff. July 30, 1979; Oct. 15, 1979; Dec. 17, 1993, eff. Feb. 1, 1994; Dec. 6, 2006, eff. immediately.

Formerly Ill.Rev.Stat.1991, ch. 110A, ¶ 316.

Committee Comments
(Revised 1979)

This rule providing for appeal by certificate of importance from the Appellate Court is former Rule 32(2) without change in substance except that the time for filing is slightly changed. It is measured in multiples of 7 days and the periods run from the date the judgment is entered. The revision makes it clear that application for a certificate of importance may be included in a petition for rehearing or may be filed separately within the time specified. It is important to notice, however, that the application does not extend the time for petitioning the Supreme Court to grant leave to appeal as a matter of discretion. It may therefore be more convenient and prudent, if a petition for rehearing is to be filed, to join the application for certificate of importance with the petition for rehearing.

In 1979, Rule 342 was amended to provide that, with the exception of stated documents (see Rule 342(a)), no portions of the record shall be reproduced, and that, absent an order of the reviewing court, no abstract shall be prepared and filed. The last sentence of Rule 316 was amended to reflect this change in the practice. See the committee comments to Rule 342.

(December 17, 1993)

It is well established that typewritten documents are accepted for filing in the reviewing courts and that professionally printed documents are not necessary.

The rule is amended to be consistent with the time frame of Rule 315(b).

Rule 317. Appeals from the Appellate Court to the Supreme Court as of Right

Appeals from the Appellate Court shall lie to the Supreme Court as a matter of right in cases in which a statute of the United States or of this state has been held invalid or in which a question under the Constitution of the United States or of this state arises for the first time in and as a result of the action of the Appellate Court. The appeal shall be initiated by filing a petition in the form prescribed by Rule 315, except that the petition shall be entitled "Petition for Appeal as a Matter of Right. Item (1) of the petition shall state that the appeal is taken as a matter of right and item (5) shall contain argument as to why appeal to the Supreme Court lies as a matter of right. In other respects the procedure is governed by Rule 315. If leave to appeal is to be sought in the alternative, the request therefor must be included in the same petition, and item (1) thereof shall include an alternative prayer for leave to appeal, and item (5) the argument as to why in the alternative leave to appeal should be allowed as a matter of sound judicial discretion. When both appeal as a matter of right and leave to appeal are sought, both requests will be disposed of by a single order. If the court allows the petition, briefs, and abstracts in cases in which they are required, shall be filed as provided in the case of appeal by leave under Rule 315.

Amended June 26, 1970, effective July 1, 1970; amended July 30, 1979, effective October 15, 1979; amended February 10, 2006, effective July 1, 2006.

Formerly Ill.Rev.Stat.1991, ch. 110A, ¶ 317.

Committee Comments
(Revised 1979)

This rule provides, in the language of the Constitution (art. VI, § 4(c)), for appeals as of right from the Appellate Court in cases in which "a question under the Constitution of the United States or of this State arises for the first time in and as a result of the action of the Appellate Court." The procedure in such cases will be similar to that provided in Rule 315 for petitions for leave to appeal, except that the petition need only contain argument as to why appeal lies to the Supreme Court as a matter of right. Prior to the adoption of this rule effective January 1, 1967, such appeals were taken by notice of appeal. (See former Rule 32(3).) The experience of the Supreme Court was that this procedure was often invoked improperly, a fact which the court would not usually discover until full briefs on the merits were filed and the case was scheduled for oral argument. The time of counsel and of the court is saved by giving the court an opportunity to determine this preliminary question on the basis of a petition filed in advance.

The rule was amended in June 1970 (a) to make mandatory the provision that if leave to appeal is to be sought in the alternative to appeal as of right, the requests for both alternatives are to appear in the same petition, and (b) to provide expressly that if there are requests for both an appeal as of right and an appeal by leave, the court will dispose of both requests in a single order.

In 1979, Rule 342 was amended to provide that, with the exception of stated documents (see Rule 342(a)), no portions of the record shall be reproduced, and that, absent an order of the reviewing court, no abstract shall be prepared and filed. The last sentence of Rule 317 was amended to reflect

this change in the practice. See the committee comments to Rule 342.

Rule 318. General Rules Governing All Appeals from the Appellate Court to the Supreme Court

(a) Relief to Other Parties. In all appeals, by whatever method, from the Appellate Court to the Supreme Court, any appellee, respondent, or coparty may seek and obtain any relief warranted by the record on appeal without having filed a separate petition for leave to appeal or notice of cross-appeal or separate appeal.

(b) Interlocutory Review. The review of cases at an interlocutory stage is not favored, and a failure to seek review when the Appellate Court's disposition of the case is not final does not constitute a waiver of the right to present any issue in the appropriate court thereafter.

(c) Appellate Court Briefs. If it is important for the Supreme Court to know the contentions of any party in the Appellate Court, copies of the pertinent Appellate Court briefs certified by the clerk of that court may be filed in the Supreme Court.

(d) Fees. In appeals taken from the Appellate Court, the clerk of that court is entitled to receive from the party appealing only the fees allowed by law for his certificate and copy of proceedings had in the Appellate Court and the reasonable cost of sending the record from the clerk's office, either by mail or express, to the clerk of the Supreme Court.

Amended Dec. 17, 1993, eff. Feb. 1, 1994.

Formerly Ill.Rev.Stat.1991, ch. 110A, ¶ 318.

Committee Comments

This rule is taken without major change from former Rules 32(1), 32(4), 32(5) and 39(2). Paragraph (c) differs from the last mentioned rule in that it dispenses with the need for obtaining leave of the Supreme Court in order to have briefs in the Appellate Court certified to the Supreme Court. In addition it deletes the requirement of former Rule 39 that the Appellate Court briefs shall be filed only "if it is important to know the position taken by any party in the Appellate Court."

Rules 319, 320. Reserved

PART C. RECORD ON APPEAL

Rule 321. Contents of the Record on Appeal

The record on appeal shall consist of the judgment appealed from, the notice of appeal, and the entire original common law record, unless the parties stipulate for, or the trial court, after notice and hearing, or the reviewing court, orders less. The common law record includes every document filed and judgment and order entered in the cause and any documentary exhibits offered and filed by any party. Upon motion the reviewing court may order that other exhibits be included in the record. The record on appeal shall also include any report of proceedings prepared in accordance with Rule 323. There is no distinction between the common law record and the report of proceedings for the purpose of determining what is properly before the reviewing court.

Amended eff. July 30, 1979; Oct. 15, 1979; Dec. 17, 1993, eff. Feb. 1, 1994.

Formerly Ill.Rev.Stat.1991, ch. 110A, ¶ 321.

Committee Comments
(Revised 1979)

As originally adopted, Rule 321 provided that the record on appeal consisted of "the judgment appealed from, the notice of appeal, and other parts of the trial court record designated in the praecipes." (36 Ill.2d R. 321.) Rule 322 set forth the procedure for the filing of praecipes by the parties designating the parts of the record to be included. In 1979 Rule 321 was amended to provide that unless the parties stipulate for less or the trial or reviewing court orders less, the entire original common law trial record will be transmitted to the reviewing court. Reference to praecipes was deleted, and Rule 322 was abrogated.

While Rule 321, as amended, permits the trial or the reviewing court, or the parties by stipulation, to order that less than the "entire original common law trial court record" be transmitted to the reviewing court, it makes it plain that such portions of the entire trial record as are transmitted should be original papers, and this is underscored by the deletion in Rule 324 of the provision permitting the trial or reviewing court to order otherwise, and the deletion in Rule 331 of the phrase "unless the record contains no original papers."

(December 17, 1993)

This rule is amended to describe the contents of the common law record, including any documentary exhibits in the trial court, and to provide that the reviewing court upon motion may order that other exhibits, including physical exhibits and evidence, be included in the record on appeal.

Rule 322. Repealed effective Oct. 15, 1979

Rule 323. Report of Proceedings

(a) Contents; Preparation. A report of proceedings may include evidence, oral rulings of the trial judge, a brief statement of the trial judge of the reasons for his decision, and any other proceedings that the party submitting it desires to have incorporated in the record on appeal. The report of proceedings shall include all the evidence pertinent to the issues on appeal. There shall be only a single report of proceedings if more than one appeal is taken.

Within the time for filing the docketing statement under Rule 312 the appellant shall make a written request to the court reporting personnel as defined in Rule 46 to prepare a transcript of the proceedings that appellant wishes included in the report of proceedings. Within 7 days after service on the appellee of the docketing statement and a copy of the request for transcript the appellee may serve on the appellant a designation of additional portions of the proceedings that the appellee deems necessary for inclusion in the report of proceedings. Within 7 days after service of such designation the appellant shall request the court reporting personnel to include the portions of the proceedings so designated or make a motion in the trial court for an order that such portions not be included unless the cost is advanced by the appellee.

The entire expense of incorporating unnecessary and immaterial matter in the report of proceedings may be assessed by the reviewing court as costs against the party who designated that matter, irrespective of how the appeal is decided.

(b) Certification and Filing. Court reporting personnel who transcribe a report of proceedings shall certify to its accuracy and shall notify all parties that the report of proceedings has been completed and is ready for filing. A report of proceedings may be filed without further certification if, within 14 days of the date on which notice of its completion was sent to the parties, no party has objected, citing alleged inaccuracies involving matters of substance. If objections are noted, the report of proceedings shall be submitted, upon notice given by the party seeking certification, to the judge before whom the proceedings occurred or the judge's successor (or if that is impossible because of the judge's absence or sickness or other disability, then, to any other judge of the court) for the judge's certificate of correctness of those items the accuracy of which has been disputed by any party, and shall be filed, duly certified, in the trial court within 49 days after the filing of the notice of appeal. If, however, the parties so stipulate, a report of proceedings may be filed without certification.

(c) Procedure If No Verbatim Transcript Is Available (Bystander's Report). If no verbatim transcript of the evidence of proceedings is obtainable the appellant may prepare a proposed report of proceedings from the best available sources, including recollection. In any trial court, a party may request from the court official any audiotape, videotape or other recording of the proceedings. The court official or any person who prepared and kept, in accordance with these rules, any audiotape, videotape, or other report of the proceedings shall produce a copy of such materials to be provided at the party's expense. Such material may be transcribed for use in preparation of a bystander's report. The proposed report shall be served on all parties within 28 days after the notice of appeal is filed. Within 14 days after service of the proposed report of proceedings, any other party may serve proposed amendments or an alternative proposed report of proceedings. Within 7 days thereafter, the appellant shall, upon notice, present the proposed report or reports and any proposed amendments to the trial court for settlement and approval. The court, holding hearings if necessary, shall promptly settle, certify, and order filed an accurate report of proceedings. Absent stipulation, only the report of proceedings so certified shall be included in the record on appeal.

(d) Agreed Statement of Facts. The parties by written stipulation may agree upon a statement of facts material to the controversy and file it without certification in lieu of and within the time for filing a report of proceedings.

(e) Extension of Time. The reviewing court or any judge thereof may extend the time for filing, in the trial court, the report of proceedings or agreed statement of facts or for serving a proposed report of proceedings, on notice and motion filed in the reviewing court before the expiration of the original or extended time, or on notice and motion filed within 35 days thereafter. Motions for extensions of time shall be supported by an affidavit showing the necessity for extension, and motions made after expiration of the original or extended time shall be further supported by a showing of reasonable excuse for failure to file the motion earlier. A copy of any motion for extension of time shall be served on the clerk preparing the record on appeal.

Amended eff. Oct. 21, 1969; Jan. 1, 1970; July 1, 1971; July 30, 1979; Oct. 15, 1979; Jan. 5, 1981, eff. Feb. 1, 1981; Feb. 19, 1982, eff. April 1, 1982; Oct. 25, 1990, eff. Nov. 1, 1990; Dec. 17, 1993, eff. Feb. 1, 1994; eff. Sept. 23, 1996; amended Dec. 13, 2005, eff. immediately.

Formerly Ill.Rev.Stat.1991, ch. 110A, ¶ 323.

Committee Comments
(Revised February 1982)

This rule is based upon former Rules 36(1)(c) and (d), and 36–1(3)(c), as they existed before 1967, with certain provisions added to make the paragraph a complete statement as to the contents of the report of proceedings and the procedure for having it approved and filed.

Paragraph (a)

Paragraph (a), as originally adopted, was based upon former Rule 36(1)(c). The provision that the report of proceedings shall include "all the evidence pertinent to the issues on appeal" was new. The second paragraph was added in 1979 and is designed to assure early settlement of the contents of the report of proceedings. Formerly the failure of the appellant to order necessary parts of the proceedings transcribed and included would not be apparent until the report of proceedings was presented to the trial judge for certification, which, under paragraph (b) could take place late in the 49 day period allowed for the filing of the report of proceedings. The new provision, patterned in part on Rule 10(b) of the Federal Rules of Appellate Procedure, gives the appellee early notice of any omissions and avoids the alternatives of late motions

for extension of time and over designation out of an abundance of caution, the first productive of unnecessary delay in the hearing of the appeal and the second unnecessary expense. See the committee comments to Rule 330.

Paragraph (b)

Paragraph (b) is also derived from former Rule 36(1)(c). The 49-day (instead of 50-day) time period follows the principle of multiples of seven. The words "in the trial court" were inserted in 1969 to state the existing practice. (See Rule 608(b).) In 1967, paragraph (b) was amended to provide for stipulations dispensing with the necessity of certification. The last sentence of this paragraph, added in 1969, is based upon Federal Rule of Appellate Procedure 11(a).

Paragraph (c)

Paragraph (c) is taken from former Rule 36–1(3)(c), which was included by the Illinois Supreme Court in Rule 36–1 as a part of the "expeditious and inexpensive" appeal procedure instituted May 18, 1964, in appeals from cases assignable to magistrates. The comments of the Illinois Supreme Court Rules Committee to Rule 36–1 (53 Ill.B.J. 18 (1964)) indicate the common-law background of the procedure outlined in this paragraph. The changes in substance in the revised paragraph are the deletion of the requirement that the trial court settle and certify the report and order it filed within 14 days after presentation in favor of an admonition that it do so "promptly", and the insertion of the words "holding hearings if necessary" in the last sentence to make explicit what was implied in the former rule. In 1971, the time within which the appellant's proposed report of proceedings must be served was increased from 7 to 14 days and the last sentence of the paragraph was added to make it explicit that after a report of proceedings has been settled or agreed upon, only that report is to be included in the record on appeal.

Paragraph (d)

Paragraph (d) is a simplified version of former Rule 36–1(d). If the parties agree upon a statement of facts, it is filed in lieu of the report of proceedings and the time requirements for the report of proceedings apply. The words "without certification" were added in 1971.

Paragraph (e)

Paragraph (e) is derived from the final paragraph of former Rule 36(1)(c). The main point of the 1981 amendment is to place the sole authority for granting extensions of time under this rule in the reviewing court. The rule contains a "safety valve" which did not appear in the former rule, allowing the court to extend the time on motion filed within 35 days after the expiration of the time for filing the report of proceedings, supported by a showing of reasonable excuse. The former rule allowed no relief, however compelling the circumstances, once the time period had expired. The last sentence, as amended in 1981, also contains a requirement that any motion for extension of time be supported by a showing of necessity. This is in line with the general policy of deciding cases on appeal expeditiously; unnecessary delay is not favored. In 1971, paragraph (e) was amended to make it explicit that the reviewing court may extend the time for serving a proposed report of proceedings under paragraph (c) as well as for filing the report of proceedings. This amendment is consonant with other amendments made in 1979 placing in the reviewing court the general supervision of the progress of the appeal. See the committee comments to Rule 303(f).

(December 17, 1993)

Paragraph (a) is amended to require that the appellant's written request for preparation of the report of proceedings be made within the applicable time for filing the docketing statement under new Rule 312. Previously the request was to be made within 14 days of the filing of the notice of appeal regardless of whether the appeal was direct or interlocutory in nature. The requirement that appellant serve notice of the request upon all parties is now contained in Rule 312. The provision for assessment of costs of incorporating unnecessary matters was taken from former Rule 330.

Paragraph (c), as amended, now contains the appellation "Bystander's Report," clarifies that the proposed report of proceedings shall be served on all parties, and reallocates the times for preparing and serving the proposed report and any proposed amendments or alternative report, without lengthening the overall time for the procedure.

Rule 324. Preparation and Certification by the Circuit Clerk of the Record on Appeal

The clerk of the trial court shall prepare, bind, and certify the record on appeal. The record shall be arranged in three sections: the common law record, the report of proceedings, and the trial exhibits. The common law record and report of proceedings shall be in chronological order. Beginning with the common law record, each separately bound volume of the common law record and report of proceedings shall be numbered consecutively. All pages of the common law record shall be numbered consecutively with the letter "C" preceding the number of each page. All pages of the report of proceedings shall be numbered consecutively by volume. In lieu of renumbering the pages of exhibits, a list of exhibit numbers shall be provided. No bound volume of the record shall exceed 250 pages, and each volume shall be securely bound. There shall be only one record on appeal even if more than one appeal is taken. The certificate shall be in the form prescribed below, and a copy shall be delivered to appellant at the time the record is forwarded to the reviewing court. The clerk shall accept for inclusion in the record or a supplemental record an original or a copy of any filing that carries a filing stamp of the clerk of the circuit court without any need for further authentication. Notice of filing must be given to all parties of record.

Appeal to the _____ Court of Illinois

_____ District

From the Circuit Court of the _____ Judicial Circuit

_____ County, Illinois

[Names of all plaintiffs, including intervening plaintiffs]

v.

Circuit Court No. _____
Trial Judge _____
Reviewing Court No. _____

[Names of all defendants, including intervening or impleaded defendants]

(The designations of appellant, appellee, cross-appellant, and cross-appellee may be added to follow the trial court designations. If not all plaintiffs or all defendants are appellants or appellees, the names of those who are should be included parenthetically just below the title.)

CERTIFICATION OF RECORD

The record has been prepared and certified in the form required for transmission to the reviewing court. It consists of:

_____ volume/s of Common Law Record

_____ volume/s of Report of Proceedings

_____ volume/s or description of Exhibits

(Here set forth a detailed table of contents of the record on appeal.)

Kindly acknowledge receipt of this record on the attached copy of this letter.

I do further certify that this certification of the record pursuant to Supreme Court Rule 324 issued out of my office this _____ day of _____, 20 ___.

_____
Clerk of the Circuit Court

cc: _____

Appellant's Attorney

_____

Address

_____

City, State & Zip

Received this above record this _____ day of _____, 20 ___.

_____

Clerk of the Reviewing
Court

Amended Oct. 21, 1969, eff. Jan. 1, 1970; July 30, 1979, eff. Oct. 15, 1979; July 1, 1985, eff. Aug. 1, 1985; April 10, 1987, eff. Aug. 1, 1987; Dec. 17, 1993, eff. Feb. 1, 1994; May 30, 2008, eff. immediately; Oct. 15, 2015, eff. Jan. 1, 2016.

Formerly Ill.Rev.Stat.1991, ch. 110A, ¶ 324.

Committee Comments
(Revised July 30, 1979)

This rule was based in part on former Rules 36(1)(b) and (2)(a), and was in part new in 1967. As originally adopted, it provided in part that "[u]nless otherwise ordered by the trial or reviewing court, the original papers in the trial court record shall be used and copies need not be furnished by the parties." Thus the use of the original papers was permissive, though the contemplation was that in most instances original papers would be used. In 1979 this provision was deleted and Rule 321 was amended to provide that the record on appeal shall consist of the "entire original trial court record," unless the parties stipulate for or the trial or reviewing court orders "less." See the committee comments to Rule 321.

Commentary
(December 17, 1993)

This rule is amended to explain more specifically the manner in which the record on appeal shall be prepared. The circuit clerk now is required to provide the reviewing court with an inventory of exhibits, and the rule establishes a 250–page limit per volume of record to make the record easier to use.

Rule 325. Transmission of Record on Appeal or Certificate in Lieu of Record

Upon payment of the estimated prescribed fee, and estimated transportation costs, the clerk shall transmit the record to the reviewing court or, upon request, deliver it to the appellant for transmission. At the request of any party, to facilitate work on the appeal, the clerk of the trial court shall deliver to the reviewing court a certificate that the record has been prepared and certified in the form required for transmission to the reviewing court. The timely filing of the certificate in the reviewing court shall be considered the filing of the record on appeal. The certificate in lieu of record shall be in the following form:

Appeal to the _____ Court of
Illinois _____ District

From the Circuit Court of the _____ Judicial
Circuit _____ County, Illinois

[Names of all plaintiffs,
including intervening plaintiffs]

	Circuit Court No. _____
v.	Trial Judge _____
	Reviewing Court No. _____

[Names of all defendants,
including intervening or
impleaded defendants]

(The designations of appellant, appellee, cross-appellant, and cross-appellee may be added to follow the trial court designations. If not all plaintiffs or all defendants are appellants or appellees, the names of those who are should be included parenthetically just below the title.)

CERTIFICATE IN LIEU OF RECORD

I, _____, clerk of the circuit court in said county and State and keeper of the records, files, and seal of the court, do hereby certify that the record on appeal in the above-captioned matter has been prepared and certified in the form required for transmission to the reviewing court.

(Here set forth a detailed table of contents of the record on appeal.)

I further certify that the record on appeal has this date been delivered to _____.

_____

_____

_____

I do further certify that this certificate in lieu of record pursuant to Supreme Court Rule 325 issued out of my office this _____ day of _____, 20 ___.

_____
Clerk of the Circuit Court

Amended October 21, 1969, effective January 1, 1970; amended July 1, 1985, effective August 1, 1985; April 10, 1987, effective August 1, 1987; December 17, 1993, effective February 1, 1994; May 30, 2008, effective immediately.

Formerly Ill.Rev.Stat.1991, ch. 110A, ¶ 325.

Committee Comments
(Revised October 21, 1969)

This rule, based on former Rules 36(2)(c) and 36–1(4), with some additions and changes, recognizes the existing practice of transmission of the record to the reviewing court by a party and affirmatively requires the clerk to deliver the record to the appellant for transmission upon request and payment of the prescribed fee. If such a request is not made but the fee is paid, the clerk is to transmit the record himself. The procedure provided for in the second and third sentences of this rule for filing a certificate in lieu of the record was initiated in 1964 by former Rule 36–1(4) for cases assignable to magistrates. The new procedure eliminates the wasteful and time consuming step of sending the record to the reviewing court and then immediately having it sent back to the appellant, who normally needs it to prepare the excerpts from record or abstract and his brief. The requirement of filing the record can be met under the new rule by the filing of the certificate obtained from the clerk of the trial court. The appellant can then retain the record on appeal and either file it with his brief or, as will often be convenient, turn it over to the appellee for the latter's use during the writing of his brief. Rule 326 requires that the record be delivered to the reviewing court at the time the reply brief is due or earlier if the reviewing court so orders.

The requirement that a copy of the notice of appeal be sent to the clerk of the reviewing court with the certificate, added in 1969, is for the convenience of the clerk. Failure to comply, or late compliance, with this requirement would not affect the timeliness of the filing of the certificate.

(December 17, 1993)

Rule 325 is amended to require the clerk of the circuit court to deliver the certificate in lieu of record directly to the reviewing court for filing, which is consistent with the circuit clerk's responsibility of delivering the record to the reviewing court. Previously, the certificate was delivered to appellant, who then had the responsibility of filing it with the reviewing court, a circuitous procedure. The provision that a copy of a notice of appeal be sent to the reviewing court with the certificate is eliminated as unnecessary because the reviewing court already would have received the notice of appeal under Rules 303 or 307.

Rule 326. Time for Filing Record on Appeal

Except as provided in Rules 306, 307, 308 and 335, the record on appeal or certificate in lieu thereof shall be filed in the reviewing court within 63 days after the filing of the notice of appeal, or the last notice of appeal if more than one appeal is taken, or, if the time for filing a report of proceedings has been extended, within 14 days after the expiration of the extended time. If a certificate is filed in lieu of the record, the appellant, or the trial court clerk at appellant's request, shall deliver the record to the reviewing court at the time the reply brief is due or earlier if the reviewing court so orders. Extensions of time for filing the record or certificate may be granted by the reviewing court or a judge thereof on motion made before the expiration of the original or extended time or on motion filed within 35 days thereafter supported by a showing of reasonable excuse for failure to file the motion earlier. The movant shall serve a copy of any motion for extension of time on the clerk preparing the record on appeal.

Amended eff. Oct. 21, 1969; Jan. 1, 1970; Dec. 17, 1993, eff. Feb. 1, 1994.

Formerly Ill.Rev.Stat.1991, ch. 110A, ¶ 326.

Committee Comments
(Revised October, 1969)

This rule is based on former Rule 36(2)(d) and (e). Provision is made for the certificate procedure. Time periods are in multiples of seven. The 35-day "safety-valve" provision is similar to the one applicable to the report of proceedings in Rule 323(e).

The insertion in 1969 of the words "or the last notice of appeal if more than one appeal is taken" in the first sentence is based upon Federal Rule of Appellate Procedure 11(a). The 1969 amendment to the rule also requires the delivery of the record to the reviewing court at the time the reply brief is due rather than 14 days thereafter, as formerly.

Rule 327. Notice of Filing Record

Upon the filing of the record on appeal or the certificate in lieu of record, whichever occurs first, the clerk of the reviewing court shall provide notice of filing to all parties to the appeal.

Amended eff. Oct. 21, 1969; Jan. 1, 1970; July 30, 1979; Oct. 15, 1979; July 1, 1985, eff. Aug. 1, 1985; Dec. 17, 1993, eff. Feb. 1, 1994.

Formerly Ill.Rev.Stat.1991, ch. 110A, ¶ 327.

Committee Comments
(Revised July 1, 1985)

This rule requires that upon filing the record on appeal in the reviewing court the appellant shall serve notice of the filing on the other parties to the appeal and send a copy of the notice to the reviewing court. This notice is important because the briefing schedule is framed in terms of the due date of the briefs rather than the date of service of each successive brief, and the due date of the first brief is marked in terms of the date on which the record is filed. Until 1979, it was provided in this rule that after the filing of the record and the payment of the prescribed fee the case should be docketed and that the notice include the docket number. These provisions were eliminated in that year because of the provision in amended Rule 303(f) for the docketing of the appeal at an earlier stage of the proceedings. (See the committee comments to Rule 303(f).) Notice of the docket number is no longer required because it will appear on the docketing statement served under Rule 303(g).

The 1985 change is intended to make the automated record-keeping system in the appellate and supreme courts operate more smoothly.

(December 17, 1993)

This amendment simplifies and clarifies the notification process by requiring the clerk of the reviewing court to give notice of the filing of the record on appeal or certificate in lieu of record to all parties.

Rule 328. Supporting Record

Any party seeking relief from the reviewing court before the record on appeal is filed shall file with his or her application an appropriate supporting record containing enough of the trial court record to show an appealable order or judgment, a timely filed and served notice of appeal (if required for appellate jurisdiction), and any other matter necessary to the application made. The supporting record must be authenticated by the certificate of the clerk of the trial court or by the affidavit of the attorney or party filing it. The supporting record shall bear a cover page with a caption of the appeal. The cover page shall be clearly labelled "Supporting Record." The numbering of volumes and pages of the supporting record shall conform to the requirements of Rule 324.

Adopted Dec. 17, 1993, eff. Feb. 1, 1994.

Committee Comments

(December 17, 1993)

The new rule on supporting record is an adaptation of former Rule 328, "Short Record," which was repealed in 1979 and incorporated into Rule 361. This rule provides the requirements for a uniform, limited supporting record, which a party is required to file in various situations under a number of different rules.

Rule 329.   Supplemental Record on Appeal

The record on appeal shall be taken as true and correct unless shown to be otherwise and corrected in a manner permitted by this rule. Material omissions or inaccuracies or improper authentication may be corrected by stipulation of the parties or by the trial court, either before or after the record is transmitted to the reviewing court, or by the reviewing court or a judge thereof. Any controversy as to whether the record accurately discloses what occurred in the trial court shall be submitted to and settled by that court and the record made to conform to the truth. If the record is insufficient to present fully and fairly the questions involved, the requisite portions may be supplied at the cost of the appellant. If necessary, a supplemental record may be certified and transmitted. The clerk of the circuit court shall prepare a bound and certified supplemental record which shall be filed in the reviewing court upon order issued pursuant to motion.

Amended May 28, 1982, eff. July 1, 1982; amended October 14, 2005, eff. January 1, 2006.

Formerly Ill.Rev.Stat.1991, ch. 110A, ¶ 329.

Committee Comments

(Revised May 1982)

This rule is a comprehensive provision covering amendment of the record on appeal, correction of improper authentication, and the settling of any questions concerning whether the record conforms to the truth. It contains portions of former Rule 36(3) and (4). Under this sweeping provision, it will be possible to supply omissions, correct inaccuracies or improper authentication, or settle any controversy as to whether the record on appeal accurately discloses what occurred at the trial by the procedure that will most appropriately solve the particular problem. In view of the liberal terms of this paragraph, the rather elaborate provisions of former Rule 36(4), requiring that a claim as to improper authentication be raised by motion before or at the time of the filing of the brief of the party making the claim, were eliminated as no longer necessary. Unless there is some real prejudice involved, there will be no incentive for claiming improper authentication.

Rule 329 was amended in 1982 to permit a single judge of the reviewing court to correct the record.

Rule 330.   Captions in Reviewing Courts

(a) Any document, other than a brief (see Rule 341(b)) or a preprinted form, filed in a reviewing court shall contain a caption that includes:

(1) the number of the case in the reviewing court;

(2) the name of the reviewing court, with identification of district and division, where applicable;

(3) the name of the case as it appeared in the trial court, except that the status of each party in the reviewing court shall also be indicated (e. g., plaintiff-appellant). In the case of an action for direct review in the appellate court of a final administrative decision, the parties shall be designated as petitioner(s) and respondent(s) (see Rule 335);

(4) the name of the court (or agency) from which the case was brought and the docket number in that court (or agency), and when applicable in the Supreme Court, the name of the court (or agency) where the case originated and the docket number in that court (or agency);

(5) the name of the trial judge entering the judgment to be reviewed; and

(6) the title of the document.

(b) In all appeals filed from proceedings under the Mental Health and Developmental Disabilities Code,[1] the Mental Health and Developmental Disabilities Confidentiality Act,[2] or from actions for collection of fees for mental health services, the recipient of services shall be identified by first name and last initial or by initials only. The preferred method is first name and last initial. The alternative method of initials only is to be used when, due to an unusual first name or spelling, the preferred method would create a substantial risk of revealing the recipient's identity. The name of the involved recipient of services shall not appear on any documents filed with the Appellate Court or any subsequent court.

Adopted Dec. 17, 1993, eff. Feb. 1, 1994; amended eff. Oct. 1, 2001.

[1] 405 ILCS 5/1–100 et seq.
[2] 740 ILCS 110/1 et seq.

Committee Commentary [New Rule 330]

This rule has been added to encourage uniformity and requires the use of complete captions on virtually all documents filed in the reviewing court.

Paragraph (b) was added effective October 1, 2001, to help protect the identities of recipients of mental health services. The amendment requires that only their first name and last initial, or their initials, appear on documents filed with the Appellate Court or any subsequent court. The requirement covers the parties' briefs, motions, and other similar papers. The amendment does not require deletion of names from the trial record in preparing the record on appeal, nor does it address the means by which the Appellate Court or a subsequent court maintains the confidentiality of documents appearing in the record.

Committee Commentary [Repealed Rule 330]
(December 17, 1993)

The provisions of this former rule have been incorporated into Rule 323(a).

Rule 331. Return of Record on Appeal

The record on appeal shall be returned by the clerk of the reviewing court to the clerk of the trial court after the final decision of the reviewing court.

Amended eff. July 30, 1979; Oct. 15, 1979.

Formerly Ill.Rev.Stat.1991, ch. 110A, ¶ 331.

Committee Comments
(Revised 1979)

As originally adopted this rule provided that the record should be returned "unless the record contains no original papers." It was thought at the time that while the record normally would consist primarily of original papers, there would be occasions when the trial court would order otherwise or because in the county in which the trial court sat it was considered desirable to keep original papers available for title searches. In 1979, Rule 321 was amended to provide that the record on appeal shall consist of the entire original common law trial record, unless the parties stipulate for less or the trial or reviewing court orders "less." Thus there will be no case in which the record contains no original papers and the phrase quoted above was deleted.

Rules 332 to 334. Reserved

Rule 335. Direct Review of Administrative Orders by the Appellate Court

The procedure for a statutory direct review of orders of an administrative agency by the Appellate Court shall be as follows:

(a) The Petition for Review. Unless another time period is provided specifically by the law authorizing review, the petition for review shall be filed in the Appellate Court within 35 days from the date that a copy of the order or decision sought to be reviewed was served upon the party affected by any order or decision of the administrative agency, and shall specify the parties seeking review and shall designate the respondent and the order or part thereof to be reviewed. The agency and all other parties of record shall be named respondents. The form of the petition shall be as follows:

IN THE APPELLATE COURT OF ILLINOIS
FOR THE _____ DISTRICT

[Name of Petitioner],
    Petitioner,

v.   Petition for Review
[Names of Agency and Other of Order of the
Parties of Record],[(1)]   [Name of Agency]
    Respondent.   And Docket Number

[Name of Petitioner] hereby petitions the court for review of the order [or part of the order] of the [name of agency] which [describe the order or part as to which review is sought] entered on _____, 19 __

_____

Attorney for Petitioner
Address:

(b) Service. The petitioner shall serve the petition for review on the agency and on all other parties of record to the proceeding before the agency in the manner prescribed for serving and proving service of a notice of appeal in Rule 303(c).

(c) Other Parties. If any respondent other than the agency wishes to participate in the proceeding in the Appellate Court, that respondent shall file a written appearance, and those who do shall be parties in the Appellate Court.

(d) The Record. The entire record before the administrative agency shall be the record on review unless the agency and the petitioner stipulate to omit portions. Omitted portions shall be transmitted to the Appellate Court at any time on the request of the agency, the petitioner or any other party, which request shall be served on all parties, or on order of the court. Either the original or a certified copy of the record shall be filed with the Appellate Court. As near as may be possible, the record shall contain, be arranged, prepared, bound, numbered and certified as required for the record on appeal under Rules 321 through 325.

(e) Time for Filing Record.

(1) The agency shall file the record or the certificate described in subparagraph (2) within 35 days after the filing of the petition for review. Extensions of time for filing the record or certificate may be granted by the reviewing court or a judge thereof on motion made before the expiration of the original or extended time or on motion filed within 35 days thereafter supported by a showing of reasonable excuse for failure to file the motion earlier.

(2) In lieu of filing the record within the time specified in subparagraph (1), the agency may, for the purpose of aiding the parties in preparation of briefs, excerpts or abstracts, file with the reviewing court a certificate that the record has been prepared and is available in the form prescribed by paragraph (d). The timely filing of the certificate in the reviewing court shall be considered the filing of the record.

(3) If a certificate is filed in lieu of the record, the record shall be filed no later than the date upon which the reply brief is due or earlier if the reviewing court so orders.

(f) Time for Filing Briefs. The time for filing briefs specified in Rule 343 begins to run from the day the record or the certificate in lieu thereof is filed.

(g) Stay. Application for a stay of a decision or order of an agency pending direct review in the Appellate Court shall ordinarily be made in the first instance to the agency. A motion for stay may be made to the Appellate Court or to a judge thereof, but the motion shall show that application has been made to the agency and denied, with the reasons, if any, given by it for denial, or that application to the agency for the relief sought was not practicable. The motion shall also show the reasons for the relief requested and the facts relied upon, and if the facts are subject to dispute the motion shall be supported by affidavit. With the motion shall be filed such parts of the record as are relevant to the relief sought. Reasonable notice of the motion shall be given to all parties to the proceeding in the Appellate Court. The court may condition relief under this rule upon the filing of a bond or other appropriate security.

(h) In any proceeding for the review of a decision by the Illinois State Labor Relations Board, the Illinois Local Labor Relations Board, or the Illinois Educational Labor Relations Board, a cross-petition for enforcement may be filed by the Board in accordance with the procedures set forth in Rule 361 governing motion practice in the Appellate Court, except that no proposed order shall be submitted.

(i) Application of other Rules and Administrative Review Law.

(1) Insofar as appropriate, the provisions of Rules 301 through 373 (except for Rule 326) are applicable to proceedings under this rule. As used in any applicable rule, the term "appellant" includes a petitioner and the term "appellee" includes a respondent in proceedings to review or enforce agency orders.

(2) Sections 3–101, 3–108(c), 3–109, 3–110, and 3–111 of the Code of Civil Procedure are applicable to proceedings to review orders of the agency. The Appellate Court has all of the powers which are vested in the circuit court by the above enumerated sections.

(j) Return of the Record on Appeal. The record on appeal shall be returned by the clerk of the reviewing court to the clerk of the administrative agency after the final decision of the reviewing court.

Adopted eff. July 1, 1971. Amended May 28, 1982, eff. July 1, 1982; April 27, 1984, eff. July 1, 1984; Dec. 17, 1993, eff. Feb. 1, 1994; Oct. 15, 2015, eff. Jan. 1, 2016.

Formerly Ill.Rev.Stat.1991, ch. 110A, ¶ 335.

Committee Comments
(Revised December 17, 1993)

The General Assembly has provided by law that a final order of the Pollution Control Board (415 ILCS 5/41 (West 1992)), a judgment concerning disclosure of campaign contributions and expenditures from the State Board of Elections (10 ILCS 5/9–22 (West 1992)), a final order of the Illinois State Labor Relations Board, Illinois Local Labor Relations Board (5 ILCS 315/11 (West 1992)) or the Illinois Educational Labor Relations Board (115 ILCS 5/16 (West 1992)), a decision from the Illinois Human Rights Commission (775 ILCS 5/8–111 (West 1992)), any order or decision of the Illinois Commerce Commission (220 ILCS 5/10–201 (West 1992)), final orders of the Illinois Gaming Board (230 ILCS 10/17.1 (West 1992)), final decisions of the Property Tax Appeal Board where a change in assessed valuation of $300, 000 or more was sought (35 ILCS 205/111.4 (West 1992 Supp.)) and a certain initial license issuance by the Director of the Department of Nuclear Safety and in connection therewith certain determinations of the Low–Level Radioactive Waste Disposal Facility Siting Commission (420 ILCS 20/8 (West 1992)) may be appealed directly to the Appellate Court.

Rule 335 prescribes the procedure for the review of orders of any agency which the legislature has assigned to the Appellate Court.

The rule is based upon the procedures followed under the Administrative Review Act, the Illinois rules governing appeals, and the Federal Rules of Appellate Procedure which relate to review of administrative orders by an appellate court. The orders of many Federal agencies have long been directly reviewed by the United States Courts of Appeals.

Only a few provisions of the rule require comment.

Since the petition for review serves the function of the notice of appeal, and nothing else, it should in form be as simple as the notice of appeal, as it is in the Federal practice. The statement of the questions to be presented for review is left to the appellant's brief as in other appeals and for the same reasons.

The Illinois practice of permitting parties before the administrative agency to become parties before the Appellate Court merely on filing of a notice of appearance is preferable to the Federal practice of requiring a motion to intervene.

Under both Illinois and Federal appellate practice and under the Illinois Administrative Review Act the entire record before the agency is the record before the reviewing court, wherever that record may be at any particular time. The rule is designed to insure that the record will be available to the parties when needed for the preparation of briefs, as under present Rule 325 for ordinary appeals, and to the reviewing court when it is needed there. Any portions of the record not already filed in the Appellate Court shall be transmitted thereto on request of the court, the agency, or any party. Since the report of the proceedings before the administrative agency will normally have been transcribed and be available by the time of the administrative decision, a shorter period for filing the record is allowed than in other Illinois appeals. This also conforms to the public interest in expediting review of these cases.

In 1984 subparagraph (d) was amended to require that the agency should arrange, prepare, bind, and certify the record, as near as possible, in the way the record on appeal must be prepared under Rule 324.

Commentary
(December 17, 1993)

Paragraph (h) is included to indicate that petitions for enforcement of labor board orders may be brought in the Appellate Court (see *Central City Education Association v. Illinois Educational Labor Relations Board* (1992), 149 Ill. 2d 496) and are treated as motions before the reviewing court without the need for formal briefing.

Rules 336 to 340. Reserved

PART D. BRIEFS

Rule 341. Briefs

(a) Form of Briefs. Briefs shall be produced in clear, black print on white, opaque, unglazed paper, 8½ by 11 inches, and paginated. Only one side of the paper may be used. The text must be double-spaced; however, headings may be single-spaced. Margins must be at least 1½ inch on the left side and 1 inch on the other three sides. Briefs shall be safely and securely bound on the left side in a manner that does not obscure the text. Quotations of two or more lines in length may be single-spaced; however, lengthy quotations are not favored and should be included only where they will aid the court's comprehension of the argument. Footnotes are discouraged but, if used, may be single-spaced.

Documents may be produced by a word-processing system, typewritten, or commercially printed, and reproduced by any process that provides clear copies consistent with the requirements of this rule. Typeface must be 12–point or larger throughout the document, including quoted material and any footnotes. Condensed type is prohibited. Carbon copies are not permitted.

(b) Length of Briefs.

(1) Length Limitation. The brief of appellant and brief of appellee shall each be limited to 50 pages, and the reply brief to 20 pages. Alternatively, the brief of appellant and brief of appellee shall each be limited to no more than 15,000 words, and the reply brief to 7,000 words. This length limitation excludes pages and words contained in the Rule 341(d) cover, the Rule 341(h)(1) statement of points and authorities, the Rule 341(c) certificate of compliance, the certificate of service, and those matters to be appended to the brief under Rule 342(a). Cross-appellants and cross-appellees shall each be allowed an additional 30 pages, or alternatively 8,400 words, and the cross-appellant's reply brief shall not exceed 20 pages, or alternatively 7,000 words.

(2) Motions. Motions to file a brief in excess of the length limitation of this rule are not favored. Such a motion shall be filed not less than 10 days before the brief is due or not less than 5 days before a reply brief is due and shall state the excess number of pages or words requested and the specific grounds establishing the necessity for excess pages or words. The motion shall be supported by affidavit or verification by certification under Section 1–109 of the Code of Civil Procedure of the attorney or unrepresented party. Any affidavit shall be sworn to before a person who has authority under the law to administer oaths.

(c) Certificate of Compliance. The attorney or unrepresented party shall submit with the brief his or her signed certification that the brief complies with the form and length requirements of paragraphs (a) and (b) of this rule, as follows:

I certify that this brief conforms to the requirements of Rules 341(a) and (b). The length of this brief, excluding the pages or words contained in the Rule 341(d) cover, the Rule 341(h)(1) statement of points and authorities, the Rule 341(c) certificate of compliance, the certificate of service, and those matters to be appended to the brief under Rule 342(a), is ___ pages or words.

(d) Covers. The cover of the brief shall contain: the number of the case in the reviewing court and the name of that court; the name of the court or administrative agency from which the case was brought; the name of the case as it appeared in the lower tribunal, except that the status of each party in the reviewing court shall also be indicated (*e.g.*, plaintiff–appellant); the name of the trial judge entering the judgment to be reviewed; and the individual names and addresses of the attorneys and their law firm (or of the party if the party has no attorney) filing the brief shall also be stated.

The colors of the covers of the documents shall be: abstract, gray; appellant's brief or petition, white; appellee's brief or answer, light blue; appellant's reply brief, light yellow; reply brief of appellee, light red; petition for rehearing, light green; answer to petition for rehearing, tan; and reply on rehearing, orange. If a separate appendix is filed, the cover shall be the same color as that of the brief which it accompanies.

(e) Number of Copies To Be Filed and Served; Proof of Service. Except as provided hereafter nine copies of each brief shall be filed in appeals to the Appellate Court. In proceedings in the Appellate Court to review orders of the Illinois Workers' Compensation Commission, 15 copies of each brief shall be filed. In appeals to the Supreme Court, 20 copies of each brief shall be filed. Three copies (or one copy if by email service) shall be served upon each other party to the appeal represented by separate counsel. If the Attorney General and the State's Attorney both appear for a party, each shall be served with three copies (or one copy if by e-mail service). Proof of service shall be filed with all briefs.

(f) References to Parties. In the brief the parties shall be referred to as in the trial court, *e.g.*, plaintiff and defendant, omitting the words appellant and appellee and petitioner and respondent, or by using actual names or descriptive terms such as "the employee," "the injured person," "the taxpayer," "the railroad," etc.

In all appeals involving juveniles filed from proceedings under the Juvenile Court Act or the Adoption Act, and in all appeals under the Mental Health and Developmental Disabilities Code,[1] the Mental Health and Developmental Disabilities Confidentiality Act,[2] or from actions for collection of fees for mental health services, the respective juvenile or recipient of mental-health services shall be identified by first name and last initial or by initials only.

The preferred method is the first name and last initial. The alternative method of initials only is to be used when, due to an unusual first name or spelling, the preferred method would create a substantial risk of revealing the individual's identity. The name of the involved juvenile or recipient of services shall not appear in the brief.

(g) Citations. Citations shall be made as provided in Rule 6.

(h) Appellant's Brief. The appellant's brief shall contain the following parts in the order named:

(1) A summary statement, entitled "Points and Authorities," of the points argued and the authorities cited in the Argument. This shall consist of the headings of the points and subpoints as in the Argument, with the citation under each heading of the authorities relied upon or distinguished, and a reference to the page of the brief on which each heading and each authority appear. Cases shall be cited as near as may be in the order of their importance.

(2) An introductory paragraph stating (i) the nature of the action and of the judgment appealed from and whether the judgment is based upon the verdict of a jury, and (ii) whether any question is raised on the pleadings and, if so, the nature of the question.

Illustration:

"This action was brought to recover damages occasioned by the alleged negligence of the defendant in driving his automobile. The jury rendered a verdict for the plaintiff upon which the court entered the judgment from which this appeal is taken. No questions are raised on the pleadings."

(3) A statement of the issue or issues presented for review, without detail or citation of authorities.

Illustration:

Issue Presented for Review:

"Whether the plaintiff was guilty of contributory negligence as a matter of law."

[or]

"Whether the trial court ruled correctly on certain objections to evidence."

[or]

"Whether the jury was improperly instructed."

The appellant must include a concise statement of the applicable standard of review for each issue, with citation to authority, either in the discussion of the issue in the argument or under a separate heading placed before the discussion in the argument.

(4) A statement of jurisdiction:

(i) In a case appealed to the Supreme Court directly from the trial court or as a matter of right from the Appellate Court, a brief statement under the heading "Jurisdiction" of the jurisdictional grounds for the appeal to the Supreme Court.

(ii) In a case appealed to the Appellate Court, a brief, but precise statement or explanation under the heading "Jurisdiction" of the basis for appeal including the supreme court rule or other law which confers jurisdiction upon the reviewing court; the facts of the case which bring it within this rule or other law; and the date that the order being appealed was entered and any other facts which are necessary to demonstrate that the appeal is timely. In appeals from a judgment as to all the claims and all the parties, the statement shall demonstrate the disposition of all claims and all parties. All facts recited in this statement shall be supported by page references to the record on appeal.

(5) In a case involving the construction or validity of a statute, constitutional provision, treaty, ordinance, or regulation, the pertinent parts of the provision verbatim, with a citation of the place where it may be found, all under an appropriate heading, such as "Statutes Involved." If the provision involved is lengthy, its citation alone will suffice at this point, and its pertinent text shall be set forth in an appendix.

(6) Statement of Facts, which shall contain the facts necessary to an understanding of the case, stated accurately and fairly without argument or comment, and with appropriate reference to the pages of the record on appeal, *e.g.*, R. C7, or R. 7, or to the pages of the abstract, *e.g.*, A. 7. Exhibits may be cited by reference to pages of the abstract or of the record on appeal or by exhibit number followed by the page number within the exhibit, *e.g.*, Pl. Ex. 1, p. 6.

(7) Argument, which shall contain the contentions of the appellant and the reasons therefor, with citation of the authorities and the pages of the record relied on. Evidence shall not be copied at

length, but reference shall be made to the pages of the record on appeal or abstract, if any, where evidence may be found. Citation of numerous authorities in support of the same point is not favored. Points not argued are waived and shall not be raised in the reply brief, in oral argument, or on petition for rehearing.

(8) A short conclusion stating the precise relief sought, followed by the names of counsel as on the cover.

(9) An appendix as required by Rule 342.

(i) Briefs of Appellee and Other Parties. The brief for the appellee and other parties shall conform to the foregoing requirements, except that items (2), (3), (4), (5), (6) and (9) of paragraph (h) of this rule need not be included except to the extent that the presentation by the appellant is deemed unsatisfactory.

(j) Reply Brief. The reply brief, if any, shall be confined strictly to replying to arguments presented in the brief of the appellee and need contain only Argument.

(k) Supplemental Brief on Leave to Appeal. A party allowing a petition for leave to appeal or for appeal as a matter of right or an answer thereto to stand as his or her main brief, may file a supplemental brief, so entitled, containing additional material, and omitting any of the items set forth in paragraph (h) of this rule to the extent that they are adequately covered in the petition or answer. The Points and Authorities in the supplemental brief need relate only to the contents of that brief.

(l) Copy of Document in Electronic Format. In addition to the number of copies required to be filed and served in accordance with this rule, the brief may be furnished on any removable media, such as floppy disk or CD–ROM, acceptable to the clerk of the reviewing court in Adobe Acrobat and served on each party to the appeal. The electronic document may but need not contain the required appendix. A copy of a brief in electronic format shall be filed upon request of the court or a judge thereof.

Amended October 21, 1969, effective January 1, 1970; July 30, 1979, effective October 15, 1979; January 5, 1981, effective February 1, 1981; February 19, 1982, effective April 1, 1982; May 28, 1982, effective July 1, 1982; April 27, 1984, and May 16, 1984, effective July 1, 1984; April 10, 1987, effective August 1, 1987; May 21, 1987, effective August 1, 1987; June 12, 1987, effective immediately; May 18, 1988, effective August 1, 1988; January 20, 1993, effective immediately; December 17, 1993, effective February 1, 1994; May 20, 1997, effective July 1, 1997; April 11, 2001, effective immediately; October 1, 2001, effective immediately; May 24, 2006, effective September 1, 2006; March 16, 2007, effective immediately; June 4, 2008, effective July 1, 2008; Feb. 6, 2013, eff. immediately; Dec. 9, 2015, eff. Jan. 1, 2016.

Formerly Ill.Rev.Stat.1991, ch. 110A, ¶ 341.

[1] 405 ILCS 5/1–100 et seq.
[2] 740 ILCS 110/1 et seq.

In an order entered December 18, 1981, the Illinois Supreme Court provided that, effective March 1, 1982, briefs which fail to comply with Rule 341d requiring official citations to Illinois cases will not be accepted by the clerk for filing.

Committee Comments

This rule was based upon former Supreme Court Rule 39, effective until January 1, 1967, which in turn was based upon former Uniform (and later Second, Third, Fourth, and Fifth District) Appellate Court Rule 7. There were no major changes.

Paragraph (a)

This paragraph deals with the length of briefs and the use of footnotes. It is derived from the second, third, and fourth sentences of former Rule 39(1). Three printed pages will normally contain approximately as many words as four unprinted pages, so the length limitations are substantially the same for printed and unprinted briefs.

The provision that footnotes are to be in the same size type as required for the text of the brief was deleted. Footnotes are to be used sparingly. Rule 344(b) prescribes 10–point type on 11–point slugs, instead of the 11–point type used in the body. This use of smaller type is conventional in the printing of legal texts, law reviews, the opinions of the Supreme Court of the United States, and other comparable materials. It is believed that the limited use of this slightly smaller type will not impose a burden on the courts.

In 1984 subsection (a) was amended to reduce from 75 to 50 the number of pages allowed to be in a printed brief and from 100 to 75 the number allowed in a brief that is not printed, and excludes from that page limitation those matters which are required by Rule 342(a) to be appended thereto.

Paragraph (b)

This is a revision of former Rule 40(1).

Paragraph (c)

This paragraph is derived in part from the first sentence of former Rule 39(1), except that it recognizes certain existing practices not permitted by the former rule if it was read literally. One is the use of the designations "appellant" and "appellee," together with the designation of the party in the trial court, in the title of the case appearing in the caption. The other is that the parties may be referred to by actual names or descriptive terms instead of as plaintiff or defendant, which in many instances is desirable to avoid confusion.

The paragraph was amended effective October 1, 2001, to help protect the identities of recipients of mental health services. The amendment requires that only their first name and last initial, or their initials, appear on documents filed with the Appellate Court or any subsequent court. The requirement covers the parties' briefs, motions, and other similar papers. The amendment does not require deletion of names from the trial record in preparing the record on appeal, nor does it address the means by which the Appellate Court or a subsequent court maintains the confidentiality of documents appearing in the record.

Paragraph (d)

Effective January 20, 1993, the requirements applicable to citations to cases, textbooks and statutes were placed in Rule 6, which is applicable to all documents filed in court, including briefs.

Paragraph (e)

Paragraph (e) is a substantial revision of portions of former Rule 39.

In 1981 the subparagraphs were restructured to make "Points and Authorities" the first part of the brief, so that it might act as a table of contents.

Subparagraph (1) is based upon the first three sentences of the paragraph designated II of former Rule 39(1). The revised provision specifically relates the Points and Authorities to the Argument. The same headings of the points and subpoints are to be used both here and in the Argument. The former provision that the three cases most relied on shall be cited first under each point was deleted in favor of the last sentence of subparagraph (e), which provides for ranking cases "as near as may be in the order of their importance."

The "introductory paragraph" provided for in subparagraph (2) will ordinarily not be captioned as such in the brief. As the illustration shows, the introductory paragraph is for the purpose of informing the court of the general area of the law in which the case falls, whether there was a jury trial, and whether there is a pleading question and if so what it is. The practice of many lawyers was to include in the statement of "The Nature of the Action" called for by the former rule much more detail than the courts wanted at this place in the brief.

The former requirement that "The Nature of the Case" include a statement of the party's "theory of the case" also produced much more detail than the rule contemplated.

Subparagraph (3) substitutes for the "theory of the case" a statement of "the issue or issues presented for review." Again, the court does not want detail at this point in the brief, as the illustration in the rule following this subparagraph attempts to make clear. The statement of the issue presented for review is not to be an elaborately framed legal question. Its purpose is to give the court a general idea of what the case is about. The court is not ready at this stage to appreciate the details. It should be noticed, for example, that the first alternative illustration of a statement of the issue presented for review does not state what conduct it is that one of the parties contends is contributory negligence as a matter of law. The second alternative does not describe the objections or the evidence to which they relate. The third alternative does not describe the instruction of which the complaint is made.

Subparagraph (4) is in part based upon former Rule 28–1, B. A similar provision appears in the rules of the Supreme Court of the United States. (Rule 40, 1(b).) In cases appealed to the Illinois Supreme Court as of right, it is important that the court be satisfied at the outset that jurisdiction exists. (See the comments to Rule 302.)

Subparagraph (4)(ii) was expanded effective February 1, 1994, to provide more comprehensive examples of what must be included in the statement demonstrating jurisdiction in the Appellate Court.

Subparagraph (5) is a combination of the third paragraph of former Rule 39(1) and paragraph 1(c) of Rule 40 of the rules of the Supreme Court of the United States.

Subparagraph (6) was based upon the paragraph numbered III of former Rule 39(1). The provision with respect to the citation of exhibits was new, as were the illustrations as to the form of the citations to the record. This subparagraph was amended in 1979 to delete reference to the preparation of excerpts from record to reflect the amendment of Rule 342 to eliminate the preparation and duplication of excerpts from the record except for the inclusion of copies of stated documents as an appendix to the brief, and to eliminate the preparation and filing of an abstract except on order of the reviewing court. (See Rule 342(a).) Because the elimination of excerpts and an abstract in most cases lends added importance to the accuracy and fairness with which the facts are stated in the brief, the first sentence of the subparagraph was amended to emphasize this point. A similar amendment was made to Rule 315(b)(4). See the committee comments to Rule 342.

Subparagraph (7) is a revision of the paragraph numbered IV of former Rule 39(1). The description of what the Argument is to contain is somewhat amplified. The provision admonishing against citation of numerous authorities was new. The limitation of the Argument to points made and cases cited in the Points and Authorities is no longer appropriate, since the Points and Authorities is to be derived from the Argument. The former provision that a point "made but not argued may be considered waived" was changed to the affirmative statement of the last sentence of the paragraph that failure to argue results in waiver and, further, that a point that has not been argued shall not be raised subsequently.

Subparagraph (8), requiring a short conclusion stating the precise relief sought, was new. It is customary to include a conclusion in a brief, but the relief sought is not always stated in the conclusion. This provision requires the party to end his brief by telling the court what relief he wants.

Paragraph (f)

The predecessor of this paragraph is the second paragraph following the paragraph numbered IV in former Rule 39(1). The new provision is simplified. The requirement that the appellee's brief state the propositions relied upon to sustain the judgment "as far as practicable, in the same order as the points of appellant" was not brought forward into the present rule. When the nature of the subject matter permits, counsel will normally follow the order established by his opponent in the interest of making his brief as convenient as possible for the court to use. Sometimes effective advocacy requires that a different order be adopted. In the opinion of the committee it is not possible to regulate this matter by rule.

Paragraph (g)

Paragraph (g) is the last paragraph of former Rule 39 (1), without change of substance.

Paragraph (h)

Paragraph (h) as it appeared in the revised rules effective January 1, 1967, was deleted in October 1969, as unnecessary in light of paragraph (b) of Rule 343, adopted at that time.

What is now paragraph (h) was paragraph (i) of the revision adopted effective January 1, 1967, and was new at that time, although it provides specifically for a practice that was often employed under the former rules. This paragraph makes clear the extent to which the requirements of Rule 341 apply to a supplemental brief filed in supplement of, rather than in lieu of, a petition for leave to appeal or an answer that party has allowed to stand as his main brief.

Order entered May 24, 2006—M.R. 20959

By order (M.R. 20959) of the Supreme Court concerning appellate briefs (order entered May 24, 2006, effective immediately), the Court provided:

"In re Appellate Briefs

The clerks of the reviewing courts are directed, to the extent practicable, to refuse to file any brief that does not comply with the rules of this court specifying, inter alia, the form and length of a brief on appeal."

Rule 342. Appendix to the Brief; Abstract

(a) **Appendix to the Brief.** The appellant's brief shall include, as an appendix, a table of contents to the appendix, a copy of the judgment appealed from, any opinion, memorandum, or findings of fact filed or entered by the trial judge or by any administrative agency or its officers, any pleadings or other materials from the record which are the basis of the appeal or pertinent to it, the notice of appeal, and a complete table of contents, with page references, of the record on appeal. The table shall state:

(1) the nature of each document, order, or exhibit, e.g., complaint, judgment, notice of appeal, will, trust deed, contract, and the like;

(2) in the case of pleadings, motions, notices of appeal, orders, and judgments, the date of filing or entry; and

(3) the names of all witnesses and the pages on which their direct examination, cross-examination, and redirect examination begin.

In addition, in cases involving proceedings to review orders of the Illinois Workers' Compensation Commission, the appellant's brief shall also include as part of the appendix copies of decisions of the arbitrator and the Commission.

The appellee's brief may include in a supplementary appendix other materials from the record which also are the basis of the appeal or are essential to any understanding of the issues raised in the appeal.

The pages of the appendix shall be numbered consecutively with the letter "A" preceding the number of each page. If an appendix is voluminous, it may be bound separately from the brief and labeled "Separate Appendix."

(b) **Abstract.** No abstract of the record on appeal shall be filed unless the reviewing court orders that one shall be filed, in which event the appellant shall file the abstract with the brief and the following provisions shall be applicable:

(1) The abstract shall refer to the pages of the record by numerals on the margin.

(2) It shall be preceded by a table of contents conforming with the requirements of paragraph (a) above, except that the page references to items included in the abstract shall be to abstract pages, and page references to the record pages of omitted items shall be prefixed by "R" (*e.g.*, R ___).

(3) If the record contains the evidence it shall be condensed in narrative form so as to present clearly and concisely its substance. Actual quotations may be used in lieu of a narrative for any portion of the evidence.

(4) Matters in the record on appeal not necessary for a full understanding of the question presented for decision shall not be abstracted.

(5) The abstract will be taken as sufficient unless the appellee files an additional abstract with his brief.

(c) **Cases Brought to Supreme Court from Appellate Court.** In cases brought to the Supreme Court from the Appellate Court, copies of any abstract filed in the Appellate Court shall be filed in the Supreme Court without change. Upon request and to the extent practicable, the clerk of the Appellate Court shall provide the appellant with the copies of any abstract filed in that court for transmission to the Supreme Court as a part of the 20 copies required to be filed with the brief in the Supreme Court.

(d) **Entire Record Available.** The entire record on appeal, whether or not abstracted, is available to the reviewing court for examination or reference. Omission of any relevant portion of the record from the abstract shall not prejudice a party unless the reviewing court finds that there has been no good-faith effort to comply with this rule.

(e) Costs. The actual and reasonable cost of producing an abstract required by the reviewing court to be filed, or additional abstract proved by affidavit satisfactory to the clerk of the reviewing court, shall be taxed as costs in the case; but the cost of including unnecessary matter in the abstract or additional abstract may be disallowed as costs.

Amended eff. Oct. 21, 1969; Jan. 1, 1970; July 30, 1979; Oct. 15, 1979; June 1, 1984, eff. July 1, 1984; May 18, 1988, eff. Aug. 1, 1988; Dec. 17, 1993, eff. Feb. 1, 1994; amended Oct. 15, 2004, eff. Jan. 1, 2005.

Formerly Ill.Rev.Stat.1991, ch. 110A, ¶ 342.

Committee Comments

(Revised June 1, 1984)

Rule 342 was substantially rewritten in 1979. Prior to 1964 it was required that the appellant prepare and file an abstract of the record on appeal. In that year former Rule 36–1 was adopted (29 Ill.2d R. 36–1), giving the appellant in appeals referable to magistrates the option of substituting for the abstract excerpts from the record, containing the judgment or order appealed from, the notice of appeal, and "the parts of the record deemed essential for the judges of the reviewing court to read in order to decide the issues presented" (29 Ill.2d R. 36–1(8)). Provision was made for an exchange of designations of items to be included in the excerpts, the excerpts to be filed by the appellant no later than 14 days after the due date of the appellee's brief. At the time it was thought that reproduction of the actual pages from the record was at once less time consuming, and therefore less expensive, than the preparation of a narrative statement, and also more accurate. Rule 342, effective January 1, 1967, extended the provision for the filing of excerpts from record to cover all appeals. Extensive amendments were adopted effective January 1, 1970.

As revised in 1979, Rule 342 requires that the appellant include in its brief an appendix containing a copy of the judgment appealed from, any opinion, memorandum, or findings of fact filed or entered by the trial judge, the notice of appeal, and a table of contents of the record (paragraph (a)). Otherwise it is not required that any parts of the record be duplicated. All reference to excerpts of record were therefore deleted. The contemplation is that in most instances the appeal will be heard on the original papers. It is provided, however, that the reviewing court may order that an abstract be prepared and filed. Therefore the provisions of the rule governing the contents, form, and filing of an abstract are retained. Appropriate changes were made in other rules that included reference to the preparation and filing of excerpts from the record. (See Rules 306, 307, 308, 317, 344, 607, and 612.) Since in most cases there will no longer be either abstract or excerpts, the duty of the parties to make a fair and accurate statement of the facts in their briefs, always important, has become even more so, and this duty has been emphasized by amendment to Rules 315(b)(4) and 341(e)(6).

In 1984 subparagraph (a) was amended to require that copies of the decisions of both the arbitrator and the Commission be included in the appendix in all cases involving proceedings to review orders of the Industrial Commission.

(December 17, 1993)

A separate table of contents to the appendix is added as a requirement under paragraph (a). The rule also provides that all pages of the appendix must be numbered to permit easy reference.

Rule 343. Times for Filing and Serving Briefs

(a) Time. Except as provided in subparagraph (b) below and elsewhere in these rules (see Rules 306, 307, 308, 315, and 317), the brief of the appellant shall be filed in the reviewing court within 35 days from the filing of the record on appeal. Within 35 days from the due date of the appellant's brief, or in the case of multiple appellants, the latest due date of any appellant's brief, the appellee shall file his or her brief in the reviewing court. Within 14 days from the due date of the appellee's brief, or in the case of multiple appellees, the latest due date of any appellee's brief, the appellant may file a reply brief.

(b) Cross–Appeals and Separate Appeals. Unless otherwise ordered by the reviewing court or a judge thereof, briefs of cross-appellants and separate appellants shall be filed as follows:

(1) *Cross–Appeals.* A cross-appellant shall file a single brief as appellee and cross-appellant at the time his or her brief as appellee is due; the appellant's answer to the arguments on the cross-appeal shall be included in appellant's reply brief, which shall be filed within 35 days from the due date of the single brief filed by the cross-appellant; and the cross-appellant may file a reply brief confined strictly to replying to those arguments raised on the cross-appeal within 14 days after the due date of the appellant's reply brief.

(2) *Separate Appeals.* A separate appellant shall follow the same briefing schedule as prescribed for the appellant. All appellees shall file their briefs within 35 days of the due date of appellants' briefs. Any replies may be filed within 14 days of the due date of appellees' briefs.

(c) Extending or Shortening Time. The reviewing court or a judge thereof, *sua sponte* or upon the motion of a party supported by affidavit or verification by certification under section 1–109 of the Code of Civil Procedure showing a good cause, may extend or shorten the time of any party to file a brief. (See Rule 361.)

Amended October 21, 1969, effective January 1, 1970; amended effective September 1, 1974; amended December 17, 1993, effective February 1, 1994; amended May 24, 2006, effective September 1, 2006; amended March 26, 2008, effective July 1, 2008.

Formerly Ill.Rev.Stat.1991, ch. 110A, ¶ 343.

Committee Comments

(March 26, 2008)

Paragraph (b)(1) was amended to make clear that the appellant has 35 days from the due date of the single brief filed by the cross-appellant to file a reply brief that includes the appellant's answer to the arguments on the cross-appeal rather than the 14 days generally allowed for filing reply briefs set forth in paragraph (a). This amendment makes no substantive change to this rule.

Order entered May 24, 2006—M.R. 20959

By order (M.R. 20959) of the Supreme Court concerning appellate briefs (order entered May 24, 2006, effective immediately), the Court provided:

"In re Appellate Briefs

The clerks of the reviewing courts are directed, to the extent practicable, to refuse to file any brief that does not comply with the rules of this court specifying, inter alia, the form and length of a brief on appeal."

See Illinois Supreme Court Order M.R. 20959 under Rule 341.

The Illinois Supreme Court, in an order entered Nov. 9, 1982, provided that when the appellant fails to file a brief when due, the clerk is directed to enter an order that the appeal be dismissed for want of compliance with this rule, unless within 14 days of the entry date of that order, the appellant obtains an order extending the filing time or permitting the filing of the brief instanter.

Where the appellee has not filed a brief when due, the clerk is directed to enter an order that the case be taken on the brief of the appellant, unless within 14 days of the entry of that order, the appellee obtains an order extending the filing time or permitting filing of the brief instanter.

Committee Comments

(Revised September 1, 1974)

This rule, governing the times for filing and serving briefs in all reviewing courts, is based in part upon former Supreme Court Rules 41(2) and (4) and Second, Third, Fourth, and Fifth District (and earlier Uniform) Appellate Court Rule 9. The provision in the former rule that if a brief or abstract was not filed within the time prescribed the appeal would be dismissed on the call of the docket was omitted as both too strict and unnecessary. The court has the inherent power to dismiss an appeal for any breach of its rules, although a less drastic remedy would normally suffice. In the rare instances in which a brief of an appellant is inexcusably not filed on time, the court can exercise this power without any provision in the rule specifically authorizing it to do so.

The committee recommended 35 days as the time period for the main briefs best calculated to fit the requirements of the bar and the reviewing courts. The committee recognized the importance of providing a long enough period to permit the preparation of a brief in the ordinary case without the necessity of an extension of time and a short enough period to permit prompt disposition of the business of the reviewing courts. Five weeks would seem to be a realistic compromise. The time for filing the reply brief was fixed at 14 days, consistent with the multiples-of-seven policy.

The rule establishes the time for filing briefs in all cases on appeal from final judgments of the circuit court, whether to the Appellate Court (Rules 303 and 304), or directly to the Supreme Court (Rule 302). It applies to appeals from orders of the circuit court granting a new trial (Rule 306) and to interlocutory appeals by permission (Rule 308), subject to the provisions in those rules measuring the 35 days allowed for the filing of the appellant's brief from the date of the order allowing the appeal, rather than from the filing of the record on appeal. Rule 307 provides for a special, shorter timetable for the filing of briefs in interlocutory appeals as of right. Appeals from the Appellate Court to the Supreme Court on certificate (Rule 316) are governed by Rule 343, but appeals from the Appellate Court to the Supreme Court on petition for leave to appeal (Rule 315) or petition for appeal as a matter of right (Rule 316) are governed by the provisions of Rule 315(g), which sets forth the timetable for filing briefs in such cases. Paragraph (c) of Rule 343 is applicable to all appeals.

In 1969 former paragraph (b) was relettered (c) and present paragraph (b) was inserted to provide the bar with explicit directions as to the briefs on cross-appeals and separate appeals.

The rule was amended in 1974 to delete material referring to appeals on petition for leave to appeal. This material was placed in Rules 306, 308, and 315. As part of the same amendment the words "with proof of service" were deleted and Rule 344(a) amended to set forth the requirement of filing proof of service.

(December 17, 1993)

Paragraph (a) has been modified to make clear that only one brief need be filed when responding to multiple briefs of opponents filed at separate times.

Paragraph (b)(2) has been changed to eliminate the former practice of automatic staggering of the briefing schedule in cases involving separate appeals.

Rule 344. Repealed and Reserved May 24, 2006, eff. Sept. 1, 2006

Rule 345. Briefs Amicus Curiae

(a) **Leave or Request of Court Necessary.** A brief *amicus curiae* may be filed only by leave of the court or of a judge thereof, or at the request of the court. A motion for leave must be accompanied by the proposed brief and shall state the interest of the applicant and explain how an *amicus* brief will assist the court.

(b) Forms; Conditions; Time. A brief of an *amicus curiae* shall follow the form prescribed for the brief of an appellee, shall identify the *amicus* as such on the cover of the brief, and shall conform to any conditions imposed by the court. Unless the court or a judge thereof specifies otherwise, it shall be filed on or before the due date of the initial brief of the party whose position it supports. The color of the cover shall be the same as that of the party's brief whose position it supports.

(c) Oral Argument. *Amicus curiae* will not be allowed to argue orally.

Amended Feb. 19, 1982, eff. April 1, 1982; May 28, 1982, eff. July 1, 1982; Dec. 17, 1993, eff. Feb. 1, 1994; amended Dec. 6, 2005, eff. immediately; amended Sept. 20, 2010, eff. immediately.

Formerly Ill.Rev.Stat.1991, ch. 110A, ¶ 345.

Committee Comments
(Revised May 1982)

Rule 345 was new in 1967. It conformed generally to the practice in the Supreme Court prior to its adoption. As originally adopted, paragraph (b) provided that "[t]he court shall fix the time and conditions for the filing of the *amicus curiae* brief." In the original committee comments, however, it was noted that "if feasible, the *amicus curiae* brief should be filed at the same time as the brief of the party whose position is being supported." In 1980, the rule was amended to elevate this admonition to a requirement, "unless the court specifies otherwise." The rule was also amended in 1980 to prohibit *amicus curiae* from arguing orally Rules 345(a) and (b) were amended in 1982 to permit a single judge to grant leave to file a brief *amicus curiae* and to alter the date for its filing.

Rules 346 to 350. Reserved

PART E. ORAL ARGUMENT

Rule 351. Sequence and Manner of Calling Cases for Oral Argument

Cases in the reviewing court shall be numbered in the order in which they are docketed. They shall be called for argument or submitted without argument in the sequence and manner provided by the administrative orders of the court. The clerk shall give counsel advance notice as to when the case is to be argued, the amount of time for oral argument, and the requirement of advance registration, if any. The hour set shall be as definite as the business of the court permits. Counsel shall acknowledge receipt of the notice of oral argument and advise the clerk if they intend to argue.

Amended Dec. 17, 1993, eff. Feb. 1, 1994.

Formerly Ill.Rev.Stat.1991, ch. 110A, ¶ 351.

Committee Comments

This rule replaces former Rule 42. Applicable to all reviewing courts, it leaves each court free to provide by administrative orders for the sequence and manner of calling cases for oral argument. The provision as to the notice to be given by the clerk to counsel is new. The last sentence is also new. If the business of the court permits it to set arguments for two or more starting times during the day, there will be a substantial saving of time and expense to counsel and parties.

Rule 352. Conduct of Oral Arguments

(a) Request; Waiver; Dispensing With Oral Argument. A party shall request oral argument by stating at the bottom of the cover page of his or her brief that oral argument is requested, or, if the party has allowed a petition for leave to appeal or answer to stand as his or her brief, by mailing to the clerk and to opposing parties, within the time in which the party could have filed a further brief, a notice requesting oral argument. If any party so requests, all other parties may argue without an additional request. No party may argue unless that party has filed a brief as required by the rules and paid any fee required by law. A party who has requested oral argument and who thereafter determines to waive oral argument shall promptly notify the clerk and all other parties. Any other party who has filed a brief without requesting oral argument may then request oral argument upon prompt notice to the clerk and all other parties.

After the briefs have been filed, the court may dispose of any case without oral argument if no substantial question is presented, but this power should be exercised sparingly.

(b) Length. Unless the court otherwise orders, each side shall be allowed not to exceed 20 minutes for its main argument. In all cases, the appellant shall have not to exceed an additional 10 minutes strictly confined to rebuttal. If only one side argues, the argument shall not exceed 15 minutes. The court may grant additional time on motion filed in advance of the date fixed for hearing if it appears that additional time is necessary for the adequate presentation of the case. A party is not obliged to use all of the time allowed, and the court may terminate the argument whenever in its judgment further argument is unnecessary.

(c) Reading Prohibited. Reading at length from the record, briefs, or authorities cited will not be permitted.

(d) Divided Arguments. No more than two counsel will be heard from each side except by leave of court, which will be granted when there are several parties on the same side with diverse interests. Divided arguments are not favored and care shall be taken to avoid duplication of arguments.

(e) Multiple Parties. If a case involves appeals by more than one party the sequence of oral argument shall be as the parties agree or as the court directs.

(f) Limitation on Briefs and Memoranda. No brief or memorandum shall be filed after the due date of the reply brief or after oral argument except by leave of court or a judge thereof.

(g) When Oral Argument Not Requested. If a case is submitted to the court without request for oral argument, it shall be decided on the briefs unless the court orders oral argument.

Amended effective July 1, 1975; May 28, 1982, effective July 1, 1982; June 19, 1989, effective August 1, 1989; August 18, 1989, effective September 1, 1989; December 17, 1993, effective February 1, 1994; Feb. 6, 2013, eff. immediately.

Formerly Ill.Rev.Stat.1991, ch. 110A, ¶ 352.

Committee Comments

(Revised July 1, 1975)

This rule is based upon former Supreme Court Rule 43. See also former Second, Third, Fourth, and Fifth District (and earlier Uniform) Appellate Court Rule 13(4).

Paragraph (a)

Paragraph (a) is based largely upon the first paragraph of former Rule 43. The last two sentences are new; the former provision did not require notice of an election to waive oral argument, but provided that if a party appeared at the argument and the other party failed to appear, the party who appeared could argue anyway. The new provision, stated in the last two sentences of the paragraph, requires prompt notice of waiver and a prompt notice by the opposite party if he desires oral argument.

The last paragraph was added in 1975. As to the length of argument, see comment to paragraph (b).

Paragraph (b)

This paragraph is based in part upon the second paragraph of former Rule 43. The provision for requesting additional time by motion filed in advance of the date fixed for hearing is new. The final sentence, which reminds counsel that he need not use all the time allowed and which provides that the court may terminate the argument whenever in its judgment further argument is unnecessary, is also new.

Paragraph (a) limits the power of the court to deny permission to argue orally to cases in which it is determined that no substantial question is presented, and cautions that the power to dispense with oral argument is to be used sparingly. Paragraph (b), on the other hand, leaves the court free to limit the length of the argument in advance, as well as to terminate it once it has begun. When argument is to be limited in advance, ordinarily counsel should be notified reasonably in advance of the date set for argument.

Paragraph (c)

This provision is taken from former Second, Third, Fourth, and Fifth District (and earlier Uniform) Appellate Court Rule 13(4), second paragraph, last sentence.

Paragraph (d)

This paragraph is based upon the first sentence of the third paragraph of former Rule 43 and paragraph 4 of Rule 44 of the Rules of the Supreme Court of the United States.

Paragraph (e)

This paragraph is new.

Paragraph (f)

This paragraph is derived from the second sentence of former Supreme Court Rule 43 (which did not provide for the filing of another brief upon leave of court or a judge thereof) and the last paragraph of former Second, Third, Fourth, and Fifth District (and earlier Uniform) Appellate Court Rule 13(4).

Paragraph (g)

This paragraph is new.

Rules 353 to 360. Reserved

PART F.   OTHER PROVISIONS

Rule 361.   Motions in Reviewing Court

(a) Content of Motions; Supporting Record; Other Supporting Papers. Unless another form is elsewhere prescribed by these rules, an application for an order or other relief shall be made by filing a motion. Motions shall be in writing and shall state the relief sought and the grounds therefor. If the record has not been filed the movant shall file with the motion an appropriate supporting record (Rule 328). When the motion is based on facts that do not appear of record it shall be supported by affidavit. Argument not contained in the motion may be made in a supporting memorandum.

If counsel has conferred with opposing counsel and opposing counsel has no objection to the motion, that fact should be stated in the motion in order to allow the court to rule upon the motion without waiting until the time for filing responses has passed.

(b) In Appellate Court; In Supreme Court While in Session. If the motion is filed in the Appellate Court, or in the Supreme Court while in session, the motion shall be served, presented, and filed as follows:

(1) The motion, together with proof of service, shall be filed with the clerk. Service and filing will be excused only in case of necessity.

(2) Responses to a motion shall be in writing and be filed, with proof of service, within 5 days after personal, e-mail or facsimile service of the motion, or 10 days after mailing of the motion if service is by mail, or 10 days after delivery to a third-party

commercial carrier if service is by delivery to a third-party commercial carrier, or within such further time as the court or a judge thereof may allow. Except by order of court, replies to responses will not be allowed and oral arguments on motions will not be heard.

(3) Motions, supporting papers, and responses filed in the Supreme Court shall consist of an original and one copy and in the Appellate Court an original and three copies (in workers' compensation cases arising under Rule 22(g) an original and five copies). A proposed order phrased in the alternative (e.g., "Allowed" or "Denied") shall be submitted with each motion, and a copy shall be served upon all counsel of record. A copy of the style of such orders may be obtained from the clerk's office. No motion shall be accepted by the clerk unless accompanied by such a proposed order.

(c) **In Supreme Court While Not in Session.**

(1) If a rule provides that relief may be granted "by the court or a justice thereof," the motion shall be directed to only one justice. Such a motion shall be directed to the justice of the judicial district involved or, in Cook County, to the justice designated to hear motions. For the second, third, fourth, and fifth judicial districts, the original motion and one copy shall be filed with the clerk in Springfield, together with a proof of service and a proposed order in compliance with paragraph (b)(3). The response to a motion shall be directed to the justice within the time provided in paragraph (b)(2), and the original and one copy shall be filed with the clerk in Springfield. For the first judicial district (Cook County), the motion and one copy, together with a proof of service and a proposed order, shall be filed with the clerk in the Chicago satellite office. The deputy clerk will direct the motion to the justice designated to hear motions. Responses to a motion shall be filed with the clerk in the Chicago satellite office within the time provided in paragraph (b)(2).

(2) If the motion seeks relief that under these rules requires action by the full court, and the case arises from the second, third, fourth, or fifth judicial district, the movant shall file the original and eight copies with the clerk in Springfield. Responses to a motion and eight copies shall be filed with the clerk in Springfield within the time provided in paragraph (b)(2) or, if applicable, within the time provided in Rule 381 or 383. If the case arises from the first judicial district (Cook County), the movant shall file an original and eight copies with the clerk in the Chicago satellite office. Responses to a motion and eight copies shall be filed with the clerk in Chicago within the time provided in paragraph (b)(2) or, if applicable, within the time provided in Rule 381 or 383. Regardless of district, a proof of service in the form required in the preceding shall accompany the motion.

(d) **When Acted Upon.** Except in extraordinary circumstances, or where opposing counsel has indicated no objections, no motion will be acted upon until the time for filing responses has expired.

(e) **Corrections.** The clerk is authorized to make corrections in any document of a party to any pending case upon receipt of written request from that party together with proof that a copy of the request has been transmitted to all other parties.

(f) **Motions for Extensions of Time.** Motions for extensions of time shall be supported by affidavit or verification by certification under section 1–109 of the Code of Civil Procedure of counsel or the party showing the number of previous extensions granted and the reason for each extension. Any affidavit shall be sworn to before a person who has authority under the law to administer oaths.

(g) **Emergency Motions and Bail Motions.** Each District of the Appellate Court shall promulgate and publish rules setting forth the procedure for emergency motions, including notice requirements. Subject to the rules of each District, an emergency motion must specify the nature of the emergency and the grounds for the specific relief requested. Except in the most extreme and compelling circumstances, a motion for an extension of time will not be considered an emergency. Motions regarding bail in criminal cases or bonds in civil and criminal cases shall be considered emergency motions if so designated by the movant.

(h) **Dispositive Motions.**

(1) Dispositive motions in the Appellate Court should be ruled upon promptly after the filing of the objection to the motion, if any. A dispositive motion may be taken with the case where the court cannot resolve the motion without consideration of the full record on appeal and full briefing of the merits.

(2) For purposes of this Rule 361(h), "dispositive motion" means any motion challenging the Appellate Court's jurisdiction or raising any other issue that could result in the dismissal of any portion of an appeal or cross appeal without a decision on the merits of that portion of the appeal or cross-appeal.

(3) A dispositive motion shall include:

(a) a discussion of the facts and issues on appeal sufficient to enable the court to consider the dispositive motion;

(b) a discussion of the facts and law supporting the dismissal of the appeal or cross-appeal or portion thereof prior to a determination of the appeal on the merits;

(c) a discussion of the relationship, if any, of the purported dispositive issue to the other issues on appeal;

(d) an appropriate supporting record containing (i) if the record on appeal has not yet been filed, the parts of the trial court record necessary to support the dispositive motion; and (ii) if necessary, any evidence of relevant matters not of record in accordance with Rule 361(a).

(4) An objection to a dispositive motion shall address each of the required portions of the motion, and if the record on appeal has not yet been filed, shall include any parts of the trial court record not submitted by the movant that is necessary to oppose the motion, and may include evidence of relevant matters not of record in accordance with Rule 361(a).

(5) The Appellate Court may order additional briefing, record submissions, or oral argument as it deems appropriate.

Amended Sept. 29, 1978, eff. Nov. 1, 1978; July 30, 1979, eff. Oct. 15, 1979; Jan. 5, 1981, eff. Feb. 1, 1981; May 28, 1982, eff. July 1, 1982; June 15, 1982, eff. July 1, 1982; Aug. 9, 1983, eff. Oct. 1, 1983; Aug. 30, 1983, eff. Oct. 1, 1983; Feb. 27, 1987, eff. April 1, 1987; Dec. 17, 1993, eff. Feb. 1, 1994; eff. Oct. 1, 1998; May 25, 2001; Oct. 14, 2005, eff. Jan. 1, 2006; May 24, 2006, eff. Sept. 1, 2006; eff. Dec. 29, 2009; March 14, 2014, eff. immediately; Dec. 11, 2014, eff. Jan. 1, 2015.

Formerly Ill.Rev.Stat.1991, ch. 110A, ¶ 361.

Committee Comments
(Revised May 1982)

Rule 361 replaced former section 86.1 of the Civil Practice Act, former Supreme Court Rule 49, former Rule 3 of the First District Appellate Court, and former Rule 5 of the other districts (earlier Uniform Appellate Court Rule 5). It applies to motions in all reviewing courts. Except for the provisions as to time, the rule made no substantial change in the preexisting practice. The argument in support of a motion, if not set forth in the motion itself, is to be submitted in a memorandum in support of the motion, rather than in a document entitled "suggestions." The time provisions are designed to insure that the other parties have an opportunity to file objections. The number of copies of documents conforms to former requirements in the Supreme Court and all Appellate Court districts except the First District, which required an original and two copies. The additional copy gives the clerk one for his file. Paragraph (f) was new.

Paragraph (g) was added in 1978, extending to civil cases a requirement formerly appearing in Rule 610(3) (58 Ill.2d R. 610(3)), applicable only to criminal appeals.

Two clarifying changes were made in 1979. The first sentence of paragraph (a) was added to make it explicit that, unless otherwise provided for, all applications for relief are to be made by motion, and the provisions of former Rule 328, abrogated in 1979, were in substance transferred to paragraph (a) of this rule, where they appear as the third sentence. The "short record" under the former practice is called a "supporting record" in recognition of the fact that such a record serves the sole purpose of supporting the motion and not as a basis for docketing an appeal as the "short record" was under Rule 327 before its amendment in 1979.

In 1981, paragraph (c) was amended to require that copies of motions directed to a justice when the court is not in session must be sent to the other justices at their district chambers whenever the motion seeks relief that will require action by the full court. In 1982, it was amended to clarify this requirement.

(December 17, 1993)

The rule has been reorganized and nonsubstantive additions are made. Reference to the former motion call practice of the Supreme Court in the First District has been deleted.

(January 1, 2006)

Paragraph (h) was added effective January 1, 2006, to address the concerns of the bench and bar with respect to dispositive motions in the Appellate Court. Where a straightforward dispositive issue exists, such as an easily determinable lack of appellate jurisdiction, taking the motion with the case delays the final resolution of the case and greatly increases the burden on all parties by forcing them unnecessarily to brief and argue the merits of the appeal. Paragraph (h) requires that dispositive motions provide the necessary context, including those portions of the record that are necessary to resolve the motion. Where such context is provided, the rule provides that the court should resolve the dispositive motion "promptly after the filing of the objection, if any."

Rule 362. Amendment of Pleadings and Process in the Reviewing Courts

(a) Application. Any party who seeks on appeal to amend his or her pleadings or the process in the record on appeal shall present a written application therefor, supported by affidavit. No application shall be presented until the record on appeal is on file.

(b) Showing Necessary. The application, and the affidavit in support thereof, must show the amendment to be necessary, that no prejudice will result to the adverse party if the amendment sought is permitted, and that the issues sought to be raised by the amendment are supported by the facts in the record on appeal. The amended pleading or process shall be presented with the application.

(c) Service. A copy of the application and affidavit in support thereof must be served upon the other parties and proof of service filed at the time the application and affidavit are filed.

(d) Objections. The opposing party shall have five days in which to file objections, service of which shall be made upon the applicant, and proof of service filed with the clerk of the reviewing court.

(e) Time. No application for amendment of pleadings or process will be considered if made after the cause has been submitted for decision.

(f) On Court's Own Motion. The reviewing court may, of its own motion, before or after submission of the case for decision, order amendment to be made.

Amended Dec. 17, 1993, eff. Feb. 1, 1994.

Formerly Ill.Rev.Stat.1991, ch. 110A, ¶ 362.

Committee Comments

This is former Rule 50 without change of substance.

Rule 363. Inspection of Original Exhibits on Appeal

Whenever, in the opinion of the reviewing court, an inspection of an original exhibit not in the record on appeal is important to a correct decision of the appeal, the court may enter an order for its transmission, safekeeping, and return. The clerk of the reviewing court will receive the exhibit and hold it subject to the order.

Amended Dec. 17, 1993, eff. Feb. 1, 1994.

Formerly Ill.Rev.Stat.1991, ch. 110A, ¶ 363.

Committee Comments

This is former Rule 51, but specifically limited to original *exhibits*; the former language was "original paper."

(December 17, 1993)

The rule is changed to reflect that the reviewing court, rather than the trial court, is responsible for securing exhibits the reviewing court may wish to examine on appeal.

Rule 364. Privacy Protection for Documents Filed in Courts of Review

Text of rule added effective July 1, 2016.

(a) Applicability.

(1) Any document, including exhibits, containing personal identifiers shall not be filed with a court of review except as provided in paragraph (c). This rule applies to paper and electronic filings.

(2) This rule does not apply to documents in cases filed confidentially or to any document filed under seal.

(b) Personal identifiers, for purposes of this rule, are defined as follows:

(1) Social Security and individual taxpayer-identification numbers;

(2) driver's license and state identification card numbers;

(3) financial account numbers;

(4) debit and credit card numbers; and

(5) for a juvenile or recipient of mental health services involved in a proceeding referenced in Rule 341(f), the name of the individual.

(c) The filing of a document containing personal identifiers is permissible if redacted, by using the letter "x" in place of each omitted digit or character, and shall only include:

(1) the last four digits of the Social Security or individual taxpayer-identification number;

(2) the last four digits of the driver's license or state identification card number;

(3) the last four digits of the financial account number;

(4) the last four digits of the debit and credit card number; and

(5) in appeals filed from proceedings referenced in Rule 341(f), rather than redaction, the respective juvenile or recipient of mental health services shall be identified by first name and last initial, except that initials only shall be used when, due to an unusual first name or spelling, using the first name and last initial would create a substantial risk of revealing the individual's identity.

(d) When the filing of personal identifiers is required by law, ordered by the court, or otherwise necessary to effect disposition of a matter, the party filing the document shall file a form in substantial compliance with the appended "Notice Of Confidential Information Within Court Filing," along with the number of copies required for motions pursuant to Rule 361. Proof of service, as provided by Rule 12, shall be filed with the notice. The notice shall contain the personal identifiers in issue, and shall be filed under seal by the clerk immediately upon filing. Thereafter, the notice and any attachments thereto shall remain under seal and not available for public access, except as the court or a justice thereof may order.

After the notice containing the personal identifier has been filed under seal, subsequent documents filed in the case shall include only redacted personal identifiers and, if necessary, appropriate reference to the sealed document containing the personal identifier.

If any of the personal identifiers in the sealed filing subsequently requires amendment or updating, the responsible party shall file the amended or additional information by filing a separate "Notice Of Confidential Information Within Court Filing" form.

(e) The clerk of the reviewing court is not required to review documents or exhibits for compliance with this rule.

(f) If a document or exhibit is filed containing personal identifiers, a party or any other person whose information has been included may file a motion pursuant to Rule 361 requesting that the court order redaction or the proper designation pursuant to this rule. The motion shall be filed under seal, and the clerk of the reviewing court shall remove the document or exhibit containing the personal identifier from public access pending the court's ruling on the motion. A motion requesting redaction or the proper designation pursuant to this rule shall have attached a copy of the redacted version of the document. If the court or a judge thereof allows the motion, the clerk shall retain the unredacted copy under seal and the redacted copy shall become available for public access.

Appendix

Case Number in the Reviewing Court

Name of Reviewing Court (Include Appellate District, if applicable)

Case Title (Complete)	)	Appeal from Circuit Court of _____ County
	)	Lower Court Case No. _____
	)	Trial Judge _____

NOTICE OF CONFIDENTIAL INFORMATION WITHIN COURT FILING

Pursuant to Illinois Supreme Court Rule 364(d), the filer of a document containing personal identifiers required by law, ordered by the court, or otherwise necessary to effect disposition of a matter shall, at the time of such filing, include this confidential information form which identifies the personal identifier redacted from such filing pursuant to Rule 364(d), and which will be redacted from future filings to protect the subject personal identifier. **This personal identifier information will not be available to the public and this document will be sealed by the clerk of the reviewing court.**

Party/Individual Information:

1. Name: _____
    Address: _____
               _____
    Phone: _____
    SSN: _____

Other personal identifiers as defined in Rule 364(b), to the extent applicable:

2. Name: _____
    Address: _____
               _____
    Phone: _____
    SSN: _____

Other personal identifier information as defined in Rule 364(b), to the extent applicable:

(Attach additional pages, if necessary.)
Adopted Dec. 3, 2015, eff. July 1, 2016.

Rule 365. Appeal to Wrong Court

If a case is appealed to either the Supreme Court or the Appellate Court, or the wrong district of the Appellate Court, which should have been appealed to a different court, the case shall be transferred to the proper court, and the clerk shall transmit the record on appeal and all other papers filed in the case, with the order of transfer, to the clerk of the proper court. That clerk shall file the record and other papers upon receiving them, without charging an additional filing fee, and the case shall then proceed as if it had been appealed to the proper court in the first instance. Any bond executed in such a transferred case is binding on the parties thereto with the same force and effect as if given in a case appealed directly to the court to which the case is transferred.

Amended Dec. 17, 1993, eff. Feb. 1, 1994.

Formerly Ill.Rev.Stat.1991, ch. 110A, ¶ 365.

Committee Comments

Paragraph (a) is former Rule 28–1(D), which belongs here rather than in the rule relating to direct appeals to the Supreme Court. Paragraph (b) is section 86 of the Civil Practice Act, which covers the same ground as former Rule 47.

(December 17, 1993)

Paragraph (a) concerning collateral attack and waiver is deleted because it is an outdated vestige of practice under Illinois' former Constitution.

This rule is expanded to permit limited, intra-district transfers when appeals are docketed in the wrong appellate court district.

Rule 366. Powers of Reviewing Court—Scope of Review and Procedure—Lien of Judgment

(a) Powers. In all appeals the reviewing court may, in its discretion, and on such terms as it deems just,

(1) exercise all or any of the powers of amendment of the trial court;

(2) allow substitution of parties by reason of marriage, death, bankruptcy, assignment, or any other cause, allow new parties to be added or parties to be dropped, or allow parties to be rearranged as appellants or appellees, on such reasonable notice as it may require;

(3) order or permit the record to be amended by correcting errors or by adding matters that should have been included;

(4) draw inferences of fact; and

(5) enter any judgment and make any order that ought to have been given or made, and make any other and further orders and grant any relief, including a remandment, a partial reversal, the order of a partial new trial, the entry of a remittitur, or the enforcement of a judgment, that the case may require.

(b) Scope of Review

(1) *General.*

(i) *Error of Law.* Any error of law affecting the judgment or order appealed from may be brought up for review.

(ii) *Error of Fact.* Any error of fact, in that the judgment or order appealed from is not sustained by the evidence or is against the weight of the evidence, may be brought up for review.

(2) *Scope and Procedure on Review in Jury Cases.* In jury cases the following rules govern:

(i) *Instructions.* No party may raise on appeal the failure to give an instruction unless the party shall have tendered it.

(ii) *Remittitur.* Consenting to a remittitur as a condition to the denial of a new trial does not preclude the consenting party from asserting on appeal that the amount of the verdict was proper. No cross-appeal is required.

(iii) *Post–Trial Motion.* A party may not urge as error on review of the ruling on the party's post-trial motion any point, ground, or relief not specified in the motion.

(iv) *Review of Conditional Rulings on Post–Trial Motion.* The reviewing court, if it determines to reverse an unconditional ruling of the trial court on a post-trial motion, may review and determine any conditional rulings made by the trial court on other questions raised by the motion. No cross-appeal is required.

(3) *Scope and Procedure on Review in Nonjury Cases.* In nonjury cases the following rules govern:

(i) *Special Findings and Motions Unnecessary.* No special findings of fact, certificate of evidence, propositions of law, motion for a finding, or demurrer to the evidence is necessary to support the judgment or as a basis for review. The sufficiency of the evidence to support the judgment is subject to review without formal action to preserve the question.

(ii) *Post Judgment Motions.* Neither the filing of nor the failure to file a post judgment motion limits the scope of review.

(iii) *Procedure When Judgment at Close of Plaintiff's Case is Reversed.* If a judgment entered in favor of the defendant pursuant to a motion for a finding or judgment at the close of plaintiff's case is reversed on appeal, the case shall be remanded with directions to proceed as though the motion had been denied by the trial court or waived.

(c) Lien of Judgment. If the reviewing court enters final judgment and orders its enforcement, a certificate or certified copy of the judgment may be filed in the office of the recorder of deeds of any county in which real estate of the judgment debtor is situated and, in case of registered land, a memorial thereof entered upon the register of the last certificate of the title to be affected, and the judgment shall thereupon have the same force and effect as a lien upon the real estate, as if the judgment had been originally rendered by a court in that county.

Amended Oct. 21, 1969, eff. Jan. 1, 1970; May 28, 1982, eff. July 1, 1982; Dec. 17, 1993, eff. Feb. 1, 1994.

Formerly Ill.Rev.Stat.1991, ch. 110A, ¶ 366.

Committee Comments

(Revised July 1, 1971)

As adopted effective January 1, 1967, this rule was former section 92 of the Civil Practice Act, as amended in 1965 (Ill.Rev.Stat.1965, ch. 110, par. 92), without change of substance.

The last sentence of former section 92(3)(b) and section 89 of the Civil Practice Act provided in substance that if in a nonjury law case the Appellate Court found a material fact contrary to the finding of the trial court, the Appellate Court's finding was conclusive on the Supreme Court. The provisions were repealed by the General Assembly in 1965 because they were in conflict with the broad appellate powers conferred on the Supreme Court by the Judicial Article. Laws of 1965, p. 2543, §§ 1, 2.

Paragraph (b)

Subparagraph (1) was paragraph (b) in the 1967 revision. The words "in any civil case" were deleted from new paragraph (i) in 1969 as unnecessary.

Subparagraphs (2) and (3) were added in 1969. They are taken from the provisions in the Civil Practice Act on scope of review and related procedure in jury and nonjury cases, mentioned below.

Subparagraphs (2)(i), (ii) and (iii) are taken from sections 67(3), 68.1(7), and 68.1(2) of the Civil Practice Act (Ill.Rev.Stat.1969, ch. 110, pars. 67(3), 68.1(7), and 68.1(2)), respectively, without change of substance. Subparagraph 2(iv) is based on section 68.1(6) of the Act.

Subparagraph (2)(v) is new. It abrogates the ruling in *Keen v. Davis*, 108 Ill.App.2d 55, 63–64 (5th Dist. 1969), denying reviewability, on the appeal from an order allowing a new trial, of questions raised by other rulings of the trial court on the post-trial motion. Once the appeal is allowed, the whole case is before the reviewing court, and efficient judicial administration is advanced by disposing of all questions presented by the record. See also Rule 306(a)(2).

Subparagraph (3)(i) combines paragraphs (3) and (4) of section 64 of the Civil Practice Act (Ill.Rev. Stat.1967, ch. 110, pars. 64(3), (4)) without change in substance.

Subparagraphs (3)(ii) and (iii) are, respectively, the last sentence of section 68.3(1) and the last sentence of section 64(5) of the Civil Practice Act (Ill.Rev.Stat.1969, ch. 110, pars. 68.3(1), 64(5)) without change of substance.

(December 17, 1993)

Paragraph (b)(2)(v) is deleted because Rule 306 contains a substantively identical provision.

Rule 367. Rehearing in Reviewing Court

(a) Time; Length. A petition for rehearing may be filed within 21 days after the filing of the judgment, unless on motion the time is shortened or enlarged by the court or a judge thereof. Motions to extend the time for petitioning for rehearing are not favored and will be allowed only in the most extreme and compelling circumstances. Unless authorized by the court or a judge thereof, the petition shall be limited to 27 pages, or alternatively 8,000 words, and in either case be supported by a certificate of compliance in accordance with Rule 341(c).

(b) Contents. The petition shall state briefly the points claimed to have been overlooked or misapprehended by the court, with proper reference to the particular portion of the record and brief relied upon, and with authorities and argument, concisely stated in support of the points. Reargument of the case shall not be made in the petition.

(c) Form; Copies; Service; Notification of Reporter. The number of copies of the petition, and of any answer or reply (see paragraph (d)), the form, cover and service shall conform to the requirements for briefs (see Rule 341), except that, in the Supreme Court, petitions for rehearing shall be delivered or mailed by first-class mail or delivered by third-party commercial carrier, and a copy of the petition or any motion seeking to change the time for filing the petition shall also be delivered or mailed by first-class mail or delivered by third-party commercial carrier to the Reporter of Decisions, 207 W. Jefferson, Suite 305, Bloomington, Illinois 61701, and a certificate of mailing or delivery shall be supplied to the clerk of the Supreme Court.

(d) Answer; Reply; Oral Argument. No answer to a petition for rehearing will be received unless requested by the court or unless the petition is granted. No substantive change in the relief granted or denied by the reviewing court may be made on denial of rehearing unless an answer has been requested. If the petition is granted or if an answer is requested, the opposing party shall have 21 days from the request or the granting of the rehearing to answer the petition, and petitioner shall have 14 days after the due date of the answer within which to file a reply. Unless authorized by the court or a judge thereof, the answer shall be limited to 27 pages, or alternatively 8,000 words, the reply shall be limited to 10 pages, or alternatively 3,500 words, and each must be supported by a certificate of compliance in accordance with Rule 341(c). Three copies (or one copy if by e-mail service) of each shall be served on opposing counsel and proof of service filed with the clerk. The original briefs of the parties, and the petition for rehearing, the answer, and the reply shall stand as briefs on the rehearing. Oral argument will be permitted only if ordered by the court on its own motion.

(e) Limitation on Petitions in Appellate Court. When the Appellate Court has acted upon a petition for rehearing and entered judgment on rehearing no further petitions for rehearing shall be filed in that court.

Amended Oct. 1, 1976, eff. Nov. 15, 1976; Feb. 19, 1982, eff. April 1, 1982; April 10, 1987; June 12, 1987, eff. Aug. 1, 1987; Dec. 17, 1993, eff. Feb. 1, 1994; Oct. 14, 2005, eff. Jan. 1, 2006; May 24, 2006, eff. Sept. 1, 2006; Dec. 29, 2009; eff. immediately; Dec. 11, 2014, eff. Jan. 1, 2015; Dec. 9, 2015, eff. Jan. 1, 2016; Mar. 8, 2016, eff. immediately

Formerly Ill.Rev.Stat.1991, ch. 110A, ¶ 367.

Commentary
(December 17, 1993)

The rule is modified to reflect that all types of reviewing court dispositions are subject to the rehearing procedures and time limits (see *Woodson v. Chicago Board of Education* (1993), 154 Ill. 2d 391).

Committee Comments
(Revised February 1982)

This rule is based upon former Rule 44.

Paragraph (a)
As adopted in 1967, paragraph (a) changed the time limit provided in former Rule 44 to 21 days in accordance with the general principle that time periods should be multiples of seven days. The flat prohibition against extensions of time appearing in former Rule 44 was removed in favor of a statement that extensions were not favored. In 1976, the paragraph was amended to strengthen the language disfavoring extensions of time.

Paragraph (b)
This paragraph is the second and third sentences of former Rule 44(1) without change of substance.

Paragraph (c)
This paragraph was derived from a part of the first sentence of former Rule 44(1) and the third sentence of paragraph (2) of that rule. There was no change of substance until 1982, when the rule was reworded to specifically require that the parties furnish the Reporter of Decisions a copy of any rehearing petition or any motion seeking to change the time for filing a rehearing petition.

Paragraph (d)
This paragraph is based primarily upon former Rule 44(3). It does not change the preexisting practice.

Paragraph (e)
This new provision is applicable only to the Appellate Court. When that court has twice considered a case, once initially and a second time on rehearing, there would seem to be no need for further consideration, especially when there is a higher court from which relief can be sought. See Rules 315(b), 316, and 317 as to the date from which the time for seeking Supreme Court review begins to run.

Rule 368. Issuance, Stay, and Recall of Mandates from Reviewing Court

(a) Issuance; Stay on Petition for Rehearing. The clerk of the reviewing court shall transmit to the circuit court the mandate of the reviewing court, with notice to the parties, not earlier than 35 days after the entry of judgment unless the court orders otherwise. The timely filing of a petition for rehearing will stay the mandate until disposition of the petition unless otherwise ordered by the court. If the petition is denied, the mandate shall issue not earlier than 35 days after entry of the order denying the petition unless the court upon motion orders the time shortened or enlarged.

(b) Stay When Review by Supreme Court Is Sought. In cases in which an injunction has been modified or set aside by the Appellate Court, that court's mandate may be stayed only upon order of that court, the Supreme Court or a judge of either court. In all other cases, the mandate is stayed automatically if, before it may issue, a party who is entitled to seek review by the Supreme Court files a petition in the Supreme Court for such review. The stay is effective until the expiration of the time to seek review, and, if review is timely sought, until disposition of the case by the Supreme Court. The Supreme Court, the Appellate Court, or a judge of either court may, upon motion, order otherwise or stay the mandate upon just terms.

(c) Stay or Recall by Order. The Appellate Court, the Supreme Court, or a judge of either court may, upon just terms, stay the issuance of or recall any mandate of the Appellate Court until the time for seeking review by the Supreme Court expires, or if review is timely sought, until it is granted or refused, or if review is granted, until final disposition of the case by the Supreme Court. The stay may apply to any judgment entered or standing affirmed in any court pursuant to the mandate of the Appellate Court. In cases in which review by the Supreme Court of the United States may be sought, the court whose decision is sought to be reviewed or a judge thereof, and in any event the Supreme Court of Illinois or a judge thereof, may stay or recall the mandate, as may be appropriate.

Amended December 17, 1993, effective February 1, 1994; amended February 10, 2006, effective July 1, 2006.

Formerly Ill.Rev.Stat.1991, ch. 110A, ¶ 368.

Committee Comments

This rule is principally derived from section 82(4) of the Civil Practice Act and former Supreme Court Rule 45, Rule 10 of the First Appellate District, and Rule 16 of the other Appellate Districts (earlier Uniform Appellate Court Rule 16). The rule is made the same for the Supreme and Appellate Courts.

Paragraph (a)

Paragraph (a) enlarges the minimum time for issuance of a mandate from 15 to 21 days, but reduces the time after denial of rehearing from 10 to 7 days in the Appellate Court and, in the Supreme Court, from the period until the end of the term, or 15 days if the denial was during vacation, to 7 days. There is no good reason for delay after rehearing is denied. Issuance of the mandate in the Supreme Court is no longer tied in to the close of the term of court. The mandate is to be issued automatically by the clerk of the reviewing court.

Paragraph (b)

Paragraph (b) removes from the automatic stay provision of the superseded Appellate Court rules (Rule 10 of the First District, Rule 16 of the other districts) cases in which the Appellate Court sets aside or modifies an injunction. The Committee believes that in view of the nature and gravity of injunctive relief it is wrong to provide for the automatic continuance of an injunction that presumptively was erroneously issued, in whole or in part, and that such an injunction should be continued in effect only if one of the reviewing courts or a judge thereof determines that it should be.

The provision of the former rules for an automatic stay in other cases (unless the Supreme or Appellate Court or a judge of either otherwise orders) is retained. The affidavit filed to obtain the automatic stay may be that of the party or his attorney, and need not be executed by both as under the former rules.

Paragraph (c)

Paragraph (c) simplifies section 82(4) of the Practice Act to make it clear that the Supreme Court, the Appellate Court, or a judge of either, when appropriate, has discretion to grant a stay upon just terms until final disposition of the case, whether by the Illinois Supreme Court or the Supreme Court of the United States.

Rule 369. Filing of Mandate in Circuit Court and Proceedings Thereafter

(a) Filing of Mandate. The clerk of the circuit court shall file the mandate promptly upon receiving it.

(b) Dismissal or Affirmance. When the reviewing court dismisses the appeal or affirms the judgment and the mandate is filed in the circuit court, enforcement of the judgment may be had and other proceedings may be conducted as if no appeal had been taken.

(c) Remandment. When the reviewing court remands the case for a new trial or hearing and the mandate is filed in the circuit court, the case shall be reinstated therein upon 10 days' notice to the adverse party.

Amended May 28, 1982, eff. July 1, 1982.

Formerly Ill.Rev.Stat.1991, ch. 110A, ¶ 369.

Committee Comments

This rule is a revision of and supersedes section 88 of the Civil Practice Act. Changes have been made in the light of the provision in Rule 368 for automatic issuance of the mandate.

Rule 370. Process in Reviewing Court

(a) Form. The form of process in reviewing courts shall be, as near as may be, to similar process issued by the circuit court and may be prescribed by administrative orders of the reviewing courts.

(b) Execution and Return. Process in reviewing courts shall be executed and returned in the same manner as process in the circuit court is executed and returned unless the court orders otherwise.

Formerly Ill.Rev.Stat.1991, ch. 110A, ¶ 370.

Committee Comments

This Rule is a revision of section 91 of the Civil Practice Act and former Rule 2(5). The provision for the prescribing of the form of process by administrative orders of the reviewing courts is new, but should result in no change in practice.

Rule 371. Repealed eff. Feb. 1, 1994

Rule 372. Removing Records from Reviewing Court

(a) Work on Appeal. Prior to the due date of the reply brief, any party to the appeal may, for the purpose of work on the appeal, request, in writing, the clerk of the reviewing court to transmit the record on appeal to the clerk of the trial court or to the party's attorney. The clerk shall comply with the request, without the necessity of obtaining an order of court, by sending the record to the clerk of the trial court or the attorney, charges collect. Upon receiving the record on appeal, the clerk of the trial court or the attorney is responsible for its safekeeping and shall return the record to the clerk of the reviewing court by prepaid mail or express not later than the day upon which the reply brief is due. The parties may unbind the record for the purpose of photocopying, but the party responsible for unbinding the record must restore it to its original condition.

(b) Other. Except as otherwise provided in this rule, no record shall be taken from the files of the reviewing court except on leave granted by the court, or a judge thereof. The clerk shall report promptly to the court every violation of this rule.

Amended Jan. 5, 1981, eff. Feb. 1, 1981; Dec. 17, 1993, eff. Feb. 1, 1994.

Formerly Ill.Rev.Stat.1991, ch. 110A, ¶ 372.

Committee Comments

(Revised January 5, 1981)

This is substantially former Supreme Court Rule 54 and Rule 20 of the Second, Third, Fourth and Fifth Appellate Court Districts, made applicable to all reviewing courts. A change permits the clerk to transmit the record directly to the attorney who will be using it, and not merely to the clerk of the trial court, who would then in normal course let the attorney have it. For many years prior to the adoption of this rule the clerk of the Appellate Court for the First District was authorized to permit temporary withdrawal of the record by attorneys who needed to use it in preparing their briefs and abstracts. The bar did not abuse this privilege.

With the elimination of "excerpts from record" in 1979, paragraph (a) of Rule 372 was amended in

1981 to substitute the due date of the reply brief for the due date of the excerpts from record as a base for the time limit imposed on requests under the paragraph. Since under the prior practice both the reply brief and the excerpts from record were due 14 days after the due date of the appellee's brief, the 1981 amendment does not effect a change in the practice.

Rule 373. Date of Filing Papers in Reviewing Court; Certificate or Affidavit of Mailing

Unless received after the due date, the time of filing records, briefs or other papers required to be filed within a specified time will be the date on which they are actually received by the clerk of the reviewing court. If received after the due date, the time of mailing, or the time of delivery to a third-party commercial carrier for delivery to the clerk within three business days, shall be deemed the time of filing. Proof of mailing or delivery to a third-party commercial carrier shall be as provided in Rule 12(b)(3). This rule also applies to a motion directed against the judgment and to the notice of appeal filed in the trial court.

Amended Jan. 5, 1981, eff. Feb. 1, 1981; July 1, 1985, eff. Aug. 1, 1985; Dec. 17, 1993, eff. Feb. 1, 1994; Dec. 29, 2009, eff. immediately; Sept. 19, 2014, eff. immediately.

Formerly Ill.Rev.Stat.1991, ch. 110A, ¶ 373.

Committee Comments

(Revised July 1, 1985)

Rule 373 was new in 1967. It was designed to make it unnecessary for counsel to make sure that briefs and other papers mailed before the filing date actually reach the reviewing court within the time limit. Receipt of the paper in the clerk's office a day or two later will not delay the appeal. As originally adopted the rule provided that the time of mailing might be evidenced by the post mark affixed by a United States Post Office. Because of problems with the legibility of post marks, and delay in affixing them in some cases, the rule was amended in 1981 to provide for the use of affidavits of mailing or United States Postal Service certificates of mailing.

The 1985 amendment regarding the recording of a filing date was intended to simplify record keeping in the appellate and supreme courts.

(December 17, 1993)

The rule is revised to make the method of proof of mailing consistent with practice under Rule 12.

Reference to the notice of appeal coming within the scope of the rule is a reflection of existing law (see *Harrisburg–Raleigh Airport Authority v. Department of Revenue* (1989), 126 Ill.2d 326).

(December 29, 2009)

The rules on service and filing have been revised to provide for sending documents via third-party commercial carrier. Under these rules, the term "delivery" refers to all the carrier's standard pick-up methods, such as dropping a package in a UPS or FedEx box or with a UPS or FedEx contractor.

Rule 374. Costs in the Reviewing Courts

(a) Except as otherwise provided by law, if an appeal is dismissed, costs shall be taxed against the appellant unless otherwise agreed by the parties or excused by the court for good cause shown; if a judgment is affirmed, costs shall be taxed against the appellant unless excused by the court for good cause shown; if a judgment is reversed, costs shall be taxed against the appellee unless excused by the court for good cause shown; if a judgment is affirmed or reversed in part or is vacated, costs shall be allowed only as ordered by the court.

(b) The following costs are taxable:

(1) filing fees paid to the clerk of the reviewing court;

(2) appearance fees in the reviewing court;

(3) the fee paid to the clerk of the trial court (but not to court reporter) for preparing the record for appeal;

(4) the actual and reasonable costs of printing or otherwise producing necessary copies of an abstract requested by the reviewing court pursuant to Rule 342 (however, the clerk of the reviewing court will not tax costs for unnecessary matters included in the abstracts, nor will the clerk allow costs for additional abstract without order of court); and

(5) the actual and reasonable cost of printing, or otherwise producing necessary copies of briefs authorized by these rules (the cost of including unnecessary matters or arguments may be disallowed as costs).

(c) An appellant or an appellee, as the case may be, who desires costs to be taxed, shall state them in an itemized and verified bill of costs which should be filed with the clerk of the reviewing court, with proof of service, within 14 days after rehearing is denied or barred. Any objections to the bill of costs must be filed within 10 days after service of the bill of costs, unless the time is extended by the court. If objections are filed to the bill of costs, the clerk of the reviewing court will refer said bill and objections to the court for disposition. If no objections are filed to the bill of costs, the clerk of the reviewing court shall tax the costs.

(d) Costs pursuant to this rule shall not be taxed against any public, municipal, governmental, or quasi-municipal corporation, or against any public officer in that person's official capacity for the benefit of the public.

Added Feb. 19, 1982, eff. April 1, 1982. Amended Dec. 17, 1993, eff. Feb. 1, 1994.

Formerly Ill.Rev.Stat.1991, ch. 110A, ¶ 374.

Rule 375. Failure to Comply With Rules; Frivolous Appeals—Sanctions

(a) **Failure to Comply With Appeals Rules.** If after reasonable notice and an opportunity to respond, a party or an attorney for a party or parties is determined to have wilfully failed to comply with the appeal rules, appropriate sanctions may be imposed upon such a party or attorney for the failure to comply with these rules. Appropriate sanctions for violations of this section may include an order that a party be barred from presenting a claim or defense relating to any issue to which refusal or failure to comply with the rules relates, or that judgment be entered on that issue as to the other party, or that a dismissal of a party's appeal as to that issue be entered, or that any portion of a party's brief relating to that issue be stricken. Additionally, sanctions involving an order to pay a fine, where appropriate, may also be ordered against any party or attorney for a party or parties.

(b) **Appeal or Other Action Not Taken in Good Faith; Frivolous Appeals or Other Actions.** If, after consideration of an appeal or other action pursued in a reviewing court, it is determined that the appeal or other action itself is frivolous, or that an appeal or other action was not taken in good faith, for an improper purpose, such as to harass or to cause unnecessary delay or needless increase in the cost of litigation, or the manner of prosecuting or defending the appeal or other action is for such purpose, an appropriate sanction may be imposed upon any party or the attorney or attorneys of the party or parties. An appeal or other action will be deemed frivolous where it is not reasonably well grounded in fact and not warranted by existing law or a good-faith argument for the extension, modification, or reversal of existing law. An appeal or other action will be deemed to have been taken or prosecuted for an improper purpose where the primary purpose of the appeal or other action is to delay, harass, or cause needless expense.

Appropriate sanctions for violation of this section may include an order to pay to the other party or parties damages, the reasonable costs of the appeal or other action, and any other expenses necessarily incurred by the filing of the appeal or other action, including reasonable attorney fees.

A reviewing court may impose a sanction upon a party or an attorney for a party upon the motion of another party or parties, or on the reviewing court's own initiative where the court deems it appropriate. If the reviewing court initiates the sanction, it shall require the party or attorney, or both, to show cause why such a sanction should not be imposed before imposing the sanction. Where a sanction is imposed, the reviewing court will set forth the reasons and basis for the sanction in its opinion or in a separate written order.

Adopted June 19, 1989, eff. Aug. 1, 1989. Amended Dec. 17, 1993, eff. Feb. 1, 1994.

Formerly Ill.Rev.Stat.1991, ch. 110A, ¶ 375.

Committee Comments
(August 1, 1989)

Paragraph (a) is intended to cover those situations where a party or his attorney or both fail to comply with the appeals rules. The sanctions under this paragraph are intended to apply in those circumstances where the party or attorney wilfully fails to comply with the rules. No sanction is intended to be imposed under this paragraph for an inadvertent violation of the appeals rules. No formal hearing process is envisioned before a sanction will be imposed, rather any sanction imposed will be by a procedure summary in nature and will not involve the formalities required in procedures for citations of contempt of court. (See *People v. Waldron* (1986), 114 Ill.2d 295.) However, the sanctions imposed under this paragraph are only those that would be typically inherently available to a reviewing court in enforcing its rules, and the impositions of small fines similar to those imposed for petty offenses. (See old section of Title 18 of the United States Code, Crimes & Criminal Procedure, 18 U.S.C. § 1 (1982) (repealed October 30, 1984); Pub.L. 98–596, § 8, 98 Stat. 3138 (1984); see also Ill.Rev.Stat.1987, ch. 38, par. 1005–5–1; Ill.Rev.Stat. 1987, ch. 24, pars. 1–2–1, 1–2–1.1.) Furthermore, before any sanction is imposed, a party and/or attorney will receive notice of the violation and a reasonable opportunity to correct it.

Paragraph (b) is derived from the current appellate Rule 38 of the Federal Rules of Appellate Procedure, section 1912 of the Judicial Code (28 U.S.C. § 1912) and section 1927 of the Judicial Code (28 U.S.C. § 1927). It is also similar to the requirements set forth in Rule 7–102 of the Illinois Code of Professional Responsibility and Rule 3.1 of the ABA Model Rules of Professional Conduct, and adopts a modified version of Federal Rule 11. Moreover, appeals courts have been recognized to have inherent authority to impose sanctions for taking a frivolous appeal or for abusive tactics in the conduct of the appeal. See *Roadway Express Inc. v. Piper* (1980), 447 U.S. 752, 65 L.Ed.2d 488, 100 S.Ct. 2455.

However, this paragraph relates not only to frivolous appeals, *i.e.*, those without merit and no chance of success, but also to appeals which are conducted in a frivolous manner, *i.e.*, those whose primary purpose is to delay enforcement of the judgment, to cause a party to incur unnecessary expense, or which are generally prosecuted in bad faith. The determination that the appeal is frivolous or the conduct is improper is based on an objective standard of conduct, *viz.*, an appeal will be found to be frivolous if a reasonable prudent attorney would not in good faith have brought such an appeal, or the appeal conduct will be found to be improper if a reasonable prudent attorney would not have engaged in such conduct. If an appeal is found to be frivolous, or the conduct improper, the subjective

nature of the conduct is then important to determine the appropriate nature and amount of the sanction. A party or attorney will be given notice before any sanction is imposed, either by the motion of an aggrieved party or by a rule to show cause issued by the court. A party or attorney who is a subject of a proposed sanction where the proposed sanction is initiated by the court is entitled to respond before any sanction is imposed. If a sanction is imposed, as noted, the court in its opinion or in a separate written order will provide a statement of reasons or basis for the imposed sanction.

Under paragraph (b), a penal fine may be imposed if the conduct in a particular case also constitutes a violation of the civil appeals rules as set forth in paragraph (a) above.

(December 17, 1993)

The rule has been modified to make clear that any action pursued in the reviewing court is subject to sanctions if the conduct constitutes a violation of the rule.

Rules 376 to 380.   Reserved

PART G.   ORIGINAL ACTIONS IN SUPREME COURT

Rule 381.   Original Actions in the Supreme Court Pursuant to Article VI, Section 4(a), of the Constitution

(a) Motion for Leave to File; Only Issues of Law Considered. Proceedings in the supreme court in original actions in cases relating to revenue, *mandamus*, prohibition, or *habeas corpus*, and as may be necessary to the complete determination of any case on review, shall be instituted by filing a motion, supported by explanatory suggestions, for leave to file a complaint seeking appropriate relief. Only issues of law will be considered. The proposed complaint shall be sworn to and shall contain or have attached to it the lower court records or other pertinent material that will fully present the issues of law. If the motion is filed when the court is not in session and the case arises from the second, third, fourth, or fifth judicial district, the movant shall file the original and eight copies with the clerk in Springfield. If the case arises from the first judicial district (Cook County), the movant shall file the original motion and eight copies with the clerk in the Chicago satellite office.

(b) Service of Process. A copy of the motion together with the proposed complaint shall be served upon the other party or parties, including the nominal party or parties, and proof of service shall be filed at the time the motion is filed.

(c) Judge a Nominal Party. In an original action to review a judge's judicial act the judge is a nominal party, only, in the proceeding, and need not respond to the motion or complaint unless instructed to do so by the court. The judge's failure to do so will not admit any allegation. Counsel for the prevailing party may file appropriate papers for that party but shall not file any paper in the name of the judge.

(d) Objections to Motion. The respondent shall have 7 days after personal, e-mail or facsimile service of the motion, or 14 days after mailing of the motion if service is by mail, or 14 days after delivery to a third-party commercial carrier if service is by delivery to a third-party commercial carrier, or within such further time as the court or a judge thereof may allow to file any objections to the motion, and service shall be made upon the movant and proof of service filed with the clerk of the court. Oral argument on the motion shall be permitted as the court may allow.

(e) Briefs. If the motion is allowed, briefs conforming to the requirements of Rules 341 through 344 shall be filed in support of the pleadings, within the time fixed by the court on motion of any party or on its own motion. On notice to the court and the other party or parties, the plaintiff or defendant may allow his or her original papers to stand as his or her brief without order of court.

Amended eff. May 27, 1969; June 25, 1971, eff. July 1, 1971; Jan. 5, 1981, eff. Feb. 1, 1981; Feb. 19, 1982, eff. April 1, 1982; Feb. 27, 1987, eff. April 1, 1987; Dec. 17, 1993, eff. Feb. 1, 1994; eff. March 1, 2001; eff. Dec. 29, 2009; March 14, 2014, eff. immediately; Dec. 9, 2015, eff. Jan. 1, 2016.

Formerly Ill.Rev.Stat.1991, ch. 110A, ¶ 381.

Committee Comments

(Revised January 5, 1981)

Paragraphs (a), (b) and (c)

Prior to the adoption of the Constitution of 1970, the original jurisdiction rule necessarily was concerned with the only original jurisdiction cases authorized by the Constitution of 1870, which was limited to actions relating to revenue, *mandamus*, prohibition and *habeas corpus*. The new Constitution vests original and exclusive jurisdiction in the Supreme Court in other classes of cases in which factual issues might arise. Rule 381 would be inappropriate for such cases. Paragraph (a) has, therefore, been modified to limit Rule 381 to the traditional original actions to which it has previously applied, which are now covered by article VI, section 4(a), of the 1970 Constitution. A new Rule 382 provides for cases arising by virtue of the new mandatory exclusive original jurisdiction vested in the Supreme Court by articles IV and V of the 1970 Constitution.

The procedure in original actions was unchanged in substance by this rule, as adopted effective January 1, 1967, though it is spelled out in more detail than it was in former Rule 46, which governed until that date. Effective January 1, 1964, the paragraph of the former rule requiring original proceedings relating to the revenue to be brought at least twenty days before the first day of the term, unless the cause is continued, was deleted as unnecessary. Matters relating to the closing of the issues, the briefing schedule, and the holding of an oral argument are left to the discretion of the Supreme Court.

Paragraph (a) was amended in 1981 to add the penultimate sentence, requiring that when the motion is filed when the court is not in session a copy shall be sent to each of the justices at his district chambers. See the committee comments to Rule 361(c).

Paragraph (d)

Paragraph (d) was added to Rule 381 in May, 1969, to protect the judge whose action is being reviewed from becoming personally involved as a party in litigation in which his role is solely judicial. The amendment makes it unnecessary for the judge to choose between the alternatives of retaining counsel of his own or being represented by counsel for the successful party. "A judge will thus be guarded from engaging in ex parte discussions with counsel or aligning himself even temporarily with one side in pending litigation." *Rapp v. Van Deusen* (3d Cir. 1965), 350 F.2d 806, 813. See also *General Tire & Rubber Co. v. Watkins* (4th Cir. 1966), 363 F.2d 87, 89. See also Rule 21 of the Federal Rules of Appellate Procedure.

Rule 382. Original Actions in the Supreme Court Pursuant to Article IV, Section 3, and Article V, Section 6(d), of the Constitution

(a) Institution of Proceedings. Proceedings in the Supreme Court when the court has original and exclusive jurisdiction under article IV, section 3, and article V, section 6(d), of the Constitution, which relate to redistricting of the General Assembly and to the ability of the Governor to serve or resume office, shall be instituted by filing a motion for leave to file a complaint, which motion shall be accompanied by the complaint and a brief in support of the motion. The complaint may be supported by affidavits or other pertinent documents.

(b) Subsequent Procedure. Thereafter the case shall proceed in the manner ordered by the court. Whenever appropriate, and subject to order of the court, the rules governing cases in the circuit court shall serve as a guide to the procedure to be followed. The court may dispose of the case on the papers filed or may order further briefing or may order oral argument on the motion for leave to file or on the complaint or on the pleadings or on the pleadings supplemented by pertinent documentary evidence, or may call for additional evidence and for briefs and argument after such evidence has been received. If the court determines that disputed issues of material fact must be resolved on the basis of oral testimony, it may appoint a judge or retired judge of any Illinois court to take testimony and to report his findings of fact and recommendations to the Supreme Court.

(c) Briefs, Pleadings, and Other Documents. Briefs, pleadings, and other documents filed with the Supreme Court in cases covered by this rule shall, to the extent appropriate, conform to Rules 341 through 344.

Adopted June 25, 1971, eff. July 1, 1971. Amended Dec. 17, 1993, eff. Feb. 1, 1994.

Formerly Ill.Rev.Stat.1991, ch. 110A, ¶ 382.

Committee Comments
(July 1, 1971)

This rule is based in part upon Rule 381 and in part upon Rule 9 of the United States Supreme Court Rules and the practice thereunder, which enables that Court to deal with original cases involving factual issues requiring the taking of evidence. The object is to give the Court complete flexibility as to the procedure to be followed, depending upon the circumstances of the particular case. The procedures most likely to be employed, which have been employed by the United States Supreme Court, are specifically described because of the unfamiliarity of some of such procedures in prior Illinois practice.

The defendant need take no action until the Supreme Court indicates what is appropriate. If the Court deems the complaint obviously insufficient on its face, it may dispose of the case without calling the defendant to do anything. It may request the defendant to file either an answer to the complaint or a brief, in part depending on whether factual issues are presented. Because of the constitutional prohibition against "fee officers in the judicial system" (art. VI, sec. 14), the evidence must be taken by an active or retired judge, who will be already receiving a State salary, rather than by a master.

Rule 383.   Motions for Supervisory Orders

(a) A motion requesting the exercise of the Supreme Court's supervisory authority shall be supported by explanatory suggestions and shall contain or have attached to it the lower court records or other pertinent material that will fully present the issues, authenticated as required by Rule 328.

(b) A copy of the motion, explanatory suggestions, and all supporting papers must be served upon the other parties, including the nominal party or parties, and proof of service filed at the time the motion is filed.

(c) A person whose act is the subject of this proceeding shall be designated as a respondent. A respondent need not respond to the motion unless instructed to do so by the court, and failure to respond will not admit any of the allegations contained in the motion. The prevailing party or parties below shall file appropriate papers for that respondent but shall not file any paper in the name of the respondent.

(d) The prevailing party below shall have 7 days after personal, e-mail or facsimile service of the motion, or 14 days after mailing of the motion if service is by mail, or 14 days after delivery of the motion to a third-party commercial carrier if service is by delivery to a third-party commercial carrier, or within such

further time as the court or a judge thereof may allow, to file any objections to the motion, and service shall be made upon the movant and proof of service filed with the clerk of the court.

(e) Illegible copies of papers shall not be received. If the motion is filed when the court is not in session and the case arises from the second, third, fourth, or fifth judicial district, the movant shall file the original and eight copies with the clerk in Springfield. If the case arises from the first judicial district (Cook County), the movant shall file the original motion and eight copies with the clerk in the Chicago satellite office.

(f) Oral argument shall be permitted only if requested by the court.

Adopted Aug. 9, 1983, eff. Oct. 1, 1983. Amended Feb. 27, 1987, eff. April 1, 1987; Dec. 17, 1993, eff. Feb. 1, 1994; March 1, 2001, eff. immediately; Dec. 29, 2009, eff. immediately; Feb. 10, 2014, eff. immediately; March 14, 2014, eff. immediately; Dec. 9, 2015, eff. Jan. 1, 2016.

Formerly Ill.Rev.Stat.1991, ch. 110A, ¶ 383.

Committee Comments

This procedure is intended to discourage a practice which has developed since 1971 by which parties petition for leave to file a petition for mandamus or, *in the alternative,* for a supervisory order, in cases in which mandamus would be an inappropriate remedy.

Rule 384.   Proceedings for the Transfer and Consolidation of Multicircuit Actions

(a) Motion to Consolidate—Transfer. When civil actions involving one or more common questions of fact or law are pending in different judicial circuits, and the supreme court determines that consolidation would serve the convenience of the parties and witnesses and would promote the just and efficient conduct of such actions, the supreme court may, on its own motion or on the motion of any party filed with the supreme court, transfer all such actions to one judicial circuit for consolidated pretrial, trial, or post-trial proceedings.

(b) Pretrial Consolidation—Remandment. Unless the action is terminated or unless otherwise ordered by the supreme court, an action transferred for pretrial proceedings only shall, at or before the conclusion of those pretrial proceedings, be remanded to the circuit from which it was transferred. However, the supreme court may, on its own initiative or at the request of the transferee circuit court, separate any claim, cross-claim, counterclaim or third-party claim and remand such claims at any time.

(c) Procedure.

(1) *General.* Except as otherwise provided hereafter, procedures for processing motions for consolidation filed under this rule shall, to the extent feasible, follow the procedures set forth in Rule 383, "Motions for Supervisory Orders."

(2) *Notice to Clerks.* A party filing a motion to consolidate shall file a copy of such motion with the clerk of the circuit court of each circuit in which the actions to be consolidated are pending, and shall include an appendix to such motion specifying the county in which each such case is pending and the names and file numbers of all cases to be consolidated.

(3) *Notice to Parties.* Service on other parties shall be as provided in Rule 383(b).

(4) *Oral Argument.* If the supreme court requests oral argument on the motion to consolidate, the clerk of the supreme court shall so notify the clerk of each affected circuit court and the attorney(s) for each affected party.

(5) *Procedures—Orders to Consolidate.* If the supreme court grants a motion to consolidate or if the supreme court initiates a consolidation of cases at the circuit court level, the clerk of the supreme court shall send a copy of the court's order to the clerk of each affected circuit court and to the attorney(s) for each affected party. The clerks of the circuit courts from which a transfer is ordered shall promptly certify and transfer to the clerk of the circuit court to which the transfer is ordered all papers in the affected cases and in this and all other respects the cases shall be treated as if there had been an intrastate transfer on the grounds of *forum non conveniens*. See Rule 187(c).

Adopted Oct. 25, 1990, eff. Nov. 1, 1990.

Formerly Ill.Rev.Stat.1991, ch. 110A, ¶ 384.

Committee Comment

This rule is new and is based upon Title 28, section 1407, of the United States Code, which establishes the procedure in the Federal courts for the transfer of civil actions involving one or more common questions of fact, pending in different districts, to one district for coordination or consolidated pretrial proceedings. This new rule provides for similar procedures in Illinois for the transfer of related cases pending in different judicial circuits within the State. The rule, however, not only covers cases involving common questions of fact, but includes cases which involve common questions of law as well. Additionally, this rule, unlike 28 U.S.C. § 1407, also provides for the transfer of the related cases, where appropriate, for trial or post-trial proceedings and not just for transfers for pretrial proceedings.

Another major departure from the Federal procedures set forth in section 1407 is that transfers in Illinois will be made by the supreme court and not a judicial panel. This was considered required by the Illinois Constitution (Ill. Const. 1970, art. VI, § 4) and is more consistent with current Illinois practice. In an attempt to adhere to current Illinois practice, the rule provides that, to the extent feasible, motions processed under the new rule shall follow the procedures set forth in Rule 383, "Motions for Supervisory Orders." Further, where a transfer is ordered by the supreme court the clerks of the courts affected shall treat the case as if there had been an intrastate transfer on the grounds of *forum non conveniens* under Rule 187(c).

Section (c)(2) is new and does not have a counterpart in Rule 383. Section (c)(2) requires a party filing a motion to consolidate to also file a copy of the motion and an appendix specifying the county in which each case is pending and the names and file numbers of all the cases consolidated, with the clerk of the circuit court, where the asserted related actions are pending. Also, in section (c)(4), this rule specifically directs the clerk of the supreme court to notify the clerks of the affected circuits and the parties if the supreme court requests oral argument. This is also the case under section (c)(5) of the rule where the supreme court grants a motion to consolidate, the supreme court clerk again is directed to notify the affected circuit court clerks and the parties.

Rules 385 to 400. Reserved

ARTICLE IV. RULES ON CRIMINAL PROCEEDINGS IN THE TRIAL COURT

Rule
451.   Instructions.
452 to 470.   Reserved.

PART D.   POST-CONVICTION PROCEEDINGS

471.   Transcripts for Poor Persons Bringing Post–Convic-
         tion Proceedings.
472 to 500.   Reserved.

PART A.   WAIVERS AND PLEAS

Rule 401.   Waiver of Counsel

(a) **Waiver of Counsel.** Any waiver of counsel shall be in open court. The court shall not permit a waiver of counsel by a person accused of an offense punishable by imprisonment without first, by addressing the defendant personally in open court, informing him of and determining that he understands the following:

    (1) the nature of the charge;

    (2) the minimum and maximum sentence prescribed by law, including, when applicable, the penalty to which the defendant may be subjected because of prior convictions or consecutive sentences; and

    (3) that he has a right to counsel and, if he is indigent, to have counsel appointed for him by the court.

(b) **Transcript.** The proceedings required by this rule to be in open court shall be taken verbatim, and upon order of the trial court transcribed, filed and made a part of the common law record.

Amended June 26, 1970, eff. Sept. 1, 1970; June 28, 1974, eff. Sept. 1, 1974; Sept. 29, 1978, eff. Nov. 1, 1978; amended April 27, 1984, eff. July 1, 1984.

Formerly Ill.Rev.Stat.1991, ch. 110A, ¶ 401.

Committee Comments

(Revised April 27, 1984)

Rule 401, as adopted in 1967 (36 Ill. 2d R. 401), covered (1) waiver of indictment, (2) waiver of counsel, (3) pleas of guilty, and (4) the requirement of representation by counsel in open court on a guilty plea or waiver of counsel or waiver of indictment by persons under 18 years of age. In 1970, items (3) and (4) were transferred to Rules 402 and 403 respectively (43 Ill. 2d Rules 402, 403), and waiver of counsel and waiver of indictment were separated into separate lettered paragraphs (a) and (b), respectively (43 Ill. 2d R. 401(a), (b)), in order to give a clearer and more specific statement of the requirements for each type of waiver, since in a given case both waivers might not occur, or might occur at different times. In 1975, the Code of Criminal Procedure of 1963 was amended to abolish the requirement of indictment, and in 1978, to reflect this change, paragraph (b) of Rule 401 (58 Ill. 2d R. 401) was rescinded and former paragraph (c) became the present paragraph (b).

With regard to waiver of counsel, the 1970 amendments made no major change in substance, although they made explicit some requirements that were only implicit in the rule as originally adopted. For example, Rule 401 as originally adopted merely stated that the defendant must understand "the consequences [of the charges against him] if found guilty" (36 Ill. 2d R. 401(b)), while paragraph (a)(2) defines these consequences. The definition is the same as in Rule 402, paragraph (a)(2), concerning admonition of the consequences when a plea of guilty is accepted. See the committee comments to Rule 402.

Original Rule 401 (36 Ill. 2d R. 401), and Rule 401(a), as amended in 1970 (43 Ill. 2d R. 401(a)), required waiver of counsel only in cases in which the defendant was accused of a crime punishable by imprisonment in the penitentiary. In 1974, this paragraph of the rule was amended (58 Ill. 2d R. 401(a)) to conform to the decision of the Supreme Court of the United States in *Argersinger v. Hamlin* (1972), 407 U.S. 25, in which it was held that no imprisonment may be imposed, absent a knowing and intelligent waiver, unless the defendant was represented by counsel at his trial.

The present paragraph (b) is derived from the last two sentences of paragraph (b) of former Rule 401 (36 Ill. 2d R. 401).

[1984 Amendment]

In 1984 paragraph (b) was amended to require transcription of the verbatim report of waiver proceedings only when ordered by the trial court. This brings Rule 401(b) into line with Rule 402(e), which requires transcription of guilty plea proceedings in felony cases to be transcribed only when ordered by the trial court.

Rule 402.   Pleas of Guilty or Stipulations Sufficient to Convict

In hearings on pleas of guilty, or in any case in which the defense offers to stipulate that the evidence is sufficient to convict, there must be substantial compliance with the following:

(a) **Admonitions to Defendant.** The court shall not accept a plea of guilty or a stipulation that the evidence is sufficient to convict without first, by addressing the defendant personally in open court, informing him or her of and determining that he or she understands the following:

    (1) the nature of the charge;

    (2) the minimum and maximum sentence prescribed by law, including, when applicable, the penalty to which the defendant may be subjected because of prior convictions or consecutive sentences;

    (3) that the defendant has the right to plead not guilty, or to persist in that plea if it has already been made, or to plead guilty; and

    (4) that if he or she pleads guilty there will not be a trial of any kind, so that by pleading guilty he or she waives the right to a trial by jury and the right to be confronted with the witnesses against

him or her; or that by stipulating the evidence is sufficient to convict, he or she waives the right to a trial by jury and the right to be confronted with any witnesses against him or her who have not testified.

(b) Determining Whether the Plea is Voluntary. The court shall not accept a plea of guilty without first determining that the plea is voluntary. If the tendered plea is the result of a plea agreement, the agreement shall be stated in open court. The court, by questioning the defendant personally in open court, shall confirm the terms of the plea agreement, or that there is no agreement, and shall determine whether any force or threats or any promises, apart from a plea agreement, were used to obtain the plea.

(c) Determining Factual Basis for Plea. The court shall not enter final judgment on a plea of guilty without first determining that there is a factual basis for the plea.

(d) Plea Discussions and Agreements. When there is a plea discussion or plea agreement, the following provisions, in addition to the preceding paragraph of this rule, shall apply:

(1) The trial judge shall not initiate plea discussions. Upon request by the defendant and with the agreement of the prosecutor, the trial judge may participate in plea discussions. Prior to participating in the plea discussions, the trial judge shall admonish the defendant and inquire as to the defendant's understanding of the following:

That the defendant's attorney has requested that the trial judge participate in the conference to determine whether or not the charge(s) which is/are pending against the defendant can be resolved by a plea of guilty;

That during the course of the conference the prosecutor will be present and advise the judge of the facts of the case as contained in the police reports or conversations with witnesses, that the defendant's attorney will also be present and will advise the judge of any information the defendant may have concerning the circumstances which led to the defendant's arrest in the case.

That without the conference, the judge would not learn about this information unless the case proceeded to trial.

That the judge will also learn whether the defendant has a prior criminal history, his or her driving record, whether the defendant has any alcohol or drug problem, the defendant's work history, family situation, and other things which would bear on what, if any punishment should be imposed upon the defendant as a result of his or her plea of guilty to one or more of these charges.

That these are things that the judge would not learn about unless the case went to trial and the defendant was found guilty.

That at the end of the conference, the judge may make a recommendation as to what an appropriate sentence would be.

That the defendant or the prosecutor is free to accept or reject the judge's recommendation. However, if the defendant rejects the judge's recommendation and he or she wishes to have a trial on the charges, the defendant may not obtain another judge solely on the basis that the judge participated in the conference and is aware of the facts and circumstances surrounding the incident as well as the defendant's background. This means that the defendant will be waiving his or her right to request a substitution of judge based upon the judge's knowledge of the case.

That knowing all of these things the defendant still wishes that the judge participate in this conference.

(2) If a tentative plea agreement has been reached by the parties which contemplates entry of a plea of guilty in the expectation that a specified sentence will be imposed or that other charges before the court will be dismissed, the trial judge may permit, upon request of the parties, the disclosure to him or her of the tentative agreement and the reasons therefor in advance of the tender of the plea. At the same time the trial judge may also receive, with the consent of the defendant, evidence in aggravation or mitigation. The judge may then indicate to the parties whether he or she will concur in the proposed disposition; and if the judge has not yet received evidence in aggravation or mitigation, he or she may indicate that his or her concurrence is conditional on that evidence being consistent with the representations made. If the judge has indicated his or her concurrence or conditional concurrence, the judge shall so state in open court at the time the agreement is stated as required by paragraph (b) of this rule. If the defendant thereupon pleads guilty, but the trial judge later withdraws his or her concurrence or conditional concurrence, the judge shall so advise the parties and then call upon the defendant either to affirm or to withdraw his or her plea of guilty. If the defendant thereupon withdraws his or her plea, the trial judge shall recuse himself or herself.

(3) If the parties have not sought or the trial judge has declined to give his or her concurrence or conditional concurrence to a plea agreement, the judge shall inform the defendant in open court at the time the agreement is stated as required by paragraph (b) of this rule that the court is not bound by the plea agreement, and that if the defendant persists in his or her plea the disposition may be different from that contemplated by the plea agreement.

(e) Transcript. In cases in which the defendant is charged with a crime punishable by imprisonment in the penitentiary, the proceedings required by this rule to be in open court shall be taken verbatim, and upon order of the trial court transcribed, filed, and made a part of the common law record.

(f) Plea Discussions, Plea Agreements, Pleas of Guilty Inadmissible Under Certain Circumstances. If a plea discussion does not result in a plea of guilty, or if a plea of guilty is not accepted or is withdrawn, or if judgment on a plea of guilty is reversed on direct or collateral review, neither the plea discussion nor any resulting agreement, plea, or judgment shall be admissible against the defendant in any criminal proceeding.

Adopted June 26, 1970, eff. Sept. 1, 1970. Amended eff. Sept. 17, 1970; Jan. 5, 1981, eff. Feb. 1, 1981; May 20, 1997, eff. July 1, 1997; April 26, 2012, eff. July 1, 2012.

Formerly Ill.Rev.Stat.1991, ch. 110A, ¶ 402.

Committee Comments
(Revised May 1997)

The procedure on pleas of guilty was previously dealt with briefly in former Rule 401, paragraph (b). More extended and specific treatment of this subject is now required for at least two reasons. For one, the Supreme Court of the United States has recently held that it is a violation of due process to accept a guilty plea in State criminal proceedings without an affirmative showing, placed on the record, that the defendant voluntarily and understandingly entered his plea of guilty. (*Boykin v. Alabama* (1969), 395 U.S. 238.) For another, increased attention has recently been given to the long-standing practice of pleading guilty as a consequence of a prior agreement between the prosecution and defense concerning the disposition of the case; it is generally conceded that "plea discussions" and "plea agreements" are often appropriate, but that such procedures should not be concealed behind an in-court ceremony at which the defendant sometimes seems to think that he is expected to state falsely that no promises were made to him. (See American Bar Association Project on Minimum Standards for Criminal Justice, Standards Relating to Pleas of Guilty (Approved Draft 1968); Enker, *Perspectives on Plea Bargaining*, in The President's Commission on Law Enforcement and Administration of Justice, Task Force Report (1967): The Courts.) Two major objectives of new Rule 402 are: (1) to insure compliance with the *Boykin* requirements; and (2) to give visibility to the plea-agreement process and thus provide the reviewing court with a record containing an accurate and complete account of all relevant circumstances surrounding the guilty plea. See *United States v. Jackson* (7th Cir.1968), 390 F.2d 130.

Paragraph (a) sets forth the admonitions which must be given to the defendant to insure that his guilty plea is intelligently and understandingly made, as required by *Boykin*. Subparagraph (1) requires that the defendant be informed of the nature of the charge, as now also required by section 113–1 of the Code of Criminal Procedure of 1963. Subparagraph (2) requires that the defendant also be informed of the minimum and maxi-

mum sentences prescribed by law; this deviation from section 113–4(c) of the Code, which only expressly requires explanation of the "maximum penalty provided by law," is based upon the assumption that notice of both the minimum and maximum will give the defendant a more realistic picture of what might happen to him. (See ABA Standards Relating to Pleas of Guilty 28 (Approved Draft 1968).) Subparagraphs (3) and (4) cover the requirements enumerated in *Boykin*, namely, that the record on a guilty plea affirmatively show a waiver of "three important federal rights": the privilege against self-incrimination; the right to trial by jury; and the right to confront one's accusers.

The 1997 amendment was added to require that admonitions be given in cases in which the defense offers to stipulate to the sufficiency of the evidence to convict. See *People v. Horton*, 143 Ill.2d 11 (1991).

Paragraph (b) requires a determination that the guilty plea is voluntary by inquiry of the defendant as to whether any force or threats or promises were made to him. This is now accepted practice, see, e.g., *People v. Darrah* (1965), 33 Ill.2d 175, 210 N.E.2d 478, although not expressly required by Code section 113–4. In contrast to current practice, paragraph (b) also requires that if the tendered plea is the result of a plea agreement, then the agreement must be stated in open court. It is important to give visibility to the plea-agreement process in this way, as otherwise the defendant may feel required to state falsely that no promises were made and the plea may later be subject to collateral attack.

Paragraph (c) requires that the court determine there is a factual basis for the plea. Such inquiry is not uncommon in current practice, but heretofore has not been specifically required by law. The language of paragraph (c) is based upon the recent revision of Rule 11 of the Federal Rules of Criminal Procedure, and, as is true under the Federal rule, no particular kind of inquiry is specified; the court may satisfy itself by inquiry of the defendant or the attorney for the government, by examination of the presentence report, or by any other means which seem best for the kind of case involved. For a statement of the value of such a procedure, see ABA Standards Relating to Pleas of Guilty 30–34 (Approved Draft 1968).

Underlying paragraph (d), concerning plea discussions and plea agreements, is the notion that it is sometimes permissible for a defendant to plead guilty pursuant to a prior agreement that the prosecution will obtain, seek, or not oppose a certain disposition. For one assessment of various reasons upon which such practices may be legitimately based, see ABA Standards Relating to Pleas of Guilty 36–52 (Approved Draft 1968).

Subparagraph (1) of paragraph (d) prohibits the trial judge from initiating plea discussions.

Under subparagraph (d)(2), the judge, if he considers it appropriate, may be advised, in advance of the plea, of the tentative plea agreement and indicate his conditional concurrence or (if, with consent of the defendant, he then receives evidence in aggravation or mitigation) concurrence. Such concurrence or conditional concurrence is to be stated for the record when the plea is received, but if the judge later determines before sentencing that a more severe disposition is called for he must so advise the defendant and give him an opportunity to withdraw the plea. If the defendant does withdraw his plea under these circumstances, it would be inappropriate for the same judge to be involved in the trial of the case, so he is required to recuse himself. If, however, the defendant elects not to withdraw his plea, the judge is not required to recuse himself. Under subparagraph (3), where there is a plea agreement but no concurrence or conditional concurrence by the judge (either because the parties have not sought it or the judge has declined to give it), the judge is required to advise the defendant that he is not bound by the agreement stated in court at the time of the plea. This caution will remove any possibility of an inference by the defendant that the judge's awareness of the agreement indicates concurrence in it. See *People v. Baldridge* (1960), 19 Ill.2d 616, 169 N.E.2d 353.

Paragraph (e) is derived from former Rule 401. It was amended in 1981 to leave within the court's discretion the question of whether the proceedings shall be transcribed. The requirement that they shall be taken verbatim remains.

Paragraph (f) adopts the prevailing view that once a guilty plea has been annulled by withdrawal or other means, it should not be subsequently admissible against the defendant in criminal proceedings. (See *People v. Haycraft* (1966), 76 Ill.App.2d 149, 221 N.E.2d 317.) It follows that a plea discussion which has not resulted in a still-effective guilty plea should likewise be inadmissible, for otherwise defendants could engage in plea discussions only at their peril.

Rule 402A. Admissions or Stipulations in Proceedings to Revoke Probation, Conditional Discharge or Supervision

In proceedings to revoke probation, conditional discharge or supervision in which the defendant admits to a violation of probation, conditional discharge or supervision, or offers to stipulate that the evidence is sufficient to revoke probation, conditional discharge or supervision, there must be substantial compliance with the following.

(a) Admonitions to Defendant. The court shall not accept an admission to a violation, or a stipulation that the evidence is sufficient to revoke, without first addressing the defendant personally in open court, and informing the defendant of and determining that the defendant understands the following:

(1) the specific allegations in the petition to revoke probation, conditional discharge or supervision;

(2) that the defendant has the right to a hearing with defense counsel present, and the right to appointed counsel if the defendant is indigent and the underlying offense is punishable by imprisonment;

(3) that at the hearing, the defendant has the right to confront and cross-examine adverse witnesses and to present witnesses and evidence in his or her behalf;

(4) that at the hearing, the State must prove the alleged violation by a preponderance of the evidence;

(5) that by admitting to a violation, or by stipulating that the evidence is sufficient to revoke, there will not be a hearing on the petition to revoke probation, conditional discharge or supervision, so that by admitting to a violation, or by stipulating that the evidence is sufficient to revoke, the defendant waives the right to a hearing and the right to confront and cross-examine adverse witnesses, and the right to present witnesses and evidence in his or her behalf; and

(6) the sentencing range for the underlying offense for which the defendant is on probation, conditional discharge or supervision.

(b) Determining Whether Admission Is Voluntary. The court shall not accept an admission to a violation, or a stipulation sufficient to revoke without first determining that the defendant's admission is voluntary and not made on the basis of any coercion or promise. If the admission or tendered stipulation is the result of an agreement as to the disposition of the defendant's case, the agreement shall be stated in open court. The court, by questioning the defendant personally in open court, shall confirm the terms of the agreement, or that there is no agreement, and shall determine whether any coercion or promises, apart from an agreement as to the disposition of the defendant's case, were used to obtain the admission.

(c) Determining Factual Basis for Admission. The court shall not revoke probation, conditional discharge or supervision on an admission or a stipulation without first determining that there is a factual basis for the defendant's admission or stipulation.

(d) Application of Rule 402. The provisions of Rules 402(d), (e), and (f) shall apply to proceedings on a petition to revoke probation, conditional discharge or supervision.

Adopted Oct. 20, 2003, eff. Nov. 1, 2003.

Committee Comments
(October 20, 2003)

This rule follows the mandate expressed in *People v. Hall*, 198 Ill. 2d 173 (2001).

Rule 403. Pleas and Waivers by Persons Under 18

A person under the age of 18 years shall not, except in cases in which the penalty is by fine only, be permitted to enter a plea of guilty or to waive trial by jury, unless he is represented by counsel in open court.

Adopted June 26, 1970, eff. Sept. 1, 1970. Amended Aug. 9, 1983, eff. Oct. 1, 1983.

Formerly Ill.Rev.Stat.1991, ch. 110A, ¶ 403.

Committee Comments
(June, 1970)

This rule is derived from former Rule 401, paragraph (c). The only change in substance is the insertion of the phrase "except in cases in which the penalty is by fine only," qualifying the requirement of representation by counsel when a person under 18 enters a plea of guilty or waives jury trial. This change conforms to section 113–5 of the Code of Criminal Procedure of 1963.

See also Committee Comments to Rule 401.

Rules 404 to 410. Reserved

PART B. DISCOVERY

REVISED RULES AS TO DISCOVERY IN CRIMINAL CASES

Order Adopting Supreme Court Rules for Discovery and Procedure Before Trial in Criminal Cases

Rules 411–415 are adopted effective October 1, 1971. The committee comments to these rules are ordered filed. These rules govern all further proceedings in cases then pending, except when, in the opinion of the trial, Appellate or Supreme Court, the application of the new rules in a particular case then pending would not be feasible or would work an injustice, in which case former procedures apply.

Present Rule 411 (Voir Dire Examination) and present Rule 412 (Opening Statements) are redesignated Rules 431 and 432, respectively. Rules 418 through 430, 435, and 437 through 450 remain reserved.

Rule 411. Applicability of Discovery Rules

These rules shall be applied in all criminal cases wherein the accused is charged with a felony, and all juvenile delinquency cases wherein the accused is charged with an offense that would be a felony if committed by an adult. They shall become applicable following indictment or information or petition for adjudication of wardship and shall not be operative prior to or in the course of any preliminary hearing. Adopted eff. Oct. 1, 1971. Amended March 1, 2001, eff. immediately, except when in the opinion of the Trial, Appellate, or Supreme Court the application of the amended provisions in a particular case pending at the time of the amendment becomes effective would not be feasible or would work an injustice, in which case former procedures would apply; Dec. 9, 2011, eff. immediately.

Formerly Ill.Rev.Stat.1991, ch. 110A, ¶ 411.

Committee Comments
(October 1, 1971)

To avoid confusion, the Committee rejected the A.B.A. Standard which called for the application of discovery rules in "all serious criminal cases." No such standard exists in Illinois and the application of the discovery rules is extended to all offenses carrying a possible penalty of penitentiary imprisonment. The use of the extensive discovery procedures prescribed in these rules at preliminary stages of the criminal trial would serve no valid purpose and their use is confined to post-indictment procedures. The Committee considered but unanimously declined to make the rules applicable in juvenile court proceedings since the nature of such proceedings generally does not require discovery rules. However, if such proceedings become more adversary in nature, it may be desirable or necessary to apply the rules to them at some future date. In any event, the requirements of *In Re Gault*, (1967) 387 U.S. 1, must be met.

Special Supreme Court Committee on Capital Cases
(March 1, 2001)

Rule 411, as amended, makes criminal discovery rules applicable to the sentencing hearing in a capital case. A capital sentencing hearing is a unique and complex proceeding, which often takes place immediately following trial on the merits. Allowing pretrial discovery for capital sentencing will assist counsel in preparing for this critical stage of a capital trial and prevent delay and disruption of the sentencing hearing. See also Rule 416(c) (pretrial notice of aggravating factors the State will rely upon in sentencing).

The amendment to Rule 411 does not create new forms of discovery. Instead, the amendment extends the application of existing discovery methods to capital sentencing hearings. The committee notes that any discovery rule that requires disclosure by the defense is subject to constitutional limitations and limitations based on attorney-client or other privilege. Existing discovery rules expressly mention constitutional limitations on defense disclosures (see, e.g., Rule 413) and provide that attorney work product is not subject to disclosure by the State or the defense (Rule 412(j)).

The committee found that the existing discovery rules and associated case law would adequately address constitutional and privilege-based objections to pretrial disclosure of sentencing information by the defense. However, constitutional and privilege-based limitations on discovery do not preclude the possibility that pretrial disclosure of defense sentencing information could directly or indirectly aid the State's case on the merits. The extension of discovery procedures to capital sentencing is not intended to provide such an advantage to the State.

In the event the defense objects to disclosure of specific sentencing information on the ground that disclosure would harm the defense case on the merits, the trial court should take any action necessary to prevent that harm. Options available to the trial court include excision of objectionable material pursuant to Rule 415(e) and the use of protective orders to defer disclosure or restrict the use of information disclosed (Rule 415(d)). *In camera* review of a claim of potential harm from disclosure of sentencing information (Rule 415(f)) may be appropriate to prevent disclosure of defense theories or strategy, or where the identity of a defense sentencing witness is unknown to the State.

Rule 412. Disclosure to Accused

(a) Except as is otherwise provided in these rules as to matters not subject to disclosure and protective orders, the State shall, upon written motion of defense counsel, disclose to defense counsel the following material and information within its possession or control:

(i) the names and last known addresses of persons whom the State intends to call as witnesses, together with their relevant written or recorded statements, memoranda containing substantially verbatim reports of their oral statements, and a list of memoranda reporting or summarizing their oral statements. Upon written motion of defense counsel memoranda reporting or summarizing oral statements shall be examined by the court *in camera* and if found to be substantially verbatim reports of oral statements shall be disclosed to defense counsel;

(ii) any written or recorded statements and the substance of any oral statements made by the accused or by a codefendant, and a list of witnesses to the making and acknowledgment of such statements;

(iii) a transcript of those portions of grand jury minutes containing testimony of the accused and relevant testimony of persons whom the prosecuting attorney intends to call as witnesses at the hearing or trial;

(iv) any reports or statements of experts, made in connection with the particular case, including results of physical or mental examinations and of scientific tests, experiments, or comparisons, and a statement of qualifications of the expert;

(v) any books, papers, documents, photographs or tangible objects which the prosecuting attorney intends to use in the hearing or trial or which were obtained from or belong to the accused; and

(vi) any record of prior criminal convictions, which may be used for impeachment, of persons whom the State intends to call as witnesses at the hearing or trial.

If the State has obtained from the defendant, pursuant to Rule 413(d), information regarding defenses the defendant intends to make, it shall provide to defendant not less than 7 days before the date set for the hearing or trial, or at such other time as the court may direct, the names and addresses of witnesses the State intends to call in rebuttal, together with the information required to be disclosed in connection with other witnesses by subdivisions (i), (iii), and (vi), above, and a specific statement as to the substance of the testimony such witnesses will give at the trial of the cause.

(b) The State shall inform defense counsel if there has been any electronic surveillance (including wiretapping) of conversations to which the accused was a party, or of his premises.

(c) Except as is otherwise provided in these rules as to protective orders, the State shall disclose to defense counsel any material or information within its possession or control which tends to negate the guilt of the accused as to the offense charged or which would tend to reduce his punishment therefor. The State shall make a good-faith effort to specifically identify by description or otherwise any material disclosed pursuant to this section based upon the information available to the State at the time the material is disclosed to the defense. At trial, the defendant may not offer evidence or otherwise communicate to the trier of fact the State's identification of any material or information as tending to negate the guilt of the accused or reduce his punishment.

(d) The State shall perform its obligations under this rule as soon as practicable following the filing of a motion by defense counsel.

(e) The State may perform these obligations in any manner mutually agreeable to itself and defense counsel or by:

(i) notifying defense counsel that material and information, described in general terms, may be inspected, obtained, tested, copied, or photographed, during specified reasonable times; and

(ii) making available to defense counsel at the time specified such material and information, and suitable facilities or other arrangements for inspection, testing, copying and photographing of such material and information.

(f) The State should ensure that a flow of information is maintained between the various investigative personnel and its office sufficient to place within its possession or control all material and information relevant to the accused and the offense charged.

(g) Upon defense counsel's request and designation of material or information which would be discoverable if in the possession or control of the State, and which is in the possession or control of other governmental personnel, the State shall use diligent good-faith efforts to cause such material to be made available to defense counsel; and if the State's efforts are unsuccessful and such material or other governmental personnel are subject to the jurisdiction of the court, the court shall issue suitable subpoenas or orders to cause such material to be made available to defense counsel.

(h) **Discretionary Disclosures.** Upon a showing of materiality to the preparation of the defense, and if the request is reasonable, the court, in its discretion, may require disclosure to defense counsel of relevant material and information not covered by this rule.

(i) Denial of Disclosure. The court may deny disclosure authorized by this rule and Rule 413 if it finds that there is substantial risk to any person of physical harm, intimidation, bribery, economic reprisals, or unnecessary annoyance or embarrassment resulting from such disclosure which outweighs any usefulness of the disclosure to counsel.

(j) Matters Not Subject to Disclosure.

(i) *Work Product.* Disclosure under this rule and Rule 413 shall not be required of legal research or of records, correspondence, reports or memoranda to the extent that they contain the opinions, theories or conclusions of the State or members of its legal or investigative staffs, or of defense counsel or his staff.

(ii) *Informants.* Disclosure of an informant's identity shall not be required where his identity is a prosecution secret and a failure to disclose will not infringe the constitutional rights of the accused. Disclosure shall not be denied hereunder of the identity of witnesses to be produced at a hearing or trial.

(iii) *National Security.* Disclosure shall not be required where it involves a substantial risk of grave prejudice to national security and where a failure to disclose will not infringe the constitutional rights of the accused. Disclosure shall not thus be denied hereunder regarding witnesses or material to be produced at a hearing or trial.

Adopted eff. Oct. 1, 1971. Amended Oct. 1, 1976, eff. Nov. 15, 1976; June 15, 1982, eff. July 1, 1982; March 1, 2001, eff. immediately, except when in the opinion of the Trial, Appellate, or Supreme Court the application of the amended provisions in a particular case pending at the time the amendment becomes effective would not be feasible or would work an injustice, in which case former procedures would apply.

Formerly Ill.Rev.Stat.1991, ch. 110A, ¶ 412.

Committee Comments
(October 1, 1971)

Paragraph (a). It is intended that the disclosures required by this paragraph be implemented as a matter of course, and without time-consuming recourse to the courts. The discovery is not intended to be "automatic," in the sense that the State is not required to furnish information without any request by the defense counsel. It is recognized that in many cases discovery will be neither necessary nor wanted; paragraph (a), therefore, reflects the Committee's opinion that the choice of discovery or no discovery under this rule be within the discretion of defense counsel. By requiring the motion to be made in writing, rather than allowing oral motions, the Committee expressed the intent that certainty was necessary in order to prevent later disputes. Paragraph (a), subparagraph (i), enlarges upon the Code of Criminal Procedure of 1963, § 114-9(a). In addition to requiring production of a list of intended witnesses and their last known addresses (in the case of a police officer his official address

shall be sufficient), the State will also be expected to produce these witnesses' prior statements. *People v. Moses,* 11 Ill.2d 84, 142 N.E.2d 1 (1957), and decisions thereunder required the State to tender to defense counsel all such statements when the witness was tendered for cross-examination. Nothing herein changes the types of material that are to be provided; only the time of their disclosure is changed. By requiring disclosure prior to trial, it is hoped that the fruits of discovery can be harvested. Or in the event the parties have been unable to arrange a guilty plea or a dismissal, the disclosure assures defense counsel adequate time to prepare. Pre-trial disclosure of this nature not only affords defense counsel adequate opportunity to investigate the case, but also ensures the end of untimely interruptions at trial occasioned by disclosures of statements at trial. The A.B.A. Standard limited production of witnesses' statements to those in written or recorded form. Paragraph (a), subparagraph (i) requires the additional production of any substantially verbatim report of an oral statement by a witness. The State is also obliged to produce a list of all memoranda reporting or summarizing oral statements whether or not the memoranda appears to the State to be substantially verbatim reports of such statements. The defense is then entitled, upon filing of a written motion, to have the court examine the memoranda listed by the State. If the court finds that the memoranda do contain substantially verbatim reports of witness statements, the memoranda will be disclosed to defense counsel. This additional requirement serves two purposes. First, it ensures that the final responsibility for determining what is producible rests with the court. Second, it establishes, as a matter of record, the contents of the State's file with respect to reports of witness statements and thereby facilitates appellate review of contested questions of discovery under this subsection.

Paragraph (a), subparagraph (ii), is substantially § 114–10(a) of the Code of Criminal Procedure of 1963. Because of the decision in *Miranda v. Arizona,* 384 U.S. 436, 16 L.Ed.2(d) 694, 86 S.Ct. 1601 (1966), uncertainty as to the proper definition of "confession" exists. To ensure uniformity the Committee therefore chose to make all statements, not only confessions, discoverable. The availability of all such statements will also enable defense counsel to better prepare the case. The major change in prior law is that provision which makes discoverable the prior statements, etc., of all the accused's codefendants. If an informed motion for severance or excision of a codefendant's statement to remove prejudice is to be properly made, defense counsel must be able to obtain all of the codefendant's statements.

Paragraph (a), subparagraph (iii), adopts the A.B.A. Standard for production of grand jury minutes. In terms of Illinois practice, it makes mandatory disclosure of what is now discretionary under the second sentence of § 112–6(b) of the Code of Criminal Procedure of 1963. Such full disclosure is now required in a number of other jurisdictions, including California, Iowa, Kentucky and Minnesota.

In paragraph (a), subparagraph (iv), the Committee chose to adopt the Standard recommended by the A.B.A. There should be no problem of tampering with or misuse of the information, and without the opportunity to examine such evidence prior to trial defense counsel has the very difficult task of rebutting evidence of which he is unaware. In the interest of fairness paragraph (a), subparagraph (iv), requires the disclosure of all such results and reports, whether the result or report is "positive," or "negative," and whether or not the State intends to use the report at trial. If the State has the opportunity to view the results of any such examination the same opportunity should enure to defense counsel. No relevancy limitation is included; the only requirement is that the examination, etc. have been made "in connection with" the case. This subparagraph, and the others in this paragraph, are intended to supplement Rule 412(c), which requires the State to disclose any results, etc., which tend to negate the guilt of the accused or would tend to reduce his punishment were he convicted.

Paragraph (a), subparagraph (v), is identical to the A.B.A. Standard for production of books, papers, documents, photographs and tangible objects.

Paragraph (a), subparagraph (vi), differs from the A.B.A. Standards in that it is limited to prior convictions which may be used for impeachment purposes in Illinois. The Committee could discern no valid reason why this information should not be disclosed to the defense prior to trial when such information is in the possession or control of the State.

Paragraph (b) is included to expose for appropriate challenge an important collateral constitutional question. The nature of the exposure is designed to ensure the confidentiality of the information, and to provide flexibility in the releasing of the information, but to permit the litigation of any issues which those facts may present at a time when such litigation is most economical for the process. The necessity of the revelation of the existence of electronic surveillance has been recognized, and *in camera* hearings on the question of suppression of such evidence might be necessary. (*Alderman v. United States*, 394 U.S. 165, 22 L.Ed. 2d 176, 89 S.Ct. 961 (1969).) Because of the small number of cases in which such activity is involved, the Committee chose to put the burden on the State to inform defense counsel, rather than to require the submission of a motion.

Paragraph (c) is included to comply with the constitutional requirement that the prosecution disclose, "evidence favorable to an accused * * * where the evidence is material either to guilt or to punishment." (*Brady v. Maryland*, 373 U.S. 83, 87, 10 L.Ed.2d 215, 218, 83 S.Ct. 1194, 1196–97 (1963).) Although the pretrial disclosure of material is now not constitutionally required, it is clear that, if a conviction is to be valid, the material must be disclosed so that the defense can make use of it. In providing for pretrial disclosure, this paragraph permits adequate preparation for, and minimizes interruptions of, a trial, and assures informed pleas by the accused.

Paragraph (d) differs from the A.B.A. Standards only to require the State to perform its obligations as soon as is practicable following defense counsel's motion for discovery, rather than as soon as is practicable following his request for discovery. This change was made to accommodate the procedures of Rule 412(a), which require the filing of a written motion to initiate most discovery. More precision in describing the standard for performance was not deemed feasible for a rule that would be applied in such a wide variety of situations.

Paragraph (e) is designed to provide an orderly procedure for disclosure by the State. It delimits the extent of its responsibility to notifying defense counsel, only in general terms, as to the existence and availability of the material and information. The State need not send copies to defense counsel and it need not point out the significance of various items. It must, however, make the material available at specified and reasonable times, and permit—and provide suitable facilities or other arrangements for—inspection, testing, copying and photographing the material or information. If the State should desire to delay or restrict discovery it can seek a protective order therefor (Rule 415(d)) at the time of defense counsel's original motion or at any time following. Access to material by a defense expert must be permitted, sufficient to allow him to reach conclusions regarding the State's examining or testing techniques and results. Where feasible, defense counsel should have the opportunity to have a test made by his chosen expert, either in the State's laboratory or in his own laboratory using a sufficient sample.

Paragraph (f) is designed to deal with the problem of the extent to which the State can be expected to know of the existence of material or information which it is obligated to disclose. In discharging its duties it should know, or seek to know, of the existence of material or information at least equal to that which it should disclose to defense counsel. The formulation of a rule such as this means especially that the State should not discourage the flow of information to it from investigative personnel in order to avoid having to make disclosure. Supplementing paragraph (f) are Rules 412(g), dealing with material held by other government personnel, and 415(b), dealing with the State's continuing duty to disclose new information of which it learns. The Committee chose not to include a rule similar to A.B.A. Standard 2.1(d), which describes persons whose possession or control of material and information could be imputed to the prosecutor. It is assumed that this paragraph and the paragraphs cited in this Comment will be sufficient to guide a court in determining if proper disclosure has been made.

Paragraph (g) is part of the attempt to delineate the scope of the State's responsibilities for obtaining information which it is obligated to disclose to defense counsel. It complements the requirement in Rule 412(F), that it ensure the flow of information between the prosecutor and investigative personnel. Since the State's obligations are not limited to revealing only what happens to come within its possession or control, it is expected that the State will attempt to obtain material not within its possession but of which it has knowledge. Accordingly, this paragraph is primarily concerned with material of which the State does not have knowledge but of which defense counsel is aware; and therefore the burden is upon defense counsel to make the request and to designate the material or information which he wishes to inspect. This paragraph avoids placing the burden on the prosecutor, in the first instance, of canvassing all governmental agencies which might conceivably possess information relevant to the defendant. Paragraph (g) is not intended to enlarge the scope of discovery but merely to deal with problems of implementation. It is, therefore, limited to material or information "which would be discoverable if in the possession or control of the State."

Paragraph (h) of this rule authorizes discovery only if the court so orders within the exercise of its discretion; discovery will only be allowed when defense counsel can show that what he seeks is material to the preparation of the defense. Though there was some opinion in the Committee that the production of items and the performance of duties required in paragraphs 412(a) through (g) would result in adequate discovery in most cases, by providing for mandatory discovery the Committee did not intend to bar discovery of any other matters which the defense might find useful. To deal with such a broad area, however, it is believed that the criteria here set forth and the discretionary power accorded to the court provide a satisfactory balance between the needs of the State and the needs of the defense.

Paragraph (i). Although the A.B.A. Standards combine the provisions of this paragraph with the provisions of paragraph 412(h), the Committee separated the paragraphs. By separating the two paragraphs it was felt that there would be no confusion in the application of the court's right to deny disclosure. Paragraph (i) is intended not only to be used by the court in conjunction with the discretionary disclosures provided for in paragraph 412(h), but is also to be applied whenever the risks of disclosure outweigh the advantages of such disclosure to the defense or State.

Under paragraph (j), subparagraph (i), the material which is protected is primarily that which is protected from civil discovery under the doctrine of *Hickman v. Taylor*, 329 U.S. 495 (1947). But rather than merely indicate that "work product" is exempted from discovery the Committee chose instead to define it in such a way as to provide guidance to those who will administer and carry out the disclosures provided for in these rules.

Paragraph (j), subparagraph (ii). The value of informants to effective law enforcement is so highly regarded that encouragement of their use, through protection of their identity, has resulted in the development of one of the few privileges accorded to the State. The public interest in protecting the sources of information concerning the commission of crimes is served by providing for the non-disclosure of the identity of informants except when compelling circumstances require it. Disclosure should only be required when constitutional problems are raised or when the informant's identity is to be disclosed at trial (although a protective order under

Rule 414(d) might still be in order). The cases which have established this privilege include *McCray v. Illinois*, 386 U.S. 300 (1967); *Roviaro v. United States*, 353 U.S. 53 (1957); *People v. White*, 16 N.Y.2d 270, 266 N.Y.S.2d 100, 213 N.E.2d 438 (1965); and *Commonwealth v. Carter*, 208 Pa.Super. 245, 222 A.2d 475 (1966), aff'd mem., 209 Pa.Super. 732, 226 A.2d 215 (1967).

Paragraph (j), subparagraph (iii). While a defendant has a constitutional right to information which tends to negate his guilt or mitigate his punishment (*Brady v. Maryland*, 373 U.S. 83 (1963)), and to be confronted with the witnesses against him (*Jencks v. United States*, 353 U.S. 657 (1957)), and to any other information the withholding of which might violate his constitutional rights, he has no such right to information which does not affect his constitutional rights. This subparagraph, therefore, permits non-disclosure if disclosure would involve a substantial risk of grave prejudice to national security, and if such non-disclosure does not violate a constitutional right of the defendant. If the State intends to use the information or material at trial it should be disclosed to defendant prior to trial unless the State obtains a protective order delaying disclosure.

Special Supreme Court Committee on Capital Cases
(March 1, 2001)

In developing the specific-identification proposal, the committee was concerned with the possibility that information that clearly tends to be exculpatory or mitigating would not be disclosed or would be lost among other information. Examples of information that clearly tends to be exculpatory or mitigating include: a statement that a person other than the defendant committed the crime, a statement that the act that caused death was committed by an accomplice, or a preliminary scientific test result that is not inculpatory, and some types of impeachment evidence, such as certain prior convictions of State witnesses, information concerning promises or expectations of leniency for a State witness, or prior inaccurate or unsuccessful attempts at identification of the perpetrator by an occurrence witness. The purpose of the specific-identification requirement is to reinforce the duty to disclose and reduce the chance of pretrial or trial error with respect to this type of evidence.

The amendment to paragraph (c) requires a "good-faith" effort to specifically identify exculpatory and mitigating materials "based on information available to the State at the time the material is disclosed to the defense." Thus, the duty to specifically identify is not as broad as the duty to disclose under Rule 412(c). See Rule 416(g), committee comments. The good-faith standard is intended to avoid creating an impossible burden for the prosecution. A "good-faith" effort by prosecutors would include the specific identification of information that clearly tends to be exculpatory or mitigating. The amended rule is not intended to require that prosecutors specifically identify materials with remote or speculative exculpatory or mitigating value. The need to specifically identify materials falling between the extremes will depend upon the facts of the case.

The language stating that the duty to identify exculpatory or mitigating information must be viewed in light of the information available to the State when the material is disclosed to the defense is significant for several reasons. First, the information available to the State when disclosure is made will guide the determination of whether the State has made a good-faith effort to specifically identify exculpatory or mitigating information. Failure to identify information that can be characterized as exculpatory or mitigating only when viewed in light of the defense's theory of the case cannot be seen as evidence of failure to comply with the rule when the State was not aware of the defense theory. Second, placing the focus of the inquiry regarding compliance with the rule on information available at the time of disclosure to the defense is intended to avoid a standard based on hindsight evaluation of the exculpatory or mitigating value of information. Thus, a prosecutor's failure to identify information should not be second-guessed based on defense theories revealed after the information has been disclosed, unexpected events at trial, or new theories suggested after the trial.

The committee notes that in light of new evidence received or events at trial, materials that had no exculpatory value when initially disclosed could be viewed as exculpatory later in the trial process. The committee did not intend that the duty to specifically identify exculpatory or mitigating information would be subject to continuous updating.

The specific identification of potentially exculpatory or mitigating material by the prosecution pursuant to paragraph (c) is not an admission by the State for any purpose. Neither the terms or manner of the specific identification by the prosecution nor the fact that the prosecution has made the specific identification are relevant or admissible for the purposes of trial on the merits or sentencing. In addition, specific identification of materials pursuant to paragraph (c) does not imply that the material will be admissible as evidence.

Rule 413. Disclosure to Prosecution

(a) The person of the accused. Notwithstanding the initiation of judicial proceedings, and subject to constitutional limitations, a judicial officer may require the accused, among other things, to:

(i) appear in a line-up;

(ii) speak for identification by witnesses to an offense;

(iii) be fingerprinted;

(iv) pose for photographs not involving reenactment of a scene;

(v) try on articles of clothing;

(vi) permit the taking of specimens of material under his fingernails;

(vii) permit the taking of samples of his blood, hair and other materials of his body which involve no unreasonable intrusion thereof;

(viii) provide a sample of his handwriting; and

(ix) submit to a reasonable physical or medical inspection of his body.

(b) Whenever the personal appearance of the accused is required for the foregoing purposes, reasonable notice of the time and place of such appearance shall be given by the State to the accused and his counsel, who shall have the right to be present. Provision may be made for appearances for such purposes in an order admitting the accused to bail or providing for his release.

(c) Medical and scientific reports. Subject to constitutional limitations, the trial court shall, on written motion, require that the State be informed of, and permitted to inspect and copy or photograph, any reports or results, or testimony relative thereto, of physical or mental examinations or of scientific tests, experiments or comparisons, or any other reports or statements of experts which defense counsel has in his possession or control, including a statement of the qualifications of such experts, except that those portions of reports containing statements made by the defendant may be withheld if defense counsel does not intend to use any of the material contained in the report at a hearing or trial.

(d) Defenses. Subject to constitutional limitations and within a reasonable time after the filing of a written motion by the State, defense counsel shall inform the State of any defenses which he intends to make at a hearing or trial and shall furnish the State with the following material and information within his possession or control:

(i) The names and last known addresses of persons he intends to call as witnesses, together with their relevant written or recorded statements, including memoranda reporting or summarizing their oral statements, any record of prior criminal convictions known to him; and

(ii) any books, papers, documents, photographs, or tangible objects he intends to use as evidence or for impeachment at a hearing or trial;

(iii) and if the defendant intends to prove an alibi, specific information as to the place where he maintains he was at the time of the alleged offense.

(e) Additional disclosure. Upon a showing of materiality, and if the request is reasonable, the court in its discretion may require disclosure to the State of relevant material and information not covered by this rule.

Adopted eff. Oct. 1, 1971. Amended Oct. 1, 1976, eff. Nov. 15, 1976; June 15, 1982, eff. July 1, 1982.

Formerly Ill.Rev.Stat.1991, ch. 110A, ¶ 413.

Committee Comments
(October 1, 1971)

Paragraphs (a) and (b) provide for procedures to secure evidence from or involving the use of defendant's person consistent with the rules enunciated in *Gilbert v. California*, 388 U.S. 263 (1967) and cases cited therein. See also *Williams v. United States*, 419 F.2d 740 (D.C.Cir.1970) (bail order may provide for appearance of defendant for line-up).

Paragraph (c) provides for the production of medical and scientific evidence in the possession or control of defense counsel. Such evidence does not fall within the attorney-client privilege (*People v. Speck*, 41 Ill.2d 177), nor does such evidence involve self-incrimination unless it is based upon statements made by defendant. Where statements of defendant are involved they may be excised from reports. When defense counsel intends to use the scientific or medical evidence based upon the defendant's statements to the expert, excision shall not be made.

Paragraph (d) requires that defense counsel inform the State of any defenses he intends to offer. The notice of defenses includes both affirmative defenses, *i.e.*, insanity, and nonaffirmative defenses, *i.e.*, consent to intercourse in rape cases. The notice may include alternative and inconsistent defenses. In addition, defense counsel must produce a list of witnesses and their statements, along with any records or physical evidence he intends to use and any record of prior convictions, known to him. The general justifications for discovery in criminal cases apply to discovery against the defense. Such discovery eliminates unfair surprise and allows the opposing party to establish the truth or falsity of the defense. In addition, discovery against the defense eliminates the argument that criminal discovery is a one-way street. The discovery provisions with respect to the defense case are based upon two further premises: (1) when defense counsel receives full discovery of the evidence the State will introduce, he can then determine what defenses he can offer to that evidence and (2) only when defense counsel states his defense or defenses can the trial court make a full and fair determination of whether the dictates of *Brady v. Maryland*, 373 U.S. 83 (1963), have been fully met.

Paragraph (e) allows the court to order additional discovery not covered by the remainder of the rule but only upon a showing of materiality and reasonableness. The provision is parallel to Rule 412(h).

Rule 414.   Evidence Depositions

(a) If it appears to the court in which a criminal charge is pending that the deposition of any person other than the defendant is necessary for the preservation of relevant testimony because of the substantial possibility it would be unavailable at the time of hearing or trial, the court may, upon motion and notice to both parties and their counsel, order the taking of such person's deposition under oral examination or written questions for use as evidence at a hearing or trial.

(b) The taking of depositions shall be in accordance with rules providing for the taking of depositions in civil cases, and the order for the taking of a deposition may provide that any designated books, papers, documents or tangible objects, not privileged, be produced at the same time and place.

(c) If a witness is committed for failure to execute a recognizance to appear to testify at a hearing or trial, the court on written motion of the witness and upon notice to the State and defense counsel may order that his deposition be taken, and after the deposition has been subscribed, the court may discharge the witness.

(d) Rule 207—Signing and Filing Depositions— shall apply to the signing and filing of depositions taken pursuant to this rule.

(e) The defendant and defense counsel shall have the right to confront and cross-examine any witness whose deposition is taken. The defendant and defense counsel may waive such right in writing, filed with the clerk of the court.

(f) If the defendant is indigent, all costs of taking depositions shall be paid by the county wherein the criminal charge is initiated. If the defendant is not indigent the costs shall be allocated as in civil cases. Adopted eff. Oct. 1, 1971.

Formerly Ill.Rev.Stat.1991, ch. 110A, ¶ 414.

Committee Comments
(October 1, 1971)

The Committee chose not to include depositions for discovery purposes, but did decide to follow the unmistakable trend and provide for depositions to preserve testimony. This rule allows both the State and defense counsel to take such depositions and use the testimony as evidence at a hearing or trial in situations where the potential witness will be unable to appear at hearing or trial for any reason. The deposition is not taken by right but is subject to court approval. Notice should be taken of the fact that depositions may be taken by written questions as well as by oral examination.

Paragraph (c) provides for the taking of a deposition in circumstances which most other jurisdictions have recognized as a necessary use of depositions. In order to prevent unnecessary incarceration, a judge may permit the deposition of a witness committed for failure to execute a recognizance to appear.

Paragraphs (e) and (f) protect the defendant's constitutional rights. Paragraph (e) protects his rights of confrontation and cross-examination, and paragraph (f) assures equal protection to those indigents whose defense requires the taking of a deposition.

Rule 415.   Regulation of Discovery

(a) Investigations Not to be Impeded. Except as is otherwise provided as to matters not subject to disclosure and protective orders, neither the counsel for the parties nor other prosecution or defense personnel shall advise persons having relevant material or information (except the accused) to refrain from discussing the case with opposing counsel or showing opposing counsel any relevant material, nor shall they otherwise impede opposing counsel's investigation of the case.

(b) Continuing Duty to Disclose. If, subsequent to compliance with these rules or orders pursuant thereto, a party discovers additional material or information which is subject to disclosure, he shall promptly notify the other party or his counsel of the existence of such additional material, and if the additional material or information is discovered during trial, the court shall also be notified.

(c) Custody of Materials. Any materials furnished to an attorney pursuant to these rules shall remain in his exclusive custody and be used only for the purposes of conducting his side of the case, and shall be subject to such other terms and conditions as the court may provide.

(d) Protective Orders. Upon a showing of cause, the court may at any time order that specified disclosures be restricted or deferred, or make such other order as is appropriate, provided that all material and information to which a party is entitled must be disclosed in time to permit counsel to make beneficial use thereof.

(e) Excision. When some parts of certain material are discoverable under these rules, and other parts not discoverable, as much of the material should be disclosed as is consistent with the rules. Excision of certain material and disclosure of the balance is preferable to withholding the whole. Material excised pursuant to judicial order shall be sealed, impounded and preserved in the records of the court, to be made available to the reviewing court in the event of an appeal.

(f) In Camera Proceedings. Upon request of any person, the court may permit any showing of cause for denial or regulation of disclosures, or portion of such showing, to be made *in camera*. A record shall be made of such proceedings. If the court enters an order granting relief following a showing *in camera*, the entire record of such showing shall be sealed, impounded, and preserved in the records of the court, to be made available to the reviewing court in the event of an appeal.

(g) Sanctions.

(i) If at any time during the course of the proceedings it is brought to the attention of the court that a party has failed to comply with an applicable discovery rule or an order issued pursuant thereto, the court may order such party to permit the discovery of material and information not previously disclosed, grant a continuance, exclude such evidence, or enter such other order as it deems just under the circumstances.

(ii) Wilful violation by counsel of an applicable discovery rule or an order issued pursuant thereto may subject counsel to appropriate sanctions by the court.

Adopted eff. Oct. 1, 1971.

Formerly Ill.Rev.Stat.1991, ch. 110A, ¶ 415.

Committee Comments
(October 1, 1971)

Paragraph (a). One barrier to pretrial investigation and meaningful discovery procedures is the practice of some attorneys of advising witnesses not to cooperate with opposing counsel. This paragraph is included to provide that discovery shall not be frustrated by improper conduct of counsel or the various agents of counsel.

Paragraph (b) is modeled after Fed.R.Crim.P. 16(c). This paragraph is intended to permit thorough preparation and to minimize paperwork and delay. After discovery has been conducted as provided, any additional material or information acquired by either side which is subject to disclosure should be automatically and promptly disclosed. The notification required by this paragraph is intended to make such disclosures as simple and easy as possible.

Paragraph (c). If the materials to be provided were to become, in effect, matters of public availability once they had been turned over to counsel for the limited purposes which pretrial disclosures are designed to serve, the administration of criminal justice would likely be prejudiced. Accordingly, this paragraph establishes a mandatory requirement in every case that the material which an attorney receives shall remain in his exclusive custody. While he will undoubtedly have to show it to, or at least discuss it with others, he is not permitted to furnish them with copies or let them take it from his office. It should be noted that this paragraph also applies to the State. Nothing in this paragraph should be interpreted to prevent counsel from having tests performed by experts on materials furnished by opposing counsel or from having experts examine reports received from opposing counsel. Tangible objects, such as guns, knives, clothing, not subject to duplication but furnished for purposes of testing, etc., should be returned to the furnishing party when such testing or inspection is completed. If not returned routinely the last phrase permits the court to so order, in addition to any other terms and conditions provided.

Paragraph (d). In order that legitimate needs of exceptional cases will not shape discovery policy and result in denial of discovery in all cases, this paragraph is designed to provide sufficient flexibility to meet such exceptional needs. This paragraph, adapted from Fed.R.Crim.P. 16(e), permits application by the party concerned to the court for a protective order adjusting the time, place, recipient, or use of the disclosures as are necessary in a particular case. It is anticipated that it will ordinarily be needed with respect to those matters for which discovery is mandatory, rather than matters where the court has discretion in allowing discovery under Rule 412(h). While the protective order is designed to permit flexibility, it is to be used under a policy of as full and as early discovery as possible; it is not intended to permit denial of disclosure, although it may result in deferral until a later time. The disclosure must be made in time for a party to make beneficial use of it. Normal use of the protective order will be made when there is substantial risk to any person of physical harm, intimidation, bribery, or economic reprisals which outweigh any usefulness of disclosure to the defendant or State.

Paragraph (e). Occasions will arise when material will contain information which is both discoverable and nondiscoverable. This paragraph recognizes the right of a party to excise, or have excised, the nondiscoverable portion. The procedure under this paragraph is different from that under the Jencks Act, 18 U.S.C. § 3500(c), and under present Illinois practice, only in giving approval to a party excising portions of material without court supervision. Approval of counsel's independent conduct is consistent with the purpose of expediting the discovery process, but it is expected that in many cases counsel will seek a decision by the court, and that, in any event, he will be held accountable for excisions, if they are challenged by opposing counsel. The only change from the A.B.A. Standards is the requirement that the material excised pursuant to a judicial order not only be sealed, but also impounded and preserved.

Paragraph (f) provides for preserving the confidentiality of material at such times as the trial court is called upon to decide whether to require its disclosure. In issuing protective orders under paragraph (d), allowing excision of portions of material under paragraph (e), or in otherwise deciding that certain material is not subject to disclosure, the trial court must have an opportunity to examine, in private, the particular material as well as the reasons for non-disclosure. The purpose of issuing such rulings would often be defeated if the hearing were to be held in open court. To protect the litigants from error by the trial court, provision is made for the making and preserving of a record of all such proceedings for purposes of appeal.

Through paragraph (g), the Committee intended to emphasize that these discovery rules must be enforced. Rather than attempt to provide specific sanctions for specific violations, the Committee deemed it wise to leave the sanctions to the discretion of the trial court. This paragraph does contain one provision not present in the A.B.A. Standards. If justified, under the circumstances, the court may exclude evidence which a party has failed to disclose under applicable discovery rules. The Committee felt that such a device is a useful sanction, and that even though some problems may arise in applying it against the accused, the sanction can be applied in some situations. In this regard this paragraph conforms to Fed.R.Crim.P. 16(g), and further guarantees the expedition of the discovery process. The sanctions listed are not exclusive.

Rule 416. Reserved

Rule 417. DNA Evidence

(a) **Statement of Purpose**. This rule is promulgated to produce uniformly sufficient information to allow a proper, well-informed determination of the admissibility of DNA evidence and to insure that such evidence is presented competently and intelligibly. The rule is designed to provide a minimum standard for compliance concerning DNA evidence, and is not intended to limit the production and discovery of material information.

(b) **Obligation to Produce.** In all felony prosecutions, post-trial and post-conviction proceedings, the proponent of the DNA evidence, whether prosecution or defense, shall provide or otherwise make available to the adverse party all relevant materials, including, but not limited to the following:

(i) Copies of the case file including all reports, memoranda, notes, phone logs, contamination records, and data relating to the testing performed in the case.

(ii) Copies of any autoradiographs, lumigraphs, DQ Alpha Polymarker strips, PCR gel photographs and electropherograms, tabular data, electronic files and other data needed for full evaluation of DNA profiles produced and an opportunity to examine the originals, if requested.

(iii) Copies of any records reflecting compliance with quality control guidelines or standards employed during the testing process utilized in the case.

(iv) Copies of DNA laboratory procedure manuals, DNA testing protocols, DNA quality assurance guidelines or standards, and DNA validation studies.

(v) Proficiency testing results, proof of continuing professional education, current curriculum vitae and job description for examiners, or analysts and technicians involved in the testing and analysis of DNA evidence in the case.

(vi) Reports explaining any discrepancies in the testing, observed defects or laboratory errors in the particular case, as well as the reasons for those and the effects thereof.

(vii) Copies of all chain of custody documents for each item of evidence subjected to DNA testing.

(viii) A statement by the testing laboratory setting forth the method used to calculate the statistical probabilities in the case.

(ix) Copies of the allele frequencies or database for each locus examined.

(x) A list of all commercial or in-house software programs used in the DNA testing, including the name of the software program, manufacturer and version used in the case.

(xi) Copies of all DNA laboratory audits relating to the laboratory performing the particular tests.

Adopted March 1, 2001, effective immediately, except when in the opinion of the trial, Appellate, or Supreme Court the application of the new rule in a particular case pending at the time the rule becomes effective would not be feasible or would work an injustice, in which case former procedures would apply.

Committee Comments

Special Supreme Court Committee on Capital Cases
(March 1, 2001)

The standardized disclosures required by Rule 417 are intended to provide the information necessary for a full understanding of DNA test results, and to aid litigants and the courts in determining the admissibility of those results. The rule requires disclosure of information that is, or should be, readily available from any laboratory performing DNA testing. Standardized disclosure requirements should also make responses to disclosure requests less burdensome for laboratory personnel.

In drafting the rule, the committee considered court opinions from several jurisdictions that established guidelines for pretrial disclosures regarding DNA evidence. See, *e.g.*, *People v. Castro*, 144 Misc. 2d 956, 978–9, 545 N.Y.S.2d 985, 999 (1989); *People v. Perry*, 586 So. 2d 242, 255 (Ala. 1991); *Polk v. State*, 612 So. 2d 381, 394 (Miss. 1992). Rule 417 draws from those opinions, but also reflects the committee's examination of current practices in forensic science.

The disclosures required by the rule can be crucial in any trial in which the discovery rules for criminal cases apply, and also in related post-trial and post-conviction proceedings (including a proceeding on a motion for DNA testing not available at the time of trial to establish actual innocence (725 ILCS 5/116–3)). Therefore, the rule requires production of information regarding DNA testing by the proponent of DNA evidence in any felony trial, and in all related post-trial or post-conviction proceedings. While the disclosures required under the rule encompass the technologies presently utilized (restriction fragment length polymorphism, polymerase chain reaction, short tandem repeats, etc.), production is not limited to those techniques. Because the rule provides no limitation upon the specific information or materials to be provided, it is designed to encompass future techniques that may be developed in the testing of DNA evidence.

Rules 418 to 429. Reserved

PART C. TRIALS

Rule 430. Trial of Incarcerated Defendant

An accused shall not be placed in restraint of any form unless there is a manifest need for restraint to protect the security of the court, the proceedings, or to prevent escape. Persons charged with a criminal offense are presumed innocent until otherwise proven guilty and are entitled to participate in their defense as free persons before the jury or bench. Any deviation from this right shall be based on evidence specifically considered by the trial court on a case-by-case basis. The determination of whether to impose a physical restraint shall be limited to trial proceedings in which the defendant's innocence or guilt is to be determined, and does not apply to bond hearings or other instances where the defendant may be required to appear before the court prior to a trial being commenced. Once the trial judge becomes aware of restraints, prior to allowing the defendant to appear before the jury, he or she shall conduct a separate hearing on the record to investigate the need for such restraints. At such hearing, the trial court shall consider and shall make specific findings as to:

(1) the seriousness of the present charge against the defendant;

(2) defendant's temperament and character known to the trial court either by observation or by the testimony of witnesses;

(3) defendant's age and physical attributes;

(4) defendant's past criminal record and, more particularly, whether such record contains crimes of violence;

(5) defendant's past escapes, attempted escapes, or evidence of any present plan to escape;

(6) evidence of any threats made by defendant to harm others, cause a disturbance, or to be self-destructive;

(7) evidence of any risk of mob violence or of attempted revenge by others;

(8) evidence of any possibility of any attempt to rescue the defendant by others;

(9) size and mood of the audience;

(10) physical security of the courtroom, including the number of entrances and exits, the number of guards necessary to provide security, and the adequacy and availability of alternative security arrangements.

After allowing the defendant to be heard and after making specific findings, the trial judge shall balance these findings and impose the use of a restraint only where the need for restraint outweighs the defendant's right to be free from restraint.

Adopted March 22, 2010, eff. July 1, 2010.

Commentary

(March 22, 2010)

This rule codifies the holdings in *People v. Boose*, 66 Ill. 2d 261 (1977), and *People v. Allen*, 222 Ill. 2d 340 (2006).

Rule 431. Voir Dire Examination

(a) The court shall conduct *voir dire* examination of prospective jurors by putting to them questions it thinks appropriate, touching upon their qualifications to serve as jurors in the case at trial. The court may permit the parties to submit additional questions to it for further inquiry if it thinks they are appropriate and shall permit the parties to supplement the examination by such direct inquiry as the court deems proper for a reasonable period of time depending upon the length of examination by the court, the complexity of the case, and the nature of the charges. Questions shall not directly or indirectly concern matters of law or instructions. The court shall acquaint prospective jurors with the general duties and responsibilities of jurors.

(b) The court shall ask each potential juror, individually or in a group, whether that juror understands and accepts the following principles: (1) that the defendant is presumed innocent of the charge(s) against him or her; (2) that before a defendant can be convicted the State must prove the defendant guilty beyond a reasonable doubt; (3) that the defendant is not required to offer any evidence on his or her own behalf; and (4) that if a defendant does not testify it cannot be held against him or her; however, no inquiry of a prospective juror shall be made into the defendant's decision not to testify when the defendant objects.

The court's method of inquiry shall provide each juror an opportunity to respond to specific questions concerning the principles set out in this section.

Formerly Supreme Court Rule 411, eff. Jan. 1, 1967. Redesignated as Rule 431, eff. Oct. 1, 1971. Amended April 3, 1997, eff. May 1, 1997; March 21, 2007, eff. May 1, 2007; April 26, 2012, eff. July 1, 2012.

Formerly Ill.Rev.Stat.1991, ch. 110A, ¶ 431.

Committee Comments

The new language is intended to ensure compliance with the requirements of *People v. Zehr,* 103 Ill.2d 472 (1984). It seeks to end the practice where the judge makes a broad statement of the applicable law followed by a general question concerning the juror's willingness to follow the law.

Rule 432. Opening Statements

Opening statements in criminal cases are governed by rule 235.

Formerly Supreme Court Rule 412, eff. Jan. 1, 1967. Redesignated as Rule 432, eff. Oct. 1, 1971.

Formerly Ill.Rev.Stat.1991, ch. 110A, ¶ 432.

Rule 433. Impeachment of Witnesses—Hostile Witnesses

The impeachment of witnesses and the examination of hostile witnesses in criminal cases is governed by Rule 238.

Adopted Sept. 29, 1978, eff. Nov. 1, 1978. Amended Feb. 19, 1982, eff. April 1, 1982.

Formerly Ill.Rev.Stat.1991, ch. 110A, ¶ 433.

Rule 434. Jury Selection

(a) Impaneling Juries. In criminal cases the parties shall pass upon and accept the jury in panels of four, commencing with the State, unless the court, in its discretion, directs otherwise, and alternate jurors shall be passed upon separately.

(b) Names and Addresses of Prospective Jurors. Upon request, the parties shall be furnished with a list of prospective jurors with their addresses, if known.

(c) Challenging Prospective Jurors for Cause. Each party may challenge jurors for cause. If a prospective juror has a physical impairment, the court shall consider such prospective juror's ability to perceive and appreciate the evidence when considering a challenge for cause.

(d) Peremptory Challenges. A defendant tried alone shall be allowed seven peremptory challenges in a case in which the punishment may be imprisonment in the penitentiary, and five in all other cases; except that, in a single trial of more than one defendant, each defendant shall be allowed five peremptory challenges in a case in which the punishment may be imprisonment in the penitentiary, and three in all other cases. If several charges against a defendant or defendants are consolidated for trial, each defendant shall be allowed peremptory challenges upon one charge only, which single charge shall be the charge against that defendant authorizing the greatest maximum penalty. The State shall be allowed the same number of peremptory challenges as all of the defendants.

(e) Selection of Alternate Jurors. After the jury is impaneled and sworn the court may direct the selection of alternate jurors, who shall take the same oath as the regular jurors. Each party shall have one additional peremptory challenge for each alternate juror. If before the final submission of a cause a member of the jury dies or is discharged he shall be replaced by an alternate juror in the order of election.

JUSTICE SIMON, dissenting [March 27, 1985 amendment]:

The motivation for the idea of reducing the number of peremptory challenges in criminal cases was to alleviate the practice of using peremptory challenges to exclude black persons from service on juries solely because of their race. I do not believe that this is the proper remedy for what I perceive to be an existing, serious and evil practice.

This court should not tamper, by rule, with the number of peremptory challenges allowed because this is a decision that historically has been made by the General Assembly. We should therefore leave any change to that body. In 1983, our chief justice recommended to the legislature a reduction in the number of peremptory challenges permitted by statute in criminal cases. Before considering any independent action we should allow the legislature ample time to consider the wisdom of, and to act on, that recommendation.

Presently, the General Assembly has before it three separate bills designed to prevent the use of peremptory challenges to exclude persons from juries because of their race or sex. House Bills 319 and 325 both would require clerks to keep records of the sex and race of jurors removed by peremptory challenges. House Bill 324 would require prosecutors to state their reasons for using peremptory challenges when the defendant requests an explanation or on the court's own motion in cases where the defendant or the court believes that peremptory challenges are being used to exclude persons on the sole basis of race. I would allow the legislature ample time to consider these approaches and any others developed during its consideration of the problem of excluding persons from juries because of their race before we attempt to solve it in the fashion proposed by this rule.

I find it peculiar that the court is reducing the number of peremptory challenges presently available in criminal cases in the guise of dealing with the problem of excluding persons from juries because of their race. This court has consistently denied there is any such problem in Illinois. For example, in *People v. Mack* (1984), 105 Ill.2d 103, this court said:

> "Regardless of the many emotional arguments on this question that have been raised in this court and in our appellate court, there is just no evidence that blacks are systematically and purposefully excluded from serving on juries in Cook County where the defendants are black." *People v. Mack* (1984), 105 Ill.2d 103, 122.

I have argued that in many cases in this State black persons have been excluded by prosecutors from juries for no other reason than that they are black. There is a problem in many counties in Illinois, and the proper way to attack it is for trial judges to put a stop to it whenever they observe prosecutors using peremptory challenges to exclude persons from the *voir dire* because they are black. The solution approved by the United States Court of Appeals for the Second Circuit in *McCray v. Abrams* (2d Cir. Dec. 22, 1984), 750 F.2d 1113, will be more effective in stopping this pernicious practice than trying to stop it by reducing the number of peremptory challenges. See also *People v. Wheeler* (1978), 22 Cal.3d 258, 148 Cal.Rptr. 890, 583 P.2d 748; *Commonwealth v. Soares* (1979), 377 Mass. 461, 387 N.E.2d 499, *cert. denied* (1979), 444 U.S. 881, 62 L.Ed.2d 110, 100 S.Ct. 170; *State v. Crespin* (N.M.App.1980), 94 N.M. 486, 612 P.2d 716; *State v. Neil* (Fla.1984), 457 So.2d 481; *People v. Payne* (1983), 99 Ill.2d 135, 140 (Simon, J., dissenting); *People v. Frazier* (1984), 127 Ill.App.3d 151.

The reduction in the number of peremptory challenges given to a criminal defendant in capital cases is also a matter of concern from the standpoint of fairness. A prosecutor has the opportunity to select a jury which is strongly in favor of the death sentence by challenging for cause potential jurors who express equivocal or ambivalent views about imposing a death sentence. (See *Witherspoon v. Illinois* (1968), 391

U.S. 510, 20 L.Ed.2d 776, 88 S.Ct. 1770.) Curtailing the number of peremptory challenges available to a defendant in a capital case decreases the defendant's opportunity to exclude prospective jurors who demonstrate unusual zeal in favor of the death sentence, and thus could diminish the viability of his constitutional right to trial by jury as required by the Constitution.

In addition, I question how effective the change the court has adopted will be in preventing exclusion of persons from jury service solely because of their race. Fourteen peremptory challenges in a capital case will still permit any prosecutor who is bent on excluding black persons the opportunity to eliminate many otherwise qualified jurors solely because of their race. Therefore, I recommend that this court attack this pattern of abuse head on instead of circuitously. We should do it by forbidding the use of peremptory challenges based on race and leave to the General Assembly its traditional role in setting the number of legitimate peremptory challenges permitted in criminal cases.

Finally, I question why it is necessary to place, in our rules, new Rules 434(b), (c) and (e), which merely duplicate what is already in the Code of Criminal Procedure of 1963 (Ill.Rev.Stat.1983, ch. 38, par. 115–4).[1] This appears to be needless repetition.

Adopted February 19, 1982, effective April 1, 1982; amended March 27, 1985, effective May 1, 1985; Feb. 6, 2013, eff. immediately.

Formerly Ill.Rev.Stat.1991, ch. 110A, ¶ 434.
[1] 725 ILCS 5/115–4.

Committee Comments
(March 27, 1985)

This 1985 amendment incorporates many of the purely procedural aspects of jury selection now contained in section 115–4 of the Code of Criminal Procedure of 1963 (Ill.Rev.Stat.1983, ch. 38, par. 115–4). This 1985 amendment also reduces from 20 to 14 the number of peremptory challenges permitted to be exercised by either the defendant or the State in a capital case in which only one defendant is on trial (and from 12 to 8 the number allowed each defendant and the State when two or more defendants are tried jointly for such an offense). It also reduces from 10 to 7 the number of peremptory challenges allowed when one defendant is tried for an offense which may be punishable by imprisonment in the penitentiary (and from 6 to 5 the number allowed each defendant and the State when two or more defendants are joined for trial in a case in which each is charged with an offense which may be punishable by imprisonment in the penitentiary).

Rule 435. Reserved

Rule 436. Separation and Sequestration of Jury in Criminal Cases; Admonition by Court

(a) In criminal cases, either before or after submission of the cause to the jury for determination, the trial court may, in its discretion, keep the jury together in the charge of an officer of the court, or the court may allow the jurors to separate temporarily outside the presence of a court officer, overnight, on weekends, on holidays, or in emergencies.

(b) The jurors shall, whether permitted to separate or kept in charge of officers, be admonished by the trial court that it is their duty (1) not to converse with anyone else on any subject connected with the trial until they are discharged; (2) not to knowingly read or listen to outside comments or news accounts of the procedure until they are discharged; (3) not to discuss among themselves any subject connected with the trial, or form or express any opinion on the cause until it is submitted to them for deliberation; and (4) not to view the place where the offense was allegedly committed.

Adopted May 20, 1997, eff. July 1, 1997.

Committee Comments

This proposed rule is intended to allow jurors to go home for an evening, weekend, holiday, or emergency and dispense with the need to accommodate the jurors in a hotel overnight, even if the cause has been submitted to them for final deliberation. The Code of Criminal Procedure presently requires "an officer of the court * * * to keep [jurors] together and prevent conversation between the jurors and others" (except interpreters), after final submission of the cause to the jury for determination. 725 ILCS 5/115–4. This proposed rule provides that in appropriate cases, jurors may separate temporarily after being admonished with regard to their duties. It does away with the blanket requirement that they be sequestered and guarded.

Rules 437 to 450. Reserved

Rule 451. Instructions

(a) Use of IPI Criminal Instructions; Requirements of Other Instructions. Whenever Illinois Pattern Jury Instructions, Criminal, contains an instruction applicable in a criminal case, giving due consideration to the facts and the governing law, and the court determines that the jury should be instructed on the subject, the IPI Criminal instruction shall be used, unless the court determines that it does not accurately state the law. The most current version of the IPI Criminal instructions is maintained on the Supreme Court website. Whenever IPI Criminal does not contain an instruction on a subject on which the court determines that the jury should be instructed, the instruction given on that subject should be simple, brief, impartial, and free from argument.

(b) Court's Instructions. At any time before or during the trial, the court may direct counsel to prepare designated instructions. Counsel shall comply with the direction, and copies of instructions so prepared shall be marked "Court's Instructions." Counsel may object at the conference on instructions

to any instruction prepared at the court's direction, regardless of who prepared it, and the court shall rule on these objections as well as objections to other instructions. The grounds of the objections shall be particularly specified.

(c) Section 2–1107 of the Code of Civil Procedure to Govern. Except as otherwise provided in these rules, instructions in criminal cases shall be tendered, settled, and given in accordance with section 2–1107 of the Code of Civil Procedure,[1] but substantial defects are not waived by failure to make timely objections thereto if the interests of justice require. The court shall instruct the jury after the arguments are completed, or, in its discretion, at the close of all the evidence.

(d) Procedure. The court shall be provided an original and a copy of each instruction, and a copy shall be delivered to each opposing counsel. In addition to numbering the copies and indicating who tendered them, as required by section 2–1107 of the Code of Civil Procedure, the copy shall contain a notation substantially as follows:

"IPI Criminal No. ___" or "IPI Criminal No. ___ Modified" or "Not in IPI Criminal"

as the case may be. All objections made at the conference and the rulings thereon shall be shown in the report of proceedings.

(e) Instructions Before Opening Statements. After the jury is selected and before opening statements, the court may orally instruct the jury as follows:

(i) On cautionary or preliminary matters, including, but not limited to, the burden of proof, the believability of witnesses, and the receipt of evidence for a limited purpose.

(ii) On the issue of substantive law applicable to the case, including, but not limited to, the elements of the offense. When requested by the defendant, the court may instruct the jury on the elements of an affirmative defense. Nothing in this rule is intended to eliminate the giving of written instructions at the close of the trial in accord with paragraph (c).

(f) Instructions During Trial. Nothing in the rule is intended to restrict the court's authority to give any appropriate instruction during the course of the trial.

(g) Proceedings When an Enhanced Sentence is Sought. When the State intends, for the purpose of sentencing, to rely on one or more sentencing enhancement factors which are subject to the notice and proof requirements of section 111–3(c–5) of the Code of Criminal Procedure, the court may, within its discretion, conduct a unitary trial through verdict on the issue of guilt and on the issue of whether a sentencing enhancement factor exists. The court may also, within its discretion, upon motion of a party, conduct a bifurcated trial. In deciding whether to conduct such a bifurcated trial, the court must first hold a pretrial hearing to determine if proof of the sentencing enhancement factor is not relevant to the question of guilt or if undue prejudice outweighs the factor's probative value. Such bifurcated trial shall be conducted subject to the following:

(1) The court shall first conduct a trial through verdict on the issue of guilt under the procedures applicable to trials in other cases.

(2) If a guilty verdict is rendered, the court shall then conduct a separate proceeding before the same jury, or before the court if a jury was waived at trial or is waived for purposes of the separate proceeding. This separate proceeding shall be confined to the issue of whether the sentencing enhancement factor exists. The order in which the parties may present evidence and argument and the rules governing admission of evidence shall be the same as at trial, with the burden remaining on the State to prove the factor beyond a reasonable doubt. After the evidence is closed, the submission and giving of instructions shall proceed in accordance with paragraphs (a), (b), (c) and (d) of this rule.

(3) The court may enter a directed verdict or judgment notwithstanding the verdict respecting any fact at issue in the separate proceeding.

Amended June 19, 1968, effective January 1, 1969; February 19, 1982, effective April 1, 1982; May 28, 1982, effective July 1, 1982; May 20, 1997, effective July 1, 1997; February 10, 2006, effective July 1, 2006; Feb. 6, 2013, eff. immediately; April 8, 2013, eff. immediately.

Formerly Ill.Rev.Stat.1991, ch. 110A, ¶ 451.
[1] 735 ILCS 5/2–1107.

Committee Comments

This amendment gives the trial court the option of formally instructing the jury at the close of the evidence prior to closing arguments. It also expressly authorizes the trial court to orally instruct the jury prior to opening statements concerning cautionary and preliminary matters and on key issues of substantive law, such as the elements of the offense or of an affirmative defense. The amendments also recognize that it may become necessary for the trial court to give appropriate instructions during the course of the trial to guide the jurors in their consideration of the evidence.

(February 10, 2006)

Paragraph (g)

In response to the Supreme Court's decision in *Apprendi v. New Jersey,* 530 U.S. 466, 147 L. Ed.

2d 435, 120 S. Ct. 2348 (2000), the Illinois legislature adopted Illinois Code of Criminal Procedure section 111–3(c–5) (725 ILCS 5/111–3(c–5)), which sets notice and proof requirements for sentencing enhancement factors in nondeath penalty cases. However, this section does not specify how the sentencing enhancements are to be tried when the trier of fact is a jury. Rule 451 (a) provides a basis for trial courts to utilize special interrogatories when the sentencing enhancement factor is to be proven during a unitary trial.

The Supreme Court Committee on Jury Instructions in Criminal Cases recommended the adoption of a rule which would provide that bifurcated trials as well as unitary trials are authorized, and that trial courts have discretion in deciding which to conduct.

Because bifurcating a trial generally causes additional inconvenience to the jury, the witnesses, and/or the parties, and causes additional cost to the parties and/or the taxpayers, paragraph (g) makes unitary trials the presumptive option. Before a court orders a bifurcated trial, the court must find that having a unitary trial might cause prejudice and that this risk outweighs the additional difficulties associated with a bifurcated trial. Paragraph (g) does not apply when the court serves as trier of fact on sentencing enhancement factors. Whether to bifurcate in that circumstance involves different considerations.

Rules 452 to 470. Reserved

PART D. POST–CONVICTION PROCEEDINGS

Rule 471. Transcripts for Poor Persons Bringing Post–Conviction Proceedings

If a petition filed under the provisions of article 122 of the Code of Criminal Procedure of 1963,[1] dealing with post-conviction hearings, alleges that the petitioner is unable to pay the costs of the proceeding, the trial court may order that the petitioner be permitted to proceed as a poor person and order a transcript of the proceedings resulting in the conviction delivered to petitioner in accordance with paragraph (b) of Rule 607.

Formerly Ill.Rev.Stat.1991, ch. 110A, ¶ 471.
[1] 725 ILCS 5/122–1 et seq.

Committee Comments

This is paragraph (1) of former Rule 27–1 with necessary minor changes but no changes of substance.

Rules 472 to 500. Reserved

ARTICLE V. RULES ON TRIAL COURT PROCEEDINGS IN TRAFFIC AND CONSERVATION OFFENSES, ORDINANCE OFFENSES, PETTY OFFENSES, AND CERTAIN MISDEMEANORS—BAIL SCHEDULES

PART A. GENERAL

Rule
501. Definitions.
502. Reserved.
503. Multiple Charges Under These Rules.
504. Appearance Date.
505. Notice to Accused.
506 to 525. Reserved.

PART B. BAIL SCHEDULES

526. Bail Schedule–Traffic Offenses.
527. Bail Schedule—Conservation Offenses.
528. Bail Schedule—Ordinance Offenses, Petty Offenses, Business Offenses and Certain Misdemeanors.

PART C. FINES, PENALTIES AND COSTS—10% DEPOSIT STATUTE

529. Fines, Penalties and Costs on Written Pleas of Guilty in Minor Traffic and Conservation Offenses.
530. Applicability of 10% Cash Deposit Statute.
531 to 550. Reserved.

PART D. REQUIRED COURT APPEARANCES, FORMS AND PROCEDURES

551. Traffic and Conservation Offenses for Which a Court Appearance is Required.
552. Uniform Tickets–Processing.
553. Posting Bail or Bond.
554. Substitution of Cash Bail.
555. Returning Bail or Documents.
556. Procedure if Defendant Fails to Appear.
557 to 569. Reserved.

PART E. RULES AND PROCEDURES FOR NON–TRAFFIC/NON–CONSERVATION ORDINANCE VIOLATIONS

570. Applicability.
571. Code of Civil Procedure to Apply.
572. Form of Charging Document.
573. Service of the Charging Document.
574. Opportunity to Settle.
575. Appearance of Defendant, Answer; Failure to Appear; Discovery and Pretrial Procedures.
576. Right to Counsel.
577. Jury Trial.
578. Burden of Proof.
579. Disposition and Appeal.
580 to 600. Reserved.

Date Effective

Article V was adopted by Supreme Court order on October 26, 1967, effective January 1, 1968.

The following order was entered December 22, 1981, adopting revised Rules 501 through 556:

IN THE SUPREME COURT OF ILLINOIS ORDER

The revised rules attached hereto and hereinafter adopted, relating to procedures in traffic cases, conservation cases, quasi-criminal cases and certain misdemeanors, were prepared by the Conference of Chief Circuit Judges and, at the request of that conference, are adopted by the Supreme Court of Illinois.

Revised Rules 501 through 556, attached hereto, are hereby adopted effective January 15, 1982.

These revised Rules 501 through 556 will govern trial court proceedings in traffic cases, conservation cases, municipal ordinance cases, and such misdemeanor cases as are covered thereby which are commenced after these rules take effect. They will also govern further proceedings in such actions then pending except when, in the opinion of the trial, appellate or supreme court, the application of the new rules in a particular action then pending would not be feasible or would work an injustice, in which cases the former procedure applies.

Dated: December 22, 1981

PART A. GENERAL

Rule 501. Definitions

(a) Bond Certificates. Bail security documents which also guarantee payment of judgments for fines, penalties and costs, not to exceed $140 for any single offense or $500 for multiple offenses arising out of the same occurrence (auto bond certificates), or not to exceed $500 for any single offense covered by Rule 526(b)(1) (truck bond certificates), which are issued or guaranteed, in counties other than Cook, by companies or membership associations authorized to do so by the Director of Insurance, State of Illinois, under regulations issued by this court. (Note: Copies of these regulations may be obtained by writing to: Director, Administrative Office of the Illinois Courts, 3101 Old Jacksonville Road, Springfield, IL 62704–6488.) The privilege of issuing bond certificates for use in Cook County shall be governed by rule of the Circuit Court of Cook County. (Note: Copies of the Cook County rule may be obtained by writing to: Office of the Chief Judge, Richard J. Daley Center, Chicago IL 60602.)

(b) Cash or Cash Bail. United States currency; transfer of United States currency by means of credit cards, debit cards, or electronic fund transfer; traveler's checks issued by major banks or express companies which, alone or in combination with currency, total the exact amount required to be deposited as bail; and negotiable drafts on major credit card companies, under conditions approved by the Administrative Director.

(c) Conservation Offense. Any case charging a violation listed below, except any charge punishable upon conviction by imprisonment in the penitentiary:

(1) The Fish and Aquatic Life Code, as amended (515 ILCS 5/1–1 *et seq.*);

(2) The Wildlife Code, as amended (520 ILCS 5/1.1 *et seq.*);

(3) The Boat Registration and Safety Act, as amended (625 ILCS 45/1–1 *et seq.*);

(4) The Park District Code, as amended (70 ILCS 1205/1–1 *et seq.*);

(5) The Chicago Park District Act, as amended (70 ILCS 1505/0.01 *et seq.*);

(6) The State Parks Act, as amended (20 ILCS 835/0.01 *et seq.*);

(7) The State Forest Act, as amended (525 ILCS 40/0.01 *et seq.*);

(8) The Forest Fire Protection District Act, as amended (425 ILCS 40/0.01 *et seq.*);

(9) The Snowmobile Registration and Safety Act, as amended (625 ILCS 40/1–1 *et seq.*);

(10) The Endangered Species Protection Act, as amended (520 ILCS 10/1 *et seq.*);

(11) The Forest Products Transportation Act, as amended (225 ILCS 740/1 *et seq.*);

(12) The Timber Buyers Licensing Act, as amended (225 ILCS 735/1 *et seq.*);

(13) The Downstate Forest Preserve District Act, as amended (70 ILCS 805/0.001 *et seq.*);

(14) The Exotic Weed Act, as amended (525 ILCS 10/1 *et seq.*);

(15) The Ginseng Harvesting Act, as amended (525 ILCS 20/0.01 *et seq.*);

(16) The Cave Protection Act, as amended (525 ILCS 5/1 *et seq.*);

(17) Any regulations, proclamations or ordinances adopted pursuant to any code or act named in this Rule 501(c);

(18) Ordinances adopted pursuant to the Counties Code for the acquisition of property for parks or recreational areas (55 ILCS 5/5–1005(18));

(19) The Recreational Trails of Illinois Act, as amended (20 ILCS 862/1 *et seq.*);

(20) The Herptiles–Herps Act, as amended (510 ILCS 68/1–1 et seq.).

(d) Driver's License. A current driver's license or temporary visitor's driver's license issued by the Secretary of State of Illinois. However, restricted driving permits, monitoring device driving permits, instruction permits, probationary licenses or temporary licenses issued under chapter 6 of the Illinois Vehicle Code, as amended (625 ILCS 5/6–100 *et seq.*) shall not be accepted in lieu of or in addition to bail amounts established in Rule 526.

(e) Unit of Local Government. Any county, municipality, township, special district, or unit designated as a unit of local government by law.

(f) Traffic Offense. Any case which charges a violation of any statute, ordinance or regulation relating to the operation or use of motor vehicles, the use of streets and highways by pedestrians or the operation of any other wheeled or tracked vehicle, including cases charging violations under chapter 6 of the Illinois Vehicle Code, as amended (625 ILCS 5/6–100 *et seq.*), but excluding cases in which a ticket was served by "tie-on," "hang-on," or "appended" methods and cases charging violations of:

(1) Section 9–3 (b) of the Criminal Code of 1961, as amended (reckless homicide) (720 ILCS 5/9–3(b));

(2) Section 12–5 of the Criminal Code of 1961, as amended (reckless conduct) (720 ILCS 5/12–5);

(3) Article I of chapter 4 of the Illinois Vehicle Code, as amended (anti–theft laws) (625 ILCS 5/4–100 *et seq.*);

(4) Any charge punishable upon conviction by imprisonment in the penitentiary;

(5) "Jay walking" ordinances of any unit of local government;

(6) Any conservation offense (see Rule 501(c)).

(g) Promise to Comply. An option available to Illinois residents and residents of other member jurisdictions of the Nonresident Violator Compact of 1977 (625 ILCS 5/6–800 *et seq.*) to obtain release from custody without bail following arrests on view for minor traffic offenses (see 625 ILCS 5/6–306.4(a) or 6–308(a)) by signing a written promise to comply with the terms of the Uniform Citation and Complaint (625 ILCS 5/6–306.4 or 6–308). Residents of Illinois not charged with a petty traffic violation, and nonresidents charged with traffic offenses specified in section 6–306.4(b) of the Illinois Vehicle Code, as amended (625 ILCS 6–306.4(b)), shall not be released on a promise to comply, but must post bail or secure release in accordance with these rules.

(h) Individual Bond. Bonds authorized without security for persons arrested for or charged with offenses covered by Rules 526, 527 and 528 who are unable to secure release from custody under these rules (see Rule 553(d)).

Amended effective Oct. 7, 1970; Jan. 31, 1972, eff. March 1, 1972; Feb. 17, 1977, eff. April 1, 1977, in counties other than Cook, eff. July 1, 1977, in Cook County; Dec. 22, 1981, eff. Jan. 15, 1982; April 27, 1984, eff. July 1, 1984; March 27, 1985, eff. May 1, 1985; June 26, 1987, eff. Aug. 1, 1987; June 19, 1989, eff. Aug. 1, 1989; Dec. 7, 1990, eff. Jan. 1, 1991; June 12, 1992, eff. July 1, 1992; May 24, 1995, eff. Jan. 1, 1996; Sept. 30, 2002, eff. immediately; June 11, 2009, eff. immediately; Aug. 6, 2010, eff. Sept. 15, 2010; Dec. 12, 2013, eff. Jan. 1, 2014; June 11, 2014, eff. July 1, 2014; Dec. 30, 2014, eff. Jan. 1, 2015; Oct. 15, 2015, eff. immediately.

Formerly Ill.Rev.Stat. 1991, ch. 110A, ¶ 501.

Committee Comments

Paragraph (a)

Paragraph (a) is new, but incorporates by reference Paragraph 13.12 of the Cook County rules and Sections 6 and 6A of Paragraph F of the former Supreme Court rule. It appears to the Committee that only companies or membership associations which wish to issue bond certificates are particularly interested in the regulations under which they might be authorized to do so. The Supreme Court has adopted Sections 6 and 6A of the former Supreme Court rule as Administrative Regulations and has expressly stated that these new rules do not supersede Paragraph 13.12 of the Cook County rule.

Paragraph (b)

The Committee defines a credit card or debit card as follows: any instrument or device whether known as a credit card, secured credit card, charge plate, prepaid card, debit card, automated teller machine card, smart card or by any other name issued, with or without fee, by an issuer for the use of the card holder, to obtain credit, money, goods, services, or anything else of value. (Source: Illinois Credit Card and Debit Card Act (720 ILCS 250/2.03, 2.15) and Local Governmental Acceptance of Credit Cards Act (50 ILCS 345/10)).

The Committee defines "electronic fund transfer" as a nonpaper transaction that is electronically processed for the purpose of instructing or authorizing a financial institution to debit an account for the purpose of posting bail consistent with these rules.

Paragraph (c)

Paragraph (c) is new. With specific exceptions, persons charged with a violation of the Uniform Act Regulating Traffic on Highways have the statutory option of depositing a chauffeur's or operator's license in lieu of other security (Section 6–306(a), Illinois Motor Vehicle Law, as amended by HB 620, approved Aug. 7, 1967). The Supreme Court may require however that, in specified cases, a driver's license must be deposited in addition to a cash deposit on bail amounts fixed by rule or order (Section 6–306(b), Illinois Motor Law, as amended, *supra.*) The rules so provide. See rule 526(d). Failure to appear after notice when a driver's license has been deposited in lieu of bail, shall result in mandatory suspension of the driver's license. See rule 556(a). (Section 6–306(c)(2), Illinois Motor Vehicle Law, as amended, *supra.*) Similar provisions will be continued under the new Drivers License Act (Chap. 6A, Illinois Motor Vehicle Law) which was approved August 17, 1967 (HB 1951) and which becomes effective January 1, 1969. The term "driver's license" no longer includes drivers' licenses issued by states other than the State of Illinois. Under Section 1 of Paragraph F of the former Supreme Court rule, an offender was given an option of depositing a license certificate issued by "any ... state requiring the same for operation of motor vehicle...." Experience has shown that ac-

cepting out-of-state drivers' licenses in lieu of cash bail was, at best, tenuous security to insure a nonresident's appearance.

Paragraph (d)

Paragraph (d) is derived from Paragraph 13.2 of the Cook County rule and Paragraph B of the former Supreme Court rule, without change.

Paragraph (e)

Paragraph (e) is derived in part from Section 4 of Paragraph F of the former Supreme Court rule which excepted the following cases from applicability under the rule: "... cases wherein the traffic summons (ticket) is served by the 'tie-on', 'hang-on' or 'appended' method, and ... alleged violation of the ordinances of a municipality, commonly referred to as the 'Jay Walking Ordinance'." The remainder of the rule is new. The Cook County rule applied to "... criminal and quasi-criminal offenses in Cook County, other than felonies, in cases in which bail has not been set by a judge or magistrate...." Parking violations were also covered by the Cook County rule and Paragraph 13.14 of those rules (which was not superseded by the order adopting these Supreme Court rules) authorized and directed the Chief Judge to establish "... a schedule of penalties and procedures for violation of municipal parking ordinances." It appears that other circuits could also promulgate rules similar to Cook County's Paragraph 13.14 and that part of General Order No. 7 (para. 1(b)) which implements that rule. It has been suggested that, unless otherwise specifically provided, the Code of Criminal Procedure of 1963 does not apply to "traffic offense" proceedings. The Code of Criminal Procedure applies to "criminal proceedings" (Ill.Rev.Stat.1965, ch. 38, par. 100–2). "Criminal proceedings" can be fairly defined as prosecutions for violations of the general criminal laws. Cf. Village of Park Forest v. Jay D. Bragg, (1967) Ill.Sup.Ct. No. 40193. Traffic offenses, as defined by this paragraph, are not violations of the general criminal laws but are, rather, a hybrid class of regulatory and penal offenses, encompassing violations of state statutes, municipal ordinances and regulations relating to the operation and use of motor vehicles, etc. As may also be true in the case of "conservation offenses", (see comment under par. (c)) "traffic offenses" may now constitute a *sui generis* class of regulatory and penal offenses, which, in the absence of specific statutes to the contrary, are subject, exclusively, to procedures established by Supreme Court rule or order.

Rule 502. Reserved

Rule 503. Multiple Charges Under These Rules

(a) **Amount of Bail–Hearing Date.** Police officers should refrain from issuing multiple citations for offenses arising out of the same occurrence. A person arrested and charged with more than one offense arising out of the same occurrence when the bail is established for each such offense under Rule 526, 527 or 528 shall be released from custody as follows:

(1) If bail for each such offense is established by Rule 526, and the accused is eligible for release on

each charge by a promise to comply pursuant to section 6–306.4 or 6–308 of the Illinois Vehicle Code, as amended (625 ILCS 5/6–306.4 or 6–308), he or she may elect to be released by executing the written promise on the complaint copy; a court appearance shall be required on each charge.

(2) In all other cases, the accused shall be released from custody after posting bail on the charge for which the highest bail is required, and, except as provided below, a court appearance shall be required on each charge. Whether a court appearance will be required for any other offenses charged at the same time as an offense requiring bail under Rule 526(b)(1) will be determined without regard to such truck violations. A separate bail shall be required for each case involving truck violations under Rule 526(b)(1) or similar municipal ordinances, and all such charges may be satisfied without a court appearance under Rule 529.

(3) No court appearance shall be required under this rule where all charges are traffic and conservation offenses which may be satisfied without a court appearance under Rule 529 and the accused elects to post separate cash bail on each such charge.

(4) No court appearance shall be required under this rule where all charges are traffic offenses which may be satisfied without a court appearance under Rule 529, the separate bails required for all such charges do not exceed $500, and the accused has deposited an approved bond certificate in lieu of bail; in such event, if the accused does not appear on the date set for appearance, or any date to which the case(s) may be continued, it shall be presumed he has elected to post separate bails and consented to the entry of *ex parte* judgment on each such charge (see Rule 556(b)).

All such charges, whenever practicable, should be set for hearing on the same day in the same court, to be disposed of at the same time (see Rule 501(b) for definition of "Cash Bail").

(b) New Bail–Application of Bail and Return of Balance. After final disposition of a charge for which bail was posted, the court shall set new bail in a single amount to cover any concurrent charges which may be continued for further hearing at a future date. The clerk may apply any cash or security originally posted as bail to payment of any fine, penalties and costs due on the charge for which bail was originally posted or any other charge disposed of at the same time, but shall return any remaining balance to the accused and shall not retain the balance to apply, in whole or in part, to any new bail set by the court, without the consent of the accused.

Amended eff. Oct. 7, 1970; Feb. 17, 1977, eff. April 1, 1977, in counties other than Cook, effective July 1, 1977, in Cook County; Dec. 22, 1981, eff. Jan. 15, 1982; April 27, 1984, eff. July 1, 1984; June 26, 1987, eff. Aug. 1, 1987; June 19, 1989, eff. Aug. 1, 1989; Dec. 7, 1990, eff. Jan. 1, 1991; June 12, 1992, eff. July 1, 1992; Sept. 30, 2002, eff. immediately; June 11, 2009, eff. immediately; Aug. 6, 2010, eff. Sept. 15, 2010; Dec. 30, 2014, eff. Jan. 1, 2015.

Formerly Ill.Rev.Stat.1991, ch. 110A, ¶ 503.

Committee Comments
Paragraph (a)

Paragraph (a) is derived from the first two sentences of paragraph 13.10 of the Cook County rule and expands, substantially, the sense of Section 1(c) of Paragraph F of the former Supreme Court rule. However, the rule now applies only to multiple traffic and conservation charges.

Paragraph (b)

Paragraph (b) is derived from the second paragraph of paragraph 13.10 of the Cook County rule, but expands those provisions and details the procedure to be followed after final disposition of the charge for which bail was originally posted. Bail in a single amount should hereafter be set for all continued charges. When more than one such charge is continued, it is suggested that the clerk make copies of the receipt for bail or the bond and place one copy in each offense file. The second sentence of this paragraph was inserted to clarify the responsibility of the clerks where new bail has been set and a cash balance remains from the bail originally deposited (or any balance after fines and costs, if any, have been deducted). Posting new bail is the defendant's responsibility. This rule would not preclude the defendant from instructing the clerk to apply the original cash bail (or any balance) to any new bail set on the continued charges.

Rule 504. Appearance Date

The date set by the arresting officer or the clerk of the circuit court for an accused's first appearance in court shall be not less than 14 days but within 60 days after the date of the arrest, whenever practicable. It is the policy of this court that, if the arresting agency has been exempted from the requirements of Rule 505, an accused who appears and pleads "not guilty" to an alleged traffic or conservation offense punishable by fine only should be granted a trial on the merits on the appearance date or, if the accused demands a trial by jury, within a reasonable time thereafter. A failure to appear on the first appearance date by an arresting officer from a Rule 505 exempted agency shall, in and of itself, not normally be considered good cause for a continuance.

Adopted Oct. 26, 1967, eff. Jan. 1, 1968. Amended eff. Oct. 7, 1970; Feb. 17, 1977, eff. April 1, 1977, in counties other than Cook, eff. July 1, 1977, in Cook County; Dec. 22, 1981, eff. Jan. 15, 1982; Nov. 21, 1988, eff. Dec. 1, 1988; June 19, 1989, eff. Aug. 1, 1989; May 24, 1995, eff. Jan. 1, 1996.

Formerly Ill.Rev.Stat.1991, ch. 110A, ¶ 504.

Committee Comments

The first sentence of this rule is derived from Paragraph 13.9 of the Cook County rule, except that the time limit between the date of arrest and the first court appearance is extended from not more than 30 days, whenever practicable, to not more than 45 days, whenever practicable. Paragraph E of the former Supreme Court rule also provided that the defendant's appearance in court should be set for not less than 10 nor more than 30 days after the date of the issuance of the summons. However, the words "whenever practicable" did not appear in the downstate rule. The Committee feels that a 35-day period between the date of arrest and the date of first court appearance will make it somewhat easier for law enforcement officers to set at least one court date each 35 days for appearance on tickets which they have issued.

Traditionally, and as a matter of practice, in Cook County, if a police officer fails to appear to prosecute his case on the appearance date which he established in the ticket, the case is dismissed for want of prosecution. On the contrary, however, Paragraph E of the former Supreme Court rule expressly provided that the police officer would not be required to appear on the date he set for defendant's first appearance. Defendants who appeared and pleaded "not guilty" were instructed that their plea would be entered and, usually, the case was continued to a future date on which the police officer would be required to appear. Some defendants had to make two or more court appearances to answer the same charge. Where a defendant was a resident of a county other than the county in which he was required to appear, he had to travel long distances to make a second appearance on the same charge. The second sentence of this rule is new and sets forth as the policy of the Supreme Court that a defendant who pleads "not guilty" should be granted a trial on the merits on the date the police officers set for defendant's first court appearance.

The third sentence relates to Rule 505, which is also new. See comment under Rule 505.

Rule 505. Notice to Accused

When issuing a Uniform Citation and Complaint, a conservation complaint or a Notice to Appear in lieu of either, the officer shall also issue a written notice to the accused in substantially the following form:

AVOID MULTIPLE COURT APPEARANCES

If you intend to plead "not guilty" to this charge, or if, in addition, you intend to demand a trial by jury, so notify the clerk of the court at least 10 days (excluding Saturdays, Sundays or holidays) before the day set for your appearance. A new appearance date will be set, and arrangements will be made to have the arresting officer present on that new date. Failure to notify the clerk of either your intention to plead "not guilty" or your intention to demand a jury trial may result in your having to return to court, if you plead "not guilty" on the date originally set for your court appearance.

Upon timely receipt of notice that the accused intends to plead "not guilty," the clerk shall set a new appearance date not less than 7 days nor more than 60 days after the original appearance date set by the arresting officer or the clerk of the circuit court, and notify all parties of the new date and the time for appearance. If the accused demands a trial by jury, the trial shall be scheduled within a reasonable period. In order to invoke the right to a speedy trial, the accused if not in custody must file an appropriate, separate demand, as provided in section 103–5 of the Code of Criminal Procedure of 1963, as amended (725 ILCS 5/103–5). The proper prosecuting attorney shall be served with such separate written demand for speedy trial. If the accused fails to notify the clerk as provided above, the arresting officer's failure to appear on the date originally set for appearance may be considered good cause for a continuance. Any state agency or any unit of local government desiring to be exempt from the requirements of this Rule 505 may apply to the Conference of Chief Circuit Judges for an exemption. Adopted Oct. 26, 1967, eff. Jan. 1, 1968. Amended eff. Oct. 7, 1970; Feb. 17, 1977, eff. April 1, 1977, in counties other than Cook, eff. July 1, 1977, in Cook County; Dec. 22, 1981, eff. Jan. 15, 1982; April 27, 1984, eff. July 1, 1984; June 26, 1987, eff. Aug. 1, 1987; June 19, 1989, eff. Aug. 1, 1989; May 24, 1995, eff. Jan. 1, 1996.

Formerly Ill.Rev.Stat.1991, ch. 110A, ¶ 505.

Committee Comments

See comment under Rule 504. This rule is new and takes into consideration the unique situation in which the State Highway Police, for all practical purposes, find it impossible to appear on the first date which they set for defendant's appearance. State Highway Police jurisdiction and responsibility is statewide. Officers traveling from Cairo to Chicago for duty in riot areas or some other such activity have a duty to issue traffic tickets to violators that they may observe at any place along the route. This may result in a State Police officer's having to write tickets returnable, in some unusual cases, in up to 25 counties in any given 35-day period. This situation is particularly acute when aircraft observation officers and radar officers travel from county to county and issue, or cause to be issued, tickets returnable in 25 or 30 counties in large areas of the State. The State Highway Police have consistently maintained that requiring officers to appear in several counties each month would substantially deplete the law enforcement effectiveness of the State Highway Police.

The rule provides that the Illinois State Highway Police shall be the only police agency authorized to issue written notice requiring the defendant to notify the clerk of his intention to plead not guilty and request trial by jury. The procedure is incorporated as an exception for the Illinois State Highway Police only because of the peculiar circumstance of their statewide jurisdiction. It was deemed unnecessary and undesirable to require the circuit clerks of the several counties to accept, receive, record, and issue notices concerning each traffic ticket issued by every police officer. The Committee is aware of the fact that police in very small towns and villages may have difficulty adjusting to the requirement that they appear on the date set for first appearance of each traffic and conservation defendant. On the other hand, however, municipal and county police officers are responsible only in one county, all tickets issued by them are returnable at some place within the boundaries of that one county. Their burden, regardless how difficult, will not amount to the same burden which would be faced by State Police Officers, each of whom usually covers several counties.

Cook County is excepted from the provisions of this rule.

Rules 506 to 525. Reserved

PART B. BAIL SCHEDULES

Note

NOTE: The bail provisions of Rules 526, 527 and 528 do not apply to arrests on warrant. Bail is preset to avoid undue delay in freeing certain persons accused of an offense when, because of the hour or the circumstances, it is not practicable to bring the accused before a judge. When the accused is actually brought before a judge, the bail amounts specified in these rules do not control. Nothing in these rules is intended to limit a peace officer's discretion to issue a Notice to Appear in an appropriate case (725 ILCS 5/107–12).

Committee Comments

This NOTE is derived from but expands, somewhat, Paragraph 13.1 of the Cook County rule and a similar NOTE which appeared in Section 1, Paragraph F of the former Supreme Court rule. The Committee felt that this NOTE would make it clear that the bail provisions of rules 526, 527 and 528 are only applicable when bail has not been set by a judge. There apparently has been some misunderstanding about this. Whether or not, under any given circumstances, it is "practicable" to bring an offender before a judge to have bail set will be a matter of judgment for the arresting officer. In an ordinary case, slight inconvenience, alone, may make it impracticable to do so. However, where the circumstances surrounding the violation are aggravated or where the violation was particularly dangerous, the police officer may decide that the desirability of having a bail hearing before a judge may outweigh the inconvenience to himself or the alleged offender. For example, if a person is arrested for removing one plant from a state forest in violation of Section 8 of An Act in relation to State forests, operation of forest tree nurseries and providing penalties in connection therewith, approved July 2, 1925, as amended (Ill.Rev.Stat.1965, ch. 57½, para. 29), the circumstances would clearly warrant release on $25 cash bail under rule 527(b). On the other hand, if a person were arrested for tearing up and destroying a large number of plants in a state forest, the circumstances might warrant an appearance before a judge for a hearing to set bail. The hour of the day and the availability of a judge or magistrate are of paramount importance in determining practicability. Of course, the defendant has the right to insist upon being brought before a judge for a hearing to set bail (Ill.Rev.Stat.1965, ch. 16, para. 83).

Rule 526. Bail Schedule–Traffic Offenses

(a) **Bail in Minor Traffic Offenses.** Unless released on a written promise to comply and except as provided in paragraphs (b), (c), (d) and (f) of this rule a person arrested for a traffic offense and personally served by the arresting officer with a Citation and Complaint shall post bail in the amount of $120 in one of the following ways: (1) by posting $120 cash bail (see Rule 501(b) for definition of "Cash Bail"); or (2) by depositing, in lieu of such amount, an approved bond certificate; or (3) by depositing, in lieu of such amount, a current Illinois driver's license.

(b) **Bail in Certain Truck Offenses.**

(1) Persons charged with a violation of section 3–401(d) or 15–111 of the Illinois Vehicle Code, as amended (truck overweight) (625 ILCS 5/3–401(d) or 5/15–111), charged with a violation of section 15–112(e) of the Illinois Vehicle Code, as amended (gross weight) (625 ILCS 5/15–112(e)), or charged with a violation punishable by fine pursuant to sections 15–113.1, 15–113.2 or 15–113.3 of the Illinois Vehicle Code, as amended (permit moves) (625 ILCS 5/15–113.1 *et seq.*), unless released on a written promise to comply, shall post cash bail in an amount equal to the amount of the minimum fine fixed by statute, plus penalties and costs (see Rule 501(b) for definition of "Cash Bail"). The accused may, in lieu of cash bail, deposit a money order issued by a money transfer service company which has been approved by the Administrative Director under regulations issued by this court. The money order shall be made payable to the clerk of the circuit court of the county in which the violation occurred. When the bail for any offense hereunder does not exceed $500, the accused may, at his option, deposit a truck bond certificate in lieu of bail.

(2) Persons charged with violating section 15–112(g) of the Illinois Vehicle Code, as amended, by refusing to stop and submit a vehicle and load to weighing after being directed to do so by an officer, or with violating section 15–112(g) by removing all or part of the load prior to weighing shall post bail in the amount of $1,200 (625 ILCS 5/15–112(g)).

(c) **Bail in Other Traffic Offenses (Rules of the Road).** Except as provided in paragraph (e) of this rule, persons charged with violations of the following sections of the Illinois Vehicle Code, unless released on a written promise to comply, shall post bail in the amount specified:

ILCS	Description	Bail
(1) 625 ILCS 5/11–601	Speeding, but only when more than 20 mph over the posted limit but not more than 25 mph over the posted limit	$140
(2) 625 ILCS 5/11–601.5	Speeding, but only when 26 mph over the posted limit but less than 35 mph over the posted limit	$1,500
	Speeding, but only when 35 mph or more over the posted limit	$2,000
(3) 625 ILCS 5/11–204	Fleeing or Attempting to Elude Police Officer	$2,000
(4) Blank		

ILCS	Description	Bail
(5) 625 ILCS 5/11–501	Misdemeanor Driving Under Influence of Alcohol or Drugs or with 0.08 or more Blood- or Breath Alcohol Concentration	$3,000
(6) 625 ILCS 5/11–503	Reckless Driving	$2,000
(7) 625 ILCS 5/11–506	Street Racing	$2,000
(8) 625 ILCS 5/12–603.1	Use of Safety Belts, Driver or Passenger	$60

(d) Bail in Other Traffic Offenses (Vehicle Title & Registration Law).

Except as provided in paragraph (e) of this rule, persons charged with violations of the following sections of the Illinois Vehicle Code shall post bail in the amount specified:

ILCS	Description	Bail
(1) 625 ILCS 5/3–707	Operating Without Insurance	$2,000
(2) 625 ILCS 5/3–708	Operating when Registration Suspended for Non–insurance	$3,000
(3) 625 ILCS 5/3–710	Display of False Insurance Card	$2,000

(e) Driver's License or Bond Certificate in Lieu of or in Addition to Bail.

An accused who has a valid Illinois driver's license may deposit his driver's license in lieu of the bail specified in subparagraphs (2), (3), and (6) of Rule 526(c) and subparagraphs (1) and (3) of Rule 526(d). In lieu of posting the cash amount specified in subparagraphs (5) and (7) of Rule 526(c) or subparagraph (2) of Rule 526(d), an accused must post $1,000 bail and his current Illinois driver's license. Persons who do not possess a valid Illinois driver's license shall post bail in the amounts specified in Rule 526(c) or 526(d).

(f) Bail in Other Traffic Offenses (Driver Licensing Law).

Persons charged with violations of the following sections of the Illinois Vehicle Code shall post bail in the amount specified:

ILCS	Description	Bail
(1) 625 ILCS 5/6–301	Unlawful Use of License	$1,500
(2) 625 ILCS 5/6–303	Misdemeanor Driving With Suspended or Revoked License under the following circumstances:	$1,500
See article VI, "Penalties," Illinois Vehicle Code (625 ILCS 5/6–601)	(a) All cases other than those where the license is suspended for failure to appear	
	(b) License suspended for failure to appear (see Rule 526(a))	
(3) 625 ILCS 5/6–304.1	Permitting Driving Under Influence of Alcohol or Drugs	$1,500
(4) 625 ILCS 5/6–101	Unlicensed Driving, under the following circumstances:	$1,500
See article VI, "Penalties," Illinois Vehicle Code (625 ILCS 5/6–601)	(a) All cases other than those charging license expired for less than one year	
	(b) License expired less than one year (see Rule 526(a))	
(5) 625 ILCS 5/6–507	Commercial Driver's License	$1,500

(g) Bail for Traffic Offenses Defined by Ordinance.

Bail for traffic offenses defined by any ordinances of any unit of local government which are similar to those described in this Rule 526 shall be the same amounts as provided for in this rule.

Adopted Oct. 26, 1967, eff. Jan. 1, 1968. Amended eff. Oct. 7, 1970; Jan.31, 1972, eff. March 1, 1972; February 17, 1977, eff. April 1, 1977, in counties other than Cook, eff. July 1, 1977, in Cook County; Sept. 29, 1978, eff. Nov. 1, 1978; Sept.20, 1979, eff. Oct. 15, 1979; Dec. 22, 1981, eff. Jan. 15, 1982; April 27, 1984, eff. July 1, 1984; March 27, 1985, eff. May 1, 1985; June 26, 1987, eff. August 1, 1987; June 19, 1989, eff. Aug. 1, 1989; Jan. 11, 1990, eff. immediately; Dec. 7, 1990, eff. Jan. 1, 1991; June 12, 1992, eff. July 1, 1992; Sept. 27, 1993, eff. Oct. 1, 1993; April 11, 2000, eff. immediately; Sept. 30, 2002, eff. immediately; Dec. 5, 2003, eff. immediately; May 30, 2008, eff. immediately; June 11, 2009, eff. immediately; June 3, 2010, eff. Sept. 15, 2010; Dec. 7, 2011, eff. immediately; Dec. 12, 2013, eff. Jan. 1, 2014; Dec. 30, 2014, eff. Jan. 1, 2015.

Formerly Ill.Rev.Stat.1991, ch. 110A, ¶ 526.

For applicability of bail provisions to arrests on warrant, see ILCS S.Ct. Art. V, Pt. B.

ADMINISTRATIVE REGULATIONS

These Regulations were adopted as such by the Supreme Court in its order of October 26, 1967 adopting Rules 501 et seq. The Regulations were formerly sections 6 and 6A of paragraph F of the prior Rule which became effective February 15, 1964 and which was superseded by Rule 501 et seq.

Sec. 6. Bond Certificate. A "Bond Certificate", as such term is used in this rule, shall be a certificate issued or guaranteed by any company or membership association which has been authorized to issue the same as provided in this Section 6.

(a) Any surety or insurance company or any membership association which is a licensee in good standing under the Bail Bond Act, approved June 29, 1931, as amended, [Ill.Rev.Stat.1963, chap. 38, pars. 627c–627o] may apply to the Director of Insurance of the State of Illinois, who is hereby designated by the Court for this purpose, for authority to issue or guarantee Bond Certificates guaranteeing the payment of a judgment for fine and cost not in excess of $25.00.

(b) The applicant shall deposit and maintain with the Director of Insurance of the State of Illinois

(1) a sum of Twenty Five Thousand Dollars ($25,000) in good and merchantable securities having a fair market value of Twenty Five Thousand Dollars (which deposit shall be in addition to the deposit required under said Bail Bond Act) and of the kind or kinds authorized as deposits for professional bondsmen under Section 12 of said Bail Bond Act as security for the payment of such judgments not in excess of $25.00, including ex parte judgment for failure of any certificate holder to appear in court, entered in cases in which such Bond Certificates have been deposited as bail, and

(2) a written Guarantee

(A) undertaking to pay every such judgment which shall have become final, to the Clerk of the Circuit Court in which such judgment is entered within twenty days after receipt of a notice from said Clerk of the entry of such judgment and that the same has become final, such notice to be given within three (3) years after entry of such judgment, and to furnish to said Clerks, for use in notifying the applicant of the entry of judgments with respect to which the applicant is obligated, addressed envelopes with postage prepaid or business reply envelopes requiring no postage,

(B) in the event of the failure to pay such judgment within such twenty-day period, authorizing the said Director of Insurance pursuant to the order of any judge, associate judge or magistrate of the Circuit Court of the county in which such judgment shall have been entered to sell so much of the securities deposited with him as shall be necessary to make payment of (1) such judgment and to pay the same to the Clerk of said Circuit Court, and (2) the costs and expenses incident to such sale; and further agreeing that upon such payments the Director of Insurance shall be released and exonerated from any further liability with respect to such payments,

(C) agreeing to restore said deposit of security upon ten days' notice from the Director of Insurance if such deposit shall diminish for any reason so that its fair market value is less than $25,000.

(D) agreeing that upon the expiration of one year following termination of its authority to issue Bond Certificates an accounting shall be made of its liability with respect to Bond Certificates issued prior to the date of such termination of authority and so much of said deposit of securities as shall be necessary to satisfy such liability (including costs and expenses incident to the sale of such securities) shall be applied to such liability, and agreeing that upon such payment to satisfy such liability the Director of Insurance shall be released and exonerated from any further liability with respect to such payments,

(E) agreeing that the Guarantee shall be liberally construed to impose liability upon it as an issuer of Bond Certificates in accordance with the purpose and intent of this Rule of Court, and that every Bond Certificate issued by it or with respect to which it assumes liability by such Guarantee, regardless of the form or language employed therein, shall be construed as if it contained in express language the liability intended by this Rule of Court to be imposed upon a company or association authorized to issue such Bond Certificates, and that every such Bond Certificate issued by it or with respect to which it assumes liability under said Guarantee, regardless of the form or language employed therein, shall be construed with respect to cases arising in the State of Illinois, on and after January 1, 1964, as if it provided as follows:

"BOND CERTIFICATE
This is to certify that

_____
(Name of Issuer)

in accordance with the rules of the Supreme Court of Illinois, does hereby guarantee the appearance of the within named holder of this Bond Certificate (whose signature is hereto affixed) in the Circuit Court of any county of Illinois, when arrested for any traffic violation punishable by fine only, committed prior to the date of certificate expiration, which expiration date is indicated on the reverse side hereof, by guaranteeing the payment of any judgment not in excess of $25.00, including ex parte judgment for failure of said holder to appear in court, rendered against said holder with respect to the traffic violation for which this Bond Certificate was deposited as bond."

(F) agreeing that whenever any such Bond Certificate shall have been accepted in Illinois as bond to guarantee the appearance of any person named therein or on any identification card incorporated by reference therein in the Circuit Court of any county of Illinois for a traffic violation alleged to have been committed prior to the date of expiration of such Bond Certificate shown or referred to thereon, such company or association shall be liable thereon to the extent and subject to the conditions and terms of said Guarantee and of this Rule of Court, and

(G) agreeing that whenever an arresting officer accepts as bail a Bond Certificate which shall appear to be a genuine Bond Certificate issued to the person depositing it with the officer and to have been issued by or guaranteed by such company or association, such company or association shall be liable thereon, notwithstanding that such Bond Certificate shall be a forgery or counterfeit or otherwise not genuine, or shall have been lost or stolen or misappropriated or obtained by fraud by the person depositing it with such officer, in all respects and to the same extent and subject to the same conditions and terms as if said Bond Certificate were in all respects genuine and a certificate which the depositor thereof was entitled to use for such purpose, provided that the arresting officer shall have had exhibited to him, as provided by Section 1 of Part F of this Rule, an operator's or chauffeur's license certificate which shall appear to have been issued to the person so arrested.

(c) If the application is approved, the Director of Insurance will authorize the issuance of Bond Certificates by the applicant, will issue an appropriate certificate evidencing such authority, and will authorize the applicant to notify the Clerks of the Circuit Courts that Bond Certificates with respect to which such applicant has assumed liability shall be accepted by officials as bond for the appearance of the holders thereof arising from traffic violations punishable by fine only as provided in Part F of this Rule. Upon receipt of such notice the Clerks of the Circuit Court shall in turn give such notice to all officials authorized to accept bail in traffic cases.

(d) Whenever any such company or association shall violate the terms of its said written Guarantee with respect to the restoration and maintenance of its deposit with the Director of Insurance of the State of Illinois the Director of Insurance may revoke the authority of such company or association hereunder and suspend the acceptance of its Bond Certificate as bail.

(e) When authority is revoked as to any company or association with respect to the issuance of Bond Certificates, notice of such action shall be given by the said Director of Insurance to the Administrative Director under Article VI, Section 2 of the Illinois Constitution (Judicial Article) who shall notify the Clerks of all the Circuit Courts who in turn shall give such notice to all officials authorized to accept bail in traffic cases.

(f) Any order revoking such authority shall provide for the payment of (1) all unpaid judgments then unsatisfied; (2) those entered within one year following such order of revocation in cases in which such Bond Certificates were deposited as bail prior to the entry of such order; and (3) those entered not later than 60 days following such order of revocation, irrespective of the dates upon which the Bond Certificates were deposited as bail and even if such Bond Certificates were deposited after the entry of such order of revocation. From time to time the Director of Insurance pursuant to orders of any judge, associate judge or magistrate of any Circuit Court which shall have entered such final judgment shall sell so much of the securities as may be required to satisfy (1) such unpaid judgments and (2) the costs and expenses incident to such sale, and upon such payments the Director of Insurance shall be released and exonerated from any further liability with respect thereto. After such payments the balance of securities deposited or the proceeds therefrom shall be returned to the depositor, and the Director of Insurance shall have no further liability with respect to such deposits.

Sec. 6A. Truck Bond Certificates. A "Truck Bond Certificate", as such term is used in this Rule, shall be a certificate issued or guaranteed by any company or membership association which has been authorized to issue the same as provided in this Section 6A.

(a) Any surety or insurance company or any membership association which is a licensee in good standing under the Bail Bond Act, approved June 29, 1931, as amended, may apply to the Director of Insurance of the State of Illinois, who is hereby designated by the Court for this purpose, for authority to issue or guarantee Truck Bond Certificates guaranteeing the payment of a judgment for fine and costs not in excess of $100.

(b) The applicant shall deposit and maintain with the Director of Insurance of the State of Illinois

(1) a sum of Fifty Thousand Dollars ($50,000) in good merchantable securities having a fair market value of Fifty Thousand Dollars ($50,000) (which deposit shall be in addition to the deposit required under said Bail Bond Act) and of the kind or kinds authorized as deposits for professional bondsmen under Section 12 of said Bail Bond Act as security for the payment of such judgments not in excess of $100, including ex parte judgment for failure of any certificate holder to appear in court, entered in cases in which such Truck Bond Certificates have been deposited as bail, and

(2) a written Guarantee, satisfactory to the Director of Insurance, by which such company or association undertakes to perform agreements in all respects similar to those undertaken by companies or associations filing written agreements with the Director of Insurance pursuant to Section 6 of Part F of this Rule, with variations necessary to carry out the intent that under this Section 6A the deposit of securities required shall be $50,000 (rather than $25,000) and that the judgments guaranteed with respect to offenses enumerated in Section 3 of Part F of this Rule shall be $100 and the judgments guaranteed

with respect to offenses referred to in Section 1 of Part F of this Rule shall be $25.

(c) If the application is approved, the Director of Insurance will authorize the issuance of Truck Bond Certificates by the applicant, will issue an appropriate certificate evidencing such authority, and authorize the applicant to notify the Clerks of the Circuit Courts that Truck Bond Certificates with respect to which such applicant has assumed liability shall be accepted by officials as bond for the appearance of the holders thereof arising from traffic violations punishable by fine only as provided in Part F of this Rule. Upon receipt of such notice the Clerks of the Circuit Court shall in turn give such notice to all officials authorized to accept bail in traffic cases.

(d) Whenever any such company or association shall violate the terms of its said written Guarantee with respect to the restoration and maintenance of its deposit with the Director of Insurance of the State of Illinois the Director of Insurance may revoke the authority of such company or association hereunder and suspend the acceptance of its Truck Bond Certificate as bail.

(e) When authority is revoked as to any company or association with respect to the issuance of Truck Bond Certificates, notice of such action shall be given by the said Director of Insurance to the Administrative Director under Article VI, Section 2 of the Illinois Constitution (Judicial Article) who shall notify the Clerks of all the Circuit Courts who in turn shall give such notice to all officials authorized to accept bail in traffic cases.

(f) Any order revoking such authority shall provide for the payment of (1) all unpaid judgments then unsatisfied; (2) those entered within one year following such order of revocation in cases in which such Truck Bond Certificates were deposited as bail prior to the entry of such order; and (3) those entered not later than 60 days following such order of revocation, irrespective of the dates upon which the Truck Bond Certificates were deposited as bail and even if such Truck Bond Certificates were deposited after the entry of such order of revocation. From time to time the Director of Insurance pursuant to orders of any judge, associate judge or magistrate of any Circuit Court which shall have entered such final judgment shall sell so much of the securities as may be required to satisfy (1) such unpaid judgments and (2) the costs and expenses incident to such sale, and upon such payments the Director of Insurance shall be released and exonerated from any further liability with respect thereto. After such payments the balance of securities deposited or the proceeds therefrom shall be returned to the depositor, and the Director of Insurance shall have no further liability with respect to such deposits.

Committee Comments

Paragraph (a)

Paragraph (a) is derived from Section 1, Paragraph F of the former Supreme Court rule and Paragraph 13.4 of the Cook County rule. Drivers' licenses issued by foreign jurisdictions will, however, no longer be accepted in lieu of cash bail, as they had been under the former Supreme Court rule. See the comment under rule 501(c).

Paragraph (b)

Paragraph (b)(1) is derived from Section 3(a), Paragraph F of the former Supreme Court rule and Paragraph 13.5 of the Cook County rule, except that the Cook County rule provided that bail would be in the fixed amount of $100 rather than the amount of the fine fixed by statute, plus costs. Paragraph (b)(2) is derived from Section 3(b), Paragraph F of the former Supreme Court rule. There was no similar provision in the Cook County rule. Paragraph (b)(3) restates, with minor changes, Section 3(c) of Paragraph F of the former Supreme Court rule.

Paragraph (c)

Paragraph (c) is derived from Section 2, Paragraph F of the former Supreme Court rule. The Committee felt that setting out the U.A.R.T. citation, the Ill.Rev.Stat. reference and a description of the offense makes the rule more understandable and easier to administer on the street. Section 2, Paragraph F of the former Supreme Court rule provided that bail in an amount greater than $25 would be required for violation of certain sections of the U.A.R.T. and for violation of Section 6–303 of the Illinois Motor Vehicle Law (license violations). (Note: See paragraph (e) of this rule). The Cook County rule did not establish bail for specific violations of the U.A.R.T. but, rather, apparently relied on the provisions of Subparagraph (c) of Paragraph 13.6 which set bail in the amount of $200 for any misdemeanor punishable by fine or imprisonment in a penal institution other than the penitentiary, or both. Paragraph (c)(2), is new and establishes bail in the amount of $50 cash for violation of Section 47.2 of the U.A.R.T. House Bill 1377, approved July 20, 1967, transferred the prohibition against illegal possession or transportation of alcoholic liquor from the Dram Shop Act to the U.A.R.T. and established as a penalty a fine not less than $25 nor more than $500. Speeding over 21 miles per hour in excess of the posted limit (Paragraph (c)(1)), drag racing under Section 48.1 of the U.A.R.T. (Paragraph (c)(7)) and "Fleeing or attempting to Elude Police Officer"—Section 22.01 U.A.R.T. (Ill.Rev.Stat.1965, ch. 95½, para. 119.1) (Paragraph (c)(3)) are all new provisions. It appears to the Committee that the increased bail amount for certain speeding violations under paragraph (c)(1) is warranted. Previously, defendants going at even extraordinary high speeds could nonetheless be released on bail of $25. Because speeding violations (and other relatively minor U.A.R.T. offenses) may now be punished by jail sentences. (HB 1606, 75th General Assembly), the bail ($50) can not be required to be cash bail, as has been provided for cases punishable by fine only.

Paragraph (d)

This paragraph is new and provides that a driver's license may be deposited in lieu of the bail specified in subparagraphs (c)(1), (c)(2) or (c)(3) of rule 526 and that, if a defendant elects to take advantage of the 10% deposit provisions of Section 110–7 of the Code of Criminal Procedure, he must, if charged with a violation set forth in subparagraph (c)(4) through (c)(7) of rule 526 deposit his valid, current Illinois driver's license in addition to the 10% deposit. If the violator cannot or does not deposit a current, valid Illinois driver's license he must post the full cash amount of the pre-set bail, if he wishes to take advantage of the pre-set bail provisions, rather than waiting to be brought before a judge for a bail hearing. This bail structure is new. The provision that a driver may deposit his Illinois driver's license in lieu of the bail required by sub-paragraphs (c)(1), (c)(2) and (c)(3) is required by Section 6–306(a) of the Illinois Motor Vehicle Law.

Paragraph (e)

Paragraph (e) is derived in part from Section 2, Paragraph F of the former Supreme Court rule and specifies bail for certain license violations. Under the former Supreme Court rule, the only license violation for which bail was pre-set was Section 6–303 of the Illinois Motor Vehicle Law (driving with a suspended or revoked license). Bail for such offense was set at $500 for residents of Illinois. However, there was no specific pre-set bail provision for any license violations by non-residents.

Paragraph (f)

Paragraph (f) is new and provides that bail for ordinance offenses similar to statutory traffic offenses shall be the same as provided elsewhere in this rule.

Rule 527. Bail Schedule—Conservation Offenses

(a) General. Except as provided in paragraphs (b), (c), (d), (e), (f), and (g) of this Rule 527, a person arrested for a conservation offense and personally served by the arresting officer with a conservation complaint shall post cash bail in the amount of $ 120 (see Rule 501(b) for definition of "Cash Bail").

(b) Bail for Specified Violations of the Wildlife Code. Persons arrested for a conservation offense listed below and personally served by the arresting officer with a conservation complaint shall post bail in the amount specified:

WILDLIFE CODE

ILCS	Description	Bail
520 ILCS 5/2.9	Unlawful Taking or Possession of Wild Turkeys out of Season	$1,500
520 ILCS 5/2.16	Unlawful Sale or Barter of Game Birds	$1,500
520 ILCS 5/2.18	Unlawful Taking of Migratory Game Birds	$1,500
520 ILCS 5/2.24	Unlawful Taking or Possessing of Deer out of Season	$1,500
520 ILCS 5/2.25	Unlawful Taking or Possessing of Deer out of Season	$1,500
520 ILCS 5/2.29	Unlawful Sale or Barter of Game Animals	$1,500
520 ILCS 5/2.30	Unlawful Taking of Furbearing Mammals	$1,500
520 ILCS 5/2.33a(k)	Possession of Green Hides	$1,500

(c) Bail for Specified Violations of the Boat Registration and Safety Act. Persons arrested for a conservation offense listed below and personally served by the arresting officer with a conservation complaint shall post bail in the amount specified:

BOAT REGISTRATION AND SAFETY ACT

ILCS	Description	Bail
625 ILCS 45/5–1	Careless Operation of Motorboat	$1,500
625 ILCS 45/5–16(A)	Operating Motorboat Under the Influence of Liquors or Drugs	$2,000
625 ILCS 45/5–22	Failure to Yield to Emergency Watercraft	$1,500

(d) Bail for Specified Violations of the Snowmobile Registration and Safety Act. Persons arrested for a conservation offense listed below and personally served by the arresting officer with a conservation complaint shall post bail in the amount specified:

SNOWMOBILE REGISTRATION AND SAFETY ACT

ILCS	Description	Bail
625 ILCS 40/3–10	Falsification or Alteration	$1,500
625 ILCS 40/5–1(B)	Reckless, Negligent or Careless Operation of Snowmobile	$1,500
625 ILCS 40/5–7(a)	Operating Snowmobile Under the Influence of Liquor or Drugs	$2,000

(e) Bail for Specified Violations of the Fish and Aquatic Life Code. Persons arrested for a conservation offense listed below and personally served by the arresting officer with a conservation complaint shall post bail in the amount specified:

FISH AND AQUATIC LIFE CODE

ILCS	Description	Bail
515 ILCS 5/10–140	Dip Net Without Commercial License	$1,500
515 ILCS 5/15–5	Failure to Have Required Commercial Fishing License	$1,500
515 ILCS 5/15–10	Failure to Have Required Commercial Musselor License	$1,500
515 ILCS 5/20–90	Aquaculture Permit	$1,500

(f) Bail for Specified Violations of the Forest Products Transportation Act. Persons arrested for a conservation offense listed below and personally served by the arresting officer with a conservation complaint shall post bail in the amount specified:

FOREST PRODUCTS TRANSPORTATION ACT

ILCS	Description	Bail
225 ILCS 740/5	Transportation of Forest Products Without Consent	$1,500

(g) Bail for Class A Misdemeanors. Persons arrested for any conservation offense classified as a Class A misdemeanor and personally served by the arresting officer with a conservation complaint shall post bail in the amount of $1,500, except as may be provided in paragraphs (b), (c), (d), (e), and (f).

Adopted Oct. 26, 1967, eff. Jan. 1, 1968. Amended eff. October 7, 1970; January 31, 1972, eff. March 1, 1972; February 17, 1977, eff. April 1, 1977, in counties other than Cook, eff. July 1, 1977, in Cook County; December 22, 1981, eff. January 15, 1982; April 27, 1984, eff. July 1, 1984; March 27, 1985, eff. May 1, 1985; June 26, 1987, eff. August 1, 1987; June 19, 1989, eff. August 1, 1989; June 12, 1992, eff. July 1, 1992; September 30, 2002, eff. immediately; Dec. 6, 2006, eff. immediately; June 11, 2009, eff. immediately; June 3, 2010, eff. September 15, 2010; Dec. 12, 2013, eff. Jan. 1, 2014.

Formerly Ill.Rev.Stat.1991, ch. 110A, ¶ 527.

For applicability of bail provisions to arrests on warrant, see ILCS S.Ct. Art. V, Pt. B.

Committee Comments

This rule is new. The rule establishes bail in specific amounts for violation of specified conservation offenses and establishes general bail provisions for remaining conservation offenses.

Rule 528. Bail Schedule—Ordinance Offenses, Petty Offenses, Business Offenses and Certain Misdemeanors

(a) **Offenses Punishable by Fine Not to Exceed $1,000.** Bail for offenses (other than traffic or conservation offenses), including ordinance violations, punishable only by a fine which does not exceed $1,000 shall be $120.

(b) **Offenses Punishable by Fine in Excess of $1,000.** Bail for offenses (other than traffic or conservation offenses) punishable only by a fine which exceeds $1,000 shall be $1,500.

(c) **Certain Other Offenses.** Bail for any other offenses, including violation of any ordinance of any unit of local government (other than traffic or conservation offenses) punishable by fine or imprisonment in a penal institution other than the penitentiary, or both, shall be $1,500, except as provided in paragraph (d) of this Rule 528 and except that bail for Class C misdemeanors shall be $120.

(d) **Domestic Violence Offenses.** No bail is established under these rules as provided in section 110–15 of the Code of Criminal Procedure of 1963 (725 ILCS 5/110–15) for the offense of domestic battery (720 ILCS 5/12–3.2), a violation of an order of protection (720 ILCS 5/12–30), or any similar violation of a local ordinance. Bail for these offenses shall be set by the court pursuant to statute.

Adopted Oct. 26, 1967, eff. Jan. 1, 1968. Amended eff. Oct. 7, 1970; Feb. 17, 1977, eff. April 1, 1977, in counties other than Cook, eff. July 1, 1977, in Cook County; Dec. 22, 1981, eff. Jan. 15, 1982; June 12, 1992, eff. July 1, 1992; March 19, 1997, eff. April 15, 1997; Oct. 22, 1999, eff. Dec. 1, 1999; amended June 3, 2010, effective September 15, 2010.

Formerly Ill.Rev.Stat.1991, ch. 110A, ¶ 528.

For applicability of bail provisions to arrests on warrant, see ILCS S.Ct. Art. V, Pt. B.

Committee Comments
Paragraph (a)

Paragraph (a) is derived from Section 1, Paragraph I of the former Supreme Court rule and Paragraph 13.6(a) of the Cook County rule. The paragraph is applicable only to municipal ordinance offenses punishable by fine. As a general matter, it appears that municipal ordinance offenses may be punishable directly only by a fine; incarceration is usually available as a "penalty" only in the event an offender is unable to pay the fine. (See Sections 1–2–1 and 1–2–9 of the Illinois Municipal Code, as amended (Ill.Rev.Stat.1965, ch. 34, para. 437 and

438.) However, in at least one instance the Legislature has expressly granted counties of more than 500,000 persons authority to pass ordinances which may be directly punishable by a fine of a jail sentence up to six months (e.g., Sections 1 and 2 of An Act to provide for the Licensing and regulation of food service establishments in counties of over 500,000 population and providing penalty for violation thereof, approved Aug. 6, 1963 (Ill.Rev.Stat. 1965, ch. 34, para. 439 and 440). For an example of an ordinance which, on its face, would call for possible jail sentence as a direct penalty see the violation: inciting to Riot, etc. (Section 193–1.1 of the Ordinances of the City of Chicago).

Paragraph (b)

Paragraph (b) is derived from Paragraph 13.6(b) of the Cook County rule and Section 2, Paragraph I of the former Supreme Court rule and provides preset bail amounts for statutory offenses (other than Traffic or Conservation offenses) punishable by fine only. The exception setting $25 bail for one type of Disorderly Conduct is derived from Paragraph 13.6(b) of the Cook County rule. No similar exception was contained in the Supreme Court rule. The exception setting $25 bail for a Curfew violation is new. In view of the fact that the 10% deposit provision of the Code of Criminal Procedure will not apply to cases punishable by fine only. (See rule 530), the Committee felt that the establishment of $50 cash bail (with two exceptions in the amount of $25) would comport favorably with the $1,000 bail established for offenses punishable by fine and/or imprisonment in a penal institution other than the penitentiary to which the 10% provisions are applicable.

Paragraph (c)

Paragraph (c) is derived from Paragraph 13.6(c) of the Cook County rule and Section 3 of Paragraph I of the former Supreme Court rule and provides pre-set bail amounts for statutory offenses (other than Traffic or Conservation offenses) punishable by fine or imprisonment in a penal institution other than the penitentiary. Under both the former Supreme Court rule and the Cook County rule, a general ($200) bail paragraph was followed by a list of more serious offenses for which higher amounts of bail were required.

PART C. FINES, PENALTIES AND COSTS—10% DEPOSIT STATUTE

Rule 529. Fines, Penalties and Costs on Written Pleas of Guilty in Minor Traffic and Conservation Offenses

(a) **Traffic Offenses.** All traffic offenses, except those requiring a court appearance under Rule 551 and those involving offenses set out in Rule 526(b)(1), may be satisfied without a court appearance by a written plea of guilty, with the exception of electronic pleas unless authorized by the Supreme Court, and payment of fines, penalties and costs, equal to the bail required by Rule 526 unless an order of failure to appear to answer the charge has been entered pursuant to Rule 556(a), in which case the fine, penalties and costs shall be equal to the amount of the required bail, plus an additional penalty of $35. The balance remaining after deducting the amounts required by sections 27.3a and 27.3c of the Clerks of Courts Act (705 ILCS 105/27.3a, 27.3c) shall be distributed as follows:

(1) 44.5% shall be disbursed to the entity authorized by law to receive the fine imposed in the case;

(2) 16.825% shall be disbursed to the State Treasurer; and

(3) 38.675% shall be disbursed to the county's general corporate fund.

No other fines, fees, penalties or costs shall be assessed in any case which is disposed of on a written plea of guilty without a court appearance under paragraph (a) of Rule 529. A charge of violating section 3–401(d), 15–111 or offenses punishable by fine pursuant to sections 15–113.1, 15–113.2 or 15–113.3 of the Illinois Vehicle Code (truck overweight and permit moves) (625 ILCS 5/15–111, 15–113.1 through 15–113.3), or similar municipal ordinances, may be satisfied without a court appearance by a written plea of guilty and payment of the minimum fine fixed by statute, plus all applicable penalties and costs (see Rule 526(b)(1)). Fines, penalties, and costs shall be disbursed by the clerk pursuant to statute.

(b) Conservation Offenses. Conservation offenses for which $120 cash bail is required under Rule 527 may be satisfied without a court appearance by a written plea of guilty, with the exception of electronic pleas unless authorized by the Supreme Court, and payment of fines, penalties and costs, equal to the cash bail required by Rule 527. The balance remaining after deducting the amounts required by sections 27.3a and 27.3c of the Clerks of Courts Act (705 ILCS 105/27.3a, 27.3c) shall be distributed as follows:

(1) 67% shall be disbursed to the entity authorized by law to receive the fine imposed in the case;

(2) 16.825% shall be disbursed to the State Treasurer; and

(3) 16.175% shall be disbursed to the county's general corporate fund.

No other fines, fees, penalties or costs shall be assessed in any case which is disposed of on a written plea of guilty without a court appearance under paragraph (b) of this Rule 529.

(c) Supervision on Written Pleas of Guilty. In counties designated by the Conference of Chief Circuit Judges, the circuit court may by rule or order authorize the entry of an order of supervision under section 5–6–3.1 of the Unified Code of Corrections (730 ILCS 5/5–6–3.1), for traffic offenses satisfied pursuant to paragraph (a) of this Rule 529. Such circuit court rule or order may include but does not require a program by which the accused, upon payment of the fines, penalties and costs equal to bail required by Rule 526, agrees to attend and successfully complete a traffic safety program approved by the court under standards set by the Conference. The accused shall be responsible for payment of any traffic safety program fees. If the accused fails to file a certificate of successful completion on or before the termination date of the supervision order, the supervision shall be summarily revoked and conviction entered. Any county designated by the Conference pursuant to this rule may opt-out of this rule upon notification to the Conference by the chief judge of the circuit and rescinding any rule or order entered to establish supervision on written pleas of guilty.

(d) The provisions of Supreme Court Rule 402 relating to pleas of guilty do not apply in cases where a defendant enters a guilty plea under this rule. The clerk of the circuit court shall disburse fines, penalties, and costs as provided for in paragraph (a) of this Rule 529.

Adopted Oct. 26, 1967, eff. Jan. 1, 1968. Amended eff. Oct. 7, 1970; Feb. 17, 1977, eff. April 1, 1977, in counties other than Cook, eff. July 1, 1977, in Cook County; amended Sept. 20, 1979, eff. Oct. 15, 1979; Dec. 22, 1981, eff. Jan. 15, 1982; April 27, 1984, eff. July 1, 1984; March 27, 1985, eff. May 1, 1985; June 26, 1987, eff. Aug. 1, 1987; June 19, 1989, eff. Aug. 1, 1989; Dec. 20, 1991, eff. Jan. 1, 1992; June 12, 1992, eff. July 1, 1992; amended Jan. 20, 1993, eff. immediately; amended May 24, 1995, eff. Jan. 1, 1996; amended April 1, 1998, eff. immediately; March 16, 2001, eff. immediately; amended Dec. 5, 2003, eff. Jan. 1, 2004; Aug. 6, 2010, eff. Sept. 15, 2010; Dec. 7, 2011, eff. immediately.

Formerly Ill.Rev.Stat.1991, ch. 110A, ¶ 529.

Committee Comments
Paragraph (a)

Paragraph (a) is derived from Paragraph G of the former Supreme Court rule and provisions relating to fines (not costs) in General Order No. 7 of the Circuit Court of Cook County, dated Jan. 2, 1964, establishing a schedule of fines for certain traffic violations. Overweight violations may now be satisfied, without a court appearance, by a written plea of guilty and payment of a fine in the amount fixed by statute, plus costs. Neither the former Supreme Court rule nor the Cook County rule had contained a similar provision. The Committee felt that there is no substantial reason to require a court appearance on an overweight violation, providing that a written plea of guilty is submitted and the appropriate fine and costs are paid by the violator. The fine schedule now provides that the offense of speeding more than 10 but not more than 20 miles per hour over the speed limit may be satisfied upon a written plea of guilty, without a court appearance, by payment of a fine at the rate of $1 for each mile per hour in excess of the speed limit, plus costs. Under both the former Supreme Court rule and General Order No. 7 of the Circuit Court of Cook County, dated Jan. 2, 1964, the maximum speed which would allow settlement by plea without a court appearance was not more than 15 miles per hour over the speed limit.

It should be noted that the schedule of fines payable upon a written plea of guilty, without a court appearance, is related to the rule on mandatory court appearances (Rule 551). Rule 551 not only requires a court appearance, on a speeding violation when the speed is 21 miles per hour or more over the posted limit, but for any alleged U.A.R.T. offense, if the charge follows any conviction for violating the U.A.R.T. during a preceding one year period. See Comment under Rule 551(c).

Paragraph (b)

Paragraph (b) is new and establishes a schedule of fixed fines and costs for minor violations of conservation statutes and ordinances. The fine amounts for conservation offenses are based on minimum amounts of fines provided for in the various statutes.

Paragraph (c)

Paragraph (c) does not specify the amount of costs to be charged, but merely defines what cases will be considered "minor" traffic, conservation or municipal ordinance cases for the purposes of applying the $5 costs provided for by statute in counties of the first and second class. Section 14(b)(3) of "An Act concerning fees and to classify the several counties of this state with reference thereto," approved March 20, 1872, as amended by HB 2245, approved September 1, 1967. Costs for Cook County, which is a third class county, will be set by Circuit Court rule or order. It is anticipated that the costs specified in this paragraph will be exclusive and that no additional fees or costs will be imposed on written pleas of guilty, or on any findings of guilty in cases which could have been satisfied without a court appearance.

Committee Comments
(December 5, 2003)

Under present Supreme Court Rule 529 (Fines, Penalties and Costs on Written Pleas of Guilty in Minor Traffic and Conservation Offenses), cash bail is distributed on pleas of guilty, where a court appearance is not required, by deducting applicable costs, including clerk's fees (705 ILCS 105/27.1a, 27.2 or 27.2a, as the case may be), Automation Fee (705 ILCS 105/27.3a), Document Storage Fee (705 ILCS 105/27.3c) and Fee to Finance the Court System (55 ILCS 5/5–110). The balance is then distributed by the clerk to the Traffic and Criminal Conviction Surcharge (TCCS) and LEADS Maintenance Fund (730 ILCS 5/5–9–1(c)), Driver's Education Fund (Driver's Ed) (625 ILCS 5/16–104a), Violent Crime Assistance Fund (VCVA) (725 ILCS 240/10(b)) (VCVA is not assessed in speeding violation cases), Trauma Center Fund (625 ILCS 5/16–104(b)), if applicable, and the entity entitled to receive the fine.

The proposed amendments to Rules 529(a) and 529(b) would exclude electronic pleas and eliminate itemized distribution by the clerk of the funds noted above and, instead, after first deducting the Automation Fee and Document Storage Fee, distribute the bail for traffic offenses along the present line of section 27.6 of the Clerk's of Court Act (705 ILCS 105/27.6) in the following percentages: 44.5% to the entity entitled to receive the fine, 38.675% to the county's general fund, and 16.825% to the state Treasurer. Under Rule 529(b), since conservation offenses are not included under section 27.6, bail would be distributed as follows: 67% to the entity entitled to receive the fine, 16.175% to the county's general fund, and 16.825% to the state Treasurer, which is similar to the current disbursal of these amounts.

The $5 Fee to Finance the Court System (55 ILCS 5/5–1101) is distributed to the county's general fund under the present rule on an itemized basis, and would be included in the 38.675% disbursed to the county's general fund under proposed amended Rule 529(a).

The Court Security Fee (55 ILCS 5/5–1103) is not included either in present Rule 529, or the proposed amendment, since the statute requires a court appearance by the violator before the assessment of this fee.

By way of background, the percentage distribution formula under 705 ILCS 105/27.6 became effective on January 1, 1993, and has been adopted for the assessment of fines, fees, costs and forfeitures in 10 counties throughout the state, including Cook County, for violations of the Vehicle Code.

Supreme Court Rule 526 (Bail Schedules–Traffic Offenses), Rule 527 (Bail Schedule–Conservation Offenses) and Rule 529 (Fines, Penalties and Costs on Written Pleas of Guilty in Minor Traffic and Conservation Offenses), among others, were amended on June 12, 1992, effective July 1, 1992, increasing bail in minor traffic cases from $50 to $75 and from $75 to $95 since the amount of fines received by the municipalities was being reduced by legislative "add-ons."

The committee does not believe Supreme Court Rule 529, in its present form, provides adequate direction to the circuit clerks in the distribution of funds under this rule. For instance, a problem arises in the calculation of the TCCS/LEADS Fund which requires the court to assess an additional penalty of $5 for each $40, or fraction thereof, of fine imposed, and the Driver's Ed Fund and VCVA, which requires the court to assess an additional penalty of $4 for each $40, or fraction thereof, of fine imposed. This, by necessity, involves the use of a multiplier. To arrive at the multiplier, the clerk must divide the fine by 40 when a fine plus costs is assessed, or follow the method prescribed under 730 ILCS 5/5–9–1(c) (TCCS/LEADS Maintenance Fund), 725 ILCS 240/10(b) (VCVA) and 625 ILCS 5/16–104a (Drivers's Ed) when the court levies "a gross amount for fine, costs, fees and penalties." The committee concluded that an assessment under Rule 529 was not a "levy of a gross amount."

Under the current rule, the fine is represented as the "balance of the bail," and is the amount remaining after deducting various costs and fees. Therefore, since the court has not assessed a specific fine, the clerk has no exact amount to divide by 40 and is left to reach his or her own conclusion as the correct multiplier. In certain instances if the clerk computes these additional penalties with a multiplier of 1, it results in a fine which is greater that $40; if a multiple of 2 is used, it results in a fine of less than $40.

Chief Justice Benjamin K. Miller, in the Supreme Court's Annual Report to the Legislature dated January 31, 1991, discussed the "plethora of user fees and surcharges enacted by the General Assembly," then concluded that "[t]he complexity of the structure of various charges is such that they are not uniform, and are confusing. It has been impossible for the court system to apply the charge in a consistent and coherent manner."

The Article V Committee agrees, and in order to enhance uniformity and consistency throughout the state in the disbursement of fines, costs, penalties and forfeitures under Rule 529, it recommends a percentage disbursal of funds upon pleas of guilty in traffic and conservation cases which are satisfied without a court appearance by the violator. The committee believes this disbursal, which would be made monthly to all entities, would be fair to all concerned, increase the efficiency of the clerks, and substantially reduce the possibility of error.

As an example of the continuing dilemma facing the circuit clerks, Public Act 93–32, effective June 20, 2003, directs that an "additional penalty of $4.00 shall be assessed by the court imposing a fine (upon a plea or finding of guilty in all traffic, criminal, conservation and local ordinance cases)." The funds are to be remitted by the circuit clerk to the state Treasurer and deposited in the Traffic and Criminal Surcharge Fund. The committee concluded the additional penalty under this act could not be collected or distributed under Rules 529 and 556 since the total amount of bail was already exhausted by other fines, fees and costs and the act itself provides that the additional penalty "shall not reduce or affect the distribution of any other fine, costs, fees and penalties." The committee felt the only way to obtain the funds required under Public Act 93–32 would be: (1) order the offender to appear in court for the assessment of the $4 additional penalty, or (2) increase the amount of bail under Rule 526. It considered the first option to be counterproductive. As to the second option, the committee noted Justice Heiple's dissent when bail was increased under Rule 526 in 1992. In his dissent, he stated, "[W]hile the original purpose of enacting and enforcing highway traffic laws was public safety, this purpose has, in substantial measure, given way to the purpose of earning bounty revenues of government. Any bail figure, to the extent it exceeds the amount necessary to insure the presence of the defendant in court, in a misuse and abuse of the bail process." The committee, after discussion, is not recommending the increase of bail under Rules 526 and 527.

The committee was also concerned about the 10 counties which distribute gross fines and costs pursuant to 705 ILCS 105/27.6, since this distribution would include money collected by the circuit clerk as a result of forfeiture of bonds, ex parte judgments or guilty pleas pursuant to Rule 529. Public Act 93–32 directs the court to assess an additional penalty; section 27.6 provides that "(f) or offenses

subject to this section, judges shall impose one total sum of money payable for violations. The circuit clerk may add on no additional amounts except for amounts that are required by Sections 27.3a and 27.3c of this Act." The inconsistency between the two acts places the circuit clerks in a quandary, particularly in those counties operating under section 27.6.

The committee has recommended the circuit clerks be given a clear and definite direction concerning distribution of funds under this rule and believes the proposed amendment would provide that direction.

Rule 530. Applicability of 10% Cash Deposit Statute

The 10% cash deposit provision of section 110–7 of the Code of Criminal Procedure of 1963, as amended (725 ILCS 5/110–7), applies in every case in which the amount of bail under these rules is $1,200 or more, except those cases involving truck violations under Rule 526(b)(1) or similar municipal ordinances.

Adopted Oct. 26, 1967, eff. Jan. 1, 1968. Amended eff. October 7, 1970; February 17, 1977, eff. April 1, 1977, in counties other than Cook, eff. July 1, 1977, in Cook County; December 22, 1981, eff. January 15, 1982; April 27, 1984, eff. July 1, 1984; June 26, 1987, eff. August 1, 1987; June 19, 1989, eff. August 1, 1989; June 12, 1992, eff. July 1, 1992; September 30, 2002, eff. immediately; amended June 3, 2010, eff. September 15, 2010.

Formerly Ill.Rev.Stat.1991, ch. 110A, ¶ 530.

Committee Comments

In both the former Supreme Court rule and the Cook County rule there were paragraphs entitled "Non-Applicable Statutes" (Downstate—Paragraph J; Cook County—Paragraph 13.7). This rule makes the 10% cash deposit provisions of Section 110–7 of the Code of Criminal Procedure inapplicable to any offense punishable by fine only. A driver's license must be deposited in addition to a 10% cash deposit, if a violator takes advantage of pre-set bail specified in rule 526(c)(4) through 526(c)(7). Those offenses are: Leaving the scene of an accident where death or injury resulted; Driving while under the influence of liquor or drugs; Reckless driving, and Drag racing.

Rules 531 to 550. Reserved

PART D. REQUIRED COURT APPEARANCES, FORMS AND PROCEDURES

Rule 551. Traffic and Conservation Offenses for Which a Court Appearance is Required

A court appearance is required for:

(a) All alleged Class A and Class B misdemeanor violations of the Illinois Vehicle Code, as amended (625 ILCS 5/1–100 *et seq.*).

(b) All alleged violations of the following specified sections:

ILCS	Description
625 ILCS 5/3–707	Operating Without Insurance
625 ILCS 5/3–708	Operating When Registration Suspended for Noninsurance
625 ILCS 5/6–101	No Valid Driver's License
625 ILCS 5/6–104	Violation of Classification
625 ILCS 5/6–113	Operating in Violation of Restricted License or Permit
625 ILCS 5/6–301	Unlawful Use of License or Permit
625 ILCS 5/11–409	Making False Report
625 ILCS 5/11–1414(a)	Passed School Bus–Loading or Unloading
625 ILCS 5/15–112(g)	Refusal to stop and submit vehicle and load to weighing after being directed to do so by an officer, or removal of load prior to weighing
625 ILCS 5/15–301(j)	Violation of Excess Size or Weight Permit

(c) All alleged violations of the Child Passenger Protection Act, as amended (625 ILCS 25/1 *et seq.*).

(d) Any traffic offense which results in an accident causing the death of any person or injury to any person other than the accused.

(e) Conservation offenses for which more than $120 bail is required under Rule 527, or for which civil penalties are required under section 20–35 of the Fish and Aquatic Life Code, as amended (515 ILCS 5/20–35), or section 3.5 of the Wildlife Code, as amended (520 ILCS 5/3.5).

(f) Offenses arising from multiple charges as provided in Rule 503.

(g) Violation of any ordinance of any unit of local government defining offenses comparable to those specified in subparagraphs (a), (b), (c), (d) and (h) of this Rule 551.

(h) Any minor traffic offense where the statutory minimum fine is greater than $95, except those offenses involving truck violations under Rule 526(b)(1) or similar municipal ordinances.

Adopted Oct. 26, 1967, eff. Jan. 1, 1968. Amended eff. October 7, 1970; February 17, 1977, eff. April 1, 1977, in counties other than Cook, eff. July 1, 1977, in Cook County; September 20, 1979, eff. October 15, 1979; December 22, 1981, eff. January 15, 1982; April 27, 1984, eff. July 1, 1984; March 27, 1985, eff. May 1, 1985; June 26, 1987, eff. August 1, 1987; June 19, 1989, eff. August 1, 1989; December 7, 1990, eff. January 1, 1991; June 12, 1992, eff. July 1, 1992; May 24, 1995, eff. January 1, 1996; March 26, 1996, eff. May 1, 1996; September 30, 2002, eff. immediately; August 6, 2010, effective September 15, 2010; Dec. 12, 2013, eff. Jan. 1, 2014.

Formerly Ill.Rev.Stat.1991, ch. 110A, ¶ 551.

Committee Comments

Paragraph (a)

Paragraph (a) is derived from Paragraph G of the former Supreme Court rule and Cook County General Order No. 7, dated January 2, 1964. Court appearances will be required for alleged violations of Chapters 3, 5, 6 and 8 of the Illinois Motor Vehicle Law. Chapter 4 of the Illinois Motor Vehicle Law is not covered by these rules. (See rule 501(e)).

Paragraph (b)

Specific violations of the U.A.R.T. which will now require a court appearance are reduced in number from the numerous specific violations which formerly required a court appearance under both the former Supreme Court rule and Cook County General Order No. 7. It should be noted that law enforcement officers have no discretion to determine whether a particular violation should or should not require a court appearance. If the violation does not require a court appearance under these rules, the police officer may not require the offender to appear.

Paragraph (c)

Paragraph (c) is new. Second or subsequent violations of any provision of the U.A.R.T., during any one year period, are subject to increasingly higher penalties. (Ill.Rev.Stat.1965, ch. 95½, para. 234, as amended 1967, House Bill 1606, approved Aug. 17, 1967.) Unless a court appearance is required for such second and subsequent violations, a defendant could plead guilty in writing and, without a court appearance, pay the fixed minimum fine ($10), plus costs (See Rule 529(a)). The fixed fine ($10) would not be equal to the minimum fines required by statute for second and subsequent U.A.R.T. offenses during a one year period. It is, at this time, virtually impossible for the police to determine a violator's prior conviction record on the street, although it may soon be feasible through use of radios and computers. The bail for minor violations whether a first offense or a second or subsequent offense remains the same ($25). However, it is anticipated that the police will check prior convictions within 5 days after arrest and file their report as part of the record, so that a repeating violator cannot cop a plea for $10, plus costs.

Paragraph (d)

Paragraph (d) is new and requires a court appearance for any traffic offense which results in an accident causing injury to or the death of any person. The Committee also considered a proposal to require a court appearance for any alleged offense involving property damage in excess of $100 value. However, it was felt that such a provision would be extremely difficult to enforce. It would require police officers to make accurate evaluations of the dollar amount of property damages involved in any given accident, at the time of the accident.

Paragraph (e)

Paragraph (e) is new. Conservation offenses for which more than $35 cash bail is required under Rule 527 are the more serious conservation violations.

Paragraph (f)

Paragraph (f) is derived from similar provisions which existed in both the former Supreme Court rule and in Cook County General Order No. 7, dated Jan. 2, 1964.

Rule 552. Uniform Tickets–Processing

Uniform Citation and Complaint forms and conservation complaints shall be in forms which may, from time to time, be approved by the Conference of Chief Circuit Judges and filed with this court. The uniform forms shall be adapted for use by municipalities. The arresting officer shall complete the form or ticket and, within 48 hours after the arrest, shall transmit the portions entitled "Complaint" and "Disposition Report" and, where appropriate, "Report of Conviction," either in person or by mail, to the clerk of the circuit court of the county in which the violation occurred. Each Uniform Citation and Complaint form and conservation complaint shall upon receipt by the clerk be assigned a separate case number, chronologically, including multiple citations issued to the same accused for more than one offense arising out of the same occurrence (see Rule 503(a)). A final disposition noted on the reverse side of the "Complaint" shall be evidence of the judgment in the case. Upon final disposition of each case, the clerk shall execute the "Disposition Report" and promptly forward it to the law enforcement agency that issued the ticket. On a plea or finding of guilty in any traffic case, the clerk shall also execute the "Report of Conviction" portion of the Uniform Citation and Complaint, if and as applicable, and such other reports as required by section 6–204 of the Illinois Vehicle Code, as amended (625 ILCS 5/6–204) and promptly forward same to the Secretary of State. This rule does not prohibit the use of electronic or mechanical systems of record keeping, transmitting or reporting.

Adopted Oct. 26, 1967, eff. Jan. 1, 1968. Amended eff. October 7, 1970; February 17, 1977, eff. April 1, 1977, in counties other than Cook, eff. July 1, 1977, in Cook County; December 22, 1981, eff. January 15, 1982; April 27, 1984, eff. July 1, 1984; March 27, 1985, eff. May 1, 1985; June 26, 1987, eff. August 1, 1987; June 19, 1989, eff. August 1, 1989; September 30, 2002, eff. immediately.

Formerly Ill.Rev.Stat.1991, ch. 110A, ¶ 552.

Committee Comments

This rule incorporates the 1967 changes to Section 111–3 of the Code of Criminal Procedure of 1963 (House Bill 2241, 75th General Assembly) which provides that uniform traffic tickets and uniform conservation tickets shall be in a form approved by the Conference of Chief Circuit Judges and filed with the Supreme Court. That Act further provides that such uniform tickets need not be verified unless the defendant expressly requests verification.

There is no constitutional mandate that complaints be verified. People v. Harding, 1966, 34 Ill.2d 475. It was apparently felt that doing away with the statutory necessity of verification and placing the burden on the defendant to expressly request verification would be desirable, because close

to 2 million traffic tickets are processed annually. The remainder of this rule is adapted from paragraph D of the former Supreme Court rule and instructs the police and the circuit clerks on handling various copies of the uniform tickets.

Rule 553. Posting Bail or Bond

(a) By Whom and Where Taken. The several circuit clerks, deputy circuit clerks and law enforcement officers designated by name or office by the chief judge of the circuit are authorized to let to bail any person arrested for or charged with an offense covered by Rules 526, 527 and 528. Upon designation by the chief judge of the circuit, bail may be taken in accordance with this article in any county, municipal or other building housing governmental units, police station, sheriff's office or jail, district headquarters building of the Illinois State Police, weigh station, or portable scale unit established for enforcement of truck violations under Rule 526(b)(1) or similar municipal ordinances. Bail deposits by credit card, debit card or by any other electronic means may only be accepted upon the approval of the chief judge and the circuit clerk's ability to accept such deposits. Individual bonds under paragraph (d) of this rule may additionally be taken as designated by the chief judge of the circuit.

(b) Copy of Bond–Receipt for Cash Bail. A carbon copy of the bond or an official receipt showing the amount of cash bail posted, specifying the time and place of court appearance, shall be furnished to the accused and shall constitute a receipt for bail. The bond or cash bail, or both, shall be delivered to the office of the circuit clerk of the county in which the violation occurred within 48 hours of receipt or within the time set for the accused's appearance in court, whichever is earlier (see Rule 501(b) for definition of "Cash Bail").

(c) Driver's License or Bond Certificate. If an accused deposits a driver's license with the arresting officer in lieu of bail or in addition to bail, or deposits a bond certificate, the arresting officer shall note that fact on the accused's copy of the ticket and transmit the driver's license or bond certificate to the clerk within the time provided in paragraph (b) of this rule.

(d) Individual Bond. Persons arrested for or charged with an offense covered by Rules 526, 527 and 528 who are unable to secure release from custody under these rules may be released by giving individual bond (in the amount required by this article) by those law enforcement officers designated by name or office by the chief judge of the circuit, except when the accused is (1) unable or unwilling to establish his identity or submit to being fingerprinted as required by law, (2) is charged with an offense punishable by imprisonment and will pose a danger to any person or the community, or (3) elects release on separate bail under Rule 503(a)(3) or 503(a)(4). Persons required to deposit both bail and driver's license under Rule

526(e) may be released on $1,000 individual bond and their current Illinois driver's license. If authorized by the chief judge of the circuit, individual bonds under this paragraph (d) may be executed by signing the citation or complaint agreeing to comply with its conditions.

(e) Alternative Procedure in Minor Cases–Counties Other Than Cook. In any case, excluding citations written by local law enforcement in Cook County, in which the bail or bond specified by Rule 526, 527 or 528 does not exceed $200 in United States currency, an accused not required to be fingerprinted may post bond by giving the United States currency to the sworn law enforcement officer. The officer shall provide the accused with a copy of the citation duly noted with the amount of the United States currency posted as bond. The accused shall then be released from custody. In such cases, the officer will deliver the appropriate portions(s) of the ticket along with the United States currency as bond(s) to the clerk of the circuit court or a designated building approved by the issuing law enforcement agency and approved by the receiving law enforcement agency before the end of his or her current tour of duty.

Adopted Oct. 26, 1967, eff. Jan. 1, 1968. Amended eff. Oct. 7, 1970; Feb. 17, 1977, eff. April 1, 1977, in counties other than Cook, eff. July 1, 1977, in Cook County; Oct. 17, 1979, eff. Nov. 15, 1979; Dec. 22, 1981, eff. Jan. 15, 1982; June 26, 1987, eff. Aug. 1, 1987; Dec. 7, 1990, eff. Jan. 1, 1991; June 12, 1992, eff. July 1, 1992; May 24, 1995, eff. Jan. 1, 1996; June 11, 2009, eff. immediately; Aug. 6, 2010, eff. Sept. 15, 2010; Dec. 7, 2011, eff. immediately.

Formerly Ill.Rev.Stat.1991, ch. 110A, ¶ 553.

Committee Comments

Paragraph (a)

Paragraph (a) is derived with only minor changes from Section 13.3 of the Cook County rules. No similar provision was in effect downstate.

Paragraph (b)

Paragraph (b) is derived from Section 13.8 of the Cook County rule and incorporates the sense of various provisions of the downstate rule.

Paragraph (c)

Paragraph (c) is derived from Section 1(a) of Paragraph F of the former Supreme Court rule and Paragraph 13.11 of the Cook County rule. The violator's copy of the Uniform Ticket constitutes the receipt required by section 6–306(c)(1) of the Illinois Motor Vehicle Law, as amended 1967, (H.B. 620, approved Aug. 7, 1967).

Paragraph (d)

Paragraph (d) repeats provisions found in Section 1(b) of Paragraph F of the former Supreme Court rule and Paragraph 13.4(d) of the Cook County rule, but extends the availability of individual bond to a juvenile defendant to any case rather than only to those cases in which the maximum penalty might be

by fine alone. It further provides that a juvenile defendant should execute the bond in the amount required by the rules rather than requiring that he execute the bond in a specific amount (formerly $25, downstate; $100 in Cook County).

Paragraph (e)

Paragraph (e) continues, for counties other than Cook, the practice of "bail by mail" (See Section 1(b), Paragraph F—former Supreme Court rule), which has been in effect downstate for several years. The only significant change in the bail by mail procedure is that the stamped envelope which the defendant uses to transmit his bail to the clerk is to be provided by the arresting officer. In the past no provision has required the officer to make an envelope or a stamp available to an alleged offender.

Rule 554. Substitution of Cash Bail

(a) Not sooner than 10 court days after arrest and not later than 3 court days before the date set for appearance in court, an accused who deposited his driver's license or a bond certificate in lieu of cash bail, or who was released on Notice to Appear, promise to comply, or individual bond under Rule 553(d), may recover either his license or bond certificate or further secure his release by substituting cash bail in the amount required by this article with the clerk of the circuit court of the county in which the violation occurred; provided, however, that no driver's license required to be deposited under subparagraph (e) of Rule 526 may be recovered under this rule. The clerk may waive the time limits specified by this rule.

(b) In all cases in which a court appearance is not required under Rule 551, an accused who desires to satisfy the charge but is unwilling to plead guilty may substitute cash bail under paragraph (a) of this rule; in such event, if the accused does not appear on the date set for appearance, or any date to which the case may be continued, it shall be presumed he has consented to the entry of an *ex parte* judgment (see Rule 556(b)).

Adopted Oct. 26, 1967, eff. Jan. 1, 1968. Amended eff. Oct. 7, 1970; Feb. 17, 1977, eff. April 1, 1977, in counties other than Cook, eff. July 1, 1977, in Cook County; Dec. 22, 1981, eff. Jan. 15, 1982; April 27, 1984, eff. July 1, 1984; June 26, 1987, eff. Aug. 1, 1987; Aug. 21, 1996, eff. immediately.

Formerly Ill.Rev.Stat.1991, ch. 110A, ¶ 554.

Committee Comments

This rule is derived, in part, from Section 5(a) of Paragraph F of the former Supreme Court rule. However, the rule now provides that the license or bond certificate can be redeemed only by substituting cash bail in the "appropriate" amount. The time limits specified are for the clerk's convenience. He may waive them.

Rule 555. Returning Bail or Documents

(a) **Court Appearance.** A defendant who personally appears in court on the date on which his case is finally disposed of shall, upon payment of any fines, penalties and costs which may be assessed against him upon a plea or finding of guilty, or as a condition of an order of supervision under section 5–6–3.1 of the Unified Code of Corrections, as amended (730 ILCS 5/5–6–3.1), recover unless otherwise provided by law his driver's license (unless revoked or suspended) or the bond certificate deposited by him. Cash bail, or any balance due the defendant, shall be refunded to the defendant by the clerk as soon as practicable after the disposition of the charges.

(b) **Written Plea of Guilty.** In any case that can be disposed of on a written plea of guilty without a court appearance under Rule 529, the defendant may submit his written plea of guilty and pay the prescribed fines, penalties and costs to the clerk of the circuit court of the county in which the violation occurred not earlier than 10 court days after arrest, and not later than 3 court days before the date set for appearance, unless the clerk waives these time limits. If cash bail was posted, the clerk shall apply the amount necessary to pay prescribed fines, penalties and costs. If a driver's license or bond certificate was deposited, the full amount of the prescribed fines, penalties and costs must be paid to the clerk. Upon receiving payment in full, the clerk shall unless otherwise provided by law return the driver's license or bond certificate to the defendant. A written plea of guilty may be mailed to the clerk of the circuit court of the county in which the violation occurred. If the plea is accompanied by the full amount of the prescribed fines, penalties and costs, the clerk shall mail to the defendant any driver's license or bond certificate deposited in lieu of bail.

Adopted Oct. 26, 1967, eff. Jan. 1, 1968. Amended eff. October 7, 1970; February 17, 1977, eff. April 1, 1977, in counties other than Cook, eff. July 1, 1977, in Cook County; December 22, 1981, eff. January 15, 1982; April 27, 1984, eff. July 1, 1984; June 26, 1987, eff. August 1, 1987; June 19, 1989, eff. August 1, 1989; September 30, 2002, eff. immediately.

Formerly Ill.Rev.Stat.1991, ch. 110A, ¶ 555.

Committee Comments

Paragraph (a)

Paragraph (a) is derived from Section 5(c), Paragraph F of the former Supreme Court rule. These provisions are primarily for the instruction of the clerk. The last sentence was added because clerks cannot, practicably, return cash bail at the time of the court appearance. Cash bail is customarily returned by mail, in the form of a check.

Paragraph (b)

Paragraph (b) is derived from Section 5(b) of Paragraph F of the former Supreme Court rule. The earliest date on which a written plea may be submitted is lengthened from 3 days to 5 days in order to accommodate problems which may arise where the circuit clerk's office has several branches and the file has to be transported within the county. Five days between arrest and the first day for accepting pleas also allows time to check prior convictions. See Comment under rule 551(c). The penultimate sentence of paragraph (b) provides that in counties other than Cook a written plea of guilty may be mailed to the clerk. Cook County, because of tremendous volume, does not accept pleas of guilty by mail. Downstate counties have traditionally accepted these pleas of guilty (any payment of fine and costs) by mail as a convenience to defendants. There has always been some question as to whether the defendant or the clerk ought properly pay the cost of mailing the balance of the cash bail or the driver's license or bond certificate, after a written plea of guilty has been mailed to the clerk. The last sentence of Paragraph (b) made it clear that the clerk will, hereafter, have the responsibility of mailing the cash bail, driver's license or bond certificate.

Rule 556. Procedure if Defendant Fails to Appear

(a) **Promise to Comply or Driver's License Deposited.** If a person accused of a traffic offense has executed a written promise to comply (see Rule 501(g)), or deposited his driver's license in lieu of or in addition to cash bail or cash deposit and bond, and does not appear on the date set for appearance, or any date to which the case may be continued, the court shall continue the case for a minimum of 30 days and require a notice of the continued court date to be sent to the defendant at his last known address. The clerk shall notify the defendant of the court's order. If the defendant does not appear on the continued court date or, within that period, satisfy the court that his appearance is impossible and without any fault on his part, the court shall enter an order of failure to appear to answer the charge(s). A verified charge may be filed (if none has previously been filed) and a summons or warrant of arrest for the defendant may be issued. Within 21 days after the date to which the case had been continued, the clerk shall notify the Secretary of State of the court's order. The Secretary of State shall, in the case of an Illinois licensed driver who has deposited his driver's license, immediately suspend the defendant's driving privileges in accordance with sections 6–306.3 or 6–308 of the Illinois Vehicle Code, as amended (625 ILCS 5/6–306.3 or 6–308); if the defendant is not an Illinois licensed driver or resident the Secretary of State shall notify the appropriate driver's licensing authority pursuant to the Nonresident Violator Compact of 1977, as amended (625 ILCS 5/6–800 *et seq.*). The clerk of the circuit court shall notify the Secretary of State of the final disposition of the case as provided in Rule 552 when the defendant has appeared and otherwise satisfied his obligations following an order of failure to appear under this paragraph (a). The court may in lieu of the foregoing procedure, enter an *ex parte* judgment of conviction against any accused charged with an offense punishable by a fine only and in so doing shall assess fines, penalties and costs in an amount equal to the cash bail required by this article. Payment received for fines, penalties, and costs assessed following the entry of an *ex parte* judgment shall be disbursed by the clerk pursuant to Rule 529. The clerk of the court shall notify the Secretary of State of the conviction pursuant to Rule 552, and if the accused is an Illinois registered driver, the clerk shall notify the Secretary of State of the unsatisfied judgment pursuant to section 6–306.6(a) of the Illinois Vehicle Code, as amended (625 ILCS 5/6–306.6(a)).

(b) Court Appearance Not Required–Cash Bail Posted or Bond Certificate Deposited. In all cases in which a court appearance is not required under Rule 551 and cash bail is posted or a bond certificate deposited, the defendant shall be provided with a statement, in substantially the following form, on the "Complaint" or on the bond form:

In the event you fail to appear in court to answer a charge that does not require you to appear in court, you thereby consent to the entry of a judgment against you in the amount of all applicable fines, penalties and costs, and the application of the cash bail or other security you have deposited to their payment and satisfaction."

If the defendant does not appear on the date set for appearance, or any date to which the case may be continued, the court may enter an *ex parte* judgment against the defendant assessing fines, penalties and costs in an amount equal to the cash bail required by this article. The clerk of the circuit court shall apply the cash bail or security in payment thereof pursuant to Rule 529.

(c) Court Appearance Required—Cash Bail Posted or Bond Certificate Deposited. If a defendant fails to appear on the date set for appearance, or any date to which the case may be continued, and a court appearance is required, the court shall enter an order declaring the bail to be forfeited and continue the case for a minimum of 30 days. Notice of such order of forfeiture shall be mailed forthwith to the accused at his last known address. If the accused does not appear on the continued court date or, within that period, satisfy the court that his appearance is impossible and without any fault on his part, the court shall enter judgment in accordance with sections 110–7 and 110–8 of the Code of Criminal Procedure of 1963, as amended (725 ILCS 5/110–7, 110–8). In addition to forfeiture, a verified charge may be filed and a summons or warrant of arrest may issue. The court may, with the concurrence of the prosecuting agency, in lieu of the foregoing procedure, enter an *ex parte* judgment of conviction against any accused charged with an offense punishable by a fine only and in so doing shall assess fines, penalties and costs in an amount equal to the cash bail required by this article. Pay-

ment received for fines, penalties, and costs assessed following the entry of an *ex parte* judgment shall be disbursed by the clerk pursuant to Rule 529. The clerk of court shall notify the Secretary of State of the conviction pursuant to Rule 552 and of any unsatisfied judgment pursuant to section 6–306.6(a) of the Illinois Vehicle Code, as amended (625 ILCS 5/6–306.6(a)).

(d) Individual Bonds. In all cases in which a defendant released by giving individual bond under Rule 553(d) fails to appear on the date set for appearance, or any date to which the case may be continued, the court shall enter an order declaring the bond to be forfeited and continue the case for a minimum of 30 days. Notice of such order of forfeiture shall be mailed forthwith to the accused at his last known address. If the accused does not appear on the continued court date or, within that period, satisfy the court that his appearance is impossible and without any fault on his part, the court shall enter judgment in accordance with section 110–8 of the Code of Criminal Procedure of 1963, as amended (725 ILCS 5/110–8). In addition to forfeiture, a verified charge may be filed and a summons or warrant of arrest may issue. The court may in lieu of the foregoing procedure, enter an *ex parte* judgment of conviction against any accused charged with an offense punishable by a fine only and in so doing shall assess fines, penalties and costs in an amount equal to the cash bail required by this article. Payment received for fines, penalties, and costs assessed following the entry of an *ex parte* judgment shall be disbursed by the clerk pursuant to Rule 529. The clerk of the court shall notify the Secretary of State of the conviction pursuant to Rule 552 and of the unsatisfied judgment pursuant to section 6–306.6(a) of the Illinois Vehicle Code, as amended (625 ILCS 5/6–306.6(a)).

(e) Notice to Appear. In all cases in which a defendant is issued a Notice to Appear under section 107–12 of the Code of Criminal Procedure of 1963, as amended (725 ILCS 5/107–12), and fails to appear on the date set for appearance, or any date to which the case may be continued, the court may enter an *ex parte* judgment of conviction against an accused charged with an offense punishable by a fine only and in so doing shall assess fines, penalties and costs in an amount equal to the cash bail required by this article. Payment received for fines, penalties, and costs assessed following the entry of an *ex parte* judgment shall be disbursed by the clerk pursuant to Rule 529. The clerk of the court shall notify the Secretary of State of the conviction pursuant to Rule 552 and of the unsatisfied judgment pursuant to section 6–306.6(a) of the Illinois Vehicle Code, as amended (625 ILCS 5/6–306.6(a)). In lieu of the foregoing procedure, a summons or warrant of arrest may be issued.

Adopted Oct. 26, 1967, eff. Jan. 1, 1968. Amended eff. Oct. 7, 1970; Feb. 17, 1977, eff. April 1, 1977, in counties other than Cook, eff. July 1, 1977, in Cook County; Dec. 22, 1981, eff. Jan. 15, 1982; April 27, 1984, eff. July 1, 1984; June 26, 1987, eff. Aug. 1, 1987; June 19, 1989, eff. Aug. 1, 1989; Dec. 7, 1990, eff. Jan. 1, 1991; May 24, 1995, eff. Jan. 1, 1996; Oct. 22, 1999, eff. Dec. 1, 1999; December 5, 2003, eff. January 1, 2004; Dec. 30, 2014, eff. Jan. 1, 2015.

Formerly Ill.Rev.Stat.1991, ch. 110A, ¶ 556.

Committee Comments
(December 5, 2003)

Supreme Court Rule 556 ("Procedure if Defendant Fails to Appear") delineates several procedures if the defendant fails to appear after depositing a driver's license in lieu of bond, executes a written promise to comply, posts bond or issued a notice to appear.

The rule provided that the court may "enter an *ex parte* judgment of conviction against any accused charged with an offense punishable by a fine only and in so doing shall assess fines, penalties and costs in an amount not to exceed the cash bail required by this article." Rule 556 does not detail the specific costs and penalties, or their amounts, in the entry of *ex parte* judgments. The clerk is then left with deciding which costs, fees and additional penalties (and their amounts) should be applied. This is currently being determined on a county by county basis.

The committee concluded that distribution under Rule 556 was not a "levy of a gross amount."

See Rule 529, Committee Comments.

The committee believes that consistency and uniformity in disbursing funds from *ex parte* judgments was of the utmost importance in the efficient administration of justice and recommends that the fines, penalties and costs assessed by equal to bail, and the distribution of those amounts should be pursuant to Supreme Court Rule 529(a). The State's Attorney fee, if any, would be included within the county's 38.675% distribution.

Rules 557 to 569. Reserved

PART E. RULES AND PROCEDURES FOR NON–TRAFFIC/NON–CONSERVATION ORDINANCE VIOLATIONS

Rule 570. Applicability

Rules 570 through 579 are applicable to the prosecution, through the judicial system, of violations of ordinances passed pursuant to section 5–1113 of the Counties Code (55 ILCS 5/5–1113), section 1–2–1 of the Illinois Municipal Code (65 ILCS 5/1–2–1), and section 11–1301 of the Illinois Vehicle Code (625 ILCS 5/11–1301) or home rule authority for which the penalty does not include the possibility of a jail term. These rules shall not apply to administrative adjudications.

Adopted Dec. 7, 2011, eff. immediately.

Committee Comment
(December 7, 2011)

Rules 570 through 579 apply to the prosecution of ordinance violations not punishable by a jail term and other than traffic and conservation offenses. These rules also apply to parking offenses. Violations of ordinances punishable by a jail term are to be prosecuted in accordance with the rules of criminal procedure. 65 ILCS 5/1–2–1.1. Nothing in these rules is intended to limit the ability to proceed through an administrative process or other alternative methods of resolving ordinance violations.

Rule 570 establishes the applicability of the ordinance violation prosecutions which are prosecuted through the judicial system to ordinances passed pursuant to the Counties Code (55 ILCS 5/5–1113 (ordinance and rules to execute powers; limitations on punishments)), the Illinois Municipal Code (65 ILCS 5/1–3–1 (ordinances and rules; fines or penalties; limitations on punishment)), and home rule authority where the penalty does not include jail time.

Rule 570 would exclude from these rules ordinance violations heard by the administrative adjudication process.

Rule 571. Code of Civil Procedure to Apply

Except as specifically stated herein or in existing statutes, the Code of Civil Procedure shall apply in all ordinance prosecutions to which these rules apply. Adopted Dec. 7, 2011, eff. immediately.

Committee Comment
(December 7, 2011)

This rule builds on the holdings of both *City of Danville vs. Hartshorn*, 53 Ill. 2d 399 (1973) and *Village of Park Forest v. Walker*, 64 Ill. 2d 286 (1976), in which the Supreme Court held that the Civil Practice Act applied to ordinance violations where the penalty is a fine only. Persons charged with violating municipal ordinances have a right to trial by jury if a written jury demand along with the jury fee is filed and paid at the time of first appearance under provisions of section 2–1105 of the Code of Civil Procedure. But under Supreme Court Rule 201(h), discovery in ordinance prosecution cases where the penalty is a fine only, is allowed only by leave of court. Before and after the *Hartshorn* decision, courts have struggled to decide what portions of the Code of Civil Procedure apply to ordinance violation prosecutions. It is the intent of Rule 571 to clarify that the Code of Civil Procedure applies to all ordinance violation proceedings under Rules 570 through 579, except as otherwise provided by Supreme Court Rules such as Rule 201(h).

Rule 572. Form of Charging Document

(a) A prosecution for an ordinance violation for which the penalty does not include the possibility of a jail term may be initiated by a charging document such as a Notice to Appear, Citation, Ticket, or Complaint or combination of the same. The charging document shall be signed by an attorney representing the plaintiff, or by a peace officer or a code enforcement officer authorized by the plaintiff to sign the charging document. The charging document shall be verified as provided in section 1–109 of the Code of Civil Procedure (735 ILCS 5/1–109). Such charging document or combination of documents shall contain at least the following:

1. The name of the prosecuting entity;

2. The name of the defendant and his or her address, if known;

3. The nature of the offense and a reference to the relevant ordinance;

4. A statement whether the defendant is required to appear in court and, if so, the date, time and place of appearance;

5. If applicable, the steps the defendant can take to avoid an otherwise required appearance; and

6. A statement that the defendant may demand a jury trial by filing a jury demand and paying a jury demand fee when entering his or her appearance, plea, answer to the charge, or other responsive pleading.

(b) The following statement(s) shall also appear on the charging document or combination of documents listed in (a) above in the event a warrant or default judgment will be sought by the prosecuting entity:

1. A statement that a default judgment may be entered in the event the person fails to appear in court or answer the charge made on the date set for the defendant's court appearance or any date to which the case is continued. The statement must also contain the specific amount of any default judgment.

2. A statement that an arrest warrant may issue if the defendant fails to appear at any hearing.

(c) Multiple Violations. Multiple violations of automobile parking offenses may be contained in a single count. Violations of the same offense occurring on different days, or violations of ordinances which carry a per day fine, may be stated in one count even though each violation or day upon which a violation occurs carries a separate fine. Such separate violations and fines must be clearly stated.

(d) Prayer for Relief. It shall be sufficient for the prosecuting entity to generally pray for a penalty range between the minimum and maximum penalties authorized by the corporate authorities of the prosecuting entity.

(e) Amendments. The charging document may be amended at any time, before or after judgment, to conform the pleadings to the proofs on just and reasonable terms. However, the amount of any default judgment appearing on the charging document under Rule 572(b) may not be amended after the entry of such judgment, without notice to defendant.

Adopted Dec. 7, 2011, eff. immediately.

Committee Comment
(December 7, 2011)

Many prosecuting entities have created hybrid complaints that serve both as notice to appear and the charging document itself, similar to a traffic citation. Since an ordinance violation prosecution incorporates aspects of both criminal and civil procedures, the more general term "charging document" phrase is used.

(a) Rule 572 is intended to provide flexibility in the initiation of an ordinance violation prosecution. The Municipal Code states that "the first process shall be a summons or a warrant." 65 ILCS 5/1–2–9.

Many prosecuting entities, however, begin with a "Notice to Appear" which is provided for in the Code of Criminal Procedure, 725 ILCS 5/1 07–12: (a) Whenever a peace officer is authorized to arrest a person without a warrant he may instead issue to such a person a notice to appear *** (c) Upon failure of the person to appear a summons or warrant of arrest may issue." A notice to appear "is a means by which a person may be brought before the court without the inconvenience of immediate arrest ***. Such a notice may be issued whenever a peace officer has probable cause to make a warrantless arrest." *People v. Warren*, 173 Ill. 2d 348, 357 (1996).

The purpose of this rule is to continue to allow prosecuting entities to utilize the most efficient means of initiating ordinance violation proceedings. "Notices to Appear" are an appropriate and reasonable means of informing defendants of charges against them and are similar to citations issued in traffic cases.

This does not prohibit a prosecuting entity from obtaining an arrest warrant based upon probable cause, as authorized in section 1–2–9 of the Municipal Code (65 ILCS 5/1–2–9).

This rule also makes it clear that an attorney need not sign the charging document in every case. This is especially important where the process is initiated by a nonattorney such as a police officer or code enforcement officer.

(b) This section provides for issuance of default judgments or warrants upon a failure to appear.

(c) This is intended to minimize paperwork and codify the decision in *Village of Oak Park v. Flanagan*, 35 Ill. App. 3d 6 (1st Dist. 1975). The Village of Oak Park case involved prosecution for multiple parking tickets in which the court held that a computer printout was sufficient to comply with the requirements of pleading for ordinance violations. Note, however, this rule is not meant to contravene the one act, one crime rule identified in *Village of Sugar Grove v. James Rich*, 347 Ill. App. 3d 689 (1st Dist. 2004).

(d) Section 2–604 of the Code of Civil Procedure requires a "specific" prayer for relief. 735 ILCS 5/2–604. This paragraph is intended to make it clear that a prayer for a penalty within the penalty range authorized by the ordinance is sufficiently specific to advise the defendant of the maximum penalty to which they are exposed.

(e) Section 2–616(a) of the Code of Civil Procedure specifically permits amendments to civil pleadings at various times. 735 ILCS 5/2–616(a). The purpose is to avoid minor errors in the charging document being a cause of a finding of not guilty when a violation has been proved by the requisite proof. The last sentence enforces the requirement of Rule 572(b) that if the prosecuting entity will seek a default judgment, it must state the specific amount in the charging document or combination of documents served upon the defendant.

Rule 573. Service of the Charging Document

The charging document, including a notice to appear, may be served by hand delivery by a peace officer, code enforcement officer, or as otherwise authorized by law. Where the fine would not be in excess of $750 for a municipal ordinance offense, service of summons may be made by certified mail, return receipt requested, as authorized in section 1–2–9.1 of the Municipal Code (65 ILCS 5/1–2–9.1) whether service is to be within or without the state. Parking tickets should include a certification that the ticket was either placed on the vehicle or hand delivered to the driver. This rule does not prohibit initiating prosecution by any other means authorized by statute.

Adopted Dec. 7, 2011, eff. immediately.

Committee Comments
(December 7, 2011)

Service of process in civil actions generally is covered in Supreme Court Rules 101 through 110. Many ordinance prosecutions are initiated by code enforcement officers, *e.g.*, building safety inspectors for property maintenance violations or animal control officers for animal ordinance violations.

The final sentence makes it clear that this rule allowing for the initiation of prosecution by a Notice to Appear does not abrogate the opportunity to initiate a prosecution as provided in section 1–2–9 of the Municipal Code (65 ILCS 5/1–2–9), namely, by summons or warrant.

Rule 574. Opportunity to Settle

An opportunity to avoid a court appearance through settlement of the dispute may be provided for by ordinance. The manner and time limit for settlement before which a court appearance will be required may be set forth in the charging document.

Adopted Dec. 7, 2011, eff. immediately.

Committee Comment
(December 7, 2011)

This rule permits settlement of a violation. This allows for more efficient processing and court time management.

Rule 575. Appearance of Defendant, Answer; Failure to Appear; Discovery and Pretrial Procedures

(a) A defendant responding to a charging document for an ordinance violation may appear and enter a plea, file an answer to the charge, or file other responsive pleadings. A Not Guilty plea will be construed as a general denial. The defendant need not file a written answer unless ordered to do so by the Court.

(b) In the event the defendant fails to appear at any proceeding for which the Court has not excused the defendant's appearance, an arrest warrant may issue, or default judgment may be entered. If such judgment is entered, the defendant shall be mailed written notice to the defendant's last known address of: (1) the amount of the judgment, (2) if applicable, the date by which such judgment must be paid, and (3) that a motion to vacate judgment must be filed within 30 days of the date of the mailing of the written notice. "Defendant's last known address" shall be presumed to be the address provided by the defendant himself or herself upon actual delivery of the charging document.

(c) A party may make a motion for summary judgment prior to any trial on the merits.

(d) In prosecutions for violations of ordinances, no discovery procedures shall be allowed prior to trial except by leave of court.

Adopted Dec. 7, 2011, eff. immediately.

Committee Comment
(December 7, 2011)

(a) The purpose of this section is to provide for a simple process for those who appear to answer a charge and also in determining the effect of a failure to appear for an ordinance violation charge. Supreme Court Rule 286(a) provides for a general denial in small claims cases and this rule provides a similar procedure for ordinance violations. Supreme Court Rule 556(a) permits the entry of default judgment in traffic cases. This rule provides a similar procedure for ordinance violations.

(b) This section provides for procedures to follow in the event of a Defendant's failure to appear at any proceeding for which the Court has not previously excused the appearance.

(c) *Village of Beckmeyer v. Wheelan*, 212 Ill. App. 3d 287 (5th Dist. 1991), provides for summary judgment motions in ordinance violation cases.

(d) Supreme Court Rule 201(h) provides: "In suits for violation of municipal ordinances where the penalty is a fine only no discovery procedure shall be used prior to trial except by leave of court. This rule extends the application of the rule to cases in which penalties may include public service work and restitution in addition to fines."

Rule 576. Right to Counsel

A defendant has a right to be represented by an attorney; however, there shall be no right to appointment of counsel in suits for violation of ordinances for which the penalty does not include the possibility of a jail term.

Adopted Dec. 7, 2011, eff. immediately.

Committee Comment

(December 7, 2011)

This rule reiterates the long held principle that the right to a court appointed counsel does not attach where there is no possibility of being sentenced to a jail term as a penalty for the underlying offense. See *City of Urbana v. Andre N.B.*, 211 Ill. 2d 456 (2004); *City of Danville v. Clark*, 63 Ill. 2d 408 (1976).

Rule 577.   Jury Trial

Either party shall have the right to trial by a jury. The prosecuting entity shall make its jury demand at the time the action is commenced. The defendant shall make his or her jury demand and pay the jury demand fee at the time of entering his or her appearance, plea, answer to the charge, or other responsive pleading. Failure to pay the required jury fee to the clerk of the circuit court at the time of entering his or her initial appearance, or by a date ordered by the court, shall constitute a forfeiture of the right to a jury trial.

Because ordinance offenses do not provide for penalties in excess of $50,000, any jury request shall result in the matter being tried by a jury of six members.

Adopted Dec. 7, 2011, eff. immediately.

Committee Comment

(December 7, 2011)

Section 2–1105 of the Code of Civil Procedure is applicable to jury demands in ordinance violation cases. *City of Danville v. Hartshorn*, 53 Ill. 2d 399, 403 (1973). Section 103–6 of the Code of Criminal Procedure also applies to jury demands in ordinance violation cases. It provides: "every person accused of an offense shall have the right to a trial by jury unless *** (ii) the offense is an ordinance violation punishable by fine only and the defendant either fails to file a demand for a trial by jury at the time of entering his or her plea of not guilty or fails to pay to the clerk of the circuit court at the time of entering his or her plea of not guilty any jury fee required to be paid to the clerk." 725 ILCS 5/103–6; 705 ILCS 105.27.1a(w)(3).

Rule 578.   Burden of Proof

The prosecuting entity must prove the ordinance violation by a preponderance of the evidence; meaning it is more likely true than not that the violation occurred.

Adopted Dec. 7, 2011, eff. immediately.

Committee Comment

(December 7, 2011)

This rule restates case law which holds that the burden of proof in ordinance violation cases is the civil law standard of preponderance of the evidence rather than the criminal standard of beyond a reasonable doubt. *City of Mattoon v. Mentzer*, 282 Ill. App. 3d 628, 634 (4th Dist. 1996) (citing *Chicago v. Joyce*, 38 Ill. 2d 368, 373 (1967)).

Rule 579.   Disposition and Appeal

(a) Sentence. The court shall determine the amount of any fine for an ordinance violation to which these rules apply, except that any fine imposed shall not be less than the "minimum fine" authorized by ordinance. Court costs shall be imposed.

(b) Additional Conditions. In addition to any fine imposed, the court may impose a sentence including restitution, or other appropriate penalties or conditions authorized by ordinance. A sentence of conditional discharge or court supervision disposition shall be permitted by ordinance.

(c) Dispositional Considerations. The court may consider evidence and information may be offered by the parties in consideration for the penalties and/or conditions sought.

(d) Appealability. Either party shall have the right to appeal any final judgment entered in an ordinance violation case pursuant to Rule 303, "Appeals from Final Judgments of the Circuit Court in Civil Cases."

Adopted Dec. 7, 2011, eff. immediately.

Committee Comment

(December 7, 2011)

(a) In accordance with typical situations in which a range of penalties is authorized by statute, the court in *City of Chicago v. Roman*, 184 Ill. 2d 504, 511 (1998), held that the fine may not be less than the statutory minimum.

(b) Under the holding in *City of Highland Park v. Curtis*, 83 Ill. App. 2d 218, 229 (2d Dist. 1967), the court should be permitted to impose restitution. Other dispositions must be provided for by ordinance. *Village of Wheeling v. Evanger's Dog and Cat Food Co., Inc.*, 399 Ill. App. 3d 304 (1st Dist. 2010).

(c) Statutory authorization for imposition of court supervision is found in the Illinois Municipal Code (65 ILCS 5/1–1–1 *et seq.*). *Village of Wheeling v. Evanger's Dog and Cat Food Co., Inc.*, 399 Ill. App. 3d 304, 307 (1st Dist. 2010).

(d) Because ordinance violation prosecutions are "quasi-criminal in character, but civil in form," municipalities may properly appeal from a judgment in favor of a defendant. Neither double jeopardy nor Supreme Court Rule 604 bars such an appeal. *Village of Riverdale v. Irwin*, 259 Ill. App. 3d 1008, 1009 (1st Dist. 1994); *Village of Park Forest v. Bragg*, 38 Ill. 2d 225, 227 (1967).

Rules 580 to 600.   Reserved

ARTICLE VI.   APPEALS IN CRIMINAL CASES, POST–CONVICTION CASES, AND JUVENILE COURT PROCEEDINGS

Rule 601.   Supersedure of Code of Criminal Procedure of 1963

These rules supersede and replace articles 120 and 121, except sections 121–1 and 121–13 of the Code of Criminal Procedure of 1963.[1]

Amended eff. Oct. 21, 1969; Jan. 1, 1970.

Formerly Ill.Rev.Stat.1991, ch. 110A, ¶ 601.

[1] 725 ILCS 5/121–1, 5/121–13.

Committee Comments

This rule is essentially former Rule 27(1). It contains some changes in language necessitated by the fact that the new Criminal Appeals Rules are intended to supersede and replace almost all of the criminal appeals procedures contained in the Code of Criminal Procedure of 1963.

Rule 602.   Method of Review

The only method of review in a criminal case in which judgment was entered on or after January 1, 1964, shall be by appeal. The party appealing shall be known as the appellant and the adverse party as the appellee, but the title of the case shall not be changed. Review of cases in which judgments were entered before January 1, 1964, shall be governed by the time limitations in effect on December 31, 1963, and the procedure shall be as provided by the rules then in effect, * or as provided by these rules, at the option of the appellant.

May 30, 2008, effective immediately.

Formerly Ill.Rev.Stat.1991, ch. 110A, ¶ 602.

* See Ill.Rev.Stat.1963, ch. 110, which contains the former rules governing writs of error, amended or repealed January 1, 1964.

Committee Comments

This is former Rule 27(2) without change. Rule 27(2) is derived from sections 121–2 and 121–4(b) of the code.

Rule 603.   Court To Which Appeal is Taken

Appeals in criminal cases in which a statute of the United States or of this State has been held invalid shall lie directly to the Supreme Court as a matter of right. All other appeals in criminal cases shall be taken to the Appellate Court.

Amended effective July 1, 1971; October 1, 2010, effective immediately; Feb. 6, 2013, eff. immediately.

Formerly Ill.Rev.Stat.1991, ch. 110A, ¶ 603.

Committee Comments
(Revised July 1, 1971)

The rule, new in 1967, was revised in 1971, in light of the new Constitution, which limited the Supreme Court's mandatory direct appellate jurisdiction to death cases. The constitutional question basis for direct appeal was revised to limit direct appeal to cases in which a statute is held invalid. The same provision appears in Rule 302, governing civil appeals.

Rule 604.   Appeals from Certain Judgments and Orders

(a) Appeals by the State.

(1) *When State May Appeal.* In criminal cases the State may appeal only from an order or judgment the substantive effect of which results in dismissing a charge for any of the grounds enumerated in section 114–1 of the Code of Criminal Procedure of 1963; arresting judgment because of a defective indictment, information or complaint; quashing an arrest or search warrant; or suppressing evidence.

(2) *Leave to Appeal by State.* The State may petition for leave to appeal under Rule 315(a).

(3) *Release of Defendant Pending Appeal.* A defendant shall not be held in jail or to bail during

the pendency of an appeal by the State, or of a petition or appeal by the State under Rule 315(a), unless there are compelling reasons for his or her continued detention or being held to bail.

(4) *Time Appeal Pending Not Counted.* The time during which an appeal by the State is pending is not counted for the purpose of determining whether an accused is entitled to discharge under section 103B5 of the Code of Criminal Procedure of 1963.

(b) Appeals When Defendant Placed Under Supervision or Sentenced to Probation, Conditional Discharge or Periodic Imprisonment. A defendant who has been placed under supervision or found guilty and sentenced to probation or conditional discharge (see 730 ILCS 5/5–6–1 through 5–6–4), or to periodic imprisonment (see 730 ILCS 5/5–7–1 through 5–7–8), may appeal from the judgment and may seek review of the conditions of supervision, or of the finding of guilt or the conditions of the sentence, or both. He or she may also appeal from an order modifying the conditions of or revoking such an order or sentence.

(c) Appeals From Bail Orders by Defendant Before Conviction.

(1) *Appealability of Order With Respect to Bail.* Before conviction a defendant may appeal to the Appellate Court from an order setting, modifying, revoking, denying, or refusing to modify bail or the conditions thereof. As a prerequisite to appeal the defendant shall first present to the trial court a written motion for the relief to be sought on appeal. The motion shall be verified by the defendant and shall state the following:

(i) the defendant's financial condition;

(ii) his or her residence addresses and employment history for the past 10 years;

(iii) his or her occupation and the name and address of his or her employer, if he or she is employed, or his or her school, if he or she is in school;

(iv) his or her family situation; and

(v) any prior criminal record and any other relevant facts.

If the order is entered upon motion of the prosecution, the defendant's verified answer to the motion shall contain the foregoing information.

(2) *Procedure.* The appeal may be taken at any time before conviction by filing a verified motion for review in the Appellate Court. The motion for review shall be accompanied by a verified copy of the motion or answer filed in the trial court and shall state the following:

(i) the court that entered the order;

(ii) the date of the order;

(iii) the crime or crimes charged;

(iv) the amount and condition of bail;

(v) the arguments supporting the motion; and

(vi) the relief sought.

No brief shall be filed. A copy of the motion shall be served upon the opposing party. The State may promptly file an answer.

(3) *Disposition.* Upon receipt of the motion, the clerk shall immediately notify the opposing party by telephone of the filing of the motion, entering the date and time of the notification on the docket, and promptly thereafter present the motion to the court.

(4) *Report of Proceedings.* The court, on its own motion or on the motion of any party, may order court reporting personnel as defined in Rule 46 to file in the Appellate Court a report of all proceedings had in the trial court on the question of bail.

(5) *No Oral Argument.* No oral argument shall be permitted except when ordered on the court's own motion.

(d) Appeal by Defendant From a Judgment Entered Upon a Plea of Guilty. No appeal from a judgment entered upon a plea of guilty shall be taken unless the defendant, within 30 days of the date on which sentence is imposed, files in the trial court a motion to reconsider the sentence, if only the sentence is being challenged, or, if the plea is being challenged, a motion to withdraw the plea of guilty and vacate the judgment. No appeal shall be taken upon a negotiated plea of guilty challenging the sentence as excessive unless the defendant, within 30 days of the imposition of sentence, files a motion to withdraw the plea of guilty and vacate the judgment. For purposes of this rule, a negotiated plea of guilty is one in which the prosecution has bound itself to recommend a specific sentence, or a specific range of sentence, or where the prosecution has made concessions relating to the sentence to be imposed and not merely to the charge or charges then pending. The motion shall be in writing and shall state the grounds therefor. When the motion is based on facts that do not appear of record it shall be supported by affidavit unless the defendant is filing the motion *pro se* from a correctional institution, in which case the defendant may submit, in lieu of an affidavit, a certification as provided in section 1–109 of the Code of Civil Procedure (735 ILCS 5/1–109). The motion shall be presented promptly to the trial judge by whom the defendant was sentenced, and if that judge is then not sitting in the court in which the judgment was entered, then to the chief judge of the circuit, or to such other judge as the chief judge shall designate. The trial court shall then determine whether the defendant is represented by counsel, and if the defendant is indigent and desires counsel, the trial court shall appoint counsel. If the defendant is indigent, the trial court shall order a copy of the transcript as provided in Rule 402(e) be furnished the defendant without cost. The defendant's attorney shall file with the trial court a certificate stating that the attorney has consulted with the defendant either by phone, mail, electronic means or in person to ascertain defendant's contentions of error in the sentence and the entry of the plea of guilty, has examined the trial court file and both the report of proceedings of the plea of guilty and the report of proceedings in the sentencing hearing, and has made any amendments to the motion necessary for adequate presentation of any defects in those proceedings. The motion shall be heard promptly, and if allowed, the trial court shall modify the sentence or vacate the judgment and permit the defendant to withdraw the plea of guilty and plead anew. If the motion is denied, a notice of appeal from the judgment and sentence shall be filed within the time allowed in Rule 606, measured from the date of entry of the order denying the motion. Upon appeal any issue not raised by the defendant in the motion to reconsider the sentence or withdraw the plea of guilty and vacate the judgment shall be deemed waived.

The certificate of counsel shall be in the following form:

STATE OF ILLINOIS
IN THE CIRCUIT COURT OF THE _____ JUDICIAL CIR-
CUIT
COUNTY OF _____
(Or, IN THE CIRCUIT COURT OF COOK COUNTY)

PEOPLE OF THE STATE
OF ILLINOIS,

Plaintiff

vs.   CASE NO. _____

_____
Defendant

CERTIFICATE OF COUNSEL
PURSUANT TO ILLINOIS SUPREME COURT RULE 604(d)

I, _____, attorney for Defendant, certify pursuant to Supreme Court Rule 604(d) that:

1. I have consulted with the Defendant in person, by mail, by phone or by electronic means to ascertain the defendant's contentions of error in the entry of the plea of guilty and in the sentence;

2. I have examined the trial court file and report of proceedings of the plea of guilty and the report of proceedings in the sentencing hearing; and

3. I have made any amendments to the motion necessary for the adequate presentation of any defects in those proceedings.

Respectfully submitted,

_____
Date   Attorney for the Defendant

(e) Appeal From an Order Finding Defendant Unfit to Stand Trial or Be Sentenced. The defendant or the State may appeal to the Appellate Court from an order holding the defendant unfit to stand trial or be sentenced.

(f) Appeal by Defendant on Grounds of Former Jeopardy. The defendant may appeal to the Appel-

late Court the denial of a motion to dismiss a criminal proceeding on grounds of former jeopardy.

(g) Appeal From an Order Granting a Motion to Disqualify Defense Counsel. The defendant may petition for leave to appeal to the Appellate Court from an order of the circuit court granting a motion to disqualify the attorney for the defendant based on a conflict of interest. The procedure for bringing interlocutory appeals pursuant to this subpart shall be the same as set forth in Supreme Court Rule 306(c). Amended eff. July 1, 1969; Oct. 21, 1969, eff. Jan. 1, 1970; eff. Oct. 1, 1970, July 1, 1971, Nov. 30, 1972, Sept. 1, 1974, and July 1, 1975; Feb. 19, 1982, eff. April 1, 1982; June 15, 1982, eff. July 1, 1982; Aug. 9, 1983, eff. Oct. 1, 1983; April 1, 1992, eff. Aug. 1, 1992; Oct. 5, 2000, eff. Nov. 1, 2000; Feb. 1, 2005, eff. immediately; Dec. 13, 2005, eff. immediately; Feb. 10, 2006, effective July 1, 2006; Nov. 28, 2012, eff. Jan. 1, 2013; Feb. 6, 2013, eff. immediately; Dec. 11, 2014, eff. immediately; Dec. 3, 2015, eff. immediately; Mar. 8, 2016, eff. immediately.

Formerly Ill.Rev.Stat.1991, ch. 110A, ¶ 604.

Committee Comment
(February 10, 2006)
Paragraph (g)

Paragraph (g) permits interlocutory review of certain attorney disqualification orders but does not change attorney disqualification law. The circuit court still has discretion to accept or reject a defendant's conflict of interest waiver, based on consideration of the interests identified in People v. Ortega, 209 Ill. 2d 354 (2004).

Committee Comments
(February 1, 2005)

The language in paragraph (a) allowing interlocutory appeals from orders decertifying a prosecution as a capital case or finding the defendant to be mentally retarded provides for the kinds of appeals contemplated by section 9–1(h–5) of the Criminal Code of 1961 (720 ILCS 5/9–1(h–5)) and section 114–15(f) of the Code of Criminal Procedure of 1963 (725 ILCS 5/114–15(f)).

Committee Comments
(Revised July 1, 1975)

Rule 604 was amended in September 1969 to add paragraph (b), dealing with appeals when probation has been granted. The 1969 amendment made what was formerly the entirety of Rule 604 into paragraph (a) and made an appropriate change in the title of the rule.

Paragraph (a)

Subparagraph (1) of paragraph (a) is former Rule 27(4), as it existed until January 1, 1967, with slight changes in language. (Rule 27(4) was derived from sections 121–1 and 120–2 of the Code.) The rule makes it clear that an order dismissing an indictment, information or complaint for any of the grounds enumerated in section 114–1 of the Code is appealable.

Subparagraph (2) was added by amendment effective November 30, 1972.

Subparagraph (3) is former section 120–3(a) of the Code without change.

Subparagraph (4) is section 120–3(b) of the Code without change.

Paragraph (b)

Paragraph (b) is based upon sections 117–1(d) and 117–3(e) of the Code and is included in the rule in conformity with the policy of covering all appeals in the supreme court rules, as contemplated by the judicial article of the Constitution. (Ill. Const., art. VI, § 16.) Paragraph (b) was amended in 1974 to cover conditional discharge and periodic imprisonment, new forms of sentence created by the adoption in Illinois of the Unified Code of Corrections.

Paragraph (c)

Paragraph (c) was added in 1971 to establish a procedure for appeals from orders in criminal cases concerning bail. Prior to its adoption, the only avenue of relief was an original petition to the Supreme Court for a writ of *habeas corpus*. Subparagraph (c)(2) was amended in 1974 to provide that the State may file an answer.

Paragraph (d)

Paragraph (d), added in 1975, provides that before a defendant may file a notice of appeal from a judgment entered on his plea of guilty, he must move in the trial court to vacate the judgment and withdraw his plea. Issues not raised in such a motion are waived. The time within which an appeal may be taken runs from the date on which the order disposing of the motion is entered. Provision is made for appointment of counsel and provision of a free transcript of the proceedings, which, under Rule 402(e), are required to be transcribed, filed, and made a part of the common law record.

Rule 605. Advice to Defendant

(a) On Judgment and Sentence After Plea of Not Guilty.

(1) In all cases in which the defendant is found guilty and sentenced to imprisonment, probation or conditional discharge, periodic imprisonment, or to pay a fine, or in which a sentence of probation or conditional discharge has been revoked or the conditions attached to such a sentence have been modified, excluding cases in which the judgment and sentence are entered on a plea of guilty, the trial court shall, at the time of imposing sentence or modifying the conditions of the sentence, advise the defendant of the right to appeal, of the right to request the clerk to prepare and file a notice of appeal, and of the right, if indigent, to be furnished, without cost to the defendant, with a transcript of the proceedings at the trial or hearing.

(2) In addition to the foregoing rights, in cases in which the defendant has been convicted of a felony or a Class A misdemeanor or convicted of a lesser offense and sentenced to imprisonment, periodic imprisonment, or to probation or conditional discharge conditioned upon periodic imprisonment, or in which a sentence of probation or conditional discharge has been revoked or the conditions attached to such a sentence have been modified and a sentence or condition of imprisonment or periodic imprisonment imposed, the trial court shall advise the defendant of the right to have counsel appointed on appeal.

(3) At the time of imposing sentence or modifying the conditions of the sentence, the trial court shall also advise the defendant as follows:

A. that the right to appeal the judgment of conviction, excluding the sentence imposed or modified, will be preserved only if a notice of appeal is filed in the trial court within thirty (30) days from the date on which sentence is imposed;

B. that prior to taking an appeal, if the defendant seeks to challenge the correctness of the sentence, or any aspect of the sentencing hearing, the defendant must file in the trial court within 30 days of the date on which sentence is imposed a written motion asking to have the trial court reconsider the sentence imposed, or consider any challenges to the sentencing hearing, setting forth in the motion all issues or claims of error regarding the sentence imposed or the sentencing hearing;

C. that any issue or claim of error regarding the sentence imposed or any aspect of the sentencing hearing not raised in the written motion shall be deemed waived; and

D. that in order to preserve the right to appeal following the disposition of the motion to reconsider sentence, or any challenges regarding the sentencing hearing, the defendant must file a notice of appeal in the trial court within 30 days from the entry of the order disposing of the defendant's motion to reconsider sentence or order disposing of any challenges to the sentencing hearing.

(b) On Judgment and Sentence Entered on a Plea of Guilty.
In all cases in which a judgment is entered upon a plea of guilty, other than a negotiated plea of guilty, at the time of imposing sentence, the trial court shall advise the defendant substantially as follows:

(1) that the defendant has a right to appeal;

(2) that prior to taking an appeal the defendant must file in the trial court, within 30 days of the date on which sentence is imposed, a written motion asking to have the trial court reconsider the sentence or to have the judgment vacated and for leave to withdraw the plea of guilty, setting forth the grounds for the motion;

(3) that if the motion is allowed, the sentence will be modified or the plea of guilty, sentence and judgment will be vacated and a trial date will be set on the charges to which the plea of guilty was made;

(4) that upon the request of the State any charges that may have been dismissed as a part of a plea agreement will be reinstated and will also be set for trial;

(5) that if the defendant is indigent, a copy of the transcript of the proceedings at the time of the defendant's plea of guilty and sentence will be provided without cost to the defendant and counsel will be appointed to assist the defendant with the preparation of the motions; and

(6) that in any appeal taken from the judgment on the plea of guilty any issue or claim of error not raised in the motion to reconsider the sentence or to vacate the judgment and to withdraw the plea of guilty shall be deemed waived.

For the purposes of this rule, a negotiated plea is one in which the prosecution has bound itself to recommend a specific sentence, or a specific range of sentence, or where the prosecution has made concessions relating to the sentence to be imposed and not merely to the charge or charges then pending.

(c) On Judgment and Sentence Entered on a Negotiated Plea of Guilty. In all cases in which a judgment is entered upon a negotiated plea of guilty, at the time of imposing sentence, the trial court shall advise the defendant substantially as follows:

(1) that the defendant has a right to appeal;

(2) that prior to taking an appeal the defendant must file in the trial court, within 30 days of the date on which sentence is imposed, a written motion asking to have the judgment vacated and for leave to withdraw the plea of guilty, setting forth the grounds for the motion;

(3) that if the motion is allowed, the plea of guilty, sentence and judgment will be vacated and a trial date will be set on the charges to which the plea of guilty was made;

(4) that upon the request of the State any charges that may have been dismissed as a part of a plea agreement will be reinstated and will also be set for trial;

(5) that if the defendant is indigent, a copy of the transcript of the proceedings at the time of the defendant's plea of guilty and sentence will be provided without cost to the defendant and counsel will be appointed to assist the defendant with the preparation of the motions; and

(6) that in any appeal taken from the judgment on the plea of guilty any issue or claim of error not raised in the motion to vacate the judgment and to withdraw the plea of guilty shall be deemed waived.

For the purposes of this rule, a negotiated plea is one in which the prosecution has bound itself to recommend a specific sentence, or a specific range of sentence, or where the prosecution has made concessions relating to the sentence to be imposed and not merely to the charge or charges then pending.

Amended eff. June 23, 1967; June 1970, eff. Sept. 1, 1970; June 25, 1971, eff. July 1, 1971; June 28, 1974, eff. Sept. 1, 1974; eff. July 1, 1975; April 1, 1992, eff. Aug. 1, 1992; Oct. 5, 2000, eff. Nov. 1, 2000; Nov. 22, 2000, nunc pro tunc Nov. 1, 2000; Oct. 1, 2001, eff. immediately.

Formerly Ill.Rev.Stat.1991, ch. 110A, ¶ 605.

Committee Comments
(Revised July 1, 1975.)

This rule is derived from former Rule 27(6), as it existed before 1967, which in turn was derived from section 121–4(c) of the Code of Criminal Procedure. In 1967 the requirement that the stenographic transcript of the court's advice to the defendant and the defendant's answers be filed as a part of the common-law record was transferred to Rule 401, and the last sentence of the former rule was transferred to Rule 606(a).

This rule was amended in June, 1970, to add the last sentence, which requires the trial court to advise the defendant of the time within which his notice of appeal must be filed in order to preserve his right to appeal. See Rule 651(b) for a comparable provision.

The 1971 amendments remove the requirement that the court advise of their various rights defendants who plead guilty. They also extended the requirement that the advice be given in all cases, including misdemeanor cases, in which the defendant was convicted of an offense punishable by imprisonment for more than six months. In thus extending the requirement these amendments conformed the rule to the provisions of Rule 607, as amended the same year, dealing with the rights of indigents to appointed counsel and a report of proceedings. (See Committee Comments to that rule.) In 1974, Rule 607 was again amended to provide for a free transcript in all cases in which the defendant has been convicted and sentenced. Under the amended rule, however, the right to appointment of counsel is limited to cases in which the offense was a felony or a class A misdemeanor, or in which the sentence involves some imprisonment, whether imposed as a sentence or as a condition to a sentence of probation or conditional discharge. This rule was again amended to conform its provisions with those of Rule 607. The language of both rules was changed to conform with the language of the Unified Code of Corrections.

In 1975, Rule 604(d) was added to provide that before appealing a judgment and sentence entered on a plea of guilty, the defendant must move in the trial court for vacation of the judgment and to withdraw the plea of guilty. Rule 605 was amended to designate the matter then contained in the rule as paragraph (a), and to add new paragraph (b), providing that on imposition of sentence the defendant shall be advised of the requirements of Rule 604(d).

Rule 606.   Perfection of Appeal

(a) **How Perfected.**   Appeals shall be perfected by filing a notice of appeal with the clerk of the trial court. The notice may be signed by the appellant or his attorney. If the defendant so requests in open court at the time he is advised of his right to appeal or subsequently in writing, the clerk of the trial court shall prepare, sign, and file forthwith a notice of appeal for the defendant. No step in the perfection of the appeal other than the filing of the notice of appeal is jurisdictional.

(b) **Time.**   Except as provided in Rule 604(d), the notice of appeal must be filed with the clerk of the circuit court within 30 days after the entry of the final judgment appealed from or if a motion directed against the judgment is timely filed, within 30 days after the entry of the order disposing of the motion. When a timely posttrial or postsentencing motion directed against the judgment has been filed by counsel or by defendant, if not represented by counsel, any notice of appeal filed before the entry of the order disposing of all pending postjudgment motions shall have no effect and shall be stricken by the trial court. Upon striking the notice of appeal, the trial court shall forward to the appellate court within 5 days a copy of the order striking the notice of appeal, showing by whom it was filed and the date on which it was filed. This rule applies whether the timely postjudgment motion was filed before or after the date on which the notice of appeal was filed. A new notice of appeal must be filed within 30 days following the entry of the order disposing of all timely postjudgment motions. Within 5 days of its being so filed a copy of the notice of appeal or an amendment of the notice of appeal shall be transmitted by the clerk of the circuit court to the clerk of the court to which the appeal is taken. Except as provided in paragraph (c) below, and in Rule 604(d), no appeal may be taken from a trial court to a reviewing court after the expiration of 30 days from the entry of the order or judgment from which the appeal is taken. The clerk of the appellate court shall notify any party whose appeal has been dismissed under this rule.

(c) **Extension of Time in Certain Circumstances.** On motion supported by a showing of reasonable excuse for failing to file a notice of appeal on time filed in the reviewing court within 30 days of the expiration of the time for filing the notice of appeal, or on motion supported by a showing by affidavit that there is merit to the appeal and that the failure to file a notice of appeal on time was not due to appellant's culpable negligence, filed in the reviewing court within six months of the expiration of the time for filing the notice of appeal, in either case accompanied by the proposed notice of appeal, the reviewing court may grant leave to appeal and order the clerk to transmit the notice of appeal to the trial court for filing. However, when the appellant is filing the motion *pro se* from a correctional institution, the appellant may

submit, in lieu of the affidavit referred to herein, a certification as provided in section 1–109 of the Code of Civil Procedure (735 ILCS 5/1–109).

(d) **Form of Notice of Appeal.**   The notice of appeal shall be substantially in the following form:

In the Circuit Court of the _____
Judicial Circuit,
_____ County, Illinois
(Or, In the Circuit Court of Cook County, Illinois)

THE PEOPLE OF THE
STATE OF ILLINOIS,

v.   No. _____

_____

Notice of Appeal

Joining Prior Appeal / Separate
Appeal / Cross Appeal

(circle one)

An appeal is taken from the order or judgment described below.

(1) Court to which appeal is taken: _____

(2) Name of appellant and address to which notices shall be sent.

Name: _____

Address: _____ Email: _____

(3) Name and address of appellant's attorney on appeal.

Name: _____

Address: _____ Email: _____

If appellant is indigent and has no attorney, does he want one appointed?

(4) Date of judgment or order: _____

(5) Offense of which convicted _____

(6) Sentence: _____

(7) If appeal is not from a conviction, nature of order appealed from: _____

(8) If the appeal is from a judgment of a circuit court holding unconstitutional a statute of the United States or of this state, a copy of the court's findings made in compliance with Rule 18 shall be appended to the notice of appeal.

(Signed) _____
(May be signed by appellant,
attorney for appellant, or
clerk of circuit court.)

The notice of appeal may be amended as provided in Rule 303(b)(5).

(e) **Copies of Notice of Appeal to be Sent by Clerk.**

(1) *When Defendant Is Appellant and Action Is Prosecuted by the State.* When the defendant is the appellant and the action was prosecuted by the State, the clerk shall send a copy of the notice of appeal to the State's Attorney of the county in which the judgment was entered and a copy to the Attorney General at his Springfield, Illinois, office.

(2) *When Defendant Is Appellant and the Action Is Prosecuted by a Governmental Entity Other Than the State.* If the defendant is the appellant and the action was prosecuted by a governmental entity other than the State for the violation of an ordinance, the copy of the notice of appeal shall be sent to the chief legal officer of the entity (*e.g.,* corporation counsel, city attorney), or if his name and address do not appear of record, then to the chief administrative officer of the entity at his official address.

(3) *When the Prosecuting Entity Is the Appellant.* When the State or other prosecuting entity is the appellant a copy of the notice of appeal shall be sent to the defendant and a copy to his counsel.

(f) Docketing. Upon receipt of the copy of the notice of appeal transmitted to the reviewing court pursuant to paragraph (a) of this rule, or the entry of an order granting a motion for leave to appeal under paragraph (c) of this rule, the clerk of the reviewing court shall enter the appeal upon the docket.

(g) Docketing Statement; Filing Fee. Within 14 days after the filing of the notice of appeal and pursuant to notice to the appellee's attorney, the party filing the notice of appeal shall file with the clerk of the reviewing court a docketing statement, together with proof of service thereof, and the filing fee as required by Rule 313. The form and contents of the docketing statement shall be as follows:

Docket Number in the Reviewing Court

Case Title (Complete)   ) Appeal   From
) _____ County
) Circuit No. _____
) Trial Judge _____
) Date of Judgment _____
) Date of Posttrial Motion _____
) Date of Notice of Appeal _____
) Felony ( )   Misdemeanor ( )
) In Custody ( )   Out on Bond ( )

DOCKETING STATEMENT

(Criminal)

1. Full name and complete address of appellant(s) filing this statement:

Name: _____

Address: _____

Telephone: _____ Email address: _____

Counsel On Appeal for Appellant(s) filing this docketing statement:

Name: _____ ARDC # _____

Address: _____

Telephone: _____ Email address: _____

2. Full name and complete address of appellee(s):

Name: _____

Address: _____

Telephone: _____ Email address: _____

Counsel On Appeal for Appellee(s):

Name: _____

Address: _____

Telephone: _____

ARDC # if known: _____ Email address: __

Court Reporting Personnel

(If more space is needed, use other side.)

Name: _____

Address: _____

Telephone: _____ Email address: _____

General statement of issues proposed to be raised: (Failure to include an issue in this statement will not result in the waiver of the issue on appeal.)

_____

_____

_____

As _____ attorney for the appellant _____ *Pro Se* appellant, I hereby certify that on the _____ day of _____, 20 _____, I asked / made a written request to the clerk of the circuit court to prepare the record on appeal, and on the _____ day of _____, 20 _____, I made a written request to the court reporting personnel to prepare the transcript(s).

_____	_____	_____
Date	Appellant's Attorney	*Pro Se* Appellant

In lieu of court reporting personnel's signature, I have attached the written request to the court reporting personnel to prepare the transcript (s).

_____	_____	_____
Date	Appellant's Attorney	*Pro Se* Appellant

In lieu of court reporting personnel's signature, I have attached the written request to the court reporting personnel to prepare the transcript (s).

_____	_____
Date	Court Reporting Personnel or Supervisor

Amended Oct. 21, 1969, eff. Jan. 1, 1970; eff. July 1, 1971, July 1, 1975, and Feb. 17, 1977; July 15, 1979, eff. Oct, 15, 1979; April 27, 1984, eff. July 1, 1984; Aug. 27, 1999, eff. immediately; Oct. 22, 1999, eff. Dec. 1, 1999; Dec. 13, 2005, eff. immediately; July 27, 2006, eff. Sept. 1, 2006; March 20, 2009, eff. immediately; Dec. 12, 2012, eff. Jan. 1, 2013; Feb. 6, 2013, eff. immediately; Dec. 11, 2014, eff. immediately.

Formerly Ill.Rev.Stat.1991, ch. 110A, ¶ 606.

Committee Comments

(Revised 1979)

Paragraph (a)

This rule is an amalgam of former Rule 27(5)(a) and Rule 76(6), as those rules existed before 1967. Rule 27(5)(a) and Rule 27(6) were derived from sections 121–4(a), 121–4(c), and 121–12(a) of the Code of Criminal Procedure. A change of some significance made in 1967 is that the defendant may request the clerk to prepare a notice of appeal in writing any time after the court has advised him of his right to appeal. Under the former practice, the defendant was required to request the clerk to prepare the notice of appeal at the time of the admonition by the court.

Paragraph (b)

This is former Rule 27(7)(a) without substantial change. Rule 27(7)(a) was derived from section 121–4(c) of the Code.

Paragraph (c)

This paragraph was new in 1967. It was designed to provide an inexpensive and expeditious method of applying for leave to appeal after the initial 30-day period has elapsed. The practice under former Rule 27 was for the applicant for leave to appeal to prepare a petition that amounted to a complete brief on the merits. When leave is sought within 30 days after the initial period has run, the new procedure requires only a simple motion together with a showing of "reasonable excuse" for the failure to file the notice of appeal within the 30-day period. This showing ought to contain sufficient facts to show reasonable excuse and should either be certified or supported by affidavits.

As promulgated to take effect in 1967, the "reasonable excuse" standard applied to petitions made within six months of the 30-day period for the filing of a notice of appeal. In 1971, the paragraph was amended to limit this period to 30 days, making it parallel to the provisions of Rule 303(e) governing civil cases, and to provide that within six months after the expiration of the initial 30-day period for filing the notice of appeal relief can be obtained upon a showing by affidavit that there is merit in the appeal and that the failure to file the notice of appeal on time was not due to appellant's culpable negligence.

Paragraph (d)

This paragraph is new. It sets out a form for the notice of appeal. The contents of the notice of appeal are essentially those required by former Rule 27(5)(b), which was derived from section 121–4(a) of the Code. Setting out the form of the criminal notice of appeal in the rule will help the drafter of a notice of appeal, who may be the clerk or even the defendant himself, in drawing the document, which is jurisdictional.

Paragraph (e)

Prior to 1975, Rule 606(e) provided that in criminal cases a copy of the notice of appeal by a defendant should be sent to the State's Attorney of the county in which the judgment was entered and to the Attorney General at his Springfield office.

In 1973 the General Assembly provided that a municipality, by its corporate attorney, may prosecute violations of ordinances defining misdemeanors punishable by imprisonment not to exceed 6 months. Further, the 1970 Constitution of Illinois provides for adoption of such ordinances by home-rule units without statutory sanction. Thus prosecutions may be brought by a governmental entity other than the State. Paragraph (e) provides that in such circumstances the notice of appeal need not be sent to the State's Attorney, who has no function in the prosecution, or to the Attorney General, but instead will be sent to the legal officer of the prosecuting entity. In some instances the attorney for a governmental entity will make no appearance and the record will not show his name and address. In such a case, the copy of the notice of appeal must be sent to the chief administrative officer, *e.g.*, to the mayor at the city hall.

Paragraph (f)

Paragraph (f), requiring the filing of a docketing statement, was added in 1979. See the committee comments to Rule 303(g).

Paragraph (g)

Paragraph (g), requiring the filing of a docketing statement, was added in 1979. See the committee comments to Rule 303(g).

Rule 607. Appeals by Poor Persons

(a) Appointment of Counsel. Upon the filing of a notice of appeal in any case in which the defendant has been found guilty of a felony or a Class A misdemeanor, or in which he has been found guilty of a lesser offense and sentenced to imprisonment or periodic imprisonment, or to probation or conditional discharge conditioned upon periodic imprisonment, or in which a sentence of probation or conditional discharge has been revoked or the conditions attached to such a sentence modified and a sentence of imprisonment or periodic imprisonment imposed, and in cases in which the State appeals, the trial court shall determine whether the defendant is represented by counsel on appeal. If not so represented, and the court determines that the defendant is indigent and desires counsel on appeal, the court shall appoint counsel on appeal. Compensation and reimbursement for expenses of appointed attorneys shall be as provided by statute.

(b) Report of Proceedings. In any case in which the defendant has been found guilty and sentenced to imprisonment, probation or conditional discharge, or periodic imprisonment, or to pay a fine, or in which a hearing has been held resulting in the revocation of, or modification of the conditions of, probation or conditional discharge, the defendant may petition the court in which he was convicted for a report of the proceedings at his trial or hearing. If the conduct on which the case was based was also the basis for a juvenile proceeding which was dismissed so that the case could proceed, the defendant may include in his petition a request for a report of proceedings in the juvenile proceeding. The petition shall be verified by the petitioner and shall state facts showing that he was at the time of his conviction, or at the time probation or conditional discharge was revoked or its conditions modified, and is at the time of filing the petition, without financial means with which to obtain the report of proceedings. If the judge who imposed sentence or entered the order revoking probation or conditional discharge or modifying the conditions, or in his absence any other judge of the court, finds that the defendant is without financial means with which to obtain the report of proceedings at his trial or hearing, he shall order the court reporting personnel as defined in Rule 46 to transcribe an original and copy of his notes. The original and one copy of the report shall be certified by the court reporting personnel and filed with the clerk of the trial court as provided below, without charge. The clerk of the trial court shall then, upon written request of the defendant, release a copy of the report of proceedings to the defendant's attorney of record on appeal. In the event no attorney appears of record, the clerk shall, upon written request of the defendant, release the report of proceedings to the defendant, his guardian or custodian. The court reporting personnel who prepare reports of proceedings pursuant to an order under this rule shall be paid pursuant to a schedule of charges approved by the public employer and employer representative for the court reporting personnel.

(c) Filing Fees Excused. If the defendant is represented by court-appointed counsel, the clerk of the reviewing court shall docket the appeal and accept papers for filing without the payment of fees.

(d) Copies of Briefs or Petitions for Leave to Appeal. If the defendant is represented by court-appointed counsel, the clerk of the Supreme Court shall accept for filing not less than 15 legible copies of briefs or petitions for leave to appeal or answers thereto; and the clerks of the Appellate Court shall accept for filing not less than 6 legible copies of briefs.

Amended effective June 23, 1967; October 21, 1969, effective January 1, 1970; effective July 1, 1971; June 28, 1974, effective September 1, 1974; September 29, 1978, effective November 1, 1978; July 30, 1979 and September 20, 1979, effective October 15, 1979; April 7, 1993, effective June 1, 1993; September 22, 1997, effective January 1, 1998; September 30, 2002, effective immediately; December 13, 2005, effective immediately; Feb. 6, 2013, eff. immediately.

Formerly Ill.Rev.Stat.1991, ch. 110A, ¶ 607.

Committee Comments
(Revised 1979)

Paragraph (a)

As adopted effective January 1, 1967, this paragraph was former Rule 27(18) with no substantial change except to provide that counsel other than the public defender may be appointed only in the discretion of the court. Rule 27(18) was derived

from section 121–13(b) of the Code of Criminal Procedure. This provision harmonized the rule with the provisions of section 113–3 of the code, as amended by the 1965 General Assembly.

As adopted in 1967, paragraph (a) provided for the appointment of counsel on appeal only in cases in which the defendant had been convicted of a crime punishable by imprisonment in the penitentiary. In 1971, the rule was amended to extend the right to appointed counsel to cases in which the defendant had been convicted of an offense punishable by imprisonment for more than six months. The term "criminal" was dropped to make it plain that the rule applied to ordinance violation cases in which the penalty could exceed six months imprisonment. In 1974, after the decision in Argersinger v. Hamlin (1972), 407 U.S. 25, extending the right to counsel to all cases in which any imprisonment is actually imposed, paragraph (a) was amended to bring it in accord with the decision. At the same time the limitation on appointment of counsel other than the public defender was deleted.

Paragraph (b)

As adopted effective January 1, 1967, this paragraph was former Rule 27(9)(b) without substantial change. Rule 27(9)(b) was derived from earlier Rule 65–1(1), repealed effective January 1, 1964.

Like paragraph (a), this paragraph originally applied only to cases in which the defendant had been convicted of a crime punishable by imprisonment in the penitentiary. In 1971, it was amended to apply to cases in which the defendant had been convicted of an offense (including ordinance violations) punishable by more than six months imprisonment. In 1974, it was amended to conform to the requirements set out in Mayer v. City of Chicago (1971), 404 U.S. 189, where it was held that a defendant convicted of an ordinance violation punishable by fine only is entitled, if indigent, to receive a free transcript of the proceedings at the trial. As presently worded, paragraph (b) provides that a defendant found guilty of any offense and sentenced to any of the sentences provided for in the Unified Code of Corrections (see Ill.Rev.Stat.1973, ch. 38, ¶ 1005–5–3) may proceed under the rule.

Paragraph (b) was amended in October 1969 to provide explicitly that an indigent juvenile convicted of a felony after dismissal of a juvenile proceeding involving the facts on which the felony case is based is entitled to a report of proceedings of the juvenile proceeding. The need for insuring the availability of such a transcript was underscored by People v. Jiles, 43 Ill.2d 145, 251 N.E.2d 529 (1969). The reference to "a felony case" in this provision was changed in 1971 to "that case," referring to any case that falls within the general coverage of the rule, meaning, since 1974, any case in which the defendant has been found guilty of an offense and sentenced.

In 1978 paragraph (b) was amended to provide that upon written request the copy of the report of proceedings made for the defendant shall be delivered to the defendant's attorney of record, if he has one, and otherwise, on written request, released to the defendant or his guardian or custodian. This change was designed to avoid confusion over the delivery of the copy and leave a record of its delivery.

Paragraphs (c) and (d)

These provisions, new in 1967, codified existing Supreme Court practice.

In 1979, Rule 342 was amended to provide that with the exception of stated documents (see Rule 342(a)), no portions of the record shall be reproduced. Rule 317 was amended to reflect this change in the practice. See the committee comments to Rule 342.

(September 22, 1997)

This amendment of Rule 607(b) directing the preparation of an additional copy of the report of proceedings in a case in which a death sentence is imposed is a necessary complement to Rule 608, amended September 22, 1997, effective January 1, 1998, which requires the preparation and filing of a duplicate record on appeal, in addition to the original, in death sentence cases.

Rule 608. The Record on Appeal

(a) Designation and Contents. The clerk of the circuit court shall prepare the record on appeal upon the filing of a notice of appeal. The record on appeal must contain the following:

(1) a cover sheet showing the title of the case;

(2) a certificate of the clerk showing the impaneling of the grand jury if the prosecution was commenced by indictment;

(3) the indictment, information, or complaint;

(4) a transcript of the proceedings at the defendant's arraignment and plea;

(5) all motions, transcript of motion proceedings, and orders entered thereon;

(6) all arrest warrants, search warrants, consent to search forms, eavesdropping orders, and any similar documents;

(7) a transcript of proceedings regarding waiver of counsel and waiver of jury trial, if any;

(8) the report of proceedings, including opening statements by counsel, testimony offered at trial, and objections thereto, offers of proof, arguments and rulings thereon, the instructions offered and given, and the objections and rulings thereon, closing argument of counsel, communications from the jury during deliberations, and responses and supplemental instructions to the jury and objections, arguments and rulings thereon; the court reporting personnel as defined in Rule 46 shall take the record of the proceedings regarding the selection of the jury, but the record need not be transcribed unless a party designates that such proceedings be included in the record on appeal;

(9) exhibits offered at trial and sentencing, along with objections, offers of proof, arguments, and

rulings thereon; except that physical and demonstrative evidence, other than photographs, which do not fit on a standard size record page shall not be included in the record on appeal unless ordered by a court upon motion of a party or upon the court's own motion;

(10) the verdict of the jury or finding of the court;

(11) post-trial motions, including motions for a new trial, motions in arrest of judgment, motions for judgment notwithstanding the verdict and the testimony, arguments and rulings thereon;

(12) a transcript of proceedings at sentencing, including the presentence investigation report, testimony offered and objections thereto, offers of proof, argument, and rulings thereon, arguments of counsel, and statements by the defendant and the court;

(13) the judgment and sentence; and

(14) the notice of appeal, if any.

Within 14 days after the notice of appeal is filed the appellant and the appellee may file a designation of additional portions of the circuit court record to be included in the record on appeal. Thereupon the clerk shall include those portions in the record on appeal. Additionally, upon motion of a party, the court may allow photographs of exhibits to be filed as a supplemental record on appeal, in lieu of the exhibits themselves, when such photographs accurately depict the exhibits themselves. There is no distinction between the common law record and the report of proceedings, for the purpose of determining what is properly before the reviewing court.

(b) Report of Proceedings; Time. The report of proceedings contains the testimony and exhibits, the rulings of the trial judge, and all other proceedings before the trial judge, unless the parties designate or stipulate for less. It shall be certified by court reporting personnel or the trial judge and shall be filed in the trial court within 49 days after the filing of the notice of appeal. The report of proceedings shall be taken as true and correct unless shown to be otherwise and corrected in a manner permitted by Rule 329.

(c) Time for Filing Record on Appeal. The record shall be filed in the reviewing court within 63 days from the date the notice of appeal is filed in the trial court. If more than one appellant appeals from the same judgment or from different judgments in the same cause to the same reviewing court, the trial court may prescribe the time for filing the record in the reviewing court, which shall not be more than 63 days from the date the last notice of appeal is filed. If the time for filing the report of proceedings has been extended, the record on appeal shall be filed within 14 days after the expiration of the extended time.

(d) Extensions of Time. The reviewing court or any judge thereof may extend the time for filing, in the trial court, the report of proceedings or agreed statement of facts or for serving a proposed report of proceedings, on notice and motion filed in the reviewing court before the expiration of the original or extended time, or on notice and motion filed within 35 days thereafter. Motions for extensions of time shall be supported by an affidavit showing the necessity for extension, and motions made after expiration of the original or extended time shall be further supported by a showing of reasonable excuse for failure to file the motion earlier. However, when a motion for extension of time is filed *pro se* from a correctional institution, the movant may submit, in lieu of the affidavit referred to herein, a certification as provided in section 1–109 of the Code of Civil Procedure (735 ILCS 5/1–109).

Amended October 21, 1969, eff. Jan. 1, 1970; Sept. 29, 1978, eff. Nov. 1, 1978; July 30, 1979, eff. Oct. 15, 1979; Feb. 19, 1982, eff. April 1, 1982; July 3, 1986, eff. Aug. 1, 1986; Sept. 22, 1997, eff. Jan. 1, 1998; Dec. 13, 2005, eff. immediately; Feb. 6, 2013, eff. immediately; April 8, 2013, eff. immediately; Dec. 11, 2014, eff. immediately.

Formerly Ill.Rev.Stat.1991, ch. 110A, ¶ 608.

Committee Comments
(Revised July 3, 1986)

Paragraph (a)

This is former Rule 27(8) with certain changes. Former Rule 27(8) was derived from section 121–7(b) of the Code of Criminal Procedure of 1963 and earlier Rule 65–2, repealed effective January 1, 1964.

Paragraph (a) provided for the appellant, within 14 days of the filing of the notice of appeal, to file a designation of portions of the circuit court record to be included in the record on appeal. The appellee, within seven days thereafter, could file a designation of additional portions to be included. The paragraph further provided for the clerk to prepare the record on appeal containing the designated portions of the circuit court record or, if no designation was filed, to prepare a mandatory record containing the documents specified in the paragraph.

In 1986, paragraph (a) was amended to require the immediate preparation of a mandatory record on appeal, in all cases, upon the filing of the notice of appeal, without the need for any designation by the parties. The amendment expanded the portions of the circuit court record which must be included in the record on appeal and allows the parties to designate additional portions to be included.

Subsection (9) of paragraph (a) requires that the record on appeal in all cases where a sentence of death is imposed include a transcript of all proceedings regarding the selection of the jury. This subsection also requires the court reporters in other cases to take notes of the jury-selection proceedings, but the transcription of such notes is required only when requested by a party. The "proceedings regarding the selection of the jury" include the procedures set forth by the circuit court for the selection of the jury and for the exercise of peremptory challenges, the questions asked of prospective jurors, the responses thereto, questions refused by the court, along with objections, argument and rulings thereon.

Subsection (10) of paragraph (a) requires that all exhibits offered at trial and sentencing be included in the record on appeal. An exception to this requirement was added for exhibits, other than photographs, which are large, bulky or otherwise do not fit easily in the record on appeal. Examples of such exhibits include weapons, clothing, narcotics, charts and models. The court, however, should order such exhibits to be included in the record on appeal when they are relevant to the determination of an issue on appeal or needed for an understanding of the case. Photographs offered as exhibits are to be included in the record on appeal.

Paragraph (a), as amended in 1986, allows the filing of a supplemental record on appeal containing photographs of exhibits. The use of the photographs in lieu of the exhibits themselves should be permitted when the exhibits are large, bulky or otherwise do not fit easily in the record on appeal and the photographs of the exhibits are sufficient for the determination of the issues on appeal and for an understanding of the case.

Photographs of oversized photographic exhibits are permitted under this rule.

Paragraph (d)

Paragraph (d), as amended in 1979, applies to criminal cases the same time limitations on extensions of time to file the report of proceedings in the trial court and to file the record on appeal in the reviewing court imposed in civil cases by Rules 323(e) and 326.

The 1981 amendment places the sole authority for granting extensions of time under paragraph (d) in the reviewing court. (The trial judges remain vested with the authority to grant extensions in a narrow class of cases pursuant to Rule 608(c).)

The provision permitting a grant of an extension of time to file the report of proceedings or the record on appeal within 6 months after the entry of the judgment, added in 1969, was deleted by the 1979 amendments.

Committee Comments
(September 22, 1997)

This rule is amended to provide for the preparation and filing of a duplicate record in a case in which a death sentence is imposed so that the parties may use the duplicate in any collateral proceedings. The availability of a certified, duplicate record will be advantageous in situations in which post-conviction proceedings must be commenced in the trial court within the time prescribed by the Post–Conviction Hearing Act (725 ILCS 5/122–1 (West 1996)) or other papers must be filed in those proceedings and the direct appeal still is pending in the Supreme Court, rendering the record unavailable.

Photographic exhibits need not be duplicated for purposes of this amendment.

Paragraph (c) also is amended to eliminate the shorter record-filing time for capital cases, consistent with practice.

Rule 609. Stays

(a) Imprisonment or Confinement. If an appeal is taken from a judgment following which the defendant is sentenced to imprisonment or periodic imprisonment, or to probation or conditional discharge conditioned upon periodic imprisonment, or from an order revoking or modifying the conditions attached to a sentence of probation or conditional discharge and imposing a sentence of imprisonment or periodic imprisonment, the defendant may be admitted to bail and the sentence or condition of imprisonment or periodic imprisonment stayed, with or without bond, by a judge of the trial or reviewing court. Upon motion showing good cause the reviewing court or a judge thereof may revoke the order of the trial court or order that the amount of bail be increased or decreased.

(b) Other Cases. On appeals in other cases the judgment or order may be stayed by a judge of the trial or reviewing court, with or without bond. Upon motion showing good cause the reviewing court or a judge thereof may revoke the order of the trial court or order that the amount of bail be increased or decreased.

Amended October 21, 1969, effective January 1, 1970; June 28, 1974, effective September 1, 1974; Feb. 6, 2013, eff. immediately.

Formerly Ill.Rev.Stat.1991, ch. 110A, ¶ 609.

Committee Comments

(Revised September 1, 1974)

This rule is former Rule 27(16) with language changes for clarification. Rule 27(16) was derived from section 121–6 of the code. In 1974, paragraph (b) of the rule was amended to conform its language to that used in the Unified Code of Corrections, enacted effective January 1, 1973, as paragraphs 1001–1–1 through 1008–6–1 of chapter 38 of the Illinois Revised Statutes, setting forth the types of sentences available to the trial court in criminal proceedings and making provision for the modification of sentences imposed upon conditions. The 1974 amendment to the rule also permits stay of a sentence or condition of imprisonment "with or without bond."

Rule 610. Motions

Motions in reviewing courts shall be governed by Rule 361, except that in addition to the requirements set forth in Rule 361 every motion for extension of time in a criminal case shall be supported by an affidavit showing the following:

(1) the date on which counsel was engaged or appointed to prosecute the appeal;

(2) the date on which the complete record was filed in the reviewing court;

(3) the reason for the present request for an extension.

However, when a motion is filed *pro se* from a correctional institution, the movant may submit, in lieu of the affidavit referred to herein, a certification as provided in section 1–109 of the Code of Civil Procedure (735 ILCS ⁵⁄₀1–109).

The purpose of this rule is the achievement of prompt preparation and disposition of criminal cases in the reviewing courts, and motions for extension of time are looked upon with disfavor.

Amended Sept. 29, 1978, eff. Nov. 1, 1978; Dec. 11, 2014, eff. immediately.

Formerly Ill.Rev.Stat.1991, ch. 110A, ¶ 610.

Committee Comments

(Revised Sept. 29, 1978)

This rule is an amalgam of former Rules 49 and 49–1, and is applicable to criminal cases in both the Supreme Court and the Appellate Court.

Prior to amendment in 1978, paragraph (3) provided that a motion for extension of time should include the number of extensions previously obtained from the reviewing court and the reason for each such extension. In 1978, this requirement was made applicable to civil cases by the addition of Rule 361(g), and accordingly paragraph (3) was rescinded and paragraph (4) became paragraph (3). Since motions in criminal cases are generally governed by Rule 361, this makes no change in the practice in criminal appeals.

Rule 611. Oral Argument

(a) Sequence and Manner of Calling. The sequence and manner of calling cases for oral argument is governed by Rule 351 and priority shall be given to appeals in criminal cases over appeals in civil cases.

(b) Other Matters. In other respects oral argument is governed by Rule 352.

Amended Feb. 6, 2013, eff. immediately.

Formerly Ill.Rev.Stat.1991, ch. 110A, ¶ 611.

Committee Comments

This is former Rule 27(15) with language changes for clarification.

Rule 27(15) was derived in part from section 121–12(c) of the Code of Criminal Procedure of 1963.

Rule 612. Procedural Matters Which Are Governed by Civil Appeals Rules

Text of rule effective until July 1, 2016. See, also, rule effective July 1, 2016.

The following civil appeals rules apply to criminal appeals insofar as appropriate:

(a) Dismissal of appeals by the trial court: Rule 309.

(b) Appeals to the Supreme Court: Rules 302(b), 302(c), 315, 316, 317, and 318.

(c) Procedure if no verbatim transcript is available and procedure for an agreed statement of facts: Rules 323(c) and (d).

(d) Preparation and certification of record on appeal by clerk: Rule 324.

(e) Transmission of record on appeal or certificate in lieu of record: Rule 325. (If the defendant is represented by court-appointed counsel, no fees need be paid to the clerk of the trial court.)

(f) Notice of filing: Rule 327.

(g) Amendment of the record on appeal: Rule 329.

(h) Return of record on appeal: Rule 331.

(i) Contents, form, length, number of copies, *etc.,* of briefs: Rule 341.

(j) Abstract: Rule 342.

(k) Times for filing and serving briefs: Rule 343.

(*l*) Briefs *amicus curiae*: Rule 345.

(m) Inspection of original exhibits: Rule 363.

(n) Appeal to wrong court: Rule 365.

(o) Rehearing in reviewing courts: Rule 367.

(p) Issuance, stay, and recall of mandates from reviewing court: Rule 368.

(q) Process in reviewing courts: Rule 370.

(r) Removing records from the reviewing court: Rule 372.

(s) Constructive date of filing papers in reviewing court: Rule 373.

Amended October 21, 1969, effective January 1, 1970; effective January 1, 1970, and July 1, 1971; July 30, 1979, effective October 15, 1979; September 22, 1997, effective January 1, 1998; May 24, 2006, effective September 1, 2006; July 27, 2006, effective September 1, 2006; Feb. 6, 2013, eff. immediately.

Formerly Ill.Rev.Stat.1991, ch. 110A, ¶ 612.

Committee Comments
(Revised 1979)

This rule was new in 1967. It cross-refers to all of the civil appeals rules that are applicable to criminal appeals.

The references to an agreed statement of facts, as provided in Rule 323(d), and to constructive date of filing papers in the reviewing court, as provided in Rule 373, were added in 1969. The reference to Rule 302(b), which deals with bypassing the Appellate Court in appeals in cases in which the public interest requires expeditious determinations, was added in 1971.

In 1979, former paragraph (g), referring to the short record provided by repealed Rule 328, was deleted, and the successive paragraphs relettered.

Newly lettered paragraphs (j), (k), and (*l*) were amended to reflect changes in Rules 342, 343, and 344. See the committee comments to those rules.

Rule 612. Procedural Matters Which Are Governed by Civil Appeals Rules

Text of rule effective July 1, 2016. See, also, rule effective until July 1, 2016.

The following civil appeals rules apply to criminal appeals insofar as appropriate:

(a) Dismissal of appeals by the trial court: Rule 309.

(b) Appeals to the Supreme Court: Rules 302(b), 302(c), 315, 316, 317, and 318.

(c) Procedure if no verbatim transcript is available and procedure for an agreed statement of facts: Rules 323(c) and (d).

(d) Preparation and certification of record on appeal by clerk: Rule 324.

(e) Transmission of record on appeal or certificate in lieu of record: Rule 325. (If the defendant is represented by court-appointed counsel, no fees need be paid to the clerk of the trial court.)

(f) Notice of filing: Rule 327.

(g) Amendment of the record on appeal: Rule 329.

(h) Return of record on appeal: Rule 331.

(i) Contents, form, length, number of copies, *etc.,* of briefs: Rule 341.

(j) Abstract: Rule 342.

(k) Times for filing and serving briefs: Rule 343.

(*l*) Briefs *amicus curiae*: Rule 345.

(m) Inspection of original exhibits: Rule 363.

(n) Appeal to wrong court: Rule 365.

(o) Rehearing in reviewing courts: Rule 367.

(p) Issuance, stay, and recall of mandates from reviewing court: Rule 368.

(q) Process in reviewing courts: Rule 370.

(r) Removing records from the reviewing court: Rule 372.

(s) Constructive date of filing papers in reviewing court: Rule 373.

(t) Redaction of personal identifiers for documents filed in courts of review: Rule 364.

Amended October 21, 1969, effective January 1, 1970; effective January 1, 1970, and July 1, 1971; July 30, 1979, effective October 15, 1979; September 22, 1997, effective January 1, 1998; May 24, 2006, effective September 1, 2006; July 27, 2006, effective September 1, 2006; Feb. 6, 2013, eff. immediately; Dec. 3, 2015, eff. July 1, 2016.

Formerly Ill.Rev.Stat.1991, ch. 110A, ¶ 612.

Committee Comments
(Revised 1979)

This rule was new in 1967. It cross-refers to all of the civil appeals rules that are applicable to criminal appeals.

The references to an agreed statement of facts, as provided in Rule 323(d), and to constructive date of filing papers in the reviewing court, as provided in Rule 373, were added in 1969. The reference to Rule 302(b), which deals with bypassing the Appellate Court in appeals in cases in which the public interest requires expeditious determinations, was added in 1971.

In 1979, former paragraph (g), referring to the short record provided by repealed Rule 328, was deleted, and the successive paragraphs relettered. Newly lettered paragraphs (j), (k), and (*l*) were amended to reflect changes in Rules 342, 343, and 344. See the committee comments to those rules.

Rule 613. Mandate of Reviewing Court

(a) In all cases the reviewing court shall direct the appellate or trial court to proceed in accordance with the mandate.

(b) Reversal When Appellant Is Serving Sentence. If in a case on appeal the appellant is serving the sentence imposed in the trial court and the judgment is reversed and appellant ordered discharged, the clerk of the reviewing court shall at once mail to the imprisoning officer, certified mail, return receipt requested, a copy of the mandate of the reviewing court. It shall be the duty of the imprisoning officer to release appellant from custody forthwith upon receiving a certified copy of the mandate of the reviewing court. If appellant is serving the sentence and the judgment is reversed and the cause remanded to the trial court for further proceedings, the clerk of the reviewing court shall at once mail to the imprisoning officer, certified mail, return receipt requested, a copy of the mandate of the reviewing court. The imprisoning officer shall forthwith, upon receiving the certified copy of the mandate of the reviewing court, return appellant to the trial court to which the cause was remanded.

(c) Credit for Time Served Pending Appeal. In any case in which, pending appeal, an appellant serves any portion of the sentence imposed in the trial court and the judgment of the trial court is reversed by a reviewing court and a new trial ordered, the appellant shall be given credit in any subsequent sentence for the time served pending appeal.

Amended June 26, 1987, effective August 1, 1987; September 22, 1997, effective immediately; Feb. 6, 2013, eff. immediately.

Formerly Ill.Rev.Stat.1991, ch. 110A, ¶ 613.

Committee Comments

This is section 121–14 of the Code of Criminal Procedure of 1963, with some language changes for clarification. Although it was not part of former Rule 27, the Committee recommended that it be made part of the Supreme Court Rules in keeping with the effort to place all provisions concerning appellate practice in a single body of rules.

Rule 614. Notifying Prisoner of Affirmance by Appellate Court

When a judgment of conviction of a person incarcerated in a penal institution is affirmed by the Appellate Court, the clerk of that court shall at once mail to the prisoner a copy of the opinion of the court, certified mail, return receipt requested, in an envelope marked, "OFFICIAL LEGAL MAIL–ADDRESSEE MUST ACKNOWLEDGE RECEIPT IN WRITING." The clerk shall note the date of mailing upon the records of the court.

Amended June 26, 1987, eff. Aug. 1, 1987.

Formerly Ill.Rev.Stat.1991, ch. 110A, ¶ 614.

Committee Comments

This is taken from former Rule 27(13), which was adopted by the Supreme Court on January 25, 1966 because of a number of cases in which defendants represented by appointed counsel had not learned of the affirmance of their cases until after the time for filing a petition to the Supreme Court for leave to appeal had expired.

Rule 615. The Cause on Appeal

(a) Insubstantial and Substantial Errors on Appeal. Any error, defect, irregularity, or variance which does not affect substantial rights shall be disregarded. Plain errors or defects affecting substantial rights may be noticed although they were not brought to the attention of the trial court.

(b) Powers of the Reviewing Court. On appeal the reviewing court may:

(1) reverse, affirm, or modify the judgment or order from which the appeal is taken;

(2) set aside, affirm, or modify any or all of the proceedings subsequent to or dependent upon the judgment or order from which the appeal is taken;

(3) reduce the degree of the offense of which the appellant was convicted;

(4) reduce the punishment imposed by the trial court; or

(5) order a new trial.

Formerly Ill.Rev.Stat.1991, ch. 110A, ¶ 615.

Committee Comments

This is section 121–9 of the Code of Criminal Procedure of 1963 without change in substance.

Rules 616 to 650. Reserved

Rule 651. Appeals in Post–Conviction Proceedings

(a) Right of Appeal. An appeal from a final judgment of the circuit court in any post-conviction proceeding shall lie to the Appellate Court in the district in which the circuit court is located.

(b) Notice to Petitioner of Adverse Judgment. Upon the entry of a judgment adverse to a petitioner in a post-conviction proceeding, the clerk of the trial court shall at once mail or deliver to the petitioner a notice in substantially the following form:

"You are hereby notified that on _____ the court entered an order, a copy of which is enclosed herewith. You have a right to appeal to the Illinois Appellate Court in the district in which the circuit court is located. If you are indigent, you have a right to a transcript of the record of the post-conviction proceedings and to the appointment of counsel on appeal, both without cost to you. To preserve your right to appeal you must file a notice of appeal in the trial court within 30 days from the date the order was entered."

(c) Record for Indigents; Appointment of Counsel. Upon the timely filing of a notice of appeal in a post-conviction proceeding, if the trial court determines that the petitioner is indigent, it shall order that a transcript of the record of the post-conviction proceedings, including a transcript of the evidence, if any, be prepared and filed with the clerk of the court to which the appeal is taken and shall appoint counsel on appeal, both without cost to the petitioner. The record filed in that court shall contain a showing, which may be made by the certificate of petitioner's attorney, that the attorney has consulted with petitioner by phone, mail, electronic means or in person to ascertain his or her contentions of deprivation of constitutional rights, has examined the record of the proceedings at the trial, and has made any amendments to the petitions filed *pro se* that are necessary for an adequate presentation of petitioner's contentions.

(d) Procedure. The procedure for an appeal in a post-conviction proceeding shall be in accordance with the rules governing criminal appeals, as near as may be.

Amended effective January 1, 1969; October 21, 1969, effective January 1, 1970; effective July 1, 1971; November 30, 1984, effective December 1, 1984; April 26, 2012, eff. immediately; Feb. 6, 2013, eff. immediately.

Formerly Ill.Rev.Stat.1991, ch. 110A, ¶ 651.

Committee Comments
(Revised November 30, 1984)

This rule was drawn from former Rule 27–1, in effect from January 1, 1964, to January 1,1967. Paragraph (a) was added.

Paragraphs (b) and (c) were amended effective January 1, 1969, by adding the references to appointment of counsel on appeal. Minor language changes were also made at that time.

The last sentence of Rule 651(c) was added in 1969 to implement the decisions of the court with respect to the responsibilities of an attorney representing an indigent prisoner in a post-conviction

proceeding. *People v. Garrison* (1969), 43 Ill.2d 121; *People v. Jones* (1969), 43 Ill.2d 160; *People v. Slaughter* (1968), 39 Ill.2d 278, 285.

In 1971 Rule 651 was amended to provide that appeals in post-conviction proceedings lie to the Appellate Court. Prior to that time, the appeal lay directly to the Supreme Court.

Paragraphs (a), (b), and (c) were amended in 1984 by providing that appeals from post-conviction proceedings involving a judgment imposing a sentence of death shall lie directly to the Supreme Court as a matter of right.

Rules 652 to 659. Reserved

Rule 660. Appeals in Cases Arising Under the Juvenile Court Act

(a) Delinquent Minors. Appeals from final judgments in delinquent minor proceedings, except as otherwise specifically provided, shall be governed by the rules applicable to criminal cases.

(b) Other Proceedings. In all other proceedings under the Juvenile Court Act, appeals from final judgments shall be governed by the rules applicable to civil cases.

(c) All Proceedings. In all appeals filed from proceedings under the Juvenile Court Act, the minor(s) shall be identified by first name and last initial or by initials only. The preferred method is first name and last initial. The alternative method of initials only is to be used when, due to an unusual first name or spelling, the preferred method would create a substantial risk of revealing a minor's identity. The name(s) of the involved minor(s) shall not appear on any documents filed with the Appellate Court or any subsequent court.

Adopted Sept. 8, 1975, eff. Oct. 1, 1975. Amended July 1, 1985, eff. Aug. 1, 1985; October 1, 2001, eff. immediately.

Formerly Ill.Rev.Stat.1991, ch. 110A, ¶ 660.

Committee Comments

Rule 660 was added in 1975 to clarify the procedure in appeals from determinations under the Juvenile Court Act. It provides simply that appeals from determinations in delinquency proceedings are governed by the rules applicable to appeals in criminal cases, and all other appeals under the Act are governed by the rules governing appeals in civil cases.

Paragraph (b) was amended in 1985 to delete references to "minors in need of supervision," "neglected minors" and "dependent minors," because of various additions, deletions and changes in the labels which are now applied to minors who may be adjudicated wards in proceedings before the circuit court.

Paragraph (c) was added effective October 1, 2001, to help protect the identities of minors. The amendment requires that their first name and last initial, or their initials only, appear on documents filed with the Appellate Court or any subsequent court. The requirement covers the parties' briefs, motions, and other similar papers. The amendment does not require deletion of names from the trial court record in preparing the record on appeal, nor does it address the means by which the Appellate Court or a subsequent court maintains the confidentiality of documents appearing in the record.

Rule 660A. Expedited Appeals in Delinquent Minor Cases

The expedited procedures in this rule shall apply to appeals from final judgments in delinquent minor proceedings arising under the Juvenile Court Act.

(a) *Special Caption; Service of Notice of Appeal on Trial Judge.* The notice of appeal or petition for leave to appeal, docketing statement, briefs and all other notices, motions and pleadings filed by any party in relation to an appeal involving a delinquent minor case under the Juvenile Court Act shall include the following statement in bold type on the top of the front page: THIS APPEAL INVOLVES A DELINQUENT MINOR PROCEEDING UNDER THE JUVENILE COURT ACT. When the notice of appeal is filed pursuant to the provisions of Rule 606(b), it shall also be served on the trial judge.

(b) *Status Hearing in Circuit Court.* Upon receipt of the notice of appeal in a delinquent minor case arising under the Juvenile Court Act, the trial judge shall take any and all action necessary to expedite preparation of the record on appeal. The trial court shall have continuing jurisdiction for the purpose of enforcing the rules for preparation of the record. The trial court may request the assistance of the chief judge to resolve filing delays, and the chief judge shall assign or reassign the court reporting personnel's work as necessary to ensure compliance with the filing deadlines.

(c) *Record.* The record on appeal shall be filed no later than 35 days after the filing of the notice of appeal or granting of leave to appeal. Any request for extension of the time for filing shall be accompanied by an affidavit of the court clerk or court reporting personnel stating the reason for the delay, and shall be served on the trial judge and the chief judge of the circuit. Lack of advance payment shall not be a reason for noncompliance with filing deadlines for the record or transcript. Any subsequent request for an extension of time shall be made to the appellate court by written notice and motion to all parties in accordance with rules.

(d) *Time for Filing of Briefs in the Appellate Court.* Unless otherwise ordered by the appellate court, the brief of the appellant shall be filed in the reviewing court within 28 days from the filing of the record on appeal. Within 28 days from the due date of the appellant's brief, the appellee shall file a brief in the reviewing court. Within 7 days from the due date

of the appellee's brief, the appellant may file a reply brief in the reviewing court.

(e) *Oral Argument.* If oral argument is requested by a party, a reviewing court shall, no later than seven days from the due date of appellant's reply brief, determine whether the case should be called for oral argument.

(f) *Deadline for Decision.* Except for good cause shown, the appellate court shall file its decision within 150 days after the filing of the notice of appeal.

(g) *Extensions of Time Disfavored.* Requests for extensions of time are disfavored and shall be granted only for compelling circumstances.

(h) *Effective Date.* This rule shall apply to all orders in which a notice of appeal is filed after its effective date.

Adopted March 15, 2013, eff. May 1, 2013. Amended May 23, 2013, eff. July 1, 2013.

Rule 661. Appeals as Poor Persons by Minors Found to be Delinquent

Upon the filing of a notice of appeal in any proceeding in which a minor has been found to be delinquent, or in which probation or conditional discharge imposed in such a proceeding has been revoked, appointment of counsel and the provision of a transcript of the adjudicatory and dispositional hearings without cost to the minor shall be governed by Rule 607.

Adopted eff. May 29, 1968. Amended Sept. 8, 1975, eff. Oct. 1, 1975.

Formerly Ill.Rev.Stat.1991, ch. 110A, ¶ 661.

Committee Comments
(October 1, 1975)

Prior to 1975, Rule 661 set forth the procedure for obtaining counsel and a free transcript of the proceedings below in cases in which an appeal is taken from a delinquency proceeding in the Juvenile Court. This procedure was the same as that provided in Rule 607 in the case of appeals from judgments in criminal cases. In 1975, Rule 660 was added, making the rules dealing with appeals in criminal cases generally applicable to delinquency proceedings. It was thus unnecessary to repeat the substance of Rule 607 in Rule 661. Because Rule 607, by its terms, applies only to appeals from certain types of criminal cases, it was necessary to retain Rule 661 to make it plain that Rule 607 applies.

Rule 662. Adjudication of Wardship and Revocation of Probation or Conditional Discharge

(a) Adjudication of Wardship. An appeal may be taken to the Appellate Court from an adjudication of wardship in the event that an order of disposition has not been entered within 90 days of the adjudication of wardship.

(b) Revocation of Probation or Conditional Discharge. An appeal may be taken to the Appellate Court from an order revoking probation or conditional discharge in the event that an order of disposition has not been entered within 90 days from the revocation of probation or conditional discharge.

(c) Procedure. The notice of appeal in appeals under this rule shall be filed within 30 days after the expiration of the 90 days specified in this rule and not thereafter.

Added Sept. 8, 1975, eff. Oct. 1, 1975.

Formerly Ill.Rev.Stat.1991, ch. 110A, ¶ 662.

Committee Comments
(October 1, 1975)

In juvenile court proceedings, there is a two step procedure. First a hearing is held to adjudicate the subject juvenile a ward of the court; then there is a separate hearing resulting in a disposition. If the dispositional hearing and order follow closely the adjudicatory hearing and order, judicial efficiency dictates that an appeal should be taken after disposition. If there is a long delay in disposing of the case, however, Rule 662 provides that an appeal may be taken from the first order. The period set is 90 days to account for normal delay caused by administrative problems. After that period, if the dispositional hearing has not been held, the juvenile may appeal. In such a case he must file his notice of appeal within 30 days of the expiration of the period, and not after. Thus the 6 months period for application for leave to appeal provided in Rule 605(c) has no application. For similar reasons, the same provisions are applied to appeals from orders revoking probation or conditional discharge in juvenile cases.

Rule 663. Adoption–Appointment of a Guardian With Power to Consent

(a) An appeal may be taken to the Appellate Court from an order of the court empowering the guardian of the person of a minor to consent to the adoption of such a minor.

(b) The caption on an appeal taken from an order of the court empowering the guardian of the person of a minor to consent to the adoption of such a minor shall not include the name of the minor. Rather, the minor shall be identified by first name and last initial or by initials only. The preferred method is by first name and last initial. The alternative method of initials only is to be used when, due to an unusual first name or spelling, the preferred method would create a substantial risk of revealing the minor's identity.

Adopted Sept. 8, 1975, eff. Oct. 1, 1975. Amended October 1, 2001, eff. immediately.

Formerly Ill.Rev.Stat.1991, ch. 110A, ¶ 663.

Committee Comments

Rule 663, added in 1975, makes an order empowering a guardian of the person of a minor to consent to the minor's adoption appealable. See Rule 307(a)(6).

Paragraph (b) was added effective October 1, 2001, to help protect the identities of minors. The amendment requires that their first name and last initial, or their initials only, appear in the caption.

Rules 664 to 700. Reserved

ARTICLE VII. RULES ON ADMISSION AND DISCIPLINE OF ATTORNEYS

PART A. ADMISSION TO THE BAR

PART B. REGISTRATION AND DISCIPLINE OF ATTORNEYS

PART C. MINIMUM CONTINUING LEGAL EDUCATION

PART D. COMMISSION ON PROFESSIONALISM

PART A. ADMISSION TO THE BAR

Rule 701. General Qualifications

(a) Subject to the requirements contained in these rules, persons may be admitted or conditionally admitted to practice law in this State by the Supreme Court if they are at least 21 years of age, of good moral character and general fitness to practice law, and have satisfactorily completed examinations on academic qualification and professional responsibility as prescribed by the Board of Admissions to the Bar or have been licensed to practice law in another jurisdiction and have met the requirements of Rule 705.

(b) Any person so admitted to practice law in this State is privileged to practice in every court in Illinois. No court shall by rule or by practice abridge or deny this privilege by requiring the retaining of local counsel or the maintaining of a local office for the service of notices.

Amended effective October 2, 1972; April 8, 1980, effective May 15, 1980; June 12, 1992, effective July 1, 1992; March 1, 2001. The amendment to paragraph (b) shall be effective one year after its adoption, and shall apply in capital cases filed by information or indictment on or after its effective date; amended October 2, 2006, effective July 1, 2007; Feb. 6, 2013, eff. immediately.

Formerly Ill.Rev.Stat.1991, ch. 110A, ¶ 701.

Committee Comments

Special Supreme Court Committee on Capital Cases
(March 1, 2001)

The requirement that all defense counsel and assistant prosecutors appearing as lead or co-counsel in capital cases must be members of the Capital Litigation Trial Bar was adopted to improve the fairness and reliability of capital trials. The minimum qualifications for membership in the Capital Litigation Trial Bar are intended to insure that capital cases are tried by experienced, well-trained attorneys. See Rule 714. The amendment to Rule 701(b) provides the means for enforcement of the qualification standards by prohibiting an attorney who is not a member of the Capital Litigation Trial Bar from appearing as lead or co-counsel in a capital case. See also Rule 416(d). The Capital Litigation Trial Bar membership requirement does not apply to the elected or appointed State's Attorney of the county of venue or the Attorney General. In addition, Rule 701(b) does not prohibit nonmembers from participating in a capital trial in the capacity of "third chair," provided such participation by a third attorney for the prosecution or defense is under the direct supervision of qualified lead or co-counsel.

For the purposes of Rule 701(b), the definition of a "capital" case is supplied by paragraphs (c) and (d) of Rule 416. Rule 416(c) provides that the State must give notice of its intent to seek or decline to seek the death penalty as soon as practicable, and in no event later than 120 days after arraignment, unless the court directs otherwise. Rule 416(d) provides that if the State provides notice of intent to seek the death penalty or fails to provide any notice in the time allowed by Rule 416(c), the trial court must confirm that attorneys appearing in the case are properly certified members of the Capital Litigation Trial Bar. Thus, the Capital Litigation Trial Bar membership requirement of Rule 701(b) is effective upon notification that the State will seek the death penalty or expiration of the time allowed for notice under Rule 416(c) without any notice from the State, whichever occurs first.

Though the trial court will not enforce the counsel qualification standards of this rule and Rule 714 until the State provides notice of intent to seek the death penalty or the time for notice expires, in any case where the defendant may be eligible for the death penalty, defense counsel must presume the case will be capital unless the State has provided notice to the contrary. Attorneys who are not members of the Capital Litigation Trial Bar should not agree to provide representation for a defendant in a potentially capital case (*i.e.*, a case in which the defendant may be eligible for the death penalty, where the time for State notice has not expired and the State has not provided any notice with respect to its intent to seek or decline to seek the death penalty). Attorneys should also decline to provide representation as sole counsel for a defendant in a potentially capital case, unless they are properly certified as lead counsel. See Rule 714. An attorney who is not properly certified under Rule 714 should never agree to provide representation for a defendant in a potentially capital case on the assumption that the State will not seek the death penalty, or that admission to the Capital Litigation Trial Bar or proper certification will be obtained after accepting the engagement.

When considering representation of a defendant charged with first degree murder, an attorney who is not a member of the Capital Litigation Trial Bar (or does not have proper certification) should immediately determine whether the defendant may be subject to the death penalty. The attorney should ascertain, for example, whether the defendant has been denied bail because the offense is capital, or whether the charges filed or information available through reasonable investigation suggest that one of the statutory aggravating factors of section 9–1(b) of the Criminal Code of 1961 (720 ILCS 5/9–1(b)) may apply. If any information available to the attorney suggests the case is potentially capital, the attorney should decline to provide representation for the defendant. An agreement to provide limited representation in a potentially capital case should be entered into only after careful consideration of the complex practical, legal, and ethical issues involved, and full disclosure of the attorney's inability to provide representation in a capital case.

Adherence to the principles described above with respect to defense counsel in a potentially capital case will ensure fairness to the defendant, compliance with ethical responsibilities, and the proper administration of justice. Consistent with these principles, an attorney appointed for an indigent defendant in a potentially capital case should be a member of the Capital Litigation Trial Bar, certified as lead counsel. In addition, State's Attorneys are encouraged to assign assistant prosecutors who are members of the Capital Litigation Trial Bar in all potentially capital cases.

Rule 702. Board of Admissions to the Bar

(a) The Board of Admissions to the Bar shall oversee the administration of all aspects of bar admissions in this State including the character and fitness process. The board shall consist of seven members of the bar, appointed by the Supreme Court to serve staggered terms of three years. In addition, the Supreme Court shall appoint a dean of a law school located in Illinois as a non-voting *ex-officio* member of the board to serve a term of three years. Each member shall

serve until his or her successor is duly appointed and qualified. No member may be appointed to more than three full consecutive terms.

(b) A majority of the board shall constitute a quorum. A president and vice-president shall be designated by the Supreme Court and may serve only one three-year term. A secretary and treasurer shall be annually elected by the members of the board. One member may hold the office of both secretary and treasurer.

(c) The board shall audit annually the accounts of its treasurer and shall report to the court at each November term a detailed statement of its finances, together with such recommendations as shall seem advisable. All fees paid to the board in excess of its expenses shall be applied as the court may from time to time direct.

Amended June 12, 1992, eff. July 1, 1992; Dec. 30, 1993, eff. Jan. 1, 1994; Dec. 5, 2012, eff. Jan. 1, 2013; March 23, 2015, eff. July 1, 2015.

Formerly Ill.Rev.Stat.1991, ch. 110A, ¶ 702.

Rule 703. Educational Requirements

Every applicant seeking admission to the bar on examination shall meet the following educational requirements:

(a) **Preliminary and College Work.** Each applicant shall have graduated from a four-year high school or other preparatory school whose graduates are admitted on diploma to the freshman class of any college or university having admission requirements equivalent to those of the University of Illinois, or shall have become otherwise eligible for admission to such freshman class; and shall have satisfactorily completed at least 90 semester hours of acceptable college work, while in actual attendance at one or more colleges or universities approved by the Board of Admissions to the Bar. In lieu of such preliminary or college work, the board may, after due investigation, accept the satisfactory completion of the program or curriculum of a particular college or university. Proof of preliminary education may be made either by diploma showing graduation or by certificate that the applicant has become eligible for admission to such college or university, signed by the registrar thereof. Proof of the satisfactory completion of college work may be made by certificate, signed by the registrar of the college or university, that the applicant has satisfactorily completed the required college work. In lieu of the diploma and certificates described herein, the board may accept, as proof of the preliminary and college work required herein, a certificate from an approved law school that the law school has on file proof of such preliminary and college work.

(b) **Legal Education.** After the completion of both the preliminary and college work above set forth in paragraph (a) of this rule, each applicant shall have pursued a course of law studies and fulfilled the requirements for and received a first degree in law from a law school approved by the American Bar Association. Each applicant shall make proof that he has completed such law study and received a degree, in such manner as the Board of Admissions to the Bar shall require.

JUSTICE HEIPLE, dissenting [June 12, 1992 amendment]:

By the amendment to Rule 711 and by Rule 703, which was previously adopted, this court recognizes only law schools which have been approved by the American Bar Association. I both dissent and object to these rules because they represent an improper delegation of a governmental and judicial function to a trade association of lawyers.

The American Bar Association is a voluntary association of dues paying lawyers (currently $225 per annum) that exists for the benefit of its members. No lawyer is required to belong. Most do not. It clothes its parochial existence with an overlay of public activities and pronouncements designed to convince the general public that it is interested in the general welfare. That its primary focus is the benefit of its members, however, is beyond question. That the American Bar association is a trade association warrants neither commendation nor condemnation. As a trade association engaging in improving the status of lawyers and lobbying Congress and the State legislatures, it is on a par with any other trade association. It is decidedly not, however, an arm of the State of Illinois nor of this court.

It is improper for this court to assign and delegate to that organization the ultimate decisionmaking function of deciding for the State of Illinois which law schools warrant official recognition. It would be proper, of course, for this court and its Board of Law Examiners (now, Board of Admissions to the Bar) to consider and weigh the evaluations of the American Bar Association in considering which law schools are to be approved. The work of the American Bar Association in evaluating law schools could be considered as relevant evidence in that regard. No objection could be raised to that procedure.

This court, however, has no right to delegate its decisionmaking function to the American Bar Association, the Teamsters Union, the Republic of Uganda or any other such body or group. If the rule asserts a valid principle of law, then this court could as well assign all of its decisionmaking functions to others who might be considered experts in their field.

For the reasons given, I respectfully dissent.

Amended Sept. 28, 1977, eff. Oct. 15, 1977; Sept. 14, 1984; amended June 12, 1992, eff. July 1, 1992.

Formerly Ill.Rev.Stat.1991, ch. 110A, ¶ 703.

Rule 704. Qualification on Examination

(a) Every applicant for the Illinois bar examination shall file with the Board of Admissions to the Bar both a character and fitness registration application and a separate application to take the bar examination. The applications shall be in such form as the board shall prescribe and shall be subject to the fees and filing deadlines set forth in Rule 706.

(b) In the event the character and fitness registration application and the separate application to take the bar examination shall be satisfactory to the board, the applicant shall be admitted to the examination; provided, however, that the following applicants must first receive certification of good moral character and general fitness to practice law by the Committee on Character and Fitness pursuant to Rule 708 before they will be permitted to write the bar examination: (1) applicants who have been convicted of felonies; (2) applicants against whom are pending indictments, criminal informations, or criminal complaints charging felonies; (3) applicants who have been rejected, or as to whom hearings are pending, in another jurisdiction on a ground related to character and fitness; or (4) applicants admitted to practice in another jurisdiction who have been reprimanded, censured, disciplined, suspended or disbarred in such other jurisdiction or against whom are pending disciplinary charges or proceedings in that jurisdiction.

(c) The Board of Admissions to the Bar shall conduct separate examinations on academic qualification and professional responsibility. At least two academic qualification examinations shall be conducted annually, one in February and the other in July, or at such other times as the board, in its discretion, may determine. At least three professional responsibility examinations shall be conducted annually, one in March, another in August, and another in November, or at such other times as the board, in its discretion, may determine. The board may designate the Multistate Professional Responsibility Examination of the National Conference of Bar Examiners as the Illinois professional responsibility examination. The board may determine the score that constitutes a passing grade.

(d) The academic qualification examination shall be conducted under the supervision of the board, by uniform printed questions, and may be upon the following subjects: administrative law; agency and partnership; business organizations, including corporations and limited liability companies; commercial paper; conflict of laws; contracts; criminal law and procedure; family law; equity jurisprudence; evidence; federal and state constitutional law; federal jurisdiction and procedure; federal taxation; Illinois procedure; personal property, including sales and bailments; real property; secured transactions; suretyship; torts; trusts and future interests; and wills and decedents' estates. The academic qualification examination may also include a performance test.

The Board may include the Multistate Bar Examination, the Multistate Essay Examination and the Multistate Performance Test of the National Conference of Bar Examiners as components of the examination.

(e) In the event the Board of Admissions to the Bar shall find that an applicant has achieved a passing score, as determined by the board, on the academic and professional responsibility examinations, meets the requirements of these rules, and has received from the Committee on Character and Fitness its certification of good moral character and general fitness to practice law, the board shall certify to the court that these requirements have been met; the Board may also transmit to the Court any additional information or recommendation it deems appropriate.

(f) For all persons taking the bar examination after the effective date of this rule, a passing score on the Illinois bar examination is valid for four years from the last date of the examination. An applicant for admission on examination who is not admitted to practice within four years must repeat and pass the examination after filing the requisite character and fitness registration and bar examination applications and paying the fees therefor in accordance with Rule 706.

Amended eff. Oct. 2, 1972; April 8, 1980, eff. May 15, 1980; eff. June 19, 1987; June 12, 1992, eff. July 1, 1992; May 7, 1993; July 1, 1998; July 6, 2000; Dec. 6, 2001; amended October 2, 2006, eff. July 1, 2007.

Formerly Ill.Rev.Stat.1991, ch. 110A, ¶ 704.

Rule 705. Admission on Motion

Any person who, as determined by the Board of Admissions to the Bar, has been licensed to practice in the highest court of law in any United States state, territory, or the District of Columbia for no fewer than three years may be eligible for admission on motion on the following conditions:

(a) The applicant meets the educational requirements of Rule 703.

(b) The applicant meets Illinois character and fitness requirements and has been certified by the Committee on Character and Fitness.

(c) The applicant licensed to practice law for fewer than 15 years has passed the Multistate Professional Responsibility Examination in Illinois or in any jurisdiction in which it was administered.

(d) The applicant is in good disciplinary standing before the highest court of every jurisdiction in which ever admitted and is at the time of application on active status in at least one such jurisdiction.

(e) The applicant provides documentary evidence satisfactory to the Board that for at least three of the five years immediately preceding the application, he or she was engaged in the active, continuous, and lawful practice of law.

(f) The applicant has paid the fee for admission on motion in accordance with Rule 706.

(g) For purposes of this rule, the term "practice of law" shall mean:

(1) Practice as a sole practitioner or for a law firm, professional corporation, legal services office, legal clinic, or other entity the lawful business of which consists of the practice of law or the provision of legal services;

(2) Employment in a state or local court of record in a United States state, territory, or the District of Columbia as a judge, magistrate, referee or similar official, or as a judicial law clerk;

(3) Employment in a federal court of record in a United States state, territory, or the District of Columbia as a judge, magistrate, referee or similar official, or as a judicial law clerk;

(4) Employment as a lawyer for a corporation, agency, association, trust department, or other similar entity;

(5) Practice as a lawyer for a state or local government;

(6) Practice as a lawyer for the federal government, including legal service in the armed forces of the United States;

(7) Employment as a law professor at a law school approved by the American Bar Association; or

(8) Any combination of the above;

provided in each instance, however, that such employment is available only to licensed attorneys and that the primary duty of the position is to provide legal advice, representation, and/or services.

(h) For purposes of this rule, the term "active and continuous" shall mean the person devoted a minimum of 80 hours per month and no fewer than 1,000 hours per year to the practice of law during 36 of the 60 months immediately preceding the application.

(i) Except as provided in this subsection (i) and subsection (j) that follows, for purposes of this rule, the term "lawful" shall mean the practice was performed physically without Illinois and either physically within a jurisdiction in which the applicant was licensed or physically within a jurisdiction in which a lawyer not admitted to the bar is permitted to engage in such practice. An applicant relying on practice performed in a jurisdiction in which he or she is not admitted to the bar must establish that such practice is permitted by statute, rule, court order, or by written confirmation from the admitting or disciplinary authority of the jurisdiction in which the practice occurred. Practice falling within subparagraph (g)(3) or (g)(6) above shall be considered lawful practice even if performed physically without a jurisdiction in which the applicant is admitted. Practice falling within (g)(7) above shall be considered lawful practice even if performed physically without a jurisdiction in which the applicant is admitted, provided that the professor does not appear in court or supervise student court appearances as part of a clinical course or otherwise;

(j) Practice performed within Illinois pursuant to a Rule 716 license may be deemed lawful and counted toward eligibility for admission on motion, provided all other requirements of Rule 705 are met.

(k) Practice performed without Illinois and within the issuing jurisdiction pursuant to a limited or temporary license may be counted toward eligibility for admission on motion only if the limited or temporary license authorized practice without supervision in the highest court of law in the issuing jurisdiction.

(*l*) A person who has failed an Illinois bar examination administered within the preceding five years is not eligible for admission on motion.

(m) Admission on motion is not a right. The burden is on the applicant to establish to the satisfaction of the Board that he or she meets each of the foregoing requirements.

Adopted April 3, 1989, eff. immediately. Amended October 25, 1989, eff. immediately; June 12, 1992, eff. July 1, 1992; December 6, 2001, eff. immediately; September 30, 2002, eff. immediately; February 6, 2004, eff. immediately; October 1, 2010, eff. January 1, 2011; November 26, 2013, eff. immediately; Oct. 15, 2015, eff. Jan. 1, 2016.

Rule 706. Filing Deadlines and Fees of Registrants and Applicants

(a) Character and Fitness Registration. Character and fitness registration applications filed with applications to take the bar examination shall be accompanied by a registration fee of $450.

(b) Applications to Take the Bar Examination. The fees and deadlines for filing applications to take the February bar examination are as follows:

(1) $500 for applications postmarked on or before the regular filing deadline of September 1 preceding the examination;

(2) $700 for applications postmarked after September 1 but on or before the late filing deadline of November 1; and

(3) $1,000 for applications postmarked after November 1 but on or before the final late filing deadline of December 31.

The fees and deadlines for filing applications to take the July bar examination are as follows:

(1) $500 for applications postmarked on or before the regular filing deadline of February 15 preceding the examination;

(2) $700 for applications postmarked after February 15 but on or before the late filing deadline of April 1; and

(3) $1,000 for applications postmarked after April 1 but on or before the final late filing deadline of May 31.

(c) Applications for Reexamination. The fees and deadlines for filing applications for reexamination at a February bar examination are as follows:

(1) $500 for applications postmarked on or before the regular reexamination filing deadline of November 1;

(2) $850 for applications postmarked after November 1 but on or before the final late filing deadline of December 31.

The fees and deadlines for filing applications for reexamination at a July bar examination are as follows:

(1) $500 for applications postmarked on or before the regular reexamination filing deadline of May 1;

(2) $850 for applications postmarked after May 1 but on or before the final late filing deadline of May 31.

(d) Late Applications. The Board of Admissions shall not consider requests for late filing of applications after the final bar examination filing deadlines set forth in the preceding subparagraphs (b) and (c).

(e) Applications for Admission on Motion under Rule 705. Each applicant for admission to the bar on motion under Rule 705 shall pay a fee of $1,250.

(f) Application for Limited Admission as House Counsel. Each applicant for limited admission to the bar as house counsel under Rule 716 shall pay a fee of $1,250.

(g) Application for Limited Admission as a Lawyer for Legal Service Programs. Each applicant for limited admission to the bar as a lawyer for legal service programs under Rule 717 shall pay a fee of $100.

(h) Recertification Fee. Each applicant for Character and Fitness recertification shall pay a fee of $450.

(i) Payment of Fees. All fees are nonrefundable and shall be paid in advance by certified check, cashier's check or money order payable to the Board of Admissions to the Bar. Fees of an applicant who does not appear for an examination shall not be transferred to a succeeding examination.

(j) Fees to be Held by Treasurer. All fees paid to the treasurer of the Board of Admissions to the Bar shall be held by him or her subject to the order of the court.

Amended Jan. 30, 1975, eff. March 1, 1975; Oct. 1, 1982, eff. Oct. 1, 1982; June 12, 1992, eff. July 1, 1992; July 1, 1998, eff. immediately; July 6, 2000, eff. Aug. 1, 2000; Dec. 6, 2001, eff. immediately; Feb. 11, 2004, eff. July 1, 2004; Oct. 1, 2010, eff. Jan. 1, 2011; Jan. 10, 2012, eff. immediately; Nov. 26, 2013, eff. Jan. 1, 2014; Feb. 10, 2014, eff. immediately.

Rule 707. Permission for an Out–of–State Attorney to Provide Legal Services in Proceedings in Illinois

(a) Permission to Provide Legal Services in a Proceeding in Illinois. Upon filing pursuant to this rule of a verified Statement by an eligible out-of-state attorney and the filing of an appearance of an active status Illinois attorney associated with the attorney in the proceeding, the out-of-state attorney is permitted to appear as counsel and provide legal services in the proceeding without order of the tribunal. The permission is subject to termination pursuant to this rule.

(b) Eligible Out-of-State Attorney. An out-of-state attorney is eligible for permission to appear under this rule if the attorney:

(1) is admitted to practice law without limitation and is authorized to practice law in another state, territory, or commonwealth of the United States, in the District of Columbia, or in a foreign country and is not prohibited from practice in any jurisdiction or any other jurisdiction by reason of discipline, resignation with charges pending, or permanent retirement;

(2) on or after January 1, 2014, has not entered an appearance in more than five other proceedings under the provisions of this rule in the calendar year in which the Statement is filed;

(3) has not been enjoined or otherwise prohibited from obtaining permission under this rule; and

(4) has not been admitted to the practice of law in Illinois by unlimited or conditional admission. The admission of an attorney as a house counsel pursuant to Rule 716, as a legal services program lawyer pursuant to Rule 717, or as a foreign legal counsel pursuant to Rules 712 and 713 does not preclude that attorney from obtaining permission to provide legal services under this rule.

(c) Proceedings Requiring Permission. The following proceedings require permission under this rule:

(1) a case before a court of the State of Illinois;

(2) a court-annexed alternative dispute resolution proceeding; and

(3) a case before an agency or administrative tribunal of the State of Illinois or of a unit of local government in Illinois, if the representation by the out-of-state attorney constitutes the practice of law in Illinois or the agency or tribunal requires that a representative be an attorney.

The appeal or review of a proceeding before a different tribunal is a separate proceeding for purposes of this rule.

(d) Statement. The out-of-state attorney shall include the following information in the Statement and shall serve the Statement upon the Administrator of the Attorney Registration and Disciplinary Commission, the Illinois counsel with whom the attorney is associated in the proceeding, the attorney's client, and all parties to the proceeding entitled to notice:

(1) the attorney's full name, all addresses of offices from which the attorney practices law and related email addresses and telephone numbers;

(2) the name of the party or parties that the attorney represents in the proceeding;

(3) a listing of all proceedings in which the attorney has filed an appearance pursuant to this rule in the calendar year in which the Statement is filed and the ARDC registration number of the attorney, if assigned previously;

(4) a listing of all jurisdictions in which the attorney has been admitted and the full name under which the attorney has been admitted and the license or bar number in each such jurisdiction, together with a letter or certificate of good standing from each such jurisdiction, except for federal courts and agencies of the United States;

(5) a statement describing any office or other presence of the attorney for the practice of law in Illinois;

(6) a statement that the attorney submits to the disciplinary authority of the Supreme Court of Illinois;

(7) a statement that the attorney has undertaken to become familiar with and to comply, as if admitted to practice in Illinois, with the rules of the Supreme Court of Illinois, including the Illinois Rules of Professional Conduct and the Supreme Court Rules on Admission and Discipline of Attorneys, and other Illinois law and practices that pertain to the proceeding;

(8) the full name, business address and ARDC number of the Illinois attorney with whom the attorney has associated in the matter; and

(9) a certificate of service of the Statement upon all entitled to service under this rule.

(e) Additional Disclosures. The out-of-state attorney shall advise the Administrator of new or additional information related to items 4, 5 and 8 of the Statement, shall report a criminal conviction or discipline as required by Supreme Court Rule 761 and Rule 8.3(d) of the Illinois Rules of Professional Conduct, respectively, and shall report the conclusion of the attorney's practice in the proceeding. The attorney shall make these disclosures in writing to the Administrator within 30 days of when the information becomes known to the attorney. The out-of-state attorney shall provide waivers upon request of the Administrator to authorize bar admission or disciplinary authorities to disclose information to the Administrator.

(f) Fee per Proceeding. At the time of serving the Statement upon the Administrator, the out-of-state attorney shall submit to the Administrator a nonrefundable fee in the amount of $250 per proceeding, except that no fee shall be due from an attorney appointed to represent an indigent defendant in a criminal or civil case, from an attorney employed by or associated with a nonprofit legal service organization in a civil case involving the client of such a program, from an attorney providing legal services pursuant to Rule 718, or from an attorney employed by the United States Department of Justice and representing the United States. Fees shall be deposited in the disciplinary fund maintained pursuant to Rule 751(e)(6). The Attorney Registration and Disciplinary Commission shall retain $75 of each fee received under this section to fund its expenses to administer this rule. The $175 balance of each such fee shall be remitted to a trust fund established by the Attorney Registration and Disciplinary Commission for the Court's Access to Justice Commission and used at the Court's discretion to provide funding for the work of the Commission on Access to Justice and related Court programs that improve access to justice for low-income and disadvantaged Illinois residents, as well as to provide funding to the Lawyers Trust Fund of Illinois for distribution to legal aid organizations serving the State. The Court or its designee may direct the deposit of other funds into the trust fund. The Attorney Registration and Disciplinary Commission shall act in a ministerial capacity only and shall have no interest in or discretion concerning the trust fund. The Attorney Registration and Disciplinary Commission shall make payments from the trust fund pursuant to written direction from the Court or its designee. Such directions may be submitted electronically.

(g) Administrator's Review of Statement. The Administrator of the Attorney Registration and Disciplinary Commission shall conduct an inquiry into the Statement. It shall be the duty of the out-of-state attorney and Illinois attorneys to respond expeditiously to requests for information from the Administrator related to an inquiry under this section.

(h) Registration Requirement. An out-of-state attorney who appears in a proceeding pursuant to this rule shall register with the Attorney Registration and Disciplinary Commission and pay the registration fee required by Rule 756 for each year in which the attorney has any appearance of record pursuant to this rule. The attorney shall register within 30 days of the filing of a Statement pursuant to this rule if the attorney is not yet registered.

(i) Duration of Permission to Practice. The permission to practice law shall extend throughout the out-of-state attorney's practice in the proceeding unless earlier terminated. The Supreme Court, the Chief Judge of the Circuit Court for the circuit in which a proceeding is pending, or the court in which a proceeding is pending may terminate the permission to practice upon its own motion or upon motion of the Administrator if it determines that grounds exist for termination. Grounds may include, but are not limited to:

(1) the failure of the out-of-state attorney to have or maintain qualifications required under this rule;

(2) the conduct of the attorney inconsistent with Rule 5.5 or other rules of the Illinois Rules of Professional Conduct, the Supreme Court Rules on

Admission and Discipline of Attorneys or other rules of the Supreme Court, or other Illinois law and practices that pertain to the proceeding;

(3) the conduct of the attorney in the proceeding;

(4) the absence of an Illinois attorney who is associated with the out-of-state lawyer as counsel, who has an appearance of record in the proceeding, and who participates actively in the proceeding pursuant to Rule 5.5(c)(1) of the Illinois Rules of Professional Conduct;

(5) inaccuracies or omissions in the Statement;

(6) the failure of the attorney or the associated Illinois lawyer to comply with requests of the Administrator for information; or

(7) the failure of the attorney to pay the per-proceeding fee under this rule or to comply with registration requirements under Rule 756.

(j) Disciplinary Authority. The out-of-state attorney shall be subject to the disciplinary and unauthorized practice of law authority of the Supreme Court. The Administrator may institute disciplinary or unauthorized practice of law investigations and proceedings related to the out-of-state attorney. The Administrator may seek interim relief in the Supreme Court pursuant to the procedure set forth in Rule 774. The Administrator may also refer matters to the disciplinary authority of any other jurisdiction in which the attorney may be licensed.

Amended June 12, 1992, eff. July 1, 1992; amended October 2, 2006, eff. July 1, 2007; June 18, 2013, eff. July 1, 2013; May 29, 2014, eff. July 1, 2014.

Formerly Ill.Rev.Stat.1991, ch. 110A, ¶ 707.

Rule 708. Committee on Character and Fitness

(a) At the November term in each year, the Supreme Court shall appoint a Committee on Character and Fitness in each of the judicial districts of this state, comprised of Illinois lawyers. In the First Judicial District the committee shall consist of no fewer than 30 members of the bar, and in the Second, Third, Fourth and Fifth Judicial Districts, each committee shall consist of no fewer than 15 members of the bar. Unless the Court specifies a shorter term, all members shall be appointed for staggered three-year terms and shall serve until their successors are duly appointed and qualified. No member may be appointed to more than three full consecutive terms. Vacancies for any cause shall be filled by appointment of the Court for the unexpired term. The Court shall appoint a chairperson and a vice-chairperson for each committee. The chairperson may serve only one three-year term. The members of the Board of Admissions to the Bar shall be *ex-officio* members of the committees and are authorized to serve as members of hearing panels of any committee.

(b) Pursuant to the Rules of Procedure for the Board of Admissions to the Bar and the Committees on Character and Fitness, the Committee shall determine whether each applicant presently possesses good moral character and general fitness for admission to the practice of law. An applicant may be so recommended if the committee determines that his or her record of conduct demonstrates that he or she meets the essential eligibility requirements for the practice of law and justifies the trust of clients, adversaries, courts and others with respect to the professional duties owed to them. A record manifesting a failure to meet the essential eligibility requirements, including a deficiency in the honesty, trustworthiness, diligence, or reliability of an applicant, may constitute a basis for denial of admission.

(c) The essential eligibility requirements for the practice of law include the following: (1) the ability to learn, to recall what has been learned, to reason, and to analyze; (2) the ability to communicate clearly and logically with clients, attorneys, courts, and others; (3) the ability to exercise good judgment in conducting one's professional business; (4) the ability to conduct oneself with a high degree of honesty, integrity, and trustworthiness in all professional relationships and with respect to all legal obligations; (5) the ability to conduct oneself with respect for and in accordance with the law and the Illinois Rules of Professional Conduct; (6) the ability to avoid acts that exhibit disregard for the health, safety, and welfare of others; (7) the ability to conduct oneself diligently and reliably in fulfilling all obligations to clients, attorneys, courts, creditors, and others; (8) the ability to use honesty and good judgment in financial dealings on behalf of oneself, clients, and others; (9) the ability to comply with deadlines and time constraints; and (10) the ability to conduct oneself properly and in a manner that engenders respect for the law and the profession.

(d) If required by the Committee or its Rules of Procedure, each applicant shall appear before the committee of his or her district or some member thereof and shall furnish the committee such evidence of his or her good moral character and general fitness to practice law as in the opinion of the committee would justify his or her admission to the bar.

(e) At all times prior to his or her admission to the bar of this state, each applicant is under a continuing duty to supplement and continue to report fully and completely to the Board of Admissions to the Bar and to the Committee on Character and Fitness all information required to be disclosed pursuant to any and all application documents and such further inquiries prescribed by the Board and the Committee.

(f) If the Committee is of the opinion that the applicant is of good moral character and general fitness to practice law, it shall so certify to the Board of Admissions to the Bar, and the Board shall transmit such certification to the Court together with any additional information or recommendation the Board deems appropriate when all other admission requirements have been met. If the Committee is not of that

opinion, it shall file with the Board of Admissions to the Bar a statement that it cannot so certify, together with a report of its findings and conclusions.

(g) Character and Fitness certification is valid for nine months from the date of certification. An applicant who has been so certified and who has not been admitted to practice within nine months must be recertified after filing the requisite character and fitness registration and paying the fee therefor in accordance with Rule 706.

(h) An applicant who has availed himself or herself of his or her full hearing rights before the Committee on Character and Fitness and who deems himself or herself aggrieved by the determination of the committee may, on notice to the committee by service upon the Director of Administration for the Board of Admissions in Springfield, petition the Supreme Court for review within 35 days after service of the Committee's decision upon the applicant, and, unless extended for good cause shown, the Committee shall have 28 days to respond. The director shall file the record of the hearing with the Supreme Court at the time that the response of the Committee is filed.

Amended eff. Nov. 15, 1971; Oct. 2, 1972; April 10, 1987, eff. Aug. 1, 1987; June 12, 1992, eff. July 1, 1992; April 4, 1995, eff. immediately; Nov. 22, 2000, eff. Dec. 1, 2000; eff. Dec. 6, 2001, eff. immediately; Oct. 2, 2006, eff. July 1, 2007; Nov. 26, 2013, eff. Jan. 1, 2014.

Formerly Ill.Rev.Stat.1991, ch. 110A, ¶ 708.

Rule 709. Power to Make Rules, Conduct Investigations, and Subpoena Witnesses

(a) Subject to the approval of the Supreme Court, the Board of Admissions to the Bar and the Committee on Character and Fitness shall have power to make, adopt, and alter rules not inconsistent with this rule, for the proper performance of their respective functions.

(b) The Board of Admissions to the Bar and the Committee on Character and Fitness for each judicial district are hereby respectively constituted bodies of commissioners of this court, who are hereby empowered and charged to receive and entertain complaints, to make inquiries and investigations, and to take proof from time to time as may be necessary, concerning applications for admission to the bar, examinations given by or under the supervision of the Board of Admissions to the Bar, and the good moral character and general fitness to practice law of applicants for admission. They may call to their assistance in such inquiries other members of the bar and make all necessary rules and regulations concerning the conduct of such inquiries and investigations, and take the testimony of witnesses. The hearings before the commissioners shall be private unless any applicant concerned shall request that they be public. Upon application by the commissioners, the clerk of the Supreme Court shall issue subpoenas *ad testificandum*, subpoenas *duces tecum*, or *dedimus potestatem* to take depositions. Witnesses shall be sworn by a commissioner or any person authorized by law to administer oaths. All testimony shall be taken under oath, transcribed, and transmitted to the court, if requested. The commissioners shall report to the Supreme Court the failure or refusal of any person to attend and testify in response to a subpoena.

Amended eff. Nov. 15, 1971; Oct. 2, 1972; May 28, 1982, eff. July 1, 1982; June 12, 1992, eff. July 1, 1992; Dec. 6, 2001, eff. immediately; Nov. 26, 2013, eff. Jan. 1, 2014.

Formerly Ill.Rev.Stat.1991, ch. 110A, ¶ 709.

Rule 710. Immunity

Any person who communicates information concerning an applicant for admission to the Illinois bar to any member of the Illinois Board of Admissions to the Bar or to any member of the Character and Fitness Committees or to the Director of Administration, administrators, staff, investigators, agents, or attorneys of the Board or such Committees shall be immune from all civil liability which, except for this rule, might result from such communication. The grant of immunity provided by this rule shall apply only to those communications made by such persons to any member of the Illinois Board of Admissions to the Bar or to any member of the Character and Fitness Committees or to the Director of Administration, administrators, staff, investigators, agents, or attorneys of the Board or such Committees.

Adopted eff. April 4, 1995, eff. immediately. Amended Nov. 26, 2013, eff. Jan. 1, 2014.

Rule 711. Representation by Supervised Senior Law Students or Graduates

(a) Eligibility. A student in a law school approved by the American Bar Association may be certified by the dean of the school to be eligible to perform the services described in paragraph (c) of this rule, if he/she satisfies the following requirements:

(1) He/She must have received credit for work representing at least one-half of the total hourly credits required for graduation from the law school.

(2) He/She must be a student in good academic standing, and be eligible under the school's criteria to undertake the activities authorized herein.

A graduate of a law school approved by the American Bar Association who (i) has not yet had an opportunity to take the examinations provided for in Rule 704, (ii) has taken the examinations provided for in Rule 704 but not yet received notification of the results of either examination, or (iii) has taken and passed both examinations provided for in Rule 704 but has not yet been sworn as a member of the Illinois bar may, if the dean of that law school has no objection, be authorized by the Administrative Director of the Illinois Courts to perform the services described in paragraph (c) of this rule.

For purposes of this rule, a law school graduate is defined as any individual not yet licensed to practice law in any jurisdiction.

(b) Agencies Through Which Services Must Be Performed. The services authorized by this rule may only be carried on in the course of the student's or graduate's work with one or more of the following organizations or programs:

(1) a legal aid bureau, legal assistance program, organization, or clinic chartered by the State of Illinois or approved by a law school approved by the American Bar Association;

(2) the office of the public defender; or

(3) a law office of the State or any of its subdivisions.

(c) Services Permitted. Under the supervision of a member of the bar of this State, and with the written consent of the person on whose behalf he/she is acting, an eligible law student or graduate may render the following services:

(1) He/She may counsel and advise clients, negotiate in the settlement of claims, represent clients in mediation and other nonlitigation matters, and engage in the preparation and drafting of legal instruments.

(2) He/She may appear in the trial courts, courts of review and administrative tribunals of this State, including court-annexed arbitration and mediation, subject to the following qualifications:

(i) Written consent to representation of the person on whose behalf the law student or graduate is acting shall be filed in the case and brought to the attention of the judge or presiding officer.

(ii) Appearances, pleadings, motions, and other documents to be filed with the court may be prepared by the student or graduate and may be signed by him with the accompanying designation "Senior Law Student" or "Law Graduate" but must also be signed by the supervising member of the bar.

(iii) In criminal cases, in which the penalty may be imprisonment, in proceedings challenging sentences of imprisonment, and in civil or criminal contempt proceedings, the student or graduate may participate in pretrial, trial, and posttrial proceedings as an assistant of the supervising member of the bar, who shall be present and responsible for the conduct of the proceedings.

(iv) In all other civil and criminal cases in the trial courts or administrative tribunals, the student or graduate may conduct all pretrial, trial, and posttrial proceedings, and the supervising member of the bar need not be present.

(v) In matters before courts of review, the law student or graduate may prepare briefs, excerpts from the record, abstracts, and other documents filed in courts of review of the State, which may set forth the name of the student or graduate with the accompanying designation "Senior Law Student" or "Law Graduate" but must be filed in the name of the supervising member of the bar. Upon motion by the supervising member of the bar, the senior law student or law graduate may request authorization to argue the matter before the court of review. If the law student or law graduate is permitted to argue, the supervising member of the bar must be present and responsible for the conduct of the hearing.

(d) Compensation. A student or graduate rendering services authorized by this rule shall not request or accept any compensation from the person for whom he/she renders the services, but may receive compensation from an agency described in paragraph (b).

(e) Certification and Authorization.

(1) Upon request of a student or the appropriate organization, the dean of the law school in which the student is in attendance may, if he/she finds that the student meets the requirements stated in paragraph (a) of this rule, file with the Administrative Director a certificate so stating. Upon the filing of the certificate and until it is withdrawn or terminated the student is eligible to render the services described in paragraph (c) of this rule. The Administrative Director shall authorize, upon review and approval of the completed application of an eligible student as defined in paragraph (a) and the certification as described in paragraph (e), the issuance of the temporary license. No services that are permitted under paragraph (c) shall be performed prior to the issuance of a temporary license.

(2) Unless otherwise provided by the Administrative Director for good cause shown, or unless sooner withdrawn or terminated, the certificate shall remain in effect until the expiration of 24 months after it is filed, or until the announcement of the results of the first bar examination following the student's graduation, whichever is earlier. The certificate of a student who passes that examination shall continue in effect until he/she is admitted to the bar.

(3) The certificate may be withdrawn by the dean at any time, without prior notice, hearing, or showing of cause, by the mailing of a notice to that effect to the Administrative Director and copies of the notice to the student and to the agencies to which the student had been assigned.

(4) The certificate may be terminated by this court at any time without prior notice, hearing, or showing of cause. Notice of the termination may be filed with the Administrative Director, who shall notify the student and the agencies to which the student had been assigned.

(f) Application by Law Graduate. A law school graduate who wishes to be authorized to perform services described in paragraph (c) of this rule shall apply directly to the Administrative Director, with a copy to the dean of the law school from which he/she graduated.

Amended eff. May 27, 1969; July 1, 1985, eff. Aug. 1, 1985; July 3, 1986, eff. Aug. 1, 1986; June 19, 1989, eff. Aug. 1, 1989; June 12, 1992, eff. July 1, 1992; October 10, 2001; Dec. 5, 2003, eff. immediately; Feb. 10, 2006, eff. immediately; June 18, 2013, eff. July 1, 2013.

Formerly Ill.Rev.Stat.1991, ch. 110A, ¶ 711.

Committee Comments

(July 1, 1985)

This rule was amended, effective August 1, 1985, to allow the Administrative Director of the Illinois Courts to allow certain graduates of approved law schools to perform services under this rule pending their first opportunity to sit for the bar examination and to allow the Administrative Director, upon good cause shown, to extend the termination date of a certificate beyond the period prescribed by the rule. "Good cause shown" would ordinarily be limited to evidence that the licensee was unable to sit for the first bar examination offered following his graduation because of illness, a death in his family, military obligation, etc.

(June 18, 2013)

This rule was amended effective July 1, 2013, to clarify that students and law graduates may perform nonlitigation legal services under this rule. Nothing in this rule should be construed to require law students or law graduates to be certified under this rule for work, including but not limited to transactional, pretrial, and policy work, that properly may be performed by a law student or other nonlawyer under Rule 5.3 of the Illinois Rules of Professional Conduct.

Rule 712. Licensing of Foreign Legal Consultants Without Examination

(a) General Regulation. In its discretion the supreme court may license to practice as a foreign legal consultant on foreign and international law, without examination, an applicant who:

(1) has been admitted to practice (or has obtained the equivalent of such admission) in a foreign country, and has engaged in the practice of law of such country, and has been in good standing as an attorney or counselor at law (or the equivalent of either) in such country, for a period of not less than five of the seven years immediately preceding the date of his or her application, provided that admission as a notary or its equivalent in any foreign country shall not be deemed to be the equivalent of admission as an attorney or counselor at law;

(2) possesses the good moral character and general fitness requisite for a member of the bar of this state;

(3) possesses the requisite documentation evidencing compliance with the immigration laws of the United States; and

(4) intends to practice as a legal consultant in the State of Illinois and to maintain an office therefor in the State of Illinois.

(b) Reciprocity. In considering whether to license an applicant under this rule, the supreme court may in its discretion take into account whether a member of the bar of the supreme court would have a reasonable and practical opportunity to establish an office for the giving of legal advice to clients in the applicant's country of admission (as referred to in paragraphs (c)(1) and (c)(5) of this rule), if there is pending with the supreme court a request to take this factor into account from a member of the bar of this court actively seeking to establish such an office in that country which raises a serious question as to the adequacy of the opportunity for such a member to establish such an office, or if the supreme court decides to do so on its own initiative.

(c) Proof Required. An applicant to be licensed under this rule must file with the supreme court or its designee:

(1) a certificate from the authority in such foreign country having final jurisdiction over professional discipline, certifying as to the applicant's admission to practice and the date thereof and as to his or her good standing as such attorney or counselor at law or the equivalent, together with a duly authenticated English translation of such certificate if it is not in English;

(2) a letter of recommendation from one of the members of the executive body of such authority, or from one of the judges of the highest law court or court of original jurisdiction of such foreign country, together with a duly authenticated English translation of such letter if it is not in English;

(3) evidence of his or her citizenship, educational and professional qualifications, period of actual practice in such foreign country and age;

(4) the affidavits of reputable persons as evidence of the applicant's good moral character and general fitness, substantially as required by Rule 708;

(5) a summary of the laws and customs of such foreign country that relate to the opportunity afforded to members of the bar of the supreme court to establish offices for the giving of legal advice to clients in such foreign country; and

(6) a completed character and fitness registration application in the form prescribed by the Board of Admissions to the Bar and such other evidence of character, qualification and fitness as the supreme court may from time to time require and compliance with the requirements of this subsection.

(d) Waiver. Upon a showing that strict compliance with the provisions of paragraph (c)(1) or (c)(2) of this rule would cause the applicant unnecessary hardship, the supreme court may in its discretion waive or vary the application of such provisions and permit the applicant to furnish other evidence in lieu thereof.

(e) Right to Practice and Limitations on Scope of Practice. A person licensed as a foreign legal consultant under this rule may render legal services and give professional advice within this state only on the law of the foreign country where the foreign legal consultant is admitted to practice. A foreign legal consultant in giving such advice shall not quote from or summarize advice concerning the law of this state (or of any other jurisdiction) which has been rendered by an attorney at law duly licensed under the law of the State of Illinois (or of any other jurisdiction, domestic or foreign). A licensed foreign legal consultant shall not:

(1) appear for a person other than himself or herself as attorney in any court, or before any judicial officer, or before any administrative agency, in this state (other than upon admission in isolated cases pursuant to Rule 707) or prepare pleadings or any other papers or issue subpoenas in any action or proceeding brought in any such court or before any such judicial officer, or before any such administrative agency;

(2) prepare any deed, mortgage, assignment, discharge, lease or any other instrument affecting real estate located in the United States of America;

(3) prepare any will, codicil or trust instrument affecting the disposition after death of any property located in the United States of America and owned by a citizen thereof;

(4) prepare any instrument relating to the administration of decedent's estate in the United States of America;

(5) prepare any instrument or other paper which relates to the marital relations, rights or duties of a resident of the United States of America or the custody or care of the children of such a resident;

(6) render professional legal advice with respect to a personal injury occurring within the United States;

(7) render professional legal advice with respect to United States immigration laws, United States customs laws or United States trade laws;

(8) render professional legal advice on or under the law of the State of Illinois or of the United States or of any state, territory or possession thereof or of the District of Columbia or of any other jurisdiction (domestic or foreign) in which such person is not authorized to practice law (whether rendered incident to the preparation of legal instruments or otherwise);

(9) directly, or through a representative, propose, recommend or solicit employment of himself or herself, his or her partner, or his or her associate for pecuniary gain or other benefit with respect to any matter not within the scope of practice authorized by this rule;

(10) use any title other than "foreign legal consultant" and affirmatively state in conjunction therewith the name of the foreign country in which he or she is

admitted to practice (although he or she may additionally identify the name of the foreign or domestic firm with which he or she is associated); or

(11) in any way hold himself or herself out as an attorney licensed in Illinois or as an attorney licensed in any United States jurisdiction.

(f) Disciplinary Provisions. Every person licensed to practice as a foreign legal consultant under this rule shall execute and file with the Illinois Attorney Registration and Disciplinary Commission, in such form and manner as the supreme court may prescribe:

(1) the foreign legal consultant's written commitment to observe the Rules of Professional Conduct, as adopted by the Illinois Supreme Court and as it may be amended from time to time, to the extent applicable to the legal services authorized by subparagraph (e) of this rule;

(2) a duly acknowledged instrument, in writing, setting forth the foreign legal consultant's address in this state and designating the clerk of the supreme court as the foreign legal consultant's agent upon whom process may be served, with like effect as if served personally upon the foreign legal consultant, in any action or proceeding thereafter brought against the foreign legal consultant and arising out of or based upon any legal services rendered or offered to be rendered by the foreign legal consultant within or to residents of this state, whenever after due diligence service cannot be made upon the foreign legal consultant at such address or at such new address in this state as he or she shall have filed in the office of the clerk of the supreme court by means of a duly acknowledged supplemental instrument in writing; and

(3) appropriate evidence of professional liability insurance or other proof of financial responsibility, in such form and amount as the supreme court may prescribe, to assure his or her proper professional conduct and responsibility.

(g) Service of Process. Service of process on the clerk of the supreme court, pursuant to the designation filed as required by Rule 712(f)(2) above, shall be made by personally delivering to and leaving with such clerk, or with a deputy or assistant authorized by the foreign legal consultant to receive such service, at his or her office, duplicate copies of such process together with a fee of $10. Service of process shall be complete when such clerk has been so served. Such clerk shall promptly send one of such copies to the foreign legal consultant to whom the process is directed, by certified mail, return receipt requested, addressed to such foreign legal consultant at his or her address specified by the foreign legal consultant as aforesaid.

(h) Separate Authority. This rule shall not be deemed to limit or otherwise affect the provisions of Rule 704.

(i) Unauthorized Practice of Law. Any person who is licensed under the provisions of this rule shall not be deemed to have a license to perform legal services prohibited by Rule 712(e) hereof. Any person licensed hereunder who violates the provisions of Rule 712(e) is engaged in the unauthorized practice of law and may be held in contempt of the court. Such person may also be subject to disciplinary proceedings pursuant to Rule 777 and the penalties imposed by section 32–5 of the Criminal Code of 1961, as amended,[1] and section 1 of the Attorney Act (705 ILCS 205/1).

Adopted December 7, 1990, effective immediately. Amended December 6, 2001, effective immediately; May 30, 2008, effective immediately.

Formerly Ill.Rev.Stat.1991, ch. 110A, ¶ 712.

[1] 720 ILCS 5/32–5. (repealed)

Rule 713. Applications for Licensing of Foreign Legal Consultants

(a) Referral to Committee on Character and Fitness.

(1) The Committee on Character and Fitness of the judicial district in which any applicant for a license (pursuant to Rule 712) to practice as a foreign legal consultant resides shall pass upon his or her good moral character and general fitness to practice as a foreign legal consultant. The applicant shall furnish the committee with copies of the affidavits referred to in paragraphs (b)(3), (b)(4) and (b)(5) hereof. Each applicant for a license to practice as a foreign legal consultant shall appear before the committee of his district or some member thereof and shall furnish the committee such evidence of his or her good moral character and general fitness to practice as a foreign legal consultant as in the opinion of the committee would justify his or her being licensed as a foreign legal consultant.

(2) Unless otherwise ordered by the supreme court, no license to practice as a foreign legal consultant shall be granted without a certificate, from the Committee on Character and Fitness for the judicial district in which the applicant resides, certifying that the committee has found that the applicant is of good moral character and general fitness to practice as a foreign legal consultant.

(b) Documents–Affidavits and Other Proof Required. Every applicant for a license to practice as a foreign legal consultant shall file the following additional papers with his or her application:

(1) a certificate from the authority having final jurisdiction over professional discipline in the foreign country in which the applicant was admitted to practice, which shall be signed by a responsible official or one of the members of the executive body of such authority and shall be attested under the hand and seal, if any, of the clerk of such authority, and which shall certify:

(i) as to the authority's jurisdiction in such matters;

(ii) as to the applicant's admission to practice in such foreign country and the date thereof and as to his or her good standing as an attorney or counselor at law or the equivalent therein; and

(iii) as to whether any charge or complaint has ever been filed against the applicant with such authority, and, if so, the substance of each such charge or complaint and the disposition thereof;

(2) a letter of recommendation from one of the members of the executive body of such authority or from one of the judges of the highest law court or court of general original jurisdiction of such foreign country, certifying to the applicant's professional qualifications, together with a certificate under the hand and seal, if any, of the clerk of such authority or of such court, as the case may be, attesting to the office held by the person signing the letter and the genuineness of his signature;

(3) affidavits as to the applicant's good moral character and general fitness to practice as a foreign legal consultant from three reputable persons residing in this state and not related to the applicant, two or whom shall be practicing Illinois attorneys;

(4) affidavits from two attorneys or counselors at law or the equivalent admitted in and practicing in such foreign country, stating the nature and extent of their acquaintance with the applicant and their personal knowledge as to the nature, character and extent of the applicant's practice, and as to the applicant's good standing as an attorney or counselor at law or the equivalent in such foreign country, and the duration and continuity of such practice;

(5) the National Conference of Bar Examiners questionnaire and affidavit;

(6) documentation in duly authenticated form evidencing that the applicant is lawfully entitled to reside and be employed in the United States of America pursuant to the immigration laws thereof;

(7) such additional evidence as the applicant may see fit to submit with respect to his or her educational and professional qualifications and his or her good moral character and general fitness to practice as a foreign legal consultant;

(8) a duly authenticated English translation of every paper submitted by the applicant which is not in English; and

(9) a duly acknowledged instrument designating the clerk of the supreme court the applicant's agent for service of process as provided in Rule 712(f)(2).

(c) **University and Law School Certificates.** A certificate shall be submitted from each university and law school attended by the applicant, setting forth the information required by forms which shall be provided to the applicant for that purpose.

(d) **Exceptional Situations.** In the event that the applicant is unable to comply strictly with any of the foregoing requirements, the applicant shall set forth the reasons for such inability in an affidavit, together with a statement showing in detail the efforts made to fulfill such requirements.

(e) **Authority of Committee on Character and Fitness to Require Additional Proof.** The Committee on Character and Fitness may in any case require the applicant to submit such additional proof or information as it may deem appropriate.

(f) **Filing.** Every application for a license as a foreign legal consultant, together with all the papers submitted thereon, shall upon its final disposition be filed in the office of the clerk of the supreme court.

(g) **Fees of Applicants.** Each applicant for a license to practice as a foreign legal consultant on foreign or international law shall pay in advance a fee of $800. All fees shall be paid to the treasurer of the Board of Admissions to the Bar to be held by the treasurer subject to the order of the court.

(h) **Undertaking.** Prior to taking custody of any money, securities (other than unindorsed securities in registered form), negotiable instruments, bullion, precious stones or other valuables, in the course of his or her practice as a foreign legal consultant, for or on behalf of any client domiciled or residing in the United States, every person licensed to practice as a foreign legal consultant shall obtain, and shall maintain in effect for the duration of such custody, an undertaking issued by a duly authorized surety company, and approved by a justice of the supreme court, to assure the faithful and fair discharge of his or her duties and obligations arising from such custody. The undertaking shall be in an amount not less than the amount of any such money, or the fair market value of any such property other than money, of which the foreign legal consultant shall have custody, except that the supreme court may in any case in its discretion for good cause direct that such undertaking shall be in a greater or lesser amount. The undertaking or a duplicate original thereof shall be promptly filed by the foreign legal consultant with the clerk of the supreme court.

Adopted eff. Dec. 7, 1990. Amended June 12, 1992, eff. July 1, 1992; eff. Dec. 6, 2001.

Formerly Ill.Rev.Stat.1991, ch. 110A, ¶ 713.

Rule 714. Reserved

Rule 715. Admission of Graduates of Foreign Law Schools

Any person who has received his or her legal education and law degree in a foreign country may make application to the Board of Admissions to the Bar for admission to the bar upon academic qualification examination upon the following conditions:

(a) The applicant has been licensed to practice law in the foreign country in which the law degree was conferred and/or in the highest court of law in any state or territory of the United States or the District of Columbia and is in good standing as an attorney or counselor at law (or the equivalent of either) in that country or other jurisdiction where admitted to practice.

(b) The applicant has been actively and continuously engaged in the practice of law under such license or licenses for at least five of the seven years immediately prior to making application.

(c) The Board has determined that the quality of the applicant's preliminary, college and legal education is acceptable for admission to the bar of this state based upon its review and consideration of any matters deemed relevant by the Board including, but not limited to, the jurisprudence of the country in which the applicant received his or her education and training, the curriculum of the law schools attended and the course of studies pursued by the applicant, accreditation of the law schools attended by the applicant by competent accrediting authorities in the foreign country where situated, post-graduate studies and degrees earned by the applicant in the foreign country and in the United States, and the applicant's success on bar examinations in other jurisdictions in this country. Each applicant shall submit such proofs and documentation as the Board may require.

(d) The applicant has achieved a passing score as determined by the Board on the full academic qualification examination.

(e) The applicant has achieved a passing score as determined by the Board on the Multistate Professional Responsibility Examination in Illinois or in any other jurisdiction in which it was administered.

(f) The applicant meets the character and fitness standards in Illinois and has been so certified to the Board by the Committee on Character and Fitness pursuant to Rule 708.

(g) The applicant has filed the requisite character and fitness registration and bar examination applications and has paid the fees therefor in accordance with Rule 706.

Adopted October 4, 2002, effective January 1, 2003.

Rule 716. Limited Admission Of House Counsel

A person who, as determined by the Board of Admissions to the Bar, has been licensed to practice in the highest court of law in any United States state, territory, the District of Columbia, or a foreign jurisdiction, or is otherwise authorized to practice in a foreign jurisdiction, may receive a limited license to practice law in this state when the lawyer is employed in Illinois as house counsel exclusively for a single corporation, partnership, association or other legal entity (as well as any parent, subsidiary or affiliate thereof), the lawful business of which consists of activities other than the practice of law or the provision of legal services upon the following conditions:

(a) The applicant meets the educational requirements of Rule 703 or Rule 715(c) if a foreign lawyer;

(b) The applicant meets Illinois character and fitness requirements and has been certified by the Committee on Character and Fitness;

(c) The applicant licensed to practice law for fewer than 15 years has passed the Multistate Professional Responsibility Exam in Illinois or in any jurisdiction in which it was administered, or, in the case of a lawyer who has been admitted or otherwise authorized to practice only in a foreign jurisdiction, has completed the course on ethics for foreign lawyers approved by the Illinois Supreme Court Commission on Professionalism;

(d) The applicant is in good disciplinary standing before the highest court of every jurisdiction in which ever admitted and is at the time of application on active status in at least one such jurisdiction, or, in the case of a lawyer who has been admitted or otherwise authorized to practice only in a foreign jurisdiction, is not disbarred, suspended, or otherwise prohibited from practice in any jurisdiction by reason of discipline, resignation with charges pending, or permanent retirement;

(e) The applicant has paid the fee for limited admission of house counsel under Rule 706.

(f) Application requirements. To apply for the limited license, the applicant must file with the Board of Admissions to the Bar the following:

(1) A completed application for the limited license in the form prescribed by the Board;

(2) A duly authorized and executed certification by applicant's employer that:

(A) The employer is not engaged in the practice of law or the rendering of legal services, whether for a fee or otherwise;

(B) The employer is duly qualified to do business under the laws of its organization and the laws of Illinois;

(C) The applicant works exclusively as an employee of said employer for the purpose of providing legal services to the employer at the date of his or her application for licensure; and

(D) The employer will promptly notify the Clerk of the Supreme Court of the termination of the applicant's employment.

(3) Such other affidavits, proofs and documents as may be prescribed by the Board.

(g) Authority and Limitations. A lawyer licensed and employed as provided by this Rule has the authority to act on behalf of his or her employer for all purposes as if licensed in Illinois. A lawyer licensed under this rule shall not offer legal services or advice to the public or in any manner hold himself or herself out to be engaged or authorized to engage in the practice of law, except such lawyer, other than a lawyer licensed under this rule only on the basis of being admitted or authorized to practice in a foreign jurisdiction, may provide voluntary *pro bono* public services as defined in Rule 756(f).

(h) Duration and Termination of License. The license and authorization to perform legal services under this rule shall terminate upon the earliest of the following events:

(1) The lawyer is admitted to the general practice of law under any other rule of this Court.

(2) The lawyer ceases to be employed as house counsel for the employer listed on his or her initial application for licensure under this rule; provided, however, that if such lawyer, within 120 days of ceasing to be so employed, becomes employed by another employer and such employment meets all requirements of this Rule, his or her license shall remain in effect, if within said 120–day period there is filed with the Clerk of the Supreme Court: (A) written notification by the lawyer stating the date on which the prior employment terminated, identification of the new employer and the date on which the new employment commenced; (B) certification by the former employer that the termination of the employment was not based upon the lawyers character and fitness or failure to comply with this rule; and (C) the certification specified in subparagraph (f)(2) of this rule duly executed by the new employer. If the employment of the lawyer shall cease with no subsequent employment within 120 days thereafter, the lawyer shall promptly notify the Clerk of the Supreme Court in writing of the date of termination of the employment, and shall not be authorized to represent any single corporation, partnership, association or other legal entity (or any parent, subsidiary or affiliate thereof).

(3) The lawyer is suspended or disbarred from practice in any jurisdiction or any court or agency before which the lawyer is admitted.

(4) The lawyer fails to maintain active status in at least one jurisdiction, or, in the case of a lawyer who has been admitted or otherwise authorized to practice only in a foreign jurisdiction, has been disbarred, suspended, or otherwise prohibited from practice in any jurisdiction by reason of discipline, resignation with charges pending, or permanent retirement.

(i) Annual Registration and MCLE. Beginning with the year in which a limited license to practice law under this rule is granted and continuing for each subsequent year in which house counsel continues to practice law in Illinois under the limited license, house counsel must register with the Attorney Registration and Disciplinary Commission and pay the fee for active lawyers set forth in Rule 756 and fully comply with all MCLE requirements for active lawyers set forth in Rule 790 *et seq.*

(j) Discipline. A lawyer licensed under this rule shall be subject to the jurisdiction of the Court for disciplinary purposes to the same extent as all other lawyers licensed to practice law in this state.

(k) Credit toward Admission on Motion. The period of time a lawyer practices law while licensed under this rule may be counted toward eligibility for admission on motion, provided all other requirements of Rule 705 are met.

(*l*) Newly Employed House Counsel. A lawyer who is newly employed as house counsel in Illinois shall not be deemed to have engaged in the unauthorized practice of law in Illinois prior to licensure under this rule if application for the license is made within 90 days of the commencement of such employment.

Adopted Feb. 11, 2004, eff. July 1, 2004. Amended March 26, 2008, eff. July 1, 2008; Oct. 1, 2010, eff. Jan. 1, 2011; Dec. 9, 2011, eff. July 1, 2012; April 8, 2013, eff. immediately; Nov. 26, 2013, eff. immediately; Oct. 15, 2015, eff. Jan. 1, 2016.

Rule 717. Limited Admission of Legal Service Program Lawyers

(a) Eligibility. A lawyer admitted to the practice of law in another state or the District of Columbia who meets the educational requirements of Rule 703 may receive a limited license to practice law in this state when the lawyer is employed in Illinois for an organized legal service, public defender or law school clinical program providing legal assistance to indigent persons.

(b) Application Requirements. To qualify for the license the applicant must file with the Board of Admissions to the Bar the following:

(1) A completed application for the limited license and a completed character and fitness registration application in the form prescribed by the Board.

(2) A certificate of good standing from the highest court of each jurisdiction of admission.

(3) A certificate from the disciplinary authority of each jurisdiction of admission which:

(a) states that the applicant has not been suspended, disbarred or disciplined and that no charges of professional misconduct are pending; or

(b) identifies any suspensions, disbarments, or disciplinary sanctions and any pending charges.

(4) A duly authorized and executed certification by the applicant's employer that:

(a) it is engaged in the practice of law for the rendering of legal services to indigent persons;

(b) it is duly qualified to do business under the laws of its organization and the laws of Illinois;

(c) the applicant will work exclusively as an employee of said employer, noting the date employment is expected to commence; and

(d) it will promptly notify the Clerk of the Supreme Court of the termination of the applicant's employment.

(5) Such other affidavits, proofs and documentation as may be prescribed by the Board.

(6) The requisite fees in accordance with Rule 706.

(c) Character and Fitness Approval. Each applicant for a limited license under this rule must receive certification of good moral character and general fitness to practice law by the Committee on Character and Fitness in accordance with the provisions of Rule 708.

(d) Certification by the Board. In the event the Board of Admissions to the Bar shall find that the applicant meets the requirements of this rule and has received from the Committee on Character and Fitness its certification of good moral character and general fitness to practice law, the Board shall certify to the Court that such applicant is qualified for licensure.

(e) Limitation of Practice. A lawyer while in the employ of an employer described in subparagraph (a) of this rule may perform legal services in this state solely on behalf of such employer and the indigent clients represented by such employer. In criminal cases classified as felonies, the lawyer may participate in the proceedings as an assistant of a supervising member of the bar who shall be present and responsible for the conduct of the proceedings.

(f) Duration and Termination of License. The license and authorization to perform legal services under this rule shall terminate upon the earliest of the following events:

(1) Eighteen months after admission to practice under this rule.

(2) The lawyer is admitted to the general practice of law under any other rule of this Court.

(3) The lawyer ceases to be employed for the employer listed on his or her initial application for licensure under this rule.

(4) Withdrawal of an employer's certification filed pursuant to subparagraph (b)(4) of this rule. An employer may withdraw certification at any time without cause being stated.

(g) Annual Registration. Once the Court has conferred a limited license to perform legal services under this rule, the lawyer must register with the Attorney Registration and Disciplinary Commission and pay the fee for active lawyers set forth in Rule 756 for the year in which the license is conferred and for any subsequent year into which the limited license extends.

(h) Discipline. All lawyers licensed under this rule shall be subject to the jurisdiction of the Court for disciplinary purposes to the same extent as all other lawyers licensed to practice law in this state.

(i) No Credit Toward Admission on Motion. The period of time a lawyer practices law while licensed under this rule shall not be counted toward his or her eligibility for admission on motion under Rule 705.
Adopted February 11, 2004, effective July 1, 2004.

Rule 718. Provision of Legal Services Following Determination of Major Disaster

(a) Determination of existence of major disaster. Solely for purposes of this rule, this Court shall determine when an emergency affecting the justice system, as a result of a natural or other major disaster has occurred.

(b) Temporary practice in this jurisdiction following major disaster. Following the determination of an emergency affecting the justice system in this jurisdiction pursuant to paragraph (a) of this rule, or a determination that persons displaced by a major disaster in another jurisdiction and residing in this jurisdiction are in need of pro bono services and the assistance of lawyers from outside of this jurisdiction is required to help provide such assistance, a lawyer authorized to practice law in another United States jurisdiction, and not disbarred, suspended from practice or otherwise restricted from practice in any jurisdiction, may provide legal services in this jurisdiction on a temporary basis. Such legal services must be provided on a *pro bono* basis without compensation, expectation of compensation or other direct or indirect pecuniary gain to the lawyer. Such legal services shall be assigned and supervised through an established not-for-profit bar association, *pro bono* program or legal services program or through such organization(s) specifically designated by this Court.

(c) Temporary practice in this jurisdiction following major disaster in another jurisdiction. Following the determination of a major disaster in another United States jurisdiction, a lawyer who is authorized to practice law and who principally practices in that affected jurisdiction, and who is not disbarred, suspended from practice or otherwise restricted from practice in any jurisdiction, may provide legal services in this jurisdiction on a temporary basis. Those legal services must arise out of and be reasonably related to that lawyer's practice of law in the jurisdiction, or area of such other jurisdiction, where the major disaster occurred.

(d) Duration of authority for temporary practice. The authority to practice law in this jurisdiction granted by paragraph (b) of this rule shall end when this Court determines that the conditions caused by the major disaster in this jurisdiction have ended except that a lawyer then representing clients in this jurisdiction pursuant to paragraph (b) is authorized to continue the provision of legal services for such time as is reasonably necessary to complete the representation, but the lawyer shall not thereafter accept new clients. The authority to practice law in this jurisdiction granted by paragraph (c) of this rule shall end 60 days after this Court declares that the conditions caused by the major disaster in the affected jurisdiction have ended.

(e) Legal services in proceedings in Illinois. The authority granted by this rule permits the provision of legal services in proceedings within Illinois only as follows:

(1) by permission under Rule 707; or

(2) if this Court, in any determination made under paragraph (a), grants blanket permission to provide legal services in all or designated proceedings in this jurisdiction to lawyers providing legal services pursuant to paragraph (b).

(f) Disciplinary authority and registration requirement. Lawyers providing legal services in this jurisdiction pursuant to paragraphs (b) or (c) are subject to this Court's disciplinary authority and the Rules of Professional Conduct of this jurisdiction as provided in Rule 8.5 of the Rules of Professional Conduct. Lawyers providing legal services in this jurisdiction under paragraphs (b) or (c) shall, within 30 days from the commencement of the provision of legal services, file a registration statement with the Clerk of this Court, unless all of the lawyer's legal services authorized under this rule are also permitted under Rule 707, in which case the attorney need only register annually with the ARDC. The registration statement shall be in a form prescribed by this Court. Any lawyer who provides legal services pursuant to this rule shall not be considered to be engaged in the unlawful practice of law in this jurisdiction.

(g) Notification to clients. Lawyers authorized to practice law in another United States jurisdiction who provide legal services pursuant to this rule shall inform clients in this jurisdiction of the jurisdiction in which they are authorized to practice law, any limits of that authorization, and that they are not authorized to practice law in this jurisdiction except as permitted by this rule. They shall not state or imply to any person that they are otherwise authorized to practice law in this jurisdiction.

Adopted eff. April 4, 2012. Amended June 18, 2013, eff. July 1, 2013.

Committee Comments
(April 4, 2012)

[1] A major disaster in this or another jurisdiction may cause an emergency affecting the justice system with respect to the provision of legal services for a sustained period of time interfering with the ability of lawyers admitted and practicing in the affected jurisdiction to continue to represent clients until the disaster has ended. When this happens, lawyers from the affected jurisdiction may need to provide legal services to their clients, on a temporary basis, from an office outside their home jurisdiction. In addition, lawyers in an unaffected jurisdiction may be willing to serve residents of the affected jurisdiction who have unmet legal needs as a result of the disaster or, though independent of the disaster, whose legal needs temporarily are unmet because of disruption to the practices of local lawyers. Lawyers from unaffected jurisdictions

may offer to provide these legal services either by traveling to the affected jurisdiction or from their own offices or both, provided the legal services are provided on a *pro bono* basis through an authorized not-for-profit entity or such other organization(s) specifically designated by this Court. A major disaster includes, for example, a hurricane, earthquake, flood, wildfire, tornado, public health emergency or an event caused by terrorists or acts of war.

[2] Under paragraph (a), this Court shall determine whether a major disaster causing an emergency affecting the justice system has occurred in this jurisdiction, or in a part of this jurisdiction, for purposes of triggering paragraph (b) of this rule. This Court may, for example, determine that the entirety of this jurisdiction has suffered a disruption in the provision of legal services or that only certain areas have suffered such an event. The authority granted by paragraph (b) shall extend only to lawyers authorized to practice law and not disbarred, suspended from practice or otherwise restricted from practice in any other manner in any other jurisdiction.

[3] Paragraph (b) permits lawyers authorized to practice law in an unaffected jurisdiction, and not disbarred, suspended from practice or otherwise restricted from practicing law in any other manner in any other jurisdiction, to provide *pro bono* legal services to residents of the affected jurisdiction following determination of an emergency caused by a major disaster; notwithstanding that they are not otherwise authorized to practice law in the affected jurisdiction. Other restrictions on a lawyer's license to practice law that would prohibit that lawyer from providing legal services pursuant to this rule include, but are not limited to, probation, inactive status, disability inactive status or a nondisciplinary administrative suspension for failure to complete continuing legal education or other requirements. Lawyers on probation may be subject to monitoring and specific limitations on their practices. Lawyers on inactive status, despite being characterized in many jurisdictions as being "in good standing," and lawyers on disability inactive status are not permitted to practice law. Public protection warrants exclusion of these lawyers from the authority to provide legal services as defined in this rule. Lawyers permitted to provide legal services pursuant to this rule must do so without fee or other compensation, or expectation thereof. Their service must be provided through an established not-for-profit organization that is authorized to provide legal services either in its own name or that provides representation of clients through employed or cooperating lawyers. Alternatively, this court may instead designate other specific organization(s) through which these legal services may be rendered. Under paragraph (b), an *emeritus* lawyer from another United States jurisdiction may provide *pro bono* legal services on a temporary basis in this jurisdiction provided that the *emeritus* lawyer is authorized to provide *pro bono* legal services in that jurisdiction pursuant to that jurisdiction's *emeritus* or *pro bono* practice rule. Lawyers may also be authorized to provide legal services in

this jurisdiction on a temporary basis under Rule 5.5(c) of the Illinois Rules of Professional Conduct.

[4] Lawyers authorized to practice law in another jurisdiction, who principally practice in the area of such other jurisdiction determined by this Court to have suffered a major disaster, and whose practices are disrupted by a major disaster there, and who are not disbarred, suspended from practice or otherwise restricted from practicing law in any other manner in any other jurisdiction, are authorized under paragraph (c) to provide legal services on a temporary basis in this jurisdiction. Those legal services must arise out of and be reasonably related to the lawyer's practice of law in the affected jurisdiction. For purposes of this rule, the determination of a major disaster in another jurisdiction should first be made by the highest court of appellate jurisdiction in that jurisdiction. For the meaning of "arise out of and reasonably related to," see Rule 5.5 Comment [14] of the Illinois Rules of Professional Conduct.

[5] Emergency conditions created by major disasters end, and when they do, the authority created by paragraphs (b) and (c) also ends with appropriate notice to enable lawyers to plan and to complete pending legal matters. Under paragraph (d), this Court determines when those conditions end only for purposes of this rule. The authority granted under paragraph (b) shall end upon such determination except that lawyers assisting residents of this jurisdiction under paragraph (b) may continue to do so for such longer period as is reasonably necessary to complete the representation. The authority created by paragraph (c) will end 60 days after this Court makes such a determination with regard to an affected jurisdiction.

[6] Paragraphs (b) and (c) do not authorize lawyers to appear in the courts of this jurisdiction. Court appearances are subject to the *pro hac vice* admission rules of the particular court. This Court may, in a determination made under paragraph (e)(2), include authorization for lawyers who provide legal services in this jurisdiction under paragraph (b) to appear in all or designated courts of this jurisdiction without need for such *pro hac vice* admission. If such an authorization is included, any *pro hac vice* admission fees shall be waived. A lawyer who has appeared in the courts of this jurisdiction pursuant to paragraph (e) may continue to appear in any such matter notwithstanding a declaration under paragraph (d) that the conditions created by major disaster have ended. Furthermore, withdrawal from a court appearance is subject to Rule 1.16 of the Illinois Rules of Professional Conduct.

[7] Authorization to practice law as a foreign legal consultant or in-house counsel in a United States jurisdiction offers lawyers a limited scope of permitted practice and may therefore restrict that person's ability to provide legal services under this rule.

Rule 719. Admission of Military Spouse Attorneys From Other Jurisdictions

(a) **Eligibility.** A lawyer admitted to the practice of law in another state or the District of Columbia who meets the educational requirements of Rule 703 may receive a license to practice law in this state if the lawyer is:

(1) identified by the Department of Defense (or, for the Coast Guard when it is not operating as a service in the Navy, by the Department of Homeland Security) as the spouse of a service member of the United States Uniformed Services; and/or is a party to a civil union with a service member pursuant to the Illinois Religious Freedom Protection and Civil Union Act; and

(2) is residing—or intends, within the next six months, to be residing—in Illinois due to the service member's military orders for a permanent change of station to the State of Illinois.

(b) **Application Requirements.** To qualify for the license the applicant must file with the Board of Admissions to the Bar the following:

(1) a completed application for license and a completed character and fitness registration application in the form prescribed by the Board;

(2) a certificate of good standing from the highest court of each jurisdiction of admission;

(3) a certificate from the disciplinary authority of each jurisdiction of admission which:

(a) states that the applicant has not been suspended, disbarred or disciplined and that no charges of professional misconduct are pending; or

(b) identifies any suspensions, disbarments, or disciplinary sanctions and any pending charges;

(4) a copy of the service member's military orders reflecting a permanent change of station to a military installation in Illinois; and

(5) such other affidavits, proofs and documentation as may be prescribed by the Board.

(c) **Fee Waiver.** The requisite fees in accordance with Rule 706 will be waived for all lawyers complying with the requirements of Rule 719.

(d) **Character and Fitness Approval.** Each applicant for a license under this rule must receive certification of good moral character and general fitness to practice law by the Committee on Character and Fitness in accordance with the provisions of Rule 708.

(e) **Certification by the Board.** In the event the Board of Admissions to the Bar shall find that the applicant meets the requirements of this rule and has received from the Committee on Character and Fitness its certification of good moral character and general fitness to practice law, the Board shall certify to the Court that such applicant is qualified for licensure.

(f) **Duration and Termination of License.** The license and authorization to perform legal services under this rule shall be limited by the earliest of the following events:

(1) the service member is no longer a member of the United States Uniformed Services;

(2) the military spouse attorney is no longer married to the service member;

(3) a change in the service member's military orders reflecting a permanent change of station to a military installation other than Illinois, except that if the service member has been assigned to an unaccompanied or remote assignment with no dependants authorized, the military spouse attorney may continue to practice pursuant to the provisions of this rule until the service member is assigned to a location with dependants authorized; or

(4) the lawyer is admitted to the general practice of law under any other rule of this Court.

In the event that any of the events listed in subparagraph (f)(1)–(3) occur, the attorney licensed under this rule shall notify the clerk of the Supreme Court of the event in writing within one year of the date upon which the event occurs and upon such notification, the license and authorization to perform services under this rule shall be terminated.

(g) Annual Registration. Once the Court has conferred a license to perform legal services under this rule, the lawyer must register with the Attorney Registration and Disciplinary Commission and pay the fee for active lawyers set forth in Rule 756 for the year in which the license is conferred and for any subsequent year into which the license extends.

(h) Discipline. All lawyers licensed under this rule shall be subject to the jurisdiction of the Court for disciplinary purposes to the same extent as all other lawyers licensed to practice law in this state.

(i) Credit Toward Admission on Motion. The period of time a lawyer practices law while licensed under this rule shall be counted toward his or her eligibility for admission on motion under Rule 705. Adopted June 18, 2013, eff. July 1, 2013.

Rule 720. Reserved

Rule 721. Professional Service Corporations, Professional Associations, Limited Liability Companies, and Registered Limited Liability Partnerships for the Practice of Law

(a) Professional service corporations formed under the Professional Service Corporation Act (805 ILCS 10/1 *et seq.*), professional associations organized under the Professional Association Act (805 ILCS 305/0.01 *et seq.*), limited liability companies organized under the Limited Liability Company Act (805 ILCS 180/1–1 *et seq.*), or registered limited liability partnerships organized under the Uniform Partnership Act (1997) (805 ILCS 206/100 *et seq.*), or professional corporations, professional associations, limited liability companies, or registered limited liability partnerships formed under similar provisions of successor Acts to any of the

foregoing legislation or under similar statutes of other states or jurisdictions of the United States, may engage in the practice of law in Illinois provided that

(1) each natural person shall be licensed to practice law who is (A) a shareholder, officer, or director of the corporation (except the secretary of the corporation), member of the association, member (or manager, if any) of the limited liability company, or partner of the registered limited liability partnership, (B) a shareholder, officer, or director of a corporation (except the secretary of the corporation), member of an association, member (or manager, if any) of a limited liability company, or partner of a registered limited liability partnership that itself is a shareholder of a corporation, member of an association, member (or manager, if any) of a limited liability company, or partner of a registered limited liability partnership engaged in the practice of law, or (C) engaged in the practice of law and an employee of any such corporation, association, limited liability company, or registered limited liability partnership; and

(2) one or more persons shall be members of the bar of Illinois, and engaged in the practice of law in Illinois, who are either (A) shareholders of the corporation, members of the association or limited liability company, or partners of the registered limited liability partnership permitted to engage in the practice of law in Illinois hereunder, or (B) shareholders of a corporation, members of an association or limited liability company, or partners in a registered limited liability partnership permitted to engage in the practice of law in Illinois hereunder that itself is a shareholder of the corporation, member of the association or limited liability company, or partner of the registered limited liability partnership permitted to engage in the practice of law in Illinois hereunder; and

(3) the corporation, association, limited liability company, or registered limited liability partnership shall do nothing which, if done by an individual attorney, would violate the standards of professional conduct applicable to attorneys licensed by this court; and

(4) no natural person shall be permitted to practice law in Illinois who is a shareholder, officer, director of the corporation, member of the association, member (or manager, if any) of the limited liability company, or partner of the registered limited liability partnership, or an employee of the corporation, association, limited liability company, or registered limited liability partnership, unless that person is either a member of the bar in Illinois or specially admitted by court order to practice in Illinois.

(b) This rule does not diminish or change the obligation of each attorney engaged in the practice of law in behalf of the corporation, association, limited liability company, or registered limited liability partnership to conduct himself or herself in accordance with the standards of professional conduct applicable to attorneys licensed by this court. Any attorney who by act or omission causes the corporation, association, limited liability company, or registered limited liability partnership to act in a way which violates standards of professional conduct, including any provision of this rule, is personally responsible for such act or omission and is subject to discipline therefor. Any violation of this rule by the corporation, association, limited liability company, or registered limited liability partnership is a ground for the court to terminate or suspend the right of the corporation, association, limited liability company, or registered limited liability partnership to practice law or otherwise to discipline it.

(c) No corporation, association, limited liability company, or registered limited liability partnership shall engage in the practice of law in Illinois, or open or maintain an establishment for that purpose in Illinois, without a certificate of registration issued by this court.

(d) Unless the corporation, association, limited liability company, or registered limited liability partnership maintains minimum insurance or proof of financial responsibility in accordance with Rule 722, the articles of incorporation or association or organization, or the partnership agreement, shall provide, and in any event the shareholders of the corporation, members of the association or limited liability company, or partners of the registered limited liability partnership shall be deemed to agree by virtue of becoming shareholders, members, or partners, that all shareholders, members, or partners shall be jointly and severally liable for the acts, errors, and omissions of the shareholders, members, or partners, and other employees of the corporation, association, limited liability company, or registered limited liability partnership, arising out of the performance of professional services by the corporation, association, limited liability company, or registered limited liability partnership while they are shareholders, members, or partners.

(e) An application for registration shall be in writing signed by an authorized shareholder of the corporation, member of the association or limited liability company, or partner of the registered limited liability partnership, and filed with the clerk of this court with a fee of $50. The application shall contain the following:

(1) the name and street address of the corporation, association, limited liability company, or registered limited liability partnership in the State of Illinois;

(2) the statute under which it is formed;

(3) the names and addresses of the shareholders of the corporation, members of the association or limited liability company, or partners of the registered limited liability partnership;

(4) a statement of whether the corporation, association, limited liability company, or registered limited liability partnership is on a calendar or fiscal year basis and if fiscal, the closing date;

(5) a statement that each shareholder, officer, and director of the corporation (except the secretary of the corporation), each member of the association, each member (and each manager, if any) of the limited liability company, or each partner of the registered limited liability partnership is a member of the bar of each jurisdiction in which such person practices law and that no disciplinary action is pending against any of them; and

(6) such other information and documents as the court may from time to time require.

(f) A certificate of registration shall continue in effect until it is suspended or revoked, subject, however, to renewal annually on or before January 31 of each year. The application for renewal shall contain the information itemized in paragraph (e) of this rule and be signed by an authorized shareholder, member, or partner and filed with the clerk of this court with a fee of $40. No certificate is assignable.

(g) Nothing in this rule modifies the attorney-client privilege.

(h) To the extent that the provisions of this rule or Rule 722 are inconsistent with any provisions of the Professional Service Corporation Act, the Professional Association Act, the Limited Liability Company Act, or the Uniform Partnership Act, such provisions of said acts shall have no application.

Adopted eff. March 18, 1969. Amended Oct. 21, 1969, eff. Nov. 15, 1969; Oct. 1, 1976, eff. Nov. 15, 1976; Feb. 19, 1982, eff. April 1, 1982; Oct. 9, 1984, eff. Nov. 1, 1984; Feb. 5, 1997, eff. March 1, 1997; April 1, 2003, eff. July 1, 2003; May 20, 2008, effective immediately; Sept. 30, 2009, effective immediately.

Formerly Ill.Rev.Stat.1991, ch. 110A, ¶ 721.

Committee Comments
(April 1, 2003; Revised December 5, 2003)

As amended, Rule 721: (i) includes registered limited liability partnerships among the kinds of entities that may engage in the practice of law in Illinois; (ii) facilitates registration and renewal by permitting a single authorized member of such law firms to execute the application for registration or renewal; and (iii) clarifies that a corporation, association, limited liability company, or registered limited liability partnership formed under the laws of this state or similar statutes of other states or jurisdictions of the United States can itself be a shareholder of a corporation, member of an association or limited liability company, or partner of a registered limited liability partnership that is registered under the rule.

Rule 722.   Limited Liability Legal Practice

(a) For purposes of this rule:

(1) "Limited liability entity" means a corporation, association, limited liability company, or registered limited liability partnership engaged in the practice of law in Illinois pursuant to Rule 721.

(2) "Owner" means a shareholder, member, manager, or partner of a limited liability entity.

(3) "Wrongful conduct" means acts, errors, or omissions in the performance of professional services by any owners or employees of a limited liability entity while they were affiliated with that entity.

(b) The liability, if any, of owners of a limited liability entity, for a claim asserted against the limited liability entity or any of its owners or employees arising out of wrongful conduct, shall be determined by the provisions of the statute under which the limited liability entity is organized if that entity maintains minimum insurance or proof of financial responsibility, as follows:

(1) "Minimum insurance" means a professional liability insurance policy applicable to a limited liability entity, and any of its owners or employees, for wrongful conduct. Such insurance shall exist, in one or more policies, with respect to claims asserted during an annual policy period due to alleged wrongful conduct occurring during the policy period and the previous six years. Such policies shall have a minimum amount of insurance of $100,000 per claim and $250,000 annual aggregate, times the number of lawyers in the firm at the beginning of the annual policy period, provided that the firm's insurance need not exceed $5,000,000 per claim and $10,000,000 annual aggregate. Evidence of any such minimum insurance shall be provided with each application for registration or renewal pursuant to Rule 721 by means of an affidavit or a verification by certification under section 1–109 of the Code of Civil Procedure of an authorized shareholder, member, or partner that his or her firm maintains the minimum insurance required by this rule. For purposes of Rules 721(d) and 722, the minimum amount of insurance required shall not be affected: (A) by any exceptions or exclusions from coverage that are customary with respect to lawyers professional liability insurance policies; (B) if, with respect to a particular claim, the limited liability entity fails to maintain insurance for wrongful conduct occurring before the annual policy period, so long as insurance coverage in the amount specified in this rule exists with respect to the claim in question; or (C) if, during an annual policy period, the per claim or annual aggregate limits are exceeded by the amounts of any claims, judgments, or settlements. If evidence of insurance is provided with a registration or renewal application pursuant to Rule 721 and it is ultimately determined that the limited liability entity failed to maintain minimum insurance during the period covered by that registration or renewal, unless such failure is fraudulent or wilful the joint and several liability of the owners for a claim arising out of wrongful conduct shall be limited to the minimum per claim amount of insurance applicable to the limited liability entity under this rule.

(2) Owners of a limited liability entity that has obtained minimum insurance shall be jointly and severally liable, up to the amount of the deductible or retention, for any claims arising out of wrongful conduct unless the limited liability entity has also provided proof of financial responsibility in a sum no less than the amount of the deductible or retention.

(3) "Proof of financial responsibility" means funds that are specifically designated and segregated for the satisfaction of any judgments against a limited liability entity, and any of its owners or employees, entered by or registered in any court of competent jurisdiction in Illinois, arising out of wrongful conduct. At the beginning of an annual period covered by a certificate of registration pursuant to Rule 721, such funds shall be in a sum no less than the minimum required annual aggregate for minimum insurance by that limited liability entity, unless the proof of financial responsibility is provided solely to apply to the deductible or retention pertaining to the applicable minimum insurance, in which case the funds shall be no less than the amount of the deductible or retention. During the annual period covered by a certificate of registration pursuant to Rule 721, such funds may be used only to satisfy any judgments against the limited liability entity, and any of its owners or employees, entered by or registered in any court of competent jurisdiction in Illinois, arising out of wrongful conduct. Such funds may be in any of the following forms: (A) deposit in trust or in bank escrow of cash, bank certificates of deposit, or United States Treasury obligations; (B) a bank letter of credit, or (C) a surety bond. Evidence of any such proof of financial responsibility shall be provided with each application for registration or renewal pursuant to Rule 721 by means of an affidavit or a verification by certification under section 1–109 of the Code of Civil Procedure of an authorized shareholder, member, or partner that his or her firm maintains the funds required by this rule. Otherwise minimum proof of financial responsibility remains minimum, for purposes of this rule, if the individual or combined amount of any judgments during the annual period covered by the certificate of registration exceeds the amount of the segregated funds.

(4) If a limited liability entity maintains minimum insurance or proof of financial responsibility at the time that a bankruptcy case is commenced with respect to that entity, it shall be deemed to do so with respect to claims asserted after the commencement of the bankruptcy case.

(c) Nothing in this rule or any law under which a limited liability entity is organized shall relieve any lawyer from personal liability for claims arising out of acts, errors, or omissions in the performance of professional services by the lawyer or any person under the lawyer's direct supervision and control.

Adopted April 1, 2003, effective July 1, 2003. Amended March 15, 2004, effective immediately.

Committee Comments
(April 1, 2003)

Rule 721 imposes joint and several liability on lawyers with an ownership interest in law firms organized under statutes that purport to limit vicarious liability, for claims arising out of the performance of professional services by any firm lawyers or employees, unless the firm maintains minimum insurance or proof of financial responsibility in accordance with Rule 722. For lawyers with an ownership interest in such firms to obtain the limited liability authorized by statute, Rule 722 imposes additional obligations, beyond any statutory requirements, to provide sufficient professional liability insurance or other funds to protect clients with such claims.

Rules 721 and 722 do not reduce lawyers' liability for their own professional conduct or that of persons under their direct supervision and control. Nor do these rules affect lawyers' ethical responsibilities for their own conduct, or that of their law firm or their firm's lawyers or employees, under Rules 5.1, 5.2, or 5.3 of the Rules of Professional Conduct.

Rules 723 to 729. Reserved

Rule 730. Group Legal Services

No attorney shall participate in a plan which provides group legal services in this State unless the plan has been registered as hereinafter set forth:

(a) The plan shall be registered in the office of the Administrator of the Attorney Registration and Disciplinary Commission within 15 days of the effective date of the plan on forms supplied by the Administrator.

(b) Amendments to any plan for group legal services and to any other documents required to be filed upon registration of a plan, made subsequent to the registration of the plan, shall be filed in the office of the Administrator no later than 30 days after the adoption of the amendment.

(c) The Administrator shall maintain an index of the plans registered pursuant to this rule. All documents filed in compliance with this rule shall be deemed public documents and shall be available for public inspection during normal business hours.

(d) Neither the Commission nor the Administrator shall approve or disapprove of any plan for group legal services or render any legal opinion regarding any plan. The registration of any plan under this rule shall not be construed to indicate approval or disapproval of the plan.

(e) Plans existing on the effective date of this order shall be registered on or before June 1, 1977.

(f) Subsequent to initial registration, all such plans shall be registered annually on or before July 1 on forms supplied by the Administrator. Plans initially registered prior to July 1, 1977, need not be registered again until July 1, 1978.

Adopted April 21, 1977, eff. May 1, 1977. Amended Sept. 28, 1994, eff. Oct. 1, 1994.

Formerly Ill.Rev.Stat.1991, ch. 110A, ¶ 730.

Rules 731 to 750. Reserved

PART B. REGISTRATION AND DISCIPLINE OF ATTORNEYS

Rules of the Attorney Registration and Disciplinary Commission, are set out following the Illinois Supreme Court Rules.

ORDER ADOPTING PART B OF ARTICLE VII OF THE SUPREME COURT RULES

In re: Registration and Discipline of Attorneys

It is ordered that the attached rules [Rules 751 to 756] are adopted as Rules of this Court to be effective February 1, 1973.

It is further ordered that pending disciplinary matters shall be governed by existing rules until further order of this Court.

ORDER OF JUNE 1, 1973 AMENDING ORDER ADOPTING PART B. OF ARTICLE VII OF THE SUPREME COURT RULES

The order of January 24 [25], 1973, [adopting part B. of Article VII of the Supreme Court Rules] requiring that pending disciplinary matters shall be governed by existing rules, is amended as follows:

1. All disciplinary matters undertaken by the Chicago Bar Association and the Illinois State Bar Association prior to February 1, 1973, shall proceed through the inquiry process under rules in effect prior to February 1, 1973.

2. Complaints on such matters shall be voted and prepared in accordance with the rules in effect prior to February 1, 1973. However, complaints may be drawn, naming the Administrator of the new disciplinary system as complainant, and referred to him for prosecution before the appropriate Hearing Board established by Rule 753 of the Court. The hearing and review of complaints, drawn in the name of the Administrator, shall be governed by Rules 751–768 of the Court and the Rules of the Disciplinary Commission issued pursuant thereto.

3. Complaints heretofore voted but with respect to which no hearing has commenced shall likewise be referred to the Administrator for prosecution before the appropriate Hearing Board established by Rule 753 of the Court. The Administrator shall be substituted as the complainant in all such cases. The hearing and review of such complaints shall be governed by Rules 751–768 of the Court and the Rules of the Disciplinary Commission issued pursuant thereto.

4. No complaints shall be referred to the Administrator in which a hearing has commenced.

5. In all matters in which a complaint has been voted and a hearing has commenced, the hearing and review shall be governed by the rules in effect prior to February 1, 1973.

Rule 751. Attorney Registration and Disciplinary Commission

(a) Authority of the Commission. The registration of, and disciplinary proceedings affecting, members of the Illinois bar, and unauthorized practice of law proceedings instituted under the authority of Rule 752(a), shall be under the administrative supervision of an Attorney Registration and Disciplinary Commission. Any lawyer admitted in another United States jurisdiction who provides legal services on a temporary basis in Illinois pursuant to Rule 5.5 of the Illinois Rules of Professional Conduct shall be subject to the administrative supervision of the Attorney Registration and Disciplinary Commission to the same extent as a lawyer licensed to practice law in this state. The authority granted in this paragraph to the Attorney Registration and Disciplinary Commission related to the unauthorized practice of law proceedings shall be independent of that granted by statute, regulation, or other legal authority to any governmental agency, entity, or individual to pursue action relating to the unauthorized practice of law, including but not limited to any action by the Illinois Attorney General or State's Attorney, or any action filed pursuant to the Illinois Attorney Act (705 ILCS 205/1).

(b) Membership and Terms. The Commission shall consist of four members of the Illinois bar and three nonlawyers appointed by the Supreme Court. One member shall be designated by the court as chairperson and one member shall be designated by the court as vice-chairperson. Unless the court specifies a shorter term, all members shall be appointed for three-year terms and shall serve until their successors are appointed. Any member of the Commission may be removed by the court at any time, without cause.

(c) Compensation. None of the members of the Commission shall receive compensation for serving as such, but all members shall be reimbursed for their necessary expenses.

(d) Quorum. Four members of the Commission shall constitute a quorum for the transaction of business. The concurrence of four members shall be required for all action taken by the Commission.

(e) Duties. The Commission shall have the following duties:

(1) to appoint, with the approval of the Supreme Court, an administrator to serve as the principal executive officer of the registration and disciplinary system. The Administrator shall receive such compensation as the Commission authorizes from time to time;

(2) to make rules for disciplinary and unauthorized practice of law proceedings not inconsistent with the rules of this court;

(3) to supervise the activities of the Administrator; supervision of the Administrator shall include review, after the fact, of representative samples of investigative matters concluded by the Administrator without reference to the Inquiry Board;

(4) to authorize the Administrator to hire attorneys, investigators and clerical personnel and to set the salaries of such persons;

(5) to appoint from time to time, as it may deem appropriate, members of the bar to serve as commissioners in addition to those provided for in Rule 753;

(6) to collect and administer the disciplinary fund provided for in Rule 756, to collect and remit to the Lawyers' Assistance Program Fund the fee described in Rule 756(a)(1) and the Lawyers' Assistance Program Act (30 ILCS 105/5.570 [1]), to collect and remit to the Lawyers Trust Fund the fee described in Rule 756(a)(1), to collect and remit to the Supreme Court Commission on Professionalism the fee described in Rule 756(a)(1) and, on or before April 30 of each year, file with the court an accounting of the monies received and expended for disciplinary activities and fees remitted to the Lawyers' Assistance Program Fund, the Lawyers Trust Fund, and the Supreme Court Commission on Professionalism, and a report of such activities for the previous calendar year, which shall be published by the court, and there shall be an independent annual audit of the disciplinary fund as directed by the court, the expenses of which shall be paid out of the fund;

(7) to submit an annual report to the court evaluating the effectiveness of the registration and disciplinary system and recommending any changes it deems desirable; and

(8) to develop a comprehensive orientation program for new members of the Inquiry Board and implement that program.

Adopted Jan. 25, 1973, eff. Feb 1, 1973. Amended eff. May 17, 1973, April 1, 1974, and May 21, 1975; Aug. 9, 1983, eff. Oct. 1, 1983; April 10, 1987, eff. Aug. 1, 1987; June 4, 1987, eff. immediately; March 17, 1988, eff. immediately; Oct. 13, 1989, eff. immediately; Oct. 4, 2002, eff. immediately; Sept. 29, 2005, eff. immediately; July 1, 2009, eff. Jan. 1, 2010; Dec. 7, 2011, eff. immediately; Jan. 17, 2013, eff. immediately.

Formerly Ill.Rev.Stat.1991, ch. 110A, ¶ 751.
[1] 30 ILCS 105/5.570, as enacted by P.A. 92–747, § 90.

Rule 752. Administrator

Subject to the supervision of the Commission, the Administrator shall:

(a) On his own motion, on the recommendation of an Inquiry Board or at the instance of an aggrieved party, investigate conduct of attorneys licensed in Illinois and attorneys admitted in another United States jurisdiction who provide legal services on a temporary basis in Illinois pursuant to Rule 5.5 of the Illinois Rules of Professional Conduct, whose conduct tends to defeat the administration of justice or to bring the courts or the legal profession into disrepute, and investigate allegations of the unauthorized practice of law, including investigations involving disbarred lawyers and other persons, entities, or associations that are not authorized to practice law by this court.

(b) Assist each Inquiry Board in its investigations and prosecute disciplinary cases before the Hearing Boards, the Review Board and the court and prosecute unauthorized practice of law proceedings pursuant to Rule 779;

(c) Employ at such compensation as may be authorized by the Commission, such investigative, clerical and legal personnel as may be necessary for the efficient conduct of his office;

(d) Discharge any such personnel whose performance is unsatisfactory to him; and

(e) Maintain such records, make such reports and perform such other duties as may be prescribed by the Commission from time to time.

Adopted Jan. 25, 1973, eff. Feb. 1, 1973. Amended eff. May 17, 1973, and April 1, 1974; March 17, 1988, eff. immediately; Dec. 7, 2011, eff. immediately.

Formerly Ill.Rev.Stat.1991, ch. 110A, ¶ 752.

Rule 753. Inquiry, Hearing and Review Boards

(a) Inquiry Board

(1) There shall be an Inquiry Board. It shall consist of members of the bar of Illinois and nonlawyers appointed by the Commission to serve annual terms as commissioners of the court. Nonlawyer members shall be appointed to the Board in a ratio of two lawyers for each nonlawyer. The Commission may appoint as many members of the Board as it deems necessary to carry on the work of the Board.

(2) The Board shall inquire into and investigate matters referred to it by the Administrator. The Board may also initiate investigations on its own motion and may refer matters to the Administrator for investigation.

(3) After investigation and consideration, the Board shall dispose of matters before it by voting to dismiss the charge, to close an investigation, to file a complaint with the Hearing Board, or to institute unauthorized practice of law proceedings.

(4) The Board may act in panels. Each panel shall consist of two lawyers and one nonlawyer as designated by the Commission. The Commission shall designate one of the members of each panel as chairman. The majority of a panel shall constitute a quorum and the concurrence of a majority shall be necessary to a decision.

(b) Filing a Complaint.
A disciplinary complaint voted by the Inquiry Board shall be prepared by the Administrator and filed with the Hearing Board. The complaint shall reasonably inform the attorney of the acts of misconduct he is alleged to have committed.

(c) Hearing Board

(1) There shall be a Hearing Board. It shall consist of members of the bar of Illinois and nonlawyers appointed by the Commission to serve annual terms as commissioners of the court. Members shall be appointed to the Board in a ratio of two lawyers for each nonlawyer.

(2) The Hearing Board may act in panels of not less than three members each, as designated by the Commission. The Commission shall also designate one of the lawyer members of each panel as chairperson. The majority of a panel shall constitute a quorum and the concurrence of a majority shall be necessary to a decision. In the absence of the chairperson of a panel at a hearing, the lawyer member present shall serve as acting chairperson.

(3) The hearing panels shall conduct hearings on complaints filed with the Board and on petitions referred to the Board. The panel shall make findings of fact and conclusions of fact and law, together with a recommendation for discipline, dismissal of the complaint or petition, or nondisciplinary disposition. The Hearing Board may order that it will administer a reprimand to the respondent in lieu of recommending disciplinary action by the court.

(4) The scheduling of matters before the Board shall be in accordance with Commission rules.

(5) Proceedings before the Board, including discovery practice, shall be in accordance with the Code of Civil Procedure and the rules of the supreme court as modified by rules promulgated by the Commission pursuant to Supreme Court Rule 751(a). Information regarding prior discipline of a respondent will not be divulged to a hearing panel until after there has been a finding of misconduct, unless that information would be admissible for reasons other than to show a propensity to commit the misconduct in question.

(6) Except as otherwise expressly provided in these rules, the standard of proof in all hearings shall be clear and convincing evidence.

(d) Review of Hearing Board Reports

(1) *Review Board.* There shall be a nine-member Review Board which shall be appointed by the court. Appointments shall be for a term of three years or until a successor is appointed. Appointments to the Review Board shall be staggered, so that the terms of three members are scheduled to expire each year. No member shall be appointed for more than three consecutive three-year terms. One member shall be designated by the court as chairperson and one member may be designated by the court as vice-chairperson. The Review Board shall function in panels of three, presided over by the most senior member of the panel. The concurrence of two members of a panel shall be necessary to a decision.

(2) *Exceptions; Agreed Matters.* Reports of the Hearing Board shall be docketed with the Review Board upon the filing of a notice of exceptions by either party. The respondent or the Administrator may file exceptions to the report of the Hearing

Board with the Review Board within 21 days of the filing of the report in the Commission. If neither the respondent nor the Administrator files a notice of exceptions to the Hearing Board report, and the report recommends action by the court, the clerk of the Attorney Registration and Disciplinary Commission shall submit the report of the Hearing Board to the court as an agreed matter. Upon the submission of any matter as an agreed matter, the clerk of the Commission shall give notice to the parties of that submission. Within 21 days after submission of the report to the court, the Administrator shall file a motion to approve and confirm the report of the Hearing Board. No response to this motion shall be filed unless ordered by the court on its own motion or pursuant to a motion for leave to respond. Upon receipt of the motion to approve and confirm, the court may enter a final order as recommended by the Hearing Board or as otherwise determined by the court, order briefs or oral argument or both, or remand the matter with directions to the Hearing Board or the Review Board.

(3) *Action by the Review Board.* The Review Board may approve the findings of the Hearing Board, may reject or modify such findings as it determines are against the manifest weight of the evidence, may make such additional findings as are established by clear and convincing evidence, may approve, reject or modify the recommendations, may remand the proceeding for further action or may dismiss the proceeding. The Review Board may order that it will administer a reprimand to the respondent in lieu of recommending disciplinary action by the court. A copy of the report or order of the Review Board shall be served on the respondent and the Administrator.

(e) Review of Review Board Reports

(1) *Petition for Leave to File Exceptions.* Reports or orders of the Review Board shall be reviewed by the court only upon leave granted by the court or upon the court's own motion. Either party may petition the court for leave to file exceptions to the order or report of the Review Board. The petition shall be filed within 35 days of the filing of the order or report in the Commission. The supreme court, or a justice thereof, on motion supported by affidavit or verification by certification under section 1–109 of the Code of Civil Procedure may extend the time for petitioning for leave to file exceptions, but such motions are not favored and will be allowed only in the most extreme and compelling circumstances. (See Rule 361.)

(2) *Grounds for Petition for Leave to File Exceptions.* Whether a petition for leave to file exceptions will be granted is a matter of sound judicial discretion. The following, while neither controlling nor fully measuring the court's discretion, indicate the character of the reasons which will be considered; the general importance of the question presented; the existence of a conflict between the report of the Review Board and prior decisions of the court; and the existence of a substantial disparity between the discipline recommended and discipline imposed in similar cases.

(3) *Contents of Petition for Leave to File Exceptions.* The petition for leave to file exceptions shall contain, in the following order:

(a) a request for leave to file exceptions;

(b) a statement of the date upon which the report of the Review Board was filed;

(c) a statement of the points relied upon for rejection of the report of the Review Board;

(d) a fair and accurate statement of the facts, which shall contain the facts necessary to an understanding of the case, without argument or comment, with appropriate references to the record by transcript page and exhibit number;

(e) a short argument (including appropriate authorities) stating why review by the supreme court is warranted and why the decision of the Review Board should be rejected; and

(f) a copy of the reports of the Hearing and Review Boards and proposed exceptions shall be appended to the petition. The petition shall otherwise be prepared, served, and filed in accordance with requirements for briefs as set forth in Rule 341.

(4) *Answer.* The opposing party need not but may file an answer, with proof of service, within 14 days after the expiration of the time for the filing of the petition. The supreme court, or a justice thereof, on motion supported by affidavit or verification by certification under section 1–109 of the Code of Civil Procedure may extend the time for filing an answer, but such motions are not favored and will be allowed only in the most extreme and compelling circumstances. (See Rule 361.) An answer shall set forth reasons why the petition should not be granted, and shall conform, to the extent appropriate, to the form specified in this rule for the petition, omitting the first four items set forth in paragraph (3) except to the extent that correction of the petition is considered necessary. The answer shall otherwise be prepared, served, and filed in accordance with the requirements for briefs as set forth in Rule 341. No reply to the answer shall be filed.

(5) *Ruling on Petition.*

(a) If the court allows exceptions to an order or report of the Review Board, it may:

(i) enter a final order as recommended by the Review Board or as otherwise determined by the court;

(ii) enter an order remanding the matter with directions to the Hearing Board or the Review Board; or

(iii) accept the matter for further consideration.

If the case is accepted for further consideration, the clerk of the Attorney Registration and Disciplinary Commission shall transmit the record of the case to the court. Either party may assert error in any ruling, action, conclusion or recommendation of the Review Board without regard to whether the party filed exceptions. The petition for leave to file exceptions allowed by the court shall stand as the brief of the appellant. Remaining briefs shall be prepared, filed, and served in compliance with Rules 341 and 343. The parties shall not be entitled to oral argument before the court as of right. Oral argument may be requested in accordance with Rule 352.

(b) If the court denies leave to file exceptions, it may:

(i) enter a final order as recommended by the Review Board or as otherwise determined by the court; or

(ii) enter an order remanding the matter with directions to the Hearing Board or the Review Board.

(6) *Agreed Matters.* If a petition for leave to file exceptions is not timely filed and if the report of the Review Board recommends action by the court, the clerk of the Attorney Registration and Disciplinary Commission shall submit the report of the Review Board together with a copy of the report of the Hearing Board to the court as an agreed matter. Upon the submission of any matter as an agreed matter, the clerk of the Commission shall give notice to the parties of that submission. Within 21 days after submission of the report to the court, the Administrator shall file a motion to approve and confirm the report of the Review Board. No response to this motion shall be filed unless ordered by the court on its own motion or pursuant to a motion for leave to respond. Upon receipt of the motion to approve and confirm, the court may enter a final order of discipline as recommended or as otherwise determined by the court, order briefs or oral argument or both, or remand the matter with directions to the Hearing Board or the Review Board.

(7) *Finality of Review Board Decision.* If exceptions are not filed and the order or report of the Review Board does not recommend disciplinary action by the court, the order or report of the Review Board shall be final.

(f) Duty of Respondent or Petitioner. It shall be the duty of the respondent or petitioner who is the subject of any investigation or proceeding contemplated by these rules to appear at any hearing at which his presence is required or requested. Failure to comply, without good cause shown, may be considered

as a separate ground for the imposition of discipline or denial of a petition.

Adopted Jan. 25, 1973, eff. Feb. 1, 1973. Amended eff. May 17, 1973, April 1, 1974, and May 21, 1975; Oct. 1, 1976, eff. Nov. 15, 1976; Aug. 9, 1983, eff. Oct. 1, 1983; July 1, 1985, eff. Aug. 1, 1985; Oct. 13, 1989, eff. immediately; Oct. 16, 1990, eff. Nov. 1, 1990; May 26, 1993, eff. immediately; Oct. 15, 1993, eff. immediately; Dec. 30, 1993, eff. Jan. 1, 1994; Feb. 2, 1994, eff. immediately; Dec. 1, 1995, eff. immediately; June 29, 2006, eff. Sept. 1, 2006; Dec. 7, 2011, eff. immediately; Mar. 18, 2016, eff. immediately.

Formerly Ill.Rev.Stat.1991, ch. 110A, ¶ 753.

Rule 754. Subpoena Power

(a) **Power to Take Evidence.** The Administrator, the Inquiry Board and the Hearing Board are empowered to take evidence of respondents, petitioners and any other attorneys or persons who may have knowledge of the pertinent facts concerning any matter which is the subject of an investigation or hearing.

(b) **Issuance of Subpoenas.** The clerk of the court shall issue a subpoena *ad testificandum* or a subpoena *duces tecum* as provided below:

(1) upon request of the Administrator related to an investigation conducted pursuant to Rules 752, 753, 759, 767, 779, or 780 or related to a deposition or hearing before the Hearing Board; the Administrator may use a subpoena in an investigation conducted pursuant to Rule 753 until such time as a complaint is filed with the Hearing Board;

(2) upon request of the Inquiry or Hearing Board related to a proceeding pending before the Board;

(3) upon request of the respondent or the petitioner related to a deposition or hearing before the Hearing Board;

(4) upon request of the Administrator related to the investigation or review of a Client Protection Claim; or

(5) upon the request of the Administrator in aid of a person or entity authorized to compel a witness to appear by the laws governing lawyer discipline or disability investigations and proceedings in another jurisdiction, for that person or entity to compel a witness to appear in the county in Illinois in which the witness resided, is employed, or is served with the subpoena and to give testimony and/or produce documents, to the same extent authorized in the discipline or disability investigation and/or proceeding of the other jurisdiction. The person or entity seeking the issuance of a subpoena shall provide to the Administrator proof of authority to compel the attendance of the witness under the laws of the other jurisdiction.

(c) **Fees and Costs.** Respondents and petitioners shall not be entitled to a witness fee or reimbursement for costs to comply with any subpoena issued pursuant to this rule. All other persons shall be entitled to payment for fees, mileage and other costs as provided by law. Such payments shall be made by the Commission for a subpoena issued at the instance of the Administrator, the Inquiry Board or the Hearing Board. Such payments shall be made by the respondent or the petitioner for a subpoena issued at his instance.

(d) **Judicial Review.** A motion to quash a subpoena issued pursuant to this rule shall be filed with the court. Any person who fails or refuses to comply with a subpoena may be held in contempt of the court.

(e) **Enforcement.** A petition for rule to show cause why a person should not be held in contempt for failure or refusal to comply with a subpoena issued pursuant to this rule shall be filed with the court. Unless the court orders otherwise, the petition shall be referred to the chief judge of the circuit court of Cook County or Sangamon County or any other judge of those circuits designated by the chief judge. The designated judge shall be empowered to entertain petitions, hear evidence, and enter orders compelling compliance with subpoenas issued pursuant to this rule. When a petition is referred to the circuit court, the following procedures should be followed:

(1) The Clerk of the Supreme Court shall forward a copy of the petition for rule to show cause to the designated judge of the circuit court and, at the same time, shall send notice to the party who filed the petition and all persons upon whom the petition was served that the matter has been referred to the circuit court. The notice shall name the judge to whom the matter has been referred and state the courthouse at which proceedings pertaining to the petition will be heard.

(2) Any answer to the petition or other responsive pleading shall be filed with the Clerk of the Supreme Court and a copy of such answer or other pleading shall be delivered to the judge to whom the matter has been referred by mailing or hand delivering the copy to the chambers of the designated judge. The proof of service for such answer or other responsive pleading shall state that delivery to the designated judge was made in accordance with this rule.

(3) Proceedings on the petition before the designated judge, including scheduling of hearings and time for serving notices of hearing, shall be governed by the rules of the circuit court in which the designated judge sits, unless otherwise ordered by the judge.

(4) The designated judge may enter any order available to the circuit court in the exercise of its authority to enforce subpoenas, including orders for confinement or fines. If the judge finds an attorney in contempt for failure to comply with a subpoena issued pursuant to this rule, in addition to entertaining any other order, the judge may also recommend that the court suspend the attorney from the practice of law in this State until the attorney complies

with the subpoena. Upon issuance of such a recommendation by the designated judge, the Administrator shall file with the Clerk of the Supreme Court a petition seeking implementation of the recommendation of suspension.

Adopted Jan. 25, 1973, eff. Feb. 1, 1973. Amended May 21, 1975; June 12, 1987, eff. Aug. 1, 1987; Nov. 29, 1990, eff. Dec. 1, 1990; March 28, 1994, eff. immediately; April 1, 1994, eff. immediately; Dec. 7, 2011; eff. immediately; April 8, 2013, eff. immediately.

Formerly Ill.Rev.Stat.1991, ch. 110A, ¶ 754.

Rule 755. Assistance of Members of the Bar— Rule Making Power of Boards

(a) **Assistance of Bar.** The Commission and the inquiry, hearing and review boards may call to their assistance other members of the bar.

(b) **Supplementary Rules.** Subject to the approval of the Commission, the inquiry, hearing and review boards may make supplementary rules concerning the procedures before the respective boards.

Adopted Jan. 25, 1973, eff. Feb. 1, 1973. Amended Aug. 9, 1983, eff. Oct. 1, 1983.

Formerly Ill.Rev.Stat.1991, ch. 110A, ¶ 755.

Rule 756. Registration and Fees

(a) **Annual Registration Required.** Except as hereinafter provided, every attorney admitted to practice law in this state shall register and pay an annual registration fee to the Commission on or before the first day of January. Every out-of-state attorney permitted to appear and provide legal services in a proceeding pursuant to Rule 707 shall register for each year in which the attorney has such an appearance of record in one or more proceedings. Annual registration fees and penalties paid for the year or prior years shall be deemed earned and non-refundable on and after the first day of January. Except as provided below, all fees and penalties shall be retained as a part of the disciplinary fund. The following schedule shall apply beginning with registration for 2017 and until further order of the court:

(1) No registration fee is required of an attorney admitted to the bar less than one year before the first day of January for which the registration fee is due; an attorney admitted to the bar for more than one year but less than three years before the first day of January for which the registration fee is due shall pay an annual registration fee of $121; an out-of-state attorney permitted to appear and provide legal services pursuant to Rule 707 shall pay a registration fee of $121 for each year in which the attorney's appearance is of record in one or more such proceedings if a per-proceeding fee is required in any such proceeding under Rule 707(f); an attorney admitted to the bar for more than three years before the first day of January for which the regis-

tration fee is due shall pay an annual registration fee of $385, out of which $10 shall be remitted to the Lawyers' Assistance Program Fund, $95 shall be remitted to the Lawyers Trust Fund, $25 shall be remitted to the Supreme Court Commission on Professionalism, and $25 shall be remitted to the Client Protection Program Trust Fund. For purposes of this rule, the time shall be computed from the date of the attorney's initial admission to practice in any jurisdiction in the United States.

(2) An attorney in the Armed Forces of the United States shall be exempt from paying a registration fee until the first day of January following discharge.

(3) No registration fee is required of any attorney during the period he or she is serving in one of the following offices in the judicial branch:

(A) in the office of justice, judge, associate judge or magistrate of a court of the United States of America or the State of Illinois; or

(B) in the office of judicial law clerk, administrative assistant, secretary or assistant secretary to such a justice, judge, associate judge or magistrate, or in any other office included within the Supreme Court budget that assists the Supreme Court in its adjudicative responsibilities, provided that the exemption applies only if the attorney is prohibited by the terms of his or her employment from actively engaging in the practice of law.

(4) Upon written application and for good cause shown, the Administrator may excuse the payment of any registration fee in any case in which payment thereof will cause undue hardship to the attorney.

(5) An attorney may advise the Administrator in writing that he or she desires to assume inactive status and, thereafter, register as an inactive status attorney. The annual registration fee for an inactive status attorney shall be $121. Upon such registration, the attorney shall be placed upon inactive status and shall no longer be eligible to practice law or hold himself or herself out as being authorized to practice law in this state, except as is provided in paragraph (k) of this rule. An attorney who is on the master roll as an inactive status attorney may advise the Administrator in writing that he or she desires to resume the practice of law, and thereafter register as active upon payment of the registration fee required under this rule and submission of verification from the Director of MCLE that he or she has complied with MCLE requirements as set forth in Rule 790 *et seq*. If the attorney returns from inactive status after having paid the inactive status fee for the year, the attorney shall pay the difference between the inactive status registration fee and the registration fee required under paragraphs (a)(1) through (a)(3) of this rule. Inactive status under this rule does not include inactive disability status as described in Rules 757 and 758.

Any lawyer on inactive disability status is not required to pay an annual fee.

(6) An attorney may advise the Administrator in writing that he or she desires to assume retirement status and, thereafter, register as a retired attorney. Upon such registration, the attorney shall be placed upon retirement status and shall no longer be eligible to practice law or hold himself or herself out as being authorized to practice law in this state, except as is provided in paragraph (k) of this rule. The retired attorney is relieved thereafter from the annual obligation to register and pay the registration fee. A retired attorney may advise the Administrator in writing that he or she desires to register as an active or inactive status lawyer and, thereafter so register upon payment of the fee required for the current year for that registration status, plus the annual registration fee that the attorney would have been required to pay if registered as active for each of the years during which the attorney was on retirement status. If the lawyer seeks to register as active, he or she must also submit, as part of registering, verification from the Director of MCLE of the lawyer's compliance with MCLE requirements as set forth in Rule 790 *et seq*.

(7) An attorney who is on voluntary inactive status pursuant to former Rule 770 who wishes to register for any year after 1999 shall file a petition for restoration under Rule 759. If the petition is granted, the attorney shall advise the Administrator in writing whether he or she wishes to register as active, inactive or retired, and shall pay the fee required for that status for the year in which the restoration order is entered. Any such attorney who petitions for restoration after December 31, 2000, shall pay a sum equal to the annual registration fees that the attorney would have been required to pay for each full year after 1999 during which the attorney remained on Rule 770 inactive status without payment of a fee.

(8) Permanent Retirement Status. An attorney may file a petition with the court requesting that he or she be placed on permanent retirement status. All of the provisions of retirement status enumerated in Rule 756(a)(6) shall apply, except that an attorney who is granted permanent retirement status may not thereafter change his or her registration designation to active or inactive status, petition for reinstatement pursuant to Rule 767, or provide *pro bono* services as otherwise allowed under paragraph (k) of this rule.

(A) The petition for permanent retirement status must be accompanied by a consent from the Administrator, consenting to permanent retirement status. The Administrator may consent if no prohibitions listed in subparagraph (a)(8)(B) of this rule exist. If the petition is not accompanied by a consent from the Administrator, it shall be denied.

(B) An attorney shall not be permitted to assume permanent retirement status if:

1. there is a pending investigation or proceeding against the attorney in which clear and convincing evidence has or would establish that:

a. the attorney converted funds or misappropriated funds or property of a client or third party in violation of a rule of the Illinois Rules of Professional Conduct;

b. the attorney engaged in criminal conduct that reflects adversely on the attorney's honesty in violation of Rule 8.4(b) of the Illinois Rules of Professional Conduct; or

c. the attorney's conduct resulted in or is likely to result in actual prejudice (loss of money, legal rights, or valuable property rights) to a client or other person, unless restitution has been made; or

2. the attorney retains an active license to practice law in any jurisdictions other than the State of Illinois.

(C) If permanent retirement status is granted, any pending disciplinary investigation of the attorney shall be closed and any proceeding against the attorney shall be dismissed. The Administrator may resume such investigations pursuant to Commission Rule 54 and may initiate additional investigations and proceedings of the attorney as circumstances warrant. The permanently retired attorney shall notify other jurisdictions in which the he or she is licensed to practice law of his or her permanent retirement in Illinois. The permanently retired attorney may not reactivate a license to practice law or obtain a license to practice law in any other jurisdiction.

(b) The Master Roll. The Administrator shall prepare a master roll of attorneys consisting of the names of attorneys who have registered and have paid or are exempt from paying the registration fee and of recently admitted attorneys who are not yet required to register. The Administrator shall maintain the master roll in a current status. At all times a copy of the master roll shall be on file in the office of the clerk of the court. An attorney who is not listed on the master roll is not entitled to practice law or to hold himself or herself out as authorized to practice law in this state. An attorney listed on the master roll as on inactive or retirement status shall not be entitled to practice law or to hold himself or herself out as authorized to practice law in Illinois, except as is provided in paragraph (k) of this rule.

(c) Registration.

(1) Each attorney is obliged to register on or before the first day of January of each year unless the attorney is on retirement status pursuant to paragraph (a)(6) of this rule, has been allowed to assume permanent retirement status pursuant to paragraph (a)(8) of this rule, or has been placed on inactive status pursuant to former Rule 770, except that an attorney not authorized to practice law due to discipline or disability inactive status is not required to register until the conclusion of the discipline or disability inactive status.

(2) Registration requires that the attorney provide all information specified under paragraphs (c) through (g) of this rule. An attorney's registration shall not be complete until all such information has been submitted.

(3) On or before the first day of November of each year, the Administrator shall send to each attorney on the Master Roll a notice of the annual registration requirement. The notice may be sent to the attorney's listed Master Roll mail or email address. Failure to receive the notice shall not constitute an excuse for failure to register.

(4) Each attorney must submit registration information by means of the ARDC online registration system or other means specified by the Administrator. Registration payments may be submitted online, by check sent through the mail to the address designated by the Administrator, or through other means authorized by the Administrator.

(5) Each attorney shall update required registration information within 30 days of any change, except for those attorneys relieved of the registration obligation under a provision of this rule.

(6) Except as otherwise provided in this rule or Supreme Court Rule 766, information disclosed under paragraphs (c) through (g) shall not be confidential.

(d) Disclosure of Trust Accounts. Each lawyer shall identify any and all accounts maintained by the lawyer during the preceding 12 months to hold property of clients or third persons in the lawyer's possession in connection with a representation, as required under Rule 1.15(a) of the Illinois Rules of Professional Conduct, by providing the account name, account number and financial institution for each account. For each account, the lawyer shall also indicate whether each account is an IOLTA account, as defined in Rule 1.15(i)(2) of the Illinois Rules of Professional Conduct. If a lawyer does not maintain a trust account, the lawyer shall state the reason why no such account is required.

(e) Disclosure of Malpractice Insurance. Each lawyer shall disclose whether the lawyer has malpractice insurance on the date of the registration, and if so, shall disclose the dates of coverage for the policy. The Administrator may conduct random audits to assure the accuracy of information reported. Each lawyer shall maintain, for a period of seven years from the date the coverage is reported, documentation showing the name of the insurer, the policy number, the amount of coverage and the term of the policy, and shall produce such documentation upon the Administrator's request. The requirements of this subsection shall not apply to attorneys serving in the office of justice, judge, associate judge or magistrate as defined in subparagraph (a)(3) of this rule on the date of registration.

(f) Disclosure of Voluntary *Pro Bono* Service. Each lawyer shall report the approximate amount of his or her *pro bono* legal service and the amount of qualified monetary contributions made during the preceding 12 months.

(1) *Pro bono* legal service includes the delivery of legal services or the provision of training without charge or expectation of a fee, as defined in the following subparagraphs:

(a) legal services rendered to a person of limited means;

(b) legal services to charitable, religious, civic, community, governmental or educational organizations in matters designed to address the needs of persons of limited means;

(c) legal services to charitable, religious, civic, or community organizations in matters in furtherance of their organizational purposes; and

(d) training intended to benefit legal service organizations or lawyers who provide *pro bono* services.

In a fee case, a lawyer's billable hours may be deemed *pro bono* when the client and lawyer agree that further services will be provided voluntarily. Legal services for which payment was expected, but is uncollectible, do not qualify as *pro bono* legal service.

(2) *Pro bono* legal service to persons of limited means refers not only to those persons whose household incomes are below the federal poverty standard, but also to those persons frequently referred to as the "working poor." Lawyers providing *pro bono* legal service need not undertake an investigation to determine client eligibility. Rather, a good-faith determination by the lawyer of client eligibility is sufficient.

(3) Qualified monetary contribution means a financial contribution to an organization as enumerated in subparagraph (1)(b) which provides legal services to persons of limited means or which contributes financial support to such an organization.

(4) As part of the lawyer's annual registration fee statement, the report required by subsection (f) shall be made by answering the following questions:

(a) Did you, within the past 12 months, provide any *pro bono* legal services as described in subparagraphs (1) through (4) below? Yes No If no, are you prohibited from providing legal services because of your employment?

___ Yes ___ No

If yes, identify the approximate number of hours provided in each of the following categories where the service was provided without charge or expectation of a fee:

(1) hours of legal services to a person/persons of limited means;

(2) hours of legal services to charitable, religious, civic, community, governmental or educational organizations in matters designed to address the needs of persons of limited means;

(3) hours of legal services to charitable, religious, civic or community organizations in furtherance of their organizational purposes; and

(4) hours providing training intended to benefit legal service organizations or lawyers who provide *pro bono* services.

Legal services for which payment was expected, but is not collectible, do not qualify as *pro bono* services and should not be included.

(b) Have you made a monetary contribution to an organization which provides legal services to persons of limited means or which contributes financial support to such organization? Yes No

If yes, approximate amount: $ _____.

(5) Information provided pursuant to this subsection (f) shall be deemed confidential pursuant to the provisions of Rule 766, but the Commission may report such information in the aggregate.

(g) Practice Related Information. Each attorney shall provide the following practice related information:

(1) An address, email address, and telephone number designated by the attorney as the attorney's listings on the Master Roll;

(2) The attorney's residential address, which shall be deemed to be the address required by paragraph (g)(1) above if the attorney has not provided such an address;

(3) The name of all other states of the United States in which the lawyer is licensed to practice law; and

(4) For attorneys on active status and engaged in the practice of law, the type of entity at which the attorney practices law, the number of attorneys in that organization, the principal areas of law in which the attorney practices, and whether that organization has established a written succession plan.

Information provided pursuant to paragraphs (g)(2) and (g)(4) of this rule shall be deemed confidential pursuant to this rule. Information pursuant to paragraph (g)(1) shall be confidential pursuant to this rule for a lawyer registered under paragraph (a)(5) or (a)(6) of this rule, on inactive status pursuant to former Rule 770, on permanent retirement status under paragraph (a)(8) of this rule, or exempt from payment of a fee under paragraph (a)(3) of this rule. The Administrator may release confidential information under paragraph (g)(1) of this rule upon written application demonstrating good cause and the absence of risk of harm to the lawyer. The Commission may report in the aggregate information made confidential by paragraph (g).

(h) Removal from the Master Roll. On or after February 1 of each year the Administrator shall remove from the master roll the name of any person who has not registered for that year. A lawyer will be deemed not registered for the year if the lawyer has not paid all required fees and has not provided the information required by paragraphs (c) through (g) of this rule. Any person whose name is not on the master roll and who practices law or who holds himself or herself out as being authorized to practice law in this state is engaged in the unauthorized practice of law and may also be held in contempt of the court.

(i) Reinstatement to the Master Roll. An attorney whose name has been removed from the master roll solely for failure to register and pay the registration fee may be reinstated as a matter of course upon registering and paying the registration fee prescribed for the period of his suspension, plus the sum of $25 per month for each month that such registration fee is delinquent.

(j) No Effect on Disciplinary Proceedings. The provisions of this rule pertaining to registration status shall not bar, limit or stay any disciplinary investigations or proceedings against an attorney except to the extent provided in Rule 756(a)(8) regarding permanent retirement status.

(k) *Pro Bono* Authorization for Inactive and Retired Status Attorneys and Attorneys Admitted in Other States.

(1) Authorization to Provide *Pro Bono* Services. An attorney who is registered as inactive or retired under Rule 756(a)(5) or (a)(6), or an attorney who is admitted in another state and is not disbarred or otherwise suspended from practice in any jurisdiction shall be authorized to provide *pro bono* legal services under the following circumstances:

(a) without charge or an expectation of a fee by the attorney;

(b) to persons of limited means or to organizations, as defined in paragraph (f) of this rule; and

(c) under the auspices of a sponsoring entity, which must be a not-for-profit legal services organization, governmental entity, law school clinical program, or bar association providing *pro bono* legal services as defined in paragraph (f)(1) of this rule.

(2) Duties of Sponsoring Entities. In order to qualify as a sponsoring entity, an organization must submit to the Administrator an application identifying the nature of the organization as one described in section (k)(1)(c) of this rule and describing any program for providing *pro bono* services which the entity sponsors and in which attorneys covered under paragraph (k) may participate. In the application, a responsible attorney shall verify that the program will provide appropriate training and support and malpractice insurance for volunteers and that the sponsoring entity will notify the Administrator as soon as any attorney authorized to provide services under this rule has ended his or her participation in the program. The organization is required to provide malpractice insurance coverage for any attorneys participating in the program and must inform the Administrator if the organization ceases to be a sponsoring entity under this rule.

(3) Procedure for Attorneys Seeking Authorization to Provide *Pro Bono* Services. An attorney admitted in Illinois who is registered as inactive or retired, or an attorney who is admitted in another state but not Illinois, who seeks to provide *pro bono* services under this rule shall submit a statement to the Administrator so indicating, along with a verification from a sponsoring entity or entities that the attorney will be participating in a *pro bono* program under the auspices of that entity. An attorney who is seeking authorization based on admission in another state shall also disclose all other state admissions and whether the attorney is the subject of any disbarment or suspension orders in any jurisdiction. The attorney's statement shall include the attorney's agreement that he or she will participate in any training required by the sponsoring entity and that he or she will notify the Administrator within 30 days of ending his or her participation in a *pro bono* program. Upon receiving the attorney's statement and the entity's verification, the Administrator shall cause the master roll to reflect that the attorney is authorized to provide *pro bono* services. That authorization shall continue until the end of the calendar year in which the statement and verification are submitted, unless the lawyer or the sponsoring entity sends notice to the Administrator that the program or the lawyer's participation in the program has ended.

(4) Renewal of Authorization. An attorney who has been authorized to provide *pro bono* services under this rule may renew the authorization on an annual basis by submitting a statement that he or she continues to participate in a qualifying program, along with verification from the sponsoring entity that the attorney continues to participate in such a program under the entity's auspices and that the attorney has taken part in any training required by the program. An attorney who is seeking renewal based on admission in another state shall also affirm that the attorney is not the subject of any disbarment or suspension orders in any jurisdiction.

(5) Annual Registration for Attorneys on Retired Status. Notwithstanding the provisions of Rule 756(a)(6), a retired status attorney who seeks to provide *pro bono* services under this rule must register on an annual basis, but is not required to pay a registration fee.

(6) MCLE Exemption. The provisions of Rule 791 exempting attorneys from MCLE requirements by reason of being registered as inactive or retired shall apply to inactive or retired status attorneys authorized to provide *pro bono* services under this rule, except that such attorneys shall participate in training to the extent required by the sponsoring entity.

(7) Disciplinary Authority. Lawyers admitted in another state who are providing legal services in this jurisdiction pursuant to this paragraph are subject to this Court's disciplinary authority and the Rules of Professional Conduct of this jurisdiction, as provided in Rule 8.5 of the Rules of Professional Conduct of 2010. Any lawyer who provides legal services pursuant to this rule shall not be considered to be engaged in the unlawful practice of law in this jurisdiction.

Adopted Jan. 25, 1973, eff. Feb. 1, 1973. Amended eff. May 17, 1973, April 1, 1974, and Feb. 17, 1977; Aug. 9, 1983, eff. Oct. 1, 1983; April 27, 1984, and June 1, 1984, eff. July 1, 1984; July 1, 1985, eff. Aug. 1, 1985; eff. Nov. 1, 1986; Dec. 1, 1988, eff. Dec. 1, 1988; Nov. 20, 1991, eff. immediately; June 29, 1999, eff. Nov. 1, 1999; July 6, 2000, eff. Nov. 1, 2000; July 26, 2001, eff. immediately; Oct. 4, 2002, eff. immediately; June 15, 2004, eff. Oct. 1, 2004; May 23, 2005, eff. immediately; Sept. 29, 2005, eff. immediately; June 14, 2006, eff. immediately; Sept. 14, 2006, eff. immediately; March 26, 2008, eff. July 1, 2008; July 29, 2011, eff. Sept. 1, 2011; June 5, 2012, eff. immediately; June 21, 2012, eff. immediately; Nov. 28, 2012, eff. immediately; April 8, 2013, eff. immediately; July 1, 2013, eff. immediately; June 18, 2013, eff. July 1, 2013; March 14, 2014, eff. immediately; June 23, 2014, eff. immediately; Feb. 2, 2015, eff. immediately; May 27, 2015, eff. June 1, 2015; April 1, 2016, eff. immediately.

Committee Comments
(April 27, 1984)

Subparagraph (d) was amended in 1984 to change from April 1 to February 1 the date on which the Administrator will remove from the master roll persons who have not registered. In 1984 paragraph headings were added to subparagraphs (c), (d) and (e).

The amendments to this rule effective October 1, 1983 formally implement a change made in the fee schedule provided for in this rule effective on October 1, 1982. The modification increases the fees of all but the newer attorneys from $30 to $40, increases the fees of the newer attorneys from $15 to $20 and reduces from five years to three years after the year in which the attorney is admitted the time during which a newer attorney pays the smaller fee. The amendment also eliminates a variety of obsolete provisions and makes certain stylistic changes.

(June 14, 2006)

Paragraph (f) is derived from the findings of the Special Supreme Court Committee on *Pro Bono* Publico Legal Service. The Special Committee recognized the vast unmet and burgeoning legal needs of persons of limited means in Illinois, and the unique role that lawyers play in providing greater access to these critical legal services. Therefore, the rule is established to serve as an annual reminder to the lawyers of Illinois that *pro bono* legal service is an integral part of a lawyer's professionalism.

Through this annual reminder, the primary intended goal is to increase the delivery of legal services directly to persons of limited means in paragraph (f)(1)(a). While the provision of legal services as defined in the other categories is laudable and beneficial to local communities and various organizations, the vast unmet need calls out for increased direct legal services to persons of limited means and support of the organizational infrastructure providing those legal services.

Paragraph (f) is not intended to impose upon lawyers a mandatory duty to provide *pro bono* service but, rather, is intended to impose a mandatory reporting requirement. The rule was drafted to encompass a broad spectrum of *pro bono* legal opportunities, including not only traditional services, but also training and monetary contributions.

Paragraph (f)(4)(b). Certain lawyers are prohibited from performing legal services by constitutional, statutory, rule, or other regulatory prohibitions. Members of the legal profession who fall into these exempt categories are encouraged to make a financial contribution to support the provision of legal services to persons of limited means. They are also encouraged to participate in training programs for volunteer attorneys.

(April 8, 2013)

Paragraph (j) is not intended to apply to attorneys who are otherwise authorized to provide *pro bono* service in Illinois, including house counsel admitted under Rule 716.

Rule 757. Transfer to Disability Inactive Status Upon Involuntary Commitment or Upon Judicial Determination of Legal Disability Because of Mental Condition

If an attorney admitted to practice in this State has been, because of mental condition, judicially declared to be a person under legal disability or in need of mental treatment, or has been involuntarily committed to a hospital on such grounds, the court shall enter an order transferring the attorney to disability inactive status until the further order of the court.

Any disciplinary proceeding which may be pending against the attorney shall be stayed while he is on disability inactive status.

No attorney transferred to disability inactive status may engage in the practice of law until restored to active status by order of the court.

Adopted March 30, 1973, eff. April 1, 1973. Amended Sept. 8, 1975, eff. Oct. 1, 1975; May 28, 1982, eff. July 1, 1982; June 29, 1999, eff. Nov. 1, 1999.

Formerly Ill.Rev.Stat.1991, ch. 110A, ¶ 757.

Rule 758. Mental Disability or Addiction to Drugs or Intoxicants

(a) **Petition.** If the Inquiry Board has reason to believe that an attorney admitted to practice in this State is incapacitated from continuing to practice law by reason of mental infirmity, mental disorder, or addiction to drugs or intoxicants, the Administrator shall file a petition with the Hearing Board requesting a hearing to determine whether the attorney is incapacitated and should be transferred to disability inactive status pending the removal of the disability, or be permitted to continue to practice law subject to conditions imposed by the court.

(b) **Hearing and Review Procedure.** The hearing and review procedure shall be the same as provided in Rule 753 for disciplinary cases. The Administrator and the attorney may consent to a transfer to disability inactive status under the procedure set forth in Rule 762(a).

(c) **Transfer to Disability Inactive Status.** If the court determines that the attorney is incapacitated from continuing to practice law, the court shall enter an order transferring the attorney to disability inactive status until further order of the court. The court may impose reasonable conditions upon an attorney's continued practice of law warranted by the circumstances.

(d) **Stay of Disciplinary Proceedings.** Disciplinary proceedings pending against the attorney shall be stayed while the attorney is on disability inactive status.

(e) **Practice of Law Prohibited.** No attorney transferred to disability inactive status may engage in the practice of law until restored to active status by order of the court.

Adopted March 30, 1973, eff. April 1, 1973. Amended Sept. 8, 1975, eff. Oct. 1, 1975; June 1, 1984, eff. July 1, 1984; Oct. 16, 1990, eff. Nov. 1, 1990; June 29, 1999, eff. Nov. 1, 1999.

Formerly Ill.Rev.Stat.1991, ch. 110A, ¶ 758.

Rule 759. Restoration to Active Status

(a) **Petition.** An attorney transferred to disability inactive status under the provisions of Rules 757, 758 or, prior to November 1, 1999, pursuant to Rule 770 may file a petition with the court for restoration to active status. The petition must be accompanied by verification from the Director of MCLE that the attorney has complied with MCLE requirements as set forth in Rule 790 *et seq.* and verification from the Administrator that the attorney has reimbursed the Client Protection Program for all payments arising from petitioner's conduct pursuant to Rule 780(e). A copy of the petition shall be served on the Administrator, who shall have 21 days to answer the petition. If the Administrator consents or fails to file exceptions in the answer to the petition, the court may order that the petitioner be restored to active status without a

hearing. If the Administrator excepts to the petition in the answer, the petition and answer shall be referred to the Hearing Board, which shall hear the matter.

(b) **Hearing and Review Procedure.** The hearing and review procedure shall be the same as provided in Rule 753 for disciplinary cases.

(c) **Disposition.** The court may impose reasonable conditions upon an attorney's restoration to active status as may be warranted by the circumstances. A restoration ordered under this rule shall be effective seven days after entry of the court's order allowing the petition provided that the petitioner produces to the Administrator within the seven days verification from the Director of MCLE that the attorney has complied with MCLE requirements as set forth in Rule 790 >et seq.

(d) **Resumption of Disciplinary Proceedings.** If an attorney is restored to active status, disciplinary proceedings pending against the attorney may be resumed.

Adopted March 30, 1973, eff. April 1, 1973. Amended Sept. 8, 1975, eff. Oct. 1, 1975; June 1, 1984, eff. July 1, 1984; Oct. 16, 1990, eff. Nov. 1, 1990; June 29, 1999, eff. Nov. 1, 1999; Sept. 29, 2005, eff. immediately; Feb. 9, 2015, eff. immediately.

Formerly Ill.Rev.Stat.1991, ch. 110A, ¶ 759.

Rule 760. Appointment of Medical Experts

(1) In any proceeding under Rules 757, 758, or 759, upon motion of the Administrator or the attorney, the court may order a mental or physical examination of the attorney. Such examination shall be conducted by a member of a panel of physicians chosen for their special qualifications by the Administrative Office of the Illinois Courts.

(2) The examining physician shall prepare a report of his examination, and copies of the report shall be given to the court, the Hearing Board, the Administrator, and the attorney.

(3) The Administrator, the attorney, or the Hearing Board may call the examining physician to testify. A physician so called shall be subject to cross-examination.

(4) The cost of the examination and the witness fees of the physician, if called to testify, shall be paid from the Disciplinary Fund.

Adopted March 30, 1973, eff. April 1, 1973. Amended Sept. 8, 1975, eff. Oct. 1, 1975; March 19, 1997, eff. April 15, 1997; amended eff. Dec. 16, 2010.

Formerly Ill.Rev.Stat.1991, ch. 110A, ¶ 760.

Rule 761. Conviction of Crime

(a) **Notification.** It is the duty of an attorney admitted in this State who is convicted in any court of a felony or misdemeanor to notify the Administrator of the conviction in writing within 30 days of the entry of the judgment of conviction. The notification is required:

(1) Whether the conviction results from a plea of guilty or of *nolo contendere* or from a judgment after trial; and

(2) Regardless of the pendency of an appeal or other post-conviction proceeding.

(b) Conviction of Crime Involving Moral Turpitude. If an attorney is convicted of a crime involving fraud or moral turpitude, the Administrator shall file a petition with the court alleging the fact of such conviction and praying that the attorney be suspended from the practice of law until further order of the court. A certified copy of the judgment of conviction shall be attached to the petition and shall be *prima facie* evidence of the fact that the attorney was convicted of the crime charged. Upon receipt of the petition the court shall issue a rule to show cause why the attorney should not be suspended from the practice of law until the further order of the court. After consideration of the petition and the answer to the rule to show cause, the court may enter an order, effective immediately, suspending the attorney from the practice of law until the further order of the court.

(c) Conviction of Crime Not Involving Moral Turpitude. If an attorney is convicted of a crime that does not involve fraud or moral turpitude, the Administrator shall refer the matter to the Inquiry Board.

(d) Hearing. Where an attorney has been convicted of a crime involving fraud or moral turpitude, a hearing shall be conducted before the Hearing Board to determine whether the crime warrants discipline, and, if so, the extent thereof.

(1) If the attorney has not appealed from the conviction, the Administrator shall file a complaint with the Hearing Board alleging the fact of the conviction.

(2) If the attorney has appealed from the conviction, the hearing shall be delayed until completion of the appellate process unless the attorney requests otherwise. If after the completion of the appellate process the conviction has not been reversed, the attorney shall notify the Administrator within 30 days of the mandate being filed in the trial court that the conviction was affirmed. Upon becoming aware that the conviction has been affirmed, the Administrator shall file a complaint with the Hearing Board as described in (1) above.

(e) Time of Hearing. Hearings pursuant to this rule shall commence within 60 days after the complaint is filed.

(f) Proof of Conviction. In any hearing conducted pursuant to this rule, proof of conviction is conclusive of the attorney's guilt of the crime.

(g) Hearing and Review Procedure. The hearing and review procedure shall be the same as provided in Rule 753 for disciplinary cases.

Adopted March 30, 1973, eff. April 1, 1973. Amended eff. July 16, 1973; amended Sept. 8, 1975, eff. Oct. 1, 1975; Aug. 9, 1983, eff. Oct. 1, 1983; June 1, 1984, eff. July 1, 1984.

Formerly Ill.Rev.Stat.1991, ch. 110A, ¶ 761.

Rule 762. Disbarment and Other Discipline on Consent

(a) Disbarment on Consent. If, while any charge of misconduct is under investigation or pending against him before the Inquiry Board, Hearing Board or Review Board, an attorney files with the court a motion to strike his name from the roll of attorneys admitted to practice law in this State, the clerk of the court shall immediately file with the Administrator a copy of the motion. Within 21 days thereafter the Administrator shall file with the court and serve upon the attorney respondent a statement of charges which shall set forth a description of the evidence which would be presented against the attorney respondent if the cause proceeded to hearing and the findings of misconduct which that evidence would support. Within 14 days after the statement of charges is filed with the court, the attorney respondent shall file with the court his affidavit stating that:

(1) he has received a copy of the statement of charges;

(2) if the cause proceeded to a hearing, the Administrator would present the evidence described in the statement of charges, and that evidence would clearly and convincingly establish the facts and conclusions of misconduct set forth in the statement of charges; except that in cases where the charges are based upon a judgment of conviction of a crime, it shall be sufficient that the attorney respondent state that if the matter proceeded to hearing, the judgment of conviction would be offered into evidence and would constitute conclusive evidence of his guilt of the crime for purposes of disciplinary proceedings;

(3) his motion is freely and voluntarily made; and

(4) he understands the nature and consequences of his motion.

If the attorney respondent fails to file the required affidavit within the 14-day period provided above, or in the event the affidavit does not contain the statements required by subparagraphs (1), (2), (3) and (4) above, the court may deny the attorney's motion to strike his name from the roll of attorneys admitted to practice law in this State. If the court allows the motion, the facts and conclusions of misconduct set forth in the Administrator's statement of charges shall be deemed established and conclusive in any future disciplinary proceedings related to the attorney, including any proceedings under Rule 767.

(b) Other Discipline on Consent.

(1) *Petition.* The Administrator and respondent may submit a proceeding to the court as an agreed matter by way of petition to impose discipline on consent under the following circumstances:

(a) during the pendency of a proceeding before the court; or

(b) during the pendency of a proceeding before the Review, Hearing or Inquiry Boards and with the approval of the board before which the proceeding is pending.

(2) *Content of Petition.* The petition shall be prepared by the Administrator and shall set forth the misconduct and a recommendation for discipline.

(3) *Affidavit.* Attached to the petition shall be an affidavit executed by the attorney stating that:

(a) he has read the petition;

(b) the assertions in the petition are true and complete;

(c) he joins in the petition freely and voluntarily; and

(d) he understands the nature and consequences of the petition.

The affidavit may recite any other facts which the attorney wishes to present to the court in mitigation.

(4) *Submission to Court.* The Administrator shall file the petition and affidavit with the Clerk of the court. The clerk shall submit the matter to the court as an agreed matter.

(5) *Action on Petition.* The court may allow the petition and impose the discipline recommended in the petition. Otherwise, the court shall deny the petition. If the petition is denied, the proceeding will resume as if no petition had been submitted. No admission in the petition may be used against the respondent. If the proceeding resumes before the Inquiry or Hearing Board, the proceeding will be assigned to a different panel of the board.

Adopted March 30, 1973, eff. April 1, 1973. Amended eff. May 21, 1975; Oct. 13, 1989; Jan. 5, 1993.

Formerly Ill.Rev.Stat.1991, ch. 110A, ¶ 762.

Rule 763. Reciprocal Disciplinary Action

If an attorney licensed to practice law in Illinois and another jurisdiction is disciplined in the other jurisdiction, the attorney may be subjected to the same or comparable discipline in Illinois, upon proof of the order of the other jurisdiction imposing the discipline. For purposes of this rule, "other jurisdiction" is defined as the District of Columbia; a country other than the United States; a state, province, territory, or commonwealth of the United States or another country.

The Administrator shall initiate proceedings under this rule by filing a petition with the court, to which a certified copy of the order of the other jurisdiction is attached, together with proof of service upon the attorney. Within 21 days after service of a copy of the petition upon him the attorney may request in writing a hearing on the petition. If the court allows the request for a hearing, the hearing shall be held before the Hearing Board no less than 14 days after notice thereof is given to the attorney respondent and the Administrator. At the hearing the attorney may be heard only on the issues as to (1) whether or not the order of the other jurisdiction was entered; (2) whether it applies to the attorney; (3) whether it remains in full force and effect; (4) whether the procedure in the other jurisdiction resulting in the order was so lacking in notice or opportunity to be heard as to constitute a deprivation of due process of law; and (5) whether the conduct of the attorney warrants substantially less discipline in Illinois.

If an attorney is suspended until further order of the Court or disbarred in Illinois pursuant to this rule, reinstatement in Illinois shall be governed by the provisions of Rule 767.

Nothing in this rule shall prohibit the institution of independent disciplinary proceedings in this State against any attorney based upon his conduct in another jurisdiction, and, in the event the Administrator elects to proceed independently, any discipline imposed in this State shall not be limited to the discipline ordered by the other jurisdiction.

Adopted March 30, 1973, eff. April 1, 1973. Amended Sept. 21, 1994, eff. Oct. 1, 1994; Feb. 9, 2015, eff. immediately.

Formerly Ill.Rev.Stat.1991, ch. 110A, ¶ 763.

Rule 764. Duties of a Disciplined Attorney and Attorneys Affiliated with Disciplined Attorney

An attorney who is disbarred, disbarred on consent, or suspended for six months or more shall comply with each of the following requirements. Compliance with each requirement shall be a condition to the reinstatement of the disciplined attorney. Failure to comply shall constitute contempt of court.

Any and all attorneys who are affiliated with the disciplined attorney as a partner or associate shall take reasonable action necessary to insure that the disciplined attorney complies with the provisions of paragraphs (a), (b), (c), (d), and (e) below. Within 35 days of the effective date of the order of discipline, each affiliated attorney or a representative thereof shall file with the clerk of the supreme court and serve upon the Administrator a certification setting forth in detail the actions taken to insure compliance with paragraphs (a), (b), (c), (d), and (e) below.

(a) Maintenance of Records. The disciplined attorney shall maintain:

(1) files, documents, and other records relating to any matter which was the subject of a disciplinary investigation or proceeding;

(2) files, documents, and other records relating to any and all terminated matters in which the disciplined attorney represented a client at any time prior to the imposition of discipline;

(3) files, documents, and other records of pending matters in which the disciplined attorney had some responsibility on the date of, or represented a client during the year prior to, the imposition of discipline;

(4) all financial records related to the disciplined attorney's practice of law during the seven years preceding the imposition of discipline, including but not limited to bank statements, time and billing records, checks, check stubs, journals, ledgers, audits, financial statements, tax returns and tax reports; and

(5) all records related to compliance with this rule.

(b) Withdrawal from Law Office and Removal of Indicia as Lawyer. Upon entry of the final order of discipline, the disciplined attorney shall not maintain a presence or occupy an office where the practice of law is conducted. The disciplined attorney shall take such action necessary to cause the removal of any indicia of the disciplined attorney as lawyer, counsellor at law, legal assistant, legal clerk, or similar title.

(c) Notification to Clients. Within 21 days after the entry of the final order of discipline, the disciplined attorney shall notify, by certified mail, return receipt requested, all clients whom the disciplined attorney represented on the date of the imposition of discipline, of the following:

(1) the action taken by the supreme court;

(2) that the disciplined attorney may not continue to represent them during the period of discipline;

(3) that they have the right to retain another attorney; and

(4) that their files, documents, and other records are available to them, designating the place where they are available.

(d) List of Clients. Within 21 days after the effective date of an order of discipline, the disciplined attorney shall file with the clerk of the supreme court and serve upon the Administrator an alphabetical list of the names, addresses, telephone numbers and file numbers of all clients whom the disciplined attorney represented on the date of, or during the year prior to, the imposition of discipline. At the same time, the disciplined attorney shall serve upon the Administrator a copy of each notification served pursuant to paragraph (c) above.

(e) Notification to Courts. Within 21 days of the effective date of the order of discipline, the disciplined attorney shall file a notice before the court in all pending matters in which the disciplined attorney is counsel of record and request withdrawal of his appearance. The notice shall advise the court of the action taken by the supreme court. The notice shall be served upon the disciplined attorney's former client and all other parties who have entered an appearance.

(f) Notification to Others. Within 21 days of the effective date of the order of discipline, the disciplined attorney shall, by certified mail, return receipt requested, notify the following of the action taken by the supreme court and his inability, during the period of discipline, to practice law in the State of Illinois:

(1) all attorneys with whom the disciplined attorney was associated in the practice of law on the effective date of the order of discipline;

(2) all attorneys of record in matters in which the disciplined attorney represented a client on the effective date of the order of discipline;

(3) all parties not represented by an attorney in matters in which the disciplined attorney represented a client on the effective date of the order of discipline;

(4) all other jurisdictions in which the disciplined attorney is licensed to practice law;

(5) all governmental agencies before which the disciplined attorney is entitled to represent a person.

(g) Affidavit of Disciplined Attorney. Within 35 days after the effective date of an order of discipline, the disciplined attorney shall file with the clerk of the supreme court and serve upon the Administrator an affidavit stating:

(1) the action the disciplined attorney has taken to comply with the order of discipline;

(2) the action the disciplined attorney has taken to comply with this rule;

(3) the arrangements made to maintain the files and other records specified in paragraph (a) above;

(4) the address and telephone number at which subsequent communications may be directed to him; and

(5) the identity and address of all other State, Federal, and administrative jurisdictions to which the disciplined attorney is admitted to practice law.

(h) Compensation Arising from Former Law Practice. Provided that the disciplined attorney complies with the provisions of this rule, the disciplined attorney may receive compensation on a *quantum meruit* basis for legal services rendered prior to the effective date of the order of discipline. The disciplined attorney may not receive any compensation related to the referral of a legal matter to an attorney or attributed to the "good will" of his former law office.

(1) *Matters in which Legal Proceedings Instituted.* The disciplined attorney shall not receive any compensation regarding a matter in which a legal proceeding was instituted at any time prior to the imposition of discipline without first receiving approval of the tribunal.

(2) *Other Aspects of Former Law Office.* The disciplined attorney shall not receive any compensation related to any agreement, sale, assignment or transfer of any aspect of the disciplined attorney's former law office without first receiving the approval of the supreme court. Prior to entering into any such transaction, the disciplined attorney shall file a petition in the supreme court and serve a copy upon the Administrator. The petition shall disclose fully the transaction contemplated, shall attach any and all related proposed agreements and documents, and shall request approval of the transaction. The Administrator shall answer or otherwise plead to the petition within 28 days of service of the petition on the Administrator. If the supreme court determines that an evidentiary hearing is necessary, it may refer the matter to the circuit court for hearing.

(i) Change of Address or Telephone Number. Within 35 days of any change of the disciplined attorney's address or telephone number during the period of discipline, the disciplined attorney shall notify the Administrator of the change.

(j) Modification of Requirements. On its own motion or at the request of the Administrator or respondent, the supreme court may modify any of the above requirements.

Adopted March 30, 1973, eff. April 1, 1973. Amended Oct. 20, 1989, eff. Nov. 1, 1989; amended eff. Aug. 27, 1990.

Formerly Ill.Rev.Stat.1991, ch. 110A, ¶ 764.

Rule 765. Service

(a) Method of Service. Service of any notice, complaint, petition, subpoena, pleading or document in proceedings under these rules may be made in any manner authorized by the Code of Civil Procedure [1] or rules of this court or by delivery of any such notice, complaint, petition, subpoena, pleading, or document to the address listed on the master roll for the attorney.

(b) Substitute Service. The failure of any attorney to provide the Administrator with a registration address shall be deemed an appointment by such attorney of the clerk of the Illinois Supreme Court to be the attorney's agent upon whom may be served any notice, complaint, petition, subpoena, pleading or other document under these rules. Service upon the clerk may be made by filing the document with the clerk of the supreme court, together with an affidavit setting forth facts showing that, upon inquiry as full as circumstances permit, the attorney cannot be located, and by mailing the documents by certified mail, proper postage prepaid, return receipt requested, to the last known address of the attorney.

Adopted March 30, 1973, eff. April 1, 1973. Amended eff. May 21, 1975; amended May 28, 1982, eff. July 1, 1982; Oct. 16, 1990, eff. Nov. 1, 1990.

Formerly Ill.Rev.Stat.1991, ch. 110A, ¶ 765.
[1] 735 ILCS 5/1–101 et seq.

Committee Comments

In 1990, Rule 765 was revised to provide for service of notices, pleadings and other documents by lawful means other than personal service on an attorney, and for appointment of the clerk of the supreme court as the agent of any attorney who fails to provide the Administrator with a registration address.

These revisions will reduce the expenses incurred in personally serving hundreds of documents, such as notices, complaints, petitions, subpoenas and rules to show cause, and the delays which result from locating and perfecting service on attorneys who attempt to avoid service. Because the revised rule allows for service to be perfected by delivery of an item to a registration address, resources presently committed to serving recalcitrant attorneys could be devoted to conducting investigations and reducing unnecessary delay in processing charges.

Additionally, the revised rule allows for service to be obtained on attorneys who fail to register or who fail to give the Administrator a registration address by filing documents with the clerk of the supreme court. The revision is modeled, in part, on the Illinois Vehicle Code, which provides that use of a vehicle on Illinois roads constitutes consent to the appointment of the Secretary of State as an agent for the service of process (see Ill.Rev.Stat.1989, ch. 95½, par. 10–301), and in part on similar rules in use in Indiana and Ohio (Indiana Admission and Discipline Rule 23, § 12; Ohio Grievance Rule 5; see *Matter of Carmody* (Ind.1987), 513 N.E.2d 649; *Columbus Bar Association v. Gross* (1982), 2 Ohio St.3d 5, 441 N.E.2d 570; see also *Bell Federal Savings & Loan Association v. Horton* (1978), 59 Ill.App.3d 923, 376 N.E.2d 1029).

Rule 766. Confidentiality and Privacy

(a) Public Proceedings. Proceedings under Rules 751 through 780 shall be public with the exception of the following matters, which shall be private and confidential:

(1) investigations conducted by the Administrator;

(2) proceedings before the Inquiry Board;

(3) proceedings pursuant to Rule 753 before the Hearing Board prior to the service of a complaint upon the respondent;

(4) information pursuant to which a board or the court has issued a protective order;

(5) deliberations of the Hearing Board, the Review Board and the court;

(6) proceedings before the Hearing and Review Boards pursuant to Rule 758;

(7) proceedings pursuant to Rule 760;

(8) deliberations of the Commission and minutes of Commission meetings;

(9) deliberations related to a claim submitted under the Client Protection Program;

(10) information concerning trust accounts provided by lawyers as part of the annual registration pursuant to Rule 756(d); and

(11) information concerning *pro bono* services and monetary contributions in support of *pro bono* services provided by lawyers as part of the annual registration pursuant to Rule 756(f).

(b) Disclosures of Confidential Information.

(1) *Public Information of Misconduct.* Where there is public information of allegations which, if true, could result in discipline, the Administrator, with the approval of the court or a member thereof, and in the interest of the public and the legal profession, may disclose whether the matter is being investigated.

(2) *Disclosures in the Interests of Justice.* In the interests of justice and on such terms as it deems appropriate the court or a member thereof may authorize the Administrator to produce, disclose, release, inform, report or testify to any information, reports, investigations, documents, evidence or transcripts in the Administrator's possession.

(3) *Referral to Lawyers' Assistance Program.* When an investigation by the Administrator reveals reasonable cause to believe that a respondent is or may be addicted to alcohol or other chemicals, is or may be abusing the use of alcohol or other chemicals, or is or may be experiencing a mental health condition or other problem that is impairing the respondent's ability to practice law, the information giving rise to this belief may be communicated to the Lawyers' Assistance Programs, Inc., or comparable organization designed to assist lawyers with substance abuse or mental health problems.

Adopted March 30, 1973, eff. April 1, 1973. Amended eff. April 1, 1974; Sept. 28, 1976, eff. Nov. 15, 1976; June 1, 1984, eff. July 1, 1984; eff. Oct. 13, 1989; March 28, 1994; amended Nov. 19, 2004, eff. Jan. 1, 2005; amended March 29, 2006, eff. immediately; amended June 14, 2006, eff. immediately.

Formerly Ill.Rev.Stat.1991, ch. 110A, ¶ 766.

Rule 767. Reinstatement

(a) Petition. An attorney who has been disbarred, disbarred on consent or suspended until further order of the court may file his verified petition with the clerk of the court seeking to be reinstated to the roll of attorneys admitted to practice law in this State. No petition shall be filed within a period of five years after the date of an order of disbarment, three years after the date of an order allowing disbarment on consent, two years after the date of an order denying a petition for reinstatement, or one year after an order allowing the petition for reinstatement to be withdrawn. No petition for reinstatement shall be filed by an attorney suspended for a specified period

and until further order of the court, until the specified period of time has elapsed. The petition shall include the information specified by Commission rule.

(b) Presentation of Petition. An attorney who has been disbarred, disbarred on consent or suspended until further order of the court may present to the Administrator a copy of the petition he proposes to file with the clerk within 120 days prior to the date on which the petition may be filed.

(c) Costs. The petition shall be accompanied by a receipt showing payment to the Commission of a $500 deposit to be applied against the costs, as defined in Rule 773, necessary to the investigation, hearing and review of the petition. If the costs exceed the amount of the deposit, the petitioner shall pay the excess at the conclusion of the matter pursuant to the procedures of Rule 773. If the deposit exceeds the costs, the excess shall be refunded to the petitioner.

(d) Notice of Petition. The Administrator shall give notice to the following:

(1) the chief judge of each circuit in which the petitioner maintained an office or engaged in the practice of law;

(2) the president of each local or county bar association in each county in which the petitioner maintained an office or engaged in the practice of law.

(e) Form of Notice. The notice shall be in substantially the following form:

NOTICE OF PETITION FOR REINSTATEMENT AS ATTORNEY

_____, who was licensed to practice law in the State of Illinois on _____ and who was (suspended from the practice of law on _____) (disbarred on _____), has filed (has stated his intention to file) in the Supreme Court of Illinois a petition for readmission to the practice of law in Illinois. A hearing on that petition will be held.

Any person desiring to be heard or having relevant information may communicate with the Administrator of the Attorney Registration and Disciplinary Commission at (insert address and telephone number of Administrator's office concerned).

(f) Factors to be Considered. The petition shall be referred to a hearing panel. The panel shall consider the following factors, and such other factors as the panel deems appropriate, in determining the petitioner's rehabilitation, present good character and current knowledge of the law:

(1) the nature of the misconduct for which the petitioner was disciplined;

(2) the maturity and experience of the petitioner at the time discipline was imposed;

(3) whether the petitioner recognizes the nature and seriousness of the misconduct;

(4) when applicable, whether petitioner has made restitution;

(5) the petitioner's conduct since discipline was imposed; and

(6) the petitioner's candor and forthrightness in presenting evidence in support of the petition.

(g) Report of Hearing Panel. The hearing panel shall make a report of its findings and recommendations. A copy of the report shall be served upon the petitioner and upon the Administrator.

(h) Hearing and Review Procedure. The hearing and review procedure shall be the same as provided in Rule 753 for disciplinary cases.

Adopted March 30, 1973, eff. April 1, 1973. Amended Sept. 8, 1975, eff. Oct. 1, 1975; amended eff. Feb. 17, 1977; amended May 26, 1978, eff. July 1, 1978; Aug. 9, 1983, eff. Oct. 1, 1983; June 1, 1984, eff. July 1, 1984; amended May 23, 2005, eff. immediately.

Formerly Ill.Rev.Stat.1991, ch. 110A, ¶ 767.

Commentary

(May 23, 2005)

Paragraph (c) is amended to provide that the procedures of Rule 773 to recover costs are applicable in all respects to a reinstatement proceeding.

Rule 768.　Notification of Disciplinary Action

Upon the date on which an order of this court disbarring or suspending an attorney, or transferring him to disability inactive status becomes final, the clerk shall forthwith mail a copy of the order to the attorney, the presiding judge of each of the Illinois Appellate Court Districts, the chief judge of each of the judicial circuits of Illinois, the chief judge of each of the United States district courts in Illinois, and the chief judge of the United States Court of Appeals for the Seventh Circuit. The Administrator shall forthwith provide a copy of the order to each other jurisdiction in which the attorney is known to be licensed to practice law and to the National Regulatory Data Bank administered by the American Bar Association.

Adopted March 30, 1973, eff. April 1, 1973. Amended June 29, 1999, eff. Nov. 1, 1999; Feb. 9, 2015, eff. immediately.

Formerly Ill.Rev.Stat.1991, ch. 110A, ¶ 768.

Rule 769.　Maintenance of Records

It shall be the duty of every attorney to maintain originals, copies or computer-generated images of the following:

(1) records which identify the name and last known address of each of the attorney's clients and which reflect whether the representation of the client is ongoing or concluded; and

(2) all financial records related to the attorney's practice, for a period of not less than seven years, including but not limited to bank statements, time and billing records, checks, check stubs, journals, ledgers, audits, financial statements, tax returns and tax reports.

Adopted Oct. 20, 1989, eff. Nov. 1, 1989. Amended July 18, 1990, eff. Aug. 1, 1990; amended April 1, 2003, effective immediately.

Formerly Ill.Rev.Stat.1991, ch. 110A, ¶ 769.

Committee Comments

(April 1, 2003)

This amendment gives attorneys the option of maintaining records in forms that save space and reduce cost without increasing the risk of premature destruction. For example, CDs and DVDs have a normal life exceeding seven years, so an attorney might use them to maintain financial records. At present, however, floppy disks, tapes, hard drives, zip drives, and other magnetic media have insufficient normal life to meet the requirements of this rule.

Rule 770.　Types of Discipline

Conduct of attorneys which violates the Rules of Professional Conduct contained in article VIII of these rules or which tends to defeat the administration of justice or to bring the courts or the legal profession into disrepute shall be grounds for discipline by the court. Discipline may be:

(a) disbarment;

(b) disbarment on consent;

(c) suspension for a specified period and until further order of court;

(d) suspension for a specified period of time;

(e) suspension until further order of the court;

(f) suspension for a specified period of time or until further order of the court with probation;

(g) censure; or

(h) reprimand by the court, the Review Board or a hearing panel.

Adopted May 26, 1978, effective July 1, 1978; amended June 3, 1980, effective July 1, 1980; amended August 9, 1983, effective October 1, 1983; amended October 13, 1989, effective immediately; amended and renumbered March 23, 2004, effective April 1, 2004.

Formerly Ill.Rev.Stat.1991, ch. 110A, ¶ 770.

Commentary

(March 23, 2004)

Effective April 1, 2004, former Rule 771 ("Types of Discipline") was renumbered as Rule 770 and a new Rule 771 ("Finality of Orders and Effective Date of Discipline") was adopted.

Rule 771. Finality of Orders and Effective Date of Discipline

(a) Finality. All orders imposing discipline pursuant to these rules, except orders entered in cases that were accepted by the court for further consideration pursuant to Rule 753(e)(5)(a)(iii), are final when filed by the clerk of the court, and the mandates in all such cases shall issue at the time the orders are filed. No petition for rehearing pursuant to Rule 367 may be filed in such a case, nor will any motion or other paper submitted after an order is filed automatically stay or recall the court's mandate. The finality of orders imposing discipline entered in cases accepted by the court for further consideration pursuant to Rule 753(e)(5)(a)(iii) shall be governed by Rules 367 and 368.

(b) Effective Date. Unless otherwise ordered by the court or unless governed by Rules 367 and 368, all orders of discipline are effective when filed by the clerk of the court, except that orders of suspension for a specified period of time which do not continue until further order of court or any orders of suspension which are stayed, in part, by a period of probation become effective 21 days after the date they are filed by the clerk of the court.

(c) Interim Suspension. Unless otherwise ordered by the court, all interim suspension orders imposed under Rule 761 or Rule 774 and all subsequent disciplinary orders entered while the lawyer is on interim suspension are effective when filed by the clerk of the court.

Adopted March 23, 2004, effective April 1, 2004.

Formerly Ill.Rev.Stat.1991, ch. 110A, ¶ 771.

Commentary

(March 23, 2004)

Effective April 1, 2004, a new Rule 771 ("Finality of Orders and Effective Date of Discipline") was adopted and the former Rule 771 ("Types of Discipline") was renumbered as Rule 770.

Rule 772. Probation

(a) Qualifications. The court may order that an attorney be placed on probation if the attorney has demonstrated that he:

(1) can perform legal services and the continued practice of law will not cause the courts or profession to fall into disrepute;

(2) is unlikely to harm the public during the period of rehabilitation and the necessary conditions of probation can be adequately supervised;

(3) has a disability which is temporary or minor and does not require treatment and transfer to disability inactive status; and

(4) is not guilty of acts warranting disbarment.

Probation shall be ordered for a specified period of time or until further order of the court in conjunction with a suspension which may be stayed in whole or in part.

(b) Conditions. The order placing an attorney on probation shall state the conditions of probation. The conditions shall take into consideration the nature and circumstances of the misconduct and the history, character and condition of the attorney. The following conditions, and such others as the court deems appropriate, may be imposed:

(1) periodic reports to the Administrator;

(2) supervision over trust accounts as the court may direct;

(3) satisfactory completion of a course of study;

(4) successful completion of the multistate Professional Responsibility Examination;

(5) restitution;

(6) compliance with income tax laws and verification of such to the Administrator;

(7) limitations on practice;

(8) psychological counseling and treatment;

(9) the abstinence from alcohol or drugs; and

(10) the payment of disciplinary costs.

(c) Administration. The Administrator shall be responsible for the supervision of attorneys placed on probation. Where appropriate, he may recommend to the court modification of the conditions and shall report to the court the probationer's failure to comply with the conditions of probation. Upon a showing of failure to comply with the conditions of probation, the court shall issue a rule to show cause why probation should not be revoked and the stay of suspension vacated.

Adopted Aug. 9, 1983, eff. Oct. 1, 1983. Amended June 29, 1999, eff. Nov. 1, 1999.

Formerly Ill.Rev.Stat.1991, ch. 110A, ¶ 772.

Rule 773. Costs

(a) Costs Defined. Costs may include the following expenses reasonably and necessarily incurred by the Administrator in connection with the matter: witness fees; duplication of documents necessary to the prosecution of the case; travel expenses of witnesses; bank charges for producing records; expenses incurred in the physical or mental examination of a respondent attorney; fees of expert witnesses; and court reporting expenses except the cost of transcripts of proceedings before the hearing board or review board where the Administrator takes exception to the findings and recommendation of the hearing board or review board, which shall be paid by the Administrator unless the Administrator prevails, at least in part, before the reviewing board or this court, in which case the Administrator may include the transcript costs in the statement of costs subject to the limitations of section (c) of this rule. If both the Administrator and respondent take exception to the findings and recommendation of the hearing board or review board, the cost of the transcript may be taxed to the nonprevailing party. If the Administrator and the respondent each prevail in part, the Administrator may include the costs of transcripts in the statement of costs, subject to the limitations of section (c) of this rule.

(b) Duty of Respondent. It is the duty of a respondent to reimburse the Commission for costs not to exceed $1,000 and for such additional amounts as the court may order on the motion of the Administrator for good cause shown, which may include (1) costs incurred in the investigation, hearing and review of matters brought pursuant to article VII of these rules which result in the imposition of discipline, (2) costs involved in the investigation of alleged violations of the terms and conditions of any such disciplinary order, when such violations are later proved, (3) costs involved in any proceedings for the enforcement of any rule, judgment or order of this court which was made necessary by any act or omission on the part of the respondent, (4) costs incurred to compel the appearance of respondent and to transcribe respondent's testimony when the appearance followed respondent's failure to comply with a request from the Inquiry Board or Administrator to provide information concerning a matter under investigation, and (5) costs incurred to obtain copies of records from a financial institution, when the institution's production of the records followed respondent's failure to comply with a request from the Inquiry Board or the Administrator to provide those records.

(c) Statement of Costs. After the imposition of discipline by the court, the Administrator shall prepare an itemized statement of costs, not to exceed $1,000, which shall be made a part of the record. A copy of the statement shall be served on the respondent. The Administrator may petition the court for costs reasonably and necessarily incurred by the administrator in excess of $1,000, which may be allowed for good cause shown. Costs up to $1,000 shall be paid by the respondent within 30 days of service of the statement. Costs in excess of $1,000 shall be paid by the respondent within 30 days of the order allowing the petition for excess costs.

(d) Assessment of Costs. If the respondent contests the amount of the costs or fails to pay the costs within 30 days of service of the statement or order allowing excess costs, the Administrator may petition the court for an order and judgment assessing costs against the respondent and directing the respondent to pay the costs, in full or in part, to the Commission. Costs shall be paid by the respondent attorney within 30 days after the entry of the order and judgment assessing costs. Proceedings for the collection of costs assessed against the respondent attorney may be initiated by the Administrator on the order and judgment

entered by the court. A petition for reinstatement pursuant to Rule 767 must be accompanied by a receipt verifying payment of any costs imposed in connection with prior disciplinary proceedings involving the petitioner.

JUSTICE McMORROW dissents from this amendment of Rule 773.

Adopted Aug. 9, 1983, eff. Oct. 1, 1983. Amended June 1, 1984, eff. July 1, 1984; Feb. 21, 1986, eff. Aug. 1, 1986; eff. Oct. 13, 1989; Oct. 5, 2000, eff. Nov. 1, 2000; Nov. 22, 2000, nunc pro tunc Nov. 1, 2000.

Formerly Ill.Rev.Stat.1991, ch. 110A, ¶ 773.

Rule 774. Interim Suspension

(a) Grounds for Suspension. During the pendency of a criminal indictment, criminal information, disciplinary proceeding or disciplinary investigation, the court on its own motion, or on the Administrator's petition for a rule to show cause, may suspend an attorney from the practice of law until further order of the court. The petition shall allege:

(1) the attorney-respondent has been formally charged with the commission of a crime which involves moral turpitude or reflects adversely upon his fitness to practice law, and there appears to be persuasive evidence to support the charge; or

(2) a complaint has been voted by the Inquiry Board; the attorney-respondent has committed a violation of the Rules of Professional Conduct which involves fraud or moral turpitude or threatens irreparable injury to the public, his or her clients, or to the orderly administration of justice; and there appears to be persuasive evidence to support the charge.

(b) Form and Service of Petition. The petition shall be verified or supported by affidavit or other evidence and shall be filed with the clerk. The petition shall be served personally upon the respondent. If the respondent is unavailable or respondent's whereabouts is unknown, the respondent shall be served by mailing a copy of the petition by ordinary mail to respondent's last address shown on the master roll.

(c) Suspension Order and Conditions of Suspension. The court may make such orders and impose such conditions on the interim suspension as it deems necessary to protect the interest of the public and the orderly administration of justice, including but not limited to:

(1) Notification to clients of the respondent's interim suspension;

(2) Audit of the respondent's books, records, and accounts;

(3) Appointment of a trustee to manage respondent's affairs; and

(4) Physical and mental examination of the respondent.

Adopted June 1, 1984, eff. July 1, 1984. Amended eff. March 25, 1991.

Formerly Ill.Rev.Stat.1991, ch. 110A, ¶ 774.

Rule 775. Immunity

Any person who submits a claim to the Client Protection Program or who communicates a complaint concerning an attorney or allegations regarding the unauthorized practice of law to the Attorney Registration and Disciplinary Commission, or its administrators, staff, investigators or any member of its boards, shall be immune from all civil liability which, except for this rule, might result from such communications or complaint. The grant of immunity provided by this rule shall apply only to those communications made by such persons to the Attorney Registration and Disciplinary Commission, its administrators, staff, investigators and members of its boards.

Adopted Oct. 13, 1989, eff. immediately. Amended March 28, 1994, eff. immediately; Dec. 7, 2011, eff. immediately.

Formerly Ill.Rev.Stat.1991, ch. 110A, ¶ 775.

Rule 776. Appointment of Receiver in Certain Cases

(a) Appointment of Receiver. Where it comes to the attention of the circuit court in any judicial circuit from any source that a lawyer in the circuit is unable properly to discharge his responsibilities to his clients due to disability, disappearance or death, and that no partner, associate, executor or other responsible party capable of conducting the lawyer's affairs is known to exist, then, upon such showing, the presiding judge in the judicial circuit in which the lawyer maintained his practice, or the supreme court, may appoint an attorney from the same judicial circuit to serve as a receiver to perform certain duties hereafter enumerated. Notice of such appointment shall be made promptly to the Administrator of the Attorney Registration and Disciplinary Commission either at his Chicago or Springfield office, as appropriate. A copy of said notice shall be served on the affected attorney at his or her last known residence.

(b) Duties of the Receiver. As expeditiously as possible, the receiver shall take custody of and make an inventory of the lawyer's files, notify the lawyer's clients in all pending cases as to the lawyer's disability, or inability to continue legal representation, and recommend prompt substitution of attorneys, take appropriate steps to sequester client funds of the lawyer, and to take whatever other action is indicated to protect the interests of the attorney, his clients, or other affected parties. A copy of the appointing order shall be served on the affected attorney at his or her last known residence address.

(1) The attorney appointed to serve as receiver shall be designated from among members of the bar from the same judicial circuit who are not representing any party who is adverse to any known client of the disabled, absent or deceased lawyer, and who have no adverse interest or relationship with that lawyer or his estate which would affect the receiver's ability to perform the duties above enumerated.

(2) An attorney appointed as receiver may decline the appointment for personal or professional reasons. If no available members of the bar from the same judicial circuit can properly serve as receiver as a result of personal or professional obligations, the Administrator of the Attorney Registration and Disciplinary Commission shall be appointed to serve as receiver.

(3) Any objections by or on behalf of the disabled, absent, or deceased lawyer, or any other interested party to the appointment of or conduct by the receiver shall be raised and heard in the appointing court prior to or during the pendency of the receivership.

(c) Effect of Appointment of Receiver. Where appropriate, a receiver appointed by the court pursuant to this rule may apply to the court for a stay of any applicable statute of limitation, or limitation on time for appeal; or to vacate or obtain relief from any judgment, for a period not to exceed 60 days. An application to the court setting forth reasons for such application shall constitute a pleading sufficient to toll any limitations period. For good cause shown, such stay may be extended for an additional 30 days.

(d) Liability of Receiver. A receiver appointed pursuant to this rule shall:

(1) not be regarded as having an attorney-client relationship with the clients of the disabled, absent or deceased lawyer, except that the receiver shall be bound by the obligations of confidentiality imposed by the Rules of Professional Conduct with respect to information acquired as receiver;

(2) have no liability to the clients of the disabled, absent or deceased lawyer except for injury to such clients caused by intentional, willful or gross neglect of duties as receiver; and

(3) except as herein provided, be immune to separate suit brought by or on behalf of the disabled, absent, or deceased lawyer.

(e) Compensation of the Receiver.

(1) The receiver shall normally serve without compensation.

(2) On application by the receiver, with notice to the Administrator of the Attorney Registration and Disciplinary Commission, and upon showing by the receiver that the nature of the receivership was extraordinary and that failure to award compensation would work substantial hardship on the receiv-

er, the court may award reasonable compensation to the receiver to be paid out of the Disciplinary Fund, or any other fund that may be designated by the supreme court. In such event, compensation shall be awarded only to the extent that the efforts of the receiver have exceeded those normally required in an amount to be determined by the court.

(f) Termination of Receivership. Upon completion of the receiver's duties as above enumerated, he shall file with the appointing court a final report with a copy thereof served upon the Administrator of the Attorney Registration and Disciplinary Commission. Adopted Oct. 20, 1989, eff. Nov. 1, 1989. Amended eff. March 25, 1991.

Formerly Ill.Rev.Stat.1991, ch. 110A, ¶ 776.

Rule 777. Registration of, and Disciplinary Proceedings Relating to, Foreign Legal Consultants

(a) Supervision and Control of Foreign Legal Consultants. The registration of, and disciplinary proceedings affecting, persons who are licensed (pursuant to Rule 712) to practice as foreign legal consultants shall be subject to the supreme court rules (Rule 751 *et seq.*) and to the rules of the Attorney Registration and Disciplinary Commission relating to the registration and discipline of attorneys. As used in those rules, the terms "attorney" and "attorney and counselor at law" shall include foreign legal consultants except to the extent that those rules concern matters unrelated to the permissible activities of foreign legal consultants.

(b) Issuance of Subpoenas by Clerk Relating to Investigation of Foreign Legal Consultants. Upon application by the Administrator or an Inquiry Board, disclosing that the Administrator or Inquiry Board is conducting an investigation of either professional misconduct on the part of a foreign legal consultant or the unlawful practice of law by a foreign legal consultant, or of a Hearing Board that it is conducting a hearing relating thereto, or upon application by a respondent, the clerk of this court shall be empowered to issue subpoenas for the attendance of witnesses and the production of books and papers before the Administrator or Inquiry Board or Hearing Board.

(c) Issuance of Subpoenas by Clerk Relating to Investigation of Wrongfully Representing Himself as a Foreign Legal Consultant. Upon application by the Administrator or an Inquiry Board disclosing that it has reason to believe that a person, firm or corporation other than a foreign legal consultant is unlawfully practicing or assuming to practice law as a foreign legal consultant and that it is conducting an investigation thereof, or of a Hearing Board that it is conducting a hearing relating thereto, or upon application by any respondent, the clerk of this court shall be empowered to issue subpoenas for the attendance of witnesses and production of books and papers before

the Administrator or Inquiry Board or Hearing Board.

(d) Taking Evidence. The Administrator or Inquiry Board conducting an investigation and any Hearing Board conducting a hearing pursuant to this rule is empowered to take and transcribe the evidence of witnesses, who shall be sworn by any person authorized by law to administer oaths.

(e) Disciplinary Procedure. Disciplinary proceedings and proceedings under Rules 757, 758, or 759 against any foreign legal consultant shall be initiated and conducted in the manner and by the same agencies as prescribed by law for such proceedings against those admitted as attorneys. Adopted eff. Dec. 7, 1990. Amended eff. Dec. 16, 2010.

Formerly Ill.Rev.Stat.1991, ch. 110A, ¶ 777.

Rule 778. Retention of Records by Administrator

(a) Retention of Records. The Administrator is permitted to retain the record of investigation for all matters resulting in the imposition of discipline as defined by Rule 770, for investigations which have been stayed or deferred by the transfer of the attorney to disability inactive status, or for investigations that have resulted in the filing of unauthorized practice of law proceedings.

(b) Expungement. The Administrator shall expunge the record of an investigation concluded by dismissal or closure by the Administrator or Inquiry Board three years after the disposition of the investigation, unless deferral of expunction is warranted under paragraph (c). Expungement shall consist of the Administrator's destruction of the investigative file and other related materials maintained by the Administrator relating to the attorney, including any computer record identifying the attorney as a subject of an investigation.

(c) Deferral of Expungement of Investigative Materials. Expungement of an investigative file and all related materials under paragraph (b) shall be deferred until the passage of three years from the later of the following events:

(1) the conclusion of any pending disciplinary or disability proceeding related to the attorney before the Hearing or Review Boards or the Court; or

(2) the termination of any previously imposed sanction (including suspension, disbarment or probation) or the restoration of the attorney from disability inactive to active status; or

(3) the termination of any permanent retirement status related to the attorney. Adopted Jan. 5, 1993, eff. immediately. Amended June 29, 1999, eff. Nov. 1, 1999; Dec. 7, 2011, eff. immediately; June 5, 2012, eff. immediately.

Formerly Ill.Rev.Stat.1991, ch. 110A, ¶ 778.

Rule 779. Unauthorized Practice of Law Proceedings

(a) Proceedings against Suspended Illinois Lawyers and Out of State Lawyers. Unauthorized practice of law proceedings authorized by the Inquiry Board against an Illinois attorney who is suspended or against a lawyer licensed in another jurisdiction in the United States shall be instituted by the Administrator by the filing of a disciplinary complaint before the Hearing Board, and the hearing and review procedure shall be governed by Rule 753.

(b) Proceedings Against Disbarred Illinois Lawyers and Unlicensed Persons. Unauthorized practice of law proceedings authorized by the Inquiry Board against an Illinois attorney who is disbarred or disbarred on consent or against a person, entity or association that is not licensed to practice law in any other United States' jurisdiction may be brought by the Administrator as civil and/or contempt actions pursuant to the rules of this court, its inherent authority over the practice of law, or other laws of the State related to the unauthorized practice of law. Proceedings shall be commenced in the circuit court for the circuit in which venue would be proper under the Code of Civil Procedure (735 ILCS 5/2–101 *et seq.*), unless venue is fixed by a specific law governing the proceedings, in which case that venue provision controls. The circuit court is authorized to enter a final judgment disposing of the case. Appeals from that judgment are governed by Rule 301 of this court.
Adopted Dec. 7, 2011, eff. immediately.

Rule 780. Client Protection Program

(a) There is established under the auspices of the Attorney Registration and Disciplinary Commission a Client Protection Program to reimburse claimants from the Client Protection Program Trust Fund for losses:

(1) caused by dishonest conduct committed by lawyers admitted to practice law in the State of Illinois; or

(2) involving unearned, unrefunded fees paid to lawyers admitted to practice law in the State of Illinois who later died or were transferred to disability inactive status.

(b) The purpose of the Client Protection Program is to promote public confidence in the administration of justice and the integrity of the legal profession by reimbursing losses, as defined in Rule 780(a), occurring in the course of a lawyer-client or fiduciary relationship between the lawyer and the claimant.

(c) Reimbursements of losses by the Program shall be within the sole discretion of the Commission, and not a matter of right. No person shall have a right in the Program as a third-party beneficiary or otherwise, either before or after the allowance of a claim. The determination of the Commission shall be final and shall not be subject to judicial review.

(d) The Client Protection Program shall be funded by an annual assessment as provided in rule 756. The Commission shall establish by rule the maximum amount which any one claimant may recover from the Program and may establish the aggregate maximum which may be recovered because of the conduct of any one lawyer.

(e) A lawyer who is the subject of a claim that results in reimbursement to a claimant shall be liable to the Program for restitution. Disciplinary orders imposing suspension or probation shall include a provision requiring the disciplined lawyer to reimburse the Client Protection Program Trust Fund for any payments arising from his or her conduct prior to the termination of the period of suspension or probation. Prior to filing a petition for reinstatement or restoration to active practice, a petitioner shall reimburse the Client Protection Program Trust Fund for all payments arising from petitioner's conduct. The petition must be accompanied by a statement from the Administrator indicating that all such payments have been made.

(f) The Commission may make rules related to the investigation and consideration of a Client Protection Program claim.
Adopted eff. March 28, 1994, effective immediately; amended Sept. 14, 2006, eff. immediately; Feb. 9, 2015, eff. immediately.

PART C. MINIMUM CONTINUING LEGAL EDUCATION

Preamble

The public contemplates that attorneys will maintain certain standards of professional competence throughout their careers in the practice of law. The following rules regarding Minimum Continuing Legal Education are intended to assure that those attorneys licensed to practice law in Illinois remain current regarding the requisite knowledge and skills necessary to fulfill the professional responsibilities and obligations of their respective practices and thereby improve the standards of the profession in general.

Rule 790. Title and Purpose

These rules shall be known as the Minimum Continuing Legal Education Rules ("Rules"). The purpose of the Rules is to establish a program for Minimum Continuing Legal Education ("MCLE"), which shall operate as an arm of the Supreme Court of Illinois.
Adopted September 29, 2005, effective immediately.

Rule 791. Persons Subject to MCLE Requirements

(a) Scope and Exemptions

These Rules shall apply to every attorney admitted to practice law in the State of Illinois, except for the following persons, who shall be exempt from the Rules' requirements:

(1) All attorneys on inactive or retirement status pursuant to Supreme Court Rules 756(a)(5) or (a)(6), respectively, or on inactive status pursuant to the former Supreme Court Rule 770 or who have previously been placed on voluntarily removed status by the Attorney Registration and Disciplinary Commission ("ARDC");

(2) All attorneys on disability inactive status pursuant to Supreme Court Rules 757 or 758;

(3) All attorneys serving in the office of justice, judge, associate judge, or magistrate of any federal or state court;

(4) All attorneys serving in the office of judicial law clerk, administrative assistant, secretary, or assistant secretary to a justice, judge, associate judge or magistrate of any federal court or any court of the State of Illinois, or in any other office included within the Supreme Court budget that assists the Supreme Court in its adjudicative responsibilities, provided that the exemption applies only if the attorney is prohibited by the terms of his or her employment from actively engaging in the practice of law;

(5) All attorneys licensed to practice law in Illinois who are on active duty in the Armed Forces of the United States, until their release from active military service and their return to the active practice of law;

(6) An attorney otherwise subject to this rule is entitled to an exemption if the attorney meets all of these criteria:

(i) the attorney is a member of the bar of another state which has a comparable minimum continuing legal education requirement or is licensed to practice law under a limited license issued by another state which has a comparable minimum continuing legal education requirement;

(ii) the individual attorney's only or primary office is in that other state or, if the attorney has no office, the individual attorney's only or primary residence is in that state;

(iii) the attorney is required by that state to complete credits to be in compliance with the continuing legal education requirements established by court rule or legislation in that state; and

(iv) the attorney has appropriate proof that he or she is in full compliance with the continuing legal education requirements established by court rule or legislation in that state; and

(7) In rare cases, upon a clear showing of good cause, the Minimum Continuing Legal Education Board ("Board") may grant a temporary exemption to an attorney from the Minimum Continuing Legal Education ("MCLE") requirements, or an extension of time in which to satisfy them. Good cause for an exemption or extension may exist in the event of illness, financial hardship, or other extraordinary or extenuating circumstances beyond the control of the attorney. Attorneys denied a temporary exemption or extension may request reconsideration of the initial decision made by the Director of MCLE ("Director") by filing a request in a form approved by the Board (or a substantially similar form) no later than 30 days after the Director's initial decision. The Director shall decide the request for reconsideration within 30 days of its receipt, and promptly notify the attorney. If the Director denies the request, the attorney shall have 30 days from the date of that denial to submit an appeal to the full Board for consideration at its next scheduled Board meeting. Submission of a request for reconsideration or an appeal does not stay any MCLE compliance deadlines or MCLE fee payments.

(b) Full Exemptions

An attorney shall be exempt from these Rules for an entire reporting period applicable to that attorney, if:

(1) The attorney is exempt from these Rules pursuant to paragraphs (a)(1), (a)(2), (a)(3), (a)(4),(a)(5), or (a)(6), on the last day of that reporting period; or

(2) The attorney is exempt from these Rules pursuant to paragraphs (a)(1), (a)(2), (a)(3), (a)(4), (a)(5), or (a)(6), for at least 365 days of that reporting period; or

(3) The attorney receives a temporary exemption from the Board pursuant to paragraph (a)(7), for that reporting period.

(c) Partial Exemptions

An attorney who is exempt from these Rules for more than 60, but less than 365, days of a two-year reporting period, and who is not exempt for the entire reporting period pursuant to paragraph (b), shall be required to earn one-half of the CLE activity hours that would otherwise be required pursuant to Rule 794(a) and (d).

(d) Nonexemptions

An attorney who is exempt from these Rules for less than 61 days during a two-year reporting period, and who is not exempt for the entire reporting period pursuant to paragraph (b), shall be required to earn all of the CLE activity hours required pursuant to Rule 794(a) and (d).

(e) Resuming Active Status

An attorney who was exempt from these Rules, pursuant to paragraphs (b)(1) or (b)(2), above, for the attorney's last completed reporting period because the attorney was on inactive, retirement or disability inactive status pursuant to Supreme Court Rules 756(a)(5) or (a)(6), 757 or 758, shall upon return to active status, have 24 months to complete the deferred CLE requirements, not to exceed two times the requirement for the current two-year reporting period, in addition to the CLE credit required for the current two-year reporting period.

(f) Attorneys on Discipline Status

Paragraphs (f)(1) and (2) shall apply to attorneys on discipline status for reporting periods ending June 30, 2012, and thereafter.

(1) Discipline Imposed Pursuant to Rule 770(a), (b), (c) and (e)

(i) An attorney whose discipline is imposed pursuant to Rule 770(a), (b), (c) and (e) is not required to comply with the MCLE requirements for any reporting period in which the discipline is in effect.

(ii) If the attorney is reinstated to the master roll by order of the Supreme Court ("Court"), the attorney must thereafter earn no less than 30 hours of MCLE credit and no more than 90 hours of MCLE credit which will be set by the MCLE Board based on the length of the attorney's discipline and whether credits need to be earned for the current reporting period. Those MCLE credits shall be earned and reported to the MCLE Board no later than 365 days after entry of the order reinstating the attorney to the master roll. The attorney shall contact the MCLE Board promptly after entry of the order reinstating the attorney to the master roll to establish the number of credits that need to be earned by the attorney. The attorney may apply any MCLE credits earned while the discipline imposed pursuant to Rule 770(a), (b), (c) or (e) was in effect. If the attorney does not earn the needed credits and report no later than 365 days after entry of the order reinstating the attorney to the master roll, the attorney shall pay a late fee, in an amount as set by the Board in the Court-approved fee schedule, and the attorney shall be referred to the ARDC pursuant to Rule 796(e). A reinstated attorney then needs to comply with the MCLE requirements for the two-year reporting period that begins after the attorney's reinstatement and all reporting periods thereafter.

(2) Discipline Pursuant to Rule 770(d), (f), (g) and (h)

An attorney whose discipline is imposed pursuant to Rule 770(d), (f), (g) and (h) is required to comply with the MCLE requirements for all reporting periods in which the discipline is in effect.

(g) Foreign Legal Consultants

Beginning with the reporting period ending June 30, 2012 and thereafter, the MCLE Rules do not apply to foreign legal consultants licensed under Rule 712. Adopted Sept. 29, 2005, eff. immediately. Amended Dec. 6, 2005, eff. immediately; Feb. 10, 2006, eff. immediately; Sept. 27, 2011, eff. immediately; Dec. 7, 2011, eff. immediately; June 5, 2012, eff. immediately.

Rule 792. The MCLE Board

(a) Administration

The administration of the program for MCLE shall be under the supervision of the Minimum Continuing Legal Education Board ("Board").

(b) Selection of Members; Qualifications; Terms

(1) The Board shall consist of nine members, appointed by the Supreme Court ("Court"). At least one member may be a nonattorney and at least one member shall be a circuit court judge. The Executive Director of the Supreme Court Commission on Professionalism and the Administrator of the Attorney Registration and Disciplinary Commission shall serve as *ex-officio* members in addition to the nine members appointed by the Court but shall have no vote.

(2) To be eligible for appointment to the Board, an attorney must have actively practiced law in Illinois for a minimum of 10 years.

(3) Three members, including the chairperson, shall initially be appointed to a three-year term. Three members shall be appointed to an initial two-year term, and three members shall be appointed to an initial one-year term. Thereafter, all members shall be appointed or reappointed to three-year terms.

(4) Board members shall be limited to serving three consecutive three-year terms.

(5) No individual may be appointed to the Board who stands to gain financially, directly or indirectly, from accreditation or other decisions made by the Board.

(6) Any member of the Board may be removed by the Court at any time, without cause.

(7) Should a vacancy occur, the Court shall appoint a replacement to serve for the unexpired term of the member.

(8) Board members shall serve without compensation, but shall be reimbursed for reasonable and necessary expenses incurred in performing their official duties, including reasonable travel costs to and from Board meetings.

(9) The chairperson and vice-chairperson shall be designated by the Court. Other officers shall be elected by the members of the Board at the first meeting of each year.

(c) Powers and Duties

The Board shall have the following powers and duties:

(1) To recommend to the Court rules and regulations for MCLE not inconsistent with the rules of the Court and these Rules, including fees sufficient to ensure that the MCLE program is financially self-supporting; to implement MCLE rules and

regulations adopted by the Court; and to adopt forms necessary to insure attorneys' compliance with the rules and regulations.

(2) To meet at least twice a year, or more frequently as needed, either in person, by conference telephone communications, or by electronic means. Six members of the Board shall constitute a quorum for the transaction of business. A majority of the quorum present shall be required for any official action taken by the Board.

(3) To accredit commercial and noncommercial continuing legal education ("CLE") courses and activities, and to determine the number of hours to be awarded for attending such courses or participating in such activities.

(4) To review applications for accreditation of those courses, activities or portions of either that are offered to fulfill the professional responsibility requirement in Rule 794(d)(1) for conformity with the accreditation standards and hours enumerated in Rule 795, exclusive of review as to substantive content. Those courses and activities determined to be in conformance shall be referred to the Supreme Court Commission on Professionalism for substantive review and approval as provided in Rules 799(c)(5) and (d)(6)(i). Professional responsibility courses or activities approved by both the Commission on Professionalism and the MCLE Board as specified in this subsection shall be eligible for accreditation by the MCLE Board.

(5) To submit an annual report to the Court evaluating the effectiveness of the MCLE Rules and the quality of the CLE courses, and presenting the Board's recommendations, if any, for changes in the Rules or their implementation, a financial report for the previous fiscal year, and its recommendations for the new fiscal year. There shall be an independent annual audit of the MCLE fund as directed by the Court, the expenses of which shall be paid out of the fund. The audit shall be submitted as part of the annual report to the Court.

(6) To coordinate its administrative responsibilities with the Attorney Registration and Disciplinary Commission ("ARDC"), and to reimburse expenses incurred by the ARDC attributable to enforcement of MCLE requirements.

(7) To take all action reasonably necessary to implement, administer and enforce these rules and the decisions of the MCLE Director, staff and Board.

(8) To establish policies and procedures for notification and reimbursement of course fees, if appropriate, in those instances where course accreditation is withheld or withdrawn.

(d) Administration

The Board shall appoint, with the approval of the Supreme Court, a Director of MCLE ("Director") to serve as the principal executive officer of the MCLE program. The Director, with the Board's authorization, will hire sufficient staff to administer the program. The Board will delegate to the Director and staff authority to conduct the business of the Board within the scope of this Rule, subject to review by the Board. The Director and staff shall be authorized to acquire or rent physical space, computer hardware and software systems and other items and services necessary to the administration of the MCLE program.

(e) Funding

The MCLE program shall initially be funded in a manner to be determined by the Court. Thereafter, funding shall be derived solely from the fees charged to CLE providers and from late fees and reinstatement fees assessed to individual attorneys. This schedule of CLE provider fees, late fees, and reinstatement fees must be approved by the Court, and any reference in these Rules to a fee assessed or set by the Board means a fee based on the Court-approved fee schedule. The Board may elect to charge fees up to the amount approved by the Court and the Board may, as it deems appropriate, charge fees less than the amount approved by the Court.

Adopted Sept. 29, 2005, eff. immediately. Amended Dec. 6, 2005, eff. immediately; June 5, 2007, eff. immediately; Nov. 23, 2009, eff. Dec. 1, 2009; Sept. 27, 2011, eff. immediately; Jan. 17, 2013, eff. immediately; Nov. 19, 2015, eff. immediately.

Rule 793. Requirement for Newly–Admitted Attorneys

(a) Scope

Except as specified in paragraph (f), every Illinois attorney admitted to practice on or after October 1, 2011, must complete the requirement for newly-admitted attorneys described in paragraph (c).

(b) Completion Deadline

The requirements established in paragraphs (c), (f) and (h) must be completed by the last day of the month that occurs one year after the newly-admitted attorney's admission to practice in Illinois.

(c) Elements of the Requirement for Newly–Admitted Attorneys

The requirement for newly-admitted attorneys includes three elements:

(1) A Basic Skills Course of no less than six hours covering topics such as practice techniques and procedures under the Illinois Rules of Professional Conduct, client communications, use of trust accounts, attorneys' other obligations under the Court's Rules, required record keeping, professional responsibility topics (which may include professionalism, diversity issues, mental illness and addiction issues and civility) and may cover other rudimentary elements of practice. The Basic Skills Course must include at least six hours approved for profes-

sional responsibility credit. An attorney may satisfy this requirement by participating in a mentoring program approved by the Commission on Professionalism pursuant to Rule 795(d)(12); and

(2) At least nine additional hours of MCLE credit. These nine hours may include any number of hours approved for professional responsibility credit;

(3) Reporting to the MCLE Board as required by Rule 796.

(d) Exemption From Other Requirements

During this period, the newly-admitted lawyer shall be exempt from the other MCLE requirements. A newly-admitted attorney may earn carryover credit as established by Rule 794(c)(2).

(e) Initial Reporting Period

The newly admitted attorney's initial two-year reporting period for complying with the MCLE requirements contained in Rule 794 shall commence, following the deadline for the attorney to complete the newly-admitted attorney requirement, on the next July 1 of an even-numbered year for lawyers whose last names begin with a letter A through M, and on the next July 1 of an odd-numbered year for lawyers whose last names begin with a letter N through Z.

(f) Prior Practice

(1) Attorneys admitted to the Illinois bar before October 1, 2011

The newly-admitted attorney requirements of Rule 793(c) do not apply to attorneys who are admitted in Illinois before October 1, 2011, and after practicing law in other states for a period of one year or more. Attorneys shall report this prior practice exemption to the MCLE Board under Rule 796. Thereafter, such attorneys will be subject to MCLE requirements under the appropriate schedule for each attorney.

(2) Attorneys admitted to the Illinois bar on October 1, 2011, and thereafter

The newly-admitted attorney requirements of Rule 793(c) do not apply to attorneys who: (i) were admitted in Illinois on October 1, 2011, and thereafter; and (ii) were admitted in Illinois after practicing law in other states for a period of at least one year in the three years immediately preceding admission in Illinois. Instead, such attorneys must complete 15 hours of MCLE credit (including four hours of professional responsibility credits) within one year of the attorney's admission to practice in Illinois. Such attorneys shall report compliance with this requirement to the MCLE Board under Rule 796. Thereafter, such attorneys will be subject to the MCLE requirements under the appropriate schedule for each attorney.

(g) Approval

The Basic Skills Course shall be offered by CLE providers, including "in-house" program providers, authorized by the MCLE Board after its approval of the provider's planned curriculum and after approval by the Commission on Professionalism of the professional responsibility credit. Courses shall be offered throughout the state and at reasonable cost.

(h) Applicability to Attorneys Admitted after December 31, 2005, and before October 1, 2011

Attorneys admitted to practice after December 31, 2005, and before October 1, 2011, have the option of completing a Basic Skills Course totaling at least 15 actual hours of instruction as detailed under the prior Rule 793(c) or of satisfying the requirements of paragraph (c).

Adopted Sept. 29, 2005, eff. immediately. Amended Sept. 27, 2011, eff. immediately.

Rule 794. Continuing Legal Education Requirement

(a) Hours Required

Except as provided by Rules 791 or 793, every Illinois attorney subject to these Rules shall be required to complete 20 hours of CLE activity during the initial two-year reporting period (as determined on the basis of the lawyer's last name pursuant to paragraph (b), below) ending on June 30 of either 2008 or 2009, 24 hours of CLE activity during the two-year reporting period ending on June 30 of either 2010 or 2011, and 30 hours of CLE activity during all subsequent two-year reporting periods.

(b) Reporting Period

The applicable two-year reporting period shall begin on July 1 of even-numbered years for lawyers whose last names begin with the letters A through M, and on July 1 of odd-numbered years for lawyers whose last names begin with the letters N through Z.

(c) Carryover of Hours

(1) For attorneys with two-year reporting periods

All CLE hours may be earned in one year or split in any manner between the two-year reporting period.

(i) If an attorney earns more than the required CLE hours in the two-year reporting periods of July 1, 2006, through June 30, 2008, or July 1, 2007, through June 30, 2009, the attorney may carry over a maximum of 10 hours earned during that period to the next reporting period, except for professional responsibility credits referred to in paragraph (d).

(ii) If an attorney earns more than the required CLE hours in the two-year reporting periods of July 1, 2008, through June 30, 2010, or July 1, 2009, through June 30, 2011, and all reporting periods thereafter, the attorney may carry over to the next reporting period a maximum of 10 hours, including hours approved for professional responsibility credit. Professional responsibility credit carried over to the next reporting period may be used to meet the professional responsibility requirement of the next reporting period.

(2) For newly-admitted attorneys subject to Rule 793

(i) For an attorney admitted to practice in Illinois on January 1, 2006, through June 30, 2009, such newly-admitted attorney may carry over to his or her first two-year reporting period a maximum of 10 CLE hours (except for professional responsibility credits referred to in paragraph (d)) earned after completing the newly-admitted attorney requirement pursuant to Rule 793.

(ii) For an attorney admitted to practice in Illinois on July 1, 2009, and thereafter, such newly-admitted attorney may carry over to his or her first two-year reporting period a maximum of 15 CLE hours earned in excess of those required by Rule 793(c) or Rule 793(f)(2) if those excess hours were earned after the attorney's admission to the Illinois bar and before the start of the attorney's first two-year reporting period. Those carryover hours may include up to six hours approved for professional responsibility credit. Professional responsibility credit carried over to the next reporting period may be used to meet the professional responsibility requirement of the next reporting period.

(3) An attorney, other than a newly admitted attorney, may carry over to his or her first two-year reporting period a maximum of 10 CLE activity hours (except for professional responsibility credits referred to in paragraph (d)) earned between January 1, 2006, and the beginning of that period.

(d) Professional Responsibility Requirement

(1) A minimum of four of the total hours required for the first two reporting periods must be in the area of professionalism, diversity issues, mental illness and addiction issues, civility, or legal ethics. Beginning with the reporting periods ending on June 30 of either 2012 or 2013, in which 30 hours of CLE are required, and for all subsequent reporting periods, a minimum of six of the total CLE hours required must be in such areas.

(2) Such credit may be obtained either by:

(i) Taking a separate CLE course or courses, or participating in other eligible CLE activity under these Rules, specifically devoted to professionalism, diversity issues, mental illness and addiction issues, civility, or legal ethics; or

(ii) Taking a CLE course or courses, or participating in other eligible CLE activity under these Rules, a portion of which is specifically devoted to professionalism, diversity issues, mental illness and addiction issues, civility, or legal ethics credit. Only that portion of a course or activity specifically devoted to professionalism, diversity issues, mental

illness and addiction issues, civility, or legal ethics shall receive CLE credit for the professional responsibility requirement of this paragraph.

Adopted Sept. 29, 2005, eff. immediately. Amended Oct. 1, 2010, eff. immediately; Sept. 27, 2011, eff. immediately.

Rule 795. Accreditation Standards and Hours

(a) Standards

Eligible CLE courses and activities shall satisfy the following standards:

(1) The course or activity must have significant intellectual, educational or practical content, and its primary objective must be to increase each participant's professional competence as an attorney.

(2) The course or activity must deal primarily with matters related to the practice of law.

(3) The course or activity must be offered by a provider having substantial, recent experience in offering CLE or demonstrated ability to organize and effectively present CLE. Demonstrated ability arises partly from the extent to which individuals with legal training or educational experience are involved in the planning, instruction and supervision of the activity.

(4) The course or activity itself must be conducted by an individual or group qualified by practical or academic experience. The course or activity, including the named advertised participants, must be conducted substantially as planned, subject to emergency withdrawals and alterations.

(5) Thorough, high quality, readable and carefully prepared written materials should be made available to all participants at or before the time the course is presented, unless the absence of such materials is recognized as reasonable and approved by the Board.

(6) Traditional CLE courses or activities shall be conducted in a physical setting conducive to learning. The course or activity may be presented by remote or satellite television transmission, telephone or videophone conference call, videotape, film, audio tape or over a computer network, so long as the Board approves the content and the provider, and finds that the method in question has interactivity as a key component. Such interactivity may be shown, for example, by the opportunity for the viewers or listeners to ask questions of the course faculty, in person, via telephone, or on-line; or through the availability of a qualified commentator to answer questions directly, electronically, or in writing; or through computer links to relevant cases, statutes, law review articles, or other sources.

(7) The course or activity must consist of not less than one-half hour of actual instruction, unless the Board determines that a specific program of less than one-half hour warrants accreditation.

(8) A list of the names of all participants for each course or activity shall be maintained by the provider for a period of at least three years. The provider shall issue a certificate, in written or electronic form, to each participant evincing his or her attendance. Such lists and certificates shall state the number of CLE hours, including professionalism, diversity issues, mental illness and addiction issues, civility, or legal ethics CLE hours, earned at that course or activity.

(b) Accredited CLE Provider

The Board may extend presumptive approval to a provider for all of the CLE courses or activities presented by that provider each year that conform to paragraph (a)'s Standards (1) through (8), upon written application to be an "Accredited Continuing Legal Education Provider." Such accreditation shall constitute prior approval of all CLE courses offered by such providers. However, the Board may withhold accreditation or limit hours for any course found not to meet the standards, and may revoke accreditation for any organization which is found not to comply with standards. The Board shall assess an annual fee, over and above the fees assessed to the provider for each course, for the privilege of being an "Accredited Continuing Legal Education Provider."

(c) Accreditation of Individual Courses or Activities

(1) Any provider not included in paragraph (b) desiring advance accreditation of an individual course or other activity shall apply to the Board by submitting a required application form, the course advance accreditation fee set by the Board, and supporting documentation no less than 45 days prior to the date for which the course or activity is scheduled. Documentation shall include a statement of the provider's intention to comply with the accreditation standards of this Rule, the written materials distributed or to be distributed to participants at the course or activity, if available, or a detailed outline of the proposed course or activity and list of instructors, and such further information as the Board shall request. The Board staff will advise the applicant in writing within 30 days of the receipt of the completed application of its approval or disapproval.

(2) Providers denied approval of a course or activity shall promptly provide written notice of the Board's denial to all attorneys who requested Illinois MCLE credit for the course. Providers denied approval of a course or activity or individual attorneys who have attended such course or activity may request reconsideration of the Board's initial decision by filing a form approved by the Board no later than 30 days after the Board's initial decision. The Director shall consider the request within 30 days of its receipt, and promptly notify the provider and/or the individual attorney. If the Director denies the request, the provider shall have 30 days from the

date of that denial to submit an appeal to the Board for consideration at the next scheduled Board meeting. Submission of a request for reconsideration or an appeal does not stay any MCLE submission deadlines or fee payments.

(3) Providers who do not seek prior approval of their course or activity may apply for approval for the course or activity after its presentation by submitting an application provided by MCLE staff, the supporting documentation described above, and the accreditation fee set by the Board.

(4) A list of the names of participants shall be maintained by the provider for a period of three years. The provider shall issue a certificate, in written or electronic form, to each participant evincing his or her attendance. Such lists and certificates shall state the number of CLE hours, including professionalism, diversity issues, mental illness and addiction issues, civility, or legal ethics CLE hours, earned at that course or activity.

(5) An attorney may apply to the Illinois MCLE Board for accreditation of an individual out-of-state CLE course if the following provisions are satisfied: (i) the attorney participated in the course either in person or via live audio or video conference; (ii) (a) for a course held in person in a state with a comparable MCLE requirement, the course must be approved for MCLE credit by that state; or (b) for a course held in person in a state or the District of Columbia without a comparable MCLE requirement, the course must be approved for MCLE credit by at least one other state with a comparable MCLE requirement; or (c) for a course attended by live audio or video conference, the course must be approved for MCLE credit by at least one other state with a comparable MCLE requirement; and (iii) the course provider has chosen not to seek accreditation of the course for Illinois MCLE credit.

(d) Nontraditional Courses or Activities

In addition to traditional CLE courses, the following courses or activities will receive CLE credit:

(1) "In–House" Programs. Attendance at "in-house" seminars, courses, lectures or other CLE activity presented by law firms, corporate legal departments, governmental agencies or similar entities, either individually or in cooperation with other such entities, subject to the following conditions:

(i) The CLE course or activity must meet the rules and regulations for any other CLE provider, as applicable.

(ii) Specifically, the course or activity must have significant intellectual, educational or practical content, its primary objective must be to increase the participant's professional competence as an attorney, and it must deal primarily with matter related to the practice of law, professionalism, diversity issues, mental illness and addiction issues, civility or ethical obligations of attorneys.

No credit will be afforded for discussions relating to the handling of specific cases, or issues relating to the management of a specific law firm, corporate law department, governmental agency or similar entity.

(iii) The course or activity shall be submitted for approval on an individual course or activity basis rather than on a Presumptively Accredited Continuing Legal Education Provider basis.

(iv) The application, including all written materials or an abstract thereof, should be filed with the Board at least 30 days prior to the date on which the course or activity is to be held in order for a prior determination of acceptability to be made. However, prior approval by the Board shall not be required.

(v) Only courses or activities that have at least five attorney participants shall qualify for CLE credit. The attorneys need not be associated with the same firm, corporation or governmental agency.

(vi) Experienced attorneys must contribute to the teaching, and efforts should be made to achieve a balance of in-house and outside instructors.

(vii) The activity must be open to observation, without charge, by members of the Board or their designates.

(viii) The activity must be scheduled at a time and location so as to be free of interruptions from telephone calls and other office matters.

(ix) A list of the names of participants shall be maintained by the provider for a period of three years. The provider shall issue a certificate, in written or electronic form, to each participant evincing his or her attendance. Such lists and certificates shall state the number of CLE hours, including professionalism, diversity issues, mental illness and addiction issues, civility, or legal ethics CLE hours, earned at that activity.

(x) The Board may impose a fee, similar to the fees assessed on traditional CLE providers, on the provider of an in-house program for programs involving payments to the provider.

(2) Law School Courses. Attendance at J.D. or graduate level law courses offered by American Bar Association ("ABA") accredited law schools, subject to the following conditions:

(i) Credit ordinarily is given only for courses taken after admission to practice in Illinois, but the Board may approve giving credit for courses taken prior to admission to practice in Illinois if giving credit will advance CLE objectives.

(ii) Credit towards MCLE requirements shall be for the actual number of class hours attended, but the maximum number of credits that may be earned during any two-year reporting period by attending courses offered by ABA accredited law schools shall be the minimum number of CLE hours required by Rules 794(a) and (d).

(iii) The attorney must comply with registration procedures of the law school, including the payment of tuition.

(iv) The course need not be taken for law school credit towards a degree; auditing a course is permitted. However, the attorney must comply with all law school rules for attendance, participation and examination, if any, to receive CLE credit.

(v) The law school shall give each attorney a written certification evincing that the attorney has complied with requirements for the course and attended sufficient classes to justify the awarding of course credit if the attorney were taking the course for credit.

(3) Bar Association Meetings. Attendance at bar association or professional association meetings at which substantive law, matters of practice, professionalism, diversity issues, mental illness and addiction issues, civility, or legal ethics are discussed, subject to the requirements for CLE credit defined in paragraphs (a)(1) through (a)(2) above. The bar or professional association shall maintain a list of the names of all attendees at each meeting for a period of three years and shall issue a certificate, in written or electronic form, to each participant evincing his or her attendance. Such lists and certificates shall state the number of CLE hours, including professionalism, diversity issues, mental illness and addiction issues, civility, or legal ethics CLE hours, earned at that meeting.

(4) Cross–Disciplinary Programs. Attendance at courses or activities that cross academic lines, such as accounting-tax seminars or medical-legal seminars, may be considered by the Board for full or partial credit. Purely nonlegal subjects, such as personal financial planning, shall not be counted towards CLE credit. Any mixed-audience courses or activities may receive credit only for sessions deemed appropriate for CLE purposes.

(5) Teaching Continuing Legal Education Courses. Teaching at CLE courses or activities during the two-year reporting term, subject to the following:

(i) Credit may be earned for teaching in an approved CLE course or activity. Presentations shall be counted at the full hour or fraction thereof for the initial presentation; a repeat presentation of the same material shall be counted at one-half; no further hours may be earned for additional presentations of the same material.

(ii) Time spent in preparation for a presentation at an approved CLE activity shall be counted at six times the actual presentation time.

(iii) Authorship or coauthorship of written materials for approved CLE activities shall qualify for CLE credit on the basis of actual preparation time, but subject to receiving no more than 10 hours of credit in any two-year reporting period.

(6) Part–Time Teaching of Law Courses. Teaching at an ABA–accredited law school, or teaching a law course at a university, college, or community college, subject to the following:

(i) Teaching credit may be earned for teaching law courses offered for credit toward a degree at a law school accredited by the ABA, but only by lawyers who are not employed full-time by a law school. Full–time law teachers who choose to maintain their licenses to practice law are fully subject to the MCLE requirements established herein, and may not earn any credits by their ordinary teaching assignments. Presentations shall be counted at the full hour or fraction thereof for the initial presentation; a repeat presentation of the same material shall be counted at one-half; no further hours may be earned for additional presentations of the same material. Teaching credit may be earned by appearing as a guest instructor, moderator, or participant in a law school class for a presentation which meets the overall guidelines for CLE courses or activities, as well as for serving as a judge at a law school moot court argument. Time spent in preparation for an eligible law school activity shall be counted at three times the actual presentation time. Appearing as a guest speaker before a law school assembly or group shall not count toward CLE credit.

(ii) Teaching credit may be earned for teaching law courses at a university, college, or community college by lawyers who are not full-time teachers if the teaching involves significant intellectual, educational or practical content, such as a civil procedure course taught to paralegal students or a commercial law course taught to business students. Presentations shall be counted at the full hour or fraction thereof for the initial presentation; a repeat presentation of the same material shall be counted at one-half; no further hours may be earned for additional presentations of the same material.

(7) Legal Scholarship. Writing law books and law review articles, subject to the following:

(i) An attorney may earn credit for legal textbooks, casebooks, treatises and other scholarly legal books written by the attorney that are published during the two-year reporting period.

(ii) An attorney may earn credit for writing law-related articles in responsible legal journals or other legal sources, published during the two-year reporting period, that deal primarily with matters related to the practice of law, professionalism, diversity issues, mental illness and addiction issues, civility, or ethical obligations of attorneys. Republication of any article shall receive no additional CLE credits unless the author made substantial revisions or additions.

(iii) An attorney may earn credit towards MCLE requirements for the actual number of hours spent researching and writing, but the maximum number of credits that may be earned during any two-year reporting period on a single publication shall be one-half the minimum number of CLE hours required by Rules 794(a) and (d). Credit is accrued when the eligible book or article is published, regardless whether the work in question was performed in the then-current two-year reporting period. To receive CLE credit, the attorney shall maintain contemporaneous records evincing the number of hours spent on a publication.

(8) Pro Bono Training. Attendance at courses or activities designed to train lawyers who have agreed to provide pro bono services shall earn CLE credit to the same extent as other courses and seminars.

(9) Bar Review Courses. Attendance at bar review courses before admission to the Illinois Bar shall not be used for CLE credit.

(10) Reading Legal Materials. No credit shall be earned by reading advance sheets, newspapers, law reviews, books, cases, statutes, newsletters or other such sources.

(11) Activity of Lawyer–to–Lawyer Mentoring. Lawyers completing a comprehensive year-long structured mentoring program, as either a mentor or mentee, may earn credit equal to the minimum professional responsibility credit during the two-year reporting period of completion, provided that the mentoring plan is preapproved by the Commission on Professionalism, the completion is attested to by both mentor and mentee, and completion occurs during the first three years of the mentee's practice in Illinois. For reporting periods ending in 2011 or earlier, the maximum number of professional responsibility credit hours shall be four. Beginning with the reporting periods ending on June 30 of either 2012 or 2013, in which 30 hours of CLE are required, the maximum number of credit hours available shall be six.

(e) Credit Hour Guidelines

Hours of CLE credit will be determined under the following guidelines:

(1) Sixty minutes shall equal one hour of credit. Partial credit shall be earned for qualified activities of less than 60 minutes duration.

(2) The following are not counted for credit: (i) coffee breaks; (ii) introductory and closing remarks; (iii) keynote speeches; (iv) lunches and dinners; (v) other breaks; and (vi) business meetings.

(3) Question and answer periods are counted toward credit.

(4) Lectures or panel discussions occurring during breakfast, luncheon, or dinner sessions of bar association committees may be awarded credit.

(5) Credits are determined by the following formula: Total minutes of approved activity *minus* minutes for breaks (as described in paragraph (e)(2)) *divided by* 60 *equals* maximum CLE credit allowed.

(6) Credits merely reflect the maximum that may be earned. Only actual attendance or participation earns credit.

(f) Financial Hardship Policy

The provider shall have available a financial hardship policy for attorneys who wish to attend its courses, but for whom the cost of such courses would be a financial hardship. Such policy may be in the form of scholarships, waivers of course fees, reduced course fees, or discounts. Upon request by the Board, the provider must produce the detailed financial hardship policy. The Board may require, on good cause shown, a provider to set aside without cost, or at reduced cost, a reasonable number of places in the course for those attorneys determined by the Board to have good cause to attend the course for reduced or no cost.

Adopted September 29, 2005, effective immediately; amended October 4, 2007, effective immediately; October 12, 2010, effective immediately; September 27, 2011, effective immediately; Feb. 6, 2013, eff. immediately.

Rule 796. Enforcement of MCLE Requirements

(a) Reporting Compliance

(1) Notice of Requirement to Submit MCLE Certification

The MCLE Board shall send to attorneys as set forth in (i), (ii) and (iii) below a notice of requirement to submit an MCLE certification ("Initial MCLE Notice"). The attorney's certification shall state whether the attorney complied with these Rules, has not complied with these Rules or is exempt.

(i) Newly-admitted attorney requirement

On or before the first day of the month preceding the end of an attorney's newly-admitted attorney requirement reporting period, the Director shall mail or email to the attorney, at a mailing or email address maintained by the ARDC, an Initial MCLE Notice.

(ii) Two-year reporting period and deferred credits requirements

On or before May 1 of each two-year reporting period, the Director shall mail or email to the attorney, at a mailing or email address maintained by the ARDC, an Initial MCLE notice.

(iii) Attorneys Known to be Exempt or Removed for MCLE Noncompliance

An Initial MCLE Notice need not be sent to an attorney known by the Director to be fully exempt from these Rules pursuant to Rule 791(b) or to an attorney who has already been removed from the master roll of attorneys due to the attorney's failure to comply with the MCLE requirements for two consecutive reporting periods or more.

(2) Every Illinois attorney who is either subject to these Rules or who is sent an MCLE Initial Notice shall submit a certification to the Board, by means of the Board's online reporting system or other means specified by the Director, within 31 days after the end of the attorney's reporting period. It is the responsibility of each attorney on the master roll to notify the ARDC of any change of address or email address. Failure to receive an Initial MCLE Notice shall not constitute an excuse for failure to file the certification.

(b) Failure to Report Compliance

Attorneys who fail to submit an MCLE certification within 31 days after the end of their reporting period, or who file a certification within 31 days after the end of their reporting stating that they have not complied with these Rules during the reporting period, shall be mailed or emailed a notice by the Director to inform them of their noncompliance. Attorneys shall be given 61 additional days from the original certification due date provided in Rule 796(a)(2) to achieve compliance and submit a certification, by means of the Board's online reporting system or other means specified by the Director, stating that they have complied with these Rules or are exempt. The Director shall not send a notice of noncompliance to attorneys whom the Director knows, based on the status of the attorneys' licenses as inactive, retirement, disability inactive, judicial or military with the ARDC, are fully exempt from these Rules.

(c) Grace Period

Attorneys given additional time pursuant to paragraph (b) to comply with the requirements of these Rules may use that "grace period" to attain the adequate number of hours for compliance. Credit hours earned during a grace period may be counted toward compliance with the previous reporting period requirement, and hours in excess of the requirement may be used to meet the current reporting period's requirement. No attorney may receive more than one grace period with respect to the same reporting period, and the grace period shall not be extended if the Director fails to send, or the attorney fails to receive, a notice pursuant to paragraph (b).

(d) Late Fees

(1) Attorneys who are not fully exempt under Rule 791(a)(1), (2), (3) or (5) and who, for whatever reason, fail to submit an MCLE certification pursuant to Rule 796(a)(2) within 31 days after the end of their reporting period, and who are sent a notice of noncompliance from the Director pursuant to para-

graph (b), shall pay a late fee, in an amount to be set by the Board. The Director shall not assess a late fee to an attorney whom the Director knows, based on the status of the attorney's license as inactive, retirement, disability inactive, judicial or military with the ARDC, are fully exempt from these Rules.

(2) Attorneys who submit an MCLE certification to the Board within 31 days after their reporting period ends and who certify that they failed to comply with these Rules during the applicable reporting period, shall pay a late fee, in an amount to be set by the Board that is less than the late fee imposed pursuant to paragraph (d)(1).

(e) Failure to Comply or Failure to Report

The Director shall refer to the ARDC the names of attorneys who were mailed or emailed a notice of noncompliance and who, by the end of their grace periods, failed either: (1) to comply or to report compliance with the requirements of these Rules to the MCLE Board; or (2) to report an exemption from the requirements of these Rules to the MCLE Board. The Director shall also refer to the ARDC the names of attorneys who, by the end of their grace period, failed to pay any outstanding MCLE fee. The ARDC shall then send notice, by mail or email, to any such attorneys that they will be removed from the master roll on the date specified in the notice, which shall be no sooner than 21 days from the date of the notice, because of their failure to comply or report compliance, failure to report an exemption, or failure to pay an outstanding MCLE fee. The ARDC shall remove such attorneys from the master roll of attorneys on the date specified in the notice unless the Director certifies before that date that an attorney has complied. Such removal is not a disciplinary sanction.

(f) Recordkeeping and Audits

(1) Each attorney subject to these Rules shall maintain, for three years after the end of the relevant reporting period, certificates of attendance received pursuant to Rules 795(a)(8), (c)(4), (d)(1)(ix), (d)(2)(v), (d)(3), as well as sufficient documentation necessary to corroborate CLE activity hours earned pursuant to Rules 795(d)(4) through (d)(9).

(2) The Board may conduct a reasonable number of audits, under a plan approved by the Court. At least some of these audits shall be randomly selected, to determine the accuracy of attorneys' certifications of compliance or exemption. With respect to audits that are not randomly selected, in choosing subjects for those audits the Board shall give increased consideration to attorneys who assumed inactive or retirement status under Supreme Court Rule 756(a)(5) or (a)(6), and were thereby fully or partially exempt from these Rules pursuant to Rule 791(b) or (c), and who subsequently resumed active status.

(3) The ARDC may investigate an attorney's compliance with these Rules only upon referral from the Director; the ARDC will not investigate an attorney's compliance with these Rules as part of its other investigations. When the Director refers a matter to the ARDC, the investigation, and any resulting prosecution, shall be conducted in accordance with the rules pertaining to ARDC proceedings.

(g) Audits That Reveal an Inaccurate Certification

(1) If an audit conducted pursuant to paragraph (f)(2) reveals that the attorney was not in compliance with or exempt from these Rules for any reporting period for which the attorney had filed a certification of compliance or exemption, the Director shall provide the attorney with written notice containing: (i) the results of the audit, specifying each aspect of the Rules with which the attorney did not comply or the reason why the attorney is not exempt; (ii) a summary of the basis of that determination; and (iii) a deadline, which shall be at least 30 days from the date of the notice, for the attorney to file a written response if the attorney objects to any of the contents of the notice.

(2) After considering any response from the attorney, if the Board determines that the attorney filed an inaccurate certification, the attorney shall be given 60 days in which to file an amended certification, together with all documentation specified in paragraph (f)(1), demonstrating full compliance with the applicable MCLE requirements. The attorney also shall pay a late fee in an amount to be set by the Board. The assessment of a late fee is not a disciplinary sanction.

(3) If the results of the audit suggest that the attorney willfully filed a false certification, the Board through its Director shall provide that information to the ARDC.

(h) Reinstatement

An attorney who has been removed from the master roll due to noncompliance with these Rules may be reinstated by the ARDC, upon recommendation of the Board. Such recommendation may be made only after the removed attorney files a certification which the Board determines shows full compliance with the applicable MCLE requirements for each reporting period for which the attorney was removed from the master roll due to MCLE noncompliance. To be reinstated, the attorney shall pay a reinstatement fee for each reporting period for which the attorney was removed from the master roll due to MCLE noncompliance with the request, in an amount to be set by the Board. The Board may elect to cap the total amount of the reinstatement fee when an attorney has been removed from the master roll due to MCLE noncompliance in more than six consecutive reporting periods. The attorney must also meet any further conditions and pay any additional fees as may be required by Rule 756. The removed attorney may attain the necessary credit hours during the period of removal to meet the requirements for the years of noncompliance. Excess hours earned during the period of removal, however, may not be counted towards meeting the current or future reporting periods' requirements.

Adopted Sept. 29, 2005, eff. immediately. Amended Oct. 5, 2006, eff. immediately; Sept. 27, 2011, eff. immediately; Nov. 19, 2015, eff. Feb. 1, 2016.

Rule 797. Confidentiality

All files, records and proceedings of the Board must be kept confidential, and may not be disclosed except (a) in furtherance of the duties of the Board, (b) upon written request and consent of the persons affected, (c) pursuant to a proper subpoena *duces tecum*, or (d) as ordered by a court of competent jurisdiction.

Adopted September 29, 2005, effective immediately.

Rule 798. Reserved

PART D. COMMISSION ON PROFESSIONALISM

Rule 799. Supreme Court Commission on Professionalism

(a) Purpose

The Supreme Court Commission on Professionalism is hereby established in order to promote among the lawyers and judges of Illinois principles of integrity, professionalism and civility; to foster commitment to the elimination of bias and divisiveness within the legal and judicial systems; and to ensure that those systems provide equitable, effective and efficient resolution of problems and disputes for the people of Illinois.

(b) Membership and Terms

(1) The Court shall appoint 14 members to the Commission, one of whom shall be designated the Chair and one of whom shall be designated the Vice–Chair. The Director of the Minimum Continuing Legal Education Program and the Administrator of the Attorney Registration and Disciplinary Commission shall serve as *ex-officio* members in addition to the 14 members appointed by the Court but shall have no vote.

(2) In addition to the members described above, the Chief Justice may invite to serve on the Commission a judge of the United States District Courts located in Illinois.

(3) The appointed members of the Commission shall be selected with regard to their reputations for professionalism, and for their past contributions to the bar and to their communities, to the extent feasible, the appointees should reflect a diversity of geography, practice areas, race, ethnicity, and gender.

(4) Members of the Commission shall be appointed for terms of three years, except that in making initial appointments to the Commission, the Court may limit appointments to ensure that the terms of the Commission's members are staggered, so that no more than one third of the members' terms expire in any given year.

(5) None of the members of the Commission shall receive compensation for their service, but all members shall be reimbursed for their necessary expenses.

(c) Duties

The Commission's duties shall include:

(1) Creating and promoting an awareness of professionalism by all members of the Illinois bar and bench;

(2) Gathering and maintaining information to serve as a resource on professionalism for lawyers, judges, court personnel, and members of the public;

(3) Developing public statements on principles of ethical and professional responsibility for distribution to the bench and bar for purposes of encouraging, guiding and assisting individual lawyers, law firms and bar associations on the ethical and professional tenets of the profession;

(4) Assisting CLE providers with the development of courses and activities offered to fulfill the professional responsibility requirement for minimum continuing legal education under Rule 794(d)(1);

(5) Determining and publishing criteria for, monitoring, coordinating, and approving, courses and activities offered to fulfill the professional responsibility requirement for minimum continuing legal education under Rule 794(d)(1);

(6) Reviewing and approving the content of courses and activities offered to fulfill the professional responsibility requirement for minimum continuing legal education under Rule 794(d)(1) and forwarding the Commission's determination to the Minimum Continuing Legal Education (MCLE) Board;

(7) Monitoring activities related to professionalism outside the State of Illinois;

(8) Collaborating with law schools in the development and presentation of professionalism programs for law student orientation and other events as coordinated with law school faculty;

(9) Facilitating cooperation among practitioners, bar associations, law schools, courts, civic and lay

organizations and others in addressing matters of professionalism, ethics, and public understanding of the legal profession; and

(10) Recommending to the Court other methods and means of improving the profession and accomplishing the purposes of this Commission.

The Commission shall have no authority to impose discipline upon any member of the Illinois bar or bench, or to exercise any duties or responsibilities belonging to either the Judicial Inquiry Board, the Attorney Registration and Disciplinary Commission, the Board of Admissions to the Bar, or the MCLE Board.

(d) Administration

(1) The Commission shall have the authority to appoint, with the approval of the Supreme Court, an Executive Director, who shall be an attorney who is an active member in good standing of the Illinois bar. The Executive Director shall have the authority to hire such additional staff as necessary to perform the Commission's responsibilities.

(2) The Commission shall meet at least twice a year and at other times at the call of the Chair. A majority of its members shall constitute a quorum for any action. Meetings may be held at any place within the state and may also be held by means of telecommunication that permits reasonably accurate and contemporaneous participation by the members attending by such means.

(3) The Chair may appoint committees of members and assign them to such responsibilities, consistent with the purposes, powers and duties of the Commission, as the Chair may deem appropriate.

(4) The Commission shall file annually with the Court an accounting of the monies received and expended for its activities, and there shall be an annual independent audit of the funds as directed by the court, the expenses of which shall be paid out of the fund.

(5) The Commission shall submit an annual report to the Court describing and evaluating the effectiveness of its activities.

(6) Approving CLE Programs.

(i) The Commission shall receive from the MCLE Board applications for accreditation of those courses and activities offered to fulfill the professional responsibility requirement for minimum continuing legal education under Rule 794(d)(1). The Commission shall establish procedures for approval of such courses or activities consistent with the criteria published under paragraph (c)(5) of this rule. Professional responsibility courses and activities, the content of which is approved by the Commission, shall be forwarded to the MCLE Board for accreditation. Absent Commission approval, such courses and activities are not eligible for CLE accreditation. The Commission shall complete its review as expeditiously as possible and with regard to the applicable time lines contained in Rule 795.

(ii) Providers that have been designated "Accredited Continuing Legal Education Providers" under Rule 795(b) must, in addition to that accreditation, obtain Commission approval of any course or activity offered to fulfill the professional responsibility requirement of Rule 794(d)(1), but will not be required to pay an accreditation fee in addition to the fee the provider has paid to the Minimum Continuing Legal Education Board.

(e) Funding

The Commission shall be funded by an annual assessment as provided in Rule 756.

Adopted Sept. 29, 2005, eff. immediately. Amended Dec. 6, 2005, eff. immediately; June 5, 2007, eff. immediately; Sept. 27, 2011, eff. immediately; June 5, 2012, eff. immediately; Jan. 18, 2013, eff. immediately.

ARTICLE VIII. ILLINOIS RULES OF PROFESSIONAL CONDUCT [REPEALED]

EDITORIAL COMMENT

The Illinois Rules of Professional Conduct were formerly contained in Illinois Revised Statutes 1991, Chapter 110A, following ¶ 777.

The Illinois Rules of Professional Conduct, adopted Feb. 8, 1990, eff. Aug. 1, 1990 were repealed by Order M.R. 3140 and replaced by the Illinois Rules of Professional Conduct of 2010, eff. Jan. 1, 2010.

Rules 1.1 to 8.5. Repealed eff. Jan. 1, 2010

ARTICLE VIII. ILLINOIS RULES OF PROFESSIONAL CONDUCT OF 2010

EDITORIAL COMMENT

The Illinois Rules of Professional Conduct were formerly contained in Illinois Revised Statutes 1991, Chapter 110A, following ¶ 777.

The Illinois Rules of Professional Conduct of 2010 are adopted, eff. Jan. 1, 2010, by order of the Supreme Court of the State of Illinois dated July 1, 2009 (M.R. 3140). The Illinois Rules of Professional Conduct as adopted Feb. 8, 1990, eff. Aug. 1, 1990 were repealed by Order M.R. 3140 and replaced by the Illinois Rules of Professional Conduct of 2010.

Former Provisions

Former Article VIII, the Code of Professional Responsibility, consisting of Canons 1 to 9 and Rules 1–101 to 9–102, was repealed effective August 1, 1990.

Preamble: a Lawyer's Responsibilities

[1] A lawyer, as a member of the legal profession, is a representative of clients, an officer of the legal system and a public citizen having special responsibility for the quality of justice.

[2] As a representative of clients, a lawyer performs various functions. As advisor, a lawyer provides a client with an informed understanding of the client's legal rights and obligations and explains their practical implications. As advocate, a lawyer zealously asserts the client's position under the rules of the adversary system. As negotiator, a lawyer seeks a result advantageous to the client but consistent with requirements of honest dealings with others. As an evaluator, a lawyer acts by examining a client's legal affairs and reporting about them to the client or to others.

[3] In addition to these representational functions, a lawyer may serve as a third-party neutral, a nonrepresentational role helping the parties to resolve a dispute or other matter. Some of these Rules apply directly to lawyers who are or have served as third-party neutrals. See, *e.g.*, Rules 1.12 and 2.4. In addition, there are Rules that apply to lawyers who are not active in the practice of law or to practicing lawyers even when they are acting in a nonprofessional capacity. For example, a lawyer who commits fraud in the conduct of a business is subject to discipline for engaging in conduct involving dishonesty, fraud, deceit or misrepresentation. See Rule 8.4.

[4] In all professional functions a lawyer should be competent, prompt and diligent. A lawyer should maintain communication with a client concerning the representation. A lawyer should keep in confidence information relating to representation of a client except so far as disclosure is required or permitted by the Rules of Professional Conduct or other law.

[5] A lawyer's conduct should conform to the requirements of the law, both in professional service to clients and in the lawyer's business and personal affairs. A lawyer should use the law's procedures only for legitimate purposes and not to harass or intimidate others. A lawyer should demonstrate respect for the legal system and for those who serve it, including judges, other lawyers and public officials. While it is a lawyer's duty, when necessary, to challenge the rectitude of official action, it is also a lawyer's duty to uphold legal process.

[6] As a public citizen, a lawyer should seek improvement of the law, access to the legal system, the administration of justice and the quality of service rendered by the legal profession. As a member of a learned profession, a lawyer should cultivate knowledge of the law beyond its use for clients, employ that knowledge in reform of the law and work to strengthen legal education. In addition, a lawyer should further the public's understanding of and confidence in the rule of law and the justice system because legal institutions in a constitutional democracy depend on popular participation and support to maintain their authority.

[6A] It is also the responsibility of those licensed as officers of the court to use their training, experience, and skills to provide services in the public interest for which compensation may not be available. It is the responsibility of those who manage law firms to create an environment that is hospitable to the rendering of a reasonable amount of uncompensated service by lawyers practicing in that firm. Service in the public interest may take many forms. These include but are not limited to *pro bono* representation of persons unable to pay for legal services and assistance in the organized bar's efforts at law reform. An individual lawyer's efforts in these areas is evidence of the lawyer's good character and fitness to practice law, and the efforts of the bar as a whole are essential to the bar's maintenance of professionalism. To help monitor and quantify the extent of these activities, and to encourage an increase in the delivery of legal services to persons of limited means, Illinois Supreme Court Rule 756(f) requires disclosure with each lawyer's annual registration with the Illinois Attorney Registration and Disciplinary Commission of the approximate amount of his or her *pro bono* legal service and the approximate amount of qualified monetary contributions. See also Committee Comment (June 14, 2006) to Illinois Supreme Court Rule 756(f).

[6B] The absence from the Illinois Rules of a counterpart to ABA Model Rule 6.1 regarding *pro bono* and public service should not be interpreted as limiting the responsibility of lawyers to render uncompensated service in the public interest. Rather, the rationale is that this responsibility is not appropriate for disciplinary rules because it is not possible to articulate an appropriate disciplinary standard regarding *pro bono* and public service.

[7] Many of a lawyer's professional responsibilities are prescribed in the Rules of Professional Conduct, as well as substantive and procedural law. However, a lawyer is also guided by personal conscience and the approbation of professional peers. A lawyer should strive to attain the highest level of skill, to improve the law and the legal profession and to exemplify the legal profession's ideals of public service.

[8] A lawyer's responsibilities as a representative of clients, an officer of the legal system and a public citizen are usually harmonious. Thus, when an opposing party is well represented, a lawyer can be a zealous advocate on behalf of a client and at the same time assume that justice is being done. So also, a lawyer can be sure that preserving

client confidences ordinarily serves the public interest because people are more likely to seek legal advice, and thereby heed their legal obligations, when they know their communications will be private.

[9] In the nature of law practice, however, conflicting responsibilities are encountered. Virtually all difficult ethical problems arise from conflict between a lawyer's responsibilities to clients, to the legal system and to the lawyer's own interest in remaining an ethical person while earning a satisfactory living. The Rules of Professional Conduct often prescribe terms for resolving such conflicts. Within the framework of these Rules, however, many difficult issues of professional discretion can arise. Such issues must be resolved through the exercise of sensitive professional and moral judgment guided by the basic principles underlying the Rules. These principles include the lawyer's obligation zealously to protect and pursue a client's legitimate interests, within the bounds of the law, while maintaining a professional, courteous and civil attitude toward all persons involved in the legal system.

[10] The legal profession is largely self-governing. Although other professions also have been granted powers of self-government, the legal profession is unique in this respect because of the close relationship between the profession and the processes of government and law enforcement. This connection is manifested in the fact that ultimate authority over the legal profession is vested largely in the courts.

[11] To the extent that lawyers meet the obligations of their professional calling, the occasion for government regulation is obviated. Self-regulation also helps maintain the legal profession's independence from government domination. An independent legal profession is an important force in preserving government under law, for abuse of legal authority is more readily challenged by a profession whose members are not dependent on government for the right to practice.

[12] The legal profession's relative autonomy carries with it special responsibilities of self-government. The profession has a responsibility to assure that its regulations are conceived in the public interest and not in furtherance of parochial or self-interested concerns of the bar. Every lawyer is responsible for observance of the Rules of Professional Conduct. A lawyer should also aid in securing their observance by other lawyers. Neglect of these responsibilities compromises the independence of the profession and the public interest which it serves.

[13] Lawyers play a vital role in the preservation of society. The fulfillment of this role requires an understanding by lawyers of their relationship to our legal system. The Rules of Professional Conduct, when properly applied, serve to define that relationship.

SCOPE

[14] The Rules of Professional Conduct are rules of reason. They should be interpreted with reference to the purposes of legal representation and of the law itself. Some of the Rules are imperatives, cast in the terms "shall" or "shall not." These define proper conduct for purposes of professional discipline. Others, generally cast in the term "may," are permissive and define areas under the Rules in which the lawyer has discretion to exercise professional judgment. No disciplinary action should be taken when the lawyer chooses not to act or acts within the bounds of such discretion. Other Rules define the nature of relationships between the lawyer and others. The Rules are thus partly obligatory and disciplinary and partly constitutive and descriptive in that they define a lawyer's professional role. Many of the Comments use the term "should." Comments and the Preamble and Scope do not add obligations to the Rules but provide guidance for practicing in compliance with the Rules.

[15] The Rules presuppose a larger legal context shaping the lawyer's role. That context includes court rules and statutes relating to matters of licensure, laws defining specific obligations of lawyers and substantive and procedural law in general. The Comments are sometimes used to alert lawyers to their responsibilities under such other law.

[16] Compliance with the Rules, as with all law in an open society, depends primarily upon understanding and voluntary compliance, secondarily upon reinforcement by peer and public opinion and finally, when necessary, upon enforcement through disciplinary proceedings. The Rules do not, however, exhaust the moral and ethical considerations that should inform a lawyer, for no worthwhile human activity can be completely defined by legal rules. The Rules simply provide a framework for the ethical practice of law.

[17] Furthermore, for purposes of determining the lawyer's authority and responsibility, principles of substantive law external to these Rules determine whether a client-lawyer relationship exists. Most of the duties flowing from the client-lawyer relationship attach only after the client has requested the lawyer to render legal services and the lawyer has agreed to do so. But there are some duties, such as that of confidentiality under Rule 1.6, that attach when the lawyer agrees to consider whether a client-lawyer relationship shall be established. See Rule 1.18. Whether a client-lawyer relationship exists for any specific purpose can depend on the circumstances and may be a question of fact.

[18] Under various legal provisions, including constitutional, statutory and common law, the responsi-

bilities of government lawyers may include authority concerning legal matters that ordinarily reposes in the client in private client-lawyer relationships. For example, a lawyer for a government agency may have authority on behalf of the government to decide upon settlement or whether to appeal from an adverse judgment. Such authority in various respects is generally vested in the attorney general and the state's attorney in state government, and their federal counterparts, and the same may be true of other government law officers. Also, lawyers under the supervision of these officers may be authorized to represent several government agencies in intragovernmental legal controversies in circumstances where a private lawyer could not represent multiple private clients. These Rules do not abrogate any such authority.

[19] Failure to comply with an obligation or prohibition imposed by a Rule is a basis for invoking the disciplinary process. The Rules presuppose that disciplinary assessment of a lawyer's conduct will be made on the basis of the facts and circumstances as they existed at the time of the conduct in question and in recognition of the fact that a lawyer often has to act upon uncertain or incomplete evidence of the situation. Moreover, the Rules presuppose that whether or not discipline should be imposed for a violation, and the severity of a sanction, depend on all the circumstances, such as the willfulness and seriousness of the violation, extenuating factors and whether there have been previous violations.

[20] Violation of a Rule should not itself give rise to a cause of action against a lawyer nor should it create any presumption in such a case that a legal duty has been breached. In addition, violation of a Rule does not necessarily warrant any other nondisciplinary remedy, such as disqualification of a lawyer in pending litigation. The Rules are designed to provide guidance to lawyers and to provide a structure for regulating conduct through disciplinary agencies. They are not designed to be a basis for civil liability. Furthermore, the purpose of the Rules can be subverted when they are invoked by opposing parties as procedural weapons. The fact that a Rule is a just basis for a lawyer's self-assessment, or for sanctioning a lawyer under the administration of a disciplinary authority, does not imply that an antagonist in a collateral proceeding or transaction has standing to seek enforcement of the Rule. Nevertheless, since the Rules do establish standards of conduct by lawyers, a lawyer's violation of a Rule may be evidence of breach of the applicable standard of conduct.

[21] The Comment accompanying each Rule explains and illustrates the meaning and purpose of the Rule. The Preamble and this note on Scope provide general orientation and are instructive and not directive. The Comments are intended as guides to interpretation, but the text of each Rule is authoritative.

Rule 1.0. Terminology

(a) "Belief" or "believes" denotes that the person involved actually supposed the fact in question to be true. A person's belief may be inferred from circumstances.

(b) "Confirmed in writing," when used in reference to the informed consent of a person, denotes informed consent that is given in writing by the person or a writing that a lawyer promptly transmits to the person confirming an oral informed consent. See paragraph (e) for the definition of "informed consent." If it is not feasible to obtain or transmit the writing at the time the person gives informed consent, then the lawyer must obtain or transmit it within a reasonable time thereafter.

(c) "Firm" or "law firm" denotes a lawyer or lawyers in a law partnership, professional corporation, sole proprietorship or other association authorized to practice law; or lawyers employed in a legal services organization or the legal department of a corporation or other organization.

(d) "Fraud" or "fraudulent" denotes conduct that is fraudulent under the substantive or procedural law of the applicable jurisdiction and has a purpose to deceive.

(e) "Informed consent" denotes the agreement by a person to a proposed course of conduct after the lawyer has communicated adequate information and explanation about the material risks of and reasonably available alternatives to the proposed course of conduct.

(f) "Knowingly," "known," or "knows" denotes actual knowledge of the fact in question. A person's knowledge may be inferred from circumstances.

(g) "Partner" denotes a member of a partnership, a shareholder in a law firm organized as a professional corporation, or a member of an association authorized to practice law.

(h) "Reasonable" or "reasonably" when used in relation to conduct by a lawyer denotes the conduct of a reasonably prudent and competent lawyer.

(i) "Reasonable belief" or "reasonably believes" when used in reference to a lawyer denotes that the lawyer believes the matter in question and that the circumstances are such that the belief is reasonable.

(j) "Reasonably should know" when used in reference to a lawyer denotes that a lawyer of reasonable prudence and competence would ascertain the matter in question.

(k) "Screened" denotes the isolation of a lawyer from any participation in a matter through the timely imposition of procedures within a firm that are reasonably adequate under the circumstances to protect information that the isolated lawyer is obligated to protect under these Rules or other law.

(*l*) "Substantial" when used in reference to degree or extent denotes a material matter of clear and weighty importance.

(**m**) "Tribunal" denotes a court, an arbitrator in a binding arbitration proceeding or a legislative body, administrative agency or other body acting in an adjudicative capacity. A legislative body, administrative agency or other body acts in an adjudicative capacity when a neutral official, after the presentation of evidence or legal argument by a party or parties, will render a binding legal judgment directly affecting a party's interests in a particular matter.

(**n**) "Writing" or "written" denotes a tangible or electronic record of a communication or representation, including handwriting, typewriting, printing, photostating, photography, audio or video recording and electronic communications. A "signed" writing includes an electronic sound, symbol or process attached to or logically associated with a writing and executed or adopted by a person with the intent to sign the writing.

Adopted July 1, 2009, eff. Jan. 1, 2010. Amended Oct. 15, 2015, eff. Jan. 1, 2016.

Comment

Confirmed in Writing

[1] If it is not feasible to obtain or transmit a written confirmation, if required, at the time the client gives informed consent, then the lawyer must obtain or transmit it within a reasonable time thereafter. If a lawyer has obtained a client's informed consent, and written confirmation is required, the lawyer may act in reliance on that consent so long as it is confirmed in writing within a reasonable time thereafter.

Firm

[2] Whether two or more lawyers constitute a firm within paragraph (c) can depend on the specific facts. For example, two practitioners who share office space and occasionally consult or assist each other ordinarily would not be regarded as constituting a firm. However, if they present themselves to the public in a way that suggests that they are a firm or conduct themselves as a firm, they should be regarded as a firm for purposes of the Rules. The terms of any formal agreement between associated lawyers are relevant in determining whether they are a firm, as is the fact that they have mutual access to information concerning the clients they serve. Furthermore, it is relevant in doubtful cases to consider the underlying purpose of the Rule that is involved. A group of lawyers could be regarded as a firm for purposes of the Rule that the same lawyer should not represent opposing parties in litigation, while it might not be so regarded for purposes of the Rule that information acquired by one lawyer is attributed to another.

[3] With respect to the law department of an organization, including the government, there is ordinarily no question that the members of the department constitute a firm within the meaning of the Rules of Professional Conduct. There can be uncertainty, however, as to the identity of the client. For example, it may not be clear whether the law department of a corporation represents a subsidiary or an affiliated corporation, as well as the corporation by which the members of the department are directly employed. A similar question can arise concerning an unincorporated association and its local affiliates.

[4] Similar questions can also arise with respect to lawyers in legal aid and legal services organizations. Depending upon the structure of the organization, the entire organization or different components of it may constitute a firm or firms for purposes of these Rules.

Fraud

[5] When used in these Rules, the terms "fraud" or "fraudulent" refer to conduct that is characterized as such under the substantive or procedural law of the applicable jurisdiction and has a purpose to deceive. This does not include merely negligent misrepresentation or negligent failure to apprise another of relevant information. For purposes of these Rules, it is not necessary that anyone has suffered damages or relied on the misrepresentation or failure to inform.

Informed Consent

[6] Many of the Rules of Professional Conduct require the lawyer to obtain the informed consent of a client or other person (*e.g.*, a former client or, under certain circumstances, a prospective client) before accepting or continuing representation or pursuing a course of conduct. See, *e.g.*, Rules 1.2(c), 1.6(a) and 1.7(b). The communication necessary to obtain such consent will vary according to the Rule involved and the circumstances giving rise to the need to obtain informed consent. The lawyer must make reasonable efforts to ensure that the client or other person possesses information reasonably adequate to make an informed decision. Ordinarily, this will require communication that includes a disclosure of the facts and circumstances giving rise to the situation, any explanation reasonably necessary to inform the client or other person of the material advantages and disadvantages of the proposed course of conduct and a discussion of the client's or other person's options and alternatives. In some circumstances it may be appropriate for a lawyer to advise a client or other person to seek the advice of other counsel. A lawyer need not inform a client or other person of facts or implications already known to the client or other person; nevertheless, a lawyer who does not personally inform the client or other person assumes the risk that the client or other person is inadequately informed and the consent is invalid. In determining whether the information and explanation provided are reasonably adequate, relevant factors include whether the client or other person is experienced in legal matters generally and in making decisions of the type involved, and whether the client or other person is independently represented by other counsel in giving the consent. Normally, such persons need less information and explanation than others, and generally a client or other person who is independently

represented by other counsel in giving the consent should be assumed to have given informed consent.

[7] Obtaining informed consent will usually require an affirmative response by the client or other person. In general, a lawyer may not assume consent from a client's or other person's silence. Consent may be inferred, however, from the conduct of a client or other person who has reasonably adequate information about the matter. Rule 1.5(e) requires that a person's consent be confirmed in writing. For a definition of "writing" and "confirmed in writing," see paragraphs (n) and (b). Other Rules require that a client's consent be obtained in a writing signed by the client. See Rules 1.5(c), 1.8(a) and (g). For a definition of "signed," see paragraph (n).

Screened

[8] This definition applies to situations where screening of a personally disqualified lawyer is permitted to remove imputation of a conflict of interest under Rules 1.10, 1.11, 1.12 or 1.18.

[9] The purpose of screening is to assure the affected parties that confidential information known by the personally disqualified lawyer remains protected. The personally disqualified lawyer should acknowledge the obligation not to communicate with any of the other lawyers in the firm with respect to the matter. Similarly, other lawyers in the firm who are working on the matter should be informed that the screening is in place and that they may not communicate with the personally disqualified lawyer with respect to the matter. Additional screening measures that are appropriate for the particular matter will depend on the circumstances. To implement, reinforce and remind all affected lawyers of the presence of the screening, it may be appropriate for the firm to undertake such procedures as a written undertaking by the screened lawyer to avoid any communication with other firm personnel and any contact with any firm files or other information, including information in electronic form, relating to the matter, written notice and instructions to all other firm personnel forbidding any communication with the screened lawyer relating to the matter, denial of access by the screened lawyer to firm files or other information, including information in electronic form, relating to the matter, and periodic reminders of the screen to the screened lawyer and all other firm personnel.

[10] In order to be effective, screening measures must be implemented as soon as practical after a lawyer or law firm knows or reasonably should know that there is a need for screening.

Comment adopted July 1, 2009, eff. Jan. 1, 2010. Amended Oct. 15, 2015, eff. Jan. 1, 2016.

Rule 1.1. Competence

A lawyer shall provide competent representation to a client. Competent representation requires the legal knowledge, skill, thoroughness and preparation reasonably necessary for the representation.

Adopted July 1, 2009, eff. Jan. 1, 2010.

Comment
Legal Knowledge and Skill

[1] In determining whether a lawyer employs the requisite knowledge and skill in a particular matter, relevant factors include the relative complexity and specialized nature of the matter, the lawyer's general experience, the lawyer's training and experience in the field in question, the preparation and study the lawyer is able to give the matter and whether it is feasible to refer the matter to, or associate or consult with, a lawyer of established competence in the field in question. In many instances, the required proficiency is that of a general practitioner. Expertise in a particular field of law may be required in some circumstances.

[2] A lawyer need not necessarily have special training or prior experience to handle legal problems of a type with which the lawyer is unfamiliar. A newly admitted lawyer can be as competent as a practitioner with long experience. Some important legal skills, such as the analysis of precedent, the evaluation of evidence and legal drafting, are required in all legal problems. Perhaps the most fundamental legal skill consists of determining what kind of legal problems a situation may involve, a skill that necessarily transcends any particular specialized knowledge. A lawyer can provide adequate representation in a wholly novel field through necessary study. Competent representation can also be provided through the association of a lawyer of established competence in the field in question.

[3] In an emergency a lawyer may give advice or assistance in a matter in which the lawyer does not have the skill ordinarily required where referral to or consultation or association with another lawyer would be impractical. Even in an emergency, however, assistance should be limited to that reasonably necessary in the circumstances, for ill-considered action under emergency conditions can jeopardize the client's interest.

[4] A lawyer may accept representation where the requisite level of competence can be achieved by reasonable preparation. This applies as well to a lawyer who is appointed as counsel for an unrepresented person. See also Rule 6.2.

Thoroughness and Preparation

[5] Competent handling of a particular matter includes inquiry into and analysis of the factual and legal elements of the problem, and use of methods and procedures meeting the standards of competent practitioners. It also includes adequate preparation. The required attention and preparation are determined in part by what is at stake; major litigation and complex transactions ordinarily require more extensive treatment than matters of lesser complexity and consequence. An agreement between the lawyer and the client regarding the scope of the representation may limit the matters for which the lawyer is responsible. See Rule 1.2(c).

Retaining Or Contracting With Other Lawyers

[6] Before a lawyer retains or contracts with other lawyers outside the lawyer's own firm to provide or assist in the provision of legal services to a client, the lawyer should ordinarily obtain in-

formed consent from the client and must reasonably believe that the other lawyers' services will contribute to the competent and ethical representation of the client. See also Rules 1.2(e) and Comment [15], 1.4, 1.5(e), 1.6, and 5.5(a). The reasonableness of the decision to retain or contract with other lawyers outside the lawyer's own firm will depend upon the circumstances, including the education, experience and reputation of the nonfirm lawyers; the nature of the services assigned to the nonfirm lawyers; and the legal protections, professional conduct rules, and ethical environments of the jurisdictions in which the services will be performed, particularly relating to confidential information.

[7] When lawyers from more than one law firm are providing legal services to the client on a particular matter, the lawyers ordinarily should consult with each other and the client about the scope of their respective representations and the allocation of responsibility among them. See Rule 1.2. When making allocations of responsibility in a matter pending before a tribunal, lawyers and parties may have additional obligations that are a matter of law beyond the scope of these Rules.

Maintaining Competence

[8] To maintain the requisite knowledge and skill, a lawyer should keep abreast of changes in the law and its practice, including the benefits and risks associated with relevant technology, engage in continuing study and education and comply with all continuing legal education requirements to which the lawyer is subject

Comment adopted July 1, 2009, eff. Jan. 1, 2010. Amended Oct. 15, 2015, eff. Jan. 1, 2016.

Rule 1.2. Scope of Representation and Allocation of Authority Between Client and Lawyer

(a) Subject to paragraphs (c) and (d), a lawyer shall abide by a client's decisions concerning the objectives of representation and, as required by Rule 1.4, shall consult with the client as to the means by which they are to be pursued. A lawyer may take such action on behalf of the client as is impliedly authorized to carry out the representation. A lawyer shall abide by a client's decision whether to settle a matter. In a criminal case, the lawyer shall abide by the client's decision, after consultation with the lawyer, as to a plea to be entered, whether to waive jury trial and whether the client will testify.

(b) A lawyer's representation of a client, including representation by appointment, does not constitute an endorsement of the client's political, economic, social or moral views or activities.

(c) A lawyer may limit the scope of the representation if the limitation is reasonable under the circumstances and the client gives informed consent.

(d) A lawyer shall not counsel a client to engage, or assist a client, in conduct that the lawyer knows is criminal or fraudulent, but a lawyer may

(1) discuss the legal consequences of any proposed course of conduct with a client,

(2) counsel or assist a client to make a good-faith effort to determine the validity, scope, meaning or application of the law, and

(3) counsel or assist a client in conduct expressly permitted by Illinois law that may violate or conflict with federal or other law, as long as the lawyer advises the client about that federal or other law and its potential consequences.

(e) After accepting employment on behalf of a client, a lawyer shall not thereafter delegate to another lawyer not in the lawyer's firm the responsibility for performing or completing that employment, without the client's informed consent.

Adopted July 1, 2009, eff. Jan. 1, 2010. Amended Oct. 15, 2015, eff. Jan. 1, 2016.

Comment

Allocation of Authority between Client and Lawyer

[1] Paragraph (a) confers upon the client the ultimate authority to determine the purposes to be served by legal representation, within the limits imposed by law and the lawyer's professional obligations. The decisions specified in paragraph (a), such as whether to settle a civil matter, must also be made by the client. See Rule 1.4(a)(1) for the lawyer's duty to communicate with the client about such decisions. With respect to the means by which the client's objectives are to be pursued, the lawyer shall consult with the client as required by Rule 1.4(a)(2) and may take such action as is impliedly authorized to carry out the representation.

[2] On occasion, however, a lawyer and a client may disagree about the means to be used to accomplish the client's objectives. Clients normally defer to the special knowledge and skill of their lawyer with respect to the means to be used to accomplish their objectives, particularly with respect to technical, legal and tactical matters. Conversely, lawyers usually defer to the client regarding such questions as the expense to be incurred and concern for third persons who might be adversely affected. Because of the varied nature of the matters about which a lawyer and client might disagree and because the actions in question may implicate the interests of a tribunal or other persons, this Rule does not prescribe how such disagreements are to be resolved. Other law, however, may be applicable and should be consulted by the lawyer. The lawyer should also consult with the client and seek a mutually acceptable resolution of the disagreement. If such efforts are unavailing and the lawyer has a fundamental disagreement with the client, the lawyer may withdraw from the representation. See Rule 1.16(b)(4). Conversely, the client may resolve the disagreement by discharging the lawyer. See Rule 1.16(a)(3).

[3] At the outset of a representation, the client may authorize the lawyer to take specific action on the client's behalf without further consultation. Absent a material change in circumstances and subject to Rule 1.4, a lawyer may rely on such an advance

714

authorization. The client may, however, revoke such authority at any time.

[4] In a case in which the client appears to be suffering diminished capacity, the lawyer's duty to abide by the client's decisions is to be guided by reference to Rule 1.14.

Independence from Client's Views or Activities

[5] Legal representation should not be denied to people who are unable to afford legal services, or whose cause is controversial or the subject of popular disapproval. By the same token, representing a client does not constitute approval of the client's views or activities.

Agreements Limiting Scope of Representation

[6] The scope of services to be provided by a lawyer may be limited by agreement with the client or by the terms under which the lawyer's services are made available to the client. When a lawyer has been retained by an insurer to represent an insured, for example, the representation may be limited to matters related to the insurance coverage. A limited representation may be appropriate because the client has limited objectives for the representation. In addition, the terms upon which representation is undertaken may exclude specific means that might otherwise be used to accomplish the client's objectives. Such limitations may exclude actions that the client thinks are too costly or that the lawyer regards as repugnant or imprudent.

[7] Although this Rule affords the lawyer and client substantial latitude to limit the representation, the limitation must be reasonable under the circumstances. If, for example, a client's objective is limited to securing general information about the law the client needs in order to handle a common and typically uncomplicated legal problem, the lawyer and client may agree that the lawyer's services will be limited to a brief telephone consultation. Such a limitation, however, would not be reasonable if the time allotted was not sufficient to yield advice upon which the client could rely. Although an agreement for a limited representation does not exempt a lawyer from the duty to provide competent representation, the limitation is a factor to be considered when determining the legal knowledge, skill, thoroughness and preparation reasonably necessary for the representation. See Rule 1.1.

[8] All agreements concerning a lawyer's representation of a client must accord with the Rules of Professional Conduct and other law. See, *e.g.*, Rules 1.1, 1.8 and 5.6, and Supreme Court Rules 13(c)(6) and 137(e).

Criminal, Fraudulent and Prohibited Transactions

[9] Paragraph (d) prohibits a lawyer from knowingly counseling or assisting a client to commit a crime or fraud. This prohibition, however, does not preclude the lawyer from giving an honest opinion about the actual consequences that appear likely to result from a client's conduct. Nor does the fact that a client uses advice in a course of action that is criminal or fraudulent of itself make a lawyer a party to the course of action. There is a critical distinction between presenting an analysis of legal aspects of questionable conduct and recommending

the means by which a crime or fraud might be committed with impunity.

[10] Paragraph (d)(3) was adopted to address the dilemma facing a lawyer in Illinois after the passage of the Illinois Compassionate Use of Medical Cannabis Pilot Program Act effective January 1, 2014. The Act expressly permits the cultivation, distribution, and use of marijuana for medical purposes under the conditions stated in the Act. Conduct permitted by the Act may be prohibited by the federal Controlled Substances Act, 21 U.S.C. §§ 801–904 and other law. The conflict between state and federal law makes it particularly important to allow a lawyer to provide legal advice and assistance to a client seeking to engage in conduct permitted by Illinois law. In providing such advice and assistance, a lawyer shall also advise the client about related federal law and policy. Paragraph (d)(3) is not restricted in its application to the marijuana law conflict. A lawyer should be especially careful about counseling or assisting a client in other contexts in conduct that may violate or conflict with federal, state, or local law.

[11] When the client's course of action has already begun and is continuing, the lawyer's responsibility is especially delicate. The lawyer is required to avoid assisting the client, for example, by drafting or delivering documents that the lawyer knows are fraudulent or by suggesting how the wrongdoing might be concealed. A lawyer may not continue assisting a client in conduct that the lawyer originally supposed was legally proper but then discovers is criminal or fraudulent. The lawyer must, therefore, withdraw from the representation of the client in the matter. See Rule 1.16(a). In some cases, withdrawal alone might be insufficient. It may be necessary for the lawyer to give notice of the fact of withdrawal and to disaffirm any opinion, document, affirmation or the like. See Rule 4.1. In such situations, the lawyer should also consider whether disclosure of information relating to the representation is appropriate. See Rule 1.6(b).

[12] Where the client is a fiduciary, the lawyer may be charged with special obligations in dealings with a beneficiary.

[13] Paragraph (d) applies whether or not the defrauded party is a party to the transaction. Hence, a lawyer must not participate in a transaction to effectuate criminal or fraudulent avoidance of tax liability. Paragraph (d) does not preclude undertaking a criminal defense incident to a general retainer for legal services to a lawful enterprise. The last clause of paragraph (d) recognizes that determining the validity or interpretation of a statute or regulation may require a course of action involving disobedience of the statute or regulation or of the interpretation placed upon it by governmental authorities.

[14] If a lawyer comes to know or reasonably should know that a client expects assistance not permitted by the Rules of Professional Conduct or other law or if the lawyer intends to act contrary to the client's instructions, the lawyer must consult with the client regarding the limitations on the lawyer's conduct. See Rule 1.4(a)(5).

[15] The prohibition stated in paragraph (e) has existed in Illinois ethics rules and in the prior Code since 1980. It is intended to curtail abuses that occasionally occur when a lawyer attempts to transfer complete or substantial responsibility for a matter to an unaffiliated lawyer without the client's awareness or consent. The Rule is designed to clarify the lawyer's obligation to complete the employment contemplated unless the client gives informed consent to substitution by an unaffiliated lawyer. The Rule is not intended to prohibit lawyers from hiring lawyers outside of their firm to perform certain services on the client's or the law firm's behalf. Nor is it intended to prevent lawyers from engaging lawyers outside of their firm to stand in for discrete events in situations such as personal emergencies, illness or schedule conflicts.

Comment adopted July 1, 2009, eff. Jan. 1, 2010. Amended June 14, 2013, eff. July 1, 2013; Oct. 15, 2015, eff. Jan. 1, 2016.

Rule 1.3. Diligence

A lawyer shall act with reasonable diligence and promptness in representing a client.
Adopted July 1, 2009, eff. Jan. 1, 2010.

Comment

[1] A lawyer should pursue a matter on behalf of a client despite opposition, obstruction or personal inconvenience to the lawyer, and take whatever lawful and ethical measures are required to vindicate a client's cause or endeavor. A lawyer must also act with commitment and dedication to the interests of the client and with zeal in advocacy upon the client's behalf. A lawyer is not bound, however, to press for every advantage that might be realized for a client. For example, a lawyer may have authority to exercise professional discretion in determining the means by which a matter should be pursued. See Rule 1.2. The lawyer's duty to act with reasonable diligence does not require the use of offensive tactics or preclude the treating of all persons involved in the legal process with courtesy and respect.

[2] A lawyer's work load must be controlled so that each matter can be handled competently.

[3] Perhaps no professional shortcoming is more widely resented than procrastination. A client's interests often can be adversely affected by the passage of time or the change of conditions; in extreme instances, as when a lawyer overlooks a statute of limitations, the client's legal position may be destroyed. Even when the client's interests are not affected in substance, however, unreasonable delay can cause a client needless anxiety and undermine confidence in the lawyer's trustworthiness. A lawyer's duty to act with reasonable promptness, however, does not preclude the lawyer from agreeing to a reasonable request for a postponement that will not prejudice the lawyer's client.

[4] Unless the relationship is terminated as provided in Rule 1.16, a lawyer should carry through to conclusion all matters undertaken for a client. If a lawyer's employment is limited to a specific matter, the relationship terminates when the matter has been resolved. If a lawyer has served a client over a substantial period in a variety of matters, the client sometimes may assume that the lawyer will continue to serve on a continuing basis unless the lawyer gives notice of withdrawal. Doubt about whether a client-lawyer relationship still exists should be clarified by the lawyer, preferably in writing, so that the client will not mistakenly suppose the lawyer is looking after the client's affairs when the lawyer has ceased to do so. For example, if a lawyer has handled a judicial or administrative proceeding that produced a result adverse to the client and the lawyer and the client have not agreed that the lawyer will handle the matter on appeal, the lawyer must consult with the client about the possibility of appeal before relinquishing responsibility for the matter. See Rule 1.4(a)(2). Whether the lawyer is obligated to prosecute the appeal for the client depends on the scope of the representation the lawyer has agreed to provide to the client. See Rule 1.2.

[5] To prevent neglect of client matters in the event of a sole practitioner's death or disability, the duty of diligence may require that each sole practitioner prepare a plan, in conformity with applicable rules, that designates another competent lawyer to review client files, notify each client of the lawyer's death or disability, and determine whether there is a need for immediate protective action. See Illinois Supreme Court Rule 776, Appointment of Receiver in Certain Cases.

Rule 1.4. Communication

(a) A lawyer shall:

(1) promptly inform the client of any decision or circumstance with respect to which the client's informed consent, as defined in Rule 1.0(e), is required by these Rules;

(2) reasonably consult with the client about the means by which the client's objectives are to be accomplished;

(3) keep the client reasonably informed about the status of the matter;

(4) promptly comply with reasonable requests for information; and

(5) consult with the client about any relevant limitation on the lawyer's conduct when the lawyer knows that the client expects assistance not permitted by the Rules of Professional Conduct or other law.

(b) A lawyer shall explain a matter to the extent reasonably necessary to permit the client to make informed decisions regarding the representation.
Adopted July 1, 2009, eff. Jan. 1, 2010.

Comment

[1] Reasonable communication between the lawyer and the client is necessary for the client effectively to participate in the representation.

Communicating with Client

[2] If these Rules require that a particular decision about the representation be made by the client, paragraph (a)(1) requires that the lawyer promptly consult with and secure the client's consent prior to taking action unless prior discussions with the client have resolved what action the client wants the lawyer to take. For example, a lawyer who receives from opposing counsel an offer of settlement in a civil controversy or a proffered plea bargain in a criminal case must promptly inform the client of its substance unless the client has previously indicated that the proposal will be acceptable or unacceptable or has authorized the lawyer to accept or to reject the offer. See Rule 1.2(a).

[3] Paragraph (a)(2) requires the lawyer to reasonably consult with the client about the means to be used to accomplish the client's objectives. In some situations-depending on both the importance of the action under consideration and the feasibility of consulting with the client-this duty will require consultation prior to taking action. In other circumstances, such as during a trial when an immediate decision must be made, the exigency of the situation may require the lawyer to act without prior consultation. In such cases the lawyer must nonetheless act reasonably to inform the client of actions the lawyer has taken on the client's behalf. Additionally, paragraph (a)(3) requires that the lawyer keep the client reasonably informed about the status of the matter, such as significant developments affecting the timing or the substance of the representation.

[4] A lawyer's regular communication with clients will minimize the occasions on which a client will need to request information concerning the representation. When a client makes a reasonable request for information, however, paragraph (a)(4) requires prompt compliance with the request, or if a prompt response is not feasible, that the lawyer, or a member of the lawyer's staff, acknowledge receipt of the request and advise the client when a response may be expected. A lawyer should promptly respond to or acknowledge client communications.

Explaining Matters

[5] The client should have sufficient information to participate intelligently in decisions concerning the objectives of the representation and the means by which they are to be pursued, to the extent the client is willing and able to do so. Adequacy of communication depends in part on the kind of advice or assistance that is involved. For example, when there is time to explain a proposal made in a negotiation, the lawyer should review all important provisions with the client before proceeding to an agreement. In litigation a lawyer should explain the general strategy and prospects of success and ordinarily should consult the client on tactics that are likely to result in significant expense or to injure or coerce others. On the other hand, a lawyer ordinarily will not be expected to describe trial or negotiation strategy in detail. The guiding principle is that the lawyer should fulfill reasonable client expectations for information consistent with the duty to act in the client's best interests, and the client's overall requirements as to the character of representation. In certain circumstances, such as

when a lawyer asks a client to consent to a representation affected by a conflict of interest, the client must give informed consent, as defined in Rule 1.0(e).

[6] Ordinarily, the information to be provided is that appropriate for a client who is a comprehending and responsible adult. However, fully informing the client according to this standard may be impracticable, for example, where the client is a child or suffers from diminished capacity. See Rule 1.14. When the client is an organization or group, it is often impossible or inappropriate to inform every one of its members about its legal affairs; ordinarily, the lawyer should address communications to the appropriate officials of the organization. See Rule 1.13. Where many routine matters are involved, a system of limited or occasional reporting may be arranged with the client.

Withholding Information

[7] In some circumstances, a lawyer may be justified in delaying transmission of information when the client would be likely to react imprudently to an immediate communication. Thus, a lawyer might withhold a psychiatric diagnosis of a client when the examining psychiatrist indicates that disclosure would harm the client. A lawyer may not withhold information to serve the lawyer's own interest or convenience or the interests or convenience of another person. Rules or court orders governing litigation may provide that information supplied to a lawyer may not be disclosed to the client. Rule 3.4(c) directs compliance with such rules or orders.

Comment adopted July 1, 2009, eff. Jan. 1, 2010. Amended Oct. 15, 2015, eff. Jan. 1, 2016.

Rule 1.5. Fees

(a) A lawyer shall not make an agreement for, charge, or collect an unreasonable fee or an unreasonable amount for expenses. The factors to be considered in determining the reasonableness of a fee include the following:

(1) the time and labor required, the novelty and difficulty of the questions involved, and the skill requisite to perform the legal service properly;

(2) the likelihood, if apparent to the client, that the acceptance of the particular employment will preclude other employment by the lawyer;

(3) the fee customarily charged in the locality for similar legal services;

(4) the amount involved and the results obtained;

(5) the time limitations imposed by the client or by the circumstances;

(6) the nature and length of the professional relationship with the client;

(7) the experience, reputation, and ability of the lawyer or lawyers performing the services; and

(8) whether the fee is fixed or contingent.

(b) The scope of the representation and the basis or rate of the fee and expenses for which the client will be responsible shall be communicated to the

717

client, preferably in writing, before or within a reasonable time after commencing the representation, except when the lawyer will charge a regularly represented client on the same basis or rate. Any changes in the basis or rate of the fee or expenses shall also be communicated to the client.

(c) A fee may be contingent on the outcome of the matter for which the service is rendered, except in a matter in which a contingent fee is prohibited by paragraph (d) or other law. A contingent fee agreement shall be in a writing signed by the client and shall state the method by which the fee is to be determined, including the percentage or percentages that shall accrue to the lawyer in the event of settlement, trial or appeal; litigation and other expenses to be deducted from the recovery; and whether such expenses are to be deducted before or after the contingent fee is calculated. The agreement must clearly notify the client of any expenses for which the client will be liable whether or not the client is the prevailing party. Upon conclusion of a contingent fee matter, the lawyer shall provide the client with a written statement stating the outcome of the matter and, if there is a recovery, showing the remittance to the client and the method of its determination.

(d) A lawyer shall not enter into an arrangement for, charge, or collect:

(1) any fee in a domestic relations matter, the payment or amount of which is contingent upon the securing of a divorce or upon the amount of alimony or support, or property settlement in lieu thereof; or

(2) a contingent fee for representing a defendant in a criminal case.

(e) A division of a fee between lawyers who are not in the same firm may be made only if:

(1) the division is in proportion to the services performed by each lawyer, or if the primary service performed by one lawyer is the referral of the client to another lawyer and each lawyer assumes joint financial responsibility for the representation;

(2) the client agrees to the arrangement, including the share each lawyer will receive, and the agreement is confirmed in writing; and

(3) the total fee is reasonable.

Adopted July 1, 2009, eff. Jan. 1, 2010.

Comment

Reasonableness of Fee and Expenses

[1] Paragraph (a) requires that lawyers charge fees that are reasonable under the circumstances. The factors specified in (1) through (8) are not exclusive. Nor will each factor be relevant in each instance. Paragraph (a) also requires that expenses for which the client will be charged must be reasonable. A lawyer may seek reimbursement for the cost of services performed in-house, such as copying, or for other expenses incurred in-house, such as telephone charges, either by charging a reasonable

amount to which the client has agreed in advance or by charging an amount that reasonably reflects the cost incurred by the lawyer.

Basis or Rate of Fee

[2] When the lawyer has regularly represented a client, they ordinarily will have evolved an understanding concerning the basis or rate of the fee and the expenses for which the client will be responsible. In a new client-lawyer relationship, however, an understanding as to fees and expenses must be promptly established. Generally, it is desirable to furnish the client with at least a simple memorandum or copy of the lawyer's customary fee arrangements that states the general nature of the legal services to be provided, the basis, rate or total amount of the fee and whether and to what extent the client will be responsible for any costs, expenses or disbursements in the course of the representation. A written statement concerning the terms of the engagement reduces the possibility of misunderstanding.

[3] Contingent fees, like any other fees, are subject to the reasonableness standard of paragraph (a) of this Rule. In determining whether a particular contingent fee is reasonable, or whether it is reasonable to charge any form of contingent fee, a lawyer must consider the factors that are relevant under the circumstances. Applicable law may impose limitations on contingent fees, such as a ceiling on the percentage allowable, or may require a lawyer to offer clients an alternative basis for the fee. Applicable law also may apply to situations other than a contingent fee, for example, government regulations regarding fees in certain tax matters.

Terms of Payment

[4] A lawyer may require advance payment of a fee, but is obliged to return any unearned portion. See Comments [3B] through [3D] to Rule 1.15 and Rule 1.16(d). A lawyer may accept property in payment for services, such as an ownership interest in an enterprise, providing this does not involve acquisition of a proprietary interest in the cause of action or subject matter of the litigation contrary to Rule 1.8 (i). However, a fee paid in property instead of money may be subject to the requirements of Rule 1.8(a) because such fees often have the essential qualities of a business transaction with the client.

[5] An agreement may not be made whose terms might induce the lawyer improperly to curtail services for the client or perform them in a way contrary to the client's interest. For example, a lawyer should not enter into an agreement whereby services are to be provided only up to a stated amount when it is foreseeable that more extensive services probably will be required, unless the situation is adequately explained to the client. Otherwise, the client might have to bargain for further assistance in the midst of a proceeding or transaction. However, it is proper to define the extent of services in light of the client's ability to pay. A lawyer should not exploit a fee arrangement based primarily on hourly charges by using wasteful procedures.

Prohibited Contingent Fees

[6] Paragraph (d) prohibits a lawyer from charging a contingent fee in a domestic relations matter when payment is contingent upon the securing of a divorce or upon the amount of alimony or support or property settlement to be obtained. This provision does not preclude a contract for a contingent fee for legal representation in connection with the recovery of postjudgment balances due under support, alimony or other financial orders because such contracts do not implicate the same policy concerns.

Division of Fee

[7] A division of fee is a single billing to a client covering the fee of two or more lawyers who are not in the same firm. A division of fee facilitates association of more than one lawyer in a matter in which neither alone could serve the client as well, or referral of a matter where appropriate, and often is used when the fee is contingent and the division is between a referring lawyer and a trial specialist. Paragraph (e) permits the lawyers to divide a fee either on the basis of the proportion of services they render or, where the primary service performed by one lawyer is the referral of the client to another lawyer, if each lawyer assumes financial responsibility for the representation as a whole. In addition, the client must agree to the arrangement, including the share that each lawyer is to receive, and the agreement must be confirmed in writing. Contingent fee agreements must be in a writing signed by the client and must otherwise comply with paragraph (c) of this Rule. Joint financial responsibility for the representation entails financial responsibility for the representation as if the lawyers were associated in a general partnership. See *In re Storment*, 203 Ill. 2d 378 (2002). A lawyer should only refer a matter to a lawyer whom the referring lawyer reasonably believes is competent to handle the matter. See Rule 1.1.

[8] Paragraph (e) does not prohibit or regulate division of fees to be received in the future for work done when lawyers were previously associated in a law firm, or payments made pursuant to a separation or retirement agreement.

Disputes over Fees

[9] If a procedure has been established for resolution of fee disputes, such as an arbitration or mediation procedure established by law or rule, the lawyer must comply with the procedure when it is mandatory, and, even when it is voluntary, the lawyer should conscientiously consider submitting to it. Law may prescribe a procedure for determining a lawyer's fee, for example, in representation of an executor or administrator, a class or a person entitled to a reasonable fee as part of the measure of damages. The lawyer entitled to such a fee and a lawyer representing another party concerned with the fee should comply with the prescribed procedure.

Rule 1.6.   Confidentiality of Information

(a) A lawyer shall not reveal information relating to the representation of a client unless the client gives informed consent, the disclosure is impliedly authorized in order to carry out the representation, or the

disclosure is permitted by paragraph (b) or required by paragraph (c).

(b) A lawyer may reveal information relating to the representation of a client to the extent the lawyer reasonably believes necessary:

(1) to prevent the client from committing a crime in circumstances other than those specified in paragraph (c);

(2) to prevent the client from committing fraud that is reasonably certain to result in substantial injury to the financial interests or property of another and in furtherance of which the client has used or is using the lawyer's services;

(3) to prevent, mitigate or rectify substantial injury to the financial interests or property of another that is reasonably certain to result or has resulted from the client's commission of a crime or fraud in furtherance of which the client has used the lawyer's services;

(4) to secure legal advice about the lawyer's compliance with these Rules;

(5) to establish a claim or defense on behalf of the lawyer in a controversy between the lawyer and the client, to establish a defense to a criminal charge or civil claim against the lawyer based upon conduct in which the client was involved, or to respond to allegations in any proceeding concerning the lawyer's representation of the client;

(6) to comply with other law or a court order; or

(7) to detect and resolve conflicts of interest if the revealed information would not prejudice the client.

(c) A lawyer shall reveal information relating to the representation of a client to the extent the lawyer reasonably believes necessary to prevent reasonably certain death or substantial bodily harm.

(d) Information received by a lawyer participating in a meeting or proceeding with a trained intervener or panel of trained interveners of an approved lawyers' assistance program, or in an intermediary program approved by a circuit court in which nondisciplinary complaints against judges or lawyers can be referred, shall be considered information relating to the representation of a client for purposes of these Rules.

(e) A lawyer shall make reasonable efforts to prevent the inadvertent or unauthorized disclosure of, or unauthorized access to, information relating to the representation of a client.

Adopted July 1, 2009, eff. Jan. 1, 2010. Amended Oct. 15, 2015, eff. Jan. 1, 2016.

Comment

[1] This Rule governs the disclosure by a lawyer of information relating to the representation of a client during the lawyer's representation of the client. See Rule 1.18 for the lawyer's duties with

respect to information provided to the lawyer by a prospective client, Rule 1.9(c)(2) for the lawyer's duty not to reveal information relating to the lawyer's prior representation of a former client and Rules 1.8(b) and 1.9(c)(1) for the lawyer's duties with respect to the use of such information to the disadvantage of clients and former clients.

[2] A fundamental principle in the client-lawyer relationship is that, in the absence of the client's informed consent, the lawyer must not reveal information relating to the representation. See Rule 1.0(e) for the definition of informed consent. This contributes to the trust that is the hallmark of the client-lawyer relationship. The client is thereby encouraged to seek legal assistance and to communicate fully and frankly with the lawyer even as to embarrassing or legally damaging subject matter. The lawyer needs this information to represent the client effectively and, if necessary, to advise the client to refrain from wrongful conduct. Almost without exception, clients come to lawyers in order to determine their rights and what is, in the complex of laws and regulations, deemed to be legal and correct. Based upon experience, lawyers know that almost all clients follow the advice given, and the law is upheld.

[3] The principle of client-lawyer confidentiality is given effect by related bodies of law: the attorney-client privilege, the work product doctrine and the rule of confidentiality established in professional ethics. The attorney-client privilege and work product doctrine apply in judicial and other proceedings in which a lawyer may be called as a witness or otherwise required to produce evidence concerning a client. The rule of client-lawyer confidentiality applies in situations other than those where evidence is sought from the lawyer through compulsion of law. The confidentiality rule, for example, applies not only to matters communicated in confidence by the client but also to all information relating to the representation, whatever its source. A lawyer may not disclose such information except as authorized or required by the Rules of Professional Conduct or other law. See also Scope.

[4] Paragraph (a) prohibits a lawyer from revealing information relating to the representation of a client. This prohibition also applies to disclosures by a lawyer that do not in themselves reveal protected information but could reasonably lead to the discovery of such information by a third person. A lawyer's use of a hypothetical to discuss issues relating to the representation is permissible so long as there is no reasonable likelihood that the listener will be able to ascertain the identity of the client or the situation involved.

Authorized Disclosure

[5] Except to the extent that the client's instructions or special circumstances limit that authority, a lawyer is impliedly authorized to make disclosures about a client when appropriate in carrying out the representation. In some situations, for example, a lawyer may be impliedly authorized to admit a fact that cannot properly be disputed or to make a disclosure that facilitates a satisfactory conclusion to a matter. Lawyers in a firm may, in the course of the firm's practice, disclose to each other information relating to a client of the firm, unless the client has instructed that particular information be confined to specified lawyers.

Disclosure Adverse to Client

[6] Although the public interest is usually best served by a strict rule requiring lawyers to preserve the confidentiality of information relating to the representation of their clients, the confidentiality rule is subject to limited exceptions. Paragraph (c) recognizes the overriding value of life and physical integrity and requires disclosure reasonably necessary to prevent reasonably certain death or substantial bodily harm. Such harm is reasonably certain to occur if it will be suffered imminently or if there is a present and substantial threat that a person will suffer such harm at a later date if the lawyer fails to take action necessary to eliminate the threat. Thus, a lawyer who knows from information relating to a representation that a client or other person has accidentally discharged toxic waste into a town's water must reveal this information to the authorities if there is a present and substantial risk that a person who drinks the water will contract a life-threatening or debilitating disease and the lawyer's disclosure is necessary to eliminate the threat or reduce the number of victims.

[6A] Paragraph (b)(1) preserves the policy of the 1980 Illinois Code of Professional Responsibility and the 1990 Illinois Rules of Professional Conduct that permitted a lawyer to reveal the intention of a client to commit a crime. This general provision would permit disclosure where the client's intended conduct is a crime, including a financial crime, and the situation is not covered by paragraph (c).

[7] Paragraph (b)(2) is a limited exception to the rule of confidentiality that permits the lawyer to reveal information to the extent necessary to enable affected persons or appropriate authorities to prevent the client from committing fraud, as defined in Rule 1.0(d), that is reasonably certain to result in substantial injury to the financial or property interests of another and in furtherance of which the client has used or is using the lawyer's services. Such a serious abuse of the client-lawyer relationship by the client forfeits the protection of this Rule. The client can, of course, prevent such disclosure by refraining from the wrongful conduct. Like paragraph (b)(1), paragraph (b)(2) does not require the lawyer to reveal the client's misconduct, but the lawyer may not counsel or assist the client in conduct the lawyer knows is criminal or fraudulent. See Rule 1.2(d). See also Rule 1.16 with respect to the lawyer's obligation or right to withdraw from the representation of the client in such circumstances, and Rule 1.13(c), which permits the lawyer, where the client is an organization, to reveal information relating to the representation in limited circumstances.

[8] Paragraph (b)(3) addresses the situation in which the lawyer does not learn of the client's crime or fraud until after it has been consummated. Although the client no longer has the option of preventing disclosure by refraining from the wrongful conduct, there will be situations in which the loss suffered by the affected person can be prevented, rectified or mitigated. In such situations, the law-

yer may disclose information relating to the representation to the extent necessary to enable the affected persons to prevent or mitigate reasonably certain losses or to attempt to recoup their losses. Paragraph (b)(3) does not apply when a person who has committed a crime or fraud thereafter employs a lawyer for representation concerning that offense.

[9] A lawyer's confidentiality obligations do not preclude a lawyer from securing confidential legal advice about the lawyer's personal responsibility to comply with these Rules. In most situations, disclosing information to secure such advice will be impliedly authorized for the lawyer to carry out the representation. Even when the disclosure is not impliedly authorized, paragraph (b)(4) permits such disclosure because of the importance of a lawyer's compliance with the Rules of Professional Conduct.

[10] Where a legal claim or disciplinary charge alleges complicity of the lawyer in a client's conduct or other misconduct of the lawyer involving representation of the client, the lawyer may respond to the extent the lawyer reasonably believes necessary to establish a defense. The same is true with respect to a claim involving the conduct or representation of a former client. Such a charge can arise in a civil, criminal, disciplinary or other proceeding and can be based on a wrong allegedly committed by the lawyer against the client or on a wrong alleged by a third person, for example, a person claiming to have been defrauded by the lawyer and client acting together. The lawyer's right to respond arises when an assertion of such complicity has been made. Paragraph (b)(5) does not require the lawyer to await the commencement of an action or proceeding that charges such complicity, so that the defense may be established by responding directly to a third party who has made such an assertion. The right to defend also applies, of course, where a proceeding has been commenced.

[11] A lawyer entitled to a fee is permitted by paragraph (b)(5) to prove the services rendered in an action to collect it. This aspect of the Rule expresses the principle that the beneficiary of a fiduciary relationship may not exploit it to the detriment of the fiduciary.

[12] Other law may require that a lawyer disclose information about a client. Whether such a law supersedes Rule 1.6 is a question of law beyond the scope of these Rules. When disclosure of information relating to the representation appears to be required by other law, the lawyer must discuss the matter with the client to the extent required by Rule 1.4. If, however, the other law supersedes this Rule and requires disclosure, paragraph (b)(6) permits the lawyer to make such disclosures as are necessary to comply with the law.

Detection of Conflicts of Interest

[13] Paragraph (b)(7) recognizes that lawyers in different firms may need to disclose limited information to each other to detect and resolve conflicts of interest, such as when a lawyer is considering an association with another firm, two or more firms are considering a merger, or a lawyer is considering the purchase of a law practice. See Rule 1.17, Comment [7]. Under these circumstances, lawyers

and law firms are permitted to disclose limited information, but only once substantive discussions regarding the new relationship have occurred. Even limited information should be disclosed only to the extent reasonably necessary. Moreover, the disclosure of any information is prohibited if it would prejudice the client (e.g., disclosure would compromise the attorney-client privilege; the fact that a corporate client is seeking advice on a corporate takeover that has not been publicly announced; that a person has consulted a lawyer about the possibility of divorce before the person's intentions are known to the person's spouse; or that a person has consulted a lawyer about a criminal investigation that has not led to a public charge). Under those circumstances, paragraph (a) prohibits disclosure unless the client or former client gives informed consent. A lawyer's fiduciary duty to the lawyer's firm may also govern a lawyer's conduct when exploring an association with another firm and is beyond the scope of these Rules.

[14] Paragraph (b)(7) does not restrict the use of information acquired by means independent of any disclosure pursuant to paragraph (b)(7). Paragraph (b)(7) also does not affect the disclosure of information within a law firm when the disclosure is otherwise authorized, see Comment [5], such as when a lawyer in a firm discloses information to another lawyer in the same firm to detect and resolve conflicts of interest that could arise in connection with undertaking a new representation.

[15] A lawyer may be ordered to reveal information relating to the representation of a client by a court or by another tribunal or governmental entity claiming authority pursuant to other law to compel the disclosure. Absent informed consent of the client to do otherwise, the lawyer should assert on behalf of the client all nonfrivolous claims that the order is not authorized by other law or that the information sought is protected against disclosure by the attorney-client privilege or other applicable law. In the event of an adverse ruling, the lawyer must consult with the client about the possibility of appeal to the extent required by Rule 1.4. Unless review is sought, however, paragraph (b)(6) permits the lawyer to comply with the court's order.

[16] Paragraph (b) permits disclosure only to the extent the lawyer reasonably believes the disclosure is necessary to accomplish one of the purposes specified. Where practicable, the lawyer should first seek to persuade the client to take suitable action to obviate the need for disclosure. In any case, a disclosure adverse to the client's interest should be no greater than the lawyer reasonably believes necessary to accomplish the purpose. If the disclosure will be made in connection with a judicial proceeding, the disclosure should be made in a manner that limits access to the information to the tribunal or other persons having a need to know it and appropriate protective orders or other arrangements should be sought by the lawyer to the fullest extent practicable.

[17] Paragraph (b) permits but does not require the disclosure of information relating to a client's representation to accomplish the purposes specified in paragraphs (b)(1) through (b)(7). In exercising

the discretion conferred by this Rule, the lawyer may consider such factors as the nature of the lawyer's relationship with the client and with those who might be injured by the client, the lawyer's own involvement in the transaction and factors that may extenuate the conduct in question. A lawyer's decision not to disclose as permitted by paragraph (b) does not violate this Rule. Disclosure may be required, however, by other Rules. Some Rules require disclosure only if such disclosure would be permitted by paragraph (b). See Rules 1.2(d), 4.1(b), and 8.1. Rules 3.3 and 8.3, on the other hand, requires disclosure in some circumstances regardless of whether such disclosure is permitted by this Rule. See Rule 3.3(c).

Withdrawal

[17A] If the lawyer's services will be used by a client in materially furthering a course of criminal or fraudulent conduct, the lawyer must withdraw, as stated in Rule 1.16(a)(1). The lawyer may give notice of the fact of withdrawal regardless of whether the lawyer decides to disclose information relating to a client's representation as permitted by paragraph (b). The lawyer may also withdraw or disaffirm any opinion or other document that had been prepared for the client or others. Where the client is an organization, the lawyer must also consider the provisions of Rule 1.13.

Acting Competently to Preserve Confidentiality

[18] Paragraph (e) requires a lawyer to act competently to safeguard information relating to the representation of a client against unauthorized access by third parties and against inadvertent or unauthorized disclosure by the lawyer or other persons who are participating in the representation of the client or who are subject to the lawyer's supervision. See Rules 1.1, 5.1 and 5.3. The unauthorized access to, or the inadvertent or unauthorized disclosure of, information relating to the representation of a client does not constitute a violation of paragraph (e) if the lawyer has made reasonable efforts to prevent the access or disclosure. Factors to be considered in determining the reasonableness of the lawyer's efforts include, but are not limited to, the sensitivity of the information, the likelihood of disclosure if additional safeguards are not employed, the cost of employing additional safeguards, the difficulty of implementing the safeguards, and the extent to which the safeguards adversely affect the lawyer's ability to represent clients (e.g., by making a device or important piece of software excessively difficult to use). A client may require the lawyer to implement special security measures not required by this Rule or may give informed consent to forgo security measures that would otherwise be required by this Rule. Whether a lawyer may be required to take additional steps to safeguard a client's information in order to comply with other law, such as state and federal laws that govern data privacy or that impose notification requirements upon the loss of, or unauthorized access to, electronic information, is beyond the scope of these Rules. For a lawyer's duties when sharing information with nonlawyers outside the lawyer's own firm, see Rule 5.3, Comments [3]–[4].

[19] When transmitting a communication that includes information relating to the representation of a client, the lawyer must take reasonable precautions to prevent the information from coming into the hands of unintended recipients. This duty, however, does not require that the lawyer use special security measures if the method of communication affords a reasonable expectation of privacy. Special circumstances, however, may warrant special precautions. Factors to be considered in determining the reasonableness of the lawyer's expectation of confidentiality include the sensitivity of the information and the extent to which the privacy of the communication is protected by law or by a confidentiality agreement. A client may require the lawyer to implement special security measures not required by this Rule or may give informed consent to the use of a means of communication that would otherwise be prohibited by this Rule. Whether a lawyer may be required to take additional steps in order to comply with other law, such as state and federal laws that govern data privacy, is beyond the scope of these Rules.

Former Client

[20] The duty of confidentiality continues after the client-lawyer relationship has terminated. See Rule 1.9(c)(2). See Rule 1.9(c)(1) for the prohibition against using such information to the disadvantage of the former client.

Lawyers' Assistance and Court Intermediary Programs

[21] Information about the fitness or conduct of a law student, lawyer or judge may be received by a lawyer while participating in an approved lawyers' assistance program. Protecting the confidentiality of such information encourages law students, lawyers and judges to seek assistance through such programs. Without such protection, law students, lawyers and judges may hesitate to seek assistance, to the detriment of clients and the public. Similarly, lawyers participating in an approved intermediary program established by a circuit court to resolve nondisciplinary issues among lawyers and judges may receive information about the fitness or conduct of a lawyer or judge. Paragraph (d) therefore provides that any information received by a lawyer participating in an approved lawyers' assistance program or an approved circuit court intermediary program will be protected as confidential client information for purposes of the Rules. See also Comment [5] to Rule 8.3.

Comment adopted July 1, 2009, eff. Jan. 1, 2010. Amended Oct. 15, 2015, eff. Jan. 1, 2016.

Rule 1.7. Conflict of Interest: Current Clients

(a) Except as provided in paragraph (b), a lawyer shall not represent a client if the representation involves a concurrent conflict of interest. A concurrent conflict of interest exists if:

(1) the representation of one client will be directly adverse to another client; or

(2) there is a significant risk that the representation of one or more clients will be materially limited by the lawyer's responsibilities to another client, a former

client or a third person or by a personal interest of the lawyer.

(b) Notwithstanding the existence of a concurrent conflict of interest under paragraph (a), a lawyer may represent a client if:

(1) the lawyer reasonably believes that the lawyer will be able to provide competent and diligent representation to each affected client;

(2) the representation is not prohibited by law;

(3) the representation does not involve the assertion of a claim by one client against another client represented by the lawyer in the same litigation or other proceeding before a tribunal; and

(4) each affected client gives informed consent.

Adopted July 1, 2009, eff. Jan. 1, 2010.

Comment

General Principles

[1] Loyalty and independent judgment are essential elements in the lawyer's relationship to a client. Concurrent conflicts of interest can arise from the lawyer's responsibilities to another client, a former client or a third person or from the lawyer's own interests. For specific Rules regarding certain concurrent conflicts of interest, see Rule 1.8. For former client conflicts of interest, see Rule 1.9. For conflicts of interest involving prospective clients, see Rule 1.18. For a definition of "informed consent" see Rule 1.0(e).

[2] Resolution of a conflict of interest problem under this Rule requires the lawyer to: (1) clearly identify the client or clients; (2) determine whether a conflict of interest exists; (3) decide whether the representation may be undertaken despite the existence of a conflict, i.e., whether the conflict is consentable; and (4) if so, consult with the clients affected under paragraph (a) and obtain their informed consent. The clients affected under paragraph (a) include both of the clients referred to in paragraph (a)(1) and the one or more clients whose representation might be materially limited under paragraph (a)(2).

[3] A conflict of interest may exist before representation is undertaken, in which event the representation must be declined, unless the lawyer obtains the informed consent of each client under the conditions of paragraph (b). To determine whether a conflict of interest exists, a lawyer should adopt reasonable procedures, appropriate for the size and type of firm and practice, to determine in both litigation and nonlitigation matters the persons and issues involved. See also Comment to Rule 5.1. Ignorance caused by a failure to institute such procedures will not excuse a lawyer's violation of this Rule. As to whether a client-lawyer relationship exists or, having once been established, is continuing, see Comment to Rule 1.3 and Scope.

[4] If a conflict arises after representation has been undertaken, the lawyer ordinarily must withdraw from the representation, unless the lawyer has obtained the informed consent of the client under the conditions of paragraph (b). See Rule 1.16.

Where more than one client is involved, whether the lawyer may continue to represent any of the clients is determined both by the lawyer's ability to comply with duties owed to the former client and by the lawyer's ability to represent adequately the remaining client or clients, given the lawyer's duties to the former client. See Rule 1.9. See also Comments [5] and [29].

[5] Unforeseeable developments, such as changes in corporate and other organizational affiliations or the addition or realignment of parties in litigation, might create conflicts in the midst of a representation, as when a company sued by the lawyer on behalf of one client is bought by another client represented by the lawyer in an unrelated matter. Depending on the circumstances, the lawyer may have the option to withdraw from one of the representations in order to avoid the conflict. The lawyer must seek court approval where necessary and take steps to minimize harm to the clients. See Rule 1.16. The lawyer must continue to protect the confidences of the client from whose representation the lawyer has withdrawn. See Rule 1.9(c).

Identifying Conflicts of Interest: Directly Adverse

[6] Loyalty to a current client prohibits undertaking representation directly adverse to that client without that client's informed consent. Thus, absent consent, a lawyer may not act as an advocate in one matter against a person the lawyer represents in some other matter, even when the matters are wholly unrelated. The client as to whom the representation is directly adverse is likely to feel betrayed, and the resulting damage to the client-lawyer relationship is likely to impair the lawyer's ability to represent the client effectively. In addition, the client on whose behalf the adverse representation is undertaken reasonably may fear that the lawyer will pursue that client's case less effectively out of deference to the other client, i.e., that the representation may be materially limited by the lawyer's interest in retaining the current client. Similarly, a directly adverse conflict may arise when a lawyer is required to cross-examine a client who appears as a witness in a lawsuit involving another client, as when the testimony will be damaging to the client who is represented in the lawsuit. On the other hand, simultaneous representation in unrelated matters of clients whose interests are only economically adverse, such as representation of competing economic enterprises in unrelated litigation, does not ordinarily constitute a conflict of interest and thus may not require consent of the respective clients.

[7] Directly adverse conflicts can also arise in transactional matters. For example, if a lawyer is asked to represent the seller of a business in negotiations with a buyer represented by the lawyer, not in the same transaction but in another, unrelated matter, the lawyer could not undertake the representation without the informed consent of each client.

Identifying Conflicts of Interest: Material Limitation

[8] Even where there is no direct adverseness, a conflict of interest exists if there is a significant risk that a lawyer's ability to consider, recommend or carry out an appropriate course of action for the client will be materially limited as a result of the lawyer's other responsibilities or interests. For example, a lawyer asked to represent several individuals seeking to form a joint venture is likely to be materially limited in the lawyer's ability to recommend or advocate all possible positions that each might take because of the lawyer's duty of loyalty to the others. The conflict in effect forecloses alternatives that would otherwise be available to the client. The mere possibility of subsequent harm does not itself require disclosure and consent. The critical questions are the likelihood that a difference in interests will eventuate and, if it does, whether it will materially interfere with the lawyer's independent professional judgment in considering alternatives or foreclose courses of action that reasonably should be pursued on behalf of the client.

Lawyer's Responsibilities to Former Clients and Other Third Persons

[9] In addition to conflicts with other current clients, a lawyer's duties of loyalty and independence may be materially limited by responsibilities to former clients under Rule 1.9 or by the lawyer's responsibilities to other persons, such as fiduciary duties arising from a lawyer's service as a trustee, executor or corporate director.

Personal Interest Conflicts

[10] The lawyer's own interests should not be permitted to have an adverse effect on representation of a client. For example, if the probity of a lawyer's own conduct in a transaction is in serious question, it may be difficult or impossible for the lawyer to give a client detached advice. Similarly, when a lawyer has discussions concerning possible employment with an opponent of the lawyer's client, or with a law firm representing the opponent, such discussions could materially limit the lawyer's representation of the client. In addition, a lawyer may not allow related business interests to affect representation, for example, by referring clients to an enterprise in which the lawyer has an undisclosed financial interest. See Rule 1.8 for specific Rules pertaining to a number of personal interest conflicts, including business transactions with clients. See also Rule 1.10 (personal interest conflicts under Rule 1.7 ordinarily are not imputed to other lawyers in a law firm).

[11] When lawyers representing different clients in the same matter or in substantially related matters are closely related by blood or marriage, there may be a significant risk that client confidences will be revealed and that the lawyer's family relationship will interfere with both loyalty and independent professional judgment. As a result, each client is entitled to know of the existence and implications of the relationship between the lawyers before the lawyer agrees to undertake the representation. Thus, a lawyer related to another lawyer, *e.g.*, as parent, child, sibling or spouse, ordinarily may not represent a client in a matter where that lawyer is representing another party, unless each client gives informed consent. The disqualification arising from a close family relationship is personal and ordinarily is not imputed to members of firms with whom the lawyers are associated. See Rule 1.10.

[12] A lawyer is prohibited from engaging in sexual relationships with a client unless the sexual relationship predates the formation of the client-lawyer relationship. See Rule 1.8(j).

Interest of Person Paying for a Lawyer's Service

[13] A lawyer may be paid from a source other than the client, including a co-client, if the client is informed of that fact and consents and the arrangement does not compromise the lawyer's duty of loyalty or independent judgment to the client. See Rule 1.8(f). If acceptance of the payment from any other source presents a significant risk that the lawyer's representation of the client will be materially limited by the lawyer's own interest in accommodating the person paying the lawyer's fee or by the lawyer's responsibilities to a payer who is also a co-client, then the lawyer must comply with the requirements of paragraph (b) before accepting the representation, including determining whether the conflict is consentable and, if so, that the client has adequate information about the material risks of the representation.

Prohibited Representations

[14] Ordinarily, clients may consent to representation notwithstanding a conflict. However, as indicated in paragraph (b), some conflicts are nonconsentable, meaning that the lawyer involved cannot properly ask for such agreement or provide representation on the basis of the client's consent. When the lawyer is representing more than one client, the question of consentability must be resolved as to each client.

[15] Consentability is typically determined by considering whether the interests of the clients will be adequately protected if the clients are permitted to give their informed consent to representation burdened by a conflict of interest. Thus, under paragraph (b)(1), representation is prohibited if in the circumstances the lawyer cannot reasonably conclude that the lawyer will be able to provide competent and diligent representation. See Rule 1.1 (competence) and Rule 1.3 (diligence).

[16] Paragraph (b)(2) describes conflicts that are nonconsentable because the representation is prohibited by applicable law. For example, in some states substantive law provides that the same lawyer may not represent more than one defendant in a capital case, even with the consent of the clients, and under federal criminal statutes certain representations by a former government lawyer are prohibited, despite the informed consent of the former client. In addition, decisional law in some states limits the ability of a governmental client, such as a municipality, to consent to a conflict of interest.

[17] Paragraph (b)(3) describes conflicts that are nonconsentable because of the institutional interest in vigorous development of each client's position when the clients are aligned directly against each other in the same litigation or other proceeding before a tribunal. Whether clients are aligned directly against each other within the meaning of this

paragraph requires examination of the context of the proceeding. Although this paragraph does not preclude a lawyer's multiple representation of adverse parties to a mediation (because mediation is not a proceeding before a "tribunal" under Rule 1.0(m)), such representation may be precluded by paragraph (b)(1).

Informed Consent

[18] Informed consent requires that each affected client be aware of the relevant circumstances and of the material and reasonably foreseeable ways that the conflict could have adverse effects on the interests of that client. See Rule 1.0(e) (informed consent). The information required depends on the nature of the conflict and the nature of the risks involved. When representation of multiple clients in a single matter is undertaken, the information must include the implications of the common representation, including possible effects on loyalty, confidentiality and the attorney-client privilege and the advantages and risks involved. See Comments [30] and [31] (effect of common representation on confidentiality).

[19] Under some circumstances it may be impossible to make the disclosure necessary to obtain consent. For example, when the lawyer represents different clients in related matters and one of the clients refuses to consent to the disclosure necessary to permit the other client to make an informed decision, the lawyer cannot properly ask the latter to consent. In some cases the alternative to common representation can be that each party may have to obtain separate representation with the possibility of incurring additional costs. These costs, along with the benefits of securing separate representation, are factors that may be considered by the affected client in determining whether common representation is in the client's interests.

[20] Reserved.

Revoking Consent

[21] A client who has given consent to a conflict may revoke the consent and, like any other client, may terminate the lawyer's representation at any time. Whether revoking consent to the client's own representation precludes the lawyer from continuing to represent other clients depends on the circumstances, including the nature of the conflict, whether the client revoked consent because of a material change in circumstances, the reasonable expectations of the other clients and whether material detriment to the other clients or the lawyer would result.

Consent to Future Conflict

[22] Whether a lawyer may properly request a client to waive conflicts that might arise in the future is subject to the test of paragraph (b). The effectiveness of such waivers is generally determined by the extent to which the client reasonably understands the material risks that the waiver entails. The more comprehensive the explanation of the types of future representations that might arise and the actual and reasonably foreseeable adverse consequences of those representations, the greater the likelihood that the client will have the requisite understanding. Thus, if the client agrees to consent

to a particular type of conflict with which the client is already familiar, then the consent ordinarily will be effective with regard to that type of conflict. If the consent is general and open-ended, then the consent ordinarily will be ineffective, because it is not reasonably likely that the client will have understood the material risks involved. On the other hand, if the client is an experienced user of the legal services involved and is reasonably informed regarding the risk that a conflict may arise, such consent is more likely to be effective, particularly if, *e.g.*, the client is independently represented by other counsel in giving consent and the consent is limited to future conflicts unrelated to the subject of the representation. In any case, advance consent cannot be effective if the circumstances that materialize in the future are such as would make the conflict nonconsentable under paragraph (b).

Conflicts in Litigation

[23] Paragraph (b)(3) prohibits representation of opposing parties in the same litigation, regardless of the clients' consent. On the other hand, simultaneous representation of parties whose interests in litigation may conflict, such as coplaintiffs or codefendants, is governed by paragraph (a)(2). A conflict may exist by reason of substantial discrepancy in the parties' testimony, incompatibility in positions in relation to an opposing party or the fact that there are substantially different possibilities of settlement of the claims or liabilities in question. Such conflicts can arise in criminal cases as well as civil. The potential for conflict of interest in representing multiple defendants in a criminal case is so grave that ordinarily a lawyer should decline to represent more than one codefendant. On the other hand, common representation of persons having similar interests in civil litigation is proper if the requirements of paragraph (b) are met.

[24] Ordinarily a lawyer may take inconsistent legal positions in different tribunals at different times on behalf of different clients. The mere fact that advocating a legal position on behalf of one client might create precedent adverse to the interests of a client represented by the lawyer in an unrelated matter does not create a conflict of interest. A conflict of interest exists, however, if there is a significant risk that a lawyer's action on behalf of one client will materially limit the lawyer's effectiveness in representing another client in a different case; for example, when a decision favoring one client will create a precedent likely to seriously weaken the position taken on behalf of the other client. Factors relevant in determining whether the clients need to be advised of the risk include: where the cases are pending, whether the issue is substantive or procedural, the temporal relationship between the matters, the significance of the issue to the immediate and long-term interests of the clients involved and the clients' reasonable expectations in retaining the lawyer. If there is significant risk of material limitation, then absent informed consent of the affected clients, the lawyer must refuse one of the representations or withdraw from one or both matters.

[25] When a lawyer represents or seeks to represent a class of plaintiffs or defendants in a class-

action lawsuit, unnamed members of the class are ordinarily not considered to be clients of the lawyer for purposes of applying paragraph (a)(1) of this Rule. Thus, the lawyer does not typically need to get the consent of such a person before representing a client suing the person in an unrelated matter. Similarly, a lawyer seeking to represent an opponent in a class action does not typically need the consent of an unnamed member of the class whom the lawyer represents in an unrelated matter.

Nonlitigation Conflicts

[26] Conflicts of interest under paragraphs (a)(1) and (a)(2) arise in contexts other than litigation. For a discussion of directly adverse conflicts in transactional matters, see Comment [7]. Relevant factors in determining whether there is significant potential for material limitation include the duration and intimacy of the lawyer's relationship with the client or clients involved, the functions being performed by the lawyer, the likelihood that disagreements will arise and the likely prejudice to the client from the conflict. The question is often one of proximity and degree. See Comment [8].

[27] For example, conflict questions may arise in estate planning and estate administration. A lawyer may be called upon to prepare wills for several family members, such as husband and wife, and, depending upon the circumstances, a conflict of interest may be present. In estate administration the identity of the client may be unclear under the law of a particular jurisdiction. Under one view, the client is the fiduciary; under another view the client is the estate or trust, including its beneficiaries. In order to comply with conflict of interest rules, the lawyer should make clear the lawyer's relationship to the parties involved.

[28] Whether a conflict is consentable depends on the circumstances. For example, a lawyer may not represent multiple parties to a negotiation whose interests are fundamentally antagonistic to each other, but common representation is permissible where the clients are generally aligned in interest even though there is some difference in interest among them. Thus, a lawyer may seek to establish or adjust a relationship between clients on an amicable and mutually advantageous basis; for example, in helping to organize a business in which two or more clients are entrepreneurs, working out the financial reorganization of an enterprise in which two or more clients have an interest or arranging a property distribution in settlement of an estate. The lawyer seeks to resolve potentially adverse interests by developing the parties' mutual interests. Otherwise, each party might have to obtain separate representation, with the possibility of incurring additional cost, complication or even litigation. Given these and other relevant factors, the clients may prefer that the lawyer act for all of them.

Special Considerations in Common Representation

[29] In considering whether to represent multiple clients in the same matter, a lawyer should be mindful that if the common representation fails because the potentially adverse interests cannot be reconciled, the result can be additional cost, embarrassment and recrimination. Ordinarily, the lawyer will be forced to withdraw from representing all of the clients if the common representation fails. In some situations, the risk of failure is so great that multiple representation is plainly impossible. For example, a lawyer cannot undertake common representation of clients where contentious litigation or negotiations between them are imminent or contemplated. Moreover, because the lawyer is required to be impartial between commonly represented clients, representation of multiple clients is improper when it is unlikely that impartiality can be maintained. Generally, if the relationship between the parties has already assumed antagonism, the possibility that the clients' interests can be adequately served by common representation is not very good. Other relevant factors are whether the lawyer subsequently will represent both parties on a continuing basis and whether the situation involves creating or terminating a relationship between the parties.

[30] A particularly important factor in determining the appropriateness of common representation is the effect on client-lawyer confidentiality and the attorney-client privilege. With regard to the attorney-client privilege, the prevailing rule is that, as between commonly represented clients, the privilege generally does not attach. Hence, it should generally be assumed that if litigation eventuates between the clients, the privilege will not protect any such communications, and the clients should be so advised.

[31] As to the duty of confidentiality, continued common representation will almost certainly be inadequate if one client asks the lawyer not to disclose to the other client information relevant to the common representation. This is so because the lawyer has an equal duty of loyalty to each client, and each client has the right to be informed of anything bearing on the representation that might affect that client's interests and the right to expect that the lawyer will use that information to that client's benefit. See Rule 1.4. The lawyer should, at the outset of the common representation and as part of the process of obtaining each client's informed consent, advise each client that information will be shared and that the lawyer will have to withdraw if one client decides that some matter material to the representation should be kept from the other. In limited circumstances, it may be appropriate for the lawyer to proceed with the representation when the clients have agreed, after being properly informed, that the lawyer will keep certain information confidential. For example, the lawyer may reasonably conclude that failure to disclose one client's trade secrets to another client will not adversely affect representation involving a joint venture between the clients and agree to keep that information confidential with the informed consent of both clients.

[32] When seeking to establish or adjust a relationship between clients, the lawyer should make clear that the lawyer's role is not that of partisanship normally expected in other circumstances and, thus, that the clients may be required to assume

greater responsibility for decisions than when each client is separately represented. Any limitations on the scope of the representation made necessary as a result of the common representation should be fully explained to the clients at the outset of the representation. See Rule 1.2(c).

[33] Subject to the above limitations, each client in the common representation has the right to loyal and diligent representation and the protection of Rule 1.9 concerning the obligations to a former client. The client also has the right to discharge the lawyer as stated in Rule 1.16.

Organizational Clients

[34] A lawyer who represents a corporation or other organization does not, by virtue of that representation, necessarily represent any constituent or affiliated organization, such as a parent or subsidiary. See Rule 1.13(a). Thus, the lawyer for an organization is not barred from accepting representation adverse to an affiliate in an unrelated matter, unless the circumstances are such that the affiliate should also be considered a client of the lawyer, there is an understanding between the lawyer and the organizational client that the lawyer will avoid representation adverse to the client's affiliates, or the lawyer's obligations to either the organizational client or the new client are likely to limit materially the lawyer's representation of the other client.

[35] A lawyer for a corporation or other organization who is also a member of its board of directors should determine whether the responsibilities of the two roles may conflict. The lawyer may be called on to advise the corporation in matters involving actions of the directors. Consideration should be given to the frequency with which such situations may arise, the potential intensity of the conflict, the effect of the lawyer's resignation from the board and the possibility of the corporation's obtaining legal advice from another lawyer in such situations. If there is material risk that the dual role will compromise the lawyer's independence of professional judgment, the lawyer should not serve as a director or should cease to act as the corporation's lawyer when conflicts of interest arise. The lawyer should advise the other members of the board that in some circumstances matters discussed at board meetings while the lawyer is present in the capacity of director might not be protected by the attorney-client privilege and that conflict of interest considerations might require the lawyer's recusal as a director or might require the lawyer and the lawyer's firm to decline representation of the corporation in a matter.

Rule 1.8. Conflict of Interest: Current Clients: Specific Rules

(a) A lawyer shall not enter into a business transaction with a client or knowingly acquire an ownership, possessory, security or other pecuniary interest adverse to a client unless:

(1) the transaction and terms on which the lawyer acquires the interest are fair and reasonable to the client and are fully disclosed and transmitted in writing in a manner that can be reasonably understood by the client;

(2) the client is informed in writing that the client may seek the advice of independent legal counsel on the transaction, and is given a reasonable opportunity to do so; and

(3) the client gives informed consent, in a writing signed by the client, to the essential terms of the transaction and the lawyer's role in the transaction, including whether the lawyer is representing the client in the transaction.

(b) A lawyer shall not use information relating to representation of a client to the disadvantage of the client unless the client gives informed consent, except as permitted or required by these Rules.

(c) A lawyer shall not solicit any substantial gift from a client, including a testamentary gift, or prepare on behalf of a client an instrument giving the lawyer or a person related to the lawyer any substantial gift unless the lawyer or other recipient of the gift is related to the client. For purposes of this paragraph, related persons include a spouse, child, grandchild, parent, grandparent or other relative or individual with whom the lawyer or the client maintains a close, familial relationship.

(d) Prior to the conclusion of representation of a client, a lawyer shall not make or negotiate an agreement giving the lawyer literary or media rights to a portrayal or account based in substantial part on information relating to the representation.

(e) A lawyer shall not provide financial assistance to a client in connection with pending or contemplated litigation, except that:

(1) a lawyer may advance court costs and expenses of litigation, the repayment of which may be contingent on the outcome of the matter; and

(2) a lawyer representing an indigent client may pay court costs and expenses of litigation on behalf of the client.

(f) A lawyer shall not accept compensation for representing a client from one other than the client unless:

(1) the client gives informed consent;

(2) there is no interference with the lawyer's independence of professional judgment or with the client-lawyer relationship; and

(3) information relating to representation of a client is protected as required by Rule 1.6.

(g) A lawyer who represents two or more clients shall not participate in making an aggregate settlement of the claims of or against the clients, or in a criminal case an aggregated agreement as to guilty or *nolo contendere* pleas, unless each client gives informed consent, in a writing signed by the client. The lawyer's disclosure shall include the existence and nature of all the claims or pleas involved and of the participation of each person in the settlement.

(h) A lawyer shall not:

(1) make an agreement prospectively limiting the lawyer's liability to a client for malpractice unless the client is independently represented in making the agreement; or

(2) settle a claim or potential claim for such liability with an unrepresented client or former client unless that person is advised in writing of the desirability of seeking and is given a reasonable opportunity to seek the advice of independent legal counsel in connection therewith.

(i) A lawyer shall not acquire a proprietary interest in the cause of action or subject matter of litigation the lawyer is conducting for a client, except that the lawyer may:

(1) acquire a lien authorized by law to secure the lawyer's fee or expenses; and

(2) contract with a client for a reasonable contingent fee in a civil case.

(j) A lawyer shall not have sexual relations with a client unless a consensual sexual relationship existed between them when the client-lawyer relationship commenced.

(k) While lawyers are associated in a firm, a prohibition in the foregoing paragraphs (a) through (i) that applies to any one of them shall apply to all of them.

Adopted July 1, 2009, eff. Jan. 1, 2010.

Comment

Business Transactions Between Client and Lawyer

[1] A lawyer's legal skill and training, together with the relationship of trust and confidence between lawyer and client, create the possibility of overreaching when the lawyer participates in a business, property or financial transaction with a client, for example, a loan or sales transaction or a lawyer investment on behalf of a client. The requirements of paragraph (a) must be met even when the transaction is not closely related to the subject matter of the representation, as when a lawyer drafting a will for a client learns that the client needs money for unrelated expenses and offers to make a loan to the client. The Rule applies to lawyers engaged in the sale of goods or services related to the practice of law, for example, the sale of title insurance or investment services to existing clients of the lawyer's legal practice. It also applies to lawyers purchasing property from estates they represent. It does not apply to ordinary fee arrangements between client and lawyer, which are governed by Rule 1.5, although its requirements must be met when the lawyer accepts an interest in the client's business or other nonmonetary property as payment of all or part of a fee. In addition, the Rule does not apply to standard commercial transactions between the lawyer and the client for products or services that the client generally markets to others,

for example, banking or brokerage services, medical services, products manufactured or distributed by the client, and utilities' services. In such transactions, the lawyer has no advantage in dealing with the client, and the restrictions in paragraph (a) are unnecessary and impracticable.

[2] Paragraph (a)(1) requires that the transaction itself be fair to the client and that its essential terms be communicated to the client, in writing, in a manner that can be reasonably understood. Paragraph (a)(2) requires that the lawyer inform the client in writing that the client may seek the advice of independent legal counsel and provide a reasonable opportunity for the client to do so. Paragraph (a)(3) requires that the lawyer obtain the client's informed consent, in a writing signed by the client, both to the essential terms of the transaction and to the lawyer's role. When necessary, the lawyer should discuss both the material risks of the proposed transaction, including any risk presented by the lawyer's involvement, and the existence of reasonably available alternatives and should explain why the advice of independent legal counsel is desirable. See Rule 1.0(e) (definition of informed consent). The common law regarding business transactions between lawyer and client may impose additional requirements, such as encouraging the client to seek independent legal counsel, in lawyer liability and other nondisciplinary contexts.

[3] The risk to a client is greatest when the client expects the lawyer to represent the client in the transaction itself or when the lawyer's financial interest otherwise poses a significant risk that the lawyer's representation of the client will be materially limited by the lawyer's financial interest in the transaction. Here the lawyer's role requires that the lawyer must comply, not only with the requirements of paragraph (a), but also with the requirements of Rule 1.7. Under that Rule, the lawyer must disclose the risks associated with the lawyer's dual role as both legal adviser and participant in the transaction, such as the risk that the lawyer will structure the transaction or give legal advice in a way that favors the lawyer's interests at the expense of the client. Moreover, the lawyer must obtain the client's informed consent. In some cases, the lawyer's interest may be such that Rule 1.7 will preclude the lawyer from seeking the client's consent to the transaction.

[4] If the client is independently represented in the transaction, paragraph (a)(2) of this Rule is inapplicable, and the paragraph (a)(1) requirement for full disclosure is satisfied either by a written disclosure by the lawyer involved in the transaction or by the client's independent counsel. The fact that the client was independently represented in the transaction is relevant in determining whether the agreement was fair and reasonable to the client as paragraph (a)(1) further requires.

Use of Information Related to Representation

[5] Use of information relating to the representation to the disadvantage of the client violates the lawyer's duty of loyalty. Paragraph (b) applies when the information is used to benefit either the lawyer or a third person, such as another client or

business associate of the lawyer. For example, if a lawyer learns that a client intends to purchase and develop several parcels of land, the lawyer may not use that information to purchase one of the parcels in competition with the client or to recommend that another client make such a purchase. The Rule does not prohibit uses that do not disadvantage the client. For example, a lawyer who learns a government agency's interpretation of trade legislation during the representation of one client may properly use that information to benefit other clients. Paragraph (b) prohibits disadvantageous use of client information unless the client gives informed consent, except as permitted or required by these Rules. See Rules 1.2(d), 1.6, 1.9(c), 3.3, 4.1(b), 8.1 and 8.3.

Gifts to Lawyers

[6] A lawyer may accept a gift from a client, if the transaction meets general standards of fairness. For example, a simple gift such as a present given at a holiday or as a token of appreciation is permitted. If a client offers the lawyer a more substantial gift, paragraph (c) does not prohibit the lawyer from accepting it, although such a gift may be voidable by the client under the doctrine of undue influence, which treats client gifts as presumptively fraudulent. In any event, due to concerns about overreaching and imposition on clients, a lawyer may not suggest that a substantial gift be made to the lawyer or for the lawyer's benefit, except where the lawyer is related to the client as set forth in paragraph (c).

[7] If effectuation of a substantial gift requires preparing a legal instrument such as a will or conveyance the client should have the detached advice that another lawyer can provide. The sole exception to this Rule is where the client is a relative of the donee.

[8] This Rule does not prohibit a lawyer from seeking to have the lawyer or a partner or associate of the lawyer named as executor of the client's estate or to another potentially lucrative fiduciary position. Nevertheless, such appointments will be subject to the general conflict of interest provision in Rule 1.7 when there is a significant risk that the lawyer's interest in obtaining the appointment will materially limit the lawyer's independent professional judgment in advising the client concerning the choice of an executor or other fiduciary. In obtaining the client's informed consent to the conflict, the lawyer should advise the client concerning the nature and extent of the lawyer's financial interest in the appointment, as well as the availability of alternative candidates for the position.

Literary Rights

[9] An agreement by which a lawyer acquires literary or media rights concerning the conduct of the representation creates a conflict between the interests of the client and the personal interests of the lawyer. Measures suitable in the representation of the client may detract from the publication value of an account of the representation. Paragraph (d) does not prohibit a lawyer representing a client in a transaction concerning literary property from agreeing that the lawyer's fee shall consist of a share in ownership in the property, if the arrangement conforms to Rule 1.5 and paragraphs (a) and (i).

Financial Assistance

[10] Lawyers may not subsidize lawsuits or administrative proceedings brought on behalf of their clients, including making or guaranteeing loans to their clients for living expenses, because to do so would encourage clients to pursue lawsuits that might not otherwise be brought and because such assistance gives lawyers too great a financial stake in the litigation. These dangers do not warrant a prohibition on a lawyer lending a client court costs and litigation expenses, including the expenses of medical examination and the costs of obtaining and presenting evidence, because these advances are virtually indistinguishable from contingent fees and help ensure access to the courts. Similarly, an exception allowing lawyers representing indigent clients to pay court costs and litigation expenses regardless of whether these funds will be repaid is warranted.

Person Paying for a Lawyer's Services

[11] Lawyers are frequently asked to represent a client under circumstances in which a third person will compensate the lawyer, in whole or in part. The third person might be a relative or friend, an indemnitor (such as a liability insurance company) or a co-client (such as a corporation sued along with one or more of its employees). Because third-party payers frequently have interests that differ from those of the client, including interests in minimizing the amount spent on the representation and in learning how the representation is progressing, lawyers are prohibited from accepting or continuing such representations unless the lawyer determines that there will be no interference with the lawyer's independent professional judgment and there is informed consent from the client. See also Rule 5.4(c) (prohibiting interference with a lawyer's professional judgment by one who recommends, employs or pays the lawyer to render legal services for another).

[12] Sometimes, it will be sufficient for the lawyer to obtain the client's informed consent regarding the fact of the payment and the identity of the third-party payer. If, however, the fee arrangement creates a conflict of interest for the lawyer, then the lawyer must comply with Rule. 1.7. The lawyer must also conform to the requirements of Rule 1.6 concerning confidentiality. Under Rule 1.7(a), a conflict of interest exists if there is significant risk that the lawyer's representation of the client will be materially limited by the lawyer's own interest in the fee arrangement or by the lawyer's responsibilities to the third-party payer (for example, when the third-party payer is a co-client). Under Rule 1.7(b), the lawyer may accept or continue the representation with the informed consent of each affected client, unless the conflict is nonconsentable under that paragraph.

Aggregate Settlements

[13] Differences in willingness to make or accept an offer of settlement are among the risks of common representation of multiple clients by a single

lawyer. Under Rule 1.7, this is one of the risks that should be discussed before undertaking the representation, as part of the process of obtaining the clients' informed consent. In addition, Rule 1.2(a) protects each client's right to have the final say in deciding whether to accept or reject an offer of settlement and in deciding whether to enter a guilty or *nolo contendere* plea in a criminal case. The rule stated in this paragraph is a corollary of both these Rules and provides that, before any settlement offer or plea bargain is made or accepted on behalf of multiple clients, the lawyer must inform each of them about all the material terms of the settlement, including what the other clients will receive or pay if the settlement or plea offer is accepted. See also Rule 1.0(e) (definition of informed consent). Lawyers representing a class of plaintiffs or defendants, or those proceeding derivatively, may not have a full client-lawyer relationship with each member of the class; nevertheless, such lawyers must comply with applicable rules regulating notification of class members and other procedural requirements designed to ensure adequate protection of the entire class.

Limiting Liability and Settling Malpractice Claims

[14] Agreements prospectively limiting a lawyer's liability for malpractice are prohibited unless the client is independently represented in making the agreement because they are likely to undermine competent and diligent representation. Also, many clients are unable to evaluate the desirability of making such an agreement before a dispute has arisen, particularly if they are then represented by the lawyer seeking the agreement. This paragraph does not, however, prohibit a lawyer from entering into an agreement with the client to arbitrate legal malpractice claims, provided such agreements are enforceable and the client is fully informed of the scope and effect of the agreement. Nor does this paragraph limit the ability of lawyers to practice in the form of a limited-liability entity, where permitted by law, provided that each lawyer remains personally liable to the client for his or her own conduct and the firm complies with any conditions required by law, such as provisions requiring client notification or maintenance of adequate liability insurance. Nor does it prohibit an agreement in accordance with Rule 1.2 that defines the scope of the representation, although a definition of scope that makes the obligations of representation illusory will amount to an attempt to limit liability.

[15] Agreements settling a claim or a potential claim for malpractice are not prohibited by this Rule. Nevertheless, in view of the danger that a lawyer will take unfair advantage of an unrepresented client or former client, the lawyer must first advise such a person in writing of the appropriateness of independent representation in connection with such a settlement. In addition, the lawyer must give the client or former client a reasonable opportunity to find and consult independent counsel.

Acquiring Proprietary Interest in Litigation

[16] Paragraph (i) states the traditional general rule that lawyers are prohibited from acquiring a proprietary interest in litigation. Like paragraph (e), the general rule has its basis in common law champerty and maintenance and is designed to avoid giving the lawyer too great an interest in the representation. In addition, when the lawyer acquires an ownership interest in the subject of the representation, it will be more difficult for a client to discharge the lawyer if the client so desires. The Rule is subject to specific exceptions developed in decisional law and continued in these Rules. The exception for certain advances of the costs of litigation is set forth in paragraph (e). In addition, paragraph (i) sets forth exceptions for liens authorized by law to secure the lawyer's fees or expenses and contracts for reasonable contingent fees. The law of each jurisdiction determines which liens are authorized by law. These may include liens granted by statute, liens originating in common law and liens acquired by contract with the client. When a lawyer acquires by contract a security interest in property other than that recovered through the lawyer's efforts in the litigation, such an acquisition is a business or financial transaction with a client and is governed by the requirements of paragraph (a). Contracts for contingent fees in civil cases are governed by Rule 1.5.

Client–Lawyer Sexual Relationships

[17] The relationship between lawyer and client is a fiduciary one in which the lawyer occupies the highest position of trust and confidence. The relationship is almost always unequal; thus, a sexual relationship between lawyer and client can involve unfair exploitation of the lawyer's fiduciary role, in violation of the lawyer's basic ethical obligation not to use the trust of the client to the client's disadvantage. In addition, such a relationship presents a significant danger that, because of the lawyer's emotional involvement, the lawyer will be unable to represent the client without impairment of the exercise of independent professional judgment. Moreover, a blurred line between the professional and personal relationships may make it difficult to predict to what extent client confidences will be protected by the attorney-client evidentiary privilege, since client confidences are protected by privilege only when they are imparted in the context of the client-lawyer relationship. Because of the significant danger of harm to client interests and because the client's own emotional involvement renders it unlikely that the client could give adequate informed consent, this Rule prohibits the lawyer from having sexual relations with a client regardless of whether the relationship is consensual and regardless of the absence of prejudice to the client.

[18] Sexual relationships that predate the client-lawyer relationship are not prohibited. Issues relating to the exploitation of the fiduciary relationship and client dependency are diminished when the sexual relationship existed prior to the commencement of the client-lawyer relationship. However, before proceeding with the representation in these circumstances, the lawyer should consider whether the lawyer's ability to represent the client will be materially limited by the relationship. See Rule 1.7(a)(2).

[19] When the client is an organization, paragraph (j) of this Rule prohibits a lawyer for the

organization (whether inside counsel or outside counsel) from having a sexual relationship with a constituent of the organization who supervises, directs or regularly consults with that lawyer concerning the organization's legal matters.

Imputation of Prohibitions

[20] Under paragraph (k), a prohibition on conduct by an individual lawyer in paragraphs (a) through (i) also applies to all lawyers associated in a firm with the personally prohibited lawyer. For example, one lawyer in a firm may not enter into a business transaction with a client of another member of the firm without complying with paragraph (a), even if the first lawyer is not personally involved in the representation of the client. The prohibition set forth in paragraph (j) is personal and is not applied to associated lawyers.

Rule 1.9. Duties to Former Clients

(a) A lawyer who has formerly represented a client in a matter shall not thereafter represent another person in the same or a substantially related matter in which that person's interests are materially adverse to the interests of the former client unless the former client gives informed consent.

(b) A lawyer shall not knowingly represent a person in the same or a substantially related matter in which a firm with which the lawyer formerly was associated had previously represented a client

(1) whose interests are materially adverse to that person; and

(2) about whom the lawyer had acquired information protected by Rules 1.6 and 1.9(c) that is material to the matter; unless the former client gives informed consent.

(c) A lawyer who has formerly represented a client in a matter or whose present or former firm has formerly represented a client in a matter shall not thereafter:

(1) use information relating to the representation to the disadvantage of the former client except as these Rules would permit or require with respect to a client, or when the information has become generally known; or

(2) reveal information relating to the representation except as these Rules would permit or require with respect to a client.

Adopted July 1, 2009, eff. Jan. 1, 2010.

Comment

[1] After termination of a client-lawyer relationship, a lawyer has certain continuing duties with respect to confidentiality and conflicts of interest and thus may not represent another client except in conformity with this Rule. Under this Rule, for example, a lawyer could not properly seek to rescind on behalf of a new client a contract drafted on behalf of the former client. So also a lawyer who has prosecuted an accused person could not properly represent the accused in a subsequent civil action

against the government concerning the same transaction. Nor could a lawyer who has represented multiple clients in a matter represent one of the clients against the others in the same or a substantially related matter after a dispute arose among the clients in that matter, unless all affected clients give informed consent. See Comment [9]. Current and former government lawyers must comply with this Rule to the extent required by Rule 1.11.

[2] The scope of a "matter" for purposes of this Rule depends on the facts of a particular situation or transaction. The lawyer's involvement in a matter can also be a question of degree. When a lawyer has been directly involved in a specific transaction, subsequent representation of other clients with materially adverse interests in that transaction clearly is prohibited. On the other hand, a lawyer who recurrently handled a type of problem for a former client is not precluded from later representing another client in a factually distinct problem of that type even though the subsequent representation involves a position adverse to the prior client. Similar considerations can apply to the reassignment of military lawyers between defense and prosecution functions within the same military jurisdictions. The underlying question is whether the lawyer was so involved in the matter that the subsequent representation can be justly regarded as a changing of sides in the matter in question.

[3] Matters are "substantially related" for purposes of this Rule if they involve the same transaction or legal dispute or if there otherwise is a substantial risk that confidential factual information as would normally have been obtained in the prior representation would materially advance the client's position in the subsequent matter. For example, a lawyer who has represented a businessperson and learned extensive private financial information about that person may not then represent that person's spouse in seeking a divorce. Similarly, a lawyer who has previously represented a client in securing environmental permits to build a shopping center would be precluded from representing neighbors seeking to oppose rezoning of the property on the basis of environmental considerations; however, the lawyer would not be precluded, on the grounds of substantial relationship, from defending a tenant of the completed shopping center in resisting eviction for nonpayment of rent. Information that has been disclosed to the public or to other parties adverse to the former client ordinarily will not be disqualifying. Information acquired in a prior representation may have been rendered obsolete by the passage of time, a circumstance that may be relevant in determining whether two representations are substantially related. In the case of an organizational client, general knowledge of the client's policies and practices ordinarily will not preclude a subsequent representation; on the other hand, knowledge of specific facts gained in a prior presentation that are relevant to the matter in question ordinarily will preclude such a representation. A former client is not required to reveal the confidential information learned by the lawyer in order to establish a substantial risk that the lawyer has

confidential information to use in the subsequent matter. A conclusion about the possession of such information may be based on the nature of the services the lawyer provided the former client and information that would in ordinary practice be learned by a lawyer providing such services.

Lawyers Moving Between Firms

[4] When lawyers have been associated within a firm but then end their association, the question of whether a lawyer should undertake representation is more complicated. There are several competing considerations. First, the client previously represented by the former firm must be reasonably assured that the principle of loyalty to the client is not compromised. Second, the rule should not be so broadly cast as to preclude other persons from having reasonable choice of legal counsel. Third, the rule should not unreasonably hamper lawyers from forming new associations and taking on new clients after having left a previous association. In this connection, it should be recognized that today many lawyers practice in firms, that many lawyers to some degree limit their practice to one field or another, and that many move from one association to another several times in their careers. If the concept of imputation were applied with unqualified rigor, the result would be radical curtailment of the opportunity of lawyers to move from one practice setting to another and of the opportunity of clients to change counsel.

[5] Paragraph (b) operates to disqualify the lawyer only when the lawyer involved has actual knowledge of information protected by Rules 1.6 and 1.9(c). Thus, if a lawyer while with one firm acquired no knowledge or information relating to a particular client of the firm, and that lawyer later joined another firm, neither the lawyer individually nor the second firm is disqualified from representing another client in the same or a related matter even though the interests of the two clients conflict. See Rule 1.10(b) for the restrictions on a firm once a lawyer has terminated association with the firm.

[6] Application of paragraph (b) depends on a situation's particular facts, aided by inferences, deductions or working presumptions that reasonably may be made about the way in which lawyers work together. A lawyer may have general access to files of all clients of a law firm and may regularly participate in discussions of their affairs; it should be inferred that such a lawyer in fact is privy to all information about all the firm's clients. In contrast, another lawyer may have access to the files of only a limited number of clients and participate in discussions of the affairs of no other clients; in the absence of information to the contrary, it should be inferred that such a lawyer in fact is privy to information about the clients actually served but not those of other clients.

[7] Independent of the question of disqualification of a firm, a lawyer changing professional association has a continuing duty to preserve confidentiality of information about a client formerly represented. See Rules 1.6 and 1.9(c).

[8] Paragraph (c) provides that information acquired by the lawyer in the course of representing a client may not subsequently be used or revealed by the lawyer to the disadvantage of the client. However, the fact that a lawyer has once served a client does not preclude the lawyer from using generally known information about that client when later representing another client.

[9] The provisions of this Rule are for the protection of former clients and can be waived if the client gives informed consent. With regard to the effectiveness of an advance waiver, see Comment [22] to Rule 1.7. With regard to disqualification of a firm with which a lawyer is or was formerly associated, see Rule 1.10.

Rule 1.10. Imputation of Conflicts of Interest: General Rule

(a) While lawyers are associated in a firm, none of them shall knowingly represent a client when any one of them practicing alone would be prohibited from doing so by Rules 1.7 or 1.9, unless the prohibition is based on a personal interest of the prohibited lawyer and does not present a significant risk of materially limiting the representation of the client by the remaining lawyers in the firm.

(b) When a lawyer has terminated an association with a firm, the firm is not prohibited from thereafter representing a person with interests materially adverse to those of a client represented by the formerly associated lawyer and not currently represented by the firm, unless:

(1) the matter is the same or substantially related to that in which the formerly associated lawyer represented the client; and

(2) any lawyer remaining in the firm has information protected by Rules 1.6 and 1.9(c) that is material to the matter.

(c) A disqualification prescribed by this Rule may be waived by the affected client under the conditions stated in Rule 1.7.

(d) The disqualification of lawyers associated in a firm with former or current government lawyers is governed by Rule 1.11 and with former judges, arbitrators, mediators or other third-party neutrals is governed by Rule 1.12.

(e) When a lawyer becomes associated with a firm, no lawyer associated in the firm shall knowingly represent a person in a matter in which that lawyer is disqualified under Rule 1.9 unless the personally disqualified lawyer is timely screened from any participation in the matter and is apportioned no part of the fee therefrom.

Adopted July 1, 2009, eff. Jan. 1, 2010.

Comment

Definition of "Firm"

[1] For purposes of the Rules of Professional Conduct, the term "firm" denotes lawyers in a law partnership, professional corporation, sole proprietorship or other association authorized to practice

law; or lawyers employed in a legal services organization or the legal department of a corporation or other organization. See Rule 1.0(c). Whether two or more lawyers constitute a firm within this definition can depend on the specific facts. See Rule 1.0, Comments [2] through [4].

Principles of Imputed Disqualification

[2] The rule of imputed disqualification stated in paragraph (a) gives effect to the principle of loyalty to the client as it applies to lawyers who practice in a law firm. Such situations can be considered from the premise that a firm of lawyers is essentially one lawyer for purposes of the rules governing loyalty to the client, or from the premise that each lawyer is vicariously bound by the obligation of loyalty owed by each lawyer with whom the lawyer is associated. Paragraph (a) operates only among the lawyers currently associated in a firm. When a lawyer moves from one firm to another, the situation is governed by Rules 1.9(b) and 1.10(b).

[3] The rule in paragraph (a) does not prohibit representation where neither questions of client loyalty nor protection of confidential information are presented. Where one lawyer in a firm could not effectively represent a given client because of strong political beliefs, for example, but that lawyer will do no work on the case and the personal beliefs of the lawyer will not materially limit the representation by others in the firm, the firm should not be disqualified. On the other hand, if an opposing party in a case were owned by a lawyer in the law firm, and others in the firm would be materially limited in pursuing the matter because of loyalty to that lawyer, the personal disqualification of the lawyer would be imputed to all others in the firm.

[4] The rule in paragraph (a) also does not prohibit representation by others in the law firm where the person prohibited from involvement in a matter is a nonlawyer, such as a paralegal or legal secretary. Nor does paragraph (a) prohibit representation if the lawyer is prohibited from acting because of events before the person became a lawyer, for example, work that the person did while a law student. Such persons, however, ordinarily must be screened from any personal participation in the matter to avoid communication to others in the firm of confidential information that both the nonlawyers and the firm have a legal duty to protect. See Rules 1.0(k) and 5.3.

[5] Rule 1.10(b) operates to permit a law firm, under certain circumstances, to represent a person with interests directly adverse to those of a client represented by a lawyer who formerly was associated with the firm. The Rule applies regardless of when the formerly associated lawyer represented the client. However, the law firm may not represent a person with interests adverse to those of a present client of the firm, which would violate Rule 1.7. Moreover, the firm may not represent the person where the matter is the same or substantially related to that in which the formerly associated lawyer represented the client and any other lawyer currently in the firm has material information protected by Rules 1.6 and 1.9(c).

[6] Rule 1.10(c) removes imputation with the informed consent of the affected client or former client under the conditions stated in Rule 1.7. The conditions stated in Rule 1.7 require the lawyer to determine that the representation is not prohibited by Rule 1.7(b) and that each affected client or former client has given informed consent to the representation. In some cases, the risk may be so severe that the conflict may not be cured by client consent. For a discussion of the effectiveness of client waivers of conflicts that might arise in the future, see Rule 1.7, Comment [22]. For a definition of informed consent, see Rule 1.0(e).

[7] Where a lawyer has joined a private firm after having represented the government, imputation is governed by Rule 1.11(b) and (c), not this Rule. Under Rule 1.11(d), where a lawyer represents the government after having served clients in private practice, nongovernmental employment or in another government agency, former-client conflicts are not imputed to government lawyers associated with the individually disqualified lawyer. Where a lawyer has joined a private firm after having been a judge or other adjudicative officer or law clerk to such person or an arbitrator, mediator or other third-party neutral, imputation is governed by Rule 1.12, not this Rule.

[8] Where a lawyer is prohibited from engaging in certain transactions under Rule 1.8, paragraph (k) of that Rule, and not this Rule, determines whether that prohibition also applies to other lawyers associated in a firm with the personally prohibited lawyer.

[9] Where the conditions of paragraph (e) are met, imputation is removed and consent is not required. Requirements for screening procedures are stated in Rule 1.0(k). This paragraph does not prohibit a lawyer from receiving a salary or partnership share established by independent agreement, but that lawyer may not receive compensation directly relating the lawyer's compensation to the fee in the matter in which the lawyer is disqualified. Nonconsensual screening in such cases adequately balances the interests of the former client in protecting its confidential information, the interests of the current client in hiring the counsel of its choice (including a law firm that may have represented the client in similar matters for many years), and the interests of lawyers in career mobility, particularly when they are moving involuntarily.

Rule 1.11. Special Conflicts of Interest for Former and Current Government Officers and Employee

(a) Except as law may otherwise expressly permit, a lawyer who has formerly served as a public officer or employee of the government:

(1) is subject to Rule 1.9(c); and

(2) shall not otherwise represent a client in connection with a matter in which the lawyer participated personally and substantially as a public officer or employee, unless the appropriate government agency gives its informed consent to the representation.

(b) When a lawyer is disqualified from representation under paragraph (a), no lawyer in a firm with which that lawyer is associated may knowingly undertake or continue representation in such a matter unless:

(1) the disqualified lawyer is timely screened from any participation in the matter and is apportioned no part of the fee therefrom; and

(2) written notice is promptly given to the appropriate government agency to enable it to ascertain compliance with the provisions of this Rule.

(c) Except as law may otherwise expressly permit, a lawyer having information that the lawyer knows is confidential government information about a person acquired when the lawyer was a public officer or employee may not represent a private client whose interests are adverse to that person in a matter in which the information could be used to the material disadvantage of that person. As used in this Rule, the term "confidential government information" means information that has been obtained under governmental authority and which, at the time this Rule is applied, the government is prohibited by law from disclosing to the public or has a legal privilege not to disclose and which is not otherwise available to the public. A firm with which that lawyer is associated may undertake or continue representation in the matter only if the disqualified lawyer is timely screened from any participation in the matter and is apportioned no part of the fee therefrom.

(d) Except as law may otherwise expressly permit, a lawyer currently serving as a public officer or employee:

(1) is subject to Rules 1.7 and 1.9; and

(2) shall not:

(i) participate in a matter in which the lawyer participated personally and substantially while in private practice or nongovernmental employment, unless the appropriate government agency gives its informed consent; or

(ii) negotiate for private employment with any person who is involved as a party or as lawyer for a party in a matter in which the lawyer is participating personally and substantially, except that a lawyer serving as a law clerk to a judge, other adjudicative officer or arbitrator may negotiate for private employment as permitted by Rule 1.12(b) and subject to the conditions stated in Rule 1.12(b).

(e) As used in this Rule, the term "matter" includes:

(1) any judicial or other proceeding, application, request for a ruling or other determination, contract, claim, controversy, investigation, charge, accusation, arrest or other particular matter involving a specific party or parties, and

(2) any other matter covered by the conflict of interest rules of the appropriate government agency.
Adopted July 1, 2009, eff. Jan. 1, 2010.

Comment

[1] A lawyer who has served or is currently serving as a public officer or employee is personally subject to the Rules of Professional Conduct, including the prohibition against concurrent conflicts of interest stated in Rule 1.7. In addition, such a lawyer may be subject to statutes and government regulations regarding conflict of interest. Such statutes and regulations may circumscribe the extent to which the government agency may give consent under this Rule. See Rule 1.0(e) for the definition of informed consent.

[2] Paragraphs (a)(1), (a)(2) and (d)(1) restate the obligations of an individual lawyer who has served or is currently serving as an officer or employee of the government toward a former government or private client. Rule 1.10 is not applicable to the conflicts of interest addressed by this Rule. Rather, paragraph (b) sets forth a special imputation rule for former government lawyers that provides for screening and notice. Because of the special problems raised by imputation within a government agency, paragraph (d) does not impute the conflicts of a lawyer currently serving as an officer or employee of the government to other associated government officers or employees, although ordinarily it will be prudent to screen such lawyers.

[3] Paragraphs (a)(2) and (d)(2) apply regardless of whether a lawyer is adverse to a former client and are thus designed not only to protect the former client, but also to prevent a lawyer from exploiting public office for the advantage of another client. For example, a lawyer who has pursued a claim on behalf of the government may not pursue the same claim on behalf of a later private client after the lawyer has left government service, except when authorized to do so by the government agency under paragraph (a). Similarly, a lawyer who has pursued a claim on behalf of a private client may not pursue the claim on behalf of the government, except when authorized to do so by paragraph (d). As with paragraphs (a)(1) and (d)(1), Rule 1.10 is not applicable to the conflicts of interest addressed by these paragraphs.

[4] This Rule represents a balancing of interests. On the one hand, where the successive clients are a government agency and another client, public or private, the risk exists that power or discretion vested in that agency might be used for the special benefit of the other client. A lawyer should not be in a position where benefit to the other client might affect performance of the lawyer's professional functions on behalf of the government. Also, unfair advantage could accrue to the other client by reason of access to confidential government information about the client's adversary obtainable only through the lawyer's government service. On the other hand, the rules governing lawyers presently or formerly employed by a government agency should not be so restrictive as to inhibit transfer of employment to and from the government. The govern-

ment has a legitimate need to attract qualified lawyers as well as to maintain high ethical standards. Thus a former government lawyer is disqualified only from particular matters in which the lawyer participated personally and substantially. The provisions for screening and waiver in paragraph (b) are necessary to prevent the disqualification rule from imposing too severe a deterrent against entering public service. The limitation of disqualification in paragraphs (a)(2) and (d)(2) to matters involving a specific party or parties, rather than extending disqualification to all substantive issues on which the lawyer worked, serves a similar function.

[5] When a lawyer has been employed by one government agency and then moves to a second government agency, it may be appropriate to treat that second agency as another client for purposes of this Rule, as when a lawyer is employed by a city and subsequently is employed by a federal agency. However, because the conflict of interest is governed by paragraph (d), the latter agency is not required to screen the lawyer as paragraph (b) requires a law firm to do. The question of whether two government agencies should be regarded as the same or different clients for conflict of interest purposes is beyond the scope of these Rules. See Rule 1.13 Comment [9].

[6] Paragraphs (b) and (c) contemplate a screening arrangement. See Rule 1.0(k) (requirements for screening procedures). These paragraphs do not prohibit a lawyer from receiving a salary or partnership share established by independent agreement, but that lawyer may not receive compensation directly relating the lawyer's compensation to the fee in the matter in which the lawyer is disqualified.

[7] Notice, including a description of the screened lawyer's prior representation and of the screening procedures employed, generally should be given as soon as practicable after the need for screening becomes apparent.

[8] Paragraph (c) operates only when the lawyer in question has knowledge of the information, which means actual knowledge; it does not operate with respect to information that merely could be imputed to the lawyer.

[9] Paragraphs (a) and (d) do not prohibit a lawyer from jointly representing a private party and a government agency when doing so is permitted by Rule 1.7 and is not otherwise prohibited by law.

[10] For purposes of paragraph (e) of this Rule, a "matter" may continue in another form. In determining whether two particular matters are the same, the lawyer should consider the extent to which the matters involve the same basic facts, the same or related parties, and the time elapsed.

Rule 1.12. Former Judge, Arbitrator, Mediator or Other Third–Party Neutral

(a) Except as stated in paragraph (d), a lawyer shall not represent anyone in connection with a matter in which the lawyer participated personally and substantially as a judge or other adjudicative officer or

law clerk to such a person or as an arbitrator, mediator or other third-party neutral, unless all parties to the proceeding give informed consent.

(b) A lawyer shall not negotiate for employment with any person who is involved as a party or as lawyer for a party in a matter in which the lawyer is participating personally and substantially as a judge or other adjudicative officer or as an arbitrator, mediator or other third-party neutral. A lawyer serving as a law clerk to a judge or other adjudicative officer may negotiate for employment with a party or lawyer involved in a matter in which the clerk is participating personally and substantially, but only after the lawyer has notified the judge or other adjudicative officer.

(c) If a lawyer is disqualified by paragraph (a), no lawyer in a firm with which that lawyer is associated may knowingly undertake or continue representation in the matter unless:

(1) the disqualified lawyer is timely screened from any participation in the matter and is apportioned no part of the fee therefrom; and

(2) written notice is promptly given to the parties and any appropriate tribunal to enable them to ascertain compliance with the provisions of this Rule.

(d) An arbitrator selected as a partisan of a party in a multimember arbitration panel is not prohibited from subsequently representing that party.

Adopted July 1, 2009, eff. Jan. 1, 2010.

Comment

[1] This Rule generally parallels Rule 1.11. The term "personally and substantially" signifies that a judge who was a member of a multimember court, and thereafter left judicial office to practice law, is not prohibited from representing a client in a matter pending in the court, but in which the former judge did not participate. So also the fact that a former judge exercised administrative responsibility in a court does not prevent the former judge from acting as a lawyer in a matter where the judge had previously exercised remote or incidental administrative responsibility that did not affect the merits. Compare the Comment to Rule 1.11. The term "adjudicative officer" includes such officials as judges pro tempore, referees, special masters, hearing officers and other parajudicial officers, and also lawyers who serve as part-time judges.

[2] Like former judges, lawyers who have served as arbitrators, mediators or other third-party neutrals may be asked to represent a client in a matter in which the lawyer participated personally and substantially. This Rule forbids such representation unless all of the parties to the proceedings give their informed consent. See Rule 1.0(e) and (b). Other law or codes of ethics governing third-party neutrals may impose more stringent standards of personal or imputed disqualification. See Rule 2.4.

[3] Although lawyers who serve as third-party neutrals do not have information concerning the parties that is protected under Rule 1.6, they typically owe the parties an obligation of confidentiality

under law or codes of ethics governing third-party neutrals. Thus, paragraph (c) provides that conflicts of the personally disqualified lawyer will be imputed to other lawyers in a law firm unless the conditions of this paragraph are met.

[4] Requirements for screening procedures are stated in Rule 1.0(k). Paragraph (c)(1) does not prohibit the screened lawyer from receiving a salary or partnership share established by independent agreement, but that lawyer may not receive compensation directly related to the matter in which the lawyer is disqualified.

[5] Notice, including a description of the screened lawyer's prior representation and of the screening procedures employed, generally should be given as soon as practicable after the need for screening becomes apparent.

Rule 1.13. Organization as Client

(a) A lawyer employed or retained by an organization represents the organization acting through its duly authorized constituents.

(b) If a lawyer for an organization knows that an officer, employee or other person associated with the organization is engaged in action, intends to act or refuses to act in a matter related to the representation that is a violation of a legal obligation to the organization, or a crime, fraud or other violation of law that reasonably might be imputed to the organization, and that is likely to result in substantial injury to the organization, then the lawyer shall proceed as is reasonably necessary in the best interest of the organization. Unless the lawyer reasonably believes that it is not necessary in the best interest of the organization to do so, the lawyer shall refer the matter to higher authority in the organization, including, if warranted by the circumstances, to the highest authority that can act on behalf of the organization as determined by applicable law.

(c) Except as provided in paragraph (d), if

(1) despite the lawyer's efforts in accordance with paragraph (b) the highest authority that can act on behalf of the organization insists upon or fails to address in a timely and appropriate manner an action or a refusal to act, that is clearly a crime or fraud, and

(2) the lawyer reasonably believes that the crime or fraud is reasonably certain to result in substantial injury to the organization,

then the lawyer may reveal information relating to the representation whether or not Rule 1.6 permits such disclosure, but only if and to the extent the lawyer reasonably believes necessary to prevent substantial injury to the organization.

(d) Paragraph (c) shall not apply with respect to information relating to a lawyer's representation of an organization to investigate an alleged crime, fraud or other violation of law, or to defend the organization or an officer, employee or other constituent associated with the organization against a claim arising out of an alleged crime, fraud or other violation of law.

(e) A lawyer who reasonably believes that he or she has been discharged because of the lawyer's actions taken pursuant to paragraphs (b) or (c), or who withdraws under circumstances that require or permit the lawyer to take action under either of those paragraphs, shall proceed as the lawyer reasonably believes necessary to assure that the organization's highest authority is informed of the lawyer's discharge or withdrawal.

(f) In dealing with an organization's directors, officers, employees, members, shareholders or other constituents, a lawyer shall explain the identity of the client when the lawyer knows or reasonably should know that the organization's interests are adverse to those of the constituents with whom the lawyer is dealing.

(g) A lawyer representing an organization may also represent any of its directors, officers, employees, members, shareholders or other constituents, subject to the provisions of Rule 1.7. If the organization's consent to the dual representation is required by Rule 1.7, the consent shall be given by an appropriate official of the organization other than the individual who is to be represented, or by the shareholders. Adopted July 1, 2009, eff. Jan. 1, 2010.

Comment

The Entity as the Client

[1] An organizational client is a legal entity, but it cannot act except through its officers, directors, employees, shareholders and other constituents. Officers, directors, employees and shareholders are the constituents of the corporate organizational client. The duties defined in this Comment apply equally to unincorporated associations. "Other constituents" as used in this Comment means the positions equivalent to officers, directors, employees and shareholders held by persons acting for organizational clients that are not corporations.

[2] When one of the constituents of an organizational client communicates with the organization's lawyer in that person's organizational capacity, the communication is protected by Rule 1.6. Thus, by way of example, if an organizational client requests its lawyer to investigate allegations of wrongdoing, interviews made in the course of that investigation between the lawyer and the client's employees or other constituents are covered by Rule 1.6. This does not mean, however, that constituents of an organizational client are the clients of the lawyer. The lawyer may not disclose to such constituents information relating to the representation except for disclosures explicitly or impliedly authorized by the organizational client in order to carry out the representation or as otherwise permitted by Rule 1.6.

[3] When constituents of the organization make decisions for it, the decisions ordinarily must be accepted by the lawyer even if their utility or prudence is doubtful. Decisions concerning policy and operations, including ones entailing serious risk,

are not as such in the lawyer's province. Paragraph (b) makes clear, however, that when the lawyer knows that the organization is likely to be substantially injured by action of an officer or other constituent that violates a legal obligation to the organization or is a crime, fraud or other violation of law that might be imputed to the organization, the lawyer must proceed as is reasonably necessary in the best interest of the organization. As defined in Rule 1.0(f), knowledge can be inferred from circumstances, and a lawyer cannot ignore the obvious.

[4] In determining how to proceed under paragraph (b), the lawyer should give due consideration to the seriousness of the misconduct and its consequences, the responsibility in the organization and the apparent motivation of those involved, the policies of the organization concerning such matters, and any other relevant considerations. Ordinarily, referral to a higher authority would be necessary. In some circumstances, however, it may be appropriate for the lawyer to ask the constituent to reconsider the matter; for example, if the circumstances involve a constituent's innocent misunderstanding of law and subsequent acceptance of the lawyer's advice, the lawyer may reasonably conclude that the best interest of the organization does not require that the matter be referred to higher authority. If a constituent persists in conduct contrary to the lawyer's advice, it will be necessary for the lawyer to take steps to have the matter reviewed by a higher authority in the organization. If the matter is of sufficient seriousness and importance or urgency to the organization, referral to higher authority in the organization may be necessary even if the lawyer has not communicated with the constituent. Any measures taken should, to the extent practicable, minimize the risk of revealing information relating to the representation to persons outside the organization. Even in circumstances where a lawyer is not obligated by Rule 1.13 to proceed, a lawyer may bring to the attention of an organizational client, including its highest authority, matters that the lawyer reasonably believes to be of sufficient importance to warrant doing so in the best interest of the organization.

[5] Paragraph (b) also makes clear that when it is reasonably necessary to enable the organization to address the matter in a timely and appropriate manner, the lawyer must refer the matter to higher authority, including, if warranted by the circumstances, the highest authority that can act on behalf of the organization under applicable law. The organization's highest authority to whom a matter may be referred ordinarily will be the board of directors or similar governing body. However, applicable law may prescribe that under certain conditions the highest authority reposes elsewhere, for example, in the independent directors of a corporation.

Relation to Other Rules

[6] The authority and responsibility provided in this Rule are concurrent with the authority and responsibility provided in other Rules. In particular, this Rule does not limit or expand the lawyer's responsibility under Rules 1.8, 1.16, 3.3 or 4.1.

Paragraph (c) of this Rule supplements Rule 1.6(b) by providing an additional basis upon which the lawyer may reveal information relating to the representation, but does not modify, restrict, or limit the provisions of Rule 1.6(b). Under Paragraph (c) the lawyer may reveal such information only when the organization's highest authority insists upon or fails to address threatened or ongoing action that is clearly a crime or fraud, and then only to the minimum extent the lawyer reasonably believes necessary to prevent reasonably certain substantial injury to the organization. It is not necessary that the lawyer's services be used in furtherance of the crime or fraud, but it is required that the matter be related to the lawyer's representation of the organization. If the lawyer's services are being used by an organization to further a crime or fraud by the organization, Rules 1.6(b)(1), 1.6(b)(2) or 1.6(b)(3) may permit the lawyer to disclose confidential information. In such circumstances Rule 1.2(d) may also be applicable, in which event, withdrawal from the representation under Rule 1.16(a)(1) may be required. Because the lawyer may reveal information relating to the representation outside the organization under paragraph (c) only in circumstances involving a crime or fraud, the lawyer may be required to act under paragraph (b) in situations that arise out of violations of law that do not constitute a crime or fraud even though disclosure outside the organization would not be permitted by paragraph (c).

[7] Paragraph (d) makes clear that the authority of a lawyer to disclose information relating to a representation in circumstances described in paragraph (c) does not apply with respect to information relating to a lawyer's engagement by an organization to investigate an alleged violation of law or to defend the organization or an officer, employee or other person associated with the organization against a claim arising out of an alleged crime, fraud or other violation of law. This is necessary in order to enable organizational clients to enjoy the full benefits of legal counsel in conducting an investigation or defending against a claim.

[8] A lawyer who reasonably believes that he or she has been discharged because of the lawyer's actions taken pursuant to paragraph (b) or (c), or who withdraws in circumstances that require or permit the lawyer to take action under either of these paragraphs, must proceed as the lawyer reasonably believes necessary to assure that the organization's highest authority is informed of the lawyer's discharge or withdrawal, and what the lawyer reasonably believes to be the basis for his or her discharge or withdrawal.

Government Agency

[9] The duty defined in this Rule applies to governmental organizations. Defining precisely the identity of the client and prescribing the resulting obligations of such lawyers may be more difficult in the government context and is a matter beyond the scope of these Rules. See Scope [18]. Although in some circumstances the client may be a specific agency, it may also be a branch of government, such as the executive branch, or the government as a whole. For example, if the action or failure to

act involves the head of a bureau, either the department of which the bureau is a part or the relevant branch of government may be the client for purposes of this Rule. Moreover, in a matter involving the conduct of government officials, a government lawyer may have authority under applicable law to question such conduct more extensively than that of a lawyer for a private organization in similar circumstances. Thus, when the client is a governmental organization, a different balance may be appropriate between maintaining confidentiality and assuring that the wrongful act is prevented or rectified, for public business is involved. In addition, duties of lawyers employed by the government or lawyers in military service may be defined by statutes and regulation. This Rule does not limit that authority. See Scope.

Clarifying the Lawyer's Role

[10] There are times when the organization's interest may be or become adverse to those of one or more of its constituents. In such circumstances the lawyer should advise any constituent, whose interest the lawyer finds adverse to that of the organization of the conflict or potential conflict of interest, that the lawyer cannot represent such constituent, and that such person may wish to obtain independent representation. Care must be taken to assure that the individual understands that, when there is such adversity of interest, the lawyer for the organization cannot provide legal representation for that constituent individual, and that discussions between the lawyer for the organization and the individual may not be privileged.

[11] Whether such a warning should be given by the lawyer for the organization to any constituent individual may turn on the facts of each case.

Dual Representation

[12] Paragraph (g) recognizes that a lawyer for an organization may also represent a principal officer or major shareholder.

Derivative Actions

[13] Under generally prevailing law, the shareholders or members of a corporation may bring suit to compel the directors to perform their legal obligations in the supervision of the organization. Members of unincorporated associations might have a corresponding right. Where permitted, such an action may be brought nominally by the corporation or unincorporated association, but usually is, in fact, a legal controversy over management of the organization.

[14] The question can arise whether counsel for the organization may defend such an action. The proposition that the organization is the lawyer's client does not alone resolve the issue. Most derivative actions are a normal incident of an organization's affairs, to be defended by the organization's lawyer like any other suit. However, if the claim involves serious charges of wrongdoing by those in control of the organization, a conflict may arise between the lawyer's duty to the organization and the lawyer's relationship with the board. In those circumstances, Rule 1.7 governs who should represent the directors and the organization.

Rule 1.14. Client With Diminished Capacity

(a) When a client's capacity to make adequately considered decisions in connection with a representation is diminished, whether because of minority, mental impairment or for some other reason, the lawyer shall, as far as reasonably possible, maintain a normal client-lawyer relationship with the client.

(b) When the lawyer reasonably believes that the client has diminished capacity, is at risk of substantial physical, financial or other harm unless action is taken and cannot adequately act in the client's own interest, the lawyer may take reasonably necessary protective action, including consulting with individuals or entities that have the ability to take action to protect the client and, in appropriate cases, seeking the appointment of a guardian ad litem, conservator or guardian.

(c) Information relating to the representation of a client with diminished capacity is protected by Rule 1.6. When taking protective action pursuant to paragraph (b), the lawyer is impliedly authorized under Rule 1.6(a) to reveal information about the client, but only to the extent reasonably necessary to protect the client's interests.

Adopted July 1, 2009, eff. Jan. 1, 2010.

Comment

[1] The normal client-lawyer relationship is based on the assumption that the client, when properly advised and assisted, is capable of making decisions about important matters. When the client is a minor or suffers from a diminished mental capacity, however, maintaining the ordinary client-lawyer relationship may not be possible in all respects. In particular, a severely incapacitated person may have no power to make legally binding decisions. Nevertheless, a client with diminished capacity often has the ability to understand, deliberate upon, and reach conclusions about matters affecting the client's own well-being. For example, children as young as five or six years of age, and certainly those of ten or twelve, are regarded as having opinions that are entitled to weight in legal proceedings concerning their custody. So also, it is recognized that some persons of advanced age can be quite capable of handling routine financial matters while needing special legal protection concerning major transactions.

[2] The fact that a client suffers a disability does not diminish the lawyer's obligation to treat the client with attention and respect. Even if the person has a legal representative, the lawyer should as far as possible accord the represented person the status of client, particularly in maintaining communication.

[3] The client may wish to have family members or other persons participate in discussions with the lawyer. When necessary to assist in the representation, the presence of such persons generally does not affect the applicability of the attorney-client evidentiary privilege. Nevertheless, the lawyer must keep the client's interests foremost and, except for protective action authorized under para-

graph (b), must to look to the client, and not family members, to make decisions on the client's behalf.

[4] If a legal representative has already been appointed for the client, the lawyer should ordinarily look to the representative for decisions on behalf of the client. In matters involving a minor, whether the lawyer should look to the parents as natural guardians may depend on the type of proceeding or matter in which the lawyer is representing the minor. If the lawyer represents the guardian as distinct from the ward, and is aware that the guardian is acting adversely to the ward's interest, the lawyer may have an obligation to prevent or rectify the guardian's misconduct. See Rule 1.2(d).

Taking Protective Action

[5] If a lawyer reasonably believes that a client is at risk of substantial physical, financial or other harm unless action is taken, and that a normal client-lawyer relationship cannot be maintained as provided in paragraph (a) because the client lacks sufficient capacity to communicate or to make adequately considered decisions in connection with the representation, then paragraph (b) permits the lawyer to take protective measures deemed necessary. Such measures could include: consulting with family members, using a reconsideration period to permit clarification or improvement of circumstances, using voluntary surrogate decisionmaking tools such as durable powers of attorney or consulting with support groups, professional services, adult-protective agencies or other individuals or entities that have the ability to protect the client. In taking any protective action, the lawyer should be guided by such factors as the wishes and values of the client to the extent known, the client's best interests and the goals of intruding into the client's decisionmaking autonomy to the least extent feasible, maximizing client capacities and respecting the client's family and social connections.

[6] In determining the extent of the client's diminished capacity, the lawyer should consider and balance such factors as: the client's ability to articulate reasoning leading to a decision, variability of state of mind and ability to appreciate consequences of a decision; the substantive fairness of a decision; and the consistency of a decision with the known long-term commitments and values of the client. In appropriate circumstances, the lawyer may seek guidance from an appropriate diagnostician.

[7] If a legal representative has not been appointed, the lawyer should consider whether appointment of a guardian ad litem, conservator or guardian is necessary to protect the client's interests. Thus, if a client with diminished capacity has substantial property that should be sold for the client's benefit, effective completion of the transaction may require appointment of a legal representative. In addition, rules of procedure in litigation sometimes provide that minors or persons with diminished capacity must be represented by a guardian or next friend if they do not have a general guardian. In many circumstances, however, appointment of a legal representative may be more expensive or traumatic for the client than circumstances in fact require. Evaluation of such circumstances is a matter entrusted to the professional judgment of the lawyer. In

considering alternatives, however, the lawyer should be aware of any law that requires the lawyer to advocate the least restrictive action on behalf of the client.

Disclosure of the Client's Condition

[8] Disclosure of the client's diminished capacity could adversely affect the client's interests. For example, raising the question of diminished capacity could, in some circumstances, lead to proceedings for involuntary commitment. Information relating to the representation is protected by Rule 1.6. Therefore, unless authorized to do so, the lawyer may not disclose such information. When taking protective action pursuant to paragraph (b), the lawyer is impliedly authorized to make the necessary disclosures, even when the client directs the lawyer to the contrary. Nevertheless, given the risks of disclosure, paragraph (c) limits what the lawyer may disclose in consulting with other individuals or entities or seeking the appointment of a legal representative. At the very least, the lawyer should determine whether it is likely that the person or entity consulted with will act adversely to the client's interests before discussing matters related to the client. The lawyer's position in such cases is an unavoidably difficult one.

Emergency Legal Assistance

[9] In an emergency where the health, safety or a financial interest of a person with seriously diminished capacity is threatened with imminent and irreparable harm, a lawyer may take legal action on behalf of such a person even though the person is unable to establish a client-lawyer relationship or to make or express considered judgments about the matter, when the person or another acting in good faith on that person's behalf has consulted with the lawyer. Even in such an emergency, however, the lawyer should not act unless the lawyer reasonably believes that the person has no other lawyer, agent or other representative available, except when that representative's actions or inaction threaten immediate and irreparable harm to the person. The lawyer should take legal action on behalf of the person only to the extent reasonably necessary to maintain the status quo or otherwise avoid imminent and irreparable harm. A lawyer who undertakes to represent a person in such an exigent situation has the same duties under these Rules as the lawyer would with respect to a client.

[10] A lawyer who acts on behalf of a person with seriously diminished capacity in an emergency should keep the confidences of the person as if dealing with a client, disclosing them only to the extent necessary to accomplish the intended protective action. The lawyer should disclose to any tribunal involved and to any other counsel involved the nature of his or her relationship with the person. The lawyer should take steps to regularize the relationship or implement other protective solutions as soon as possible. Normally, a lawyer would not seek compensation for such emergency actions taken.

Rule 1.15. Safekeeping Property

(a) A lawyer shall hold property of clients or third persons that is in a lawyer's possession in connection with a representation separate from the lawyer's own property. Funds shall be deposited in one or more separate and identifiable interest- or dividend-bearing client trust accounts maintained at an eligible financial institution in the state where the lawyer's office is situated, or elsewhere with the informed consent of the client or third person. For the purposes of this Rule, a client trust account means an IOLTA account as defined in paragraph (j)(2), or a separate, interest-bearing non–IOLTA client trust account established to hold the funds of a client or third person as provided in paragraph (f). Funds of clients or third persons shall not be deposited in a non-interest-bearing or non-dividend-bearing account. Other, tangible property shall be identified as such and appropriately safeguarded. Complete records of client trust account funds and other property shall be kept by the lawyer and shall be preserved for a period of seven years after termination of the representation.

Maintenance of complete records of client trust accounts shall require that a lawyer:

(1) prepare and maintain receipt and disbursement journals for all client trust accounts required by this Rule containing a record of deposits and withdrawals from client trust accounts specifically identifying the date, source, and description of each item deposited, and the date, payee and purpose of each disbursement;

(2) prepare and maintain contemporaneous ledger records for all client trust accounts showing, for each separate trust client or beneficiary, the source of all funds deposited, the date of each deposit, the names of all persons for whom the funds are or were held, the amount of such funds, the dates, descriptions and amounts of charges or withdrawals, and the names of all persons to whom such funds were disbursed;

(3) maintain copies of all accountings to clients or third persons showing the disbursement of funds to them or on their behalf, along with copies of those portions of clients' files that are reasonably necessary for a complete understanding of the financial transactions pertaining to them;

(4) maintain all client trust account checkbook registers, check stubs, bank statements, records of deposit, and checks or other records of debits;

(5) maintain copies of all retainer and compensation agreements with clients;

(6) maintain copies of all bills rendered to clients for legal fees and expenses;

(7) prepare and maintain reconciliation reports of all client trust accounts, on at least a quarterly basis, including reconciliations of ledger balances with client trust account balances;

(8) make appropriate arrangements for the maintenance of the records in the event of the closing, sale, dissolution, or merger of a law practice.

Records required by this Rule may be maintained by electronic, photographic, or other media provided that printed copies can be produced, and the records are readily accessible to the lawyer.

Each client trust account shall be maintained only in an eligible financial institution selected by the lawyer in the exercise of ordinary prudence.

(b) A lawyer may deposit the lawyer's own funds in a client trust account for the sole purpose of paying bank service charges on that account, but only in an amount necessary for that purpose.

(c) A lawyer shall deposit in a client trust account funds received to secure payment of legal fees and expenses, to be withdrawn by the lawyer only as fees are earned and expenses incurred. Funds received as a fixed fee, a general retainer, or an advance payment retainer shall be deposited in the lawyer's general account or other account belonging to the lawyer. An advance payment retainer may be used only when necessary to accomplish some purpose for the client that cannot be accomplished by using a security retainer. An agreement for an advance payment retainer shall be in a writing signed by the client that uses the term "advance payment retainer" to describe the retainer, and states the following:

(1) the special purpose for the advance payment retainer and an explanation why it is advantageous to the client;

(2) that the retainer will not be held in a client trust account, that it will become the property of the lawyer upon payment, and that it will be deposited in the lawyer's general account;

(3) the manner in which the retainer will be applied for services rendered and expenses incurred;

(4) that any portion of the retainer that is not earned or required for expenses will be refunded to the client;

(5) that the client has the option to employ a security retainer, provided, however, that if the lawyer is unwilling to represent the client without receiving an advance payment retainer, the agreement must so state and provide the lawyer's reasons for that condition.

(d) Upon receiving funds or other property in which a client or third person has an interest, a lawyer shall promptly notify the client or third person. Except as stated in this Rule or otherwise permitted by law or by agreement with the client, a lawyer shall promptly deliver to the client or third person any funds or other property that the client or third person is entitled to receive and, upon request by the client or third person, shall promptly render a full accounting regarding such property.

(e) When in the course of representation a lawyer is in possession of property in which two or more persons (one of whom may be the lawyer) claim interests, the property shall be kept separate by the lawyer until the dispute is resolved. The lawyer shall promptly distribute all portions of the property as to which the interests are not in dispute.

(f) All funds of clients or third persons held by a lawyer or law firm which are nominal in amount or are expected to be held for a short period of time, including advances for costs and expenses, and funds belonging in part to a client or third person and in part presently or potentially to the lawyer or law firm, shall be deposited in one or more IOLTA accounts, as defined in paragraph (j)(2). A lawyer or law firm shall deposit all funds of clients or third persons which are not nominal in amount or expected to be held for a short period of time into a separate interest- or dividend-bearing client trust account with the client designated as income beneficiary. Funds of clients or third persons shall not be deposited in a non-interest-bearing or non-dividend-bearing account. Each IOLTA account shall comply with the following provisions:

(1) Each lawyer or law firm in receipt of nominal or short-term client funds shall establish one or more IOLTA accounts with an eligible financial institution authorized by federal or state law to do business in the state of Illinois and which offers IOLTA accounts within the requirements of this Rule as administered by the Lawyers Trust Fund of Illinois.

(2) Eligible institutions shall maintain IOLTA accounts that pay the highest interest rate or dividend available from the institution to its non–IOLTA account customers when IOLTA accounts meet or exceed the same minimum balance or other account eligibility guidelines, if any. In determining the highest interest rate or dividend generally available from the institution to its non–IOLTA accounts, eligible institutions may consider factors, in addition to the IOLTA account balance, customarily considered by the institution when setting interest rates or dividends for its customers, provided that such factors do not discriminate between IOLTA accounts and accounts of non–IOLTA customers, and that these factors do not include that the account is an IOLTA account.

(3) An IOLTA account that meets the highest comparable rate or dividend standard set forth in paragraph (f)(2) must use one of the identified account options as an IOLTA account, or pay the equivalent yield on an existing IOLTA account in lieu of using the highest-yield bank product:

(a) a checking account paying preferred interest rates, such as money market or indexed rates, or any other suitable interest-bearing deposit account offered by the eligible institution to its non–IOLTA customers.

(b) for accounts with balances of $100,000 or more, a business checking account with automated investment feature, such as an overnight sweep and investment in repurchase agreements fully collateralized by U.S. Government securities as defined in paragraph (h).

(c) for accounts with balances of $100,000 or more, a money market fund with, or tied to, check-writing capacity, that must be solely invested in U.S. Government securities or securities fully collateralized by U.S. Government securities, and that has total assets of at least $250 million.

(4) As an alternative to the account options in paragraph (f)(3), the financial institution may pay a "safe harbor" yield equal to 70% of the Federal Funds Target Rate or 1.0%, whichever is higher.

(5) Each lawyer or law firm shall direct the eligible financial institution to remit monthly earnings on the IOLTA account directly to the Lawyers Trust Fund of Illinois. For each individual IOLTA account, the eligible financial institution shall provide: a statement transmitted with each remittance showing the name of the lawyer or law firm directing that the remittance be sent; the account number; the remittance period; the rate of interest applied; the account balance on which the interest was calculated; the reasonable service fee(s) if any; the gross earnings for the remittance period; and the net amount of earnings remitted. Remittances shall be sent to the Lawyers Trust Fund electronically unless otherwise agreed. The financial institution may assess only allowable reasonable fees, as defined in paragraph (j)(8). Fees in excess of the earnings accrued on an individual IOLTA account for any month shall not be taken from earnings accrued on other IOLTA accounts or from the principal of the account.

(g) A lawyer or law firm should exercise reasonable judgment in determining whether funds of a client or third person are nominal in amount or are expected to be held for a short period of time. No charge of ethical impropriety or other breach of professional conduct shall attend to a lawyer's or law firm's exercise of reasonable judgment under this rule or decision to place client funds in an IOLTA account or a non–IOLTA client trust account on the basis of that determination. Ordinarily, in determining the type of account into which to deposit particular funds for a client or third person, a lawyer or a law firm shall take into consideration the following factors:

(1) the amount of interest which the funds would earn during the period they are expected to be held and the likelihood of delay in the relevant transaction or proceeding;

(2) the cost of establishing and administering the account, including the cost of the lawyer's services;

(3) the capability of the financial institution, through subaccounting, to calculate and pay interest

earned by each client's funds, net of any transaction costs, to the individual client.

(h) All trust accounts, whether IOLTA or non–IOLTA, shall be established in compliance with the following provisions on dishonored instrument notification:

(1) A lawyer shall maintain trust accounts only in eligible financial institutions that have filed with the Attorney Registration and Disciplinary Commission an agreement, in a form provided by the Commission, to report to the Commission in the event any properly payable instrument is presented against a client trust account containing insufficient funds, irrespective of whether or not the instrument is honored. Any such agreement shall apply to all branches of the financial institution and shall not be canceled except upon 30 days notice in writing to the Commission. The Commission shall annually publish a list of financial institutions that have agreed to comply with this rule and shall establish rules and procedures governing amendments to the list.

(2) The overdraft notification agreement shall provide that all reports made by the financial institution shall be in the following format:

(a) In the case of a dishonored instrument, the report shall be identical to the overdraft notice customarily forwarded to the depositor, and should include a copy of the dishonored instrument, if such a copy is normally provided to depositors; and

(b) In the case of instruments that are presented against insufficient funds but which instruments are honored, the report shall identify the financial institution, the lawyer or law firm, the account number, the date of presentation for payment and the date paid, as well as the amount of overdraft created thereby. Such reports shall be made simultaneously with, and within the time provided by law for, notice of dishonor, if any. If an instrument presented against insufficient funds is honored, then the report shall be made within five banking days of the date of presentation for payment against insufficient funds.

(3) Every lawyer practicing or admitted to practice in this jurisdiction shall, as a condition thereof, be conclusively deemed to have consented to the reporting and production requirements mandated by this Rule.

(4) Nothing herein shall preclude a financial institution from charging a particular lawyer or law firm for the reasonable cost of producing the reports and records required by paragraph (h) of this Rule. Fees charged for the reasonable cost of producing the reports and records required by paragraph (h) are the sole responsibility of the lawyer or law firm, and are not allowable reasonable fees for IOLTA accounts as those are defined in paragraph (j)(8).

(i) A lawyer who learns of unidentified funds in an IOLTA account must make periodic efforts to identify and return the funds to the rightful owner. If after 12 months of the discovery of the unidentified funds the lawyer determines that ascertaining the ownership or securing the return of the funds will not succeed, the lawyer must remit the funds to the Lawyers Trust Fund of Illinois. No charge of ethical impropriety or other breach of professional conduct shall attend to a lawyer's exercise of reasonable judgment under this paragraph (i).

A lawyer who either remits funds in error or later ascertains the ownership of remitted funds may make a claim to the Lawyers Trust Fund, which after verification of the claim will return the funds to the lawyer.

(j) Definitions

(1) "Funds" denotes any form of money, including cash, payment instruments such as checks, money orders or sales drafts, and electronic fund transfers.

(2) "IOLTA account" means a pooled interest- or dividend-bearing client trust account, established with an eligible financial institution with the Lawyers Trust Fund of Illinois designated as income beneficiary, for the deposit of nominal or short-term funds of clients or third persons as defined in paragraph (f) and from which funds may be withdrawn upon request as soon as permitted by law.

(3) "Eligible financial institution" is a bank or a savings bank insured by the Federal Deposit Insurance Corporation or an open-end investment company registered with the Securities and Exchange Commission that agrees to provide dishonored instrument notification regarding any type of client trust account as provided in paragraph (h) of this Rule; and that with respect to IOLTA accounts, offers IOLTA accounts within the requirements of paragraph (f) of this Rule.

(4) "Properly payable" refers to an instrument which, if presented in the normal course of business, is in a form requiring payment under the laws of this jurisdiction.

(5) "Money market fund" is an investment company registered under the Investment Company Act of 1940, as amended, that is qualified to hold itself out to investors as a money market fund or the equivalent of a money market fund under Rules and Regulations adopted by the Securities and Exchange Commission pursuant to said Act.

(6) "U.S. Government securities" refers to U.S. Treasury obligations and obligations issued by or guaranteed as to principal and interest by any AAA–rated United States agency or instrumentality thereof. A daily overnight financial repurchase agreement ("repo") may be established only with an institution that is deemed to be "well capitalized" or

"adequately capitalized" as defined by applicable federal statutes and regulations.

(7) "Safe harbor" is a yield that if paid by the financial institution on IOLTA accounts shall be deemed as a comparable return in compliance with this Rule. Such yield shall be calculated as 70% of the Federal Funds Target Rate as reported in the Wall Street Journal on the first business day of the calendar month.

(8) "Allowable reasonable fees" for IOLTA accounts are per-check charges, per deposit charges, a fee in lieu of a minimum balance, federal deposit insurance fees, automated investment ("sweep") fees, and a reasonable maintenance fee, if those fees are charged on comparable accounts maintained by non–IOLTA depositors. All other fees are the responsibility of, and may be charged to, the lawyer or law firm maintaining the IOLTA account.

(9) "Unidentified funds" are amounts accumulated in an IOLTA account that cannot be documented as belonging to a client, a third person, or the lawyer or law firm.

(k) In the closing of a real estate transaction, a lawyer's disbursement of funds deposited but not collected shall not violate his or her duty pursuant to this Rule 1.15 if, prior to the closing, the lawyer has established a segregated Real Estate Funds Account (REFA) maintained solely for the receipt and disbursement of such funds, has deposited such funds into a REFA, and:

(1) is acting as a closing agent pursuant to an insured closing letter for a title insurance company licensed in the State of Illinois and uses for such funds a segregated REFA maintained solely for such title insurance business; or

(2) has met the "good-funds" requirements. The good-funds requirements shall be met if the bank in which the REFA was established has agreed in a writing directed to the lawyer to honor all disbursement orders drawn on that REFA for all transactions up to a specified dollar amount not less than the total amount being deposited in good funds. Good funds shall include only the following forms of deposits: (a) a certified check, (b) a check issued by the State of Illinois, the United States, or a political subdivision of the State of Illinois or the United States, (c) a cashier's check, teller's check, bank money order, or official bank check drawn on or issued by a financial institution insured by the Federal Deposit Insurance Corporation or a comparable agency of the federal or state government, (d) a check drawn on the trust account of any lawyer or real estate broker licensed under the laws of any state, (e) a personal check or checks in an aggregate amount not exceeding $5,000 per closing if the lawyer making the deposit has reasonable and prudent grounds to believe that the deposit will be irrevocably credited to the REFA, (f) a check drawn on the account of or issued by a lender approved by the United States Department of Housing and Urban Development as either a supervised or a nonsupervised mortgagee as defined in 24 C.F.R. § 202.2, (g) a check from a title insurance company licensed in the State of Illinois, or from a title insurance agent of the title insurance company, provided that the title insurance company has guaranteed the funds of that title insurance agent. Without limiting the rights of the lawyer against any person, it shall be the responsibility of the disbursing lawyer to reimburse the trust account for such funds that are not collected and for any fees, charges and interest assessed by the paying bank on account of such funds being uncollected.

Adopted July 1, 2009, eff. Jan. 1, 2010. Amended Nov. 23, 2009, eff. Jan. 1, 2010; July 1, 2011, eff. Sept. 1, 2011; April 7, eff. July 1, 2015.

Comment

[1] A lawyer should hold property of others with the care required of a professional fiduciary. Securities should be kept in a safe deposit box, except when some other form of safekeeping is warranted by special circumstances. All property that is the property of clients or third persons, including prospective clients, must be kept separate from the lawyer's business and personal property and, if monies, in one or more client trust accounts. Client trust accounts should be made identifiable through their designation as "client trust account" or "client funds account" or words of similar import indicating the fiduciary nature of the account. Separate trust accounts may be warranted when administering estate monies or acting in similar fiduciary capacities. A lawyer should maintain on a current basis complete records of client trust account funds as required by paragraph (a), including subparagraphs (1) through (8). These requirements articulate recordkeeping principles that provide direction to a lawyer in the handling of funds entrusted to the lawyer by a client or third person. Compliance with these requirements will benefit the attorney and the client or third party as these fiduciary funds will be safeguarded and documentation will be available to fulfill the lawyer's fiduciary obligation to provide an accounting to the owners of the funds and to refute any charge that the funds were handled improperly.

[2] While normally it is impermissible to commingle the lawyer's own funds with client funds, paragraph (b) provides that it is permissible when necessary to pay bank service charges on that account. Accurate records must be kept regarding which part of the funds are the lawyer's.

[3] Lawyers often receive funds from which the lawyer's fee will be paid. The lawyer is not required to remit to the client funds that the lawyer reasonably believes represent fees owed. However, a lawyer may not hold funds to coerce a client into accepting the lawyer's contention. The disputed portion of the funds must be kept in a trust account and the lawyer should suggest means for prompt resolution of the dispute, such as arbitration. The

undisputed portion of the funds shall be promptly distributed. Specific guidance concerning client trust accounts is provided in the Client Trust Account Handbook published by the Illinois Attorney Registration and Disciplinary Commission as well as on the website of the Illinois Attorney Registration and Disciplinary Commission.

[3A] Paragraph (c) relates to legal fees and expenses that have been paid in advance. The reasonableness, structure, and division of legal fees are governed by Rule 1.5 and other applicable law.

[3B] Paragraph (c) must be read in conjunction with *Dowling v. Chicago Options Associates, Inc.,* 226 Ill. 2d 277 (2007). In *Dowling*, the Court distinguished different types of retainers. It recognized advance payment retainers and approved their use in limited circumstances where the lawyer and client agree that a retainer should become the property of the lawyer upon payment. Prior to *Dowling*, the Court recognized only two types of retainers. The first, a general retainer (also described as a "true," "engagement," or "classic" retainer) is paid by a client to the lawyer in order to ensure the lawyer's availability during a specific period of time or for a specific matter. This type of retainer is earned when paid and immediately becomes property of the lawyer, regardless of whether the lawyer ever actually performs any services for the client. The second, a "security" retainer, secures payment for future services and expense, and must be deposited in a client trust account pursuant to paragraph (a). Funds in a security retainer remain the property of the client until applied for services rendered or expenses incurred. Any unapplied funds are refunded to the client. Any written retainer agreement should clearly define the kind of retainer being paid. If the parties agree that the client will pay a security retainer, that term should be used in any written agreement, which should also provide that the funds remain the property of the client until applied for services rendered or expenses incurred and that the funds will be deposited in a client trust account. If the parties' intent is not evident, an agreement for a retainer will be construed as providing for a security retainer.

[3C] An advance payment retainer is a present payment to the lawyer in exchange for the commitment to provide legal services in the future. Ownership of this retainer passes to the lawyer immediately upon payment; and the retainer may not be deposited into a client trust account because a lawyer may not commingle property of a client with the lawyer's own property. However, any portion of an advance payment retainer that is not earned must be refunded to the client. An advance payment retainer should be used sparingly, only when necessary to accomplish a purpose for the client that cannot be accomplished by using a security retainer. An advance payment retainer agreement must be in a written agreement signed by the client that contains the elements listed in paragraph (c). An advance payment retainer is distinguished from a fixed fee (also described as a "flat" or "lump-sum" fee), where the lawyer agrees to provide a specific service (*e.g.*, defense of a criminal charge, a real estate closing, or preparation of a will or trust) for a fixed amount. Unlike an advance payment retainer, a fixed fee is generally not subject to the obligation to refund any portion to the client, although a fixed fee is subject, like all fees, to the requirement of Rule 1.5(a) that a lawyer may not charge or collect an unreasonable fee.

[3D] The type of retainer that is appropriate will depend on the circumstances of each case. The guiding principle in the choice of the type of retainer is protection of the client's interests. In the vast majority of cases, this will dictate that funds paid to retain a lawyer will be considered a security retainer and placed in a client trust account, pursuant to this Rule.

[4] Paragraph (e) also recognizes that third parties may have lawful claims against specific funds or other property in a lawyer's custody, such as a client's creditor who has a lien on funds recovered in a personal injury action. A lawyer may have a duty under applicable law to protect such third-party claims against wrongful interference by the client. In such cases, when the third-party claim is not frivolous under applicable law, the lawyer must refuse to surrender the property to the client until the claims are resolved. A lawyer should not unilaterally assume to arbitrate a dispute between the client and the third party, but, when there are substantial grounds for dispute as to the person entitled to the funds, the lawyer may file an action to have a court resolve the dispute.

[5] The obligations of a lawyer under this Rule are independent of those arising from activity other than rendering legal services. For example, a lawyer who serves only as an escrow agent is governed by the applicable law relating to fiduciaries even though the lawyer does not render legal services in the transaction and is not governed by this Rule.

[6] Paragraphs (a), (f) and (g) requires that nominal or short-term funds belonging to clients or third persons be deposited in one or more IOLTA accounts as defined in paragraph (j)(2) and provide that the interest earned on any such accounts shall be submitted to the Lawyers Trust Fund of Illinois. The Lawyers Trust Fund of Illinois will disburse the funds so received to qualifying organizations and programs to be used for the purposes set forth in its by-laws. The purposes of the Lawyers Trust Fund of Illinois may not be changed without the approval of the Supreme Court of Illinois. The decision as to whether funds are nominal or short-term shall be in the reasonable judgment of the depositing lawyer or law firm. Client and third-person funds that are neither nominal or short-term shall be deposited in separate, interest- or dividend-bearing client trust accounts for the benefit of the client as set forth in paragraphs (a) and (f).

[7] Paragraph (h) requires that lawyers maintain trust accounts only in financial institutions that have agreed to report trust account overdrafts to the ARDC. The trust account overdraft notification program is intended to provide early detection of problems in lawyers' trust accounts, so that errors by lawyers and/or banks may be corrected and serious lawyer transgressions pursued.

[8] Paragraph (i) applies when accumulated balances in an IOLTA account cannot be documented as belonging to an identifiable client or third party, or to the lawyer or law firm. This paragraph provides a mechanism for a lawyer to remove these funds from an IOLTA account when, in the lawyer's reasonable judgment, further efforts to account for them after a period of 12 months are not likely to be successful. This procedure facilitates the effective management of IOLTA accounts by lawyers; addresses situations where an IOLTA account becomes the responsibility of a lawyer's successor, law partner, or heir; and supports the provision of civil legal aid in Illinois.

The Lawyers Trust Fund of Illinois will publish instructions for lawyers remitting unidentified funds. Proceeds of unidentified funds received under paragraph (i) will be distributed to qualifying organizations and programs according to the purposes set forth in the by-laws of the Lawyers Trust Fund. When a lawyer learns that funds have been remitted in error or later identifies the owner of remitted funds, the lawyer may make a claim to the Lawyers Trust Fund for the return of the funds. After verification of the claim, the Lawyer Trust Fund will return the funds to the lawyer who then ensures the funds are restored to the owner.

Paragraph (i) relates only to unidentified funds, for which no owner can be ascertained. Unclaimed funds in client trust accounts—funds whose owner is known but have not been claimed—should be handled according to applicable statutes including the Uniform Disposition of Unclaimed Property Act (765 ILCS 1025 et seq.).

[9] Paragraph (j) provides definitions that pertain specifically to Rule 1.15. Paragraph (1) defines expansively the meaning of "funds," to include any form of money, including electronic fund transfers. Paragraph (2) defines an IOLTA account and paragraph (3) defines an eligible financial institution for purposes of the overdraft notification and IOLTA programs. Paragraph (4) defines "properly payable," a term used in the overdraft notification provisions in paragraph (h)(1). Paragraphs (5) through (8) define terms pertaining to IOLTA accounts. Paragraph (9) defines "unidentified funds" as that term is used in paragraph (i).

[10] Paragraph (k) applies only to the closing of real estate transactions and adopts the "good-funds" doctrine. That doctrine provides for the disbursement of funds deposited but not yet collected if the lawyer has already established an appropriate Real Estate Funds Account and otherwise fulfills all of the requirements contained in the Rule.

Commentary adopted July 1, 2009, eff. Jan. 1, 2010. Amended July 1, 2011, eff. Sept. 1, 2011; April 7, 2015, eff. July 1, 2015.

Rule 1.16. Declining or Terminating Representation

(a) Except as stated in paragraph (c), a lawyer shall not represent a client or, where representation has commenced, shall withdraw from the representation of a client if:

(1) the representation will result in violation of the Rules of Professional Conduct or other law;

(2) the lawyer's physical or mental condition materially impairs the lawyer's ability to represent the client; or

(3) the lawyer is discharged.

(b) Except as stated in paragraph (c), a lawyer may withdraw from representing a client if:

(1) withdrawal can be accomplished without material adverse effect on the interests of the client;

(2) the client persists in a course of action involving the lawyer's services that the lawyer reasonably believes is criminal or fraudulent;

(3) the client has used the lawyer's services to perpetrate a crime or fraud;

(4) the client insists upon taking action that the lawyer considers repugnant or with which the lawyer has a fundamental disagreement;

(5) the client fails substantially to fulfill an obligation to the lawyer regarding the lawyer's services and has been given reasonable warning that the lawyer will withdraw unless the obligation is fulfilled;

(6) the representation will result in an unreasonable financial burden on the lawyer or has been rendered unreasonably difficult by the client; or

(7) other good cause for withdrawal exists.

(c) A lawyer must comply with applicable law requiring notice to or permission of a tribunal when terminating a representation. When ordered to do so by a tribunal, a lawyer shall continue representation notwithstanding good cause for terminating the representation.

(d) Upon termination of representation, a lawyer shall take steps to the extent reasonably practicable to protect a client's interests, such as giving reasonable notice to the client, allowing time for employment of other counsel, surrendering papers and property to which the client is entitled and refunding any advance payment of fee or expense that has not been earned or incurred. The lawyer may retain papers relating to the client to the extent permitted by other law.

Adopted July 1, 2009, eff. Jan. 1, 2010.

Comment

[1] A lawyer should not accept representation in a matter unless it can be performed competently, promptly, without improper conflict of interest and to completion. Ordinarily, a representation in a matter is completed when the agreed-upon assistance has been concluded. See Rules 1.2(c) and 6.5. See also Rule 1.3, Comment [4].

Mandatory Withdrawal

[2] A lawyer ordinarily must decline or withdraw from representation if the client demands that the lawyer engage in conduct that is illegal or violates the Rules of Professional Conduct or other law. The lawyer is not obliged to decline or withdraw

simply because the client suggests such a course of conduct; a client may make such a suggestion in the hope that a lawyer will not be constrained by a professional obligation.

[3] When a lawyer has been appointed to represent a client, withdrawal ordinarily requires approval of the appointing authority. See also Rule 6.2. Similarly, court approval or notice to the court is often required by applicable law before a lawyer withdraws from pending litigation. Difficulty may be encountered if withdrawal is based on the client's demand that the lawyer engage in unprofessional conduct. The court may request an explanation for the withdrawal, while the lawyer may be bound to keep confidential the facts that would constitute such an explanation. The lawyer's statement that professional considerations require termination of the representation ordinarily should be accepted as sufficient. Lawyers should be mindful of their obligations to both clients and the court under Rules 1.6 and 3.3.

Discharge

[4] A client has a right to discharge a lawyer at any time, with or without cause, subject to liability for payment for the lawyer's services. Where future dispute about the withdrawal may be anticipated, it may be advisable to prepare a written statement reciting the circumstances.

[5] Whether a client can discharge appointed counsel may depend on applicable law. A client seeking to do so should be given a full explanation of the consequences. These consequences may include a decision by the appointing authority that appointment of successor counsel is unjustified, thus requiring self-representation by the client.

[6] If the client has severely diminished capacity, the client may lack the legal capacity to discharge the lawyer, and in any event the discharge may be seriously adverse to the client's interests. The lawyer should make special effort to help the client consider the consequences and may take reasonably necessary protective action as provided in Rule 1.14.

Optional Withdrawal

[7] A lawyer may withdraw from representation in some circumstances. The lawyer has the option to withdraw if it can be accomplished without material adverse effect on the client's interests. Withdrawal is also justified if the client persists in a course of action that the lawyer reasonably believes is criminal or fraudulent, for a lawyer is not required to be associated with such conduct even if the lawyer does not further it. Withdrawal is also permitted if the lawyer's services were misused in the past even if that would materially prejudice the client. The lawyer may also withdraw where the client insists on taking action that the lawyer considers repugnant or with which the lawyer has a fundamental disagreement.

[8] A lawyer may withdraw if the client refuses to abide by the terms of an agreement relating to the representation, such as an agreement concerning fees or court costs or an agreement limiting the objectives of the representation.

Assisting the Client Upon Withdrawal

[9] Even if the lawyer has been unfairly discharged by the client, a lawyer must take all reasonable steps to mitigate the consequences to the client. The lawyer may retain papers as security for a fee only to the extent permitted by law. See Rule 1.15.

Refund of Unearned Fees

[10] See Comments [3B] through [3D] to Rule 1.15 and Rule 1.16(d).

Rule 1.17. Sale of Law Practice

A lawyer or a law firm may sell or purchase, and the estate of a deceased lawyer or the guardian or authorized representative of a disabled lawyer may sell, a law practice, including good will, if the following conditions are satisfied:

(a) The seller ceases to engage in the private practice of law in the geographic area in which the practice has been conducted;

(b) The entire practice is sold to one or more lawyers or law firms;

(c) The seller gives written notice to each of the seller's clients regarding:

(1) the proposed sale;

(2) the client's right to retain other counsel or to take possession of the file; and

(3) the fact that the client's consent to the transfer of the client's files will be presumed if the client does not take any action or does not otherwise object within ninety (90) days of receipt of the notice.

If a client cannot be given notice, the representation of that client may be transferred to the purchaser only upon entry of an order so authorizing by a court having jurisdiction. The seller may disclose to the court *in camera* information relating to the representation only to the extent necessary to obtain an order authorizing the transfer of a file.

(d) The fees charged clients shall not be increased by reason of the sale.

Adopted July 1, 2009, eff. Jan. 1, 2010.

Comment

[1] The practice of law is a profession, not merely a business. Clients are not commodities that can be purchased and sold at will. Pursuant to this Rule, when a lawyer or an entire firm ceases to practice and other lawyers or firms take over the representation, the selling lawyer or firm may obtain compensation for the reasonable value of the practice as may withdrawing partners of law firms. See Rules 5.4 and 5.6.

Termination of Practice by the Seller

[2] The requirement that all of the private practice be sold is satisfied if the seller in good faith makes the entire practice available for sale to the purchasers. The fact that a number of the seller's clients decide not to be represented by the purchas-

ers but take their matters elsewhere, therefore, does not result in a violation. Return to private practice as a result of an unanticipated change in circumstances does not necessarily result in a violation. For example, a lawyer who has sold the practice to accept an appointment to judicial office does not violate the requirement that the sale be attendant to cessation of practice if the lawyer later resumes private practice upon being defeated in a contested or a retention election for the office or resigns from a judiciary position.

[3] The requirement that the seller cease to engage in the private practice of law does not prohibit employment as a lawyer on the staff of a public agency or a legal services entity that provides legal services to the poor, or as in-house counsel to a business.

[4] The Rule permits a sale of an entire practice attendant upon retirement from the private practice of law within the jurisdiction. Its provisions, therefore, accommodate the lawyer who sells the practice on the occasion of moving to another state. Some states, like Illinois, are so large that a move from one locale therein to another is tantamount to leaving the jurisdiction in which the lawyer has engaged in the practice of law. To also accommodate lawyers so situated, the Rule also permits the sale of the practice when the lawyer leaves the geographic area rather than the jurisdiction. In such cases, it is advisable for the parties' agreement to define the geographic area.

[5] Reserved.

Sale of Entire Practice

[6] The Rule requires that the seller's entire practice be sold. The prohibition against sale of less than an entire practice protects those clients whose matters are less lucrative and who might find it difficult to secure other counsel if a sale could be limited to substantial fee-generating matters. The purchasers are required to undertake all client matters in the practice, subject to client consent. This requirement is satisfied, however, even if a purchaser is unable to undertake a particular client matter because of a conflict of interest.

Client Confidences, Consent and Notice

[7] Negotiations between seller and prospective purchaser prior to disclosure of information relating to a specific representation of an identifiable client no more violate the confidentiality provisions of Model Rule 1.6 than do preliminary discussions concerning the possible association of another lawyer or mergers between firms, with respect to which client consent is not required. See Rule 1.6(b)(7). Providing the purchaser access to information beyond that allowed by Rule 1.6(b)(7), such as the client's file, requires client consent. The Rule provides that before such information can be disclosed by the seller to the purchaser the client must be given actual written notice of the contemplated sale, including the identity of the purchaser, and must be told that the decision to consent or make other arrangements must be made within 90 days. If nothing is heard from the client within that time, consent to the sale is presumed.

[8] A lawyer or law firm ceasing to practice cannot be required to remain in practice because some clients cannot be given actual notice of the proposed purchase. Since these clients cannot themselves consent to the purchase or direct any other disposition of their files, the Rule requires an order from a court having jurisdiction authorizing their transfer or other disposition. The Court can be expected to determine whether reasonable efforts to locate the client have been exhausted, and whether the absent client's legitimate interests will be served by authorizing the transfer of the file so that the purchaser may continue the representation. Preservation of client confidences requires that the petition for a court order be considered *in camera*.

[9] All elements of client autonomy, including the client's absolute right to discharge a lawyer and transfer the representation to another, survive the sale of the practice.

Fee Arrangements Between Client and Purchaser

[10] The sale may not be financed by increases in fees charged the clients of the practice. Existing arrangements between the seller and the client as to fees and the scope of the work must be honored by the purchaser.

Other Applicable Ethical Standards

[11] Lawyers participating in the sale of a law practice are subject to the ethical standards applicable to involving another lawyer in the representation of a client. These include, for example, the seller's obligation to exercise competence in identifying a purchaser qualified to assume the practice and the purchaser's obligation to undertake the representation competently (see Rule 1.1); the obligation to avoid disqualifying conflicts, and to secure the client's informed consent for those conflicts that can be agreed to (see Rule 1.7 regarding conflicts and Rule 1.0(e) for the definition of informed consent); and the obligation to protect information relating to the representation (see Rules 1.6 and 1.9).

[12] If approval of the substitution of the purchasing lawyer for the selling lawyer is required by the rules of any tribunal in which a matter is pending, such approval must be obtained before the matter can be included in the sale (see Rule 1.16).

Applicability of the Rule

[13] This Rule includes the sale of a law practice of a deceased or disabled lawyer. Thus, the seller may be represented by a nonlawyer representative not subject to these Rules. Since, however, no lawyer may participate in a sale of a law practice which does not conform to the requirements of this Rule, the representatives of the seller as well as the purchasing lawyer can be expected to see to it that they are met.

[14] Admission to or retirement from a law partnership or professional association, retirement plans and similar arrangements, and a sale of tangible assets of a law practice, do not constitute a sale or purchase governed by this Rule.

[15] This Rule does not apply to the transfers of legal representation between lawyers when such transfers are unrelated to the sale of a practice.

Comment adopted July 1, 2009, effective Jan. 1, 2010. Amended Oct. 15, 2015, eff. Jan. 1, 2016.

Rule 1.18. Duties to Prospective Client

(a) A person who consults with a lawyer about the possibility of forming a client-lawyer relationship with respect to a matter is a prospective client.

(b) Even when no client-lawyer relationship ensues, a lawyer who has learned information from a prospective client shall not use or reveal that information, except as Rule 1.9 would permit with respect to information of a former client.

(c) A lawyer subject to paragraph (b) shall not represent a client with interests materially adverse to those of a prospective client in the same or a substantially related matter if the lawyer received information from the prospective client that could be significantly harmful to that person in the matter, except as provided in paragraph (d). If a lawyer is disqualified from representation under this paragraph, no lawyer in a firm with which that lawyer is associated may knowingly undertake or continue representation in such a matter, except as provided in paragraph (d).

(d) When the lawyer has received disqualifying information as defined in paragraph (c), representation is permissible if:

(1) both the affected client and the prospective client have given informed consent, or

(2) the lawyer who received the information took reasonable measures to avoid exposure to more disqualifying information than was reasonably necessary to determine whether to represent the prospective client; and that lawyer is timely screened from any participation in the matter and is apportioned no part of the fee therefrom.

Adopted July 1, 2009, eff. Jan. 1, 2010. Amended Oct. 15, 2015, eff. Jan. 1, 2016.

Comment

[1] Prospective clients, like clients, may disclose information to a lawyer, place documents or other property in the lawyer's custody, or rely on the lawyer's advice. A lawyer's consultations with a prospective client usually are limited in time and depth and leave both the prospective client and the lawyer free (and sometimes required) to proceed no further. Hence, prospective clients should receive some but not all of the protection afforded clients.

[2] Not all persons who communicate information to a lawyer are prospective clients. A person becomes a prospective client by consulting with a lawyer about the possibility of forming a client-lawyer relationship with respect to a matter. Whether communications, including written, oral, or electronic communications, constitute a consultation depends on the circumstances. For example, a consultation is likely to have occurred if a lawyer, either in person or through the lawyer's advertising in any medium, specifically requests or invites the submission of information about a potential representation without clear and reasonably understandable warnings and cautionary statements that limit the lawyer's obligations, and a person provides information in response. See also Comment [4]. In contrast, a consultation does not occur if a person provides information to a lawyer in response to advertising that merely describes the lawyer's education, experience, areas of practice, and contact information, or provides legal information of general interest. A person who communicates information unilaterally to a lawyer, without any reasonable expectation that the lawyer is willing to discuss the possibility of forming a client-lawyer relationship, is not a "prospective client." Moreover, a person who communicates with a lawyer for the purpose of disqualifying the lawyer is not a "prospective client."

[3] It is often necessary for a prospective client to reveal information to the lawyer during an initial consultation prior to the decision about formation of a client-lawyer relationship. The lawyer often must learn such information to determine whether there is a conflict of interest with an existing client and whether the matter is one that the lawyer is willing to undertake. Paragraph (b) prohibits the lawyer from using or revealing that information, except as permitted by Rule 1.9, even if the client or lawyer decides not to proceed with the representation. The duty exists regardless of how brief the initial conference may be.

[4] In order to avoid acquiring disqualifying information from a prospective client, a lawyer considering whether or not to undertake a new matter should limit the initial consultation to only such information as reasonably appears necessary for that purpose. Where the information indicates that a conflict of interest or other reason for non-representation exists, the lawyer should so inform the prospective client or decline the representation. If the prospective client wishes to retain the lawyer, and if consent is possible under Rule 1.7, then consent from all affected present or former clients must be obtained before accepting the representation.

[5] A lawyer may condition a consultation with a prospective client on the person's informed consent that no information disclosed during the consultation will prohibit the lawyer from representing a different client in the matter. See Rule 1.0(e) for the definition of informed consent. If the agreement expressly so provides, the prospective client may also consent to the lawyer's subsequent use of information received from the prospective client.

[6] Even in the absence of an agreement, under paragraph (c), the lawyer is not prohibited from representing a client with interests adverse to those of the prospective client in the same or a substantially related matter unless the lawyer has received from the prospective client information that could be significantly harmful if used in the matter.

[7] Under paragraph (c), the prohibition in this Rule is imputed to other lawyers as provided in Rule 1.10, but, under paragraph (d)(1), imputation may be avoided if the lawyer obtains the informed consent of both the prospective and affected clients. In the alternative, imputation may be avoided if the conditions of paragraph (d)(2) are met and all dis-

qualified lawyers are timely screened. See Rule 1.0(k) (requirements for screening procedures). Paragraph (d)(2) does not prohibit the screened lawyer from receiving a salary or partnership share established by independent agreement, but that lawyer may not receive compensation directly related to the matter in which the lawyer is disqualified.

[8] Reserved.

[9] For the duty of competence of a lawyer who gives assistance on the merits of a matter to a prospective client, see Rule 1.1. For a lawyer's duties when a prospective client entrusts valuables or papers to the lawyer's care, see Rule 1.15.

Comment adopted July 1, 2009, eff. Jan. 1, 2010. Amended Oct. 15, 2015, eff. Jan. 1, 2016.

Rule 2.1. Advisor

In representing a client, a lawyer shall exercise independent professional judgment and render candid advice. In rendering advice, a lawyer may refer not only to law but to other considerations such as moral, economic, social and political factors, that may be relevant to the client's situation.

Adopted Feb. 8, 1990, eff. Aug. 1, 1990. Revised July 1, 2009, eff. Jan. 1, 2010.

Comment

Scope of Advice

[1] A client is entitled to straightforward advice expressing the lawyer's honest assessment. Legal advice often involves unpleasant facts and alternatives that a client may be disinclined to confront. In presenting advice, a lawyer endeavors to sustain the client's morale and may put advice in as acceptable a form as honesty permits. However, a lawyer should not be deterred from giving candid advice by the prospect that the advice will be unpalatable to the client.

[2] Advice couched in narrow legal terms may be of little value to a client, especially where practical considerations, such as cost or effects on other people, are predominant. Purely technical legal advice, therefore, can sometimes be inadequate. It is proper for a lawyer to refer to relevant moral and ethical considerations in giving advice. Although a lawyer is not a moral advisor as such, moral and ethical considerations impinge upon most legal questions and may decisively influence how the law will be applied.

[3] A client may expressly or impliedly ask the lawyer for purely technical advice. When such a request is made by a client experienced in legal matters, the lawyer may accept it at face value. When such a request is made by a client inexperienced in legal matters, however, the lawyer's responsibility as advisor may include indicating that more may be involved than strictly legal considerations.

[4] Matters that go beyond strictly legal questions may also be in the domain of another profession. Family matters can involve problems within the professional competence of psychiatry, clinical psychology or social work; business matters can involve problems within the competence of the accounting profession or of financial specialists. Where consultation with a professional in another field is itself something a competent lawyer would recommend, the lawyer should make such a recommendation. At the same time, a lawyer's advice at its best often consists of recommending a course of action in the face of conflicting recommendations of experts.

Offering Advice

[5] In general, a lawyer is not expected to give advice until asked by the client. However, when a lawyer knows that a client proposes a course of action that is likely to result in substantial adverse legal consequences to the client, the lawyer's duty to the client under Rule 1.4 may require that the lawyer offer advice if the client's course of action is related to the representation. A lawyer ordinarily has no duty to initiate investigation of a client's affairs or to give advice that the client has indicated is unwanted, but a lawyer may initiate advice to a client when doing so appears to be in the client's interest.

Rule 2.2. Reserved

Rule 2.3. Evaluation for Use by Third Persons

(a) A lawyer may provide an evaluation of a matter affecting a client for the use of someone other than the client if the lawyer reasonably believes that making the evaluation is compatible with other aspects of the lawyer's relationship with the client.

(b) When the lawyer knows or reasonably should know that the evaluation is likely to affect the client's interests materially and adversely, the lawyer shall not provide the evaluation unless the client gives informed consent.

(c) Except as disclosure is authorized in connection with a report of an evaluation, information relating to the evaluation is otherwise protected by Rule 1.6.

Adopted July 1, 2009, eff. Jan. 1, 2010.

Comment

Definition

[1] An evaluation may be performed at the client's direction or when impliedly authorized in order to carry out the representation. See Rule 1.2. Such an evaluation may be for the primary purpose of establishing information for the benefit of third parties; for example, an opinion concerning the title of property rendered at the behest of a vendor for the information of a prospective purchaser, or at the behest of a borrower for the information of a prospective lender. In some situations, the evaluation may be required by a government agency; for example, an opinion concerning the legality of the securities registered for sale under the securities laws. In other instances, the evaluation may be required by a third person, such as a purchaser of a business.

[2] A legal evaluation should be distinguished from an investigation of a person with whom the lawyer does not have a client-lawyer relationship.

For example, a lawyer retained by a purchaser to analyze a vendor's title to property does not have a client-lawyer relationship with the vendor. So also, an investigation into a person's affairs by a government lawyer, or by special counsel by a government lawyer, or by special counsel employed by the government, is not an evaluation as that term is used in this Rule. The question is whether the lawyer is retained by the person whose affairs are being examined. When the lawyer is retained by that person, the general rules concerning loyalty to client and preservation of confidences apply, which is not the case if the lawyer is retained by someone else. For this reason, it is essential to identify the person by whom the lawyer is retained. This should be made clear not only to the person under examination, but also to others to whom the results are to be made available.

Duties Owed to Third Person and Client

[3] When the evaluation is intended for the information or use of a third person, a legal duty to that person may or may not arise. That legal question is beyond the scope of this Rule. However, since such an evaluation involves a departure from the normal client-lawyer relationship, careful analysis of the situation is required. The lawyer must be satisfied as a matter of professional judgment that making the evaluation is compatible with other functions undertaken in behalf of the client. For example, if the lawyer is acting as advocate in defending the client against charges of fraud, it would normally be incompatible with that responsibility for the lawyer to perform an evaluation for others concerning the same or a related transaction. Assuming no such impediment is apparent, however, the lawyer should advise the client of the implications of the evaluation, particularly the lawyer's responsibilities to third persons and the duty to disseminate the findings.

Access to and Disclosure of Information

[4] The quality of an evaluation depends on the freedom and extent of the investigation upon which it is based. Ordinarily a lawyer should have whatever latitude of investigation seems necessary as a matter of professional judgment. Under some circumstances, however, the terms of the evaluation may be limited. For example, certain issues or sources may be categorically excluded, or the scope of search may be limited by time constraints or the noncooperation of persons having relevant information. Any such limitations that are material to the evaluation should be described in the report. If after a lawyer has commenced an evaluation, the client refuses to comply with the terms upon which it was understood the evaluation was to have been made, the lawyer's obligations are determined by law, having reference to the terms of the client's agreement and the surrounding circumstances. In no circumstances is the lawyer permitted to knowingly make a false statement of material fact or law in providing an evaluation under this Rule. See Rule 4.1.

Obtaining Client's Informed Consent

[5] Information relating to an evaluation is protected by Rule 1.6. In many situations, providing an evaluation to a third party poses no significant risk to the client; thus, the lawyer may be impliedly authorized to disclose information to carry out the representation. See Rule 1.6(a). Where, however, it is reasonably likely that providing the evaluation will affect the client's interests materially and adversely, the lawyer must first obtain the client's consent after the client has been adequately informed concerning the important possible effects on the client's interests. See Rules 1.6(a) and 1.0(e).

Financial Auditors' Requests for Information

[6] When a question concerning the legal situation of a client arises at the instance of the client's financial auditor and the question is referred to the lawyer, the lawyer's response may be made in accordance with procedures recognized in the legal profession. Such a procedure is set forth in the American Bar Association Statement of Policy Regarding Lawyers' Responses to Auditors' Requests for Information, adopted in 1975.

Rule 2.4. Lawyer Serving As Third–Party Neutral

(a) A lawyer serves as a third-party neutral when the lawyer assists two or more persons who are not clients of the lawyer to reach a resolution of a dispute or other matter that has arisen between them. Service as a third-party neutral may include service as an arbitrator, a mediator or in such other capacity as will enable the lawyer to assist the parties to resolve the matter.

(b) A lawyer serving as a third-party neutral shall inform unrepresented parties that the lawyer is not representing them and shall explain to them the difference between the lawyer's role as a third-party neutral and a lawyer's role as one who represents a client.

Adopted July 1, 2009, eff. Jan. 1, 2010.

Comment

[1] Alternative dispute resolution has become a substantial part of the civil justice system. Aside from representing clients in dispute-resolution processes, lawyers often serve as third-party neutrals. A third-party neutral is a person, such as a mediator, arbitrator, conciliator or evaluator, who assists the parties, represented or unrepresented, in the resolution of a dispute or in the arrangement of a transaction. Whether a third-party neutral serves primarily as a facilitator, evaluator or decisionmaker depends on the particular process that is either selected by the parties or mandated by a court.

[2] The role of a third-party neutral is not unique to lawyers, although, in some court-connected contexts, only lawyers are allowed to serve in this role or to handle certain types of cases. In performing this role, the lawyer may be subject to court rules or other law that apply either to third-party neutrals generally or to lawyers serving as third-party neutrals. Lawyer-neutrals may also be subject to various codes of ethics.

[3] Unlike nonlawyers who serve as third-party neutrals, lawyers serving in this role may experience unique problems as a result of differences between the role of a third-party neutral and a lawyer's service as a client representative. The potential for confusion is significant when the parties are unrepresented in the process. Thus, paragraph (b) requires a lawyer-neutral to inform unrepresented parties that the lawyer is not representing them. For some parties, particularly parties who frequently use dispute-resolution processes, this information will be sufficient. For others, particularly those who are using the process for the first time, more information will be required. The lawyer should inform unrepresented parties of the important differences between the lawyer's role as third-party neutral and a lawyer's role as a client representative, including the inapplicability of the attorney-client evidentiary privilege. The extent of disclosure required under this paragraph will depend on the particular parties involved and the subject matter of the proceeding, as well as the particular features of the dispute-resolution process selected.

[4] A lawyer who serves as a third-party neutral subsequently may be asked to serve as a lawyer representing a client in the same matter. The conflicts of interest that arise for both the individual lawyer and the lawyer's law firm are addressed in Rule 1.12.

[5] Lawyers who represent clients in alternative dispute-resolution processes are governed by the Rules of Professional Conduct. When the dispute-resolution process takes place before a tribunal, as in binding arbitration (see Rule 1.0(m)), the lawyer's duty of candor is governed by Rule 3.3. Otherwise, the lawyer's duty of candor toward both the third-party neutral and other parties is governed by Rule 4.1.

Rule 3.1.   Meritorious Claims and Contentions

A lawyer shall not bring or defend a proceeding, or assert or controvert an issue therein, unless there is a basis in law and fact for doing so that is not frivolous, which includes a good-faith argument for an extension, modification or reversal of existing law. A lawyer for the defendant in a criminal proceeding, or the respondent in a proceeding that could result in incarceration, may nevertheless so defend the proceeding as to require that every element of the case be established.
Adopted July 1, 2009, eff. Jan. 1, 2010.

Comment

[1] The advocate has a duty to use legal procedure for the fullest benefit of the client's cause, but also a duty not to abuse legal procedure. The law, both procedural and substantive, establishes the limits within which an advocate may proceed. However, the law is not always clear and never is static. Accordingly, in determining the proper scope of advocacy, account must be taken of the law's ambiguities and potential for change.

[2] The filing of an action or defense or similar action taken for a client is not frivolous merely because the facts have not first been fully substantiated or because the lawyer expects to develop vital evidence only by discovery. What is required of lawyers, however, is that they inform themselves about the facts of their clients' cases and the applicable law and determine that they can make good-faith arguments in support of their clients' positions. Such action is not frivolous even though the lawyer believes that the client's position ultimately will not prevail. The action is frivolous, however, if the lawyer is unable either to make a good-faith argument on the merits of the action taken or to support the action taken by a good-faith argument for an extension, modification or reversal of existing law.

[3] The lawyer's obligations under this Rule are subordinate to federal or state constitutional law that entitles a defendant in a criminal matter to the assistance of counsel in presenting a claim or contention that otherwise would be prohibited by this Rule.

Rule 3.2.   Expediting Litigation

A lawyer shall make reasonable efforts to expedite litigation consistent with the interests of the client.
Adopted July 1, 2009, eff. Jan. 1, 2010.

Comment

[1] Dilatory practices bring the administration of justice into disrepute. Although there will be occasions when a lawyer may properly seek a postponement for personal reasons, it is not proper for a lawyer to routinely fail to expedite litigation solely for the convenience of the advocates. Nor will a failure to expedite be reasonable if done for the purpose of frustrating an opposing party's attempt to obtain rightful redress or repose. It is not a justification that similar conduct is often tolerated by the bench and bar. The question is whether a competent lawyer acting in good faith would regard the course of action as having some substantial purpose other than delay. Realizing financial or other benefit from otherwise improper delay in litigation is not a legitimate interest of the client.

Rule 3.3.   Candor Toward the Tribunal

(a) A lawyer shall not knowingly:

(1) make a false statement of fact or law to a tribunal or fail to correct a false statement of material fact or law previously made to the tribunal by the lawyer;

(2) fail to disclose to the tribunal legal authority in the controlling jurisdiction known to the lawyer to be directly adverse to the position of the client and not disclosed by opposing counsel; or

(3) offer evidence that the lawyer knows to be false. If a lawyer, the lawyer's client, or a witness called by the lawyer, has offered material evidence and the lawyer comes to know of its falsity, the lawyer shall take reasonable remedial measures, including, if necessary, disclosure to the tribunal. A lawyer may refuse to offer evidence, other than the testimony of a

defendant in a criminal matter, that the lawyer reasonably believes is false.

(b) A lawyer who represents a client in an adjudicative proceeding and who knows that a person intends to engage, is engaging or has engaged in criminal or fraudulent conduct related to the proceeding shall take reasonable remedial measures, including, if necessary, disclosure to the tribunal.

(c) The duties stated in paragraphs (a) and (b) continue to the conclusion of the proceeding, and apply even if compliance requires disclosure of information otherwise protected by Rule 1.6.

(d) In an *ex parte* proceeding, a lawyer shall inform the tribunal of all material facts known to the lawyer that will enable the tribunal to make an informed decision, whether or not the facts are adverse.

Adopted July 1, 2009, eff. Jan. 1, 2010.

Comment

[1] This Rule governs the conduct of a lawyer who is representing a client in the proceedings of a tribunal. See Rule 1.0(m) for the definition of "tribunal." It also applies when the lawyer is representing a client in an ancillary proceeding conducted pursuant to the tribunal's adjudicative authority, such as a deposition. Thus, for example, paragraph (a)(3) requires a lawyer to take reasonable remedial measures if the lawyer comes to know that a client who is testifying in a deposition has offered evidence that is false.

[2] This Rule sets forth the special duties of lawyers as officers of the court to avoid conduct that undermines the integrity of the adjudicative process. A lawyer acting as an advocate in an adjudicative proceeding has an obligation to present the client's case with persuasive force. Performance of that duty while maintaining confidences of the client, however, is qualified by the advocate's duty of candor to the tribunal. Consequently, although a lawyer in an adversary proceeding is not required to present an impartial exposition of the law or to vouch for the evidence submitted in a cause, the lawyer must not allow the tribunal to be misled by false statements of law or fact or evidence that the lawyer knows to be false.

Representations by a Lawyer

[3] An advocate is responsible for pleadings and other documents prepared for litigation, but is usually not required to have personal knowledge of matters asserted therein, for litigation documents ordinarily present assertions by the client, or by someone on the client's behalf, and not assertions by the lawyer. Compare Rule 3.1. However, an assertion purporting to be on the lawyer's own knowledge, as in an affidavit by the lawyer or in a statement in open court, may properly be made only when the lawyer knows the assertion is true or believes it to be true on the basis of a reasonably diligent inquiry. There are circumstances where failure to make a disclosure is the equivalent of an affirmative misrepresentation. The obligation prescribed in Rule 1.2(d) not to counsel a client to commit or assist the client in committing a fraud

applies in litigation. Regarding compliance with Rule 1.2(d), see the Comment to that Rule. See also the Comment to Rule 8.4 (b).

Legal Argument

[4] Legal argument based on a knowingly false representation of law constitutes dishonesty toward the tribunal. A lawyer is not required to make a disinterested exposition of the law, but must recognize the existence of pertinent legal authorities. Furthermore, as stated in paragraph (a)(2), an advocate has a duty to disclose directly adverse authority in the controlling jurisdiction that has not been disclosed by the opposing party. The underlying concept is that legal argument is a discussion seeking to determine the legal premises properly applicable to the case.

Offering Evidence

[5] Paragraph (a)(3) requires that the lawyer refuse to offer evidence that the lawyer knows to be false, regardless of the client's wishes. This duty is premised on the lawyer's obligation as an officer of the court to prevent the trier of fact from being misled by false evidence. A lawyer does not violate this Rule if the lawyer offers the evidence for the purpose of establishing its falsity.

[6] If a lawyer knows that the client intends to testify falsely or wants the lawyer to introduce false evidence, the lawyer should seek to persuade the client that the evidence should not be offered. If the persuasion is ineffective and the lawyer continues to represent the client, the lawyer must refuse to offer the false evidence. If only a portion of a witness's testimony will be false, the lawyer may call the witness to testify but may not elicit or otherwise permit the witness to present the testimony that the lawyer knows is false.

[7] The duties stated in paragraphs (a) and (b) apply to all lawyers, including defense counsel in criminal cases. In some jurisdictions, however, courts have required counsel to present the accused as a witness or to give a narrative statement if the accused so desires, even if counsel knows that the testimony or statement will be false. The obligation of the advocate under the Rules of Professional Conduct is subordinate to such requirements. See also Comment [9].

[8] The prohibition against offering false evidence only applies if the lawyer knows that the evidence is false. A lawyer's reasonable belief that evidence is false does not preclude its presentation to the trier of fact. A lawyer's knowledge that evidence is false, however, can be inferred from the circumstances. See Rule 1.0(f). Thus, although a lawyer should resolve doubts about the veracity of testimony or other evidence in favor of the client, the lawyer cannot ignore an obvious falsehood.

[9] Although paragraph (a)(3) only prohibits a lawyer from offering evidence the lawyer knows to be false, it permits the lawyer to refuse to offer testimony or other proof that the lawyer reasonably believes is false. Offering such proof may reflect adversely on the lawyer's ability to discriminate in the quality of evidence and thus impair the lawyer's effectiveness as an advocate. Because of the special protections historically provided criminal defen-

dants, however, this Rule does not permit a lawyer to refuse to offer the testimony of such a client where the lawyer reasonably believes but does not know that the testimony will be false. Unless the lawyer knows the testimony will be false, the lawyer must honor the client's decision to testify. See also Comment [7].

Remedial Measures

[10] Having offered material evidence in the belief that it was true, a lawyer may subsequently come to know that the evidence is false. Or, a lawyer may be surprised when the lawyer's client, or another witness called by the lawyer, offers testimony the lawyer knows to be false, either during the lawyer's direct examination or in response to cross-examination by the opposing lawyer. In such situations or if the lawyer knows of the falsity of testimony elicited from the client during a deposition, the lawyer must take reasonable remedial measures. In such situations, the advocate's proper course is to remonstrate with the client confidentially, advise the client of the lawyer's duty of candor to the tribunal and seek the client's cooperation with respect to the withdrawal or correction of the false statements or evidence. If that fails, the advocate must take further remedial action. If withdrawal from the representation is not permitted or will not undo the effect of the false evidence, the advocate must make such disclosure to the tribunal as is reasonably necessary to remedy the situation, even if doing so requires the lawyer to reveal information that otherwise would be protected by Rule 1.6. It is for the tribunal then to determine what should be done-making a statement about the matter to the trier of fact, ordering a mistrial or perhaps nothing.

[11] The disclosure of a client's false testimony can result in grave consequences to the client, including not only a sense of betrayal but also loss of the case and perhaps a prosecution for perjury. But the alternative is that the lawyer cooperate in deceiving the court, thereby subverting the truth-finding process which the adversary system is designed to implement. See Rule 1.2(d). Furthermore, unless it is clearly understood that the lawyer will act upon the duty to disclose the existence of false evidence, the client can simply reject the lawyer's advice to reveal the false evidence and insist that the lawyer keep silent. Thus the client could in effect coerce the lawyer into being a party to fraud on the court.

Preserving Integrity of Adjudicative Process

[12] Lawyers have a special obligation to protect a tribunal against criminal or fraudulent conduct that undermines the integrity of the adjudicative process, such as bribing, intimidating or otherwise unlawfully communicating with a witness, juror, court official or other participant in the proceeding, unlawfully destroying or concealing documents or other evidence or failing to disclose information to the tribunal when required by law to do so. Thus, paragraph (b) requires a lawyer to take reasonable remedial measures, including disclosure if necessary, whenever the lawyer knows that a person, including the lawyer's client, intends to engage, is engaging or has engaged in criminal or fraudulent conduct related to the proceeding.

Duration of Obligation

[13] A practical time limit on the obligation to rectify false evidence or false statements of law and fact has to be established. The conclusion of the proceeding is a reasonably definite point for the termination of the obligation. A proceeding has concluded within the meaning of this Rule when a final judgment in the proceeding has been affirmed on appeal or the time for review has passed.

***Ex Parte* Proceedings**

[14] Ordinarily, an advocate has the limited responsibility of presenting one side of the matters that a tribunal should consider in reaching a decision; the conflicting position is expected to be presented by the opposing party. However, in any *ex parte* proceeding, such as an application for a temporary restraining order, there is no balance of presentation by opposing advocates. The object of an *ex parte* proceeding is nevertheless to yield a substantially just result. The judge has an affirmative responsibility to accord the absent party just consideration. The lawyer for the represented party has the correlative duty to make disclosures of material facts known to the lawyer and that the lawyer reasonably believes are necessary to an informed decision.

Withdrawal

[15] Normally, a lawyer's compliance with the duty of candor imposed by this Rule does not require that the lawyer withdraw from the representation of a client whose interests will be or have been adversely affected by the lawyer's disclosure. The lawyer may, however, be required by Rule 1.16(a) to seek permission of the tribunal to withdraw if the lawyer's compliance with this Rule's duty of candor results in such an extreme deterioration of the client-lawyer relationship that the lawyer can no longer competently represent the client. Also see Rule 1.16(b) for the circumstances in which a lawyer will be permitted to seek a tribunal's permission to withdraw. In connection with a request for permission to withdraw that is premised on a client's misconduct, a lawyer may reveal information relating to the representation only to the extent reasonably necessary to comply with this Rule or as otherwise permitted by Rule 1.6.

Rule 3.4. Fairness to Opposing Party and Counsel

A lawyer shall not:

(a) unlawfully obstruct another party's access to evidence or unlawfully alter, destroy or conceal a document or other material having potential evidentiary value. A lawyer shall not counsel or assist another person to do any such act;

(b) falsify evidence, counsel or assist a witness to testify falsely, or offer an inducement to a witness that is prohibited by law;

(c) knowingly disobey an obligation under the rules of a tribunal, except for an open refusal based on an assertion that no valid obligation exists;

(d) in pretrial procedure, make a frivolous discovery request or fail to make reasonably diligent effort to comply with a legally proper discovery request by an opposing party;

(e) in trial, allude to any matter that the lawyer does not reasonably believe is relevant or that will not be supported by admissible evidence, assert personal knowledge of facts in issue except when testifying as a witness, or state a personal opinion as to the justness of a cause, the credibility of a witness, the culpability of a civil litigant or the guilt or innocence of an accused; or

(f) request a person other than a client to refrain from voluntarily giving relevant information to another party unless:

(1) the person is a relative or an employee or other agent of a client; and

(2) the lawyer reasonably believes that the person's interests will not be adversely affected by refraining from giving such information.

Adopted July 1, 2009, eff. Jan. 1, 2010.

Comment

[1] The procedure of the adversary system contemplates that the evidence in a case is to be marshalled competitively by the contending parties. Fair competition in the adversary system is secured by prohibitions against destruction or concealment of evidence, improperly influencing witnesses, obstructive tactics in discovery procedure, and the like.

[2] Documents and other items of evidence are often essential to establish a claim or defense. Subject to evidentiary privileges, the right of an opposing party, including the government, to obtain evidence through discovery or subpoena is an important procedural right. The exercise of that right can be frustrated if relevant material is altered, concealed or destroyed. Applicable law in many jurisdictions makes it an offense to destroy material for purpose of impairing its availability in a pending proceeding or one whose commencement can be foreseen. Falsifying evidence is also generally a criminal offense. Paragraph (a) applies to evidentiary material generally, including computerized information. Applicable law may permit a lawyer to take temporary possession of physical evidence of client crimes for the purpose of conducting a limited examination that will not alter or destroy material characteristics of the evidence. In such a case, applicable law may require the lawyer to turn the evidence over to the police or other prosecuting authority, depending on the circumstances.

[3] With regard to paragraph (b), it is not improper for a lawyer to pay a witness or prospective witness the reasonable expenses incurred in providing evidence or to compensate an expert witness on terms permitted by law. Expenses paid to a witness or prospective witness may include reimbursement for reasonable charges for travel to the place of a deposition or hearing or to the place of consultation with the lawyer and for reasonable related out-of-pocket costs, such as for hotel, meals, or child care, as well as compensation for the reasonable value of time spent attending a deposition or hearing or in consulting with the lawyer. An offer or payment of expenses may not be contingent on the content of the testimony or the outcome of the litigation, or otherwise prohibited by law.

[4] Paragraph (f) permits a lawyer to advise employees of a client to refrain from giving information to another party, for the employees may identify their interests with those of the client. See also Rule 4.2.

Rule 3.5. Impartiality and Decorum of the Tribunal

A lawyer shall not:

(a) seek to influence a judge, juror, prospective juror or other official by means prohibited by law;

(b) communicate *ex parte* with such a person during the proceeding unless authorized to do so by law or court order;

(c) communicate with a juror or prospective juror after discharge of the jury if:

(1) the communication is prohibited by law or court order;

(2) the juror has made known to the lawyer a desire not to communicate; or

(3) the communication involves misrepresentation, coercion, duress or harassment; or

(d) engage in conduct intended to disrupt a tribunal.

Adopted July 1, 2009, eff. Jan. 1, 2010.

Comment

[1] Many forms of improper influence upon a tribunal are proscribed by criminal law. Others are specified in the Illinois Code of Judicial Conduct, with which an advocate should be familiar. A lawyer is required to avoid contributing to a violation of such provisions. See Rule 8.4(f).

[2] During a proceeding a lawyer may not communicate *ex parte* with persons serving in an official capacity in the proceeding, such as judges, masters or jurors, unless authorized to do so by law or court order.

[3] A lawyer may on occasion want to communicate with a juror or prospective juror after the jury has been discharged. The lawyer may do so unless the communication is prohibited by law or a court order but must respect the desire of the juror not to talk with the lawyer. The lawyer may not engage in improper conduct during the communication.

[4] The advocate's function is to present evidence and argument so that the cause may be decided according to law. Refraining from abusive or obstreperous conduct is a corollary of the advocate's right to speak on behalf of litigants. A lawyer may stand firm against abuse by a judge but should avoid reciprocation; the judge's default is no justifi-

cation for similar dereliction by an advocate. An advocate can present the cause, protect the record for subsequent review and preserve professional integrity by patient firmness no less effectively than by belligerence or theatrics.

[5] The duty to refrain from disruptive conduct applies to any proceeding of a tribunal, including a deposition. See Rule 1.0(m).

Rule 3.6. Trial Publicity

(a) A lawyer who is participating or has participated in the investigation or litigation of a matter shall not make an extrajudicial statement that the lawyer knows or reasonably should know will be disseminated by means of public communication and would pose a serious and imminent threat to the fairness of an adjudicative proceeding in the matter.

(b) Notwithstanding paragraph (a), a lawyer may state:

(1) the claim, offense or defense involved and, except when prohibited by law, the identity of the persons involved;

(2) information contained in a public record;

(3) that an investigation of a matter is in progress;

(4) the scheduling or result of any step in litigation;

(5) a request for assistance in obtaining evidence and information necessary thereto;

(6) a warning of danger concerning the behavior of a person involved, when there is reason to believe that there exists the likelihood of substantial harm to an individual or to the public interest; and

(7) in a criminal case, in addition to subparagraphs (1) through (6):

(i) the identity, residence, occupation and family status of the accused;

(ii) if the accused has not been apprehended, information necessary to aid in apprehension of that person;

(iii) the fact, time and place of arrest; and

(iv) the identity of investigating and arresting officers or agencies and the length of the investigation.

(c) Notwithstanding paragraph (a), a lawyer may make a statement that a reasonable lawyer would believe is required to protect a client from the substantial undue prejudicial effect of recent publicity not initiated by the lawyer or the lawyer's client. A statement made pursuant to this paragraph shall be limited to such information as is necessary to mitigate the recent adverse publicity.

(d) No lawyer associated in a firm or government agency with a lawyer subject to paragraph (a) shall make a statement prohibited by paragraph (a).

Adopted July 1, 2009, eff. Jan. 1, 2010.

Comment

[1] It is difficult to strike a balance between protecting the right to a fair trial and safeguarding the right of free expression. Preserving the right to a fair trial necessarily entails some curtailment of the information that may be disseminated about a party prior to trial, particularly where trial by jury is involved. If there were no such limits, the result would be the practical nullification of the protective effect of the rules of forensic decorum and the exclusionary rules of evidence. On the other hand, there are vital social interests served by the free dissemination of information about events having legal consequences and about legal proceedings themselves. The public has a right to know about threats to its safety and measures aimed at assuring its security. It also has a legitimate interest in the conduct of judicial proceedings, particularly in matters of general public concern. Furthermore, the subject matter of legal proceedings is often of direct significance in debate and deliberation over questions of public policy.

[2] Special rules of confidentiality may validly govern proceedings in juvenile, domestic relations and mental disability proceedings, and perhaps other types of litigation. Rule 3.4(c) requires compliance with such rules.

[3] The Rule sets forth a basic general prohibition against a lawyer's making statements that the lawyer knows or should know would pose a serious and imminent threat to the fairness of an adjudicative proceeding. Recognizing that the public value of informed commentary is great and the likelihood of prejudice to a proceeding by the commentary of a lawyer who is not involved in the proceeding is small, the Rule applies only to lawyers who are, or who have been involved in the investigation or litigation of a case, and their associates.

[4] Paragraph (b) identifies specific matters about which a lawyer's statements would not ordinarily be considered to pose a serious and imminent threat to the fairness of an adjudicative proceeding, and should not in any event be considered prohibited by the general prohibition of paragraph (a). Paragraph (b) is not intended to be an exhaustive listing of the subjects upon which a lawyer may make a statement, but statements on other matters may be subject to paragraph (a).

[5] There are, on the other hand, certain subjects that would pose a serious and imminent threat to the fairness of a proceeding, particularly when they refer to a civil matter triable to a jury, a criminal matter, or any other proceeding that could result in incarceration. These subjects relate to:

(1) the character, credibility, reputation or criminal record of a party, suspect in a criminal investigation or witness, or the identity of a witness, or the expected testimony of a party or witness;

(2) in a criminal case or proceeding that could result in incarceration, the possibility of a plea of guilty to the offense or the existence or contents of any confession, admission, or statement given by a defendant or suspect or that person's refusal or failure to make a statement;

(3) the performance or results of any examination or test or the refusal or failure of a person to submit to an examination or test, or the identity or nature of physical evidence expected to be presented;

(4) any opinion as to the guilt or innocence of a defendant or suspect in a criminal case or proceeding that could result in incarceration;

(5) information that the lawyer knows or reasonably should know is likely to be inadmissible as evidence in a trial and that would, if disclosed, create a substantial risk of prejudicing an impartial trial; or

(6) the fact that a defendant has been charged with a crime, unless there is included therein a statement explaining that the charge is merely an accusation and that the defendant is presumed innocent until and unless proven guilty.

[6] Another relevant factor in determining prejudice is the nature of the proceeding involved. Criminal jury trials will be most sensitive to extrajudicial speech. Civil trials may be less sensitive. Nonjury hearings and arbitration proceedings may be even less affected. The Rule will still place limitations on prejudicial comments in these cases, but the likelihood of prejudice may be different depending on the type of proceeding.

[7] Finally, extrajudicial statements that might otherwise raise a question under this Rule may be permissible when they are made in response to statements made publicly by another party, another party's lawyer, or third persons, where a reasonable lawyer would believe a public response is required in order to avoid prejudice to the lawyer's client. When prejudicial statements have been publicly made by others, responsive statements may have the salutary effect of lessening any resulting adverse impact on the adjudicative proceeding. Such responsive statements should be limited to contain only such information as is necessary to mitigate undue prejudice created by the statements made by others.

[8] See Rule 3.8(f) for additional duties of prosecutors in connection with extrajudicial statements about criminal proceedings. *Cf. Devine v. Robinson*, 131 F. Supp. 2d 963 (N.D. Ill. 2001).

Rule 3.6 of the Rules of Professional Conduct was originally amended October 22, 1999, effective December 1, 1999; however, the Supreme Court of Illinois stayed the effect and enforcement of this rule until further order of the Court. The Supreme Court announced March 16, 2000, that the November order "staying the force and effect" of the October order "is lifted," and that the amended rules "are effective immediately."

Rule 3.7. Lawyer As Witness

(a) A lawyer shall not act as advocate at a trial in which the lawyer is likely to be a necessary witness unless:

(1) the testimony relates to an uncontested issue;

(2) the testimony relates to the nature and value of legal services rendered in the case; or

(3) disqualification of the lawyer would work substantial hardship on the client.

(b) A lawyer may act as advocate in a trial in which another lawyer in the lawyer's firm is likely to be called as a witness unless precluded from doing so by Rule 1.7 or Rule 1.9.

Adopted July 1, 2009, eff. Jan. 1, 2010.

Comment

[1] Combining the roles of advocate and witness can prejudice the tribunal and the opposing party and can also involve a conflict of interest between the lawyer and client.

Advocate–Witness Rule

[2] The tribunal has proper objection when the trier of fact may be confused or misled by a lawyer serving as both advocate and witness. The opposing party has proper objection where the combination of roles may prejudice that party's rights in the litigation. A witness is required to testify on the basis of personal knowledge, while an advocate is expected to explain and comment on evidence given by others. It may not be clear whether a statement by an advocate-witness should be taken as proof or as an analysis of the proof.

[3] To protect the tribunal, paragraph (a) prohibits a lawyer from simultaneously serving as advocate and necessary witness except in those circumstances specified in paragraphs (a)(1) through (a)(3). Paragraph (a)(1) recognizes that if the testimony will be uncontested, the ambiguities in the dual role are purely theoretical. Paragraph (a)(2) recognizes that where the testimony concerns the extent and value of legal services rendered in the action in which the testimony is offered, permitting the lawyers to testify avoids the need for a second trial with new counsel to resolve that issue. Moreover, in such a situation the judge has firsthand knowledge of the matter in issue; hence, there is less dependence on the adversary process to test the credibility of the testimony.

[4] Apart from these two exceptions, paragraph (a)(3) recognizes that a balancing is required between the interests of the client and those of the tribunal and the opposing party. Whether the tribunal is likely to be misled or the opposing party is likely to suffer prejudice depends on the nature of the case, the importance and probable tenor of the lawyer's testimony, and the probability that the lawyer's testimony will conflict with that of other witnesses. Even if there is risk of such prejudice, in determining whether the lawyer should be disqualified, due regard must be given to the effect of disqualification on the lawyer's client. It is relevant that one or both parties could reasonably foresee that the lawyer would probably be a witness. The conflict of interest principles stated in Rules 1.7, 1.9 and 1.10 have no application to this aspect of the problem.

[5] Because the tribunal is not likely to be misled when a lawyer acts as advocate in a trial in which another lawyer in the lawyer's firm will testify as a necessary witness, paragraph (b) permits the lawyer to do so except in situations involving a conflict of interest.

Conflict of Interest

[6] In determining if it is permissible to act as advocate in a trial in which the lawyer will be a necessary witness, the lawyer must also consider that the dual role may give rise to a conflict of interest that will require compliance with Rules 1.7 or 1.9. For example, if there is likely to be substantial conflict between the testimony of the client and that of the lawyer the representation involves a conflict of interest that requires compliance with Rule 1.7. This would be true even though the lawyer might not be prohibited by paragraph (a) from simultaneously serving as advocate and witness because the lawyer's disqualification would work a substantial hardship on the client. Similarly, a lawyer who might be permitted to simultaneously serve as an advocate and a witness by paragraph (a)(3) might be precluded from doing so by Rule 1.9. The problem can arise whether the lawyer is called as a witness on behalf of the client or is called by the opposing party. Determining whether or not such a conflict exists is primarily the responsibility of the lawyer involved. If there is a conflict of interest, the lawyer must secure the client's informed consent. In some cases, the lawyer will be precluded from seeking the client's consent. See Rule 1.7. See Rule 1.0(e) for the definition of "informed consent."

[7] Paragraph (b) provides that a lawyer is not disqualified from serving as an advocate because a lawyer with whom the lawyer is associated in a firm is precluded from doing so by paragraph (a). If, however, the testifying lawyer would also be disqualified by Rule 1.7 or Rule 1.9 from representing the client in the matter, other lawyers in the firm will be precluded from representing the client by Rule 1.10 unless the client gives informed consent under the conditions stated in Rule 1.7.

Rule 3.8. Special Responsibilities of a Prosecutor

The duty of a public prosecutor is to seek justice, not merely to convict. The prosecutor in a criminal case shall:

(a) refrain from prosecuting a charge that the prosecutor knows is not supported by probable cause;

(b) make reasonable efforts to assure that the accused has been advised of the right to, and the procedure for obtaining, counsel and has been given reasonable opportunity to obtain counsel;

(c) not seek to obtain from an unrepresented accused a waiver of important pretrial rights, such as the right to a preliminary hearing;

(d) make timely disclosure to the defense of all evidence or information known to the prosecutor that tends to negate the guilt of the accused or mitigates the offense, and, in connection with sentencing, disclose to the defense and to the tribunal all unprivileged mitigating information known to the prosecutor, except when the prosecutor is relieved of this responsibility by a protective order of the tribunal;

(e) not subpoena a lawyer in a grand jury or other criminal proceeding to present evidence about a past or present client unless the prosecutor reasonably believes:

(1) the information sought is not protected from disclosure by any applicable privilege;

(2) the evidence sought is essential to the successful completion of an ongoing investigation or prosecution; and

(3) there is no other feasible alternative to obtain the information;

(f) except for statements that are necessary to inform the public of the nature and extent of the prosecutor's action and that serve a legitimate law enforcement purpose, refrain from making extrajudicial comments that pose a serious and imminent threat of heightening public condemnation of the accused and exercise reasonable care to prevent investigators, law enforcement personnel, employees or other persons assisting or associated with the prosecutor in a criminal case from making an extrajudicial statement that the prosecutor would be prohibited from making under Rule 3.6 or this Rule.

(g) When a prosecutor knows of new, credible and material evidence creating a reasonable likelihood that a convicted defendant did not commit an offense of which the defendant was convicted, the prosecutor shall:

(1) promptly disclose that evidence to an appropriate court or authority, and

(2) if the conviction was obtained in the prosecutor's jurisdiction,

(i) promptly disclose that evidence to the defendant unless a court authorizes delay, and

(ii) undertake further reasonable investigation, or make reasonable efforts to cause an investigation, to determine whether the defendant was convicted of an offense that the defendant did not commit.

(h) When a prosecutor knows of clear and convincing evidence establishing that a defendant in the prosecutor's jurisdiction was convicted of an offense that the defendant did not commit, the prosecutor shall seek to remedy the conviction.

(i) A prosecutor's judgment, made in good faith, that evidence does not rise to the standards stated in paragraphs (g) or (h), though subsequently determined to have been erroneous, does not constitute a violation of this rule.

Adopted July 1, 2009, eff. Jan. 1, 2010. Amended Oct. 15, 2015, eff. Jan. 1, 2016.

Committee Comments

Special Supreme Court Committee on Capital Cases
(March 1, 2001)

Paragraph (a) of Rule 3.8 is substantially similar to Standard 3–1.2(c) of the American Bar Association (ABA) Standards for Criminal Justice (3d ed. 1993); however, paragraph (a) of Rule 3.8 restates a principle that is far older than the ABA standard. In 1924, the Illinois Supreme Court reversed a conviction for murder, noting that:

"The State's attorney in his official capacity is the representative of all the people, including the defendant, and it was as much his duty to safeguard the constitutional rights of the defendant as those of any other citizen." *People v. Cochran*, 313 Ill. 508, 526 (1924).

In 1935, the United States Supreme Court described the duty of a federal prosecutor in the following passage:

"The United States Attorney is the representative not of an ordinary party to a controversy, but of a sovereignty whose obligation to govern impartially is as compelling as its obligation to govern at all; and whose interest, therefore, in a criminal prosecution is not that it shall win a case, but that justice shall be done. As such, he is in a peculiar and very definite sense the servant of the law, the twofold aim of which is that guilt shall not escape or innocence suffer. He may prosecute with earnestness and vigor-indeed, he should do so. But, while he may strike hard blows, he is not at liberty to strike foul ones. It is as much his duty to refrain from improper methods calculated to produce a wrongful conviction as it is to use every legitimate means to bring about a just one." *Berger v. United States*, 295 U.S. 78, 88, 79 L. Ed. 1314, 1321, 55 S. Ct. 629, 633 (1935).

Paragraph (a) of Rule 3.8 does not set an exact standard, but one good prosecutors will readily recognize and have always adhered to in the discharge of their duties. Specific standards, such as those in Rules 3.3, 3. 4, 3.5, 3.6, the remaining paragraphs of Rule 3.8, and other applicable rules provide guidance for specific situations. Paragraph (a) of Rule 3.8 is intended to remind prosecutors that the touchstone of ethical conduct is the duty to act fairly, honestly, and honorably.

Comment

[1] A prosecutor has the responsibility of a minister of justice and not simply that of an advocate. This responsibility carries with it specific obligations to see that the defendant is accorded procedural justice and that guilt is decided upon the basis of sufficient evidence.

[1A] The first sentence of Rule 3.8 restates an established principle. In 1924, the Illinois Supreme Court reversed a conviction for murder, noting that:

"The state's attorney in his official capacity is the representative of all the people, including the defendant, and it was as much his duty to safeguard the constitutional rights of the defendant as those of any other citizen." *People v. Cochran*, 313 Ill. 508, 526 (1924).

In 1935, the United States Supreme Court described the duty of a federal prosecutor in the following passage:

"The United States Attorney is the representative not of an ordinary party to a controversy, but of a sovereignty whose obligation to govern impartially

is as compelling as its obligation to govern at all; and whose interest, therefore, in a criminal prosecution is not that it shall win a case, but that justice shall be done. As such, he is in a peculiar and very definite sense the servant of the law, the twofold aim of which is that guilt shall not escape or innocence suffer. He may prosecute with earnestness and vigor-indeed, he should do so. But, while he may strike hard blows, he is not at liberty to strike foul ones. It is as much his duty to refrain from improper methods calculated to produce a wrongful conviction as it is to use every legitimate means to bring about a just one." *Berger v. United States*, 295 U.S. 78, 88, 79 L. Ed. 1314, 1321, 55 S. Ct. 629, 633 (1935).

The first sentence of Rule 3.8 does not set an exact standard, but one good prosecutors will readily recognize and have always adhered to in the discharge of their duties. Specific standards, such as those in Rules 3.3, 3.4, 3.5, 3.6, the remaining paragraphs of Rule 3.8, and other applicable rules provide guidance for specific situations. Rule 3.8 is intended to remind prosecutors that the touchstone of ethical conduct is the duty to act fairly, honestly, and honorably.

[2] In Illinois, a defendant may waive a preliminary hearing and thereby lose a valuable opportunity to challenge probable cause. Accordingly, prosecutors should not seek to obtain waivers of preliminary hearings or other important pretrial rights from unrepresented accused persons. Paragraph (c) does not apply, however, to an accused appearing pro se with the approval of the tribunal. Nor does it forbid the lawful questioning of an uncharged suspect who has knowingly waived the rights to counsel and silence.

[3] The exception in paragraph (d) recognizes that a prosecutor may seek an appropriate protective order from the tribunal if disclosure of information to the defense could result in substantial harm to an individual or to the public interest.

[4] Paragraph (e) is intended to limit the issuance of lawyer subpoenas in grand jury and other criminal proceedings to those situations in which there is a genuine need to intrude into the client-lawyer relationship.

[5] Paragraph (f) supplements Rule 3.6, which prohibits extrajudicial statements that pose a serious and imminent threat of prejudicing an adjudicatory proceeding. In the context of a criminal prosecution, a prosecutor's extrajudicial statement can create the additional problem of increasing public condemnation of the accused. Although the announcement of an indictment, for example, will necessarily have severe consequences for the accused, a prosecutor can, and should, avoid comments which have no legitimate law enforcement purpose and have a substantial likelihood of increasing public opprobrium of the accused. Nothing in this Comment is intended to restrict the statements which a prosecutor may make which comply with Rule 3.6(b) or 3.6(c). *Cf. Devine v. Robinson*, 131 F. Supp. 2d 963 (N.D. Ill. 2001).

[6] Like other lawyers, prosecutors are subject to Rules 5.1 and 5.3, which relate to responsibilities

regarding lawyers and nonlawyers who work for or are associated with the lawyer's office. Paragraph (f) reminds the prosecutor of the importance of these obligations in connection with the unique dangers of improper extrajudicial statements in a criminal case. In addition, paragraph (f) requires a prosecutor to exercise reasonable care to prevent persons assisting or associated with the prosecutor from making improper extrajudicial statements, even when such persons are not under the direct supervision of the prosecutor. Ordinarily, the reasonable care standard will be satisfied if the prosecutor issues the appropriate cautions to law- enforcement personnel and other relevant individuals.

[7] When a prosecutor knows of new, credible and material evidence creating a reasonable likelihood that a person outside the prosecutor's jurisdiction was convicted of a crime that the person did not commit, paragraph (g) requires prompt disclosure to the court or other appropriate authority, such as the chief prosecutor where the conviction occurred. If the conviction was obtained in the prosecutor's jurisdiction, paragraph (g) requires the prosecutor to examine the evidence and undertake further reasonable investigation to determine whether the defendant is in fact innocent or make reasonable efforts to cause another appropriate authority to undertake the necessary investigation, and to promptly disclose the evidence to the court and, absent court-authorized delay, to the defendant. Consistent with the objectives of Rules 4.2 and 4.3, disclosure to a represented defendant must be made through the defendant's counsel, and, in the case of an unrepresented defendant, would ordinarily be accompanied by a request to a court for the appointment of counsel to assist the defendant in taking such legal measures as may be appropriate.

[8] Under paragraph (h), once the prosecutor knows of clear and convincing evidence that the defendant was convicted of an offense that the defendant did not commit, the prosecutor must seek to remedy the conviction. Necessary steps may include disclosure of the evidence to the defendant, requesting that the court appoint counsel for an unrepresented defendant and, where appropriate, notifying the court that the prosecutor has knowledge that the defendant did not commit the offense of which the defendant was convicted.

Comment adopted July 1, 2009, eff. Jan. 1, 2010. Amended Oct. 15, 2015, eff. Jan. 1, 2016.

Rule 3.8 of the Rules of Professional Conduct was originally amended October 22, 1999, effective December 1, 1999; however, the Supreme Court of Illinois stayed the effect and enforcement of this rule until further order of the Court. The Supreme Court announced March 16, 2000, that the November order "staying the force and effect" of the October order "is lifted," and that the amended rules "are effective immediately."

Rule 3.9. Advocate in Nonadjudicative Proceedings

A lawyer representing a client before a legislative body or administrative agency in a nonadjudicative proceeding shall disclose that the appearance is in a representative capacity and shall conform to the provisions of Rules 3.3(a) through (c) and 3.4(a) through (c).

Adopted July 1, 2009, eff. Jan. 1, 2010. Amended Nov. 23, 2009, eff. Jan. 1, 2010.

Comment

[1] In representation before bodies such as legislatures, municipal councils, and executive and administrative agencies acting in a rulemaking or policymaking capacity, lawyers present facts, formulate issues and advance argument in the matters under consideration. The decisionmaking body, like a court, should be able to rely on the integrity of the submissions made to it. A lawyer appearing before such a body must deal with it honestly and in conformity with applicable rules of procedure. See Rules 3.3(a) through (c) and 3.4(a) through (c).

[2] Lawyers have no exclusive right to appear before nonadjudicative bodies, as they do before a court. The requirements of this Rule therefore may subject lawyers to regulations inapplicable to advocates who are not lawyers. However, legislatures and administrative agencies have a right to expect lawyers to deal with them as they deal with courts.

[3] This Rule only applies when a lawyer represents a client in an official hearing or meeting of a governmental agency or a legislative body to which the lawyer or the lawyer's client is presenting evidence or argument. It does not apply to representation of a client in otherwise permitted lobbying activities, a negotiation or other bilateral transaction with a governmental agency or in connection with an application for a license or other privilege or the client's compliance with generally applicable reporting requirements, such as the filing of income-tax returns. Nor does it apply to the representation of a client in connection with an investigation or examination of the client's affairs conducted by government investigators or examiners. Representation in such matters is governed by Rules 4.1 through 4.4.

Rule 4.1. Truthfulness in Statements to Others

In the course of representing a client a lawyer shall not knowingly:

(a) make a false statement of material fact or law to a third person; or

(b) fail to disclose a material fact when disclosure is necessary to avoid assisting a criminal or fraudulent act by a client, unless disclosure is prohibited by Rule 1.6.

Adopted July 1, 2009, eff. Jan. 1, 2010.

Comment

Misrepresentation

[1] A lawyer is required to be truthful when dealing with others on a client's behalf, but generally has no affirmative duty to inform an opposing party of relevant facts. A misrepresentation can occur if the lawyer incorporates or affirms a statement of another person that the lawyer knows is

false. Misrepresentations can also occur by partially true but misleading statements or omissions that are the equivalent of affirmative false statements. For dishonest conduct that does not amount to a false statement or for misrepresentations by a lawyer other than in the course of representing a client, see Rule 8.4.

Statements of Fact

[2] This Rule refers to statements of fact as well as law. Whether a particular statement should be regarded as one of fact can depend on the circumstances. Under generally accepted conventions in negotiation, certain types of statements ordinarily are not taken as statements of material fact. Estimates of price or value placed on the subject of a transaction and a party's intentions as to an acceptable settlement of a claim are ordinarily in this category, and so is the existence of an undisclosed principal except where nondisclosure of the principal would constitute fraud. Lawyers should be mindful of their obligations under applicable law to avoid criminal and tortious misrepresentation.

Crime or Fraud by Client

[3] Under Rule 1.2(d), a lawyer is prohibited from counseling or assisting a client in conduct that the lawyer knows is criminal or fraudulent. Paragraph (b) states a specific application of the principle set forth in Rule 1.2(d) and addresses the situation where a client's crime or fraud takes the form of a lie or misrepresentation. Ordinarily, a lawyer can avoid assisting a client's crime or fraud by withdrawing from the representation. Sometimes it may be necessary for the lawyer to give notice of the fact of withdrawal and to disaffirm an opinion, document, affirmation or the like. In extreme cases, substantive law may require a lawyer to disclose information relating to the representation to avoid being deemed to have assisted the client's crime or fraud. If the lawyer can avoid assisting a client's crime or fraud only by disclosing this information, then under paragraph (b) the lawyer is required to do so, unless the disclosure is prohibited by Rule 1.6.

Rule 4.2. Communication with Person Represented by Counsel

In representing a client, a lawyer shall not communicate about the subject of the representation with a person the lawyer knows to be represented by another lawyer in the matter, unless the lawyer has the consent of the other lawyer or is authorized to do so by law or a court order.

Adopted July 1, 2009, eff. Jan. 1, 2010.

Comment

[1] This Rule contributes to the proper functioning of the legal system by protecting a person who has chosen to be represented by a lawyer in a matter against possible overreaching by other lawyers who are participating in the matter, interference by those lawyers with the client-lawyer relationship and the uncounselled disclosure of information relating to the representation.

[2] This Rule applies to communications with any person who is represented by counsel, including counsel in a limited scope representation pursuant to Rule 1.2(c), concerning the matter to which the communication relates.

[3] The Rule applies even though the represented person initiates or consents to the communication. A lawyer must immediately terminate communication with a person if, after commencing communication, the lawyer learns that the person is one with whom communication is not permitted by this Rule.

[4] This Rule does not prohibit communication with a represented person, or an employee or agent of such a person, concerning matters outside the representation. For example, the existence of a controversy between a government agency and a private party, or between two organizations, does not prohibit a lawyer for either from communicating with nonlawyer representatives of the other regarding a separate matter. Nor does this Rule preclude communication with a represented person who is seeking advice from a lawyer who is not otherwise representing a client in the matter. A lawyer may not make a communication prohibited by this Rule through the acts of another. See Rule 8.4(a). Parties to a matter may communicate directly with each other, and a lawyer is not prohibited from advising a client concerning a communication that the client is legally entitled to make. Also, a lawyer having independent justification or legal authorization for communicating with a represented person is permitted to do so.

[5] Communications authorized by law may include communications by a lawyer on behalf of a client who is exercising a constitutional or other legal right to communicate with the government. Communications authorized by law may also include investigative activities of lawyers representing governmental entities, directly or through investigative agents, prior to the commencement of criminal or civil enforcement proceedings. When communicating with the accused in a criminal matter, a government lawyer must comply with this Rule in addition to honoring the constitutional rights of the accused. The fact that a communication does not violate a state or federal constitutional right is insufficient to establish that the communication is permissible under this Rule.

[6] A lawyer who is uncertain whether a communication with a represented person is permissible may seek a court order. A lawyer may also seek a court order in exceptional circumstances to authorize a communication that would otherwise be prohibited by this Rule, for example, where communication with a person represented by counsel is necessary to avoid reasonably certain injury.

[7] In the case of a represented organization, this Rule prohibits communications with a constituent of the organization who supervises, directs or regularly consults with the organization's lawyer concerning the matter or has authority to obligate the organization with respect to the matter or whose act or omission in connection with the matter may be imputed to the organization for purposes of civil or criminal liability. Consent of the organization's lawyer is not required for communication with a

former constituent. If a constituent of the organization is represented in the matter by his or her own counsel, the consent by that counsel to a communication will be sufficient for purposes of this Rule. Compare Rule 3.4(f). In communicating with a current or former constituent of an organization, a lawyer must not use methods of obtaining evidence that violate the legal rights of the organization. See Rule 4.4.

[8] The prohibition on communications with a represented person only applies in circumstances where the lawyer knows that the person is in fact represented in the matter to be discussed. This means that the lawyer has actual knowledge of the fact of the representation; but such actual knowledge may be inferred from the circumstances. See Rule 1.0(f). Thus, the lawyer cannot evade the requirement of obtaining the consent of counsel by closing eyes to the obvious.

[8A] For purposes of this Rule, when a person is being represented on a limited basis under Rule 1.2(c), a lawyer is only deemed to know that the person is represented by another lawyer, and the subject of that representation, upon receipt of (i) a proper Notice of Limited Scope Appearance under Supreme Court Rule 13(c)(6), or (ii) with respect to a matter not involving court proceedings, written notice advising that the client is being represented by specified counsel with respect to an identified subject matter and time frame. A lawyer is permitted to communicate with a person represented under Rule 1.2(c) outside the subject matter or time frame of the limited scope representation.

[9] In the event the person with whom the lawyer communicates is not known to be represented by counsel in the matter, the lawyer's communications are subject to Rule 4.3.

[Comment adopted July 1, 2009, effective January 1, 2010. Amended June 14, 2013, eff. July 1, 2013.]

Rule 4.3. Dealing With Unrepresented Person

In dealing on behalf of a client with a person who is not represented by counsel, a lawyer shall not state or imply that the lawyer is disinterested. When the lawyer knows or reasonably should know that the unrepresented person misunderstands the lawyer's role in the matter, the lawyer shall make reasonable efforts to correct the misunderstanding. The lawyer shall not give legal advice to an unrepresented person, other than the advice to secure counsel, if the lawyer knows or reasonably should know that the interests of such a person are or have a reasonable possibility of being in conflict with the interests of the client.

Adopted July 1, 2009, eff. Jan. 1, 2010.

Comment

[1] An unrepresented person, particularly one not experienced in dealing with legal matters, might assume that a lawyer is disinterested in loyalties or is a disinterested authority on the law even when the lawyer represents a client. In order to avoid a misunderstanding, a lawyer will typically need to identify the lawyer's client and, where necessary,

explain that the client has interests opposed to those of the unrepresented person. For misunderstandings that sometimes arise when a lawyer for an organization deals with an unrepresented constituent, see Rule 1.13(f).

[2] The Rule distinguishes between situations involving unrepresented persons whose interests may be adverse to those of the lawyer's client and those in which the person's interests are not in conflict with the client's. In the former situation, the possibility that the lawyer will compromise the unrepresented person's interests is so great that the Rule prohibits the giving of any advice, apart from the advice to obtain counsel. Whether a lawyer is giving impermissible advice may depend on the experience and sophistication of the unrepresented person, as well as the setting in which the behavior and comments occur. This Rule does not prohibit a lawyer from negotiating the terms of a transaction or settling a dispute with an unrepresented person. So long as the lawyer has explained that the lawyer represents an adverse party and is not representing the person, the lawyer may inform the person of the terms on which the lawyer's client will enter into an agreement or settle a matter, prepare documents that require the person's signature and explain the lawyer's own view of the meaning of the document or the lawyer's view of the underlying legal obligations.

Rule 4.4. Respect for Rights of Third Persons

(a) In representing a client, a lawyer shall not use means that have no substantial purpose other than to embarrass, delay, or burden a third person, or use methods of obtaining evidence that violate the legal rights of such a person.

(b) A lawyer who receives a document or electronically stored information relating to the representation of the lawyer's client and knows that the document or electronically stored information was inadvertently sent shall promptly notify the sender.

Adopted July 1, 2009, eff. Jan. 1, 2010. Amended Oct. 15, 2015, eff. Jan. 1, 2016.

Comment

[1] Responsibility to a client requires a lawyer to subordinate the interests of others to those of the client, but that responsibility does not imply that a lawyer may disregard the rights of third persons. It is impractical to catalogue all such rights, but they include legal restrictions on methods of obtaining evidence from third persons and unwarranted intrusions into privileged relationships, such as the client-lawyer relationship.

[2] Paragraph (b) recognizes that lawyers sometimes receive a document or electronically stored information that was mistakenly sent or produced by opposing parties or their lawyers. A document or electronically stored information is inadvertently sent when it is accidentally transmitted, such as when an email or letter is misaddressed or a document or electronically stored information is accidentally included with information that was intention-

ly transmitted. If a lawyer knows that such a document or electronically stored information was sent inadvertently, then this Rule requires the lawyer to promptly notify the sender in order to permit that person to take protective measures. Whether the lawyer is required to take additional steps, such as returning the document or electronically stored information, is a matter of law beyond the scope of these Rules, as is the question of whether the privileged status of a document or electronically stored information has been waived. Similarly, this Rule does not address the legal duties of a lawyer who receives a document or electronically stored information that the lawyer knows may have been inappropriately obtained by the sending person. For purposes of this Rule, "document or electronically stored information" includes, in addition to paper documents, email and other forms of electronically stored information, including embedded data (commonly referred to as "metadata"), that is subject to being read or put into readable form. Metadata in electronic documents creates an obligation under this Rule only if the receiving lawyer knows that the metadata was inadvertently sent to the receiving lawyer.

[3] Some lawyers may choose to return a document or delete electronically stored information unread, for example, when the lawyer learns before receiving it that it was inadvertently sent. Where a lawyer is not required by applicable law to do so, the decision to voluntarily return such a document or delete electronically stored information is a matter of professional judgment ordinarily reserved to the lawyer. See Rules 1.2 and 1.4.

Comment adopted July 1, 2009, eff. Jan. 1, 2010. Amended Oct. 15, 2015, eff. Jan. 1, 2016.

Rule 5.1. Responsibilities of Partners, Managers, and Supervisory Lawyers

(a) A partner in a law firm, and a lawyer who individually or together with other lawyers possesses comparable managerial authority in a law firm, shall make reasonable efforts to ensure that the firm has in effect measures giving reasonable assurance that all lawyers in the firm conform to the Rules of Professional Conduct.

(b) A lawyer having direct supervisory authority over another lawyer shall make reasonable efforts to ensure that the other lawyer conforms to the Rules of Professional Conduct.

(c) A lawyer shall be responsible for another lawyer's violation of the Rules of Professional Conduct if:

(1) the lawyer orders or, with knowledge of the specific conduct, ratifies the conduct involved; or

(2) the lawyer is a partner or has comparable managerial authority in the law firm in which the other lawyer practices, or has direct supervisory authority over the other lawyer, and knows of the conduct at a time when its consequences can be avoided or mitigated but fails to take reasonable remedial action.

Adopted July 1, 2009, eff. Jan. 1, 2010.

Comment

[1] Paragraph (a) applies to lawyers who have managerial authority over the professional work of a firm. See Rule 1.0(c). This includes members of a partnership, the shareholders in a law firm organized as a professional corporation, and members of other associations authorized to practice law; lawyers having comparable managerial authority in a legal services organization or a law department of an enterprise or government agency; and lawyers who have intermediate managerial responsibilities in a firm. Paragraph (b) applies to lawyers who have supervisory authority over the work of other lawyers in a firm.

[2] Paragraph (a) requires lawyers with managerial authority within a firm to make reasonable efforts to establish internal policies and procedures designed to provide reasonable assurance that all lawyers in the firm will conform to the Rules of Professional Conduct. Such policies and procedures include those designed to detect and resolve conflicts of interest, identify dates by which actions must be taken in pending matters, account for client funds and property and ensure that inexperienced lawyers are properly supervised.

[3] Other measures that may be required to fulfill the responsibility prescribed in paragraph (a) can depend on the firm's structure and the nature of its practice. In a small firm of experienced lawyers, informal supervision and periodic review of compliance with the required systems ordinarily will suffice. In a large firm, or in practice situations in which difficult ethical problems frequently arise, more elaborate measures may be necessary. Some firms, for example, have a procedure whereby junior lawyers can make confidential referral of ethical problems directly to a designated senior partner or special committee. See Rule 5.2. Firms, whether large or small, may also rely on continuing legal education in professional ethics. In any event, the ethical atmosphere of a firm can influence the conduct of all its members and the partners may not assume that all lawyers associated with the firm will inevitably conform to the Rules.

[4] Paragraph (c) expresses a general principle of personal responsibility for acts of another. See also Rule 8.4(a).

[5] Paragraph (c)(2) defines the duty of a partner or other lawyer having comparable managerial authority in a law firm, as well as a lawyer who has direct supervisory authority over performance of specific legal work by another lawyer. Whether a lawyer has supervisory authority in particular circumstances is a question of fact. Partners and lawyers with comparable authority have at least indirect responsibility for all work being done by the firm, while a partner or manager in charge of a particular matter ordinarily also has supervisory responsibility for the work of other firm lawyers engaged in the matter. Appropriate remedial action by a partner or managing lawyer would depend on the immediacy of that lawyer's involvement and the seriousness of the misconduct. A supervisor is required to intervene to prevent avoidable consequences of misconduct if the supervisor knows that

the misconduct occurred. Thus, if a supervising lawyer knows that a subordinate misrepresented a matter to an opposing party in negotiation, the supervisor as well as the subordinate has a duty to correct the resulting misapprehension.

[6] Professional misconduct by a lawyer under supervision could reveal a violation of paragraph (b) on the part of the supervisory lawyer even though it does not entail a violation of paragraph (c) because there was no direction, ratification or knowledge of the violation.

[7] Apart from this Rule and Rule 8.4(a), a lawyer does not have disciplinary liability for the conduct of a partner, associate or subordinate. Whether a lawyer may be liable civilly or criminally for another lawyer's conduct is a question of law beyond the scope of these Rules.

[8] The duties imposed by this Rule on managing and supervising lawyers do not alter the personal duty of each lawyer in a firm to abide by the Rules of Professional Conduct. See Rule 5.2(a).

Rule 5.2. Responsibilities of a Subordinate Lawyer

(a) A lawyer is bound by the Rules of Professional Conduct notwithstanding that the lawyer acted at the direction of another person.

(b) A subordinate lawyer does not violate the Rules of Professional Conduct if that lawyer acts in accordance with a supervisory lawyer's reasonable resolution of an arguable question of professional duty.

Adopted July 1, 2009, eff. Jan. 1, 2010.

Comment

[1] Although a lawyer is not relieved of responsibility for a violation by the fact that the lawyer acted at the direction of a supervisor, that fact may be relevant in determining whether a lawyer had the knowledge required to render conduct a violation of the Rules. For example, if a subordinate filed a frivolous pleading at the direction of a supervisor, the subordinate would not be guilty of a professional violation unless the subordinate knew of the document's frivolous character.

[2] When lawyers in a supervisor-subordinate relationship encounter a matter involving professional judgment as to ethical duty, the supervisor may assume responsibility for making the judgment. Otherwise a consistent course of action or position could not be taken. If the question can reasonably be answered only one way, the duty of both lawyers is clear and they are equally responsible for fulfilling it. However, if the question is reasonably arguable, someone has to decide upon the course of action. That authority ordinarily reposes in the supervisor, and a subordinate may be guided accordingly. For example, if a question arises whether the interests of two clients conflict under Rule 1.7, the supervisor's reasonable resolution of the question should protect the subordinate professionally if the resolution is subsequently challenged.

Rule 5.3. Responsibilities Regarding Nonlawyer Assistance

With respect to a nonlawyer employed or retained by or associated with a lawyer:

(a) a partner, and a lawyer who individually or together with other lawyers possesses comparable managerial authority in a law firm shall make reasonable efforts to ensure that the firm has in effect measures giving reasonable assurance that the person's conduct is compatible with the professional obligations of the lawyer;

(b) a lawyer having direct supervisory authority over the nonlawyer shall make reasonable efforts to ensure that the person's conduct is compatible with the professional obligations of the lawyer; and

(c) a lawyer shall be responsible for conduct of such a person that would be a violation of the Rules of Professional Conduct if engaged in by a lawyer if:

(1) the lawyer orders or, with the knowledge of the specific conduct, ratifies the conduct involved; or

(2) the lawyer is a partner or has comparable managerial authority in the law firm in which the person is employed, or has direct supervisory authority over the person, and knows of the conduct at a time when its consequences can be avoided or mitigated but fails to take reasonable remedial action.

Adopted July 1, 2009, eff. Jan. 1, 2010. Amended Oct. 15, 2015, eff. Jan. 1, 2016.

Comment

[1] Paragraph (a) requires lawyers with managerial authority within a law firm to make reasonable efforts to ensure that the firm has in effect measures giving reasonable assurance that nonlawyers in the firm and nonlawyers outside the firm who work on firm matters act in a way compatible with the professional obligations of the lawyer. See Comment [6] to Rule 1.1 and Comment [1] to Rule 5.1. Paragraph (b) applies to lawyers who have supervisory authority over such nonlawyers within or outside the firm. Paragraph (c) specifies the circumstances in which a lawyer is responsible for the conduct of such nonlawyers within or outside the firm that would be a violation of the Rules of Professional Conduct if engaged in by a lawyer.

Nonlawyers Within the Firm

[2] Lawyers generally employ assistants in their practice, including secretaries, investigators, law student interns, and paraprofessionals. Such assistants, whether employees or independent contractors, act for the lawyer in rendition of the lawyer's professional services. A lawyer must give such assistants appropriate instruction and supervision concerning the ethical aspects of their employment, particularly regarding the obligation not to disclose information relating to representation of the client, and should be responsible for their work product. The measures employed in supervising nonlawyers

should take account of the fact that they do not have legal training and are not subject to professional discipline.

Nonlawyers Outside the Firm

[3] A lawyer may use nonlawyers outside the firm to assist the lawyer in rendering legal services to the client. Examples include the retention of an investigative or paraprofessional service, hiring a document management company to create and maintain a database for complex litigation, sending client documents to a third party for printing or scanning, and using an Internet-based service to store client information. When using such services outside the firm, a lawyer must make reasonable efforts to ensure that the services are provided in a manner that is compatible with the lawyer's professional obligations. The extent of this obligation will depend upon the circumstances, including the education, experience and reputation of the nonlawyer; the nature of the services involved; the terms of any arrangements concerning the protection of client information; and the legal and ethical environments of the jurisdictions in which the services will be performed, particularly with regard to confidentiality. See also Rules 1.1, 1.2, 1.4, 1.6, 5.4(a), and 5.5(a). When retaining or directing a nonlawyer outside the firm, a lawyer should communicate directions appropriate under the circumstances to give reasonable assurance that the nonlawyer's conduct is compatible with the professional obligations of the lawyer.

[4] Where the client directs the selection of a particular nonlawyer service provider outside the firm, the lawyer ordinarily should agree with the client concerning the allocation of responsibility for monitoring as between the client and the lawyer. See Rule 1.2. When making such an allocation in a matter pending before a tribunal, lawyers and parties may have additional obligations that are a matter of law beyond the scope of these Rules.

Comment adopted July 1, 2009, eff. Jan. 1, 2010. Amended Oct. 15, 2015, eff. Jan. 1, 2016.

Rule 5.4. Professional Independence of a Lawyer

(a) A lawyer or law firm shall not share legal fees with a nonlawyer, except that:

(1) an agreement by a lawyer with the lawyer's firm, partner, or associate may provide for the payment of money, over a reasonable period of time after the lawyer's death, to the lawyer's estate or to one or more specified persons;

(2) a lawyer who purchases the practice of a deceased, disabled, or disappeared lawyer may, pursuant to the provisions of Rule 1.17, pay to the estate or other representative of that lawyer the agreed-upon purchase price;

(3) a lawyer or law firm may include nonlawyer employees in a compensation or retirement plan, even though the plan is based in whole or in part on a profitsharing arrangement; and

(4) a lawyer may share court-awarded legal fees with a nonprofit organization that employed, retained or recommended employment of the lawyer in the matter.

(b) A lawyer shall not form a partnership with a nonlawyer if any of the activities of the partnership consist of the practice of law.

(c) A lawyer shall not permit a person who recommends, employs, or pays the lawyer to render legal services for another to direct or regulate the lawyer's professional judgment in rendering such legal services.

(d) A lawyer shall not practice with or in the form of a professional corporation or association authorized to practice law for a profit, if:

(1) a nonlawyer owns any interest therein, except that a fiduciary representative of the estate of a lawyer may hold the stock or interest of the lawyer for a reasonable time during administration;

(2) a nonlawyer is a corporate director or officer thereof or occupies the position of similar responsibility in any form of association other than a corporation; or

(3) a nonlawyer has the right to direct or control the professional judgment of a lawyer.

Adopted July 1, 2009, eff. Jan. 1, 2010.

Comment

[1] The provisions of this Rule express traditional limitations on sharing fees. These limitations are to protect the lawyer's professional independence of judgment. Where someone other than the client pays the lawyer's fee or salary, or recommends employment of the lawyer, that arrangement does not modify the lawyer's obligation to the client. As stated in paragraph (c), such arrangements should not interfere with the lawyer's professional judgment.

[2] This Rule also expresses traditional limitations on permitting a third party to direct or regulate the lawyer's professional judgment in rendering legal services to another. See also Rule 1.8(f) (lawyer may accept compensation from a third party as long as there is no interference with the lawyer's independent professional judgment and the client gives informed consent).

Rule 5.5. Unauthorized Practice of Law; Multijurisdictional Practice of Law

(a) A lawyer shall not practice law in a jurisdiction in violation of the regulation of the legal profession in that jurisdiction, or assist another in doing so.

(b) A lawyer who is not admitted to practice in this jurisdiction shall not:

(1) except as authorized by these Rules or other law, establish an office or other systematic and continuous presence in this jurisdiction for the practice of law; or

(2) hold out to the public or otherwise represent that the lawyer is admitted to practice law in this jurisdiction.

(c) A lawyer admitted in another United States jurisdiction, and not disbarred or suspended from practice in any jurisdiction, may provide legal services on a temporary basis in this jurisdiction that:

(1) are undertaken in association with a lawyer who is admitted to practice in this jurisdiction and who actively participates in the matter;

(2) are in or reasonably related to a pending or potential proceeding before a tribunal in this or another jurisdiction, if the lawyer, or a person the lawyer is assisting, is authorized by law or order to appear in such proceeding or reasonably expects to be so authorized;

(3) are in or reasonably related to a pending or potential arbitration, mediation, or other alternative dispute resolution proceeding in this or another jurisdiction, if the services arise out of or are reasonably related to the lawyer's practice in a jurisdiction in which the lawyer is admitted to practice and are not services for which the forum requires pro hac vice admission; or

(4) are not within paragraphs (c)(2) or (c)(3) and arise out of or are reasonably related to the lawyer's practice in a jurisdiction in which the lawyer is admitted to practice.

(d) A lawyer admitted in another United States jurisdiction or admitted or otherwise authorized to practice in a foreign jurisdiction, and not disbarred or suspended from practice in any jurisdiction or the equivalent thereof, may provide legal services through an office or other systematic and continuous presence in this jurisdiction that:

(1) are provided to the lawyer's employer or its organizational affiliates and are not services for which the forum requires pro hac vice admission; or

(2) are services that the lawyer is authorized by federal or other law or rule to provide in this jurisdiction.

(e) For purposes of paragraph (d), the foreign lawyer must be a member in good standing of a recognized legal profession in a foreign jurisdiction.

Adopted July 1, 2009, eff. Jan. 1, 2010. Amended Oct. 15, 2015, eff. Jan. 1, 2016.

Comment

[1] A lawyer may practice law only in a jurisdiction in which the lawyer is authorized to practice. A lawyer may be admitted to practice law in a jurisdiction on a regular basis or may be authorized by court rule or order or by law to practice for a limited purpose or on a restricted basis. Paragraph (a) applies to unauthorized practice of law by a lawyer, whether through the lawyer's direct action or by the lawyer assisting another person.

[2] The definition of the practice of law is established by law and varies from one jurisdiction to another. Whatever the definition, limiting the practice of law to members of the bar protects the public against rendition of legal services by unqualified persons. This Rule does not prohibit a lawyer from employing the services of paraprofessionals and delegating functions to them, so long as the lawyer supervises the delegated work and retains responsibility for their work. See Rule 5.3.

[3] A lawyer may provide professional advice and instruction to nonlawyers whose employment requires knowledge of the law; for example, claims adjusters, employees of financial or commercial institutions, social workers, accountants and persons employed in government agencies. Lawyers also may assist independent nonlawyers, such as paraprofessionals, who are authorized by the law of a jurisdiction to provide particular law-related services. In addition, a lawyer may counsel nonlawyers who wish to proceed *pro se*. See Supreme Court Rule 137(e) (lawyer may help draft a pleading, motion or other paper filed by a *pro se* party). See also Supreme Court Rule 13(c)(6) (lawyer may make a limited scope appearance in a civil proceeding on behalf of a *pro se* party).

[4] Other than as authorized by law or this Rule, a lawyer who is not admitted to practice generally in this jurisdiction violates paragraph (b)(1) if the lawyer establishes an office or other systematic and continuous presence in this jurisdiction for the practice of law. Presence may be systematic and continuous even if the lawyer is not physically present here. Such a lawyer must not hold out to the public or otherwise represent that the lawyer is admitted to practice law in this jurisdiction. See also Rules 7.1(a) and 7.5(b).

[5] There are occasions in which a lawyer admitted to practice in another United States jurisdiction, and not disbarred or suspended from practice in any jurisdiction, may provide legal services on a temporary basis in this jurisdiction under circumstances that do not create an unreasonable risk to the interests of their clients, the public or the courts. Paragraph (c) identifies four such circumstances. The fact that conduct is not so identified does not imply that the conduct is or is not authorized. With the exception of paragraphs (d)(1) and (d)(2), this Rule does not authorize a U.S. or foreign lawyer to establish an office or other systematic and continuous presence in this jurisdiction without being admitted to practice generally here.

[6] There is no single test to determine whether a lawyer's services are provided on a "temporary basis" in this jurisdiction, and may therefore be permissible under paragraph (c). Services may be "temporary" even though the lawyer provides services in this jurisdiction on a recurring basis, or for an extended period of time, as when the lawyer is representing a client in a single lengthy negotiation or litigation.

[7] Paragraphs (c) and (d) apply to lawyers who are admitted to practice law in any United States jurisdiction, which includes the District of Columbia and any state, territory or commonwealth of the United States. Paragraph (d) also applies to law-

yers admitted or otherwise authorized to practice in a foreign jurisdiction. The word "admitted" in paragraphs (c), (d) and (e) contemplates that the lawyer is authorized to practice in the other jurisdiction and excludes a lawyer who while technically admitted is not authorized to practice.

[8] Paragraph (c)(1) recognizes that the interests of clients and the public are protected if a lawyer admitted only in another jurisdiction associates with a lawyer licensed to practice in this jurisdiction. For this paragraph to apply, however, the lawyer admitted to practice in this jurisdiction must actively participate in and share responsibility for the representation of the client.

[9] Lawyers not admitted to practice generally in a jurisdiction may be authorized by law or order of a tribunal or an administrative agency to appear before the tribunal or agency. This authority may be granted pursuant to formal rules governing admission pro hac vice or pursuant to informal practice of the tribunal or agency. Under paragraph (c)(2), a lawyer does not violate this Rule when the lawyer appears before a tribunal or agency pursuant to such authority. To the extent that a court rule or other law of this jurisdiction requires a lawyer who is not admitted to practice in this jurisdiction to obtain admission pro hac vice before appearing before a tribunal or administrative agency, this Rule requires the lawyer to obtain that authority.

[10] Paragraph (c)(2) also provides that a lawyer rendering services in this jurisdiction on a temporary basis does not violate this Rule when the lawyer engages in conduct in anticipation of a proceeding or hearing in a jurisdiction in which the lawyer is authorized to practice law or in which the lawyer reasonably expects to be admitted pro hac vice. Examples of such conduct include meetings with the client, interviews of potential witnesses, and the review of documents. Similarly, a lawyer admitted only in another jurisdiction may engage in conduct temporarily in this jurisdiction in connection with pending litigation in another jurisdiction in which the lawyer is or reasonably expects to be authorized to appear, including taking depositions in this jurisdiction.

[11] When a lawyer has been or reasonably expects to be admitted to appear before a court or administrative agency, paragraph (c)(2) also permits conduct by lawyers who are associated with that lawyer in the matter, but who do not expect to appear before the court or administrative agency. For example, subordinate lawyers may conduct research, review documents, and attend meetings with witnesses in support of the lawyer responsible for the litigation.

[12] Paragraph (c)(3) permits a lawyer admitted to practice law in another jurisdiction to perform services on a temporary basis in this jurisdiction if those services are in or reasonably related to a pending or potential arbitration, mediation, or other alternative dispute resolution proceeding in this or another jurisdiction, if the services arise out of or are reasonably related to the lawyer's practice in a jurisdiction in which the lawyer is admitted to practice. The lawyer, however, must obtain admission

pro hac vice in the case of a court-annexed arbitration or mediation or otherwise if court rules or law so require.

[13] Paragraph (c)(4) permits a lawyer admitted in another jurisdiction to provide certain legal services on a temporary basis in this jurisdiction that arise out of or are reasonably related to the lawyer's practice in a jurisdiction in which the lawyer is admitted but are not within paragraphs (c)(2) or (c)(3). These services include both legal services and services that nonlawyers may perform but that are considered the practice of law when performed by lawyers.

[14] Paragraphs (c)(3) and (c)(4) require that the services arise out of or be reasonably related to the lawyer's practice in a jurisdiction in which the lawyer is admitted. A variety of factors evidence such a relationship. The lawyer's client may have been previously represented by the lawyer, or may be resident in or have substantial contacts with the jurisdiction in which the lawyer is admitted. The matter, although involving other jurisdictions, may have a significant connection with that jurisdiction. In other cases, significant aspects of the lawyer's work might be conducted in that jurisdiction or a significant aspect of the matter may involve the law of that jurisdiction. The necessary relationship might arise when the client's activities or the legal issues involve multiple jurisdictions, such as when the officers of a multinational corporation survey potential business sites and seek the services of their lawyer in assessing the relative merits of each. In addition, the services may draw on the lawyer's recognized expertise developed through the regular practice of law on behalf of clients in matters involving a particular body of federal, nationally uniform, foreign, or international law.

[15] Paragraph (d) identifies two circumstances in which a lawyer who is admitted to practice in another United States or a foreign jurisdiction, and is not disbarred or suspended from practice in any jurisdiction or the equivalent thereof, may establish an office or other systematic and continuous presence in this jurisdiction for the practice of law. Pursuant to paragraph (c) of this Rule, a lawyer admitted in any U.S. jurisdiction may also provide legal services in this jurisdiction on a temporary basis. Except as provided in paragraphs (d)(1) and (d)(2), a lawyer who is admitted to practice law in another United States or foreign jurisdiction and who establishes an office or other systematic or continuous presence in this jurisdiction must become admitted to practice law generally in this jurisdiction.

[16] Paragraph (d)(1) applies to a U.S. or foreign lawyer who is employed by a client to provide legal services to the client or its organizational affiliates, i.e., entities that control, are controlled by, or are under common control with the employer. This paragraph does not authorize the provision of personal legal services to the employer's officers or employees. The paragraph applies to in-house corporate lawyers, government lawyers and others who are employed to render legal services to the employer. The lawyer's ability to represent the employer outside the jurisdiction in which the lawyer is

licensed generally serves the interests of the employer and does not create an unreasonable risk to the client and others because the employer is well situated to assess the lawyer's qualifications and the quality of the lawyer's work.

[17] If an employed lawyer establishes an office or other systematic presence in this jurisdiction for the purpose of rendering legal services to the employer, the lawyer may be subject to registration or other requirements, including assessments for client protection funds and mandatory continuing legal education. See Illinois Supreme Court Rules 706(f), (g), 716, and 717 concerning requirements for house counsel and legal service program lawyers admitted to practice in other jurisdictions who wish to practice in Illinois.

[18] Paragraph (d)(2) recognizes that a U.S. or foreign lawyer may provide legal services in a jurisdiction in which the lawyer is not licensed when authorized to do so by federal or other law, which includes statute, court rule, executive regulation or judicial precedent.

[19] A lawyer who practices law in this jurisdiction pursuant to paragraphs (c) or (d) or otherwise is subject to the disciplinary authority of this jurisdiction. See Rule 8.5(a).

[20] In some circumstances, a lawyer who practices law in this jurisdiction pursuant to paragraphs (c) or (d) may have to inform the client that the lawyer is not licensed to practice law in this jurisdiction. For example, that may be required when the representation occurs primarily in this jurisdiction and requires knowledge of the law of this jurisdiction. See Rule 1.4(b).

[21] Paragraphs (c) and (d) do not authorize communications advertising legal services in this jurisdiction by lawyers who are admitted to practice in other jurisdictions. Whether and how lawyers may communicate the availability of their services in this jurisdiction is governed by Rules 7.1 to 7.5.

[22] Paragraph (e) recognizes the importance of the structure and procedures of the legal system in a foreign jurisdiction in assuring that a foreign lawyer is qualified to practice in Illinois. Application of paragraph (e) requires recognition that structure and procedures vary among foreign jurisdictions. Where members of the profession in the foreign jurisdiction are admitted or authorized to practice as lawyers or counselors at law or the equivalent, and are subject to effective regulation and discipline by a duly constituted professional body or a public authority, paragraph (e) is satisfied. Where the legal system does not have such structure and procedures, other attributes of the system must be considered to determine whether they supply assurances of an appropriate legal background. In addition, a foreign lawyer must satisfy the requirements of Illinois Supreme Court Rule 716 to be admitted as house counsel.

Comment adopted July 1, 2009, eff. Jan. 1, 2010. Amended June 14, 2013, eff. July 1, 2013; Oct. 15, 2015, eff. Jan. 1, 2016.

Rule 5.6. Restrictions on Right to Practice

A lawyer shall not participate in offering or making:

(a) a partnership, shareholders, operating, employment, or other similar type of agreement that restricts the right of a lawyer to practice after termination of the relationship, except an agreement concerning benefits upon retirement; or

(b) an agreement in which a restriction on the lawyer's right to practice is part of the settlement of a client controversy.

Adopted July 1, 2009, eff. Jan. 1, 2010.

Comment

[1] An agreement restricting the right of lawyers to practice after leaving a firm not only limits their professional autonomy but also limits the freedom of clients to choose a lawyer. Paragraph (a) prohibits such agreements except for restrictions incident to provisions concerning retirement benefits for service with the firm.

[2] Paragraph (b) prohibits a lawyer from agreeing not to represent other persons in connection with settling a claim on behalf of a client.

[3] This Rule does not apply to prohibit restrictions that may be included in the terms of the sale of a law practice pursuant to Rule 1.17.

Rule 5.7. Reserved

Rule 6.1. Reserved

Rule 6.2. Accepting Appointments

A lawyer shall not seek to avoid appointment by a tribunal to represent a person except for good cause, such as:

(a) representing the client is likely to result in violation of the Rules of Professional Conduct or other law;

(b) representing the client is likely to result in an unreasonable financial burden on the lawyer; or

(c) the client or the cause is so repugnant to the lawyer as to be likely to impair the client-lawyer relationship or the lawyer's ability to represent the client.

Adopted July 1, 2009, eff. Jan. 1, 2010.

Comment

[1] A lawyer ordinarily is not obliged to accept a client whose character or cause the lawyer regards as repugnant. The lawyer's freedom to select clients is, however, qualified. All lawyers have a responsibility to assist in providing *pro bono* publico service. See Preamble. An individual lawyer fulfills this responsibility by accepting a fair share of unpopular matters or indigent or unpopular clients. A lawyer may also be subject to appointment by a court to serve unpopular clients or persons unable to afford legal services.

Appointed Counsel

[2] For good cause a lawyer may seek to decline an appointment to represent a person who cannot

afford to retain counsel or whose cause is unpopular. Good cause exists if the lawyer could not handle the matter competently, see Rule 1.1, or if undertaking the representation would result in an improper conflict of interest, for example, when the client or the cause is so repugnant to the lawyer as to be likely to impair the client-lawyer relationship or the lawyer's ability to represent the client. A lawyer may also seek to decline an appointment if acceptance would be unreasonably burdensome, for example, when it would impose a financial sacrifice so great as to be unjust.

[3] An appointed lawyer has the same obligations to the client as retained counsel, including the obligations of loyalty and confidentiality, and is subject to the same limitations on the client-lawyer relationship, such as the obligation to refrain from assisting the client in violation of the Rules.

Rule 6.3. Membership in Legal Services Organization

A lawyer may serve as a director, officer or member of a not-for-profit legal services organization, apart from the law firm in which the lawyer practices, notwithstanding that the organization serves persons having interests adverse to a client of the lawyer. The lawyer shall not knowingly participate in a decision or action of the organization:

(a) if participating in the decision or action would be incompatible with the lawyer's obligations to a client under Rule 1.7; or

(b) where the decision or action could have a material adverse effect on the representation of a client of the organization whose interests are adverse to a client of the lawyer.

Adopted July 1, 2009, eff. Jan. 1, 2010.

Comment

[1] Lawyers should be encouraged to support and participate in not-for-profit legal service organizations. A lawyer who is an officer or a member of such an organization does not thereby have a client-lawyer relationship with persons served by the organization. However, there is potential conflict between the interests of such persons and the interests of the lawyer's clients. If the possibility of such conflict disqualified a lawyer from serving on the board of a legal services organization, the profession's involvement in such organizations would be severely curtailed.

[2] It may be necessary in appropriate cases to reassure a client of the organization that the representation will not be affected by conflicting loyalties of a member of the board. Established, written policies in this respect can enhance the credibility of such assurances.

Rule 6.4. Law Reform Activities Affecting Client Interests

A lawyer may serve as a director, officer or member of an organization involved in reform of the law or its administration notwithstanding that the reform may affect the interests of a client of the lawyer. When the lawyer knows that the interests of a client may be materially benefitted by a decision in which the lawyer participates, the lawyer shall disclose that fact but need not identify the client.

Adopted July 1, 2009, eff. Jan. 1, 2010.

Comment

[1] Lawyers involved in organizations seeking law reform generally do not have a client-lawyer relationship with the organization. Otherwise, it might follow that a lawyer could not be involved in a bar association law reform program that might indirectly affect a client. See also Rule 1.2(b). For example, a lawyer specializing in antitrust litigation might be regarded as disqualified from participating in drafting revisions of rules governing that subject. In determining the nature and scope of participation in such activities, a lawyer should be mindful of obligations to clients under other Rules, particularly Rule 1.7. A lawyer is professionally obligated to protect the integrity of the program by making an appropriate disclosure within the organization when the lawyer knows a private client might be materially benefitted.

Rule 6.5. NonProfit and Court–Annexed Limited Legal Services Programs

(a) A lawyer who, under the auspices of a program sponsored by a nonprofit organization or court, provides short-term limited legal services to a client without expectation by either the lawyer or the client that the lawyer will provide continuing representation in the matter:

(1) is subject to Rules 1.7 and 1.9(a) only if the lawyer knows that the representation of the client involves a conflict of interest; and

(2) is subject to Rule 1.10 only if the lawyer knows that another lawyer associated with the lawyer in a law firm is disqualified by Rule 1.7 or 1.9(a) with respect to the matter.

(b) Except as provided in paragraph (a)(2), Rule 1.10 is inapplicable to a representation governed by this Rule.

Adopted July 2, 2009, eff. Jan. 1, 2010.

Comment

[1] Legal services organizations, courts and various nonprofit organizations have established programs through which lawyers provide short-term limited legal services-such as advice or the completion of legal forms-that will assist persons to address their legal problems without further representation by a lawyer. In these programs, such as legal-advice hotlines, advice-only clinics or pro se counseling programs, a client-lawyer relationship is established, but there is no expectation that the lawyer's representation of the client will continue beyond the limited consultation. Such programs are normally operated under circumstances in which

it is not feasible for a lawyer to systematically screen for conflicts of interest as is generally required before undertaking a representation. See, *e.g.*, Rules 1.7, 1.9 and 1.10.

[2] A lawyer who provides short-term limited legal services pursuant to this Rule must secure the client's informed consent to the limited scope of the representation. See Rule 1.2(c). If a short-term limited representation would not be reasonable under the circumstances, the lawyer may offer advice to the client but must also advise the client of the need for further assistance of counsel. Except as provided in this Rule, the Rules of Professional Conduct, including Rules 1.6 and 1.9(c), are applicable to the limited representation.

[3] Because a lawyer who is representing a client in the circumstances addressed by this Rule ordinarily is not able to check systematically for conflicts of interest, paragraph (a) requires compliance with Rules 1.7 or 1. 9(a) only if the lawyer knows that the representation presents a conflict of interest for the lawyer, and with Rule 1.10 only if the lawyer knows that another lawyer in the lawyer's firm is disqualified by Rules 1.7 or 1.9(a) in the matter.

[4] Because the limited nature of the services significantly reduces the risk of conflicts of interest with other matters being handled by the lawyer's firm, paragraph (b) provides that Rule 1.10 is inapplicable to a representation governed by this Rule except as provided by paragraph (a)(2). Paragraph (a)(2) requires the participating lawyer to comply with Rule 1.10 when the lawyer knows that the lawyer's firm is disqualified by Rules 1.7 or 1.9(a). By virtue of paragraph (b), however, a lawyer's participation in a short-term limited legal services program will not preclude the lawyer's firm from undertaking or continuing the representation of a client with interests adverse to a client being represented under the program's auspices. Nor will the personal disqualification of a lawyer participating in the program be imputed to other lawyers participating in the program.

[5] If, after commencing a short-term limited representation in accordance with this Rule, a lawyer undertakes to represent the client in the matter on an ongoing basis, Rules 1.7, 1.9(a) and 1.10 become applicable.

Rule 7.1. Communications Concerning a Lawyer's Services

A lawyer shall not make a false or misleading communication about the lawyer or the lawyer's services. A communication is false or misleading if it contains a material misrepresentation of fact or law, or omits a fact necessary to make the statement considered as a whole not materially misleading.
Adopted July 1, 2009, eff. Jan. 1, 2010.

Comment

[1] This Rule governs all communications about a lawyer's services, including advertising permitted by Rule 7.2. Whatever means are used to make

known a lawyer's services, statements about them must be truthful.

[2] Truthful statements that are misleading are also prohibited by this Rule. A truthful statement is misleading if it omits a fact necessary to make the lawyer's communication considered as a whole not materially misleading. A truthful statement is also misleading if there is a substantial likelihood that it will lead a reasonable person to formulate a specific conclusion about the lawyer or the lawyer's services for which there is no reasonable factual foundation.

[3] An advertisement that truthfully reports a lawyer's achievements on behalf of clients or former clients may be misleading if presented so as to lead a reasonable person to form an unjustified expectation that the same results could be obtained for other clients in similar matters without reference to the specific factual and legal circumstances of each client's case. Similarly, an unsubstantiated comparison of the lawyer's services or fees with the services or fees of other lawyers may be misleading if presented with such specificity as would lead a reasonable person to conclude that the comparison can be substantiated. The inclusion of an appropriate disclaimer or qualifying language may preclude a finding that a statement is likely to create unjustified expectations or otherwise mislead the public.

[4] See also Rule 8.4(e) for the prohibition against stating or implying an ability to influence improperly a government agency or official or to achieve results by means that violate the Rules of Professional Conduct or other law.

Comment adopted July 1, 2009, eff. Jan. 1, 2010. Amended Oct. 15, 2015, eff. Jan. 1, 2016.

Rule 7.2. Advertising

(a) Subject to the requirements of Rules 7.1 and 7.3, a lawyer may advertise services through written, recorded or electronic communication, including public media.

(b) A lawyer shall not give anything of value to a person for recommending the lawyer's services except that a lawyer may

(1) pay the reasonable costs of advertisements or communications permitted by this Rule;

(2) pay the usual charges of a legal service plan or a not-for-profit lawyer referral service;

(3) pay for a law practice in accordance with Rule 1.17; and

(4) refer clients to another lawyer or a nonlawyer professional pursuant to an agreement not otherwise prohibited under these Rules that provides for the other person to refer clients or customers to the lawyer, if

(i) the reciprocal referral agreement is not exclusive, and

(ii) the client is informed of the existence and nature of the agreement.

(c) Any communication made pursuant to this Rule shall include the name and office address of at least one lawyer or law firm responsible for its content. Adopted July 1, 2009, eff. Jan. 1, 2010.

Comment

[1] To assist the public in learning about and obtaining legal services, lawyers should be allowed to make known their services not only through reputation but also through organized information campaigns in the form of advertising. Advertising involves an active quest for clients, contrary to the tradition that a lawyer should not seek clientele. However, the public's need to know about legal services can be fulfilled in part through advertising. This need is particularly acute in the case of persons of moderate means who have not made extensive use of legal services. The interest in expanding public information about legal services ought to prevail over considerations of tradition. Nevertheless, advertising by lawyers entails the risk of practices that are misleading or overreaching.

[2] This Rule permits public dissemination of information concerning a lawyer's name or firm name, address, email address, website, and telephone number; the kinds of services the lawyer will undertake; the basis on which the lawyer's fees are determined, including prices for specific services and payment and credit arrangements; a lawyer's foreign language ability; names of references and, with their consent, names of clients regularly represented; and other information that might invite the attention of those seeking legal assistance.

[3] Questions of effectiveness and taste in advertising are matters of speculation and subjective judgment. Some jurisdictions have had extensive prohibitions against television and other forms of advertising, against advertising going beyond specified facts about a lawyer, or against "undignified" advertising. Television, the Internet, and other forms of electronic communication are now among the most powerful media for getting information to the public, particularly persons of low and moderate income; prohibiting television, Internet, and other forms of electronic advertising, therefore, would impede the flow of information about legal services to many sectors of the public. Limiting the information that may be advertised has a similar effect and assumes that the bar can accurately forecast the kind of information that the public would regard as relevant. But see Rule 7.3(a) for the prohibition against a solicitation through a real-time electronic exchange initiated by the lawyer.

[4] Neither this Rule nor Rule 7.3 prohibits communications authorized by law, such as notice to members of a class in class action litigation.

Paying Others to Recommend a Lawyer

[5] Except as permitted under paragraphs (b)(1)–(b)(4), lawyers are not permitted to pay others for recommending the lawyer's services or for channeling professional work in a manner that violates Rule 7.3. A communication contains a recommendation if it endorses or vouches for a lawyer's credentials, abilities, competence, character, or other professional qualities. Paragraph (b)(1), however, allows a lawyer to pay for advertising and communications permitted by this Rule, including the costs of print directory listings, on-line directory listings, newspaper ads, television and radio airtime, domain-name registrations, sponsorship fees, Internet-based advertisements, and group advertising. A lawyer may compensate employees, agents and vendors who are engaged to provide marketing or client development services, such as publicists, public-relations personnel, business-development staff and website designers. Moreover, a lawyer may pay others for generating client leads, such as Internet-based client leads, as long as the lead generator does not recommend the lawyer, any payment to the lead generator is consistent with Rules 1.5(e) (division of fees) and 5.4 (professional independence of the lawyer), and the lead generator's communications are consistent with Rule 7.1 (communications concerning a lawyer's services). To comply with Rule 7.1, a lawyer must not pay a lead generator that states, implies, or creates a reasonable impression that it is recommending the lawyer, is making the referral without payment from the lawyer, or has analyzed a person's legal problems when determining which lawyer should receive the referral. See also Rule 5.3 for the duties of lawyers and law firms with respect to the conduct of nonlawyers; Rule 8.4(a) for the duty to avoid violating the Rules through the acts of another.

[6] A lawyer may pay the usual charges of a legal service plan or a not-for-profit lawyer referral service. A legal service plan is a prepaid or group legal service plan or a similar delivery system that assists people who seek to secure legal representation. A lawyer referral service, on the other hand, is any organization that holds itself out to the public as a lawyer referral service. Such referral services are understood by the public to be consumer-oriented organizations that provide unbiased referrals to lawyers with appropriate experience in the subject matter of the representation and afford other client protections, such as complaint procedures or malpractice insurance requirements. Consequently, this Rule only permits a lawyer to pay the usual charges of a not-for-profit lawyer referral service.

[7] A lawyer who accepts assignments or referrals from a legal service plan or referrals from a lawyer referral service must act reasonably to assure that the activities of the plan or service are compatible with the lawyer's professional obligations. See Rule 5.3. Legal service plans and lawyer referral services may communicate with the public, but such communication must be in conformity with these Rules. Thus, advertising must not be false or misleading, as would be the case if the communications of a group advertising program or a group legal services plan would mislead the public to think that it was a lawyer referral service sponsored by a state agency or bar association. Nor could the lawyer allow in-person, telephonic, or real-time contacts that would violate Rule 7.3.

[8] A lawyer also may agree to refer clients to another lawyer or a nonlawyer professional, in return for the undertaking of that person to refer clients or customers to the lawyer. Such reciprocal referral arrangements must not interfere with the

lawyer's professional judgment as to making referrals or as to providing substantive legal services. See Rules 2.1 and 5.4(c). Except as provided in Rule 1.5(e), a lawyer who receives referrals from a lawyer or nonlawyer professional must not pay anything solely for the referral, but the lawyer does not violate paragraph (b) of this Rule by agreeing to refer clients to the other lawyer or nonlawyer professional, so long as the reciprocal referral agreement is not exclusive and the client is informed of the referral agreement. Conflicts of interest created by such arrangements are governed by Rule 1.7. Reciprocal referral agreements should not be of indefinite duration and should be reviewed periodically to determine whether they comply with these Rules. This Rule does not restrict referrals or divisions of revenues or net income among lawyers within firms comprised of multiple entities.

Comment adopted July 1, 2009, eff. Jan. 1, 2010. Amended Oct. 15, 2015, eff. Jan. 1, 2016.

Rule 7.3. Solicitation of Clients

(a) A lawyer shall not by in-person, live telephone or real-time electronic contact solicit professional employment when a significant motive for the lawyer's doing so is the lawyer's pecuniary gain, unless the person contacted:

(1) is a lawyer; or

(2) has a family, close personal, or prior professional relationship with the lawyer.

(b) A lawyer shall not solicit professional employment by written, recorded or electronic communication or by in-person, telephone or real-time electronic contact even when not otherwise prohibited by paragraph (a), if:

(1) the target of the solicitation has made known to the lawyer a desire not to be solicited by the lawyer; or

(2) the solicitation involves coercion, duress or harassment.

(c) Every written, recorded or electronic communication from a lawyer soliciting professional employment from anyone known to be in need of legal services in a particular matter shall include the words "Advertising Material" on the outside envelope, if any, and at the beginning and ending of any recorded or electronic communication, unless the recipient of the communication is a person specified in paragraphs (a)(1) or (a)(2).

(d) Notwithstanding the prohibitions in paragraph (a), a lawyer may participate with a prepaid or group legal service plan operated by an organization not owned or directed by the lawyer that uses in-person or telephone contact to solicit memberships or subscriptions for the plan from persons who are not known to need legal services in a particular matter covered by the plan.

Adopted July 1, 2009, eff. Jan. 1, 2010. Amended Oct. 15, 2015, eff. Jan. 1, 2016.

Comment

[1] A solicitation is a targeted communication initiated by the lawyer that is directed to a specific person and that offers to provide, or can reasonably be understood as offering to provide, legal services. In contrast, a lawyer's communication typically does not constitute a solicitation if it is directed to the general public, such as through a billboard, an Internet banner advertisement, a website or a television commercial, or if it is in response to a request for information or is automatically generated in response to Internet searches.

[2] There is a potential for abuse when a solicitation involves direct in-person, live telephone or real-time electronic contact by a lawyer with someone known to need legal services. These forms of contact subject a person to the private importuning of the trained advocate in a direct interpersonal encounter. The person, who may already feel overwhelmed by the circumstances giving rise to the need for legal services, may find it difficult fully to evaluate all available alternatives with reasoned judgment and appropriate self-interest in the face of the lawyer's presence and insistence upon being retained immediately. The situation is fraught with the possibility of undue influence, intimidation, and over-reaching.

[3] This potential for abuse inherent in direct in-person, live telephone or real time electronic solicitation justifies its prohibition, particularly since lawyers have alternative means of conveying necessary information to those who may be in need of legal services. In particular, communications can be mailed or transmitted by email or other electronic means that do not involve real-time contact and do not violate other laws governing solicitations. These forms of communications and solicitations make it possible for the public to be informed about the need for legal services, and about the qualifications of available lawyers and law firms, without subjecting the public to direct in-person, telephone or real-time electronic persuasion that may overwhelm a person's judgment.

[4] The use of general advertising and written, recorded or electronic communications to transmit information from lawyer to the public rather than direct in-person, live telephone or real-time electronic contact, will help to assure that the information flows cleanly as well as freely. The contents of advertisements and communications permitted under Rule 7.2 can be permanently recorded so that they cannot be disputed and may be shared with others who know the lawyer. This potential for informal review is itself likely to help guard against statements and claims that might constitute false and misleading communications, in violation of Rule 7.1. The contents of direct in-person, live telephone or real-time electronic contact can be disputed and may not be subject to third-party scrutiny. Consequently, they are much more likely to approach (and occasionally cross) the dividing line between accurate representations and those that are false and misleading.

[5] There is far less likelihood that a lawyer would engage in abusive practices against a former

client, or a person with whom the lawyer has close personal or family relationship, or in situations in which the lawyer is motivated by considerations other than the lawyer's pecuniary gain. Nor is there a serious potential for abuse when the person contacted is a lawyer. Consequently, the general prohibition in Rule 7.3(a) and the requirements of Rule 7.3(c) are not applicable in those situations. Also, paragraph (a) is not intended to prohibit a lawyer from participating in constitutionally protected activities of public or charitable legal-service organizations or bona fide political, social, civic, fraternal, employee or trade organizations whose purposes include providing or recommending legal services to their members or beneficiaries.

[6] But even permitted forms of solicitation can be abused. Thus, any solicitation which contains information which is false or misleading within the meaning of Rule 7.1, which involves coercion, duress or harassment within the meaning of Rule 7.3(b)(2), or which involves contact with someone who has made known to the lawyer a desire not to be solicited by the lawyer within the meaning of Rule 7.3(b)(1) is prohibited. Moreover, if after sending a letter or other communication as permitted by Rule 7.2 the lawyer receives no response, any further effort to communicate with the recipient of the communication may violate the provisions of Rule 7.3(b).

[7] This Rule is not intended to prohibit a lawyer from contacting representatives of organizations or groups that may be interested in establishing a group or prepaid legal plan for their members, insureds, beneficiaries or other third parties for the purpose of informing such entities of the availability of and details concerning the plan or arrangement which the lawyer or lawyer's firm is willing to offer. This form of communication is not directed to people who are seeking legal services for themselves. Rather, it is usually addressed to an individual acting in a fiduciary capacity seeking a supplier of legal services for others who may, if they choose, become prospective clients of the lawyer. Under these circumstances, the activity which the lawyer undertakes in communicating with such representatives and the type of information transmitted to the individual are functionally similar to and serve the same purpose as advertising permitted under Rule 7.2.

[8] The requirement in Rule 7.3(c) that certain communications be marked "Advertising Material" does not apply to communications sent in response to requests of potential clients or their spokespersons or sponsors. General announcements by lawyers, including changes in personnel or office location, do not constitute communications soliciting professional employment from a client known to be in need of legal services within the meaning of this Rule.

[9] Paragraph (d) of this Rule permits a lawyer to participate with an organization which uses personal contact to solicit members for its group or prepaid legal service plan, provided that the personal contact is not undertaken by any lawyer who would be a provider of legal services through the plan. The organization must not be owned by or directed (whether as manager or otherwise) by any lawyer or law firm that participates in the plan. For example, paragraph (d) would not permit a lawyer to create an organization controlled directly or indirectly by the lawyer and use the organization for the in-person or telephone solicitation of legal employment of the lawyer through memberships in the plan or otherwise. The communication permitted by these organizations also must not be directed to a person known to need legal services in a particular matter, but is to be designed to inform potential plan members generally of another means of affordable legal services. Lawyers who participate in a legal service plan must reasonably assure that the plan sponsors are in compliance with Rules 7.1, 7.2 and 7.3(b). See 8.4(a).

Comment adopted July 1, 2009, eff. Jan. 1, 2010. Amended Oct. 15, 2015, eff. Jan. 1, 2016.

Rule 7.4. Communication of Fields of Practice and Specialization

(a) A lawyer may communicate the fact that the lawyer does or does not practice in particular fields of law.

(b) The Supreme Court of Illinois does not recognize certifications of specialties in the practice of law, nor does it recognize certifications of expertise in any phase of the practice of law by any agency, governmental or private, or by any group, organization or association. A lawyer admitted to engage in patent practice before the United States Patent and Trademark Office may use the designation "Patent Attorney" or a substantially similar designation.

(c) Except when identifying certificates, awards or recognitions issued to him or her by an agency or organization, a lawyer may not use the terms "certified," "specialist," "expert," or any other, similar terms to describe his qualifications as a lawyer or his qualifications in any subspecialty of the law. If such terms are used to identify any certificates, awards or recognitions issued by any agency, governmental or private, or by any group, organization or association, the reference must meet the following requirements:

(1) the reference must be truthful and verifiable and may not be misleading in violation of Rule 7.1;

(2) the reference must state that the Supreme Court of Illinois does not recognize certifications of specialties in the practice of law and that the certificate, award or recognition is not a requirement to practice law in Illinois.

Adopted July 1, 2009, eff. Jan. 1, 2010.

Comment

[1] Paragraph (a) of this Rule permits a lawyer to indicate areas of practice in communications about the lawyer's services. If a lawyer practices only in certain fields, or will not accept matters except in a specified field or fields, the lawyer is permitted to so indicate.

[2] Paragraph (b) states the general policy of the Supreme Court of Illinois not to recognize certifica-

tions of specialties or expertise, except that it recognizes that admission to patent practice before the Patent and Trademark Office confers a long-established and well-recognized status. The omission of reference to lawyers engaged in trademark or admiralty practice that were contained in the prior rule is not intended to suggest that such lawyers may not use terms such as "Trademark Lawyer" or "Admiralty" to indicate areas of practice as permitted by paragraph (a).

[3] Paragraph (c) permits a lawyer to state that the lawyer is certified, is a specialist in a field of law, or is an "expert" or any other similar term, only if certain requirements are met.

Rule 7.5. Firm Names and Letterheads

(a) A lawyer shall not use a firm name, letterhead or other professional designation that violates Rule 7.1. A trade name may be used by a lawyer in private practice if it does not imply a connection with a government agency or with a public or charitable legal services organization and is not otherwise in violation of Rule 7.1.

(b) A law firm with offices in more than one jurisdiction may use the same name or other professional designation in each jurisdiction, but identification of the lawyers in an office of the firm shall indicate the jurisdictional limitations on those not licensed to practice in the jurisdiction where the office is located.

(c) The name of a lawyer holding a public office shall not be used in the name of a law firm, or in communications on its behalf, during any substantial period in which the lawyer is not actively and regularly practicing with the firm.

(d) Lawyers may state or imply that they practice in a partnership or other organization only when that is the fact.

Adopted July 1, 2009, eff. Jan. 1, 2010.

Comment

[1] A firm may be designated by the names of all or some of its members, by the names of deceased members where there has been a continuing succession in the firm's identity or by a trade name such as the "ABC Legal Clinic." A lawyer or law firm may also be designated by a distinctive website address or comparable professional designation. Although the United States Supreme Court has held that legislation may prohibit the use of trade names in professional practice, use of such names in law practice is acceptable so long as it is not misleading. If a private firm uses a trade name that includes a geographical name such as "Springfield Legal Clinic," an express disclaimer that it is a public legal aid agency may be required to avoid a misleading implication. It may be observed that any firm name including the name of a deceased partner is, strictly speaking, a trade name. The use of such names to designate law firms has proven a useful means of identification. However, it is misleading to use the name of a lawyer not associated

with the firm or a predecessor of the firm, or the name of a nonlawyer.

[2] With regard to paragraph (d), lawyers sharing office facilities, but who are not in fact associated with each other in a law firm, may not denominate themselves as, for example, "Smith and Jones," for that title suggests that they are practicing law together in a firm.

Rule 7.6. Reserved

Rule 8.1. Bar Admission and Disciplinary Matters

An applicant for admission to the bar, or a lawyer in connection with a bar admission application or in connection with a disciplinary matter, shall not:

(a) knowingly make a false statement of material fact; or

(b) fail to disclose a fact necessary to correct a misapprehension known by the person to have arisen in the matter, or knowingly fail to respond to a lawful demand for information from an admissions or disciplinary authority, except that this Rule does not require disclosure of information otherwise protected by these Rules or by law.

Adopted July 1, 2009, eff. Jan. 1, 2010.

Comment

[1] The duty imposed by this Rule extends to persons seeking admission to the bar as well as to lawyers. Hence, if a person makes a material false statement in connection with an application for admission, it may be the basis for subsequent disciplinary action if the person is admitted, and in any event may be relevant in a subsequent admission application. The duty imposed by this Rule applies to a lawyer's own admission or discipline as well as that of others. Thus, it is a separate professional offense for a lawyer to knowingly make a misrepresentation or omission in connection with a disciplinary investigation of the lawyer's own conduct. Paragraph (b) of this Rule also requires correction of any prior misstatement in the matter that the applicant or lawyer may have made and affirmative clarification of any misunderstanding on the part of the admissions or disciplinary authority of which the person involved becomes aware.

[2] This Rule is subject to the provisions of the Fifth Amendment of the United States Constitution and corresponding provisions of state constitutions. A person relying on such a provision in response to a question, however, should do so openly and not use the right of nondisclosure as a justification for failure to comply with this Rule.

[3] A lawyer representing an applicant for admission to the bar, or representing a lawyer who is the subject of a disciplinary inquiry or proceeding, is governed by the Rules applicable to the client-lawyer relationship, including Rule 1.6 and, in some cases, Rule 3.3.

Rule 8.2. Judicial and Legal Officials

(a) A lawyer shall not make a statement that the lawyer knows to be false or with reckless disregard as to its truth or falsity concerning the qualifications or integrity of a judge, adjudicatory officer or public legal officer, or of a candidate for election or appointment to judicial or legal office.

(b) A lawyer who is a candidate for judicial office shall comply with the applicable provisions of the Code of Judicial Conduct.

Adopted July 1, 2009, eff. Jan. 1, 2010.

Comment

[1] Assessments by lawyers are relied on in evaluating the professional or personal fitness of persons being considered for election or appointment to judicial office and to public legal offices, such as attorney general, prosecuting attorney and public defender. Expressing honest and candid opinions on such matters contributes to improving the administration of justice. Conversely, false statements by a lawyer can unfairly undermine public confidence in the administration of justice.

[2] When a lawyer seeks judicial office, the lawyer should be bound by applicable limitations on political activity.

[3] To maintain the fair and independent administration of justice, lawyers are encouraged to continue traditional efforts to defend judges and courts unjustly criticized.

Rule 8.3. Reporting Professional Misconduct

(a) A lawyer who knows that another lawyer has committed a violation of Rule 8.4(b) or Rule 8.4(c) shall inform the appropriate professional authority.

(b) A lawyer who knows that a judge has committed a violation of applicable rules of judicial conduct that raises a substantial question as to the judge's fitness for office shall inform the appropriate authority.

(c) This Rule does not require disclosure of information otherwise protected by the attorney-client privilege or by law or information gained by a lawyer or judge while participating in an approved lawyers' assistance program or an intermediary program approved by a circuit court in which nondisciplinary complaints against judges or lawyers can be referred.

(d) A lawyer who has been disciplined as a result of a lawyer disciplinary action brought before any body other than the Illinois Attorney Registration and Disciplinary Commission shall report that fact to the Commission.

Adopted July 1, 2009, eff. Jan. 1, 2010.

Comment

[1] Self-regulation of the legal profession requires that members of the profession initiate disciplinary investigation when they know of a violation of the Rules of Professional Conduct. See *In re Himmel*,

125 Ill. 2d 531 (1988). Lawyers have a similar obligation with respect to judicial misconduct. An apparently isolated violation may indicate a pattern of misconduct that only a disciplinary investigation can uncover. Reporting a violation is especially important where the victim is unlikely to discover the offense.

[2] A report about misconduct is not required where it would involve disclosure of information protected by the attorney-client privilege or by law. However, a lawyer should encourage a client to consent to disclosure where prosecution would not substantially prejudice the client's interests.

[3] If a lawyer were obliged to report every violation of the Rules, the failure to report any violation would itself be a professional offense. Such a requirement existed in many jurisdictions but proved to be unenforceable. This Rule limits the reporting obligation to those offenses that a self-regulating profession must vigorously endeavor to prevent. A measure of judgment is, therefore, required in complying with the provisions of this Rule. A report should be made to the Illinois Attorney Registration and Disciplinary Commission unless some other agency is more appropriate in the circumstances. See *Skolnick v. Altheimer & Gray*, 191 Ill. 2d 214 (2000). Similar considerations apply to the reporting of judicial misconduct.

[4] The duty to report professional misconduct does not apply to a lawyer retained to represent a lawyer whose professional conduct is in question or to a lawyer consulted in a professional capacity by another lawyer on whether the inquiring lawyer has a duty to report a third party lawyer's professional misconduct. Such a situation is governed by the Rules applicable to the client-lawyer relationship.

[5] Information about a lawyer's or judge's misconduct or fitness may be received by a lawyer in the course of that lawyer's participation in an approved lawyers' or judges' assistance program or an approved intermediary program. In these circumstances, providing for an exception to the reporting requirements of paragraphs (a) and (b) of this Rule encourages lawyers and judges to seek treatment or assistance through such programs. Conversely, without such an exception, lawyers and judges may hesitate to seek assistance from these programs, which may then result in additional harm to their professional careers and additional injury to the welfare of clients and the public. See also Comment [19] to Rule 1.6.

[6] Rule 8.3(d) requires a lawyer to bring to the attention of the Illinois Attorney Registration and Disciplinary Commission any disciplinary sanction imposed by any other body against that lawyer. The Rule must be read in conjunction with Illinois Supreme Court Rule 763.

Rule 8.4. Misconduct

It is professional misconduct for a lawyer to:

(a) violate or attempt to violate the Rules of Professional Conduct, knowingly assist or induce another to do so, or do so through the acts of another.

(b) commit a criminal act that reflects adversely on the lawyer's honesty, trustworthiness, or fitness as a lawyer in other respects.

(c) engage in conduct involving dishonesty, fraud, deceit, or misrepresentation.

(d) engage in conduct that is prejudicial to the administration of justice.

(e) state or imply an ability to influence improperly a government agency or official or to achieve results by means that violate the Rules of Professional Conduct or other law.

(f) knowingly assist a judge or judicial officer in conduct that is a violation of applicable rules of judicial conduct or other law. Nor shall a lawyer give or lend anything of value to a judge, official, or employee of a tribunal, except those gifts or loans that a judge or a member of the judge's family may receive under Rule 65(C)(4) of the Illinois Code of Judicial Conduct. Permissible campaign contributions to a judge or candidate for judicial office may be made only by check, draft, or other instrument payable to or to the order of an entity that the lawyer reasonably believes to be a political committee supporting such judge or candidate. Provision of volunteer services by a lawyer to a political committee shall not be deemed to violate this paragraph.

(g) present, participate in presenting, or threaten to present criminal or professional disciplinary charges to obtain an advantage in a civil matter.

(h) enter into an agreement with a client or former client limiting or purporting to limit the right of the client or former client to file or pursue any complaint before the Illinois Attorney Registration and Disciplinary Commission.

(i) avoid in bad faith the repayment of an education loan guaranteed by the Illinois Student Assistance Commission or other governmental entity. The lawful discharge of an education loan in a bankruptcy proceeding shall not constitute bad faith under this paragraph, but the discharge shall not preclude a review of the lawyer's conduct to determine if it constitutes bad faith.

(j) violate a federal, state or local statute or ordinance that prohibits discrimination based on race, sex, religion, national origin, disability, age, sexual orientation or socioeconomic status by conduct that reflects adversely on the lawyer's fitness as a lawyer. Whether a discriminatory act reflects adversely on a lawyer's fitness as a lawyer shall be determined after consideration of all the circumstances, including: the seriousness of the act; whether the lawyer knew that the act was prohibited by statute or ordinance; whether the act was part of a pattern of prohibited conduct; and whether the act was committed in connection with the lawyer's professional activities. No charge of professional misconduct may be brought pursuant to this paragraph until a court or administrative agency of competent jurisdiction has found that the lawyer has

engaged in an unlawful discriminatory act, and the finding of the court or administrative agency has become final and enforceable and any right of judicial review has been exhausted.

(k) if the lawyer holds public office:

(1) use that office to obtain, or attempt to obtain, a special advantage in a legislative matter for a client under circumstances where the lawyer knows or reasonably should know that such action is not in the public interest;

(2) use that office to influence, or attempt to influence, a tribunal to act in favor of a client; or

(3) represent any client, including a municipal corporation or other public body, in the promotion or defeat of legislative or other proposals pending before the public body of which such lawyer is a member or by which such lawyer is employed.

Adopted July 1, 2009, eff. Jan. 1, 2010.

Comment

[1] Lawyers are subject to discipline when they violate or attempt to violate the Rules of Professional Conduct, knowingly assist or induce another to do so or do so through the acts of another, as when they request or instruct an agent to do so on the lawyer's behalf. Paragraph (a), however, does not prohibit a lawyer from advising a client concerning action the client is legally entitled to take.

[2] Many kinds of illegal conduct reflect adversely on fitness to practice law, such as offenses involving fraud and the offense of willful failure to file an income tax return. However, some kinds of offenses carry no such implication. Traditionally, the distinction was drawn in terms of offenses involving "moral turpitude." That concept can be construed to include offenses concerning some matters of personal morality, such as adultery and comparable offenses, that have no specific connection to fitness for the practice of law. Although a lawyer is personally answerable to the entire criminal law, a lawyer should be professionally answerable only for offenses that indicate lack of those characteristics relevant to law practice. Offenses involving violence, dishonesty, breach of trust, or serious interference with the administration of justice are in that category. A pattern of repeated offenses, even ones of minor significance when considered separately, can indicate indifference to legal obligation.

[3] A lawyer who, in the course of representing a client, knowingly manifests by words or conduct, bias or prejudice based upon race, sex, religion, national origin, disability, age, sexual orientation or socioeconomic status, violates paragraph (d) when such actions are prejudicial to the administration of justice. Legitimate advocacy respecting the foregoing factors does not violate paragraph (d). A trial judge's finding that peremptory challenges were exercised on a discriminatory basis does not alone establish a violation of this Rule.

[4] A lawyer may refuse to comply with an obligation imposed by law upon a good-faith belief that no valid obligation exists. The provisions of Rule

1.2(d) concerning a good-faith challenge to the validity, scope, meaning or application of the law apply to challenges of legal regulation of the practice of law.

[5] Lawyers holding public office assume legal responsibilities going beyond those of other citizens. A lawyer's abuse of public office can suggest an inability to fulfill the professional role of lawyers. The same is true of abuse of positions of private trust such as trustee, executor, administrator, guardian, agent and officer, director or manager of a corporation or other organization.

Rule 8.5. Disciplinary Authority; Choice of Law

(a) Disciplinary Authority. A lawyer admitted to practice in this jurisdiction is subject to the disciplinary authority of this jurisdiction, regardless of where the lawyer's conduct occurs. A lawyer not admitted in this jurisdiction is also subject to the disciplinary authority of this jurisdiction if the lawyer provides or offers to provide any legal services in this jurisdiction. A lawyer may be subject to the disciplinary authority of both this jurisdiction and another jurisdiction for the same conduct.

(b) Choice of Law. In any exercise of the disciplinary authority of this jurisdiction, the rules of professional conduct to be applied shall be as follows:

(1) for conduct in connection with a matter pending before a tribunal, the rules of the jurisdiction in which the tribunal sits, unless the rules of the tribunal provide otherwise; and

(2) for any other conduct, the rules of the jurisdiction in which the lawyer's conduct occurred, or, if the predominant effect of the conduct is in a different jurisdiction, the rules of that jurisdiction shall be applied to the conduct. A lawyer shall not be subject to discipline if the lawyer's conduct conforms to the rules of a jurisdiction in which the lawyer reasonably believes the predominant effect of the lawyer's conduct will occur.

Adopted July 1, 2009, eff. Jan. 1, 2010.

Comment
Disciplinary Authority

[1] It is longstanding law that the conduct of a lawyer admitted to practice in this jurisdiction is subject to the disciplinary authority of this jurisdiction. Extension of the disciplinary authority of this jurisdiction to other lawyers who provide or offer to provide legal services in this jurisdiction is for the protection of the citizens of this jurisdiction. Reciprocal enforcement of a jurisdiction's disciplinary findings may advance the purposes of this Rule, subject always to the need to avoid unjust results. For purposes of reciprocal discipline, suspension of the privilege to provide legal services on a temporary basis, pursuant to Rule 5.5(c) shall not necessarily be considered equivalent to suspension of licensure for a lawyer admitted to practice in this jurisdiction. The fact that the lawyer is subject to

the disciplinary authority of this jurisdiction may be a factor in determining whether personal jurisdiction may be asserted over the lawyer for civil matters.

Choice of Law

[2] A lawyer may be potentially subject to more than one set of rules of professional conduct which impose different obligations. The lawyer may be licensed to practice in more than one jurisdiction with differing rules, or may be admitted to practice before a particular court with rules that differ from those of the jurisdiction or jurisdictions in which the lawyer is licensed to practice. Additionally, the lawyer's conduct may involve significant contacts with more than one jurisdiction.

[3] Paragraph (b) seeks to resolve such potential conflicts. Its premise is that minimizing conflicts between rules, as well as uncertainty about which rules are applicable, is in the best interest of both clients and the profession (as well as the bodies having authority to regulate the profession). Accordingly, it takes the approach of (i) providing that any particular conduct of a lawyer shall be subject to only one set of rules of professional conduct, (ii) making the determination of which set of rules applies to particular conduct as straightforward as possible, consistent with recognition of appropriate regulatory interests of relevant jurisdictions, and (iii) providing protection from discipline for lawyers who act reasonably in the face of uncertainty.

[4] Paragraph (b)(1) provides that as to a lawyer's conduct relating to a proceeding pending before a tribunal, the lawyer shall be subject only to the rules of the jurisdiction in which the tribunal sits unless the rules of the tribunal, including its choice of law rule, provide otherwise. As to all other conduct, including conduct in anticipation of a proceeding not yet pending before a tribunal, paragraph (b)(2) provides that a lawyer shall be subject to the rules of the jurisdiction in which the lawyer's conduct occurred, or, if the predominant effect of the conduct is in another jurisdiction, the rules of that jurisdiction shall be applied to the conduct. In the case of conduct in anticipation of a proceeding that is likely to be before a tribunal, the predominant effect of such conduct could be where the conduct occurred, where the tribunal sits or in another jurisdiction.

[5] When a lawyer's conduct involves significant contacts with more than one jurisdiction, it may not be clear whether the predominant effect of the lawyer's conduct will occur in a jurisdiction other than the one in which the conduct occurred. So long as the lawyer's conduct conforms to the rules of a jurisdiction in which the lawyer reasonably believes the predominant effect will occur, the lawyer shall not be subject to discipline under this Rule. With respect to conflicts of interest, in determining a lawyer's reasonable belief under paragraph (b)(2), a written agreement between the lawyer and client that reasonably specifies a particular jurisdiction as within the scope of that paragraph may be considered if the agreement was obtained with the client's informed consent confirmed in writing.

[6] If two admitting jurisdictions were to proceed against a lawyer for the same conduct, they should, applying this Rule, identify the same governing ethics rules. They should take all appropriate steps to see that they do apply the same rule to the same conduct, and in all events should avoid proceeding against a lawyer on the basis of two inconsistent rules.

[7] The choice of law provision applies to lawyers engaged in transnational practice, unless international law, treaties or other agreements between competent regulatory authorities in the affected jurisdictions provide otherwise.

Comment adopted July 1, 2009, eff. Jan. 1, 2010. Amended Oct. 15, 2015, eff. Jan. 1, 2016.

Comment
(February 14, 1995)

(a) *Source*

The first sentence of Rule 8.5 is substantially equivalent to the rule as originally issued on February 8, 1990, to be effective August 1, 1990, which read as follows:

"A lawyer admitted to practice in this jurisdiction is subject to the disciplinary authority of this jurisdiction although engaged in practice elsewhere."

This language was identical with the American Bar Association (ABA) Model Rule language as it then stood.

The present language of Illinois Rule 8.5 is substantially identical with the present ABA Model Rule language, as amended August 11, 1993.

The ABA Model Rule language is followed by an extensive "Comment" which is not adopted in Illinois.

(b) *Illinois Code of Professional Responsibility Provisions*

The Illinois Code had no provisions relating to this subject.

(c) *Other Comment*

Paragraph (a) restates longstanding law. Nothing contained in Rule 8.5 abrogates the jurisdiction of the Illinois courts or the Attorney Registration and Disciplinary Commission over Illinois lawyers no matter where they practice: the rule simply directs which law or code of conduct should guide an Illinois tribunal when dealing with attorney conduct in an interstate transaction.

The rule does not purport to direct such tribunals when the transaction in question involves jurisdictions outside the United States.

In subparagraph (b)(2)(ii), the "jurisdiction in which the lawyer principally practices" refers to the jurisdiction in which the lawyer's principal office is located; the provisions of the subparagraph relating to the "predominant effect" of "particular conduct" shall apply solely to circumstances where there is a single jurisdiction, in which the lawyer is licensed, which experiences that "predominant effect." Where no such single jurisdiction can be determined, as in a large multistate transaction, then the applicable rules of conduct would be those of the jurisdiction of principal practice.

ARTICLE IX. CHILD CUSTODY OR ALLOCATION OF PARENTAL RESPONSIBILITIES PROCEEDINGS

PART A. RULES OF GENERAL APPLICATION TO CHILD CUSTODY OR ALLOCATION OF PARENTAL RESPONSIBILITIES PROCEEDINGS

Rule 900. Purpose and Scope

(a) **Purpose.** Trial courts have a special responsibility in cases involving the care and custody or allocation of parental responsibilities of children. When a child is a ward of the court, the physical and emotional well-being of the child is literally the business of the court. The purpose of this article (Rules 900 *et seq.*) is to expedite cases affecting the custody or allocation of parental responsibilities of a child, to ensure the coordination of custody or allocation of parental responsibilities matters filed under different statutory Acts, and to focus child custody or allocation of parental responsibilities proceedings on the best interests of the child, while protecting the rights of other parties to the proceedings.

(b)(1) Definitions. For the purposes of this article, "child custody or allocation of parental responsibilities proceeding" means an action affecting child custody or allocation of parental responsibilities, visitation, or parenting time. "Relocation" means an action involving relocation of a minor child pursuant to section 609.2 of the Illinois Marriage and Dissolution of Marriage Act (750 ILCS 5/609). "Child" means a person who has not attained the age of 18.

(b)(2) Part A. *Scope.* Rules 900 through 920, except as stated therein, apply to all child custody or allocation of parental responsibilities proceedings initiated under article II, III, or IV of the Juvenile Court Act of 1987, the Illinois Marriage and Dissolution of Marriage Act, the Uniform Child Custody Jurisdiction and Enforcement Act, the Illinois Parentage Act of 2015, the Illinois Domestic Violence Act of 1986 and article 112A of the Code of Criminal Procedure of 1963, and guardianship matters involving a minor under article XI of the Probate Act of 1975.

(b)(3) Part B. *Scope of Rules 921 through 940.* Rules 921 through 940 apply to allocation of parental responsibilities proceedings initiated under the Illinois Marriage and Dissolution of Marriage Act, and the Illinois Parentage Act of 2015.

(b)(4) Part C. *Scope of Rule 942.* Rule 942 applies to child custody proceedings under articles II, III, and IV of the Juvenile Court Act of 1987.

(c) Applicability of Other Rules. Applicable provisions of articles I and II of these rules shall continue to apply in child custody or allocation of parental responsibilities proceedings except as noted in this article.

Adopted February 10, 2006, effective July 1, 2006. Amended July 1, 2013, eff. Sept. 1, 2013; Mar. 8, 2016, eff. immediately.

Committee Comments

(Revised March 8, 2016)

Special Supreme Court Committee
on Child Custody Issues

Rule 900 emphasizes the importance of child custody or allocation of parental responsibilities proceedings and highlights the purpose of the rules that follow, which is to ensure that child custody and allocation of parental responsibilities proceedings are expeditious, child-focused and fair to all parties.

The rules in the 900 series were written by the Special Supreme Court Committee on Child Custody Issues. The Special Committee was appointed shortly after our Supreme Court adopted the rules promulgated by the Special Supreme Court Committee on Capital Cases. See Rule 43 (judicial

seminars on capital cases), Rule 411 (applicability of discovery rules to capital sentencing hearings), Rule 412(c) (State identification of material that may be exculpatory or mitigating), Rule 417 (DNA evidence), and Rules 701(b) and 714 (Capital Litigation Bar). These rules were designed to improve pretrial and trial procedures in capital cases. In appointing the Special Committee on Child Custody Issues, our Supreme Court indicated its strong desire to address problems which were apparent in the most significant cases courts must decide—those involving child custody or allocation of parental responsibilities.

Our Supreme Court and legislature have repeatedly stressed the need for child custody or allocation of parental responsibilities proceedings to be handled expeditiously, with great emphasis on the best interest of the child. As pointed out by our Supreme Court in *In re D.F.*, 208 Ill. 2d 223, 241 (2003), the Juvenile Court Act of 1987 (705 ILCS 405/2–14(a)), sets forth the "legislature's stated policy and purpose of expediting juvenile court proceedings and seeking permanency for children in a 'just and speedy' manner." Similarly, the Illinois Marriage and Dissolution of Marriage Act (750 ILCS 5/606(a)) provides: "Custody proceedings shall receive priority in being set for hearing." As explained by our Supreme Court in *In re A.W.J.*, 197 Ill. 492, 497–98 (2001): "Like proceedings under the Adoption Act (750 ILCS 50/1 *et seq.* (West 1994)) and the Juvenile Court Act of 1987 (705 ILCS 405/2–1 *et seq.* (West 1994)) custody proceedings under the Marriage and Dissolution Act are guided by the overriding lodestar of the best interests of the child or children involved."

The Special Committee noted that proceedings under the Adoption Act "shall receive priority over other civil cases in being set for hearing," and that appealable orders under the Adoption Act "shall be prosecuted and heard on an expedited basis." 750 ILCS 50/20.

The Special Committee also noted that, effective July 1, 2004, our Supreme Court adopted Rule 306 A, Expedited Appeals in Child Custody Cases. Rule 306 A (f) provides that "Except for good cause shown, the appellate court shall issue its decision within 150 days after the filing of the notice of appeal." Rule 306 A (h) provides in part: "Requests for continuance are disfavored and shall be granted only for compelling circumstances."

Paragraph (b)(1) defines "Child custody or allocation of parental responsibilities proceedings" broadly for the purposes of the rules. The broad definition is important, because the need to expedite custody and allocation of parental responsibilities decisions applies to all types of custody and allocation of parental responsibilities cases and coordination of these cases is essential.

The rest of Rule 900(b) sets out the scope of the Committee's other rule proposals.

Paragraph (b)(2) explains that Part A of the rules, consisting of Rules 900 through 920, is applicable to all child custody and allocation of parental responsibilities proceedings, except as noted. Rules 909 through 920 are reserved.

Paragraph (b)(3) explains that Part B of the rules, consisting of Rules 921 through 940, deals with dissolution of marriage and paternity cases. Rules 925 through 940 are reserved.

Paragraph (b)(4) explains that Part C of the rules, consisting only of Rule 942, Court Family Conferences, applies to nondelinquency juvenile cases.

Other Supreme Court rules will continue to apply in child custody or allocation of parental responsibilities proceedings unless noted.

The 900 series of rules does not address proceedings arising under the Adoption Act (750 ILCS 50/1 *et seq.*). The Special Committee believes that adoption is qualitatively different from the child custody and allocation of parental responsibilities proceedings addressed in the Rule 900 series. Consequently, any rule changes applicable to proceedings under the Adoption Act will be addressed separately.

The Illinois Marriage and Dissolution of Marriage Act, Pub. Act 99–90 (eff. Jan. 1, 2016) (amending 750 ILCS 5/101 *et seq.*), has changed the terms "Custody," "Visitation" (as to parents) and "Removal" to "Allocation of Parental Responsibilities," "Parenting Time" and "Relocation." These rules are being amended to reflect those changes. The rules utilize both "custody" and "allocation of parental responsibilities" in recognition that some legislative enactments covered by the rules utilize the term "custody" while the Illinois Marriage and Dissolution of Marriage Act and the Illinois Parentage Act of 2015 utilize the term "allocation of parental responsibilities." The Special Committee has attempted to adhere to the usage found in the applicable legislative enactments.

Rule 901. General Rules

(a) Expedited Hearings. Child custody and allocation of parental responsibilities proceedings shall be scheduled and heard on an expedited basis. Hearings in child custody and allocation of parental responsibilities proceedings shall be held in strict compliance with applicable deadlines established by statute or by this article.

(b) Setting of Hearings. Hearings in child custody and allocation of parental responsibilities proceedings shall be set for specific times. At each hearing, the next hearing shall be scheduled and the parties shall be notified of the date and time of the next hearing. Hearings rescheduled following a continuance shall be set for the earliest possible date.

(c) Continuances. Parties, witnesses and counsel shall be held accountable for attending hearings in child custody and allocation of parental responsibilities proceedings. Continuances shall not be granted in child custody and allocation of parental responsibilities proceedings except for good cause shown and may be granted if the continuance is consistent with the health, safety and best interests of the child. The

party requesting the continuance and the reasons for the continuance shall be documented in the record.

(d) In any child custody, allocation of parental responsibilities, or relocation proceeding taken under advisement by the trial court, the trial judge shall render its decision as soon as possible but not later than 60 days after the completion of the trial or hearing.

(e) Appeals. Appeals from orders entered in child custody and allocation of parental responsibilities proceedings shall be pursuant to the applicable civil appeals rules. All such proceedings shall be expedited according to Rule 311(a).

Adopted February 10, 2006, eff. July 1, 2006. Amended February 26, 2010, eff. immediately; Mar. 8, 2016, eff. immediately.

Committee Comments
(Revised March 8, 2016)

Special Supreme Court Committee
on Child Custody Issues

Rule 901 includes procedures that are designed and proven to expedite child custody and allocation of parental responsibilities proceedings.

Paragraph (a) requires strict compliance with statutory and rule based deadlines for child custody and allocation of parental responsibilities proceedings.

Paragraphs (b) and (c) concerning the setting of hearings and limitations on continuances should help to significantly reduce delays in child custody and allocation of parental responsibilities proceedings.

Paragraph (d) requires timely disposition of cases taken under advisement by the trial court.

Rule 902. Pleadings

(a) Complaint or Petition. The initial complaint or petition in a child custody or allocation of parental responsibilities proceeding shall state (1) whether the child involved is the subject of any other child custody or allocation of parental responsibilities proceeding pending before another division of the circuit court, or another court or administrative body of Illinois or of any other state, an Indian tribe, or a foreign country and (2) whether any order affecting the custody, allocation of parental responsibilities, visitation, or parenting time of the child has been entered by the circuit court or any of its divisions, or by another court or administrative body of Illinois or of any other state, an Indian tribe, or a foreign country. If any child custody or allocation of parental responsibilities proceeding is pending with respect to the child, or any order has been entered with respect to the custody, allocation of parental responsibilities, visitation, or parenting time of the child, the initial complaint or petition shall identify the tribunal involved and the parties to the action.

(b) Verification of Initial Complaint or Petition. The plaintiff or petitioner in a child custody or allocation of parental responsibilities proceeding shall verify the pleadings required by paragraph (a) of this rule. If the plaintiff or petitioner is a public agency, the verification shall be on information and belief of the attorney filing the pleading and shall state that reasonable efforts were made to obtain all information relevant to the matters verified.

(c) Answer or Appearance. In a child custody or allocation of parental responsibilities proceeding the defendant's (or respondent's) answer, if required, shall include a verified disclosure of any relevant information known to the defendant (or respondent) regarding any pending proceedings or orders described in paragraph (a) of this rule. Any defendant or respondent who appears but is not required to file an answer in the child custody or allocation of parental responsibilities matter shall be questioned under oath by the court at the party's first appearance before the court regarding any proceedings or orders described in paragraph (a) of this rule.

(d) Continuing Duty. The parties have a continuing duty to disclose information relating to other pending child custody or allocation of parental responsibilities proceedings or any existing orders affecting the custody, allocation of parental responsibilities, visitation, or parenting time of the child, and shall immediately disclose to the court and the other parties to the proceeding any such information obtained after the initial pleadings, answer or appearance.

Adopted February 10, 2006, effective July 1, 2006. Amended Mar. 8, 2016, eff. immediately.

Committee Comments

(Revised March 8, 2016)

Special Supreme Court Committee
on Child Custody Issues

The purpose of Rule 902 is to ensure that the trial court is aware of all custody and allocation of parental responsibilities proceedings and orders relating to the child who is before the court. The Special Committee found that child custody and allocation of parental responsibilities, visitation and parenting time may be the subject of multiple proceedings and orders. Rule 902 addresses the problem of multiple proceedings that may occur intrastate and intra-circuit. Multiple proceedings may arise intra-circuit when parties file for relief under different statutory provisions (*e.g.*, an abuse case and a simultaneous guardianship case).

Paragraph (a) provides that the initial pleading of a party to a custody or allocation of parental responsibilities proceeding must include information regarding other pending custody or allocation of parental responsibilities proceedings and prior orders relating to custody, allocation of parental responsibilities, visitation or parenting time. Information in paragraph (a) may be submitted to the court in a joint filing including the information

required by section 209(a) of the Uniform Child–Custody and Enforcement Act (750 ILCS 36/209(a)).

Paragraph (b) requires that the pleadings required by paragraph (a) of this rule be verified by the plaintiff or petitioner in child custody or allocation of parental responsibilities proceedings.

Paragraph (c) provides that parties not required to file pleadings may be questioned by the trial court regarding other pending matters and prior orders.

Paragraph (d) provides that all parties have a continuing duty to disclose such matters to the court.

Requiring disclosure of other proceedings and orders should minimize the possibility of inconsistent child custody or allocation of parental responsibilities orders and help to prevent forum shopping.

Rule 903. Assignment and Coordination of Cases

Whenever possible and appropriate, all child custody and allocation of parental responsibilities proceedings relating to an individual child shall be conducted by a single judge. Each judicial circuit shall adopt a rule or order providing for assignment and coordination of child custody and allocation of parental responsibilities proceedings. Assignments in child custody and allocation of parental responsibilities proceedings shall be in accordance with the circuit rule or order then in force.

Adopted February 10, 2006, effective July 1, 2006. Amended Mar. 8, 2016, eff. immediately

Committee Comments

(Revised March 8, 2016)

Special Supreme Court Committee
on Child Custody Issues

Rule 903 encourages the assignment of all custody and allocation of parental responsibilities proceedings concerning a child to a single judge. The rule does not mandate consolidation of child custody or allocation of parental responsibilities proceedings, because consolidation may be inadvisable in certain cases. Moreover, in some counties mandatory consolidation may be impracticable because of the arrangement of courtrooms and facilities.

Rule 903 encourages the consolidation of cases by requiring that the judicial circuits adopt rules or orders concerning the assignment and coordination of child custody and allocation of parental responsibilities proceedings, and by providing that the assignment of child custody and allocation of parental responsibilities proceedings will be in accordance with those rules.

Commentary adopted February 10, 2006, effective July 1, 2006.

Rule 904. Case Management Conferences

In child custody proceedings other than cases under articles II, III and IV of the Juvenile Court Act of 1987, and cases under the Illinois Marriage and Dissolution of Marriage Act and the Illinois Parentage Act of 1984 provided for under Part B of this article (see Rule 923), an initial case management conference pursuant to Rule 218 shall be held not later than 90 days after the petition or complaint has been served upon the respondent. If not previously resolved, the court shall address the appointment of a guardian *ad litem* or counsel for the child and counsel for any indigent party entitled to the assistance of appointed counsel at the initial case management conference.

Adopted February 10, 2006, effective July 1, 2006.

Committee Comments
Special Supreme Court Committee on Child Custody Issues

Case management conferences provide an effective way for the trial court to simplify issues and expedite cases. Rule 904 provides that an initial case management conference will be held within 90 days after the petition or compliant has been served upon the respondent in child custody proceedings not covered by other rules.

Special rules regarding conferences are included in Parts B and C of the Rule 900 series: Rule 923 addresses case management conferences in dissolution of marriage and paternity cases. Rule 942 authorizes the use of Court Family Conferences in abuse and neglect cases.

Rule 905. Mediation

(a) Each judicial circuit shall establish a program to provide mediation for cases involving the custody or allocation of parental responsibilities of a child or relocation of a child or visitation or parenting time issues (whether or not the parties have been married). In addition to the minimum requirements set forth in subparagraph (b)(2) of Rule 99, local circuit court rules for mediation in child custody, allocation of parental responsibilities, relocation, visitation, and parenting time cases shall address: (i) mandatory training for mediators; (ii) limitation of the mediation program to child custody, allocation of parental responsibilities, relocation, visitation, and parenting time issues; (iii) (unless otherwise provided for in this article) standards to determine which child custody, allocation of parental responsibilities, relocation, visitation, and parenting time issues should be referred to mediation and the time for referral; and (iv) excuse from referral to mediation if the court determines an impediment to mediation exists. The immunity and approval requirements of subparagraph (b)(1) of Rule 99 shall apply to mediation programs for child custody, allocation of parental responsibilities, relocation, visitation, and parenting time matters.

(b) Each judicial circuit shall establish a program to provide mediation for dissolution of marriage and paternity cases involving the custody, allocation of parental responsibilities of a child, relocation of a child, visitation or parenting time issues (whether or not the parties have been married). In addition to the minimum requirements set forth in subparagraph (b)(2) of Rule 99, local circuit court rules for mediation in dissolution of marriage and paternity cases shall address: (i) mandatory expertise requirements of a mediator; (ii) mandatory training for mediators; (iii) limitation of the mediation program to child custody, allocation of parental responsibilities, relocation, visitation, and parenting time issues; and (iv) referral of child custody, allocation of parental responsibilities, relocation, visitation, and parenting time issues to mediation, pursuant to Rule 923(a)(3), unless the court determines an impediment to mediation exists. The immunity and approval requirements of subparagraph (b)(1) of Rule 99 shall apply to mediation programs for child custody, allocation of parental responsibilities, relocation, visitation, and parenting time matters. In cases where a litigant can only communicate in a language other than English, the court will make a good-faith effort to provide a mediator, and a *pro bono* attorney where applicable, and/or an interpreter who speaks the language of the litigant who needs English assistance.

(c) Every judicial circuit shall file a quarterly report with the Administrative Office of the Illinois Courts setting out the number of custody, allocation of parental responsibilities, visitation, parenting time, and relocation cases referred to mediation, the number of custody, allocation of parental responsibilities, visitation, parenting time, and relocation cases where mediation was referred but did not proceed, the number of cases referred on a *pro bono* basis, the number of cases where there was a full settlement, the number of cases where there was a partial settlement, and the percentage of cases wherein the parties were satisfied or unsatisfied with the process. Every judicial circuit shall require the completion of a mediation report filled out by a mediator on every custody, allocation of parental responsibilities, visitation, parenting time, and relocation case referred to mediation as well as the parties' evaluation of the mediation on forms prescribed by the Administrative Office of the Illinois Courts. The information contained in the mediator and parties' evaluation reports shall remain confidential and shall only be utilized for administrative and statistical purposes as well as the court's review of the efficacy of the mediation program.

(d) In addition to meeting the requirements of Rule 905(a), (b), and (c), local circuit rules may also impose other requirements as deemed necessary by the individual circuits.

Adopted February 10, 2006, effective January 1, 2007. Amended May 19, 2006, effective January 1, 2007; July 1, 2013, eff. Sept. 1, 2013; Mar. 8, 2016, eff. immediately.

Committee Comments
(Revised March 8, 2016)

Special Supreme Court Committee on Child Custody Issues

The Committee believes mediation can be useful in nearly all contested custody or allocation of parental responsibilities proceedings. Mediation can resolve a significant portion of custody and allocation of parental responsibilities disputes and often has a positive impact even when these issues are not resolved. The process of mediation focuses the parties' attention on the needs of the child and helps parties to be realistic in their expectations regarding custody or allocation of parental responsibilities.

Many counties and judicial circuits have had mandatory mediation programs in place in their domestic relations courts for years. Cook County and Du Page County have utilized mandatory mediation programs for more than a decade. To date, these mandatory mediation programs have been implemented by the judicial circuits under the auspices of Rule 99, Mediation Programs.

Rule 905 requires each judicial circuit to establish a mediation program for child custody and allocation of parental responsibilities proceedings. Local circuit court rules will address the specifics of the mediation programs. The Cook County model for mediation programs, which provides county-employed mediators at no cost to the parties, may not be financially or administratively feasible for every circuit. Alternatively, some circuits have required approved mediators to mediate a certain number of reduced fee or *pro bono* cases per year as identified by the court. The individual judicial circuits may implement rules which are particularly appropriate for them, including provisions specifying responsibility for mediation costs.

Paragraph (a) applies to cases involving custody, allocation of parental responsibilities, visitation, or parenting time issues, other than those arising in dissolution of marriage and paternity cases. It requires local circuit court rules to address mandatory training for mediators and limits the mediation program to issues involving child custody, allocation of parental responsibilities, visitation, and parenting time. Paragraph (a) also requires local circuit court rules to set standards to use in determining which child custody, allocation of parental responsibilities, visitation, and parenting time issues should be referred to mediation and also address when the referral will be made.

Paragraph (b) provides for mediation of disputed custody, allocation of parental responsibilities, visitation, parenting time, and relocation issues in dissolution of marriage and paternity cases. The timing and manner of referral to mediation in dissolution of marriage and paternity cases is provided for in Rule 923.

Parties may be excused from referral under both paragraphs (a) and (b) if the court determines an impediment to mediation exists. Such impediments may include family violence, mental or cognitive impairment, alcohol abuse or chemical dependency, or other circumstances which may render mediation inappropriate or would unreasonably interfere with the mediation process.

Date effective

Publisher's Note: the May 19, 2006 amendment, effective January 1, 2007, changed the effective date of the February 10, 2006 enactment of this rule from July 1, 2006 to January 1, 2007.

Rule 906. Attorney Qualifications and Education in Child Custody, Allocation of Parental Responsibilities, Visitation, and Parenting Time Matters

(a) Statement of Purpose. This rule is promulgated to insure that counsel who are appointed by the court to participate in child custody, allocation of parental responsibilities, visitation, and parenting time matters, as delineated in Rule 900(b)(2), possess the ability, knowledge, and experience to do so in a competent and professional manner. To this end, each circuit court of this state shall develop a set of qualifications and educational requirements for attorneys appointed by the court to represent children in child custody and allocation of parental responsibilities cases and guardianship cases when custody or visitation is an issue and shall further develop a plan for the procurement of qualified attorneys in accordance with the plan.

(b) Submission of Qualifications and Plan. The Chief Judge of a judicial circuit shall be responsible for the creation of the qualifications and Plan and for submitting them to the Conference of Chief Judges for approval. The Chief Judges of two or more contiguous judicial circuits may submit a Plan for the creation of a single set of qualifications and Plan encompassing those judicial circuits or encompassing contiguous counties within the circuits.

(c) Qualifications and Plan. The qualifications shall provide that the attorney is licensed and in good standing with the Illinois Supreme Court. Certification requirements may address minimum experience requirements for attorneys appointed by the court to represent minor children. In addition, the qualifications may include one or all of the following which are recommended: (1) Prior to appointment the attorney shall have 10 hours in the two years prior to the date the attorney qualifies for appointment in approved continuing legal education courses in the following areas: child development; roles of guardian *ad litem* and child representative; ethics in child custody and allocation of parental responsibilities cases; relevant substantive state, federal, and case law in custody, allocation of parental responsibilities, visitation, and parenting time matters; family dynamics, including substance abuse, domestic abuse, and mental health issues. (2) Periodic continuing education in approved child related courses shall be required to maintain qualification as an attorney eligible to be appointed by the court in child custody, allocation of parental responsibilities, visitation, and parenting time cases. (3) Requirements for initial pro bono representation. (4) Attorneys who work for governmental agencies may meet the requirements of this rule by attending appropriate in-house legal education classes.

(d) Conference of Chief Judges Review and Approval. The Conference of Chief Judges shall review and approve the Plan or may request that the Chief Judge modify the submitted list of qualifications and Plan. Upon approval, the Chief Judge of each circuit shall be responsible for administering the program and insuring compliance. An attorney approved to be appointed by the Court to participate in child custody, allocation of parental responsibilities, visitation, and parenting time matters under a Plan approved in one county or judicial circuit shall have reciprocity to participate in child custody, allocation of parental responsibilities, visitation, and parenting time matters in other counties and judicial circuits in Illinois.

Adopted February 10, 2006, effective July 1, 2006. Amended Mar. 8, 2016, eff. immediately.

Committee Comments
(Revised March 8, 2016)
Special Supreme Court Committee on Child Custody Issues

Paragraph (a) requires each judicial circuit to establish qualifications and educational requirements for attorneys who are appointed by a court to represent children in child custody and allocation of parental responsibilities proceedings. The circuits would also be required to establish a plan for procuring the services of qualified attorneys for child custody and allocation of parental responsibilities cases.

Paragraph (b) requires that attorney qualification and procurement plans be submitted to the Conference of Chief Circuit Judges for approval. It also provides that attorney qualification and procurement plans may be drafted to apply to contiguous circuits or to contiguous counties within two or more circuits.

Paragraph (c) specifies that attorneys appointed to represent children must be licensed and in good standing as attorneys. It also provides that the qualifications and standards must include a minimum experience requirement, and may include criteria concerning initial and continuing legal education requirements and requirements for initial *pro bono* representation. Attorneys approved under a circuit plan would be eligible for appointment in cases in other areas of the state on the basis of reciprocity.

In writing Rule 906, the Special Committee considered Rule 714, Capital Litigation Trial Bar, which imposes minimum requirements upon trial counsel in order to insure that counsel who participate in capital cases possess the ability, knowledge and experience to do so in a competent and professional manner. The Special Committee believes that cases involving child custody, allocation of parental responsibilities, visitation and parenting time issues demand the same high standards of advocacy as do capital cases.

The Special Committee is mindful that many judicial circuits will find it very difficult to find funds to pay for the plans under which counsel are appointed. Ideally, the State would provide sufficient funding to reimburse the private attorneys who are appointed by the court. In the absence of such funding, the individual judicial circuits will need to be innovative in meeting the financial requirements of the plans. In addition to requiring the parties to pay for the appointed lawyer's services, the local rules could provide for the targeting of court filing fees. Voluntary *pro bono* service is also strongly encouraged.

Rule 907. Minimum Duties and Responsibilities of Attorneys for Minor Children

(a) Every child representative, attorney for a child and guardian *ad litem* shall adhere to all ethical rules governing attorneys in professional practice, be mindful of any conflicts in the representation of children and take appropriate action to address such conflicts.

(b) Every child representative, attorney for a minor child and guardian *ad litem* shall have the right to interview his or her client(s) without any limitation or impediment. Upon appointment of a child representative, attorney for the child or guardian *ad litem*, the trial court shall enter an order to allow access to the child and all relevant documents.

(c) As soon as practicable, the child representative, attorney for the child or guardian *ad litem* shall interview the child, or if the child is too young to be interviewed, the attorney should, at a minimum, observe the child. The child representative, attorney for the child or guardian *ad litem* shall also take whatever reasonable steps are necessary to obtain all information pertaining to issues affecting the child, including interviewing family members and others possessing special knowledge of the child's circumstances.

(d) The child representative, attorney for the child or guardian *ad litem* shall take whatever reasonable steps are necessary to determine what services the family needs to address the custody or allocation of parental responsibilities dispute, make appropriate recommendations to the parties, and seek appropriate relief in court, if required, in order to serve the best interest of the child.

(e) The child representative, attorney for the child or guardian *ad litem* shall determine whether a settlement of the custody or allocation of parental responsibilities dispute can be achieved by agreement, and, to the extent feasible, shall attempt to resolve such disputes by an agreement that serves the best interest of the child.

Adopted February 10, 2006, effective July 1, 2006. Amended Mar. 8, 2016, eff. immediately.

Committee Comments
Special Supreme Court Committee on Child Custody Issues

Rule 907 establishes minimum standards of practice for attorneys who represent children.

Paragraph (a) sets out the responsibility of an attorney representing a child in any capacity to act in accordance with the rules of ethics and avoid conflicts of interest.

Paragraphs (b) and (c) provide guidance on the attorney's essential duty of investigation: the duty to determine the child's circumstances and the family's needs. In aid of this duty, the rule provides specifically that an attorney has the right to interview a child client without limitation or impediment. Paragraph (b) also provides that the trial court shall enter an order allowing the child representative, attorney for the child or guardian *ad litem* access to all relevant documents.

Paragraph (d) addresses advocacy. The attorney for a child is required to make appropriate recommendations to the parties, seek resolution by agreement where it is in the best interests of the child, and seek relief on behalf of the child in court, when needed.

The Special Committee is aware that the American Bar Association and the National Conference of Commissioners on Uniform State Laws have taken the position that there should be three distinct types of appointments: (1) a child's attorney, who provides independent legal counsel in the same manner as to an adult client; (2) a "best interest attorney," such as Illinois' child representatives, who provide independent legal services for the child's best interests but who does not make general "recommendations"; (3) a guardian *ad litem*, who gathers information for the court and helps identify other needed services for the child or family.

In its Standards of Practice for Attorneys Representing Children in Custody Cases, the ABA recommended that attorneys not serve as GALs unless they do so as would a non-lawyer. However, the Illinois Marriage and Dissolution of Marriage Act mandates that GALs appointed under the Act be attorneys and that they may actually act in *loco parentis* for the child. See 750 ILCS 5/506. It is the position of the Special Committee that none of these concerns require changes in the language of Rule 907 or any other rule.

Rule 908. Judicial Training on Child Custody and Allocation of Parental Responsibilities Issues

(a) Meeting the challenge of deciding child custody and allocation of parental responsibilities cases fairly and expeditiously requires experience or training in a broad range of matters including, but not limited to: (1) child development, child psychology and family dynamics; (2) domestic violence issues; (3) alternative dispute resolution strategies; (4) child sexual abuse issues; (5) financial issues in these matters; (6) addiction and treatment issues; (7) statutory time limitations; and (8) cultural and diversity issues.

(b) Judges should have experience or training in the matters described in paragraph (a) of this rule before hearing these cases. Before a judge is assigned to hear child custody cases or allocation of parental responsibilities cases, the Chief Judge of the judicial circuit should consider the judge's judicial and legal experience, any prior training the judge has completed and any training that may be available to the judge before he or she will begin hearing these cases.

(c) Judges who, by specific assignment or otherwise, may be called upon to hear child custody or allocation of parental responsibilities cases should participate in judicial education opportunities available on these topics, such as attending those sessions or por-

tions of the Education Conference, presented bi-annually at the direction of the Supreme Court, which address the topics described in paragraph (a) of this rule. Judges may also elect to participate in any other Judicial Conference Judicial Education Seminars addressing these topics, participate in other judicial education programs approved for the award of continuing judicial education credit by the Supreme Court, complete individual training through the Internet, computer training programs, video presentations, or other relevant programs. The Chief Judges of the judicial circuits should make reasonable efforts to ensure that judges have the opportunity to attend programs approved for the award of continuing judicial education credit by the Supreme Court which address the topics and issues described in paragraph (a) of this rule.

Adopted February 10, 2006, effective July 1, 2006. Amended May 19, 2006, effective July 1, 2006; Mar. 8, 2016, eff. immediately.

Committee Comments

(Revised March 8, 2016)

Special Supreme Court Committee
on Child Custody Issues

Proposed Rule 908 recognizes the complexity of child custody and allocation of parental responsibilities cases and the broad range of experience and training that would be helpful to judges hearing these cases.

Paragraph (b) requires that chief judges consider a judge's experience and training before the judge is assigned to hear such cases. This provision does not establish a mandatory prerequisite to such an assignment.

Paragraph (c) requires that trial judges who will hear child custody and allocation of parental responsibilities cases should participate in Judicial Education opportunities on these type of matters. The proposed rule encourages personal attendance at seminars, but emphasizes that other forms of training may be used.

PART B. ALLOCATION OF PARENTAL RESPONSIBILITIES PROCEEDINGS UNDER THE ILLINOIS MARRIAGE AND DISSOLUTION OF MARRIAGE ACT AND THE ILLINOIS PARENTAGE ACT OF 1984

Rule 921. General Provisions

In addition to the rules in Part A of this article, the rules in this Part B shall apply to allocation of parental responsibilities proceedings filed under the Illinois Marriage and Dissolution of Marriage Act, and the Illinois Parentage Act of 1984.

Adopted February 10, 2006, effective July 1, 2006. Amended Mar. 8, 2016, eff. immediately.

Committee Comments
(Revised March 8, 2016)
Special Supreme Court Committee on Child Custody Issues

Rule 921 establishes the scope of Part B, which includes Rules 921 through 924. Rules 925 through 940 are Reserved. Rules 921 through 924 apply to allocation of parental responsibilities proceedings filed under the Illinois Marriage and Dissolution of Marriage Act, and the Illinois Parentage Act of 1984. The requirements of Rules 921 through 924 are in addition to the requirements of Part A found in Rules 900 through 908 as applicable.

Rule 922.   Time Limitations

All allocation of parental responsibilities proceedings under this rule in the trial court shall be resolved within 18 months from the date of service of the petition or complaint to final order. In the event this time limit is not met, the trial court shall make written findings as to the reason(s) for the delay. The 18–month time limit shall not apply if the parties, including the attorney representing the child, the guardian *ad litem* or the child representative, agree in writing and the trial court makes a written finding that the extension of time is for good cause shown. In the event the parties do not agree, the court may consider whether an extension of time should be allowed for good cause shown.
Adopted February 10, 2006, effective July 1, 2006. Amended Mar. 8, 2016, eff. immediately.

Committee Comments
(Revised March 8, 2016)
Special Supreme Court Committee on Child Custody Issues

Rule 922 provides that allocation of parental responsibilities matters in dissolution of marriage and paternity cases must be resolved within 18 months. Written findings are required if the deadline is not met, and extensions of the time limit may only be granted for good cause shown, on written finding by the trial court.

Rule 923.   Case Management Conferences

(a) Initial Conference. In an allocation of parental responsibilities proceeding under this part, an initial case management conference pursuant to Rule 218 shall be held not later than 90 days after service of the petition or complaint is obtained. In addition to other matters the court may choose to address, the initial conference shall cover the following issues:

(1) *Parenting Education.* The parents shall show proof of completion of an approved parenting education program as required by Rule 924, provide a fixed schedule for compliance, or show cause to excuse compliance;

(2) *Allocation of Parental Responsibilities and Parenting Plan.* The parents shall provide the court with an agreed order regarding allocation of parental responsibilities and an agreed parenting plan, if there is an agreement. In the event that the parents do not agree to a parenting plan, then each parent must submit a proposed parenting plan to the Court within 120 days after service or filing of a petition for allocation of parental responsibilities;

(3) *Mediation.* If there is no agreement regarding allocation of parental responsibilities or a parenting plan or both, the court shall schedule the matter for mediation in accordance with Rule 905(b) and shall advise each parent of the responsibilities imposed upon them by the pertinent local court rules.

(b) A full case management conference shall be held not later than 30 days after mediation has been completed. In addition to other matters the court may choose to address at the conference, and if the court has not appointed counsel previously, the court shall address whether to appoint an attorney for the child or a guardian *ad litem* or a child representative in accordance with section 506 of the Illinois Marriage and Dissolution of Marriage Act (750 ILCS 5/506).
Adopted February 10, 2006, effective July 1, 2006. Amended Mar. 8, 2016, eff. immediately.

Committee Comments
(Revised March 8, 2016)
Special Supreme Court Committee on Child Custody Issues

Paragraph (a) provides that an initial case management conference is required within 90 days after service of a petition or complaint is obtained in a dissolution of marriage case involving a child or in a paternity case. At the initial conference the trial court will ensure compliance with parenting education requirements (Rule 924) and determine whether the parents have agreed to the allocation of parental responsibilities and parenting plan. Parents not in agreement regarding allocation of parental responsibilities and parenting plan issues at the time of the initial case management conference will be referred to mediation. The trial court may also use the initial case management conference to address other matters it deems proper.

Each judicial circuit which currently has a mediation program has a provision in their local circuit court rules explaining how parents whose children are the subject of an allocation of parental responsibilities dispute must comply with the circuit court rules. These rules vary from judicial circuit to judicial circuit. In Cook County, parents are required to attend the mediation session but, if they do not agree with the mediator's decision, the parents merely bring this fact to the attention of the circuit court. In Du Page County, if the parents do not agree on allocation of parental responsibilities after they have completed the requirements of the mediation program, they may be required to see a clinical psychologist for a mandatory evaluation. Another difference between the judicial circuits is how the costs of mediation are paid. While many mediation programs impose costs, the Cook County Circuit Court's Marriage and Family Counseling Service is free.

Paragraph (a)(3) supports the Special Committee's goal of allowing the individual judicial circuits to adopt rules and set up programs which best suit that circuit's needs.

Paragraph (b) provides that in cases referred to mediation under the rule, a full case management conference is required within 30 days after mediation is completed. At the full case management conference, the court will consider, inter alia, the appointment of counsel for the child as provided in section 506 of the Illinois Marriage and Dissolution of Marriage Act (750 ILCS 5/506).

Rule 924. Parenting Education Requirement

(a) **Program.** Each circuit or county shall create or approve a parenting education program consisting of at least four hours covering the subjects of parenting time and allocation of parental responsibilities and their impact on children.

(b) **Mandatory Attendance.** Except when excused by the court for good cause shown, all parties shall be required to attend and complete an approved parenting education program as soon as possible, but not later than 60 days after an initial case management conference. In the case of a default or lack of jurisdiction over the respondent, only the petitioning party is required to attend but if the respondent later enters an appearance or participates in postjudgment proceedings, then the party who has not attended the program shall attend. The court shall not excuse attendance unless the reason is documented in the record and a finding is made that excusing one or both parents from attendance is in the best interests of the child.

(c) **Sanctions.** The court may impose sanctions on any party willfully failing to complete the program.
Adopted February 10, 2006, effective July 1, 2006. Amended Mar. 8, 2016, eff. immediately.

Committee Comments
(Revised March 8, 2016)

Special Supreme Court Committee
on Child Custody Issues

Parenting education can have a very positive impact on the outcome of an child custody allocation of parental responsibilities proceeding. Parenting education encourages parents to think about the impact of their actions on their children and teaches parents to deal with adult problems in ways that avoid harm to their children.

Paragraph (a) requires each judicial circuit or county to create or approve a parenting education program and sets out the minimum requirements of such a program. Individual judicial circuits or counties may permit the circuit courts to impose additional educational requirements on one or all of the parties.

Paragraph (b) requires parenting education for all dissolution of marriage cases involving a child and all parentage cases, absent good cause shown. Compliance with the parenting education requirement will be reviewed at the initial case management conference. Parents are expected to complete parenting education not later than 60 days after the initial case management conference.

Paragraph (c) provides that sanctions may be imposed on parties who willfully fail to comply with the parenting education requirement.

PART C. CHILD CUSTODY PROCEEDINGS UNDER ARTICLES II, III AND IV OF THE JUVENILE COURT ACT OF 1987

Rule 941. General Provisions

In addition to the rules in part A of this article, the rules in this part C shall apply to child custody proceedings filed under articles II, III and IV of the Juvenile Court Act of 1987.
Adopted February 10, 2006, effective July 1, 2006.

Rule 942. Court Family Conferences

(a) **Abuse Neglect, and Dependency Cases.** In cases under articles II, III, and IV of the Juvenile Court Act of 1987, on motion of any party or on its own motion, the court may in its discretion hold a Court Family Conference in accordance with this rule.

(b) **Initial Conference**

(1) *Time.* At the temporary custody hearing, or as soon thereafter as possible, the court shall set the date and time for an initial Court Family Conference. The initial Court Family Conference shall be held not less than 56 days after the Temporary Custody Hearing.

(2) *Parties.* All parties shall appear at the initial Court Family Conference except the minor, who may appear in person or through a guardian *ad litem* or his or her attorney. The caseworker assigned to the case must also appear. If no party objects, a foster parent may participate in the Conference. If any party objects, the court in its discretion may exclude the foster parent but the foster parent retains the right to be heard by the court before the end of the proceedings. The court may in its discretion allow other persons interested in the minor to attend the Conference at the request of the child or a parent. The failure of any party (with the exception of the child or his or her guardian *ad litem* or attorney) to appear shall not prevent the court from proceeding with the Court Family Conference.

(3) *Record.* If all parties are present for the initial Court Family Conference, the court shall conduct the Conference off the record, and at the conclusion of the Conference summarize the Conference for the record. If the parents are not present,

the Court shall conduct the entire Conference on the record.

(4) *Disclosure of Service Plan.* The Illinois Department of Children and Family Services or its assigns shall provide the most recent service plan to all parties seven days before the initial Court Family Conference. In the event that the service plan has not been filed with the court prior to the initial Court Family Conference, the court shall convene the initial Court Family Conference and discussion shall focus on services that would appropriately be included in the plan. Such discussion should ensure that the family and the caseworker have a clear understanding of the expectations of the court.

(5) *Issues.*

(A) The discussion at the initial Court Family Conference shall focus on eliminating the causes or conditions that contributed to the findings of probable cause and, if applicable, the existence of urgent and immediate necessity. If possible, at the conclusion of the discussion the court shall set a target date for return home or case closure. If the court determines that setting a target date for return home or case closure is not possible or is premature, the court, during the discussion, shall make clear to the parties and the caseworker what needs to be accomplished before the court will consider setting a target return home date.

(B) The discussion at the initial Court Family Conference shall include the services contained in the service plan for the parents and the child. The needs of the child and visitation plans between the parent and the child and between the child and any siblings shall also be discussed.

(C) The discussion shall include any other matters that the court, in its discretion, deems relevant.

(6) *Other Issues.* At the initial Court Family Conference, the court may address case management issues that would be appropriate for consideration at a subsequent Court Family Conference.

(7) *Order.* At the conclusion of the initial Court Family Conference, the court shall enter an order approving the service plan or setting forth any changes the court requires to be made to the service plan.

(c) Subsequent Court Family Conferences. Court Family Conferences may be held after the initial Conference as the court deems necessary. At a subsequent Court Family Conference, the court has the authority to make orders relating to case management as is provided for in other civil cases by Rule 218. In the court's discretion, matters considered at the initial Conference may be reviewed at any subsequent Conference.

(d) Concurrent Hearings. The initial Court Family Conference may be held concurrently with any

hearing held within the required time. Subsequent Court Family Conferences may be held concurrently with any other hearing on the case.

(e) Confidentiality. With the exception of statements that would support new allegations of abuse or neglect, statements made during an off the record portion of an initial or subsequent Court Family Conference shall be inadmissible in any administrative or judicial proceeding. If the court refers to any specific statements made by the parents in its summary of the off the record portion of the Conference or in the order entered following the Conference, upon objection of the parents, such references shall be stricken.
Adopted February 10, 2006, effective July 1, 2006.

Committee Comments
Special Supreme Court Committee on Child Custody Issues

A Court Family Conference is intended to be an opportunity for the trial court, the parents, the caseworker and the child or child's representative to discuss the court process, and the meaning, intent and practicality of the service plan; to discuss and ensure the safety of the child; to cooperatively discuss goals; and ultimately, to expedite resolution of the case through reunification of the family or other appropriate action. Paragraph (a) authorizes the use of Court Family Conferences in abuse, neglect and dependency cases.

Paragraph (b)(1) provides that a Court Family Conference will be held not less than 56 days after the Temporary Custody Hearing in cases when the court determines it is appropriate to do so.

Paragraph (b)(2) provides that all parties are required to appear at a Court Family Conference, except the minor, who may appear through a guardian *ad litem* or through counsel. The assigned caseworker must also appear, and a foster parent may appear, absent objection by a party.

Paragraph (b)(3) provides that statements made at Court Family Conferences are confidential and may not be used subsequently, except for statements that may provide the basis for a new allegation of abuse or neglect. The Court Family Conference will be off the record unless the parents are not present. Upon completion of an off the record Conference, the court will summarize the matter for the record.

Paragraph (b)(4) provides that the most recent service plan is to be provided to the parties seven days prior to the Conference. At the initial Conference the service plan is discussed, with the purpose of ensuring that the caseworker and the parents clearly understand the expectations of the court.

Paragraph (b)(5) addresses the issues which should be discussed at the Court Family Conference, with an emphasis on the parties, the court and the service providers sharing information in an open and expeditious manner.

Paragraph (b)(7) provides that the court may approve the service plan or order changes to the plan at the conclusion of an initial Court Family Conference.

Paragraph (c) allows subsequent Court Family Conferences, and the combination of initial or subsequent Court Family Conferences with other hearings in the case. Subsequent Court Family Conferences may address any issues that could be considered in a case management conference under Rule 218.

Paragraph (d) provides that Court Family Conferences may be held at the same time that the court conducts any other hearing. As the rules of evidence apply to hearings, but do not apply to Court Family Conferences, it is incumbent upon the circuit court to only consider properly admissible evidence when determining the result of the hearing.

In order to promote an open and honest discourse at an initial or subsequent Court Family Conference, Paragraph (e) provides that statements made during the off the record portion of the Conference shall be inadmissible in any administrative or judicial proceeding. The only exception to this confidentiality requirement is when the statements at the Conference would support new allegations of abuse or neglect.

ARTICLE X. ILLINOIS SUPREME COURT COMMISSION ON ACCESS TO JUSTICE

Rule
10–100. Illinois Supreme Court Commission on Access to Justice.
10–101. Standardized Forms.

Rule 10–100. Illinois Supreme Court Commission on Access to Justice

(a) Purpose.

The Illinois Supreme Court Commission on Access to Justice is established to promote, facilitate, and enhance equal access to justice with an emphasis on access to the Illinois civil courts and administrative agencies for all people, particularly the poor and vulnerable. The purpose is to make access to justice a high priority for everyone in the legal system and, to the maximum extent possible, the Commission is intended to complement and collaborate with other entities addressing access to justice issues.

(b) Membership and Terms.

(1) The Illinois Supreme Court shall appoint seven members to the Commission. In addition, the Illinois Bar Foundation, The Chicago Bar Foundation, Lawyers Trust Fund of Illinois, and the Illinois Equal Justice Foundation shall have the right to appoint one member each. The commission shall be composed of five members of the judiciary, five lawyers, and one member who is not a lawyer. The Chief Justice of the Illinois Supreme Court shall appoint a person to serve as chair of the commission from among the members of the commission.

(i) The Illinois Supreme Court Commission on Access to Justice may, at its discretion, appoint separate specialized working groups and members to assist it in the carrying out of the purposes of the commission. Specialized groups may include, for example, Education, Court Rules/Procedures, Resources, Standardized Forms, and New Initiatives. These groups shall focus on particular issues within the working group's area of concentration. Membership within these specialized groups may be composed of both members and nonmembers of the Illinois Access to Justice Commission.

(2) Appointed members shall be selected based on their dedication to the purposes and goals of the Commission. The potential appointee's contributions to the bar and community and demonstrated commitment to providing legal services to the underserved also shall be considered.

(3) Members of the Commission shall be appointed for terms of three years, except that in making initial appointments to the Commission, the Court may make appointments for one-year or two-year terms to ensure that the terms of the Commission's members are staggered, so that no more than one third of the members' terms expire in any given year.

(4) Members shall not be compensated for their contributions, but may be reimbursed for their necessary expenses.

(c) Duties.

In realizing the purpose of the Commission, the duties may include:

(1) encouraging means by which individuals can find proper legal representation in the judicial system;

(2) maintaining circuit court and community support and assistance so that the existing legal self-help centers in all Illinois counties can remain effective and accessible;

(3) collaborating with the circuit courts to develop standard guidelines and judicial education programs regarding interaction between self-represented litigants, judges, clerks, and other court personnel;

(4) creating standardized forms for simpler civil legal problems and basic procedural functions that, while not required for use by all litigants, would be required for courts to accept for filing throughout the state to ease the difficulty in self-representation;

(5) addressing language barriers in the courtroom;

(6) addressing the issue of accessibility to the courts, particularly in rural areas of Illinois;

(7) recognizing judges, attorneys, clerks, or other court personnel for their contributions of leadership and commitment to access to justice;

(8) recommending legislation, court rules, codes of conduct, policies, appropriations, and systematic changes that will open greater access to the courts, as needed;

(9) working with law schools in the development and furtherance of court-based programs that enhance equal access to justice;

(10) monitoring and sharing information on equal justice activities of similar entities in Illinois and in states outside of Illinois;

(11) expanding social work and social services in the court system for the purposes of addressing access to justice for individuals with special needs;

(12) supporting and guiding circuit court efforts to increase access through court-based information systems, Web sites, social media, and other technology platforms;

(13) researching and developing information by which the Commission's purpose can be made successful;

(14) promoting and supporting *pro bono* efforts in the state and fostering judicial and circuit court support for *pro bono* efforts throughout the state; and

(15) recommending to the Supreme Court other methods and means of improving the purposes and goals laid out in section (a) above.

(d) Administration.

(1) The Commission shall meet twice a year, at a minimum, and at other times at the request of the chair.

(2) A majority of its members in attendance at a meeting shall constitute a quorum. Meetings may be held at any place within the state and may also be held by means of telecommunication.

(3) The chair may appoint committees of members and assign them responsibilities consistent with the purposes and duties of the Commission.

(4) The Commission shall submit an annual report to the Court reporting on its activities and finances in the previous year and describing future goals for the upcoming year.

(5) The Commission shall appoint, with the approval of the Supreme Court, an Executive Director to serve as the principal executive officer to support the Commission's purpose and carry out its duties. The Executive Director, with the Commission's ap-proval, may hire sufficient staff as necessary to assist in fulfilling the Commission's duties.

(6) Support for the Commission will be provided through in-kind and financial support from a combination of private and public sources.

Adopted June 13, 2012, eff. immediately. Amended April 8, 2013, eff. immediately.

Rule 10–101. Standardized Forms

(a) The Illinois Supreme Court Commission on Access to Justice shall establish a process to develop and approve standardized, legally sufficient forms for areas of law and practice where the Commission determines that there is a high volume of self-represented litigants and that standardized forms will enhance access to justice.

(b) The Commission shall establish a process for publication, review and approval of any proposed standardized form in accordance with the Supreme Court's administrative order regarding standardized forms.

(c) Standardized forms approved by the Commission may be used by any party wherever they are applicable and must be accepted for filing and use by all courts.

(d) Courts may not require that parties use an altered standardized form except that a court may modify a standardized form order as necessary or appropriate to adjudicate a particular issue, claim or action.

(e) A party may supplement a standardized court form with additional material as long as the form is not altered.

Adopted Nov. 28, 2012, eff. immediately.

Committee Comment
(November 28, 2012)

(a) This rule and the Court's accompanying administrative order were adopted to set out a formal process for the development, review and approval of standardized forms for use in the Illinois courts. Utilizing standardized forms in areas of law and practice where there is a high volume of self-represented litigants in the Illinois courts will enhance access to justice for these litigants and at the same time will improve the overall administration of justice.

(b) An open and inclusive process for the development of standardized forms will be necessary to achieve the goals of this rule.

(c) Standardized forms can only be effective if they are required to be accepted by all courts in the state. Technology and assistance that can make forms more user-friendly and accessible for people without lawyers and allow for necessary translations into other languages and formats cannot be efficiently provided if there are multiple variations of the same forms.

(d) For the same reasons noted in comment (c), allowing courts to require alterations of standardized forms would defeat the purposes of having standardized forms. The one exception is for court orders where findings or particular rulings from the court may need to be added to standard form orders.

(e) In some cases, such as an action involving a written contract, an exhibit may be necessary for a pleading to be legally sufficient. Litigants may wish to include other exhibits or supporting information with a complaint or filing as well. For privacy and other practical reasons, it also may be advisable that certain confidential, personal or private information be submitted through a supplementary process rather than included in a standardized form. All pleadings, exhibits or other supporting information filed with the court must be consistent with the requirements of Supreme Court Rule 15 (social security numbers in pleadings and related matters) and Supreme Court Rule 138 (personal identity information).

ILLINOIS RULES OF EVIDENCE

Including Amendments Received Through April 1, 2016

ARTICLE I. GENERAL PROVISIONS

Explanatory Notes

On January 1, 2011, by order of the Illinois Supreme Court, the Illinois Rules of Evidence will govern proceedings in the courts of Illinois except as otherwise provided in Rule 1101.

Rule 101. Scope

These rules govern proceedings in the courts of Illinois to the extent and with the exceptions stated in Rule 1101. A statutory rule of evidence is effective unless in conflict with a rule or a decision of the Illinois Supreme Court.

Adopted September 27, 2010, eff. January 1, 2011. Comment amended Jan. 6, 2015, eff. immediately.

COMMENT

Rule 101 provides that a statutory rule of evidence is effective unless in conflict with an Illinois Supreme Court rule or decision. There is no current statutory rule of evidence that is in conflict with a rule contained in the Illinois Rules of Evidence.

Rule 102. Purpose and Construction

These rules shall be construed to secure fairness in administration, elimination of unjustifiable expense and delay, and promotion of growth and development of the law of evidence to the end that the truth may be ascertained and proceedings justly determined.

Adopted September 27, 2010, eff. January 1, 2011.

Rule 103. Rulings on Evidence

(a) Effect of Erroneous Ruling. Error may not be predicated upon a ruling which admits or excludes evidence unless a substantial right of the party is affected, and

(1) Objection. In case the ruling is one admitting evidence, a timely objection or motion to strike appears of record, stating the specific ground of objection, if the specific ground was not apparent from the context; or

(2) Offer of Proof. In case the ruling is one excluding evidence, the substance of the evidence was made known to the court by offer or was apparent from the context within which questions were asked.

(b) Preserving a Claim of Error for Appeal.

(1) Civil and Criminal Cases. In civil and criminal trials where the court has not made a previous ruling on the record concerning the admission of evidence, a contemporaneous trial objection or offer of proof must be made to preserve a claim of error for appeal.

(2) Criminal Cases. In criminal trials, once the court rules before or at trial on the record concerning the admission of evidence, a contemporaneous trial objection or offer of proof need not be renewed to preserve a claim of error for appeal.

(3) Civil Cases. In civil trials, even if the court rules before or at trial on the record concerning the admission of evidence, a contemporaneous trial objection or offer of proof must be made to preserve a claim of error for appeal.

(4) Posttrial Motions. In all criminal trials and in civil jury trials, in addition to the requirements provided above, a claim of error must be made in a posttrial motion to preserve the claim for appeal. Such a motion is not required in a civil nonjury trial.

(c) Record of Offer and Ruling. The court may add any other or further statement which shows the character of the evidence, the form in which it was offered, the objection made, and the ruling thereon. It may direct the making of an offer in question and answer form.

(d) Hearing of Jury. In jury cases, proceedings shall be conducted, to the extent practicable, so as to prevent inadmissible evidence from being suggested to the jury by any means, such as making statements or offers of proof or asking questions in the hearing of the jury.

(e) Plain Error. Nothing in this rule precludes taking notice of plain errors affecting substantial rights although they were not brought to the attention of the court.

Adopted September 27, 2010, eff. January 1, 2011. Amended Oct. 15, 2015, eff. immediately.

Rule 104.   Preliminary Questions

(a) Questions of Admissibility Generally. Preliminary questions concerning the qualification of a person to be a witness, the existence of a privilege, or the admissibility of evidence shall be determined by the court, subject to the provisions of subdivision (b). In making its determination, the court is not bound by the rules of evidence except those with respect to privileges.

(b) Relevancy Conditioned on Fact. When the relevancy of evidence depends upon the fulfillment of a condition of fact, the court shall admit it upon, or subject to, the introduction of evidence sufficient to support a finding of the fulfillment of the condition.

(c) Hearing of Jury. Hearings on the admissibility of confessions shall in all cases be conducted out of the hearing of the jury. Hearings on other preliminary matters shall be so conducted when the interests of justice require, or when an accused is a witness and so requests.

(d) Testimony by Accused. The accused does not, by testifying upon a preliminary matter, become subject to cross-examination as to other issues in the case.

(e) Weight and Credibility. This rule does not limit the right of a party to introduce before the jury evidence relevant to weight or credibility.

Adopted September 27, 2010, eff. January 1, 2011

Rule 105.   Limited Admissibility

When evidence which is admissible as to one party or for one purpose but not admissible as to another party or for another purpose is admitted, the court, upon request, shall restrict the evidence to its proper purpose or scope and instruct the jury accordingly.

Adopted September 27, 2010, eff. January 1, 2011.

Rule 106.   Remainder of or Related Writings or Recorded Statements

When a writing or recorded statement or part thereof is introduced by a party, an adverse party may require the introduction at that time of any other part or any other writing or recorded statement which ought in fairness to be considered contemporaneously with it.

Adopted September 27, 2010, eff. January 1, 2011.

ARTICLE II.   JUDICIAL NOTICE

Rule 201.   Judicial Notice of Adjudicative Facts

(a) Scope of Rule. This rule governs only judicial notice of adjudicative facts.

(b) Kinds of Facts. A judicially noticed fact must be one not subject to reasonable dispute in that it is either (1) generally known within the territorial jurisdiction of the trial court or (2) capable of accurate and ready determination by resort to sources whose accuracy cannot reasonably be questioned.

(c) When Discretionary. A court may take judicial notice, whether requested or not.

(d) When Mandatory. A court shall take judicial notice if requested by a party and supplied with the necessary information.

(e) Opportunity to be Heard. A party is entitled upon timely request to an opportunity to be heard as to the propriety of taking judicial notice and the tenor of the matter noticed. In the absence of prior notification, the request may be made after judicial notice has been taken.

(f) Time of Taking Notice. Judicial notice may be taken at any stage of the proceeding.

(g) Informing the Jury. In a civil action or proceeding, the court shall inform the jury to accept as conclusive any fact judicially noticed. In a criminal case, the court shall inform the jury that it may, but is not required to, accept as conclusive any fact judicially noticed.

Adopted September 27, 2010, eff. January 1, 2011

ARTICLE III.   PRESUMPTIONS IN CIVIL ACTIONS AND PROCEEDINGS

Rule 301.   Presumptions in General in Civil Actions and Proceedings

In all civil actions and proceedings not otherwise provided for by rule, statute or court decision, a presumption imposes on the party against whom it is directed the burden of going forward with evidence to rebut or meet the presumption, but does not shift to such party the burden of proof in the sense of the risk of nonpersuasion, which remains throughout the trial upon the party on whom it was originally cast.

Adopted September 27, 2010, eff. January 1, 2011.

ARTICLE IV. RELEVANCY AND ITS LIMITS

Rule 401. Definition of "Relevant Evidence"

"Relevant evidence" means evidence having any tendency to make the existence of any fact that is of consequence to the determination of the action more probable or less probable than it would be without the evidence.

Adopted September 27, 2010, eff. January 1, 2011.

Rule 402. Relevant Evidence Generally Admissible; Irrelevant Evidence Inadmissible

All relevant evidence is admissible, except as otherwise provided by law. Evidence which is not relevant is not admissible.

Adopted September 27, 2010, eff. January 1, 2011.

Rule 403. Exclusion of Relevant Evidence on Grounds of Prejudice, Confusion, or Waste of Time

Although relevant, evidence may be excluded if its probative value is substantially outweighed by the danger of unfair prejudice, confusion of the issues, or misleading the jury, or by considerations of undue delay, waste of time, or needless presentation of cumulative evidence.

Adopted September 27, 2010, eff. January 1, 2011.

Rule 404. Character Evidence not Admissible to Prove Conduct; Exceptions; Other Crimes

(a) Character Evidence Generally. Evidence of a person's character or a trait of character is not admissible for the purpose of proving action in conformity therewith on a particular occasion, except:

(1) *Character of Accused.* In a criminal case, evidence of a pertinent trait of character offered by an accused, or by the prosecution to rebut the same;

(2) *Character of Alleged Victim.* In a criminal case, and subject to the limitations imposed by section 115–7 of the Code of Criminal Procedure (725 ILCS 5/115–7), evidence of a pertinent trait of character of the alleged victim of the crime offered by an accused, or by the prosecution to rebut the same, or evidence of a character trait of peacefulness of the alleged victim offered by the prosecution in a homicide or battery case to rebut evidence that the alleged victim was the first aggressor;

(3) *Character of Witness.* Evidence of the character of a witness, as provided in Rules 607, 608, and 609.

(b) Other Crimes, Wrongs, or Acts. Evidence of other crimes, wrongs, or acts is not admissible to prove the character of a person in order to show action in conformity therewith except as provided by sections 115–7.3, 115–7.4, and 115–20 of the Code of Criminal Procedure (725 ILCS 5/115–7.3, 725 ILCS 5/115–7.4, and 725 ILCS 5/115–20). Such evidence may also be admissible for other purposes, such as proof of motive, opportunity, intent, preparation, plan, knowledge, identity, or absence of mistake or accident.

(c) In a criminal case in which the prosecution intends to offer evidence under subdivision (b), it must disclose the evidence, including statements of witnesses or a summary of the substance of any testimony, at a reasonable time in advance of trial, or during trial if the court excuses pretrial notice on good cause shown.

Adopted September 27, 2010, eff. January 1, 2011.

Comment

Evidence of character or a trait of character of a person for the purpose of proving that the person acted in conformity therewith on a particular occasion is not admissible, except in a criminal case to the extent provided for under Rule 404(a)(1) (regarding the character of the accused), and under Rule 404(a)(2) (regarding the character of the alleged victim). Rule 404(b) renders inadmissible evidence of other crimes, wrongs, or acts to prove the character of a person in order to show action in conformity therewith, but allows proof of other crimes, wrongs, or acts where they are relevant under statutes related to certain criminal offenses, as well as for other purposes, such as proof of motive, opportunity, intent, preparation, plan, knowledge, identity, or absence of mistake or accident.

Rule 405.   Methods of Proving Character

(a) Reputation or Opinion. In all cases in which evidence of character or a trait of character of a person is admissible, proof may be made by testimony as to reputation, or by testimony in the form of an opinion.

(b) Specific Instances of Conduct.

(1) In cases in which character or a trait of character of a person is an essential element of a charge, claim, or defense, proof may also be made of specific instances of that person's conduct;   and

(2) In criminal homicide or battery cases when the accused raises the theory of self-defense and there is conflicting evidence as to whether the alleged victim was the aggressor, proof may also be made of specific instances of the alleged victim's prior violent conduct.

Adopted September 27, 2010, eff. January 1, 2011.

Comment

Specific instances of a person's conduct as proof of a person's character or trait of character are not generally admissible as proof that the person acted in conformity therewith.   Specific instances of a person's conduct are admissible, however, under Rule 405(b)(1), as proof of a person's character or a trait of character only in those limited cases (such as negligent entrustment, negligent hiring, and certain defamation actions), when a person's character or a trait of character is an essential element of a charge, claim, or defense.   Specific instances of conduct are also admissible under Rule 405(b)(2) in criminal homicide or battery cases when the accused raises the theory of self-defense and there is conflicting evidence as to whether the alleged victim was the aggressor.

Rule 406.   Habit; Routine Practice

Evidence of the habit of a person or of the routine practice of an organization, whether corroborated or not and regardless of the presence of eyewitnesses, is relevant to prove that the conduct of the person or organization on a particular occasion was in conformity with the habit or routine practice.

Adopted September 27, 2010, eff. January 1, 2011.

Rule   407.   Reserved. [Subsequent   Remedial Measures]

Rule 408.   Compromise and Offers to Compromise

(a) Prohibited Uses. Evidence of the following is not admissible on behalf of any party, when offered to prove liability for, invalidity of, or amount of a claim that was disputed as to validity or amount, or to impeach through a prior inconsistent statement or contradiction:

(1) furnishing or offering or promising to furnish— or accepting or offering or promising to accept—a valuable consideration in compromising or attempting to compromise the claim; and

(2) conduct or statements made in compromise negotiations regarding the claim.

(b) Permitted Uses. This rule does not require the exclusion of any evidence otherwise discoverable merely because it is presented in the course of settlement negotiations.   This rule also does not require exclusion if the evidence is offered for purposes not prohibited by subdivision (a).   Examples of permissible purposes include proving a witness' bias or prejudice; negating an assertion of undue delay; establishing bad faith; and proving an effort to obstruct a criminal investigation or prosecution.

Adopted September 27, 2010, eff. January 1, 2011.

Rule 409.   Payment of Medical and Similar Expenses

In addition to the provisions of section 8–1901 of the Code of Civil Procedure (735 ILCS 5/8–1901), evidence of furnishing or offering or promising to pay medical, hospital, or similar expenses occasioned by an injury is not admissible to prove liability for the injury.

Adopted September 27, 2010, eff. January 1, 2011.

Rule 410.   Inadmissibility of Pleas, Plea Discussions, and Related Statements

Evidence of a plea discussion or any resulting agreement, plea, or judgment is not admissible in any criminal proceeding against the defendant who made the plea or was a participant in the plea discussions under the following circumstances:

(1) a plea of guilty which is not accepted or is withdrawn;

(2) a plea of nolo contendere;

(3) any statement made in the course of any proceedings under Illinois Supreme Court Rule 402 regarding either of the foregoing pleas; or

(4) any statement made in the course of a plea discussions which does not result in a plea of guilty, or which results in a plea of guilty which is not accepted or is withdrawn, or which results in a judgment on a plea of guilty which is reversed on direct or collateral review.

Adopted September 27, 2010, eff. January 1, 2011.   Amended Oct. 15, 2015, eff. immediately.

Rule 411.   Liability Insurance

Evidence that a person was or was not insured against liability is not admissible upon the issue whether the person acted negligently or otherwise wrongfully.   This rule does not require the exclusion of evidence of insurance against liability when offered

for another purpose, such as proof of agency, ownership, or control, or bias or prejudice of a witness.
Adopted September 27, 2010, eff. January 1, 2011.

Rule 412. Prior Sexual Activity or Reputation as Evidence

Evidence of the sexual activity or reputation of a
person alleged to be a victim of a sexual offense is
inadmissible:

(a) in criminal cases, as provided for and subject to
the exceptions in section 115–7 of the Code of Criminal Procedure of 1963 (725 ILCS 5/115–7);

(b) in civil cases, as provided for and subject to the
exceptions in section 8–2801 of the Code of Civil
Procedure (735 ILCS 5/8–2801).
Adopted Oct. 15, 2015, eff. immediately.

Rule 413. Evidence of Other Offenses in Crimi-nal Cases

(a) **Evidence in Certain Cases.** In a criminal case
for an offense set forth in section 115–7.3 of the Code

of Criminal Procedure of 1963 (725 ILCS 5/115–7.3),
evidence of the defendant's commission of another
offense or offenses set forth in section 115–7.3 is
admissible, as provided in section 115–7.3.

(b) **Evidence in Domestic Violence Cases.** In a
criminal case for an offense related to domestic violence as set forth in section 115–7.4 of the Code of
Criminal Procedure of 1963 (725 ILCS 5/115–7.4),
evidence of the defendant's commission of another
offense or offenses of domestic violence is admissible,
as provided in section 115–7.4.

(c) **Evidence of Prior Convictions.** In a criminal
case for the type of offenses set forth in section
115–20 of the Code of Criminal Procedure of 1963 (725
ILCS 5/115–20), evidence of the defendant's conviction
for an offense set forth in that section is admissible
when the victim is the same person who was the
victim of the previous offense that resulted in the
conviction of the defendant, as provided in section
115–20.
Adopted Oct. 15, 2015, eff. immediately.

ARTICLE V. PRIVILEGES

Rule 501. General Rule

Except as otherwise required by the Constitution of
the United States, the Constitution of Illinois, or
provided by applicable statute or rule prescribed by
the Supreme Court, the privilege of a witness, person,
government, state, or political subdivision thereof shall
be governed by the principles of the common law as
they may be interpreted by Illinois courts in the light
of reason and experience.
Adopted September 27, 2010, eff. January 1, 2011.

Rule 502. Attorney–Client Privilege and Work Product; Limitations on Waiver

The following provisions apply, in the circumstances
set out, to disclosure of a communication or information covered by the attorney-client privilege or work-
product protection.

(a) **Disclosure Made in an Illinois Proceeding or
to an Illinois Office or Agency; Scope of a Waiver.**
When the disclosure is made in an Illinois proceeding
or to an Illinois office or agency and waives the
attorney-client privilege or work-product protection,
the waiver extends to an undisclosed communication
or information in any proceeding only if:

(1) the waiver is intentional;

(2) the disclosed and undisclosed communications
or information concern the same subject matter;
and

(3) they ought in fairness to be considered together.

(b) **Inadvertent Disclosure.** When made in an
Illinois proceeding or to an Illinois office or agency,
the disclosure does not operate as a waiver in any
proceeding if:

(1) the disclosure is inadvertent;

(2) the holder of the privilege or protection took
reasonable steps to prevent disclosure; and

(3) the holder promptly took reasonable steps to
rectify the error, including (if applicable) following
Supreme Court Rule 201(p).

(c) **Disclosure Made in a Federal or Another
State's Proceeding or to a Federal or Another
State's Office or Agency.** When the disclosure is
made in a federal or another state's proceeding or to a
federal or another state's office or agency and is not
the subject of a court order concerning waiver, the
disclosure does not operate as a waiver in an Illinois
proceeding if the disclosure:

(1) would not be a waiver under this rule if it had
been made in an Illinois proceeding; or

(2) is not a waiver under the law governing the
federal or state proceeding where the disclosure
occurred.

(d) **Controlling Effect of a Court Order.** An
Illinois court may order that the privilege or protection is not waived by disclosure connected with the
litigation pending before the court—in which event
the disclosure is also not a waiver in any other proceeding.

(e) **Controlling Effect of a Party Agreement.** An
agreement on the effect of disclosure in an Illinois

proceeding is binding only on the parties to the agreement, unless it is incorporated into a court order.

(f) Definitions. In this rule:

(1) "attorney-client privilege" means the protection that applicable law provides for confidential attorney-client communications; and

(2) "work-product protection" means the protection that applicable law provides for tangible material (or its intangible equivalent) prepared in anticipation of litigation or for trial.

Adopted Nov. 28, 2012, eff. Jan. 1, 2013.

ARTICLE VI. WITNESSES

Rule 601. General Rule of Competency

Every person is competent to be a witness, except as otherwise provided by these rules, by other rules prescribed by the Supreme Court, or by statute.

Adopted September 27, 2010, eff. January 1, 2011.

Rule 602. Lack of Personal Knowledge

A witness may not testify to a matter unless evidence is introduced sufficient to support a finding that the witness has personal knowledge of the matter. Evidence to prove personal knowledge may, but need not, consist of the witness' own testimony. This rule is subject to the provisions of Rule 703, relating to opinion testimony by expert witnesses.

Adopted September 27, 2010, eff. January 1, 2011.

Rule 603. Oath or Affirmation

Before testifying, every witness shall be required to declare that the witness will testify truthfully, by oath or affirmation, administered in a form calculated to awaken the witness' conscience and impress the witness' mind with the duty to do so.

Adopted September 27, 2010, eff. January 1, 2011.

Rule 604. Interpreters

An interpreter is subject to the provisions of these rules relating to qualification as an expert and the administration of an oath or affirmation to make a true translation.

Adopted September 27, 2010, eff. January 1, 2011.

Rule 605. Competency of Judge as Witness

The judge presiding at the trial may not testify in that trial as a witness. No objection need be made in order to preserve the point.

Adopted September 27, 2010, eff. January 1, 2011.

Rule 606. Competency of Juror as Witness

(a) At the Trial. A member of the jury may not testify as a witness before that jury in the trial of the case in which the juror is sitting. If the juror is called so to testify, the opposing party shall be afforded an opportunity to object out of the presence of the jury.

(b) Inquiry Into Validity of Verdict or Indictment. Upon an inquiry into the validity of a verdict or indictment, a juror may not testify as to any matter or statement occurring during the course of the jury's deliberations or to the effect of anything upon that or any other juror's mind or emotions as influencing the juror to assent to or dissent from the verdict or indictment or concerning the juror's mental processes in connection therewith. But a juror may testify (1) whether any extraneous prejudicial information was improperly brought to the jury's attention, (2) whether any outside influence was improperly brought to bear upon any juror, or (3) whether there was a mistake in entering the verdict onto the verdict form. A juror's affidavit or evidence of any statement by the juror may not be received concerning a matter about which the juror would be precluded from testifying.

Adopted September 27, 2010, eff. January 1, 2011.

Rule 607. Who May Impeach

The credibility of a witness may be attacked by any party, including the party calling the witness, except that the credibility of a witness may be attacked by the party calling the witness by means of a prior inconsistent statement only upon a showing of affirmative damage. The foregoing exception does not apply to statements admitted pursuant to Rules 801(d)(1)(A), 801(d)(1) (B), 801(d)(2), or 803.

Adopted September 27, 2010, eff. January 1, 2011.

Rule 608. Evidence of Character of Witness for Truthfulness or Untruthfulness

The credibility of a witness may be attacked or supported by evidence in the form of opinion or reputation, but subject to these limitations: (1) the evidence may refer only to character for truthfulness or untruthfulness, and (2) evidence of truthful character is admissible only after the character of the witness for truthfulness has been attacked by opinion or reputation evidence or otherwise.

Adopted September 27, 2010, eff. January 1, 2011. Amended Jan. 6, 2015, eff. immediately.

Rule 609. Impeachment by Evidence of Conviction of Crime

(a) General Rule. For the purpose of attacking the credibility of a witness, evidence that the witness has been convicted of a crime, except on a plea of nolo contendere, is admissible but only if the crime, (1) was punishable by death or imprisonment in excess of one year under the law under which the witness was convicted, or (2) involved dishonesty or false statement regardless of the punishment unless (3), in either case, the court determines that the probative value of the evidence of the crime is substantially outweighed by the danger of unfair prejudice.

(b) Time Limit. Evidence of a conviction under this rule is not admissible if a period of more than 10 years has elapsed since the date of conviction or of the release of the witness from confinement, whichever is the later date.

(c) Effect of Pardon, Annulment, or Certificate of Rehabilitation. Evidence of a conviction is not admissible under this rule if (1) the conviction has been the subject of a pardon, annulment, certificate of rehabilitation, or other equivalent procedure, and (2) the procedure under which the same was granted or issued required a substantial showing of rehabilitation or was based on innocence.

(d) Juvenile Adjudications. Evidence of juvenile adjudications is generally not admissible under this rule. The court may, however, allow evidence of a juvenile adjudication of a witness other than the accused if conviction of the offense would be admissible to attack the credibility of an adult and the court is satisfied that admission in evidence is necessary for a fair determination of the issue of guilt or innocence.

(e) Pendency of Appeal. The pendency of an appeal therefrom does not render evidence of a conviction inadmissible. Evidence of the pendency of an appeal is admissible.

Adopted September 27, 2010, eff. January 1, 2011. Comment amended Jan. 6, 2015, eff. immediately.

Rule 610. Religious Beliefs or Opinions

Evidence of the beliefs or opinions of a witness on matters of religion is not admissible for the purpose of showing that by reason of their nature the witness' credibility is impaired or enhanced.

Adopted September 27, 2010, eff. January 1, 2011.

Rule 611. Mode and Order of Interrogation and Presentation

(a) Control by Court. The court shall exercise reasonable control over the mode and order of interrogating witnesses and presenting evidence so as to (1) make the interrogation and presentation effective for the ascertainment of the truth, (2) avoid needless consumption of time, and (3) protect witnesses from harassment or undue embarrassment.

(b) Scope of Cross–Examination. Cross-examination should be limited to the subject matter of the direct examination and matters affecting the credibility of the witness, which include matters within the knowledge of the witness that explain, qualify, discredit or destroy the witness's direct testimony. The court may, in the exercise of discretion, permit inquiry into additional matters as if on direct examination.

(c) Leading Questions. Leading questions should not be used on the direct examination of a witness except as may be necessary to develop the witness' testimony. Ordinarily leading questions should be permitted on cross-examination. When a party calls a hostile or an unwilling witness or an adverse party or an agent of an adverse party as defined by section 2–1102 of the Code of Civil Procedure (735 ILCS 5/2–1102), interrogation may be by leading questions.

Adopted September 27, 2010, eff. January 1, 2011. Amended Oct. 15, 2015, eff. immediately.

Rule 612. Writing Used to Refresh Memory

If a witness uses a writing to refresh memory for the purpose of testifying, either—

(1) while testifying, or

(2) before testifying, an adverse party is entitled to have the writing produced at the hearing, to inspect it, to cross-examine the witness thereon, and to introduce in evidence for the purpose of impeachment those portions which relate to the testimony of the witness. If it is claimed that the writing contains matters not related to the subject matter of the testimony the court shall examine the writing in camera, excise any portions not so related, and order delivery of the remainder to the party entitled thereto. Any portion withheld over objections shall be preserved and made available to the appellate court in the event of an appeal. If a writing is not produced or delivered pursuant to order under this rule, the court shall make any order justice requires, except that in criminal cases when the prosecution elects not to comply, the order shall be one striking the testimony or, if the court in its discretion determines that the interests of justice so require, declaring a mistrial.

Adopted September 27, 2010, eff. January 1, 2011.

Rule 613. Prior Statements of Witnesses

(a) Examining Witness Concerning Prior Statement. In examining a witness concerning a prior statement made by the witness, whether written or not, the statement need not be shown nor its contents disclosed to the witness at that time, but on request the same shall be shown or disclosed to opposing counsel.

(b) Extrinsic Evidence of Prior Inconsistent Statement of Witness. Extrinsic evidence of a prior inconsistent statement by a witness is not admissible unless the witness is first afforded an opportunity to explain or deny the same and the opposing party is afforded an opportunity to interrogate the witness thereon, or the interests of justice otherwise require. This provision does not apply to statements of a party-opponent as defined in Rule 801(d)(2).

(c) Evidence of Prior Consistent Statement of Witness. A prior statement that is consistent with the declarant-witness's testimony is admissible, for rehabilitation purposes only and not substantively as a hearsay exception or exclusion, when the declarant testifies at the trial or hearing and is available to the opposing party for examination concerning the statement, and the statement is offered to rebut an express or implied charge that:

(i) the witness acted from an improper influence or motive to testify falsely, if that influence or motive did not exist when the statement was made; or

(ii) the witness's testimony was recently fabricated, if the statement was made before the alleged fabrication occurred.

Adopted September 27, 2010, eff. January 1, 2011. Amended Jan. 6, 2015, eff. immediately; Oct. 15, 2015, eff. immediately.

Rule 614. Calling and Interrogation of Witnesses by Court

(a) Calling by Court. The court may, on its own motion or at the suggestion of a party, call witnesses, and all parties are entitled to cross-examine witnesses thus called.

(b) Interrogation by Court. The court may interrogate witnesses, whether called by itself or by a party.

(c) Objections. Objections to the calling of witnesses by the court or to interrogation by it may be made at the time or at the next available opportunity when the jury is not present.

Adopted September 27, 2010, eff. January 1, 2011.

Rule 615. Exclusion of Witnesses

At the request of a party the court shall order witnesses excluded so that they cannot hear the testimony of other witnesses, and it may make the order of its own motion. This rule does not authorize exclusion of (1) a party who is a natural person, or (2) an officer or employee of a party which is not a natural person designated as its representative by its attorney, or (3) a person whose presence is shown by a party to be essential to the presentation of the party's cause, or (4) a person authorized by law to be present.

Adopted September 27, 2010, eff. January 1, 2011.

ARTICLE VII.   OPINIONS AND EXPERT TESTIMONY

Rule 701.   Opinion Testimony by Lay Witnesses

If the witness is not testifying as an expert, the witness' testimony in the form of opinions or inferences is limited to those opinions or inferences which are (a) rationally based on the perception of the witness, and (b) helpful to a clear understanding of the witness' testimony or the determination of a fact in issue, and (c) not based on scientific, technical, or other specialized knowledge within the scope of Rule 702.

Adopted September 27, 2010, eff. January 1, 2011.

Rule 702.   Testimony by Experts

If scientific, technical, or other specialized knowledge will assist the trier of fact to understand the evidence or to determine a fact in issue, a witness qualified as an expert by knowledge, skill, experience, training, or education, may testify thereto in the form of an opinion or otherwise. Where an expert witness testifies to an opinion based on a new or novel scientific methodology or principle, the proponent of the opinion has the burden of showing the methodology or scientific principle on which the opinion is based is sufficiently established to have gained general acceptance in the particular field in which it belongs.

Adopted September 27, 2010, eff. January 1, 2011.

Comment

Rule 702 confirms that Illinois is a *Frye* state. The second sentence of the rule enunciates the core principles of the *Frye* test for admissibility of scientific evidence as set forth in *Donaldson v. Central Illinois Public Service Co.*, 199 Ill.2d 63, 767 N.E.2d 314 (2002).

Rule 703.   Bases of Opinion Testimony by Experts

The facts or data in the particular case upon which an expert bases an opinion or inference may be those perceived by or made known to the expert at or before the hearing. If of a type reasonably relied upon by experts in the particular field in forming opinions or inferences upon the subject, the facts or data need not be admissible in evidence.

Adopted September 27, 2010, eff. January 1, 2011.

Rule 704. Opinion on Ultimate Issue

Testimony in the form of an opinion or inference otherwise admissible is not objectionable because it embraces an ultimate issue to be decided by the trier of fact.

Adopted September 27, 2010, eff. January 1, 2011.

Rule 705. Disclosure of Facts or Data Underlying Expert Opinion

The expert may testify in terms of opinion or inference and give reasons therefor without first testifying to the underlying facts or data, unless the court requires otherwise. The expert may in any event be required to disclose the underlying facts or data on cross-examination.

Adopted September 27, 2010, eff. January 1, 2011.

ARTICLE VIII. HEARSAY

Rule 801. Definitions

The following definitions apply under this article:

(a) **Statement.** A "statement" is (1) an oral or written assertion or (2) nonverbal conduct of a person, if it is intended by the person as an assertion.

(b) **Declarant.** A "declarant" is a person who makes a statement.

(c) **Hearsay.** "Hearsay" is a statement, other than one made by the declarant while testifying at the trial or hearing, offered in evidence to prove the truth of the matter asserted.

(d) **Statements Which Are Not Hearsay.** A statement is not hearsay if

(1) **Prior Statement by Witness.** In a criminal case, the declarant testifies at the trial or hearing and is subject to cross-examination concerning the statement, and the statement is

(A) inconsistent with the declarant's testimony at the trial or hearing, and—

(1) was made under oath at a trial, hearing, or other proceeding, or in a deposition, or

(2) narrates, describes, or explains an event or condition of which the declarant had personal knowledge, and

(a) the statement is proved to have been written or signed by the declarant, or

(b) the declarant acknowledged under oath the making of the statement either in the declarant's testimony at the hearing or trial in which the admission into evidence of the prior statement is being sought or at a trial, hearing, or other proceeding, or in a deposition, or

(c) the statement is proved to have been accurately recorded by a tape recorder, video-tape recording, or any other similar electronic means of sound recording; or

(B) one of identification of a person made after perceiving the person.

(2) **Statement by Party–Opponent.** The statement is offered against a party and is (A) the party's own statement, in either an individual or a representative capacity, or (B) a statement of which the party has manifested an adoption or belief in its truth, or (C) a statement by a person authorized by the party to make a statement concerning the subject, or (D) a statement by the party's agent or servant concerning a matter within the scope of the agency or employment, made during the existence of the relationship, or (E) a statement by a coconspirator of a party during the course and in furtherance of the conspiracy, or (F) a statement by a person, or a person on behalf of an entity, in privity with the party or jointly interested with the party.

Adopted September 27, 2010, eff. January 1, 2011. Amended Oct. 15, 2015, eff. immediately.

Rule 802. Hearsay Rule

Hearsay is not admissible except as provided by these rules, by other rules prescribed by the Supreme Court, or by statute as provided in Rule 101.

Adopted September 27, 2010, eff. January 1, 2011.

Rule 803. Hearsay Exceptions; Availability of Declarant Immaterial

The following are not excluded by the hearsay rule, even though the declarant is available as a witness:

(1) *Reserved.* [Present Sense Impressions].

(2) *Excited Utterance.* A statement relating to a startling event or condition made while the declarant was under the stress of excitement caused by the event or condition.

(3) *Then Existing Mental, Emotional, or Physical Condition.* A statement of the declarant's then existing state of mind, emotion, sensation, or physical condition (such as intent, plan, motive, design, mental feeling, pain, and bodily health), but not including:

(A) a statement of memory or belief to prove the fact remembered or believed unless it relates to the execution, revocation, identification, or terms of declarant's will; or

(B) a statement of declarant's then existing state of mind, emotion, sensation, or physical condition to prove the state of mind, emotion, sensation, or physical condition of another declarant at that time or at any other time when such state of the other declarant is an issue in the action.

(4) *Statements for Purposes of Medical Diagnosis or Treatment.* (A) Statements made for purposes of medical treatment, or medical diagnosis in contemplation of treatment, and describing medical history, or past or present symptoms, pain, or sensations, or the inception or general character of the cause or external source thereof insofar as reasonably pertinent to diagnosis or treatment but, subject to Rule 703, not including statements made to a health care provider consulted solely for the purpose of preparing for litigation or obtaining testimony for trial, or (B) in a prosecution for violation of sections 11–1.20, 11–1.30, 11–1.40, 11–1.50, or 11–1.60 of the Criminal Code of 1961 (720 ILCS 5/11–1.20, 11–1.30, 11–1.40, 11–1.50, 11–1.60), or for a violation of the Article 12 statutes in the Criminal Code of 1961 that previously defined the same offenses, statements made by the victim to medical personnel for purposes of medical diagnoses or treatment including descriptions of the cause of symptom, pain or sensations, or the inception or general character of the cause or external source thereof insofar as reasonably pertinent to diagnosis or treatment.

(5) *Recorded Recollection.* A memorandum or record concerning a matter about which a witness once had knowledge but now has insufficient recollection to enable the witness to testify fully and accurately, shown to have been made or adopted by the witness when the matter was fresh in the witness' memory and to reflect that knowledge correctly.

(6) *Records of Regularly Conducted Activity.* A memorandum, report, record, or data compilation, in any form, of acts, events, conditions, opinions, or diagnoses, made at or near the time by, or from information transmitted by, a person with knowledge, if kept in the course of a regularly conducted business activity, and if it was the regular practice of that business activity to make the memorandum, report, record or data compilation, all as shown by the testimony of the custodian or other qualified witness, or by certification that complies with Rule 902(11), unless the source of information or the method or circumstances of preparation indicate lack of trustworthiness, but not including in criminal cases medical records. The term "business" as used in this paragraph includes business, institution, association, profession, occupation, and calling of every kind, whether or not conducted for profit.

(7) *Absence of Entry in Records Kept in Accordance With the Provisions of Paragraph (6).* Evi-dence that a matter is not included in the memoranda reports, records, or data compilations, in any form, kept in accordance with the provisions of paragraph (6), to prove the nonoccurrence or nonexistence of the matter, if the matter was of a kind of which a memorandum, report, record, or data compilation was regularly made and preserved, unless the sources of information or other circumstances indicate lack of trustworthiness.

(8) *Public Records and Reports.* Records, reports, statements, or data compilations, in any form, of public offices or agencies, setting forth (A) the activities of the office or agency, or (B) matters observed pursuant to duty imposed by law as to which matters there was a duty to report, excluding, however, police accident reports and in criminal cases medical records and matters observed by police officers and other law enforcement personnel, unless the sources of information or other circumstances indicate lack of trustworthiness.

(9) *Records of Vital Statistics.* Facts contained in records or data compilations, in any form, of births, fetal deaths, deaths, or marriages, if the report thereof was made to a public office pursuant to requirements of law.

(10) *Absence of Public Record or Entry.* To prove the absence of a record, report, statement, or data compilation, in any form, or the nonoccurrence or nonexistence of a matter of which a record, report, statement, or data compilation, in any form, was regularly made and preserved by a public office or agency, evidence in the form of a certification in accordance with Rule 902, or testimony, that diligent search failed to disclose the record, report, statement, or data compilation, or entry.

(11) *Records of Religious Organizations.* Statements of births, marriages, divorces, deaths, legitimacy, ancestry, relationship by blood or marriage, or other similar facts of personal or family history, contained in a regularly kept record of a religious organization.

(12) *Marriage, Baptismal, and Similar Certificates.* Statements of fact contained in a certificate that the maker performed a marriage or other ceremony or administered a sacrament, made by a clergyman, public official, or other person authorized by the rules or practices of a religious organization or by law to perform the act certified, and purporting to have been issued at the time of the act or within a reasonable time thereafter.

(13) *Family Records.* Statements of fact concerning personal or family history contained in family Bibles, genealogies, charts, engravings on rings, inscriptions on family portraits, engravings on urns, crypts, or tombstones, or the like.

(14) *Records of Documents Affecting an Interest in Property.* The record of a document purporting to establish or affect an interest in property, as proof of

the content of the original recorded document and its execution and delivery by each person by whom it purports to have been executed, if the record is a record of a public office and an applicable statute authorizes the recording of documents of that kind in that office.

(15) *Statements in Documents Affecting an Interest in Property.* A statement contained in a document purporting to establish or affect an interest in property if the matter stated was relevant to the purpose of the document, unless dealings with the property since the document was made have been inconsistent with the truth of the statement or the purport of the document.

(16) *Statements in Ancient Documents.* Statements in a document in existence 20 years or more the authenticity of which is established.

(17) *Market Reports, Commercial Publications.* Market quotations, tabulations, lists, directories, or other published compilations, generally used and relied upon by the public or by persons in particular occupations.

(18) *Reserved.* [Learned Treatises].

(19) *Reputation Concerning Personal or Family History.* Reputation among members of a person's family by blood, adoption, or marriage, or among a person's associates, or in the community, concerning a person's birth, adoption, marriage, divorce, death, legitimacy, relationship by blood, adoption, or marriage, ancestry, or other similar fact of personal or family history.

(20) *Reputation Concerning Boundaries or General History.* Reputation in a community, arising before the controversy, as to boundaries of or customs affecting lands in the community, and reputation as to events of general history important to the community or State or nation in which located.

(21) *Reputation as to Character.* Reputation of a person's character among associates or in the community.

(22) *Judgment of Previous Conviction.* Evidence of a final judgment, entered after a trial or upon a plea of guilty, adjudging a person guilty of a crime punishable by death or imprisonment in excess of one year, to prove any fact essential to sustain the judgment, but not including, when offered by the Government in a criminal prosecution for purposes other than impeachment, judgments against persons other than the accused. The pendency of an appeal may be shown but does not affect admissibility.

(23) *Judgment as to Personal, Family or General History, or Boundaries.* Judgments as proof of matters of personal, family or general history, or boundaries, essential to the judgment, if the same would be provable by evidence of reputation.

(24) *Receipt or Paid Bill.* A receipt or paid bill as prima facie evidence of the fact of payment and as prima facie evidence that the charge was reasonable. Adopted September 27, 2010, eff. January 1, 2011. Amended April 26, 2012, eff. immediately.

Rule 804. Hearsay Exceptions; Declarant Unavailable

(a) **Definition of Unavailability.** "Unavailability as a witness" includes situations in which the declarant-

(1) is exempted by ruling of the court on the ground of privilege from testifying concerning the subject matter of the declarant's statement; or

(2) persists in refusing to testify concerning the subject matter of the declarant's statement despite an order of the court to do so; or

(3) testifies to a lack of memory of the subject matter of the declarant's statement; or

(4) is unable to be present or to testify at the hearing because of death or then existing physical or mental illness or infirmity; or

(5) is absent from the hearing and the proponent of a statement has been unable to procure the declarant's attendance (or in the case of a hearsay exception under subdivision (b)(2), (3), or (4), the declarant's attendance or testimony) by process or other reasonable means.

A declarant is not unavailable as a witness if exemption, refusal, claim of lack of memory, inability, or absence is due to the procurement or wrongdoing of the proponent of a statement for the purpose of preventing the witness from attending or testifying.

(b) **Hearsay Exceptions.** The following are not excluded by the hearsay rule if the declarant is unavailable as a witness:

(1) *Former Testimony.* Testimony given as a witness (A) at another hearing of the same or a different proceeding, or in an evidence deposition taken in compliance with law in the course of the same or another proceeding, if the party against whom the testimony is now offered, or, in a civil action or proceeding, a predecessor in interest, had an opportunity and similar motive to develop the testimony by direct, cross, or redirect examination, or (B) in a discovery deposition as provided for in Supreme Court Rule 212(a)(5).

(2) *Statement Under Belief of Impending Death.* In a prosecution for homicide, a statement made by a declarant while believing that the declarant's death was imminent, concerning the cause or circumstances of what the declarant believed to be impending death.

(3) *Statement Against Interest.* A statement which was at the time of its making so far contrary to the declarant's pecuniary or proprietary interest, or so far tended to subject the declarant to civil or criminal liability, or to render invalid a claim by the declarant

against another, that a reasonable person in the declarant's position would not have made the statement unless believing it to be true. A statement tending to expose the declarant to criminal liability and offered in a criminal case is not admissible unless corroborating circumstances clearly indicate the trustworthiness of the statement.

(4) *Statement of Personal or Family History.*

(A) A statement concerning the declarant's own birth, adoption, marriage, divorce, legitimacy, relationship by blood, adoption, or marriage, ancestry, or other similar fact of personal or family history, even though declarant had no means of acquiring personal knowledge of the matter stated; or

(B) a statement concerning the foregoing matters, and death also, of another person, if the declarant was related to the other by blood, adoption, or marriage or was so intimately associated with the other's family as to be likely to have accurate information concerning the matter declared.

(5) *Forfeiture by Wrongdoing.* A statement offered against a party that has engaged or acquiesced in wrongdoing that was intended to, and did, procure the unavailability of the declarant as a witness.

Adopted September 27, 2010, eff. January 1, 2011.

Rule 805. Hearsay Within Hearsay

Hearsay included within hearsay is not excluded under the hearsay rule if each part of the combined statements conforms with an exception to the hearsay rule provided in these rules.

Adopted September 27, 2010, eff. January 1, 2011.

Rule 806. Attacking and Supporting Credibility of Declarant

When a hearsay statement, or a statement defined in Rule 801(d)(2)(C), (D), (E), or (F), has been admitted in evidence, the credibility of the declarant may be attacked, and if attacked may be supported, by any evidence which would be admissible for those purposes if declarant had testified as a witness. Evidence of a statement or conduct by the declarant at any time, inconsistent with the declarant's hearsay statement, is not subject to any requirement that the declarant may have been afforded an opportunity to deny or explain. If the party against whom a hearsay statement has been admitted calls the declarant as a witness, the party is entitled to examine the declarant on the statement as if under cross-examination.

Adopted September 27, 2010, eff. January 1, 2011.

ARTICLE IX. AUTHENTICATION AND IDENTIFICATION

Rule

Rule 901. Requirement of Authentication or Identification

(a) **General Provision.** The requirement of authentication or identification as a condition precedent to admissibility is satisfied by evidence sufficient to support a finding that the matter in question is what its proponent claims.

(b) **Illustrations.** By way of illustration only, and not by way of limitation, the following are examples of authentication or identification conforming with the requirements of this rule:

(1) *Testimony of Witness With Knowledge.* Testimony that a matter is what it is claimed to be.

(2) *Nonexpert Opinion on Handwriting.* Nonexpert opinion as to the genuineness of handwriting, based upon familiarity not acquired for purposes of the litigation.

(3) *Comparison by Trier or Expert Witness.* Comparison by the trier of fact or by expert witnesses with specimens which have been authenticated.

(4) *Distinctive Characteristics and the Like.* Appearance, contents, substance, internal patterns, or other distinctive characteristics, taken in conjunction with circumstances.

(5) *Voice Identification.* Identification of a voice, whether heard firsthand or through mechanical or electronic transmission or recording, by opinion based upon hearing the voice at any time under circumstances connecting it with the alleged speaker.

(6) *Telephone Conversations.* Telephone conversations, by evidence that a call was made to the number assigned at the time by the telephone company to a particular person or business, if (A) in the case of a person, circumstances, including self-identification, show the person answering to be the one called, or (B) in the case of a business, the call was made to a place of business and the conversation related to business reasonably transacted over the telephone.

(7) *Public Records or Reports.* Evidence that a writing authorized by law to be recorded or filed and in fact recorded or filed in a public office, or a purported public record, report, statement, or data compilation, in any form, is from the public office where items of this nature are kept.

(8) *Ancient Documents or Data Compilation.* Evidence that a document or data compilation, in any form, (A) is in such condition as to create no suspicion concerning its authenticity, (B) was in a place where it, if authentic, would likely be, and (C) has been in existence 20 years or more at the time it is offered.

(9) *Process or System.* Evidence describing a process or system used to produce a result and showing that the process or system produces an accurate result.

(10) *Methods Provided by Statute or Rule.* Any method of authentication or identification provided by statute or by other rules prescribed by the Supreme Court.

Adopted September 27, 2010, eff. January 1, 2011.

Rule 902. Self–Authentication

Extrinsic evidence of authenticity as a condition precedent to admissibility is not required with respect to the following:

(1) *Domestic Public Documents Under Seal.* A document bearing a seal purporting to be that of the United States, or of any State, district, Commonwealth, territory, or insular possession thereof, or the Panama Canal Zone, or the Trust Territory of the Pacific Islands, or of a political subdivision, department, officer, or agency thereof, and a signature purporting to be an attestation or execution.

(2) *Domestic Public Documents Not Under Seal.* A document purporting to bear the signature in the official capacity of an officer or employee of any entity included in paragraph (1) hereof, having no seal, if a public officer having a seal and having official duties in the district or political subdivision of the officer or employee certifies under seal that the signer has the official capacity and that the signature is genuine.

(3) *Foreign Public Documents.* A document purporting to be executed or attested in an official capacity by a person authorized by the laws of a foreign country to make the execution or attestation, and accompanied by a final certification as to the genuineness of the signature and official position (A) of the executing or attesting person, or (B) of any foreign official whose certificate of genuineness of signature and official position relates to the execution or attestation or is in a chain of certificates of genuineness of signature and official position relating to the execution or attestation. A final certification may be made by a secretary of an embassy or legation, consul general, consul, vice consul, or consular agent of the United States, or a diplomatic or consular official of the foreign country assigned or accredited to the United States. If reasonable opportunity has been given to all parties to investigate the authenticity and accuracy of official documents, the court may, for good cause shown, order that they be treated as presumptively authentic without final certification or permit them to be evidenced by an attested summary with or without final certification.

(4) *Certified Copies of Public Records.* A copy of an official record or report or entry therein, or of a document authorized by law to be recorded or filed and actually recorded or filed in a public office, including data compilations in any form, certified as correct by the custodian or other person authorized to make the certification, by certificate complying with paragraph (1), (2), or (3) of this rule or complying with any statute or rule prescribed by the Supreme Court.

(5) *Official Publications.* Books, pamphlets, or other publications purporting to be issued by public authority.

(6) *Newspapers and Periodicals.* Printed materials purporting to be newspapers or periodicals.

(7) *Trade Inscriptions and the Like.* Inscriptions, signs, tags, or labels purporting to have been affixed in the course of business and indicating ownership, control, content, ingredients, or origin.

(8) *Acknowledged Documents.* Documents accompanied by a certificate of acknowledgment executed in the manner provided by law by a notary public or other officer authorized by law to take acknowledgments.

(9) *Commercial Paper and Related Documents.* Commercial paper, signatures thereon, and documents relating thereto to the extent provided by general commercial law.

(10) *Presumptions Under Statutes.* Any signature, document, or other matter declared by statutes to be presumptively or prima facie genuine or authentic.

(11) *Certified Records of Regularly Conducted Activity.* The original or a duplicate of a record of regularly conducted activity that would be admissible under Rule 803(6) if accompanied by a written certification of its custodian or other qualified person that the record

    (A) was made at or near the time of the occurrence of the matters set forth by, or from information transmitted by, a person with knowledge of these matters;

    (B) was kept in the course of the regularly conducted activity; and

    (C) was made by the regularly conducted activity as a regular practice.

The word "certification" as used in this subsection means with respect to a domestic record, a written declaration under oath subject to the penalty of perjury and, with respect to a record maintained or located in a foreign country, a written declaration signed in a country which, if falsely made, would subject the maker to criminal penalty under the laws of the country. A party intending to offer a record into evidence under this paragraph must provide written notice of that intention to all adverse parties, and must make the record and certification available for inspection sufficiently in advance of their offer into evidence to provide an adverse party with a fair opportunity to challenge them.

Adopted September 27, 2010, eff. January 1, 2011.

Rule 903. Subscribing Witness' Testimony Unnecessary

The testimony of a subscribing witness is not necessary to authenticate a writing unless required by the laws of the jurisdiction whose laws govern the validity of the writing.

Adopted September 27, 2010, eff. January 1, 2011.

ARTICLE X. CONTENTS OF WRITINGS, RECORDINGS AND PHOTOGRAPHS

Rule
1001. Definitions.
1002. Requirement of Original.
1003. Admissibility of Duplicates.
1004. Admissibility of Other Evidence of Contents.
1005. Public Records.
1006. Summaries.
1007. Testimony or Written Admission of Party.
1008. Functions of Court and Jury.

Rule 1001. Definitions

For purposes of this article the following definitions are applicable:

(1) *Writings and Recordings*. "Writings" and "recordings" consist of letters, words, sounds, or numbers, or their equivalent, set down by handwriting, typewriting, printing, photostating, photographing, magnetic impulse, mechanical or electronic recording, or other form of data compilation.

(2) *Photographs*. "Photographs" include still photographs, X-ray films, video tapes, motion pictures and similar or other products or processes which produce recorded images.

(3) *Original*. An "original" of a writing or recording is the writing or recording itself or any counterpart intended to have the same effect by a person executing or issuing it. An "original" of a photograph includes the negative or any print therefrom. If data are stored in a computer or similar device, any printout or other output readable by sight, shown to reflect the data accurately, is an "original."

(4) *Duplicate*. A "duplicate" is a counterpart produced by the same impression as the original, or from the same matrix, or by means of photography, including enlargements and miniatures, or by mechanical or electronic re-recording, or by chemical reproduction, or by other equivalent techniques which accurately reproduces the original.

Adopted September 27, 2010, eff. January 1, 2011.

Rule 1002. Requirement of Original

To prove the content of a writing, recording, or photograph, the original writing, recording, or photograph is required, except as otherwise provided in these rules or by statute.

Adopted September 27, 2010, eff. January 1, 2011.

Rule 1003. Admissibility of Duplicates

A duplicate is admissible to the same extent as an original unless (1) a genuine question is raised as to the authenticity of the original or (2) in the circumstances it would be unfair to admit the duplicate in lieu of the original.

Adopted September 27, 2010, eff. January 1, 2011.

Rule 1004. Admissibility of Other Evidence of Contents

The original is not required and other evidence of the contents of a writing, recording, or photograph is admissible if—

(1) *Originals Lost or Destroyed*. All originals are lost or have been destroyed, unless the proponent lost or destroyed them in bad faith; or

(2) *Original Not Obtainable*. No original can be obtained by any available judicial process or procedure; or

(3) *Original in Possession of Opponent*. At a time when an original was under the control of the party against whom offered, that party was put on notice, by the pleadings or otherwise, that the contents would be a subject of proof at the hearing; or

(4) *Collateral Matters*. The writing, recording, or photograph is not closely related to a controlling issue.

Adopted September 27, 2010, eff. January 1, 2011.

Rule 1005. Public Records

The contents of an official record, or of a document authorized to be recorded or filed and actually recorded or filed, including data compilations in any form, if otherwise admissible, may be proved by copy, certified as correct in accordance with Rule 902 or testified to be correct by a witness who has compared it with the original. If a copy which complies with the foregoing cannot be obtained by the exercise of reasonable diligence, then other evidence of the contents may be given.

Adopted September 27, 2010, eff. January 1, 2011.

Rule 1006. Summaries

The contents of voluminous writings, recordings, or photographs which cannot conveniently be examined in court may be presented in the form of a chart, summary, or calculation. The originals, or duplicates, shall be made available for examination or copying, or both, by other parties at reasonable time and place. The court may order that they be produced in court.

Adopted September 27, 2010, eff. January 1, 2011.

Rule 1007. Testimony or Written Admission of Party

Contents of writings, recordings, or photographs may be proved by the testimony or deposition of the party against whom offered or by that party's written admission, without accounting for the nonproduction of the original.

Adopted September 27, 2010, eff. January 1, 2011.

Rule 1008. Functions of Court and Jury

When the admissibility of other evidence of contents of writings, recordings, or photographs under these rules depends upon the fulfillment of a condition of fact, the question whether the condition has been fulfilled is ordinarily for the court to determine in accordance with the provisions of Rule 104(a). However, when an issue is raised (a) whether the asserted writing ever existed, or (b) whether another writing, recording, or photograph produced at the trial is the original, or (c) whether other evidence of contents correctly reflects the contents, the issue is for the trier of fact to determine as in the case of other issues of fact.

Adopted September 27, 2010, eff. January 1, 2011.

ARTICLE XI. MISCELLANEOUS RULES

Rule
1101. Applicability of Rules.
1102. Title.

Rule 1101. Applicability of Rules

(a) Except as otherwise provided in paragraphs (b) and (c), these rules govern proceedings in the courts of Illinois.

(b) **Rules Inapplicable.** These rules (other than with respect to privileges) do not apply in the following situations:

(1) **Preliminary Questions of Fact.** The determination of questions of fact preliminary to admissibility of evidence when the issue is to be determined by the court under Rule 104.

(2) **Grand Jury.** Proceedings before grand juries.

(3) **Miscellaneous Proceedings.** Proceedings for extradition or rendition; preliminary examinations in criminal cases; sentencing, conditional discharge or supervision; postconviction hearings; issuance of warrants for arrest, criminal summonses, and search warrants; and proceedings with respect to release on bail or otherwise, and contempt proceedings in which the court may act summarily.

(c) **Small Claims Actions.** These rules apply to small claims actions, subject to the application of Supreme Court Rule 286(b).

Adopted September 27, 2010, eff. January 1, 2011. Amended April 8, 2013, eff. immediately; Jan. 6, 2015, eff. immediately.

Rule 1102. Title

These rules may be known and cited as the Illinois Rules of Evidence.

Adopted September 27, 2010, eff. January 1, 2011.

RULES OF THE ATTORNEY REGISTRATION AND DISCIPLINARY COMMISSION

Including Amendments Received Through April 1, 2016

ARTICLE I. GENERAL

Rule 1. Preamble

It is the policy of the Commission that disciplinary and unauthorized practice of law matters be handled expeditiously, with due regard to the right of the respondent to have adequate time to prepare his defense. The courts, the public, the bar, and the respondents have a vital interest in an early determination of any charge which bears upon the fitness of an attorney to practice his profession or an allegation of unauthorized practice of law. The elimination of unnecessary delay was a major objective of the Court in creating the Commission and in establishing the office of Administrator. Implementation of this objective is one of the principal purposes of the following rules.

Adopted eff. April 19, 1985. Amended Dec. 7, 2011, eff. immediately.

Rule 2. Definitions

As used in these rules:

(a) Misconduct. Misconduct is behavior of an attorney which violates the Illinois Code of Professional Responsibility or which tends to defeat the administration of justice or to bring the Courts or legal profession into disrepute.

(b) Charge. A charge is information which may constitute an allegation of misconduct by an attorney or an allegation of unauthorized practice of law.

(c) Chair. The Chair is a person designated by the Commission to serve as chairperson of an Inquiry Board panel or a Hearing Board panel.

(d) Respondent. A respondent is an attorney charged with misconduct or under investigation by the Administrator or a person, whether an individual, entity or association, charged with the unauthorized practice of law or under investigation under an allegation of the unauthorized practice of law.

(e) Complaining Witness. A complaining witness is a person who makes a charge of misconduct or an allegation of the unauthorized practice of law.

(f) Clerk. The Clerk of the Commission is the person designated by the Administrator to receive, keep and maintain the files, pleadings, records, documents, evidence and other papers of the various panels and boards related to the work of the Commission and its Boards.

Adopted eff. April 19, 1985. Amended eff. July 25, 1986; April 15, 1994; Dec. 7, 2011, eff. immediately.

Rule 3. Construction

The masculine form of a word includes the feminine. Except for proper nouns, the singular form includes the plural and the plural the singular.

Adopted eff. April 19, 1985.

Rule 4. Term Limits

(a) General Rule. Commission appointments of board members shall be limited to nine consecutive annual terms, except as otherwise provided in this rule.

(b) Applicability of Term Limits. Except as provided in paragraphs (c) and (d) of this rule, term limits apply to consecutive appointments of board members to the same position on the same board. An appointment to a different position or to a different board or an appointment following a break in service of at least one year shall be deemed to be the first appointment toward the nine consecutive appointment term limit for that position. The Inquiry Board, the Hearing Board, the Oversight Committee, the Client Protection Review Panel and any other body established by the Commission pursuant to these rules shall be deemed different boards. The positions of chair and of member of a panel of any of these bodies shall be deemed different. Term limits shall not affect an appointment that continues until further order pending the completion of the Commission's annual appointment process.

(c) Chairs of Hearing Board Panels. Commission appointments of Chairs of Hearing Board panels shall not be subject to term limits.

(d) **Implementation.** The term limit provisions of this rule shall be implemented over a five year period, beginning with appointments for 2013.
Adopted Jan. 2, 2012, eff. Feb. 28, 2013.

ARTICLE II.   INVESTIGATIONS BY THE ADMINISTRATOR

Rule
51. Initiation of an Investigation.
52. Charges.
53. Duty of Attorneys.
54. Closure by Administrator.
55. Reference to Inquiry Board.
56 to 100.   Reserved.

Rule 51.   Initiation of an Investigation

The Administrator may initiate an investigation on his own motion based upon information from any source.
Adopted eff. April 19, 1985.

Rule 52.   Charges

Charges received by the Administrator shall be in writing, shall identify the respondent and the person making the charge, and shall be sufficiently clear to apprise the respondent of the misconduct or unauthorized practice charged. In his discretion, the Administrator may provide assistance at his office to persons desiring to make a charge and may furnish forms for that purpose. The Administrator is not required to investigate any charge which does not meet the requirements of this rule, although in his discretion he may do so.
Adopted eff. April 19, 1985. Amended eff. Dec. 7, 2011, eff. immediately.

Rule 53.   Duty of Attorneys

The Administrator may request the respondent, or any other attorney who may have knowledge of pertinent facts, to provide information, in writing, concerning the matter under investigation. Such requests by the Administrator may be made by letter. It shall be the duty of every attorney admitted to practice in this state to respond within 14 days to any such request from the Administrator.
Adopted eff. April 19, 1985.

Rule 54.   Closure by Administrator

When the Administrator concludes that there is insufficient evidence to establish that the respondent has engaged in misconduct or to establish an allega-

Rules 5 to 50.   Reserved

tion of unauthorized practice of law, the Administrator shall close the investigation. The Administrator shall notify the complaining witness of his decision to close an investigation. Closure by the Administrator shall not bar the Administrator from resuming the investigation if circumstances warrant. The Administrator shall report to the Commission actions taken under this rule.
Adopted eff. April 19, 1985. Amended eff. July 25, 1986; Oct. 21, 1988; Dec. 7, 2011, eff. immediately.

Rule 55.   Reference to Inquiry Board

When the Administrator concludes that there is sufficient evidence to establish that the respondent engaged in misconduct or the unauthorized practice of law or the Administrator believes consideration by the Inquiry Board is warranted, the Administrator shall refer the matter to the Inquiry Board. At the time the referral is made, the Administrator shall send notice of the referral to the respondent. The notice shall state the date upon which the Inquiry Board is scheduled to consider the matter, shall state that a complaint may be voted or unauthorized practice of law proceedings may be authorized, and shall include information as to how the respondent may request an appearance before the Inquiry Board. In any matter as to which the respondent has not previously been afforded an opportunity to respond, the notice shall include information as to how a response may be submitted, and in cases where the respondent has previously been afforded an opportunity to respond, the notice shall contain information as to how the respondent can submit any additional information to be considered by the Inquiry Board. The notice shall be sent by regular mail, postage prepaid, addressed to the respondent at the address shown on the Master Roll, or if the respondent's name does not appear on the Master Roll, at his last known business address or residence address.
Adopted eff. April 19, 1985. Amended eff. Oct. 21, 1988; May 1, 2001; Dec. 7, 2011, eff. immediately.

Rules 56 to 100.   Reserved

ARTICLE III.   THE INQUIRY BOARD

Rule
101. Organization.
102. Function and Procedure of Inquiry Board.

Rule
103. Inquiry Panel Agenda.
104. Prompt Disposition.

Rule
105.   Deleted.
106.   Right to Counsel.
107.   Notification to Complaining Witness.
108.   Determination to Defer Further Proceedings.
109 to 200.   Reserved.

Rule 101.   Organization

The Inquiry Board shall act in panels composed of two lawyers and one nonlawyer. Two members of the panel shall constitute a quorum. The concurrence of two members shall be necessary to a decision by the panel. The decision of a panel shall be the decision of the Inquiry Board. In the absence of the chair of a panel at a meeting, the members present shall designate one of the members as acting chair. A panel may reconsider its decision to dismiss an investigation, to close an investigation or to vote a complaint prior to the filing of the complaint with the clerk of the Commission, or to institute unauthorized practice of law proceedings prior to the institution of those proceedings.

Adopted eff. April 19, 1985. Amended eff. July 25, 1986; April 15, 1994; Dec. 7, 2011, eff. immediately.

Rule 102.   Function and Procedure of Inquiry Board

The Board shall determine whether there is sufficient evidence for the filing of a complaint or petition with the Hearing Board or unauthorized practice of law proceedings. The Board shall review the investigation made by the Administrator. The Board may direct any additional investigation it deems appropriate and require the attendance of witnesses before it or one of its members. Where the Board deems appropriate, it may allow or require the appearance of the respondent, but the Board shall not be required to allow the respondent's appearance. The Board shall not determine the merits of the charge or conduct adversary hearings. The Board is not required to hear the testimony of witnesses. The Board may determine to defer further proceedings where warranted by the circumstances as set forth in Rule 108.

Adopted eff. April 19, 1985. Amended eff. July 25, 1986; July 9, 1990, eff. July 12, 1990; May 1, 2001; Dec. 7, 2011, eff. immediately.

Rule 103.   Inquiry Panel Agenda

The Administrator shall: (a) prepare an agenda in advance for each meeting of a panel; and (b) maintain minutes of the meeting, indicating the disposition of each investigation on the agenda, whether a complaint shall be voted, unauthorized practice of law proceedings shall be authorized, the investigation dismissed, the investigation closed, or the matter continued for further action.

Adopted eff. April 19, 1985. Amended eff. July 25, 1986; Dec. 7, 2011, eff. immediately.

Rule 104.   Prompt Disposition

Investigations before the Board shall be disposed of promptly.

Adopted eff. April 19, 1985. Amended eff. July 25, 1986.

Rule 105.   Deleted eff. May 1, 2001

Rule 106.   Right to Counsel

If respondent appears before a panel, or one of its members, he may be represented by counsel.

Adopted eff. April 19, 1985. Amended eff. July 25, 1986.

Rule 107.   Notification to Complaining Witness

The Administrator shall notify the complaining witness of the decision of the Inquiry Board.

Adopted eff. April 19, 1985. Amended eff. July 25, 1986.

Rule 108.   Determination to Defer Further Proceedings

(a) Deferral. With the agreement of the Administrator and the attorney, the Inquiry Board may determine to defer further proceedings pending the attorney's compliance with conditions imposed by the Board for supervision of the attorney for a specified period of time not to exceed one year unless extended by the Inquiry Board prior to the conclusion of the specified period. Proceedings may not be deferred under the provisions of this Rule if:

(1) the conduct under investigation involves misappropriation of funds or property of a client or a third party;

(2) the conduct under investigation involves a criminal act that reflects adversely on the attorney's honesty;

(3) the conduct under investigation resulted in or is likely to result in actual prejudice (loss of money, legal rights or valuable property rights) to a client or other person, unless restitution is made a condition of deferral; or

(4) the attorney has previously been disciplined or placed on supervision as provided in this Rule.

(b) Conditions. Such conditions shall take into consideration the nature and circumstances of the conduct under investigation by the board and the history, character and condition of the attorney. The conditions may include, but are not limited to, the following:

(1) periodic reports to the Administrator;

(2) supervision of the attorney's practice or accounting procedures;

(3) satisfactory completion of a course of study;

(4) successful completion of the Multistate Professional Responsibility Examination;

(5) compliance with the provisions of the Rules of Professional Conduct;

(6) restitution;

(7) psychological counseling or treatment; and

(8) abstinence from alcohol or drugs.

(c) Affidavit. Prior to the Inquiry Board entering its determination to defer further proceedings, the attorney shall execute an affidavit setting forth the following:

(1) the nature of the conduct under investigation by the Inquiry Board as admitted by the attorney;

(2) the conditions to be imposed by the Inquiry Board for supervision of the attorney;

(3) that the attorney does not object to the conditions to be imposed;

(4) that the attorney understands that should he fail to comply with the conditions imposed by the Inquiry Board a formal complaint may be voted and filed with the Hearing Board;

(5) that the admissions by the attorney with respect to his or her conduct may be introduced as evidence in any further proceedings before the Hearing or Review Board; and

(6) that the attorney joins in the Inquiry Board's determination freely and voluntarily, and understands the nature and consequences of the Board's action.

(d) Supervision. The Administrator shall be responsible for the supervision of the conditions imposed by the Inquiry Board. Where appropriate, he may recommend to the Board modifications of the conditions and shall report to the Board the attorney's failure to comply with the conditions or to cooperate with the Administrator. Upon a showing of the attorney's failure to comply with conditions, the Board may request that any deferred matters be returned to its agenda for future consideration.

(e) Compliance. Upon the attorney's successful compliance with the conditions imposed by the Inquiry Board, the Board shall dismiss or close the investigations pending before it at the time it determined to defer further consideration.

Adopted July 9, 1990, eff. July 12, 1990. Amended eff. Oct. 23, 1992.

Rules 109 to 200. Reserved

ARTICLE IV. THE HEARING BOARD

Rule 201. Organization

The Hearing Board shall act in panels composed of two lawyers and one nonlawyer. The Commission will designate one of the lawyer members as Chair of the panel. Two members of the panel shall constitute a quorum. The Administrator and the respondent may consent to a hearing before one member of the panel; however, the concurrence of two members of a panel shall be necessary to a decision. In the absence of the Chair at a hearing, the remaining lawyer member shall serve as acting chair. The decision of the panel shall be the decision of the Hearing Board.

Adopted eff. April 19, 1985. Amended eff. July 25, 1986; April 15, 1994.

Rules 202 to 210. Reserved

Rule 211. Preparation and Form of Complaint

A complaint voted by the Inquiry Board shall be prepared by the Administrator and captioned "In the Matter of Attorney Respondent. No. _____," The complainant shall be the Administrator. The complaint shall contain a concise statement of the facts constituting the alleged misconduct.

Adopted eff. April 19, 1985.

Rule 212. Docketing and Assignment to Panel for Hearing

The complaint shall be filed with the Clerk. The Clerk shall docket the complaint and shall assign the matter to a hearing panel in accordance with procedures and policies established by the Commission. If any member of the panel is unavailable to hear the matter, the Clerk shall assign another member of the Board to serve on the panel hearing the matter. Adopted eff. April 19, 1985. Amended Dec. 11, 1992, eff. March 1, 1993.

Rule 213. Reserved

Rule 214. Service of Complaint

The Clerk shall cause a copy of the complaint, a copy of these rules and a notice of the hearing to be served on the respondent within or without the State of Illinois as follows:

(a) By Personal Service. Personal service shall be made by leaving a copy with the respondent personally; or

(b) By Mail Service. If a person authorized to make personal service, as provided in Rule 215 below, files with the Hearing Board his affidavit that the respondent (1) resides out of the state, (2) has left the state, (3) on due inquiry cannot be found, or (4) is concealed within the state so that process cannot be served upon him, the Administrator shall serve the respondent by ordinary mail, postage fully prepaid, directed to the respondent at the address shown on the Master Roll or if he is not listed on the Master Roll at his last known business or residence address. The Administrator's certificate of mailing is sufficient proof of service. Adopted eff. April 19, 1985.

Rule 215. Persons Authorized to Make Service

Personal service may be made:

(1) By a member of the Administrator's staff;

(2) By the Sheriff of any county in which the respondent is found;

(3) At the direction of the chair of the hearing panel to which a matter is assigned, by any member of the bar of this state; or

(4) In another state, by any resident of the state who, by the laws or rules of court of that state, is authorized to serve process in disciplinary proceedings. Adopted eff. April 19, 1985.

Rules 216 to 230. Reserved

Rule 231. Return Date

The respondent shall answer the complaint within 21 days after personal service or within 28 days after the date of mailing when service is by mail. Respondent shall include in a separate section in the answer the following information related to respondent's professional background:

a. whether respondent has ever been admitted to practice law before any other state court, federal court or administrative agency or admitted before the bar of any foreign country and, if so, the identity of each such court, jurisdiction or agency; the year of each such admission; the full name under which respondent was admitted and any subsequent name changes; and any bar or registration number assigned; and

b. whether respondent has ever received any other professional license or certificate and, if so, the identity of each such issuing entity; the year of issuance of each such license or certificate; the full name under which the license or certificate was issued to respondent and any subsequent name changes; and any certificate or registration number assigned. Adopted eff. April 19, 1985. Amended eff. March 31, 1995; Sept. 14, 2012, eff. Jan. 1, 2013.

Rule 232. Pleadings Subsequent to the Complaint

The original of each pleading subsequent to the complaint shall be filed by the pleader with the Clerk. A copy of any pleading filed shall be served in the manner prescribed for the service of papers by the rules of the Supreme Court. Adopted eff. April 19, 1985.

Rule 233. Answer to be Specific

The answer shall specifically admit or deny each allegation of the complaint. Every allegation not specifically denied is deemed admitted unless the answer states the reason the respondent is unable to make a specific denial. Adopted eff. April 19, 1985.

Rule 234. Replies

No reply shall be filed by the Administrator. Any new matter alleged in the respondent's answer shall be deemed denied. Adopted eff. April 19, 1985.

Rule 235. Motions

All motions shall be made in writing prior to hearing. Rulings on motions shall be made by the chair of the panel or in a manner as the chair shall determine. No oral arguments shall be allowed on motions. The movant may submit written authority in support of the motion and the other party may submit counter authority within 7 days after receipt of the movant's authority. To facilitate the development of a full evidentiary record in matters other than default proceedings, dispositive motions such as those seeking summary judgment or dismissal prior to completion of the evidentiary record on charges shall not be permitted. This rule is not intended to prevent motions pursuant to Illinois Supreme Court Rules 201 and 219 or motions for a directed finding at hearing.

Adopted eff. April 19, 1985. Amended eff. Sept. 1, 2012.

Rule 236. Failure to Answer

When the respondent fails to answer the complaint, as required by Rules 231 through 233, upon motion of the Administrator and notice to the respondent, all factual allegations and disciplinary charges shall be deemed admitted, and no further proof shall be required. A respondent who has failed to answer timely may seek leave of the hearing panel to vacate an order of default and file an answer upon a showing that his failure to answer was a result of mistake, inadvertence, surprise or excusable neglect. At any hearing in which the allegations of the complaint have been deemed admitted, the respondent and Administrator shall be limited to presenting evidence of aggravating and mitigating factors and arguments regarding the form and amount of discipline to be imposed. No hearing shall be conducted within twenty-eight days of the entry of an order vacating an order of default.

Adopted eff. April 19, 1985. Amended eff. Oct. 21, 1988; Sept. 14, 2012, eff. Jan. 1, 2013.

Rule 237. Master File

The original of the complaint and all subsequent pleadings and other documents shall be filed with the Clerk and maintained in a master file.

Adopted eff. April 19, 1985.

Rules 238 to 250. Reserved

Rule 251. Discovery

(a) Except as provided herein, discovery practice shall be in accordance with the Code of Civil Procedure [1] and the Rules of the Supreme Court. Written interrogatories shall not be served by any party without leave of the chair of the hearing panel and upon good cause shown. At any time after the respondent has been served, either party may request admissions of fact and genuineness of documents pursuant to Supreme Court Rule 216. Discovery shall be filed with the clerk of the Commission, with the exception of discovery depositions and items produced pursuant to discovery requests.

(b) **Work Product.**

(1) The Administrator and the respondent shall be entitled to a work product privilege for materials prepared by their respective counsel or counsel's agents, including employed or independently retained paralegals and investigators, in anticipation of proceedings under Supreme Court Rules 751 et seq., or for purposes of proceedings pending under those Rules. Work product includes, but is not limited to, notes and memoranda prepared by counsel or counsel's agents of witnesses' oral statements

which are not verbatim and which have not been reviewed, altered, corrected or signed by the witness, except that the privilege does not extend to those portions of memoranda of investigators and paralegals that provide the investigator's or paralegal's summary of the statements of those interviewed and other factual information.

(2) Neither the Administrator nor the respondent shall be compelled to disclose work product in the course of discovery under these rules except upon a showing of the absolute impossibility of securing similar information from other sources. If the Chair determines that there is no possibility of the requesting party securing similar information from another source, the Chair may order the other party to produce for *in camera* review the work product that contains the otherwise unobtainable information with proposed redactions of mental impressions, characterizations, theories, instructions to staff that reveal investigative or litigation strategy, and litigation plans, as well as factual information otherwise obtainable. Having so ordered, the Chair shall review the work product material and the proposed redactions, and, thereafter, order disclosure of only otherwise unobtainable factual information.

(3) Disclosure or production of information or materials to a Respondent, Petitioner, or the Administrator during an investigation or proceeding does not constitute subject matter waiver of the party's work product privilege.

Adopted eff. April 19, 1985. Amended eff. April 1, 1996; Sept. 30, 2005; Oct. 26, 2012, eff. Feb. 1, 2013.

[1] 735 ILCS 5/1–101 et seq.

Rule 252. Deleted effective Sept. 1, 2012.

Rule 253. Disclosure of Witnesses

(a) Within 28 days of service of the complaint upon respondent, the Administrator and the attorney—respondent shall file a report disclosing the name, address and telephone numbers of persons who have knowledge of facts which are the subject of the proceeding, and identifying the subject matter of their knowledge. The Administrator and attorney—respondent have a duty to seasonably supplement or amend any prior answer or response whenever new or additional information subsequently becomes known to that party. The Administrator and attorney—respondent shall disclose to all parties of record any reports about the case received from an expert witness who will testify at hearing within a reasonable time after receipt of the report.

(b) The Hearing Board shall not allow the Administrator or the attorney—respondent to offer the testimony of any person whose identity and location is not disclosed in a report pursuant to this rule, but the Hearing Board shall not bar testimony of a witness based upon the adequacy of the disclosure of the subjects of the witness' testimony, absent a showing of substantial prejudice by the party seeking to bar the testimony. The Hearing Board shall not allow the Administrator or the attorney—respondent to offer the testimony of any expert witness who provided a report to the party calling that expert witness, if that report has not been timely disclosed to all other parties.

Adopted eff. April 24, 1987. Amended eff. Sept. 30, 2005.

Rules 254 to 259. Reserved

Rule 260. Prehearing Conferences

(a) **Pre-hearing Conferences.** As soon as practicable after the filing of the petition, answer or after the time for filing an answer has elapsed, a member of the Hearing Board who has been designated Chair in the case shall schedule and preside over a pre-hearing conference. All pre-hearing conferences may take place at the offices of the Attorney Registration and Disciplinary Commission or by telephone, as determined by the Chair. The respondent or petitioner, counsel for respondent or petitioner if any, and counsel for the Administrator shall personally attend all pre-hearing conferences unless excused by the Chair.

(b) **Objectives.** The Chair is responsible for bringing the case to a full and fair hearing in a timely and efficient manner. In furtherance of this responsibility, the Chair shall conduct prehearing conferences to consider and take action regarding:

(1) the formulation and simplification of the issues;

(2) the elimination of frivolous charges or defenses;

(3) the necessity of amendments to the pleadings;

(4) entry into stipulations regarding undisputed evidence and obtaining prehearing rulings on the admissibility of evidence;

(5) the identification and limitation of witnesses, including character or expert witnesses;

(6) the possibility of discipline on consent pursuant to Supreme Court Rule 762;

(7) the supervision of discovery;

(8) the scheduling of the hearing; and

(9) any other matters which may aid in the disposition of the action.

(c) **Scheduling Order.** In all cases where a complaint has been filed pursuant to Supreme Court Rules 753 or 761, the Chair shall enter a scheduling order, as soon as practicable, establishing dates certain for the following matters and any other matters the Chair deems appropriate:

(1) the filing of an answer if none has been filed;

(2) the filing of reports pursuant to Commission Rule 253 if none has been filed;

(3) the filing of motions pursuant to Commission Rules 235 and 236;

(4) retention of counsel by *pro se* respondents;

(5) a discovery cut-off date, including specific dates for document production and depositions as deemed necessary by the Chair. However, all discovery shall be completed no later than 14 days prior to the date set for hearing;

(6) the filing of stipulations;

(7) the exchange of exhibits;

(8) the filing of a joint motion for approval to file petition to impose discipline on consent pursuant to Supreme Court Rule 762(b);

(9) hearing date.

(d) **Additional Pre-hearings.** The Chair may modify the scheduling order and hold additional prehearing conferences as deemed necessary.

(e) **Order.** For each pre-hearing conference, the Chair shall enter an order reciting any action taken by the Chair and reciting any agreements made by the Administrator and the respondent or petitioner and approved by the Chair.

(f) **Sanctions.** The Chair shall, in addition to any other sanctions authorized by Supreme Court Rule or Commission Rule, make and enforce all rules and orders necessary to compel compliance with this rule.

(Adopted eff. March 10, 1987. Amended eff. Oct. 21, 1988; April 15, 1994; May 1, 2001; Sept. 1, 2012.)

Rule 261. Substitution and Recusal of Hearing Chair and Panel Members

(a) **In General.** Substitution of the Chair of the Hearing panel assigned to a case may be requested consistent with the provisions of Section 5/2-1001 of the Code of Civil Procedure. Parties may request substitution of Hearing panel members other than the Chair due to the involvement of the panel member, as provided in Section 5/2-1001(a)(1), or for cause, as provided in Section 5/2-1001(a)(3). Motions for a substitution of a Chair for cause shall be heard by the Chair of the full Hearing Board or another Chair designated by him. Motions for substitution of a panel member other than the Chair shall be heard by the Chair assigned to the case.

(b) **After Denial of Approval to File Consent Petition.** Whenever a panel denies a motion for leave to file a petition presented pursuant to Supreme Court Rule 762(b), the members of that panel shall recuse themselves from further proceedings in the case and the case shall be assigned to a different panel of the Hearing Board.

Adopted eff. May 1, 2001.

Rules 262 to 270. Reserved

Rule 271. Deleted effective Oct. 21, 1988

Rule 272.   Continuances

The Chair may continue a hearing or pre-hearing conference at the Chair's discretion. No hearing or pre-hearing conference shall be continued at the request of any party except upon written motion supported by affidavit. No hearing shall be continued at the request of a party except under extraordinary circumstances. Engagement of counsel shall not be deemed an extraordinary circumstance. No pre-hearing conference shall be continued at the request of a party except for good cause.

(Adopted eff. April 19, 1985. Amended eff. March, 10, 1987; April 15, 1994; Sept. 1, 2012.)

Rule 273.   Evidence

The admissibility of matters offered in evidence in proceedings brought pursuant to these rules shall be governed by the Code of Civil Procedure[1] and Rules of the Supreme Court. An affidavit or letter which attempts to establish the character or reputation of a respondent or petitioner shall not be admitted. Evidence concerning the character or reputation of a respondent or petitioner may be limited by the hearing panel as the interest of justice requires.

Adopted eff. April 19, 1985.

[1] 735 ILCS 5/1–101 et seq.

Rule 274.   Hearings to be Continuous

Hearings shall continue from day to day until the taking of evidence has been completed. Hearings may be held on Saturday.

Adopted eff. April 19, 1985.

Rule 275.   Exclusion of Witnesses

Upon motion of either party, the hearing panel may exclude witnesses from the hearing.

Adopted May 11, 1990, eff. June 1, 1990.

Rule 276.   Exhibits

Each party must appear at hearing with all documentary exhibits prepared in the following manner:

(a) The first page of each exhibit or group exhibit shall be labeled as Administrator's Exhibit (Adm. Ex.), Respondent's Exhibit (Resp. Ex.), or Petitioner's Exhibit (Pet. Ex.), with the appropriate number of the exhibit.

(b) Any exhibit that contains more than one page shall be bound, stapled or otherwise fastened permanently, and shall have all pages of that exhibit consecutively numbered.

(c) Prior to the start of the hearing, each party shall tender to the Chair, on a form provided by the Clerk, a table of the exhibits the party plans to offer. A copy of the table shall be served upon opposing counsel.

(d) At the close of evidence and before the hearing is adjourned, it shall be the duty of each party to assure that all exhibits that were admitted into evidence for that party and all exhibits that were the subject of an offer of proof by that party during the hearing have been delivered to the Chair in a form consistent with this rule.

Adopted eff. June 30, 1995.

Rule 277.   Prior Discipline

If the hearing panel concludes that the Administrator has established that the respondent engaged in misconduct, the Chair shall enter an order directing the Administrator to file within seven days copies of any orders or opinions imposing discipline on the respondent, that are not already in evidence. At the same time, the Administrator may file written argument not to exceed five pages in length regarding the effect to be given to the prior discipline. Within seven days after the filing of prior disciplinary orders or opinions, the respondent may file a written argument not to exceed five pages in length regarding the effect to be given to the prior discipline.

Adopted May 11, 1990, eff. June 1, 1990.

Rules 278 to 280.   Reserved

Rule 281.   Report of the Hearing Board

The report of the Hearing Board shall be prepared by the panel as soon as practicable after completion of the hearing. The report shall be filed with the Clerk. The Clerk shall serve a copy upon the respondent and the Administrator.

Adopted eff. April 19, 1985.

Rule 282.   Reprimands

The hearing panel may order that it will administer a reprimand to respondent. The reprimand shall include a description of the respondent's misconduct and the reasons for the reprimand.

(a) Order. The order and the proposed reprimand shall be filed with the Clerk. The order shall designate the time and place for the delivery of the proposed reprimand, not less than 21 days after the filing of the order. The Clerk shall serve a copy of the order and proposed reprimand upon the respondent and the Administrator.

(b) Exceptions. The respondent or the Administrator may, within 21 days thereafter, file exceptions to the order with the Review Board as provided by Supreme Court Rule 753(e). Upon the filing of exceptions, the matter shall be reviewed by the Review Board. If no exceptions are filed, the order shall become final.

(c) Delivery. The hearing panel shall deliver the reprimand to the respondent orally and in writing.

(d) Subsequent Disciplinary Proceedings. The reprimand may be admitted into evidence in any subsequent disciplinary proceeding relating to the respondent in accordance with Supreme Court Rule 753(c)(5) and Commission Rule 277 and 314.

Adopted eff. April 19, 1985. Amended May 11, 1990, eff. June 1, 1990.

Rule 283. Notification to Complaining Witness

The Administrator shall notify the complaining witness of the action taken by the Hearing Board.

Adopted eff. April 19, 1985.

Rule 284. Post–Trial Procedures

(a) **Post–Trial Motions.** Except as provided herein, post-trial motions shall not be filed with or considered by the Hearing Board. A matter which might otherwise be presented by post-trial motion may be the subject of an exception filed with the Review Board. Motions for an extension of the time within which to file exceptions to the report of the Hearing Board shall be ruled upon by the chair of the hearing panel which prepared the report.

(b) **Closing Argument.** The Hearing Board shall not allow or consider written summations, written closing argument or post-trial memoranda.

Adopted eff. April 19, 1985. Amended eff. July 25, 1986.

Rules 285 to 290. Reserved

Rule 291. Perpetuating Testimony

(a) **Petition.** The Administrator, an attorney, or any person who is or has been the subject of proceedings pursuant to these rules or the disciplinary rules of the Supreme Court may file with the Clerk a petition for an order authorizing the petitioner to take a deposition for the purpose of perpetuating testimony. The petition shall be captioned "In the Matter of Attorney–Respondent No. _____." The petition shall state: (i) the name and address of the person to be examined; (ii) the facts which the petitioner desires to establish by the proposed testimony; and (iii) the reasons for perpetuating the testimony.

(b) **Service on the Administrator.** Service on the Administrator shall be made by mailing or delivering the original and two copies of the petition to the office of the Administrator in Springfield or Chicago directed to the attention of the Clerk of the Commission.

(c) **Service on an Attorney or Other Person.** Service of the petition on an attorney or other person shall be made in the same manner provided by Rules 214 and 215 for service of a complaint.

(d) **Filing and Docketing by Clerk.** Upon receipt of the petition, the Clerk shall file and docket it. If the matter which is the subject of the petition has been assigned to a hearing panel, the Clerk shall assign the petition to the chair of that panel. If the matter which is the subject of the petition has not been assigned to a hearing panel, the Clerk shall assign the petition to a chair of a hearing panel in accordance with procedures and policies established by the Commission.

(e) **Order and Examination.** If the chair of the hearing panel assigned to hear the petition determines that the perpetuation of the testimony may prevent a failure or delay of justice, he shall designate or describe the persons whose depositions are to be taken specifying the subject matter of the examination and whether the depositions shall take upon oral examination or written questions and fixing the time, place and conditions of the examination. The order shall be filed with the Clerk who shall notify the parties of the entry of the order.

Adopted eff. April 19, 1985. Amended Dec. 11, 1992, eff. March 1, 1993.

Rules 292 to 300. Reserved

ARTICLE V.   THE REVIEW BOARD

Rule 301. Review of Hearing Board Report, Notice of Exceptions

(a) **Method of Review.** Every report of the Hearing Board is reviewable by the Review Board as of right.

(b) **Time; Filing.** Review is initiated by filing a Notice of Exceptions with the Clerk of the Commission within 21 days of service of the Hearing Board Report to the parties. The party who files a Notice of Exceptions first shall be considered the appellant. The appellee need not file a Notice of Exceptions to assert additional error but shall assert any such additional error within his brief.

(c) **Form and Contents of Notice of Exceptions.** The Notice of Exceptions shall bear the title and number of the matter, naming and designating the parties in the same manner as before the Hearing Board and adding the further designation "appellant" or "appellee" (e.g. respondent—appellant). The Notice of Exceptions shall be titled as such and specify the Hearing Board Report or portion thereof excepted to and the relief sought from the Review Board, as well as the signature and address of each appellant or his or her attorney.

Adopted eff. April 19, 1985. Amended eff. Jan. 15, 1988; Feb. 2, 1994.

Rule 302. Briefs

(a) **Time.** Unless the Review Board orders otherwise, the brief of the appellant shall be filed with the Clerk of the Commission no later than 35 days after the date that the Notice of Exceptions is due. Within 35 days from the due date of the appellant's brief, the appellee shall file a brief with the Clerk. Within 14 days from the due date of the appellee's brief, the appellant may file a reply brief. Should the appellee raise additional errors in his brief, the appellant's reply brief shall also address those errors, shall be designated as the appellant-cross-appellee's reply brief, and shall be filed within 14 days of the filing of the appellee's brief. The appellee may file a reply brief confined strictly to replying to the appellant's argument on the additional errors within 14 days after the due date of the appellant-cross-appellee's reply brief. If the brief of the Appellee raises additional errors in his brief, the cover of the brief shall be captioned: Brief of Appellee. Cross Relief Requested. Should the Review Board allow a brief to be filed after the date it is due, the Review Board may extend the due date of any subsequent brief as necessary.

(b) **Number of Copies and Service.** The original and one copy of each brief shall be filed with the Clerk of the Commission. In addition, the party shall serve three copies upon the other party to review. Proof of service shall be filed with all briefs.

(c) **Extensions.** The Review Board may upon the motion of a party extend the time to file a brief. The motion must be accompanied by a supporting affidavit showing the number of previous extensions granted and the reason for each extension. Such motions are not favored and will be allowed only in the most extreme and compelling circumstances. The original and one copy of the motion shall be filed with the Clerk of the Commission. In addition, the party shall serve one copy upon the other party to review. A notice of filing with proof of service shall be filed with all motions.

(d) **Page Limitations and Format Requirements.** Unless authorized by the Review Board, the appellant's brief and the appellee's brief, excluding appendices, shall each be limited to 50 pages, and the reply brief shall be limited to 20 pages. Neither narrow margins nor any other device shall be employed to evade the page limitation. Footnotes, if any, shall be used sparingly. The text of all briefs must be double-spaced, except for headings, quotations, and footnotes. At least 12-point type must be used in the body of briefs, and at least 10-point type must be used for footnotes. A motion to authorize the filing of briefs in excess of the limitations of this rule shall be filed before the brief is due and shall state the maximum number of pages requested. Motions to allow additional pages are not favored, and the specific grounds establishing the necessity for excess pages shall be clearly set forth in an affidavit filed in support of the motion.

(e) **Cover.** The cover of each brief shall contain the number of the matter, the status of each party at the Review Board level (e.g. respondent-appellant, Administrator–appellee), the individual names and addresses of the attorneys (or of the party if he or she is appearing pro se) filing the brief, and if desired, of their law firm, shall also be stated. The colors of the covers of the documents shall be: appellant's brief or petition, white; appellee's brief or answer, light blue; appellant's reply brief, light yellow; appellee's reply brief, light red.

(f) **Contents of Appellant's Brief.** The appellant's brief shall contain the following parts in the order named:

(1) A summary statement, entitled "Points and Authorities," of the points argued and the authorities cited in the Argument. This shall consist of the headings of the points and subpoints as in the Argument, with the citation under each heading of the authorities relied upon or distinguished and a reference to the page of the brief on which each heading and each authority appear. Cases shall be cited as near as may be in the order of their importance.

(2) An introductory paragraph stating (i) the nature of the matter and of the recommendation appealed from, and (ii) whether any question is raised on the pleadings, and if so, the nature of the question.

(3) A statement of the legal issue or issues presented for review, without detail or citation of authorities.

(4) A Statement of Facts, which shall contain the facts necessary to an understanding of the case, stated accurately and fairly without argument or comment, and with appropriate reference to the pages of the record on appeal. Exhibits may be cited by reference to pages of the record on appeal or by exhibit number followed by the page number within the exhibit.

(5) Argument, which shall contain the contentions of the party and the reasons therefor, with citation of the authorities and the pages of the record relied on. Evidence shall not be copied at length, but reference shall be made to the pages of the record on appeal where evidence may be found. Citation of numerous authorities in support of the same point is not favored. Points not argued are waived and shall not be raised in the reply brief or oral argument.

(6) A short conclusion stating the precise relief sought, followed by the names of counsel as on the cover.

(7) An appendix containing the Hearing Board Report, the Notice of Exceptions, an index of the record, and the full text of each Rule of Professional Conduct at issue and related Comments.

(g) **Briefs of Appellee.** The brief for the appellee and other parties shall conform to the foregoing requirements, except that items (f)(2), (f)(3), (f)(4), and (f)(7) of this rule need not be included except to the extent that the presentation by the appellant is deemed unsatisfactory.

(h) **Reply Briefs.** The reply brief, if any, shall be confined strictly to replying to arguments presented in the brief of the appellee and need only contain Argument.

(i) **Nonconforming Briefs.** The Review Board may strike any brief or portion thereof that does not conform to the Rules, or take any other action authorized by precedent of the Supreme Court or Appellate Court for enforcing the requirements pertaining to the form and content of briefs, including refusing to review arguments not supported by citation to the record or legal precedent.

(j) **Failure to File.** If the appellant fails to file a brief within the time set by this rule or any additional time which the Review Board allows, the Review Board shall strike the exceptions of that appellant and the matter shall proceed as if those exceptions had not been filed.

Adopted eff. April 19, 1985. Amended Dec. 1, 1995, eff. immediately; May 31, 2005; June 12, 2009, eff. Jan. 1, 2010; June 27, 2011, eff. Sept. 1, 2011; Sept. 14, 2012, eff. Feb. 1, 2013.

Rule 303. Reserved.

Rule 304. Oral Arguments

(a) **Request; Waiver; Dispensing with Oral Argument.** A party shall request oral argument by stating at the bottom of the cover page of the brief that oral argument is requested. If any party so requests and the Review Board grants oral arguments, all other parties may argue without an additional request. No party may argue unless a brief is filed as required by the rules. A party who has requested and been granted oral argument and who thereafter determines to waive oral argument shall promptly notify the Clerk of the Commission and the other party in writing no later than fourteen days before the date of the argument. Any party who has filed a brief without requesting oral argument may then request oral argument upon prompt notice to the Clerk and all other parties.

In determining whether to allow or require oral argument, the Review Board may consider whether oral argument would be necessary for consideration of the issues presented for review.

When oral argument is not requested, the matter shall be decided on the briefs unless the Review Board orders oral argument.

(b) **Length.** Unless the Review Board otherwise orders, each side shall argue for not more than 20 minutes, with an additional ten minutes rebuttal for the party with the right to close. The Review Board may grant additional time on motion filed with the Clerk of the Commission in advance of the date fixed for argument if it appears that additional time is necessary for the adequate presentation of the case. A party is not obliged to use all of the time allowed, and the Review Board may terminate the argument whenever in its judgment further argument is unnecessary.

(c) **Reading Prohibited.** Reading at length from the record, briefs, or authorities cited will not be permitted.

(d) **Sequence and Manner of Calling Matters for Oral Argument.** Matters shall be called for argument in accordance with procedures and policies established by the Commission.

Adopted eff. April 19, 1985. Amended eff. Feb. 2, 1994.

Rules 305 to 310. Reserved

Rule 311. Review Board Report

The report of the Review Board shall address the issues raised by the parties and need not address any portion of the Hearing Board report with which the parties have not taken issue. The Review Board report may consist of the adoption of the Hearing Board report. Unanimous reports shall be submitted in the name of the Review Board Panel. When there is a divided vote, the members constituting the majority and the member dissenting or concurring in part shall be named. Any member dissenting or concurring in part may submit a statement of position within a reasonable time following the filing of the report.

Adopted eff. April 19, 1985. Amended eff. Feb. 2, 1994.

Rule 312. Reprimands

The Review Board may order that it will administer a reprimand to respondent. The reprimand shall include a description of the respondent's misconduct and the reasons for the reprimand.

(a) **Order.** The order and proposed reprimand shall be filed with the Clerk. The order shall designate the time and place for the delivery of the proposed reprimand, not less than 21 days after the filing of the order and proposed reprimand upon the respondent and the Administrator.

(b) **Exceptions.** The respondent or the Administrator may, within 21 days thereafter, file exceptions or petition the Court for leave to file exceptions to the order as provided by Supreme Court Rule 753(e). Upon the filing of exceptions or a petition for leave to file exceptions, the proceeding in the Review Board shall be stayed pending action by the Supreme Court. If no exceptions are filed, the order shall become final.

(c) Delivery. The Review Board shall deliver the reprimand to the respondent orally and in writing.

(d) Subsequent Disciplinary Proceedings. The reprimand may be admitted in evidence in any subsequent disciplinary proceeding relating to the respondent in accordance with Supreme Court Rule 753(c)(5) and Commission Rule 277 and 314.

Adopted eff. April 19, 1985. Amended May 11, 1990, eff. June 1, 1990.

Rule 313. Notification to Complaining Witness

The Administrator shall notify the complaining witness of the action taken by the Review Board.

Adopted eff. April 19, 1985.

ARTICLE VI.   REINSTATEMENT

Rule 400. Presentation of Petition

In accordance with Supreme Court Rule 767(b), an attorney who has been disbarred, disbarred on consent, or suspended until further order of the court may present to the Administrator a copy of the petition he proposes to file with the clerk of the Court within 120 days prior to the date on which the petition may be filed.

Adopted eff. April 15, 1994.

Rule 401. Form of Petition

A petition pursuant to Supreme Court Rule 767 shall restate subparagraphs (1) through (25) contained in Rule 402 below. The petitioner's response shall follow each restated subparagraph, except that, with respect to subparagraphs (2), (3), (4), (7), (8) (20), (22), and (23), the response may be "submitted under separate cover to the Administrator," provided that the required information and/or documents are delivered to the Administrator on the same date and by the same method as is used for filing the petition with the Court or presenting the petition to the Administrator. For the purpose of Rule 402 the term "period of discipline" means the interval between the date an attorney is disbarred, disbarred on consent or suspended until further order of the court and the date

Rule 314.   Prior Discipline

In the event the Hearing Board did not find misconduct, but the Review Board concludes that the Administrator has established that the respondent engaged in misconduct, the Chair shall enter an order directing the Administrator to file within seven days copies of any orders or opinions imposing discipline on the respondent, that are not already in evidence. At the same time, the Administrator may file written argument not to exceed five pages in length regarding the effect to be given to the prior discipline. Within seven days after the filing of prior disciplinary orders or opinions, the respondent may file a written argument not to exceed five pages in length regarding the effect to be given to the prior discipline.

Adopted May 11, 1990, eff. June 1, 1990.

Rules 315 to 399.   Reserved

his verified petition seeking to be reinstated on the roll of attorneys is filed with the Clerk of the Court.

Adopted eff. April 19, 1985. Amended June 12, 2009, eff. Jan. 1, 2010.

Rule 402.   Content of Petition

The petition shall contain petitioner's response to the following:

(1) The date on which discipline was imposed. If there was a reported opinion, the volume and page number;

(2) The age, residence address and telephone number of the petitioner;

(3) The name, age and address of all dependents of the petitioner;

(4) During the period of discipline, the address of each residence of the petitioner, including temporary and part-time residences, and the dates of each residence;

(5) During the period of discipline, the name and address of each employer, associate or partner of the petitioner; the dates of each employment, association, or partnership; the positions occupied and titles held; the name and address of the immediate supervisor; and the reason for leaving the employment, association or partnership;

(6) A statement including the case caption, general nature, dates and disposition of every civil or criminal action which pended during the period of discipline to which petitioner was either a party or claimed an interest;

(7) A statement of the monthly earnings and other income of the petitioner and the sources from which all earnings and income were derived during the period of discipline;

(8) A statement of assets and financial obligations of the petitioner during the period of discipline, the dates when acquired or incurred, the names and address of all creditors;

(9) Whether the discipline was related to a misappropriation or failure to account for any monies, a financial benefit to petitioner or a financial detriment to anyone, and a statement of the amounts involved, held or received by petitioner and the details of any restitution or accounting, including the dates and amounts, and the names and addresses of the persons to whom such restitution or accounting was made;

(10) During the period of discipline, whether the petitioner sought or obtained assistance, consultation or treatment for a mental or emotional disorder or for addiction to drugs or alcohol, and the name and address of each provider of services, and the services rendered, their duration and purpose;

(11) During the period of discipline, whether the petitioner was admitted to any institution, as an in-patient or out-patient, for a mental or emotional disorder or for addiction to drugs or alcohol, and the name and address of each institution, the date of petitioner's admission and discharge, the purpose of the admission, the diagnosis reached and the treatment rendered;

(12) A copy of petitioner's written authorization and consent to the Court and the Administrator to secure copies of all reports and records relating to the services referred to in subparagraphs (10) and (11) above;

(13) During the period of discipline whether the petitioner applied for admission or reinstatement to practice as an attorney in any court and the caption and details of the application or petition;

(14) Whether the petitioner has ever applied for a license or certificate relating to any business or occupation;

(15) During the period of discipline, whether petitioner engaged in the practice of law in any jurisdiction, and all material facts of the practice;

(16) During the period of discipline, whether the petitioner's name appeared together with the designation "lawyer," "attorney-at-law," "counselor at law" or similar description on any door or window, or any building, legal or telephone directory, and all facts relating to the listing, including its location, the place, and duration;

(17) All facts relating to petitioner's compliance with Supreme Court Rules 764, 773 and 780;

(18) All material facts upon which the petitioner relies to establish fitness to resume the practice of law;

(19) The address and telephone number for each location where petitioner maintained an office, business or engaged in the practice of law from the date of the petitioner's admission to the practice of law to the date the petition is filed with the Clerk of the Court.

(20) The names and addresses of all financial institutions at which petitioner had, or was signatory to, accounts, safety deposit boxes, deposits or loans during the period of discipline; the number of each account, box, deposit or loan; the date each account, box, deposit or loan was opened, approved or made; and the date each account, box or loan was closed, discharged or paid;

(21) A copy of petitioner's written consent to the Court and Administrator to secure copies of all statements, records of accounts, cancelled checks and loan records in the financial institutions listed in response to sub-paragraph (20);

(22) Copies of petitioner's federal and state income tax returns for each of the five years immediately preceding the date the petition is filed and for each year, or part of a year, during the period of discipline and, in an appropriate form, petitioner's written consent to the Court and the Administrator to secure copies of the original returns;

(23) Copies of other tax returns, individual, partnership, corporate or fiduciary, which petitioner is entitled to inspect pursuant to the provisions of the Internal Revenue Code and appropriate state laws or regulations and, in an appropriate form, petitioner's written consent to the Court and the Administrator to secure copies of the original returns;

(24) A copy of petitioner's written consent to the Court and the Administrator to examine and secure copies of any records relating to any criminal investigation of petitioner, including but not limited to grand jury minutes, presentence investigations and probation and parole records; and

(25) A copy of current photographs, not smaller than three inches by three inches, of petitioner, front and side views; and

(26) The originals of the items required in paragraphs 12, 21, 24 and 25 shall be provided to the Administrator at the time the petition is served upon the Administrator.

Adopted eff. April 19, 1985. Amended July 9, 1990, eff. July 12, 1990; amended eff. April 15, 2004.

Rules 403 to 410. Reserved

Rule 411. Filing of Petition

(a) **Clerk of the Commission.** The petitioner shall deliver four copies of the petition to the clerk of the Commission and shall deposit $500 with the Commission to be applied against the costs, as defined in Supreme Court Rule 773 and required in Supreme Court Rule 767(c).

(b) **Service upon the Administrator.** The petitioner shall serve two copies of the petition upon the

Administrator no later than the date the petition is filed with the clerk of the Commission.

(c) Clerk of the Court. Within seven days after the copies of the petition have been received by the clerk of the Commission, the petitioner shall file with the clerk of the Court the original petition, accompanied by a receipt verifying payment of the $500 deposit to the Commission pursuant to Supreme Court Rule 767(c), payment of any costs imposed in connection with prior proceedings involving the petitioner pursuant to Supreme Court Rules 773 and/or 767, and reimbursement by petitioner for all Client Protection payments arising from petitioner's conduct pursuant to Supreme Court Rule 780(e).

Adopted eff. April 19, 1985. Amended eff. April 15, 1994; Sept. 30, 2005.

Rule 412. Assignment to Chair

Upon receipt of notification from the Supreme Court that the petition has been filed with the clerk of the Court, the clerk of the Commission shall docket the petition and shall assign the matter to a Chair of the Hearing Board in accordance with procedures and policies established by the Commission.

Adopted eff. April 19, 1985. Amended eff. April 15, 1994; Sept. 30, 2005.

Rule 413. Prehearing Conference

Within sixty days after the petition is filed with the clerk of the Commission, the hearing panel shall conduct a prehearing conference to determine the date by which the Administrator must file any written objections to the petition and the date of the hearing.

Adopted eff. April 19, 1985. Amended eff. April 15, 1994.

Rule 414. Investigation by Administrator; Objections and Participation in Hearing

The Administrator shall conduct an investigation into any matter raised by the petition and may file with the clerk of the Commission written objections to the petition within the time specified by the hearing panel. The Administrator shall have a right to participate in the hearing.

Adopted eff. April 19, 1985. Amended eff. April 15, 1994.

Rule 415. Hearing and Review Procedure

In accordance with Supreme Court Rule 767(h), the hearing and review procedure shall be the same as provided in Supreme Court Rule 753 for disciplinary cases.

Adopted eff. April 15, 1994.

Rules 416 to 500. Reserved

ARTICLE VII. CLIENT PROTECTION PROGRAM

Rule 501. Eligible Claims

The Commission may consider a claim if the claimant complies with procedures established by the Commission and if the following conditions exist:

(a) The claimant experienced a loss of money or property, excluding loss of profit, consequential damages, interest, and costs of recovery; and

(b) The loss arose out of or during the course of a lawyer–client relationship between the lawyer and the claimant related to a matter in this state, or a fiduciary relationship between the lawyer and the claimant that is related to the practice of law in this state; and

(c) The loss was caused by the intentional dishonesty of the lawyer and the claim was not based on negligence; and

(d) There is no reasonably available collateral source for reimbursement to the claimant, such as insurance, surety, bond, or some other fund; and

(e) Reasonable efforts have been made by the claimant to exhaust administrative and civil remedies; and

(f) The lawyer was licensed to practice law in this state at the time of the misconduct or was licensed within three years prior to the misconduct; and

(g) The claim was filed within three years after the date the claimant knew or should have known of the dishonest conduct, or within one year after the date the lawyer was disciplined or died, whichever is later;

(h) The dishonest conduct occurred on or after January 1, 1984;

(i) The lawyer involved has been disciplined by the Supreme Court of Illinois or has died;

(j) The claimant has cooperated fully with disciplinary and law enforcement officials.

Adopted eff. March 28, 1994. Amended eff. March 31, 1997; May 31, 2000.

Rule 502. Excluded Claims

Notwithstanding the provisions of Commission Rule 501, a claim is not eligible for payment to the extent that it involves any one of the following factors:

(a) Losses incurred by spouses, children, parents, grandparents, siblings, partners, associates and employees of the lawyer(s) causing the losses;

(b) Losses covered by any bond, surety agreement, or insurance contract, to the extent covered thereby, including any loss to which any bonding agent, surety or insurer is subrogated, to the extent of that subrogated interest;

(c) Losses incurred by any financial institution which are recoverable under a bond or an insurance or surety contract;

(d) Losses incurred by any business entity controlled by the lawyer or any person or entity described in Commission Rule 502(a), (b), or (c);

(e) Losses incurred by any governmental entity or agency.

Adopted eff. March 28, 1994.

Rule 503. Claims Payments Discretionary

(a) In cases of extreme hardship or special and unusual circumstances, the Commission may, in its discretion, recognize a claim which would otherwise be excluded under these rules.

(b) In cases where it appears that there will be unjust enrichment, or the claimant unreasonably or knowingly contributed to the loss, the Commission may, in its discretion, deny the claim.

Adopted eff. March 28, 1994.

Rule 504. Form of Claim

The Administrator shall investigate a claim if it is submitted on a form approved by the Commission. The Administrator may, as a matter of discretion, investigate claims which are not filed on the claim form approved by the Commission.

Adopted eff. March 28, 1994.

Rule 505. Content of Claim Form

(a) The claim form shall require that the claimant provide the following information:

(1) The name, address and telephone number of the claimant;

(2) The name, address and telephone number of the lawyer or lawyers whose dishonest conduct caused the loss;

(3) A statement of when the claimant hired the lawyer, the date on which the loss occurred, the date upon which any attorney–client relationship with the lawyer ended, and the date upon which the claimant discovered the loss;

(4) A detailed description of what the lawyer did which was dishonest and the amount of the loss caused by the dishonesty, together with a copy of all documentation which supports the claim;

(5) A description of what the claimant has done to recover the loss, including whether the claimant

has sued the lawyer or otherwise made a claim against the lawyer or the lawyer's assets;

(6) A statement of whether the claimant has contacted appropriate criminal authorities regarding prosecution. If so, the statement should include copies of any related materials. If the answer is no, the statement should include an explanation of why such action has not been taken;

(7) A statement of the extent to which the loss has caused the claimant any special hardship;

(8) A statement of the extent to which the claimant has cooperated with disciplinary authorities;

(9) A statement of any relationship between the claimant and the lawyer; and

(10) An agreement to execute any subrogation or like agreements, to the extent that the client protection program makes any payment to the claimant.

(b) The claimant shall sign the claim form.

Adopted eff. March 28, 1994.

Rule 506. Claims Procedure

If the attorney whose conduct is the subject of the claim has already been disciplined by the Supreme Court of Illinois, or has died, the Administrator shall commence an investigation of the claim. The investigation shall be concluded as soon as is practicable. If the attorney has not been disciplined and has not died, the Administrator shall hold the claim in abeyance, pending conclusion of the disciplinary proceedings. During the abeyance, the Administrator may gather facts underlying the claim. As part of the investigation, the Administrator shall send a copy of the claim to the lawyer whose conduct is alleged to have caused the loss at his or her last registered or known address and shall request from the attorney a full statement of the facts related to the claim. The attorney has a duty to respond to the request and to cooperate with any further requests. The Administrator shall conduct a complete investigation and shall prepare and submit to the Commission a report addressing the factors identified in Commission Rules 501, 502 and 503.

Adopted eff. March 28, 1994. Amended eff. Dec. 1, 1994.

Rule 507. Determination

(a) Payment of a claim shall be made only on affirmative vote of four members of the Commission. The decision to pay a claim shall be reflected in an order of the Commission.

(b) In determining the amount of any payment, the Commission may consider:

(1) Monies available and likely to become available for payment of claims;

(2) The size and number of claims presented and likely to be presented in the future;

(3) The amount of a claimant's loss compared with losses sustained by others;

(4) The comparative hardship suffered by a claimant because of a loss;

(5) The total amount of losses caused by the dishonest conduct of any one lawyer;

(6) The culpability or negligence of the claimant contributing to the loss;

(7) The extent to which there is a collateral source for reimbursement to the claimant;

(8) The effort made by the claimant to exhaust administrative and civil remedies;

(9) Other factors as appear to be just and proper.

(c) The Commission order shall be filed with the Clerk.

Adopted eff. March 28, 1994. Amended eff. Dec. 1, 1994.

Rule 508. Request for Reconsideration: Assignment to Panel

The Clerk shall provide a copy of the Commission's order to the claimant and the lawyer who is the subject of the claim. Within 21 days of the mailing of the order, the claimant or the lawyer may request reconsideration of the order by sending such a written request to the Clerk. The request shall state the basis of the request for reconsideration and whether a hearing is requested. If no request is received within the stated time, the order shall become final. If a request is received, the Clerk shall forward the request to the Commission. The Commission may assign the request to a panel designated by the Commission to review the request. The panel shall be composed of two lawyers and one non-lawyer, and may be a panel of the Inquiry or Hearing Panel.

Adopted eff. March 28, 1994. Amended eff. Dec. 1, 1994.

Rule 509. Review by Panel

At the Commission's request, the panel shall review the report submitted by the Administrator and the request for reconsideration. The Administrator shall assist the panel. The panel may consider any and all information obtained by the Administrator during the investigation and may request the Administrator to conduct additional investigation. The panel may convene a hearing at which both the claimant and the lawyer may appear. Hearings shall be informal. The Chair of the panel shall preside at the hearing. The panel shall prepare a report and recommendation to the Commission. The report of the panel shall address those factors identified in Commission Rules 501, 502 and 503.

Adopted eff. March 28, 1994. Amended eff. Dec. 1, 1994.

Rule 510. Payment of Claims

The Administrator shall pay claims out of the Client Protection Trust Fund in accordance with an order of the Commission. The maximum payment to any one claimant arising from a claim shall be $100.00. The Commission shall require as a condition of payment that the claimant execute such instruments, take such action or enter into such agreements as the Commission requires, including assignments, subrogation agreements, and trust agreements. Aggregate payments arising from the conduct of any one attorney shall not exceed $1,000,000.

Adopted eff. March 28, 1994. Amended eff. Oct. 15, 1998; eff. April 1, 2003; Dec. 8, 2006, eff. Jan. 31, 2007; eff. March 31, 2009; Feb. 24, 2014, eff. March 20, 2014.

Rule 511. Restitution and Subrogation

(a) The Commission may bring such action as it deems advisable to enforce restitution obligations against the lawyer whose conduct gave rise to the payment of a claim.

(b) As a condition of reimbursement, a claimant shall be required to provide the Commission with a transfer of the claimant's rights, to the extent of a claim payment, against the lawyer, the lawyer's legal representative, estate or assigns or any third party or entity who may be liable for the claimant's loss.

(c) Upon commencement of an action by the Commission as subrogee or assignee of a claim, the Administrator shall advise the claimant, who may then join in such action to recover the claimant's unreimbursed losses.

(d) In the event that the claimant commences an action to recover unreimbursed losses against the lawyer or another entity who may be liable for the claimant's loss, the claimant shall be required to notify the Commission of such action.

(e) The claimant shall be required to agree to cooperate in all efforts that the Commission undertakes to achieve restitution for the Disciplinary Fund.

Adopted eff. March 28, 1994.

Rule 512. Compensation For Representing Claimants

No lawyer shall accept any payment for representing a claimant in a claim before the Client Protection Fund.

Adopted eff. March 28, 1994.

ARTICLE VIII. ETHICS INQUIRY PROGRAM

Rule 601. Establishment of Program

There is established under the auspices of the Commission an Ethics Inquiry Program. The Administrator shall employ Ethics Inquiry Counsel, who shall respond to ethics inquiries.

Adopted eff. March 31, 1995.

Rule 602. Purpose of Program

The purpose of the program is to provide information to attorneys and other members of the public so that the inquirer may identify and determine the Rules of Conduct which apply to an attorney's actions. The goal of the program is to assist attorneys in conducting themselves within the bounds of the Illinois Rules of Professional Conduct, thereby enhancing the quality of the representation provided by Illinois attorneys.

Adopted eff. March 31, 1995.

Rule 603. The Ethics Inquiry

Any Illinois attorney or other member of the public may make an ethics inquiry by telephone to the Commission's designated ethics inquiry telephone line. The inquiry may request assistance in identifying an applicable rule of conduct. If the inquiry presents a set of facts, those facts shall be presented in hypothetical format.

Adopted eff. March 31, 1995.

Rule 604. Response of Ethics Inquiry Program

Ethics Inquiry Counsel shall provide general information and research assistance regarding ethics issues under Illinois law. Ethics Inquiry Counsel shall not provide legal advice or advisory opinions. Before rendering assistance to an inquirer, the Ethics Inquiry Counsel shall advise each inquirer that only legal research assistance is being furnished, that no legal opinion is being rendered, and that the inquirer is responsible for making his or her own final judgment on the ethical issue presented.

Adopted eff. March 31, 1995.

Rule 605. Inadmissibility of Inquiry Communications

Neither the fact that an inquiry has been made nor its content nor the response thereto shall be admissible in any attorney discipline proceeding.

Adopted eff. March 31, 1995.

Rule 606. Records; Disclosure

Ethics Inquiry Counsel shall not make or maintain any record of the identity of an inquirer or the substance of a specific inquiry or response. Ethics Inquiry Counsel shall keep records of the number of inquiries and the nature and type of inquiries and responses. Such records shall be used solely to aid the Commission in developing the Ethics Inquiry Program and developing additional educational programs. Such records shall be privileged from disclosure in any attorney disciplinary proceeding.

Adopted eff. March 31, 1995.

THE BOARD OF ADMISSIONS TO THE BAR AND THE COMMITTEES ON CHARACTER AND FITNESS FOR THE STATE OF ILLINOIS RULES OF PROCEDURE

Including Amendments Received Through April 1, 2016

RULE 1. CHARACTER AND FITNESS COMMITTEES

Rule 1.1. Appointment and Term

The appointment and terms of the members of the Committees on Character and Fitness for the five Judicial Districts shall be as provided by Supreme Court Rule 708 (a). Any member whose term has expired and who has an uncompleted assignment as a member of an Inquiry Panel or a Hearing Panel may, at the discretion of the Committee Chair, continue to serve until conclusion of the assignment.

October 2, 2006, eff. July 1, 2007.

Rule 1.2.   Mandatory Annual Meeting

In January or February of each year, the members of each Committee shall meet in person to consider and review all pending matters and the objectives and work of the Committee for the ensuing year. The meeting shall be scheduled in advance by the Chair of the Committee with assistance from the Board's staff in Springfield.

October 2, 2006, eff. July 1, 2007.

Rule 1.3.   Expenses of the Committees

Subject to the prior approval of the Board, all reasonable costs and expenses of the Committees shall be reimbursed by the Board.

October 2, 2006, eff. July 1, 2007.

RULE 2.   DIRECTOR OF ADMINISTRATION

Rule 2.1.   Director of Administration

The Illinois Board of Admissions to the Bar (Board) shall appoint a Director of Administration (Director), who, subject to the supervision of the Board, shall oversee the administration of all aspects of bar admissions, including the character and fitness process. The Director shall receive such compensation as the Board authorizes.

October 2, 2006, eff. July 1, 2007.

Rule 2.2.   Duties of Director

Subject to the direction of the Board, the Director shall:

(1) conduct examinations on academic qualification and professional responsibility in accordance with Supreme Court Rule 704; (2) receive, process, investigate, and review all materials, documentation, and information submitted by and concerning all law student registrants (registrants), and all applicants for admission, including limited admission, to the bar (applicants), pursuant to Supreme Court Rules 704, 705, 712, 713, 715, 716, and 717; (3) maintain the records of the Character and Fitness Committees and assist each Committee in its investigation and evaluation of registrants and applicants; (4) employ, at such compensation as may be authorized by the Board, such administrative, clerical, investigative, and legal personnel as may be necessary for the efficient conduct of the office; (5) discharge any such personnel whose performance is unsatisfactory; and (6) maintain such records, make such reports, and perform such other duties as may be required by the Board.

October 2, 2006, eff. July 1, 2007.

RULE 3.   CHARACTER AND FITNESS REGISTRATION

Rule 3.1.   Character and Fitness Registration by Law Students Prior to and Apart from a Bar Examination

Rule 3.1a.   Timely Registration by First Year Law Students

Every student attending law school who intends to take the Illinois bar examination shall file with the Board at its office in Springfield a character and fitness registration application in the form prescribed by the Board and thereby become a "law student registrant" or "registrant." Such application may be timely filed no later than the first day of March following the law student's commencement of law school; provided, however, that a student who commences law school after the first day of January and before the first day of March in any calendar year may timely file such application no later than the first day of July following the student's commencement of law school. A character and fitness registration application timely filed by a law student shall be accompanied by the nominal timely filing fee provided by Supreme Court Rule 706(a).

Rule 3.1b.   Late Registration by First and Second Year Law Students

A character and fitness registration application may also be filed after the applicable filing deadline, upon payment of the late filing fee provided by Supreme Court Rule 706(a), by any first or second year law student seeking to initiate the character and fitness process prior to and separate from his or her registration for an Illinois bar examination.

Rule 3.1c.   Restricted Late Registration by Third Year Law Students

Third year law Students and others likely eligible to register for one of the next two succeeding bar examinations may not file a character and fitness registration application apart from an application to take a bar examination application without the prior written authorization of the Board on the basis of recently occurring or recently discovered matters of significant character and fitness concern. Any such authorized late registration application shall be accompanied by the late filing fee provided by Supreme Court Rule 706(a).

Rule 3.1d.   Separate Bar Examination Application is Required

A law student registrant's character and fitness application is not an application to take the Illinois bar examination or for admission to the Illinois bar unless and until the registrant files a separate application to take the bar examination in the form prescribed by the Board. Any such application to take the bar examination shall be accompanied by the filing fee provided by Supreme Court Rule 706(b).

October 2, 2006, eff. July 1, 2007.

Rule 3.2. Character and Fitness Registration by Other Applicants

At the time of making application to take the bar examination, application for admission on motion, application for limited admission under Rule 717, or application on any other basis permitted by these Rules, any applicant who has not previously filed a character and fitness registration application shall file with the Board at its office in Springfield a character and fitness registration application in the form prescribed by the Board together with such additional proofs and documentation as the Board may require; any such application shall be accompanied by the appropriate filing fee(s) provided by Supreme Court Rule 706.

October 2, 2006, eff. July 1, 2007.

Rule 3.3. Attorneys' Questionnaire

Every applicant for admission on examination, admission on motion, or limited admission under Rule 717, who has been admitted to the bar of another jurisdiction shall file, in addition to all other proofs required, an Attorneys' Questionnaire in the form prescribed by the Board, together with documentary evidence as to the standing of the applicant in each jurisdiction in which the applicant has been admitted to practice.

October 2, 2006, eff. July 1, 2007.

Rule 3.4. Continuing Obligation to Report

Every law student registrant and applicant for admission on examination, admission on motion, limited admission under Rule 717, or application on any other basis permitted by these Rules has a continuing obligation to report promptly to the Board any change or addition to the information provided in his or her character and fitness questionnaire including without limitation changes in address, email address, phone number(s), and employment, as well as criminal charges, disciplinary proceedings, traffic violations, parking violations not paid on receipt, and any other occurrence or event that could bear upon character and fitness or the ability of the Board to communicate with the registrant, the applicant, or any person or entity named in his or her application.

October 2, 2006, eff. July 1, 2007.

Rule 3.5. Additional Questionnaire

Every law student registrant and applicant for admission on examination, admission on motion, limited admission under Rule 717, or application on any other basis permitted by these Rules shall file an Additional Questionnaire in the form prescribed by the Board as a supplement to the character and fitness questionnaire most recently filed upon the request of the Board or the Committee as well as under the following circumstances:

a. When 9 or more months have elapsed between the date a registrant or applicant was recommended for certification by the Committee and the date the registrant or applicant is otherwise eligible for admission to the bar;

b. when 9 or more months have elapsed between the date a registrant or applicant filed his or her most recent character and fitness questionnaire and the date the registrant or applicant submits a written request for reactivation of his or her application pursuant to Rule 10.2;

c. when a registrant or applicant requests a hearing pursuant to Rule 9.2g;

d. when a registrant or applicant is notified that his or her petition for new hearing has been granted pursuant to Rule 13; and

e. when an applicant who previously registered for an Illinois bar examination makes application for a subsequent bar examination;

provided, however, that if 3 or more years have elapsed since the registrant or applicant last filed a long form Character and Fitness Questionnaire, such registrant or applicant shall file a current long form Character and Fitness Questionnaire rather than an Additional Questionnaire.

October 2, 2006, eff. July 1, 2007.

RULE 4. APPLICATION TO TAKE THE BAR EXAMINATION

Rule 4. Application to Take the Bar Examination

Every applicant for the Illinois bar examination shall file with the Board at its office in Springfield an application to take the bar examination in the form prescribed by the Board. Applications shall be filed, and fees paid as provided in Supreme Court Rule 706.

October 2, 2006, eff. July 1, 2007.

RULE 5. PROCESSING OF CHARACTER AND FITNESS REGISTRATION APPLICATIONS

Rule 5. Processing of Character and Fitness Registration Applications

With regard to each character and fitness registration application, Additional Questionnaire, and Attorneys' Questionnaire received, the Director shall cause a character investigation and report to be prepared by the transmittal of requests for pertinent information to appropriate persons and entities, including but not limited to employers, former employers, colleges and universities, law schools, other bar admitting authorities, courts, law enforcement agencies, creditors, credit reporting agencies, former spouses and character references.

October 2, 2006, eff. July 1, 2007.

RULE 6. CHARACTER AND FITNESS REQUIREMENTS

Rule 6.1. Committee Determination of Requisite Character and Fitness

The Committee shall determine whether to recommend to the Board that a law student registrant or applicant presently possesses the requisite character and fitness for admission to the practice of law. If the Committee deems it necessary or appropriate under the circumstances, it shall conduct further investigation of the registrant or applicant before ascertaining his or her character and fitness. The registrant or applicant has the burden to prove by clear and convincing evidence that he or she has the requisite character and fitness for admission to the practice of law.

October 2, 2006, eff. July 1, 2007.

Rule 6.2. Recommendation for Certification

A registrant or applicant may be recommended for certification to the Board if the Committee determines that his or her record of conduct demonstrates that he or she meets the essential eligibility requirements for the practice of law and justifies the trust of clients, adversaries, courts and others with respect to the professional duties owed to them. A record manifesting a failure to meet the essential eligibility requirements, including a deficiency in the honesty, trustworthiness, diligence, or reliability of a law student registrant or applicant may constitute a basis for denial of admission.

October 2, 2006, eff. July 1, 2007.

Rule 6.3. Eligibility Requirements

The essential eligibility requirements for the practice of law include the following: (1) the ability to learn, to recall what has been learned, to reason, and to analyze; (2) the ability to communicate clearly and logically with clients, attorneys, courts, and others; (3) the ability to exercise good judgment in conducting one's professional business; (4) the ability to conduct oneself with a high degree of honesty, integrity, and trustworthiness in all professional relationships and with respect to all legal obligations; (5) the ability to conduct oneself with respect for and in accordance with the law and the Illinois Rules of Professional Conduct; (6) the ability to avoid acts that exhibit disregard for the health, safety, and welfare of others; (7) the ability to conduct oneself diligently and reliably in fulfilling all obligations to clients, attorneys, courts, creditors, and others; (8) the ability to use honesty and good judgment in financial dealings on behalf of oneself, clients, and others; (9) the ability to comply with deadlines and time constraints; and (10) the ability to conduct oneself properly and in a manner that engenders respect for the law and the profession.

October 2, 2006, eff. July 1, 2007.

Rule 6.4. Cause for Further Detailed Inquiry

The revelation or discovery of any of the following should be treated as cause for further detailed inquiry before the Committee decides whether the law student registrant or applicant possesses the requisite character and fitness to practice law: (a) unlawful conduct; (b) academic misconduct; (c) making false statements, including omissions; (d) misconduct in employment; (e) acts involving dishonesty, fraud, deceit or misrepresentation; (f) abuse of legal process; (g) neglect of financial responsibilities; (h) neglect of professional obligations; (i) violation of an order of a court; (j) evidence of conduct indicating instability or impaired judgment; (k) denial of admission to the bar in another jurisdiction on character and fitness grounds; (l) disciplinary action by a lawyer disciplinary agency or other professional disciplinary agency of any jurisdiction; (m) acts constituting the unauthorized practice of law; (n) failure to comply with the continuing duty of full disclosure to the Board and the Committee subsequent to the date of registration or application.

October 2, 2006, eff. July 1, 2007.

Rule 6.5. Prior Misconduct, Factors Considered

In determining whether to recommend to the Board that the present character and fitness of a registrant or applicant qualifies him or her for admission to the practice of law, the Committee shall consider the following factors in assigning weight and significance to prior misconduct (a) age at the time of the conduct; (b) recency of the conduct; (c) reliability of the information concerning the conduct; (d) seriousness of the conduct; (e) factors underlying the conduct; (f) cumulative effect of the conduct; (g) ability and willingness to accept responsibility for the conduct; (h) candor in the admissions process; (i) materiality of any omissions or misrepresentations; (j) evidence of rehabilitation; and (k) positive social contribution since the conduct.

October 2, 2006, eff. July 1, 2007.

Rule 6.6. Certification; Additional Information or Recommendation

Provided that all other conditions for admission have been met, upon receipt from the Committee of a recommendation for certification pursuant to these Rules, the Board shall transmit such certification to the Supreme Court together with any additional information or recommendation the Board may deem appropriate. A copy of the Board's recommendation, if any, shall be mailed to the applicant, his or her counsel, if any, and to the Committee Chair.

October 2, 2006, eff. July 1, 2007.

RULE 7. CONDITIONAL ADMISSION

Rule 7.1. Conditional Admission

In its sole discretion, the Committee on Character and Fitness may recommend to the Board that an applicant be admitted to the bar on a conditional basis in accordance with these Rules. The terms and conditions of a recommendation for conditional admission shall be set forth in a written Consent Agreement signed by the Committee, the applicant, and the Director. An applicant may be considered or recommended for conditional admission at the discretion of the Committee.

October 2, 2006, eff. July 1, 2007.

Rule 7.2. Limited Purpose of Conditional Admission

As provided by Rule 7.3, conditional admission may be employed to permit an applicant who currently satisfies character and fitness requirements to practice law while his or her continued participation in an ongoing course of treatment or remediation for previous misconduct or unfitness is monitored to protect the public. Conditional admission is neither to be used as a method of achieving fitness nor as a method of monitoring the behavior of all applicants who have rehabilitated themselves from misconduct or unfitness. Conditional admission may be employed only when an applicant has been engaged in a sustained and effective course of treatment or remediation for a period of time sufficient to demonstrate his or her commitment and progress but not yet sufficient to render unlikely a recurrence of the misconduct or unfitness.

October 2, 2006, eff. July 1, 2007.

Rule 7.3. Limited Circumstances under which conditional admission may be considered

The Committee on Character and Fitness may recommend that an applicant be admitted to the bar conditioned on the applicant's compliance with relevant conditions prescribed by the Committee if the applicant currently satisfies all requirements for admission to the bar and possesses the requisite good moral character and fitness for admission, except that he or she is engaged in a sustained and effective course of treatment for or remediation of

    a. substance abuse or dependence;

    b. a diagnosed mental or physical impairment that, should it reoccur, would likely impair the applicant's ability to practice law or pose a threat to the public; or

    c. neglect of financial affairs,

that previously rendered him or her unfit for admission to the bar, and the applicant has been engaged in such course of treatment or remediation for no fewer than 6 continuous months, if the subject of treatment is substance abuse or dependence or mental or physical impairment, and no fewer than 3 continuous months if the subject of remediation is neglect of financial affairs. Absent recent lapses, recent failures, or evidence that a lapse or failure is presently likely to occur, an applicant who has engaged in such sustained and effective course of treatment or remediation for at least 24 continuous months may not be conditionally admitted.

October 2, 2006, eff. July 1, 2007.

Rule 7.4. Recommendation of Inquiry Panel or Hearing Panel

Rule 7.4a. A recommendation that an applicant be admitted to the bar on a conditional basis can be made only after the applicant has personally met with all members of a 3 person Inquiry Panel appointed in accordance with these Rules. A majority of the Inquiry Panel shall constitute a quorum, and the concurrence of a majority shall be necessary to a recommendation.

Rule 7.4b. A recommendation for conditional admission may also be made by the members of a Hearing Panel; provided, however, that the applicant did not decline to consider or consent to conditional admission at the Inquiry Panel level. A majority of the Hearing Panel shall constitute a quorum, and the concurrence of a majority shall be necessary to a recommendation.

October 2, 2006, eff. July 1, 2007.

Rule 7.5. Report of Recommendation of Inquiry Panel to Full Committee

In the event that a majority of the members of an Inquiry Panel votes to recommend the conditional admission of an applicant, the Inquiry panel shall report to the full Committee the vote, the matters of concern, the nature, substance, and duration of the course of treatment or remediation in which the applicant is engaged, complete and detailed information regarding the applicant's progress in connection therewith including any lapses or failures, the panel's general recommendation regarding the terms and conditions of admission, any additional facts relevant to the recommendation, and confirmation of the applicant's consent to admission on a conditional basis. The full Committee shall then determine whether the recommendation of the Inquiry Panel should be affirmed or denied.

October 2, 2006, eff. July 1, 2007.

Rule 7.6. Review of Recommendation of Inquiry Panel by Full Committee and Preparation of Written Report

Rule 7.6a. If the report to the full Committee is made and discussed at a meeting of the full Committee, members of the Inquiry Panel may participate in the discussion of the matter, but shall not be entitled to vote. Five members of the Committee who were not members of the Inquiry Panel shall constitute a quorum, and the concurrence of a majority of the members who are present and entitled to vote shall be necessary to a decision. If the recommendation of the Inquiry Panel is affirmed, within 21 days after such affirmation the Chair of the Inquiry Panel shall prepare and submit to the Director a written report containing all of the information required by Rule 7.5.

Rule 7.6b. If the report to the full Committee is not made and discussed at a meeting of the full Committee, within 21 days after the vote of the Inquiry Panel, the Chair of the Inquiry Panel shall prepare and submit to the Director a written report containing all of the information required by Rule 7.5. The Director shall then forward the report to all remaining members of the Committee, along with a request for the vote of each member as to whether the recommendation of the panel should be affirmed or denied. The concurrence of a majority of the remaining members of the Committee shall be necessary to a decision.

Rule 7.6c. If the recommendation of the Inquiry Panel is denied by the full Committee, within 21 days of such denial, the Chair or Vice Chair of the full Committee shall prepare and submit to the Director a brief written report containing the reason for the denial. The application shall thereafter be further considered in accordance with Rules 9.2f *et seq.*

October 2, 2006, eff. July 1, 2007.

Rule 7.7. Preparation and Execution of Consent Agreement

Upon receipt of the written report and recommendation of an Inquiry Panel for conditional admission and its affirmation by the full Committee as hereinabove provided, or upon receipt of the written report and recommendation for conditional admission of a Hearing Panel, the Director shall prepare and submit to the Chair of the panel that recommended conditional admission the Consent Agreement setting forth the terms and conditions of admission. The original Consent Agreement shall be signed by the Chair of the Inquiry Panel or Hearing Panel that recommended conditional admission, the applicant, and the Director.

October 2, 2006, eff. July 1, 2007.

Rule 7.8. Authorized Conditions of Admission

An applicant's admission may be conditioned on the applicant's submitting to specified alcohol, drug, or mental health treatment; medical, psychological, or psychiatric care; participation in group therapy or support; debt management counseling; random chemical screening; and supervision, monitoring, mentoring, or other conditions deemed appropriate by the Committee on Character and Fitness. The conditions shall be tailored to deter and detect conduct or conditions that pose a risk to clients or the public, to ensure continued abstinence, payment, treatment, counseling, and other support and shall, when appropriate, take into consideration the recommendations of qualified professionals regarding treatment and remediation.

October 2, 2006, eff. July 1, 2007.

Rule 7.9. Length of Conditional Period

The period of conditional admission shall not exceed 24 months, unless the Court orders otherwise. The filing of a petition to extend the period or a petition to revoke admission shall extend the period of conditional admission until the Court enters a final order on the petition.

October 2, 2006, eff. July 1, 2007.

Rule 7.10. Submission of Recommendation, Report, and Consent Agreement to Supreme Court

The Director shall submit to the Court copies of the recommendation and report of the Committee, the executed Consent Agreement, the Board's certification that the applicant is otherwise qualified for admission to the bar, relevant information from the applicant's character and fitness file, and any additional information or recommendation the Board deems appropriate. A copy of the executed Consent Agreement and the Board's recommendation, if any, shall be mailed to the applicant.

October 2, 2006, eff. July 1, 2007.

Rule 7.11. Supreme Court Review of Recommendation, Report and Consent Agreement

Rule 7.11a. If the Court determines that the applicant qualifies for admission on the terms and conditions set forth in the Consent Agreement, the Court shall enter an Order requiring the applicant to comply with such terms and conditions for the period specified immediately following the date of his or her admission to the bar. In this event, copies of the Court Order, the signed Consent Agreement, and the recommendation and report of the Committee shall be mailed to the Attorney Registration and Disciplinary Commission (ARDC).

Rule 7.11b. If the Court denies the recommendation for conditional admission, 6 months after the date of the denial the applicant may file with the Board a supplement to his or her previous character and fitness questionnaire in the form prescribed by the Board along with his or her personal affidavit describing the extent, if any, to which s/he has in the interim engaged in a course of treatment for, or remediation of, the misconduct or unfitness that was the basis of the recommendation. Following Investigation and report of the supplemental materials, the application shall be considered further in accordance with these Rules by the Inquiry Panel or Hearing Panel that previously recommended conditional admission.

October 2, 2006, eff. July 1, 2007.

Rule 7.12. Monitoring Compliance with Consent Agreement Following Conditional Admission

If the applicant is conditionally admitted to the bar, the Administrator of ARDC shall monitor his or her compliance with the terms and conditions of the Consent Agreement throughout the period of conditional admission. The Administrator may take such action as is necessary to monitor compliance with the terms of the Consent Agreement, including without limitation referral for monitoring by a lawyer assistance program or other monitoring authority, requiring the conditionally admitted lawyer to make periodic appearances before a monitoring agent or entity, requiring the lawyer to submit physical or written evidence or other verification of compliance with the Consent Agreement, and requiring the lawyer to submit to an assessment by a medical professional.

October 2, 2006, eff. July 1, 2007.

Rule 7.13. Reporting Changed Circumstances or Noncompliance with Consent Agreement

Rule 7.13a. When the Administrator or the conditionally admitted lawyer identifies a change in circumstances that impacts the efficacy of the terms and conditions of the Consent Agreement, the Administrator or the conditionally admitted lawyer may report the change to the Court and petition the Court to modify the terms or conditions affected by the changed circumstances.

Rule 7.13b. When a conditionally admitted lawyer fails to comply with the Consent Agreement, the Administrator shall, where warranted, file with the Court a report of the noncompliance and a petition for revocation, modification, or extension of conditional admission. The petition shall be served upon the lawyer, who shall file a response within 21 days following service of the petition. If the Court determines there is a material dispute of fact, the Court shall refer the case to a panel of the ARDC Hearing Board, which shall set the matter for hearing on a date within 90 days of the Order referring the case to the panel. The Administrator must prove the violation(s) of the Consent Agreement by a preponderance of the evidence. The Hearing Board panel shall resolve all disputes of fact and file its findings with the Court within 45 days of the date the hearing concludes. Upon consideration of the pleadings and, where applicable, the findings of the Hearing Board panel, the Court shall determine whether to continue or revoke the lawyer's conditional admission license and, if not revoked, whether to modify conditions or extend the period of conditional admission.

October 2, 2006, eff. July 1, 2007.

Rule 7.14. Reapplication Following Revocation of Conditional Admission License

An applicant whose conditional admission license has been revoked may reapply for admission to the bar, but not within 2 years of the order revoking the conditional admission license, unless the Court orders otherwise. The applicant shall file a character and fitness registration application in the form prescribed by the Board together with such additional proofs and documentation as the Board may require and his or her personal affidavit describing the extent, if any, to which he or she has in the interim engaged in a course of treatment for, or remediation of, the misconduct or unfitness that was the basis of revocation of the conditional admission license. Following preparation of a character and fitness investigation and report in accordance with these Rules, the reapplication and materials shall be assigned for character and fitness review directly to an Inquiry Panel, if the original recommendation for conditional admission was made at the Inquiry Panel level, or to a Hearing Panel, if the original recommendation for conditional admission was made by a Hearing Panel. To the extent possible, the original Inquiry Panel or Hearing Panel shall be reconstituted; any unavailable member of the original panel shall be replaced by another member of the Committee.

October 2, 2006, eff. July 1, 2007.

Rule 7.15. Costs of Conditional Admission

The applicant shall promptly pay directly or reimburse the Board for costs incurred for evaluation and testing in connection with Committee consideration of substance abuse or dependency, diagnosed mental impairment, or diagnosed medical disorder prior to the submission of a recommendation for conditional admission to the Court. The Board may agree to postpone reimbursement for such costs on the basis of compelling evidence of inability to pay; provided, however, in that event the repayment of such costs shall be incorporated into the Consent Agreement as a condition of compliance. Costs incurred after the applicant is conditionally admitted to the bar shall be defined and paid in accordance with Supreme Court Rule 773.

October 2, 2006, eff. July 1, 2007.

Rule 7.16. Confidentiality

All information related to the conditional admission of an applicant including without limitation the fact of conditional admission and the existence and terms of the written Consent Agreement shall be confidential. An Order of the Court revoking a conditional admission license, however, shall be a matter of public record.

October 2, 2006, eff. July 1, 2007.

RULE 8. INITIAL REVIEW OF CHARACTER AND FITNESS REGISTRATION APPLICATIONS

Rule 8.1. [Interim Approval]

If the character and fitness application, investigation, and report of a law student registrant or an applicant for admission or limited admission to the bar raise no character and fitness concerns, as determined by the Director after review of said application and materials, the Director may recommend to the Board the interim approval of the law student registrant or the certification of the applicant; in this event, upon the request of any Character and Fitness Committee, the Director shall provide monthly notice to the Committee of all such recommendations.

October 2, 2006, eff. July 1, 2007.

Rule 8.2. [Evaluation of Application that Raises Character and Fitness Concerns]

If the character and fitness application, investigation, and report of a law student registrant or an applicant for admission or limited admission to the bar raise character and fitness concerns, the Director shall forward the application and materials for evaluation in accordance with Supreme Court Rules 708 and 709 to a member of the Committee in the District in which the registrant or applicant receives mail or as otherwise determined by the Board; *provided, however,* that a character and fitness registration application falling within the purview of Supreme Court Rule 704(b) or otherwise containing matters of significant character and fitness concern shall instead be assigned directly to an Inquiry Panel, the members and Chair of which may be appointed by the Committee Chair of that District or by the Director, for evaluation and review as provided in Rule 9.2a *et seq.* Character and fitness registration applications that have been assigned to a member of the Character and Fitness Committee or to an Inquiry Panel in one District shall not be reassigned to another District.

October 2, 2006, eff. July 1, 2007.

RULE 9. CONSIDERATION OF CHARACTER AND FITNESS REGISTRATION APPLICATIONS

Rule 9.1. Consideration of Application by Committee Member

Each character and fitness registration application assigned to a Committee member shall be reviewed by the member, and the law student registrant or applicant shall be required to appear in person before the member to discuss the application and the materials submitted and gathered in connection therewith. The registrant or applicant shall provide to the member any further information or documentation requested and shall cooperate with any further investigation undertaken by the member.

Rule 9.1a. Recommendation for Interim Certification of a Law Student Registrant

The Director, as provided in Rule 8.1, or the Committee member who has received assignment of an application and completed a review thereof, as hereinabove provided, may recommend to the Board the interim certification of the law student registrant, in which case the registrant shall be so notified in writing. Any such interim approval shall be tentative and subject to withdrawal on the basis of new information disclosing facts existing or conduct engaged in by the registrant prior to the registrants's admission to the

bar including the cumulative effect of such new information or conduct.

Rule 9.1b. Recommendation for Certification of Other Applicants

The Director, as provided in preceding Rule 8.1, or the member of the committee who has reviewed the application of an applicant for admission on examination, for admission on motion, for limited admission under Rule 717, or for admission on any other basis permitted by these Rules may recommend to the Board the certification of the applicant. The applicant may thereafter be recommended by the Board for admission to the bar if all other requirements for admission have been met.

October 2, 2006, eff. July 1, 2007.

Rule 9.2. Appointment of Inquiry Panel

If a member is not prepared to recommend the interim certification of a law student registrant or the certification of an applicant, then the Chair of the Committee shall assign the application to an Inquiry Panel for further review and examination. The Inquiry Panel shall consist of the member to whom the matter was originally assigned, as panel Chair, and two additional members of the Committee appointed by the Committee Chair. A majority of the Inquiry Panel shall constitute a quorum, and the concurrence of a majority shall be necessary to a decision.

Rule 9.2a. Inquiry Panel Review

Each member of the Inquiry Panel shall review the application and the registrant or applicant shall be required to appear in person before all members of the panel to discuss the application and the materials submitted and gathered in connection therewith. The registrant or applicant shall provide to the panel any further information or documentation requested and shall cooperate with any further investigation undertaken by the panel.

Rule 9.2b. Declination to Certify

In the event that a majority of the members of an Inquiry Panel votes to withhold the certification of a registrant or an applicant, within 21 days after such vote the Chair of the Inquiry Panel shall prepare and submit to the Director a written report advising the Inquiry Panel vote, the matters of concern, and the basis for the declination to certify.

Rule 9.2c. Report of Inquiry Panel Recommendation for Certification to Full Committee

In the event that a majority of the members of an Inquiry Panel votes to recommend the interim certification of a registrant or the certification of an applicant to the Board, the panel shall report the vote, the matters of concern, and the basis for the recommendation for certification to the full Committee. The full Committee shall then determine whether the recommendation of the Inquiry Panel should be affirmed or denied.

Rule 9.2d. Review of Recommendation of Inquiry Panel by Full Committee and Preparation of Written Report

Rule 9.2d.i. If the report to the full Committee is made and discussed at a meeting of the full Committee, members of the Inquiry Panel may participate in the discussion of the matter, but shall not be entitled to vote. Five members of the Committee who were not members of the Inquiry Panel shall constitute a quorum, and the concurrence of a majority of the members who are present and entitled to vote shall be necessary to a decision. If the recommendation of the Inquiry Panel is affirmed, within 21 days after such affirmation the Chair of the Inquiry Panel shall prepare and submit to the Director a written report advising the matters of concern, the basis for the recommendation for certification, and the full Committee's affirmation of the recommendation of the panel.

Rule 9.2d.ii. If the report to the full Committee is not made and discussed at a meeting of the full Committee, within 21 days after the vote of the Inquiry Panel, the Chair of the Inquiry Panel shall prepare and submit to the Director a written report advising the Inquiry Panel vote, the matters of concern, and the basis for the recommendation for certification. The Director shall then forward the written report to all remaining members of the Committee, along with a request for the vote of each member as to whether the recommendation of the Panel should be affirmed or denied. The concurrence of a majority of the remaining members of the Committee shall be necessary to a decision.

Rule 9.2d.iii. If the recommendation of the Inquiry Panel is denied by the full Committee, within 21 days after such denial, the Chair of the full Committee shall prepare and submit to the Director a written report advising the matters of concern and the basis for the declination to certify.

Rule 9.2.e Upon receipt by the Director of the written report and recommendation of an Inquiry Panel for the interim certification of a registrant and its affirmation by the full Committee as hereinabove provided, the registrant shall be accorded interim approval and so advised in writing. Upon receipt by the Director of such report and recommendation and such affirmation for the certification of an applicant, the applicant may thereafter be recommended by the Board for admission to the bar if all other admission requirements have been met.

Rule 9.2f. Upon receipt by the Director of a written report advising an Inquiry Panel's vote to withhold certification or a written report advising a vote of the full Committee to deny an Inquiry Panel's recommendation for certification, the registrant or applicant shall thereafter be notified in writing of the Committee's declination to certify and provided with a copy of the report of the Inquiry Panel or of the Committee. The notice shall also advise the right of the registrant or applicant to submit a written request for hearing within 21 days of the date of the mailing of the notice and include instructions for doing so. If the registrant or applicant fails properly to request a hearing within 21 days of the date of the mailing of the notice, his or her application shall be placed on inactive status and made subject to the requirements of Rule 10.2.

Rule 9.2g. In the event the registrant or applicant properly requests a hearing, he or she shall also promptly complete and file an Additional Questionnaire pursuant to Rule 3.5c. Upon receipt of the written request for hearing and the properly completed and filed Additional Questionnaire, the Director shall cause a supplemental character investigation and report to be prepared pursuant to Rule 5. The Director shall then notify the Chair of the Committee of the request for hearing and request the appointment of a Hearing Panel.

October 2, 2006, eff. July 1, 2007.

Rule 9.3. Appointment of Hearing Panel

The Chair of the Committee shall appoint a Hearing Panel from the remaining members of the Committee, none of whom have been members of the Inquiry Panel, to consider formally the application. A hearing will thereafter be scheduled on a date certain no fewer than 75 days after receipt of the properly completed and filed Additional Questionnaire. The Chair of the Committee shall chair the Hearing Panel or shall designate a member of the panel as Chair. The Hearing Panel shall consist of five members of the Committee, and four members of the panel shall constitute a quorum. Following the hearing, the Hearing Panel shall prepare or cause to be prepared Findings and Conclusions together with a recommendation for or against the certification of the registrant or applicant.

Rule 9.3a. Notice of Hearing. No fewer than 21 days prior to the hearing to be conducted by the Hearing Panel, the Panel shall cause a Notice to be sent to the registrant or applicant by mail containing:

1. the date, time, and place of such hearing;

2. the disclosure of matters adverse to the registrant or applicant;

3. if such matters were based in full or in part upon statements from other persons, the names of such persons;

4. confirmation of the right of the registrant or applicant to be represented by counsel, at his or her own expense, to examine and cross-examine witnesses, to adduce evidence bearing upon the aforesaid adverse matters and upon his or her character and fitness, and for such purposes to make reasonable use of the Committee's subpoena powers under Rule 9.3c;

5. confirmation of the right of the registrant or applicant or of his or her counsel, if any, to inspect

prior to the hearing his or her character and fitness file; and

  6. a copy of these Rules.

Rule 9.3b. The hearing before the Hearing Panel shall be private unless the registrant or applicant requests that it be public. Subject to the approval of the Board, the Director shall appoint counsel from among the members of the bar to prepare and present the matters adverse to the law student registrant or applicant. The Hearing Panel shall not be bound by the formal rules of evidence. It may in its discretion take evidence in other than testimonial form, having the right to rely upon records and other materials furnished to the Hearing Panel in response to its requests for assistance in its inquiries pursuant to these Rules and Supreme Court Rule 709. It may further in its discretion determine whether any evidence to be taken in testimonial form shall be taken in person at the hearing or upon deposition, but all testimonial evidence shall, in either event, be taken under oath. The matters to be considered by the Hearing Panel need not be limited to the matters of concern set forth in the notice to the law student registrant or applicant of the matters adverse to the law student registrant or applicant. A complete stenographic record of the hearing shall be kept, and a transcript may be ordered by the law student registrant or applicant at his or her expense.

Rule 9.3c. The Committee shall, upon request of any member or of the law student registrant or the applicant, apply to the Clerk of the Supreme Court for the issuance of subpoenas or writs for the taking of testimony at its hearings or upon evidence depositions and shall, upon like request, report to said Court the failure or refusal of any person to attend and testify in response to any such subpoena or writ. The taking of depositions shall be limited to evidence depositions where permitted by the Committee under the criteria set forth in Supreme Court Rule 212(b).

Rule 9.3d. The Hearing Panel members shall confer and deliberate among themselves at the conclusion of the hearing and subsequent thereto as necessary. The Panel may vote at the conclusion of the hearing or may defer the vote to a later date not more than 45 days after conclusion of the hearing or 45 days after the record of the hearing is closed, whichever shall later occur, at which time a vote of the Hearing Panel shall be taken. The members may vote by mail, email, fax, or telephone. The registrant or applicant shall be recommended for certification to the Board only upon receiving at least three affirmative votes.

Rule 9.3e. If the Hearing Panel shall vote to recommend the certification of the registrant or applicant to the Board, within 45 days thereafter, or, in the event of special circumstances, within such additional period of time as may be approved by the full Committee, the Chair of the Hearing Panel shall cause to be prepared and submitted to the Director for transmittal to the Court the Findings and Conclusions of the Committee. The Findings and Conclusions shall contain a synopsis of the contents of the application, a full and fair explication of each of the matters of concern, and, with regard to each such matter, the basis for the recommendation of certification; if the vote of the panel is less than unanimous, the Findings and Conclusions shall include a clear and concise statement of the concern(s) and conclusion(s) of the minority. The Director shall thereafter transmit such Findings and Conclusions to the Court together with any recommendation and information the Board may deem appropriate to submit. A copy of the report and the Board's recommendation, if any, shall be mailed to the law student registrant or applicant and to his or her counsel if any; a copy of any Board recommendation shall also be submitted to the Committee.

Rule 9.3f. If the Hearing Panel shall vote not to recommend the certification of the law student registrant or applicant, within 45 days thereafter, or, in the event of special circumstances, within such additional period of time as may be approved by the full Committee, the Chair of the Hearing Panel shall cause to be prepared and submitted to the Director for transmittal to the law student registrant or applicant the Findings and Conclusions of the Committee. The Findings and Conclusions of the Committee shall thereafter be served on the law student registrant or applicant by mail to the address designated by the law student registrant or applicant for receipt of notices, and the date of service shall be the date of mailing; a copy of the Findings and Conclusions of the Committee shall also be mailed to counsel for the registrant or applicant, if any.

Rule 9.3g. Prior to the mailing of the written Findings and Conclusions of the Committee to the law student registrant or applicant, the deliberation and decision of the Hearing Panel shall remain confidential.

October 2, 2006, eff. July 1, 2007.

RULE 10. STATUS OF CERTAIN CHARACTER AND FITNESS REGISTRATION APPLICATIONS

Rule 10.1. [Tentative Recommendation Pending Examination Results]

Each recommendation for the certification of an applicant for admission on examination prior to the announcement of the results of such examination shall be a tentative recommendation. At the discretion of the Committee, in the event an applicant for admission upon examination has failed to pass the examination, no further action as to such applicant need be taken thereafter by the Committee or any Panel thereof until such time as the Committee shall be advised that the applicant has passed a subsequent examination.

October 2, 2006, eff. July 1, 2007.

Rule 10.2. [Failure to Provide Requested Information or Documentation, Inactive Status]

The character and fitness registration application of a registrant or applicant who without reasonable explanation has failed to provide requested information or documentation for a period of more than 90 days shall be placed on inactive status. Such application may be returned to active status only upon the written request of the registrant or applicant, which request shall include all previously requested information and documentation and satisfactorily address all previously outstanding matters of character and fitness concern, and the registrant or applicant shall be so advised in writing. If 9 or more months have passed since the date the registrant or applicant filed his or her most recent character and fitness questionnaire, the registrant or applicant must also properly complete and file an Additional Questionnaire pursuant to Rule 3.5b.

October 2, 2006, eff. July 1, 2007.

RULE 11. CONFIDENTIALITY

Rule 11. Confidentiality

All information received by the Board or a Committee on Character and Fitness or any agent of the Board or Committee pertaining to a law student registrant or applicant is subject to a quasi-judicial privilege. Such information shall be held in confidence and shall not be disclosed except as follows: (a) The name, date of birth, and Social Security number of a law student registrant or applicant and the date of his or her application, may be made available for placement in a national data bank operated by or on behalf of the National Conference of Bar Examiners; (b) Information requested by the Attorney Registration and Disciplinary Commission in connection with disciplinary proceedings, reinstatement proceedings, or investigations regarding the unauthorized practice of law shall be released by the Board in response to a subpoena issued by that agency; (c) Reports to the Supreme Court or any information required by the Supreme Court at any time shall be filed with the Court; (d) Information shall be released in response to a written request from the National Conference of Bar Examiners or from other bar admitting authorities when accompanied by an authorization for the release of such information duly executed by the person about whom such information is sought; (e) Information concerning a law student registrant or applicant shall be released by the Board in response to a subpoena issued in connection with the criminal investigation or prosecution of such law student registrant or applicant; (f) matters of concern raised by a law student registrant's or applicant's investigation and report may be disclosed to the registrant or applicant upon consideration of the registrant's or applicant's file pursuant to Rules 9.1 or 9.2 by a Committee member or an Inquiry Panel; (g) except

as provided in preceding subparagraph (f), the Committee shall disclose to the law student registrant or applicant the contents of his or her character and fitness file only as provided by Rule 9.3a and Rule 9.3b, which documents shall thereafter become a part of the record before the Supreme Court in the event the law student registrant or applicant files a petition for review pursuant to Supreme Court Rule 708(e).

October 2, 2006, eff. July 1, 2007.

RULE 12. APPEALS

Rule 12. Appeals

Any law student registrant or applicant who has received an unfavorable recommendation from the Committee may file an appropriate petition for review by the Supreme Court with the Clerk of the Court in Springfield in accordance with Supreme Court Rule 708(e).

October 2, 2006, eff. July 1, 2007.

RULE 13. NEW HEARINGS

Rule 13.1. [Time to Petition to Character and Fitness Committee]

Any law student registrant or applicant who has been denied certification as hereinabove provided may petition the Character and Fitness Committee issuing the denial for a new hearing, but not within two years of the date the Committee mailed its Findings and Conclusions to the law student registrant or applicant, unless a shorter time is allowed by the decision of the Committee. If the registrant or applicant petitions the Supreme Court for relief from such denial pursuant to Rule 12, and the Court denies the petition, the foregoing two year period shall commence on the date of the Order of the Court, unless a shorter time is allowed by the Court. If the Committee recommends the certification of a registrant or applicant who is subsequently denied interim certification or admission by the Supreme Court, the registrant or applicant may petition the Committee that conducted the original hearing for a new hearing but not within two years of the date of the order of denial, unless a shorter time is allowed by the Court.

October 2, 2006, eff. July 1, 2007.

Rule 13.2. [Petition for New Hearing, Activities and Conduct of the Law School Applicant or Registrant]

No petition for a new hearing will be considered unless it shall include a showing of the activities and conduct of the law student registrant or applicant since, and the circumstances and conditions arising after, the last action of the Committee or of the Court, all of which must be fully set forth in the petition for new hearing.

October 2, 2006, eff. July 1, 2007.

Rule 13.3. [Denial of Petition]

The Committee may deny the petition for new hearing without hearing testimony of witnesses, if the petition does not meet the foregoing requirements of this Rule and if the petition does not set forth substantial new matter which would *prima facie* overcome the reasons for the previous denial and establish that the law student registrant or applicant now has the good moral character and general fitness to practice law which would justify certification. If the Committee determines that the petition complies with this Rule and sets forth such substantial new matter, the petition shall be granted. Such determination shall be made by majority vote of the full Committee at a meeting conducted in person or by telephone conference at which a quorum is present within 45 days after service of the petition for new hearing upon the Committee. The members present at the meeting may also vote by mail, email, fax, or telephone.

October 2, 2006, eff. July 1, 2007.

Rule 13.4. [Grant of Petition; Additional Questionnaire; Supplemental Integration]

In the event the petition is granted, the registrant or applicant shall be so notified by mail, and he or she shall promptly complete and file an Additional Questionnaire pursuant to Rule 3.5d. Upon receipt of the properly completed and filed Additional Questionnaire, the Director shall cause a supplemental character investigation and report to be prepared pursuant to Rule 5. A new hearing shall thereafter be scheduled and held pursuant to the requirements of Rules 9.3 *et seq.* To the extent possible, the original Hearing Panel shall be reconvened for the purpose of the new hearing. Any unavailable member of the original panel shall be replaced by another member of the Committee.

October 2, 2006, eff. July 1, 2007.

RULE 14. SERVICE

Rule 14. Service

All notices, reports, and other documents and items, including Findings and Conclusions of the Committee, required to be mailed or delivered under these Rules, may be sent by United States mail, postage prepaid, or by any private courier or delivery service approved by the Board, costs prepaid by the sender. The date of service is the date of depositing such items in the United States mails or tendering to the courier or delivery service as appropriate.

October 2, 2006, eff. July 1, 2007.

ADMINISTRATIVE AND PROCEDURAL RULES OF THE ILLINOIS APPELLATE COURT FIRST DISTRICT

Including Amendments Received Through April 1, 2016

ADMINISTRATIVE RULES

Rule 1. Organization

A. Court to Sit in Divisions; Presiding Judges.

This Court shall sit in divisions in such numbers as from time to time shall be determined by the Supreme Court. Each division is included within the term "Court" as used in these rules unless the context indicates otherwise. The judges in each division shall each year select one of their number to serve as presiding judge for a term of one year.

B. Executive Committee.

There shall be an Executive Committee of the entire Court composed of one judge from each division, selected by the judges in the division. Each member shall serve for a term of one year, but may succeed himself or herself when the individual division shall so decide. The Executive Committee shall exercise general administrative authority over the business of the Court and annually shall elect one of its members to be chairperson. The Executive Committee shall select one of its members to act as vice-chairperson, who shall automatically take over the duties of the chairperson of the Executive Committee whenever the chairperson is incapacitated or otherwise unavailable.

C. Court Sessions; Three Judges Must Participate in Every Decision.

The Court shall be in session throughout the year and each division shall sit periodically as its judicial business requires. Three judges must participate in the disposition of every case and the concurrence of two shall be necessary to a disposition. Between sittings of a division, any judge of the division may decide any motion of course and also may enter any order which might have been entered under the practice previously existing in the Appellate Court or now existing in the Supreme Court of Illinois.

D. Sitting of a Division.

For the purpose of calling cases and motions, and hearing oral argument, the division will sit on such days of the week as may be determined by the Executive Committee. The sitting of a division may be varied by the division, subject to the general authority of the Executive Committee.

Amended eff. Aug. 12, 1974; amended eff. Sept. 1, 2004.

Formerly Ill.Rev.Stat.1991, ch. 110A, ¶ 801.

Rule 2. Rules Governing the Assignment and Management of Cases in the First District

Section

I. General Rules Concerning the Retention and Assignment of Cases.

II. Panel Designations.

III. Compensatory Reduction for Industrial Commission Cases.

IV. Assignment of Non-Ready Cases for Motion Purposes and Motion Practice Generally.

V. Management of Non-Ready Cases.

VI. Priority of This Rule.

§ I. General Rules Concerning the Retention and Assignment of Cases

A. CASES RETAINED ON DECEMBER 2, 1996 AND ON FUTURE ROTATION DATES.

Upon the rotation of the judges of the First District on December 2, 1996, and on every annual rotation date thereafter, each judge shall retain the following categories of cases:

(1) Assigned cases then under advisement (including cases in which oral arguments have been heard and non-oralled cases in which opinions or orders have been circulated or are in circulation);

(2) Previously assigned ready cases;

(3) Previously assigned Research ready cases;

(4) *Anders/Finley* cases assigned to a designated judge;

(5) Previously assigned non-ready cases where petitions for leave to appeal have been allowed under Rule 306 or where permissive interlocutory appeals have been allowed under Rule 308;

(6) Previously assigned non-ready cases related to a case previously disposed of by an opinion or a Rule 23 order authored by the assigned judge who is still a member of this court;

(7) Previously assigned non-ready cases in which an order has been entered expediting briefing and/or oral argument;

(8) Assigned cases which have been disposed of by an opinion or a Rule 23 order, but for which no mandate has yet issued.

(9) Assigned, non-ready cases under Supreme Court Rule 306A, Expedited Appeals in Child Custody Cases, involving initial final child custody orders, orders modifying child custody where a change of custody has been granted, final orders of adoption and final orders terminating parental rights.

B. ASSIGNMENT OF READY AND *ANDERS/FINLEY* CASES AS OF DECEMBER 2, 1996.

Commencing on December 2, 1996, cases that have attained ready status shall be randomly assigned, for dispositional purposes, to a designated judge, together with a panel as provided in section II below, only after the director of Research has determined which cases will be taken by Research. Thereafter, each case shall be categorized as a "ready civil case," a "ready criminal case," or a "ready Research case." When a motion to withdraw as counsel under *Anders* or *Finley* is filed, the case shall be categorized as an "*Anders/Finley*" case. Such ready and *Anders/Finley* cases shall be assigned to a designated judge and a panel through computerized random selection, balanced for annual equalization among the judges of this court in each of the four categories listed above.

"Designated judge," as used above and throughout this Rule, refers to the judge assigned to author a decision, provided that the judge writes on behalf of a majority of the panel.

C. ASSIGNMENT OF CASES INVOLVING DISCRETIONARY APPEALS.

When the division to which a case is assigned for motion purposes grants a discretionary appeal pursuant to Supreme Court Rules 306 or 308, the case shall be randomly assigned by computer to a designated judge and a panel in that division for dispositional purposes. When the case attains ready status, the designated judge shall be credited with a ready civil case.

D. ASSIGNMENT OF RELATED AND CONSOLIDATED CASES.

(1) *Related Cases*

When it is determined that a case is related to a case previously disposed of by an opinion or Rule 23 order authored by a judge who is still a member of this court, it shall be assigned to that judge as the designated judge and a panel as provided in section II below. When such a case attains ready status, the designated judge shall be credited with a ready case in the appropriate category (*i.e.*, civil, criminal, Research or *Anders/Finley*). If the authoring judge of a disposed of case is no longer a member of this court, any case related to that disposed case shall be treated as any other case.

(2) *Consolidated Cases*

When a non-ready case is consolidated with an earlier filed non-ready case, both cases shall be assigned for motion purposes to the division in which the earlier filed case is assigned. When a non-ready case is consolidated with a ready case, the non-ready case shall be reassigned for motion and dispositional purposes to the designated judge and the panel to which the ready case is assigned, without regard to which case has the lower number.

E. ASSIGNMENT OF EXPEDITED CASES.

When a division to which a case is assigned for motion purposes allows a motion to expedite the filing of briefs and/or the setting of oral argument, the case shall be randomly assigned by computer to a designated judge and a panel in that division for dispositional purposes. When the case attains ready status, the designated judge shall be credited with a ready case in the appropriate category (*i.e.*, civil, criminal, or Research).

§ II. Panel Designations

When a case is assigned to a designated judge pursuant to this Rule, regardless of its characterization as criminal, civil, Research, or *Anders/Finley*, in addition to its assignment to the designated judge, two other judges shall be assigned by number, through computerized random selection, to constitute a panel to consider that case. Thereafter, except for a realignment of the panel due to recusals, any opinion or Rule 23 order entered in a non-oralled case shall be rendered by the assigned panel. Also with due regard to scheduling considerations, every effort shall be made to conform oral argument settings to the assigned panel.

"Scheduling considerations," as used above, shall include, but not be limited to the following circumstances: where there is a need, in the opinion of the designated judge, to set a case for prompt hearing on an accelerated or expedited case; where an assigned member of the panel is unavailable due to recusal, illness, or vacation; where there are no ready cases to be heard on a given oral argument date; where, in the opinion of the designated judge, adherence to panel designations would unduly delay the hearing of a case.

Effective December 2, 1996, each judge is assigned a number from 1 to 4, in accordance with the order in which judges are listed within each division in M.R. 1062, the September 25, 1996 order of the supreme court. (The listing is set forth below.) Thereafter, each judge shall retain the assigned number upon rotation to a different division. Except for cases then under advisement, when a judge rotates to a different division, the cases accompanying that judge shall retain their numerical panel designations and a new panel, bearing the same number designations, shall be constituted for that case within the new division. Likewise, each judge who rotates into a different division shall replace, on an assigned panel for each case, the departing judge who bears the same number.

When a judge is transferred into a different division to replace another judge, outside the regular rotation system, the transferred judge shall assume the number of the replaced judge, and, if a change of numbers has occurred, the presiding judge of the division shall randomly assign judges of that division, in rotation and by number, to constitute panels for the cases accompanying the transferred judge.

Numerical Listing of Judges pursuant to Section II of the Rule Governing the Assignment and Management of Cases Incorporated by Reference in the Rule

(Note: The names in parentheses refer to the Judges' numerical assignments as of July 2004)

1. Hon. Calvin C. Campbell (Hon. Denise O'Malley)	1. Hon. Anne M. Burke (Hon. Mary Jane Theis)
2. Hon. Robert C. Buckley (Hon. Joseph Gordon)	2. Hon. David Cerda (Hon. Alan J. Greiman)
3. Hon. Sheila M. O'Brien (Hon. Margaret S. McBride)	3. Hon. Warren D. Wolfson (Hon. Patrick J. Quinn)
4. Hon. Michael J. Gallagher (Hon. Jill K. McNulty)	4. Hon. Daniel J. McNamara (Hon. Allen Hartman)

1. Hon. Gino L. DiVito (Hon. Anne M. Burke)	1. Hon. Leslie Elaine South (Hon. Calvin C. Campbell)
2. Hon. John P. Tully (Hon. Rodolfo Garcia)	2. Hon. Thomas E. Hoffman (Hon. P. Scott Neville)
3. Hon. Thomas R. Rakowski (Hon. Warren D. Wolfson)	3. Hon. John N. Hourihane (Hon. Sheila M. O'Brien)
4. Hon. Jill K. McNulty (Hon. Robert Cahill)	4. Hon. Allen Hartman (Hon. Ellis E. Reid)

1. Hon. William Cousins, Jr. (Hon. Leslie E. South)	1. Hon. Mary Jane Theis (Hon. Margaret O'Mara Frossard)
2. Hon. Joseph Gordon (Hon. Thomas E. Hoffman)	2. Hon. Alan J. Greiman (Hon. John P. Tully)
3. Hon. Marvin Leavitt (Hon. Themis Karnezis)	3. Hon. Patrick J. Quinn (Hon. James Fitzgerald Smith)
4. Hon. Robert Cahill (Hon. Shelvin Louise M. Hall)	4. Hon. Morton Zwick (Hon. Michael J. Gallagher)

§ III. Compensatory Reduction for Industrial Commission Cases

When any member of this court is assigned to author an opinion or Rule 23 order as a member of the Industrial Commission Panel, the most recent prior assigned ready civil or criminal case shall be removed from that judge's case inventory and randomly reassigned as provided by this Rule.

§ IV. Assignment of Non–Ready Cases for Motion Purposes and Motion Practice Generally

On December 2, 1996, all cases not listed in section 1(A) of this Rule shall become unassigned cases, and all such cases and all new cases docketed thereafter, shall be evenly assigned, through computerized random selection, among the six divisions for motion purposes only. Except for transfers due to consolidations, recusals, or related case purposes, the assignment of these cases to a division for motion purposes shall remain fixed until the case is assigned to a designated judge, regardless of the rotation or transfer of judges between the divisions.

§ V. Management of Non–Ready Cases

A staff motions attorney designated by this court shall be required to examine the notice of appeal and the docketing statement for each new appeal filed. When that attorney determines that there is a question as to the court's jurisdiction to hear a given appeal, he or she shall notify the Chairman of the Executive Committee. If the Chairman of the Executive Committee agrees with the staff attorney's assessment, the appellant shall be ordered to file a jurisdictional statement within 21 days, or within any period of time deemed reasonable.

The clerk of the court shall advise the presiding judges, at regular intervals set by the presiding judges, of any case assigned to their respective divisions for motion purposes in which the record is 56 days or more past due or the appellant's or appellee's brief is 35 days or more past due, and no motion for an extension is pending. It shall thereupon be the responsibility of the division to enter an order directing the filing of the record or brief, or, in civil cases, to consider dismissing the appeal for want of prosecution, or to take the case on appellant's brief only. When the division enters an order that a case is to be taken on the appellant's brief only, the clerk shall immediately designate the case as ready, determine whether it will be taken by Research, and randomly assign it in accordance with the provisions of this Rule.

§ VI. Priority of this Rule

To the extent that this Rule may be in conflict with any previous Rule of this court, the provisions of this Rule shall govern over the other Rule.

Amended eff. Aug. 12, 1974; Feb. 20, 1976; Oct. 1, 1979; Jan. 1, 1984; amended eff. Sept. 1, 2004.

Formerly Ill.Rev.Stat.1991, ch. 110A, ¶ 802.

Rule 3. Docketing, Numbering and Assigning Cases

A. Docketing and Numbering of Cases. Each case in this Court shall, upon the transmittal of the notice of appeal, or upon the filing of a motion for leave to file a late notice of appeal, filing of a Rule 306 petition, filing of a Rule 308 application, filing of a Rule 604(c) bail motion, or filing of a Petition for Review in appeals filed pursuant to Supreme Court Rule 335, be given a permanent number. The title of the case and its number shall be entered upon the clerk's docket as soon as possible. All cases shall be numbered consecutively in the order of presentation of one of the documents identified above to the clerk for filing.

B. Assignment of Cases. All cases shall be assigned by computerized random assignment to a division, in motion status, upon transmittal of the notice of appeal or the filing of one of the documents set forth in paragraph A, with the exception of cases filed under Supreme Court Rule 306A (involving initial final child custody orders, orders modifying child custody where a change of custody has been granted, final orders of adoption and final orders terminating parental rights), which shall be randomly assigned by computer to a justice of the court upon transmittal of the

notice of appeal or the filing of one of the documents set forth in paragraph A.

C. Transfer or Reassignment of Cases. The Executive Committee may, in its discretion, at any time transfer or reassign any case to a different division. Cases that are consolidated, and related cases, will be reassigned to the division having the lowest permanent docket number as long as such reassignment is consistent with the General Rules Concerning Retention and Assignment of Cases.

Amended eff. Aug. 12, 1974; July 1, 1977; Sept. 1, 1978; amended eff. Sept. 1, 2004.

Formerly Ill.Rev.Stat.1991, ch. 110A, ¶ 803.

Rule 4. Motion Practice

A. General Motion Practice. Motions must comply with Supreme Court Rule 361 and be filed as follows:

(1) Original and three (3) copies of the motion, with proof of service attached at the back of the original and each copy of the motion. The proof of service shall specify the method of delivery (personal or by mail, or by facsimile as permitted by Supreme Court Rule 11), the date served, and the name and address of the party (or the party's attorney) served. Motions must be arranged in four complete sets.

(2) One (1) proposed order for the Court to sign, reciting the relief requested, and phrased in the alternative, i.e., ALLOWED/DENIED. The proposed order should not be attached to the motion.

(3) Where a draft order consists of more than one page, a portion of the order, not just the Justices' signature lines, must appear on the last page. Page numbers must appear at the bottom of each page of a multiple page order. The Appellate Court number must appear at the top of each page.

B. Assignment of Motions. Motions will be directed to the division to which the case has been assigned. In an emergency, if all the judges of the assigned division are unavailable, a motion may be ruled upon by any other division or judge designated by the Chairperson of the Executive Committee. If the Chairperson of the Executive Committee is unavailable, then any other member of the Executive Committee may make that designation. If no member of the Executive Committee is available, then any judge may rule on an emergency motion.

C. Motion Titles Must Indicate the Specific Nature of the Relief Sought. Motion titles shall reflect the precise nature of the relief sought, i.e., "Motion for Extension of Time to File the Appellant's Brief" rather than just "Motion" or "Motion for Extension of Time".

D. Motions for Extension of Time. Motions for extension of time should be filed prior to the due date. Such motions should ask for a specific due date (i.e., extension to and including January 15, 2003), not a certain number of additional days (i.e., an additional 15 days). The extended due date requested shall be at least fourteen (14) days after the original due date, to avoid having the requested new date expire before the order granting the extension is entered (the divisions generally rule on routine motions once a week).

A motion for extension of time should be supported by an affidavit as required by Supreme Court Rule 361(f).

E. Instanter Motions. If a party is seeking to file a record, supplemental record, briefs or other documents instanter, the title of the motion and body of the accompanying proposed order should include the word "instanter". The record, supplemental record, briefs or other documents which the party is seeking to file <u>must</u> accompany the instanter motion.

F. Motions for Stay. A motion requesting a stay of proceedings in the Appellate Court, along with the proposed order submitted with the motion, shall include a provision that a status report will be prepared and filed with the Court on or before a date certain.

A status report shall be in the form of a motion, and shall be titled as "Motion to File Status Report". Each status report shall include a provision for filing an updated status report on a date certain, and that provision shall also be included in the proposed order submitted with the Motion to File Status Report.

G. A Motion Shall Not Contain a Response to a Different Motion; A Response to a Motion Shall Not Contain a New Motion. A motion shall not include both a request for relief and a response to a different motion previously filed. The motion and the response must be filed separately. Similarly, in responding to a motion, the party filing the response should not include in the response a new motion or request for its own relief. A motion separate from the response must be filed.

H. Mailing of Orders. Upon the Court ruling on any motion, the Clerk shall cause a copy of the order entered to be mailed to all attorneys or parties pro se of record. However, neither the failure of the Clerk to mail the copy, nor the failure of the attorney or party pro se to receive the copy, shall affect the force, validity or effect of the order.

I. Motions for Clarification. Proposed orders submitted with a Motion for Clarification must specify the relief being requested upon clarification rather than just indicating allowed/denied.

Amended eff. Aug. 12, 1974; amended eff. Sept. 1, 2004; amended June 9, 2008, eff. July 1, 2008.

Formerly Ill.Rev.Stat.1991, ch. 110A, ¶ 804.

Rule 5. Motions Filed in the Appellate Court Prior to the Transmittal of the Notice of Appeal or Notice of Interlocutory Appeal by the Circuit Court

For those appeals initiated by filing a Notice of Appeal or Notice of Interlocutory Appeal in the Circuit Court, the Appellate Court can take no action until it receives a Notice of Appeal or Notice of Interlocutory Appeal that has been file-stamped by the Circuit Court. This applies to Motions for Stay under Supreme Court Rule 305 as well as all other motions. If, before the Circuit Court has transmitted the file-stamped Notice of Appeal or Notice of Interlocutory Appeal to the Appellate Court, a party needs to file a motion or other document in the Appellate Court, the party shall:

(1) provide a file-stamped copy of the Notice of Appeal or Notice of Interlocutory Appeal to the Clerk of the Appellate Court, along with an additional filing such as a docketing statement, appearance, or motion (the Appellate Court will not docket an appeal and issue an appeal number solely on the basis of being presented with a Notice of Appeal or Notice of Interlocutory Appeal, unless the Notice was transmitted by the Clerk of the Circuit Court); and

(2) pay the required docketing or appearance fee. Presentation to the Clerk of the Appellate Court of a file-stamped copy of a Notice of Appeal, or Notice of Interlocutory Appeal, and/or presentation of the Notice of Filing the Notice of Appeal, or Notice of Interlocutory Appeal, pursuant to Supreme Court Rule 303(c), are not sufficient bases for the Appellate Court to docket an appeal and issue an Appellate Court number.

Effective Sept. 1, 2004; amended June 9, 2008, effective July 1, 2008.

Rule 6. Emergency Motions

No emergency motion may be filed in the Appellate Court unless the appeal has been docketed pursuant to First District Rule 3 (Docketing, Numbering and Assigning Cases) or Rule 5 (Motions Filed in the Appellate Court Prior to the Transmittal of the Notice of Appeal by the Circuit Court).

The words "Emergency Motion" must appear in the title. The Appellate Court Clerk, upon receiving a filing titled "Emergency Motion", shall immediately direct that filing to the justices of the division to which the appeal has been assigned. If the emergency motion requires action by the Court by a certain date or time, that information must be set forth in the first paragraph of the motion. The motion shall specify the nature of the emergency and the grounds for the specific relief requested. The movant shall attach to the motion a copy of all Circuit Court and Appellate Court documents, including orders, relevant to the motion.

The party filing the emergency motion shall immediately personally serve all other parties, if possible, or otherwise immediately serve the other parties by facsimile or overnight mail. The type of service made shall be specifically noted on the Certificate of Service.

Emergency motions should only be filed when a matter involves a genuine emergency. Motions for extensions of time to file a record or a brief are <u>not</u> considered emergencies.

The Court may (1) enter an order requesting a response by a specific date; (2) wait for the time provided by Supreme Court Rule for a response to expire; (3) enter an order resolving the motion; or (4) take whatever action is deemed appropriate.

Effective Sept. 1, 2004.

Rule 7. Amending a Notice of Appeal or Notice of Cross–Appeal

If the time to file an amended Notice of Appeal (or Notice of Cross-Appeal) as of right under Supreme Court Rule 303b(4) has expired, and a party files a motion in the Appellate Court pursuant to that rule to amend the Notice of Appeal (or Notice of Cross-Appeal), the party must specify the information being corrected.

The party shall state in both the title of the motion to amend, and the proposed order submitted with the motion, the amendment being requested, i.e., "Motion to Amend the Trial Court Number to _____", or "Motion to Amend the Date of the Trial Court's Judgment To _____".

Similarly, a timely amended Notice of Appeal (or Notice of Cross-Appeal) filed with the Clerk of the Circuit Court should specify the amendment being made.

Effective Sept. 1, 2004.

Rule 8. Appeals Under Supreme Court Rules 306, 307(d), 308, and 604(c)–Filing Requirements

When filing a Petition for Leave to Appeal under Supreme Court Rule 306,[1] an appeal relating to Temporary Restraining Orders under Supreme Court Rule 307(d), an Application for Leave to Appeal under Supreme Court Rule 308, or a Verified Motion for Review of a bail order under Supreme Court Rule 604(c), a party shall specify on the cover page of the Petition, Application or Verified Motion the Supreme Court Rule pursuant to which the document is being filed.

Parties filing an Application or Petition under Supreme Court Rules 306, 307(d), or 308, or a Verified Motion for Review under Supreme Court Rule 604(c), shall file an original and three copies with proof of service attached. If the supporting record for an Application or Petition is based on an attorney's or party's affidavit, four copies of the supporting record must be filed, and a copy provided to every other party. If the supporting record has been prepared, bound and certified by the Clerk of the Circuit Court, no additional copies need be submitted to the Appellate Court, or served on other parties.

If a party elects to allow his or her petition or answer to stand as his or her brief, he or she must comply with the notice and filing requirements of Supreme Court rule 306 (i).

Effective September 1, 2004.

[1] Under amendments to Supreme Court Rule 306(a)(5), effective January 1, 2004, a party filing a petition for leave to appeal from an interlocutory order affecting the care and custody of unemancipated minors under Supreme Court Rule 306(a)(5) must also file a notice of interlocutory appeal with the Clerk of the Circuit Court within the time allowed for filing the petition for leave to appeal. See Rule 306(b) for the expedited filing requirements.

Rule 9. Docketing Statements and Appearances; Fees

The Clerk's Office may accept docketing statements for filing beyond the fourteen (14) day due date, for a reasonable time, without motion.

The docketing statement may serve as the appearance for the appellant or petitioner.

Appellees and respondents are encouraged to file an appearance with the Clerk of the Appellate Court as soon as possible so as to become a party of record entitled to receive notification from the Court of any orders entered. The fact that an appellant or petitioner has indicated on the docketing statement the appellee's or respondent's name, or the name of the appellee's or respondent's attorney, does not constitute an appearance for the appellee or respondent.

<u>Docketing Fee/Appearance Fee Must Be Paid by Each Law Firm</u>

Each law firm that appears by way of the docketing statement, appearance form, pro hac vice motion and/or as amicus must pay the appropriate fee to be of record and receive copies of the Court's orders.

The Appellant's docketing fee for a criminal case is $25. The Appellee's appearance fee for a criminal case is $15.

The Appellant's docketing fee for a civil case is $25. The Appellee's appearance fee for a civil case is $15.

Effective September 1, 2004; amended June 9, 2008, effective July 1, 2008. Amended eff. Jan. 1, 2009.

Rule 10. Address Changes—Attorneys and Non–Imprisoned Parties

All attorneys, as well as all parties representing themselves, shall immediately notify the Appellate Court Clerk by letter of any change of address.

A copy of the letter shall be served on all parties.

Effective September 1, 2004.

Rule 11. Address Notification for Defendants in Criminal Matters

Within 14 days of the filing of the appellee's brief in any criminal matter, counsel for the defendant(s)[1] shall serve notice on the Clerk of the Appellate Court, stating the case title, Appellate Court and Circuit Court numbers, the defendant's name and Department of Corrections number, and the defendant's then current address. The notice shall be titled "NOTICE OF CRIMINAL DEFENDANT'S CURRENT ADDRESS".

Thereafter, counsel shall immediately serve the Clerk of the Appellate Court with notice of any subsequent change of the defendant's address. Such subsequent notice(s) shall be titled "NOTICE OF SUBSEQUENT CHANGE OF ADDRESS OF A CRIMINAL DEFENDANT".

A Certificate of Service showing that service has been made on all other parties shall be attached to all such notices.

If a defendant in a criminal matter is not represented by counsel, then it is that defendant's responsibility to initially advise the Clerk of the Appellate Court by letter of his or her case title, Appellate Court and Circuit Court numbers, Department of Corrections number, and his or her address if that information does not appear on the notice of appeal. Such defendants must thereafter immediately notify the Clerk by letter of any change of address and must identify the Appellate Court case numbers of all active appeals in which the defendant is representing himself.

Effective September 1, 2004.

1 As used in this rule, the word "defendant" refers to all non-prosecuting parties in criminal matters, regardless of whether such party is identified in the pleadings as the plaintiff or defendant, petitioner or respondent, or appellant or appellee.

Rule 12. Substitution or Withdrawal of Counsel

Attorneys seeking to withdraw or to be substituted as counsel must file a motion consistent with Supreme Court Rule 13(c).

If, however, an attorney is appearing as additional, not substituted, counsel, the attorney may simply file an appearance form titled "Additional Appearance", with a proof of service and payment of the appropriate fee.

Where the substitution of one law firm for another law firm is simultaneous, if the original law firm has paid the fee, the substituted law firm does not need to also pay a fee. If the substitution is not simultaneous, a fee will be required from the law firm that appears at a date after the prior attorney has withdrawn.

Effective September 1, 2004; amended June 9, 2008, effective July 1, 2008.

Rule 13. Waiver of Fees

The Appellate Court's fees are automatically waived in criminal and juvenile delinquency appeals for the State's Attorney, the State Appellate Defender and the Public Defender only. Fees are automatically waived in civil cases only for the State's Attorney and the Public Guardian, when the Public Guardian is representing a minor. Fees in both criminal and civil cases are waived for the Illinois Attorney General.

In all other appeals, all parties not identified in the preceding paragraph shall either pay the appropriate fee or file a motion requesting that the fee be waived.

Information Required for Waiver of Fees

A party seeking to proceed as a poor person must file a motion supplying the financial information that is required by Supreme Court Rule 298. An updated Circuit Court indigency form may be attached in support of the motion.

Effective September 1, 2004; amended June 9, 2008, effective July 1, 2008.

Rule 14. Custody Cases Expedited Under Supreme Court Rule 306A—Mandatory Procedures For Custody Cases Involving (1) Initial Final Custody Orders, (2) Orders Modifying Child Custody Where a Change of Custody has been Granted, (3) Final Orders of Adoption and (4) Final Orders Terminating Parental Rights; Applicability of Supreme Court Rule 306A to Petitions for Leave to Appeal Allowed Under Supreme Court Rule 306(a)(5)

A. Record on Appeal—Due Date.

In the four types of custody cases enumerated in Supreme Court Rule 306A, the record on appeal shall be filed within 35 days of the filing of the notice of appeal pursuant to Supreme Court Rule 306A, subsection (e).

Any initial motion for extension of time to file the record filed in the Circuit Court pursuant to Rule 306A, as well as the ruling on such motion, must be immediately served on the Clerk of the Appellate Court by counsel for the moving party, or by the party who filed the motion if the party is not represented by counsel.

All subsequent motions for extension of time, which must be filed in the Appellate Court, as well as the rulings on such motions, must be immediately served on the trial judge and the chief judge of the Circuit Court by counsel for the moving party, or by the party who filed the motion if the party is not represented by counsel.

B. Briefing Schedule.

The appellant's brief shall be filed within 21 days from the filing of the record on appeal. Within 21 days from the due date of the appellant's brief, or in the case of multiple appellants, the latest due date of any appellant's brief, the appellee shall file his or her brief. Within 14 days from the due date of the appellee's brief, or in the case of multiple appellees, the latest due date of any appellee brief, the appellant may file a reply brief.

C. Requests for Extensions.

In accordance with Supreme Court Rule 306A(h), requests for a continuance may only be granted upon written motion by counsel or the party requesting the continuance. Such motions will not be favored, except for good cause shown.

D. Decision Due Date.

Pursuant to Supreme Court Rule 306A, section (f), except for good cause shown, the Appellate Court shall issue its decision within 150 days after the filing of the notice of appeal.

E. Applicability of This Rule to Petitions Allowed Under Supreme Court Rule 306(a)(5).

If a petition for leave to appeal an interlocutory order affecting the care and custody of unemancipated minors filed pursuant to Supreme Court Rule 306(a)(5) is allowed, then the time for filing any additional record under Supreme Court Rule 306(g), and for either filing a notice of election to stand on the petition or for filing a brief under Supreme Court Rule 306(h), shall be the same as the time permitted for the filing of the record and the filing of briefs under Supreme Court Rule 306A, except that the time for such filings shall begin to run from the date that the petition was granted rather than the date that the Notice of Appeal was filed.

Except for good cause shown, the Appellate Court shall issue its decision within 150 days after entering the order allowing the 306(a)(5) petition for leave to appeal.

Effective: July 1, 2004.

Rule 15. Accelerating the Appeal

A party seeking to have an appeal expedited shall file a motion pursuant to Supreme Court Rule 311.

Parties seeking to expedite the briefing schedule, the setting of oral argument, or the filing of the decision shall file a motion setting forth the reasons to expedite.

Appellant, when moving the Court to expedite the briefing, must state when the complete record and appellant's brief will be filed. Communication with the Clerk of the Circuit Court as to record preparation is necessary. If the appellant is seeking leave to prepare and file a supporting record supported by affidavit of the attorney or party in lieu of the bound, certified record prepared by the Circuit Court Clerk, the appellant must explain why the preparation of the record by the Circuit Court Clerk is not practical.

Effective September 1, 2004.

Rule 16. Prehearing Conferences

Motions for a Rule 310 conference shall be directed to the Chairman of the Executive Committee for consideration.

Effective September 1, 2004.

Rule 17. Filing Documents Under Seal

No record, exhibit, or brief may be filed under seal in the Appellate Court, unless the Appellate Court has first given leave for filing under seal, notwithstanding that the material was filed under seal in the Circuit Court.

A motion will specify exactly what will be filed under seal and identify by name the persons to whom the party wants to restrict access to the sealed documents.

Effective September 1, 2004.

Rule 18. Records—Filing, Withdrawing and Returning Records on Appeal

A. Filing the Record—Notice of Filing.

Upon filing the record in the Appellate Court, the appellant, petitioner, or the administrative agency (in a Supreme Court Rule 335 appeal) shall serve a notice of filing on the other parties to the appeal. The notice of filing shall indicate the number of volumes being filed.

B. Withdrawing and Returning A Record Before A Case is Fully Briefed or Otherwise Ready.

Prior to the due date of the reply brief, any party of record may sign out the record for purposes of working on the appeal. If a party of record is not represented by counsel, then the signature of the party of record, along with the party's address and telephone number, shall serve as a written request under Supreme Court Rule 372(a). If a party of record is represented, then the signature of the party's attorney of record, along with the attorney's address and telephone number, shall serve as a written request under Supreme Court Rule 372(a). A party shall return the record to the Clerk's Office when it files its brief.

If a certificate in lieu of record has been filed, the record, at the latest, shall be presented upon the filing of the reply brief, or the due date for filing a reply brief.

C. Withdrawing the Record After a Case is Fully Briefed or is Otherwise Ready.

No one, including the parties and their attorneys, may withdraw the record from the Clerk's Office from the time the case has been fully briefed or deemed "ready" by the Court until issuance of the mandate, except by permission of the Court. Permission to withdraw the record may be requested by motion, or by letter submitted to the division clerk for the appropriate division. Proof of service must accompany such motion or letter.

The Court may refuse to allow the record to be withdrawn, may allow the record to be viewed in the Clerk's Office only, or may allow the record to be withdrawn.

Effective September 1, 2004.

Rule 19. Supplemental Records

A bound and certified record prepared by the Clerk of the Circuit Court, or administrative agency in an appeal under Supreme Court Rule 335, that is filed in the Appellate Court, First District, is considered to be the complete record. Any record subsequently prepared shall be a supplemental record and shall also be bound and certified. A record cannot be supplemented with documents attached to a motion seeking leave to supplement the record, since such documents have not been bound and certified.

The trial court retains jurisdiction regarding supplemental record preparation. Therefore, motions for leave to file a supplemental record should be filed in the first instance in the trial court. Such motions may be filed initially in the Appellate Court only if the movant shows that filing a motion in the trial court would not be practical or that the trial court has denied the motion to supplement the record in whole or in part.

Once the a supplemental record has been bound and certified, a motion must be filed in the Appellate Court seeking leave to file the supplemental record instanter. The bound and certified supplemental record must be submitted with the motion. Both the motion to supplement the record instanter, and the proposed order submitted with the motion, shall specify the number of volumes, boxes, etc., of supplemental record that the party is seeking leave to file.

Presentation of a stipulation with the bound and certified supplemental record alone is not sufficient; the Appellate Court requires a motion for leave to file the supplemental record instanter.
Effective September 1, 2004.

Rule 20. Supporting Records Under Rule 328

When a Supreme Court Rule 328 supporting record is prepared pursuant to attorney or party affidavit, the party submitting the supporting record shall submit four (4) copies of the supporting record with any filing, whether it be a Rule 306, Rule 307(d) or Rule 308 appeal, or any other filing asking for relief. If the supporting record has been prepared, bound and certified by the Clerk of the Circuit Court, no additional copies need be submitted to the Appellate Court, or served on other parties.

The movant shall include in the supporting record all relevant court orders.

Service of a supporting record prepared pursuant to attorney or party affidavit shall be made on all parties.
Effective September 1, 2004.

Rule 21. Record Preparation—Exclusion of Physical Evidence and Exhibits; Records to Consist of Original Documents

A. Exclusion of Physical Evidence and Exhibits.

The Clerk of the Circuit Court shall not send to this Court with the record on appeal any physical evidence included in the record as an exhibit, except that evidence of a descriptive or documentary nature, such

as papers or photographs, shall still be included in the record on appeal.

If any exhibit or physical evidence not included in the record pursuant to this Rule is required for consideration on appeal, the Circuit Court may forward such exhibit to the Clerk of the Appellate Court upon order of the Appellate Court entered on the Court's own motion or pursuant to the motion of any party.

B. Record to Consist of Original Documents.

In preparing the record on appeal, the Circuit Court shall include only original documents from the Circuit Court Clerk's file and not photocopies, unless original papers do not exist.
Effective September 1, 2004.

Rule 22. Trial Judge to be Identified

The name of the Circuit Court judge whose ruling is being appealed should appear on the notice of appeal, as well as on motions and the cover pages of the briefs.
Effective September 1, 2004.

Rule 23. Corrections to Briefs or Other Documents

The Clerk's Office shall not correct any documents. If the corrections sought to be made are minor, then the party seeking to make the corrections should send a letter to the Clerk of the Appellate Court identifying the changes to be made. The letter shall evidence that all parties to the appeal were sent a copy of the letter. The Clerk's office will notify the party seeking to make the changes when the briefs will be available for that party to come to the Clerk's office to effectuate the changes outlined in the letter. Briefs or documents to which minor changes have been made will not be re-stamped, nor will the individual pages on which the minor changes are found be stamped.

If major changes to a brief or other documents are necessary, then the party seeking to make the changes should file a motion seeking leave to withdraw the briefs or other documents and file substituted briefs or documents, indicating generally the changes to be made and the date on which the substituted briefs or documents will be filed. The substituted briefs or other documents will be stamped as of the date that they are filed. The motion to withdraw and substitute should indicate whether the original briefs or other documents should be returned to the party filing the motion or discarded by the Clerk's Office.
Effective September 1, 2004.

Rule 24. Tapes of Oral Arguments

Tapes of oral arguments are for the Court's use. No tape of an oral argument will be made available except by leave of Court, which shall be requested by motion. The Court may refuse the request, allow the parties to listen to the tape at the Court, or enter any other order deemed appropriate.

Effective September 1, 2004.

Rule 25. Law Bulletin Notification of Oral Arguments and Decisions

The Appellate Court, First District, publishes in the Chicago Daily Law Bulletin notices of the oral arguments scheduled and the future filings of the Court's decisions. This publication shall constitute official notice of such arguments and filings.

However, the failure of the Clerk to provide notice, and/or of the Chicago Daily Law Bulletin to publish such notice, shall not impair the force, validity or effect of the oral argument schedules or future filings.

Effective September 1, 2004.

Rule 26. Oral Argument Notification and Notice of the Filings of a Decision; Decisions Not to be Mailed

A. Oral Argument Notification.

If the Court determines that an oral argument shall be held in an appeal, the Clerk's office shall provide written notification to the parties or their attorneys of record, or, if the matter involves an emergency, oral notification, of the scheduling of the oral argument.

If written notification is provided, the parties or their attorneys are required to promptly return to the Clerk's Office the acknowledgment form that accompanies the notice of argument.

Parties must serve a copy of the executed acknowledgment form on all other parties or their attorneys of record.

Failure of the Clerk's Office to provide written or oral notification of a scheduled oral argument shall not affect the scheduled oral argument.

B. Notice of the Filing of a Decision.

The Clerk's Office shall provide written notification of the Court's filing of an opinion, Rule 23 order, or summary order to the parties or their attorneys of record.

However, the failure of the Clerk to provide written notification of the filing of an opinion, Rule 23 order or summary order shall not impair the force, validity or effect of the filing.

C. Decisions Not to be Mailed.

The Clerk's office shall not mail copies of decisions. Copies of decisions shall be available in the Clerk's office at no charge to the attorneys and parties of record. Non–parties may obtain copies in the Clerk's office at a cost of $.25 per page.

Effective September 1, 2004.

Rule 27. Mandates

The Clerk of the Appellate Court issues the mandate to the Clerk of the Circuit Court, who files the mandate and spreads it of record. Certified copies of the filed mandate shall be requested from the Clerk of the Circuit Court, not the Clerk of the Appellate Court.

A party seeking to have the mandate issue fewer than 21 days from the entry of judgment shall file a motion with the Appellate Court.

For immediate issuance of the mandate once 21 days have elapsed after the entry of a judgment, a party may submit a letter to the Clerk of the Appellate Court stating that no Petition for Rehearing, no Affidavit of Intent, no Petition for Leave to Appeal, and no Motion for Extension of Time for Filing a Petition for Leave to Appeal has been filed, and requesting that the mandate issue as soon as possible. The letter shall be served on all parties.

Effective September 1, 2004.

Rule 28. Cases Affirmed or Remanded by the Supreme Court

A. Cases Affirmed by the Supreme Court.

When a judgment of this Court is affirmed by the Supreme Court on appeal, or the appeal is dismissed, and the mandate of the Supreme Court is filed in this Court, the Clerk of this Court shall issue this Court's mandate.

B. Cases Remanded By the Supreme Court.

When a judgment of this Court is reversed by the Supreme Court and the case is remanded to this Court pursuant to the Supreme Court's mandate, the Supreme Court's judgment shall be reflected in the Appellate Court records. If the Supreme Court specifies the judgment to be entered by this Court, this Court will enter an order consistent with the Supreme Court judgment. If the Supreme Court does not specify what judgment is to be entered here, this Court may file any order it deems appropriate and/or entertain motions from the parties.

Effective September 1, 2004.

Rule 29. Dismissal of Appeals by the Trial Court

When an appeal has been dismissed in the trial court pursuant to Supreme Court Rule 309 (civil appeals), or Rule 606(b) (criminal appeals), the Circuit Court shall transmit such dismissal orders to the Appellate Court pursuant to Supreme Court Rules 309 and 606(b). In addition, the parties shall send to the Clerk of the Appellate Court a file-stamped copy of the Rule 309 or Rule 606(b) order of dismissal.

Effective September 1, 2004.

Rule 30. Bonds in Civil Cases

A. Obtaining a Bond in the Appellate Court.

Consistent with Supreme Court Rule 305, applications for, and approval of, bonds should initially be sought in the Circuit Court.

If approval of a bond is sought in the Appellate Court, the party seeking the bond shall file a motion in the Appellate Court to have the amount of the bond set.

If the Appellate Court allows the motion and sets the amount of the bond, the party seeking the bond, after obtaining a bond in the amount ordered, shall present the bond to the Clerk of the Appellate Court, who shall take the bond to an Appellate Court Justice for approval. Unless otherwise requested by a party in its motion for bond and approved by the Appellate Court in its order allowing a bond, only surety bonds may be presented to the Appellate Court for approval.

B. Original Bonds Approved in the Appellate Court to be Filed in the Circuit Court.

In accordance with Supreme Court Rule 305(m), all original bonds approved by the Appellate Court shall be returned to the party that requested the bond. That party shall then file the original bond with the Clerk of the Circuit Court.

Effective July 1, 2004.

Rule 31. Criminal Defendants' Mail

A. Mail Concerning *Anders/Finley* Cases and Cases Where Defendant is Pro Se.

1. Mail reasonably related to *Anders* and *Finley* motions, including responses to such motions, should be mailed to, and will be handled by, the Clerk's office.

2. Mail from a defendant who has been allowed by the Appellate Court to proceed pro se should be mailed to, and will be handled by, the Clerk's office.

B. Mail Concerning General Correspondence and Inquiries that are Not Case Specific.

The Clerk of the Appellate Court will review all general correspondence, inquiries and other mail that is not case specific to determine whether the matters addressed should be handled by the Clerk's office or directed elsewhere.

C. Mail Concerning Appeals Where the Defendant is Represented by Counsel.

In cases where the defendant is represented by retained or appointed counsel, the defendant must send all mail, including correspondence, motions, requests for briefs, requests for status and other documents to his or her attorney. Copies of such mail shall not be sent to the Clerk's office. Counsel shall review all mail and timely respond or file the documents in the Appellate Court, if appropriate. If counsel determines that the matter should be handled by the Clerk's office, counsel shall forward the document to the Clerk's office with a brief explanation as to why the the matter could not be handled by counsel.

Mail sent by defendants to the Clerk's office in cases where a defendant is represented by counsel shall not be considered by the Clerk and shall be returned to the defendant.

D. Other Mail.

The Clerk of the Appellate Court shall determine by whom mail not covered by the preceding paragraphs should be handled.

Effective September 1, 2004.

Rule 32. Court's Computer Information

The Court's computer system and the information contained in that system may not be printed out and provided to any party or his or her attorney, or the general public.

Effective September 1, 2004.

Rule 33. Records Not to be Photocopied by the Clerk's Office

The Clerk's office for the Appellate Court, First District, may not photocopy bound and certified records for any party or non-party. Pursuant to Supreme Court Administrative Order M.R. 10958, the Clerk's office may photocopy other documents filed in the Clerk's office at a charge of $.25 per page. This charge is not waived for parties who have been allowed to proceed as poor persons.

Effective September 1, 2004.

Rule 34. Repeal of Prior Administrative and Procedural Rules and Resolutions, and Adoption of New Administrative and Procedural Rules

Except for Rule 14 (expedited custody cases) and Rule 30 (bonds in civil cases), all prior Administrative and Procedural Rules and Resolutions previously in force and effect in the Illinois Appellate Court, First District, are hereby repealed as of September 1, 2004. The new Administrative and Procedural Rules, except Rules 14 and 30, are effective September 1, 2004, and shall govern all matters, whether already pending or filed on or after September 1, 2004, unless, in regard to pending matters, application of the new rules would not be feasible or would result in an injustice, in which case the party or parties affected may file a motion seeking to have the repealed rule or resolution apply.

In regard to Rules 14 and 30, those rules remain effective as of July 1, 2004.

Effective September 1, 2004.

Rule 35. Clerk's Office not to Assist with Document Preparation; Clerk's Office not to Provide Legal Advice; Proof of Service Required

No member of the Clerk's office, including any attorneys employed in that office, may prepare any documents for any party or attorney, or review any documents for any party or attorney, other than to determine whether the documents may be accepted for filing.

The fact that a document is accepted for filing by the Clerk's office does not mean that the document complies with all applicable Supreme Court Rules, First District Rules, and relevant statutes or case law.

No member of the Clerk's office, including any attorneys employed in that office, may provide legal advice to any party or attorney.

The Clerk's office cannot accept any documents for filing that are not accompanied by a Proof of Service. The Clerk and the Clerk's staff are prohibited from serving any documents on behalf of any party, even if the party has been allowed by the Court to proceed as a poor person and/or is incarcerated.

Effective January 1, 2005; amended June 9, 2008, effective July 1, 2008.

Rule 36. Restrictions on the Clerk's Office's use of Mail, Faxes, and Telephones on Behalf of Parties or Their Attorneys; Advanced Payment Required for Copies of Documents

The clerk's office may not forward mail on behalf of any party or attorney (except as provided in Rule 31, Criminal Defendants' Mail). Parties and their attorneys may not send faxes to the clerk's office, nor request the clerk's office to send faxes on their behalf, unless so requested by the Court. Parties and their attorneys may not request the clerk's office to make telephone calls on their behalf. The Clerk's office is not permitted to accept any collect calls.

Where a request is made for copies of documents in the Clerk's office, no copies will be made unless the person making the request first pays the appropriate fee.

Effective January 1, 2005; amended June 9, 2008, effective July 1, 2008.

Rule 37. Settlement Conference Program

A. PROGRAM GOALS.

The primary purpose of the Settlement Conference Program is to provide the parties to certain civil appeals pending in the First District of the Illinois Appellate Court with a forum to explore settlement in compliance with Supreme Court Rule 310.1. The program also provides the parties with an opportunity to limit and simplify the issues on appeal and has the potential for reducing the court's calendar.

B. DEFINITIONS.

The following terms, when used in this rule, shall have the meanings hereinafter ascribed to them, except when the context requires otherwise.

1. *Court.* "Court" means the First District of the Illinois Appellate Court.

2. *Appellate Mediator.* "Appellate Mediator" means an individual appointed by the settlement administrator to preside over a settlement conference following training provided by the Administrative Office of the Illinois Courts.

3. *Mediation Committee.* "Mediation Committee" means the committee of judges of this court appointed to administer and oversee the operation of the Settlement Conference Program.

4. *Settlement Administrator.* "Settlement Administrator" means the attorney designated by the court to assist the mediation committee in administering the Settlement Conference Program.

5. *Executive Committee.* "Executive Committee" means the Executive Committee of the First District of the Illinois Appellate Court.

C. ADMINISTRATION.

The Settlement Conference Program shall be administered by a mediation committee consisting of six judges of this Court, one from each division, appointed by the executive committee for one year terms effective September 1st of each year. The members of the mediation committee shall select one of their number to serve as the chairman. The mediation committee shall be assisted in its duties by a settlement administrator designated by the chairman of the executive committee.

D. APPELLATE MEDIATORS.

1. *Qualifications.* Current judges of this court and retired supreme, appellate, and circuit court judges are qualified to serve as mediators in the Settlement Conference Program. Attorneys who have been licensed to practice law in the State of Illinois for a minimum of 10 years and who have participated in more than five appeals before any state or federal appellate court are qualified to serve as mediators in the Settlement Conference Program.

2. *Appointment.* Any person possessing the qualifications to serve as an appellate mediator as set forth in the preceding paragraph may apply to the mediation committee for appointment. Appellate mediators shall be approved by and serve at the pleasure of the mediation committee. The mediation committee shall maintain a current roster of all individuals that have been approved to serve as appellate mediators. The roster shall indicate each individual's area(s) of expertise.

3. *Assignment.* Upon the transfer of an appeal to the settlement conference docket as hereinafter provided, the settlement administrator shall select an appellate mediator from the roster maintained by the mediation committee and assign that individual to the case. However, under no circumstances shall a judge of this court be assigned as an appellate mediator to any case that has been assigned to him or her for dispositional purposes. The settlement administrator shall make every reasonable effort to suitably match appellate mediators with cases that fall within their areas of expertise.

4. *Compensation.* Judges of this Court serving as appellate mediators shall receive no additional compensation. All other individuals serving as appellate

mediators shall be compensated at the rate of $125.00 per hour. Special consent must be obtained from the chairman of the mediation committee for any appellate mediator other than a judge of this court to devote more than three hours to any assigned case.

E. APPLICABILITY.

The Settlement Conference Program shall be applicable to appeals in accordance with Supreme Court Rule 310.1(b).

Appeals which have been assigned to a judge of this court for dispositional purposes are not eligible for inclusion in the Settlement Conference Program without the approval of the judge to whom the case is so assigned. Appeals brought pursuant to Supreme Court Rules 304(b)(2) and (5), 306, 307(a)(2) through (7), inclusive, and 308 and appeals which have been placed on an accelerated docket pursuant to Supreme Court Rule 311 shall not be assigned to the Settlement Conference Program unless the presiding judge of the division to which the case is assigned recommends it for inclusion within the program or the judge to whom the case has been assigned for dispositional purposes, if any, approves of the assignment.

F. CASE SELECTION.

1. *Settlement Status Report.* An appellant in a civil appeal filed with this court may file a "Settlement Status Report" in the form attached to this rule with the clerk of this court contemporaneously with the filing of the docketing statement. Consistent with the provisions of paragraph F2 below, nothing herein precludes this court from entertaining a "Settlement Status Report" requesting that this case be assigned to the Settlement Conference Program when filed by any party at any time. Notice of the filing of a "Settlement Status Report", along with a copy of same, shall be served upon all parties in accordance with the provisions of Supreme Court Rule 11.

2. *Motions for Assignment to the Settlement Conference Program.* On his or her own motion or on motion of any party, the presiding judge of the division to which a case is assigned may, with the approval of the judge to whom the case may have been assigned for dispositional purposes, if any, recommend to the mediation committee that a civil appeal be assigned to the Settlement Conference Program. When filed by a party, such motion shall be accompanied by a "Settlement Status Report" as provided in paragraph F1 above.

3. *Mediation Committee Review.* Upon receipt of a "Settlement Status Report" requesting assignment of a case to the Settlement Conference Program or a recommendation from a presiding judge of this court, the clerk of this court shall transmit a copy of the "Settlement Status Report" or recommendation to each member of the mediation committee, and, in the case of a "Settlement Status Report", to the presiding judge of the division to which the case is assigned. If the case has been previously assigned to a judge of

this court for dispositional purposes, the presiding judge of the division shall forward a copy of the "Settlement Status Report" to the judge to whom the case is assigned.

Within 10 days of the delivery of copies of the "Settlement Status Report" or recommendation from a presiding judge to the members of the mediation committee, the Mediation Committee shall evaluate the case to determine if the case is eligible for assignment to the Settlement Conference Program. If the case is eligible, the Mediation Committee shall so notify the chairman of the executive committee. Upon such notice, the chairman of the executive committee shall enter an order assigning the case to the Settlement Conference Program, transferring it to a settlement docket to be maintained and monitored by the mediation committee, and staying the filing of the record and/or briefs pending further order of court.

4. *Notification.* Upon the entry of an order assigning a case to the Settlement Conference Program, the settlement administrator shall immediately assign an appellate mediator to the case and the clerk of this court shall forward a written notice to the parties and the appellate mediator informing them that the case has been selected for inclusion in the Settlement Conference Program and that an appellate mediator has been appointed.

5. *Objection to Assignment.* Any party to an appeal may object to the case being assigned to the Settlement Conference Program by submitting a written objection to the settlement administrator. Such objections shall be submitted no later than 10 court days after the date upon which the clerk of this court mailed the written notice to the parties informing them that the case was selected for inclusion in the program. Copies of the objection need not be served on any opposing party or counsel; rather, upon receipt of any such objection, the settlement administrator shall send a written notice to all parties and the appellate mediator, informing them that an objection has been received and that, as a consequence, the case will be removed from the Settlement conference Program. With the mailing of such a notice, the appointment of the appellate mediator shall be considered terminated without fee. The settlement administrator shall deliver a copy of the objection to the chairman of the executive committee, who shall, unless otherwise directed by the chairman of the Mediation Committee, enter an order removing the case from the Settlement Conference Program, reassigning the case to the division of this court to which it was assigned prior to its assignment to the program, and reestablishing a record and/or briefing schedule. Thereafter, the clerk of this court shall mail a copy of such order to each party.

Objections filed pursuant to the terms of this section shall not be placed in the file of the case maintained by the clerk of this court and the name of the party filing the objection shall remain confidential. A separate confidential file containing objections shall be maintained by the settlement administrator, who shall not permit access thereto without an order entered by the chairman of the executive committee.

G. SETTLEMENT CONFERENCES.

1. *Scheduling.* Within 21 days of the assignment of a case to the Settlement Conference Program and provided that no timely objection to such assignment has been received, the settlement administrator, after consulting with the appellate mediator, shall furnish the parties with a written notice containing three proposed dates when the appellate mediator is available for an initial settlement conference. These dates shall be no earlier than 7 days and no later than 21 days after the date on which the notice of proposed dates is mailed. Within 5 days of the mailing of the notice of proposed dates, the parties shall advise the settlement administrator of their preferences as to a date. If a party fails to so notify the settlement administrator of a preferred date, it shall be presumed that the party is available for the initial conference on any of the suggested dates. Thereafter, the settlement administrator shall promptly select one of the proposed dates, taking into consideration, to the extent possible, the parties' preferences and notify the parties and the appellate mediator of the date of the initial settlement conference. The scheduling of any settlement conferences after the initial conference shall be made at the direction of the appellate mediator in consultation with the attorneys representing the parties, with notice to the special administrator.

2. *Location of Settlement Conferences.* All settlement conferences shall be held in rooms provided for that purpose at 160 N. LaSalle Street, Chicago, Illinois.

3. *Participation.* Participation by all parties to an appeal assigned to the Settlement Conference Program is mandatory unless or until the case has been removed from the program by order of the chairman of the executive committee. Unless ordered otherwise by the appellate mediator, parties may be represented at settlement conferences by their attorneys of record. Each attorney representing a client at a settlement conference must be able to contact his or her client by telephone during the conference. If the party is a corporation, partnership, or other body or organization, the attorney attending the conference must be able to contact a person having settlement authority.

4. *Role of the Appellate Mediator.* The appellate mediator's role is to preside over settlement conferences, facilitate the voluntary resolution of the case, assist the parties in simplifying issues, and set the dates for continued settlement conferences provided no date for any settlement conference may be extended for more than 45 days after assignment of the case to the Settlement Conference Program unless approved by the chairman of the Executive Committee. The appellate mediator has the authority to terminate the settlement conference at any time that, in his or her opinion, the process has become unproductive for any reason. If the appellate mediator does terminate a settlement conference, he or she shall so notify the settlement administrator in writing. Promptly thereafter, the chairman of the executive committee shall enter an order removing the case from the Settlement Conference Program, reassigning the case to the division from which it came, and reestablishing a record and/or briefing schedule.

5. *Nature of the Conference.* The settlement conference shall be an informal confidential meeting presided over by the appellate mediator. The agenda for the conference shall be set by the appellate mediator, who may request that the parties complete and file with the settlement administrator a pre-conference memorandum on forms approved by the mediation committee. The sequence of presentation at a settlement conference shall be at the discretion of the appellate mediator, and he or she shall be at liberty during the course of a scheduled conference to speak to the parties separately.

H. SETTLEMENT AGREEMENTS.

1. *Dismissals.* If the settlement conference results in the settlement of the case and the parties agree to dismiss the appeal, the parties shall execute a stipulation to dismiss and file same with the clerk of this court. Upon the filing of a stipulation to dismiss, an order dismissing the appeal shall be entered by three judges assigned to the mediation committee.

2. *Agreements to Narrow Issues.* If the settlement conference does not result in the settlement of the case, but the parties do agree to narrow the issues on appeal, they shall memorialize their agreement in writing and prepare a proposed order reciting the terms thereof. If the order is approved by the mediation committee, it shall be entered by three judges assigned to the mediation committee and shall be binding upon the parties unless modified by subsequent order of this court. Upon the entry of an order approving the parties' agreement to narrow the issues on appeal, the chairman of the executive committee shall enter an order removing the case from the Settlement Conference Program, reassigning the case to the division of this court to which it was assigned prior to its assignment to the program, and reestablishing the filing of the record and/or briefing schedule.

I. CONFIDENTIALITY.

The settlement conference and all documents prepared by the parties, the appellate mediator and the settlement administrator shall be confidential. No transcript or recording shall be made of any settlement conference and no mention of the settlement discussions shall be made in any brief filed with this court or in oral argument. Except for orders entered by this court and written stipulations and agreements entered into by the parties, documents prepared by the parties and received by the appellate mediator or the settlement administrator as part of the Settlement Conference Program shall not be filed of record with the clerk of this court and, upon the dismissal of the case or its removal from the Settlement Conference Program, which ever is first to occur, shall be destroyed by the settlement administrator.

J. SANCTIONS.

Failure to participate in a settlement conference in good faith, failure to attend a regularly scheduled settlement conference, or failure to comply with the rules of this court applicable to settlement conferences may subject a party to the imposition of sanctions under Supreme Court Rule 375.

K. STATISTICAL REPORTING.

The settlement administrator shall maintain statistics as to the number and type of cases which are: considered by the mediation committee for inclusion in the Settlement Conference Program; assigned to the Settlement Conference Program; removed from the program on the objection of a party; removed from the program without any settlement having been reached; dismissed by agreement of the parties while assigned to the program; and removed from the program after the entry of an order narrowing the issues on appeal. The settlement administrator shall report those statistics to the members of this court annually and to the Director of the Administrative Office of the Illinois Courts annually.

Effective January 1, 2005.

IN THE APPELLATE COURT OF ILLINOIS FIRST DISTRICT

)	Appellate Court # _____
)	Trial Court # _____
)	Trial Judge _____
)	

SETTLEMENT STATUS REPORT

Is there a potential for settlement of this case through assignment to the Settlement Conference Program pursuant to Illinois Supreme Court Rule 310.1?

Yes _____   No _____

If yes, the undersigned requests that this matter be scheduled for a Settlement Conference Program pursuant to Illinois Supreme Court Rule 310.1 and First District Illinois Appellate Court Rule 37.

Nature of this Cause of Action (check appropriate box):

☐ Tort   ☐ Contract   ☐ Probate
☐ Other (if so, briefly specify) _____

Brief statement of pertinent issues (50 words or less): _____

_____

Attorney(s) for Appellant(s)/Appellee(s)
Name _____
Address _____
Telephone Number ____

Name, address and phone number of appellant/appellee attorney(s):

Name _____
Address _____
Telephone Number ____

Rule 38. Briefs

A. No Briefs May Filed Until Record is Filed. No party may file a brief unless the record (or Certificate in Lieu of Record) has been filed.

B. Page Limits/Orders for Supplemental Briefs. When the Court issues an order allowing a supplemental brief to be filed, the supplemental brief shall be limited to 20 pages unless the party files a motion seeking additional pages in advance of the filing of the supplemental brief. A party filing a Motion for Leave to File A Supplemental Brief must include in the proposed order a date by which the Supplemental Brief will be filed if the order is allowed.

C. Parties Who Have Appeared But Will Not be Filing A Brief. Any party who has filed an appearance but will not be submitting a brief shall send a letter to the Clerk of the Appellate Court on or before the date the party's brief would have been due advising that no brief will be filed by that party. All counsel must be copied on the letter.

D. Adopting the Brief of Another Party. If a party intends to adopt the brief of another party, the party seeking to adopt the brief shall file a motion to adopt within 14 days of the filing of the brief being adopted.

Adopted June 9, 2008, effective July 1, 2008.

UNIFORM ADMINISTRATIVE AND PROCEDURAL RULES APPELLATE COURTS SECOND, THIRD, FOURTH, AND FIFTH DISTRICTS

Including Amendments Received Through April 1, 2016

The Uniform Rules set out herein were adopted April 14, 1967, effective January 1, 1967.

Rule 1. Sessions

(1) The Court of each District shall be in session throughout the year, as its judicial business requires, and shall sit periodically for the purpose of hearing oral arguments at the direction of the Presiding Judge thereof.

Formerly Ill.Rev.Stat.1991, ch. 110A, ¶ 901.

Rule 2. Call of Cases

(2) The Presiding Judge of each respective District shall determine the days the Court shall sit for the purpose of hearing oral arguments and shall so inform its Clerk, who shall forthwith prepare a call of cases as directed by the Presiding Judge, indicating thereon the general number of the case, the respective names of the parties—appellant and appellee—the order in which the several cases will be called for argument and submission, and the day and hour the Court will sit. When so prepared, the Clerk shall forthwith send a copy of such call to counsel of record representing the respective parties in each of the several cases appearing on such call, or to the litigant if not represented by counsel. At least seven (7) days shall intervene between the date the Clerk mails a copy of the call to the respective attorneys and the date the case is subject to call.

Formerly Ill.Rev.Stat.1991, ch. 110A, ¶ 902.

Rule 3. Hearing

(3) The Court shall hear the oral arguments in such cases pursuant to such call. The Presiding Judge shall call the cases in the order listed by the Clerk, and the call shall continue until all of the listed cases are heard and submitted for opinion.

Formerly Ill.Rev.Stat.1991, ch. 110A, ¶ 903.

Rule 4. Assignment of Number to Cause

(4) Every cause or proceeding, upon the filing of the initial instrument or record on appeal, shall be given a general number by the Clerk, which it shall permanently retain.

Formerly Ill.Rev.Stat.1991, ch. 110A, ¶ 904.

Rule 5. Library

(5) The Clerk of each respective District is hereby designated as the Librarian of the Court for such District, and he shall not permit any person, except Judges of the Court, to take any book from the library without the consent of the Court or of the Presiding Judge. No book shall be marked or underlined, and no page shall be folded down. Any person who violates the provisions of this rule may be held in contempt of the Court.

Formerly Ill.Rev.Stat.1991, ch. 110A, ¶ 905.

Rule 6. Repeal of Prior Administrative Rules and Adoption of New Rules

(6) All Administrative Rules heretofore in force and effect in the Second, Third, Fourth and Fifth Appellate Court Districts are hereby repealed; and these Administrative Rules are adopted, effective January 1, 1967, in lieu of all Administrative Rules heretofore in force.

Formerly Ill.Rev.Stat.1991, ch. 110A, ¶ 906.

Rule 7. Practice and Procedure

(7) The Rules of Practice & Procedure heretofore adopted by the respective Courts of the Second, Third, Fourth and Fifth Appellate Court Districts, effective January 1, 1956, together with all amendments thereto, be, and the same are hereby set aside and rescinded. Practice in said Appellate Court Districts of the State of Illinois shall be governed by the Rules of Practice promulgated by the Supreme Court of the State of Illinois, effective January 1, 1967, and the order of the Supreme Court adopting such Rules dated November 28, 1966.

Formerly Ill.Rev.Stat.1991, ch. 110A, ¶ 907.

Rule 8. Citation of Opinions

(8) The opinions of the Illinois Appellate Court which have been published in abstract form only, shall not be cited in the briefs of litigants unless the entire text of said abstract opinion is appended to the brief. When on oral argument counsel cites authorities from other jurisdictions, he shall provide this Court with four (4) copies of the full text of such authorities. Amended in 1977.

Formerly Ill.Rev.Stat.1991, ch. 110A, ¶ 908.

Rule 9. Excerpts from the Record

(9) Pursuant to the provisions of Supreme Court Rule 342(b), the Clerks of said respective Districts, upon request of the appellant, may prepare and file excerpts from the record, as provided in said Rule 342, upon the advance payment to said Clerk of the sum of twenty-five (25) cents per page therefor. It shall be the obligation of counsel for appellant and for appellee to prepare the Table of Contents as required by Rule 342(d).

Formerly Ill.Rev.Stat.1991, ch. 110A, ¶ 909.

Rule 10. Filing of Order

(10) The respective Clerks of the Second, Third, Fourth and Fifth Appellate Court Districts are hereby directed to file and enter this Administrative and Procedural order of record as of January 1, 1967, and to forthwith file a certified copy thereof with the Administrative Director of the Illinois Supreme Court.

Formerly Ill.Rev.Stat.1991, ch. 110A, ¶ 910.

APPELLATE COURT RULES, SECOND DISTRICT

Including Amendments Received Through April 1, 2016

Article
I. General Rules.
II. Building Rules.
III. Personnel Rules.

Effective June 4, 2013 (Rescinds Prior Rules effective October 4, 2011)

Explanatory Notes

Supreme Court Rule 22(h) authorizes this court to adopt rules that are consistent with the Illinois Supreme Court Rules and Illinois statutes. The Uniform Administrative and Procedural Rules Appellate Courts Second, Third, Fourth, and Fifth Districts (the Uniform Administrative Rules) also provide rules for this court. To facilitate the administration of justice, the Illinois Appellate Court, Second District (the Court), hereby enacts the following rules (the Local Rules) in addition to the Supreme Court Rules and the Uniform Administrative Rules. In the event of a conflict, the Supreme Court Rules and the Uniform Administrative Rules shall control. All prior rules issued by the Court are hereby rescinded.

Adopted effective Oct. 4, 2011. Amended effective March 4, 2014.

Preamble

These Local Rules are set forth to facilitate the administration of justice in the Court. The Court may at its discretion alter, suspend, rescind, or waive these Local Rules, in whole or in part, as the ends of justice require.

Adopted effective Oct. 4, 2011.

ARTICLE I. GENERAL RULES

Rule 101. Filing materials with the Court

(a) Materials (including but not limited to records, exhibits, briefs, motions, and memoranda) to be filed with the Court must be directed to the Clerk's Office either by personal delivery, or by U.S. Mail or third-party commercial carrier, at the following address:

Clerk of the Illinois Appellate Court, Second District

55 Symphony Way

Elgin, Illinois 60120

(b) Except as provided in Supreme Court Rule 341(*l*) and Local Rule 111, the Court does not accept electronic filings.

(c) The Court's acceptance of a filing does not itself establish that the filing is timely or otherwise complies with the Supreme Court Rules or any other applicable rule.

(d) The Clerk's Office will not correct any filings on any party's behalf.

(1) If a party seeks to make typographical corrections to a filing, then the party seeking to make the corrections must file a motion in the Clerk's Office identifying the changes to be made. If the motion is granted, the Clerk's Office will notify the party seeking to make the corrections of a time when the filing will be available for that party to come to the Clerk's Office to effectuate the corrections outlined in the motion.

(2) If a party seeks to make substantive changes to a filing, then the party seeking to make the changes must file a motion seeking leave to withdraw the filing and to file a substitute.

Adopted eff. Oct. 4, 2011. Amended eff. June 4, 2013; March 4, 2014.

Rule 102. Requirements for Documents Filed With the Court

(a) All documents filed with the Court, including motions, must comply with the formatting guidelines of Supreme Court Rules 341(a), (f), and (g).

(b) Every document filed in the Court shall be personally signed by at least one attorney of record and shall list that person's professional address. Parties who are not represented by an attorney shall sign their names and provide their addresses.

Adopted eff. Oct. 4, 2011.

Rule 103. Motions for Extension of Time

(a) A party moving for an extension of time must comply with Supreme Court Rules 361(a) and (f) and, where applicable, 610. In addition to the information required by those rules, the movant's affidavit must provide:

(1) The number of days requested and the number of days granted on each of the previous motions for extension of time filed by the movant, and the total number of days granted on all of those previous motions;

(2) The total number of days requested and the total number of days granted on all of the previous motions for extension of time filed by other parties;

(3) The number of days that will have elapsed from the date of filing of the notice of appeal to the date that the case will be ready for disposition, pursuant to Local Rule 105 or 107, if the present extension and no further extension is granted; and

(4) In a criminal case, the status of the defendant's sentence (where applicable) or, in any case that may become moot due to the passage of time on appeal, the date on which the appeal may become moot.

(b) A motion for an extension of time should be filed, where practicable, at least 10 days prior to the date to be extended if served by mail or by third-party commercial carrier or at least 5 days prior to the date to be extended if served personally, by facsimile, or by e-mail.

(c) Motions for extension of time in cases accelerated pursuant to Supreme Court Rule 311(a) or 660A and/or Local Rule 106 must comply with subsection (a) of this Local Rule and Local Rule 106(d).

Adopted eff. Oct. 4, 2011. Amended eff. June 4, 2013.

Rule 104. Records on Appeal not to Include Physical Evidence or Photostatic Copies

(a) The circuit clerks of the respective counties within the Second District of the Illinois Appellate Court are not to send to the Court any physical evidence included in the record. Examples of such evidence that should not be sent are: weapons, narcotics or drug paraphernalia, materials marked as "biohazard," and x-rays. Evidence of a descriptive or documentary nature, including video recordings, audio recordings, and photographs, should be included in the record on appeal. If physical evidence is required for consideration of an appeal, the Court, *sua sponte* or upon motion of a party, will direct the circuit court to transfer such evidence.

(b) Except where the circuit clerks are to submit electronic records pursuant to Local Rule 111, the circuit clerks are to submit records containing the original documents from the circuit court's file, and not photostatic copies. However, photostatic copies may be submitted if:

(1) The original papers of the record do not exist; or

(2) The Chief Judge of the circuit from which the appeal originates files a letter with the Court stating good cause why the original is not available and why a photostatic copy of the record should be filed in its stead. Whether the letter filed by the Chief Judge states good cause shall be determined by the Court.

Adopted eff. Oct. 4, 2011. Amended eff. June 4, 2013; July 22, 2014.

Rule 105. Disposition of Cases

(a) Where no appellee's brief is timely filed, a case will be considered ready for disposition two weeks after the day the brief is due to be filed, unless a timely motion for extension of time to file the appellee's brief is filed. If a timely motion or timely motions for extension of time are filed but no brief is subsequently timely filed, the case will be considered ready for disposition two weeks after the due date determined by the resolution of the motion or motions for extension.

(b) All other cases will be considered ready for disposition upon the timely filing of the appellant's reply brief (or cross-reply brief, if applicable). Where no reply brief (or cross-reply brief) is timely filed, a case will be considered ready for disposition on the day the reply brief (or cross-reply brief) is due to be filed, unless a timely motion for extension of time to file the reply brief (or cross-reply brief) is filed. If a timely motion or timely motions for extension of time are filed but no reply brief (or cross-reply brief) is subsequently timely filed, the case will be considered ready for disposition as of the due date determined by the resolution of the motion or motions for extension.

Adopted eff. Oct. 4, 2011. Amended eff. June 4, 2013.

Rule 106. Certain Cases Accelerated

(a) In addition to the categories of cases listed in Supreme Court Rules 311(a) and 660A, the Court will also accelerate appeals from orders granting or denying petitions for removal.

(b) In order to expedite appeals under Supreme Court Rules 311(a) and 660A and this Local Rule, parties may file memoranda in lieu of formal briefs. Such memoranda need not comply with all the requirements applicable to formal briefs but must comply with the requirements of Supreme Court Rules 341(a), (b), (d), (e), (f), (g), and (j), and Local Rule 102.

(c) Unless the Court orders otherwise, all cases listed in Supreme Court Rule 311(a) shall adhere to the following schedule:

(1) The record on appeal (or certificate in lieu of record), including the common-law record and the transcript of proceedings, shall be filed no later than 35 days after the filing of the notice of appeal. Any request for extension of the time for filing shall be accompanied by an affidavit of the court clerk or court reporter stating the reason for the delay, and shall be served on the trial judge and the chief judge of the circuit. Lack of advance payment shall

not be a reason for noncompliance with filing deadlines.

(2) The appellant's brief or memorandum in lieu of a formal brief must be filed within 21 days of the filing of the record or certificate with the Court.

(3) The appellee's brief or memorandum in lieu of a formal brief must be filed within 21 days thereafter.

(4) Any reply brief or memorandum in lieu of a formal brief must be filed within 7 days thereafter.

(5) In the case of a cross-appeal, the cross-reply brief or memorandum in lieu of a formal brief must be filed within 7 days thereafter.

(d) Unless the Court orders otherwise, all cases listed in Supreme Court Rule 660A shall adhere to the following schedule:

(1) The record on appeal (or certificate in lieu of record), including the common-law record and the transcript of proceedings, shall be filed no later than 35 days after the filing of the notice of appeal. Any request for extension of the time for filing shall be accompanied by an affidavit of the court clerk or court reporter stating the reason for the delay, and shall be served on the trial judge and the chief judge of the circuit. Lack of advance payment shall not be a reason for noncompliance with filing deadlines.

(2) The appellant's brief or memorandum in lieu of a formal brief must be filed within 28 days of the filing of the record or certificate with the Court.

(3) The appellee's brief or memorandum in lieu of a formal brief must be filed within 28 days thereafter.

(4) Any reply brief or memorandum in lieu of a formal brief must be filed within 7 days thereafter.

(5) In the case of a cross-appeal, the cross-reply brief or memorandum in lieu of a formal brief must be filed within 7 days thereafter.

(e) Motions for extension of time are disfavored and shall be granted only for compelling circumstances.

(1) A motion for an extension must comply with Local Rule 103(a).

(2) When a motion for an extension is based on a delay in the preparation of the record, the motion shall detail the proceedings at the status hearing required by Supreme Court Rule 311(a)(3) or 660A(b), including the trial court's determination of the status of the case, the trial judge's actions to expedite the preparation of the record, and whether the trial judge has requested the chief judge's assistance in resolving any filing delays. The motion shall also attach a file-stamped copy of any order entered at the status hearing and an affidavit of the clerk or court reporter stating the reason for the delay.

(3) A motion for an extension must be filed at least 10 days prior to the date to be extended if served by mail or by third-party commercial carrier or at least 5 days prior to the date to be extended if served personally, by facsimile, or by e-mail.

(4) The Court may require a personal appearance by the attorney or party requesting the extension.

(f) Motions should be served personally, by facsimile, or by e-mail whenever possible.

(g) Before filing any motion, a party shall confer with opposing counsel and inquire as to whether opposing counsel intends to file an objection. The results of that inquiry shall be stated in the motion. Adopted eff. Oct. 4, 2011. Amended eff. June 4, 2013; March 4, 2014; July 22, 2014; Oct. 6, 2015.

Rule 107. Disposition of Accelerated Cases

(a) Where no appellee's brief is timely filed, a case accelerated pursuant to Supreme Court Rule 311(a) or 660A and/or Local Rule 106 will be considered ready for disposition three days after the day that the brief is due to be filed, unless a timely motion for extension of time to file the appellee's brief is filed. If a timely motion or timely motions for extension of time are filed but no appellee's brief is subsequently timely filed, the case will be considered ready for disposition three days after the due date determined by the resolution of the motion or motions for extension.

(b) All other accelerated cases will be considered ready for disposition upon the timely filing of the appellant's reply brief (or cross-reply brief, if applicable). Where no reply brief (or cross-reply brief) is timely filed, a case will be considered ready for disposition on the due date for the reply brief (or cross-reply brief), unless a timely motion for extension of time is filed. If a timely motion or timely motions for extension are filed but no reply brief (or cross-reply brief) is subsequently timely filed, the case will be considered ready for disposition as of the due date determined by the resolution of the motion or motions for extension.

Adopted eff. Oct. 4, 2011. Amended eff. June 4, 2013.

Rule 108. Emergency Motions

Pursuant to Supreme Court Rule 361(g), emergency motions shall be filed and disposed of as follows:

(a) An emergency motion may be filed only if an appeal has been docketed. The title of the motion shall include the words "Emergency Motion." If the motion requires the Court to act within a specific time, that information shall be set out in the first paragraph of the motion. The motion shall specify the nature of the emergency and the grounds for the specific relief requested. The motion shall also state what relief was sought in the circuit court or why no relief was sought in that court. The movant shall attach to the motion a copy of every circuit court and appellate court document relevant to the motion. An emergency motion should be filed only when it involves a genuine emergency.

(b) The movant shall immediately serve the motion on every other party personally, by facsimile, or by e-mail. The type of service made shall be specifically noted on the proof of service filed with the motion.

(c) Except in extraordinary circumstances necessitating an earlier ruling on the motion, or unless opposing counsel has indicated no objection to the motion, the Court will allow any non-moving party 3 days to respond to an emergency motion.

Adopted eff. Oct. 4, 2011. Amended eff. June 4, 2013.

Rule 109. Length and Substance of Oral Arguments

(a) Each side will receive a total of 15 minutes to present its main argument, and the appellant or appellants will receive a total of 5 additional minutes to present rebuttal.

(b) Oral arguments shall omit the recitation of the facts and the procedural history of the case except to the extent necessary to frame the issues that are presented on appeal.

Adopted eff. Oct. 4, 2011.

Rule 110. Availability and Copying of Materials

(a) The Clerk's Office will not photocopy for any party or non-party any documents filed with the Clerk's Office. These restrictions may be waived by the Court on motion.

(b) Any filed materials, not including those filed under seal or impounded, will be made available for review upon request by any party or non-party. Parties may request filed materials from the record of any appeal to which they are a party, and the materials will be made available as soon as practicable pursuant to Supreme Court Rule 372. Non–parties may view filed materials by making a written request to the Clerk at least 7 days before the date on which the non-party desires to view the materials. Before making such materials available to non-parties, the Court may conduct its own review and redact any sensitive information appearing on the materials. The Court may also monitor any review of the materials in order to ensure the integrity of the documents and the privacy of such sensitive information.

(c) The Court's computer system and the information contained in that system, including but not limited to internal electronic communications and internal administrative documents, will not be printed out or provided to any party or his or her attorney, or to the general public.

Adopted eff. Oct. 4, 2011. Amended eff. June 4, 2013; Feb. 3, 2015.

Rule 111. Electronic Records on Appeal

(a) In all cases in which the notice of appeal is filed on or after June 1, 2014, the circuit clerks of Boone, Carroll, De Kalb, Du Page, Jo Daviess, Kendall, Lake, Lee, McHenry, Ogle, Stephenson, and Winnebago Counties shall electronically transfer records on appeal (common–law records and reports of proceedings) to the Clerk of the Court via i2file.net. In all cases in which the notice of appeal is filed on or after October 1, 2014, the circuit clerk of Kane County shall electronically transfer records on appeal (common–law records and reports of proceedings) to the Clerk of the Court via i2file.net. The electronic reports of proceedings shall be formatted with text searchable by both word and phrase. Except as provided by Local Rule 104(a), the circuit clerks shall transfer exhibits physically, not electronically.

(b) Upon request by the Clerk of the Court, the circuit clerks shall create and transport to the Clerk of the Court the paper copy of the record on appeal, prepared and certified in accordance with the Supreme Court Rules. Otherwise, the circuit clerks shall not create paper records on appeal but shall retain original common-law records and reports of proceedings in accordance with the Supreme Court Rules.

(c) Throughout the duration of an appeal, the Clerk of the Court shall retain an unmodified copy of the electronic record on appeal and, where the paper copy of the record on appeal has been requested and prepared, the paper copy of the record on appeal, in accordance with the Supreme Court Rules. After the Court issues its mandate in the appeal, the Clerk of the Court may delete the copy of the electronic record on appeal and shall transport to the circuit clerk any paper record created at the Court's request and the exhibits.

(d) When a party requests the record on appeal from the Court, that party will receive a copy of the electronic record on appeal. If a party submits to the Clerk of the Court a written request for the paper record on appeal, the Clerk of the Court shall immediately forward that request to the circuit clerk with a direction to immediately create and transport the paper record on appeal pursuant to this Local Rule. The written request shall include: (1) the full name of the case on appeal (and, if applicable, the case(s) with which the case is consolidated); (2) the appellate case number(s); (3) the circuit case number(s); and (4) the requesting party's name, address, phone number, and e-mail address. The Clerk of the Court shall not send the paper record on appeal, as opposed to a copy thereof, to any correctional institution.

(e) A party who wishes to access the electronic record on appeal must register a user name and a password and provide a valid e-mail address at i2file.net. The party then must make a written request through i2file.net in the standard pdf format and in the form prescribed by the Court.

(f) Upon receipt of a written request for access to the electronic record on appeal, the Clerk of the Court shall have the sole authority to grant or deny access to the electronic record on appeal and, if granted, may deny or revoke future access to the electronic record on appeal.

(g) Upon receipt of a copy of the electronic record on appeal, a party may search, bookmark, and annotate that copy, which need not be returned to the Court. All markings shall be secure and shall be unique to that copy. When that copy is deleted, all markings shall be destroyed. No party shall view or access another party's copy.

(h) Upon the grant of a motion to supplement the electronic record on appeal, the supplement shall be prepared as a separate volume. The volume shall be paginated with consecutive numbers starting with the next number following the last number in the preceding volume.

(i) If an electronic record on appeal includes documents that are impounded, sealed, or otherwise protected, an Impounded Table of Contents will list all such documents according to the dates they were filed with the circuit clerk. The electronic record on appeal shall contain, as applicable, separate volumes entitled Impounded Common Law Record and Impounded Report of Proceedings. The Impounded Common Law Record shall be paginated with consecutive numbers starting with one, with an "IC" preceding each page number, and shall contain no more than 250 pages per volume. The Impounded Report of Proceedings shall follow the same requirements, except that an "IR" shall precede each page number.

(j) In all appeals, except as provided below, any party or attorney of record on appeal wishing to access impounded or sealed documents in the electronic record on appeal must move to access those documents. Upon written motion supported by affidavit, specifying the basis for access, the Court, in its sole discretion, shall grant or deny authorization to access any such documents. However, in criminal appeals, and in all appeals under Supreme Court Rules 311(a) and 660A, attorneys of record on appeal may access, without motion, all impounded documents in the electronic record on appeal. Such access without motion does not extend to *sealed* documents in the electronic record on appeal.

Adopted eff. Oct. 4, 2011. Amended eff. Nov. 1, 2012; June 4, 2013; March 4, 2014; July 22, 2014; Feb. 3, 2015; Oct. 6, 2015.

ARTICLE II. BUILDING RULES

Rule 201.   Clerk's Office Hours of Operation

Except in extraordinary circumstances, the Clerk's Office will be open for the transaction of public business from 8:30 a.m. to 4:30 p.m. each day, except Saturdays, Sundays, and those legal holidays determined by the Illinois Supreme Court.

Adopted eff. Oct. 4, 2011. Amended eff. June 4, 2013.

Rule 202.   No Smoking in the Courthouse

Smoking is not allowed in the courthouse.

Adopted eff. Oct. 4, 2011.

ARTICLE III. PERSONNEL RULES

Rule 301.   Restrictions on Communication With Court Staff

The members of the Court's staff will not render legal opinions or advice to litigants or potential litigants before the Court, or their counsel. All litigants and potential litigants before the Court, and their counsel, shall be cognizant of these restrictions if they have occasion to communicate with the Court's staff.

Adopted eff. Oct. 4, 2011.

APPELLATE COURT ORDERS, THIRD DISTRICT

Including Amendments Received Through April 1, 2016

Administrative Order One

The Circuit Clerks of the respective counties within the Third District of the Illinois Appellate Court are requested not to send to this Court with the record on appeal any physical evidence included in the record as an exhibit. Evidence of a descriptive or documentary nature, such as papers or photographs, should still be included in the record on appeal. If an exhibit of physical evidence is required for consideration on appeal, the Circuit Clerk may forward to the Clerk of this Court such exhibit only upon the written request of one of the Justices of this Court.

It is the further order of this Court that in preparing the record on appeal, Circuit Clerks are to submit for filing records containing the original documents from the Circuit Clerk's file and not photostatic copies unless such original papers do not exist.

ENTERED: April 29, 1980

Administrative Order Twenty–Seven

IT IS THIS DAY ORDERED BY THE COURT THAT video and audio tapes included as part of the record on appeal are not to be released to the parties or their attorneys. If the parties or their attorneys need to review such tapes they may do so at the circuit court, if the court has such equipment available, or at this court. Alternatively, the circuit court may provide the parties or their attorneys duplicates of the original tapes if it desires to provide this service. If the circuit court does not wish to provide this service, it may send the tapes to this court and this court will, upon request, provide duplicates of the tapes for a fee commensurate with the cost of production thereof.

ENTERED: May 20, 1992.

Administrative Order Thirty–Four

THE THIRD DISTRICT APPELLATE COURT finds that a problem exists with regard to non-exempt appellants failing to pay the circuit courts of this district for the preparation of the record on appeal. The Court further finds that the circuit courts are nonetheless preparing the records and filing them with this Court in the belief that this Court may find them in contempt for failing to do so. This Court hereby declares that it will not require the circuit courts of this appellate district to prepare and file the record on appeal in any case where the appellant is required to pay a record-preparation fee but has failed to do so.

ENTERED: May 11, 1994.

Administrative Order Thirty–Six

When filing an Emergency Motion, the moving party must notify the opposing party or attorney by telephone prior to filing and transmit by facsimile a copy to the opposing party or attorney. This requirement does **not** excuse the moving party from complying with the normal notice requirements. Emergency motions shall be filed in this court by personal delivery or, if that is impractical, by overnight mail. They shall be prominently labelled as **"EMERGENCY"** Motions.

ENTERED: January 19, 1995.

Administrative Order Thirty–Seven

THE THIRD DISTRICT APPELLATE COURT finds that a problem exists with regard to non-exempt appellants failing to pay court reporters for preparation of reports of proceedings. The Court further finds that court reporters are nonetheless preparing reports of proceedings in the belief that this Court may find them in contempt for failing to do so. This Court hereby declares that it will not require court reporters to prepare reports of proceedings in any case where the appellant is required to pay a preparation fee but has failed to do so.

ENTERED: June 21, 1995.

Administrative Order Thirty–Eight

THE THIRD DISTRICT APPELLATE COURT will, effective this date, accept condensed Reports of Proceedings in which four transcript pages are compressed onto a single page. If the party paying for the reports of proceedings objects to the compressed format, the court reporters shall use the standard format.

ENTERED: July 18, 1995.

Administrative Order Thirty–Nine

IT IS THIS DAY ORDERED BY THE COURT that Briefs filed in the Third District Appellate Court shall contain Statements of Facts NOT EXCEEDING FIFTEEN PAGES in length.

ENTERED: October 11, 1995.

Administrative Order Forty–Three

IT IS THIS DAY ORDERED BY THE COURT that Motions and Responses thereto filed in the Third District Appellate Court shall NOT EXCEED EIGHT PAGES in length. Moreover, they shall be neatly and legibly produced on paper 8–½ by 11 inches, double spaced, with the text in type not smaller than standard elite typewriting and not to exceed 6 by 8–½ inches.

Administrative Order Forty–Seven

(Modified May 19, 2010)

Pursuant to our authority under Supreme Court Rule 311(a)(6) to adopt mandatory procedures to ensure completion of Rule 311(a) appeals within 150 days after the filing of the notice of appeal, we hereby adopt the following local rules. These rules augment Rule 311(a) and will not excuse noncompliance with its specific terms.

1. The clerk of each circuit court in the Third District is ordered to:

A. Post a notice informing all attorneys and parties of the need to include the following statement in bold type on every document: **THIS APPEAL INVOLVES A QUESTION OF CHILD CUSTODY, ADOPTION, TERMINATION OF PARENTAL RIGHTS OR OTHER MATTER AFFECTING THE BEST INTERESTS OF A CHILD.**

B. Stamp every document, including but not limited to the notice of appeal and the record, which the circuit court clerks transmit to this court in a case falling within the scope of Supreme Court Rule 311(a), with the following statement in bold type: **THIS APPEAL INVOLVES A QUESTION OF CHILD CUSTODY, ADOPTION, TERMINATION OF PARENTAL RIGHTS OR OTHER MATTER AFFECTING THE BEST INTERESTS OF A CHILD.**

2. Extensions for preparation of the record on appeal shall be allowed only for the most compelling circumstances. Pursuant to paragraph (a)(4) of Rule 311, the trial court has the authority to allow one extension. In no event shall that extension total more than 10 days. The circuit court shall immediately notify the clerk of this court when any extension is granted and the length of such extension.

3. In order to expedite these appeals, the circuit court clerk is encouraged to file a certificate in lieu of record with this court in compliance with Supreme Court Rule 325 and to transmit the record directly to the appellant's attorney. The attorneys are encouraged to transmit the record directly between themselves with a notice to the clerk of this court of the date and method of transmission.

4. From the date the record on appeal is filed with this court, the appellant shall file his or her brief within 14 days; the appellee shall file his or her brief within 14 days from the appellant's due date; and the appellant shall file his or her reply brief, if any, within 7 days from the appellee's due date. Where there are multiple appellants or appellees, their briefs shall be due on the same dates.

5. Briefs complying with Supreme Court Rules 341 and 342 shall be filed in all appeals.

6. This court will look with extreme disfavor upon any requests for extensions in the briefing schedule and will grant such requests only for the most compelling circumstances. As with all appeals, the briefing schedule will continue to run while any motions are pending.

7. Motions and responses thereto shall be filed by facsimile or in person with this court and shall be served upon the opposing party by facsimile or in person. Additionally, a hard copy shall be mailed to the court at the time of the facsimile transmission. The proof of service shall state that service by facsimile or in person has been made upon the opposing party and this court, and that a hard copy has been mailed to the court if the filing was by facsimile. The opposing party shall file its response, if any, within three days. Again, it should be noted that motions do not stay or extend the filing schedule.

ENTERED: May 19, 2010.

Administrative Order Forty–Eight

Illinois Supreme Court Rule 341(e)(3) states that "[t]he appellant must include a concise statement of the applicable standard of review for each issue, with citation to authority, either in the discussion of the issue in the argument or under a separate heading placed before the discussion in the argument." This Court hereby orders that the appellant shall set forth the standard of review under a separate section entitled "Standard of Review." This section shall appear at the beginning of the arguments on each issue raised. If the appellee disagrees with the standard of review set forth by the appellant, appellee shall so indicate and shall likewise set forth its version of the applicable standard of review in a separate section at the beginning of each issue's argument section.

Setting forth the standard of review separately will aid this Court in determining prior to submission of the case whether this requirement has been met. Moreover, the appellee and the Court will be able to more easily determine the appellant's contention regarding the applicable standard of review.

ENTERED: October 7, 2004.

Administrative Order Fifty–Two

Pursuant to Supreme Court Rule 341(1), appellants and appellees are encouraged to file five (5) electronic copies of their briefs on CD–ROM disks, along with the usual nine (9) paper copies. Electronic briefs shall be presented in Adobe Acrobat format. The appellant shall file its electronic copies with its reply brief so that both the original brief and the reply brief are on one disk. Likewise, cross-appellants shall file their electronic copies with their cross-reply briefs.

ENTERED: October 12, 2006.

Administrative Order Fifty–Seven

IT IS THIS DAY ORDERED BY THE COURT that when the appendix to a brief exceeds 20 pages, the party shall separately bind the entire appendix and provide the Court with nine copies. The appendix shall in all other ways comply with Supreme Court Rule 342(a).

ENTERED: May 19, 2010.

ADMINISTRATIVE AND PROCEDURAL RULES OF THE ILLINOIS APPELLATE COURT, FOURTH DISTRICT

Including Amendments Received Through April 1, 2016

GENERAL PROCEDURES

Rule
1. Filing and Form of Documents Filed in the Appellate Court.
2. Appearance and Withdrawal of Attorneys.
3. Address Changes.
4. Contents of the Record on Appeal.
5. Review of Administrative Orders.
6. Briefs.
7. Filing Fees and Reproduction of Materials.
8. Motions.
9. Emergency Motions.
10. Disposition of Cases.
11. Mandatory Accelerated Disposition of Child Custody Appeals.
12. Appeals Advanced in Delinquent Minor Cases.
13. Accelerated Case Timetable for Cases Other than Appeals Filed Under Rules 311(a) and 660A.
14. Disposition of Accelerated Cases.
15. Oral Arguments.
16. Rehearing.
17. Recording of Proceedings.
18. Workers' Compensation Commission Appeals.
19. Fourth District Appellate Courthouse Building.
20. Personnel.
21. Electronic Records on Appeal.

Rule 1. Filing and Form of Documents Filed in the Appellate Court

Documents and materials including, but not limited to, the original common law record (Supreme Court Rule 321), exhibits, motions, briefs and any and all other materials must be forwarded to the Appellate Court Clerk's office either by personal delivery or by the United States Postal Service or similar courier.

For physical delivery by private courier:	For United States Postal Service mail
Fourth District Appellate Court Clerk	Fourth District Appellate Court Clerk
201 West Monroe Street	201 West Monroe Street
Springfield, Illinois 62704	Post Office Box 19206
	Springfield, Illinois 62794–9206

Unless received after the due date, documents and materials required to be filed within a specified time will be deemed filed upon receipt by the Appellate Court Clerk (Supreme Court Rule 373). If received after the due date, the time of mailing shall be deemed the time of filing. Proof of mailing shall be as provided in Supreme Court Rule 12.

All documents filed with the Fourth District Appellate Court, including motions, must comply with supreme court rules and must be signed by at least one attorney of record and shall list that person's professional physical address, email address and Illinois Attorney Registration and Disciplinary Commission number. Parties not represented by an attorney shall sign their name and provide a contact address and email address, if possible.

Adopted eff. March 1, 2010. Amended eff. Jan. 1, 2012; Nov. 15, 2014; April 1, 2015.

Rule 2. Appearance and Withdrawal of Attorneys

Attorneys shall file a written appearance or other pleading before addressing the Court unless presenting a motion for leave to appear by intervention or otherwise. Procedures for withdrawal shall be consistent with Supreme Court Rule 13(c).

Adopted eff. March 1, 2010.

Rule 3. Address Changes

All attorneys, as well as all pro se parties, shall immediately notify the Appellate Court Clerk in writing of any change of address. A copy of the letter shall be served on all parties of record.

Adopted eff. March 1, 2010. Amended eff. April 1, 2015.

Rule 4. Contents of the Record on Appeal

The record on appeal shall consist of the judgment from which the appeal is taken, the notice of appeal, and the entire original common law record. The common law record includes every document filed, judgment or order entered in the cause, all documentary exhibits offered and filed and the report of proceedings (Supreme Court Rule 321).

The contents of the record on appeal are specified in Supreme Court Rules 321 and 608. Rule 608(a)(10) requires that all exhibits offered at trial and sentencing be included in the record on appeal.

Exceptions:

(a) Physical evidence

Examples of physical evidence that **should not** be sent to the reviewing Court are weapons, narcotics, drug paraphernalia, clothing or other physical evidence. Photographs offered as exhibits are to be included in the record on appeal.

If physical evidence is required for consideration by the reviewing Court of the case on appeal, the Court, on its own motion or upon motion of a party, will direct the Circuit Court Clerk to transfer such evidence.

Exhibits of a descriptive or documentary nature including video recordings, audio recordings, computer media such as disks or flash drives **should be sent** to the Appellate Court.

The use of photographs in lieu of the exhibits themselves is permitted when the exhibits are large, bulky or otherwise do not fit easily into the record on appeal and the photographs of the exhibits are sufficient for the determination of the issues on appeal and for an understanding of the case.

(b) Pornographic evidence

Transmission of any materials through the United States Postal Service that are pornographic in nature must follow the protocol from the United States Attorney's office requiring that such materials be double-wrapped with the inner wrapper clearly marked "to be opened by addressee only, contains pornographic evidence" or a similar statement that describes what is being transmitted. The outer wrapping on which the address is printed should be sent via United States Mail and should require a signature release. The address should state the specific individual to whom the package is to be delivered.

To send parcels containing pornographic material to the Fourth District Appellate Court of Illinois, address the outer package as directed in paragraph number 1, General Procedures.

In preparation of the record on appeal, the Circuit Court Clerks within the Fourth Appellate District of Illinois are to submit records containing the original documents, not copies of the original documents. However, copies may be submitted if:

1) The original papers of the record do not exist, or

2) The Chief Judge of the circuit from which the appeal originates files a letter with the stating good cause why the original is not available and why a copy of the record should be accepted by the Appellate Court instead. Whether the letter filed by the Chief Judge states good cause shall be determined by the Appellate Court.

The record on appeal shall be prepared in accordance with Supreme Court Rules 323, 324 and 325. Upon transmittal of the prescribed fees by the appellant, the Circuit Court Clerk shall forward the record to the Appellate Court, or upon request, provide it to the appellant for delivery to the Appellate Court (Supreme Court Rule 325).

At the request of any party, the clerk of the trial court shall deliver to the Appellate Court a certificate that the record has been prepared and certified in the form required. The timely filing of the certificate in lieu of record shall be considered the filing of the record on appeal (Supreme Court Rule 325).

Adopted eff. March 1, 2010. Amended eff. Nov. 15, 2014; April 1, 2015.

Rule 5.   Review of Administrative Orders

The procedure for direct review of Administrative Orders by the Appellate Court is defined in Supreme Court Rule 335.

Adopted eff. March 1, 2010.

Rule 6.   Briefs

All briefs filed with the Fourth District Appellate Court must be signed by at least one attorney of record and shall list that person's professional physical address, email address and Attorney Registration and Disciplinary Commission number. Parties not represented by an attorney shall sign their name and provide a contact address and telephone number. The form, length, number of copies, format of briefs, and time deadlines, must comply with Supreme Court Rules 341 through 345.

Adopted eff. March 1, 2010. Amended eff. Jan. 1, 2012; Nov. 15, 2014; April 1, 2015.

Rule 7.   Filing Fees and Reproduction of Materials

As of 1/1/2015, in all cases docketed in the Appellate Court, all appellants or cross-appellants shall pay a filing fee of $50. All appellees, upon entry of appearance or filing any paper, shall pay a $30 fee as required by section 705 of the Appellate Court Act (705 ILCS 15/28) and Supreme Court Rule 313, and Court Administrative Order M. R. 3140.

The Clerk's office will not photocopy bound and certified records for any party or non-party. Reproductions of other documents filed with the Appellate Court Clerk may be requested and, if the request is granted, will be provided at the cost of $0.25 per page (Supreme Court Administrative Order M.R. 10958).

Filed materials, including those that may not be photocopied, will be made available for review upon request with the exception of cases involving minor(s). The Court may monitor any review of materials to ensure the integrity of the record.

The Court's computer system and the information contained in that system, including but not limited to internal electronic court communications and internal administrative documents, will not be printed or provided to any party, his or her attorney, or the general public.

Adopted eff. March 1, 2010. Amended eff. Jan. 1, 2012; May 1, 2013; Nov. 15, 2014; April 1, 2015.

Rule 8. Motions

Motion titles shall reflect the precise nature of the relief sought, such as "Motion for Extension of Time to File the Appellant's Brief" rather than merely "Motion" or "Motion for Extension of Time."

Motions shall be in writing and shall state the relief sought and the grounds therefor. When the motion is based on facts that do not appear of record, the motion shall be supported by affidavit. If counsel has conferred with opposing counsel and opposing counsel has no objection to the motion, that fact should be stated in the motion and affidavit in order to allow the Court to rule on the motion. The procedures for motions are specified in Supreme Court Rules 361 and 610.

Adopted eff. March 1, 2010.

Rule 9. Emergency Motions

Emergency motions shall be filed and proceed pursuant to Supreme Court Rule 361(g). No emergency motion may be filed in the Appellate Court unless the appeal has been docketed following receipt of a filed notice of appeal or interlocutory petition under applicable supreme court rules.

The words "Emergency Motion" must appear in the title. The Appellate Court Clerk, upon receiving a filing entitled "Emergency Motion," shall immediately direct that filing to the Court's motions judge. If the emergency motion requires action by the Court by a certain date or time, that information must be set forth in the first paragraph of the motion. The motion shall specify the nature of the emergency and the grounds for the specific relief requested.

The movant shall attach to the motion a copy of all Circuit Court and Appellate Court documents, including orders, relevant to the motion. The party filing the emergency motion shall immediately personally serve all other parties, if possible, or otherwise immediately serve all other parties by facsimile or overnight mail. The type of service made shall be specifically indicated on the Certificate of Service.

Emergency motions shall only be filed when a matter involves a genuine emergency. Motions for extension of time to file a record or brief are not considered emergencies.

Upon receipt of an Emergency Motion, the Court may

  1. Enter an order requesting a response by a specific date or time;

  2. Wait for the time provided by supreme court rule for expiration of time for a response.

  3. Enter an order resolving the motion; or

  4. Take whatever action is deemed appropriate.

Adopted eff. March 1, 2010.

Rule 10. Disposition of Cases

Where no appellee brief is timely filed, a case will be considered ready for submission to the Court five days after the day the brief is due to be filed, unless a timely motion for extension of time to file the brief is filed. If a timely motion for extension of time is filed, but no brief is subsequently timely filed, the case will be considered ready for submission to the Court on the due date determined by the resolution of the motion(s) for extension.

All other cases will be considered ready for disposition upon the timely filing of the appellant reply brief (or cross-reply brief). Where no reply brief (or cross-reply brief) is timely filed, a case will be considered ready for disposition on the day the reply brief (or cross-reply brief) is due to be filed, unless a timely motion for extension is filed.

If a timely motion for extension is filed but no reply brief (or cross-reply brief) is subsequently timely filed, the case will be considered ready for disposition as of the due date determined by the resolution of the motion or motions for extension. See last page of this document[1] for appeal time schedule.

Adopted eff. March 1, 2010. Amended eff. Oct. 1, 2013; Nov. 15, 2014; April 1, 2015.

[1] See schedule following last rule.

Rule 11. Mandatory Accelerated Disposition of Child Custody Appeals

The expedited procedures in Rule 311(a) shall apply to appeals from final orders in child custody cases and to interlocutory appeals in child custody cases from which leave to appeal has been granted pursuant to Rule 306(a)(5). If the appeal is taken from a judgment or order affecting other matters, issues or decisions affecting the rights of persons other than the child, the court may handle all pending issues using the expedited rules in Rule 311(a), unless doing so will delay the decision on the child custody appeal.

In order to expedite appeals under Rule 311(a), parties may file memoranda in lieu of formal briefs. Such memoranda must comply with the requirements of Supreme Court Rules 341(a), (b), (c), (d), (e), (f), (g) and (j).

Adopted eff. March 1, 2010. Amended eff. Nov. 15, 2014; April 1, 2015.

Rule 12. Appeals Advanced in Delinquent Minor Cases

The expedited procedures in Supreme Court Rule 660A shall apply to appeals from final judgments in delinquent minor proceedings arising under the Juvenile Court Act.

Adopted eff. Oct. 1, 2013.

Rule 13. Accelerated Case Timetable for Cases Other than Appeals Filed Under Rules 311(a) and 660A

All accelerated cases must adhere to the following due date schedule:

1. The record on appeal (or certificate in lieu of record) and the report of proceedings shall be filed no later than 35 days after the filing of the notice of appeal. Any request for extension of the time for filing shall be accompanied by an affidavit of the court clerk or court reporter stating the reason for the delay, and shall be served on the trial judge and the chief judge of the judicial circuit.

2. The appellant brief or memorandum in lieu of a formal brief must be filed within 21 days of the filing of the record or certificate in the Appellate Court.

3. The appellee brief or memorandum in lieu of a formal brief must be filed within 21 days thereafter.

4. Any reply brief or memorandum in lieu of a formal brief must be filed within 7 days thereafter.

5. In the case of a cross-appeal, the cross-reply brief or memorandum in lieu of a formal brief must be filed within 7 days thereafter.

Requests for continuance are disfavored and shall be granted only for compelling circumstances (Supreme Court Rule 311a(7)).

When a motion requesting a continuance is based on a delay in the preparation of the record, the motion shall detail the proceedings at the status hearing required by Supreme Court Rule 311(a)(3), including the trial court's determination of the record and whether the trial judge has requested the chief judge's assistance in resolving any filing delays. The motion shall also attach a file-stamped copy of any order entered at the status hearing and an affidavit of the clerk or court reporter stating the reason for the delay.

Former Rule 12 adopted eff. March 1, 2010. Renumbered as Rule 13 eff. Oct. 1, 2013. Amended eff. Nov. 15, 2014; April 1, 2015.

Rule 14. Disposition of Accelerated Cases

Where no appellee brief is timely filed, an accelerated case will be considered ready for disposition 3 days after the day that the brief is due to be filed, unless a timely motion for extension of time to file the appellee brief is filed. If a timely motion for extension of time is filed but no appellee brief is subsequently timely filed, the case will be considered ready for disposition 3 days after the due date determined by the resolution of the motion or motions for extension of time.

All other accelerated cases will be considered ready for disposition upon the timely filing of the appellant reply brief (or cross-reply brief, if applicable). Where no reply brief (or cross-reply brief) is timely filed, a case will be considered ready for disposition on the due date for the reply brief (or cross-reply brief) unless a timely motion for extension of time is filed.

If a timely motion for extension is filed but no reply brief (or cross-reply brief) is subsequently timely filed, the case will be considered ready for disposition as of the due date determined by the resolution of the motion or motions for extension of time.

Former Rule 13 adopted eff. March 1, 2010. Renumbered as Rule 14 eff. Oct. 1, 2013. Amended eff. Nov. 15, 2014; April 1, 2015.

Rule 15. Oral Arguments

Cases in the Appellate Court shall be called for argument or submitted without argument in the sequence and manner provided by Supreme Court Rules 351 and 352.

Appellant(s) and appellee(s) shall receive a total of 20 minutes for oral argument. The appellant(s) will receive a total of 5 additional minutes to present rebuttal. Oral argument shall omit the recitation of the facts and procedural history of the case except to the extent necessary to frame the issues that are presented on appeal.

In workers' compensation cases, the appellant(s) and appellee(s) shall receive a total of 15 minutes for oral argument with 5 additional minutes to present rebuttal for appellant.

Former Rule 14 adopted eff. March 1, 2010. Renumbered as Rule 15 eff. Oct. 1, 2013.

Rule 16. Rehearing

A petition for rehearing may be filed within 21 days after the filing of the judgment (Supreme Court Rule 367).

Former Rule 15 adopted eff. March 1, 2010. Renumbered as Rule 16 eff. Oct. 1, 2013.

Rule 17. Recording of Proceedings

Audio recordings of all oral arguments in the Illinois Appellate Court are available at www.state.il.us/court http://www.state.il.us/court

Former Rule 16 adopted eff. March 1, 2010. Renumbered as Rule 17 eff. Oct. 1, 2013. Amended eff. Nov. 15, 2014; April 1, 2015.

Rule 18. Workers' Compensation Commission Appeals

A five-judge panel of the Appellate Court will sit as the Workers' Compensation Commission division of each district of the Appellate Court and will hear and decide all appeals involving review of orders from the Workers' Compensation Commission. (Supreme Court Rule 22 (i)).

Former Rule 17 adopted eff. March 1, 2010. Renumbered as Rule 18 eff. Oct. 1, 2013.

Rule 19. Fourth District Appellate Courthouse Building

The Fourth District Appellate Court Clerk's office is open for the transaction of business from 8:30 a.m. to 4:30 p.m. each day except Saturdays, Sundays and legal holidays as determined by the Illinois Supreme Court.

Former Rule 18 adopted eff. March 1, 2010. Renumbered as Rule 19 eff. Oct. 1, 2013.

Rule 20. Personnel

The members of the Fourth District Appellate Court staff are precluded from providing legal advice to litigants, potential litigants, or their counsel.

Former Rule 19 adopted eff. March 1, 2010. Renumbered as Rule 20 eff. Oct. 1, 2013.

Rule 21. Electronic Records on Appeal

Effective December 1, 2011, when the record on appeal is filed by the Circuit Court Clerk electronically, as authorized by the Supreme Court of Illinois, any party to the appeal may request access to the electronic record on appeal. This section of the Fourth District Appellate Court local rules is in addition to all existing Supreme Court Rules governing the appellate process, and in all instances of conflict, the Supreme Court rules control.

*The Fourth District Appellate Court is presently conducting a pilot project for electronic transmission of the Record on Appeal with Adams, Moultrie and Logan Counties.

a. Any party who wishes to access an electronic copy of the Record on Appeal must register with the Appellate Court Clerk pursuant to the Clerk's required registration process.

b. The Appellate Court Clerk will acknowledge successful registration, when complete, and respond to the requesting party electronically.

c. Upon receipt of any party's request for access to the electronic record on appeal, the Fourth District Appellate Court shall, in its own discretion, grant or deny authorization to access the electronic Record on Appeal as offered by the Appellate Court Clerk at a designated secured web site http://www.judici.com Any copy of the electronic record downloaded by either party need not be returned to the Court.

d. In its sole discretion, the Court may revoke future access to an electronic record, or any portion thereof.

e. In preparation of the Record on Appeal the Circuit Court Clerk shall label documents in the common law record's Table of Contents exactly as titled. The more descriptive the title of the document, the more efficient the electronic Record on Appeal in navigation and location of specific contents. Example:

"Motion to Compel Production of Tax and Financial Information" rather than simply **Motion**.

f. If the Record on Appeal includes an impounded document, protected document, or document filed under seal or other restriction, the document(s) shall be referenced in the Electronic Record on Appeal PDF file's Table of Contents. Such references within the electronic Record on Appeal shall advise that the document filed on that date was impounded, sealed or otherwise secured by the trial court.

During the process of preparation of the Record on Appeal, the Circuit Court Clerk shall create a separate secured volume or PDF file as part of the Record on Appeal entitled "Secured Record on Appeal" in which any such secured document(s) within the common law record or any secured exhibits or reports of proceedings shall be placed. The Table of Contents of the PDF file in the "Secured Record on Appeal" shall index the documents contained within it.

Both the Record on Appeal and the separate PDF file entitled "Secured Record on Appeal," if any, shall be transmitted together by the Circuit Court Clerk to the Fourth District Appellate Court on or before the due date of the record on appeal.

g. A party to an appeal wishing to access the "Secured Record on Appeal," or any portion thereof, must move to unseal or view the documents within it. Upon proper motion supported by affidavit justifying such access, the Court, in its sole discretion, shall grant or deny access to such document(s) within the "Secured Record on Appeal" PDF file.

h. Upon grant of any motion to supplement the Record on Appeal, the supplement shall be prepared as a separate PDF file by the Circuit Court Clerk. The supplement PDF file shall be titled as such by the Circuit Court Clerk and transmitted electronically in the same manner as the Record on Appeal to the Fourth District Appellate Court Clerk.

i. When labeling transcripts in the Reports of Proceedings section of the Record on Appeal, the Circuit Court Clerk shall include in description the date of the court proceeding and the last name of the court reporter that certified the transcript.

j. Whenever possible the Circuit Clerk shall request and obtain the transcripts from the court reporter(s) in a format which allows the transcript text to be searched, copied and pasted when working with the electronic Record on Appeal, as this significantly enhances the utility of the record.

k. When creating the Table of Contents of the Exhibits the Circuit Court Clerk shall use the exhibit number and party offering the exhibit.

l. Photographic exhibits shall be scanned and included in the electronic record. Any photographs larger than 8 ½ × 11 inches that cannot be successfully scanned shall remain in the possession of the Circuit Court Clerk and shall be listed in the Table of Contents of the Exhibits. The Index or Table of Contents of the Record on Appeal shall advise as to which exhibits, if any, were retained by the Circuit Court Clerk by insertion of a page in proper sequential order stating what the exhibit is and that it was retained by the Circuit Clerk.

m. The Circuit Court Clerk shall insert a page into the Table of Contents of the Exhibits for any exhibit(s) that were offered by a party in the circuit court proceedings but were not allowed by the trial court. The inserted page shall state that the exhibit was offered but not allowed. Example:

"People's Exhibit #12—Not Admitted,"
or similar language.

n. Exhibits of a descriptive or documentary nature including video recordings, audio recordings, computer media such as discs or flash drives that cannot be included in the electronic record **should be sent** to the Appellate Court via other delivery method. Those exhibits shall be listed in the Table of Contents of the Exhibits which shall advise which exhibits, if any, were unable to be included in the electronic record and the date they were sent to the Appellate Court, and the delivery method.

o. The clerk shall include in the package(s) of such descriptive or documentary exhibit item(s) a receipt to be signed by the Appellate Clerk and returned to the Circuit Court Clerk confirming receipt by the Appellate Court Clerk of the package, its contents, and the date received.

p. Any physical exhibits such as clothing, weapons, drugs, documents too large or bulky to scan or other **physical** exhibits shall remain in the custody of the Circuit Court Clerk unless or until requested by the Appellate Court. The Table of Contents of the Exhibits in the electronic record shall advise which such exhibits were unable to be included in the electronic record. Physical Exhibits retained by the Circuit Court Clerk such weapons, drugs, etc. shall be listed in the Table of Contents of the Exhibits with a page inserted describing the exhibit and that it was retained by the Circuit Clerk. Example:

"People's Exhibit #14—knife—retained by the Circuit Court Clerk," or similar language.

Former Rule 20 adopted eff. Dec. 1, 2011. Amended eff. May 1, 2013. Renumbered as Rule 21 eff. Oct. 1, 2013. Amended eff. Nov. 15, 2014.

Time Schedule for an Appeal

DAY 0	An appealable order is entered.
DAY 30	The notice of appeal must be filed in the Circuit Court within 30 days of the entry of an appealable order. **The filing of the notice of appeal begins a new time schedule.**
DAYS 0–7	The notice of appeal must be filed, with proof of service, in the Appellate Court.
DAY 1 to 14	Appellant orders transcripts and requests the circuit clerk to prepare the Record on Appeal.
DAY 14	Docketing statement must be filed in the Appellate Court.
DAY 49	Report of proceedings filed with Circuit Court Clerk (seven weeks after notice of appeal.)
DAY 63	Record on appeal must be filed in the Appellate Court (nine weeks after notice of appeal.) **The filing of the record begins a new time schedule.**
DAY 0	The record or certificate in lieu of record must be filed in the Appellate Court.
35 DAYS	The appellant brief is due 35 days (five weeks) after the record is filed.
35 DAYS	The appellee brief must be filed 35 days (five weeks) after the due date of the appellant brief.
14 DAYS	The appellant reply brief must be filed 14 days (two weeks) after the due date of the appellee brief.

The case proceeds to oral or nonoral calendar.

APPELLATE COURT ORDERS,
FIFTH DISTRICT

Including Amendments Received Through April 1, 2016

Order 05–01–95

IN THE
APPELLATE COURT OF ILLINOIS
FIFTH DISTRICT

ADMINISTRATIVE ORDER

This matter has been considered on the court's own motion, and the court, being advised in the premises, finds:

That a problem exists with respect to certain non-exempt appellants who fail to pay either the court reporter for preparation of the transcripts of proceedings or the circuit clerk for preparation of the record on appeal;

That some court reporters and circuit clerks are nonetheless preparing transcripts of proceedings and the record on appeal, respectively, in the belief that their failure to do so may subject them to a finding of contempt of the appellate court.

IT IS THEREFORE ORDERED that this court hereby declares that it will not require court reporters to prepare transcripts of proceedings or circuit clerks to prepare the record on appeal in any case where the appellant is required to pay a record-preparation fee but has failed to do so.

ENTERED: May 1, 1995.

Order 01–03–06

IN THE
APPELLATE COURT OF ILLINOIS
FIFTH JUDICIAL DISTRICT

ADMINISTRATIVE ORDER

Pursuant to Supreme Court Rule 361(g), effective January 1, 2006, the Fifth District is charged with promulgating and publishing local rules governing emergency motions, including bail motions. Accordingly, the procedure for seeking emergency relief by motion shall be in the manner as prescribed herein.

An appeal must be properly docketed in this court before a movant can seek emergency relief by motion. However, an appeal may be docketed on the strength of an emergency motion that is accompanied by a supporting record (see Supreme Court Rule 328) that includes, at a minimum, file-stamped copies of the notice of appeal, the order or judgment from which the appeal is taken, post-trial motions if any, and the orders disposing of post-trial motions.

Any motion seeking emergency relief must be titled as an emergency motion and must be filed with the clerk of the court. An emergency motion may be filed by facsimile.

An emergency motion must be accompanied by personal service, facsimile service in the manner prescribed by Supreme Court Rule 12(b), or by overnight mail.

Except in the most extreme and compelling circumstances, a motion seeking an extension of time will not be treated as an emergency motion.

The court may order a response to an emergency motion, hold the motion until the time for responding expires, rule on the motion prior to the time for filing an objection if warranted by extraordinary circumstances (see Supreme Court Rule 361(d)), or take whatever action it deems appropriate.

ENTERED: January 3, 2006, effective January 3, 2006.

Order 10–29–09

IN THE
APPELLATE COURT OF ILLINOIS
FIFTH JUDICIAL DISTRICT

ADMINISTRATIVE ORDER

This matter has been considered on the court's own motion and pursuant to Supreme Court Rule 22(h) (Official Reports Advance Sheet No. 26 (December 17, 2008)), which authorizes this court to adopt rules governing civil and criminal cases which are consistent with Illinois Supreme Court Rules and the statutes of this state; and the court, being advised in the premises, finds:

That docket sheet entries are a part of the basic court record in the lower court;

That in some of the circuit courts in the counties within the Fifth District of the Illinois Appellate Court, docket entries are no longer handwritten or typed on a docket sheet but instead are entered into a computer;

That in some counties these computerized docket sheets are printed out and made a part of the record. However, in some counties the computerized docket sheets are not made a part of the record and are available only upon request of the circuit clerk; and

That to facilitate the administration of justice, the Illinois Appellate Court, Fifth District, hereby enacts the following rule with respect to docket sheet entries.

IT IS THEREFORE ORDERED that when preparing the record on appeal for transmission to this court, the Circuit Clerks of the respective counties within the Fifth District of the Illinois Appellate Court should include within the record all docket entries, including those generated by a computer.

ENTERED: October 29, 2009.

Order 04–01–10

IN THE
APPELLATE COURT OF ILLINOIS
FIFTH JUDICIAL DISTRICT

ADMINISTRATIVE ORDER

Pursuant to our authority under Supreme Court Rule 311(a)(6) to adopt mandatory procedures to ensure completion of Rule 311(a) appeals within 150 days after the filing of the notice of appeal, we hereby adopt the following local rules.

Mandatory Procedures for Custody Cases Expedited Under Supreme Court Rule 311(a)

Record on Appeal

Due Date.

In appeals from final orders in child custody cases and interlocutory appeals in child custody cases from which leave to appeal has been granted pursuant to Rule 306(a)(5), the record on appeal shall be filed within 35 days of the filing of the notice appeal pursuant to Supreme Court Rule 311(a)(4)

Requests for Extensions

Extensions for preparation of the record on appeal shall be allowed only for the most compelling circumstances. Pursuant to 311(a)(4), the trial court has the authority to allow one extension of time to file the record. In no event shall that extension total more than 10 days. Any order entered by the circuit court granting an extension must be immediately served on the Clerk of the Appellate Court by counsel for the moving party, or by the party who filed the motion if the party is not represented by counsel,

Filing the Record

In order to expedite appeals under 311 (a), the circuit clerk is encouraged to file a certificate in lieu of record with this court in compliance with Supreme Court Rule 325 and to transmit the record directly to appellant's attorney. The attorneys are encouraged to transmit the record directly between themselves with a notice to the clerk of this court of the date and method of transmission.

Briefs

Schedule

- Appellant's opening brief shall be filed within 21 days of the filing of the record or certificate in lieu in the Appellate Court.

- Appellee's answer brief shall be filed within 21 days of the due date of appellants brief

- Appellant's reply brief, if any, shall be filed within 7 days of the due date of appellee's brief.

- In the case of a cross-appeal, the cross-reply brief shall be filed within 7 days of the due date of appellant's reply brief

Requests for Extension

This court will look with extreme disfavor upon any requests for extensions in the briefing schedule and will grant such requests only for the most compelling circumstances.

Whenever possible, motions for extension of time to file a brief and responses thereto shall be filed by facsimile or in person with this court and shall be served on the opposing party by facsimile or in person. In addition, a hard copy shall be mailed to the court at the time of the facsimile transmission. The proof of service shall state that service by facsimile or in person has been made upon the opposing party and this court, and that a hard copy has been mailed to the court if the filing was by facsimile. The opposing party shall file its response, if any, within three days. As with all appeals, motions do not stay the filing schedule and the briefing schedule will continue to run while any motions are pending,

If a petition for leave to appeal pursuant to Supreme Court Rule 306(a)(5) is granted, the time for filing a notice of election to stand on the petition or answer or for filing a new brief shall begin to run from the date that the petition is granted. In order to allow a petition or answer to stand as a brief, the party must notify the other parties and the clerk of this court on or before the due date of the brief, ENTERED: April 1, 2010.

Order 04–01–10(b)

IN THE
APPELLATE COURT OF ILLINOIS
FIFTH JUDICIAL DISTRICT

ADMINISTRATIVE ORDER

This matter has been considered on the court's own motion; and pursuant to Supreme Court Rule 311(a); and the court, being advised in the premises, finds;

That on May 1, 1995, this court entered an administrative order concerning a problem of appellants in civil appeals who are not otherwise entitled to a free record on appeal and fail to pay either the official court reporter for preparation of transcripts of proceedings or the circuit clerk for preparation of the record on appeal. The administrative order declared that under such circumstances court reporters were not required to prepare transcripts of proceedings and circuit clerks were not required to prepare records on appeal until payment was advanced;

That Supreme Court Rule 311(a) does not relieve an appellant who must otherwise pay for a transcript of proceeding or a record on appeal of that burden.

However, paragraph (a)(4) of the rule provides that "[l]ack of advance payment shall not be a reason for noncompliance with filing deadlines for the record or transcript," Accordingly, our administrative order is amended to comport with the new rule.

IT IS THEREFORE ORDERED that this court declares that it will not require court reporters and circuit clerks to prepare transcripts of proceedings and the record on appeal in any civil case not governed by Supreme Court Rule 311(a) where the appellant is required to pay a record preparation fee but has failed to do so.

ENTERED: November 22, 2004. REVISED: April 1, 2010.

CONSOLIDATED INDEX TO CHAPTER 735, CIVIL PROCEDURE, AND COURT RULES

References are either to Chapter, Act and Section, or to Court Rule

Abbreviations

App.Ct.First Dist. Rule . . . . .Administrative and Procedure Rules of the Illinois Appellate Court, First District

App.Ct.Fourth Dist. Rule . . . . .Administrative and Procedural Rules of the Illinois Appellate Court, Fourth District

App.Ct.Second Dist. Rule . . . . .Appellate Court Rules, Second District

Bar Admis. Rule . . . . .Rules of Procedure for the Board of Admissions to the Bar and Committees on Character and Fitness

Dis. Com. Rule . . . . .Rules of the Attorney Registration and Disciplinary Commission

Evid Rule . . . . .Rules of Evidence

RPC Rule . . . . .Rules of Professional Conduct

S.Ct. CJC Rule . . . . .Supreme Court Rules Code of Judicial Conduct

S.Ct. Rule . . . . .Supreme Court Rules

Unif. App. Rule . . . . .Uniform Administrative and Procedural Rules, Appellate Courts, Second, Third, Fourth and Fifth Districts

ATTORNEYS—Cont'd

Appointments—Cont'd

Receivers and receivership, **S.Ct. Rule 776**

Arbitration and award, adverse or pecuniary interest, **RPC Rule 1.12**

Assignments, office or practice, disciplined attorneys, **S.Ct. Rule 764**

Assistance,

Disciplinary proceedings, **S.Ct. Rule 755**

Nonlawyers, powers and duties, **RPC Rule 5.3**

Associate judges, registration fees, **S.Ct. Rule 756**

Associations, professional associations, **S.Ct. Rule 721**

Audits and auditors,

Books and papers, interim suspensions from practice of law, **S.Ct. Rule 774**

Continuing education, **S.Ct. Rule 796**

Disciplinary fund, **S.Ct. Rule 751**

Authority, allocation, **RPC Rule 1.2**

Bad checks, trust accounts, **RPC Rule 1.15**

Bar admission, **Bar Admis. Rule 1.1 et seq.**

Boards and commissions,

Admissions, **S.Ct. Rule 702 et seq.**

Disciplinary proceedings, generally, post

MCLE board, continuing education, **S.Ct. Rule 792**

Professionalism commission, **S.Ct. Rule 799**

Terms of office, disciplinary proceedings, **Dis. Com. Rule 4**

Bribery and corruption,

Advertisements, **RPC Rule 7.2**

Judges or court officials, **RPC Rule 3.5**

Briefs, generally, this index

Business and commerce, adverse or pecuniary interest, **RPC Rule 1.8**

Campaign contributions, misconduct, **RPC Rule 8.4**

Candor, **RPC Rule 3.3**

Censure, **S.Ct. Rule 770**

Certificates and certification, **S.Ct. Rules 704, 708**

Fitness, admission to bar, **S.Ct. Rule 704 et seq.**

Licenses and permits, fees, **S.Ct. Rule 313**

Character and reputation,

Inquiries and investigations, **S.Ct. Rule 709**

Privileges and immunities, disclosure, **S.Ct. Rule 710**

Claim determination, client protection program, **Dis.Com. Rule 507**

Client protection program, **S.Ct. Rule 780; Dis. Com. Rule 501 et seq.**

Claims, payment, **Dis.Com. Rule 510**

Discretionary nature, **Dis.Com. Rule 503**

Confidential or privileged information, deliberations, **S.Ct. Rule 766**

Determination of claim, **Dis.Com. Rule 507**

Eligible clients, **Dis.Com. Rule 501**

Excluded claims, **Dis.Com. Rule 502**

Form of claim, **Dis.Com. Rule 504**

Contents, **Dis.Com. Rule 505**

ATTORNEYS—Cont'd

Client protection program—Cont'd

Payment, claims, **Dis.Com. Rule 510**

Discretionary nature, **Dis.Com. Rule 503**

Privileges and immunities, claimants, **S.Ct. Rule 775**

Procedure for claims, **Dis.Com. Rule 506**

Representation of claimants, compensation, **Dis.Com. Rule 512**

Request for reconsideration, claim determination, **Dis.Com. Rule 508**

Restitution, **Dis.Com. Rule 511**

Review by panel, claim determination, **Dis.Com. Rule 509**

Subpoenas, investigation of claims, **S.Ct. Rule 754**

Subrogation, **Dis.Com. Rule 511**

Clients,

Confidential or privileged information, **RPC Rule 1.6**

Property, safekeeping, **RPC Rule 1.15**

Records and recordation, **S.Ct. Rule 769**

Client or third party property, **RPC Rule 1.15**

Evidence, **735 ILCS 5/8–2005**

Fees, inflation, **735 ILCS 5/8–2006**

Code of Judicial Conduct. Judges, this index

College education, **S.Ct. Rule 703**

Committees, character and fitness, **S.Ct. Rule 708**

Admission to the bar, **Bar Admis. Rule 1.1 et seq.**

Communications,

Clients, **RPC Rule 1.4**

Represented parties, **RPC Rule 4.2**

Services of attorneys, **RPC Rule 7.1 et seq.**

Compensation and salaries. Attorneys Fees, generally, this index

Competent representation of clients, **RPC Rule 1.1**

Complaint, against attorneys, agreements limiting, **RPC Rule 1.8**

Compromise and settlement,

Adverse or pecuniary interest, **RPC Rule 1.8**

Limitations, practice of law, **RPC Rule 5.6**

Restrictions, right to practice, **RPC Rule 5.6**

Computers, records and recordation, client records, **735 ILCS 5/8–2005**

Conditional admission to bar, **S.Ct. Rule 701; Bar Admis. Rule 7.1 et seq.**

Conduct before tribunals, **RPC Rule 3.3**

Confidential or privileged information,

Admission to the bar,

Character and fitness, **Bar Admis. Rule 11**

Conditional admission, **Bar Admis. Rule 7.16**

Clients, **RPC Rule 1.6**

Continuing education, **S.Ct. Rule 797**

Disciplinary proceedings, **S.Ct. Rule 766**

Discovery, **S.Ct. Rule 201**

Government information, successive private employment, conflict of interest, **RPC Rule 1.11**

Lawyers assistance program, disclosure, **S.Ct. Rule 766**

BRIEFS—Cont'd

Size, books and papers, filing, **S.Ct. Rule 10**

Supreme court, original jurisdiction, **S.Ct. Rule 382**

BROADCASTING

Radio. Television and Radio, generally, this index

Television and Radio, generally, this index

BROKERS

Insurance Producers, generally, this index

BROTHERS AND SISTERS

Relatives, generally, this index

BUFFALO GROVE

Eminent domain, quick take, **735 ILCS 30/25-7-103.105**

BUILDING

Construction, generally, this index

BUILDING CODES

Actions and proceedings, continuances, violations, **735 ILCS 5/2-1007**

Actions for violation, continuances, **735 ILCS 5/2-1007**

Continuance, actions for violations, **735 ILCS 5/2-1007**

Crimes and offenses, continuances, actions for violations, **735 ILCS 5/2-1007**

Regulation of construction, continuance, violations, actions for, **735 ILCS 5/2-1007**

BUILDINGS

Attachment, watercraft, **735 ILCS 5/4-201**

Codes. Building Codes, generally, this index

Condominiums, generally, this index

Construction, generally, this index

Courthouses, generally, this index

Housing, generally, this index

Safety. Building Codes, generally, this index

School Buildings and Grounds, generally, this index

Zoning and Planning, generally, this index

BULLS

Animals, generally, this index

BURDEN OF PROOF

Evidence, this index

BUREAUS

Administrative Review, generally, this index

BURGLARY

Limitation of civil actions, **735 ILCS 5/13-202.1**

Residential burglary, limitation of civil actions, **735 ILCS 5/13-202.1**

BUSINESS AND COMMERCE

Aliases. Assumed or Fictitious Names, generally, this index

Assumed or Fictitious Names, generally, this index

Attorneys, adverse or pecuniary interest, **RPC Rule 1.8**

BUSINESS AND COMMERCE—Cont'd

Corporations, generally, this index

Crimes and offenses. Fraud, generally, this index

Electronic Transactions, generally, this index

Fictitious names. Assumed or Fictitious Names, generally, this index

Fraud, generally, this index

Judges, this index

Limited Liability Companies, generally, this index

Names. Assumed or Fictitious Names, generally, this index

Organizations,

  Associations and Societies, generally, this index

  Corporations, generally, this index

  Limited Liability Companies, generally, this index

  Partnerships, generally, this index

Partnerships, generally, this index

Products Liability, generally, this index

Professional Associations, generally, this index

Zoning and Planning, generally, this index

BUSINESS CORPORATION ACT

Corporations, generally, this index

BUSINESS OFFENSES

Crimes and Offenses, generally, this index

BUSINESS ORGANIZATIONS

Associations and Societies, generally, this index

Corporations, generally, this index

Limited Liability Companies, generally, this index

Partnerships, generally, this index

BUSINESS RECORDS

Accounts and Accounting, generally, this index

Evidence, **S.Ct. Rule 236**

CABINS

Mobilehomes and Mobilehome Parks, generally, this index

CABLE TELEVISION

See, also, Public Utilities, generally, this index

Confidential or privileged information, **735 ILCS 5/8-901 et seq.**

CALENDARS

Case management conferences, **S.Ct. Rule 218**

Rules of court, powers and duties, **735 ILCS 5/1-104**

CAMERAS

Photography and Pictures, generally, this index

CANAL BOATS

Ships and Shipping, generally, this index

CANALS

Eminent domain, **735 ILCS 30/10-5-10**

Floods and Flood Control, generally, this index

Harbors and Ports, generally, this index

CANNABIS

Definitions, eviction, emergency proceedings, **735 ILCS 5/9-118**

PERSONAL PROPERTY—Cont'd
Motor Vehicles, generally, this index
Ne Exeat, generally, this index
Orders of court, relief petition, **735 ILCS 5/2–1401**
Pleadings, property rights trial, **735 ILCS 5/12–202**
Replevin, generally, this index
Rights, trial, **735 ILCS 5/12–201 et seq.**
Subpoenas, property rights, trial, **735 ILCS 5/12–203**
Title to Property, generally, this index
Trial, rights, **735 ILCS 5/12–201 et seq.**
Wills, generally, this index

PERSONAL REPRESENTATIVES
Probate Proceedings, this index

PERSONNEL
Officers and Employees, generally, this index

PERSONS
Definitions,
Discovery, foreign states, **735 ILCS 35/2**
Foreign money claims, **735 ILCS 5/12–655**
Fraudulently obtained public funds, **735 ILCS 5/20–101**
Limitation of actions, construction, **735 ILCS 5/13–214**
Strategic lawsuits against public participation, **735 ILCS 110/10**

PERSONS WITH DISABILITIES
Handicapped Persons, generally, this index
Hearing Impaired Persons, generally, this index
Mentally Retarded and Developmentally Disabled Persons, generally, this index

PERU
Eminent domain, quick take, **735 ILCS 30/25–7–103.63**

PETIT JURORS
Jury, generally, this index

PETS
Animals, generally, this index

PEYOTE
Controlled Substances, generally, this index

PHENCYCLIDINE
Controlled Substances, generally, this index

PHENOBARBITAL
Controlled Substances, generally, this index

PHILANTHROPIC ORGANIZATIONS
Charities, generally, this index

PHOTOGRAPHY AND PICTURES
Courts, **S.Ct. CJC Rule 63**
Definitions, evidence, **Evid. Rule 1001**
Evidence, **Evid. Rule 1001 et seq.**
Records, **735 ILCS 5/8–401**
Judges, courts, **S.Ct. CJC Rule 63**

PHOTOGRAPHY AND PICTURES—Cont'd
Personal property, exemptions, **735 ILCS 5/12–1001 et seq.**

PHRASES
Words and Phrases, generally, this index

PHYSICAL DISABILITY
Handicapped Persons, generally, this index

PHYSICAL EXAMINATIONS
Attorneys,
Attendance, discovery, **735 ILCS 5/2–1003**
Orders of court, motions by administrator or attorney, **S.Ct. Rule 760**
Confidential or privileged information, terrorism, exemptions, **735 ILCS 5/8–802**
Discovery, **735 ILCS 5/2–1003; S.Ct. Rule 215**
Exemptions, terrorism, confidential or privileged information, **735 ILCS 5/8–802**
Reports, discovery, **S.Ct. Rule 215**
Rules of court, discovery, **S.Ct. Rule 215**
Terrorism, confidential or privileged information, exemptions, **735 ILCS 5/8–802**
Witnesses, discovery, **S.Ct. Rule 215**

PHYSICAL RESTRAINTS
Trial, inmates, **S.Ct. Rule 430**

PHYSICALLY HANDICAPPED PERSONS
Handicapped Persons, generally, this index

PHYSICIANS AND SURGEONS
Actions and proceedings. Medical Malpractice, generally, this index
Affidavits, malpractice actions, consulting physicians, **735 ILCS 5/2–622**
Confidential or privileged information, **735 ILCS 5/8–802**
Exemptions, **735 ILCS 5/8–802**
Patients, **735 ILCS 5/8–802**
Terrorism, exemptions, **735 ILCS 5/8–802**
Consultants, affidavits, malpractice, **735 ILCS 5/2–622**
Depositions, **S.Ct. Rule 204**
Evidence,
Malpractice, res ipsa loquitur, **735 ILCS 5/2–1113**
Privileged communications, **735 ILCS 5/8–802**
Examinations and examiners. Physical Examinations, generally, this index
Exemptions, confidential or privileged information, **735 ILCS 5/8–802**
Fees, mental or physical examination of attorney, physicians testifying, **S.Ct. Rule 760**
Homicides, privileged communications, exceptions, **735 ILCS 5/8–802**
Judgments and decrees, reduction, medical malpractice, **735 ILCS 5/2–1205**
Limitations, injury or death, **735 ILCS 5/13–212**
Malpractice. Medical Malpractice, generally, this index
Medical Malpractice, generally, this index